ਪੰਜਾਬੀ-ਅੰਗਰੇਜ਼ੀ : ਅੰ

PUNJABI-ENGLISH
ENGLISH-PUNJABI
DICTIONARY

ਪੰਜਾਬੀ-ਅੰਗਰੇਜ਼ੀ : ਅੰਗਰੇਜ਼ੀ-ਪੰਜਾਬੀ ਕੋਸ਼

PUNJABI-ENGLISH
ENGLISH-PUNJABI
DICTIONARY

Compiled by
Dr. K.K. Goswami

Hippocrene Books, Inc.
New York

© 2000 Dr. K.K. Goswami

First Published	2002
First Reprint	2004
Second Reprint	2007
Third Reprint	2009

ISBN 978-0-7818-0940-5

Published in arrangement with:
UBS Publishers' Distributors Pvt. Ltd.
5 Ansari Road, New Delhi-110 002, India

For information, address:
Hippocrene Books, Inc.
171 Madison Avenue
New York, NY 10016

Cataloging-in-Publication Data available from the Library of Congress.

Printed in India

Dedicated to

The Punjabi Speakers

as well as

the lovers of

Punjabi Language and Culture

in

India and abroad.

PREFACE

Punjabi is one of the national languages of multilingual India. It has a long tradition and cultural identity. The vital characteristic of language needs constant change and modification in its vocabulary repository. Therefore, dictionary work is necessary for the development of the language. The present Punjabi-English and English-Punjabi dictionary has been developed on this point of view.

This is a dictionary with a difference in that it makes a truly linguistic approach to Punjabi lexicography. This is a medium sized dictionary having two parts — one from Punjabi to English and second from English to Punjabi. It comprises well over 25,000 entries (round about 11,000 entries from Punjabi and 14,000 entries from English), which one comes across most frequently during contact with people or in literature today. These are explained firstly in main meaning and then in various nuances and their modern renderings are set out in all accuracy. Efforts have also been made to add idioms or idiomatic usages. Meanings of a word have been arranged on the basis of their frequencies. Some words have quite a large number of meanings but some have given exhaustive signification.

This dictionary is meant for a foreign learner but will it also be of immense use to the general reader as well as the students who are called upon to translate in both languages; i.e., English and Punjabi. Hence, this dictionary has a special purpose, that it teaches both Punjabi and English. Rather, it teaches Punjabi to English speakers and English to Punjabi speakers.

There is a lack of standardization in the Punjabi writing system; therefore, we do not find homogeneity in Punjabi spellings. However, the pronunciation of English words has been transcribed in Gurmukhi letters of Punjabi in the common script, not in the International Phonetic Alphabets System because this dictionary is mainly meant for the common reader and not for the linguists or the language experts and scholars.

The transliteration system adopted for indicating the pronunciation of Punjabi words in the dictionary is based on principles which are, by an large, accepted by modern scholars and Orientalists. Even then, efforts have been made to standardize the spellings and meanings of Punjabi words as prevalent in the standard books. The significant feature of the sound patterns of Punjabi is the existence of the tone. Therefore, Punjabi is also called as a tonal language. The tones are phonetic realizations of pitch and duration which roughly correspond to the gh, jh, dh, dh, bh (the aspirated voiced sounds) series of consonants of Hindi and other North Indian languages.

It gives me great pleasure to acknowledge the assistance I have received from a number of Punjabi scholars and speakers. I owe a debt of gratitude to my friends Dr. Thakur Dass and Dr. R.C. Garg who gave fruitful suggestions for this work. I express my love and affections to my children Namrata, Gaurav and Mudita who are always prepared to help me a lot in my academic works.

I express my sincere thanks to Sardar Jaswant Singh 'Ajit' who has not only read the proofs efficiently but has also given valuable suggestions in the finalization of the dictionary.

I am also thankful to M/s Rachna Enterprises, especially Smt. Manorama Aggarwal, who took lot of pain to ensure the correct composing of the dictionary.

Every effort has been made to make the dictionary useful to the learners and translators of Punjabi and English languages.

Krishan Kumar Goswami

Points to be Noted on Transcription of English and Punjabi Pronunciation

1. All main or primary entries have the phonetic transcription but the derived words begining with swing dash (~) are not transcribed because of the economy.

2. Nasalized vowel has mostly been taken as Gurmukhi ਟਿੱਪੀ / ˙ / and ਬਿੰਦੀ /ੱ/, as ਚੰਗਾ, ਨੀਂਦਰ. English word 'fund' and 'banned' have been transcribed as ਫੰਡ and ਬੈਂਡ respectively.

3. The addak / ˙ / sign has been used in the germinated or over stressed syllables e.g. ਸੱਚ, ਪੱਕਾ.

4. English words ending with 'r' in spelling but pronounced when followed by a vowel sound have been represented as /ਅ*/ e.g. brother /ਬਰਅਦਅ*/, here /ਹਿਅ*/. In the middle of the word, 'r' is mostly represented as /:/ e.g. pierce /'ਪਿਅ:ਸ/.

5. When a consonant occurs initially in the second syllable as 'measure', it is transcribed as /'ਮੈਯ਼ਅ*/ whereas in 'yes', it is transcribed as /ਯੈਸ/. Here, in measure, ਯ਼ is fricative and in yes, ਯ is semivowel.

6. In the word 'Singh' /ਸਿੰਙ/, ng word final combination has been represented by Gurmukhi velar nasal consonant /ਙ/.

7. When an entry is used on different parts of speech with differing pronunciations, the transcriptions are provided after the entry in the order of parts of speech as shown after the transcription, such as Conflict /ਕੋਨਫ਼ਲਿਕਟ, ਕਅਨ'ਫ਼ਲਿਕਟ/. Here /ਕੋਨਫ਼ਲਿਕਟ/ is noun and /ਕਅਨ'ਫ਼ਲਿਕਟ/ is a verb.

8. If a given sound in the transcription is put in the bracket, this sound is often omitted in pronunciation, such as maladjustment /'ਮੈਲਅ'ਜਅੱਸ(ਟ)ਮਅੰਟ/.

9. English distinguishes between the initial consonantal sounds in

the pair 'vent' and 'went' which are transcribed as ਵ਼ and ਵ. A dot under ਵ has been put to make the sound of English fricative V effective possibly.

10. The tone bearing consonants of Punjabi have been transcribed in the traditional style with a diacritic mark upon them, such as gh́, jh́, ḍh́, dh́, bh́ for the common reader, although these can be transcribed as k+tone, ch+tone, ṭ+tone, t+tone and p+tone sounds (such as ḱora, ćhagg, ṭol, ṭaan and ṕaajjee respectively) for the linguists, language experts and language teachers. In the final position, they indicate high tone on the preceding vowels and aspiration form is not given, such as ਮਾਘ (maag), ਦੂਧ (dud), ਲਾਭ (laab).

11. Subscript of ਰ /r/ in the clusters of sounds has been used by adding to the bottom of the letters, such as /ਪ੍ਰ/ in ਪ੍ਰੇਮ (prem).

12. Similarly, subscript of ਹ /h/ is added to the letters ਨ੍ਹ, ਲ੍ਹ, ੜ੍ਹ to denote the high tone, such as ਚਿੰਨ੍ਹ (chinnh) sign, ਕਿਲ੍ਹਾ (kilhaa) fort, ਦ੍ਰਿੜ੍ਹਤਾ (drirhtaa) determination.

13. Subscript of ਵ (w) has also been added to the letter ਸ in some of the Sanskrit borrowings to denote the semivowel's sound, such as ਸ੍ਵਰ, ਸ੍ਵਦੇਸ਼ੀ.

14. The variations found in the vocabulary of Punjabi has also been given in one entry e.g. ਉਸਤਾਦਗੀ~ਉਸਤਾਦੀ, ਦੇਸ਼ੀ~ਦੇਖੀ, ਨਾਲਸ਼~ਨਾਲਿਸ਼.

15. The grammatical categories have also been provided after the transcribed phonetic form. But the derived forms have not been provided with the grammatical categories as a measure of economy.

ਸੰਖੇਪ (ਪੰਜਾਬੀ ਵਿਚ)
Abbreviations in Punjabi

ਅਪ੍ਰ	ਅਪ੍ਰਚਲਤ
ਇਤਿ	ਇਤਿਹਾਸਕ
ਸਿਖਿ	ਸਿਖਿਆ-ਸ਼ਾਸਤਰ
ਸੰਗੀ	ਸੰਗੀਤ
ਕਾ	ਕਾਨੂੰਨ
ਕਾਵਿ	ਕਾਵਿਕ, ਕਾਵਿ-ਸ਼ਾਸਤਰ
ਗਣਿ	ਗਣਿਤ
ਚਿਕਿ	ਚਿਕਿਤਸਾ
ਜੀਵ	ਜੀਵ-ਵਿਗਿਆਨ
ਜੋ	ਜੋਤਸ਼
ਤਰਕ	ਤਰਕ-ਸ਼ਾਸਤਰ
ਦਰਸ਼	ਦਰਸ਼ਨ-ਸ਼ਾਸਤਰ
ਧੁਨੀ	ਧੁਨੀ-ਵਿਗਿਆਨ
ਬਹੁ	ਬਹੁਵਚਨ
ਪ੍ਰਾ	ਪ੍ਰਾਚੀਨ
ਬਾਈ	ਬਾਈਬਲ
ਬੋਲ	ਬੋਲ-ਚਾਲ
ਭਾਸ਼ਾ	ਭਾਸ਼ਾ-ਵਿਗਿਆਨ
ਭੂ	ਭੂਗੋਲ
ਭੌ	ਭੌਤਕ-ਵਿਗਿਆਨ
ਮਨੋ	ਮਨੋ-ਵਿਗਿਆਨ
ਰਸਾ	ਰਸਾਇਨ-ਵਿਗਿਆਨ
ਲਾਖ	ਲਾਖਣਕ
ਵਿਆ	ਵਿਆਕਰਣ

Abbreviations in English
(Parts of speech)

a	adjective	F	French
adv	adverb	L	Latin
conj	conjunction	pl.	plural
interj	interjection	pred.	predicate
n	noun	pref.	prefix
v	verb	pron.	pronoun
aux	auxiliary	usu	usually

symbols

~ represents the first part of the entry/word.

* represents the pronunciation of 'ra'.

: represents the pronunciation of 'r'.

Phonetic Transliteration of English words in Gurmukhi Script

Effort has been made to follow the standard English pronunciation of both vowels and consonants. However, some of the exceptions and additional symbols are to be followed :

Vowel

(Initial and combined with a consonant)

ਅੰ	*a* in agenda; *u* in but; *o* in come;	ਅਜੇਂਡਾ, ਬੱਟ, ਕੰਮ
	er in maker; *e* in broken	ਮੇਕਅੰ, ਬ੍ਰੋਕਨ
ਅ*	*ear* in earth; *ir* in bird; *ere* in where	ਅ*ਥ, ਬ*ਡ, ਵੇਅ*
	or in word; *ur* in turn	ਵ*ਡ, ਟ*ਨ
ਆ	*ar* in car	ਕਾ*
ਔ	*o* in office, on, not	ਔਫਿਸ, ਔਨ, ਨੌਟ
	aw in law.	ਲੌ
ਆਇ	*i* in idea, line	ਆਇਡਅ, ਲਾਇਨ
ਅਉ	*o* in home, *oa* in boat, *ou* in mould	ਹਅਉਮ, ਬਅਉਟ, ਮਅਉਲਡ
ਆਉ	*ou* in house	ਹਾਉਸ
ਐ	*e* in egg, memory	ਐਗ, ਮੈਂਮਅਰਿ
	a in act, man, abject	ਐਕਟ, ਮੈਨ, ਐਬਜੈਕਟ
ਏਇ	*a* in age	ਏਇਜ

Consonant

ਟ and ਡ	the English *t* and *d* are neither dental nor cerebal; *t* is alveolar, *d* is a dental fricative.	
	th in theory, filth	ਥਿਅਰਿ; ਫਿਲਥ
	th in father, this	ਫਾ*ਦ, ਦਿਸ
	ng in making, kingdom	ਮੇਕਿਙ, ਕਿਙਡਮ
Si and Su	*si* in occasion,	ਅ'ਕੇਇਯ਼ਨ
	su in pleasure	ਪਲੈੱਯ਼ਅ*

Phonetic Transcription of Punjabi words in Roman Script

Vowel (ਸਵਰ)

Punjabi shape	English sign	Matra	Word	
ਅ	a	∅	ਅਮੀਰ (ameer)	ਰਸ (ras)
ਆ	aa	ਾ	ਆਸ (aas)	ਰਾਸ (raas)
ਇ	i	ਿ	ਇਕ (ik)	ਸਿਰ (sir)
ਈ	ee	ੀ	ਈਸਾ (eesaa)	ਰੀਸ (rees)
ਏ	e	ੇ	ਏਲਚੀ (elchee)	ਕੇਸ (kes)
ਐ	ae	ੈ	ਐਸ਼ (aesh)	ਖੈਰ (khair)
ਉ	u	ੁ	ਉਮਰ (umar)	ਸੁਰ (sur)
ਊ	oo	ੂ	ਊਤ (oot)	ਸੂਮ (soom)
ਓ	o	ੋ	ਓਸ (os)	ਮੋਰ (mor)
ਔ	au	ੌ	ਔਖ (aukh)	ਖੌਫ (khauf)

Consonant (ਵਿਅੰਜਨ)

Punjabi shape	English sign	Word	
ਸ	s	ਸਸ	(sas)
ਹ	h	ਹਰਮ	(haram)
ਕ	k	ਕਾਰ	(kaar)
ਖ	kh	ਖੀਰ	(kheer)
ਗ	g	ਗਰਮ	(garam)
ਘ	gh'	ਘਰ	(gh'ar)
ਙ	–		–
ਚ	ch	ਚਾਬੀ	(chaabee)
ਛ	chh	ਛੇਤੀ	(chhetee)
ਜ	j	ਜਾਪ	(jaap)
ਝ	jh'	ਝੂਠ	(jh'oot)
ਞ	nj		–

ਟ	ṭ	ਟਮਾਟਰ	(ṭmaaṭar)
ਠ	ṭh	ਠਾਠ	(ṭhaaṭ)
ਡ	ḍ	ਡਾਕ	(ḍaak)
ਢ	ḍh'	ਢਾਬਾ	(ḍh'aabaa)
ਣ	ṇ	ਲੂਣ	(looṇ)
ਤ	t	ਤੀਰ	(teer)
ਥ	th	ਥਣ	(thaṇ)
ਦ	d	ਦੂਰ	(door)
ਧ	dh'	ਧਰਮ	(dh'aram)
ਨ	n	ਨਰਮ	(naram)
ਪ	p	ਪੁੱਤ	(putt)
ਫ	ph	ਫਾਟਕ	(phaaṭak)
ਬ	b	ਬੀਬਾ	(beebaa)
ਭ	bh'	ਭੋਗ	(bh'og)
ਮ	m	ਮਸ	(mas)
ਯ	y	ਯਾਰੀ	(yaaree)
ਰ	r	ਰਸਮ	(rasam)
ਲ	l	ਲਾਲਾ	(laalaa)
ਵ	v (w)	ਵੈਰ	(vair)
ੜ	ṛ	ਮਾੜਾ	(maaṛaa)

ਪੰਜਾਬੀ-ਅੰਗਰੇਜ਼ੀ ਕੋਸ਼

ੳ

ੳ First letter of Gurmukhi alphabets, pronounced as 'uṛa'; a vowel.

ਉਸਤਤ, ਉਸਤਤਿ, ਉਸਤਤੀ (ustat, ustati, ustatee) n f Praise, appreciation, eulogy; ~ਗੀਤ Psalm.

ਉਸਤਰਾ (ustra) n m Razor, blade; ~ਫੇਰਨ To shave, to swindle.

ਉਸਤਾਦ (ustaad) n a Teacher, instructor, tutor, master; Expert; Clever, cunning, tricky.

ਉਸਤਾਦਗੀ (ustaadgee) n f Teacher-ship, tutorship, guidance, mastery, artfulness; Tact, clever-ness, prudence. Also ਉਸਤਾਦੀ

ਉਸ਼ਨਾਕ (ushnaak) a Wise, intelligent, sharp, witty, active, clever, prudent.

ਉਸ਼ਨਾਕੀ (ushnaakeė) n f Wisdom, intelligence, cleverness, prudence.

ਉਸਰਨ (usaran) n f Growth, growing.

ਉਸਰਨਾ (usarnaa) v To grow, to develop, to be built up.

ਉਸ਼ਾ (ushaa) n f Dawn.

ਉਸਾਸ (usaas) n Breath, expiration; Sigh.

ਉਸਾਰਨਾ (usaarnaa) v To construct, to build.

ਉਸਾਰਾ (usaaraa) n m Porch, vestibule, room built on top floor.

ਉਸਾਰੀ (usaaree) n Construction, structure, act of building.

ਉਰ (oh) pron He, she, it, they.

ਉਹ-ਹੋ (o'ho) interj. Oh!

ਉਹਨਾਂ (o'nā) pron They.

ਉਹਲਾ (ohlaa) n Aside, secret, curtain.

ਉਹਲੇ (ohle) n Out of side, aside, concealed, behind the scene.

ਉਹੀ, ਓਹੀ (uhi, ohi) a The same, ibid. Also ਉਹੋ

ਉਕਸਣਾ (ukasṇaa) v To be excited, to be agitated, to be kindled.

ਉਕਸਾਉਣਾ (udksaauṇaa) v To instigate, to stimulate, to excite, to kindle.

ਉਕਸਾਹਟ (uksaahaṭ) n f Excitement, instigation, stimulation, temptation.

ਉਕਤਾਉਣਾ (uktaauṇaa) v To bore, to feel melancholy, to be dejected, to be tired of, to be weary.

ਉਕਤੀ (uktee) n f Maxim, aphorism; Speech.

ਉੱਕਰ (ukkar) adv Similar, like the same, in the same way;

Engrave, inscribe.

ਉਕਰਨਾ (ukarnaa) *v* To engrave, to inscribe, to etch, to pendown.

ਉਕਰਾਈ (ukraaee) *n f* Carving, inscription or embossing, act of engraving; Wages for carving.

ਉਕੜ-ਦੁਕੜ (ukaṛ-dukaṛ) *a adv* Haphazard; Haphazardly.

ਉਕੜੂ (ukaṛoo) *a* Posture of sitting on hams with soles of feet on the ground, bent or tilted forward. Also **ਉਕੜ**

ਉੱਕਾ (ukkaa) *a* Wholly, Quite, at all; ~ਹੀ Out and out; ~ਪੁਕਾ The whole, complete, the only, in lumpsum.

ਉਕਾਉਣਾ (ukkaunaa) *v* To cause, to miss, to omit.

ਉਕਾਈ (ukaaee) *n f* Error, mistake, default, blunder, lapse, omission.

ਉੱਖਲ (ukkhal) *n m* Lubber, large wooden morter for pounding grains.

ਉਖਲੀ (ukhalee) *n f* Small wooden or stone mortar for pounding grains.

ਉਖੜਨਾ (ukharnaa) *v* To be uprooted, to be dislocated, to be dislodged, to be unhinged.

ਉਖਾੜਨਾ (ukhaarnaa) *v* To uproot, to dislocate, to disjoin, to tear up.

ਉੱਗਣਾ (uggṇaa) *v* To grow, to crop up, to germinate.

ਉਗਰ (ugar) *a* Austere; Fierce, wrathful; Intense; ~ਤਾ Fierceness, intensity, tersocity, terror, wrathfulness; ~ਵਾਦ Terrorism; ~ਵਾਦੀ Militant, terrorist, extremist.

ਉਗਰਾਹੀ (ugraahee) *n f* Collection (of donation or subscription), realization.

ਉਗਰਾਹੁਣਾ (ugraauṇaa) *v* To collect, to realize, to encash.

ਉੱਗਲਨਾ (uggalnaa) *v* To disclose, to reveal (a secret or misappropriated property).

ਉੱਗਲੱਛਣਾ (uglacchṇaa) *v* To vomit, disgorge, throw out; To disclose, to reveal (secret or misappropriated property).

ਉੱਂਗਲ (ungal) *n f* Finger; ~ਕਰਨੀ To hint, to blot, to defame.

ਉੱਂਗਲੀ (unglee) *n f* Finger; ~ਕਰਨੀ To hint, to point out, to censure; ~ਧਰਨੀ To select, to choose; ~ਫੜਨੀ To give or receive support or helping hand; ~ਮੂੰਹ ਵਿਚ ਪਾਉਣੀ To wonder, to be astonished, to be amazed.

ਉਗਾਉਣਾ (ugaauṇaa) *v* To grow, to cause, to raise.

ਉਗਾਹ (ugaah) *n m* Witness. Also ਗਵਾਹ

ਉਗਾਲ (ugaal) *n* Vomit, spit; ~ਦਾਨ Spittoon, cuspidor.

ਉਗਾਲਣਾ (ugaalṇaa) *v* To chew the cud.

ਉਗਾਲੀ (ugaaḷee) *n f* Cud; Cud-chewing, ruminating, mastication.

ਉਘਰਨਾ (ugharnaa) *v* To intimidate, to bully by showing a fist, to blow a fist in anger.

ਉਘਲਾਉਣਾ (ughlaauṇaa) *v* To doze, to slumber.

ਉਘਲਨਾ (ughalnaa) *v* To become clear, to be exposed, to be uncovered, to be disclosed, to be revealed.

ਉਂਘਾ (unghaa) *a* Famous, reputed, well-known, eminent, prominent, popular.

ਉਘਾੜ (ughaaṛ) *n m* Disclosure, exposure, divulgence, manifestation. Also ਉਘਾੜਾ

ਉਘਾੜਨਾ (Ughaaṛnaa) *v* To disclose, to expose, to lay bear, to uncover, to divulge (secret).

ਉਘੇੜਨਾ (ugheṛnaa) *v* To open (eyes or door), to uncover (deceit, conspiracy); To separate maize from cob.

ਉੱਚ (uchch) *a* Exalted, high, superior, grand; ~ਨੀਚ Up and

down, rise and fall.

ਉਚਕਟਾ (uchakṇaa) *v* To jump, to bounce, to startle.

ਉੱਚੱਕਾ (uchakkaa) *n m* Robber, thief, pickpocket.

ਉਚਕਾਉਣਾ (uchkaauṇaa) *v* To cause, to startle.

ਉਚਟਨਾ (uchatṇaa) *v* To be displeased, to grow tired, to be fed up.

ਉਚਤਮ (uchatam) *a* Superb, supreme, highest, maximum, super, excellent.

ਉੱਚਤਾ (uchchtaa) *n f* Superiority, transcendence, transcedency; ~ਭਾਵ Superiority complex.

ਉੱਚਰ (uchchar) *v* To Speak out, to utter, to spell-out.

ਉਚਰਨਾ (ucharnaa) *v* To say, to speak, to utter, to pronounce, to sermonize.

ਉਚੜਨਾ (ucharṇaa) *v* To be separated, to be bruised.

ਉਚੜਵਾਂ (Ucharvaan) *a* Movable; Portable.

ਉੱਚਾ (uchchaa) *a* Tall, high, lofty, noble, loud, elevated, eminent; ~ਸੁਨਣਾ To be hard of hearing, ~ਹਥ ਹੋਣਾ To have an upper hand, to be winning; ~ਚੜ੍ਹਨਾ To rise, to climb, ~ਨੀਵਾਂ Uneven;

~ਹੋਣਾ To pick up a quarrel, ~ਬੋਲ Tall talk. Also ਉੱਚੀ

ਉਚਾਈ (uchaaee) *n f* Height, altitude, rise, elevation, loudness.

ਉਚਾਟ (uchaat) *n m* Indifference, dejection, restlessness; ~ਹੋਣਾ To lose interest, to be indifferent, to grow tired.

ਉਚਾਰ (uchaar) *n m* Speech, utterance.

ਉਚਾਰਨ (uchaaran) *n m* Pronunciation, articulation.

ਉਚਾਲਾ (uchaalaa) *n m* Instigation.

ਉਚਾਵਾਂ (uchaavaan) *a* Portable; ~ਚੁੱਲ੍ਹਾ Portable oven, fickle minded.

ਉਚਾਵੀਂ (uchaaveen) *a* Movable.

ਉਚਿਤ (uchit) *a* Reasonable, proper, appropriate, fit, legitimate; ~ਤਾ Legitimacy, appropriateness, justification.

ਉਚੇਚ (uchech) *n m* Formality.

ਉਚੇਚਾ (uchechaa) *a adv* Special, particular, exclusive; Specially, particularly.

ਉਚੇੜਨਾ (Uchernaa) *v* To separate forcibly, to strip off, to pluck, to disunite.

ਉਛਲਣਾ (uchhalnaa) *v* To jump, to leap, to hop, to spring up.

ਉਛਾਹ (uchhaah) *n m* Enthusiasm, zeal, zest. Also ਉਤਸਾਹ

ਉਛਾਲ (Uchhaal) *n f* Buoyancy, upthrust.

ਉਛਾਲਨਾ (Uchhaalnaa) *v* To throw up, to toss up, to hurl; ਪਗੜੀ~To disgrace, to defame.

ਉਛਾਲਾ (uchhaalaa) *n m* Jump, upward, thrust.

ਉਛਾੜ (uchhaar) *n m* Cover, casing, covering, covor (for a pillow or quilt).

ਉੱਜਡ (Ujjad) *a* Rustic, unrefined, foolish, rash, clownish, inconsiderate.

ਉਜ਼ਰ (Uzar) *n f* Objection, excuse, plea; ~ਦਾਰੀ Objection filed in court.

ਉਜਰਤ (Ujarat) *n f* Remuneration, wages, emoluments, pay, fee.

ਉਜਰਤੀ (Ujaratee) *a* Paid, on wages, remunerative.

ਉਜਲ (Ujal) *a* Clear, sparking, shining, bright, radiant, brilliant, elegant; ~ਦੀਦਾਰ Good-looking, handsome, well-dressed, smart; ~ਤਾ Elegance, serenity, purity.

ਉਜਲਾ (Ujlaa) *a* Pure, clean, shining, bright, luminous, radiant.

ਉਜੜਨਾ (Ujarnaa) *v* To be destroyed or ruined, to perish, to be laid waste.

ਉਜੜ-ਪੁਜੜ (Ujar-Pujar) *n m* Vandalism.

ਉਜੜਿਆ (Ujariaa) *a* Destroyed, laid

waste, uprooted; ~ਉਜੜਿਆ ਨਗਰ Ghost town.

ਉਜਾਗਰ (Ujaagar) *a* Famous, popular, well-known, renowned, bright.

ਉਜਾਲਾ (Ujaalaa) *n m* Light, daybreak, dawn, splendour; ~ਹੋਣਾ To dawn.

ਉਜਾੜ (Ujaaṛ) *n f a* Desert, lonely place, solitude; Desolate, ruined, deserted.

ਉਜਾੜਨਾ (Ujaaṛnaa) *v* To ruin, to wreck, to destroy, to ravage, to devastate.

ਉਜਾੜਾ (ujaaṛaa) *n m* Destruction, ruination, devastation; ~ਕਰਨਾ To destroy, to lay waste, to ruin.

ਉਜਾੜੂ (ujaaṛoo) *a* Wastrel, spendthrift, extravagant, squanderer.

ਉਜੇਬਾ (Ujebaa) *a* Like that, such as, that, similar. Also ਉੱਵੇਂ

ਉੱਝ (Unjh) *adv* Otherwise.

ਉਟੇਕਣਾ (Uṭeknaa) *v* To quarrel, to strike, to hit query, question.

ਉਟਕਣਾ (Uṭaknaa) *v* To go astray.

ਉਠ (Uth) *v* Rise, stand up; ~ਖੜੋਣਾ/ ਖੜੋਣਾ To stand up, to rise, to get up, to wake up, to become alert; ~ਜਾਣਾ To go away, to run away, to die; ~ਬੈਠਣਾ To wake up, to sit

up in bed, to be well.

ਉਠਕ-ਬੈਠਕ (Uṭhak-baeṭhak) *n* Company, close acquaintance.

ਉਠਣਾ (Uṭhanaa) *v* To rise, to get up, to wake up, to stand up, to grow.

ਉਠਵਾਉਣਾ (Uṭhwaaunaa) *v* To help or cause, to carry.

ਉਠਵਾਈ (Uṭhwaaee) *n f* Wages for carrying.

ਉਠਾ (Uṭhhaa) *n m* Swelling, sore, boil, rise. Also ਉਠਾਅ

ਉਠਾਉਣਾ (Uṭhaaunaa) *v* To awaken, to carry, to remove, to suffer, to bear, to loft, to raise, to elevate. Also ਉਠਾਣਾ

ਉਠਾਊ (Uṭhaau) *n v* Move from the spot; Take it away.

ਉਠਾਈਗੀਰ (Uṭhaaeegeer) *n m* Petty thief. Also ਉਠਾਈਗੀਰਾ

ਉਡਣਾ (udnaa) *v a* To fly, to soar, to disappear, to vanish, to explode, to volatilize, to difuse in air, flying fast.

ਉਡਦੀ ਖਬਰ (Uḍdee khabar) *n f* Hearsay, rumour, uncertified report, doubtful news.

ਉਡਦੇ ਫਿਰਨਾ (Uḍde phirnaa) *v* To roam about in delight, to reel lost in delight.

ਉਡਕੇ ਲਿਆਉਣਾ (Uḍke liaaunaa) *v* To

do or bring instantly or enthusiastically.

ਉੱਡਰ (uddar) *n m* Otter.

ਉਡਵਾਉਣਾ (udvaaunaa) *v* To let fly, to cause to fly, to waste, to squander, to dissipate, to diffuse in air, to entice, to blow up, to destroy; ਗੁੱਡੀ ~ To fly the kite. Also **ਉਡਾਉਣਾ**

ਉਡਾਊ (udaaoo) *a* Spendthrift, lavish; Squanderer, extravagant.

ਉਡਾਣ (udaan) *n f* Flight.

ਉਡਾਰ (udaar) *a* Capable for flying.

ਉਡਾਰੀ (udaree) *n f* Flight, act of flying, sortie; ~ਮਾਰਨੀ To fly away, to take to flight, to disappear, to vanish.

ਉਡਾਰੂ (udaaroo) *n a* Flier, pilot, aeronaut, aviator, airman; Wilful; ~ਹੋ ਜਾਣਾ To slip away, to disappear.

ਉਡੀਕ (udeek) *n f* Wait, waiting expectation.

ਉਡੀਕਣਾ (Udeeknaa) *v* To wait, to say, to expect.

ਉਣ (un) *v* Weave, knit.

ਉਣੰਜੁਵਾਂ (unajva) *a m* Forty-nine.

ਉਣੰਜਾ (unaja) *a* Forty-nine.

ਉਣਤਾਲੀ (untalee) *a* Thrity-nine.

ਉਣਤਾਲੀਵਾਂ (untaliva) *a* Thrity-ninth.

ਉਣਤੀ (untee) *n f* Process, design or pattern of knitting, texture.

ਉਣੱਤੀ (unattee) *a* Twenty-nine.

ਉਣਨਾ (unnaa) *v* To knit, to weave.

ਉਣਵਾਈ (unavaaee) *n f* Knitting, weaving, wages for knitting or weaving. Also **ਉਣਾਈ**

ਉਣਾਸੀ (unaasee) *a* Seventy-nine.

ਉਣਾਹਠ (unaath) *a* Fifty-nine.

ਉਣਾਨਵੇਂ (unaanve) *a* Eighty-nine.

ਉਤਸਵ (uttasav) *n m* Festival, function, festivity, fete, rejoicing; Occasion, opportunity.

ਉਤਸਾਹ (utsaah) *n m* Zeal, zest, incentive, enthusiasm, eagerness; ~ਜਨਕ Encouraging, inspiring, inspirational; ~ਦੇਣਾ/ਵਧਾਉਣਾ To inspire, to enthuse, to encourage; ~ਭੰਗ Discouraging, demoralising, demoralisation.

ਉਤਸੁਕ (utasuk) *a* Keen, eager, curious.

ਉਤਸੁਕਤਾ (utasuktaa) *n f* Curiosity, eagerness, yearning, keeness.

ਉਤਕੰਠਾ (utakanthaa) *n f* Longing, craving, passion, solitude.

ਉਤਪਤੀ (utpatee) *n f* Birth, production, reproduction, origin, growth, derivation.

ਉਤਪੰਨ (utpann) *a* Created, born, produced; ~ਹੋਣਾ To grow, to comeforth, to take berth.

ਉਤਪਾਤ (utpaat) *n m* Cicisbeo.

ਉਤਪਾਦਕ (utpaadak) *n a m* Producer;

Productive, generative.

ਉਤਪਾਦਨ (utpaadan) *n m* Production, output.

ਉੱਤਮ (uttam) *a* Good, of good quality, best, highest, top, perfect, supreme, superior, excellent, superb; **~ਪੁਰਖ** (gr.) First person.

ਉੱਤਰ (uttar) *v m n* Get down; Answer, reply; **ਸੋੜਵੇਂ~** Replication, retort.

ਉੱਤਰ (uttar) *n m* North.

ਉਤਰ-ਅਧਿਕਾਰੀ (uttar-adhikaree) *n m* Descendant, successor, inheritor.

ਉਤਰਦਾਇਕ (uttardaayik) *a* Answerable, accountable, responsible. Also **ਉਤਰਾਦਾਈ**

ਉਤਰਨਾ (utarnaa) *v* To descend, to dismount, to disembark, to come down, to diminish, to decrease, to fall in value, to decay, to fade, to be copied, to subside.

ਉਤਰਵਰਤੀ (utarvartee) *a* Subsequent, latter; successor.

ਉਤਰਵਾਈ (utarvaaee) *n f* Wages or act of bringing down or unloading, unloading.

ਉਤਰਾਉ (utraau) *n f* Inclination, slope, descent.

ਉਤਰਾਅ-ਚੜ੍ਹਾਅ (utraa-charaa) *n m* Fluctuation, rise and fall.

ਉਤਰਾਈ (utraaee) *n f* Decline, declination, regress, descent, slope.

ਉਤਰਾਧਿਕਾਰ (utraadhikaar) *n m* Inheritence.

ਉਤਰਾਧਿਕਾਰੀ (utraadhikaaree) *n m* Successor.

ਉਤਰਾਧੀ (utraadhee) *a* Belonging to the north.

ਉਤਰਾਰਧ (utraaradh) *a m* Latter-half.

ਉਤਰੀ (utree) *a* Northern, northly.

ਉੱਤਰੋਤਰ (utrottar) *a adv* Successive, successively .

ਉਤਲਾ (utlaa) *a* Upper, over and above the income, additional; External, outward; **~ਦਿਲੋਂ** Superficially, insincerely, in a light manner. Also **ਉਤਲੇ**

ਉਤਾਣਾ (utaanaa) *v* To lie facing downward or upside down.

ਉਤਾਰ (utaar) *n m* Fall, slope, decline, descent, decrease, reduction; **~ਚੜ੍ਹਾਓ** Ups and downs, ascent and descent, rise and fall.

ਉਤਾਰਨਾ (utaarnaa) *v* To copy, to help in descending, to cast off, to take off, to degrade, to lower, to bring down, to unload, to dismount, to dethrone, to remove, to dislocate, to cause, to disembark.

ਉਤਾਰਾ (utaaraa) *n m a* Copy, halting place, stage (Journey), a bent upon, determined, intent, dead set, ready for; ~**ਕਰਨਾ** To stay, to sojourn, to prepare a copy; ~**ਕਰਾਉਣਾ** To lodge, to accommodate, to get a copy made.

ਉਤਾਰੂ (utaroo) *n a* Hurry, haste, hastiness, impatience; Impatient, anxious, rash, speedy, quick, hasty, swift, one who can do things quickly.

ਉਤਾੜ (utaaṛ) *n m* Upstream, upland, highland, elevated region.

ਉੱਤੇ (utte) *prep* Upon, on, over, above, upward, on the top.

ਉਤੇਜਕ (utejak) *a* Stimulant, stimulating, exciting, provocating, provocative, inspiring.

ਉਤੇਜਨਾ (utejnaa) *n f* Excitement, provocation, stimulation, inspiration.

ਉਤੇੜਨਾ (uteṛnaa) *v* To dilate.

ਉੱਤੋਂ (utton) *prep* From above.

ਉਥਲ-ਪੁਥਲ (uthal-puthal) *n f* Upheaval, turmoil.

ਉਥਲਣਾ (uthalṇaa) *v* To turn over.

ਉਥਾਈਂ (uthaaeen) *a* Exactly there, there, at that very place.

ਉਥਾਨ (uthaan) *n m* Pitch, rise; ~**ਪਤਨ** Fluctuation, rise and fall.

ਉਥਾਨਕਾ (uthaankaa) *n m* Preface, foreword, introduction, prelude.

ਉਥਾਪਨ (uthaapan) *n m* Dissolution.

ਉਥਾਪਣਾ (uthaapaṇaa) *v* To transplant.

ਉਥੇ (uthe) *adv* At that place, there, over there.

ਉਥੋਂ (uthon) *adv* From there, from that place.

ਉਦਕ (udak) *n m* Water.

ਉਦਕਰਥ (udkarath) *n* Creation.

ਉਦਗਮ (udgam) *n m* Origin, rising, upcoming.

ਉਦਗਾਰ (udgaar) *n m* Inner feelings, sentiments.

ਉਦਘਾਟਨ (udghaaṭan) *n m* Inauguration, opening, ceremony; ~**ਕਰਤਾ** Inaugurator, release, uncovering; ~**ਕਰਨਾ** To inaugurate, to declare open, to expose, to exhibit, to bring to view.

ਉੱਦਘਾਟਨੀ (udghaatanee) *a* Inauguratory, inaugural; ~**ਭਾਸ਼ਨ** Inaugural speech.

ਉਦਮ (udaṁ) *n m* Effort, exertion, endeavour, industry, diligence.

ਉਦਮੀ (udamee) *a* Industrious, enterprising, diligent.

ਉਦਯੋਗ (udyog) *n m* Industry, enterprise.

ਉਦਯੋਗਿਕ (udyogik) *a* Industrial.

ਉਦਯੋਗੀ (udyogee) *n m* Industrialist.

ਉਦਰ (udar) *n m* Abdomen, belly, womb, stomach, livelihood.

ਉਦਰੇਵਾਂ (udarevaan) *n m* Homesickness; Longing, yearning.

ਉਦਾਸ (udaas) *a* Sad, dejected, sorrowful, disconsolate, sullen, dull, rueful.

ਉਦਾਸੀ (udaasee) *n f* Sadness, cheerlessness, sorrow, depression, dejection, melancholy.

ਉਦਾਸੀਨ (udaaseen) *a* Neutral, apathetic.

ਉਦਾਸੀਨਤਾ (udaaseentaa) *n f* Apathy, depression, dejection etc.

ਉਦਾਹਰਣ (udaaharaṇ) *n m* Example, illustration, instance.

ਉਦਾਤ (udaat) *a n* Sublime.

ਉਦਾਤੀਕਰਣ (udaateekaraṇ) *n m* Sublimation; ~ਕਰਨਾ To sublimate.

ਉਦਾਰ (udaar) *a* Liberal, generous, large hearted, open minded, bounteous, bountiful, benevolent, humane; ~ਤਾ Magnaminity, catholicity, liberality, bounty; ~ਵਾਦ Liberalism; ~ਵਾਦੀ Liberal, Liberalist.

ਉਦਾਲਾ (udaalaa) *n m* Environment, neighbourhood, surroundings.

ਉਦਿਆਨ (udiyaan) *n m* Garden, orchard, forest; Solitude, deserted place.

ਉਦੇ (ude) *n m* Rising, dawn; ~ਹੋਣਾ To rise.

ਉਦੇਸ਼ (udesh) *n m* Aim, purpose.

ਉਦੇਸ਼ਾਤਮਕ (udeshaatmak) *a* Purposive, purfroseful, teteological.

ਉਦੋਂ (udon) *adv* Then, at that time; ~ਕਾ Since then, from that time.

ਉਧਰ (udhar) *adv* There, on that side, in that direction, yonder ; ~ਤੋਂ From that side.

ਉਧਰਣ (udharaṇ) *n m* Deliverance, redemption, salvation.

ਉਧਰਨਾ (udharnaa) *v* To be redeemed, to be rescued, to attain salvation, to be liberated.

ਉਧਰਿਤ (udharit) *a* Based, on the basis of.

ਉਧਰੋਂ (udhron) *adv* From that side, from there.

ਉਧਲਣਾ (udhalṇaa) *v* To run away with some one to elope.

ਉਧੜਨਾ (udharnaa) *v* To be unsewn, to be encorded, to be unstitched, to be unravelled, to be unstrung, to be ripped.

ਉਧੜਵਾਉਣਾ (udharvaauṇaa) *v* To get unstitched, to get uncorded.

ਉਧੜਾਈ (udharaaee) *n f* Wages for

unstitching or uncording, act of unstitching or uncording.

ਉਧਾਰ (udhaar) *n a m* Loan, credit; ~**ਦੇਣਾ** To give on credit; To loan; ~**ਲੈਣਾ** To take on credit, to borrow; ~**ਪੱਟਾ** Debenture.

ਉਧਾਰਾ (udhaaraa) *a* On loan, borrowed.

ਉੱਧਾਰ (uddhaar) *n m* Salvation, redemption, deliverance; Reformation, uplift; ~**ਕਰਨਾ** To redeem, to uplift; ~**ਨਾ** To liberate, to redeem, to discharge, to save.

ਉਧਾਲਣਾ (udhaalṇaa) *v* To abduct, to kidnap, to seduce.

ਉਧਾਲਾ (udhaalaa) *n m* Elopement, abduction, act of running away with someone.

ਉਧੇੜਬੁਣ (udherbuṇ) *n m* Indecision, planning indecisively, perplexity.

ਉਧੇੜਨਾ (udhernaa) *v* To unsew, to remove the seams, to unravel, to rip, to unweave, to undo.

ਉੱਨ (un) *n f* Wool; ~**ਵਰਗਾ** Woolly.

ਉਨਸ (unas) *n f* Attachment, love, sociability.

ਉਨਸਰੀ (unasaree) *n f* A fruit of blackberry, *Rubus flavus*; A fruit of yellow berry, *Rubus fructicosa*.

ਉੱਨਤ (unnat) *a* Developed, thriving, ameliorated, improved,

advanced.

ਉਨਤੀ (unati) *n m* Uplift, progress, advancement, evolution, improvement, development, amelioration; ~**ਸ਼ੀਲ** Progressive, growing, developing; ~**ਕਰਨੀ** To progress, to improve, to develop, to rise, to thrive, to advance.

ਉਨੱਤੀ (unattee) *a* Twenty-nine.

ਉਨਮੱਤ (unmatt) *a* Intoxicated, frenzied, insane.

ਉਨਮਨਾ (unmanaa) *a* Absent-minded, agitated; ~**ਅਵਸਥਾ** A stage of mind (according to yoga).

ਉਨਮਾਦ (unmaad) *n m* Insanity, frenzy intoxication.

ਉਨਾਬੀ (unnabi) *a* Maroon.

ਉੱਨੀ (unni) *a* Nineteen.

ਉ ਨੀਂਦਾ (uneendaa) *n m* Sleeplessness, insomnia.

ਉਨੀਵਾਂ (univān) *a* Nineteenth. Also **ਉਨੀਆਂ**

ਉਨ੍ਹਾਂ (unaan) *pr* Them, those.

ਉਨ੍ਹਾਲਾ (unhaalaa) *n m* Summer, hot weather.

ਉਪ (upa) *a* (*Prefix for*) Deputy, Vice, Sub-, *Pre;* ~**ਅੰਗ** Appendage; ~**ਸਰਗ** Prefix; ~**ਕਲਪਟਾ** Hypothesis.

ਉਪਸੰਹਾਰ (upsanhaar) *n m* Denouement, end.

ਉਪਸਥਿਤ (upasthit) *a* Present.

ਉਪਸਥਿਤਿ (upasthiti) *n f* Presence, attendance.

ਉਪਹਾਸ (uphaas) *n m* Joke, jest, ridicule, satire.

ਉਪਹਾਸੀ (uphaasee) *a* Satirical, ridiculous, jovial.

ਉਪਹਾਰ (uphaar) *n m* Present, gift.

ਉਪਕਰਣ (upkaran) *n m* Instrument, apparatus.

ਉਪਕਾਰ (upkaar) *a* Beneficence, kindness, help, assistance; Benefactor, philanthrope, benevolent.

ਉਪਖੇਤਰ (upkhetar) *n m* Sub-area.

ਉਪਗ੍ਰਹਿ (upgreh) *n m* Satellite, moon.

ਉਪਚਾਰ (upchaar) *n m* Treatment remedy.

ਉਪਚਾਰੀ (upchaaree) *a n* Remedial; Fellow who treats or administers treatment.

ਉਪਚੇਤਨ (upchetan) *a* Subconscious.

ਉਪਜ (upaj) *n f* Produce, crop, yield, result, product, out-turn, out-put, growth, original idea.

ਉਪਜਣਾ (upajnaa) *v* To grow, to be born, to shoot forth, to originate.

ਉਪਜਾਉਣਾ (upjaaunaa) *v* To produce, to cultivate.

ਉਪਜਾਊ (upjaaoo) *a* Fertile, rich, productive, vegetative, fecund; ~ਪਣ Producer, cultivator.

ਉਪਜੀਵਕਾ (upjeevakaa) *n f* Vocation, profession, livelihood, subsistence.

ਉਪੱਦਰ (upaddar) *n m* Tyranny, oppression, turbulence, crime, persecution, outrage, rowdyism.

ਉਪੱਦਰੀ (upaddaree) *a n* Rowdy, mischievous; Rioter.

ਉਪਦੇਸ਼ (updesh) *n m* Precept, teaching, preaching, advice, counsel, lecture, sermon; ~ਦੇਣਾ To sermonise, to teach, to lecture, to preach, to advise; ~ਵਾਦ Didacticism; ~ਕ Lecturer, sermonizer, preceptor, preacher; ~ਣ (fem) Lecturer.

ਉਪਧਾਰਾ (updhaaraa) *n* Sub-clause.

ਉਪਨਗਰ (upnagar) *n m* Suburb; suburban.

ਉਪਨਾਮ (upnaam) *n m* Nick name, alias, surname.

ਉਪਨਿਆਸ (Upaniyaas) *n m* Novel, fiction; ~ਕਾਰ Novelist, fiction writer; ~ਕਾਰੀ Fiction-writing.

ਉਪਨਿਯਮ (upniyam) *n m* Subrule.

ਉਪਨਿਵੇਸ਼ (upnivesh) *n m* Colony; ~ਵਾਦ Colonialism.

ਉਪਭੋਗ (upbhog) *n m* Consumption; ~ਕਰਨਾ To consume; ~ਤਾ Consumer.

ਉਪਮਾ (upmaa) *n f* Comparison,

simile, analogy; Praise, eulogy.

ਉਪਮਾਉਨਾ (upmaaunaa) *v* To compare; To praise, to eulogize.

ਉਪਮਾਨ (upmaan) *n m* (poetics) That with which comparison is made.

ਉਪਯੋਗ (upyog) *n m* Use, utilisation.

ਉਪਯੋਗਤਾ (upyogtaa) *n f* Utility service, usefulness; ~**ਵਾਦ** Utilitarianism; ~**ਵਾਦੀ** Utilitarian.

ਉਪਯੋਗੀ (upyogee) *adv* Useful, serviceable.

ਉਪਰ (upar) *adv* Above, up, upon, on, over, on the top; ~**ਸੁੱਟਣਾ** To toss, to throw up; ~**ਚੜ੍ਹਨਾ** To climb, to ascend, to rise; ~**ਤੋਂ** From above; Successively, continuously, one after the other; ~**ਥੱਲੇ ਕਰਨਾ** To scatter things, to disarrange; ~**ਵਲ** Upwards.

ਉਪਰੰਤ (uprant) *adv* After, next, since, afterwards.

ਉਪਰਲਾ (uparlaa) *a* Upper, extra; External, superficial, outward; ~**ਖਰਚਾ** Overhead cost or expenses. Also **ਉਪਰਲੀ**

ਉਪਰੀ ਆਮਦਨ (upree aamdan) *n f* Tips, income through unfair means, income in addition to salary.

ਉਪਰਲੇ (uparle) *a* Extra, overhead (charges), seniors.

ਉਪਰਾਉ (Upraau) *n m* Aloofness, estrangement.

ਉਪਰਾਉਨਾ (upraaunaa) *v* To estrange, to make oneself appear, a stranger, to stand aloof.

ਉਪਰਾਮ (upraam) *a* Despondent, sick, disgusted, dejected, disconsolate; ~**ਹੋਣਾ** To become sad, to be distracted, to turn one's, mind from the material objects; ~**ਤਾ** Sadness, despondency, distraction, act of turning one's mind from the world despair.

ਉਪਰਾਲਾ (upraalaa) *n m* Effort; Suggestion, means, method.

ਉਪਰੋਂ (upron) *adv* From above; ~**ਉਪਰੋਂ** Formally, as a formality; ~ **ਲੰਘ ਜਾਣਾ** To run over; To supersede.

ਉਪਲਾ (uplaa) *n m* Dried cake of cow-dung. Also **ਪਾਥੀ**

ਉਪੜਨਾ (uparnaa) *v* To reach, to arrive.

ਉਪਾਉ (upaau) *n m* Remedy; Step; Means, measures, contrivance, plan.

ਉਪਾਸ਼ਕ (upaashak) *n m* Worshipper, adorer, devotee

ਉਪਾਸ਼ਨਾ (upaashnaa) *n f* Worship, devotion, adoration.

ਉਪਖਿਆਨ (upakhiaan) *n m* Legend, anecdote, episode.

ਉਪਾਧ (upaadh) *n* Trouble, riots, upheaval.

ਉਪਾਧਿਆਇ (upaadhiai) *n m* Spiritual, preceptor, teacher.

ਉਪਾਧੀ (upaadhee) *n f* Degree, epithet, nick-name, title, designation; ~ਦਾ Root of the trouble, basis of the upheaval.

ਉਪਾਰਜਿਤ (upaarjit) *a* Acquired.

ਉਪਾਰਨਾ (upaarnaa) *v* To break (fast).

ਉਪਾਵਣਹਾਰ (upaavanhaar) *n* Creator, maker.

ਉਪੇਖਿਆ (upekhiaa) *n f* Neglect, negligence, ingoring, disregard.

ਉਫ (uf) *int* oh! alas!

ਉਫਰਾਉ (ufraau) *a* Swellings, rising.

ਉਫਲਨਾ (ufalnaa) *v* To rebound, to spring.

ਉਬਸਨਾ (ubasnaa) *v* To putrefy, to become mouldy

ਉਬਸਾਉਨਾ (ubasaaunaa) *v* To cause to putrefy.

ਉਬਕ (ubak) *n m* Vomit.

ਉਬਾਕੀ (ubaakee) *n f* Vomit, vomiting.

ਉਬਕਾਈ (ubkaaee) *n f* Retching, nausea.

ਉਬਲਨਾ (ubalnaa) *n a* To boil, to be boiled, to simmer, to bubble, to be enraged.

ਉਬਲਦਾ (ubaldaa) *a v* Ebullient, boiling, very hot; To cause to boil.

ਉਬਾਸੀ (ubaasee) *n f* Yawn, gape.

ਉਬਾਕ (ubaak) *n f a* Retching, vomitting sensation; Spasm; Nausea.

ਉਬਾਕਨਾ (ubaakanaa) *v* To retch; To vomit, to regurgitate.

ਉਬਾਰ (ubaar) *v m* Deliverance, liberation, upward projection.

ਉਬਾਰਨਾ (ubaarnaa) *v* To deliver, to liberate, to lift or project upward, to salvage, to redeem.

ਉਬਾਲ (ubaal) *n m* Ebullition, boiling simmering, spurt, Passion; ~ਉਠਨਾ/ਆਉਨਾ To boil, rising of passions or sentiments.

ਉਬਾਲਨਾ (ubaalnaa) To boil, boiling.

ਉਭਾਰਨਾ (ubh'arnaa) *v* To swell, to rase; To boil over; To excite; To bounce; To bulge; To heave, to protrude; To make prominent.

ਉਭਰਵਾਂ (ubharvaā) *a* Protruding, bulging, swollen, embossed.

ਉਭਰਿਆ (ubhariaa) *v a* Risen, protructed, boiled over; ~ਧੈਂਦਾ Flanged bottom.

ਉਭੜਵਾਹੇ (ubharvaahe) *adv* With a start; Spontaneously.

ਉਭਾ (ubhaa) *n a* East, short (breath); ~ਸਾਹ Groan, sigh.

ਉਭਾਸਰਨਾ (ubhaasarnaa) *v* To speak out, to speak up, to spell out ones trouble moaringly.

ਉਭਾਨ (ubhaan) *n* Tree *Populus eupharatica.*

ਉਭਾਰ (ubhaar) *n m* Prominence, swelling, profuberance, bulge, rise, boil; Bossing.

ਉਭਾਰਨਾ (ubhaarnaa) *v* To excite, to swell, to raise, to arouse, to rouse, to incite, to instigate.

ਉਮਸ (umas) *n f* Sultriness, mugginess.

ਉਮੰਗ (umang) *n f* Ambition, hope, passion, longing, desire, exultation.

ਉਮਡਣਾ (umadṇaa) *v* To overflow, to overwhelm, to swell, to gush out, to gather quickly.

ਉਮਤ (umat) *n m* Followers, people of the same belief, off spring, pupils.

ਉਮਦਾ (umdaa) *a* Better, good, nice.

ਉਮਰ (umar) *n f* Age, lifetime, life; ~ਢਲਣੀ To age; ~ਕੈਦ Life sentence; ~ਕੈਦੀ Life convict; ~ਪਟਾ Lease for life; ~ਭਰ (ਸਾਰੀ ਉਮਰ) For life, through out life.

ਉਮਰਾ (ਉਮਰਾਉ) (umraa) *n* Courtiers, nobes.

ਉੱਮੁਲਣਾ (ummalṇaa) *v* To gush out, to spring forth.

ਉਮਾਹ (umaah) *n m* Ambition, excessive joy, exuberance.

ਉਮੀ (umee) *a* Illiterate, uneducated.

ਉਮੀਆ (umeeaa) *n m* Wheat or barley roasted in the ear.

ਉਮੀਦ (umeed) *n f* Hope, confidence, expectation, reliance; ~(ਉਮੀਦਾਂ) ਤੇ ਪਾਣੀ ਫਿਰਨਾ All hopes to be dashed to the ground. Also ਉਮੈਦ

ਉਮੀਦਵਾਰ (Umeedvaar) *n m* Candidate, applicant, expectant, hopeful.

ਉਮੀਦਵਾਰੀ (Umeedvaaree) *n f* Hopefulness, pregnancy, expectancy.

ਉਰ (ur) *n m* Heart, breast, bosom.

ਉਰਸਾ (ursaa) *n m* A stone on which a brahmin grinds sandalwood.

ਉਰਲ-ਪਰਲ (ural-paral) *n m* (articles) Superfluous, meaningless, additional; ~ਕੰਮ Superfluous work.

ਉਰਲਾ (urlaa) *a* Belonging to this side, on the nearer side. Also ਉਰਲੀ

ਉਰਵਾਰ (urvaar) *prep* On this side; ~ਪਾਰ Through to the other side, across.

ਉਰਾਂ (uraan) *a* On this side, here, higher, nearer.

ਉਰੇ (ure) *adv* Here, near, on this side; ~ਪਰੇ Out of the way, hidden; ~ਪਰੇ ਹੋਣਾ To elope, to be somewhere nearby, to go or be out of sight, to hide, to go underground.

ਉਰਾਰ (uraar) *n m* On this bank or nearer side of a river or canal or pitch or tank etc.

ਉਰਿਓਂ (uriōn) *adv* From a nearer place.

ਉਰੇਰੇ (urere) *adv* A little on this side, a little nearer.

ਉਲਕਾ (ulkaa) *n* Meteor. Also **ਉਲਕਾਪਾਤ**

ਉਲੰਘਨਾ (ulanghnaa) *n f* Violation, contravention; Transgression, intringement, contravention; ~**ਕਰਨੀ** To violate, to transgress, to intringe, to contravene.

ਉਲਝਨ (uljhaṇ) *n f* Tangle, complication, confusion, fix, intricacy, entanglement, dilemma, perplexity.

ਉਲਝਨਾ (uljhṇaa) *v* To be involved or entangled, to be confused or puzzled, to dispute, to enter into a dispute.

ਉਲਝਾਉ (uljhaau) *n m* Entanglement, involvement, involution, confusion, perplexity.

ਉਲਝਾਉਣਾ (uljhaauṇaa) *v* To entangle to complicate, to involve, to confuse, to perplex.

ਉਲਟ (ulaṭ) *n a m* Inverse, reverse, change inversion, Opposite, reversed, contrary; ~**ਜਾਣਾ** To be turned over, to capsize; ~**ਤੋਰ ਤੇ**

Conversely; ~**ਪੁਲਟ** Upside down, topsy turvy, in disorderly manner; ~**ਪੈਠੀ ਪਰਤ** To return without a pause; ~(**ਉਲਟੇ**) **ਬਾਂਸ ਬਰੇਲੀ ਨੂੰ** To carry coal to new castle.

ਉਲਟਣਾ (ulaṭṇaa) *v* To upset, to invert, to reverse, to turn upside down, to be upset, to be inverted.

ਉਲਟਵਾਂ (ulaṭvaan) *a* Inversive. Also **ਉਲਟਵੀਂ**

ਉਲਟਾ (ulṭaa) *a adv* Opposite, converse reversed, overturned, inverse, inverted; On the contrary; ~**ਸਮਝਣਾ** To misunderstand; ~**ਚਲਾਉਣਾ** To drive backward; ~**ਚੋਰ ਕੋਤਵਾਲ ਨੂੰ ਡਾਂਟੇ** The case of thief threatening a policeman; ~**ਜਮਾਨਾ** Preposterous times; ~**ਤਵਾ** Jet black, coal black.

ਉਲਟਾਉ (ultaau) *n m* Inversion, overturning.

ਉਲਟਾਉਣਾ (ultaaunaa) *v* To reverse, to invert, to upset, to overturn, to interchange; ~**ਪੁਲਟਾਉਣਾ** Topsy turvy, disconnected.

ਉਲਟੀ (ulṭee) *n f a* Vomit; Contrary, capsized, overturned, inverted upside down, inverse, inside out; ~**ਕਰਨੀ** To vomit; ~**ਪੱਟੀ ਪੜ੍ਹਾਉਣੀ** To mislead, to misguide, to poison the mind; ~**ਮਾਲਾ ਫੇਰਨੀ** To invoke a curse; ~ਉਲਟੀ ਸਮਝ Perverted mind, perversion; ~ਸਿੱਧੀ Absurd, irrelevant; ~ ਸੁਣਾਉਣਾ To insult, to scold, to revile.

ਉਲਥਾ (ulthaa) *n m* Translation, rendering version; ~ਕਰਨਾ To translate, to interpret, to render; ~ਕਾਰ Translator.

ਉਲੱਦਣਾ (uladdṇaa) *v* To pour, to invert, to overturn, to reveal (the secrets).

ਉਲਫ਼ਤ (ulfat) *n f* Love.

ਉਲਰਨਾ (ularnaa) *a* To tilt, to sway, to lurch, to lean, to be off-balance, to bound.

ਉਲਰਵਾਂ (ularvaan) *a* Tipped, off-balance.

ਉਲਰਿਆ (ulariaa) *a* Tilted, off-balance.

ਉਲਾਹਮਾ (ulahmaa) *n m* Reproof, complaint, blame. Also ਉਲਾਂਭਾ

ਉਲਾਹੁਣਾ (ulaahuṇaa) *v* To mourn for the dead.

ਉਲਾਂਘ (ulaangh) *n f* Jump, pace, stride, long step.

ਉਲਾਰ (ulaar) *a n m* unbalanced, off balance, tilted, depressed by weight on oneside, lopsided, raised in a threatening manner; Tilt, inclination.

ਉਲਾਰਨਾ (ulaarnaa) *v* To tilt, to sway.

ਉੱਲੀ (ullee) *n f* Fungus, mould,

mildew.

ਉਲੀਕਣਾ (uleekṇaa) *v* To draw, to outline, to sketch, to trace, to portray.

ਉੱਲੂ (ulloo) *n m* Owl; Foolish, simpleton; ~ਸਿੱਧਾ ਕਰਨਾ To grind one's own axe, to take some work; ~ਦਾ ਪੱਠਾ Idiot, dullard, an arrant fool, silly fellow, fool; ~ਬਣਨਾ To be fooled; ~ਬੋਲਣੇ To be deserted (place).

ਉਲੇਹੜਨਾ (uleharnaa) *v* To hem.

ਉਵੇਂ (ooven) *adv* Likewise, so, similarly, by the way, in that way.

ਉੜਦ (uṛad) *n f* Horse bean.

ਉੜਾਕ (oṛaak) *a* Haughty, insolent, disrespectful.

ਊਸ਼ਾ (ushaa) *n f* Early morning, redness of dawn.

ਊਗਲ (ugal) *n f* Buckwheat.

ਊਂਘ (oongh) *n f* Doze, slumber.

ਊਂਘਣਾ (oonghṇaa) *v* To doze, to feel sleepy, to slumber.

ਊਜ (ooj) *n f* Imputation, blame, aspersion, allegation.

ਊਜਣ (oojaṇ) *n f* Grain, *Hordeum caeleste.*

ਊਟ-ਪਟਾਂਗ (oot-paṭaang) *n* Nonsense, irrelevant or absurd talk.

ਊਠ (ooṭh) *n m* Camel; ~ਦੇ ਮੂੰਹ ਜੀਰਾ A drop in the ocean; ~ਕਿਸ ਕਰਵਟ

ਬੈਠਦਾ ਹੈ Wait and see how things turn out.

ਉਠਕ-ਬੈਠਕ (ooṭhak-baeṭhak) *n f* Sitting and standing, sit-ups.

ਉਠਨੀ (ooṭhnee) *n f* Dromedary, she camel.

ਉੂਣ (ooṇ) *n f* Deficiency, shortage.

ਉੂਣਤਾਈ (ooṇtaaee) *n f* Flaw, defect, shortcoming lack.

ਉੂਣਾ (ooṇaa) *a* Deficient, defective, incomplete.

ਉੂਤ (oot) *a* Foolish, stupid, rude, childless; ~ਜਾਣਾ To die issueless; ~ਪੁਣਾ Foolishness, stupidity.

ਉੂਦ (ood) *n f* Aloe, Eaglewood.

ਉੂਦ-ਬਞਾਉ (ood-balaau) *n m* Otter, an aquatic cat.

ਉੂਦਾ (ooda) *a* Violet, of the colour of a brinjal.

ਉੂਧਮ (oodham) *n m* Uproar, agitation, noise, revolt, rebellion, disturbance, furore, riot, pandemonium, turmoil; ~ਮਚਾਉਣਾ To create disturbance, to make noise, to agitate.

ਉੁੱਧਾ (oondhaa) *a* Overturned, upside down.

ਉੂਰਜਾ (oorjaa) *n f* Energy, power.

ਉੂਰਾ (ooraa) *a n m* Incomplete, uneducated; Reel, bobbin, winder, windlass. Also ਉੂਰੀ

ਉੂਲ-ਜਲੂਲ (ool-jalool) *a* Senseless (talk),

nonsense, absurd.

ਉੂੜਾ-ਐੜਾ (oora-aera) *n m* Alphabets; ~ਨਾ ਜਾਣਨਾ To be illiterate, to be unlettered, to be ignorant.

ਓਅੰਕਾਰ (ounkaar) *n m* God, Saviour of all.

ਓਹਦਾ (ōda) *pron* Same as ਓਸਦਾ

ਓਹਲਾ (ōla) *n m* cover, veil, screen, protection, support, refuge; Privacy, secrecy.

ਓਹਲਾ (ohlaa) *n m* Cover, secret, refuge, protection; ~ਕਰਨਾ To conceal, to keep secret; ~ਦੇਣਾ To give refuge, to keep secret.

ਓਹੜ-ਪੋਹੜ (ohar-pohar) *n m* First aid.

ਓਹੋ (oho) *pron* The same, the very fellow.

ਓਕ (ok) *n f* Cuplike shape of a hand to drink water.

ਓਕੜਾ (okraa) *a* Strong, headstrong.

ਓਗਰਾ (ograa) *n m* A type of coarse grain; Rice-water.

ਓਛਾ (ochhaa) *a* Mean, narrow-minded, undignified, shallow.

ਓਝਰੀ (ojhree) *n f* Stomach, intenstine.

ਓਝਲ (ojhal) *a* Behind the scene, out of sight, concealed; Retirement; ~ਹੋਣਾ To disappear, to be out of sight; ~ਕਰਨਾ To conceal.

ਓਝਾ (ojhaa) *n m* Occultist, necromanner, witch doctor.

ਓਟ (oṭ) *n f* Protection, shelter, refuge, shadow, screen, partition.

ਓਟਣਾ (otṇaa) *v* To shelter, to give refuge; To confess (to a crime), to accept responsibllity (for a crime).

ਓਥੇ (othe) *adv* There, at the place.

ਓਥੋਂ (otheōn) *adv* From there.

ਓਦਨ (odaṇ) *adv* On that day.

ਓਦਰਨਾ (odarnaa) *v* To become sad in separation, to become eager, to meet, to long for, to yearn.

ਉਦਰੇਵਾਂ (udervaan) *n m* Longing for meeting depression as a result of separation from a dear relation, homesickness.

ਓਦਾਂ (odaan) *adv* Like that, in that way; otherwise.

ਓਦੋਂ (oden) *adv* Then, at that time.

ਓਪਰਲਾ (oparlaa) *adv* Belonging to the other side.

ਓਪਰਾ (opraa) *a* Stranger, unfamiliar, outsider, alien; ~ਪਣ Otherness strangeness, unfamiliarity, alienation.

ਓਭੜ (ōbhaṛ) *a* Unknown, stranger.

ਓਲਾ (oḷa) *n m* Hail-stone.

ਓੜਨੀ (orṇee) *n f* Cover, headgear, veil, wrapper.

ਅ

ਅ Vowel, second letter of Gurmukhi letter pronounced as airaa.

ਅਉਸਰ (ausar) *n m* Opportunity occasion, time.

ਅਉਗੁਣ (augun) *n m* Vice, fault, defect, shortcoming.

ਅਉਤ (aut) *a* Issueless, rude.

ਅਉਧ (audh) *n f* Term, tenure, age, life span.

ਅਇਆਨਾ (aiaanaa) *a m* Infant, child, ignorant, innocent.

ਅਇਆਲੀ (aiaalee) *n m* Shepherd.

ਅੰਸ (ansh) *n m* Part, constituent, degree, numerator.

ਅੰਸ (ans) *n f* Progeny, lineal descendant, offspring, progeny.

ਅਸ਼ਕ (ashak) *n m* Tear.

ਅੰਸ਼ਕਾਲੀ (anshkaalee) *a* Part time.

ਅਸੰਖ (asankh) *a* Countless, infinite, innumerable.

ਅਸੰਗਤ (asangat) *a* Irrelevant, inconsistant, incoherant.

ਅਸ਼ੱਗਨ (ashaggan) *n m* Ill omen, inauspicious omen.

ਅਸਚਰਜ (ascharaj) *n a m* Wonder, astonishment; Wonderful, astonishing; ~ਜਨਕ Surprising, astonishing, marvellous.

ਅਸ਼ਟਾਮ (ashtaam) *n m* Stamp paper, stamp, bond.

ਅਸਤਬਲ (astabal) *n m* Stable.

ਅਸਤਬਾਜ਼ੀ (astabaazee) *n f* Fireworks.

ਅਸਤਰ (astar) *n m* Missile, weapon; Inner coating, lining of a garment.

ਅਸਤੀਫ਼ਾ (asteefaa) *n m* Resignation; ~ਦੇਣਾ To Resign.

ਅਸੰਤੁਸ਼ਟ (asantusht) *a* Dissatisfied, displeased, discontented.

ਅਸੰਤੋਖ (asantokh) *n m* Dissatisfaction, discontentment.

ਅਸਥਾਈ (asathai) *a* Temporary, impermanent, transitory.

ਅਸਥਾਨ (asthaan) *n m* Place, position room, residence, space.

ਅਸਥਾਪਤ (asthaapat) *a* Installed, established, appointed.

ਅਸਥਾਪਨ (asathapan) *n m* Installation.

ਅਸਥਾਪਨਾ (asathapana) *n f* Establishment, instalment.

ਅਸਪਸ਼ਟ (aspasht) *a* Ambigious, vague, obscure, dubious imperceptible, illegible, not clear; ~ਤਾ Lack of clarity, obscureness, vagueness, ambiguity.

ਅਸਪਾਤ (aspaat) *n m* Steel.

ਅਸਬਾਬ (asbaab) *n m* Luggage, baggage, reasons, causes.

ਅਸੰਭਵ (asambhav) *a* Impossible, impracticable, improbable.

ਅਸਮਤ (asmat) *n f* Modesty, chastity.

ਅਸਮਤਾ (asamtaa) *n f* Inequality, dissimilarity.

ਅਸਮਰਥ/ਅਸਮਰਥਕ (asmarath/ asmarathak) *a* Incapable, unable, incompetent, weak, Impotent.

ਅਸਮਾਨ (asmaan) *n m* Sky, heaven; ~ਸਿਰ ਤੇ ਚੁਕਣਾ To create havoc, to make exclusive noise; ~ਟੁਟ ਪੈਣਾ To be struck by calamity; ~ਤੇ ਉਡਣਾ To be proud; ~ਤੇ ਚੜ੍ਹਨਾ To be too proud, to be too vain; ~ਤੋਂ ਡਿਗਣਾ To fall from a great height; ~ਨੂੰ ਟਾਕੀ ਲਾਉਣੀ To be crafty.

ਅਸਮਾਨੀ (asmaanee) *a* Sky blue, azure, heavenly.

ਅਸਰ (asar) *n m* Effect, influence, impression; Result, consequence; ~ਦਾਇਕ Effective, impressive, forceful, influential.

ਅਸਲ (asal) *a* Real, true, pure de facto, capital, amount.

ਅਸਲਾ (aslaa) *n* (1) Arms, military weapons; (2) Root, source, origin.

ਅਸਲੀ (aslee) *a* Original, real, true, pure, unadulterated.

ਅਸਲੀਅਤ (asliyat) *n f* Reality, fact, actuality.

ਅਸ਼ਲੀਲ (ashleel) *a* Obscene, vulgar, indecent; ~ਲਿਖਤ Pornography.

ਅਸਵਾਰ (aswaar) *n m* Rider.

ਅਸ਼ਾਂਤੀ (ashaantee) *n f* Disorder, disquiet, dissatisfaction.

ਅਸਾਧ (asaadh) *a* Incurable, Incorrigible, desperate.

ਅਸਾਧਾਰਨ (asaadhaaran) *a* Uncommon, extraordinary, unusual, abnormal, a typical.

ਅਸਾਨ (asaan) *a* Easy, facile.

ਅਸਾਰ (asaar) *n a* (1) Traces, signs, characteristics; (2) Width; Meaningless, unreal.

ਅਸਾਵਧਾਨ (asaawdhaan) *a* Careless, inadvertent.

ਅਸਾਵਧਾਨੀ (asavdani) *n f* Inattention, inattentiveness, heedlessness, carelessness, inadvertence, inadvertency.

ਅਸਿੱਖ (asikkh) *a* Unteachable, untutored; Not sikh-like.

ਅਸੀਂ (aseen) *pron* We.

ਅੱਸੀ (assee) *a* eighty.

ਅਸੀਸ (asees) *n m* Blessing, benediction.

ਅਸੁਧ (ashudh) *a* Impure, adulterated; Wrong, incorrect.

ਅਸ਼ੁਧੀ (ashudhee) *n f* Mistake, error, inaccuracy, misprint; ~ਪਤਰ Errata, erratum.

ਅਸੁਰ (asur) *n m* Demon, devil, satan.

ਅਸੂਝ (asoojh) *n* Indicretion.

ਅਸੂਲ (asool) *n m* Principal, rule, law, theory, doctrine, canon; ~ਨ On principle, in principle.

ਅਸੂਲੀ (asuli) *a* Principled, morally correct or vaild, righteous.

ਅਹੰਕਾਰ (ahāankaar) *n m* Same as ਅਹੰ; Pride, arrogance, conceit.

ਅਹੰਕਾਰੀ (ahāankaari) *a* Proud, arrogant, conceited.

ਅਹਿਦ (ahed) *n m* Resolve, vow, determination, promise.

ਅਹਿਮ (ahem) *a* Important, essential, significant, momentous.

ਅਹਿੰਸਾ (ahinsaa) *n f* Non-violence.

ਅਹਿਮਕ (ahemak) *n m* Fool, stupid; ~ਪੁਣਾ Foolishness stupidity.

ਅਹਿਮੀਅਤ (ahimeeyat) *n f* Importance, significance.

ਅਹਿੱਲ (ahill) *a* Immovable, employee, agent, public servant, petty official.

ਅਹਿਲਕਾਰ (ahilkaar) *n m* Official, clerk in a court of law.

ਅਹੁਦਾ (auhdaa) *n m* Rank, post.

ਅਹੂਤੀ (ahootee) *n f* Oblation, burnt offering, immolation.

ਅੰਕ (ank) *n m* (1) Numeral, number, mark, figure; (2) Letter of the alphabet; (3) Act (of a drama); (4) Issue (of a newspaper or magazine).

ਅਕਸ (aks) *n m* Reflection, reflected image.

ਅਕਸਰ (aksar) *adv* Often, frequently, mostly.

ਅਕਸਰੀਅਤ (aksareeat) *n f* Majority.

ਅੱਕਣਾ (akkaṇaa) *v* To be fed up, to be bored, tired (of), irritated.

ਅਕਦ/ਅਗਦ (akad/agad) *n* Marriage.

ਅਕਲ (akal) *n f* Wisdom, intelligence, sense, head, reason; ~ਟਿਕਾਣੇ ਲਾਉਣੀ To set right, to bring sense, to cut to size; ~ਮੰਦ Wise, sensible; ~ਤੇ ਪਥਰ ਪੈਣੇ To be out of one's head, to be bereft of all intellect; ~ਤੇ ਪੜਦਾ ਪੈਣਾ To be stupid; ~ਦਾ ਅੰਨ੍ਹਾ Fool, block head, stupid; ~ਦਾ ਦੁਸ਼ਮਣ Silly, stupid; ~ਦਾ ਪੂਰਾ Foolish (sarcastically); ~ਦੁੜਾਉਣੀ To think, to reason.

ਅਕਾ (akaa) *n* Boredom, tedium, iksomeness, wearisomeness, nuisance, annoyance, exasperation.

ਅਕਾਉਣਾ (akaauṇaa) *a* Boring, monotonous, tedious, dreary.

ਅਕਾਉ (akaaoo) *a* Boring, dreary.

ਅਕਾਰਥ (akaarath) *a* Useless, fruitless, unprofitable; ~ਜਾਣਾ To go waste, to be wasted.

ਅਕਾਰਨ (akaaran) *a adv* Without cause, unprovoked, needless, groundless, unnecessary, unwarranted; Needlessly, unnecessarily.

ਅਕਾਲ (akaal) *a n m* Untimely, before time, immortal, timeless, god; ~ਪੁਰਖ God, not affected by death or time; ~ਚਲਾਣਾ ਕਰਨਾ To pass away, to die, to breathe one's last away.

ਅਕਾਲੀ (akaalee) *a m* Divine, a sect of the sikhs.

ਅਕੀਦਾ (akeedaa) *n* Faith, belief, doctrine, principle.

ਅਕੇਵਾਂ (akevaan) *n* Boredom, tendium, weariness, exasperation.

ਅੱਖ (akkh) *n f* Eye; ~ਆਉਣੀ To have sore eye; ~ਨਾ ਚੁਕਣੀ To be ashamed, not to look up; ~ਬਚਾਉਣੀ To avoid notice, to slip away, to blink; ~ਮਚੋਲੀ Hide and seek; ~ਲੜਨੀ To fall in love.

ਅਖੰਡ (akhand) *a* Indivisible, undivided; continuous, whole entire, uninterrupted; ~ਪਾਠ Uninterrupted recitation, non-stop recital of Sikh or Hindu scripture.

ਅਖਤਿਆਰ (akhtiyaar) *n m* Authority, competency, right, discretion.

ਅਖਬਾਰ (akhbaar) *n m* Newspaper.

ਅੱਖਰ (akkhar) *n m* Letter, character (of alphabet); Syllable; ~ਕ੍ਰਮ Alphabetical order.

ਅੱਖਰੀ (akkharee) *a* Pertainning to letters, literal.

ਅੱਖਰੋਟ (akhrot) *n m* Walnut.

ਅਖਵਾਉਣਾ (akhvaaunaa) *v* Get communicated or recommended; To be called, to cause to say.

ਅਖੜ (akhar) *a* Rude, haughty, quarrelsome, obstinate, wild, impolite, rough, uncivilized; ~ਪੁਣਾ Brusqness, stubborness, arrogance.

ਅਖਾਣ (akhaan) *n m* Proverb, saying, aphorism, adage.

ਅਖਾੜਾ (akhaaraa) *n m* Arena, wrestling place, plaestra, amphitheatre.

ਅਖੀਰ (akheer) *n adv f* End, extreme; Limit; Atlast.

ਅਖੁੱਟ (akhutt) *a* Boundless, inexhaustible.

ਅੱਗ (agg) *n a f* Fire, heat, flame, jealousy, passion; Burning, very hot; ~ਤੇ ਤੇਲ ਪਾਉਣਾ To add fuel to the fire; ~ਤੇ ਪਾਣੀ ਪਾਉਣਾ To pacify, to calm down; ~ਤੇ ਲੇਟਣਾ To be uneasy, to be restless; ~ਦੇਣੀ To light the pyre, to perform funeral rites; ~ਪਾਣੀ ਦਾ ਵੈਰ Innate mutual hostility; ~ਬਗੋਲਾ ਹੋਣਾ To fly into rage; ~ਭੜਕਾਉਣੀ To excite.

ਅੰਗ (ang) *n m* Limb, part, portion, fraction, division; Member.

ਅਗਰ (agar) *n conj f* Front; If, in case; ~ਗਾਮੀ Forerunner, progressive, foremost, precedent.

ਅੰਗਰੇਜ਼ (angrez) *n m* Englishman, The English, Britisher.

ਅੰਗਰੇਜ਼ੀ (angrezee) *a n m* English, British; English language.

ਅਗਵਾ (agwaa) *n m* Abduction; ~ਕਰਨਾ To abduct, to hijack.

ਅਗਵਾਈ (agwaaee) *n f* Guidance, leadership; ~ਕਰਨਾ To lead, to guide, to provide leadership.

ਅਗਵਾਨੀ (agvaanee) *n f* Welcome, reception; ~ਕਰਨੀ To welcome, to receive, to usher.

ਅਗਵਾੜਾ (agvaaraa) *n m* Front side, front portion, foreground, front, facade.

ਅਗੜ-ਪਿਛੜ (aggar-picchar) *adv* One after the other, one behind the other, successively, in quick succession.

ਅਗੜਮ-ਬਗੜਮ (agaram-bagram) *a* Worthless, absurd, irrelevant.

ਅੰਗੜਾਈ (angraaee) *n f* Stretching of the limbs.

ਅਗਾਂਹ (agaanha) *a m* Forword, onward, future, more; ~ਚਲਣਾ To march forward.

ਅਗਾੜੀ (agaaree) *n f* Front position, forepart, future; Rope with which horse is tied; ~ ਪਿਛਾੜੀ One behind the other, forward and backward.

ਅੰਗੀ (angee) *n f* Brassiere, bodice.

ਅੰਗੀਠੀ (angeethee) *n f* Furnace, fire pot, stove, heater.

ਅੰਗੂਠਾ (angoothaa) *n m* Thumb, the great toe; ~ਵਿਖਾਉਣਾ To defy, to challenge.

ਅਗੂੰਠੀ (angoothee) *n m* Finger ring, ring.

ਅੰਗੂਰ (angoor) *n m* Grapes, vines, scale.

ਅਗੇ (agge) *adv* Before, in front, onward; ~ਅਗੇ Ahead, forward, a course of time; ~ਕਰਨਾ To present, to put forward, to push forward; ~ਦੌੜ ਪਿਛੇ ਚੋੜ Haste makes waste; ~ਨਿਕਲਣਾ To surpass, to cross, to advance,

to overtake; ~ਵਧਣਾ To progress,
to proceed, to improve.

ਅਗੇਤਰ (agetar) *n* Prefix, affix.

ਅੰਗੋਛਾ (angochhaa) *n m* Towel, any
piece of cloth for wiping.

ਅਚੰਭਾ (achambhaa) *n m* Wonder,
ashtonishment, amazement,
marvel.

ਅਗੇਤ (aget) *n m* Early time,
earliness, advance (in relation to
sowing operation); Prefix.

ਅਗੇਰੇ (agere) *adv* Forward, further
on, more forward, more to the
front.

ਅਗੋਂ (aggon) *adv f* From the front,
from the opposite direction; Next,
hereafter, henceforth; ~ਪਿੱਛੋਂ
sooner or later; From anyside.

ਅਚਨਚੇਤ (achanchet) *adv* Suddenly,
all of a sudden, without warning,
abruptly, unexpectedly,
precipitately.

ਅਚਰਜ (acharaj) *a* Wondeful,
ashtonishing, strange, amazing,
marvellous.

ਅਚਰ (achar) *a* Inanimate; ~ਚਰ
Animate and inanimate.

ਅਚਲ (achal) *a* Immovable, static,
stationary, constant, invariable,
fixed, motionless, Invariant,
constant.

ਅਚਾਨਕ (achaanak) *a* Suddenly, by
chance, unexpectedly, all of a
sudden.

ਅਚਾਰ (achaar) *n m* Pickles.

ਅਚੇਤ (achet) *a* Senseless,
unconscious, inattentive; ~ਅਵਸਥਾ
Trance.

ਅੱਛਾ (achhaa) *a* Good, nice,
pleasant, fine; Well, alright; ~ਹੋਣਾ
To recover, to be healed; ~ਕਰਨਾ
To cure, to heal.

ਅਛੂਤ (achhoot) *a* Untouchable.

ਅੱਜ (ajj) *adv* Today, This day, now;
~ਕਲ Now a days, in a few days.

ਅਜਨਬੀ (ajanabee) *n m* Stranger,
unfamiliar, alien.

ਅਜਪਾ (ajapaa) *a* Unrecited,
unpronounced, unutterable.

ਅਜਬ (ajab) *a* Curious, rare, strange,
wonderfull.

ਅਜ਼ਮਤ (azamat) *n f* Honour, dignity,
greatness.

ਅਜ਼ਮਾਇਸ਼ੀ (azmayishee) *a*
Probationary, on probation.

ਅਜਲਾਸ (ajlaas) *n m* Session.

ਅਜ਼ਾਦੀ (azaadee) *n f* Freedom,
independence, liberty. Also
ਆਜ਼ਾਦੀ

ਅਜ਼ਾਬ (azaab) *n m* Torture, torment,
suffering, pain.

ਅੰਜਾਮ (anjaam) *n m* Consequence,

end, result, outcome.

ਅਜ਼ੀਜ਼ (azeez) *a* Dear, son.

ਅਜੀਬ (ajeeb) *a* Strange, wonderful, peculiar.

ਅਜ਼ੀਮ (azeem) *a* Great, grand, huge, stupendous.

ਅਜੁੜਵਾਂ (ajurvaan) *a* Incompatible; Not matching; Different; Disjointed, disconnected, separate.

ਅਜੇ (aje) *adv* Yet, still, as yet.

ਅਜੋਕਾ (ajokaa) *a* Upto date, of present date, modern.

ਅਟਕ (atak) *n* Hindrance, obstacle, impediment, bar, hitch, hurdle.

ਅਟਕਲ (atakal) *n f* Guess, conjecture, rough estimate; Rough and ready solution, trial and error method.

ਅਟਕਣਾ (atakanaa) *v* To stop, to halt, to stay, to stick, to be hindered.

ਅਟਕਾ (atka) *n m* Stoppage, obstruction, delay, interruption, impediment, hinderance.

ਅਟਕਾਉਣਾ (atkaaunaa) *v* To stop, obstruct, impede, retard, delay, interrupt.

ਅਟਾ-ਸਟਾ (attaa-sattaa) *adv* Rough estimate.

ਅਟਾਰੀ (ataaree) *n f* Mansion, loft.

ਅਟੇਰਨਾ (aternaa) *v* To bring under control, to influence.

ਅੱਠ (atth) *a* eight.

ਅੱਠਤਰ (athattar) *v* seventy-eight.

ਅਠਵੰਞਾ (athvanjaa) *a* fifty-eight.

ਅਠਾਈ (athaaee) *a* twenty-eight.

ਅਠਿਆਨੀ (athiaanee) *n f* Eight anna coin, half rupee, fifty paisa coin.

ਅਡਣਾ (adnaa) *v* To spread, to open.

ਅੰਡਾ (andaa) *n m* Egg.

ਅੱਡਾ (addaa) *n m* Stand, station, base, rendezvous; ~ਜਮਾਉਣਾ To settle down, to set up a base.

ਅੱਡਾਣਾ (adaanaa) *n m* Obstruction.

ਅੱਡੀ (addee) *n f* Heel, spur; ~ਨਾ ਲਾਉਣਾ To take no rest, not to pause.

ਅਡੋਲ (adol) *a* Steady, unshaken, immovable.

ਅਣਹੋਣੀ (anhonee) *a* Impossible, unfamiliar, improbable.

ਅਣਖ (anakkh) *n* Self-respect, self honour.

ਅਣਗਿਣਤ (anginat) *a* Innumberable, countless.

ਅਣਚਾਹਿਆ (anchahiyaa) *a* Undesired, unwanted.

ਅਣਛਪਿਆ (anchhapiyaa) *a* Unpublished, unprinted.

ਅਣਡਿਠ (andith) *a* Unseen.

ਅਣਬਣ (anban) *n f* Discord, quarrel.

ਅਣਮੋਲ (anmol) *a* Precious invaluable, priceless.

ਅਣ-ਵਿਆਹਿਆ (aṇviaahiaa) *n a m* Bachelor; Unmarried.

ਅਣੂ (aṇoo) *n m* Molecule, smallest particle.

ਅੱਤ (att) *a* Too much, very, excess.

ਅੰਤਮ (antam) *a* Last.

ਅੰਤਰ (antar) *n a Prep m* Difference, Spacing, contrast; Internal, inner; Between, amongst; ~ਸੂਝ Intuition; ~ਧਿਆਨ Lost in meditation, invisible; ~ਬੋਧ Inner knowledge, self realisation, intuition.

ਅੰਤਰਜਾਮੀ (antarjaamee) *n m* The supreme spirit; Omniscient.

ਅਤਰ (attar) *n m* Scent, perfume, essence, otto; ~ਦਾਨੀ Perfumᴄbox.

ਅੰਤਰਰਾਸ਼ਟਰੀ (antarraashtree) *a* International.

ਅੰਤਰਾ (antraa) *n* Part of a song or hymn.

ਅਤਾ-ਪਤਾ (ataa-pataa) *n m* Whereabouts, information.

ਅਤਿਵਾਦ (ativaad) *n m* Terrorism.

ਅਤੇ (ate) *Prop* And, as well as.

ਅੱਥਰੂ (atthroo) *n m* Tear.

ਅਦਨਾ (adnaa) *a* Small, poor, inferior.

ਅਦਬ (adab) *n m* (1) Respect, civility; (2) Literature.

ਅਦਬੀ (adbee) *a* Literary.

ਅਦਰਕ (adarak) *n f* Ginger.

ਅੰਦਰ (andar) *n adv m* Inside, interior room, in, inside, within; ~ਅੰਦਰ Internally, mentally; ~ਖਾਤੇ Secretly, confidentially; ~ਖਾਨੇ/ਗਤੀ Surreptitously, clandestinely, under the table.

ਅੰਦਰੋ-ਅੰਦਰ (andro-andar) *adv* Secretly, internally.

ਅੰਦਰਲਾ (andarlaa) *a n m* Internal, interior, inner, intrinsic; Mind.

ਅਦਲ (adal) *n* Justice, equity; ~ਬਦਲ Exchange, alteration.

ਅਦਾ (adaa) *n f* Grace, beauty; Coquetry, gesture, expression; ~ਕਾਰ Actor, performer; ~ਕਾਰੀ Acting, performance.

ਅੰਦਾਜ਼ (andaaz) *n m* Style, manners, mode.

ਅੰਦਾਜ਼ਨ (andaazan) *adv* Approximately, nearly, roughly.

ਅੰਦਾਜ਼ਾ (andaazaa) *n m* Guess, estimate.

ਅਦਾਰਾ (adaaraa) *n m* Institution.

ਅਦਾਲਤ (adaalat) *n f* Court, tribunal.

ਅਦਾਲਤੀ (adaaltee) *a* Judicial, pertaining to court.

ਅਦਾਵਤ (adaavat) *n* Enmity, hostility.

ਅੰਦੇਸ਼ਾ (andeshaa) *n m* Apprehension, fear, scare.

ਅੱਧ (addh) *prop* Half; ~ਪਕਾ Half

baked, semi-ripe; ~**ਰੰਗ** Paralysis, hemiplegia.

ਅੰਧਰਾਤਾ (andhrata) Night blindness.

ਅੱਧਾ (addhaa) *a* Half.

ਅਧਾਨ (adhaan) *n* Pregnancy, conception.

ਅੰਧਾ (andhaa) *a* Blind, rash; ~**ਧੁੰਦ** Blindly, rashly, excessively, unwittingly. Also **ਅੰਨ੍ਹਾ**

ਅੰਧਾਰ (andhaar) *n m* Gloom, anarchy.

ਅਧਿਅਕਸ਼ (adhiyaksh) *n m* Head, president, chairman.

ਅਧਿਆਇ (adhiyae) *n m* Chapter, portion.

ਅਧਿਆਪਕ (adhiyaapak) *n m* Teacher, tutor, instructor, professor, educator, pedagogue, percepter.

ਅਧਿਆਪਨ (adhiyaapan) *n m* Teaching.

ਅੰਧਿਆਰਾ (andhiyaraa) *n m* Darkness, obscurity.

ਅਧਿਐਨ (adhiyan) *n m* Study, learning, perusal.

ਅਧਿਕਾਰ (adhikaar) *n m* Right, authority, privilege, title, power, claim.

ਅਧਿਕਾਰੀ (adhikaaree) *n m* Officer, authority, entitled.

ਅਧੀਨ (adheen) *a n f* Dependent; Slave, servant, ~**ਗੀ** Subordination, submission, humility, meekness.

ਅਧੀਰਾਜ (adheeraj) *n m* Emperor, ruler, sovereign.

ਅਧੂਰਾ (adhooraa) *a* Incomplete, unfinished, half-done; ~**ਪਣ** Incompletion.

ਅੱਧੋ-ਅੱਧ (addho-addh) *n m* Half and half, fifty-fifty.

ਅੰਨ (ann) *n m* Grain, corn, food; ~**ਦਾਤਾ** God, farmer.

ਅਨਸਰ (ansar) *n m* Element.

ਅਨਹੋਣਾ (anhonaa) *a* Impossible, improbable, unpromising.

ਅਨਘੜ (anaghar) *a* Crude, rough, uncivilised, primitive, unchiselled.

ਅਨਜਾਣ (Anajaan) *a n m* Innocent, unknown, unacquainted, ignorant; Stranger.

ਅਨੰਦ (anand) *n m* Pleasure, joy, happiness, delight, tranquility, comfort; ~**ਕਾਰਜ** Marriage ceremony.

ਅਨਪੜ੍ਹ (anapadh) *a* Uneducated, illiterate; ~**ਤਾ** Illiteracy.

ਅਨਾਜ (anaaj) *n m* Grain, corn.

ਅਨਾਥ (anaath) *a* Orphan, destitute, desolate, poor, unprotected.

ਅਨਾਦ/ਅਨਾਦੀ (anaad/anaadee) *a* Eternal, uncreated, ever existant; God.

ਅਨਾਦਰ (anaadar) *n m* Insult, disrespect, irreverence.

ਅਨਾਨਾਸ (anaanaas) *n m* Pine apple.

ਅਨਾਰ (anaar) *n m* Pomegranate.

ਅਨਾੜੀ (Anaaṛee) *a n m* Inexpert, clumsy, unskilled, artless; Simpleton, novice.

ਅਨੁਸ਼ਾਸਨ (anushaasan) *n m* Discipline.

ਅਨੁਸੂਚੀ (anusoochee) *n f* Schedule.

ਅਨੁਦਾਨ (anudaan) *n m* Grant, subsidy.

ਅਨੁਪਾਤ (Anupaat) *n m* Ratio, proportion.

ਅਨੁਪੂਰਕ (Anupoorak) *a* Suplementary.

ਅਨੁਭਵ (anubhav) *n m* Feeling, perception, sensation, experience, cognition.

ਅਨੁਯਾਈ (anuyaaee) *n m* Follower, disciple, adherent.

ਅਨੁਵਾਦ (anuvaad) *n m* Translation, interpretation, adaptation.

ਅਨੁਵਾਦਕ (anuvaadak) *n m* Translator, interpreter.

ਅੰਨ੍ਹਾ (annaa) *n m a* Blindman; Blind; ਅਕਲ ਦਾ~ Fool; ~ਦੀਵਾ Dimlight; (ਅੰਧਾ)~ਧੁੰਦ Recklessly, indiscreatly, at random, indiscriminately.

ਅੰਨ੍ਹੇਰ (anner) *n m* Injustice, tyranny, darkness; ~ਗਰਦੀ Anarchy,

lawlessness, mismanagement.

ਅੰਨ੍ਹੇਵਾਹ (annevaah) *adv* Blindly, rashly recklessly, slapdash.

ਅਪੰਗ (apang) *a* Crippled, disabled, handicapped.

ਅਪਜਸ (apjas) *n m* Infame, notoriety, ignominy, ill fame, ill repute, defamation, slander, calumny.

ਅਪੱਣਤ (apaṇatt) *n* Intimacy, familiarity, affection, attachment.

ਅਪਣਾ (apṇaa) *a* Own. Also ਆਪਣਾ

ਅਪਣਾਉਣਾ (apṇaauṇaa) *v* To own, to declare or claim as one's own, to acknowledge, to adopt, to espouse.

ਅਪਮਾਨ (apmaan) *n m* Insult, dishonour, disrespect, slur; ~ਕਰਨਾ To insult, to disgrace, to stigmatise.

ਅਪ੍ਰਵਾਨ (apravaan) *a* Unapproved, unacceptable.

ਅਪਰਾਧ (apraadh) *n m* Crime, offence, sin, transgression, fault.

ਅਪਰਾਧੀ (apraadhee) *a m* Criminal, offender, guilty, delinquent.

ਅਪਵਾਦ (apvaad) *n m* Exception, reproach.

ਅਪਵਿਤਰ (apvitar) *a* Impure, unholy, defiled.

ਅੱਪੜ (appaṛ) *a n v* Fallow; Uncultivated land; Reach

(Imperative).

ਅਪੜਨਾ (aparnaa) v To arrive, to reach, to approach.

ਅਪੁੱਠਾ (apuṭṭhaa) a Perverse, backwards, upside down.

ਅਫ਼ਸਰ (afsar) n m Officer, boss.

ਅਫ਼ਸਾਨਾ (afsaanaa) n m Fiction, story, tale; ~ਨਵੀਸ Fiction writer.

ਅਫ਼ਸੋਸ (afsos) n m Sorrow, regret; ~ਨਾਕ Deplorable.

ਅਫਰਾ (aphraa) n m Flatulence, bloat, bloating. Also ਅਫ਼ਾਰਾ

ਅਫਰਾ-ਤਫ਼ਰੀ (afraa-tafree) n f Stampede.

ਅਫ਼ਲਾਤੂਨ (aflatoon) n m Plato (the philospher); A clever person.

ਅਫ਼ਲਾਤੂਨੀ (aflatoonee) a Platonic; clever, smart.

ਅਫ਼ਵਾਹ (afvaah) n f Rumour, hearsay, unverified statement.

ਅਫ਼ੀਮ (afeem) n f Opium.

ਅਫ਼ੀਮੀ (afeemee) a n Opium eater or addict; Lazy or whimsical person.

ਅੰਬ (amb) n m Mango.

ਅੰਬਰ (ambar) n m Cloud, sky.

ਅੰਬੜੀ (ambaree) n f Mamma, mother.

ਅੰਬਣਾ (ambṇaa) v To get tried, fatigued, exhausted; (for a limb or muscle) To get numb.

ਅੱਬਾ (abbaa) n m Father.

ਅਬਾਦੀ (abbadee) n f Population, habitation, census.

ਅੰਬਾਰ (ambaar) n m Heap, stock, multitude, lump.

ਅਬੂਝ (aboojh) a Subtle, unintelligible, unwise.

ਅਭੰਗ (abhang) a Indivisible, unbroken, unimpaired.

ਅਭਾਗਾ (abhaagaa) a Unlucky, unfortunate, miserable.

ਅਭਿਆਸ (abhiyaas) n m Practice, exercise, training, rehearsal.

ਅਭਿੰਨ (abhinn) a Integral, indistinguishable, similar.

ਅਭਿਨੇਤਾ (abhinetaa) n m Actor.

ਅਭਿਨੇਤਰੀ (abinetree) n f Actress.

ਅਭਿਮਾਨ (abhimaan) n m Pride, arrogance, haughtiness, vanity, ego.

ਅਭਿਲਾਖਾ (abhilaakhaa) n f Desire, wish, craving.

ਅਮਨ (aman) n m Peace, tranquility.

ਅਮਰ (amar) a Eternal, immortal, undying.

ਅਮਲ (amal) n m Action, conduct, habit; ~ਕਰਨਾ To act upon, to carry out, to execute, to follow; ~ਵਿਚ ਲਿਆਉਣਾ To implement; To put into practice.

ਅਮਲਾ (amlaa) n m Subordinate staff,

personal staff.

ਅੰਮਾ (ammaa) *n f* Mother; ~ਜਾਏ Brothers.

ਅਮਾਨਤ (amaanat) *n m* Trust, deposit, faith; ~ਦਾਰ Trustee; Trust worthy ~ਵਿਚ ਖ਼ਿਆਨਤ Breach of trust; ~ਨਾਮਾ Trust deed.

ਅਮਾਨਤੀ (amaantee) *a* Keeper of safe deposits, trustee.

ਅਮਾਮ (amaam) *n m* Priest, spiritual guide, successor of prophet mohammad.

ਅਮੀਰ (ameer) *n a m* Chief, nobleman; Rich.

ਅਮੋਲ (amol) *a* Precious, invaluable.

ਅੰਮ੍ਰਿਤ (ammrit) *n m* Nectar, ambrosia, panacea, holywater, water of life baptism or initiation ceremony; ~ਛਕਣਾ To undergo initiation ceremony of the Khalsa; ~ਧਾਰੀ duly baptised (Sikh).

ਅੱਯਾਸ਼ (ayyaash) *n a* Voluptuary, debauch, lewd.

ਅੱਯਾਸ਼ੀ (ayyaashee) *n a f* Profigacy, dissipation, pleasure-seeking, love of pleasure, voluptuousness, voluptuosity, dissoluteness.

ਅਰਸ਼ (arash) *n m* Sky, heaven; God's abode.

ਅਰਸਾ (arsaa) *n m* Duration, period, span of time, time-span.

ਅਰਕ (arak) *n* Distilled product, distillated, extract; ~ਕਢਣਾ To distil; To cause to perspire, to tire out; ~ਦਾਨੀ Fancy container for ~ਅਰਕ for perfumes.

ਅਰਜ਼ (araz) *n f* request, supplication, solicitation, petition, appeal, entreaty; ~ਕਰਨੀ To make a request, to request, to supplicate, to petition, to appeal, to entreat; Petitioner, supplicant.

ਅਰਜ਼ੀ (arzee) *n f* Written request, application; Petition, representation.

ਅਰਜ਼ੀਨਵੀਸ (arzeenavees) *n m* Petition writer, writer of petitions and other legal documents or private accounts, scribe.

ਅਰਜ਼ੀਨਵੀਸੀ (arzeenaveesee) *n f* Profession or art of writing petitions.

ਅਰਥ (arath) *n m* Meaning, purpose, intention, interpretation; Finance; ~ਵਿਗਿਆਨ Semantics; ~ਸ਼ਾਸਤਰ Economics.

ਅਰਥੀ (arthee) *n f* Bier, hearse.

ਅਰਦਲੀ (ardlee) *n m* Orderly, attendant, peon.

ਅਰਦਾਸ (ardaas) *n f* Prayer, request, supplication, offering to a deity.

ਅਰਬ (arab) *a n* A thousand million;

Arabia (country's name).

ਅਰਮਾਨ (armaan) *n m* Desire, longing, aspiration; Sorrow.

ਅਰੜਾਉਣਾ (arṛaauṇaa) *v* To cry hoarsely or at the highest pitch, to blubber; (of cattle) To low, to moo.

ਅਰਾਧਨਾ (araadhnaa) *n f* Worship, prayer.

ਅਰਾਮ (araam) *n m* Rest, comfort, ease; ~**ਤਲਬ** or **ਪਰਸਤ** Lazy, ease lovings, idolent; ~**ਪਰਸਤੀ** Indolence, sloth, laziness.

ਅਲਸਾਉਣਾ (alsaauṇaa) *v* To dose, to relax, to laze.

ਅਲੜ (allaṛ) *a* Immature, childish, foolish, young.

ਅਲਖ (alakh) *n f* Invocation.

ਅਲਜ਼ਾਮ (alzaam) *n m* Blame, censure, accusation.

ਅਲਬੇਲਾ (albelaa) *a* Carefree, jaunty, bonny.

ਅਲਮਸਤ (almast) *adv* Carefree.

ਅਲਮ-ਗਲਮ (alam-glam) *n m* Knick-knack, miscellaneous articles.

ਅਲਮਾਰੀ (almaaree) *n f* Almirah, bookshelf.

ਅੱਲਾ (allaa) *n m* God.

ਅਲਾਉਣਾ (alaauṇaa) *v* To say, to speak out.

ਅਲਾਪ (alaap) *n m* Talk, dialogue, conversation, song.

ਅਲਾਪਣਾ (alaapṇaa) *v* To speak out, to say, to sing.

ਅਲਾਮਤ (alaamat) *n f* Sign, indication, symptom, characteristic.

ਅਲਾਲਤ (alaalat) *n f* Disease, ailment, indisposition, sickness.

ਅਲੂਆ (alloonaa) *a* (lit hairless), young, unfledged, tender, adolescent, immature.

ਅਲੂਣਾ (alloonaa) *a* Without salt, unsalted, tasteless.

ਅਲੋਚਕ (alochak) *n m* Critic, reviewer.

ਅਲੋਚਨਾ (alochnaa) *n f* Criticism, review, critique.

ਅਵਤਾਰ (avtaar) *n m* Incarmation.

ਅਵਤਾਰੀ (avtaaree) *n m* Incarnated, superhuman.

ਅੱਵਲ (avval) *a* First, topmost, foremost, principal.

ਅਵਾਈ (avaaee) *n f* Rumour, hearsay.

ਅਵਾਜ਼ (avaaz) *n f* Sound, voice.

ਅਵਾਮ (avaam) *n m* People, masses.

ਅਵਾਰਗੀ (avaargee) *n f* vagrancy, vagabondage, wandering.

ਅਵਾਰਾ (avaaraa) *a* Vagrant, vegabond, loafer, errant; ~**ਪਣ** Vagabondage. Also **ਆਵਾਰਾ**

ਅਵੇਰ (aver) *n f* Delay, lateness.

ਅੜ (aṛ) *n f* Stubbornness,

obstinacy, obdurateness.

ਅੜੰਗਾ (aṛangaa) *n m* Obstacle, entanglement; Difficult or problematic situation; **~ਪਾਉਣਾ** To make things difficult, to create problems, to oppose; **~ਪੈਣਾ** Difficult situation arisen or be created.

ਅੜਚਨ (aṛachan) *n f* Difficulty, obstruction, problem.

ਅੜਨਾ (aṛnaa) *v* To stop, to resist, to baulk on.

ਅੜੀਅਲ (aṛiyal) *a* Stubborn, inflexible, mulish.

ਆਂ (aan) *n m* Mucus.

ਆਇਆ (aaiyaa) *n* Maid servant.

ਆਸ (aas) *n f* Hope, trust, faith, expectation, longing, reliance.

ਆਸ਼ਕ (aashak) *n m* Lover, sweet heart, paramour.

ਆਸਣ (aasaṇ) *n m* Seat, place, yogic posture; **~ਉਖੜਨਾ** To be thrown out of gear, to be dislodged; **~ਡੋਲਣਾ** Seat or throne to be shaky, to get panicky.

ਆਸਤੀਨ (aasteen) *n f* Sleeve; **~ਚੜ੍ਹਾਉਣੀ** To threaten, to get ready (to fight); **~ਦਾ ਸੱਪ** Serpent in the bosom, a foe in the guise of a friend.

ਆਸ਼ਨਾ (aashnaa) *n f* Friend, lover,

acquaintance.

ਆਸ਼ਨਾਈ (aashnaaee) *n f* Love affairs, courtship, friendship.

ਆਸਰਾ (aasraa) *n m* Protection, Dependence, backing, hope.

ਆਸਾਨ (aasaan) *a* Easy, convenient, light.

ਆਸਾਰ (aasaar) *n m* Sign, traces, symptoms, indications, effects.

ਆਸ਼ਿਆਨਾ (aashiaanaa) *n m* Nest, resting place.

ਆਹ (aah) *n f* Sigh.

ਆਹਰ (aahar) *n m* Impulse, enthusiasm, zeal, occupation, activity.

ਆਹਲਕ (aahlak) *n m* Laziness, sloth, sluggishness, indolence.

ਆਹੜਤ (aaharat) *n f* Commission, brokerage.

ਆਹੜਤੀ (aaharatee) *n m* Commision agent, broker.

ਆਹੋ (aaho) *adv* Yes.

ਆਕੜ (aakaṛ) *n f* Haughtiness, arrogance, stiffness, pride, coquetry.

ਆਕੜਨਾ (aakaṛnaa) *v* To stiffen, to become starchy or stiff; To be proud, arrogant, supercilious, overbearing, haughty; To behave in a haughty manner, to take airs.

ਆਕਾ (aakaa) *n m* master, employer.

ਆਕੀ (aakee) *a* Rebel, defiant, disobedient, recalcitrant.

ਆਖਣਾ (aakhṇaa) *v* To say, to tell, to ask; ਰੋਟੀ~To invite to lunch or dinner.

ਆਖਰ (aakhar) *n adv* The end, limit; In or at the end, at last, ultimately.

ਆਖਰੀ (aakhree) *a* Last, ultimate, final, decisive.

ਆਂਗਣ (aangaṇ) *n m* Compound, courtyard.

ਆਗਤ (aagat) *n f* Arrival, income, proceeds.

ਆਗਿਆ (aagiaa) *n f* Permission, order, command, instruction; ~ਕਰਨੀ To order, to command; ~ਦੇਣੀ To permit, to sanction, to approve; ~ਵਿਚ ਰਹਿਣਾ To be loyal, obedient, subservient.

ਆਗੂ (aagoo) *n m* Leader, guide, captain, forerunner.

ਆਚਰਣ (aacharaṇ) *n m* Conduct, character, behaviour, demeanour, practice, custom.

ਆਚਾਰੀਆ (aachaariyaa) *n* Professor; A religious orator.

ਆਜਜ਼ (aajaz) *a* Helpless, humble, incapable.

ਆਟਾ (aaṭaa) *n m* Flour.

ਆੜ (aaḍ) *a* Channel, water-channel.

ਆਂਢ (aanḍh) *n* Knot; Joint, relation, connection.

ਆਂਢ-ਗੁਆਂਢ (aanḍh-guaanḍh) *n m* Neighbourhood, surrounding, vicnity, environment.

ਆਤਸ਼ (aatash) *n* Fire, flame; ~ਬਾਜ਼ੀ Firework, pyrotechmy; ~ਮਜ਼ਾਜ Hot tempered.

ਆਤੰਕ (aatank) *n m* Terror; ~ਵਾਦ Terrorism.

ਆਤਮ (aatam) *n* Self, life; ~ਸੰਘਰਸ਼ Self struggle; ~ਹਤਿਆ/ਘਾਤ Suicide; ~ਕਥਾ Autobiography.

ਆਤਮਾ (aatmaa) *n f* The soul, spirit.

ਆਦਤ (aadat) *n f* Habit, nature, characteristic.

ਆਦਮ (aadam) *n m* Adam, man, mankind, the first man; ~ਖੋਰ Maneater, connibal.

ਆਦਮੀ (aadmee) *n m* Man, Person.

ਆਦਮੀਅਤ (aadmeeyat) *n f* Humanity, civility, good breeding.

ਆਂਦਰ (aandar) *n f* Intestine.

ਆਦਰ (aadar) *n m* Respect, honour.

ਆਦਰਸ਼ (aadarsh) *n m* Ideal, model, standard, goal, aim.

ਆਦਲ (addal) *a* Accustomed habituated.

ਆਦੀ (aadee) *a* Accustomed, habituated.

ਆਨ (aan) *n f* Honour, grace, dignity; ~ਸ਼ਾਨ Glory, splendour, grandeur, pomp, lustre; ~ਬਾਨ Grandeur, pomp and show.

ਆਨਾ (aanaa) *n m* Eyeball; Anna (a coin) sixteenth part of a rupee.

ਆਨਾ-ਕਾਨੀ (aanaa-kaanee) *n f* Deliberate delay, neglact or refusal, procrastination, finding, excuses, avoidance.

ਆਪੱਤੀ (aappatee) *n f* Objection, catastrophe; ~ਜਨਕ Objectionable.

ਆਪਾ (aapaa) *n m* Selfhood, one's own existence, one's own self; ~ਖੋਣਾ To lose consciousness of one's self, to become abnormal; ~ਧਾਪੀ Race for promotion, personal anxiety or interest.

ਆਪੇ (aape) *adv* Automatically; ~ਤੋਂ ਬਾਹਰ ਹੋਣਾ To be in fury, to lose senses, to lose self control.

ਆਫ਼ਤ (aafat) *n f* Calamity, misfortune, disaster, misery.

ਆਫਰਨਾ (aapharnaa) *v* To swell out, to boast, to be gorged, to swagger.

ਆਬ (aab) *n* Water, lustre.

ਆਬਸ਼ਾਰ (aabshaar) *n* Waterfall, cascade.

ਆਬਕਾਰੀ (aabkaaree) *n f* Excise, distillery.

ਆਬਰੂ (aabroo) *n f* Honour, character.

ਆਬੋਹਵਾ (aabo-hawaa) *n f* Climate.

ਆਮ (aam) *a* Common, general, ordinary, undistinguished; Plenty, abundant, plentiful, easily available, frequent.

ਆਮਦ (aamad) *n f* Arrival.

ਆਮਦਨ (aamdan) *n f* Income; Profit. Also ਆਮਦਨੀ.

ਆਯਾਤ (aayaat) *n m* Imports.

ਆਰਸੀ (aarsee) *n m* Looking glass, mirror set in a ring.

ਆਰਜ਼ੀ (aarzee) *a* Temporary, provisional.

ਆਰਜੂ (aarzoo) *n f* Desire, wish, expectation, hope, longing, yearning, aspiration.

ਆਰਾ (aaraa) *n m* Pit-saw, lumberman's saw, sawing machine, sawmill, lumber mill.

ਆਰੀ (aaree) *n f* Small hand saw.

ਆਲਸੀ (aalsee) *a* Idle, lazy, sluggish, lethargic.

ਆਲ੍ਹਣਾ (aalhṇaa) *n m* Nest.

ਆਲਮ (aalam) *n m* State, condition, universe, world; A learned scholar.

ਆਲਾ (aalaa) *n* Asylum, abode.

ਆਲੀਸ਼ਾਨ (aaleeshaan) *a* Splendid, magnificent.

ਆਲੂ (aaloo) *n m* Potato.

ਆਵਾ (aavaa) *n m* Kiln, brick kiln.

ਆਵਾ-ਜਾਈ (aavaa jaaee) *n f* Traffic, frequenting transport and communication.

ਆੜ (aar) *n f* Shelter, curtain, hindrance, wall, screen.

ਆੜੁਤ (aarhat) *n f* Brokerage, agency, commission.

ਆੜੀ (aaree) *n m* Friend, companion teammate.

ਐਸ਼ (aesh) *n f* Pleasure, luxury, delight; ~ ਪਰਸਤ, ~ਪੱਠਾ Enjoyment, loving, pleasure, voluptuous, prifilgate.

ਐਂਠ (aenth) *n f* Uppishness, arrogance, presumptuousness.

ਐਤਵਾਰ (aetwaar) *n m* Sunday.

ਐਥੇ (aethe) *adv* Here, at this place.

ਐਥੋਂ (aethon) *adv* From here.

ਐਨਾ (aenaa) *a adv* This much, so much.

ਐਬ (aeb) *n m* Defect, vice, fault drawback.

ਐਰਾ-ਗੈਰਾ (aeraa-gaeraa) *n m* Stranger, alien.

ਐਲਾਨ (aelaan) *n m* Announcement, proclamation.

ਐਵੇਂ (aiven) *a* Gratis, by the way; Free of cost.

ਔਸਤ (ausat) *n f* Average, mean; ~ਨ On the average.

ਔਸਰ (ausar) *n m* Opportunity, occasion, time.

ਔਕੜ (aukar) *n* Difficulty, dilemma.

ਔਂਕੜ (aunkar) *n* Short vowel or maatra indicated by (ੁ) and wirtten below a letter in Gurmukhi script.

ਔਖ (aukh) *n f* Difficulty, trouble, discomfort.

ਔਖਾ (aukhaa) *a* Difficult, arduous, uncomfortable.

ਔਘਟ (aughat) *n a* Crisis; Difficult, rugged, uneven, inaccessible.

ਔਜ਼ਾਰ (auzaar) *n m* Tool, instrument, implement.

ਔਤ (aut) *a* Issueless, childless. Also ਔਤਰਾ

ਔਥੇ (authe) *adv* There, at that place (pointing out); Also ਉਥੇ and ਐਥੇ

ਔਰਤ (aurat) *n f* Women, lady, female, wife.

ਔਲਾਦ (aulaad) *n f* Children, offspring, progeny generation.

ਔੜ (aur) *n f* Drought, scarcity, dearth, dire need.

ਔੜਾ (auraa) *n m* Obstacle, hitch.

ੲ

ੲ Third letter of Gurmukhi alphabets pronounced as eeṛee.

ੲਿਆਣਾ (iaaṇaa) *n m* Child, infant.

ੲਿਆਲੀ (iyaalee) *n m* Shepherd, goat herd.

ੲਿਸ਼ਕ (ishak) *n m* Love, passion, amour; ~ਮਿਜ਼ਾਜੀ Carnal love, lust.

ੲਿਸ਼ਤਿਹਾਰ (ishitihaar) *n m* Poster, notice, advertisement, bill.

ੲਿਸਤਿਕਬਾਲ (istikbaal) *n m* Welcome.

ੲਿਸਤ੍ਰੀ (istree) *n f* Women, female, wife; Smoothing iron.

ੲਿਸਥਿਰ (isthir) *a* Still, motionless, unmoving.

ੲਿਸਰਾਰ (israar) *n m* Insistance.

ੲਿਸ਼ਾਰਾ (ishaaraa) *n m* Sign, hint, mark; ~ਕਰਨਾ To point out, to indicate.

ੲਿਹਸਾਨ (ehesaan) *n m* Favour, obligation, courtesy, kindness; ~ਮੰਦ Grateful, thankful, obliged.

ੲਿਹਤਿਆਤ (ehetiaat) *n m* Precaution, care; ~ਨ As a precaution, cautiously.

ੲਿਹਾਤਾ (ihaataa) *n m* Compound, campus.

ੲਿੱਕ (ik) *a pref adv* One, a, an, united; Signifying unity, uniformity or continuity; Uniformly, constantly, continuously, consistently; ~ਸਾਰ Continuously, uninterruptedly, in the same breath; ~ਸਾਰ Uniform, similar, throughout constant, continuous; ~ਸੁਰ In unison, harmonious, consonant; Of the same opinion, unanimous, united; ~ਕਰਨਾ To unite, unify, bring to gether; To combine, to mix, to amalgamate, to integrate; ~ਜੁਟ United; ~ਤਰਫ਼ਾ One-sided, partial; Ex parte; ~ਦਮ One breath; At once, immediately, instantly, forthwith; Suddenly, all at once; ~ਮਿੱਕ Completely united, closely mixed, indistinguishable.

ੲਿੱਕਠ (ikaṭh) *n m* Unity, harmony, harmoniousness; Assembly, assemblage, gathering, meeting; Funeral feast and congregation *usually* held after the death of old heads of families.

ੲਿਕੱਠਾ (ikaṭhaa) *a adv* Collected,

united, amass, collectively.

ਇਕਤੰਤਰ (ikatantar) *n m* Monocracy.

ਇਕਬਾਲ (ikbaal) *n m* Greatness, eminence, dignity; Confession.

ਇਕਰਾਰ (ikraar) *n m* Agreement, assurance, undertaking, commitment; Promise; ~ਨਾਮਾ Agreement, contract.

ਇਕਲਾ (ikalaa) *a* Alone, single, one only, single-handed, unaided or unaccompanied, all by oneself.

ਇਕਲੌਤਾ (iklautaa) *a* Only, lonely, solitary.

ਇਕਾਸੀ (ikaasee) *a* Eighty-one.

ਇਕਾ-ਦੁਕਾ (ikaa-dukaa) *a* A few, rare, sporadic.

ਇਕਾਨਵਾਂ (ikaanvaan) *a* Ninety-first.

ਇਕੀ (ikee) *a* Twenty-one.

ਇੱਕੋ (ikko) *a* Only one; ~ਇੱਕ The only, the only one; ~ਜਿਹਾ Similar, identical, alike.

ਇਖ਼ਤਿਆਰ (ikhtiaar) *n m* Authority discretion, choice, right.

ਇਖ਼ਲਾਕ (ikhlaak) *n m* Manners, morality, ethics.

ਇਜ਼ਤ (izat) *n f* Honour, dignity, glory, grandeur, respect, esteem; ~ਦਾਰ Respectable, honourable.

ਇਜਾਜ਼ਤ (ijaazat) *n f* Permission.

ਇਜਾਰਾ (ijaaraa) *n m* Lease,

monopoly.

ਇੱਟ (iṭṭ) *n f* Brick; ~ਘੜੇ ਦਾ ਵੈਰ Arch enmity; ~ਨਾਲ ਇੱਟ ਵਜਾਉਣੀ To raze to the ground, to bring ruination.

ਇਤਹਾਦ (ithaad) *n m* Unity, alliance.

ਇੰਤਕਾਮ (intkaam) *n m* Revenge.

ਇੰਤਕਾਲ (intkaal) *n m* Death.

ਇੰਤਖ਼ਾਬ (intkhaab) *n m* Selection.

ਇੰਤਜ਼ਾਮ (intzaam) *n m* Arrangement, management, order.

ਇੰਤਜ਼ਾਮੀਆ (intzaamia) *a* Executive, administrative, managerial; Executive committee, management, managing committee.

ਇੰਤਜ਼ਾਰ (intzaar) *n f* Waiting, expectation, looking for.

ਇਤਫ਼ਾਕੀਆ (itfaakiaa) *a* Accidentical, by chance, casual.

ਇਤਬਾਰ (itbaar) *n m* Reliance, trust, confidence.

ਇਤਮੀਨਾਨ (itminaan) *n m* Satisfaction.

ਇਤਰਾਜ਼ (itraaz) *n m* Objection, point of order.

ਇਤਲਾਹ (itlaah) *n f* Information, intimation, report; ~ਕਰਨੀ/ਦੇਣੀ To intimate to inform; ~ਨਾਮਾ Written information.

ਇਤਿਹਾਸ (itihaas) *n m* History, chronicle, annals, tradition; ~ਕਾਰ Historian; Chronicler.

ਇਤਹਾਦ (itihaad) *n m* Unity, union, alliance, coalition, concord, association.

ਇਤਹਾਦੀ (itahaadee) *n m a* Ally, confederate; Allied.

ਇੰਦਰੀ (indree) *n f* Generative organ.

ਇਨਸਾਨ (insaan) *n m* Man, mankind, humanbeing, mankind; A virtuous or cuetureo person.

ਇਨਸਾਨੀਅਤ (insaaniat) *n f* Humanness, humanity, human nature; Virtuousness, right conduct, propriety; Mankind.

ਇਨਸਾਫ਼ (insaaf) *n m* Justice, fairness, fairplay, impartiality; ~ਪਸੰਦ Impartial, lover of justice.

ਇਨਕਲਾਬ (inklaab) *n m* Revolution, change.

ਇਨਕਾਰ (inkaar) *n m* Refusal, denial, dissention, objection; ~ਕਰਨਾ To refuse, to deny, to disobey.

ਇੰਨਾ (innaa) *adv* So much, this much that.

ਇਨਾਇਤ (inaayit) *n f* Benevolence, generosity, grace.

ਇਨਾਮ (inaam) *n m* Prize, gift, reward.

ਇਬਾਦਤ (ibaadat) *n f* Prayer, worship, devotion.

ਇਮਤਿਹਾਨ (imtihaan) *n m* Examination, test, investigation, trial.

ਇਮਦਾਦ (imdaad) *n f* Help, assistance, aid, succour, support.

ਇਮਾਨ (imaan) *n m* Faith, belief. Also ਈਮਾਨ

ਇਮਾਰਤ (imaarat) *n f* Building.

ਇਰਾਦਾ (iraadaa) *n m* Intention, idea, purpose, mind.

ਇੱਲ (ill) *n f* Kite (a bird).

ਇਲਹਾਮ (ilhaam) *n m* Prophecy, revelation.

ਇਲਜ਼ਾਮ (ilzaam) *n m* Allegation, blame, charge.

ਇੱਲਤ (illat) *n f* Bad habit, mischief; ~ਕਰਨੀ To make mischief, to frolic; ~ਪੈਣੀ To develop a bad habit.

ਇਲਮ (ilam) *n m* Knowledge, education, learning, science; ~ਹੋਣਾ To have knowledge, to have information, to be aware of.

ਇਲਾਹੀ (ilhaahee) *a* Celestial, divine.

ਇਲਾਕਾ (ilaakaa) *n m* Area, territory, jurisdiction, ward; ~ਈ Territorial, regional.

ਇਲਾਜ (ilaaj) *n m* Treatment, remedy, cure.

ਇਲਾਨ (ilan) *n m* declaration, proclamation, announcement, promulgation; **~ਕਰਨਾ** To declare, proclaim, announce, promulgate.

ਇਲਾਨੀਆ (ilaaniaa) *adv* Openly, publicly, by proclamation.

ਇਲਾਵਾ (ilava) *adv* Besides, in addition to, over and above.

ਇਵਜ (evaz) *n m* Return, exchange, replacement; **~ਵਿੱਚ** In return for, in exchange, in place of, as a substitute.

ਇਵਜ਼ਾਨਾ (ivazana) *n m* compensation, recompense, reparation.

ਈਰਖਾ (eerkhaa) *n f* Jealousy, envy, malice, malevolence.

ਏਕਣ (aekaṇ) *adv* Like this.

ਏਕਮ (ekam) *n f* One, first (data).

ਏਕਾ (aekaa) *n m* Unity, one.

ਏਡਾ (eḍaa) *adv* So much, this much.

ਏਦੂੰ (edoon) *adv* Compared to this, from this.

ਏਲਚੀ (elchee) *n m* Ambassador, messenger of some empire or a country.

ਸ

ਸ Fourth letter of Gurmukhi alphabets, pronounced as sassa.

ਸ਼ਊਰ (shaoor) *n m* Etiquette.

ਸੱਸ (sass) *n f* Mother-in-law.

ਸੰਸਕ੍ਰਿਤੀ (sanskriti) *n f* Culture.

ਸੰਸਕਾਰ (sanskaar) *n m* Sacrament, rite, ceremony, (last rite); Refinement; Mental impression; There are sixteen Hindu ceremonies.

ਸਸਕਾਰ (saskaar) *n m* Cremation.

ਸ਼ਸਤਰ (shastar) *n m* Weapon, arms, instrument.

ਸਸਤਾ (sastaa) *a* Cheap, trivial, easy.

ਸੰਸਥਾ (sansthaa) *n f* Institution, organisation, concern.

ਸੰਸਥਾਨ (sansthaan) *n m* Institute, Institution.

ਸੰਸਦ (sansad) *n f* Parliament.

ਸੰਸਾ (sansaa) *n m* Doubt, fear, suspicion, uncertainty.

ਸੰਸਾਰ (sansaar) *n m* Universe, world.

ਸੰਸਾਰਿਕ (sansaarik) *a* Worldly, mundane, physical, temporal, pertaining to mundane existence.

ਸੰਸਾਰੀ (sansaaree) *a* Of this world, worldly, mortal (usually for person).

ਸ਼ਸ਼ੋਪੰਜ (shashopanj) *n m* Hesitation, indecision, perplexity, hesitancy.

ਸਹਾਇਤਾ (sahaayitaa) *n f* Assistance, help, aid, succour; ~ਕਰਨੀ or ਦੇਣੀ To assist, to help, to support, to succour.

ਸ਼ਹਾਦਤ (shahaadat) *n f* Martyrdom; testimony, evidence.

ਸਹਾਈ (sahaaee) *a* (one) who provides help, assistance or support; conducive; ~ਹੋਣਾ To go to one's help, to come to one's resuce, to be conducive to.

ਸਹਾਰਨਾ (sahaarnaa) *v* To endure, to bear, to suffer; To support, to hold, to sustain.

ਸਹਾਰਾ (sahaaraa) *n m* Support, assistance, help, shoulder, succour, aid.

ਸ਼ਹਿ (sheh) *n* Instigation, incitement.

ਸਹਿਆ (sahiaa) *n m* Rabbit, hare.

ਸਹਿਹੋਂਦ (saihond) *n* Coexistence, symbiosis.

ਸਹਿਕਣਾ (saihkaṇaa) *v* To long for, to wish to have.

ਸਹਿਕਰਮੀ (saihkarmee) *n m* Colleague, officemate.

ਸਹਿਕਾਰ (saihkaar) *n m* Cooperation,

collaboration. Also **ਸਹਿਕਾਰਿਤਾ**

ਸਹਿਕਾਲੀ (saihkaalee) *a* Contemporary, coeval.

ਸਹਿਗਾਨ (saihgaaṇ) *n* Chorus.

ਸਹਿਚਾਰਤਾ (saihchartaa) *n* *f* Association.

ਸਹਿਜ (Saihj) *a* Natural, native, cognate, easy.

ਸਹਿਣਾ (saihṇaa) *v* To bear, to endure, to suffer, to sustain.

ਸਹਿਨਸ਼ੀਲ (saihnsheel) *a* Tolerable, forbearing, endurable, moderate.

ਸਹਿਮਣਾ (saihmṇaa) *v* To be afraid, overawed; To wince, to finch to recoil.

ਸਹੀ (sahee) *n* *a* *m* Signature, attestation; Correct, accurate, right.

ਸ਼ਹੀਦ (shaheed) *n* Martyr.

ਸੰਹੁ (sanhu) *n* *f* Oath, vow, pledge, affirmation.

ਸਹੁਰ (sauhr) *n* *m* Husband.

ਸਹੁਰਾ (sauhraa) *n* *m* Father-in-law.

ਸਹੂਲਤ (sahoolat) *n* *f* Facility, ease.

ਸਹੇਲੀ (sahelee) *n* *f* Female friend of a lady or girl. Also **ਸਹੇਲੜੀ**

ਸਹੇੜਨਾ (saherṇaa) *v* To contract, to enter into relationship with; To acquire, to own, to adopt.

ਸੱਕ (sakk) *n* *m* Bark, peel, sliver, splinter, spill; Bark of a particular plant used, usually by women to clean teeth and mouth and as a cosmetic for colouring lips and gums.

ਸੰਕਟ (sankaṭ) *n* *m* Distress, crisis, agony, calamity, danger; **~ਕਾਲ** Emergency; **~ਮਈ** Dangerous, hazardous.

ਸਕੱਤਰ (sakatar) *n* *m* Secretary.

ਸੱਕਤਰੇਤ (sakatteret) *n* *m* Secretarial job or duties.

ਸ਼ਕਤੀ (shaktee) *n* *f* Power, strength, vigour, might, capacity, energy, potency, calibre, force.

ਸੰਕਰ (sankar) *a* Hybrid, integrade, crossbreed.

ਸ਼ੱਕਰ (shakkar) *n* *f* Sugar, rawsugar.

ਸ਼ਕਲ (shakal) *n* *f* Figure, shape, form face, appearance.

ਸੰਕਲਨ (sankalan) *n* *m* Compilation, collection, consolidation.

ਸ਼ੰਕਾ (shankaa) *n* *f* Doubt, suspicion, disbelief, suspense.

ਸਕਾਰਥ (sakaarath) *a* Purposeful, meaningful.

ਸਕਾਰਨਾ (sakaarna) *v* To accept, to approve, to endorse.

ਸਕਾਰਾ (sakaaraa) *n* *m* Commission (for encashment).

ਸ਼ੱਕੀ (shakkee) *a* Doubtful, sceptic.

ਸੰਕੀਰਨ (sankeeran) *a* Narrow, Parochial, complex; ~ਤਾ Narrowness, pettiness, meaness, complexity.

ਸਕੂਨ (sakoon) *n m* Peace; ~ਮਿਲਣਾ To have peace; To feel relieved.

ਸੰਕੇਤ (sanket) *n m* Sign, symbol, code, hint, suggestion; ~ਕਰਨਾ To point out, to hint, to allude.

ਸ਼ਖਸ (shakhs) *n m* Person, individual.

ਸੱਖਣਾ (sakhnaa) *a* Hollow, vacant, empty.

ਸਖਤ (sakhat) *a* Hard, harsh, stiff, rigid, cruel.

ਸਖਾਵਤ (sakhaawat) *n f* Generasity, munificance, charity.

ਸੰਖਿਆ (sankhiaa) *n f* Number, sum, calculation.

ਸਖੀ (sakhee) *a* Generous, liberal, bountiful.

ਸੰਖੇਪ (sankhep) *n a m* Abridgement, brevity, precis, resume, synopsis, abstract; brief, short, concise, extract.

ਸੰਗ (sang) *n m* Association, company, friendship.

ਸੰਗਤ (sangat) *n f* Company, association; Religious congregation; (math) Correspondence.

ਸੰਗਤਰਾ (sangtaraa) *n m* Orange, *Citrus aurantium, Citrus sinesis.*

ਸੰਗਠਨ (sangathan) *n m* Organisation.

ਸੰਗਣਾ (sangnaa) *v* To feel shy, to hesitate, to be bashfull.

ਸੰਗਦਿਲ (sangdil) *a* Cruel.

ਸਗਨ (sagan) *n m* Presage, augury, portent; Gift in cash made to bride or bridegroom on the occasion of betrothal or marriage, or to a child on its birth; ~ਪਾਉਣਾ To give a monetary gift on an auspicious occassion.

ਸੰਗਮ (sangam) *n m* Junction, union, juncture, confluence.

ਸੰਗਲ (sangal) *n f* Chain, signal.

ਸਗਾਈ (sagaaee) *n f* Betrothal, engagement.

ਸ਼ਗਿਰਦ (shagird) *n m* Pupil, student.

ਸੰਗੀਤ (sangeet) *n m* Music.

ਸੰਗੀਨ (Sangeen) *a* Severe, serious, intense, heavy.

ਸੰਗ੍ਰਹਿ (sangreh) *n m* Collection, compilation.

ਸਗੋਂ (sagon) *adv conj* But, rather, on the contrary.

ਸੰਘ (sangh) *n m* (1) Throat, gullet; (2) Association, organisation, guild.

ਸੰਘਾਰ (sanghaar) *n m* Massacre, annihilation.

ਸੱਚ (Sachch) *n a m* Truth; Right; True.

ਸੱਚਾਈ (sachaaee) *n f* Truth, fact, sincerity, veracity. Also ਸਚਿਆਈ

ਸੰਚਾਰ (sanchaar) *n m* Communication, propagation, penetration.

ਸੰਚਾਲਕ (sanchaalak) *n m* Director, conductor.

ਸੱਜਣ (sajjaṇ) *n m* Virtuous man; Respectable person; Well wisher friend; Lover.

ਸੰਜਮ (sanjam) *n m* Restraint, discipline, soberness, brevity.

ਸੱਜਾ (Sajja) *a n f* Right; Decoration.

ਸਜ਼ਾ (sazaa) *n f* Punishment, penalty.

ਸਜਾਉਣਾ (sajaauṇaa) *v* To decorate, to adorn, to beautify, to embellish, to grace, to equip.

ਸਜਾਵਟ (sajaawaṭ) *n f* Decoration, Adornment, display, embellishment.

ਸੰਜੀਦਗੀ (sanjeedgee) *n f* Seriousness.

ਸੰਜੀਦਾ (sanjeedaa) *a* Serious, soleman.

ਸਜੀਲਾ (sajeelaa) *a* Handsome, beautiful, graceful, well-shaped.

ਸੱਜੂ (sajoo) *a* Right handed; Rightist.

ਸੰਜੋਗ (sanjog) *n m* Chance, opportunity, luck; Coherence, cohesion, event; Association.

ਸੰਝ (sanjh) *n f* Evening, sunset.

ਸੱਟ (saṭṭ) *n f* Stroke, hit, injury; ~ਮਾਰਨੀ or ਲਾਉਣੀ To strike, to whack, to blow.

ਸੱਟਾ (saṭṭaa) *n m* Speculation, business at stock exchange, forward dealing; Wild guess, bluff; Gambling; ~ਬਜ਼ਾਰ Stock exchange.

ਸੱਟੇਬਾਜ਼ (saṭṭebaaz) *n m* Speculator; bluff, bluffer.

ਸੱਟੇਬਾਜ਼ੀ (saṭṭebaazee) *n f* Speculation; Bluffing.

ਸੱਠ (saṭṭh) *a* sixty.

ਸੰਢਾ (sandhaa) *a* Stout, strong, robust; Bull.

ਸਤ (sat) *n m* Essence, juice, sap.

ਸੱਤ (satt) *a n* seven.

ਸੰਤ (sant) *n m* Saint, holy man, a pious or deeply religious person; An ascetic, mendicant; ~ਬਾਣੀ Utterances esp hymns of saints.

ਸਤਕਾਰ (satkaar) *n m* Respect, honour, reverence, hospitality, veneration, treatment.

ਸਤੱਰ (satarr) *n m* Standard, level, degree of excellence.

ਸਤਵੰਤ (satwant) *a* Virtuous.

ਸਤਾਉਣਾ (Sataauṇaa) *v* To tease, to torture, to harass, to oppress, to torment, to vex.

ਸਤਾਈ (sataee) *a* twenty-seven.

ਸੰਤਾਨ (santaan) *n m* Children, issue, offspring, progeny.

ਸ਼ਤਾਨ (shataan) *n m* Satan, devil.

ਸੰਤਾਪ (santaap) *n m* Distress, agony, sorrow, repentance, woe.

ਸ਼ਤਾਬੀ (shataabee) *adv* Quickly, hastily.

ਸਤਿਆ (satiaa) *a* Teased, vexed.

ਸੱਤਿਆ (sattiaa) *n m* Strength, power, truth, virtue.

ਸਤਿਆਨਾਸ (satiaanaas) *n m* Ruin, destruction.

ਸ਼ਤੀਰ (shateer) *n m* Beam, log, sleeper.

ਸੰਤੁਸ਼ਟੀ (santushtee) *n m* Satisfaction, satiation.

ਸੰਤੋਖ (ਸੰਤੋਸ਼) (santokh/santosh) *n m* Satisfaction, contentment, patience, complacence, gratification, comfort.

ਸਥਾਪਨਾ (sthaapnaa) *n m* Installing, foundation, establishing.

ਸਦਕਾ (Sadkaa) *n m adv* Alm, secrifice; Due to, for the sake of, because of.

ਸੱਦਣਾ (sadnaa) *n m* To call, to invite.

ਸਦਮਾ (sadmaa) *n m* Shock, blow, trauma; Sorrow, grief, bereavement; ~ਪਹੁੰਚਣਾ To suffer shock or trauma; ~ਪਹੁੰਚਾਉਣਾ To cause, to shock.

ਸਦਰ (sadar) *n m* President, chairman, chairperson.

ਸਦਾ (sadaa) *adv* Always, perpetually, constantly.

ਸੱਦਾ (saddaa) *n m* Invitation, call.

ਸਦਾਕਤ (sadaakat) *n m* Truth.

ਸਦਾਰਤ (sdaarat) *n f* Presidentship, chairmanship, headship.

ਸਦਾਚਾਰ (sadaachaar) *n m* Virtue, morality, etiquette, conduct.

ਸੰਦੂਕੜੀ (sandookaree) *n f* Small box. Also ਸੰਦੂਕ

ਸੰਧੂਰ (sandoor) *n m* Vermillion, red lead; ~ਦਾਨੀ Casket for containing vermilion.

ਸਨਕ (sanak) *n f* Mania, fad, sneering.

ਸਨਕੀ (sankee) *a* Whimisical, capricious, eccentric, idiosyncratic, cranky; Daft, crazy; Cynic, cynical.

ਸਨਤ (sanat) *n m* Industry; ~ਕਾਰ industrialist.

ਸਨਤੀ (sanatee) *a* Industrial; ~ਕਰਨ industrialisation.

ਸਨਦ (sanad) *n m* Certificate, testimonial.

ਸਨਮ (sanam) *n m* Sweet heart, beloved; Statue.

ਸਨਮਾਨ (sanmaan) *n m* Honour,

respect.

ਸਨਮੁਖ (sanmukh) *adv* Before, in front of, facing.

ਸ਼ਨਾਖਤ (shanaakht) *n f* Indentification.

ਸੰਨਾਟਾ (sannaataa) *n m* Absolute silence, stillness, quiet.

ਸਨਾਤਨ (Sanaatan) *a* Ancient, eternal, classical, premedieval, traditional.

ਸੰਨਿਆਸ (sanniyaas) *n m* Asceticism, renunciation, monasticism.

ਸਨੇਹਾ (sanehaa) *n m* Message esp. oral communication, information; ~ਘੱਲਣਾ To send a message; ~ਦੇਣਾ To give or deliver a message.

ਸੱਪ (sapp) *n m* Snake, serpent, viper; ~ਸੁੰਘਣਾ To be rendered still.

ਸਪਰੇਟਾ (sapretaa) *n m* Skimmed milk.

ਸ਼ਪਾਸ਼ਪ (shapaashap) *adv* Quickly, hurriedly.

ਸੰਪਾਦਕ (sampaadak) *n m* Editor.

ਸੰਪਾਦਕੀ (Sampaadkee) *n f* Editorial.

ਸਪੋਲੀਆ (sapoliyaa) *n a m* Small snake, untrustworthy, dangerous.

ਸਫਰ (safar) *n m* Journey, travel.

ਸਫ਼ਾ (safaa) *n m* Page, leaf.

ਸਫ਼ਾਇਆ (saffaaiaa) *n m* Elimination, extinction, annihilation, eradication.

ਸਫ਼ਾਈ (safaaee) *n f* Cleanliness, cleanness, hygiene, sanitation; Evidence or statement in defence esp. During a court case, defence, exculpation, vindication.

ਸਫ਼ਾਰਸ਼ (safaarash) *n f* Recommendation.

ਸਫ਼ਾਰਤ (safaarat) *n* Embassy, diplomatic mission; ~ਖ਼ਾਨਾ Embassy (building of office).

ਸਫ਼ੀਰ (safeer) *n m* Ambassador, envoy.

ਸਫ਼ੈਦ (safaid) *a* White, blank; ~ਝੂਠ Blatant lie, white lie.

ਸਫ਼ੈਦਾ (safaedaa) *n m* Eucalyptus, white paint in paste form, putty, white lead; Zinc oxide; Whitish variety of mango or of muskmelon.

ਸਫ਼ੈਦੀ (safaedee) *n f* Whiteness; White wash; White of egg.

ਸਬਕ (sabak) *n m* Lesson, lecture, moral.

ਸਬਜ਼ (sabaz) *a* Green fresh, verdant, unripe.

ਸ਼ਬਜ਼ੀ (saubzee) *n f* Vegetable, greenery, herbage.

ਸ਼ਬਦ (sabad) *n m* Sound, voice, religious hymn, word; ~ਜੋੜ

Spelling; ~ਕੋਸ਼ Dictionary.

ਸਬੱਬ (sabab) *n m* Reason, cause, excuse, ground, basis.

ਸਬਰ (sabar) *n m* Patience, contentment.

ਸ਼ਬਾਬ (shabaab) *n m* Youth.

ਸਬੀਲ (sabeel) *n m* plan, scheme.

ਸਬੂਤ (saboot) *n m* Evidence, proof.

ਸੰਭਲਨਾ (sambhalna) *v* To be alert, to be cautious.

ਸਭਾ (sabhaa) *n f* Association, assembly, society, convention, board, meeting.

ਸੰਭਾਲ (sambhaal) *n f* Care, control, upkeep, supervision.

ਸੰਭਾਲਨਾ (sambhaalnaa) *v* To protect, to nourish, to support, to retain, to sustain, to prop.

ਸਭਿਅਤਾ (sabhiyataa) *n f* Civilization, decency, politeness, etiquette.

ਸ਼ਮਸ਼ਾਨ (shamshaan) *n m* Cemetry, cremation ground.

ਸਮੱਸਿਆ (samasiyaa) *n f* Problem, dilemma.

ਸ਼ਮਸ਼ੀਰ (shamsheer) *n f* Sword.

ਸਮਝ (samajh) *n f* Understanding, comprehension, sense, knowledge; ~ਦਾਰ Intelligent, wise.

ਸਮਝਨਾ (samajhnaa) *v* To understand, to comprehend, to think, to suppose, to deem, to taken for.

ਸਮਝਾਉਣਾ (samjhaaunaa) *v* To explain, to instruct, to advise, to inculcate, to cause to understand.

ਸਮਝੌਤਾ (samjhautaa) *n m* Agreement, treaty, negotiation, compromise, concilliation, understanding.

ਸਮਰਥ (samrath) *a* Capable, fit.

ਸਮਰਥਨ (samarathan) *n m* Support, backing, agreement.

ਸਮਰਥਾ (samarthaa) *n f* Ability, power, competence, capacity, strength, vitality, vigour, might...

ਸਮਰਪਣ (samarpan) *n m* Dedication, surrender.

ਸਮਰੂਪਤਾ (samrooptaa) *n f* Similarity, homomorphism.

ਸਮਾ (samaa) *n m* Time, moment, period, season.

ਸਮਾਗਮ (samaagam) *n m* Assembly, meeting, conference, celebration.

ਸਮਾਚਾਰ (samaachaar) *n m* News, message, information, report; ~ਪਤਰ Newspaper.

ਸਮਾਜ (samaaj) *n m* Society, community institution, assembly.

ਸਮਾਧਾਨ (samdhaan) *n m* Solution.

ਸਮਾਪਟ (samaapan) *n m* Completion,

conclusion, termination, valedictory.

ਸਮਾਪਤੀ (smaaptee) *n f* Completion, end, expiry, termination.

ਸਮਾਯੋਜਨ (smaayojan) *n m* Adjustment.

ਸਮਾਰਕ (smaarak) *n m* Memorial.

ਸਮਾਲੋਚਨਾ (samaalochnaa) *n* Criticism, commentry.

ਸ਼ਮੀਜ (shameez) *n f* Bodice, brassiere, feminine underwear.

ਸਮੁੰਦਰ (samunder) *n m* Sea, ocean.

ਸਮੇਟਣਾ (sametnaa) *v* To collect, to gather, to amass, to fold up, to finish.

ਸਰ (sar) *n m* Tank, pond.

ਸਰਸਰਾਉਣਾ (sarsraaunaa) *v* To rustle.

ਸਰਸਰੀ (sarsaree) *a n f* Cursory, superficial, hurried; Summary (trial) haste, hurry.

ਸਰਹੱਦ (sarhadd) *n f* Boundary, frontier, limit.

ਸਰਹਾਣਾ (sarhaanaa) *n m* Pillow.

ਸਰਕਣਾ (sarknaa) *v* To move, to slide, to crawl, to slip, to creep.

ਸਰਕਾਉਣਾ (sarkaaunaa) *v* To shift, to displace, to push ahead.

ਸਮਗਰੀ (samaggree) *n f* Material, ingredients, stuff, equipment, tools, appliances, provisions (collectively).

ਸਮਾਉਣਾ (samauna) *v* To be adjusted or accommodated, to be absorbed, assimilated, imbibed; To combine; To be contained, held; To permeate, pervade.

ਸਮਾਗਮ (samaagam) *n m* Function, celebration; Gathering, reunion.

ਸਮਾਧ (samaadh) *n* Tomb, sepulchre, shrine raised over the ashes of a deceased person.

ਸਮਾਧੀ (samadāi) *n f* Deep meditation, contemplation, concentration as a mystic exercise or experience, trance; Sitting posture for meditation; Shrine raised over the ashes of a deceared great man, tomb.

ਸਮੀਖਿਆ (sameekhiaa) *n f* Review, careful, detailied or critical study, critique, commentary, analysis; ~ਸ਼ਾਸਤਰ Criticism, art of criticism; ~ਕਰਨੀ To review, criticise, comment upon, to conduct a thorough study (of or about)

ਸਮੋਸਾ (samosaa) *n m* A kind of roasted sandwich, a snack.

ਸਮੋਣਾ (samonaa) *v* To absorb, subsume, assimilate, incorporate.

ਸੱਯਾਹ (sayyaa) *n m* Traveller, tourist, explorer.

ਸੱਯਾਦ (sayyaad) *n m* Bird-catcher, fowler, hunter.

ਸਰਕਾਰ (sarkaar) *n f* Government, administrator, master.

ਸਰਕਾਰੀ (sarkaaree) *a* Of pertaining to government, governmental, official, public, state.

ਸਰਗਨਾ (sarganaa) *n m* leader, head, chief, (usually of a group of criminals of rebels).

ਸਰਗਰਮ (sargaram) *a* Active, actively engaged, zealously busy; enthusiastic, intent, energetic, dilligent.

ਸਰਗਰਮੀ (sargarmee) *n f* Zeal, passion, activity.

ਸ਼ਰਣ (sharaṇ) *n f* Shelter, refuge, protection.

ਸ਼ਰਤ (sharat) *n f* Condition, bet, stipulation.

ਸਰਦਾਰ (sardaar) *n m* Chief, leader, eminent person, foreman.

ਸਰਦੀ (sardee) *n f* Winter, coldness, cold, chilliness.

ਸ਼ਰਧਾ (shardhaa) *n f* Faith, trust, belief, reliance.

ਸਰਪ੍ਰਸਤ (sarprast) *n m* Guardian, patron.

ਸਰਫ਼ (saraf) *n m* Expenditure, expense.

ਸਰਫ਼ਾ (sarfaa) *n m* Saving, economy.

ਸ਼ਰਬਤ (sharbat) *n m* Syrup, sweet drink.

ਸਰਬੱਤ (sarbatt) *adv* All & sundary, all.

ਸ਼ਰਮ (sharam) *n f* Shame, modesty, bashfulness; ~ਨਾਕ Shameful, disgraceful.

ਸ਼ਰਮਾਕਲ (sharmaakal) *a* Shy, modest, bashful.

ਸ਼ਰਮੀਲਾ (sharmeelaa) *a* Shy, bashful.

ਸਰਲ (saral) *a* Plain, straight, easy, upright, simple, honest; ~ਤਾ Simplicity.

ਸਰਾਂ (saraan) *n f* Inn, tavern.

ਸਰਾਹੁਣਾ (sraahuṇaa) *v* To praise, to admire, to applaud, to appreciate, to laud, to eulogize: Also ਸਲਾਹੁਣਾ

ਸਰਾਪ (sraap) *n m* Curse.

ਸ਼ਰਾਫ਼ਤ (shraafat) *n f* Nobility, gentlemanliness, politeness.

ਸ਼ਰਾਬ (shraab) *n f* Liqour, wine, alcohal.

ਸ਼ਰਾਰਤ (shraarat) *n f* Mischief, vice, villainy, wickedness.

ਸ਼ਰਾਰਤੀ (shraartee) *n m* Mischievous, wicked.

ਸ਼ਰੀਕ (shreek) *n m* Partner, relative, friend; Included.

ਸ਼ਰੀਕਾ (shreekaa) *n m* Relationship, companionship.

ਸ਼ਰੀਫ਼ (shreef) *a n* Noble, gentle, holy; Nobleman.

ਸਰੀਰ (sreer) *n m* Body, physique person; ~ਤਿਆਗਣਾ to pass away, to die.

ਸ਼ਰੀਰ (shreer) *a* Mischievous, vicious, wicked.

ਸਰੋਕਾਰ (sarokaar) *n m* Concern, relation, interest.

ਸਰੋਪਾ (saropaa) *n m* Robe of honour.

ਸਰੋਵਰ (sarovar) *n m* Tank, lake, a large pond.

ਸਲਾਹ (slaah) *n m* Advice, counsel; Consulation; Opinion; ~ਕਾਰ adviser, consultant, counsellor.

ਸਲਾਖ਼ (salaakh) *n f* Rod, bar. Also ਸਰੀਆ

ਸਲਾਨਾ (slaanaa) *a* Annual, yearly.

ਸਲਾਮ (slaam) *n m* Salutation, compliments, adieu, goodbye.

ਸਲਾਮਤ (slaamat) *a* Safe, sound.

ਸਲੀਕਾ (sleekaa) *n m* Etiquette, decorum.

ਸਲੂਕ (salook) *n m* Behaviour, conduct, treatment, mode.

ਸਲੂਣਾ (saloonaa) *n m* Cooked vegetable dish; Saltish, saline; Tasty, savoury; ~ਪਣ Saltishness, salinity; Saltish taste.

ਸਲੋਨਾ (Saloonaa) *a* Charming.

ਸਵਰਗ (Sawarag) *n m* Heaven, paradise; Happiness; ~ਵਾਸ Death, demise, heavenly abode.

ਸਵਾਇਆ (swaaiaa) *a* One and a quarter times, informal, a little, in a small quantity.

ਸਵਾਸ (swaas) *n f* Breath, respiration.

ਸਵਾਹ (swaah) *n m* Ash, dust.

ਸਵਾਂਗ (swaang) *n m* Imitation, mimicry, drama, mockery, disguise, burlesque, mosquerade, folk play, fancy dress. Also ਸਾਂਗ

ਸੰਵਾਦ (sanwaad) *n m* Dialogue, conversation, correspondence, intelligence, information; ~ਦਾਤਾ Correspondent, pressmen.

ਸਵਾਦ (swaad) *n m* Taste, flavour; Relish pleasure, savour, delight.

ਸਵਾਦੀ (swaadee) *a* Tasteful, delicious, amorous.

ਸਵਾਰਥ (swaarath) *n m* Self-interest, selfishness, desire.

ਸਵਾਰਥੀ (swaarthee) *a* Selfish, selfseeking.

ਸੰਵੀਧਾਨ (sanvidhaan) *n m* Constitution.

ਸਵੀਕਾਰ (saweekar) *n m a* Assent, acceptance, agreement, promise; Accepted.

ਸਵੀਕਾਰਨਾ (sweekaarnaa) *v* To accept, to consent, to agree.

ਸੜਕ (sarak) *n f* Road, path, highway.

ਸੜਨਾ (sarnaa) *v* To rot, to decay, to perish, to burn.

ਸੜਾਂਹਦ (sraanhd) *n f* Stench, purtrid smell, putrefaction, disagreeable. Also ਸੜਿਆਂਦ

ਸਾਇਤ (saait) *n f* Time, moment (auspicious).

ਸਾਹ (saah) *n m* Breath, respite, rest, relaxation; ~ਆਉਣਾ To regain breath; To breathe easily or freely, to feel respite, to relax; ~ਸੁੱਕਣਾ To be frightened; ~ਘੁਟਣਾ To feel suffocation; ~ਚੜ੍ਹਨਾ To breathe heavily; To be out of breath; ~ਫੁਲਣਾ To breathe hard, heavily or rapidly, to feel difficulty in breathing, to be out of breath, with slight exertion; ~ਲੈਣਾ To breathe; To have respite to take rest, to relax after exertion, to take a breather; To wait; ~ਵਿਚ ਸਾਹ ਆਉਣਾ To breathe easily (after tension), to feel relief (following despair).

ਸ਼ਾਹ (shah) *n m* Money lender, banker, merchant, richman, king, gentleman, shopkeeper.

ਸ਼ਾਹਾਨਾ (shaahaanaa) *a* Regal, royal, majestic, princely.

ਸਾਹਿੱਤ (saahit) *n m* Literature; ~ਕਾਰ Literateur, writer, man of letters.

ਸਾਹਿਲ (saahil) *n m* Sea coast, sea shore.

ਸ਼ਾਹੂਕਾਰ (shaahookaar) *n m* Richman, wealthy, person, banker, moneylender.

ਸ਼ਾਹੂਕਾਰਾ (shaahookaaraa) *n m* Money lending, business, banking profession.

ਸਾਖ (saakh) *n f* Credibility, trust.

ਸ਼ਾਖ (shaakh) *n f* Branch, bough, sect, offshoot.

ਸਾਖਰ (saakhar) *a* Literate; ~ਤਾ literacy.

ਸਾਖਿਆਤ (sakhiaat) *a* Present, visible, manifest, in person, in conrete form.

ਸ·ਖੀ (saakhee) *n f* Story, anecdote *usu.* Connected with a holy person; Evidence, testimony; Witness, deponent, testifier.

ਸਾਗ (saag) *n m* Green leafy vegetable; A dish of vegetables.

ਸ਼ਾਗਿਰਦ (shaagird) *n m* Disciple, pupil, follower, student.

ਸਾਜ਼ਸ਼ (saazash) *n f* Conspiracy, intrigue, plot, complot collusion; ~ਕਰਨੀ To conspire, to plot, to complot, to collude, to intrigue.

ਸਾਜ਼ਬਾਜ਼ (saazbaaz) *n f* Illegal or secret contacts, collusion, conspiracy.

ਸਾਂਝ (saanjh) *n* Partnership, share, association.

ਸਾਂਝਾ (saanjhaa) *a* Common.

ਸ਼ਾਂਤੀ (shaantee) *n f* Peace, tranquility.

ਸਾਥੀ (saathee) *n m* Companion, comrade, associate, partisan.

ਸਾਦਗੀ (saadgee) *n f* Simplicity, plainness, homliness.

ਸਾਧਣਾ (saadhnaa) *v* To achieve, to resolve, to settle, to gain.

ਸਾਧਨ (saadhan) *n m* Channel, means, resource, equipment, accomplishment, device, medium.

ਸਾਧੂ (saadhoo) *n a m* Saint, hermit, sage, monk, ascetic, mendicant; Pious, holy, virtuous.

ਸ਼ਾਨ (shaan) *n f* Glory, grandeur, splendour, majesty, elegance, magnificence, dignity, lustre, embellishment.

ਸਾਨੀ (saanee) *a* Equal; Identical.

ਸਾਫ਼ (saaf) *a* Clean, clear, neat, distinct, vivid; Legible, intelligible; Unobstructed, smooth, frank, straightforward; Blatant, obvious; Cloudless; ~ਸਾਫ਼ Quite clear, categorical, frank, frankly, flatly; Lucidly, clearly; ~ਸੁਥਰਾ Clean, neat and clean, tidy; ~ਕਰਨਾ To clean, to wash, to cleanse, to rub, to scrub, to wipe, to mop; To clear, to clarify, to purify, to depurate, to refine; To spruce up, tidy up; To dress (meal); ~ਦਿਲ Honest, uprightness, guilelessness, candour.

ਸਾਫ਼ਗੋ (saafgo) *a* Truthful, frank; Upright, candid; ~ਈ Truthfulness, frankness, candour, uprightness, rectitude.

ਸਾਫ਼ਾ (saafaa) *n m* Turban, washcloth.

ਸਾਬਕ (saabak) *a* Former, ex-.

ਸਾਬਣ (saaban) *n m* Soap.

ਸਾਬਤ (saabat) *a* Complete, whole, full, compact.

ਸਾਂਭ (saambh) *n m* care, caretaking, maintenance, upkeep; Protection, custody, looking after; Preservation, conservation; ~ਕੇ ਰੱਖਣਾ To preserve, keep in good condition or safely.

ਸਾਂਭਣਾ (sambhnaa) *v* To secure, to keep safely; To occupy forcibly.

ਸਾਮੰਤ (saamant) *n m f* Feudal lord, mandarin, satrap, noble.

ਸਾਮੂਣਾ (saamanaa) *n m* Encounter,

confrontation, front, opposition;
~ਕਰਨਾ To face, to oppose, to
fight, to stand upto.

ਸਾਮ੍ਹਣੇ (saamane) *adv* In front of,
opposite, before, face to face,
in the presence of; ~ਹੋਣਾ To be
in front, to be present.

ਸ਼ਾਮਤ (shaamat) *n f* Misfortune,
illluck, misadventure, adversity,
disaster, affliction.

ਸਾਮਾਨ (samaan) *n m* Goods, stock,
material, apparatus.

ਸਾਰਨਾ (saarnaa) *v* To avail, to
accomplish, to complete, to
arrange.

ਸਾਰਨੀ (saarnee) *n f* Table, list.

ਸਾਲਣ (saalan) *n m* Meat, fish or
vegetable curry.

ਸਾਲਮ (saalam) *a* Complete, uncut,
undivided, full, whole.

ਸਾਲਾ (saalaa) *n m* Brother-in-law,
wife's brother.

ਸਾਲਾਨਾ (saalaanaa) *a* Annual, yearly.

ਸਾਵਧਾਨੀ (saavdhaanee) *n* Vigilance,
alertness, consciousness.

ਸਾਂਵਲਾ (saanwlaa) *a* Dark
complexioned, tawny.

ਸਾੜਨਾ (saarnaa) *v* To burn, to char,
to cremate, to rot.

ਸਿਆਸਤ (siaasat) *n f* Politics; ~ਦਾਨ
Politician.

ਸਿਆਹੀ (siaahee) *n f* Ink; Darkness.

ਸਿਆਣਨਾ (siaannaa) *v* To recognise,
to identify.

ਸਿਆਣਪ (siaanap) *n m* Wisdom,
intelligence, dexterity, cleverness.

ਸਿਆਣਾ (siaanaa) *a* Wise, intelligent,
sagacious, prudent,
circumspect, sensible; Physician;
Old person.

ਸਿਆਪਾ (siaapaa) *n m* Mourning,
wailing; ~ਪਾਉਣਾ To creat
problem; ~ਪੈਣਾ To be in trouble

ਸਿਆਲ (siaal) *n m* Winter, cold
season.

ਸਿਸਕਣਾ (sisaknaa) *v* To sob, to
flutter, on the death bed.

ਸਿਸਕਾਰਨਾ (siskaarnaa) *v* To hiss, to
produce a hissing sound.

ਸਿਸਕੀ (siskee) *n f* Sobbing, sighing.

ਸਿਹਤ (sihat) *n f* Health; Physical
fitness.

ਸਿਹਾਰੀ (sihaaree) *n f* Vowel sign ਇ
in Gurmukhi script.

ਸਹੇੜਨਾ (sahernaa) *v* To adopt, to
acquire, to take responsibility of.

ਸਿੱਕ (sikk) *n f* Longing, yearning,
love, desire.

ਸ਼ਿਕਸਤ (shikast) *n f* Defeat, failure.

ਸ਼ਿਕੰਜਵੀ (shikanjavee) *n f* Lemon
juice.

ਸ਼ਿਕੰਜਾ (shikanjaa) *n m* Clamp, press,

rack, torture.

ਸਿਕੜਾ (siknaa) *v* To yearn, to be fond of.

ਸਿੱਕੜਾ (sikknaa) *v* To long, to yearn, to desire, to hope.

ਸਿਕਰੀ (sikree) *n f* Dandruff, scurf.

ਸਿਕਵਾਉਣਾ (sikvaaunaa) *v* To get some thing warmed, heated or baked. Also **ਸਿਕਾਉਣਾ**

ਸਿੱਕਾ (sikkaa) *n m* Coin.

ਸ਼ਿਕਾਇਤ (shikaayit) *n f* Complaint, grievance, ailment, accusation.

ਸ਼ਿਕਾਰ (shikaar) *n m* Prey, victim, chase, quarry.

ਸਿੱਖ (sikh) *n f* Sikh (Community), pupil; Advice, instruction.

ਸਿਖਣਾ (sikhnaa) *v* To learn, to acquire knowledge or skill, to receive training.

ਸਿਖਲਾਈ (sikhlaaee) *n f* Instruction, training, teaching, schooling.

ਸਿਖਿਆ (sikhiaa) *n f* Education, schooling, tutuion, instruction, training, advice, teaching, precept: **~ਸਿਖਾਇਆ** Already trained; Under instigation; **~ਸ਼ਾਸਤਰ** Pedagogy, paedantics, theory and art of teaching; **~ਦੇਣਾ** To advise, to instruct, to educate, to train.

ਸਿਖਾਉਣਾ (sikhaaunaa) *v* To teach, to

instruct, to train, to educate.

ਸਿਟਣਾ (sitnaa) *v* To throw, to drop.

ਸਿਤਮ (sitam) *n m* Tyranny, oppression.

ਸਿਥਲ (sithal) *a* Inactive, ineffective, dormant, feeble, weak, weary, sickly; **~ਤਾ** Inactiveness, infirmity, laxity, inertia, weariness, dormancy, sickliness.

ਸਿਧੱੜ (siddhar) *a* Simple, simlpleton.

ਸਿੱਧਾ (siddhaa) *a* Straight, direct, plain, simple, erect, innocent.

ਸਿਧਾਉਣਾ (sidhaaunaa) *v* To tame, to domesticate.

ਸਿਧਾਂਤ (sidhaant) *n m* Theory, principle, doctrine, axiom, thesis.

ਸਿਧਾਰਨਾ (sidhaarnaa) *v* To depart, to proceed; **ਪਰਲੋਕ~** To die, to breathe one's last.

ਸਿਪਾਹਸਲਾਰ (sipaahslaar) *n m* Commander, general, commander-in-chief.

ਸਿਪਾਹੀ (sipaahee) *n m* Soldier, constable.

ਸਿਫ਼ਤ (sifat) *n f* Glorification, Praise, attribution, appreciation.

ਸਿਫ਼ਰ (sifar) *n f* Zero, nil, naught, cypher.

ਸਿਮਟਣਾ (simatnaa) *v* To contract, to shrink, to shrivel.

ਸਿਮਰਨ (simaran) *n m*

Rememberance, recollection, memory.

ਸਿਮਰਨਾ (simaranaa) v To remember, to recollect, to meditate.

ਸਿਰ (sir) *n m* Head, top, apex; ~ਉੱਚਾ ਕਰਨਾ To stand up with honour; ~ਅੱਖਾਂ ਤੇ With pleasure, most cordially, most cheerfully; ~ਸਿਹਰਾ Credit; ~ਸਾਰਾਹ To damn; ~ਖਪਾਈ Wearisome labour, irritation, idle talk, drudgery; ~ਖਾਣਾ To bore, to vex, to tease, to bother; ~ਖੇਹ ਪੈਣੀ To be insulted, to be disgraced; ~ਘੁਮਣਾ To feel giddy; ~ਚੁਕਣਾ To rebel, to rise against; ~ਚੜਨਾ To be impudent, to become arrogant; ~ਤੇ ਬਣਨੀ To be in trouble; ~ਤੇ ਭੂਤ ਸਵਾਰ ਹੋਣਾ To be crazy, to be under obsession; ~ਨਿਵਾਉਣਾ To salute, to bow in abeisance; ~ਨੀਵਾਂ ਹੋਣਾ To be disgraced, to be ashamed, to lose face; ~ਪਿਟਣਾ To lament; ~ਪੈਰ ਨਾ ਹੋਣਾ Not in order; ~ਫਿਰਨਾ To go mad, to run amuck; ~ਭਾਰੀ ਹੋਣਾ to have, an headache; ~ਮਾਰਨਾ To workhard, to make diligent search.

ਸਿਰੜੀ (sirṛee) a Obstinate, stubborn; Hardworking.

ਸਿਰਾ (siraa) *n m* Side, end, apex, edge, margin, point.

ਸਿਲ (sil) *n f* Stone slab, flat piece of rock; ~ਵੱਟਾ Stone and pestle, grinding stone.

ਸਿਲਸਿਲਾ (silsilaa) *n m* Series, sequence, concatenation; Serial order, arrangement, der, system.

ਸਿਲਸਿਲੇਵਾਰ (silsilevaar) *a adv* Serial, serially arranged, concatenate, consecutive, successive; In a row, serially, consecutively, successively; ~ਕਰਨਾ To serialise, to arrange serially or in a particular order.

ਸਿਲਮਾ (silmaa) *n m* Fine gold, silver or copper wire or thread used in embroidery or filigree; ~ਸਿਤਾਰਾ Ornamentation, embellishment.

ਸਿਲਾ (silaa) *n m* Consequence; Reward, recompense, requital; ~ਦੇਣਾ To reward, to recompense or repay, to requite.

ਸਿਆ (sia) *n m* Mild, pleasant warmth (provided by sunshine during winter), sun.

ਸ਼ੀਸ਼ਾ (sheeshaa) *n m* Mirror, looking glass, glass, pane.

ਸ਼ੀਸ਼ੀ (sheeshee) *n f* Small bottle.

ਸੀਟੀ (seetee) *n f* Whistle, buzzer

ਸੀਨਾ (seenaa) *n m* Chest, bosom,

breast; ~ਜ਼ੋਰ Aggressor.

ਸੀਮਾ (seemaa) *n f* Border, demarcation, limit, precinct, landmark.

ਸੀਖ (seekh) *n f* (1) Advice, instruction (2) Metallic rod or bar skewer; (3) Match stick; ~ਕਬਾਬ Minced meat roasted on a skewer, seekh kebab, shashlick.

ਸੀਮਿਤ (seemit) *a* Limited, finite.

ਸੀਰਤ (seerat) *n f* Temperament.

ਸੀਰਾ (seera) *n m* a Semi-solid or liquid dish of roasted wheat flour mixed with boiled, sweetened water; Syrup; Treacle; Molasses.

ਸੁਆਹ (suaah) *n m* Ash, ashes, cinder.

ਸੁਆਉਣਾ (suaaunaa) *v* (1) To assist (an animal) to clave or foal; (2) To lull or make (one) to sleep; (3) To get (a garment) stitched.

ਸੁਆਗਤ (suaagat) *n* Welcome, reception, acceptance. Also ਸਵਾਗਤ

ਸਵਾਗਤੀ (suaagatee) *n m* Receptionist.

ਸੁਆਦ (suaad) *n m* Taste, relish, pleasure, delight.

ਸੁਆਰਨਾ (suaarnaa) *v* To improve, refine, reform, repair; To accomplish or help in accomplishing; To clean, brush up, spruce, to adorn, to decorate; To repair, to set right, to remove fault or defect.

ਸੁਆਲ (suaal) *n m* Question, problem, sum, querry, interrogation, demand; ~ਜੁਆਬ Question-answer, controversy, interlocution, discussion, wrangling, querrel, dispute; ~ਪਾਉਣਾ To put a question, to request, to demand, to set a problem. Also ਸਵਾਲ

ਸੁਆਲੀ (suaalee) *n m* Beggar.

ਸੁਸਤੀ (sustee) *n f* Laziness, slowness, lethargy, idleness, indolence, dullness, negligence.

ਸੁਹੰਢਣਾ (suhandhnaa) *a* Durable, long lasting.

ਸੁਹੰਪ (suhannap) *n m* Beauty, prettiness, comeliness, handsomensss, physical charm, attractiveness, grace

ਸੁਹਣਾ (suhnaa) *a* Charming, beautiful, handsome, graceful.

ਸੁਹਬਤ (sobat) *n f* Company, society, association.

ਸੁਹਰਤ (suharat) *n f* Fame, reputation, celebrity.

ਸੁਹਾਗ (suhaag) *n m* Married state of a woman while her husband is alive, bliss of married life; Ornaments worn by women only while their husbands are alive; Nuptial song; ~ਉਜੜਨਾ To become a widow; ~ਗੀਤ Nuptial song; ~ਭਾਗ good fortune, bliss of married women; ~ਰਾਤ The first night of the newly weds sharing a bed.

ਸੁਹਾਗਣ (suhaagan) n f Married or fortunate women, a woman whose hasband is alive.

ਸੁਹਾਗਾ (suhaagaa) n m Borax, tincal orrispowder.

ਸੁਹੇਲਾ (suhelaa) a m Easy; Comfortable, soothing.

ਸੁਕਣਾ (suknaa) v To wither, to dry, to evaporate, to be lean and thin, to emaciate.

ਸ਼ੁਕਰੀਆ (shukriyaa) n m Thanks.

ਸੁਕੜਨਾ (Sukarnaa) v To shrink, to contract.

ਸੁਕਾ (sukaa) a Dry, withered, anhydrous, arid, blank.

ਸੁਕਾਉਣਾ (sukaaunaa) v To dry, to air, to dehydrate, to evaporate, desicate, to cause, to wither.

ਸੁਕੇੜਨਾ (sukernaa) v To compress, to deflate, to shrink; To collect.

ਸੁਖ (sukh) n m Comfort, amenity, ease, pleasure, delight, good health; ~ਦਾਈ Comfortable, soothing; ~ਦੁਖ Ups and downs.

ਸੁਖਾਉਣਾ (sukhaaunaa) v To agree, to suit, to soothe, to relieve pain.

ਸੁਗੰਦ (sugand) n f Oath, conjuration.

ਸੁਗੰਧ (sugandh) n f Fragrance, incense, odour, smell, perfume, aroma.

ਸੁਗਮ (sugam) a Facile, easy, exoteric, feasible.

ਸ਼ੁਗਲ (shugal) n m Hobby, avocation, amusement, recreation, pastime.

ਸੁੰਗੜਨਾ (sungarnaa) v To shrink, contract, to shrivel, to pucker.

ਸੁੰਗੜਾ (sungraa) n m Shrinkage, contraction (extent of).

ਸੁਗਾਤ (sugaat) n f Gift, present, curio, speciality.

ਸੁੰਘਣਾ (sunghnaa) v To smell, to sniff, to nose, to scent.

ਸੁਘੜ (sughar) a Elegent, sensible, competent, skillful, accomplished, decorous, virtuous; ~ਤਾ Accomplishment, intelligence, adroitness; Competence; ~ਸੁਜਾਨ Intelligent; Virtuous.

ਸੁੱਚਾ (suchchaa) a Pure, chaste, genuine, clean, unpolluted.

ਸੁਚੇਤ (suchet) a Cautious, alert, mindful, attentive, awake, aware, conscious, careful, watchful, wakeful, vigilant.

ਸੁੰਜ (sunj) *n f* Inhabitation, desolation, emptiness.

ਸੁਜਣਾ (sujṇaa) *v* To swell, to be puffed, to be angry.

ਸੁੱਜਾ (sujjaa) *a* Swollen, inflamed, tumid, turgid, turgent.

ਸੁਝਣਾ (sujhṇaa) *v* To Strike, to occur suddenly, to come to mind, at once.

ਸੁੰਞ (sunñ) *n f* Vaccum, vacuity, void, emptiness, vacant place, desolation, vacancy, nothingness; Lonelinesss, lonesomeness.

ਸੁੰਞਾ (suñaa) *a* Vacant, solitary, lone, deserted, naked.

ਸੁਟਣਾ (suṭṇaa) *v* To throw, to discard, to fling.

ਸੁੰਡ (sunḍ) *n f* Trunk of an elephant.

ਸੁੰਢ (sundh) *n f* Dry ginger.

ਸੁਣਕਣਾ (suṇakṇaa) *v* To blow the nose.

ਸੁਣਨਾ (suṇnaa) *v* To hear, to listen, to attend, to heed.

ਸੁਣਵਾਈ (suṇvaaee) *n f* Hearing *esp* of petition in law suit.

ਸੁਣਾਉਣਾ (suṇaaunaa) *v* To tell, to repeat, to read out, to say, to relate, to narrate.

ਸੁਤੰਤਰ (sutantar) *a* Independent, free, self-governing, unrestrained, uncontrolled; ~ਤਾ Independence, freedom, liberty.

ਸੁੱਥਣ (sutthaṇ) *n f* Trousers usually worn by females. (Also called **ਸਲਵਾਰ**)

ਸੁਥਰਾ (suthraa) *a* Neat, clean, pure, orderly, chaste; ~ਪਣ Neatness, cleanliness, tidiness.

ਸੁੰਦਰ (sundar) *a* Beautiful, handsome, elegant, grand, pretty, fair, fine, bonny; ~ਤਾ Beauty, hand someness, grace, prettiness.

ਸੁਦਰਸ਼ਨ (sudarshan) *a* Elegant, beautiful, good-looking; ~ਚੱਕਰ Mythical ring-shaped weapon wielded by Lord Krishana.

ਸੁਦਾਈ (shudaaee) *a* Eccentric insane, crazy, loony, mad.

ਸੁਦਾਗਰ (sudaagar) *n m* Merchant, trader.

ਸੁੱਧ (suddh) *n f* Intelligence, sensation, attention, care, consciousness, feeling; ਬੁੱਧ~ Commonsense, sensibility, persence of mind; ~ਲੈਣੀ To remember to enquire after; ਬੇ~ Senseless.

ਸੁਧ (shudh) *a* Pure, uncorrupt, unpolluted, chaste, sanctified, pure; ~ਕਰਨਾ To purify, to chestena, to modify. Also ਸੁਧ

ਸੁੰਧਕ (sundhak) *n f* Information, clue, trace, hint, intelligence; ~ਲੈਣੀ To gather information, to try, to findout, to spy.

ਸੁਧਰਨਾ (sudharnaa) *v* To be improved, reformed, rectified or mended, to improve, to get better.

ਸੁਧਾਰ (sudhaar) *n f* Reforms, improvement, correction, reformation.

ਸੁਧਾਣਾ (sudhaanaa) *v* To tame, to train.

ਸੁਧਾਰਨਾ (sudhaarnaa) *v* To amend, to reform, to correct, to improve, to rectify, to renovate, to refine

ਸੁੱਧੀ (suddhee) *n f* Purification, purity, ablution, santification.

ਸੁੰਨ (sunn) *a* (1) Void, emptiness, absolute silence, (2) Benumbed, insane deed; ~ਹੋਣਾ To be benumed, to be stunned.

ਸੁਨਸਾਨ (sunsaan) *a* Desolate, barren, dreary, lonely.

ਸੁਨੇਹਾ (sunehaa) *n m* Message.

ਸੁਪਨਾ (supnaa) *n m* Dream, vision.

ਸੁਪਾਰੀ (supari) *n f* Betel nut, arecanut; Betel-palm, *Areca catechu.*

ਸੁਬਕ (subak) *a* Thin, slender, slim,

lean, delicate; Fast, swift-footed, agile.

ਸੁਬ੍ਹਾ (shubbaa) *n m* Doubt, distrust suspicion.

ਸੁਬੜਾ (subṛaa) *n m* A skin disease of chickenpox type.

ਸੁਭਾਉ (subhaau) *n m* Habit, nature, temperament, disposition, habitual behaviour, habitude; Character, mentality. Also ਸੁਭਾਅ

ਸੁਭਾਗ (subhaag) *n m* Good luck, good fortune, felicity; Lucky, fortunate.

ਸੁਯੋਗ (suyog) *a* Worthy, befitting, deserving; Acuminous.

ਸੁਰ (sur) *n m* (1) Angel, god; (2) Tune, melody, note; Cadence, tone, pitch; Musical sound or voice; ~ਸੰਗਮ Symphony; ~ਤਾਲ Musical rhythm, cadence; ~ਮਿਲਾਉਣਾ To harmonise, attune; *fig* To agree to, to chime in.

ਸੁਰਕੀ (surkee) *n f* Sip; Sound produced by sipping a liquid too hot for gulping; Slurp.

ਸੁਰਖ (surakh) *a* Red, scarlet.

ਸੁਰਖਾਬ (surkhaab) *n m* Ruddy sheldrake; ~ਦਾ ਪਰ ਲਗਣਾ To assume a novel or special position.

ਸੁਰਖੀ (surkhee) *n f* Redness, red

colour, pink-coloured face powder, reddle, ruddle; Headline, heading, title, caption, rubric.

ਸੁਰਗ (surag) *n f* Paradise, heaven, Elysium, Olympus, abode of God or gods, the next world.

ਸੁਰੰਗ (surang) *n f* Tunnel, mine, subterraneous.

ਸੁਰਜੀਤ (surjeet) *a* Alive.

ਸੁਰਤ (surat) *n f* Awareness, attention, awakening, presence of mind, reflection, sense.

ਸੁਰਮਾ (surma) *n m* Antimony or collyrium powder; Graphite, plumbago rod in a lead pencil, lead of a pencil.

ਸੁਰਾਹੀ (suraahee) *n f* Flagon, flask.

ਸੁਰਾਖ (suraakh) *n m* Hole, perforation, orifice, aperture, cavity, bore; ~ਕਰਨਾ/ ~ਕੱਢਣਾ To make, dig or pierce a hole to perforate, to bore; ~ਦਾਰ Perforated.

ਸੁਰਾਗ (suraag) *n m* Clue, trace, hint, sign, lead, leading intelligence; ~ਕੱਢਣਾ To trace, to spy.

ਸੁਰੀਲਾ (sureelaa) *a* Melodious, musical, harmonious, sonorous, sweet.

ਸੁਲਾਹ (sulaah) *n f* Agreement, rapprochment, peace; ~ਕਰਨੀ

To make peace, to come, to terms, to compromise, to settle (dispute), to conclude peace treaty. Also ਸੁਲ੍ਹਾ

ਸੁਲੱਖਣਾ (sulakhṇaa) *a* Fortunate, happy, gentle.

ਸੁਲਗਾਉਣਾ (sulgaauṇaa) *v* To inflame, to kindle, to light, to fan.

ਸੁਲੱਛਣਾ (sulachhṇaa) *a* Good natured, good mannered.

ਸੁਲਝਣਾ (sulajhnaa) *v* To be settled, to be unravelled.

ਸੁਲਝਾਉਣਾ (suljhaauṇaa) *v* To disentangle, to unravel, to straighten, to solve.

ਸੁਲਤਾਨ (sultaan) *n m* King, emperor, ruler, sultan.

ਸੁਲਫਾ (sulfaa) *n* A small ball of crude tobacco or charas, an intoxicating drug.

ਸੁਵੰਨਾ (suannaa) *a m* Of good colour, pleasing to the eye.

ਸੁਵੱਲਾ (suvallaa) *a m* Cheap, lowpriced, inexpensive.

ਸੁਵਾਸ (suvaas) *n m* Fragrance, aroma, perfume, scent.

ਸੁੜਕਣਾ (suṛakṇaa) *v* To slurp, to drink noisily.

ਸੂਆ (sooaa) *n m* Packing needle; Injection; Poker; Watercourse, canal distributory.

ਸੂਈ (sooee) *n f* Needle, pin, pointer.

ਸੂਹ (sooh) *n m* Clue, trace, inkling; Information, tip-off, news, intelligence; Acquaintance; **~ਕੱਢਣੀ** To trace out, to find a clue, to detect, to spy, to find out; **~ਮਿਲਣੀ/ ~ਲੱਗਣੀ** To get an inkling of; **~ਲੈਣੀ** To snoop, to sneak, to try, to find-out.

ਸੂਖਮ (sukham) *a* Fine, slender, delicate, light, subtle, imperceptible, abstract, tenuous, mysterious; **~ਤਾ** Fineness, delicacy, lightness, subtlety, abstractness, mysteriousness, perspicacity.

ਸੂਚਨਾ (soochnaa) *n f* Information, notice, announcement, warning, notification, report, intimation.

ਸੂਚੀ (soochee) *n f* List, schedule, table, inventory, catalogue; **~ਕਾਰ** Tabulator; **~ਬੱਧ** Tabulated, catalogued.

ਸੂਜੀ (soojee) *n f* Coarsly ground flour of wheat.

ਸੂਝ (soojh) *n f* Sensibility, insight, perception, intelligence, discretion acumen; **~ਵਾਨ** Intelligent, shrewd.

ਸੂਣਾ (sooṇaa) *v* (for cattle) To clave, (for horse) to foal, to give birth,

reproduce, multiply.

ਸੂਤ (soot) *n m adv* Yarn esp cotton yarn; Cord or line used by carpenters and masons; Unit of measurement,1/8th of an inch; Correct, proper; manageable, properly aligned or adjusted, in working order, slighty, a little distance.

ਸੂਤਕ (sootak) *n m* Child birth, impurity or uncleanliness associated by Hindu custom with birth in a house.

ਸੂਤਰ (sootar) *n m* Formula, maxim, brief precept, aphorism; **~ਧਾਰ** Stage manager, director, controller, wirepuller (in a puppet show), puppeteer; Moderator.

ਸੂਤਰੀ (sootree) *a* Pronged, point (formula, policy or programme), starand; **~ਕਰਨ** Formulation.

ਸੂਤਲੀ (sootlee) *n f* Twine string, pack thread.

ਸੂਤੀ (sootee) *a* Cotton, made of cotton.

ਸੂਦ (sood) *n m* Interest, profit on cash loan, rate of interest, name of a Khatri subcaste; **~ਖੋਰ** Usurer, moneylender; **~ਖੋਰੀ** Usury, moneylending.

ਸੂਫ਼ੀ (soofee) *a* Holy, pious, sober;

~ਆਨਾ Pertaining to Sufis or Sufism; Sober, simple.

ਸੂਬਾ (soobaa) *n m* Province; ~(ਸੂਬੇ) ਦਾਰ Governor.

ਸੂਮ (soom) *n m* Miser, niggard, stingy, hunks.

ਸੂਰਜ (sooraj) *n m* The sun.

ਸੂਰਤ (soorat) *n f* Form, figure; Face, visage, countenance, appearance; Situation, circumstance; Instance, case; Means, method, wayout.

ਸੂਰਮਾ (soormaa) *a* Brave, bold, hero, warrior.

ਸੂਲ (sool) *n m* Thorn, spike.

ਸੂਲੀ (soolee) *n f* The cross, crucifix, any cross; *fig* Torturous situation or life, torture; ~ਚੜ੍ਹਾਉਣਾ To crucify; ~ਤੇ ਟੰਗਣਾ To troture.

ਸੇਕਣਾ (seknaa) *v* To warm, to bask, to foment.

ਸੇਕਾ (sekaa) *n m* Heat, warmth.

ਸੇਖੀ (shekhee) *n f* Boast, brag, bravado, vaunt.

ਸੇਜ (sej) *n f* Bed *esp* a soft or decorated one, particularly one laid for a couple to lie on or in.

ਸੇਣਾ (senaa) *v* To foster, to brood.

ਸੇਧਣਾ (sedhnaa) *v* To aim at; To straighten, to align.

ਸ਼ੇਰ (sher) *n* Lion, tiger; ~ਨ· Lioness tigress.

ਸੇਵਾ (sevaa) *n f* Service, attendance, duty, worship; ~ਦਾਰ Servant, worker (paid or free). Same as ਸੇਵਕ

ਸੈ (shai) *n f* Thing, object, article.

ਸੈਂਕੜਾ (sainkraa) *n m a* ·Hundred, century (of runs); Percent.

ਸ਼ੈਤਾਨ (shaitan) *n m* Satan, devil.

ਸ਼ੈਦਾਈ (shaidaaee) *n m* Lover, love crazy.

ਸੈਨਾ (sainaa) *n f* Army, military, force, regiment, troop; ~ਪਤੀ Commander-in-chief, supreme commander.

ਸੈਨਿਕ (sainik) *n m* Soldier militaryman.

ਸੈਰ (sair) *n f* Walk, excursion, stroll, outing, promenade; ~ਗਾਹ A place for excursion or walk, park, tourist resort.

ਸੈਲਾਨੀ (sailaanee) *a* Jovial, rambler, traveller, tourist, vagrant, fond of excursion.

ਸੈਲਾਬ (sailaab) *n m* Flood.

ਸੋਹਣਾ (sohnaa) *a m* Beautiful, handsome, good-looking, comely, shapely, lovely, charming, pretty, cute; Grand, graceful, elegant, attractive, pleasing.

ਸ਼ੋਹਦਾ (shohdaa) *a* Innocent, poor fellow.

ਸ਼ੋਕ (shok) *n m* Grief, sorrow.

ਸ਼ੋਖ (shokh) *a* Brilliant, sancy, mercurial, audacious, cheeky, sportive.

ਸੋਗ (sog) *n m* Lamentation, mourning, sadness, sorrow, grief, woe; ~ਮਈ Sorrowful, grievous, melancholy.

ਸੋਚ (soch) *n f* Thought, anxiety, consideration, apprehension, reason, thinking, contemplation; ~ਸਮਝ Understanding, prudence, carefulness; ~ਵਿਚਾਰ Consideration, consultation, circumspection.

ਸੋਚਣਾ (sochnaa) *v* To think, to contemplate, to imagine, to suppose, to consider, to conceive.

ਸੋਜ (soj) *n f* Swelling, tumidity; ~ਚੜੂਲੀ To swell.

ਸੋਜ਼ਸ਼ (sozash) *n f* Inflammation, burning sensation.

ਸੋਟਾ (sotaa) *n m* Club, batton, stick; Staff, bludgeon.

ਸੋਤਾ (sotaa) *n m* Source, spring.

ਸੋਧਣਾ (sodhnaa) *v* To revise, to rectify, to correct, to amend, to purify, to purge.

ਸੋਨਾ (sonaa) *n m* Gold, riches.

ਸ਼ੋਰ (shor) *n m* Noise, clamor, cry, blatancy.

ਸ਼ੌਕ (shauk) *n m* Liking, fondness, zest, inclination, interest.

ਸੌਖਾ (saukhaa) *a* Easy, convenient.

ਸੰਗਾਤ (saugaat) *n f* Present, gift.

ਸੌਣਾ (saunaa) *v* To Sleep, to down.

ਸੌਦਾ (saudaa) *n m* Merchandise, bargain, business, transaction; ~ਗਰ Trader, merchant.

ਸੰਦਾਈ (saudaaee) *n m* Mad, crazy.

ਸੰਪਣਾ (saupnaa) *v* To entrust, to handover, to consign, to concede, to give charge.

ਸੰੜ (saur) *n f* Pinch, tightness.

ਸੰੜਾ (sauraa) *a* Close, narrow, tight, cramped; ~ਪਨ Closeness, narrowness.

ਹ

ਹ Fifth letter of Gurmukhi alphabets, pronounced as hahaa.

ਹਉਕਾ (haukaa) *n m* Sigh, moan, suspiration; **~ਭਰਨਾ** To heave a sigh, to moan, to groan, to suspire.

ਹਉਆ (hauaa) *n m* Object of fear or terror, bugbear, betenoire.

ਹੰਸ (hans) *n m* Swan, goose; Religious soul.

ਹੱਸਣਾ (hassnaa) *v n a* To laugh, to smile, to cut a joke, to make fun of; One who is always laughing, cheerful, jolly, jovial.

ਹਸਤਾਖਰ (hastaakhar) *n m* Signature, autograph.

ਹਸਤੀ (hastee) *n f* Position, personality, dignity; Life, existence.

ਹਸਦ (hasad) *n f* Envy, jealousy; **~ਕਰਨਾ** Envy, to be jealous.

ਹਸਪਤਾਲ (haspataal) *n m* Hospital, dispensary, infiremary.

ਹਸਮੁਖ (hasmukh) *a* Cheerful, blithesome, jolly, jovial, gay, jocose jocular, vivacious, risible.

ਹਸ਼ਰ (hashar) *n m* Result, end, doomsday.

ਹਸਰਤ (hasrat) *n f* Regret, sorrow, grief; Desire.

ਹਸਾਉਣਾ (hasaaunaa) *v* To make one laugh, to cause laughter, to amuse, tickle; Comic, comical, funny, amusing, humorous, witty, laughable, ludicrous.

ਹਸਾਣ (hasaan) *n m* Act or process of laughing.

ਹੱਕ (hakk) *n m a* Right, claim; ad just, true, proper; **~ਦਬਾਉਣਾ** To usurp a right; **~ਦਾਰ** Entitled, claimant, deserving; **~ਦਾਰੀ** Entitlement, title, claim.

ਹੱਕਣਾ (hakknaa) *v* To drive, to urge on , to push, to goad. Also **ਹਿਕਣਾ**

ਹਕਲਾ (haklaa) *n m* Stammer.

ਹਕਲਾਉਣਾ (haklaaunaa) *v* To stammer.

ਹੱਕਾ-ਬੱਕਾ (hakkaa-bakkaa) *a* Stunned, perplexed, bewildered, confused, stupefied.

ਹੰਕਾਰ (hankaar) *n m* Pride, egoism, haughtiness, arrogance.

ਹੰਕਾਰੀ (hankaaree) *a* Proud, vain, arrogant, haughty, conceited, pompous, egoistic.

ਹਕਾਰਤ (hakaarat) *n f* Contempt, hatred disdain.

ਹਕੀਕਤ (hakeekat) *n f* Reality, fact, truth.

ਹਕੀਕੀ (hakeekee) *a* Real, actual, true; Veritable; Own.

ਹਕੀਮ (hakeem) *n m* Physician, medico, doctor; ~ਨੀਮ Quack, charlatan.

ਹਕੂਮਤ (hakoomat) *n f* Government, administration, rule, authority.

ਹਗਣਾ (hagnaa) *v* To exrcete, to ease oneself.

ਹੰਗਾਮਾ (hangaamaa) *n m* Disturbance, uproar, tumult.

ਹੰਘਾਲਣਾ (hanghalnaa) *v* To cleanse, to rinse, to swill.

ਹਚਕੋਲਾ (hachkaulaa) *n m* Swing, push, jolt.

ਹੰਜ (hanj) *n m* Tears. Also ਹੰਜੂ

ਹੱਜ (hajj) *n m* Purpose, use; Pilgrimage to mecca.

ਹਜ਼ਮ (hazam) *a* Digested, usurped.

ਹਜ਼ਰਤ (hazrat) *n m a* Majesty, dignity, highness; Clever, cunning (metaphorically).

ਹਜਾਮ (hajaam) *n m* Barber, hair dresser.

ਹਜਾਮਤ (hajaamat) *n f* Shaving, Hair cutting.

ਹਜੂਮ (hajoom) *n m* Crowd, multitude.

ਹਟਕਣਾ (hataknaa) *v* To check, to restrain, to dissuade.

ਹਟਣਾ (hatnaa) *v* To go back, to withd raw, to return, to shift, to recede, to give way, to deviate.

ਹੱਟਾ (hattaa) *n m* Big shop, emporium.

ਹੱਟਾ-ਕੱਟਾ (hattaa-kattaa) *a* Strong, stout, robust, vigorous.

ਹਟਾਉਣਾ (hataaunaa) *v* To remove, to repulse, to drive away, to push back, to sack.

ਹੱਟੀ (hattee) *n f* Shop.

ਹੱਠ (haatth) *n m* Obstinacy, insistence, tenacity, stubbornness, disobedience.

ਹੱਠੀ (hatthee) *a* Obstinate stubborn, dogmatist, disobedient.

ਹੱਡ (hadd) *n m* Bone; Skeleton of animal; ~ਸੇਕਣੇ To beat, to give a thrashing; ~ਭੰਨਣੇ To work hard, toil, to drudge; ~ਭੰਨਵਾਂ Toilsome, arduous, strenuous, laborious, bone-breaking.

ਹੱਡੀ (Haddee) *n f* Bone; ~ਉਤਰਨੀ For bone or joint to be dislocated.

ਹੰਡੋਲਾ (handolaa) *n m* Cradle, swing, storm.

ਹੰਢਾਉਣਾ (handhaaunaa) *v a* To wear out, to use till it is worn out.

ਹੱਤਕ (hattak) *n f* Insult, disrespect, disgrace, dishonour.

ਹੱਤਿਆ (hattiaa) *n f* Murder,

assasination, killing, slaughter, homicide; **~ਕਰਨੀ** To commit, to kill, butcher, assassinate, slaughter; **~ਕਾਂਡ** Murder story, massacre, carnage.

ਹਤਿਆਰਾ (hatiaaraa) *n m a* Murderer, assassin, murderous, ferocious, bloody.

ਹੱਥ (Hatth) *n m* Hand, arm; **~ਉੱਚਾ ਹੋਣਾ** To have an upper hand; **~ਸਾਫ਼ ਕਰਨਾ** To steal, to swindle, to misappropriate; **~ਕਟ ਜਾਣੇ** To be rendered helpless; **~ਖਿਚਣਾ** To avoid, to desist, to withdraw; **~ਖੁਲ੍ਹਾ ਹੋਣਾ** To be bounteous, to have enough money; **~ਗਰਮ ਕਰਨਾ** To bribe; **~ਚੁਕਣਾ** To assault, to strike, to beat; **~ਜੋੜਨਾ** To pray, to beg pardon; **~ਆਉਣਾ** To come under the control of; **~ਜੋੜਨੇ** To fold one's hand in respect, prayer or supplication, to beg, to entreat, to pray; To beg; To be excused, to express inabilite; **~ਤੰਗ ਹੋਣਾ** To be tight financially, to be short of money, to be penniless; **~ਦਾ ਸੁਚਾ** Honest, in dealing; **~ਦੀ ਮੈਲ** Wealth, money; **~ਪਾਉਣਾ** To interfere; **~ਪੀਲੇ ਕਰਨਾ** To marry (daughter or Sister); **~ ਫੇਰਨਾ** To rob; **~ਮਲਣਾ** To repent, to be sorry;

~ਲੰਮੇ ਹੋਣੇ To have a long reach; **~ਕੰਡੇ** Secret contrivances.

ਹਥਕੜੀ (hathkaṛee) *n f* Handcuff, manacies.

ਹੱਥਨੀ (hatthṇee) *n f* Female elephant.

ਹੱਥਾ (hatthaa) *n m* Handle; **~ਪਾਈ** Fight, scuffle, violence.

ਹਥਿਆਉਣਾ (hathiaauṇaa) *v* To grab, to seize.

ਹਥਿਆਰ (hathiaar) *n m* Weapon, arms, tools, instruments; **~ਸੁੱਟਣੇ** To surrender, capitulate, to accept defeat, to surrender arms, to throw down arms; **~ਬੰਦ** Armed.

ਹੱਥੀ (hatthee) *n f* Handle, grip.

ਹਥੇਲੀ (hathelee) *n f* Palm, metacarpus.

ਹਥੌੜਾ (hathauṛaa) *n m* Hammer.

ਹੱਦ (hadd) *n f* Limit, border, limitations, boundary; **~ਕਰਨੀ/~ਕਰ ਦੇਣੀ** To do something unusual, amazing, wonderful, laudable, or improper; **~ਬੰਦੀ** Demarcation, delimitation.

ਹਦਵਾਣਾ (hadwaaṇaa) *n m* Watermelon.

ਹੰਦਾ (handaa) *n m* Cooked food collected daily by priests.

ਹਦਾਇਤ (hadaait) *n f* Instruction, guidance, direction. Also **ਹਦੈਤ**

ਹਨੇਰ (haner) *n* Darkness, misrule, tyranny, calamity, lawlessness; Injustice; ~ਖਾਤਾ Mismanagement, confusion; ~ਗਰਦੀ Anarchy, lawlessness.

ਹਨੇਰਾ (haneraa) *a* Dark, gloom, foggy, obscure; ~ਘੁੱਪ Blinding darkness.

ਹਨੇਰੀ (haneree) *n f* Dust-storm, wind-storm, tornado, hurricane; ~ਕੋਠੀ Dark cell, dungeon.

ਹਨੇਰੇ (Hanere) *a* Dark; ~ਸਵੇਰੇ At odd hours; ~ਵਿਚ ਤੀਰ ਚਲਾਉਣਾ To strike without taking aim; ~ਵਿਚ ਰਖਣਾ To keep in the dark, to keep ignorant, to keep uninformed.

ਹਪਣਾ (hapnaa) *v* To gulp, to swallow whole.

ਹਫਣਾ (haphnaa) *v* To be out of breath, to breathe heavily, to pant.

ਹਫਤਾ (Haftaa) *n m* Week; ~ਵਾਰ weekly. Also ਹਫਤੇਵਾਰ

ਹਫੜਾ-ਦਫੜੀ (haphra-daphree) *n f* Confusion, commotion, panic, bustle, stampede, hurry, haste, furmoil, flurry.

ਹਫੀਮ (Hafeem) *n f* Opium.

ਹਬਸ਼ੀ (habshee) *n m* Negro, negroid, an African, Abyssinian or Ethiopean.

ਹਬਕਾ (habkaa) *n m* Jerk; Sudden attack of sorrow, shock.

ਹੰਬਣਾ (hambanaa) *n m* Spring, jump, determined effort *esp.* after tiredness, sheer will.

ਹੰਬਾਉਣਾ (hambaaunaa) *v* To tire out, to exhaust.

ਹਮਸ਼ਕਲ (hamshakal) *a* Similar, resembling.

ਹਮਸਾਇਆ (hamsaaiyaa) *n m* Neighbour.

ਹਮਜੋਲੀ (hamjolee) *n m* Chum, nearest friend.

ਹਮਦਰਦੀ (hamdardee) *n f* Sympathy.

ਹਮਰਾਜ਼ (hamraaz) *n m* Confidant, confident.

ਹਮਲ (hamal) *n m* Pregnancy; ~ਗਿਰਨਾ Abortion, miscarriage.

ਹਮਲਾ (hamlaa) *n m* Attack, invasion, assault; ~ਕਰਨਾ To attack, to invade.

ਹਮਵਤਨ (hamwatan) *n m a* Countryman *or* country woman, compatriot, fellow citizen.

ਹਮਾਇਤ (hamayit) *n f* Support, protection, patronage, abetment; Sympathy.

ਹਮਾਕਤ (hamaakat) *n f* Stupidity, folly, foolishness.

ਹਮਾਮ (hamaam) *n m* Hot or turkish bath, a metallic drum with a tap.

ਹਮਾਮ-ਦਸਤਾ (hamaam-dastaa) *n m*

Pestle and mortar.

ਹਮੇਸ਼ਾ (hameshaa) *adv* Always, ever, perpetually

ਹਯਾ (hayaa) *n f* Modesty, coyness, sense of shameness; **ਬੇ~** Shameless, immodest.

ਹਰ (har) *a pref* Each, every, any; **~ਇਕ** Each one, everyone, all and sundry; **~ਹੀਲੇ** By all or any means; **~ਕੋਈ** Everyone, any Tom, Dick or Harry; **~ਜਾਈ** Fickle, inconstant (male lover); **~ਥਾਂ** Everywhere; **~ਦਮ** Always; **~ਦਿਲ ਅਜ਼ੀਜ਼** Popular, likeable, favourite of one and all; **~ਵਾਰੀ** Each or every time.

ਹਰਕਤ (harkat) *n f* Movement, motion, gesture, action.

ਹਰਕਾਰਾ (harkaaraa) *n m* Courier, postman, messenger, carrier.

ਹਰਜ (haraj) *n m* Loss, waste (of time, money or effort); **~ਕਰਨਾ** To waste.

ਹਰਜਾਈ (harjaae) *n m* Omnipresent.

ਹਰਜਾਨਾ (harjaanaa) *n m* Damage, compensation, indemnity.

ਹਰਣ (haraṇ) *n m* Kidnapping, abduction, removal.

ਹਰਨ (haran) *n m* Deer, antelope; **~ਹੋ ਜਾਣਾ** To run away. Also **ਹਿਰਨ**

ਹਰਣਾ (harṇaa) *v* To abduct, to kidnap.

ਹਰਫ਼ (haraf) *n m* Alphabetical letter, particle, word.

ਹਰਫ਼ਨ ਮੌਲਾ (harfan maulaa) *a m* Master or jack of all trades, versatile.

ਹਰਮ (haram) *n m* Harem, seragilo, inner apartments of a house.

ਹਰਵਾਉਣਾ (harvaauṇaa) *v* To cause defeat, to defeat through someone else; Also **ਹਰਾਉਣਾ**

ਹਰਾ (haraa) *a* Green, fresh, verdant.

ਹਰਾਉਣਾ (haraaunaa) *v* To defeat.

ਹਰਾਸਤ (haraasat) *n f* Custody, arrest, care. Also **ਹਿਰਾਸਤ**

ਹਰਾਮ (haraam) *a* Improper, unlawful, sinful, prohibited; **~ਖੋਰ** Corrupt person; **~ਜ਼ਾਦਾ** Illegitimate, bastard, rascal, scoundral.

ਹਰਾਮੀ (haraamee) *n m a* Rascal; *a* Illegal, illegitimate, bastard.

ਹਰਾਰਤ (haraarat) *n f* Heat, light, fever, feverishness, temperature.

ਹੱਲ (hall) *n m* Solution; Plough.

ਹਲਕ (halak) *n m* Throat.

ਹਲਕਣਾ (halkṇaa) *v* To go mad.

ਹਲਕਾ (halkaa) *a* Light, easy, soft, cheap.

ਹਲਚਲ (halchal) *n m* Commotion, tumult, agitation, disorder.

ਹਲਦੀ (haldee) *n f* Turmeric, *Curcuma longa.*

ਹਲਫ਼ (halaf) *n m* Oath, vow; **~ਨਾਮਾ**

Affidavit.

ਹਲਫ਼ੀਆ ਬਿਆਨ (halfiaa biaan) *n m* statement on oath, affidavit, deposition; **~ਬਿਆਨ ਦੇਣ ਵਾਲਾ** Deponent; **~ਬਿਆਨ ਦੇਣਾ** To depose.

ਹਲਵਾ (halwa) *n m* Pudding, Sweetmeat.

ਹਲਵਾਈ (halwaaee) *n m* Confectioner, sweet seller.

ਹੱਲਾ (hallaa) *n m* Assault, attack, noise, uproar, tumult.

ਹਲਾ (halaa) *n pron* All right, agreed; **~ਸ਼ੇਰੀ** Encouragement, abetment, incitement, instigation; **~ਸ਼ੇਰੀ ਦੇਣੀ** To encourage, to abet, to incite, to instigate.

ਹੱਲਾ (halla) *n m* Attack, assault, charge; noise, uproar; **~ਕਰਨਾ** To make noise; same as **ਹੱਲਾ ਬੋਲਣਾ**; **~ਗੁੱਲਾ** Noise, din, uproar, merrymaking, revel, mirth.

ਹਲਾਉਣਾ (halaaunaa) *v* To Shake, to mix, to move.

ਹਲਾਲ (halaal) *a* Legal, lawful, legitimate; Slaughtered.

ਹਲੂਨਣਾ (haloonnaa) *v* To shake, to give a jolt.

ਹਲੂਣਾ (haloonaa) *n m* Jerk, joilt, shaking up; Swaying motion, swing; **~ਦੇਣਾ** To shake, sway,

swing.

ਹਵਸ (hawas) *n f* Lust, longing, yearning, overambition.

ਹਵਾ (hawaa) *n* Air, wind, atmosphere; Reputation; **~ਕੱਢਣਾ** To deflate; **~ਕਰਨਾ** To fan; **~ਖਾਣੀ** To go for a walk; **~ਪਾਣੀ** Climate.

ਹੱਵਾ (havaa) *n f* Eve, the first woman

ਹਵਾਈ (hawaaee) *a* Airy, aerial; Flase; **~ਅੱਡਾ** Aerodrome; **~ਕਿਲਾ** Fertile ambition; **~ਜਹਾਜ** Aeroplane.

ਹਵਾਲ (hawaal) *n m* News; Condition; **~ਦਾਰ** Sergeant, lower police officer.

ਹਵਾਲਾ (hawaalaa) *n m* Reference, mention, example; **~ਦੇਣਾ** To refer, to mention, to quote.

ਹਵਾਲਾਤ (hawaalaat) *n m* Lock up, jail.

ਹਵਾਲੇ (havaale) *a* In custody (of); **~ਕਰਨਾ** To hand over, deliver, give, entrust.

ਹਵਾੜ (havaar) *n m* Steam, visible evaporation, vapours or particles; hot breath; *fig* Suppressed or latent feeling esp. Anger; **~ਕੱਢਣੀ** to let out steam; To give vent to anger or hurt feelings to leak out a secret, to have catharsis; **~ਲੈਣੀ** To inhale steam, to have steam fomentation; *fig* To pry or spy.

ਹਵੇਲੀ (havelee) *n f* Large walled house, mansion.

ਹੜਤਾਲ (hartaal) *n m* Strike.

ਹੜਪਣਾ (harapnaa) *v* To gulp, to usurp.

ਹੜਬੜੀ (harbaree) *n f* Confusion, melee, pell-mell; consternation.

ਹੜ੍ਹ (har) *n m* Flood, deluge, inundation; ~ਆਉਣਾ To be flooded; ~ਮਾਰ Damage or destruction caused by flood.

ਹਾਏ (haae) *interj* An expression of pain, pleasure, grief or anxiety depending on intonation; Oh, ah, alack, alas; *n f* Cry of pain.

ਹਾਏਂ (haaen) *interj* Interrogative expression, what? is it?

ਹਾਸਾ (haasaa) *n m* Laughter, fun, joke, giggle, mockery, amusement.

ਹਾਸ਼ੀਆ (haashiyaa) *n m* Margin, edging, side, border, commentary.

ਹਾਹਾਕਾਰ (haahaakaar) *n m* Lamentation.

ਹਾਕਮ (haakam) *n m* Ruler, governor, officer, magistrate, administrator; Welider of authority to give command or order.

ਹਾਜਤ (haajat) *n f* (1) Need, necessity, want, requirement; (2) Call of nature; ~ਹੋਣੀ To need,

want, require to feel need; To feel call of nature.

ਹਾਜਮਾ (haajmaa) *n m* Digestion, digestive power, assimilation. Also **ਹਾਜ਼ਮਾ**

ਹਾਜਰ (haajar) *a* Present, in attendance, ready, readily available; ~ਹੋਣਾ To be present, to present oneself, to attend, to appear; ~ਕਰਨਾ To present, to produce, to supply, to make available; ~ਜਵਾਬ Ready or nimble-witted; ~ਜਵਾਬੀ Ready or nimble wit, wittiness; Repartee; ~ਨਾਜ਼ਰ present, manifest, immanent, omnipresent. Also **ਹਾਜ਼ਰ**

ਹਾਜਰੀ (haajree) *n f* (1) Presence, attendance; rollcall; (2) *informal* breakfast, light meal; ~ਪੁਕਾਰਨੀ To take roll-call, to call the roll; ~ਭਰਨੀ To be in attendance, to be at someone's beck and call; to go and meet; to record attendance ~ਲਾਉਣੀ To call and to mark attendance. Also **ਹਾਜ਼ਰੀ**

ਹਾਜਰੀਨ (haajreen) *n pl m* Audience, assembly of listeners or spectators viewers. Also **ਹਾਜ਼ਰੀਨ**

ਹਾਣ (haan) *n m* Equality or near equality in age, coetaneousness.

ਹਾਣੀ (haanee) *n m* One's equal in

age; companion, pal, mate; lover.

ਹਾਣਨ (haanan) *n f* Lady equal in age, lady mate of a lady.

ਹਾਥੀ (haathee) *n m* Elephant.

ਹਾਦਸਾ (haadsaa) *n m* Accident, casualty.

ਹਾਨੀ (haanee) *n f* Loss, harm, disadvantage, damage; ~ਕਾਰਕ harmful, disadvantageous, adverse, detrimental.

ਹਾਮਲਾ (haamlaa) *a* Pregnant.

ਹਾਮੀ (haamee) *n f* Consent, assent, acceptance, support; ~ਭਰਨਾ To support, to second, to back up, to advocate.

ਹਾਰ (haar) *n* (1) Defeat, loss, frustration, rout; (2) Necklace, wreath; ~ਸਿੰਗਾਰ Ornamentation, adornment, make-up, cosmetics; ~ਪਾਉਣਾ To garland; ~ਖਾਣੀ To be defeated, to lose, to be overpowered.

ਹਾਰਨਾ (haarnaa) *v* To lose, to fail, to abandon.

ਹਾਲ (haal) *n m a* Condition , state, Situation; News; Hall; Recent, current, present.

ਹਾਲਤ (haalat) *n f* Condition, state, situation, position, circumstances, stage.

ਹਾਵੀ (haavee) *a* dominant, predominant, overbearing, overwhelming; ~ਹੋਣਾ To dominate, predominate, to overbear, to overwhelm; To excel; To defeat.

ਹਾੜਨਾ (haarnaa) *v* To estimate, to guess at, to measure.

ਹਾੜ੍ਹ (haar) *n m* Fourth month of Bikrami calendar (mid-June to mid-July); Summer.

ਹਿੱਸਾ (hissa) *n m* share, part, portion, quota, contribution.

ਹਿਸਾਬ (hisaab) *n m* Account, Calculation, mathematics, arithmatics, computation; ~ਕਿਤਾਬ Account, Book keeping, reckoning; ~ਚੁਕਾਉਣਾ To clear, liquidate or settle account; ~ਦੇਣਾ To render account; ~ਲਾਉਣਾ To Calculate, to reckon, to estimate.

ਹਿੱਕ (hikk) *n f* Breast, bosom, chest.

ਹਿਕਣਾ (hiknaa) *v* To drive (animal), to goad, to urge on. Also ਹੱਕਣਾ

ਹਿੰਗ (hing) *n f* Asafoetida; ~ਲਗੇ ਨਾ ਫਟਕੜੀ *ph* Without cost or trouble.

ਹਿਚਕ (hichak) *n f* Hestiation, reluctance; Wavering, uacillation, uncertainty.

ਹਿਕਮਤ (hikmat) *n f* Wisdom

philosophy, physic, art of healing.

ਹਿਚਕਿਚਾਉਣਾ (hichkichaaunaa) *v* To hesitate, to waver, to vacillate, to falter. Also **ਹਿਚਕਿਚਾਣਾ**

ਹਿਚਕੀ (hichkee) *n f* Hiccough, sobbing, convulsion.

ਹਿਚਕੋਲਾ (hichkaulaa) *n m* Jolt, jerk, shock.

ਹਿੱਜਾ (hijjaa) *n m* Spelling.

ਹਿਣਹਿਣਾਉਣਾ (hiṇhiṇaaunaa) *v* To neigh (of horse).

ਹਿੱਤ (hitt) *n m Prep* Interest, affection, sincerity, gain; For.

ਹਿੱਤੂ (hittoo) *n m* Sincere, well-wisher, benefactor.

ਹਿੰਦਸਾ (hindsaa) *n m* Figure, digit.

ਹਿੰਦੁਸਤਾਨ (hindustaan) *n m* India.

ਹਿਫ਼ਾਜ਼ਤ (hifaazat) *n m* Safety, protection; ~**ਕਰਨੀ** To protect, to guard, to keep in safe custody; ~**ਵਿਚ ਲੈਣਾ** To take into custody, to provide protection.

ਹਿੰਮਤ (himmat) *n f* Courage, bravery, enterprise.

ਹਿਮਾਇਤ (himayit) *n m* Support, backing, help, aid, partisanship.

ਹਿਰਸ (hiras) *n f* Ambition, yearning, acquisitiveness, lust, desire, greed, avarice.

ਹਿਰਸੀ (hirsee) *a* Greedy, ambitious,

covetous, avaricious.

ਹਿਰਖ (hirakh) *n m* Anger, irritation, displeasure, rage, complaint, grumble. Also **ਹਰਖ**

ਹਿਲਣਾ (hilṇaa) *v* To move, to shake, to swing, to be dislocate.

ਹਿਲਾਉਣਾ (hillaunaa) *v* To shake, to toss to nod; To tame, to domesticate.

ਹੀਆ (heeaa) *n m* Heart, spirit; boldness, courage, guts.

ਹੀਂਗਣਾ (heengṇaa) *v* To bray, to cry.

ਹੀਜੜਾ (heejṛaa) *n m* Eunuch.

ਹੀਣਤਾ (heeṇtaa) *n f* Inferiority, abjectness, lowness.

ਹੀਣਾ (heeṇaa) *a* Low, poor, menial craven.

ਹੀਰਾ (heeraa) *n m a* Diamond, gem, pearl, jewel; Precious, costly, unique.

ਹੀਲ-ਹੁਜਤ (heel-hujat) *n f* Pretext, evasion, quirk, pretence.

ਹੀਲਾ (heelaa) *n f* Pretext, pretence, contrivance, way, effort, attempt.

ਹੁੱਸੜ (husaṛ) *n m* Sultriness, stuffiness, stuffy weather; tiredness, tedium, boredom, impatience.

ਹੁਸੜਨਾ (husaṛnaa) *v* To long for, to feel uneasy.

ਹੁਸ਼ਿਆਰ (hushiaar) *a* Intelligent,

smart, competent; clever, shrewd, cunning; sensible, vigilant, cautious.

ਹੁਕਮ (hukam) *n m* Order, command, mandate, sanction; ~**ਅਦੂਲੀ** disobedience, defiance; ~**ਨਾਮਾ** Warrent, decree; ~**ਰਾਨ** Ruler, king, emperor.

ਹੁੱਕਾ (hukkaa) *n m* Smoking pipe, hookah; hubble-bubble; ~**ਪਾਣੀ** Social relations; ~**ਪਾਣੀ ਬੰਦ ਕਰਨਾ** To ostracise; ~**ਪੀਣਾ** To smoke hubble, bubble.

ਹੁੰਗਾਰਾ (hungaaraa) *n m* Monosyllabic response indicating assent or listener's attention, response or reaction, mostly in positive concurrence; ~**ਭਰਨਾ** To respond, to express support or concurrence.

ਹੁੱਜਤ (hujjat) *n m* Argument, controversy, disputartion, excuse; joke, sarcasm; ~**ਬਾਜ਼ੀ** Pointless agrumentation; Jocularity, waggishness.

ਹਜੂਮ (hajoom) *n m* Crowd.

ਹੁੱਟਣਾ (hutnaa) *v* To feel tired, to be fatigued, to be weary.

ਹੁਣ (hun) *adv* Now, at present.

ਹੁਣੇ (hune) *adv* Just now, this very moment, presently; ~**ਹੁਣੇ** Just

now, a little while ago.

ਹੁਨਰ (hunar) *n m* Accomplishment, craft, art, skill, talent; ~**ਮੰਦ** Skilful, meritorious.

ਹੁਨਾਲ (hunaal) *n m* Summer. Also **ਹੁਨਾਲਾ**

ਹੁਬਕਣਾ (hubaknaa) *v* To sob, to blubber, to snivel.

ਹੁਮਹੁਮਾਉਣਾ (humhumaaunaa) *v* To gather eagerly in large number.

ਹੁਲਸਾਉਣਾ (hulsaaunaa) *v* To be pleased, to be elated, to please.

ਹੁਲਣਾ (hulnaa) *v* To spread.

ਹੁਲੜ (hular) *n m* Tumult, uproar, disturbance, commotion, riot; ~**ਬਾਜ਼** Disturbance maker, rioter

ਹੁਲਾਸ (hulaas) *n m* Joy, elation, cheerfulness, buoyancy, incentive.

ਹੁਲੀਆ (huliaa) *n m* Appearance, shape, features, description, descriptive roll.

ਹੁਰਕ (hurak) *n f* Longing, wish *esp* unfulfilled persistent expectation.

ਹੁਕਣਾ (hooknaa) *v* To raise, to utter cry fo pain.

ਹੂੰਝਣਾ (hoonjnaa) *v* To flush out, to scavenge, to sweep, to broom.

ਹੂਟਾ (hoonaa) *n m* Swing.

ਹੂਬਹੂ (hoobahoo) *adv* Exactly, actual, similar, graphic.

ਹੂਰ (hoor) *n f* Nymph, fairy of

paradise.

ਹੇਕੜੀ (hekree) *n f* Arrogance, show of strength.

ਹੇਠ (heṭh) *adv* Below, under, beneath.

ਹੇਠਲਾ (Heṭhlaa) *adv* Bottom, lower, subordinate.

ਹੇਰਨਾ (hernaa) *v* To look, to search; To blockade

ਹੇਰ-ਫੇਰ (her-pher) *n* Exchange, reciprocation, shuffle, disorder, quirk.

ਹੇਰਾ-ਫੇਰੀ (heraa-pheree) *n f* Embezzlement; deceit; trickery, pettifoggery, chicanery, gimmick, gimmickry; ~ਕਰਨੀ To embezzle; to deceive, to trick, to cheat, to pettifog.

ਹੈਸੀਅਤ (heseeat) *n f* Position, status, capacity.

ਹੈਰਤ (hairat) *n f* Ashtonishment, surprise, wonder.

ਹੈਰਾਨ (hairaan) *a* Surprised, perplexed, perturbed. worried.

ਹੈਰਾਨੀ (hairaanee) *n f* Surprise.

ਹੈਵਾਨ (haivaan) *n m* Rute, rustic, beast.

ਹੈਵਾਨੀਅਤ (haivaaniyat) *n f* Animal nature, animality, brutishness, beastliness.

ਹੋਕਾ (haukaa) *n m* Announcement, public proclamation.

ਹੋਰ (hor) *adv* More, other, additional.

ਹੋਸ਼ (hosh) *n m* Consciousness, sense, awakening; ~ਉਡਣੇ To be surprised, baffled, afraid or frightened;   ~ਹਵਾਸ Consciousness, awareness, understanding, mental faculties, senses; ~ਠਿਕਾਣੇ ਕਰਨੇ To teach one a lesson, to bring one to one's senses.

ਹੋਛਾ (hochhaa) *a* Blunt, brusque, frivolous, flippant, uncivil, ill-mannered, undignified, mean.

ਹੋਣੀ (honee) *n f* Fate, destiny, predestination, the inevitable, appointed lot.

ਹੋੜ (hor) *n f* Competition.

ਹੌਸਲਾ (haunslaa) *n m* Courage, moral, spirit.

ਹੌਂਕਣਾ (haunknaa) *v* To breath quickly, to gast, to puff, to pant.

ਹੌਕਾ (haukaa) *n m* Sigh.

ਹੌਲ (haul) *n m* Fear, dread, terror, panic; ~ਪੈਣਾ To be terror-stricken.

ਹੌਲਣਾ (haulnaa) *v* To be frightened, to be horrified.

ਹੌਲਾ (haulaa) *a m* Light, undignified, easy, soft, sad, cheap; ~ਪਣ Lightness, pettiness, cheapness.

ਹੌਲੀ (haulee) *a f* Slow, mild, gradual.

ਕ

ਕ Sixth letter of Gurmukhi alphabets, pronounced as 'Kakkaa'.

ਕਉਲ (kaul) *n m* Promise; Brass bowl.

ਕਉਆ (kauaa) *n n* Crow.

ਕਸ਼ (kash) *n m* Puff, inhalation of tobacco, smoke; ~ਲਾਉਣਾ To smoke.

ਕਸ਼ਸ਼ (kashash) *n f* Attraction, tension. Also; ਕਸ਼ਿਸ਼

ਕਸਕ (kasak) *n f* Pang, twinge, spasm; Heartache, heartburning, anguish; grudge, enmity, jealousy; ~ਕੱਢਲੀ To Avenge, to retaliate.

ਕਸ਼ਟ (kasht) *n m* Hardship, agony, toil, tribulation.

ਕੱਸਣਾ (kassṇaa) *v* To tighten, to clamp, to band, to clinch.

ਕਸਬਣ (kasban) *n f* Whore, prostitute.

ਕਸਬਾ (kasbaa) *n m* Town, townlet.

ਕਸਮ (kasam) *n f* Oath; ~ਖਾਣੀ To swear; ~ਦੁਆਉਣੀ To administer an oath.

ਕਸ਼ਮਕਸ਼ (kashmakash) *n f* Struggle, tension, dilemma; ~ਵਿੱਚ ਪੈਣਾ To be double minded.

ਕਸਰ (kasar) *n f* Default, deficiency, dearth, fraction, indisposition; ~ਕੱਢਣੀ To make up the loss; ~ਪੂਰੀ ਕਰਨੀ To make up the deficit; ~ਲਗਣੀ To incur a loss.

ਕਸਰਤ (kasrat) *n f* Exercise, sport, athletics, practice; ~ਕਰਨੀ To take exercise.

ਕਸਵਾਉਣਾ (kasvaauṇaa) *v* To get tightened.

ਕੱਸਾ (kassaa) *a m* Deficient, less, short.

ਕਸਾਈ (kasaaee) *n m a* (1) Butcher; (2) Tightening, act of drawing out; (3) Cruel, merciless; ~ਪੁਣਾ Butcher's trade; Cruelty, mercilessness, pitiless nature, stone-heartedness.

ਕਸੀਦਾ (kaseedaa) *n m* Embroidery, needlework, broche.

ਕਸੈਲਾ (kasailaa) *a* Bitter, pungent, astringent; ~ਪਨ Bitterness, pungentness.

ਕਸੌਟੀ (kasautee) *n f* Criterion, norm, touch stone, proof, test.

ਕਹਾਉਣਾ (kahaauṇaa) *v* To get some thing communicated, to cause or get someone say something, to be called, to be named. Also **ਅਖਵਾਉਣਾ**

ਕਹਾਣੀ (kahaanee) *n f* Story, tale, episode, fable; **~ਕਾਰ** Storywriter.

ਕਹਾਵਤ (kahaavat) *n f* Proverb, saying, maxim, dictum.

ਕਹਿਕਸ਼ਾਂ (kahekashaan) *n f* Rainbow.

ਕਹਿਕਹਾ (kahekahaa) *n m* Loud laughter.

ਕਹਿਣਾ (kahenaa) *v* To say, to speak, to tell, to utter, to address, to relate; **~ਸੁਣਨਾ** To counsel, to chat.

ਕਹਿਰ (kaehr) *n m* Wrath, anger, rage, ire; oppression; calamity, (divine) chastisement.

ਕਹਿਲਾਵਾ (kahelaavaa) *n m* Invitation, summon.

ਕਕੱਰ (kakkar) *n m* Frost, rime, glazedice.

ਕੰਕਰ (kankar) *n m* Small piece of stone, pebble, gravel, shingle.

ਕੰਕਰੀ (kankree) *n f* Pebble, small gravel.

ਕਕਰੀਲਾ (kakreelaa) *a m* Frosty, icycold, covered with frost.

ਕੱਕਾ (kakkh) *n m* Browm haired, golden (hair), auburn, blonde; The letter ਕ

ਕਕਾਰ (kakkar) *n m* The five symbols of Sikh faith, all with ਕ (k) in initial position-*Kachhaa*, underwear;

Karaa, steel bangle; *Kirpaan*, sword or dagger; *Kes*, untrimmed hair; and *Kanghaa*, comb.

ਕਕੋਰੀਆ (kakoriaa) *a* Blue eyed.

ਕੱਖ (kakkh) *n m* Straw, piece of chaff dry stalk of grass.

ਕੰਗਣ (kangan) *n m* Bracelet, bangle, ornament for wrist.

ਕੰਗਲਾ (kanglaa) *a* Poor, beggerly.

ਕੰਗਾਲ (kangaal) *a n* Poor, penniless, beggarly; Bankrupt.

ਕੰਘਾ (kanghaa) *n m* Comb.

ਕੰਘੀ (kanghee) *n f* Comb; **~ਪੱਟੀ** Hairdressing, make-up.

ਕੱਚ (kachch) *n m* Glass, sound of crushing or piercing, crudity, rawness, unripeness. inexperience; **~ਪੱਕ** Uncertainity.

ਕਚਹਿਰੀ (kachheree) *n f* Court, assembly, public office.

ਕਚਕਚ (kachkach) *n f* Excessive talk, foolish talk.

ਕਚਪਕਾ (kachpakka) *a m* Not fully ripe; half-baked.

ਕਚਰਾ (kachraa) *n m* Debris, rubbish, embryo.

ਕੱਚਾ (kachchaa) *a* Unripe, raw, unbaked, inexperienced, undeveloped, green, weak; **~ਕਾਗਜ਼** Provisional document;

~ਚਿੱਠਾ Inside story, naked truth, real tale; ~ਪੱਕਾ Undecided, undetermined, uncertain.

ਕਚਿਆਉਣਾ (kachiaaunaa) v To feel embarrassed, to feel ashamed.

ਕਚਾਵਾ (kachaavaa) n m Saddle (for came); pack-frame (for donkey), packsaddle.

ਕਚੂਮਰ (kachoomar) n m Anything cut into small pieces or crushed badly.

ਕੱਛਾ (kachhaa) n m Underwear, shorts.

ਕੱਛਣਾ (kachhnaa) v To measure (land).

ਕਛਾਉਣਾ (kachhaunaa) v to get measured.

ਕਛਾਰ (kachhaar) n f Marshy land.

ਕੱਛੀ (kachhee) n f Underwear of a child.

ਕੰਜ (kanj) n f A small girl; ~ਕੁਆਰੀ Innocent virgin; Barren.

ਕੰਜਕ (kanjak) n f Innocent virgin girl.

ਕੰਜਣਾ (kanjnaa) v To cover, to veil, to enshroud.

ਕੰਜਰ (kanjar) n m A man dealing with prostitutes, man with no respect, shameless man; ~ਖਾਨਾ Brothel, bawdy house, house of ill fame; ~ਪੁਣਾ Prostitution; shamelessness, utter lack of selfrespect.

ਕੰਜਰੀ (kanjree) n f Prostitute.

ਕੰਜੂਸ (kanjoos) n m a Miser, miserly, stingy, hunks.

ਕੰਜੂਸੀ (kanjoosee) n f Miserliness, niggardliness, stinginess, skimpiness,

ਕਟਣਾ (katnaa) v To cut, to bite, to chop, to intersect, to deduct, to strike out.

ਕਟਵਾਈ (katvaaee) n Cutting, mowing, reaping.

ਕੱਟੜ (katar) a Staunch, dogmatic, orthodox, bigot, fanatic, intolerant, fundamentalist; ~ਤਾ Dogmatism, fundamentalism; ~ਪੰਥੀ Orthodox, fanatic, fundamentalist (person) ਕੱਟੜ

ਕਟਾਰ (kataar) n Dagger, dirk, poniard.

ਕਟਾਰੀ (kataaree) n Dagger, dirk, poniard.

ਕਟੌਰਾ (katauraa) n m Bowl, cup,

ਕਟੌਰੀ (katauree) n f Small bowl, goblet of metal.

ਕਟੌਤੀ (katautee) n f Discount, commission, deduction.

ਕੰਠ (kanth) n m a Throat, committed to memory; ~ਮਾਲਾ Necklace; ~ਲਾਉਣਾ To embrace.

ਕਠਪੁਤਲੀ (kathputlee) n f Puppet; fig

a subservient, obsequious person, stooge, underling, accomplice.

ਕੰਠੀ (kanṭhee) *n f* Pearl necklace, an ornament for the neck..

ਕਠੋਰ (kaṭhor) *a* Hard, harsh, rough, severe, rigid, stern, unbending; ~ਤਾ Hardness, rigidity, harshness

ਕੰਡ (kanḍ) *n f* Back; behind, rear; ~ਕਰਨਾ To desert, To withdraw support; ~ਪਿੱਛੇ Behind the back; ~ਲਗਣੀ To be defeated; ~ਵਿਖਾਉਣੀ To flee, to show one's back.

ਕੰਡਾ (kanḍaa) *n m* (1) Thorn, fork, hindrance, impediment; (2) Big scale or balance, weighing machine.

ਕੰਡੀ (kanḍee) *n f* Small weighing scale.

ਕੱਢਣਾ (kadhnaa) *v* To draw forth, to oust, to turn out, to expel, to solve a question; To embroider.

ਕੰਢਾ (kanḍhaa) *n m* Shore, coast; Edge, verge, margin.

ਕਢਾਉਣਾ (kadhaaunaa) *v* To get embroided.

ਕਢਾਈ (kadhaaee) *n f* Embroidary.

ਕਣ (kaṇ) *n f* Particle, seed, grain.

ਕਣਕ (kaṇak) *n f* Wheat.

ਕਣੀ (kaṇee) *n f* Rain drop, Broken rice.

ਕੱਤਣਾ (kattṇaa) *v* To spin.

ਕਤਰਨਾ (katarnaa) *v* To cut, to trim, to chop, to strip.

ਕਤਰਨੀ (katarnee) *n f* Scissors.

ਕਤਰਾ (katraa) *n m* Drop.

ਕਤਰਾਉਣਾ (katraaunaa) *v* (1) To avoid, to shirk, to fudge, to dodge; (2) To get something cut, clipped.

ਕਤਲ (katal) *n m* Murder, slaughter; ~ਕਰਨਾ To murder, to assassinate, to kill, to slay.

ਕਤਾਰ (kataar) *n f* Row, line, series, order.

ਕਤੂਰਾ (katooraa) *n m* Pup, cur, whelp.

ਕਥਾ (kathaa) *n f* Sermon, tale, anecdote, narrative.

ਕੱਦ (kadd) *n m* Height, stature, size, magnitude; ~ਆਵਰ tall

ਕਦਮ (kadam) *n f* Step, foot.

ਕਦਰ (kadar) *n f* Respect, value, worth, merit, deference; ~ਕਰਨੀ To respect, to honour, to appreciate; ~ਦਾਨ Patron, connoisseur.

ਕਦਾਚਾਰ (kadaachaar) *n m* Misconduct, delinquency, bad behaviour.

ਕਦਾਵਰ (kadaavar) *a* Stalwart, hefty, tall.

ਕਦੀ (kadee) *adv* Sometimes, seldom, ever, on some occasion.

ਕਦੀਮ (kadeem) *a* Ancient, old.

ਕਦੂ (kaddoo) *n m a* Gourd, pumkin, cucurbit; Dull, simpleton, foolish; ~ਕਸ਼ Grater.

ਕੰਧ (kandh) *n f* Wall.

ਕੰਧਾ (kandhaa) *n m* Shoulder.

ਕੰਧੀ (kandhee) *n f* Bank (of a river), border, margin.

ਕੰਧੂਈ (kandhooee) *n f* Darning needle

ਕੰਨ (kann) *n m* Ear; ~ਹੋ ਜਾਣੇ To be alert, to learn a lesson, to know; ~ਕੱਟਣਾ To excel in cunning or cleverness; ~ਕਰਨੇ To warn; To be attentive; ~ਖੜੇ ਹੋਣੇ To be alarmed; ~ਖਾਣਾ To make much noise, to vex; ~ਧਰਨਾ to listen attentively; ~ਨਾ ਧਰਨਾ To pay deaf ears to; ~ਪੈਣਾ To hear a rumour.

ਕਨਪੇੜਾ (kanperaa) *n m* Swelling behind the ears, mumps.

ਕਨਾਤ (kanaat) *n f* Canopy, canvas wall.

ਕੰਨੂਨ (kanoon) *n m* Law, statute, regulation, legislation, rule; ~ਛਾਂਟਣਾ To argue unnecessarily; ~ਦਾਨ Jurist, lawyer, legal expert; ~ਨ According to or as per law; ~ਬਣਾਉਣਾ To legistate, to make

law Also ਕਾਨੂੰਨ

ਕਨੂੰਨੀ (kanoonee) *a* legal, lawful, legitimate, dejure; pettifogger.

ਕਪਟ (kapaṭ) *n m* Fraud, deceit, trick, cajolery, malice, guile; ~ਤਾ Deceitfulness.

ਕਪਣਾ (kapṇaa) *v* To cut, to chop

ਕਪਤਾਨ (kaptaan) *n m* Captain.

ਕੰਪਨ (kampan) *n m* Shivering, trembling, vibration.

ਕਪੜਾ (kapṛaa) *n m* Clothing, cloth, dress, fabric, apparel.

ਕਪਾਹ (kapaah) *n f* Cotton.

ਕਪਾਲ (kapaal) *n m* Skull, head; fate, destiny.

ਕਪੂਰ (kapoor) *n m* Camphor.

ਕਪੂਰਾ (kapooraa) *n m* Testicle or kidney of male goat.

ਕਫ਼ਨ (kafan) *n m* Coffin, shroud, pall.

ਕਫ਼ਾਇਤ (kafaait) *n f* Thrift, economy, sufficiency; ~ਕਰਨੀ To economise.

ਕੰਭਖਤ (kambhakhat) *a* Unfortunate, unlucky.

ਕੰਭਖਤੀ (kambhakhtee) *n f* Misfortune, wretchedness, adversity.

ਕਬਜ਼ (kabaz) *n f* Constipation, catching, seizure; ~ਕੁਸ਼ਾ Laxative, purgative, digestive.

ਕਬਜ਼ਾ (kabzaa) *n m* (1) Seizure, hold, occupancy, possession,

(2) Handle, grip; Hinge; ~ਕਰਨਾ To occupy, to possess, to seize, to conquer.

ਕਬਜ਼ੀ (Kabzee) *n f* Constipation.

ਕੰਬਣਾ (kambnaa) *v* To tremble, to shiver, to shake, to shudder.

ਕੰਬਣੀ (kambanee) *n f* Trembling motion, tremble, shiver, vibration, shudder, tremor. Also ਕਾਂਬਾ

ਕਬਰ (kabar) *n f* Tomb, grave; ~ਸਤਾਨ Graveyard, cemetry.

ਕੰਬਲ (kambal) *n f* Blanket, wollen sheet.

ਕਬਾਇਲੀ (kabaailee) *a* Tribal; Tribesman; The tribals.

ਕਬਾਬ (kabaab) *n m* Roasted meat, roast.

ਕਬਾਲਾ (kabaalaa) *n m* Transfer, sale deed.

ਕਬਾੜ (kabaar) *n m* Junk, Useless broken material; ~ਖਾਨਾ Junk store.

ਕਬਾੜਾ (kabaaraa) *n m* Turmoil, Ruination.

ਕਬਾੜੀ (kabaaree) *n m* Junkman, dealer in second hand & useless material.

ਕਬਿੱਤ (kabitt) *n m* Poetry, verse.

ਕਬੀਲਾ (kabeelaa) *n m* Tribe, clan.

ਕਬੂਤਰ (Kabootar) *n m* Pigeon; ~ਖਾਨਾ Pigeon house, loft.

ਕਬੂਲ (kabool) *a* Accepted, confessed; ~ਕਰਨਾ To confess, to admit, to accept.

ਕਬੂਲਣਾ (kaboolnaa) *v* To confess, to accept.

ਕਮ (kam) *a* Less, little; ~ਉਮਰ Adolescent; ~ਅਕਲ Stupid, feeble minded.

ਕੰਮ (kamm) *n m* Work, business, task, act, action, service, deed, occupation, purpose; ~ਆਉਣਾ To be use, to be helpful; ~ਕੱਢਣਾ To have one's purpose served; ~ਕਰਨਾ To work, to serve, To labour, to be busy.

ਕਮਜ਼ਾਤ (kamzaat) *a* Of low birth or caste, mean, base, ignoble.

ਕਮਜ਼ੋਰ (kamzor) *a* Weak, insecure, feeble; Impotent.

ਕਮਜ਼ੋਰੀ (kamzoree) *n f* Weakness, feebleness, infirmity, debility, fragility; Impotence; *Hyposthenia*.

ਕਮਰ (kamar) *n f* Waist, loins; ~ਸਿੱਧੀ ਕਰਨਾ To relax; ~ਕਸਣੀ To get ready, to gird up one's loins; ~ਟੁੱਟਣੀ To be discouraged, to lose support.

ਕਮਰਾ (kamraa) *n m* Room, chamber, closet.

ਕਮਲ (kamal) *n m* Lotus.

ਕਮਲਾ (kamlaa) *n f a* Beautiful lady,

the goddess lakshmi; Insane
mad, crazy.

ਕਮਾਉਣਾ (kamaaunaa) *v* To earn, to
acquire, to gain.

ਕਮਾਉ (kamaau) *a* Earning, earner,
bread-winner, hard-working,
industrious.

ਕਮਾਈ (kamaaee) *n f* Earning,
wages, gain.

ਕਮਾਦ (kamaad) *n m* Sugercane.

ਕਮਾਨੀ (kamaanee) *n f* Spring.

ਕਮਾਲ (kamaal) *n m* Miracle,
accomplishment, excellence,
perfection.

ਕਮੀ (kamee) *n f* Want, dearthy,
paucity, shortfall, decrease.

ਕਮੀਜ਼ (kameez) *n f* Shirt.

ਕਮੀਨਾ (kameenaa) *a* Mean, base,
low; ~**ਪਨ** Meanness.

ਕਮੇਰਾ (kameraa) *n m* Worker,
labourer.

ਕਰਜ਼ (karaz) *n m* Debit, loan, credit;
~**ਦਾਰ** Debitor, indebted. Also
ਕਰਜ਼ਾ

ਕਰਜ਼ਾਈ (karzaaee) *n m* Borrower,
indebtor.

ਕਰਨੀ (karnee) *n f* Deed, doing,
performance.

ਕਰਤਬ (kartab) *n m* Skill, trick, action,
jugglery, performance.

ਕਰਤਾਰ (kartaar) *n m* God, the

creator.

ਕਰਤੂਤ (kartoot) *n f* Misconduct,
misdeed, action.

ਕਰਨਹਾਰ (karnanhaar) *a n m* Doer,
creator; God.

ਕਰਨਾ (karnaa) *v* To do, to act,
perform; To practice (as in **ਪੀਆ
ਕਰਦਾ** used to drink or usually
drank).

ਕਰਨੀ (karnee) *n f* Deeds, actions,
conduct, practice.

ਕਰਨੈਲ (karnail) *n m* colonel.

ਕ੍ਰਮ (kram) *n m* Grade, Sequence,
series; ~**ਸੰਖਿਆ** Serial number.

ਕਰਮ (karam) *n* (1) Action, deed,
performance, (2) destiny, fate;
(3) Object (gr) ; ~**ਸ਼ਾਲਾ** Workshop;
~**ਚਾਰੀ** Official, servant, worker.

ਕਰਵਟ (karvat) *n f* Side, back.

ਕਰੜਾ (karraa) *a* Hard, strong, harsh,
stiff, strict, tough, inflexible,
difficult; ~**ਈ** Toughness, stiffness,
hardness, strictness.

ਕਰਾਉਣਾ (kaaraaunaa) *v* To get or
have (something) done; to assist
in doing something. Also **ਕਰਵਾਉਣਾ**

ਕਰਾਏਦਾਰ (karaaedaar) *n m* Tenant,
hirer, lodger.

ਕਰਾਹੁਣਾ (krahunaa) *v* To groan, to
cry in pain, to moan.

ਕਰਾਮਾਤ (kraamaat) *n f* Miracle,

wonder, magic.

ਕਰਾਮਾਤੀ (karaamaatee) *a* Miraculous, thaumaturgic miracle-maker, thaumaturge.

ਕਰਾਰ (karaar) *n m* Promise, undertaking, word of honour; stability, satisfaction, mental calm.

ਕਰਾਰਾ (kraaraa) *a* Crisp, spicy, piquant, Strong.

ਕਰਾੜ (kraar̤) *a* Miser, thrifty; Money-lender; Petty shopkeeper, small businessman.

ਕਰਿਆਨਾ (kariyaanaa) *n* Grocery, provision.

ਕਰੀਚਣਾ (kareechnaa) *v* To grind, to gnash, grit (teeth).

ਕਰੀਬ (kareeb) *adv* Near, near about, close to, not far; About, nearly, approximately.

ਕਰੀਬਨ (kareeban) *adv* Nearly, approximately, roughly, almost.

ਕਰੀਬੀ (kareebee) *a* Near, close, (relation or place); nearness, closeness.

ਕਰੀਮ (kareem) *a* Kind, benign, benevolent, compassionate, bounteous, bountiful, clement; An attribute of God.

ਕਰੀੜਨਾ (kreer̤naa) *v* To grind (teeth), to gnash.

ਕਰੇੜਨਾ (karer̤naa) *v* To scrape.

ਕਰੋਸ਼ੀਆ (karoshiaa) *n m* Crochet, crochet-needle.

ਕਰੋਧ (krodh) *n m* Anger, wrath, rage, fury, resentment.

ਕਰੋੜ (karor) *a* Crore, ten million; ~**ਪਤਿ** Multi-millionaire, a very rich person.

ਕੱਲ (kall) *n m* Tomorrow, yesterday.

ਕਲਹ (kalah) *n f* Clash, quarrel, scrimmage.

ਕਲੰਕ (kalank) *n m* Blemish, stigma, moral stain, blot, smudge, splodge smirch, smear; taint; ignominy disgrace.

ਕਲਤਰ (kalatar) *n f* Wife.

ਕਲਪਣਾ (kalapṇaa) *v* To lament, to grieve.

ਕਲਪਾਉਣਾ (kalpaauṇaa) *v* To cause grief or annoyance, to vex, to annoy, to irritate, to torment.

ਕਲਫ਼ (kalaf) *n f* Starch, farina; hairdye.

ਕਲਬੂਤ (kalboot) *n m* Frame, body, mould; last, shoe-stretcher.

ਕਲਮ (kalam) *n f* Pen; Reed; Cutting, graft; Wedge; Unshaved tuft of hair near the temples; ~**ਕਰਨਾ** To cut, to sever; ~**ਘੜਨੀ** To sharpen reed-pen; ~**ਚਲਾਉਣੀ** To exercise authority, to issue order or judgement; ~**ਫੇਰਨੀ** To delete, erase, to cancel, to strike out, to bring to nothing, to destory; ~ਲਾਉਣੀ To plant a cutting; to graft; ~ਦਾਨ Ink-stand, inkpot stand.

ਕਲਮਾ (kalmaa) *n m* Muhammadan's sacred formula; speech, utterance, sentence.

ਕਲਮੀ (kalmee) *a* Written; grafted, (fruit) bone by a grafted tree; crystalline.

ਕਲਪਨਾ (kalpnaa) *n f* Imagination, assumption, notion, hypothesis, supposition, fancy, dream.

ਕਲਮੂੰਹਾ (kalmoonhaa) *a* Swart, swarthy.

ਕੱਲ੍ਹ (kallh) *n m* Yesterday, tomorrow; ~ਕੱਲ੍ਹ ਕਰਨਾ To go on postponing, delaying; ~ਪਰਸੋਂ A few day back.

ਕਲ੍ਹਾ (kalhaa) *n f* Quarrel, tussle, conflict, discord, trouble.

ਕਲਾ (kalaa) *n f* Art, skill, craft, fine, art, machine; Supernatural, power; Phase of moon; ~ਬਾਜ Acrobat, gymnast; ~ਬਾਜ਼ੀ Acrobatic feat, somersault; volteface; Acrobatics, gymnastics.

ਕੱਲਾ (kallaa) *a* Alone, lonely, single, solitary, lone. Also ਇਕੱਲਾ

ਕਲਾਮ (kalaam) *n m* Utterance, speech; sacred text; poem, verse, poetic work.

ਕਲਾਵਾ (kalaavaa) *n m* Armful; grip with both arms extended, encirclement with arm; Hug embrace.

ਕਲਿਆਣ (kaliyaan) *n m* Welfare, benediction, success; ~ਕਾਰੀ Auspicious, blissful, benedictory.

ਕਲੂਟਾ (kalootaa) *a* Dark, complexioned.

ਕਲੇਸ਼ (kalesh) *n m* Anguish, distress, trouble, agony, affliction, torment.

ਕਲੇਜਾ (kalejaa) *n m* Liver, bosom, heart, courage; ~ਸਾੜਨਾ To give pain, to torment, to cause jealousy.

ਕਲੇਜੀ (kalejee) *n f* Liver of slaughtered bird or animal.

ਕਵਾਰਾ (kawaaraa) *n m* Bachelor, unmarried youth.

ਕਵਿਤਾ (kavitaa) *n f* Poetry, poem, verse.

ਕੜਕ (karak) *n m* Crash, Cracking sound, sound of breaking up.

ਕੜਕਣਾ (karaknaa) *a* To crackle, to thunder, to chuck.

ਕੜਛਾ (karchhaa) *n m* Large cooking spoon, ladle.

ਕੜਛੀ (karchhee) *n f* Cooking or serving, spoon, ladle.

ਕੜਨਾ (karnaa) *a* To tie, to fasten or bind tightly.

ਕੜ੍ਨਾ (karhnaa) *v* To boil, to rise

ਕੜਾ (karaa) *n m* A metallic, metal ring, wrislet; Hard; Stout.

ਕੜਾਹ (karaah) *n m* Pudding of flour, sugar and butter.

ਕੜਾਹਾ (karaahaa) *n m* Cauldron, large frying pan.

ਕੜਾਹੀ (karaahee) *n f* Frying pan, stewpan.

ਕੜਾਕਾ (karakaa) *n m* Cracking sound; Intenseness; ~ਦਾਰ Crisp.

ਕਾਂ (kaan) *n* Crow. Also ਕਾਉਂ

ਕਾਇਦਾ (kaaidaa) *n m* (1) Custom, base, rule, law, practice, good manner, (2) Primer, elementary text book.

ਕਾਇਲ (kaail) *a* Convinced, subdued; ~ਹੋਣਾ To be convinced, the impressed, to believe.

ਕਾਈ (kaaee) *n f* Moss, fungus.

ਕਾਸਦ (kaasad) *n m* Messenger, ambassador. Also ਕਾਸਿਦ

ਕਾਸ਼ਤ (kaashat) *n f* Cultivation, sowing, tilage, tilth; ~ਕਰਨਾ To cultivate, grow, produce; to till, to plough; ~ਕਾਰ Cultivatior, farmer, agriculturist; ~ਕਾਰੀ

Farming, agriculture, cultivation.

ਕਾਸਬੀ (kaasbee) *n m* Weaver.

ਕਾਹਲ (kaahal) *a* Lazy, lethargic, slothful, indolent.

ਕਾਹਲੀ (kaahlee) *a* Hurriedly, hastly, quickly, fast.

ਕਾਹਨੂੰ (kaahnoo) *adv* Why, what for.

ਕਾਹਲਾ (kaahlaa) *a* Hasty, impetuous.

ਕਾਹਵਾ (kahwaa) *n m* Tea without milk, coffee.

ਕਾਕੜਾ (kaakraa) *n m* Measles.

ਕਾਗਜ਼ (kaagaz) *n m* Paper, Written document.

ਕਾਂਗੜੀ (kanngree) *n f* Warming pan.

ਕਾਟ (kaat) *n* Cut, dissection, cutting, wound, deduction.

ਕਾਠ (kaath) *n f* Wood, timber.

ਕਾਠੀ (kaathee) *n f* (1) Saddle; (2) Frame, appearance, body, shape.

ਕਾਣ (kaan) *n m* Defect, blemish, crookedness.

ਕਾਣਾ (kaanaa) *a* One eyed.

ਕਾਤਲ (kaatal) *n m* Murderer, assassin, killer.

ਕਾਤੀ (kaatee) *n f* Scissors, dagger, Shears.

ਕਾਦਰ (kaadar) *a* Almighty, potent, all powerful; creator or lord of creation; God. Also ਕੁਦਰਤ

ਕਾਨਾਫੂਸੀ (kanaaphoosee) *n* Whisper,

Secret talk in a low tone.

ਕਾਫ਼ਰ (kaafar) *n m* Atheist, infidel, heretic, agnostic, non-believer in God or in Islamic; Renegade, apostate.

ਕਾਫ਼ਲਾ (kaaflaa) *n m* Caravan.

ਕਾਫ਼ੀ (kafee) *a n m* Sufficient, enough, adequate; Coffee.

ਕਾਬਜ਼ (kaabaz) *a* In possession, possessing, holding, in occupation, occupant.

ਕਾਬਲ (kabal) *n m* Able, capable, competent, qualified, worthy, deserving, fit, intelligent, learned, meritorious.

ਕਾਬਲੀਅਤ (kableeyat) *n f* Ability, worthiness, capacity.

ਕਾਬੂ (kaboo) *n m* Control, hold, command, power.

ਕਾਮਯਾਬ (Kaamyaab) *a* Successful; ~ਹੋਣਾ To be successful, to succeed.

ਕਾਮਰੀ (kaamree) *n m* Blanket.

ਕਾਮਲ (kaamal) *a* Perfect, complete, expert, accomplished.

ਕਾਰਸਤਾਨੀ (kaarastaanee) *n f* Mischief, doing, conspiracy.

ਕਾਰਕੁਨ (kaarkun) *n m* Worker, member, agent, clerk.

ਕਾਰਖਾਨਾ (kaarkhaanaa) *n m* Mill, factory.

ਕਾਰਗਰ (kaargar) *a* Effective, beneficial.

ਕਾਰਗੁਜ਼ਾਰ (kaarguzaar) *n m* Performer, worker.

ਕਾਰਗੁਜ਼ਾਰੀ (kaarguzaaree) *n f* Performance, work, achievement.

ਕਾਰਜ (kaaraj) *n m* Action, work, business, transaction, task; ~ਸਾਧਕ Useful, instrumental, officiating, executive; ~ਭਾਰ Work load, responsibility; ~ਵਾਹਕ Acting, officiating, temporary, adhoc.

ਕਾਰਨ (kaaran) *n m* Cause, reason, motive, ground; purpose; factor responsible for; Because of, due to, owing to, by reason of, by virtue of.

ਕਾਰਨਾਮਾ (kaarnaamaa) *n m* Achievement, adventure, feat, laudable deed.

ਕਾਰਵਾਈ (kaarvaaee) *n f* Proceedings; action, activity.

ਕਾਰਿੰਦਾ (kaarindaa) *n m* Agent, worker.

ਕਾਰੀਗਰ (kaareegar) *n m* Workman, artisan, mechanic, craftsman.

ਕਾਰੀਗਰੀ (kaareegaree) *n f* Skill, workmanship, mastery, proficiency, adroitness, dexterity.

ਕਾਰੋਬਾਰ (kaarobaar) *n m* Occupation, business.

ਕਾਲ (kaal) *n* (1) Time, period, era; (2) Death, famine; (3) Tense(gr); ~**ਕੋਠੜੀ** Dungeon, dark cell.

ਕਾਲਖ (kaalakh) *n f* Soot, smudge, blot, stain.

ਕਾਲਾ (kaalaa) *a m* Black, dark; ~**ਸੱਪ** Adder; ~**ਚੋਰ** Notorious thief; ~**ਨੀਲਾ** unfair, ugly; ~**ਮੋਤੀਆ** Glaucoma.

ਕਾਲੀ (kaalee) *a f* Black, dusky, dark; ~**ਮਿਰਚ** Black pepper.

ਕਾਵਿ (kaavi) *n m* Poetry, poesy, poetic literature, poetic composition or work; ~**ਸ਼ਾਸਤਰ** Poetics, prosody, treatise on versification; ~**ਕਲਾ** Art of poetry, poetic art; ~**ਚੋਰੀ** Plagiarism; ~**ਰਚਨਾ** Versification, poetic work or composition.

ਕਾੜ੍ਹਨਾ (kaarhnaa) *v* To boil thoroughly, to boil on low heat for a long time, to decoct.

ਕਾੜ੍ਹ (kaarhaa) *n m* Decoction, herbs or drugs decocted in water; Intensily hot; Sultry weather.

ਕਿਆਰਾ (kiara) *n m* Plot, subdivison of a field.

ਕਿਆਮਤ (kiyaamat) *n f* Calamity, oppression, doom, annihilation.

ਕਿਸ਼ਤ (kisht) *n f* Instalment.

ਕਿਸ਼ਤੀ (kishtee) *n f* Boat dinghy, canoe.

ਕਿਸਮ (kisam) *n f* Type, variety, kind, class.

ਕਿਸਮਤ (kismat) *n f* Fate, fortune, luck.

ਕਿੱਸਾ (kissaa) *n m* Story; ~**ਤਮਾਮ ਕਰਨਾ** To put on end to , to wind up.

ਕਿਸਾਨ (kisaan) *n* Farmer, peasant, agriculturist, cultivator.

ਕਿਹੜਾ (kehraa) *pron* Which, what, who?

ਕਿਕਣ (kikan) *adv* How?

ਕਿਕਲੀ (kiklee) *n f* A kind of folk dance performed by females; a peal of laughter.

ਕਿਚਕਿਚਾਉਣਾ (kichkichaaunaa) *v* To grind or gnash teeth in anger.

ਕਿਣਕਾ (kiṇkaa) *n m* Particle, speck, granule, broken piece of grain; Atom.

ਕਿਤਾਬ (kitaab) *n f* Book, publication; ~**ਚਾ** Booklet, pamphlet.

ਕਿਤਾਬੀ (kitaabee) *a* Bookish.

ਕਿਥੇ (kithe) *adv* Where?

ਕਿੱਦਣ (kiddaṇ) *adv* When, on what day or date.

ਕਿਧਰੇ (kidhre) *adv* Perchance, possibly.

ਕਿਧਰੋਂ (kindron) *adv* Wherefrom, from

which side or direction, from where?

ਕਿਨਵਾਂ (kinvaan) *a* Which one, where (in a series or sequence).

ਕਿਨ੍ਹੇ (kinne) *pron* Who, which one (in subjective case).

ਕਿਨਾਰਾ (kinaaraa) *n m* Bank, shore coast; Border, side hem. Also ਕੰਢਾ

ਕਿਨਾਰਾਕਸ਼ੀ (kinaaraakashee) *n m* Standing apart, dissociation.

ਕਿਨਾਰੀ (kinaaree) *n f* Hem, edging, lace, fringe, tatting.

ਕਿਰਕਿਰਾ (kirkiraa) *a* Spoiled, gritty, sandy.

ਕਿਰੱਤਗ (kirtagg) *a* Obliged, grateful; ~ਤਾ Gratitude, obligation. Also ਕ੍ਰਿਤਗਤਾ

ਕਿਰਤਘਣ (kiratghaṇ) *a* Ungrateful, unthankful. Also ਕ੍ਰਿਤਘਣ

ਕਿਰਤਾਰਥ (kirataarath) *a* Obliged, grateful, gratified.

ਕਿਰਪਾ (kirpaa) *n f* Kindness, benignity, compassion; favour, benevolence, beneficence, benefaction; mercy, grace, graciousness; ~ਕਰ ਕੇ Kindly, please; ~ਕਰਨੀ To be kind, benign; to favour, oblige, bestow benefaction or benefit, to do a good turn, to do favour.

·ਕਿਰਦਾਰ (kirdaar) *n m* Role, character.

ਕਿਰਪਾਨ (kirpaan) *n f* Sword.

ਕਿਰਪਾਲਤਾ (kirpaaltaa) *n f* Graciousness, beneficence.

ਕਿਰਲਾ (kirlaa) *n m* Big lizzard.

ਕਿਰਲੀ (kirlee) *n f* Lizzard.

ਕਿਰਾਇਆ (kiraayiaa) *n m* Rent, fare, hiring or Conveyance charges. Also ਕਰਾਇਆ

ਕਿੱਲ (kill) *n f* Iron nail, pin, tack.

ਕਿਲਾ (killaa) *n m* Fort, garrison, castle, citadel.

ਕਿਲਕਾਰੀ (kilkaaree) *n f* Outcry, joyful shriek.

ਕਿਲੱਤ (killat) *n f* Deficiency, scarcity, want, shortage, paucity, dearth.

ਕਿੱਲੀ (killee) *n f* Peg, trenail.

ਕਿਵਾੜ (kivaaṛ) *n m* Door, gate.

ਕਿੜਕਿੜ (kiṛkiṛ) *n f* Cracking sound.

ਕੀ (kee) *pron* What, whether. Also ਕੀਹ

ਕੀਕਣ (keekan) *adv* How, in what way. Also ਕੀਕੂੰ

ਕੀਨਾ (keenaa) *n m* Malice, spite, rancour, vindictiveness, vindictive feelling; ~ਰੱਖਣਾ To harbour Malice To be vindictive, rancorous

ਕੀਮਖਾਬ (keemkhaab) *n m* Costly silken cloth, brocade.

ਕੀਮਾ (keemaa) *n m* Minced meat.

ਕੀਰਤ (keerat) *n m* Reputation.

ਕੀਰਤਨ (kirtan) *n m* Hymn singing, devotional singing in praise of deity; ~ਕਰਨਾ To Perform hymn.

ਕੀਰਤੀ (keertee) *n f* Glory, fame, reputation, praise.

ਕੀੜਾ (Keeṛaa) *n m* Insect, worm, vermin.

ਕੁਸਕਣਾ (kusakṇaa) *v* To speak meekly, to utter a word.

ਕੁਸੰਗਤ (kusangat) *n f* Bad company.

ਕੁਸ਼ਤੀ (kushtee) *n f* Wrestling, duel.

ਕੁਹਾੜਾ (kuhaaraa) *n m* Large axe.

ਕੁਹਾੜੀ (kuhaaree) *n f* Small axe, chopper, hatchet.

ਕੁੱਕੜ (kukkaṛ) *n m* Cock; ~ਖਾਨਾ Poultry farm.

ਕੁੱਕੜੀ (kukkree) *n f* Hen; bobbin.

ਕੁੱਖ (kukkh) *n f* Womb, cavity; ~ਹਰੀ ਹੋਣੀ To be pregnant, to bear a child.

ਕੁਚੱਜਾ (kuchajjaa) *n m* Awkwardness, clumsiness, lack of proper manner or method; tactlessness.

ਕੁੱਚਲਣਾ (kuchalṇaa) *v* To crush, to squash, to run over, to tread.

ਕੁੱਛੜ (kuchchhaṛ) *n f* Lap, bosom, haunch.

ਕੁੰਜੀ (kunjee) *n f* Key, note, annotation of a book.

ਕੁੱਝ (kujh) *a* Some, a little, something.

ਕੁਟਣਾ (kuṭṇaa) *v* To beat, to thrash, to pound, to cudgel.

ਕੁਟਾਈ (kuṭaaee) *n f* Beating, thrashing.

ਕੁੰਡਲ (kundal) *n m* Curl lock (of hair), ringlet; coil, spiral; noose of rope; large heavy ear-ring; curlicue curlycue; ~ਦਾਰ Curly, coiled, spiralled.

ਕੁੰਡਲੀ (kundlee) *n f* Small coil or ring; Horoscope.

ਕੁੰਡਾ (kundaa) *n m* Bolt, hook, chain, hatchet.

ਕੁੰਡੀ (Kundee) *n f* Bolt, hook, chain, staple.

ਕੁਤਪੁਣਾ (kutpuṇaa) *n m* Wrangling, querrel, meanness, doglike behaviour.

ਕੁਤਰਨਾ (kutarnaa) *v* To gnaw, to cut into small pieces.

ਕੁੱਤਾ (kuttaa) *n m* Dog, a low and mean person.

ਕੁਤਾਹੀ (kutaahee) *n f* Carelessness, deficiency, want, decrease.

ਕੁੱਤੀ (kuttee) *n f* Bitch.

ਕੁਦਣਾ (kudṇaa) *v* To jump, to leap, to dance, to hop.

ਕੁੰਦਨ (kundan) *n m* Pure gold; Pure, good, honest; in perfect health.

ਕੁਦਰਤ (kudarat) *n f* Nature, divinity, power; ~ਨ Naturally, by chance, coincidently.

ਕੁਦਰਤੀ (kudartee) *a* Natural, divine; innate; unexpected; By chance, naturally.

ਕੁਨਬਾ (kunbaa) *n m* Family, kinsfolk.

ਕੁੱਪਤ (kupatt) *n m* Quarrel, altercation, wrangle, brawl, squabble; dishonourable or disorderly behaviour.

ਕੁੱਪਤਾ (kupattaa) *a* Quarrelsome, wrangler, squabbler; spoilsport.

ਕੁੱਪਾ (kuppaa) *n m* Large vessel made from raw hide (for holding and carrying oil); Any large container, canister; Fat, corpulent, bulky.

ਕੁੱਪੀ (kuppee) *n f* Lubricating can, Oil container, oil-can.

ਕੁਫਰ (kufar) *n m* Atheism, disbelief, unbelief in the existence of God, blasphemy

ਕੁੱਬ (kubb) *n f* Bend, curve, curvature; bend or crook in body, hump, hunch; **~ਕੱਢਣਾ** To remove bending, to straighten.

ਕੁਮਲਾਉਣਾ (kumlaaunaa) *v* To fade, to wither, to shrivel, to lose luster.

ਕੁਰਸੀ (kursee) *n f* Chair, seat; authority.

ਕੁਰਕੀ (kurkee) *n f* Attachment, seizure.

ਕੁਰਬਾਨ (kurbaan) *a* Sacrificed,

martyred; **~ਹੋਣਾ** To die for, to become a martyr, to give one's life for.

ਕੁਰਬਾਨੀ (kurbaanee) *n f* Sacrifice.

ਕੁਰਲਾਉਣਾ (kurlaaunaa) *v* To moon, to groan, to cry.

ਕੁਰੇਦਨਾ (kurednaa) *v* To scrape, to scratch.

ਕੁੱਲ (kull) *n m* Dynasty, ancestry, family, lineage caste, race.

ਕੁਲਛਣਾ (kulachhnaa) *a* Ill mannered, ill-bred.

ਕੁਲਟਾ (kultaa) *n f* Prostitute, bad women.

ਕੁਲਾਂਚ (kulaanch) *n f* Jump, hop, bound.

ਕੁੜੱਕੀ (kurkkee) *n f* Trap, net.

ਕੁੜਮ (kuram) *n m* Father-in-law of one's son or daughter.

ਕੁੜਮਾਈ (kurmaaee) *n f* Betrothal, engagement.

ਕੁੜਨਾ (kurnaa) *v* To pine, to grieve, to feel displeased.

ਕੁੜੀ (kuree) *n f* Girl, daughter virgin.

ਕੁਹਣੀ (kuhnee) *n* Elbow, ancon.

ਕੂਕ (kook) *n f* Whistle, shout, complaint, woes.

ਕੂਕਣਾ (kooknaa) *v* To Scream, to cry, to sob, to shout.

ਕੂਕਾਂ (kookaan) *n f* Screams, cries.

ਕੂਚਨਾ (koochnaa) *v* To cleanse thoroughly by scrubbing.

ਕੂਚੀ (koochee) *n f* Brush, swab.

ਕੂਤਨਾ (kootnaa) *v* To evaluate, to estimate.

ਕੂੜ (koor) *n m* Lie, falsehood.

ਕੂੜਾ (kooraa) *n m* a Waste, rubbish, trash, sweepings, Liar; False, lying.

ਕੇਸ (kes) *n m* Hair.

ਕੇਸਰ (kesar) *n m* Saffron, *Crocus stivus.*

ਕੇਂਦਰ (kendar) *n m* Centre, core, nucleus; centroid; focus; head quarters; the central government; ~ਮੁਖੀ Centripetal.

ਕੇਂਦਰੀ (kendree) *a* Central, centric, core, main, nuclear.

ਕੈਦੀ (kaidee) *n m* Prisoner, detainee, captive; convict.

ਕੈਫ਼ੀਅਤ (kaifiat) *n f* State condition, well-being; remarks, detail, statement.

ਕੇਰਨਾ (kernaa) *v* To pour, to scatter, to spread, to drop.

ਕੈ (kai) *n f* Vomitting.

ਕੈਂਚੀ (kainchee) *n f* Scissors.

ਕੈਦ (kaid) *n m* Imprisonment, restraint, confinement; ~ਖਾਨਾ Prison, jail, gaol.

ਕੋਇਲ (koil) *n f* Cuckoo, nightingale.

ਕੋਇਲਾ (koilaa) *n m* Charcoal, coal.

ਕੋਸ਼ (kosh) *n m* Dictionary, lexicon, Treasure.

ਕੋਸਨਾ (kosnaa) *v* To curse, to damn, to execrate, to imprecate.

ਕੋਸਾ (kosaa) *a* Luke warm, tepid.

ਕੋਸ਼ਿਸ਼ (koshish) *n f* Attempt, endeavour.

ਕੋਹ (kōh) *n m* Mountain; A unit of distance approximately equal to 24 kilometres; ~ਸਤਾਨ Mountainous country, hilly tract, mountain range.

ਕੋਹਨਾ (kohnaa) *v* To torture, to slay, to kill.

ਕੋਹਰਾ (kohraa) *n m* frost.

ਕੋਹਲੂ (kohloo) *n m* Oil press.

ਕੋਹੜਾ (kohraa) *n m* Leper.

ਕੋਕਾ (kokaa) *n m* Small nil, nosepin.

ਕੋਝਾ (kojhaa) *a* Ugly, unseemly, awkward.

ਕੋਠੜੀ (kothree) *n f* Room, cabin, cell, closet.

ਕੋਠਾ (kothaa) *n m* House, terrace, upper storey.

ਕੋਠੀ (kothee) *n f* Banglow, mansion, masonary house.

ਕੋਠੇਲਾ (kothelaa) *n m* Young camel (Two year old).

ਕੋਣ (kon) *n m* Angle.

ਕੋਤਵਾਲ (kotwaal) *n m* Chief Police

Officer, Police Inspector.

ਕੋਤਵਾਲੀ (kotwaalee) *n f* Police station.

ਕੋਤਾਹੀ (kotaahee) *n f* Negligance, default.

ਕੋਫਤ (koft) *n f* Botheration, hardship, trouble.

ਕੋਰਮਾ (kormaa) *n m* Curry, cooked meat.

ਕੋਰਾ (koraa) *a* Fresh, new, unused, unwashed, foolish, stupid; ~ਜਵਾਬ Flat refusal, blank reply.

ਕੌਡੀ (kaudee) *n f* Small sea shell, cowrie.

ਕੌਮ (kaum) *n f* Nation, creed, tribe, clan, sect, caste.

ਕੌਮੀ (kaumee) *a* National; ~ਅਤ Nationality.

ਕੌਲ (kaul) *n m* Promise, word, consent, agreement.

ਕੌੜਾ (kauraa) *a* Bitter, acrimonious, pungent; ~ਪਣ Bitterness.

ਕੌੜੀ (kauree) *n m* Score; Cowrie.

ਖ

ਖ Seventh letter of Gurmukhi alphabets pronounced as khakhaa.

ਖਉ (khau) *n m* Destruction, annihilation, hardship, decay, decline, danger. Also ਖੈ

ਖਸਖਸ (khas khas) *n f* Poppy seed. Also ਖਸਖਾਸ

ਖਸਣਾ (khasṇaa) *v* To Snatch, to deprive, to seize.

ਖਸਤਾ (khastaa) *a* Crisp, broken, dilapidated, poor, miserable; ~ਹਾਲ Miserable, wretched, pitiable.

ਖਸਮ (khasam) *n m* Husband, owner, master, lord; ~ਕਰਨਾ To marry, to remarry; ~ਖਾਣੀ Widow, devourer of husband.

ਖਸਮਾਨਾ (khasmaanaa) *n m* Husbandhood; Protection, patronage, refuge.

ਖਸਰਨਾ (khasarnaa) *v* To rub, to wipe, to scour.

ਖਸਰਾ (khasraa) *n m* Measles.

ਖੱਸੀ (khassee) *a* Sterilized, castrated, impotent, stoneless; ~ਕਰਨਾ To castrate, to sterilise, emasculate.

ਖਸੂਸੀਅਤ (khasoosiat) *n* Special quality, charactersitic or trait, properly, peculiarity.

ਖਹਿਣਾ (khaihṇaa) *v* To rub, to push with body, to jostle, to provoke or start a quarrel, to pick up quarrel, to bicker, to wrangle.

ਖਹਿਬੜਨਾ (khaibarnaa) *v* To altercate, to quarrel, to squabble, to wrangle.

ਖਹਿੜਾ (khairaa) *n m* Urging, impulsion, insistence, persistent entreaty; ~ਛਡਾਉਣਾ To disentangle, to disengage, oneself from, to get rid of.

ਖਹੁਰਾ (khauraa) *a* Hard, rough, coarse; hot-tempered, harsh, menacing.

ਖੱਖਰ (khakkhar) *n f* Hives of wasps.

ਖੰਗਾਲਣਾ (khangaalṇaa) *v* To rinse, to cleanse.

ਖੰਘ (khang) *n f* Cough, coughing.

ਖੰਘਣਾ (khangh'ṇaa) *v* To cough.

ਖੰਘਾਰ (khangh'aar) *n m* Sputum, phlegm.

ਖੰਘਾਰਨਾ (khangh'aarnaa) *v* To cough, to discharge phlegm.

ਖੱਚ (khachch) *n f* Noise, trouble,

vexation.

ਖਚਰ (khachar) *n m* Mule; ~ਪੁਣਾ Cleverness, williness; Wickedness.

ਖਚਰਾ (khachraa) *a* Mulish, deceitful, perverse.

ਖੰਜਰ (khanjar) *n m* Dagger.

ਖੱਜਲ (khajjal) *a* Ruined, wretched, forlorn, distressed.

ਖਜ਼ਾਨਚੀ (khazaanchee) *n m* Treasurer, cashier, bursar.

ਖ਼ਜ਼ਾਨਾ (khazaanaa) *n m* Treasury, repository, store, magazine.

ਖ਼ਜ਼ਾਬ (khazaab) *n m* Dye, hairdye.

ਖੱਜੀ (khajjee) *n f* Date, palm.

ਖਜੂਰ (khajoor) *n m* Date, Phoenix dactylifera.

ਖਟਕਣਾ (khatakṇaa) *v* To prick, to be terrified, to be offended.

ਖਟਕਾ (khatkaa) *n m* Apprehension, suspicion, anxiety, doubt, fear.

ਖਟਕਾਉਣਾ (khatkaaunaa) *v* To knock, to strike.

ਖਟਖਟਾਉਣਾ (khatkhataaunaa) *v* To knock, to thump, to rap

ਖਟਣਾ (khatṇaa) *v* To gain, to benefit, to earn.

ਖਟਪਟ (khatpat) *n f* Estrangement, alienation, quarrel, conflict, disagreement, strained relations.

ਖਟਮਲ (khatmal) *n m* Bug, bedbug,

Cimex lectularius.

ਖਟਵਾਉਣਾ (khatvaaunaa) *v* To cause to earn.

ਖੱਟਣਾ (khattṛaa) *n m* Plain bed.

ਖੱਟਾ (khattaa) *a n m* Sour, acidic, sharp; Ferment, curd (yoghurt); A little curd added to milk to curdle or coagulate it.

ਖਟਾਈ (khtaaaee) *n f* Sourness, acidity.

ਖਟਾਸ (khataas) *n f* Sourness, acidity.

ਖਟਿਆ (khatiaa) *a* Earned

ਖੱਟੀ (khatee) *n f* Earning, income, gain, emoluments.

ਖਟੀਕ (khateek) *n m* Tanner.

ਖੰਡ (khanḍ) *n f* (1) Sugar; (2) Portion, part, region, piece, segment.

ਖੱਡ (khaḍḍ) *n m* Pit, ditch, ravine.

ਖੰਡਾ (khanḍaa) *n m* Broad sword.

ਖੱਡਾ (khaḍḍaa) *n m* Pit, ditch, dugout; cavity, concavity. Also ਖੱਡਾ

ਖੱਡੀ (khaḍḍee) *n f* Loom, Weaver's pit.

ਖਤ (khat) *n m* (1) Letter, a note; Handwriting; (2) line; shave.

ਖ਼ਤਮ (khatam) *a* Ended, finished, concluded, complete; ~ਹੋਣਾ To be completed, to be finished; to come to an end, to exhaust, to expire; ~**ਕਰ ਦੇਣਾ** To kill, to murder; ~**ਕਰਨਾ** To finish, to exhaust, to come to an end, to kill.

ਖਤਰਨਾਕ (khatarnaak) *a* Dangerous, risky, critical, alarming, serious.

ਖਤਰਾ (khatraa) *n m* Danger, jeopardy, peril, risk.

ਖਤੂੰਗੜਾ (khatoongṛaa) *n m* Young donkey.

ਖੰਦਕ (khandak) *n f* Deep ditch, trench.

ਖੱਦਰ (khaddar) *n m* Coarse cotton cloth.

ਖਦੇੜਨਾ (khadeṛnaa) *v* To cast out, to rout.

ਖੰਨੀ (khannee) *a* Half, quarter (loaf)

ਖੱਪ (khapp) *n f* Noise, fuss; ~**ਖਾਨਾ** Pointless, talk, noisy scene.

ਖਪਣਾ (khapnaa) *v* To worry, to be spent, to be destroyed.

ਖਪਤ (khapat) *n f* Sale, consumption, expenditure; ~**ਕਾਰ** Consumer.

ਖਪਤੀ (khaptee) *a* Crack, insane, crazy, obsessed.

ਖਪਰੈਲ (khaprail) *n m* Tiled hut.

ਖਪਾਉਣਾ (khapaaunaa) *v* (1) To tease, to vex; (2) To finish, to consume; To employ; (3) To destroy.

ਖੱਪੀ (khappee) *a* Noisy, bothersome, quarrelsome, prone to raise noise.

ਖਫ਼ਾ (khaffaa) *a* Angry, annoyed, unhappy, displeased; Estranged.

ਖੱਬਚੂ (khabchoo) *a n* Left handed.

ਖਬਰ (khabar) *n f* News, report, information; **ਉਡਦੀ**~ Hearsay, rumour, doubtful news uncertified report; ~**ਦਾਰ** Alert, vigilant, watchful, cautious; Beware.

ਖਬਰੇ (khabre) *adv* Perhaps, may be, could be, possibly.

ਖੱਬਾ (khabbaa) *a* Left, left handed.

ਖੱਬੀਸ (khabbees) *a m* Miser; Wicked, vile.

ਖੰਭ (khamb) *n m* Wing, feather.

ਖੰਭਾ (khambhaa) *n m* Pillar, post.

ਖਮਿਆਜ਼ਾ (khamiaazaa) *n m* Consequence, compensatory.

ਖਮੀਰ (khameer) *n m* Leaven, yeast, barm; Fermentation, bacterization.

ਖਮੀਰਾ (khameeraa) *a* Fermented, leavended.

ਖਮੋਸ਼ੀ (khamoṣi) *n m* Silence, quiet, quietude, muteness, speechlessness, dumbness.

ਖਰ (khar) *n m f* Ass, donkey; foolish, stupid.

ਖਰਚਾ (kharchaa) *n m* Expenditure,

charges, cost, overhead expeness; costs (in law suit); subsistence money paid to separated spouse, alimony. Also **ਖਰਚ**

ਖਰਬ (kharab) *a* One hundred thousand million; 100,000,000,00.

ਖਰਾ (kharaa) *a* Pure, genuine, real, sincere, true, unadulterated, plainspeaking; ~**ਪਨ** purity, geniuneness.

ਖਰਾਇਤ (kharaait) *n f* Charity, alms. Also **ਖੈਰਾਤ**

ਖਰਾਇਤੀ (kharaaitee) *a* Charitable

ਖਰਾਸ਼ (kharaash) *n f* Abrasion, bruise scratch.

ਖਰਾਂਟ (kharaant) *a* Cunning, crafty, clever, smart, mischievous, deceitful; ~**ਪੁਣਾ** Cunningness, craftiness, cleverness, mischievousness, deceitfulness.

ਖਰਾਬ (kharaab) *a* Bad, defective, spoiled, nasty, sinful, wicked.

ਖਰੀਦ (khareed) *n f* Purchase, buying, shopping; ~**ਦਾਰ** Customer, buyer; ~**ਦਾਰੀ** Purchase, buying.

ਖਰੀਦਣਾ (khareednaa) *v* To buy, to purchase.

ਖਰੂੰਡ (kharoond) *n f* Scratch, caused by finger nails or paws or claws.

ਖਰੋਚਣਾ (kharochnaa) *v* To Scratch, to scrape.

ਖਲ (khal) *n f* Oil cake.

ਖੱਲ (khall) *n f* Skin, hide, bellows; ~**ਲਾਹੁਣੀ** To skin, to flay, to peel off skin; To beat, to thrash ruthlessly.

ਖਲਕ (khalak) *n f* Creation, creatures, created.

ਖਲਕਤ (khalkat) *n f* People, crowd, world.

ਖਲਬਲੀ (khalbalee) *n f* Disturbance, commotion, agitation, outrage.

ਖਲਲ (khalal) *n m* Obstruction, interruption, disturbance, confusion.

ਖਲੜ (khallar) *n m* Large or thick hide.

ਖਲੜੀ (khalree) *n f* Skin.

ਖੱਲਾ (khallaa) *n m* Shoe.

ਖਲ੍ਹਾਰਨਾ (khalihaarnaa) *v* To make one stay, to cause to stop, to halt.

ਖਲੋਣਾ (khalonaa) *v* To stand; To halt, to stop or wait, to be or stay erect without support; To be stable.

ਖਲੋਤਾ (khalotaa) *a* Stagnant, standing; ~**ਪਾਣੀ** Staganant water

ਖੜਕਣਾ (kharaknaa) *v* To rattle, to clank, to clink, to jingle, to ring, to tinkle; To clatter; To be knocked, thumped, tapped; To talk in a rage; To cross swords.

ਖੜਕਾ (kharkaa) *n m* Rattling, clattering sound, noise (as of bang, knock, etc); ~ਦੜਕਾ Threatening noise, show of force to create fear or awe; Brave posture; public disturbance, disorder.

ਖੜਕਾਉਣਾ (kharkaaunaa) *v* To knock, to rap, to tap; To ring, rattle; To thump; To shake, To beat producing ratting or clanking noise; To thrash, to chastise.

ਖੜਗ (kharag) *n f* sword.

ਖੜਨਾ (kharnaa) *v* To take away, to carry away.

ਖੜਾਉਣਾ (kharaaunaa) *v* To lose, to be deprived of.

ਖੜਾਵਾਂ (kharaawaan) *n f* Wooden sandles, wooden shoes.

ਖਾਈ (khaaee) *n f* Ditch, trench, pit, groove.

ਖਾਸ (khaas) *a* Special, particular, specific, peculiar, proper, Chief. Also ਖਸੂਸੀ

ਖਾਂਸੀ (khaansee) *n f* Cough; ਕਾਲੀ ~Whooping Cough.

ਖਾਸੀਅਤ (khaasiyat) *n f* Quality, peculiarity, natural disposition.

ਖਾਮਖਾਹ (khaamkhaa) *adv* Uncalled for, without reason or justification or provocation, unjustly, unjustifiably; Also ਖ਼ਾਮਖਾਹ

ਖਾਹਿਸ਼ (khaahish) *n f* Passion, desire, wish, longing, will aspiration; ~ਮੰਦ Willing, desirous.

ਖਾਕ (khaak) *n f* Ashes, earth, nothing; ~ਛਾਨਨੀ To labour in vain; ~ਵਿਚ ਰਲਨਾ To die, to perish; ~ਵਿਚ ਰੁਲਨਾ To be miserable, to live in misery.

ਖਾਕਾ (khaakaa) *n m* Sketch, outline map; Plan, rough plan; Also ਖ਼ਾਕਾ

ਖਾਕੀ (khaakee) *a* Of the dust colour, dusty, greyish brown; Made of earth, material (as against ਨੂਰੀ-Spiritual); Also ਖ਼ਾਕੀ

ਖਾਣ (khaan) *n f* Mine, mineral deposits or source; Abundant stock, store, treasure.

ਖਾਣਾ (khaanaa) *v n m* To eat, to dine, to take, to consume, to ingest; To suffer, endure (defeat, beating, deceit); To embezzle, to misappropriate; To take (oath); To corrode, to erode; Meal, dinner, feast, fare, food, diet, grub, repast.

ਖਾਤਮਾ (khaatmaa) *n m* End, death, annihitation.

ਖ਼ਾਤਰ (khaatar) *n f* Hospitality, Service; ~ਤਵਾਜ਼ਾ Hospitality; ~ਦਾਰੀ Hospitality, servitude, warm reception.

ਖ਼ਾਤਾ (khaataa) *n f* Account, Account book; ~ਵਹੀ Ledger.

ਖਾਤੀ (khaatee) *n m* Carpenter, woodcutter, carver, engraver.

ਖਾਦ (khaad) *n f* Manure, fertilizer, waste, dung.

ਖ਼ਾਦਮ (khaadam) *n m* Servant, attendant.

ਖ਼ਾਨਸਾਮਾ (khaansaamaa) *n m* Butler, steward.

ਖ਼ਾਨਦਾਨ (khaandaan) *n m* Family, race, dynasty.

ਖ਼ਾਨਦਾਨੀ (khaandaanee) *a* Hereditary, ancestral, of good birth, blue blooded; ~ਆਦਮੀ Noble man;~ ਵੈਰ vendetta.

ਖ਼ਾਨਾ (khanaa) *n m* House, chamber compartment, column, cell receptacle; ~ਖ਼ਰਾਬੀ Ruin, destruction; ~ਪੂਰੀ Filling in the blanks; ~ਬਦੋਸ਼ Nomad, nomadic; Vagaboned.

ਖ਼ਾਬ (khaab) *n m* Dream.

ਖ਼ਾਮੀ (khaamee) *n f* Defect, drawback, flaw.

ਖ਼ਾਮੋਸ਼ੀ (khaamoshee) *n f* Silence, reticence.

ਖ਼ਾਰਸ਼ (khaarash) *n f* itch, scabbies; Also ਖ਼ਾਰਸ਼

ਖ਼ਾਰਜ (khaaraj) *a* Discharged, dismissed, expelled; ~ਕਰਨਾ To discharge, to expel, to rusticate.

ਖ਼ਾਰਾ (khaaraa) *a n m* Saltish; Alkaline, saline, hardstone.

ਖਾਲਸਾ (khaalsaa) *n m* Pure; Sikh.

ਖ਼ਾਲਿਸ (khaalis) *a* Pure, genuine, real, undulterated. Also ਖ਼ਾਲਸ

ਖ਼ਾਲੀ (khaalee) *a* Empty, vacant, blank, void; ~ਕਰਨਾ To vacate, to clear.

ਖ਼ਾਵੰਦ (khaawand) *n m* Husband, lord, master.

ਖ਼ਾੜਕੂ (khaarkoo) *a* Courageous, bold, brave; dreaded, feared, dominating, terrorist, militant.

ਖਾੜੀ (khaaree) *n f* Gulf, bay, creek, oceanic channel.

ਖਿਆਨਤ (khiaanat) *n f* Dishonesty, misappropriation, breach of trust, embezzlement.

ਖਿਆਲ (khiyaal) *n m* Idea, belief, imagination, opinion, conception, impression, thought; ~ਨਾ ਕਰਨਾ To ignore, to overlook, to be careless; ~ਨਾ ਰਹਿਣਾ To forget; ~ਰਖਣਾ To take care of, to bear in mind.

ਖਿਆਲੀ (khiyaalee) *a* Imaginary, Idle,

visionary, dreamy.

ਖਿਸਕਣਾ (khisaknaa) v To slip, to steal away.

ਖਿਸਕਾਉਣਾ (khiskaaunaa) v To remove, to move, to draw back.

ਖਿਸਕੂ (khiskoo) a Truant, shirker, malingere; inconsistent, fickle, inconstant.

ਖਿੱਚ (khichch) n f Fascination, attraction, lure, affinity; Tension, strain.

ਖਿਚਣਾ (khichnaa) v To draw, to pull, to drag, to attract, to suck up.

ਖਿਚੜੀ (khichree) n f Dish of rice & pulse, a mixed heap, hotch-potch.

ਖਿਚਾਈ (khichaaee) n f Haulage.

ਖਿਜ਼ਾਬ (khizaab) n m Hair-dye.

ਖਿੱਝ (khijjh) n f Irritation, annoyance, vexation.

ਖਿੱਝਣਾ (khijjhnaa) v To be irritated, to be angry, to be annoyed, to be vexed.

ਖਿੰਡਣਾ (khindnaa) v To Scatter, to disperse, to diffuse, to adjourn.

ਖਿੰਡਾਉਣਾ (khindaaunaa) v To spread, to scatter, to break, to disperse.

ਖਿਡਾਰ (khidaar) n m Player.

ਖਿਡੌਣਾ (khidaunaa) n m Toy, plaything.

ਖਿਤਾਬ (khitaab) n m Title, surname, address.

ਖਿਦਮਤ (khidmat) n f Service, duty, appointment.

ਖਿਦੇੜਨਾ (khidernaa) v To push back.

ਖਿਨ (khin) n m Moment, instant.

ਖਿਮਾ (khimaa) n f Excuse, apology, pardon, forgiveness.

ਖਿਲੰਦੜਾ (khilandraa) a Playful, gamester, frolicsome.

ਖਿਲਾਫ਼ (khilaaf) a Contrary, opposite, against, adverse.

ਖਿਲਾਰ (khilaar) n m Spread, dissémination, expansion, dispersal.

ਖਿੱਲੀ (khillee) n f Jest, laughter, mockery, humour, fun, joke, ridicule.

ਖਿਲੇਰਨਾ (khilearnaa) v To scatter, to disperse.

ਖਿੜਕੀ (khirkee) n f Window, venthole.

ਖਿੜਖਿੜਾਉਣਾ (khirkhiraaunaa) v To laugh, to bloom, to delight.

ਖਿੜਨਾ (khirnaa) v To blossom, to be cheerful, to be delighted.

ਖੀਸਾ (kheesaa) n m Pocket, bag.

ਖੀਰ (kheer) n f Rice pudding, rice cooked in sweetened milk; Milk.

ਖੁਆਉਣਾ (khuaaunaa) v To feed, to cause to eat.

ਖੁਆਰ (khuaar) *a* Disgraced, dishonoured, inconvenienced.

ਖੁਆਰੀ (khuaaree) *n f* Disgrace, dishonour, humiliation, wretchedness.

ਖੁਸ਼ (khush) *a* Glad, happy, pleased, cheerful, gay, delighted, humorous; ~ਹਾਲ Fortune, Prosperous, happy; ~ਗਵਾਰ Pleasant, soothing, healthy.

ਖੁਸ਼ੀ (khushee) *n f* Joy, happiness, pleasure, cheerfulness, gaiety.

ਖੁਸ਼ਕ (khushak) *a* Dry, withered, arid.

ਖੁਸ਼ਕੀ (khushkee) *n f* Dryness, dryland, drought.

ਖੁਸ਼ਖਤ (khushkhat) *n m* Fine writing.

ਖੁਸਣਾ (khusnaa) *v* To be snatched, To be taken away by force, to be seized, plundered, robbed, lost.

ਖੁਸ਼ਬੂ (khushboo) *n m* Fragrance, odour, scent, flavour, perfume.

ਖੁਸਰਾ (khusraa) *n m* Eunuch, hermaphrodite.

ਖੁਸ਼ਾਮਦ (khushaamad) *n f* Flattery, sycophancy.

ਖੁਜਲਾਉਣਾ (khujlaaunaa) *v* To scratch, to itch.

ਖੁਟਕਣਾ (khutakanaa) *v* To strike, to apprehend, to be in doubt.

ਖੁਟਣਾ (khutnaa) *v* To be finished, to end, to be fully consumed.

ਖੁੱਡ (khudd) *n* Hole, pit, narrow cave.

ਖੁਣਸ (khunas) *n f* Animosity, rancour, malice, enmity, ill will.

ਖੁਣਨਾ (khunnaa) *v* To dig, to engrave, to sink.

ਖੁਤਖੁਤੀ (khutkhutee) *n f* Hesitation, fear.

ਖੁਦਕੁਸ਼ੀ (khudkushee) *n f* Suicide.

ਖੁਦਗਰਜ਼ (khudgarz) *a* Selfish.

ਖੁਦਗਰਜ਼ੀ (khudgarzee) *n f* Selfishness.

ਖੁਦਦਾਰ (khuddaar) *a* Self-respecting.

ਖੁਦਦਾਰੀ (khudaaree) *n f* Self-respect, self-esteem, sense of honour.

ਖੁਦ-ਬਖੁਦ (khudbakhud) *adv* Automatically, of or by oneself, of one's own volition, in voluntarily, by itself; Also ਖੁਦਬਖੁਦ

ਖੁਦਾ (khudaa) *n m* God, almighty, lord; ~ਵੰਦ God, lord, master.

ਖੁਦਾਈ (khudaaee) *n f* Excavation, digging, engraving.

ਖੁੰਧਕ (khundhak) *n f* Provocation, irritation.

ਖੁਨਕ (khunak) *a* Cold, chilled.

ਖੁਫੀਆ (khufiaa) *a* Disguised, secret, Confidential, hidden.

ਖੁੰਬ (khumb) *n f* Mushroom, agaricus.

ਖੁਭਣਾ (khubhṇaa) *v* To thrust, to push, press (into); To penetrate, pierce, enter, prick.

ਖੁਭੋਣਾ (khubhoṇaa) *v* To thrust, to push, press (into); To penertrate, to pierce, enter prick.

ਖੁਮਾਰੀ (khumaaree) *n f* Intoxication, drowsiness, hangover.

ਖੁਰ (khur) *n m* Hoof, cloven.

ਖੁਰਕ (khurak) *n f* Itch, scabies.

ਖੁਰਕਣਾ (khuraknaa) *v* To itch, to scratch.

ਖੁਰਚਣਾ (khurachṇaa) *v* To erase, to raze, to scrape.

ਖੁਰਦਬੀਨ (khuradbeen) *n m* Microscope.

ਖੁਰਦਰਾ (khurdaraa) *a* Rough, uneven, not smooth, coarse, not soft, crude; ~ਪਣ Roughness, coarseness.

ਖੁਰਪਾ (khurpaa) *n m* Weeding Knife, hoeing implement.

ਖੁਰਪੀ (khurpee) *n f* Small weeding tonife.

ਖੁਰਾ (khura) *n m* Footprint, footmark, trace, track.

ਖੁਰਾਕ (khuraak) *n f* Diet, food, Sustenance, victuals, dose.

ਖੁਰਾਂਟ (khuraanṭ) *a* Experienced, old, snob.

ਖੁਲਣਾ (khulnaa) *v* To open, to get loose, to be untied, to be exposed.

ਖੁਲਾਸਾ (khulaasaa) *n m* Abstract, summary, gist, substance, essence, outline, inference.

ਖੁਸਟ (khoosaṭ) *a* Decrepit, haggard.

ਖੂਹ (khooh) *n m* Well.

ਖੂਹੀ (khooee) *n f* Narrow well.

ਖੂਨ (khoon) *n m* Blood, murder; ~ਸਫੇਦ ਹੋਣਾ To become inhumane, to loose natural affection; ~ਕਰਨਾ To murder; ~ਪਸੀਨਾ ਇਕ ਕਰਨਾ To work hard, to toil; ~ਪਸੀਨੇ ਦੀ ਕਮਾਈ Hard-earned money; ~ਪੀਣਾ To harass continually, to suck blood

ਖੂਨੀ (khoonee) *n m* Murderer, assassin.

ਖੂਬੀ (khoobee) *n f* Virtue, grace, beauty, quality, merit.

ਖੇਹ (kheh) *n f* Dust, ash; ~ਖਾਣਾ Adulterous, immoral person. ~ਛਾਣਨੀ To wander fruitlessly.

ਖੇਚਲ (khechal) *n f* Inconvenience, pains, trouble; ~ਕਰਨੀ To take Trouble, to bother.

ਖੇਡ (kheḍ) *n f* Play, game, fun, sport, pastime, show.

ਖੇਡਣਾ (kheḍṇaa) *v* To play, to act.

ਖੇਤ (khet) *n m* Farm, cultivated land, battle field.

ਖੇਤਰ (khetar) *n m* Region, sphere,

realm, field, land; ~ਵਲ Area.

ਖੇਤੀ (khetee) *n m* Farming, agriculture, crop; ~ਬਾੜੀ Agriculture.

ਖੇਪ (khep) *n* A load carried in one trip; Merchandise.

ਖੇਰ (khair) *n f* Well-being, welfare, health and happiness; Catechu (tree) *Accacia catechu.*

ਖੇਰਾਤ (khairaat) *n f* Alms, Charity.

ਖੋਖਲਾ (khokhlaa) *a* Hollow, empty, excavated.

ਖੋਖਾ (khokhaa) *n m* Empty cartridge or shell, fired case; Wooden packing case; Cabin, hut.

ਖੋਜ (khoj) *n f* Search, enquiry, discovery, investigation, a hunt.

ਖੋਜਣਾ (khojnaa) *v* To search, to trace, to discover to investigate, to seek.

ਖੋਟ (khot) *n m* Impurity, defect, adulteration, flaw, deception,

blemish.

ਖੋਟਾ (khotaa) *a* Impure, defective, false, malicious, adulterated.

ਖੋਤਾ (khotaa) *n m* Ass, donkey.

ਖੋਦਣਾ (khodnaa) *v* To dig, to engrave.

ਖੋਪੜੀ (khopree) *n f* Skull, scalp, pate, cranium. Also ਖੋਪਰੀ

ਖੋਪਾ (khopaa) *n m* Coconut, copra.

ਖੋਭਣਾ (khobhnaa) *v* To thrust, to push in, to drive in, to stab, prick, pierce.

ਖੋਲਣਾ (kholnaa) *v* To open, to loose, to untie, to detach, to reveal, to unravel

ਖੌਫ਼ (khauf) *n m* Fear, terror, dread, apprehension, misgiving, dismay, alarm; ~ਨਾਕ Fearsome, dreadful, terrible, terrifying.

ਖੌਲਣਾ (khaulnaa) *v* To boil, to bubble, to be excited, to be agitated.

ਗਾ

ਗ Eighth letter of Gurmukhi alphabets, pronounced as 'gaggaa'

ਗਉਂ (gaun) *n m* Act of going, Expedience, self-interest, selfishness; **~ਕੱਢਣਾ** To achieve one's own objectives, to watch self interest.

ਗਊ (gau) *n f* Cow; Gentle, meek; **~ਸ਼ਾਲਾ** Charitable home for old uncared for cows; **~ਮਾਸ** Beef.

ਗਸ਼ (gush) *n m* Fainting, swoon, stupor.

ਗਸ਼ਤ (gasht) *n f* Patrolling walk, stroll, circuit; **~ਕਰਨੀ** To patrol, to wander, to go round; **~ਚਿੱਠੀ** Circular letter, circular.

ਗਸ਼ਤੀ (gashtee) *a* Mobile, circular.

ਗਹਿਣੇ (gahene) *n* Ornaments, jewellery; **~ਰਖਣਾ** To pawn, to mortgage.

ਗੰਧਲਣਾਂ (ganghalnaa) *v* (For water) To become turbid, muddy, dirty, roily.

ਗੰਧਲਿਆ (ganghaliaa) *a* Turbid, muddy, dirty.

ਗੱਚਣਾ (gachchnaa) *v* To dig up (plant) alongwith earth covering its roots.

ਗੰਜ (ganj) *n f* Baldness; Grain market, small colony.

ਗਜ਼ (gaz) *n m* Yard, spike.

ਗਜਣਾ (gajnaa) *v* To thunder, to roar, to howl.

ਗ਼ਜ਼ਬ (gazab) *n m* Outrage, violence; Injustice; Something strange.

ਗਜਰਾ (gajraa) *n m* Armlet, bangles, chaplet, necklace.

ਗ਼ਜ਼ਲ (gazal) *n f* Ode, sonnet, lyric, poem.

ਗੰਜਾ (ganjaa) *a* Bold, scalp head.

ਗਟਕਣਾ (gataknaa) *v* To gulp, to swallow.

ਗੱਟਾ (gatta) *n m* Stopper, cork, plug; sprag.

ਗਠ (gath) *n f* Knot, node.

ਗਠਣਾ (gathnaa) *v* To tie, to join, to sew, to organize.

ਗੱਠਾ (gatthaa) *n* Package; Onion.

ਗੱਠੜ (gathar) *n m* A big packet, a large bundle, bale.

ਗਠੜੀ (gathree) *n f* Bundle

ਗਠੀਲਾ (gatheelaa) *a* Muscular, compact, well-built.

ਗੱਡਣਾ (gadnaa) *v* To bury, to fix, to plant, to entomb.

ਗਡਰੀਆ (gaḍariyaa) *n m* Shepherd, grazier.

ਗੱਡਾ (gaḍḍa) *n m* Bullock-cart.

ਗੰਡਾਸਾ (gaṇḍaasaa) *n m* Sickle, axe for chopping fodder, hatchet.

ਗੱਡੀ (gaḍḍee) *n f* Cart, carriage, train, car, wagon.

ਗੰਢ (gandh) *n f* Bundle, pack, parcel, bale, knot.

ਗੰਢਣਾ (gandhṇaa) *v* To patch, to mend, to cobble, to repair.

ਗੰਢਵਾਉਣਾ (gandhvaauṇaa) *v* To get something repaired, mended, bobbled. Also ਗੰਢਾਉਣਾ

ਗੰਢਵਾਈ (gandhwaaee) *n f* Wages for repairing. Also ਗੰਢਾਈ

ਗੰਢਾ (gandhaa) *n m* Onion.

ਗੰਣਨਾ (gaṇṇna) *n f* Counting, enumeration, calculation.

ਗਣਿਤ (gaṇit) *n m* Arithmatic, calculation.

ਗਤ (gat) *n f* Condition, state, plight.

ਗੱਤਾ (gattaa) *n m* Card, cardboard.

ਗਤਕਾ (gatka) *n m* Sword play, sword practice with wooden swords or sticks; fencing, swordsmanship.

ਗਤੀ (gatee) *n f* Movement, motion, speed, velocity; ~ਸ਼ੀਲ Dynamic, kinetic; ~ਹੀਨ Static, motionless.

ਗੰਦ (gand) *n m* Impurity, refuse, dirt, filth, foulness; ~ਗੀ Dirt, filth, foulness.

ਗੱਦ (gadd) *n m* Prose; ~ਕਾਰ Prose-writer.

ਗਦਗਦ (gadgad) *a* Joyful, delighted, very happy.

ਗੰਦਮ (gandam) *n f* Wheat, Triticum stivum.

ਗ਼ਦਰ (gandar) *n m* Mutiny, revolt, rebellion; ~ਮਚਣਾ To occur chaos, to mutiny.

ਗੰਦਲ (gandal) *n f* Tender stem, stalk or shoot.

ਗੱਦਾ (gadda) *n m* Cushion, padded seat or mattress, pallet.

ਗੰਦਾ (gandaa) *a* Dirty, filthy, nasty, contaminated, impure.

ਗੱਦਾਰ (gaddaar) *a n m* Threacherous, turncoat; Traitor, disloyal.

ਗੱਦਾਰੀ (gaddaaree) *n f* Treachery, disloyalty, treason.

ਗੱਦੀ (gaddee) *n f* Pad, cushion, seat; Throne; Seat of temporal or spiritual authority.

ਗਦੇਲਾ (gadelaa) *n m* Cushion, quilt.

ਗੰਧ (gandh) *n f* Smell, odour.

ਗੰਧਕ (gandhak) *n f* Sulphur, brimstone; ~ਦਾ ਤੇਜ਼ਾਬ Sulphuric acid.

ਗੰਧਲਾ (gandhlaa) *a* Fragrant, sweet-smelling.

ਗਧਾ (gadhaa) *n m* Ass, donkey; Fool, stupid fellow.

ਗੰਨਾ (ganna) *n m* Sugarcane.

ਗਨੀਮਤ (ganeemat) *n f* Plunder, boon, blessing; Satisfaction.

ਗਨੇਰੀ (ganeree) *n f* Small bit of sugarcane.

ਗੱਪ (gapp) *n f* Gossip, chat, false report, rumour.

ਗੱਪੀ (gappee) *a m* Gossipy, boaster.

ਗਪੋੜ (gapor) *n m* Rumour, boastful gossip.

ਗਫ਼ਲਤ (gafalat) *n f* Carelessness, indifference, negligence.

ਗੱਫਾ (gapphaa) *n m* A lion's share, a big morsel.

ਗਬਨ (gaban) *n m* Embezzlement, misappropriation, fraud.

ਗੱਭਣ (gabbhan) *a* Pregnant mostly for cattles.

ਗਭਰੂ (gabhroo) *n m* Youngman, husband.

ਗੰਭੀਰ (gambheer) *a* Serious, sober, reserve, contemplative.

ਗਮ (gam) *n m* Grief, sorrow, woe, anxiety.

ਗਮਲਾ (gamlaa) *n* Flowerpot, vase.

ਗ੍ਰਹਿ (greh) *n m* Planet.

ਗ੍ਰਹਿਣ (grehn) *n m* Eclipse.

ਗ੍ਰਾਰਕ (garak) *a* Immersed, sunk.

ਗਰਕਣਾ (garaknaa) *v* To perish, to sink.

ਗਰਜ (garaj) *n f* Thunder, roar, gnarl, bellow.

ਗ੍ਰਰਜ਼ (garaz) *n f* Need, object, interest, selfishness, concern; ~ਮੰਦ Self interested, needy, destitute. Also ਗਰਜ

ਗਰਜਣਾ (garajnaa) *v* To thunder, to howl, to gnarl.

ਗ੍ਰਰਜ਼ੀ (garzee) *a* Needy, selfish.

ਗ੍ਰੰਥ (granth) *n m* Book, scripture of the sikhs.

ਗ੍ਰੰਥੀ (granthee) *n m* Priest (in Sikh religion).

ਗ੍ਰਰਦਨ (gardan) *n f* Neck; ~ਉਡਾਉਣੀ To behead, to chop off head.

ਗ੍ਰਰਦਾਨਣਾ (gardaannaa) *v* To involve, to implicate.

ਗਰਭ (garabh) *n m* Preganancy, conception, womb, gestation; ~ਪਾਤ Miscarriage, abortion, feticide, aborticide.

ਗਰਮ (garam) *a* Hot, warm; ~ਜੋਸ਼ੀ enthusiasm, warmth, warmheartedness, cordiality; ~ਮਿਜ਼ਾਜ Short tempered, hot headed, short-tempered, touchy, irritable.

ਗਰਮਾਗਰਮੀ (garmaagarmee) *n f* Excitement, heated exchange.

ਗਰਮੀ (garmee) *n f* Heat, warmth, passion, summer.

ਗਰਾਰਾ (garara) *n m* (1) Loose-fitting trousers; (2) Gargle.

ਗਰਾਰੀ (graaree) *n f* Pinion, pulley, gear.

ਗਿ੍ਫ਼ਤਾਰ (griftaar) *a* Arrested, captured. Also ਗਿਰਫ਼ਤਾਰ

ਗਿ੍ਫ਼ਤਾਰੀ (griftaaree) *n m* Arrest, capture. Also ਗਿਰਫ਼ਤਾਰੀ

ਗ਼ਰੀਬ (gareeb) *a* Poor, needy, helpless; Meek.

ਗਰੂਰ (garoor) *n m* Pride, vanity.

ਗੋਹ (groh) *n m* Company, group, gang. Also ਗਰੋਹ

ਗੱਲ (gall) *n f* Talk, dialogue, affair.

ਗਲ (gal) *n m* Throat, larynx, neck.

ਗਲਣਾ (galnaa) *v* To rot, to compose, to decay, to dissolve.

ਗ਼ਲਤ (galat) *a* Wrong, mistaken, faulty, incorrect, erroneous; ~ਸਮਝਣਾ To misunderstand, misapprehend, misjudge; ~ਸਲਤ Confused, jumbled, disordered, involved; ~ਧਾਰਨਾ misconception; ~ਫ਼ਹਮੀ Misunderstanding, misapprehension; disagreement, dissension; smugness.

ਗਲਤੀ (galti) *n f* Mistake, error, inaccuracy, misconception, misunderstanding, misjudgement; wrong-doing, blunder; Lapse, omission; ~ਦਾ ਪੁਤਲਾ Fallible, liable to err.

ਗੱਲਾਂ (gallaan) *n f* Idle talk.

ਗਾਲਾ (galaa) *n m* Throat.

ਗੱਲਾ (gallaa) *n m* Corn, grain harvest.

ਗੱਲਾ (gallaa) *n m* Money, box, safe, a chest for money.

ਗਲਾਉਣਾ (galaaunaa) *v* To melt, to fuse.

ਗਲਾਸ (glaas) *n m* Tumbler, glass.

ਗਲਾਸੀ (glaasee) *n f* Small tumbler.

ਗਲਿਆਰਾ (galiaaraa) *n m* Corridor, gallery.

ਗਲੀ (galee) *n f* Street, lane, passage.

ਗਲੀਚਾ (galeechaa) *n m* Carpet.

ਗਲੀਜ਼ (galeez) *a* Dirty, filthy.

ਗਵੱਈਆ (gavvaiyaa) *n m* Singer, vocalist, musician.

ਗਵਾਹ (gawaah) *n m* Witness, deponent.

ਗਵਾਹੀ (gawahee) *n m* Testimony, deposition, evidence.

ਗਵਾਚਣਾ (gwaachnaa) *v* To be lost.

ਗਵਾਂਢ (gawaandh) *n m* Neighbourhood.

ਗਵਾਂਢੀ (gawaandhee) *n m*

Neighbour.

ਗੰਵਾਰ (ganwaar) *a* Rustic, uncivilized, crude, vulgar; ~ਪੁਣਾ Vulgarity, rusticity.

ਗੜਕਣਾ (garaknaa) *v* To roar, to boil.

ਗੜਪਣਾ (garapnaa) *v* To swallow.

ਗੜਬੜੀ (garbaree) *n f* Confusion, disorder.

ਗੜਵਾ (garvaa) *n m* Medium-size pitcher like metal vessel.

ਗੜਵੀ (garvee) *n f* A small pitcher like metal vessel.

ਗਾਂ (gaan) *n f a* Cow; Meak, poor; ~ਦਾ ਮਾਸ Beef.

ਗਾਉਣਾ (gaaunaa) *v* To sing, to chant.

ਗਾਇਬ (gaaib) *a* Vanished, invisible.

ਗਾਹਕ (gaak) *n m* Customer, buyer, client.

ਗਾਹਕੀ (gaahkee) *n f* Purchase, sale, demand.

ਗਾਗਰ (gaagar) *n f* Metalic pitcher, water utensil; ~ਵਿਚ ਸਾਗਰ Too much in a few words.

ਗਾਚਨੀ (gaachnee) *n f* Yellow clay; fuller's earth.

ਗਾਚੀ (gaachee) *n f* Cake, sapling with earth round the roots.

ਗਾਜਰ (gaajar) *n f* Carrot.

ਗਾਟਾ (gaataa) *n m* Neck.

ਗਾਣਾ (gaanaa) *n* Song, singing, tune.

ਗਾਥਾ (gaathaa) *n m* Tale, narrative, a story.

ਗਾਦ (gaad) *n f* Silt, sediments, lees.

ਗਾਬ (gaab) *n f* Silt, mud, mire.

ਗਾਰ (gaar) *n f* Cave, hollow.

ਗਾਰਦ (gaarad) *n f* Guard, group of soldiers or police men deployed for protection.

ਗਾਰਾ (gaaraa) *n m* Morter of mud used as building material.

ਗਾਲ੍ਹੜ (gaallar) *n m* Squirrel.

ਗਾਲ੍ਹੀ (gaalee) *n f* Abuse.

ਗਾਲਣਾ (gaalnaa) *v* To melt, to decompose, to dissolve.

ਗਾਲੜੀ (gaalree) *a* Talkative.

ਗਾੜਾ (gaaraa) *a* Dense, thick intense, stiff, concentrated.

ਗਿਆਨ (giyaan) *n m* Knowledge; ~ਧਿਆਨ Meditation, spiritual pursuit.

ਗਿਆਨੀ (giyaanee) *n m a* Scholar philosopher, sage; Learned, intelligent.

ਗਿੱਚੀ (gichchee) *n f* Neck, nape.

ਗਿਜ਼ਾ (gizaa) *n f* Diet, food.

ਗਿੱਝਣਾ (gijjhnaa) *v* To be accustomed to, to get used to.

ਗਿਟਕ (gitak) *n f* Stone of fruit, endocarp.

ਗਿਟਮਿਟ (giṭmiṭ) *n f* Talk, conversation in an unfamiliar language English; Unintelligible talk.

ਗਿੱਟਾ (giṭṭaa) *n m* Ankle.

ਗਿੱਠ (giṭṭh) *n* Span, measure of length equal to stretched hand, about 9 inches; Fully stretched hand or palm.

ਗਿੱਠਾ (giṭṭha) *a* Dwarfish, dwarf, pigmy, midget, shorty, Tom Thumb. Also ਗਿਠਮੁਠੀਆ

ਗਿਣਤੀ (giṇtee) *n f* Number, count, calculation, roll call.

ਗਿਣਨਾ (giṇnaa) *v* To Count, to compute, to enumerate.

ਗਿਦੜ (gidaṛ) *n m a* Jackal; Coward.

ਗਿੱਧ (giddh) *n m* Vulture.

ਗਿਰਗਟ (girgaṭ) *n f* Chameleon.

ਗਿਰਨਾ (girnaa) *v* To fall, to drop, to stumble, to collapse.

ਗਿਰਾਂ (giraan) *n m* Village.

ਗਿੱਲਾ (gillaa) *a* Wet, damp.

ਗਿਲਾ (gilaa) *n m* Reproach, complaint, grievance; ~ਸ਼ਿਕਵਾ Informal complaint.

ਗਿਲਾਫ਼ (gilaaf) *n m* Cover, covering.

ਗਿੜਗੜਾਉਣਾ (girgraauṇaa) *v* To beseech earnestly, to grovel, to request very humbly.

ਗਿੜਨਾ (girnaa) *v* To revolve, to rotate, to turn.

ਗੀਗਾ (geegaa) *n m* Beloved child infant, innocent.

ਗੀਂਢਾ (geeṇdhaa) *a* Short (person); Shorty, short and stout.

ਗੁਆਉਣਾ (guaauṇaa) *v* To lose, to waste, to miss, to forfeit.

ਗੁਆਂਢ (guaandh) *n m* Neighbourhood, Vicinage.

ਗੁਆਂਢੀ (guaandhee) *n m* Neighbour.

ਗੁਸਤਾਖ਼ (gustaakh) *a* Arrogant, impolite, rude, haughty, impudent; ~ਗੁਸਤਾਖੀ (gustaakhee) Arrogance, impoliteness, rudeness.

ਗੁਸਲ (gusal) *n m* Bath, purification; ~ਖਾਨਾ Bathroom.

ਗੁੱਸਾ (gussaa) *n m* Anger, rage, wrath, fury.

ਗੁਸੈਲ (gusail) *a* Wrathful, passionate, irritable.

ਗੁੰਗਾ (gungaa) *a* Dumb, mute, speechless.

ਗੁੱਗਾ (guggaa) *n m* Snake.

ਗੁੱਛਾ (gucchaa) *n m* Bunch, cluster, bouquet.

ਗੁਜ਼ਰ (guzar) *n m* Livelihood.

ਗੁਜ਼ਰਨਾ (guzarnaa) *v* To pass, To expire, to die, to pass away.

ਗੁਜ਼ਰਾਨ (guzraan) *n f* Living, livelihood.

ਗੁੰਜਾਇਸ਼ (gunjaaish) *n f* Capacity,

margin, accommodation, profit.

ਗੁਜ਼ਾਰਸ਼ (guzzarash) *n f* Request, petition, representation.

ਗੁਜ਼ਾਰਾ (guzaaraa) *n m* Living, maintenance, livelihood, Sustenance, adjustment; ~ਕਰਨਾ To subsist, to reconcile, to manage, to adjust.

ਗੁੰਝਲ (gunjhal) *n f* Entangled knot, snarl, entanglement; complication, knotty problem; intricacy, puzzlement, perplexity; enigma, puzzle; ~ਦਾਰ Entangled, snarled, tangled, complicated, knotty; intricate, puzzling, perplexing.

ਗੁੰਝਲਣਾ (gunjhalṇaa) *v* To become snarled; To get entangled, involved, jumbled, enmeshed, to become problematic; to be confused, confounded, perplexed.

ਗੁੰਝਾ (gujjhaa) *a* Hidden, secret, invisible, surreptitious, covert, concealed; obscure, mysterious.

ਗੁਟ (guṭ) *n m* Group, faction, clique, coterie, combine, gang, bloc.

ਗੁਟਕਾ (guṭkaa) *n m* Manual, handbook, Small piece (of wood).

ਗੁੱਡਾ (guddaa) *n m* Doll, kite.

ਗੁੰਡਾ (gundaa) *n m a* Scoundrel, rogue, hooligan, rascal; Wicked, knavish.

ਗੁੱਡੀ (guḍḍee) *n f* Doll, kite, child's puppet.

ਗੁਣ (guṇ) *n m* Virtue, quality, excellence, merit, worth.

ਗੁਣਗੁਣਾ (guṇguṇaa) *a* Luke warm.

ਗੁਣਗੁਣਾਉਣਾ (guṇguṇaauṇaa) *v* To murmur, to mutter, to hum, to buzz, to Snuffle.

ਗੁੱਤ (gutt) *n f* Plait, braid.

ਗੁੱਥਲੀ (gutthlee) *n f* Bag, money bag.

ਗੁੱਥੀ (gutthee) *n f* A riddle, knot, enigma.

ਗੁੰਦਣਾ (gundṇaa) *v* To weave, to plait, to braid, to interlace.

ਗੁਦਾਮ (gudaam) *n m* Godown, Store, warehouse, depot, granary.

ਗੁਨਾਹ (gunaah) *n m* Fault, guilt, offence, crime.

ਗੁਪਤ (gupat) *a* Secret, concealed, hidden, private, mysterious, covert, latent.

ਗੁਫ਼ਤਗੂ (guftagoo) *n f* Dialogue, conversation, chat.

ਗੁਫਾ (gufaa) *n f* Cave, den, cavern.

ਗੁੰਬਦ (gumbad) *n m* Dome, vault.

ਗੁਬਾਰ (gubaar) *n m* Dust, dirt; Perplexity, suppressed, anger.

ਗੁਬਾਰਾ (gubaaraa) *n m* Balloon.

ਗੁੰਮਨਾਮ (gummnaam) *a* Anonymous, unknown, obscure, unimportant.

ਗੁਮਰ (gumar) *n m* Pride, vanity, envy, wish to wreck vengeance.

ਗੁਮਰਾਹ (gumraah) *a* Astray, stranded, following wrong or evil path, misled, erring, wandering, aberrant.

ਗੁਮਾਉਣਾ (gumaaunaa) *v* To lose, to misplace.

ਗੁਮਾਸ਼ਤਾ (gumaashtaa) *n m* Agent, manager, representative.

ਗੁਮਾਨ (gumaan) *n m* Pride, haughtiness, imagination, guess.

ਗੁਰ (gur) *n m* Formula, tip, method.

ਗੁਰਗਾਬੀ (gurgabi) *n f* Pumps; lowcut shoes without fastening; pump shoes.

ਗੁਰਦਾ (gurdaa) *n m* Kideny; courage, pluck, fearlessness; forbearaṇce, patience, endurance.

ਗਰਮੁਖ (gurmukh) *a* Guru-oriented, pious, religious, devout, virtuous; A good, model or ideal Sikh, a noble person.

ਗੁੱਰਾਉਣਾ (gurraauṇaa) *v* To roar, to growl, to howl.

ਗੁਰੂ (guroo) *n m* Spiritual guide, teacher, tutor, instructor; (planet) Jupiter; ~ਘੰਟਾਲ Perfect, rascal, reprobate.

ਗੁਲਸ਼ਨ (gulshan) *n m* Flower garden.

ਗੁਲਜ਼ਾਰ (gulzaar) *n m* Garden.

ਗੁਲਦਸਤਾ (guldastaa) *n m* Bunch of flowers, bouquet, nosegay.

ਗੁਲਦਾਨ (guldaan) *n m* Glowervase, flowerpot, snuff dish.

ਗੁਲਫਾਮ (gulpham) *a* Handsome, beautiful.

ਗੁਲਾਬ (gulaab) *n m* Rose.

ਗੁਲਾਮ (gulaam) *n m* Slave, bondman, servant.

ਗੁਲਿਸਤਾਨ (gulistaan) *n m* Garden.

ਗੁੱਲੀ ਡੰਡਾ (gullee ḍanḍaa) *n m* Tipcat.

ਗੁਲਬੰਦ (gulband) *n m* Muffler, scarf, necktie, neckcloth.

ਗੁਲੇਲ (gulel) *n f* Pelletbow, catapult; ~ਚੀ Person using or adept in the use of pellet bow or gulel.

ਗੁੜ (guṛ) *n m* Rawsugar, molasses, lumped brown sugar, jaggery.

ਗੁੜਕਣਾ (guṛaknaa) *v* To cackle, to chuckle.

ਗੁੜ੍ਹਨਾ (guṛhnaa) *v* To digest, to realise.

ਗੂੰਹ (goonh) *n m* Exereta, faces.

ਗੂੰਜ (goonj) *n f* Echo, resonance, resounding.

ਗੂੰਜਣਾ (goonjṇaa) *v* To resound, to echo.

ਗੂੰਦ (goond) *n f* Gum, glue.

ਗੂੜ੍ਹ (gooṛh) *n m* Close intimacy, fastness or deepness (colour), profundity.

ਗੂੜ੍ਹਾ (gooṛhaa) *a* Deep, fast, dark (colour); intense (love, friendship); profound.

ਗੇਂਦ (Gend) *n* Ball; ~ਬੱਲਾ Cricket (game).

ਗੇੜਾ (geṛaa) *n m* Turn, rotation, circuit; chance, opportunity, vicissistude.

ਗੇਂਦਾ (gendaa) *n m* Marigold flower.

ਗੈਂਡਾ (gaindaa) *n m* Rhinoceros.

ਗੈਰ (gair) *a* Stranger, alien, foreign, other, non, lack; ~ਅਬਾਦ Barren, unpopulated; ~ਸਰਕਾਰੀ Non-Government, private; ~ਹਾਜ਼ਰ Absent; ~ਕਾਨੂੰਨੀ Illegal, unlawful; ~ਜ਼ਿੰਮੇਵਾਰ Irresponsible; ~ਮਾਮੂਲੀ Extrordinary, excellent, strange.

ਗੈਰਤ (gairat) *n f* Shame, modesty, honour.

ਗੋਸ਼ਟੀ (goshṭee) *n f* Seminar, symposium; conversation, discussion.

ਗੋਸ਼ਤ (gosht) *n m* Meat, flesh.

ਗੋਸ਼ਾ (goshaa) *n m* Corner, angle, a private place.

ਗੋਹਾ (gohaa) *n m* Cowdung, Ordure.

ਗੋਗੜ (gogaṛ) *n f* Pot belly, paunch.

ਗੋਗਾ (gogaa) *n m* Rumour.

ਗੋਡਾ (goḍaa) *n m* knee.

ਗੋਤਾ (gotaa) *n m* Dip, drive immersion; ~ਖੋਰ diver.

ਗੋਦੀ (godee) *n f* Lap; ~ਪਾਉਣਾ To give away for adoption; Dock; ~ਮਜ਼ਦੂਰ Docker; ~ਵਾੜਾ Dockyard.

ਗੋਰਾ (gora) *a n m* White, fair, skinned, beautiful; Whiteman, Europeon.

ਗੋਲ (gol) *a n m* Round, circular, globular; Goal (in hockey); ~ਕਰਨਾ To score a goal, to embezzle, to evade, to avoid, not to implement; ~ਮਾਲ Confusion, mess, something fishy; ~ਮੋਲ Round, global; Vague, ambiguous, fat.

ਗੋਲਕ (golak) *n f* Moneybox, charitybox, cashchest.

ਗੋਲਾਬਾਰੀ (golaabaaree) *n f* Bombardment, shelling.

ਗੋਲਾਬਾਰੂਦ (golaabaarood) *n m* Ammunition.

ਗੌਣ (gauṇ) *n m a* Song, secondary auxiliary, minor.

ਗੌਰ (gaur) *n m* Consideration, close attention.

ਗੌਰਵ (gaurav) *n m* Glory, dignity.

ਘ

ਘ Ninth letter of Gurmukhi alphabets, pronounced as ghaghaa.

ਘਉਣਾ (ghaunaa) *v* To grind, to pestle.

ਘਉਂ-ਘੱਪ (ghaoon-ghapp) *a* Disappeared, stolen, embezzled; ~ਕਰਨਾ To embezzle, steal, misappropriate, spend, waste, fritter away.

ਘਸਣਾ (ghasnaa) *v* To rub, to wear out, to impair.

ਘੱਸਾ (ghassaa) *n m* Push with hip, powerful hard rub, jostle, jerk.

ਘਸਰ (ghasar) *n f* Abrasion, bruise, scratch, rub; ~ਮਸਰ Dallying, dilly-dallying, delaying; ~ਮਸਰ ਕਰਨਾ To dilly-dally, to delay, procrastinate, to try to avoid doing something.

ਘਸਾਈ (ghasaaee) *n m a* Work of rubbing, friction; Hard labour, depreciation.

ਘਸਿਆਰਾ (ghasiaaraa) *n m a* Grass cutter, Mean, lower person (proverbial).

ਘਸੀਟਣਾ (ghaseetnaa) *v* To pull, to drag, to scribble.

ਘਸੁੰਨ (ghasunn) *n* Clenched fist, blow with clenched fist, box, punch, buffet, jab, fisticuff; ~ਜੜਨਾ/ ~ਫੇਰਨਾ/ ~ਮਾਰਨਾ To box punch, jab, buffet, pummel, fisticuff.

ਘਸੋੜਨਾ (ghsornaa) *v* To thrust, to penetrate.

ਘਰਾਰਾ (ghraaraa) *n* Petticoat.

ਘੱਗਾ (ghaggaa) *a* Hoarse.

ਘਗਿਆਉਣਾ (ghagiaaunaa) *v* To implore.

ਘਚੋਰ (ghachor) *n m* Dark, narrow nock.

ਘਚੋਲਣਾ (ghacholnaa) *v* To foul, to mix, to make turbid.

ਘਚੋਲਾ (ghacholaa) *n m* Confusion, disorder, bungling.

ਘਟਣਾ (ghatnaa) *v* To decrease, to fall, to lessen, to shorten; To happen, to take place.

ਘਟਨਾ (ghatnaa) *n f* Incident, occurrence, happening, event, accident, chance, occasion.

ਘੰਟਾ (ghantaa) *n m* Bell, hour, gong.

ਘੱਟਾ (ghattaa) *n f* Cloudiness, dust.

ਘਟਾ (ghataa) *n f* Shortness, deficiency; decline (as of age or day); contraction, shrinkage.

ਘਟਾਉਣਾ (ghataaunaa) *v* To deduct,

to diminish, to reduce, to subtract, to decrease.

ਘਟਾਟੋਪ (ghaṭaaṭop) *n m* Gathering of dark clouds in the sky; A covering for a palanquin or carriage.

ਘੰਟੀ (ghanṭee) *n f* Bell tinkle, call bell, telephone bee; Sound of bell ringing, tintunnabulation; instructional period.

ਘਟੀਆ (ghaṭiyaa) *a* Inferior, cheap, worthless, inexpensive.

ਘੰਡ (ghanḍ) *n m a* Rascal, wicked, villainous, rough, reprobate; **~ਪੁਣਾ** Wickedness, villainousness.

ਘੰਡੀ (ghanḍee) *n f* Adam's apple, larynx, uvula, sound box.

ਘੰਦੂਈ (ghandooee) *n f* Big needle.

ਘਨਚਕਰ (ghanchakar) *a m* Blockhead.

ਘਪਲਾ (ghaplaa) *n m* Bungling, mess, confusion.

ਘਬਰਾਉਣਾ (ghabraauṇaa) *v* To be bewildered, to be baffled, to be confused, to be disturbed, to be puzzled, to be perturbed.

ਘਮੰਡ (ghamanḍ) *n m* Pride, haughtiness, arrogance, conceit, elation.

ਘਮੰਡੀ (ghamanḍee) *a* Proud, haughty, arrogant, lofty,

conceited.

ਘਰ (ghar) *n m* Home, house, dwelling, residence, family; **~ਆਬਾਦ ਕਰਨਾ** To marry, to build a family; **~ਸਿਰ ਤੇ ਚੁਕਣਾ** To create too much noise; **~ਜਵਾਈ** Resident son-in-law; **ਡਾਕ~** Post office; **~ਭਰਨਾ** to amass wealth; **~ਦੀ ਖੇਤੀ** Easy to procure, handy; **~ਦੀ ਗਲ** Family affair, easy job, mutual affair; **~ਪੂਰਾ ਹੋਣਾ** To be satisfied; To be compensated; **~ਵਾਲਾ** Husband, owner, master of the house; **~ਵਾਲੀ** wife, mistress of the house.

ਘਰੂਟਣਾ (gharooṭnaa) *v* To scratch (with nail).

ਘਰੋੜਨਾ (gharorṇaa) *v* to scrub, to scrape, to rasp.

ਘਲਣਾ (ghalṇaa) *v* To send, to despatch, to forward, to remit, to transmit.

ਘੱਲੂਘਾਰਾ (ghalooghaaraa) *n m* Holocaust, massacre, great destruction, deluge, genocide, slaughter.

ਘੜਨਾ (gharnaa) *v* To mould, to fabricate, to coin, to frame, to fashion, to construct.

ਘੜਮੱਸ (gharmass) *n f* Milling crowd, stampede, confusion, tumult;

~ਪੈਣੀ Stampede to occur or be caused.

ਅੜਵੰਜੀ (gharvanjee) *n f* Pitcher-stand.

ਅੜਵਾਉਣਾ (gharvaaunaa) *v* To get something manufactured by cutting, etc.

ਘੜਾ (ghraa) *n m* Pitcher, waterpot.

ਘੜਿਆਲ (ghrriyaal) *n m* (1) Big bell, big gong; (2) Crocodile, alligator.

ਘੜੀ (gharee) *n f* Watch, clock; Small pitcher or water pot; Moment, 24 minute (measure of time); ਔਖੀ~ Time of crisis; ~ਘੜੀ Time and again; ~ਮੁੜੀ Again and again, time and again.

ਘਾਈ (ghaaee) *n f* loincloth.

ਘਾਹ (ghaah) *n f* Grass, fodder, straw; ~ਖੋਦਣਾ To idle away time, to undertake a petty job; ~ਵਢਣਾ To do a job in hurried manner.

ਘਾਘ (ghaagh) *a* Shrewd, cunning, experienced

ਘਾਟ (ghaat) *n* (*m*) Quay, jetty, bathing place on the bank of river; (*f*) Shortage, want, deficiency, dearth, decrease, scarcity. ~ਘਰ Dwelling; ~ਘਾਟ ਦਾ ਪਾਣੀ ਪੀਣਾ To get varied experience, to wander from place to place.

ਘਾਟਾ (ghaataa) *n m* Loss, deficiency, deficit, decline, falling, inadequacy.

ਘਾਟੀ (ghaatee) *n f* Valley, dale, pass, gorge.

ਘਾਣੀ (ghaanee) *n f* Oil mill, oilpress.

ਘਾਬਰਨਾ (ghaabarnaa) *v* To feel perplexed, to be confused, to be anxious.

ਘਾਮੜ (ghaamar) *n m a* Blockhead, idiot, dull, idiotic, dullard.

ਘਾਲ (ghaal) *n* Toil, hard task, painful, service, effort, labour.

ਘਿਓ (ghio) *n m* Butter oil, clarified butter; ~ਸ਼ਕਰ ਹੋਣਾ To have intimate association.

ਘਿਸਨਾ (ghisnaa) *v* To be warn out, to wear out.

ਘਿੱਗੀ (ghigee) *n* Hiccup caused by crying and sobbing; ~ਬੰਝ ਜਾਨੀ To cry hoarse, to cry one's heart out.

ਘਿਚ-ਪਿਚ (ghich-pich) *n* Illegible scribble, careless scrawl; ~ਕਰਨੀ/ ~ਮਾਰਨੀ To write badly, illegibly. Also ਘਿਚ-ਮਿਚ

ਘਿਰਨਾ (ghirnaa) *n f* Hatred, contempt, scorn, abhorrence.

ਘਿਰਨਾ (ghirnaa) *v* To be surrounded, cornered, brought to bay, encircled.

ਘਿਰਨੀ (ghirnee) *n f* Pulley, wheel.

ਘੀਸੀ (gheesee) *n f* Rubbing of buttocks on the ground.

ਘੁਸਣਾ (ghusṇaa) *v* To enter, to pentrate, to go in forcibly or without permission, to transgress, to trespass; To interfere, to meddle.

ਘੁੱਸਣਾ (ghussṇaa) *v* To err, to make a mistake; to miscalcuate; to miss (the right way); to be lost or stranded.

ਘੁਸਬੈਠ (ghusbaeṭh) *n f* Intrusion, infiltration.

ਘੁਸਬੈਠੀਆ (ghusbaeṭhiaa) *n* infiltratior, intruder.

ਘੁਸਮੁਸਾ (ghusmusaa) *n m a* Semidark, semi-darkness (as at dawn, or dusk); Dim, foggy or shadowy light, dusky, somewhat dark; Twilight, crepuscular.

ਘੁਸੜਨਾ (ghusaṛnaa) *v* To insert, to thrust, to pierce, to penetrate.

ਘੁਸਾਉਣਾ (ghusaauṇaa) *v* To cause to enter, to shirk, to mislead, to miss.

ਘੁੰਗਰੂ (ghungroo) *n m* Small bells; An ornament worn round the ankle; The ratling sound of a dying person.

ਘੁੱਗੂ (ghugoo) *n m* Owl.

ਘੁੱਟ (ghuṭṭ) *n f* One sip, drought.

ਘੁੱਟਣ (ghuṭṭan) *n f* Tightness, suffocation, stifle.

ਘੁਟਣਾ (ghuṭnaa) *v* To press, to copmress, to squeeze, to tighten.

ਘੁੰਡ (ghunḍ) *n m* Veil.

ਘੁੰਡੀ (ghunḍee) *n f* Knot, button; Trick, problem, complication.

ਘੁਣ (ghuṇ) *n m* Worm that infest wood; Decaying disease, diminishing process.

ਘੁਤਰ (ghutar) *n f* Any point of criticism, fault, blemish, shortcoming, defect, weakness; ~ਕੱਢਣੀ To find fault, to criticise.

ਘੁੰਨਾ (ghunnaa) *a* Deceitful, cunning.

ਘੁਪ (ghup) *a* Dark, dense.

ਘੁੰਮਕੜ (ghummakaṛ) *n m* Wanderer, rover, traveller.

ਘੁੰਮਣਾ (ghummṇaa) *v* To circulate, to revolve, to rotate, to spin, to roam.

ਘੁੰਮਰ (ghummar) *n m* Circular dance; Whirlpool spin, twirl.

ਘੁਮਾਉਣਾ (ghumaauṇaa) *v* To rotate, to revolve, to spin, to whisk.

ਘੁਮੇਰ (ghumer) *n m* Dizziness, giddiness, vertigo.

ਘੁਰਕਣਾ (ghurakṇaa) *v* To chide, to scold, to reprimand, to threaten.

ਘੁਰਨਾ (ghurnaa) *n m* Den, lair, hiding place, dugout, pit made by animals with their paws.

ਘੁਰਾੜੇ (ghuraaṛe) *n m* Snorings.

ਘੁਲਣਾ (ghulṇaa) *v* To dissolve, to wrestle, to combat.

ਘੁੜਸਵਾਰ (ghuṛswaar) *n m* Horseman, horse rider, cavalier.

ਘੁੜਸਾਲ (ghuṛsaal) *n f* Horse stable.

ਘੂਸ (ghoos) *n f* Bribe, illegal gratification.

ਘੂਕਣਾ (ghookṇaa) *v* To spin, to rotate, to produce whirling sound or buzzing sound. Also ਘੂਰਕਣਾ

ਘੂਰਨਾ (ghoornaa) *v* To stare, to frown; To look lustfully; To scorn, to rebuke.

ਘੇਰਨਾ (ghernaa) *v* To circumference, to surround, to fence, to blockade, to round up, to close.

ਘੇਰਾ (gheraa) *n m* Circumference, circuit, gamut, ambit, circle, periphery, closing.

ਘੋਸ਼ਣਾ (ghoshṇaa) *y n f* Announcement, proclamation; ~ਪੱਤਰ Manifasto.

ਘੋਗਾ (ghogaa) *n m* Sea-shell; Oyster, whelk, snail.

ਘੋਟਣਾ (ghotṇaa) *v n m* To choke, to cram, to learn by rote, to repeat; To pound, to rub, to grind, to bruise, to polish; A short round club with which spice or Bhangs is ground.

ਘੋਟਾ (ghotaa) *n m* Cramming, learn by heart.

ਘੋਪਣਾ (ghopṇaa) *v* To stab, to thrust into.

ਘੋਲ (ghol) *n m* Duel, wrestling, struggle, conflict, combat, solution.

ਘੋਲੀ (gholee) *n m* Wrestler.

ਘੋਲਣਾ (gholṇaa) To dissolve.

ਘੋੜਾ (ghroaa) *n m* Horse; Steed, chess knight; Trigger, gun-lock.

ਘੋੜੀ (ghoṛee) *n* Mare; female horse; A marriage song; Crutch; Hammer of a gun; Portable wooden platform, stand for woof; ~ਚੜੂਨਾ A marriage ceremony in which the bridegroom ride a mare while going to bride's place.

ਘੌਲ (ghaul) *n f* Laziness, negligence; Carelessness, indifference, dilly-dally, indolence; ~ਕਰਨੀ To delay through laziness, to dilly-dally, to neglect.

ਘੌਲੀ (ghaulee) *a* Lazy, indolent, negligent, sluggard, careless; indifferent.

ਙ

ਙ Tenth letter of Gurmukhi alphabets, pronounced as 'ngaa'.

ਚ

ਚ Eleventh letter of Gurmukhi alphabets, pronounced as 'chachchaa'.

ਚਸਕਾ (chaskaa) *n m* Relish, taste; Habit, addiction; Pleasure, ardent desire; ~ਬਾਜ਼ Voluptuous, sensual.

ਚਸਕੇਖੋਰ (chaskekhor) *a* Greedy, having weakness for or easily tempted by something, such as spicy, juicy, eatables.

ਚਸਕੇਦਾਰ (chaskedaar) *a* Spicy, delicious, tempting; appetizing.

ਚਸ਼ਮਦੀਦ (chashamdeed) *a* Seen, witnessed; ~ਗਵਾਹ Eye-witness

ਚਸ਼ਮਾ (chashmaa) *n m* (1) Spring; (2) Spectacles, goggles, glasses.

ਚਹਿਕਣਾ (chahekṇaa) *v* To chirp, to warble. Also ਚਹਿਚਹਾਉਣਾ

ਚਹੇਤਾ (chahetaa) *a* Favourite

ਚਕਣਾ (chakṇaa) *v* To lift, to raise; To incite, to instigate.

ਚਕਨਾਚੂਰ (chaknaachoor) *n m* splintered, broken to pieces; Dead tired.

ਚਕਮਾ (chakmaa) *n m* Trick, deception, temptation.

ਚੱਕਰ (chakkar) *n m* Circle, whirlwind, circular path, wheel, rotation, spin; ~ਆਉਣੇ To feel giddy; ~ਖਾਣਾ To be perplexed, to be confounded, to whirl; To rotate; ~ਚਲਾਉਣਾ To launch a tricky move; ~ਮਾਰਨੇ To come again and again; ~ਵਿਚ ਪੈਣਾ To suffer harrassment, to be taken into; ~ਦਾਰ Spirally, circuitous; ~ਵਰਤੀ Emperor, universal monarch.

ਚਕਰਾਉਣਾ (chakraauṇaa) *v* To be bewildered, to be confused.

ਚਕਲਾ (chaklaa) *n m* (1) An open space, a brothel, bagino; (2) flat round disc used for flattening bread.

ਚਕਲੀ (chaklee) *n f* A disc, pulley.

ਚੱਕ (chakk) *n m* (1) A bite or cut made with teeth; (2) Potter's wheel; (3) Village in canal colony; A compact piece of agriculture land; ~ਮਾਰਨਾ To bite, to take a bite; ~ਬੰਦੀ Demarcation of agricultural land; Divison of land into compact portions.

ਚਕਾਚੌਂਧ (chakaachaundh) *n m* Dazzle, brilliance.

ਚੱਕੀ (chakkee) *n f* A grinding mill,

handmill; Cake.

ਚਖਣਾ (chakhnaa) *v* To taste, to relish, to eat.

ਚੰਗਾ (changaa) *a* Good, nice, fine salutary; ~ਭਲਾ Healthy, hale & hearty.

ਚੰਗਿਆਈ (changiaaee) *n f* Goodness.

ਚੰਗੇਰ (changer) *n f* A broad shallow, basket woven of bamboos etc.

ਚੰਗੇਰਾ (changeraa) *a* Better, superior, preferable.

ਚੰਘਿਆੜਨਾ (changhìaarnaa) *v* To roar, to trumpet.

ਚੰਚਲ (chanchal) *a* Unsteady, agile, inconstant, volatile, restless, energetic, playful, fickle.

ਚੱਜ (chajj) *n m* Dexterity, conduct, good behaviour, rules of etiquette.

ਚਟਣਾ (chatnaa) *v* To lick, to lap; To fondle, to embezzle.

ਚਟਕ (chatak) *n m* Smack, crash; ~ਮਟਕ Brilliance, lustre, brightness, glitter.

ਚਟਕਣਾ (chataknaa) *v* To snap, to crack, to be split, to burst.

ਚਟਕਾਰਨਾ (chatkaarnaa) *v* To produce sound by snapping the tongue.

ਚਟਕੀਲਾ (chatakeelaa) *a* Relishing, pungent, flavoury, appetising.

ਚਟਨੀ (chatnee) *n f* Sauce, condiment.

ਚਟ ਪੁੰਜੀਆ (chatpunjiyaa) *a* Mean; Poor.

ਚਟਪਟਾ (chatpataa) *a* Spicy, saucy, pungent, delicious.

ਚਟਵਾਈ (chatwaaee) *n f* Act of licking.

ਚਟਾਈ (chataaee) *n f* Mat.

ਚਟਾਕ (chataak) *n m* Crack or sudden sharp noise as of a slap or whip; scar, patch, a healed wound.

ਚਟਾਕਾ (chataakaa) *n m* A Smack, crack, explosion.

ਚਟਾਨ (chataan) *n f* Rock.

ਚੱਟੀ (chattee) *n f* Fine, loss; Surcharge, expenditure; Punishment, penalty.

ਚੱਠ (chatth) *n m* Inauguration, house warming function.

ਚੰਡਾਲ (chandaal) *n m* Merciless, a wretch; Untouchable, a low born, an inferior caste; ~ਚੋਕੜੀ Bunch of rascals or bad characters; ~ਪੁਣਾ Meaness mercilessness.

ਚੰਡੂ (chandoo) *n* Smoking Opium; ~ਖਾਨਾ Place for opium smokers; rumour manufacturing centre; ~ਬਾਜ਼ Opium addict; rumour monger.

ਚਤਰ (chatar) *a* Intelligent, shrewd, wise, sagacious, smart, ingeneous; Clever, cunning, sky, crafty, skillful, deft, adept.

ਚਤਰਾ (chatraa) *a* Cleaver, cunning, smart.

ਚੰਦਨ (chandan) *n m* Sandalwood.

ਚੰਦਰ (chandar) *n m* Moon.

ਚੱਦਰ (chaddar) *n f* A bed sheet, wrap.

ਚੰਦਰਾ (chandraa) *a* (1) Ill omened; evil, bad; (2) Hailstone, painful inflammation.

ਚੰਦਾ (chandaa) *n m* Contribution collection, subscription.

ਚੰਨ (chann) *a n m* Beautiful, pleasure giving; Moon

ਚਪਟਾ (chaptaa) *a* Flat, level, even, horizontal, plane.

ਚੰਪਤ (champat) *a* Disappeared, hidden, vanished, out of sight.

ਚਪਲ (chapal) *a* Playful, volatile, tricky, quick, brisk.

ਚੱਪਲ (chappal) *n f* A footwear, chappal.

ਚਪੜ-ਚਪੜ (chapar-chapar) *n f* Sound of lapping or eating; nonsensical talk, chatter, jabber; ~ਕਰਨੀ To lap or eat noisily; to chatter, jabber.

ਚਪੜਾਸ (chapraas) *n f* Post or function of a peon, peonage.

ਚਪੜਾਸੀ (chapraasee) *n m* Peon, official attendant or messenger.

ਚੱਪਾ (chappa) *a* One fourth, fourth part; Paddle, oar; ~ਚੱਪਾ Every little space; ~ਚੱਪਾ ਛਾਣ ਮਾਰਨਾ To make a thorough search.

ਚਪਾਤੀ (chapaatee) *n f* Bread; a thin cake.

ਚੱਪੂ (chappoo) *n m* An oar, a paddle.

ਚਪੇੜ (chaper) *n m* A slap, smack, blow; Risk, loss.

ਚੱਬਣਾ (chabbnaa) *v* To chew, to munch, to masticate.

ਚੰਬੜ (chambar) *n m* Clinging, clasping, adhesion.

ਚੰਬੜਨਾ (chambarnaa) *v* To stick, to cling, to hold fast, to adhere.

ਚਬੂਤਰਾ (chabootraa) *n m* Platform, dais, stage, terrace, stand.

ਚੰਭਲਾਉਣਾ (chambhlaaunaa) *v* To instigate, to excite, to spoil.

ਚੱਮ (chamm) *n m* Leather, skin, hide, felt; ~ਉਧੇੜਨਾ To thrash, to flog, to beat mercilessly.

ਚਮਕ (chamak) *n f* Brilliance, lustre, shine, illumination, gleam, flash; ~ਦਮਕ Splendour, brightness; ~ਦਾਰ Bright, shining, luminous.

ਚਮਕਣਾ (chamaknaa) *v* To sparkle,

to flash, to shine, to glow, to twinkle.

ਚਮਗਾਦੜ (chamgaadar) *n m* Bat, a vampire.

ਚਮਚ (chamach) *n m* Spoon.

ਚਮਚਾ (chamchaa) *n m* Spoon; Scoop; Tout, protege; ~ਗੀਰੀ Sycophancy, obsequiousness.

ਚਮਨ (chaman) *n m* Small garden, a lawn.

ਚਮੜਾ (chamṛaa) *n* Leather.

ਚਮੜੀ (chamṛee) *n f* Skin.

ਚਰਸ (charas) *n f* Intoxicating drug of hemp.

ਚਰਕਣਾ (charaknaa) *v* To creak.

ਚਰਖੜੀ (charkhṛee) *n f* Pulley.

ਚਰਖਾ (charkhaa) *n m* Spinning wheel.

ਚਰਖੀ (charkhee) *n f* Pulley, spindle, a small spinning wheel.

ਚਰਚਾ (charchaa) *n f* Talk, discussion, report, remark, mention, rumour

ਚਰਨਾ (charnaa) *v* To graze, to pasture, to feed.

ਚਰਬੀ (charbee) *n f* Fat, grease, tallow.

ਚਰਵਾਹਾ (charwaahaa) *n m* Herdman, grazier.

ਚਰਾਉਣਾ (charaaunaa) *v* To graze, to pasture.

ਚਰਿੱਤਰ (charittar) *n m* Character,

conduct, behaviour, nature, habit, act, deed, custom.

ਚਰੋਕਣਾ (charoknaa) *a* Pretty old.

ਚਲਣ (chalan) *n m* Motion, conduct, method, habit, custom; ~ਸਾਰ Durable.

ਚਲਣਾ (chalnaa) *v* To walk, to move, to proceed, to go, to flow, to be in vogue.

ਚਲਦਾ (chaldaa) *a* Moving, in motion, on the move; Serviceable, in working order; Continuing, continued, ongoing, current; ~ਪੁਰਜਾ Component in motion or in working order; Clever, smart, resourceful, cunning; ~ਫਿਰਦਾ Mobile; Paddler; Active.

ਚਲਾਕ (chalaak) *a* Clever, cunning, nimble, artful, tricky.

ਚਲਾਣਾ (chalaanaa) *n m* Departure, exodus, passing away; ~ਕਰ ਜਾਣਾ To die, to pass away.

ਚੱਲਿਤਰ (chalitar) *n m* Trick, artifice, guile, pretence, coquetry; ~ਕਰਨਾ To beguile, to trick.

ਚੜਨਾ (charnaa) *v* To ascend, to rise, to go up, to climb, to mount, to ride (horse); ਦਿਨ~ Day break.

ਚੜ੍ਹਾਈ (charhaaee) *n f* Ascent, rise, invasion, attack, push.

ਚੜ੍ਹਾਵਾ (charaawaa) *n m* Offering to

a god; Exaltation, oblation.

ਚਾ (chaa) *n f* (1) Eagerness, ambition, zest, enthusiasm; (2) Tea.

ਚਾਹ (chaah) *n f* Desire, aspiration, will, longing.

ਚਾਹਤ (chaahat) *n f* Fondness, desire longing.

ਚਾਹੁਣਾ (chaahuṇaa) *v* To desire, to like, to crave, to need, to require, to ask for.

ਚਾਕਰੀ (chaakree) *n f* Service, menialship, attendance.

ਚਾਕੂ (chaakoo) *n m* Knife.

ਚਾਚਾ (chaachaa) *n m* Uncle, father's younger brother.

ਚਾਟ (chaaṭ) *n f* A kind of pungent, sour delicacy; Taste, liking, addiction, (bad) habit, weakness (for) allurement, temptation; ~**ਲੱਗਣੀ/ਚਾਟ ਲੱਗਣਾ** To be addicted to, to fall for, to be allured or tempted to a bad habit.

ਚਾਂਟਾ (chaanṭaa) *n m* Slap.

ਚਾਦਰ (chaadar) *n f* Bed sheet, bedspread, coverlet; ~**ਪਾਉਣੀ** To marry (a window) Through a ceremony; ~**ਵੇਖ ਕੇ ਪੈਰ ਪਸਾਰਨਾ** To cut coat according to one's cloth.

ਚਾਂਦਨੀ (chaandnee) *n f* Moonlight; canopy, bed sheet.

ਚਾਂਦੀ (chandee) *n f* Silver.

ਚਾਨਣ (chaananṇ) *n m* Light, sunshine, brightness.

ਚਾਪਲੂਸ (chaaploos) *n m* Flatterer, servile, wheedler.

ਚਾਬਕ (chaabak) *n f* Lash, whip, a thrash.

ਚਾਬੀ (chaabee) *n f* Key; ~**ਘੁਮਾਉਣੀ** To tutor; to turn the key.

ਚਾਰਪਾਈ (chaarpaaee) *n f* Cot.

ਚਾਰਾ (chaaraa) *n m* Fodder, pasture; Lure; Remedy.

ਚਾਲ (chaal) *n f* Motion, movement walk, gait; Habit, procedure; Tradition, custom, manner; ~**ਢਾਲ** Gait, fashion, manner; ~**ਬਾਜ਼** Deceitful, cunning, tricker.

ਚਾਲੂ (chaaloo) *n m* In vogue, current, prevalent; ~**ਕਰਨਾ** To promote, to promulgate.

ਚਾਵਲ (chaawal) *n m* Rice. Also **ਚੌਲ**

ਚਾੜ੍ਹਨਾ (chaaṛnaa) *v* To lift, to raise, to offer, to ascend; To cook.

ਚਾੜੀ (chaaṛee) *n f* Bribe; Flatter.

ਚਿੱਕ (chikk) *n f* Curtain or screen made of split bamboo sticks; Thin mortar of mud, mire.

ਚਿਕਣਾ (chiknaa) *a* Greasy, oily, smooth.

ਚਿਕਨਾਈ (chiknaaee) *n f* Fatness, greasiness, lubricant.

ਚਿੱਕੜ (chikkaṛ) *n f* Filth, mire, mud, clay, marsh, morass.

ਚਿਕਿਤਸਾ (chikitsaa) *n f* Medical science, treatment.

ਚਿਖਾ (chikhaa) *n f* A funeral pyre.

ਚਿੰਗਾਰੀ (chingaaree) *n f* Spark.

ਚਿਘਾਉਣਾ (chighaauṇaa) *v* To jeer, to huff, to mock.

ਚਿੰਘਾੜ (chinghaaṛ) *n f* Shrill cry, a scream, the trumppeting of an elephant.

ਚਿੰਘਾੜਨਾ (chingaaṛnaa) *v* To trumpet, to scream.

ਚਿਚਲਾਉਣਾ (chichlaauṇaa) *v* To cry out, to squeal, to hoot, to howl, to yell, to shriek.

ਚਿਚੜ (chichaṛ) *n m* A louse or tick which sticks to the body of cattle.

ਚਿਟਕਨਾ (chiṭaknaa) *v* To crack.

ਚਿਟਕਨੀ (chiṭkanee) *n f* Bolt, catch-bar.

ਚਿਟਕਾ (chiṭkaa) *n m* Glare of the sun.

ਚਿੱਟਾ (chiṭṭaa) *a* White, fair, milky; ~ਪਣ Whiteness.

ਚਿੱਠਾ (chiṭṭhaa) *n m* Memorandum of accounts, balance sheet, account book, cheap pamphlet, invoice.

ਚਿੱਠੀ (chiṭṭhee) *n m* Letter, a written note, document, circular; ~ਚਪੱਠੀ Correspondence, letter writing; ~ਰਸਾਨ Postman.

ਚਿਨਨਾ (chinnaa) *v* To decorate, to arrange in an orderly manner; To lay (bricks).

ਚਿਨਾਈ (chinaaee) *n f* Masonary assortment, building work.

ਚਿਤ (chit) *n* Mind, attention; ~ਲਾਉਣਾ to concertrate, to pay heed to; ~ਵਿਚ ਬਿਠਾਉਣਾ To love; ~ਕਬਰਾ Dappled, speckled, spotted

ਚਿੰਤਨ (chintan) *n m* Contemplation, thinking, reflection.

ਚਿੱਤਰ (chittar) *n m* A picture, illustration, painting, diagram; ~ਕਾਰ Artist, painter; ~ਪਟ Screen. Also **ਚਿਤ੍ਰ**

ਚਿਤਰਾ (chitraa) *n m* Leopard, panther.

ਚਿਤਰੀ ਵਾਲਾ (chitree waalaa) *n* Spotted, speckled (banana).

ਚਿਤੜ (chitaṛ) *n m* Buttock, posterior, bottom.

ਚਿੰਤਾ (chintaa) *n f* Worry, pensiveness, anxiety, doubt, thought.

ਚਿਤਾਉਣਾ (chitaaunaa) *v* To remind, to prompt.

ਚਿਤਾਰਨਾ (chitaarnaa) *v* To remember, to recollect, to entertain, to suppose.

ਚਿਤੇਰਾ (chiteraa) *n m* Painter.

ਚਿੱਥਣਾ (chitthnaa) *v* To munch, to crush with teeth, to masticate, to chew.

ਚਿੰਦੀ (chindee) *n f* Rag, small piece of cloth.

ਚਿੰਨੂ (chinnh) *n m* Sign, symbol, token, emblem, badge.

ਚਿਪਕਣਾ (chipaknaa) *v* To stick, to adhere.

ਚਿਪਚਿਪਾ (chipchipaa) *a* Greasy, waxy, adhesive, gummy, viscid.

ਚਿੰਬੜਨਾ (chimbarnaa) *v* To cling, to adhere, to embrace.

ਚਿਰਕ (chirak) *n f* Delay.

ਚਿਰਨਾ (chirnaa) *v* To be torn, to be sawn, to be split.

ਚਿਰਾਗ਼ (chiraag) *n m* Lamp.

ਚਿਰੋਕਣਾ (chiroknaa) *adv* Since, long, of old.

ਚਿਲਕਣਾ (chilaknaa) *v* To shine, to glitter, to glow, to brighten.

ਚਿਲਮ (chilam) *n f* An earthen pipe where fire & tobacco are placed for smoking.

ਚਿਲਮਚੀ (chilamchee) *n f* A wash basin.

ਚਿਲਮਨ (chilman) *n f* Bamboo curtain.

ਚਿੜ (chir) *n f* Irritation, vexation, detestation, fretfulness; ~ਚਿੜਾ Irritable ill-tempered, peevish,

short tempered; ~ਚਿੜਾਹ ਟ Peevishness, irritability, sourness, fretfulness.

ਚਿੜਨਾ (chirnaa) *v* To be irritated, to be chafed.

ਚਿੜਾਉਣਾ (chiraaunaa) *v* To vex, to chafe, to irritate, to provoke, to jeer at, to tease.

ਚਿੜੀ (chiree) *n f* Female sparrow; The shuttle cock; To club suit in playing cards; ~ਛਿੱਕਾ Badminton.

ਚੀਕ (cheek) *n f* Scream, shriek, yell, shrill cry.

ਚੀਕਣਾ (cheeknaa) *v a* To scream, to yell, to shout, to cry; Soapy, oily, slippery.

ਚੀਚੀ (cheechee) *n m* Smallest finger of hand.

ਚੀਜ਼ (cheez) *n* A thing, article, a commodity, a substance.

ਚੀਥੜਾ (cheethraa) *n m* Rag, a tatterred garment.

ਚੀਨੀ (cheenee) *n f* Sugar; Chinese national; ~ਮਿਟੀ China clay.

ਚੀਪੜ (cheepar) *a* Miser.

ਚੀਰਨਾ (cheernaa) *v* To saw, to tear, to rip, to rive.

ਚੀਰਾ (cheeraa) *n m* A cut, an incision, operation.

ਚੀਲ (cheel) *n f* A kite.

ਚੀੜਾ (chirhaa) *a* Hard, rigid, stiff;

gummy, gluey, glutinous; Fussy, difficult to deal with, hard bargainer; Firm, tough, resolute; Stingy, miser.

ਚੁਆਉਣਾ (chuaauṇaa) v To get (A milk animal) milked; to drip something (on to).

ਚੁਆਤੀ (chuaatee) n f Spark, ember, small smouldring piece of wood; fire brand; inciter.

ਚੁਸਕੀ (chooskee) n Sip.

ਚੁਸਤੀ (chustee) n f Activity, alertness, readiness, promptness.

ਚੁਹਲ (chuhal) n f Merriment, festivity, sportiveness, blandishment; ~ਬਾਜ਼ Sportive.

ਚੁੱਕ (chukk) n f Stiffening of or pain in back muscles or backbone; spinal disorder or dislocation; ~ਕੱਢਣੀ To treat or heal spinal disorder; ~ਪੈਣੀ To suffer from spinal dislocation; ~ਦੇਣਾ To lift, to raise; ~ਲੈਣਾ To lift, pick up, take up; to steal; to carry.

ਚੁੱਕਣਾ (chukkṇaa) v To lift, to arouse, to carry, to excite.

ਚੁਕੰਨਾ (chukannaa) a Alert, active, vigilant, cautions.

ਚੁਕਵਾਈ (chukwaaee) n f Act of lifting, porterage.

ਚੁੰਗ (chung) n f Retail; customer; Something given to a customer gratis as bonus on purchases; A handful, a pinch, a bit.

ਚੁਗਣਾ (chugṇaa) v To peck, to pick food with beak.

ਚੁਗ਼ਲ (chugal) n m Tell-tale backbiting; Block head, owl, fool; ~ਖ਼ੋਰ Backbiter, sycophant.

ਚੁਗਲੀ (chuglee) n f An instance of backbiting, false and malicious report; ~ਕਰਨੀ To backbite.

ਚੁਗਿਰਦਾ (chugirdaa) n m Boundary, ambit, surrounding perimeter.

ਚੁੰਗੀ (chungee) n f Toll, octroi, cess, excise duty.

ਚੁੰਝ (chunjh) n f Beak; Nib, corner; Pointed end.

ਚੁਟਕਾਰਨਾ (chuṭkaarnaa) v To flick

ਚੁਟਕੀ (chuṭkee) n f A pinch, fillip, a snapping with finger.

ਚੁਣਨਾ (chuṇnaa) v To select, to pick, to sort, to choose, to arrange.

ਚੁਤ (chut) n f Vagina.

ਚੁਤੜ (chutaṛ) n m Buttocks, rumps, hips.

ਚੁਧਰੰਮਾ (chudharmmaa) n m Leadership.

ਚੁੰਧਲਾਉਣਾ (chundhlaauṇaa) v To dazzle.

ਚੁੰਨ੍ਹਾ (chunnhaa) a Bleary eyed, purblind, having Small eyes.

ਚੁੰਨੀ (chunnee) *n m* A head cloth for women.

ਚੁੱਪ (chupp) *a* Silent, mute, mum, speechless; ~ਚਾਪ In silence; ~ਚੁਪੀਤਾ Without uttering a single word.

ਚੁਪਾਲ (chupaal) *n m* Meeting place for village elders or assembly.

ਚੁਫੇਰੇ (chuphere) *adv* Around, all around. Also ਚੁਗਿਰਦੇ

ਚੁੰਬਕ (chumbak) *n m* Magnet, loadstone.

ਚੁਬਾਰਾ (chubaaraa) *n m* An attic, upper storey, summer house, upper open room.

ਚੁਬੁਰਜੀ (chuburjee) *n* Pavillion.

ਚੁਭਣਾ (chubhnaa) *v* To pierce, to sting.

ਚੁਭਨ (chubhan) *n f* Pricking, lingering pain, irritation.

ਚੁਮਣਾ (chumnaa) *v* To kiss, to suckle, to osculate, to lip.

ਚੁੰਮੀ (chummee) *n m* Kiss, osculation.

ਚੁਰਸਤਾ (churastaa) *n m* A crossing.

ਚੁਰਕਣਾ (churaknaa) *v* To be dysenteric.

ਚੁਰਾਉਣਾ (churaaunaa) *v* To steal, to pilfer, to thieve.

ਚੁਰੇੜਾ (chureraa) *a* Broader, wider.

ਚੁਲਬੁਲਾ (chulbulaa) *a* Vivacious, agile, mercurial, restless.

ਚੁਲਬੁਲਾਉਣਾ (chulbulaaunaa) *v* To be playful, to be fidgety, to be restless.

ਚੁਲੀ (chulee) *n f* A mouthful of liquid, oblation.

ਚੁੜਨਾ (churnaa) *v* To be an invalid, to linger a painful life.

ਚੁੜੈਲ (churail) *n f* Witch, hag, hobgoblim, female giant.

ਚੂਸਣਾ (choosnaa) *v* To suck, to suckle, to sip.

ਚੂਹਾ (choohaa) *n m* Mouse, rat.

ਚੂਕ (chook) *n f* Error, blunder, mistake, fault.

ਚੂਕਣਾ (chooknaa) *v* To err, to blunder, to fail, to miss.

ਚੂਚਾ (choochaa) *n m* Chicken, squeaker.

ਚੂੰਢੀ (choondhee) *n f* Pinch, clothe-spin, paper clip.

ਚੂਨਾ (choonaa) *n m* Lime, mortar.

ਚੂਰਨ (chooran) *n m* A powder (especially of medicine).

ਚੂਰਾ (chooraa) *n m* Sawdust, powder.

ਚੂਰੀ (chooree) *n m* Crushed bread mixed with ghee and sugar.

ਚੂੜੀ (chooree) *n f* Bangle, bracelet, spire, pitch.

ਚੇਹਰਾ (chehraa) *n m* Face, appearance.

ਚੇਚਕ (chechak) *n f* Small pox.

ਚੇਤਨਾ (chetnaa) *v* To recollect, to remember, to be alert.

ਚੇਤਨ (chetan) *n m a* Conscious soul, a living being; Conscious, alert, cautious, observant.

ਚੇਤਨਾ (chetnaa) *n f* Consciousness, awareness, sentiency, under-standing.

ਚੇਪਣਾ (chepnaa) *v* To paste, to stick, to glue.

ਚੇਪੀ (chepee) *n f* Sticker, patch, a piece of cloth or paper.

ਚੇਲਾ (chelaa) *n m* A pupil, follower, disciple.

ਚੈਨ (chain) *n m* Rest, tranquility, ease, relief, repose, piece.

ਚੋਖਾ (chokhaa) *a* Sufficient, enough, ample, tolerable.

ਚੋਗਾ (choga) *n m* Birdfeed, bait.

ਚੋਟ (chot) *n f* Wound, hurt, blow, bruise, percussion; Ironical remark; **ਡੰਕੇ ਦੀ~** Openly, challengingly.

ਚੋਟਾ (chotaa) *n m* Thief, pilferer, rascal.

ਚੋਟੀ (chotee) *n f* Top knot, a plait, pig tail; Summit, top, peak, vertex crest; A female thief.

ਚੋਣ (chon) *n m* Choice, selection, election, option, pick; **ਉਪ~** Bye election; **~ਹਲਕਾ** Constituency, electorate.

ਚੋਣਵਾਂ (chonwaan) *a* Selected, chosen, selective.

ਚੋਪੜਨਾ (choparnaa) To butter, to besmear, to anoint.

ਚੋਰ (Chor) *n m* Thief, burglar, pilferer, swindler; **~ਬਜ਼ਾਰ** Black market; **~ਦਰਵਾਜ਼ਾ** Backdoor.

ਚੋਰੀ (choree) *n m* Theft, burglary; **~ਚੋਰੀ** Seretly, privately; **~ਛਿਪੇ** Stealthly.

ਚੋਲਾ (cholaa) *n m* A long robe worn by saints; Shirts; Human body; **~ਛਡਣਾ** To die; **~ਬਦਲਣਾ** To be reborn; To change physical frame.

ਚੋਲੀ (cholee) *n f* Bodice, blouse, vest, corset.

ਚੌਸਰ (chausar) *n m* Chess, chess board.

ਚੌਕ (chauk) *n m* Public square, cross road, road junction, crossing, plaza.

ਚੌਕਸ (chaukas) *a* Alert, careful, watchful, vigilant.

ਚੌਕਸੀ (chauksee) *n f* Alertness, carefulness, watchfulness, vigilance, wariness, precaution, circumspection.

ਚੌਂਕਣਾ (chaunknaa) *v* To stratle, to be astonished.

ਚੌਕੰਨਾ (chaukannaa) *a* Cautious, alert.

ਚੌਕੜੀ (chaukaṛee) *n f* Posture of sitting cross-legged.

ਚੌਕਾ (chaukaa) *n m* Kitchen, clean place for cooking.

ਚੌਕੀ (chaukee) *n f* Stool, a small wooden chair with no arm; ~ਦਾਰ Watchman.

ਚੌਧਰੀ (chaudharee) *n m* Chieftain, headman, leader.

ਚੌਪੜ (chaupaṛ) *n m* Dice, chess.

ਚੌਪਾਲ (chaupaal) *n m* Rural meeting place.

ਚੌਰਸ (chauras) *a* Flat, plane, square, smooth, oblong.

ਚੌਲ (chaul) *n m* Rice. Also ਚਾਵਲ

ਚੌੜ (chauṛ) *n m a* Spoiling, destruction, ruin; Wasted, spoiled; ~ਕਰਨਾ To spoil, to damage, to waste.

ਚੌੜਾ (chauṛaa) *a* Broad, wide, open, flat.

ਚੌੜਾਈ (chauṛaaee) *n f* Width, breadth, span, extension.

ਛ

ਛ Twelfth letter of Gurmukhi alphabets, pronounced as 'chhachhaa'.

ਛਕਣਾ (chhaknaa) *v* To eat satisfactorily, to be gratified; To deceive, to cheet.

ਛਕੜਾ (chhakraa) *n m* Cart, van, truck, wagon.

ਛੱਕਾ (chhakkaa) *n m* A group of six, Sixer, sixth at cards.

ਛਕਾਉਣਾ (chhakaaunaa) *v* To satiate, to serve; To deceive.

ਛੰਗਵਾਉਣਾ (chhangvaaunaa) *v* To get trimmed, to get pruned.

ਛਛੂੰਦਰ (chhachhoondar) *n m* Muskrat, mole.

ਛਛੋਹਰਾ (chhachhohraa) *a m* Sordid, trifling, shallow, childish, light headed.

ਛੱਜ (chhajj) *n m* Winnowing basket, winnower; ~ਛੱਜ ਰੋਣਾ To weep bitterly.

ਛਜਲੀ (chhajlee) *n f* Hood (of a Snake).

ਛੱਜਾ (chhajjaa) *n m* Balcony, gallery-shelf, penthouse, brim.

ਛਟਣਾ (chhatnaa) *v* To remove dust from the grain, to slander, to husk, to thresh.

ਛੱਡਣ (chhaddan) *n m* Quittance.

ਛੰਡਣਾ (chhandnaa) *v* To dust, to toss, to reprimand.

ਛੱਡਣਾ (chhadnaa) *v* To leave, to relinquish, to remit, to renounce, to quit, to release, to vacate, to forgo.

ਛਣਕ (chhanak) *n f* Clang, clink, jingle, sound produced by clattering of metal or coin.

ਛਣਕਣਾ (chhanaknaa) *v* To clatter, to clink, to babble.

ਛਣਨਾ (channaa) *v* To be sieved, strained; (for cloth, garment) to get worn out, thinned.

ਛੱਤ (chhatt) *n f* Roof, ceiling, storey.

ਛਤਰੀ (chhatree) *n f* Umbrella, parachute, dome.

ਛਤਰੇ (chhatre) *n m* Locks of hair.

ਛੱਤਾ (chhattaa) *n m* Beehive, honey comb.

ਛੰਨ (chhann) *n f* Small hut, thatched roof.

ਛੰਨਾ (chhannaa) *n m* Bowl, cup.

ਛੱਪਰ (chhappar) *n m* Thatched roof or shed, booth.

ਛੱਪਰੀ (chhappree) *n f* Cottage, hut,

shed, hovel.

ਛਪਵਾਉਣਾ (chhapvaaunaa) v To cause to be printed or embossed or stamped.

ਛਪਵਾਈ (chhapvaaee) n f Printing.

ਛੱਪੜ (chhappar) n m Pool, Pond.

ਛਪੜੀ (chhapree) n f Small, pond, puddle, cesspool.

ਛਪਾਕੀ (chhapaakee) n f White gum, erysipelas.

ਛਬੀਲ (chhabeel) n f Place where water is distributed gratuitously.

ਛਬੀਲਾ (chhabeelaa) a Elegant, handsome, beautiful, graceful.

ਛਮਕ (chhamak) n f Stick, cane; ~ਛੱਲੋ A passionate woman, a beautiful girl.

ਛਲ (chhal) n m Deception, dodge, trap, trick, fraud.

ਛਲਕਣਾ (chhalaknaa) v To spill, to overflow, to wobble, to shake.

ਛੱਲਾ (chhallaa) n m Plain ring worn on fingers, annulus.

ਛੱਲੀ (chhallee) n f Corncob of maize; spool; Enlarged spleen; Stiffened muscle.

ਛਲਾਵਾ (chhalaawaa) n m Illusion, hallucination, dodge.

ਛਲੀਆ (chhaliyaa) a Artful, crafty, fraudulent, cunning, tricky, deceitful, cheat.

ਛੜ (chhar) n f Bale, pole, staff (of a flag); Shaft (of spear).

ਛੜਾ (chharaa) n m a Bachelor, unmarried; Single, lone; ~ਛਾਂਟ All alone.

ਛੜੀ (chharee) n f A rod, cane, good, stick.

ਛਾਂ (chhaan) n f Shade. Also ਛਾਂਉਂ

ਛਾਉਣੀ (chhaaunee) n Cantonment, Permanant military camp or barrack; Encampment. Also ਛੌਣੀ

ਛਾਈ (chhaaee) n f Dark, spot, pimples; Ashes.

ਛਾਹ (chhaah) n f Butter milk, whey.

ਛਾਂਟਣਾ (chhaatnaa) v To select, to pick, to retrench, to clip, to choose, to sort out (mail).

ਛਾਣ (chaan) v Residue, refuse after sieving; bran; ~ਮਾਰਨਾ To search, explore, look for thoroughly.

ਛਾਣਨਾ (chhaannaa) v To filter, to percolate; To screen, to sieve, to sift.

ਛਾਣਨੀ (chhaannee) n f Sieve, bolter.

ਛਾਣਬੀਣ (chhaanbeen) n f Probe, scrutiny, sifting.

ਛਾਤੀ (chhaatee) n f Chest, breast, bosom, heart, bust; ~ਤਾਣਨਾ To stretch out one's chest; To offer a brave front, to face boldly.

ਛਾਪਣਾ (chhaapnaa) v To print, to

publish.

ਛਾਪਾ (chhaapaa) *n m* Sudden attack, surprise attack, surprise visit; ~ਮਾਰਨਾ To raid; to attack suddenly; To surprise.

ਛਾਬੜੀ (chhaabree) *n f* Small basket; ~ਵਾਲਾ Hawker, pedlar.

ਛਾਬਾ (chhaabaa) *n m* Small basket; A pan of weighing scale.

ਛਾਰ (chhaar) *n f* Alkali; Ashes, dirt.

ਛਾਲ (chhaal) *n f* Bark, peel; Jump, plunge; ~ਮਾਰਨਾ To jump, to leap, to skip.

ਛਾਲਾ (chhaalaa) *n m* Boil, burn, pock, skin-blister.

ਛਿਆਸੀ (chhiaasee) *a* Eighty-six.

ਛਿਆਲੀ (chiaalee) *a* Forty-six. Also ਛਤਾਲੀ

ਛਿੱਕਣਾ (chhiknaa) *v* To seneeze.

ਛਿੱਕਾ (chikkaa) *n m* Cup-shaped network with strings for fasterning over animal's mouth against its damaging crops or for hanging eatables to protect them against cats, mice or ants; Tennis or badminton racket.

ਛਿਜਣਾ (chhijnaa) *v* To decrease, to lessen, to waste away.

ਛਿੱਟ (chhitt) *n f* Drop, splash.

ਛਿਟਣਾ (chhitnaa) *v* To spatter.

ਛਿੱਟਾ (chhittaa) *n m* Water splash,

spray, shower.

ਛਿਣਕਣਾ (chhinaknaa) *v* To sprinkle.

ਛਿਤਰ (chhittar) *n m* Used foot wear, worn out shoes; ~ਮਾਰਨਾ To beat with shoes.

ਛਿੱਥਾ (chhitthaa) *a* Annoyed, angry, abashed, peevish.

ਛਿਦਣਾ (chhidnaa) *v* To be perforated, to be piered with holes, to be wounded.

ਛਿੱਦਰ (chhiddar) *n m* Mistake, omission; Hole, slot.

ਛਿਨ (chhin) *n m* A moment.

ਛਿੰਨ-ਭਿੰਨ (chhinn-bhinn) *a* Decomposed, scattered, cut.

ਛਿਨਾਲ (chhinaal) *n f* A Strumpet, harolt, prostitute.

ਛਿਪਾਉਣਾ (chhipaaunaa) *v* To hide, to conceal, to cover.

ਛਿੱਲ (chhil) *n f* Skin, bark, peel, shell, husk, rind. Also ਛਿਲਕਾ

ਛਿਲਣਾ (chhilnaa) *v* To peel, to raze, to rind, to pare, to chisel, to shell.

ਛਿੱਲੜ (chhillar) *n m* Rind, skin, crust, husk.

ਛਿੜ (chhir) *n f* Start; ~ਜਾਣਾ To straggle, to disperse, to dissolve, to break out (war).

ਛਿੜਕਣਾ (chhiraknaa) *v* To sprinkle, to scatter, to spray.

ਛਿੜਨਾ (chhirnaa) *v* Beginning, to

continue, to start, to go for a grazing.

ਛੁਹਰ (chuhar) *n m* A lad, boy, youngster.

ਛੁਹਾਉਣਾ (chhuhaaunaa) *v* To touch.

ਛੁਹਾਰਾ (chhuhaaraa) *n m* Dried date, palm.

ਛੁਟਕਣਾ (chhutaknaa) *v* To slip, to break loose, to abscise.

ਛੁਟਕਾਰਾ (chhutkaaraa) *n m* Rescue, escape, release, exemption, discharge, acquittal.

ਛੁਟਣਾ (chhutnaa) *v* To get rid of , to be discharged, to escape, to slip away, to break loose.

ਛੁੱਟੜ (chhutar) *a* Divorced, derelict, woman abandoned by the husband.

ਛੁੱਟੀ (chhuttee) *n f* Leave, vacation, holiday, intermission.

ਛੁਡਾਉਣਾ (chhudaaunaa) *v* To save, to liberate, to get discharged, to get removed, to disentangle.

ਛੁਪਣਾ (chhupnaa) *v* To hide, to disappear, to be concealed.

ਛੁਰਾ (chhuraa) *n m* A long knife, chopper, dagger.

ਛੁਰੀ (chhuree) *n f* A knife.

ਛੁੱਛਾ (chhuchhaa) *a* Empty, unfilled or partly filled (vessel); Vain (person), hollow, mean.

ਛੂਤ (chhoot) *n f* Infection, contagion, contamination;   **~ਛਾਤ** Untouchability, (now legally banned in India).

ਛੇਕ (chhek) *n m* Hole, gap, loophole, flaw, puncture, cut.

ਛੇਕਣਾ (chheknaa) *v* To ostracise, excommunicate, to boycott; To ignore, to disown.

ਛੇਕੜ (chhekar) *adv* At last, ultimately, in the long run.

ਛੇਤੀ (chhetee) *n a* Expeditiousness briskness, promptness, haste, soon, shortly; **~ਕਰਨਾ** To make haste, to expedite, to speed up; **~ਨਾਲ** Swiftly, quickly.

ਛੇੜਨਾ (chhernaa) *v* To tease, to chaff, to harass, to irritate.

ਛੈਣੀ (chhainee) *n* Chisel, graver.

ਛੋਕਰਾ (chhokraa) *n* Boy, lad, youngster.

ਛੋਟਾ (chhotaa) *a* Small, little, short, junior, subordinate, tiny.

ਛੋਲਾ (chholaa) *n m* Gram, chick-pea.

ਛੋਲੀਆ (chholiaa) *n m* Green gram.

ਛੋੜਨਾ (chhornaa) *v* To release, to leave, to relinquish, to renounce, to forego.

ਛੌਂਕਣਾ (chhaunknaa) *v* To fry and season with spices.

ਜ

ਜ Thirteenth letter of Gurmukhi alphabets, pronounced as 'jajjaa'.

ਜਈ (jaee) *n f* Oat.

ਜਸ (jas) *n m* Fame, reputation, praise, glory, splendour.

ਜਸ਼ਨ (jashan) *n m* Feast, celebration, merriment.

ਜਸੂਸ (jasoos) *n m* Spy, informer, detective. Also ਜਾਸੂਸ

ਜਸੂਸੀ (jasoosee) *a n f* Detective, detecting; Espionage, spying.

ਜਹੰਨਮ (jahannam) *n m* Hell, inferno.

ਜਹਾਜ (jahaaj) *n m* Ship, steamer, vessel, launch, liner; Aeroplane, aircraft; ~ਅਸਲਾ Air crew; (ਜਹਾਜੀ) ~ਬੇੜਾ Fleet; Navy; Armada; ~ਰਾਨ Sailor; Flier; ~ਰਾਨੀ Shipping, naval, nautical.

ਜਹਾਂ (jahaan) *n m* World; ~ਗੀਰ World conquerer. Also ਜਹਾਨ

ਜਹਾਦ (jahaad) *n m* Holywar, crusade.

ਜਹਾਲਤ (jahaalat) *n f* Stupidity, ignorance.

ਜ਼ਹਿਮਤ (zhemat) *n f* Botheration, affliction, perplexity, difficulty, calamity.

ਜ਼ਹਿਰ (zaher) *n m* Poison, venom.

ਜ਼ਹੀਨ (zaheen) *a* Intelligent, sagacious.

ਜ਼ਹੂਰ (Jahoor) *n* Manifestation, presence, appearance. Also ਜ਼ਹੂਰ

ਜਕ (jak) *n f* Shyness, hesitation, disgrace, disilusion.

ਜਕੜ (jakaṛ) *n f* Grip, hold.

ਜਕੜਨਾ (jakaṛnaa) *v* To grip, to tie up, to fasten tightly.

ਜ਼ਕਾਤ (zakaat) *n f* Alms, charity, tax, customs duty.

ਜੱਕੋ-ਤੱਕਾ (jakko-takkaa) *n m* Hesitation, reluctance, double mindedness, indecision, quandary, irresoluteness, ambivalence, dilemma; ~ਕਰਨਾ To hesitate, dither, procrastinate, to be double minded, irresolute, ambivalent.

ਜੱਖਣਾ (jakkhaṇaa) *n f* Existence; Essence.

ਜ਼ਖ਼ਮ (zakham) *n m* Wound, cut.

ਜ਼ਖ਼ਮੀ (zakhmee) *a* Wounded, hurt.

ਜ਼ਖੀਰਾ (zakheeraa) *n m* Store house, reservoir, hoard, repository, stock.

ਜਗ (jag) *n m* (1) World, universe,

cosmos; (2) Jug; ~ਹਸਾਈ Public disgrace, derision, contempt, infamy.

ਜੰਗ (jang) *n f* Battle, war, fight, compaign; ~ਕਰਨੀ To fight, to wage war; ~ਛੇੜਨੀ To declare war (against), To go to the war (with); ~ਬੰਦੀ Ceasefire, trace.

ਜਗ੍ਹਾ (jaggaah) *n f adv* Place, locality, location, space, station, post; Instead of. Also ਜਗਹਾ

ਜੰਗਜੂ (jangajoo) *n m* Warrior, fighter.

ਜਗਣਾ (jagnaa) *v* To burn, to light.

ਜਗਤ (jagat) *n m* World, universe.

ਜਗਮਗ (jagmag) *a* Shining, gleaming, glimmering.

ਜਗਮਗਾਉਣਾ (jagmagaaunaa) *v* To shine, to gleam, to glitter, to sparkle.

ਜਗਰਾਤਾ (jagraataa) *n m* Sleeplessness, nightly vigil, keeping awake throughout the night singing hymns.

ਜੰਗਲ (jangal) *n m* Forest, woods, wilderness.

ਜੰਗਲਾ (janglaa) *n m* Railing, fencing, palisade.

ਜੰਗਲੀ (janglee) *a* Wild, savage, barbarion.

ਜਗਾਉਣਾ (jagaaunaa) *v* To awaken, to raise, to wake up, to burn, to

light, to illuminate.

ਜੰਗਾਲ (jangaal) *n m* Rust, verdigris, corrosion.

ਜੰਗੀ (jangee) *a* Martial, gigantic, brave, warlike.

ਜਗੀਰ (jageer) *n f* Manor, estate, rent, free land, grant, feud; ~ਦਾਰ Landlord, grantee. Also ਜਾਗੀਰ

ਜੰਘ (jangh) *n f* Leg, thigh.

ਜਚਗੀ (jachgee) *n f* Maternity, childbirth; Period of confinement for delivery and convalescence thereafter.

ਜਚਣਾ (jachnaa) *v* To suit, to match, to befit.

ਜੱਚਾ (zachchaa) *n f* Woman who has just delivered a child; ~ਖਾਨਾ Maternity home.

ਜੰਞ (janj) *n f* Marriage party; ~ਚੜੂਨੀ To depart for marriage; ~ਘਰ Place where marriage party is stayed.

ਜਜ਼ਬਾ (jazbaa) *n m* Feeling, emotion, sentiment.

ਜਜਮਾਨ (jajmaan) *n m* Host.

ਜੰਜਾਲ (janjaal) *n m* Trouble, difficulty, perflexity, fix.

ਜੱਜੀ (jajjee) *n f* Office, post; Function of Judge.

ਜਜ਼ੀਆ (jaziaa) *n m* Toll tax, capitation tax.

ਜ਼ੰਜੀਰ (zanjeer) *n f* Chain, Zipper.

ਜਜ਼ੀਰਾ (jazeera) *n m* Island.

ਜੰਝੂ (janjoo) *n m* The sacred thread worn by Hindus.

ਜੰਝ (janj) *n m* Marriage party, marriage procession led by the bridegroom.

ਜੰਝੂ (janju) *n* Sacred thread (worn by Hindus as mark of initiation).

ਜੱਟ (jaṭṭ) *n m* Name of an agricultural class of northwestern India; A member of this class; Farmer, agriculturist, peasant.

ਜਟਾ (jaṭaa) *n f* Strand of matted hair, elf-lock.

ਜਣਨਾ (Jaṇnaa) *v* To give birth to, to procreate, to bear, to bring forth, to breed.

ਜਣਨੀ (jaṇnee) *n f* Mother, projentrix.

ਜਣਾ (jaṇaa) *n* Man, individual, chap, husband.

ਜਤਨ (jatan) *n a m* Effort, attempt, diligence, endeavour, exertion; ~ਸ਼ੀਲ Endeavouring, attempting, trying on the job; Industrious.

ਜੰਤਰ (jantar) *n m* Instrument, implement, apparatus, machine.

ਜੰਤ੍ਰਿਕ (jantric) *a* Mechanical.

ਜੰਤਰੀ (jantree) *n f* Calendar, almanac.

ਜਤਾਉਣਾ (jataaunaa) *v* To remind, to

inform, to evince, to caution.

ਜਤੀ (jatee) *n m* Ascetic, chaste.

ਜੰਤੂ (jantoo) *n m* Animal, creature.

ਜਥਾ (Jathaa) *n m* Group, squad, corps, company, batch.

ਜਥੇਦਾਰ (jathedaar) *n m* Leader of a group.

ਜਥੇਬੰਧ (jatheband) *a* Organised, grouped, united, embodied as a working group.

ਜਥੇਬੰਦੀ (jathebandee) *n f* Organisation, union, grouping.

ਜੰਦਰਾ (jandraa) *n m* Lock, machine.

ਜੱਦੀ (jaddee) *a* Ancestral, hereditary, patrimonial.

ਜਦੀਦ (jadeed) *a* Fresh, new, recent, modern.

ਜਦੋਂ (jadon) *adv* When; ~ਕਦੀ/ ~ਕਦੇ/ ~ਜਦੋਂ Whenever, as and when; ~ਤਾਈਂ/ ~ਤੀਕ Until, till, as long as, till such time as; ~ਵੀ Whenever.

ਜ਼ਨ (zan) *n f* Woman, wife; ~ਮੁਰੀਦ Henpecked husband, cuckold.

ਜਨ (jan) *n m* A person, individual, mankind; ~ਸੰਖਿਆ Population; ~ਗਣਨਾ Census; ~ਤੰਤਰ Democracy.

ਜੰਨਤ (jannat) *n f* Paradise, heaven.

ਜਨਮ (Janam) *n m* Birth, origin; ~ਕੁੰਡਲੀ Horoscope, birth chart; ~ਜਾਤ Inborn, inherent; ~ਦਾਤਾ

Creator, father, god.

ਜਨਾਹ (janaah) *n m* Adulterer, fornicatior. Also ਜ਼ਨਾਹ

ਜਨਾਜ਼ਾ (janaazaa) *n m* Hearse, coffin, bier, funeral procession.

ਜਨਾਨਾ (zanaanaa) *a* Feminine, female.

ਜ਼ਨਾਨੀ (zanaanee) *n f* wife, women.

ਜਨੂੰਨ (jannoon) *n m* Mania, lunacy.

ਜਪ (jap) *n m* Meditate, repeat; Recitation or silent repetition of God's name, mystical formula or prayer; ~ਮਾਲਾ Rosary.

ਜਪਣਾ (japṇaa) *v* To repeat god's name mentally or orally in low tone; To tell one's beads.

ਜੱਫਾ (japphaa) *n m* Holding tightly by waist, a tight embrace.

ਜਬਤ (zabat) *n m* Forfeiture, control, self-command.

ਜਬਰ (jabar) *n m* Compulsion, coercion, opression, tyranny; ~ਕਰਨਾ To coerce, to oppress, to tyrannize; ~ਦਸਤ Strong, powerful, vigorous; ~ਨ By force, forcibly, illegally.

ਜਬਰੀ (jabree) *adv* Forcibly, coercive, repressive, compulsorily.

ਜ਼ਬਾਨ (zabaan) *n f* Tongue, dialect, language, speech, promise; ~ਖੋਲ੍ਹਣੀ To speak out; ~ਤੇ ਚੜ੍ਹਨਾ To be the subject of talk; ~ਦਰਾਜ਼ੀ Loquaciousness, rudeness, impertinence; ~ਦਾ ਕੋੜਾ Bitter tongued; ~ਦੇਣੀ To promise; ~ਲੜਾਉਣੀ To argue, to confort.

ਜ਼ਬਾਨੀ (jabaanee) *adv* Orally, verbally; Mentally; By word of mouth.

ਜਮ (jam) *n m* Messenger of death; God of death, yama. Also ਜਮਕਾਲ

ਜੰਮ (jamm) *a* Native (of), born (in).

ਜਮ੍ਹਾਂ (jamaa) *n m a* Accumulation, sum total; Accumulated, collected; ~ਹੋਣਾ To assemble, to collect; ~ਕਰਾਉਣਾ To deposit; ~ਖੋਰੀ Hoarding.

ਜਮਹੂਰੀ (janahooree) *a* Democratic; ~ਅਤ Democracy.

ਜਮਘਟਾ (jamghaṭṭaa) *n m* Crowd, throng, multitude, large assemblage.

ਜੰਮਣਾ (jammṇaa) *v* (1) To take birth, to be born; To take root, to sprout, to germinate; To give birth, to bear, to beget; To procreate; (2) To freeze, to condense; To congeal, to coalgulate, to curdle; To set, to settle.

ਜਮਦੂਤ (jamdoot) *n m* Angel of death.

ਜਮਾਉਣਾ (jamaauṇaa) *v* To beget, to

produce, to create, to breed, to grow.

ਜਮਾਤ (jamaat) *n f* Class, party, group, society.

ਜਮਾਤੀ (jamaatee) *n m* Classfellow, classmate.

ਜਮਾਂਦਰੂ (jamaandroo) *a* Congential, innate, inbred, inborn, since birth; Natural.

ਜਮਾਦਾਰ (jamaadaar) *n m* (1) A junior commissioned military rank (now **ਨਾਇਬ ਸੂਬੇਦਾਰ** in India); (2) Mate, supervisor of labour gang or squad; (3) Scavenger, sweeper.

ਜਮਾਦਾਰਨੀ (jamaadarnee) *n f* A female scavenger, sweeper.

ਜਮਾਦਾਰੀ (jamadari) *n f* Rank, post, job of junior military, commissioned officer, supervisory etc.

ਜ਼ਮਾਨਤ (zamaanat) *n f* Bond, security, guarantee, bail; **~ਨਾਮਾ** Security bond.

ਜ਼ਮਾਨਾ (zamaanaa) *n m* Times, age, period, present day world; **~ਸਾਜ** Worldly wise, time server, prudent, clever, cunning. Also **ਜਮਾਨੇਸਾਜ਼**

ਜਮਾਲ (jamaal) *n m* Beauty, splendour, grandeur, elegance.

ਜ਼ਮੀਨ (zameen) *n f* Earth, land.

ਜ਼ਮੀਰ (zameer) *n f* Conscience.

ਜ਼ਰ (zar) *n m* Gold, wealth. Also **ਜ਼ਰ**

ਜ਼ਰਖੇਜ (zarkhez) *a* Productive, fertile.

ਜ਼ਰਦ (zarad) *a* Pale, yellow.

ਜ਼ਰਦਾ (jardaa) *n m* Powdered tobacco.

ਜ਼ਰਾ (zaraa) *a adv* Little, a little, somewhat.

ਜ਼ਰਾਇਤ (zarraait) *n f* Agriculture, farming.

ਜੱਰਾਹ (jarrah) *n m* Surgeon.

ਜ਼ਰੀਆ (zariaa) *n m* Means.

ਜ਼ਰੂਰ (zaroor) *adv* Certainly, surely, doubtless, necessarily, essentially.

ਜ਼ਰੂਰਤ (zaroorat) *a* Need, necessity, want, requirement.

ਜ਼ਰੂਰੀ (zarooree) *a* Necessary, essential, requisite.

ਜਲ (jal) *n m* Water, aqua; **~ਘਰ** Waterworks; **~ਥਲ** Inundation, flood; **~ਧਾਰਾ** Water current; **~ਨਿਕਾਸ** Sewerage, dewatering; **~ਵਾਯੂ** Climate.

ਜਲਸਾ (jalsaa) *n m* Gathering, conference, a meeting, a sitting, festivity.

ਜਲਜ਼ਲਾ (jalzalaa) *n m* Earthquake.

ਜਲਣਾ (jalṇaa) *v* To burn; To inflame, to be enkindled; To be jealous.

ਜਲਦਬਾਜ਼ (jaldbaz) *a* Prone to hasty

decision or action; Reckless, brash, impetuous, rash. Also **ਜਲਦਬਾਜ਼**

ਜਲਦੀ (jaldee) *n f* Hurry, quickness, speediness, haste.

ਜਲਵਾ (jalva) *n m* Splendour, glitter, resplendence, glow; Grace, pleasing glimpse or sight.

ਜਲਾਪਾ (jalaapaa) *n m* Heart burning; Jealousy. Also **ਸਾੜਾ**

ਜਲਾਲ (jalaal) *n m* Splendour, glory, diginty, majesty.

ਜਲਾਲਤ (zalaalat) *n f* Meanness, disgrace, wretchedness.

ਜ਼ਲੀਲ (zaleel) *a* Mean; Disgraced, humiliated; ~**ਕਰਨਾ** To humiliate, to dishonour, to mortify.

ਜਲੂਸ (jaloos) *n m* Procession, pageant.

ਜਲੇਪਾ (jalepaa) *n m* Jealousy.

ਜਵਾਈ (jawaaee) *n m* Son-in-law.

ਜਵਾਹਰ (jawahhar) *n m* Jewel, gem, precious stone.

ਜਵਾਨ (jawaan) *a n m* Young, youthful; Youth, youngman.

ਜਵਾਨੀ (jawaanee) *n f* Stage of life between boyhood and middle age, youth, youthfulness, manhood, prime, full bloom, maturity; Adolescence, puberty; **ਚੜ੍ਹਦੀ~** Early youth, early

manhood, adolescence; **ਢਲਦੀ~** Middle age; ~**ਚੜ੍ਹਨਾ** To become youth to come of prime age.

ਜਵਾਬ (Jawaab) *n m* Answer, reply; Defense, refusal; ~**ਸਵਾਲ** Discussion, altercation; ~**ਮਿਲਣਾ** To get a refusal, to be dismissed; ~**ਦੇ ਜਾਣਾ** To break down, to collapse; ~**ਤਲਬੀ** Explanation; ~**ਦੇਹ** Accountable, answerable.

ਜਵਾਬੀ (jawaabee) *a* Reply paid, reciprocal, counter, corresponding.

ਜਵਾਂਮਰਦ (jawaanmarad) *a* Manly, brave person.

ਜਵਾਂਮਰਦੀ (jawaanmardee) *n f* Manliness, courage, bravery, virility, vigour.

ਜਵਾਰ (javar) *n f* a kind of Indian millet sorghum; ~**ਭਾਟਾ** Tide, tidal waves, ebb and flow, rise and fall of seas; Spring or neap tides.

ਜਵਾਲ (jawaal) *n f* Downfall, decline.

ਜਵਾਲਾ (jawaalaa) *n f* Flame, fire, blaze; ~**ਮੁਖੀ** A volcano.

ਜੜ (jaṛ) *n a* Foundation, basis, root, source, origin, root cause; Senseless, numb, dumb, inert, inanimate, irrational; ~**ਤਾ** Inanimate state, inertia.

ਜੜਤ (jaṛat) *n f* Inlaying, insetting,

embedding, fixing; Inlay or inset work.

ਜੜਨਾ (jarnaa) *v* To fit, to strike, to set (jewels), to join.

ਜੜੀ (jaree) *n f* Herb medicainal herb. Also **ਜੜੀ ਬੂਟੀ**

ਜਾਇਆ (jaaiyaa) *n m* Born, son, offspring.

ਜ਼ਾਇਆ (zaaiyaa) *a* Waste, wasted in vain; ~**ਹੋਣਾ** To go waste, to be in vain.

ਜ਼ਾਇਕਾ (zaaikaa) *n m* Taste.

ਜਾਇਦਾਦ (jaaidaad) *n f* Property, estate, assets.

ਜਾਸਤੀ (jastee) *n f* High handedness, excess, oppression, injustice.

ਜਾਹਲ (jaahal) *a* Vulgar, unrefined, uncultured, untutored, lacking sophistication, uneducated, illiterate, ignorant, backward, stupid, rustic, boorish, uncivilized.

ਜਾਗਣਾ (jaagnaa) *v* To get up from the bed, to awake, to rise.

ਜਾਂਗਲੀ (jaanglee) *a* Wild, bestial, aboriginal, sylvan.

ਜਾਂਘੀਆ (jaanghiaa) *n m* Shorts, underwear, napkin (for child).

ਜਾਂਚ (jaanch) *n f* Trial, audit, inspection, investigation, scrutiny, assessment.

ਜਾਂਚਣਾ (jaanchnaa) *v* To examine, to calculate, to scrutinize, to inspect, to ascertain, to question.

ਜਾਚਨਾ (jaachnaa) *n f* Prayer.

ਜਾਣਕਾਰ (jaankaar) *a* Who knows, knower, knowing, knowledgeable, well-informed, familiar, conversant, acquainted; Cognisant.

ਜਾਣਕਾਰੀ (jaankaaree) *n f* Knowledge, information, familiarity, conversance, acquaintance, exeprience, understanding.

ਜਾਣਨਾ (jaannaa) *v* To know, to see, to consider, to comprehend.

ਜਾਣਾ (jaanaa) *v* To go, to depart, to continue.

ਜਾਤਕ (jaatak) *n m* Child, new born babe.

ਜਾਤਰੀ (jaatree) *n m* Traveller, pilgrim.

ਜ਼ਾਤੀ (zaatee) *a* Personal, self, individual, specific.

ਜਾਦੂ (jaadoo) *n m* Magic, charm, spell, black art, enchantment; ~**ਗਰ** Magician, wizard; ~**ਟੂਣਾ** Sorcery, black art.

ਜਾਨ (jaan) *n f* Life, essence, vital force, spirit, strength; ~**ਉੱਤੇ ਖੇਡਣਾ** To be ready, to stake one's life; ~**ਸੁਕਣੀ** To be much afraid or worried; ~**ਕਢਣੀ** To put too much trouble, to kill; ~ਖਪਾਉਣੀ To work very hard; ~ਦੇਣੀ To die, to scrifice one's life; ~ਪੈਣੀ To come to life, to get relief; ~ਸ਼ੀਨ Successor'e heir; ~ਦਾਰ Organic, living; ~ਬਾਜ਼ Brave, courageous; ~ਮਾਰੀ Hard work.

ਜਾਨਵਰ (jaanwar) *n m* Animal, beast.

ਜਾਨੀ (jaanee) *a* Dear, love, beloved, sweet heart; ~ਦੁਸ਼ਮਨ Deadly foe; ~ਦੋਸਤ Fast friend, bosom friend.

ਜਾਪਣਾ (jaapṇaa) *v* To feel, to appear, to seem.

ਜ਼ਾਫ਼ਰਾਨ (zaafraan) *n* Saffron.

ਜ਼ਾਬਤਾ (zaabtaa) *n m* Control, code, procedure, discipline.

ਜ਼ਾਬਰ (zaabar) *a* Oppressor, tyrant.

ਜਾਮ (jaam) *n* (1) Wine glass, bowl; (2) Fruit jam; (3) Traffic jam.

ਜਾਮਾ (jaamaa) *n m* Garment, robe, gown, vestment.

ਜਾਰੀ (jaaree) *a* Continued, in force, running, current; ~ਕਰਨਾ To issue, to commence, to enforce; ~ਰਖਣਾ To continue, to carry on, to sustain.

ਜਾਲ (jaal) *n m* Net, web, trap, mesh, network.

ਜਾਲ੍ਹ (jaalh) *n m* Forgery, deception; ~ਸਾਜ Forger; ~ਸਾਜ਼ੀ Forgery.

ਜਾਲਣਾ (jaalṇaa) *v* To burn, to ignite,

to light; To vex, to irritate; To endure, to suffer.

ਜ਼ਾਲਮ (zaalam) *a* Tyrannical, barbarous, cruel, oppressive, brutal.

ਜਾਲਾ (jaalaa) *n m* Cobweb, net moss, spider's web; ਅਖਾਂ ਦਾ~ Cataract.

ਜਾਲੀ (jaalee) *n f* Network, snood, gauze, lattice; ~ਦਾਰ Gauzy, neted, latticed.

ਜਾਲ੍ਹੀ (jaalhee) *a* Forged, fake, fobricate, spurious. Also ਜਾਅਲੀ

ਜਾੜਾ (jaaṛaa) *n m* Winter, cold weather.

ਜਿਉਣਾ (jiuṇaa) *v* To live, to exist, to be alive.

ਜਿਸ (jis) *pron* Who, which, that; Whom, where, what (other than interrogative); ~ਕਰਕ/ ~ਕਾਰਨ Wherefor; ~ਤੇ Whereon, whereupon, where at; ~ਥਾਂ Where; ~ਦਮ When; ~ਨਾਲ Whereby, where with, with which or wnom; ~ਨੂੰ Whom; ~ਵੇਲੇ When, at the time when.

ਜਿਸਮ (jisam) *n m* Body; ~ਮਾਨੀ Corporol.

ਜਿਹੜਾ (jeṛa) *pron* Who, which, that, what; ~ਕਿਹੜਾ Anyone, anybody; Any Tom, Dick or Harry.

ਜਿਹਾ (jihaa) *adv* Like, similar, as;

~ਕਿਹਾ Howsoever.

ਜ਼ਿਕਰ (zikar) *n m* Mention, cursory remarks.

ਜਿਕਣ (jikaṇ) *adv* According as, as if, for instance, for example.

ਜਿਗਰ (jigar) *n m* Liver, bile; ~ਦਾ ਟੁਕੜਾ Son, life.

ਜਿਗਰਾ (jigraa) *n m* Courage, bravery, patience, perseverance.

ਜਿਗਰੀ (jigree) *a* Intimate, friendly.

ਜਿੱਚ (jichch) *a* Vexed, annoyed, irritated, sullen, peeved, peevish. Also ਜਿੱਚ

ਜਿੱਜੀ (jijjee) *n f* Thick or dried nasal mucus.

ਜਿਠਾਣੀ (jiṭhaaṇee) *n* Wife of husband's elder brother, sister-in-law.

ਜਿਠੇਰਾ (jiṭheraa) *a* Elder.

ਜਿਤਨਾ (jitnaa) *v* To win, to conquer, to vanquish.

ਜਿੱਥੇ (jitthe) *adv* Where; ~ਕਿੱਥੇ Wherever; ~ਵੀ Wheresoever.

ਜਿੱਥੋਂ (jithon) *adv* From where, whence.

ਜ਼ਿਦ (zid) *n f* Obstinancy, persistance, stubbornness; ~ਲ Obstinate, bull headed.

ਜਿੱਦਣ (jiddaṇ) *adv* On the day when (ਜਿਸ+ਦਿਨ) on (a specified or appointed) day.

ਜ਼ਿੰਦਗੀ (zindagee) *n* Life, age, lifetime; ~ਹਰਾਮ ਹੋਣੀ To be miserable; ~ਦੇ ਦਿਨ ਕਟਣੇ To simply exist, to carry on somehow.

ਜ਼ਿੰਦਾ (zindaa) *a* Living, animate; ~ਦਿਲ Lively, vivacious, gay, buoyant; ~ਦਿਲੀ Vivacity, liveliness, gaiety, blithness; ~ਬਾਦ Long live, may....live long. Also ਜਿੰਦਾ

ਜਿੱਦੀ (ziddee) *a* Obstinate, pertinacious, stiff, stubborn.

ਜਿੰਨ (jinn) *n m* Ghost, devil, demon.

ਜ਼ਿਬਾਹ (zibbaah) *n m* Act of killing or slaughtering.

ਜ਼ਿੰਮਾ (zimaa) *n m* Responsibility, undertaking, trust, charge, accountability, liability, onus; ~ਵਾਰ Responsible liable.

ਜ਼ਿਮੀਂਦਾਰ (zimeendaar) *n m* Landlord, landholder.

ਜ਼ਿਮੀਂਦਾਰਾ (zimeendaaraa) *a n m* Pertaining to agriculture or farming.

ਜ਼ਿਮੀਂਦਾਰੀ (zimeendaaree) *n f* Landlordism, landed estate; Agriculture, farming.

ਜ਼ਿੰਮੇ (zime) *adv* Under responsibility, incharge; ~ਵਾਰ Responsible, liable.

ਜ਼ਿੱਲਤ (zillat) *n f* Insult, disgrace,

dishonour.

ਜਿਲਦ (jilad) *n f* Binding (of book), cover, ligament; **~ਸਾਜ਼** Bookbinder.

ਜ਼ਿਲ੍ਹਾ (zillaa) *n m* District, commune.

ਜਿੱਲਾ (jillaa) *a* Lazy, lethargic, sluggish.

ਜਿਵੇਂ (jiven) *adv* As, in the manner of; As if, as though, so to say, for example, for instance; **~ਕਿ** As it were; For example, for instance; **~ਕਿਵੇਂ** Somehow, somehow or the other, by any means, by hook or crook, by means fair or foul, howsoever.

ਜੀ (Jee) *n m v* Mind, heart, soul, live; Intial term 'yes', 'sir' etc; **~ਆਉਣਾ** To fall in love with; **~ਸੜ ਜਾਣਾ** To be grieved; **~ਕਡਣਾ** To take courage; **~ਕਰਨਾ** To desire; **~ਖੱਟਾ ਹੋਣਾ** To feel disgusted; **~ਖੋਲ ਕੇ** Freely, heartly; **~ਚੁਰਾਉਣਾ** To shirk, to desist from work; **~ਤਰਸਣਾ** To long, to yearn; **~ਫਿਕਾ ਹੋਣਾ** To be disenchanted; **~ਭਰ ਆਉਣਾ** To be moved to tears; **~ਭਰਨਾ** To be fully satisfied; **~ਰਖਣਾ** To gratify, to appeas; **~ਲਾਉਣਾ** To pay attention to.

ਜੀਭ (jeebh) *n f* Tongue; **~ਚਲਤੀ** To have a fluent tongue; **~ਚਲਾਉਣੀ**

To talk too much; **~ਪਕੜਨੀ** To silent, to stop speaking.

ਜੀਵ (jeev) *n m* Creature, animal, mortal, soul.

ਜੀਵਨ (jeevan) *n m* Life, existence; **~ਸਾਥੀ** Life partner, husband.

ਜੀਵਨੀ (jeevnee) *n f* Biograply.

ਜ਼ੁਕਾਮ (zookaam) *n m* Cold, coryza.

ਜੁਗਤ (jugat) *n f* Method, manner, way, skill, skillfulness, knack; Tool; Device, contrivance; Plan, scheme, expedient.

ਜੁਗਨੀ (jugnee) *n f* A mode of Punjabi folk song; A heart shaped ornament for the neck.

ਜੁਗਨੂੰ (jugnoon) *n m* Glow-worm, firefly, glowfly, lightning bug.

ਜੁਗਾਲਣਾ (jugaalṇaa) *v* To chew.

ਜੁਗਾਲੀ (jugaalee) *n f* The chewing of the cud, rumination.

ਜੁਗਾੜ (jugaaṛ) *n m* Manoeuvre, contrivance, arrangement.

ਜੁਝਾਰੂ (juhjaaru) *a n m* Fighter, valiant; Heroic, militant, aggressive, vigorously combative; Intreped, fearless.

ਜੁਟਣਾ (juṭṇaa) *v* To unite, to be assembled; To entangled, to cohabit; To be ivolved in something with determination and vigour, to work seriously.

ਜੁਤਣਾ (jutṇaa) *v* To be yoked, to be engaged in a work.

ਜੁੱਤੀ (juttee) *n f* Shoe, boot, slipper.

ਜੁਦਾ (judaa) *a* Seperate, distinct, different, apart.

ਜੁਦਾਈ (judaaee) *n f* Separation from a dear one.

ਜੁੱਧ (juddh) *n m* Battle, fighting, war, skirmish, hostilities, armed encounter, warfare, combat action or engagement; ~ਕਰਨਾ To fight, to fight a war; ~ਛਿੜਨਾ For war to break out or commence; ~ਦਾ ਮੈਦਾਨ Battlefield.

ਜੁੰਬਸ਼ (jumbash) *n f* Movement; Motion.

ਜੁਰਮ (juram) *n m* Crime, offence, charge, fault, guilt.

ਜੁਰਮਾਨਾ (jurmaanaa) *n m* Fine, penalty.

ਜੁਰਾਬ (juraab) *n f* One of a pair of socks or stockings; Usually ਜੁਰਾਬਾਂ

ਜ਼ੁਲਫ਼ (zulaf) *n f* Curl, lock of hair, ringlet, tress.

ਜ਼ੁਲਮ (zulam) *a* Tyranny, cruelty, oppression, brutality, outrage.

ਜ਼ੁਲਮੀ (zulamee) *n m* Tyrannical, oppressive.

ਜੁਲਾਹਾ (julaahaa) *n m a* Weaver; Timid, fool.

ਜੁੜਨਾ (jurnaa) *v* To be joined, to be united, to collect, to associate, to get together.

ਜੁੜਵਾਂ (jurvaan) *a* Twin, conjoint, synthetic, cohesive.

ਜੂੰ (joon) *n f* A louse, pediculus.

ਜੂਆ (juaa) *n m* Gambling, dice, any game of chance played with stakes; Grave risk; ~ਖਾਨਾ Gambling house, gamblers'den.

ਜੂਝਣਾ (joojhṇaa) *v* To fight, to struggle.

ਜੂਠ (jooth) *n f* Garbage, refuse, leavings, ort, offal, leftover.

ਜੂਠਾ (joothaa) *a* Polluted, contaminated by taste or touch, partially eaten or drunk.

ਜੂੜਨਾ (joornaa) *v* To bind, to yoke, to tie.

ਜੂੜਾ (jooraa) *n m* Tuft, knot of braided hair, top knot.

ਜੇਠ (jeth) *n m* Elder brother of husband, brother-in-law.

ਜੇਠਾ (jethaa) *a* First born, senior.

ਜੇਬ (jeb) *n m* Pocket, pouch.

ਜ਼ੇਵਰ (zevar) *n m* Ornaments, jewellary.

ਜੋਸ਼ (josh) *n m* Zeal, enthusiasm, passion, emotion, fervency excitement, upsurge.

ਜੋਖਣਾ (jokhṇaa) *v* To estimate, to

weigh, to appraise, to span.

ਜੋਗੀ (jogee) *n m* Ascetic, saint, devotee.

ਜੋਟਾ (jotaa) *n m* Twosome, duo, couple, pair.

ਜੋਣਾ (jonaa) *v* To yoke, harness, to press into work, to engage, to force.

ਜੋਤਸ਼ (jotash) *n m* Astrology, astronomy.

ਜੋਤਸ਼ੀ (jotshee) *n m* Astrologer, fortune teller.

ਜੋਤਣਾ (jotnaa) To yoke, to harness. Also **ਜੋਣਾ** and **ਵਾਹੁਣਾ**

ਜੋਬਨ (joban) *n m* Lustre, bloom of youth, brilliance, puberty.

ਜੋਰ (zor) *n m* Strength, force, power, effort, influence, vigour, vitality, momentum, pressure, impetus; **~ਚਲਣਾ** To have sway; **~ਜੋਰ ਦਾ** Bitterly, intense; **~ਦੇਣਾ** To emphasize; **~ਮਾਰਨਾ** To try

level best, to compel, to make frantic efforts; **~ਅਜ਼ਮਾਈ** Trial of strength; **~ਸ਼ੋਰ** Zest, enthusiasm; **~ਜ਼ਬਰ** Oppression; **~ਜ਼ਬਰਦਸਤੀ** Duress, coercion; **~ਦਾਰ** Vigorous, energetic, powerful.

ਜੋਰਾਵਰ (joraavar) *a* (For persons) strong, powerful, mighty; Bully.

ਜੋਰੂ (joroo) *n f* Wife, life partner.

ਜੋੜ (jor) *n m* Joint, sum, addition, tally, connection, total, match, relevancy, bond, fellow; **~ਦਾਰ** Having joints, not of one piece, seamy.

ਜੋੜਨਾ (jornaa) *v* To join, to sum up, to link, to collect, to cement, to gather, to set, to connect, to paste, to attach, to unite.

ਜੋੜਾ (joraa) *n m* Couple, pair, twin.

ਜੌਹਰ (jauhar) *n m* Excellence, talent, essence.

ਜੌਹਰੀ (jauhree) *n m* Jeweller.

ਝ

ਝ The fourteenth letter of Gurmukhi alphabets, pronouned as 'Jhajhaa'.

ਝਉਣਾ (jhaunaa) v To wither, to sage, to lose heart.

ਝਉਲਾ (jhaulaa) n m Glimpse, glance.

ਝਈ (jhaee) n f Sudden, furious attack, charge; Gritting teeth in anger; Crouching; ~ਲੈ ਕੇ ਪੈਣਾ To attack suddenly or furiously.

ਝੱਸਣਾ (jhasnaa) v To rub, to massage, (with oil, etc.).

ਝਕ (jhak) n f Shyness, hesitation, timidity. Also ਝਿਝਕ

ਝਕਝੋਰਨਾ (jhakjhornaa) v To jerk, to shake violently.

ਝਕਣਾ (jhaknaa) v To hesitate, to feel shy, to blench, to quail.

ਝਕਾਉਣਾ (jhakaaunaa) v To tease, to tentalize, to dodge.

ਝੰਕਾਰ (jhankaar) n f Jingling sound, tinkling sound.

ਝੱਕੀ (jhakkee) a Hesitant, shy, reluctant, diffident.

ਝਕੋਲਣਾ (jhakolnaa) v To Shake, to stir.

ਝਖ (jhakh) n m Nonsensical talk;

~ਮਾਰਨਾ To waste time for nothing.

ਝਖਮਾਰ (jhakhmaar) a To shake, to rock, swing; To muddle, to rinse. Also ਘਰੋਲਣਾ

ਝਖਣਾ (jhakhnaa) v To rave.

ਝੱਖੜ (jhakhar) n m a Storm, strong wind, tempest, gust, hurricane, gust; Crazy, cranky, whimsical.

ਝੰਖਾਰ (jhankhaar) n f Interwined branches, of bushes.

ਝੱਗ (jhagg) n m Foam, scum, lather, spume; ~ਦਾਰ Foamy, frothy; Lathery.

ਝਗੜਨਾ (jhagarnaa) v To quarrel, to wrangle, to altercate, to squabble, to dispute.

ਝਗੜਾ (jhagraa) n m Conflict, quarrel, tussel, dispute, altercation, wrangling; ~ਲੂ Contentious, rowdy, quarrelsome, bellicose.

ਝੱਗਾ (jhaggaa) n m Frock, a loose garment for babies, shirt.

ਝੰਜਟ (jhanjat) n m Botheration, encumberance, perplexity, difficulty.

ਝੱਜਰ (jhajjar) n m Small porous earthen pitcher with a long neck.

ਤੌਬਾ (taubaa) *n f* Penitence, repentence, determination never to do again bad some things; ~ਕਰਨੀ To forswear, to repent, to vow never to repeat; ~ਤੋਬਾ An expression of horror. Also ਤੋਬਾ

ਤੌਰ (taur) *n m* Method, mode, manner, fashion, way; ~ਤਰੀਕਾ Behaviour, conduct.

ਤੌਲੀਆ (tauliaa) *n m* Towel.

ਤੌਲੇ (taule) *adv* Hastily, quickly, hurriedly.

ਤੌੜਾ (tauṛaa) *n m* Earthern cooking pot.

ਥ

ਥ Twenty second letter of Gurmukhi alphabets, pronounced as 'thathaa'.

ਥਹੀ (thaee) *n f* Pile; Wad; Small heap or stack.

ਥਹੁ (Thaho) *n m* Inkling, clue, trace, location, information; Recollection, memory; method; ~ਪਤਾ Address, location; ~ਟਿਕਾਣਾ Whereabout, place; ~ਲਾਉਣਾ To Trace, to locate, to discover.

ਥਕਣਾ (thaknaa) *v* To be tired, to be weary, to be fatigued.

ਥਕਾਊ (thakaaoo) *a* Tiring, wearing, wearying, gruelling, wearisome, fatiguing, tiresome; Exasperating, irksome, tedious.

ਥਕਾਉਣਾ (thakaaunaa) *v* To tire, to weary, to fatigue.

ਥਕਾਵਟ (thakaavat) *n f* Weariness, fatigue, exhaustion, tiresomeness; ~ਲਗਣਾ To get tired, to get exhausted.

ਥਣ (than) *n m* Teat, udder, breast.

ਥੱਥਲਾ (thathlaa) *n m* Stammerer; Also ਥੱਥਾ

ਥਥਲਾਉਣਾ (thathlaaunaa) *v* To stammer, to lisp.

ਥੱਥਾ (thathaa) *a* Stammerer, stutterer.

ਥਪਕਣਾ (thapaknaa) *v* To pat, to soothe, to solace, to tap.

ਥਪਕੀ (thapkee) *n f* Pat, stroke.

ਥਪਣਾ (thapnaa) *v* To dab, to be smear, to impose, to apportion.

ਥੱਪੜ (thappar) *n m* Slap, spank, flap.

ਥਪੇੜਾ (thaperaa) *n m* Forceful slap; Also ਥਪੇੜ

ਥੱਬਾ (thabbaa) *n m* Heap, pile (grass or vegetable or papers), united bundle.

ਥੱਬੀ (thabbee) *n m* A smaller bundle or pile.

ਥੰਮ੍ਹ (thamm) *n m* Pillar, Support, post.

ਥੰਮ੍ਹਣਾ (thammnaa) *v* To stop, to cease, to support, to restrain.

ਥਰਕਣਾ (tharaknaa) *v* To tremble, to shake, to quake, to waver.

ਥਰਥਰਾਉਣਾ (tharthraaunaa) *v* To tremble, to quiver, to shiver, to shake, to trill, to vibrate.

ਥਲ (thal) *n m* Place, dryland, sandy region; ~ਸੈਨਾ Army, land forces.

ਥਲਕਾ (thalkaa) *n m* Sensation; ~ਮਚਾ

ਦੇਣਾ To create sensation.

ਥਲਾ (thallaa) *n m* Base, basement, plinth, ground, footing, bottom, lower part.

ਥੱਲੇ (thalle) *adv* Under, beneath, below.

ਥੜ੍ਹਾ (tharraa) *n m* Platform, dais, stage, rostrum.

ਥਾਂ (thaan) *n f* Place, locality, site, spot, situation, venue, room; ~ਦੇਣੀ To accommodate, to house, to make room; ~ਬਦਲੀ Transfer, replacement, displacement; ~ਮੱਲਣੀ To occupy, to supplant.

ਥਾਉਂ (thaaun) *adv* Instead of, in place of, for.

ਥਾਹ (thaah) *n f* Bottom, depth, limit; ~ਪਾਉਣੀ To understand, to fathom; ~ਲੜਨੀ To seek refuge.

ਥਾਣਾ (thaanaa) *n m* Police station.

ਥਾਨੇਦਾਰ (thaanedaar) *n m* Police inspector office incharge of a police station.

ਥਾਨ (thaan) *n m* Roll of cloth (20 to 40 metres); Place, spot, site.

ਥਾਪਣਾ (thaapnaa) *v* To appoint, to fix, to engage, to install, to set.

ਥਾਲੀ (thaalee) *n f* Metal plate, small dish; ~ਦਾ ਬੈਗੰਣ Fickel person.

ਥਿਤ (thit) *n f* Date.

ਥਿੰਦ (thind) *n f* Grease, Wax. Also

ਥਿੰਧ

ਥਿੰਦਾ (thindaa) *a* Greasy, oily.

ਥਿੰਦਿਆਈ (thindiaaee) *n f* Greasiness, oilness, lubricity.

ਥਿੜਕਣ (thirkan) *n f* Deviation, slipping, aberration.

ਥਿੜਕਨਾ (thiraknaa) *v* To err, to be unsettled, to stagger, to slip, to stumble.

ਥਿੜਕਵਾਂ (thirkvaan) *a* Stumbling, staggering, unstable; uneven, rough slippery (ground or path).

ਥੁਕ (thuk) *n f* Spit, saliva, sputum; ~ਕੇ ਚਟਣਾ To break one's promise; ~ਦੇਣਾ To spit, to leave, to give up; ~ਲਾਉਣੀ To deceive, to dupe, to cheat.

ਥੁਕਣਾ (thuknaa) *v* To spit, to spittle, to curse.

ਥੁਥਨੀ (thuthnee) *n f* Animal's mouth; snout, muzzle. Also ਥੁਥਨੀ

ਥੁੰਨ (thunn) *n m* snout; ~ਮੂੰਨ Silent, slullen, illhumoured.

ਥੁੜ (thur) *n f* Want, scarcity, paucity, dearth, inadequacy, need, rarity, shortage.

ਥੁੜਨਾ (thurnaa) *v* To be in want, to feel hard up.

ਥੈਲਾ (thailaa) *n m* Sack, large bag.

ਥੈਲੀ (thailee) *n f* Small bag, pouch, purse, follicle, alary.

ਥੋਕ (thok) *a* Wholesale, bulk.

ਥੋਥਾ (thothaa) *a* Hollow, empty, worthless; **~ਪਣ** Hollowness, emptiness, vacuousness.

ਥੋਥੜਾ (thothṛaa) *n m* Snout of beast, puffed face.

ਥੋਪਣਾ (thopṇaa) *v* To foist upon, to impose upon.

ਥੋੜਾ (thoṛaa) *a* Small, inadequate, little, insufficient, meagre; **~ਥੋੜਾ** By & by, in small amounts; **~ਬਹੁਤਾ** More or less about.

ਥੌਹ (thau) *n m* Memory, recollection; estimate, measure; **~ਟਿਕਾਣਾ** Whereabouts; address; **~ਲਾਉਣਾ** Estimate, assess, to have or get a measure of.

ਦ

ਦ Twenty third letter of Gurmukhi alphabets, pronouned as 'daddaa'.

ਦਇਆ (daiaa) *n f* Pity, compassion, mercy, clemency, kindness, sympathy; **~ਲੂ/~ਵਾਨ** Merciful, kind, compassionate, gracious.

ਦਸਖਤ (daskhat) *n m* Signature, handwriting. Also **ਦਸਤਖਤ**

ਦੱਸਣਾ (dassṇaa) *v* To tell, to direct, to imply, to inform, to intimate, to acquaint.

ਦਸਤ (dast) *n m* (1) Hand; (2) Loose motion, dysentry, diarrhoea; **~ਕਾਰ** Handicraftman, artisan; **~ਕਾਰੀ** Handicraft, handwork; **~ਗੀਰ** Helper, supporter, succourer; **~ਲਗਨੇ** To suffer from diarrhoea.

ਦਸਤਕ (dastak) *n f* Knock, knocking.

ਦਸਤਰਖਾਨ (dastarkhaan) *n m* Dining table; Table cloth of a dining table.

ਦਸਤਾ (dastaa) *n m* Quire (of paper); Grip, helve, shank, handle of an instrument; Pounder, pestle; Troop, corps, squad.

ਦਸਤਾਨਾ (dastanaa) *n m* Glove, guantlet.

ਦਸਤਾਰ (dastaar) *n f* Turban; **~ਬੰਦੀ** Turban ceremony; Consecration.

ਦਸਤਾਵੇਜ਼ (dastavez) *n m* Document, deed, bond; **~ਖਾਨਾ** Archives.

ਦਸਤੀ (dastee) *a adv* Manual, hand made, through hand; Per bearer.

ਦਸਤੂਰ (dastoor) *n m* Custom, fashion, mode, method, manner, convention.

ਦਸਤੂਰੀ (dasturee) *n f* Customary, legal; Customary commission, perquisite.

ਦਸ਼ਮਲਵ (dashamlav) *n m* Decimal, decimal point.

ਦਸ਼ਮਿਕ (dashmik) *a* Decimal.

ਦਸ਼ਾ (dashaa) *n f* Condition, state, circumstance, position.

ਦਸਾਉਰੀ (dasauree) *a* Imported, foreign. Also **ਦਸੌਰੀ**

ਦਸ਼ਾਬਦੀ (dashabdee) *n f* Decade.

ਦਸੋਰ (dasor) *n m* Foreign country, alien land.

ਦਹਾਈ (dahaaee) *n f* Place and value of tens digit in a number.

ਦਹਾਕਾ (dahaakaa) *n m* Tens, decade.

ਦਹਾੜਨਾ (dahaaṛnaa) *v* To roar.

ਦਹਿਸ਼ਤ (daheshat) *n f* Terror, panic, awe, dread, fear; **~ਗਰਦ** Terrorist; **~ਗਰਦੀ** Terrorism; **~ਗੋਜ਼** Horrible; **~ਨਾਕ** Fearful, Terrible, dreadful.

ਦਹਿਲਣਾ (dahelnaa) *v* To tremble with fear, to be terrified, to dread, to get freightened.

ਦਹਿਲੀਜ਼ (dahileez) *n f* Doorsill, threshold. Also **ਦਲ਼੍ਹੀਜ਼**

ਦਹੀ (dahee) *n n* Curd, youghurt, coagulated milk; **~ਜਮਾਉਣਾ** To curdle.

ਦਹੇਜ (dahej) *n* Dowry. Also **ਦਹੇਜ਼**

ਦਕਿਆਨੂਸ (dakiaanoos) *n m a* Stereotyped natured man, hackneyed viewed man.

ਦਕਿਆਨੂਸੀ (dakiaanoosee) *a* Stereotyped or hackneyed; outdated, obsolete, conservative.

ਦਖਣ (dakhaṇ) *n m* The south, Deccan.

ਦਖਣਾ (dakhṇaa) *n f* Donation, charity, alms. Also **ਦੱਛਣਾ**

ਦਖਲ (dakhal) *n m* Interference, intervention, intrusion, intermission, occupancy, possesion; **~ਅੰਦਾਜੀ** Interference, intervention, meddling; **~ਦੇਣਾ** To interfere, to invene, to interpose, to meddle.

ਦੰਗ (dang) *a* Astonished, amazed, wonder-struck; **~ਕਰਨਾ** To astonish, to surprise.

ਦੰਗਈ (dangaee) *n m* Riotous person or mob, one causing or taking part in hooligan, rioter.

ਦਗਣਾ (dagṇaa) *v* To be fired, to sparkle, to be kindled.

ਦੰਗਲ (dangal) *n m* Arena, wrestling tournament.

ਦੰਗਲੀ (danglee) *a* Qurrelsome.

ਦਗਾ (dagaa) *n m* Betrayel, deceit, disloyalty, cheating; **~ਬਾਜ਼** Betrayer, deceiver, disloyal, treacherous.

ਦੰਗਾ (dangaa) *n m* Riot, turbulance, disturbance, hub-hub; **~ਫਸਾਦ** Riot, rowdyism, turbulance.

ਦੰਡ (danḍ) *n m* Punishment, penalty, sentence, fine. Also **ਡੰਨ**

ਦੰਤ (dant) *a* Mammoth.

ਦੰਦ (dand) *n m* Tooth; **ਹਾਥੀ ਦੇ~**Tusk; **~ਕਢਣੇ** To extract teeth, to smirk, to laugh, teething; **~ਸਾਜ਼** Dentist; **~ਕਥਾ** Hearsay; **~ਖਟੇ ਕਰਨੇ** To discourage, to defeat; **~ਨਿਕਲਣੇ** To teethe.

ਦਦਿਆਹੁਰਾ (dadiahura) *n m* Husband's grand father.

ਦਦੇਹਸ (dadehas) *n f* Grandmother-in-law; mother of father-in-law.

ਦੰਦੇਹਾਰ (dandehaar) *a* Dented, dentale, denticulate, toothed, serrated.

ਦਨਾ (danaa) *n m* Wise, intelligent, knowledgeable; wiseacre.

ਦਨਾਈ (danaaee) *n f* Wisdom; intelligence.

ਦਫ਼ਤਰ (daftar) *n m* Office, bureau; ~ਸ਼ਾਹੀ Bureaucracy.

ਦਫ਼ਤਰੀ (daftaree) *a n m* Official, ministerial, record keeper; Book-binder.

ਦਫ਼ਨ (dafan) *a* Buried, entombed.

ਦਫ਼ਨਾਉਣਾ (dafnaaunaa) *v* To bury, to entomb.

ਦਫ਼ਾ (dafaa) *n f a* (1) Clause, section of law; (2) A Single term, One time, one turn; ~ਲਾਉਣੀ To frame a charge; Out of the way; ~ਕਰਨਾ To remove, to repel, to bundle off.

ਦਫ਼ੇਦਾਰ (dafedaar) *n m* Corporal.

ਦਬਕਣਾ (dabaknaa) *v* To hide (in fear), to lurk, to crouch.

ਦਬਕਾ (dabkaa) *n m* Verbal threat, chiding, snub; Cellar, vault.

ਦਬਕਾਉਣਾ (dabkaaunaa) *v* To threaten, to intimidate, to snub, to bully.

ਦਬਣਾ (dabnaa) *v* To bury, to entomb; To press, to supress, to crush, to succumb; To conceal.

ਦਬਦਬਾ (dabdabaa) *n m* Sway, grandeur.

ਦਬਾਉਣਾ (dabaaunaa) *v* To press, to overpower, to compel, to bury, to crush. Also ਦਬਾਣਾ

ਦਬੀਰ (dabeer) *n m* Scribe, writer, clerk.

ਦਬੂ (daboo) *a* Recessive, servile.

ਦਬੇਲ (dabel) *a* Servile, timid, depressed, under dog; ~ਕਰਨਾ To tame.

ਦਬੋਚਣਾ (dabochnaa) *v* To catch hold of, to suppress.

ਦੰਭ (damb) *n m* Hypocrisy, dissimulation, fraud.

ਦੰਭੀ (dambee) *a* Hypocrite, coxcomb, ostentations.

ਦਮ (dam) *n m* Breath, endurance; ~ਤੋੜਨਾ To die, to breathe one's last; ~ਭਰ ਲਈ for a while, for a short duration Instant, moment; ~ਮਾਰਨਾ To boast; ~ਲਾਉਣਾ To smoke; ~ਲੈਣਾ To take rest.

ਦਮਕ (damak) *n f* Lustre, brilliance.

ਦਮਕਣਾ (damaknaa) *v* To shine, to glitter.

ਦਮਦਮਾ (damdamaa) *n m* Mound, battery, raised platform; Temporary resting place.

ਦਮਨ (daman) *n m* Repression, subjugation; ~ਕਰਨਾ To suppress, to crush, to subjugate; to quell.

ਦਮੜਾ (damṛaa) *n m* Rupee, wealth.

ਦਮਾ (damaa) *n m* Asthma.

ਦਮਾਮਾ (damaamaa) *n m* Large kettle drum, pomp and show.

ਦਰ (dar) *n* (1) Door, gate; (2) Rate, price.

ਦਰਸ਼ਕ (darshak) *n m* Spectator, on-looker, visitor, sightseer.

ਦਰਸ਼ਨ (darshan) *n m* (1) Philosophy; (2) Face, view, sight, appearance, glimpse, holy presence; ~ਸ਼ਾਸਤਰ Philosophy.

ਦਰਸ਼ਨੀ (darshanee) *a* Worthseeing, good looking, handsome, beautiful.

ਦਰਕ (darak) *n m* Fear; Loose motion caused by intense fear; Crack, fissure.

ਦਰਕਣਾ (darknaa) *v* To be cracked, to be split, to be freightened.

ਦਰਕਾਰ (darkaar) *n m a* Need, necessity; A needed, necessary, required.

ਦਰਕਿਨਾਰ (darkinaar) *adv* Apart from, not to speak of, besides.

ਦਰੱਖਤ (darakkhat) *n m* Tree.

ਦਰਖਾਸਤ (darkhaast) *n f* Application, appeal, petition, request; ~ਕਰਤਾ Applicant, appellant.

ਦਰਗੜੀ (daragḍee) *a* Half backed.

ਦਰਗਾਹ (dargaah) *n f* Tomb of a saint, shrine, mosque, threshold, court of law.

ਦਰਜ (daraj) *a* Entered, registered.

ਦਰਜਨ (darjan) *n f* Dozen, twelve in number.

ਦਰਜਾ (darjaa) *n m* Class, degree, rank, category, standard, grade, division.

ਦਰਜ਼ੀ (darjee) *n m* Tailor; ~ਗੀਰੀ Tailoring.

ਦਰਜੇਦਾਰ (darjedaar) *a* Graduated, marked with degrees.

ਦਰਜੇਵਾਰ (darjewaar) *adv a* Gradually, gradual.

ਦਰਦ (darad) *n m* Pain, ache, pathos, agony, pity, mercy, sympathy; ਬੇ~ Hard hearted, pitiless; ~ਨਾਕ painful, dreadful, pitiable; ~ਵੰਡਾਉਣਾ To sympathize.

ਦਰਦੀ (dardee) *a* Sympathiser.

ਦਰਪਣ (darpaṇ) *n m* Mirror, looking glass.

ਦਰਬ (darb) *n m* Wealth, riches, property.

ਦਰਬਾਨ (darbaan) *n m* Gatekeeper;

watchman, gateman, janitor.

ਦਰਬਾਰ (darbaar) *n m* Royal court, hall of audience.

ਦਰਬਾਰੀ (darbaaree) *n m a* Courtier, related to court.

ਦਰਮਿਆਨ (darmiaan) *n m adv* Centre, middle; Amid, between, in the course of, amongst, amidst.

ਦਰਮਿਆਨਾ (darmiaanaa) *a* Average, moderate, middle.

ਦ੍ਰਵ (drav) *n m* Liquid, fluid; ~**ਸੀਲ** Fusible.

ਦਰਵਾਜ਼ਾ (darwaazaa) *n m* Door, gate, entrance. Also **ਦਰ-ਦਵਾਰ**

ਦਰਵੇਸ਼ (darvesh) *n m* Hermit, a muslim saint, mendicant, recluse, beggar.

ਦਰੜ (darar) *a* Coarsely ground, crushed; crushed grain (used as cattle feed); ~**ਫਰੜ** Crushed partly or superficially; (something) done haphazardly, half-baked.

ਦਰੜਨਾ (dararnaa) *v* To crush, grind; to destroy, annihilate.

ਦੱਰਾ (darraa) *n m* Mountain pass, pass.

ਦਰਾਣੀ (daraanee) *n f* Sister-in-law, wife of husband's younger brother.

ਦਰਾੜ (daraar) *n f* Fissure, crevice, cleft, crack, slit, opening; rift, chink; Distance or break (in relations).

ਦਰਿਆ (dariaa) *n m* River, stream; ~**ਦਿਲ** Large-hearted, generous, benevolent, charitable; ~**ਦਿਲੀ** Large-heartedness, generosity, benevolence, charitableness.

ਦਰਿਆਈ (dariaaee) *a* Riverine, fluvial, riparian.

ਦਰਿੰਦਾ (darindaa) *n m* Carnivorous animal, carnivore, any dangerous or ferocious animal, beast.

ਦਰੀ (daree) *n f* Cotton mat or carpet, durrie.

ਦਰੁਸਤ (darust) *a* Correct, right, accurate, true, proper, fit, precise; ~**ਕਰਨਾ** To correct, to amend; to rectify, to adjust, to repair, to set or put right, to improve; to chasten.

ਦਰੋਗਾ (darogaa) *n m* Superintendent; jailor, inspector; Sub-inspector of police, station house officer.

ਦਲ (dal) *n m* Party, organised band, group or team; Armed force, fighting force, army, troop; Swarm, multitude.

ਦਲਣਾ (dalṇaa) *a* To grind coarsely, to bruise with millstones, to crush, to pulverise; To annihilate, destroy.

ਦਲਦਲ (daldal) *n f* Marsh, swamp, bog, marshland; Quagmire, quag.

ਦੱਲਾ (dallaa) *n m* Pimp, procurer, pander, panderer, go-between, tout procuress.

ਦਲਾਲ (dalaal) *n m* Broker, middleman, commission-agent.

ਦਲਾਲੀ (dalaalee) *n f* Profession of ਦਲਾਲ Brokerage, commission.

ਦਲਾਵਰ (dalaavar) *a* Brave. Also ਦਲੇਰ

ਦਲਿੰਦਰ (dalidar) *n m* Sloth, lethargy, laziness, idleness, indolence, sluggishness.

ਦਲਿੰਦਰੀ (daliddaree) *a* Wretched, poor, lethargic, lazy.

ਦਲੀਲ (daleel) *n f* Argument, plea, reason, consideration.

ਦਲੇਰ (daler) *a* Brave, bold, courageous, daring, valiant, dashing; ~ਨਾ Courageous, undaunting.

ਦਲੇਰੀ (daleree) *n f* Valour, courage, boldness, bravery, generosity.

ਦਵਾ (davaa) *n f* Cure, remedy, drug, medicine; ~ਖ਼ਾਨਾ Dispensary, pharmacy; ~ਦਾਰੂ Medication, treatment.

ਦਵਾਈ (dawaee) *n f* Medicine, drug; ~ਕਰਨਾ To treat, to medicate.

ਦਵਾਤ (dwaat) *n f* Inkpot, Inkstand.

ਦਵਾਰ (dwaar) *n m* Gate, door, passage; ~ਪਾਲ Gatekeeper. Also ਦੁਆਰ and ਦਰਵਾਜ਼ਾ

ਦੜਕਾਉਣਾ (daṛkaauṇaa) *v* To snub, to awe.

ਦੜਨਾ (darnaa) *v* To hide, to remain inactive, to keep silent.

ਦੜਬਾ (darbaa) *n m* Hen house, hen-coop, roost, loft.

ਦੜਾ (daraa) *n m* Mixed grain, fruit, etc; any impure, mixed, adulterated or sub-standard stuff. Also called ਦੜੇ ਦਾ ਮਾਲ A kind of gambling. Also called ਸੱਟਾ

ਦਾਅ (daa) *n m* (1) Opportunity, manoevre, trick (in wrestling also), (2) strategem; (3) Turn, bet, stake, wager; ~ਮਾਰਨਾ To make use of a trick. Also ਦਾਉ

ਦਾਅਵਾ (daawaa) *n m* claim, law suit, case, demand; ~ਕਰਨਾ To sue, to claim. Also ਦਾਹਵਾ and ਦਾਵਾ

ਦਾਇਰਾ (daairaa) *n m* Circle, sphere, ring, circuit, society, club.

ਦਾਈ (daaee) *n f* Nurse, midwife.

ਦਾਸ (daas) *n m* Slave, servant, bondsman; ~ਤਾ Slavery, bondage, servitude.

ਦਾਸਤਾਨ (daastaan) *n f* Tale, story, incident.

ਦਾਹ (daah) *n m* Cremation, burning; ~ਸੰਸਕਾਰ Funeral ceremony.

ਦਾਹਵਤ (dahwat) *n f* Invitation, party; ~ਦੇਣਾ To give a feast/party.

ਦਾਖ (daakh) *n f* Dry grape, currant.

ਦਾਖਲ (daakhal) *a* Entered, inserted, admitted; ~ਹੋਣਾ To enter, to introduce; ~ਕਰਨਾ To admit, to enrol.

ਦਾਖਲਾ (dakhlaa) *n m* Admission, entry, entrance, enrolment.

ਦਾਗ (daag) *n m* Stain, spot, blemish, stigma, scar, blot, mark, burn.

ਦਾਗਨਾ (daagnaa) *v* To burn, to fire, to stain, to stigmatize.

ਦਾਜ (daaj) *n m* Dowry, bride's portion.

ਦਾਣਾ (daanaa) *n m* Grain, seed, granule; pellet, shot; bird or cattle-feed, provender; A unit, single (fruit etc.); Pimple, sore, eruption (as in chickenpox); ~ਪਾਣੀ Victuals; Livelihood; Fate;

~ਮੰਡੀ Grain market.

ਦਾਤਣ (daatan) *n f* Twing or walnut bark used for cleansing teeth.

ਦਾਤਰ (daatar) *n m* A falciform kitchen implement for cutting vegetables.

ਦਾਤਰੀ (daatree) *n f* Sickle, scythe, reaping hook.

ਦਾਤਾਰ (dataar) *n m* Giver, an attribution to God.

ਦਾਂਦ (daand) *n m* Ox, bull.

ਦਾਦ (daad) *n f* (1) Ringworm; (2) Praise, appreciation; ~ਦੇਣੀ To appreciate, to backup, to applause; ~ਫ਼ਰਿਆਦ Petition, complaint.

ਦਾਦਕਾ (daadkaa) *a* Paternal.

ਦਾਦਕੇ (daadke) *n m* Paternal home or village; Paternal ancestors

ਦਾਦਰ (daadar) *n m* Frog

ਦਾਦਾ (daadaa) *n m* Paternal grand father.

ਦਾਨ (daan) *n m* Donation, alms, charity, benefaction, gift.

ਦਾਨਸ਼ਮੰਦ (daanashmand) *a n* Wise, intelligent, prudent, a wise person, intellectual.

ਦਾਨਸ਼ੀਲ (daansheel) *a* Charitable, liberal, bountiful, munificent, generous, benevolent.

ਦਾਨਵ (daanav) *n m* Devil, demon,

evil spirit, ghost, giant.

ਦਾਨਾਹ (daanaah) *a* Wise, learned, sensible; ~ਈ Wisdom, sagacity, prudence. Also ਦਾਨਾ

ਦਾਬ (daab) *n f* Impression, pressure, suppression; Layer.

ਦਾਬਾ (daabaa) *n m* Coercion, imposition; Warning, threat; ~ਪਾਉਣਾ To dominate, to impose.

ਦਾਮ (daam) *n m* Price, value, rate.

ਦਾਮਨ (daaman) *n m* Skirt of garment, foot-hill; ~ਛੁੜਾਉਣਾ To get rid of.

ਦਾਰੂ (daaroo) *n f* Medicine, drug; Alcohal, wine, liquour.

ਦਾਰੋਮਦਾਰ (daaromadaar) *n m* Dependence, reliance.

ਦਾਲ (daal) *n f* Pulse, split grain; ~ਨਾ ਗਲਣਾ To be unsuccessful.

ਦਾਵਾ (daawaa) *n m* Claim, suit, legal, action. Also ਦਾਅਵਾ

ਦਾਵੇਦਾਰ (daavedaar) *n m* Claimant, plaintiff.

ਦਾੜ੍ਹ (daarh) *n f* Grinder tooth, cheek tooth, tricuspid.

ਦਾੜ੍ਹਨਾ (darhnaa) *v* To chew, to devour.

ਦਾੜ੍ਹੀ (daarhee) *n f* Beard; ~ਹੱਥ ਲਾਉਣਾ To beg, to appeal abjectly; ~ਖੋਹਣੀ To insult, to disgrace.

ਦਿਓਰ (dior) *n m* Husband's younger brother; brother-in-law.

ਦਿਆਨਤ (diaanat) *n f* Honesty, truthfulness; ~ਦਾਰ Honest, truthful; ~ਦਾਰੀ Honesty, moral integrity.

ਦਿਆਲ (diaal) *a* Merciful, kind, gracious, benign; ~ਤਾ Kindness, compassion, mercy. Also ਦਿਆਲੂ

ਦਿਸਣਾ (disṇaa) *v* To be seen, to appear.

ਦਿੱਸ (diss) *n f* Appearance, looks, aspect, visual impression.

ਦਿਸ਼ਾ (dishaa) *n f* Direction, side, region.

ਦਿਹਾਤ (dihaat) *n m* Village, country side.

ਦਿਹਾਤੀ (dihaatee) *n m a* Villager; Rural, rustic.

ਦਿਹਾੜੀ (dihaaṛee) *n f* Daily wages, day's labour.

ਦਿੱਕ (dikk) *n m a* Tuber culosis, hectic fever; Vexed, annoyed, teased, bothered; ~ਤਪ Tuberculosis.

ਦਿੱਕਤ (dikkat) *n f* Difficulty, trouble.

ਦਿਖਾਉਣਾ (dikhaauṇaa) *v* To show, to display, to exhibit, to expose.

ਦਿਖਾਵਾ (dikhaavaa) *n m* Show, display, ostentation hypocrisy, exhibition.

ਦਿਦਾਰ (didaar) *n m* Look, sight. Also ਦੀਦਾਰ

ਦਿਨ (din) *n m* Day, suitable occasion, luck; ~ਕਟਣਾ To pass time in misery; ~ਗੁਜ਼ਾਰਨਾ To idle, to waste time; ~ਚੜ੍ਹਨਾ Rising of sun; ~ਫਿਰਨੇ To begin, to prosper; ~ਰਾਤ At all time, day & night, always; ~ਦਿਹਾੜੇ In broad day light.

ਦਿਮਾਗ (dimaag) *n m* Brain, head, mind, intellect, arrogance; ~ਹੋਣਾ To be proud, to be arrogant; ~ਲੜਾਉਣਾ To cudgel one's brain, to think on a subject carefully.

ਦਿਮਾਗ਼ੀ (dimaagee) *a* Mental, intellectual, cerebral, brilliant.

ਦਿਲ (dil) *n m* Heart, mind, will, courage; ~ਉਚਾਟ ਹੋਣਾ To be disgusted; ~ਸਾਫ਼ ਹੋਣਾ To have no reservation; ~ਹਾਰਨਾ To lose heart; ~ਹੌਲਾ ਹੋਣਾ To feel easy; ~ਕਰਨਾ To aspire, to wish; ~ਖੱਟਾ ਹੋਣਾ To sicken; ~ਛੋਟਾ ਕਰਨਾ To be dejected, to feel disheartened; ~ਟੁਟਣਾ To lose courage, to be distracted; ~ਢਾਹੁਣਾ To sadden, to deject; ~ਤੋਂ ਦੂਰ ਹੋਣਾ To forget; ~ਦੇਣਾ To fall in love with; ~ਰਖਣਾ To oblige, to comply with one's wishes; ~ਲਗਣਾ To be attached to, to be fond of; ~ਵਿਚ ਰਖਣਾ To keep secret, not to divulge; ~ਬਰ Sweetheart, beloved, paramour; ~ਲਗੀ Joke, amusement.

ਦਿਲਾਸਾ (dilaasaa) *n m* Consolation, solace, encouragement.

ਦਿਲਾਵਰ (dilaavar) *a* Brave, courageous. Also ਦਲਾਵਰ

ਦਿਵਾਰ (divaar) *n f* Wall. Also ਦਿਵਾਲ

ਦਿਲੀ (dilee) *a* Hearty, sincere, cordial warm-hearted.

ਦਿਲੋਂ (dilon) *adv* Heartily, sincerely, earnestly, whole-heartedly; From the bottom of one's heart.

ਦਿਵਾਉਣਾ (divaaunaa) *v* To cause to give, to assist in getting, to get one something from someone else, to procure for.

ਦਿਵਾਲਾ (divaalaa) *n m* Bankruptcy, insolvency, liquidation.

ਦਿਵਾਲੀ (divaalee) *n f* Festival of lamps; Feast; ~ਆ Bankrupt, Insolvent. Also ਦੀਵਾਲੀ

ਦੀਆ (deeaa) *n m* Earthern lamp; ~ਬਾਲਣਾ To light a lamp; ~ਸਲਾਈ Match stick. Also ਦੀਵਾ

ਦੀਗਰ (deegar) *a* Other, another, more.

ਦੀਦ (deed) *n f* Sight, glance, show; consideration, modesty.

ਦੀਦਾ (deedaa) *n m* Eye, orb.

ਦੀਨ (deen) *n m* Poor, needy, meek, humble; Religion, faith; ~ਈਮਾਨ Virtue religion; ~ਤਾ Humility, modesty; ~ਬੰਧੂ God, friend of the poor.

ਦੀਮਕ (deemak) *n f* White ant.

ਦੀਵਟ (deevat) *n f* Lamp stand.

ਦੀਵਾਨ (deewan) *n m* Minister, royal court; Congregation; ~ਖਾਨਾ Court chamber, audience hall. Also ਦਿਵਾਨ

ਦੀਵਾਨਗੀ (deevaangee) *n f* Madness, lunacy, insanity. Also ਦਿਵਾਨਗੀ

ਦੀਵਾਨਾ (deevaanaa) *n m* Insane, lunatic, mad. Also ਦਿਵਾਨਾ

ਦੁਆ (duaa) *n f* Prayer; Supplication, blessing; ~ਦੇਣਾ To bless; ~ਸਲਾਮ Greetings, salutation, compliments.

ਦੁਸ਼ਟ (dushṭ) *n m* Rascal, villain, scoundral; ~ਤਾ Meanness, wickedness, rascality, villainy.

ਦੁਸ਼ਮਣ (dushmaṇ) *n m* Enemy, foe.

ਦੁਸ਼ਮਨੀ (dushmaṇee) *n f* Enmity, animosity; ਖਾਨਦਾਨੀ ~Vendetta.

ਦੁਸ਼ਵਾਰ (dushwaar) *a* Difficult.

ਦੁਸ਼ਵਾਰੀ (dushwaaree) *n f* Difficulty.

ਦੁਸ਼ਾਲਾ (dushaalaa) *n m* Shawl, embroidered wrapper.

ਦੁਹਣਾ (duhṇaa) *v* To milk. Also ਦੋਹਣਾ

ਦੁਹਰਾ (duhraa) *a* Double, duplicate, two fold.

ਦੁਹਰਾਉ (duhraau) *n m* Repetition, revision, iteration, tautology.

ਦੁਹਰਾਉਣਾ (duhraauṇaa) *v* To repeat, to revise, to recapitulate, to reiterate, to go over, to echo. Also ਦੋਹਰਾਉਣਾ

ਦੁਹਾਈ (duhaaee) *n f* Cry for help, appeal, invocation, clamour; ~ਦੇਣੀ To call upon, to make an appeal.

ਦੁਹਾਜੂ (duhaaju) *n m* One who is married a second time.

ਦੁਕਾਨ (dukaan) *n f* Shop, warehouse; - ਚਲਾਉਣਾ To run a shop; ~ਵਧਾਉਣਾ to close a shop; ~ਦਾਰ Shopkeeper; ~ਦਾਰੀ Business, Shopkeeping.

ਦੁਖ (dukh) *n m* Suffering, grief, distress, misery, hardship, tribulation, pain, trouble, agony; ~ਉਠਾਉਣਾ To suffer; ~ਦੇਣਾ To torment, to harass.

ਦੁਖਣਾ (dukhṇaa) *v* To ache, to pain, to hurt.

ਦੁਖੜਾ (dukhṛaa) *n m* Tale of sufferings, grievance, trouble.

ਦੁਖਾਉਣਾ (dukhaauṇaa) *v* To inflict pain, to hurt, to torment.

ਦੁਖਾਂਤ (dukhaaant) *n m* Tragic end,

tragedy; tragic play.

ਦੁਖੀਆ (dukhiaa) *a* Unfortunate, troubled, grieved, sorrowful, miserable, sufferer. Also ਦੁਖੀ

ਦੁਚਿੱਤਾ (duchittaa) *a* In two minds, double-minded, diffident, hesitant.

ਦੁੱਛਤਾ (duchhattaa) *a* Double-storey (building).

ਦੁਤਰਫ਼ਾ (dutarfaa) *a* Mutual, reciprocal.

ਦੁੱਧ (duddh) *n m* Milk, sap, juice of some plants & trees; ~ਉਤਰਨਾ Lactation; ~ਪਿਆਉਣਾ To suckle; ~ਵਾਲਾ Milkman.

ਦੁਧਾਰਾ (dudhaaraa) *a* Double-edged (weapon).

ਦੁੱਧਲ (duddhal) *a* High-yielding (milch cattle).

ਦੁਨੀਆ (duniaa) *n f* The world, cosmos, people; ~ਦਾਰ Worldlywise; ~ਦਾਰੀ Worldliness.

ਦੁਪਹਿਰ (dupehr) *n f* Noon, midday

ਦੁੱਪਟਾ (dupattaa) *n m* Veil, wrapper.

ਦੁਫਾੜ (duphaaṛ) *n m* Two fragments, thing cut into two.

ਦੁਬਲਾ (dublaa) *a* Thin, lean, slim, slender; ~ਪਤਲਾ Slender, scrawny.

ਦੁੰਬਾ (dumbaa) *n m* Fat-tailed ram.

ਦੁਬਾਰਾ (dubaaraa) *a* Again, for the second time.

ਦੁਭਾਸ਼ੀਆ (dubhaashiyaa) *n m* Interpreter.

ਦੁਮ (dum) *n f* Tail, end; ~ਕਟਾ Bob tailed; ~ਦਾਰ Tailed, with tail.

ਦੁਮੰਜ਼ਲਾ (dummanzalaa) *a* Double storeyed.

ਦੁਰਕਾਰਨਾ (durkaarnaa) *v* To condemn, to repulse, to spurn.

ਦੁਰਗਤ (durgat) *n f* Dishonour, disgrace, insult, humiliation.

ਦੁਰਗੰਧ (durgandh) *n f* Bad smell, stench, fetid odour.

ਦੁਰਜਨ (durjan) *n m* Rascal, scounderal, mischief maker.

ਦੁਰਬਲ (durbal) *a* Weak, frail, slender, invalid, lean, thin, poor; ~ਤਾ Infirmity, feebleness, weakness; debility.

ਦੁਰਮਤ (durmat) *n f* Evilmindedness, wickedness.

ਦੁਰਲਭ (durlabh) *a* Rare, scare, unattainable.

ਦੁਰਾਚਾਰ (duraachaar) *n m* Malpractice, corruption, misconduct.

ਦੁਲਹਨ (dulhan) *n f* Bride, newly married woman.

ਦੁਲਾਰ (dulaar) *n m* love, affection, fonding.

ਦੁੜਾਉਣਾ (duṛaauṇaa) *v* To make or get one run; To chase, drive away.

ਦੂਸ਼ਣ (dooshaṇ) *n m* Flaw, defect, blot, stigma; blame, accusation, calumny, slander; Pollution, contamination, defilement.

ਦੂਜ (dooj) *n f* Second date, second day of lunar for night; Second turn (in game).

ਦੂਜਾ (doojaa) *a* Second, next, another.

ਦੂਣਾ (dooṇaa) *a* Double, two times, twofold, twice in size or quantity.

ਦੂਤ (doot) *n m* Envoy, consul, messenger, courtier, ambassador; ਰਾਜ~ Ambassador, royal envoy ਦੇਵ~ Angel of God; ਜਮ~ Angel of death.

ਦੂਧੀਆ (doodhiaa) *a* Milky, white.

ਦੂਰ (door) *n a* Distance; Discount, far; Away; ~ਹੁੰਦੇ ਜਾਣਾ To recede; ~ਹੋਣਾ To be away; ~ਕਰਨਾ To remove, to repel; ~ਰਹਿਣਾ To stand off, to avoid; ~ਅੰਦੇਸ਼ Farsighted; ~ਦੂਰ Widely apart.

ਦੂਰਬੀਨ (doorbeen) *n f* Telescope.

ਦੂਰੀ (dooree) *n f* Distance, farness, expanse, remoteness; estrangement.

ਦੂਲ੍ਹਾ (dulhaa) *n m* Bridegroom.

ਦੇਸ (des) *n m* Country, motherland, fatherland, territory, region; ~ਨਿਕਾਲਾ Deportation, exile, externment; ~ਵਾਸੀ Native, countrymen. Also ਦੇਸ਼

ਦੇਸੀ (desee) *a* Native, home made, local, indigenous; ~ਸ਼ਕਰ Jaggery; ~ਖੰਡ Brown sugar; ~ਬੋਲੀ Vernacular.

ਦੇਹਾਂਤ (dehaant) *n m* Death, demise.

ਦੇਖਣਾ (dekhṇaa) *v* To see, to look to, to observe, to seek, to find, to take care, to examine.

ਦੇਖ-ਰੇਖ (dekh-rekh) *n f* .Care, supervision; ~ਕਰਨਾ To look after, to supervise.

ਦੇਖ-ਭਾਲ (dekh-bhaal) *n f* Supervision, Inspection, observation, reconnaissance.

ਦੇਖਿਆ-ਭਾਲਿਆ (dekhiaa-bhaaliaa) *a* Familiar, tried, tested.

ਦੇਗ (deg) *n f* Kettle, large narrow-mouthed cooking vessel, offering; ~ਚੀ Small cooking pot, kettle. Also ਦੇਗਚਾ

ਦੇਣ (deṇ) *n m* Debt, liability, due, contribution; ~ਵਾਲਾ Payer, debtor, bestower; ~ਹਾਰ Giver, worth giving; ~ਦਾਰ Debtor, indebted, liable; ~ਦਾਰੀ Debt, accountability.

ਦੇਣਾ (deṇaa) v To give, to pay, to offer, to grant, to allow, to bestow, to entrust, to hand over, to impart, to accord; ਸੰਹੁ~ To administer an oath.

ਦੇਰ (der) n f Delay, lateness; ~ਬਾਦ Later on. Also ਦੇਰੀ

ਦੇਵ (dev) n m God, Holy spirit, deity; ~ਅਸਥਾਨ Temple; ~ਤਾ God, deity, divinity, angel; ~ਦਰਸ਼ਨ Visitation; ~ਦੂਤ Mercury; ~ਲ Temple.

ਦੇਵਰ (devar) n m Brother-in-law, younger brother of husband; Also ਦਿਉਰ

ਦੇਵੀ (devee) n m Goddess, pious lady.

ਦੈਵੀ (daivee) a Angelic, celestial, heavenly, divine, superhuman.

ਦੋਸ਼ (dosh) n m Fault, flaw, defect, offence, sin; ~ਸਿੱਧੀ Conviction; ~ਲਾਉਣਾ To blame, to accuse. Also ਦੇਖ

ਦੋਸਤ (dost) n m Friend, lover; ~ਨਾ Friendly; ~ਤੀ Friendship.

ਦੋਸ਼ੀ (doshee) a n m Accused,

culpable, delinquent; Criminal, culprit. Also ਦੋਖੀ

ਦੋਗਲਾ (doglaa) n m a Bastard; illegitimate, half-bred, mongrel; ~ਪਣ Hybridness, illegitimacy, double dealing.

ਦੌਰ (daur) n m Era, period; Phase, stage; Course, bout, circuit.

ਦੌਰਾ (dauraa) n m (1) Fit, paroxysm, spasm; (2) Tour, translocation; ~ਕਰਨਾ To go round, to tour; ~ਪੈਣਾ To suffer fits.

ਦੌਰਾਨ (dauraan) n m adv Duration, During, meantime.

ਦੌਲਤ (daulat) n f Wealth, property, money; ~ਖਾਨਾ Residence, house; ~ਮੰਦ Rich, wealthy.

ਦੌਲਾ ਮੌਲਾ (daulaa-maulaa) n m Simp-leton,. goose.

ਦੌੜ (dauṛ) n f Run, race, gallop; ~ਜਾਣਾ To run away; ~ਦਾ ਘੋੜਾ Race horse.

ਦੌੜਨਾ (dauṛnaa) v To run, to gallop, to speed up, to race.

ਦੌੜੀਆ (dauṛiaa) n m Runner, racer, sprinter.

ਧ

ਧ Twenty fourth letter of Gurmukhi alphabets, pronounced as 'dhaddhaa' (a tone marker).

ਧਸਣਾ (dhasnaa) *v* To thrust in, to enter, to penetrate, to sink, to go deep into.

ਧਸਾਉਣਾ (dhasaaunaa) *v* To pierce, to thrust, to penetrate.

ਧਸੋੜਨਾ (dhasornaa) *v* To penetrate, pierce, thrust, push or force into.

ਧਕਣਾ (dhaknaa) *v* To push, to oust, to thrust.

ਧਕ-ਧਕ (dhak-dhak) *n f* Palpitation, heart beat, fear, anxiety.

ਧਕਮ ਧਕਾ (dhakkam-dhakkaa) *n m* Hustle, Pushing and jostling, great rush.

ਧੱਕੜ (dhakkar) *a* Aggressive, violent, domineering, usurpur; ~ਰੱਵਈਆ Aggressive attitude, unreasonable attitude.

ਧੱਕਾ (dhakkaa) *n m* Jerk, push, jolt, shock, concussion, coercion, aggression, impulse, stroke; ~ਦੇਣਾ To push, to jerk.

ਧੱਕੇਸ਼ਾਹੀ (dhake shaahee) *n f* High handedness, despotism.

ਧੱਕੇਬਾਜ਼ੀ (dhake-baazee) *n f* Force, violence, oppression.

ਧੱਕੇਲਣਾ (dhakelnaa) *v* To push, to shave, to thrust.

ਧੱਖ (dhakkh) *n f* Louse egg, young louse.

ਧਗੜਾ (dhagraa) *n m* Paramour.

ਧਣਨਾ (dhannaa) *v* To fertilize, to impregnate, to inseminate.

ਧੱਦਰ (dhaddar) *n f* Shingles, herpes, zoster; Ringworm, tinea.

ਧੰਦਾ (dhandaa) *n m* Profession, occupation, avocation, business. Also ਧੰਧਾ

ਧੰਨ (dhann) *n a* God bless you! Well done! Bravo!; ~ਧੰਨ Applause, accolade; ~ਭਾਗ Fortunately ~ਵਾਦ Thanks.

ਧਨ (dhan) *n m a* Wealth, property, money, capital, riches; Plus, positive; ~ਨੀਤੀ Fiscal policy; ~ਵਾਨ Rich, wealthy, affluent.

ਧਨੁਸ਼ (dhanush) *n m* Bow; ਇੰਦਰ~ Rainbow; ~ਧਾਰੀ Archer. Also ਧਨੁਖ

ਧੱਫੜ (dhapphar) *n m* Nettle rash, swelling due to biting of an insect.

ਧੱਬਾ (dhabbaa) *n m* Spot, stain, blot.

ਧੱਮ (dhamm) *n f* Thud, dull sound.

ਧਮਕਣਾ (dhamaknaa) To thump, to arrive suddenly; ਆ~ To appear unexpectedly or surprisingly.

ਧਮਕਾਉਣਾ (dhamkaaunaa) *v* To threaten, to chide, to intimidate.

ਧਮਕਾਊ (dhamkaau) *a* Threatening, frightening, intimidating, daunting.

ਧਮਕੀ (dhamkee) *n f* Threat, menace, bullying, intimidation.

ਧਮਾਕਾ (dhamaakaa) *n m* Explosion, thunder, thump, bump, crash.

ਧਰਤੀ (dhartee) *n f* Earth, land, soil, ground; ~ਮਾਤਾ Mother land.

ਧਰਨਾ (dharnaa) *n m v* Picket; To keep, to put, to place, to lay.

ਧਰਮ (dharam) *n m* Religion, duty, righteousness, sect, faith, belief; ~ਅਸਥਾਨ Holy place, religious place; ~ਸ਼ਾਸਤਰ Scriptures; ~ਸ਼ਾਲਾ Inn, pilgrims house; ~ਨਿਰਪੇਖਤਾ Secularism; ~ਪਤਨੀ Wife; ~ਬਦਲੀ Conversion.

ਧਰਮਾਤਮਾ (dharmaatmaa) *a* Pious, holy, virtuous, godly, religious.

ਧਰਵਾਉਣਾ (dharvaaunaa) *v* To get placed, to have something put down.

ਧਰਾਤਲ (dharaatal) *n m* Land surface, area.

ਧਰੀਕਣਾ (dhareeknaa) *n* To drag, to pull along a surface.

ਧੜ (dhar) *n m* Trunk of body, body.

ਧੜਕਣ (dharkan) *n f* Beating of the heart, palpitation, pulsation.

ਧੜਕਣਾ (dharaknaa) *v* To palpitate, to throb, to beat, to pulsate, to be terrified.

ਧੜਕਾ (dharkaa) *n m* Fear, palpitation, suspense, apprehension.

ਧੜੰਮ (dhrumm) *n* Thud, Thump. Also ਧੜਾਮ

ਧੜੱਲੇਦਾਰ (dharalledaar) *a* Forceful, vehement impressive.

ਧੜਾ (dharaa) *n m* Group, party, side; counterpoise, counter balance; ~ਧੜ Quickly, incessantly, continously.

ਧੜਾਕਾ (dharaakaa) *n m* Thump, crash, explosion, out bust.

ਧੜੇਬਾਜ਼ (dharebaaz) *a f* Partisan, factious, cliquish.

ਧੜੇਬਾਜ਼ੀ (dharebaazee) *n f* Partisanship, factionalism, party spirit.

ਧਾਉਣਾ (dhaaunaa) *v* To run, to hasten, to hurry.

ਧਾਕ (dhaak) *n f* Awe, fear, terror, grandeur, fame, credit.

ਧਾਗਾ (dhaagaa) *n m* Thread, cord; ~ਪੋਣਾ To needle, to thread.

ਧਾਂਤ (dhaant) *n f* Semen. Also ਧਾਤ

ਧਾਤ (dhaat) *n f* Metal, mineral; Semen; ਕਚੀ~ Ore; ਖੁਲ੍ਹੀ~ Bullion; ਮਿਸ਼ਰਤ~ Alloy.

ਧਾਤੂ (dhaatoo) *n m* Root of a word, stem, element, constituent.

ਧਾਂਦਲੀ (dhaandlee) *n f* Anarchy, disorder, disturbance; ~ਮਚਾਉਣੀ To create disturbance.

ਧਾਨ (dhaan) *n m* Paddy, husky rice, rice plant.

ਧਾਰ (dhaar) *n* (1) Edge, sharpness, line; (2) Limit, trend, current, stream; ~ਲਾਉਣੀ To sharpen; ~ਕਢਣੀ To milk; ਤੇਜ਼~ Torent, strong current; ~ਮਾਰਨੀ To urinate, to damn care.

ਧਾਰਣਾ (dhaarṇaa) *n f* Conception, notion, assumption.

ਧਾਰਨਾ (dharnaa) *v* To determine, to resolve, to assume, to imagine.

ਧਾਰਾਵਾਹਿਕ (dhaaraavaahik) *a* Serial, serialised, continued.

ਧਾਰੀ (dhaaree) *n f* Suff stripe, line, streaker; Meaning wielder or bearer such as ਪਗੜਧਾਰੀ, ਜਟਾਧਾਰੀ; ~ਦਾਰ Striped, streaked, striated.

ਧਾਵਾ (dhaavaa) *n m* Raid, attack, assault, invasion, incursion.

ਧਾੜਵੀ (dhaarvee) *n m* Robber, raider, dacoit, plunderer, marauder, mugger.

ਧਾੜਾ (dhaaraa) *n m* Raid, robbery, dacoity loot, spoil, plunder, extortion, exploitation.

ਧਿਆਉਣਾ (dhiaauṇaa) *v* To meditate (upon), to contemplate, to reflect, to remember, to repeat (the name of Diety).

ਧਿਆਨ (dhiaan) *n m* Attention, meditation, absorption; ~ਕਰਨਾ To pay attention to, to take care; ~ਦੇਣਾ To pay heed, to attend; ~ਮੋੜਨਾ To divert attention; ~ਯੋਗ Note worthy, remarkable.

ਧਿਕਾਰ (dhikaar) *n f* Curse, seproach, scorn, rebuke, phew! fie!

ਧਿਕਾਰਨਾ (dhikaarnaa) *v* To reproach, to curse, to anthematize.

ਧਿੰਗਾਣਾ (dhingaaṇaa) *n m* Use of force, wrong injustice, oppression.

ਧਿੰਗਾਣੇ (dhingaaṇe) *adv* By force, forcibly, unjustly, wrongfully.

ਧਿਜਾਉਣ (dhijaaun) *v* To comfort, console; To win or build up confidence, to reassure; To coax, to inveigle.

ਧੀ (dhee) *n f* Daughter.

ਧੀਮਾ (dheemaa) *a* Slow, mild, gentle, tardy, dim, feeble, faint.

ਧੀਰ (dheer) *n m* Patience, consolation, endurance, forbearance, solace. Also ਧੀਰਜ

ਧੀਰੇ (dheere) *adv* Slowly, lightly, gently, gradually, carefully; ~ਧੀਰੇ Little by little, step by step.

ਧੁਆਂਖ (dhuaankh) *n f* Soot, smoke-deposit, smut.

ਧੁੱਸਾ (dhussaa) *n m* Rough, coarse woolen blanket.

ਧੁਖਣਾ (dhukhnaa) *v* To ignite, to smoulder, to burn without flame, to take fire.

ਧੁਤਕਾਰਨਾ (dhutkaarnaa) *v* To rebuke, to chide, to rebuff.

ਧੁੰਦ (dhund) *n f* Mist, fog, haziness.

ਧੁੰਦਲਕਾ (dhundalkaa) *n m f* Dusk, haziness, fogginess, semi darkness.

ਧੁੰਦਲਾ (dhundlaa) *a* Foggy, dim, dull, blurred, shabby, doubtful, pale, smoky; ~ਪਣ Fogginess, mistiness, vagueness.

ਧੁਨ (dhun) *n f* Single mindedness, zeal, passion, abosorption in thought or action.

ਧੁਨਣਾ (dhunnaa) *v* To muzzle.

ਧੁਨੀ (dhunee) *n f* Tune, musical mode, musical sound, tone, melody, sound, speech-sound; ~ਵਿਗਿਆਨ Musicology, phonology, phonemics, phonetics.

ਧੁੰਨੀ (dhunnee) *n f* Navel, umbilicus.

ਧੁੱਪ (dhupp) *n f* Sunshine, sunlight, sun.

ਧੁੰਮ (dhumm) *n f* Frame, reputation, show, bustle.

ਧੁਰ (dhur) *n f adv* Extremity; Right from or upto; ਅਗਲਾ~ Foremost.

ਧੁਰਾ (dhuraa) *n f* Axle, shaft, hub, pivot.

ਧੂੰਆ (dhooaan) *n m* Smoke, fume; ~ਧਾਰ Full of smoke; High flown (speech), heavy (rain). Also ਧੂੰ

ਧੂਪ (dhoop) *n f* Incense, perfume, olibanum.

ਧੂ (dhoo) *n f* Pull; attraction, pang, pain; Spasm.

ਧੂਣਾ (dhoonaa) *v* To pull, to drag, to haul, to pull up, haul up, admonish, reprove; To manhandle; To snatch.

ਧੂਣੀ (dhoonee) *n f* Open fire, with straw; Fire kept going by ascetics practising austerities; Incense burning; ~ਬਾਲ਼ਣੀ To make an open fire; ~ਰਮਾਉਣੀ To make and maintain fire burning (by ascetics), to become an ascetic, to practise austerities.

ਧੂਮ (dhoom) *n f* Comet; Reputation, fame; ~ਧਾਮ Pomp and show, boom, tumplt.

ਧੂੜ (dhoor) *n f* Dust, grit; fine powder; ~ਉੱਡਣੀ For dust to blow or rise.

ਧੇਤੇ (dhete) *n m pl.* Members of daugher-in-law's family collectively. see ਪੁਤੇਤੇ

ਧੋਖਾ (dhokhaa) *n m* Deception, deceit, fraud, delusion, hoax, dupe.

ਧੋਣਾ (dhonaa) *v* To wash, to cleanse, to flush, to launder.

ਧੋਤੀ (dhotee) *n* Cloth worn round the waiste.

ਧੋਬੀ (dhobee) *n m* Washerman, launderer.

ਧੌਂਸ (dhauns) *n f* Bullying, awe, threat, bluster, swagger.

ਧੌਣ (dhaun) *n f* Neck; ~ਸੁਟਣੀ To lose heart, to be depressed; ~ਧੱਪਾ scuffle, row.

ਧੌਲਾ (dhaulaa) *a* Grey, white, hoary.

ਨ

ਨ Twenty fifth letter of the Gurmukhi alphabets, pronounced as 'nannaa'.

ਨਸ (nas) *n f* Vein, nerve, sinew.

ਨਸ਼ਈ (nashai) *a* Drunk, intoxicated, inebriate, under influence of drink; alcoholic, drunkard; drug-addict.

ਨਸ਼ਟ (nasht) *a* Lost, ruined, destroyed, smashed, demolished.

ਨੱਸਣਾ (nassnaa) *v* To run, to flee, to decamp.

ਨਸਬੰਦੀ (nasbandee) *n f* vasectomy.

ਨਸਲ (nasal) *n f* Race, breed, clan, genealogy, species, generation.

ਨਸਲੀ (naslee) *a* Racial.

ਨਸ਼ਾ (nashaa) *n m* Intoxication, stimulation, booze; ~ਬੰਦੀ prohibition.

ਨਸਾਉਣਾ (nasaaunaa) *v* To make run, to make one give up.

ਨਸੀਹਤ (naseehat) *n f* Advice, counsel, instruction.

ਨਸੀਬ (naseeb) *n* Destiny, fortune, fate, luck, lot. Also **ਨਸੀਬਾ**

ਨਸ਼ੀਲਾ (nasheelaa) *a* Intoxicating, inebriant.

ਨੱਹਕ (nahakk) *a* unjustly, without justification, undeservedly, unjustifiably, wrongly.

ਨਾਉਣਾ (nhaaunaa) *v* To bathe, to take bath; Also **ਨੁਉਣਾ**

ਨਹਿਰ (naher) *n f* Stream, canal, water way.

ਨਹੀਂ (naheen) *a* No, not, nay, refusal.

ਨਹੁੰ (nahun) *n m* Finger nail, nail.

ਨਹੂਸਤ (nahoosat) *n f* Inauspiciousness, bad luck.

ਨਹੂਸਤੀ (nahoostee) *n* Inauspicious, ill omened.

ਨੱਕ (nakk) *n m* Noise, organ; ~ਹੇਠਾਂ under the very nose of, in the presence of; ~ਰੱਖ ਲੈਣਾ To keep up one's prestige; ~ਰਗੜਨਾ To be seech humbly, to eat humble pie; ~ਵਢਣਾ To inflict humiliation, to dishonour; ~ਵਢਿਆ ਜਾਣਾ To be insulted, to be disgraced; ~ਵਾਲਾ Honourable, having prestige, ~ਵਿਚ ਦਮ ਕਰਨਾ To harass, to tease incessantly.

ਨਕਸ਼ (naksh) *n m* Impression, sign, features, apprearance.

ਨਕਸ਼ਾ (nakshaa) *n m* Map, chart, layout plan, sketch, model, design, contour; ~ਕਸ਼ Cartographer; ~ਨਵੀਸ Tracer, draftsman; ~ਪੁਸਤਕ

Atlas

ਨਕਸੀਰ (nakseer) *n f* Bleeding from nose.

ਨਕਚੂੰਡੀ (nakchoondee) *n f* Clamp, clip, paper clip; Pincers.

ਨਕਦ (nakad) *n m adv* Cash; In cash; Ready money; ~ਨਰੈਟ Hardcash; Mammon, god of riches. Also ਨਗਦ

ਨਕਲ (nakal) *n f* Copy, duplicate, transcription, mimicry, parody; ~ਕਰਨਾ To copy, to imitate, to mimic; ~ਚੀ Imitator, mimic, buffon; ~ਨਵੀਸ Copyist.

ਨਕਲੀ (naklee) *a* False, fictitous, artificial, rake, imitative.

ਨਕਾਸ਼ੀ (nakaashee) *n f* Painting, drawing, engraving.

ਨਕਾਬ (nakaab) *n m* Veil, mask; ~ਪੋਸ਼ Masked.

ਨਕਾਰਨਾ (nkaarnaa) *v* To reject, to dishonour.

ਨਕਾਰਾ (nakaaraa) *a* useless, valueless, unfit, good for nothing, of no use, rotter; ~ਪਣ Disability, indolence, handicap.

ਨਕੇਲ (nakel) *n f* Cavesson, camel's nose band; ~ਪਾਉਣੀ To put nosebar; to check, to restrain.

ਨਕੌੜਾ (nakauraa) *n m* Large or fat nose; noseband.

ਨਖੱਟੂ (nakhattoo) *a* Non-earning, worthless.

ਨਖਰਾ (nakhraa) *n m* Coquetry, pretence, trick.

ਨਖਲਿਸਤਾਨ (nakhlistaan) *n m* Oasis.

ਨਖਿੱਧ (nakhiddh) *a* Worthless, unworthy, inferior, wretched.

ਨਖੇੜਨਾ (nakhernaa) *v* To disunite, to disjoin, to separate, to individualize, to detach, to sunder, to divorce.

ਨੱਗ (nagg) *n m* Item, package, piece.

ਨਗ (nag) *n m* Precious stone.

ਨੰਗ (nang) *n m* Nudity, nakedness; Poverty, destitution; ~ਧੜੰਗ Absolute make, starked nude.

ਨਗਮਾ (nagmaa) *n m* Song, melody.

ਨਗਰ (nagar) *n m* City, town, borough; ~ਨਿਗਮ Municipal corporation; ~ਪਤੀ Mayor; ~ਪਾਲਕਾ Municipal committee.

ਨੰਗਾ (nangaa) *a* Naked, bare, nude, unclad, unclothed, undressed, shameless; ਕਰਨਾ~ To denude, to unclothe, to strip, to undress, to expose; ਭੁੱਖਾ~ Poor, destitude.

ਨਗਾਰਾ (nagaaraa) *n m* Kettle drum.

ਨਗੀਨਾ (nageenaa) *n m* Gem, a precious stone set in ring.

ਨੱਚਣਾ (nachchnaa) *v* To dance, to fret.

ਨਚੋੜ (nachor) *n m* Gist, sum, substance, summary, digest; ~ਕੱਢਣਾ To condense, to abbreviate.

ਨਚੋੜਨਾ (nachornaa) *v* To compress, to rinse, to squeeze, to wring.

ਨਛੱਤਰ (nachhattar) *n m* Star, planet; zodic sign; Position of moon in lunar orbit.

ਨਜ਼ਦੀਕ (nazdeek) *a* Near, adjacent, close, in vicinity. Also **ਨਜੀਕ**

ਨਜ਼ਮ (nazam) *n f* Verse, poetry, poem.

ਨਜ਼ਰ (nazar) *n f* Present, gift, cosecration, dedication; Sight, vision, look, glance, attension, evil eye; ~**ਕਰਨਾ** To present, to offer, to devote; ~**ਆਉਣਾ** To come in sight, to be seen, to appear; ~**ਅੰਦਾਜ਼ ਕਰਨਾ** To ignore, to take no notice of; ~**ਚੜ੍ਹਨਾ** To be in one's good books; ~**ਮਾਰਨੀ** To glance, to go through, to survey; ~**ਰਖਣਾ** To watch, to care; ~**ਬਟੂ** To avert the evil eye; ~**ਬੰਦੀ** Detention, confinement.

ਨਜ਼ਰਾਨਾ (nazraanaa) *n m* Present, gift.

ਨਜ਼ਰੀਆ (nazariaa) *n m* Approach, point of view, attitude.

ਨਜ਼ਲਾ (nazlaa) *n m* Bad cold, catarrh, flu.

ਨਜ਼ਾਕਤ (nazaakat) *n f* Delicacy, elegance, coquetry.

ਨਜਾਤ (najaat) *n f* Release, salvation, freedom, emancipation, rid.

ਨਜ਼ਾਰਾ (nazaaraa) *n m* Sight, view, scene, glance, vista.

ਨਜਿੱਠਣਾ (najitthnaa) *v* To fulfil, to perform, to endure, to tackle, to settle, to conclude, to dispose of.

ਨਜੂਮ (najoom) *n m* Astronomy, astrology; Fortune-telling, fore-telling, predictor.

ਨਜੂਮੀ (najoomee) *n m* Astrologer, fortune teller, star gazer, augur.

ਨਠਣਾ (nathnaa) *v* To flee, to run.

ਨਢਰੀ (nadharee) *n f* Girl, damsel, lass, young woman.

ਨੱਢਾ (naddhaa) *n m* Boy, youth, youngman.

ਨੱਢੀ (naddhee) *n f* Youngwoman, damsel.

ਨਤੀਜਾ (nateejaa) *n m* Result, consequence, conclusion, inference. .

ਨੱਥ (natth) *n f* Nose ring.

ਨੱਥਣਾ (natthnaa) *v* To have the nose pierced, to bring under control, to ring (the nose).

ਨਥਨਾ (nathnaa) *n m* Nostril; ~**ਫੁਲਣਾ** To get angry.

ਨੱਥੀ (natthee) *a* Attached, appended, enclosed.

ਨੱਥੂ-ਖੈਰਾ (natthoo-khaeraa) *n m* Any Tom, Dick or Harry.

ਨਦਾਨ (nadaan) *a* Ignorant, innocent, foolish.

ਨਦਾਨੀ (nadaanee) *n f* Innocence, ignorance, foolishness.

ਨਦੀ (nadee) *n f* River, rivulet, small stream; ~ਤਲ River bed.

ਨਨਾਣ (nanaan) *n f* Husband's sister, sister in law. Also ਨਣਾਨ

ਨਪਣਾ (napnaa) *v* To catch, to nip, to press, to cover; To be measured.

ਨਪੀੜਨਾ (napeernaa) *v* To squeeze, to compress, to press.

ਨਪੂਤਾ (napootaa) *a* Issueless, having no son.

ਨਫਰਤ (nafrat) *n f* Hatred, scorn, contempt, aversion, disgust.

ਨਫਾ (nafaa) *n m* Profit, gain, benefit, advantage; ~ਖੋਰ Profiteer; ~ਖੋਰੀ Profiteering.

ਨਫਾਸਤ (nafaasat) *n f* Decency, etiquette, nicety.

ਨਫੀ (nafee) *a n f* Negative, minus, subtracted; Subtration, reduction.

ਨਫੀਸ (nafees) *a* Nice, decent, delicate.

ਨਬਜ਼ (nabaz) *n f* Pulse (of the hand); ~ਵੇਖਣੀ To feel the pulse.

ਨੰਬਰ (nambar) *n m* Number, marks, score; ~ਦੇਣੇ To evaluate, to award marks; ~ਫੇਰਨਾ To dial; ~ਦਾਰ Village headman.

ਨੰਬਰੀ (numbree) *a* Regular, established, numbered.

ਨਬਾਲਗ਼ (nabaalag) *a* Minor, ward.

ਨਬੇੜਨਾ (nabernaa) *v* To settle, to finish, to end, to conclude.

ਨਮਕ (namak) *n m* Salt; ~ਹਰਾਮ Disloyal, unfaithful; ~ਹਲਾਲ Loyal, faithful; ~ਛਿੜਕਣਾ To add insult to injury.

ਨਮਕੀਨ (namkeen) *a* Saltish, saline, beautiful, handsome.

ਨਮੀ (namee) *n f* Moisture, dampness, humidity.

ਨਮੂਨਾ (namoonaa) *n m* Model, sample, specimen, pattern, design, type, example.

ਨਰਕ (narak) *n m* Hell, inferno, very dirty place.

ਨਰਮ (naram) *a* Soft, gentle, mild, tender, delicate; ~ਦਿਲ Kind hearted.

ਨਰਾਜ਼ (naraaz) *a* Displeased, estranged, angry, offended, annoyed, unhappy; ~ਕਰਨਾ To displease, to offend, to annoy, to rub one up the wrong way. Also ਨਾਰਾਜ਼

ਨਰਾਜ਼ਗੀ (naraazgee) *n f* Displeasure, estrangement, anger, unhappiness. Also ਨਾਰਾਜ਼ਗੀ

ਨਰੇਲ (narel) *n m* Coconut, coconut

palm. Also **ਨਾਰੀਅਲ**

ਨਲਕਾ (nalkaa) *n m* Water tap, hand pump.

ਨਲੀ (nalee) *n f* Snot; Tube, pipe.

ਨਲੈਕ (nalaik) *a* Duffer, incompetent, inefficient, unworthy.

ਨਵਾਂ (nawaan) *a* New, fresh, recent, novel, modern; ~**ਨਕੋਰ** Brand new, unused, fresh.

ਨਵਾਬ (nawaab) *n m* Baron, nawab.

ਨਵਾਬੀ (nawaabee) *n f* Nawabship.

ਨਵੇਕਲਾ (naveklaa) *a* Isolated, separate, sole, solitary, exclusive, alone; ~**ਪਣ** Exculsiveness, isolation.

ਨਰੋਆ (naroaa) *n m* Funeral, bier, hearse.

ਨਾਂ (naan) *n m* Name, fame, reputation; ~**ਹੋਣਾ** To win credit, to be famous; ~**ਦੇਣਾ** To label, to name; Also **ਨਾਉਂ** and **ਨਾਮ**

ਨਾ (naa) *a adv n* No; Not, nay; Refusal, denial. Also **ਨਾਂਹ**

ਨਾਉ (naao) *n f* Boat, sailing, vessel. Also **ਨਾਵ**

ਨਾਅਰਾ (naaraa) *n m* Slogan, war cry.

ਨਾਇਬ (naaib) *a* Assistant, deputy.

ਨਾਈ (naaee) *n m* Barber, hair dresser.

ਨਾਸ (naas) *n m* Destruction, annihilation, ruin, waste. Also **ਨਾਸ਼**

ਨਾਸਤਕ (naastak) *n m* Infidel, atheist, unbeliever, heretic, sceptic

ਨਾਸ਼ਤਾ (naashtaa) *n m* Breakfast, light refreshment.

ਨਾਸੂਰ (naasoor) *n m* Ulcer, cancer.

ਨਾਹਕ (naahak) adv *a* Invain; Undeserved.

ਨਾਕਾ (naakaa) *n* Barrier, block, barricade; ~**ਬੰਦੀ** Blockade.

ਨਾਕਾਮ (naakaam) *a* Unsuccessful; ~**ਯਾਬੀ** Defeat, failure.

ਨਾਖੁਨ (naakhun) *n m* Nail.

ਨਾਗ (naag) *n m* Snake, serpent; A cruel personal.

ਨਾਗਰਿਕ (naagrik) *n m* Citizen, city dweller; ~**ਤਾ** Citizenship.

ਨਾਗਾ (naagaa) *a n m* Vacant, blank; Omission, absence, suspension; Fast, starvation.

ਨਾਚ (naach) *n m* Dance, ballet; ~**ਘਰ** Ball room.

ਨਾਜ਼ (naaz) *n m* Delicacy, gracefulness, fonding, blandishment; ~**ਨੀਨ** Delicate woman, beautiful damsel.

ਨਾਜਾਇਜ਼ (naajaaiz) *a* Improper, illigitimate, unbecoming, illicit.

ਨਾਟਕ (naatak) *n m* Drama, play; ~**ਕਾਰ** Dramatist, playwright.

ਨਾਤਾ (naataa) *n m* Relationship, alliance.

ਨਾਦਮ (naadam) *a* Ashamed.

ਨਾਦਰ (naadar) *a* Rare, uncommon.

ਨਾਨਕਾ (naankaa) *a* Belonging to maternal grandfather's family or village.

ਨਾਨਾ (naanaa) *n m* Maternal grandfather.

ਨਾਨੀ (naanee) *n f* Maternal grandmother; ~ਯਾਦ ਆਉਣੀ To be at one's wit's ends, to be in great trouble; ~ਯਾਦ ਕਰਾਉਣੀ To teach one a lesson.

ਨਾਪ (naap) *n m* Measurement, scale.

ਨਾਪਣਾ (naapṇaa) *a* To measure; to weigh.

ਨਾਪਾਕ (naapaak) *a* Polluted, unholy, unclean.

ਨਾਫ਼ਰਮਾਨ (naafarmaan) *a* Disobedience, insubordination.

ਨਾਫ਼ਰਮਾਨੀ (naafarmaanee) *n f* Disobedience, insubordination.

ਨਾਬਾਲਗ (naabaalag) *a* Under age; Minor.

ਨਾਬੀਨਾ (naabeenaa) *a* Blind.

ਨਾਭ (naabh) *n f* Navel, hilum, nucleus. Also ਨਾਭੀ

ਨਾਮ (naam) *n m* Name, designation, Fame; Reality, godi; ~ਕਮਾਉਣਾ To earn name and fame; ~ਲੇਵਾ Descendant, follower.

ਨਾਮਜ਼ਦ (naamzad) *a n* Nominated,

designated; Nominee; ~ਕਰਨਾ To nominate, to designate, to appoint; ~ਗੀ Nomination.

ਨਾਮਣਾ (namṇaa) *n m v* Renown, fame, honour; To designate.

ਨਾਮਰਦ (naamarad) *a* Impotent, cowardly, eunuch.

ਨਾਮਵਰ (naamvar) *a* Renowned, famous.

ਨਾਮਾ (naamaa) *n* Letter, epistle; Cash; *As suffix* meaning letter, document or book such as ਹੁਕਮਨਾਮਾ, ਸ਼ਾਹਨਾਮਾ

ਨਾਮਾਕੂਲ (naamaakool) *a* unreasonable, stupid, foolish.

ਨਾਮਾਨਿਗਾਰ (naamaanigaar) *n m* Correspondent, Press Reporter.

ਨਾਮਾਵਲੀ (naamaavalee) *n f* List of names, schedule, catalogue, nominal roll.

ਨਾਮੀ (naamee) *a* Famous, reputed, renowned, notorious; ~ਗਰਾਮੀ Famous, well-known.

ਨਾਮੁਰਾਦ (naamuraad) *a* Issueless, childless, unlucky, ill-omened.

ਨਾਯਾਬ (naayaab) *a* Rare, scarce.

ਨਾਰ (naar) *n f* Woman, wife.

ਨਾਰਾਜ਼ਗੀ (naaraazgee) *n f* Anger, displeasure, resentment.

ਨਾਰੀ (naaree) *n f* Women, female, eve.

ਨਾਰੀਅਲ (naarial) *n m* Coconut; *Cocos*

nucifera. Also **ਨਰੈਲ**

ਨਾਲ (naal) *n f adv prep* Barrel, pipe, tube; Alongwith, accompanying; By the side of; ~**ਹੋਣਾ** To accompany, to side; ~**ਦਾ** Adjacent, near, immediate; ~**ਨਾਲ** Along, neck to neck; ~**ਨਾਲ ਰਹਿਣਾ** To live together, to shadow; ~**ਲਗਣਾ** To touch, to cohere, to conjoin; ~**ਲਾਉਣਾ** To attach.

ਨਾਲਸ਼ (naalash) *n f* Law suit, complaint. Also **ਨਾਲਿਸ਼**

ਨਾਲ (naall) *n f* Horse shoe, hoof.

ਨਾਲਾ (naalaah) *n m* Big drain, water-course, sewer, gutter, channel, canal, rivulet; Trouser string.

ਨਾਲਾਇਕ (naalaaik) *a* Unitelligent, dull, obtuse, stupid; Intefficient; incapable.

ਨਾਲਾਇਕੀ (naalaiki) *a* Dullness, obtuseness, stupidity; Ineffciency.

ਨਾਲੀ (naalee) *n f* Drain, sewer, gutter, pipe, tube, channel; **ਬੰਦੂਕ ਦੀ**~ Barrel (of gun).

ਨਾਲੇ (naale) *adv* With, therewith; too, also, besides, at the same time.

ਨਾਂਵ (naanv) *n gr.* Noun, name; ~**ਰੂਪ** Declension.

ਨਾਵਾਂ (naavaan) *n m* Money; Entry, name.

ਨਾਵਿਕ (naavik) *a* Nautical, naval.

ਨਾੜ (naar) *n f* Pulse, vein.

ਨਾੜਾ (naaraa) *n m* Trouser string, Drawer string; Bamboo pole.

ਨਾੜੀ (naaree) *n f* Blood vessel, vein, pulse, nerve.

ਨਿਓਣਾ (nuinaa) *v* To bow, to stop, to bend.

ਨਿਓਲਾ (niolaa) *n m* Mongoose.

ਨਿਆਂ (niaan) *n m* Justice, logic, equity; ~**ਅਧੀਨ** Sub-judice; ~**ਕਾਰ** Judge; Justice. Also **ਨਿਆਉਂ**, **ਨਿਆਇ**

ਨਿਆਸ (niaas) *n m* Deposit; something entrusted for state-keeping; Pledge, investment.

ਨਿਆਂਸ਼ੀਲ (niaansheel) *a* Just, judicious, equitable; ~**ਤਾ** Justness, judiciousness.

ਨਿਆਂਹੀਣ (niaanheen) *a* Unjust, unfair inequitable; ~**ਤਾ** Unjustness; unfairness, inequity, inequitableness.

ਨਿਆਜ਼ (niaaz) *n m* Offering, prayer, dedication, devotion, petition.

ਨਿਆਣਾ (niaanaa) *a n m* Young, underage; Baby, infant, child.

ਨਿਆਮਤ (niaamat) *n f* Gift, present, blessing.

ਨਿਆਰਾ (niaaraa) *a* Uncommon, distinct, seperate; ~**ਪਣ** Uncommonness peculiarity, distinctness.

ਨਿਸੰਗ (nishang) *adv a* Certainly, without doubt; Shameless, impudent, outspoken, unhesitating, bold.

ਨਿਸਚਾ (nishchaa) *n m* Faith, certainty belief, determination.

ਨਿਸਚਿਤ (nishchit) *a* Definite, settled, resolved, sure, decided, determined, specific, certain.

ਨਿਸ਼ਠਾ (nishṭhaa) *n f* Allegiance, faith; ~ਪੂਰਵਕ Loyally, faithfully; ~ਵਾਨ Faithful, religious (person).

ਨਿਸਤਾਰਨਾ (nistaarnaa) *v* To liberate, to save, to redeem.

ਨਿਸਤਾਰਾ (nistaaraa) *n m* Salvation, liberation, emancipation, release, redemption, reclamation.

ਨਿਸਫਲ (nisphal) *a* Fruitless, useless, abortive, infructuous.

ਨਿਸਬਤ (nisbat) *n* Relation, proportion, comparison, connection; ~ਨ Comparatively, proportionately, relatively.

ਨਿਸਰਣ (nisaraṇ) *n m* Growth.

ਨਿਸਰਨਾ (nisarnaa) *v* To come up, to spring up, to blossom, to grow.

ਨਿਸ਼ਾਨ (nishaan) *n f* Flag, banner, emblem, symbol, sign, mark, stamp, impression, standard; ~ਚੀ Marksman sriper; ~ਦੇਹੀ

Demarcation.

ਨਿਸ਼ਾਨਾ (nishaanaa) *n m* Aim, mark, target, goal; ~ਮਾਰਨਾ To hit, to aim, to direct.

ਨਿਸ਼ਾਨੀ (nishaanee) *n f* Token, sign, symptom, indication, momento.

ਨਿਹੰਗ (nihang) *n m a* A sect of baptised Sikh, without taint, pure.

ਨਿਹਥਾ (nihathaa) *a* Unarmed, without means, empty handed; ~ਕਰਨਾ To disarm.

ਨਿਹਾਲ (nihaal) *a* Happy, delighted, exalted, satisfied. Also **ਨਿਹਾਲਾ**

ਨਿਹੋਰਾ (nihoraa) *n m* Complaint, reproach.

ਨਿਕਦਰੀ (nikadree) *n f* Degradation, devaluation.

ਨਿਕੰਮਾ (nikammaa) *a* Useless, idle, adject, worthless, valueless, ineffective.

ਨਿੱਕਰ (nikkar) *n f* Shorts, knicker.

ਨਿਕਲਣ (nikalaṇ) *n f* Emergence, exit.

ਨਿਕਲਣਾ (nikalṇaa) *v* To come out, to go out, to evolve, to germinate, to emanate, to derive, to issue, to be published.

ਨਿਕੜਾ (nikṛaa) *a* Small in stature, diminutive.

ਨਿੱਕਾ (nikkaa) *a* Small, little, petty, short.

ਨਿਕਾਸ (nikaas) *n m* Outlet, exit,

emergence, opening, emanation, evacuation, derivation.

ਨਿਕਾਸੀ (nikaasee) *n m* Out-turn, clearance, vacated.

ਨਿਕਾਹ (nikaah) *n m* Nuptial, muslim marriage.

ਨਿਖੱਟੂ (nikhattoo) *a* Worthless, unemployed, idle.

ਨਿਖਰਨਾ (nikharnaa) *v* To brighten up, to be clear, to be cleansed.

ਨਿਖੜਨਾ (nikharnaa) *v* To be separated, to come apart, to diverge.

ਨਿਖਾਰ (nikhaar) *n m* Whiteness, brightness, lustre, elegance.

ਨਿਖਾਰਨਾ (nikhaarnaa) *v* To cleanse, to brighten, to bleach, to purify.

ਨਿਖੇੜਨਾ (nikhernaa) *v* To separate, to differentiate, to select.

ਨਿਖੇੜਾ (nikheraa) *n m* Distinction, differentiation, separation.

ਨਿਗਮ (nigam) *n m* Corporation, corporate body.

ਨਿੱਗਰ (niggar) *a* Solid, hard, heavy, massy, sound, concrete, tangible, strong; ~ਤਾ Solidness, compactness, hardness.

ਨਿਗਰਾਨ (nigraan) *n m a* Supervisor, controller manager, caretaker, watch; Invigilator, surveillan.

ਨਿਗਰਾਨੀ (nigraanee) *n f* Observation, supervision, invigilation, watch, surveiliace, custody, upkeep; ~ਕਰਨਾ To watch, to look after; ~ਵਿਚ ਰਖਣਾ To keep under surveillance.

ਨਿਗਲਣਾ (nigalnaa) *v* To swallow, to gulp, to eat, to embezzle.

ਨਿਗਹਬਾਨ (nigahbaan) *n m* Protector, guardian.

ਨਿਗਹਬਾਨੀ (nigahbaanee) *n* Protection, guard, supervision.

ਨਿਗਾਹ (nigaah) *n f* Sight, vision.

ਨਿਗੂਣੀ (nigoonee) *a* Paltry, of little value.

ਨਿਘਰਨਾ (nigharnaa) *v* To be destroyed, to be immesed, to be swallowed, to be overwhelmed.

ਨਿਘਰਾ (nighraa) *a* Homeless, waif.

ਨਿੱਘਾ (nigghaa) *a* Moderately, warm, magnanimous, patient, self-controlling.

ਨਿਘਾਸ (nighaas) *n m* Warmth; Profit.

ਨਿਘਾਰਨਾ (nigaarnaa) *v* To cause to sink, submerge.

ਨਿਚਲਾ (nichlaa) *a* Lower, under.

ਨਿਚੁੜਨਾ (nichurnaa) *v* To drip, to be squeezed dry. Also **ਨਿਚੜਨਾ**

ਨਿਚੋੜ (nichor) *n m* Gist, essence, resume, quiteessence, summary.

ਨਿਚੋੜਨਾ (nichornaa) *v* To squeeze, to wring, to press, to pour out.

ਨਿੱਛ (nichchh) *n f* Sneeze; ~ਮਾਰਨੀ To

sneeze.

ਨਿਛਾਵਰ (nichhaawar) *n m* Sacrifice, offering.

ਨਿਜਾਤ (nijaat) *n f* Salvation, freedom. Also **ਨਜਾਤ**

ਨਿਜ਼ਾਮ (nizaam) *n m* Ruler, management, rule.

ਨਿਜੀ (nijee) *a* Personal, private, own, self.

ਨਿਝਕ (nijhak) *a* unhesitating, unabashed, forward, bold, fearless, reckless; Frank.

ਨਿਡਰ (niḍar) *a* Fearless, dauntless, undaunted, intrepid; ~**ਤਾ** Fearlessness, temerity, interpidity.

ਨਿਢਾਲ (niḍhaal) *a* Exhausted, depressed, weak, helpless, invalid.

ਨਿਤ (nit) *adv* Always, ever; ~**ਨੇਮ** Daily, routine.

ਨਿਤਰਨਾ (nitarnaa) *v* To be clarified, to be seprated, To be decanted.

ਨਿਤਾਣਾ (nitaaṇaa) *a* Weak, faint, powerless, feeble, sinewless, infirm.

ਨਿਤਾਰਨਾ (nitaarnaa) *v* To clarify, to decant, to winnow, to refine.

ਨਿੰਦਕ (nindak) *n m* Caluminator, defamer, slanderer, censorious, vilifier, backbiter.

ਨਿੰਦਣਾ (nindṇaa) *v* To defame, to

vilify, to blaspheme, to censure, to condemn, to slander, to dispraise.

ਨਿੰਦਰਾਉਣਾ (nidaraunaa) *v* To feel sleepy; to make sleepy, to cause sleep.

ਨਿੰਦਰਾਇਆ (ninderaaiaa) *a* Sleepy, drowsy, slumberous, somnolent.

ਨਿੰਦਾ (nindaa) *n f* Censure, blasphemy, reproach, slander, backbiting; ~**ਕਰਨਾ** To condemn.

ਨਿੰਦਿਤ (nindit) *a* Criticised, condemned, malgned, columniated, defamed.

ਨਿਧੜਕ (nidharak) *a* Fearless, bold, dauntless, outspoken; ~**ਤਾ** Fearlessness, audaciousness.

ਨਿਪਟਣਾ (nipatṇaa) *v* To settle, to tackle, to decide.

ਨਿਪਟਾਰਾ (niptaaraa) *n m* Disposal, settlement; ~**ਕਰਨਾ** To settle, to dispose of, to finish, to decide.

ਨਿਪੁੱਤਾ (niputtaa) *a* Sonless, without male issue.

ਨਿਪੁੰਨ (nipunṇ) *a* Adept, proficient, skilful, expert; ~**ਤਾ** Efficiency, mastery.

ਨਿਬੰਧ (nibandh) *n m* Essay, treatise, article, thesis; ~**ਕਾਰ** Essayist, essay writer.

ਨਿਬੜਨਾ (nibarnaa) *v* To be settled,

to be brought to an issue, to be decided, to be finished.

ਨਿੰਬੂ (nimboo) *n m* Lime, lemon.

ਨਿਬੇੜਨਾ (nibernaa) *v* To finish, to end, to settle, to execute, to perform, to dispose of.

ਨਿਬੇੜਾ (niberaa) *n m* End, finish, settlement, conclusion; Speed or pace of executing a task.

ਨਿਭਣਾ (nibhnaa) *v* To pull on, to carry on, to finish.

ਨਿਭਾਣਾ (nibhaanaa) *v* To perform, to accomplish, to conduct, to keep one's faith. Also **ਨਿਭਾਉਣਾ**

ਨਿੰਮ (nimm) *n f* Margosa tree; *Azadirachta indica.*

ਨਿੰਮਾ (nimmaa) *a* Dim, low, abscure, dubious.

ਨਿਮੰਤਰਨ (nimantaran) *n m* Invitation; ~**ਪੱਤਰ** Invitation card.

ਨਿਮਰਤਾ (nimartaa) *n f* Modesty, courtesy, humbleness, meekness.

ਨਿੰਮਲ (nimmal) *a* Cloudless, clear, fair. Also **ਨਿੰਬਲ**

ਨਿਮਾਣਾ (nimaanaa) *a* Humble, simple, meek, poor, devoid of pride.

ਨਿਯਤ (niyat) *a* Fixed, settled, prescribed, appointed; ~**ਕੰਮ** Assignment, allotted task.

ਨਿਯੰਤਰਣ (niyantran) *n m* Control,

Management, restrain.

ਨਿਯਮ (niyam) *n m* Rule(s), norm, principle, canon.

ਨਿਯਮਿਤ (niyamat) *a* Regular, lawful, methodical.

ਨਿਯੁਕਤ (niyukta) *a* Appointed; ~**ਕਰਨਾ** To appoint.

ਨਿਯੁਕਤੀ (niyukti) *n f* Appointment, nomination.

ਨਿਰੰਕਾਰ (nirankaar) *a* Formless; The Formless One, God.

ਨਿਰਖ (nirakh) *n m* Rate, price, cost, current market rate.

ਨਿਰਖਣਾ (nirakhnaa) *v* To see, to look, to appreciate, to ascertain.

ਨਿਰੱਖਰ (nirakkhar) *a* Illiterate, unlettered; ~**ਤਾ** Illiteracy.

ਨਿਰਗੁਣ (nirgun) *a* Absolute, virtueless, formless, transcendent, without qualities, unskilled.

ਨਿਰਛਲ (nirchhal) *a* Candid, frank, naive, sincere, guileless, unsophisticated.

ਨਿਰੰਜਨ (niranjan) *a* Formless; The formless one, God.

ਨਿਰਜਨ (nirjan) *a* Unpopulated, desolate, uninhabited.

ਨਿਰਣਾ (nirnaa) *n m* Decision, verdict, judgement, conclusion. Also **ਨਿਰਨਾ**

ਨਿਰੰਤਰ (nirantar) *a adv* Continous,

incessant, ceaseless, perpetual, constant, consecutive, uninterrupted; Ceaselessly; ~ਤਾ Continuity, continuum, uninterruptedness.

ਨਿਰਦਈ (nirdaee) *a* Cruel, merciless, callous, ruthless, brutal, stern.

ਨਿਰਦੇਸ਼ (nirdesh) *n m* Direction, reference; ~ਕ Director, supervisor.

ਨਿਰਦੋਸ਼ (nirdosh) *a* Faultless, innocent, inculpable, guiltless, correct.

ਨਿਰਧਨ (nirdhan) *a* Poor, penniless; ~ਤਾ Poverty, pauperism.

ਨਿਰਨਾ (nirnaa) *a* Empty stomach, taking no food. Also **ਨਿਰਣਾ**

ਨਿਰਨਾਇਕ (nirnaaik) *a* Decisive, affirmative.

ਨਿਰਪੱਖ (nirpakkh) *a* Impartial, unbiased, unprejudiced, neutral; ~ਤਾ Neutrality.

ਨਿਰਪੇਖ (nirpekh) *a* Absolute, neutral, independent.

ਨਿਰਬਲ (nirbal) *a* Weak, powerless, frail, decrepit; ~ਤਾ Weakness, fraility.

ਨਿਰਭੈ (nirbhai) *a* Fearless, dauntless, bold, intrepid; ~ਤਾ Fearlessness, dauntlessness, intrepidity, boldness,

indomitability.

ਨਿਰਮਲ (nirmal) *a* Clear, transparent, pure, spotless, unpolluted, clean, lucid, crystalline; ~ਤਾ Cleanliness, purity, transparency.

ਨਿਰਮਾਣ (nirmaan) *n m* Construction, manufacture, production.

ਨਿਰਮੂਲ (nirmool) *a* Baseless, groundless.

ਨਿਰਮੋਹੀ (nirmohee) *a* Indifferent, without love and affection.

ਨਿਰਲੇਪ (nirlep) *a* Neutral, disinterested; ਗੁਟ~ Non-aligned.

ਨਿਰਵਾਸੀ (nirvaasee) *a* Non-resident.

ਨਿਰਵਾਚਨ (nirvaachan) *n m* Election.

ਨਿਰਵਾਣ (nirvaan) *n m* Emancipation, salvation, denouement, freedom from worldly concern. Also **ਨਿਰਵਾਨ**

ਨਿਰਵੈਰ (nirvair) *a* Without malice, without hatred, free from animosity.

ਨਿਰਾ (niraa) *a adv* More, simple, unalloyed, only, sheer; Entirely, merely, simply.

ਨਿਰਾਸ (niraas) *a* Disappointed; Despaired, disconsolate; ~ਤਾ Despair, frustration, dejection. Also **ਨਿਰਾਸ਼ਾ**

ਨਿਰਾਹਾਰ (niraahaar) *a* Fasting, without meals.

ਨਿਰਾਕਾਰ (niraakaar) *a* Incorporeal, formless.

ਨਿਰਾਦਰ (niraadar) *n m* Insult, dishonour, disrespect.

ਨਿਰਾਦਰੀ (niraadaree) *n f* Disgrace, disrespect, insult, abasement, blasphemy.

ਨਿਰਾਲਾ (niraalaa) *a* Peculiar, extraordinary, excellent, odd strange, rare, distinct; ~ਪਣ Strangeness, unusualness, peculiarity.

ਨਿਰੀਖਕ (nireekhak) *n m* Inspector, supervisor, invigilator, observer.

ਨਿਰੀਖਣ (nireekhan) *n m* Observation, inspection, invigilation. .

ਨਿਰੋਧ (nirodh) *n m* Restriction, obstruction, repression; Condom.

ਨਿਰੋਲ (nirol) *a* Unadurated, unmixed, clear, pure.

ਨਿਲੱਜ (nillaj) *a* Shameless, devoid of a sense of honour, immodest, brazen faced impudent.

ਨਿਲੰਬਨ (nilamban) *n m* Suspension.

ਨਿਲਾਮੀ (nillaamee) *n f* Auction.

ਨਿਵਾਉਣਾ (nivaaunaa) *v* To cause, to bend, to humble, to bring under descipline.

ਨਿਵਾਸ (nivass) *n m* Residence, house, dwelling quarter, habitation, domicile. Also ਨਿਵਾਸਾ

ਨਿਵਾਸੀ (nivaasee) *n m* Resident, inhabitant, dweller, citizen.

ਨਿਵਾਜਣਾ (nivaajnaa) *v* To honour, to dignify, to crown.

ਨਿਵਾਣ (nivaan) *n f* Slope, drop, downward, lowness, valley, depression.

ਨਿਵਾਰਨ (nivaaran) *n m* Healing, prevention, hindering or removing, eradication.

ਨਿਵਾਰਨਾ (nivaarnaa) *v* To heal, to prevent, to remove, to eradicate.

ਨਿਵਾਲਾ (nivaalaa) *n m* Morsel, mouthful.

ਨਿਵੇਦਨ (nivedan) *n m* Request, appeal, petition, representation; ~ਪੱਤਰ Application.

ਨੀਅਤ (neeyat) *n f* Intention, motive, desire, aim, purpose. Also ਨੀਤ, ਨੀਯਤ

ਨੀਂਹ (neenh) *n f* Foundation, base, basemen, bottom.

ਨੀਂਗਰ (neengar) *n m* Boy, child, infant, toddler.

ਨੀਚ (neech) *a* Mean, vile, low, humble, inferior, slavish, sordid, disgraceful; ~ਤਾ Meaness, degeneracy, vulgarity.

ਨੀਝ (neejh) *n f* Sharp look, close inspection; ~ਸ਼ਾਲਾ Observatory.

ਨੀਤੀ (neetee) *n f* Policy, diplomacy,

prudence, counsel, politics; ~ਵਾਨ Poltician, statesman, moralist.

ਨੀਂਦ (neend) n f Sleep, slumber; ਡੂੰਘੀ~ Coma.

ਨੀਮ (neem) a prep Half, middle; Quasi, semi, demi; ~ਗਰਮ Lukewarm; ~ਪਾਗਲ Half mad.

ਨੀਲ (neel) n m a Bruise, blue; Indigo; Ten billion, 10,000,000,000,000 ~ਕੰਠ Blue Jay.

ਨੀਲਮ (neelam) n m Gem, sapphire.

ਨੀਲਾ (neelaa) a Blue, bluish, azure; ਅਸਮਾਨੀ~ Sky blue.

ਨੀਵਾਂ (neevaan) a Low, lower; ~ਕਰਨਾ To lower, to demean.

ਨੁਸਖਾ (nuskhaa) n m Prescription, recipe, treatise.

ਨੁਸ਼ਾਦਰ (nushaadar) n m Ammonium chloride.

ਨੁਹਾਰ (nuhaar) n f Appearance, features, countenance, outline, face, similitude.

ਨੁਕਸ (nukas) n m Defect, fault, flaw, snag, lacuna, weakness, blemish; ~ਕੱਢਣਾ To find fault, to pick holes, to carp; ~ਦਾਰ Defective, faulty.

ਨੁਕਸਾਨ (nuksaan) n m Loss, harm, damage, deficiency.

ਨੁਕਤਾ (nuktaa) n m Point, dot; ~ਚੀਨ Critic, faultfinder; ~ਚੀਨੀ Criticism,

fault finding.

ਨੁੱਕਰ (nukkar) n m Corner, extremity, nook, apex of an angel.

ਨੁਕੀਲਾ (nukeelaa) a Pointed, sharp, barbed, angular.

ਨੁਮਾਇੰਦਗੀ (numaindagee) n Representation; representativeness; ~ਕਰਨਾ To represent.

ਨੁਮਾਇੰਦਾ (numaindaa) n m Representative, deputy, agent.

ਨੁਚੜਨਾ (nucharnaa) v To exude.

ਨੁਮਾਇਸ਼ (numaaish) n f Show, exhibition, display, demonstration.

ਨੂੰਹ (noonh) n f Daughter-in-law, Son's wife.

ਨੂਰ (noor) n m Light, splendour, brilliance.

ਨੂਰੀ (nooree) a Bright, lustrous.

ਨੇਸਤੀ (nestee) n f Laziness, lethargy langour; Non-existence, nothingness.

ਨੇਸਤੋਨਾਬੂਦ (nestonaabood) a Fully destroyed, utterly devastated.

ਨੇਹੁੰ (nehun) n m Love, affection.

ਨੇਕ (nek) a Good, kind, virtuous; ~ਦਿਲ Sincere, honest; ~ਨਾਮ Renowned, famous; ~ਨਾਮੀ Fame, good reputation; ~ਨੀਅਤੀ Honesty, integrity, rectitude.

ਨੇਕੀ (nekee) n f Goodness, virtue,

kindness.

ਨੇਜ਼ਾ (nezaa) *n m* Long spear, lance.

ਨੇਤਰ (netar) *n m* Eye.

ਨੇਤਾ (netaa) *n m* Leader, chief, directing head; Demogogue; Torchbearer; ~ਗੀਰੀ Leadership, demogogy.

ਨੇਂਦਰਾ (nendraa) *n m* Contribution to a wedding feast. Also ਨਿਊਂਦਾ

ਨੇਮਾਵਲੀ (nemaavalee) *n f* Code, directory.

ਨੇੜੇ (nere) *adv* Near, close by, beside, at hand.

ਨੋਕ (nok) *n f* Point, end, tip, angle; ~ਝੋਕ Mutual repartee, pleasantry; ~ਦਾਰ Pointed, angular, sharp, conical, barbed.

ਨੋਚਣਾ (nochṇaa) *v* To pinch, to tear, to scratch, to pluck.

ਨੋਟ (noṭ) *n m* Note, noting, minutes; Currency note; ~ਕਰਨਾ To note, to note down, to take notes, to write; To take notice, to be warned.

ਨੌਕਰ (haukar) *n m* Servant, attendant, domestic employees; ~ਸ਼ਾਹੀ Bureaucracy.

ਨੌਕਰੀ (naukree) *n f* Service, employment, job, post.

ਨੌਕਾ (naukaa) *n f* Boat.

ਨੌਗਾ (naugaa) *n m* Portion, share, lot; Allotment, quota.

ਨੌਜਵਾਨ (naujawaan) *n m a* Youth, youngman; Youthful.

ਨੌਬਤ (naubat) *n f* Turn time, opportunity, state, condition.

ਨੌਲਖਾ (naulakhaa) *a* Very valuable, costing nine lakhs currency, priceless.

ਨੌਲੀ (naulee) *n f* Nose, turned up nose.

ਨੌਲਨਾ (naulnaa) *v* To abuse, to rebuke, to scold, to reprove, to revile at.

ਪ

ਪ Twenty sixth letter of Gurmukhi alphabets, pronounced as 'pappaa'.

ਪਉਂਚਾ (paunchaa) *n m* Talon, opening of trousers. Also **ਪੱਚਾ**

ਪਉਲਾ (paulaa) *n m* Shoe, footwear.

ਪਉੜੀ (pauṛee) *n f* Stanza.

ਪਸ਼ਚਾਤਾਪ (pashchaataap) *n m* Repetence, remorse, penitence, expiation.

ਪਸਤੌਲ (pastaul) *n f* Pistol, revolver.

ਪਸੰਦ (pasand) *n m* Choice, liking, approval, selection; **ਆਰਾਮ~** Easy going; **ਮਨ~** Favourite.

ਪਸੰਦੀਦਾ (pasandeedaa) *a* Liked, favourite, chosen.

ਪਸਪਾ (paspaa) *a* Stepping backward, running away, fleeing; **~ਕਰਨਾ** To make one run away, to defeat, to rout.

ਪਸ਼ਮ (pasham) *n f* Soft wool, fur; **~ਦਾਰ** wooly.

ਪਸ਼ਮੀਨਾ (pashmeenaa) *n m* Soft fine wool, fur.

ਪਸਰਨਾ (pasarnaa) *v* To Spread out, to expand, to be stretched out.

ਪਸਲੀ (paslee) *n f* Rib.

ਪਸ਼ਾਬ (pashaab) *n m* Urine; **~ਕਰਨਾ** To make water, to urinate; **~ਖ਼ਾਨਾ** Urinal. Also **ਪਿਸ਼ਾਬ**

ਪਸਾਰਨਾ (pasaarnaa) *v* To spread, to extend, to stretch, to diffuse.

ਪੰਸਾਰੀ (pansaaree) *n m* Grocer, druggist, spice seller, apothecary. Also **ਪੰਸਾਰੀ** or **ਪਨਸਾਰੀ**

ਪਸੀਜਣਾ (paseejṇaa) *v* To deliquesce, to be compassionate, to relent, to prespire.

ਪਸੀਨਾ (paseenaa) *n m* Sweat, prespiration; **~ਆਉਣਾ** To sweat, prespire.

ਪਸ਼ੂ (pashoo) *n m* Animal, beast, brute, cattle, quadruped; **~ਪਾਲਣ** Animal husbandry, cattle, breeding.

ਪਸ਼ੇਮਾਨ (pashemaan) *a* Sorry, ashamed, penitent, regretful, remorseful repentent.

ਪਹਾੜ (pahaaṛ) *n m* Mountain; **~ਟੁੱਟ ਪੈਣਾ** Advent of calamity.

ਪਹਾੜਾ (pahaaṛaa) *n m* Multiplication table.

ਪਹਾੜੀ (pahaaṛee) *n m a* Hill, hillock; Hilly, alpine, mountainous; **~ਦੱਰਾ** Revine, mountain pass.

ਪਹਿਨਣਾ (pahinṇaa) *v* To wear, to

put on, to dress.

ਪਹਿਰਾ (paheraa) *n m* Watch, escort, guard, patrol; ~**ਦੇਣਾ** To keep watch, to guard.

ਪਹਿਰਾਵਾ (paheraawaa) *n m* Dress, fashion, costume, attire.

ਪਹਿਲ (pahel) *n f* Priority, preference, precedence; ~**ਕਰਨਾ** To lead, to forestall.

ਪਹਿਲਵਾਨ (pahelwaan) *n m* Wrestler, champion, athlete.

ਪਹਿਲਾਂ (pahelaan) *adv* At first, formerly, previously, before; ~**ਆਉਣਾ** To precede, to come early.

ਪਹਿਲਾ (pahelaa) *a* First, primary, maiden, former, previous; ~**ਭਾਸ਼ਣ** Maiden speech.

ਪਹੀਆ (pahiyaa) *n m* Wheel, cart track.

ਪਹੁੰਚ (pahunch) *n f* Arrival, access, acknowledgement, approach, receipt.

ਪਹੁੰਚਾ (paunchaa) *n m* Claw, paw; Hand, wrist; Lower opening of trousers or shorts.

ਪਹੁੰਚਣਾ (pahunchnaa) *v* To reach, to arrive at, to attain.

ਪਹੇਲੀ (pahelee) *n f* Riddle, quiz.

ਪਕਣਾ (paknaa) *v* To ripen, to be cooked, to bake.

ਪਕਵਾਨ (pakwaan) *n m* Cooked delicacies, bakemeats, pastry, fried cakes, sweatmeats.

ਪਕੜ (pakar) *n f* Hold, seizure, catch, bout, clasp, clamp, influence; ~**ਲੈਣਾ** To catch, to arrest, to clutch, to hold, to grasp; ~**ਵਿਚ ਆਣਾ** Come in one's hold.

ਪਕੜਨਾ (pakarnaa) *v* To catch, to arrest, to hold, to seize, to grip.

ਪੱਕਾ (pakkaa) *a* Cooked, ripe, strong, perfect, firm, established, tight, permanent, certain, sure, resolute, stable, hard, solid; ~**ਕਰਨਾ** To confirm, to harden, to affirm, to stabilize; ~**ਖਾਣਾ** Fried cooked food; ~**ਦੋਸਤ** Fast friend; ~**ਰੰਗ** Fast colour; ~**ਮਾਲ** Finished goods.

ਪਕਾਉਣਾ (pakaaunaa) *v* To cook, to bake, to fry, to ripen, to make firm.

ਪਕਿਆਈ (pakiaaee) *n f* Hardness firmness, strength; Steadfastness.

ਪਖੰਡ (pakhand) *n m* Hypocricy, humbug, deceit, prudery, pretence.

ਪਖੰਡੀ (pakhandee) *a* Imposter, cheat, hypocrite; Imposter, deceitful, dissembler. Also **ਪਖੰਡਣ** (*f*)

ਪਖਪਾਤ (pakkhpaat) *n m* Partiality, favour, bias, partisanship, nepotism.

ਪਖਵਾੜਾ (pakhwaaṛaa) *n m* Fortnight, lunar fortnight.

ਪੱਖਾ (pakkhaa) *n m* Fan, propeller.

ਪਖਾਵਜ (pakhaavaj) *n m* A kind of drum.

ਪੱਖੀ (pakkhee) *a n m f* Partial, biased; Supporter, co-party man; Partisan; Bird; Hand fan.

ਪੰਖੇਰੂ (pankheroo) *n m* Bird, winged animal; Spirit.

ਪੱਗ (pagg) *n f* Turban; ~ਲਾਹੁਣੀ To insult; ~ਵਟਾਉਣੀ To make friends with.

ਪੰਗਤ (pangat) *n f* Line, row, column.

ਪਗੜੀ (pagṛee) *n f* Turban, imprest; ~ਉਛਾਲਣੀ To ridicule; ~ਪੈਰਾਂ ਤੇ ਰਖਣਾ To submit, to beg mercy; ~ਲਾਹੁਣੀ To disgrace, to insult. Also **ਪੱਗ**

ਪੰਗਾ (pangaa) *n m* Briar, thorn, splinter, prickle.

ਪੰਗੇਬਾਜ਼ (Pangebaaz) *n m* Problematist, quarrelsome.

ਪੰਘਰਨਾ (pangharnaa) *v* To melt, to fuse, to liquefy, to smell.

ਪੰਘੂੜਾ (panghooṛaa) *n m* Cradle, crib.

ਪਚਨਾ (pachnaa) *v* To be digested, to be consumed.

ਪੰਚਮ (pancham) *a* Fifth (note in music) high pitched, sharp.

ਪੰਚਰ (panchar) *n m* Puncture in rubber tube or bladder punctured; ~ਲਾਉਣਾ To mend, to repair, to puncture.

ਪਚਾਉਣਾ (pachaauṇaa) *v* To digest, to assimilate; ਪੈਸਾ~ To embezzle money.

ਪੱਛਣਾ (pachchhṇaa) *v* To scarify, to make incision, to incise.

ਪਛਤਾਉਣਾ (pachhtaauṇaa) *v* To repent, to grieve, to regret.

ਪਛਤਾਵਾ (pachhtaavaa) *n* Repentence, regret, remorse, grief, penetence, ruefulness.

ਪੱਛਮੀ (pachhmee) *a* Western.

ਪਛੜਨਾ (pachhaṛnaa) *v* To lag behind, to fall behind.

ਪਛਾਣ (pachaaṇ) *n f* Recognition, acquaintance, identification.

ਪਛਾਣਨਾ (pachaaṇnaa) *v* To identify, to recognise, to distinguish, to perceive, to make out.

ਪਛਾੜਨਾ (pachhaarṇaa) *v* To over power, to prostrate, to defeat, to overthrow.

ਪੰਛੀ (panchhee) *n m* Bird; ~ਵਿਗਿਆਨ Ornithology.

ਪੱਛੀ (pachchhee) *n f* Small basket, sugarcane rind.

ਪੱਜ (pajj) *n m* Excuse, pretence, pretext.

ਪੰਜਾ (panjaa) *n m* Paw, claw, grip; The figure 5.

ਪਜਾਮਾ (pajaamaa) *n m* Trousers.

ਪੰਜੇਬ (panjeb) *n f* Anklet, tinkling silver ornament.

ਪਟਕਣਾ (paṭaknaa) *v* To knock down, to overthrow, to dash against.

ਪਟਕਾ (paṭkaa) *n m* A waist cloth, turban, sash, belt, girdle.

ਪਟੜਾ (paṭraa) *n m* Wooden plank, wash board.

ਪਟੜੀ (paṭree) *n f* Way, pavement, footpath; Silver ornament;~ਬੈਠਣਾ To have harmonious relations.

ਪਟਾ (paṭaa) *n m* Strap, badge, dog-coller; Lease deed.

ਪਟਾਕ (paṭaak) *n m* Crash, explosion, thump.

ਪਟਾਕਾ (paṭaakaa) *n m* cracker.

ਪਟਾਕਣਾ (paṭaaknaa) *v* To talk incessantly.

ਪੱਟੀ (paṭṭee) *n f* Bandage, cloth or metal strip; ਹਵਾਈ~ Air strep; ~ਪੜ੍ਹਾਨਾ To tutor; ਉਲਟੀ~ਪੜ੍ਹਾਨਾ To misguide.

ਪੱਠਾ (paṭṭhaa) *n m* Muscles, tendon, sinew; A robust youngman; Young wrestler; A fodder plant or grass.

ਪਠਾਰ (paṭhaar) *n m* Plateau.

ਪਠੋਰਾ (paṭhoraa) *n m* Young goat;

Kid.

ਪੰਡ (panḍ) *n f* Bundle, package, bale burden.

ਪੰਡਾਲ (panḍaal) *n m* Sitting place for marriage or public meeting.

ਪਤ (pat) *n f* Honour, respect; ~ਲਾਹੁਣੀ To dishonour, to disgrace.

ਪੱਤ (patt) *n m* Leaf. Also ਪੱਤਾ

ਪਤੰਗ (patang) *n f* Kite.

ਪਤੰਗਾ (patangaa) *n m* Worm, moth, spark, live coal.

ਪੱਤਰ (pattar) *n m* Letter, foliage, document, deed, leaf, paper, newspaper, periodical.

ਪਤਲਾ (patlaa) *a* Thin, lean, slim, weak, diluted, watery; ~ਪਣ Thinness, leanness.

ਪਤਲੂਣ (patloon) *n f* Pantaloons.

ਪਤਾ (pataa) *n m* Address, knowledge, information, trace; ~ਲਗਣਾ To know.

ਪੱਤਾ (pattaa) *n m* Card, leaf.

ਪਤਾਸਾ (pataasaa) *n m* A kind of sweet meat prepared by sugar only.

ਪਤਾਲ (pataal) *n m* Hell, lower world, infernal regions, nadir, hader.

ਪੰਤਾਲੀ (pantaalee) *a* Forty-five. Also ਪੰਜਤਾਲੀ

ਪਤਾਲੂ (pataaloo) *n m* Testes, testicles.

ਪਤਿਆਉਣਾ (patiaaunaa) v To confide in, to trust, to belive, to depend on, to appease, to soothe.

ਪਤੀ (patee) n m Husband, master; ਸੈਨਾ~ Commander; ਰਾਸ਼ਟ੍~ President; ~ਬ੍ਰਤਾ Chaste woman; A woman faithful to her husband.

ਪੱਤੀ (pattee) n f Portion, share, division.

ਪਤੀਜਣਾ (pateejanaa) v To be reassured, satisfied or trustful, to be persuaded.

ਪਤੀਲਾ (pateelaa) n m Cooking pot, cooking vessel.

ਪੱਤੇਬਾਜ਼ (pattebaaz) a Tricksy, trickster, cheat, deceiver, swindler.

ਪੱਤੇਬਾਜ਼ੀ (pattebaazee) n f Trickery, cheating, swindling.

ਪੰਥ (panth) n m Religious sect, way, path, custom.

ਪੱਥਣਾ (patthnaa) v To make or mould with strokes of hand (bricks, cowdung cakes, etc.)

ਪੱਥਰ (patthar) n m a Stone, gem; Hard, heavy; ~ਤੇ ਲੀਕ Certainly; ~ਦਾ ਕੋਲਾ Hard coke; ~ਦਾ ਫ਼ਰਸ਼ Pavement; ~ਦਿਲ Hard hearted; ~ਮਾਰਨਾ To stone, to pelt.

ਪਥਰਾਉਣਾ (pathraaunaa) v To become hard, to be dead, to calcify, to fossilize, to become insipid.

ਪੱਥਰੀ (patthree) n f Flint, small stone, gallstone, stone in kidney.

ਪਥਰੀਲਾ (pathreelaa) a Strony, full of stones.

ਪੱਥਲਣਾ (pathallanaa) v To turn over, to cause to turn, to overturn.

ਪਥੇਰਾ (patheraa) n m Brick-maker.

ਪਦ (pad) n (1) Foot; Foot step; (2) Couplet, stanza, verse; Expression, word form; (3) Post, rank, degree, status; ~ਉਨਤੀ Promotion; ~ਅਧਿਕਾਰੀ Officer, official.

ਪੱਦ (padd) n m Fart, passing wind noisily through anus; ~ਮਾਰਨਾ To fart, to pass wind.

ਪੱਦਣਾ (paddnaa) v To pass wind; To show fear or cowardice, to behave cowardly.

ਪੰਦਰਾਂ (pandraan) a Fifteenth.

ਪਦਵੀ (padvee) n f Position, rank, degree, status, designation.

ਪਦਾਉਣਾ (padaaunaa) v To weary out, to reduce, to frighten, to cause to pass the wind.

ਪਦਾਰਥ (padaarath) n m Thing, stuff, object, substance, matter, material, food; ~ਵਾਦ Matrialism.

ਪੰਧ (pandh) n m Journey, route,

distance, passage, path, way; ~ਕਰਨਾ To travel.

ਪੱਧਤੀ (paddhatee) *n f* System, method; Custom; Ritual.

ਪੱਧਰ (paddhar) *n f* Level, plane, evenness; Standard, measure, norm, stratum.

ਪਧਰਾ (padhraa) *a* Smooth, even, easy, level, plain, flat, simple.

ਪੰਨਾ (pannaa) *n m* Leaf, page, foil; Emerald.

ਪਨਾਹ (panaah) *n f* Refuge, asylum, protection, shelter; ~ਦੇਣੀ To give refuge, to shelter; ਬੇ~ Unlimited, infinite, too much.

ਪਨੀਰ (paneer) *n m* Cheese.

ਪਪੜੀ (papṛee) *n f* Crust.

ਪੱਪੀ (pappee) *n f* Kiss.

ਪਪੀਹਾ (papeehaa) *n m* Rain bird.

ਪਪੀਤਾ (papeetaa) *n m* Papaya, papaw.

ਪੱਬ (pabb) *n m* Foot, fore part of the foot, toe; Water-lily.

ਪਰ (par) *n m conj Prep adv* Feather, wing; But, however; On, at; Last, bygone; ~ਉਪਕਾਰ Benevolence, philanthropy; Beneficence; ~ਅਧੀਨ (ਪਰਾਧੀਨ) Dependent, slave.

ਪ੍ਰਸੰਸਾ (prasansaa) *n f* Praise, applause, eulogy, admiration, appreciation. Also ਪਰਸੰਸਾ

ਪ੍ਰਸੰਗ (prasang) *n m* Context, theme, topic, incident, anecdote. Also ਪਰਸੰਗ

ਪਰਸਣਾ (parasṇaa) *v* To touch, to feel.

ਪ੍ਰਸਤਾਵ (prastaav) *n m* Proposal, motion, proposition, resolution, essay; ~ਕ Mover, proposer; ~ਨਾ Prologue, preface, foreward, introduction.

ਪ੍ਰਸੰਨ (prasann) *a* Glad, happy, delighted; ~ਤਾ Happiness, joy, merriment.

ਪ੍ਰਸ਼ਨ (prashan) *n m* Question, enquiry, problem; ~ਪੱਤਰ Question paper.

ਪਰਸਪਰ (parsapar) *a* Mutual, reciprocal, respective.

ਪ੍ਰਸ਼ਾਸਨ (prashaasan) *n m* Administration. Also ਪਰਸ਼ਾਸਨ

ਪ੍ਰਸਾਦ (prasaad) *n m* Kindness, favour, boon, blessing, food offered to god, communion food. Also ਪਰਸਾਦ

ਪ੍ਰਸਾਰ (prasaar) *n m* Extension, transmission, propagation.

ਪ੍ਰਸਾਰਣ (prasaaraṇ) *n m* Broadcast, transmission, propagation. Also ਪਰਸਾਰਣ

ਪ੍ਰਸਿੱਧ (prasiddh) *a* Famous, eminent, known, renowned, reputed,

distinguished, popular. Also
ਪਰਸਿੱਧ

ਪ੍ਰਸੂਤ (prasoot) *n m* Maternity,
childbirth. Also **ਪਰਸੂਤ**

ਪਰਸੋਂ (parsoon) *a* Day after
tomorrow, day before yesterday.

ਪਰਾਂ (praan) *adv* Beyond, farther,
ahead, at a distance.

ਪਰਹੇਜ਼ (parhez) *n m* Forbearance,
abstinence, prevention,
avoidance.

ਪ੍ਰਕਾਸ਼ (prakaash) *n m* Light, day
light.

ਪਰਕੋਟਾ (parkotaa) *n m* Parapet,
rampart.

ਪਰਖ (parakh) *n f* Trial, examination,
criticism, probation.

ਪਰਖਣਾ (parakhnaa) *v* To test, to
examine, to evaluate, to review, to
assess genuineness.

ਪਰਗਟ (pargat) *a* Apparent, clear,
disclosed, overt, known, obvious,
visible; ~**ਕਰਨਾ** To disclose, to
express, to manifest, to unveil, to
expose, to reveal. Also **ਪ੍ਰਗਟ**

ਪ੍ਰਗਤੀ (pragatee) *n f* Progress,
growth.

ਪਰਚਣਾ (parchnaa) *v* To be amused,
to be satisfied, to be entertained,
to be diverted, to be engaged.

ਪਰਚੱਲਤ (parchallat) *a* Current,

prevailing, in vogue.

ਪਰਚਾ (parchaa) *n m* Examination
paper; Newspaper, tabloid; Bill,
invoice.

ਪਰਚਾਉਣਾ (parchaaunaa) *v* To amuse,
to entertain, to divert, assuage,
console satisfy.

ਪਰਚਾਰ (parchaar) *n m* Propgation,
publicity, preaching, promulgation,
spreading. Also **ਪ੍ਰਚਾਰ**

ਪਰਚੂਣ (parchoon) *n f a* Grocery; In
retail.

ਪਰਛੱਤੀ (parchhattee) *n f* Loft.

ਪਰਛਾਵਾਂ (parcchavaan) *n m* Shadow,
shade, rejection.

ਪਰਜਾ (parjaa) *n f* Public, people,
subjects, tenants, dependents,
followers; ~**ਤੰਤਰ** Republic,
democracy.

ਪਰਤ (parat) *n f* Fold, layer, stratum,
crust; Copy, transcript; ~**ਦਾਰ**
Stratified, laminated.

ਪਰਤੱਖ (partakkh) *a* Direct, obvious,
evident, clear, overt, visible, red;
~**ਹੋਣਾ** To materialize; ~**ਕਰਨਾ** To
actualize, to invoke.

ਪਰਤਣਾ (partanaa) *v* To turn, to
return, to revert, to recede, to
get back.

ਪਰਤੰਤਰ (partantar) *a* Dependent,
subdued; ~**ਤਾ** Dependence,

reliance.

ਪਰਤਾਉਣਾ (partaaunaa) *v* To return, to turn over, to refund, to test, to experiment.

ਪਰਤਾਪ (partaap) *n m* Splendour, brilliance, glory, warmth.

ਪਰਤਾਵਾ (partaavaa) *n m* Trial, experiment, examination, test.

ਪ੍ਰਤਿਨਿਧ (pratinidh) *n m* Representative.

ਪ੍ਰਤਿਪੂਰਕ (pratipoorak) *a* Compensatory.

ਪ੍ਰਤਿਯੋਗਤਾ (pratiyogtaa) *n m* Competition.

ਪ੍ਰਤਿਵਾਦ (prativaad) *n m* Refutation, argument, protest.

ਪ੍ਰਤੀਕ (prateek) *n m* Symbol, sign, emblem; **~ਸ਼ਾਸਤਰ** Symbolics; **~ਵਾਦ** Symbolism.

ਪ੍ਰਤੀਖਿਆ (prateekhiyaa) *n f* Wait, expectation.

ਪਰਦਖਣਾ (pardakhnaa) *n m* Circumambulation, perambulation.

ਪਰਦਾ (pardaa) *n m* Curtain, screen, mask, veil, fold, partition wall, privacy, concealment, disguise; **~ਉਠਣਾ** Curtain to be raised; To be uncovered, to be disclosed; **~ਉਠਾਉਣਾ** To raise curtain, to reveal; **~ਕਰਨਾ** To draw a curtain or veil, to conceal, to hide from view.

ਪਰਦੇਸ (pardes) *n m* Foreign country.

ਪਰਧਾਨ (pardhaan) *n m* President, chairman, chief. Also **ਪ੍ਰਧਾਨ**

ਪਰਨਾਲਾ (parnaalaa) *n m* Gutter, spout, drain for leaving off water from roof.

ਪਰਪੰਚ (parpanch) *n m* Deceit, falsehood, treachery; The world.

ਪਰਪੰਰਾ (parampraa) *n f* Tradition, convention, aeon.

ਪਰਫੁੱਲਤ (parphullat) *a* Glad, happy, pleased, flourishing.

ਪ੍ਰਬੰਧ (prabandh) *n m* Management, organisation, administration, arrangement, system.

ਪ੍ਰਬਲ (prabal) *a* Strong, mighty, powerful, violent, dominant.

ਪਰਭਾਤ (prabhaat) *n f* Dawn, early morning. Also **ਪ੍ਰਭਾਤ**

ਪਰਭਾਵ (parbhaav) *n m* Influence, effect, impression, sway; **~ਸ਼ਾਲੀ** Effective, impressive, influential, inspiring; **~ਹੀਣ** Ineffective; **ਵਾਦ** Impressionism. Also **ਪ੍ਰਭਾਵ**

ਪਰਮਾਣ (parmaan) *n m* Proof, example, authority, illustration; **~ਪੱਤਰ** Certificate.

ਪਰਮਾਣੂ (parmaanoo) *n m* Atom; **~ਸ਼ਕਤੀ** Atomic energy.

ਪਰਮਾਤਮਾ (parmaatmaa) *n m* God, the supreme being.

ਪਰਮਾਰਥ (parmaarath) *n m* Virtue, the subtle truth, salvation, the first object, the best end.

ਪ੍ਰਯਤਨ (prayatan) *n m* Effort, endeavour, attempt, struggle.

ਪ੍ਰਯੋਗ (prayog) *n m* Experiment, usage.

ਪਰਲੋ (parlo) *n f* Doomsday, the day of last judgement, final destruction or end of the universe; Great widespread calamity.

ਪਰਲੋਕ (parlok) *n m* The other or the next world, the hereafter; ~ਸਿਧਾਰਨਾ To die, pass away, to breathe one's last, to expire, decease; ~ਗਮਨ Death, decease.

ਪਰਵਰ (parvar) *a* Patron, nourisher; ~ਦਗਾਰ Providence, God.

ਪਰਵਰਿਸ਼ (parvarish) *n m* Nourishment, fostering, patronising, support.

ਪਰਵਾਸ (parvaas) *n m* Migration.

ਪਰਵਾਸੀ (parvaasee) *a* Migrant, emigrant, resident in foreign country.

ਪਰਵਾਹ (parvaah) *n f* Care, concern, attention, anxiety, regard; ~ਕਰਨੀ To heed, to be care (about), to pay attention; ਬੇ~ Careless, indifferent, unmindful, unreflecting.

ਪਰਵਾਨ (parvaan) *a* Accepted, acknowledged, true, just; ਗੀ~ Approval, acceptence, sanction, recognition; ~ਚੜੂਨਾ To grow up, to be accepted.

ਪਰਵਾਨਾ (parvaanaa) *n* Moth, butterfly, lover; Note, warrant, written order.

ਪਰਵਾਰ (parvaar) *n m* Family, household, relation; ~ਨਿਯੋਜਨ Family planning. Also ਪਰਿਵਾਰ

ਪਰਾਂ (paraan) *adv* Away, beyond, further on, off, far, apart.

ਪਰਾਇਆ (praaiaa) *a* Stranger, foreign, alien.

ਪ੍ਰਾਸਚਿਤ (praaschit) *n m* Repentence, atonement, expiation.

ਪ੍ਰਾਹੁਣਾ (praahunaa) *n m* Guest, visitor.

ਪ੍ਰਾਣ (praan) *n m* Breath, life, soul courage, energy; ~ਦੇਣਾ To give up life; ~ਲੈਣਾ To kill.

ਪ੍ਰਾਣੀ (praanee) *n m a* Animal, living creature, man or woman; Living, alive, animate.

ਪ੍ਰਾਂਤ (praant) *n m* Province.

ਪ੍ਰਾਤ (praat) *n f* Large brass dish, kneeding pan.

ਪਰਾਂਦਾ (praandaa) *n m* Bandeau, braid, coloured yarn for tying up hair. Also **ਪਰਾਂਦੀ**

ਪਰਾਰ (paraar) *n adv* Year before last.

ਪ੍ਰਾਰਥਨਾ (praarthnaa) *n f* Prayer, request, entreaty, submission.

ਪ੍ਰਾਲਬਧ (praalabdh) *n m* Fortune, fate.

ਪਰਿਣਾਮ (parinaam) *n m* Conclusion, consequence, result.

ਪਰਿੰਦਾ (parindaa) *n m* Bird.

ਪਰਿਭਾਸ਼ਾ (paribhaashaa) *n f* Definition.

ਪਰੀ (paree) *n f* Fairy, nymph, elf, sprite; Very beautiful or graceful woman.

ਪਰੀਖਿਆ (pareekhiaa) *n f* Examination test, enquiry, investigation.

ਪ੍ਰੀਤ (preet) *n f* Love, affection, attachment.

ਪ੍ਰੀਤਮ (preetam) *a m n* Dearest, dear; Lover, paramour, beloved, husband.

ਪਰੇ (pare) *adv* Beyond, younder, at a distance.

ਪਰੇਸ਼ਾਨ (pareshaan) *a* Perplexed, confused, troubled, distressed.

ਪਰੇਸ਼ਾਨੀ (pareshaanee) *n f* Confusion, perplexity, distraction, trouble, harassment, vexation, distress.

ਪ੍ਰੇਤ (pret) *n m* Ghost, evil spirit, fiend, deceased. Also **ਪਰੇਤ**

ਪ੍ਰੇਮ (prem) *n m* Love, affection. Also **ਪਰੇਮ**

ਪ੍ਰੇਰਨਾ (prernaa) *n f* Inspiration, incentive, motivation.

ਪ੍ਰੇਰਿਤ (prerit) *a* Induced, motivated; ~**ਕਰਨਾ** To inspire.

ਪ੍ਰੋਸਣਾ (prosanaa) *v* To serve meal, to set at the dining table.

ਪਰੋਖ (parokh) *a* Indirect, not visible.

ਪ੍ਰੋਣਾ (pronaa) *v* To thread, to string, to needle. Also **ਪਰੋਣਾ**

ਪਰੌਂਠਾ (paraunthaa) *n m* Indian loaf inlaid with butter and then fried.

ਪਲ (pal) *n m* Moment, second, twinkling of an eye.

ਪਲਸੇਟਾ (palsetaa) *n m* Turning from side to side when lying, tripping (as wrestlers); ~**ਮਾਰਨਾ** To take a sideways roll or turn.

ਪਲਕ (palak) *n f* Eye lid, eye lash, moment, twinkling of an eye; ~**ਝਪਕਣੀ** To wink, to blink; ~**ਲਾਉਣੀ** To sleep.

ਪਲੰਘ (palangh) *n m* Sleeping couch, bed.

ਪਲਟਣ (paltan) *n f* Battalion, infantry, regiment, corps, brigade, platoon. Also **ਪਲਟਨ**

ਪਲਟਣਾ (paltnaa) *v* To overturn, to return, to upset, to convert, to retreat, to turnover, to reverse.

ਪਲਟਾ (paltaa) *n m* Turn, change, retaliation, alteration, conversion.

ਪਲਟਾਉਣਾ (paltaaunaa) *v* To alter, to change, to reverse, to retract, to retrace, to turn.

ਪਲਣਾ (palnaa) *v* To be nourished, to be reared, to grow, to develop.

ਪਲੰਦਾ (palandaa) *n m* Parcel, bundle, pad, wad.

ਪਲੜਾ (palraa) *n m* Pan (of a scale or balance). Also **ਪਲਾ**

ਪੱਲਾ (palla) *n m* Border of a cloth, lap, skirting; ~**ਛੱਡਣਾ** To let one go; ~**ਛੁਡਾਉਣਾ** To get rid of; ~**ਫੜਨਾ** To catch or hold; To shelter.

ਪਲਾਂਘ (palaangh) *n f* Long step, leap, jump, bounce.

ਪਲਾਲ (palaal) *n m* Vain talking, bragging, idle or random speech.

ਪਲੀਤ (paleet) *a* Impure, unclean, polluted, filthy.

ਪਲੀਤਾ (paleetaa) *n m* Torch, gun cotton; ~**ਲਾਉਣਾ** To ignite, to incite.

ਪੱਲੂ (palloo) *n m* Border of a garment, hem of cloth, sail, bunt, lappet.

ਪਲੇਠ (paleth) *a* First born. Also **ਪਲੇਠੀ ਦਾ, ਪਲੇਠਾ**

ਪਲੇਥਣ (palethan) *n* Dry flour dusted at the time of rolling bread,

powder, dredge.

ਪਵਿਤਰ (pavitar) *a* Pure, sacred, holy, spotless, solemn, sanctified; ~**ਅਸਥਾਨ** Shrine; ~**ਆਤਮਾ** Holy spirit; ~**ਯਾਦਗਾਰਾਂ** Relics.

ਪੜਸੰਗ (parsaang) *n* Ladder.

ਪੜਚੋਲ (parchol) *n f* Investigation, inquiry; Criticism, verification; ~**ਕਰਨੀ** To inquire into, to investigate, to comment, to verify.

ਪੜਚੋਲੀਆ (parcholiaa) *n m* Investigator, researcher.

ਪੜਛੱਤੀ (parcchattee) *n f* Shelf made under the roof, attic, loft.

ਪੜਤਾ (partaa) *n m* Cost price; ~**ਖਾਣਾ** To gain a suitable profit.

ਪੜਤਾਲ (partaal) *n f* Enquiry, checking, scrutiny, verification, investigation, search, audit; **ਅਦਾਲਤੀ~** Inquisition.

ਪੜਤਾਲਣਾ (partaalnaa) *v* To check, to verify, to audit. Also **ਪੜਤਾਲ ਕਰਨਾ**

ਪੜ੍ਹੰਦੜ (parhandar) *adv* Readable; ~**ਨਾਟਕ** Closet play.

ਪੜਦਾਦਾ (pardaadaa) *n* Great-grand father, father's grandfather.

ਪੜ੍ਹਨਾ (parhnaa) *v* To read, to learn, to study, to go through, to recite.

ਪੜਨਾਨਾ (parnaanaa) *n m* Great-grand father, mother's grand father.

ਪੜਪੋਤਾ (parpotaa) *n m* Great-grandson, son's grandson, grand son's son.

ਪੜ੍ਨਾ (parhnaa) *v* To read, study, learn, to recite.

ਪੜ੍ਹਾਉਨਾ (parhaaunaa) *v* To teach, educate, to tutor; To instruct, train in reading and writing; To have someone educated.

ਪੜ੍ਹਾਈ (parhaaee) *n* Education, study, learning; Teaching, tution.

ਪੜ੍ਹਾਕੂ (parhaakoo) *a n m* Studious; student.

ਪੜੋਸ (paros) *n m* Neighbourhood, vicinity.

ਪਾਂ (paan) *n f* Itch, scabies, pus; ~ਮਾਰਿਆ Scabious.

ਪਾਉਨਾ (paaunaa) *v* To find, to get, to obtain, to add, to pour, to mix, to put on (clothes).

ਪਾਉਲੀ (paulee) *n m* Weaver; 25 paise coin. Also ਪੌਲੀ

ਪਾਏਦਾਨ (paaedaan) *n m* Footboard, footrest, doormat.

ਪਾਏਦਾਰ (paaedaar) *a* Durable, lasting, strong.

ਪਾਸਾ (paasaa) *n m* Side, direction, face, quarter, aspect, dimension; ~ਪਲਟਨਾ To change sides; ~ਬਦਲਨਾ To turn round.

ਪਾਗਲ (paagal) *a n m* Insane, mad, crazy, loony, lunatic, fool; Madman, lunatic; ~ਖ਼ਾਨਾ Lunatic asylum, mental hospital, bedlam; ~ਪਣ Madness, lunancy.

ਪਾਚਨ (paachan) *a n m* Digestive; Digestion, assimilation.

ਪਾਜੀ (paajee) *a* Mean, wicked, rascal, vile.

ਪਾਟਨਾ (paatnaa) *v* To be torn, to split, to burst, to cleave, to be broken.

ਪਾਟਾ (paataa) *v* Torn, rent, split; ~ਪੁਰਾਣਾ Worn-out, old (garment) rag, tatters.

ਪਾਠ (paath) *n m* Lesson, text, chapter of a book, religious study; ~ਸ਼ਾਲਾ School; ~ਕ Reader, scholar; ~ਕ੍ਰਮ Syllabus; ~ਪੁਸਤਕ Text book.

ਪਾਣੀ (paanee) *n m* Water, Adam's scale Adam's ale; ~ਚੜ੍ਹਾਉਨਾ To glid, to polish; ~ਫਿਰਨਾ To be undone, to be destroyed; ~ਫੇਰਨਾ To spoil, to shatter, to submerg; ~ਭਰਨਾ To serve, to draw water; ~ਵਾਂਗ ਰੋੜਨਾ (ਪੈਸਾ) To spend lavishly.

ਪਾਤਸ਼ਾਹ (paatshaah) *n m* King, emperor, sovereign, monarch; ~ਤ Empire, government.

ਪਾਤਸ਼ਾਹੀ (paatshaahee) *n f* Kingship,

kingdom, dominion, empire, rule government; Kingly, imperial, regal, royal.

ਪਾਦਰੀ (paadree) *n m* Priest, clergyman, chaplain, bishop, pastor, padre; **~ਸੰਸਥਾ** Holy orders.

ਪਾਂਧੀ (paandhee) *n m* Traveller.

ਪਾਪ (paap) *n m* Sin, vice, evil, guilt, crime, fault, impiety; **~ਕਰਨਾ** To commit a sin.

ਪਾਪੜ (paapar) *n m* Thin crisp cake made of pulse.

ਪਾਪੀ (paapee) *n m a* Sinner, criminal, wretched; Sinful, immoral, vicious, impious.

ਪਾਬੰਦੀ (paabandee) *n* Restriction, check, ban, abidance, limitation, punctuality.

ਪਾਮਰ (paamar) *a* Mean, base, low, wicked, vile.

ਪਾਮਾਲ (paamaal) *a* Trampled; ravaged, destroyed, ruined, devastated, laid, waste; **~ਕਰਨਾ** To damage, to destroy, trample, ruin, devastate, crush, to lay waste, to ravage.

ਪਾਰ (paar) *n m* The opposite bank, far side; Limit, bound; Across, over, beyond, on the far side; **~ਉਤਾਰਾ** Salvation, liberation;

Success; **~ਕਰਨਾ** To cross, to take across, to kill.

ਪਾਰਸ (paaras) *n m* Touchstone; **~ਪੱਥਰ** Philosopher's stone (which converts any metal into gold on touching).

ਪਾਰਖੂ (paarkhoo) *n m* Evaluator, assayer, critic, connoisseur.

ਪਾਰਾ (paaraa) *n m* Mercury, quick silver, hydrargyrum.

ਪਾਰਾਵਾਰ (paaraawaar) *n m* Farthest limit, expanse, vastness.

ਪਾਲਣ (paalaṇ) *n m* Nourishing, bringing up, upbringing, nurture; Observing, obeying, execution, carrying out; **~ਹਾਰ** Nourisher, breeder, nurturer, sustainer, protector, God. Also **ਪਾਲਨ**

ਪਾਲਣਾ (paalṇaa) *v* To nourish, to nurse, to bring up, to nurture, to breed, to tame, to feed, to foster, to rear.

ਪਾਲਤੂ (paaltoo) *a* Domesticated, tame, pet.

ਪਾਲਾ (paalaa) *n m* Frost, cold, chilly weather; **~ਮਾਰਨਾ** To feel afraid.

ਪਾਵਲੀ (paavlee) *n m* Weaver.

ਪਾਵਾ (paavaa) *n m* Leg of a piece of furniture.

ਪਾੜ (paar) *n m* Breach, gap, opening, hole, fissure; Split charm, rent, cut, gash, slash.

ਪਾੜਨਾ (paarṇaa) v To tear, to split, to rip, to rend, to divide.

ਪਾੜਾ (paaṛaa) n m Gap, difference, distance; Furrows.

ਪਿਉ (pio) n m Father, sire, male parent.

ਪਿਆਉਣਾ (piaauṇaa) v To serve (water or other liquid); To water to get or cause one to drink, to serve drinks.

ਪਿਆਉ (piaao) n m Stall for serving water free to the needy.

ਪਿਆਜ (piaaj) n m Onion, *Allium cepa*.

ਪਿਆਦਾ (piaadaa) n m Foot soldier, footman, court mesenger or attendent; (in chess) pawn.

ਪਿਆਸਾ (piaasaa) n m Thirsty, desirous of.

ਪਿਆਰ (piaar) n m Affection, love, regard.

ਪਿਆਲਾ (piaalaa) n m Cupbowl, goblet, chalice, powder-pan.

ਪਿਸਣਾ (pisṇaa) v To be ground, to be pulverised.

ਪਿਸਾਈ (pisaae) n f Act of grinding, wages of grinding.

ਪਿਸ਼ਾਬ (pishaab) n m Urine, piss; ~ਖਾਨਾ Urinal.

ਪਿੱਸੂ (pissoo) n m Flea, gnat.

ਪਿਘਲਣਾ (pighalṇaa) v To melt, to dissolve, to be moved.

ਪਿਚਕਣਾ (pichakṇaa) v To be squeezed, to shrival.

ਪਿਚਕਾਉਣਾ (pichkaauṇaa) v To squeeze, compress, constrict, press, to cause to shrink, shrivel, contract.

ਪਿੱਛਲਗ (pichchhlag) n m Henchman, appendent, follower, satellite.

ਪਿਛਲਾ (pichhlaa) a Last, back, past, late, previous, subsequent, former.

ਪਿਛਵਾੜਾ (pichhwaaṛaa) n m Rear, back.

ਪਿਛਾ (pichhaa) a The back part, rear, chase, following, posterior, buttocks.

ਪਿਛੇ (pichchhe) adv Behind, afterwards, on the backside; ~ਪਿਛੇ At one's heels, in the wake of.

ਪਿਛੋਂ (pichchhon) adv Afterwards, subsequently, at the back, from behind.

ਪਿਛੋਕਾ (pichhokaa) n m Antecedents, ancestors.

ਪਿੰਜਰ (pinjar) n f Rib, skelton, carcass, anatomy.

ਪਿੰਜਰਾ (pinjraa) n m Cage, trap.

ਪਿੰਜਵਾਉਣਾ (pinjwaauṇaa) v To get the cotton carded for spinning.

ਪਿਟਣਾ (pitṇaa) v n m To lament by beating breast; Trouble, agony, mourning, lamentation.

ਪਿਟਵਾਉਣਾ (pitvaauṇaa) v To get someone beaten up.

ਪਿੱਠ (pitṭh) n f Back, behind; ~ਠੋਕਣੀ To encourage, to praise, to pat on the back, to bolster up; ~ਤੇ ਹੋਣਾ To support, to assist; ~ਦੇਣੀ To leave, to depart, to run away, to desert; ~ਪਿੱਛੇ Behind one's back; ~ਪਿੱਛੇ ਕਹਿਣਾ To back bite; ~ਲਾਉਣੀ To defeat, to floor; ~ਵਿਖਾਉਣੀ To turn tail, to flee from the battle field.

ਪਿੱਠੂ (pitṭhoo) n m Basket, pannier, pack carrier; Comrade, assistant.

ਪਿੰਡ (pinḍ) n m Village; Heap, lump, cake or ball of meal.

ਪਿੰਡਾ (pinḍaa) n m Body; ~ਛੁੜਾਣਾ To get rid of.

ਪਿੱਤ (pitt) n f Prickly heat.

ਪਿੱਤਰ (pittar) n m Ancestors, forefathers.

ਪਿੱਤਲ (pittal) n m Brass.

ਪਿਤਾ (pitaa) n m Father, dad, daddy.

ਪਿਦਣਾ (pidṇaa) v To run hither or thither in game.

ਪਿਦਾਉਣਾ (pidaauṇaa) v To weary, to vex, to defeat in game.

ਪਿੱਦੀ (piddee) a Tomtit.

ਪਿੰਨਣਾ (pinnanaa) a To beg, to ask for alms.

ਪਿੰਨਾ (pinnaa) n m Ball, thread ball.

ਪਿਲਪਿਲਾ (pilpilaa) a Soft, flabby, flaccid, plump, pulpy, lymphetic; ~ਪਣ Flabbiness, softness.

ਪੀਸਣਾ (peesṇaa) v To grind, to reduce, to powder, to mill, to gnash (teeth). Also ਪੀਹਣਾ

ਪੀਂਘ (peengh) n f Swing, trapeze; Rainbow.

ਪੀਂਘਾ (peenghaa) n m Hammock.

ਪੀਚਣਾ (peechnaa) v To absorb, to soak, to moistened, to be hard and tight.

ਪੀੜਾ (peeḍaa) a Firm, solid; ~ਪਣ Toughness, hardness.

ਪੀਣਾ (peeṇaa) v To drink, to absorb, to suppress (an emotion); ਸਿਗਰਟ~ To smoke.

ਪੀਪ (peep) n f Pus.

ਪੀਪਾ (peepaa) n m Cask, tin, can, butt, barrel.

ਪੀਲਾ (peelaa) a Yellow, pale, bleak; ~ਪਣ Paleness, yellowness.

ਪੀਲੀਆ (peeliya) n m Jaundice, xanthosis.

ਪੀੜ (peeṛ) n f Pain, ache, anguish, affliction, ailment.

ਪੀੜੀ (peeṛhee) n f Generation, race,

descent; A wooden or iron stool, small square.

ਪੀੜਾਂ (peeṛaan) *n f* Pain, labour throes.

ਪੁਆੜਾ (poaaṛaa) *n m* Dispute, quarrel, wrangle, discord, trouble, inconvenience; **~ਪਾਊਣਾ** To create or cause dispute.

ਪੁਸ਼ਟ (pushṭ) *a* Nourishing; Strong, muscular, stout, virile.

ਪੁਸ਼ਟੀ (pushtee) *n f* Support, ratification, aid, affirmation; **~ਕਰਨੀ** To confirm, to corroborate.

ਪੁਸ਼ਤ (pusht) *n f* Generation, ancestry; **~ਦਰ ਪੁਸ਼ਤੁ** Generation to generation.

ਪੁਸਤਕ (pustak) *n f* Book, volume.

ਪੁਸ਼ਾਕ (pushaak) *n f* Dress, costume, garment, clothes, array. Also **ਪੋਸ਼ਾਕ**

ਪੁਕਾਰਨਾ (pukaarnaa) *v* To shout, to call out, to exclaim, to evoke.

ਪੁਗਣਾ (pugṇaa) *v* To arrive, to mature, to end, to reach destination.

ਪੁਗਾਉਣਾ (pugaauṇaa) *v* To terminate, to make one succeed.

ਪੁਚਕਾਰਨਾ (puchkaarnaa) *v* To pat, to caress, to fondle, to blandish, to produce a hissing sound from lips.

ਪੁਚਾਉਣਾ (puchaauṇaa) *v* To convey, to transmit, to extend, to carry, to cause to reach.

ਪੁਛ (puchh) *n f* Enquiry, investigation question, querry, question; **~ਹੋਣੀ** To be sought after, to be in demand, to be important enough; **~ਗਿਛ** Investigation, interrogation.

ਪੁਛਣਾ (puchhṇaa) *v* To enquire, to ask, to question.

ਪੁੰਜ (punj) *n m* Heap, mass, aggregate, embodiment.

ਪੁਜਣਾ (pujṇaa) *v* To reach, to get at, to arrive, to come.

ਪੁਟਣਾ (puṭṇaa) *v* To dig, to pull out, to uproot, to excavate.

ਪੁੱਠ (puṭṭh) *n f* Hip, buttock; Backside, reverse side.

ਪੁੱਠਾ (puṭṭhaa) *a* Reversed, contrary, upside down, indirect.

ਪੁਣਨਾ (puṇnaa) *v* To filter, to strain, to abuse.

ਪੁੱਤਰ (puttar) *n m* Son.

ਪੁਤਰੇਲਾ (putrelaa) *n m* Adopted son, adoptee.

ਪੁਤਲਾ (putlaa) *n m* Idol, image, effigy, personification, incarnation.

ਪੁਤਲੀ (putlee) *n f* Doll, puppet; Pupil of the eye.

ਪੁੰਨ (punn) *n m* Charity, alms, virtuous deed, dole, benefiction.

ਪੁਨਿਆਂ (puniaan) *n f* Full moon night.

ਪੁਰਖ (purakh) *n m* Man, male, person, individual, mankind.

ਪੁਰਨੂਰ (purnoor) *a* Full of light, radiant, brilliant, resplendent.

ਪੁਰਵਾਉਣਾ (purvaunaa) *v* To get (pit, ditch, form etc.) filled up.

ਪੁਰਾਣਾ (puraanaa) *a* Old, aged, ancient, antique, chronic.

ਪੁਲ (pul) *n m* Bridge, pons; ਤਰੀਫ਼ ਦੇ~ਬੰਨੁਣਾ To praise too much.

ਪੁਲੰਦਾ (pulandaa) *n m* Bundle, wad, sheaf.

ਪੁਲਾੜ (pulaar) *n m* Space, cosmos.

ਪੁੜਾ (puraa) *n m* Large packet.

ਪੁੜੀ (puree) *n f* Small parcel, wrapper of paper, dose of medicine.

ਪੂਛ (poochh) *n f* Tail, hanger-on; Importance; ~ਲ Tail; Parasite.

ਪੂਜਣਾ (poojnaa) *a* To worship, to rever, to adore, to respect.

ਪੂਜਾ (poojaa) *n f* Worship, adoration, veneration, respect, devotion; ~ਭੇਟ Offering.

ਪੂੰਜੀ (poonjee) *n f* Capital, wealth, principal assets, stock; ~ਵਾਦ Capitalism.

ਪੂੰਝਣਾ (poonjhnaa) *v* To wipe, to clean, to scrub, to efface.

ਪੂਰਨ (pooran) *a* Full, entire, complete, perfect,

complementary.

ਪੂਰਨਾ (poornaa) *v* To fill, to blow, to fulfil, to finish, to complete.

ਪੂਰਾ (pooraa) *a* Full, complete, total, whole, entire, thorough, all, perfect, adequate; ~ਸੂਰਾ Self-contained, just enough; ~ਪੂਰਾ Out and out, exhaustive, all out, adequate.

ਪੇਸ਼ਕਸ਼ (peshkash) *n f* Offer, present.

ਪੇਸ਼ਗੀ (peshgee) *n f* Advance, earnest money.

ਪੇਸ਼ਤਰ (peshtar) *adv* Before, earlier than, ahead of.

ਪੇਸ਼ਬੰਦੀ (peshbandee) *n f* Forestalling, anticipation, precaution.

ਪੇਸ਼ਾ (peshaa) *n m* Profession, trade, occupation, vocation, pursuit; Prostitution, harlotry; ~ਵਰ Professional career.

ਪੇਸ਼ੀ (peshee) *n f* Presence, trial, hearing of law suit; ~ਆਂ Muscles; ~ਨ ਗੋਈ Prediction.

ਪੇਕਾ (pekaa) *n m a* Parent's house; Paternal.

ਪੇਚ (pech) *n m* Screw; ~ਕਸ Screw driver; ~ਦਾਰ Zigzag, complex, twisted.

ਪੇਚਸ (pechas) *n f* Dysentery.

ਪੇਚਾ (pechaa) *n m* Tangle,

entanglement, involvement, convolution, complication; ~ਪਾਉਣਾ To entangle, complicate.

ਪੇਚੀਦਗੀ (pecheedgee) *n f* Complexity, intricacy, complication.

ਪੇਚੀਦਾ (pecheedaa) *a* Complex, complicated.

ਪੇਟ (peṭ) *n m* Stomach, abdomen, belly, womb, capacity; ~ਹੋ ਜਾਣਾ To conceive, to get pregnant; ~ਕਟਣਾ To starve one self; ~ਖਾਲੀ ਕਰਨਾ To relieve nature; ~ਪੂਜਾ ਕਰਨਾ To eat.

ਪੇਟੀ (peṭee) *n f* Belt, gridle; Box, chest, big trunk.

ਪੇਟੂ (peṭoo) *a n m* Glottonous, ravenous, rapacious, vocacious; Glutton, epicure.

ਪੇਂਡੂ (pendoo) *n m a* Village, peasant; Rustic, rural, agrestic; ~ਕਾਵਿ Pastoral poetry; ~ਬੋਲੀ Patois; ~ਲਹਿਜਾ Brogue.

ਪੈਸਾ (paesaa) *n m* Pice, money, wealth, paisa; ~ਉਡਾਉਣਾ To spend money lavishly; ~ਖਾ ਜਾਣਾ To misappropriate money; ~ਖੁਆਉਣਾ To bribe; ~ਬਣਾਉਣਾ To mint money; ~ਲਾਉਣਾ To invest money.

ਪੈਗੰਬਰ (paegambar) *n m* Prophet, apostle, messenger of God.

ਪੈਗ਼ਾਮ (paegaam) *n m* Message, embassy.

ਪੈਜ (paej) *n f* Honour, fair name; Vow, promise.

ਪੈਂਠ (paenṭh) *a n* Dominating influence; Reputation, awe, strong impression or effect; Sixty five.

ਪੈਂਡਾ (paenḍaa) *n m* Distance, trek, passage, journey.

ਪੈਂਤੜਾ (paentṛaa) *n* Strategy, position, posture, attitude.

ਪੈਦਲ (paedal) *adv a* Marching, foot(man); Onfoot, afoot.

ਪੈਦਾ (paedaa) *a* Born, produced, begotton; ~ਇਸ਼ Birth, creation, production; ~ਹੋਣਾ To be produced, to grow, to be born; ~ਕਰਨਾ To produce, to earn, to father, to breed; ~ਵਾਰ Produce, yield, crop, output, product, production.

ਪੈਮਾਇਸ਼ (paemaaish) *n f* Measurement, survey.

ਪੈਮਾਨਾ (paemaanaa) *n m* Scale, measure, instrument for measuring.

ਪੈਰ (paer) *n m* Foot, footprint, step, traces; ~ਉਖੜਨੇ To be uprooted; ~ਚਟਣੇ To fawn; ~ਚੁਮਣੇ To worship, to show reverence; ~ਜੰਮਣੇ To be well-settled, to be firmly lodged;

~ਪਸਾਰ ਕੇ ਸੋਣਾ To enjoy a carefree sleep; ~ਭਾਰੀ ਹੋਣੇ To be pregnant.

ਪੈਰਵੀ (paervee) *n f* Pursuit, follow up, prosecution, following, conduct.

ਪੋਸਣਾ (posṇaa) *v* To nourish, to rear, to develop, to tame.

ਪੋਸਤੀ (postee) *n m a* Lazy person; One addicted to poppy pods.

ਪੋਹਣਾ (pohṇaa) *v* To cause sensation, feeling or pain, to affect; To be felt.

ਪੋਟਲੀ (poṭlee) *n f* Small bundle or package tied in cloth piece; Cavity, gland, follicute.

ਪੋਣਾ (poṇaa) *n m* (1) Straining cloth, dish cloth, kitchen napkin; perforated stone screen; (2) enclosure in a bathing tank meant exclusively for ladies.

ਪੋਚਣਾ (pochṇaa) *v* To smear, to daub, to coat, to besmear.

ਪੋਚਾ (pochaa) *n m* Daub, dab, coating plaster; ~ਪਾਚੀ

Camouflage.

ਪੋਤਰਾ (potraa) *n m* Grand son.

ਪੋਤੜਾ (potṛaa) *n m* Babycloth, napkin, diapers, nappies.

ਪੋਥਾ (pothaa) *n m* Big book, voluminous book, tome.

ਪੋਥੀ (pothee) *n f* Book, tract.

ਪੋਪਲਾ (poplaa) *a* Toothless, shrivelled.

ਪੋਲ (pol) *n m* Hollow, space; Pole, vacuity, vacuousness.

ਪੋਲਾ (polaa) *a* Soft, hollow, porous, placid, vacuous; ~ਪਣ Hollowness, weakness, flaccidness.

ਪੌਣ (pauṇ) *n f* Air, wind, breeze.

ਪੌਦ (paud) *n f* Saplings, vegetation, plantation.

ਪੌਦਾ (paudaa) *n* Plant, sapling, young tree.

ਪੌਰਾਣਿਕ (pauraanik) *a* Mythological, legendary.

ਪੌਲਾ (paulaa) *n m* One foot of shoe.

ਪੌੜੀ (pauṛee) *n f* Ladder; Progression; ~ਦਾਰ Terraced.

ਫ

ਫ Twenty seventh letter of Gurmukhi alphabets, pronounced as 'phaphaa'.

ਫਸਣਾ (phasṇaa) *v* To be entrapped, to be ensnared, to be caught, to get into a difficulty, to be entangled, to be involved.

ਫਸਤਾ (fastaa) *n m* Dispute, quarrel; **~ਮੁਕਾਉਣਾ** To finish, to put an end, to kill.

ਫਸਲ (fasal) *n f* Harvest, crop, produce, season.

ਫਸਲੀ (faslee) *a* Seasonal, pertaining to a crop.

ਫਸਾਉਣਾ (phasaauṇaa) *v* To implicate, to ensnare, to trap, to entangle. Also **ਫਾਹਉਣਾ**

ਫਸਾਹਤ (fasaahat) *n f* Sweet talk.

ਫਸਾਦ (fasaad) *n m* Dispute, quarrel, disturbance, faction, riot, agitation; **~ਛੇੜਨਾ** To create disturbance; **~ਦੀ ਜੜ** Root cause and trouble.

ਫਸਾਨਾ (fasaanaa) *n m* Story, narrative, fiction.

ਫਸੀਲ (faseel) *n m* Rampart, boundary.

ਫਹਾ (phahaa) *n m* Sticking, a flock of cotton or cloth impregnated with medicine to paste on a wound. Also **ਫਹਿਆ**

ਫਹਿਰਿਸਤ (faherisht) *n f* List, catalogue.

ਫੱਕ (phakk) *n f* Fine chaff of rice or barley.

ਫੱਕ (fakk) *a* Discoloured.

ਫੱਕਣਾ (phaknaa) *v* To put something powdered into mouth from the palm, to waste.

ਫਕਤ (fakat) *adv* Only, merely.

ਫੱਕਰ (phakkar) *n m* Abuse, foul language, meaningless or useless or useless chatter. Also **ਫੱਕੜ**

ਫੱਕੜ (phakkaṛ) *n m* Carefree, poor, mendicant, hermit; **~ਪੁਣਾ** Carelessness, carefreeness.

ਫੱਕੀ (phakkee) *n f* Medicinal powder.

ਫਕੀਰ (fakeer) *n m* Hermit, mendicant, sadhu, recluse, beggar.

ਫਕੀਰੀ (fakeeree) *a* Life of a fakir, reclusion, anchoritism, mendicancy.

ਫਖਰ (fakhar) *n m* Pride, justified, righteous. Also **ਫਖ਼ਰ**

ਫੱਗ (phagg) *n m* Feather.

ਫਜ਼ਲ (fazal) *n m* Favour, kindness, grace, bounty.

ਫਜ਼ਾ (fazaa) *n f* Atmosphere, climate, weather; Situation.

ਫਜ਼ੀਹਤ (fazeehat) *n f* Discomfiture, insult, disgrace.

ਫਜ਼ੀਲਤ (fazeelat) *n f* Importance, greatness, dignity.

ਫਜ਼ੂਲ (fazool) *a* Surplus, excess, useless, worthless; ~ਖਰਚ Extravagant; ~ਖਰਚੀ Extravagance.

ਫਟ (phat) *n m adv* Wound, cut, crack; Quickly, instantly, hastily.

ਫਟਕਣ (phatkan) *n m* Flutter; Chaff separated from grain in winnowing.

ਫਟਕਣਾ (phataknaa) *v* To winnow, to shake, to flutter; To throb.

ਫਟਣਾ (phatnaa) *v* To be torn, to burst, to explode, to be cut, to turn sour; ਛਾਤੀ ਦਾ~ To have unbearable sorrow.

ਫੱਟਾ (phattaa) *n m* A plank, wooden board, board, sign board.

ਫੱਟੀ (phattee) *n f* Small plank, school boy's board to write on.

ਫਟੀਕ (phateek) *n f* Fatigue.

ਫੰਡਣਾ (phandnaa) *v* To beat, to scold, to winnow, to dust.

ਫਣ (phan) *n m* Expanded hood of snake. Also ਫਨ

ਫਣੀਅਰ (phaneear) *n m* Hooded snake, cobra.

ਫਤਿਹ (phate) *n f* Victory, success, triumph; Sikh salutation or greeting.

ਫਤੂਹੀ (fatoohee) *n f* A waist coat, a sleeveless coat.

ਫਤੂਰ (fatoor) *n m* Infirmity, disturbance, defect, interruption.

ਫੱਦ (phadd) *n m* Toothless gum.

ਫੰਦਣਾ (phandnaa) *v* To trap, to ensnare. Also ਫੰਧਣਾ

ਫੱਦੜ (phaddar) *a* Very fat and ugly, worthless.

ਫੰਦਾ (phandaa) *n m* A snare, a loop, a knot, trap.

ਫਨ (fan) *n m* Skill, art; ~ਕਾਰ Artisan, artist, craftman, expert.

ਫਨਾਹ (fanaah) *n m* Destruction, ruin, devastation.

ਫਫੜਾ (phaphraa) *n m* Deceit, fraud; Flattery, sycophancy, hypocrisy.

ਫਫੇਕੁੱਟ (phaphekut) *a* Deceitful, wily, cunning, hypocrite.

ਫਫੇਕੁਟਣੀ (phaphekutnee) *n f* Old talkative and cunning woman. Also ਫਫੇਕੁਟਣਾ

ਫਫੋਲਾ (phapholaa) *n m* Blister, scald, boiled, an eruption.

ਫਬਣਾ (phabṇaa) *v* To look well, to suit, to benefit, to appear beautiful.

ਫਰ (phar) *n m* Fur, soft wool on the body of sheep etc.

ਫਰਸ਼ (farash) *n m* Floor, pavement.

ਫ਼ਰਸਾ (pharsaa) *n m* Battle axe.

ਫ਼ਰਹੰਗ (farhang) *n m* Lexicon, key note, commentary.

ਫ਼ਰਕ (farak) *n m* Difference, deficiency, discrepancy, variance, disparity, destinction; ~ਪੈਣਾ To differ, to be displeased,

ਫਰਕਣਾ (pharakṇaa) *v* To tremble, to vibrate, to quiver, to throb, to flutter, to beat, to wink.

ਫ਼ਰੰਗੀ (farangee) *n m* A foreigner, an English man.

ਫ਼ਰਜ਼ (faraz) *n m* Duty, moral duty, responsibility, obligation; ~ਕਰਨਾ To assume, to suppose.

ਫ਼ਰਜ਼ੰਦ (farzand) *n m* Son.

ਫ਼ਰਜ਼ੀ (farzee) *a* Fictitious, hypothetical, assumed, supposed.

ਫਰੰਟ (farant) *a* Opponent, one who opposes; Warfront; Disobedient; ~ਹੋਣਾ To stand against, to revolt, to oppose.

ਫ਼ਰਦ (farad) *n f* A list, a catalogue, document, sheet of wool or paper.

ਫ਼ਰਮਾ (farmaa) *n m* Frame, format.

ਫ਼ਰਮਾਉਣਾ (farmaauṇaa) *v* To order, to command, speak. Also **ਫ਼ਰਮਾਣਾ**

ਫ਼ਰਮਾਇਸ਼ (farmaaish) *n f* Command, order, recommendation, royal edict; ~ਕਰਨੀ To ask for, to request, to order.

ਫ਼ਰਮਾਨ (farmaan) *n f* A royal command, order. Also **ਫ਼ਰਮਾਣ**

ਫ਼ਰਮਾਂਬਰਦਾਰ (farmaanbardaar) *a* Obedient, dutiful, loyal.

ਫ਼ਰਮਾਬਰਦਾਰੀ (farmaabardaaree) *n* Obedience, dutifulness, compliance, docility; Loyality.

ਫ਼ਰਲੋ (farlo) *n f* Absence without leave, furlough.

ਫੱਰਾ (pharraa) *n m* Banner, penant, any loose paper.

ਫ਼ਰਾਸ਼ (faraash) *n m* Personal attendant, a servant who spreads carpets or fixes tents etc ; Floorer.

ਫ਼ਰਾਖ (faraakh) *a* Open, spacious, commodious; ~ਦਿਲ Open-hearted, large hearted, generous, liberal; ~ਦਿਲੀ Open or large-heartedness, generosity, generousness, liberality.

ਫ਼ਰਾਟਾ (faraataa) *n m* Rush, puff, sound of anything rushing or fluttering.

ਫ਼ਰਾਰ (faraar) *a* Absconding, at large, fugitive.

ਫ਼ਰਿਆਦ (fariyaad) *n f* A request, a complaint; A petition, exclaiming for help.

ਫ਼ਰਿਆਦੀ (fariyaadee) *a* Suppliant, petitioner, appellant.

ਫ਼ਰਿਸ਼ਤ (ferisht) *n f* List, catalogue. Also ਫ਼ਹਿਰਿਸ਼ਤ

ਫ਼ਰਿਸ਼ਤਾ (farishtaa) *n m* An angel, a messenger of God.

ਫ਼ਰੇਬ (fareb) *n m* Fraud, deception, trick, treachery.

ਫ਼ਰੇਬੀ (farebee) *a* Fraudulant, deceptive cunning, artful.

ਫਰੋਲਣਾ (pharolnaa) *v* To search, to probe.

ਫਲ (phal) *n m* (1) Fruit; (2) Consequence, reward, yield, profit, produce; (3) Blade of instrument or weapon, a plough share, a point of piercing instrument; ਖੇਤਰ~ Area; ਗੁਣਨ ~Product; ~ਦੇਣਾ To yield fruit; ~ਦਾਰ Fruitful, productive, profitable.

ਫਲਸਫਾ (phalasaphaa) *n m* Philosophy. Also ਫ਼ਲਸਫ਼ਾ

ਫਲਸਫ਼ਾਨਾ (phalasphaanaa) *a* Philosophical.

ਫਲਸਫ਼ੀ (phalasphee) *n m* philosopher.

ਫਲਕ (phalak) *n m* Sky, heaven; Facet, plane.

ਫਲਣਾ (phalnaa) *v* to be fruitful, to bear fruit.

ਫਲਾਂਘ (phalaangh) *n f* Leap, jump.

ਫਲਾਣਾ (falaanaa) *n m* Such a one, so and so; ~ਢੀਂਗੜਾ Such and such, any Tom, dick or harry. Also ਫਲਾਂ

ਫਲੀ (phalee) *n f* Pod, seed pod, bean, silique.

ਫਲੂਸ (faloos) *n m* Balloon.

ਫੜ੍ਹ (pharh) *n f* Boast, false pomp, a bet; ~ਬਾਜ਼ Boastful, vaunta braggart; ~ਬਾਜ਼ੀ Bragging, boasting, vaunting; ~ਮਾਰਨੀ To boast, to talk tall.

ਫੜਕ (pharak) *n m* Writhing, flutter; ~ਉਠਣਾ To be thrilled, to be aroused emotionally.

ਫੜਕਣ (pharkan) *n f* Flutter, flap, throb, pulsation, palpitation, quiver, tremor.

ਫੜਕਣਾ (pharaknaa) *v* To pulsate, to throb, to flutter, to writhe.

ਫੜਨਾ (pharnaa) *v* To catch hold of, to seize, to grapple, to arrest, to catch, to hold.

ਫੜਫੜਾਉਣਾ (pharpharaaunaa) *v* To flutter, to flap, to flicker, to throb.

ਫ਼ਾਇਦਾ (faaidaa) *n m* Profit, gain, benefit, dividend, advantage.

ਫਾਸਣਾ (phaasṇaa) *v* To entrap.

ਫ਼ਾਸਲਾ (faaslaa) *n m* Distance, space, gap, interval.

ਫਾਂਸੀ (phaansee) *n f* Execution, gallows, death by hanging; **~ਲੱਗਣਾ** To be hanged till death; **~ਲਾਉਣਾ** To hang, to execute death sentence.

ਫਾਹ (phaah) *n m* Snaring, hanging; **~ਦੇਣਾ** To strangle. Also **ਫਾਹਾ**

ਫਾਕਾ (phaakaa) *n m* Fast, going without food; **~ਕਸ਼ੀ** Starvation, hunger; fasting; **~ਕਰਨਾ** To fast, to go without food, to observe fast, to miss a meal.

ਫ਼ਾਜ਼ਿਲ (faazil) *a* Proficient, learned, scholar.

ਫਾਂਟ (phaanṭ) *n f* Beating, division, slice, scrap, chip.

ਫਾਟਕ (phaaṭak) *n m* Door, gate, drive way, postern; Barrier (at rail/road crossing).

ਫਾਂਟਣਾ (phaanṭṇaa) *v* To beat, to punish.

ਫਾੜੀ (phaaḍee) *a* Lazy, slack, sluggish, lethargic.

ਫ਼ਾਨੀ (faanee) *a* Mortal, temporal, perishable, destructible.

ਫ਼ਾਨੂਸ (faanoos) *n m* Chandelier; Any light with translucent glass housing.

ਫ਼ਾਰਗ (faarag) *a* Free. Also **ਫ਼ਾਗਿਰ**

ਫਾਲਜ (phaalaj) *n m* Paralysis, hemiplegia.

ਫਾਲਤੂ (faaltoo) *a* Extra, spare, excess, useless, worhtless.

ਫਾੜ (phaaṛ) *n m* A fragment, a piece, dissection.

ਫਾੜਨਾ (phaaṛnaa) *v* To tear, to chop (wood), to cut, to burst open, to cleave, to split, to saw.

ਫਾੜੀ (phaaṛee) *n f* Fragment, segment, natural section (as of certain fruits like orange); Slice, splinter, piece.

ਫਿਸਣਾ (phisṇaa) *v* To be shrivlled, to be crushed, to discharge matter.

ਫਿਸਲਣਾ (phisalṇaa) *v* To slip, to glide, to incline, to be degraded.

ਫ਼ਿਕਰ (fikar) *n f* Care, worry, concern, anxiety, consideration; **~ਮੰਦ** Anxious, worried, pensive.

ਫ਼ਿਕਰਾ (fikraa) *n m* Sentence, a string of words.

ਫਿੱਕਾ (phikkaa) *a* Tasteless, insipid, dim, pale, light, vapid, unkind, devoid of radiance; **~ਪਣ** Tastelessness, paleness, dimness, indifference.

ਫਿਟਕਾਰ (phiṭkaar) *n f* Disdain, chiding, scolding, censure, curse, reproof, rebuking.

ਫਿਟਕਾਰਨਾ (phiṭkaarnaa) *v* To rebuke, to chide, to scold, to censure, to repudiate, to insult.

ਫਿੱਟਣਾ (phiṭṇaa) *v* To be overfed, to become bulky or hefty; To become proud or overbearing; To turn sour, to curdle or split.

ਫਿਟਾਉਣਾ (phitaauṇaa) *v* To split (milk) into curd and whey, to cause (milk) to be split, to curdle (milk); To make fat or proud.

ਫਿਟਿਆ (phiṭiaa) *a* Spoilt, egoistic, haughty, turned sour, curdled, precipitated.

ਫਿੱਡਾ (phiḍḍaa) *a* Deformed, clubfooted, snub-nosed.

ਫ਼ਿਤਰਤ (fitarat) *n f* Nature, disposition.

ਫ਼ਿਦਾ (fidaa) *a* Infatuated, devoted.

ਫਿਰਕਣੀ (phirkaṇee) *n f* Any rotating disc of a machine, fly-wheel.

ਫ਼ਿਰਕਾ (firkaa) *n m* Sect, tribe, clan; **~ਪ੍ਰਸਤੀ** Communalism, sectarianism.

ਫਿਰਕੀ (phirkee) *n f* Bobbin, spool, reel; pulley; A paper toy stuck at the end of a stick so that it rotates as the child holding it runs.

ਫਿਰਨਾ (phirnaa) *v* To whirl, to go round, to be rotated, to roam, to be circulated, to walk about, to travel; **ਉਡਦੇ~** To roam about in delight, to feel lost in delight; **ਦਿਨ~**To take a favourable turn.

ਫਿਰਾਉਣਾ (phiraauṇaa) *v* To rotate, to roll, to shift; **ਅੱਖਾਂ~** To turn away one's eyes.

ਫ਼ਿਰੌਤੀ (firautee) *n f* Ransom.

ਫਿਲਹਾਲ (philhaal) *adv* For the time being, for the present.

ਫਿਲਫ਼ੌਰ (filfaur) *adv* Immediately.

ਫੀਤਾ (pheetaa) *n m* Measuring tape, ribbon, lace, strip of cloth.

ਫ਼ੀਲ (feel) *n m* Elephant; **~ਖਾਨਾ** Stable for elephants.

ਫੁਸਕਣਾ (phusakṇaa) *v* To wail, to weep, to cry in low tone.

ਫੁਸਲਾਉਣਾ (phuslaauṇaa) *v* To lure, to fondle, to allure, to coax. Also **ਫੁਸਲਾਣਾ** or **ਫਾਹੁਣਾ**

ਫੁਸਲਾਹਟ (phuslaahat) *n f* Inducement, cajolery, temptation, seduction, allurement.

ਫ਼ੁਹਸ਼ (fuhash) *a* Indecent, immodest, obscene, vulgar. Also **ਫੁਹਸ**

ਫੁਹਾਰ (phuhaar) *n f* Drizzle; spray.

ਫੁਹਾਰਾ (phuhaaraa) *n m* Fountain; watering pot, sprinkler; Jet, discharge of liquid in fine spray or gush.

ਫੁਕਣਾ (phuknaa) *v* To be burnt, to burn, to be reduced to ashes, to be destroyed, to be wasted.

ਫੁੰਕਾਰ (phunkaar) *n f* Hissing sound (of snake), loud and strong breathing.

ਫੁੰਕਾਰਨਾ (phunkaarnaa) *v* To give out a hissing sound, to hiss.

ਫੁੰਕਾਰਾ (phunkaaraa) *n m* Hissing or hissing sound as of snake; Snort.

ਫੁਟ (phut) *n f* Discord, disunion, disagreement; ~ਪੈਣੀ To be disunited, to be divided in opinion.

ਫੁਟਕਲ (phutkal) *a* Miscellaneous, retail, separate, not enmass.

ਫੁੱਟਣਾ (phutnaa) *v* To sprout, to burgeon, to ratoon; To go away; To run away, to flee, to disappear. Also **ਟੁੱਟਣਾ**

ਫੁੱਟਾ (phuttaa) *n m* Foot ruler.

ਫੁੰਡਣਾ (phundnaa) *v* To strike, to shoot.

ਫੁਦਕਣਾ (phudaknaa) *v* To leap, to hop, to jump.

ਫੁੱਫੜ (phupphar) *n m* Husband of father's sister; Uncle.

ਫੁੰਮਣ (phumman) *n m* Tassel, cockade (satirically, lovingly used for young man).

ਫੁਰਸਤ (fursat) *n f* Spare time, vacant hour, leisure.

ਫੁਰਤੀ (phurtee) *n f* Promptness, smartness, quickness, nimbleness; ~ਨਾਲ Smartly, quickly; ~ਲਾ Smart, prompt, active, nimble.

ਫੁੱਲ (phull) *n m* Flower, blossom; Light, Residual bones of a person after cremation; ~ਵਾੜੀ Flower bed.

ਫੁਲਕਾ (phulkaa) *n m* Light Indian bread, loaf, same as **ਚਪਾਤੀ**

ਫੁਲਝੜੀ (phuljharee) *n f* A kind of firework emiting bright sparks; Slang. beautiful woman, sparkling beauty.

ਫੁਲਣਾ (phulnaa) *v* To swell, to be puffed, to bloom, to flower, to be happy.

ਫੁਲਾਉਣਾ (phulaaunaa) *v* To inflate, to puff up.

ਫੁਲਾਦ (phulaad) *n m* Steel.

ਫੁਲਾਦੀ (phulaadee) *a* Of or like steel, steely; Strong, tough.

ਫੁਲੇ (phule) *n m* Pop corn.

ਫੁੜਕਣਾ (phuraknaa) *v* To fall insensitive or unconscious, to flutter or writhe, to death, to die.

ਫੂਹੜ (phoohar) *n m* Crude matress.

ਫੂਕ (phook) *n f* Air blown with mouth or inflator; Puff, whiff, blow; ~ਕੱਢਣੀ

To deflate, to demoralise, to bewilder, to frighten; ~ਦੇਣੀ To flatter, to elate, to incite; ~ਨਿਕਲਣੀ To be deflated; ~ਫੂਕ ਕੇ ਪੈਰ ਰੱਖਣਾ To be very careful or cautious; ~ਭਰਨੀ/~ਦੇਣੀ To inflate, to fill with air, to pump air (into); ~ਮਾਰਨੀ To blow (in order to make fire or to warm up (skin), to puff; To blow off (as flame or candle) to puff, to whiff.

ਫੂਕਣਾ (phooknaa) v To blow, to whiff, to burn, to waste, to reduce to ashes.

ਫੇਹਣਾ (phehnaa) v To crush, to crack, to squeeze, to trample.

ਫੇਫੜਾ (phephraa) n m Lung.

ਫੇਰ (pher) n m adv Turn, rotation; Change, vicissitude; Later, in future, afterwards; Then, thereafter; Once again; Once more.

ਫੇਰਨਾ (phernaa) v To revolve, to rotate, to circulate, to return; ਪਾਣੀ~ To undo.

ਫੇਰੀ (pheree) n f Circuit, hawking, going round; ~ਵਾਲਾ Pedlar, hawker.

ਫੇਰੇ (phere) n m pl Rounds, circumambulation; ~ਲੈਣੇ To marry.

ਫੇੜਨਾ (phernaa) v To harm, to spoil,

to do an evil turn.

ਫੈਸਲਾ (faislaa) n Decision, judgement, settlement, arbitration, agreement; ~ਕਰਨਾ To settle, to decide; ~ਹੋਣਾ To come to a mutual agreement.

ਫੈਂਟਣਾ (phaintnaa) v To shuffle (cards), to beat.

ਫੈਲਣਾ (phailnaa) v To be stread, to expand, to be propagated.

ਫੈਲਾਉ (phaelaau) v To spread, extend, expand, dilate, open out; To scatter disperse; To diffuse, radiate; To become widely known (as news), to be disseminated, propagated, publicised; To be unfolded and stretched.

ਫੋਸ (phos) n m Fresh dung, excreta of an animal. Also ਫੋਸੀ

ਫੋਸੜ (phosar) a Worthless, lazy, sluggish, lethargic.

ਫੋਕਟ (phokat) a Useless, of no value.

ਫੋਕਾ (phokaa) a Hollow, tasteless, insipid.

ਫੋਗ (phog) n f Dregs, residual remains after extracting juice or essence. Also ਫੋਕ

ਫੋਤਾ (fotaa) n m Testicle.

ਫੋਲਣਾ (pholnaa) v To search, to expose, to find out, to scatter.

ਮਜ਼ਹਬੀ (mazhabee) *a* Religious; ~ਲੜਾਈ Crusade.

ਮੰਜਾ (manjaa) *n m* Cot, four poster.

ਮਜ਼ਾ (mazaa) *n m* Taste, fun, pleasure, deliciousness; ~ਚਖਾਉਣਾ To teach a lesson, to punish.

ਮਜ਼ਾਕ (mazaak) *n m* Joke, jest, witticism.

ਮਜ਼ਾਕੀਆ (mazaakiaa) *a* Witty, jovial, jolly, humorous, joker.

ਮਜ਼ਾਜ (mazaaj) *n m* Nature, pride, haughtness, health.

ਮਜ਼ਾਰ (mazaar) *n f* Tomb, grave, shrine.

ਮਜਾਲ (majaal) *n f* Strength, power, ability, daring.

ਮਜੀਠਾ (majeethaa) *a* Red, deep red.

ਮਜ਼ੀਦ (mazeed) *a* Additional, supplementary.

ਮਜ਼ੇਦਾਰ (mazedaar) *a* Delicious, tasty, tasteful, relishing, enjoyable, pleasant, delightful, scrumptious.

ਮੱਝ (majj) *n m* Adult female buffalo.

ਮੱਟ (matt) *n m* Large earthern pot, pitcher. Also ਮਟਕਾ

ਮਟਕਣਾ (mataknaa) *v* To flirt, to walk sprightly.

ਮਟਕਾਉਣਾ (matkaaunaa) *v* To wink, to coquette. Also ਮਟਕਾਣਾ

ਮਟਕੀ (matkee) *n f* Pitcher.

ਮੱਠ (matth) *n m* Monastry, convent, abbey, hermitage.

ਮੱਠਾ (matthaa) *n m a* Churned curd, butter milk; Slow, lazy.

ਮੱਠੀ (mathee) *n f* Small-sized crisp, round, flat, fried bread.

ਮੰਡਣਾ (mandnaa) *v* To fill in, to affirm, to thrust, to crush, to starch cloth.

ਮੰਡਪ (mandap) *n m* Canopy, pavillion, temple, dome.

ਮੰਡਲ (mandal) *n m* Board, Division, association, sphere, circle, circumference.

ਮੰਡਲਾਉਣਾ (mandlaaunaa) *v* To hover, to move about, to flutter about. Also ਮੰਡਲਾਣਾ

ਮੰਡਲੀ (mandlee) *n f* Group, gang, band coterie, clique; Choir; Trupe.

ਮੱਡੀ (maddee) *n f* Household luggage.

ਮੰਡੀ (mandee) *n f* Market, mart, trading centre; Cattle fair.

ਮਣਕਾ (mankaa) *n m* Bead, perforated jewl, stone, etc.

ਮਣੀ (manee) *n f* Semen; Jewel, gem, precious stone.

ਮਤ (mat) *n m* Belief, dogma, theory, view, doctrine, faith, religion.

ਮੱਤ (matt) *n f* Advice, opinion, thought, sense, understanding; ~ਦੇਣੀ To advise; ~ਭੇਦ Differences, dissent; ~**ਦਾਤਾ** Voter, elector ~**ਦਾਨ** Poll.

ਮਾਤਹਿਤ (maateht) *a* Subordinate. Also **ਮਤਹਿਤ**

ਮੰਤਰ (mantar) *n m* Incantaton, spell, counsel, vedic text or hymn.

ਮੰਤਰੀ (mantree) *n m* Minister, adviser, counsellor.

ਮਤਰੇਆ (matreaa) *a* Step brother, sister, etc. Also **ਮਤੇਆ**

ਮਤਲਬ (matlab) *n m* Meaning, purpose, idea, object, motive, intention; ~**ਦਾ ਯਾਰ** Fair weather friend; ~**ਪ੍ਰਸਤੀ** Selfishness; **ਬੇ~** Unmeaningly.

ਮਤਲਬੀ (matlabee) *a* Selfish, self-seeking, self-interested

ਮਤਵਾਤਰ (matvaatar) *adv* Constantly, without break, incessantly, continually, continuously, uninterruptedly.

ਮਤਵਾਲਾ (matwaalaa) *a* Intoxicated, tipsy, Insane; Carefree; ~**ਪਣ** Insanity.

ਮਤਾ (mataa) *n m* Resolution, motion, source of thought.

ਮਥਣਾ (mathṇaa) *v* To churn. Also **ਰਿੜਕਣਾ**

ਮਥਾ (matthaa) *n m* Forehead, top, front; ~**ਟੇਕਣਾ** To pay respect; ~**ਪਿਟਣਾ** To lament, to wail; ~**ਮਾਰਨਾ**

To try to convince, to argu, to talk one's head off.

ਮੰਦ (mand) *a* Slow, mild, dull; ~**ਹਾਲੀ** Bad days, hard time, poverty distitution.

ਮਦ (mad) *n m* Intoxication, wine, madness; Ecstasy; ~**ਹੋਸ਼** Intoxicated, drunk, unconscious in ecstacy.

ਮਦਤ (madat) *n f* Help, assistance, aid, support; ~**ਗਾਰ** Helper, supporter. Also **ਮਦਦ**

ਮੰਦਾ (mandaa) *a* Dull, feeble, slow, bad, ill.

ਮਦਾਨ (maadaan) *n m* Plain; Open ground of field, (play) ground; (battle) field; Arena.

ਮਧਰਾ (madhraa) *a* Short statured, dwarf; ~**ਪਣ** Short stature, low height.

ਮਧਾਣੀ (madhaaṇee) *n f* Chrun, churning stick or staff.

ਮਧੁਰ (madhur) *a* Mellodious, sweet, pleasant, soft; ~**ਤਾ** Euphony, sweetness, mellifluence, softness.

ਮਧੂ (madhoo) *n f* Honey; ~**ਮੱਖੀ** Bee.

ਮਧੋਲਣਾ (madholṇaa) *v* To crumple, to crush in hands or under feet, to spoil, to use carelessly (cloth or paper).

ਮਨ (man) *n m* Mind, soul, heart,

intention, desire, wish, purpose, intellect; ~ਫੇਰਨਾ To turn one's mind from; ~ਭਰ ਜਾਣਾ To be fed up, wearied, satiated; ~ਮਾਰਨਾ To control one's mind or passion; to be patient, diligent.

ਮਨਸਬ (mansab) *n m* Office, rank, post; ~ਦਾਰ Official; Magistrate.

ਮਨਸ਼ਾ (manshaa) *n f* Wish, desire, will, purpose, motive, intention.

ਮਨਸੂਖ (mansookh) *a* Rescinded, annulled, cancelled; ~ਕਰਨਾ To cancel, to annual, to rescind.

ਮਨਸੂਖੀ (mansookhee) *n f* Cancellation, annulment, abrogation, revocation, invalidation.

ਮਨਸੂਬਾ (mansoobaa) *n m* Plan, intention.

ਮਨਹੂਸ (manhoos) *a* Inauspicious, illomened, unlucky, boding ill.

ਮਨੱਕਾ (mankkaa) *a* Dried grape, raisin or currant.

ਮਨਹੂਸੀਅਤ (manhoosiat) *n f* Inauspiciousness.

ਮਨਚਲਾ (manchalaa) *a* Fearless, assiduos, bold.

ਮਨਜ਼ੂਰ (manzoor) *a* Accepted, agreeable.

ਮਨਜ਼ੂਰੀ (manzooree) *n f* Acceptance, sanction, consent, approval.

ਮੰਨਣਾ (mannnaa) *v* To agree, to profess, to accept, to assent, to acknowledge, to accede.

ਮੰਨਤ (mannat) *n f* Vow, promise, decision to offer something to a deity after fulfilment of desire.

ਮਨਨ (manan) *n m* Thought, reflection, contemplation, internalization, thinking process; Deliberation.

ਮੰਨਵਾਉਣਾ (manvaaunaa) *v* To make one to agree, to persuade one to accept.

ਮਨ੍ਹਾਂ (manhaan) *a* Forbidden, prohibited; ~ਕਰਨਾ To forbid.

ਮਨਾਉਣਾ (manaaunaa) *v* To persuade, to appease, to reconcile.

ਮਨਾਹੀ (manaahee) *n f* Restraint, ban, prohibition.

ਮਨੁੱਖ (manukkh) *n m* Man, person, human being; ~ਤਾ Humanity, manhood, civility.

ਮਨੋਹਰ (manohar) *a* Alluring, beautiful, elegant, lovely, pleasing, fascinating, attractive.

ਮਨੋਰੰਜਨ (manoranjan) *n m* Recreation.

ਮਨੋਰਥ (manorath) *n m* Wish, hope, desire, purpose, aim.

ਮਨੌਤੀ (manautee) *n f* Postulate,

axiom something assumed without proof; promise, vow. Also **ਸੁੱਖਣਾ** or **ਮੰਨਤ**

ਮਫ਼ਰੂਰ (mafroor) *a* Absconder, underground.

ਮਮਟੀ (mamtee) *n f* A small room built above the first storey, loft.

ਮੰਮਾ (mammaa) *n m* Breast, teat.

ਮਮਿਆਉਣਾ (mamiaauṇaa) *v* (for goats) To bleat.

ਮਰਹੂਮ (marhoom) *a* Late, dead, expired.

ਮਰਕਜ਼ (markaz) *n m* Centre, axis.

ਮਰਕਜ਼ੀ (markazee) *a* Central.

ਮਰਘਟ (marghaṭ) *n m* Cemetary, grave yard.

ਮਰਜ਼ (maraz) *n f* Disease, ailment, illness.

ਮਰਜ਼ੀ (marzee) *n f* Willingness, desire, inclination.

ਮਰਜੀਵੜਾ (marjeevaṛaa) *n m a* Parsimonious, living poorly, stingy, miser; (One) ready to lay down one's life for a cause.

ਮਰਤਬਾ (martabaa) *n m* Turn, post, position, status.

ਮਰਦ (marad) *n m* Man, a brave person, husband.

ਮਰਦਾਨਾ (mardaanaa) *a* Male, masculine, manlike, manly. Also **ਮਰਦਾਵਾਂ**

ਮਰਦਮਸ਼ੁਮਾਰੀ (mardamshumaaree) *n f* Census.

ਮਰਦੂਦ (mardood) *a* Damned, contemptable, despised, wicked.

ਮਰਨ (maran) *n m* Death; **~ਹਾਰ**, **~ਕਿਨਾਰੇ** Death bed, dying.

ਮਰਨਾ (marnaa) *v* To die, to succumb, to pass away, to expire, to fade.

ਮਰਮਰ (marmar) *n m* Marble.

ਮਰਮਰੀ (marmaree) *a* Marble, white, snow-white; Soft, tender; Made of marble.

ਮਰਯਾਦਾ (maryaadaa) *n f* Decorum, custom, tradition, propriety of conduct, practice; **~ਹੀਣ** Wanton, unconventional. Also **ਮਰਿਆਦਾ**

ਮਰਲਾ (marlaa) *n m* A unit of area measuring 1/160th of an acre; 5 yards square or 25 square yards.

ਮਰੀਅਲ (mariyal) *a* Sickly, feeble, weak.

ਮਰੀਜ਼ (mareez) *n m* Patient, sick, ill, diseased (person).

ਮਰੁੰਡਣਾ (marunḍṇaa) *v* To yank, to pluck, to rip, to tweak (top of plants or flowers)

ਮਰੋੜ (maroṛ) *n m* Twist, tortion, contortion, tweak; Stufy, oppressive, hot and windless weather; Loose motions preceded by contortion and pain in stomach; Tenesmus; Dysentery.

ਮਰੋੜਨਾ (marornaa) v To twist, to wring, to contrast.

ਮਰੋੜਾ (maroraa) n m Twist, dysentery.

ਮਲਕ (malak) n m King, chieftain, noble; Angel; Name of a Khatri subcaste.

ਮਲਕਾ (malkaa) n f Queen, empress.

ਮਲਕੀਅਤ (malkiat) n f Possesion, ownership; Property.

ਮਲੰਗ (malang) n m Fakir, Muslim mendicant; Carefree, indifferent to life; ~ਪੁਣਾ Mendicancy, mendicity; Carefreeness, indifference or indifferent attitude towards life.

ਮਲਣਾ (malnaa) v To rub, to massage, to anoint, to pound; To clean (untensils); To wring (hands); ਹੱਥ~ To regret, to chafe. Also ਮਲਨਾ

ਮੱਲਣਾ (mallnaa) v To occupy (seat, land etc.), to posses illegally.

ਮਲਬਾ (malbaa) n m Refuse, debris, rubbish.

ਮਲੱਪ (malapp) n m Stomach worm, round worm nematode, ascarid,

Ascaris lumbricoides.

ਮਲ੍ਹਮ (malham) n f Ointment, salve, unguent; ~ਪੱਟੀ Dressing.

ਮਲਮਲ (malmal) n f Muslin, linen.

ਮਲਾਈ (malaaee) n f Cream (of milk), essence.

ਮਲਾਹ (malaah) n m Boatman, sailor, oarsman, rower; ~ਗੀਰੀ Boatmanship.

ਮਲਾਮਤ (malaamat) n f Reproach, rebuke, accusation, censure, scolding, chiding.

ਮਲਾਲ (malaal) n m Remorse, dejection, sorrow, regret, compunction.

ਮਲੀਆਮੇਟ (maliaamet) a Totally or completely destroyed, devastated, exterminated, ruined; ~ਕਰਨਾ To destroy completely, to raze to ground.

ਮਲੀਦਾ (maleedaa) a n m Crushed, mashed, reduced to pulp; Eatable thing.

ਮਲੂਕ (malook) a Tender, slender, delicate, unfit for hand work.

ਮਲੇਛ (malechh) a n m Wicked, of low caste; Barbarian, outcaste, sinful person.

ਮਵਾਦ (mavaad) n m Pus, purulent matter. Also ਮੁਆਦ

ਮਵੇਸ਼ੀ (maveshee) n m Cattle, beast.

ਮੜ੍ਹਨਾ (maṛhnaa) *v* To wrap, to surround with a layer, to entrust.

ਮੜ੍ਹੀ (maṛhee) *n f* Funeral pyre; memorial built at site of cremation.

ਮਾਂ (maan) *n f* Mother; ~ਜਾਇਆ Brother; ~ਜਾਈ Sister; ~ਪਿਉ Parents.

ਮਾਊਂ (maaun) *a n f* Coward, timid; simpleton, foolish; Mum, silent, cat, cat's mew.

ਮਾਅਨਾ (maaynaa) *n m* Meaning.

ਮਾਇਆ (maaiaa) *n f* Money, illusion, magical power of deity; ~ਵਾਦ Illusionism. Also ਮਾਯਾ

ਮਾਈ (maaee) *n f* Mother, old woman.

ਮਾਸ (maas) *n m* Flesh, meat; Month; ~ਖੋਰ Carnivorous.

ਮਾਸਟਰ (maasṭar) *n m* Teacher, master.

ਮਾਸਟਰੀ (mastree) *n f* Teaching profession, mastership.

ਮਾਸਾਹਾਰੀ (maasaahaaree) *a* Non-vegetarian.

ਮਾਸਿਕ (maasik) *a* Monthly, per month.

ਮਾਹ (maah) *n m* Month; ~ਵਾਰ Monthly; ~ਵਾਰੀ Menses, monthly.

ਮਾਹੀ (maahee) *n m* (1) Fish; Boatman. Also ਮਾਸ਼ਕੀ (2) Lover beloved, husband. Also ਮਾਰੀਆ;

~ਗੀਰ Fisherman. Also ਮਾਛੀ

ਮਾਹੋਲ (maahol) *n m* Environment, atmosphere.

ਮਾਕੂਲ (maakool) *a* Reasonable, proper, befitting, correct.

ਮਾਚਸ (maachas) *n f* Match-box, match stick, lucifer match.

ਮਾਂਜਣਾ (maanjṇaa) *v* To scrub, to cleanse, to scour.

ਮਾਜਰਾ (maajraa) *n m* Happening, occurence, incident, matter, news.

ਮਾਂਝੀ (maanjhee) *n m* Boatsman, ferryman, steersman.

ਮਾਠਣਾ (maṭhṇaa) *v* To acquire by stratagem or deceit, to swindle, to wangle; To buy very cheap.

ਮਾਣ (maṇ) *n m* Respect, regard, honour, esteem; Self-respect; Pride, arrogance, conceit; ~ਹਾਨੀ Loss of self-respect, humilliation, disgrace, insult; ~ਕਰਨਾ To be proud, to be proud of; to respect, to honour.

ਮਾਤਮ (maatam) *n m* Death, bereavement; ~ਕਰਨਾ To mourn, to lament; ~ਪੁਰਸੀ Consolence.

ਮਾਤਾ (maataa) *n f* Mother; Small pox; ~ਨਿਕਲਣੀ To have attack of small pox.

ਮਾਨਤਾ (maantaa) *n f* Recognition.

ਮਾਪ (maap) *n m* Measurement, size, dimensions.

ਮਾਪਣਾ (maapṇaa) *v* To measurer, to take measurement.

ਮਾਫ਼ (maaf) *a* Pardoned, excused; ~ਕਰਨਾ To pardon, to condone, to remit, to excuse.

ਮਾਫ਼ਕ (maafak) *a* Suitable, agreeable, fit, favourable, like.

ਮਾਫ਼ੀ (maafee) *n f* Pardon, remission; ~ਨਾਮਾ Written apology, request for pardon.

ਮਾਮਲਾ (maamlaa) *n m* Affair, matter, problem, business. Also ਮੁਆਮਲਾ

ਮਾਮੂਲ (maamool) *n m* Routine.

ਮਾਮੂਲੀ (maamoolee) *a* Ordinary, common, petty, insignificant, trivial, customary.

ਮਾਯੂਸ (maayoos) *a* Disappointed, frustrated.

ਮਾਯੂਸੀ (maayoosee) *n f* Disappointment, frustration.

ਮਾਰ (maar) *n f* Beating, blow, range; ~ਸੁਟਣਾ To kill, to put to death; ~ਕਾਟ Riot, flight; ~ਧਾੜ Robbery, spoilation; ~ਲੈਣਾ To conquer, to embezzle.

ਮਾਰਕਾ (maarkaa) *n m* Mark, sign, trade mark.

ਮਾਰਗ (maarag) *n m* Path, way, road, passage, channel.

ਮਾਰਨਾ (maarnaa) *v* To kill, to beat, to hit, to conquer, to embezzle.

ਮਾਰਫ਼ਤ (maarfat) *prep* Through, by, care of, via.

ਮਾਲ (maal) *n m* Public revenue, luggage, goods, commodity, money, wares; ~ਅਸਬਾਬ Luggage; ~ਅਫ਼ਸਰ Revenue officer; ~ਖ਼ਜ਼ਾਨਾ Treasury; ~ਖ਼ਾਨਾ Ware house, store house; ~ਗੱਡੀ Goods train; ~ਦਾਰ Wealthy; ~ਮਤਾ Wealth, effects; ~ਗੁਦਾਮ Godown.

ਮਾਲਸ਼ (maalash) *n f* Rubbing of oil on body, massage.

ਮਾਲਸ਼ੀਆ (malshiaa) *a n m* Masseur.

ਮਾਲਕ (maalak) *n m* Owner, master, lord, proprieter, husband; ~ਣ Matron; Housewife; Land lady.

ਮਾਲਕੀ (maalkee) *n f* Ownership.

ਮਾਲਾ (maalaa) *n f* Garland, rosary; ~ਮਾਲ Very rich, very wealthy.

ਮਾਲੀ (maalee) *n m a* Gardner; Recuniary, fiscal.

ਮਾੜਾ (maaṛaa) *a* Weak, poor, bad, very little; ~ਮੋਟਾ Ordinary, cheap, to some extent.

ਮਾੜੀ (maaṛee) *n f* Mansion, attic, a small room on the roof of house.

ਮਿਆਦ (miaad) *n f* Duration, time, term, tenure, period; Durability.

ਮਿਆਦੀ (miyaadee) *a* Periodical, for

a fixed period; ~ਬੁਖਾਰ Typhoid.

ਮਿਆਨ (miyaan) *n f* Sheath, scabbard.

ਮਿਆਰ (miyaar) *n m* Standard.

ਮਿਆਰੀਕਰਨ (miaareekaran) *n m* Standardization.

ਮਿਸਤਰੀ (mistree) *n m* Craftman, artisan; ਰਾਜ~ Mason.

ਮਿਸਰੀ (misree) *n f* Sugar candy.

ਮਿਸਲ (misal) *n f* File of office or court.

ਮਿਸਾਲ (misaal) *n f* Example, instance; ਬੇ~ Unparalled, unmatched, unique, unexample.

ਮਿੱਸੀ (missee) *a* Mixed; ~ਰੋਟੀ Bread by mixing wheat flour and gram flour.

ਮਿਹਣਾ (mehnaa) *v* To reproach, to chide, to upraide.

ਮਿਹਤਰ (mehatar) *n m* Sweeper, scavenger.

ਮਿਹਤਰਾਨੀ (mehtaraanee) *n* Female sweeper.

ਮਿਹਨਤ (mehnat) *n f* Labour, hard work, toil, effort.

ਮਿਹਨਤਾਨਾ (mehnatanaa) *n m* Wages, remuneration.

ਮਿਹਨਤੀ (mehnatee) *a* Labourious, industrious, hardworking.

ਮਿਹਮਾਨ (mehmaan) *n m* Guest; ~ਦਾਰੀ Hospitality, feast, treat;

Being a guest. Also ਮਹਿਮਾਨ

ਮਿਹਮਾਨੀ (mehmaanee) *n f* Hospitality, care and service of quests.

ਮਿਹਰ (mehar) *n f* Kindness, mercy, compassion; ~ਬਾਨ Kind, merciful, compassionate; ~ਬਾਨੀ kindness, benevolence.

ਮਿਕਦਾਰ (mikdaar) *n f* Quantity, amount, proportion.

ਮਿਜ਼ਾਜ (mizaaj) *n m* Temprament, mood; Disposition, nature.

ਮਿੱਝ (mijj) *n f* Marrow, pitch, pulp; ~ਕੱਢਣੀ To crush, squeze, press hard, to beat severely, to whop; ~ਨਿਕਲਣੀ To be reduced, to pulp, to be throughly beaten or defeated, to be crushed under heavy weight or excessive work.

ਮਿੰਟ (mint) *n m* Minute.

ਮਿਟਣਾ (mitnaa) *v* To be erased, to be wiped out, to be effaced.

ਮਿਟਾਉਣਾ (mitaaunaa) *v* To erase, to wipe out, to efface, to annihilate, to blot out, to destroy, to expunge.

ਮਿਟਿਆਲਾ (mitiaalaa) *a* Grey, dusty, dust coloured.

ਮਿੱਟੀ (mittee) *n f* Clay, dust, earth, dust, soil, ashes; ~ਖਰਾਬ ਹੋਣੀ To be humiliated; ~ਦਾ ਤੇਲ Kerosene oil; ~ਦਾ ਮਾਧੋ Dunce, Simpleton, nitwit fool; ~ਦੇ ਮੁੱਲ Damn cheap; ~ਪਾਉਣੀ To hush up; ~ਵਿਚ ਮਿਲਾਉਣਾ To ruin, to raze to the ground.

ਮਿੱਠਾ (mitthaa) a Sweet, delicious; ~ਸ Sweetness.

ਮਿਠਿਆਈ (mithiaaee) n f Sweetmeat, confectionary, candy.

ਮਿੱਡਾ (middaa) a Snub-nosed, snubby.

ਮਿੱਤਰ (mittar) n m Friend, comrade, companion; ~ਘਾਤ Cheating a friend; ~ਤਾ Friendship.

ਮਿਤੀ (mitee) n f Date.

ਮਿਥਣਾ (mithnaa) v To decide, to arrange, to allot, to allocate, to imagine.

ਮਿਥਿਆ (mithiaa) a n f Untrue, false; Lie, delusion, falsehood.

ਮਿਧਣਾ (midhnaa) v To crush (under feet), to trample, to pound.

ਮਿੰਨਤ (minnat) n m Request, entreaty, supplication.

ਮਿਮਿਆਉਣਾ (mimiaaunaa) v To bleat, to supplicate.

ਮਿਰਗ (mirag) n m Deer, antelope. Also ਮ੍ਰਿਗ

ਮਿਰਗੀ (mirgee) n f Epilpsy, apoplexy.

ਮਿਰਚ (mirach) n f Chilli; ਕਾਲੀ~ Pepper; ਲਾਲ~ Capsicum.

ਮਿਰਤਕ (mirtak) n a Dead person, corpse; Deceased, lifeless.

ਮਿਰਤੂ (mritoo) n f Death, mortality, thanatos; ~ਦੰਡ Death sentence, capital punishment, death penalty.

ਮਿਲਣ (milan) n m Meeting, union, mixing, contact; ~ਸਾਰ Sociable, qourteous.

ਮਿਲਣਾ (milnaa) v To meet, to come across, to mix, to merge, to tally, to assamble, to mingle; ~ਜੁਲਣਾ To meet cordially.

ਮਿਲਣੀ (milnee) n f Formal or ceremonial meeting and embracing by relations of bride and bridegroom.

ਮਿਲਾਉਣਾ (millaaunaa) v To mix, to blend, to affiliate, to adjust, to associate, to compare, to incorporate; ਅੱਖ~ To see face to face. Also ਮਿਲਾਣਾ

ਮਿਲਾਪ (milaap) n m Union, concord, meeting, social intercourse; ~ੜਾ Sociable, amiable, courteous.

ਮਿਲਾਵਟ (milaavat) n f Adulteration, blend, additive; ~ਕਰਨਾ To adulterate.

ਮਿਲਾਵਟੀ (milaavatee) a Adulterated.

ਮਿਲੀ-ਭਗਤ (milee-bhagat) n f Collusion, conspiracy, secret

understanding.

ਮੀਸਣਾ (meesṇaa) *a* Perverse, taciturn, not disposed to answer.

ਮੀਂਹ (meenh) *n* Rain.

ਮੀਚਣਾ (meechṇaa) *v* To close, to shut (eyes).

ਮੀਟਣਾ (meeṭṇaa) *v* To shut or close (as eye, palm, book, etc).

ਮੀਨਾ (meenaa) *n m* A type of precious stone of blue colour used in inset work; **~ਕਾਰ** Artist or craftsman skilled in inset work in metal, stone or stucco; a painter of intricate designs; **~ਕਾਰੀ** Inset work in stone, stucco or metal; painting or any other visual art in intricate designs.

ਮੀਨਾਰ (meenaar) *n f* Tower, minaret.

ਮੁਅੱਤਲ (muattal) *a* Suspended.

ਮੁਅੱਤਲੀ (muattalee) *n m* Suspension.

ਮੁਆਇਨਾ (muaainaa) *n m* Inspection, visitation, visit.

ਮੁਆਫ਼ਕ (muaafak) *a* Agreeable, likeable, favourable; Suitable; Effective.

ਮੁਆਵਜ਼ਾ (muaavazaa) *n m* Compensation; **~ਦੇਣਾ** To, compensate, to indemnify.

ਮੁਸ਼ਕ (mushak) *n f* Smell, odour, fragrance; Stink, reek, stench, malodour.

ਮੁਸ਼ਕਣਾ (mushakṇaa) *v* To give out offensive odour, to come in heat (animals).

ਮੁਸ਼ੱਕਤ (mushakat) *n f* Hard work, labour, toil.

ਮੁਸਕਰਾਹਟ (muskaraahaṭ) *n f* Smile.

ਮੁਸ਼ਕਲ (mushkal) *a n f* Difficult, intricate; Hard, Difficulty, trouble, hardship.

ਮੁਸ਼ਟੰਡਾ (mushṭanḍaa) *a* Stout, robust, wicked, strong & powerful (not in good sense).

ਮੁਸਣਾ (musṇaa) *v* To be deprived of, to be cheated, to be pilfered, to be stolen.

ਮੁਸੱਦੀ (musaddee) *n m* Learned man, head man in King's household, chief writer.

ਮੁਸੱਰਤ (musarrat) *n f* Happiness, gladness, delight.

ਮੁਸੱਨਫ਼ (musannaf) *n m* Author, writer.

ਮੁਸਲਮਾਨ (musalmaan) *n m* Mohammedan, muslim.

ਮੁਸਾਫ਼ਰ (musaafar) *n m* Traveller, passenger, wayfarer; **~ਖ਼ਾਨਾ** Waiting room, inn, serai; The transient world.

ਮੁਸਾਫ਼ਰੀ (musaafaree) *n f* Travel, traveling, journeying.

ਮੁਸੀਬਤ (museebat) *n f* Trouble,

misfortune, calamity, adversity; ~ਕਟਣੀ To suffer or undergo adversity; ~ਦਾ ਮਾਰਿਆ Afflicted by misfortune; ~ਦੇ ਦਿਨ Calamitous days.

ਮੁਹਤਾਜ (muhtaaj) *a* Needy, dependent, poor.

ਮੁਹੱਬਤ (muhabbat) *n f* Love, affection.

ਮੁਹੱਬਤੀ (muhabbatee) *a* Close, affectionate, friendly.

ਮੁਹਰ (muhar) *n f* Seal, stamp, gold coin; ~ਬੰਦ Sealed. Also ਮੋਹਰ

ਮੁਹਲਤ (muhalat) *n f* Reprieve, duration, limit of, leisure.

ਮੁਹੱਲਾ (muhalla) *n m* Particular portion of town, mohallaa.

ਮੁਹਾਸਾ (muhaasaa) *n m* Acne.

ਮੁਹਾਣਾ (muhaanaa) *n m* Mouth of river. Also ਮੁਹਾਨਾ

ਮੁਹਾਂਦਰਾ (muhaandraa) *n m* Feature (facial), appearance, face, visage, form.

ਮੁਹਾਰਤ (muhaarat) *n f* Expertise, expertness. Also ਮਹਾਰਤ

ਮੁਹਾਲ (muhaal) *a* Difficult, absurd.

ਮੁਹਾਵਰਾ (muhaavraa) *n m* Idiom, usage.

ਮੁਹਿੰਮ (muhimm) *n f* Compaign, attack, arduous task, expedition.

ਮੁਕਟ (mukaṭ) *n m* Crown, crest, diadem.

ਮੁਕਣਾ (mukṇaa) *v* To end, to come to an end, to be finished.

ਮੁਕਤ (mukat) *a n m* Free, freed, released; Liberated, emancipated, redeemed; Liberated person.

ਮੁਕਤੀ (muktee) *n f* Liberation, release, redemption, salvation, riddance; ~ਦਾਤਾ Redeemer, liberator, saviour.

ਮੁਕਦਮਾ (mukadmaa) *n m* Law suit, a case; ~ਕਰਨਾ; To sue, to file a case; ~(ਮੇ) ਬਾਜ਼ੀ Litigation.

ਮੁਕੱਦਰ (mukaddar) *n m* Fortune, destiny, fate.

ਮੁਕੰਮਲ (mukammal) *a* Complete, completed, finished, finalised; entire, whole.

ਮੁਕਰਨਾ (mukarnaa) *v* To go back upon, to back out, to retreat.

ਮੁਕੱਰਰ (mukarrar) *a* Appointed, assigned, nominated, detailed; fixed, settled; Once again, once more, repeat, say again; ~ਕਰਨਾ To appoint, nominate, to assign, to fix, to determine, to set.

ਮੁੱਕਾ (mukkaa) *n m* Fist, blow with a fist; ~(ਕੇ) ਬਾਜ਼ Boxer; ~ਬਾਜ਼ੀ Boxing.

ਮੁਕਾਉਣਾ (mukaauṇaa) *v* To bring to

an end, to complete, to finish, to
spend, to consume.

ਮੁਕਾਣ (mukaaṇ) *n f* Consoling,
condolence. Also ਮੁਕਾਣੇ

ਮੁਕਾਬਲਾ (mukaabalaa) *n* Competition, encounter, comparison,
opposition.

ਮੁਕਾਮ (mukaam) *n m* Place, locale,
site, halting place.

ਮੁਕਾਲਾ (mukaalaa) *n m* Disgrace,
dishonour; Stigma.

ਮੁਖ (mukkh) *a* Main, chief, principal,
premier, first, topmost, head,
leading; ~ਮੰਤਰੀ Chief minister.

ਮੁਖਤਸਰ (mukhatsar) *a* Brief, short,
abridged, condensed.

ਮੁਖਤਾਰ (mukhtaar) *n m* Attorney,
agent.

ਮੁਖਤਾਰੀ (mukhtaaree) *n f* Independent control, absolute authority;
~ਨਾਮਾ Power of attorney; Also
ਮੁਖਤਿਆਰ

ਮੁਖਬਰ (mukhbar) *n m* Spy, reporter,
informer.

ਮੁਖਬਰੀ (mukhbaree) *n f* Tattle, tattl-
ing, telling on.

ਮੁਖੜਾ (mukhṛaa) *n m* Mouth, face.

ਮੁਖਾਲਫ਼ (mukhaalaf) *a n m* Opposite,
antagonistic; Opponent;
Adversary; ~ਤ Opposition.

ਮੁਖੀ (mukhee) *a* Head, chief; ~ਆ

Head, leader, chief.

ਮੁਖੋਟਾ (mukhoṭaa) *n m* Mask.

ਮੁਗਾਲਤਾ (mugaaltaa) *n m*
Misunderstanding. Also ਭੁਲੇਖਾ

ਮੁਚਨਾ (muchnaa) *v* To sprain.

ਮੁੱਚਲਕਾ (muchchalkaa) *n m* Bond,
agreement, binding.

ਮੁੱਛ (muchchh) *n f* Moustaches,
whiskers; ~ਉਖੇੜਨੀ To humiliate;
~ਵਿਲੀ ਹੋਣੀ To be dishonoured;
~ਾਂ To cut, to secure by fraud;
~ਲ Person having long or thick
moustaches.

ਮੁਜਰਮ (mujaram) *n m* Criminal,
offender.

ਮੁਜਰਮਾਨਾ (mujarmaanaa) *a* Criminal.

ਮੁਜਰਾ (mujraa) *n m* Professional
singing and dancing by
prostitutes.

ਮੁਜਾਹਿਦ (mujaahid) *n m* Crusader.

ਮੁਜ਼ਾਹਿਰਾ (muzaahiraa) *n m*
Demonstration.

ਮੁੰਜੀ (munjee) *n f* Rice, paddy.

ਮੁਟਾਪਾ (muṭaapaa) *n m* Fatness,
corpulence.

ਮੁਟਿਆਰ (muṭiaar) *n f* Damsel,
maiden, a young woman.

ਮੁੱਠ (muṭṭh) *n f a* Clutch, grip, fist;
Handful; ~ਭੇੜ Tussle, encounter,
clash, skirmish. Also ਮੁੱਠੀ

ਮੁੱਠਾ (muṭṭhaa) *n m* Handle of

instrument, haft, bundle.

ਮੁੱਠੀ (mutthee) *n* Grip, fist; ~**ਭਰ** Very few, a little.

ਮੁੰਡਨ (mundan) *n m* Tonsure; ~**ਕਰਨਾ** To tonsure.

ਮੁੰਡਾ (mundaa) *n m* Boy, lad, urchin; Lame; ~**ਖੁੰਡਾ** Boy irresponsible fellow.

ਮੁੰਡੀ (mundee) *n f* Head and neck.

ਮੁੱਢ (muddh) *n f* Root, origin, begining; ~**ਲਾ** Elementary, initial, primary, preliminary, original.

ਮੁਤਲਕ (mutalak) *adv* About, concerning, regarding, in connection with.

ਮੁਤਵਾਤਰ (mutvaatar) *adv* Constantly, continuously, continually, incessantly, without break.

ਮੁਤਾਸਰ (mutaasar) *a* Affected, influenced; impressed, moved.

ਮੁਤਾਬਕ (mutaabak) *a* Corrresponding, suitable, coinciding, resembling, conforming, similar; according to, in accordance with, as per, as stated (by); On or under the authority of.

ਮੁਤਾਲਬਾ (mutaalbaa) *n m* Demand.

ਮੁਥਾਜ (muthaaj) *a* Needy, in want, poor, indigent, destitute, dependent.

ਮੁਥਾਜਗੀ/ਮੁਥਾਜੀ   (muthaajgee/

muthaajee) *n f* Need, want, poverty, indigence, distitution.

ਮੁੱਦਈ (muddaee) *n m* Plaintiff, prosecutor, complainant.

ਮੁੱਦਤ (muddat) *n f* Time, duration, space of time.

ਮੁੰਦਰੀ (mundaree) *n f* Ring, finger ring.

ਮੁਧਾਉਣਾ (mudhaaunaa) *v* To invert, to turn upside down.

ਮੁੰਨਣਾ (munnnaa) *v* To shave; to cheat.

ਮੁਨਾਦੀ (munaadee) *n f* Proclamation by beat of drum.

ਮੁਨਾਫ਼ਾ (munaafaa) *n m* Profit, gain; ~**ਖੋਰ** Profiteer.

ਮੁਨਿਆਰੀ (muniaaree) *n f* General stores, general merchandise, grocery.

ਮੁੱਨੀ (munnee) *n f* A small girl, a small support. Also **ਮੁੱਨਾ**

ਮੁਨੀ (munee) *n m* Ascetic, hermit, saint.

ਮੁਨੀਮ (muneem) *n* Accountant.

ਮੁਨੀਮੀ (muneemee) *n f* Accountancy, Book keeping.

ਮੁਫ਼ਤ (mufat) *a* Free, gratis.

ਮੁਫ਼ੀਦ (mufeed) *a* Beneficial, useful.

ਮੁਬਾਰਕ (mubaarak) *n f a* Congratulation, welcome, felicitation; Blessed, auspicious, happy.

ਮੁਮਕਿਨ (mumkin) *a* Possible, feasible.

ਮੁਯੱਸਰ (muyassar) *a* Available, obtainable, accessible; ~ਕਰਨਾ To provide, to make available.

ਮੁਰਸ਼ਦ (murshad) *n m* Spiritual teacher, preceptor.

ਮੁਰਕਣਾ (muraknaa) *v a* To be twisted, to writhe, to snap; Crisp.

ਮੁਰਗਾ (murgaa) *n m* Cock, rooster, broiler, male chicken.

ਮੁਰਗੀ (murgee) *n f* Hen, female chicken; ~ਪਾਲਣ Poultry farming; ~ਖ਼ਾਨਾ Poultry shed, poultry farm.

ਮੁਰਝਾਉਣਾ (murjhaaunaa) *v* To wither, to fade, to droop, to become dejected.

ਮੁਰਦਨੀ (murdanee) *n f* Gloomy countenance, gloom, lifelessness, listlessness.

ਮੁਰਦਾ (murdaa) *n m a* Corpse, dead body, carcass; Lifeless, deceased; ~ਘਰ Mortuary; ~ਰ Lifeless, dead.

ਮੁਰੱਬਾ (murabbaa) *n m* (1) Jam marmalade; (2) Square.

ਮੁਰੱਮਤ (murammat) *n m* Repair; Beating.

ਮੁਰਮੁਰਾ (murmuraa) *n m a* Parched millet or maize; Crisp.

ਮੁਰਲੀ (murlee) *n f* Flute, pipe.

ਮੁਰੱਵਤ (muravvat) *n f* Goodness, compassion, benevolence, accommodativeness, obliging

nature.

ਮੁਰਾਦ (muraad) *n f* Wish, desire; ~ਮੰਗਣੀ To pray for boon.

ਮੁਰੀਦ (mureed) *n m* Follower, pupil, devotee, disciple.

ਮੁੱਲ (mull) *n m* Cost, rate, price, value, worth; ~ਘਟਾਉਣਾ To devalue; ~ਚੁਕਾਉਣਾ To settle the price.

ਮੁਲਕ (mulak) *n m* Country, realm, domain; region. Also ਮੁਲਖ

ਮੁਲਜ਼ਮ (mulzam) *n m* Accused.

ਮੁਲਤਵੀ (multavee) *a* Adjourned, postponed; ~ਕਰਨਾ To adjourn.

ਮੁਲੰਮਾ (mulammaa) *n m* Gilding, plating; False, outward show; Speciousness.

ਮੁਲਾਇਮ (mulaaim) *a* Tender, soft, gentle; ~ਕਰਨਾ To soften.

ਮੁਲਾਹਜਾ (mulaahjaa) *n m* Consideration, kindness, concession, regard.

ਮੁਲਾਹਜ਼ਾ (mulaahzaa) *n* Inspection; ~ਕਰਨਾ To inspect.

ਮੁਲਾਕ਼ਾਤ (mulaakaat) *n f* Visit, meeting, interview.

ਮੁਲਾਕਾਤੀ (mulaakaatee) *n m* Visitor, acquaintance.

ਮੁਲਾਜ਼ਮ (mulaazam) *n m* Servant.

ਮੁੜ (mur) *adv* Again; ~ਮੁੜ Repeatedly, again and again.

ਮੁੜਨਾ (murnaa) *v* To come back, to

return; To turn, to bend.

ਮੁੰਡਾ (Mundaa) *n m* Boy, son; bridegroom.

ਮੂੰਹ (moonh) *n m* Mouth, face, countenance; ~ਸਿਊਣਾ To make silent; ~ਸੁਕਣਾ To become thinner, to feel thirsty; ~ਸੁਜਾਊਣਾ To get displeased; ~ਕਾਲਾ ਕਰਨਾ To have illegitimate sex relations; ~ਚਟਣਾ To lick, to fondle; ~ਜ਼ਬਾਨੀ Oral; ~ਤਕਣਾ To graze, to scare in astonishment; ~ਫਟ Blunt, insolent, abusive; ~ਫੇਰ ਲੈਣਾ To shun, to abstain from; ~ਮੋੜਨਾ To desert, to refrain from; ~ਲੁਕਾਊਣਾ To hide, to avoid.

ਮੂਤ (moot) *n m* Urine. Also ਮੂਤਰ

ਮੂਰਖ (moorakh) *a* Foolish, stupid, silly, idiotic, dunce; ~ਤਾ Stupidity, foolishness.

ਮੂਰਛਾ (moorchhaa) *n* Fainting, coma, unconsciousness, insensibility, swoon.

ਮੂਰਤ (moorat) *n f* Portrait, form, picture.

ਮੂਰਤੀ (murtee) *n f* Idol, effigy, statue; ~ਕਾਰ Iconographer; ~ਪੂਜਾ Idol worship, idolatory.

ਮੂਲ (mool) *n m a* Root, source, base, original, principal; Substantive; ~ਅਧਿਕਾਰ Fundamental right; ~ਧਨ

Capital; ~ਲਾਗਤ Basic cost.

ਮੂਲੀ (moolee) *n f* Radish, *Raphanus sativs.*

ਮੂਰ੍ਹ (moorh) *n m a* Simpleton, fool, nincompoop; Foolish, stupid, demented.

ਮੇਸਣਾ (mesnaa) *v* To rub off, to erase, to blot out.

ਮੇਹਰੂ (mehroo) *n f* Buffaloes.

ਮੇਖ (mekh) *n f* Nail, hob nail, pegcotter, brad.

ਮੇਚ (mech) *n m* Measurement, size; fit, fitting, matching; ~ਲੈਣਾ To take measurement (for garments, shoes etc.)

ਮੇਚਣਾ (mechnaa) *v* To measure, to take a measurement.

ਮੇਜ਼ (mez) *n f* Table; ~ਪੋਸ਼ Table cloth; ~ਬਾਨ Host.

ਮੇਟਣਾ (metnaa) *v* To rub off, to erase, to delete, to wipe, to anihilate.

ਮੇਮਣਾ (memnaa) *n m* Lamb.

ਮੇਲ (mel) *n m* Association intimacy; Connection, harmony; Correspondence, match; Guests collected as marriage or other family function.

ਮੇਲਣਾ (melnaa) *v* To gather, to sweep, to mix; To cause to meet, to match.

ਮੇਲਾ (melaa) *n m* Fair, assembliage; ~ਠੇਲਾ Fanfare, hustle and bustle.

ਮੇਲਾਨ (melaan) *n m* Comparison, tally.

ਮੇਵਾ (mewaa) *n m* Dry fruit.

ਮੈਕਾ (maikaa) *n m* Wife's paternal house.

ਮੈਦਾਨ (maidaan) *n m* Open field, ground; ~ਮਾਰਨਾ To win, to go to answer the call of nature.

ਮੈਦਾਨੀ (maidaanee) *a* Plain, pertaining to plain.

ਮੈਲ (mail) *n f* Dirt, mud, filth, rust; ~ਖੋਰਾ Dust coloured, gray, colour that would not look dirty soon.

ਮੈਲਾ (mailaa) *a* Dirty, muddy, unclean; Feaces, filth; ~ਕੁਚੈਲਾ Dingy, dirty, polluted.

ਮੋਹ (moh) *n m* Attachment, attraction, infatuation, fondness, affection, love.

ਮੋਹਣਾ (mohṇaa) *v a* To attract, infatuate, to fascinate, to enchant, to charm, to enamour; Attractive, fascinating, charming, handsome, beautiful.

ਮੋਹਰਲਾ (moharlaa) *adv* Earlier, first, foremost, front, leading.

ਮੋਹਰੀ (mohṛee) *n f* Small wooden pillar.

ਮੋਹਿਤ (mohit) *a* Enchanted, allured fascinated.

ਮੋਂਗਾ (mongaa) *n m* Coral.

ਮੋਚ (moch) *n f* Sprain, twist.

ਮੋਚਣਾ (mochṇaa) *v* To pull out.

ਮੋਚੀ (mochee) *n m* Shoemaker, Cobbler.

ਮੋਟੜ (moṭaṛ) *n m* Fat person.

ਮੋਟਾ (moṭaa) *a m* Fat, corpulent, heavy, coarse, fleshy; ~ਝੋਟਾ Rough, coarse; ~ਤਾਜ਼ਾ Plump, robust.

ਮੋਟੀ (moṭee) *a* fat; ~ਅਕਲ Poor intelligence, dim wittedness, dullness, obtuseness; ~ਸਾਮੀ Rich wealthy, affluent, opulent person.

ਮੋਢਾ (moḍhaa) *n m* Shoulder.

ਮੋਤੀ (motee) *n m* Pearl; ~ਆ Light yellow; Jasmine ~ਆ ਬਿੰਦ Cataract.

ਮੋਦੀ (modee) *n m* Storekeeper, grain dealer, steward.

ਮੋਨਾ (monaa) *n m* Clean shaven, (one) with cropped hair.

ਮੋਮ (mom) *n f* Wax, tallow; ~ ਜਾਮਾ Oil cloth, waterproof cloth; ~ਹੋ ਜਾਣਾ To be softened, to melt; ~ਦਿਲ Soft hearted, kind, merciful; ~ਬਤੀ Candle.

ਮੋਮੀ (momee) *a* Waxy, waxen.

ਮੋਰ (moṛ) *n m* Peacock.

ਮੋਰਚਾ (morchaa) *n m* Trench, defence post; ~ਬੰਦੀ Entrenchment; ~ਮਾਰਨਾ To win, to be successful.

ਮੋਰੀ (moree) *n f* Hole, sewer.

ਮੋੜ (moṛ) *n m* Bend, turn of road, twist; ~ਤੋੜ Distortion; ~ਦਾਰ Zigzag.

ਮੋੜਨਾ (moṛnaa) *v* To return, to bend, to twist.

ਮੌਸਮ (mausam) *n* *m* Weather, season.

ਮੌਕਾ (maukaa) *n* *m* Opportunity, chance, occasion, situation; ~ਪ੍ਰਸਤ Opportunist.

ਮੌਜ (mauj) *n* *f* Enjoyment, pleasure, delight, emotion, wave.

ਮੌਜੀ (maujee) *a* Gayful, mirthful, jovial, Carefree (fellow).

ਮੌਜਾ (mauzaa) *n* *m* Sock, stocking. Also ਮੌਜਾ

ਮੌਜੂਦ (maujood) *a* Present, existing, at hand.

ਮੌਜੂਦਗੀ (maujoodgee) *n* *f* Presence.

ਮੌਜੂਦਾ (maujooda) *a* Present, current, modern, existing.

ਮੌਤ (maut) *n* *f* Death, demise, calamity, mortality.

ਯ

ਯ Thirty first letter of Gurmukhi alphabets, pronounced as 'yayyaa', semivowel.

ਯਹੂਦੀ (yahoodee) *n m* Jew.

ਯਕ (yak) *a* One, uni.

ਯਕਸਾਂ (yaksaan) *a adv* Similar, uniform, equal; ~ਕਰਨਾ To equalize, to level.

ਯਕਸਾਰਤਾ (yaksaartaa) *n f* Uniformity, similarity.

ਯਕਸਮਾਨ (yaksamaan) *a* Homogeneous.

ਯਕਜ਼ਬਾਨ (yakazabaan) *a adv* With singular voice.

ਯਕਤਰਫ਼ਾ (yaktarfaa) *a* Unilateral, one sided.

ਯਕਦਮ (yakdam) *a* Immediately.

ਯਕਮੁਸ਼ਤ (yakmusht) *adv* In one instalment, as a whole.

ਯਕਲਖ਼ਤ (yaklakht) adv All of a sudden, suddenly.

ਯਕੜ (yakar) *n m* Meaningless or nonsensical, talk; gossip; ~ਬਾਜ਼ Chatterer, chatterbox, gossiper, tale-teller; ~ਮਾਰਨਾ To talk uselessly.

ਯੱਕਾ (yakkaa) *n m* Tonga, ace; ~ਯਕ All of a sudden.

ਯਕੀਨ (yakeen) *n m* Confidence, assurance, faith, certainty; ~ਕਰਨਾ To believe, to have faith; ~ਨ Surely, certainly, definitely.

ਯੱਖ (yakkh) *n m a* Ice, snow; Ice cold.

ਯੱਗ (yagg) *n m* Oblation, religious sacrifice.

ਯਤਨ (yatan) *n m* Effort, attempt, endeavour.

ਯੰਤਰ (yantar) *n m* Instrument, implement, machine.

ਯੰਤਰੀਕਰਨ (yantreekaran) *n m* Mechanisation.

ਯਤੀਮ (yateem) *n m* Orphan, fatherless child; ~ਖ਼ਾਨਾ Orphanage.

ਯਥਾ ਸਥਿਤੀ (yathaa sthitee) *n f* Status quo.

ਯਥਾਰਥ (yathaarath) *n m a* Reality, fact; Real, accurate, actual; ~ਤਾ Reality; ~ਵਾਦ Realism.

ਯੱਭ (yabbh) *n m* Trouble, difficulty problem, nuisance, contention, wrangling; ~ਲ Stupid, foolish.

ਯਮਲਾ (yamlaa) *a* Fool, stupid, unintelligent; clever but pretending to be a simpleton.

ਯਰਕਣਾ (yarkanaa) *v* To cower, to

shy away, to be bullied.

ਯਰਕਾਉਣਾ (yarkaaunaa) *v* To bully, to cow down.

ਯਰਕਾਨ (yarkaan) *n m* Jaundice.

ਯਰਕੂ (yarkoo) *a* Timid, coward, cowardly.

ਯਰਾਨਾ (yaraanaa) *n m* Friendship, love, association, illegal love affairs. Also **ਯਾਰੀ**

ਯਾਚਨਾ (yaachnaa) *n f* Appeal, petition, request.

ਯਾਤਰਾ (yaatraa) *n f* Journey, pilgrimage, travel; **~ਭਾਸ਼ਨ** Travelogue.

ਯਾਤਰੀ (yaatree) *n m* Pilgrim, traveller.

ਯਾਦ (yaad) *n f* Memory, recollection, remembrance; **~ਆਉਣਾ** To remember; **~ਕਰਨਾ** To call; **~ਦਿਲਾਉਣਾ** To remind; **~ਰਖਣਾ** To bear in mind, to remember;

~ਗਾਰ Memorial, commemoration.

ਯਾਦਾਸ਼ਤ (yaadaasht) *n f* Memory.

ਯਾਨੀ (yaanee) *adv* Namely, that is, that is to say, meaning therby, I mean.

ਯਾਰ (yaar) *n m* Lover, friend, companion, paramour.

ਯੁਕਤ (yukat) *a* Combined, united, fitted with.

ਯੁਗ (yug) *n m* Epoch, era, period, age.

ਯੁੱਧ (yuddh) *n m* War, battle, combat, hostilities; **~ਵਿਰਾਮ** Truce; **~ਖੇਤਰ** Warfield; **~ਬੰਦੀ** Truce; **~ਭੂਮੀ** Battle field.

ਯੋਗ (yog) *a* Suitable, qualified, capable; Yoga; **~ਦਾਨ** Contribution.

ਯੋਜਨਾ (yojnaa) *n f* Plan, scheme; **~ਬੱਧ** Planned.

ਯੋਨੀ (yonee) *n f* Vegina, Source.

ਰ

ਰ Thirty second letter of Gurmukhi alphabets, pronounced as 'raaraa'.

ਰਈਸ (raees) *n m* Nobleman, rich person; ~ਜ਼ਾਦਾ Son of a rich person.

ਰਈਸੀ (raeesee) *n f* Richness, nobility.

ਰਸ (ras) *n m* Juice, taste, essence, pleasure, enjoyment; ~ਹੀਣ Tasteless; ~ਦਾਰ Juicy, full of juice.

ਰਸ਼ਕ (rashak) *n m* Envy, emulation.

ਰਸਣਾ (rasṇaa) *v* To be absorbed or throughly mixed, to mix well socially, to be come intimate, to be reconciled; to become smooth-running (for machines or parts).

ਰਸਤਾ (rastaa) *n m* Road, street, way, path, route.

ਰਸਦ (rasad) *n f* Provision, supplies, ration, store.

ਰਸਨਾ (rasnaa) *n f* Tongue.

ਰਸਮ (rasam) *n f* Custom, practice, ritual, ceremony, rite.

ਰਸਮੀ (rasmee) *a* Customary, ceremonial.

ਰੱਸਾ (rassaa) *n m* Rope; ~ਕਸ਼ੀ Tug of war; ~ਪਾਉਣਾ To tie with a rope; to control.

ਰਸਾਤਲ (rasaatal) *n m* Under world, hell, lowest layer.

ਰਸਾਲਾ (rasaalaa) *n m* (1) Cavalry, battalion; (2) Journal, magazine.

ਰਸਿਕ (rasik) *n m* Admirer, lover, amorist, gallant; Amorous; Lover of beauty, music, dance, etc., pleasure-loving, libertine; ~ਤਾ Amorousness, taste for good things of life, love for life, arts or pleasure, libertinism.

ਰੱਸੀ (rasee) *n f* Cord, string, twine.

ਰਸੀਦ (raseed) *n f* Receipt, acknowledgement, a note.

ਰਸੀਲਾ (raseelaa) *a* Amorous, delicious, tasty, sweet, attractive. Also **ਰਸੀਲੀ**

ਰਸੂਖ (rasookh) *n m* Influnce, access, friendship.

ਰਸੂਲ (rasool) *n m* Prophet, messenger of god.

ਰਸੋਈ (rasooee) *n f* Kitchen; ~ਆ Cook.

ਰਹੱਸ (raihass) *n m* Secret, mystery, enigma; ~ਮਈ Mysterious, mystical; ~ਵਾਦ Mysticism.

ਰਹਿਣਾ (raihṇaa) *v* To stay, to reside, to remain, to live, to dwell.

ਰਹਿਨ (raihn) *a* Mortgaged; ~ਕਰਨਾ To

mortgage.

ਰਹਿਨੁਮਾ (raihnumaa) *n m* Guide; ~ਈ Guidance.

ਰਹਿਬਰ (raihbar) *n m* Leader.

ਰਹਿਬਰੀ (raihbaree) *n f* Guidance, lead.

ਰਹਿਮ (raihm) *n m* Pity, mercy, kindness, compassion, sympathy; ~ਤ Mercy, pity, compassion.

ਰਕਸ (rakas) *n m* dance.

ਰਕਤ (rakat) *n m* Blood; ~ਦਾਨ Blood donation.

ਰਕਬਾ (rakbaa) *n m* Area.

ਰਕਮ (rakam) *n f* Sum, money.

ਰਕਾਬ (rakaab) *n f* Stirrup; ~ਤੇ ਪੈਰ ਰਖਣਾ To mount a horse.

ਰਕਾਬੀ (rakaabee) *n f* Plate, saucer, platter.

ਰਖਸ਼ਕ (rakshak) *n m* Protector, saviour.

ਰਖਣਾ (rakhṇaa) *v* To keep, to put, to place, to lay, to insert, to hold, to possess, to have, to contain, to engage.

ਰਖਵਾਲਾ (rakhwaalaa) *n m* Guard, guardian, keeper, protector.

ਰਖਿਆ (rakhiyaa) *n f* Safety, patronage, protection; ~ਕਰਨੀ To preserve.

ਰਖੇਲ (rakhel) *n f* Keep, Concubine, mistress.

ਰਗ (rag) *n f* Vein, nerve, artery, streak; ~ਫੜਨੀ To understand trait or nature of.

ਰੰਗ (rang) *n m* Colour, complexion, paint, dye; Merriment; ~ਉਡਣਾ To fade, to lose lustre, to turn pale with fear; ~ਚੜ੍ਹਉਣਾ Colour, coloured stale; ~ਦਾਰ Coloured; ~ਨਿਕਲਣਾ To have a clear glossy complexion; ~ਸ਼ਾਲਾ Theatre; ~ਸਾਜ਼ Painter, Dyer; ~ਬਰੰਗਾ Variegated, colourful, multicoloured; ~ਭੂਮੀ Stage, theatre; ~ਵਾਈ Act of dyeing; ~ਮੰਚ Stage; ~ਰੰਗੀਲਾ Colourful, pleasure seeking, attractive; ~ਰਲੀਆਂ Merriment, mirth; ~ਰੂਪ Beauty, appearance, mode; ~ਰੇਜ਼ Dyer.

ਰੰਗਣਾ (rangṇaa) *v* To dye, to colour, to paint, to stain.

ਰੰਗਰੂਟ (rangrooṭ) *n m* Novice, recruit, newly recruited soldier.

ਰਗੜ (ragaṛ) *n f* Friction, abrasion, concussion, bruise.

ਰਗੜਨਾ (ragaṛnaa) *v* To rub, to scrub, to grate, to grind, to wear out

ਰਗੜਾ (ragṛaa) *n m* Quarrel, rubbing, wrangling; ~ਮਾਰਨਾ To bruise, to scrap, to hit.

ਰੰਗੀਨ (rangeen) *a* Coloured, dyed, painted, mirthful.

ਰੰਗੀਨੀ (rangeenee) *n f* Colour, bright colouring, florid style; Merriment, colourfulness.

ਰੰਗੀਲਾ (rangeelaa) *a* Colourful, jovial, loving, merry, showy; ~ਪਨ Colourfulness, merriment, joviality.

ਰਚਣਾ (rachnaa) *v* To create, to make, to form, to permeate, to write (a book, poem etc).

ਰਚਨਾ (rachnaa) *n f* Creation, workmanship, literary composition; ~ਕਾਰ Creator, writer, workman; ~ਤਮਕ Constructive, compositional, creative; ~ਵਲੀ Writings.

ਰਛਕ (rachhak) *n* Preserver, defender, nourisher, helper. Also ਰਛਪਾਲ

ਰੱਛਾ (rachchhaa) *n* Protection. Also ਰਛਿਆ or ਰਖਿਆ

ਰੰਜ (ranj) *n m* Grief, sorrow, pain, sadness, displeasure.

ਰੰਜਸ਼ (ranjash) *n f* Ill feeling, animus, estragement.

ਰੰਜਕ (ranjak) *a* Gladdening, delighting, recreative.

ਰੱਜਣਾ (rajjnaa) *v* To eat to the fill, to be satisfied, to be satiated.

ਰਜਮੰਟ (rajmant) *n m* Regiment.

ਰਜ਼ਾ (razaa) *n f* Will, God's pleasure, assent, consent, premission; ~ਕਾਰ Volunteer; ~ਮੰਦ Willing, consenting;

~ਮੰਦੀ Willingness; Agreement.

ਰਜਾਉਣਾ (rajaaunaa) *v* To fill, to satisfy, to satiate, to feed to the full.

ਰਜ਼ਾਈ (razaaee) *n f a* Quilt; Satisfied, happy.

ਰਜੂਹ (rajooh) *n m* Intension, inclination, aptitude, interest.

ਰਟਣਾ (ratnaa) *v* To learn by rote, to repeat, to cram, to mug up.

ਰੱਟਾ (rattaa) *n m* (1) Cramming, learning by rote; (2) Quarrel, trouble.

ਰੰਡਾ (randaa) *n m* Widower.

ਰੰਡੀ (randee) *n f* (1) Widow, (2) Prostitute; ~ਬਾਜ਼ੀ Adultery, prostitution; ~ਰੋਣਾ Constant whimpering, crying, complaining or nagging.

ਰੰਡੇਪਾ (randepaa) *n m* Widowhood.

ਰਣ (ran) *n m* Battle, war, combat; ~ਜੋਧਾ Warrior; ~ਭੂਮੀ Battle field; ~ਨੀਤੀ Strategy.

ਰਣਵਾਸ (ranvaas) *n m* Harem, seraglio, inner part of palace.

ਰਤ (rat) *a* Occupied, engaged, busy, absorbed; *Used as suffix also as* ਕਾਰਜ~ engaged in work.

ਰੱਤ (ratt) *n f* Blood; ~ਹੀਣ Bloodless, pale; ~ਪੀਣਾ Blood sucker, cruel, brutal.

ਰਤਨ (ratan) *n m* Gem, jewel, ruby.

ਰਤਨਾਕਰ (ratanaakar) *n m* Ocean, mine or jewels.

ਰਥ (rath) *n m* Chariot; Carriage car; ~ਵਾਨ Charioteer.

ਰੱਦ (radd) *a* Cancelled, refuted, null and void, rejected, repealed; ~ਕਰਨਾ To annul, to reject, to cancel, to set aside, to nullify.

ਰੰਦਣਾ (randnaa) *v* To Smooth, to plane.

ਰੰਦਾ (randaa) *n m* Carpenter's plane, jack plane, router place.

ਰੱਦੀ (raddee) *a n f* Waste, useless, worthless, rejected; Waste paper, refuse.

ਰੰਨ (rann) *n f* Woman, lady, wife.

ਰਨ (ran) *n m* Run, (cricket).

ਰਪਟੀਆ (rapteeiaa) *n m* Reporter; Informer.

ਰਪਟ (rapat) *n f* Report, information.

ਰਫ਼ਤਾਰ (raftaar) *n f* Speed.

ਰਫੜ (raphar) *n m* Quarrel. Also ਰਫੜਾ

ਰਫ਼ੀਕ (rafeek) *n m* Companion.

ਰਫ਼ੂ (rafoo) *n m* Darning, patching; ~ਕਰਨਾ To darn; ~ਗਾਰ Darner; ~ਚਕਰ Runaway, absconding; ~ਹੋਣਾ To run away, to disappear, to escape, to show a clean pair of heels.

ਰੱਬ (rabb) *n m* God; Lord, divinity, providence; ~ਰਜ਼ਾ Will of God; ~ਰਾਖਾ May God be with you.

ਰੱਬੀ (rabbee) *a* Divine, godly, providential.

ਰੰਭਣਾ (rambhnaa) *v* To bellow.

ਰਮਣਾ (ramnaa) *v* To wander, to rove about, to go away, to depart, to be absorbed.

ਰਮਣੀਕ (ramneek) *a* Beautiful, captivating, pleasing, pleasurable, pleasant, enjoyable, delightful (for place, landscape).

ਰਮਤਾ (ramtaa) *a* Wandering, wanderer, roving, rover.

ਰਲਣਾ (ralnaa) *v* To mix, to be intermixed, to resemble.

ਰਲਾਉਣਾ (ralaaunaa) *v* To mix, to adulterate, to blend.

ਰਵਈਆ (ravaiyaa) *n m* Attitude, behaviour, trend.

ਰਵਾ (ravaa) *n m a* Pedigree, lineage, ancestry, breed; Granulated form of wheat flour, semolina; Proper justifiable, lawful.

ਰਵਾਂ (ravaan) *a* Flowing, running, moving; (for machinery or equipment) moving or working smoothly.

ਰਵਾਇਤ (ravaait) *n f* Tradition, legend, history.

ਰਵਾਦਾਰ (ravaadaar) *a* Just, liberal,

responsible, considerate.

ਰਵਾਦਾਰੀ (ravaadaaree) *n f* Justness, liberality, liberalism, broad-mindedness, considerateness, catholicity.

ਰਵਾਨਗੀ (ravaangee) *n f* Departure, setting out, going.

ਰੜਕ (raṛak) *n f* Irritation, rankle, pain animosity; Deficiency, shortage, shortcoming; **~ਕੱਢਣੀ** To act with rancour, to give expression to enmity, to retaliate; To treat irritation or pain; **~ਰੱਖਣੀ** To harbour rancour, animosity or rankle or pain.

ਰਵਾਨਾ (ravaanaa) *a* Departed, proceeding to; **~ਹੋਣਾ** To start, to depart, to flow; **~ਕਰਨਾ** To despatch, to send, to remit.

ਰਵਾਨੀ (ravaanee) *n f* Fluency, flow, course, going.

ਰੜਕਣਾ (raṛaknaa) *v* To munch, to eat with noise, to torment.

ਰੜਕਾ (raṛkaa) *n m* Broom.

ਰੜਕਾਉਣਾ (raṛkaaunaa) *v* To be fried, to be thoroughly baked, parched or cooked; To be slightly overcooked or overbaked.

ਰੜ੍ਹਨਾ (raṛhnaa) *v* To be fried, to be thoroughly baked, parched or cooked; To be slightly overcooked or overbaked.

ਰੜਾ (raṛaa) *a* Plain, bare ground, clear, clean.

ਰਾਉ (raao) *n m* King, prince, chieftain

ਰਾਇਜ (raaij) *a* Current, in vogue, in fashion, in practice, prevalent; **~ਕਰਨਾ** To put or bring into vogue in fashion or in practice; To introduce, to enforce.

ਰਾਈ (raaee) *n f* Mustard, charlock, *Brassica arvensis.*

ਰਾਏ (raae) *n f* Opinion, view, advice, counsel; **~ਦੇਣੀ** To advise.

ਰਾਸ਼ਟਰ (raashṭar) *n m* Nation, territory; Country; **~ਗਾਨ** National anthem; **~ਪਣ** Nationhood; **~ਪਤੀ** President; **~ਵਾਦ** Nationalism.

ਰਾਸ਼ਟਰੀ (raashtree) *a* National.

ਰਾਸ਼ਟਰੀਕਰਨ (raashtreekaran) *n m* Nationalization.

ਰਾਹ (raah) *n f* Path, way, road; Custom, manner, method; **~ਕੱਢਣਾ** To find a way out; **~ਤੇ ਆਉਣਾ** To be reformed; **~ਦਸਣਾ** To guide, to lead; **~ਵੇਖਣਾ** To wait for, to expect; **~ਗੀਰ** Traveller, pedestrian, wayfarer; **~ਜ਼ਨ** Robber, highwayman; **~ਦਾਰੀ** Toll-tax, transit duties.

ਰਾਹਤ (raahat) *n f* Relief, compensation, aid to victims of calamities.

ਰਾਹੀ (raahee) *n m* Traveller, wayfarer.

ਰਾਹੁਣਾ (raahunaa) *v* To sow, to

cultivate.

ਰਾਖ (raakh) *n f* Ashes; ~**ਕਰਨਾ** To reduce to ashes.

ਰਾਖਸ਼ (raakhash) *n m* Demon; A giant; A monster, wicked person.

ਰਾਖਵਾਂ (raakhwaan) *a* Reserved. Also **ਰਾਖਵੀਂ**

ਰਾਖਾ (raakhaa) *n m* Guard, protector, keeper, watchman.

ਰਾਗ (raag) *n m* Music, melody, singing; ~**ਅਲਾਪਣਾ** To relate one's own account; ~**ਰੰਗ** Merriment, dance and music; Fun and frolic; ~**ਣੀ** Musical mode.

ਰਾਗੀ (raagee) *n m* Singer, musician.

ਰਾਜ (raaj) *n* (1) Kingdom, goverment, rule, regiment; (2) Mason, brick layer; ~**ਸੀ** Political; ~**ਸੂਚਨਾ** Communique; ~**ਕਾਜ** Goverment; ~**ਕੁਮਾਰ** Prince; ~**ਕੁਮਾਰੀ** Princess; ~**ਕੋਸ਼** Exchequer, treasury; ~**ਗੱਦੀ** Throne; ~**ਗਰਦੀ** Anarchy, misrule, revolution; ~**ਗੀਰੀ** Mansory; ~**ਤੰਤਰ** Monarchy; ~**ਤਿਲਕ** Coronation; ~**ਦਰਬਾਰ** Royal court; ~**ਦਰਬਾਰੀ** Courtier; ~**ਦੂਤ** Ambassader; ~**ਦੂਤਾਵਾਸ** Embassy; ~**ਧ੍ਰੋਹ** Sedition, rebellion, conspiracy; ~**ਧਾਨੀ** Capital; ~**ਨੀਤਕ** Politician; ~**ਨੀਤਿਕ** Political; ~**ਨੀਤੀ** Politics, state policy; ~**ਪੱਤਰ** Gazette; ~**ਪੱਥ** Highway; ~**ਪਾਲ**

Dominion, kingdom; ~**ਪਾਲ** Governor; ~**ਵੰਸ਼** Imperial dynasty.

ਰਾਜ਼ (raaz) *n m* Secret, mystery; ~**ਕਾਰ** Confident; One who knows secret.

ਰਾਜਾ (raajaa) *n m* King, ruler, sovereign, rajah, monarch; Barber.

ਰਾਜ਼ੀ (raazee) *a* Willing, agreed, reconciliated, complacent, satisfied, contented; ~**ਹੋਣਾ** To agree, to consent, to be pleased; ~**ਖੁਸ਼ੀ** Hale and hearty, safe and sound; ~**ਨਾਮਾ** Deed of compromise, writ filed in court.

ਰਾਂਝਾ (raanjhaa) *n m* Title of a lover of heer, beloved.

ਰਾਤ (raat) *n f* Night; ~**ਦਿਨ** Day and night; Always; **ਰਾਤੋਂ**~ During night.

ਰਾੜ (raar) *n f* Quarrel, wrangle, dispute.

ਰਾੜਨਾ (raarhnaa) *v* To roast.

ਰੜੀਆ (raariaa) *n m a* Quarrelsome person, disputant.

ਰਿਆ (riaa) *n* concession, partiality.

ਰਿਆਇਆ (riaaiyaa) *n f* The public, subject.

ਰਿਆਇਤ (riyaait) *n f* Concession, relaxation, favour, partiality; ~**ਕਰਨੀ** To remit, to relax, to show favour.

ਰਿਆਇਤੀ (riyaaitee) *a* Concessional.

ਰਿਆਸਤ (riyaasat) *n f* Estate,

deminion, territory.

ਰਿਆਸਤੀ (riyaasatee) *a* Dominational,
territorial.

ਰਿਆਕਾਰ (riaakaar) *a* cheat.

ਰਿਆਕਾਰੀ (riaakaaree) *a* Fraud,
hypocrisy, deciutfulness.

ਰਿਆਜ਼ (riaaz) *n m* Regular practice.

ਰਿਸਣਾ (risnaa) *v* To ooze, to leak, to
drip, to exude.

ਰਿਸ਼ਤਾ (rishtaa) *n m* Relationship,
connection, betrotheral,
engagement; ~(ਤੇ)ਦਾਰ Relative, kith
and kin, a relation; ~(ਤੇ)ਦਾਰੀ
Relationship.

ਰਿਸ਼ਵਤ (rishwat) *n f* Bribe, illegal
gratification; ~ਖੋਰੀ Bribery,
corruption.

ਰਿਸਾਲਾ (risaalaa) *n m* (1) Cavalry, a
cavalry regiment; (2) Magazine,
journal, periodical.

ਰਿਸ਼ੀ (rishee) *n m* Saint, religious
person. Also ਰਿਖੀ

ਰਿਹਾ (rihaa) *a* Released, discharged;
~ਕਰਨਾ To liberate, to release, to
free; ~ਈ Release, acquittal,
deliverance.

ਰਿਹਾਇਸ਼ (rihaaish) *n f* Residence, stay,
dwelling; ~ਗਾਹ Place of residence,
lodging, inn. Also ਰਹਾਇਸ਼

ਰਿਹਾਇਸ਼ੀ (rihaaishee) *a* Residential.
Also ਰਹਾਇਸ਼ੀ

ਰਿਕਤ (rikt) *a* vacant, unfilled, empty,
blank; ~ਅਸਥਾਨ Vacancy, gap;
~ਅਸਾਮੀ Vacancy, vacant post.

ਰਿੱਛ (richchh) *n m* Bear.

ਰਿਜ਼ਕ (rizak) *n m* Food, provision, daily
bread, subsistence.

ਰਿੱਝਣਾ (rijhnaa) *v* To boil, to be boiled,
or throughly cooked, to simmer;
To rage to simmer with anger, to
be angry or sullen, to sulk.

ਰਿਝਾਉਣਾ (rijhaaunaa) *v* To allure, to
captivate, to please, to charm, to
bewitch.

ਰਿਣ (rin) *n m* Debt, obligation; ~ਪਤਰ
Debenture.

ਰਿਣਾਤਮਕ (rinaatmak) *a* Negative:

ਰਿਣੀ (rinee) *n m a* Debtor; Indebted,
obliged.

ਰਿਤੁ (ritoo) *n f* Season, weather;
Blood, menses.

ਰਿੰਦ (rind) *n m* Quarrelsome, rascal,
infidel, scoundre, drunkard.

ਰਿਵਾਜ (rivaaj) *n m* Custom, fashion,
pratice, usage.

ਰਿਵਾਜੀ (rivaajee) *a* customary,
ritualistic.

ਰਿੜ੍ਹਨਾ (rirhnaa) *v* To slide, to slip, to
glide, to roll.

ਰਿੜ੍ਹਵਾਂ (rirhvaan) *a* Slopy, inclined.

ਰਿੜਕਣਾ (riraknaa) *v n* To churn;
Churning, process churn.

ਰਿੜ੍ਹਨਾ (rirhnaa) *v* To roll, to slide, to slipdown or forward; To crawl; To roller-skate; To creep.

ਰੀਸ (rees) *n f* Emulation, habit of copying, following a precept; ~ਕਰਨੀ To vie with, to copy, to imitate.

ਰੀਂਗਣਾ (reengnaa) *v* To creep, to crawl.

ਰੀਝ (reejh) *n f* Ardent desire, fondness or wish, longing, craving.

ਰੀਝਣਾ (reejhnaa) *v* To be pleased, to be captivated, to be gratified, to be satisfied.

ਰੀਤ (reet) *n f* Custom, ceremony, rite, ritual, mode, manner.

ਰੀਤੀ (reetee) *n f* Custom, style; ~ਰਿਵਾਜ customs, traditions.

ਰੀਲ (reel) *n f* Reel, spool, cassette.

ਰੀੜ੍ਹ (reerh) *n* Back bone, spinal column, spine.

ਰੁਸਣਾ (rusnaa) *v* To be displeased, to be angry. Also ਰੁਸ ਜਾਣਾ

ਰੁਸ਼ਨਾਈ (rushnaaee) *n* (1) Light, brightness, glow, illumination, refulgence, radiance; (2) Ink, black ink.

ਰੁਸਵਾ (ruswaa) *a* Disgraced, ignominious, dishonoured, humiliated, infamous; ~ਈ Infamy, disgrace, ignominy, humiliation.

ਰੁਸੇਵਾਂ (rusevaan) *n m* Annoyance, vexation, anger, rage, displeasure.

ਰੁਹਬ (ruhb) *n m* Influence, dignity, state; ~ਦਾਰ Dignified, influential, impressive. Also ਰੋਹਬ, ਰੋਹਬਦਾਰ

ਰੁਹਾਨੀ (ruhaanee) *a* Spiritual; ~ਅਤ Spirituality. Also ਰੂਹਾਨੀ

ਰੁਕਣਾ (ruknaa) *v* To stop, to halt, to stay, to refrain.

ਰੁੱਕਾ (rukkaa) *n m* Note, scrap, letter, a piece of paper on which message in written.

ਰੁਕਾਵਟ (rukaawat) *n f* Check, restriction, resistance, obstruction, obstacle, hindrance, blockade, barrier; ~ਪਾਉਣੀ To obstruct, to hinder, to block.

ਰੁੱਖ (rukkh) *n m* Tree.

ਰੁਖ (rukh) *n m* Face, side, aptitude, direction, countenance; ~ਕਰਨਾ To proceed toward.

ਰੁਖਸਤ (rukhsat) *n f* Departure, leave, furlough; ~ਹੋਣਾ To depart, to take leave; ~ਕਰਨਾ To see off, to send away, to discharge.

ਰੁਖੜਾ (rukhraa) *a n m* Weak dry, tasteless, rude, impolite, rough; Tree.

ਰੁੱਖਾ (rukkhaa) *a* Harsh, rough, austere, inhospitable, rude, dry rugged; ~ਬੀ Harshness, roughness, dryness, indifference.

ਰੁਚੀ (ruchee) *n f* Interest, inclination, taste, liking, tendency, aptitude.

ਰੁਜ਼ਗਾਰ (ruzgaar) *n m* Service, occupation, trade, profession, empolyment, job. Also **ਰੋਜ਼ਗਾਰ**

ਰੁਜ਼ਾਨਾ (ruzaanaa) *a* Daily, everyday. Also **ਰੋਜ਼ਾਨਾ**

ਰੁਝਣਾ (rujhnaa) *v* To get busy, to be engaged.

ਰੁਝਾਉਣਾ (rujhaaunaa) *v* To engage, to engross, to make one busy.

ਰੁਝਾਨ (rujhaan) *n m* Aptitude.

ਰੁਠਣਾ (ruṭṭhnaa) *v* To be displeased, to get angry, to be annoyed.

ਰੁੱਠਾ (ruṭṭhaa) *a* Displeased, angry, annoyed. Also **ਰੁਠੜਾ**

ਰੁੰਡ-ਮੁੰਡ (runḍ-munḍ) *a* Truncated, doddered.

ਰੁਣ-ਝੁਣ (ruṇ-jhuṇ) *n* Jingling, tinkling sound, singing, soft humming; ~ਕਰਨਾ To jingle, to sing soft.

ਰੁਤ (rut) *n f* Season.

ਰੁਤਬਾ (rutbaa) *n m* Status, rank, dignity, degree.

ਰੁੰਦਣਾ (rundnaa) *v* To be trampled, to be trodden.

ਰੁਦਨ (rudan) *n m* Wailing, weeping, lamentation, shedding tears.

ਰੁੱਧਣਾ (ruddhnaa) *v* To be engaged, to be occupied, to be in use.

ਰੁੱਧਾ (ruddhaa) *a* Busy, engaged, occupied.

ਰੁਬਾਈ (rubaaee) *n f* Stanza of four lines, a form of poetry.

ਰੁਮਕਣਾ (rumaknaa) *v* To blow slowly or elegantly.

ਰੁਮਕਾ (rumkaa) *n m* Puff of breeze, gust.

ਰੁਮਾਂਸ (rumaans) *n m* Romance.

ਰੁਮਾਂਚ (rumaanch) *n m* Thrill, rapture; ~ਕ/ਕਾਰੀ Horrifying, terrifying.

ਰੁਮਾਲ (rumaal) *n m* Handkercheif, searf.

ਰੁਮਾਲਾ (rumaalaa) *n m* Piece of cloth, to cover holy book, Guru Granth sahib.

ਰੁਲਣਾ (rulnaa) *v* To be trampled, to be uncared, to rot.

ਰੁਲਦਾ-ਖੁਲਦਾ (ruldaa-khuldaa) *v* In the state of neglect, uncared for.

ਰੁਲਾਉਣਾ (rulaaunaa) *v* To neglect, to desolate, to leave uncared, to winnow, to be wasted.

ਰੁੜ੍ਹਨਾ (rurhnaa) *v* To flow, to float, to glide, to be washed away, to flux

ਰੂੰ (roon) *n m* Cleaned cotton; ~ਕਤਣਾ To spin.

ਰੂ (roo) *n f* Face; ~ਬਰੂ in front of, in the presence of before.

ਰੂਆਂ (rooaan) *n m* Small body hair;

trichome.

ਰੂਸੀ (roosee) *n f* (1) Dandruff; (2) Russian language, people of Russia.

ਰੂਹ (rooh) *n m* Soul, spirit, life.

ਰੂਪ (roop) *n m* Form, countenance, beauty; ~**ਹੀਣ** Formless; ~**ਰੰਗ** Appearance, look, features; ~**ਰੇਖਾ** Outlines, synopsis, blue print; ~**ਵਾਦ** Formalism; ~**ਵਾਨ** Handsome, good looking, beautiful; ~**ਵਿਗਿਆਨ** Morphology.

ਰੂਪਾਤਮਕ (roopaatmak) *a* Formal.

ਰੂਪਕ (roopak) *n m* Allegory, metaphor; ~**ਰੇੜਿਓ** Radio drama or play.

ਰੂਪਾਂਤਰ (roopaantar) *n m* Adaptation allotropic form; (gr) inflexion; ~**ਨ** Metamorphism, modification, version, adaptation.

ਰੂਪੋਸ਼ (rooposh) *a* Disappeared, absconding, hiding, underground, fugitive, runaway; With face covered.

ਰੂੜੀ (roorhee) *n m* Convention, motif, tradition; ~**ਗਤ** Conventional traditional, stereotype; ~**ਮੁਕਤ** Unconventional; ~**ਵਾਦ** Conservatism; ~**ਵਾਦੀ** Conservative.

ਰੇਸ਼ਮ (resham) *n m* Silk.

ਰੇਸ਼ਮੀ (reshmee) *a* Silken.

ਰੇਸ਼ਾ (rashaa) *n m* Fibre, filament; Cold, bad cold, catarrh.

ਰੇਹੜ (rehar) *n m* Course of stream, flow of water, torrent.

ਰੇਹੜਾ (rehraa) *n m* Cart. Also **ਰੇੜ੍ਹਾ**

ਰੇਹੜੀ (rehree) *n f* Small cart, hand cart. Also **ਰੇੜ੍ਹੀ**

ਰੇਖਾ (rekhaa) *n f* Line; Fate, destiny; ~**ਚਿੱਤਰ** Diagram, pen portrait.

ਰੇਖਾਤਮਕ (rekhaatmak) *a* Linear.

ਰੇਗ (reg) *n f* Sand, silt; ~**ਮਾਰ** Sand paper.

ਰੇਗਿਸਤਾਨ (registaan) *n m* Desert, sandy place.

ਰੇਗਿਸਤਾਨੀ (registaanee) *a* Desert.

ਰੇਚਕ (rechak) *a* Purgative.

ਰੇਤ (ret) *n f* Sand. Also **ਰੇਤਾ**

ਰੇਤਣਾ (retnaa) *v* To rasp, to file.

ਰੇਤਲਾ (retlaa) *a* Sandy; Silty; ~**ਪੱਥਰ** Sandstone.

ਰੇਤੀ (retee) *n f* File, rasp, file.

ਰੇਲ (rel) *n f* Railway train; ~**ਪਟੜੀ** Railway track, railway line. Also **ਰੇਲ ਗੱਡੀ**

ਰੇਲਣਾ (relnaa) *v* To heap up, to shove together.

ਰੇਲ-ਪੇਲ (rel-pel) *n f* Crowd, rush, abudance, overcrowding, hustle and bustle.

ਰੇਲਾ (relaa) *n m* Flood, torrent, rush, push.

ਰੇੜੂ (rerh) *n m* Incline, flow.

ਰੇੜੂਨਾ (rerhnaa) *v* To roll, to move someting forward.

ਰੇੜਕਾ (rerkaa) *n m* Contention, quarrel, causeless dispute.

ਰੈਣ (rain) *n m* Night; ~ਬਸੇਰਾ Night's stay; Temporary stay.

ਰੈਤਾ (raitaa) *n m* Curd salad, vegetable etc. picked and spiced in curd.

ਰੋਸ਼ਨ (roshan) *a* Lighted, illuminated, bright, conspicuous.

ਰੋਸ਼ਨੀ (roshnee) *n f* Light, brightness, eyesight, lamp.

ਰੋਹ (roh) *n m* Anger, rage, fury.

ਰੋਹੇ (rohe) *n m* Trachoma.

ਰੋਕ (rok) *n f* (1) Cash, money; (2) Hindrance, restraint, barrier, interception; ~ਟੋਕ restriction, destruction, resistance.

ਰੋਕਨਾ (roknaa) *v* To stop, to check, to hinder, to restrict, to obstruct, to ban.

ਰੋਕੜ (rokar) *n f* Ready money, cash, fund; ~ਖਾਤਾ cash book, cash account.

ਰੋਗ (rog) *n m* Disease, sickness, illness, ailment, disorder, defect; ~ਗ੍ਰਸਤ III, morbid; ~ਣ Ailing woman, patient; Sick.

ਰੋਗਨ (rogan) *n m* Varnish, polish, oil paint.

ਰੋਚਕ (rochak) Interesting, sweet, piquant, I appetising; ~ਤਾ liveliness.

ਰੋਜ਼ (roz) *n ad* Day; Everyday, daily; ~ਨਾਮਚਾ Da / dairy, logbook; ~ਬਰੋਜ਼ Daily, day by day.

ਰੋਜ਼ਾ (rozaa) *n m* Fast, fasting day; ~ਰਖਣਾ To observe a fast.

ਰੋਜ਼ੀ (rozee) *n f* Occupation, daily food, means of sustenance.

ਰੋਟ (rot) *n m* Thick loaf, thick bread.

ਰੋਟੀ (rotee) *n f* Bread, roasted cake, loaf, livelihood; ~ਦਾਲ ਚਲਾਉਣੀ To subsist.

ਰੋਡਾ (rodaa) *n m* Shaven head, bald with shaven head.

ਰੋਣ (ron) *n m* Weeping, crying, wailing, blubber, lamentation; tears; ~ਧੋਣ Wailing, lamentation, intense grief, unrestrained crying, mourning.

ਰੋਣਾ (ronaa) *v* To weep, to wail, to cry, to lament, to grieve.

ਰੋਂਦੂ (rondoo) *a* Weepy, weeper, foul player, player who cheats.

ਰੋਪਣਾ (ropnaa) *v* To plant, to transplant, to sow.

ਰੋਲਣਾ (rolnaa) *v* To pick over, to overcome, to subdue.

ਰੋੜਾ (roraa) *n m* Pebble, gravel,

brickbat, fragments of stone; ~ਅਟਕਾਉਣਾ To blockade, to put obstacles. Also ਰੋੜ

ਰੋੜ੍ਹਨਾ (rorhnaa) v To sweep away, to wash away.

ਰੌਣਕ (raunak) n f Splendour, elegance, mirth, embellishment.

ਰੌਣਕੀ (raunkee) a Gay, jovil, jolly, joyous, cheerful, humorous, witty.

ਰੌਂਦਣਾ (raudnaa) v To trample crush under feet; to spoil, to destroy.

ਰੌਲਾ (raulaa) n m Clamour, tumlut, uproar; ~ਗੌਲਾ Fuse, noise, confusion.

ਲ

ਲ Thirty third letter of Gurmukhi alphabets, pronounced as 'lallaa'.

ਲਈ (laee) *Prep* For, to, for the sake of, in order to, for the purpose of.

ਲਸੰਸ (lasans) *n m* Licence; ~ਦਾਰ Licensee, licence holder.

ਲਸ਼ਕਰ (lashkar) *n m* Army, artillery men, host.

ਲਸਲਸਾ (laslasaa) *a* Sticky, viscid.

ਲੱਸੀ (lassee) *n f* Buttermilk, whey, Drink by churning curd with water.

ਲਹਾਉਣਾ (lahaaunaa) *v* To help in bringing down, unloading.

ਲਹਾਈ (lahaaee) *n f* Descent, recession, unloading, bringing down; Insult, disgrace.

ਲਹਿਕਣਾ (laheknaa) *v* To wave, to quiver, to glitter.

ਲੰਹਿਗਾ (lahengaa) *n m* Skirt, petticoat.

ਲਹਿਜਾ (lahejaa) *n m* Accent, tone. Also ਲਹਿਜ਼ਾ

ਲਹਿਣਾ (lahenaa) *n m v* Luck, an outstanding debt; To get down, to come down, to descend.

ਲਹਿੰਦੀ (lahindee) *n m* A language spoken in West Punjab (now in Pakistan).

ਲਹਿਰ (laher) *n f* Wave, surge, surf, whim, rapture; Movement; ~ਕਾਰ Wavy, undulating.

ਲਹਿਰਾਉਣਾ (laheraaunaa) *v* To wave, to flutter, to ripple, to fluctuate.

ਲਹਿਰੀ (laehree) *a* Jovil, merry, gay, carefree, playful; Eccentric, whimsical; Unconventional.

ਲਹੁੜਾ (lahuṛaa) *a* Younger, junior.

ਲਹੂ (lahoo) *n m* Blood; ~ਦੀ ਹੋਲੀ Carnival of bloodshed; ~ਦੇ ਘੁਟ ਪੀਣੇ To suppress anger; ~ ਠੰਡਾ ਹੋਣਾ To be bereft of passion, to lose sense of respect; ~ਲੁਹਾਨ steeped in blood, covered with blood.

ਲੱਕ (lakk) *n m* Waist, girdle; ~ਸਿੱਧਾ ਕਰਨਾ To rest, to lie down; ~ਟੁਟਣਾ To be disappointed; ~ਬੰਨ੍ਹਣਾ Gird up to loins, to get ready.

ਲਕਸ਼ (lakash) *n m* Aim, object, objective target.

ਲਕਣਾ (laknaa) *v* To lap, To lick up.

ਲਕਵਾ (lakwaa) *n m* Paralysis, palsy; ~ਮਾਰਨਾ To be paralysed.

ਲਕੜ (lakaṛ) *n f* Wood, log, timber, firewood; ~ਹਾਰਾ Woodcutter; ~ਮੰਡੀ Timber market. Also ਲਕੜੀ

ਲਕੜਬੱਘਾ (lakaṛ bagghaa) *n m* Hyaena, jaguar.

ਲੰਕਾ (lankaa) *n m* Ceylon, Srilanka country.

ਲਕੀਰ (lakeer) *n f* Line, stripe, furrow; ~**ਕਾਰ** Lined streaked, striped; ~**ਦਾ ਫ਼ਕੀਰ** Traditionalist, slave of tradition or custom.

ਲੱਖ (lakkh) *a* Lac, one hundred thousand ~**ਪਤੀ** Millionaire, rich.

ਲਖਣਾ (lakhṇaa) *v* To understand, to comperhend.

ਲਖਾਉਣਾ (lakhaauṇaa) *v* To cause to understand; To explain.

ਲੰਗ (lang) *n m* Lameness, limp. Also **ਲੰਝ**

ਲੰਗੜਾ (langṛaa) *a n m* Crippled; Lame, cripple; ~**ਉਣਾ** To limp.

ਲੱਗਣਾ (laggṇaa) *v* To pinch, to have painful sensation, to cause irritation.

ਲਗਣਾ (lagṇaa) *v* To be applied, to be attached, to touch, to cast; **ਅੱਖ**~ To sleep; **ਅੱਗ**~ To catch fire; **ਆਖੇ**~ To obey; **ਪਾਲਾ**~ To feel cold; **ਰੁਪਿਆ**~ Spending of much money.

ਲਗਨ (lagan) *n f* Attachment, affection, devotion; Auspicious time. Also **ਲਗਾਨ**

ਲਗਭਗ (lagbhag) *adv* Approximately, almost, nearly, about.

ਲੰਗਰ (langar) *n m* (1) Anchor; Kedge, (2) Public kitchen; Free community kitchen.

ਲਗਵਾਉਣਾ (lagvaauṇaa) *v* To get planted, to get engaged, to get posted.

ਲੰਗੜਾਉਣਾ (langṛaauṇaa) *v* To limp, to cripple. Also **ਲੰਡਾਉਣਾ**

ਲਗਾਉਣਾ (lagaauṇaa) *v* To employ, to fix, to appoint, to engage, to apply.

ਲਗਾਤਾਰ (lagaataar) *adv* Continuously, incessantly, consecutively.

ਲਗਾਨ (lagaan) *n m* Revenue, rent.

ਲਗਾਮ (lagaam) *n f* Bridle, hit and reins; **ਬੇ**~ **ਹੋਣਾ** To be out of control.

ਲੰਗੂਰ (langoor) *n m* Ape, monkey, gorilla.

ਲੰਗੋਟ (langoṭ) *n m* Loin cloth; **ਸੁੱਚਾ**~ Sexually rightness; ~**ਦਾ ਕੱਚਾ** lustful having sex weakness. Also **ਲੰਗੋਟਾ**

ਲੰਗੋਟੀ (langoṭee) *n f* Loin cloth; ~**ਵਿਚ ਮਸਤ** Carefree in adversity; ~**ਆ (ਯਾਰ)** Intimate (friend), chum, bosom or fast (friend).

ਲੰਘਣਾ (langhṇaa) *v* To pass, to cross, to transgress.

ਲੰਘਾਉਣਾ (langhaauṇaa) *v* To pass through, to help in passing.

ਲੰਘਾਈ (langhaaee) *n f* Toll tax; Charges of getting some one to across through; Process of getting some one to pass through.

ਲਘੂ (laghoo) *a* Small, short, trivial.

ਲਚਕ (lachak) *n f* Elasticity, resilence, softness; ~ਦਾਰ Elastic, flexible.

ਲਚਕਣਾ (lachaknaa) *v* To bend, to spring.

ਲਚਕਾ (lachkaa) *n m* Jolt, flirtation.

ਲਚਕੀਲਾ (lackkeelaa) *a* Elastic, flexible, resilient, spring. Also ਲਚੀਲਾ

ਲਚਰ (lachar) *a* Lewd, obscene, foolish; ~ਪੁਣਾ Lewdness, obscenity, foolishness.

ਲੱਛਣ (lachchhan) *n m* Traits, qualities, character, sign, attribute; Features. Also ਲੱਖਣ

ਲੱਛਾ (lachchhaa) *n m* Bundle, coil, bunch.

ਲਛੇਦਾਰ (lachchhedaar) *a* With fine shreds, pleasant to hear, verbose.

ਲੱਜਾ (lajjaa) *n f* Shyness, modesty, shame, pudency, coyness. Also ਲੱਜ or ਲਜਿਆ

ਲੱਜ਼ਤ (lazzat) *n f* Taste; Flavour; Pleasure; ~ਦਾਰ Tasty, delicious, tasteful.

ਲਜਿਆਉਣਾ (lajiaaunaa) *v* To feel shy, to be abashed, to be ashamed.

ਲਜ਼ੀਜ਼ (lazeez) *a* Tasty, delicious, flavoursome.

ਲਜੀਲਾ (lajeelaa) *a* Coy, shy.

ਲਟ (lat) *n f* (1) Lock (of hair), ringlet; (2) Flame; ~ਲਟ In full swing, shining brightly.

ਲਟਕ (latak) *n f* Coquetry, love, affected gait.

ਲਟਕਣ (latkan) *n f* Pendulum, pendent, locket, embellishment.

ਲਟਕਣਾ (lataknaa) *v* To hang, to be postponed, to swing, to be kept waiting.

ਲਟਕਾਉਣਾ (latkaaunaa) *v* To hang, to suspend, to dangle, to put off.

ਲੱਟਰ (lattar) *a* Vagabond, loafer.

ਲਟਾਪਟਾ (lataapataa) *v* Miscellaneous items, odds and ends, paraphernalia.

ਲੱਟੂ (lattoo) *n m* Top, (child's) plummet. Also ਲਾਟੂ

ਲੱਠ (latth) *n m* Wooden axle, cudgel, club, stick; ~ਬਾਜ਼ Cudgel fighter. Also (ਲਠੈਠ); ~ਮਾਰ Oppressive, violent, uncouth.

ਲੰਡ (land) *n m* Penis.

ਲੰਡੇ (lande) *n f* Trader's script, script of Lahanda language.

ਲਤ (lat) *n f* Leg; ~ਅੜਾਉਣੀ To interfere; ~ਖਾਣੀ To be kicked; ~ਮਾਰਨੀ To kick, to put hindrance.

ਲੱਤਾ (lattaa) *n m* Tatter, rag.

ਲਤਾਫ਼ਤ (lataafat) *n f* Delicacy, grace.

ਲਤਾੜ (lataar) *n f* Scolding.

ਲਤਾੜਨਾ (lataarnaa) *v* To scold, to insult, to trample under foot.

ਲਤੀਫ਼ਾ (lateefaa) *n m* Witty remark,

joke, jest, tit bit; ~(ਭੋ) ਬਾਜ਼ Witticist, humorist.

ਲੱਥਪੱਥ (lathpath) *a* Besmeared, soaked, steeped. Also **ਲਤਪਤ**

ਲਦਣਾ (ladṇaa) *v* To load, to burden, to feight, to be laden.

ਲਦਵਾਉਣਾ (ladvaauṇaa) *v* To cause or help loading. Also **ਲਦਾਉਣਾ**

ਲਦਾਨ (ladaan) *n m* Loading.

ਲਪਕ (lapak) *n f* Flash, swiftness.

ਲਪਕਣਾ (lapakṇaa) *v* To rush forth, to flash, to walk fast.

ਲੰਪਟ (lampaṭ) *a* Sexual, lustful, dissolute, wanton.

ਲਪਟ (lapaṭ) *n f* Blast of wind, odour, a swift form of fire.

ਲੱਪੜ (lappaṛ) *n m* Slap, smack; ~ਲਪੜ Non sensical talk, chatter.

ਲਪੇਟ (lapet) *n f* Envelopment, engulfment, fold, entanglement, convolution.

ਲਪੇਟਣਾ (lapeṭṇaa) *v* To wrap, to roll up, to coil, to pack, to embosom, to envelop.

ਲਫੰਗਾ (lafangaa) *n m* Vagabond, loafer, having loose character.

ਲਫਜ਼ (lafaz) *n m* Word, term, phrase; Saying; ~ਬ ਲਫ਼ਜ਼ Word by word, verbatum.

ਲਫਟੈਨ (laftain) *n m* Lieutenant. Also **ਲਫਟੰਟ**

ਲਫਾਫਾ (lafaafaa) *n m* Envelope, paperbag; Outward show.

ਲੰਬ (lamb) *n m* Perpendicular; ~ਕਾਰ Perpendicular, vertical, longitudinal.

ਲਬ (lab) *n m* Lib, saliva, edge.

ਲੰਬੜ (lambaṛ) *n m* Leader, chief; ~ਦਾਰ village headman.

ਲੰਬਾ (lambaa) *a* Tall, long; ~ਚੌੜਾ Huge, vast; ~ਈ Length, tallness. Also **ਲੰਮਾ**

ਲਬਾਦਾ (labaadaa) *n m* Clock, greatcoat, pelisee; Disguise.

ਲਬਾਲਬ (labaalab) *a adv* Brimful, upto the brim or top.

ਲੰਬੂ (lamboo) *n m* A very tall man; Big fire, conflagration.

ਲੰਬੂਤਰਾ (lambootraa) *a* Oblong, elongated, long.

ਲਬੇੜਨਾ (labeṛnaa) *v* To soak, to drench, to smear.

ਲਭਣਾ (labhṇaa) *v* To search, to find out, to get, to be discovered.

ਲਮ੍ਹਾ (lamhaa) *n m* Moment, instant.

ਲਮਕਣਾ (lamakṇaa) *v* To hang, to swing, to be suspended.

ਲਮਕਾਉਣਾ (lamkaauṇaa) *v* To hang, to suspend, to delay, to prolong.

ਲਮਢੀਂਗ (lamḍheeng) *a* Awkwardly tall.

ਲਮੂਤਰਾ (lamootraa) *a* Tallish, longish.

ਲਰਜ਼ਣਾ (larazṇaa) *v* To tremble, to vibrate, to throb.

ਲਲ੍ਹਕ (lalhak) *n f* Longing, intense desire, yearning, craving.

ਲਲਕਾਰ (lalkaar) *n f* Challenge, call, bawl, threat.

ਲਲਕਾਰਨਾ (lalkaarnaa) *v* To challenge, to threaten, to bawl.

ਲਲਕਾਰਾ (lalkaaraa) *n m* Shout, whoop, bawl, threatening or challenging cry.

ਲਲਚਾਉਣਾ (lalchaauṇaa) *v* To tempt, to allure, to long for, to covet.

ਲਲੂ (laloo) *a* Ordinary, simpleton; ~ਪੰਜੂ Tom dick and Harry.

ਲਲੋ-ਪੱਤੋ (lalo patto) *n f* Flattery, wheeding.

ਲਵਾਉਣਾ (lavaauṇaa) *v* To get sharpened, to get affixed, to get registered.

ਲੜ (laṛ) *n m* End or corner (of a cloth or garment); ~ਫੜਨਾ To take refuge.

ਲੜਕਪਨ (laṛakpan) *n m* Childhood, boyhood, frivolity.

ਲੜਕਾ (laṛkaa) *n m* Boy, son, child; Bridegroom.

ਲੜਕੀ (laṛkee) *n f* Girl, daughter.

ਲੜਖੜਾਉਣਾ (laṛkhaṛaauṇaa) *v* To stagger, to falter, to reel.

ਲੜਨਾ (laṛnaa) *v* To quarrel, to fight, to bite, to sting, to struggle.

ਲੜਾਈ (laṛaaee) *n f* Battle, fight, quarrel, clash, encounter; ~ਝਗੜਾ Quarrel, dispute, bickering, altercation.

ਲੜਾਕਾ (laṛaakaa) *a* Quarrelsome, belligerent, militant, pugnacious, fighter; ~ਪਣ Quarrelsomeness, pugnacity, militancy. Also ਲੜਾਕੂ

ਲੜਾਕੀ (laṛaakee) *a n f* Quarrelsome (woman), shrewish; Virago.

ਲੜੀ (laṛee) *n f* Chain, series, row, a string or pearls, link.

ਲਾਉਣਾ (laauṇaa) *v* To fix, to appoint, to assign, to plant.

ਲਾਇਕ (laaik) *a* Able, capable, fit, intelligent.

ਲਾਇਕੀ (laaikee) *n f* worthiness, worth, suitability, fitness.

ਲਾਇਲਾਜ (laailaaj) *a* Incurable, irremediable, hopeless.

ਲਾਈਨ (laain) *n f* Line; ਗੱਡੀ ਦੀ~ Railway track; ~ਦਾਰ Striped, ruled.

ਲਾਸ਼ (laash) *n f* Deadbody, carcass.

ਲਾਸਾਨੀ (laasaanee) *a* Unequalled, unparalleled, unmatched.

ਲਾਹਨਤ (laahnat) *n f* Scolding, reproof, reproach, condemnation, curse; ~ਦਾ ਮਾਰਿਆ Damned; ~ਮੁਲਾਮਤ Censure, scolding, reproach, rebuke. Also ਲਾਨ੍ਹਤ

ਲਾਖ (laakh) *n f* Shellac, sealing wax; Lac, hundred thousand.

ਲਾਗਤ (laagat) *n f* Cost, outlay, investment, expenditure.

ਲਾਗਤਬਾਜ਼ੀ (laagatbaazee) *n f* Enmity, grudge.

ਲੰਗਰੀ (laangree) *n m* Cook.

ਲਾਗਾ (laagaa) *n m* Nearness, closeness, vicinity, proximity; ~ਬੰਨਾ Relation, connection; surroundings, vicinity.

ਲਾਗੂ (laagoo) *a* Applicable, relevant; In force, enforced.

ਲਾਗੇ (laage) *adv* Near, near by, close by.

ਲਾਂਘਾ (lavanghaa) *n m* Thorough fare, passage, vestibule.

ਲਾਚਾਰ (laachaar) *a* Helpless, compelled, destitute, forlorn.

ਲਾਚਾਰੀ (laachaaree) *n f* Helplessness, handicap.

ਲਾਜ (laaj) *n f* Modesty, shyness, shame, pudicity bashfulness; ~ਰਖਣੀ To protect one's honour.

ਲਾਜ਼ਮ (laazam) *a* Necessary, essential, compulsory.

ਲਾਜ਼ਮੀ (laazmee) *a* Compulsory, mandatory, obligatory.

ਲਾਟ (laat) *n m* (1) Governor, lord; (2) Flame, blaze.

ਲਾਟਰੀ (laatree) *n f* Lottery.

ਲਾਠੀ (laathee) *n f* Stick, club, cudgel.

ਲਾਡ (laad) *n m* Love, fonding; caressing, endearment; ~ਕਰਨਾ To fondle, to caress; ~ਲਾ Dear, darling, pet.

ਲਾਪਤਾ (laapataa) *a* Disappeared, unknown, absconding.

ਲਾਪਰਵਾਹ (laaparwaah) *a* Careless, negligent, headless, reckless.

ਲਾਪਰਵਾਹੀ (laaparwaahee) *n f* Carelessness, inattentiveness.

ਲਾਭ (laabh) *n m* Advantage, profit, gain, dividend, use, benefit; ~ਦਾਇਕ (ਕਾਰੀ) Useful, fruitful, beneficial, advantageous, profitable.

ਲਾਂਭੇ (laambhe) *adv* Aside, away.

ਲਾਮ (laam) *n f* Army, crowd, brigade; War; Host; ~ਬੰਦੀ Mobilization, *levy en masse*.

ਲਾਰ (laar) *n f* Saliva.

ਲਾਰਾ (laaraa) *n* False promise, false hope, an excuse.

ਲਾਲ (laal) *a n m* Red, angry; Darling, son, boy; Ruby; ~ਬੁਝੱਕੜ A wiseacre; A conceited fool; ~ਮਿਰਚ Chilly.

ਲਾਲਸਾ (laalsaa) *n f* Longing, craving, ardent desire, ambition, yearning

ਲਾਲਚ (laalach) *n m* Greed, temptation, avarice.

ਲਾਲਚੀ (lalchee) *a* Greedy, priggish,

avaricious.

ਲਾਲਟੈਨ (laaltain) *n f* Lantern.

ਲਾਲਾ (laalaa) *n m* Address term for shopkeeper, businessman, oldman, father etc.

ਲਾਲੀ (laalee) *n f* Redness, crimson hue; A kind of myna.

ਲਾਵਾ (laavaa) *n m* Lava.

ਲਾਵਾਂ (laavaan) *n pl f* Circum ambulations in marriage ceremony; ~ਲੈਆਂ To marry. Also **ਲਾਂ** or **ਲਾਂਵ**

ਲਾਵਾਰਸ (laavaaras) *a* Heirless, orphan, unclaimed.

ਲਾੜਾ (laaṛaa) *n m* Bridegroom.

ਲਾੜੀ (laaṛee) *n f* Bride.

ਲਿਆਉਣਾ (liaaunaa) *v* To bring, to fetch, to carry over.

ਲਿਆਕਤ (liaakat) *n f* Ability, calibre, worth, proficiency, capability, skill.

ਲਿਸ਼ਕ (lishak) *n f* Shine, sheen, glitter, lustre; ~ਦਾਰ Shinning, glossy.

ਲਿਸ਼ਕਾਰ (lishkaar) *n f* Flash, reflection, bright reflecting light. Also **ਲਿਸ਼ਕਾਰਾ**

ਲਿਸ਼ਕਣਾ (lishaknaa) *v* To shine, to glitter, to sparkle.

ਲਿੱਸਾ (lissaa) *a* weak, pale, feeble; ~ਪਣ Thinness, weakness. Also **ਲਿੱਸਣ**

ਲਿਹਾਜ਼ (lihaaz) *n m* Consideration, deference, favour, indulgence.

ਲਿਹਾਜ਼ਾ (lihaazaa) *conj adv* Accordingly, therefore.

ਲਿਖਣਾ (likhnaa) *v* To write, to inscribe, to take down, to note down; ~ਪੜ੍ਹਨਾ Study, reading and writing.

ਲਿਖਵਾਉਣਾ (likhvaaunaa) *v* To get written, to dictate. Also **ਲਿਖਾਉਣਾ**

ਲਿਖਾਈ (likhaaee) *n f* Writing, art of writing, wages for writing.

ਲਿਖਾਪੜ੍ਹੀ (likhaaparhee) *n f* Correspondence, written negotiation.

ਲਿੰਗ (ling) *n m* Sex, gender, the male organ.

ਲਿੰਗੀ (lingee) *a* Sexual.

ਲਿਟ (liṭ) *n f* Lock, wisp or strand of hair.

ਲਿਟਣਾ (liṭnaa) *v* To lie down.

ਲਿਟਾਉਣਾ (liṭaaunaa) *v* To lay down, to cause to lie down.

ਲਿੱਤਰ (littar) *n m* Old and nearly worn out shoes. Also **ਛਿਤਰ**

ਲਿਤਾੜਨਾ (litaaṛnaa) *v* To trample under feet, to scold.

ਲਿੱਦ (lidd) *n f* Horse-turd, dung of ass or elephant; ~ਕਰਨਾ To act tamely.

ਲਿਪਟਨਾ (lipaṭnaa) *v* To cling, to embrace, to be coiled round.

ਲਿਫਣਾ (liphaṇaa) *v* To bend, to stoop; To yield, submit; To relent.

ਲਿਫ਼ਾਫ਼ਾ (lifaafaa) *n m* Envelope, wrapper.

ਲਿੰਬਣਾ (limbṇaa) *v* To plaster.

ਲਿਬੜਨਾ (limbaṛnaa) *v* To smear.

ਲਿਬਾਸ (libaas) *n m* Dress, apparel, raiment, clothing, garb, vestment, attire.

ਲਿਬੇੜਨਾ (liberṇaa) *v* To besmear, to daub, to soil. Also ਲਬੇੜਨਾ

ਲਿਲੁਕ (lilhak) *n f* Cry, lament, scream; humble or abject entaty or appeal.

ਲਿਲਾਟ (lilaaṭ) *n m* Forehead, destiny. Also ਲਲਾਟ

ਲੀਕ (leek) *n f* Line, mark, trace.

ਲੀਕਣਾ (leekṇaa) *v* To rule, to draw lines, to spoil.

ਲੀਖ (leekh) *n f* Egg of a louse, nit.

ਲੀਚੜ (leechaṛ) *a* Niggardly, mean, bad paymaster.

ਲੀਰ (leer) *n f* Rag, shred; ~ਲੀਰ ਹੋਣਾ To be torn into rags.

ਲੀੜਾ (leeṛaa) *n m* Torn out, cloth, garment.

ਲੁਹਾਉਣਾ (luhaauṇaa) *v* To get unloaded, to help in unloading.

ਲੁਹਾਰ (luhaar) *n m* Blacksmith, ironsmith. Also ਲੋਹਾਰ

ਲੁਹਾਰਾ (luhaaraa) *n m* Job of blacksmith.

ਲੁਕਣਾ (lukṇaa) *v* To be concealed, to hide.

ਲੁਕਾਉਣਾ (lukaauṇaa) *v* To hide, to conceal, to cover.

ਲੁਗਾਤ (lugat) *n f* Dictionary, lexicon, glossary.

ਲੁੱਗਾ (luggaa) *a* Deserted, vacated, empty, bare (house), unoccupied and unguarded.

ਲੁਗਾਈ (lugaaee) *n f* Wife, woman.

ਲੁੰਗੀ (lungee) *n f* Striped, chequered or embroidered sheet for use as garment for lower body.

ਲੁੱਚਾ (luchchaa) *a* Wicked, shameless, knave, corrupt; Vagabond, scamp.

ਲੁੰਜਾ (lunjaa) *a* Crippled, having an arm or leg crippled, disabled.

ਲੁੱਝਣਾ (lujjṇaa) *v* To quarrel, to fight, to provoke.

ਲੁਟਣਾ (lutṇaa) *v* To plunder, to rob, to ravage, to ransack, to loot, to devastate.

ਲੁਟੇਰਾ (luṭeraa) *n m* Robber, plunderer, highwayman.

ਲਡਾਉਣਾ (luḍaauṇaa) *v* To swing, to oscillate.

ਲੁਤਫ਼ (lutaf) *n m* Enjoyment, pleasure, grace, taste.

ਲੁਪਤ (lupt) *a* Concealed, hidden, disguised, missing.

ਲੁਭਾਉਣਾ (lubhaauṇaa) *v* To allure, to

entice, to captivate, to be charmed. Also ਲੁੜਾਣਾ

ਲੁੜਕਣਾ (lurhaknaa) *v* To roll, to be upset.

ਲੁੜੀਂਦਾ (lureendaa) *a* Wanted, required, needed, necessary, needful, desired.

ਲੂੰ (loon) *n m* Short hair on the body.

ਲੂਸਣਾ (loosanaa) *v* To be scorched; to feel burning sensation; to sulk, to be sulky, to smoulder with envy or jealousy.

ਲੂਣ (loon) *n m* Salt, sodium chloride; ~ਤੇਲ Articles of bare subsistence, bread and butter; ~ਮਿਰਚ ਲਾਉਣੀ To season or smear with salt and pepper; To state or report (an incident) in exaggerated or interesting manner, to exaggerate.

ਲੂੰਬੜ (loombar) *n m* Fox.

ਲੂਲ੍ਹਾ (loolhaa) *a n m* Maimed, crippled; Cripple.

ਲੇਸ (les) *n f* Sticking fluid, adhesiveness; ~ਦਾਰ sticky, gummy.

ਲੇਖ (lekh) *n f* Composition, essay, article, writing; Destiny, fate; ~ਕ Writer; ~ਨੀ Pen, style.

ਲੇਖਾ (lekhaa) *n m* An account, calculation; ~ਕਾਰ Accountant; ~ਜੋਖਾ Assessment.

ਲੇਟਣਾ (letnaa) *v* To lie down, to roll; to rest or relax lying down; to sleep, to wallow.

ਲੇਪ (lep) *n m* Layer, coat, spread (of plaster, ointment, etc); ~ਕਰਨਾ To spread or daub with; ~ਲਾਉਣਾ To flatter; To cheat.

ਲੇਪਣਾ (lepnaa) *v* To be smear, to embalm, to paint, to plaster.

ਲੇਫ਼ (lef) *n m* Quilt.

ਲੇਲਾ (lelaa) *n m* Lamb.

ਲੈਣ-ਦੇਣ (lain-den) *n m* Trade, commerce, give and take, transaction, exchange, barter; Business, relations, dealings; ~ਕਰਨਾ To transact business, to have commercial relations; To compromise, to give and take.

ਲੈਣਾ (lainaa) *v* To get, to receive, to take, to hold, to acquire.

ਲੋਈ (loee) *n f* A thin blanket or wrapper; People, public.

ਲੋਹਾ (lohaa) *n m* Iron; ~ਲੈਣਾ To wage a war.

ਲੋਕ (lok) *n m* People, mankind, public, folk, world; ~ਸਭਾ House of people; ~ਸੇਵਕ Public servant; ~ਹਿੱਤ Public interest; ~ਕਥਾ Folk tale; ~ਗਾਥਾ Ballad; ~ਰਾਜ Democracy.

ਲੋਕਾਚਾਰ (lokaachaar) *n m* Fashion, custom, convention, ethos; Public opinion.

ਲੋਚ (loch) *n f* Flexibility, elasticity, tenderness; ~**ਦਾਰ** Tender, flexible, soft, elastic. Also **ਲਚਕ**

ਲੇਟਣਾ (lotnaa) *v* To roll, to somersault.

ਲੋਟਾ (lotaa) *n m* Small metal pot.

ਲੋਥ (loth) *n f* Corpse, dead body, carcass; ~**ੜਾ** Lump of flesh.

ਲੋਭ (lobh) *n m* Greed, temptation, allurement.

ਲੋਭੀ (lobhee) *a* Greedy, voracious.

ਲੋੜ (lor) *n f* Need, want, necessity.

ਲੋੜਨਾ (lornaa) *v* To search, to need, to expect.

ਲੋੜ੍ਹ (lorhaa) *n m* Tragedy, calamity; Atrocity, oppression; Storm; Deluge.

ਲੌਂਡਾ (laundaa) *n m* Boy, lad, slave.

ਲੌਂਡੀ (laundee) *n f* Slave girl, bond maid.

ਵ

ਵ Thirty fourth letter of Gurmukhi alphabets, pronounced as 'vaavaa'.

ਵੱਸ (vass) *n m v* Power, control, will; To over power, to bring under control, to tame.

ਵੱਸਣਾ (vassṇaa) *v* To dwell, to reside, to lodge; To rain.

ਵਸਲ (vasal) *n m* Union, meeting, copulation.

ਵਸਵਸਾ (vasvasaa) *n m* Apprehension, misgiving, anxiety, doubt, trepidation.

ਵਸਾਉਣਾ (vasaauṇaa) *v* To populate, to colonise, to shower.

ਵਸਾਹ (vasaah) *n m* Trust, credit, reliance; ~ਖਾਣਾ To trust, to rely, to have faith.

ਵਸਾਲ (vasaal) *n m* Union, meeting, cohabitation.

ਵਸੀਅਤ (vaseeat) *n f* Will, legacy, bequest; ~ਕਰਨੀ To bequeath; ~ਨਾਮਾ Will testament.

ਵਸੀਕਾ (vaseekaa) *n m* Bond, written agreement; ~ਨਵੀਸ Deed writer.

ਵਸੀਕਾਰ (vaseekaar) *n m* Control, authority.

ਵਸੀਲਾ (vaseelaa) *n m* Support, means.

ਵਸੂਲ (vasool) *a* Obtained, collected, received, realised; ~ਕਰਨਾ To collect, to realise, to fetch.

ਵਸੂਲੀ (vasoolee) *n f* Realisation of dues, recovery, collection of dues.

ਵਸੇਬਾ (vasebaa) *n m* Living, life with peace and honour, peaceful and honourable living.

ਵਹਾਉਣਾ (vahaauṇaa) *v* To cause or make to flow, to float, to pour, to spill; to waste, to squander.

ਵਹਿਸ਼ਤ (vaheshat) *n f* Savagery, madness, rudeness, wildness.

ਵਹਿਸ਼ੀ (vaheshee) *a n m* Savage, rude, uncivilized; Barbarian, savage, brute.

ਵਹਿਣਾ (vehṇaa) *v* To float, to flow.

ਵਹਿਣੀ (vaojṇee) *n f* Drain, gutter, sewer, duct.

ਵਹਿਮ (vahem) *n m* False notion, whim, fallacy, misunderstanding, apprehension, doubt.

ਵਹਿਮੀ (vahemee) *a* Whimsical, suspecious.

ਵਹਿੜ (vaheṛ) *n f* Young cow; ~ਕਾ Calf, young ox.

ਵਹੀ (vahee) *n f* Accountbook, recordbook, record of debts and debtors; ~ਖਾਤਾ Cashbook, cash account, ledger of transactions.

ਵਹੁਟੀ (vahuṭee) *n f* Wife, bride.

ਵਕਤ (vakat) *n m* Time, season, opportunity, circumstances; ~ਕਟਣਾ To pass the time; ~ਸਿਰ In all time, timely; ~ਬੇਵਕਤ At all times, at odd hours. Also **ਵਖਤ**

ਵਕਤਾ (vaktaa) *n m* Speaker, orator.

ਵਕਤੀ (vaktee) *a* Occassional, timely, momentary, temporary, transient, impermanent.

ਵਕਫ਼ (wakaf) *a n m* Reserved, allocated; Charitable, endowment, trust; ~ਨਾਮਾ Deed of reservation.

ਵਕਫ਼ਾ (wakfaa) *n m* Interval, recess, intermission, period.

ਵੱਕਾਰ (vakkaar) *n m* Prestige, honour, dignity

ਵਕਾਲਤ (vakaalat) *n m* Advocacy, pleadership, lawyer profession; ~ਨਾਮਾ Power of attorney given by client to advocate.

ਵਕੀਲ (vakeel) *n m* Lawyer, pleader, advocate, counsel.

ਵਖਰਾ (vakhraa) *a* Separate, distinctive, isolated; ~ਪਣ Distinctness, separateness.

ਵਖਾਣ (vakhaaṇ) *n m* Description, explanation.

ਵਖਾਣਨਾ (vakhaaṇnaa) *v* To describe, to relate, to explain.

ਵੱਖੀ (vakkhee) *n f* Side.

ਵੰਗ (vang) *n f* Glass bangle.

ਵਗਣਾ (vagṇaa) *v* To flow, to blow.

ਵਗਾਰ (vagaar) *n f* Forced or unpaid labour, bonded labour.

ਵੰਗਾਰ (vangaar) *n f* Challenge; ~ਮੰਨਣੀ To accept a challenge.

ਵੰਗਾਰਨਾ (vangaarnaa) *v* To challenge

ਵਚਨ (vachan) *n* (gr) (1) Number; singular number; ਬਹੁ~ plural number; (2) Speech, word, utterance, talk, promise; ~ਬੱਧ Committed.

ਵੰਚਿਤ (vanchit) *a* Deprived; ~ਕਰਨਾ To deprive.

ਵੱਛਾ (vachchhaa) *n m* Calf.

ਵੰਜਣਾ (vanjṇaa) *v* To go, to part.

ਵਜਣਾ (vahṇaa) *v* To chime, to produce sound, to ring, to be struck; ਨਾਂ ~To be famous.

ਵਜਨ (vazan) *n m* Weight, burden, measure; ~ਦਾਰ Heavy, weighty.

ਵੰਜਾਉਣਾ (vanjaauṇaa) *v* To lose, to waste, to destroy.

ਵਜਾਉਣਾ (vajaauṇaa) *v* To play on a musical instrument; ਢੋਲ~ To beat a drum; ਹੁਕਮ~ To execute an order.

ਵਜ਼ਾਹਤ (vazaahat) *n f* Explanation,

elaboration, clarification; ~ਕਰਨਾ To
elaborate, to explicate, to clarify.

ਵਜ਼ਾਰਤ (vazaarat) *n f* Ministry, cabinet;
Ministership.

ਵਜ਼ੀਫ਼ਾ (vazeefaa) *n m* Scholarship,
stipend.

ਵਜ਼ੀਰ (vazeer) *n m* Minister.

ਵਜ਼ੀਰੀ (vazeeree) *n m* Ministership.

ਵਜ਼ੀਰੇ-ਆਲ੍ਹਾ (vazeeree-aalhaa) *n m*
Chief minister.

ਵਜ਼ੀਰੇ-ਆਜ਼ਮ (vazeere-aazam) *n m*
Prime minister.

ਵਜੂਦ (vajood) *n m* Existence, body.

ਵੱਟਕ (vattak) *n f* Sale proceeds,
takings.

ਵਟਣਾ (vatnaa) *v* To twist, to interwine,
to be exchanged.

ਵੱਟਾ (vattaa) *n m* Stone, weight,
measure, brickbat, discount; ~ਸੱਟਾ
Exchange in trade, barter; ~ਖਾਤਾ
Bad debt account, dead loss.

ਵਟਾਂਦਰਾ (vataandraa) *n m* Exchange,
barter, replacement.

ਵੰਡਣਾ (vandnaa) *v* To divide, to
distribute, to split, to allocate.

ਵੱਡਾ (vaddaa) *a n* Elder, great,
senior, major; Share; ~ਦਿਨ
Christmas day.

ਵੰਡਾਉਣਾ (vandaaunaa) *v* To divide, to
distribute, to cause to be divided.

ਵਡਿਆਉਣਾ (vadiaaunaa) *v* To praise,

to applaud, to puff up.

ਵਡਿਆਈ (vadiaaee) *n f* Praise,
eulogy, greatness, excellence.

ਵੰਡੀਜਣਾ (vandeejnaa) *v* To be split.

ਵੱਡੀ ਮਾਤਾ (vaddee maataa) *n f* Small
pox.

ਵਡੇਰਾ (vaderaa) *n m a* Ancestor,
forefather; Larger, greater.

ਵੱਢਣਾ (vaddhnaa) *v* To cut, to
amputate, to abscind.

ਵੱਢੀ (vaddhee) *n f* Bribe, hush money,
illegal gratification; ~ਖੋਰੀ Bribery;
~ਦੇਣੀ To bribe.

ਵਣ (van) *n m* Wood, jungle, forest.

ਵਣਗੀ (vangee) *n f* Sample,
specimen.

ਵਣਜ (vanaj) *n m* Business, trade,
commerce.

ਵਤਨ (vatan) *n m* Motherland,
fatherland, native country, one's
own country, homeland.

ਵਤਨੀ (vatnee) *n m* Countryman,
fellow countryman, compatriot,
fellow citizen.

ਵਤੀਰਾ (vateeraa) *n m* Behaviour,
treatment, attitude.

ਵਧਣਾ (vadhnaa) *v* To increase, to
grow, to enlarge, to lengthen, to
approach; ~ਫੁਲਣਾ To grow, to
multiply.

ਵਧਾਉਣਾ (vandhaaunaa) *v* To extend,

to produce, to enhance, to enlarge, to exaggerate, to magnify.

ਵਧਾਈ (vadhaaee) *n f* Congratulation, felicitation.

ਵਧੀਆ (vadhiaa) *a* Fine, nice, excellent, superior; **~ਪਨ** Excellence, superiosity.

ਵਧੀਕ (vadheek) *adv* More, extra, in excess.

ਵਧੀਕੀ (vadheekee) *n f* Outrage, oppression.

ਵੰਨ ਸੁਵੰਨਾ (vann suvannaa) *adv* Of different shapes, of various kinds, variegated.

ਵੰਨਗੀ (vangee) *n f* Sample.

ਵਪਾਰ (vapaar) *n m* Business, trade; **~ਕ** Commercial, mercantile.

ਵਪਾਰੀ (vapaaree) *n m* Trader, businessman.

ਵਫਦ (vafad) *n f* Delegation.

ਵਫ਼ਾ (vafaa) *n f* Sincerity, fidelity, fulfilment of promise, **~ਦਾਰ** Faithful, loyal; **~ਦਾਰੀ** Loyalty, allegiance, faithfulness.

ਵਫ਼ਾਤ (vafaat) *n f* Death, demise.

ਵਰ (var) *n m* (1) Bridegroom, husband; (2) Boon, blessing, favour, solicitation.

ਵਰਸਣਾ (varasnaa) *v* To rain.

ਵਰਸ਼ਾ (varshaa) *n f* Rain. Also **ਵਰਖਾ**

ਵਰਸਾਉਣਾ (varsaaunaa) *v* To shower boons, benefaction or blessings. Also **ਵਰ ਦੇਣਾ**

ਵਰਕ (varak) *n m* Leaf (of gold, silver or tin).

ਵਰਕਾ (varkaa) *n m* Leaf (of book, etc.) folio; Piece of paper.

ਵਰਗ (varag) *n m* Square, a class, group, genus; **~ਸੰਘਰਸ਼** Class struggle; **~ਹੀਣ** Classless; **~ਭੇਦ** Class distinction, discrimination.

ਵਰਗਲਾਉਣਾ (varglaaunaa) *v* To seduce, to instigate, to coax.

ਵਰਗਾ (vargaa) *a* Similar, resembling, like.

ਵਰਜ਼ਸ਼ (varzash) *n f* Physical exercise, gymnastics (athletic).

ਵਰਜਣਾ (varjanaa) *v* To check, to forbid, to prohibit, to debar.

ਵਰਜਿਤ (varjit) *a* Forbidden, prohibited, banned, taboo, proscribed.

ਵਰਣ (varan) *n m* (1) Colour, caste; (2) Speech sound, a letter of alphabet; **~ਸੰਕਰ** Hybrid; **~ਹੀਨ** Casteless.

ਵਰਣਨ (varnan) *n m* Description, account, narration; **~ਕਰਨਾ** To describe, to narrate, to relate.

ਵਰਤ (varat) *n m* Fast; **~ਰਖਣਾ** To keep fast; **~ਲੈਣਾ** To take a fast.

ਵਰਤਨ (vartaṇ) *n m* Treatment, dealings, use, business.

ਵਰਤਨਾ (vartaṇaa) *v* To use, to treat.

ਵਰਤਾਉਨਾ (vartaaunaa) To distribute.

ਵਰਦੀ (vardee) *n f* Uniform, dress.

ਵਰਧਨ (vardhan) *n m* Enhancement, increase, propagation.

ਵਰਜਾਮ (varlyaam) *n m* Brave person, hero.

ਵਰ੍ਹਾ (varhaa) *n m* Year.

ਵਰੀ (varee) *n f* Dresses, ornaments presented to bride by her in-laws.

ਵਲ (val) *a n m* Hale and hearty; Method, tact; Twist, coil, turn; ~ਹੋ ਜਾਣਾ To recoup, to recover health; ~ਪਾਉਨਾ To spiral, to make a loop.

ਵੱਲ (vall) *adv* On the side of, in The direction of, towards, against.

ਵਲਵਲਾ (valvalaa) *n m* Excitement, passion, sentimentality.

ਵਲਾਉਨਾ (valaaunaa) *v* To coil, to wrap round, to twist, to coax.

ਵਲਾਇਤ (valaait) *n f* Foreign country, alien country.

ਵਲਾਇਤੀ (vallaitee) *a* Foreign, European, Englishman. Also ਵਲੈਤੀ

ਵਲੀ (valee) *n m* Hermit, saint.

ਵਲੂੰਧਰ (valoondhar) *n m* Scratch.

ਵਲੂੰਧਰਨਾ (valoondharnaa) *v* To. scratch, to claw.

ਵਲੇਟਨਾ (valheṭnaa) *v* To fold, to wrap, to gird.

ਵੱਲੋਂ (valon) *adv* From, on behalf of, from the side of.

ਵੜਨਾ (varnaa) *v* To enter, to pierce, to step, to penetrate.

ਵਾਇਦਾ (vaaidaa) *n m* Promise; ~ਸ਼ਿਕਨ Promise breaker; ~ਖਿਲਾੜੀ Violation of commitment.

ਵਾਈ (vaaee) *n f* Flatulence.

ਵਾਸਕਟ (waaskaṭ) *n m* Waist coat.

ਵਾਸਤਾ (vaastaa) *n m* Concern, relation, connection.

ਵਾਸਨਾ (vaasnaa) *n f* Lust, sensuality, desire, smell; ~ਮਈ Sensual, lusty.

ਵਾਹਿਗੁਰੂ (vaheguru) *n m* God, Almighty.

ਵਾਹਿਜਾਤ (vahiyaat) *a* Absurd, worthless.

ਵਾਗੁਨਾ (vaahuṇaa) *v* To plough, to till, to drive, (car, tonga etc), to discharge.

ਵਾਕਫ (vaakaf) *n m a* Acquaintance; Conversant, knowing, aware of; ਨਾ~ Ignorant, unknown.

ਵਾਕਫੀਅਤ (vaafiat) *n f* Acquaintance, knowledge. Also ਵਾਕਫੀ

ਵਾਕਿਆ (vaakiaa) *n m* Event, incident, happening, news.

ਵਾਗ (vaag) *n f* Rein; ~ਗੁੰਦਣੀ To braid.

ਵਾਚਨਾ (vaachnaa) *v* To read, recite, study.

ਵਾਛੜ (vaachhaṛ) *n f* Shower, rain.

ਵਾਜਬ (vaajab) *a* Reasonable, proper, fit, suitable.

ਵਾਜਬੀ (vaajbee) *a* Reasonable.

ਵਾਜਾ (vaajaa) *n m* Harmonium, musical instrument, band.

ਵਂਜਾ (vaanjaa) *a* Without, devoid of, lacking.

ਵਾਜ਼ਿਆ (vaaziaa) *a* Evident, clear, manfest, lucid; Explained, described, elucidated.

ਵਂਝਾ (vaanjhaa) *a* Bereft, divested, without.

ਵਾਢਾ (vaadhaa) *n m* Cut, mark of cutting.

ਵਾਣ (vaaṇ) *n m* Coarse twine for cot.

ਵਾਤਾਵਰਣ (vaataavaraṇ) *n m* Atmosphere, surroundings, climate.

ਵਾਦੀ (vaadee) *n f* Valley, vale.

ਵਾਧਾ (vaadhaa) *n m* Increase, extension, promotion, increment.

ਵਾਧੂ (vaadhoo) *a* Superfluous, not needed, in excels.

ਵਾਪਸ (vaapas) *a* Returned, given back; ~ਆਉਣਾ To come back, to return; ~ਦੇਣਾ To take back, to withdraw.

ਵਾਪਸੀ (vaapsee) *n f* Return, reversion.

ਵਾਪਰਨਾ (vaaparnaa) *v* To happen, occur, to come to pass, to take place, to befall.

ਵਾਬਸਤਾ (vaabastaa) *a* Connected, attached, linked, conjoint, conjunct, associated.

ਵਾਯੂ (vayoo) *n f* Air, wind.

ਵਾਰ (vaar) *n m* (1) Blow, attack, stroke; (2) Day; (3) Turn; Layer; (4) Sacrificing; Ballad.

ਵਾਰਸ (vaaras) *n m* Heir, successor; ~ਹੋਣਾ To succeed, to inherit.

ਵਾਰਸੀ (vaarsee) *n f* Inheriance, succession.

ਵਾਰਸ਼ਿਕ (vaarshik) *a* Yearly, annual.

ਵਾਰਤਾ (vaartaa) *n f* Negotiation, narrative, news, report; ~ਲਾਪ Dialogue, conversation, discourse.

ਵਾਰਦਾਤ (vaardaat) *n f* Incident, happening, affray, skirmish.

ਵਾਰਨਾ (vaarnaa) *v* To sacrifice, to devote, to offer something to deity.

ਵਾਲ (vaal) *n m* Hair; ~ਸੰਵਾਰਨਾ To comb the hair; ~ਵਾਲ ਬਚਣਾ To have a narrow escape.

ਵਾਲੀ (vaalee) *n m* Master, owner, lord, ruler, protector, guardian.

ਵਾਵੇਲਾ (vaavelaa) *n m* Hue and cry, outcry, clamour, lamentation.

ਵਾੜਨਾ (vaaṛnaa) *v* To thrust into, to stuff, to penetrate.

ਵਿਅਕਤਿਤਵ (viyaktitv) *n m* Personality.

ਵਿਅਕਤੀ (viyaktee) *n m* Person, individual; ~ਕਰਨ Individualisation; ~ਗਤ Personal, individual.

ਵਿਅੰਗ (viang) *n m* Irony, sarcasm, joke.

ਵਿਅਰਥ (viyarth) *a adv* Useless, fruitless, null; In vain, to no effect.

ਵਿਆਹ (viaah) *n m* Marriage, wedding, matrimony; ~ਕਰਨਾ To marry.

ਵਿਆਂਹਦੜ (viaanhdar) *n m* Bride, bridegroom, About to be married.

ਵਿਆਹੁਣਾ (viaahunaa) *v* To marry, to wed.

ਵਿਆਕਰਨ (viaakaaran) *n m* Grammar, Science of language.

ਵਿਆਕੁਲ (viaakul) *a* Confounded, distempered, impatient, agitated.

ਵਿਆਖਿਆ (viaakhiyaa) *n f* Elucidation, description, explanation; ~ਕਰਨੀ To elucidate, to expound, to interpret, to describe; ~ਪਰਕ Interpretative; ~ਤਮਕ Explanatory, elucidatory; ~ਨ Speech, ration, discourse.

ਵਿਆਜ (viaaj) *n m* Interest; ~ਖੋਰੀ Usury.

ਵਿਆਪਤ (viaapat) *a* Diffused, pervading, spread.

ਵਿਸਤਾਰ (vistaar) *n m* Extersion, expansion, elaboration, detail; ~ਕ Amplifying, amplifier; ~ਪੂਰਬਕ Indetail; ~ਵਾਦ Expansionism.

ਵਿ ਸਥਾਪਿਤ(visthaapit) *a* Displaced.

ਵਿਸਫੋਟ (visphot) *n m* Explosion, violent out burst.

ਵਿਸਰਜਨ (visarjan) *n m* Adjournment.

ਵਿਸਰਣ (visaran) *n m* Forgetfulness, forgetting.

ਵਿਸਰਨਾ (visarnaa) *v* To forget, to be forgotten.

ਵਿਸ਼ਰਾਮ (vishraam) *n m* Rest, repose, relaxation, stop; ~ਚਿੰਨ੍ਹ Punctuation.

ਵਿਸ਼ਵ (vishw) *n m* World, universe, cosmos; ~ਕੋਸ਼ Encyclopaedia; ~ਵਿਦਿਆਲਾ University.

ਵਿਸ਼ਵਾਸ (vishwass) *n m* Faith, belief, trust, reliance; ~ਕਰਨਾ To believe, to trust, to rely, to accredit; ~ਘਾਤ Betrayal, treason, deception, violation of trust; ~ਪਤਰ Credentials; ~ਪਾਤਰ Faithfully. Also ਵਿਸਾਹ

ਵਿਸਾਰਨਾ (visaarnaa) *v* To forget.

ਵਿਸ਼ੈਲਾ (vishailaa) *a* Poisonous, virose, toxic.

ਵਿਹਲੜ (vehlar) *a* Idle, unoccupied, unemployed, indolent, lazy, slothful.

ਵਿਹਲਾ (vehlaa) *a* Leisured, unoccupied, idle, unemployed, unengaged, not busy, relaxing.

ਵਿਕਣਾ (viknaa) *v* To be sold, to sell.

ਵਿੱਕਰੀ (vikkree) *n f* Sale, quantity sold, sale proceeds.

ਵਿਕਲਪ (vikalap) *n m* Alternation; alternate.

ਵਿਕਾਸ (vikaas) *n m* Development, evolution; ~ਸ਼ੀਲ Developing; evolving; ~ਵਾਦ Evolution.

ਵਿਖਾਉਣਾ (vikhaaunaa) *v* To show.

ਵਿਖਾਈ (vikjaaee) *n f* Showing, unveiling.

ਵਿਗੜਨਾ (vigarnaa) *v* To be spoiled, to be damaged, to be deteriorate.

ਵਿੰਗਾ (vingaa) *a* crooked, bent, not straight; ~ਤੜਿੰਗਾ Curved, wavy, uneven.

ਵਿਗਾੜ (vigaar) *n m* Breach, discord rupture, damage, disorder, deformity, impairment.

ਵਿਗਾੜਨਾ (vigaarnaa) *v* To spoil, to demage, to destory, to bungle.

ਵਿਗਿਆਨ (vigiaan) *n m* Science; ਅਰਥ~ Economics; ਸਮਾਜ~ Sociology; ਭਾਸ਼ਾ~ Lingiustics; ਪ੍ਰਾਣੀ~ Zoology; ਮਨੋ~ Psychology; ਰਸਾਇਣ~ Chemistry.

ਵਿਗਿਆਨਿਕ (vigiaanik) *a* Scientific.

ਵਿਗਿਆਨੀ (vigiaanee) *n m* Scientist.

ਵਿਗਿਆਪਨ (vigiaapan) *n m* Advertisement.

ਵਿਘਟਨ (vighaṭan) *n m* Disintegration, disorganisation, dissociation.

ਵਿਘਨ (vighan) *n m* Hitch, interruption, obtacle, hindrance.

ਵਿਚ (vich) Prep Inside, in, into; ~ਕਾਰ Among, during, in between, intermediate.

ਵਿਚਰਨਾ (vicharnaa) *v* To wander, to stroll about, to go.

ਵਿਚਾਰ (vichaar) *n m* Notion, idea, feeling, consideration, opinion, view, judgement; ~ਸ਼ੀਲ Deliberative; ~ਕਰਨਾ To consider, to ponder, to calculate; ~ਮੂਲਕ Ideational; ~ਵਾਨ Thinker, philosopher.

ਵਿਚਾਰਾ (vichaaraa) *a* Helpless, poor, wretched.

ਵਿਚਾਰਲਾ (vichaarlaa) *a* Middle, intermediate. Also ਵਿਚਾਲਾ

ਵਿਚੋਲਾ (vicholaa) *n m* Mediator, middleman.

ਵਿਛਣਾ (vichhnaa) *v* To be spread, to be stretched.

ਵਿਛੜਨਾ (vichharnaa) *v* To be separate, to part.

ਵਿਛਾਉਣਾ (vichhaaunaa) *v n m* To spread; Bedding.

ਵਿਛੋੜਾ (vichhoraa) *n m* Separation, parting, detachment.

ਵਿਜੈ (vijai) *n f* Conquest, victory.

ਵਿਜੋਗ (vijog) *n m* Separation, disunion, absence.

ਵਿੱਤ (vitt) *n m* Finance.

ਵਿਥ (vitth) *n f* Distance, difference, space.

ਵਿਦਰੋਹੀ (vidrohee) *a* Rebellious.

ਵਿਦਵਾਨ (vidwaan) *n m* Scholar, learned person.

ਵਿਦਾ (vidaa) *n f* Farewell, adieu, departure; ~ਈ Parting, departure, send off.

ਵਿਦਿਆ (vidiyaa) *n f* Education, instruction, learning, knowledge, study; ~ਰਥੀ Student, pupil; ~ਲਾ School, educational institution.

ਵਿਦੂਸ਼ਕ (vidooshak) *n m* Buffon, clown.

ਵਿਦੇਸ਼ (videsh) *n m* Foreign country.

ਵਿਦੇਸ਼ੀ (videshee) *n m a* Foreigner; Foreign, aline.

ਵਿਧਾਤਾ (vidhaataa) *n m* Maker, God, providence.

ਵਿਧਾਨ (vidhaan) *n m* Legislation, constitution.

ਵਿਧੀ (vidhee) *n f* Method, manner.

ਵਿਨ੍ਹੰਣਾ (vinnhnaa) *v* To pierce, to perforate.

ਵਿਨਾਸ਼ (vinaash) *n m* Destruction, ruin, annihilation, disaster.

ਵਿਪਖ (vipakh) *n m* Opposition.

ਵਿੱਪਖੀ (vipakhee) *a* Opponent, antagonist, antagonistic; Hostile, opposing.

ਵਿਫਲ (viphal) *a* Unsuccessful, fruitless, vain; ~ਤਾ Failure, uselessness.

ਵਿਭਚਾਰ (vibhchaar) *n m* Adultery, fornication, prostitution.

ਵਿਭਾਗ (vibhaag) *n m* Department.

ਵਿਭਾਗੀ (vibhaagee) *a* Departmental.

ਵਿਭਾਜਨ (vibhaajan) *n m* Division.

ਵਿਮਾਨ (vimaan) *n m* Aeroplane; ~ਚਾਲਣ Aerial navigation; ~ਚਾਲਕ Pilot.

ਵਿਮੋਚਨ (vimochan) *n m* Release, acquittal.

ਵਿਰਲਾ (virlaa) *a* Rare.

ਵਿਰਾਸਤ (viraasat) *n f* Inheritance, heredity, legacy.

ਵਿਰਾਨਾ (viraanaa) *n m* Ruins, deserted place.

ਵਿਰਾਮ (viraam) *n m* Stoppage, respite, cessation, prorogation.

ਵਿਰੇਚਨ (virechan) *n m* Purgation.

ਵਿਰੋਧ (virodh) *n m* Hostility, resistance, discord, opposition, discrepancy contradiction, constrast.

ਵਿਰੋਧੀ (virodhee) *a n m* Opposing, antagonistic; Hostile.

ਵਿਲਕਣਾ (vilaknaa) *v* To sob, to weep, to lament, to cry.

ਵਿਵਹਾਰ (vivhaar) *n m* Behaviour; Conduct

ਵਿਵਾਦ (vivaad) *n m* Controversy, dispute; ~ਗ੍ਰਸਤ disputed, controversial.

ਵਿਵੇਕ (vivek) *n m* Discretion, reason; ~ਸ਼ੀਲ Rational; ~ਹੀਨ Irrational, unreasonable.

ਵਿਵੇਕੀ (vivekee) *a* Discretionary.

ਵੀ (vee) *adv* As well as, even.

ਵੀਹ (veeh) *a* Twenty.

ਵੀਟਣਾ (veetnaa) *v* To spill, to throw away.

ਵੀਰ (veer) *n m* a Brother; Brave, gallant, valiant.

ਵੀਰਾਨ (veeraan) *a* Deserted, desolate, uninhabitated; ~ਕਰਨਾ To lay waste, to devastate.

ਵੇਸਣ (vesan) *n m* Gramflour.

ਵੇਖਣਾ (vekhnaa) *v* To see, to look, to observe, to view.

ਵੇਚਣਾ (vechnaa) *v* To sell, to dispose of, to vend.

ਵੇਦੀ (vedee) *n f* Altar.

ਵੇਰਵਾ (vervaa) *n m* Detail, particulars, description.

ਵੇਲਾ (velaa) *n m* Time, hour, occasion; **ਵੱਡਾ**~ Morning.

ਵੇੜਨਾ (vernaa) *v* To encircle, to enclose, to collect (scattered animals), to hem in fold.

ਵੇੜ੍ਹਾ (verhaa) *n m* Compound, courtyard; Patio.

ਵੈਣ (vain) *n m* Dirge, funeral song, threnody.

ਵੈਰ (vair) *n m* Enmity, ill will, hostility; **ਜੱਦੀ**~ Vendetta; ~**ਕੱਢਣਾ** To take revenge, to retaliate; ~**ਮੁੱਲ ਲੈਣਾ** To create bad bood.

ਵੈਰੀ (vairee) *n m* Enemy, foe, hostile person.

ਵੈਰਾਗ (vairaag) *n m* Renunciation, alienation, dejection, disconsolation.

ੜ

ੜ Thirtyfifth letter of Gurmukhi alphabets, pronounced as 'ṛaaṛaa'.

ੜਾੜ (ṛaaṛ) *n f* Quarrel, dispute, wrangle, fight.

ENGLISH-PUNJABI
DICTIONARY

ENGLISH-PUNJABI
DICTIONARY

A

A, **a** (ਏਇ) *n* ਰੋਮਨ ਵਰਣਮਾਲਾ ਦਾ ਪਹਿਲਾ ਅੱਖਰ, ਪਹਿਲੀ ਗੱਲ

a, **an** (ਅ, ਅਨ) *a* ਇਕ, ਕੋਈ ਇਕ, ਕੋਈ; ਫ਼ੀ, ਪ੍ਰਤੀ

A 1, A one (ਏਇ'ਵਅੱਨ) *a* ਉੱਤਮ, ਸ੍ਰੇਸ਼ਠ

aback (ਅ'ਬੈਕ) adv ਪਿੱਛੇ, ਪਿਛਲੇ ਪਾਸੇ, ਪਿਠ, ਵੱਲ, ਹਟਦਾ, ਪਿਛਾਂਹ ਨੂੰ; **taken~** ਹੈਰਾਨ , ਡੌਰ-ਭੌਰ, ਚਕ੍ਰਿਤ

abandon (ਅ'ਬੈਂ ਡਅਨ)*v n* ਛੱਡਣਾ, ਛੱਡ ਦੇਣਾ; ਤੱਜਣਾ, ਤਿਆਗਣਾ, (ਦੇ) ਹਵਾਲੇ ਕਰਨਾ, ਖਹਿੜਾ ਛੱਡ ਦੇਣਾ, ਕਿਸੇ ਜਜ਼ਬੇ ਜਾਂ ਵਾਸਨਾ ਅਧੀਨ ਹੋਣਾ, ਸਾਥ ਛੱਡਣਾ; ਤਿਆਗ; **~ed** ਛੱਡਿਆ, ਤਿਆਗਿਆ, ਵੀਰਾਨ, ਤੱਜਿਆ, ਲੁੱਚਾ-ਲਫ਼ੰਗਾ; **~ment** ਤਿਆਗ, ਛੱਡ-ਛਡਾ; ਬੇਪਰਵਾਹੀ

abase (ਅ'ਬੇਇਸ) *v* ਨਿਰਾਦਰੀ ਕਰਨੀ, ਬੇਕਦਰੀ ਕਰਨੀ; **~ment** ਨਿਰਾਦਰੀ, ਅਨਾਦਰ, ਬੇਕਦਰੀ

abask (ਅ'ਬਾਸਕ) *adv* ਧੁੱਪੇ

abate (ਅ'ਬੇਇਟ) *v* ਘਟਾਉਣਾ, ਘਟਣਾ, ਮੱਧਮ ਕਰਨਾ, ਮੱਧਮ ਹੋਣਾ, ਮੱਠਾ ਕਰਨਾ, ਮੱਠਾ ਪੈਣਾ, (ਰੋਗ ਦਾ) ਘੱਟ ਹੋਣਾ, ਮੋੜਾ ਪੈਣਾ; ਕਟੌਤੀ ਕਰਨੀ; **~ment** ਕਮੀ

abbe (ਐਬੇਇ) *n* ਮਹੰਤ

abbey (ਐਬਿ) *n* ਮੱਠ

abbot (ਐਬਅਟ) *n* ਮਹੰਤ, ਮੱਠ ਦਾ ਸੁਆਮੀ

abbreviate (ਅ'ਬਰੀਵ੍ਇਏਇਟ) *v a* ਸੰਖੇਪ ਕਰਨਾ, ਛੋਟਾ ਰੂਪ ਦੇਣਾ; ਸਾਰ ਕੱਢਣਾ; ਸੰਖਿਪਤ, ਸੰਖੇਪ; **~d** ਸੰਖਿਪਤ, ਸੰਖੇਪ, ਕੱਟਿਆ-ਵੱਢਿਆ

abbreviation (ਅਬਰੀਵਿਏਇਸ਼ਨ) *n* ਛੋਟਾ ਰੂਪ, ਸੰਖੇਪ, ਸੰਖਿਪਤ ਰੂਪ

ABC (ਏਇ ਬੀ ਸੀ) *n* ਵਰਣਮਾਲਾ, ਊੜਾ-ਐੜਾ; ਵਿਸ਼ੈ ਸਬੰਧੀ ਮੁੱਢਲੀਆ ਗੱਲਾਂ, ਆਰੰਭਕ ਜਾਣਕਾਰੀ

abdicate ('ਐਬਡਿਕੇਇਟ) *v* ਪਦ ਜਾਂ ਅਧਿਕਾਰ ਦਾ ਤਿਆਗਣਾ, ਰਾਜ-ਕਾਜ ਤਿਆਗਣਾ

abdication ('ਐਬਡਿ'ਕੇਇਸ਼ਨ) *n* ਪਦ-ਤਿਆਗ, ਰਾਜ-ਤਿਆਗ

abdomen ('ਐਬਡਅਮਅਨ) *n* ਢਿੱਡ, ਉਦਰ; ਕੀੜਿਆਂ ਆਦਿ ਦਾ ਬੂੰਡਾ

abdominal ('ਐਬ'ਡੌਮਿਨਲ) *a* ਢਿੱਡ ਦਾ, ਢਿੱਡ ਨਾਲ ਸਬੰਧਤ

abdominous (ਐਬ'ਡੌਮਿਨਅਸ) *a* ਢਿੱਡਲ, ਵੱਡੇ ਢਿੱਡ ਵਾਲਾ

abduct (ਅਬਡਅੱਕਟ) *v* ਅਗਵਾ ਕਰਨਾ, ਅਪਹਰਣ ਕਰਨਾ, ਉਧਾਲਣਾ; **~ion** ਉਧਾਲਾ, ਅਗਵਾ, ਅਪਹਰਣ; ਸਰੀਰਕ ਅੰਗ ਦੇ ਟਿਕਾਣੇ ਤੋਂ ਹਟਣ ਦੀ ਕਿਰਿਆ; (ਤਰਕ) ਸੰਦੇਹਜਨਕ ਅਨੁਮਾਨ; **~or** ਉਧਾਲੂ, ਅਗਵਾ ਕਰਤਾ, ਭਜਾ ਲੈ ਜਾਣ ਵਾਲਾ; ਉੱਤਰਿਆ ਅੰਗ

abeyance (ਅ'ਬੇਇਅੰ ਸ) *n* ਮੁਲਤਵੀ ਕਰਨਾ, ਅੱਗੇ ਪਾਉਣ, ਆਰਜ਼ੀ ਰੋਕ, ਅਟਕਾਉ

abhor (ਅਬ'ਹੋ*) *v* ਘਿਰਣਾ ਕਰਨੀ, ਨਫ਼ਰਤ ਕਰਨੀ; **~rence** ਸਖ਼ਤ ਨਫ਼ਰਤ, ਘਿਰਣਾ; **~rent** ਘਿਣਾਉਣਾ, ਘਿਰਣਾਜਨਕ, ਭ੍ਰਿਸ਼ਟ, ਤਿਰਸਕਾਰਯੋਗ; ਅਸੰਗਤ, ਬੇਮੇਲ, ਅਢੁੱਕਵਾਂ

abide (ਅ'ਬਾਇਡ) *v* ਟਿਕੇ ਰਹਿਣਾ, ਸਥਿਰ ਰਹਿਣਾ, ਕਾਇਮ ਰਹਿਣਾ ਜਾਂ ਰੱਖਣਾ; ਸਹਿਣਾ,

ਝੱਲਣਾ, ਪਾਬੰਦ ਰਹਿਣਾ, ਪੱਕੇ ਰਹਿਣਾ, ਪਾਲਣਾ
ਕਰਨੀ

abiding (ਅ'ਬਾਇਡਿੰਛ) *a* ਪੱਕਾ, ਸਥਿਰ, ਟਿਕਵਾਂ,
ਚਿਰਸਥਾਈ, ਕਾਇਮ ਰਹਿਣ ਵਾਲਾ

ability (ਅ'ਬਿਲਅਟਿ) *n* ਯੋਗਤਾ, ਕਾਬਲੀਅਤ,
ਲਿਆਕਤ, ਕੁਸ਼ਲਤਾ, ਪ੍ਰਵੀਣਤਾ, ਸਮਰੱਥਾ, ਬਲ,
ਹੈਸੀਅਤ; ਪ੍ਰਤਿਭਾ

abject (ਐਬਜੈੱਕਟ) *a v n* ਨੀਚ, ਕਮੀਨਾ, ਮੰਦਾ,
ਹੀਣ, ਘਟੀਆ, ਮਾੜਾ, ਕਮੀਨਾ ਆਦਮੀ; ~ion
ਘਟੀਆਪਣ, ਖੁਆਰੀ; ~ness ਨੀਚਤਾ, ਹੀਣਤਾ

abjure (ਅਬ'ਜੁਅ*) *v* (ਤੋਂ) ਤੋਬਾ ਕਰਨੀ, (ਦੀ)
ਸਹੁੰ ਪਾਉਣੀ

ablative (ਐਬਲਅਟਿਵ੍) *a n* (ਵਿਆ) ਅਪਾਦਾਨ
ਕਾਰਕ, ਸੰਸਕ੍ਰਿਤ ਵਿਆਕਰਨ ਵਿਚ ਪੰਜਵੀਂ
ਵਿਭਕਤੀ

ablaze (ਅਬਲੇਇਜ਼) *a adv pred* ਮੱਚਦਾ,
ਭੜਕਦਾ, ਉਤੇਜਤ

able ('ਏਇਬਲ) *a* ਯੋਗ, ਸਮਰੱਥ, ਪ੍ਰਵੀਣ,
ਲਾਇਕ, ਕਾਬਲ, ਕੁਸ਼ਲ, ਗੁਣੀ; ਹੰਢਿਆ;
~bodied ਤਕੜਾ, ਰਿਸ਼ਟ-ਪੁਸ਼ਟ, ਬਲਵਾਨ

ablution (ਅ'ਬਲੂਸ਼ਨ) *n* (ਆਮ ਤੌਰ ਤੇ ਬਹੁ
ਵਚਨ) ਪੂਜ-ਇਸ਼ਨਾਨਾ, ਨਹਾਉਣ-ਧੋਣ, ਵੁਜ਼ੂ,
ਸ਼ੁੱਧੀ

abnegate ('ਅਬੈਨਿਗੇਇਟ) *v* ਮਨ ਮਾਰਨਾ,
ਪਰਹੇਜ਼ ਕਰਨਾ, ਛੱਡ ਦੇਣਾ, (ਅਧਿਕਾਰ ਆਦਿ
ਨੂੰ) ਤਿਆਗਣਾ

abnegation (ਐਬਨਗੇਸ਼ਨ) *n* ਸੰਜਮ, ਪਰਹੇਜ਼,
ਤਿਆਗ

abnormal (ਐਬ'ਨੌਰਮਲ) *a* ਅਸਾਧਾਰਨ ,
ਵਿਲੱਖਣ, ਵਚਿੱਤਰ, ਅਸੁਭਾਵਕ, ਅਸਚਰਜ,
ਨਿਯਮ ਵਿਰੁੱਧ, ਕਸੂਤਾ, ਕੁਢੱਬਾ; ~ity

ਅਸਧਾਰਨਤਾ, ਵਿਲੱਖਣਤਾ, ਵਿਚਿੱਤਰਤਾ,
ਅਸੁਭਾਵਕਤਾ, ਬੇਕਾਇਦਗੀ, ਅਸਚਰਜਤਾ,
ਵੱਖਰਾਪਣ

aboard (ਅ'ਬੋ:ਡ) *adv prep* (ਜਹਾਜ਼ ਜਾਂ
ਗੱਡੀ) ਵਿਚ; (ਇਕ ਜਹਾਜ਼ ਦਾ ਦੂਜੇ ਜਹਾਜ਼ ਦੇ)
ਨੇੜੇ (ਹੋਣਾ), ਨਾਲ ਨਾਲ

abode (ਅੁ'ਬਅਉਡ) *n* ਘਰ, ਨਿਵਾਸ-ਸਥਾਨ,
ਮਕਾਨ ; ਟਿਕਾਣਾ, ਰਹਿਣ ਦੀ ਥਾਂ, ਰਿਹਾਇਸ਼

abolish (ਅ'ਬੌਲਿਸ਼) *v* ਅੰਤ ਕਰਨਾ, ਮਨਸੁਖ
ਕਰਨਾ, ਬੰਦ ਕਰਨਾ, ਹਟਾਉਣਾ, ਰੱਦਣਾ
(ਰਿਵਾਜ ਆਦਿ ਨੂੰ) ਤੋੜਨਾ; ~ment ਅੰਤ,
ਖ਼ਾਤਮਾ, ਮਨਸੁਖੀ, ਸੰਕੁੜੀ; (ਗੁਲਾਮੀ ਦੀ ਪ੍ਰਥਾ
ਦਾ) ਕਾਨੂੰਨ ਰਾਹੀਂ ਅੰਤ

abominable (ਅ'ਬੌਮਿਨਅਬਲ) *a* ਘਿਰਣਾਜ ਨਕ,
ਗੰਦ, ਕੁਹਜਾ, ਨਿੰਦਾਯੋਗ, ਭੈੜਾ ; ਕੁਲੱਛਣਾ

abomination (ਅ'ਬੌਮਿ'ਨੇਇਸ਼ਨ) *n* ਘਿਰਣਾ,
ਨਫ਼ਰਤ, ਕੁਰਹਿਤ; ਘਿਰਣਾਯੋਗ ਕੰਮ ਜਾਂ ਆਦਤ

aboriginal ('ਐਬਅ'ਰਿਜਅਨਲ) *n a*
ਆਦਿਵਾਸੀ, ਮੁਢਲੀ ਵਸਤੁ ਜਾਂ ਚੀਜ਼, ਪ੍ਰਾਚੀਨ,
ਜਾਂਗਲੀ; ~ity ਆਦਿਕਾਲੀਨਤਾ; ~s
ਆਦਿਵਾਸੀ, ਕਿਸੇ ਦੇਸ਼ ਦੇ ਮੂਲ ਵਸਨੀਕ

aborigines ('ਐਬਅ'ਰਿਜਅਨੀਜ਼) *n pl*
ਆਦਿਵਾਸੀ, ਪੁਰਾਣੇ ਜਾਂਗਲੀ ਲੋਕ

abort (ਅ'ਬੋਟ) *v* (ਪਸ਼ੂਆਂ ਦਾ) ਤੂਣਾ, ਗਰਭਪਾਤ
ਹੋਣਾ; ਮੁਰਝਾ ਜਾਣਾ; (ਯੋਜਨਾ ਆਦਿ) ਤਿਰਸ਼
ਫਿਸ ਹੋਣਾ, ਠੱਪ ਹੋਣਾ; ~ion ਪਸ਼ੂਆਂ ਦੇ ਤੂਣ
ਦੀ ਕਿਰਿਆ, ਗਰਭਪਾਤ

abound (ਅ'ਬਾਉਂਡ) *v* ਭਰਪੂਰ ਹੋਣਾ, ਬਹੁਤਾਤ
ਹੋਣੀ, ਕਾਫ਼ੀ ਹੋਣਾ, ਰੱਜੇ-ਪੁੱਜੇ ਹੋਣਾ, ਕਿਸੇ ਸਥਾਨ
ਦਾ ਭਰਿਆ ਹੋਣਾ, ਛਲਕਣਾ

about (ਅ'ਬਾਉਟ) *adv prep* ਸੰਬੰਧ ਵਿਚ,

ਬਾਰੇ, ਵਿਸ਼ੇ ਵਿਚ, ਬਾਬਤ; ਪ੍ਰਿਮ ਕੇ, ਲਗਭਗ, ਤੇ, ਲਾਗੇ, ਕੋਲ, ਦੁਆਲੇ, ਚੁਫੇਰੇ, ਇੱਧਰ-ਉੱਧਰ, ਨੇੜੇ-ਤੇੜੇ; **be~** ਕਰਨ ਲੱਗਣਾ, ਆਹਰ ਵਿਚ ਹੋਣਾ; **bring~** ਕਰਾਉਣਾ, ਕਰਵਾ ਲੈਣਾ, ਹੋਂਦ ਵਿਚ ਲਿਆਉਣਾ; **go~** ਕਰਨ ਲੱਗਣਾ, ਕਰਨ ਦੇ ਆਹਰ ਵਿਚ ਲੱਗਣਾ

above (ਅ'ਬਅੱਵ੍) *adv prep* ਉੱਤੇ, ਉੱਪਰ, ਉਤਾਂਹ, ਉੱਪਰ ਲਿਖਤ, ਉਪਰੋਕਤ, ਉਕਤ, ਸਿਰ ਉੱਤੇ, ਕੰਠੇ ਉੱਤੇ, ਉਤਲੇ ਪਾਸਿਓਂ ਆਉਂਦਾ (ਪਾਣੀ, ਨਦੀ, ਸੜਕ), ਆਕਾਸ਼ ਵਿਚ; ਪਰਲੋਕ ਵਿਚ; **~all** ਸਭ ਤੋਂ ਵੱਧ ਇਹ ਕਿ; **~board** ਖੁੱਲ੍ਹਮ-ਖੁੱਲ੍ਹਾ, ਸਪਸ਼ਟ ਰੂਪ ਵਿਚ, ਪਰਗਟ ਰੂਪ ਵਿਚ, ਖਰਾ, ਈਮਾਨਦਾਰ; **~ground** ਜੀਉਂਦਾ-ਜਾਗਦਾ, ਜਾਨਦਾਰ; **~mentioned** ਉੱਤੇ ਦੱਸਿਆ ਜਾਂ ਦਿੱਤਾ, ਉਪਰੋਕਤ, ਉਕਤ, ਉਪਰਲਿਖਤ; **~measure** ਅਣਮਿਣਵਾਂ, ਬੇਹਿਸਾਬ, ਬੇਹੱਦ; **~par** ਅੰਕਤ ਮੁੱਲ ਤੋਂ ਵੱਧ, ਸਧਾਰਨ ਤੋਂ ਵਧੇਰੇ, ਵਧ ਕੇ; **over and~** ਇਸ ਤੋਂ ਇਲਾਵਾ, ਇਸ ਤੋਂ ਛੁੱਟ, ਅਤੇ ਨਾਲ ਹੀ

abrasion (ਅਬਰੇਇਯਨ) *n* ਰਗੜ, ਘਸਤ, ਘਿਸਾਈ, ਖੁਰਕ; ਖੁਰਚਨ ਨਾਲ ਪਿਆ ਜ਼ਖਮ

abrasive (ਅਬਰੇਇਸਿਵ੍) *a n* ਘਸਵਾਂ; ਰਗੜਨ ਵਾਲੀ ਵਸਤੂ

abreast (ਅਬਰੈਸਟ) *adv* ਨਾਲ-ਨਾਲ, ਬਰਾਬਰ ਤੇ; ਸਮੇਂ ਦੇ ਨਾਲ ਜਾਂ ਅਨੁਸਾਰ

abridge (ਅ'ਬਰਿਜ) *v* ਸੰਖੇਪ ਕਰਨਾ, ਛੋਟਾ ਕਰਨਾ, ਘਟਾਉਣਾ, ਖੁਲਾਸਾ ਕਰਨਾ; (ਅਧਿਕਾਰ ਜਾਂ ਵਸਤੂ) ਵਾਂਝਿਆ ਕਰਨਾ; **~d** ਸੰਖਿਪਤ, ਛੋਟਾ; **~ment** ਸੰਖੇਪ, ਖੁਲਾਸਾ, ਨਿਚੋੜ, ਸਾਰ; ਸੰਖੇਪੀਕਰਨ

abroad (ਅ'ਬਰੋਡ੍) *adv n* ਬਾਹਰ, ਪਰਦੇਸ,

ਦੂਰ-ਦੁਰਾਡੀ ਥਾਂ

abrogate (ˈਐਬਰਅ(ਉ)ˈਗੇਇਸ਼ਟ) *v* ਰੱਦ ਕਰਨਾ, ਮਨਸੂਖ ਕਰਨਾ, ਨਿਰਾਕਰਨ ਕਰਨਾ, (ਕਾਨੂੰਨ ਆਦਿ ਰਿਵਾਜ ਨੂੰ) ਹਟਾ ਦੇਣਾ, ਭੰਗ ਕਰਨਾ, ਬੰਦ ਕਰਨਾ; **~d** ਰੱਦਿਆ, ਹਟਾਇਆ

abrogation (ˈਐਬਰਅ(ਉ)ˈਗੇਇਸ਼ਨ) *n* ਖੰਡਨ , ਮਨਸੂਖੀ, ਨਿਰਾਕਰਨ, ਅੰਤ

abrupt (ਅ'ਬਰਅੱਪਟ) *a n* ਅਚਨਚੇਤ, ਅਚਾਨਕ; ਅਸੰਗਤ; ਬੇਢੰਗਾ, ਬੇਜੋੜ; (ਚੜ੍ਹਾਈ) ਸੁਖੜ, (ਬਨ) ਰੁੰਡ, (ਧਰਤੀ ਵਿਚੋਂ) ਅਚਨਚੇਤ ਫੁੱਟਿਆ ਹੋਇਆ

abruption (ਅ'ਬਰਅੱਪਸ਼ਨ) *n* ਨਿਖੇਤਰ , ਕਿਸੇ ਅੰਗ ਦੇ ਝੜਨ ਦੀ ਕਿਰਿਆ

abruptly (ਅ'ਬਰਅੱਪਟਲਿ) *adv* ਅਚਾਨਕ, ਝਟਪਟ

abscond (ਅ'ਬਸਕੌਂਡ੍) *v* ਫਰਾਰ ਹੋ ਜਾਣਾ, ਭਗੌੜਾ ਹੋਣਾ, ਨਠ ਜਾਣਾ, ਚੋਰੀ ਛਿੱਪੀ ਭੱਜ ਜਾਣਾ, ਕਾਨੂੰਨ ਦੀ ਮਾਰ ਤੋਂ ਬਚਣ ਲਈ ਕਿਧਰੇ ਲੁਕ-ਛਿਪ ਜਾਣਾ; **~ence** ਫਰਾਰੀ, ਭਗੌੜਾਪਨ; **~er** ਭਗੌੜਾ, ਫਰਾਰ, ਕਾਨੂੰਨ ਦੀ ਮਾਰ ਤੋਂ ਬਚਣ ਲਈ ਛਿਪਿਆ

absence (ˈਐਬਸਅੰਸ) *n* ਗੈਰਹਾਜ਼ਰੀ, ਅਣਉਪਸਥਿਤੀ; ਅਣਹੋਂਦ, ਘਾਟ; ਅਭਾਵ ਬੇਧਿਆਨੀ, ਬੇਖ਼ਿਆਲੀ

absent (ਅਬ'ਸੈਂਟ) *v a* ਗੈਰਹਾਜ਼ਰ ਹੋਣਾ, ਗਾਇਬ ਹੋਣਾ, ਲੁਕ ਜਾਣਾ; ਗੈਰਹਾਜ਼ਰ, ਅਣਉਪਸਥਿਤ, ਅਚੇਤ, ਬੇਧਿਆਨ; **~ee** ਗੈਰਹਾਜ਼ਰ ਵਿਅਕਤੀ; **~minded** ਬੇਧਿਆਨਾ, ਅਚੇਤ, ਅਵੇਸਲਾ, ਭਰਾਂਤ ਚਿੱਤ, ਭੁੱਲਿਆ-ਭੁੱਲਿਆ; **~mindedness** ਬੇਧਿਆਨੀ, ਭਰਾਂਤੀ, ਅਚੇਤਤਾ, ਅਵੇਸਲਾਪਣ

absolute (ˈਐਬਸਅਲੂਟ) *a* ਪੂਰਾ, ਨਿਰਾ, ਉੱਕਾ

ਕੇਵਲ; ਨਿਰਪੇਖ, ਪੂਰਨ , ਸੰਪੂਰਨ; ਸਰਬ ਅਧਿਕਾਰੀ; ~ly ਪੂਰਨਭਾਂਤ, ਪੂਰੀ ਤਰ੍ਹਾਂ, ਪਰਮ, ਆਪਣੇ ਆਪ, ਬਿਲਕੁਲ, ਸੁਤੰਤਰਤਾ ਨਾਲ ਬਿਨਾ ਕਿਸੇ ਸ਼ਰਤ ਤੋਂ, ਮੂਲੋਂ, ਉੱਕਾ ਹੀ; ~ness ਨਿਰਪੇਖਤਾ, ਅਸੀਮਤਾ, ਨਿਰੰਕੁਸ਼ਤਾ, ਖ਼ੁਦਮੁਖ਼ਤਾਰੀ, ਪੂਰਨ ਅਧਿਕਾਰ

absorb (ਐਬ'ਸੋਬ) v ਹਜ਼ਮ ਕਰਨਾ, ਰਚ ਲੈਣਾ, ਆਤਮਸਾਤ ਕਰਨਾ, ਲੀਨ ਕਰਨਾ, ਸਮਾ ਲੈਣਾ, ਖਪਾ ਲੈਣਾ, ਤਦਰੂਪ ਕਰਨਾ; ~ed ਚੁਸਿਆ, ਇਕਮਿਕ ਕੀਤਾ; ਰਚਿਆ; ਰਚਾਇਆ, ਲੀਨ, ਮਸਤ, ਮਗਨ ; (ਜਿਵੇਂ ਸਿਆਹੀ-ਚੂਸ); ~ing ਮਨਮੋਹਕ, ਆਕਰਸ਼ਕ, ਮਨਮੋਹਣਾ, ਰੋਚਕ, ਦਿਲ-ਖਿੱਚਵਾਂ, ਦਿਲਚਸਪ

absorption (ਅਬ'ਸੋ:ਪਸ਼ਨ) n ਚੂਸਣ, ਸੋਖਣ ਜਾਂ ਹਜ਼ਮ ਕਰਨ , ਜਜ਼ਬ ਹੋਣਾ

abstain (ਅਬ'ਸਟੇਇਨ) v ਪਰਹੇਜ਼, ਕਰਨਾ, ਦੂਰ ਰਹਿਣਾ, ਅਲੱਗ , ਪਰੇ ਰਹਿਣਾ, ਬਚਣਾ, ਲਾਂਭੇ ਰਹਿਣਾ, ਪਾਸੇ ਰਹਿਣਾ, ਗੁਰੇਜ਼ ਕਰਨਾ

abstract ('ਐਬਸਟਰੈਕਟ, ਐਬ'ਸਟਰੈਕਟ) a n v ਭਾਵਵਾਚੀ, ਭਾਵ-ਮਈ, ਸੂਖਮ, ਅਮੂਰਤ, ਅਭੌਤਕ, ਅਵਿਅਕਤ, ਨਿਰਪੇਖ, ਸੰਖਿਪਤ, ਤੱਤ, ਸਾਰ, ਖੁਲਾਸਾ, ਸਾਰਾਂਸ਼, ਸੰਖੇਪ; ਅਸਪਸ਼ਟ, ਸਾਰ-ਸੂਚੀ; ਸਾਰ ਕੱਢਣਾ; ~ed ਮਗਨ, ਲੀਨ ਅਮੂਰਤੀਕ੍ਰਿਤ; ਸੰਖੇਪੀਕ੍ਰਿਤ; ਅਲੱਗ ਕੀਤਾ, ਘਟਾਇਆ; ~ion ਕਲਪਨਾ, ਅਮੂਰਤਤਾ; ਬੇਖਬਰੀ, ਬੇਖਿਆਲੀ, ਕਢਾਅ

absurd (ਅਬ'ਸਅ:ਡ) a ਹਾਸੋਹੀਣਾ, ਬੇਢੰਗਾ, ਬੇਤੁਕਾ, ਬੇਢੱਬਾ, ਉਟ-ਪਟਾਂਗ, ਬੇਹੁਦਾ, ਲੱਚਰ ਫ਼ਜ਼ੂਲ; ~ity ਵਿਅਰਥਤਾ, ਵਿਵੇਕਹੀਣਤਾ

abundance (ਅਬਅੰਡਅੰਸ) n ਬਹੁਲਤਾ, ਬਹੁਤਾਤ, ਭਰਮਾਰ; ਸਮਰਿਧੀ

abundant (ਅਬਅੰਡਅੰਟ) a ਭਰਪੂਰ, ਬਹੁਤ, ਘਣਾ, ਮਾਲਾਮਾਲ, ਵਾਫ਼ਰ, ਅਤੀਅਧਿਕ, (ਨਾਲ) ਪਰਿਪੂਰਨ

abuse (ਅ'ਬਯੂਸ) n v ਗਾਲ੍ਹ, ਬਦਜ਼ਬਾਨੀ, ਦੁਰਵਿਹਾਰ, ਦੁਰਵਰਤੋਂ, ਦੁਰਪ੍ਯੋਗ; ਦੁਰਵਰਤੋਂ ਕਰਨੀ, ਅਜੋਗ ਵਰਤੋਂ; ਬੁਰਾ ਭਲਾ ਆਖਣਾ, ਗਾਲ੍ਹ ਕੱਢਣੀ

abusive (ਅਬਯੂਸਿਵ) a ਅਸ਼ਲੀਲ, ਬਦਜ਼ਬਾਨ ਅਪਮਾਨਜਨਕ, ਨਿੰਦਾਪੂਰਨ; ~ness ਅਸ਼ਲੀਲਤਾ, ਅਪਮਾਨ, ਬਦਜ਼ਬਾਨੀ

abyss (ਅ'ਬਿਸ) ਡੂੰਘ, ਰਸਾਤਲ, ਨਰਕ; ਖਾਈ

academic (ਐਕਅ'ਡੈਮਿਕ) a n ਵਿੱਦਿਅਕ, ਇਲਮੀ, ਸਿਧਾਂਤਕ, ਸ਼ਾਸਤਰੀ, ਅਕਾਦਮਿਕ; ਅਫ਼ਲਾਤੂਨ ਦੀ ਅਕਾਦਮੀ ਦਾ ਮੈਂਬਰ; ~council ਵਿੱਦਿਆ-ਪਰਿਸ਼ਦ; ~year ਵਿੱਦਿਅਕ-ਸਾਲ

academy (ਅ'ਕੈਡਅਮਿ) n ਅਕਾਦਮੀ; ਪਲੇਟੋਵਾਦ, ਪਲੇਟੋਵਾਦੀ; ਸਿੱਖਿਆ-ਸੰਸਥਾ, ਵਿਸ਼ੇਸ਼ ਪ੍ਰਕਾਰ ਦੇ ਹੁਨਰ ਦੀ ਸਿੱਖਿਆ ਦੇਣ ਦੀ ਥਾਂ

accede (ਐਕ'ਸੀਡ) v ਸਵੀਕਾਰ ਕਰਨਾ, ਮਨਜ਼ੂਰ ਕਰਨਾ, ਕਬੂਲ ਕਰਨਾ, ਸੰਮਿਲਤ ਹੋਣਾ, ਸਹਿਮਤ ਹੋਣਾ, ਮੰਨਣਾ, ਰਾਜ਼ੀ ਹੋਣਾ, ਮੰਨ ਲੈਣਾ, ਗ੍ਰਹਿਣ ਕਰਨਾ

accelerate (ਅਕ'ਸੈੱਲਅਰੇਇਟ) v ਚਾਲ ਵਧਾ-ਉਣੀ, ਗਤੀ ਤੇਜ਼ ਕਰਨੀ, ਵੇਗਮਈ ਹੋਣਾ, ਜਲਦੀ ਕਰਨਾ; ~d ਤੀਬਰ, ਵੇਗਮਈ, ਤੇਜ਼, ਤੀਖਣ

acceleration (ਅਕ'ਸੈੱਲਅਰੇਇਸ਼ਨ) n ਗਤੀ ਵਿਚ ਵਾਧਾ, ਗਤੀ-ਵਰਧਨ, ਵੇਗ-ਵ੍ਰਿਧੀ

accelerator (ਅਕ'ਸੈੱਲਅਰੇਇਟਅਾ") n ਗਤੀ ਵਰਧਕ, ਵੇਗ-ਵਰਧਕ, ਐਕਸਲਰੇਟਰ

accent ('ਐਕ'ਸੈਂਟ/ਐਕ'ਸੈਂਟ) *n v* ਸਵਰ, ਸੁਰ; ਸੁਰਘਾਤ, ਧੁਨੀ-ਚਿੰਨ੍ਹ, ਸਵਰ-ਚਿੰਨ੍ਹ; ਲਹਿਜ਼ਾ, ਸਵਰ-ਉਚਾਰਨਾ

accept (ਅਕ'ਸੈਂਪਟ) *v* ਸਵੀਕਾਰ ਕਰਨਾ, ਅੰਗੀਕਾਰ ਕਰਨਾ, ਪਰਵਾਨ ਕਰਨਾ, ਮੰਨਣਾ, ਮਨਜ਼ੂਰ ਕਰਨਾ, ਲੈਣਾ, ਗ੍ਰਹਿਣ ਕਰਨਾ; **~able** ਸਵੀਕਾਰ ਕਰਨਯੋਗ, ਮੰਨਣਯੋਗ, ਪਰਵਾਨ ਕਰਨਯੋਗ; **~ance** ਸਵੀਕ੍ਰਿਤੀ, ਮਨਜ਼ੂਰੀ, ਪਰਵਾਨਗੀ, ਰਜ਼ਾਮੰਦੀ, ਮਾਨਤਾ, ਹੁੰਡੀ ਦੀ ਸਵੀਕ੍ਰਿਤੀ; **~ed** ਸਵੀਕ੍ਰਿਤ, ਮਨਜ਼ੂਰ, ਪਰਵਾਨਤ, ਮੰਨਿਆ ਹੋਇਆ

access (ਐਕਸੈੱਸ) *n* ਪਹੁੰਚ, ਰਸਾਈ, ਪ੍ਰਵੇਸ਼, ਸਬੀਲ, ਉਪਾਉ; **~aibility** ਸੁਲੱਭਤਾ, ਪ੍ਰਵੇਸ਼-ਯੋਗਤਾ, ਪਹੁੰਚ-ਯੋਗਤਾ, ਸੁਗਮਤਾ

accessible (ਅਕਸੈੱਸਅਬਲ) *a* ਸੁਲੱਭ, ਪ੍ਰਵੇਸ਼ਯੋਗ, ਸੁਗਮ

accessory (ਅਕ'ਸੈੱਸਅਰਿ) *n a* ਉਪਸਾਧਨ; ਗੌਣ, ਸਹਾਇਕ, ਪੂਰਕ

accident ('ਐਕਸਿਡਅੰਟ) *n* ਦੁਰਘਟਨਾ, ਹਾਦਸਾ, ਘਟਨਾ, ਇਤਫ਼ਾਕ, ਵਾਕਿਆ; ਘੇਤਰਤੀਬੀ, ਕ੍ਰਮਹੀਨਤਾ; **~al** ਇਤਫ਼ਾਕੀਆ, ਰੱਬ-ਸਬੱਧੀ; ਅਕਾਰਨ, ਅਣਅਵੱਸ਼ਕ,

acclaim (ਅ'ਕਲੇਇਮ) *n v* ਜੈਕਾਰਾ, ਧੰਨ ਧੰਨ, ਜੈ-ਧੁਨੀ, ਸ਼ਲਾਘਾ, ਵਾਹ-ਵਾਹ ਕਰਨੀ, ਉਸਤਤ ਕਰਨੀ, ਸਲਾਹੁਣਾ; **~ation** ਸਮਰਥਨ, ਜੈ-ਧੁਨੀ, ਵਿਜੈ-ਘੋਸ਼ਣਾ, ਉਸਤਤ, ਸ਼ਲਾਘਾ, ਸਲਾਹੁਤਾ, ਜੈ ਜੈ ਕਾਰ

accommodate (ਅ'ਕੌਮਅਡੇਇਟ) *v* (ਦੀ) ਵਿਵਸਥਾ ਕਰਨਾ, ਮੁਆਫ਼ਕ ਕਰਨਾ, ਥਾਂ ਦੇਣੀ, ਸਮਾਈ ਕਰਨਾ, (ਹਾਲਾਤ ਆਦਿ ਨਾਲ) ਸਮਝੌਤਾ ਕਰਵਾਉਣਾ, ਅਨੁਕੂਲ ਕਰਨਾ

accommodating (ਅ'ਕੌਮਅਡੇਇਟਿਙ) *a* ਲਿਹਾਜ਼ ਪਾਲਣ ਵਾਲਾ, ਨਰਮ ਸੁਭਾਅ ਵਾਲਾ, ਲਚਕੀਲਾ, ਉਦਾਰ, ਮਿਹਰਬਾਨ, ਝੱਲਣ ਵਾਲਾ, ਮਿਲਾਪੜਾ, ਕੰਮ ਆਉਣ ਵਾਲਾ

accomodation (ਅ'ਕੌਮਅ'ਡੇਇਸ਼ਨ) *n* ਰਿਹਾਇਸ਼, ਨਿਵਾਸ, ਠਾਹਰ; (ਹਾਲਾਤ ਆਦਿ ਨਾਲ) ਸਮਝੌਤਾ, ਅਨੁਕੂਲਤਾ

accompany (ਅ'ਕਾਂਮਪਅਨਿ) *v* ਸਾਥ ਹੋਣਾ, ਸੰਗ ਕਰਨਾ, ਸਾਥ ਦੇਣਾ, (ਕਿਸੇ ਦੇ) ਨਾਲ ਜਾਣਾ, ਸ਼ਾਮਲ ਹੋਣਾ,

accomplish (ਅ'ਕਾਂਮਪਲਿਸ਼) *v* ਸਿਰੇ ਚਾੜ੍ਹਨਾ, ਪੂਰਾ ਕਰਨਾ, ਸੰਪੂਰਨ ਕਰਨਾ, ਸੰਪੰਨ ਕਰਨਾ, ਸਮਾਪਤ ਕਰਨਾ, ਨਿਬੇੜਨਾ; **~ed** ਨਿਪੁੰਨ, ਸੁੱਘੜ, ਸੁਰੱਜਾ, ਗੁਣਵਾਨ, ਸ਼ਾਇਸਤਾ, ਸਿਸ਼ਟ; **~ment** ਪੂਰਤੀ, ਸਿੱਧੀ; ਗੁਣ ਪ੍ਰਾਪਤੀ, ਕਮਾਲ

accord (ਅ'ਕੋਡ) *v* ਸਵੀਕ੍ਰਿਤੀ ਦੇਣੀ, ਪਰਵਾਨਗੀ ਦੇਣੀ, ਇਕ ਮੱਤ ਹੋਣਾ, ਮੇਲ ਖਾਣਾ; ਮੁਤਾਬਕ ਹੋਣਾ; ਅਨੁਕੂਲ ਹੋਣਾ, ਇਕ ਰੂਪ ਹੋਣਾ, ਇਕ ਸੁਰ ਹੋਣਾ; ਮਰਜ਼ੀ, ਸਵੀਕ੍ਰਿਤੀ, ਪਰਵਾਨਗੀ; ਮਿਲਾਪ, ਸੰਧੀ, ਇਕਰਾਰਨਾਮਾ; **~ance** ਇਕ ਰਾਇ, ਇਕ ਮੱਤ; ਮੇਲ-ਮਿਲਾਪ, ਪਰਵਾਨਤਾ, ਰਾਜ਼ੀਨਾਮਾ, ਮੁਤਾਬਕ, ਅਨੁਸਾਰ; **In ~ance with** ਦੇ ਅਨੁਸਾਰ, ਦੇ ਅਨੁਰੂਪ, ਦੇ ਮੁਤਾਬਕ

according (ਅ'ਕੋਡਿਙ) *adv* ਅਨੁਸਾਰ, ਮੁਤਾਬਕ, ਜਿਹਾ ਕਿ, ਵਾਂਗ, ਜਿਵੇਂ ਕਿ; **~as** ਜਿਵੇਂ ਕਿ, ਜਿਸ ਤਰ੍ਹਾਂ, ਮਾਨੋ; **~to** ਦੇ ਅਨੁਸਾਰ, ਦੇ ਮੁਤਾਬਕ; **~ly** ਇਸ ਲਈ, ਇਸ ਅਨੁਸਾਰ, ਸੋ; ਤਦਾਨੁਕੂਲ, ਤਦਾਨੁਰੂਪ

account (ਅ'ਕਾਉਂਟ) *n v* ਹਿਸਾਬ-ਕਿਤਾਬ, ਲੇਖਾ, ਚਿੱਠਾ, ਜਮ੍ਹਾਂ-ਖ਼ਰਚ, ਖਾਤਾ, ਕੈਫ਼ੀਅਤ, ਤਫ਼ਸੀਲ, ਬਿਰਤਾਂਤ, ਵਿਵਰਣ; ਗਿਣਤੀ ਕਰਨੀ, ਗਿਣਨਾ;

ਕਰਨ, ਨਮਿਤ; ਲੇਖਾਜੋਖਾ ਵੇਖਣ, ਵਿਚਾਰ
ਕਰਨ'; give ~ of ਸਪਸ਼ਟ ਕਰਨ, ਕਾਰਨ
ਦੱਸਣਾ; keep ~s ਹਿਸਾਬ ਕਿਤਾਬ ਕਰਨ; on
~ of ਦੇ ਕਾਰਨ, ਫਲਸਰੂਪ; on no~ ਕਦੀ ਨਹੀਂ;
ਕਿਸੇ ਤਰ੍ਹਾਂ ਵੀ ਨਹੀਂ; take into~ ਵਿਚਾਰਨਾ,
ਧਿਆਨ ਵਿਚ ਰੱਖਣਾ; ~able ਉੱਤਰਦਾਈ,
ਜ਼ੁੰਮੇਵਾਰ, ਜਵਾਬਦੇਹ; ~ancy ਲੇਖਾਕਾਰੀ,
ਹਿਸਾਬ-ਕਿਤਾਬ, ਮੁਨੀਮੀ, ਲੇਖਾ ਸ਼ਾਸਤਰ,
ਗਿਣਤੀ-ਵਿਗਿਆਨ; ~ant ਲੇਖਾਕਾਰ, ਮੁਨੀਮ,
ਮੁਨਸ਼ੀ, ਹਿਸਾਬ-ਕਿਤਾਬ ਰੱਖਣ ਵਾਲਾ

accredit (ਅ'ਕਰੈਡਿਟ) *v* ਮਨਜ਼ੂਰ ਕਰਨਾ, ਸਵੀਕਾਰ
ਕਰਨਾ, ਅਧਿਕਾਰ ਦੇਣਾ, ਸਬੰਧ ਜੋੜਨਾ, ਮਾਨਤਾ
ਦੁਆਉਣਾ, ਮਾਨ ਦੇਣਾ; ~ed ਮਕਬੂਲ,
ਪਰਵਾਨਤ, ਅਧਿਕਾਰ-ਪ੍ਰਾਪਤ, ਪ੍ਰਤਿਸ਼ਠਾਵਾਨ;
ਕਬੂਲ

accrete (ਅ'ਕਰੀਟ) *adv v* ਇਕੱਤਰ ਕਰਨਾ,
ਜੋੜਨਾ, ਜੁੜਵਾਂ, ਸੰਯੁਕਤ, ਵਧਵਾਂ

accretion (ਅ'ਕਰੀਸ਼ਨ) *n* ਵਿਕਾਸ, ਵ੍ਰਿਧੀ,
ਸਹਿਵਰਧਨ, ਫੈਲਾਉ; ਪੌਦਿਆਂ ਦਾ ਉੱਗ ਕੇ ਗੁੱਛਾ-
ਮੁੱਛਾ ਹੋ ਜਾਣ ਦੀ ਕ੍ਰਿਆ; ਮਿਲਾਪ, ਇਕਮਿਕਤਾ

accumulate (ਅ'ਕਯੂਮਯੂਲੇਇਟ) *v* ਜੋੜਨਾ, ਜਮ੍ਹਾਂ
ਕਰਨਾ, ਸੰਗ੍ਰਹਿ ਕਰਨਾ ਜਾਂ ਹੋਣਾ, ਸੰਚਤ ਕਰਨਾ,
ਸਮੇਟਣਾ, ਢੇਰ ਲਾਉਣਾ, ਸੰਕਲਤ ਕਰਨਾ, ਵਧਦੇ
ਜਾਣਾ

accumulation (ਅ'ਕਯੂਮਯੂ'ਲੇਇਸ਼ਨ) *n* ਸਮੂਹ,
ਪੁੰਜ, ਇਕੱਠ, ਢੇਰ, ਅੰਬਾਰ, ਸੰਗ੍ਰਹਿ

accumulative (ਅ'ਕਯੂਮਯੂ'ਲਅਟਿਵ੍) *a*
ਇਕੱਠਾ, ਸੰਚਤ

accuracy ('ਏਕਯੁਰਅਸਿ) ਦਰੁਸਤੀ, ਸ਼ੁੱਧਤਾ,
ਸਚਾਈ, ਸੁਨਿਸ਼ਚੱਤਤਾ

accurate ('ਏਕਯੁਰਅਟ) *a* ਸ਼ੁੱਧ, ਠੀਕ, ਸਹੀ,

ਦਰੁਸਤ; ਸਰੇਤ, ਸਾਵਧਾਨ

accusation ('ਏਕਯੂ'ਜ਼ੇਇਸ਼ਨ) *n* ਦੋਸ਼-ਆਰੋਪਣ,
ਇਲਜ਼ਾਮ, ਦੂਸ਼ਨ, ਤੁਹਮਤ

accuse (ਅ'ਕਯੂਜ਼) *v* ਉਜ ਲਾਉਣੀ, ਦੋਸ਼
ਲਾਉਣਾ, ਤੁਹਮਤ ਲਾਉਣੀ, ਇਲਜ਼ਾਮ ਲਾਉਣਾ,
ਮੱਥੇ ਮੜ੍ਹਨਾ; ~d ਦੋਸ਼ੀ, ਅਪਰਾਧੀ, ਮੁਲਜ਼ਮ

accustom (ਅ'ਕਅੱਸਟਅਮ) *v* ਆਦੀ ਕਰਨਾ,
ਆਦਤ ਪਾਉਣੀ, ਰੀਝਾਉਣਾ, ਸੁਭਾਅ ਪਾਉਣਾ;
~ed ਆਦੀ, ਗਿੱਝਿਆ

ace (ਏਇਸ) *n* ਇਕ, ਇਕਾਈ; ਤਾਸ਼ ਦੀ ਯੱਕਾ

ache (ਏਇਕ) *n v* ਦਰਦ, ਪੀੜ, ਵੇਦਨਾ, ਕਸਕ,
ਹੂਕ, ਦੁਖਣਾ, ਦਰਦ ਹੋਣਾ, ਪੀੜ ਹੋਣੀ, ਸੂਲ
ਉੱਠਣੀ, ਰੀਸ ਪੈਣੀ

achieve (ਅ'ਚੀਵ) *v* ਪ੍ਰਾਪਤ ਕਰਨਾ, ਪਾਉਣਾ,
ਸਿਰੇ ਚਾੜ੍ਹਨਾ, ਨਿਬੇੜਤਾ, ਮਨੋਰਥ ਪ੍ਰਾਪਤ ਕਰਨਾ;
~ment ਪ੍ਰਾਪਤੀ, ਸਿੱਧੀ, ਪੂਰਤੀ, ਪੂਰਨਤਾ,
ਕਾਮਯਾਬੀ, ਸਫਲਤਾ

acid ('ਏਸਿਡ) *n a* ਤੇਜ਼ਾਬ, ਖੱਟਾ ਪਦਾਰਥ, ਤੁਰਸ਼,
ਸਿਰਕਈ, ਤੇਜ਼ਾਬੀ; ਵਿਅੰਗਮਈ, ਚੁੱਭਵਾਂ(ਬੋਲ);
~ify ਤੇਜ਼ਾਬੀ ਬਨਣਾ ਜਾਂ ਬਣਾਉਣਾ; ~ity
ਤੇਜ਼ਾਬੀਅਤ; ਅਮਲਤਾ; ਖਟਾਸ, ਤੁਰਸ਼ੀ

acknowledge (ਅ'ਕਨੌਲਿਜ) *v* ਸਵੀਕਾਰ
ਕਰਨਾ; ਪ੍ਰਸੰਸਾ ਕਰਨਾ, ਪਰਵਾਨ ਕਰਨਾ; ਪਹੁੰਚ
ਦੇਣਾ, ਰਸੀਦ ਦੇਣਾ; ਮਾਨਤਾ ਦੇਣੀ, ਕਦਰ
ਕਰਨਾ; ਹਾਮੀ ਭਰਨਾ; ~d ਸਵੀਕ੍ਰਿਤ, ਪਰਵਾਨਤ
ਮੰਨਿਆ, ਜਾਨਿਆ; ~ment ਸਨਮੁੱਖੀ, ਹਾਮੀ,
ਰਸੀਦ, ਆਧਾਰ; ਕਦਰ; ਪਹੁੰਚ, ਪ੍ਰਾਪਤੀ-ਸੂਚਨਾ

acoustic/-al (ਅ'ਕੁਸਟਿਕ/ਅ'ਕੁਸਟਿਕਲ) *a*
ਸੁਨਣ ਸਬੰਧੀ, ਕੰਨਾਂ ਸਬੰਧੀ, ਧੁਨੀ ਸਬੰਧੀ,
ਸੁਵਣੀ; ~s ਸ੍ਰਵਣ ਵਿਗਿਆਨ; (ਕਮਰੇ ਦਾ)
ਧੁਨੀ-ਗੁਣ

acquaint (ਅ'ਕਵੇਇੰਟ) *v* ਵਾਕਫੀ ਕਰਾਉਣੀ, ਖ਼ਬਰ ਦੇਣੀ, ਪਰਿਚੈ ਦੇਣਾ, ਪਰਿਚਿਤ ਕਰਨਾ; ਜਾਣਕਾਰੀ ਪ੍ਰਾਪਤ ਕਰਨੀ ਜਾਂ ਕਰਾਉਣੀ, ਸੂਚਨਾ ਦੇਣੀ, ਸੂਚਤ ਕਰਨਾ ਜਾਂ ਹੋਣਾ, ਜਤਲਾਉਣਾ, ਜਾਣੂ ਕਰਨਾ, ਵਾਕਫੀ ਕਰਾਉਣੀ, ਖ਼ਬਰ ਦੇਣੀ; ~ance ਜਾਣ-ਪਛਾਣ, ਜਾਣਕਾਰੀ, ਵਾਕਫੀਅਤ, ਪਰਿਚਯ; ਜਾਣਕਾਰ, ਵਾਰਫ਼; ਜਾਣੂ; ਪਰਿਚਿਤ, ਗਿਆਤ, ਸੂਚਤ; ~ed ਪਰਿਚਿਤ, ਗਿਆਤ, ਸੂਚਤ

acquire (ਅ'ਕਵਾਇਆ*) *v* ਲੈਣਾ, ਹਾਸਲ ਕਰਨਾ, ਗ੍ਰਹਿਣ ਕਰਨਾ, ਪ੍ਰਾਪਤ ਕਰਨਾ, ਪਾਉਣਾ, ਮਾਲਕ ਬਣਨਾ, ਕਬਜ਼ਾ ਲੈਣਾ; ~d ਪ੍ਰਾਪਤ, ਅਰਜਤ, ਗ੍ਰਹਿਤ, ਕਮਾਇਆ

aquisition ('ਐਕਵਿ'ਜ਼ਿਸ਼ਨ) *n* ਪ੍ਰਾਪਤੀ, ਗ੍ਰਹਿਣ, ਉਪਲਬਧੀ, ਲੱਭਤ, ਕਮਾਈ

acquit (ਅ'ਕਵਿਟ) *v* ਬਰੀ ਕਰਨਾ, ਰਿਹਾ ਕਰਨਾ, ਛੱਡਣਾ, ਦੋਸ਼-ਮੁਕਤ ਕਰਨਾ, ਕਰਤੱਵ ਪੂਰਾ ਕਰਨਾ, (ਫ਼ਰਜ਼) ਅਦਾ ਕਰਨਾ, ਨਿਭਾਉਣਾ; ~tal ਰਿਹਾਈ, ਛੁਟਕਾਰਾ, ਮੁਕਤੀ, ਅਪਰਾਧ-ਮੁਕਤੀ, ਖ਼ਲਾਸੀ, ਨਿਸਤਾਰ; ~tance ਰਿਹਾਈ, ਨਿਸਤਾਰਾ, ਅਪਰਾਧ-ਮੁਕਤੀ; ਅਦਾਇਗੀ, (ਕਰਜ਼ੇ ਤੋਂ) ਛੁਟਕਾਰਾ, ਚੁਕੰਤੀ, ਬੇਬਾਕੀ, ~ted ਛੁਟਿਆ, ਬਰੀ, ਰਿਹਾ, ਵਿਮੁਕਤ

acre ('ਏਇਕਅ*) *n* ਏਕੜ, 4840 ਵਰਗ ਗਜ਼; ~age (ਏਕੜਾਂ ਵਿਚ) ਖੇਤਰਫਲ; ਮਾਮਲਾ ਫ਼ੀ ਏਕੜ

acrid ('ਐਕਰਿਡ) *a* ਕੌੜਾ, ਤਲਖ਼ ਮਿਜ਼ਾਜ, ਉਤੇਜਕ, ਤਿੱਖਾ, ਤੇਜ਼-ਤਬੀਅਤ, ਚਿੜਚੜਾ; ~ity ਤੀਖਣਤਾ, ਤਿੱਖਾਪਣ, ਤੇਜ਼ੀ, ਖਟਿਆਈ, ਖਰੂਵਾਪਣ

acrimonious (ਐਕਰਿ'ਮਅਊਨਯਅਸ) *a* ਤੇਜ਼,

ਕੌੜਾ, ਕਾਵੜ, ਤਲਖ਼, ਖਰੂਵਾ, ਤੀਖਣ, ਚਿੜਚੜਾ

acrimony (ਐਕਰਿਮਅਨਿ) *n* (ਸੁਭਾਅ ਦੀ) ਤਲਖ਼ੀ, ਕੁੜੱਤਣ, ਕਟੁਤਾ

across (ਅ'ਕਰੌਸ) *adv prep a* ਪਾਰ, ਆਰ-ਪਾਰ, ਸਨਮੁਖ, ਸਾਮੁਣੇ, ਦੂਜੇ ਪਾਸੇ; ਆੜਾ, ਤਿਰਛਾ

act (ਐਕਟ) *n v* (1) ਅਧਿਨਿਯਮ; (2) ਨਾਟਕ ਦਾ ਅੰਕ; (3) ਕੰਮ, ਕਾਰਜ, ਕਾਜ, ਕਿਰਿਆ, ਕਰਤੱਵ, ਕਾਰਵਾਈ; ਵਿਹਾਰ ਕਰਨਾ, ਕਰਤੱਵ ਪਾਲਣਾ; ਅਭਿਨੈ ਕਰਨਾ; ~able ਕਰਨ ਯੋਗ, ਕਰਤੱਵ ਯੋਗ, ਵਿਹਾਰ ਯੋਗ, ਅਭਿਨੈ ਯੋਗ; ~ing ਅਦਾਕਾਰੀ, ਨਟਬਾਜ਼ੀ, ਅਭਿਨੈ, ਦਿਖਾਵਾ; ਕਾਰਜ; ਕਿਰਿਆਸ਼ੀਲਤਾ; ~or ਕਰਤਾ, ਨਟ, ਅਦਾਕਾਰ, ਅਭਿਨੇਤਾ, ਨਾਟਕ ਦਾ ਪਾਤਰ, ਐਕਟਰ

action (ਐਕਸ਼ਨ) *n v* ਅਮਲ, ਕੰਮ, ਕਾਰਜ ਕਿਰਿਆ, ਕਾਰਵਾਈ; ਵਿਹਾਰ; ਢੰਗ, ਹਰਕਤ; ਮੁਕੱਦਮਾ; ਪ੍ਰਭਾਵ; ਜੁੱਧ; ਦਾਅਵਾ ਕਰਨਾ, ਕਿਸੇ ਦੇ ਵਿਰੁਧ ਕਾਨੂੰਨੀ ਮੁਕੱਦਮਾ ਕਰਨਾ

active (ਐਕਟਿਵ) *a* ਕਿਰਿਆਸ਼ੀਲ, ਫੁਰਤੀਲਾ, ਉੱਦਮੀ, ਚੁਸਤ, ਜਾਗਰੂਕ, ਪ੍ਰਭਾਵਸ਼ਾਲੀ, ਸਾਹਸੀ ~voice ਕਰਤਰੀਵਾਚ; ~ity ਸਰਗਰਮੀ, ਚੁਸਤੀ, ਫੁਰਤੀ, ਰੁਝੇਵਾਂ, ਵਿਵਸਾਏ; ਮਿਹਨਤ

actual (ਐਕਚੁਅਲ) *a* ਵਾਸਤਵਿਕ, ਯਥਾਰਥ, ਸੱਚਾ, ਸਹੀ, ਠੀਕ, ਅਸਲੀ, ਪ੍ਰਚਲਤ, ਚਾਲੂ; ~ity ਯਥਾਰਥਕਤਾ, ਸੱਤੋਤਾ, ਵਾਸਤਵਿਕਤਾ, ਅਸਲੀਅਤ, ਸੱਚਾਈ, ਮੌਜੂਦਾ ਹਾਲਾਤ; ~ly ਸਚਮੁੱਚ, ਅਸਲ ਵਿਚ, ਦਰਅਸਲ, ਵਾਸਤਵਿਕ ਤੌਰ ਤੇ

acute (ਅ'ਕਯੂਟ) *a* ਤਿੱਖਾ, ਤੇਜ਼, ਚਤਰ, ਤੀਬਰ, ਸਖ਼ਤ, ਪ੍ਰਚੰਡ, ਸੰਵੇਦਨਸ਼ੀਲ, ਅਤੀ ਅਵੱਸ਼ਕ; ~ness ਤੀਬਰਤਾ, ਤੀਖਣਤਾ, ਤਿੱਖਾਪਣ, ਤੇਜ਼ੀ

A.D. ('ਏਇ'ਡੀ) (L) Anno Domini ਦਾ

ਸੰਖੇਪ, (ਭਗਵਾਨ ਈਸਾ ਦੇ ਵਰ੍ਹੇ ਵਿਚ) ਸੰਨ ਈਸਵੀ

adam ('ਐਡ਼ਅਮ) *n* ਬਾਬਾ ਆਦਮ, ਆਦਿ ਪੁਰਸ਼

adamant ('ਐਡ਼ਅਸਅੰਟ) *a n* ਦ੍ਰਿੜ੍ਹ, ਅਟਲ; ਕਰੜੀ ਵਸਤੁ; ਚੁੰਬਕ ਪੱਥਰ

Adam's apple (,'ਐਡ਼ਅਮਜ਼'ਐਪਲ) ਘੰਡੀ

adapt (ਅ'ਡੈਪਟ) *v* ਅਨੁਕੂਲ ਕਰਨਾ, ਮੁਆਫ਼ਕ ਬਣਾਉਣਾ, ਰੂਪ ਦੇ ਅਨੁਸਾਰ ਕਰਨਾ, ਇਕ ਤਰ੍ਹਾਂ ਦਾ ਬਣਾਉਣਾ, ਮੇਲਣਾ, ਢਾਲਣਾ; ~**ability** ਢਲ ਜਾਣ ਦਾ ਗੁਣ, ਅਨੁਕੂਲਤਾ, ਅਨੁਕੂਲਣ ਯੋਗਤਾ; ~**ation** ਅਨੁਕੂਲਣ, ਕਿਸੇ ਸ਼ਕਲ ਦਾ ਰੂਪਾਂਤਰ, ਰੂਪ ਅਨੁਕੂਲ, ਮੇਲ

add (ਐਡ) *v* ਜੋੜਨਾ, ਵਧਾਉਣਾ, ਮਿਲਾਣਾ, ਜਾਮੂੰ ਕਰਨਾ, ਸੰਮਿਲਤ ਕਰਨਾ, ਮਿਲਾਉਣਾ; ~**endum** ਜੋੜ, ਵਾਧਾ, ਯੋਗ, ਅੰਤਕਾ; ~**er** ਰਕਮਾਂ ਜੋੜਨ ਵਾਲਾ ਆਦਮੀ; ਇਕ ਤਰ੍ਹਾਂ ਦਾ ਜ਼ਹਿਰੀਲਾ ਸੱਪ

addict (ਅ'ਡਿਕਟ, 'ਐਡ਼ਿਕਟ) *v n* ਆਪਣੇ ਆਪ ਨੂੰ ਆਦਤ ਪਾਉਣੀ, ਗਿੱਝਣਾ, ਆਦੀ ਹੋਣਾ; ਅਮਲੀ, ਨਸ਼ੱਈ; ~**ed** ਆਦੀ, ਅਮਲੀ, ਨਸ਼ੱਈ, ਵਿਸ਼ੇਗ੍ਰਸਤ, ਲਿਪਤ; ~**ion** ਝੱਸ, ਵਾਦੀ

addition (ਅ'ਡਿਸ਼ਨ) *n* ਸੰਕਲਨ, ਜੋੜ, ਜਾਮੂੰ, ਵਾਧਾ, ਅਧਿਕਤਾ, ਯੋਗ, ਜੋੜਨ ਦਾ ਕੰਮ, ਜੁੜਾਈ; ~**al** ਵਾਧੂ, ਵਧੀਕ, ਅਧਿਕਤਰ; (ਪਹਿਲਾਂ ਵਾਲੀ ਚੀਜ਼ ਆਦਿ ਤੋਂ) ਇਲਾਵਾ, ਅਤਿਰਿਕਤ, ਅਨੁਪੂਰਕ

address (ਅ'ਡਰੈੱਸ) *n v* (1) ਸਿਰਨਾਵਾਂ ਪਤਾ; (2) ਵਿਆਖਿਆਨ, ਸੰਬੋਧਨ; (3) ਅਭਿਨੰਦਨ-ਪੱਤਰ; (4) ਮੁਹਾਰਤ, ਸਲੀਕਾ; ਸੰਬੋਧਤ ਕਰਨਾ, ਪਤਾ ਲਿਖਣਾ, ਵਿਆਖਿਆਨ ਦੇਣਾ, ਭਾਸ਼ਣ ਦੇਣਾ; ਮੁਖ਼ਾਤਬ ਹੋਣਾ; ~**ee** ਸਿਰਨਾਵਾਂਦਾਰ, (ਮਨੀ ਆਰਡਰ ਜਾਂ ਚਿੱਠੀ) ਪ੍ਰਾਪਤ ਕਰਨ ਵਾਲਾ, ਪ੍ਰਾਪਤ

ਕਰਤਾ; ~**er** ਪੱਤਰ ਭੇਜਣ ਵਾਲਾ, ਬੇਨਤੀ ਕਨ ਵਾਲਾ, ਸੰਬੋਧਨ ਕਰਤਾ, ਮੁਖ਼ਾਤਬ ਕਰਨ ਵਾਲਾ

adept ('ਐਡ਼ੈਪਟ) *a n* ਨਿਪੁੰਨ, ਕਾਰੀਗਰ, ਪ੍ਰਵੀਨ, ਉਸਤਾਦ, ਤਾਕ, ਮਾਹਰ ਕੀਮੀਆਗਰ

adequacy (ਐਡ਼ਿਕਵਅਸਿ) *n* ਯੋਗਤਾ, ਸਮਰਥਾ, ਢੁੱਕਵਾਂਪਣ, ਚੋਖਾਪਣ

adequate ('ਐਡ਼ਿਕਵਅਟ) *a* ਕਾਫ਼ੀ, ਪੂਰਾ, ਲੋੜ-ਅਨੁਸਾਰ, ਉਪਯੁਕਤ, ਚੋਖਾ, ਢੁੱਕਵਾਂ, ਮੁਨਾਸਬ; ~**ly** ਪੂਰਾ-ਪੂਰਾ, ਕਾਫ਼ੀ, ਪੂਰੇ ਤੌਰ ਤੇ

adhere (ਅਡ'ਹਿਅ*) *v* ਡਟੇ ਰਹਿਣਾ, ਜੰਮੇ ਰਹਿਣਾ, ਚਿੰਬੜਨਾ, ਜੁੜ ਜਾਣਾ, ਦ੍ਰਿੜ੍ਹ ਰਹਿਣਾ; ਪਾਲਣ ਕਰਨਾ, ਅਨੁਸਰਨ ਕਰਨਾ, ਸਾਥ ਦਿੰਦੇ ਰਹਿਣਾ; ~**nce** ਹਿਮਾਇਤ, ਲਗਾਉ, ਦ੍ਰਿੜ੍ਹਤਾ, ਸਮਰਥਨ, ਚਿਪਕਾਓ; ਪਾਲਣ; ਨਿਸ਼ਠਾ; ~**nt** ਪੈਰੋਕਾਰ, ਹਿਮਾਇਤੀ, ਸਹਾਇਕ, ਸਮਰਥਕ, ਅਨੁਗਾਮੀ; ਸਬੰਧਤ

adhesive (ਅਡ'ਹਿਸਿਵ) *a* ਚਿਪਕੀਲਾ, ਗੂੰਦ ਵਾਲਾ ਚਿਪਕਵਾਂ, ਚਿਪਚਿਪਾ, ਚੇਪਦਾਰ; ~**ness** ਚਿਪਚਿਪਾਹਟ

ad hoc ('ਐਡ਼'ਹੌਕ) (*L*) *a* ਉਚੇਚਾ, ਖ਼ਾਸ ਮਤਲਬ ਲਈ, ਤਦ-ਅਰਥੀ

adieu (ਅ'ਡਯੂ) *n* ਅਲਵਿਦਾ, ਰੱਬ ਰਾਖਾ, ਅੱਲਾ ਬੇਲੀ

ad infinitum (ਐਡ਼'ਇਨਫ਼ਿ'ਨਾਇਟਅਮ) (*L*) *adv* ਹਮੇਸ਼ਾ ਲਈ, ਸਦੀਵੀ; ਅਨੰਤ ਤਕ

ad interim (ਐਡ਼'ਇਨਟਅਰਿਮ) (*L*) *adv* ਵਿਚਕਾਰਲੇ ਸਮੇਂ ਲਈ, ਅਲਪਕਾਲੀਨ, ਅਸਥਾਈ

adjacent (ਅ'ਜੇਇਸਅੰਟ) *n* ਲਾਗਲਾ, ਜੁੜਵਾਂ, ਸਮੀਪਵਰਤੀ, ਨੇੜਲਾ, ਨਾਲ, ਲੱਗਵਾਂ

adject (ਅ'ਜੈਕਟ) *v* ਜੋੜਨਾ, ਮਿਲਾਉਣਾ ~**ival** ਵਿਸ਼ੇਸ਼ਣੀ, ਵਿਸ਼ੇਸ਼ਣ ਸਬੰਧੀ, ਗੁਣਵਾਚਕ; ~**ive**

ਵਿਸ਼ੇਸ਼ਣ, ਗੁਣਵਾਚਕ ਸ਼ਬਦ

adjoin (ਅ'ਜੌਇਨ) *v* ਮਿਲਿਆ ਹੋਣਾ, ਜੁੜਿਆ ਹੋਣਾ, ਮਿਲਾਉਣਾ, ਸੰਯੁਕਤ ਕਰਨਾ, ਪਾਸ ਲਿਆਉਣਾ, ਮੇਲ ਕਰਨਾ, ਜੋੜਨਾ, ਨੱਥੀ ਕਰਨਾ; **~ing** ਕੋਲ ਦਾ, ਕੋਲ ਵਾਲਾ, ਨਾਲ ਲਗਦਾ, ਨਾਲ ਦਾ, ਨਾਲ ਵਾਲਾ, ਜੁੜਿਆ

adjourn (ਅ'ਜਅ:ਨ) *v* ਮੁਲਤਵੀ ਕਰਨਾ, ਸਥਗਤ ਕਰਨਾ, ਅੱਗੇ ਪਾਉਣਾ; **~ment** ਅੱਗੇ ਪਾ ਦੇਣ, ਮੁਲਤਵੀ ਕਰਨ, ਕਾਰਜ-ਸਥਗਨ

adjudge (ਅ'ਜਅੱਜ) *v* ਨਿਆਂ-ਨਿਰਣਾ ਕਰਨਾ, ਫ਼ੈਸਲਾ ਕਰਨਾ, ਦੰਡ ਦਾ ਹੁਕਮ ਦੇਣਾ, ਤਜਵੀਜ਼ ਕਰਨਾ, ਰਾਇ ਦੇਣੀ; **~ment** ਨਿਆਂ-ਨਿਰਣਾ, ਫ਼ੈਸਲਾ, ਹੁਕਮ

adjudicate (ਅ'ਜੂਡਿਕੇਇਟ) *v* ਫ਼ੈਸਲਾ ਕਰਨਾ, ਨਿਰਣਾ ਦੇਣਾ, ਨਿਬੇੜਨਾ, ਨਿਪਟਾਰਾ ਕਰਨਾ

adjudication (ਅ'ਜੂਡਿ'ਕੇਇਸ਼ਨ) *n* ਫ਼ੈਸਲਾ, ਨਿਆਂ ਨਿਰਣਾ, ਅਦਾਲਤੀ ਹੁਕਮ

adjunct (ਐ'ਜਅੰਕਟ) *n* ਸਹਾਇਕ; ਅਧੀਨ ਵਸਤੂ; ਜੋੜ, ਸੰਯੁਕਤ ਪਦਾਰਥ

adjust (ਅ'ਜਅੱਸਟ) *v* ਤਰਤੀਬ ਦੇਣੀ, ਇਕਸਾਰ ਕਰਨਾ, ਠੀਕ ਕਰਨਾ ਅਨੁਕੂਲ ਕਰਨਾ, ਮਿਲਾਉਣਾ, ਸਮਾਯੋਜਨ ਕਰਨਾ, ਵਿਵਸਥਿਤ ਕਰਨਾ; **~ment** ਤਰਕੀਬ, ਅਨੁਕੂਲਤਾ, ਸਮਾਯੋਜਨ, ਸਮਾਧਾਨ, ਸਮਝੌਤਾ

administer (ਅਡ'ਮਿਨਿਸਟਅ*) *v* ਪ੍ਰਬੰਧ ਕਰਨਾ, ਇੰਤਜ਼ਾਮ ਕਰਨਾ, ਬੰਦੋਬਸਤ ਕਰਨਾ, ਵਿਵਸਥਾ ਕਰਨੀ, (ਕਸਮ) ਚੁਕਾਉਣੀ; ਪ੍ਰਦਾਨ ਕਰਨਾ, (ਦਵਾਈ) ਦੇਣੀ ਜਾਂ ਖਵਾਉਣੀ

administration (ਅਡ'ਮਿਨਿ'ਸਟਰੇਇਸ਼ਨ) *n* ਪ੍ਰਸ਼ਾਸਨ, ਸੰਚਾਲਨ, ਪ੍ਰਬੰਧ, ਇੰਤਜ਼ਾਮ, ਸਰਕਾਰ

administrative (ਅਡ'ਮਿਨਿ'ਸਟਰਅਟਿਵ਼) *a* ਪ੍ਰਸ਼ਾਸ਼ਕੀ, ਪ੍ਰਸ਼ਾਸਨ-ਸਬੰਧੀ; ਪ੍ਰਬੰਧਕੀ, ਇੰਤਜ਼ਾਮੀਆ

administrator (ਅਡ'ਮਿਨਿਸਟਰੇਇਟਅ*) *n* ਪ੍ਰਸ਼ਾਸਕ, ਪ੍ਰਬੰਧਕ, ਪ੍ਰਬੰਧ-ਕਰਤਾ, ਨਾਜ਼ਮ, ਸਰਬਰਾਹ, ਮੁੰਤਜ਼ਿਮ, ਵਿਵਸਥਾਪਕ

admirable ('ਐਡਮ(ਅ)ਰਅਬਲ) *a* ਪ੍ਰਸੰਸਾਯੋਗ, ਪ੍ਰਸੰਸਨੀ, ਅਦਭੁਤ, ਅਸਚਰਜ-ਜਨਕ, ਅਪੂਰਵ, ਸ਼ਲਾਘਾਯੋਗ, ਸਲਾਹੁਣਯੋਗ, ਅਤੀ ਉੱਤਮ, ਸ੍ਰੇਸ਼ਠ, ਵਧੀਆ

admiral ('ਐਡਮ(ਅ)ਰ(ਅ)ਲ) *n* ਨੌ-ਸੈਨਾਪਤੀ, ਜੰਗੀ ਬੇੜੇ ਦਾ ਸਰਦਾਰ

admiration (ਐਡਮਅ'ਰੇਇਸ਼ਨ) *n* ਸ਼ਲਾਘਾ, ਤਾਰੀਫ਼, ਪ੍ਰਸੰਸਾ; ਅਚੰਭਾ

admire (ਅਡ'ਮਾਇਅ*) *v* ਪ੍ਰਸੰਸਾ ਕਰਨਾ; ਸਲਾਹੁਣਾ, ਸ਼ਲਾਘਾ ਕਰਨੀ, ਸਿਫ਼ਤ ਕਰਨੀ, ਗੁਣ ਗਾਉਣਾ; **~r** ਪ੍ਰਸੰਸਕ, ਆਸ਼ਕ

admissibility (ਅਡ'ਮਿਸਅ'ਬਿਲਅਟਿ) *n* ਯੋਗਤਾ, ਮੰਨਣ-ਯੋਗਤਾ, ਮਾਨਤਾ, ਪ੍ਰਮਾਣਕਤਾ

admissible (ਅਡ'ਮਿਸਅਬਲ) *a* ਦਾਖ਼ਲੇ ਯੋਗ, ਮੰਨਣ ਯੋਗ, ਜਾਇਜ਼, ਗ੍ਰਹਿਣ ਕਰਨ ਯੋਗ, ਸਵੀਕਾਰ ਕਰਨ ਯੋਗ

admission (ਅਡ'ਮਿਸ਼ਨ) *n* ਦਾਖਲਾ, ਪ੍ਰਵੇਸ਼, ਪਹੁੰਚ, ਪਰਵਾਨਗੀ, ਸਵੀਕ੍ਰਿਤੀ, ਅਨੁਮਤੀ; ਇਕਬਾਲ; ਪ੍ਰਵੇਸ਼-ਸ਼ੁਲਕ, ਭਰਤੀ

admit (ਅਡ'ਮਿਟ) *v* ਦਾਖ਼ਲ ਕਰਨਾ, ਪ੍ਰਵੇਸ਼ ਕਰਨਾ ਜਾਂ ਕਰਾਉਣਾ, ਆਉਣ ਦੇਣਾ, ਪ੍ਰਵੇਸ਼ ਦੇਣਾ, ਆਗਿਆ ਦੇਣੀ, ਮੰਨਣਾ, ਸਵੀਕਾਰ ਕਰਨਾ, ਇਕਬਾਲ ਕਰਨਾ, ਭਰਤੀ ਕਰਨਾ; **~tance** ਪ੍ਰਵੇਸ਼, ਦਾਖ਼ਲਾ, ਪ੍ਰਵੇਸ਼ ਦੀ ਅਨੁਮਤੀ, ਅੰਗੀਕਰਨ

admix (ਐਡਮਿਕਸ) *v* ਮਿਲਣਾ, ਮਿਲਾਉਣਾ, ਰਲਣਾ, ਰਲਾਉਣਾ, ਮਿਸ਼ਰਣ ਕਰਨਾ, ਮਿਸ਼ਰਤ

ਹੋਣਾ, ਘੋਲ ਦੇਣਾ, ਘੁਲ ਜਾਣਾ, ਰਲ ਮਿਲ
ਜਾਣਾ; ~ture ਮਿਲਾਵਟ, ਮਿਸ਼ਰਨ, ਰਲਾ

admonish (ਅਡ'ਮੌਨਿਸ਼) *v* ਤਾੜਨਾ ਕਰਨੀ,
ਤੰਬੀਹ ਕਰਨਾ, ਝਾੜ ਪਾਉਣੀ, ਚੇਤਾਵਨੀ ਦੇਣੀ,
ਚੁਕੰਨਾ ਕਰਨਾ, ਜਤਾਉਣਾ, ਸੁਚੇਤ ਕਰਨਾ,
ਧਿਆਨ ਦਿਵਾਉਣਾ; ~ment ਝਿੜਕ, ਡਾਂਟ-
ਡਪਟ, ਚੇਤਾਵਨੀ, ਤੰਬੀਹ, ਤਾੜਨਾ

admonition (ਐਡਮਅ(ਉ)'ਨਿਸ਼ਨ) *n*
ਚਿਤਾਵਨੀ, ਤੰਬੀਰ, ਤਾੜਨਾ

ado (ਅ'ਡੂ) *n* ਝਮੇਲਾ, ਬਖੇੜਾ, ਪੁਆੜਾ, ਕਲਹ

adolescence (ਐਡਾਅ(ਉ)'ਲੈੱਸੰਸ) *n*
ਅੱਲੜ੍ਹਪਨ, ਗਭਰੇਟ-ਉਮਰ, ਮੁਟਿਆਰ-
ਅਵਸਥਾ, ਜੋਬਨ, ਕਿਸ਼ੋਰਅਵਸਥਾ

adolesent ('ਐਡਅ(ਉ)'ਲੈੱਸੰਟ) *a n* ਕਿਸ਼ੋਰ,
ਅੱਲੜ੍ਹ (ਵਿਅਕਤੀ); ਨਵ-ਯੁਵਤੀ, ਨਵ-ਯੁਵਕ

adopt (ਅ'ਡੌਪਟ) *v* ਅਪਨਾਉਣਾ; ਧਾਰਨਾ, ਗ੍ਰਹਿਣ
ਕਰਨਾ, ਲੈਣਾ, ਪ੍ਰਾਪਤ ਕਰਨਾ, ਗੋਦੀ ਲੈਣਾ,
ਮੁਤਬੰਨਾ ਬਣਾਉਣਾ; ~ion ਗੋਦੀ ਲੈਣ;
ਅੰਗੀਕਰਨ, ਗ੍ਰਹਿਣ, ਚੋਣ

adorn (ਅ'ਡੋਨ) *v* (ਗਹਿਣਿਆਂ ਨਾਲ) ਸਜਾਉਣਾ,
ਸੰਵਾਰਨਾ, ਸ਼ਿੰਗਾਰਨਾ, ਅਲੰਕਰਤ ਕਰਨਾ,
ਸੁਸ਼ੋਭਤ ਕਰਨਾ; ~ment ਸ਼ਿੰਗਾਰ, ਸਜਾਵਟ,
ਅਲੰਕਰਣ

adrift (ਅ'ਡਰਿਫਟ) *adv a* ਡਾਵਾਂਡੋਲ, ਨਿਥਾਵਾਂ,
ਅਸਥਿਰ, ਭਟਕਦਾ, ਵਹਿੰਦਾ ਹੋਇਆ

adroit (ਅ'ਡਰੌਇਟ) *a* ਹੁਸ਼ਿਆਰ, ਚਲਾਕ, ਚੰਟ,
ਲਿਫਤਾ, ਚਤਰ, ਰੁਸਤ, ਫੁਰਤੀਲਾ

adult (ਅ'ਡਅੱਲਟ) *a n* ਬਾਲਗਾ, ਪ੍ਰੋੜ੍ਹ, ਸਿਆਣਾ,
ਗੱਭਰੂ

adulterant (ਅ'ਡਅੱਲਟਅਰਅਨਟ) *a n* ਮਿਲਾਵਟ
ਵਾਲਾ, ਖੋਟਾ, ਰਲੇ ਵਾਲਾ, ਮਿਲਾਵਟ, ਖੋਟ

adulterate (ਅ'ਡਅੱਲਟਰੇਇਟ) *v a* ਮਿਲਾਵਟ
ਕਰਨਾ, ਖੋਟ ਰਲਾਉਣਾ, ਰਲਾਵਟ ਕਰਨੀ;
ਅਸ਼ੁਧ, ਭ੍ਰਿਸ਼ਟ, ਖੋਟਾ, ਨਕਲੀ, ਬਣਾਉਟੀ,
ਹਰਾਮੀ, ਵਿਭਚਾਰੀ

adulteration (ਅ'ਡਅੱਲਟਰਇਸ਼ਨ) *n* ਮਿਲਾਵਟ,
ਖੋਟ, ਰਲਾ

adulterer (ਅ'ਡਅੱਲਟਅਰਅ*) *n* ਵਿਭਾਚਾਰੀ,
ਜ਼ਨਕਾਰ, ਦੁਰਾਚਾਰੀ, ਪਰ-ਇਸਤਰੀਗਾਮੀ

adulteress (ਅ'ਡਅੱਲਟਅਰਿਸ) *a* ਯਾਰਨੀ,
ਵਿਭਚਾਰਨ, ਦੁਰਾਚਾਰਨ, ਬਦਕਾਰ, ਪਰ-
ਪੁਰਸ਼ਗਾਮਨ (ਇਸਤਰੀ)

adultery (ਅ'ਡਅੱਲਟਅਰਿ) *n* ਬਦਕਾਰੀ,
ਹਰਾਮਕਾਰੀ, ਵਿਭਚਾਰੀ, ਪਰ-ਗਾਮਨ

advance (ਅਡ'ਵਾਂਸ) *v n* ਅੱਗੇ ਵਧਣਾ, ਧਾਵਾ
ਬੋਲਣਾ; ਤਰੱਕੀ ਕਰਨੀ, ਉੱਨਤੀ ਕਰਨੀ, ਵਿਕਾਸ
ਕਰਨਾ; ਪੇਸ਼ਗੀ ਦੇਣੀ, ਸਾਈ ਦੇਣੀ; ਪ੍ਰਸਤੁਤ
ਕਰਨਾ, ਉਧਾਰ ਦੇਣਾ; ਪਹਿਲ, ਪੇਸ਼ਗੀ, ਸਾਈ;
~d ਉੱਨਤ, ਵਿਕਸਤ, ਵਧਿਆ, ਉੱਚ; ~ment
ਉੱਨਤੀ, ਤਰੱਕੀ, ਵਾਧਾ, ਪੇਸ਼ਗੀ

advantage (ਐਡ'ਵਾਂਟਿਜ) *n v* ਲਾਭ, ਨਫ਼ਾ,
ਫ਼ਾਇਦਾ, ਬਿਹਤਰੀ, ਮਹੱਤ, ਭਲਾਈ, ਲਾਭ,
ਪਹੁੰਚਾਉਣਾ, ਲਾਭਕਾਰੀ ਹੋਣਾ, ਹਿਤਕਾਰੀ ਹੋਣਾ;
~ous ਲਾਭਕਾਰੀ, ਫ਼ਾਇਦੇਮੰਦ, ਲਾਹੇਵੰਦ,
ਉਪਜੋਗੀ, ਅਨੁਕੂਲ; ~ously ਲਾਭਦਾਇਕ
ਢੰਗ ਨਾਲ, ਉਪਜੋਗੀ ਤੌਰ ਤੇ

adventure (ਅਡ'ਵੈਂਚਅ*) *n v* ਸਾਹਸ, ਜਾਂਬਾਜ਼ੀ,
ਖਤਰੇ ਵਾਲਾ ਕੰਮ, ਔਖਾ ਕੰਮ; ਖ਼ਤਰਾ ਸਹੇੜਨ,
ਸੰਕਟ ਵਿਚ ਪੈ ਜਾਣਾ, ਹਿੰਮਤ ਕਰਨਾ, ਬੀੜਾ ਚੁੱਕਣਾ
ਜਾਂ ਉਠਾਉਣਾ; ~r (ਆਦਮੀ) ਸਾਹਸੀ, ਜਾਂਬਾਜ਼,
ਹਿੰਮਤੀ, ਸਿਰਲੱਥ, ਸੱਟੇਬਾਜ਼ (ਵਿਅਕਤੀ),
ਤਿਕੜਮਬਾਜ਼

adventurours (ਅਡ'ਵੈਂਚਰਅਸ) *a* ਸੂਰਮਾ, ਬੀਰ, ਸਾਹਸੀ, ਹਿੰਮਤੀ, ਦਲੇਰ, ਜਾਂਬਾਜ਼, ਪਰਾਕਰਮੀ

adverb (ਐਡਵਅ:ਬ) *n* ਕਿਰਿਆ-ਵਿਸ਼ੇਸ਼ਣ

adversary (ਐਡਵਅਸ(ਅ)ਰਿ) *n* ਵਿਰੋਧੀ, ਪ੍ਰਤੀਪੱਖੀ, ਵੈਰੀ, ਹਰੀਫ਼

adverse (ਐਡਵਅ:ਸ) *a* ਉਲਟ, ਹਾਨੀਕਾਰਕ, ਵਿਰੁੱਧ, ਵਿਪਰੀਤ, ਪ੍ਰਤੀਕੂਲ; ਅਣ-ਸੁਖਾਵਾਂ; **~ly** ਪ੍ਰਤੀਕੂਲ ਰੂਪ ਵਿਚ, ਵਿਰੋਧੀ ਤੌਰ ਤੇ, ਮੰਦੇ (ਭਾਗਾਂ) ਨਾਲ

adversity (ਐਡ'ਵਅ:ਸਅਟਿ) *n* ਬਿਪਤਾ, ਪ੍ਰਤੀਕੂਲਤਾ, ਸੰਕਟ, ਆਫ਼ਤ, ਦੁਰਭਾਗ, ਬੁਰੇ ਦਿਨ, ਮੁਸੀਬਤ, ਮੰਦਹਾਲੀ

advertise (ਐਡਵ੍ਅਟਾਇਜ਼) *v* ਇਸ਼ਤਹਾਰ ਦੇਣਾ, ਪ੍ਰਚਾਰ ਕਰਨਾ, ਫੈਲਾਉਣਾ, ਮਸ਼ਹੂਰ ਕਰਨਾ, ਖ਼ਬਰ ਦੇਣੀ, ਸੂਚਤ ਕਰਨਾ, ਇਤਲਾਹ ਦੇਣੀ, ਵਿਗਿਆਪਨ ਕਰਨਾ ਜਾਂ ਦੇਣਾ; **~ment** ਇਸ਼ਤਿਹਾਰ, ਵਿਗਿਆਪਨ, ਆਮ ਇਤਲਾਹ, ਸੂਚਨਾ, ਐਲਾਨ

advice (ਅਡ'ਵ੍ਇਸ) *n* ਸਲਾਹ, ਰਾਇ, ਮਸ਼ਵਰਾ, ਨਸੀਹਤ; ਸੰਮਤੀ ਉਪਦੇਸ਼; ਸੂਚਨਾ, ਸਮਾਚਾਰ; **~s** ਬਿਲਟੀਆਂ, ਮਾਲ ਭੇਜਣ ਦੀਆਂ ਰਸੀਦਾਂ, ਵਿਹਾਰਕ ਸੂਚਨਾਵਾਂ

advisable (ਅਡ'ਵਾਇਜ਼ਅਬਲ) *a* ਯੋਗ, ਮੁਨਾਸਬ, ਉਚਿਤ, ਢੁੱਕਵਾਂ, ਉਪਯੁਕਤ

advise (ਅਡ'ਵਾਇਜ਼) *v* ਸਲਾਹ ਦੇਣੀ, ਮਸ਼ਵਰਾ ਦੇਣਾ, ਨਸੀਹਤ ਦੇਣੀ; ਸਿਫ਼ਾਰਸ਼ ਕਰਨੀ, ਉਪਯੁਕਤ ਦੱਸਣਾ; ਸੂਚਨਾ ਦੇਣੀ, ਸੂਚਤ ਕਰਨਾ; **~r** ਸਲਾਹਕਾਰ, ਮੰਤਰੀ, ਮਸ਼ੀਰ, ਪਰਾਮਰਸ਼ ਕਰਤਾ

advocate (ਐਡਵਅਕਅਟ) *n v* ਵਕੀਲ, ਐਡਵੋਕੇਟ; ਸਮਰਥਕ, ਪ੍ਰਤੀਨਿਧ, ਬਸੀਠ; ਵਕਾਲਤ ਕਰਨਾ, ਹਿਮਾਇਤ ਕਰਨਾ

aegis ('ਈਜਿਸ) *n* ਸਰਪਰਸਤੀ; ਰੱਖਿਆ; ਆਸਰਾ, ਯੂਨਾਨੀ ਦੇਵਤਿਆਂ ਦੀ ਢਾਲ

aerial (ਏਅਰਿਅਲ) *a n* ਹਵਾਈ, ਹਵਾ-ਸਬੰਧੀ, ਹਵਾ ਵਾਂਗ ਸੂਖਮ, ਖਿਆਲੀ, ਕਾਲਪਨਕ; ਆਕਾਸ਼ੀ, ਵਾਯੂਮੰਡਲੀ; ਏਰੀਅਲ (ਰੇਡੀਓ ਦਾ), ਲਹਿਰਾਂ ਨੂੰ ਇਕੱਠਾ ਕਰਨ ਵਾਲੀ ਤਾਰ

aerobus (ਏਅਰੋਬਅਸ) *n* ਵਾਯੂਯਾਨ, ਹਵਾਈ-ਗੱਡੀ

aerodrome (ਏਅਰੋਡਰਅਉਮ) *n* ਹਵਾਈ-ਅੱਡਾ, ਹਵਾਈ-ਜਹਾਜ਼ਾਂ ਦਾ ਅੱਡਾ

aerogram (ਏਅਰੋਗਰੈਮ) *n* ਹਵਾਈ-ਪੱਤਰ, ਹਵਾਈ ਤਾਕ, ਵਾਇਰਲੈਸ ਨਾਲ ਭੇਜੀ ਤਾਕ

aeroplane (ਏਅਰੋਪਲੇਇਨ) *n* ਹਵਾਈ-ਜਹਾਜ਼, ਵਿਮਾਨ, ਉਡਣ ਖਟੋਲਾ,

aesthetic (ਈਸ'ਥੈਟਿਕ) *n* ਸੁਹਜਵਾਦੀ, ਸੁਹਜਾਤਮਕ, ਸੁਹਜ ਭਰਿਆ, ਸੁੰਦਰਤਾਮਈ

afar (ਅ'ਫ਼ਾ*) *adv* ਦੂਰ, ਦੂਰ ਤੀਕ; **~from** ਦੂਰ ਤੋਂ, ਦੂਰੋਂ

affair (ਅ'ਫ਼ੇਅ*) *n* ਕਾਰ-ਵਿਹਾਰ, ਮਾਮਲਾ, ਸਮੱਸਿਆ, ਕਾਰਜ, ਕੰਮ, ਕਾਰੋਬਾਰ, ਸਮਾਰੋਹ, ਆਸ਼ਕੀ, ਪ੍ਰੇਮ ਸਬੰਧ, ਯਾਰੀ

affect (ਅ'ਫ਼ੈਕਟ) *v* ਅਸਰ ਕਰਨਾ, ਪ੍ਰਭਾਵ ਪਾਉਣਾ, ਮਨ ਵਿਚ ਬੈਠਣਾ; ਪੁਹਣਾ, ਵਰਤੋਂ ਕਰਨਾ, (ਬੀਮਾਰੀ ਦਾ) ਲੱਗਣਾ, ਚੁੱਭਣਾ; ਵਰਤਣਾ, ਵਿਹਾਰ ਕਰਨਾ; ਕੰਮ ਵਿਚ ਲਿਆਉਣਾ, ਵਿਖਾਵਾ ਕਰਨਾ; **~ation** ਆਡੰਬਰ, ਦੰਭ, ਖੇਖਣ, ਬਣਾਵਟ, ਦਿਖਾਵਾ, ਨਖ਼ਰਾ, ਛਲ, ਕਪਟ, ਬਹਾਨਾ; **~ed** ਭਾਵਾਤਮਕ ਢੌਂਗੀ, ਪਖੰਡੀ, ਕਪਟੀ, ਆਡੰਬਰੀ, ਆਡੰਬਰਪੂਰਨ, ਬਣਾਉਟੀ, ਕਲਪਤ, ਦਿਖਾਵੇ ਦਾ; ਪ੍ਰਭਾਵਤ, ਗ੍ਰਸਤ; ਪ੍ਰਭਾਵੀ; **~ive** ਪ੍ਰਭਾਵੀ, ਭਾਵਾਤਮਕ

affection (ਅ'ਫੈਕੱਸ਼ਨ) n ਸਨੇਹ, ਪਰੇਮ, ਮੋਹ, ਪਰੀਤ, ਲਾਡ, ਸਦਭਾਵਨਾ; ~ate ਸਨੇਹੀ, ਪਰੇਮੀ, ਪਰੀਤਵਾਨ, ਲਾਡਲਾ, ਚਾਹੁਣਵਾਲਾ, ਸਨੇਹਪੂਰਨ; ~ately ਪਿਆਰ ਨਾਲ, ਸਨੇਹ ਨਾਲ, ਪਰੇਮ ਨਾਲ, ਚਾਹ ਕੇ, ਮੋਹਤ ਹੋ ਕੇ

affidavit (ਐਫ਼ਿ'ਡੇਇਵਿਟ) n ਹਲਫ਼, ਹਲਫ਼ਨਾਮਾ, ਹਲਫ਼ੀਆ ਬਿਆਨ

affilate (ਅ'ਫ਼ਿਲਿਏਇਟ) v ਮਿਲਾਉਣਾ, ਨਾਲ ਜੋੜਨ, ਸ਼ਾਮਲ ਕਰਨਾ, ਜੋੜ ਦੇਣਾ, ਸਬੰਧ ਜੋੜਨਾ

affiliation (ਅ'ਫ਼ਿਲਿ'ਏਇਸ਼ਨ) n ਮੇਲ, ਲਗਾਓ, ਸਬੰਧ; ਸਬੰਧਨ, ਸਬੰਧੀ-ਕਰਨ; ਮੁਤਬੰਨਾ ਬਣਾਉਣਾ

affinity (ਅ'ਫ਼ਿਨਅਟਿ) n ਨੇੜਨਾ, ਲਗਾਓ, ਸਾਂਝ, ਨਾਤਾ, ਵਿਵਾਹ-ਸਬੰਧ, ਨੇੜੇ ਦਾ ਸਬੰਧ, ਆਕਰਸ਼ਣ, ਸੁਭਾਅ ਜਾਂ ਆਚਾਰ-ਵਿਚਾਰ ਦੀ ਇਕਰੂਪਤਾ; ਸਮਰੂਪਤਾ

affirm (ਅ'ਫ਼ਅਃਮ) v ਪੱਕ ਕਰਨਾ, ਪੁਸ਼ਟੀ ਕਰਨੀ, ਤਸਦੀਕ ਕਰਨੀ, ਦ੍ਰਿੜ ਹੋਣਾ, ਹਾਮੀ ਭਰਨੀ, ਸਮਰਥਨ ਕਰਨਾ

affix (ਅ'ਫ਼ਿਕਸ, 'ਐਫ਼ਿਕਸ) v n ਜੋੜਨਾ, ਬੰਨ੍ਹਣਾ, ਨੰਥੀ ਕਰਨਾ, ਚਿਪਕਾਉਣਾ, ਲਾਉਣਾ; ਜੋੜ, ਯੋਗ, ਅਗੇਤਰ-ਪਿਛੇਤਰ

affluence ('ਐਫ਼ਲੂਅੰਸ) a ਬਹੁਲਤਾ, ਇਫ਼ਰਾਤ, ਸੰਪੰਨਤਾ, ਸਮਰਿਧੀ, ਧਨ, ਦੌਲਤਮੰਦੀ, ਖ਼ੁਸ਼ਹਾਲੀ, ਅਮੀਰੀ

afford (ਅ'ਫ਼ੋ'ਡ) v ਕਰ ਸਕਣਾ, ਸਾਰ ਸਕਣਾ, ਸਮਰੱਥਾ ਰੱਖਣਾ, ਸਮਰੱਥ, ਹੋਣਾ, ਪ੍ਰਦਾਨ ਕਰਨਾ, ਪੁਗਾਉਣਾ, ਵਾਰਾ ਖਾਣਾ, ਪੁੱਗ ਸਕਣਾ, ਸਾਧਨ ਇਕੱਠੇ ਕਰਨੇ

afforest (ਐ'ਫ਼ੋਰਿਸਟ) v ਬਿਰਛ ਲਾਉਣਾ, ਜੰਗਲ ਉਗਾਉਣਾ; ~ation ਰੁੱਖ ਜਾਂ ਬਿਰਛ ਲਾਉਣ ਦਾ ਕੰਮ, ਜੰਗਲਾਉਣ

affront (ਅ'ਫ਼ਰਅੰਟ) v n ਮੁਕਾਬਲਾ ਕਰਨਾ; ਨਿਰਾਦਰ ਕਰਨਾ, ਅਪਮਾਨਤ ਕਰਨਾ, ਪੱਤ ਲਾਹੁਣੀ; ਅਪਮਾਨ, ਤਿਰਸਕਾਰ, ਅਵੱਗਿਆ

afloat (ਅ'ਫ਼ਲਅਉਟ) adv a ਤਰਦਾ, ਵਗਦਾ, ਪਰਵਾਹਤ; ਜਹਾਜ਼ ਵਿਚ, ਪ੍ਰਚਲਤ, ਵਗਿੰਦਾ ਹੋਇਆ

afoot (ਅ'ਫ਼ੁਟ) n a ਪੈਦਲ, ਪਿਆਦਾ; ਚਲਦਾ ਹੋਇਆ, ਚਲਿਤ

afore (ਅਫ਼ੋ*) adv ਪਹਿਲਾ, ਸਾਮ੍ਹਣੇ, ਅਗੇ, ਮੁਹਰੇ; ਪੂਰਵ ਕਾਲ ਵਿਚ; ~said ਉਕਤ, ਪੂਰਵ ਕਥਿਤ

afraid (ਅ'ਫ਼ਰੇਇਡ) a ਡਰਿਆ, ਭੈਭੀਤ, ਸਹਿਮਿਆ, ਠਠੰਬਰਿਆ, ਤ੍ਰਹਿਆ, ਤ੍ਰਸਤ, ਛਹਿਆ

afresh (ਅ'ਫ਼ਰੈਸ਼) adv ਨਵੇਂ ਸਿਰਿਓਂ, ਨਵੇਂ ਸਿਰੇ ਤੋਂ, ਪੁਨਰ, ਦੁਬਾਰਾ, ਮੁਢੋਂ

after ('ਆਫ਼ਟਾ*) a adv prep conj ਮਗਰਲਾ, ਮਗਰੋਂ ਦਾ, ਪਿਛੋਂ ਦਾ, ਪਰਵਰਤੀ, ਬਾਅਦ, ਪਿੱਛੋਂ, ਉਪਰੰਤ, ਪਿੱਛੋਂ, ਬਾਅਦ ਵਿਚ; ਪਿਛੇ ਪਿਛੇ, ਫਿਰ ਵੀ, ਇੰਨਾ ਕੁਝ ਹੋਣ ਤੇ ਵੀ, ਜਦ; ~math ਸਿੱਟਾ, ਨਤੀਜਾ, ਪਰਿਣਾਮ; ~noon ਲੋਢਾ ਵੇਲਾ, ਤੀਜਾ ਪਹਿਰ, ਦੁਪਹਿਰ ਪਿੱਛੋਂ ਦਾ ਸਮਾਂ

again (ਅ'ਗੇਇਨ) adv ਫਿਰ, ਦੁਬਾਰਾ, ਮੁੜ ਕੇ, ਨਵੇਂ ਸਿਰਿਓਂ, ਪੁਨਰ

against (ਅ'ਗੇਨਸਟ) prep conj ਵਿਰੁੱਧ, ਵਿਪਰੀਤ, ਖ਼ਿਲਾਫ਼, ਉਲਟ, ਪ੍ਰਤੀਕੂਲ, ਮੁਕਾਬਲੇ ਵਿਚ, ਟਾਕਰੇ ਵਿਚ, ਬਦਲੇ

age (ਏਇਜ) n v ਉਮਰ, ਆਯੂ, ਅਵਸਥਾ, ਜੀਵਨ-ਕਾਲ; ਕਾਲ, ਯੁੱਗ, ਪੀੜ੍ਹੀ, ਸਮਾਂ, ਜ਼ਮਾਨਾ; ਬੁਢੇਪਾ; ~d ਬੁੱਢਾ, ਬਿਰਧ, ਪੁਰਾਣਾ; ~less ਨਿੱਤ ਨਵਾਂ, ਸਦਾ ਜਵਾਨ, ਸਦਾ ਨਵੀਨ; ~old ਪੁਰਾਤਨ,

ਪ੍ਰਾਚੀਨ, ਪੁਰਾਣੀ

agency (ਏਇਜੰਸਿ) *n* ਸ਼ਾਖ; ਆਤ੍ਰ; ਸਾਧਨ, ਸਬੰਧ, ਏਜੰਸੀ

agenda (ਅ'ਜੈਨਡਆ) *n* ਕਾਰਜ-ਸੂਚੀ, ਕਾਰਜਕ੍ਰਮ, ਏਜੰਡਾ

agent ('ਏਇਜਅੰਟ) *n* ਪ੍ਰਤੀਨਿਧ, ਆਤੂਤੀ, ਦਲਾਲ, ਮੁਖਤਾਰ, ਕਾਰਿੰਦਾ, ਕਾਰਜ-ਕਰਤਾ

aggravate ('ਐਗਰਅਵ੍ਰੇਇਟ) *v* ਵਧਾਉਣਾ, ਵਪਰੇ ਵਿਗਾੜਨਾ; ਗੰਭੀਰ ਹੋਣਾ ਜਾਂ ਬਣਾਉਣਾ, ਚਿੜਾਉਣਾ, ਤੰਗ ਕਰਨਾ

aggravating ('ਐਗਰਅਵ੍ਰੇਇਟਿਙ) *a* ਤੰਗ ਕਰਨ ਵਾਲਾ, ਸਤਾਊ

aggravation ('ਐਗਰਅਵ੍ਰੇਇਸ਼ਨ) *n* ਵਿਗਾੜ, ਗੰਭੀਰਤਾ

aggregate ('ਐਗਰਿਗਅਟ, 'ਐਗਰਿਗੇਇਟ) *a n v* ਕੁੱਲ ਜੋੜ; ਸਮੂਹ, ਭੀੜ, ਸਮੁਦਾਇ; ਕੁੱਲ, ਇਕੱਠਾ, ਸੰਕਲਤ, ਏਕੀਕ੍ਰਿਤ; ਸਮੂਹੀਕ੍ਰਿਤ ਹੋਣਾ, ਇਕੱਠੇ ਹੋਣਾ, ਜਮ੍ਹਾਂ ਹੋਣਾ ਜਾਂ ਕਰਨਾ ਢੇਰ ਲਗਾਉਣਾ

aggress (ਅ'ਗਰੈੱਸ) *v* ਹਮਲਾ ਕਰਨਾ, (ਛੇੜ-ਛਾੜ ਵਿਚ) ਪਹਿਲ ਕਰਨੀ; ~**ion** ਹੱਲਾ, ਹਮਲਾ, ਚੜ੍ਹਾਈ, ਧਾਵਾ, ਆਕਰਮਣ; ਵਧੀਕੀ, ਵਾਧਾ, ਧੱਕਾ; ~**ive** ਹੱਲੇ ਲਈ ਤਿਆਰ ਰਹਿਣ ਵਾਲਾ, ਹਮਲੇ-ਸਬੰਧੀ, ਹੱਲੇ ਬਾਰੇ, ਆਕਰਮਣ-ਸ਼ੀਲ, ਉੱਦਮਸ਼ੀਲ; ~**or** ਹਮਲਾਵਰ, ਵਿਰੋਧੀ, ਲੜਾਕਾ, ਵਧੀਕੀ ਕਰਨ ਵਾਲਾ

aggrieve (ਅ'ਗਰੀਵ੍) *v* ਦੁਖਾਉਣਾ, ਦੁੱਖ ਦੇਣਾ, ਕਸ਼ਟ ਦੇਣਾ, ਦੁਖੀ ਕਰਨਾ, ਤੰਗ ਕਰਨਾ

aghast (ਅ'ਗਾਸਟ) *a* ਹੱਕਾ-ਬੱਕਾ, ਹੈਰਾਨ, ਵਿਸਮਤ, ਡੌਰ-ਭੌਰ, ਘੌਂਦਲਿਆ

agile ('ਐਜਾਇਲ) *a* ਚੁਸਤ, ਫੁਰਤੀਲਾ

agility (ਅ'ਜਿਲਅਟਿ) *n* ਚੁਸਤੀ, ਚਲਾਕੀ, ਫੁਰਤੀ, ਤੀਬਰਤਾ

agitate ('ਐਜਿਟੇਇਟ) *v* ਭੜਕਾਉਣਾ, ਉਕਸਾਉਣਾ, ਭਖਾਉਣਾ, ਉਤੇਜਤ ਕਰਨਾ; ਅੰਦੋਲਨ ਕਰਨਾ, ਹਲਚਲ ਕਰਨਾ; ਸੰਘਰਸ਼ ਕਰਨਾ; ~**d** ਉਤੇਜਤ, ਭੜਕਿਆ, ਸਤਾਇਆ, ਦੁਖੀ

agitation ('ਐਜਿ'ਟੇਇਸ਼ਨ) *n* ਅੰਦੋਲਨ, ਗੜਬੜ, ਵਿਆਕੁਲਤਾ, ਉਕਸਾਹਟ, ਹਲਚਲ, ਕਲਹ, ਉਤੇਜਨਾ

agitator ('ਐਜਿਟੇਇਟਆ*) *n* ਅੰਦੋਲਨ-ਕਰਤਾ, ਅੰਦੇਲਕ; ਹਲਚਲ ਪੈਦਾ ਕਰਨ ਵਾਲਾ, ਅੰਦੋਲਨਕਾਰੀ, ਉਪਦਰਵੀ

agony ('ਐਗਅਨਿ) *n* ਮਾਨਸਕ ਪੀੜ, ਵੇਦਨਾ, ਸੰਤਾਪ, ਚਿੰਤਾ, ਤਸੀਹਾ, ਸਰੀਰਕ ਕਸ਼ਟ; ਸੰਘਰਸ਼

agree (ਅ'ਗਰੀ) *v* ਮੰਨਣਾ, ਰਜ਼ਾਮੰਦ ਹੋਣਾ, ਹਾਮੀ ਭਰਨਾ, ਸਹਿਮਤ ਹੋਣਾ, ਰਾਜ਼ੀ ਹੋਣਾ, ਸਹਿਮਤੀ ਦੇਣਾ; ਤੈ ਕਰਨਾ; ~**able** ਅਨੁਕੂਲ; ਅਨੁਸਾਰ, ਅਨੁਰੂਪ, ਰਾਜ਼ੀ, ਸਹਿਮਤ; ਸੁਖਾਵਾਂ, ਰਮਣੀਕ, ਮਨੋਹਰ; ~**ment** ਸਹਿਮਤੀ, ਰਜ਼ਾਮੰਦੀ; ਮੇਲ; ਅਨੁਰੂਪਤਾ; ਸਮਝੌਤਾ, ਰਾਜ਼ੀਨਾਮਾ, ਇਕਰਾਰਨਾਮਾ

agricultural ('ਐਗਰਿ'ਕਲਚੱ(ਅ)ਰਲ) *a* ਵਾਹੀ ਦਾ, ਭੋਂ ਦਾ, ਖੇਤੀਬਾੜੀ ਦਾ, ਕਿਰਸਾਣੀ ਦਾ; ~**ist** ਵਾਹਕ, ਕਿਸਾਨ, ਜ਼ਿਮੀਂਦਾਰ

agriculture ('ਐਗਰਿਅੱਲਚਆ*) *n* ਖੇਤੀਬਾੜੀ, ਵਾਹੀ, ਕਾਸ਼ਤਕਾਰੀ, ਖੇਤੀ, ਕਿਰਸਾਨੀ, ਕ੍ਰਿਸੀ

agriculturist ('ਐਗਰਿ'ਕੱਅੰਚਅਰਿਸਟ) *n* ਕਿਰਸਾਣ, ਕਿਸਾਨ, ਜ਼ਮੀਨ ਵਾਹੁਣ ਜੀ ਬੀਜਣ ਵਾਲਾ, ਕਾਸ਼ਤਕਾਰ, ਖੇਤੀਬਾੜੀ ਕਰਨ ਵਾਲਾ

ahead (ਐ'ਹੈੱਡ) *adv pred a* ਅੱਗੇ, ਅਗਾੜੀ, ਸਾਮੂਟੇ, ਅਗਾਂਹ, ਅੱਗੇ, ਵੱਲ; ਤੇਜ਼ ਕਦਮਾਂ ਨਾਲ, ਤੀਬਰ ਗਤੀ ਨਾਲ, ਵਧਦੇ ਹੋਏ

aid (ਏਇਡ) *v n* ਸਹਾਇਤਾ ਕਰਨੀ, ਮਦਦ ਕਰਨੀ, ਉਪਕਾਰ ਕਰਨਾ; ਸਹਾਇਤਾ, ਮਦਦ

aide-de-camp ('ਏਇਡਡਅ'ਕੈਂਪ) *n* ਸੈਨਾਪਤੀ ਦਾ ਸਹਾਇਕ ਅਧਿਕਾਰੀ, ਏਡੀਕਾਂਗ, ਅੰਗ-ਸੇਵਕ

ail (ਏਇਲ) *v* ਕਸ਼ਟ ਦੇਣਾ, ਪੀੜਤ ਹੋਣਾ, ਦੁੱਖ ਦੇਣਾ ਜਾਂ ਹੋਣਾ, ਰੋਗੀ ਹੋਣਾ; **~ing** ਬੀਮਾਰ, ਦੁਖੀ, ਰੋਗੀ, ਪੀੜਤ; **~ment** ਤਬੀਅਤ ਦੀ ਖ਼ਰਾਬੀ

aim (ਏਇਮ) *n v* ਨਿਸ਼ਾਨਾ, ਟੀਚਾ, ਉਦੇਸ਼ ਮਨਸ਼ਾ; ਨਿਸ਼ਾਨਾ ਬਨਣਾ, ਵਾਰ ਕਰਨਾ, ਚੇਸ਼ਟਾ ਕਰਨੀ; **~less** ਮਨੋਰਥਹੀਣ, ਨਿਰਉਦੇਸ਼; **~lessness** ਅਟਕਣ, ਉਦੇਸ਼ਹੀਣਤਾ

air (ਏਅ) *a n* ਹਵਾ, ਵਾਯੂ; ਵਾਤਾਵਰਣ, ਵਾਯੂ-ਮੰਡਲ; ਰੰਗ ਢੰਗ, ਨਖ਼ਰਾ; ਹਵਾ ਵਿਚ ਰਖਣਾ, ਹਵਾ ਲੁਆਉਣਾ, ਹਵਾ ਖਾਣਾ, ਪਰਗਟਾਉਣਾ; **in the~** ਅਫ਼ਵਾਹ, ਅਵਾਈ; **on the~** ਰੇਡੀਓ ਤੋਂ ਬੋਲਦੇ ਹੋਏ; **open~** ਖੁੱਲ੍ਹ-ਬਹਾਰਾ, ਖੁਲ੍ਹੀ ਥਾਂ; **~base** ਹਵਾਈ ਅੱਡਾ; **~conditioned** ਵਾਯੂ-ਅਨੁਕੂਲਤ; **~craft** ਹਵਾਈ ਜਹਾਜ਼, ਵਿਮਾਨ; **~field** ਹਵਾਈ-ਅੱਡਾ; **~force** ਹਵਾਈ ਸੈਨਾ, ਵਾਯੂ ਸੈਨਾ; **~line** ਹਵਾਈ ਕੰਪਨੀ, ਵਾਯੂ-ਮਾਰਗ **~mail** ਹਵਾਈ ਡਾਕ; **~port** ਹਵਾਈ ਅੱਡਾ; **~way** ਹਵਾ ਦੇ ਆਉਣ-ਜਾਣ ਦਾ ਰਾਹ; ਵਾਯੂਮਾਰਗ, ਖਾਣਾਂ ਵਿਚ ਹਵਾ ਆਉਣ ਜਾਣ ਲਈ ਬਣਿਆ ਰਸਤਾ; **~iness** ਹੋਛਾਪਣ; ਦਿਖਾਵਾ; **~less** ਹਵਾ ਰਹਿਤ, ਦਮ ਘੋਟੂ; **~y** ਹਲਕਾ, ਹੋਲਾ, ਹਵਾਈ, ਖੁੱਲ੍ਹਾ, ਹਵਾਦਾਰ, ਪ੍ਰਸੰਨਚਿੱਤ, ਬੁਲੰਦ, ਉੱਚਾ; ਬਾਰੀਕ, ਪਤਲਾ, ਨਿਰਰਥਕ; ਜਿੰਦਾਦਿਲ, ਰੰਗੀਲਾ

alarm (ਅ'ਲਾਮ) *n v* ਚੇਤਾਵਨੀ, ਖ਼ਤਰੇ ਦਾ ਘੁੱਗੂ, ਬਿਗਲ, ਅਲਾਰਮ, ਖ਼ਬਰਦਾਰ ਕਰਨਾ, ਚੇਤਾਵਨੀ ਦੇਣਾ, ਡਰਾ ਦੇਣਾ, ਤ੍ਰਬਕਾ ਦੇਣਾ, ਹਾਲ ਦੁਹਾਈ ਪਾਉਣੀ, ਟਣਟਣਾਉਣਾ, ਅਲਾਰਮ ਬੋਲਣਾ; ਵਿਆਕੁਲ ਕਰਨਾ, ਉਤੇਜਤ ਕਰਨਾ; **~clock** ਅਲਾਰਮ-ਘੜੀ; **~ed** ਡਰਿਆ, ਭੈ-ਭੀਤ, ਘਬਰਾਇਆ, ਸਹਿਮਿਆ; **~ing** ਖ਼ਤਰਨਾਕ, ਚਿੰਤਾਜਨਕ, ਡਰਾਉਣਾ, ਤ੍ਰਾਹ ਕੱਢ ਦੇਣ ਵਾਲਾ

alas (ਅ'ਲੈਸ) *interj* ਉਹੋ, ਅਫ਼ਸੋਸ! ਹਾਏ! ਹਾਏ-ਹਾਏ!

ablum ('ਐਲਬਅਮ) *n* ਐਲਬਮ, ਚਿੱਤਰਾਵਲੀ, ਚਿੱਤਰ-ਪੁਸਤਕ

alcohol (ਐਲਕਅਹੌਲ) *n* ਮਦਸਾਰ; ਸਪਿਰਿਟ; ਅਲਕੋਹਲ

alert (ਅ'ਲਅ:ਟ) *a n v* ਚੌਕੰਨਾ, ਖ਼ਬਰਦਾਰ, ਚੌਕਸ; ਚੇਤਾਵਨੀ, ਸੰਕਟ ਸਮੇਂ ਦੀ ਸੂਚਨਾ; ਸਾਵਧਾਨ ਕਰਨਾ, ਸਚੇਤ ਕਰਨਾ; **~ness** ਸਾਵਧਾਨੀ, ਚੇਤਨਤਾ, ਖ਼ਬਰਦਾਰੀ, ਤਕੜਾਈ, ਤਿਆਰੀ

algebra ('ਐਲਜਿਬਰਅ) *n* ਬੀਜ ਗਣਿਤ, ਅਲਜਬਰਾ

alias ('ਏਇਲਿਅਸ) *n* ਉਪਨਾਮ, ਅੱਲ, ਉਰਫ਼, ਅਸਲੀ ਨਾਂ ਤੋਂ ਬਿਨਾਂ ਕੋਈ ਦੂਜਾ ਨਾਂ

alien ('ਏਇਲਯਅਨ) *a n* ਬਾਹਰਲਾ ਵਿਦੇਸ਼ੀ, ਓਪਰਾ, ਪਰਾਇਆ, ਬੇਗਾਨਾ, ਨਾਵਾਕਫ਼; ਅਸੰਗਤ, ਬਾਹਰੀ ਵਿਅਕਤੀ

alike (ਅ'ਲਾਇਕ) *a adv* ਤੁੱਲ, ਵਰਗਾ, ਮਿਲਦਾ-ਜੁਲਦਾ, ਸਮਾਨ, ਉਹੋ ਜਿਹਾ, ਉਵੇਂ ਹੀ, ਉਸੇ ਤਰ੍ਹਾਂ

alive (ਅ'ਲਾਇਵ੍) *a* ਜੀਉਂਦਾ, ਜੀਉਂਦਾ-ਜਾਗਦਾ, ਜੀਵਤ; ਫੁਰਤੀਲਾ, ਸਜੀਵ; ਵਰਤਮਾਨ, ਸਾਵਧਾਨ, ਸੋਝੀਵਾਨ, ਚੇਤਨ; ਛੋਹਲਾ, ਭਰਪੂਰ

all (ਆੱਲ) *a n adv* ਸਾਰਾ, ਸਾਰੇ ਦਾ ਸਾਰਾ, ਪੂਰਾ, ਸਮੁੱਚਾ, ਸਰਬ, ਕੁਲੱ, ਬਿਲਕੁਲ, ਸਭ ਕੁਝ,

ਪੂਰੀ ਤਰ੍ਹਾਂ

allay (ਅ'ਲੇਇ) *v* ਮੱਠਾ ਕਰਨਾ, (ਪੀੜ ਆਦਿ ਦਾ) ਘਟਾਉਣਾ, (ਤੇਹ ਦਾ) ਹਟਾਉਣਾ, ਦੂਰ ਕਰਨਾ, (ਦੰਗੇ ਫ਼ਸਾਦ ਨੂੰ) ਦਬਾ ਦੇਣਾ

allegation ('ਏਲਿ'ਗੇਇਸ਼ਨ) *n* ਦੋਸ਼, ਇਲਜ਼ਾਮ, ਦਾਵਾ; ਦੂਸ਼ਨ, ਉਜ

allegiance (ਅ'ਲੀਜੀਅਨਸ) *n* ਤਾਬੇਦਾਰੀ, ਵਫ਼ਾਦਾਰੀ, ਨਿਮਕ ਹਲਾਲੀ, ਰਾਜ-ਭਗਤੀ, ਸੁਆਮੀ-ਭਗਤੀ; **oath of~** ਵਫ਼ਾਦਾਰੀ ਦੀ ਸੌਂਗਧ, ਹਲਫ਼ੇ-ਵਫ਼ਾਦਾਰੀ

allegory ('ਐਲਿਗਾਅਰਿ) *n* ਰੂਪਕ, ਦੁਅਰਥੀ ਗੱਲ ਜਾਂ ਬਿਆਨ, ਦੂਹਰੇ ਭਾਵ ਵਾਲੀ ਕਵਿਤਾ; ਦ੍ਰਿਸ਼ਟਾਂਤ, ਪ੍ਰਤੀਕ

allergy ('ਐਲਅ*ਜਿ) *n* ਜਿਸਮ ਉੱਤੇ ਪਿਆ ਬਾਹਰਲਾ ਅਸਰ ਜੋ ਕਿਸੇ ਬੀਮਾਰੀ ਦਾ ਕਾਰਨ ਬਣੇ, ਅਤੀ ਸੰਵੇਦਨਸ਼ੀਲਤਾ, ਐਲਰਜੀ

alley (ਐਲਿ) *n* ਗਲੀ, ਭੀੜੀ ਗਲੀ, ਪਟੜੀ, ਤੰਗ ਰਸਤਾ, ਲਾਂਘਾ, ਪਗਡੰਡੀ; **blind~** ਬੰਦ ਗਲੀ

alliance (ਅ'ਲਾਇਅੰਸ) *n* ਗੱਠਜੋੜ, ਸੰਧੀ, ਮਿੱਤਰਤਾ, ਭਾਈ-ਵਾਲੀ, ਸਾਕਾਦਾਰੀ, ਨਾਤਾ, ਰਿਸ਼ਤਾ

allied (ਅ'ਲਾਇਡ) *a* ਸਬੰਧਤ, ਨਾਲ ਦਾ ਸਬੰਧ, ਜੁੜਿਆ ਹੋਇਆ, ਸਮਾਨ

alliteration (ਅ'ਲਿਟਅ'ਰੇਇਸ਼ਨ) *n* ਅਨੁਪ੍ਰਾਸ, ਵਰਣਆਵ੍ਰਿਤੀ

allocate ('ਐਲਅ(ਉ)ਕੇਇਟ) *v* ਵੰਡ ਦੇਣਾ, ਵੰਡੀ ਪਾਉਣੀ, ਟਿਕਣਾ, ਮਿੱਥਣਾ; ਨਿਸ਼ਚਤ ਕਰਨਾ, ਨਿਰਧਾਰਤ ਕਰਨਾ, ਹਿੱਸਾ ਕੱਢਣਾ, ਹਿੱਸੇ ਵੰਡਣੇ; ਸਥਾਨ ਨਿਯੁਕਤ ਕਰਨਾ

allocation ('ਐਲਅ(ਉ)'ਕੇਇਸ਼ਨ) *n* ਵੰਡਾਰਾ, ਬਟਵਾਰਾ, ਹਿੱਸੇ-ਵੰਡ, ਵੰਡ

allot (ਅ'ਲੌਟ) *v* ਹਿੱਸੇ-ਪਾਉਣਾ, ਵੰਡ ਕੇ ਦੇਣਾ, ਗੁਣੇ ਪਾਉਣਾ, ਟਿਕਣਾ, ਮਿੱਥਣਾ; ਵੰਡਣਾ, ਮੁਕੱਰਰ ਕਰਨਾ, ਅਲਾਟ ਕਰਨਾ; **~ment** ਹਿੱਸੇ-ਵੰਡ, ਵੰਡਾਰਾ, ਵਿਤਾਜਨ; ਨਿਰਧਾਰਨ; ਹਿੱਸਾ, ਨਿਰਧਾਰਤ ਭਾਗ; ਪ੍ਰਾਪਤਬੱਧ, ਭਾਗਾ, ਕਿਸਮਤ, ਨਸੀਬ; **~tee** ਵੰਡ-ਪਾਤਰ, ਜਿਸ ਨੂੰ ਚੀਜ਼ ਦਾ ਹਿੱਸਾ ਵੰਡ ਕੇ ਦਿੱਤਾ ਜਾਵੇ, ਅਲਾਟੀ

allow (ਅ'ਲਾਉ) *v* ਆਗਿਆ ਦੇਣੀ, ਇਜਾਜ਼ਤ ਦੇਣੀ, ਮੰਨਣਾ, ਜੋਗ ਮੰਨਣਾ; ਸਹਾਰਨਾ, ਝੱਲਣਾ; ਘਟਾਉਣਾ, ਕਾਟ ਕੱਟਣੀ, ਪ੍ਰਬੰਧ ਕਰਨਾ

alloy (ਅ'ਲੌਇ) *n v* ਮਿਸ਼ਰਤ ਧਾਤ, ਧਾਤ-ਮਿਸ਼ਰਨ, ਖੋਟ, ਮਿਲਾਵਟ, ਰਲਾ; ਮਿਸ਼ਰਨ ਕਰਨਾ; ਖੋਟ ਮਿਲਾਉਣੀ, ਖੋਟ ਮਿਲਾਉਣੀ, ਮਿਲਾਵਟ ਕਰਨੀ; ਖੋਟਾ ਬਣਾਉਣਾ; ਮੁੱਲ ਘਟਾਉਣਾ

allure (ਅ'ਲਯੁਅ*) *v n* ਭਰਮਾਉਣਾ, ਲਾਲਚ ਦੇਣਾ, ਵਰਗਲਾਉਣਾ, ਛਲਣਾ, ਮੋਹ ਲੈਣਾ, ਆਕਰਸ਼ਤ ਕਰਨਾ, ਰੀਝਾਉਣਾ, ਲਾਲਚ, ਲੋਭ, ਛਲ, ਆਕਰਸ਼ਨ, ਖਿਚ; **-ment** ਲੋਭ, ਲਾਲਚ, ਲਲਚਾਉ, ਖਿਚਾਉ, ਰੀਝ, ਰੀਝਾਉ, ਆਕਰਸ਼ਨ; ਮੋਹ

alluring (ਅ'ਲਯੁਅਰਿਙ) *a* ਮੋਹਕ, ਆਕਰਸ਼ਕ

allusion (ਅ'ਲੂਯ਼ਨ) *n* ਸੰਕੇਤ, ਰਮਜ਼, ਹਵਾਲਾ, ਗੁੱਝਾ ਇਸ਼ਾਰਾ, ਨਿਰਦੇਸ਼ ਸੰਦਰਤ, ਇਸ਼ਾਰੇ ਦੀ ਗੱਲ, ਗੁੱਝੀ ਗੱਲ

alma mater ('ਐਲਮਅ'ਮਾਟਅ*) *n* ਮਾਤਰੀ ਸੰਸਥਾ, ਆਪਣਾ ਕਾਲਜ ਜਾਂ ਵਿਦਿਆਲਾ, ਯੂਨੀਵਰਸਿਟੀਆਂ ਅਤੇ ਕਾਲਜਾਂ ਲਈ ਵਰਤਿਆ ਜਾਂਦਾ ਆਦਰਸੂਚਕ ਸ਼ਬਦ

almighty (ਅਲ'ਮਾਇਟਿ) *a adv* ਸਰਬਸ਼ਕਤੀਮਾਨ; (ਅਪ) ਮਹਾਂ

almirah ('ਐਲਮਿਰਅ) *n* ਅਲਮਾਰੀ

almond ('ਆਮਅਨਡ) *n* ਬਦਾਮ, ਬਦਾਮ ਵਰਗੀ

ਚੀਜ਼; ~oil ਬਦਾਮ-ਰੋਗਨ

almost ('ਓਲਮਅਉਸਟ) *adv* ਲਗਭਗ, ਕਰੀਬ

ਕਰੀਬ, ਤਕਰੀਬਨ

alms (ਆਮ) *n* ਭਿਖਿਆ, ਖ਼ੈਰਾਤ, ਖ਼ੈਰ, ਦਾਨ

aloft (ਅ'ਲੋਫ਼ਟ) *adv* ਉਤਾਂਹ, ਉੱਚਾ, ਉੱਚੇ ਦਾਅ,

ਉੱਪਰ ਨੂੰ (ਜਾਂ ਵੱਲ), ਆਕਾਸ਼ ਵਿਚ, ਹਵਾ ਵਿਚ

alone (ਅ'ਲਅਉਨ) *adv a* ਇਕੱਲਾ, ਇਕੋ ਹੀ,

ਇਕਾਕੀ, ਕੱਲਾ-ਸੁਕੱਲਾ, ਇਕੋ-ਇਕ, ਛੜਾ,

ਨਿਰਾ; ਸਿਰਫ਼; ਅਦੁੱਤੀ, ਲਾਸਾਨੀ, ਬੇਜੋੜ;

leave~ ਇਕੱਲੇ ਛੱਡਣਾ

along (ਅ'ਲੋਙ) *a adv prep* ਨਾਲ, ਨਾਲ-

ਨਾਲ, ਲਾਗੋ-ਲੁਾਗੋ, ਕੰਢੇ; ਇਕ ਸਿਰੇ ਤੋਂ ਦੂਜੇ ਸਿਰੇ

ਤਕ, ਪੂਰੀ ਲੰਬਾਈ ਵਿਚ ਜਾਂ ਲੰਬਾਈ ਦੇ ਕੁਝ

ਭਾਗ ਵਿਚ, ਅਗਾਂਹ, ਅਗਾਂਹ ਵੱਲ (ਨੂੰ),

ਸਿੱਧਾ; all~ ਹਰ ਵੇਲੇ, ਹਰ ਮੌਕੇ, ਪੂਰੇ ਸਮੇਂ

ਲਈ, ਅੰਤ ਤਕ, ਤੋੜ ਤਕ; ~side ਬਗਲ ਵਿਚ,

ਨੇੜੇ, ਨਿਕਟ, ਕੋਲ, ਪਾਸ, ਬਰਾਬਰ-ਬਰਾਬਰ;

~with ਨਾਲ-ਨਾਲ, ਸੰਗ-ਸੰਗ, ਨਾਲ ਹੀ

aloof (ਅ'ਲੂਫ਼) *adv* ਅਲੱਗ, ਔਡ, ਵੱਖ, ਪਰਾਂ,

ਦੂਰ; ਨਿਆਰਾ, ਅਲਹਿਦਾ, ਨਿਵੇਕਲਾ; ਲਾਂਭੇ

aloud (ਅ'ਲਾਉਡ) *adv* ਉੱਚੀ ਅਵਾਜ਼ ਵਿਚ,

ਉੱਚਾ ਬੋਲ ਕੇ, ਸਪਸ਼ਟ ਰੂਪ ਵਿਚ, ਖੁੱਲ੍ਹਮ-ਖੁੱਲ੍ਹਾ,

ਪਰਗਟ ਰੂਪ ਵਿਚ

alphabet ('ਐਲਫ਼ਅਬੇਟ) *n* ਵਰਨਮਾਲਾ, ਉੱਤ-

ਐੜਾ; ਪੈਂਤੀ, ਮੁੱਢਲੇ ਸਿਧਾਂਤ, ਮੁੱਢ; ~tical ਵਰਨ-

ਕ੍ਰਮ-ਸਬੰਧ, ਵਰਨਮਾਲਾ ਦਾ, ਵਰਨਾਤਮਕ

already (ਅਲ'ਰੈੱਡੀ) *adv* ਪਹਿਲਾਂ ਹੀ, ਪਹਿਲਾਂ

ਤੋਂ ਹੀ, ਅੱਗੇ ਹੀ, ਹੁਣੇ, ਹੁਣ ਤੀਕ, ਹੁਣ ਤਾਈਂ

also (ਅਲਸਅਉ) *adv* ਵੀ, ਨਾਲੇ, ਨਾਲ ਹੀ,

ਅਤੇ, (ਇਸ ਤੋਂ) ਇਲਾਵਾ

altar ('ਅਲਟ*) *n* ਵੇਦੀ, ਕੁਰਬਾਨਗਾਹ, ਉਹ ਥਾਂ

ਜਿਥੇ ਕੁਰਬਾਨੀ ਦਿੱਤੀ ਜਾਵੇ

alter ('ਅਲਟਅ*) *v* ਬਦਲਉਣਾ, ਬਦਲ ਦੇਣਾ,

ਰੂਪਾਂਤਰ ਕਰਨਾ, ਪਰਿਵਰਤਨ ਕਰਨਾ; ~ation

ਤਬਦੀਲੀ, ਪਰਿਵਰਤਨ, ਪਲਟਾ, ਰੂਪਾਂਤਰ;

~nate ਬਦਲਵਾਂ, ਪਰਤਵਾਂ, ਇਕ ਦੂਜੇ ਦੇ ਪਿੱਛੇ

ਆਉਣਾ, ਵਾਰੀ ਵਾਰੀ ਆਉਣਾ ਜਾਂ ਰਖੱਣਾ, ਬਦਲ

ਬਦਲ ਕੇ ਆਉਣਾ; ਫੇਰਵਾਂ, ਏਕਾਂਤਰ, ਹਰ ਦੂਜਾ,

ਵਟਾਵਾਂ, ਇਵਜ਼ੀ; ~nately ਵਾਰੀ ਵਾਰੀ, ਬਦਲ

ਕੇ, ਇਕ ਪਿੱਛੋਂ ਦੂਜਾ; ~native ਫੇਰਵਾਂ, ਬਦਲਵਾਂ

ਬਦਲੇ ਦਾ ਵਟਾਵਾਂ, ਦੂਜੀ ਸੂਰਤ, ਆਖ਼ਰੀ ਤਰੀਕਾ,

ਦੋਹਾਂ ਵਿਚੋਂ ਇਕ, ਇਹ ਜਾਂ ਉਹ, ਬਦਲ

although (ਅਲ'ਦਅਉ) *conj* ਭਾਵੇਂ, ਹਾਲਾਂਕਿ,

ਜਦੋਂ ਕਿ, ਤਾਂ ਵੀ, ਚਾਹੇ

altitude ('ਐਲਟਿਟਯੂਡ) *n* ਉਚਾਨ, ਉਚਾਈ

ਉੱਚੀ ਥਾਂ, ਮਹੱਤਾ, ਸ੍ਰੇਸ਼ਠਤਾ; (ਗਣਿ) ਖੜੀ

ਲੰਬਾਈ, ਅਵਲੰਬ, ਉਚਾਈ, ਸਾਗਰ ਤਟ ਤੋਂ

ਉਚਾਈ

altogether (ਓਲਟਅ'ਗੈਦਅ*) *adv* ਸਾਰੇ ਦਾ

ਸਾਰਾ, ਉੱਕਾ-ਪੁੱਕਾ, ਸਭ ਮਿਲਾ ਕੇ, ਪੂਰੀ ਤਰ੍ਹਾਂ,

ਨਿਰਾ, ਬਿਲਕੁਲ

always ('ਓਲਵ੍ਵਿਜ਼) *adv* ਸਦਾ, ਨਿੱਤ, ਹਮੇਸ਼ਾ,

ਹਰ ਸਮੇਂ, ਹਰ ਦਮ, ਹਰ ਵੇਲੇ, ਨਿਰੰਤਰ

a.m. (ਏਇ'ਐੱਮ) (L) ਪੂਰਬ-ਦੁਪਹਿਰ

amalgam (ਅ'ਮੈਲਗਅਮ) *n* ਮਿਲਾਵਟ, ਰਲਾ,

ਮਿਸ਼ਰਣ; ਕਿਸੇ ਧਾਤ ਦਾ ਪਾਰੇ ਨਾਲ ਮਿਸ਼ਰਣ;

~ate ਰਲਾਉਣਾ, ਮਿਲਾਉਣਾ, ਰਲਣਾ, ਮਿਲਣਾ,

ਸਾਂਝ ਪਾਉਣੀ, ਕਿਸੇ ਧਾਤ ਨੂੰ ਪਾਰੇ ਨਾਲ

ਮਿਲਾਉਣਾ, ਮਿਸ਼ਰਤ ਕਰਨਾ ਜਾਂ ਹੋਣਾ; ~ated

ਮਿਲਿਆ-ਜੁਲਿਆ, ਮਿਸ਼ਰਤ, ਇਕੱਠ, ਸੰਯੋਜਤ;

~ation ਮਿਲਾਵਟ, ਰਲਾ, ਮਿਸ਼ਰਨ, ਇਕੱਠ, ਸਾਂਝ, ਸੰਜੋਜਨ, ਯੋਗ, ਜਾਤੀ-ਮਿਸ਼ਰਨ, ਧਾਤੂ-ਮਿਸ਼ਰਨ

amass (ਅ'ਮੈਸ) *v* ਜੋੜਨਾ, ਸਮੇਟਨਾ, ਇਕੱਠਾ ਕਰਨਾ, ਸੰਚਤ ਕਰਨਾ, ਇਕੱਤਰ ਕਰਨਾ, ਸੰਗ੍ਰਹ ਕਰਨਾ, ਢੇਰ ਲਾਉਣਾ

amateur ('ਐਮਅਟਅ*) *n* ਗੈਰ-ਪੇਸ਼ਾਵਰ, ਸ਼ੁਕੀਨ, ਕਲਾ-ਪਰੇਮੀ

amaze (ਅ'ਮੇਇਜ਼) *n* ਹੈਰਾਨ ਕਰਨਾ, ਅਚੰਭਾ ਪੈਦਾ ਕਰਨਾ, ਵਿਸਮਤ ਕਰਨਾ, ਹੱਕਾ ਬੱਕਾ ਕਰਨਾ, ਚਕਰਾਉਣਾ; ~d ਡੌਰ-ਭੌਰ, ਭੌਚੱਕਾ, ਹੱਕਾ-ਬੱਕਾ, ਅਚੰਭਤ, ਵਿਸਮਤ; ~ment ਵਿਸਮੈ, ਹੈਰਾਨੀ, ਅਚੰਭਾ, ਅਸਚਰਜਤਾ, ਚਮਤਕਾਰ

amazing (ਐ'ਮੇਇਜ਼ਿੰਡ) *a* ਅਸਚਰਜ, ਵਿਸਮੈਕਾਰ, ਵਿਸਮਾਦੀ, ਅਜੀਬ, ਹੈਰਾਨਕੁਨ

ambassador (ਐਮ'ਬੈਸਅਡਅ*) *n* ਸਫ਼ੀਰ, ਰਾਜਦੂਤ, ਏਲਚੀ, ਦੂਤ

ambiguity ('ਐਮਬਿ'ਗਾਯੂਅਟਿ) *n* ਸੰਦੇਹ, ਸ਼ੱਕ, ਦੁਅਰਥਤਾ, ਅਸਪਸ਼ਟਤਾ, ਗੋਲ-ਮੋਲ ਗੱਲ, ਵਕਰੋਕਤੀ

ambiguous (ਐਂ'ਬਿਗਾਯੂਅਸ) *a* ਦੁਅਰਥੀ, ਸੰਦੇਹ-ਯੁਕਤ, ਅਸਪਸ਼ਟ, ਦੂਹਰੇ ਮਤਲਬ ਵਾਲਾ, ਅਨਿਸ਼ਚਤ, ਸ਼ੱਕ ਵਾਲਾ, ਮਸ਼ਕੂਕ

ambit (ਐਂਬਿਟ) *n* ਦਾਇਰਾ, ਘੇਰਾ, ਆਲਾ-ਦੁਆਲਾ

ambition (ਐਂ'ਬਿਸ਼ਨ) *n* ਅਭਿਲਾਸ਼ਾ, ਆਕਾਂਖਿਆ; ਤਾਂਘ, ਇੱਛਾ, ਚਾਹ, ਲਾਲਸਾ, ਦਾਇਆ, ਟੀਚਾ ਨਿਸ਼ਾਨਾ

ambitious (ਐਂ'ਬਿਸ਼ਸ) *a* ਅਭਿਲਾਸ਼ੀ, ਚਾਹਵਾਨ, ਤਾਂਘੀ, ਆਕਾਂਖਿਆਵਾਨ; ਜੋਸ਼ ਭਰਿਆ, ਉਤਸ਼ਾਹਪੂਰਨ; ਸ਼ਾਨਦਾਰ

ambulance ('ਐਂਬਯੁਲਅਨਸ) *n* ਹਸਪਤਾਲੀ-

ਗੱਡੀ, ਐਂਬੁਲੈਂਸ

ambush ('ਐਂਬੁਸ਼) *v n* ਘਾਤ ਲਾਉਣੀ, ਛਹਿ ਕੇ ਬੈਠਨਾ, ਘਾਤ ਵਿਚ ਬੈਠਨਾ, ਤਾੜ, ਛਹਿ, ਘਾਤ, ਦਾਅ, ਘਾਤਸਥਾਨ, ਘਾਤ ਲਾਉਣ ਵਾਲੀ ਸੈਨਕ ਟੁਕੜੀ

amend (ਅ'ਮੈਂਡ) *v* ਸੋਧਣਾ, ਸੁਧਾਰਨਾ, ਸੰਸ਼ੋਧਨ ਕਰਨਾ, ਤਰਮੀਮ ਕਰਨਾ, ਸੁਧਾਰਨਾ, ਸਊਰਨਾ; ~able ਸੁਧਾਰਨਯੋਗ, ਸੋਧਣਯੋਗ; ~ed ਸੋਧਿਆ, ਸੰਸ਼ੋਧਿਆ, ਸੁਧਰਿਆ; ~ment ਸੰਸ਼ੋਧਨ, ਤਰਮੀਮ, ਸ਼ੋਧ, ਸੁਧਾਰ

amiable ('ਏਇਮਯਅਬਲ) *a* ਮਿਲਾਪੜਾ, ਖ਼ੁਸ਼ਮਿਜਾਜ, ਮਿਲਣਸਾਰ

amicability ('ਐਮਿਕਅ'ਬਿਲਅਟਿ) *n* ਮਿਤਰਤਾ, ਸੁਹਿਰਦਤਾ, ਮੇਲ-ਮਿਲਾਪ, ਸੱਜਣਤਾ

amicable ('ਐਮਿਕਅਬਲ) ਸਨੇਹਪੂਰਨ, ਮੈਤਰੀਪੂਰਨ, ਦੋਸਤਾਨਾ, ਸੁਹਿਰਦਤਾਪੂਰਨ, ਮੇਲ-ਮਿਲਾਪ ਵਾਲਾ, ਅਪਣੱਤ ਵਾਲਾ

amicably ('ਐਮਿਕਅਬਲਿ) *adv* ਸੁਹਿਰਦਤਾ ਨਾਲ, ਦੋਸਤਾਨਾ ਤੌਰ ਤੇ

amid, -st (ਅਮਿਡ, ਅ'ਮਿਡਅਸਟ/ *prep* ਵਿਚ, ਵਿਚਕਾਰ, ਦਰਮਿਆਨ, ਅੰਦਰ

amiss (ਅ'ਮਿਸ) *adv* ਨਾਕਸ, ਬੇਰੁਖਾ, ਕਸੂਤਾ, ਬੇਮੇਕਾ, ਬੇਤੁਕਾ, ਘਾਟੇਵੰਦਾ, ਭੁੱਲ-ਭੁਲੇਖੇ, ਗਲਤੀ ਨਾਲ, ਵਿਰੋਧੀ ਭਾਵ ਨਾਲ

amity ('ਐਮਅਟਿ) *n* ਮਿਤਰਤਾ, ਸੱਜਣਤਾ, ਸੁਹਿਰਦਤਾ, ਦੋਸਤੀ, ਮੇਲ-ਮਿਲਾਪ, ਸਨੇਹ-ਭਾਵ

ammunition ('ਐਮਯੁ'ਨਿਸ਼ਨ) *n* ਬਾਰੂਦ, ਗੋਲੀ-ਸਿੱਕਾ, ਗੋਲਾ-ਬਾਰੂਦ, ਜੰਗੀ ਸਾਮਾਨ

among, -st (ਅ'ਮਅੱਙ, ਅ'ਮਅੱਙਅਸਟ) *prep* ਵਿਚ, ਵਿਚਾਲੇ, ਸਭ ਵਿਚ, ਗਿਣਤੀ ਵਿਚ, ਤੁਲਨਾ ਵਿਚ, ਮਿਲਾ ਕੇ, ਆਪਸ ਵਿਚ, ਪਰਸਪਰ

amount (ਅ'ਮਾਉਂਟ) *n v* ਧਨ-ਰਾਸ਼ੀ, ਰਕਮ, ਪੂੰਜੀ, ਕੁੱਲ ਧਨ, ਕੁੱਲ ਜੋੜ; ਮਾਤਰਾ; ਜੋੜ ਬਣਨਾ, ਜੋੜ ਹੋਣਾ; ਬਣਨਾ, ਭਾਵ ਅਰਥ ਹੋਣੇ; ਬਰਾਬਰ ਹੋਣਾ, ਕੁੱਲ ਜੋੜ ਹੋਣਾ

ample ('ਐਂਪਲ) *a* ਚੋਖਾ, ਬਹੁਤ, ਕਾਫ਼ੀ, ਖੁੱਲ੍ਹਾ, ਵੱਡਾ, ਮੋਕਲਾ, ਵਿਸਤਰਤ

amplification ('ਐਂਪਲਿਫ਼ਿ'ਕੇਇਸ਼ਨ) *n* ਵਾਧਾ, ਵਿਸਤਾਰ, ਫੈਲਾਵਟ; ਫੈਲਾਉ

amplifier ('ਐਂਪਲਿਫ਼ਾਇਆ*) *n* ਧੁਨੀਵਰਧਕ ਜੰਤਰ, ਐਂਪਲੀਫ਼ਾਇਰ

amplify ('ਐਂਪਲਿਫ਼ਾਇ) *v* ਵਧਾਉਣਾ, ਵਿਸਤਾਰ ਦੇਣਾ, ਖੁੱਲ੍ਹਾ ਕਰਨਾ, ਖੋਲ੍ਹ ਕੇ ਦੱਸਣਾ, ਵਿਸਤਾਰ-ਪੂਰਵਕ ਵਰਤਨ ਕਰਨਾ; ਧੁਨੀ ਵਿਸਤਾਰ ਕਰਨਾ

amply ('ਐਂਪਲਿ) *a* ਕਾਫ਼ੀ, ਬਹੁਤਾ, ਵਿਸਤਾਰ ਨਾਲ

amputate ('ਐਂਪਯੂਟੇਇਟ) *v* ਸਰੀਰ ਦੇ ਕਿਸੇ ਅੰਗ ਨੂੰ ਵੱਢਣਾ

amputation ('ਐਂਪਯੂ'ਟੇਇਸ਼ਨ) *n* ਅੰਗਛੇਦ, ਅੰਗ ਕਟਣ ਦੀ ਕਿਰਿਆ

amputator ('ਐਂਪਯੂਟੇਇਟਆ*) *n* ਅੰਗ-ਵੱਢਣ ਵਾਲਾ, ਅੰਗ-ਕਟਾਈ ਕਰਨ ਵਾਲਾ, ਅੰਗ ਛੇਦਕ

amuck (ਅ'ਮੱਕ) *adv* ਪਾਗਲਾਂ ਵਾਂਗ, ਪਾਗਲ ਹੋ ਕੇ, ਅਨਿਵਾਹ

amuse (ਅ'ਮਯੂਜ਼) *v* ਪਰਚਾਉਣਾ, ਖ਼ੁਸ਼ ਕਰਨਾ, ਮਨੋਰੰਜਨ ਕਰਨਾ, ਵਿਚਾਰਾਂ ਜਾਂ ਵਾਸਨਾਵਾਂ ਨੂੰ ਜਗਾਉਣਾ; ~ment ਦਿਲਪਰਚਾਵਾ, ਮਨੋਰੰਜਨ, ਖੇਡ-ਤਮਾਸ਼ਾ, ਹਾਸਾ-ਮਖੌਲ, ਦਿਲਲਗੀ

amusing (ਅ'ਮਯੂਜ਼ਿਙ) *a* ਵਿਨੋਦਕ, ਮਨੋਹਰ, ਖ਼ੁਸ਼ ਕਰਨ ਵਾਲਾ, ਸੰਤੋਖਜਨਕ

anaemia (ਅ'ਨੀਮਯਅ) *n* ਸਰੀਰ ਵਿਚ ਲਹੂ ਦਾ ਘਾਟਾ, ਭੁੱਸ, ਰਕਤਹੀਨਤਾ

analogy (ਅ'ਨੈਲਅਜਿ) *n* ਸਦ੍ਰਿਸ਼ਤਾ; ਦ੍ਰਿਸ਼ਟਾਂਤ, ਉਪਮਾ, ਸਮਾਨਤਾ, ਇਕਰੂਪਤਾ, ਸਮਰੂਪਤਾ, ਦਲੀਲਬਾਜ਼ੀ ਦਾ ਢੰਗ, ਅਨੁਪਾਤ, ਨਿਸਬਤ

analyse (ਐਨਅਲਾਇਜ਼) *v* ਨਿਖੇੜਨਾ, ਨਿਖੇੜ ਕਰਨਾ, ਵਿਸ਼ਲੇਸ਼ਣ ਕਰਨਾ, ਪੜਤਾਲ ਕਰਨਾ, ਪਰਖਣਾ, ਛਾਣਬੀਣ ਕਰਨੀ, (ਵਿਆਕਰਣ) ਵਾਕ-ਵੰਡ ਕਰਨੀ, ਤੱਤ-ਨਿਖੇੜਨਾ

analysis (ਅ'ਨੈਲਅਸਿਸ) *n* ਵਿਸ਼ਲੇਸ਼ਣ, ਨਿਖੇੜ, ਛਾਣਬੀਣ, ਅੰਗ-ਨਿਖੇੜ, ਵਾਕ-ਵੰਡ, ਤੱਤ ਦਾ ਨਿਖੇੜ

analyst ('ਐਨਅਲਿਸਟ) *n* ਵੰਡਕਾਰ, ਵਿਸ਼ਲੇਸ਼ਕ

analytical ('ਐਨਅ'ਲਿਟਅਕਲ) *a* ਨਿਖੇੜਵਾਂ, ਵਿਸ਼ਲੇਸ਼ਣੀ, ਵਿੱਛੇਦਾਤਮਕ, ਵਿਸ਼ਲੇਸ਼ਣਪੂਰਨ, ਵਿਯੋਗਾਤਮਕ

anarch ('ਐਨਾਕ) *n* ਅਰਾਜਕ, ਬਾਗੀ, ਵਿਦਰੋਹ ਦਾ ਨੇਤਾ; ~ist ਅਰਾਜਕਤਾਵਾਦੀ, ਵਿਦਰੋਹਵਾਦੀ; ~y ਅਰਾਜਕਤਾ, ਰਾਜਹੀਨਤਾ, ਰਾਜ-ਰੌਲਾ, ਰਾਜਗਰਦੀ, ਸ਼ਾਸਨਹੀਨਤਾ, ਹਨੇਰਗਰਦੀ

ancestor ('ਐਨਸੈਸਟਆ*) *n* ਪੂਰਵਜ, ਵਡੇਰਾ, ਵੱਡਾ-ਵਡੇਰਾ, ਪਿਤਰ, ਬਜ਼ੁਰਗ, ਪਿਉ-ਦਾਦਾ

anchor (ਐਙਕਅ*) *n v* ਲੰਗਰ, ਆਸਰਾ, ਸਹਾਰਾ, ਭਰੋਸਾ; ਜਹਾਜ਼ ਦਾ ਲੰਗਰ ਸੁਟਣਾ, ਠਹਿਰਨਾ, ਜੁੜਨਾ, ਬੰਨ੍ਹ ਦੇਣਾ, ਰੋਕ ਦੇਣਾ

ancient ('ਏਇਨਸ਼ਅੰਟ) *a* ਪ੍ਰਾਚੀਨ, ਪੁਰਾਤਨ, ਕਦੀਮੀ, ਬੜਾ ਪੁਰਾਣਾ, ਬੁੱਢਾ; ਪੁਰਾਣੇ ਵਿਚਾਰਾਂ ਵਾਲਾ

ancillary (ਐਨ'ਸਿਲਅਰਿ) *a* ਸਹਾਇਕ, ਅਨੁਸੰਗੀ, ਅਧੀਨ

anecdote ('ਐਨਿਕ'ਡਅਉਟ) *n* ਹਿਕਾਇਤ, ਚੁਟਕਲਾ

anew (ਅ'ਨਯੂ) *adv* ਨਵੇ ਸਿਰਿਓਂ; ਮੁੜ ਕੇ, ਦੂਜੀ ਵਾਰ, ਫੇਰ, ਮੁੜੋਂ

angel ('ਏਇੰਜਲ) *n* ਦੇਵਤਾ, ਫ਼ਰਿਸ਼ਤਾ, ਨਬੀ, ਰਸੂਲ, ਦੇਵਦੂਤ; ਪੈਗੰਬਰ; ਸੁੰਦਰ ਤੇ ਮਾਸੂਮ ਮਨੁੱਖ; ~of death ਜਮਦੂਤ, ਅਜ਼ਰਾਈਲ ਫ਼ਰਿਸ਼ਤਾ; ~ic ਅਲੌਕਕ

anger ('ਐਂਗਾ*) *n V* ਗੁੱਸਾ, ਰੋਹ, ਕਰੋਧ, ਨਰਾਜ਼ਗੀ; ਗੁੱਸੇ ਕਰਨਾ, ਨਰਾਜ਼ ਕਰਨਾ, ਰੁਸਾ ਦੇਣਾ

angle ('ਐਂਗਲ) *n V* (1) ਕੋਣ, ਜ਼ਾਵੀਆ, ਨੁੱਕਰ, ਖੂੰਜ, ਗੁੰਠ, ਕੈਨਾ, ਦ੍ਰਿਸ਼ਟੀਕੋਣ; (2) ਮੱਛੀਆਂ ਫੜਨ ਵਾਲੀ ਕੁੰਡੀ; **obtuse~** ਅਧਿਕ ਕੋਣ, ਚੌੜਾ ਕੋਣ; **right~** ਸਮਕੋਣ, ਰਾਸ ਕੋਣ

Anglican ('ਐਂਗਲਿਕਅਨ) *a n* ਇੰਗਲਿਸਤਾਨ ਦੇ ਪ੍ਰੋਟੈਸਟੈਂਟ ਮੱਤ ਨੂੰ ਮੰਨਣ ਵਾਲਾ, ਅੰਗਲੀਕੀ

angry ('ਐਂਗਰਿ) *a* ਗੁੱਸੇ, ਖਫ਼ਾ; ਨਰਾਜ਼, ਅਪ੍ਰਸੰਨ; ਕਰੋਧਿਆ, ਗੁਸੈਲਾ, ਚਿੜਚੜਾ; ਸੜਿਆ-ਭੁੰਜਿਆ

angular ('ਐਂਗਯੁਲਅ*) *a* ਨੁੱਕਰਦਾਰ, ਨੁਕਰੀਲਾ, ਕੋਣੀ, ਕੋਣਕ; ਨੁੱਕਰ ਤੇ ਸਥਿਤ, ਤਿੱਖੇ ਮੋੜ ਵਾਲਾ, ਕੋਣ ਨਾਲ ਨਾਪਿਆ; ਪਤਲਾ, ਮਾੜਾ, ਕਰੜਾ

animal ('ਐਨਿਮਲ) *n a* ਜਾਨਵਰ, ਪਸ਼ੂ, ਢੰਗਰ, ਪ੍ਰਾਣੀ, ਜੀਵ, ਜੀਵ-ਜੰਤ, ਹੈਵਾਨ, ਜਾਨਵਰਾਂ ਵਰਗਾ, ਪਸ਼ੂ ਬਿਰਤੀ ਵਾਲਾ, ਕਾਮੀ, ਜੰਗਲੀ-ਮਨੁੱਖ

animate ('ਐਨਿਮਅਟ,'ਐਨਿਮੇਇਟ) *a v* ਸਜੀਵ, ਸਚੇਤ, ਚੇਤਨ, ਜੀਵਤ, ਜਾਨਦਾਰ, ਚੁਸਤ, ਉਤਸ਼ਾਹੀ; ਜਿਵਾਲਣਾ, ਜਿੰਦ ਪਾਉਣੀ, ਜੋਸ਼ ਭਰਨਾ, ਹੌਸਲਾ ਵਧਾਉਣਾ

animation ('ਐਨਿਮੇਇਸ਼ਨ) *n* ਸਜੀਵਤਾ, ਜੋਸ਼, ਉਤਸ਼ਾਹ; ਜੀਵੰਤ-ਚਿਤਰ; ਲੋਰ, ਤਰੰਗ

animosity ('ਐਨਿ'ਮੌਸਅਟਿ) *n* ਵੈਰ-ਭਾਵ, ਦੁਸ਼ਮਨੀ, ਖੁਨਸ

ankle ('ਐਂਕਲ) *n* ਗਿੱਟਾ, ਟਖਣਾ; **~t** ਪਾਜ਼ੇਬ,

ਝਾਂਜਰ, ਪਾਇਲ; ਫੋਜੀ ਪੱਟੀਆਂ, ਬਾਂਕ

annals ('ਐਨਲਜ਼) *n (pl)* ਸਾਲਨਾਮਾ; ਇਤਿਹਾਸਕ ਲੇਖਾਂ ਦਾ ਸੰਗ੍ਰਹ, ਇਤਿਹਾਸ, ਤਾਰੀਖ਼

annex (ਅ'ਨੈੱਕਸ) *v n* ਮਿਲਾ ਲੈਣਾ, ਸੰਯੁਕਤ ਕਰਨਾ, ਸ਼ਾਮਲ ਕਰਨਾ, ਨੱਥੀ ਕਰਨਾ, ਜੋੜਨਾ; ਵਧਾ ਲੈਣਾ

annex (e) ('ਐਨੈੱਕਸ) *n* ਵਾਧਾ, ਪੂਰਕ, ਅੰਸ਼, ਅੰਤਕਾ, ਉਪਭਵਨ, ਕਿਸੇ ਮਕਾਨ ਨਾਲ ਮਿਲਦਾ ਹਿੱਸਾ, ਛੋਟਾ ਮਕਾਨ; **~ture** ਅਨੁਲੱਗ

annihilate (ਅ'ਨਾਇਅਲੇਇਟ) *v* ਮਿਟਾਉਣਾ, ਨਸ਼ਟ ਕਰਨਾ, ਜੜ੍ਹੋਂ ਪੁੱਟਣਾ ਸਰਬਨਾਸ਼ ਕਰਨਾ, ਖੇ ਕਰਨਾ, ਸੰਘਾਰਨਾ

annihilation (ਅ'ਨਾਇਅ'ਲੇਇਸ਼ਨ) *n* ਤਬਾਹੀ, ਬਰਬਾਦੀ, ਸਰਬਨਾਸ਼, ਸੱਤਿਆਨਾਸ, ਸੰਘਾਰ, ਖੇ, (ਧਰਮ) ਸਰੀਰ ਆਤਮਾ ਦਾ ਨਾਸ਼, ਪਰਲੋ, ਸੂੰਨ ਅਵਸਥਾ

anniversary ('ਐਨਿ'ਵਅਃਸ(ਅ)ਰਿ) *n* ਵਰ੍ਹੇਗੰਢ; ਸਾਲ-ਗਿਰ੍ਹਾ, ਜਰਖੰਤੀ, ਬਰਸੀ, ਵਾਰਸ਼ਕ ਉਤਸਵ, ਸਾਲਾਨਾ ਪੁਰਬ

Anno Domini ('ਐਨਅ(ਉ)'ਡੌਮਿਨਾਇ) *(L) phr (A.D)* ਸੰਨ ਈਸਵੀ ਵਿਚ, ਈਸਵੀ ਵਿਚ, ਈਸਾ ਦੇ ਜਨਮ ਬਾਅਦ

annotate ('ਐਨਅ(ਉ)ਟੇਇਟ) *v* ਵਿਆਖਿਆ ਕਰਨੀ, ਟੀਕਾ ਕਰਨਾ

annotation ('ਐਨਅ(ਉ)'ਟੇਇਸ਼ਨ) *n* ਟੀਕਾ, ਵਿਆਖਿਆ, ਭਾਸ਼

announce (ਅ'ਨਾਉਂਨਸ) *v* ਐਲਾਨ ਕਰਨਾ, ਘੋਸ਼ਣਾ ਕਰਨੀ, ਖ਼ਬਰ ਦੇਣੀ, ਹੋਕਾ ਦੇਣਾ, ਸੂਚਤ ਕਰਨਾ; **~ment** ਐਲਾਨ, ਘੋਸ਼ਣਾ, ਸੂਚਨਾ, ਹੋਕਾ; **~r** ਬੋਸ਼ਕ ਅਨਾਉਂਸਰ

annoy (ਅ'ਨੋਇ) *v* ਤੰਗ ਕਰਨਾ, ਚਿੜੁਾਉਣਾ,

ਖਿਝਾਉਣਾ, ਪਰੇਸ਼ਾਨ ਕਰਨਾ, ਜ਼ਿਦ ਕਰਨਾ;
~ance ਖਿਝ, ਚਿੜ੍ਹ, ਅਕੇਵਾਂ, ਪਰੇਸ਼ਾਨੀ,
ਛੇੜਛਾੜ, ਉਲਝਨਾਹਟ

annual ('ਐਨਯੁਅਲ) *a n* ਸਾਲਾਨਾ, ਵਾਰਸ਼ਕ;
ਵਰਸ਼ਜੀਵੀ, ਸਾਲਾਨਾ ਪਰਚਾ

annuity (ਅ'ਨਯੂਇਟੀ) *n* ਵਾਰਸ਼ਕ ਵਜ਼ੀਫਾ,
ਤਨਖ਼ਾਹ ਆਦਿ, ਵਾਰਸ਼ਕੀ, ਸਾਲਾਨਾ

annul (ਅ'ਨੱਲ) *v* ਰੱਦ ਕਰਨਾ, ਮਨਸੂਖ਼ ਕਰਨਾ,
ਮੇਟਣਾ, ਨਾਜਾਇਜ਼ ਕਰਾਰ ਦੇਣਾ; ~ment
ਮਨਸੂਖੀ, ਰੱਦਣ, ਖੰਡਨ, ਅੰਤ

annulate ('ਐਨਯੁਲੇਇਟ) *a* ਗੋਲਾਈਦਾਰ,
ਛੱਲੇਦਾਰ, ਚੂੜੀਦਾਰ

anoint (ਅ'ਨੌਇੰਟ) *v* ਚੋਪੜਨਾ, ਤੇਲ ਮਲਣਾ,
ਮਾਲਸ਼ ਕਰਨੀ; ਮੁਲਾਇਮ ਬਣਾਉਣਾ

anomaly (ਅ'ਨੈਮਅਲਿ) *n* ਅਸੰਗਤੀ ਬੇਤਰਤੀਬੀ,
ਅਟਮੇਲ, ਬਿਖਮਤਾ, ਅਨਿਯਮਤਤਾ

anonym ('ਐਨਅਨਿਮ) ਅਗਿਆਤ ਨਾਂ, ਉਪਨਾਮ;
~ous ਅਗਿਆਤ ਲੇਖਕ ਦਾ, ਅਨਾਮ,
ਗੁਮਨਾਮ; ~ously ਗੁਮਨਾਮ ਤੌਰ ਤੇ

answer (ਆਨਸਅ*) *n v* ਜਵਾਬ, ਉੱਤਰ; ਪ੍ਰਤੀ-
ਕਿਰਿਆ, ਹੱਲ, ਨਿਵਾਰਣ; ਜਵਾਬ ਦੇਣਾ, ਉੱਤਰ
ਦੇਣਾ, ਹੱਲ ਕਰਨਾ, ਜਵਾਬਦੇਹ, ਜ਼ੁੰਮੇਵਾਰ ਹੋਣਾ;
~able ਜਵਾਬਦੇਹ, ਉਤਰਦਾਈ, ਜ਼ੁੰਮੇਵਾਰ

ante-room ('ਐਨਟਿਰੁਮ) *n* ਡਿਊੜ੍ਹੀ, ਬੈਠਕ,
ਬਾਹਰਲਾ ਕਮਰਾ

anthem ('ਐਂਥਅਮ) *n* ਗੀਤ, ਤਰਾਨਾ, ਭਜਨ,
ਪਰਮਾਤਮਾ ਦੀ ਉਸਤਤੀ, ਖ਼ੁਸ਼ੀ ਦਾ ਗੀਤ

anthropology ('ਐਂਥਰਅ'ਪੌਲਅਜਿ) *n* ਮਾਨਵ-
ਵਿਗਿਆਨ

anti (ਐਂਟਿ) *pref* ਵਿਰੋਧ, ਵਿਪਰੀਤ; ~biotic
ਰੋਗਾਣੂਨਾਸ਼ਕ; ਰੋਗਾਣੂਨਾਸ਼ਕ ਦਵਾਈ; ~body

ਪ੍ਰਤੀ ਪਿੰਡ, ਲਹੂ ਦੇ ਅਜਿਹੇ ਅੰਸ਼ ਜੋ ਕੁਝ ਹੋਰ
ਅੰਸ਼ਾਂ ਦਾ ਨਾਸ਼ ਕਰਦੇ ਹਨ; ਰੋਗਨਾਸ਼ਕ ਅੰਸ਼;
~clockwise ਪੁੱਠਾ ਰੋਜ਼ਾ

anticipant (ਐਂਟਿ'ਸਿਪਅੰਟ) *n a* ਆਸਵੰਦ

anticipate (ਐਂਟਿ'ਸਿਪੇਇਟ) *v* ਪੂਰਵ ਗਿਆਨ
ਹੋਣਾ, ਅਗਾਊਂ ਜਾਨਣਾ, ਅੱਗੇ ਹੋਣਾ, ਪਹਿਲ
ਕਰਨੀ, ਆਸ ਰੱਖਣੀ; ਉਡੀਕਣਾ

anticipation (ਐਂਟਿਸਿ'ਪੇਇਸ਼ਨ) *n* ਪੂਰਵ
ਅਨੁਸਾਰ, ਪੂਰਵ ਧਾਰਣਾ, ਪੂਰਵ-ਗਿਆਨ;
ਪੂਰਵ-ਆਸ, ਪੇਸ਼ਬੰਦੀ, ਉਡੀਕ

antipathy (ਐਂ'ਟਿਪਅਥਿ) *n* ਘਿਰਣਾ; ਵੈਰ,
ਵਿਰੋਧ, ਵੈਰ-ਭਾਵ, ਦਵੈਖ-ਭਾਵ

antique (ਐਂ'ਟੀਕ) *a n* ਪੁਰਾਤਨ, ਪ੍ਰਾਚੀਨ,
ਕਦੀਮੀ; ਪੁਰਾਣੇ ਢੰਗ ਦਾ, ਪਰੰਪਰਾਵਾਦੀ,
ਰੂੜ੍ਹੀਵਾਦੀ, ਪੁਰਾਤਨ ਕਲਾ ਦੇ ਨਮੂਨੇ

antiquity (ਐਂ'ਟਿਕਵਅਟਿ) *n* ਪ੍ਰਾਚੀਨ ਕਾਲ,
ਪੂਰਵ-ਕਾਲ, ਪੁਰਾਤਨਤਾ, ਪ੍ਰਾਚੀਨਤਾ, ਪ੍ਰਾਚੀਨ-
ਯੁੱਗ, ਆਦਿਕਾਲ, ਪੁਰਾਣੇ ਆਦਮੀ, ਵੱਡ ਵਡੇਰੇ;
ਪੁਰਾਣੇ ਰੀਤੀ ਰਿਵਾਜ, ਪੰਰਪਰਾਵਾਂ, ਪੁਰਾਣੀਆਂ
ਘਟਨਾਵਾਂ, ਪ੍ਰਾਚੀਨ ਲੱਭਤਾਂ

antitheist ('ਐਂਟਿ'ਥਿਇਸਟ) *n* ਨਾਸਤਕ,
ਈਸ਼ਵਰ ਵਿਰੋਧੀ, ਖ਼ੁਦਾ ਤੋਂ ਮੁਨਕਰ

antithesis (ਐਂ'ਟਿਥਿਸਿਸ) *n* ਪ੍ਰਤੀਕੂਲਤਾ, ਮੱਤਭੇਦ,
ਪ੍ਰਤੀਪੱਖ, ਵਿਰੋਧ ਅਲੰਕਾਰ, ਵਿਪਰੀਤਤਾ

antonym (ਐਂਟਅਨਿਮ) *n* ਉਲਟ-ਭਾਵੀ ਸ਼ਬਦ,
ਵਿਪਰੀਤ-ਅਰਥ ਬੋਧਕ ਸ਼ਬਦ, ਵਿਰੋਧੀ ਅਰਥਾਂ
ਵਾਲਾ ਸ਼ਬਦ, ਵਿਪਰਯਾਯ

anxiety (ਐਙ'ਜ਼ਾਇਅਟਿ) *n* ਚਿੰਤਾ, ਫ਼ਿਕਰ,
ਪਰੇਸ਼ਾਨੀ, ਵਿਆਕੁਲਤਾ; ਤੋਖਲਾ; ਉਤਸੁਕਤਾ,
ਤਾਂਘ

anxious ('ਐਙ(ਕ)ਸ਼ਅਸ) *a* ਉਤਸੁਕ,

ਉਤਾਵਲਾ; ਬੇਚੈਨ, ਬੇਤਾਬ

any ('ਐਨਿ) *a pron* ਇਕ, ਕੋਈ, ਕੁਝ ਥੋੜ੍ਹਾ ਜਿਹਾ, ਕੋਈ ਵੀ, ਕੁਝ ਵੀ, ਹਰ ਇਕ, ਜੋ ਵੀ, ਜਿਹੜਾ ਵੀ; ~**body** ਕੋਈ ਬੰਦਾ, ਕੋਈ ਮਨੁੱਖ, ਕੋਈ ਵੀ, ਫ਼ਲਾਣਾ-ਢਿਮਕਾ; ~**how** ਕਿਸੇ ਤਰ੍ਹਾਂ, ਕਿਸੇ ਨਾ ਕਿਸੇ ਤਰੀਕੇ ਨਾਲ, ਜਿਵੇਂ ਕਿਵੇਂ ਵੀ, ਕਿਸੇ ਵੀ ਹਾਲਤ ਵਿਚ; ~**thing** ਕੋਈ ਸ਼ੈ ਜਾਂ ਵਸਤੂ, ਕੋਈ ਵੀ ਚੀਜ਼, ਕੁਝ ਵੀ, ਕੋਈ ਇਕ ਚੀਜ਼, ਹਰ ਚੀਜ਼; ~**where** ਕਿਧਰੇ; ਕਿਤੇ, ਕਿਸੇ ਥਾਂ, ਕਿਤੇ ਵੀ, ਹੋਰ ਥਾਂ, ਸਾਰੇ ਹੀ, ਸਭ ਥਾਂ; **at~time** ਕਿਸੇ ਵੇਲੇ, ਕਿਸੇ ਸਮੇਂ

apart (ਅ'ਪਾਟ) *adv* ਇਕ ਬੰਨੇ, ਵੱਖਰਾ, ਅੱਡ, ਲਾਂਭੇ, ਵੱਖ-ਵੱਖ, ਦੂਰੀ ਰੱਖ ਕੇ, ਫ਼ਾਸਲੇ ਉੱਤੇ; **set~** ਵੱਖਰਾ ਰੱਖਣਾ, ਬਚਾ ਕੇ ਰੱਖ ਲੈਣਾ

apartheid (ਅ'ਪਾਟਹੇਇਟ) *n* ਨਸਲੀ ਵਿਤਕਰਾ, ਭੇਦ ਭਾਵ ਵਾਲਾ ਵਰਤਾਉ

apartment (ਅ'ਪਾ*ਟਮਅੰਟ) *n* ਕਮਰਾ, ਕੋਠਾ, ਮਕਾਨ

apathetic ('ਐਪਅ'ਥੈੱਟਿਕ) *a* ਉਦਾਸੀਨ, ਲਾਪਰਵਾਹ, ਉਤਸ਼ਾਹਹੀਨ; ਨਿਰਪੱਖ, ਹਿਰਦੇਹੀਨ

apathy ('ਐਪਅਥਿ) *n* ਲਾਪਰਵਾਹੀ, ਰੁੱਖਾਪਨ, ਕੋਰਾਪਨ; ਅਲੇਪਤਾ, ਵੈਰਾਗ, ਬੇਦਿਲੀ, ਉਤਸ਼ਾਹ-ਹੀਨਤਾ, ਨਿਰਦਇਤਾ

ape (ਏਇਪ) *n v* ਇਕ ਪੁੱਛਹੀਨ ਬਾਂਦਰ; ਨਕਲੀਆ, ਸਾਂਗ ਲਾਉਣਾ, ਨਕਲ ਉਤਾਰਨੀ; **to play the ~** ਨਕਲ ਕਰਨਾ, ਬਾਂਦਰ ਵਾਂਗੂ ਨਕਲ ਕਰਨਾ

apex ('ਏਇਪਿਕਸ) *n* ਸਿਖਰ, ਉਤਲੀ ਨੋਕ, ਸਿਰ-ਬਿੰਦੂ, ਟੀਸੀ-ਪੱਥਰ

aphasia (ਅ'ਫ਼ੇਇਜ਼ਯਅ) *n* ਗੂੰਗਾਪਨ, ਦਿਮਾਗ਼ ਨੂੰ ਸੱਟ ਲੱਗਣ ਕਰਕੇ ਬੋਲਣਾ ਬੰਦ ਹੋ ਜਾਣ ਦਾ ਰੋਗ

Apollo (ਅ'ਪੌਲਅਉ) *n* ਯੂਨਾਨ ਦਾ ਸੂਰਜ ਦੇਵਤਾ; ਸੂਰਜ; ਅਤੀ ਸੁੰਦਰ ਵਿਅਕਤੀ

apologize (ਅ'ਪੌਲਅਜਾਇਜ਼) *v* ਮਾਫ਼ੀ ਮੰਗਣਾ, ਖ਼ਿਮਾਂ ਜਾਚਨਾ ਕਰਨੀ, ਭੁੱਲ ਮੰਨਣੀ

apologue ('ਐਪਅਲੌਗ) ਨੀਤੀ ਕਥਾ, ਇਖ਼ਲਾਕੀ ਕਿੱਸਾ, ਸਿਖਆਦਾਇਕ ਕਥਾ

apology (ਅ'ਪੌਲਅਜਿ) *n* ਖ਼ਿਮਾਜਾਚਨਾ, ਭੁੱਲ ਦੀ ਸੋਧ; ਸਫ਼ਾਈ

apostle (ਅ'ਪੌਸਲ) *n* ਪੈਗ਼ੰਬਰ, ਰਸੂਲ, ਇਸਾਈ ਧਰਮ ਪਰਚਾਰਕ

apparatus ('ਐਪਅ'ਰੇਇਟਅਸ) *n* ਉਪਕਰਣ, ਵਿਗਿਆਨਕ ਜੰਤਰ ਆਦਿ, ਸਾਮਾਨ, ਸੰਦ ਹਥਿਆਰ, ਔਜ਼ਾਰ; ਸਰੀਰ ਦੇ ਅੰਗ-ਜੋੜ

apparent (ਅੱ'ਪੈਰਅੰਟ) *a* ਦਿਸਦਾ, ਜਾਪਦਾ; ਪ੍ਰਤੱਖ, ਸਪਸ਼ਟ; ~**ly** ਜ਼ਾਹਰਾ ਤੌਰ ਤੇ, ਵੇਖਣ ਵਿਚ; ਸਪਸ਼ਟ ਰੂਪ ਵਿਚ, ਵਿਖਾਵੇ ਨੂੰ

appeal (ਅ'ਪੀਲ) *n v* ਅਪੀਲ, ਪੁਨਰ-ਵਿਚਾਰ ਪ੍ਰਾਰਥਨਾ; ਪੁਨਰ-ਵਿਚਾਰ, ਅਪੀਲ ਕਰਨੀ, ਪ੍ਰਾਰਥਨਾ ਕਰਨੀ, ਮਿੰਨਤ ਕਰਨੀ; ~**ing** ਦਿਲ ਖਿਚਵਾਂ, ਆਕਰਸ਼ਕ

appear (ਅ'ਪਿਅ*) *v* ਹਾਜ਼ਰ ਹੋਣਾ; ਪੇਸ਼ ਆਉਣਾ (ਕਾ), ਉਪਸਥਿਤ ਹੋਣਾ; ਬੈਠਣਾ (ਪਰੀਖਿਆ ਵਿਚ); ~**ance** ਪ੍ਰਤੱਖਤਾ, ਆਗਮਨ, ਹਾਜ਼ਰੀ, ਉਪਸਥਿਤੀ, ਪੇਸ਼ੀ (ਕਾ); ਰੂਪ, ਸੂਰਤ, ਦਰਸ਼ਨ, ਦ੍ਰਿਸ਼ਟੀ-ਭਰਮ

appease (ਅਪੀਜ਼) *v* ਪ੍ਰਸੰਨ ਕਰਨਾ, ਮਨਾਉਣਾ, ਰਾਜ਼ੀ ਕਰਨਾ, ਸ਼ਾਂਤ ਕਰਨਾ, ਦਿਲਾਸਾ ਦੇਣਾ; ਠੰਢਾ ਕਰਨਾ, ਸੰਤੁਸ਼ਟ ਕਰਨਾ, ਪਤਿਆਉਣਾ

appellant (ਅ'ਪੈਲਅੰਟ) *n a* ਅਪੀਲ-ਸਬੰਧੀ, ਪੁਨਰਆਵੇਦਨ ਸਬੰਧੀ; ਅਪੀਲ-ਕਰਨਾ

appellate (ਅ'ਪੈਲਅਟ) *a* ਮੁੜ, ਵਿਚਾਰਨਯੋਗ,

ਪੁਨਰਵਿਚਾਰਕ, ਅਪੀਲ ਸੁਣਨ ਜਾਂ ਕਰਨ ਵਾਲਾ

append (ਅ'ਪੈਂਡ) *v* ਜੜਨਾ, ਲਾਉਣਾ, ਮਿਲਾਉਣਾ, ਨੱਥੀ ਕਰਨਾ, ਟਾਂਕਣਾ, ਸੰਯੁਕਤ ਕਰਨਾ; ~**age** ਜੋੜ, ਵਾਧਾ, ਸਹਾਇਕ, ਜ਼ਮੀਮਾ, ਉਪਕਰਣ, ਗੌਣ-ਅੰਗ

appendicitis (ਅ'ਪੈਂਡਿ'ਸਾਇਟਿਸ) *n* ਕੁਲੰਜ, ਅੰਤੜੀਆਂ ਦੀ ਸੋਜ਼ਸ

appendix (ਅ'ਪੈਂਡਿਕਸ) *n* ਅੰਤਕਾ, ਪੂਰਕ ਭਾਗ, ਜ਼ਮੀਮਾ, ਸਹਾਇਕ ਭਾਗ

appetite ('ਐਪਿਟਾਇਟ) *n* ਭੁੱਖ, ਲਾਲਸਾ, ਚਾਹ, ਤਾਂਘ

appetize ('ਐਪਿਟਾਇਜ਼) *v* ਭੁੱਖ ਲਾਉਣਾ, ਇੱਛਾ ਜਗਾਉਣੀ, ਰੁਚਤ ਕਰਨਾ

appetizing ('ਐਪਿਟਾਇਜ਼ਿੰਗ) *a* ਭੁੱਖ-ਵਧਾਊ

applaud (ਅ'ਪਲੌਡ) *a* ਪ੍ਰਸੰਸਾ ਕਰਨਾ, ਸਲਾਹੁਣਾ, ਤਾੜੀ ਵਜਾਉਣਾ, ਵਾਹਵਾ ਕਰਨੀ

applause (ਅ'ਪਲੌਜ਼) *n* ਪ੍ਰਸੰਸਾ, ਉਸਤਤੀ, ਸਾਬਾਸ਼, ਵਾਹ ਵਾਹ, ਤਾੜੀ

apple ('ਐਪਲ) *n* ਸੇਬ, ਸਿਉਂ; ~**cart** ਯੋਜਨਾ, ਵਿਉਂਤ, ਸਕੀਮ; ~**pie order** ਚੀਜ਼ਾਂ ਦਾ ਥਾਂ ਸਿਰ ਹੋਣਾ, ਪੂਰਨ ਸ਼ਾਂਤੀ, ਮੁਕੰਮਲ ਪ੍ਰਬੰਧ

appliance (ਅ'ਪਲਾਇਅੰਨਸ) *n* ਉਪਕਰਣ, ਸਾਧਨ, ਉਪਾਉ; ਪ੍ਰਯੋਗ, ਵਰਤੋਂ

applicability ('ਐਪਲਿਕਅਬਿਲਅਟਿ) *n* ਉਚਿਤਤਾ, ਅਨੁਕੂਲਤਾ, ਯੋਗਤਾ

applicable ('ਐਪਲਿਕਅਬਲ) *a* ਮੁਨਾਸਬ, ਉਚਿਤ, ਲਾਗੂ ਹੋਣ ਯੋਗ, ਅਨੁਕੂਲ, ਪ੍ਰਸੰਗ-ਅਨੁਕੂਲ, ਯੋਗ, ਠੀਕ, ਢੁੱਕਦਾ

applicant ('ਐਪਲਿਕਅੰਟ) *n* ਨਿਵੇਦਕ, ਜਾਚਕ, ਆਵੇਦਕ, ਬਿਨਕਾਰ, ਦਰਖ਼ਾਸਤ ਕਰਨ ਵਾਲਾ, ਬੇਨਤੀ ਕਰਨ ਵਾਲਾ; ਉਮੀਦਵਾਰ

application ('ਐਪਲਿਕੇਇਸ਼ਨ) *n* (1) ਅਰਜ਼ੀ, ਦਰਖ਼ਾਸਤ, ਬਿਨੈ-ਪੱਤਰ, ਨਿਵੇਦਨ-ਪੱਤਰ, ਪ੍ਰਾਰਥਨਾ-ਪੱਤਰ; (2) ਉੱਦਮ, ਉਦਯੋਗ, ਮਿਹਨਤ; (3) ਉਚਿਤਤਾ; ਪ੍ਰਸੰਗਕਤਾ, ਸੁਸੰਗਤ

applied (ਅ'ਪਲਾਇਡ) *a* ਲਾਗੂ ਕੀਤਾ ਹੋਇਆ, ਪ੍ਰਾਯੋਗਿਕ

apply (ਅ'ਪਲਾਇ) *v* (1) ਵਰਤੋਂ ਵਿਚ ਲਿਆਉਣਾ, (2) ਵਰਤਣਾ, ਲਾਗੂ ਕਰਨਾ; ਅਰਜ਼ੀ ਦੇਣੀ, ਦਰਖ਼ਾਸਤ ਦੇਣੀ, ਪ੍ਰਾਰਥਨਾ ਕਰਨੀ; (3) ਸਬੰਧਤ ਹੋਣਾ, ਸਬੰਧ ਰੱਖਣਾ, ਧਿਆਨ ਲਗਾਉਣਾ

appoint (ਅ'ਪੌਇੰਟ) *v* ਨਿਯੁਕਤ ਕਰਨਾ, ਨਿਯਤ ਕਰਨਾ, ਥਾਪਣਾ, ਨੌਕਰੀ ਤੇ ਲਾਉਣਾ; ਨਿਸ਼ਚਤ ਕਰਨਾ; ਸੰਕੇਤ ਕਰਨਾ; ~**ed** ਨਿਯੁਕਤ; ਨਿਯਤ, ਲੱਗਿਆ ਹੋਇਆ; ~**ee** ਨਿਯੁਕਤੀ; ਨਿਯੁਕਤ; ~**ment** ਨਿਯੁਕਤੀ; (ਮਿਲਣ ਦਾ) ਇਕਰਾਰ

apportion (ਅ'ਪੌਸ਼ਨ) *v* ਹਿੱਸੇ ਕਰਨਾ, ਵੰਡਣਾ, ਹਿੱਸੇ ਅਨੁਸਾਰ ਸੌਂਪਣਾ, ਬਰਾਬਰ ਬਰਾਬਰ ਹਿੱਸਾ ਦੇਣਾ; ~**ment** ਵੰਡ, ਤਕਸੀਮ

apposite ('ਐਪਅ(ਉ)ਜ਼ਿਟ) *a* ਯੋਗ, ਉਚਿਤ, ਢੁਕਵਾਂ

apposition ('ਐਪਅ(ਉ)'ਜ਼ਿਸ਼ਨ) *n* ਵਾਧਾ, ਕੋਲ ਕੋਲ ਰੱਖਣ ਦੀ ਕਿਰਿਆ; ਮੁਹਰਬੰਦੀ, ਕਾਰਕ ਸਬੰਧ

appraisal, appraisement (ਅ'ਪਰੇਇਜ਼ਲ, ਅ'ਪਰੇਇਜ਼ਮੰਅੰਟ) *n* ਮੁਲਾਂਕਣ, ਮੁੱਲ-ਨਿਰਧਾਰਨ; ਅੰਦਾਜ਼ਾ

appraise (ਅ'ਪਰੇਇਜ਼) *v* ਮੁਲ ਪਾਉਣਾ, ਅੰਕਣਾ, ਮੁਲਾਂਕਣ ਕਰਨਾ, ਅੰਦਾਜ਼ਾ ਲਗਾਉਣਾ

appreciate (ਅ'ਪਰੀਸ਼ਿਏਇਟ) *v* ਪ੍ਰਸੰਸਾ ਕਰਨੀ, ਕਦਰ ਕਰਨੀ; ਮੁਲਾਂਕਣ ਕਰਨਾ

appreciation (ਅ'ਪਰੀਸ਼ਿ'ਏਇਸ਼ਨ) *n* ਪ੍ਰਸੰਸਾ, ਵਰਤੋਂ, ਅਨੁਭਵ

apprehend ('ਐਪਰਿ'ਹੈਂਡ) *v* ਮਹਿਸੂਸ ਕਰਨਾ, ਅਨੁਭਵ ਕਰਨਾ, ਸ਼ੰਕਾ ਕਰਨਾ; ਡਰਨਾ ਜਾਂ ਡਰਾਉਣਾ, ਭੈ ਖਾਣਾ; ਬੰਦੀ ਬਣਾਉਣਾ, ਗਰਿਫ਼ਤਾਰ ਕਰਨਾ, (ਪੁਲੀਸ ਦਾ) ਫੜਨਾ

apprehensibility ('ਐਪਰਿ'ਹੈਂਸਿ'ਬਿਲਅਟਿ) *n* ਸਮਝਣਯੋਗਤਾ, ਸੁਬੋਧਤਾ; ਗੋਚਰਤਾ, ਬੋਧ, ਸਮਝ

apprehensible ('ਐਪਰਿ'ਹੈਂਸਿਬਲ) *a* ਸੁਬੋਧ, ਸਮਝਣਯੋਗ, ਗੋਚਰ, ਅਨੁਭਵ ਦੇ ਯੋਗ

apprehension ('ਐਪਰਿ'ਹੈਂਸ਼ਨ) *n* (1) ਸਮਝ, ਬੋਧ, ਸੂਝ, ਪਕੜ, ਜਾਣਕਾਰੀ; (2) ਸ਼ੰਕਾ; ਡਰ; ਹਿਰਾਸਤ, ਗਰਿਫ਼ਤਾਰੀ, ਪਕੜ; ਘੇਰਾ

apprentice (ਅ'ਪਰੈਂਟਿਸ) ਸਿਖਾਂਦਰੂ, ਸ਼ਾਗਿਰਦ, ਸ਼ਿਲਪ-ਸਿਖਿਆਰਥੀ

apprise (ਅ'ਪਰਾਇਜ਼) *v* ਸੂਚਨਾ ਦੇਣਾ, ਦੱਸਣਾ, ਖ਼ਬਰ ਦੇਣੀ, ਜਾਣਕਾਰੀ ਰੱਖਣਾ

approach (ਅ'ਪਰਅਉਚ) *v n* ਕੋਲ ਜਾਣਾ, ਬਰਾਬਰ ਹੋਣਾ, ਪ੍ਰਵੇਸ਼, ਹਾਜ਼ਰੀ, ਪਹੁੰਚਣਾ, ਅੱਪੜਨਾ, ਮਿਲਦਾ-ਜੁਲਦਾ ਹੋਣਾ; **~ability** ਸਮੀਪਤਾ, ਨਿਕਟਤਾ; ਮਿਲਣਸਾਰੀ, ਰਸਾਈ ਯੋਗਤਾ, ਪਹੁੰਚ

appropriate (ਅ'ਪਰਅਉਪਰਿਅਟ, ਅ'ਪਰਅਉਪਰਿਏਇਟ) *a* ਢੁੱਕਵਾਂ, ਉਚਿਤ, ਅਨੁਕੂਲ, ਠੀਕ, ਸਬੰਧਤ, ਉਪਯੁਕਤ

appropriation (ਅ'ਪਰਅਉਪਰਿ'ਏਇਸ਼ਨ) *n* ਵਰਤੋਂ, ਵਿਹਾਰ, ਪ੍ਰਯੋਗ, ਇਸਤੇਮਾਲ; ਮਲਕੀਅਤ; ਚੋਰੀ; ਅਨੁਕੂਲਤਾ

approval (ਅ'ਪਰੂਵ੍ਲ) *n* ਮਨਜ਼ੂਰੀ, ਸੰਮਤੀ, ਪਰਵਾਨਗੀ, ਆਗਿਆ, ਅਨੁਮਤੀ, ਪਸੰਦ

approve (ਅ'ਪਰੂਵ੍) *v* ਮਨਜ਼ੂਰ ਕਰਨਾ, ਪਰਵਾਨ ਕਰਨਾ; ਸਵੀਕਾਰ ਕਰਨਾ, ਤਾਈਦ ਕਰਨੀ; ਪਸੰਦ ਕਰਨਾ, ਠੀਕ ਸਮਝਣਾ

approximate (ਅ'ਪਰੌਕਸਿਮਅਟ, ਅ'ਪਰੌਕਸਿਮੇਇਟ) *a v* ਲਗਭਗ, ਬਿਲਕੁਲ ਨੇੜੇ, ਅਨੁਰੂਪ, ਕਰੀਬਨ, ਅੰਦਾਜ਼ਾ ਲਾਉਣਾ, ਅਨੁਮਾਨ ਲਾਉਣਾ

apt (ਐਪਟ) *a* ਯੋਗ, ਕਾਬਲ; ਉਚਿਤ, ਢੁਕਵਾਂ, ਠੀਕ, ਮੁਨਾਸਬ; **~ly** ਯੋਗ ਤਰੀਕੇ ਨਾਲ, ਠੀਕ ਢੰਗ ਨਾਲ, ਚਤਰਾਈ ਨਾਲ, ਮੁਨਾਸਬ ਤੌਰ ਤੇ; **~ness** ਯੋਗਤਾ, ਉਚਿਤਤਾ, ਚਤੁਰਤਾ; **~itude** ਯੋਗਤਾ, ਕਾਬਲੀਅਤ; ਝੁਕਾਉ, ਰੁਝਾਣ, ਰੁਚੀ

arbitrary ('ਆਬਿਟਰਅਰਿ) *a* ਆਪ-ਹੁਦਰਾ, ਮਨ ਮੰਨਿਆ, ਧੱਕੇਸ਼ਾਹੀ ਵਾਲਾ

arbitration ('ਆਬਿ'ਰੇਈਸ਼ਨ) *n* ਪੰਚ ਦਾ ਫ਼ੈਸਲਾ, ਸਾਲਸੀ-ਫ਼ੈਸਲਾ, ਵਿਚੋਲਪੁਣਾ

arbitrator ('ਆਬਿਟਰੇਇਟਅ*) *n* ਵਿਚੋਲਾ, ਸਾਲਸ, ਪੰਚ, ਨਿਰਣਾ ਕਰਨ ਵਾਲਾ

arch (ਆਚ) *n a v* (1) ਡਾਟ, ਮਹਿਰਾਬ, ਮਹਿਰਾਬਦਾਰ, (2) ਛੱਤ, ਚਾਪ, ਕੌਸ; (3) ਪ੍ਰਧਾਨ, (4) ਮਹਾਂ ਮੱਕਾਰ, ਛਟਿਆ, ਖ਼ਚਰਾ, ਚਲਾਕ, ਗੁਰੂ ਘੰਟਾਲ

archaeology (ਆਕਿ'ਔਲਅਜਿ) *n* ਪੁਰਾਤੱਤਵ ਵਿਗਿਆਨ

archetype ('ਆਕਿਟਾਇਪ) *n* ਆਦਿ ਰੂਪ, ਮੂਲ ਰੂਪ, ਅਸਲੀ ਨਮੂਨਾ; ਮੂਲ ਆਦਰਸ਼

arch-fiend ('ਆਚ'ਫ਼ੀਨਡ) *n* ਸ਼ੈਤਾਨ

ardour ('ਆਡਅ*) *n* ਤੇਜ਼ੀ, ਪ੍ਰਚੰਡਤਾ, ਤੀਬਰਤਾ, ਉਮੰਗ, ਤੇਜ਼ ਗਰਮੀ, ਲਗਨ, ਧੁਨ, ਸਰਗਰਮੀ

area ('ਏਅਰਿਅ) *n* ਖੇਤਰਫਲ, ਰਕਬਾ; ਇਲਾਕਾ; ਖੇਤਰ

arena (ਐ'ਰੀਨਅ) *n* ਅਖਾੜਾ, ਕਾਰਜ-ਖੇਤਰ; ਰਣ-ਖੇਤਰ, ਰੰਗ-ਭੂਮੀ

arguable ('ਆਗਯੁਅਬਲ) *a* ਵਿਵਾਦਪੂਰਨ,

ਵਿਵਾਦਯੋਗ, ਵਿਚਰਯੋਗ

argue ('ਆਰਗਨੁ) v ਦਲੀਲ ਦੇਣੀ, ਤਰਕ-ਵਿਤਰਕ ਕਰਨਾ, ਵਾਦ-ਵਿਵਾਦ ਕਰਨਾ, ਬਹਿਸ ਕਰਨੀ; ਇਤਰਾਜ਼ ਕਰਨਾ, ਵਿਰੋਧ ਕਰਨਾ; ਸਿੱਧ ਕਰਨਾ; ਸੰਕੇਤ ਦੇਣਾ

argument ('ਆਰਗਨੁਮੈਂਟ) n ਦਲੀਲ, ਦਾਅਵਾ, ਹੁੱਜਤ, ਤਰਕ, ਪ੍ਰਮਾਣ, ਤਰਕ-ਪ੍ਰਣਾਲੀ, ਵਾਦ-ਵਿਵਾਦ; **~ation** ਬਹਿਸ, ਵਿਵਾਦ, ਤਰਕ, ਖੰਡਨ-ਮੰਡਨ, ਤਰਕ-ਵਿਤਰਕ

arid ('ਐਰਿਡ) a ਮਾਰੂ, ਬੰਜਰ, ਵੀਰਾਨ, ਨਿਰਜਲ

arise (ਅ'ਰਾਇਜ਼) v ਉੱਠਨਾ ਉੱਠ ਖੜੋਣਾ, ਮੁੜ ਪੈਦਾ ਹੋਣਾ, ਨਿਕਲਣਾ, ਉਤਪੰਨ ਹੋਣਾ, ਜਾਗਣਾ; ਦਿਸਣਾ

arising (ਅ'ਰਾਇਜ਼ਿੰਗ) a ਉਤਪੰਨ, ਨਿਕਲਦਾ, ਰੁੜਦਾ, ਉੱਠਦਾ

aristocracy ('ਐਰਿ'ਸਟੋਕਰਅਸਿ) n ਕੁਲੀਨ-ਵਰਗ, ਕੁਲੀਨ-ਤੰਤਰ

aristocrat ('ਐਰਿਸਟਅਕਰੈਟ) n ਕੁਲੀਨ, ਰਈਸ

arithmetic (ਅ'ਰਿਥਮਅਟਿਕ) n ਹਿਸਾਬ, ਗਿਣਤੀ, ਲੇਖ; ਹਿਸਾਬ ਦੀ ਪੋਥੀ

ark (ਆ*ਕ) n v ਪੇਟੀ, ਸੰਦੂਕ, ਬਕਸ; ਬੇੜੀ, ਨਾਵ; (ਹਜ਼ਰਤ ਨੂਹ ਦੀ ਬੇੜੀ)

arm (ਆ*ਮ) n v ਬਾਂਹ, ਭੁਜਾ, ਬਾਜ਼ੂ, ਪਸੂ ਦੀਆਂ ਮੂਹਰਲੀਆਂ ਲੱਤਾਂ; ਰੁੱਖ ਦਾ ਮੋਟਾ ਟਾਹਣ; ਕਮੀਜ਼ ਦੀ ਬਾਂਹ; ਹਥਿਆਰ, ਸ਼ਕਤੀ; ਹਥਿਆਰ ਬੰਦ ਕਰਨਾ ਜਾਂ ਹੋਣਾ, ਸ਼ਸਤਰ ਧਾਰਨੇ; **~pit** ਕੱਛਾਂ ਬਗਲਾਂ; **~ful** ਗਲਵੱਕੜੀ ਵਿਚ ਸਮਾਉਣ ਯੋਗ; **~less** ਨਿਹੱਥਾ, ਬੇਹਥਿਆਰ, ਬਾਂਹ ਹੀਣ; **~let** ਬਾਜ਼ੂਬੰਦ

armament ('ਆ*ਮਅਮਅੰਟ) n ਜੁੱਧ ਦਾ ਸਾਮਾਨ, ਜੰਗੀ-ਸਾਮਾਨ, ਸ਼ਸਤਰਬੱਧ ਫ਼ੌਜ;

ਹਥਿਆਰਬੰਦੀ, ਹਥਿਆਰਬੰਦ ਹੋਣ ਦਾ ਕੰਮ, ਸ਼ਸਤਰੀ-ਕਰਨ

armory ('ਆ*ਮਅਰਿ) n ਸ਼ਸਤਰ ਰੱਖਣ ਜਾਂ ਬਣਾਉਣ ਵਾਲਾ ਕਾਰਖ਼ਾਨਾ, ਅਸਲ੍ਹਾਖ਼ਾਨਾ

armour ('ਆ*ਮਅ) n v ਕਵਚ, ਜ਼ਰਾ ਬਕਤਰ

arms (ਆ*ਮਜ਼) n pl ਸ਼ਸਤਰ, ਹਥਿਆਰ

army ('ਆ*ਮਿ) n ਸੈਨਾ, ਫ਼ੌਜ, ਲਸ਼ਕਰ

aroma n (ਅ'ਰਅਉਮਅ) n ਮਹਿਕ, ਸੁਗੰਧ

around (ਅ'ਰਾਉੱਡ) adv prep ਹਰ ਪਾਸੇ, ਚਾਰੇ ਪਾਸੇ, ਇੱਧਰ-ਉੱਧਰ, ਆਸਪਾਸ, ਲਗਭਗ, ਕਰੀਬ ਕਰੀਬ, ਚਾਰੇ ਪਾਸਿਓਂ ਘੇਰਿਆ

arouse (ਅ'ਰਉਜ਼) v ਜਗਾਉਣਾ, ਭੜਕਾਉਣਾ, ਉਭਾਰਨ, ਉਕਸਾਉਣਾ, ਕਿਰਿਆਸ਼ੀਲ ਬਣਾਉਣਾ, ਜਾਗਰਤ ਕਰਨਾ, ਜੋਸ਼ ਦਿਵਾਉਣਾ

arrange (ਅ'ਰੇਂਜ) v ਵਿਉਂਤਣਾ, ਵਿਉਂਤ-ਬੱਧ ਕਰਨਾ, ਤਰਤੀਬ ਦੇਣਾ; ਵਿਵਸਥਿਤ ਕਰਨਾ, ਪ੍ਰਬੰਧ ਕਰਨਾ; **~ment** ਵਿਉਂਤ, ਇੰਤਜ਼ਾਮ, ਪ੍ਰਬੰਧ, ਵਿਵਸਥਾ

array (ਅ'ਰੇਇ) v n ਸੰਵਾਰਨਾ, ਸਜਾਉਣਾ, ਅੱਲਕਰਤ ਕਰਨਾ; ਫ਼ੌਜ ਦੀ ਹਥਿਆਰਬੰਦੀ, ਫ਼ੌਜੀ ਤਾਕਤ, ਲਸ਼ਕਰ

arrear ('ਅਰਿਅ*) n ਬਕਾਇਆ ਰਕਮ, ਬਕਾਇਆ, ਉਗਰਾਹੁਣਯੋਗ ਕਰਜ਼ਾ ਜਾਂ ਧਨ; ਪਛੜਿਆ ਕੰਮ

arrest (ਅ'ਰੈੱਸਟ) v n ਬੰਦੀ ਬਣਾਉਣਾ, ਗਿਰਫ਼ਤਾਰ ਕਰਨਾ, ਖਿੱਚਣਾ, ਲੁਭਾਉਣਾ; ਗਿਰਫ਼ਤਾਰੀ, ਹਿਰਾਸਤ, ਪਕੜ

arrival (ਅ'ਰਾਇਵਲ) n ਪਹੁੰਚ, ਆਗਮਨ, ਢੁਕਾਉ ਆਮਦ, ਹਾਜ਼ਰੀ

arrive (ਅ'ਰਾਇਵੑ) v ਆਉਣਾ, ਪਹੁੰਚਨਾ, ਆ ਹਾਜ਼ਰ ਹੋਣਾ, ਅੱਪੜਨਾ, ਮੰਜ਼ਲ ਤੇ ਪਹੁੰਚਣਾ

arrogance ('ਐਰਅਗਰਾਂਸ) *n* ਹੰਕਾਰ, ਘਮੰਡ, ਅਭਿਮਾਨ, ਗਰਬ, ਗਰੂਰ, ਆਕੜ

arrogant ('ਐਰਅਗਅੰਟ) *a* ਮਾਣ-ਮੱਤਾ, ਹੰਕਾਰੀ, ਅਭਿਮਾਨੀ, ਗੁਮਾਨੀ, ਆਕੜ ਖ਼ਾਂ, ਘਮੰਡੀ

arrogate ('ਐਰਅ(ਉ)ਗੇਇਟ) *v* ਝੂਠਾ ਹੱਕ ਜਮਾਉਣਾ, ਝੂਠਾ ਦਾਅਵਾ ਕਰਨਾ

arrow ('ਐਰਅਉ) *n* ਤੀਰ, ਬਾਣ, ਕਾਨੀ; ਤੀਰ ਦਾ ਨਿਸ਼ਾਨ, ਤੀਰ ਦਾ ਚਿੰਨ੍ਹ

art (ਆ*ਟ) *n* ਕਲਾ, ਹੁਨਰ, ਸ਼ਿਲਪ; ਕਾਰੀਗਰੀ, ਉਸਤਾਦੀ, ਕੁਸ਼ਲਤਾ; ਮੱਕਾਰੀ, ਚਾਲ; **~ful** ਗੁਣੀ, ਹੁਨਰੀ; ਕਪਟੀ, ਚਾਲਬਾਜ਼, ਚੰਟ

arthritis (ਆ*ਥਰਾਇਟਅਸ) *n* ਗਠੀਆ, ਜੋੜਾਂ ਦੇ ਦਰਦ ਜਾਂ ਸੋਜਸ਼ ਦੀ ਬੀਮਾਰੀ

article ('ਆ*ਟਿਕਲ) *n v* (1) ਪਦਾਰਥ, ਵਸਤੂ, ਚੀਜ਼; (2) ਧਾਰਾ, ਦਫ਼ਾ, ਅੰਸ਼, ਭਾਗ; (3) ਲੇਖ, ਨਿਬੰਧ; ਦਫ਼ਾ ਲਗਾਉਣੀ, ਨਿਯੰਤਰਨ ਰੱਖਣਾ, ਹਿੱਸਿਆਂ ਵਿਚ ਵੰਡਣਾ; ਧਰਮ ਸਿਧਾਂਤ, ਸੂਤਰ, ਨਿਯਮ; ਜੁਧ-ਨਿਯਮ

articulate (ਆ'ਟਿਕਯੁਲੇਇਟ) *v a* ਗੰਢਣਾ, ਜੋੜਨਾ, ਗੰਢ ਦੇਣੀ, ਜੋੜ ਪਾਉਣਾ; ਸਾਫ਼ ਬੋਲਣਾ, ਗੰਢਦਾਰ, ਜੋੜਦਾਰ; (ਬੋਲਣ ਵਿਚ) ਸਾਫ਼-ਸਪੱਸ਼ਟ

articulation (ਆ'ਟਿਕਯੁਲੇ'ਇਸ਼ਨ) *n* ਜੋੜਬੰਦੀ, ਜੋੜ ਗੰਢ; ਸਪੱਸ਼ਟ ਪਰਗਟਾਉ

artificial ('ਆਟਿ'ਫ਼ਿਸ਼ਲ) *a* ਨਕਲੀ, ਬਣਾਵਟੀ, ਝੂਠਾ, ਅਵਾਸਤਵਿਕ, ਮਿਥਿਆ; **~ity** ਨਕਲ, ਝੂਠ, ਬਣਾਵਟ, ਅਵਾਸਤਵਿਕਤਾ

artillery (ਆ'ਟਿਲਅਰਿ) *n* ਤੋਪਖ਼ਾਨਾ

artisan ('ਆਟਿ'ਜ਼ੈਨ) *n* ਦਸਤਕਾਰ, ਸ਼ਿਲਪਕਾਰ

artist ('ਆਟਿਸਟ) *n* ਕਲਾਕਾਰ, ਕਾਰੀਗਰ, ਗੁਣੀ

artiste (ਆ'ਟੀਸਟ) *n* ਨਾਚੀ, ਗਾਇਕਾ

artistry ('ਆਟਿਸਟਰਿ) *n* ਕਲਾਕਾਰੀ, ਫ਼ਨਕਾਰੀ,

ਕਲਾਕੌਸ਼ਲਤਾ, ਕਾਰੀਗਰੀ

artless ('ਆਟਲਿਸ) *a* ਕਲਾਹੀਨ, ਅਸੱਭਿਅ; ਅਨਾੜੀ, ਮੂਰਖ, ਬੁੱਧੂ; ਨਿਸ਼ਕਪਟ, ਛਲ ਰਹਿਤ, ਸੱਚਾ, ਸਿੱਧਾ-ਸਾਦਾ, ਭੋਲਾ-ਭਾਲਾ, ਕੁਦਰਤੀ, ਸੁਭਾਵਕ

arts (ਆ*ਟਸ) *n pl* ਲਲਿਤ ਕਲਾਵਾਂ, ਸ਼ੁੱਧ ਸਾਇੰਸਾਂ ਦੇ ਵਿਪਰੀਤ ਸਮਾਜਕ ਵਿਗਿਆਨਾਂ ਦੇ ਵਿਸ਼ੇ

as (ਐਜ਼) *a conj* ਜਿਵੇਂ, ਉਸੇ ਤਰ੍ਹਾਂ; ਕਿਉਂਕਿ, ਇਸ ਲਈ ਕਿ, ਤਾਂ ਜੋ

ascend (ਅੱਸੈਂਡ) *v* ਉੱਤਰਨਾ, ਉਪਰ ਜਾਣਾ, ਉਦੇ ਹੋਣਾ, ਉੱਚਾ-ਉਠਣਾ, ਉੱਨਤੀ ਕਰਨਾ, (ਧੁਨੀ ਜਾਂ ਆਵਾਜ਼ ਦਾ) ਉੱਚ ਹੋਣਾ, (ਤਖ਼ਤ ਤੇ) ਬੈਠਣਾ, ਬਿਰਾਜਣਾ

ascertain (ਐਸਅ'ਟੇਇਨ) *v* ਨਿਰਣਾ ਕਰਨਾ, ਨਿਸ਼ਚਾ ਕਰਨਾ, ਜਾਣਨਾ; ਜਾਂਚਣਾ, ਪਤਾ ਲਾਉਣਾ

ascetic (ਅ'ਸੈਟਿਕ) *n a* ਤਿਆਗੀ, ਵਿਰਾਗੀ, ਤਪੱਸਵੀ; ਇਕਾਂਤਵਾਸੀ, ਸਾਧਕ

ash (ਐਸ਼) *n* ਸੁਆਹ, ਭਸਮ, ਰਾਖ; **~tray** ਰਾਖਦਾਨੀ, ਸੁਆਹ ਪਾਉਣ ਵਾਲੀ ਤ੍ਰੇ (ਸਿਗਰਟ ਆਦਿ ਦੀ); **~es** ਅਸਥੀਆਂ, ਮੁਰਦੇ ਦੀ ਮਿੱਟੀ, ਸੁਆਹ

ashame (ਅ'ਸ਼ੇਇਮ) *v* ਸ਼ਰਮਿੰਦਾ ਕਰਨਾ ਜਾਂ ਹੋਣਾ, ਲੱਜਤ ਕਰਨਾ ਜਾਂ ਹੋਣਾ; **~d** ਪਸ਼ੇਮਾਨ, ਲੱਜਾਵਾਨ, ਸ਼ਰਮਿੰਦਾ

ashore (ਅ'ਸ਼ੋਰ) *adv* ਕਿਨਾਰੇ ਤੇ, ਤੱਟ ਉੱਤੇ, ਕੰਢੇ ਉੱਤੇ

aside (ਅ'ਸਾਇਡ) *adv n* ਅੱਡ, ਵੱਖ, ਦੂਰ, ਜੁਦਾ, ਇਲਾਵਾ, ਬਿਨਾਂ; (ਨਾਟਕ) ਇਕਾਂਤ-ਕਥਨ, ਪਰੋਖ ਜਤਨ

ask (ਆਸਕ) *v* ਪੁੱਛਣਾ, ਉੱਤਰ ਮੰਗਣਾ, ਬੇਨਤੀ

ਕਰਨ, ਸੱਦਾ ਦੇਣਾ, ਬੁਲਾਉਣਾ, ਜ਼ਰੂਰਤ
ਸਮਝਣਾ, ਚਾਹੁਣਾ, ਮੰਗਣਾ

asleep (ਅ'ਸਲੀਪ) *adv* ਸੁੱਤਾ, ਸੁਪਤ,
ਨੀਂਦਗ੍ਰਸਤ, ਨੀਂਦ ਵਿਚ

aspect ('ਐਸਪੈਕਟ) *n* ਪਹਿਲੂ, ਪੱਖ; ਦ੍ਰਿਸ਼ਟੀਕੋਣ,
ਨਜ਼ਰੀਆ; ਹਾਲਤ

aspersion (ਅ'ਸਪਅਃਸ਼ਨ) *v* ਤੁਹਮਤ, ਉਜ,
ਇਲਜ਼ਾਮ

aspirant (ਅ'ਸਪਾਇਰਅੰਟ) *n* ਆਕਾਂਖੀ,
ਇੱਛਾਵਾਨ, ਅਭਿਲਾਸ਼ੀ, ਉਮੀਦਵਾਰ

aspirate ('ਐਸਪਅਰੇਇਟ) *n v* (ਭਾਸ਼ਾ)
ਮਹਾਂਪ੍ਰਾਣ, ਹਕਾਰ; ਬਰਤਨ ਨੂੰ ਹਵਾ ਰਹਿਤ ਕਰਨ

aspiration ('ਐਸਪਅ'ਰੇਇਸ਼ਨ) *n* ਤਾਂਘ;
ਆਕਾਂਖਿਆ, ਆਰਜ਼ੂ, ਇੱਛਾ, ਅਭਿਲਾਸ਼ਾ;
(ਭਾਸ਼ਾ) ਮਹਾਂ-ਪ੍ਰਾਣਤਾ, ਹਾ ਦੀ ਧੁਨੀ

aspire (ਅ'ਸਪਾਇਅ*) *v* ਇੱਛਾ ਕਰਨੀ, ਤਾਂਘਣਾ,
ਆਕਾਂਖਿਆ ਕਰਨੀ

ass (ਐਸ) *n* ਖੋਤਾ, ਗਧਾ; ਮੂਰਖ ਮਨੁੱਖ, ਖਰ

assail (ਅ'ਸੇਇਲ) *v* ਧਾਵਾ ਕਰਨਾ, ਹਮਲਾ
ਕਰਨਾ; ਚੜ੍ਹਾਈ ਕਰਨਾ, (ਕੰਮ ਨੂੰ) ਦ੍ਰਿੜ੍ਹਤਾ-
ਪੂਰਵਕ ਕਰਨਾ

assassin (ਅ'ਸੈਸਿਨ) *n* ਕਾਤਲ, ਖੂਨੀ, ਹਤਿਆਰਾ,
ਘਾਤਕ; **~ate** (ਛਿਪ ਕੇ) ਹੱਤਿਆ ਕਰਨੀ,
ਵਿਸਾਹਘਾਤ ਕਰਕੇ ਮਾਰਨਾ, ਖੂਨ ਕਰਨਾ, ਮਾਰ
ਦੇਣਾ; **~ation** ਛਲ-ਘਾਤ, ਗੁਪਤ-ਘਾਤ, ਕਤਲ,
ਹੱਤਿਆ; (ਚਰਿੱਤਰ) ਬਦਨਾਮੀ

assault (ਅ'ਸੋਲਟ) *n v* ਧਾਵਾ, ਚੜ੍ਹਾਈ, ਹਮਲਾ;
ਹਮਲਾ ਕਰਨਾ, ਧਾਵਾ ਬੋਲਣਾ; ਬਲਾਤਕਾਰ ਕਰਨਾ

assay (ਅ'ਸੇਇ) *n* ਪਰੀਖਿਆ, ਕਸਵੱਟੀ, ਪਰਖ,
ਪੜਤਾਲ, ਜਾਂਚ, ਅਜ਼ਮਾਈਸ਼

assemblage (ਅਸੈਂਬਲਿਜ) *n* ਸਭਾ, ਇਕੱਠ,

ਇਕੱਤਰਤਾ, ਜਮ-ਘਟਾ

assemble (ਅਸੈਂਬਲ) *v* ਇਕੱਠਾ ਕਰਨ, ਇਕੱਤਰ
ਕਰਨ, ਇਕੱਠਾ ਹੋਣ, ਜੋੜਨਾ

assembly (ਅ'ਸੈਂਬਲਿ) *n* ਸਭਾ, ਇਕੱਠ,
ਸੰਮੇਲਨ, ਮਹਿਫਲ, ਮਜਲਸ, ਸੰਘ

assent (ਅ'ਸੈਂਟ) *v n* ਹਾਮੀ ਭਰਨੀ, ਰਜ਼ਾਮੰਦ
ਹੋਣਾ, ਸਹਿਮਤ ਹੋਣਾ, ਪਰਵਾਨ ਕਰਨਾ, ਕਬੂਲ
ਕਰਨਾ; ਸਹਿਮਤੀ, ਮਨਜ਼ੂਰੀ

assert (ਅ'ਸਅਃਟ) *v* ਨਿਸਚੇ ਪੂਰਵਕ ਕਹਿਣਾ,
ਜੋਸ਼ ਨਾਲ ਕਹਿਣਾ; ਦਾਅਵਾ ਕਰਨਾ, ਹੱਕ
ਜਮਾਉਣਾ

assertive (ਅ'ਸਅਃਟਿਵ) *a* ਨਿਸਚੇਆਤਮਕ,
ਹਠਧਰਮੀ ਵਾਲਾ; **~ness** ਦ੍ਰਿੜ੍ਹਤਾ, ਪਕਿਆਈ;
ਦਾਅਵਾਗੀਰੀ

assess (ਅ'ਸੈਸ) *v* ਨਿਯਤ ਕਰਨਾ, ਨਿਰਧਾਰਨ,
ਨਿਸ਼ਚਤ ਕਰਨਾ, ਦੰਡ ਲਾਉਣਾ, ਕਰ ਲਾਉਣਾ;
ਅਨੁਮਾਨਣਾ, ਅਨੁਮਾਨ ਲਾਉਣਾ; **~able** ਨਿਯਤ
ਕਰਨ ਯੋਗ; ਟੈਕਸ ਲਾਉਣ ਯੋਗ; **~ee** ਕਰਦਾਤਾ,
ਜਿਸ ਤੋਂ ਹਾਲਾ ਜਾਂ ਟੈਕਸ ਵਸੂਲਿਆ ਜਾਵੇ;
~ment ਕਰ-ਨਿਰਧਾਰਨ, ਮੁਲਾਂਕਣ, ਲਗਾਨ,
ਜਮਾਂਬੰਦੀ; **~or** (ਕਰ) ਨਿਰਧਾਰਕ, ਅਨੁਮਾਨਕਰਤਾ

assets (ਐਸੈੱਟਸ) *n pl* ਜਾਇਦਾਦ, ਕੁਲ
ਅਸਾਸਾ, ਸੰਪਤੀ; ਵਿਸ਼ੇਸ਼ਤਾ, ਚੰਗਿਆਈ

assign (ਅ'ਸਾਇਨ) *v* ਸੌਂਪਣਾ, ਸਪੁਰਦ ਕਰਨਾ,
ਨਿਸ਼ਚਤ ਕਰਨਾ; ਦੇਣਾ, ਵੰਡਣਾ, ਮੁਕੱਰਰ ਕਰਨਾ,
ਦੱਸਣਾ, ਨਿਰਦੇਸ਼ਨ ਕਰਨਾ, ਦੇ ਦੇਣਾ; **~able**
ਸੌਂਪਣ ਯੋਗ, ਨਿਸ਼ਚਤ ਕਰਨ ਯੋਗ, ਨਿਰਧਾਰਨ-
ਯੋਗ; **~ment** ਸਪੁਰਦਗੀ, ਸੌਂਪਿਆ ਹੋਇਆ
ਕੰਮ

assimilate (ਅ'ਸਿਮਿਲੇਇਟ) *v* ਇਕਮਿਕ ਹੋਣਾ,
ਰਚਾ ਲੈਣਾ, ਸਮਾ ਜਾਣਾ, ਆਤਮਸਾਤ ਕਰਨਾ,

ਮਿਲਾ ਲੈਣਾ; ਪਰ ਜਾਣਾ

assist (ਅ'ਸਿਸਟ) *v* ਸਹਾਇਤਾ ਦੇਣੀ ਜਾਂ ਕਰਨੀ, ਸਹਿਯੋਗ ਦੇਣਾ, ਹੱਥ ਵਟਾਉਣਾ

associate (ਅ'ਸਅਉਸ਼ਿਦੇਇਟ, ਅ'ਸਅਉਸ਼ਿਅਟ) *v n a* ਰਲਾਉਣਾ, ਸ਼ਾਮਲ ਕਰਨਾ, ਸ਼ਰੀਕ ਕਰਨਾ, ਭਾਈਵਾਲ ਬਣਾਉਣਾ, ਸਹਿਕਾਰੀ ਬਣਨਾ; ਸਹਿਯੋਗੀ, ਸਹਿਕਾਰੀ; ਹਿੱਸਾਇਤੀ, ਸਹਾਇਕ

association (ਅ'ਸਅਉਸਿ'ਏਇਸ਼ਨ) *n* ਸਭਾ, ਸੰਸਥਾ, ਸਮਾਜ, ਸੰਘ; ਮੇਲ-ਜੋਲ, ਸੰਗਤ

assume (ਅ'ਸਯੂਮ) *v* ਧਾਰਨਾ, ਲੈਣਾ, ਧਾਰਨ ਕਰਨਾ, ਅਪਨਾਉਣਾ, ਹੱਥ ਵਿਚ ਲੈਣਾ; ਮੰਨਣਾ, ਫਰਜ਼ ਕਰਨਾ

assumption (ਅ'ਸਅੰਪਸ਼ਨ) *n* ਧਾਰਨਾ; ਜ਼ੁੰਮੇਵਾਰੀ ਲੈਣ ਦੀ ਕਿਰਿਆ; ਧਾਰਨ

assumptive (ਅ'ਸਅੰਪਟਿਵ਼) *a* ਦੰਭੀ; ਫਰਜ਼ੀ, ਕਲਪਤ; ਮੰਨਿਆ

assurance (ਅ'ਸ਼ੋਰਅੰਸ) *n* ਵਿਸ਼ਵਾਸ, ਯਕੀਨ, ਜ਼ਮਾਨਤ, ਤਸੱਲੀ, ਭਰੋਸਾ; ਬੀਮਾ

assure (ਅ'ਸ਼ੋ*) ਵਿਸ਼ਵਾਸ ਦਿਵਾਉਣਾ, ਭਰੋਸਾ ਦਿਵਾਉਣਾ ਪੱਕਾ ਕਰਨਾ, ਤਸੱਲੀ ਕਰ ਲੈਣੀ

asterisk (ਐਸਟਅ(ਅ)ਰਿਸਕ) *n v* ਤਾਰਾ-ਚਿੰਨ੍ਹ; ਤਾਰੇ ਦਾ ਨਿਸ਼ਾਨ (*), ਤਾਰਿਕ, ਤਾਰਾ; ਤਾਰਾ-ਚਿੰਨ੍ਹ ਅੰਕਤ ਕਰਨਾ

asthma (ਐਸਥਮਅ) *a* ਦਮਾ, ਸਾਹ ਦਾ ਰੋਗ

astonish (ਅ'ਸਟੌਨਿਸ਼) *v* ਅਚੰਭੇ ਵਿਚ ਪਾਉਣਾ, ਹੈਰਾਨ ਕਰਨਾ, ਵਿਸਮਤ ਕਰਨਾ, ਦੰਗ ਕਰਨਾ, ਹੈਰਤ ਵਿਚ ਪਾਉਣਾ; ~**ed** ਹੈਰਾਨੀ ਭਰਿਆ, ਹੈਰਾਨਕੁਨ, ਅਸਚਰਜਜਨਕ, ਵਿਸਮਤ, ਹੱਕਾ ਬੱਕਾ, ਦੰਗ; ~**ing** ਅੰਚਭਾਕਾਰੀ, ਹੈਰਾਨਕੁਨ, ਅਸਚਰਜ ਕਰਨ ਵਾਲਾ, ਵਿਸਮਾਦ ਵਿਚ ਲੈ ਜਾਣ ਵਾਲਾ; ~**ment** ਹੈਰਾਨੀ, ਅਸਚਰਜਤਾ, ਅਚੰਭਾ

astound (ਅ'ਸਟਉਂਡ) *v* ਹੈਰਾਨ ਕਰਨਾ, ਹੱਕਾ ਬੱਕਾ ਕਰਨਾ, ਤ੍ਰਾਹ ਕੱਢਣਾ

astray (ਅ'ਸਟਰੇਇ) *adv a* ਗੁਮਰਾਹ, ਭੁੱਲਿਆ ਭਟਕਿਆ, ਔਝੜ ਪਿਆ, ਕੁਰਾਹੀਆ

astringe (ਅ'ਸਟਰਿੰਜ) *v* ਸੰਕੁਚਤ ਕਰਨਾ, ਘੁੱਟ ਕੇ ਬੰਨ੍ਹਣਾ, ਕਸਣਾ, ਸੁੰਗੜਨਾ

astrologer (ਅ'ਸਟਰੌਲਅਜਅ*) *a* ਜੋਤਸ਼ੀ, ਨਜੂਮੀ

astrology (ਅ'ਸਟਰੌਲਅਜਿ) *n* ਜੋਤਸ਼, ਜੋਤਸ਼ ਵਿੱਦਿਆ, ਨਜੂਮ, ਨਜੂਮ ਦਾ ਗਿਆਨ

astronomy (ਅ'ਸਟਰੌਨਅਮਿ) *n* ਖਗੋਲ-ਵਿਗਿਆਨ, ਤਾਰਾ-ਵਿਗਿਆਨ, ਨਛੱਤਰ ਵਿਗਿਆਨ, ਗ੍ਰਹਿਵਿੱਦਿਆ, ਖਗੋਲ-ਸ਼ਾਸਤਰ

asylum (ਅ'ਸਾਇਲਅਮ) *n* ਅਨਾਥ-ਆਸ਼ਰਮ, ਦੀਨ-ਆਸ਼ਰਮ, ਸ਼ਰਨ, ਪਨਾਹ, ਸਹਾਰਾ

at (ਐਟ) *perp* ਉੱਤੇ, 'ਤੇ, ਉੱਤੇ ਵੱਲ, ਉੱਪਰ; ~**all** ਬਿਲਕੁਲ, ਹਰ ਤਰ੍ਹਾਂ; ~ **home** ਉਚੇਚ ਰਹਿਤ ਦਾਅਵਤ; ~ **once** ਫੌਰਨ, ਇਕ ਦਮ, ਤੁਰੰਤ; ~ **one** ਸਮਝੌਤੇ ਤੇ ਸੰਮਤੀ ਨਾਲ, ਇਕਸਾਰ; ~ **random** ਅਟਕਲ-ਪੱਚੂ; ~ **sea** ਉਲਝਿਆ ਹੋਣਾ, ਸਮਝਦੇ ਨਾ ਹੋਣਾ

atheism ('ਏਇਥਿਇਜ਼(ਅ)ਮ) *n* ਨਾਸਤਕਤਾ, ਨਾਸਤਕ ਮੱਤ, ਰੱਬ ਨਾ ਮੰਨਣ ਦਾ ਵਾਦ

atheist ('ਏਇਥਿਇਸਟ) *n* ਨਾਸਤਕ, ਅਨੀਸ਼ਵਰਵਾਦੀ, ਕਾਫ਼ਰ, ਮੁਨਕਰ

athlete ('ਐਥਲੀਟ) *n* ਖਿਡਾਰੀ, ਪਹਿਲਵਾਨ, ਕਸਰਤ ਕਰਨ ਵਾਲਾ, ਰਿਸ਼ਟ ਪੁਸ਼ਟ ਆਦਮੀ, ਹੱਟਾ ਕੱਟਾ

athletic (ਐਥਲੈਟਿਕ) *a n* ਕਸਰਤੀ, ਸਰੀਰਕ ਕਸਰਤ ਦਾ, ਰਿਸ਼ਟ-ਪੁਸ਼ਟ, ਕਸਰਤ ਬਾਰੇ; (ਬ ਵ) ਕਸਰਤ-ਅਭਿਆਸ, ਕਸਰਤ, ਵਰਜ਼ਸ਼

atlas ('ਐਟਲਅਸ) *n* ਐਟਲਸ, ਭੂ-ਚਿਤਰਾਵਲੀ, ਮਾਨ ਚਿਤਰਾਵਲੀ, ਗਰਦਨ ਦੀ ਹੱਡੀ ਜਿਸ ਉੱਤੇ ਖੋਪੜੀ ਟਿਕੀ ਹੁੰਦੀ ਹੈ

atmophere ('ਐਟਮਅਸਫ਼ਿਅ*) *n* ਵਾਯੂ-ਮੰਡਲ, ਵਾਤਾਵਰਨ; ਹਾਲਤ, ਪਰਿਸਥਿਤੀਆਂ; ਆਲਾ-ਦੁਆਲਾ, ਹਵਾ, ਵਾਯੂ

atom ('ਐਟਮ) *n* ਪਰਮਾਣੂ, ਅਣੂ, ਕਣ, ਜ਼ੱਰਾ, ਸੂਖਮ ਅੰਸ਼; ~ic ਪਰਮਾਣੂ ਬਾਰੇ, ਪਰਮਾਣਵੀ, ਪਰਮਾਣੂ, ਰੂਪ, ਪਰਮਾਣੂ-ਸਬੰਧੀ; ਸੂਖਮ; ~bomb ਅਣੂ ਬੰਬ; ~y ਪਰਮਾਣੂ; ਛੋਟੀ ਵਸਤੂ, ਪਿੰਜਰ, ਢਾਂਚਾ, ਨਿਰਬਲ ਸਰੀਰ

atone (ਅ'ਟਅਉਨ) *v* ਪ੍ਰਾਸ਼ਚਿਤ ਕਰਨਾ; ~ment ਹਰਜਾਨਾ, ਪ੍ਰਾਸ਼ਚਿਤ(ਪ੍ਰ) ਸੁਲ੍ਹਾ-ਸਫ਼ਾਈ

atrocious (ਅ'ਟਰਅਉਸ਼ਅਸ) *a* ਅੱਤਿਆਚਾਰੀ, ਦੁਸ਼ਟ, ਜਾਬਰ; ਬੇਦਰਦ, ਜ਼ਾਲਮ

atrocity (ਅ'ਟਰੌਸਅਟਿ) *n* ਘੋਰ ਅੱਤਿਆਚਾਰ, ਜ਼ੁਲਮ, ਪਾਪ

attach (ਅ'ਟੈਚ) *v* ਜੋੜਨਾ ਬੰਨ੍ਹਣਾ, ਨੱਥੀ ਕਰਨਾ; ਮਿਲਾਉਣਾ; ਸੰਯੁਕਤ ਕਰਨਾ, ਸੰਮਿਲਤ ਹੋਣਾ, (ਕਾਨੂੰਨੀ ਅਧਿਕਾਰ; ਕਿਸੇ ਵਿਅਕਤੀ ਦੀ ਜਾਇਦਾਦ ਨੂੰ) ਜ਼ਬਤ ਕਰਨਾ; ~able ਕੁਰਕੀ ਯੋਗ; ~ed ਨਾਲ ਲੱਗਾ, ਨੱਥੀ ਕੀਤਾ, ਨਾਲ ਲੱਗਵਾਂ, ਲਾਗਲਾ; (ਕ) ਕੁਰਕ ਕੀਤਾ; ~ment ਮੋਹ, ਪਰੇਮ, ਸਨੇਹ, ਨਿਸ਼ਠਾ, ਲਗਾਉ; ਸੰਯੋਜਤ ਵਸਤੂ, ਯੋਗ, ਸਬੰਧ, ਬੰਧਨ; ਕੁਰਕੀ, ਜ਼ਬਤੀ

attache (ਅ'ਟੈਸ਼ੇਇ) *n* ਰਾਜਦੂਤ-ਸਹਿਕਾਰੀ, ਅਤਾਸ਼ੇ, ਅਟੈਚੀ; ~ case ਬਕਸਾ, ਅਟੈਚੀਕੇਸ

attack (ਅ'ਟੈਕ) *v n* ਧਾਵਾ ਬੋਲਣਾ, ਆਕਰਮਣ ਕਰਨਾ, ਚੜ੍ਹਾਈ ਕਰਨੀ; ਹਾਨੀਕਾਰਕ ਹੋਣਾ, ਦੋਸ਼ ਲਾਉਣਾ, ਹਮਲਾ, ਧਾਵਾ, ਚੜ੍ਹਾਈ, ਆਕਰਮਣ

attain (ਅ'ਟੇਇਨ) *v* ਪ੍ਰਾਪਤ ਕਰਨਾ, ਪਾ ਲੈਣਾ, ਹਾਸਲ ਕਰਨਾ, ਪੁੱਜ ਜਾਣਾ, ਪਹੁੰਚਣਾ; ਸਿੱਧ ਕਰਨਾ; ~able ਪ੍ਰਾਪਤ ਕਰਨ ਯੋਗ, ਪਾਉਣ ਯੋਗ; ~ment ਲਾਭ, ਪ੍ਰਾਪਤੀ, ਉਪਲਬਧੀ, ਸਿੱਧੀ; ਪ੍ਰਾਪਤ-ਵਸਤੂ

attempt (ਅ'ਟੈਂਪਟ) *v n* ਜਤਨ ਕਰਨਾ, ਕੋਸ਼ਿਸ਼ ਕਰਨਾ, ਉੱਦਮ ਕਰਨਾ, ਜਾਂਚਣਾ, ਹਮਲਾ ਕਰਨਾ; ਕੋਸ਼ਿਸ਼, ਜਤਨ, ਉੱਦਮ, ਪ੍ਰਯਾਸ; ਆਕਰਮਣ

attend (ਅ'ਟੈਂਡ) *v* ਹਾਜ਼ਰ ਹੋਣਾ, ਮੌਜੂਦ ਰਹਿਣਾ, ਸੇਵਾ ਵਿਚ ਪੁੱਜਣਾ; ਸੇਵਾ ਕਰਨਾ, ਦਿਲ ਲਾਉਣਾ, ਜੁਟ ਜਾਣਾ, ਸਾਥ ਦੇਣਾ, ਸੰਗ ਕਰਨਾ, ਨਾਲ ਰਹਿਣਾ; ਹੱਥ ਵਿਚ ਲੈਣਾ; ~ance ਹਾਜ਼ਰੀ, ਮੌਜੂਦਗੀ, ਉਪਸਥਿਤੀ; ਹਾਜ਼ਰੀ; ~ant ਦਾਸ, ਨੌਕਰ, ਚਾਕਰ, ਅਰਦਲੀ, ਸੇਵਾਦਾਰ ਸੇਵਕ, ਸਹਿਗਾਮੀ; ਸਬੰਧਤ, ਉਪਸਥਿਤ, ਹਾਜ਼ਰ

attention (ਅ'ਟੈਂਸ਼ਨ) *n* ਧਿਆਨ, ਖ਼ਿਆਲ, ਸਾਵਧਾਨੀ, ਇਕਾਗਰਤਾ, ਤਵੱਜੁਹ (ਵ) ਸ਼ਿਸ਼ਟਾਚਾਰ, ਆਦਰ ਸਤਿਕਾਰ

attentive (ਅ'ਟੈਂਟਿਵ) *a* ਚੌਕਸ, ਸਾਵਧਾਨ, ਚੇਤਨ, ਸਚੇਤ, ਜਾਗਰੂਕ, ਇਕਾਗਰ; ~ness ਸਾਵਧਾਨੀ, ਚੇਤਨਤਾ, ਇਕਾਗਰਚਿੱਤਤਾ; ਸ਼ਿਸ਼ਟਤਾ

attest (ਅ'ਟੈਸਟ) *v* ਤਸਦੀਕ ਕਰਨੀ, ਪ੍ਰਮਾਣਤ ਕਰਨਾ, ਗਵਾਹੀ ਦੇਣੀ, ਸਾਖੀ ਭਰਨਾ, ਸਹੁੰ ਚੁਕਟੀ, ਹਲਫ਼ ਲੈਣਾ; ~ation ਪ੍ਰਮਾਣੀਕਰਨ, ਤਸਦੀਕ, ਪ੍ਰਮਾਣ, ਸਾਖੀ, ਗਵਾਹੀ, ਪ੍ਰਮਾਣ-ਪੱਤਰ; ~ed ਤਸਦੀਕ ਕੀਤਾ, ਪ੍ਰਮਾਣਕ

attic (ਐਟਿਕ) *n* ਅਟਾਰੀ

attire (ਅ'ਟਾਇਅ*) *v n* ਪੁਸ਼ਾਕ ਪਹਿਨਣੀ, ਕੱਪੜੇ

attitude (ਐਟਿਟਯੂਡ) *n* ਰੁਖ, ਰਵੱਯਾ; ਮਨੋ-ਬਿਰਤੀ ਰਵੱਈਆ, ਵਿਚਾਰ, ਅੰਦਾਜ਼, ਬਿਰਤੀ; ਰੰਗ-ਢੰਗ; ਵਿਚਾਰ ਭਾਵ (ਰਾਏ), ਸਥਿਤੀ

attract (ਅ'ਟਰੈਕਟ) *v* ਖਿੱਚਣਾ, ਆਕਰਸ਼ਤ ਕਰਨਾ, ਲੁਭਾਉਣਾ, ਮੋਹਣਾ, ਧਿਆਨ ਖਿੱਚਣਾ; **~ion** ਆਕਰਸ਼ਣ, ਖਿੱਚ, ਮੋਹ, ਆਕਰਮਣ ਸ਼ਕਤੀ, ਕਸ਼ਸ਼; **~ive** ਮਨੋਹਰ, ਆਕਰਸ਼ਕ, ਦਿਲਚਸਪ, ਮਨੋਰੰਜਕ

attribute (ਐਟਰਿਬਯੂਟ, ਅ'ਟਰਿਬਯੂਟ) *n v* ਗੁਣ, ਵਿਸ਼ੇਸ਼ਤਾ ਦੱਸਣਾ, ਸਬੰਧ ਦੱਸਣਾ, ਸਰਬੰਧ ਦੱਸਣਾ; ਨਾਂ ਲਗਾਉਣਾ, ਮਨਸੂਬਾ ਕਰਨਾ, ਮੱਥੇ ਮੜ੍ਹਨਾ

attributive (ਅ'ਟਰਿਬਯੂਟਿਵ) *a* ਗੁਣਵਾਚਕ

attune (ਅ'ਟਯੂਨ) *v* ਇਕ ਸੁਰ ਕਰਨਾ, ਮਿਲਾਉਣਾ; ਅਨੁਕੂਲ ਕਰਨਾ

auction ('ਓਕਸ਼ਨ) *n v* ਨੀਲਾਮੀ, ਬੋਲੀ; ਨੀਲਾਮੀ ਕਰਨਾ

audacity (ਓ'ਡੈਸਅਟਿ) *n* ਬੇਬਾਕੀ, ਦਲੇਰੀ, ਨਿਰਭੈਤਾ ਨਿਡਰਤਾ; ਢੀਠਪੁਣਾ

audible ('ਓਡਿਬਲ) *a* ਸੁਣਨ ਯੋਗ, ਸਪੱਸ਼ਟ, ਸੁਵਣ-ਗੋਚਰ, ਸੁਵਣੀ

audience ('ਓਡਯਅੰਸ) *n* ਸਰੋਤਾ-ਗਣ; ਸਰੋਤੇ, ਸਭਾ; ਸੁਣਵਾਈ, ਮੁਲਾਕਾਤ; ਪਾਠਕ-ਗਣ, ਦਰਸ਼ਕ-ਗਣ

audit ('ਓਡਿਟ) *n* ਲੇਖਾ-ਪਰੀਖਿਆ, ਲੇਖਾ-ਪੜਤਾਲ

auditor (ਓ'ਡਿਟਅ*) *n* ਲੇਖਾ-ਪਰੀਖਿਅਕ

auditorium ('ਓਡਿ'ਟੋਰਿਅਮ) *n* ਸਭਾਭਵਨ, ਜਲਸਾ ਘਰ, ਆਡੀਟੋਰੀਅਮ

auditory ('ਓਡਿਟ(ਅ)ਰਿ) *a* ਸੁਣਨ ਬਾਰੇ, ਸੁਣਨ ਸਬੰਧੀ, ਸੁਵਣਾਤਮਕ

augment /'ਓਗਸੈਂਟ, 'ਓਗਮਅੰਟ) *v n* ਵਧਾਉਣਾ, ਵਾਧਾ ਕਰਨਾ, ਅਧਿਕ ਕਰਨਾ, ਜ਼ਿਆਦਾ ਕਰਨਾ, ਸਵਰ-ਆਗਮ, ਵਾਧਾ, ਵ੍ਰਿਧੀ

august, August (ਓ'ਗਅੱਸਟ,'ਓਗਅਸਟ) *a n* ਪੂਜਨੀਕ, ਸਤਿਕਾਰ ਯੋਗ, ਉਚੀ ਸ਼ਾਨ ਵਾਲਾ, ਮਹਾਨ; ਅਗਸਤ ਮਹੀਨਾ

aunt ('ਆਂਟ) *n* ਚਾਚੀ, ਤਾਈ, ਮਾਮੀ, ਭੂਆ, ਫੁੱਫੀ, ਮਾਸੀ

aura ('ਓਰਅ) *n* ਨੂਰ, ਆਭਾ ਮੰਡਲ ਸੁਗੰਧ, ਕੰਬਣੀ, ਥਰਥਰੀ, ਝਰਨਾਟ; ਕੰਨਾਂ ਸਬੰਧੀ, ਕੰਨਾਂ ਦਾ, ਸੁਣੀ ਹੋਈ

aurora (ਓ'ਰੋਰਅ) *n* ਪ੍ਰਭਾਤ, ਪਹੁ-ਫੁਟਾਲਾ, ਤੜਕਾ, ਸਰਘੀ ਵੇਲਾ

auspice ('ਓਸਪਿਸ) *n* ਸ਼ਗਨ, ਮਹੂਰਤ; ਸ਼ੁਭ ਅਤੇ ਸ੍ਰੇਸ਼ਠ ਅਗਵਾਈ

auspicious (ਓ'ਸਪਿਸ਼ਅਸ) *a* ਸ਼ੁਭ ਲਗਨ ਵਾਲਾ, ਚੰਗੇ ਮਹੂਰਤ ਵਾਲਾ, ਸੁਲੱਖਣਾ, ਸੁਭਾਗਸ਼ਾਲੀ, ਕਲਿਆਣਕਾਰੀ, ਮੁਬਾਰਕ

austere (ਓ'ਸਟਿਅ*) *a* ਅਤੀ-ਸੰਜਮੀ, ਸਾਦਗੀ-ਪਸੰਦ; ਕੱਟੜ; ਕਠੋਰ-ਤਪੱਸਿਆ ਕਰਨਾ ਵਾਲਾ, ਦ੍ਰਿੜ੍ਹ ਰੂਪ ਵਿਤ, ਤੀਖਣ; ਗੰਭੀਰ

austerity (ਓ'ਸਟੈਰਅਟਿ) *n* ਸਾਦਗੀ, ਸਿੱਧਾਪਣ; ਕਠੋਰਤਾ, ਸਾਧਨਾ, ਤਪੱਸਿਆ, ਦ੍ਰਿੜ੍ਹ ਸਦਾਚਾਰ

authentic (ਓ'ਥੈਂਟਿਕ) *n* ਭਰੋਸੇਯੋਗ, ਮੰਨਣ ਯੋਗ, ਵਿਸ਼ਵਾਸਪੂਰਨ, ਅਸਲੀ, ਮੌਲਕ, ਵਾਸਤਵਿਕ; **~ate** ਪ੍ਰਮਾਣਤ ਕਰਨਾ; **~ity** ਪ੍ਰਮਾਣਕਤਾ, ਵਾਸਤਵਿਕਤਾ, ਪ੍ਰਮਾਣਸਿੱਧਤਾ, ਸਚਾਈ

author ('ਓਥਅ*) *v* ਲੇਖਕ, ਲਿਖਾਰੀ, ਕਰਤਾ, ਰਚਨਹਾਰ, ਗ੍ਰੰਥਕਾਰ; ਮੋਢੀ, ਉਤਪਾਦਕ

authority (ਓ'ਥੋਰਿਟਅਟਿ) *n* ਅਧਿਕਾਰ, ਇਖ਼ਤਿਆਰ, ਪ੍ਰਭੂਤਾ; ਅਹੁਦੇਦਾਰ, ਪਦ-ਅਧਿਕਾਰੀ, ਪ੍ਰਮਾਣ, ਵਿਸ਼ੇਸ਼ੱਗ

authorize ('ਓਥਅਰਾਇਜ਼) *v* ਅਧਿਕਾਰ ਦੇਣਾ, ਇਖ਼ਤਿਆਰ ਦੇਣਾ, ਮੁਖ਼ਤਾਰ ਬਣਾਉਣਾ

authorship ('ਓਥਅ:ਸ਼ਿਪ) *n* ਗ੍ਰੰਥਕਾਰੀ, ਕਰਤ੍ਰਿਤਵ

auto ('ਓਟਅਉ) *n* (ਬੋਲ) ਸਵੈਚਾਲਕ ਗੱਡੀ, ਆਟੋ

autobiographer ('ਓਟਅ(ਉ)ਬਾਇ'ਔਗਰਅਫ਼ਅ*) *n* ਆਤਮ-ਕਥਾਕਾਰ, ਆਤਮ-ਕਥਾ-ਲੇਖਕ, ਸਵੈ-ਜੀਵਨੀਕਾਰ

autobiography ('ਓਟਅ(ਉ),ਬਾਇਅ(ਉ)ਗਰੈਫ਼ਿ) *n* ਆਪਬੀਤੀ, ਆਤਮ-ਕਥਾ, ਸਵੈਜੀਵਨੀ

autocracy (ਓ'ਟੌਕਰਅਸਿ) *n* ਖ਼ੁਦਮੁਖ਼ਤਾਰੀ, ਏਕਤੰਤਰ, ਨਿਰੰਕੁਸ਼ਤਾ; ਪ੍ਰਭਾਵ, ਦਬਦਬਾ

autocrat ('ਓਟਅ(ਉ)ਕਰੈਟ) *n* ਖ਼ੁਦਮੁਖ਼ਤਾਰ, ਬਾਦਸ਼ਾਹ, ਨਿਰੰਕੁਸ਼ ਸ਼ਾਸਕ

autograph ('ਓਟਅਗਰਾਫ਼) *n* ਆਪਣੇ ਹਸਤਾਖ਼ਰ, ਦਸਤਖ਼ਤ, ਹੱਥ-ਲਿਖਤ

automatic (ਓਟਅ'ਮੈਟਿਕ) *a* ਸਵੈਚਲਤ, ਆਪਣੇ ਆਪ ਚੱਲਣ ਜਾਂ ਕੰਮ ਕਰਨ ਵਾਲੀ

automobile ('ਓਟਅਮਅ(ਉ)ਬੀਲ) *n* ਮੋਟਰ ਜਾਂ ਕਾਰ

autonomy (ਓ'ਟੌਅਮਿ) *n* ਖ਼ੁਦਮੁਖ਼ਤਾਰੀ, ਵਿਅਕਤੀਗਤ ਸੁਤੰਤਰਤਾ, ਸਵਾਧੀਤਨਾ, ਸਵਰਾਜ

autumn ('ਓਟਅਮ) *n* ਪਤਝੜ ਦੀ ਰੁੱਤ, ਖ਼ਿਜ਼ਾਂ ਦਾ ਮੌਸਮ; ਖਰੀਫ (ਫ਼ਸਲ)

auxiliary ('ਓਗ'ਜ਼ਿਲਜਅਰਿ) *n a* ਸਹਾਈ, ਉਪਕਾਰੀ, ਸਹਾਇਕ

avail (ਅ'ਵੇਇਲ) *v* ਕੰਮ ਵਿਚ ਲਿਆਉਣਾ, ਫ਼ਾਇਦਾ ਉਠਾਉਣਾ, ਮਦਦ ਦੇਣੀ, ਸਹਾਈ, ਹੋਣਾ, ਕੰਮ ਆਉਣਾ; **to be of no ~** ਕਿਸੇ ਕੰਮ ਦਾ ਨਾ ਹੋਣਾ, ਨਿਕੰਮਾ; **of no ~** ਵਿਅਰਥ, ਨਿਸਫਲ, ਬੇਮਤਲਬ; **to ~ oneself of** ਤੋਂ (ਜਾਂ) ਦੈ ਲਾਭ ਉਠਾਉਣਾ; **~ability** ਪ੍ਰਾਪਤ, ਸੁਲੱਭਤਾ; ਉਪਲਬਧੀ; **~able** ਪ੍ਰਾਪਤ, ਮੌਜੂਦ, ਸੁਲੱਭ, ਲੱਭਦਾ, ਉਪਲਬਧ

avalanche ('ਐਵ੍ਅਲਾਂਸ਼) *n* ਬਰਫ਼ ਦਾ ਤੋਦਾ ਜੋ ਹੇਠਾਂ ਡਿਗ ਪੈਂਦਾ ਹੈ

avarice ('ਐਵ੍ਅਰਿਸ) *n* ਲੋਭ, ਲਾਲਚ, ਤ੍ਰਿਸ਼ਨਾ, ਹਿਰਸ

avenge ('ਅ'ਵੈਂਜ) *v* ਬਦਲਾ ਲੈਣਾ, ਕਿੜ ਕੱਢਣੀ, ਇੰਤਕਾਮ ਲੈਣਾ

avenue ('ਐਵ੍ਅਨਯੂ) *n* ਛਾਂਦਾਰ ਮਾਰਗ, ਪ੍ਰਵੇਸ਼ ਮਾਰਗ, ਕੁੰਜ ਗਲੀ

average ('ਐਵ੍(ਅ)ਰਿਜ) *n v a* ਔਸਤ, ਮੱਧਮਾਨ, ਸਧਾਰਨਤਾ; ਔਸਤ ਕੱਢਣੀ; ਸਧਾਰਨ ਪੱਧਰ ਦਾ ਅਨੁਮਾਨ ਲਾਉਣਾ; ਸਧਾਰਨ, ਔਸਤ ਦਰਜੇ ਦਾ, ਮਾਮੂਲੀ

averse (ਅ'ਵ੍ਅ:ਸ) *a* ਵਿਰੁੱਧ, ਵਿਪਰੀਤ, ਪ੍ਰਤੀਕੂਲ, ਖਿਲਾਫ਼, ਉਲਟ

aversion (ਅ'ਵ੍ਅ:ਸ਼ਨ) *n* ਬੇਮੁਖਤਾ, ਅਰੁਚੀ, ਵਿਰਕਤੀ, ਵਿਰੋਧ, ਨਰਾਜ਼ਗੀ

avert (ਅ'ਵ੍ਅ:ਟ) *v* ਦੂਰ ਕਰਨਾ, ਫੇਰਨਾ, ਟਾਲਣਾ, ਹਟਾਉਣਾ, ਮੋੜ ਲੈਣਾ, ਫੇਰ ਦੇਣਾ, ਟਾਲ ਦੇਣਾ

aviation ('ਏਇਵ੍ਏਇਸ਼ਨ) *n* ਚਿੜੀਆਘਰ, ਵਿਮਾਨ ਸੰਚਾਲਨ, ਹਵਾਈ ਜਹਾਜ਼ ਚਲਾਉਣ ਦੀ ਕਿਰਿਆ

avication ('ਐਵ੍ਅ(ਉ)'ਕੇਇਸ਼ਨ) *n* ਪੇਸ਼ਾ, ਧੰਦਾ, ਕੰਮ; ਸ਼ੁਗਲ

avoid ('ਅ'ਵੌਇਡ) *v* ਪਰਹੇਜ਼ ਕਰਨਾ; ਟਾਲਣਾ, ਬਚਣਾ, ਕਿਨਾਰਾ ਕਰਨਾ

await (ਅ'ਵੇਇਟ) *v* ਉਡੀਕਣਾ, ਇੰਤਜ਼ਾਰ ਕਰਨਾ, ਪ੍ਰਤੀਖਿਆ ਕਰਨੀ, ਰਾਹ ਤੱਕਣਾ, ਆਸਰਾ ਦੇਖਣਾ

awake (ਅ'ਵੇਇਕ) *a v* ਜਾਗਰਤ, ਜਾਗਰੁਕ; ਸਾਵਧਾਨ; ਉਠਣਾ, ਜਾਗਣਾ; ਉਤਸ਼ਾਹ ਦੇਣਾ,

ਸਾਵਧਾਨ ਹੋਣਾ, ਜਗਾਉਣਾ, ਸਚੇਤ ਕਰਨਾ, ਜਾਗਰਤ ਹੋਣਾ

award (ਅ'ਵੋ:ਡ) *v n* ਨਿਰਣਾ ਦੇਣਾ, ਪ੍ਰਦਾਨ ਕਰਨਾ, ਸਮਰਪਣ ਕਰਨਾ, ਸੌਂਪਣਾ, ਦੇਣਾ; ਪੰਚ-ਨਿਰਣਾ, ਫ਼ੈਸਲਾ; ਇਨਾਮ, ਪੁਰਸਕਾਰ, ਜੁਰਮਾਨਾ

aware (ਅ'ਵੇਇਆ*) *a* ਸਚੇਤ, ਸਾਵਧਾਨ, ਚੁਕੰਨਾ, ਹੁਸ਼ਿਆਰ, ਜਾਣਕਾਰ

away (ਅ'ਵੇਇ) *adv* ਦੂਰ, ਗ਼ੈਰਹਾਜ਼ਰ, ਪਰੇ, ਦੂਰੀ ਤੇ; ਅਲੱਗ, ਫ਼ਾਸਲੇ ਤੇ; ਨਿਰੰਤਰ, ਲਗਾਤਾਰ, ਹਮੇਸ਼ਾ

awe (ਓ) *n v* ਵਿਸਮਯ, ਰੁਅਬ, ਖੌਫ਼, ਡਰ; ਭਉ; ਭੈ; ਵਿਸਮਤ ਕਰ ਦੇਣਾ, ਭੈਭੀਤ ਕਰਨਾ

awful ('ਓਫ਼ੁਲ) *a* ਡਰਾਉਣਾ, ਰੋਹਬ ਵਾਲਾ; ਆਦਰ-ਯੋਗ, ਮਹਿਮਾਪੂਰਨ, ਮਹਾਨ; **~ly** ਡਰ

ਨਾਲ, ਬਹੁਤ, ਅਧਿਕ

awhile (ਅ'ਵਾਇਲ) *adv* ਕੁਝ ਚਿਰ ਲਈ, ਥੋੜੀ ਦੇਰ ਲਈ

awkward ('ਓਕਵਾ*ਡ) *a* ਬੇਡੌਲ, ਕਰੂਪ, ਕੋਝਾ; ਭੱਦਾ ਅਨਾੜੀ, ਕਠਨ; ਭਿਆਨਕ, ਡਰਾਵਣਾ

awry (ਅ'ਰਾਇ) *adv* ਭੁੱਲ ਕੇ, ਟੇਢੇ ਢੰਗ ਨਾਲ

axe (ਐਕਸ) *n* ਕੁਹਾੜੀ, ਤੇਸੀ

axiom ('ਐਕਸਿਅਮ) *n* ਅਟੱਲ ਸਚਾਈ, ਪ੍ਰਮਾਣ, ਪ੍ਰਸਿਧ ਸਿਧਾਂਤ; ਫ਼ਾਰਮੂਲਾ, ਸੂਤਰ, ਸੂਕਤੀ, ਕਥਨ, ਵਾਕ, ਗੱਲ

axis ('ਐਕਸਿਸ) *n* ਕੇਂਦਰ, ਧੁਰਾ, ਧੁਰੀ

axle ('ਐਕਸਲ) *n* ਧੁਰਾ, ਧੁਰੀ, ਕਿੱਲੀ

ayah ('ਆਇਆ) *n* ਆਯਾ, ਦਾਈ

azure ('ਐਨ਼ਅ*) *n* ਅਸਮਾਨੀ, ਰੰਗ, ਨਿਰਮਲ ਆਕਾਸ਼, ਚਮਕਦਾਰ ਨੀਲਾ ਰੰਗ

B

B, b (ਬੀ) *n* ਰੋਮਨ ਵਰਣਮਾਲਾ ਦਾ ਦੂਜਾ ਅੱਖਰ;
ਸਰਗਮ ਦੀ ਸੱਤਵੀਂ ਸੁਰ; ਦੂਜੀ ਚੀਜ਼

B. A. (ਬੀਏਇ) *a n* ਬੀ.ਏ. ਦੀ ਡਿਗਰੀ; ਬੀ.ਏ.
ਪਾਸ

baa (ਬਾ) *n v* ਭੈਂ-ਭੈਂ (ਭੇਡ ਦੀ), ਮੈਂ-ਮੈਂ; ਭੈਂ-ਭੈਂ
ਕਰਨਾ, ਮਿਆਂਕਣਾ, ਮਿਮਿਆਉਣਾ

babble ('ਬੈਬਲ) *v n* ਬੁਡਬੁਡਾਉਣਾ, ਲੁਤਰ-
ਲੁਤਰ ਕਰਨਾ, ਟੈਂ-ਟੈਂ ਕਰਨਾ; ਬਕਣਾ; ਬੜ-ਬੜ,
ਬਾਂ-ਬਾਂ, ਯੱਕੜ

babbling ('ਬੈਬਲਿਙ) *n a* ਬਕਵਾਸ, ਬੁੜਬੁੜਾਹਟ

babe ('ਬੇਇਬ) *n* ਬਾਲ, ਬਾਲਕ, ਬੱਚਾ, ਕਾਕਾ,
ਕਾਕੀ, ਨਿਆਣਾ, ਗੀਗਾ, ਭੋਲਾ ਆਦਮੀ, ਅਨਾੜੀ

babel ('ਬੇਇਬਲ) *n* ਬਾਬਲ ਦਾ ਵੱਡਾ ਮੁਨਾਰਾ;
ਰੌਲਾ-ਰੱਪਾ, ਕਾਵਾਂ-ਰੌਲੀ, ਚੀਕ-ਚਿਹਾੜਾ

baboon (ਬਅਬੂਨ) *n* ਲੰਗੂਰ

babouche (ਬਅਬੂਸ਼) *n* ਸਲੀਪਰ, ਚੱਪਲ

baby ('ਬੇਇਬਿ) *n* ਬੱਚਾ, ਬਾਲ, ਨਿੱਕੂ, ਕਾਕਾ,
ਨਿਆਣਾ, ਛੋਟੂ, ਗੀਗਾ; ਕੋਈ ਬਹੁਤ ਛੋਟੀ
ਚੀਜ਼

bachelor ('ਬੈਚਅਲਅ*) *n* ਕੰਵਾਰਾ, ਛੜਾ,
ਬ੍ਰਹਮਚਾਰੀ; ਯੂਨੀਵਰਸਿਟੀ ਦੀ ਪਹਿਲੀ ਡਿਗਰੀ
ਪ੍ਰਾਪਤ ਵਿਅਕਤੀ; (ਇਤਿ) ਜੋਧਾ, ਦੂਜੇ ਦੇ ਝੰਡੇ
ਹੇਠ ਕੰਮ ਕਰਨ ਵਾਲਾ ਸੂਰਬੀਰ

back (ਬੈਕ) *n a adv* (1) ਪਿਠ, ਕੰਢ, ਪਿੱਛਾ
(2) ਲਲਾਰੀ ਦਾ ਵੱਡਾ ਤਸਲਾ; ਤਗਾਰ; ਕੁੰਡਾ;
ਬੱਠਲ, ਟੱਬ, ਪਹਿਲਾਂ ਜੇਹੀ ਹਾਲਤ ਵਿਚ; ਪੱਠਾ,
ਪਿਛਲਾ; ਪਿੱਛੇ, ਪਿਛਾਂਗ, ਪੁਰਾਣੇ ਜ਼ਮਾਨੇ ਵਿਚ;
ਸਮਰਥਨ ਕਰਨਾ, ਪਿੱਠ ਠੋਕਣੀ, ਪੁਸ਼ਟੀ ਕਰਨੀ;

ਤਸਦੀਕ ਕਰਨਾ; ਪਿੱਛੇ ਹਟਣਾ; ਘੋੜਾ ਫੇਰਨਾ;
~ground ਪਿਛੋਕੜ, ਪਿੱਠ-ਭੂਮੀ, ਆਧਾਰ; ਪਿੱਛੇ
ਦਾ ਹਿੱਸਾ; **~log** ਰਹਿੰਦਾ ਕੰਮ; **~side** ਪਿੱਛਾ,
ਚਿੱਤੜ; **~water** ਰੁਕਿਆ ਪਾਣੀ, ਬੰਦ ਪਾਣੀ;
ਸਮੁੰਦਰ ਦੀ ਖਾੜੀ; **~out of** ਮੁਕਰਨਾ, ਪਿੱਛੇ
ਹਟਣਾ, ਆਪਣੀ ਗਲ ਤੋਂ ਫਿਰ ਜਾਣਾ; **~up** ਪਿੱਠ
ਠੋਕਣੀ, ਸਮਰਥਨ ਕਰਨਾ, ਹੌਸਲਾ ਵਧਾਉਣਾ
ਸਹਾਇਤਾ ਕਰਨਾ ਹਾਮੀ ਭਰਨੀ ਸ਼ਹਿ ਦੇਣੀ; **to
the ~ bone** ਪੂਰੀ ਤਰ੍ਹਾਂ; **turn one's~upon**
ਪਿੱਠ ਦਿਖਾਉਣਾ, ਭੱਜ ਨਿਕਲਣਾ, ਛੱਡ ਕੇ ਨੱਠ
ਜਾਣਾ **~ing** ਆਸਰਾ, ਟੇਕ, ਹਿਮਾਇਤ, ਪੁਸ਼ਟੀ

backward ('ਬੈਕਵਅ*ਡ) *a adv* ਪਛੜਿਆ;
ਪਿੱਛੇ; ਪਿਛਾਂਹ ਵੱਲ; ਭੈੜੀ ਹਾਲਤ ਵਿਚ;
ਉਲਟਿਆ; ਪਿੱਛੇ ਰਿਹਾ; **~classes** ਪੱਛੜੀਆਂ
ਸ੍ਰੇਣੀਆਂ; **~ness** ਪਛੜਾਪਣ, ਪਛੜੇਵਾਂ;
ਉਲਟਾਪਣ

bacon ('ਬੇਇਕ(ਅ)ਨ) *n* ਸੂਰ ਦਾ ਮਾਸ

bacteria (ਬੈਕ'ਟਿਅਰਿਆ) (becterium ਦਾ
pl) *n* ਜੀਵਾਣੂ, ਰੋਗਾਣੂ; **~l** ਜਰਾਸੀਮੀ; ਰੋਗਾਣੂ
ਸਬੰਧੀ

bad (ਬੈਡ') *a n* ਬੁਰਾ, ਖੋਟਾ, ਨਿਕੰਮਾ, ਘਟੀਆ,
ਨੀਚ, ਭੈੜਾ, ਹੋਛਾ, ਕਮੀਨਾ, ਚੰਦਰਾ,
ਬਦਕਾਰ; **~ly** ਭੈੜੀ ਤਰ੍ਹਾਂ, ਬੁਰੀ ਤਰ੍ਹਾਂ;
ਅਸਫਲਤਾ ਨਾਲ, ਮੰਦੇ ਹਾਲ; ਅਨਾੜੀਆਂ ਵਾਂਗ,
ਗ਼ਲਤੀ ਨਾਲ; **~ness** ਭੈੜ; ਬੁਰਾਈ, ਖੋਟ,
ਬੁਰੀ ਹਾਲਤ; ਨੁਕਸ, ਦੋਸ਼, ਖ਼ਰਾਬੀ, ਖੋਟਾਪਣ,
ਬਿਪਤਾ, ਦੁਰਗਤੀ, ਦੁਸ਼ਟਤਾ

badge (ਬੈਜ) *n* ਬਿੱਲਾ, ਨਿਸ਼ਾਨ, ਪ੍ਰਤੀਕ, ਪੱਟਾ

badminton ('ਬੈਡਮਿੰਟਅਨ) *n* ਬੈਡ-ਮਿੰਟਨ, ਚਿੜੀ-ਛਿੱਕਾ (ਇਕ ਖੇਡ); ਸ਼ਰਦਾਈ ਜੋ ਸ਼ਰਾਬ, ਸੋਡਾ ਤੇ ਖੰਡ ਰਲਾ ਕੇ ਬਣਦੀ ਹੈ

baffle ('ਬੈਫ਼ਲ) *v n* ਘਬਰਾਉਣਾ, ਮੱਤ ਮਾਰ ਦੇਣੀ; ਚਕਰਾ ਦੇਣਾ, ਰੁਕਾਵਟ ਪਾਉਣੀ, ਰੋੜਾ ਅਟਕਾਉਣਾ, ਨਿਸਫਲ ਕਰ ਦੇਣਾ; ਹੈਰਾਨ ਕਰਨ ਵਾਲਾ, ਘਬਰਾ ਦੇਣ ਵਾਲਾ, ਰੋੜਾ ਅਟਕਾਉਣ ਵਾਲਾ

bag (ਬੈਗ) *n* ਥੈਲਾ, ਥੈਲੀ, ਬੋਰਾ, ਝੋਲਾ, ਗੁੱਥੀ, ਗਾਂ ਦਾ ਲੇਵਾ; ਕੀੜਿਆਂ ਜਾਂ ਮੱਖੀਆਂ ਦੇ ਸ਼ਰੀਰ ਵਿਚ ਜ਼ਹਿਰ ਜਾਂ ਸ਼ਹਿਦ ਦੀ ਥੈਲੀ; ਅੱਖ ਦੇ ਥੱਲੇ ਉਭਰੀ ਥਾਂ; ਜਿਤਣਾ ਜਾ ਪ੍ਰਾਪਤ ਕਰਨਾ (ਇਨਾਮ ਦਾ), ਥੈਲੇ ਵਿਚ ਪਾਉਣਾ, ਫਸਾਉਣਾ, ਸ਼ਿਕਾਰ ਮਾਰਨਾ, ਹਥਿਆ ਲੈਣਾ, ਝੋਲ ਪੈਣੀ, ਭਟਕਣਾ; **let the cat out of the~** ਭੇਦ ਖੋਲ੍ਹਣਾ, ਬਿੱਲੀ ਥੈਲਿਉਂ ਬਾਹਰ ਕੱਢਣਾ

baggage ('ਬੈਗਿਜ) *n a* ਸਫ਼ਰੀ ਸਾਮਾਨ, ਫ਼ੌਜੀ ਸਾਮਾਨ, ਮਾਲ, ਵਸਤ-ਵਲੇਵਾ, ਖੁਥਭ੍ਰ ਤੀਵੀਂ

bagging ('ਬੈਗਿੜ) *n* ਸਾਮਾਨ ਅਸਬਾਬ, ਮਾਲ-ਅਸਬਾਬ; ਥੈਗ ਬਣਾਉਣ ਵਾਲਾ ਟਾਟ

bail (ਬੇਇਲ) *v n* ਜ਼ਮਾਨਤ, ਜ਼ਾਮਨੀ; ਜ਼ਾਮਨ; ਕ੍ਰਿਕਟ ਦੀ ਖੇਡ ਵਿੱਚ ਵਿਕਟਾਂ ਦੇ ਉੱਪਰ ਦੀ ਗੁੱਲੀ; ਜ਼ਮਾਨਤ ਤੇ ਛੱਡਣਾ, ਮੁਚੱਲਕਾ ਲੈਣਾ

bailment ('ਬੇਇਲਮਅੰਟ) *n* ਜ਼ਮਾਨਤ, ਜ਼ਾਮਨੀ

bake (ਬੇਇਕ) *v* ਪਕਾਉਣਾ, ਰਾਤੂਨਾ; ਸੇਕਣਾ; ਭੁਨਣਾ; ਪੱਕ ਜਾਣਾ

baker ('ਬੇਇਕਅਾ*) *n* ਨਾਨਬਾਈ, ਤੰਦੂਰੀਆ, ਰੋਟੀ ਵਾਲਾ

balance ('ਬੈਲਅੰਸ) *n v* ਤੱਕੜੀ, ਕੰਡਾ, (ਘੜੀ ਦਾ) ਕਮਾਨੀਲੀਵਰ, ਬਾਲ ਕਮਾਨੀ; ਸੰਤੁਲਨ, ਬਰਾਬਰੀ, ਬਾਕੀ; ਬੱਚਤ; (ਜੋ) ਤੁਲਾ ਰਾਸ਼ੀ: ਕਿਸੇ ਵਸਤੂ ਦਾ ਬਾਕੀ ਭਾਗ; ਤੋਲਣਾ, ਵੱਜਣ ਕਰਨਾ, ਹਿਸਾਬ ਬਰਾਬਰ ਕਰਨਾ, ਇਕ ਜਿਹਾ ਕਰਨਾ, ਜੋੜ ਮਿਲਾਉਣਾ; ਡੋਲਣਾ; **~d** ਸੰਤੁਲਤ; **~sheet** ਆਮਦਨ-ਖਰਚ ਦਾ ਚਿੱਠਾ; **lose one's~** ਡੋਲ ਜਾਣਾ, ਘਬਰਾਹਟ ਵਿਚ ਦਿਲ ਛੱਡ ਜਾਣਾ

balcony ('ਬੈਲਕਅਾਨਿ) *n* (ਉੱਪਰਲੀ ਮੰਜ਼ਲ ਦਾ) ਛੱਜਾ, ਬਾਲਕੋਨੀ

bald (ਬੋਲਡ) *a* ਗੰਜਾ, ਰੋਡਾ, ਕੋਰਾ, ਫਿੱਕਾ; ਸ਼ਰੀਰ ਤੇ ਵਿਸ਼ੇਸ਼ ਕਰਕੇ ਚਿਹਰੇ ਉੱਪਰ ਚਿੱਟੇ ਦਾਗ਼ ਵਾਲਾ ਘੋੜਾ, ਪੰਖਹੀਣ, ਬੰਜਰ, ਗੰਜੀ ਭੌਂ; **~head** ਗੰਜੇ ਸਿਰ ਵਾਲਾ; **~ness** ਗੰਜ, ਰੋਡ, ਘੋਨ, ਰੁੱਖਪਣ

bale (ਬੇਇਲ) *n v* ਗੰਠ, ਪੰਡ, ਦੁੱਖ, ਪਾਪ, ਬੁਰਾਈ, ਬਿਪਤਾ, ਕਸ਼ਟ, ਕਲੇਸ਼, ਕਠਨਾਈ, ਤਕਲੀਫ਼, ਤਬਾਹੀ; ਗੰਠ ਬੰਨ੍ਹਣੀ, ਗੰਠ ਬਣਾਉਣਾ; **~ful** ਮਨਹੂਸ, ਕਸ਼ਟਕਾਰੀ, ਸੋਗੀ, ਹਾਨੀਕਾਰਕ

ball (ਬੋਲ) *n v* ਗੇਂਦ, ਖੇਹਨੂੰ, ਖਿਦੋ, ਪਿੰਨਾ; (ਪਿਸਤੌਲ ਜਾਂ ਬੰਦੂਕ ਦੀ) ਗੋਲੀ, (ਤੋਪ ਦਾ) ਗੋਲਾ, ਬਾਰੂਦ ਦਾ ਗੋਲਾ; ਉੱਨ ਦਾ ਗੋਲਾ, ਡੋਰ ਦਾ ਗੋਲਾ; ਅੱਖ ਦਾ ਡੇਲਾ; ਅਸਮਾਨੀ ਗ੍ਰਹਿ (ਚੰਦ, ਸੂਰਜ, ਤਾਰੇ ਆਦਿ), (ਕ੍ਰਿਕਟ ਵਿਚ) ਇਕ ਵਾਰ ਸੁਟਿਆ ਗੋਂਦ; ਬਾਲ-ਨ੍ਰਿਤ, ਵਲੇਟਣਾ, ਗੋਲ-ਮੋਲ ਹੋ ਜਾਣਾ; ਗੋਲਾ ਬਣਾਉਣਾ **have the ~ at one's feet** ਸਫਲਤਾ ਦਾ ਸੌਕਾ; **keep the ~ rolling, keep up the ~** ਸਿਲਸਲਾ ਜਾਰੀ ਰੱਖਣਾ; **~room** ਨਾਚ-ਘਰ; **~open the ~** ਨਾਚ ਆਰੰਭ ਕਰਨਾ; ਕੰਮ ਸ਼ੁਰੂ ਕਰਨਾ

ballad (ਬੈਲਅਡ) *n* ਗਾਥਾ-ਕਾਵਿ, ਜਜ਼ਬੇ ਭਰਿਆ ਗੀਤ, ਬੈਲੇਡ; **~monger** ਭੱਟ, ਬੈਂਤਬਾਜ਼

ballet ('ਬੈਲੇਇ) *n* ਸੰਗੀਤਕ ਨਾਚ, ਰਾਸ-ਲੀਲ੍ਹਾ,

ਸਮੂਹ-ਨ੍ਰਿਤ; ~**girl** ਮੰਚ ਦੀ ਨਾਚੀ, ਸੰਗੀਤਕ ਨਾਟ ਦੀ ਨਰਤਕੀ

balloon (ਬਅ'ਲੂਨ) *n v* ਗੁਬਾਰਾ, ਝੁਕਾਨਾ, ਬੈਲੂਣ; ਬੁਰਜ; ਸ਼ੀਸ਼ੇ ਦਾ ਗਲੋਬ, (ਇਮਾਰਤ) ਲਾਟੂ ਜਾਂ ਗੁੰਬਦ; ਗੁਬਾਰੇ ਵਿਚ ਚੜ੍ਹਨਾ ਜਾਂ ਉਡਣਾ; ਗੁਬਾਰੇ ਵਾਂਗ ਫੁੱਲ ਜਾਣਾ

ballot ('ਬੈਲਅਟ) *n v* ਲੁਕਵੀਂ ਵੋਟ; ਗੁਪਤ ਦਿੱਤੇ ਗਏ ਮੱਤ; ਲਾਟਰੀ ਕੱਢਣ ਦਾ ਢੰਗ; ਗੁਪਤ ਰਾਇ ਦੇਣੀ, ਗੁਪਤ ਮੱਤ ਦੁਆਰਾ ਚੁਣਨਾ, ਚੋਣ ਕਰਨੀ ~**box** ਵੋਟ-ਸੰਦੂਕੜੀ, ਚੋਣ ਪੇਟੀ, ਬੈਲਟ ਬਾਕਸ; ~**paper** ਵੋਟ ਪਾਉਣ ਵਾਲੀ ਪਰਚੀ, ਗੁਪਤ ਪਰਚੀ

balm (ਬਾਮ) *n v* ਮਲ੍ਹਮ, ਖ਼ਸ਼ਬੂਦਾਰ ਲੇਪ; ਠੰਢ ਪਾਊ ਅਸਰ, ਤਸਕੀਨ, ਸੁਗੰਧਤ ਮਲ੍ਹਮ ਦਾ ਲੇਪ ਕਰਨਾ, ਤਸੱਲੀ ਦੇਣੀ, ਸੁਗੰਧ ਫੈਲਾਉਣੀ

bamboo (ਬੈਮ'ਬੂ) *n* ਬਾਂਸ, ਵੰਝ, ਵੇਟੂ; ਬਾਂਸ ਦੀ ਸੋਟੀ

ban (ਬੈਨ) *v n* ਮਨ੍ਹਾਂ ਕਰਨਾ, ਰੋਕਣਾ, ਮਨਾਹੀ ਕਰਨਾ; ਸਰਾਪ ਦੇਣਾ; ਛੇਕਣਾ; ਕਾਨੂੰਨੀ ਰੋਕ, ਬੰਦਸ਼, ਮਨਾਹੀ; ਲਾਨ੍ਹਤ-ਮਲਾਮਤ; ਸਰਾਪ; ਦੇਸ਼-ਨਿਕਾਲਾ

banal (ਬਅ'ਨਾਲ) *adv* ਤੁੱਛ, ਮਾਮੂਲੀ

banana (ਬਅ'ਨਾਨਅ) *n* ਕੇਲਾ

band (ਬੈਂਡ) *n* (1) ਵਾਜਾ, ਬੀਨ-ਵਾਜਾ, ਬੈਂਡ; ਸੰਗੀਤ-ਮੰਡਲੀ; (2) ਟੋਲੀ, ਜੱਥਾ; (3) ਪੱਟੀ, ਫੀਤਾ; ਚੁਪਟੀ ਪੱਟੀ; ਅੰਗੂਠੀ, ਛੱਲਾ; ਰੱਸੀ ਜਾਂ ਪੱਟੀ ਬੰਨ੍ਹੁਤੀ; ਸੰਗਠਨ ਕਰਨਾ, ਜਥੇਬੰਦੀ ਕਰਨੀ; ਧਾਰੀਆਂ ਪਾਉਣੀਆਂ; ~**box** ਕਾਗ਼ਜ਼ ਜਾਂ ਗੱਤੇ ਦਾ ਡੱਬਾ; ~**master** ਬੈਂਡ ਵਜੇ ਵਾਲਿਆਂ ਦਾ ਆਗੂ

bandage ('ਬੈਨਡਿਜ) *n v* (ਜ਼ਖ਼ਮ ਆਦਿ ਤੇ

ਬੰਨ੍ਹਣ ਵਾਲੀ) ਪੱਟੀ; ਅੱਖਾਂ ਤੇ ਬੰਨ੍ਹਣ ਵਾਲੀ ਪੱਟੀ; ਪੱਟੀ ਕਰਨੀ; ਪੱਟੀ ਬੰਨ੍ਹਣੀ

bandaging (ਬੈਂਡਿਜਿਙ) *n* ਮੱਲ੍ਹਮ ਪੱਟੀ

bandit (ਬੈਂਡਿਟ) *n* ਡਾਕੂ ਡਕੈਤ, ਲੁਟੇਰਾ; ਧਾੜਵੀ

bandog (ਬੈਂਡੋਗ) *n* ਸ਼ਿਕਾਰੀ ਕੁੱਤਾ, ਖੋਜੀ ਕੁੱਤਾ

bane (ਬੇਇਨ) *n* ਜ਼ਹਿਰ, ਵਿਸ਼, ਵਿਹੁ; ਤਬਾਹੀ, ਬਰਬਾਦੀ; ਤਬਾਹੀ ਦਾ ਕਾਰਨ; ~**ful** ਜ਼ਹਿਰੀਲਾ, ਵਿਸ਼ੈਲਾ, ਵਿਹੁਲਾ, ਦੁਖਦਾਈ, ਵਿਨਾਸ਼ੀ, ਖਤਰਨਾਕ; ~**fulness** ਵਿਨਾਸ਼, ਖ਼ਤਰਾ, ਬਰਬਾਦੀ

bang (ਬੈਙ) *n v adv int* ਖੜਾਕ, ਖੜਕਾ, ਧਮਾਕਾ, ਬੰਦੂਕ ਚੱਲਣ ਦੀ ਅਵਾਜ਼, ਠਾਹ; ਠੋਕਣਾ, ਖੜਾਕ ਨਾਲ ਮਾਰਨਾ, ਜ਼ੋਰ ਨਾਲ ਮਾਰਨਾ, ਕੁੱਟਣਾ, ਮਾਰਨਾ-ਪਿੱਟਣਾ; (with a~) ਧੜੰਮ ਕਰਕੇ, ਠਾਹ ਕਰਕੇ; ਯਕਾਯਕ, ਪੂਰਾ ਪੂਰਾ, ਮੁਕੰਮਲ ਤੌਰ ਤੇ

bangle (ਬੈਙਗਲ) *n v* ਚੂੜੀ, ਵੰਗਾ, ਕੜਾ, ਕੰਗਣ; ~**d** ਚੂੜੀਦਾਰ, ਚੂੜੀਵਾਲਾ, ਕੜੇਦਾਰ

banish (ਬੈਨਿਸ਼) *v* ਦੇਸ਼ ਨਿਕਾਲਾ ਦੇਣਾ, ਬਨਵਾਸ ਦੇਣਾ, ਦਿਲੋਂ ਕੱਢ ਦੇਣਾ, ਦੂਰ ਕਰ ਦੇਣਾ; ~**ment** ਦੇਸ਼ ਨਿਕਾਲਾ, ਜਲਾਵਤਨੀ, ਨਿਰਵਾਸਨ

bank (ਬੈਙਕ) *n* (1) ਕੰਢਾ ਬਣਾਉਣਾ, ਕਿਨਾਰੇ ਦਾ ਕੰਮ ਕਰਨਾ; ਢੇਰ ਲੱਗਾਨਾ, ਤੋਦਾ ਬਣ ਜਾਣਾ; ਕੰਢਾ, ਕਿਨਾਰਾ, ਕੰਧੀ, ਬੰਨਾ, ਵੱਟ; ਟਿੱਬਾ; (2) ਬੈਂਕ, ਰੁਪਏ ਲੈਣ-ਦੇਣ ਦੀ ਥਾਂ, ਸ਼ਾਹੂਕਾਰਾ, ਸਰਾਫ਼ਾ; ਜੁਏ ਤੇ ਲੱਗੀ ਕੁੱਲ ਰਕਮ; **to break the ~** ਜੁਏ ਵਿਚ ਜਿੱਤਣਾ; ~ **on** ਨਿਰਭਰ ਕਰਨਾ, ਆਸਾਂ ਬੰਨ੍ਹਣੀਆਂ, ਉਮੀਦਾਂ ਰੱਖਣੀਆਂ; ~**bill** ਚੈਕ, ਹੁੰਡੀ; ~ **note** ਹੁੰਡੀ; ~ **paper** ਬੈਂਕ ਦੇ ਨੋਟ ਜਿਹੜੇ ਲੋਕਾਂ ਵਿਚ ਚਲਦੇ ਹੋਣ, ਇਕ ਵਧੀਆ ਕਿਸਮ ਦਾ ਕਾਗ਼ਜ਼; ~ **rate** ਬੈਂਕ-ਦਰ; ~**er** ਸ਼ਾਹੂਕਾਰ, ਮਹਾਜਨ, ਸਰਾਫ਼, ਬੈਂਕ ਦਾ ਪ੍ਰਬੰਧਕ; ਜੂਆ

ਖਿਡਾਉਣ ਵਾਲਾ; ~ing ਸ਼ਾਹੂਕਾਰਾ, ਬੈਂਕਿੰਗ, ਬੈਂਕ-ਵਪਾਰ

bankrupt (ਬੈਙ੍ਕਰਅੱਪਟ) *n v* ਦਿਵਾਲੀਆ, ਸੱਖਣਾ, ਹੀਣਾ; ਦਿਵਾਲਾ ਕੱਢਣਾ; ਦਿਵਾਲੀਆ ਬਣਾਉਣਾ; ~cy ਦਿਵਾਲਾਪਨ, ਸਤਿਆਨਾਸ, ਤਬਾਹੀ, ਸੰਪੂਰਨ ਨਾਸ

banner (ਬੈਨਅ*) (ਸਮਰਾਟ, ਰਾਜਾ, ਸਰਦਾਰ ਦਾ) *n* ਝੰਡਾ, ਨਿਸ਼ਾਨ; ~ed ਝੰਡੇ ਵਾਲਾ, ਝੰਡੇਦਾਰ; ~headline (ਅਖ਼ਬਾਰ ਦੀ) ਵੱਡੀ ਸੁਰਖੀ

banquet (ਬੈਙ੍ਕਵਿਟ) *n v* ਮਹਾਂ-ਭੋਜ, ਦਾਅਵਤ, ਜ਼ਿਆਫ਼ਤ, ਖਾਣੇ ਵਿਚ ਹਿੱਸਾ ਲੈਣਾ, ਖਾਣਾ ਕਰਨਾ, ਪੇਟ ਭਰਨਾ

banquette (ਬੈਙ੍ਕੈਟ) *n* ਗੋਲੇ ਵਰ੍ਹਾਉਣ ਲਈ ਕਿਲ੍ਹੇ ਅੰਦਰ ਉਚੀ ਥਾਂ, ਫ਼ਰਾਂਸੀਸੀ ਗੱਡੀਆਂ ਵਿਚ ਡਰਾਈਵਰ ਦੇ ਪਿੱਛੇ ਬੈਠਣ ਦੀ ਥਾਂ

baptism (ਬੈਪਟਿਜ਼(ਅ)ਮ) *n* ਬਪਤਿਸਮਾ, ਇਸਾਈ ਧਰਮ ਵਿਚ ਪ੍ਰਵੇਸ਼ ਕਰਨ ਦਾ ਸੰਸਕਾਰ, ਨਾਮਕਰਨ ਸੰਸਕਾਰ, ਦੀਖਿਆ, ਪਾਹੁਲ

baptist (ਬੈਪਟਿਸਟ) *n* ਬਪਤਿਸਮਾ ਕਰਨ ਵਾਲਾ, ਇਸਾਈ ਮੱਤ ਦੀ ਦੀਖਿਆ ਦੇਣ ਵਾਲਾ

baptize (ਬੈਪਟਾਈਜ਼) *v* ਬਪਤਿਸਮਾ ਦੇਣਾ, ਅੰਮ੍ਰਿਤ ਛਕਾਉਣਾ, ਪਾਹੁਲ ਦੇਣੀ, ਸ਼ੁੱਧ ਕਰਨਾ, ਪਦਵੀ ਵਧਾਉਣੀ

bar (ਬਾ*) *n v* (1) ਸਰੀਆ, ਸੀਖ, ਸਲਾਖ, ਛੜ (ਧਾਤੂ, ਲਕੱੜੀ, ਸਾਬਣ ਆਦਿ ਦਾ) ਡੰਡਾ, (2) ਫੀਤੇ ਉਤੇ ਚਾਂਦੀ ਦੀ ਪੱਟੀ, ਰੰਗ ਆਦਿ ਦੀ ਪੱਟੀ, ਰੋਕ (ਜਿਵੇਂ ਹੁੰਗੀ ਦੀ); (3) ਸ਼ਰਾਬ ਘਰ, ਬਾਰ, ਜਲਪਾਨ ਘਰ; (4) ਵਕੀਲਾਂ ਦੀ ਸ਼੍ਰੇਣੀ; ਅਦਾਲਤ ਵਿਚ ਕੈਦੀਆਂ ਦੇ ਖੜੇ ਹੋਣ ਦੀ ਥਾਂ, ਮੁਜਰਮ ਦਾ ਕਟਹਿਰਾ; ਪਾਰਲੀਮੈਂਟ ਹਾਲ ਵਿਚ ਉਹ ਜੰਗਲਾ ਜਿਸ ਤੋਂ ਬਿਨਾਂ

ਕੋਈ ਨਹੀਂ ਜਾ ਸਕਦਾ; ਦਾਅਵੇ ਜਾਂ ਕਾਨੂੰਨ ਦੀ ਵਰਤੋਂ ਵਿਚ ਰੁਕਾਵਟ, ਅੜਿਕਾ, ਅਦਾਲਤੀ ਕਾਰਵਾਈ ਰੋਕਣ ਦੀ ਬਹਿਸ; (5) (ਸੰਗੀ) ਲਿਪੀ ਵਿਚ ਤਾਲ ਲਈ ਸਿੱਧੀ ਖੜੀ ਲਕੀਰ

barb (ਬਾਬ) *n v* (1) ਮੱਛੀ ਦੇ ਬਾਰੀਕ ਕੰਡੇ, ਬਰਛੇ ਜਾਂ ਤੀਰ ਦੀ ਨੋਕ, ਸੂਲ, ਮੱਛੀ ਫੜਨ ਵਾਲੀ ਕੁੰਡੀ; (2) ਹੂਕ ਲਗਾਉਣਾ; ਚੋਭ, ਪੀੜ; ਸੂਲ ਚੁਭਾਉਣਾ, ਸੂਲ ਲਗਾਉਣਾ

barbarian (ਬਾਬੇਅਰਿਅਨ) *n a* ਵਹਿਸ਼ੀ, ਅਸੱਭਿਅ, ਜਾਂਗਲੀ, ਉਜੱਡ, ਗੰਵਾਰ (ਵਿਅਕਤੀ); (ਇਤਿ) ਗੈਰਕਾਨੂਨੀ; ਗੈਰਇਸਾਈ; ਵਿਦੇਸੀ

barbaric (ਬਾਬੈਰੀਕ) *a* ਵਹਿਸ਼ੀ, ਮਲੇਛ, ਗੰਵਾਰ; ਜਾਂਗਲੀ; (ਇਤਿ) ਗੈਰਯੂਨਾਨੀ, ਗੈਰਇਸਾਈ; ਅਸੱਭਿਅ, ਬਰਬਰ, ਵਿਦੇਸੀ

barbarism (ਬਾਬਾਰਿਜ਼(ਅ)ਮ) *n* ਕਰੂਰਤਾ, ਵਹਿਸ਼ੀਪੁਣਾ, ਜਾਂਗਲੀਪੁਣਾ, ਉਜੱਡਪੁਣਾ, ਗੰਵਾਰਪੁਣਾ, ਅਸੱਭਿਅਤਾ, ਅਸ਼ਿਸ਼ਟਤਾ, ਅਗਿਆਨ, ਬਰਬਰ ਅਵਸਥਾ

barbarity (ਬਾਬੈਰਅਟਿ) *n* ਰਾਕਸ਼-ਪੁਣਾ, ਜ਼ੁਲਮ, ਜਬਰ, ਜਾਂਗਲੀਆਂ ਵਰਗਾ ਅੱਖੜਪਣ, ਨਿਰਦਇਅਤਾ, ਬਰਬਰਤਾ, ਅਸੱਭਿਅ ਅਵਸਥਾ; ਗੰਵਾਰੂ ਸ਼ੈਲੀ

barbarous (ਬਾਬ(ਅ)ਰਅਸ) *a* ਜਾਂਗਲੀ, ਉਜੱਡ, ਵਹਿਸ਼ੀ, ਨਿਰਦਈ, ਜ਼ਾਲਮ, ਅਸੱਭਿਅ ਸੁਭਾਅ ਵਾਲਾ, ਅਸ਼ਿਸ਼ਟ; ~ness ਨਿਰਦਇਅਤਾ, ਅਸੱਭਿਅਤਾ, ਬਰਬਰਤਾ

barbed (ਬਾਬਡ) *a* ਕੰਡਿਆਲੀ, ਕੰਡਿਆ ਵਾਲਾ, ਉਲਝਿਆ; ~wire ਕੰਡਿਆਂ ਵਾਲੀ ਤਾਰ, ਕੰਡਿਆਲੀ ਤਾਰ

barber (ਬਾਬਅ*) *n* ਨਾਈ, ਹੱਜਾਮ

bard (ਬਾਡ) *n* (1) ਢਾਡੀ, ਭੱਟ, ਗਵੱਈਆ;

ਪੁਰਾਤਨ ਕਵੀ, ਗੀਤਕਾਰ; (2) ਜੰਗੀ ਘੋੜੇ ਦੀ
ਛਾਤੀ ਅਤੇ ਪਿੱਠ ਦੀ ਸੰਜੋਅ ਜਾਂ ਕਵਚ

bare (ਬੇਇਆ*) a v (1) ਨੰਗਾ, ਅਲਾਣਾ,
ਅਣਕੱਜਿਆ, ਖੁੱਲ੍ਹੇ-ਮੂੰਹ, ਗੰਜਾ; (2) ਮਾਤਰ,
ਕੇਵਲ, ਸੁੰਨ, ਨਿਰਾ, ਸਿਰਫ਼, ਅਲਪ; (3) ਰੁੱਖ-
ਹੀਣ, ਬੰਜਰ; ਨੰਗਾ ਕਰਨਾ, ਭੇਤ ਖੋਲ੍ਹਣਾ; ਪਰਗਟ
ਕਰਨਾ, ਪਰਦਾ ਲਾਹੁਣਾ, ਉਘੇੜਨਾ; **~backed**
ਬਿਨਾ ਕਾਠੀਓਂ (ਘੋੜਾ), ਅਲਾਣਾ, ਨੰਗੇ-ਪਿੰਡੇ;
~bone ਦੁਬਲਾ ਪਤਲਾ, ਜਿਸ ਦੀਆਂ ਹੱਡੀਆਂ
ਨਿਕਲੀਆਂ ਹੋਣ; **~footed** ਨੰਗੇ ਪੈਰ, ਨੰਗੀ ਪੈਰੀਂ;
~headed ਨੰਗੇ ਸਿਰ

barely (ਬੇਅ*ਲਿ) adv ਮਸਾਂ ਹੀ, ਮੁਸ਼ਕਲ ਨਾਲ;
ਕੇਵਲ, ਮਾਤਰ; ਸਪਸ਼ਟ, ਖੁੱਲ੍ਹਮ-ਖੁੱਲ੍ਹਾ

bargain (ਬਾ*ਗਿਨ) n v ਸੌਦਾ, ਸੌਦੇਬਾਜ਼ੀ, ਸੱਟਾ,
ਮਾਲ, ਖਰਾ ਸੌਦਾ, ਚੰਗੀ ਖ਼ਰੀਦ; ਸੌਦਾ ਕਰਨਾ,
ਮੁੱਲ ਕਰਨਾ, ਸੌਦਾ ਮੁਕਾਉਣਾ, ਤਹਿ ਕਰਨਾ,
ਠਹਿਰਾਉਣਾ; **a~** ਚੰਗਾ ਜਾਂ ਮੁਨਾਫ਼ੇ ਵਾਲਾ ਸੌਦਾ;
~into the ਝੁੰਗੇ ਵਿਚ, ਮੁਫ਼ਤ ਵਿਚ, ਸੱਦੀ
ਵੱਜੋਂ; **strike a~** ਸੌਦਾ ਪੱਕਾ ਕਰਨਾ

bark (ਬਾ:ਕ) n v (1) ਛਿੱਲ, ਛਿਲਕਾ, ਕੁਨੀਨ;
ਖੱਲ, ਚਮੜੀ; ਰੁੱਖ ਦੀ ਛਿੱਲੜ ਲਾਹੁਣਾ, ਛਿਲਕਾ
ਉਤਾਰਨਾ, ਤਹਿ ਜਮਾਉਣਾ; ਘਿਸਣਾ, ਛਿੱਲਣਾ;
(2) ਭੌਂਕ, ਭੌਂਕਣ ਦੀ ਆਵਾਜ਼, ਬੰਦੂਕ ਚੱਲਣ
ਦੀ ਆਵਾਜ਼, ਖੰਘੂਰਾ; ਭੌਂਕਣਾ, ਘੁਰਕਣਾ, ਘੁਰਕ
ਕੇ ਬੋਲਣਾ, ਖੰਘੂਰਨਾ, ਚਿੜਚੜਾ ਕੇ ਜਾਂ
ਚੀਨ੍ਹਤਾਈ ਕੇ ਲਹਿਜੇ ਵਿਚ ਬੋਲਣਾ

barley (ਬਾ:ਲਿ) n ਜੌਂ, ਜੌਂ ਦਾ ਦਾਣਾ, ਜੌਂ ਦਾ
ਕਸੀਰ, ਸਿੱਟਾ ਜਾਂ ਬੱਲੀ; **~ corn** ਜੌਂ, ਜੌਂ ਦਾ
ਦਾਣਾ, ਜੌਂ ਦੀ ਫ਼ਸਲ; **~ meal** ਸੱਤੂ

barometer (ਬਅਾ*ਰੌਮਿਟਅ*) n ਬੈਰੋਮੀਟਰ, ਹਵਾ
ਦਬਾ ਮਾਪਕ, ਹਵਾ ਦੇ ਦਬਾ ਨੂੰ ਮਿਲੀਦਾ ਅਤੇ

ਆਉਣ ਵਾਲੇ ਮੌਸਮ ਅਤੇ ਸਮੁੰਦਰ ਤੋਂ ਉਚਾਈ
ਦਾ ਪਤਾ ਲਾਉਣ ਵਾਲਾ, ਇਕ ਆਲਾ ਜਾਂ ਜੰਤਰ

baron (ਬੈਰ(ਅ)ਨ) n (ਇੰਗਲੈਂਡ ਵਿਚ) ਅਮੀਰ ਨੂੰ
ਲਾਰਡ ਦਾ ਖ਼ਿਤਾਬ ਮਿਲਿਆ ਹੋਵੇ, ਸਾਮੰਤ,
ਜਾਗੀਰਦਾਰ; ਨਵਾਬ, ਬੈਰਨ, ਛੋਟਾ ਲਾਰਡ

barrack (ਬੈਰਅਕ) n v ਸੈਨਾ ਨਿਵਾਸ, ਬੈਰਕ,
ਫ਼ੌਜੀਆਂ ਦੇ ਇਕੱਠੇ ਰਹਿਣ ਲਈ ਬਣੇ ਹੋਏ ਵੱਡੇ
ਕਮਰੇ, ਨਿਵਾਸ, ਬੈਰਕਾਂ ਵਿਚ ਰੱਖਣਾ, ਥਾਂ
ਦੇਣੀ; (ਕ੍ਰਿਕਟ ਦੀ ਖੇਡ ਆਦਿ ਵਿਚ) ਮਖੌਲ
ਕਰਨਾ, ਅਵਾਜ਼ਾਂ ਕੱਸਣੀਆਂ

barrage (ਬੈਰਾਯ਼) n ਬੰਨ੍ਹ, ਬੰਧ ਬੰਦੂਕਾਂ ਦੀ
ਬੁਛਾੜ, ਬਾਰੂ; ਹਮਲਾ ਕਰਨ ਅਤੇ ਰੋਕਣ ਲਈ
ਬਣਾਈ ਗਈ ਰੋਕ, ਆੜ

barrel (ਬੈਰ(ਅ)ਲ) n v ਪੀਪਾ, ਕੁੱਪਾ, ਘੜੀ ਦਾ
ਇਕ ਪੁਰਜ਼ਾ; ਬੰਦੂਕ ਦੀ ਨਾਲੀ; ਸ਼ੇਰ ਅਤੇ ਘੋੜੇ
ਦਾ ਲੱਕ ਅਤੇ ਪਿੱਠ; ਸਿੱਧਾ ਖੜ੍ਹਾ ਸਰੀਰ;
ਪੀਪਿਆਂ ਵਿਚ ਭਰਨਾ ਜਾਂ ਰੱਖਣਾ; **~led**
ਨਲੀਦਾਰ, ਪੀਪੇ ਵਿਚ ਬੰਦ (ਸ਼ਰਾਬ); **double**
~ gun ਦੋ ਨਾਲੀ ਬੰਦੂਕ

barren (ਬੈਰ(ਅ)ਨ) a n ਬਾਂਝ, ਸੰਢ; ਅਫਲ;
(ਜ਼ਮੀਨ) ਬੰਜਰ, ਅਣਉਪਜਾਊ; ਵਿਅਰਥ,
ਥੋੜ੍ਹਾਇੰਦਾ, ਖ਼ੁਸ਼ਕ, ਜ਼ਮੀਨ

barricade (ਬੈਰਿ'ਕੇਇਡ) n v ਨਾਕਾਬੰਦੀ, ਕੱਚੀ
ਮੋਰਚਾਬੰਦੀ, ਅੜਿੱਕਾ, ਆੜ, ਰੋਕ; ਨਾਕਾਬੰਦੀ
ਕਰਨੀ, ਮੋਰਚਾਬੰਦੀ ਕਰਨੀ, ਕੱਚੇ ਮੋਰਚੇ
ਬਣਾਉਣੇ, ਬਚਾਉ ਕਰਨਾ, (ਸੜਕ) ਰੋਕ ਦੇਣਾ,
ਆੜ ਪਾਉਂਦੀ, ਰੁਕਾਵਟ ਪਾਉਂਦੀ

barrier (ਬੈਰਿਅ)* n v ਰੋਕ, ਵਾੜ, ਜੰਗਲਾ,
ਚੁੰਗੀ, ਫਾਟਕ, ਨੇਜ਼ਾਬਾਜ਼ੀ ਦਾ ਕਟਹਿਰਾ, ਆੜ;
ਰੋਕ ਲਾਉਂਦੀ, ਬੰਦ ਕਰਨਾ

barring (ਬਾਰਿਙ) prep ਛੱਡ ਕੇ, ਸਿਵਾਏ,

ਤੋਂ ਛੁੱਟ

barrow ('ਬੈਰਅਉ) *n* ਸਮਾਧੀਆਂ ਦਾ ਟਿੱਲਾ, ਕਬਰਾਂ ਦੇ ਉਪਰਲਾ ਸਿੱਟੀ ਦਾ ਢੇਰ

barter ('ਬਾਟਅ*) *n v* ਵੱਟਾ-ਸੱਟਾ, ਵਟਾਂਦਰਾ; ਵੱਟਾ-ਸੱਟਾ ਕਰਨਾ, ਇਕ ਚੀਜ਼ ਦੇ ਕੇ ਬਦਲੇ ਵਿਚ ਦੂਜੀ ਲੈਣੀ, ਚੀਜ਼ ਬਦਲੇ ਚੀਜ਼ ਲੈਣੀ ਦੇਣੀ

base (ਬੇਇਸ) *n adv v* ਆਧਾਰ, ਥੱਲਾ, ਤਲਾ; ਨੀਂਹ, ਬੁਨਿਆਦ; ਮੂਲ ਤੱਤ, (ਬਨ) ਜੋੜ; ਖਾਰ; (ਸੈਨਾ) ਬੇਸ, ਅੱਡਾ; ਕਮੀਨਾ, ਪਤਿਤ, ਨੀਚ; ਬਦਜ਼ਾਤ; ਥੋਟਾ, ਮਧਰਾ, ਮਾੜਾ, ਨਕਾਰਾ; ਨੀਂਹ ਰੱਖਣੀ, ਸਥਾਪਤ ਕਰਨਾ, ਆਧਾਰ ਬਣਾਉਣਾ, ਆਧਾਰਤ ਕਰਨਾ; **~less** ਬੇਬੁਨਿਆਦ, ਨਿਰਮੂਲ, ਆਧਾਰਹੀਨ, ਸਾਰਹੀਨ; **~lessness** ਨਿਰਮੂਲਤਾ; **~ment** ਭੋਰਾ, ਤਹਿਖ਼ਾਨਾ; ਤਲ, ਥੱਲਾ

bash (ਬੈਸ਼) *v* ਜ਼ੋਰ ਨਾਲ ਮਾਰਨਾ; **~ful** ਸ਼ਰਮਾਕਲ, ਸ਼ਰਮੀਲਾ, ਸੰਗਾਊ, ਲੱਜਾਵਾਨ; **~fully** ਸ਼ਰਮ ਨਾਲ, ਸੰਗਦਿਆਂ; **~ness** ਸ਼ਰਮ, ਸੰਗ, ਲੱਜਾ; **~less** ਬੇਸ਼ਰਮ, ਬੇਹਯਾ, ਨਿਰਲੱਜ

basic (ਬੇਇਸਿਕ) *a* ਆਧਾਰੀ, ਮੂਲ, ਮੁੱਢਲਾ, ਅਰੰਭਕ, ਪ੍ਰਧਾਨ (ਧਾਤੂ); (ਰਸਾ) ਖਾਰ-ਯੁਕਤ; **~education** ਬੁਨਿਆਦੀ ਸਿੱਖਿਆ, ਮੁੱਢਲੀ ਸਿੱਖਿਆ; **~pay** ਮੂਲ ਤਨਖ਼ਾਹ

basin ('ਬੇਇਸਨ) *n* ਚਿਲਮਚੀ, ਹੌਜ਼ੀ, ਦੌਰਾ, ਬੇਸਿਨ, ਕੁੰਡ; ਗੋਲ ਜਾਂ ਅੰਡਾ-ਕਾਰ ਨਦੀ-ਖੇਤਰ; ਜ਼ਮੀਨ ਨਾਲ ਘਿਰੀ ਹੋਈ ਬੰਦਰਗਾਹ, ਬਣਾਉਟੀ ਬੰਦਰਗਾਹ; ਨਦੀ-ਲਾਂਘਾ, ਵਹਾਉ-ਸਥਾਨ; ਕੇਂਦਰ ਵੱਲ ਝੁਕਿਆ ਪੱਥਰਾਂ ਦਾ ਢਾਂਚਾ

basis ('ਬੇਇਸਿਸ) *n (pl* bases*)* ਨੀਂਹ, ਬੁਨਿਆਦ, ਆਧਾਰ; ਮੂਲ, ਮੂਲ-ਆਧਾਰ; ਮੂਲ ਸਿਧਾਂਤ; ਫ਼ੌਜੀ ਅੱਡਾ

bask (ਬਾਸਕ) *v* ਧੁੱਪ ਸੇਕਣੀ, ਨਿੱਘ ਮਾਣਨਾ

basket ('ਬਾਸਕਿਟ) *n v* ਟੋਕਰਾ, ਟੋਕਰੀ, ਪਟਾਰਾ, ਪਟਾਰੀ, ਛਾਬਾ, ਛਿੱਕੂ, ਚੰਗੇਰ, ਪੱਛੀ; ਕਿਸੇ ਵਸਤੂ ਨੂੰ ਟੋਕਰੀ ਵਿਚ ਰੱਖਣਾ; ਪਟਾਰੀ ਪਾਉਣਾ; **~ball** ਖਿੰਡ-ਛਿੰਡ, ਗੇਂਦ, ਬਾਸਕਟ ਬਾਲ

bastard ('ਬਾਸਟਅ*ਡ) *n a* ਹਰਾਮੀ, ਨਜਾਇਜ਼ ਸੰਬੰਧ ਤੋਂ ਪੈਦਾ ਹੋਇਆ (ਬੱਚਾ), ਵਰਨਸੰਕਰ; ਕਮੀਨਾ, ਨੀਚ, ਹਰਮਜ਼ਾਦਾ, ਖੋਟਾ, ਦੋਗਲਾ

bat (ਬੈਟ) *n v* (1) ਚਮਗਿੱਦੜ, ਚਾਮ-ਚੜਿੱਕ, ਖੱਚੜ ਔਰਤ; (2) (ਕ੍ਰਿਕਟ ਦਾ) ਬੱਲਾ, ਬੈਟ; ਬੱਲੇ ਨਾਲ ਖੇਡਣਾ, ਬੱਲਾ ਮਾਰਨਾ, ਇਨਿੰਗ ਕਰਨਾ, ਵਾਰੀ ਲੈਣੀ

batch (ਬੈਚ) *n* ਜੱਥਾ, ਟੋਲੀ, ਸਮੂਹ, ਦਲ, ਰੋਟੀਆਂ ਦਾ ਪੂਰ; ਘਾਣ; (ਇਕੋ ਹੀ) ਜੱਥੇ ਵਿਚ; ਵਰਗਾ ਵਿਚ

bate (ਬੇਇਟ) *v n* ਸ਼ਕਤੀਹੀਨ ਹੋ ਜਾਣਾ, ਜ਼ੋਰ ਘਟ ਜਾਣਾ, ਘਟਾਉਣਾ; (1) ਚਮੜਾ ਸਾਫ਼ ਕਰਨ ਲਈ ਖਾਰ ਵਾਲਾ ਘੋਲ; (2) ਕਰੋਧ, ਗੁੱਸਾ

bath, Bath (ਬਾਥ) *n v* ਇਸ਼ਨਾਨ, ਨਹਾਉਣ-ਘੋਟ, ਗੁਸਲ, ਇਸ਼ਨਾਨ ਕਰਨ ਦਾ ਪਾਣੀ; ਨਹਾਉਣ ਦਾ ਭਾਂਡਾ, ਟੱਬ; ਗੁਸਲਖ਼ਾਨਾ; ਇਸ਼ਨਾਨ ਘਰ, ਹਮਾਮ; ਇਸ਼ਨਾਨ ਕਰਨਾ, ਨਹਾਉਣਾ; **~ing** ਨਹਾਉਣ-ਘੋਟ, ਇਸ਼ਨਾਨ; **~room** ਗੁਸਲਖ਼ਾਨਾ, ਇਸ਼ਨਾਨ ਘਰ

bathe (ਬੇਇਦ) *v* ਇਸ਼ਨਾਨ ਕਰਨਾ ਜਾਂ ਕਰਾਉਣਾ, ਨਹਾਉਣਾ, ਨੁਹਾਲਣਾ; ਟੁੱਭੀ ਲਾਉਣੀ, ਪਾਣੀ ਨਾਲ ਧੋਣਾ, ਧੁੱਪ ਲਗਵਾਉਣਾ

batman ('ਬੈਟਮਅਨ) *n* ਫ਼ੌਜੀ ਅਫ਼ਸਰ ਦਾ ਅਰਦਲੀ

baton ('ਬੈਟ(ਅ)ਨ) *n v* ਪੁਲੀਸ ਦੇ ਸਿਪਾਹੀ ਦਾ ਡੰਡਾ, ਬੈਂਤ; (ਸੰਗੀਤ ਨਿਰਦੇਸ਼ਕ ਦੀ ਤਾਲ ਦੇਣ

ਲਈ) ਛੜੀ; ਡੰਡੇ ਨਾਲ ਮਾਰਨ

batsman ('ਬੈਟਸਮਅਨ) *n* ਬੱਲੇਬਾਜ਼, ਗੇਂਦ ਮਾਰਨ ਵਾਲਾ ਖਿਡਾਰੀ; ਸਮੁੰਦਰੀ ਜਹਾਜ਼ ਉੱਤੇ ਉੱਤਰਨ ਵਾਲੇ ਹਵਾਈ ਜਹਾਜ਼ ਨੂੰ ਬੱਲੇ ਨਾਲ ਸੰਕੇਤ ਕਰਨ ਵਾਲਾ

battalion (ਬੈਅ'ਟੈਲਯਅਨ) *n* (ਫ਼ੌਜੀ) ਦਸਤਾ, ਪਲਟਨ, ਸੈਨਕ ਦਲ, ਬਟੈਲੀਅਨ

batten ('ਬੈਟਨ) *v n* ਕਿਸੇ ਚੀਜ਼ ਨੂੰ ਲੱਕੜੀ ਦੀਆਂ ਫੱਟੀਆਂ ਨਾਲ ਪੱਕਾ ਕਰਨਾ, ਫ਼ਰਸ਼ ਬਣਾਉਣਾ, ਚੱਕਣ ਕੱਸਣਾ, ਪੁਸ਼ਟਾ; ਬਿਜਲੀ ਦੀਆਂ ਤਾਰਾਂ ਲਈ ਲਕੜੀ ਦੀ ਫੱਟੀ

batter ('ਬੈਟਅ*) *v n* ਫੈਂਟਣਾ; ਸੂਰਤ ਵਿਗਾੜ ਦੇਣਾ, ਤੇੜ ਦੇਣਾ; ਢਾਹ ਸੁੱਟਣਾ, ਮਾਰ ਮਾਰ ਕੇ ਭੋਗ ਦੇਣਾ, ਖੁੰਭ ਠੱਪਣੀ; ਅੱਖਰਾਂ ਦੀ ਪਲੇਟ, ਪੀਠੀ ਦਾਲ ਦੀ; ਢਾਲ, ਸਲਾਮੀ

battery ('ਬੈਟਅਰਿ) (ਸੈਨਾ) ਤੋਪਖ਼ਾਨਾ, ਮੋਰਚਾ; (ਕਾ) ਧੌਲ-ਧੱਪਾ, ਮਾਰ ਕੁੱਟ; (ਬਿਜਲੀ) ਬੈਟਰੀ

batting ('ਬੈਚਿਙ) *n* ਬੱਲਾਬਾਜ਼ੀ; ਰੂੰ ਦੀ ਤਹਿ

battle ('ਬੈਟਲ) *n v* ਲੜਾਈ, ਜੁੱਧ, ਸੰਗਰਾਮ; ਸੰਘਰਸ਼; ਜਿੱਤ; ਲੜਾਈ ਕਰਨਾ, ਜੁੱਧ ਵਿਚ ਸ਼ਾਮਲ ਹੋਣਾ, ਸੰਘਰਸ਼ ਕਰਨਾ, ਮੁਕਾਬਲਾ ਕਰਨਾ; ~field ਲੜਾਈ ਦਾ ਮੈਦਾਨ ਜੁੱਧ-ਖੇਤਰ, ਰਣਭੂਮੀ

bawd (ਬੋਡ) *n* ਭੜੂਆ, ਵੇਸਵਾ, ਦੱਲੀ, ਫੱਢੇ-ਕੁੱਟਣੀ; ਗੰਦੀ ਗੱਲ, ਅਸ਼ਲੀਲ ਕਥਨ; ~iness ਅਸ਼ਲੀਲਤਾ, ਅਸ਼ਲੀਲ ਕਥਨ

bawl (ਬੋਲ) *v* ਕੂਕਣਾ, ਚੀਕਣਾ; ਧਾਹਾਂ ਮਾਰਨੀਆਂ, ਵਿਰਲਾਪ ਕਰਨਾ; ਵਰੂ ਪੈਣਾ

bay (ਬੇਇ) *n* (1) ਖਾੜੀ, ਖਲੀਜ; (2) ਜੈ ਮਾਲਾ, ਵਿਜੈ ਮੁਕਟ, ਤੇਜ-ਪੱਤਰ; (3) (ਸੈਨਾ ਵਿਚ) ਖਾਈ (ਵਿਚ ਚੱਲਣ) ਦਾ ਰਸਤਾ; (4) ਰੇਲਵੇ-ਲਾਈਨ ਦੇ ਸ਼ੁਰੂ ਜਾਂ ਅੰਤ ਤੇ ਬਣਿਆ

ਪਲੈਟਫ਼ਰਮ; (5) ਸ਼ਿਕਾਰੀ ਕੁੱਤਿਆਂ ਦੀ ਭੌਂਕ, ਭੌਂ-ਭੌਂ, ਭੌਂਕਣ, ਭੌਂਕਣਾ; ~salt ਸਮੁੰਦਰੀ ਲੂਣ, ਖਾੜੀ ਲੂਣ; be at~ ਘਿਰ ਜਾਣਾ, ਫਸ ਜਾਣਾ; ~leaf ਤੇਜ-ਪੱਤਰ

bazooka (ਬਅ'ਜ਼ੂਕਅ) *n* ਟੈਂਕ-ਤੋੜ ਰਾਕਟ, ਬਝੂਕਾ

be (ਬੀ) *v (substantive, copulative & auxiliary)* ਹੋਣਾ, ਹਾਜ਼ਰ ਹੋਣਾ, ਜਿਉਂਦੇ ਹੋਣਾ, ਜਾਰੀ ਰਹਿਣਾ, ਆ ਪੈਣਾ, ਸੰਭਾਵਨਾ ਜਾਂ ਆਸ ਦਾ ਹੋਣਾ

beach (ਬੀਚ) *n v* ਸਮੁੰਦਰ ਜਾਂ ਦਰਿਆ ਦਾ ਕੰਢਾ, ਦਰਿਆ ਦੇ ਕਿਨਾਰੇ ਦੇ ਕੰਕਰ ਜਾਂ ਗੀਟੇ; ਕਿਨਾਰੇ ਉੱਤੇ ਲੰਗਰ ਸੁੱਟਣਾ

beacon ('ਬੀਕ(ਅ)ਨ) *n v* ਚਾਨਣ-ਮੁਨਾਰਾ, ਆਕਾਸ਼ਦੀਪ, ਪਥ-ਪਰਦਰਸ਼ਕ, ਸਿਗਨਲ-ਸਟੇਸ਼ਨ; ਪਤਾ ਦੇਣਾ, ਰੌਸ਼ਨੀ ਦਿਖਾਉਣਾ, ਰਸਤਾ ਦੱਸਣਾ, ਖ਼ਤਰਾ ਦੱਸਣ ਲਈ ਇਸ਼ਾਰਾ ਕਰਨਾ, ਅਗਵਾਈ ਕਰਨੀ; ਚਾਨਣ ਦੇ ਖੰਭੇ ਲਾਉਣੇ

bead (ਬੀਡ) *n v* ਮਣਕਾ, ਸਿਮਰਨੀ ਜਾਂ ਮਾਲਾ ਦਾ ਦਾਣਾ; ਬੂੰਦ, ਬੁਲਬੁਲਾ, ਮਣਕੇਦਾਰ ਉਸਾਰੀ; (ਬੰਦੂਕ ਦੀ) ਮੱਖੀ; ਪੂਜਾ, ਪ੍ਰਾਰਥਨਾ; ਗੁੰਦਣਾ, ਲੜੀ ਬਣਾਉਣਾ

beak (ਬੀਕ) *n* ਚੁੰਝ; ਨੁਕੀਲੀ ਨੱਕ; ਬੂਥੀ

beam (ਬੀਮ) *n v* (1) ਸ਼ਤੀਰ, ਬਾਲਾ; ਲੰਗਰ ਦਾ ਦਸਤਾ; ਲੱਠ, ਹਲ ਦੀ ਵੇਲ; ਤੱਕੜੀ ਦੀ ਡੰਡੀ; ਗੱਡੀ ਦਾ ਪੂਰਾ; (2) ਚਾਨਣ ਦੀ ਕਿਰਨ, ਚਿਹਰੇ ਦੀ ਰੌਣਕ, ਖ਼ੁਸ਼ੀ, ਦਮਕ; ਖਿੜਨਾ ਰਮਕਣਾ, ਜਗਮਗਾ ਉੱਠਣਾ; ~lessing ਪ੍ਰਕਾਸ਼ਮਾਨ, ਦਮਕਦਾ; ਆਨੰਦ ਮਗਨ; ~les ਪ੍ਰਕਾਸ਼ਰਹਿਤ

bean (ਬੀਨ) *n* ਰਵਾਂਹ, ਲੋਬੀਆ, ਸੇਮ, ਕਾਫ਼ੀ

ਹੋਰਨਾਂ ਪੌਦਿਆਂ ਦੇ ਬੀਜ

bear (ਬੇਅ*) *n* ਰਿੱਛ, ਭਾਲੂ; ਉਜੱਡ ਜਾਂ ਰੁੱਖ ਮਨੁੱਖ; (ਸੱਟ) ਮਾਂਦਰੀਆ; ਸਹਿਣਾ, ਸਹਾਰਨਾ, ਝੱਲਣਾ, ਝੋਗਣਾ; ਪੈਦਾ ਕਰਨਾ; ਚੁੱਕਣਾ, ਚੁੱਕ ਕੇ ਲੈ ਜਾਣਾ, ਭਾਰ ਉਠਾਉਣਾ; ਰੁਖ ਕਰਨਾ; **~able** ਸਹਿਣਯੋਗ, ਸਹਾਰਨਯੋਗ

beard (ਬਿਅ*ੱਡ) *n v* ਦਾੜ੍ਹੀ, ਬੁੰਬਲ; ਸਖਤ ਵਾਲ; ਦਾੜ੍ਹੀ ਫੜਨਾ ਜਾਂ ਖਿਚਣਾ, ਨਿਰਾਦਰ ਕਰਨਾ; ਸਾਮੁਣਾ ਕਰਨਾ, ਵੰਗਾਰਨਾ

bearer ('ਬੇਅਰਅ*) *n* ਬਹਿਰਾ (ਹੋਟਲ ਦਾ); ਕੁਲੀ, ਵਾਹਕ, ਚੁੱਕਣ ਵਾਲਾ, ਕਹਾਰ, ਖਤ ਲੈ ਜਾਣ ਵਾਲਾ, ਸੇਵਕ, ਅੰਗ-ਰਖਿਅਕ; ਫਲਦਾਰ ਰੁੱਖ, ਫਲਤ ਵਾਲਾ ਪੌਦਾ

beast (ਬੀਸਟ) *n* ਪਸ਼ੂ, ਜਾਨਵਰ; ਘਿਰਨਾਯੋਗ ਮਨੁੱਖ, ਪਸ਼ੂ ਬਿਰਤੀ ਦਾ ਮਨੁੱਖ, ਜਾਂਗਲੀ, ਉੱਜਡ, ਹੈਵਾਨ; **~ly** ਪਸ਼ੂਹਾਰ, ਪਸ਼ੂ ਵਰਗਾ; ਗੰਦਾ, ਘਿਰਨਯੋਗ; ਲੂਚਾ, ਵਹਿਸ਼ੀ

beat (ਬੀਟ) *v n* ਮਾਰਨਾ, ਕੁੱਟਣਾ, ਮਾਰ-ਕੁਟਾਈ ਕਰਨੀ, ਹਰਾਉਣਾ; ਜਿਚ ਕਰਨਾ, ਮਾਤ ਕਰਨਾ; ਪਰ ਮਾਰਨਾ, ਫੜਫੜਨਾ; (ਢੋਲ) ਥਪਥਪਾਉਣਾ, ਵਜਾਉਣਾ; (ਦਿਲ) ਧੜਕਣਾ; ਧਕੇਲਣਾ, ਹੱਕਣਾ; ਕੁੰਦਣਾ, ਫੁਦਕਣਾ, ਸ਼ਿਕਾਰੀ ਵਲ ਲਿਆਉਣ ਲਈ ਰੋਲਾ ਪਾਉਣਾ; ਚੋਟ, ਸੱਟ (ਢੋਲ ਜਾਂ ਨਗਾਰੇ ਉੱਤੇ); (ਬੈਂਡ ਮਾਸਟਰ ਦੇ) ਡੰਡੇ ਦੀ ਗਤੀ, ਇਸ਼ਾਰਾ; (ਘੜੀ ਆਦਿ) ਹਿਲਜੁਲ, ਦਿਲ ਦੀ ਧੜਕਣ, ਸਿਪਾਹੀ ਦੀ ਗਾਸ਼ਤ, ਦੌਰਾ, ਰੌਂਦ, ਫੇਰੀ; ਇਲਾਕਾ; **~ing** ਦੰਡ, ਸਜ਼ਾ, ਫਿਟਕਾਰ, ਕੁੱਟ, ਪਿਟਾਈ; **~about the bush** ਉਰਲੀਆਂ ਪਰਲੀਆਂ ਮਾਰਨੀਆਂ, ਘੱਤਖੀਆਂ ਮਾਰਨਾ; **~back and blue** ਬਹੁਤਾ ਮਾਰਨਾ; **~one's brains** ਮਗਜ਼ ਖਪਾਈ ਕਰਨੀ, ਸਿਰ ਖਪਾਉਣਾ; **~the breast** ਛਾਤੀ

ਪਿੱਟਣਾ, ਦੁਹੱਥੜੀ ਪਿੱਟਣਾ

beau (ਬਅਉ) *n* ਬਾਂਕਾ, ਛੈਲੋਂ, ਅਲਬੇਲਾ, ਛਬੀਲਾ, ਆਸ਼ਕ, ਦਿਲਦਾਰ, ਢੋਲਾ, ਪਰੇਮੀ; **~ish** ਛੈਲ-ਛਬੀਲਾ, ਰੰਗ-ਰੰਗੀਲਾ; **~monde** ਫੈਸ਼ਨੇਬਲ ਸੁਸਾਇਟੀ, ਫੈਸ਼ਨਦਾਰ ਦੁਨੀਆ, ਸ਼ੁਕੀਨ ਲੋਕ

beauteous ('ਬਯੂਟਿਅਸ) *a* (ਕਵਿਤਾ ਵਿਚ) ਰੁਪਵੰਤ, ਸੁੰਦਰ, ਸੋਹਣਾ, ਖ਼ੂਬਸੂਰਤ, ਰਸਮਈ, ਮਨੋਹਰ, ਹੁਸੀਨ

beautician ('ਬਯੂ'ਟਿਸ਼ਨ) *n* ਸਿੰਗਾਰਕਰਤਾ, ਸਿੰਗਾਰ ਕੇਂਦਰ ਨੂੰ ਚਲਾਉਣ ਵਾਲਾ

beautiful ('ਬਯੂਟਿਫ਼ੁੱਲ) *a* ਸੋਹਣਾ, ਸੁੰਦਰ, ਖ਼ੂਬਸੂਰਤ, ਮਨਮੋਹਣਾ, ਰੁਪਵੰਤ, ਰੁਪਵਾਨ

beauty ('ਬਯੂਟਿ) *n* ਰੁਪ, ਸੁੰਦਰਤਾ-ਖ਼ੂਬਸੂਰਤੀ, ਮਨੋਹਰਤਾ, ਰਮਣੀਕਤਾ, ਜੋਬਨ, ਹੁਸਨ; ਛਬ, ਜਮਾਲ, ਸ਼ੋਭਾ; ਪਰੀ, ਸੁੰਦਰੀ, ਸੁੰਦਰ ਗੁਣ, ਚੰਗੀ ਝਾਕੀ; **~parlour** ਸਿੰਗਾਰ ਕਲਾ ਕੇਂਦਰ, ਫੈਸ਼ਨੇਬਲ ਵਾਲ ਬਣਾਉਣ ਦੀ ਦੁਕਾਨ, (ਇਸਤਰੀਆਂ ਦੇ) ਚਿਹਰੇ ਸੁੰਦਰ ਬਣਾਉਣ ਦੀਆਂ ਵਿਧੀਆਂ ਦੀ ਥਾਂ; **~spot** ਦਰਸ਼ਨੀ ਥਾਂ; ਤਿਲ, ਸਰੀਰ ਦੇ ਉੱਪਰ ਸੁੰਦਰਤਾ ਦਾ ਨਿਸ਼ਾਨ

becall (ਬਿਕੋਲ) *v* ਗਾਲ੍ਹ ਕੱਢਣੀ, ਕੋੜੇ ਸ਼ਬਦ ਕਹਿਣੇ

because (ਬਿ'ਕੌਜ਼) *adv conj* ਕਿਉਂਕਿ, ਕਿਉਂਜੋ, ਇਸ ਲਈ ਕਿ, ਇਸ ਕਰਕੇ

beck (ਬੈਕ) *v n* ਸੰਕੇਤ ਕਰਨਾ, ਇਸ਼ਾਰਾ ਕਰਨਾ, ਮੂਕ ਭਾਸ਼ਾ ਵਿਚ ਆਖਣਾ; ਸਿਰ ਹਿਲਾਉਣਾ; (1) ਇਸ਼ਾਰਾ, ਗੁੱਝਾ ਇਸ਼ਾਰਾ, ਸੰਕੇਤ; ਆਦੇਸ਼, ਹੁਕਮ; (2) ਰਜ਼ਮਾ, ਪਹਾੜੀ ਨਦੀ ਜਾਂ ਨਾਲਾ; **to have at one's~** ਇਸ਼ਾਰਿਆਂ ਤੇ ਨਚਾਉਣਾ, ਉਂਗਲੀਆਂ ਤੇ ਨਚਾਉਣਾ

becket (ਬੈਕਿਟ) n ਹੁੱਕ, ਖੂੰਟੀ

beckon ('ਬੇਕ(ਅ)ਨ) v ਇਸ਼ਾਰੇ ਨਾਲ ਬੁਲਾਉਣਾ, ਇਸ਼ਾਰੇ ਰਾਹੀਂ ਧਿਆਨ ਖਿਚਣਾ; ਕਿਸੇ ਨੂੰ ਇਸ਼ਾਰਾ ਕਰਨਾ

become (ਬਿ'ਕਅੱਮ) v ਹੋਣਾ, ਬਣ ਜਾਣਾ; ਯੋਗ ਕਰਨਾ, ਠੀਕ ਹੋਣਾ; ਜਚਣਾ, ਫਬਣਾ

becoming (ਬਿ'ਕਅੱਮਿਙ) a ਸੁਹਾਵਣਾ, ਫਬਵਾਂ; ਅਨੁਰੂਪ, ਉਪਯੁਕਤ, ਢੁੱਕਵਾਂ, ਉਚਿਤ; ~ly ਯੋਗ ਤਰੀਕੇ ਨਾਲ, ਉਚਿਤ ਢੰਗ ਅਨੁਸਾਰ, ਢੁਕਵੇਂ ਤੌਰ ਤੇ, ਚੰਗੀ ਤਰ੍ਹਾਂ ਨਾਲ; ~ness ਢੁੱਕਵਾਂਪਣ, ਉਚਿਤਤਾ, ਅਨੁਰੂਪਤਾ

bed (ਬੈੱਡ) n ਬਿਸਤਰਾ; ਵਿਛਾਈ, ਗੱਦਾ; ਸੇਜ, ਪਲੰਘ, ਚਾਰਪਾਈ, ਮੰਜਾ; ਨੀਂਹ, ਤਲਾ, ਬੁਨਿਆਦ, ਤਹਿ; ਕਿਆਰੀ; ਥੱਲਾ, ਤਲ; ਬਿਲੀਅਰਡ ਖੇਡ ਦੀ ਮੇਜ਼; ਤੋਪ ਗੱਡੀ ਦਾ ਵਿਚਕਾਰਲਾ ਹਿੱਸਾ; ਬਿਸਤਰੇ ਉੱਤੇ ਸੌਣਾ ਜਾਂ ਸੁਲਾਉਣਾ; ਪੌਦਾ ਲਗਾਉਣਾ, ਜਮਾਉਣਾ, ਤਹਿ ਜਮਾਉਣੀ, ਤਹਿ ਦੇਣੀ, ਤਹਿ ਜੰਮਣਾ, ਫਕਣਾ, ਜੜਨਾ; ~bug ਖਟਮਲ; ~of roses ਫੁੱਲਾਂ ਦੀ ਸੇਜ, ਆਨੰਦਮਈ ਅਵਸਥਾ (ਜੀਵਨ ਦੀ); ~ridden ਰੋਗੀ, ਬੀਮਾਰ, ਮੰਜੇ ਪਿਆ; ~rock ਦਰਿਆ ਦੀ ਤਹਿ ਵਿਚਲੀ ਚਟਾਨ; ਮੂਲ ਸਿਧਾਂਤ, ਬੁਨਿਆਦੀ ਅਸੂਲ; ~sore ਮੰਜੇ ਤੇ ਬਹੁਤਾ ਪਏ ਰਹਿਣ ਕਰਕੇ ਹੋ ਜਾਣ ਵਾਲਾ ਜ਼ਖਮ ਜਾਂ ਘਾਉ; ~stead ਪਲੰਘ, ਚਾਰਪਾਈ

bedaub (ਬਿ'ਡੋਬ) v ਰੰਗਣਾ, ਰੰਗ ਥਪਣਾ, ਰੰਗ ਚੜ੍ਹਾਉਣਾ; ਸ਼ੋਖ ਜਾਂ ਭੜਕੀਲੇ ਰੰਗਾਂ ਵਾਲੇ ਕੱਪੜੇ ਪਾਉਣਾ

bedding (ਬੈੱਡਿਙ) n ਬਿਸਤਰਾ, ਗੱਦਾ; ਪਰਾਲੀ

bedlam ('ਬੈੱਡਲਅਮ) n ਰੌਲਾ-ਰੱਪਾ, ਖੱਪ, (ਪ੍ਰਾ) ਪਾਗਲਖ਼ਾਨਾ; ~ism ਹੁੱਲੜਬਾਜ਼ੀ; ~ite ਝੱਲਾ, ਦਿਵਾਨਾ, ਬੌਲਾ; ਸਨਕੀ

bee (ਬੀ) n ਸ਼ਹਿਦ ਦੀ ਮੱਖੀ, ਮਧੂ ਮੱਖੀ; ਉੱਦਮੀ ਪੁਰਖ; ਮਜਲਸ, ਮਹਿਫ਼ਲ; ~hive ਮਖੀਰ, ਮਖਿਆਲ ਖੱਗਾ, ਛੱਤਾ; ~s wax ਮੋਮ; ~keeping ਮਧੂ-ਮੱਖੀ ਪਾਲਣ

beef (ਬੀਫ਼) n (ਖਾਣ ਲਈ) ਗਾਂ, ਮੱਝ ਜਾਂ ਬੈਲ ਦਾ ਮਾਸ; (ਮਨੁੱਖਾਂ ਦੀ) ਸਰੀਰਕ ਸ਼ਕਤੀ, ਮੋਟੀ ਤਾਜ਼ੀ ਗਾਂ, ਬਲਦ; ~up ਮਜ਼ਬੂਤ ਕਰਨਾ; ~y ਰਿਸ਼ਟ-ਪੁਸ਼ਟ, ਪੀਢਾ, ਠੋਸ, ਮੋਟਾ ਤਾਜ਼ਾ, ਪੱਕਾ ਕਾਠੀ ਵਾਲਾ

beep (ਬੀਪ) n ਟੀਂ ਟੀਂ ਦੀ ਅਵਾਜ਼

beer (ਬਿਅ*) n ਜੌਂ ਦੀ ਸ਼ਰਾਬ, ਬੀਅਰ

beet (ਬੀਟ) n ਚੁਕੰਦਰ

beetle (ਬੀਟਲ) n adv ਹਵੇਜ਼ਾ; ਮੂੰਗਲੀ, ਮੋਹਲਾ, ਭੂੰਡ, ਬੀਂਡਾ; ਮੱਥੇ ਤੇ ਵੱਟ ਪਾਈ, ਉਲਰਿਆ; ਬਾਹਰ ਨੂੰ ਨਿਕਲੀਆਂ ਭਵਾਂ, ਅਗਾਂਹ ਨੂੰ ਵਧੀ ਹੋਈ (ਚਟਾਨ); ਸਿਰ ਤੇ ਉਲਰਨਾ

befall (ਬਿ'ਫੋਲ) v ਵਾਪਰਨਾ, ਬੀਤਣਾ, ਆਪਣਾ ਹੋ ਜਾਣਾ

befit (ਬਿ'ਫ਼ਿਟ) v ਫਬਣਾ, ਢੁਕਣਾ, ਠੀਕ ਜੱਚਣਾ; ~ting (ਬਿ'ਫ਼ਿਟਿਙ) ਢੁਕਵਾਂ, ਠੀਕ, ਉਚਿਤ, ਯੋਗ ਉਪਯੁਕਤ

befool (ਬਿ'ਫ਼ੂਲ) v ਬੁੱਧੂ ਬਣਾਉਣਾ, ਸੋਂਜੂ ਉਡਾਉਣਾ, ਮੂਰਖ ਬਣਾਉਣਾ; ਠੱਗਣਾ, ਧੋਖਾ ਦੇਣਾ

before (ਬਿ'ਫ਼ੋ*) adv prep conj ਪਹਿਲਾਂ, ਅੱਗੋਂ ਪਹਿਲਾਂ ਤੋਂ, ਸਾਮ੍ਹਣੇ, ਮੂਹਰੇ, ਅੱਗੇ, ਇਸ ਤੋਂ ਪਹਿਲਾ ਕਿ, ਜਦ ਤਕ

befriend (ਬਿ'ਫ਼ਰੈਂਡ) v ਮਿੱਤਰ ਬਣਾ ਲੈਣਾ, ਦੋਸਤੀ ਕਾਇਮ ਕਰਨੀ, ਮਿੱਤਰਾਂ ਵਾਲਾ ਵਿਹਾਰ ਕਰਨਾ, ਸਹਾਇਤਾ ਕਰਨੀ, ਸਾਥ ਦੇਣਾ

beg (ਬੈਗ) v ਭਿਖ ਮੰਗਲੀ, ਤਰਲਾ ਕਰਨਾ, ਮਿੰਨਤ

ਕਰਨੀ, ਖ਼ੈਰ ਮੰਗਣਾ, ਬੇਨਤੀ ਕਰਨੀ; ਮੰਗ ਪਿੰਨ ਕੇ ਗੁਜ਼ਾਰਾ ਕਰਨਾ; ਕੁੱਤੇ ਦਾ ਅਗਲਾ ਪੈਰ ਚੁੱਕਣਾ

beget (ਬਿਗੈੱਟ) *v* ਜੰਮਣਾ, ਜਟਨਾ, ਪੈਦਾ ਕਰਨਾ, ਜਨਮ ਦੇਣਾ; ਕਾਰਨ ਹੋਣਾ

beggar (ਬੇਗੱਅ*) *n v* ਭਿਖਾਰੀ, ਮੰਗਤਾ; ਭਿਖ-ਮੰਗਾ, ਕੰਗਾਲ ਕਰ ਦੇਣਾ, ਮੰਗਤਾ ਬਣਾ ਦੇਣਾ, ਖ਼ਾਕ-ਸ਼ਾਹ ਕਰ ਦੇਣਾ; ਮਾਤ ਕਰਨਾ; **~s must not be choosers** ਮੰਗਤਿਆਂ ਦੀ ਚੋਣ ਦੀ ਕੋਈ ਮਹੱਤਾ ਨਹੀਂ, ਪੁੰਨ ਦੀ ਗਾਂ ਦੇ ਦੰਦ ਨਹੀਂ ਵੇਖੀਦੇ; **~y** ਕੰਗਾਲੀ, ਗ਼ਰੀਬੀ, ਅਤੀ ਨਿਰਧਨਤਾ; ਜ਼ਲਾਲਤ; ਫਕੀਰੀ

begin (ਬਿ'ਗਿਨ) *v* ਸ਼ੁਰੂ ਕਰਨਾ, ਆਰੰਭ ਕਰਨਾ, ਪਹਿਲ ਕਰਨੀ, ਪਹਿਲਾ ਕਦਮ ਚੁੱਕਣਾ, ਛੋਹਣਾ; **~ner** ਆਰੰਭਕ, ਮੋਢੀ, ਸ਼ੁਰੂ ਕਰਨ ਵਾਲਾ, ਛੋਹਣ ਵਾਲਾ, ਨਵ-ਸਿਖਅਕ, ਸਿਖਿੰਦੜ, ਸਿਖਾਂਦਰੁ, ਨੋਂਜਵਾਨ; **~ning** ਆਰੰਭ, ਸ਼ੁਰੂ, ਮੁੱਢ, ਕਿਸੇ ਵਸਤੂ ਦੇ ਸ਼ੁਰੂ ਦਾ ਹਿੱਸਾ, ਮੂਲ ਕੇਂਦਰ

begone (ਬਿਗੌਨ) *v imperat* (ਪ੍) ਦੂਰ ਹੋ, ਦੱਫਾ ਹੋ, ਪਰੇ ਹਟ

begrudge (ਬਿ'ਗਰਅੱਜ) *v* ਈਰਖਾ ਕਰਨੀ, ਕਿਸੇ ਨਾਲ ਵੈਰ ਰੱਖਣਾ, ਦਿਲ ਵਿਚ ਕਿਸੇ ਵਿਰੋਧ ਰਗ਼ੜਕ ਰੱਖਣੀ

beguile (ਬਿ'ਗਾਇਲ) *v* ਕਪਟ ਕਰਨਾ, ਧੋਖਾ ਦੇਣਾ; ਠੱਗਣਾ; ਦਿਲ ਲੁਭਾਉਣਾ

behalf (ਬਿਹਾਫ਼) *n* ਹਿਤ, ਪੱਖ, ਸਮਰਥਨ, ਤਰਫ਼; **on or in ~ of** ਨਿਮਿਤ, ਦੇ ਵੱਲੋਂ; ਵਾਸਤੇ, ਲਈ, ਖ਼ਾਤਰ

behave (ਬਿ'ਹੇਇਵ) *v* ਸਲੂਕ ਕਰਨਾ, ਪੇਸ਼ ਆਉਣਾ; ਸਲੀਕਾ ਕਰਨਾ, ਕਿਸੇ ਆਦਮੀ ਜਾਂ ਮਸ਼ੀਨ ਦਾ ਠੀਕ ਕੰਮ ਕਰਨਾ

behaviour (ਬਿ'ਹੇਵਿਯਅ*) *n* ਵਤੀਰਾ, ਰਵੱਈਆਂ; ਵਰਤਾਉ, ਸਲੂਕ; ਢੰਗ, ਚਾਲ-ਚਲਣ, ਚਾਲ-ਢਾਲ, ਲੱਛਣ, ਚਰਿੱਤਰ, ਸ਼ਿਸ਼ਟਾਚਾਰ, ਮਸ਼ੀਨ ਜਾਂ ਕਿਸੇ ਪਦਾਰਥ ਦੇ ਕੰਮ ਕਰਨ ਦਾ ਢੰਗ

behead (ਬਿ'ਹੈੱਡ) *v* ਸਿਰ ਲਾਹੁਣਾ, ਸਿਰ ਕਲਮ ਕਰਨਾ

behest (ਬਿਹੈੱਸਟ) *n* ਹੁਕਮ, ਆਗਿਆ, ਆਦੇਸ਼, ਫ਼ਰਮਾਨ

behind (ਬਿ'ਹਾਇੰਡ) *prep adv n* ਪਿੱਛੇ, ਪਛੜਿਆ ਹੋਇਆ, ਬਾਅਦ ਵਿਚ, ਪਿੱਛੇ, ਥੱਲੇ, ਉਹਲੇ ਵਿਚ, ਲੁਕਿਆ ਹੋਇਆ; ਪਿੱਛਲਾ ਹਿੱਸਾ, ਚਿੱਤੜ

behold (ਬਿ'ਹਅਉਲਡ) *v* ਦੇਖਣਾ, ਤੱਕਣਾ, ਧਿਆਨ ਕਰਨਾ

being (ਬੀਇੰਡ) *n* ਹੋਂਦ, ਹਸਤੀ, ਵਿਅਕਤੀ, ਵਜੂਦ **the Supreme B~** ਈਸ਼ਵਰ, ਪਰਮ ਸੱਤਾ

belated (ਬਿ'ਲੇਇਟਿਡ) *a* ਪਛੜਿਆ, ਚਿਰਕਾ ਪੁੱਜਾ, ਵਿਲੰਬਤ, ਜਿਸ ਨੂੰ ਰਸਤੇ ਵਿਚ ਰਾਤ ਪੈ ਜਾਏ, ਬਹੁਤ ਦੇਰ ਕਰ ਆਇਆ

belch (ਬੈਲੱਚ) *v n* ਡਕਾਰ ਮਾਰਨਾ, ਡਕਾਰਨਾ; ਤਤ੍ਹਾ-ਤਤ੍ਹ ਕੱਢਣਾ, ਨਸ਼ੇ ਵਿਚ ਬੁੜ-ਬੁੜਾਉਣਾ; ਗੰਦੀਆਂ ਗਾਲ੍ਹਾਂ ਕਢੱਣੀਆਂ; ਡਕਾਰ; ਗਰਜ, ਗੜ-ਬੜ

beldam(e) (ਬੈਲੱਡਅਮ) *n* ਬੁਢੱੜੀ, ਬੁੱਢੀ ਤੀਵੀਂ; ਡੈਣ, ਲੜਾਕੀ ਤੀਵੀਂ, ਭੂਤਨੀ, ਕਰੂਪ ਬੁੱਢੀ ਇਸਤਰੀ

beleaguer (ਬਿ'ਲੀਗਅ*) *v* ਘੇਰ ਲੈਣਾ, ਘੇਰਾ ਪਾਉਣਾ, ਘੇਰਨਾ

belial (ਬੀਲਯਅਲ) *n* ਦੈਂਤ, ਪਰੇਤ, ਸ਼ੈਤਾਨ,

ਰਾਕਸ਼ਸ, ਦੁਰਾਚਾਰੀ ਵਿਅਕਤੀ, ਦੁਸ਼ਟ, ਪਾਪੀ

belie (ਬੀਲਾਇ) *v* ਝੂਠ ਬੋਲਣਾ, ਝੂਠਾ ਕਰਨਾ, ਝੁਠਲਾਉਣਾ, ਨਿੰਦਾ ਕਰਨਾ, ਕਲੰਕ ਆਰੋਪਣ ਕਰਨਾ, ਵਡਾ ਨਾ ਕਰਨਾ

belief (ਬੀ'ਲੀਫ਼) *n* ਵਿਸ਼ਵਾਸ, ਨਿਸ਼ਚੈ, ਸ਼ਰਧਾ, ਭਰੋਸਾ, ਇਮਾਨ, ਵਿਚਾਰ, ਧਰਮ, ਮੱਤ, ਰਾਏ ਖ਼ਿਆਲ

believable (ਬਿ'ਲੀਵਅਬਲ) *a* ਵਿਸ਼ਵਾਸ ਕਰਨਯੋਗ, ਮੰਨਣਯੋਗ, ਭਰੋਸੇਯੋਗ

believe (ਬਿ'ਲੀਵ) *v* ਵਿਸ਼ਵਾਸ ਕਰਨਾ, ਭਰੋਸਾ ਕਰਨਾ, ਮੰਨਣਾ; ਰਾਏ ਰੱਖਣੀ, ਖ਼ਿਆਲ ਕਰਨਾ, ਸਮਝਣਾ

believer (ਬਿ'ਲੀਵਅ*) *n* ਮੰਨਣ ਵਾਲਾ; ਸ਼ਰਧਾਲੂ, ਉਪਾਸਕ, ਆਸਤਕ, ਵਿਸ਼ਵਾਸੀ, ਆਪਣੇ ਧਰਮ ਵਿਚ ਵਿਸ਼ਵਾਸ ਰੱਖਣ ਵਾਲਾ

believing (ਬਿ'ਲੀਵਿੰਡ) *a* ਵਿਸ਼ਵਾਸੀ

bell (ਬੈਲ) *n v* ਘੰਟਾ, ਘੰਟੀ, ਟੱਲੀ, ਘੁੰਗਰੂ, ਟੱਲ, ਘੜਿਆਲ, ਘੰਟੇ ਵਰਗੀ ਵਸਤੂ; ਬੈਰਾ; ਘੰਟੀ ਬੰਨ੍ਹਣੀ, ਘੰਟੀ ਲਾਉਣੀ; ~boy ਹੋਟਲ ਵਿਚ ਨੇਕਰ

belladonna (ਬੈਲਅ'ਡੋਨਅ) *n* ਧਤੂਰਾ, ਬੈਲਡੋਨਾ, ਭਲਾਵਾ; ਸੱਮ੍ਹ (ਭਲਾਵਿਆਂ ਦੀ)

belle (ਬੈਲ) *n* ਸੁੰਦਰੀ, ਇਸਤਰੀ, ਰੂਪਵਤੀ, ਹੁਸੀਨ, ਗੋਰੀ; ਕਿਸੇ ਥਾਂ ਦੀ ਸਭ ਤੋਂ ਸੁਹਣੀ ਇਸਤਰੀ

bellicose (ਬੈਲਿਕਅਉਸ) *a* ਲੜਾਕਾ, ਲੜਨ ਨੂੰ ਤਿਆਰ, ਫ਼ਸਾਦੀ, ਦੰਗਈ

bellicosity (ਬੈਲਿਕੌਸਅਟਿ) *n* ਜੁਧ-ਪਰੇਮ, ਦੰਗੇਬਾਜ਼ੀ, ਲੜਾਕਾਪਨ

belligerent (ਬਿ'ਲਿਜਅਰੌਂਟ) *n a* ਲੜਾਕਾ, ਜੋਧਾ, ਬੀਰ, ਜੁੱਧਕਾਰ, ਦੁਸ਼ਮਣ, ਵੈਰੀ

bellow (ਬੈਲੋਅਉ) *v n* ਰੰਭਣਾ, ਅਡਿੰਗਣਾ; ਗੱਜਣਾ, ਡਬਕ ਮਾਰਨਾ; ਕਰੋਧ ਵਿਚ ਜ਼ੋਰ ਨਾਲ ਬੋਲਣਾ; ਚਿਲਾਉਣਾ, ਕੜਕਣਾ; (ਦੁੱਖ ਨਾਲ) ਚੀਖਣਾ; ਤੋਪ ਦੀ ਆਵਾਜ਼, ਗਰਜ

bellows (ਬੈਲੋਅਉਜ਼) *n pl* ਧੋੱਕਣੀ, ਧੁਕਨੀ, ਕੈਮਰੇ ਦਾ ਫੈਲਣ ਵਾਲਾ ਹਿੱਸਾ, ਵਾਜੇ ਦਾ ਪੱਖ, ਫੇਫੜੇ

belly (ਬੈਲੀ) *n v* ਪੇਟ, ਢਿੱਡ, ਕੁੱਖ, ਗੋਗੜ, ਉਦਰ; ਸਾਮੁਣੇ ਦਾ, ਆਂਤਰਿਕ ਜਾਂ ਘੱਲੇ ਦਾ ਤਲ ਫੁੱਲਣਾ, ਹਵਾ ਭਰ ਜਾਣਾ, ਆਫਰਨਾ

belong (ਬਿ'ਲੈਂਡ) *v* ਸਬੰਧ ਹੋਣਾ, ਸਬੰਧਤ ਹੋਣਾ, ਕਿਸੇ ਦਾ ਹੋਣਾ, ਕਿਸੇ ਦਾ ਕਬਜ਼ਾ ਹੋਣਾ; ਵਾਸੀ ਹੋਣਾ

below (ਬਿ'ਲਅਉ) *adv prep* ਹੇਠਾਂ, ਥਲੇ, ਮਕਾਨ ਦੀ ਹੇਠਲੀ ਛੱਤ; ਪਾਤਾਲ ਵਿਚ, ਨੀਚਤਾ ਵਲ; ~one's breath ਬਹੁਤ ਹੌਲੀ ਜੇਹੇ, ਧੀਮੀ ਆਵਾਜ਼ ਵਿਚ

belt (ਬੈਲੱਟ) *n v* ਪੇਟੀ, ਕਮਰਬੰਦ, ਤੜਾਗੀ; ਖੇਤਰ, ਇਲਾਕਾ, ਮੰਡਲ, ਹਲਕਾ, ਤਸਮਾ, ਮਸ਼ੀਨ ਚਲਾਉਣ ਦਾ ਪਟੱ; ਪੇਟੀ ਬੰਨ੍ਹਣੀ; ਬੰਨ੍ਹਣਾ; ਰੰਗ ਨਾਲ ਗੋਲ ਘੇਰਾ ਬਣਾਉਣਾ; ਪੇਟੀ ਨਾਲ ਮਾਰਨਾ

bemean (ਬਿ'ਮੀਨ) *v* ਨਿਰਾਦਰੀ ਕਰਨੀ, ਬੇਇੱਜ਼ਤੀ ਕਰਨੀ, ਪੱਤ ਲਾਹੁਣੀ

bemoan (ਬਿ'ਮਅਉਨ) *v* ਰੋਣਾ, ਪਿਟੱਣਾ, ਕੁਰਲਾਉਣਾ, ਵਿਰਲਾਪ ਕਰਨਾ, ਮਾਤਮ ਕਰਨਾ, ਅਫ਼ਸੋਸ ਜ਼ਾਹਰ ਕਰਨਾ

bemock (ਬਿ'ਮੋਕ) *v* ਮਖ਼ੌਲ ਕਰਨਾ, ਹਾਸਾ ਉਡਾਉਣਾ, ਖਿੱਲੀ ਉਡਾਉਣਾ, ਪਰਿਹਾਸ ਕਰਨਾ

bench (ਬੈਂਚ) *n* ਬੈਂਚ, ਕਾਠ ਦੀ ਲੰਬੀ ਕੁਰਸੀ, ਚੌਂਕੀ, ਤਖ਼ਤਪੋਸ਼, ਬੱਡੂ, ਮੰਚ; ਕਚਹਿਰੀ ਦੇ ਹਾਕਮ, ਜੱਜ; ਪੀਠ, ਅਦਾਲਤ; ਕੁੱਤਿਆਂ ਨੂੰ ਰੱਖਣ ਦਾ ਘਰ

bend (ਬੈਂਡ) *v* ਮੋੜਨਾ, ਫੇਰਨਾ, ਵਿੰਗਾ ਕਰਨਾ, ਝੁਕਾਉਣਾ; (ਆਦਰ ਵਜੋਂ), ਝੁਕਣਾ, ਨਿਵਣਾ, ਨਿਵਾਉਣਾ; ਲਿਫਣਾ, ਲਿਫਾਉਣਾ, ਪਕੀ ਕਰ ਲੈਣੀ, ਵਸ ਵਿਚ ਲਿਆਉਣਾ; ਗੰਢ ਮਾਰਨੀ; ਵਲ-ਵਿੰਗ; ਗੰਢ; ਕਿਸੇ ਚੀਜ਼ ਦਾ ਮੁੜਿਆ ਹੋਇਆ ਹਿੱਸਾ; ਟੁਕੜਾ; ਸਮਾਨਾਂਤਰ ਮੁੱਖ ਰੇਖਾਵਾਂ; ~ing ਝੁਕਾਉ

beneath (ਬਿ'ਨੀਥ) *adv prep* ਥੱਲੇ, ਥੱਲੇ ਵੱਲ

benediction (ਬੈਨਿ'ਡ਼ਿਕਸ਼ਨ) *n* ਆਸ਼ੀਰਵਾਦ, ਅਸੀਸ, ਵਰ; ਸ਼ੁਭ-ਅਸੀਸ, ਸ਼ੁਭ ਕਾਮਨਾ, ਈਸ਼ਵਰੀ ਕਿਰਪਾ, ਕਲਿਆਣ

benedictive (ਬੈਨਿ'ਡ਼ਿਕਟਿਵ) *a* ਆਸ਼ੀਰਵਾਦੀ, ਮੰਗਲਵਾਦੀ

benedictory (ਬੈਨਿ'ਡ਼ਿਕਟਅਰਿ) *a* ਕਲਿਆਣਕਾਰੀ; ਅਸੀਸ ਸਬੰਧੀ, ਸ਼ੁਭ-ਇਛਾ ਸਬੰਧੀ

benefaction (ਬੈਨਿ'ਫੈਕਸ਼ਨ) *n* ਪੁੰਨ, ਦਾਨ, ਉਪਕਾਰ, ਧਰਮ-ਅਰਥ ਖ਼ਰਾਇਤ, ਭਲਾਈ, ਕਲਿਆਣ, ਸਹਾਇਤਾ

benefactor (ਬੈਨਿ'ਫੈਕਟਅਾ*) *n* ਦਾਤਾ, ਦਾਨੀ; ਉਪਕਾਰੀ, ਭਲਾ ਕਰਨ ਵਾਲਾ, ਸਰਪਰਸਤ

beneficial (ਬੈਨਿ'ਫ਼ਿਸ਼ਲ) *a* ਗੁਣਕਾਰੀ, ਲਾਹੇਵੰਦ, ਫ਼ਾਇਦੇਮੰਦ, ਕਲਿਆਣਕਾਰੀ, ਸਹਾਇਕ, ਹਿਤਕਾਰੀ; (ਕਾ) ਜਾਇਦਾਦ ਦੇ ਲਾਭ ਨਾਲ ਸਬੰਧਤ

beneficiary (ਬੈਨਿ'ਫ਼ਿਸ਼ਅਰਿ) *n a* ਲਾਭ ਪ੍ਰਾਪਤ ਕਰਨ ਵਾਲਾ, ਦਾਨ ਦਾ ਪਾਤਰ; (ਕਾ) ਜਾਗੀਰਦਾਰ, ਲਾਭ ਦਾ ਹੱਕ ਲੈਣ ਵਾਲਾ

benefit (ਬੈਨਿਫ਼ਿਟ) *n v* ਲਾਭ, ਫ਼ਾਇਦਾ, ਨਫ਼ਾ; ਹਿਤ, ਭਲਾਈ, ਭੱਤਾ, ਵਜ਼ੀਫ਼ਾ, ਗੁਜਾਰਾ; ਭਲਾ ਕਰਨਾ, ਉਪਕਾਰ, ਫ਼ਾਇਦਾ ਪ੍ਰਚਾਉਣਾ, ਫ਼ਾਇਦਾ ਉਠਾਉਣਾ, ਲਾਭ ਲੈਣਾ

benevolence (ਬਿ'ਨੈਵ਼ਅਲਅੰਸ) *n* ਦਇਆਲਤਾ, ਕਿਰਪਾ, ਮਿਹਰ, ਕਿਰਪਾਲਤਾ, ਉਦਾਰਤਾ, ਪਰਉਪਕਾਰਤਾ, ਦਿਆਲੂ ਸੁਭਾਅ

benevolent (ਬਿ'ਨੈਵ਼ਅਲਅੰਟ) *a* ਦਇਆਵਾਨ, ਦਿਆਲੂ, ਕਿਰਪਾਲੂ, ਉਪਕਾਰੀ, ਉਦਾਰ-ਚਿੰਤ, ਹਿਤੈਸ਼ੀ, ਸ਼ੁਭ-ਚਿੰਤਕ

benight (ਬਿ'ਨਾਇਟ) *v* ਹਨੇਰਾ ਕਰਨਾ, ਅੰਧਕਾਰ ਫੈਲਾਉਣਾ, ਨਿਰਾਸ ਕਰਨਾ

benign (ਬਿ'ਨਾਇਨ) *a* ਕਿਰਪਾਲੂ, ਦਿਆਲੂ, ਨੇਕ-ਦਿਲ; ਸੁਲਖਣਾ, ਗੁਣਕਾਰੀ; (ਬੀਮਾਰੀ) ਘੱਟ ਦੁੱਖਦਾਈ

benumb (ਬਿ'ਨਅੱਮ) *v* ਸੁੰਨ ਕਰਨਾ, ਨਕਾਰਾ ਕਰਨਾ, ਸ਼ਕਤੀਹੀਨ ਕਰਨਾ, ਅਕੜਾਉਣਾ

bequeath (ਬਿ'ਕਵੀਦ) *v* ਵਸੀਅਤ ਕਰ ਜਾਣਾ, ਸੰਕਲਪਣਾ; ਹਵਾਲੇ ਕਰਨਾ

bequest (ਬਿ'ਕਵੈਸੱਟ) *n* ਵਸੀਅਤਨਾਮਾ; ਵਸੀਅਤ, ਵਸੀਅਤ ਰਾਹੀਂ ਮਿਲਿਆ ਮਾਲ; ਵਿਰਸਾ;

berate (ਬਿ'ਰੇਇਟ) *v* ਝਿੜਕਣਾ, ਝਾੜਨਾ, ਝੰਬਣਾ, ਗੁੱਸੇ ਹੋਣਾ, ਬੁਰਾ ਭਲਾ ਕਹਿਣਾ, ਫਜੀਹਤ ਕਰਨਾ

berceuse (ਬੇਅ'ਸਅਃਜ਼) *(F) n* ਲੋਰੀ

bereav (ਬਿ'ਰੀਵ) *v* ਮਰ ਜਾਣਾ (ਕਿਸੇ ਸਬੰਧੀ ਪਿਆਰੇ ਦਾ) ਖੋਰ ਲੈਣਾ, ਵਿਹੂਣਾ ਕਰਨਾ, ਵਾਂਝਿਆਂ ਕਰਨਾ; ~ment ਸੋਗ, ਮਾਤਮ (ਮੌਤ ਉੱਤੇ)

bereft (ਬਿ'ਰੈੱਫਟ) *a* ਵਾਂਝਾ, ਵੰਚਤ, (ਇਕੱਲਾ) ਛੱਡਿਆ, ਨਿਆਸਰਾ, ਸ਼ੋਕ-ਅਵਸਥਾ ਵਿਚ

berg (ਬਅਰਗ) *n* ਬਰਫ਼ ਦਾ ਤੋਦਾ

berm (ਬਅਰਮ) *n* ਪਟੜੀ, ਸੜਕ ਜਾਂ ਨਹਿਰ ਦਾ ਕਿਨਾਰਾ

berry (ਬੈਰਿ) *n v* ਬੇਰ, ਰਸ-ਭਰੀ, ਕਣਕ ਦਾ ਬੀ, ਦਾਣਾ, ਇਕ ਕਿਸਮ ਦੀ ਮੱਛੀ ਦਾ ਅੰਡਾ; ਫਲ ਲੱਗਣਾ; ਬੇਰ ਚੁਗਾਣਾ

berserk (ਬਅ'ਜ਼ਅਰਕ) *a* ਪਾਗਲ, ਵਹਿਸ਼ੀ, ਜਨੂੰਨੀ

berth (ਬਅਰਥ) *n v* (ਜਹਾਜ਼ ਜਾਂ ਰੇਲ ਵਿਚ) ਸੌਣ ਲਈ ਥਾਂ; ਬਰਥ, ਸਮੁੰਦਰੀ ਜਹਾਜ਼ ਦੇ ਲੰਗਰ ਲਾਉਣ ਦੀ ਥਾਂ; (ਕਿਸੇ ਚੀਜ਼ ਲਈ) ਠੀਕ ਥਾਂ, ਨੇਕਰੀ, ਆਸਾਮੀ; (ਠੀਕ ਥਾਂ ਤੇ) ਲੰਗਰ ਸੁੱਟਣਾ, ਸੌਣ ਲਈ ਥਾਂ ਦੇਣੀ, ਟਿਕਾਣਾ ਕਰਨਾ

beseech (ਬਿ'ਸੀਚ) *v* ਬੇਨਤੀ ਕਰਨਾ, ਪ੍ਰਾਰਥਨਾ ਕਰਨਾ, ਤਰਲੇ ਕਰਨੇ, ਮਿੰਨਤ ਕਰਨੀ

beset (ਬਿ'ਸੈੱਟ) *v* ਘੇਰ ਲੈਣਾ; ਰਾਹ ਰੋਕ ਲੈਣਾ, ਮੱਲ ਲੈਣਾ; ਹੱਲਾ ਕਰਨਾ, ਟੁੱਟ ਕੇ ਜਾ ਪੈਣਾ; ਕਾਬੂ ਪਾ ਲੈਣਾ; ਜਿਚ ਕਰਨਾ

beside (ਬਿ'ਸਾਇਡ) *prep* ਨੇੜੇ, ਪਾਸ, ਕੋਲ, ਆਸ ਪਾਸ, ਕਿਨਾਰੇ ਦੇ

besides (ਬਿ'ਸਾਇਡਜ਼) *prep adv* ਇਸ ਤੋਂ ਛੁੱਟ, ਇਸ ਤੋਂ ਇਲਾਵਾ, ਨਾਲੇ, ਹੋਰ, ਸਿਵਾਏ, ਅਤਿਰਿਕਤ

besiege (ਬਿ'ਸੀਜ) *v* ਘੇਰਾ ਪਾਉਣਾ, ਘੇਰਨਾ, ਘੇਰ ਲੈਣਾ, ਭੀੜ ਕਰਨੀ; **~ment** ਘੇਰਾ, ਕਿਲ੍ਹਾਬੰਦੀ

besigh (ਬਿ'ਸਾਇ) *v* ਠੰਢਾ ਸਾਹ ਲੈਣਾ, ਆਹ ਭਰਨੀ

besmear (ਬਿ'ਸਮਿਅਰ) *v* ਲੇਪ ਕਰਨਾ, ਚੋਪੜਨਾ, ਪੋਚਣਾ, ਮਲਣਾ, ਧੱਬਾ ਲਾਉਣਾ, ਕਾਲਖ ਲਾਉਣੀ, ਕਲੰਕਤ ਕਰਨਾ

bespectecled (ਬਿ'ਸਕਪੈੱਕਟਅਲੇਡ) *a* ਐਨਕ ਵਾਲਾ, ਐਨਕਦਾਰ ਚਸ਼ਮਾ ਪਹਿਨੇ ਹੋਏ

best (ਬੈਸੱਟ) *a adv (superl of good,*

well) ਸਭ ਤੋਂ ਚੰਗਾ, ਚੰਗੇ ਤੋਂ ਚੰਗਾ; ਵਧੀਆ, ਸ੍ਰੇਸ਼ਠ, ਪਰਮ; ਸਭ ਤੋਂ ਚੰਗੀ ਤਰ੍ਹਾਂ; **be at one's ~** (ਹੁਨਰ) ਸਿਖਰ ਤੇ ਹੋਣਾ; **make the~of things** ਹਰ ਅਵਸਥਾ ਤੋਂ ਲਾਭ ਉਠਾਉਣਾ; ਕਿਸੇ ਕਿਸਮ ਦਾ ਕੰਮ ਕੱਢਣਾ

bestain (ਬਿ'ਸਟੇਇਨ) *v* ਦਾਗ ਲਾਉਣਾ, ਧੱਬਾ ਲਾਉਣਾ, ਕਲੰਕਤ ਕਰਨਾ

bestow (ਬਿ'ਸਟਅਉ) *v* ਪ੍ਰਦਾਨ ਕਰਨਾ, (ਭੇਟ) ਦੇਣਾ, ਅਰਪਣ ਕਰਨਾ; ਬਖ਼ਸ਼ਣਾ, ਜਮ੍ਹਾਂ ਕਰਨਾ, ਟਿਕਾਉਣਾ

bet (ਬੈੱਟ) *n v* ਸ਼ਰਤ; ਦਾਉ, ਬਾਜ਼ੀ; ਸ਼ਰਤ ਲਾਉਣਾ, ਬਾਜ਼ੀ ਲਾਉਣੀ, ਜੂਆ ਖੇਡਣਾ

betel ('ਬੀਟਲ) *n* ਪਾਨ-ਪੱਤਾ, ਤੰਬੋਲ; **~nut** ਸੁਪਾਰੀ

betray (ਬਿ'ਟਰੇਇ) *v* ਵਿਸ਼ਵਾਸਘਾਤ ਕਰਨਾ, ਬੇਵਫ਼ਾਈ ਕਰਨਾ; ਧਰੋਹ ਕਰਨਾ, ਭੇਤ ਖੋਲ੍ਹਣਾ; ਪਰਗਟ ਕਰਨਾ; **~al** ਵਿਸ਼ਵਾਸਘਾਤ; ਧਰੋਹ, ਬੇਵਸਾਹੀ; ਭੇਤ ਖੋਲ੍ਹਣਾ; **~er** ਵਿਸ਼ਵਾਸਘਾਤੀ, ਵਿਸ਼ਵਾਸਘਾਤਕ, ਧਰੋਹੀ

betroth (ਬਿ'ਟਰਅਉਦ) *v* ਮੰਗਣੀ ਕਰਨੀ; **~al** ਮੰਗਣੀ, ਕੁੜਮਾਈ, ਸਗਾਈ, ਸ਼ਗਨ

better (ਬੈੱਟਅ*) adv. adv. n v* ਚੰਗੇਰਾ, ਭਲੇਰਾ, ਬਿਹਤਰ; ਚੰਗੇਰਾ ਬਣਾਉਣਾ, ਸੁਧਾਰ ਕਰਨਾ; ਉੰਨਤੀ ਕਰਨਾ, (ਕਿਸੇ ਨਾਲੋਂ) ਵਧ ਜਾਣਾ; **~ment** ਭਲਾਈ, ਸੁਧਾਰ, ਉੰਨਤੀ, ਬਿਹਤਰੀ

between (ਬਿਟਵੀਨ) *a prep* ਵਿਚ, ਵਿਚਕਾਰ; ਮੱਧ ਵਿਚ, ਵਿਚ-ਵਿਚਾਲੇ, ਦਰਮਿਆਨ, ਅੰਦਰ, ਆਪੋ ਵਿਚ

beverage (ਬੈੱਵ(ਅ)ਰਿਜ) *n* ਸ਼ਰਬਤ, ਪੀਣ ਵਾਲੀ ਚੀਜ਼ (ਸ਼ਰਾਬ ਆਦਿ)

beware (ਬਿ'ਵੇਅ*) v* ਸਚੇਤ ਰਹਿਣਾ, ਖ਼ਬਰਦਾਰ

ਰਹਿਣਾ, ਚੌਕਸ ਰਹਿਣਾ, ਸਾਵਧਾਨ ਹੋਣਾ

bewilder (ਬਿ'ਵਿਲਡਅ*) *v* ਬੌਂਦਲਾਉਣਾ, ਭਰਕਾਉਣਾ; ਉਲਝਣ ਵਿਚ ਪਾਉਣਾ ਘਬਰਾ ਦੇਣਾ, ਹੈਰਾਨ ਕਰਨਾ, ਮੱਤ ਮਾਰ ਦੇਣੀ, ਭੁਲਾਉਣਾ, ਭਟਕਾਉਣਾ; **~ed** ਘਬਰਾਇਆ, ਵਿਆਕੁਲ; **~ment** ਘਬਰਾਹਟ, ਪਰੇਸ਼ਾਨੀ, ਹੈਰਾਨੀ, ਵਿਆਕੁਲਤਾ

beyond (ਬਿ'ਯੌਂਡ) *adv prep n* ਪਰਲੇ ਪਾਸੇ, ਪਾਰ, ਦੂਜੇ ਪਾਸੇ, ਉਸ ਪਾਸੇ; ਉਧਰ, ਪਰ੍ਹਾਂ; ਤੋਂ ਵਧੇਰੇ, ਪਹੁੰਚ ਤੋਂ ਬਾਹਰ, ਅਧਿਕ; ਅੱਗਾ

bi (ਬਾਇ) *prefix* ਦੋ ਗੁਣਾ, ਦੋ ਗੁਣੀ (ਵਸਤੂ), ਦੋ ਵਾਰ ਹੋਣ ਵਾਲਾ

biangular ('ਬਾਈ'ਐਙਗਯੁਲਅ*) *a* ਦੋ ਕੋਣੀ, ਦੋ ਕੋਣਾਂ ਵਾਲਾ

biannual ('ਬਾਈ'ਐਨਯੁਅਲ) *a* ਸਾਲ ਵਿਚ ਦੋ ਵਾਰੀ, ਛਿਮਾਹੀ

bias (ਬਾਇਅਸ) *n v* ਪੱਖਪਾਤ, ਧੜੇਬਾਜ਼ੀ, ਤਰਫ਼ਦਾਰੀ, ਲਿਹਾਜ਼; ਪੱਖ ਪਾਲਣਾ, ਨਾਜਾਇਜ਼ ਪ੍ਰਭਾਵ ਪਾਉਣਾ

bibilographer ('ਬਿਬਲਿਔਗਰਾਫ਼*) *n* ਪੁਸਤਕ ਸੂਚੀਕਾਰ; ਗ੍ਰੰਥ-ਵਿਗਿਆਨੀ

bibilography ('ਬਿਬਲਿ'ਔਗਰਅਫ਼ਿ) *n* ਪੁਸਤਕ-ਸੂਚੀ, ਗ੍ਰੰਥ-ਸੂਚੀ, ਪੁਸਤਕਮਾਲਾ

bicoloured ('ਬਾਇ'ਕਲਅੱਡ) *a* ਦੋ-ਰੰਗਾ, ਦੋ ਰੰਗਾਂ ਵਾਲਾ

bicycle (ਬਾਇਸਿਕਲ) *v* ਸਾਈਕਲ; ਬਾਈਸਿਕਲ ਚਲਾਉਣਾ

bid (ਬਿਡ) *n v* (ਨੀਲਾਮੀ ਦੀ) ਬੋਲੀ; ਸੱਦਾ, ਬੁਲਾਵਾ; ਹੁਕਮ ਦੇਣਾ, ਸੱਦਾ ਦੇਣਾ, ਨਿਮੰਤਰਤ ਕਰਨਾ; ਨੀਲਾਮੀ ਵਿਚ ਬੋਲੀ ਦੇਣੀ, (ਤਾਸ਼ ਦੀ ਖੇਡ ਵਿਚ) ਸਰਾਂ ਮਿਥਣੀਆਂ, ਤੁਰਮ ਬੋਲਣਾ, ਬੁਰਦ ਲਾਉਣੀ, (ਵਿਦਾਈ ਵੇਲੇ) ਨਮਸਕਾਰ ਕਹਿਣਾ; **~der** ਬੋਲੀ ਦੇਣ ਵਾਲਾ

biennial (ਬਾਇ'ਐਨਿਅਲ) *a* ਦੋ ਸਾਲ ਵਿਚ ਹੋਣ ਵਾਲਾ, ਦੋ-ਬਰਸੀ, ਦੋ-ਸਾਲਾ ਬਿਰਛ ਜਾਂ ਪੌਦਾ ਜਿਹੜਾ ਦੋ ਵਰ੍ਹੇ ਰਹੇ ਜਾਂ ਦੂਜੇ ਸਾਲ ਫੁੱਲ ਤੇ ਫਲ ਦੇਵੇ

bier (ਬਿਅ*) ਅਰਥੀ, ਮੁਰਦਾ ਲੈ ਜਾਣ ਵਾਲੀ ਗੱਡੀ, ਜਨਾਜ਼ਾ, ਤਖ਼ਤਾ, ਤਾਬੂਤ, ਬਿਬਾਣ

bifurcate ('ਬਾਇਫ਼ਅਕੇਇਟ) *v a* ਦੋ ਹਿੱਸਿਆਂ ਵਿਚ ਵੰਡਣਾ, ਦੋ ਫਾਂਕਾਂ ਕਰਨੀਆਂ, ਦੁਫਾਂਟਣਾ, ਦੁਫਾੜ ਕਰਨਾ ਜਾਂ ਹੋਣਾ, ਦੋਫਾੜਾ

bifurcation ('ਬਾਇਫ਼ਆ'ਕੇਇਸ਼ਨ) *n* ਦੁਸਾਂਗ, ਦੁਫਾਂਟਣ; ਫਾਂਟ, ਦੋ ਸ਼ਾਖ਼ਾਂ ਵਿਚ ਵੰਡ, ਦੋ ਸ਼ਾਖ਼ਾਂ ਜਾਂ ਉਨ੍ਹਾਂ ਵਿਚੋਂ ਇਕ

big (ਬਿਗ) *a v* ਵੱਡਾ, ਵਿਸ਼ਾਲ; ਮਹਾਨ, ਮੁਖੀਆ; ਫੁੱਲਿਆ; ਉਭਰਿਆ; ਪੂਰਨ, ਉਦਾਰ; ਉੱਚਾ; **~bellied** ਗਰਭਵਤੀ; **~talk** ਸ਼ੇਖ਼ੀ ਮਾਰਨਾ;

bigamy ('ਬਿਗਅਮਿ) *n* ਦੁਪਤਨੀਤਵ, ਇਕ ਪਤੀ ਦਾ ਪਤਨੀ ਦੇ ਹੁੰਦੇ ਹੋਏ ਦੂਜਾ ਵਿਆਹ

bigot ('ਬਿਗਅਟ) *n* ਕੱਟੜਪੰਥੀ, ਤੁਅੱਸਬੀ, ਹਠਧਰਮੀ; **~ry** ਕੱਟੜਪੁਣਾ, ਤੁਅੱਸਬ, ਹਠਧਰਮੀ

billingual (ਬਾਇ'ਲਿਙਗਵਲ) *a* ਦੁਭਾਸ਼ੀਆ, ਦੋ ਭਾਸ਼ਾਵਾਂ ਲਿਖਣ, ਬੋਲਣ ਜਾਂ ਜਾਣਨ ਵਾਲਾ

bill (ਬਿਲ) *n* (1) ਬੀਜਕ, ਹੁੰਡੀ, ਹਿਸਾਬ ਦੀ ਪਰਚੀ, ਰਸੀਦ, ਬਿਲ; (2) ਵਿਧੇਕ (ਕਾ); (3) ਇਸ਼ਤਿਹਾਰ; (4) ਗੰਡਾਸਾ, ਫਰਸਾ, ਲੰਗਰ ਦੀ ਫਾਲ ਦੀ ਨੋਕ; ਚੁੰਝਾਂ ਭਰਨੀਆਂ, ਲਾਡ ਕਰਨਾ, ਚੁੰਮਣਾ-ਚੱਟਣਾ; **~and coo** ਪਿਆਰ ਕਰਨਾ, ਕਲੋਲ ਕਰਨਾ, ਇਕ ਦੂਜੇ ਨੂੰ ਚੁੰਮਣਾ; **~book** ਵਹੀ ਖਾਤਾ, ਬਿਲ ਕੱਟਣ ਵਾਲੀ ਕਾਪੀ; **~of exchange** ਹੁੰਡੀ; **~sticking** ਇਸ਼ਤਿਹਾਰ ਲਾਉਣਾ

billion ('ਬਿਲਯਅਨ) *n* ਇਕ ਅਰਬ

binary ('ਬਾਇਨਰਿ) *a n* ਦੂਹਰਾ, ਜੋੜੇਦਾਰ, ਦੋ-ਅੰਗੀ, ਯੁਗਮ; **~system** ਦੋ ਆਧਾਰੀ ਪ੍ਰਣਾਲੀ

bind (ਬਾਈਂਡ) *v* ਜਿਲਦ ਬੰਨ੍ਹਣਾ, ਪੱਟੀ ਬੰਨ੍ਹਣਾ, ਗੋਟਾ ਕਿਨਾਰੀ ਲਗਾਉਣਾ, ਅਧਿਕਾਰ ਨੂੰ ਵਰਤਣਾ, ਲਾਗੂ ਕਰਨਾ, ਪੱਕਾ ਕਰਨਾ, ਪੱਕਾ ਕਰਾਉਣਾ; ਜੁੜਨਾ, ਸੰਯੁਕਤ ਹੋਣਾ; **~er** ਬੰਨ੍ਹਣ ਵਾਲਾ, ਜਿਲਦਸਾਜ਼; ਅਖਬਾਰ ਜਾਂ ਕਾਗ਼ਜ਼ਾਂ ਨੂੰ ਰੱਖਣ ਲਈ ਫਾਈਲ; **~ing** ਜਿਲਦਸਾਜ਼ੀ, ਪੱਟੀ, ਗੋਟਾ, ਬੰਧਨ, ਬੰਦਸ਼

binocular ('ਬਿ'ਨੋਂਕਲ) *n* ਦੂਰਬੀਨ, ਦੋ-ਨੇਤਰੀ, ਦੋ-ਅੱਖੀ

bio ('ਬਾਇਅਉ) ਜੀਵ, ਜਾਨਦਾਰ, ਪ੍ਰਾਣੀ; **~chemistry** ਜੀਵ-ਰਸਾਇਣਕੀ; **~physics** ਜੀਵ-ਭੌਤਕੀ; **~scope** ਚਲ-ਚਿੱਤਰਪਟ

biography (ਬਾਇ'ਔਗਰਅਫ਼ਿ) *n* ਜੀਵਨੀ, ਜੀਵਨਬਿਰਤਾਂਤ, ਜੀਵਨ-ਕਥਾ, ਜੀਵਨ-ਚਰਿੱਤਰ

biology (ਬਾਇ'ਔਲਅਜਿ) *n* ਜੀਵ-ਵਿਗਿਆਨ

bipartite ('ਬਾਈ'ਪਾਟਾਇਟ) *a* ਦੋ-ਪੱਖ, ਦੋ-ਭਾਗੀ, ਦੋ-ਖੰਡਕੀਆ

bipartition ('ਬਾਇਪਾ'ਟਿਸ਼ਨ) *n* ਦੋ-ਹਿੱਸਿਆਂ ਵਿਚ ਵੰਡ, ਦੁਤਾਜਨ

bipolar (ਬਾਇ'ਪਅਉਲਅ*) *a* ਦੋ-ਧਰੁਵੀ

bird (ਬਅ*ਡ) *n v* ਪੰਛੀ, ਪੰਖੇਰੂ, ਮੁਟਿਆਰ; (ਅਪ) ਚੂਰਾ, ਕੁੜੀ; ਪੰਛੀਆਂ ਦਾ ਸ਼ਿਕਾਰ ਕਰਨਾ ਜਾਂ ਫਸਾਉਣਾ; **~'s eye view** ਪੰਛੀ-ਝਾਤ

birth (ਬਅਃਥ) *n* ਜਨਮ, ਪੈਦਾਇਸ਼ ਜੂਨ, ਉਤਪਤੀ, ਆਰੰਭ, ਮੂਲ; ਨਸਲ, ਜਾਤੀ; ਕੁਲੀਨਤਾ; **~control** ਸੰਤਾਨ-ਸੰਜਮ; **~day** ਜਨਮ-ਦਿਨ, ਵਰ੍ਹੇ-ਗੰਢ; **~place** ਜਨਮ-ਭੂਮੀ, ਜਨਮ-ਸਥਾਨ;

~rate ਜੰਮਣ-ਦਰ, ਜਨਮ ਦਰ; **~right** ਜਮਾਂਦਰੂ ਹੱਕ, ਪੈਦਾਇਸ਼ੀ ਹੱਕ

biscuit (ਬਿਸਕਿਟ) *n* ਬਿਸਕੁਟ, ਖਤਾਈ

bisect (ਬਾਈਸੈਂਕਟ) *v* ਦੋ-ਟੁੱਕ ਕਰਨਾ, ਅੱਧੋ-ਅੱਧ ਕਰਨਾ, ਦੋ ਹਿੱਸਿਆਂ ਵਿਚ ਕੱਟਣਾ, ਵਿਚੋਂ ਟੁੱਕਣਾ

bishop ('ਬਿਸ਼ਅਪ) *n* (1) ਵੱਡਾ ਪਾਦਰੀ, ਬਿਸ਼ਪ; (2) ਮਸਾਲੇਦਾਰ ਸ਼ਰਾਬ; ਟੋਪੀ ਵਰਗੀ ਸ਼ਕਲ ਦਾ, (ਸ਼ਤਰੰਜ ਵਿਚ) ਫੀਲਾ

bit (ਬਿਟ) *n v* (1) ਟੁਕੜਾ, ਟੋਟਾ; ਗਰਾਹੀ, ਬੁਰਕੀ, ਟੁੱਕਰ, ਟੁੱਕ; (2) ਛੋਟਾ ਸਿੱਕਾ; (3) ਲਗਾਮ ਦਾ ਕੰਡਿਆਲਾ; ਚਾਬੀ ਦੇ ਦੰਦ; ਸੰਨ੍ਹੀ ਦਾ ਸਿਰਾ; ਵਰਮੇ ਦੀ ਅਟੀ, ਨੋਕ, ਸਿਰਾ; ਰੋਕ; ਲਗਾਮ ਦਾ ਆਦੀ ਬਣਾਉਣਾ; ਕਾਬੂ ਪਾਉਣਾ, ਰੋਕਣਾ, ਵਸ ਵਿਚ ਕਰਨਾ

bitch (ਬਿਚ) *n* ਕੁੱਤੀ; ਲੂੰਬੜੀ; ਲੁੱਚੀ ਰੰਨ

bite (ਬਾਇਟ) *n v* ਕੱਟਣਾ, ਵੱਢਣਾ, ਦੰਦੀ ਵੱਢਣੀ, ਤੋੜਨਾ, ਡੰਗਣਾ; ਚਾਰੇ ਤੇ ਮੂੰਹ ਮਾਰਨਾ; ਘੋਰਨਾ, ਖਾਰਨਾ

biting ('ਬਾਇਟਿਙ) *a* ਤੇਜ਼, ਤਿਖਾ, ਤੀਬਰ, ਵੱਢਦਾ, ਚੁਭਵਾਂ, ਕਾਟਵਾਂ

bitter (ਬਿਟਅ*) *a* ਕੌੜਾ ਤਿੱਖਾ, ਕੁੜ੍ਹੰਗਾ; ਦੁਖਾਵਾਂ; **~ness*** ਕੜੂਤਾ, ਤੀਖਣਤਾ, ਕਠੋਰਤਾ, ਕੁੜੱਤਣ, ਤਿਖਾਪਣ

bi-weekly ('ਬਾਇ'ਵਿਕਲਿ) *a* ਦੋ-ਸਪਤਾਹਕ

bizarre (ਬਿ'ਜ਼ਾ*) *a* ਅਦਭੁਤ, ਅਨੋਖਾ, ਵਿਲੱਖਣ

black (ਬਲੈਕ) *a n v* ਕਾਲਾ, ਮੁਸ਼ਕੀ, ਸ਼ੁੰਦਲਾ; ਮੈਲਾ, ਗੰਦਾ, ਮਲੀਨ (ਕੱਪੜਾ, ਹੱਥ); ਹਨੇਰਾ; ਪਾਪੀ, ਅਤੀਅੰਤ ਬੁਰਾ; ਨਿਰਾਸ਼ਾਜਨਕ, ਡਰਾਉਣਾ; ਧੱਬਾ; ਕਾਲਖ, ਕਾਲਾ ਰੰਗ; ਕਾਜਲ, ਹਬਸ਼ੀ; ਕਾਲੀ ਚਮੜੀ ਵਾਲਾ; ਕਾਲਾ ਕਰਨਾ; ਰੰਗ ਚੜ੍ਹਾਉਣਾ, ਕਾਲੀ ਪਾਲਸ਼ ਕਰਨਾ; **~ and**

blue ਮਾਰ ਕੁਟਾਈ ਨਾਲ ਪਏ ਨੀਲ; ~ and white ਸਾਦਾ, ਲਿਖਿਆ ਹੋਇਆ, ਸਿਆਹੀ ਨਾਲ ਲਿਖਿਆ; ਕਾਲੀ ਅਤੇ ਚਿੱਟੀ ਤਸਵੀਰ; ~art ਜਾਦੂ; ਟੂਣਾ; ~board ਬਲੈਕ ਬੋਰਡ; ~draught ਜੁਲਾਬ; ~list ਅਪਰਾਧੀਆਂ ਦੀ ਸੂਚੀ, ਕਾਨੂੰਨ ਤੋੜਨ ਵਾਲਿਆਂ ਦੀ ਸੂਚੀ, ਸ਼ੱਕੀ ਲੋਕਾਂ ਦੀ ਸੂਚੀ; ~mail ਭੇਤ ਲੁਕਾਈ ਰੱਖਣ ਦੀ ਵੱਢੀ, ਬਲੈਕਮੇਲ; ~market ਚੋਰ-ਬਜ਼ਾਰੀ; ~out ਆਰਜ਼ੀ ਹਨੇਰਾ, ਬਲੈਕ ਆਊਟ; ਚੇਤਨਾ ਸ਼ਕਤੀ ਦਾ ਅਭਾਵ, ਨ੍ਹੇਰਨੀ; ~smith ਲੁਹਾਰ; ~en ਕਾਲਾ ਕਰਨਾ ਜਾਂ ਹੋਣਾ, ਕੰਲਕ ਲਗਾਉਣਾ, ਬਦਨਾਮੀ ਕਰਨੀ, ਨਿੰਦਣਾ, ਬੁਰਾ ਕਹਿਣਾ; ~ness ਅੰਧਕਾਰ, ਕਾਲਾਪਣ, ਸਿਆਹੀ, ਕਾਲਿਮਾ

bladder (ਬਲੈਡਾਅ') *n* ਭੁਕਨਾ; ਫੁੱਲੀ ਹੋਈ ਖ਼ਾਲੀ ਚੀਜ਼, ਬਲੈਡਰ; ਮਸਾਨਾ, ਹਵਾ ਦਾ ਥੈਲਾ, ਫਲੂਸ; ਗਾਲੜੀ ਮਨੁੱਖ, ਬਾਤੂਨੀ

blade (ਬਲੇਇਡ) *n* ਪੱਤਰ, ਪੱਤੀ, ਤ੍ਰਿਣ; (ਚਾਕੂ, ਤਲਵਾਰ, ਛੁਰੀ, ਕਹੀ, ਚੱਪੂ ਆਦਿ ਦਾ) ਫਲ; ਤਲਵਾਰ, (ਹਜ਼ਾਮਤ ਕਰਨ ਵਾਲਾ) ਬਲੇਡ; ਬੱਲੇ ਜਾਂ ਚੱਪੂ ਦੀ ਥਾਪੀ; ਮੋਢੇ ਦੀ ਚੌੜੀ ਹੱਡੀ; ਤਿੱਖਾ ਬੰਦਾ, ਛੁਰੀ

blame (ਬਲੇਮ) *v n* ਦੋਸ਼ ਲਾਉਣਾ, ਦੋਸ਼ ਥੱਪਣਾ, ਭੰਡਣਾ, ਉਜ ਲਾਉਣੀ, ਨਿੰਦਾ ਕਰਨੀ, ਅਪਰਾਧੀ ਠਹਿਰਾਉਣਾ; ਦੋਸ਼, ਐਬ, ਇਲਜ਼ਾਮ; ~less ਬਿਦੋਸ਼ਾ, ਨਿਦੋਸ਼ਾ, ਬੇਕਸੂਰ, ਨਿਰਦੋਸ਼

blandish (ਬਲੈਂਡਿਸ਼) *v* ਪਸਮਾਉਣਾ, ਭਰਮਾਉਣਾ, ਚਾਪਲੂਸੀ ਕਰਨਾ

blank (ਬਲੈਂਕ) *n a* ਖ਼ਾਲੀਪਣ, ਕੋਰਾ, ਸਾਦਾ (ਕਾਗ਼ਜ਼), ਖ਼ਾਲੀ, ਫੋਕਾ, ਬਿਨਾ ਦਸਤਖ਼ਤ ਤੋਂ; ਉੱਕਾ, ਨਿਰਾ; ~cheque ਕੋਰਾ ਚੈੱਕ; ~ness ਖ਼ਾਲੀਪਣ, ਕੋਰਾਪਣ, ਸਾਦਾਪਣ; ਘਬਰਾਹਟ

blanket ('ਬਲੈਂਕਿਟ) *n v* ਕੰਬਲ, ਝੁੱਲ; ਕੰਬਲ ਨਾਲ ਕੱਜਣਾ; ਹਵਾ ਰੋਕਣੀ

blaspheme (ਬਲੈਸਾਫ਼ੀਮ) *v* ਬੇਅਦਬੀ ਕਰਨੀ, ਕੁਫ਼ਰ ਤੋਲਣਾ, ਕੁਧਰਮੀ ਗੱਲਾਂ ਕਰਨੀਆਂ, ਬੇਅਦਬੀ ਦੇ ਸ਼ਬਦ ਵਰਤਣੇ

blasphemous (ਬਲੈਸਫ਼ਅਮਅਸ) *a* ਰੱਬ-ਨਿੰਦਕ, ਪਖੰਡੀ; ਕਾਫ਼ਰ, ਕੁਫ਼ਰੀ

blasphemy ('ਬਲੈਸਫ਼ਅਮਿ) *n* ਕੁਫ਼ਰ, ਕੁਫ਼ਰ ਦੇ ਲਫ਼ਜ਼, ਬੇਅਦਬੀ

blast (ਬਲਾਸਟ) *n v* (ਹਵਾ ਦਾ ਤੇਜ਼) ਬੁੱਲਾ, ਝੋਕਾਂ; ਬੰਬ ਦੇ ਫਟਣ ਦਾ ਧਮਾਕਾ, ਭੜਕ; (ਬਾਰੂਦ ਨਾਲ) ਉਡਾਉਣਾ; ਸਤਿਆ ਸੁਆਹ ਕਰਨਾ, ਝੁਲਸਾਉਣਾ, ਝੁਲਸ ਦੇਣਾ

blatancy ('ਬਲੇਇਟਅੰਸਿ) *n* ਹੁੱਲੜਬਾਜ਼ੀ, ਸ਼ੋਰ-ਸ਼ਰਾਬਾ

blatant ('ਬਲੇਇਟਅੰਟ) *a* ਰੌਲਾ-ਪਾਊ, ਖਪ ਪਾਉਣ ਵਾਲਾ

blaze (ਬਲੇਇਜ਼) *n v* ਭਾਂਬੜ, ਲਾਟ, ਲਪਟ, ਲੂੰਆ, ਜੋਸ਼, ਭੜਕ; ਤੜਕ-ਭੜਕ, ਠਾਠ-ਬਾਠ, ਜਗ-ਮਗ, ਚਕਾਚੌਂਧ, ਲਾਟਾਂ ਨਾਲ ਬਲਣਾ; ਜੋਸ਼ ਵਿਚ ਲਾਉਣਾ, ਭੜਕ ਉੱਠਣਾ; ਚਮਕ ਪੈਣਾ

bleach (ਬਲੀਚ) *v n* ਰੰਗ ਉਡਾਉਣਾ, ਖੁੰਭ ਕਰਨਾ, ਚਿਟਿਆਉਣਾ; ਚਿੱਟਾ ਕਰਨਾ ਪੋਣ ਦਾ ਮਸਾਲਾ; ~ing ਸਫ਼ੈਦ ਕਰਨ ਦੀ ਕਿਰਿਆ, ਕੱਪੜਿਆਂ ਨੂੰ ਸਫ਼ੈਦ ਕਰਨ ਦੀ ਕਲਾ; ~ing-power (ਰਸਾ) ਕਲੋਰੀਨ ਅਤੇ ਆਕਸੀਜਨ ਦਾ ਮਿਸ਼ਰਣ, ਚੂਨੇ ਦਾ ਕਲੋਰਾਈਡ, ਰੰਗ ਉਡਾਉਣ ਵਾਲਾ ਪਾਊਡਰ, ਸਿਠਾ ਸੋਡਾ

bleak (ਬਲੀਕ) *a n* ਵੀਰਾਨ, ਬੇਰੰਗ, ਫਿੱਕਾ, ਪੀਲਾ; ਉਦਾਸ, ਉਤਸ਼ਾਹਹੀਣ; ਠੰਢਾ, ਨੰਗਾ,

ਖੁੱਲ੍ਹਾ (ਮੈਦਾਨ ਆਦਿ); ਭਿੰਨ-ਭਿੰਨ ਪ੍ਰਕਾਰ ਦੀਆਂ ਛੋਟੀਆਂ ਮੱਛੀਆਂ

bleed (ਬਲੀਡ) v ਲਹੂ ਵਗਣਾ ਜਾਂ ਵਗਾਉਣਾ; ਖ਼ੂਨ ਹੋਣਾ, ਲਹੂ ਚੁਸਣਾ

blench (ਬਲੈਂਚ) v ਝਿਜਕਣਾ, ਸਹਿਮਣਾ, ਸੰਕੋਚ ਵਿਚ ਹੋਣਾ, ਪਿਛੇ ਹਟਣਾ; ਜਾਨ ਬੁੱਝ ਕੇ ਅਨਜਾਨ ਬਨਣਾ, ਅੱਖ ਬਟਾਉਣਾ, ਕੰਨੀ ਕਤਰਾਉਣਾ; ਟਾਲਣਾ

blend (ਬਲੈਂਡ) v n ਰਲਾਉਣਾ; ਘੋਲਨਾ, ਘੁਲਨਾ, ਮਿਲਾਉਣਾ; ਇਕ ਦੂਜੇ ਵਿਚ ਮਿਲਾਵਟ

bless (ਬਲੈੱਸ) v ਅਸੀਸ ਦੇਣੀ, ਵਰ ਦੇਣਾ, ਆਸ਼ੀਰਵਾਦ ਦੇਣੀ (ਪਿਤਾ, ਭਾਈ ਆਦਿ ਦੀ), ਰੱਬੀ ਮਿਹਰ ਮੰਗਣੀ; ਨਿਹਾਲ ਕਰਨਾ, ਮਿਹਰ ਕਰਨੀ; ~**ed** ਪਵਿੱਤਰ, ਪਾਵਨ, ਮੁਬਾਰਕ, ਪੁਨੀਤ, ਧੰਨ, ਸੁਭਾਗਸ਼ਾਲੀ; ਪੂਜਨੀਕ; ~**ing** ਅਸੀਸ, ਅਸ਼ੀਰਵਾਦ, ਵਰਦਾਨ, ਬਰਕਤ, ਦੁਆ, ਰਹਿਮਤ, ਮਿਹਰ, ਫ਼ਜ਼ਲ

blind (ਬਲਾਇੰਡ) a v n ਅੰਨ੍ਹਾ, ਨੇਤਰਹੀਨ, ਮਨਾਖ਼; ਅਗਿਆਨੀ, ਬੁੱਧੂ; ਅੰਨ੍ਹੇ-ਵਾਹ, ਬੇਮਤਲਬ; ਅੰਧ ਕਰਨਾ; ਧੋਖ ਦੇਣਾ; ~**born** ਜਨਮਾਂਧ, ਜਨਮ ਤੋਂ ਅੰਨ੍ਹਾ; ~**follower** ਪਿੱਛ-ਲੱਗ, ਬਿਨਾਂ ਸੋਚੇ ਸਮਝੇ ਪਿੱਛੇ ਲੱਗਣ ਵਾਲਾ, ਅੰਧ ਵਿਸ਼ਵਾਸੀ; ~**ly** ਅੱਖਾਂ ਬੰਦ ਕਰਕੇ, ਬਿਨਾਂ ਸੋਚੇ ਸਮਝੇ; ~**ness** ਅੰਨ੍ਹਾਪਣ; ਮੂਰਖਤਾ, ਅਗਿਆਨ, ਦ੍ਰਿਸ਼ਟੀ-ਹੀਣਤਾ, ਅਸਾਵਧਾਨੀ

blink (ਬਲਿੰਕ) v n ਅੱਖ ਝਮਕਣੀ, ਝਲਕਾਰਾ ਮਾਰਨਾ, ਪਲਕ ਮਾਰਨਾ; ਧਿਆਨ ਨਾ ਦੇਣਾ, ਟਾਲਣਾ, ਨਜ਼ਰੋਂ ਓਹਲੇ ਕਰ ਜਾਣਾ; ਝਲਕ, ਝਲਕਾਰਾ, ਦੂਰ ਦੀ ਬਰਫ਼ ਦਾ ਲਿਸ਼ਕਾਰਾ

bliss (ਬਲਿਸ) n ਆਨੰਦ, ਸਰੂਰ, ਆਤਮਕ ਸੁਖ; ਸੁਰਗ; ~**ful** ਆਨੰਦਪੂਰਨ, ਆਨੰਦਤ, ਸੁਖੀ,

ਮਗਨ, ਵਿਸਮਾਦੀ; ~**fully** ਪਰਮਆਨੰਦੀ ਸਖਿਤੀ ਵਿਚ, ਆਨੰਦਪੂਰਵਕ ਹਾਲਤ ਵਿਚ

blitz (ਬਲਿਟਸ) n v ਤਗੜਾ ਤੇ ਅਚਾਨਕ ਹਮਲਾ, ਤਿੱਖਾ ਹਮਲਾ, (ਰਾਜਨੀਤੀ ਵਿਚ) ਡੂੰਘੀ ਚਾਲ; ਹਮਲੇ ਨਾਲ ਤਬਾਹੀ ਕਰਨੀ

blizzard ('ਬਲਿਜ਼ਅਡ) n ਬਰਫ਼ ਦਾ ਤੇਜ਼ ਤੂਫ਼ਾਨ, ਬਰਫ਼ੀਲਾ ਤੂਫ਼ਾਨ, ਬਰਫ਼ਾਨੀ ਹਨੇਰੀ

bloc (ਬਲੌਕ) n ਦਲ, ਗੁੱਟ, (ਰਾਜਸੀ) ਦਲਾਂ ਦਾ ਸੰਗਠਨ

block (ਬਲੌਕ) n v (ਲੱਕੜ ਦਾ) ਅੱਡਾ (ਜਿਸ ਉੱਤੇ ਰੱਖ ਕੇ ਲੱਕੜ ਰੰਦਦੇ ਜਾਂ ਠੋਕਦੇ ਹਨ); ਮਕਾਨਾਂ ਦਾ ਸਿਲਸਲਾ, ਬਲਾਕ, ਮਹੱਲਾ; ਰੋਕ; (ਪਾਰਲੀਮੈਂਟ) ਬਿਲ ਦਾ ਵਿਰੋਧ ਕਰਨ ਦੀ ਸੂਚਨ; ਅਟਕਾਉਣਾ, ਰੋਕ ਪਾਉਣੀ, ਰੋਕਣਾ, ਘੇਰਨਾ, ਬੰਦ ਕਰਨਾ; ~**ade** ਘੇਰਾ, ਨਾਕਾਬੰਦੀ, ਡੱਕਾ; ਘੇਰਾ ਘੱਤਣਾ, ਨਾਕਾਬੰਦੀ ਕਰਨੀ, ਡੱਕਾ ਲਾਉਣਾ, ਰੋਕਣਾ, ਰਾਹ ਰੋਕਣਾ; ~**ed** ਰੁਕਿਆ ਹੋਇਆ; ~**head** ਮੂਰਖ, ਉੱਜ, ਉੱਲੂ-ਬਾਟਾ, ਮੂੜ੍ਹ; ~**ish** ਮੂਰਖ, ਬੁੱਧੂ, ਹਠੀ, ਕਠੋਰ ਹਿਰਦਾ

blood (ਬਲਅੱਡ) n v ਲਹੂ, ਖ਼ੂਨ; ਰੱਤ; ਅੰਗੂਰ ਜਾਂ ਕਿਸੇ ਬੂਟੇ ਦਾ ਰਸ; ਨਸਲ, ਵੰਸ; ਉਕਸਾਉਣਾ, ਉਤੇਜਤ ਕਰਨਾ; ~**is thicker than water** ਆਪਣਾ ਆਪਣਾ ਗ਼ੈਰ ਗ਼ੈਰ; ~**pressure** ਬਲੱਡ-ਪ੍ਰੈਸ਼ਰ, ਲਹੂ ਦਾ ਦਬਾ; ~**shed** ਖ਼ੂਨ-ਖ਼ਰਾਬਾ; ~**sucker** ਰੱਤ-ਪੀਣਾ, ਲਹੂ-ਚੂਸ, ਜੋਕ, ਜਾਬਰ, ਜਰਵਾਣਾ, ਜ਼ਾਲਮ; ~**thirsty** ਲਹੂ-ਤਿਹਾਇਆ, ਖ਼ੂਨੀ, ਜ਼ਾਲਮ; ~**worm** ਲਾਲ ਕੀੜਾ; **blue~** ਉੱਚੇ ਖ਼ਾਨਦਾਨ ਵਿਚ ਪੈਦਾਇਸ, ਕੁਲੀਨਤਾ; **half~** ਸੌਤੇਲਾ; **hot~ed** ਅਤੀ ਕਰੋਧੀ; **young~** ਨਵਯੁਵਕ, ਨਵਾਂ ਸਦੱਸ

bloom (ਬਲੂਮ) *n v* ਫੁੱਲ, ਪੁਸ਼ਪ; ਬਹਾਰ; ਜੋਬਨ, ਜਵਾਨੀ, ਚਮਕ, ਤੇਜ, ਲਾਲੀ, ਰੌਣਕ, ਤਾਜ਼ਗੀ; ਮੁਨੱਕਾ ਕਿਸ਼ਮਿਸ਼; ਫੁੱਲਣਾ, ਪੂਰੇ ਜੋਬਨ ਵਿਚ ਆਉਣਾ, ਪ੍ਰਫੁੱਲਤ ਹੋਣਾ, ਬਹਾਰ ਆਉਣੀ; **~y** ਪ੍ਰਫੁਲਤ, ਖਿੜਿਆ

blossom ('ਬਲੌਸ(ਅ)ਮ) *n v* ਬੂਟੇ ਦੀ ਕਲੀ, ਸ਼ਗੂਫ਼ਾ; ਹੋਣਹਾਰਪੁਣਾ, ਵਧਣ ਮੌਲਣ ਦੇ ਦਿਨ, ਜੋਬਨ; ਖਿੜਨਾ (ਫੁੱਲ ਦਾ), ਫੁੱਲ ਲੱਗਣੇ

blot (ਬਲੌਟ) *n v* ਧੱਬਾ, ਡੱਬ, ਦਾਗ਼; ਕਲੰਕ, ਦੋਸ਼, ਔਗੁਣ, ਨੁਕਸ, ਐਬ, ਧੱਬਾ ਲੱਗਣਾ; ਧੱਬੇ ਲਾਉਣਾ; ਸਿਆਹੀ-ਚੂਸ ਨਾਲ ਸੁਕਾਉਣਾ

blow (ਬਲਅਉ) *v* (ਹਵਾ ਦਾ) ਚੱਲਣਾ, ਝੁੱਲਣਾ, ਰੁਮਕਣਾ; ਆਰਗਨ ਵਾਜਾ ਵਜਾਉਣਾ; ਧੌਂਕਣੀ ਨਾਲ ਹਵਾ ਦੇਣਾ, ਧੌਂਕਣਾ; ਸਾਹ ਬਾਹਰ ਕੱਢਣਾ, ਫੂਕ ਮਾਰਨਾ; ਉਡਾਉਣਾ; ਧਿਕਾਰਨਾ; **~out** ਬੁਝਾਉਣਾ; **~pipe** ਫੂਕਣੀ, ਧੌਂਕਣੀ

blowze (ਬਲਾਉਜ਼) *n* ਕੋਝੀ ਔਰਤ

blue (ਬਲੂ) ਨੀਲਾ, ਅਸਮਾਨੀ; ਨੀਲਾ ਰੰਗ; ਨੀਲ; ਨੀਲੱਤਣ; ਨੀਲਾ, ਕੱਪੜਾ, ਅਸਮਾਨ; ਸਮੁੰਦਰ; **~moon** ਅਣਘਟੀ ਘਟਨਾ; **once in a ~moon** ਕਦੇ ਕਦੇ, ਭੁੱਲੇ ਭਟਕੇ

bluff (ਬਲੱਫ) *v n* ਉੱਲੂ ਬਣਾਉਣਾ, ਮੂਰਖ ਬਣਾਉਣਾ, ਰੋਅਬ ਪਾਉਣ ਦੀ ਨੀਤੀ ਅਪਨਾਉਣਾ; ਗਿੱਦੜ ਭਬਕੀ, ਫੋਕੀ ਧੌਂਸ

blunder ('ਬਲਅੰਡਅ*) *v n* ਭਾਰੀ ਭੁੱਲ ਕਰਨੀ, ਗੜਬੜ ਕਰਨੀ, ਵਿਗਾੜ ਦੇਣਾ, ਖ਼ਰਾਬ ਕਰਨਾ; ਭਾਰੀ ਭੁੱਲ, ਗ਼ਲਤੀ, ਦੋਸ਼; ਅਸ਼ੁੱਧੀ

blunt (ਬਲਅੰਟ) *a n v* ਖੁੰਢਾ, ਕੁੰਦ; ਦੋ-ਟੱਕ; ਕੋਰਾ, ਰੁਖਾ, ਖਰਾ-ਖਰਾ, ਮੂੰਹ-ਫੱਟ, ਮੋਟੀ ਖੰਦੂਈ, ਛੋਟਾ ਸੂਆ; ਨਕਦ ਮਾਲ; ਖੁੰਢਾ ਕਰਨਾ, ਮੱਤ ਮਾਰਨਾ; ਕਮਜ਼ੋਰ ਕਰਨਾ; **~ness** ਖੁੰਢਾਪਣ, ਸਪਸ਼ਟਵਾਦਤਾ; ਅੱਖੜਪਣ

blur (ਬਲਅ:*) *n v* ਧੁੰਦਲਾਪਣ, ਅਸਪਸ਼ਟਤਾ; ਸਿਆਹੀ ਆਦਿ ਦਾ ਦਾਗ਼, ਧੱਬਾ; ਧੁੰਦਲਾਪਣ, ਧੁੰਦਲਾ ਕਰ ਦੇਣਾ, ਅਸਪਸ਼ਟ ਕਰਨਾ; ਧੱਬੇ ਪੈਣੇ

blush (ਬਲਅੱਸ਼) *n v* ਸ਼ਰਮਾ ਜਾਣਾ, ਸ਼ਰਮਾਉਣਾ, ਲਜਾਉਣਾ, ਸੰਕੋਚਣਾ; ਸ਼ਰਮ ਦੀ ਲਾਲੀ; ਝਲਕ, ਝਾਂਕੀ; **~ing** ਲੱਜਾਇਆ

board (ਬੋ:ਡ) *n v* ਬੋਰਡ, ਪਟੜਾ, ਫੱਟਾ, ਤਖਤਾ; ਜਹਾਜ਼ ਦਾ ਤਖ਼ਤਾ; ਰੰਗ-ਮੰਚ; ਮੰਡਲੀ; ਫੱਟਿਆਂ ਨਾਲ ਕੱਜਣਾ; ਗੱਡੀ ਜਾਂ ਜਹਾਜ਼ ਤੇ ਚੜ੍ਹਨਾ

boast (ਬਅਉਸਟ) *n v* ਸ਼ੇਖੀ, ਡੀਂਗ, ਫੜ; ਡੀਂਗ ਮਾਰਨੀ, ਸ਼ੇਖੀ ਮਾਰਨੀ, ਫੜ ਮਾਰਨੀ; **~ful** ਸ਼ੇਖ਼ੀ-ਖ਼ੋਰਾ, ਹੰਕਾਰੀ, ਫੜ-ਮਾਰ, ਗੱਪੀ; **~ing** ਸ਼ੇਖੀਬਾਜ਼ੀ, ਡੀਂਗਬਾਜ਼ੀ

boat (ਬਅਉਟ) *n v* ਬੇੜੀ, ਕਿਸ਼ਤੀ, ਨਾਵ, ਜਹਾਜ਼; ਬੇੜੀ ਵਿਚ ਜਾਣਾ, ਬੇੜੀ ਦੀ ਸੈਰ ਕਰਨੀ, ਬੇੜੀ ਚਲਾਉਣਾ; **~man** ਮੱਲਾਹ, ਖੇਵਟ; ਮਾਂਝੀ

bob (ਬੌਬ) *n v* ਵਾਲਾਂ ਦੀ ਲਟ, ਪਟੇ, ਲਟਕਣ; ਪਟੇ ਰਖਣੇ, ਛਾਂਗਣੇ ਮੂੰਹ ਨਾਲ ਫੜਨਾ, ਉਛਲਣਾ, ਕੁੱਦਣਾ, ਭੁੜਕਣਾ, ਟੱਪਣਾ; **~tail** ਦੁਮਕਟੀ; ਦੁਮਕਟਾ (ਪਸ਼ੂ)

bodice ('ਬੌਡਿਸ) *n* ਚੋਲੀ, ਅੰਗੀ, ਕੁੜਤੀ, ਬੰਡੀ

body ('ਬੌਡਿ) *n v* ਸਰੀਰ, ਤਨ, ਦੇਹ, ਪਿੰਡਾ; ਮਨੁੱਖ, ਬੰਦਾ, ਵਿਅਕਤੀ; ਲਾਸ਼, ਲੋਥ, ਲਿਖਤ ਜਾਂ ਮਜ਼ਮੂਨ ਦਾ ਪ੍ਰਧਾਨ ਅੰਗ; ਚੋਲੀ, ਧੜ; ਰੂਪ ਦੇਣਾ; ਆਕਾਰ ਚਿਤਵਨਾ, ਵਜੂਦ ਵਿਚ ਲਿਆਉਣ; **~guard** ਅੰਗ-ਰਖਿਅਕ, ਬਾਡੀਗਾਡ

bogie ('ਬਅਉਗਿ) *n* ਬੋਗੀ, ਰੇਲ ਦਾ ਡੱਬਾ

bogle ('ਬਅਉਗਲ) *n* ਭੂਤ, ਪਰੇਤ, ਹਊਆ; ਧੋਖਾ, ਚਿੜੀਆਂ ਨੂੰ ਡਰਾਉਣ ਲਈ ਖੇਤ ਵਿਚ

ਰੱਖੀ ਵਸਤੂ

bogus ('ਬਅਉਗਸ) *a* ਬਣਾਉਟੀ, ਨਕਲੀ, ਜਾਅਲੀ, ਮਿਥਿਆ, ਝੂਠੀ; ਨਿਕੰਮਾ

boil (ਬੌਇਲ) *n v* ਛਾਲਾ, ਉਠਾਅ; ਉਬਲਣਾ, ਉਬਾਲਣਾ, ਖੌਲਣਾ, ਉਬਾਲਾ ਆਉਣਾ; ਜੋਸ਼ ਖਾਣਾ; ਕੜ੍ਹਨਾ, ਕਾੜ੍ਹਨਾ; ਉਬਾਲਾ, ਉਬਾਲ; ਉਬਾਲ-ਦਰਜਾ; **~er** ਉਬਾਲਣ ਵਾਲਾ ਵੱਡਾ ਪਤੀਲਾ; ਭੱਠੀ

bold (ਬਅਉਲਡ) *a* ਦਲੇਰ, ਬਹਾਦਰ; ਹਿੰਮਤੀ, ਧੜੱਲੇਦਾਰ, ਜ਼ੋਰਦਾਰ, ਗਤੀਸ਼ੀਲ, ਬੇ-ਬਾਕ; ਸਪਸ਼ਟ; **~ness** ਹੌਸਲਾ; ਸਾਹਸ, ਨਿਡਰਤਾ, ਦਲੇਰੀ, ਸਪਸ਼ਟਤਾ

bolt (ਬਅਉਲਟ) *n v* ਚਿਟਕਣੀ; ਜੰਦਰੇ ਦੀ ਝੜ; ਕਾਬਲਿਆਂ ਨਾਲ ਕੱਸਣਾ; ਚਿਟਕਣੀ ਮਾਰਨੀ, ਬੰਦ ਕਰਨਾ (ਦਰਵਾਜ਼ਾ), ਨੱਠ ਜਾਣਾ, ਨਿਗਲ ਜਾਣਾ, ਹੜੱਪ ਕਰ ਜਾਣਾ; **~from the blue** ਦੈਵੀ ਆਪੱਤੀ, ਅਚਿੰਤੇ ਬਾਜ, ਅਚਾਨਕ, ਘਟਨਾ, ਅਚਨਚੇਤ ਮੁਸੀਬਤ

bomb (ਬੌਮ) *n v* ਬੰਬ ਦਾ ਗੋਲਾ; ਬੰਬ ਮਾਰਨਾ, ਬੰਬਾਰੀ ਕਰਨਾ, ਬੰਬ ਚਲਾਉਣਾ, ਗੋਲੇ ਵਰ੍ਹਾਉਣਾ; **~ard** ਬੰਬ ਮਾਰ ਕੇ ਨਾਸ ਕਰਨਾ, ਗੋਲੀਆਂ ਜਾਂ ਗੋਲੇ ਵਰ੍ਹਾਉਣਾ, ਗੋਲਾਬਾਰੀ ਕਰਨੀ; **~er** ਬੰਬਾਰੀ ਕਰਨ ਵਾਲਾ ਜਹਾਜ਼, ਗੋਲਾ ਮਾਰ, ਬੰਬ ਸੁੱਟਣ ਵਾਲਾ ਫ਼ੌਜੀ

bonafide ('ਬਅਉਨ'ਅਫ਼ਾਇਡਿ) *a* ਅਸਲੀ, ਵਾਸਤਵਿਕ, ਪ੍ਰਮਾਣਕ, ਸਦਭਾਵੀ, ਨਿਸ਼ਕਪਟ

bonanza (ਬਅ(ਉ)'ਨੈਂਜ਼ਅ) *n* ਗੱਫਾ

bond (ਬੌਂਡ) *n v* (1) ਸਬੰਧ, ਜੋੜ; (2) ਬੰਨ੍ਹਣ, ਕੈਦ; (3) ਇਕਰਾਰਨਾਮਾ, ਮੁਚੱਲਕਾ, ਲਿਖਤ, ਅਸ਼ਟਾਮ, ਬਾਂਡ; ਬੰਨ੍ਹਣਾ, ਜੋੜਨਾ; ਉਧਾਰ ਲਿਖਤ ਕਰਨਾ; ਚੁੰਗੀ ਲੱਗਾਣ ਵਾਲੇ ਮਾਲ ਨੂੰ ਮਾਲਗੁਦਾਮ ਵਿਚ ਬੰਦ ਰੱਖਣਾ; **~holder** ਬਾਂਡਧਾਰੀ, ਜਿਸ ਪਾਸ ਇਕਰਾਰਨਾਮੇ ਦੀ ਲਿਖਤ ਹੋਵੇ; **~age** ਬੰਨ੍ਹਣ, ਬੰਦਸ਼, ਬੰਧੇਜ, ਬੰਦੀ, ਪਾਬੰਦੀ, ਅਧੀਨਤਾ, ਦਾਸਤਾ, ਗ਼ੁਲਾਮੀ, ਕੈਦ; **~man** ਦਾਸ, ਗ਼ੁਲਾਮ; **~woman** ਦਾਸੀ

bone (ਬਅਉਨ) *n v* ਹੱਡੀ, ਅਸਥੀ; ਪਸ਼ੂਆਂ ਦੇ ਸੁੱਕੇ ਪਿੰਜਰ, ਅਸਥੀਆਂ, ਫੁੱਲ; (ਅਪ) ਚੋਰੀ ਕਰਨਾ, ਚੁਰਾਉਣਾ; **~head** (ਅਪ) ਮੂਰਖ, ਬੁੱਧੂ, ਮੂੜ੍ਹ ਵਿਅਕਤੀ, ਉੱਲੂ; **~of contention** ਲੜਾਈ-ਝਗੜੇ ਦੀ ਜੜ੍ਹ; **flesh and~** ਹੱਡੀਆਂ ਦੀ ਮੁੱਠ

bonfire ('ਬੌਨ'ਫ਼ਾਇਅ*) *n* ਧੂੰਈ; ਲੋਹੜੀ, ਉਸਤਵ-ਅਗਨੀ, ਪੁਰਬ-ਅਗਨੀ, ਭਾਂਬੜ; ਕੂੜਾ-ਕਰਕਟ ਸਾੜਨ ਲਈ ਬਾਲੀ ਅੱਗ

bonne (ਬੌਨ) *n* ਖਿਡਾਵੀ, ਨੌਕਰਾਣੀ, ਆਯਾ, ਦਾਸੀ

bonnet ('ਬੌਨਿਟ) *n v* ਤੀਵੀਆਂ ਦੀ ਅੰਗਰੇਜ਼ੀ ਟੋਪੀ, ਮਰਦਾਂ ਦੀ ਟੋਪੀ, ਬੋਨਟ; ਸਿਰ ਤੇ ਟੋਪੀ ਰਖਣੀ; ਟੋਪੀ ਨਾਲ ਮੂੰਹ ਢਕਣਾ, ਅੱਖਾਂ ਤੀਕ ਖਿੱਚ ਕੇ ਟੋਪੀ ਲਿਆਉਣੀ

bonny ('ਬੌਨਿ) *a* ਸੋਹਣਾ, ਸੁੰਦਰ; ਅਲਬੇਲਾ

bonus ('ਬਅਉਨਅਸ) *n* ਬੋਨਸ, ਵਾਧੂ ਨਫਾ, ਝੂੰਗ

bon voyage ('ਬੌਨਵ੍ਵਾ'ਯਾਯ਼) *(F)* ਰੱਬ ਰਾਖਾ! ਅਲਵਿਦਾ! ਯਾਤਰਾ ਸੰਬੰਧੀ ਸ਼ੁਭ ਕਾਮਨਾਵਾਂ

bony ('ਬਅਉਨਿ) *a* ਹੱਡੀ, ਹੱਡੀ ਵਰਗਾ, ਨਿਰਾ ਹੱਡੀਆਂ ਦਾ, ਦੁਬਲਾ-ਪਤਲਾ, ਕਮਜ਼ੋਰ

boo (ਬੂ) *n v int* ਅਨਾੜੀ, ਬੇਸਮਝ, ਮੂਰਖ, ਘਿਰਣਾ ਸੂਚਕ ਸ਼ਬਦ (ਕਹਿਣਾ), ਧਿੱਕ ਕਰਨਾ, ਧਿੱਕਾਰਨਾ, ਛੀ ਛੀ (ਕਰਨਾ), ਓਇ ਓਇ! ਹੁਸ਼ (ਕਰਨਾ)

booby ('ਬੂਬਿ) *n* ਬੁੱਧੂ, ਸਿੱਧੜ, ਭੋਲਾ, ਲੋਲ੍ਹੂ, ਹੱਸ ਜਾਤੀ ਦੀ ਕਿਸਮ ਦਾ ਇਕ ਸਮੁੰਦਰੀ ਪੰਛੀ

boodle ('ਬੂਡਲ) *n* ਭੀੜ, ਜੁੰਡੀ, ਦਲ, ਸਮੂਹ, ਝੁੰਡ

boohoo ('ਬੂਹੂ) *n v* ਕੁਰਲਾਹਟ, ਹਾਲਦੁਹਾਈ, ਗਲਾ ਫਾੜ ਕੇ ਰੋਣ ਦੀ ਧੁਨੀ; ਕੁਰਲਾਉਣਾ, ਉੱਚੀ ਉੱਚੀ ਰੋਣਾ

book (ਬੁਕ) *n v* ਪੁਸਤਕ, ਕਿਤਾਬ, ਪੋਥੀ, ਗ੍ਰੰਥ; ਤਾਲਿਕਾ, ਸੂਚੀ; ਧਾਰਮਕ ਗ੍ਰੰਥ, ਵਹੀ, ਵਹੀ ਖਾਤਾ; ਅੰਕਤ ਕਰਨਾ, ਰਜਿਸਟਰ ਤੇ ਚਾੜ੍ਹਨਾ, ਨਿਯਤ ਕਰਨਾ, ਬੁੱਕ ਕਰਨਾ, ਨਾਂ ਲਿਖ ਲੈਣਾ, ਕੰਮ ਕਾਜ ਨਿਯਤ ਕਰਨਾ; ~**binder** ਜਿਲਦਸਾਜ਼; ~**binding** ਜਿਲਦਸਾਜ਼ੀ; ~**case** ਕਿਤਾਬ-ਦਾਨ, ਕਿਤਾਬਾਂ ਦੀ ਅਲਮਾਰੀ; ~**keeper** ਹਿਸਾਬ-ਕਿਤਾਬ ਰੱਖਣ ਵਾਲਾ; ~**keeping** ਵਹੀ-ਖਾਤਾ, ਹਿਸਾਬ-ਕਿਤਾਬ; ~**let** ਕਿਤਾਬਚਾ; ~**of fate** ਕਰਮ-ਲੇਖ, ਕਰਮਾਂ ਦੇ ਲੇਖ; ~**post** ਬੁਕ ਪੋਸਟ, ਡਾਕ ਰਾਹੀਂ ਛਪੀ ਕਿਤਾਬ ਆਦਿ ਭੇਜਣਾ; ~**seller** ਕਿਤਾਬਾਂ ਵੇਚਣ ਵਾਲਾ, ਕੁਤਬ-ਫ਼ਰੋਸ਼; ~**shelf** ਕਿਤਾਬਾਂ ਦੀ ਦੁਕਾਨ; ~**worm** ਕਿਤਾਬੀ ਕੀੜਾ ਪੜਾਕੂ; **bring to~** ਗ਼ਲਤੀ ਲਈ ਸਜ਼ਾ ਦੇਣੀ; ਜਵਾਬਦੇਹੀ ਕਰਨੀ; **be in bad ~s** ਕਿਸੇ ਦੀਆਂ ਨਜ਼ਰਾਂ ਵਿਚ ਗਿਰ ਜਾਣਾ; ~**ing-clerk** ਟਿਕਟ-ਬਾਬੂ

boom (ਬੂਮ) *n v* ਗਰਜ, ਗਰੂੰਜ, ਤੇਜ਼ੀ, ਚੜ੍ਹਤ, ਬੰਦਰਗਾਹੀ ਰੋਕ, ਗੱਜਣਾ

boon (ਬੂਨ) *n* ਵਰ, ਵਰਦਾਨ, ਸੁਗਾਤ, ਦਾਨ, ਅਸੀਸ; (ਅਪ) ਪ੍ਰਾਰਥਨਾ, ਘੇਨਤੀ

boor (ਬੂਅ*) *n* ਉਜੱਡ, ਗੰਵਾਰ, ਅਸਭਿਆ, ਪੇਂਡੂ, ਅਵੇਸਾ ~**ish** ਗੰਵਾਰ; ਉਜੱਡ, ਜੰਗਲੀ; ~**ishness** ਗੰਵਾਰੁਪਣ; ਉਜੱਡਪੁਣਾ

boost (ਬੂਸਟ) *n v* ਵਾਧਾ, ਇਸ਼ਤਿਹਾਰਬਾਜ਼ੀ, ਢੰਢੋਰਾ ਪਿਟਣਾ, ਗੁਣ-ਗਾਇਨ ਕਰਨਾ, ਵਧਾ ਚੜ੍ਹਾ ਕੇ ਦੱਸਣਾ, ਵਡਿਆਉਣਾ

booster ('ਬੂਸਟਅ*) *n* ਸ਼ਕਤੀਵਰਧਕ, ਬੂਸਟਰ; ਹੱਲਾਸ਼ੇਰੀ ਦੇਣ ਵਾਲਾ

boot (ਬੂਟ) *n v* ਬੂਟ, (ਠੁੰਡ) ਮਾਰਨਾ, ਜੁੱਤੀ ਪਾਉਣੀ; ~**legger** ਸ਼ਰਾਬ ਨੂੰ ਚੋਰੀ ਛਿਪੇ ਲਿਆਉਣ ਤੇ ਵੇਚਣ ਵਾਲਾ; ਸ਼ਰਾਬ ਦਾ ਚੋਰ ਵਪਾਰੀ; ~**legging** ਨਾਜਾਇਜ਼ ਸ਼ਰਾਬ ਦਾ ਵਪਾਰ; ~**licker** ਚਾਪਲੂਸ, ਖ਼ੁਸ਼ਾਮਦੀ, ਜੁੱਤੀਚੱਟ

booth (ਬੂਦ) *n* ਬੂਥ, ਖੇਖਾ, ਸਟਾਲ, ਅਸਥਾਈ ਨਿਵਾਸ, ਛੱਪਰ, ਅਸਥਾਈ ਦੁਕਾਨ; ਮੇਲੇ ਦੀ ਹੱਟੀ, ਡੇਰਾ

booty ('ਬੂਟਿ) *n* ਲੁੱਟ, ਲੁੱਟ ਦਾ ਮਾਲ; ਲਾਭ, ਫ਼ਾਇਦਾ

border ('ਬੋਡਅ*) *n a v* ਸਰਹੱਦ, ਸੀਮਾ, ਹੱਦ, ਕਿਨਾਰਾ, ਹਾਸ਼ੀਆ; ਹੱਦਬੰਦੀ ਕਰਨੀ, ਵਲਣਾ, ਵਾੜ ਲਗਾਉਣਾ, ਹਾਸ਼ੀਆ ਲਾਉਣਾ; ਕਿਨਾਰੀ ਲਾਉਣੀ, ਮਗ਼ਜ਼ੀ ਲਾਉਣੀ; ਮਿਲਾਉਣਾ, ਜੋੜਨਾ, ਲਗਾਉਣਾ, ਸੰਜੋਗ ਕਰਨਾ

bore (ਬੋ:) *v n* (1) ਛੇਕ ਕਰਨਾ, ਵਰਮੇ ਨਾਲ ਮੋਰੀ ਕੱਢਣੀ, ਵਰਮਾਉਣਾ, ਖੋਖਲਾ ਕਰਨਾ, (ਖੂਹ) ਪੁੱਟਣਾ, ਰਾਹ ਬਣਾਉਣਾ; (2) ਤੰਗ ਕਰਨਾ; ਮਗ਼ਜ਼-ਚੱਟਣਾ, ਅਕਾਉਣਾ, ਪਰੇਸ਼ਾਨ ਕਰਨਾ; ਛੇਕ, ਮੋਰੀ; ਬੰਦੂਕ ਦੀ ਨਾਲੀ ਦਾ ਵਿਆਸ; ਪਾਣੀ ਦਾ ਪਤਾ ਲਗਾਉਣ ਲਈ ਜ਼ਮੀਨ ਵਿਚ ਕੀਤੀ ਗਈ ਮੋਰੀ; ਖੋਜ-ਤਬੇਲਾ, ਮਗ਼ਜ਼-ਚੱਟ, ਤੰਗ ਕਰਨ ਵਾਲਾ, ਬਾਤੂਨੀ; ~**dom** ਅਕੇਵਾਂ, ਉਕਤਾਹਟ

boring ('ਬੋਰਿੰਗ) *a* ਨੀਰਸ

borough ('ਬਅੱਰਅ) *n* (ਪੁਰਾਣਾ ਅਰਥ) ਆਬਾਦੀ, ਨਗਰ; (ਸੰਸਦ ਆਦਿ) ਚੋਣ ਹਲਕਾ

borrow ('ਬੌਰਅਉ) *v* ਉਧਾਰ ਲੈਣਾ; ਕਰਜ਼ਾ ਲੈਣਾ; ਮਾਂਗਵਾਂ ਲੈਣਾ; ਅਪਣਾਉਣਾ; **~er** ਉਧਾਰ ਲੈਣ ਵਾਲਾ, ਕਰਜ਼ਦਾਰ

bosom ('ਬੁਜ਼(ਅ)ਮ) *n* ਸੀਨਾ, ਛਾਤੀ, ਦਿਲ; ਅੰਦਰਲਾ ਹਿੱਸਾ; ਆਲਿੰਗਨ; ਖ਼ਿਆਲ

botany ('ਬੌਟਅਨਿ) *n* ਬਨਸਪਤੀ-ਵਿਗਿਆਨ

bote (ਬਅਉਟ) *n* ਮੁਆਵਜ਼ਾ, ਨੁਕਸਾਨ ਦੀ ਤਲਾਫ਼ੀ, ਨੁਕਸਾਨ ਦੀ ਪੂਰਤੀ

bother (ਬੌਦਅ*) *v n* ਔਖਾ ਕਰਨਾ; ਵਿਆਕੁਲ ਕਰਨਾ, ਅਕਾਉਣਾ, ਕਸ਼ਟ ਉਠਾਉਣਾ, ਜਿੱਚ ਕਰਨਾ, ਖਿਝਣਾ; ਝਮੇਲਾ, ਬਖੇੜਾ, ਪਰੇਸ਼ਾਨੀ, ਕਸ਼ਟ, ਜ਼ਹਿਮਤ; **~ation** ਚਿੰਤਾ, ਝੰਜਟ, ਝਮੇਲਾ, ਬਖੇੜਾ, ਅਕੇਵਾਂ ਸਿਰ-ਖਪਾਈ

bottle (ਬੌਟਲ) *n* ਬੋਤਲ, ਸ਼ੀਸ਼ੀ, ਕੁੱਪੀ; ਬੋਤਲ ਵਿਚ ਬੰਦ ਕਰਨਾ; (ਕਿਸੇ ਵਿਅਕਤੀ ਨੂੰ) ਉੱਤੋਂ ਜਾ ਫੜਨਾ, ਝਪਟਣਾ

bottom (ਬੌਟ(ਅ)ਮ) *n a v* ਤਹਿ, ਆਧਾਰ ਪੇਂਦਾ; (ਕੁਰਸੀ ਆਦਿ ਦੀ) ਚਿੱਤੜ, ਆਸਣ; **~neck** ਭੀੜਾ ਰਾਹ; ਰੁਕਾਵਟ, ਅੜਚਣ ਨੀਂਹ, ਗਹਿਰਾਈ; ਸਹਿਣ-ਸ਼ੀਲਤਾ; ਬੁਨਿਆਦੀ, ਆਧਾਰਕ, ਸਭ ਤੋਂ ਹੇਠਲਾ, ਅੰਤਮ, ਅਖੀਰੀ, ਪਿਛਲਾ, ਛੇਕੜਲਾ; ਟਿਕਣਾ, ਆਧਾਰਤ ਕਰਨਾ, ਤਹਿ ਤਕ ਪੁੱਜਣਾ, ਵਾਸਤਵਿਕ ਗੱਲ ਨੂੰ ਲਭਣਾ; **~less** ਨਿਰਾਧਾਰ, ਬੇ-ਬੁਨਿਆਦ, ਬੇਪੇਂਦਾ, ਅਥਾਹ, ਅਗਮ, ਅਸਗਾਹ, ਅਤਲ

bough (ਬਾਓ) *n* ਟਾਹਣੀ, ਡਾਲੀ, ਸ਼ਾਖ਼ਾ, ਲਗਰ; ਜਹਾਜ਼ ਦੇ ਦੋਵੇਂ ਪਾਸਿਆਂ ਦਾ ਹਿੱਸਾ

boulder (ਬਅਉਲਡਅ*) *n* ਗੋਲ ਪੱਥਰ

boulevard (ਬੂਲਅਵ੍ਹਾਡ) *(F) n* ਛਾਂਦਾਰ ਸੜਕ; ਜਰਨੈਲੀ ਸੜਕ, ਸ਼ਾਹ ਰਾਹ

bounce (ਬਾਉਂਸ) *v n adv* ਟੱਪਣਾ, ਉਛਲਣਾ, ਉਭਰਨਾ; ਕੁੜਕਣਾ; ਗੁੱਸੇ ਜਾਂ ਜੋਸ਼ ਵਿਚ ਉਛਲ ਪੈਣਾ; ਡੀਂਗ ਮਾਰਨੀ, ਫੜ ਮਾਰਨੀ; ਟੱਪੀ; ਫੜ੍ਹ, ਅੱਤਕਥਨੀ; **~r** ਗੱਪੀ, ਸ਼ੇਖ਼ੀ-ਖੋਰ, ਝੂਠਾ ਭਾਸ਼ਣ, ਨਾਟਕ ਵਿਚ ਸ਼ੋਰ-ਸ਼ਰਾਬਾ ਬੰਦ ਕਰਾਉਣ ਵਾਲਾ ਪਹਿਰੇਦਾਰ

bound (ਬਾਉਂਡ) *n v* ਹੱਦ, ਸੀਮਾ, ਬੰਨਾ; ਰੁਕਾਵਟ; ਟੱਪੀ, ਟਪੋਸੀ, ਛਲਾਂਗ, ਚੌਕੜੀ, ਉਛਾਲ ਹਦਾਂ ਬੰਨ੍ਹਣੀਆਂ, ਪ੍ਰਤੀਬੰਧ ਲਗਾਉਣਾ, ਹੱਦਬੰਦੀ ਕਰਨੀ, ਘੇਰਨਾ, ਸੀਮਾ ਨਿਰਧਾਰਤ ਕਰਨਾ, ਕੁੱਦਣਾ, ਉਛਲਣਾ, ਟੱਪਣਾ, ਛਾਲ ਮਾਰਨਾ, ਚੌਕੜੀ ਮਾਰਨਾ; ਟੱਪਾ ਖਾਣਾ; ਬੰਨ੍ਹਿਆ ਹੋਇਆ, ਮਜਬੂਰ; **out of ~s** ਸੀਮਾ ਤੋਂ ਬਾਹਰ, ਵਿਵਰਜਤ; **~ary** ਸਰਹੱਦ, ਸੀਮਾ, ਹੱਦ ਦੀ ਨਿਸ਼ਾਨੀ ਜਾਂ ਲੀਕ, ਹੱਦ-ਬੰਨਾ, ਕਿਨਾਰਾ, ਵੱਟ, ਵਾੜ

bounteous (ਬਾਉਂਟਿਅਸ) *a* ਦਿਆਲੂ, ਦਾਨੀ, ਸਖੀ, ਉਦਾਰ, ਕਿਰਪਾਲੂ, ਪਰਉਪਕਾਰੀ; **~ness** ਉਦਾਰਤਾ, ਕਿਰਪਾਲਤਾ

bountiful (ਬਾਉਂਟਿਫ਼ੁਲ) *a* ਕਾਫ਼ੀ, ਚੋਖਾ ਸਾਰਾ; ਦਿਆਲੂ, ਖੁੱਲ੍ਹਦਿਲਾ ਕਿਰਪਾਲੂ, ਹਿਤਕਾਰੀ, ਪਰਉਪਕਾਰੀ

bounty (ਬਾਉਂਟਿ) *n* ਦਾਤ, ਬਖ਼ਸ਼ੀਸ਼; ਉਦਾਰਤਾ, ਖੁੱਲ੍ਹ-ਦਿਲੀ, ਸਰਕਾਰੀ ਮਦਦ, ਆਰਥਕ ਸਹਾਇਤਾ

bouquet (ਬੁ'ਕੇਇ) *n* ਗੁਲਦਸਤਾ, ਬੁਕੇ; ਸ਼ਰਾਬ ਦੀ ਸੁਗੰਧੀ

bourgeois ('ਬੋਯ਼ਵਾ) *n a* ਮੱਧਵਰਗੀ ਪਰੰਪਰਾਵਾਦੀ ਵਿਅਕਤੀ, ਮੱਧ ਸ਼੍ਰੇਣੀ ਦਾ ਸਦੱਸ

boutique (ਬੂ'ਟੀਕ) *n* ਫ਼ੈਸ਼ਨਦਾਰ ਕੱਪੜਿਆਂ ਦੀ ਹੱਟੀ, ਬੁਟੀਕ

bow (ਬਅਉ) *n v* (1) ਕਮਾਨ, ਧਨੁਖ, ਕੁਮਾਣੀ; (2) ਅਸਮਾਨੀ ਪੀਂਘ, ਇੰਦਰ ਧਨੁਖ; (3) ਪ੍ਰਣਾਮ, ਨਮਸਕਾਰ, ਸਿਰ-ਝੁਕਾਈ;

ਨਿਵਣਾ, ਸਿਜਦਾ ਕਰਨਾ, ਪ੍ਰਣਾਮ ਕਰਨਾ, ਝੁਕਣਾ, ਸਲਾਮ ਕਰਨਾ, ਕੋਡਾ ਹੋਣਾ, ਸਿਜਦਾ; ~man ਤੀਰ-ਅੰਦਾਜ਼

bowel (ਬਾਉਅਲ) *n* ਅੰਦਰ, ਆਂਤੜੀ, (*in pl*) ਆਂਦਰਾਂ, ਆਂਤੜੀਆਂ, ਸਰੀਰ ਦਾ ਅੰਦਰਲਾ ਹਿੱਸਾ; ਕਿਸੇ ਵਸਤੂ ਦਾ ਅੰਦਰਲਾ ਭਾਗ; ਕੋਮਲ ਭਾਵ, ਦਇਆ, ਤਰਸ

bowl (ਬਅਉਲ) *n* ਕਟੋਰਾ, ਪਿਆਲਾ, ਠੂਠਾ, ਛੰਨਾ, ਚਿੱਪੀ; ਲੱਕੜ ਦੀ ਬਣੀ ਅਜੇਹੀ ਗੋਂਦ; ਡ੍ਰਿਕ ਡ੍ਰਿਕ ਦੀ ਖੇਡ ਖੇਡਣੀ, (ਕ੍ਰਿਕਟ ਵਿਚ) ਗੇਂਦ ਸੁੱਟਣੀ; ~er ਗੇਂਦਬਾਜ਼, ਬਾਉਲਰ; ~ing ਗੇਂਦਬਾਜ਼ੀ

box (ਬੌਕਸ) *n v* (1) ਸੰਦੂਕ, ਸੰਦੂਕੜੀ, ਪੇਟੀ, ਡੱਬਾ, ਤਿਜੋਰੀ, ਥਕਸਾ, (2) ਨਾਟਕਘਰ, ਸ਼ਰਾਬਘਰੇ ਜਾਂ ਹੋਟਲ ਵਿਚ ਬੈਠਣ ਦਾ ਵੱਖਰਾ ਕਮਰਾ, ਮੁਜਰਮ ਦਾ ਕਟਹਿਰਾ; (3) ਅਗਨਿ, ਮੁੱਕਾ, ਚਪੇੜ, ਥੱਪੜ, ਤਮਾਚਾ, ਚਾਂਟਾ; ਸੰਦੂਕ ਵਿਚ ਰੱਖਣਾ, (ਅਦਾਲਤ) ਵਿਚ ਕਾਗ਼ਜ਼ ਦਾਖ਼ਲ ਕਰਨੇ, ਖ਼ਾਨਿਆਂ ਵਿਚ ਵੰਡਣਾ; ਚਪੇੜ ਮਾਰਨੀ, ਮੁੱਕੇਬਾਜ਼ੀ ਦੀ ਖੇਡ ਵਿਚ ਅਗਨਿ ਮਾਰਨੇ; ~er ਮੁੱਕੇ-ਬਾਜ਼; ਦਰਮਿਆਨੇ ਕੱਦ ਦਾ ਚਿਕਣੇ ਵਾਲਾਂ ਵਾਲਾ ਇਕ ਕੁੱਤਾ; ~ing ਮੁੱਕੇਬਾਜ਼ੀ; ~box-office (ਬੌਕਸ-ਔਫ਼ਿਸ) (ਥੀਏਟਰ ਦਾ) ਟਿਕਟ-ਘਰ

boy (ਬੌਇ) *n* ਮੁੰਡਾ, ਲੜਕਾ, ਨੱਢਾ; ਛੋਟੂ; ਬੈਹਰਾ, ਨੌਕਰ; ~hood ਲੜਕਪਨ; ~ish ਮੁੰਡਿਆਂ ਵਰਗਾ, ਬਚਗਾਨਾ, ਬੱਚਿਆਂ ਵਾਂਗ; ~ishness ਸਾਹਸ, ਮੁੰਡਪੁਣਾ, ਲੜਕਪਨ, ਬਚਗਾਨਾਪਨ

boycott (ਬੌਇਕੌਟ) *v n* ਛੇਕਣਾ, ਭਾਈਚਾਰੇ ਜਾਂ ਬਰਾਦਰੀ ਵਿਚੋਂ ਕੱਢ ਦੇਣਾ; ਬਾਈਕਾਟ ਕਰਨਾ; ਬਾਈਕਾਟ; ਕੱਟੀ

bra (ਬਰਾ) *n* (ਬੋਲ) ਅੰਗੀ

brace (ਬਰੇਇਸ) *v n* ਬੰਨ੍ਹਣਾ, ਕਸਣਾ, ਜਕੜਨਾ;

(ਆਪਣੇ ਆਪ ਨੂੰ) ਤਕੜਾ ਜਾਂ ਤਿਆਰ ਕਰਨਾ, ਤੁੰਨਣਾ; ਤਣੀ, ਡੋਰੀ, ਪੱਟੀ, ਪਤਲੂਨ ਦੇ ਗੈਲਸ; ਜਕੜਨ, ਚਿੰਨ੍ਹ (), {} ਜੋੜ; ~let ਕੰਗਣ, ਚੂੜੀ; ਹੱਥਕੜੀ

bracket ('ਬਰੈਕਿਟ) *n v* ਕਮਾਨੀ ਦਾ ਨਿਸ਼ਾਨ ਜਿਸ ਵਿਚ ਸ਼ਬਦਾਂ ਜਾਂ ਅੰਕਾਂ ਨੂੰ ਘੇਰਿਆ ਜਾਂਦਾ ਹੈ : (), {}, []; ਚੰਦਮਾਰੀ ਵਿਚ ਦੋ ਬਿੰਦੂਆਂ ਦੀ ਦੂਰੀ, ਤੋਪਗੱਡੀ ਦੀ ਟੇਕ, ਥੈਕਟ, ਕਮਾਨੀ, ਦੀਵਾਰਗੀਰ; ਗੁੱਟਬੰਦੀ ਕਰਨਾ

brain (ਬਰੇਇਨ) *n v* ਦਿਮਾਗ਼, ਮਗ਼ਜ਼, ਭੇਜਾ; ਅਕਲ, ਸਮਝ, ਚਿਤ, ਬੁੱਧੀ; ਸੋਚ ਸ਼ਕਤੀ, ਬੋਧਕ-ਸ਼ਕਤੀ; ਵਿਚਾਰ ਕੇਂਦਰ; ~less ਮੂਰਖ, ਮੂੜ੍ਹ, ਬੇਅਕਲ, ਬੁੱਧੂ

brake (ਬਰੇਇਕ) *v n* ਸਣ ਕੁੱਟਣੀ; ਬਰੇਕ ਲਾਉਣੀ; ਪਹੀਏ ਆਦਿ ਨੂੰ ਰੋਕਣਾ, ਰੋਕ ਲਗਾਉਣਾ, ਸਣ ਆਦਿ ਕੁੱਟਣ ਦਾ ਜੰਤਰ, ਦੰਦਲ-ਮੁੰਗਲੀ, ਬਰੇਕ, ਰੋਕ, ਹੇੜਾ, ਅਟਕਣੀ

branch (ਬਰਾਂਚ) *n v* ਟਾਹਣੀ, ਸ਼ਾਖ਼, ਡਾਲੀ, ਕਿਸੇ ਸਭਾ, ਬੈਂਕ ਆਦਿ ਦੀ ਸ਼ਾਖ਼ਾ; ਸ਼ਾਖ਼ ਨਿਕਲਣੀ, ਟਹਿਣੀਆਂ ਵਿਚ ਜਾਂ ਸ਼ਾਖ਼ਾਵਾਂ ਵਿਚ ਵੰਡਣਾ; ਵੇਲ ਬੂਟੇ ਕੱਢਣਾ

brand (ਬਰੈਂਡ) *n v* ਮਾਰਕਾ; ਛਾਪ; ਚੁਆਤੀ, ਬਲਦੀ ਲੱਕੜ, ਮਸ਼ਾਲ; ਮਾਰਕਾ ਲਾਉਣ ਵਾਲੀ ਗਰਮ ਛਾਪ; ਕਲੰਕ ਦਾ ਟਿੱਕਾ; ਦਾਗ਼ਣਾ, ਡੰਮ੍ਹਣਾ, ਤੱਤੇ ਲੋਹੇ ਨਾਲ ਨਿਸ਼ਾਨ ਲਾਉਣਾ, ਮਨ ਵਿਚ ਬਿਠਾਉਣਾ, ਪੱਕਾ ਕਰਨਾ, ਕਲੰਕਤ ਕਰਨਾ; ~new ਅਤ-ਨਵੀਨ, ਨਵਾਂ ਨਿਛੋਹ, ਨਵਾਂ ਨਿਕੋਰ

brass (ਬਰਾਸ) *n* ਪਿੱਤਲ; ਪਿੱਤਲ ਦਾ ਪੱਤਰਾ; ਰੁਪਿਆ ਪੈਸਾ; ਢੀਠਪੁਣਾ, ਬੇ-ਹਯਾਈ

brave (ਬਰੇਇਵ) *a n v* ਦਲੇਰ, ਸੂਰਵੀਰ, ਵਰਿਆਮ, ਸੂਰਾ, ਤਕੜਾ, ਹਿੰਮਤੀ, ਬਹਾਦਰ,

ਸਾਹਸੀ; ਟਾਕਰੇ ਤੇ ਡਟ ਜਾਣਾ

bravo (ਬਰਾʼਵ੍ਹਅਉ) *int n* (1) ਵਾਹ-ਵਾ! ਬੱਲੇ
ਬੱਲੇ! ਸ਼ਾਵਾ! ਸ਼ਾਵਾ! ਸ਼ਾਬਾਸ਼! (2) ਹਤਿਆਰਾ,
ਡਾਕੂ, ਪੇਸ਼ਾਵਰ ਖੂਨੀ

breach (ਬਰੀਚ) *n v* ਉਲੰਘਣ, ਭੰਗ, ਨੇਮ-ਭੰਗ;
ਮੋਰੀ, ਪਾੜਾ, ਲੜਾਈ-ਝਗੜਾ, ਵਿਗਾੜ;
(ਸਮੁੰਦਰੀ) ਲਹਿਰਾਂ ਦਾ ਟਕਰਾਉਣਾ, ਦਰਾੜ ਪੈਦਾ
ਕਰਨਾ; ~of the peace ਸ਼ਾਂਤੀ-ਭੰਗ, ਦੰਗਾ,
ਫਸਾਦ

bread (ਬਰੈੱਡ) *n* ਰੋਟੀ, ਡਬਲ ਰੋਟੀ; ਰੋਜ਼ੀ,
ਉਪਜੀਵਕਾ, ਗੁਜ਼ਾਰਾ; ~and butter ਰੋਜ਼ੀ-
ਰੋਟੀ, ਦਾਲ ਫੁਲਕਾ, ਉਪਜੀਵਕਾ

breadth (ਬਰੈੱਟਥ) *n* ਚੌੜਾਈ, ਬਰ, ਅਰਜ਼ ਪੱਟ
(ਕੱਪੜੇ ਦਾ) ਪਾਟ; ਪੇਟ (ਨਦੀ ਦਾ); ਦੂਰੀ,
ਵਿੱਥ, ਫ਼ਾਸਲਾ, ਵਿਸਤਾਰ

break (ਬਰੇਇਕ) *v* ਤੋੜਨਾ, ਭੰਨਣਾ, ਟੁੱਟਣਾ,
ਭੱਜਣਾ, ਟੋਟੇ ਕਰਨਾ, ਚੂਰ ਚੂਰ ਕਰਨਾ; ਭੰਗ
ਕਰਨਾ, ਖੰਡਤ ਕਰਨਾ, ਉਲੰਘਣਾ; ਉਜਾੜਨਾ;
ਤੋੜਨਾ, ਰੋਕਣਾ ਜਾਂ ਟੇਕਣਾ, ਪ੍ਰਭਾਵਹੀਨ ਹੋਣਾ,
ਤਰੱਟੀ ਚੀੜ ਹੋਲੀ ਜਾਂ ਕਰਨੀ; ਰੁਕਣਾ, ਮੁੱਕ ਜਾਣਾ,
ਬੰਦ ਹੋਣਾ; ~able ਟੁੱਟਣ-ਫੁੱਟਣ ਵਾਲਾ, ਭੁੱਟਲ;
ਟੁੱਟਣ-ਫੁੱਟਣ ਵਾਲੀਆਂ ਚੀਜ਼ਾਂ ~down ਨਾਸ,
ਫਹਿ-ਢੇਰੀ, ਰੁਕਾਵਟ, ਠਹਿਰਾਉ, (ਸਿਹਤ ਦੀ)
ਖੀਂਤਾ, ਨਿਸੱਤਾ, ਭੰਗ ਹੋ ਜਾਣਾ; ਬੰਦ ਹੋ ਜਾਣਾ;
~news ਖ਼ਬਰ ਦੇਣਾ; ~open (ਦਰਵਾਜ਼ਾ) ਤੋੜ
ਕੇ ਅੰਦਰ ਆਉਣਾ; ~up ਕਮਜ਼ੋਰ ਹੋਣਾ, ਨਿਰਬਲ
ਹੋਣਾ, ਚੂਰ ਹੋਣਾ, ਥੱਕ-ਟੁੱਟ ਜਾਣਾ, ਖਿੰਡ-ਪੁੰਡ
ਜਾਣਾ, ਵਿਚਰਨ, ਅੰਗ, ਨਿਖੇੜ

breakfast (ʼਬਰੈੱਕਫਅਸਟ) *n v* ਨਾਸ਼ਤਾ; ਫ਼ਾਹ
ਵੇਲਾ; ਨਾਸ਼ਤਾ ਕਰਨਾ ਜਾਂ ਕਰਵਾਉਣਾ, ਫ਼ਾਹ
ਵੇਲਾ ਖਾਣਾ ਜਾਂ ਖਵਾਉਣਾ

breast (ਬਰੈੱਸਟ) *n v* ਛਾਤੀ, ਹਿੱਕ; ਸੀਨਾ, ਥਣ,
ਦੁੱਧੀ; ਹਿਰਦਾ; ਦਿਲ, ਵਲਵਲਾ, ਭਾਵਨਾਵਾਂ
ਸਾਮ੍ਹਣਾ ਕਰਨਾ, ਆਹਮੋ-ਸਾਹਮਣੇ ਹੋਣਾ; ਬਹਿਸ
ਕਰਨਾ

breath (ਬਰੈੱਥ) *n* ਸਾਹ, ਦਮ, ਸੁਆਸ, ਪ੍ਰਾਣ,
ਹਵਾ ਦਾ ਬੁੱਲਾ; ਫੂਕ; ਮੂੰਹ ਦੀ ਹਵਾੜ, ਫੁਸ-
ਫੁਸ; ਛਿਣ, ਪਲ; ~less ਨਿਰਜੀਵ, ਬੇਜਾਨ,
ਬੇਦਮ, ਮਰਿਆ ਹੋਇਆ, ਟੁੱਟੇ ਸਾਹ, ਸਹੋ-ਸਾਹ,
ਹੌਂਕਦਾ, ਹੁਸੜਵਾਂ

breathe (ʼਬਰੀਦ) *v* ਸਾਹ ਲੈਣਾ, ਜੀਉਂਦੇ ਹੋਣਾ,
ਜੀਉਣਾ; ਪਰਗਟ ਕਰਨਾ; ਮਹਿਕਣਾ

breech (ਬਰੀਚ) *n v* (ਪ੍ਰ) ਚਿੱਤੜ, ਪਿੱਛਾ; ਬੰਦੂਕ,
ਤੋਪ ਦਾ ਪਿੱਛਲਾ ਹਿਸਾ; ਬਿਰਜਮ ਪਾਉਣੀ

breed (ਬਰੀਡ) *v n* ਜਣਨਾ, (ਸੰਤਾਨ) ਜਮਾਉਣਾ,
ਜਨਮ ਦੇਣਾ, ਉਪਜਾਉਣਾ, ਗਰਭਿਤ ਕਰਨਾ,
ਉਤਪਾਦਨ ਕਰਨਾ, ਫਲ ਹੋਣਾ, ਪਾਲਣਾ;
ਵਧਾਉਣਾ, ਫੈਲਾਉਣਾ; ਸਿਧਾਉਣਾ, ਤਿਆਰ
ਕਰਨਾ; ਸਿਖਾਉਣਾ, ਪੜ੍ਹਾਉਣਾ, ਤਿਆਰ ਕਰਨਾ;
ਉਠਣਾ, ਨਿਕਲਣਾ; ਨਸਲ, ਜਾਤੀ

breeze (ਬਰੀਜ਼) *n* (1) ਰੁਮਕਦੀ ਹਵਾ, ਮੱਠੀ
ਹਵਾ; (2) ਵੱਡ-ਮੱਖੀ, ਮੱਖ; ਇਕ ਵੱਡੀ ਮੱਖੀ;
(ਬੋਲ) ਨੋਕ-ਝੋਂਕ

brethren (ʼਬਰੈੱਦਰਅਨ) *n* ਭਾਈਬੰਦ, ਧਰਮ
ਭਾਈ

brevity (ਬਰੈੱਵ੍ਹਅਟਿ) *v n* ਸੰਖੇਪਤਾ, ਥੁੜ੍ਹ, ਛੋਟੀ
ਅਵਧੀ, ਅਲਪਕਾਲ

bribe (ਬਰਾਇਬ) *n v* ਰਿਸ਼ਵਤ, ਵੱਢੀ; ਵੱਢੀ
ਦੇਣੀ ਲੋੜ ਦੇਣਾ, ਮੁੱਠੀ ਗਰਮ ਕਰਨੀ; ~ry
ਰਿਸ਼ਵਤ ਖੋਰੀ

brick (ਬਰਿਕ) *n v* ਇੱਟ, ਇੱਟਾਂ ਨਾਲ ਚਿਣਾਈ
ਕਰਨੀ, ਇੱਟਾਂ ਨਾਲ ਭਰ ਦੇਣਾ; ~bat ਹੋਣਾ,

ਢੀਮ; ਨਿਰਾਦਰੀ; **~kiln** ਇੱਟਾਂ ਦਾ ਭੱਠਾ; **~work** ਚਿਣਾਈ, ਇੱਟਾਂ ਦੀ ਉਸਾਰੀ

bride (ਬਰਾਇਡ) *n v* ਵਹੁਟੀ, ਲਾੜੀ, ਵਿਆਂਹਦੜ, ਦੁਲਹਨ; ਸੱਜ-ਵਿਆਹੀ (ਨਾਟਕ ਵਿਚ) ਵਹੁਟੀ ਦਾ ਰੂਪ ਧਾਰਨ ਕਰਨਾ ਜਾਂ ਕਰਾਉਣਾ; **~groom** ਵਰ, ਦੁੱਲਾ, ਲਾੜਾ, ਨੀਂਗਰ

bridge (ਬਰਿਜ) *n v* ਪੁਲ; ਜਹਾਜ਼ ਦੇ ਅਧਿਕਾਰੀ ਲਈ ਵਿਚਕਾਰਲਾ ਥੜ੍ਹਾ, ਸਾਰੰਗੀ ਆਦਿ ਦੀ ਘੋੜੀ, (ਨੱਕ ਦੀ) ਘੋੜੀ, ਬ੍ਰਿਜ, ਤਾਸ਼ ਦੀ ਇਕ ਖੇਡ, ਪੁਲ ਬੰਨ੍ਹਣਾ; ਪੁਲ ਬੰਨ੍ਹ ਕੇ ਪਾਰ ਕਰਨਾ

bridle ('ਬਰਾਇਡਲ) *n v* ਲਗਾਮ; ਕਾਬੂ, ਰੋਕ; ਲੰਗਰ ਦੀ ਜ਼ੰਜੀਰ; ਲਗਾਮ ਪਾਉਣੀ ਜਾਂ ਚਾੜ੍ਹਨੀ, ਕਾਬੂ ਕਰਨਾ, ਰੋਕਣਾ

brief (ਬਰੀਫ਼) *a n v* ਸਾਰ, ਬਿਊਰਾ, ਖ਼ੁਲਾਸਾ; ਸੰਖੇਪ, ਸੰਕੁਚਤ, ਮੋਟਾ-ਮੋਟਾ, ਦੋ ਹਰਫ਼ੀ, ਥੋੜ੍ਹ-ਚਿਰਾ; (ਕ) ਵਕੀਲਾਂ ਲਈ ਕਿਸੇ ਮੁਕੱਦਮੇ ਦੇ ਮੋਟੇ ਮੋਟੇ ਨੁਕਤੇ; (ਪੋਪ ਵੱਲੋਂ) ਹੁਕਮਨਾਮਾ,

brigade (ਬਰਿ'ਗੇਇਡ) *n v* ਫ਼ੌਜ ਦੀ ਟੁਕੜੀ; ਸੰਗਠਤ ਜੱਥਾ; ਬਰਿਗੇਡ ਬਣਾਉਣਾ; ਪਲਟਣ ਦੇ ਰੂਪ ਵਿਚ ਸੰਗਠਤ ਕਰਨਾ

brigand ('ਬਰਿਗਅੰਡ) *n* ਡਕੈਤ, ਡਾਕੂ, ਧਾੜਵੀ, ਰਾਹ-ਮਾਰ

bright (ਬਰਾਇਟ) *a adv* ਟਮਕਦਾ, ਲਿਸ਼ਕਦਾ, ਰੌਸ਼ਨ, ਸਾਫ਼, ਭੜਕੀਲਾ, ਚਮਕਦਾਰ, ਹਸਮੁਖ, ਤੇਜਸਵੀ, ਉਜਲ; ਉਤਸ਼ਾਹੀ, ਚੜ੍ਹਦੀਆਂ ਕਲਾਂ ਵਿਚ; **~en** ਚਮਕਾਉਣਾ ਜਾਂ ਚਮਕਣਾ, ਲਿਸ਼ਕਾਉਣਾ ਜਾਂ ਲਿਸ਼ਕਣਾ, ਪ੍ਰਕਾਸ਼ਮਾਨ ਕਰਨਾ ਜਾਂ ਹੋਣਾ, **~ness** ਖ਼ੁਸ਼ਦਿਲੀ; ਪ੍ਰਕਾਸ਼ ਤੇਜ, ਨਿਰਮਲਤਾ, ਉਜਲਾਪਣ, ਚਮਕ, ਚਮਕ-ਦਮਕ, ਤੜਕ-ਭੜਕ

brilliance ('ਬਰਿਲਯੰਸ) *n* ਚਮਕ, ਦਮਕ, ਛਬ,

ਆਭਾ, ਝਲਕ, ਪ੍ਰਤਿਭਾ

brilliant ('ਬਰਿਲਯਅੰਟ) *a n* ਚਮਕੀਲਾ, ਭੜਕੀਲਾ, ਚਮਕਦਾਰ, ਰੌਸ਼ਨ; ਬੁੱਧੀਮਾਨ; ਹਸਮੁਖ; ਪ੍ਰਸਿਧ, ਸ਼ੋਖ,

brindled ('ਬਰਿੰਡਲਡ) *a* ਚਿਤ-ਕਬਰਾ, ਡੱਬ-ਖੜੱਬਾ

bring (ਬਰਿਙ) *v* ਲਿਆਉਣਾ, ਲੈ ਜਾਣਾ, ਢੋਣਾ, ਉਪਜਾਉਣਾ, ਪੇਸ਼ ਕਰਨਾ, ਸਾਮੂਟੇ ਰੱਖਣਾ, ਪ੍ਰਸਤੁਤ ਕਰਨਾ; **~about** ਕਾਰਨ ਹੋਣਾ, (ਨੂੰ) ਵਜੂਦ ਵਿਚ ਲਿਆਉਣਾ; (ਜਹਾਜ਼ ਨੂੰ) ਮੋੜਨਾ; **~down** ਮਾਣ ਘਟਾਉਣਾ, (ਕੀਮਤ) ਘੱਟ ਕਰਨਾ, ਮਾਰ ਮੁਕਾਉਣਾ, ਸੱਟ ਮਾਰਨੀ, ਸਜ਼ਾ ਦਿਵਾਉਣੀ; **~forth** ਜਣਨਾ, ਪੈਦਾ ਕਰਨਾ, ਸਾਮੂਟੇ ਲਿਆਉਣਾ; **~forward** ਅੱਗੇ ਲਿਆਉਣਾ, (ਕਿਤਾਬ ਦੇ) ਅਗਲੇ ਸਫ਼ੇ ਉੱਤੇ ਲਿਆਉਣਾ; **~home to** ਸਿੱਧ ਕਰਨਾ, ਪੂਰੀ ਤਰ੍ਹਾਂ ਸਮਝਾ ਦੇਣਾ, ਦਿਮਾਗ਼ ਵਿਚ ਬਿਠਾ ਦੇਣਾ; **~off** ਸਫਲ ਬਣਾਉਣਾ; ਬਚਾ ਲਿਆਉਣਾ; **~out** (ਪੁਸਤਕ ਦਾ)ਪ੍ਰਕਾਸ਼ਤ ਕਰਨਾ; ਕੱਢਣਾ, ਨਸ਼ਰ ਕਰਨਾ, ਸਾਫ਼ ਸਾਫ਼ ਪਰਗਟ ਕਰਨਾ, ਭਾਂਡਾ ਫੋੜਨਾ; **~up** ਉਗਾਉਣਾ, ਪਾਲਣਾ, ਪੋਸਣਾ, ਸਿਖਾਉਣਾ; ਮੁਕੱਦਮਾ ਚਲਾਉਣਾ

brinjal ('ਬਰਿੰਜਲ) *n* ਬੈਂਗਣ, ਵਤਾਊਂ

brink (ਬਰਿੰਕ) *n* ਕੰਢਾ; ਸਿਰਾ

brisk (ਬਰਿਸਕ) *a v* ਤੇਜ਼, ਕਿਰਿਆਸ਼ੀਲ, ਚੁਸਤ, ਛੁਹਲਾ, ਫੁਰਤੀਲਾ, ਚਲਾਕ, ਜੋਸ਼ ਦੇਣ ਵਾਲਾ; ਤੇਜ਼ ਹੋਣਾ ਜਾਂ ਕਰਨਾ, ਫੁਰਤੀਲਾ ਹੋਣਾ ਜਾਂ ਕਰਨਾ; **~ness** ਸਫੁਰਤੀ, ਤੀਬਰਤਾ, ਤੇਜ਼ੀ, ਚੁਸਤੀ, ਫੁਰਤੀ

bristle ('ਬਰਿਸਲ) *n v* ਕਰੜਾ ਵਾਲ, ਮੋਟਾ ਜਾਂ ਖਰ੍ਹਵਾ ਵਾਲ, ਸੂਰ ਦਾ ਵਾਲ; ਕਰੜਾ ਜਾਂ ਖਰ੍ਹਵਾ

ਹੋ ਜਾਣਾ, ਗੁੱਸੇ ਨਾਲ ਲੂੰ ਖੜ੍ਹੇ ਹੋ ਜਾਣੇ, ਤਾਅ
ਵਿਚ ਆ ਜਾਣਾ

British ('ਬਰਿਟਿਸ਼) *a* ਬਰਤਾਨਵੀ, ਬਰਤਾਨੀਆ ਦਾ,
ਅੰਗਰੇਜ਼ਾਂ ਦਾ; **~er** ਬਰਤਾਨੀਆ ਦਾ ਵਸਨੀਕ

brittle ('ਬਰਿਟਲ) *a* ਭੁਰਭੁਰਾ, ਕੁੜਕਵਾਂ,
ਕੁੜਕੀਲਾ, ਕਮਜ਼ੋਰ, ਮਾੜਾ, ਟੁੱਟ ਜਾਣ ਵਾਲਾ,
ਨਾਸ਼ਵਾਨ; **~ness** ਭੁਰਭੁਰਾਪਣ, ਬੇਲਚਕਪਣ,
ਕਮਜ਼ੋਰੀ

broad (ਬਰੋਡ) *a n adv* ਚੌੜਾ, ਖੁੱਲ੍ਹਾ, ਮੋਕਲਾ
ਵਿਸਤਰਤ; ਪੂਰਨ, ਭਰਿਆ; ਸਪਸ਼ਟ; ਚੌੜਾ
ਹਿੱਸਾ, ਖਿਲਾਰ; ਚੌੜਾਈ ਦੇ ਰੁਖ, ਚੌੜੇ ਦਾਅ,
ਖੁੱਲ੍ਹ-ਦਿਲਾ, ਉਦਾਰ; **~based** ਚੌੜੇ ਆਧਾਰ ਤੇ,
ਉਦਾਰ (ਦਿਲ ਦਾ), ਜਿਸਦੇ ਵਿਚ ਸੰਕੀਰਣਤਾ
ਨਹੀਂ ਹੈ; **~daylight** ਦਿਨਦੀਵੀਂ, ਦਿਨ ਦਿਹਾੜੇ;
~facts ਮੋਟੀਆਂ ਮੋਟੀਆਂ ਗੱਲਾਂ ਦਾ ਤੱਥ;
~minded ਖੁੱਲ੍ਹ-ਦਿਲਾ, ਉਦਾਰ, ਫਰਾਖ਼ ਦਿਲ;
~ly ਮੋਟੇ ਤੌਰ ਤੇ

broadcast ('ਬਰੋਡਕਾਸਟ) *n v* ਪ੍ਰਸਾਰਤ ਕਰਨਾ;
ਖ਼ਬਰ ਫੈਲਾਉਣਾ ਮਸ਼ਹੂਰ ਕਰਨਾ; ਪ੍ਰਸਾਰਨ,
ਪ੍ਰਸਾਰ, ਬ੍ਰਾਡਕਾਸਟ; ਖਿਲਾਰਨਾ

brochure (ਬਰਅਊਸ਼ਅਾ*) *n* ਕਿਤਾਬਚਾ, ਰੁਵਰਕੀ,
ਪੈਂਫਲਿਟ, ਬਰੋਸ਼ਰ

brokage ('ਬਰਉਕਿਜ) *n* ਦਲਾਲੀ, ਆੜ੍ਹਤ

broker ('ਬਰਅਉਕਅ*) ਦਲਾਲ, ਆੜ੍ਹਤੀ, ਏਜੰਟ;
ਕਬਾੜੀਆ

bronze ('ਬਰੌਂਜ਼) *n a v* ਕਾਂਹ, ਕਹਿੰਆ, ਕਾਂਸੀ;
ਕਾਂਹ ਦਾ, ਕਾਂਹੇ ਵਰਗਾ; ਕਾਂਹ ਵਰਗਾ ਬਣਾਉਣਾ,
ਕਾਂਹ ਦਾ ਰੰਗ ਦੇਣਾ, ਭੂਰਾ ਤੇ ਲਾਲ ਕਰਨਾ

brook (ਬਰੁਕ) *n v* ਨਾਲਾ, ਛੋਟੀ ਨਦੀ, ਚੋਅ,
ਵੇਈਂ; ਬਰਦਾਸ਼ਤ ਕਰਨਾ, ਸਹਿਣਾ, ਸਹਿ ਜਾਣਾ,
ਸਹਾਰਨਾ, ਝੱਲਣਾ, ਜਰ ਜਾਣਾ; **~let** ਛੋਟਾ

ਨਾਲਾ, ਵੇਈਂ

broom (ਬਰੂਮ) *n* ਬੁਹਾਰੀ, ਝਾੜੂ; ਬਹੁਕਰ ਮਾਰਨੀ
ਜਾਂ ਦੇਣੀ, ਮਾਂਜਾ ਮਾਰਨਾ

brothel ('ਬਰੌਥਲ) *n* ਚਕਲਾ, ਕੰਜਰਖਾਨਾ, ਕੋਠਾ

brother ('ਬਰਅੱਧਅ*) *n* ਭਰਾ, ਭਾਈ, ਵੀਰ,
ਸਾਥੀ, ਗੁੱਝੂ, ਮਿੱਤਰ, ਸਹਿਯੋਗੀ, ਧਰਮ ਭਰਾ,
ਦੇਸ ਵਾਸੀ, ਹਮਵਤਨ; **~in-law** ਜੀਜਾ,
ਭਣਵੱਈਆ, ਸਾਲਾ; ਜੇਠ, ਦਿਉਰ; ਸਾਂਢੂ
ਨਨਾਣਵੱਈਆ; **half~** ਮਤੇਆ ਭਰਾ; **~hood**
ਭਾਈਚਾਰਾ, ਭਾਈਬੰਦੀ, ਬਰਾਦਰੀ, ਸ਼ਰੀਕਾ

brown (ਬਰਾਉਨ) *a n v* ਭੂਰਾ, ਖ਼ਾਕੀ, ਬਦਾਮੀ,
ਸਾਂਉਲਾ, ਤਾਂਬੇ ਦਾ ਸਿੱਕਾ; ਭੂਰੇ ਜਾਂ ਖ਼ਾਕੀ
ਕੱਪੜੇ; ਭੂਰਾ ਰੋਗਨ; ਭੂਰਾ ਕਰਨਾ

bruise (ਬਰੂਜ਼) *n v* ਰਗੜ, ਝਰੀਟ, ਖਸਰ,
ਲਾਗਾ, ਸੱਟ ਲੱਗਣ ਕਰਕੇ ਪਿਆ ਨੀਲ, ਦਾਗ਼;
ਰਗੜ ਮਾਰਨੀ, ਝਰੀਟ ਪੈਣੀ; ਖਸਰ ਲੱਗਾਉਣੀ;
ਦਰੜ ਦੇਣਾ, ਛਿਤਾੜ ਦੇਣਾ, ਚੂਰ ਕਰ ਦੇਣਾ, ਫੇਹ
ਸੁੱਟਣਾ; ਲੱਕੜੀ ਜਾਂ ਧਾਤ ਉੱਤੇ ਨਿਸ਼ਾਨ
ਬਣਾਉਣਾ; **~r** ਇਨਾਮੀ, ਮੁਕਾਬਲਾ ਕਰਨ
ਵਾਲਾ, ਇਨਾਮੀ ਦੰਗਲ ਲੜਨ ਵਾਲਾ, ਪੇਸ਼ਾਵਰ
ਮੁੱਕੇਬਾਜ਼, ਪਹਿਲਵਾਨ, ਮੱਲ

brush (ਬਰੁਅੱਸ਼) *v n* ਬੁਰਸ਼ ਕਰਨਾ, ਬੁਰਸ਼ ਨਾਲ
ਸਾਫ਼ ਕਰਨਾ ਜਾਂ ਚਮਕਾਉਣਾ; ਪੂੰਝਣਾ,
ਸੰਵਾਰਨਾ, ਝਾੜਨਾ; ਝਾੜ ਬੁਰਸ਼, ਕੂਚੀ, ਜੁਲਾਹੇ
ਦਾ ਕੁੱਚ, ਚਿੱਤਰਕਾਰ ਦੀ ਵਾਲਾਂ ਵਾਲੀ ਲੇਖਣੀ

brutal ('ਬਰੂਟਲ) *a* ਜੰਗਲੀ, ਵਹਿਸ਼ੀ, ਬੇਰਹਿਮ,
ਕਰੂਰ, ਅਤਿਆਚਾਰੀ, ਜ਼ਾਲਮ; **~ity** ਨਿਰਦਇਤਾ,
ਦਰਿੰਦਗੀ, ਜ਼ੁਲਮ, ਅੱਤਿਆਚਾਰ, ਕਰੂਰਤਾ

brute (ਬਰੂਟ) *n* ਨਿਰਦਈ ਵਿੱਅਕਤੀ; ਦਰਿੰਦਾ,
ਕਰੂਰ

bubble ('ਬੱਅਬਲ) *n v* ਬੁਲਬੁਲਾ; ਉਬਾਲ, ਧੋਖਾ,

ਪਰਪੰਚ, ਖਿਆਲੀ ਮਹਿਲ; ਬੁਲਬੁਲੇ ਨਿਕਲਣੇ; ਬੁਲਬੁਲੀਆਂ ਪਾਉਣੀਆਂ, ਉੱਬਲਣਾ

buck (ਬਅੱਕ) *n v* ਚਿਕਾਰਾ, ਚੀਤਲ; ਹਿਰਨ; ਮਰਦ; ਬਾਂਕਾ, ਛੈਲ ਮਨੁੱਖ; ਹਰਨ-ਚੌਕੜੀ ਭਰਨੀ, (ਘੋੜੇ ਦਾ) ਸਿੱਖ ਪਾ ਹੋਣਾ; ਧੂਸ ਮਾਰਨੀ; ਉਤਸ਼ਾਹਤ ਹੋਣਾ, ਖ਼ੁਸ਼ੀ ਨਾਲ ਭਰ ਜਾਣਾ, ਜੋਸ਼ ਵਿਚ ਆਉਣਾ; **~up** ਹੌਸਲਾ ਵਧਾਉਣਾ, ਜੋਸ਼ ਦਿਵਾਉਣਾ, ਹੱਲਾਸ਼ੇਰੀ ਦੇਣੀ

bucket (ਬੱਅਕਿਟ) *n v* ਬਾਲਟੀ, ਡੋਲ; ਡੋਲ ਨਾਲ ਪਾਣੀ ਕੱਢਣਾ; ਘੋੜਾ ਸਰਪਟ ਦੁੜਾਉਣਾ; ਬੇੜੀ ਨੂੰ ਕਾਹਲੀ ਚੱਪੂ ਨਾਲ ਚਲਾਉਣਾ; **kick the~** ਮਰ ਜਾਣਾ

buckle ('ਬਅੱਕਲ) *n v* ਬਕਸੂਆ; ਬਕਲ; ਬਕਸੂਆ ਲਾਉਣਾ, ਬਕਸੂਏ ਨਾਲ ਜੋੜਨਾ

buckram ('ਬਅੱਕਰਅਮ) *n a v* ਬੁਕਰਮ, ਮੋਟਾ ਤੇ ਕਰੜਾ ਕੱਪੜਾ, ਸਖ਼ਤ ਪਾਬੰਦੀ (ਵਰਤਾਉ ਵਿਹਾਰ ਵਿਚ) ਕਰੜਾਈ, ਨੇਮਬੱਧਤਾ, ਆਕੜ, ਰੁਖਾਈ; ਪੀੜ੍ਹਾ, ਸਖ਼ਤ, ਪੱਕਾ

bud (ਬਅੱਡ) *n v* ਕਲੀ, ਡੋਡੀ; ਕਲੀਆਂ ਨਿਕਲਣੀਆਂ, ਕਰੂੰਬਲਾਂ ਫੁੱਟਣੀਆਂ; ਵਿਕਾਸ ਦਾ ਆਰੰਭ ਕਰਨਾ, (ਬਾਗ਼ਬਾਨੀ) ਕਲਮ ਲਾਉਣੀ; *nip in the~* ਆਰੰਭ ਵਿਚ ਹੀ ਦਬਾ ਦੇਣਾ

budge (ਬਅੱਜ) *v* ਹਟਣਾ, ਖਿਸਕਣਾ, ਟਲਣਾ, ਸਰਕਣਾ; ਹਟਾਉਣਾ ਸਰਕਾਉਣਾ, ਟਾਲਣਾ

budget ('ਬਅੱਜਿਟ) *n* ਆਮਦਨੀ ਤੇ ਖ਼ਰਚ ਦਾ ਬਿਓਰਾ, ਆਮਦਨੀ-ਖ਼ਰਚ ਦਾ ਅਨੁਮਾਨ, ਸਾਲਾਨਾ ਆਮਦਨੀ-ਖ਼ਰਚ ਦਾ ਅਨੁਮਾਨਤ ਬਿਓਰਾ, ਬਜਟ; ਕਿਸੇ ਝੋਲੇ ਜਾਂ ਗੰਢ ਵਿਚ ਪਾਈਆਂ ਵਸਤੂਆਂ; **~esimate** ਬਜਟ-ਅਨੁਮਾਨ

buffalo ('ਬਅੱਫ਼ਅਲਓੁ) *n* ਸੈਂਹ, ਮੱਝ, ਸੰਢਾ, ਸੈਂਹਾਂ

buffer ('ਬਅੱਫ਼ਅ*') ਪੁਰਾਤਨਵਾਦੀ, ਦਕਿਆਨੂਸੀ, ਆਲਸੀ ਆਦਮੀ; **~state** ਦੋ ਵਿਰੋਧੀ ਰਾਜਾਂ ਦਰਮਿਆਨ ਇਕ ਨਿਰਪੱਖ ਦੇਸ

buffet ('ਬਅੱਫ਼ਿਟ) *n v* ਖਸੂਨ, ਮੁੱਕੀ; ਸੱਟ; ਲਹਿਰਾਂ ਦਾ ਥਪੇੜਾ; (ਚੀਜੀ ਦੇ) ਭਾਂਡਿਆਂ ਦੀ ਅਲਮਾਰੀ; ਮੇਜ਼ ਤੇ ਰਖੇ ਹੋਏ ਖਾਣੇ ਨੂੰ ਆਪਣੀ ਮਰਜ਼ੀ ਨਾਲ ਲੈਣਾ; ਖਸੂਨ ਮਾਰਨਾ, ਖਸੂਨ ਵੱਜਣਾ

buffoon (ਬਅੱਫ਼ੂਨ) *n v* ਵਿਦੂਸ਼ਕ, ਨਕਲੀਆ, ਭੰਡ; ਮਸਖ਼ਰਾ; ਮਸਖ਼ਰੀ ਕਰਨੀ, ਮਖ਼ੌਲ ਕਰਨਾ, ਨਕਲ ਲਾਹੁਣੀ, ਹਾਸਾ ਕਰਨਾ; **~ery** ਹਾਸਾ-ਠੱਠਾ, ਮਖ਼ੌਲਬਾਜ਼ੀ, ਭੰਡਬਾਜ਼ੀ

bug (ਬਅੱਗ) *n* ਖਟਮਲ; ਖਬਤ, ਖੁਫ਼ੀਆ ਮਾਈਕ੍ਰੋਫ਼ੋਨ

bugger ('ਬਅੱਗਅ*') *n* (ਗਾਲ੍ਹ ਵਜੋਂ) ਮੁੰਡੇਬਾਜ; ਸ਼ੈਤਾਨ, ਲੁੱਚਾ, ਬਦਮਾਸ਼

buggy ('ਬਅੱਗਿ) *n a* (1) ਬੱਘੀ, ਪਾਲਕੀ, ਗੱਡੀ; (2) ਖਟਮਲ ਵਾਲਾ, ਮਾਝਟੂਆਂ ਭਰਿਆ

bugle ('ਬਯੂਗਲ) *n v* ਬਿਗਲ; (ਵਜਾਉਣਾ); ਬਿਗਲ ਵਜਾ ਕੇ ਸਾਵਧਾਨ ਕਰਨਾ

build (ਬਿਲਡ) *n v* ਬਨਤਰ, ਨਿਰਮਾਣ-ਸ਼ੈਲੀ, ਨਿਰਮਾਣ, ਕਾਠੀ; ਬਣਾਉਣਾ, ਰਚਣਾ, ਨਿਰਮਾਣ ਕਰਨਾ, ਘਰ ਬਣਾਉਣਾ; **~er** ਰਾਜ, ਉਸਾਰੀ ਦੇ ਕੰਮ ਦਾ ਮਾਹਰ, ਉਸਰੱਈਆ, ਨਿਰਮਾਤਾ

building ('ਬਿਲਡਿਙ) *n* ਇਮਾਰਤ, ਭਵਨ, ਮਕਾਨ, ਘਰ; ਉਸਾਰੀ, ਨਿਰਮਾਣ

bulb (ਬਅੱਲਬ) *n v* ਬਲਬ, ਬਿਜਲੀ ਦਾ ਲਾਟੂ; ਗੰਢੀ, ਗੰਢ ਬੱਝਣੀ; ਗੰਢੇ ਵਰਗਾ ਫੁੱਲਾ ਹੋਣਾ, ਖੁੰਡੀ ਬਟਨੀ

bulge (ਬਅੱਲਜ) *v n* ਉੱਭਰਨਾ, ਫੁੱਲਣਾ, ਸੁੱਜਣਾ, ਅਗਾਂਹ ਵਧੇ ਹੋਣਾ; ਫੁਲਾਉਣਾ, ਵਧਾਉਣਾ,

ਪਸਾਰਨ; ਉਭਾਰ, ਕੁੱਬ, ਬਾਹਰ ਨੂੰ ਵਧਿਆ ਹਿੱਸਾ, ਸੋਜ, ਫੁਲਾਉ

bulginess ('ਬਅੱਲਜਿਨਿਸ) *n* ਉਭਾਰ, ਫੁਲਹਟ

bulk (ਬਅੱਲਕ) *n v* ਮਿਕਦਾਰ ਮਾਤਰਾ; ਭਾਰ, ਵਿਸਤਾਰ, ਜਹਾਜ਼ ਦਾ ਭਾਰ, ਖੇਪ, ਸਮੂਹ; ਢੇਰ; ਢੀਲ, ਕੱਦ-ਬੁੱਤ, ਆਕਾਰ; ਅਧਿਕ ਭਾਗ, ਅਧਿਕ ਮਾਤਰਾ, ਵੱਡਾ ਆਕਾਰ, ਭਾਰਾ ਸਰੀਰ; in ~ਭਾਰੀ ਮਾਤਰਾ ਵਿਚ; ~y ਵੱਡੇ ਆਕਾਰ ਵਾਲਾ, ਭਾਰਾ, ਵਿਸ਼ਾਲ, ਵੱਡਾ, ਮੋਟਾ-ਤਾਜ਼ਾ

bull (ਬੁਲ) *n* ਸਾਨ੍ਹ, ਬਲਦ, ਢੱਗਾ; ਵ੍ਹੇਲ ਮੱਛੀ ਦਾ ਨਰ; ਤੇਜ਼ੜੀਆ, ਸੱਟੇਬਾਜ਼, ਭਾਅ ਤੇਜ਼ ਕਰਨ ਵਾਲਾ; ਪੋਪ ਦਾ ਫ਼ਰਮਾਨ; ਕੀਮਤਾਂ ਚੜ੍ਹਾਉਣਾ, ਸੱਟੇ ਵਿਚ ਭਾਅ ਚੜ੍ਹਾਉਣੇ ~bitch ਜੁਆਨ ਕੁੱਤੀ; ~calf ਵੱਛਾ, ਵਹਿੜਕਾ; ਸਿੱਧੜ, ਸਿਧਰਾ; ~dog ਬੁਲੀ ਕੁੱਤਾ, ਇਕ ਵੱਡੇ ਸਿਰ ਵਾਲਾ ਕੁੱਤਾ; ਜ਼ਿੱਦੀ ਮਨੁੱਖ, ਗਲ ਪੈਣ ਵਾਲਾ ਲੜਾਕਾ, ਆਦਮੀ; ~dozer ਭੋਂ ਪੱਧਰੀ ਕਰਨ ਵਾਲੀ ਮਸ਼ੀਨ; ~headed ਹਠੀ, ਜ਼ਿੱਦੀ

bullet ('ਬੁਲਿਟ) *n* ਬੰਦੂਕ, ਪਿਸਤੌਲ, ਮਸ਼ੀਨਗਨ ਆਦਿ ਦੀ ਗੋਲੀ; ~proof ਜਿਸ ਉੱਤੇ ਗੋਲੀ ਅਸਰ ਨਾ ਕਰ ਸਕੇ

bulletin ('ਬੁਲਅਟਿਨ) *n* ਸੂਚਨਾ ਪੱਤਰ, ਸਰਕਾਰੀ ਸੂਚਨਾ, ਮਹੱਤਵ ਪੂਰਣ ਘਟਨਾਵਾਂ ਬਾਰੇ ਜਾਂ ਕਿਸੇ ਰੋਗੀ ਦੀ ਹਾਲਤ ਬਾਰੇ ਸੂਚਨਾ, ਬੁਲੇਟਿਨ

bullion ('ਬੁਲਯਅਨ) *n a* ਸ਼ੁੱਧ ਸੋਨਾ ਜਾਂ ਚਾਂਦੀ; ਸੋਨੇ ਜਾਂ ਚਾਂਦੀ ਦੀ ਇੱਟ; ਧਾਤੀ ਮੁਦਰਾ; ਸਰਾਫ਼ਾ

bullock ('ਬੁਲਅਕ) *n* ਬਲਦ, ਢੱਗਾ, ਬੋਲਦ

bully (ਬੁਲਿ) *n v* ਧੌਂਸਬਾਜ਼ ਗੁੰਡਾ, ਲੜਾਕਾ, ਦੱਲਾ, ਭੜੂਆ, ਧੱਕੇਸ਼ਾਹੀ ਕਰਨ ਵਾਲਾ; ਗੁੰਡਾਗਰਦੀ ਕਰਨੀ, ਧੱਕੇਸ਼ਾਹੀ ਕਰਨੀ, ਡਰਾਉਣਾ, ਧਮਕਾਉਣਾ, ਧੌਂਸ ਜਮਾਉਣੀ

bumper ('ਬਅੱਮਪਅ*) *n* ਟੱਕਰ, ਰੋਕ; ਬੰਪਰ, ਮੋਟਰ ਦੇ ਅੱਗੇ ਲੱਗੀ ਟੱਕਰ-ਰੋਕ ਫੱਟੀ; ਬੁਰੂਕਣ ਵਾਲਾ; ~crop ਭਰਵੀਂ ਫ਼ਸਲ

bun (ਬਅੱਨ) *n* ਬੰਦ, ਮਿੱਠੀ ਡਬਲ ਰੋਟੀ; ਜਲੇਬੀ ਜੂੜਾ; ਸਹੇ ਦੀ ਪੂਛ

bunch ('ਬਅੱਚ) *n v* ਗੁੱਛਾ, ਝੁੰਡ, ਗੁੱਟ; ਸਮੂਹ, ਜੱਥਾ, ਟੋਲੀ; ਗੁੱਛਾ ਬਣਾਉਣਾ; ਕੱਪੜੇ ਸੰਭਾਲਣੇ ਜਾਂ ਇਕੱਠੇ ਕਰਨੇ; ਇਕੱਠੇ ਹੋਣਾ, ਜੁੜਨਾ; ~of fives ਮੁੱਠੀ, ਪੰਜਾ; ~of flowers ਗੁਲਦਸਤਾ

bundle ('ਬਅੱਨਡਲ) *n v* ਗੰਢ, ਪੰਡ, ਗੰਢੜੀ, ਪੋਟਲੀ, ਬੰਡਲ, ਬੱਗਾ; ਗੰਢ ਬੰਨ੍ਹਨੀ, ਪੂਲਾ ਬੰਨ੍ਹਣਾ; ਇਕ ਥਾਂ ਇਕੱਠੇ ਕਰਕੇ ਬੰਨ੍ਹਣਾ

bungalow ('ਬਅੱਙਗਅਲਅਉ) *n* ਬੰਗਲਾ, ਕੋਠੀ, ਮਹਿਮਾਨ-ਘਰ

bungle ('ਬਅੱਙਗਲ) *n v* ਖ਼ਰਾਬੀ, ਵਿਗਾੜ, ਵੱਡੀ ਭੁੱਲ; ਅਨਾੜੀਪਨ; ਕੰਮ ਵਿਗਾੜਨਾ, ਗੜਬੜ ਕਰਨਾ, ਚੌੜ-ਚੁਪੱਟ ਕਰਨਾ; ~r ਅਨਾੜੀ, ਵਿਗਾੜੂ, ਬੁੱਧੂ, ਚੌੜ-ਚਾਨਣ, ਕੁਚੱਜਾ

bungling ('ਬਅੱਙਗਲਿਙ) *n* ਗੜਬੜ, ਗੋਲ-ਮਾਲ

buoy (ਬੋਇ) *n v* ਤਰਦਾ ਪੀਪਾ ਜਾਂ ਢੋਲ, ਤਰਿੰਦਾ; ਤਰਦੇ ਰਖਣ; ਸੰਭਾਲਣਾ, ਹੌਸਲਾ ਵਧਾਉਣਾ; ~ancy ਤੈਰਨ ਦੀ ਸ਼ਕਤੀ, ਤਰਨਸ਼ੀਲਤਾ; ਲਚਕ; ਉਤਸ਼ਾਹ, ਚਾਅ, ਉਮੰਗ, ਤਰੰਗ; ~ant ਤਰਨਯੋਗ, ਤਰਨਸ਼ੀਲ, ਤਰਨਹਾਰ; ਹੌਲਾ, ਛਹਲਾ; ਲਚਕਦਾਰ, ਰੁਸਤ, ਉੱਭਰਵਾਂ, ਮੌਜੀ, ਪ੍ਰਸੰਨਚਿਤ, ਖ਼ੁਸ਼ਦਿਲ

burden ('ਬਅਃਡਨ) *n v* ਭਾਰ; ਬੋਝ, ਵਜ਼ਨ, ਜ਼ੁੰਮੇਵਾਰੀ ਰਾਗ ਜਾਂ ਗੀਤ ਦੀ ਟੇਕ; ਭਾਸ਼ਟ ਆਦਿ ਦਾ ਕੇਂਦਰੀ ਭਾਵ; ਭਾਰ ਲੱਦਣਾ, ਭਾਰ ਪਾਉਣਾ, ਦਬਾਉਣਾ, ਜ਼ੁੰਮੇਵਾਰੀ ਪਾਉਣਾ, ਦੁਖੀ ਕਰਨਾ, ਕਸ਼ਟ ਦੇਣਾ

bureau ('ਬਯੁਅਰਅਉ) *n* (*pl*~*x*) ਦਫ਼ਤਰ, ਸਰਕਾਰੀ ਮਹਿਕਮਾ, ਰਾਜਕੀ ਵਿਭਾਗ, ਕੇਂਦਰ, ਕਾਰਿਆਲਾ, ਬਿਓਰੋ; ਕਈਆਂ ਖ਼ਾਨਿਆਂ ਵਾਲਾ ਮੇਜ਼, ਲਿਖਣ ਦੀ ਥਾਂ; **~cracy** ਅਫ਼ਸਰਸ਼ਾਹੀ, ਲਾਲ ਫ਼ੀਤਾ ਸ਼ਾਹੀ, ਅਧਿਕਾਰੀ-ਵਰਗ, ਅਫ਼ਸਰ ਲੋਕ; **~crat** ਅਫ਼ਸਰਸ਼ਾਹ,

burial ('ਬੈਰਿਅਲ) *n* ਮੁਰਦਾ ਦਫ਼ਨਾਉਣ ਦੀ ਰਸਮ, ਮੁਰਦਾ ਦਬੱਣ ਦੀ ਕਿਰਿਆ; ਅਰਥੀ, ਜਨਾਜ਼ਾ; ਅੰਤਮ ਸੰਸਕਾਰ

burn *v n* ਬਾਲਣਾ, ਸਾੜਨਾ, ਲੂਹਣਾ, ਮਘਾਉਣਾ, ਜਗਾਉਣਾ, ਭੜਕਾਉਣਾ, ਬਲਣਾ, ਲੂਸਣਾ, ਸੜਨਾ, ਡੰਮ੍ਹ ਲਾਉਣਾ, ਦਾਗ਼ ਦੇਣਾ, ਦਾਗ਼ਣਾ; ਸਾੜ, ਲੂਸ, ਡੰਮ੍ਹ, ਦਾਗ਼; **~ing** ਸੜਨ, ਜਲਣ, ਸਾੜਾ, ਦਾਹ, ਝੁਲਸ; ਤਪਦਾ, ਮਘਦਾ; (ਇੱਛਾ) ਤੀਬਰ; **~glass** ਆਤਸ਼ੀ ਸ਼ੀਸ਼ਾ; **~one's fingers** ਕਿਸੇ ਦੂਜੇ ਦੇ ਝਗੜੇ ਵਿਚ ਪੈ ਕੇ ਨੁਕਸਾਨ ਉਠਾਉਣਾ; **~out** ਸਭ ਕੁਝ ਸਾੜ ਫੂਕ ਦੇਣਾ; **~the candle at both ends** ਦੁਹੀਂ ਹੱਥੀਂ ਲੁਟਾਉਣਾ, ਬਹੁਤ ਜ਼ਿਆਦਾ ਖਰਚ ਕਰਨਾ; **~the mid night oil** ਰਾਤ ਨੂੰ ਬਹੁਤ ਦੇਰ ਨਾਲ ਕੰਮ ਕਰਨਾ

bursar ('ਬਅ:ਸਅ*) *n* ਖਜ਼ਾਨਚੀ, ਵਜ਼ੀਫ਼ਾ ਲੈਣ ਵਾਲਾ ਵਿਦਿਆਰਥੀ, ਬਰਸਰ

burst (ਬਅ:ਸਟ) *v n* ਫਟਣਾ, ਵਿਸਫੋਟ ਹੋਣਾ, ਪਾਟਣਾ, ਫੁੱਟਣਾ, ਫਿੱਸ ਜਾਣਾ, ਧਮਾਕਾ ਪੈਣਾ; ਬੜੇ ਵੇਗ ਨਾਲ ਖੁਲ੍ਹਣਾ, ਪਾੜ ਕੇ ਨਿਕਲ ਜਾਣਾ; ਧਮਾਕੇ ਨਾਲ ਪਾੜਨਾ; ਵਿਸਫੋਟ, ਉਛਾਲਾ ਭੜਕ, ਧੜਾਕਾ, ਫਟਣ, ਪਾਟਣ; ਮਨੋਭਾਵਾਂ ਦਾ ਅਚਾਨਕ ਵਿਸਫੋਟ; **~into laughter** ਖਿੜ-ਖਿੜ ਕੇ ਹੱਸ ਪੈਣਾ **~into tears** ਫੁੱਟ-ਫੁੱਟ ਕੇ ਰੋਣਾ; **~out** ਫੁੱਟ ਪੈਣਾ, ਚਾਘਾਂ ਮਾਰਨੀਆਂ, ਚੀਕ ਉੱਠਣਾ, ਛਿੜ ਪੈਣਾ, (ਬੀਮਾਰੀ) ਫੁੱਟ ਪੈਣੀ; **~sides with laughing** ਹੱਸਦਿਆਂ ਹੱਸਦਿਆਂ ਢਿੱਡ ਪੀੜ ਪੈ ਜਾਣੀ, ਹੱਸਦਿਆਂ ਵੱਖੀਆਂ ਟੁੱਟਣੀਆਂ; **~up** ਫਟ ਜਾਣਾ, ਖੁੱਲ੍ਹ ਜਾਣਾ, ਧਮਾਕਾ ਹੋਣਾ, ਵਿਸਫੋਟ ਹੋਣਾ; ਤਬਾਹ ਹੋ ਜਾਣਾ; **~with joy** ਖ਼ੁਸ਼ੀ ਵਿਚ ਫੁਲੇ ਨਾ ਸਮਾਉਣਾ

bury ('ਬੈਰਿ) *v* ਦੱਬਣਾ, ਗੱਡਣਾ, ਦਫ਼ਨਾਉਣਾ, ਦਫ਼ਨ ਕਰਨਾ; ਭੁਲਾ ਦੇਣਾ, ਮਿੱਟੀ ਹੇਠਾਂ ਢੱਕ ਦੇਣਾ, ਪੂਰ ਦੇਣਾ; **~alive** ਜੀਉਂਦਾ ਦਫ਼ਨ ਕਰ ਦੇਣਾ, ਦੱਬਾ ਦੇਣਾ; **~the hatchet** ਵੈਰ ਮੁਕਾਉਣਾ, ਤਲਵਾਰ ਮਿਆਨੇ ਪਾਉਣਾ

bus (ਬਅੱਸ) *n* ਬਸ, ਲਾਰੀ, ਮੋਟਰ-ਗੱਡੀ; **miss the~** ਮੌਕਾ ਖੁੰਝਾ ਦੇਣਾ, ਉੱਕ ਜਾਣਾ

bush (ਬੁਸ਼) *n* ਝਾੜੀ, ਝਾੜੀਆਂ ਦੀ ਝੰਗੀ, ਇਸ਼ਕ ਪੇਰੇ ਦੀ ਵੇਲ ਦਾ ਗੁੱਛਾ ਸੰਘਣੇ ਲੱਛੇਦਾਰ ਵਾਲ, ਝਾਟਾ, ਸੰਘਣੀਆਂ ਮੁੱਛਾਂ; **~fighter** ਛਾਪਾਮਾਰ, ਲੁਕ-ਛੁਪ ਕੇ ਲੜਾਈ ਕਰਨ ਵਾਲਾ, ਚੋਰ-ਲੜਾਈ ਲੜਨ ਵਾਲਾ, ਗੁਰੀਲਾ; **~fighting** ਛਾਪਮਾਰ ਲੜਾਈ; ਗੁਰੀਲਾ ਜੁੱਧ; **beat about the~** ਉਰਲੀਆਂ-ਪਰਲੀਆਂ ਮਾਰਨੀਆਂ; **~y** ਝਾੜੀਦਾਰ, ਸੰਘਣਾ

business ('ਬਿਜ਼ਨਿਸ) *n* ਵਣਜ-ਵਪਾਰ; ਪੇਸ਼ਾ, ਕਾਰੋਬਾਰ; ਕੰਮ, ਧੰਦਾ, ਵਿਹਾਰ, ਕੰਮ-ਕਾਰ; ਮਾਮਲਾ, ਰੁਝੇਵਾਂ, ਕੰਮਕਾਜ; ਮਤਲਬ, ਕਾਰਜ-ਕਰਮ; ਵਿਹਾਰ, ਲੈਣ-ਦੇਣ; ਕਾਰਜ ਦੀ ਗਤੀ-ਵਿਧੀ; **~man** ਵਪਾਰੀ, ਕਾਰੋਬਾਰੀ ਆਦਮੀ, ਵਿਹਾਰ ਵਿਚ ਤਜਰਬਾਕਾਰ; **has no~to** (ਉਸ ਦਾ) ਕੋਈ ਵਾਸਤਾ ਨਹੀਂ, ਕੋਈ ਹੱਕ ਨਹੀਂ

bust (ਬਅੱਸਟ) *n v* ਵਿਅਕਤੀ ਦਾ ਧੜ, ਬੁੱਤ; ਪੁਲੀਸ ਵਲੋਂ ਛਾਪਾ ਮਾਰ ਕੇ ਫੜਨਾ

busy ('ਬਿਜ਼ਿ) *a v* ਮਸਰੂਫ਼, ਰੁੱਝਾ ਹੋਇਆ, ਲੱਗਾ

ਹੋਇਆ, ਵਿਆਸਤ; ਆਹਰੀ, ਲੀਨ, ਮਗਨ;
ਰੁਝਣਾ, ਆਹਰੇ ਲਾਉਣਾ, ਜਾਂ ਲੱਗਣਾ, ਕੰਮ
ਵਿਚ ਜੁਟਣਾ

but (ਬਅੱਟ) *conj, prep, adv. n* ਇਤਰਾਜ਼,
ਆਪੱਤੀ; ਕਿੰਤੂ, ਲੇਕਿਨ, ਕੇਵਲ; ਫਿਰ ਵੀ, ਤਾਂ ਵੀ;
ਪਰ ਇਸ ਦੇ ਨਾਲ ਹੀ, ਪਰ ਫਿਰ ਵੀ; ਆਰੋਪ

butcher (ਬੁਚਆ*) *n v* ਕਸਾਈ, ਝਟਕਈ, ਬੁੱਚੜ;
ਜਲਾਦ; ਝਟਕਾਉਣਾ, ਹੱਤਿਆ ਕਰਨੀ, ਖ਼ੂਨ
ਕਰਨਾ, ਮਾਰ ਸੁੱਟਣਾ, ਕੋਹਣਾ; ਕਰੜੀ ਨੁਕਤਾ-
ਚੀਨੀ ਕਰਨਾ; ~y ਬੁਚੜਖ਼ਾਨਾ, ਕਸਾਈਪੁਣਾ,
ਖ਼ੂਨ-ਖ਼ਰਾਬਾ, ਨਿਰਦਇਤਾ ਪੂਰਵਕ ਹਤਿਆ,
ਵੱਢ-ਟੁੱਕ

butler ('ਬਅੱਟਲਅ*) *n* ਖ਼ਾਨਸਾਮਾ, ਨੌਕਰਾਂ ਦਾ
ਮੁਖੀ, ਸ਼ਰਾਬਖ਼ਾਨੇ ਦਾ ਕਰਮਚਾਰੀ, ਰਕਾਬਦਾਰ
ਭੰਡਾਰੀ, ਖ਼ਰੋਗੀ, ~y ਭੰਡਾਰ, ਲੰਗਰ

butt (ਬਅੱਟ) *n v* ਪੀਪਾ, ਕੁੰਦਾ; ਟੱਕਰ, ਧੱਕਾ;
ਚਾਂਦਮਾਰੀ ਦਾ ਮੈਦਾਨ; ਕਿਸੇ ਹਥਿਆਰ ਜਾਂ ਸੰਦ
ਦਾ ਮੋਟਾ ਸਿਰਾ; ਹਾਸੇ-ਠੱਠੇ ਦਾ ਮੌਜੂ ਜਿਸ ਦਾ
ਮਖ਼ੌਲ ਉਡਾਇਆ ਜਾਵੇ; ਸਿਰ ਦੀ ਟੱਕਰ
ਮਾਰਨੀ, ਧੱਕਣਾ; ਬਾਹਰ ਕੱਢਣਾ

butter ('ਬਅੱਟਅ*) *n v* ਮੱਖਣ, ਸੱਖਣੀ; ਚੋਪੜਨਾ,
ਮੱਖਣ ਝੱਸਣਾ; ਚਾਪਲੂਸੀ ਕਰਨੀ, ਚਿਕਨੀਆਂ
ਚੋਪੜੀਆਂ ਗੱਲਾਂ ਕਰਨੀਆਂ; ~milk ਲੱਸੀ, ਛਾਹ

butterfly ('ਬਅੱਟਅਫ਼ਲਾਇ) *n* ਤਿਤਲੀ; ਭੰਬੀਰੀ,
ਦਿਲ ਡੁੱਬਣ ਦਾ ਭਾਵ

buttock ('ਬਅੱਟਅਕ) *n v* ਚਿੱਤੜ, ਪਿੱਛਾ, ਪੁੱਠਾ;
ਘੋਲ (ਕੁਸ਼ਤੀ) ਦਾ ਇਕ ਦਾਅ; ਪੱਟਾਂ ਤੋਂ ਫੜ ਕੇ ਸੁੱਟ
ਦੇਣਾ, ਚਿੱਤੜਾਂ ਭਾਰ ਸੁੱਟਣਾ, ਚੁੱਕ ਕੇ ਮਾਰਨਾ

button (ਬਅੱਟਨ) *n v* ਬਟਨ, ਬੀਜਾ, ਗੁਦਾਮ
ਡੋਡੀ, ਅਖਿੜੀ ਖੁੰਭ; ਬਟਨ ਬੰਦ ਕਰਨੇ;
~hole ਕਾਜ, ਬਟਨ ਮਾਰਨ ਵਾਲਾ ਸੁਰਾਖ਼

buy (ਬਾਇ) *n v* ਖ਼ਰੀਦ, ਸੌਦਾ, ਮੁੱਲ; ਖ਼ਰੀਦਣਾ,
ਮੁੱਲ ਲੈਣਾ, ਪ੍ਰਾਪਤ ਕਰਨਾ, ਕਿਸੇ ਨੂੰ ਵੱਢੀ ਦੇ
ਕੇ ਆਪਣੇ ਨਾਲ ਮਿਲਾ ਲੈਣਾ; ~off ਕੁਝ ਦੇ
ਲੈ ਕੇ ਜਾਨ ਛੁਡਾ ਲੈਣੀ; ~over ਰਿਸ਼ਵਤ ਦੇ
ਕੇ ਆਪਣੇ ਵੱਲ ਕਰ ਲੈਣਾ; ~up ਸਾਰਾ ਮਾਲ
ਖ਼ਰੀਦ ਲੈਣਾ; **a good ~** ਖਰਾ ਸੌਦਾ; ~er
ਖ਼ਰੀਦਾਰ, ਗਾਹਕ

buzz (ਬਅੱਜ਼) *n v* ਸ਼ਹਿਦ ਦੀ ਮੱਖੀ ਆਦਿ ਦੀ
ਗੂੰਜ, ਭਿਣਕ, ਭਿਣਕਾਰ, ਭਿਣਭਿਣਾਹਟ;
ਭਿਣਕਣਾ, ਭਿਣ-ਭਿਣ ਕਰਨਾ, ਗੁਣਗੁਣਾਉਣਾ;
ਗਟ ਗਟ ਪੀ ਜਾਣਾ; ਚੜ੍ਹਾ ਜਾਣਾ (ਸ਼ਰਾਬ)

buzzer ('ਬਅੱਜ਼ਅ*) *n* ਸੀਟੀ, ਜਹਾਜ਼ ਦਾ ਭੋਂਪੂ;
ਭਿਣਕਲ ਵਾਲਾ; ਸਿਗਨੇਲਰ

by (ਬਾਇ) *adv prep a* ਤੋਂ, ਬੋਂ, ਤਕ, ਤੇੜੀ;
ਦੁਆਰਾ, ਹੱਥੀਂ; ਕੋਲੋਂ, ਨਾਲ ਹੀ; ਕੋਲ, ਨੇੜੇ, ਲਾਂਗੇ,
ਵੱਲ, ਬੰਨੇ, ਪਾਸੇ; ਨਾਲ ਨਾਲ, ਵਿਚੋਂ ਦੀ; ~all
means ਜ਼ਰੂਰ, ਅਵੱਸ਼, ਨਿਸਚੇ ਹੀ, ਹਰ ਹੀਲੇ;
~gone ਬੀਤਿਆ ਕਾਲ, ਭੂਤਕਾਲ, ਅਤੀਤ,
ਪੁਰਾਣਾ; ~heart ਜ਼ਬਾਨੀ, ਮੂੰਹ ਜ਼ਬਾਨੀ; ~lane
ਗਾਲੀ, ਵੱਡੀ ਗਾਲੀ ਵਿਚੋਂ ਨਿਕਲੀ ਛੋਟੀ ਗਾਲੀ,
ਇਕ ਪਾਸੇ ਦੀ ਛੋਟੀ ਗਾਲੀ; ~name ਉਪ-ਨਾਮ,
ਅੱਲ; ~pass ਫਿਰਨੀ, ਲਾਂਭਵੀਂ ਸੜਕ, ਇਕ
ਪਾਸੇ ਦਾ ਰਾਹ, ਉਪ-ਮਾਰਗ, ਸਿੱਧਾ ਰਸਤਾ;
~path ਪਗ-ਡੰਡੀ, ਇਕ ਪਾਸੇ ਦਾ ਰਾਹ,
ਉਪਮਾਰਗ, ਸਿੱਧੀ ਡੰਡੀ; ~product ਗੌਣ-
ਉਪਜ, ਨਾਲ ਲਗਦੀ ਪੈਦਾਵਾਰ; ~way
ਉਪਮਾਰਗ; ~word ਲੋਕੋਕਤੀ, ਕਹਾਵਤ, ਅਖਾਣ

by(e) (ਬਾਇ) *a* ਉਪ, ਇਤਫ਼ਾਕੀਆ, ਜ਼ਿਮਨੀ;
~election ਉਪਚੋਣ, ਜ਼ਿਮਨੀ ਚੋਣ; ~law
ਉਪ-ਨਿਯਮ, ਜ਼ਿਮਨੀ-ਕਾਨੂੰਨ; ~bye ਰੱਬ ਰਾਖਾ!
ਅਲਵਿਦਾ!

C

C, c (ਸੀ) *n* ਰੋਮਨ ਵਰਨਮਾਲਾ ਦਾ ਤੀਜਾ ਅੱਖਰ; ਤੀਜਾ ਮਨੁੱਖ ਜਾਂ ਤੀਜੀ ਗੱਲ

cab (ਕੈਬ) *n v* ਭਾੜੇ ਦੀ ਗੱਡੀ, ਟੈਕਸੀ, ਯੱਕੇ, ਬੱਘੀ ਵਿਚ ਜਾਣਾ ਜਾਂ ਉਸਨੂੰ ਚਲਾਉਣਾ; ~man ਕੋਚਵਾਨ, ਟੈਕਸੀ-ਡਰਾਇਵਰ, ਟੈਕਸੀ ਵਾਲਾ, ਯੱਕੇ ਵਾਲਾ; ਬੱਘੀ ਵਾਲਾ

cabaret ('ਕੈਬਅਰੇਇ) *n* ਰੈਸਤੋਰਾਂ ਵਿਚ ਨਾਚ ਰੰਗ, ਮਨੋਰੰਜਨ-ਕਾਰਜ, ਕੈਬਰੇ ਨਾਚ; ਸ਼ਰਾਬਖ਼ਾਨਾ, ਮੈਖ਼ਾਨਾ

cabbage ('ਕੈਬਿਜ਼) *n* ਬੰਦ ਗੋਭੀ, ਪੱਤ ਗੋਭੀ

cabin ('ਕੈਬਿਨ) *n v* ਕੋਠੜੀ, ਝੁੱਗੀ, ਹੁਜਰਾ, ਝੌਂਪੜੀ; ਜਹਾਜ਼ ਦਾ ਖ਼ਾਨ ਜਾਂ ਸੌਣ ਦਾ ਕਮਰਾ, ਕੈਬਿਨ; (ਕੈਬਿਨ ਵਿਚ) ਬੰਦ ਕਰਨਾ, ਤੁੰਨਣਾ, ਤੰਗ ਥਾਂ ਵਿਚ ਭਰਨਾ

cabinet ('ਕੈਬਿਨਿਟ) *n* (1) ਛੋਟਾ ਕਮਰਾ, ਹੁਜਰਾ, ਖ਼ਿਲਵਤ-ਖ਼ਾਨਾ, ਨਿੱਜੀ ਕਮਰਾ; (2) ਛੋਟੀ ਅਲਮਾਰੀ, ਦਰਾਜ਼ਾਂ ਵਾਲਾ ਸੰਦੂਕ; (3) ਕਾਬੀਨਾ, ਵਜ਼ਾਰਤ, ਮੰਤਰੀ-ਮੰਡਲ; ਦੀਵਾਨ-ਖ਼ਾਸ

cable ('ਕੇਇਬਲ) *n* ਤਾਰ, ਸੰਗਲੀ, ਰੱਸੀ; ਸਮੁੰਦਰੀ-ਤਾਰ; (ਮੁੰਜ ਦਾ) ਮੋਟਾ ਰੱਸਾ, ਲੰਗਰ ਦਾ ਸੰਗਲ ਜਾਂ ਰੱਸਾ; ਵਲਦਾਰ ਨੱਕਾਸ਼ੀ; ਤਾਰ ਕਸਣਾ, ਰੱਸੀ ਕਸਣਾ ਸਮੁੰਦਰੀ ਤਾਰ ਦੇਣੀ, ਰੱਸੀ ਜਾਂ ਸੰਗਲ ਨਾਲ ਬੰਨ੍ਹਣਾ

cackle (ਕੈਕਲ) *v n* ਕੁੜ ਕੁੜ ਕਰਨਾ, ਕੁੜ-ਕੁੜਾਉਣਾ; ਬਕਵਾਸ ਕਰਨੀ; ਸ਼ੇਖੀ ਮਾਰਨੀ, ਗੱਪ ਮਾਰਨੀ; ਬਕਵਾਸ, ਸ਼ੇਖੀ, ਗੱਪ, ਬਕ-ਬਕ, ਗੱਪ-ਸੜੱਪ

cactus (ਕੈਕਟਅਸ) *n* ਥੋਹਰ, ਨਾਗ-ਫਣੀ

cad (ਕੈਡ) *n* ਕਮੀਨਾ, ਉਜੱਡ ਬੰਦਾ; ਬਸ ਦਾ ਕੰਡਕਟਰ; ਮੁੰਡੂ

cadet (ਕਅ'ਡੈਟ) *n* ਫੌਜੀ ਸਕੂਲ ਦਾ ਵਿਦਿਆਰਥੀ, ਸੈਨਾ-ਸਿਖਿਆਰਥੀ, ਕੈਡਿਟ ਛੋਟਾ ਪੁੱਤਰ ਜਾਂ ਛੋਟਾ ਭਰਾ; ~corps ਫੌਜੀ ਸਕੂਲ ਦੇ ਵਿਦਿਆਰਥੀਆਂ ਦੀ ਕੰਪਨੀ, ਕੈਡਿਟ ਕੋਰ

cadre ('ਕਾਡਅ') *n* ਸ਼੍ਰੇਣੀ, ਵਰਗਾ, ਸੰਗਠਨ, ਢਾਂਚਾ; ਸਥਾਈ ਅਮਲਾ, ਰੂਪ-ਰੇਖਾ, ਨਫ਼ਰੀ

cafe ('ਕੈਫ਼ੇਇ) *n* (F) ਕਾਹਵਾ, ਕਾਫ਼ੀ; ਕਾਹਵਾਖ਼ਾਨਾ, ਵਿਸ਼੍ਰਾਮ ਘਰ, ਕਾਫ਼ੀ ਹਾਊਸ, ਰੈਸਤੋਰਾਂ, ਕੈਫ਼ੇ; ~teria ਭੋਜਨ-ਭੰਡਾਰ, ਅੰਨ-ਪੂਰਨਾ, ਰੈਸਤੋਰਾਂ

cage ('ਕੇਇਜ) *n v* ਪਿੰਜਰਾ; ਕੈਦਖ਼ਾਨਾ ਕਟਿਹਰਾ, ਜੰਗਲਾ; ਪਿੰਜਰੇ ਪਾਉਣਾ, ਜੇਲ੍ਹ ਵਿਚ ਬੰਦ ਕਰਨਾ, ਕੈਦੀ ਬਣਾਉਣਾ

cajole (ਕਅ'ਜਅਉਲ) *v* ਫੁਸਲਾਉਣਾ, ਪਸਮਾਉਣਾ, ਪਤਿਆਉਣਾ; ਚਾਪਲੂਸੀ ਕਰਨੀ, ਪੁਰਕਾਰਨਾ, ਖ਼ੁਸ਼ਾਮਦ ਕਰਨੀ; ਝਾਸਾਂ ਦੇਣਾ; ~ment, ~ry ਚਾਪਲੂਸੀ, ਫੁਸਲਾਹਟੀ, ਬੁੱਤੀ

cake (ਕੇਇਕ) *n* ਕੇਕ, ਟਿੱਕੀ, ਕੁਲਚਾ, ਮਿੱਠੀ ਰੋਟੀ, ਮੱਠੀ, ਮੰਨ, (ਕਿਸੇ ਚੀਜ਼ ਦੀ) ਚਾਕੀ; charity~ (ਸਾਧੂ ਫ਼ਕੀਰ ਨੂੰ ਭਿੱਖਿਆ ਵਿਚ ਦਿੱਤੀ ਹੋਈ ਰੋਟੀ) ਸਧੁਕੜ, ਹੰਦਾ; to take the~ ਟਿੱਕੀ ਜਾਂ ਪੇੜੀ ਬਣਾਉਣਾ, ਟਿੱਕੀਆਂ ਜਮਾਉਣਾ, ਚਪੜੀ ਜਮਾਉਣੀ, ਪੇਪੜੀ ਬੱਝਣੀ ਬਾਜ਼ੀ ਲੈ ਜਾਣਾ, ਨਾਮਣਾ ਖੱਟਣਾ

calamity (ਕਅ'ਲੈਮਅਟਿ) *n* ਬਿਪਤਾ, ਮੁਸੀਬਤ, ਰੱਬੀ ਕਹਿਰ, ਕਸ਼ਟ, ਬਦਬਖ਼ਤੀ

calcify (ਕੈਲਸਿਫ਼ਾਇ) *v* ਪੱਥਰ ਜਾਣਾ, ਕਰੜਾ ਹੋ ਜਾਣਾ, ਸਖ਼ਤ ਕਰਨਾ, ਚੂਨਾ ਬਣ ਜਾਣਾ

calcium (ਕੈਲਸ਼ਿਅਮ) *n* ਚੂਨੇ ਦੀ ਕਿਸਮ, ਚੂਨੇ ਦਾ ਸਾਰ, ਕੈਲਸ਼ਿਅਮ

calculate (ਕੈਲਕਯੁਲੇਇਟ) *v* ਗਿਣਨਾ, ਲੇਖਾ ਕਰਨਾ, ਜਾਚਣਾ, ਹਿਸਾਬ ਲਾਉਣਾ, ਗਿਣਤੀ ਕਰਨਾ, ਅਨੁਮਾਨ ਲਾਉਣਾ, ਹੱਝਣਾ, ਅੰਕਣਾ, ਕਿਆਸ ਕਰਨਾ, ਵਿਚਰਨਾ

calculating (ਕੈਲਕਯੁਲੇਇਟਿਙ) *a* ਹਿਸਾਬੀ, ਗਿਣਤੀਆਂ ਗਿਣਨ ਵਾਲਾ, ਸੁਆਰਥੀ, ਮਤਲਬੀ

calculation (ਕੈਲਕਯੁ'ਲੇਇਸ਼ਨ) *n* ਅਨੁਮਾਨ, ਗਿਣਤੀ, ਗਣਨਾ, ਹਿਸਾਬ, ਅੰਦਾਜ਼ਾ, ਤਖ਼ਮੀਨਾ, ਕਿਆਸ, ਲੇਖਾ-ਜੋਖਾ, ਅੱਟਾ-ਸੱਟਾ; ਸੋਚ-ਵਿਚਾਰ

calculative (ਕੈਲਕਯੁਲਅਟਿਵ) *a* ਗਿਣਤੀ-ਸਬੰਧੀ, ਹਿਸਾਬੀ

calculator (ਕੈਲਕਯੁਲੇਇਟਅ*) *n* ਹਿਸਾਬੀ, ਅਨੁਮਾਨ ਲਾਉਣ ਵਾਲੀ, ਹਿਸਾਬੀ ਮਸ਼ੀਨ, ਸਵਾਲ ਕੱਢਣ ਵਾਲੀ ਮਸ਼ੀਨ; ਗਣਨ-ਜੰਤਰੀ; ~y ਗਣਨਾ-ਸਬੰਧੀ, ਗਿਣਤੀ-ਸਬੰਧੀ, ਗਣਨਾਤਮਕ

calculous (ਕੈਲਕਯੁਲਅਸ) *a* ਪੱਥਰੀਲਾ, ਕੰਕਰੀਲਾ, ਪੱਥਰੀ ਦਾ ਰੋਗੀ, ਪੱਥਰੀ ਦੀ ਬੀਮਾਰੀ ਦਾ

calculus (ਕੈਲਕਯੁਲਅਸ) *n* (ਚਿਕਿ) ਪੱਥਰੀ, ਗਣਿਤ ਦੀ ਇਕ ਸ਼ਾਖਾ, ਕੈਲਕੁਲਸ

calendar (ਕੈਲਿਨਡਅ*) *n v* ਜੰਤਰੀ, ਪੱਤਰੀ, ਕੈਲੰਡਰ, ਤਾਰੀਖ਼ਾਂ ਦਾ ਹਿਸਾਬ-ਕਿਤਾਬ, ਨਿਯਮਾਵਲੀ; ਡਾਇਰੀ; ਦਰਜ ਕਰਨਾ, ਰਜਿਸਟਰ ਵਿਚ ਚੜ੍ਹਾਉਣਾ, ਸੂਚੀ ਬਣਾਉਣੀ, ਤਰਤੀਬ ਦੇਣੀ, ਵਿਉਂਤ ਅਨੁਸਾਰ ਕਰਨਾ

calf (ਕਾਫ਼) *n* ਵੱਛਾ, ਵੱਛੀ, ਕੱਟਾ, ਕੱਟੀ, ਵਛੇਰਾ, ਵਛਿਕਾ, ਹਾਥੀ ਦਾ ਬੱਚਾ, (ਹਿਰਨੋਟਾ); ਅਸੂਝ

ਵਿਅਕਤੀ; ~'s teeth ਦੁੱਧ ਦੇ ਦੰਦ; cow in~, cow with~ ਸੂਣ ਵਾਲੀ ਗਾਂ; moon~ ਜਮਾਂਦਰੂ ਮੂਰਖ

calibre, caliber (ਕੈਲਿਬਅ*) *n* ਯੋਗਤਾ, ਹੈਸੀਅਤ, ਅਖ਼ਲਾਕੀ ਪੱਧਰ, ਵਿਆਸ, ਬੋਰ

call (ਕੋਲ) *v n* ਬੁਲਾਉਣਾ, ਪੁਕਾਰਨਾ, ਜ਼ੋਰ ਨਾਲ ਚੀਕਣਾ, ਹਾਜ਼ਰੀ ਬੋਲਣਾ, ਸੱਦਣਾ, ਬੁਲਾ ਘੱਲਣਾ, ਧਿਆਨ ਕਰਨਾ; ਚਹਿਚਹਾਟ; ਬਿਗਲ, ਜ਼ਰੂਰਤ, ਹੁਕਮ, ਦੁਹਾਈ; ਅਵਾਜ਼, (ਟੈਲੀਫ਼ੋਨ ਦੀ) ਕਾਲ, ਰਸਮੀ ਮੁਲਾਕਾਤ; ਕਸ਼ਸ਼, ਬੁਲਾਵਾ; ~a meeting ਬੈਠਕ ਬੁਲਾਉਣਾ, ਇਕੱਤਰਤਾ ਕਰਨੀ; ~a spade a spade ਸਾਫ਼-ਸਾਫ਼ ਆਖਣਾ, ਕਾਣੇ ਨੂੰ ਕਾਣਾ ਆਖਣਾ, ਸੱਚ-ਪੱਤਰ ਹੋਣਾ; ~at ਮਿਲਣ ਜਾਣਾ; ~ boy ਨੋਕਰ; ~for ਮੰਗਣਾ, ਲੈ ਆਉਣਾ, ਫ਼ਰਮਾਇਸ਼ ਕਰਨੀ, ਸੰਗ ਕਰਨੀ; ~girl ਕਾਲ ਗਰਲ, ਨੱਚਨੀ; ~in (ਡਾਕਟਰ ਆਦਿ ਨੂੰ ਇਲਾਜ ਲਈ ਸਦੱਣਾ, ਵਾਪਸ ਲੈਣਾ; ~in question (ਤੇ) ਕਿੰਤੂ ਕਰਨਾ; ~money (ਬੈਂਕ) ਕਰਜ਼ਾ ਜਾਚਣ-ਰਾਸ਼ੀ; ~names ਗਾਲੀਆਂ ਦੇਣਾ, ਗਾਲ੍ਹਾਂ ਕੱਢਣੀਆਂ, ਬੁਰਾ ਭਲਾ ਆਖਣਾ; ~on ਮਿਲਣਾ, ਮਿਲਣ ਜਾਣਾ; ~out ਲਲਕਾਰਨਾ, ਵੰਗਾਰਨਾ, ਚੁਣੌਤੀ ਦੇਣਾ; ~note ਬੁਲਾਵਾ, ਸੱਦਾ, ਚੇਤਾਵਨੀ; ~sign ਨਾਮ-ਸੰਕੇਤ, ਨਾਮ-ਚਿੰਨ੍ਹ; ~woman ਦਾਈ; ~of nature (ਟੱਟੀ ਪਿਸ਼ਾਬ ਦੀ) ਹਾਜਤ; ~roll ਹਾਜ਼ਰੀ

calligrapher (ਕਅ'ਲਿਗਰਅਫ਼ਅ*) *n* ਸੁਲੇਖਕ, ਸੁਲਿਪੀਕਾਰ, ਖ਼ੁਸ਼ਨਵੀਸ

calligraphist (ਕੈਲਿ'ਗਰਅਫ਼ਿਸਟ) *n* ਸੁਲੇਖਕ, ਕਾਤਬ, ਖ਼ੁਸ਼ਨਵੀਸ

calligraphy (ਕਅ'ਲਿਗਰਅਫ਼ਿ) *n* ਸੁਲੇਖ, ਸੁਲੇਖ-ਕਲਾ, ਸੁੰਦਰ ਲਿਖਾਈ, ਖ਼ੁਸ਼ਖ਼ਤੀ, ਖ਼ੁਸ਼ਨਵੀਸੀ

calling (ਕੋਲਿੰਡ) *n* ਬੁਲਾਵਾ, ਰੱਬੀ ਰਜ਼ਾ, ਭਾਣਾ, ਪੇਸ਼ਾ, ਪੰਦਾ, ਨੇਕ ਪੇਸ਼ਾਵਰ ਲੋਕ ਜਾਂ ਕਿਸੇ ਖ਼ਾਸ ਕਿੱਤੇ ਨਾਲ ਸਬੰਧਤ ਪੁਰਸ਼; ~list ਅਤਿਥੀ-ਸੂਚੀ, ਵਿਜ਼ਿਟਿੰਗ-ਲਿਸਟ

callous (ਕੈਲਅਸ) *a* ਕਠੋਰ, ਨਿਰਦਈ, ਪੱਥਰ-ਚਿੱਤ, ਕਰੂਰ, ਬੇਰਹਿਮ, ਬੇਦਰਦ, ਸੰਗਦਿਲ; ~ness ਨਿਰਦਇਤਾ, ਕਠੋਰਤਾ, ਸਖ਼ਤੀ, ਬੇਰਹਿਮੀ, ਕਰੜਾਈ, ਬੇਦਰਦੀ, ਸੰਗਦਿਲੀ

calm (ਕਾਮ) *n a v* ਸ਼ਾਂਤੀ, ਚੈਨ, ਖ਼ਮੋਸ਼ੀ, ਸਥਿਰਤਾ, ਟਿਕਾਉ, ਅਡੋਲਤਾ, ਸਕੂਨ, ਸ਼ਾਂਤ, ਚੁੱਪ, ਖ਼ਮੋਸ਼; ਸ਼ਾਂਤ ਕਰਨਾ, ਚੁੱਪ ਕਰਾਉਣਾ, ਟਿਕਾਉਣਾ, ਤਸੱਲੀ ਦੇਣੀ, ਖ਼ਮੋਸ਼ ਹੋਣਾ; ~ly ਧੀਰਜ ਨਾਲ, ਸ਼ਾਂਤੀ ਨਾਲ, ਸਹਿਜ ਨਾਲ; ~ness ਸ਼ਾਂਤੀ, ਖ਼ਮੋਸ਼ੀ, ਸਕੂਨ, ਧੀਰਜ, ਸਥਿਰਤਾ

camel (ਕੈਮਲ) *n* ਊਠ; ਇਕ ਮਸ਼ੀਨ ਜਿਸ ਨਾਲ ਸਮੁੰਦਰੀ ਜਹਾਜ਼ ਨੂੰ ਘੱਟ ਡੂੰਘੇ ਪਾਣੀ ਵਿਚ ਚਲਾਇਆ ਜਾਂਦਾ ਹੈ;

camouflage (ਕੈਮਅਫਲਾਯ਼) *n v* ਭੁਲਾਂਦਰਾ, ਛਲ ਦਾ ਪਰਦਾ, ਭੁਲਾਂਦਰੇ ਰਾਹੀਂ ਲੁਕਾਉਣਾ

camp (ਕੈਂਪ) *n v* ਡੇਰਾ, ਪੜਾਓ, ਛਾਉਣੀ, ਤੰਬੂ, ਸਫਰੀ ਜੀਵਨ, ਧੜਾ, ਪੱਖ; ਸੈਨਾ, ਕੈਂਪ; ਪੜਾਓ ਕਰਨਾ, ਤੰਬੂ ਲਾਉਣਾ; ਡੇਰਾ ਕਰਨਾ, ਛਾਉਣੀ ਪਾਉਣੀ

campaign (ਕੈਂਪੇਇਨ) *n v* ਅੰਦੋਲਨ; ਜੰਗ, ਮੁਹਿੰਮ, ਜੱਦੋ-ਜਹਿਦ, ਲੜਾਈ; ਫ਼ੌਜੀ ਕਾਰਵਾਈ, ਜਥੇਬੰਦ ਕਾਰਵਾਈ, ਮਹਾਨ ਉਦਮ, ਜੱਦੋ-ਜਹਿਦ ਵਿਚ ਸ਼ਾਮਲ ਹੋਣਾ, ਸੰਘਰਸ਼ ਵਿਚ ਪੈਣਾ, ਅੰਦੋਲਨ ਚਲਾਉਣਾ; ~er ਅੰਦੋਲਨਕਾਰੀ, ਮੁਹਿੰਮਬਾਜ਼, ਘੁਲਾਟੀਆ

camphor (ਕੈਮਫਅ*) *n* ਕਪੂਰ, ਮੁਸ਼ਕ ਕਾਫ਼ੂਰ

campus (ਕੈਂਪਅਸ) *n* ਇਹਾਤਾ (ਸਕੂਲ, ਕਾਲਜ, ਜਾਂ ਯੂਨੀਵਰਸਿਟੀ ਦਾ) ਕੈਂਪਸ, ਸਿੱਖਿਆ-ਸੰਸਥਾ, ਕਾਲਜ

can (ਕੈਨ) *n v aux* ਕੁੱਪਾ, ਡੋਲ, ਕਨਸਤਰ, ਪੀਪਾ, ਡੱਬਾ ਪੀਪੇ ਵਿਚ ਭਰਨਾ, ਡੋਲ ਭਰਨਾ, ਡੱਬੇ ਵਿਚ ਬੰਦ ਕਰਨਾ; ਸਕਣਾ, ਯੋਗ ਹੋਣਾ, ਹੋ ਸਕਣਾ, ਸੰਭਵ ਹੋਣਾ

canal (ਕਅਨੈਲ) *n v* ਨਹਿਰ, ਆਡ਼, ਸਰੀਰ ਦੇ ਅੰਦਰ ਭੋਜਨ ਜਾਂ ਹਵਾ ਵਾਲੀ ਨਾਲੀ; ਨਹਿਰ ਪੁੱਟਣੀ, ਨਹਿਰ ਕੱਢਣੀ; ~lize ਆਡ਼ ਜਾਂ ਨਹਿਰ ਦੀ ਖ਼ੁਦਾਈ ਕਰਨੀ, ਦਰਿਆ ਵਿਚੋਂ ਨਹਿਰ ਕੱਢਣੀ

cancel (ਕੈਂਸਲ) *v n* ਰੱਦ ਕਰਨਾ, ਮੇਟਣਾ ਕਾਟਾ ਫੇਰਨਾ, ਕੱਟਣਾ, ਲੀਕ ਫੇਰਨੀ, ਮਿਟਾ ਦੇਣਾ, ਮਨਸੂਖ ਕਰਨਾ; ਵਿਅਰਥ ਠਹਿਰਾਉਣਾ; ਰੱਦ; ~lation ਮਨਸੂਖੀ, ਨਕਾਰਨ, ਕਾਟਾ, ਕਾਟ; ਰੋਕੀਕਰਣ

cancer (ਕੈਂਸਅ*) *n* ਕੈਂਸਰ, ਰਾਜਫੋੜਾ; ਭੈੜੀ ਵਾਦੀ ਜੋ ਨਾਸੂਰ ਬਣ ਕੇ ਚੰਬੜ ਜਾਵੇ; ਭਰੰਦਰ ਫੋੜਾ; ਕਰਕ ਰਾਸ਼ੀ

candid (ਕੈਂਡਿਡ) *a* ਨਿਰਪੱਖ, ਨਿਸ਼ਕਪਟ, ਖਰਾ, ਸਪੱਸ਼ਟ, ਸੱਚਾ, ਸਾਫ਼ ਦਿਲ, ਸਾਫ਼-ਗੋ, ਨਿਰਛਲ; ~ly ਸਾਫ਼ ਸਾਫ਼, ਸਫ਼ਾਈ ਨਾਲ, ਬਿਨਾ ਲੱਗਲਬੇਰ ਦੇ, ਬੇਲਾਗ ਹੋ ਕੇ; ~ness ਸਾਫ਼-ਗੋਈ, ਸਾਫ਼-ਦਿਲੀ, ਸਚਾਈ, ਨਿਸ਼ਕਪਟਤਾ

candidate (ਕੈਂਡਿਡਅਟ) *n* ਉਮੀਦਵਾਰ; ਪਰੀਖਿਆਰਥੀ; ਚੋਣ ਉਮੀਦਵਾਰ; ਤਲਬਗਾਰ

candidature (ਕੈਂਡਿਡਅਚਅ*) *n* ਪਾਤਰਤਾ, ਉਮੀਦਵਾਰ ਹੋਣ ਦੀ ਸਥਿਤੀ

candle (ਕੈਂਡਲ) *n* ਮੋਮਬੱਤੀ; ਦੀਵਾ

candy (ਕੈਂਡਿ) *n v* ਮਿਸਰੀ, ਖੰਡ ਦੀ ਗੋਲੀ; ਮਿਸਰੀ ਬਣਾਉਣਾ

cane (ਕੇਇਨ) *n v* ਗੰਨਾ, ਨੜਾ, ਬਾਂਸ ਆਦਿ;

ਸੋਟੀ, ਬੈਂਤ, ਛਿਟੀ, ਕੁਰਸੀਆਂ ਬੁਣਨ ਵਾਲੀ
ਬੈਂਤ; ਸੋਟੀ ਜਾਂ ਬੈਂਤ ਨਾਲ ਕੁੱਟਣਾ

caning ('ਕੋਇਨਿਙ) *n* ਦੰਡ ਦੇਣ ਦੀ ਕਿਰਿਆ,
ਬੈਂਤ ਲਗਾਉਣ ਦਾ ਕੰਮ, ਬੈਂਤ ਬੁਣਨ ਦਾ ਅਮਲ

canister ('ਕੈਨਿਸਟਅ*) ਧਾਤ ਦਾ ਛੋਟਾ ਡੱਬਾ,
ਕਨਸਤਰ, ਪੀਪ, ਤੇਟਾ-ਪਾਤਰ, ਦਾਨ-ਪਾਤਰ

cannibal ('ਕੈਨਿਬਲ) *n a* ਆਦਮ-ਖੋਰ,
ਮਾਨਸਖਾਣਾ, ਮਰਦਮ-ਖੋਰ

canning ('ਕੈਨਿਙ) *n* ਡੱਬੋਬੰਦੀ

cannon ('ਕੈਨਅਨ) *n v* ਤੋਪ, ਤੋਪਖਾਨਾ, ਧੁਰੇ
ਉੱਤੇ ਆਪਣੇ ਆਪ ਘੁੰਮਣ ਵਾਲਾ ਵੇਲਣਾ, ਕੁੰਜੀ
ਦੀ ਨਾਲੀ, ਬਿਲੀਅਰਡ ਖੇਡਣ ਸਮੇਂ ਇਕੋ ਵੇਲੇ
ਦੋ ਗੋੰਦਾਂ ਦੀ ਮਾਰ; ਟੇਢਾ ਟਕਰਾਉਣਾ, ਦੋ-ਗੋੰਦੀ
ਮਾਰ ਮਾਰਨਾ, ਦੋ ਗੋੰਦਾਂ ਨੂੰ ਇੱਕਠਾ ਮਾਰਨਾ;
~**ball** ਤੋਪ ਦਾ ਗੋਲਾ

canon ('ਕੈਨਅਨ) *n* ਧਾਰਮਕ ਸਿਧਾਂਤ; ਧਰਮ-
ਸੂਤਰ, ਧਰਮ-ਆਦੇਸ਼, ਧਾਰਮਕ ਨਿਯਮ,
ਵਿਧਾਨ; ਮਾਨਦੰਡ; ਇਸਾਈਆਂ ਦੀ ਨਮਾਜ਼ ਦਾ
ਪਵਿੱਤਰ ਭਾਗ; ਛਾਪੇ ਦੇ ਸਭ ਤੋਂ ਵੱਡੇ ਅੱਖਰ;
ਪਾਦਰੀਆਂ ਦੀ ਸਭਾ ਦਾ ਸਦੱਸ; ਘੰਟਾ
ਲਟਕਾਉਣ ਵਾਲਾ ਕੜਾ; ਸੰਗੀਤ ਵਿਚ ਇਕ
ਗੀਤ; ~**ical** ਧਾਰਮਕ ਆਗਿਆ ਦੁਆਰਾ
ਨਿਯਤ, ਸ਼ਰੂਈ, ਦੀਨੀ, ਮਜ਼ਬੀ; ਧਾਰਮਕ
ਗ੍ਰੰਥ ਅਥਵਾ ਪੁਸਤਕ ਦਾ ਭਾਗ; ~**ically**
ਮਰਯਾਦਾ ਪੂਰਵਕ, ਨੇਮ ਅਨੁਸਾਰ

canopy ('ਕੈਨਅਪਿ) *n v* ਛੱਤਰ; ਮੰਡਪ, ਤੰਬੂ,
ਚੰਦੋਆ, ਬਾਰੀ ਦਾ ਛੱਜਾ; ਚੰਦੋਆ ਤਾਨਣਾ; ਛੱਤਰ
ਤਾਨਣਾ, ਛੱਪਰ ਬੰਨ੍ਹਣਾ, ਤੰਬੂ ਲਾਉਣਾ

canteen (ਕੈਨ'ਟਿਨ) *n* ਚਾਹ ਪਾਣੀ ਦੀ ਦੁਕਾਨ,
ਭੋਜਨ ਭੰਡਾਰ, ਅੰਨਪੂਰਨਾ; ਫੌਜੀਆਂ ਲਈ ਰਸਦ
ਤੇ ਸ਼ਰਾਬ ਦੀ ਦੁਕਾਨ, ਮੈਖਾਨਾ; ਜਲ-ਪਾਤਰ

canton ('ਕੈਨਟੌਨ) *n v* ਪ੍ਰਾਂਤ, ਸੂਬਾ, ਪ੍ਰਦੇਸ਼,
ਇਲਾਕਾ, ਪਰਗਨਾ; ਛਾਉਨੀ, ਸਵਿਟਜ਼ਰਲੈਂਡ
ਦੀ ਇਕ ਰਿਆਸਤ; ਫ਼ਿਰਕਾ, ਕੌਮ; ਪਰਗਨਿਆਂ
ਜਾਂ ਜ਼ਿਲ੍ਹਿਆਂ ਵਿਚ ਵੰਡਣਾ, ਛਾਉਨੀ,
(ਸਿਪਾਹੀਆਂ ਨੂੰ) ਠਹਿਰਾਉਣਾ; ~**ment** ਛਾਉਨੀ
ਵੱਡਾ ਕੈਂਪ, ਫ਼ੌਜ, ਲਸ਼ਕਰ

canvas ('ਕੈਨਵ੍ਅਸ) *n v* ਬੋਰਾ, ਟਾਟ, ਤਿਰਪਾਲ,
ਮੋਟਾ ਸੂਤੀ ਕੱਪੜਾ, ਦੌੜ ਵਾਲੀ ਕਿਸ਼ਤੀ ਦਾ
ਛੱਤਦਾਰ ਕਿਨਾਰਾ; ਤੰਬੂ; ਸ਼ਾਸਤਰਾਰਥ, ਵਾਦ-
ਵਿਵਾਦ, ਬਹਿਸ, ਮੱਤ, ਵੋਟ, ਵੋਟਾਂ ਮੰਗਣਾ,
ਜਾਚਨ ਕਰਨੀ; ~**er** ਵੋਟ ਜਾਂ ਮੱਤ ਚਾਹੁਣ ਵਾਲਾ,
ਜਾਚਕ, ਮੱਤ-ਸੰਗ੍ਰਾਹਕ; ~**ing** ਕਨਵੈਸਿੰਗ, ਵੋਟ
ਦੀ ਮੰਗ, ਮੱਤ-ਸੰਗ੍ਰਹ ਦਾ ਜਤਨ, ਜਾਚਨ

cap (ਕੈਪ) *n* ਟੋਪੀ, ਕੁੱਲਾ; ਟੋਪ, ਸਿਖਰ; ਢੱਕਣ,
ਉਛਾੜ, ਗਿਲਾਫ਼; ਸਰਦਾਰ, ਮੁਖੀਆ; ਟੋਪੀ
ਪਹਿਨਣਾ ਜਾਂ ਪਹਿਨਾਉਣਾ; ਬੰਦੂਕ ਉੱਤੇ ਟੋਪੀ
ਚੜ੍ਹਾਉਣਾ; ਸਲਾਮ ਕਰਨੀ, ਪਦਵੀ ਪ੍ਰਦਾਨ ਕਰਨਾ;
ਚੋਟੀ ਤੇ ਹੋਣਾ; ਠੋਕਰ ਲਗਾ ਦੇਣਾ, ਚੋਟ ਖਾ ਲੈਣਾ

capabillity ('ਕੋਇਪਅ'ਬਿਲਅਟਿ) *n* ਯੋਗਤਾ,
ਸਮੱਰਥਾ, ਪੂੰਜਤ, ਲਿਆਕਤ

capable ('ਕਇਪਅ'ਬਲ) *a* ਯੋਗ, ਸਮੱਰਥ,
ਬਲਵਾਨ, ਲਾਇਕ, ਗੁਣੀ, ਗੁਣਵੰਤ

capacity (ਕਅ'ਪੈਸਅਟਿ) *n* ਸਮੱਰਥਾ, ਗ੍ਰਹਿਣ-
ਸ਼ਕਤੀ, ਯੋਗਤਾ, ਗੁੰਜਾਇਸ਼; ਸਮਾਈ, ਦਰਜਾ,
ਪਦ, ਹੈਸੀਅਤ

cape (ਕੇਇਪ) *n* ਫਤੂਰੀ; ਬਾਹਵਾਂ ਤੋਂ ਬਿਨਾਂ ਕੋਟ,
ਅੰਤਰੀਪ

capital ('ਕੈਪਿਟਲ) *n a* ਮੂਲ-ਧਨ, ਪੂੰਜੀ,
ਸਰਮਾਇਆ, ਲਾਗਤ; ਰਾਜਧਾਨੀ; ਥੰਮੁ ਦਾ
ਉੱਪਰਲਾ ਹਿੱਸਾ, (ਸਜ਼ਾ) ਘਾਤਕ, ਪ੍ਰਧਾਨ,
ਮਹੱਤਪੂਰਨ, ਸਰਵੋਤਮ; ~**ism** ਪੂੰਜੀਵਾਦ,

ਸਰਮਾਏਦਾਰੀ; **~ist** ਪੂੰਜੀਵਾਦੀ, ਪੂੰਜੀਪਤੀ, ਸਰਮਾਏਦਾਰ; **~ization** ਪੂੰਜੀਕਰਣ, ਪੂੰਜੀ-ਸੰਗ੍ਰਹਣ

capitation ('ਕੈਪਿ'ਟੇਇਸ਼ਨ) *n* ਨੀਯਤ (ਫ਼ੀਸ, ਮਸੂਲ ਆਦਿ); **~tax** ਨੀਯਤਕਰ

capitulate (ਕਅ'ਪਿਅਚੁਲੇਇਟ) *v* ਆਤਮ-ਸਮਰਪਣ ਕਰਨਾ, ਅਧੀਨ ਹੋ ਜਾਣਾ, ਹਥਿਆਰ ਸੁੱਟ ਦੇਣੇ (ਕੁਝ ਸ਼ਰਤ ਤੇ)

capitulation (ਕਅ'ਪਿਚੁ'ਲੇਇਸ਼ਨ) *n* ਸਮਝੌਤਾ; ਸ਼ਰਤਾਂ ਅਧੀਨ ਸਮਰਪਣ ਸੰਧੀ; ਸਿਰਲੇਖਬੰਦੀ

caprice (ਕਅ'ਪਰੀਸ) *n* ਤਰੰਗ, ਮੌਜ, ਲਹਿਰ; ਚਪਲਤਾ, ਚੰਚਲਤਾ; ਸਨਕ

capricious (ਕਅ'ਪਰਿਸ਼ਅਸ) *a* ਤਰੰਗੀ, ਮੌਜੀ, ਲਹਿਰੀ, ਵਹਿਮੀ; ਸਨਕੀ; **~ness** ਚੰਚਲਤਾ, ਅਸਥਿਰਤਾ, ਮਨਮੌਜੀਪਣ, ਸਨਕਪੁਣਾ

capricorn ('ਕੈਪਰਿਕੋਨ) *n* ਮਕਰ ਰਾਸ਼ੀ

capsize (ਕੈਪ'ਸਾਇਜ਼) *v* (ਜਹਾਜ਼, ਕਿਸ਼ਤੀ ਦਾ) ਡੁੱਬਣਾ, ਉਲਟਾ ਹੋਣਾ, ਉਲਟਣਾ, ਪਲਟਣਾ

capsule ('ਕੈਪਸਯੂਲ) *n* ਝਿੱਲੀਦਾਰ ਥੈਲੀ; ਬੀਜ-ਕੋਸ਼; ਝਿੱਲੀ ਦੀ ਡੱਬੀ; ਫਲੀ, ਖੋਲ, ਲਿਫ਼ਾਫ਼ਾ; ਗ਼ਿਲਾਫ਼; ਡੋਡਾ, ਡੋਡੀ; ਕੈਪਸੂਲ

captain ('ਕੈਪਟਿਨ) *n v* ਕਪਤਾਨ, ਆਗੂ; ਨਾਇਕ, ਸੈਨਾ ਦਾ ਅਫ਼ਸਰ, ਸਰਦਾਰ; ਖਾਣਾਂ ਦਾ ਮੈਨੇਜਰ; ਫੋਰਮੈਨ; ਅਗਵਾਈ ਕਰਨਾ, ਮਾਰਗ-ਪਰਦਰਸ਼ਨ ਕਰਨਾ, ਰਹਿਨੁਮਾਈ ਕਰਨਾ, ਕਪਤਾਨੀ ਕਰਨਾ

caption ('ਕੈਪਸ਼ਨ) *n* ਸੁਰਖ਼ੀ, ਪੁਸਤਕ ਦਾ ਸਿਰਲੇਖ; ਕਾਨੂੰਨੀ ਗਰਿਫ਼ਤਾਰੀ, ਪਕੜ

captivate ('ਕੈਪਟਿਵੇਇਟ) *v* ਬੰਦੀ ਬਣਾਉਣਾ, ਕੈਦ ਕਰਨਾ, ਮੋਹ ਲੈਣਾ, ਮੋਹਣਾ, ਆਕਰਸ਼ਤ ਕਰਨਾ, ਖਿਚ ਲੈਣਾ

captivating ('ਕੈਪਟਿਵੇਇਟਿਙ) *a* ਮਨੋਹਰ, ਮਨਮੋਹਕ, ਆਕਰਸ਼ਕ

captivation ('ਕੈਪਟਿਵੇਇਸ਼ਨ) *n* ਮੋਹਨ, ਮਨਮੋਹਕਤਾ, ਆਕਰਸ਼ਣ; ਬੰਦੀਕਰਨ

captivity (ਕੈਪ'ਟਿਵਅਟਿ) *n* ਬੰਦੀਖ਼ਾਨਾ, ਕੈਦ, ਹਿਰਾਸਤ; ਗ਼ੁਲਾਮੀ

capture ('ਕੈਪਚਅ*) *n v* ਕਬਜ਼ਾ, ਗਰਿਫ਼ਤਾਰੀ; ਜਿੱਤਣਾ, ਕਬਜ਼ਾ ਕਰਨਾ

car (ਕਾ*) *n* ਮੋਟਰ ਕਾਰ, ਗੱਡੀ, ਰਥ, ਰੇਲ ਦਾ ਡੱਬਾ, ਉਡਣ-ਖਟੋਲੇ ਦਾ ਝੂਲਾ

carat ('ਕੈਰਅਟ) *n* ਸੋਨੇ ਤੇ ਹੀਰੇ ਤੋਲਣ ਦਾ ਤੋਲ, 3½ ਗ੍ਰੇਨ ਸੋਨੇ ਦੀ ਸ਼ੁੱਧਤਾ ਦਾ ਮਾਪ

caravan ('ਕੈਰਅਵੈਨ) *n* ਕਾਫ਼ਲਾ, ਕਾਰਵਾਨ, ਬੰਦਗੱਡੀ, ਚੱਲਦਾ ਫਿਰਦਾ ਘਰ

carbon ('ਕਾ*ਬਅਨ) *n* ਕਾਰਬਨ; ਕੋਲਾ, ਕੋਇਲਾ; ਕਾਲਖ, ਸੜੀਆਂ ਹੱਡੀਆਂ, ਪੱਥਰ ਦਾ ਕੋਲਾ, ਲੱਕੜ ਦਾ ਕੋਲਾ

carcass, carcase ('ਕਾ*ਕਅਸ) *n* ਲੋਥ, ਲਾਸ਼, ਮੁਰਦਾਰ, ਪਿੰਜਰ, ਢਾਂਚਾ

card (ਕਾ*ਡ) *n v* ਪਿੰਜਣਾ, ਧੁਣਕੁਣਾ, (ਪਿੰਜਣ ਵਾਲਾ) ਤਾੜਾ, ਧੁਣਕੁਣੀ, ਉੱਨ ਸਾਫ਼ ਕਰਨ ਵਾਲਾ ਕੰਘਾ; (ਤਾਸ਼ ਦੇ) ਪੱਤੇ, ਮੋਟੇ ਕਾਗ਼ਜ਼ ਦਾ ਟੁਕੜਾ; ਪੋਸਟ-ਕਾਰਡ, ਇਸ਼ਤਿਹਾਰ, ਉੱਨ ਸਾਫ਼ ਕਰਨੀ; **~board** ਗੱਤਾ, ਮੋਟਾ ਕਾਗ਼ਜ਼; **post~** ਪੋਸਟ ਕਾਰਡ, ਕਾਰਡ **wedding** ਵਿਵਾਹ-ਪੱਤਰ **~s** ਤਾਸ਼

cardamom ('ਕਾ*ਡਅਮਅਮ) *n* ਇਲਾਇਚੀ

cardiac ('ਕਾ*ਡਿਐਕ) *n* ਦਿਲ-ਸਬੰਧੀ, ਦਿਲੀ, ਹਿਰਦੇ ਦਾ, ਦਿਲ ਲਈ ਗੁਣਕਾਰੀ ਦਵਾਈ

cardinal ('ਕਾ*ਡਿਨਲ) *a n* ਮੌਲਕ, ਪ੍ਰਧਾਨ, ਮਹੱਤਵਪੂਰਣ, ਮੂਲ; ਛੋਟੀ ਲਾਲ ਚਿੜੀ; ਗਿਰਜੇ

ਦਾ ਮੁਖੀ, ਕਾਰਡੀਨਲ ਪਾਦਰੀ

cardiogram ('ਕਾ*ਡ਼ਿਆ(ਉ)ਗਰੈਮ) *n* ਹਿਰਦੇ-ਚਿੱਤਰ, ਦਿਲ-ਗਤੀ ਲੇਖ

cardiograph ('ਕਾ*ਡ਼ਿਆ(ਉ)ਗਰਾਫ਼) *n* ਹਿਰਦੇ ਦੀ ਧੜਕਣ ਜਾਨਣ ਵਾਲਾ ਜੰਤਰ

cardiology (ਕਾ*ਡ਼ਿ'ਔਲਅਜਿ) *n* ਹਿਰਦੇ-ਵਿਗਿਆਨ

care (ਕੇਅ*) *n* ਪਰਵਾਹ, ਧਿਆਨ, ਖ਼ਬਰਦਾਰੀ, ਚੌਕਸੀ, ਫ਼ਿਕਰ, ਤੰਰਦਦ, ਚਿੰਤਾ, ਸੋਚ, ਜ਼ੁੰਮੇਵਾਰੀ, ਡਰ, ਮਾਰਫ਼ਤ; ਚਿਤਾ ਕਰਨਾ, ਫ਼ਿਕਰ ਕਰਨਾ, ਤੰਰਦਦ ਕਰਨਾ, ਸੰਭਾਲ ਕਰਨਾ, ਚੌਕਸ ਹੋਣਾ; ਪਿਆਰ ਕਰਨਾ, ਚਾਹੁਣਾ; ਰੋਗਾਂ ਦੀ ਦੇਖ ਭਾਲ ਕਰਨੀ; ਆਦਰ ਕਰਨਾ; ~of, c/o ਮਾਰਫ਼ਤ, ਦੁਆਰਾ, ਰਾਹੀਂ; ~**taker** ਰਖਵਾਲਾ, ਨਿਗਰਾਨ, ਕਾਰਿੰਦਾ; take~of ਸੰਭਾਲਣਾ, ਧਿਆਨ ਰਖਣਾ, ਖਬਰ ਲੈਣੀ; ~**ful** ਸਚੇਤ, ਸੁਰੱਜਾ, ਸਾਵਧਾਨ ਖ਼ਬਰਦਾਰ; ~**fulness** ਸਾਵਧਾਨੀ, ਸਤਰਕਤਾ, ਹੁਸ਼ਿਆਰੀ, ਖ਼ਬਰਦਾਰੀ; ~**less** ਬੇਫ਼ਿਕਰ, ਬੇਪਰਵਾਹ, ਅਚੇਤ ਅਸਾਵਧਾਨ, ਅਣਗਹਿਲਾ, ਲਾਪਰਵਾਹ, ਬੇਖ਼ਬਰ, ਅਟਕਲ-ਪੱਚੂ; ~**lessness** ਲਾਪਰਵਾਹੀ, ਬੇਪਰਵਾਹੀ, ਅਸਾਵਧਾਨੀ, ਨਿਸਚਿੰਤਤਾ

career (ਕਅ'ਰਿਅ*) *n v* ਵਿਵਸਾਇ, ਰੋਜ਼ੀ, ਪੇਸ਼ਾ, ਚਰਿੱਤਰ, ਚਲਣ; ਜੀਵਨ-ਯਾਤਰਾ; ਗਤੀ, ਰੌ, ਚਾਲ, ਰਿਵਾਜ

caress (ਕਅ'ਰੈਸ) *n v* ਲਾਡ, ਦਿਲਾਸਾ, ਪੁਚਕਾਰ, ਪਲੋਸਣਾ, ਲਾਡ ਲਡਾਉਣਾ, ਦਿਲਾਸਾ ਦੇਣਾ, ਪੁਚਕਾਰਨਾ

cargo ('ਕਾ*ਗਅਉ) *n* ਜਹਾਜ਼ ਦਾ ਮਾਲ, ਲੱਦ, ਭਾਰ

caricature ('ਕੈਰਿਕਅਚੁਅ*) *n v* ਵਿਅੰਗ-

ਚਿੱਤਰਨ, ਉਪਹਾਸ, ਨਕਲ, ਕਾਰਟੂਨ, ਵਿਅੰਗ-ਚਿੱਤਰ ਖਿੱਚਣਾ, ਕਾਰਟੂਨ ਬਣਾਉਣਾ, ਸਾਂਗ ਲਾਉਣਾ

carnage ('ਕਾ*ਨਿਜ) *n* ਕਤਲਾਮ, ਖ਼ੂਨ ਖ਼ਰਾਬਾ, ਹੱਤਿਆ ਕਾਂਡ

carnal ('ਕਾ*ਨਲ) *n* ਭੋਗਵਿਲਾਸੀ, ਕਾਮੁਕ, ਵਿਸ਼ਈ, ਸਰੀਰਕ ਵਿਸ਼ਿਆਂ ਅਤੇ ਭੋਗਾਂ ਸਬੰਧੀ; ਸੰਸਾਰਕ, ਭੌਤਕ

carnival ('ਕਾ*ਨਿਵ਼ਲ) *n* ਇਕ ਇਸਾਈ ਤਿਉਹਾਰ; ਜਸ਼ਨ; ਰੰਗ ਰਲੀਆਂ, ਮੌਜ

carpenter ('ਕਾ*ਪੈਂਟਅ*) *n v* ਤਰਖਾਣ, ਲਕੜੀ ਦਾ ਕੰਮ ਕਰਨ ਵਾਲਾ; ਤਰਖਾਣਾ ਕੰਮ ਕਰਨਾ

carpentry ('ਕਾ*ਪੈਂਟਰਿ) *n* ਤਰਖਾਣਾ ਕੰਮ, ਲੱਕੜੀ ਦਾ ਕੰਮ

carpet ('ਕਾ*ਪਿਟ) *n v* ਗ਼ਲੀਚਾ, ਕਾਲੀਨ, ਦਰੀ, ਫ਼ਰਸ਼, ਫੁੱਲਾਂ ਜਾਂ ਘਾਹ ਦਾ ਪਲਾਟ; ਦਰੀ ਵਿਛਾਉਣਾ; ਫ਼ਰਸ਼ ਵਿਛਾਉਣਾ; (ਨੌਕਰ ਦੀ) ਝਾੜ-ਝੰਬ ਕਰਨੀ

carriage ('ਕੈਰਿਜ) *n* ਗੱਡੀ, ਬੱਘੀ; ਭਾੜਾ, ਢੁਆਈ, ਬੰਦੋਬਸਤ, ਇੰਤਜ਼ਾਮ; ਢੰਗ, ਅੰਦਾਜ਼

carrier (ਕੈਰਿਅ*) *n* ਢਕੜੇ ਵਾਲਾ, ਭਾੜੇ ਵਾਲਾ, ਗੱਡੀ ਵਾਲਾ, ਭਾਰ ਢੋਣ ਵਾਲਾ; ਕੁਲੀ, ਪਾਂਡੀ, ਮਜ਼ਦੂਰ; ਬਾਈਸਿਕਲ ਦੇ ਪਿੱਛੇ ਭਾਰ ਰੱਖਣ ਲਈ ਥਾਂ, ਕੈਰੀਅਰ

carrot ('ਕੈਰਅਟ) *n* ਗਾਜਰ

carry ('ਕੈਰਿ) *v* ਢੋਣਾ, ਲੈ ਜਾਣਾ, ਪਹੁੰਚਾਉਣਾ; ਜਿੱਤਣਾ; ~**off** ਲੈ ਭੱਜਣਾ, ਭਜਾ ਕੇ ਲੈ ਜਾਣਾ, ਜਿੱਤਣਾ; ~**on** ਜਾਰੀ ਰੱਖਣਾ, ਚੱਲਦੇ ਜਾਣਾ; ~**out** ਆਗਿਆ ਦੀ ਪਾਲਣਾ ਕਰਨਾ

cart (ਕਾ:ਟ) *n* ਗੱਡਾ, ਛਕੜਾ; ਗੱਡੇ ਲੱਦਣਾ, ਲੱਦ ਕੇ ਲੈ ਜਾਣਾ; ~**horse** ਟੱਟੂ; **bullock**~ ਬੈਲ-

ਗੱਡੀ, ਬਹਿਲੀ; ~hand ਹੱਥ-ਗੱਡੀ, ਰੇੜੀ; ~age ਭਾੜਾ

cartographer (ਕਾ'ਟੋਗਰਅਫ਼ਅ*) *n* ਨਕਸ਼ਾ-ਨਵੀਸ, ਨਕਸ਼ਾ-ਨਿਗਾਰ, ਨਕਸ਼ੇ ਬਣਾਉਣ ਵਾਲਾ

cartography (ਕਾ'ਟੋਗਰਅਫ਼ਿ) *n* ਨਕਸ਼ਾ-ਨਵੀਸੀ, ਨਕਸ਼ਾ-ਨਿਗਾਰੀ, ਨਕਸ਼ੇ ਬਣਾਉਣ ਦੀ ਵਿੱਦਿਆ

cartoon (ਕਾ'ਟੂਨ) *n v* ਕਾਰਟੂਨ, ਵਿਅੰਗ-ਚਿਤਰ; ਕਾਰਟੂਨ ਬਣਾਉਣਾ, ਵਿਅੰਗ-ਚਿਤਰ ਬਣਾਉਣਾ

cartridge ('ਕਾਟਰਿਜ) *n* ਕਾਰਤੂਸ, ਗੋਲੀਆਂ (ਬੰਦੂਕ ਆਦਿ ਦੀਆਂ); blank~ ਫੋਕਾ ਕਾਰਤੂਸ

carve (ਕਾਵ਼) *v* ਘੜਨਾ, ਤਰਾਸ਼ਣਾ, ਉਕਰਨਾ, ਸਜਾਉਣਾ, ਛੋਟੇ ਛੋਟੇ ਟੁਕੜੇ ਕਰਨਾ, ਖੋਦਣਾ; ~in ਖੋਦ ਕੇ ਬਣਾਉਣਾ

carving ('ਕਾਵ਼ਿਙ) *n* ਮੂਰਤੀ-ਕਲਾ, ਸੰਗ-ਤਰਾਸ਼ੀ, ਖੁਦਨ-ਕਲਾ; ਨੱਕਾਸ਼ੀ; ਤਰਾਸ਼, ਕਾਟ

case (ਕੇਇਸ) *n v* ਮਾਮਲਾ, ਮੁਕਦਮਾ, ਹਾਲਤ, ਸੂਰਤ, ਸਥਿਤੀ; ਕੈਦੀਅਤ; ਰੋਗੀ ਦੀ ਦਸ਼ਾ; ਘਟਨਾ; ਦਾਅਵਾ, ਖੋਲ, ਡੱਬਾ; (ਭਾਸ਼ਾ) ਕਾਰਕ; ਖੋਲ ਚੜ੍ਹਾਉਣਾ, ਗਿਲਾਫ਼ ਚੜ੍ਹਾਉਣਾ, ਡੱਬੇ ਜਾਂ ਸੰਦੂਕ ਵਿਚ ਬੰਦ ਕਰਨਾ; ~history (ਚਿਕਿ) ਰੋਗ ਬਿਰਤਾਂਤ; ~as the~ may be ਜੋ ਵੀ ਹੋਵੇ; ਜਿਸ ਤਰ੍ਹਾਂ ਵੀ ਹੋਵੇ, ਦਸ਼ਾ ਅਨੁਸਾਰ; in any~ ਹਰ ਹਾਲਤ ਵਿਚ, ਹਰ ਹੀਲੇ; in~ ਜੇ, ਜੇਕਰ; in~if ਅਜਿਹਾ ਹੋਇਆ ਤਾਂ, ਜੇ, ਅਗਰ, in~of ਇਸ ਦਸ਼ਾ ਵਿਚ, ਅਜਿਹਾ ਹੋਣ ਤੇ, ਅਵਸਥਾ ਵਿਚ; in that~ ਅਜਿਹੀ ਹਾਲਤ ਵਿਚ; in the~of ਬਾਰੇ, ਸਬੰਧੀ, ਬਾਬਤ; make out one's~ ਆਪਣੇ ਪੱਖ ਵਿਚ ਦਲੀਲਾਂ ਦੇਣੀਆਂ; ~ment ਖਿੜਕੀ

cash (ਕੈਸ਼) *n v* ਰੋਕੜ, ਨਕਦ, ਨਕਦੀ

ਕਰਵਾਉਣਾ; ~account ਰੋਕੜ-ਲੇਖਾ; ~book ਲੇਖਾ-ਵਹੀ, ਵਹੀ-ਖਾਤਾ, ਰੋਕੜ; ~crop ਵਪਾਰਕ ਫ਼ਸਲ; ~deposit ਨਕਦ ਜਮ੍ਹਾ; ~memo ਨਕਦੀ ਦੀ ਰਸੀਦ

cashier (ਕੈ'ਸ਼ਿਅ*) *n v* ਖਜ਼ਾਨਚੀ, ਰੋਕੜੀਆ; ਖ਼ਾਰਜ ਕਰਨਾ, ਨਾਉਂ ਕਟਣਾ; ਰੱਦ ਕਰਨਾ, ਮੌਕੂਫ਼ ਕਰਨਾ, ਬਰਖ਼ਾਸਤ ਕਰਨਾ

casino (ਕਅ'ਸੀਨਅਉ) *n* ਜੂਆਖ਼ਾਨਾ; ਤਾਸ਼ ਦਾ ਪੁਰਾਣਾ ਖੇਲ

cask (ਕਾਸਕ) *n* (ਲੱਕੜ ਦੀ) ਪੀਪਾ, ਲੱਕੜ ਦਾ ਛੋਟਾ ਢੋਲ

cast (ਕਾਸਟ) *v n* ਸੁੱਟਣਾ; ਦਫ਼ਾ ਕਰਨਾ; ਹਿਸਾਬ ਲਗਾਉਣਾ, ਜੋੜਨਾ, ਗਿਨਣਾ; ਢਾਲਣਾ (ਪਿਘਲੀ ਹੋਈ ਧਾਤ ਦਾ); ਪਾਉਣਾ (ਵੋਟ), ਮੁਕੱਦਮਾ ਜਿੱਤਣਾ; ਆਕਾਰ, ਰੂਪ, ਪ੍ਰਕਾਰ; ਜੋੜ; ਹਿਸਾਬ; ਢਲਾਈ; ~down ਉਦਾਸ, ਦਿਲਗੀਰ; ~about ਹੱਥ ਪੈਰ ਮਾਰਨੇ, ਭਾਲਣਾ; ~a vote ਵੋਟ ਪਾਉਣੀ, ਪਰਚੀ ਪਾਉਣੀ; ~iron ਢਲਿਆ ਲੋਹਾ; ਢਾਲੇ ਹੋਏ ਲੋਹੇ ਦਾ; ਸਖ਼ਤ, ਕਠੋਰ, ਕਰੜਾ

casting ('ਕਾਸਟਿਙ) *n* ਢਲਾਈ, ਢਲੀ ਹੋਈ ਚੀਜ਼, ਪਾਤਰ-ਵੰਡ; ~vote ਨਿਰਣਾਇਕ ਵੋਟ, ਸਭਾਪਤੀ ਦਾ ਵੋਟ ਜੋ ਦੋ ਬਰਾਬਰ ਪੱਖਿਆਂ ਦਾ ਫ਼ੈਸਲਾ ਕਰਵਾ ਦੇਵੇ

caste (ਕਾਸਟ) *n* ਵਰਨ, ਜਾਤ, ਜਾਤ-ਪਾਤ, ਕੌਮ, ਫ਼ਿਰਕਾ, ਬਰਾਦਰੀ; (ਦੂਜੇ ਦੇਸ਼ਾਂ ਵਿਚ) ਵਰਗਾ, ਸਮੂ; ~system ਜਾਤੀ-ਪ੍ਰਥਾ, ਜਾਤੀ ਪ੍ਰਣਾਲੀ; ~less ਜਾਤ ਪਾਤ ਤੋਂ ਰਹਿਤ ਵਰਨਹੀਨ

castigate ('ਕੈਸਟਿਗੇਇਟ) *v* ਫਿਟਕਾਰਨਾ; ਤਾੜਨਾ, ਚੰਡਣਾ

castigation ('ਕੈਸਟਿ'ਗੇਇਸ਼ਨ) *n* ਫਿਟਕਾਰ, ਤਾੜਨਾ, ਕੁੱਟ, ਸੁਧਾਰ, ਸੁਧਾਈ

castle ('ਕਾਸਲ) *n v* ਕਿਲ੍ਹਾ, ਗੜ੍ਹ, ਕੋਟ, ਸ਼ਤਰੰਜ ਦਾ ਰੁਖ; ਰੁਖਬੰਦੀ ਕਰਨੀ; build ~s in the air ਹਵਾਈ ਕਿਲ੍ਹੇ ਉਸਾਰਨੇ, ਖ਼ਿਆਲੀ ਪੁਲਾਉ ਪਕਾਉਣੇ

casual ('ਕੈਯੂਅਲ) *a n* ਇਤਫ਼ਾਕੀਆ, ਅਣਚੇਤੀ, ਸਬੱਬੀ, ਅਚਾਨਕ, ਬੇਕਾਇਦਾ; ਅਨਿਯਮਤ, ਅਸਾਵਧਾਨ ਬੇਢੰਗਾ; ~labourer ਦਿਹਾੜੀਦਾਰ, ਕੱਚਾ ਮਜ਼ਦੂਰ, ~ly ਸਬੱਬੀ, ਕਦੇ ਕਦੇ, ਅਚਾਨਕ ਹੀ

casualties ('ਕੈਯੂਅਲਟਿਜ਼) *n* ਮਰੇ ਹੋਏ ਜਾਂ ਘਾਇਲ ਹੋਏ ਆਦਮੀਆਂ ਦੀ ਸੰਖਿਆ

casualty (ਕੈਯੂਅਲਟਿ) *n* ਦੁਰਘਟਨਾ, ਹਾਦਸਾ; ਮੁਸੀਬਤ; ਯਾਤਨਾ; (ਜੁੱਧ ਵਿਚ) ਮਰਿਆਂ ਦੀ ਸੂਚੀ, ਘਾਇਲ ਲੋਕ; ~ward ਅਚਾਨਕ ਘਾਇਲ ਹੋਏ ਲੋਕਾਂ ਦਾ ਵਾਰਡ

cat (ਕੈਟ) *n v* ਬਿੱਲੀ; ਬਿੱਲੀ-ਪਰਵਾਰ ਦੇ ਜਾਨਵਰ; ਲੜਾਕੀ ਰੰਨ, ਲੰਗਰ ਚੁੱਕਣ ਵਾਲਾ ਸ਼ਹਤੀਰ ਉਲਟੀ ਕਰਨੀ; ਲੰਗਰ ਚੁੱਕਣਾ; ~and dog life ਕੁੱਤਿਆਂ ਬਿੱਲਿਆਂ ਵਾਲਾ ਜੀਵਨ, ਕਲ੍ਹਾ ਕਲੇਸ਼ ਦਾ ਜੀਵਨ; ~eyed ਜੋ ਹਨੇਰੇ ਵਿਚ ਵੇਖ ਸਕੇ; wild~ ਸ਼ੋਰ, ਚੀਤਾ ਆਦਿ

catalogue ('ਕੈਟਅਲੌਗ) *n v* ਨਾਮਾਵਲੀ, ਸੂਚੀ-ਪੱਤਰ, ਪੁਸਤਕ ਸੂਚੀ, ਸਾਰਨੀ, ਤਾਲਿਕਾ, ਫ਼ਹਰਿਸਤ; ਸੂਚੀ ਬਣਾਉਣਾ, ਫ਼ਹਰਿਸਤ ਵਿਚ ਦਰਜ ਕਰਨਾ

cataract ('ਕੈਟਅਰੈਕਟ) *n* ਮੋਤੀਆ ਬਿੰਦ ਝਰਨਾ, ਆਬਸ਼ਾਰ, ਪਾਣੀ ਦੀ ਚਾਦਰ, ਮੋਹਲੇਧਾਰ ਵਰਖਾ

catarrh (ਕਾ'ਟਾ*) *n* ਨਜ਼ਲਾ, ਜ਼ੁਕਾਮ, ਰੇਸ਼ਾ

catastrophe (ਕਾ'ਟੈਸਟਰਅਫ਼ਿ) *n* ਬਿਪਤਾ, ਆਫ਼ਤ, ਘੱਲੂਘਾਰਾ, ਅਨਰਥ, ਕਹਿਰ, ਉਥਲ-ਪੁਥਲ; ਬਿਪਤਾ ਭਰਿਆ ਅੰਤ, ਤਬਾਹੀ, ਨਾਟਕ ਦਾ ਦੁਖਾਂਤ

catastrophic, -al ('ਕੈਟਅ'ਸਟਰੌਫ਼ਿਕ, ਕੈਟਅ'- ਸਟਰੌਫ਼ਿਕਲ) *a* ਬਿਪਤਾਪੂਰਨ, ਤਬਾਹਕਾਰੀ

catch (ਕੈਚ) *v n* ਫੜਨਾ, ਫੜ ਲੈਣਾ, ਥੰਮ੍ਹਣਾ, ਫ਼ਾਹੁਣਾ, ਗਰਿਫ਼ਤਾਰ ਕਰਨਾ, ਝੱਪਣਾ, ਧਰਨਾ; ਝੂਠ ਲੈਣਾ; ਪਕੜ, ਫੜਾਈ; ਗਰਿਫ਼ਤਾਰੀ; ਕ੍ਰਿਕਟ ਵਿਚ ਗੇਂਦ ਬੋਚ; ਅੜਿੱਕਾ, ਅੜਾਉਣੀ; ਹਟਕੋਰਾ, ਫ਼ਾਹੁਣ ਯੋਗ ਆਦਮੀ, ਚੰਗਾ ਸ਼ਿਕਾਰ; ~ment ਅਜਿਹਾ ਖੇਤਰ ਜਿਥੇ ਮੀਂਹ ਦਾ ਪਾਣੀ ਵਹਿ ਕੇ ਨਦੀ ਵਿਚ ਆਏ; ~word ਸੂਚਕ ਸ਼ਬਦ, ਪੰਨੇ ਦੇ ਸਿਰੇ ਤੇ ਲਿਖਿਆ ਆਰੰਭਕ ਤੇ ਅੰਤਮ ਸ਼ਬਦ, ਨਾਅਰਾ; ਸੂਤਰ

catching ('ਕੈਚਿੰਗ) *a n* ਦਿਲ ਖਿੱਚਵਾਂ, ਆਕਰਸ਼ਤ; ਅਸਰਦਾਇਕ, ਪਕੜ; ਗ੍ਰਾਹੀ

categorisation ('ਕੈਟਅਗਅਰਾਇ'ਜ਼ੇਇਸ਼ਨ) *n* ਵਰਗੀਕਰਨ, ਪ੍ਰਕਾਰ-ਵੰਡ

categorise ('ਕੈਟਅਗਅਰਾਇਜ਼) *v* ਵਰਗੀਕ੍ਰਿਤ ਕਰਨਾ, ਵੰਡ ਕਰਨੀ, ਵੰਡਣਾ

category ('ਕੈਟਗਅਰਿ) *n* ਸ਼੍ਰੇਣੀ

cater ('ਕੇਇਟਅ*) *v* ਭੋਜਨ ਦਾ, ਪ੍ਰਬੰਧ ਕਰਨਾ, ਲੋੜ ਪੂਰੀ ਕਰਨਾ; ~er ਭੰਡਾਰੀ, ਭੋਜਨ ਵੰਡਣ ਵਾਲਾ, ਭੋਜਪ੍ਰਬੰਧਕ; ~ing ਭੋਜਨ-ਪ੍ਰਬੰਧ, ਆਹਾਰ-ਪ੍ਰਦਾਨ, ਖਿਲਾਈ

catharsis (ਕਅ'ਥਾਸਿਸ) *n* ਜੁਲਾਬ, ਵਿਰੇਚਨ, ਸ਼ੋਧ; ਸਰੀਰ-ਸ਼ੁੱਧੀ; ਭਾਵ-ਵਿਰੇਚਨ

cattle ('ਕੈਟਲ) *n* ਪਸ਼ੂ, ਡੰਗਰ, ਵੱਗ; ਮਾਲ

cauliflower ('ਕੌਲਿ'ਫ਼ਲਾਉਅ*) *n* ਫੁੱਲ ਗੋਭੀ

causal ('ਕੌਜ਼ਲ) *a* ਕਾਰਨਵਾਦੀ, ਕਾਰਨ-ਸਬੰਧੀ, ਕਾਰਨ

causative ('ਕੌਜ਼ਅਟਿਵ) *n* (ਬੋਲ) ਕਾਰਨਿਕ, ਕਾਰਨਕਾਰੀ, ਕਾਰਨਵਾਚਕ; ਪ੍ਰੇਰਨਾਰਥਕ

cause (ਕੌਜ਼) *n v* ਕਾਰਨ, ਸਬੱਬ, ਵਜ੍ਹਾ, ਮੂਲ ਕਰਤਾ; ਉਦੇਸ਼, ਪ੍ਰਯੋਜਨ, ਦਾਅਵਾ, ਪੱਖ; **final~** ਅੰਤਮ ਉਦੇਸ਼; **first~** ਮੂਲ ਕਾਰਨ; ਸਿਰਜਨਹਾਰ, ਪਰਮਾਤਮਾ; **show~** ਕਾਰਨ ਦੱਸਣਾ; ਕਰਾਉਣਾ, ਕਰਵਾਉਣਾ; ਪੈਦਾ ਕਰਨਾ; ਬਣਾ ਲੈਣਾ

caution ('ਕੋਸ਼ਨ) *v* ਖ਼ਬਰਦਾਰੀ, ਸਾਵਧਾਨੀ, ਚੌਕਸੀ, ਚੇਤਾਵਨੀ; ਸਿਆਣਪ; ਚੇਤਾਵਨੀ ਦੇਣੀ, ਜਤਲਾਉਣਾ, ਖ਼ਬਰਦਾਰ ਕਰਨਾ, ਆਗਾਹ ਕਰਨਾ

cautious ('ਕੋਸ਼ਅਸ) *a* ਸਾਵਧਾਨ, ਚੌਕਸ, ਖ਼ਬਰਦਾਰ, ਸਿਆਣਾ; **~ly** ਸਾਵਧਾਨੀ ਨਾਲ, ਖ਼ਬਰਦਾਰ ਹੋ ਕੇ, ਸੋਚ ਸਮਝ ਕੇ, ਧਿਆਨ ਨਾਲ; **~ness** ਹੁਸ਼ਿਆਰੀ, ਚੌਕਸੀ, ਖ਼ਬਰਦਾਰੀ, ਨਿਪੁੰਨਤਾ

cavalry ('ਕੈਵਐਰਿ) ਘੁੜਸਵਾਰ ਸੈਨਾ, (ਸਵਾਰਾਂ ਦਾ) ਰਸਾਲਾ

cave (ਕੇਇਵ੍) *n v int* ਗੁਫ਼ਾ, ਕੰਦਰਾ; ਖੋਹ; ਗ੍ਰਾਰ; ਗੁਟਬੰਦੀ; ਗੁੜ੍ਹਾ ਪੁੱਟਣੀ, ਪੋਲਾ ਕਰਨਾ; ਗੁੱਟ ਬਣਾਉਣਾ, ਅਧੀਨ ਹੋ ਜਾਣਾ; ਹਾਰ ਮੰਨਣੀ, ਵਿਗਾੜ ਦੇਣਾ; (ਸਕੂਲ ਵਿਚ ਅਧਿਆਪਕ ਦੇ ਆਣ ਦੀ ਸੂਚਨਾ ਮੁੰਡਿਆਂ ਵੱਲੋਂ) ਹੁਸ਼ਿਆਰ! ਸਾਵਧਾਨ! ਖ਼ਬਰਦਾਰ!

cavern ('ਕੈਵ੍(ਅ)ਨ) *n v* ਕੰਦਰਾ, ਖੁੰਦਰ, ਗੁੜ੍ਹਾ (ਕਾਵਿਆਈ); ਗੁੜ੍ਹਾ ਖੋਦਣਾ ਜਾਂ ਬਣਾਉਣਾ; ਕੰਦਰਾ ਵਿਚ ਬੰਨ੍ਹ ਕੇ ਰੱਖਣਾ

ceiling ('ਸਿਲਿੰਡ) *n* ਛੱਤ, ਅੰਦਰਲੀ ਛੱਤ, ਮੁੱਲ ਜਾਂ ਮਜ਼ਦੂਰੀ ਆਦਿ ਦੀ ਅੰਤਮ ਸੀਮਾ

celebrate ('ਸੈਲਿਬਰੇਇਟ) *v* (ਤਿਉਹਾਰ, ਦਿਨ) ਮਨਾਉਣਾ, ਜਸ਼ਨ ਮਨਾਉਣਾ; ਸਮਾਰੋਹ ਕਰਨਾ, ਉਤਸਵ ਮਨਾਉਣਾ, (ਧਾਰਮਕ ਰੀਤ) ਅਦਾ ਕਰਨੀ, ਪੂਜਣਾ, ਕੀਰਤੀ ਕਰਨੀ; ਜਸ ਫੈਲਾਉਣਾ, ਪ੍ਰਸਿੱਧ ਕਰਨਾ

celebrity (ਸਿ'ਲੈੱਬਰਅਟਿ) *n* ਜਸ, ਪ੍ਰਸਿੱਧੀ, ਪ੍ਰਸਿੱਧ ਵਿਅਕਤੀ

celestial (ਸਿ'ਲੈੱਸਟਯਲ) *a* ਆਕਾਸ਼ੀ, ਅਸਮਾਨੀ, ਪਵਿੱਤਰ, ਸਵਰਗੀ, ਸੁੰਦਰ, ਬ੍ਰਹਮ ਲੋਕੀ

celibacy ('ਸੈਲਿਬਅਸਿ) *n* ਕੁਆਰਾਪਣ, ਜਤ-ਸਤ, ਬ੍ਰਹਮਚਾਰੀ-ਜੀਵਨ

celibate ('ਸੈਲਿਬਅਟ) *n a* ਬ੍ਰਹਮਚਾਰੀ, ਜਤੀ-ਸਤੀ, ਕੁਆਰਾ; ਅਣ-ਵਿਆਹਿਆ (ਪੁਰਸ਼), ਅਵਿਵਾਹਤ (ਜੀਵਨ)

cell (ਸੈੱਲ) *n* ਕੋਠਰੀ; ਇਕ ਖੋਲ; ਕੋਸ਼ਾਣ, ਕੋਸ਼ਿਕਾ, ਕੁਟੀਆ, ਕੁਟੀਰ; ਸਮਾਧੀ; ਕਬਰ; **condemned~** ਕਾਲ-ਕੋਠੜੀ; **~er** ਤਹਿਖ਼ਾਨਾ, ਧਰਤੀ ਹੇਠਲਾ ਗੁਦਾਮ

cellular ('ਸੈਲਯੁਲਅ*) *a* ਖ਼ਾਨੇਦਾਰ, ਛੇਕਾਂ ਵਾਲਾ, ਜਾਲੀਦਾਰ

cement ('ਸਿ'ਮੈਨਟ) *n v* ਸੀਮਿੰਟ; ਜੋੜਨ ਦਾ ਮਸਾਲਾ; ਦੰਦ ਦਾ ਸਖ਼ਤ ਆਵਾਰਣ; ਸੀਮਿੰਟ ਲਗਾਉਣਾ

cemetery ('ਸੈਮਿਟਰਿ) *n* ਸ਼ਮਸ਼ਾਨ, ਕਬਰਸਤਾਨ

censor ('ਸੈਨਸਅ*) *n v* ਦੇਸ਼-ਨਿਰੀਖਕ, ਪੁਸਤਕਾਂ, ਸਮਾਚਾਰਾਂ ਆਦਿ ਦਾ ਸੈਂਸਰ, ਦੇਸ਼ ਲੱਭਣਾ, ਪੜਤਾਲਣਾ

censure ('ਸੈਨਸ਼ਅ*) *n v* ਨਿੰਦਾ, ਕਲੰਕ, ਮੁਜ਼ੱਮਤ, ਤਿਰਸਕਾਰ, ਝਿੜਕ, ਫਿਟਕਾਰ; ਨਿੰਦਾ ਕਰਨਾ, ਦੇਸ਼ ਕੱਢਣਾ, ਮੁਜ਼ੱਮਤ ਕਰਨਾ, ਦੇਸ਼ ਲਗਾਉਣਾ

census ('ਸੈਨਸਅਸ) *n* ਮਰਦਮ ਸ਼ੁਮਾਰੀ, ਜਨ-ਗਣਨਾ

centenary (ਸੈਂ'ਟੀਨਅਰਿ) *n a* ਸ਼ਤਾਬਦੀ ਸਮਾਰੋਹ, ਸੌ ਬਰਸੀ, ਸੌ ਸਾਲਾ ਉਤਸਵ

center (ਸੈਂਟਅ*) *n* (ਪ੍ਰ) ਕਮਰਬੰਦ

centigram ('ਸੈਂਟਿਗਰੈਮ) *n* ਸੈਂਟੀਗ੍ਰਾਮ, ਗ੍ਰਾਮ ਦਾ

ਸੌਵਾਂ ਭਾਗ

centimetre ('ਸੈਂਟਿ'ਮੀਟਅ*) *n* ਸੈਂਟੀਮੀਟਰ, ਮੀਟਰ ਦਾ ਸੌਵਾਂ ਭਾਗ

centipede ('ਸੈਂਟਿਪੀਡ) *n* ਕੰਨ ਖਜੂਰਾ

central ('ਸੈਂਟਰਲ) *a* ਕੇਂਦਰੀ ਵਿਚਕਾਰਲਾ, ਮੱਧਵਰਤੀ; ਪ੍ਰਧਾਨ, ਸਰਵ, ਪ੍ਰਮੁੱਖ, ਮੁੱਖ; ਸ਼੍ਰੋਮਣੀ, ਵੱਡਾ; ~**ideal** ਕੇਂਦਰੀ ਭਾਵ; ~**ization** ਕੇਂਦਰੀਕਰਨ; ~**ly** ਕੇਂਦਰ ਵਿਚ, ਕੇਂਦਰ ਤੋਂ

centre (ਸੈਂਟਅ*) *n a v* ਕੇਂਦਰ, ਮੱਧਵਰਤੀ ਭਾਗ, ਮਰਕਜ਼, ਕੇਂਦਰੀ ਨੁਕਤਾ; ਵਿਚਕਾਰਲੀ ਥਾਂ; ਕੇਂਦਰੀ, ਮਰਕਜ਼ੀ; ਕੇਂਦਰ ਵਿਚ ਕਰਨਾ, ਕੇਂਦਰਤ ਕਰਨਾ, ਇਕੱਠਾ ਕਰਨਾ; ~**of gravity** ਗੁਰੁਤਾ-ਕੇਂਦਰ

centrifugal (ਸੈਂ'ਟਰਿਫ਼ਯੁਗਲ) *a* ਵਿਕੇਂਦਰੀ, ਕੇਂਦਰੀ ਤੋਂ ਖਿੰਡਣ ਜਾਂ ਪਸਰਨ ਵਾਲੀ, ਅਪਕੇਂਦਰੀ; ~**force** ਅਪਕੇਂਦਰ ਸ਼ਕਤੀ, ਜਿਸ ਸ਼ਕਤੀ ਨਾਲ ਕੋਈ ਚੀਜ਼ ਆਪਣੇ ਕੇਂਦਰ ਤੋਂ ਬਾਹਰ ਜਾਂਦੀ ਹੈ

centripetal (ਸੈਂ'ਟਰਿਪਿਟਲ) *a* ਕੇਂਦਰਮੁਖੀ, ਕੇਂਦਰ ਵੱਲ ਲੈ ਜਾਣ ਵਾਲੀ

century ('ਸੈਂਚੁਰਿ) *n* ਸੈਂਕੜਾ, ਸ਼ਤਕ, ਸਦੀ, ਸੌ ਵਰ੍ਹੇ ਦਾ ਸਮਾਂ, ਸ਼ਤਾਬਦੀ

cereal ('ਸਿਅਰਿਅਲ) *n a* ਅਨਾਜ, ਗੱਲਾ; ਅੰਨ ਸਬੰਧੀ, ਅੰਨ ਦਾ

cerebral ('ਸੈਰਿਬਰ(ਅ)ਲ) *a* ਦਿਮਾਗ਼ ਦਾ, ਦਿਮਾਗ਼ੀ, ਮੂਰਧਨੀ

ceremonial ('ਸੈਰਿ'ਮਅਉਨਯਅਲ) *a n* ਰਸਮੀ, ਉਪਚਾਰਕ ਰੀਤੀ-ਅਨੁਸਾਰ, ਰੀਤੀਬੱਧ, ਮਰਜਾਦਾ-ਪੁਰਬਕ, ਸਮਰੋਹ-ਸਬੰਧੀ; ਰੀਤੀ-ਪਾਲਨ, ਪੂਜਾ, ਦਸਤੂਰ, ਸੰਸਕਾਰ, ਕਰਮਕਾਂਡ ਜਾਂ ਸੰਸਕਾਰ ਦੀ ਪੋਥੀ; ~**ly** ਰਸਮੀ ਤੌਰ ਤੇ, ਰੀਤੀ ਅਨੁਸਾਰ

ceremonious ('ਸੈਰਿ'ਮਅਉਨਯਅਸ) *a* ਰਸਮੀ,

ਉਪਚਾਰਕ, ਰਸਮਪੂਜਕ, ਰੀਤ-ਪੂਜਾਰੀ

ceremony ('ਸੈਰਿਮਅਨਿ) *n* ਧਾਰਮਕ ਰੀਤ, ਰਸਮ, ਵਿਧੀ, ਸੰਸਕਾਰ; ਸ਼ਿਸ਼ਟਾਚਾਰ

certificate ('ਸਅ'ਟਿਫ਼ਿਕਅਟ, ਸਅ'ਟਿਫ਼ਿਕੇਇਟ) *n v* ਸਨਦ, ਪ੍ਰਮਾਣ-ਪੱਤਰ, ਸਰਟਿਫ਼ਿਕੇਟ, ਪ੍ਰਸੰਸਾ-ਪੱਤਰ; ਸਨਦ ਦੇਣੀ, ਤਸਦੀਕ ਕਰਨਾ

certification ('ਸਅ:ਟਿਫ਼ਿ'ਕੇਇਸ਼ਨ) *n* ਪ੍ਰਮਾਣੀਕਰਨ

certified ('ਸਅ:ਟਿਫ਼ਾਇਡ) *a* ਪ੍ਰਮਾਣਤ, ਤਸਦੀਕਸ਼ੁਦਾ

certify ('ਸਅ:ਟਿਫ਼ਿਇ) *v* ਪ੍ਰਮਾਣਤ ਕਰਨਾ, ਪ੍ਰਮਾਣ-ਪੱਤਰ ਦੇਣਾ, ਪ੍ਰਮਾਣ-ਸਹਿਤ ਆਖਣਾ, ਵਿਸ਼ਵਾਸ ਦਿਵਾਉਣਾ

cess (ਸੈਸ) *n v* ਕਰ, ਉਪਕਰ, ਚੁੰਗੀ, ਮਹਿਸੂਲ, ਸਥਾਨਕ ਕਰ; ਕਰ ਲਾਉਣਾ, ਚੁੰਗੀ ਲਾਉਣਾ

cessation (ਸੈਸੇਇਸ਼ਨ) *n* ਠਹਿਰਾਉ, ਅੰਤ, ਖ਼ਾਤਮਾ, ਮੁਕ-ਚੁਕ, (ਜੰਗ ਦੀ) ਬੰਦੀ

chafe (ਚੇਇਫ਼) *n v* ਖਿਝ; ਰਗਾੜ; ਖਿਝਣਾ, ਖਿਝਾਉਣਾ, ਮਾਲਸ਼ ਕਰਨਾ, ਸਲਣਾ; ਖੁਜਲਾਉਣਾ, ਮਲਣ ਜਾਂ ਰਗੜਨ ਨਾਲ ਸ਼ਰੀਰ ਦਾ ਛਿਲਿਆ ਜਾਣਾ, ਚਿੜ੍ਹਨਾ, ਚਿੜ੍ਹਾਉਣਾ

chaff (ਚੈਫ਼) *n v* ਤੁਕੀ, ਛਾਲੂਰ, ਫੱਕ; ਘਾਹ-ਫੂਸ, ਕੱਖ-ਕਾਣਾ; ਛੇੜਨਾ, ਮੌਜ ਉਡਾਉਣਾ, (ਘਾਹ) ਕਟਣਾ, ਝੇੜਾਂ ਕਰਨੀਆ

chain (ਚੇਇਨ) *n v* ਬੰਧਨ, ਬੇੜੀ, ਹਥਕੜੀ, ਸੰਗਲ, ਜ਼ੰਜ਼ੀਰ, ਹਾਰ, ਲੜੀ, ਸਿਲਸਲਾ; ਜ਼ੰਜ਼ੀਰ ਨਾਲ ਬੰਨ੍ਹਣਾ, ਸੰਗਲੀ ਪਾਉਣੀ, ਹੱਥਕੜੀ ਲਾਉਣੀ, ਬੰਧਨ ਪਾਉਣੇ, ਕੁੰਡੀ ਲਾਉਣੀ; ~**smoker** ਲਗਾਤਾਰ ਸਿਗਰਟ ਪੀਣ ਵਾਲਾ

chair (ਚੇਅ*) *n v* ਕੁਰਸੀ, ਚੌਕੀ, ਗੱਦੀ; ਸਭਾਪਤੀ,

ਮੁਖੀ, (ਪ੍ਰ) ਪਾਲਕੀ, ਡੋਲੀ; ਪੀਠ; ਪ੍ਰਧਾਨਗੀ ਦੀ ਕੁਰਸੀ ਤੇ ਬਿਠਾਉਣਾ; ਅਧਿਕਾਰੀ ਬਣਾਉਣਾ; ਗੱਦੀ ਤੇ ਬਿਠਾਉਣਾ; ~man ਸਭਾਪਤੀ, ਸਦਰ, ਪ੍ਰਧਾਨ, ਚੇਅਰਮੈਨ, ਰੋਗੀ ਦੀ ਪਹੀਆਂ ਵਾਲੀ ਕੁਰਸੀ ਦਾ ਰੱਖਿਅਕ; ~ship ਪ੍ਰਧਾਨਗੀ; ~person ਪ੍ਰਧਾਨ, ਸਦਰ

chaise (ਸ਼ੇਇਜ਼)*n* ਸੈਰ-ਗੱਡੀ, ਬੱਘੀ, ਸਵਾਰੀ ਬੱਘੀ

chalk (ਚੋਕ) *n v* ਚਾਕ, ਖੜੀਆ ਮਿੱਟੀ, ਚਾਕ ਦੀ ਡਲੀ; ਖੜੀਆ ਮਿੱਟੀ ਮਲਣੀ; ~out ਖ਼ਾਕਾ ਖਿਚਣਾ, ਯੋਜਨਾ ਬਣਾਉਣੀ, ਰੁਪ-ਰੇਖਾ, ਤਿਆਰ ਕਰਨੀ

challan ('ਚਅੱਲਅਨ) *n* ਚਲਾਨ

challenge ('ਚੈਲਿਨਜ) *n* ਚੁਣੌਤੀ, ਲਲਕਾਰ, ਵੰਗਾਰ, ਮੰਗ; ਇਤਰਾਜ਼, ਉਜਰ; ਲਲਕਾਰਨਾ, ਵੰਗਾਰਨਾ, ਚੁਣੌਤੀ ਦੇਣਾ; ਉਜਰ ਕਰਨਾ; ਧਿਆਨ ਦੀ ਮੰਗ ਕਰਨੀ

chamber ('ਚੇਇਮਬਅ*) *n* ਕਮਰਾ, ਸਦਨ, ਮੰਡਲ, ਜੱਜ ਦਾ ਨਿੱਜੀ ਕਮਰਾ; ਸੰਸਦ-ਭਵਨ, ਸਭਾ-ਭਵਨ; ਘੁਰਨਾ

champagne ('ਸ਼ੈਂ'ਪੇਇਨ) *n* ਸ਼ੈਮਪੇਨ, ਫ਼ਰਾਂਸ ਵਿਚ ਬਣੀ ਸ਼ਰਾਬ

champion ('ਚੈਂਪਯਅਨ) *n* ਚੈਂਪੀਅਨ, ਜੋਧਾ, ਬਲੀ, ਸੂਰਮਾ ਮਲ; ਪੱਖੀ, ਹਿਮਾਇਤੀ, ਸਮਰਥਕ, ਹਾਮੀ; ਸਰਬ ਸਮੱਰਥ ਕਰਨਾ, ਪੱਖ ਪੂਰਨਾ, ਹਾਮੀ ਭਰਨੀ

chance (ਚਾਂਸ) *n* ਮੌਕਾ, ਅਵਸਰ ਸੰਭਾਵਨਾ; ਸੰਜੋਗ; ਇਤਫ਼ਾਕ, ਦੈਵ ਘਟਨਾ, ਭਾਗ, ਸਬੱਬ, ਭਾਟਾ; ਸੰਜੋਗ ਨਾਲ ਹੋ ਜਾਣਾ; ਅਚਾਨਕ ਵਾਪਰ ਜਾਣਾ, ਜੋਖਮ ਉਠਾਉਣਾ, ਭਾਗ ਅਜ਼ਮਾਉਣਾ; by~ ਸਹਿਜ ਸੁਭਾਅ ਦੈਵਨੇਤ ਨਾਲ, ਰੱਬ

ਸਬੱਬੀ; take one's~ ਕਿਸਮਤ ਅਜ਼ਮਾਉਣਾ

chancellor ('ਚਾਂਸਅਲਅ*) *n* ਕੁਲਪਤੀ ਕੁਨਾਧੀਪਤੀ; (ਜਰਮਨੀ ਵਿਚ) ਪ੍ਰਧਾਨ ਮੰਤਰੀ; vice~ ਕੁਲਪਤਿ, ਉਪਕੁਲਪਤੀ

chance~medley ('ਚਾਨਸ'ਮੈਂਡਲਿ) *n* (ਕਾ) ਅਟਕਾਓਪੂਣੇ ਵਿਚ ਕੀਤਾ ਗਿਆ ਅਪਰਾਧ; ਅਚਿੰਤੀ ਹੱਤਿਆ, ਅਣਗਹਿਲੀ, ਅਸਾਵਧਾਨੀ

chandelier ('ਸ਼ੈਂਡਅ'ਲਿਅ*) *n* ਝਾੜ-ਫ਼ਾਨੂਸ

change (ਚੇਇੰਜ) *n v* ਬਦਲੀ, ਤਬਦੀਲੀ, ਪਰਿਵਰਤਨ, ਉਲਟ ਫੇਰ; ਫ਼ਰਕ; ਹੇਰ ਫੇਰ; ਰੋਜ਼ਗਾਰੀ, ਭਾਨ; ਬਦਲਣਾ, ਅਦਲਾ-ਬਦਲੀ ਕਰਨੀ, ਹੇਠ ਉਪਰ ਕਰਨਾ; ਪਰਿਵਰਤਨ ਕਰਨਾ; ਲੈਣ-ਦੇਣ ਕਰਨਾ, ਨੋਟ ਜਾਂ ਸਿੱਕਾ ਤੁੜਾਉਣਾ; ਚੰਨ ਦਾ ਘਟਣਾ ਵਧਣਾ

changing ('ਚੇਇੰਜਿਙ) *a* ਬਦਲਣ ਵਾਲਾ, ਪਰਿਵਰਤਨਸ਼ੀਲ

channel ('ਚੈਨਲ) *n v* ਖਾੜੀ, ਨਹਿਰ, ਨਾਲਾ; ਖਾਲ, ਨਾਲੀ, ਆੜ, ਪ੍ਰਣਾਲੀ; ਨਲਕਾ; ਮਾਰਗ; ਦਿਸ਼ਾ ਸਾਧਨ, ਮਾਧਿਅਮ; ਨਾਲੀ ਬਣਾਉਣਾ, ਨਹਿਰ ਕੱਢਣੀ, ਹਾਸ਼ੀਆ ਬਣਾਉਣਾ; ~led ਨਾਲੀਦਾਰ

chant (ਚਾਂਟ) *n v* ਗੀਤ, ਭਜਨ, ਮੰਤਰ; ਉਸਤਤੀ; ਗੀਤ ਗਾਉਣਾ, ਭਜਨ ਗਾਉਣੇ, ਮੰਤਰ, ਉਚਾਰਨੇ, ਗਾਉਣਾ

chaos (ਕਇਔਸ) *n* ਅਵਾਰਤਫਰੀ, ਬੇਤਰਤੀਬੀ, ਧੁੰਦੂਕਾਰਾ, ਉਲਝ ਪੁੰਮੀ

chaotic ('ਕੇਇਔਟਿਕ) *a* ਗਡਮਡ, ਘਡਮਸ ਵਾਲਾ, ਉਂਗੜ-ਦੁੰਗੜ; ਅਵਿਵਸਥਿਤ

chap (ਚੈਪ) *n v* (ਬੋਲ) ਛੋਕਰਾ, ਮਨੁੱਖ; ਦਰਾੜ ਬਿਆਈ; ਜਬਾੜਾ, ਹੜਬਾ; ਫਟਣਾ, ਫੁੱਟਣਾ ਤਿੜਕਣਾ, ਟੁੱਟਣਾ, ਤਰੇੜ ਆਉਣੀ

chapel ('ਚੈਪਲ) *n* ਪੁਰਾਬਨ ਘਰ, ਪੂਜਾ ਸਥਾਨ; ਰੋਮਨ ਕੈਥੋਲਿਕ ਗਿਰਜਾ

chaplain ('ਚੈਪਲਿਨ) *n* ਪੁਰੋਹਤ, ਗਿਰਜੇ ਦਾ ਪਾਦਰੀ

chaplet ('ਚੈਪਲਿਟ) *n* ਮੁਕਟ, ਸਿਹਰਾ, ਹਾਰ, ਪੁਸ਼ਪ-ਮਾਲਾ; ਛੋਟਾ ਗਿਰਜਾ

chapman ('ਚੈਪਮਅਨ) *n* ਫੇਰੀਵਾਲਾ

chapter (ਚੈਪਟਅ*) *n* ਅਧਿਆਇ, ਕਾਂਡ, ਖੰਡ, ਪ੍ਰਕਰਨ, ਪਰਿਛੇਦ; ਪਾਦਰੀ-ਸੰਘ; ਸੰਸਦ ਦਾ ਅਧਿਨਿਯਮ

character (ਕੈਰਅਕਟਅ*) *n v* ਚਰਿੱਤਰ, ਵਿਅਕਤੀਗਤ ਵਿਸ਼ੇਸ਼ਤਾ, ਆਚਾਰ, ਆਚਰਨ, ਸਦਾਚਾਰ, ਖਸਲਤ, ਫਿਤਰਤ, ਸੁਭਾਉ, ਲੱਛਣ, ਚਿੰਨ੍ਹ, ਵਿਸ਼ੇਸ਼ ਗੁਣ, ਵਚਿੱਤਰਤਾ, ਪ੍ਰਕਾਰ, ਸ਼ੈਲੀ; ਪ੍ਰਸਿੱਧੀ, ਮਾਨ-ਮਰਯਾਦਾ; ਨੇਕਨਾਮੀ; ਅੱਖਰ, ਹਰਫ਼; ਉਕਰਨਾ; **~istic** ਖ਼ਾਸਾ, ਲੱਛਣ ਵਿਸ਼ੇਸ਼ਤਾ, ਸਿਫ਼ਤ, ਖ਼ਾਸੀਅਤ, ਸੁਭਾਉ; ਚਿੰਨ੍ਹ, ਲੱਛਣ; **~rize** ਵਿਸ਼ੇਸ਼ਤਾ ਦਾ ਵਰਣਨ ਕਰਨਾ, ਲੱਛਣ-ਚਿਤਰਨ ਕਰਨਾ; **~less** ਚਰਿਤੱਰਹੀਨ, ਬਦਚਲਨ,

charcoal (ਚਾਕਅਉਲ) *n* ਲੱਕੜੀ ਦਾ ਕੋਲਾ, ਕੋਲਾ; ਅੰਗਾਰ

charge (ਚਾਜ) *n v* ਬੋਝ, ਭਾਰ, ਖ਼ਰਚਾ, ਲਾਗਤ; ਜ਼ੁੰਮੇਵਾਰੀ, ਫ਼ਰਜ਼ ਸੌਂਪਣਾ, ਰਖਿਆ, ਸੰਭਾਲ, ਅਮਾਨਤ, ਤੁਹਮਤ; ਹੱਲਾ, ਕਾਰਤੂਸ, ਬਾਰੂਦ ਗੋਲੀ, ਸਿੱਕਾ; (ਬਿਜਲੀ) ਚਾਰਜ; ਪੂਰਾ ਪੂਰਾ ਭਕਨਾ; ਮੁੱਲ ਮੰਗਣਾ; ਖ਼ਰਚਾ ਪਾਉਣਾ; ਧਾਵਾ ਕਰਨਾ; ਦੋਸ਼ੀ ਠਹਿਰਾਉਣਾ; ਜ਼ੁੰਮੇਵਾਰੀ ਸੌਂਪਣੀ; ਸੰਭਾਲਣਾ, ਕੰਮ ਸੌਂਪਣਾ; **~able** ਹਿਸਾਬ ਵਿਚ ਗਿਣਨਯੋਗ, ਭਰਨਯੋਗ, ਦੋਸ਼ਨਯੋਗ, ਆਰੋਪਨਯੋਗ; ਮਹਿੰਗਾ; ਖ਼ਰਚਨਯੋਗ; **~less** ਕਲੰਕਰਹਿਤ; **~ness** ਵਸੂਲੀ

charge d'affaires (ਸ਼ਾਯੋਇਡੈੱਫ਼ੇਅ*) ਉਪ-ਰਾਜਦੂਤ

chariot (ਚੈਰਿਅਟ) *n v* ਰਥ, ਸੂਰਜ ਦਾ ਰਥ; ਰਥ ਵਿਚ ਲੈ ਜਾਣਾ, ਰਥ; **~eer** ਸਾਰਥੀ, ਰਥਵਾਨ

charitable (ਚੈਰਿਟਅਬਲ) *a* ਖ਼ਰੈਤੀ; ਖੁੱਲ੍ਹ-ਦਿਲਾ; ਦਾਨੀ, ਉਪਕਾਰੀ, ਸਖੀ; ਦਇਆਵਾਨ, ਕਿਰਪਾਲੂ, ਉਦਾਰ

charity (ਚੈਰਅਟਿ) *n* ਪਰਉਪਕਾਰ , ਕਿਰਪ, ਉਦਾਰਤਾ, ਦਿਆਲਤਾ, ਦਇਆ; ਦਾਨ, ਭਿੱਖਿਆ

charm (ਚਾ*ਮ) *n v* ਮਨੋਹਰਤਾ, ਲੁਭਾਇਮਾਨਤਾ, ਜਾਦੂ, ਮੰਤਰ, ਤਲਿਸਮ, ਤਵੀਤ, ਖਿੱਚ, ਕਸ਼ਸ਼; ਮੋਹ ਲੈਣਾ; ਖ਼ੁਸ਼ ਕਰਨਾ, ਆਨੰਦ ਦੇਣਾ, ਵਸ ਵਿਚ ਕਰਨਾ; ਜਾਦੂ ਦੀ ਸ਼ਕਤੀ ਪ੍ਰਾਪਤ ਕਰਨੀ; **~ing** ਮਨੋਹਰ, ਸੁਹਾਵਣਾ, ਦਿਲਕਸ਼, ਮਨਮੋਹਕ, ਸੁੰਦਰ

chart (ਚਾ*ਟ) *n v* ਚਾਰਟ, ਜਹਾਜ਼ੀਆਂ ਦਾ ਸਮੁੰਦਰੀ ਨਕਸ਼ਾ; ਰੇਖਾ-ਚਿੱਤਰ, ਸਾਰਨੀ, ਨਕਸ਼ਾ ਬਣਾਉਣਾ

charter (ਚਾਟਅ*) *n v* ਸਨਦ, ਫ਼ਰਮਾਨ, ਅਧਿਕਾਰ ਪੱਤਰ, ਪੱਟਾ, ਆਧਾਰ; ਸਨਦ ਦੇਣੀ, ਅਧਿਕਾਰ ਪੱਤਰ ਦੇਣਾ; ਪਰਵਾਨਾ ਦੇਣਾ; **~ed accountant** ਅਧਿਯਿਤ ਲੇਖਾਕਾਰ, ਚਾਰਟਰਡ ਅਕਾਉਂਟੈਂਟ

chase (ਚੇਇਜ਼) *n v* ਸ਼ਿਕਾਰ; ਬੀੜ, ਸ਼ਿਕਾਰਗਾਹ; ਪਿੱਛਾ; (ਛਪਾਈ ਵਿਚ) ਟਾਈਪ ਨੂੰ ਕਸਣ ਦਾ ਢਾਂਚਾ; ਪਿੱਛਾ ਕਰਨਾ, ਪਿੱਛੇ ਭੱਜਣਾ; ਫ਼ਰਮਾ ਕਸਣਾ; ਨੱਕਾਸ਼ੀ ਕਰਨਾ; ਸ਼ਿੰਗਾਰਨਾ

chaste (ਚੇਇਸਟ) *a* ਪਵਿੱਤਰ, (ਮਨ) ਸੁੱਚਾ, ਅਛੋਹ, ਨਿਰਮਲ, ਖ਼ਾਲਸ; ਸਤਵੰਤੀ, ਕੁਆਰਾ, ਅਣਲੱਗ

chastise (ਚੈ*ਸਟਾਇਜ਼) *v* ਦੰਡ ਦੇਣਾ, ਸਜ਼ਾ ਦੇਣੀ,

ਚੰਡਣਾ, ਖੁੰਭ ਠੱਪਣੀ, ਤਾੜਨਾ ਕਰਨੀ, ਸਿਧਾ ਕਰਨਾ

chastity (ਚੈਸਟਅਟਿ) *n* ਪਵਿੱਤਰਤਾ, ਸ਼ੁੱਧਤਾ, ਸਤ, ਕੁਆਰਾਪਣ; ਸ਼ੈਲੀ ਦੀ ਸ਼ੁੱਧੀ

chat (ਚੈਟ) *n* ਗੱਪ, ਬਾਤਚੀਤ, ਗੱਲ-ਕੱਥ, ਗੱਲਬਾਤ

chatter (ਚੈਟਅ*) *n v* ਗੱਪ, ਗੜਬੜ, ਬਕਵਾਸ; ਟੀ ਟੀ ਕਰਨਾ, ਟਰ ਟਰ ਕਰਨਾ, ਦੰਦ ਕਰੀਚਨੇ, ਪੁਰਜ਼ਿਆਂ ਦਾ ਕਿੜ ਕਿੜ ਕਰਨਾ; **~box** ਬਕਵਾਸੀ, ਗਲਾਪੜ; ਬਾਤੂਨੀ, ਗੱਪੀ

chauffeur (ਸ਼ਅਉਫ਼ਅ*) *n* ਸ਼ੋਫਰ, ਪੇਸ਼ਾਵਰ ਕਾਰ-ਡਰਾਈਵਰ

chauvinism (ਸ਼ਅਉਵਿਨਿਜ਼(ਅ)ਮ) *n* ਕੱਟੜਪੁਣਾ, ਘੋਰ ਦੇਸ਼ ਭਗਤੀ

chauvinist (ਸ਼ਅਉਵਿਨਿਸਟ) *n* ਕੱਟੜ ਦੇਸ਼ ਪਰੇਮੀ

cheap (ਚੀਪ) *a* ਸਸਤਾ, ਸੁਵੱਲਾ, ਸੁਲੱਭ, ਸਹਿਜੇ ਹੀ ਪ੍ਰਾਪਤ; ਨਿਕੰਮਾ, ਹੋਛਾ; ਮਹਤੱਵਹੀਨ; **~ly** ਸਸਤੇ ਭਾਅ ਵਿਚ, ਘਟੀਆ ਤਰੀਕੇ ਨਾਲ, ਸਸਤੇ ਢੰਗ ਨਾਲ; **~ness** ਸਸਤਾਪਣ, ਸੁਲੱਭਤਾ, ਘਟੀਆਪਣ

cheat (ਚੀਟ) *n a v* ਠੱਗੀ, ਧੋਖਾ, ਫ਼ਰੇਬ, ਛਲ; ਕਪਟ; ਠੱਗ, ਦਗ਼ੇਬਾਜ਼, ਕਪਟੀ, ਫ਼ਰੇਬੀ; ਧੋਖਾ ਦੇਣਾ, ਬੇਈਮਾਨੀ ਕਰਨੀ, ਛਲਣਾ, ਝਾਂਸਾ ਦੇਣਾ; **~er** ਧੋਖੇਬਾਜ਼, ਕਪਟੀ, ਛਲ ਕਰਨ ਵਾਲਾ, ਠੱਗ; **~ing** ਧੋਖੇਬਾਜ਼ੀ

check (ਚੈੱਕ) *n v* ਰੋਕ, ਸੰਜਮ, ਅਟਕਾਅ, ਠੱਲ੍ਹ, ਰੋਕਣਾ, ਝਿੜਕ; ਨਿਰੀਖਣ, ਜਾਂਚ, ਪੜਤਾਲ; ਚਾਰਖ਼ਾਨਾ ਕੱਪੜਾ; ਸੌਂਪਣਾ, ਜਾਂਚ ਪੜਤਾਲ ਕਰਨੀ

cheek (ਚੀਕ) *n* ਗੱਲ੍ਹ, ਰੁਖ਼ਸਾਰ; **~ness** ਗੁਸਤਾਖ਼ੀ

cheer (ਚਿਅ*) *n v* ਖ਼ੁਸ਼ੀ; ਘੱਲੇ-ਘੱਲੇ, ਖ਼ੁਸ਼ੀ ਪਰਗਟ ਕਰਨ ਵਾਲੇ ਸ਼ਬਦ; ਘੱਲੇ-ਘੱਲੇ ਕਰਨਾ, ਢਾਰਸ ਦੇਣਾ, ਪ੍ਰਸੰਨ ਕਰਨਾ; **~up** ਖ਼ੁਸ਼ ਹੋਣਾ, ਚੜ੍ਹਦੀ ਕਲਾ ਵਿਚ ਆਉਣਾ; **~ful** ਖ਼ੁਸ਼, ਪ੍ਰਫੁੱਲਤ, ਆਨੰਦ, ਹਸਦਾ-ਰਸਦਾ, ਹਸਮੁਖ, ਟਹਿਕਦਾ ਹੋਇਆ, ਆਨੰਦਕਾਰਕ, ਆਨੰਦ ਦੇਣ ਵਾਲਾ; **~fully** ਚਾਈਂ ਚਾਈਂ, ਖ਼ੁਸ਼ੀ ਖ਼ੁਸ਼ੀ, ਚਾਅ ਨਾਲ, ਦਿਲ ਨਾਲ; **~fulness** ਖ਼ੁਸ਼ੀ, ਟਹਿਕ, ਆਨੰਦ, ਪ੍ਰਸੰਨਤਾ; **~less** ਉਦਾਸ, ਨਿਮੋਝੂਣਾ, ਬੇ-ਰੌਣਕ, ਮੁਰਝਾਇਆ (ਚਿਹਰਾ)

cheese (ਚੀਜ਼) *n* ਪਨੀਰ; **bread and ~**ਦਾਲ-ਰੋਟੀ

chef (ਸ਼ੈੱਫ਼) *n* ਖਾਨਸਾਮਾ, ਮੁੱਖ ਰਸੋਈਆ

chemical (ਕੈੱਮਿਕਲ) *a n* ਰਸਾਇਣਕ, ਰਸਾਇਣ; ਰਸਾਇਣਕ ਪਦਾਰਥ

chemist (ਕੈੱਮਿਸਟ) *n* ਰਸਾਇਣ ਵਿੱਦਿਆ ਨੂੰ ਜਾਨਣ ਵਾਲਾ, ਦਵਾਈਆਂ ਵੇਚਣ ਵਾਲਾ, ਦਵਾਫ਼ਰੋਸ਼, ਕੈਮਿਸਟ; **~ry** ਰਸਾਇਣ-ਵਿਗਿਆਨ, ਰਸਾਇਣਕੀ

cheque (ਚੈੱਕ) *n* ਚੈੱਕ, ਹੁੰਡੀ; **~book** ਚੈਕਾਂ ਦੀ ਕਾਪੀ; **blank~** ਕੋਰਾ ਚੈੱਕ; **crossed~** ਰੇਖਾ-ਅੰਕਤ ਚੈੱਕ, ਨਕਦ ਭੁਗਤਾਨ ਦੀ ਥਾਂ ਖਾਤੇ ਵਿਚ ਜਮ੍ਹਾ ਹੋਣ ਵਾਲਾ ਚੈੱਕ

cherish (ਚੈੱਰਿਸ਼) *v* ਪਾਲਣ-ਪੋਸਣ ਕਰਨਾ, ਕਦਰ ਕਰਨੀ, ਹਿਤ ਕਰਨਾ, ਦਿਲ ਵਿਚ ਥਾਂ ਦੇਣੀ, ਨਿਵਾਜਣਾ

chess (ਚੈੱਸ) *n* ਸ਼ਤਰੰਜ; **~board** ਸ਼ਤਰੰਜ ਦੀ ਬਿਸਾਤ, ਸ਼ਤਰੰਜੀ; **~men** ਮੋਹਰੇ, ਗੋਟ

chest (ਚੈੱਸਟ) *n* ਛਾਤੀ, ਸੀਨਾ, ਹਿੱਕ; ਪੇਟੀ, ਸੰਦੂਕ, ਸੰਦੂਕੜੀ, ਦਰਾਜਾਂ ਵਾਲੀ ਅਲਮਾਰੀ

chew (ਚੂ) *n v* ਗੋਲੀ; ਚਿਬਣਾ, ਚਬਾਉਣਾ,

ਉਗਾਲੀ ਕਰਨੀ

chicken (ਚਿਕਿਨ) *n* ਚੂਜ਼ਾ; **~hearted** ਕਾਇਰ, ਡਰਪੋਕ; **~pox** ਛੋਟੀ ਮਾਤਾ

chickling (ਚਿਕਲਿਙ) *n* ਚੂਜ਼ਿਆਂ ਦਾ ਚੋਗਾ

chide (ਚਾਇਡ) *v* ਡਾਂਟਣਾ, ਝਾੜਨਾ

chiding (ਚਾਇਡਿਙ) *n* ਡਾਂਟ, ਝਾੜ, ਝਿੜਕ, ਘੁਰਨੀ

chief (ਚੀਫ਼) *n* ਪ੍ਰਧਾਨ, ਪ੍ਰਮੁੱਖ, ਮੁਖੀ; **~dom** ਸਰਦਾਰੀ, ਚੌਧਰ; **~tain** ਮੁਖੀਆ

child (ਚਾਇਲਡ) *n* ਬਾਲ, ਬੱਚਾ, ਬਾਲਕ; ਕਾਕਾ, ਮੁੰਡਾ, ਅੰਞਾਣਾ; ਸੰਤਾਨ, ਵੰਸ਼; **~bed** (ਪ੍ਰ) ਜਨੇਪਾ; **~'s play** ਸੌਖਾ ਕੰਮ, ਬੱਚਿਆਂ ਦਾ ਖੇਲ; **with~** ਗਰਭਵਤੀ; **~hood** ਬਚਪਨ, ਬਾਲਪਨ, ਬਾਲ-ਅਵਸਥਾ, ਛੋਟੀ ਉਮਰ; **~ish** ਬਚਗਾਨਾ, ਬੱਚੇ ਵਾਂਗ **~like** ਸਰਲ, ਭੋਲਾ; **~ness** ਬਚਗਾਨਾਪਣ

chill (ਚਿਲ) *n a v* ਸੀਤ, ਠੰਢ, ਸਰਦੀ, ਪਾਲਾ, ਕਾਂਬਾ, ਉਤਸ਼ਾਹਹੀਨਤਾ, ਉਦਾਸੀ; ਠੰਢਾ; ਠੰਢ ਲੱਗ ਜਾਣੀ, ਠਰਨਾ, ਸੁਸਤ ਹੋਣਾ, ਦਿਲ ਢਾਹੁਣਾ, ਨਿਰਾਸ ਹੋਣਾ; **~y** ਸੀਤ, ਠੰਢਾ, ਠਰਿਆ, (ਸੁਭਾਅ ਦਾ), ਰੁੱਖਾ, ਉਦਾਸੀਨ

chilli (ਚਿਲਿ) *n* ਸੁੱਕੀ ਲਾਲ ਮਿਰਚ

chimney (ਚਿਮਨਿ) *n* ਚਿਮਨੀ, ਅੰਗੀਠੀ, ਧੂੰਆਂ ਨਿਕਲਣ ਵਾਲੀ ਥਾਂ, ਤੰਗ ਦਰਾੜ

chimpanzee (ਚਿਮਪੈਂਜ਼ੀ) *n* ਬਾਂਦਰ ਦੀ ਇਕ ਨਸਲ, ਚਿੰਪਾਂਜ਼ੀ

chin (ਚਿਨ) *n* ਠੋਡੀ

chink (ਚਿੰਕ) *n v* ਝਰੋਖਾ, ਛੇਕ, ਮੋਰੀ, ਝਟਕਾਰ; ਛਣਕਣਾ, ਟੁਣਕਣਾ, ਟੁਣਕਾਰ ਹੋਣੀ

chip (ਚਿਪ) *n* ਟੁਕੜਾ, ਛਿਲਤਰ, ਗੀਟਾ, ਪਾਖੀ;

chirp (ਚਅ:ਪ) *n* ਚਹਿਚਹਾਟ, ਚੀਂ ਚੀਂ, ਚੂੰ ਚੂੰ; ਚੀਂ

ਚੀਂ ਕਰਨਾ, ਚਹਿਚਹਾਉਣਾ,

chirrup (ਚਿਰਅਪ) *v* ਚੂੰ ਚੂੰ ਕਰਨਾ; ਪੁਚਕਾਰਨਾ

chisel (ਚਿਜ਼ਲ) *n v* ਛੈਣੀ, ਰੇਰਸੀ; ਚੱਕੀ-ਰਾਹਾ; ਛਿੱਲਣਾ, ਘੜਨਾ; ਧੋਖਾ ਦੇਣਾ, ਠੱਗ ਲੈਣਾ

chit-chat (ਚਿਟਚੈਟ) *n* ਗੱਪ-ਸ਼ੱਪ, ਗੱਲਬਾਤ

chivalrous (ਸ਼ਿਵ੍ਲਰਅਸ) *a* ਬੀਰ, ਸੂਰਬੀਰ, ਬੀਰ ਕਾਲ ਦਾ; ਸੱਭਿਅ; ਸੁਆਰਥਹੀਨ, ਉਦਾਰ, ਨਿਸ਼ਕਾਮ

chivalry (ਸ਼ਿਵ੍ਲਰਿ) *n* ਘੋੜਸਵਾਰ, ਘੋੜਸਵਾਰਾਂ ਦਾ ਰਿਸਾਲਾ; ਸ਼ਿਸ਼ਟ ਜੋਧਾ, ਬੀਰਤਾ, ਸੂਰਬੀਰਤਾ

chock (ਚੌਕ) *n* ਗੁਟਕਾ, ਲੱਕੜ ਦਾ ਟੁਕੜਾ

chocolate (ਚੌਕ(ਅ)ਲਅਟ) *n a* ਚਾਕਲੇਟ (ਖਾਣ ਵਾਲੀ); ਗੁੜ੍ਹਾ ਲਾਖ ਜਾਂ ਕਥਈ (ਰੰਗ)

choice (ਚੌਇਸ) *n a* ਚੋਣ, ਚੁਣੀ ਹੋਈ ਚੀਜ਼, ਪਸੰਦ, ਛਾਂਟ; ਵਧੀਆ, ਸੰਗਤ; **at ~** ਇੱਛਾ ਅਨੁਸਾਰ, ਮਰਜ਼ੀ ਨਾਲ

choke (ਚਅਉਕ) *v n* ਗਲ ਘੁੱਟਣਾ; ਤੂੜਨਾ, ਬੰਦ ਕਰਨਾ, ਭਰ ਦੇਣਾ, ਸਾਹ ਰੋਕਣਾ; ਰੋਕਣਾ; ਰੋਕ, ਰੁਕਾਵਟ; ਚੋਕ

cholera ('ਕੌਲਅਰਅ) *n* ਹੈਜ਼ਾ

choleric ('ਕੌਲਅਰਿਕ) *a* ਚਿੜਚੜਾ, ਸੜੀਅਲ, ਖਿਝੂ, ਗੁੱਸੈਲ, ਕਰੋਪੀ, ਤੇਜ਼ ਮਿਜ਼ਾਜ

choose (ਚੂਜ਼) *v* ਚੁਣਨਾ, ਨਿਸ਼ਚਤ ਕਰਨਾ; **~r** ਚੋਣਕਾਰ, ਚੁਣਨ ਵਾਲਾ, ਪਸੰਦ ਕਰਨ ਵਾਲਾ; **~y** (ਬੋਲ) ਵਹਿਮੀ, ਸਨਕੀ

chop (ਚੌਪ) *n v* ਮਾਸ ਦਾ ਟੁਕੜਾ, ਵੱਢ, ਫੱਟ, ਕੱਟਣਾ, ਵੱਢਣਾ, ਟੁਕੜੇ ਟੁਕੜੇ ਕਰਨਾ, ਕੀਮਾ ਕਰਨਾ; (ਗੱਲ) ਟੇਕਣਾ; **~in** ਗੱਲ ਕੱਟਣੀ ਬਦਲ ਜਾਣਾ, ਬਦਲੀ ਕਰਨੀ, ਚੰਚਲ ਹੋਣਾ, ਅਸਥਿਰ ਹੋਣਾ; **~about, -round** ਦਿਸ਼ਾ ਬਦਲ ਦੇਣਾ, ਰੁਖ ਬਦਲ ਦੇਣਾ

chopper ('ਚੌਪਅ*) *n* ਛੋਟੀ ਕੁਹਾੜੀ, ਗੰਡਾਸਾ, ਟੇਕਾ

choppy ('ਚੌਪਿ) *a* (ਸਮੁੰਦਰ) ਤੂਫ਼ਾਨੀ

choral ('ਕੋਰ(ਅ)ਲ) *a* ਸਮੂਹ-ਗਾਨ ਸਬੰਧੀ

chord (ਕੋਡ) *n* ਤੰਦ, ਤਾਰ, ਡੋਰੀ, ਵਤਰ

chore (ਚੋ*) *n* ਛੋਟਾ ਮੋਟਾ, ਕੰਮ, ਨਿਤ ਦਾ ਕੰਮ

choreograph ('ਕੋਰਿਅਗਰਾਫ਼਼਼) *n* ਨ੍ਰਿਤ-ਲੇਖ; ~**y** ਨ੍ਰਿਤਲੇਖਨ

chorus ('ਕੋਰਅਸ) *n* ਸਮੂਹ-ਗਾਨ, ਸਹਿਗਾਨ, ਜੋਗੀਆਂ ਵਾਲਾ ਗੀਤ, ਨਾਚ ਮੰਡਲੀ ਦਾ ਗੀਤ

christ (ਕਰਾਇਸਟ) *n* ਹਜ਼ਰਤ ਈਸਾ, ਈਸਾ ਮਸੀਹ, ਯਸੂਹ-ਮਸੂਹ; ~**hood** ਮਸੀਹਪਣ

Christian ('ਕਰਿਸਚਨ) *n* ਇਸਾਈ, ਮਸੀਹੀ ਯਸੂਹੀ; ~**era** ਸੰਨ ਈਸਵੀ; ~**ity** ਇਸਾਈ ਮੱਤ, ਮਸੀਹੀ ਧਰਮ

Christmas ('ਕਰਿਸਮਅਸ) (Xmas) *n* ਕ੍ਰਿਸਮਸ, ਇਸਾਈਆਂ ਦਾ ਦਿਨ 25 ਦਸੰਬਰ; ~**day** ਹਜ਼ਰਤ ਈਸਾ ਦਾ ਜਨਮ ਦਿਨ, ਵੱਡਾ ਦਿਨ

chronic ('ਕਰੌਨਿਕ) *a* ਪੁਰਾਣਾ, ਦਾਇਮੀ, ਚਿਰਕਾਲੀਨ, ਪੱਕਾ

chronicle ('ਕਰੌਨਿਕਲ) *n v* ਰੋਜ਼ਨਾਮਚਾ, ਰੋਜ਼ਨਾਮਾ, ਬਿਰਤਾਂਤ; ਰੋਜ਼ਨਾਮਚਾ ਲਿਖਣਾ, ਕਹਾਣੀ ਲਿਖਣਾ

Chronicles ('ਕਰੌਨਿਕਲਜ਼) *n* ਬਾਈਬਲ ਦੇ ਦੋ ਅਧਿਆਇ

chronological ('ਕਰੌਨਅ'ਲੌਜਿਕਲ) *a* ਕਾਲ-ਕ੍ਰਮਕ

chronology (ਕਰਅ'ਨੌਲੋਜਿ) *n* ਕਾਲਕ੍ਰਮ ਅਨੁਸਾਰ ਲਿਖਣਾ, ਰੋਜ਼ਨਾਮਚਾ ਲਿਖਣਾ

chuck (ਚਅੱਕ) *int v* ਠੱਕ ਠੱਕ, ਕੱਟ ਕੱਟ, ਕੜ

ਕੜ; ਝਟਕਾਉਣਾ, ਪਰੇ ਸੁਟਣਾ; ਪਰੇ ਮਾਰਨਾ, ਭੁਆ ਕੇ ਸੁੱਟਣਾ; ਕੁਕੜੀਆਂ ਨੂੰ ਸੱਦਣ ਦੀ ਅਵਾਜ਼; ਝਟਕਾ; ਪਿਆਰਾ, ਯਾਰ, ਪਿਆਰ ਤੇ ਲਾਡ ਵਾਲਾ ਸ਼ਬਦ; ~**away** ਬਰਬਾਦ ਕਰਨਾ, ਗੁਆਉਣਾ; ~**out** (ਬੋਲ) ਗਿਚੀਓਂ ਫੜ ਕੇ ਬਾਹਰ ਕੱਢਣਾ, ਧੱਕੇ ਦੇਣਾ; ~**up** ਛੱਡ ਦੇਣਾ, ਗਲੋਂ ਲਾਹੁਣਾ; ~**y** ਪਿਆਰਾ ਬੇਟਾ

chuckle ('ਚਅੱਕਲ) *n v* ਮਿੰਨ੍ਹਾ ਮਿੰਨ੍ਹਾ ਹਾਸਾ; ਕੁਕੜੀਆਂ ਦੀ ਕੁੜ ਕੁੜ; ਕੁੜ ਕੁੜ ਕਰਨਾ; ਮੂੰਹ ਬੰਦ ਕਰ ਕੇ ਹੱਸਣਾ; ~**head**, ~**headed** ਬੁੱਧੂ, ਮੂਰਖ, ਮੋਟੀ ਮੱਤ ਵਾਲਾ

chuff (ਚਅੱਫ) *n* ਵਿਦੂਸ਼ਕ

chum (ਚਅੱਮ) *n* ਆੜੀ, ਲੰਗੋਟੀਆ ਯਾਰ; ~**up with** ਗੁੜ੍ਹੀ ਮਿੱਤਰਤਾ ਹੋਣੀ, ਗਹਿਰੀ ਦੋਸਤੀ ਹੋਣੀ; ~**my** ਮਿੱਤਰ, ਯਾਰ, ਸਾਥੀ; ਮਿਲਣਸਾਰ

chunk (ਚਅੰਕ) *a* ਮੋਟਾ ਟੁਕੜਾ, ਕੋਤਲਾ, ਫਾਂਕ,

chunky ('ਚਅੰਕਿ) *a* ਮੋਟੂ

church (ਚਅਃਚ) *n* ਗਿਰਜਾ ਘਰ, ਕਲੀਸਾ; ਪਰਮ-ਸਥਾਨ; ਇਸਾਈ ਲੋਕ; ~**ing** ਪੂਜਨ; ~**man** ਪਾਦਰੀ

churl (ਚਅਃਲ) *n* ਉਜੱਡ, ਪੇਂਡੂ, ਘਟੀਆ, ਬਦਤਮੀਜ਼, ਕੰਜੂਸ, ਮੱਖੀ-ਚੂਸ; ~**ish** ਉਜੱਡ, ਅੱਖੜ, ਗੰਵਾਰ, ਅਸ਼ਿਸ਼ਟ; ~**ishness** ਕੰਜੂਸੀ; ਅਸ਼ਿਸ਼ਟਤਾ, ਅੱਖੜਪਣ, ਉਜੱਡਤਾ

churn (ਚਅਃਨ) *n v* ਚਾਟੀ; ਦੁੱਧ ਰਿੜਕਣਾ, ਦੁੱਧ ਵਿਲੋਣਾ

cigar (ਸਿ'ਗਾ*) *n* ਸਿਗਾਰ, ਚੁਰਟ

cigarette ('ਸਿਗਅ'ਰੈੱਟ) *n* ਸਿਗਰਟ

cine ('ਸਿਨਿ) *a* ਸਿਨੇਮਾ-ਸਬੰਧੀ, ਫ਼ਿਲਮ ਦਾ

cinema ('ਸਿਨਅਮਅ) *n* ਸਿਨੇਮਾ, ਚਲ-ਚਿਤਰ, ਚਲਦੀਆਂ ਮੂਰਤਾਂ ਵਾਲਾ ਨਾਟਕ; ਸਿਨੇਮਾ-ਘਰ

cipher (ਸਾਇਫਅ*) *n* ਸੂਨ, ਨਿਕੰਮਾ, ਨਾਚੀਜ਼, ਝੀਰੋ, ਗੁਪਤ ਲਿਖਤ; ਹਿਸਾਬ ਲਾਉਣਾ; ਕਢਣਾ; ਜੋੜਨਾ

circle (ਸਅਃਕਲ) *n* ਗੋਲ ਚੱਕਰ, ਗੋਲ ਦਾਇਰਾ; ਪਰਿਕਰਮਾ, ਕੁੰਡਲ, ਛੱਲਾ, ਚੱਕਰ; ਮੰਡਲ; ਖੇਤਰ, ਹਲਕਾ; ਘੇਰਨਾ, ਵਲਣਾ, ਚੱਕਰ ਲਾਉਣਾ, ਘੁੰਮਣਾ

circuit (ਸਅਃਕਿਟ) *n* ਘੇਰਾ, ਚੱਕਰ, ਦਾਇਰਾ; ਪਰਿਕਰਮਾ; ਵਲਵੇਂਦਾਰ ਸ਼ਫ਼ਰ; ਹਲਕਾ; ਘੇਰਨਾ, ਵਲਣਾ, ਚੱਕਰ ਲਾਉਣਾ, ਘੁੰਮਣਾ, ਦੌਰਾ; **short~** ਬਿਜਲੀ ਦੀ ਰੌ ਜਾਂ ਧਾਰਾ ਦੀ ਰੁਕਾਵਟ

circular (ਸਅਃਕ੍ਯੂਲਅ*) *a n* ਗੋਲ, ਚੱਕਰਦਾਰ; ਗਸ਼ਤੀ ਪੱਤਰ; **~letter** ਗਸ਼ਤੀ ਚਿੱਠੀ

circulate (ਸਅਃਕ੍ਯੂਲੇਇਟ) *v* ਭੇਜਣਾ, ਘੁਮਾਣਾ, ਪ੍ਰਚਾਰ ਕਰਨਾ, ਸੰਚਾਰ ਕਰਨਾ; ਪ੍ਰਚਲਤ ਹੋਣਾ, ਦੌਰ ਚੱਲਣਾ, ਚੱਕਰ ਮਾਰਨਾ

circulating (ਸਅਃਕ੍ਯੂਲੇਇਟਿਙ) *a* ਗਸ਼ਤੀ, ਘੁੰਮਦਾ

circulation (ਸਅਃਕ੍ਯੂ'ਲੇਇਸ਼ਨ) *n* ਦੌਰਾ (ਖ਼ੂਨ ਦਾ), ਚੱਕਰ, ਗਸ਼ਤ, ਵਿੱਕਰੀ (ਅਖ਼ਬਾਰ; ਕਿਤਾਬਾਂ ਆਦਿ ਦੀ)

circumference (ਸਅ'ਕਅੱਮਸਫ਼(ਅ)ਰਅੰਸ) *n* ਘੇਰਾ ਘੇਰ, ਚੁਗਿਰਦਾ, ਮੰਡਲ, ਦਾਇਰਾ

circumscribe ('ਸਅਃਕਅਮਸਕਰਾਇਬ) *v* ਘੇਰਨਾ, ਅਹਾਤਾਬੰਦੀ ਕਰਨਾ, ਸੀਮਾਬੱਧ ਕਰਨਾ; ਸੀਮਤ ਕਰਨਾ, ਸੀਮਾ ਨਿਸ਼ਚਤ ਕਰਨਾ, ਨਿਯਮਤ ਕਰਨਾ

circumstance ('ਸਅਃਕਅਮਸਟਅੰਸ) *n* ਹਾਲਤ, ਸੂਰਤ, ਅਵਸਥਾ, ਸਥਿਤੀ, ਵਾਤਾਵਰਨ, ਦਸ਼ਾ; **under no ~s** ਕਦਾਚਿਤ ਨਹੀਂ, ਕਿਸੇ ਸੂਰਤ ਵੀ ਨਹੀਂ

circumstantial ('ਸਅਃਕਅਮ'ਸਟੈਂਸ਼ਲ) *a*

ਇਤਫ਼ਾਕੀਆ, ਅਚਾਨਕ; ਵੇਰਵੇ-ਸਹਿਤ; ਤਫ਼ਸੀਲਵਾਰ; ਪ੍ਰਸੰਗਕ; **~ity** ਸੰਜੋਗ; ਵਿਵਰਨਾਤਮਕਤਾ; **~ly** ਅਚਾਨਕ ਹੀ, ਸੰਜੋਗਵਸ

circumvent ('ਸਅਃਕਅਮ'ਵੈਂਟ) *v* ਫਹੁਣਾ, ਫਸਾਉਣਾ, ਛਲ ਖੇਡਣਾ, ਧੋਖਾ ਦੇਣਾ, ਝਾਂਸਾ ਦੇਣਾ

circus (ਸਅਃਕਸ) *n* ਸਰਕਸ, ਚੁਗਾਨ, ਗੋਲ ਅਖਾੜਾ, ਰੰਗ-ਮੰਡਲ

cistern ('ਸਿਸਟਅਨ) *n* ਪਾਣੀ ਦੀ ਟੈਂਕੀ, ਹੌਜ਼, ਕੁੰਡ

citadel ('ਸਿਟਅਡ(ਅ)ਲ) *n* ਗੜ੍ਹੀ, ਕਿਲ੍ਹਾ, ਕੋਟ; ਅੰਤਮ ਆਸਰਾ; ਓਟ, ਪਨਾਹ

citation (ਸਾਇਟੇਇਸ਼ਨ) *n* ਹਵਾਲਾ ਪ੍ਰਸੰਗ, ਸੰਦਰਭ; ਸੋਧਾ ਪੱਤਰ; ਪ੍ਰਮਾਣ, ਨਜ਼ੀਰ; ਸੱਦਾ

cite (ਸਾਇਟ) *v n* ਸੱਦਣਾ, ਹਵਾਲਾ ਦੇਣਾ, ਮਿਸਾਲ ਦੇਣੀ, ਉਦਾਹਰਨ ਦੇਣਾ; ਸੱਦ, ਬੁਲਾਵਾ, ਹਵਾਲਾ, ਉਦਾਹਰਨ; ਮਿਸਾਲ

citizen ('ਸਿਟਿਜ਼ਨ) *n* ਨਾਗਰਿਕ, ਸ਼ਹਿਰੀ, ਨਿਵਾਸੀ; **~ship** ਨਾਗਰਿਕਤਾ, ਸ਼ਹਿਰੀਅਤ, ਸ਼ਹਿਰੀ ਅਧਿਕਾਰ

city ('ਸਿਟਿ) *n* ਨਗਰ, ਸ਼ਹਿਰ, ਵੱਡਾ ਕਸਬਾ

civic ('ਸਿਵ੍ਕਿ) *a* ਨਾਗਰਿਕਤਾ ਸਬੰਧੀ, ਸ਼ਹਿਰੀਅਤ ਸਬੰਧੀ; ਨਾਗਰਿਕਤਾ, ਨਗਰ-ਸਬੰਧੀ, ਨਗਰ-ਪਾਲਕਾ ਸਬੰਧੀ; **~s** ਨਾਗਰਿਕ-ਸ਼ਾਸਤਰ

civil ('ਸਿਵ੍ਲ) *a* ਸੱਭਿਅ, ਸ਼ਿਸ਼ਟ; ਵਿਨੀਤ; ਅਸੈਨਕ, ਵਿਹਾਰਕ; ਦੀਵਾਨੀ; ਗ਼ੈਰ-ਫ਼ੌਜਦਾਰੀ; ਸਮਾਜਕ, ਦੀਵਾਨੀ, ਗ਼ੈਰ-ਫ਼ੌਜਦਾਰੀ; ਸਮਾਜਕ, ਕਾਨੂੰਨੀ; **~disobedience** ਸਤਿਆਗ੍ਰਹਿ, ਸਿਵਲ ਨਾਫ਼ਰਮਾਨੀ, ਨਾ ਮਿਲਵਰਤਨ; **~law** ਦੀਵਾਨੀ ਕਾਨੂੰਨ, ਨਾਗਰਿਕ ਕਾਨੂੰਨ; **~mar- riage** ਅਦਾਲਤੀ ਵਿਆਹ, ਸਿਵਲ ਮੈਰਿਜ;

~rights ਨਾਗਰਿਕ ਅਧਿਕਾਰ; ~servant ਰਾਜ ਅਧਿਕਾਰੀ; ~service ਸਰਕਾਰੀ ਨੌਕਰੀ, ਰਾਜ ਸੇਵਾ; ਸਿਵਲ-ਸਰਵਿਸ; ~war ਥਾਨਾ ਜੰਗੀ, ਘਰੇਲੂ ਜੁੱਧ, ਗ੍ਰਹਿ ਜੁੱਧ ~ian ਪ੍ਰਬੰਧ ਵਿਭਾਗ ਦਾ ਕਰਮਚਾਰੀ, ਅਸੈਨਕ ਅਧਿਕਾਰੀ; ਅਸੈਨਕ; ~ization ਸੱਭਿਅਤਾ, ਤਹਿਜ਼ੀਬ, ਸੁਘੜਤਾ, ਸੁਰੱਜ, ਮਨੁੱਖਤਾ; ਸ਼ਿਸ਼ਟਤਾ; ~ize ਸੱਭਿਅਤਾ ਸਿਖਾਉਣੀ, ਸੁਧਾਰਨਾ, ਸੁੱਘੜ ਬਣਾਉਣਾ, ਤਹਿਜ਼ੀਬ ਸਿਖਾਉਣਾ; ~ized ਸੱਭਿਅ, ਨਿਮਰ

clad (ਕਲੈੱਡ) *a* ਕੱਪੜੇ, ਪਾਏ ਹੋਏ, ਵਸਤਰਾਂ ਨਾਲ ਸਜੇ ਹੋਏ

claim (ਕਲੇਇਮ) *n v* ਹੱਕ, ਮੰਗ, ਮੁਤਾਲਬਾ, ਦਾਅਵਾ, ਹੱਕ ਜਮਾਉਣਾ, ਮੁਤਾਲਬਾ ਕਰਨਾ, ਦਾਅਵਾ ਕਰਨਾ; ~able ਹੱਕ ਯੋਗ, ਦਾਅਵਾਯੋਗ, ਆਦੇਸ਼ਯੋਗ; ~ant ਹੱਕਦਾਰ, ਦਾਅਵੇਦਾਰ

clamminess ('ਕਲੈਮਿਨੈਸ) *n* ਚਿਪਚਿਪਾਹਟ, ਲੇਸਲਾਪਨ

clamour ('ਕਲੈਂਮ') *n v* ਰੌਲਾ-ਰੱਪਾ, ਦੁਹਾਈ, ਚੀਕ-ਚਿਹਾੜਾ ਪਾਉਣਾ, ਧੱਪ ਪਾਉਣੀ

clamp (ਕਲੈੱਪ) *n v* ਜੋੜ, ਸ਼ਿਕੰਜਾ; ਢੇਰ; ਪੱਤਰਾ ਚੜ੍ਹਾਉਣਾ; ਸ਼ਿਕੰਜਾ ਕਸਣਾ; ਢੇਰ ਲਗਾਉਣਾ; ~ed ਕਸਿਆ, ਜਕੜਿਆ

clan (ਕਲੈਨ) *n* ਛਿਰਕਾ, ਕਬੀਲਾ, ਬਰਾਦਰੀ

clap (ਕਲੈੱਪ) *n v* ਤਾੜੀ, ਦਸਤਕ; ਤਾੜੀਆਂ ਮਾਰਨਾ, ਦਸਤਕ ਦੇਣਾ, ਥਪਥਪਾਉਣਾ; ~eyes on ਨਜ਼ਰ ਪੈਣਾ, ਦੇਖਣਾ

clarification ('ਕਲੈਰਿਫ਼ਿ'ਕੇਇਸ਼ਨ) *n* ਸਪਸ਼ਟੀਕਰਨ, ਸਫ਼ਾਈ

clarify ('ਕਲੈਰਿਫ਼ਾਇ) *v* ਸਪਸ਼ਟ ਕਰਨਾ, ਖੋਲ੍ਹ ਕੇ ਦੱਸਣਾ, ਸਾਫ਼ ਕਰਨਾ, ਛਾਂਟਣਾ, ਸਾਫ਼ ਹੋਣਾ, ਸੁਲਝਣਾ

clarity ('ਕਲੈਰਅਟਿ) *n* ਸਪਸ਼ਟਤਾ, ਸਫ਼ਾਈ, ਸ਼ੁੱਧਤਾ, ਸੁਅੱਛਤਾ, ਨਿਰਮਲਤਾ

clash (ਕਲੈਸ਼) *n v* ਟੱਕਰ, ਟਕਰਾ, ਲੜਾਈ, ਝੜਪ, ਮੁੱਠ-ਭੇੜ, ਖਟਪਟ, ਰੁਕਾਵਟ, ਹਮਲਾ; ਟਕਰਾਉਣਾ; ਲੜਨਾ; ਖਟਪਟਾਉਣਾ; ਰੋਕਣਾ, ਹਮਲਾ ਕਰਨਾ

clasp (ਕਲਾਸਪ) *n v* ਕੁੰਡਾ, ਬਕਸੂਆ; ਪਕੜ, ਜੱਫੀ, ਗਲਵਕੜੀ; ਬੰਦ ਕਰਨਾ, ਬੰਨ੍ਹਣਾ, ਬਕਸੂਆ ਲਾਉਣਾ, ਜੱਫੀ ਪਾਉਣਾ, ਚੰਬੜਨਾ, ਗਲ ਲਾਉਣਾ

class (ਕਲਾਸ) *n v* ਵਰਗ, ਸ਼੍ਰੇਣੀ; ਜਮਾਤ; ਦਰਜਾ, ਵਰਗੀਕਰਨ ਕਰਨਾ; ਜਮਾਤ ਵੰਡ ਕਰਨਾ, ਦਰਜੇਵਾਰ ਕਰਨਾ; ~fellow ਜਮਾਤੀ, ਹਮਜਮਾਤ, ਸਹਿਪਾਠੀ; ~room ਅਧਿਐਨ-ਕਮਰਾ, ਕਲਾਸ ਰੂਮ

classic ('ਕਲੈਸਿਕ) *a n* ਉੱਤਮ, ਟਕਸਾਲੀ, ਸ਼੍ਰੇਸ਼ਠ; ਸਨਾਤਨੀ; ਕਿਸੇ ਦੇਸ਼ ਦਾ ਪੁਰਾਤਨ ਸਾਹਿਤ; ਯੂਨਾਨੀ ਜਾਂ ਲਾਤੀਨੀ ਜਾਂ ਸੰਸਕ੍ਰਿਤ ਭਾਸ਼ਾ

classification ('ਕਲੈਸਿਫ਼ਿ'ਕੇਇਸ਼ਨ) *n* ਵਰਗੀਕਰਨ, ਸ਼੍ਰੇਣੀਕਰਨ

classifier ('ਕਲੈਸਿਫ਼ਾਇਅ') *n* ਸ਼੍ਰੇਣੀ ਜਾਂ ਵਰਗ ਵਿਚ ਰੱਖਣ ਵਾਲਾ, ਕ੍ਰਮਬੱਧ ਕਰਨ ਵਾਲਾ

classify ('ਕਲੈਸਿਫ਼ਾਇ) *v* ਵਰਗੀਕਰਨ ਕਰਨਾ, ਸ਼੍ਰੇਣੀ ਬੱਧ ਕਰਨਾ, ਦਰਜਾਬੰਦੀ ਕਰਨਾ

clatter ('ਕਲੈਟਅ') *v n* ਖੜਕਣਾ, ਖੜਕਾਉਣਾ, ਰੌਲਾ ਪੈਣਾ, ਬਕਬਕ ਕਰਨਾ, ਖੜਕਾਟ, ਰੌਲਾ, ਬਕਵਾਸ

clause (ਕਲੋਜ਼) *n* ਉਪਵਾਕ, ਛੋਟਾ ਵਾਕ; ਦਫ਼ਾ, ਸ਼ਰਤ

claw (ਕਲੋ) *n* ਪੰਜਾ, ਪੌਂਚਾ, ਨਹੁੰਦਰ; ਸੰਨੀ

clay (ਕਲੇਇ) *n* ਪਾਂਡੂ, ਚੀਕਣੀ ਮਿੱਟੀ; ~pipe ਮਿੱਟੀ ਦਾ ਹੁੱਕਾ ਜਾਂ ਪਾਈਪ

clean (ਕਲੀਨ) *a adv v n* ਸਾਫ਼, ਸੁਥਰਾ, ਸੁਅੱਛ, ਉੱਜਲ, ਨਿਰਮਲ, ਬੇਦਾਗ਼, ਉੱਤਮ; ਸਰਾਸਰ, ਨਿਰੋਲ ਸਫ਼ਾਈ ਨਾਲ; ਸਾਫ਼ ਕਰਨਾ, ਮਾਂਜਣਾ; ਉੱਜਲਾ ਕਰਨਾ, ਝਾੜਨਾ, ਸਫ਼ਾਈ, ਝਾੜ-ਪੂੰਝ; ~**tongue** ਸ਼ੁੱਭ ਬਚਨ ਬੋਲਣੇ; ~**er** ਸਾਫ਼ ਕਰਨ ਵਾਲਾ, ਝਾੜੂ ਦੇਣ ਵਾਲਾ; ਕੱਪੜੇ ਡਰਾਈਕਲੀਨ ਕਰਨ ਵਾਲਾ; ~**ing** ਸਫ਼ਾਈ; ~**liness** ਸਫ਼ਾਈ, ਸਫ਼ਾਈ ਪਸੰਦੀ; ~**ness** ਪਵਿੱਤਰਤਾ, ਨਿਰਮਲਤਾ, ਸੁਅੱਛਤਾ; ~**se** ਸਾਫ਼ ਕਰਨਾ, ਸ਼ੁੱਧ ਕਰਨਾ, ਝਾੜਨਾ, ਪੂੰਝਣਾ, ਮਾਂਜਣਾ, ਧੋਣਾ, ਪਵਿੱਤਰ ਕਰਨਾ

clear (ਕਲਿਅ*) *a v* ਸਾਫ਼, ਨਿਰਮਲ, ਬੇਦਾਗ਼, ਖਾਲਸ, ਸੁਅੱਛ, ਸਪਸ਼ਟ, ਪਰਗਟ; ਨਿਖੱਰਨ, ਸਾਫ਼ ਕਰਨਾ, ਸਾਫ਼ ਹੋਣਾ, ਨਿਰਮਲ ਹੋਣਾ, ਭੁਲੇਖਾ ਦੂਰ ਕਰਨਾ, ਨਿਰ-ਅਪਰਾਧ ਠਹਿਰਾਉਣਾ, ਰਿਹਾ ਕਰਨਾ; ~**ance** ਸਪਸ਼ਟਤਾ, ਸਫ਼ਾਈ; ਭੁਗਤਾਨ; ਭੁਗਤਾਨ ਪੱਤਰ, ਜਹਾਜ਼ ਖ਼ਾਲੀ ਹੋਣ ਦਾ ਪ੍ਰਮਾਣ-ਪੱਤਰ, ਸੋਧਨ; ਮਾਲ ਦਾ ਨਿਕਾਸ, ਡਾਕ ਦਾ ਨਿਕਾਸ; ~**away** ਲਾਂਭੇ ਕਰਨਾ, ਹਟਾਉਣਾ, ਅੱਖਾਂ ਤੋਂ ਦੂਰ ਹੋ ਜਾਣਾ; ~**ing** ਨਿਕਾਸੀ; ~**ly** ਸਾਫ਼ ਸਾਫ਼ ਸਰਮੁੱਖ, ਸਪਸ਼ਟਤਾ ਪੂਰਵਕ; ~**ness** ਸਫ਼ਾਈ, ਸੁਅੱਛਤਾ, ਸਪਸ਼ਟਤਾ, ਨਿਰਵਿਘਨਤਾ; ~**off** ਛੁਟਕਾਰਾ ਪਾਉਣਾ, ਖ਼ਲਾਸੀ ਪਾਉਣਾ; ~**up** ਹੱਲ ਕਰਨਾ, ਨਿੱਤਰ ਆਉਣਾ; ~**conscience** ਸਾਫ਼, ਜ਼ਮੀਰ; ~**sighted** ਤੇਜ਼ ਨਜ਼ਰ, ਤੀਬਰ ਦ੍ਰਿਸ਼ਟੀ

cleavage (ਕਲੀਵਿਜ) *n* ਚੀਰ, ਦਰਜ, ਵਿੱਥ; ਪਾੜਾ

cleave (ਕਲੀਵ) *v* ਚੀਰਨਾ, ਪਾੜਨਾ, ਵਫ਼ਾਦਾਰ ਰਹਿਣਾ, ਡਟੇ ਰਹਿਣਾ

cleft (ਕਲੈੱਫਟ) *n* ਦਰਾੜ, ਤੇੜ, ਦਰਜ, ਚੀਰ

clemency (ਕਲੈੱਮਅੰਸਿ) *a* ਨਰਮ-ਦਿਲੀ, ਉਦਾਰਤਾ, ਕਿਰਪਾ, ਦਇਆ, ਰਹਿਮ, ਤਰਸ

clement (ਕਲੈੱਮਅੰਟ) *a* ਨਰਮ-ਦਿਲ, ਕਿਰਪਾਲੂ, ਉਦਾਰ, ਦਇਆਸਮਈ

clergy (ਕਲਅਜਿ) *n* ਪਾਦਰੀ-ਵਰਗ, ਪਰੋਹਤ-ਵਰਗ; ਪਾਦਰੀ ਜਾਂ ਪਰੋਹਤ ਦਾ ਅਧਿਕਾਰ; ~**man** ਪਾਦਰੀ

cleric (ਕਲੈਰਿਕ) *n a* ਪਾਦਰੀ, ਪਰੋਹਤ; ਪਾਦਰੀਆਂ ਦਾ, ਪਾਦਰੀ-ਵਰਗ-ਸਬੰਧੀ; ~**al** ਪਾਰਲੀਮੈਂਟ ਆਦਿ ਵਿਚ ਪਾਦਰੀ-ਵਰਗ ਦਾ ਮੈਂਬਰ ਜਾਂ ਸਦੱਸ; ਕਲਰਕੀ, ਕਲਰਕ ਸਬੰਧੀ; ਪਾਦਰੀ ਦਾ

clerk (ਕਲ*ਕ) *a* ਮੁਨਸ਼ੀ, ਬਾਬੂ; ਲੇਖਕ; ਕਲਰਕ, ਪਾਦਰੀ; **great~** (ਪੁ) ਮਹਾਨ ਵਿਦਵਾਨ

clever (ਕਲੈੱਵੋਅ*) *n* ਚੁਸਤ, ਹੁਸ਼ਿਆਰ, ਸਰੇਤ, ਸਿਆਣਾ; ਚੁੰਟ, ਚਤਰ, ~**ness** ਚਤਰਾਈ, ਚੁਸਤੀ, ਹੁਸ਼ਿਆਰੀ, ਚਲਾਕੀ, ਪ੍ਰਵੀਣਤਾ, ਸਾਵਧਾਨੀ

cliche (ਕਲੀਸ਼ੇ) *n* ਘਸੇ-ਪਿਟੇ ਸ਼ਬਦ

cliff (ਕਲਿਫ਼) *n* ਟਿੱਲਾ, ਚਟਾਨ, ਢਲਵਾਨ, ਢਿੰਗ

climate (ਕਲਾਇਮਇਟ) *n* ਜਲਵਾਯੂ, ਪੌਣ-ਪਾਣੀ, ਆਬੋ-ਹਵਾ; ਵਾਤਾਵਰਣ, ਮਾਹੌਲ

climatic (ਕਲਾਇ'ਮੈਟਿਕ) *a* ਜਲਵਾਯੂ-ਸਬੰਧੀ

climax (ਕਲਾਇਮੈਕਸ) *n* ਸਿਖਰ, ਟੀਸੀ, ਤੇੜ; ਚਰਮ ਸੀਮਾ, ਚਰਮ ਬਿੰਦੂ

climb (ਕਲਾਇਮ) *n v* ਚੜ੍ਹਾਈ; ਉਤਕਰਸ਼; ਚੜ੍ਹਨਾ, ਉੱਨਤੀ ਕਰਨੀ; ~**er** (ਪਹਾੜ ਉੱਤੇ) ਚੜ੍ਹਨ ਵਾਲਾ, ਉੱਨਤੀ ਕਰ ਰਿਹਾ ਵਿਅਕਤੀ

cling (ਕਲਿੰਘ) *v* ਚੰਬੜਨਾ, ਲੱਗੇ ਰਹਿਣਾ, ਚਿਪਕਣਾ, ਲਿਪਟਣਾ; ਵਫ਼ਾਦਾਰ ਰਹਿਣਾ, ਡਟੇ ਰਹਿਣਾ

clinic ('ਕਲਿਨਿਕ) n ਚਕਿਤਸ਼ਾਲਾ, ਕਲਿਨਿਕ

clip (ਕਲਿਪ) n v ਚੁੰਢੀ, ਕਲਿਪ, ਚੁਟਕੀ; ਕਾਂਟ-ਛਾਂਟ; ਫੜਨਾ, ਕਸ ਕੇ ਫੜਨਾ, ਕਾਂਟ-ਛਾਂਟ ਕਰਨਾ; ~per ਕੈਂਚੀ, ਕਾਤ; ~ping ਕਟਾਈ, ਕੁਤਰਨ, ਕਾਤਰ, ਛੰਟਾਈ

clique (ਕਲੀਕ) n ਢਾਣੀ, ਜੁੰਡੀ, ਗੁਟ

cloak (ਕਲਅਉਕ) n v ਚੋਗਾ, ਅੰਗਰਖਾ, ਲਬਾਦਾ; ਆੜ, ਓਟ; ਚੋਗਾ, ਪਾਉਣਾ, ਢੱਕਣਾ; ~room ਕਲੋਕ ਰੂਮ, ਸਾਮਾਨ ਰੱਖਣ ਵਾਲਾ ਕਮਰਾ

clock (ਕਲੋਕ) n ਵੱਡੀ ਘੜੀ, ਦੀਵਾਰ-ਘੜੀ; ~tower ਘੰਟਾ ਘਰ; ~wise ਸਿਧਾ ਗੋੜਾ

clod (ਕਲੋਡ) n v (ਮਿੱਟੀ ਦਾ) ਢੇਲਾ, ਡਲਾ, ਡਲਾ ਮਾਰਨਾ; the~ ਧਰਤੀ, ਜ਼ਮੀਨ

clog (ਕਲੋਗ) n v ਡਾਹਾ; ਅੜੰਗਾ; ਖੜਾਵਾਂ; ਅੜਿੱਕਾ, ਅਟਕਾਉ, ਰੁਕਾਵਟ, ਰੋਕਣਾ; ਅੱਟ ਜਾਣਾ

close (ਕਲਅਉਸ) a adv n v ਗੁਪਤ, ਗੁੱਝ; ਨੇੜੇ, ਨਿਕਟ, ਪਾਸ; ਘਣਾ, ਘਨਿਸ਼ਠ; ਬੰਦ; ਤੰਗ, ਭੀੜਾ, ਸੌੜਾ, ਸੰਕੀਰਣ; ਸੰਕੁਚਤ; ਸੂਮ; ਸੀਮਤ; ਮੁੰਦਣਾ, ਮੀਟਣਾ, ਭੇੜਨਾ, ਬੰਦ ਕਰਨਾ, ਨੇੜੇ ਆਉਣਾ; ਭਿੜਨਾ, ਭਿੜਾਉਣਾ, ਮਿਲਣਾ, ਮਿਲ ਜਾਣਾ, ਜੜਨਾ, ਜੋੜਨਾ; ~air ਬੰਦ, ਹੁੰਮਸ, ਹੁਸੜ ਘੁਟਣ; ~by ਨੇੜੇ; ~fisted ਕੰਜੂਸ, ਮੱਖੀ ਚੂਸ, ~at hand ਪਾਸ ਹੀ, ਨੇੜੇ ਹੀ; ~in ਪਾਸ ਆਉਣਾ, ਹੌਲੀ-ਹੌਲੀ ਕੰਮ ਹੋਣਾ, ਘੇਰਨਾ, ਅਹਾਤਾਬੰਦੀ ਕਰਨਾ; ~ly ਧਿਆਨਪੂਰਵਕ, ਬਾਰੀਕੀ ਨਾਲ; ਪਾਸ ਪਾਸ, ਕਰੀਬ ਕਰੀਬ; ~ness ਨਿਕਟਤਾ, ਸਮੀਪਤਾ, ਜੋੜ; ਸਮਾਪਤੀ; ਹੁੰਮਸ, ਘੁਟਣ

closet ('ਕਲੋਜ਼ਿਟ) n ਕੋਠੜੀ, ਕਮਰਾ, ਖਿਲਵਗਾਹ; ਬਰਤਨਾਂ ਦੀ ਅਲਮਾਰੀ

closure ('ਕਲਅਉਯ਼ਅ*) n v ਬੰਦਸ਼, ਪਾਬੰਦੀ,

ਰੋਕ, ਇਹਾਤਾ; ਰੋਕਣਾ, ਬੰਦ ਕਰਨਾ

clot (ਕਲੋਟ) n v ਫੁੱਟ, ਫੁੱਟੀ, ਗੱਤਲਾ; ਘਣਚੱਕਰ, ਫੁੱਟੀ ਹੋਣਾ, ਜੰਮ ਜਾਣਾ; ~of blood ਖ਼ੂਨ ਦਾ ਗੱਤਲਾ; ~ted hair ਜਟਜੂਟ

cloth (ਕਲੋੱਥ) n ਕੱਪੜੇ, ਵਸਤਰ, ਜਾਮਾ, ਪੁਸ਼ਾਕ ਲਈ ਕੱਪੜਾ, ਪੱਟੂ, ਸ਼ਾਲ; table~ ਮੇਜ਼ ਪੋਸ਼; the~ ਪਾਦਰੀ ਦਾ ਪਦ

clothe (ਕਲਅਉਦ) v ਕੱਪੜੇ ਪਹਿਨਾਉਣਾ; ਕੱਜਣਾ, ਢਕਣਾ

clothier ('ਕਲਅਉਦਿਅ*) n ਜੁਲਾਹਾ; ਬਜਾਜ; ਵਸਤਰ-ਵਪਾਰੀ

clothing ('ਕਲਅਉਦਿੲ) n ਪੁਸ਼ਾਕ, ਵਸਤਰ

cloud (ਕਲਾਉਡ) n v ਬੱਦਲ, ਮੇਘ, ਘਟ ਘਟਾ; ਗਰਦ, ਗੁੰਦਲਕਾ; ਗੁੰਦਲਾਪਣ, ਬੱਦਲ ਛਾ ਜਾਣੇ, ਘਟਾ ਉਠਣੀ, ਨਿਰਾਸ ਹੋਣਾ; ~burst ਮੂਸਲਾਧਾਰ ਵਰਸ਼ਾ, ਤੁਫ਼ਾਨੀ ਛਹਿਬਰ; ~of words ਵਾਕ-ਜਾਲ, ਸ਼ਬਦ-ਅੜੰਬਰ, ਵਾਕ ਛਲ; in the~ ਅਵਾਸਤਵਿਕ, ਕਲਪਨਾ ਵਿਚ

clout (ਕਲਾਉਟ) n v ਟਾਕੀ, ਚੀਥੜਾ, ਪੂੰਝਣ, ਪੋਤਣਾ, ਸਾਫੀ; ਕੀਲਾ, ਟਾਕੀ ਲਾਉਣਾ, ਚੀਥੜਾ ਗੰਢਣਾ, ਪੂੰਝਣਾ

clown (ਕਲਾਉਨ) n ਉਜੱਡ, ਅਨਘੜ; ਗੰਵਾਰ; ਭੰਡ, ਨਕਲੀਆ, ਮਸਖ਼ਰਾ, ਵਿਦੂਸ਼ਕ; ~ish ਅੱਖੜ, ਉਜੱਡ, ਮਜ਼ਾਕੀਆ, ਅਸੱਭਿਅ

club (ਕਲੱਬ) n v ਕਲੱਬ, ਸਭਾ, ਡੰਡਾ, ਸੋਟਾ, ਲੱਠ, ਚਿੜੀਏ ਦਾ ਪੱਤਾ; ਡੰਡੇ ਮਾਰਨਾ, ਕੁੱਟਣਾ; ਜੋੜਨਾ, ਮਿਲਣਾ, ਸ਼ਾਮਲ ਹੋਣਾ, ਲਾਭ ਪਹੁੰਚਾਉਣਾ ~law ਜਬਰਦਸਤੀ, ਡੰਡੇ ਦਾ ਕਾਨੂੰਨ; ~s ਚਿੜੀਏ ਦਾ ਰੰਗ, ਚਿੜੀਆ

clue (ਕਲੂ) n ਉੱਘ-ਸੁੱਘ, ਭਿਣਕ, ਪਤਾ, ਨਿਸ਼ਾਨ; ~less ਬੇਨਿਸ਼ਾਨ; ਲਾਪਤਾ

clump ('ਕਲਅੰਪ) *n v* ਸਮੂਹ; ਝੁਰਮਟ; ਸੁੱਕਾ; ਘਸੁੰਨ; ਸੰਘਣੇ ਬਿਰਛ ਲਗਾਉਣਾ; ਢੇਰ ਲਗਾਉਣਾ, ਜੁੱਤੀ ਨੂੰ ਦੋਹਰਾ ਤਲਾ ਲਗਾਉਣਾ; ਘਸੁੰਨ ਮਾਰਨਾ

clumsily ('ਕਲਅੰਜ਼ਿਲਿ) *adv* ਬੇਢੰਬੇ ਢੰਗ ਨਾਲ, ਕੁਚੱਜਪੁਣੇ ਨਾਲ

clumsiness ('ਕਲਅੰਜ਼ਿਨਇਸ) *n* ਭੱਦੀਪਨ, ਅਨਾੜੀਪਨ, ਬੇਢੰਗਾਪਨ, ਅੱਖੜਪਣ

clumsy ('ਕਲਅੰਜ਼ਿ) *a* ਕੁਢੱਬਾ, ਬੇਡੌਲ, ਬੇਢੰਗਾ, ਅੱਖੜ, ਭੱਦਾ, ਅਨਾੜੀ, ਫੂਹੜ

cluster ('ਕਲਅਸਟਅ*) *n v* ਝੁਰਮਟ, ਝੁੰਮਰ, ਗੁੱਛਾ, ਝੰਡ, ਝੁਮਕਾ; ਸਮੂਹ; ਝੁੰਡ ਬਣਾਉਣਾ, ਇਕੱਠਾ ਹੋਣਾ, ਜਮ੍ਹਾ ਕਰਨਾ ਜਾਂ ਹੋਣਾ

clutch (ਕਲਅੱਚ) *n v* ਪਕੜ, ਪੰਜਾ, ਸ਼ਿਕੰਜਾ, ਕਲੱਚ; ਝਪਟਨਾ, ਘੁੱਟ ਕੇ ਫੜਨਾ, ਜਕੜ ਲਾਉਣੀ

Co (ਕਅਉ) *perf* ਨਾਲ; ਸਹਿ, ਕੰਪਨੀ ਦਾ ਸੰਖਿਪਤ ਰੂਪ; ~author ਸਹਿ-ਲੇਖਕ

coach (ਕਅਉਚ) *n v* (ਸ਼ਾਹੀ) ਗੱਡੀ, ਸਵਾਰੀ, ਗੱਡੀ, ਰੇਲ ਦਾ ਡੱਬਾ; ਸਮੁੰਦਰੀ ਜਹਾਜ਼ ਦਾ ਪਿਛਲਾ ਕਮਰਾ; ਘਰ ਪੜ੍ਹਾਉਣ ਵਾਲਾ ਅਧਿਆਪਕ; ਘਰ ਪੜ੍ਹਾਉਣਾ, ਖੇਡਣਾ ਸਿਖਾਉਣਾ; ~man ਕੋਚਵਾਨ, ਸਾਈਸ, ਚਾਲਕ; ~manship ਕੋਚਵਾਨੀ, ਸਾਈਸੀ

coal (ਕਅਉਲ) *n v* ਖਣਿਜੀ ਕੋਲਾ, ਪੱਥਰ ਦਾ ਕੋਲਾ; ~bed ਕੋਲੇ ਦੀ ਤਹਿ; ~black ਕਾਲਾ-ਸਿਆਹ, ਕਾਲਾ ਧੂਤ; ~dust ਕੋਲੇ ਦਾ ਚੂਰਾ, ਕੇਰੀ; ~field ਕੋਲਾ-ਖੇਤਰ, ਕੋਲੇ ਦੀ ਖਾਣ; ~pit ਕੋਲੇ ਦੀ ਖਾਣ; ~tar ਲੁੱਕ, ਤਾਰਕੋਲ

coalition (ਕਅਉਅ'ਲਿਸ਼ਨ) *n* ਮੇਲ; ਸੰਯੋਗ, ਸੰਧੀ, ਸੰਯੁਕਤ, ਮਿਲਾਪ, ਸਹਿਯੋਗ, ਸਹਿਮਿਲਨ, ਗਠਬੰਧਨ, ਕੋਲੀਸ਼ਨ

coarse (ਕੋ*ਸ) *a* ਘਟੀਆ, ਮੋਟਾ, ਖੁਰਦਰਾ, ਤੁੱਛ, ਸਧਾਰਨ; ਗੰਵਾਰ, ਅਸੱਭਿਆ, ਅੱਖੜ ਅਨਾੜੀ, ਭੱਦਾ

coast (ਕਅਉਸਟ) *n v* ਸਮੁੰਦਰੀ ਤਟ, ਸਮੁੰਦਰੀ ਕੰਢਾ; ਤਟ ਦੇ ਨਾਲ ਨਾਲ ਜਾਣਾ; ~guard ਤੱਟ-ਰੱਖਿਅਕ ਪੁਲੀਸ; ~line ਤੱਟ-ਰੇਖਾ; ~al ਤਟਵਰਤੀ, ਤਟੀ, ਸਾਹਲੀ, ਕਿਨਾਰੇ ਦਾ

coat (ਕਅਉਟ) *n v* ਕੋਟ; ਪਰਦਾ, ਝਿੱਲੀ; ਮੁਲੰਮਾ; ਉੱਪਰਲੀ ਤਹਿ, ਢਕੇ ਹੋਣਾ, ਮੁਲੰਮਾ ਕਰਨਾ, ਤਹਿ ਚੜ੍ਹਾਉਣਾ, ਪੋਚਣਾ, ਕਲੀ ਕਰਨਾ; ~ed ਕੋਟਧਾਰੀ, ਢੱਕਿਆ, ਪੋਚਿਆ, ਛਿਲਕੇਦਾਰ; turn one's~ ਨਮਕਹਰਾਮੀ ਕਰਨਾ, ਗ਼ਦਾਰੀ ਕਰਨਾ

coax (ਕਅਉਕਸ) *v* ਪਰਚਾਉਣਾ, ਵਲਾਉਣਾ, ਦਿਲਾਸਾ ਦੇਣਾ, ਮਨਾਉਣਾ; ਵਰਗਲਾਉਣਾ

cobble ('ਕੌਬਲ) *v* ਗੰਢਣਾ, ਗੰਢ ਤੁਪ ਕਰਨਾ, ਜੁੱਤੀਆਂ ਸਿਉਣਾ; ~r ਮੋਚੀ, ਜੁੱਤੀਆਂ ਗੰਢਣ ਜਾਂ ਸਿਉਣ ਵਾਲਾ

cobra ('ਕਅਉਬਰਾ) *n* ਫਨੀਅਰ ਕਾਲਾ ਨਾਗ

cobweb ('ਕੌਬਵੈੱਬ) *n a* ਮੱਕੜੀ ਦਾ ਜਾਲਾ, ਜਾਲ, ਫੰਦਾ; ਧੋਖਾ; ਸ਼ਬਦਜਾਲ; ਕਮਜ਼ੋਰ, ਪਤਲਾ

cock (ਕੌਕ) *n* ਕੁੱਕੜ, ਮੁਰਗਾ; ਟੂਟੀ; ਮੁੜਪੈਂਚ; ਉੱਟਪਟਾਂਗ ਗੱਲ; ਤਾਨਣਾ, ਖੜਾ ਕਰਨਾ, ਚੜ੍ਹਾਉਣਾ (ਬੰਦੂਕ ਦਾ ਘੋੜਾ); ~and bull story ਬਣਾਉਟੀ ਕਹਾਣੀ, ਮਨਘੜਤ ਕਹਾਣੀ; ~eyed ਭੈਂਗਾ, ਲਾਂਵਾਂ, ਮੂੜ, ਹਾਸੋਹੀਣਾ; ~pit ਕੁੱਕੜਾਂ ਦਾ ਅਖਾੜਾ; ਅਖਾੜਾ; ਹਵਾਈ ਜਹਾਜ਼ ਵਿਚ ਚਾਲਕ ਦੇ ਬੈਠਣ ਦੀ ਥਾਂ

cockroach ('ਕੌਕਰਅਉਚ) *n* ਤਿਲਚਟਾ, ਕਾਕਰੋਚ

cocktail ('ਕੌਕਟੇਇਲ) *n a* ਕਾਕਟੇਲ, ਰਲੀ ਮਿਲੀ ਸ਼ਰਾਬ; ਇਕ ਪ੍ਰਕਾਰ ਦਾ ਤੋੜਾ;

coco ('ਕਅਉਕਅਉ) *n* ਗਿਰੀ, ਘੇਪਾ, ਨਾਰੀਅਲ

code ('ਕਅਉਡ) *n* ਕੋਡ, ਨਿਆਇ-ਸ਼ਾਸਤਰ, ਸਦਾਚਾਰ ਦੇ ਨਿਯਮ; ਸੰਹਿਤਾ, ਕਾਨੂੰਨ ਦਾ ਗ੍ਰੰਥ, ਨਿਯਮਾਂਵਲੀ, ਵਿਧਾਨਾਂ ਜਾਂ ਨਿਯਮਾਂ ਦਾ ਸੰਗ੍ਰਹ; ਸੁਕੇਤ-ਪੱਧਤੀ; ਸੰਖਿਪਤ ਨਾਂ, ਸੰਕੇਤਾਵਲੀ; ਗੁਪਤ-ਦੇਸ਼; ਸੰਕੇਤਬੱਧ ਕਰਨਾ, ਸੰਖਿਪਤ ਕਰਨਾ; ~words ਸੰਕੇਤ-ਸ਼ਬਦ, ਸੰਕੇਤ

codification ('ਕਅਉਡਿਫ਼ਿ'ਕੇਇਸ਼ਨ) *n* ਨਿਯਮ-ਵਿਵਸਥਾ, ਕਾਨੂੰਨੀ-ਵਿਵਸਥਾ; ਸੰਹਿਤਾਕਰਨ

codified ('ਕਅਉਡਿਫ਼ਾਇਡ) *a* ਵਿਵਸਥਿਤ, ਨਿਯਮਬੱਧ, ਸੰਹਿਤਾ, ਸੰਹਿਤਾਬੱਧ

codifier ('ਕਅਉਡਿਫ਼ਾਇਆ*) *n* ਸੰਹਿਤਾਕਾਰ

codify ('ਕਅਉਡਿਫ਼ਾਇ) *v* ਨਿਯਮਤ ਕਰਨਾ, ਨਿਯਮਬੱਧ ਕਰਨਾ, ਸੰਗ੍ਰਹ ਕਰਨਾ, ਸੰਹਿਤਾਕਰਨ ਕਰਨਾ

co-education ('ਕਅਉਐਡਯੂ'ਕੇਇਸ਼ਨ) *n* ਸਾਂਝੀ ਸਿੱਖਿਆ, ਸਹਿ-ਸਿੱਖਿਆ

coerce (ਕਅਉ'ਅਃਸ) *v* ਦਬਾਉਣਾ, ਜ਼ਬਰ ਕਰਨਾ, ਬੇਵਸ ਕਰਨਾ

corecion (ਕਅਉ'ਅਃਸ਼ਨ) *n* ਦਾਬਾ, ਦਬਾਉ, ਜ਼ਬਰ, ਜ਼ਬਰਦਸਤੀ, ਵਧੀਕ, ਹਿੰਸਾ

coercive (ਕਅਉ'ਅਃਸਿਵੑ) *a* ਦਬਾਉ, ਬਲਯੁਕਤ, ਬਲਾਤਕਾਰੀ, ਦਮਨਸ਼ੀਲ; ~ness ਬਲ-ਪ੍ਰਯੋਗ, ਦਬਾਉ, ਦਮਨ

coexist ('ਕਅਉਇਗਾ'ਜ਼ਿਸਟ) *v* ਇਕ ਹੀ ਕਾਲ ਵਿਚ ਵਿਦਮਾਨ ਹੋਣਾ, ਸਮਕਾਲੀ ਹੋਣਾ; ~ence ਸਹਿਹੋਂਦ, ਸਹਿਅਸਤਿਤਵ, ਸਹਿਭਾਵ, ਸਮਕਾਲੀ ਵਿਦਮਾਨਤਾ; ~ent ਸਮਕਾਲੀਨ

coffee ('ਕੌਫ਼ਿ) *n* ਕਾਫ਼ੀ, ਕਾਹਵਾ, ਕਾਫ਼ੀ ਦਾ ਬੂਟਾ

coffer ('ਕੌਫ਼ਅ*) *n* *v* ਤਿਜੋਰੀ, ਖ਼ਜ਼ਾਨੇ ਵਾਲੀ ਅਲਮਾਰੀ, ਖ਼ਜ਼ਾਨਾ, ਕੋਸ਼, ਜਮ੍ਹਾ ਰੱਖਣਾ, ਤਿਜੋਰੀ

ਵਿਚ ਬੰਦ ਕਰਨਾ

coffin ('ਕੌਫ਼ਿਨ) *n* ਤਾਬੂਤ; ਨਿਕੰਮਾ ਜਹਾਜ਼, ਘੋੜੇ ਦਾ ਸੁੰਮ

cognition (ਕੌਗਾ'ਨਿਸ਼ਨ) *n* ਬੋਧ, ਗਿਆਨ, ਅਨੁਭਵ; ਸੰਕਲਪ; ~al ਬੋਧਾਤਮਕ ਗਿਆਨ ਸਬੰਧੀ, ਅਨੁਭੂਤੀ ਜਾਂ ਧਾਰਨਾ ਸਬੰਧੀ

cognizance ('ਕੌਗਨਿਜ਼ਅੰਸ) *n* ਗਿਆਨ; ਪਛਾਣ; ਧਿਆਨ; ਲੱਛਣ, ਚਿੰਨ੍ਹ, ਕਾਨੂੰਨੀ ਅਧਿਕਾਰ ਦਾ ਪ੍ਰਯੋਗ

cohabit (ਕਅਉ'ਹੈਬਿਟ) *v* ਪਤੀ ਪਤਨੀ ਦੀ ਤਰ੍ਹਾਂ ਰਹਿਣਾ, ਸਹਿਵਾਸ ਕਰਨਾ; ~ation ਸੰਭੋਗ, ਸਹਿਵਾਸ

co-heir, -ess ('ਕਅਉ'ਏਅ*'ਕਅਉ'ਏਅਰਿਸ) *n* ਬਰਾਬਰ ਦਾ ਹੱਕਦਾਰ, ਹਮਵਾਰਸ, ਵਿਰਸੇ ਦਾ ਹੱਕਦਾਰ

cohere (ਕਅ(ਉ)'ਹਿਅ*) *v* ਚੰਬੜਨਾ, ਜੁੜਨਾ, ਇਕਸਾਰ ਹੋਣਾ, ਸੰਗੁਕਤ ਹੋਣਾ; ~nce, ~ncy ਸੰਮਤੀ, ਸੰਸ਼ਲੇਸ਼ਣ, ਇਕੱਠ, ਇੱਕਤਰਤਾ, ਇਕਸਾਰਤਾ; ~nt ਉਚਿਤ, ਸੰਗੁਕਤ, ਚਿਹਕਿਆ, ਚੰਬੜਿਆ, ਜੁੜਿਆ, ਜੰਮਿਆ

cohesion (ਕਅ(ਉ)'ਹੀਜ਼ਨ) *n* ਜੋੜ, ਮੇਲ, ਸੰਯੋਗ, ਸੰਗੁਕਤ ਹੋਣ ਦੀ ਪ੍ਰਵਿਰਤੀ

coil (ਕੋਇਲ) *v* *n* ਕੁੰਡਲ ਬਣਾਉਣੇ, ਵਲ ਪਾਉਣੇ, ਪੇਚ ਪਾਉਣੇ; ਕੁੰਡਲ, ਵਲ, ਪੇਚ, ਲੱਛਾ, ਅੱਟੀ, ਕੁੰਡਲੀ

coin (ਕੋਇਨ) *n* *v* ਸਿੱਕਾ, ਰੁਪਇਆ, ਪੈਸਾ, ਧਨ, ਮੁਦਰਾ; ਸਿੱਕਾ ਢਾਲਣਾ ਜਾਂ ਬਣਾਉਣਾ, ਘੜਨਾ, ਟਕਸਾਲਣਾ; false~ ਖੋਟਾ ਸਿੱਕਾ, ਜਾਅਲੀ ਸਿੱਕਾ; ~age ਸਿੱਕਾ ਢਲਾਈ, ਪ੍ਰਚਲਤ ਸਿੱਕਾ ਜਾਂ ਮੁਦਰਾ; ਸਿੱਕੇ; ਘੜੇ ਗਏ ਸ਼ਬਦ; ~less ਨਿਰਧਨ, ਕੰਗਾਲ, ਗ਼ਰੀਬ

coincide ('ਕਅਉਇਨ'ਸਾਇਡ) *v* ਇਕੇ ਸਮੇਂ ਵਾਪਰਨਾ, ਰਲਣਾ-ਮਿਲਣਾ, ਮੇਲ ਖਾਣਾ, ਠੀਕ ਬੈਠਣਾ; ਸਮਕਾਲੀ ਹੋਣਾ; ਅਨੁਰੂਪ ਹੋਣਾ; **~nce** ਢੋ, ਮੇਲ, ਸੰਯੋਗ, ਸੰਕਾ-ਮੇਲ; ਅਨੁਰੂਪਤਾ; **~nt** ਸੰਯੋਗੀ, ਮਿਲਦਾ-ਜੁਲਦਾ; **~ntal** ਸੰਯੋਗੀ, ਸੁਭਾਵਕ, ਉਸੇ ਥਾਂ ਜਾਂ ਉਸੇ ਸਮੇਂ, ਸਮਕਾਲੀ

coir ('ਕੌਇਅ*) *n* ਨਾਰੀਅਲ ਦੇ ਰੇਸ਼ੇ, ਕੋਇਰ

coke (ਕਅਉਕ) *n* ਕੋਕ, ਪੱਥਰ ਦਾ ਕੋਲਾ, ਪੱਥਰੀ ਕੋਲਾ; ਇਕ ਪੇਯ

cold (ਕਅਉਲਡ) *n a* ਠੰਢ, ਸਰਦੀ, ਨਜ਼ਲਾ, ਜ਼ੁਕਾਮ; ਠੰਢਕ; ਠੰਢਾ, ਸੀਤ, ਸੀਤਲ, ਸਰਦ; ਰੁੱਖਾ, ਅਰੋਚਕ, ਕੋਰਾ, ਪ੍ਰਤੀਕੂਲ; **~blooded** ਨਿਰਦਈ, ਬੇਦਰਦ; **~bloodedness** ਨਿਰਦਇਤਾ, ਨਿਸ਼ਠੁਰਤਾ, ਬੇਰਹਿਮੀ; **~steel** ਤਲਵਾਰ, ਸੰਗੀਨ ਆਦਿ; **~war** ਸੀਤ ਜੁੱਧ, ਠੰਢੀ-ਜੰਗ; **give the~ shoulder (to)** ਬੇਰੁਖ਼ੀ ਵਰਤਣਾ

collaborate (ਕਅ'ਲੈਬਅਰੇਇਟ) *v* ਸਹਿਯੋਗ ਦੇਣਾ, ਨਾਲ ਮਿਲ ਕੇ ਕੰਮ ਕਰਨਾ, ਹੱਥ ਵਟਾਉਣਾ, ਮਿਲਵਰਤਨ ਕਰਨਾ, ਸਾਥ ਦੇਣਾ

collaboration (ਕਅ'ਲੈਬਅ'ਰੇਇਸ਼ਨ) *n* ਸਹਿਕਾਰਤਾ, ਸਹਿਯੋਗ ਜਾਂ ਮਿਲਵਰਤਨ, ਹੱਥ ਵਟਾਈ, ਸਾਂਝੀ ਪੈਦਾਵਾਰ

collapse (ਕਅ'ਲੈਪਸ) *v n* ਢਰੰਮ ਕਰਕੇ ਡਿਗ ਪੈਣਾ, ਹਿੰਮਤ ਹਾਰਨੀ, ਭੱਠਾ ਬਹਿ ਜਾਣਾ, ਬੇਹੋਸ਼ ਹੋ ਜਾਣਾ; ਨਸ਼ਟ ਹੋਣਾ, ਢਹਿ ਜਾਣਾ; ਗਿਰਾਵਟ, ਪਤਨ;

collar (ਕੋਲਅ*) *v n* ਹਸਲੀ, ਕੰਠ, ਗੁਲੂਬੰਦ, ਕਾਲਰ, ਗਲ ਪੈਣਾ, ਗਿਰੀਓਂ ਫੜਕ, ਪੇਟੇ ਪਾ ਲੈਣਾ; ਢੋਹਣਾ; ਗਰਿਫ਼ਤਾਰ ਕਰਨਾ; **~bone** ਹਸਲੀ

colleague (ਕੌਲੀਗਾ) *n* ਸਹਿਕਾਰੀ, ਸਹਿਯੋਗੀ, ਸਾਥੀ, ਭਾਈਵਾਲ

collect (ਕੌਲੇਕੰਟ) *v n* ਜੁੜਨਾ, ਜੋੜਨਾ, ਸੰਗ੍ਰਹ ਕਰਨਾ, ਇਕੱਤਰ ਕਰਨਾ, ਇਕੱਠਾ ਕਰਨਾ, ਜਮ੍ਹਾ ਕਰਨਾ, ਵਸੂਲ ਕਰਨਾ, ਉਗਰਾਹੁਣਾ; ਇਸਾਈਆਂ ਦੀ ਅਰਦਾਸ ਜੋ ਉਹ ਪਾਠ ਤੋਂ ਪਿੱਛੋਂ ਕਰਦੇ ਹਨ; **~ed** ਇਕੱਤਰਤ, ਸੰਗ੍ਰਹਤ; ਸ਼ਾਂਤ, ਧੀਰਜਵਾਨ; **~ion** ਜੋੜ, ਇਕੱਠ; ਉਗਰਾਹੀ; ਇਕੱਤਰੀਕਰਨ, ਸਮੂਹ, ਢੇਰ, ਅੰਬਾਰ; ਇਕੱਠ

collective (ਕਅ'ਲੇਕਟਿਵ) *adv* ਇਕੱਤਰਤ, ਸਮੂਹਕ, ਇਕੱਠਾ, ਰਲਵਾਂ, ਸਮੁੱਚਾ; **~ly** ਇਕੱਠੇ ਹੋ ਕੇ, ਰਲ ਕੇ, ਸਾਂਝੇ ਤੌਰ ਤੇ, ਸਮੂਹਕ ਤੌਰ ਤੇ

collector (ਕਅ'ਲੇਕਟਅ*) *n* ਜ਼ਿਲੇ ਦਾ ਮੁਖੀ, ਕੁਲੈਕਟਰ, ਡਿਪਟੀ ਕਮਿਸ਼ਨਰ, ਉਗਰਾਹੀ ਕਰਨ ਵਾਲਾ, ਵਸੂਲ ਕਰਨ ਵਾਲਾ, ਇੱਕਠ ਕਰਨ ਵਾਲਾ; ਮਸ਼ੀਨ ਦਾ ਇਕ ਪੁਰਜ਼ਾ; **~ate** ਕੁਲੈਕਟਰੀ

college (ਕੌਲਿਜ) *n* ਮਹਾਂ-ਵਿਦਿਆਲਾ, ਕਾਲਜ

collegian (ਕਅ'ਲੀਜਿਅਨ) *n* ਕਾਲਜ ਦਾ ਵਿਦਿਆਰਥੀ, ਕਿਸੇ ਕਾਲਜ ਦਾ ਸਦੱਸ

collegiate (ਕਅ'ਲੀਜਿਏਟ) *a v* ਕਾਲਜ-ਸਬੰਧੀ, ਕਾਲਜ ਦਾ; ਕਾਲਜ ਦਾ ਪਦ ਦੇਣਾ, ਕਾਲਜ ਦੀ ਸਥਿਤੀ ਪ੍ਰਦਾਨ ਕਰਨਾ, ਕਾਲਜ ਬਣਾਉਣਾ

collide (ਕਅ'ਲਾਇਡ) *n* ਭਿੜਨ, ਟੱਕਰਨਾ, ਟਕਰਾਉਣਾ, ਟੱਕਰ ਖਾਣਾ, ਵਿਰੋਧ ਹੋਣਾ, ਮੁੰਠ-ਭੇੜ ਹੋਣਾ

colliery (ਕੌਲਿਯਅਰਿ) *n* ਕੋਲੇ ਦੀ ਖਾਣ, ਕੋਲਰੀ

collision (ਕਅ'ਲਿਯਅਨ) *n* ਭੇੜ, ਟੱਕਰ, ਟਕਰਾ, ਮੁੰਠ-ਭੇੜ, ਸੰਘਰਸ਼

collocation (ਕਲਅ(ਉ)'ਕੇਇਸ਼ਨ) *n* ਸ਼ਬਦ-ਕ੍ਰਮ

colloquial (ਕਅ'ਲਅਉਕਵਿਅਲ) *a* ਲੋਕਕ, ਗੱਲ-ਬਾਤੀ, ਬੋਲਚਾਲੀ

collusion (ਕਅ'ਲੂਯਨ) *n* ਗੰਠ-ਜੋੜ, ਗਾਂਢਾ-ਸਾਂਢਾ

collusive (ਕਅ'ਲੂਸਿਵ) *a* ਫ਼ਰੇਬੀ, ਕਪਟਪੂਰਨ

colonel (ਕਅ:ਨਲ) *n* ਕਰਨੈਲ, ਕਰਨਲ

colonial (ਕਅ'ਲਅਉਨਯਅਲ) *n* ਬਸਤੀਵਾਦੀ; ~ism ਬਸਤੀਵਾਦ

colonization (ਕੌਲਅਨਾਇ'ਜ਼ੇਇਸ਼ਨ) *a n* ਬਸਤੀਕਰਨ, ਨੌਆਬਾਦਕਾਰੀ

colonize (ਕੌਲਅਨਾਇਜ਼) *n* ਨਵੀਂ ਬਸਤੀ ਵਸਾਉਣਾ, ਨਵੀਂ ਥਾਂ ਜਾ ਕੇ ਵਸ ਜਾਣਾ

colony (ਕੌਲਅਨਿ) *n* ਨਵੀਂ ਅਬਾਦੀ, ਬਸਤੀ, ਛਾਉਣੀ

colour (ਕਅੱਲਅ) *n v* ਰੰਗ, ਚਿਹਰੇ ਦੀ ਰੰਗਤ, ਰੰਗ-ਰੂਪ, ਸ਼ਕਲ-ਸੂਰਤ, ਬਾਣਾ; ਝੰਡਾ; ਬਿਲਾ, ਵਰਦੀ; ਰੰਗਣਾ, ਰੰਗ ਭਰਨਾ, ਸਚਾਈ ਨੂੰ ਛਿਪਾਉਣਾ, ਝੂਠ ਕਥਨ ਕਰਨਾ; ਲੱਜਾਉਣਾ; ਪ੍ਰਭਾਵ ਛੱਡਣਾ; ~able ਮਨੋਹਰ, ਰਮਣੀਕ, ਨਕਸ਼ੀ, ਜਾਅਲੀ; ~ed ਰੰਗੀਨ, ਰੰਗਿਆ; ~ful ਰੰਗੀਨ, ਮਨੋਰੰਜਕ, ਸੁਦਰਸ਼ਨ, ਮੋਹਕ; ~less ਬੇਰੰਗ, ਰੰਗਹੀਨ ਵਰਣਹੀਨ, ਪੀਲਾ, ਜ਼ਰਦ; ਫਿੱਕਾ, ਉਦਾਸੀਨ, ਰੁੱਖਾ; ~lessness ਰੰਗਹੀਨਤਾ, ਉਦਾਸੀਨਤਾ, ਫਿੱਕਪਣ, ਰੁੱਖਾਪਣ, ਪੀਲਾਪਣ

column (ਕੌਲਅਮ) *n* ਥੰਮੂ, ਖੰਭਾ, ਕੌਲਾ, ਲਾਠ; ਆਸਰਾ, ਟੇਕ; ਫ਼ੌਜ ਦੀ ਸਫ਼; (ਅਖ਼ਬਾਰ ਦਾ) ਕਾਲਮ; ਜਹਾਜ਼ਾਂ ਦਾ ਬੇੜਾ

columnist (ਕੌਲਅਮਨਿਸਟ) *n* ਕਿਸੇ-ਸਮਾਚਾਰ-ਪੱਤਰ ਵਿਚ ਲਗਾਤਾਰ ਲਿਖਣ ਵਾਲਾ, ਕਾਲਮਨਵੀਸ

coma (ਕਅਉਮਅ) *n* ਡੂੰਘੀ ਬੇਹੋਸ਼ੀ

comb (ਕਅਉਮ) *n v* ਕੰਘੀ, ਕੰਘਾ; ਕੁੱਕੜ ਦੀ ਕਲਗੀ, ਸ਼ਹਿਦ ਦਾ ਛੱਤਾ; ਕੂਚ ਫੇਰਨਾ, ਕੰਘੀ ਕਰਨਾ, ਸਾਫ਼ ਕਰਨਾ

combat (ਕੌਂਬੈਟ) *n v* ਲੜਾਈ, ਮੁੱਠਭੇੜ, ਟੱਕਰ; ਭਿੜਨਾ, ਘੁਲਣਾ, ਲੜਨਾ, ਮੁਕਾਬਲਾ ਕਰਨਾ; ~ive ਲੜਾਕਾ, ਰਣਸ਼ੀਲ

combination (ਕੌਂਬਿ'ਨੇਇਸ਼ਨ) *n* ਸੁਮੇਲ; ਜੋੜ, ਜੁੱਟ, ਮੇਲ, ਸੰਜੋਗ, ਇਕੱਠ

combine (ਕਅੰ'ਬਾਇਨ) *v* ਜੋੜਨਾ, ਮੇਲਣਾ, ਇਕੱਠ ਕਰਨਾ; ~d ਸੰਯੁਕਤ, ਮਿਲਿਆ, ਸੰਯੋਜਿਤ

come (ਕਅੱਮ) *v* ਆਉਣਾ, ਚੱਲਣਾ, ਅੱਗੇ ਵਧਣਾ, ਵਾਪਰਨਾ, ਹੋਣਾ, ਨਿਕਲਣਾ, ਨਿਕਾਸ ਹੋਣਾ; ~about ਵਾਪਰਨਾ, ਬੀਤਣਾ, ਹੋਣਾ; ~across ਮਿਲਣਾ, ਰੂ-ਬਰੂ ਹੋਣਾ, ਭੇਂਟ ਕਰਨਾ; ~along ਕਿਸੇ ਨਾਲ ਜਾਣਾ, ਸਾਥ ਦੇਣਾ; ~at ਗੱਲ ਸਮਝਣਾ, ਪਹੁੰਚਣਾ; ~by ਹੱਥ ਆਉਣਾ, ਪ੍ਰਾਪਤ ਕਰਨਾ; ~forward ਸਾਮ੍ਹਣੇ ਆਉਣਾ; ~in ਅੰਦਰ ਆਉਣਾ, ਘੁਸਣਾ, ਪ੍ਰਵੇਸ਼ ਕਰਨਾ; ~into ਪ੍ਰਾਪਤ ਕਰਨਾ, ਪਾਉਣਾ; ~into force ਲਾਗੂ ਹੋਣਾ; ~out ਹੜਤਾਲ ਕਰਨੀ, ਕੰਮ ਛੱਡਣਾ, ਪ੍ਰਕਾਸ਼ਤ ਹੋਣਾ; ਸਫ਼ਲ ਹੋਣਾ, ਕਾਮਯਾਬ ਹੋਣਾ; ~to ਹੋਸ਼ ਵਿਚ ਆਉਣਾ; ~to an end ਖ਼ਤਮ ਹੋ ਜਾਣਾ, ਸਮਾਪਤ ਹੋਣਾ; ~up ਚੜ੍ਹਨਾ; ~upon ਅਚਾਨਕ ਹਮਲਾ ਕਰਨਾ

comedian (ਕਅ'ਮੀਡਯਅਨ) *n* ਕਾਮੇਡੀ (ਸੁਖਾਂਤ ਨਾਟਕ) ਦਾ ਅਭਿਨੇਤਾ ਜਾਂ ਲੇਖਕ; ਠੱਠ, ਨਕਲੀਆ

comedy (ਕੌਮਅਡਿ) *n* ਨਾਚ-ਰੰਗ, ਦਿਲਲੱਗੀ, ਸੁਖਾਂਤ ਨਾਟਕ, ਕਾਮਦੀ

comely (ਕਅੱਮਲਿ) *a* ਸੋਹਣੀ (ਵਿਸ਼ੇਸ਼ ਕਰਕੇ ਜਨਾਨੀ)

comfort (ਕਅਮੱਫ਼ਅ*ਟ) *n v* ਸੁਖ, ਆਰਾਮ,

ਇਤਮੀਨਾਨ, ਦਿਲਾਸਾ, ਸੰਤੋਖ; ਸੁਖ ਦੇਣਾ,
ਆਰਾਮ ਪਹੁੰਚਾਉਣਾ, ਦਿਲਾਸਾ ਦੇਣਾ, ਤਸੱਲੀ
ਦੇਣੀ; ~able ਸੁਖਦਾਇਕ, ਆਰਾਮਦੇਹ, ਧੀਰਜ-
ਬੰਨ੍ਹਾਉ, ਸੁਖੀ, ਮੌਜੀ, ਕਾਢੀ, ਖਾਸੀ; ~ably ਸੋਖ
ਨਾਲ, ਆਰਾਮ ਨਾਲ, ਤਸੱਲੀ ਨਾਲ; ~less ਸੁਖ-
ਰਹਿਤ, ਦੁਖੀ, ਸੰਤੋਖ-ਹੀਨ

comic (ਕੌਮਿਕ) a ਸੁਖੰਤਕ, ਸੁਖਾਂਤ, ਹਸਾਉਣਾ,
ਮਸ਼ਕਰੀ ਭਰਿਆ; ~opera ਹਾਸ-ਰਸੀ ਸੰਗੀਤ-
ਨਾਟ; ~al ਹਾਸਪੂਰਨ, ਵਚਿੱਤਰ; ਅਨੋਖਾ, ਨਿਰਾਲਾ

coming (ਕਅੱਮਿਙ) n a ਆਗਮਨ, ਭਾਵੀ,
ਆਗਾਮੀ

command (ਕਅੱਮਾਂਡ) v n ਆਗਿਆ ਦੇਣੀ,
ਹੁਕਮ ਕਰਨਾ, ਕਮਾਨ ਕਰਨੀ, ਕਾਬੂ ਕਰਨਾ;
ਆਗਿਆ, ਹੁਕਮ, ਆਦੇਸ਼, ਕਮਾਨ, ਨਿਯੰਤਰਣ;
at~ ਮੁੱਠੀ ਵਿਚ, ਇਖ਼ਤਿਆਰ ਵਿਚ

commander (ਕਅੱਮਾਂਡਅ*) n ਸੈਨਾਪਤੀ,
ਫੋਜਦਾਰ, ਕਮਾਂਡਰ; ਨਾਈਟ ਦੀ ਉੱਚੀ ਉਪਾਧੀ,
ਮੁੱਖ ਸੈਨਾਪਤੀ

commandment (ਕਅੱਮਾਂ(ਡ)ਮਅੰਟ) n ਰੱਬੀ
ਹੁਕਮ, ਧਾਰਮਕ ਨਿਯਮ

commando (ਕਅੱਮਾਂਡਅਓ) n ਛਾਪਾਮਾਰ ਸੈਨਕ,
ਕਮਾਂਡੋ

commemorable (ਕਅੱਮੌਮੱਅਰਅਬਲ) a
ਯਾਦਗਾਰੀ, ਸਮਰਣੀਜ

commemorate (ਕਅੱਮੌਮੱਅਰੇਇਟ) v (ਕਿਸੇ
ਦੀ ਯਾਦ) ਮਨਾਉਣਾ, ਯਾਦਗਾਰ ਕਾਇਮ
ਕਰਨਾ; ਸਮਾਰਕ ਹੋਣਾ, ਯਾਦ ਕਰਨਾ

commemoration (ਕਅੱਮੌਮੱਅਰੇਇਸ਼ਨ) n
ਯਾਦਗਾਰ, ਯਾਦਗਾਰੀ ਕਾਰਜ

commence (ਕਅੱਮੈਂਸ) v ਸ਼ੁਰੂ ਕਰਨਾ,
ਆਰੰਭਣਾ, ਛੋਹਣਾ, ਚਲਾਉਣਾ, ਚਲੱਣਾ, ਸ਼ੁਰੂ

ਹੋਣਾ; ~ment ਸ਼ੁਰੂ, ਮੁੱਢ, ਆਰੰਭ

commend (ਕਅੱਮੈਂਡ) v ਸੌਂਪਣਾ, ਸਪੁਰਦ ਕਰਨਾ,
ਹੱਥ ਵਿਚ ਦੇਣਾ; ਪ੍ਰਸ਼ੰਸਾ ਕਰਨਾ, ਸ਼ਲਾਘਾ ਕਰਨਾ;
~able ਸੌਂਪਣਯੋਗ, ਸ਼ਲਾਘਾਯੋਗ, ਸਪੁਰਦ
ਕਰਨਯੋਗ, ਆਦਰਯੋਗ; ~ation ਸ਼ਲਾਘਾ,
ਵਡਿਆਈ, ਪ੍ਰਸ਼ੰਸਾ, ਸਿਫ਼ਾਰਿਸ਼

commensurate (ਕਅੱਮੈਂਸ਼ੁ(ਅ)ਰਅਟ) a
ਸਮਾਨ, ਅਨੁਕੂਲ, ਅਨੁਰੂਪ, ਬਰਾਬਰ

comment ('ਕੌਮੈਂਟ) n ਟਿੱਪਣੀ, ਰਾਏ; ਟੀਕਾ
ਟਿੱਪਣੀ ਕਰਨੀ, ਰਾਏ ਦੇਣੀ; ~ary ਵਿਆਖਿਆ,
ਭਾਸ਼ਣ, ਟਿੱਪਣੀ, ਸਮਾਲੋਚਨਾ; ~ator
ਟਿੱਪਣੀਕਾਰ

commerce ('ਕੌਮਅਃਸ) n ਵਣਜ, ਵਪਾਰ,
ਤਜਾਰਤ, ਸੰਪਰਕ, ਮੇਲ-ਜੋਲ; ਤਾਸ਼ ਦੀ ਇਕ
ਖੇਡ

commercial (ਕਅੱਮਅਃਸ਼ਲ) a ਵਣਜ-ਸਬੰਧੀ,
ਵਿਹਾਰਕ, ਵਪਾਰਕ, ਤਜਾਰਤੀ

commission (ਕਅੱਮਿਸ਼ਨ) n v ਦਲਾਲੀ, ਆੜ੍ਹਤ;
ਆਦੇਸ਼, ਹਿਦਾਇਤ, ਹੁਕਮ; ਆਯੋਗ, ਅਧਿਕਾਰੀ-
ਵਰਗਾ; ਅਧਿਕਾਰ ਪ੍ਰਦਾਨ ਕਰਨਾ, ਇਖ਼ਤਿਆਰ
ਦੇਣਾ, ਮੁਖਤਿਆਰ ਬਣਾਉਣਾ, ਕਿਮਸ਼ਨ ਦੇਣਾ;
ਅਫ਼ਸਰ ਬਣਾਉਣਾ; ~ed ਨਿਯੁਕਤ, ਅਧਿਲਿਤ,
ਕਿਮਸ਼ਨ ਦੁਆਰਾ ਪਰਾਪਤ; ~er ਆਯੁਕਤ,
ਕਿਮਸ਼ਨਰ; ~agent ਆੜ੍ਹਤੀਆ

commit (ਕਅੱਮਿਟ) v ਵਚਨਬੱਧ ਕਰਨਾ, ਸੌਂਪਣਾ,
ਹਵਾਲੇ ਕਰਨਾ, ਸਪੁਰਦ ਕਰਨਾ; ਪਾਬੰਦ ਹੋਣਾ,
ਅਰਪਣ ਕਰਨਾ; ~ment ਪ੍ਰਤੀਬੱਧਤਾ, ਵਚਨ-
ਬੱਧਤਾ ਪਾਬੰਦੀ, ਕੈਦ, ਵਚਨ, ਬੰਧਨ; ~ted
ਵਚਨਬੱਧ, ਪ੍ਰਤੀਬੱਧ

committee (ਕਅੱਮਿਟਿ) n ਸਮਿਤੀ, ਸਭਾ,
ਕਮੇਟੀ, ਵਿਸ਼ੇਸ਼ ਉਦੇਸ਼ ਲਈ ਸਥਾਪਤ ਸਭਾ;

joint ~ ਸੰਯੁਕਤ ਕਮੇਟੀ; **standing**~ ਸਥਾਈ
ਸਮਿਤਿ

commode (ਕਅ'ਮਅਓਡ) *n* ਦਰਾਜ਼ਾਂ ਵਾਲਾ
ਸੰਦੂਕ, ਪੇਟੀ, ਸ਼ਿੰਗਾਰ ਦੀ ਅਲਮਾਰੀ; ਟੱਟੀ
ਪਿਸ਼ਾਬ ਵਾਲਾ ਬਰਤਨ, ਕਮੋਡ

commodity (ਕਅ'ਮੋਡਅਟੀ) *n* ਚੀਜ਼, ਪਦਾਰਥ,
ਜਿਨਸ, ਵਪਾਰ ਦੀ ਵਸਤੂ, ਉਪਯੋਗੀ ਵਸਤੂ

common (ਕੋਮਨ) *a n* ਸਧਾਰਨ, ਸਾਂਝਾ, ਆਮ,
ਅਵਾਮੀ, ਮਾਮੂਲੀ, ਸੁਲਭ, ਸੰਜੁਕਤ; ਸਮਲਾਤ,
ਸਾਂਝੀ ਜ਼ਮੀਨ; ~**gender** ਨਪੁੰਸਕ ਲਿੰਗ;
~**market** ਸਾਂਝੀ ਮੰਡੀ; ~**room** ਬੈਠਕ, ਸਾਂਝਾ
ਕਮਰਾ; ~**sense** ਆਮ ਸਮਝ, ਸਧਾਰਨ ਸੂਝ;
~**wealth** ਰਾਸ਼ਟਰ-ਮੰਡਲ

commotion (ਕਅ'ਮਅਓਸ਼ਨ) *n* ਰੌਲਾ, ਹਫੜਾ-
ਦਫੜੀ, ਗੜਬੜ, ਹੁੱਲੜ, ਹਲਚਲ, ਖਲਬਲੀ

communal ('ਕੋਮਯੁਨਲ) *a* ਫਿਰਕੂ,
ਸੰਪਰਦਾਇਕ; ਸਰਵਜਨਕ, ਅਵਾਮੀ; ~**ism**
ਫਿਰਕਾਪਰਸਤੀ, ਫਿਰਕੁਪੁਣਾ, ਸੰਪਰਦਾਇਕਤਾ

commune (ਕਅਮਯੂਨ) *n v* ਪਰਗਾਣਾ,
ਪੰਚਾਇਤ; ਭੇਦ ਭਰੀ ਗਾਲ ਕਰਨੀ

communicabillity (ਕਅ'ਮਯੁਨਿਕਅ-
'ਬਿਲਅਟੀ) *n* ਸੰਚਰਨ-ਯੋਗਤਾ, ਸੰਚਰਤਾ,
ਸੰਵਾਦਸ਼ੀਲਤਾ

communicable (ਕਅ'ਮਯੂਨਿਕਅਬਲ) *a*
ਸੰਚਾਰੀ, ਸੂਚਨਾਯੋਗ, ਦੱਸਣਯੋਗ, ਪਤਾ ਦੇਣ ਦੇ
ਯੋਗ, ਕਥਨਯੋਗ

communicate (ਕਅ'ਮਯੂਨਿਕੇਇਟ) *v* ਸੰਚਾਰਨ,
ਸੂਚਤ ਕਰਨਾ, ਖ਼ਬਰ ਦੇਣੀ, ਆਵਾਜਾਈ ਦਾ
ਸਾਧਨ ਪੈਦਾ ਕਰਨਾ

communication (ਕਅ'ਮਯੂਨਿ'ਕੇਇਸ਼ਨ) *n*
ਸੰਚਾਰ, ਸੂਚਨਾ, ਖ਼ਬਰ, ਪਹੁੰਚ, ਆਵਾਜਾਈ,
ਪ੍ਰਚਾਰ, ਪ੍ਰਚਲਨ, ਸੰਪਰਕ

communicative (ਕਅਮ'ਯੂਨਿਕਅਟਿਵ) *a*
ਖ਼ਬਰ ਪੁਚਾਉਣ ਵਾਲਾ, ਸੰਚਾਰੀ; ~**ness**
ਖੁੱਲ੍ਹੀਆਂ ਗੱਲਾਂ ਕਰਨ ਦਾ ਭਾਵ

communion (ਕਅ'ਮਯੂਨਯਅਨ) *n* ਭਾਈਚਾਰਾ,
ਸੰਪਰਦਾਈ, ਸੰਗਤ; (ਇਸਾਈ ਮੱਤ) ਰੱਬੀ-ਭੋਜ;
ਸੰਪਰਕ, ਸਾਂਝ, ਰਾਬਤਾ

communique (ਕਅ'ਮਯੂਨਿਕੇਇ) *n* ਸਰਕਾਰੀ
ਐਲਾਨ, ਅਧਿਕਾਰਤ ਘੋਸ਼ਣਾ

communism ('ਕੋਮਯੁਨਿਜ਼(ਅ)ਮ) *n* ਸਾਮਵਾਦ,
ਸਾਮਵਾਦੀ ਅੰਦੋਲਨ

communist ('ਕੋਮਯੁਨਿਸਟ) *n* ਸਾਮਵਾਦੀ,
ਸਾਂਝੀਵਾਲ, ਕੀਮਿਊਨਿਸਟ

community (ਕਅ'ਮਯੂਨਅਟੀ) *n* ਭਾਈਚਾਰਾ,
ਬਰਾਬਰੀ, ਫ਼ਿਰਕਾ, ਸੰਪਰਦਾਇ; ਸਮਾਜ, ਸਮੂਹ,
ਰਾਜਨੀਤਕ, ਸਮਾਜਕ ਅਤੇ ਨਾਗਰਿਕ ਸੰਗਠਨ,

communize ('ਕੋਮਯੁਨਾਇਜ਼) *v* ਸਮੂਹੀਕਰਨ
ਕਰਨਾ, ਸਮਾਜੀਕਰਨ ਕਰਨਾ

commutable (ਕਅ'ਮਯੂਟਅਬਲ) *a*
ਵਟਾਉਣਜੋਗ

commutation (ਕੋਮਯੂ'ਟੇਇਸ਼ਨ) *n* ਵਟਾਆ

commute (ਕਅ'ਮਯੂਟ) *v* ਬਦਲਣਾ, ਵਟਾ ਲੈਣਾ;
~**r** ਰੋਜ਼ਾਨਾ ਯਾਤਰੀ

compact (ਕਅੰ'ਪੈਕਟ) *a n* ਪੁਖਤਾ, ਪੱਕਾ, ਦ੍ਰਿੜ੍ਹ,
ਠੋਸ, ਸੰਘਣਾ; ਚੁਸਤ (ਸ਼ੈਲੀ); ਸੰਧੀ, ਮੁਆਹਿਦਾ

companion (ਕੰਪੈਨਯਅਨ) *n v* ਸਾਥੀ, ਸੰਗੀ,
ਯਾਰ, ਬੇਲੀ, ਆੜੀ, ਸਹਿਕਾਰੀ, ਸਹਾਇਕ;
ਸਾਂਝੀ, ਹਿੱਸੇਦਾਰ; ਸਾਥ ਦੇਣਾ, ਨਾਲ ਹੋਣਾ, ਜੋੜ
ਮਿਲਾਉਣਾ, ਸਾਥ ਨਿਬਾਉਣਾ; ~**ship** ਜੋਟੀ,
ਯਾਰੀ, ਸਾਥ, ਸੰਗਤ, ਭਾਈਵਾਲੀ; **bad**~
ਕੁਸੰਗ, ਕੁਸੰਗਤ, ਮਾੜੀ ਸੰਗਤ

comparable ('ਕੌਂਪ(ਅ)ਰਅਬਲ) *a* ਸਮਾਨ, ਸਦ੍ਰਿਸ਼, ਬਰਾਬਰ ਦਾ, ਨਾਲ ਦਾ, ਮੁਕਾਬਲੇ ਦਾ, ਟਾਕਰੇ ਦਾ, ਮੇਚਵਾਂ

comparative (ਕਅੰਪੈਰਅਟਿਵ੍) *a* ਤੁਲਨਾਤਮਕ; ਤੁਲਨਾਵਾਚੀ; ਮੁਕਾਬਲੇ ਦਾ; ~ly ਤੁਲਨਾਤਮਕ ਤੌਰ ਤੇ, ਮੁਕਾਬਲਤਨ

compare (ਕਅੰਮ'ਪੇਅ*) *v* ਤੁਲਨਾ ਕਰਨਾ, ਉਪਮਾ ਕਰਨਾ, ਟਾਕਰਾ ਕਰਨਾ, ਮੁਕਾਬਲਾ ਕਰਨਾ, ਬਰਾਬਰੀ ਕਰਨਾ, ਤੁਲਨਾ ਹੋਣਾ, ਮਿਲਾਉਣਾ, ਮੇਲਨ ਕਰਨਾ; ਜਾਂਚਣਾ

comparison (ਕਅੰਪੈਰਿਸਨ) *n* ਤੁਲਨਾ, ਉਪਮਾ, ਬਰਾਬਰੀ, ਮੁਕਾਬਲਾ, ਟਾਕਰਾ; ਉਦਾਹਰਣ, ਮਿਸਾਲ, ਦ੍ਰਿਸ਼ਟਾਂਤ; in~with ਤੁਲਨਾ ਵਿਚ, ਮੁਕਾਬਲੇ ਵਿਚ

compart (ਕੰਪਾ*ਟ) *v* ਵਖ ਵਖ ਕਰਨਾ, ਅਲਗ ਅਲਗ ਟੁਕੜਿਆਂ ਵਿਚ ਵੰਡਣਾ; ~ment ਕਮਰਾ, ਡੱਬਾ, ਪਰੀਖਿਆ, ਵਿਚ ਕੰਪਾਰਟਮੈਂਟ, ਪਰਿਪੂਰਕ ਪਰੀਖਿਆ

compass ('ਕੰਪਅਸ) *n v* ਕੁਤਬਨੁਮਾ, ਦਿਸ਼ਾਸੂਚਕ; ਕੰਪਸ, ਪਰਕਾਰ, ਚੱਕਰ, ਘੇਰਨ, ਵਲਨਾ, ਚੱਕਰ ਕੱਟਣਾ

compassion (ਕਅੰਪੈਸ਼ਨ) *n* ਦਇਆ, ਕਿਰਪਾ, ਤਰਸ, ਦਰਦ, ਰਹਿਮ, ਰਹਿਮਦਿਲੀ; ~ate ਦਇਆ-ਵਾਨ, ਕਿਰਪਾਲੂ, ਦਿਆਲੂ; ਦਇਆ ਕਰਨੀ, ਤਰਸ ਕਰਨਾ, ਰਹਿਮ ਖਾਣਾ; ~ness ਦਇਆਸ਼ੀਲਤਾ, ਦਇਆਲਤਾ, ਕਰੁਣਾ

compatibility (ਕਅੰਪੈਟਅ'ਬਿਲਅਟਿ) *n* ਸੰਗਤੀ, ਅਨੁਕੂਲਤਾ, ਅਨੁਰੂਪਤਾ

compatible (ਕਅੰਪੈਟਅਬਲ) *a* ਅਨੁਕੂਲ, ਅਨੁਰੂਪ, ਯੋਗ, ਢੁੱਕਵਾਂ, ਮੁਨਾਸਬ, ਮੁਆਫ਼ਕ,

compatriot (ਕਅੰਪੈਟਿਰਿਅਟ) *n* ਹਮ-ਵਤਨੀ, ਵਤਨੀ, ਦੇਸ਼ਵਾਸੀ

compel (ਕਅੰਪੈੱਲ) *v* ਮਜਬੂਰ ਕਰਨਾ, ਦਬਾਉਣਾ, ਲਾਚਾਰ ਕਰਨਾ, ਬੇਵੱਸ ਕਰਨਾ

compelling (ਕਅੰਪੈੱਲਿਙ) *a* (ਕਹਾਣੀ ਆਦਿ) ਰੋਮਾਂਚਕਾਰੀ, ਜ਼ੋਰਦਾਰ, ਜ਼ੋਰਪਾਊ

compensate ('ਕੌਂਪੈਨਸੇਇਟ) *v* ਮੁਆਵਜ਼ਾ ਦੇਣਾ, ਇਵਜ਼ਾਨਾ ਦੇਣਾ, ਭਰਨਾ, ਘਾਟਾ ਪੂਰਾ ਕਰਨਾ, ਮੁਜਰਾਈ ਲੈਣਾ

compensation ('ਕੌਂਪੈਨਸੇਇਸ਼ਨ) *n* ਪੂਰਤੀ, ਯਤੜਪੂਰਤੀ, ਇਵਜ਼ਾਨਾ, ਮੁਆਵਜ਼ਾ, ਹਾਨੀ-ਪੂਰਤੀ

compensatory ('ਕੰਪਅੰਨ'ਸੇਇਟ(ਅ)ਰਿ) *a* ਮੁਜਰਾਈ ਪੂਰਕ, ਹਾਨੀਪੂਰਕ

compere ('ਕੌਂਪੇਅ*) *n v* (ਗੋਸ਼ਠੀ ਆਦਿ ਦਾ) ਸੰਚਾਲਕ; ਸੰਚਾਲਨ ਕਰਨਾ

compete (ਕਅੰਪੀਟ) *v* ਟਾਕਰਾ ਕਰਨਾ, ਰੀਸ ਕਰਨਾ; ਬਰਾਬਰੀ ਕਰਨਾ, ਮੁਕਾਬਲਾ ਕਰਨਾ, ਪ੍ਰਤੀਯੋਗਤਾ ਕਰਨਾ

competency ('ਕੌਂਮਪਿਟਅੰਸਿ) *n* ਯੋਗਤਾ, ਸਾਮੱਰਥਾ, ਸ਼ਕਤੀ

competent (ਕੌਂਮਪਿਟ(ਅੰ)ਟ) *a* ਯੋਗ, ਢੁਕਵਾਂ, ਸਾਮੱਰਥ, ਸ਼ਕਤੀਵਾਨ

competing (ਕਅੰਪੀਟਿਙ) *a* ਪ੍ਰਤੀਯੋਗੀ

competition ('ਕੌਂਪਿ'ਟਿਸ਼ਨ) *n* ਮੁਕਾਬਲਾ, ਬਰਾਬਰੀ, ਪ੍ਰਤੀਯੋਗਤਾ, ਟਾਕਰਾ

competitive (ਕਅੰਪੈੱਟਅਟਿਵ੍) *a* ਪ੍ਰਤੀਯੋਗਤਾਮੂਲਕ, ਮੁਕਾਬਲੇ ਦਾ

compilation ('ਕੌਂਪਿ'ਲੇਇਸ਼ਨ) *n* ਸੰਗ੍ਰਹ, ਸੰਕਲਨ, ਸੰਪਾਦਨ

compile (ਕਅੰਪਾਇਲ) *v* ਸੰਕਲਨ ਕਰਨਾ, ਸੰਗ੍ਰਹ ਕਰਨਾ, ਰਚਨਾ ਕਰਨਾ, ਇਕੱਤਰ ਕਰਨਾ, (ਕ੍ਰਿਕਟ ਵਿਚ) ਦੇਰ ਤਕ ਖੇਡਣਾ ਤੇ ਦੌੜਾਂ ਬਣਾਉਣਾ;

~d ਸੰਕਲਨ, ਸੰਪਾਦਤ, ਰਚਿਤ; ~r ਸੰਕਲਨ-
ਕਰਨ, ਰਚਨਾਕਾਰ

complacence (ਕਅੱਪਲੇਇਸੰਸ) a ਸੰਤੁਸ਼ਟਤਾ;
ਤ੍ਰਿਪਤੀ; ਤਸੱਲੀ, ਸ਼ਾਂਤੀ, ਇਤਮੀਨਾਨ; ਖ਼ੁਸ਼ੀ

complacent (ਕਅੱਪਲੇਇਸੰਟ) a ਸੰਤੁਸ਼ਟ, ਤ੍ਰਿਪਤ

complain (ਕਅੱਪਲੇਇਨ) v ਗਿਲਾ ਕਰਨਾ,
ਸ਼ਿਕਵਾ ਕਰਨਾ, ਸ਼ਿਕਾਇਤ ਕਰਨੀ, ਫ਼ਰਿਆਦ
ਕਰਨਾ, ਰੋਲਾ-ਪਾਉਣਾ; ~ant ਫ਼ਰਿਆਦੀ,
ਸ਼ਿਕਾਇਤ ਕਰਨ ਵਾਲਾ, ਮੁਦੱਈ; ~t ਗਿਲਾ,
ਫ਼ਰਿਆਦ, ਸ਼ਿਕਾਇਤ, ਸ਼ਿਕਵਾ

complement (ਕੌਂਪਲਿਮਅੰਟ, 'ਕੌਂਮਪਲਿਮਅੰਟ) n
v ਪੂਰਕ, ਪੂਰਤੀ ਕਰਨਾ, ਪੂਰਾ ਕਰਨਾ, ਖ਼ੁਸ਼ਹਾਲ
ਬਣਾਉਣਾ

complementary ('ਕੌਂਲਿ'ਮੈਂਟ(ਅ)ਰਿ) a ਪੂਰਕ,
ਪੂਰਾ ਕਰਨ ਵਾਲਾ, ਸਹਾਇਕ

complete (ਕਅੱਪਲੀਟ) v ਪੂਰਾ ਕਰਨਾ, ਪੂਰਤੀ
ਕਰਨਾ, ਸੰਪੂਰਨ ਕਰਨਾ, ਮੁਕਾਉਣਾ, ਸਮਾਪਤ
ਕਰਨਾ, ਭੋਗ ਪਾਉਣਾ, ਸਿਰੇ ਚੜ੍ਹਾਉਣਾ; ~ness
ਪੂਰਨਤਾ, ਸਮਾਪਤੀ, ਸੰਪੂਰਨਤਾ

completion (ਕਅੱਪਲੀਸ਼ਨ) n ਪੂਰਤੀ, ਪੂਰਨਤਾ,
ਤਕਮੀਲ, ਸਮਾਪਤੀ

complex ('ਕੌਂਪਲਕਸ) n a (1) ਗੁੰਝਲ,
ਉਲਝਣ, ਪੇਚੀਦਾ ਮਾਮਲਾ, ਜਟਿਲ ਗੱਲ;
(2) ਭਵਨ-ਸਮੂਹ; (3) ਮਨੋਗ੍ਰੰਥੀ; ਗੁੰਝਲਦਾਰ,
ਜਟਿਲ, ਉਲਝਿਆ, ਪੇਚੀਦਾ

complexion (ਕਅੱਪਲੈੱਕਸ਼ਨ) n ਰੰਗ-ਢੰਗ,
ਚੇਹਰਾ-ਮੁਹਰਾ, ਰੰਗ-ਰੂਪ, ਸਰੂਪ

complexity (ਕਅੱਪੈਲੱਕਸਅਟਿ) n ਉਲਝਣ,
ਉਲਝਾਉ, ਜਟਿਲਤਾ, ਪੇਚੀਦਗੀ, ਗੁੰਝੀ

compliance ('ਕਅੱਪਲਾਇਅੰਸ) n ਆਗਿਆ-
ਪਾਲਨ, ਹੁਕਮ ਦੀ ਤਾਮੀਲ, ਫ਼ਰਮਾਬਰਦਾਰੀ;

ਸੰਮਤੀ

complicate ('ਕੌਂਪਲਿਕੇਇਟ) v ਉਲਝਾਉਣਾ,
ਜਟਿਲ ਬਣਾਉਣਾ, ਪੇਚੀਦਾ ਬਣਾਉਣਾ; ~d
ਪੇਚੀਦਾ, ਗੁੰਝਲਦਾਰ, ਉਲਝਿਆ, ਪੇਚਦਾਰ, ਜਟਿਲ

complication ('ਕੌਂਪਲਿ'ਕੇਇਸ਼ਨ) n ਉਲਝਨ,
ਗੁੰਝਲ, ਜਟਿਲਤਾ, ਜਟਿਲ ਪ੍ਰਸ਼ਨ, ਗੁੱਥੀ

compliment (ਕੰਪਲਿਮਅੰਟ, ਕੌਂਮਪਲਿਮੈਂਟ) n v
(in pl) ਸ਼ੁਭ ਕਾਮਨਾਵਾਂ, ਸਲਾਘਾ, ਸਲਾਹੁਤਾ,
ਆਦਾਬ, ਵਡਿਆਈ; (ਪ੍) ਸੁਗਾਤ; ਸਲਾਘਾ
ਕਰਨਾ, ਸਲਾਹੁਣ, ਅਦਬ ਸਲਾਮ ਬੁਲਾਉਣਾ;
ਸੁਗਾਤ ਦੇਣੀ; ~ary ਪ੍ਰਸੰਸਾਮਈ, ਸਨਮਾਨ-
ਸੂਚਕ, ਅਭਿਨੰਦਨੀ

component (ਕਅੱਪਅਉਨਅੰਟ) n ਅੰਗ, ਹਿੱਸਾ,
ਭਾਗ, ਜੁਜ਼

compose (ਕੰਪਅਉਜ਼) v ਸੁਆਰਨਾ, ਲਿਖਣਾ,
ਸਾਹਿਤ-ਸਿਰਜਨਾ ਕਰਨੀ, ਰਚਨਾ ਕਰਨੀ,
ਨਿਰਮਾਣ ਕਰਨਾ; ਇੱਕਤਰ ਕਰਨਾ; ਕੰਪੋਜ਼ ਕਰਨਾ;
ਛਾਪੇ ਦੇ ਅੱਖਰ ਜੋੜਨਾ, ਵਿਵਸਥਿਤ ਕਰਨਾ,
ਵਿਉਂਤ ਨਾਲ ਰਖਣਾ; ਸੰਗੀਤ ਵਿਚ ਧੁਨ
ਬਣਾਉਣਾ; ਸ਼ਾਂਤ ਕਰਨਾ; ~d ਸ਼ਾਂਤ, ਅਡੋਲ;
~dness ਸ਼ਾਂਤੀ, ਗੰਭੀਰਤਾ, ਇਤਮੀਨਾਨ; ~r
ਸੰਗੀਤਕਾਰ, ਲੇਖਕ, ਰਚਨਾਕਾਰ, ਕਵੀ, ਰਚੇਤਾ

composing (ਕਅੱਪਅਉਜ਼ਿਙ੍) n ਰਚਨਾ, ਟਾਈਪ
ਨੂੰ ਜੋੜਨ ਦੀ ਕਿਰਿਆ, ਕੰਪੋਜ਼ਿੰਗ

composite (ਕੌਂਪਅਜ਼ਿਟ) n ਸੰਘਠਤ, ਮਿਸ਼ਰਤ,
ਸੰਯੋਜਤ; ~interest ਮਿਸ਼ਰਤ ਵਿਆਜ;
~sentence ਸੰਯੁਕਤ ਵਾਕ; ~word ਸਮਾਸੀ
ਸ਼ਬਦ

comprehend ('ਕੌਂਪਰਿ'ਹੈਂਡ) v ਸੰਮਿਲਤ
ਕਰਨਾ, ਗ੍ਰਹਿਤ ਕਰਨਾ, ਮਿਲਾਉਣਾ; ਅਨੁਭਵ
ਕਰਨਾ, ਸਮਝਣਾ

comprise (ਕਅੰ'ਪਰਾਇਜ਼) n ਸ਼ਾਮਲ ਕਰਨਾ,
ਮਿਲਾਉਣਾ, ਅੰਦਰ ਸਮਾਉਣਾ; ਧਾਰਨ ਕਰਨਾ

compulsion (ਕਅੰ'ਪਅੱਲਸ਼ਨ) n ਜ਼ੋਰਾਵਰੀ,
ਜ਼ਬਰਦਸਤੀ, ਜ਼ਬਰ, ਜ਼ੋਰ, ਬੰਧਨ, ਦਬਾਉ,
ਬੇਵਸੀ, ਮਜਬੂਰੀ

compulsorily (ਕਅੰ'ਪਅੱਲਸਅਰਅਲਿ) a
ਜ਼ਬਰਦਸਤੀ ਨਾਲ, ਬਲਪੂਰਵਕ, ਮਜਬੂਰਨ

compulsory (ਕਅੰ'ਪਅੱਲਸ(ਅ)ਰਿ) a ਜ਼ਰੂਰੀ,
ਅਵੱਸ਼ਕ, ਲਾਜ਼ਮੀ, ਅਨਿਵਾਰੀ; ਜ਼ਬਰੀ

compute (ਕਅੰ'ਪਯੂਟ) v ਲੇਖਾ ਕਰਨਾ, ਗਿਣਨਾ,
ਹਿਸਾਬ ਲਾਉਣਾ, ਗਿਣਤੀ ਵਿਚ ਲਿਆਉਣਾ;
~r, computor ਹਿਸਾਬ ਲਗਾਉਣ ਵਾਲਾ,
ਗਾਣਕ, ਕੰਪਿਊਟਰ

computing (ਕਅੰ'ਪਯੂਟਿਙ) n ਗਿਣਤੀ, ਗਣਨਾ,
ਹਿਸਾਬ

comrade ('ਕੌਮਰੇਇਡ) n ਸੰਗੀ, ਸਾਥੀ, ਯਾਰ,
ਹਮਦਮ, ਮਿੱਤਰ, ਕਾਮਰੇਡ; ~ship ਸੰਗ; ਸਾਥ,
ਯਾਰੀ, ਦੋਸਤੀ, ਸਿੱਤਰਤਾ

conceal (ਕਅਨ'ਸੀਲ) v ਗੁਪਤ ਰੱਖਣਾ,
ਲੁਕਾਉਣਾ, ਛੁਪਾਉਣਾ, ਢਕਣਾ, ਉਹਲੇ ਰੱਖਣਾ

concede (ਕਅਨ'ਸੀਡ) v ਮੰਨਣਾ, ਮਨਜ਼ੂਰ ਕਰਨਾ,
ਸਵੀਕਾਰ ਕਰਨਾ, ਕਬੂਲ ਕਰਨਾ; ਪ੍ਰਦਾਨ ਕਰਨਾ

concentrate ('ਕੌਨਸ(ਅ)ਨਟਰੇਇਟ) v ਕੇਂਦਰਤ
ਕਰਨਾ, ਸਹਿ-ਕੇਂਦਰ ਹੋਣਾ, ਇਕਾਗਰ ਹੋਣਾ,
ਸੰਘਣਾ ਕਰਨਾ, ਗਾੜ੍ਹਾ ਕਰਨਾ ~d ਕੇਂਦਰਤ,
ਸੰਘਣਾ

concentration ('ਕੌਨਸ(ਅ)ਨ'ਟਰੇਇਸ਼ਨ) n
ਕੇਂਦਰੀ-ਕਰਨ, ਸਹਿ-ਕੇਂਦਰੀਕਰਨ, ਇਕੱਤਰੀਕਰਨ,
ਟਿਕਾਉ

concept ('ਕੌਨਸੈੱਪਟ) n ਸੰਕਲਪ, ਧਾਰਨਾ,
ਸੰਬੋਧ; ~ion ਧਾਰਨਾ, ਖ਼ਿਆਲ, ਅਨੁਭਵ,

ਗਰਭ-ਧਾਰਨ, ਗਾਰਭਾਧਾਨ

conceptive (ਕਅਨ'ਸੈਪਟਿਵ) a ਖ਼ਿਆਲੀ,
ਅਨੁਭਵੀ, ਗਰਭ-ਸਬੰਧੀ

conceptual (ਕਅਨ'ਸੈਪਚੁਅਲ) a ਧਾਰਨਾ
ਸਬੰਧੀ, ਸੰਕਲਪਵਾਦੀ, ਤਸੱਵਰੀ

concern (ਕਨ'ਸਅ:ਨ) v ਸਬੰਧ ਰੱਖਣਾ, ਸਰੋਕਾਰ
ਜਾਂ ਵਾਸਤਾ ਰੱਖਣਾ, ਵਾਹ ਪੈਣਾ, ਲਗਾਉ
ਰੱਖਣਾ; ਦਿਲਚਸਪੀ ਲੈਣਾ; ਫ਼ਿਕਰ ਕਰਨਾ; ~ed
ਸੰਬੰਧਤ, ਪ੍ਰਸੰਗਾਬੱਧ ਚਿੰਤਤ, ਚਿੰਤਾਤੁਰ; ~ing
ਬਾਬਤ, ਬਾਰੇ, ਸਬੰਧਤ, ਵਿਸ਼ੇ ਵਿਚ, ਪ੍ਰਤੀ

concession (ਕਅਨ'ਸੈਸ਼ਨ) n ਛੋਟ, ਰਿਆਇਤ;
ਸਵੀਕਾਰਨ, ਮਾਫ਼ੀ

concise (ਕਅਨ'ਸਾਇਸ) a ਸੰਖੇਪ, ਛੋਟਾ ~ly
ਸੰੀਖਪ ਢੰਗ ਨਾਲ; ~ness ਸੰਖਿਪਤਤਾ

conclave ('ਕੌਙਕਲੇਇਵ) n ਪੋਪ ਦੀ ਚੋਣ ਲਈ
ਵੱਡੇ ਪਾਦਰੀਆਂ ਦਾ ਇਕੱਠ; ਮੁੱਖ ਰਾਜਨੀਤਕ
ਪਾਰਟੀਆਂ ਦੇ ਅਗੂਆਂ ਦਾ ਇਕੱਠ

conclude (ਕਅਨ'ਕਲੂਡ) v ਭੋਗ ਪਾਉਣਾ,
ਨਿਬੇੜਨਾ, ਮੁਕਾਉਣਾ, ਖ਼ਤਮ ਕਰਨਾ, ਪੂਰਾ
ਕਰਨਾ, ਸਿਰੇ ਚਾੜ੍ਹਨਾ; ~d ਸਮਾਪਤ; ਨਿਸ਼ਚਤ

concluding (ਕਅਨ'ਕਲੂਡਿਙ) a ਸਮਾਪਤੀ
(ਸਮਾਰੋਹ ਆਦਿ); ਅੰਤਮ (ਟਿੱਪਣੀ ਆਦਿ)

conclusion (ਕਅਨ'ਕਲੂਯ਼ਨ) n ਸਿੱਟਾ, ਨਤੀਜਾ,
ਪਰਿਣਾਮ; ਅੰਤ, ਸਮਾਪਤੀ, ਨਿਸ਼ਚਾ; ਨਿਸ਼ਕਰਸ਼;
in ~ ਉਂਤਕ, ਅੰਤ ਵਿਚ

concoct ('ਕਅਨ'ਕੌਕਟ) v ਮਨੋਂ ਘੜਨਾ, ਜੋੜਨਾ,
ਮਨੋਂ ਬਣਾਉਣਾ ~ed ਮਨਘੜਤ, ਘੜੀ ਹੋਈ,
ਜੋੜੀ ਹੋਈ

concord (ਕੌਙਕੋ*ਡ) n ਸਮਝੌਤਾ, ਸੰਧੀ; ਮੇਲ-
ਮਿਲਾਪ, ਤਰਕੀਬ, ਸਹਿਮਤੀ, ਸਿੱਤਰਤਾ; ਤਾਲ-
ਮੇਲ ~ance ਏਕਤਾ, ਸਹਿਮਤੀ, ਸਮਾਨਤਾ,

ਸਮਤਾ, ਸਦ੍ਰਿਸ਼ਤਾ, ਅਨੁਕੂਲਤਾ; ਅਨੁਲਮਤਿਕਾ

concrete ('ਕੌਂਕਰੀਟ) *a n v* ਪੱਕਾ, ਠੋਸ, ਨਿਗਰ ਪਦਾਰਥ; ਨਿਗੱਰਪੁਣਾ; ~ness ਪਕਿਆਈ, ਸਖ਼ਤਾਈ, ਠੋਸਪਣ

concur (ਕਅਨ'ਕਾ*) *v* ਸੰਮਤੀ ਰਖਣਾ, ਸਹਿਮਤ ਹੋਣਾ, ਰਾਇ ਮੇਲਣੀ, ਇਕ ਮਤ ਹੋਣਾ, ਅਨੁਕੂਲ ਹੋਣਾ; ~rence ਸੰਮਤੀ, ਸਹਿਮਤੀ, ਮਨਜ਼ੂਰੀ, ਮਿਲਵਰਤਨ; ~rent ਸਮਕਾਲੀ, ਸਹਿਵਰਤੀ, (ਸਜ਼ਾਵਾਂ) ਇਕੋ ਵੇਲੇ ਲਾਗੂ ਹੇਣ ਵਾਲੀਆਂ, ਸਹਿਗਾਮੀ ਅਨੁਸਾਰੀ, ਸੰਮਤੀ ਰਖੱਣ ਵਾਲਾ; ਸਮਾਨ; ਸਮਾਨਾਂਤਰ ਪਰਿਸਥਿਤੀ

condemn (ਕਅਨ'ਡੈੱਮ) *v* ਦੁਰਕਾਰਨਾ, ਤਿਰਸਕਾਰਨਾ, ਭੰਡਣਾ, ਰੱਦ ਕਰਨਾ; ਅਪਰਾਧੀ ਠਹਿਰਾਉਣਾ, ਦੋਸ਼ ਥਪੱਣਾ, ਸਜ਼ਾ ਸੁਣਾਉਣਾ; (ਵਿਰੁੱਧ) ਨਿਰਣਾ ਦੇਣਾ, ਬੁਰਾ-ਭਲਾ ਕਹਿਣਾ; ~able ਦੰਡ ਦੇਣਯੋਗ, ਤਿਰਸਕਾਰ ਕਰਨਯੋਗ, ਨਿੰਦਣਯੋਗ; ~ation ਦੰਡ-ਆਗਿਆ, ਸਜ਼ਾ ਦਾ ਹੁਕਮ; ਦੂਸ਼ਣ, ਨਿੰਦਾ; ~ed ਦੰਡਤ, ਨਿੰਦਤ; ਨਿਕੰਮਾ, ਨਕਾਰਾ, ਨਿਸ਼ਿਧ

condensation ('ਕੈਨਡੈਂਨ'ਸੇਇਸ਼ਨ) *n* ਸੰਖੇਪਤਾ; ਗਾੜ੍ਹਾਪਣ, ਸੰਘਣਾਪਣ, ਘਾਣ

condense (ਕਅਨ'ਡੈਂਸ) *v* ਸੰਖੇਪ ਕਰਨਾ, ਛੋਟਾ ਕਰਨਾ, ਗਾੜ੍ਹਾ ਕਰਨਾ, ਬੱਦਲਾਂ ਦਾ ਘੁਲਣਤਾ; ~d ਸੰਖਿਪਤ, ਘਣੀਭੂਤ

condiment ('ਕੌਂਡਿਮਅੰਟ) *n* ਅਚਾਰ; ~al ਮਸਾਲੇਦਾਰ, ਚਟਪਟਾ

condition (ਕਅਨ'ਡਿਸ਼ਨ) *n v* ਅਵਸਥਾ, ਦਸ਼ਾ, ਸਥਿਤੀ, ਹਾਲਤ, ਹਾਲ; ਪਰਿਸਥਿਤੀ; ਸ਼ਰਤ, ਪ੍ਰਤੀਬੰਧ; ਹੈਸੀਅਤ, ਡੀਲ-ਡੌਲ, ਰੰਗ-ਢੰਗ, (ਦਸ਼ਾ) ਠੀਕ ਕਰਨਾ, ਅਨੁਕੂਲ ਕਰਨਾ, ਗਿਝਾਉਣਾ, ਆਦਤ ਪਾਉਣਾ, ਸ਼ਰਤ ਲਾਉਣਾ; ~al ਸ਼ਰਤਬੰਧ, ਸ਼ਰਤੀਆ,

ਮਸ਼ਰੂਤ; ~ed ਅਨੁਕੂਲ, ਆਦੀ

condole (ਕਅਨ'ਡਅਉਲ) *v* ਅਫ਼ਸੋਸ ਕਰਨਾ, ਮਾਤਮ-ਪੁਰਸ਼ੀ ਕਰਨਾ, ਹਮਦਰਦੀ ਕਰਨੀ, ਪਰਚਾਉਣੀ ਕਰਨੀ; ~nce ਅਫ਼ਸੋਸ, ਮਾਤਮ, ਮਾਤਮਪੁਰਸ਼ੀ, ਪਰਚਾਉਣੀ, ਸੋਗ

condone (ਕਅਨ'ਡਉਨ) *v* ਛੋਟ ਦੇਣੀ, ਮਾਫ਼ ਕਰਨਾ ਜਾਣ ਦੇਣਾ, ਨਜ਼ਰਅੰਦਾਜ਼ ਕਰਨਾ

conduct ('ਕੌਂਡਅੱਕਟ) *n* ਵਤੀਰਾ, ਰਵੱਈਆ, ਚਾਲ-ਚਲਨ, ਆਚਰਨ, ਆਚਾਰ-ਵਿਹਾਰ, ਪ੍ਰਣਾਲੀ, ਪੱਧਤੀ

confederation (ਕਅਨ'ਫ਼ੈੱਡਅ'ਰੇਇਸ਼ਨ) *n* ਮਹਾਂਸੰਘ

confer (ਕਅਨ'ਫ਼ਅ:*) *v* (ਡਿਗਰੀ, ਪਦਵੀ, ਬਿੱਲਾ, ਖ਼ਿਤਾਬ) ਦੇਣਾ, ਪ੍ਰਦਾਨ ਕਰਨਾ; ਸਲਾਹ ਕਰਨੀ, ਮਸ਼ਵਰਾ ਕਰਨਾ

conference ('ਕੌਂਫ਼ੱਅ(ਅ)ਰਅੰਸ) *n* ਸੰਮੇਲਨ, ਕਾਨਫ਼ਰੰਸ, ਜਲਸਾ; ਸਲਾਹ, ਮਸ਼ਵਰਾ

conferment (ਕਅਨ'ਫ਼ਅਅ'ਮਅੰਟ) *n* ਪ੍ਰਦਾਨ, ਉਪਹਾਰ, ਭੇਂਟ

confess (ਕਅਨ'ਫ਼ੈੱਸ) *v* (ਅਪਰਾਧ) ਇਕਬਾਲ ਕਰਨਾ, ਮੰਨ ਜਾਣਾ; ਪਛਤਾਵਾ ਕਰਨਾ, ਤੋਬਾ ਕਰਨੀ, ਕਬੂਲਣਾ

confession (ਕਅਨ'ਫ਼ੈੱਸ਼ਨ) *n* ਇਕਬਾਲ, ਤੋਬਾ

confidant ('ਕੌਂਫ਼ਿ'ਡੈਂਟ) *n* ਵਿਸ਼ਵਾਸਪਾਤਰ, ਭਰੋਸੇਯੋਗ ਪੁਰਸ਼, ਹਮਰਾਜ਼, ਰਾਜ਼ਦਾਨ

confide (ਕਅਨ'ਫ਼ਾਇਡ) *v* ਵਿਸਾਹ ਖਾਣਾ, ਭਰੋਸਾ ਕਰਨਾ, ਭੇਤੀ ਬਣਾਉਣਾ, ਸੌਂਪਣਾ, ਹਵਾਲੇ ਕਰਨਾ; ~nce ਵਿਸ਼ਵਾਸ, ਵਿਸਾਹ, ਭਰੋਸਾ, ਯਕੀਨ, ਪ੍ਰਤੀਤੀ, ਹੀਆ; ~nt ਭਰੋਸਾ ਕਰਨ ਵਾਲਾ, ਭੇਤੀ, ਮਹਿਰਮ, ਵਿਸ਼ਵਾਸੀ, ਵਿਸ਼ਵਾਸ-ਪੂਰਨ; ~ntial ਗੁਪਤ, ਗੁੱਝਾ, ਰਹੱਸਮਈ, ਭੇਤਵਾਲੀ

configuration (ਕਅਨ'ਫ਼ਿਗਅਰਏਸ਼ਨ) *n* ਰੂਪ, ਡੀਲ-ਡੌਲ, ਰੂਪ-ਰੇਖਾ, ਨੁਹਾਰ, ਵਜ਼੍ਹਾ-ਕਤ੍ਹਾ

configure (ਕਅਨ'ਫ਼ਿਗਅ*) *v* ਰੂਪ ਦੇਣਾ, ਸ਼ਕਲ ਬਣਾਉਣੀ, ਸ਼ਕਲ ਦੇਣੀ, ਢਾਂਚਾ ਬਣਾਉਣਾ

confine ('ਕੌਨਫ਼ਾਇਨ, ਕਅਨ'ਫ਼ਾਇਨ) *n (in pl) v* ਹੱਦ, ਹੱਦ-ਬੰਨਾ, ਸੀਮਾਂਤ, ਸੀਮਾ; ਹੱਦ ਅੰਦਰ ਕਰਨਾ, ਸੀਮਾ-ਬੱਧ ਕਰਨਾ, ਘੇਰੇ ਵਿੱਚ ਰੱਖਣਾ, ਕੈਦ ਕਰਨਾ, ਰੋਕ ਰੱਖਣਾ, ਅਟਕਾਉਣਾ; **~d** ਸੀਮਤ, ਘਿਰਿਆ, ਬੰਦ, ਸੰਕੀਰਣ

confirm (ਕਅਨ'ਫ਼ਅ:ਮ) *v* ਪੁਸ਼ਟੀ ਕਰਨੀ, ਹਾਮੀ ਭਰਨੀ, ਪੱਕਾ ਕਰਨਾ, ਸਥਾਈ ਕਰਨਾ, ਤਸਦੀਕ ਕਰਨਾ, ਮਨਜ਼ੂਰੀ ਦੇਣਾ; **~ation** ਪੁਸ਼ਟੀ, ਪੁਸ਼ਟੀਕਰਨ, ਤਸਦੀਕ, ਸਮਰਥਨ, ਮਨਜ਼ੂਰੀ, ਨਾਮਕਰਨ ਸੰਸਕਾਰ; **~ative, ~atory** ਪੁਸ਼ਟੀਕਾਰਕ, ਸਮਰਥਕ, ਤਾਈਦੀ, ਹਿਮਾਇਤੀ

confiscate ('ਕੌਨਫ਼ਿਸਕੇਇਟ) *v* ਜ਼ਬਤ ਕਰਨਾ, ਕੁਰਕ ਕਰਨਾ, ਖੋਹ ਲੈਣਾ; **~d** ਜ਼ਬਤ ਕੀਤਾ, ਕੁਰਕ ਕੀਤਾ, ਖੋਹਿਆ

confiscation ('ਕੌਅਨ'ਫ਼ਿਸਕਅਨ) *n* ਜ਼ਬਤੀ, ਕੁਰਕੀ

confix (ਕਅਨ'ਫ਼ਿਕਸ) *v* ਦ੍ਰਿੜ੍ਹ ਕਰਨਾ, ਪੱਕਾ ਕਰਨਾ, ਮਜ਼ਬੂਤੀ ਨਾਲ ਜਮਾਉਣਾ

conflict ('ਕੌਨਫ਼ਲਿਕਟ, ਕਅ'ਫ਼ਲਿਕਟ) *n v* ਟਾਕਰਾ, ਕਸ਼ਮਕਸ਼, ਸੰਘਰਸ਼, ਮੁਕਾਬਲਾ, ਵਿਰੋਧ, ਦਵੰਦ, ਬਖੇੜਾ, ਝਗੜਾ, ਟਾਕਰਾ ਕਰਨਾ, ਟੱਕਰਨਾ, ਵਿਰੋਧ ਕਰਨਾ, ਝਗੜਨਾ, ਮੁਕਾਬਲਾ ਹੋਣਾ; **~ing** ਵਿਪਰੀਤ, ਪ੍ਰਤੀਕੂਲ, ਪਰਸਪਰ ਵਿਰੋਧੀ ਵਿਵਾਦਗ੍ਰਸਤ; **~ion** ਵਿਰੋਧ, ਵਿਵਾਦ, ਕਲਹ, ਟੱਕਰ, ਮੁੱਠ-ਭੇੜ ਪ੍ਰਤੀਕੂਲਤਾ; **~ive** ਵਿਵਾਦਗ੍ਰਸਤ, ਪ੍ਰਤੀਕੂਲ, ਪਰਸਪਰ ਵਿਰੋਧੀ

confluence ('ਕੌਨਫ਼ਲੁਅੰਸ) *n* ਸੰਗਮ, ਮੇਲ, ਵੇਣੀ

conform (ਕਲਨ'ਫ਼ੋਮ) *v* ਅਨੁਕੂਲ ਕਰਨਾ, ਇਕ ਸੁਰ ਹੋਣਾ, ਇਕਸਾਰ ਦੇਣਾ, ਅਨੁਸਾਰ ਕਰਨਾ, ਅਨੁਕੂਲ ਹੋਣਾ; **~ation** ਅਨੁਕੂਲੀਕਰਨ, ਅਨੁਰੂਪ; ਸਦ੍ਰਿਸ਼ਤਾ, ਬਣਾਵਟ, ਢਾਂਚਾ

conformity (ਕਅਨ'ਫ਼ੋਮਅਟਿ) *n* ਅਨੁਕੂਲਣ, ਅਨੁਰੂਪਤਾ, ਅਨੁਸਾਰਤਾ, ਮੇਲ, ਪੈਰਵੀ, ਤਾਮੀਲ, ਅਗਿਆਕਾਰਤਾ

confuse (ਕਅਨ'ਫ਼ਯੂਜ਼) *v* ਮੱਤ ਮਾਰ ਦੇਣੀ, ਭੁਚਲਾਉਣਾ, ਉਲਝਾਉਣਾ, ਪਰੇਸ਼ਾਨ ਕਰਨਾ; **~d** ਪਰੇਸ਼ਾਨ, ਘਬਰਾਇਆ ਹੋਇਆ, ਉਲਝਿਆ ਹੋਇਆ

confusing (ਕਅਨ'ਫ਼ਯੂਜ਼ਿਙ) *a* ਪਰੇਸ਼ਾਨੀ ਵਾਲਾ, ਚਕਰਾਉਣ ਵਾਲਾ, ਉਲਝਾਉਣ ਵਾਲੀ, ਭਰਮਕਾਰੀ

confusion (ਕਅਨ'ਫ਼ਯੂਜ਼ਨ) *n* ਘਬਰਾਹਟ, ਘੜਮੱਵਸ, ਹਫੜਾ ਦਫੜੀ, ਪਰੇਸ਼ਾਨੀ

congenial (ਕਅਨ'ਜੀਨਯਅਲ) *a* ਹਮਦਰਦ, ਅਨੁਸਾਰੀ, ਸੁਹਾਵਣਾ, ਅਨੁਕੂਲ, ਸੁਖਾਉਂਦਾ, ਮਨਪਸੰਦ; **~ity** ਉਚਿਤਤਾ, ਸਮਾਨਤਾ, ਹਮਜਿਨਸੀ

congratulate (ਕਅਨ'ਗਰੈਚੁਲੇਇਟ) *v* ਵਧਾਈ ਦੇਣੀ, ਮੁਬਾਰਕ ਦੇਣੀ

congratulation (ਕਅਨ'ਗਰੈਚੁ'ਲੇਇਸ਼ਨ) *n* ਵਧਾਈ, ਮੁਬਾਰਕ, ਮੁਬਾਰਕਬਾਦ

congruity (ਕੌਙ'ਗਰੂਅਟਿ) *n* ਇਕਸਾਰਤਾ, ਸਮਰੂਪਤਾ, ਅਨੁਰੂਪਤਾ, ਸਦ੍ਰਿਸ਼ਟਤਾ, ਸੰਗਤੀ

congruous ('ਕੌਙ'ਗਰੁਅਸ) *a* ਉਚਿਤ, ਢੁੱਕਵਾਂ, ਅਨੁਰੂਪ, ਅਨੁਕੂਲ, ਸਦ੍ਰਿਸ਼; ਯੁਕਤ

conjugation ('ਕੌਨਯੁ'ਗੇਇਸ਼ਨ) *n* ਸਬੰਧ, ਸੰਯੋਗ, ਮੇਲ, ਜੋੜ, ਸੰਯੋਜਨ; ਰੂਪ-ਸਾਧਨਾ; ਧਾਤੂ ਰੂਪ; ਕਿਰਿਆ-ਰੂਪ; ਭੋਗ, ਮੈਥਨ, ਜੜਾਈ, ਪੇਂਦ

conjure (ਕਅਨ'ਜੁਅ*) *v* ਵਾਸਤਾ ਪੁਆਉਣਾ,

ਬੇਨਤੀ ਕਰਨ, ਅਪੀਲ ਕਰਨ; ਜਾਦੂ ਕਰਨ,
ਰੂਹਾਂ ਨੂੰ ਬੁਲਾਉਣਾ

connect (ਕਅ'ਨੈੱਕਟ) *v* ਜੋੜਨ, ਜੁੜਨ, ਗੰਢਣਾ,
ਸਬੰਧ ਪੈਦਾ ਕਰਨ, ਮੇਲਣ; **~ed** ਸਬੰਧਤ,
ਜੁੜਿਆ, ਸੰਯੁਕਤ

connote (ਕਅ'ਨਅਉਟ) *v* ਸੰਕੇਤ ਕਰਨ, ਭਾਵ
ਪਰਗਟ ਕਰਨ, ਜਤਲਾਉਣਾ

conquer (ਕੌਙਕਅ*) *v* ਫ਼ਤਿਹ ਕਰਨਾ, ਸਰ
ਕਰਨਾ, ਜਿਤਣਾ, ਅਧੀਨ ਕਰਨਾ; **~or** ਜੇਤੂ,
ਵਿਜਈ, ਵਿਜੇਤਾ

conquest ('ਕੌਙਕਵੈੱਸਟ) *n* ਜਿਤ, ਫ਼ਤਿਹ, ਵਿਜੈ

conscience ('ਕੌਨਸ਼(ਅੰ)ਸ) *n* ਜ਼ਮੀਰ, ਈਮਾਨ,
ਅੰਤਹਕਰਣ, ਅੰਤਰ ਆਤਮ; **~less** ਬੇਈਮਾਨ,
ਅਵਿਵੇਕੀ, ਬੇਜ਼ਮੀਰ; **~ly** ਈਮਾਨਦਾਰੀ ਨਾਲ
ਵਿਵੇਕਪੂਰਵਕ; **~ness** ਈਮਾਨਦਾਰੀ, ਜ਼ਮੀਰ,
ਸਾਤਵਿਕਤਾ

conscious ('ਕੌਨਸ਼ਅਸ) *a* ਚੇਤਨ, ਸਚੇਤ,
ਸੋਝੀਵਾਨ; **~ness** ਚੇਤਨਤਾ, ਜਾਣਕਾਰੀ;
ਨਿਪੁੰਨਤਾ; ਸੋਝੀ, ਚੇਤਨਾ; ਜਾਨਕਾਰੀ, ਗਿਆਨ,
ਅਨੁਭਵ

consecutive ('ਕਅਨ'ਸੈਕਯੁਟਿਵ) *a* ਲਗਾਤਾਰ,
ਸਿਲਸਲੇਵਾਰ, ਲੜੀਵਾਰ, ਲਾਗਵੇਂ; ਨਿਰੰਤਰ;
~ly ਉਪਰੋਥਲੀ, ਨਾਲੋ ਨਾਲ, ਸਿਲਸਲੇਵਾਰ;
ਲਗਾਤਾਰ

consensus (ਕਅਨ'ਸੈੱਨੱਸਅਸ) *n* ਸਹਿਮਤੀ,
ਸਰਵਸੰਮਤੀ, ਏਕਤਾ

consent (ਕਅਨ'ਸੈਂਟ) *n v* ਰਜ਼ਾਮੰਦੀ, ਸਹਿਮਤੀ,
ਸੰਮਤੀ, ਮਨਜ਼ੂਰੀ, ਆਗਿਆ; ਰਜ਼ਾਮੰਦ ਹੋਣਾ,
ਮਨਜ਼ੂਰੀ ਦੇਣੀ, ਸਲਾਹ ਦੇਣੀ, ਸਹਿਮਤ ਹੋਣਾ,
ਸਵੀਕਾਰ ਕਰਨਾ, ਮੰਨ ਲੈਣਾ

consequence ('ਕੌਨਸਿਕਵਅੰਸ) *n* ਸਿੱਟਾ,

ਫਲ, ਪਰਿਣਾਮ, ਮਹੱਤਾ, ਮਹੱਤਵ

consequent ('ਕੌਨਸਿਕਵਅੰਟ) *n* ਸਿੱਟਾ,
ਨਤੀਜਾ, ਫਲ; **~ly** ਸਿੱਟੇ ਵਜੋਂ, ਨਤੀਜੇ ਦੇ ਤੌਰ
ਤੇ, ਫਲਸਰੂਪ

consider (ਕਅਨ'ਸਿੱਡਅ*) *v* ਸੋਚਣਾ, ਵਿਚਾਰਨਾ,
ਗੌਲਣਾ, ਧਿਆਨ ਦੇਣਾ, ਸਮਝਣਾ; **~able**
ਸੋਚਣਯੋਗ, ਵਿਚਾਰਨਯੋਗ, ਗੌਰ ਕਰਨਯੋਗ;
ਕਾਫ਼ੀ, ਬਹੁਤ; **~ably** ਢੇਰ ਸਾਰਾ, ਬਹੁਤ ਸਾਰਾ,
ਅਤੀਅੰਤ, ਅਤਿਅਧਿਕ; **~ate** ਸਚੇਤ, ਦੂਰਦਰਸ਼ੀ

consideration (ਕਅਨ'ਸਿੱਡਅ'ਰੇਇਸ਼ਨ) *n*
ਵਿਚਾਰ, ਖਿਆਲ, ਗੌਰ, ਧਿਆਨ, ਗੰਭੀਰ ਚਿੰਤਨ;
in ~ of ਨੂੰ ਧਿਆਨ ਵਿਚ ਰਖਦਿਆਂ; **take into
~** ਵਿਚਾਰ ਅਧੀਨ ਕਰਨਾ, ਗੌਰ ਕਰਨਾ; ਧਿਆਨ
ਦੇਣਾ; **under~** ਵਿਚਾਰ-ਅਧੀਨ

consign (ਕਅਨ'ਸਾਇਨ) *v* ਸੌਂਪਣਾ, ਬਖ਼ਸ਼ਣਾ,
ਹਵਾਲੇ ਕਰਨਾ, ਭੇਜਣਾ; **~ee** ਪ੍ਰਾਪਤ ਕਰਨ ਵਾਲਾ,
(ਪਾਰਸਲ) ਪ੍ਰਾਪਤ ਕਰਨ ਵਾਲਾ; **~ment** ਮਾਲ
ਭਿਜਵਾਈ, ਸਪੁਰਦਗੀ, ਸੌਂਪਿਆ ਗਿਆ ਮਾਲ

consist (ਕਅਨ'ਸਿਸਟ) *v* ਬਣਨਾ, ਬਣਿਆ ਹੋਣਾ,
ਸ਼ਾਮਲ ਹੋਣਾ; **~ence** ਘਣਤਾ, ਠੋਸਪਣ,
ਪਕਿਆਈ, ਦ੍ਰਿੜ੍ਹਤ; **~ent** ਦ੍ਰਿੜ੍ਹ, ਸਥਿਰ,
ਅਟਲ; ਅਨੁਕੂਲ

consolation ('ਕੌਨਸਅ'ਲੇਇਸ਼ਨ) *n* ਦਿਲਾਸਾ,
ਧਰਵਾਸ, ਧੀਰਜ, ਢਾਰਸ, ਤਸੱਲੀ

console (ਕਅਨ'ਸਅਉਲ) *v* ਦਿਲਾਸਾ ਦੇਣਾ,
ਢਾਰਸ ਦੇਣਾ, ਧੀਰਜ ਬੰਨ੍ਹਾਉਣਾ, ਤਸੱਲੀ ਦੇਣੀ

consolidation (ਕਅਨ'ਸੌਲਿ'ਡੇਇਸ਼ਨ) *n*
ਚੱਕਬੰਦੀ, ਮੁਰੱਬਾਬੰਦੀ

consonant ('ਕੌਨਸਅੰਟ) *a n* ਇਕ-ਸੁਰ,
ਢੁੱਕਦਾ, ਸੁਰੀਲਾ, ਮਧੁਰ; ਵਿਅੰਜਨ

consort ('ਕਨਸੋਟ) *n v* ਪਤੀ ਜਾਂ ਪਤਨੀ,

ਹਮਰਾਹੀ; ਸਾਥੀ ਜਹਾਜ਼

conspicuous (ਕਅਨ'ਸਪਿਕਯੂਅਸ) *a* ਉੱਘਾ,
ਪ੍ਰਤੱਖ, ਪਰਗਟ, ਸਪਸ਼ਟ, ਵਿਅਕਤ

conspiracy (ਕਅਨ'ਸਪਿਰਅਸਿ) *n* ਸਾਜ਼ਸ,
ਸਾਜ਼ਬਾਜ਼

conspire (ਕਅਨ'ਸਪਾਇਆ*) *v* ਸਾਜ਼ਸ ਕਰਨਾ,
ਮਨਸੂਬਾ ਬਣਾਉਣਾ, ਵਿਦਰੋਹ ਕਰਨਾ, ਸੰਮਿਲਤ
ਹੋਣਾ

constable ('ਕਅੰਨਸਟਅਬਲ) *n* ਪੁਲੀਸ ਦਾ
ਸਿਪਾਹੀ, ਕਾਨਸਟੇਬਲ, ਪੁਲਸੀਆ

constant ('ਕੌਨਸਟਅੰਟ) *a n* ਥਿਰ, ਸਥਿਰ,
ਸਥਾਈ, ਪੱਕਾ, ਦ੍ਰਿੜ, ਅਡੋਲ, ਨਿਰੰਤਰ,
ਲਗਾਤਾਰ; ਵਫ਼ਾਦਾਰ; ਸੱਚਾ, ਥਿਰ ਜਾਂ ਸਥਾਈ
ਸੰਖਿਆ (ਰਾਸਿ), ਪੱਕਾ ਨਾਪ; ~ly ਲਗਾਤਾਰ,
ਨਿਰੰਤਰ, ਨਿਤ, ਹਰਦਮ, ਮੁਤਵਾਤਰ

constipation ('ਕੌਨਸਟਿ'ਪੇਇਸ਼ਨ) *n* ਕਬਜ਼ੀ,
ਕਬਜ਼

constituency (ਕਅਨ'ਸਟਿਟਯੂਅੰਸਿ) *a n* ਚੋਣ-
ਖੇਤਰ, ਚੋਣ-ਹਲਕਾ, ਖ਼ਰੀਦਾਰ ਲੋਕ, ਗਾਹਕ-ਵਰਗਾ

constituent (ਕਅਨ'ਸਟਿਯੂਅੰਟ) *a n* ਸੰਘਟਕ;
~d ਸਥਾਪਤ, ਸੰਗਠਤ, ਨਿਯੁਕਤ, ਸੰਸਥਾਪਤ

constitute ('ਕੌਨਸਟਿਟਯੂਟ) *v* ਬਣਾਉਣਾ, ਖੜ੍ਹਾ
ਕਰਨਾ, ਕਾਨੂੰਨੀ ਰੂਪ ਦੇਣਾ, ਸਥਾਪਤ ਕਰਨਾ,
ਵਿਧਾਨਕ ਰੂਪ ਦੇਣਾ, ਸੰਸਥਾਪਨ ਕਰਨਾ

constitution ('ਕੌਨਸਟਿ'ਟਯੂਸ਼ਨ) *n* ਸੰਵਿਧਾਨ,
ਸੰਗਠਨ; ਦਸ਼ਾ; ਪੱਧਤੀ, ਰੀਤ; ਸਰੀਰ ਰਚਨਾ,
ਗਠਨ, ਬਣਾਵਟ; ਅਸੂਲ, ਸਿਧਾਂਤ

constrain (ਕਅਨ'ਸਟਰੇਇਨ) *v* ਰੋਕਣਾ, ਪਾਬੰਦੀ
ਲਾਉਣੀ, ਮਜਬੂਰ ਕਰਨਾ; ~t ਰੁਕਾਵਟ,
ਮਜਬੂਰੀ, ਪਾਬੰਦੀ, ਬੰਦਸ਼, ਨਿਯੰਤਰਨ

constrict (ਕਅਨ'ਸਟਰਿਕਟ) *v* ਸਮੇਟਣਾ,

ਸੁੰਗੋੜਨਾ, ਖਿਚਣਾ, ਦੱਬਣਾ; ਵਲਣਾ; ~ion
ਖਿਚਾਉ, ਦਬਾਅ, ਕਸ, ਸੰਕੀਰਨਤਾ

construct (ਕਅਨ'ਸਟਰਅੱਕਟ) *v* (ਇਮਾਰਤ)
ਉਸਾਰਨਾ, ਰਚਨਾ ਕਰਨਾ, ਨਿਰਮਾਣ ਕਰਨਾ, ਵਾਕ
ਬਣਾਉਣਾ; ਖ਼ਾਨਾ ਖਿਚਣਾ; ~ed ਤਿਆਰ, ਰਚਿਤ,
ਨਿਰਮਤ; ~ion ਉਸਾਰੀ, ਕਰਨ, ਬਣਾਵਟ,
ਨਿਰਮਤ ਵਸਤ; ਸ਼ਬਦ-ਯੋਜਨਾ; ~ive ਉਸਾਰੂ,
ਰਚਨਾਤਮਕ, ਨਿਰਮਾਣਸ਼ੀਲ, ਵਾਸਤਵਿਕ

consult (ਕਅਨ'ਸਅੱਲਟ) *v* ਸੰਮਤੀ ਲੈਣੀ,
ਮਸ਼ਵਰਾ ਲੈਣਾ, ਰਾਇ ਲੈਣੀ, ਸਲਾਹ ਲੈਣੀ,
ਵਿਚਾਰ ਕਰਨੀ; ~ant ਸਲਾਹਕਾਰ; ~ation
ਰਾਇ, ਸਲਾਹ, ਮਸ਼ਵਰਾ, ਸੋਚ-ਵਿਚਾਰ

consume (ਕਅਨ'ਸਯੂਮ) *v* ਖਪਾ ਦੇਣਾ, ਖ਼ਰਚ
ਕਰ ਦੇਣਾ, ਖਪਤ ਕਰਨਾ, ਵਰਤ ਲੈਣਾ,
ਉਡਾਉਣਾ; ~d ਖਪਤ ਕੀਤਾ; ~r ਖਪਤਕਾਰ,
ਉਪਭੋਗਤਾ, ਗ੍ਰਾਹਕ

consuming (ਕਅਨ'ਸਯੂਮਿਙ) *a* ਉਪਭੋਗੀ

consumption (ਕਅਨ'ਸਅੱਮਪਸ਼ਨ) *n* ਖਪਤ,
ਉਪਭੋਗ, ਖਪਾ, ਖ਼ਰਚ; ਉਜਾੜਾ, ਵਿਨਾਸ਼

contact ('ਕੌਨਟੈਕਟ) *n v* ਵਾਹ, ਮੇਲ; ਸੰਪਰਕ,
ਛੋਹ, ਸਬੰਧ, ਵਾਹ ਪੈਨਾ, ਮਿਲਣਾ, ਛੋਹਣਾ, ਪੋਦ
ਚੜ੍ਹਨੀ

contagious (ਕਅਨ'ਟੇਇਜਅਸ) *n* ਛੂਤਕਾਰੀ,
ਲਾਗ ਵਾਲਾ

contain (ਕਅਨ'ਟੇਇਨ) *v* ਸ਼ਾਮਲ ਕਰਨਾ,
ਘੇਰਨਾ, ਰੱਖਣਾ, ਘਿਰੇ ਹੋਣਾ; ਗਰਭਿਤ ਹੋਣਾ;
~er ਡੱਬਾ, ਬਕਸ਼; ~ed ਸ਼ਾਮਲ, ਸੰਮਿਲਤ

contaminate (ਕਅਨ'ਟੈਮਿਨੇਇਟ) *n* ਭ੍ਰਿਸ਼ਟ
ਕਰਨਾ, ਭਿੱਟਣਾ, ਵਿਗਾੜਨਾ, ਗੰਦਾ ਕਰਨਾ,
ਦੂਸ਼ਤ ਕਰਨਾ

contamination (ਕਅਨ'ਟੈਮਿ'ਨੇਇਸ਼ਨ) *n* ਭਿੱਟ,

ਭੂਤ, ਦੂਸ਼ਨ ਬ੍ਰਿਸ਼ਟਤਾ, ਮਿਲਾਵਟ, ਖੋਟ

contemplate (ਕੌਨਟੱਪਲੇਇਟ) *v* ਧਿਆਉਣਾ, ਕਲਪਨਾ ਕਰਨਾ, ਸੋਚਣਾ, ਵਿਚਾਰਨਾ, ਇਰਾਦਾ ਕਰਨਾ, ਇੱਛਾ ਰੱਖਣਾ

contemplation (ਕੌਨਟਅੱਪਲੇਇਸ਼ਨ) *n* ਧਿਆਨ, ਕਲਪਨਾ, ਸੋਚ, ਵਿਚਾਰ

contemplative (ਕੌਨਟਅੱਪਲੇਇਟਿਵ) *a* ਧਿਆਨੀ, ਅੰਤਰ ਧਿਆਨੀ, ਚਿੰਤਨਸ਼ੀਲ, ਸੋਚਵਾਨ, ਵਿਚਾਰਸ਼ੀਲ

contemporary (ਕੌਅਨ'ਟੈਂਪ(ਅ)ਰ(ਅ)ਰਿ) *a* ਸਮਕਾਲੀ, ਸਮਕਾਲੀਨ; ਸਮਕਾਲਕ; ਹਾਲੀ

contempt (ਕਅਨ'ਟੈਂਪਟ) *n* ਘਿਰਣਾ, ਨਫ਼ਰਤ, ਤਿਰਸਕਾਰ, ਅਪਮਾਨ, ਅਵੱਗਿਆ; **~of court** ਹੱਤਕ ਅਦਾਲਤ, ਅਦਾਲਤ ਦਾ ਅਪਮਾਨ; **~ible** ਘਿਰਨਾਯੋਗ, ਤੁੱਛ, ਨੀਚ, ਕੀਂ; **~uous** ਘਿਰਣਾ ਭਰੀ, ਹੱਤਕ ਭਰੀ

contend (ਕਅਨ'ਟੈਂਡ) *v* ਬਹਿਸ ਕਰਨਾ, ਵਾਦ-ਵਿਵਾਦ ਕਰਨਾ, ਸੰਘਰਸ਼ ਕਰਨਾ, ਹੱਥ-ਪੈਰ ਮਾਰਨਾ, ਝਗੜਨਾ, ਝੜਪਣਾ, ਉੱਤਰ ਕਰਨਾ

content (ਕੌਨਟੈਂਟ) *n v* ਤੱਤ, ਅੰਸ਼; (ਪੁਸਤਕ ਆਦਿ ਦਾ) ਵਿਸ਼ਾ ਵਸਤੂ; ਸਮਗਰੀ; ਸਬਰ, ਤ੍ਰਿਪਤੀ, ਸੰਤੁਸ਼ਟੀ; ਸੰਤੋਖੀ, ਸੰਤੁਸ਼ਟ, ਰਾਜੀ, ਤ੍ਰਿਪਤ ਕਰਨਾ, ਰਜਾਣਾ, ਰੀਝਾਉਣਾ, ਰਜ਼ਾਮੰਦ ਕਰਨਾ; **table of ~s** ਵਿਸ਼ੇ-ਸੂਚੀ; **~ed** ਤ੍ਰਿਪਤ, ਸੰਤੁਸ਼ਟ, ਰੱਜਿਆ, ਪ੍ਰਸੰਨ

contention (ਕਅਨ'ਟੈਨਸ਼ਨ) *n* ਮੁਕਾਬਲਾ, ਟਾਕਰਾ; ਵਾਦ-ਵਿਵਾਦ, ਵਿਵਾਦਗ੍ਰਸਤ ਵਿਸ਼ਾ; ਤਕਰਾਰ, ਰੇੜਕਾ

contentious (ਕਅਨ'ਟੈਨੱਸ਼ਅਸ) *a* ਵਿਵਾਦਪੂਰਨ, ਝਗੜੇ ਭਰਿਆ

contest (ਕੌਨਟੈਸਟ, ਕਅਨ'ਟੈਸੱਟ) *n v* ਸੰਘਰਸ਼,

ਮੁਕਾਬਲਾ, ਦਵੰਦ, ਪ੍ਰਤੀਯੋਗਤਾ, ਟਾਕਰਾ, ਵਿਵਾਦ; ਝਗੜਾ; ਜੱਦੋ-ਜਹਿਦ ਕਰਨਾ, ਵਿਰੋਧ ਕਰਨਾ, ਬਹਿਸ ਕਰਨਾ, ਝਗੜਨਾ; **~ant** ਪ੍ਰਤੀਯੋਗੀ, ਵਿਵਾਦ ਕਰਨ ਵਾਲਾ

context (ਕੌਨਟੈਕਸਟ) *n* ਪ੍ਰਸੰਗ, ਵਿਸ਼ਾ, ਸੰਦਰਭ

contextual (ਕਅਨ'ਟੈਕਸਟਯੂਅਲ) *a* ਸੰਬਧਤ, ਪ੍ਰਸੰਗ ਸਬੰਧੀ

contiguity ('ਕੰਨਟਿ'ਗਯੂਅਟਿ) *n* ਨਿਕਟਤਾ, ਮੇਲ, ਲਗਾਉ, ਰਾਬਤਾ

contiguous (ਕਅਨ'ਟਿਗਯੂਅਸ) *a* ਨੇੜੇ ਦਾ, ਨਿਕਟਵਰਤੀ, ਜੁੜਿਆ

contingent (ਕਅਨ'ਟਿਨਜਅੰਟ) *a* ਸਬੰਧੀ, ਇਤਫ਼ਾਕੀਆ, ਅਚਾਨਕ

continual (ਕਅਨ'ਟਿਨਯੂਅਲ) *a* ਜਾਰੀ, ਲਗਾਤਾਰ, ਅਖੰਡ, ਨਿਰੰਤਰ; **~ly** ਲਗਾਤਾਰ, ਇਕ ਰਸ, ਹਰ ਸਮੇਂ, ਨਿਰੰਤਰ

continuance (ਕਅਨ'ਟਿਨਯੂਅੰਸ) *n* ਲਗਾਤਾਰਤਾ, ਨਿਰੰਤਰਤਾ; ਸਿਲਸਲਾ, ਲੜੀ

continuation (ਕਅਨ'ਟਿਨਯੂ'ਏਇਸ਼ਨ) *n* ਲਗਾਤਾਰਤਾ, ਲੜੀਬੱਧਤਾ, ਪੁਨਰ-ਆਰੰਭ

continue (ਕਅਨ'ਟਿਨਯੂ) *v* ਜਾਰੀ ਰੱਖਣਾ, ਜਾਰੀ ਰਹਿਆ, ਚਾਲੂ ਰੱਖਣਾ, ਰੋਕ ਰੱਖਣਾ, ਠਹਿਰਾਉਣਾ; **~d** ਲਗਾਤਾਰ, ਨਿਰੰਤਰ

continuity (ਕੌਨਟਿ'ਨਯੂਅਟਿ) *n* ਲਗਾਤਾਰਤਾ, ਅਖੰਡਤਾ, ਨਿਰੰਤਰਤਾ, ਰਵਾਨੀ

continuous (ਕਅਨ'ਟਿਨਯੂਅਸ) *adv* ਲਗਾਤਾਰ, ਅਟੁੱਟ, ਅਖੰਡ, ਨਿਰੰਤਰ, ਨਿਰਵਿਘਨ; **~ly** ਲਗਾਤਾਰ, ਅਟੁੱਟ ਤਰੀਕੇ ਨਾਲ, ਸਦਾ, ਨਿਰੰਤਰ

contraception (ਕੌਨਟਰਾਅ'ਸੈਪੱਸ਼ਨ) *n* ਗਰਭ ਰੋਕ, ਗਰਭ ਨਿਰੋਧ

contraceptive ('ਕੌਨਟਰਾ'ਸੈਪਟਿਵ) n
ਗਰਭ ਰੋਕੂ, ਗਰਭ ਨਿਰੋਧਕ

contract (ਕੌਨਟਰੈਕਟ, ਕਾਨ'ਟਰੈਕਟ) n v
ਠੇਕਾ, ਇਕਰਾਰਨਾਮਾ, ਇਕਰਾਰ; ਠੇਕਾ ਦੇਣਾ ਜਾਂ
ਲੈਣਾ; ਸੁੰਗੜਨਾ, ਸਿਮਟਣਾ, ਸੰਕੋਚ ਕਰਨਾ,
ਸਕੁੰਚਿਤ ਕਰਨਾ; ਮਰੋੜਨਾ; ~ion ਸੰਕੋਚ,
ਸੁੰਗੇੜ, ਸੁੰਗੜਨ, ਸੁੰਗੜਾਉ; ਸੰਖੇਪ; ਠੇਕਾ ਕਰਨ
ਦੀ ਕਿਰਿਆ; ਸੰਕੀਰਣਤਾ; ਖਿਚੰ, ਕਸ; ~or
ਠੇਕੇਦਾਰ, ਸੰਖਿਪਤ ਕਰਨ ਵਾਲਾ

contradict (ਕੌਨਟਰਾ'ਡ੍ਰਿਕਟ) v ਖੰਡਨ ਕਰਨਾ,
ਰੱਦ ਕਰਨਾ, ਤਰਦੀਦ ਕਰਨੀ, ਮੁਕਰੱਨਾ, ਵਿਰੁੱਧ
ਆਖਣਾ; ~ion ਖੰਡਨ, ਇਨਕਾਰ, ਭਾਨੀ,
ਵਿਰੋਧ, ਤਰਦੀਦ; ~ory ਖੰਡਨਾਤਮਕ, ਅੰਤਰ-
ਵਿਰੋਧੀ, ਪਰਸਪਰ ਵਿਰੁੱਧ, ਅਸੰਗਤ, ਉਲਟਾ

contrary (ਕੌਂਟਰਾਰਿ, ਕਾਂ'ਟਰੇਰਿ) n a
ਪ੍ਰਤੀਕੂਲਤਾ, ਵਿਰੋਧ, ਵਿਪੱਖ, ਵਿਪਰੀਤਤਾ,
ਉਲਟਾਪਣ; ਉਲਟਾ, ਪ੍ਰਤੀਕੂਲ, ਵਿਰੋਧੀ,
ਅਸੰਗਤ

contrast (ਕੌਂਟਰਾਸਟ, ਕਾਂ'ਟਰਾਸਟ) n v
ਟਾਕਰਾ, ਅੰਤਰ, ਭਿੰਨਤਾ, ਫ਼ਰਕ, ਭਿੰਨ-ਭੇਦ;
ਅੰਤਰ ਹੋਣਾ, ਭਿੰਨਤਾ ਦੱਸਣੀ, ਵਖਰਾਉਣ;
~ing ਵਿਰੋਧੀ, ਵਿਖਮ

contravene ('ਕੌਨਟਰਾ'ਵੀਨ) v ਹੁਕਮ ਅਦੂਲੀ
ਕਰਨੀ, ਤੋੜਨਾ; ਖੰਡਨ ਕਰਨਾ, ਮੱਤ-ਭੇਦ ਹੋਣਾ;
ਵਿਵਾਦ ਕਰਨਾ, ਟੇਕਣਾ

contravening (ਕੌਂਟਰਾ'ਵੀਨਿਙ) a ਪਰਪਸਪਰ
ਵਿਰੋਧੀ

contribute (ਕਾਂ'ਟਰਿਬਯੂਟ) v ਚੰਦਾ ਦੇਣਾ, ਹਿੱਸਾ
ਪਾਉਣਾ, (ਪੱਤਰ-ਪੱਤਰਕਾਵਾਂ ਨੂੰ) ਲੇਖ ਭੇਜਣਾ,
ਪ੍ਰਦਾਨ ਕਰਨਾ

contribution (ਕਾਂ'ਟਰਿਬਯੂਸ਼ਨ) n ਚੰਦਾ, ਲੇਖ,

ਸਹਾਇਤਾ, ਜਜ਼ੀਆ, ਮਸੂਲ, ਯੋਗ-ਦਾਨ

contributor (ਕਾਂ'ਟਰਿਬਯੂਟ*) n ਲੇਖ ਭੇਜਣ
ਵਾਲਾ, ਯੋਗਦਾਨੀ, ਸਹਾਇਕ

control (ਕਾਨ'ਟਰਅਉਲ) n v ਕੰਟਰੋਲ, ਕਾਬੂ,
ਵਸ, ਇਖਤਿਆਰ, ਨਿਗਰਾਨੀ, ਸ਼ਾਸਨ, ਜਬਤ;
ਕਾਬੂ ਵਿਚ ਰੱਖਣਾ, ਬੰਨ੍ਹਣਾ, ਰੋਕਣਾ, ਸੰਜਮ ਕਰਨਾ,
ਵੱਸ ਵਿਚ ਕਰਨਾ; ~ler ਕੰਟਰੋਲਰ, ਨਾਜ਼ਰ

controversial (ਕੌਂਟਰਾ'ਵ੍ਯਃਸ਼ਲ) a
ਵਿਵਾਦਪੂਰਨ, ਬਹਿਸ-ਗੋਚਰਾ, ਤਕਰਾਰ ਵਾਲਾ,
ਵਿਵਾਦਗ੍ਰਸਤ

controversy (ਕੌਂਟਰਅਵ੍ਯਃਸਿ) n ਝਗੜਾ,
ਵਿਵਾਦ, ਚਰਚਾ, ਵਾਦ-ਵਿਵਾਦ, ਪ੍ਰਤੀਵਾਦ

convene (ਕਾਨ'ਵੀਨ) v ਸਮਾਗਮ ਬੁਲਾਉਣਾ,
ਇਕੱਠ ਕਰਨਾ, ਇਕੱਠੇ ਹੋਣਾ, ਜਲਸਾ ਕਰਨਾ,
ਸੱਦਣਾ; ~d ਬੁਲਾਇਆ ਗਿਆ, ਆਯੋਜਤ; ~r
ਆਯੋਜਕ, ਸਮਾਗਮਕਰਤਾ, ਸੰਯੋਜਕ

convenience (ਕਾਨ'ਵੀਨਯਅੰਸ) n ਸਹੂਲਤ,
ਆਰਾਮ, ਸੌਖ, ਲਾਭ, ਸੁੱਖ, ਸੁਵਿਧਾ

convenient (ਕਾਨ'ਵੀਨਯਅੰਟ) a ਆਰਾਮਦੇਹ,
ਸਰਲ, ਸੌਖਾ, ਲਾਹੇਵੰਦ; ਸੁਖਾਲਾ, ਅਨੁਕੂਲ,
ਉਚਿਤ, ਸੁਵਿਧਾਜਨਕ

convention (ਕਾਨ'ਵੈਨਸ਼ਨ) n ਸਮਾਗਮ,
ਸੰਮੇਲਨ, ਸਭਾ, ਸੰਸਦ; ਸਮਝੌਤਾ, ਦਸਤੂਰ, ਪ੍ਰਥਾ,
ਮਰਯਾਦਾ, ਸੰਧੀ, ਜਨ-ਸੰਮਤੀ, ਇਕਰਾਰਨਾਮਾ

conventional (ਕਾਨ'ਵੈਨਸ਼ਅਨਲ) a ਰਸਮੀ,
ਰਿਵਾਜੀ, ਰਵਾਇਤੀ, ਰੀਤਵਾਦੀ, ਰੂੜੀਵਾਦੀ,
ਮਰਯਾਦਾ-ਪੂਰਨ, ਪਰੰਪਰਾਗਤ; ~ly ਰੀਤੀ
ਅਨੁਸਾਰ, ਪ੍ਰਥਾ ਅਨੁਸਾਰ

conversant (ਕਾਨਨ'ਵ੍ਯਃਸਅੰਟ) a ਜਾਣਕਾਰ,
ਵਾਕਫ਼, ਜਾਣੂ, ਵਾਕਫ਼ਕਾਰ, ਪਰਿਚਿਤ, ਨਿਪੁੰਨ

conversation (ਕੌਨਵ੍ਯਾ'ਸੋਇਸ਼ਨ) n

ਵਾਰਤਾਲਾਪ, ਗੱਲਬਾਤ, ਗੱਲ-ਕੱਥ, ਗੁਫ਼ਤਗੂ

converse (ਕਅਨ'ਵ੍ਅਃਸ, ਕੈਨਵਅਃਸ) *v n a* ਗੱਲਾਂ ਕਰਨੀਆਂ, ਵਾਰਤਾਲਾਪ ਕਰਨੀ; ਉਲਟਾ ਮਸਲਾ, ਪਲਟਾ, ਉਲਟ, ਉਲਟਾ, ਸੁਧਾ, ਪੁੱਠਾ, ਵਿਪਰੀਤ

conversion (ਕਅਨ'ਵ੍ਅਃਸ਼ਨ) *n* ਰੂਪਾਂਤਰਣ, ਧਰਮ ਦੀ ਬਦਲੀ, ਧਰਮ-ਪਰਿਵਰਤਨ, ਪਰਿਵਰਤਨ

convert (ਕੰਨਵ੍ਅਃਟ, ਕਅਨ'ਵਅਃਟ) *n v* ਨਵ-ਧਰਮੀ, ਧਰਮ ਬਦਲਾਉਣਾ, ਧਰਮ ਵਿਚ ਸ਼ਾਮਲ ਕਰਨ; (ਵਿਚ) ਬਦਲਨਾ; ~**ed** ਪਰਿਵਰਤਤ, ਰੂਪਾਂਤਰਤ

convex (ਕੰਨ'ਵ੍ਵੈਕਸ) *a* ਉਭਰਿਆ, ਕੁੱਬਾ, ਕੁਬੰਧਰ, ਉਤੱਲ; ਉਤਾਰ, ਕੁੱਬ

convey (ਕਅਨ'ਵ੍ਏ) *v* ਲੈ ਜਾਣਾ, ਅਪੜਾ ਦੇਣਾ; ਪਹੁੰਚਾਉਣਾ, ਕਿਸੇ ਦੇ ਹੱਥੀਂ ਘੱਲਣਾ; ਹੱਥ ਬਦਲਣ; ~**ance** ਗੱਡੀ, ਢੁਆਈ, ਵਾਹਣ

convict (ਕਅਨ'ਵ੍ਵਿਕਟ, ਕੰਨਵ੍ਵਿਕਟ) *v n* ਦੋਸ਼ੀ ਠਹਿਰਾਉਣਾ, ਸਜ਼ਾ ਸੁਣਾਉਣਾ; ਮੁਜਰਮ, ਕਸੂਰਵਾਰ, ਅਪਰਾਧੀ, ਦੋਸ਼ੀ

convince (ਕਅਨ'ਵ੍ਵਿੰਸ) *v* ਨਿਸ਼ਚਾ ਕਰਵਾਉਣਾ, ਮਨਾਉਣਾ, ਮੰਨ ਲੈਣਾ

convincible (ਕਅਨ'ਵ੍ਵਿੰਸਅਬਲ) *a* ਯਕੀਨ ਕਰਨ ਲਈ ਤਿਆਰ, ਮੰਨ ਲੈਣ ਵਾਲਾ, ਮੰਨਣਯੋਗ

convincing (ਕਅਨ'ਵ੍ਵਿੰਸਿਙ) *a* ਮੰਨਣਯੋਗ, ਯਕੀਨੀ, ਵਿਸ਼ਵਾਸਮਈ

convocation (ਕੰਨਵ੍ਅ(ਓ)ਕੇਇਸ਼ਨ) *n* ਦੀਖਿਆਂਤ-ਸਮਾਰੋਹ, ਪਾਦਰੀਆਂ ਦਾ ਜਲਸਾ; ਸੱਦਾ, ਸਮਾਗਮ, ਸੰਮੇਲਨ, ਸਮਾਰੋਹ

convoy ('ਕੰਨਵ੍ਓਇ) *n v* ਵਪਾਰਕ ਬੇੜਾ, ਰੱਖਿਅਕ

ਬੇੜਾ; ਫ਼ੌਜੀ ਦਸਤਾ ਜਾਂ ਰਸਦ ਦੇ ਸਾਮਾਨ ਦਾ ਕਾਫ਼ਲਾ; ਨਿਗਰਾਨੀ; ਰੱਖਿਆ ਵਾਸਤੇ ਨਾਲ ਜਾਣਾ, ਪਰਾਹੁਣਿਆਂ ਦੀ ਅਗਵਾਈ ਕਰਨੀ

cook (ਕੁਕ) *v n* ਰੋਟੀ ਪਕਾਉਣੀ, ਭੋਜਨ ਬਣਾਉਣਾ, ਪੱਕਣਾ, ਪਕਾਉਣਾ; ਮਨਘੜਤ ਗੱਲ ਕਰਨੀ; ਰਸੋਈਆਂ, ਲਾਂਗਰੀ, ਬਾਵਰਚੀ

cool (ਕੂਲ) *n a v* ਠੰਢ, ਸੀਤਲਤਾ; ਠੰਢਾ, ਠਰੂੰਮੇ ਵਾਲਾ, ਸ਼ਾਂਤ, ਮੰਦ, ਉਤਸਾਹਹੀਣ, ਉਦਾਸੀਨ, ਸੀਤਲ, ਸੀਤ; ਠੰਢਾ ਹੋਣਾ, ਧੀਮਾ ਕਰਨਾ, ਠਰੂੰਮਾ ਦੇਣਾ, ਠਰੂੰਮਾ ਰੱਖਣਾ; ~**headed** ਸ਼ਾਂਤ, ਧੀਰਜਵਾਨ, ਠੰਢੇ ਦਿਲ ਵਾਲਾ; ~**ness** ਠੰਢਕ, ਸੀਤਲਤਾ

coolie (ਕੂਲਿ) *n* ਪਾਂਡੀ, ਕੁਲੀ, ਪੱਲੇਦਾਰ

co-operate (ਕਅਓ'ਔਪਅਰੇਇਟ) *v* ਮਿਲ ਕੇ ਕੰਮ ਕਰਨਾ, ਸਹਿਕਾਰੀ ਹੋਣਾ, ਸਹਿਯੋਗ ਦੇਣਾ, ਮਿਲਵਰਤਨ ਕਰਨੀ

co-operation (ਕਅਓ'ਔਪਅ'ਰੇਇਸ਼ਨ) *n* ਮਿਲਵਰਤਨ, ਸਹਿਕਰਤਾ, ਸਹਿਯੋਗ, ਮੇਲ-ਮਿਲਾਪ

co-operative (ਕਅਓ'ਔਪ(ਅ)ਰਅਟਿਵ੍) *a* ਸਹਿਕਾਰੀ, ਸਹਿਯੋਗੀ; ~**bank** ਸਹਿਕਾਰੀ ਬੈਂਕ, ਜ਼ਿੰਮੀਦਾਰਾ ਬੈਂਕ

co-opt (ਕਅਓ'ਔਪਟ) *v* ਨਾਮਜ਼ਦ ਕਰਨਾ, ਨਿਯੁਕਤ ਕਰਨਾ, ਨਾਲ ਰਲਾ ਲੈਣਾ, ਸੰਯੁਕਤ ਕਰਨਾ; ~**ed** ਨਿਯੁਕਤ, ਜੋੜਿਆ, ਨਾਮਜ਼ਦ ਕੀਤਾ ਹੋਇਆ

co-ordinate (ਕਅਓ'ਓਡਨਅਟ, ਕਅਓ'ਓਡਅਨਅਟ, ਕਅਓ'ਓਡਿਨੇਇਟ) *a n v* ਸਮਾਨ, ਤੁਲ ਬਰਾਬਰ; ਇਕਸਾਰ; ਉਪਵਾਕ; ਸਮਾਨ ਕਰਨਾ, ਬਰਾਬਰ ਕਰ ਦੇਣਾ; ਇਕਸਾਰ ਕਰਨਾ, ਅਨੁਸਾਰਨਾ

co-ordination (ਕਅਓ'ਓਡਿ'ਨੇਇਸ਼ਨ) *n* ਤਾਲ-

ਮੇਲ, ਅਨੁਸਰਨ, ਇਕਸਾਰਤਾ, ਮੇਲ

co-ordinator (ਕਅਉ'ਉਡਨੇਇਟਅ*) *n* ਸੰਯੋਜਕ, ਤਾਲਮੇਲ ਕਰਨ ਵਾਲਾ

copper (ਕੌਪਅ*) *n a* ਤਾਂਬਾ; ਪੈਸਾ, ਪੁਲਸੀਆ; **~smith** ਠਠਿਆਰ

copra (ਕੌਪਰਅ) *n* ਖੋਪਾ

copulate (ਕੌਪਯੁਲੇਇਟ) *v* ਸੰਭੋਗ ਕਰਨਾ, ਮੈਥੁਨ ਕਰਨਾ, ਸਹਿਵਾਸ ਕਰਨਾ

copulation (ਕੌਪਯੁ'ਲੇਇਸਨ) *n* ਸੰਜੋਗ, ਜੋੜ-ਮੇਲ, ਸੰਭੋਗ; ਮੈਥੁਨ, ਸਹਿਵਾਸ

copy (ਕੌਪਿ) *n v* ਉਤਾਰਾ, ਕਾਪੀ, ਨਕਲ, ਪਰਤ; ਉਤਾਰਨਾ, ਉਤਾਰਾ ਲਾਹੁਣਾ, ਕਾਪੀ ਕਰਨੀ, ਨਕਲ ਉਤਾਰਨੀ, ਪਰਤ ਤਿਆਰ ਕਰਨੀ, ਨਕਲ ਮਾਰਨੀ; **~right** ਉਤਾਰਾ ਅਧਿਕਾਰ, ਕਾਪੀਰਾਈਟ; **~ist** ਨਕਲ-ਨਵੀਸ, ਨਕਲ-ਉਤਾਰ; ਨਕਲਚੀ

coquetry (ਕੌਕਿਟਰਿ) *n* ਨਖ਼ਰਾ, ਨਖ਼ਰੇਬਾਜ਼ੀ, ਚੁਹਲ

coquette (ਕੌ'ਕੈਟ) *n* ਨਖ਼ਰੇਬਾਜ਼, ਚੌਂਚਲੇਬਾਜ਼, ਅਲਬੇਲਾ, ਬਾਂਕਾ

coral (ਕੌਰ(ਅ)ਲ) *n* ਮੂੰਗਾ

cord (ਕੋਡ) *n v* ਰੱਸੀ, ਡੋਰੀ, ਰੱਸਾ, ਪੱਠਾ; ਤੜ ਬੰਨ੍ਹਣਾ, ਜਕੜਨਾ

cordial (ਕੋਡਜਅਲ) *a n* ਦਿਲੀ, ਹਾਰਦਿਕ; ਨਿਸ਼ਕਪਟ, ਦੋਸਤਾਨਾ, ਸਨੇਹਪੂਰਨ, ਨਿੱਘ; **~ly** ਦਿਲੋਂ, ਪਰੇਮ ਨਾਲ, ਸੁਹਿਰਦਤਾ ਨਾਲ

core (ਕੋ*) *n v* ਗਿਰੀ, ਮਗ਼ਜ਼, ਗੁੱਦਾ, ਗੁਲੀ, ਸਾਰ, ਤੱਤ, ਗੁੱਦਾ ਕੱਢਣਾ

co-relation (ਕਅਉਰਿ'ਲੇਇਸ਼ਨ) *n* ਆਪਸੀ ਸਬੰਧ, ਪਰਸਪਰ ਸਬੰਧ

cork (ਕੋਕ) *n a v* ਕਾਕ, ਡੱਟ; ਕਾਕ ਦਾ, ਕਾਕ ਤੋਂ ਬਣਿਆ; ਕਾਕ ਲਾਉਣਾ, ਡੱਟ ਦੇਣਾ, ਟੇਢਾ ਚੱਲਣਾ, ਰੋਕਣਾ

corn (ਕੋਨ) *n v* ਦਾਣੇ, ਅੰਨ, ਅਨਾਜ, (US) ਮੱਕੀ; ਨਮਕ ਛਿੜਕਨਾ; **~flour** (ਮੱਕੀ ਆਦਿ ਦਾ) ਆਟਾ

corner (ਕੋ*ਨਅ*) *n v* ਨੁੱਕਰ, ਗੁੱਠ, ਖੂੰਜਾ, ਕੋਨਾ, ਗੋਸ਼ਾ, ਗੁਪਤ ਥਾਂ; ਨੁੱਕਰਾਂ ਕੱਢਣੀਆਂ, ਘੇਰ ਲੈਣਾ; **~boy** ਅਵਾਰਾ, ਲੋਫਰ

coronation (ਕੌਰਅ'ਨੇਇਸ਼ਨ) *n* ਰਾਜ ਤਿਲਕ, ਤਖਤ ਨਸ਼ੀਨੀ, ਤਾਜਪੋਸ਼ੀ ਦੀ ਰਸਮ

corporation (ਕੋ*ਪਅ'ਰੇਇਸ਼ਨ) *n* ਨਿਗਮ, ਮਹਾਂ-ਨਗਰ ਸਭਾ, ਕਾਰਪੋਰੇਸ਼ਨ; **~municipal** ਨਗਰਪਾਲਕਾ, ਨਿਗਮ

corps (ਕੋ*) *n* ਪਲਟਨ, ਫ਼ੌਜ ਦਾ ਦਸਤਾ, ਕੋਰ

corpse (ਕੋ*ਪਸ) *n* ਲੋਥ, ਲਾਸ਼, ਮਿਰਤਕ ਸਰੀਰ

corpus (ਕੋ*ਪਅਸ) *n* ਸਰੀਰ, ਦੇਹ, ਪੁਸਤਕਾਂ ਦਾ ਸੰਗ੍ਰਹ

correct (ਕਅ'ਰੇਕੱਟ) *a v* ਸਹੀ, ਸਿੱਧ, ਠੀਕ, ਢੁੱਕਵਾਂ, ਉਚਿਤ, ਸ਼ੁੱਧ; ਸਹੀ ਕਰਨਾ, ਠੀਕ ਕਰਨਾ, ਯੋਗ ਬਣਾਉਣਾ, ਸੁਆਰਨਾ, ਸੁਧਾਰਨਾ; **~ion** ਸੁਧਾਈ, ਸੋਧ, ਸੰਸ਼ੋਧਨ, ਦਰੁੱਸਤੀ, ਸੁਧਾਰ, ਝਿੜਕ

correlate ('ਕੌਰਅਲੇਇਟ) *v* ਸਹਿ-ਸਬੰਧਤ ਹੋਣਾ, ਪਰਸਪਰ ਸਬੰਧ ਕਾਇਮ ਕਰਨਾ, ਦੋ ਚੀਜ਼ਾਂ ਦਾ ਇਕ ਦੂਜੇ ਦੇ ਸਹਾਰੇ ਹੋਣਾ

correlation ('ਕੌਰਅ'ਲੇਇਸ਼ਨ) *n* ਪਰਸਪਰ ਸਬੰਧ, ਆਪਸੀ ਮੇਲ, ਸਹਿ-ਸਬੰਧ

correspond ('ਕੌਰਿ'ਸਪੌਂਡ) *v* ਅਨੁਸਾਰੀ ਹੋਣਾ, ਜੋੜ ਹੋਣਾ, ਬਰਾਬਰ ਹੋਣਾ; ਚਿੱਠੀ ਪੱਤਰ ਲਿਖਣਾ; **~ence** ਅਨੁਸਰਣ; ਲਿਖਤ-ਪੜ੍ਹਤ, ਪੱਤਰ ਵਿਹਾਰ, ਚਿੱਠੀ ਚਪੱਠੀ; **~ent** ਅਨੁਸਾਰੀ; ਪੱਤਰ-ਪਰੇਰਕ; ਨਾਮਾਨਿਗਾਰ, ਸੰਵਾਦਦਾਤਾ; ਆੜ੍ਹਤੀਆ

corrigendum ('ਕੌਰਿ'ਜੈਂਡਅਮ) *n* ਸ਼ੁੱਧੀ ਸੂਚੀ;

ਸੁੱਧੀ ਪੱਤਰ, ਸੰਸ਼ੋਧਨ, ਸੁਧਾਰ

corroborate (ਕਅੱਰੌਬਅਰੇਇਟ) *v* ਪ੍ਰੋੜ੍ਹਤਾ ਕਰਨੀ, ਪੱਕਾ ਕਰਨਾ, ਤਸਦੀਕ ਕਰਨੀ, ਤਾਈਦ ਕਰਨੀ, ਹਾਮੀ ਭਰਨੀ

corroborator (ਕਅੱਰੌਬਅਰੇਇਟਅ*) *n* ਪੁਸ਼ਟੀਕਾਰ, ਪੁਸ਼ਟੀ ਕਰਨ ਵਾਲਾ, ਸਾਖੀ, ਸਮਰਥਕ

corrupt (ਕਅੱਰਅੱਪਟ) *a* ਵੱਢੀ-ਖੋਰ, ਹਰਾਮ-ਖੋਰ, ਖੋਟਾ, ਮਾੜਾ; ਰਿਸ਼ਵਤਖੋਰ, ਬਦਕਾਰ; ਵੱਢੀ ਦੇਣੀ; ਵਿਗਾੜਨ, ਖਰਾਬ ਹੋਣਾ, ਢੁਕਣਾ; ~**ion** ਵੱਢੀਖੋਰੀ, ਹਰਾਮਖੋਰੀ, ਖ਼ਰਾਬੀ, ਰਿਸ਼ਵਤ ਖੋਰੀ; ਅਪਭ੍ਰਸ਼ਟ ਸ਼ਬਦ

cortege (ਕੋਂਟਿਏਜ਼) *n* ਨੌਕਰ-ਚਾਕਰ, ਅਮਲਾ-ਫੈਲਾ

cosmetic (ਕੋਜ਼ਮੈਟਿਕ) *a n* ਸ਼ੋਭਾਜਨਕ, ਸ਼ਿੰਗਾਰ ਪੂਰਨ

cosmic (ਕੋਜ਼ਮਿਕ) *a* ਬ੍ਰਹਿਮੰਡੀ

cosmonaut (ਕੋਜ਼ਮਅਨੌਟ) *n* ਪੁਲਾੜ ਯਾਤਰੀ

cosmopolitan (ਕੋਜ਼ਮਅੱਪੌਲਿਟ(ਅ)ਨ) *n* ਵਿਸ਼ਵਪ੍ਰੇਮੀ, ਵਿਸ਼ਵ ਨਾਗਰਿਕ

cosmos (ਕੋਜ਼ਮੌਸ) *n* ਬ੍ਰਹਿਮੰਡ, ਸੰਸਾਰ, ਸ੍ਰਿਸ਼ਟੀ, ਵਿਆਪਕਤਾ

cost (ਕੋਸਟ) *n v* ਮੁੱਲ, ਲਾਗਤ, ਦਾਮ, ਕੀਮਤ, ਖ਼ਰਚ; ਮੁੱਲ ਤਾਰਨਾ, ਪੈਸੇ ਖ਼ਰਚ ਕਰਨੇ, ਮੁੱਲ ਕਰਾਉਣਾ, ਕੀਮਤ ਨਿਸ਼ਚਤ ਕਰਨੀ; ~**ac-countant** ਲਾਗਤ-ਲੇਖਾਕਾਰ, ਮੁਨੀਮ, ਗਾਟਕ; ~**book** ਖਾਣ-ਖਾਤਾ, ਖਦਾਨ-ਖਾਤਾ; **at the ~ of** ਨੁਕਸਾਨ ਸਹਿ ਕੇ; **at all ~s** ਹਰ ਹਾਲਤ ਵਿਚ; ~**less** ਅਟਮੁੱਲਾ, ਮੁਫ਼ਤ; ~**ly** ਬਹੁਮੁੱਲਾ, ਕੀਮਤੀ, ਵਡਮੁੱਲਾ, ਮਹਿੰਗਾ

cosy (ਕਅਉਜ਼ਿ) *a n* ਸੁੱਖਦਾਈ (ਥਾਂ), ਨਿੱਘਾ,

ਆਰਾਮ ਦੇਹ; ਸਨੇਹਪੂਰਨ

cot (ਕੋਟ) *n* ਮੰਜਾ, ਮੰਜੀ, ਬੱਚਿਆਂ ਦਾ ਝੂਲਾ, ਖਟੋਲਾ

coterie (ਕਅਉਟਰਿ) *n* ਜੁੰਡਲੀ, ਚੰਡਾਲ-ਚੌਕੜੀ, ਟੋਲਾ

cottage (ਕੋਟਿਜ) *n* ਕੁੱਟੀ, ਕੁਟੀਆ, ਛੱਪਰ, ਝੌਂਪੜੀ, ਛੋਟਾ ਘਰ, ਪੇਂਡੂ ਮਕਾਨ

cotton (ਕੋਟਨ) *n v* ਰੂੰ, ਫੰਬਾ, ਕਪਾਹ, ਸੂਤ, ਧਾਗਾ, ਸੂਤੀ ਧਾਗਾ, ਸੂਤੀ ਕੱਪੜ; ਸੰਮਤੀ ਹੋਣੀ, ਸੁਰਮੇਲ ਹੋਣਾ, ਰਾਇ ਮਿਲਣੀ; ~**cake** ਖਲ (ਵੜੇਵਿਆਂ ਦੀ); ~**yarn** ਧਾਗਾ

cough (ਕੋਫ਼) *n v* ਖੰਘ, ਖਾਂਸੀ; ਖੰਘਾਰ; ਖੰਘਣਾ, ਖੰਘੂਰਾ ਮਾਰਨਾ, ਖੰਘਾਰਨਾ, ਖਉਂ ਖਉਂ ਕਰਨਾ

council (ਕਾਉਂਸਲ) *n* ਕੌਂਸਲ, ਸਭਾ, ਪਰਿਸ਼ਦ, ਕਮੇਟੀ, ਸਮਿਤੀ

counsel (ਕਾਉਂਸਲ) *n* ਮਸ਼ਵਰਾ, ਸਲਾਹ; ਕਾਨੂੰਨੀ ਸਲਾਹਕਾਰ, ਵਕੀਲ; ਸਲਾਹ ਦੇਣਾ, ਮਸ਼ਵਰਾ ਦੇਣਾ, ਰਾਇ ਦੇਣਾ, ਸਮਝਾਉਣਾ; ~**lor** ਸਲਾਹਕਾਰ, ਉਪਦੇਸ਼ਕ, ਵਕੀਲ

count (ਕਾਉਂਟ) *n v* ਗਿਣਤੀ, ਗਣਨਾ; ਸੰਖਿਆ, ਤਾਦਾਦ; ਕੁੱਲ ਜੋੜ, ਪੂਰਨ ਸੰਖਿਆ; ਲੇਖਾ, ਹਿਸਾਬ; ਸ਼ੁਮਾਰੀ; ~**less** ਅਣਗਿਣਤ; ਅਸੰਖ, ਸੰਖਿਆਤੀਤ, ਬੇਹਿਸਾਬ, ਬੇਸ਼ੁਮਾਰ; ਗਿਣਨਾ, ਹਿਸਾਬ ਕਰਨਾ, ਹਿਸਾਬ ਲਗਾਉਣਾ ਗਿਣਤੀ ਕਰਨਾ, ਸ਼ੁਮਾਰ ਕਰਨਾ, ਸੋਚਣਾ, ਵਿਚਾਰਨਾ, ਖ਼ਿਆਲ ਕਰਨਾ

counter (ਕਾਉਂਟ*) *n a v* (ਬੈਂਕ, ਦੁਕਾਨ ਆਦਿ ਦਾ) ਕਾਉਂਟਰ; ਜੁੱਤੀ ਦੀ ਅੱਡੀ; ਗਿਣਨ ਵਾਲਾ; ਵਿਪਰੀਤ, ਉਲਟਾ, ਪ੍ਰਤੀਕੂਲ, ਵਿਰੋਧੀ; ਦੋਹਰਾ; ਵਿਰੋਧ ਕਰਨਾ; ਰੱਦ ਕਰਨਾ, ਰੋਕਣਾ; ਵਿਪਰੀਤ ਚਲਣਾ; ~**action** ਰੋਕ, ਰੁਕਾਵਟ, ਵਿਰੋਧ;

~attack ਜਵਾਬੀ ਹਮਲਾ; ~sign ਪ੍ਰਤੀਪੁਸ਼ਟੀ ਕਰਨਾ

country ('ਕੰਟਰਿ) *n* ਦੇਸ਼, ਮੁਲਕ, ਵਤਨ; ਰਾਸ਼ਟਰ, ਪਿੰਡ, ਦੇਹਾਤੀ ਖੇਤਰ; ~side ਪਿੰਡ ਦਾ ਇਲਾਕਾ, ਪਿੰਡ

coup (ਕੂ) *n* ਚਾਲ, ਕਾਰੀ ਚੋਟ, ਰਾਜ ਪਲਟਾ

coup d'etat ('ਕੂਡੇਇ'ਟਾ) (*F*) *n* ਰਾਜ ਪਲਟਾ, ਰਾਜਗਰਦੀ

couple ('ਕੱਪਲ) *n v* ਜੋੜਾ, ਪਤੀ-ਪਤਨੀ, ਲਾੜਾ ਲਾੜੀ, ਦੰਪਤੀ; ਗੰਢਣਾ, ਸਬੰਧ ਜੋੜਨਾ, ਸੰਭੋਗ ਕਰਨਾ

couplet ('ਕੱਪਲਿਟ) ਬੈਂਤ, ਦੋਹਰਾ

coupon ('ਕੂਪੌਨ) *n* ਕੂਪਨ, ਪਰਚੀ, ਟਿਕਟ

courage ('ਕੱਰਿਜ) *n* ਹਿੰਮਤ, ਸਾਹਸ, ਹੌਸਲਾ, ਜਿਗਰਾ, ਹੀਆ, ਮਰਦਾਨਗੀ, ਬਹਾਦਰੀ

courageous (ਕਅ'ਰੇਇਜਸ) *a* ਸਾਹਸੀ, ਜਿਗਰੇ ਵਾਲਾ, ਹਿੰਮਤੀ, ਬਹਾਦਰ, ਦਲੇਰ ਦਿਲਾਵਰ; ~ness ਦਲੇਰੀ, ਨਿਰਭੀਰਤਾ, ਸਾਹਸ, ਹਿੰਮਤ, ਹੀਆ

courier (ਕੁਰਿਅ*) *n* ਹਰਕਾਰਾ

course (ਕੋ*ਸ) *n* ਪਾਠ-ਕ੍ਰਮ ਚਾਲ, ਰਫ਼ਤਾਰ, ਰਾਹ, ਰਵਸ਼; ਖੋਜ-ਦੋੜ ਦਾ ਮੈਦਾਨ; ਦਿਸ਼ਾ; ਪਾਣੀ ਦਾ ਰਾਹ, ਖਾਣੇ ਦਾ ਦੌਰ; ਰੀਤ, ਰਸਮ, ਮਾਂਚਾਰੀ; ~of action ਕਿਰਿਆ-ਵਿਧੀ; of ~ ਕੁਦਰਤੀ, ਨਿਸ਼ਚੇ ਹੀ

court (ਕੋ*ਟ) *n v* (1) ਵਿਹੜਾ, ਆਂਗਨ; (2) ਟੈਨਿਸ ਖੇਡਣ ਦਾ ਮੈਦਾਨ; (3) ਸ਼ਾਹੀ ਦਰਬਾਰ, ਦਰਬਾਰੀ, ਖ਼ੁਸ਼ਾਮਦ ਕਰਨੀ, ਚਾਪਲੂਸੀ ਕਰਨੀ, ਰੀਝਾਉਣਾ, ਪਰੇਮ ਕਰਨਾ; (4) ਅਦਾਲਤ, ਕਚਹਿਰੀ; ~yard ਵਿਹੜਾ, ਆਂਗਨ, ਦਲਾਨ, ਘਰ ਦੇ ਬਾਹਰ ਦੇ ਸਿਹਨ; civil~ ਦੀਵਾਨੀ ਅਦਾਲਤ; criminal

ਫ਼ੌਜਦਾਰੀ ਅਦਾਲਤ; high~ ਹਾਈਕੋਰਟ, ਉੱਚ ਨਿਆਇਆਲਾ; supreme~ ਸੁਪਰੀਮ ਕੋਰਟ, ਸਰਵ-ਉੱਚ ਨਿਆਇਆਲਾ; ~ship ਵਿਆਹ ਤੋਂ ਪਹਿਲਾਂ ਪਿਆਰ

courteous ('ਕਾਃਟਯਅਸ) *a* ਸ਼ਿਸ਼ਟ, ਨਿਮਰ, ਭੱਦਰ, ਮਿਲਣਸਾਰ; ਮੁਲਾਹਜ਼ੇਦਾਰ, ਬੀਬਾ

courtesy ('ਕਾਃਟਿਸਿ) *n* ਮੂੰਹ-ਮੁਲਾਹਜ਼ਾ, ਸ਼ਿਸ਼ਟਤਾ, ਭੱਦਰਤਾ, ਨਿਮਰਤਾ, ਸ਼ਰਾਫਤ

cousin ('ਕੱਜ਼ਨ) *n* ਮਸੇਰ, ਫਫੇਰ, ਚਚੇਰ ਭਰਾ ਜਾਂ ਭੈਣ

covenant ('ਕਅਵਨਅੰਟ) *n v* ਪ੍ਰਤਿੱਗਿਆ; ਇਕਰਾਰ ਨਾਮਾ; ਇਕਰਾਰ ਕਰਨਾ

cover ('ਕਅੱਵ*) *n v* ਢੱਕਣ, ਕੱਜਣ, ਉਢਾੜ ਗ਼ਿਲਾਫ਼, ਲਿਫ਼ਾਫ਼ਾ, ਮੇਜ਼ਪੋਸ਼ ਆਤ੍ਰ, ਓਟ, ਰੋਕ; ਢਕਣਾ, ਕੱਜਣਾ, ਲੁਕਾਉਣਾ, ਛੱਤਣਾ; ਛਾ ਜਾਣਾ; ਕਾਫ਼ੀ ਹੋਣਾ, ਧਨਣਾ, ਅੰਡੇ ਸਿਉਣਾ; ਸ਼ਾਮਲ ਹੋਣਾ; (ਫ਼ਾਸਲਾ ਤੈ ਕਰਨਾ; (ਵਿਸ਼ਾ ਆਦਿ) ਨਿਬਾਹੁਣਾ; ~ed ਢਕਿਆ ਹੋਇਆ, ਅਤੰਰਗਤ; ~ing ਚਾਦਰ, ਪਰਦਾ, ਆਵਰਣ; ~let ਗਿਲਾਫ਼, ਉਢਾੜ, ਚਾਦਰ

covert ('ਕਅਵਅਟ, 'ਕੱਅੱਵਅ*) *a n* ਲੁਕਵਾਂ, ਗੁੱਝਾ, ਗੁਪਤ, ਭਾਰੀ; ਓਟ, ਪਨਾਹ, ਆਸਰਾ; ~ure ਆਸਰਾ, ਪਨਾਹ; ਸੁਹਾਗ

covet ('ਕਅੱਵਿਟ) *v* ਲੋਭੀ ਹੋਣਾ, ਹਿਰਸ ਕਰਨੀ; ਤਮ੍ਹਾਂ ਕਰਨੀ, ਲਾਲਚ ਕਰਨਾ, ਚਾਹੁਣ; ~ous ਲੋਭੀ, ਹਿਰਸੀ, ਲਾਲਚੀ, ਹਵਸੀ

cow (ਕਾਉ) *n v* ਗਾਂ, ਗਊ, ਢੱਗੀ; ਡਰਾਉਣਾ, ਧਮਕਾਉਣਾ, ਝਰਕਾਉਣਾ, ਰੋਹਬ ਦੇਣਾ; ~boy ਗਵਾਲਾ, ਚਾਕ, ਪਾਲੀ, ਵਾਗੀ, ਛੇੜੂ, ਚਰਵਾਹਾ; ~dung ਗੋਹਾ, ਗੋਬਰ; ~herd ਚਰਵਾਹਾ

coward ('ਕਾਉਅਡ) *n a* ਡਰਾਕਲ, ਡਰੂ, ਡਰਪੋਕ, ਕਾਇਰ, ਬੁਜ਼ਦਿੱਲ

coy (ਕੋਇ) *a* ਸੰਗਾਊ, ਸ਼ਰਮਾਕਲ, ਲੱਜਾਵਾਨ; (ਥਾਂ) ਲੁਕਵੀਂ, ਇਕਵਾਂਝੀ

crab (ਕਰੈਬ) *n v* ਕੇਕੜਾ, ਜੰਗਲੀ ਸਿਊ; ਸੜੀਅਲ, ਭਾਰ ਚੁੱਕਣ ਵਾਲਾ ਜੰਤਰ; ਨਿੰਦਾ ਕਰਨੀ; ਖਿਝਣਾ, ਪੰਜੇ ਮਾਰਨਾ, ਪੱਜੀਆਂ ਉਡਾਉਣੀਆਂ

crack (ਕਰੈਕ) *n a v* ਦਰਜ, ਤੇੜੇ, ਦਰਾੜ, ਫੱਟ; ਧਮਾਕਾ, ਕੜਕ; ਚੋਟਵਾਂ, ਜ਼ੋਰ ਦਾ, ਨਿਪੁੰਨ; ਕੜਕਾਉਣਾ, ਤਿੜਕਾਉਣਾ, ਫੱਟ ਲਾਉਣਾ, ਤੇੜੇ ਪਾਉਣੀ; ਕੜਕਣਾ; **~a joke** ਠੱਠਾ-ਮਜ਼ਾਕ ਕਰਨਾ, ਮਖੌਲ ਕਰਨਾ; **~ed** (ਅਪ) ਪਾਗਲ, ਉਨਮੱਤ; **~er** ਪਟਾਕਾ, ਤਿੜਤਿੜੀ, ਧਮਾਕਾ, ਗੋਲਾ (ਆਤਸ਼-ਬਾਜ਼ੀ); ਕਰਾਰਾ ਬਿਸਕੁਟ; **~ers** (ਅਪ) ਝੱਲਾ, ਸਨਕੀ

cradle (ਕਰੇਇਡਲ) *n v* ਝੂਲਾ; ਖਟੋਲਾ, ਪੰਘੂੜਾ; ਪੰਘੂੜੇ ਵਿਚ ਪਾਉਣਾ, ਪਾਲਣ ਪੋਸ਼ਣ ਕਰਨਾ; **a child in~** ਦੁੱਧ ਪੀਂਦਾ ਬੱਚਾ; **from the~** ਬਚਪਨ ਤੋਂ

craft (ਕਰਾਫ਼ਟ) *n* ਪੇਸ਼ਾ, ਧੰਦਾ, ਸ਼ਿਲਪਕਾਰੀ, ਹੁਨਰਮੰਦੀ, ਕਾਰੀਗਰੀ, ਹਵਾਈ ਜਹਾਜ਼; **~swan** ਸ਼ਿਲਪਕਾਰ, ਸ਼ਿਲਪੀ, ਦਸਤਕਾਰ, ਕਾਰੀਗਰ; **~smanship** ਦਸਤਕਾਰੀ, ਕਾਰੀਗਰੀ; **~y** ਚਾਲਬਾਜ਼, ਛਲੀਆ, ਕਪਟੀ, ਫ਼ਰੇਬੀ, ਮੱਕਾਰ; ਨਿਪੁੰਨ

cram (ਕਰੈਮ) *n v* ਭੀੜ, ਜਮਘਟਾ; ਝੂਠ; ਘੋਟਾ, ਰੱਟਾ; ਤੂੜਨਾ, ਠੂਸਣਾ, ਰਟਣਾ, ਘੋਟਾ ਲਾਉਣਾ; **~mer** ਘੋਟੂ, ਰੱਟੂ

crane (ਕਰੇਇਨ) *n v* ਭਾਰ ਆਦਿ ਚੁੱਕਣ ਵਾਲਾ ਜੰਤਰ, ਕਰੇਨ; ਸਾਰਸ, ਲਮਢੀਂਗ; ਕਰੇਨ ਨਾਲ ਭਾਰ ਚੁੱਕਣਾ; ਸਾਰਸ ਵਾਂਗ ਧੌਣ ਅੱਗੇ ਨੂੰ ਕਰਨਾ

crank (ਕਰੈਂਕ) *n v a* ਧੁਰੇ ਦੀ ਕੂਹਣੀ ਦਾ ਸਿਰਾ, ਗੱਲ ਦਾ ਫੇਰ ਜਾਂ ਪੇਚ, ਕੂਹਣੀਦਾਰ ਬਣਾਉਣਾ, ਮੋੜਨਾ; (ਮਸ਼ੀਨਰੀ) ਢਿੱਲੀ; ਖ਼ਬਤੀ; **~y** ਢਿੱਲਾ, ਕਮਜ਼ੋਰ, ਬੇਢਾ, ਖ਼ਬਤੀ, ਪਾਗਲ, ਸਨਕੀ ਵਹਿਮੀ

crash (ਕਰੈਸ਼) *n v* ਤਬਾਹੀ, ਬਰਬਾਦੀ, ਧਮਾਕਾ, ਡਿੱਗਣਾ, ਟੁੱਟਣਾ

crave (ਕਰੇਇਵ) *v* ਲਾਲਸਾ ਕਰਨਾ, ਤਰਸਣਾ, ਜਾਚਨਾ ਕਰਨੀ, ਤਰਲਾ ਕਰਨਾ

craving ('ਕਰੇਇਵਿੰਡ) *n* ਲਾਲਸਾ, ਅਭਿਲਾਸ਼ਾ, ਸਿੱਕ, ਤਾਂਘ, ਲਲੂਕ

crawl *v n* ਹੌਲੀ ਹੌਲੀ ਤੁਰਨਾ, ਪੇਟ ਦੇ ਭਾਰ ਤੁਰਨਾ; ਥੋੜ੍ਹੇ ਪਾਣੀ ਵਾਲਾ ਟੋਇਆ (ਮੱਛੀਆਂ ਫੜਨ ਲਈ)

craze (ਕਰੇਇਜ਼) *v n* ਮੱਤ ਮਾਰਨੀ, ਪਾਗਲ ਬਣਾ ਦੇਣਾ; ਵਹਿਮ, ਸਨਕ, ਖ਼ਬਤ, ਪਾਗਲਪਨ

crazy ('ਕਰੇਇਜ਼ਿ) *a* ਖ਼ਬਤੀ, ਸੁਦਾਈ, ਝੱਲਾ, ਕਮਲਾ, ਠਰਕੀ, ਸਨਕੀ

cream (ਕਰੀਮ) *n v* ਮਲਾਈ; ਕਰੀਮ; ਸਾਰ, ਤੱਤ; ਮਲਾਈ ਆਉਣੀ; ਤੱਤ ਕੱਢਣਾ, ਨਿਚੋੜ ਕੱਢਣਾ

crease (ਕਰੀਸ) *n v* ਵੱਟ, ਕਰੀਜ਼, ਸਲਵਟ; ਸ਼ਿਕਨ; ਵੱਟ ਪਾਉਣੇ ਜਾਂ ਪੈਣੇ, ਸਲਵਟ ਪਾਉਣੇ

creasy ('ਕਰੀਸਿ) *a* ਭਾਨ ਵਾਲਾ, ਵੱਟਦਾਰ, ਝੁਰੜੀਆਂ ਵਾਲਾ

create (ਕਰੀ'ਏਇਟ) *v* ਉਤਪੰਨ ਕਰਨਾ, ਬਣਾਉਣਾ, ਉਪਜਾਉਣਾ, ਰਚਣਾ, ਸਿਰਜਣਾ

creation (ਕਰਿ'ਏਇਸ਼ਨ) *n* ਉਪਜ, ਰਚਨਾ, ਸਿਰਜਣਾ, ਉਤਪਤੀ, ਸ੍ਰਿਸ਼ਟੀ

creative (ਕਰੀ'ਏਇਟਿਵ) *a* ਸਿਰਜਣਾਤਮਕ, ਰਚਨਾਤਮਕ, ਸਿਰਜਣਸ਼ੀਲ, ਉਤਪਾਦਕ

creator (ਕਰਿ'ਏਇਟਆ*) *n* ਸਿਰਜਣਹਾਰ,

ਸ੍ਰਿਸ਼ਟਾ, ਕਰਤਾਰ, ਜਨਮਦਾਤਾ

creature ('ਕਰੀਚਅ*) *n* ਜੀਵ, ਜੀਊੜਾ, ਪ੍ਰਾਣੀ

creche (ਕਰੈਸ਼) *n* ਬਾਲਵਾੜੀ

credential (ਕਰਿ'ਡੈਂਸ਼ਲ) *n* ਪਰੀਚੈ ਪੱਤਰ, ਸਨਦ, ਜਾਣ ਪਛਾਣ ਦੀ ਚਿੱਠੀ, ਵਸੀਕਾ

credibility ('ਕਰੈੱਡਅ'ਬਿਲਅਟਿ) *n* ਸ਼ਾਖ, ਪ੍ਰਤੀਤ

credible ('ਕਰੈੱਡਅਬਲ) *a* ਮੰਨਣਯੋਗ, ਭਰੋਸੇਯੋਗ, ਇਤਬਾਰੀ, ਵਿਸ਼ਵਾਸਯੋਗ

credit ('ਕਰੈਡਿਟ) *n v* ਭਰੋਸਾ, ਇਤਬਾਰ, ਯਕੀਨ, ਸਾਥ; ਭਰੋਸਾ ਕਰਨਾ, ਇਤਬਾਰ ਕਰਨਾ, ਮੰਨ ਲੈਣਾ, ਲੇਖੇ ਵਿਚ ਜੋੜਨਾ, ਖਾਤੇ ਵਿਚ ਜਮ੍ਹਾਂ ਕਰਨਾ; **~account** ਵਹੀ-ਖਾਤਾ; **~bill** ਹੁੰਡੀ; **letter of~** ਹੁੰਡੀ; **~able** ਸ਼ੋਭਨੀਕ, ਪ੍ਰਸੰਸਾਯੋਗ ਵਡਿਆਉਣ ਯੋਗ; **~or** ਲੈਣਦਾਰ, (ਸ਼ਾਹੂਕਾਰ)

creed (ਕਰੀਡ) *n* ਦੀਨ, ਮੱਤ, ਧਰਮ, ਸੰਪਰਦਾਇ

creep (ਕਰੀਪ) *n v* ਝੁਣਝੁਣੀ; ਘਿਸਰਨਾ, ਪੇਟ ਦੇ ਭਾਰ ਟੁਰਨਾ, ਹੌਲੀ ਹੌਲੀ ਟੁਰਨਾ, ਜੂੰ ਦੀ ਟੋਰ ਟੁਰਨਾ, ਘਸਣਾ; **~er** ਘਸਰ ਕੇ ਟੁਰਨ ਵਾਲਾ, ਵੇਲ; **~y** ਘਸਾ ਦੇ ਟੁਰਨ ਵਾਲਾ; ਪੇਟ ਦੇ ਭਾਰ ਟੁਰਨ ਵਾਲਾ, ਸਰੀਰ ਨੂੰ ਸੁੰਨ ਕਰ ਦੇਣ ਵਾਲਾ, ਲੂੰ ਕੰਡੇ ਖੜ੍ਹੇ ਕਰਨ ਵਾਲਾ; ਸ਼ੰਕਾਜਨਕ

cremate (ਕਰਿ'ਮੇਇਟ) *v* ਸਸਕਾਰ ਕਰਨਾ, ਦਾਗ ਦੇਣਾ

cremation (ਕਰਿ'ਮੇਇਸ਼ਨ) *n* ਦਾਹ-ਸਸਕਾਰ, ਦਾਹ-ਕਿਰਿਆ

crematory (ਕਰਿਮਅਟਰਿ) *n* ਸ਼ਮਸ਼ਾਨ ਭੂਮੀ

crematorium ('ਕਰੈੱਮਅ'ਟੋਰਿਅਮ) *n* ਸ਼ਮਸ਼ਾਨ ਘਾਟ

crest (ਕਰੈਸਿਟ) *n* ਚੋਟੀ, ਸਿਖਰ; ਕਲਗ਼ੀ, ਤਾਜ

crew (ਕਰੂ) *n* ਜਹਾਜ਼ੀ ਅਮਲਾ, ਮੱਲਾਹ; ਟੋਲਾ, ਜੱਥਾ

cricket ('ਕਰਿਕਿਟ) *n* ਕ੍ਰਿਕਟ, ਬੱਲੇ ਤੇ ਗੇਂਦ ਦੀ ਖੇਡ; ਟਿੱਡਾ, ਝੀਂਗਰ

crime (ਕਰਾਇਮ) *n v* ਜੁਰਮ, ਦੋਸ਼, ਅਪਰਾਧ, ਕਾਨੂੰਨ ਵਿਰੁੱਧ ਕੰਮ; ਦੋਸ਼ੀ ਠਹਿਰਾਉਣਾ, ਦੋਸ਼, ਮੜ੍ਹਨਾ

criminal ('ਕਰਿਮਿਨਲ) *n a* ਮੁਜਰਮ, ਦੋਸ਼ੀ, ਅਪਰਾਧੀ, ਗੁਨਾਹਗਾਰ, (ਮੁਕੱਦਮਾ) ਫ਼ੌਜਦਾਰੀ

crimson ('ਕਰਿਮਜ਼ਨ) *n a v* ਊਦਾ ਰੰਗ, ਕਿਰਮਚੀ ਰੰਗ, ਗੂੜ੍ਹਾ ਲਾਲ ਰੰਗ; ਅਰਗਵਾਨੀ, ਗੂੜ੍ਹਾ ਲਾਲ ਰੰਗਣਾ

cripple ('ਕਰਿਪਲ) *v n* ਲੂਲ੍ਹਾ, ਟੁੰਡਾ, ਲੁੰਜਾ, ਲੰਗੜਾ; ਲੰਗੜਾ ਕੇ ਟੁਰਨਾ, ਨਿਰਬਲ ਕਰਨਾ, ਵਿਗਾੜਨਾ

crisis ('ਕਰਾਇਸਿਸ) *n* ਸੰਕਟ, ਔਖੀ ਘੜੀ

crisp (ਕਰਿਸਪ) *a n v* ਖ਼ਸਤਾ, ਭੁਰਭੁਰਾ, ਮੁਰਮਰਾ, ਕਰਾਰਾ, ਫੁਰਤੀਲਾ, ਵਾਲ ਘੁੰਗਰਾਲੇ ਬਣਾਉਣਾ; **~ate** ਵਲਦਾਰ, ਲਹਿਰੀਆ, ਘੁੰਗਰਾਲਾ

criterion (ਕਰਾਇ'ਟਿਅਰਿਅਨ) *n* ਮਾਪ-ਦੰਡ, ਕਸੌਟੀ, ਪਰਖ

critic ('ਕਰਿਟਿਕ) *n* ਆਲੋਚਕ, ਨੁਕਤਾਚੀਨ, ਸਮਾਲੋਚਕ, ਸਮੀਖਿਆਕਾਰ; **~al** ਆਲੋਚਨਾਤਮਕ; ਸਮਾਲੋਚਨਾਤਮਕ, ਸੰਕਟਮਈ, ਖ਼ਤਰਨਾਕ, ਨਾਜ਼ਕ; **~ism** ਆਲੋਚਨਾ, ਸਮਾਲੋਚਨਾ; ਪੜਚੋਲ, ਸਮੀਖਿਆ, ਨੁਕਤਾਚੀਨੀ; **~ize** ਨੁਕਤਾਚੀਨੀ ਕਰਨੀ, ਆਲੋਚਨਾ ਕਰਨੀ, ਛਾਣ-ਬੀਣ ਕਰਨੀ, ਨੁਕਸ ਕੱਢਣੇ

critique (ਕਰਿ'ਟੀਕ) *n* ਆਲੋਚਨਾਤਮਕ ਵਿਸ਼ਲੇਸ਼ਣ

crockery ('ਕਰੌਕਅਰਿ) *n* ਮਿੱਟੀ ਜਾਂ ਚੀਨੀ ਦੇ ਭਾਂਡੇ, ਪਿਰਚ ਪਿਆਲੀਆਂ, ਕ੍ਰਾਕਰੀ

crocodile ('ਕਰੌਕਅਡਾਇਲ) *n* ਮਗਰਮੱਛ, ਘੜਿਆਲ, ਸੰਸਾਰ

crone (ਕਰਉਨ) *n* ਬੁੱਢੀ ਠੇਰੀ, ਬੁੱਢੜੀ

crony ('ਕਰਉਨਿ) *n* ਲੰਗੋਟੀਆ ਯਾਰ, ਜਿਗਰੀ ਦੋਸਤ

crop (ਕਰੌਪ) *n v* ਫ਼ਸਲ; ਅਨਾਜ; ਖੇਤੀ ਕੱਟਣ, (ਫ਼ਸਲ) ਵੱਢਣਾ, ਕਤਰਨਾ, ਛਾਂਗਣਾ; **~up** ਪਰਗਟ ਹੋਣਾ, ਪੈਦਾ ਹੋਣਾ, ਨਿਕਲਣਾ

cross (ਕਰੌਸ) *n v* ਸੂਲੀ, ਸਲੀਬ, ਫਾਂਸੀ; ਇਸਾਈ ਧਰਮ; ਤਸੀਹਾ, ਬਿਪਤਾ, ਕਸ਼ਟ; ਦੋਗਲਾ ਪਸ਼ੂ; ਜੋੜ; ਠੱਗੀ; ਕਟਣਾ, ਕਾਟਾ ਮਾਰਨਾ, ਉਲੀਕਣਾ, ਪਾਰ ਕਰਨਾ, ਲੰਘਣਾ, ਰਾਹ ਵਿਚ ਮਿਲਣਾ; ਸੂਲੀ ਜਾਂ ਸਲੀਬ ਬਣਾਉਣਾ; ਦੋਗਲਾ ਕਰਨਾ; ਉਲਟਾ, ਵਿਰੁੱਧ, ਟੇਢਾ, ਆਢਾ, ਕਾਟਵਾਂ, ਸਲੀਬੀ, ਚਿੜਚਿੜਾ, ਕੋਂਝਾ; **~breed** ਦੋਗਲਾ; **~examination** ਜਿਰਹਾ, ਪੁੱਛ ਗਿੱਛ; **~legged** ਚੌਕੜੀ ਮਾਰ ਕੇ ਬੈਠਣਾ; **~question** ਪ੍ਰਤੀ-ਪ੍ਰਸ਼ਨ ਕਰਨਾ; ਜਿਰਹਾ ਕਰਨਾ; **~road** ਚੌਰਾਹਾ; **~way** ਪਗਡੰਡੀ; **~word** ਸ਼ਬਦ-ਪਹੇਲੀ, ਸ਼ਬਦ-ਅੜਾਉਣੀ

crow (ਕਰਅਉ) *n v* ਕਾਂ, ਕਾਂਗ, ਕਉਆ; ਬਾਂਗ; ਕੁੱਕੜ ਦਾ ਬਾਂਗ ਦੇਣਾ

crowd (ਕਰਾਉਡ) *n v* ਭੀੜ, ਜਮਘਟਾ, ਖਲਕਤ, ਬਾੜ, ਝੁਰਮਟ, ਟੋਲੀ, ਗੁਟ; ਭੀੜ ਹੋਣੀ ਜਾਂ ਕਰਨੀ, ਝੁਰਮਟ ਪੈਣਾ

crown (ਕਰਾਉਨ) *n v* ਮੁਕਟ, ਤਾਜ, ਸਿਹਰਾ, ਇਕ ਅੰਗਰੇਜ਼ੀ ਸਿੱਕਾ; ਟੇਟਣ, ਟੇਟਲੀ, ਚੁੰਡਾ, ਟੀਸੀ, ਚੋਟੀ; 15"×19" ਦਾ ਕਾਗ਼ਜ਼; ਦੰਦ ਦਾ ਮਸੂੜੇ ਤੋਂ ਬਾਹਰ ਦਾ ਭਾਗ; ਆਦਰਸ਼ ਸਥਿਤੀ; ਮੁਕਟ ਪੁਆਉਣਾ, ਸਿਹਰਾ ਬੰਨ੍ਹਣਾ, ਵਡਿਆਉਣਾ, ਦੰਦ ਮੜ੍ਹਾਉਣਾ

crumble (ਕਰਅੰਬਲ) ਚੂਰਾ ਚੂਰਾ ਹੋਣਾ, ਭੋਰਨਾ, ਭੁਰਨਾ, ਟੁੱਟਣਾ, ਤੋੜਨਾ

crusade (ਕਰੂ'ਸੇਇਡ) *n v* ਧਰਮ ਜੁੱਧ, ਮਸੀਹੀ ਜਹਾਦ; ਧਰਮ ਜੁੱਧ ਕਰਨਾ

crush (ਕਰਅੱਸ਼) *v n* ਦਲਣਾ, ਦਰੜਨਾ, ਕੁਚਲਣਾ, ਚੂਰ ਕਰਨਾ, ਮਸਲਣਾ; ਭੀੜ-ਭੜੱਕਾ, ਜਾਮਘਟਾ

crux (ਕਰਅੱਰਸ) *n* ਘੁੰਡੀ, ਗੁੱਥੀ, ਮੂਲ ਸਮੱਸਿਆ; ਪੇਚੀਦਾ ਮਾਮਲਾ

cry (ਕਰਾਇ) *n* ਚੀਕ, ਕੂਕ, ਸ਼ੋਰ, ਚੀਂਘਿਆੜ, ਰੋਣ, ਪੁਕਾਰ, ਫ਼ਰਿਆਦ, ਕੁਰਲਾਹਟ, ਲਲਕਾਰ, ਨਾਅਰਾ; ਚੀਕਣਾ, ਕੂਕਣਾ, ਚੀਂਘਿਆੜਨਾ, ਰੋਣਾ, ਵਿਲਕਣਾ, ਪੁਕਾਰਨਾ, ਢੰਡੋਰਾ ਕਰਨਾ, ਉੱਚੀ ਅਵਾਜ਼ ਦੇਣੀ; **~down** ਨਿੰਦਣਾ, ਭੰਡਣਾ; **~ing need** ਸਖ਼ਤ ਲੋੜ; **~up** ਵਧਾ ਚੜ੍ਹਾ ਕੇ ਦੱਸਣਾ, ਸੋਹਿਲੇ ਗਾਉਣੇ

crystal ('ਕਰਿਸਟਲ) *n a* ਰਵਾ, ਬਲੌਰੀ, ਰਵੇਦਾਰ, ਪਾਰਦਰਸ਼ੀ ਸ਼ੀਸ਼ਾ

cub (ਕਅੱਬ) *n* ਕਤੂਰਾ, ਬੱਚਾ (ਸ਼ੇਰ, ਰਿੱਛ ਜਾਂ ਕੁੱਤੇ ਦਾ), ਅੱਲੜ੍ਹ ਮੁੰਡਾ, ਸਕਾਉਟ ਬੱਚਾ; ਸਿਖਾਂਦਰੂ ਪੱਤਰਕਾਰ; ਬੱਚਾ ਜਣਨਾ

cube (ਕਯੂਬ) *n* ਘਣ, ਛੇ-ਬਾਹੀ ਆਕਾਰ, ਘਣਾਕਾਰ

cubicle (ਕਯੂਬਿਕਲ) *n* ਵਿਦਿਆਰਥੀਆਂ ਦਾ ਸੌਣ ਕਮਰਾ

cuckold ('ਕਅੱਕਅਉਲਡ) *n* ਭੜਵਾ

cuckoo ('ਕੁਕੁ) *n* ਬਘੀਹਾ, ਕੋਇਲ

cucumber ('ਕਯੂਕਅੱਮਬਅ") *n* ਖੀਰਾ, ਤਰ

cuddle ('ਕਅੱਡਲ) *v n* ਗਲ ਲਾਉਣਾ, ਲਾਡ ਪਿਆਰ ਕਰਨਾ, ਜੱਫੀ ਪਾਉਣਾ; ਜੱਫੀ, ਆਲਿੰਗਨ

cudgel ('ਕਅੱਜਿ(ਅ)ਲ) *n v* ਸੋਟਾ, ਡੰਡਾ; ਡੰਡੇ ਮਾਰਨਾ

cue (ਕਯੂ) *n* ਸੰਕੇਤ, ਇਸ਼ਾਰਾ; ਗੁਤ

culminate ('ਕਅੱਲਮਿਨੇਇਟ) *v* ਸਿਖਰ ਤੇ
ਪੁਜਣਾ, ਉੱਚਾ ਹੋਣਾ; ਨਤੀਜਾ ਹੋਣਾ

culmination ('ਕਅੱਲਮਿ'ਨੇਇਸ਼ਨ) *n* ਟੀਸੀ,
ਸਿਖਰ; ਨਤੀਜਾ, ਸਿੱਟਾ

culpable ('ਕਅੱਲਪਅਬਲ) *a* ਦੋਸ਼ਪੂਰਨ,
ਅਪਰਾਧੀ

culprit ('ਕਅੱਲਪਰਿਟ) *n* ਦੋਸੀ, ਅਪਰਾਧੀ, ਮੁਜਰਮ

cult (ਕਅੱਲਟ) *n* ਦੀਨ, ਮਾਰਗ, ਸੰਪਰਦਾਇ,
ਧਰਮ, ਰੀਤ, ਪੂਜਾ-ਪੱਧਤੀ

cultivate ('ਕਅੱਲਟਿਵੇਇਟ) *v* ਵਾਹੁਣਾ, ਖੇਤੀ
ਕਰਨੀ, ਸੁਆਰਨਾ, ਸਿੱਖਿਆ ਦੇਣਾ, ਧਰਤੀ
ਤਿਆਰ ਕਰਨੀ

cultivation ('ਕਅੱਲਟਿ'ਵੇਇਸ਼ਨ) *n* ਵਾਹੀ ਖੇਤੀ,
ਕਾਸ਼ਤ

cultural ('ਕਅੱਲਚ(ਅ)ਰ(ਅ)ਲ) *a* ਸਾਂਸਕ੍ਰਿਤਕ,
ਸੱਭਿਆਚਾਰਕ

culture ('ਕਅੱਲਚਅ*) *n v* ਸੰਸਕ੍ਰਿਤੀ,
ਸੱਭਿਆਚਾਰ, ਕਾਸ਼ਤਕਾਰੀ; ਖੇਤੀ ਕਰਨੀ, ਜੋਤਣਾ;
~d ਸੁਸੰਸਕ੍ਰਿਤ, ਸੱਭਿਆ, ਕੋਮਲ ਭਾਵਾਂ ਦਾ
ਸੁਆਮੀ, ਸੱਭਿਆਵਾਨ; ਬੀਜੀ ਹੋਈ ਜ਼ਮੀਨ

culvert ('ਕਅੱਲਵਅ:ਟ) *n* (ਸੜਕ ਆਦਿ ਦੀ)
ਪੁਲੀ

cumber ('ਕਅੱਮਬਅ*) *v n* ਭਾਰ ਪਾਉਣਾ,
ਰੁਕਾਵਟ ਪਾਉਣਾ; ਬੋਝ, ਰੁਕਾਵਟ

cumulate (ਕਯੂਮਯੁਲੇਇਟ) *v a* ਇਕੱਠਾ ਕਰਨਾ,
ਜਾਮ੍ਹਾਂ ਕਰਨਾ, ਢੇਰ ਲਗਾਉਣਾ; ਇਕੱਤਰਤ, ਜਾਮ੍ਹਾਂ,
ਢੇਰ ਕੀਤਾ, ਸੰਚਤ

cumulation (ਕਯੂਮਯੁ'ਲੇਇਸ਼ਨ) *n* ਸਮੂਹ, ਢੇਰ,
ਇਕੱਤਰੀਕਰਣ

cumulative (ਕਯੂਮਯੁਲ(ਅ)ਟਿਵ) *a* ਸਮੁੱਚਾ,

ਇੱਕਠਾ, ਸੰਚਤ

cunning (ਕਅੱਨਿੰਡ) *a n* ਚਲਾਕ, ਚੰਟ, ਘਾਗ,
ਉਸਤਾਦ, ਮੱਕਾਰ; ਚਲਾਕੀ, ਉਸਤਾਦੀ, ਮੱਕਾਰੀ

cup (ਕਅੱਪ) *n* ਪਿਆਲਾ, ਛੰਨਾ, ਠੂਠਾ, ਜਾਮ, ਕੱਪ; in
one's ~s ਸ਼ਰਾਬ ਦੇ ਨਸੇ ਵਿਚ, ਮਦਹੋਸ਼

cupboard (ਕਅੱਬਅਡ) *n* ਭਾਂਡਿਆਂ ਤੇ ਭੋਜਨ ਦੀ
ਅਲਮਾਰੀ

cupid (ਕਯੂਪਿਡ) *n* ਕਾਮਦੇਵ, ਸੁੰਦਰ ਮੁੰਡਾ, ਕਾਮ
ਦਾ ਰੋਮਨ ਦੇਵਤਾ

curable (ਕਯੂਅਰਅਬਲ) *a* ਠੀਕ ਹੋਣ ਯੋਗ,
ਇਲਾਜ ਯੋਗ

curative ('ਕਯੂਅਰਅਟਿਵ) *adv. n* ਰੋਗਨਾਸ਼ਕ
(ਦਵਾਈ)

curator (ਕਯੂ'ਰੇਇਅ*) *n* ਰੱਖਿਅਕ, ਪ੍ਰਬੰਧਕ,
ਵਿਵਸਥਾਪਕ

curb (ਕਅ:ਬ) *n v* ਗੰਢ, ਰੋਕ, ਅੜਾਉਣੀ,
ਰੋਕਣਾ, ਖੱਬੀ ਪਾਉਣੀ

curd (ਕਅ:ਡ) *n* ਦਹੀ

cure (ਕਯੂਅ*) *n v* ਇਲਾਜ, ਚਿਕਿਤਸਾ, ਉਪਾਅ,
ਤੰਦਰੁਸਤੀ, ਅਰੋਗਤਾ; ਇਲਾਜ ਕਰਨਾ; ਦਵਾਈ
ਦੇਣੀ, ਤੰਦਰੁਸਤ ਹੋਣਾ; ~less ਲਾਇਲਾਜ,
ਅਸਾਧ, ਨਿਰਉਪਾਇ

curfew (ਕਅ:ਫ਼ਯੂ) *n* ਕਰਫਿਊ, ਘਰਬੰਦੀ ਦਾ
ਹੁਕਮ; ~order ਕਰਫਿਊ ਦਾ ਹੁਕਮ

curio (ਕਯੂਅਰਿਅਉ) *n* ਅਨੋਖੀ ਕਲਾਕ੍ਰਿਤ

curiosity (ਕਯੂਅਰਿ'ਔਸਿਟਿ) *n* ਉਤਸੁਕਤਾ, ਪ੍ਰਬਲ
ਇੱਛਾ, ਜਿਗਿਆਸਾ, ਉਤਕੰਠ; ਅਨੋਖਾਪਣ

curious (ਕਯੂਅਰਿਅਸ) *a* ਜਿਗਿਆਸੂ, ਅਨੋਖਾ,
ਨਿਆਰਾ, ਵਿਸਮੈਜਨਕ, ਉਤਸੁਕ

curl (ਕਅ:ਲ) *n v* ਵਾਲਾਂ ਦਾ ਛੱਲਾ, ਘੁਰਾੜੂ ਜਾਂ
ਪੇਚ, ਲਿਟ ਜੁਲਫ਼; ਦੇ ਕੁੰਡਲ ਬਣਾਉਣੇ

currency (ਕਅੱਰ(ਅ)ਨਸਿ) *n* ਪ੍ਰਚਲਤ ਮੁਦਰਾ, ਸਿੱਕਾ, ਕਰੰਸੀ; ਪ੍ਰਸਾਰ, ਰਿਵਾਜ;

current ('ਕਅੱਰ(ਅ)ਨਟ) *a n* ਜਾਰੀ ਮੌਜੂਦਾ, ਵਰਤਮਾਨ, ਆਧੁਨਿਕ, ਵਿਦਮਾਨ, ਪ੍ਰਚਲਤ, ਚਲੰਤ, ਚਾਲੂ, ਪਰਵਾਹ, ਬਿਜਲੀ ਦੀ ਧਾਰਾ, ਕਰੰਟ, ਵੇਗ, ਗਤੀ; ~account ਚਾਲੂ ਲੇਖਾ

curriculum (ਕਕਅ'ਰਿਕਯਅਲਯਅਮ) *n* ਪਾਠਕ੍ਰਮ

curry (ਕਅੱਰਿ) *n v* ਸ਼ੋਰਬਾ; ਸ਼ੋਰਬਾ ਤਿਆਰ ਕਰਨਾ

curse (ਕਅਃਸ) *n* ਫਿਟਕਾਰ, ਧਿੱਕਾਰ; ਫਿਟਲਾਨ੍ਹਤ ਦੇਣਾ, ਧਿਰਕਾਰਨਾ, ਸਰਾਪਣਾ

cursory (ਕਅਃਸ(ਅ)ਰਿ) *a* ਸਰਸਰੀ, ਕਾਹਲੀ ਦਾ

curtail (ਕਅਃ'ਟੇਇਲ) *v* ਕੱਟਣਾ, ਛਾਂਟਣਾ, ਘਟਾਉਣਾ, ਸੰਖੇਪ ਕਰਨਾ; ~ment ਕਾਂਟ-ਛਾਂਟ, ਘਾਟਾ, ਛਾਂਟੀ, ਸੰਖੇਪਤਾ

curtain ('ਕਅਃਟਨ) *n v* ਪਰਦਾ, ਓਹਲਾ, ਚਿਕ ਪਰਦਾ ਡੇਗਣਾ; ਓਹਲਾ ਕਰਨਾ

curvature (ਕਅਃਵਅਚਅ) *n* ਮੋੜ, ਵਿੰਗ, ਵਕਰਤਾ

curve ('ਕਅਃਵ) *n v* ਮੋੜ, ਗੋਲਾਈ, ਵਿੰਗ, ਖ਼ਮ, ਵਕਰ; ਮੋੜਨਾ, ਗੋਲ ਕਰਨਾ; ~d ਟੇਢਾ ਵਿੰਗਾ, ਵਕਰ

cushion ('ਕੁਸ਼ਨ) *n v* ਗੱਦਾ, ਗਦੇਲਾ, ਗੱਦਾ ਲਾਉਣਾ, ਗੁਦਗੁਦਾ ਕਰਨਾ

cushy ('ਕੁਸ਼ਿ) *a* ਸੌਖਾ (ਕੰਮ), ਆਨੰਦਮਈ, ਸੁਖਦਾਇਕ

custard ('ਕਅੱਸਟਅਃਡ) *n* ਫਿਰਨੀ, ਚੌਲਾਂ ਦੇ ਆਟੇ ਅਤੇ ਦੁੱਧ ਦੀ ਖੀਰ, ਕਸਟਰਡ

custodian (ਕਅੱਸਟਅਉਡਯਅਨ) *n* ਨਿਗਰਾਨ, ਰਖਵਾਲਾ, ਦਰੋਗਾ

custody ('ਕਅੱਸਟਅਡਿ) *n* ਹਿਰਾਸਤ, ਕੈਦ, ਸਪੁਰਦਗੀ, ਨਿਗਰਾਨੀ; **take into~** ਕੈਦ ਕਰਨਾ, ਹਿਰਾਸਤ ਵਿਚ ਲੈਣਾ

custom ('ਕਅੱਸਟਅਮ) *n* (1) ਰੀਤ, ਰਿਵਾਜ, ਪ੍ਰਥਾ; ਨਿਤਨੇਮ; (2) ਵਤੀਰਾ; ਗਾਹਕੀ; (3) ਚੁੰਗੀ, ਅਯਾਤ-ਕਰ; ~er ਗਾਹਕ, ਖ਼ਰੀਦਾਰ, ਆਸਾਮੀ

cut (ਕਅੱਟ) *v n* ਕਟਣਾ, ਵਢੰਨਾ, ਟੁੱਕਣਾ, ਟੱਕ ਲਾਉਣਾ, ਘਾਉ ਲਾਉਣਾ, ਕਲਮ ਕਰਨਾ, ਛਿਲਣਾ, ਚੀਰਨਾ, ਘਟਾਉਣਾ, ਘੱਟ ਕਰਨਾ, ਟੱਕ, ਵੱਢ, ਚੀਰ, ਫੱਟ, ਕਾਂਟ-ਛਾਂਟ, ਘਾਉ; ~out ਗਾਤੇ ਨੂੰ ਕੱਟ ਕੇ ਬਣਾਇਆ ਵਿਅਕਤੀ ਆਦਿ ਦੀ ਬੁਤ; ਕਟ-ਆਉਟ; ~off ਵੱਖ ਕਰਨਾ; ਟੇਕਣਾ

cutler ('ਕਅੱਟਲਅ*) *n* ਛੁਰੀਸਾਜ਼; ~y ਛੁਰੀਸਾਜ਼ੀ; ਛੁਰੀ ਕਾਂਟੇ

cutlet ('ਕਅੱਟਲਿਟ) *n* ਕਤਲਾ, ਕਤਲੰਮਾ

cutter ('ਕਅੱਟਅ*) *n* ਟੇਕਾ; ਦਰਜ਼ੀ; ਕਤੀਆ, ਕੈਂਚੀ

cutting ('ਕਅੱਟਿਙ) *n* ਕਟਾਈ, ਕਾਤਰ, ਟੋਟਾ

cycle ('ਸਇਕਲ) *n v* ਚੱਕਰ, ਦੌਰ, ਗਰਦਿਸ਼; ਸਾਈਕਲ; ਫਿਰਨਾ, ਚੱਕਰ ਲਾਉਣੇ, ਬਾਈਸਿਕਲ ਚਲਾਉਣਾ

cyclist ('ਸਾਇਕਲਿਸਟ) *n* ਸਾਈਕਲ ਸਵਾਰ

cyclone ('ਸਾਇਕਲਅਉਨ) *n* ਸਮੁੰਦਰੀ ਝੱਖੜ, ਸਾਗਰੀ ਤੂਫ਼ਾਨ, ਚੱਕਰਦਾਰ, ਹਵਾ

cylinder ('ਸਿਲਿੰਡਅ*) *n* ਵੇਲਣ, ਵੇਲਣਾਕਾਰ ਪਦਾਰਥ; ਸਿਲੰਡਰ

cynic ('ਸਿਨਿਕ) *n* ਸਨਕੀ ਵਿਅਕਤੀ, ਨੱਕ-ਚੜ੍ਹਾ ਵਿਅਕਤੀ; ~al ਰੁੱਖਾ, ਸਨਕੀ, ਤੁਰਸ਼

cypher, cipher (ਸਾਇਫਅ*) *n* ਸਿਫ਼ਰ, ਬਿੰਦੀ

D

D, d (ਡੀ) *n* ਰੋਮਨ ਵਰਣਮਾਲਾ ਦਾ ਚੌਥਾ ਵਰਣ ਜਾਂ ਅੱਖਰ; 500 ਦਾ ਚਿੰਨ੍ਹ

dabble ('ਡੈਬਲ) *v* ਕੁਰੱਜ ਮਾਰਨਾ, ਪਾਣੀ ਵਿਚ ਹੱਥ ਪੈਰ ਮਾਰਨਾ, ਛਿੜਕਣਾ, ਛਿੱਟੇ ਮਾਰਨਾ, ਗਿੱਲਾ ਕਰਨਾ, ਖੰਗੋਲਣਾ, ਪਾਣੀ ਵਿਚੋਂ ਕੱਢਣਾ

dacoit (ਡਅ'ਕੌਇਟ) *n* ਡਾਕੂ, ਡਕੈਤ; **~y** ਡਾਕਾ, ਡਕੈਤੀ, ਧਾੜਾ

dad (ਡੈਡ) *n* ਬਾਪੂ, ਭਾਪਾ, ਅੱਬਾ; *daddy*, *dada* ਵੀ

daddle (ਡੈਡਲ) *v* ਡਗਮਗਾਉਣਾ; ਲੜਖੜਾ ਕੇ ਟੁਰਨਾ, ਝੂਮ ਝੂਮ ਕੇ ਚੱਲਣਾ

daffodil ('ਡੈਫਅਡਿਲ) *n* ਨਰਗਸੀ ਫੁੱਲ; ਹਲਕਾ ਪੀਲਾ ਰੰਗ

dagger (ਡੈਗਅ*) *n* ਛੁਰਾ, ਖੰਜਰ, ਕਟਾਰ; ***at ~s drawn*** ਜਾਨੀ ਦੁਸ਼ਮਣ, ਕੱਟੜ ਵੈਰੀ

daily ('ਡੇਇਲਿ) *adv a* ਰੋਜ਼, ਨਿੱਤ ਨਿੱਤ, ਰੋਜ਼ਾਨਾ; ਨਿਰੰਤਰ, ਦੈਨਕ (ਪੱਤਰ), ਦਿਹਾੜੀਦਾਰ

dairy ('ਡੇਅਰਿ) *n* ਦੁੱਧ-ਘਰ, ਦੁੱਧ-ਮੱਖਣ ਆਦਿ ਦੀ ਦੁਕਾਨ, ਡੇਅਰੀ

dais ('ਡਇਸ) *n* ਮੰਚ, ਚਬੂਤਰਾ, ਥੜ੍ਹਾ

dak (ਡਾਕ) *n* ਡਾਕ (ਵਿਭਾਗ)

dakota (ਡਅ'ਕਅਓਟਅ) *n* ਛੋਟਾ ਹਵਾਈ ਜਹਾਜ਼

dale (ਡੇਇਲ) *n* ਘਾਟੀ, ਵਾਦੀ, ਦੂਨ

dally (ਡੈਲਿ) *v* ਸਮਾਂ ਗੁਆਉਣਾ; ਨਖਰੇ ਕਰਨਾ; ਟਾਲਣਾ, ਢਿਲ ਕਰਨਾ; ਕਲੋਲ ਕਰਨਾ, ਚੋਹਲ ਕਰਨਾ

dam (ਡੈਮ) *n v* ਡੈਮ, ਬੰਨ੍ਹ, ਰੋਕਿਆ ਪਾਣੀ; ਬੰਨ੍ਹ ਬੰਨ੍ਹਣਾ, ਡੈਮ ਉਸਾਰਨਾ

damage ('ਡੈਮਿਜ) *n* ਹਾਨੀ ਪੂਰਤੀ, ਨੁਕਸਾਨ; ਹਰਜਾਨਾ, ਚੱਟੀ; **~able** ਹਾਨੀਕਾਰਕ, ਟੁੱਟਣਹਾਰ

dame (ਡੇਇਮ) *n* (ਉਪਾਧੀ ਵਜੋਂ) ਸਰਦਾਰਨੀ

damn (ਡੈਮ) *n v* ਫਿਟਕਾਰ, ਨਿੰਦਾ, ਧਿੱਕਾਰ, ਲਾਨ੍ਹਤ; ਫਿਟਕਾਰ ਪਾਉਣੀ; **~ation** ਫਿਟਕਾਰ, ਲਾਨ੍ਹਤ, ਧਿਰਕਾਰ, ਬਦਅਸੀਸ; **~atory** ਧਿਰਕਾਰ ਭਰਿਆ, ਘਿਰਣਾਪੂਰਨ, ਨਿੰਦਾਪੂਰਨ; **~ed** ਧਿਰਕਾਰਿਆ, ਰੱਦ ਕੀਤਾ, ਦੁਰਕਾਰਿਆ, ਨਿੰਦਤ; ਅਤੀਅੰਤ, ਅਤਿ ਅਧਿਕ

damsel ('ਡੈਮਜ਼ਲ) *n* ਮੁਟਿਆਰ, ਨੱਢੀ, ਕੁਆਰੀ, ਕੰਨਿਆ

damson ('ਡੈਮਜ਼(ਅ)ਨ) *n a* ਆਲੂਬੁਖ਼ਾਰਾ

dance (ਡਾਂਸ) *n v* ਨਾਚ, ਨ੍ਰਿਤ; ਨਾਚ ਕਰਨਾ, ਨੱਚਣਾ, ਮੁਜਰਾ ਕਰਨਾ, ਨਚਾਉਣਾ; **~r** ਨ੍ਰਿਤਕਾਰ, ਨਾਚੀ, ਨਰਤਕੀ

dancing ('ਡਾਂਸਿਙ) *n* ਨਾਚ-ਕਲਾ, ਨ੍ਰਿਤ-ਕਲਾ; **~girl** ਨਾਚੀ, ਨਰਤਕੀ

dandruff ('ਡੈਨਡਰਿਫ਼) *n* ਸਿੱਕਰੀ, ਕਰ

dandy (ਡੈਂਡਿ) *n* ਵਿਸ਼ੇਸ਼ ਕਿਸਮ ਦੇ ਮਸਤੂਲ ਦਾ ਜਹਾਜ਼, ਛੈਲ ਛਬੀਲਾ, ਬਾਂਕਾ

danger ('ਡੇਇੰਜਅ*) *n* ਭੈ, ਖ਼ਤਰਾ, ਖਟਕਾ, ਜੋਖ਼ਮ; **~ous** ਖ਼ਤਰਨਾਕ, ਭਿਆਨਕ, ਭਿਅੰਕਰ, ਡਰਾਉਣਾ

dangle ('ਡੈਂਗਲ) *v* ਪਿੱਛੇ ਪਿੱਛੇ ਫਿਰਨਾ; ਲਟਕਾਉਣਾ, ਲਟਕਣਾ; **~r** (ਆਸ਼ਕ ਆਦਿ) ਪਿੱਛਲਗ

dare (ਡੇਅ*) *v* ਹੌਸਲਾ ਕਰਨਾ, ਹਿੰਮਤ ਕਰਨੀ, ਸਾਹਸ ਕਰਨਾ

daring ('ਡੇਅਰਿੰਗ) *n a* ਦਲੇਰੀ, ਵੀਰਤਾ, ਬਹਾਦਰੀ, ਜੇਰਾ, ਹਿੰਮਤ, ਜਿਗਰੇ ਵਾਲਾ, ਨਿਡਰ, ਹਿੰਮਤੀ

dark (ਡਾਕ) *n a* ਅੰਧਕਾਰ, ਹਨੇਰਾ; ਅਗਿਆਨ, ਸਿਆਹ, ਕਾਲਾ, ਸਾਂਵਲਾ; ਅਸਪਸ਼ਟਤਾ, ਭਿਆਨਕ, ਧੁੰਧਲਾ, ਉਦਾਸ, ਗੁਪਤ; ~**blue** ਗੁੜ੍ਹਾ ਨੀਲਾ; **in the~** ਬੇਖ਼ਬਰ, ਅਨਜਾਣ; ~**en** ਧੁੰਦਲਾ ਕਰਨਾ, ਕਾਲਾ ਕਰਨਾ, ਅੰਨ੍ਹਾ ਕਰਨਾ, ਘਬਰਾਉਣਾ; ~**ness** ਹਨੇਰਾਪਨ, ਧੁੰਦਲਾਪਨ, ਅੰਧਕਾਰ, ਅਗਿਆਨ

darling ('ਡਾਲਿੰਗ) *n a* ਪਿਆਰਾ, ਪ੍ਰੀਤਮ; ਪ੍ਰਿਅ, ਲਾਡਲਾ, ਦੁਲਾਰਾ

darn (ਡਾ*ਨ) *v n* ਰਫੂ ਕਰਨਾ, ਜਾਲੀ ਪਾਉਣਾ; ~**ing** ਰਫੂ, ਰਫੂਗਰੀ

dart (ਡਾਟ) *n v* ਤੀਰ, ਬਰਛੀ; ਭਾਲਾ; ਬਾਣ; ਤੀਰ ਮਾਰਨਾ, ਬਰਛੀ ਮਾਰਨਾ, ਤੇਜ਼ੀ ਨਾਲ ਵਧਣਾ

dash (ਡੈਸ਼) *n v* ਵਕਫਾ, ਵਾਕ ਛੋੜਣ ਦਾ ਨਿਸ਼ਾਨ (—), ਅਲਪ ਮਾਤਰਾ; ਕਲਮ ਦੀ ਝਰੀਟ, ਰੰਗ ਦਾ ਛਿੱਟਾ; ਚੁਟਕੀ; ਪਾਣੀ ਦੀਆਂ ਛਲਾਂ ਦੀ ਅਵਾਜ਼; ਤੁਰਤ-ਫੁਰਤ ਕੰਮ; ਚੜ੍ਹਾਈ, ਧਾਵਾ; ਡੈਸ਼ ਲਾਉਣਾ; ਟੱਕਰ ਖਾਣਾ, ਟਕਰਾਉਣਾ ਦਬਾਉਣਾ, ਤੇਜ਼ਨ, ਮਿੱਟੀ ਵਿਚ ਮਿਲਾ ਦੇਣਾ; ਤੇਜ਼ੀ ਨਾਲ ਡਿੱਗਣਾ; ~**ing** ਉਮੰਗੀ, ਸ਼ਾਨ ਵਿਖਾਉਣ ਵਾਲਾ

data ('ਡੇਇਟਾ) *n* (*datum* ਦਾ ਬ ਵ), ਸਮਗਰੀ, ਆਧਾਰ, ਅੰਕੜੇ

date (ਡੇਇਟ) *n v* ਤਿਥੀ, ਮਿਤੀ, ਤਾਰੀਖ; ਤਾਰੀਖ ਪਾਉਣੀ; ਖਜੂਰ, ਛੁਹਾਰਾ; ~**d** ਮਿਤੀ-ਯੁਕਤ; ~**less** ਬੇਤਾਰੀਖਾ; ਆਦਿ, ਪੁਰਾਣਾ

dative ('ਡੇਇਟਿਵ) *n a* ਸੰਪਰਦਾਨ ਕਾਰਕ

daub (ਡੋਬ) *v n* ਪੋਚਣਾ, ਲਿੰਬਣਾ, ਲਘੇੜਨਾ; ਪੋਚਾ, ਭੱਦਾ ਚਿਤਰ

daughter ('ਡੋਟਅ*) *n* ਪੁੱਤਰੀ, ਬੇਟੀ, ਧੀ, ਲੜਕੀ, ਜਾਈ; ~**in-law** ਨੂੰਹ

daunt (ਡੋਂਟ) *v* ਹਿੰਮਤ ਤੋੜਨ; ਡਾਂਟਣਾ, ਧਮਕਾਉਣਾ, ਭੈ ਦੇਣਾ; ~**less** ਨਿਡਰ, ਨਿਧੜਕ

dawdle ('ਡੋਡਲ) *v* ਸਮਾਂ ਨਸ਼ਟ ਕਰਨਾ, ਅਵਾਰਾ ਘੁੰਮਣਾ, ਬੇਕਾਰ ਫਿਰਨਾ, ਸੁਸਤੀ ਕਰਨਾ

dawn (ਡੋਨ) *n v* ਪ੍ਰਭਾਤ, ਸਰਘੀ ਵੇਲਾ, ਪਹੁਫੁਟਾਲਾ, ਤੜਕਾ, ਪ੍ਰਾਤਾਕਾਲ; ਸਵੇਰ ਹੋਣਾ; ਦਿਸਣਾ, ਆਰੰਭ ਹੋਣਾ

day (ਡੇਇ) *n* ਦਿਨ, ਦਿਵਸ, ਵਾਰ; ਸਵੇਰ; ਅੱਠ ਪਹਿਰ, ਨਿਸ਼ਚਤ ਮਿਤੀ; ਦੌਰ, ਯੁੱਗ; ~**book** ਰੋਜ਼-ਨਾਮਚਾ; ~**break** ਪ੍ਰਭਾਤ, ਪਹੁ-ਫੁਟਾਲਾ; ~**light** ਚਾਨਣ, ਧੁੱਪ, ਤੜਕਾ; ~**long** ਸਾਰਾ ਦਿਨ; *better~ s* ਖ਼ੁਸ਼ਹਾਲੀ ਦਾ ਸਮਾਂ, ਚੰਗੇ ਦਿਨ

daze (ਡੇਇਜ਼) *v n* ਚਕਰਾ ਦੇਣਾ, ਚਲਿੱਤ ਕਰ ਦੇਣਾ, ਹੱਕਾ-ਬੱਕਾ ਕਰ ਦੇਣਾ, ਚੁੰਧਿਆ ਦੇਣਾ; ਹੈਰਾਨੀ

dazzle (ਡੈਜ਼ਲ) *v* ਚੁੰਧਿਆਉਣਾ, ਚਕਾਚੌਂਧ ਕਰਨਾ, ਚਕਰਾ ਦੇਣਾ, ਹੈਰਾਨ ਕਰਨਾ

dazzling (ਡੈਜ਼ਲਿੰਗ) *a* ਚੁੰਧਿਆ ਦੇਣ ਵਾਲਾ, ਪਰੇਸ਼ਾਨ ਕਰਨ ਵਾਲਾ

dead (ਡੈਡ) *a adv* ਮਰਿਆ, ਮਿਰਤਕ, ਮੁਰਦਾ; ਨਿਰਜੀਵ; ਅਚੇਤਨ, ਬੇਸੁਧ; ਅਪ੍ਰਚਲਤ, ਪ੍ਰਭਾਵਹੀਨ, ਬੀਤਿਆ, ਪੁਰਾਣਾ; ਪੂਰੇ ਤੋਰ ਤੇ, ਬਿਲਕੁਲ; ਸਰਾਸਰ; ~**against** ਸਖ਼ਤ ਵੈਰੀ; ਜਾਨੀ ਦੁਸ਼ਮਨ; ~**end** ਅੰਤਮ ਸਿਰਾ, ਬੰਦ ਗਲੀ; ~**hours** ਅੱਧੀ ਰਾਤ; ~**language** ਅਪ੍ਰਚਲਤ ਭਾਸ਼ਾ; ~**lock** ਅੜਿਕਾ; ~**shot** ਚੰਗਾ ਨਿਸ਼ਾਨੇਬੀ; ~**stock** ਡੁੱਬੀ ਰਕਮ, ਬੇਕਾਰ ਮਾਲ; ~**sure** ਪੱਕਾ ਨਿਸ਼ਚਾ; ~**wood** ਮਰਿਆ ਸੱਪ,

ਵਾਯੂ ਦਾ ਭਾਰ; **~en** ਮਾਰਨਾ, ਅਚੇਤ ਕਰਨਾ, ਸੁੰਨ ਕਰਨਾ; ਘਟ ਕਰ ਦੇਣਾ; **~ly** ਮੌਤ ਵਰਗੀ, ਅਤੀਅੰਤ, ਬਿਲਕੁਲ

deaf (ਡੈੱਫ਼) *a* ਬੋਲਾ; ਡੋਰਾ; ਬਹਿਰਾ, ਲਾਪਰਵਾਹ; **~mute** ਗੁੰਗਾ-ਬੋਲਾ ਆਦਮੀ; **~en** ਬੋਲਾ ਕਰਨਾ, ਕੰਨ ਪਾੜ ਦੇਣੇ; (ਆਵਾਜ਼) ਨਾ ਸੁਣਨ ਦੇਣੀ

deal (ਡੀਲ) *n v* ਸੌਦਾ; ਹਿੱਸਾ, ਵੰਡਾਰਾ; ਵਰਤਾਉ ਕਰਨਾ; ਸਲੂਕ ਕਰਨਾ, ਸੌਦਾ ਕਰਨਾ; **~er** ਵਪਾਰੀ, ਦੁਕਾਨਦਾਰ, ਵਿਕਰੇਤਾ; **~ing** ਲੈਣ-ਦੇਣ, ਕਾਰੋਬਾਰ, ਵਣਜ; ਵਪਾਰ; ਵਰਤਾਉ

dean (ਡੀਨ) *n* (ਯੂਨੀਵਰਸਿਟੀ ਵਿਚ) ਡੀਨ; ਵੱਡਾ ਪਾਦਰੀ, ਮੱਠ-ਅਧਿਕਾਰੀ

dear (ਡਿਅ*) *a* ਪਿਆਰਾ, ਦੁਲਾਰਾ, ਲਾਡਲਾ, ਚਹੇਤਾ; ਮਹਿੰਗਾ; **~ness** ਪ੍ਰੀਤ, ਪਰੇਮ, ਪਿਆਰ, ਮਹਿੰਗਾਈ

dearth (ਡਾਃਥ) *n* ਥੁੜ, ਕਮੀ, ਘਾਟ, ਤੋੜਾ, ਕਿੱਲਤ

death (ਡੈਥ) *n* ਦੇਹਾਂਤ, ਮੌਤ, ਮਿਰਤੂ; **~sentence** ਮੌਤ ਦੀ ਸਜ਼ਾ, ਮਿਰਤੂ ਦੰਡ; **~less** ਅਮਰ, ਸਦੀਵੀ

debacle (ਡੇਇ'ਬਾਕਲ) *n* ਪਤਨ, ਜ਼ਵਾਲ; ਭਾਜੜ

debar (ਡਿ'ਬਾ*) *n* ਵਰਜਣਾ, ਮਨ੍ਹਾਂ ਕਰਨਾ, ਰੋਕਣਾ; ਖ਼ਾਰਜ ਕਰਨਾ; ਅੜਚਨ ਪਾਉਣੀ; **~red** ਵਰਜਤ, ਵਿਵਰਜਤ; ਰੋਕਿਆ

debase (ਡਿ'ਬੇਇਸ) *v* ਮਿਲਾਵਟ ਕਰਨੀ, ਖੋਟ ਰਲਾਉਣੀ; ਮੁੱਲ ਘਟਾਉਣਾ; ਦਰਜਾ ਘੱਟ ਕਰਨਾ, ਆਦਰ ਮਾਨ ਘਟਾਉਣਾ, ਵਿਗਾੜਨਾ; **~ment** ਮਿਲਾਵਟ, ਖ਼ਰਾਬੀ, ਨੁਕਸ, ਵਿਗਾੜ, ਬੇਕਦਰੀ, ਨਿਰਾਦਰ

debatable (ਡਿ'ਬੇਇਟਅਬਲ) *a* ਵਿਵਾਦਗ੍ਰਸਤ,

ਬਹਿਸਯੋਗ, ਸ਼ਕੀ, ਸ਼ੰਕਾਪੂਰਨ

debate (ਡਿ'ਬੇਇਟ) *n v* ਬਹਿਸ, ਵਾਦ-ਵਿਵਾਦ ਵਿਚਾਰ-ਵਟਾਂਦਰਾ; ਵਿਵਾਦ ਕਰਨਾ, ਤਕਰਾਰ ਕਰਨਾ

debauch (ਡਿ'ਬੋਚ) *n v* ਭ੍ਰਿਸ਼ਟ, ਲੁੱਚਾ, ਬਦਮਾਸ਼ੀ ਕਰਨੀ, ਬਦਕਾਰੀ ਕਰਨੀ, ਅਵਾਰਾ ਬਣਾਉਣਾ; ਸਤ ਭੰਗ ਕਰਨਾ; ਫੁਸਲਾਉਣਾ; **~edness** ਭ੍ਰਿਸ਼ਟਤਾ, ਚਰਿੱਤਰਹੀਨਤਾ; **~ery** ਕਾਮ ਵਾਸ਼ਨਾ, ਅੱਯਾਸ਼ੀ, ਵਿਸ਼ਯ ਭੋਗ

debenture (ਡਿ'ਬੈਨੱਚਅ*) *n* ਇਕਰਾਰਨਾਮਾ; ਤਮੱਸਕ, ਰਿਣ ਪੱਤਰ

debit (ਡੈੱਬਿਟ) *n v* ਖ਼ਰਚ, ਉਧਾਰ, ਕਰਜ਼ਾ, ਰਿਣ, ਉਧਾਰ ਖਾਤਾ

debonair (ਡੈਬੱਅ'ਨੇਅ*) *a* ਨਿਮਰ, ਸੱਜਣ, ਭੱਦਰ, ਮਿਲਣਸਾਰ, ਸੁਸ਼ੀਲ

debris (ਡੇਇਬਰੀ) *n* ਮਲਬਾ, ਇੱਟਾਂ ਰੋੜੇ

debt (ਡੈੱਟ) *n* ਕਰਜ਼, ਰਿਣ, ਦੇਣਦਾਰੀ, ਉਧਾਰ; **~of nature** ਮੌਤ; **~ee** ਸਾਹੂਕਾਰ, ਰਿਣਦਾਤਾ; **~or** ਦੇਣਦਾਰ, ਕਰਜ਼ਦਾਰ, ਰਿਣੀ

decade (ਡੈਕੇਇਡ) *n* ਦਹਾਕਾ; ਦਸ਼ਕ, ਦਹਾਈ

decamp (ਡਿ'ਕੈਂਪ) *v* ਅਚਾਨਕ ਭੱਜ ਜਾਣਾ, ਰਫ਼ੂ ਚੱਕਰ ਹੋ ਜਾਣਾ, ਕੁਝ ਚੁਰਾ ਕੇ ਨੱਸ ਜਾਣਾ, ਡੇਰਾ ਚੁੱਕਣਾ, ਲੋਪ ਹੋਣਾ; **~ment** ਕੂਚ, ਰਵਾਨਗੀ, ਫਰਾਰੀ, ਪਲਾਇਨ

decay (ਡਿ'ਕੇਇ) *v n* ਪਤਿਤ ਹੋਣਾ, ਨਾਸ ਹੋਣਾ, ਖ਼ਰਾਬ ਹੋਣਾ, ਘਟਾਉਣਾ; ਤਬਾਹੀ, ਬਰਬਾਦੀ, ਜ਼ਵਾਲ, ਪਤਨ, ਨਾਸ

decease (ਡਿ'ਸੀਸ) *n v* ਮੌਤ, ਮਿਰਤੂ, ਦੇਹਾਂਤ, ਮਰਨਾ, ਸੁਰਗਵਾਸ ਹੋਣਾ; **~d** ਮਿਰਤਕ, ਸੁਰਗਵਾਸੀ

deceit (ਡਿ'ਸੀਟ) *n* ਕਪਟ, ਧੋਖਾ, ਛਲ, ਫ਼ਰੇਬ,

~ful ਛਲੀਆ, ਕਪਟੀ, ਮੱਕਾਰ, ਧੋਖੇਬਾਜ਼,
ਚਾਲਬਾਜ਼; ~fulness ਕਪਟਪੂਰਨਤਾ, ਛਲ,
ਦਗਾ, ਮੱਕਾਰੀ, ਧੋਖੇਬਾਜ਼ੀ, ਚਾਲਬਾਜ਼ੀ

deceive (ਡਿ'ਸੀਵ) v ਧੋਖਾ ਦੇਣਾ, ਛਲ ਕਰਨਾ,
ਛਲਣਾ, ਵਿਸ਼ਵਾਸਘਾਤ ਕਰਨਾ; ~r ਠੱਗ,
ਕਪਟੀ, ਮੱਕਾਰ, ਧੋਖੇਬਾਜ਼, ਦਗਾਬਾਜ਼

december (ਡਿ'ਸੈਂਬਅ*) n ਅੰਗਰੇਜ਼ੀ ਸਾਲ ਦਾ
ਬਾਰ੍ਹਵਾਂ ਮਹੀਨਾ, ਦਸੰਬਰ

decency (ਡੀਸੰਸਿ) n ਸੁਸ਼ੀਲਤਾ, ਸ਼ਿਸਟਤਾ;
ਸੁੱਘੜਤਾ, ਭਲਮਾਨਸੀ, ਮਰਯਾਦਾ

decent (ਡੀਸੰਟ) a ਸੁੱਘੜ, ਭਲਾ, ਸਾਊ,
ਭਲਮਾਨਸ, ਸੁਸ਼ੀਲ, ਚੰਗਾ, ਚੋਖਾ

decentralize (ਡੀ'ਸੈਂਟਰਅਲਾਇਜ਼) v
ਵਿਕੇਂਦਰੀਕਰਨ ਕਰਨਾ, ਵਿਕੇਂਦਰਤ ਕਰਨਾ; ~d
ਵਿਕੇਂਦਰੀਕ੍ਰਿਤ, ਵਿਕੇਂਦਰਤ

deceptible (ਡਿ'ਸੈੱਪਟਅਬਲ) n ਛਲਣਯੋਗ

deception (ਡਿ'ਸੈੱਪੱਸ਼ਨ) n ਕਪਟ, ਛਲ, ਧੋਖਾ,
ਝਾਂਸਾ

deceptive (ਡਿ'ਸੈੱਪਟਿਵ) a ਭਰਮਪੂਰਨ, ਕਪਟ-
ਪੂਰਨ, ਝੂਠਾ

decide (ਡਿ'ਸਾਇਡ) v ਫ਼ੈਸਲਾ ਦੇਣਾ, ਨਿਰਣਾ
ਕਰਨਾ, ਨਿਸ਼ਚਤ ਕਰਨਾ, ਤੈ ਕਰਨਾ,

deciding (ਡਿ'ਸਾਇਡਿੰਗ) a ਨਿਸ਼ਚੇਕਾਰੀ;
ਨਿਰਣਾਤਮਕ

decimal (ਡੈ'ਸਿਮਲ) n a ਦਸ਼ਮਲਵ,
ਇਸ਼ਾਰੀਆ, ਦਸ਼ਾਂਸ਼ਕ, ਦਸ਼ਮਕ, ਦਸ਼ਾਂਸ;
~system ਦਸ਼ਮਲਵ ਪ੍ਰਣਾਲੀ

decipher (ਡਿ'ਸਾਇਫ਼ਅ*) n v ਗੁਝੂ ਜਾਂ ਗੁਪਤ
ਲੇਖ ਜਾਂ ਲਿਪੀ ਦੀ ਵਿਆਖਿਆ, ਗੁਪਤ ਲੇਖ
ਵਾਚਨਾ

decision (ਡਿ'ਸਿਯ਼ਨ) n ਨਿਰਣਾ, ਫ਼ੈਸਲਾ,

ਨਿਸ਼ਚਾ, ਨਿਬੇੜਾ

decisive (ਡਿ'ਸਾਇਸਿਵ਼) a ਫ਼ੈਸਲਾਕੁਨ,
ਨਿਸ਼ਚੇਕਾਰੀ, ਨਿਰਣਾਇਕ, ਨਿਸ਼ਚਤ; ~ness
ਨਿਸ਼ਚਤਤਾ, ਨਿਸ਼ਚਾਤਮਕਤਾ, ਨਿਰਣਾਇਕਤਾ

deck (ਡੈੱਕ) n v ਜਹਾਜ਼ ਦਾ ਫ਼ਰਸ਼, ਡੈੱਕ; ਜ਼ਮੀਨ;
ਢਾ ਜਾਣਾ, ਢਕ ਲੈਣਾ; ਅਲੰਕਰਤ ਕਰਨਾ,
ਸਿੰਗਾਰਨਾ

declaim (ਡਿ'ਕਲੇਇਮ) v ਭਾਸ਼ਣ ਦੇਣਾ, ਜੋਸ਼ੀਲੀ
ਤਕਰੀਰ ਕਰਨੀ

declamation (ਡੈੱਕਲਅਮ'ਮੇਇਸ਼ਨ) n ਭਾਵੁਕ
ਭਾਸ਼ਣ; ਭਾਸ਼ਣਬਾਜ਼ੀ; ਅਲੰਕਾਰਮਈ
ਵਿਆਖਿਆਨ

declaration (ਡੈੱਕਲਅ'ਰੇਇਸ਼ਨ) n ਐਲਾਨ,
ਘੋਸ਼ਣਾ-ਪੱਤਰ, ਮਹਿਸੂਲੀ ਮਾਲ ਦਾ ਵਿਵਰਣ

declaratory (ਡਿ'ਕਲੈਰਅਟ(ਅ)ਰਿ) a ਘੋਸ਼ਕ,
ਸੂਚਕ, ਪ੍ਰਕਾਸ਼ਕ

declare (ਡਿ'ਕਲੇਅ*) v ਐਲਾਨ ਕਰਨਾ, ਘੋਸ਼ਣਾ
ਕਰਨਾ, ਬਿਆਨ ਦੇਣਾ, ਸੂਚਤ ਕਰਨਾ, ਮਹਿਸੂਲੀ
ਮਾਲ ਦਾ ਵਿਵਰਣ ਦੇਣਾ; ~d ਐਲਾਨ ਸ਼ੁਦਾ,
ਘੋਸ਼ਤ

declass (ਡੀ'ਕਲਾਸ) v ਛੇਕਣਾ, ਜਮਾਤ ਜਾਂ ਜਾਤੀ
ਵਿਚੋਂ ਕੱਢਣਾ, ਹੁੱਕਾ-ਪਾਣੀ ਬੰਦ ਕਰਨਾ

decline (ਡਿ'ਕਲਾਇਨ) n v ਪਤਨ, ਗਿਰਾਵਟ,
ਨਿਘਾਰ, ਉਤਰਾਅ;(ਭਾਅ ਦਾ) ਮੰਦਾ, ਅੰਤਮ
ਅਝੀ, ਪਤਨ ਵਲ ਜਾਣਾ; ਕੀਮਤਾਂ ਘਟਣੀਆਂ,
ਭਾਅ ਮੰਦੇ ਹੋਣੇ, ਢਲਣਾ, ਢਾਲਣਾ, ਝੁਕਾਉਣਾ;
~on ਉਤਰਨਾ

declining (ਡਿ'ਕਲਾਇਨਿੰਗ) a ਢਲਵਾਂ,
ਢਾਲਦਾਰ, ਪਤਨਸ਼ੀਲ

decode (ਡੀ'ਕਅਊਡ) v ਗੁਪਤਲੇਖ ਪੜ੍ਹਨਾ,
ਸੰਕੇਤ-ਵਾਚਨਾ

decompose (ਡੀਕਅੱ'ਪਅਉਜ਼) v ਅੰਗ-ਨਿਖੇੜ ਕਰਨ, ਅਲੱਗ ਕਰਨ, ਵਿਸ਼ਲੇਸ਼ਣ ਕਰਨ; ਗਲਣਾ, ਸੜਨ, ਗਲਾਉਣਾ

decomposition (ਡੀਕੰਪਅਜ਼ਿਸ਼ਨ) v ਵਿਖਟਣ; ਵਿਸ਼ਲੇਸ਼ਣ, ਸੜਨ, ਗਲਣ .

decontaminate (ਡੀਕਅਨ'ਟੈਮਿਨੇਇਟ) v ਰੋਗਾਨੂਰਹਿਤ ਕਰਨਾ, ਸ਼ੁੱਧ ਕਰਨਾ, ਦੋਸ਼-ਮੁਕਤ ਕਰਨਾ

decontamination (ਡੀਕੰਟੈਮਿਨੇਸ਼ਨ) n ਨਿਰਦੋਸ਼ੀਕਰਨ, ਸ਼ੁਧੀਕਰਨ, ਦੋਸ਼ਮੁਕਤੀ

decontrol (ਡੀਕੰਟਰਅਉਲ) n v ਕੰਟਰੋਲ, ਨਿਵਾਰਨ, ਵਿਨਿਯੰਤਰਣ, ਅਪਨਿਯੰਤਰਣ ਕਰਨ

decor (ਡੇਇਕੋ*) n ਸ਼ਿੰਗਾਰ, ਸਜਾਵਟ; **~ate** ਸ਼ਿੰਗਾਰਨਾ, ਸਜਾਉਣਾ, ਸੰਵਾਰਨਾ, ਤਮਗਾ ਦੇਣਾ; **~ation** ਸਜਾਵਟ, ਸ਼ਿੰਗਾਰ, ਅਲੰਕਰਨ, ਅਲੰਕਾਰ; ਸਾਜ਼; ਤਮਗਾ

decorum (ਡਿ'ਕੋਰਅਮ) n ਮਰਯਾਦਾ, ਸੁਘੜਤਾ, ਵਿਹਾਰਸ਼ੀਲਤਾ, ਸੁੱਚਜਤਾ

decoy (ਡੀ'ਕੋਇ, ਡਿ'ਕੋਇ) n v ਫੰਦਾ, ਚਾਰਾ, ਫਸਾਉਣਾ, ਧੋਖੇ ਨਾਲ ਫੜਨਾ, ਘੇਰਨਾ, ਧੋਖਾ ਦੇਣਾ

decrease (ਡੀ'ਕਰੀਸ, ਡੀਕਰੀਸ) v n ਘੱਟ ਕਰਨਾ, ਘਟਾਉਣਾ; ਕਮੀ, ਘਾਟਾ; **~d** ਘਟਿਆ

decree (ਡਿ'ਕਰੀ) n v ਫ਼ਰਮਾਨ, ਹੁਕਮ; ਰੱਜਾ, ਡਿਗਰੀ; ਰਾਜ-ਆਗਿਆ; ਹੁਕਮ ਦੇਣਾ, ਫ਼ਰਮਾਨ ਜਾਰੀ ਕਰਨਾ, ਆਗਿਆ ਦੇਣੀ, ਡਿਗਰੀ ਕਰਨੀ

decrown (ਡੀ'ਕਰਾਉਨ) v ਤਾਜ ਉਤਾਰਨਾ, ਤਾਜਹੀਨ ਕਰਨਾ

decry (ਡਿ'ਕਰਾਇ) v ਨਿੰਦਾ, ਭੰਡਣਾ, ਦੋਸ਼ ਲਗਾਉਣਾ, ਕੋਸਣਾ

dedicate (ਡੈਡਿਕੇਇਟ) v ਭੇਟਾ ਕਰਨਾ, ਅਰਪਣ ਕਰਨਾ; ਸਮਰਪਣ ਕਰਨਾ, ਪ੍ਰਦਾਨ ਕਰਨਾ, ਨਿਛਾਵਰ ਕਰਨਾ, ਸੌਂਪਣਾ; **~d** ਭੇਟਾ ਕੀਤਾ, ਸਮਰਪਤ; ਸਿਦਕਵਾਨ

dedication (ਡੈਡਿਕੇ'ਇਸ਼ਨ) n ਭੇਟਾ, ਨਜ਼ਰ, ਸਮਰਪਣ, ਸ਼ਰਧਾ

deduct (ਡਿ'ਡਅੱਕਟ) v ਘਟਾਉਣਾ, ਘਟਾ ਦੇਣਾ; ਕਟੌਤੀ ਕਰਨਾ, ਕੱਟਣਾ, ਅਨੁਮਾਨ ਕਰਨਾ; **~ion** ਕਟੌਤੀ, ਕਾਟ, ਛੋਟ; ਸਿੱਟਾ

deed (ਡੀਡ) n ਕੰਮ, ਕਾਰਜ; ਕਰਨੀ; ਦਸਤਾਵੇਜ਼, ਲਿਖਤ, ਪੱਟਾ

deem (ਡੀਮ) v ਵਿਚਾਰ ਕਰਨਾ, ਗਿਣਨਾ, ਸੋਚਣਾ, ਮੰਨਣਾ, ਸਮਝਣਾ, ਅਨੁਭਵ ਕਰਨਾ, ਅਨੁਮਾਨ ਲਾਉਣਾ

deep (ਡੀਪ) a n adv ਡੂੰਘਾ, ਅਗਾਧ, ਗੰਭੀਰ, ਗਹਿਰਾ; ਘਣਾ; ਡੁੱਬਿਆ, ਸ਼ੋਖ (ਰੰਗ), ਤੀਬਰ; ਅਤੀਅੰਤ, ਅਧਿਕ; ਸਾਗਰ, ਸਮੁੰਦਰ ਦਾ ਡੂੰਘਾ ਹਿੱਸਾ; ਗਹਿਰਾਈ ਵਿਚ; **~learning** ਅਥਾਹ ਵਿਦਵਤਾ, ਡੂੰਘਾ ਗਿਆਨ; **~interest** ਡਾਢੀ ਦਿਲਚਸਪੀ; **~rooted** ਡੂੰਘਾ, ਗਹਿਰਾ; **in~waters** ਸੰਕਟ ਵਿਚ ਫਸਿਆ; **the~** ਸਮੁੰਦਰ, ਸਾਗਰ; ਖੱਡਾ, ਟੋਆ

deer (ਡਿਅ*) n ਹਿਰਨ, ਮਿਰਗ

deface (ਡਿ'ਫ਼ੇਇਸ) v ਰੂਪ ਵਿਗਾੜਨਾ, ਕਰੂਪ ਕਰਨਾ, ਮਿਟਾਉਣਾ, ਬਦਨਾਮ ਕਰਨਾ; **~d** ਵਿਗੜਿਆ, ਕਰੂਪ, ਵਿਕਿਰਤ

defacto (ਡੇਇ'ਫ਼ੈਕਟਅਉ) adv ਯਥਾਰਥ ਵਿਚ

defalcate (ਡੇਇ'ਫ਼ੈਲਕੇਇਟ) v ਗ਼ਬਨ ਕਰਨਾ, ਖਾ ਜਾਣਾ, (ਰੁਪਏ ਦੀ) ਖਿਆਨਤ ਕਰਨੀ, ਹੜਪਣਾ, ਗੋਲਮਾਲ ਕਰਨਾ, ਮਾਰ ਲੈਣਾ

defalcation (ਡੀਫ਼ੈਲ'ਕੇਇਸ਼ਨ) n ਗ਼ਬਨ, ਘਾਲਾ-ਮਾਲਾ, ਵਿਸ਼ਵਾਸਘਾਤ

defamation (ਡੈਫ਼ਅ'ਮੇਇਸ਼ਨ) *n* ਬਦਨਾਮੀ, ਨਿਰਾਦਰ, ਤੌਹੀਨ, ਮਾਨ-ਹਾਨੀ, ਹੱਤਕ, ਬੇਇੱਜ਼ਤੀ

defamatory (ਡਿ'ਫ਼ੈਮਅਟ(ਇ)ਰਿ) *a* ਬਦਨਾਮੀ ਵਾਲਾ, ਬਦਨਾਮੀ ਦਾ, ਕਲੰਕਤਕਾਰੀ

defame (ਡਿ'ਫ਼ੇਇਮ) *v* ਬਦਨਾਮ ਕਰਨਾ, ਨਿਰਾਦਰ ਕਰਨਾ, ਭੰਡੀ ਕਰਨੀ, ਨਿੰਦਾ ਕਰਨਾ

default (ਡਿ'ਫ਼ੋਲਟ) *n v* ਉਕਾਈ, ਤਰੁਟੀ, ਭੁੱਲ ਚੁੱਕ; ਅਣਗਹਿਲੀ ਕਰਨੀ, ਅਦਾਲਤ ਵਿਚ ਹਾਜ਼ਰ ਨਾ ਹੋਣਾ, ਪੈਰਵੀ ਨਾ ਕਰਨੀ; ਹਿਸਾਬ ਨਾ ਚੁਕਾਉਣਾ; ~ed ਅਸ਼ੁੱਧ, ਦੋਸ਼ਪੂਰਨ (ਥੀਮਾ, ਕਿਸ਼ਤ ਆਦਿ); ~er (ਅਦਾਲਤ ਵਿਚ) ਗ਼ੈਰ-ਹਾਜ਼ਰ ਧਿਰ; ਭੁਗਤਾਨ ਤੋਂ ਖੁੰਝਣ ਵਾਲਾ

defeat (ਡਿ'ਫ਼ੀਟ) *n v* ਹਾਰ, ਅਸਫਲਤਾ, ਸ਼ਿਕਸਤ, ਹਰਾਉਣਾ, ਨਿਸਫਲ ਕਰਨਾ; ਪਿੱਠ ਲਾਉਣੀ; ~d ਹਾਰਿਆ, ਪਰਾਜਿਤ

defect (ਡਿਫ਼ੈਕੱਟ) *n* ਔਗੁਣ, ਵਿਕਾਰ, ਤਰੁਟੀ, ਦੋਸ਼, ਐਬ, ਨੁਕਸ, ਖ਼ਾਮੀ, ਖ਼ਰਾਬੀ, ਕਲੰਕ, ਕਮੀ; ~ion ਪੱਖ-ਤਿਆਗਾ, ਧਰਮ-ਤਿਆਗਾ, ਦਲ-ਤਿਆਗਾ

defective (ਡਿ'ਫ਼ੈਕੱਟਿਵ) *a* ਨੁਕਸਦਾਰ, ਦੋਸ਼ਪੂਰਨ, ਤਰੁਟੀਪੂਰਨ, ਖੋਟਾ, ਦਾਗ਼ੀ, ਅਪੂਰਨ

defector (ਡਿ'ਫ਼ੈਕਟਅ*) *n* ਦਲਬਦਲੂ

defence (ਡਿ'ਫ਼ੈਂਸ) *n* ਰੱਖਿਆ, ਸੁਰੱਖਿਆ, ਪ੍ਰਤੀਵਾਦ ਲੇਖ, ਬਚਾਉ, ਰੋਕ, ਆੜ, ਓਟ, ਕਿਲ੍ਹਾ-ਬੰਦੀ; line of~ ਮੋਰਚਾਬੰਦੀ

defend (ਡਿ'ਫ਼ੈਂਡ) *v* ਰੱਖਿਆ ਕਰਨਾ, ਬਚਾਉ ਕਰਨਾ; ਪ੍ਰਤੀਵਾਦ ਕਰਨਾ, ਪੱਖ-ਪੂਸ਼ਟੀ ਕਰਨੀ; ਸਫ਼ਾਈ ਪੇਸ਼ ਕਰਨਾ, ਮੁਕੱਦਮੇ ਦੀ ਜਵਾਬਦੇਹੀ ਕਰਨਾ; ਉਜ਼ਰਦਾਰੀ ਕਰਨਾ; ~able ਰੱਖਿਆ ਕਰਨ ਯੋਗ

defensive (ਡਿ'ਫ਼ੈਂਸਿਵ੍) *n a* ਬਚਾਉ, ਰੱਖਿਆ; ਰੱਖਿਅਕ, ਰੱਖਿਆਤਮਕ

defer (ਡਿ'ਫ਼ਅ*) *v* ਟਾਲਣਾ, ਲਮਕਾਉਣਾ; ਮੂਲਤਵੀ ਕਰਨਾ, ਸਥਗਤ ਕਰਨਾ; ~ment ਦੇਰੀ, ਸਥਗਨ; ~red ਮੂਲਤਵੀ ਕੀਤਾ ਗਿਆ, ਸਥਗਤ

deference (ਡੈਫ਼(ਅ)ਰ(ਅ)ਨਸ) *n* ਸਨਮਾਨ, ਆਦਰ, ਇਜ਼ਤ, ਲਿਹਾਜ਼, ਸਤਿਕਾਰ

deferent (ਡੈਫ਼(ਅ)ਰਅੰਟ) *a* ਸਨਮਾਨਤ

deferential (ਡੈਫ਼ਅ'ਰੈਂਸ਼ਲ) *a* ਆਦਰਪੂਰਨ, ਆਦਰਯੋਗ, ਮਾਨਯੋਗ

defiant (ਡਿ'ਫ਼ਾਇਅੰਟ) *a* ਵਿਰੋਧੀ, ਅੱਗਿਆਕਾਰੀ, ਗੁਸਤਾਖ਼

deficiency (ਡਿ'ਫ਼ਿਸ਼ਿੰਸਿ) *n* ਅਪੂਰਨਤਾ, ਤੋਟਾ, ਕਮੀ, ਕਸਰ, ਅਧੂਰਾਪਣ, ਨੁਕਸ, ਅਭਾਵ

deficient ('ਡਿ'ਫ਼ਿਸ਼ੰਟ) *a* ਥੋੜ੍ਹਾ, ਘੱਟ, ਅਧੂਰਾ, ਅਪੂਰਨ, ਊਣਾ, ਦੋਸ਼ਪੂਰਨ

deficit ('ਡੈਫ਼ਿਸਿਟ) *n* ਘਾਟਾ, ਤੋਟਾ, ਕਮੀ, ਨੁਕਸਾਨ, ਕਸਰ

defile (ਡਿ'ਫ਼ਾਇਲ, 'ਡੀਫ਼ਾਇਲ) *v n* ਪਾਲ ਵਿਚ ਹੋ ਕੇ ਚੱਲਣਾ; ਤੰਗ ਰਸਤਾ, ਸੰਕੀਰਨ ਘਾਟੀ, ਸੌੜਾ ਰਾਹ; ਭ੍ਰਿਸ਼ਟ ਕਰਨਾ, ਸਤ ਭੰਗ ਕਰਨਾ, ਅਪਵਿੱਤਰ ਕਰਨਾ, ਭਿੱਟਣਾ, ਦੂਸ਼ਤ ਕਰਨਾ; ~d ਦੂਸ਼ਤ, ਕਲੰਕਤ, ਭ੍ਰਿਸ਼ਟ, ਅਪਵਿੱਤਰ; ~ment ਅਪਵਿੱਤਰਤਾ, ਦੂਸ਼ਣ, ਭ੍ਰਿਸ਼ਟਤਾ, ਪਲੀਤੀ ਭਿੱਟ

definable (ਡਿ'ਫ਼ਾਇਨਅਬਲ) *a* ਪਰਿਭਾਸ਼ੀ; ਸਪਸ਼ਟ ਕਰਨ ਯੋਗ; ਪਰਿਭਾਸ਼ਾ

define (ਡਿ'ਫ਼ਾਇਨ) *v* ਪਰਿਭਾਸ਼ਾ ਦੇਣਾ, ਲੱਛਣ ਦਸੱਣਾ, ਸਪਸ਼ਟ ਅਰਥ ਦੱਸਣਾ, ਸੀਮਾ-ਅੰਕਤ ਕਰਨਾ; ~d ਪਰਿਭਾਸ਼ਤ, ਨਿਰਧਾਰਤ

definite ('ਡੈਫ਼ਿਨਿਟ) *a* ਨਿਸ਼ਚਤ, ਨਿਯਤ, ਸਪਸ਼ਟ, ਸੀਮਾਬੱਧ ਨਿਰਵੀਤ, ਮੁਕੱਰਰ; ~ly ਸਪਸ਼ਟ ਤੌਰ ਤੇ, ਬਿਲਕੁਲ

definition ('ਡਿਫ਼ਿ'ਨਿਸ਼ਨ) *n* ਪਰਿਭਾਸ਼ਾ,

ਵਿਆਖਿਆ, ਲੱਛਣ, ਅਰਥ ਨਿਰੂਪਣ

definitive (ਡਿ'ਫ਼ਿਨਿਟਿਵ਼) *a* ਨਿਯਤ, ਨਿਸ਼ਚਤ; ਨਿਰਣਾਤਮਕ

deflate (ਡਿ'ਫ਼ਲੇਇਟ) *v* ਵਧੇ ਮੁੱਲ ਨੂੰ ਘਟਾਉਣਾ, ਮੁਦਰਾ-ਸਫ਼ੀਤੀ ਵਿਚ ਕਮੀ ਕਰਨਾ; ਫੂਸ ਕਰਨਾ, ਹਵਾ ਕੱਢਣਾ

deflation (ਡਿ'ਫ਼ਲੇਇਸ਼ਨ) *n* ਮੁਦਰਾ-ਸਫ਼ੀਤੀ ਵਿਚ ਕਮੀ, ਵਧੀਆਂ ਕੀਮਤਾਂ ਦਾ ਘਟਣਾ, ਹਵਾ ਕੱਢਣ ਦੀ ਕਿਰਿਆ

deflect (ਡਿ'ਫ਼ਲੈੱਕਟ) *v* ਲਾਂਭੇ ਮੁੜਨਾ, ਖਿੱਝਕਣਾ, ਮੁੜਨਾ; **~ion, deflexion** ਪੱਥ-ਵਿਚਲਣ, ਚੁੰਬਕੀ ਸੂਈ ਦਾ ਕੇਂਦਰ-ਬਿੰਦੂ ਤੋਂ ਹਟਾਉ

deforest ('ਡੀ'ਫ਼ੌਰਿਸਟ) *v* ਜੰਗਲ ਕੱਟਣੇ; **~ation** (ਡੀ'ਫ਼ੌਰਿਸਟੇਇਸ਼ਨ) *n* ਜੰਗਲ ਵੱਢਣ

deform (ਡਿ'ਫ਼ੌਮ) *v* ਕਰੂਪ ਕਰਨਾ, ਰੂਪ ਵਿਗਾੜਨਾ, ਸਕਲ ਵਿਗਾੜਨੀ, ਬੇਢੰਗਾ ਕਰਨਾ; **~ation** ਕਰੂਪਤਾ, ਬਦਸੂਰਤੀ, ਵਿਰੂਪਤਾ, ਬੋਝ, ਸ਼ਬਦ ਦਾ ਵਿਗਾੜਿਆ ਰੂਪ; **~ed** ਬੇਢੰਗਾ, ਬੇਡੌਲ, ਵਿਰੂਪਤ

defraud (ਡਿ'ਫ਼ਰੋਡ) *v* ਛਲ ਕਰਨਾ, ਧੋਖਾ ਕਰਨਾ, ਕਪਟ ਕਰਨਾ, ਠੱਗਣਾ, ਹੱਕ ਮਾਰਨਾ

deft (ਡੈੱਫ਼ਟ) *a* ਹੁਸ਼ਿਆਰ, ਚਤਰ, ਨਿਪੁੰਨ, ਪ੍ਰਵੀਣ, ਕੁਸ਼ਲ, ਚਲਾਕ; **~ness** ਨਿਪੁੰਨਤਾ, ਚਤਰਤਾ, ਚਲਾਕੀ, ਹੁਸ਼ਿਆਰੀ

defuse ('ਡੀ'ਫ਼ਯੂਜ਼) *v* ਸੰਕਟ ਟਾਲਣਾ; (ਬੰਬ) ਨਕਾਰਾ ਕਰਨਾ

defy (ਡਿ'ਫ਼ਾਇ) *v* ਵਿਰੋਧ ਕਰਨਾ, ਅਵੱਗਿਆ ਕਰਨਾ, ਆਗਿਆ ਨੂੰ ਉਲੰਘਣਾ, ਉਪੇਖਿਆ ਕਰਨਾ, ਵੰਗਾਰਨਾ

degenerate ('ਡਿ'ਜੈੱਨੑਅਰਅਟ) *a v n* ਪਤਿਤ, ਹੀਣਾ, ਚਰਿੱਤਰਹੀਨ, ਭ੍ਰਿਸ਼ਟ, ਨੀਚ; ਨਿਘਰਿਆ,

ਵਿਗੜਿਆ; ਪਤਿਤ ਹੋਣਾ; ਪਤਿਤ ਪੁਰਸ਼

degeneration ('ਡਿ'ਜੈੱਨੑਅ'ਰੇਇਸ਼ਨ) *n* ਗਿਰਾਵਟ, ਹ੍ਰਾਸ, ਪਤਨ, ਅਧੋਗਤੀ

degradation ('ਡਿਗਰਅ'ਡੇਇਸ਼ਨ) *n* ਅਧੋਗਤੀ, ਪਤਨ, ਗਿਰਾਵਟ

degrade (ਡਿ'ਗਰੇਇਡ) *v* ਪਦ ਘਟਾਉਣਾ, ਅਪਮਾਨ ਕਰਨਾ, ਨਿਰਾਦਰ ਕਰਨਾ; ਨੈਤਕ ਪਤਨ ਹੋਣਾ, ਵਿਗਾੜਨਾ, ਪਤਿਤ ਕਰਨਾ, ਭ੍ਰਿਸ਼ਟ ਕਰਨਾ

degrading (ਡਿ'ਗਰੇਇਡਿੰਗ) *a* ਅਪਮਾਨਜਨਕ; ਹੀਨਤਾ ਭਰਿਆ, ਬੁਰਾ, ਹੱਤਕ ਭਰਿਆ, ਬੇਇੱਜ਼ਤੀ ਵਾਲਾ

degree (ਡਿ'ਗਰੀ) *n* ਦਰਜਾ, ਪਦਵੀ, ਮਾਤਰਾ; ਡਿਗਰੀ, ਸਨਦ; ਤਾਪਮਾਨ ਦੀ ਇਕਾਈ; ਉਪਾਧੀ; (ਵਿਆ) ਕੋਟੀ

degression (ਡਿ'ਗਰੈੱਸ਼ਨ) *n* ਗਿਰਾਵਟ, ਜ਼ਵਾਲ, ਪਤਨ

dehumanize ('ਡੀ'ਹਯੂਮਅਨਾਇਜ਼) *v* ਅਮਾਨਵੀ ਬਣਾਉਣਾ, ਹੀਣਾ ਕਰਨਾ, ਅਸੱਭਿਆ ਬਣਾਉਣਾ

deil (ਡੀਲ) *n* ਭੂਤ-ਪਰੇਤ, ਜਿੰਨ, ਚੁੜੇਲ

deity ('ਡੀਇਟਿ) *n* ਦੇਵਤਵ, ਦੇਵ ਸਰੂਪ, ਦੇਵਤਾ; **The D~** ਈਸ਼ਵਰ, ਰਚਨਹਾਰਾ, ਕਰਤਾਰ, ਕਰਤਾਪੁਰਖ

deject ('ਡਿ'ਜੈੱਕਟ) *v* ਦਿਲ ਤੋੜਨਾ, ਉਦਾਸ ਕਰਨਾ, ਦਿਲ ਖੱਟਾ ਕਰਨਾ, ਬੇਦਿਲ ਹੋਣਾ; **~ed** ਉਦਾਸ, ਨਿੰਮੋਝੂਣਾ, ਉਦਾਸੀਨ; **~ion** ਨਿਰਾਸਤਾ, ਉਦਾਸੀ, ਖਿੰਨਤਾ, ਗਿਲਾਨੀ

de jure ('ਡੇਇ'ਜ਼ੂਅ(ਰਿ) (*L*) *a* ਕਾਨੂੰਨੀ ਅਧਿਕਾਰ ਅਨੁਸਾਰ

delay (ਡਿ'ਲੇਇ) *v n* ਦੇਰ ਕਰਨਾ, ਰੁਕਾਵਟ ਪਾਉਣਾ, ਟਾਲਣਾ, ਲਮਕਾਉਣਾ; ਦੇਰ, ਰੁਕਾਵਟ

delegate ('ਡੈਲਿਗੇਇਟ, ਡੈਲਿਗਅਟ) *v n*

ਪ੍ਰਤਿਨਿਧ ਬਣਾਉਣਾ, ਮੁਖ਼ਤਿਆਰ ਕਰਨ; ਪ੍ਰਤੀਨਿਧ, ਏਲਚੀ, ਮੁਖ਼ਤਿਆਰ, ਡੈਲੀਗੇਟ

delegation ('ਡੈਲਿ'ਗੇਇਸ਼ਨ) *n* ਪ੍ਰਤੀਨਿਧ-ਮੰਡਲ, ਵਫ਼ਦ, ਅਧਿਕਾਰ-ਸੌਂਪਣਾ, ਸੁਪਰਦਗੀ

delete (ਡਿ'ਲੀਟ) *v* ਕੱਟਣਾ; ਮੇਟਣਾ, ਲੀਕ ਫੇਰਨੀ, ਰੱਦ ਕਰਨ; ~d ਕੱਟਿਆ

deletion (ਡਿ'ਲੀਸ਼ਨ) *n* ਕਾਟ, ਛਾਂਟ

deliberate (ਡਿ'ਲਿਬਅਰੇਇਟ) *v a* ਵਿਚਾਰ ਕਰਨਾ, ਸੋਚਣਾ, ਚਿੰਤਨ ਕਰਨਾ, ਵਿਚਾਰਨਾ, ਸਲਾਹ ਮਸ਼ਵਰਾ ਕਰਨਾ, ਰਾਇ ਲੈਣਾ

deliberation (ਡਿ'ਲਿਬਅ'ਰੇਇਸ਼ਨ) *n* ਸੋਚ-ਵਿਚਾਰ, ਸਲਾਹ-ਮਸ਼ਵਰਾ, ਵਾਦ-ਵਿਵਾਦ, ਚਰਚਾ, ਬਹਿਸ

deliberative (ਡਿ'ਲਿਬ(ਅ)ਰਟਿਵ) *a* ਵਿਚਾਰਾਤਮਕ, ਵਿਚਾਰਪੂਰਨ

delecacies ('ਡੈਲਿਕਅਸਿਜ਼) *n* ਸੁਆਦਲੀਆਂ ਚੀਜ਼ਾਂ, ਨਿਆਮਤਾਂ, ਸੁਆਦੀ ਭੋਜਨ

delicacy ('ਡੈਲਿਕਅਸਿ) *n* ਸੁਖਮਤਾ, ਬਾਰੀਕੀ, ਮਧੁਰਤਾ, ਕੋਮਲਤਾ, ਨਜ਼ਾਕਤ, ਸੁਆਦੀ ਭੋਜਨ

delicate (ਡੈਲਿਕਅਟ) *a* ਨਾਜ਼ੁਕ, ਕੋਮਲ; ਸੁਖਮ-ਗ੍ਰਾਹੀ, ਸੰਵੇਦਨਸ਼ੀਲ, ਸੁਖਮ, ਬਾਰੀਕ, ਹਲਕਾ (ਰੰਗ), ਸੁਆਦੀ (ਭੋਜਨ); ਸ਼ਰਮੀਲਾ, ਮਲੂਕ, ਕੂਲਾ

delicious (ਡਿ'ਲਿਸ਼ਿਅਸ) *a* ਸੁਆਦੀ, ਰਸੀਲਾ, ਮਿੱਠਾ, ਮਜ਼ੇਦਾਰ

delight (ਡਿਲਾਇਟ) *n a* ਪ੍ਰਸੰਨਤਾ, ਖ਼ੁਸ਼ੀ, ਆਨੰਦ; ਖ਼ੁਸ਼ ਹੋਣਾ, ਪ੍ਰਸੰਨ ਹੋਣਾ, ਆਨੰਦਤ ਹੋਣਾ; ~ed ਖ਼ੁਸ਼, ਪ੍ਰਸੰਨ; ~ful ਆਨੰਦਮਈ, ਦਿਲਚਸਪ, ਰਸੀਲਾ, ਰਮਣੀਕ; ~some ਆਨੰਦਦਾਇਕ

delimitate (ਡਿ'ਲਿਮਿਟੇਇਟ) *v* ਹੱਦਬੰਦੀ ਕਰਨਾ, ਸੀਮਾਬੰਧ ਕਰਨਾ

delimitation (ਡਿ'ਲਿਮਿ'ਟੇਇਸ਼ਨ) *n* ਹੱਦਬੰਦੀ, ਸੀਮਾ-ਨਿਰਧਾਰਨ, ਸੀਮਾ-ਨਿਰਦੇਸ਼ਨ

delineable (ਡਿ'ਲਿਨਿਅਬਲ) *a* ਰੂਪ-ਰੇਖਯੋਗ, ਵਰਣਨਯੋਗ

delineate (ਡਿ'ਲਿਨਿਏਇਟ) *v* ਵਰਣਨ ਕਰਨਾ, ਬਿਆਨ ਕਰਨਾ, ਰੇਖਾਂਤਰ ਕਰਨਾ, ਨਕਸ਼ਾ ਖਿੱਚਣਾ

delineation (ਡਿ'ਲਿਨਿ'ਏਇਸ਼ਨ) *n* ਚਿੱਤਰਨ, ਬਿਆਨ, ਰੂਪ-ਰੇਖਾ, ਖ਼ਾਕਾ, ਵਰਣਨ, ਉੱਲੇਖ, ਬਿਰਤਾਂਤ

delinquency (ਡਿ'ਲਿਡ਼ਕਵਅੰਸਿ) *n* ਖ਼ਤਾ, ਦੋਸ਼; ਭੁੱਲ; ਕੁਕਰਮ, ਅਪਰਾਧ

delinquent (ਡਿ'ਲਿਡ਼ਕਵਅੰਟ) *n* ਅਪਰਾਧੀ, ਕਸੁਰਵਾਰ, ਖ਼ਤਾਵਾਰ

deliquesce ('ਡੈਲਿ'ਕਵੈੱਸ) *v* ਤਰਲ ਹੋਣਾ, ਪਤਲਾ ਹੋ ਜਾਣਾ, ਪਿਘਲਣਾ, ਪਸੀਜਣਾ, ਘੁਲ ਜਾਣਾ; ~nce ਤਰਲਤਾ, ਦ੍ਰਵਤਾ; ਪਤਲਾਪਣ

delirium (ਡਿ'ਲਿਰਿਅਮ) *n* ਸਰਸਾਮ; ਬਕਝਵਾਦ; ਉਨਮਾਦ

deliver (ਡਿ'ਲਿਵਅ*) *v* (ਡਾਕ) ਵੰਡਣਾ; (ਚਿੱਠੀ) ਦੇਣਾ, ਸਪੁਰਦ ਕਰਨਾ, (ਭਾਸ਼ਣ) ਦੇਣਾ, ਉਤਪੰਨ ਕਰਨਾ, ਜਨਮ ਦੇਣਾ; ~y ਸਪੁਰਦਗੀ, (ਡਾਕ ਆਦਿ ਦੀ) ਵੰਡ, ਛੁਟਕਾਰਾ, ਅਰਪਣ, ਪ੍ਰਦਾਨ

dell (ਡੈੱਲ) *n* ਵਾਦੀ, ਘਾਟੀ, ਦੂਨ, ਖੱਡ

delta (ਡੈੱਲਟਾ) *n* ਯੂਨਾਨੀ ਵਰਣਮਾਲਾ ਦਾ ਚੌਥਾ ਅੱਖਰ, ਡੈਲਟਾ, ਦਹਾਨਾ

delude (ਡਿ'ਲੂਡ) *v* ਭਰਮਾਉਣਾ, ਧੋਖਾ ਦੇਣਾ, ਛਲਣਾ, ਸਬਝ ਬਾਗ਼ ਦਿਖਾਉਣਾ, ਬਹਿਕਾਉਣਾ

delusion (ਡੈ'ਲੂਯ਼ਅਨ) *n* ਵਹਿਮ, ਭੁਲੇਖਾ, ਮਾਇਆ-ਜਾਲ

delusive (ਡਿ'ਲੀਸਿਵ਼) *a* ਭਰਮਪੂਰਨ, ਮਾਇਆਵੀ

deluxe (ਡਲ'ਅਕਸ) *(F) a adv* ਬਹੁਤ ਵਧੀਆ, ਸ਼ਾਨਦਾਰ (ਢੰਗ ਨਾਲ)

delve (ਡੈੱਲਵ੍) *v* ਪੁੱਟਣਾ, ਖੋਜ ਕਰਨਾ, ਛਾਣਬੀਨ ਕਰਨੀ, ਡੁਬਕੀ ਲਾਉਣੀ, (ਸੜਕ ਆਦਿ ਦਾ) ਅਚਾਨਕ ਧਸ ਜਾਣਾ, ਬੈਠ ਜਾਣਾ, ਪ੍ਰਵੇਸ਼

demagogue ('ਡੈੱਮਅਗੌਗ) *n* ਸ਼ਬਦ-ਆਡੰਬਰੀ, ਉਸ਼ਟੰਡਬਾਜ਼ੀ; ਸਿਆਸੀ ਆਗੂ

demagogy ('ਡੈੱਮਅਗੌਗਿ) *n* ਨੇਤਾਗੀਰੀ, ਘਟੀਆ ਲੀਡਰੀ

demand (ਡਿ'ਮਾਂਡ) *n v* ਮੰਗ, ਲੋੜ, ਜ਼ਰੂਰਤ, ਦਾਅਵਾ, ਅਵੱਸ਼ਕਤਾ ਹੋਣੀ, ਮੰਗ ਕਰਨਾ, ਮੰਗਣਾ

demarcate ('ਡੀਮਾ*ਕੇਇਟ) *v* ਹੱਦ-ਬੰਦੀ ਕਰਨਾ, ਨਿਸ਼ਾਨਦੇਹੀ ਕਰਨਾ, ਸੀਮਾ ਨਿਸ਼ਚਤ ਕਰਨਾ; **~d** ਨਿਸ਼ਚਤ, ਨਿਰਧਾਰਤ, ਸੀਮਾਂਕਤ

demarcation ('ਡੀਮਾ*ਕੇਇਸ਼ਨ) *n* ਹੱਦਬੰਦੀ, ਸੀਮਾ-ਨਿਰਧਾਰਨ, ਸੀਮਾ-ਅੰਕਣ

demerit (ਡੀ'ਮੈਰਿਟ) *v* ਔਗੁਣ; ਅਯੋਗਤਾ; ਨੁਕਸ, ਖ਼ਰਾਬੀ

demise (ਡਿ'ਮਾਇਜ਼) *v n* ਇੰਤਕਾਲ ਕਰਨਾ, ਮੌਤ, ਦੇਹਾਂਤ, ਚਲਾਣਾ, ਵਸੀਅਤ ਕਰਨੀ,

demit (ਡਿ'ਮਿਟ) *v* ਤਿਆਗਣਾ, ਅਸਤੀਫ਼ਾ ਦੇਣਾ

democracy (ਡਿ'ਮੌਕਰਅਸਿ) *n* ਲੋਕਤੰਤਰ, ਜਨਤੰਤਰ, ਪਰਜਾਤੰਤਰ, ਗਣਰਾਜ

democrat ('ਡੈੱਮਅਕਰੈਟ) *n* ਲੋਕਤੰਤਰਵਾਦੀ, ਗਣ-ਤੰਤਰਵਾਦੀ, ਲੋਕਰਾਜੀ; **~ic** ਲੋਕਤੰਤਰਾਤਮਕ, ਗਣਤੰਤਰਾਤਮਕ, ਜਮਹੂਰੀ, ਲੋਕਰਾਜੀ

demolish (ਡਿ'ਮੌਲਿਸ਼) *v* ਢਾਹੁਣਾ, ਨਸ਼ਟ ਕਰਨਾ, ਪੁੱਟ ਸੁੱਟਣਾ, ਤੋੜਨਾ, ਨਿਗਲ ਜਾਣਾ, ਖਾ ਜਾਣਾ; **~ment, demoilition** ਨਾਸ਼, ਵਿਨਾਸ਼; ਖੰਡਨ

demon ('ਡੀਮਅਨ) *n* ਰਾਖਸ਼, ਸ਼ੈਤਾਨ, ਜਿੰਨ, ਦਾਨਵ, ਅਸੁਰ

demonetization ('ਡੀ'ਮਐਨਿਟਾਇ'ਜ਼ਇਸ਼ਨ) *n* ਸਿੱਕੇ ਦਾ ਅਪ੍ਰਚਲਕਰਣ

demonetize ('ਡੀ'ਮਐਨਿਟਾਇਜ਼) *v* ਸਰਕਾਰੀ ਸਿੱਕੇ ਨੂੰ ਚੱਲਣ ਤੋਂ ਹਟਾਉਣਾ, ਵਿਮੁਦਰੀਕਰਨ ਕਰਨਾ

demoniac (ਡਿ'ਮਅਉਨਿਐਕ) *a* ਦਾਨਵੀ, ਰਾਖਸ਼ੀ; **~al** ਅਸੁਰੀ; ਦਾਨਵੀ; ਰਾਖਸ਼ੀ

demonic (ਡੀ'ਮੌਨਿਕ) *a* ਭੂਤਗ੍ਰਸਤ; ਪਿਸ਼ਾਚਗ੍ਰਸਤ

demonstrate ('ਡੈੱਮਅਨਸਟਰੇਇਟ) *v* ਪਰਦਰਸ਼ਤ ਕਰਨਾ, ਨੁਮਾਇਸ਼ ਕਰਨਾ, ਮੁਜ਼ਾਹਰਾ ਕਰਨਾ, ਵਿਖਾਲਾ ਕਰਨਾ, ਪਰਦਰਸ਼ਨ ਕਰਨਾ, ਵਿਆਖਿਆ ਕਰਨਾ, ਸਿੱਧ ਕਰਨਾ, ਪ੍ਰਮਾਣਤ ਕਰਨਾ

demonstration ('ਡੈੱਮਅਨ'ਸਟਰੇਇਸ਼ਨ) *v* ਪਰਦਰਸ਼ਨ, ਨੁਮਾਇਸ਼, ਮੁਜ਼ਾਹਰਾ, ਸਪਸ਼ਟੀਕਰਨ, ਵਿਆਖਿਆ

demonstrator (ਡੈੱਮਅਨਸਟਰੇਇਟਅ*) *n* ਪਰਦਰਸ਼ਕ, ਮੁਜ਼ਾਹਰੇ ਵਿਚ ਹਿੱਸਾ ਲੈਣ ਵਾਲਾ, ਨਿਰਦੇਸ਼ਕ, ਪ੍ਰਤੀਪਾਦਕ, ਡਿਮਾਨਸਟਰੇਟਰ

demoralization (ਡਿ'ਮੌਰਅਲਾਇ'ਜ਼ੇਇਸ਼ਨ) *n* ਸਦਾਚਾਰਕ ਗਿਰਾਵਟ, ਨੈਤਕ ਪਤਨ, ਉਤਸ਼ਾਹ-ਭੰਗ, ਬੇਦਿਲੀ

demoralize (ਡਿ'ਮੈਰਅਲਾਇਜ਼) *v* ਚਰਿੱਤਰ ਭ੍ਰਿਸ਼ਟ ਕਰਨਾ, ਚਰਿੱਤਰਹੀਨ ਕਰਨਾ, ਨੈਤਕ ਪਤਨ ਕਰਨਾ, ਵਿਗਾੜਨਾ, ਨਿਰਉਤਸ਼ਾਹ ਕਰਨਾ, ਬੇਦਿਲ ਕਰਨਾ, ਮਨੋਬਲ ਡੇਗਣਾ

demote ('ਡੀ'ਮਅਉਟ) *v* ਪਦ ਘਟਾਉਣਾ, ਅਵੂੰਨਤ ਕਰਨਾ; **~d** ਅਵੂੰਨਤ

demotion ('ਡੀ'ਮਅਉਸ਼ਨ) *n* ਪਦ ਘਟਾਈ, ਅਵਨਤਿ

demur (ਡਿ'ਮਯੁਅ:) *v n* ਇਤਰਾਜ਼ ਕਰਨਾ, ਉਜ਼ਰ

ਕਰਨ, ਆਪੱਤੀ ਕਰਨੀ; ਇਤਰਾਜ਼, ਉਜ਼ਰ;
~rage ਦੇਰੀ, ਅਟਕਾਉ, ਮਾਲ ਛੁਡਾਉਣ ਵਿਚ
ਦੇਰੀ ਦਾ ਹਰਜਾਨਾ

demure (ਡਿ'ਮਯੂਅ*) n ਸ਼ਰਮਾਕਲ, ਸੰਗਾਊ,
ਸੰਕੋਚੀ, ਸ਼ਾਂਤ, ਧੀਰਜਵਾਨ

demy (ਡਿ'ਮਾਇ) n ਕਾਗ਼ਜ਼ ਦਾ ਇਕ ਨਾਪ
(17½ x 22½)

den (ਡੈਨ) n ਖੋਹ, ਘੁਰਨਾ, ਚੋਰਾਂ ਦਾ ਅੱਡਾ, ਛੋਟੀ
ਗੰਦੀ ਕੋਠੜੀ, ਗੁਫ਼ਾ

dengue ('ਡਿ'ਡਗੀ) n ਹੱਡ-ਭੰਨਵਾਂ ਬੁਖ਼ਾਰ

denial (ਡਿ'ਨਾਇਲ) n ਇਨਕਾਰ, ਨਾਂਹ, ਖੰਡਨ,
ਨਾਮਨਜ਼ੂਰੀ

denied (ਡੇ'ਨਾਇਡ) v ਵਾਂਝਾ ਰੱਖਿਆ ਗਿਆ,
ਵੰਚਤ

denigrate ('ਡੈਨਿਗਰੇਇਟ) v ਅਪਮਾਨ ਕਰਨਾ,
ਭੰਡੀ ਕਰਨੀ, ਦਾਗ਼ ਲਾਉਣਾ, ਕਲੰਕਤ ਕਰਨਾ

denigration ('ਡੈ'ਨਿ'ਗਰੇਇਸ਼ਨ) n ਨਿੰਦਾ,
ਬਦਨਾਮੀ, ਅਪਜਸ, ਅਪਮਾਨ, ਭੰਡੀ

denim (ਡੈਨਿਮ) n ਮੋਟਾ, ਨੂਸ਼ੂ ਤੇ ਰੰਗਦਾਰ ਸੂਤੀ
ਕੱਪੜਾ

denominate (ਡਿ'ਨੌਮਿ'ਨੇਇਟ) v ਨਾਂ ਰੱਖਣਾ,
ਨਾਮਕਰਨ ਕਰਨਾ, ਸੰਗਿਆ ਦੇਣੀ, ਨਾਂ ਨਾਲ
ਬੁਲਾਉਣਾ, ਬੁਲਾਉਣਾ, ਕਹਿਣਾ

denomination (ਡਿ'ਨੌਮਿ'ਨੇਇਸ਼ਨ) n ਨਾਂ,
ਸੰਗਿਆ, ਉਪਾਧੀ, (ਅਰਥ) ਮੁੱਲ-ਅੰਕ; ਜਾਤੀ;
ਪੰਥ; ਸ਼੍ਰੇਣੀ, ਧਾਰਮਕ ਸੰਪਰਦਾਇ, ਫ਼ਿਰਕਾ

denotation ('ਡੀਨਅ(ਉ)'ਟੇਇਸ਼ਨ) n ਨਾਂ
ਸੰਗਿਆ, ਪ੍ਰਤੀਕ-ਕਥਨ, ਚਿੰਨ੍ਹਾਂ ਦੁਆਰਾ
ਪਰਗਟੀਕਰਨ

denotative (ਡਿ'ਨਅਉਟਅਟਿਵ਼) a ਵਾਚਕ,
ਨਿਰਦੇਸ਼ਕ, ਸੂਚਕ, ਵਸਤੂਵਾਚੀ

denote (ਡਿ'ਨਅਉਟ) v ਨਾਂ ਦੇਣਾ; ਅਰਥ ਦੇਣਾ;
ਦੱਸਣਾ, ਵਿਅਕਤ ਕਰਨਾ, ਸੰਕੇਤ ਕਰਨਾ

denounce (ਡਿ'ਨਾਊਂਸ) n ਬੁਰਾਈ ਕਰਨਾ, ਦੋਸ਼
ਥੱਪਣਾ; ਬਦਅਸੀਸ ਦੇਣੀ, ਸੰਧੀ ਤੋੜਨ ਦੀ
ਸੂਚਨ ਦੇਣਾ; ਭਵਿੱਖਬਾਣੀ ਕਰਨਾ

dense (ਡੈਂਸ) a ਸੰਘਣਾ, ਘਣਾ; ਗਾੜ੍ਹਾ; ਜੜ੍ਹ,
ਬੁੱਧੂ

density ('ਡੈਂਸਅਟਿ) n ਸੰਘਣਾਪਣ, ਗਾੜ੍ਹਾਪਣ,
ਘਣਤਾ; ਬੁੱਧੂਪਣਾ

dental ('ਡੈਂਟਲ) a ਦੰਦਾਂ ਸਬੰਧੀ, ਦੰਦਾ ਦੇ ਇਲਾਜ
ਸਬੰਧੀ; ਦੰਤੀ

dentist ('ਡੈਨਟਿਸਟ) n ਦੰਦਾਂ ਦਾ ਡਾਕਟਰ, ਦੰਦ-
ਸਾਜ਼

denture ('ਡੈਂਚਅ*) n ਦੰਦ-ਮਾਲਾ, ਬਣਾਉਟੀ
ਦੰਦ

denude (ਡਿ'ਨਯੂਡ) v ਵਸਤਰਹੀਨ ਕਰਨਾ, ਨੰਗਾ
ਕਰਨਾ, ਨੰਗਿਆਉਣਾ

denunicate (ਡਿ'ਨਅੰਨਸਿਏਇਟ) v ਨਿੰਦਣਾ,
ਤਿਰਸਕਾਰਨਾ, ਫਿਟਕਾਰਨਾ, ਲਾਹ-ਪਾਹ ਕਰਨਾ

denunciation (ਡਿ'ਨਅੰਨਸਿ'ਏਇਸ਼ਨ) n
ਫਿਟਕਾਰ, ਨਿੰਦਾ, ਦੋਸ਼-ਆਰੋਪਣ

deny (ਡਿ'ਨਾਇ) v ਅਸਵੀਕਾਰ ਕਰਨਾ, ਨਾਮਨਜ਼ੂਰ
ਕਰਨਾ, ਨਾਂਹ ਕਰਨੀ, ਮੁੱਕਰਨਾ, ਖੰਡਨ ਕਰਨਾ

depart (ਡਿ'ਪਾਟ) v ਵਿੱਛੜਨਾ, ਵਿਦਾ ਹੋਣਾ, ਟੁਰ
ਜਾਣਾ, ਪਰਲੋਕ ਸਿਧਾਰਨਾ, ਚਲਾਣਾ ਕਰਨਾ

department (ਡਿ'ਪਾਟਮਅੰਟ) n ਵਿਭਾਗ,
ਮਹਿਕਮਾ, ਮੰਡਲ; ਅੰਗ; ~al ਵਿਭਾਗੀ,
ਮਹਿਕਮੇ ਸਬੰਧੀ; ਵਿਸ਼ੇ ਸਬੰਧੀ

departure (ਡਿ'ਪਾਚਅ*) n ਚਲਾਣਾ, ਵਿਦਾਇਗੀ,
ਕੂਚ, ਰਵਾਨਗੀ; ਮੌਤ

depend (ਡਿ'ਪੈਂਡ) v ਨਿਰਭਰ ਹੋਣਾ, ਆਸਰੇ ਹੋਣਾ,

ਅਧੀਨ ਹੋਣਾ, ਆਸਰਤ ਹੋਣਾ, ਅਵਲੰਬਤ ਹੋਣਾ;
~**able** ਵਿਸ਼ਵਾਸਯੋਗ, ਭਰੋਸੇਯੋਗ, ਨਿਰੰਤਰ
ਰਹਿਣਯੋਗ, ਆਸਰੇਯੋਗ; ~**ant** ਆਸਰਤ,
ਨਿਰੰਤਰ, ਅਧੀਨ, ਅਵਲੰਬੀ, ਸੇਵਕ; ~**ence**
ਨਿਰੰਤਰਤਾ, ਆਸਰਾ, ਭਰੋਸਾ, ਵਿਸਾਹ; ਅਧੀਨਤਾ

depict (ਡਿਪਿਕਟ) *v* ਚਿਤਰਨਾ, ਵਰਣਨ ਕਰਨਾ,
ਦਰਸਾਉਣਾ, ਚਿੱਤਰਤ ਕਰਨਾ; ~**ion** ਚਿਤਰਣ,
ਵਰਣਨ, ਪ੍ਰਸਤੁਤੀਕਰਨ

depilate (ਡੈਪਿਲੇਇਟ) *v* ਵਾਲ ਲਾਹੁਣਾ, ਮੁੰਨਣਾ

deplete (ਡਿਪਲੀਟ) *v* ਕਿਸੇ ਅੰਗ ਵਿਚੋਂ ਲਹੂ
ਕੱਢਣਾ, ਖ਼ਾਲੀ ਕਰਨਾ, ਖ਼ਰਚ ਕਰਨਾ

deplorable (ਡਿਪਲੋਰਅਬਇਲ) *a* ਦੁਖਦਾਇਕ,
ਸ਼ੋਕਪੂਰਨ, ਭੈੜਾ, ਖ਼ਰਾਬ

deplore (ਡਿਪਲੋ*) *v* ਸ਼ੋਕ ਕਰਨਾ, ਅਫ਼ਸੋਸ
ਕਰਨਾ, ਹੱਥ ਮਲਣੇ

deploy (ਡਿਪਲੋਇ) *v* ਪੰਗਤੀਬੱਧ ਕਰਨਾ, (ਫ਼ੌਜ
ਦੀ) ਪਰੁਬੰਦੀ ਕਰਨਾ; ~**ed** ਪੰਗਤੀਬੱਧ,
ਲਾਮਬੱਧ; ~**ment** ਪਾਬੰਦੀ, ਪਰੁਬੰਦੀ

deponent (ਡਿਪਅਉਨੰਟ) *n a* ਹਲਫ਼ੀਆ
ਬਿਆਨ ਦੇਣ ਵਾਲਾ, ਸ਼ਾਹਦ; ਅਭਿਸਾਕਸੀ

deport (ਡਿਪੋਟ*) *v* ਦੇਸ਼ ਨਿਕਾਲਾ ਦੇਣਾ,
ਜਲਾਵਤਨ ਕਰਨਾ

depose (ਡਿਪਅਉਜ਼) *n* ਬੇਦਖ਼ਲ ਕਰਨਾ, ਰਾਜ-
ਗੱਦੀ ਤੋਂ ਲਾਹੁਣਾ; ਹਲਫ਼ੀਆ ਬਿਆਨ ਦੇਣਾ;

deposit (ਡਿਪੌਜ਼ਿਟ) *n v* ਜਮ੍ਹਾ ਰਕਮ, ਅਮਾਨਤ;
ਰੇਤ ਜਾਂ ਮਿੱਟੀ ਆਦਿ ਦਾ ਜਮਾਉ, ਸਾਈ,
ਧਰੋਹਰ; ਜਮ੍ਹਾਂ ਕਰਾਉਣਾ, ਸਾਈ ਦੇਣੀ, ਗਿਰਵੀ
ਰੱਖਣਾ, ਪੇਸ਼ਗੀ ਦੇਣੀ, ਬਿਆਨਾ ਦੇਣਾ; ~**ory**
ਬੈਂਕ, ਗੁਦਾਮ, ਭੰਡਾਰ, ਸੰਗ੍ਰਹਸਥਾਨ, ਮਾਲਖ਼ਾਨਾ,
ਖ਼ਾਜ਼ਾਨਾ

deposition (ਡੈਪਅਜ਼ਿਸ਼ਨ) *n* ਜਮ੍ਹਾਂ; ਅਮਾਨਤ,

ਧਰੋਹਰ, ਰਾਜ ਤੋਂ ਵੰਚਤ ਕਰਨਾ, ਗਵਾਹੀ, ਹਲਫ਼ੀਆ
ਬਿਆਨ; ਸਰਮਾਇਆ, ਬਿਆਨਾ, ਸਾਈ

depot (ਡੈਪਅਉ) *n* ਗੁਦਾਮ, ਡੀਪੂ, ਮਾਲਖ਼ਾਨਾ,
ਭੰਡਾਰ, ਕੋਠੀ; ਰੰਗਰੂਟਾਂ ਦੀ ਸਿਖਲਾਈ ਵਾਲੀ
ਥਾਂ

depreciate (ਡਿਪਰੀਸ਼ਿਏਇਟ) *v* (ਘਸਾਈ
ਕਰਨਾ) ਕਦਰ ਘਟਾਉਣੀ ਜਾਂ ਘਟਣੀ, ਮੰਦਾ
ਸਮਝਣਾ, (ਰੁਪਏ ਦੀ ਕੀਮਤ) ਘਟਾਉਣੀ ਜਾਂ
ਘਟਣੀ, ਮੁੱਲ ਗਿਰਾਉਣਾ ਜਾਂ ਗਿਰਨਾ, ਭਾਅ
ਗਿਰਨੇ ਜਾਂ ਗਿਰਾਉਣੇ; ਤੁੱਛ ਸਮਝਣਾ, ਹੇਠੀ
ਕਰਨੀ ਜਾਂ ਹੋਣੀ

depreciation (ਡਿਪਰੀਸਿਏਇਸ਼ਨ) *n* ਬੇਕਦਰੀ,
ਮੰਦੀਕਰਨ, ਮੁੱਲ-ਘਾਟਾ; ਉਪੇਖਿਆ, ਭਾਅ ਵਿਚ
ਕਮੀ, ਮੁੱਲ-ਹ੍ਰਾਸ; ਘਸਾਈ

depress (ਡਿਪਰੈੱਸ) *v* (ਦਿਲ) ਢਾਹੁਣਾ, ਨੀਵਾਂ
ਕਰਨਾ; ਬਜ਼ਾਰ ਮੰਦਾ ਕਰਨਾ, ਵਪਾਰ ਦੀ
ਸਰਗਰਮੀ ਘੱਟ ਕਰਨਾ; ਉਦਾਸ ਕਰਨਾ, ਦੁਖੀ
ਕਰਨਾ, ਖਿੰਨ ਕਰਨਾ; ~**ed** ਉਦਾਸ, ਦੁਖੀ, ਖਿੰਨ
ਦਲਿਤ; ~**ion** ਉਦਾਸੀ, ਬੇਦਿਲੀ, ਵਿਸ਼ਾਦ,
ਨਿਰਉਤਸਾਹ, ਮੰਦਵਾੜਾ, ਪਤਨ, ਟੋਆ, ਸੁਰ
ਵਿਚ ਹਲਕਾਪਨ, (ਹਵਾ ਦੇ ਦਬਾ ਦਾ) ਘਟਾਉ

deprivation (ਡੈਪਰਿਵ੍ਏਇਸ਼ਨ) *n* ਵੰਚਣ,
ਬਰਤਰਫ਼ੀ, ਵਿਗੋਚਾ, ਮੱਕੂਫ਼ੀ, ਹਾਨੀ, ਲੋਪ

depute (ਡਿਪਯੂਟ) *v* ਨਿਯੁਕਤ ਕਰਨਾ, ਪ੍ਰਤੀਨਿਧ
ਨਿਯੁਕਤ ਕਰਨਾ, (ਅਧਿਕਾਰ ਕਰਨਾ) ਸੌਂਪਣਾ,
ਸਪੁਰਦ ਕਰਨਾ, ਮੁਖ਼ਤਿਆਰ ਕਰਨਾ

deprive (ਡਿਪਰਾਇਵ) *v* ਵੰਚਤ ਕਰਨਾ, ਵਾਂਝਿਆਂ
ਕਰਨਾ, ਖੋਹ ਲੈਣਾ, ਹਟਾਉਣਾ, ਲੁੱਟ ਲੈਣਾ; ~**d**
ਰਹਿਤ, ਵਿਹੂਣਾ, ਵਾਂਝਾ, ਵੰਚਤ

depth (ਡੈਪੱਥ) *n* ਡੂੰਘਾਈ, ਗਹਿਰਾਈ, ਡੂੰਘਾ
ਪਾਣੀ, ਡੂੰਮ, ਗੰਭੀਰਤਾ; ਸੂਖਮ ਬੁੱਧੀ

deputation ('ਡੇਪਯੂ'ਟੇਇਸ਼ਨ) *n* ਪ੍ਰਤੀਨਿਧ ਮੰਡਲ, ਵ੍ਫਦ, ਪ੍ਰਤੀਨਿਯੁਕਤੀ

depute (ਡਿ'ਪਯੂਟ) *v* ਪ੍ਰਤੀਨਿਯੁਕਤ ਕਰਨਾ, ਪ੍ਰਤੀਨਿਧ ਨਿਯੁਕਤ ਕਰਨਾ, ਸਪੁਰਦ ਕਰਨਾ, ਮੁਖ਼ਤਿਆਰ ਕਰਨਾ (ਅਧਿਕਾਰ) ਸੌਂਪਣਾ; **~d** ਪ੍ਰਤੀਨਿਯੁਕਤ

deputy ('ਡੇਪਯੁਟਿ) *n* ਸਹਿ, ਉਪ, ਸਹਿਕਾਰੀ, ਨਾਇਬ

derail (ਡਿ'ਰੇਇਲ) *v* ਪਟੜੀ ਤੋਂ ਲਾਹੁਣਾ; ਪਟੜੀ ਤੋਂ ਉਤਰ ਜਾਣਾ, ਅਸਲੀ ਰਾਹ ਤੋਂ ਉਖੜ ਜਾਣਾ

derange (ਡਿ'ਰੇਇੰਜ) *v* ਉਲਟ-ਪੁਲਟ ਕਰਨਾ, ਘੁੱਪੀ ਭ੍ਰਿਸ਼ਟ ਕਰਨਾ, ਪਾਗਲ ਕਰ ਦੇਣਾ, ਅੜਚਨ ਪਾਉਣੀ; **~d** ਉਲਟਾ-ਪੁਲਟਾ, ਬੇਤਰਤੀਬ, ਪਾਗਲ, ਵਿਆਕੁਲ; **~ment** ਉਲਟ-ਪੁਲਟ, ਬੇਤਰਤੀਬਾ, ਫ਼ਤੂਰ

derivation ('ਡੇਰਿ'ਵ਼ੇਇਸ਼ਨ) *n* ਵਿਉਤਪਤੀ, ਮੂਲ, ਸਰੋਤ

derivative (ਡਿ'ਰਿਵ਼ਅਟਿਵ਼) *a n* ਵਿਉਤਪਤ, (ਸ਼ਬਦ), ਵਿਉਤਪੰਨ ਤੱਤ

derive (ਡਿ'ਰਾਇਵ਼) *v* ਕੱਢਣਾ, ਉਤਪਤੀ ਹੋਣੀ, ਵਿਉਤਪੰਨ ਹੋਣਾ, ਮੂਲ ਲੱਭਣਾ, (ਸ਼ਬਦਾਂ ਦੀ) ਵਿਉਪੱਤੀ ਲੱਭਣੀ; **~d** ਉਤਪੰਨ, ਵਿਉਤਪੰਨ, ਵਿਉਤਪਾਦਤ

derogate ('ਡੇਰੋਅ(ਉ)ਗੇਇਟ) *v* ਘਟਾਉਣਾ, ਕਮੀ ਕਰਨਾ, ਅਪਮਾਨ ਕਰਨਾ, ਵੱਟਾ ਲਾਉਣਾ, ਨਿਕਦਰੀ ਹੋਣਾ, ਹੇਠੀ ਹੋਣੀ, ਅਪਮਾਨਤ ਹੋਣਾ

derogation (ਡੇਰੋਅ(ਉ)'ਗੇਇਸ਼ਨ) *n* ਅਲਪੀਕਰਨ, ਪਤਨ, ਨਿਕਦਰੀ, ਹੇਠੀ, ਗੌਰਵਹੀਨਤਾ, ਅਪਮਾਨ

derogatory (ਡਿ'ਰੌਗਅਟ(ਅ)ਰਿ) *a* ਅਪਮਾਨਜਨਕ, ਹੇਠੀ ਵਾਲੀ, ਸ਼ਾਨ ਵਿਰੁੱਧ

descend (ਡਿ'ਸੈਂਡ) *v* ਲਹਿਣਾ, ਲੱਖਣਾ, ਉੱਤਰਨਾ, ਡਿੱਗਣਾ, ਆ ਪੈਣਾ; ਪੈਣਾ, ਘਟਣਾ (ਵਰਣਨ ਵਿਚ), ਵੰਸ਼-ਕ੍ਰਮ ਅਨੁਸਾਰ ਆਉਣਾ, ਉੱਤਰ ਆਉਣਾ; **~ant** ਵੰਸ਼, ਔਲਾਦ, ਸੰਤਾਨ, ਜਾਨਸ਼ੀਨ

descent (ਡੇ'ਸੈਂਟ) *n* ਉਤਰਾਈ, ਢਲਵਾਣ, ਲਹਾਈ; ਅਚਾਨਕ ਹੱਲਾ; ਵੰਸ਼, ਕੁਲ, ਪੀੜ੍ਹੀ; ਉੱਤਪਤੀ, ਉਦਭਵ

describe (ਡਿ'ਸਕਰਾਇਬ) *v* ਵਰਣਨ ਕਰਨਾ, ਬਿਆਨ ਕਰਨਾ, ਉਲੀਕਣਾ, ਚਿਤਰਣ ਕਰਨਾ, ਅੰਕਤ ਕਰਨਾ, ਬਖਾਨਣਾ

description (ਡਿ'ਸਕਰਿਪਸ਼ਨ) *n* ਵਰਣਨ, ਬਿਆਨ, ਨਿਰੂਪਣ, ਵਿਵਰਣ, ਭਾਂਤ, ਵੰਨਗੀ, ਪ੍ਰਕਾਰ, ਸ਼੍ਰੇਣੀ

descriptive (ਡਿ'ਸਕਰਿਪਟਿਵ਼) *a* ਵਰਣਨਾਤਮਕ, ਚਿਤਰਾਤਮਕ, ਬਿਆਨੀਆ; **~ness** ਵਰਣਨਾਤਮਕਤਾ, ਬਿਆਨ

desert ('ਡੇਜ਼ਅਟ, ਡਿ'ਜ਼ਅਃਟ) *n* ਰੇਗਿਸਤਾਨ, ਮਾਰੂਥਲ, ਸੁਨਸਾਨ, ਉਜਾੜ, ਵੀਰਾਨ; ਧੋਖਾ ਦੇਣਾ, ਅਲੱਗ ਹੋਣਾ; **~ed** ਤਿਆਗਿਆ, ਇਕੱਲਵਾਂਝਾ

deserve (ਡਿ'ਜ਼ਅਃਵ਼) *v* ਸੁਯੋਗ ਹੋਣਾ, ਕਾਬਲ ਹੋਣਾ, ਪਾਤਰ ਹੋਣਾ, ਅਧਿਕਾਰੀ ਹੋਣਾ, ਲਾਇਕ ਹੋਣਾ

deserving (ਡਿ'ਜ਼ਅਃਵ਼ਿਙ) *a* ਅਧਿਕਾਰੀ, ਹੱਕਦਾਰ, ਸੁਪਾਤਰ, ਸੁਯੋਗ

design (ਡਿ'ਜ਼ਾਇਨ) *v n* (ਚਿਤਰ ਦੀ) ਰੂਪ ਰੇਖਾ ਬਣਾਉਣਾ, (ਭਵਨ ਮਕਾਨ ਆਦਿ ਦਾ) ਖ਼ਾਕਾ ਖਿੱਚਣਾ, ਕਥਾਨਕ ਜਾਂ ਆਧਾਰ ਸੋਚਣਾ, ਰੂਪ-ਰੇਖਾ ਬਣਾਉਣਾ, ਵਿਉਂਤ ਕਰਨੀ, ਇਰਾਦਾ ਕਰਨਾ, ਉਪਾਉ ਕਰਨਾ; ਆਕਾਰ, ਸਾਂਚਾ, ਢਾਂਚਾ, ਰੂਪ-ਰੇਖਾ, ਖ਼ਾਕਾ; ਨਮੂਨਾ, ਉਦੇਸ਼, ਮਨਸੂਥਾ, ਸਾਜ਼ਸ਼; **~ed** ਬਣਾਇਆ ਗਿਆ, ਕਲਪਤ, ਰੂਪਅੰਕਤ

designate (ਡੈਜ਼ਿਗਨੇਇਟ) *v a* ਨਿਯਤ ਕਰਨ, ਨਾਂ ਰੱਖਣਾ, ਮਨੋਨੀਤ ਕਰਨਾ, ਨਿਰਦਿਸ਼ਟ ਨਾਂ, ਮਨੋਨੀਤ

designation ('ਡੈਜ਼ਿਗਾ'ਨੇਇਸ਼ਨ) *n* ਨਾਂ, ਪਦਵੀ, ਅਹੁਦਾ, ਮਨੋਨੀਤ, ਪਦ-ਸੰਗਿਆ

desirable (ਡਿ'ਜ਼ਾਇਅਰਅਬਲ) *a* ਇੱਛਤ, ਲੋੜੀਂਦਾ, ਵਾਜਬੀ, ਮਨ-ਭਾਉਂਦਾ, ਵਾਂਛਤੀ

desire (ਡਿ'ਜ਼ਾਇਅ*) *n* ਚਾਹ, ਖ਼ਾਹਸ਼, ਇੱਛਾ, ਅਭਿਲਾਸ਼ਾ, ਕਾਮਨਾ, ਮਨੋਰਥ; ਚਾਹੁਣਾ, ਖ਼ਾਹਸ਼ ਕਰਨਾ, ਮੰਗ ਕਰਨਾ

desirous (ਡਿ'ਜ਼ਾਇਅਰਅਸ) *a* ਅਭਿਲਾਸ਼ੀ, ਇੱਛਕ, ਚਾਹਵਾਨ, ਇੱਛਾਵਾਨ, ਖ਼ਾਹਸ਼ਮੰਦ

desist (ਡਿ'ਜ਼ਿਸਟ) *v* ਹਟ ਜਾਣਾ, ਬਾਜ਼ ਰਹਿਣਾ, ਗੁਰੇਜ਼ ਕਰਨਾ, ਹੱਥ ਖਿੱਚਣਾ

desk (ਡੈਸਕ) *n* ਮੇਜ਼; ਡੈਸਕ; **~man** ਉਪ-ਸੰਪਾਦਕ; **the~** ਸਾਹਿਤਕ ਕੰਮ, ਦਫ਼ਤਰੀ ਕੰਮ

desolate (ਡੈਸਅਲਅਟ, 'ਡੈਸਅਲੇਇਟ) *a v* ਇੱਕਲਾ, ਲੁਗਾ, ਬੇਕਸ਼; ਉਜਾੜ, ਸੁੰਨ, ਵੀਰਾਨ, ਬੰਜਰ, ਗ਼ੈਰ-ਆਬਾਦ; ਉਜਾੜਨਾ, ਵੀਰਾਨ ਕਰਨਾ, ਗ਼ੈਰ-ਆਬਾਦ ਕਰਨਾ; ਦਿਲ ਤੋੜਨਾ, ਉਦਾਸ ਕਰਨਾ

desolation ('ਡੈਸਅਲੇਇਸ਼ਨ) *n* ਬਰਬਾਦੀ, ਵੀਰਾਨੀ, ਉਜਾੜ; ਉਦਾਸੀ, ਵਿਸ਼ਾਦ, ਨਿਰਾਸ਼ਤਾ

despair (ਡਿ'ਸਪੇਅ*) *n v* ਨਿਰਾਸ਼ਤਾ, ਆਸਹੀਣਤਾ; ਨਿਰਾਸ਼ ਹੋਣਾ, ਢੇਰੀ ਢਾਹ ਬੈਠਣਾ, ਉਮੀਦ ਛੱਡ ਬੈਠਣਾ

despatch (ਡਿ'ਸਪੈਚ) *v n* ਭੇਜਣਾ, ਬੱਲਣਾ, ਰਵਾਨਾ ਕਰਨਾ; ਮਾਰ ਮੁਕਾਉਣਾ; ਰਵਾਨਗੀ; ਖ਼ਾਤਮਾ; ਤੇਜ਼ੀ, ਫੁਰਤੀ, ਕਾਹਲ; ਸਰਕਾਰੀ ਚਿੱਠੀ; ਵੇਖੋ dispatch

desperate ('ਡੈਸਪ(ਅ)ਰਅਟ) *a* ਨਿਰਾਸ਼, ਬਿਲਕੁਲ ਮਾਯੂਸ, ਜਾਨ ਦੀ ਬਾਜ਼ੀ ਖੇਡਣ ਵਾਲਾ,

ਸਿਰਲੱਥ, ਨਿਹੰਗ, ਖ਼ਤਰਨਾਕ; **~ness, desperation** ਨਿਰਾਸ਼ਤਾ, ਬੇਬਾਕੀ; ਨਿਧੜਕਤਾ

despise (ਡਿ'ਸਪਾਇਜ਼) *v* ਨੀਚ ਸਮਝਣਾ, ਘਿਰਨਾ ਕਰਨਾ, ਤੁੱਛ ਸਮਝਣਾ, ਤਿਰਸਕਾਰ ਕਰਨਾ; **~dness** ਨੀਚਤਾ, ਘਿਰਨਾ, ਤੁੱਛਤਾ, ਤਿਰਸਕਾਰ

despite (ਡਿ:ਸਪਾਇਟ) *n prep* ਈਰਖਾ, ਕੀਨਾ, ਦਵੈਸ਼, ਘਿਰਨਾ; (ਪ੍ਰ) ਤਿਰਸਕਾਰ, ਬਾਵਜੂਦ, ਹੁੰਦੇ ਹੋਏ, ਹੋਣ ਦੇ ਬਾਵਜੂਦ; **~ful** ਦਵੈਸ਼ੀ, ਅਤਿਆਚਾਰੀ, ਅਪਮਾਨਜਨਕ, ਤਿਰਸਕਾਰਪੂਰਨ

despond (ਡਿ'ਸਪੱਡ) *v n* ਹਿੰਮਤ ਹਾਰਨਾ, ਦਿਲ ਹਾਰਨਾ, ਨਿਰਾਸ਼ ਹੋਣਾ, ਉਚਾਟ ਹੋਣਾ; ਉਦਾਸੀ, ਨਿਰਾਸ਼ਾ, ਨਿਰਾਸ਼ਤਾ (ਪ੍ਰ)

desitination ('ਡੈਸਟਿਨੇਇਸ਼ਨ) *n* ਮੰਜ਼ਲ, ਲਕਸ਼, ਨਿਯਤ ਥਾਂ, ਟਿਕਾਣਾ, ਮੰਜ਼ਲ, ਭਾਗ, ਸੰਜੋਗ

destiny ('ਡੈਸਟਿਨਿ) *n* ਤਕਦੀਰ, ਹੋਣੀ, ਸੰਜੋਗ, ਪ੍ਰਾਲਬਧ, ਤਕਦੀਰ, ਨਸੀਬ, ਭਾਗ

destitute ('ਡੈਸਟਿਟਯੂਟ) *a* ਵਾਂਝਿਆ, ਵਿਰਵਾ, ਵਰਜਤ, ਅਨਾਥ, ਮੁਥਾਜ, ਬੁੱਭਿਆ, ਸਾਧਨਹੀਨ

destroy (ਡਿ'ਸਟਰੌਇ) *v* ਬਰਬਾਦ ਕਰਨਾ, ਉਜਾੜਨਾ, ਵਿਅਰਥ ਕਰਨਾ, ਫਨਾ ਕਰਨਾ; ਅੰਤ ਕਰਨਾ, ਮੇਟਣਾ, ਨਾਸ ਕਰਨਾ; **~er** ਨਸ਼ਟ; ਪਤਿਤ

destruction (ਡਿ'ਸਟਰੱਕਸ਼ਨ) *n* ਬਰਬਾਦੀ, ਤਬਾਹੀ, ਉਜਾੜਾ, ਵਿਨਾਸ਼

destructive (ਡਿ'ਸਟਰੱਕਟਿਵ) *a* ਵਿਨਾਸ਼ਕਾਰੀ, ਨਾਸ਼ਕ, ਤਬਾਹਕੁਨ, ਸੰਘਾਰਨੀ, ਮੁਹਲਕ, ਤਖਰੀਬੀ, ਨਾਸ਼ਾਤਮਕ

detach (ਡਿ'ਟੈਚ) *v* ਨਿਖੇੜਨਾ, ਅੱਡ ਕਰਨਾ, ਜੁਦਾ ਕਰਨਾ, ਵੱਖਰਾ ਕਰਨਾ, ਅਲਗ ਕਰਨਾ; **~ed** ਦੂਜਿਆਂ ਤੋਂ ਵੱਖਰਾ, ਅੱਡਰਾ; ਨਿਰਪੱਖ; **~ment**

ਨਿਰਲੇਪਤਾ, ਵੈਰਾਗ, ਵਿਚਾਰ-ਸੁਤੰਤਰਤਾ; ਟੁਕੜੀ

detail (ਡੀਟੇਇਲ) *n* *v* ਵਿਸਤਾਰ, ਵਿਵਰਣ, ਵੇਰਵਾ; ਤਫ਼ਸੀਲ; ਦਸਤਾ; ਅੰਸ਼, ਵਿਸਤਾਰ ਨਾਲ ਵਰਨਣ ਕਰਨਾ; ਵੇਰਵਾ ਦੇਣਾ, ਘੋਲ ਕੇ ਲਿਖਣਾ; **~ed** ਵਿਸਤਾਰਤ, ਵਿਸਤਾਰ-ਪੂਰਵਕ, ਵਿਵਰਣ ਸਹਿਤ

detain (ਡਿ'ਟੇਇਨ) *v* ਰੋਕਣਾ, ਅਟਕਾਉਣਾ, ਬਿਠਾਈ ਰੱਖਣਾ, ਇੰਤਜ਼ਾਰ ਕਰਾਉਣਾ; ਬੰਨ੍ਹ ਰੱਖਣਾ, ਕੈਦ ਕਰਨਾ, ਨਜ਼ਰਬੰਦ ਕਰਨਾ; **~ed** ਰੋਕਿਆ, ਡੱਕਿਆ, ਨਜ਼ਰਬੰਦ

detect (ਡਿ'ਟੈੱਕਟ) *v* ਖੋਜ ਕੱਢਣਾ, ਸੂਹ ਕੱਢਣੀ, ਪਤਾ ਲਗਾਉਣਾ; ਤਾੜ ਲੈਣਾ; **~able** ਖੋਜਣਯੋਗ, ਸੂਹ ਕੱਢਣਯੋਗ, ਫੜਨਯੋਗ; **~ion** ਖੋਜ, ਪਕੜ, ਸੂਹ, ਲਭਾਈ; **~ive** ਖੋਜੀ, ਜਾਸੂਸ, ਗੁਪਤਚਰ, ਸੂਹੀਆ

detention, detainment (ਡਿ'ਟੈੱਨਸ਼ਨ, ਡਿ'ਟੇਇਨਮੰਏਟ) *n* ਦੇਰ; ਅਟਕਾ, ਰੋਕ, ਨਜ਼ਰਬੰਦੀ, ਗਰਿਫ਼ਤਾਰੀ

detenu, detinu ('ਡੇਇਟਾਅਨਯੂ) *n* ਨਜ਼ਰਬੰਦ, ਬੰਦੀ

deter (ਡਿ'ਟਾਅ:*) *v* ਰੋਕਣਾ, ਠਾਕਣਾ, ਬਾਜ਼ ਰੱਖਣਾ; **~ed** ਰੋਕਿਆ ਜਾਂ ਰੁਕਿਆ

deteriorate (ਡਿ'ਟਿਅਰਿਰੇਇਟ) *v* ਵਿਗਾੜਨਾ ਜਾਂ ਵਿਗੜਨਾ, ਖ਼ਰਾਬ ਕਰਨਾ

deterioration (ਡਿ'ਟਿਅਰਿਅ'ਰੇਇਸ਼ਨ) *n* ਵਿਗਾੜ, ਖ਼ਰਾਬੀ, ਗਿਰਾਵਟ, ਪਤਨ; ਗਾਲਣ

determinant (ਡਿ'ਟਾਅ:ਮਿਨੰਏਟ) *a* ਨਿਰਣਾਇਕ, ਨਿਰਲੇਕਾਰੀ; **~al** ਨਿਰਣੇਆਤਮਕ, ਨਿਰਧਾਰਨ ਸਬੰਧੀ, ਨਿਸ਼ਚਤਾਤਮਕ

determinate (ਡਿ'ਟਾਅ'ਮਿਨਅਟ) *a* ਨਿਸ਼ਚਤ, ਨਿਰਧਾਰੀ, ਨਿਰਧਾਰਤ; **~ness** ਸਥਿਰਤਾ,

ਨਿਸ਼ਚਤਤ

determination (ਡਿ'ਟਾਅ:ਮਿਨੇਇਸ਼ਨ) *n* ਪੱਕਾ ਇਰਾਦਾ, ਦ੍ਰਿੜ੍ਹਤਾ, ਨਿਸ਼ਚਾ; ਪਰਿਭਾਸ਼ਾ, ਸੀਮਾ-ਨਿਰਧਾਰਣ; ਜਾਂਚ

determine (ਡਿ'ਟਾਅ:ਮਿਨ) *v* ਪੱਕਾ ਇਰਾਦਾ ਕਰਨਾ, ਨਿਸ਼ਚਾ ਕਰਨਾ, ਠਾਨਣਾ (ਕਾ), ਸੀਮਤ ਕਰਨਾ, ਠਹਿਰਾਉਣਾ, ਫ਼ੈਸਲਾ ਕਰਨਾ, ਨਿਰਣਾ ਕਰਨਾ, ਤਸ਼ਖ਼ੀਸ ਕਰਨਾ; **~d** ਪੱਕਾ, ਦ੍ਰਿੜ੍ਹ, ਅਟੱਲ; ਨਿਸ਼ਚਤ, ਨਿਰਧਾਰਤ, ਸੀਮਤ, ਨਿਰਲੀਤ

deterred (ਡਿ'ਟਾਅ:ਡ) *a* ਰੋਕਿਆ ਜਾਂ ਰੁਕਿਆ

deterrence, determent (ਡਿ'ਟੈੱਰਅੰਸ, ਡਿ'ਟਾਅ:ਮੰਏਟ) *n* ਰੋਕ, ਰੁਕਾਵਟ, ਠੱਲ੍ਹ

detest (ਡਿ'ਟੈੱਸਟ) *v* ਘਿਰਨਾ ਕਰਨੀ, ਤਿਰਸਕਾਰਨਾ; **~ation** ਘਿਰਨਾ, ਤਿਰਸਕਾਰ, ਗਿਲਾਨੀ

dethrone (ਡਿਥਰਅਉਨ) *v* ਗੱਦੀਓਂ ਲਾਹੁਣਾ, ਪਰਭਾਵ ਜਾਂ ਜ਼ੋਰ ਘੱਟ ਕਰਨਾ

detriment ('ਡੈੱਟਰਿਮੰਏਟ) *n* ਹਾਨੀ, ਨੁਕਸਾਨ, ਹਰਜਾ; **~al** ਹਾਨੀਕਾਰਕ, ਬਾਧਕ

deuce (ਡਯੂਸ) *n* (ਤਾਸ਼ ਦੀ) ਦੁੱਕੀ; (ਟੈਨਿਸ) ਦੋਹਾਂ ਦੀ ਬਰਾਬਰੀ; ਮੁਸੀਬਤ, ਬਲਾ, ਆਫ਼ਤ; **~d** ਦਾਨਵੀ, ਵਹਿਸ਼ੀ; ਵਿਆਕੁਲਤਾ ਨਾਲ

devaluation (ਡੀ'ਵੈਲਯੂ'ਏਇਸ਼ਨ) *n* ਵਿਮੁੱਲਣ, ਅਵਮੁੱਲਣ

devalue ('ਡੀ'ਵੈਲਯੂ) *v* ਮੁਦਰਾ ਦਾ ਮੁੱਲ ਘਟਾਉਣਾ, ਵਿਮੁੱਲਣ ਕਰਨਾ, ਨਸ਼ਟ ਕਰਨਾ, ਤਬਾਹ ਕਰਨਾ

devastate ('ਡੈੱਵ੍ਹਅਸਟੇਇਟ) *v* ਉਜਾੜਨਾ, ਬਰਬਾਦ ਕਰਨਾ, ਵੀਰਾਨ ਕਰਨਾ, ਨਸ਼ਟ ਕਰਨਾ, ਤਬਾਹ ਕਰਨਾ

devastation ('ਡੈੱਵ੍ਹਅਸ'ਟੇਇਸ਼ਨ) *n* ਉਜਾੜਾ,

ਤਬਾਹੀ, ਬਰਬਾਦੀ, ਵੀਰਾਨੀ, ਉਜਾੜ, ਵਿਨਾਸ਼

develop (ਡਿ'ਵੈੱਲਅਪ) *v* ਵਧਾਉਣਾ ਜਾਂ ਵਧਣਾ, ਵਿਕਾਸ ਕਰਨ ਦਾਂ ਹੋਣਾ, ਉੱਨਤੀ ਕਰਨੀ ਜਾਂ ਹੋਣੀ; ਪ੍ਰਕਾਸ਼ਤ ਕਰਨਾ, ਫੋਟੋ ਧੋਣਾ; ਦਿਖਲਾਉਣਾ, ਪਰਦਰਸ਼ਤ ਕਰਨਾ; ਪ੍ਰੰਗਰਨ; ~ed ਵਿਕਸਤ, ਉੱਨਤ, ਪ੍ਰਫੁੱਲਤ, ਵਧਿਆ ਫੁੱਲਿਆ; ~ing ਵਿਕਾਸਸ਼ੀਲ, ਵਿਕਾਸੀ; ~ment ਵਿਕਾਸ, ਉੱਨਤੀ, ਤਰੱਕੀ; ਵਾਧਾ, ਪ੍ਰਖ਼ਤਰਗੀ; (ਫੋਟੋ) ਧੁਲਾਈ

deviate ('ਡੀਵਿ'ਏਇਟ) *v* (ਮਾਰਗ, ਸ਼ਾਸਨ, ਸੱਚਾਈ ਆਦਿ ਤੋਂ) ਹਟਣਾ, ਫਿਰ ਜਾਣਾ, ਭਟਕਣਾ, ਉਲੰਘਣ ਕਰਨਾ; ~d ਵਿਚਲਤ, ਪਥ-ਭ੍ਰਿਸ਼ਟ

deviation (ਡਿ'ਵਿ'ਏਇਸ਼ਨ) *n* ਭਟਕਣ, ਖਿਤਾਨ, ਪ੍ਰਹਨ, ਪਥ-ਭ੍ਰਸ਼ਟਤਾ, ਵਿਚਲਨ

device (ਡਿ'ਵਾਇਸ) *n* ਵਿਉਂਤ, ਢੰਗ, ਜੁਗਤ, ਤਰਕੀਬ, ਉਪਾਉ; ਮਰਜ਼ੀ, ਖ਼ੁਸ਼ੀ, ਇੱਛਿਆ; ਖ਼ਾਕਾ, ਚਿੱਤਰ

devil, The devil (ਡੈੱਵ੍ਲ) *n* ਸ਼ੈਤਾਨ, ਅਸੁਰ, ਇਬਲੀਸ, ਪਰੇਤ, ਬਦਮਾਸ਼, ਭਾੜੇ ਦਾ ਟੱਟੂ; ~ish ਸ਼ੈਤਾਨੀ, ਅਸੁਰੀ; ਭਿਆਨਕ; ਸਖ਼ਤ, ਅਤੀਅੰਤ; ~ishness ਸ਼ੈਤਾਨੀ, ਰਾਖ਼ਸ਼ਪੁਨਾ, ਪਿਸ਼ਾਚਤਾ

devolve (ਡਿ'ਵੌੱਲਵ) *v* ਸਪੁਰਦ ਕਰਨਾ ਜਾਂ ਹੋਣਾ, ਸੌਂਪਣਾ; ਹਵਾਲੇ ਕਰਨਾ ਜਾਂ ਹੋਣਾ ਵਿਰਸੇ ਵਿਚ ਮਿਲਣਾ

devote (ਡਿ'ਵੈਉਟ) *v* ਭੇਟਾ ਕਰਨਾ, ਸਮਰਪਣ ਕਰਨਾ, ਅਰਪਣ ਕਰਨਾ; ~d ਅਰਪਿਆ, ਵਕਫ਼ ਕੀਤਾ ਹੋਇਆ; ਸਰਧਾਵਾਨ, ਦ੍ਰਿੜ੍ਹ ਭਗਤ; ਉਪਾਸ਼ਕ; ~dness ਸਮਰਪਣ, ਆਤਮ-ਸਮਰਪਣ, ਭਗਤੀ, ਸ਼ਰਧਾ, ਅਨੁਰਾਗ; ~e ਸ਼ਰਧਾਲੂ, ਉਪਾਸ਼ਕ, ਭਗਤ

devotion (ਡਿ'ਵੌਉਸ਼ਨ) *n* ਸ਼ਰਧਾ, ਭਗਤੀ,

ਸਿਦਕ, ਭਗਤੀ ਭਾਵ, ਪਰੇਮ; ~al ਧਾਰਮਕ, ਭਗਤੀ ਸਬੰਧੀ, ਸ਼ਰਧਾਮਈ

dew (ਡਯੂ) *n v* ਤਰੇਲ, ਓਸ, ਸ਼ਬਨਮ, ਤੁਸ਼ਾਰ; ਟੇਪੇ, ਤਰ ਕਰਨਾ, ਤਰੇਲ ਦਾ ਬਨਣਾ

dexterous ('ਡੈਕਸਟ(ਅ)ਰਅਸ) *a* ਨਿਪੁੰਨ, ਚਤਰ, ਉਸਤਾਦ, ਫੁਰਤੀਲਾ; ਸੱਜੇ ਹੱਥ, ਸਿੱਧ ਹੱਥਾ

diabetes ('ਡਾਇਆ'ਬੀਟੀਜ਼) *n* ਸ਼ਕਰ ਰੋਗ, ਜ਼ਿਆਬਤੀਸ

diabetic (ਡਾਇਆ'ਬੈਟਿਕ) *n a* ਜ਼ਿਆਬਤੀਸ, ਸ਼ਕਰ-ਰੋਗੀ, ਸ਼ਕਰ-ਰੋਗ ਸਬੰਧੀ

diabolic,-al ('ਡਾਇਆ'ਬੌੱਲਿਕ, ਡਾਇਆ'ਬੌੱਲਿਕਲ) *a* ਸ਼ੈਤਾਨੀ, ਸ਼ੈਤਾਨ ਵਾਂਗੂ, ਰਾਖ਼ਸ਼ੀ; ਨਿਰਦਈ, ਪਾਪੀ; ਦੁਸ਼ਟ

diacritic ('ਡਾਇਆ'ਕਰਿਟਿਕ) *n* ਭੇਦ-ਸੂਚਕ

diagnose ('ਡਾਇਆਗਨਅਉਜ਼) *v* (ਰੋਗ), ਤਸ਼ਖ਼ੀਸ ਕਰਨੀ, ਜਾਂਚ ਕਰਨਾ, ਲਖਣਾ

diagnosis (ਡਾਇਆਗਨਅਉਸਿਸ) *n* ਰੋਗ ਦੀ ਪਛਾਣ, ਤਸ਼ਖ਼ੀਸ; ਰੋਗ ਦਾ ਵਰਨਣ

diagnostic ('ਡਾਇਆਗਾ'ਨੌਸਟਿਕ) *a n* ਤਸ਼ਖ਼ੀਸੀ, ਤਸ਼ਖ਼ੀਸ ਸਬੰਧੀ; ਬੀਮਾਰੀ ਦੇ ਚਿੰਨ੍ਹ, ਰੋਗ-ਲੱਛਣ

diagonal (ਡਾਇ'ਐਗਾਅਨਲ) *a n* ਆੜਾ, ਟੇਢਾ, (ਰੇਖਾ) ਦੁਸਾਰ, ਕਰਨ ਰੇਖਾ

diagram ('ਡਾਇਆਗਰੈਮ) *n* ਖ਼ਾਕਾ, ਨਕਸ਼ਾ, (ਰੇਖਾ) ਸ਼ਕਲ, ਰੇਖਾ-ਚਿੱਤਰ

dial ('ਡਾਇ(ਅ)ਲ) *n v* ਅੰਕ-ਪਟ, (ਘੜੀ ਜਾਂ ਫ਼ੋਨ ਦਾ) ਡਾਇਲ; ਭਾਢ ਦਾ ਮਾਪਕ; ਟੈਲੀਫ਼ੋਨ ਕਰਨਾ, ਡਾਇਲ ਕਰਨਾ, ਨੰਬਰ ਫੇਰਨਾ

dialect ('ਡਾਇਲੈਕਟ) *n* ਉਪਭਾਸ਼ਾ, ਬੋਲੀ

dialogue ('ਡਾਇਆਲੌਗ) *n* ਵਾਰਤਾਲਾਪ,

ਗੱਲਬਾਤ; ਸੰਬਾਦ

diameter (ਡਾਇ'ਐਮਿਟਅ*) *n* ਵਿਆਸ; ਨਾਪ ਦੀ ਇਕਾਈ

diamond ('ਡਾਇਅਮਅੰਡ) *n v* ਹੀਰਾ (ਤਾਸ਼ ਵਿਚ) ਇੱਟ ਦਾ ਪੱਤਾ (ਰੰਗ); ਹੀਰਿਆਂ ਨਾਲ ਜੜਿਆ, ਜੜਾਊ

dirarrhoea ('ਡਾਇਅ'ਰਿਅ) *n* ਦਸਤ, ਪੇਚਸ਼, ਮਰੋੜ, ਅਤਿਸਾਰ; (ਡੰਗਰਾਂ ਦੀ) ਮੋਕ

diary ('ਡਾਇਅਰਿ) *n* ਰੋਜ਼ਨਾਮਚਾ, ਦੈਨਕੀ, ਡਾਇਰੀ, ਪਤਰੀ, ਜੰਤਰੀ

dice ('ਡਾਇਸ) *n pl v* ਗੋਟੀਆਂ, ਗੋਟਾਂ, ਚੌਪੜ, (ਪਾਸਾ ਆਦਿ) ਖੇਡਣਾ; ਮਾਸ ਦੇ ਚੌਰਸ ਟੁਕੜੇ ਕਰਨਾ; ~**r** ਚੌਪੜ ਖਿਡਾਰੀ, ਜੁਆਰੀਆ, ਜੂਏਬਾਜ਼

dichotomy (ਡਾਇ'ਕੌਟਅਮਿ) *n* ਦੁਵੰਡ, ਦੁਫਾੜ, ਦੋ ਟੁਕ

dictate (ਡਿਕ'ਟੇਇਟ,'ਡਿਕਟੇਇਟ) *v n* ਬੋਲ ਕੇ ਲਿਖਾਉਣਾ; ਹੁਕਮ ਚਲਾਉਣਾ, ਬੋਲੇ ਅਨੁਸਾਰ ਲਿਖਤ; ਹੁਕਮ, ਆਦੇਸ਼

dictation (ਡਿਕ'ਟੇਇਸ਼ਨ) *n* ਇਮਲਾ; ਆਦੇਸ਼, ਹੁਕਮ

dictator ('ਡਿਕ'ਟੇਇਟਅ*) *n* ਕੁਲਮੁਖ਼ਤਾਰ, ਨਿਰੰਕੁਸ਼ ਸ਼ਾਸਕ, ਤਾਨਾਸ਼ਾਹੀ, ਬੋਲ ਕੇ ਲਿਖਾਉਣ ਵਾਲਾ

diction ('ਡਿਕਸ਼ਨ) *n* ਲਿਖਣ ਸ਼ੈਲੀ; ਬੋਲਿਆ ਵਾਕ; ਭਾਸ਼ਾ, ਭਾਸ਼ਾ ਦੀ ਸ਼ੈਲੀ; ਸ਼ਬਦ-ਚੋਣ, ਸ਼ਬਦ-ਯੋਜਨਾ; ~**ary** ਸ਼ਬਦ-ਕੋਸ਼, ਕੋਸ਼

dictum ('ਡਿਕਟਅਮ) *n* ਅਖਾਣ, ਕਹਾਵਤ, ਉਕਤੀ

didactic (ਡਿ'ਡੈਕਟਿਕ) *a* ਉਪਦੇਸ਼ਾਤਮਕ, ਸਿੱਖਿਆ-ਦਾਇਕ, ਸਿੱਖਿਆਤਮਕ; ~**ism** ਉਪਦੇਸ਼ਾਤਮਕਤਾ, ਸਿੱਖਿਆਵਾਦ

die (ਡਾਇ) *n v* ਪਾਸਾ (ਜੂਏ ਵਿਚ) ਗੀਟੀ, ਮੋਹਰਾ, ਪਾਸੇ ਦੀ ਖੇਡ; ਠੱਪਾ; ਮਰਨਾ, ਮਰ ਜਾਣਾ, ਚਲਾਣਾ ਕਰਨਾ, ਮਿਟ ਜਾਣਾ, ਖ਼ਤਮ ਹੋਣਾ, (ਬੂਟਿਆਂ ਦਾ) ਮੁਰਝਾ ਜਾਣਾ, ਕੁਮਲਾ.ਜਾਣਾ

diet (ਡਾਇਟ) *n v* ਖ਼ੁਰਾਕ, ਆਹਾਰ; ਨਿਯਮਤ ਭੋਜਨ; ਪਰਹੇਜ਼ ਵਾਲੀ, ਖ਼ੁਰਾਕ ਦੇਣੀ; ਸੱਥ, ਸਭਾ, ਮਜਲਸ

dietician (ਡਾਇਅ'ਟਿਸ਼ਨ) *n* ਆਹਾਰ-ਵਿਗਿਆਨੀ

differ ('ਡਿਫ਼ਅ*) *v* ਫ਼ਰਕ ਹੋਣਾ, ਅੰਤਰ ਹੋਣਾ, ਵੱਖ ਵੱਖ ਹੋਣਾ, ਭੇਦ ਹੋਣਾ

difference ('ਡਿਫ਼ਰ(ਅ)ਨਸ) *n* ਫ਼ਰਕ, ਅੰਤਰ, ਵਿਤਕਰਾ, ਵਖਰੇਵਾਂ, ਭੇਦ, ਭਿੰਨਤਾ; ਅਸਹਿਮਤੀ, ਮੱਤਭੇਦ, ਝਗੜਾ, ਵਿਵਾਦ; ਵਿਰੋਧ, ਪਾੜਾ; ਵਿਅਕਤੀਗਤ ਜਾਂ ਜਾਤੀਗਤ ਵਿਸ਼ੇਸ਼ਤਾ

different ('ਡਿਫ਼ਰ(ਅ)ਨਟ) *a* ਵੱਖਰਾ, ਭਿੰਨ, ਹੋਰ, ਦੂਜਾ; ਅਸਮਾਨ, ਬੇਜੋੜ, ਬੇਮੇਲ; ~**iation** ਭਿੰਨਤਾ, ਵਖਰੇਵਾਂ, ਵਿਤਕਰਾ, ਵਿਭੇਦੀਕਰਨ

difficult ('ਡਿਫ਼ਿਕ(ਅ)ਲਟ) *a* ਔਖਾ, ਕਠਨ, ਮੁਸ਼ਕਲ, ਕਰੜਾ; ਟੇਢਾ

diffidence (ਡਿਫ਼ਿਡਅੰਸ) *n* ਝਿਜਕ, ਝਾਕਾ, ਸੰਕੋਚ, ਸੰਗ, ਆਸ਼ੰਕਾ; ਆਤਮ-ਸੰਦੇਹ, ਆਪਣੇ ਆਪ ਉੱਤੇ ਵਿਸ਼ਵਾਸ ਨਾ ਹੋਣ ਦੀ ਹਾਲਤ; ਸੰਗਾਊਪਣ, ਸ਼ਰਮੀਲਾਪਣ

diffident (ਡਿਫ਼ਿਡਅੰਟ) *a* ਸੰਗਾਊ, ਸ਼ਰਮਾਕਲ, ਸੰਕੋਚਵਾਨ, ਬੇਹੌਸਲਾ; ਅਵਿਸ਼ਵਾਸੀ, ਆਤਮ ਵਿਸ਼ਵਾਸਹੀਣ

diffuse (ਡਿ'ਫ਼ਯੂਜ਼) *v a* ਖਿਲਾਰਨਾ ਜਾਂ ਖਿੱਲਰਨਾ; ਖਿੱਲਰਵਾਂ, ਵਿਸਤਰਤ, ਵਿਸਤਾਰਸ਼ੀਲ; ~**d** ਫੈਲਿਆ, ਵਿਸਤਰਤ, ਵਿਆਪਤ

diffusible (ਡਿ'ਫਯੂਅਬਲ) *a* ਖਿਲਰਨਯੋਗ ਪ੍ਰਸਾਰਨਯੋਗ

diffusion (ਡਿ'ਫ਼ਯੂਜ਼ਨ) *n* ਖਿਲਾਰ, ਫੈਲਾਉ,

ਪ੍ਰਸਾਰਨ, ਵਿਆਪਕਤਾ

dig (ਡਿਗ) *v n* ਪੁੱਟਣਾ; ਟੋਆ ਕੱਢਣਾ, ਕੱਚ ਕੇ ਸੁਟਣਾ, ਘੁਰਨਾ, ਚੋਭਣਾ, ਖੋਜ ਕਰਨੀ; ਪੁਟਾਈ, ਗੋਡੀ; ਹੁੱਝ, ਠੁੰਗਾ

digamy ('ਡਿਗਾਅਮਿ) *n* ਦੋ-ਵਿਆਹ

digest (ਡਿ'ਜੈਸਟ, 'ਡਾਇਜੈਸਟ) *v n* ਪਚਾਉਣਾ, ਹਜ਼ਮ ਕਰਨਾ, ਹਜ਼ਮ ਹੋਣਾ; ਸਹਿ ਜਾਣਾ, ਜਰ ਜਾਣਾ, ਨਾਲ ਮਿਲਾ ਲੈਣਾ; ਸੰਖੇਪ; ਸੰਖਿਪਤ, ਪੁਸਤਕ, ਖੁਲਾਸਾ; ~ion ਪਾਚਨ-ਸ਼ਕਤੀ, ਹਾਜ਼ਮਾ; ~ive ਪਚਾਉ, ਹਾਜ਼ਮੇਦਾਰ, ਹਾਜ਼ਮੇ ਲਈ ਚੰਗਾ, ਪਾਚਕ, ਪਾਚਨਸ਼ੀਲ

digit ('ਡਿਜਿਟ) *n* o ਤੋਂ 9 ਤਕ ਦਾ ਕੋਈ ਅੰਕ, ਅੰਕੜਾ; ਹੱਥ ਜਾਂ ਪੈਰ ਦੀ ਉਂਗਲ

dignify (ਡਿਗਨਿਫ਼ਾਇ) *n* ਵਡਿਆਉਣਾ, ਮਾਨ ਦੇਣਾ, ਸਨਮਾਨਤ ਕਰਨਾ, ਸ਼ਾਨ ਵਧਾਉਣੀ

dignitary (ਡਿਗਨਿਟ(ਅ)ਰਿ) *n* ਉੱਚੀ ਪਦਵੀ ਵਾਲਾ ਵਿਅਕਤੀ, ਪਤਵੰਤਾ

dignity ('ਡਿਗਨਅਟਿ) *n* ਮਾਨ, ਵਡਿਆਈ, ਪਰਤਿਸ਼ਠਾ, ਗੌਰਵ, ਪ੍ਰਤਾਪ, ਸਨਮਾਨ, ਸ਼ਾਨ

dilapidate ('ਡਿ'ਲੈਪਿਡੇਇਟ) *v* ਤੋੜਨਾ, ਭੰਨਣਾ, ਟੁੱਟ ਭੱਜ ਜਾਣਾ, ਉਜਾੜਨਾ ਜਾਂ ਉਜੜਨਾ, ਨਾਸ ਕਰਨਾ ਜਾਂ ਹੋਣਾ; ~d ਟੁੱਟਾ ਭੱਜਾ; ਭੈੜੀ ਹਾਲਤ ਵਿਚ, ਉਜੜਿਆ, ਖ਼ਸਤਾ ਹਾਲ

dilemma (ਡਿ'ਲੈੱਮਅ) *n* ਦੁਬਧਾ, ਦੁਵੱਲੀ ਔਕੜ, ਦੁਚਿੰਤੀ; ਪਰੇਸ਼ਾਨੀ

dilligence ('ਡਿਲਿਜਅੰਸ) *n* ਮਿਹਨਤ, ਘਾਲ, ਪਰਿਸ਼੍ਰਮ, ਉੱਦਮ

dilligent ('ਡਿਲਿਜਅੰਟ) *a* ਮਿਹਨਤੀ, ਪਰਿਸ਼੍ਰਮੀ, ਉੱਦਮੀ

dilly ('ਡਿਲਿ) *n* ਗੱਡੀ, ਥੈਲਾ, ਝੋਲਾ; ~dally ਢਿਲ-ਮੱਠ ਕਰਨੀ, ਟਾਲ-ਮਟੋਲ ਕਰਨਾ;

ਅਵਾਰਾਗਰਦੀ ਕਰਨਾ

dilute(ਡਾਇ'ਲਯੂਟ) *v a* ਪਤਲਾ ਕਰਨਾ, ਪਾਣੀ ਮਿਲਾ ਕੇ ਮੱਧਮ ਕਰਨਾ; (ਰੰਗ) ਫਿੱਕਾ ਕਰਨਾ; ਮੱਠਾ ਪਾ ਦੇਣਾ; ਹਲਕਾ, ਫਿੱਕਾ (ਰੰਗ); ਸੁਆਦਹੀਨ, ਪਤਲਾ

dim (ਡਿਮ) *a v* ਨਿੰਮ੍ਹਾ, ਮੱਧਮ; ਧੁੰਦਲਾ, ਅਸਪਸ਼ਟ, ਫਿੱਕਾ; ਨਿੰਮ੍ਹਾ ਕਰਨਾ ਜਾਂ ਹੋਣਾ

dimension (ਡਿ'ਮੈਨਸ਼ਨ) *n* ਪਰਿਮਾਪ, (ਲੰਬਾਈ-ਚੌੜਾਈ) ਆਯਾਮ; ~al ਨਾਪ ਸਬੰਧੀ, ਆਕਾਰ ਜਾਂ ਵਿਸਤਾਰ ਬਾਰੇ

diminish (ਡਿ'ਮਿਨਿਸ਼) *v* ਘਟਾਉਣਾ ਜਾਂ ਘਟਨਾ, ਸੰਖਿਪਤ ਕਰਨਾ; ਮੱਠਾ ਪੈਣਾ ਜਾਂ ਹੋਣਾ; ~ing ਹ੍ਰਾਸਮਾਨ, ਘਟਣ ਵਾਲਾ

dimple (ਡਿੰਪਲ) *n* ਨੇਡੀ ਦਾ ਡੂੰਘ, (ਹੱਸਣ ਲੱਗਿਆਂ) ਗੱਲ੍ਹਾਂ ਵਿਚ ਪੈਂਦਾ ਟੋਆ; ਟੋਆ ਪੈਣਾ, ਡੂੰਘ ਬਣਨਾ

dimply (ਡਿੰਪਲਿ) *a* ਡੂੰਘਦਾਰ, ਲਹਿਰਦਾਰ

din (ਡਿਨ) *n v* ਰੌਲਾ, ਸ਼ੋਰ; ਰੌਲਾ ਪਾਉਣਾ, ਸ਼ੋਰ ਕਰਨਾ, ਸਿਰ ਖਾਣਾ, ਕੰਨ ਖਾਣੇ, ਬੋਲ ਬੋਲ ਕੇ ਅਕਾ ਦੇਣਾ

dinar ('ਡੀਨਾ*) *n* ਦਿਨਾਰ (ਇਕ ਕੁਵੈਤੀ, ਇਰਾਕੀ ਅਤੇ ਇਰਾਨੀ ਸਿੱਕਾ)

dine (ਡਾਇਨ) *v* ਰੋਟੀ ਖਾਣੀ, ਭੋਜਨ ਕਰਨਾ, ਖਾਣਾ ਖਾਣਾ

dinner ('ਡਿਨਅ*) *n* ਸ਼ਾਮ ਦੀ ਦਾਅਵਤ, ਰਾਤ ਦਾ ਭੋਜਨ

dip (ਡਿਪ) *n* ਡੋਬਟਾ, ਡੋਬਾ ਦੇਣਾ; ਡੋਬ ਕੇ ਰੰਗਣਾ; ਡੁੱਬਣਾ, ਲਹਿਣਾ; ਕੜਛੀ ਨਾਲ ਕੱਢਣਾ, (ਝੰਡੇ, ਜਹਾਜ਼ ਦੇ ਪੱਲੇ ਜਾਂ ਤੱਕੜੀ ਨੂੰ) ਨੀਵਾਂ ਕਰਨਾ

diphtheria, diphtheritis (ਡਿਫ਼'ਥਿਅਰਿਅ, ਡਿਫ਼-ਥੈਰਾਇਟਿਸ) *n* ਗਲਘੋਟੂ ਰੋਗ

diphthong ('ਡਿਫਥੋਂਙ) *n* ਸੰਯੁਕਤ ਸਵਰ, ਸੰਧੀਸਵਰ

diploma (ਡਿ'ਪਲਅਉਮਅ) *n* ਸਨਦ, ਪ੍ਰਮਾਣ ਪੱਤਰ; ਰਾਜ ਪੱਤਰ, ਅਧਿਕਾਰ ਪੱਤਰ

diplomacy (ਡਿ'ਪਲੋਮਅਸਿ) *n* ਰਾਜਨੀਤੀ, ਜੁਗਤ, ਚਤਰਤਾ; ਕੂਟਨੀਤੀ

diplomat ('ਡਿਪਲਅਮੈਟ) *n* ਨੀਤੀਵਾਨ, ਸਫ਼ੀਰ, ਰਾਜਦੂਤ

dire ('ਡਾਇਅ*) *a* ਤੀਬਰ, ਘੋਰ, ਭਿਅੰਕਰ

direct (ਡਿ'ਰੈਕਟ) *v a adv* ਆਗਿਆ ਦੇਣੀ; ਨਿਰਦੇਸ਼ਨ ਦੇਣਾ, ਚਲਾਉਣਾ; ਦਿਸ਼ਾ ਪ੍ਰਦਾਨ ਕਰਨਾ; ਹੁਕਮ ਦੇਣਾ, ਆਦੇਸ਼ ਦੇਣਾ; ਸਿੱਧਾ, ਬਿਲਕੁਲ, ਕਤਈ, ਸਪਸ਼ਟ, ਸਰਲ, ਖਰਾ, ਠੀਕ; ਤੁਰਤ; **~action** ਅਮਲੀ ਕਾਰਵਾਈ

direction (ਡਿ'ਰੈਕਸ਼ਨ) *n* ਸੰਚਾਲਨ, ਨਿਰਦੇਸ਼ਨ, ਨਿਗਰਾਨੀ, ਆਦੇਸ਼; ਦਿਸ਼ਾ, ਪਹਿਲੂ

directive (ਡਿ'ਰੈਕਟਿਵ) *n a* ਨਿਰਦੇਸ਼; ਨਿਰਦੇਸ਼ਕ, ਮਾਰਗਦਰਸ਼ਕ, ਸੂਚਕ

director (ਡਿ'ਰੈਕਟਅ*) *n* ਨਿਰਦੇਸ਼ਕ, ਸੰਚਾਲਕ, ਸੂਤਰਧਾਰ, (ਫ਼ਿਲਮ) ਨਿਰਦੇਸ਼ਕ, ਨਿਰਮਾਤਾ; **~ate** ਪ੍ਰਬੰਧ ਸੰਚਾਲਕ, ਨਿਰਦੇਸ਼ਕ ਦਾ ਦਫ਼ਤਰ, ਅਧਿਕਰਤਾ ਸੰਮਤੀ, ਸੰਚਾਲਕ-ਮੰਡਲ, ਸੰਚਾਲਕ-ਪਦ; **~ship** ਸੰਚਾਲਕਤਾ, ਨਿਰਦੇਸ਼ਕਤਵ, ਸੰਚਾਲਕਪਦ; **~y** ਨਿਰਦੇਸ਼ਤਾ, ਡਾਇਰੈਕਟਰੀ, ਨਿਯਮਾਵਲੀ; ਰਾਹਨਾਮਾ; ਸੰਚਾਲਕ ਮੰਡਲ

direful ('ਡਾਇਅਫ਼ੁਲ) *a* ਘੋਰ, ਭਿਅੰਕਰ

dirt (ਡਅਃਟ) *n v* ਧੂੜ, ਚਿੱਕੜ, ਮੈਲ, ਮਲ, ਕੂੜਾ ਕਰਨਾ, ਗੰਦਗੀ; **~y** ਮੈਲਾ, ਗੰਦਾ, ਕਲੰਕਤ, ਅਪਵਿੱਤਰ, ਗੰਧਲਿਆ, ਮਿਟਿਆਲਾ; ਖ਼ਰਾਬ

disability ('ਡਿਸਅ'ਬਿਲਅਟਿ) *n* ਅਯੋਗਤਾ, ਅਸਮਰੱਥਾ; ਅੰਗਹੀਨਤਾ, ਅਪਾਜਪੁਣਾ

disable (ਡਿਸ'ਏਇਬਲ) *v* ਅਯੋਗ ਠਹਿਰਾਉਣਾ, ਅਸਮੱਰਥ ਘੋਸ਼ਤ ਕਰਨਾ; ਅੰਗਹੀਨ ਕਰਨਾ, ਨਕਾਰਾ ਕਰਨਾ, ਅਪਾਹਜ ਬਣਾ ਦੇਣਾ; **~d** ਅੰਗਹੀਨ, ਨਾਕਾਮ, ਅਪੰਗ, ਅਪਾਹਜ; **~ment** ਅਸਮਰੱਥਤਾ, ਅਸ਼ਕਤੀ, ਅਯੋਗਤਾ, ਅੰਗਹੀਨਤਾ

disadvantage ('ਡਿਸਅਡ'ਵਾਂਟਿਜ) *n* ਹਾਨੀ, ਘਾਟਾ, ਨੁਕਸਾਨ; ਦਿੱਕਤ, ਔਖਿਆਈ

disagree ('ਡਿਸਅ'ਗਰੀ) *v* ਮੱਤ-ਭੇਦ ਰੱਖਣਾ, ਅਸੰਮਤੀ ਰੱਖਣਾ, ਅਸਹਿਮਤ ਹੋਣਾ

disallow ('ਡਿਸਅ'ਲਾਉ) *v* ਅਸਵੀਕਾਰ ਕਰਨਾ, ਆਗਿਆ ਨਾ ਦੇਣੀ, ਮਨ੍ਹਾ ਕਰਨਾ, ਨਾਮਨਜ਼ੂਰ ਕਰਨਾ; **~ed** ਨਾ-ਮਨਜ਼ੂਰ, ਅਸਵੀਕ੍ਰਿਤ

disappear ('ਡਿਸਅ'ਪਿਅ*) *v* ਲੁਕਣਾ, ਲੋਪ ਹੋਣਾ, ਅੱਖਾਂ ਤੋਂ ਉਹਲੇ ਹੋਣਾ, ਗੁਆਚਣਾ, ਛਿਪ ਜਾਣਾ, ਮਿਟ ਜਾਣਾ, ਗਾਇਬ ਹੋ ਜਾਣਾ; **~ance** ਲੋਪ, ਉਹਲੇ, ਓਟ, ਅਦ੍ਰਿਸ਼ਤਾ

disappoint ('ਡਿ'ਸਅ'ਪੋਇੰਟ) *v* ਨਿਸਫਲ ਕਰਨਾ, ਆਸ ਭੰਗ ਕਰਨੀ, ਆਸ ਤੋੜਨੀ, ਨਿਰਾਸ ਕਰਨਾ; **~ed** ਨਿਰਾਸ, ਮਾਯੂਸ, ਨਾਉਮੀਦ; **~ment** ਨਿਰਾਸ਼ਤਾ, ਨਿਰਾਸ਼ਾ

disapproval ('ਡਿਸਅ'ਪਰੂਵਲ) *n* ਅਸੰਮਤੀ, ਨਾਮਨਜ਼ੂਰੀ, ਨਾ-ਪਸੰਦਗੀ

disapprove ('ਡਿਸਅ'ਪਰੂਵ੍) *v* ਅਪ੍ਰਵਾਨ ਕਰਨਾ, ਅਸੰਮਤੀ ਪਰਗਟ ਕਰਨੀ, ਵਿਰੋਧ ਕਰਨਾ, ਨਾ ਪਸੰਦ ਕਰਨਾ

disarm (ਡਿਸ'ਆਮ) *v* ਸ਼ਸਤਰਹੀਣ ਕਰਨਾ, ਬੇਬਸ ਕਰਨਾ, ਨਿਹੱਥਾ ਕਰਨਾ; **~ament** ਨਿਸ਼ਸਤਰੀਕਰਨ, ਸ਼ਸਤਰਹੀਣਤਾ, ਸ਼ਸਤਰ-ਤਿਆਗ; **~ed** ਨਿਹੱਥਾ, ਬੇਬਸ

disarrange ('ਡਿਸਅ'ਰੇਇੰਜ) *v* ਬੇਤਰਤੀਬ ਕਰਨਾ, ਅੱਗੇ ਪਿੱਛੇ ਕਰ ਦੇਣਾ, ਉਲਟ-ਪੁਲਟ

ਕਰ ਦੇਣ; ~ment ਬੇਤਰਤੀਬੀ, ਉਲਟ-ਪੁਲਟ, ਅਵਿਵਸਥਾ, ਗੜਬੜ

disarray ('ਡਿਸਅਰੇਇ) *n v* ਬੇਤਰਤੀਬੀ, ਗੜਬੜ ਉਲਟ-ਪੁਲਟ, ਉਲਟ-ਪੁਲਟ ਕਰਨਾ, ਅੱਗੇ ਪਿੱਛੇ ਕਰ ਦੇਣਾ

disassociate (ਡਿਸਅ'ਸ਼ਿਏਇਟ) *v* ਅੱਲਗ ਹੋ ਜਾਣਾ, ਨਾਤਾ ਤੋੜ ਦੇਣਾ, ਸਬੰਧ ਤੋੜ ਲੈਣਾ

disaster (ਡਿ'ਜ਼ਾਸਟਅ*) *n* ਬਿਪਤਾ, ਮੁਸੀਬਤ, ਸ਼ਾਮਤ, ਆਫ਼ਤ, ਸੰਕਟ; ~ous ਬਿਪਤਾ ਵਾਲਾ, ਮੰਦ ਭਾਗਾ, ਸੰਕਟ ਵਾਲਾ, ਘੋਰ

disband (ਡਿਸਬੈਂਡ) *n* (ਸੈਨਾ, ਪਲਟਨ) ਤੋੜ ਦੇਣੀ, ਲਾਮਬੰਦੀ ਸਮਾਪਤ ਕਰ ਦੇਣੀ; ਖਿੰਡਾ ਦੇਣਾ, ਭੰਗ ਕਰ ਦੇਣਾ, ਬਰਖ਼ਾਸਤ ਕਰ ਦੇਣਾ

disbelief ('ਡਿਸਬਿ'ਲੀਫ਼) *n* ਅਵਿਸ਼ਵਾਸ, ਬੇਯਕੀਨੀ, ਬੇਇਤਬਾਰੀ; ਬੇਪ੍ਰਤੀਤੀ; ਨਾਸਤਕਤਾ

disbelieve ('ਡਿਸਬਿ'ਲੀਵ਼) *v* ਅਵਿਸ਼ਵਾਸ ਕਰਨਾ, ਨਾ ਮੰਨਣਾ

disburse (ਡਿਸ'ਬਅਃਸ) *v* ਖ਼ਰਚ ਕਰਨਾ, ਖ਼ਰਚਣਾ, ਭੁਗਤਾਨ ਕਰਨਾ, ਅਦਾਇਗੀ ਕਰਨਾ, ਵੰਡਣੀ; ~ment ਭੁਗਤਾਨ, ਅਦਾਇਗੀ, ਖ਼ਰਚ

disc (ਡਿਸਕ) *n* ਤਵਾ, ਚੱਕਲੀ, ਤਸ਼ਤਰੀ

discard (ਡਿਸ'ਕਾਡ) *v n* ਸੁੱਟ ਪਾਉਣਾ, ਛੱਡ ਦੇਣਾ, ਬਰਖ਼ਾਸਤ ਕਰਨਾ, ਕੱਢ ਦੇਣਾ

discern (ਡਿ'ਸਅਃਨ) *v* ਵੇਖ ਲੈਣਾ, ਸਮਝ ਜਾਣਾ, ਜਾਣ ਲੈਣਾ, ਤਾੜ ਲੈਣਾ; ਜਾਂਚਣਾ

discharge (ਡਿਸ'ਚਾ*ਜ, 'ਡਿਸਚਾ*ਜ) *v n* ਬਰਖ਼ਾਸਤ ਕਰਨਾ, ਕੱਢ ਦੇਣਾ; (ਫ਼ਰਜ਼) ਨਿਭਾਉਣਾ, ਛੁਟਣਾ, (ਜਹਾਜ਼ ਆਦਿ ਤੋਂ) ਮਾਲ ਲਾਹੁਣਾ; (ਦਰਿਆ ਦਾ) ਸਮੁੰਦਰ ਵਿਚ ਡਿੱਗਣਾ; (ਕਾ) ਰਿਹਾ ਕਰਨਾ; ਬਿਜਲੀ ਖ਼ਾਰਜ ਕਰਨੀ; ਪਾਕ ਨਿਕਲਣਾ; (ਤੋਪ ਆਦਿ) ਦਾਗ਼ਣਾ ਜਾਂ ਚਲਾਉਣਾ, (ਰੋਗੀ ਨੂੰ)

ਹਸਪਤਾਲ ਵਿਚੋਂ ਜਾਣ ਦੀ ਆਗਿਆ ਦੇਣੀ; (ਨੌਕਰੀ ਤੋਂ) ਬਰਖ਼ਾਸਤਗੀ; ਰਿਹਾਈ, ਛੁਟਕਾਰਾ; ਫ਼ਰਜ਼ ਦਾ ਪਾਲਣ; ਤੋਪ ਆਦਿ ਦਾ ਫ਼ਾਇਰ; ਕਰਜ਼ ਦੀ ਅਦਾਇਗੀ; ਨਾਂ-ਕਟਾਈ; ~d ਦੋਸ਼ ਮੁਕਤ, ਸੇਵਾ ਮੁਕਤ

disciple (ਡਿ'ਸਾਇਪਲ) *n* ਚੇਲਾ, ਮੁਰੀਦ, ਸ਼ਿਸ਼, ਅਨੁਯਾਈ, ਸ਼ਾਗਿਰਦ

disciplinary ('ਡਿਸਿਪਲਿਨ(ਅ)ਰਿ) *a* ਅਨੁਸ਼ਾਸਨ-ਸਬੰਧੀ, ਨਿਯਮ ਪਾਲਣ ਸਬੰਧੀ, ਅਨੁਸ਼ਾਸਕ

discipline (ਡਿਸਿਪਲਿਨ) *n v* ਅਨੁਸ਼ਾਸਨ, ਜ਼ਬਤ, ਨਿਯਮ-ਪਾਲਣ; ਸੰਜਮ; ਵਿਸ਼ਾ-ਖੇਤਰ; ਨਿਰੰਤਰਣ; ਅਨੁਸ਼ਾਸਨ ਵਿਚ ਰੱਖਣਾ, ਸੰਜਮ ਵਿਚ ਰੱਖਣਾ, ਨਿਯਮਬੱਧ ਰੱਖਣਾ; ~d ਅਨੁਸ਼ਾਸਤ, ਨਿਰੰਤਰਤ

disclose (ਡਿਸ'ਕਲਅਉਜ਼) *v* ਪਰਗਟ ਕਰਨਾ, ਜ਼ਾਹਰ ਕਰਨਾ, ਖੋਲ੍ਹਣਾ (ਭੇਦ ਆਦਿ), ਉਘਾੜਨਾ, ਦੱਸਣਾ

disclosure (ਡਿਸ'ਕਲਅਉਜ਼ਅ*) *n* ਪਰਗਟਾਉ, ਉਘਾੜ, ਖੋਲ੍ਹਿਆ ਭੇਦ

discord ('ਡਿਸਕੋਡ, ਡਿ'ਸਕੋਡ) *n v* ਅਸਹਿਮਤੀ, ਮੱਤਭੇਦ, ਅਣ-ਬਣ, ਫੁੱਟ, ਕਲਹ, ਝਗੜਾ; ਅਸਹਿਮਤ ਹੋਣਾ; ਮੱਤਭੇਦ ਹੋਣਾ

discount (ਡਿਸਕਾਉਂਟ, ਡਿ'ਸਕਾਉਂਟ) *n v* ਕਟੌਤੀ, ਵੱਟਾ ਲਾਉਣਾ, ਕਾਟ ਕਰਨੀ; ਘਟਾਉਣਾ, ਕੱਢਣਾ, ਛੋਟੀ (ਮਾਲ) ਵੇਚਣ ਲਈ ਘੱਟ ਲਾਭ ਤੇ ਦੇ ਦੇਣਾ; ਗਿਣਤੀ ਵਿਚ ਨਾ ਰੱਖਣਾ; ਹੁੰਡੀ ਲੈਣੀ, ਹਿਸਾਬ ਵਿਚੋਂ ਕੱਢ ਦੇਣਾ

discourage (ਡਿ'ਸਕਅੱਰਿਜ) *v* ਦਿਲ ਢਾਹੁਣਾ, ਉਤਸ਼ਾਹਹੀਨ ਕਰਨਾ, ਹੌਂਸਲਾ ਢਾਹੁਣਾ, ਹਿੰਮਤ ਤੋੜਨੀ, ਨਿਰਾਸ ਕਰਨਾ; ~d ਨਿਰਉਤਸ਼ਾਹਤ, ਨਿਰਾਸ; ~ment ਉਤਸ਼ਾਹਭੰਗ, ਦਿਲਢਾਹੀ;

ਅਸਮਰਥਨ, ਹੌਸਲਾ ਸ਼ਿਕਨੀ

discouraging (ਡਿ'ਸਕਅੱਰਿਜਿਙ) *a* ਨਿਰਉਤਸ਼ਾਹ ਕਰਨ ਵਾਲਾ, ਦਿਲ ਢਾਹੁਣ ਵਾਲਾ

discourse ('ਡਿਸਕੋ'ਸ) *n v* ਪ੍ਰਵਚਨ, ਵਾਰਤਾਲਾਪ, ਵਿਆਖਿਆਨ, ਭਾਸ਼ਣ, ਪ੍ਰੋਕਤਿ

discourteous (ਡਿਸ'ਕਅ:ਟਯਅਸ) *a* ਬਦਤਮੀਜ਼, ਅੱਸਭਿਅ, ਉਜੱਡ, ਅਸ਼ਿਸ਼ਟ; **~ly** ਬਦਤਮੀਜ਼ੀ ਨਾਲ, ਅੱਸਭਿਅ ਢੰਗ ਨਾਲ; **~ness** ਅਸ਼ਿਸ਼ਟਤਾ, ਬਦਤਮੀਜ਼ੀ, ਬੇਲਿਹਾਜ਼ੀ, ਉਜੱਡਤਾ, ਕੋਰਾਪਣ

discourtesy (ਡਿਸ'ਕਅ:ਟਿਸਿ) *n* ਅਸ਼ਿਸ਼ਟਾਚਾਰ, ਦੁਸ਼ੀਲਤਾ

discover (ਡਿ'ਸਕਅੱਵ੍ਅ) *v* ਖੋਜ ਕਰਨੀ, ਲੱਭ ਲੈਣਾ, ਪਰਗਟ ਕਰਨਾ, ਭੇਦ ਖੋਲ੍ਹਣਾ, ਪਤਾ ਕਰਨਾ, ਬਾਹਰ ਕੱਢਣਾ, ਜਾਣ ਲੈਣਾ, ਪੋਲ ਖੋਲ੍ਹਣਾ; **~er** ਖੋਜੀ, ਢੂੰਡਾਊ, ਗਿਆਤਾ; **~y** ਲੱਭਤ, ਖੋਜ, ਸੋਧ, ਪ੍ਰਾਪਤੀ; ਸਪਸ਼ਟੀਕਰਨ

discredit (ਡਿਸ'ਕਰੈਡਿਟ) *n v* ਬੇਇਤਬਾਰੀ, ਅਪ੍ਰਤਿਸ਼ਠਾ, ਬਦਨਾਮੀ ਵਾਲੀ ਗੱਲ, ਬੇਪ੍ਰਤੀਤੀ ਕਰਨੀ, ਸ਼ਾਖ਼ ਘਟਾਉਣੀ

discreet (ਡਿ'ਸਕਰੀਟ) *a* ਸਿਆਣਾ, ਸੂਝਵਾਨ, ਵਿਚਾਰਵਾਨ, ਸਾਵਧਾਨ, ਗੰਭੀਰ

discrepancy (ਡਿ'ਸਕਰੈਪਅੰਸਿ) *n* ਭੁੱਲ, ਫ਼ਰਕ, ਅੰਤਰ, ਭੇਦ

discrete (ਡਿ'ਸਕਰੀਟ) *a* ਵੱਖਰਾ, ਅਲੱਗ, ਭਿੰਨ, ਖੰਡਤ

discretion (ਡਿ'ਸਕਰੈੱਸ਼ਨ) *n* ਸੂਝ, ਸਿਆਣਪ, ਵਿਵੇਕ, ਵਿਚਾਰਸ਼ੀਲਤਾ; **~ary** ਇੱਛਾ ਅਨੁਸਾਰ, ਇਖ਼ਤਿਆਰੀ, ਸਵੈਧੀਨ

discriminate (ਡਿਸਕਰਿਮਿਨਇਟ) *v* ਫ਼ਰਕ ਕੱਢਣਾ, ਨਿਤਾਰਾ ਕਰਨਾ, ਸੂਖਮ ਭੇਦ ਰੱਖਣਾ, ਵਿਸ਼ੇਸ਼ਤਾ ਦੱਸਣੀ, ਨਿਖੇੜਨਾ, ਅੰਤਰ ਹੋਣਾ, ਫ਼ਰਕ ਹੋਣਾ

discrimination (ਡਿ'ਸਕਰਿਮਿ'ਨੇਇਸ਼ਨ) *n* ਸੂਝ, ਵਿਵੇਕ, ਤਮੀਜ਼, ਵਿਤਕਰਾ, ਭੇਦ-ਭਾਵ, ਪੱਖ-ਪਾਤ; ਵਖਰੇਵਾਂ

discriminatory (ਡਿ'ਸਕਰਿਮਿਨਅਟ(ਅ)ਰਿ) *a* ਵਿਭੇਦਕ, ਵਿਭੇਦਕਾਰ, ਪੱਖਪਾਤੀ

discursion (ਯਡਿ'ਸਕਅ:ਸ਼ਨ) *n* ਵਿਵਾਦ, ਬਹਿਸ, ਤਰਕਯੁਕਤ ਵਾਰਤਾ

discursive (ਡਿ'ਸਕਅ:ਸਿਵ੍) *a* ਉਕਤੀ-ਪੂਰਨ, ਤਰਕਪੂਰਨ, ਲੰਬਾ ਚੌੜਾ; ਅਸੰਗਤ; **~ly** ਦਲੀਲ ਨਾਲ; ਬੇਤੁਕੇ ਢੰਗ ਨਾਲ; **~ness** ਤਰਕਪੂਰਣਤਾ, ਵਲ-ਫੇਰ, ਅਸੰਗਤੀ

discuss (ਡਿ'ਸਕਅੱਸ) *v* ਵਿਚਾਰਨਾ, ਵਿਚਾਰ ਵਿਮਰਸ਼ ਕਰਨਾ; ਤਰਕ ਕਰਨਾ, ਚਰਚਾ ਕਰਨੀ, ਬਹਿਸ ਕਰਨੀ; **~ion** ਬਹਿਸ, ਵਾਦ-ਵਿਵਾਦ, ਵਿਚਾਰ-ਵਟਾਂਦਰਾ, ਚਰਚਾ

disease (ਡਿ'ਜ਼ੀਜ਼) *n* ਰੋਗ, ਬੀਮਾਰੀ, ਮਰਜ਼ ਦੋਸ਼; **~d** ਰੋਗੀ, ਬੀਮਾਰ, ਮਰੀਜ਼, ਅਸੁਅਸਥ, ਰੋਗ-ਗ੍ਰਸਤ; ਦੂਸ਼ਤ

disfigure (ਡਿਸ'ਫ਼ਿਗਅ*) *v* ਸ਼ਕਲ ਵਿਗਾੜਨੀ, ਕਰੂਪ ਕਰ ਦੇਣਾ, ਬੱਜ ਲਾਉਣੀ, ਵਿਗਾੜਨਾ, ਬਦਸੂਰਤ ਬਣਾ ਦੇਣਾ

disfranchise (ਡਿਸ'ਫ਼ਰੈਨਚਾਇਜ਼) *v* ਵੋਟ ਦਾ ਹੱਕ ਖੋਹ ਲੈਣਾ, ਨਾਗਰਿਕਤਾ ਦੇ ਅਧਿਕਾਰ ਤੋਂ ਵਾਂਝਿਆਂ ਕਰ ਦੇਣਾ

disforest (ਡਿਸ'ਫ਼ੋਰਿਸਟ) *v* ਜੰਗਲ ਕੱਟਣਾ

disgrace (ਡਿਸ'ਗਰੇਇਸ) *n v* ਬੇਇੱਜ਼ਤੀ, ਬਦਨਾਮੀ, ਨਮੋਸ਼ੀ, ਨਿਰਾਦਰ; ਬੇਇੱਜ਼ਤੀ ਕਰਨੀ, ਨਿਰਾਦਰ ਕਰਨਾ, ਪਤ ਲਾਹੁਣੀ

disguise (ਡਿਸ'ਗਾਇਜ਼) *v n* ਭੇਸ ਬਦਲਣਾ ਜਾਂ

ਵਟਾਉਣਾ; ਲੁਕਾਉਣਾ; ਸਾਂਗ ਰਚਣਾ, ਢੌਂਗ
ਰਚਣਾ; ਭੇਸ; ਛਲ

disgust (ਡਿਸ'ਗਾਐਸਟ) *n v* ਉਪਰਾਮਤਾ, ਅਰੁਚੀ,
ਉਚਾਟ, ਉਕਤਾਹਟ; ਉਚਾਟ ਕਰਨਾ, ਅਕਾ ਦੇਣ;
~ed ਉਚਾਟ, ਉਪਰਾਮ, ਅੱਕਿਆ, ਉਕਤਾਉਆ;
~ful ਘਿਣਾਉਣਾ, ਅਕਾਊ, ਉਕਤਾਊ

dish (ਡਿਸ਼) *n v* ਪਿਆਲੀ, ਕੌਲੀ, ਡੂੰਘਾ ਕਟੋਰਾ,
ਪਰੋਸਿਆ ਭੋਜਨ; ਪਰੋਸਣਾ; (ਅਪ) ਠੱਗਣਾ,
ਧੋਖਾ ਦੇਣਾ; ਰਿਬ ਪੈਣਾ; ~out ਵੰਡਣਾ

disharmony (ਡਿਸ'ਹਾਮਅਨਿ) *n* ਸੁਰਹੀਣਤਾ,
ਅਨਜੋੜ, ਬੇਸੁਰਾਪਨ, ਅਸੰਗਤੀ

dishearten (ਡਿਸ'ਹਾਟਨ) *v* ਨਿਰਾਸ਼ ਕਰਨਾ,
ਨਿਰਉਤਸਾਹ ਕਰਨਾ, ਦਿਲ ਢਾਹੁਣਾ, ਹਿੰਮਤ
ਤੋੜਨੀ, ਡੁਲਾਉਣਾ; ~ment ਨਿਰਾਸ਼ਾ,
ਉਤਸਾਹਹੀਣਤਾ

dishonest (ਡਿਸ'ਔਨਿਸਟ) *a* ਖੋਟਾ, ਕਪਟੀ,
ਬੇਇਮਾਨ ਧੋਖੇਬਾਜ਼

dishonour (ਡਿਸ'ਔਨਾ*) *v n* ਬੇਇੱਜ਼ਤੀ
ਕਰਨੀ, ਨਿਰਾਦਰ ਕਰਨਾ, ਅਪਮਾਨ ਕਰਨਾ, ਪਤ
ਲਾਹੁਣਾ; ਵਾਪਸ ਮੋੜ ਦੇਣਾ; ਨਿਰਾਦਰ,
ਅਪਮਾਨ; ~ed ਅਪਮਾਨਤ, ਨਾਮਨਜ਼ੂਰ

disintergation (ਡਿਸ'ਇਨਟਿ'ਗਰੇਇਸ਼ਨ) *n*
ਵਿਭਾਜਨ, ਅਵਛੇਦਨ, ਖੰਡਨ, ਵਿਯੋਜਨ

dislike (ਡਿਸ'ਲਾਇਕ) *v n* ਘਿਰਣਾ ਕਰਨੀ,
ਨਫ਼ਰਤ ਕਰਨੀ, ਬੁਰਾ ਲੱਗਣਾ, ਨਾ ਪਸੰਦ
ਕਰਨਾ, ਘਿਰਣਾ, ਨਫ਼ਰਤ

dislocate ('ਡਿਸਲਅ(ਉ)ਕੇਇਟ) *v* ਜੋੜ ਅਲੱਗ
ਕਰਨੀ, ਸਰਕਾਉਣਾ, ਥਾਂ ਤੋਂ ਹਟਾਉਣਾ; ਸੋਚ
ਆਉਣੀ; (ਕਿਸੇ ਅੰਗ ਨੂੰ) ਅਲੱਗ ਅਲੱਗ
ਕਰਨਾ; ਉਲਟ-ਪੁਲਟ ਕਰਨਾ

dislocation ('ਡਿਸਲਅ(ਉ)'ਕੇਇਸ਼ਨ) *n* ਹੱਡੀ ਦੀ

ਉਤਰਾਈ, ਸੋਚ; ਉਲਟ-ਪੁਲਟ, ਖਲਲ,
ਗੜਬੜ, ਖ਼ਰਾਬੀ; ਵਿਸਥਾਪਨ

dislodge (ਡਿਸ'ਲੌਜ) *v* ਕੱਢ ਦੇਣਾ, ਉਖਾੜਨਾ,
ਮੋਰਚੇ ਤੋਂ ਹਟਾਉਣਾ, ਪੁੱਟ ਸੁੱਟਣਾ

disloyal ('ਡਿਸ'ਲੌਇ(ਅ)ਲ) *a* ਗ਼ਦਾਰ; ਬਾਗ਼ੀ;
ਬੇਵਫ਼ਾ

dismal ('ਡਿਜ਼ਮ(ਅ)ਲ) *a* ਸੋਗਮਈ, ਦੁੱਖਮਈ,
ਉਦਾਸੀਨ, ਬਦਕਿਸਮਤ, ਬੇਰੌਣਕ, ਸੁਨਸਾਨ,
ਵੀਰਾਨ, ਉੱਜੜਿਆ-ਪੁੱਜੜਿਆ, ਭਿਆਨਕ,
ਡਰਾਉਣਾ

dismantle (ਡਿਸ'ਮੈਂਟਲ) *v* ਵੰਚਤ ਕਰਨਾ,
(ਮੋਰਚਾਬੰਦੀ ਆਦਿ ਨੂੰ) ਤੋੜ ਦੇਣਾ; (ਜਹਾਜ਼ ਨੂੰ
ਮਸਤੂਲ, ਤੋਪ ਫ਼ੌਜ ਦੇਣਾ, ਉਪੇਣਾ

dismay (ਡਿਸ'ਮੇਇ) *v* ਮਸਤੂਲ-ਰਹਿਤ ਕਰਨਾ

dismember (ਡਿਸ'ਮੈਂਬਅ*) *v* ਟੁਕੜੇ ਟੁਕੜੇ
ਕਰਨਾ, ਬੰਦ ਬੰਦ ਕੱਟਣੇ, ਅੰਗ-ਭੰਗ ਕਰਨਾ;
ਵੰਡ ਦੇਣਾ, (ਦੇਸ਼ ਦਾ) ਬਟਵਾਰਾ ਕਰਨਾ;
~ment ਵਿਭਾਜਨ

dismiss (ਡਿਸ'ਮਿਸ) *v* ਮੌਕੂਫ਼ ਕਰਨਾ, ਕੱਢ ਦੇਣਾ,
ਬਰਖ਼ਾਸਤ ਕਰਨਾ, ਨੌਕਰੀਉਂ ਕੱਢ ਦੇਣਾ
ਸਾਮੁਖਿਓ ਹਟਾ ਦੇਣਾ, ਮੁਕੱਦਮਾ ਖ਼ਾਰਜ ਕਰਨਾ;
ਜ਼ੋਰ ਦੀ ਹਿੱਟ ਲਾਉਣੀ

dismount (ਡਿਸ'ਮਾਉਂਟ) *v* ਘੋੜੇ ਤੋਂ ਉਤਰਨਾ,
ਘੋੜੇ ਤੋਂ ਡੇਗ ਦੇਣਾ; ਉਤਰਾਈ;

disobedience (ਡਿਸਅ'ਬੀਡਯਅਸਿ) *n*
ਆਗਿਆ-ਭੰਗ, ਅਵੱਗਿਆ, ਨਾ-ਫ਼ਰਮਾਨੀ,
ਨਿਯਮ-ਉਲੰਘਨ, ਹੁਕਮ-ਅਦੂਲੀ

disobedient (ਡਿਸਅ'ਬੀਡਯਅੰਟ) *a* ਆਕੀ,
ਅਵੱਗਿਆਕਾਰੀ, ਨਾਬਰ

disobey (ਡਿਸਅ'ਬੇਇ) *v* ਆਗਿਆ ਭੰਗ ਕਰਨੀ,
ਅਵੱਗਿਆ ਕਰਨੀ, ਨਿਯਮ ਤੋੜਨਾ, ਹੁਕਮ ਨਾ

ਮੰਨਣਾ, ਨਾ-ਫ਼ਰਮਾਨੀ ਕਰਨੀ

disorder (ਡਿਸ'ਓਡਅ*) *n* ਬੇਤਰਤੀਬੀ, ਉਲਟ-ਪੁਲਟ, ਗੜਬੜ; ਹਲਚਲ; ਰੋਗ; ਉਲਟ-ਪੁਲਟ ਕਰਨਾ; **~ly** ਬੇਤਰਤੀਬ; ਉੱਗੜ-ਦੁੱਗੜ; ਅਨਿਯਮਤ, ਬੇਜ਼ਾਬਤਾ, ਬੇ-ਲਗਾਮ, ਹਫ਼ੜਾ-ਦਫ਼ੜੀ ਭਰਿਆ

disown (ਡਿਸ'ਅਉਨ) *v* ਛੱਡਣਾ, ਇਨਕਾਰ ਕਰਨੀ, ਮੁੱਕਰਨਾ, ਨਾ ਮੰਨਣਾ, ਨਾ ਅਪਨਾਉਣਾ, ਤਿਆਗਣਾ; **~ed** ਤਿਆਗਿਆ

dispel (ਡਿ'ਸਪੈੱਲ) *v* (ਭਰਮ ਜਾਂ ਭੈ ਜਾਂ ਹਨੇਰਾ) ਨਿਵਿਰਤ ਕਰਨਾ, ਹਟਾਉਣਾ, ਮਿਟਾਉਣਾ, ਦੂਰ ਕਰਨਾ, ਕੱਢਣਾ

dispensable (ਡਿ'ਸਪੈੱਸੇਬਲ) *a* (ਕਾਨੂੰਨ ਜਾਂ ਰਸਮ) ਬੇ-ਲੋੜਾ, ਗ਼ੈਰਜ਼ਰੂਰੀ; ਛੱਡੇ ਜਾਣ ਯੋਗ

dispensary (ਡਿ'ਸਪੈੱਨਸ(ਅ)ਰਿ) *n* ਦਵਾਖ਼ਾਨਾ, ਸ਼ਫ਼ਾਖ਼ਾਨਾ

dispense (ਡਿ'ਸਪੈੱਸ) *v* ਵੰਡਣਾ, ਤਕਸੀਮ ਕਰਨਾ, ਨੁਸਖ਼ੇ ਅਨੁਸਾਰ ਦਵਾਈ ਬਣਾਉਣੀ; (ਪਾਪਾਂ ਤੋਂ) ਛੋਟ ਦੇਣੀ, ਮਾਫ਼ੀ ਦੇਣੀ, ਛੱਡਣਾ, ਤਿਆਗਣਾ; (ਨੌਕਰੀ ਤੋਂ) ਛੁੱਟੀ ਦੇਣੀ

disperse (ਡਿ'ਸਪਅ:ਸ) *v* (ਰੋਸ਼ਨੀ) ਫੈਲਾਉਣਾ; ਖਿੰਡਾਉਣਾ, ਖਿੰਡਣਾ; ਸਭਾ ਉਠਾਉਣੀ

displace (ਡਿਸ'ਪਲੇਇਸ) *v* ਥਾਂ ਤੋਂ ਹਟਾਉਣਾ, ਸਰਕਾਉਣਾ, ਉਰੇ ਪਰੇ ਕਰਨਾ; ਥਾਂ ਮੱਲਣੀ, ਪਦਵੀ ਤੋਂ ਲਾਹੁਣਾ

display (ਡਿ'ਸਪਲੇਇ) *v* ਵਿਖਾਲਣਾ, ਦੱਸਣਾ, ਸਾਮੂਹੇ ਲਿਆਉਣਾ; ਵਿਖਾਲਾ ਕਰਨਾ, ਨੁਮਾਇਸ਼ ਕਰਨਾ; **~ed** ਪਰਦਰਸ਼ਤ, ਫੈਲਾਇਆ, ਦਿਖਾਇਆ

displease (ਡਿਸ'ਪਲੀਜ਼) *v* ਨਾਰਾਜ਼ ਕਰਨਾ, ਰੁਸਾਉਣਾ, ਚਿੜਾਉਣਾ; **~d** ਨਾਰਾਜ਼, ਨਾਖ਼ੁਸ਼, ਰੁੱਸਿਆ, ਅਪ੍ਰਸੰਨ

displeasing (ਡਿ'ਪਲੀਜ਼ਿਙ) *a* ਅਣਸੁਖਾਵਾਂ, ਅਰੋਚਕ, ਅਸੰਤੋਖਜਨਕ, ਅਪ੍ਰਿਯ

displeasure (ਡਿਸ'ਪਲੈੱਹ਼ਅ*) *n* ਨਾਰਾਜ਼ਗੀ, ਗੁੱਸਾ, ਬੇਆਰਾਮੀ, ਅਸੰਤੋਖ, ਅਪ੍ਰਸੰਨਤਾ

disposal (ਡਿ'ਸਪਅਉਜ਼ਲ) *n* ਸਪੁਰਦਗੀ, ਸੌਂਪਣੀ, ਸਮਰਪਣ, ਨਿਬੇੜਾ, ਨਿਪਟਾਰਾ, ਇਖ਼ਤਿਆਰ; ਇੰਤਜ਼ਾਮ; ਵਿੱਕਰੀ

disposable (ਡਿ'ਸਪਅਉਜ਼ਅਬਲ) *adv* ਇਕ ਵਾਰੀ ਵਰਤ ਕੇ ਸੁੱਟਣ ਯੋਗ

dispose (ਡਿ'ਸਪਅਉਜ਼) *v* ਥਾਂ ਸਿਰ ਜਾਂ ਠੁਕ ਸਿਰ ਰੱਖਣਾ; ਟਿਕਾਉਣਾ, ਢਾਲਣਾ, ਰੁਚੀ ਪੈਦਾ ਕਰਨੀ; ਵਿੱਕਰੀ ਕਰਨੀ; ਸਮਾਪਤ ਕਰਨਾ, ਨਸ਼ਟ ਕਰਨਾ, ਮਾਰ ਦੇਣਾ; ਫ਼ੈਸਲਾ ਕਰਨਾ, ਨਿਪਟਾਉਣਾ, ਤੈ ਕਰਨਾ, ਨਿਰਾ ਕਰਨਾ

disposition (ਡਿਸਪਅ'ਜ਼ਿਸ਼ਨ) *n* ਸੁਭਾਅ, ਮਿਜ਼ਾਜ, ਰੁਚੀ, ਤਬੀਅਤ; ਪ੍ਰਕਿਰਤੀ; ਵਿਉਂਤ, ਪ੍ਰਬੰਧ; ਅਧਿਕਾਰ

disproportion (ਡਿਸਪਰਅ'ਪੋਸ਼ਨ) *n* ਅਨੁਪਾਤ-ਹੀਨਤਾ, ਬੇਮੇਲ, ਅਸੰਗਤੀ; **~ate** ਬੇਢੰਗਾ, ਵਿਖਮ, ਬੇਮੇਲ, ਬੇਡੋਲ, ਬੇਜੋੜ, ਅਨੁਪਾਤਹੀਨ; **~ately** ਬੇਮੇਲਵੇਂ ਢੰਗ ਨਾਲ, ਅਨੁਪਾਤਹੀਨਤਾ ਨਾਲ

disprove (ਡਿਸ'ਪਰੂਵ਼) *v* ਗ਼ਲਤ ਸਾਬਤ ਕਰਨਾ, ਖੰਡਨ ਕਰਨਾ, ਝੂਠ ਸਾਬਤ ਕਰਨਾ, ਰੱਦ ਕਰਨਾ ਝੁਠਲਾਉਣਾ

disputable (ਡਿ'ਸਪਯੂਟਅਬਲ) *a* ਵਿਵਾਦਪੂਰਨ, ਸ਼ੱਕੀ, ਸੰਦੇਹੀ

dispute (ਡਿ'ਸਪਯੂਟ) *v* ਵਿਵਾਦ ਕਰਨਾ; ਝਗੜਾ ਕਰਨਾ, ਹੁੱਜਤ ਕਰਨੀ; ਬਹਿਸਣਾ, ਸੰਦੇਹ ਪਰਗਟ ਕਰਨਾ

disqualification (ਡਿਸ'ਕਵੌਲਿਫ਼ਿ'ਕੇਇਸ਼ਨ) *n*

n ਅਯੋਗਤਾ, ਨੁਕਸ, ਖਾਮੀ, ਕਮੀ, ਔਗੁਣ

disqualified (ਡਿਸ'ਕਵੈਲਿਫ਼ਾਇਡ) *a* ਅਯੋਗ
ਕਰਾਰ ਦਿੱਤਾ ਗਿਆ, ਅਯੋਗ

disqualify (ਡਿਸ'ਕਵੈਲਿਫ਼ਾਇ) *v* ਅਯੋਗ ਕਰਨਾ
ਜਾਂ ਠਹਿਰਾਉਣਾ, (ਕਾ) ਅਧਿਕਾਰ ਖੋਹ ਲੈਣਾ

disregard (ਡਿਸਰਿ'ਗਾਡ) *v n* ਧਿਆਨ ਨ ਦੇਣਾ,
ਅੱਖਾਂ ਤੋਂ ਉਹਲੇ ਕਰਨਾ, ਪਰਵਾਹ ਨਾ ਕਰਨੀ,
ਗ਼ਾਫ਼ਲਤ, ਅਣਗਹਿਲੀ, ਅਣਸੁਣੀ, ਅੱਵਗਿਆ,
ਅਨਾਦਰ, ਉਪੇਖਿਆ

disrespect (ਡਿਸ'ਰਿਸਪੈੱਕਟ) *n v* ਅਨਾਦਰ,
ਬੇਅਦਬੀ, ਗੁਸਤਾਖ਼ੀ; ਅਨਾਦਰ ਕਰਨਾ, ਅਪਮਾਨ
ਕਰਨਾ

disrupt (ਡਿਸ'ਰਅੱਪਟ) *v* ਗੜਬੜੀ ਪਾਉਣੀ, ਫੁੱਟ
ਪਾਉਣੀ, ਭੰਗ ਕਰਨਾ; ਚੀਰਨਾ; ~ion ਤੋੜ-ਫੋੜ,
ਪਾੜਾ, ਵਿਘਨ, ਗੜਬੜ; ~ive ਫੁੱਟ ਪਾਊ;
ਵਿਘਟਨਕਾਰੀ, ਵਿਨਾਸ਼ਕ

dissatisfaction[*] (ਡਿਸ'ਸੈਟਿਸ'ਫ਼ੈਕਸ਼ਨ) *n*
ਅਤ੍ਰਿਪਤੀ, ਅਸੰਤੋਸ਼, ਬੇਚੈਨੀ, ਨਾਰਾਜ਼ਗੀ

dissatisfied (ਡਿਸ'ਸੈਟਿਸ'ਫ਼ਾਇਡ) *a*
ਅਸੰਤੋਖਜਨਕ, ਅਤ੍ਰਿਪਤਕਾਰੀ

dissatisfy (ਡਿਸ'ਸੈਟਿਸਫ਼ਾਇ) *v* ਅਸੰਤੁਸ਼ਟ
ਕਰਨਾ, ਅਤ੍ਰਿਪਤ ਕਰਨਾ; ਨਾਖ਼ੁਸ਼ ਕਰਨਾ, ਨਾਰਾਜ਼
ਕਰਨਾ

dissect (ਡਿ'ਸੈੱਕਟ) *v* ਬੰਦ ਬੰਦ ਕੱਟਣਾ, ਅੰਗ
ਅੰਗ ਵੱਖ ਕਰਨਾ, ਚੀਰਨਾ, ਵਿਸ਼ਲੇਸ਼ਣ ਕਰਨਾ;
ਛਾਣਬੀਨ ਕਰਨੀ; ~ion ਅੰਗ-ਵਿੱਛੇਦ, ਚੀਰ-
ਫਾੜ, ਵਿਸ਼ਲੇਸ਼ਣ ਸੂਖਮ ਪਰੀਖਿਆ ਛਾਣਬੀਨ

disseminate (ਡਿ'ਸੈਮੀਨੇਇਟ) *v* ਖਿਲਾਰਨਾ,
ਬੀਜਣਾ, ਬਿਖੇਰਨਾ; ਪ੍ਰਚਾਰ ਕਰਨਾ, ਪ੍ਰਸਾਰ ਕਰਨਾ

dissemination (ਡਿ'ਸੈਮਿ'ਨੇਇਸ਼ਨ) *n* ਖ਼ਿਲਾਰ,
ਬੀਜਣ ਦੀ ਕਿਰਿਆ, ਵਿਕੀਰਣ; ਪ੍ਰਸਾਰ, ਪ੍ਰਚਾਰ,
ਪ੍ਰਸਾਰਣ

dissent (ਡਿ'ਸੈਂਟ) *v* ਅੰਗੀਕਾਰ ਨਾ ਕਰਨਾ, ਨਾ
ਮੰਨਣਾ, ਇਨਕਾਰ ਕਰਨਾ, ਮੱਤਭੇਦ ਰੱਖਣਾ,
ਅਸੰਮਤੀ ਰੱਖਣਾ; ਮੱਤਭੇਦ; ਅਸਹਿਮਤੀ; ~ient
ਅਸਹਿਮਤ, ਭਿੰਨ ਮੱਤਪ੍ਰਕਾਸ਼ਕ, ਬਹੁਮਤ ਵਿਰੋਧੀ

dissert (ਡਿ'ਸਅ:ਟ) *v* ਸਪਸ਼ਟ ਵਿਆਖਿਆ
ਕਰਨਾ, ਵਿਸਤਰਤ ਵਿਵੇਚਨ ਕਰਨਾ, ਵਿਵਰਣ
ਦੇਣਾ, ਬਹਿਸ ਕਰਨਾ, ਵਿਚਾਰ ਵਿਮਰਸ਼ ਕਰਨਾ

dissertation (ਡਿ'ਸਅ:ਟੇਸ਼ਨ) *a* ਖੋਜ-ਨਿਬੰਧ,
ਰਚਨਾ; ਵਿਵੇਚਨ, ਨਿਰੂਪਣ, ਵਿਆਖਿਆ,
ਵਿਚਾਰ-ਪ੍ਰਬੰਧ

dissidence (ਡਿਸਿਡਅੰਸ) *n* ਮੱਤਭੇਦ, ਵਿਰੋਧ,
ਅਸੰਮਤੀ, ਅਸਹਿਮਤੀ

dissident ('ਡਿਸਿਡਅੰਟ) *a n* ਵਿਰੋਧੀ, ਮੱਤਭੇਦੀ;
ਮੱਤਭੇਦ ਰੱਖਣ ਵਾਲਾ, ਅਸੰਮਤੀ ਰਖਣ ਵਾਲਾ

dissimilar (ਡਿ'ਸਿਮਿਲਅ*) *n* ਵਿਜਾਤੀ, ਭਿੰਨ,
ਅਸਾਵਾਂ, ਵੱਖਰਾ, ਵਿਖਮ, ਅਸਮਾਨ, ਅਸਮਰੂਪ

dissimilate (ਡਿ'ਸਿਮਿਲੇਇਟ) *n* (ਭਾਸ਼ਾ) ਅੱਖਰਾਂ
ਨੂੰ ਬਦਲਣਾ, ਧੁਨੀ-ਭੇਦ ਕਰਨਾ, ਅਸਮ ਕਰਨਾ

dissimilation (ਡਿ'ਸਿ'ਮਿਲੇਇਸ਼ਨ) *n* ਧੁਨੀ-ਭੇਦ,
ਅਸਮਤਾ

dissolute (ਡਿਸਅਲੂਟ) *a* ਅਵਾਰਾ, ਲੁੱਚਾ, ਲੰਪਟ,
ਵੈਲੀ, ਬਦਕਾਰ, ਵਿਸ਼ਈ ਦੁਰਾਚਾਰੀ; ਲਫੰਗਾ,
ਬਦਚਲਨ

dissolution (ਡਿਸਅ'ਲੂਸ਼ਨ) *n* ਦ੍ਰਵੀਕਰਨ
ਵਿਲੋਪ; ਵਿਘਟਨ, ਖ਼ਾਤਮਾ, ਲੋਪ

dissolve (ਡਿ'ਜ਼ੋਲਵ) *v* ਘੋਲਣਾ, ਘਲਣਾ,
ਗਾਲਣਾ; ਗਲਣਾ, ਪੰਘਾਰਨਾ, ਪੰਘਰਨਾ,
ਪਿਘਲਾਉਣਾ, ਪਿਘਲਣਾ; ਵਿਘਟਨ ਕਰਨਾ,
ਤੋੜਨਾ, ਅੰਤ ਕਰਨਾ, (ਮਸਲਾ) ਹੱਲ ਕਰਨਾ,
ਤੈਅ ਕਰਨਾ, ਮਿਟਾਉਣਾ; ~d ਘੁਲਿਆ,

ਘੋਲਿਆ, ਵਿਲੀਨ

distance (ਡਿਸਟਅੰਸ) *n* ਵਿੱਥ, ਫ਼ਾਸਲਾ, ਵਾਟ, ਪੰਧ, ਪੈਂਡਾ; ਪਾੜਾ, ਅੰਤਰ; ਮੁੱਦਤ; ਦੂਰ ਰੱਖਣਾ, ਪਿੱਛੇ ਛੱਡ ਜਾਣਾ, ਅੱਗੇ ਲੰਘ ਜਾਣਾ

distant (ਡਿਸਟਅੰਟ) *a* ਦੁਰੇਡਾ, ਪਰੇਡਾ, ਦੂਰਵਰਤੀ, ਵਿੱਥ ਉੱਤੇ; ਨਿੱਘ-ਰਹਿਤ

distemper (ਡਿ'ਸਟੈਂਪਅ*) *n v* ਵਿਕਾਰ, ਬਦਮਜ਼ਾਜ਼ੀ; ਪੱਕਾ ਪਲਸਤਰੀ ਰੰਗ, ਆਬਦਾਰ ਪਲਸਤਰ; ਪੱਕਾ ਰੰਗਦਾਰ ਪਲਸਤਰ ਕਰਨਾ, ਸਿਹਤ ਵਿਗਾੜਨੀ, ਦਿਮਾਗ਼ੀ ਸੰਤੁਲਨ ਵਿਗਾੜਨਾ; **~ed** ਉਲਟਾ-ਪੁਲਟਾ, ਅਸਤ-ਵਿਅਸਤ, ਕ੍ਰਮਹੀਨ, ਅਵਿਵਸਥਿਤ; ਅਸੰਜਮੀ, ਬੇਚੈਨ

distil (ਡਿ'ਸਟਿਲ) *v* ਚੋਣਾ, ਟਪਕਣਾ, ਰਿਸਣਾ; ਨਿਚੋੜਨਾ, ਖਿੱਚਣਾ, (ਅਰਕ, ਸੱਤ, ਸ਼ਰਾਬ) ਕੱਢਣਾ, ਨਿਕਲਣਾ; ਛਣਨਾ; **~ler** ਆਬਕਾਰ, ਅਰਕ ਜਾਂ ਸ਼ਰਾਬ ਕੱਢਣ ਵਾਲਾ, ਸੁਰਾਕਾਰ; **~lery** ਸ਼ਰਾਬ ਦੀ ਭੱਠੀ ਜਾਂ ਕਾਰਖ਼ਾਨਾ

distinct (ਡਿ'ਸਟਿਙਕਟ) *a* ਵੱਖਰਾ, ਅੱਡ, ਭਿੰਨ, ਨਿਵੇਕਲਾ, ਨਿਆਰਾ; ਸਪਸ਼ਟ, ਨਿਸ਼ਚਤ; ਵਿਅਕਤੀਗਤ; **~ion** ਵਖਰੇਵਾਂ, ਫ਼ਰਕ, ਭਿੰਨਤਾ, ਭੇਦ, ਨਿਖੇੜਾ, ਵਿਸ਼ੇਸ਼ਤਾ; ਮਹੱਤਾ, ਪ੍ਰਸਿੱਧੀ, ਵਡਿਆਈ, ਉੱਚ ਪਦਵੀ, ਮਰਤਬਾ, ਖ਼ਿਤਾਬ; ਵਿਅਕਤਿਤਵ; **~ive** ਵਿਸ਼ੇਸ਼, ਨਿਵੇਕਲਾ, ਖ਼ਾਸ, ਅਲੌਕਕ, ਅਲੱਗ, ਭਿੰਨ; ਮੁੱਖ, ਪ੍ਰਮੁੱਖ; **~iveness** ਵਿਸ਼ੇਸ਼ਤਾ, ਅਲੌਕਕਤਾ, ਭੇਦ, ਭਿੰਨਤਾ, ਵੱਖਰੇਵਾਂ, ਪ੍ਰਮੁੱਖਤਾ

distinguish (ਡਿ'ਸਟਿਙਗਵਿਸ਼) *v* ਵੱਖਰਾਉਣਾ, ਭਿੰਨ ਦਰਸਾਉਣਾ, ਫ਼ਰਕ ਦੇਣਾ, ਨਿਖੇੜ ਕਰਨਾ, ਛਾਂਟਣਾ, ਛਾਣਨਾ, ਉਘਾੜਨਾ, ਪ੍ਰਸਿੱਧ ਹੋਣਾ, ਪਰਗਟ ਹੋਣਾ; **~ed** ਚੋਟਵਾਂ, ਉੱਘਾ, ਪ੍ਰਸਿੱਧ, ਨਾਮੀ, ਨਾਮਵਰ, ਪ੍ਰਤਿਸ਼ਠਤ; ਵਿਸ਼ੇਸ਼, ਵਿੱਲਖਣ,

ਅਦਭੁਤ

distort (ਡਿ'ਸਟੋ'ਟ) *v* ਵਿਗਾੜਨਾ, ਮੋੜਨਾ-ਤੋੜਨਾ, ਭੰਨ-ਤੋੜ ਦੇਣਾ, ਗਲਤ ਬਿਆਨੀ ਕਰਨਾ; ਵਿਸ਼ਿਤ ਕਰਨਾ, ਵਿਰੂਪ ਕਰ ਦੇਣਾ, ਹੁਲੀਆ ਵਿਗਾੜਨਾ; **~ed** ਵਿਗਾੜਿਆ, ਵਿਸ਼ਿਤ, ਵਿਰੂਪਤ; **~ion** ਵਿਗਾੜ, ਮੋੜ-ਤਰੋੜ, ਭੰਨ-ਤੋੜ, ਗਲਤ-ਬਿਆਨੀ, ਵਿਕਾਰ, ਵਿਰੂਪੀਕਰਨ, ਵਿਰੂਪਣ, ਕਰੂਪੀਕਰਨ

distract (ਡਿ'ਸਟਰੈਕਟ) *v* ਧਿਆਨ-ਹਟਾਉਣਾ, ਉਚਾਟ ਕਰਨਾ, ਘਬਰਾ ਦੇਣਾ, ਚਿੱਤ ਭਰਮਾਉਣਾ, ਚਕਰਾ ਦੇਣਾ, ਵਿਆਕੁਲ ਕਰਨਾ; **~ion** ਬੇਧਿਆਨੀ, ਉਲਝਣ, ਵਿਆਕੁਲਤਾ, ਜਿੱਚੀ; ਵਿਘਨ, ਰੁਕਾਵਟ, ਖਲਲ, ਹਰਜ; ਦਿਲ-ਭੁਲਾਵਾ; ਉਨਮਾਦ, ਪਾਗਲਪਣ

distress (ਡਿ'ਸਟਰੈੱਸ) *n v* ਦੁੱਖ, ਕਲੇਸ਼, ਕਸ਼ਟ, ਬਿਪਤਾ, ਤੰਗੀ, ਦਿੱਕਤ; ਆਪੱਤੀ; ਪੀੜਤ ਕਰਨਾ, ਕਲਪਾਉਣਾ, ਦੁਖਾਉਣਾ, ਸਤਾਉਣਾ, ਤੰਗ ਕਰਨਾ; **~ed** ਦੁੱਖੀ, ਪੀੜਤ, ਚਿੰਤਾਤੁਰ

distributary (ਡਿ'ਸਰਿਬਯੁਟ(ਅ)ਰਿ) *n* ਨਦੀ ਜਾਂ ਨਹਿਰ ਦੀ ਸ਼ਾਖਾ, ਸਹਾਇਕ ਨਦੀ, ਰਜਵਾਹਾ

distribute (ਡਿ'ਸਟਰਿਬਯੂਟ) *v* ਵੰਡਣਾ, ਵਰਤਾਉਣਾ, ਵਿਕੀਰਨ ਕਰਨਾ; ਖਿਲਾਰਨਾ; ਵਿਭਾਜਨ ਕਰਨਾ, ਬਟਵਾਰਾ ਕਰਨਾ; ਕ੍ਰਮਵਾਰ ਕਰਨਾ; **~d** ਵੰਡਿਆ, ਵਿਭਾਜਤ, ਕ੍ਰਮਬੱਧ

distribution (ਡਿਸਟਰਿ'ਬਯੂਸ਼ਨ) *n* ਵਿਭਾਜਨ, ਵਿਤਾਰੀ, ਵੰਡ, ਬਟਵਾਰਾ, ਵਿਤਾਜਨ-ਕ੍ਰਮ

disrtibutor (ਡਿ'ਸਟਰਿਬਯੂਟਅ*) *n* ਵਰਤਾਵਾ, ਵੰਡਣ ਵਾਲਾ, ਵਿਤਰਕ, ਵਿਤਾਜਕ, ਵੰਡਾਵਾ; ਥੋਕ ਵਪਾਰੀ

district (ਡਿਸਟਰਿਕਟ) *n v* ਜ਼ਿਲ੍ਹਾ, ਇਲਾਕਾ, ਹਲਕਾ, ਮੰਡਲ, ਭੂਖੰਡ; ਤਾਲ੍ਹੁਕਾ; ਚੋਣ-ਖੇਤਰ ਜਨਪਦ

disturb (ਡਿ'ਸਟਾਃਬ) v ਵਿਘਨ ਪਾਉਣਾ, ਦਖ਼ਲ ਦੇਣਾ, ਹਲਚਲ ਮਚਾਉਣੀ, ਅਸ਼ਾਂਤ ਕਰਨਾ, ਬੇਚੈਨ ਕਰਨਾ, ਉਲਟ ਪੁਲਟ ਕਰ ਦੇਣਾ; ~ance ਵਿਘਨ, ਹਲਚਲ, ਫ਼ਸਾਦ, ਦਖ਼ਲ, ਅਸ਼ਾਂਤੀ; ਵਿਆਕੁਲਤਾ, ਖਲਬਲੀ, ਉਪੱਦਰ, ਹੁੱਲੜ, ਦੰਗਾ, ਵਿਦਰੋਹ; ~ed ਅਸ਼ਾਂਤ, ਵਿਆਕੁਲ, ਘਾਬਰਿਆ, ਬੇਚੈਨ

ditch (ਡਿਚ) a v ਖਾਈ, ਖੱਡ; ਖਾਈ ਪੁੱਟਣਾ, ਅੱਧ-ਵਿਚਾਲੇ ਛੱਡਣਾ

ditto (ਡਿਟਾਓ) a v ਉਪਰੋਕਤ, ਪਹਿਲੇ ਦੀ ਨਕਲ; ਹਾਂ ਵਿਚ ਹਾਂ ਮਿਲਾਉਣੀ, ਪੁਸ਼ਟੀ ਕਰਨੀ

ditty (ਡਿਟਿ) n ਟੱਪਾ, ਛੋਟਾ ਗੀਤ

dive (ਡਾਇਵ) v n ਟੁੱਬੀ ਮਾਰਨੀ, ਗੋਤਾ ਮਾਰਨਾ, ਡੁਬਕੀ ਲਾਉਣੀ, ਮਨ ਵਿਚ ਝਾਤੀ ਮਾਰਨਾ; ਟੁੱਬੀ, ਗੋਤਾ, ਡੁਬਕੀ, ਤਰਿਖਾਨਾ

diverge (ਡਾਇ'ਵ੍ਯਾ:ਜ*) v ਵੱਖ ਹੋਣਾ, ਅਪਸਰਣ ਕਰਨਾ, ਵਿਚਲਤ ਹੋਣਾ, ਭਟਕਾਉਣਾ, ਭਟਕਣਾ; ਰੁਖ ਫੇਰਨਾ; ~nce ਅਪਸਰਣ; ਭਟਕਣਾ; ~nt ਅਪਸਾਰੀ, ਭਟਕਣ ਵਾਲਾ, ਬਹਿਕਾਉਣ ਵਾਲਾ; ਭਿੰਨ, ਵਿਰੁੱਧ

diverse (ਡਾਇ'ਵ੍ਯਾ:ਸ) a ਵੱਖ ਵੱਖ, ਭਿੰਨ ਭਿੰਨ, ਤਰ੍ਹਾਂ ਤਰ੍ਹਾਂ ਦਾ ਵੰਨ-ਸੁਵੰਨਾ, ਅਸਮਾਨ, ਰੰਗਾ-ਬਰੰਗਾ

diversion (ਡਾਇ'ਵ੍ਯਾ:ਸ਼ਨ) n ਮੋੜ; ਵਿਚਲਨ, ਬਹਿਕਾਉ, ਭਟਕਣ, ਦਿਲ ਭੁਲਾਵਾ, ਵਿਲਾਸ

diversity (ਡਾਇਵ੍ਯਾ:ਸਅਟਿ) n ਭੇਦ, ਵਿਭਿੰਨਤਾ, ਵੰਨ-ਸੁਵੰਨਤਾ, ਅਨੇਕ ਰੂਪਤਾ, ਵਿਵਿਧਤਾ, ਰੰਗਾ-ਬਰੰਗਾਪਨ

divert (ਡਾਇ'ਵ੍ਯਾ:ਟ) v ਮੋੜਨਾ, ਫੇਰਨਾ, ਪਰੇ ਹਟਾਉਣਾ; ਟਾਲਣਾ; ਘੁਸਾਉਣਾ, ਦੂਰ ਕਰਨਾ, ਰੁਖ ਬਦਲਣਾ, ਵਰਾਉਣਾ, ਮਨੋਰੰਜਨ ਕਰਨਾ

divest (ਡਾਇ'ਵੈੱਸਟ) v ਨੰਗਾ ਕਰਨਾ, ਵਸਤਰਹੀਨ ਕਰਨਾ; ਵੰਚਤ ਕਰਨਾ, ਅਧਿਕਾਰ ਖੋਹ ਲੈਣਾ

divide (ਡਿ'ਵਾਇਡ) n v ਵੰਡ; ਵਟ, ਬੰਨ੍ਹੀ; ਵੰਡਣਾ, ਵਿਭਾਜਤ ਕਰਨਾ, ਫੁੱਟ ਪਾਉਣਾ, ਧਿਆਨ ਵਟਾਉਣਾ, ਹਿੱਸਾ ਵੰਡਣਾ; ਵੰਡਣਾ, ਤਕਸੀਮ ਕਰਨਾ; ~d ਵੰਡਿਆ ਹੋਇਆ, ਵਿਭਾਜਤ, ਵੱਖ

dividend (ਡਿ'ਵਿਡਅੰਡ) n (ਗਣਿ) ਵਾਂਡੂ, ਭਾਜ-ਅੰਕ, ਲਾਭ-ਅੰਸ਼

divider (ਡਿ'ਵਿਿਇਅ*) n ਪਾਤੂ, ਵਿਭਾਜਕ

dividing (ਡਿ'ਵਾਇਡਿਙ) a ਵਿਭਾਜਕ

divine (ਡਿ'ਵਾਇਨ) a n v ਇਸ਼ਵਰੀ; ਰੱਬੀ, ਇਲਾਹੀ, ਦੈਵੀ, ਰੂਹਾਨੀ, ਪਵਿੱਤਰ, ਧਾਰਮਕ; ~ness ਦੈਵਤਵ, ਦੈਵੀਪਨ; ਪਵਿੱਤਰਤਾ

divinity (ਡਿ'ਵਿਨਅਟਿ) n ਦੇਵਤਵ, ਦਿੱਵੀਕਰਨ, ਦਿਵਤਾ, ਇਸ਼ਵਰਤਾ; ਪੂਜਨੀਕ ਵਿਅਕਤੀ; ਧਾਰਮਕਤਾ

divisible (ਡਿ'ਵਿਜ਼ਿਅਬਲ) a ਵੰਡਣਯੋਗ, ਭਾਗ ਹੋਣ ਜੋਗ, ਵਿਭਾਜੀ

division (ਡਿ'ਵਿਯ੍ਹਨ) n ਵੰਡ, ਖੰਡਨ; ਵਿਭਾਜਨ, ਬਟਵਾਰਾ; ਵਰਗੀਕਰਨ, ਵਰਗਾ; ਤਕਸੀਮ, ਭਾਗਾ, ਸੀਮਾ, ਹੱਦ; ਖੰਡ; ਸੈਨਾ-ਦਲ, ਟੁਕੜੀ, ਡਿਵੀਜ਼ਨ; ਦਰਜਾ, ਸ਼੍ਰੇਣੀ; ~al ਵਿਭਾਗੀ, ਮੰਡਲੀ; ਅਰਥ ਭੇਦ

divorce (ਡਿ'ਵੋਸ) n ਤਲਾਕ, ਤਿਆਗ; ਤਲਾਕ ਦੇਣਾ, ਸਬੰਧ ਤੋੜਨਾ; ~e ਤਲਾਕਸ਼ੁਦਾ ਵਿਅਕਤੀ, ਤਲਾਕਸ਼ੁਦਾ ਔਰਤ

divulge (ਡਾਇ'ਵ੍ਯਅਲਜ) v (ਭੇਦ) ਖੋਲ੍ਹਣਾ, ਨਸ਼ਰ ਕਰਨਾ, ਉਘਾੜਨਾ, ਪਰਗਟ ਕਰਨਾ, ਜ਼ਾਹਰ ਕਰਨਾ; ~nce ਉਘਾੜਾ, ਪਰਗਟਾਵਾ, ਪ੍ਰਚਾਰ-ਪ੍ਰਸਾਰ

do (ਡੂ) v aux subst ਸਰਗਮ ਦਾ ਪਹਿਲਾ ਸੁਰ

ਕਰਨਾ, ਪ੍ਰਦਾਨ ਕਰਨਾ, ਦੇ ਦੇਣਾ, ਸੰਪਾਦਨ ਕਰਨਾ, ਸੰਪੰਨ ਕਰਨਾ, ਪਾਲਣ ਕਰਨਾ; ਪੂਰਾ ਕਰਨਾ. ਮੁਕੰਮਲ ਕਰਨਾ, ਮੁਰੰਮਤ ਕਰਨੀ; ਪਕਾਉਣਾ, ਪ੍ਰਸ਼ਨ ਹੱਲ ਕਰਨਾ, ਸੰਮਸਿਆ ਸੁਲਝਾਉਣੀ; ਅਨੁਵਾਦ ਕਰਨਾ; ਕੰਮ ਕਰਨਾ, ਵਧਣਾ, ਬੰਦ ਕਰਨਾ; ਚਲਾਉਣਾ, ਗੁਜ਼ਾਰਨਾ; ਉਪਯੁਕਤਾ ਕਰਨਾ, ਠੀਕ ਹੋਣਾ; **~away** ਛੁਟਕਾਰਾ ਪਾਉਣਾ, ਮੌਤ ਦੇ ਘਾਟ ਉਤਾਰਨਾ; **well-to ~** ਧਨਵਾਨ, ਖਾਂਦਾ-ਪੀਂਦਾ

doctor (ਡੌਕਟਅ*) *n* ਚਿਕਿਤਸਕ; ਡਾਕਟਰ; ਹਕੀਮ, ਵੈਦ; ਪੰਡਤ, ਵਿਦਵਾਨ, (ਅਪ, ਨੌ) ਰਸੋਈਆ; ਡਾਕਟਰ ਦੀ ਉਪਾਧੀ ਦੇਣਾ; **~ate** ਡਾਕਟਰ ਦੀ ਉਪਾਧੀ

doctrine (ਡੌਕਟਰਿਨ) *n* ਸਿੱਖਿਆ, ਵਿੱਦਿਆ, ਵਾਦ, ਮੱਤ, ਪੰਥ, ਸਿਧਾਂਤ, ਅਸੂਲ

document (ਡੌਕਯੁਮਅੰਟ, 'ਡੌਕਯੁਮੈਂਟ) *n v* ਲਿਖਤ, ਦਸਤਾਵੇਜ਼; ਲਿਖਤੀ, ਪ੍ਰਮਾਣ, ਲੇਖ-ਪੱਤਰ; **~ary** ਲੇਖ-ਬੱਧ, ਦਸਤਾਵੇਜ਼ੀ, ਤਹਿਰੀਰੀ, (ਵਾਕਿਆਤੀ ਜਾਂ ਦਸਤਾਵੇਜ਼ੀ) ਫ਼ਿਲਮ, ਵਰਿਤ-ਚਿੱਤਰ, **~ation** (ਦਸਤਾਵੇਜ਼ ਦੁਆਰਾ) ਪ੍ਰਮਾਣ, ਸਬੂਤ; ਪ੍ਰਸਤੁਤੀਕਰਨ, ਪ੍ਰਸਾਰਨ

dodge (ਡੌਜ) *n* ਟਾਲ-ਮਟੋਲ, ਖੁਸ਼ਾਉ, ਝਾਂਸਾ, ਚਲਾਕੀ; ਥਾਂ ਬਦਲ ਦੇਣਾ, ਪੈਂਤੜਾ ਬਦਲਣਾ, ਖਿਸਕਣਾ, ਕਤਰਾਉਣਾ, ਟਾਲ-ਮਟੋਲ ਕਰਨਾ; ਵਾਕ-ਚਾਤਰੀ ਕਰਨੀ, ਉਸਤਾਦੀ ਦਿਖਾਉਣਾ; ਫਿਰਾ ਕੇ ਸਵਾਲ ਪੁੱਛਣਾ

doer (ਡੂਅ*) *n* ਕਰਤਾ, ਕਾਰਕ, ਕਾਰਿੰਦਾ, ਦਾਤਾ, ਸੁਪਾਰਕ; ਹੱਲ ਕਰਨ ਵਾਲਾ

dog (ਡੌਗ) *n v a* ਕੁਕਰ, ਕੁੱਤਾ; ਤੁੱਛ ਵਿਅਕਤੀ, ਨਿਕੰਮਾ ਆਦਮੀ; ਖੋਜ ਕਰਨਾ, ਪਤਾ ਲਾਉਣਾ, ਸੁਰਾਗ ਲਾਉਣਾ, ਪਿੱਛਾ ਕਰਨਾ; ਫੜਨਾ;

ਘਟੀਆ, ਬਿਲਕੁਲ; **go to the ~s** ਨਸ਼ਟ ਹੋਣਾ, ਅਧੋਗਤ ਹੋਣਾ

dogma (ਡੌਗਮਅ) *n* ਮੱਤ-ਸਿਧਾਂਤ, ਧਰਮ-ਸਿਧਾਂਤ, ਹਠ ਧਰਮੀ; **~tic** ਸਿਧਾਂਤਆਤਮਕ, ਰੁੜ੍ਹੀਬੱਧ; ਹਠਧਰਮੀ

doldrums (ਡੌਲਡਰਅਮਜ਼) *n* ਉਦਾਸੀ, ਖਝੋਤ, ਢਹਿੰਦੀ ਕਲਾ, ਵਿਸ਼ਾਦ; ਸੁੰਨ-ਖੰਡ

dole (ਡਾਓਲ) *n v* ਰੰਜ, ਦੁੱਖ, ਸ਼ੋਕ, ਉਦਾਸੀ; ਕਲੇਸ਼, ਦਾਨ, ਤੁੱਛ ਦਾਨ; (ਪ੍ਰ) ਕਿਸਮਤ, ਵਿਤਾਗ, ਤੁੱਛ ਅੰਸ਼; ਦਾਨ ਕਰਨਾ, ਵੰਡਣਾ

doll (ਡੌਲ) *n v* ਪੁਤਲੀ, ਗੁੱਡੀ, ਗੁੱਡਾ, ਸਜਣਾ, ਸਜਾਉਣਾ, ਸ਼ਿੰਗਾਰਨਾ, ਬਣਨਾ-ਠਣਨਾ

dolly (ਡੌਲਿ) *n* ਪੁਤਲੀ, ਗੁੱਡਾ, ਗੁੱਡੀ

domain (ਡਅ(ਉ)'ਮੋਇਨ) *n* ਇਲਾਕਾ, ਜਾਗੀਰ; ਪ੍ਰਦੇਸ਼; ਕਾਰਜ-ਖੇਤਰ

dome (ਡਅਓਮ) *n* ਗੁੰਬਦ, ਮਮਟੀ; ਮਹਿਲ, ਹਵੇਲੀ; ਸਿਖਰ, ਗੋਲ ਚੋਟੀ; **~d** ਗੁੰਬਦਦਾਰ, ਮਮਟੀਵਾਲਾ, ਗੁਮਟੀਦਾਰ

domestic (ਡਅ(ਓ)'ਮੈਸਟਿਕ) *a n* ਘਰੋਗੀ, ਪਰਵਾਰਕ, ਘਰੇਲੂ; ਦੇਸੀ

domicile (ਡੌਮਿਸਾਇਲ) *n v* ਪੱਕਾ ਨਿਵਾਸ, ਘਰ, ਨਿਵਾਸ-ਸਥਾਨ, ਵਤਨ; ਵਸਣਾ, ਨਾਗਰਿਕਤਾ ਪ੍ਰਾਪਤ ਕਰਨਾ

dominance, domination (ਡੌਮਿਨੰਸ, ਡੌਮਿ'ਨੇਇਸ਼ਨ) *n* ਪ੍ਰਬਲਤਾ, ਬੋਲਬਾਲਾ

dominant (ਡੌਮਿਨਅੰਟ) *a n* ਪ੍ਰਮੁਖ; ਪ੍ਰਬਲ; ਪ੍ਰਭੁਤਾਸ਼ਾਲੀ;

dominate (ਡੌਮਿਨੇਇਟ) *v* ਪ੍ਰਭੁਤਾ ਜਮਾਉਣਾ, ਅਧਿਕਾਰ ਰੱਖਣਾ; ਪ੍ਰਬਲ ਹੋਣਾ, ਛਾ ਜਾਣਾ; ਹਾਵੀ ਹੋਣਾ

dominion (ਡਅ'ਮਿਨਯਅਨ) *n* ਪ੍ਰਭੁਤਾ, ਸੱਤਾ,

ਅਧਿਕਾਰ, ਮਲਕੀਅਤ, ਰਿਆਸਤ; ਬਾਦਸ਼ਾਹੀ;
ਅਮਲਦਾਰੀ, ਇਲਾਕਾ

don (ਡੌਨ) *n* (ਸੰਬੋਧਨ ਵਜੋਂ) ਸ੍ਰੀਮਾਨ, ਸਾਹਿਬ,
ਸਰਦਾਰ, ਭੱਦਰ ਪੁਰਸ਼, ਪ੍ਰਮੁੱਖ ਵਿਅਕਤੀ,
ਪ੍ਰਸਿੱਧੀ-ਪ੍ਰਾਪਤ ਮਨੁੱਖ, ਵਿਸ਼ਵਵਿਦਿਆਲੇ ਦਾ
ਅਧਿਅਕਸ਼ ਜਾਂ ਅਧਿਆਪਕ

donate (ਡਅ(ਓ)ਨੇਇਟ) *v* ਦਾਨ ਕਰਨਾ, ਦਾਨ
ਦੇਣਾ, ਪ੍ਰਦਾਨ ਕਰਨਾ, ਭੇਂਟ ਕਰਨਾ

donation (ਡਅ(ਓ)ਨੇਇਸ਼ਨ) *v* ਦਾਨ, ਭੇਟਾ,
ਚੰਦਾ; ਭੇਂਟ, ਉਪਹਾਰ

donkey (ਡੌਂਕਿ) *n a* ਖੋਤਾ, ਗਾਧਾ, ਖਰ;
ਅਗਿਆਨੀ ਮਨੁੱਖ, ਨਿਰਬੋਧ ਵਿਅਕਤੀ

donor (ਡਾਉਨਅ*) *n* ਦਾਨੀ, ਦਾਤਾ, ਖ਼ੂਨ ਦਾਨ
ਕਰਨ ਵਾਲਾ

doom (ਡੂਮ) *n v* ਤਕਦੀਰ, ਪਰਲੋ, ਵਿਨਾਸ਼,
ਤਬਾਹੀ, ਬਰਬਾਦੀ; ਅੰਤ, ਮਿਰਤੂ, ਮੌਤ ਦੇ ਮੂੰਹ
ਧਕੱਣਾ, ਨਿਯੁਕਤ ਕਰਨਾ, ਸਜ਼ਾ ਦਾ ਹੁਕਮ
ਸੁਣਾਉਣਾ; ~s day ਕਿਆਮਤ ਦਾ ਦਿਨ, ਪਰਲੋ
ਦਾ ਦਿਨ

door (ਡੋ*) *n* ਬੂਹਾ, ਦਰਵਾਜ਼ਾ, ਦੁਆਰ, ਕਿਵਾੜ;
ਕਪਾਟ; ਪ੍ਰਵੇਸ਼-ਪਥ, ਪ੍ਰਵੇਸ਼ ਮਾਰਗ; ~keeper
ਦਾਰਪਾਲ, ਦਰਬਾਨ; ~mat ਪਾਇਦਾਨ

dormitory (ਡੋ*ਮਅਟਰਿ) *n* ਸੌਣ-ਕਮਰਾ
(ਬੋਰਡਿੰਗ ਵਿਚ)

dose (ਡਅਉਜ਼) *n v* (ਦਵਾਈ ਦੀ) ਖ਼ੁਰਾਕ,
ਮਾਤਰਾ; ਖ਼ੁਸ਼ਾਮਦ, ਮਿਸ਼ਰਨ ਬਣਾਉਣਾ; ਦਵਾ
ਦੇਣੀ; ਖ਼ੁਰਾਕ ਪਿਆਉਣੀ

dossier (ਡੌਸਿਏਇ*) *n* ਮਿਸਲ, ਕਾਗ਼ਾਂ ਦੀ
ਫ਼ਾਈਲ; ਚਾਲ-ਚਲਣ ਦਾ ਲਿਖਤੀ ਵੇਰਵਾ,
ਗੁਪਤ ਫ਼ਾਈਲ

dot (ਡੌਟ) *n v* ਨੁਕਤਾ, ਬਿੰਦੀ, ਬਿੰਦੂ; (ਸੰਗੀ)

ਚਿੰਨ੍ਹ; (ਟੈਲੀਗ੍ਰਾਫੀ) ਸੰਕੇਤ ਚਿੰਨ੍ਹ, ਨਿੱਕੀ ਚੀਜ਼;
ਬਿੰਦੀ, ਲਾਉਣੀ, ਨੁਕਤਾ ਲਾਉਣਾ; ਚਿਤਰਨਾ,
ਨਿਸ਼ਾਨਾ ਮਾਰਨਾ

double (ਡਅੱਬਲ) *n v a* ਪ੍ਰਤੀਰੂਪ, ਪ੍ਰਤੀ ਮੂਰਤੀ;
ਨਕਲ; ਦੁਗਣਾ; ਦੂਹਰਾ; ਧੋਖੇਬਾਜ਼, ਕਪਟੀ;
ਦੁਗਣਾ ਕਰਨਾ ਜਾਂ ਹੋਣਾ, ਦੂਹਰਾ ਕਰਨਾ; ਤਹਿ
ਕਰਨਾ; ਕਸ ਕੇ ਫੜਨਾ, ਗੋਡ ਦਾ ਟੱਪ ਖਾਣਾ,
ਪਲਟਾਉਣਾ; ਦੂਣਾ, ਦੁੱਗਣਾ, ਦੂਹਰਾ, ਡਬਲ
ਸੰਦੇਹਪੂਰਨ, ਦੋ-ਅਰਥਕ; ਦੋ-ਰੰਗਾ; ਦੁਗਾਣੀ
ਸ਼ਕਤੀ ਵਾਲਾ; ਮੱਕਾਰ; ~edged ਦੋ-ਧਾਰੀ, ਦੋ-
ਰੂਪੀ, ਦੋ-ਅਕਸ਼ਰ; ~faced ਕਪਟੀ, ਕੁਟਿਲ,
ਛਲੀਆ, ਮੱਕਾਰ, ਦੁਬਾਜਰਾ

doubt (ਡਾਉਟ) *n* ਸ਼ੱਕ, ਸ਼ੰਕਾ, ਸੰਦੇਹ, ਸ਼ੁਬ੍ਹਾ, ਖੇ-
ਵਸਾਹੀ; ਅਵਿਸ਼ਵਾਸ, ਖਟਕਾ; ਸ਼ੱਕ ਕਰਨਾ,
ਦੁਬਧਾ ਵਿਚ ਹੋਣਾ; ਵਿਚਾਰ ਕਰਨਾ, ਡਰਨਾ;
~ful ਸ਼ੱਕ ਵਾਲਾ, ਸ਼ੰਕਾ ਭਰਿਆ, ਸੰਦੇਹਪੂਰਨ,
ਗ਼ੈਰਯਕੀਨੀ, ਸੰਦਿਗਧ

dove (ਡਅੱਵ) *n* ਘੁੱਗੀ, ਕੁਮਰੀ, ਫਾਖ਼ਤਾ, ਦਿਵ-
ਆਤਮਾ

down (ਡਾਊਨ) *v adv a* ਢੇਗ ਦੇਣਾ, ਪਟਕਾ ਦੇਣਾ,
ਹਰਾਉਣਾ; ਅਧੋਗਤੀ; ਹੇਠਾਂ, ਥੱਲੇ; ਉਦਾਸ,
ਦਿਲਗੀਰ ਮਸੋਸਿਆ, ਨਿਵਾਣ; get~ ਉਤਰਨਾ
shout~ ਚਿਲਾ ਚਿਲਾ ਕੇ ਚੁਪ ਕਰਾ ਦੇਣਾ; ~fall
ਗਿਰਾਵਟ, ਅਵਨਤੀ, ਤਬਾਹੀ, ਬਰਬਾਦੀ, ਨਾਸ,
(ਮੀਂਹ ਦੀ) ਬੁਛਾੜ, ਫੰਡ, ਵਾਛੜ; ~grade ਪਦ-
ਅਵਨਤੀ, ਦਰਜਾ ਘਟਾਉਣਾ; ~pour ਮੋਹਲੇਧਾਰ
ਮੀਂਹ, ਬੁਛਾੜ, ਝੜੀ; ~stairs ਹੇਠਲੀ ਛੱਤ ਉੱਤੇ,
~trodden ਕੁਚਲਿਆ, ਦਲਿਤ ਲਿਤਾੜਿਆ,
ਦਬਿਆ, ਪੀੜਤ; ~ward ਪਤਨਸ਼ੀਲ, ਅਧੋਮੁਖੀ,
ਨੀਵੇਂ ਪਾਸੇ; up and ~ਇੱਧਰ-ਉੱਧਰ; ਅੱਗੇ
ਪਿੱਛੇ, ਉੱਪਰ-ਹੇਠਾਂ

dowry ('ਡਾਉਰਿ) *n* ਦਹੇਜ-ਦਾਜ, ਕੰਨਿਆ-ਦਾਨ

doze ('ਡਅਉਜ਼) *n v* ਉਂਘ, ਝਪਕੀ, ਹਲਕੀ ਨੀਂਦ

dozen ('ਡਅੱਜ਼ਨ) *n* ਦਰਜਨ, ਬਾਰਾਂ

draft (ਡਰਾਫ਼ਟ) *n v* ਢੋਂਗੀ ਟੁਕੜੀ, ਦਸਤਾ; ਡਰਾਫ਼ਟ; ਖਰੜਾ, ਢਾਂਚਾ, ਰੂਪ-ਰੇਖਾ; ਢਾਂਚਾ ਬਣਾਉਣਾ

draftsman ('ਡਰਾਫ਼ਟਸਮਅਨ) *n* ਨਕਸ਼ਾਨਵੀਸ, ਮਾਨਚਿਤਰਕਾਰ, ਰੇਖਾਕਾਰ, ਨਕਸ਼ਾ ਬਣਾਉਣ ਵਾਲਾ, ਮਸੌਦਾਕਾਰ

drag (ਡਰੈਗ) *v n* ਘਸੀਟਣਾ, ਖਿੱਚਣਾ, ਔਖੇ ਚੱਲਣਾ; ਜਾਲ ਸੁੱਟਣਾ; ਸੁਹਾਗਾ, ਫੰਡੂ, ਕਰਾਹ; ਅੜਿੱਕਾ; ~on ਘਸੀਟਦੇ ਜਾਣਾ; ~out ਲਮਕਾਉਣਾ, ਲੰਬਾ ਕਰਨਾ, ਦੇਰ ਲਗਾਉਣਾ; ~up ਸਖਤ ਵਰਤਾਉ ਕਰਨਾ

drain (ਡਰੇਇਨ) *v n* ਪਾਣੀ ਕੱਢਣਾ, ਨਿਚੋੜਨਾ; ਕੱਢਣਾ; ਚੋਣਾ; ਨਾਲੀ, ਵਹਿਣੀ, ਮੋਰੀ; ਨਿਕਾਸ; ~age ਨਿਕਾਸ-ਪ੍ਰਬੰਧ,ਜਲ-ਪ੍ਰਣਾਲੀ, ਵਹਿਣੀਆਂ

drama (ਡਰਾਮਅ) *n* ਨਾਟਕ, ਰੂਪਕ, ਸਾਂਗ, ਰਾਸ; ਨਾਟਕ ਕਲਾ; ~itc ਨਾਟਕ ਸਬੰਧੀ, ਨਾਟਕੀ; ਅਨੋਖਾ ਵੱਖਿਤਰ; ਅਚਾਨਕ; ~tist ਨਾਟਕਕਾਰ

drastic ('ਡਰੈਸਟਿਕ) *a* ਕਠੋਰ, ਕਰੜਾ, ਸਖ਼ਤ, ਉਗਰ, ਪ੍ਰਚੰਡ

draught (ਡਰਾਫ਼ਟ) *n v* ਖਿਚਾਈ, ਘਸੀਟ; ਭਾਰ ਢੁਆਈ; ਘੁੱਟ (ਪਾਣੀ ਆਦਿ ਦਾ); ਦਵਾਈ (ਪੀਣ ਵਾਲੀ) ਦੀ ਇਕ ਖੁਰਾਕ; ਢਾਂਚਾ, ਖ਼ਾਕਾ, ਨਕਸ਼ਾ, ਰੂਪ-ਰੇਖਾ; ਖਰੜਾ; ਢੋਂਗੀ ਟੁਕੜੀ, ਢੋਂਗੀ ਦਸਤਾ; ਹੁੰਡੀ, ਚੈੱਕ; ਛਾਂਟਣਾ; ਢਾਂਚਾ ਬਣਾਉਣਾ; ~sman ਨਕਸ਼ਾਨਵੀਸ, ਖਰੜਾ ਲੇਖਕ, ਰੂਪ ਰੇਖਾ ਖਿੱਚਣ ਵਾਲਾ

draw (ਡਰੋ) *n v* ਖਿੱਚ; ਖਿਚਾਈ; (ਗਾਹਕਾਂ ਨੂੰ) ਖਿੱਚਣ ਵਾਲੀ ਵਸਤੂ, ਲਾਟਰੀ, ਖਿੱਚਣਾ, ਧੂਹਣਾ, ਘਸੀਟਣਾ; ਢੋਣਾ, ਖਿਚ ਪਾਉਣਾ, ਖਿੱਚੇ ਜਾਣਾ, ਆਕਰਸ਼ਤ ਹੋਣਾ, ਇਕੱਤਰ ਹੋਣਾ, ਇਕੱਠੇ ਹੋਣਾ; ਰਜ਼ਾਮੰਦ ਕਰਨਾ; (ਖੂਹ ਵਿਚੋਂ ਪਾਣੀ) ਕੱਢਣਾ; ਸਤ ਜਾਂ ਰਸ ਕੱਢਣਾ; (ਸਰੀਰ ਵਿਚੋਂ ਲਹੂ) ਕੱਢਣਾ, ਪ੍ਰਾਪਤ ਕਰਨਾ, ਗ੍ਰਹਿਣ ਕਰਨਾ; (ਤਾਸ਼ ਵਿਚ) ਪੱਤਾ ਕਢਵਾਉਣਾ; ਅਨੁਮਾਨ ਲਾਉਣਾ, (ਨਕਸ਼ਾ ਆਦਿ) ਖਿੱਚਣਾ, (ਤਸਵੀਰ) ਬਣਾਉਣੀ, ਦਸਤਾਵੇਜ ਤਿਆਰ ਕਰਨਾ; ਬਰਾਬਰੀ ਵਿਖਾਉਣੀ, ਹਿੱਲਣਾ-ਜੁੱਲਣਾ, ਚਲੱਣਾ; ਨੇੜੇ ਆ ਪੁੱਜਣਾ; ~attention ਧਿਆਨ ਖਿੱਚਣਾ; ~back ਘਾਟ, ਕਮੀ, ਤਰੁੱਟੀ, ਨਿਊਨਤਾ, ਨੁਕਸ, ਐਬ

drawee (ਡਰੋ'ਈ) *n* ਹੁੰਡੀ-ਗ੍ਰਾਹਕ

drawer (ਡਰੋ*) *n* (ਮੇਜ਼ ਆਦਿ ਦਾ) ਖ਼ਾਨਾ, ਦਰਾਜ, ਗ੍ਰਾਹਕ, ਹੁੰਡੀਕਰਤਾ; ਢੋਣ ਵਾਲਾ

drawing (ਡਰੋਇੰਡ) *n* ਨਕਸ਼ਾਕਸ਼ੀ; ਖਿੱਚਣ, ਨਕਸ਼ਾ, ਖ਼ਾਕਾ, ਢਾਂਚਾ; ਚਿੱਤਰ, ਤਸਵੀਰ; ਚਿੱਤਰ-ਵਿੱਦਿਆ; ~room ਬੈਠਕ; ਦਰਬਾਰ ਭਵਨ

dray (ਡਰੇਇ) *n* ਠੇਲ੍ਹਾ, ਰੇੜ੍ਹਾ

dread (ਡਰੈੱਡ) *v n a* ਡਰਨਾ, ਸਹਿਮਣਾ, ਭੈ ਖਾਣਾ; ਭੈ, ਡਰ, ਆਤੰਕ, ਖ਼ਤਰਾ; ਡਰਾਉਣੀ ਵਸਤੂ; ਭਿਆਨਕ, ਡਰਾਉਣਾ; ~ful ਭਿਆਨਕ, ਡਰਾਉਣਾ, ਖੌਫ਼ਨਾਕ, ਆਤੰਕਮਈ

dream (ਡਰੀਮ) *n v* ਸੁਪਨਾ; ਕਪੋਲ ਕਲਪਨਾ; ਸੁਪਨੇ ਵੇਖਣਾ, ਖਿਆਲੀ ਪਲਾਉ ਪਕਾਉਣੇ, ਵਿਚਾਰਾਂ ਵਿਚ ਡੁੱਬੇ ਰਹਿਣਾ

dreary ('ਡਰਿਅਰਿ) *a* ਵਿਰਾਨ, ਉਜਾੜ, ਸੁਨਸਾਨ, ਉਦਾਸ, ਫਿੱਕਾ, ਨੀਰਸ

dredge (ਡਰੈੱਜ) *n v* ਸਮੁੰਦਰ ਜਾਂ ਦਰਿਆ ਦੀ ਤਹਿ ਵਿੱਚੋਂ ਗਾਰਾ ਕੱਢਣ ਵਾਲਾ ਜੰਤਰ; ਝਾਮ; ਇਸ ਜੰਤਰ ਨਾਲ ਗਾਰਾ ਕੱਢਣਾ; (ਕਿਸੇ ਚੀਜ਼ ਉੱਤੇ ਆਟਾ, ਮੈਦਾ ਆਦਿ) ਛਿੜਕਣਾ

drench (ਡਰੈਂਚ) *v n* ਭਿਊਂ ਦੇਣਾ, ਤਰੋ ਤਰ ਕਰ ਦੇਣਾ, ਮੋਹਲੇਧਾਰ ਮੀਂਹ; ਪਸ਼ੂਆਂ ਦੀ ਦਵਾਈ ਦੀ ਖੁਰਾਕ

dress (ਡਰੈੱਸ) *v n* ਕੱਪੜੇ ਪਾਉਣੇ; (ਜ਼ਖ਼ਮ ਆਦਿ ਉੱਤੇ) ਪੱਟੀ ਬੰਨ੍ਹਣੀ; ਸਜਾਉਣਾ, ਵਾਲ ਸੰਵਾਰਨੇ, ਕੰਘੀ-ਪੱਟੀ ਕਰਨੀ; ਈਸਤਰੀ ਕਰਨੀ; ਪੁਸ਼ਾਕ, ਕੱਪੜੇ, ਵਰਦੀ, ਵਸਤਰ, ਵੇਸ, ਬਾਣਾ, ਬਾਹਰੀ ਰੂਪ, ਭੇਸ, ਰੂਪ-ਰੰਗ; **~circle** ਰੰਗ-ਭਵਨ, (ਥੀਏਟਰ) ਦੀ ਗੈਲਰੀ; **~ed** ਚੰਗੇ ਕੱਪੜੇ ਪਹਿਨੇ ਹੋਏ; **~er** ਸ਼ਿੰਗਾਰ ਮੇਜ਼, ਮਲ੍ਹਮ-ਪੱਟੀ ਕਰਨ ਵਾਲਾ, ਵਸਤਰ ਆਦਿ ਪਵਾਉਣ ਵਾਲਾ, ਬੂਟਿਆਂ ਨੂੰ ਕੱਟਣ-ਛਾਂਟਣ ਵਾਲਾ **~maker** ਦਰਜੀ, ਦਰਜਨ; **~up** ਭੇਸ ਬਣਾਉਣਾ

dressing (ਡਰੈੱਸਿਙ) *n* ਮਲ੍ਹਮ ਪੱਟੀ; ਪੁਸ਼ਾਕ ਆਦਿ ਪਹਿਨਣ, ਬੂਟਿਆਂ ਨੂੰ ਛਾਂਟਣ, ਰੁੜ੍ਹੀ ਪਾਉਣ; **~room** ਸ਼ਿੰਗਾਰ-ਕਮਰਾ

drift (ਡਰਿਫ਼ਟ) *n v* ਵਹਿਣ, ਵਹਾ, ਰੋੜ੍ਹ; ਧਾਰ; ਵੰ; ਇਕੱਠਾ ਕਰਨਾ; ਵਰਮਾ ਮਾਰਨਾ, ਛੇਕ ਕਰਨਾ, ਛੇਕ ਕੱਢਣਾ

drill (ਡਰਿਲ) *n v* ਵਰਮਾ; ਕਵਾਇਦ, ਡ੍ਰਿਲ, ਕਰੜਾ ਅਨੁਸ਼ਾਸਨ; ਵਰਮੇ ਨਾਲ ਛੇਕ ਕੱਢਣਾ; ਡ੍ਰਿਲ ਕਰਨਾ

drink (ਡਰਿਙਕ) *v n* ਪੀਣਾ; ਸ਼ਰਾਬ ਪੀਣਾ; ਪਾਣੀ ਧਾਣੀ, ਸ਼ਰਬਤ, ਜਲਪਾਨ, ਸ਼ਰਾਬ, ਨਸ਼ਾ-ਪਾਣੀ, ਦਾਰੂ; ਪੈੱਗ; **~ing water** ਪੀਣ ਵਾਲਾ ਪਾਣੀ

drip (ਡਰਿਪ) *v n* ਚੋਣਾ, ਚੋਆ ਪੈਣਾ, ਰਿਸਣਾ; ਚੋਆ

drive (ਡਰਾਇਵ) *v n* (ਮੋਟਰ ਆਦਿ) ਚਲਾਉਣਾ; ਹਿੱਕਣਾ, ਟੋਕਣਾ; ਸੁੱਟਣਾ, ਧੱਕਣਾ; ਠੋਕਣਾ (ਕਿੱਲਾ, ਕਿੱਲ ਆਦਿ), ਗੋਡਣਾ, ਛੇਕ ਕਰਨਾ; (ਕ੍ਰਿਕਟ) ਗੇਂਦ ਅਗੇ ਸੁੱਟਣੀ; ਸ਼ਕਤੀ, ਸਾਹਸ,

ਉੱਦਮ, ਧੱਕਾ, ਝਟਕਾ; ਮੋਟਰ ਦਾ ਰਸਤਾ ਜਾਂ ਸੜ੍ਹਕ; **~at** ਮਤਲਬ ਹੋਣਾ, ਭਾਵ ਹੋਣਾ; **~away** ਪਰ੍ਹੇ ਕਰਨਾ, ਭਜਾਉਣਾ, ਨਠਾਉਣਾ

drizzle (ʼਡਰਿਜ਼ਲ) *v n* ਨਿੱਕਾ ਨਿੱਕਾ ਮੀਂਹ ਵਰ੍ਹਨਾ, ਕਿਣ-ਮਿਣ ਹੋਣੀ; ਫੁਹਾਰ ਪੈਣੀ; ਫੁਰ੍ਹੂ, ਨਿੱਕਾ ਨਿੱਕਾ ਮੀਂਹ

drop (ਡਰੌਪ) *v n* ਡਿਗਣਾ, ਡੇਗਣਾ; ਚੋਣਾ, ਚੁਆਉਣਾ; ਲਹਿ ਜਾਣਾ; ਘਟਣਾ; ਪੱਛੜਨਾ, ਹੇਠਾਂ ਨੂੰ ਜਾਣਾ, ਮਰਨਾ, ਮਰ ਜਾਣਾ; ਸਮਾਪਤ ਹੋਣਾ, ਖ਼ਤਮ ਹੋ ਜਾਣਾ; (ਕੀਮਤਾਂ ਦਾ) ਡਿੱਗਣਾ, ਘੱਟ ਹੋਣਾ; ਹੰਝੂ ਸੁੱਟਣਾ; ਛੱਡ ਦੇਣਾ, ਤਿਆਗਣਾ; ਸੂਣਾ (ਭੇਡ, ਬੱਕਰੀ ਆਦਿ ਦਾ); ਕਣੀ, ਛਿੱਟ, ਬੂੰਦ, ਤੁਪਕਾ, ਖੁਟ, (ਦਵਾਈ ਦੀ) ਬੋਤੀ ਜੇਹੀ ਮਾਤਰਾ (ਬ ਵ) ਤਰਲ ਦਵਾਈ; ਸਮਾਜੀ ਗਿਰਾਵਟ ਉਤਾਰ; ਮੰਦਾ ਪੈ ਰਿਹਾ ਪਦਾਰਥ

drought, drouth (ਡਰਾਊਟ) *n* ਔੜ, ਸੋਕਾ, ਤੇਹ, ਪਿਆਸ, ਖ਼ੁਸ਼ਕੀ

drown (ਡਰਾਉਨ) *v* ਡੁੱਬਣਾ, ਡੋਬਣਾ; ਡੁੱਬ ਕੇ ਮਰਨਾ, ਗੋਤਾ ਦੇਣਾ, ਪਾਣੀ ਵਿਚ ਸੁੱਟਣਾ; ਪੂਰਾ ਭਿਊਂ ਦੇਣਾ, ਤਰ ਕਰ ਦੇਣਾ

drowse (ਡਰਾਊਜ਼) *v* ਉਂਘਣਾ, ਨਿੰਦਰਾਉਣਾ; ਨੀਂਦ ਲਿਆਉਣੀ; ਉਂਘਦਿਆਂ ਸਮਾਂ ਲੰਘਾਉਣਾ, ਆਲਸ ਪਾਉਣਾ, ਸੁਸਤੀ ਚਾਹੁਣੀ ਉਂਘ

drowsiness (ʼਡਰਾਊਜ਼ਿਨਿਸ) *n* ਸੁਸਤੀ, ਆਲਸ, ਉਂਘ

drowsy (ʼਡਰਾਊਜ਼ਿ) *a* ਉਂਘਦਾ, ਨਿੰਦਰਾਇਆ; ਆਲਸ ਵਿਚ; ਸੁਸਤ ਪਿਆ

drudge (ʼਡਰਅੱਜ) *v n* ਮਿਹਨਤ ਕਰਨੀ, ਜਾਨ ਮਾਰ ਕੇ ਕੰਮ ਕਰਨਾ, ਕਾਮਾ, ਭਾੜੇ ਦਾ ਟੱਟੂ, ਵਗਾਰ ਵਿਚ ਕੰਮ ਕਰਨ ਵਾਲਾ, ਸੇਵਕ; ਗ਼ੁਲਾਮ; **~ry** ਮਜ਼ਦੂਰੀ; ਗ਼ੁਲਾਮੀ; ਸਖ਼ਤ ਮਿਹਨਤ, ਹੱਡ

ਭੰਨਵੀਂ ਕਾਰ; ਵਗਾਰ

drug (ਡਰੱਗ) *n v* ਦਵਾਈ, ਔਸ਼ਧੀ, ਔਖਧ, ਜੜੀ ਬੂਟੀ, ਅਮਲ; ਦਵਾ ਦੇਣਾ ਪਿਆਉਣਾ, ਦਵਾਈਆਂ ਮਿਲਾਉਣਾ; ~**gist** ਦਵਾ ਫ਼ਰੋਸ਼, ਪੰਸਾਰੀ, ਦਵਾਈਆਂ ਬਣਾਉਣ ਵਾਲਾ, ਅੱਤਾਰ

drum (ਡਰੱਮ) *n v* ਢੋਲ, ਢੋਲਕੀ; ਨਗਾਰਾ; ਦਮਾਮਾ; ਕੰਨ ਦਾ ਪਰਦਾ; ਪੀਪਾ, ਬੇਲ੍ਹ ਦਾ ਉਤਲਾ ਭਾਗ; ਢੋਲ ਵਜਾਉਣਾ, ਠੱਕ-ਠੱਕ ਕਰਨਾ, ਲਗਾਤਾਰ ਠੋਕਣਾ

drunkard (ਡਰੰਅਕਅੱਡ) ਨਸ਼ੱਈ, ਨਸ਼ੇਬਾਜ਼, ਸ਼ਰਾਬੀ, ਸ਼ਰਾਬਖੋਰ

dry (ਡਰਾਇ) *a* ਸੁੱਕਾ, ਖ਼ੁਸ਼ਕ; ਲੂਹਿਆ, ਰੁੱਖਾ, ਕੋਰਾ, ਫਿੱਕਾ, ਫੇਕਾ, ਖਰੁਵਾ; ~**fruit** ਸੁੱਕਾ ਮੇਵਾ ~**ness** ਖ਼ੁਸ਼ਕੀ, ਨੀਰਸਤਾ; ਨਿਰਲੱਜਤਾ

dual (ਡਯੂਅਲ) *a n* ਦੂਹਰਾ; ਦੂਣਾ; ਦੁਵੱਲੀ; ~**ism** ਦਵੈਤਵਾਦ; ਦਵੈਤ

dubious (ਡਯੂਬਯਅਸ) *a* ਸੰਦੇਹ-ਜਨਕ, ਅਸਪਸ਼ਟ, ਧੁੰਦਲਾ, ਅਨਿਸ਼ਚਤ; ਦੋ-ਅਰਥੀ, ਸ਼ੰਕੇ ਵਾਲਾ

duck (ਡਅੱਕ) *n v* ਬੱਤਖ਼, ਮੁਰਗਾਬੀ; ਮੋਟਾ ਸੂਤੀ ਕਪੜਾ; ਕਬੂਤਰੀ; ਚੁੱਭੀ ਮਾਰਨੀ, ਗੋਤਾ ਮਾਰਨਾ; ਸਿਰ ਨਿਵਾਉਣਾ, ਗੋਤਾ ਦੇਣਾ, ਚੁੱਭੀ ਲਵਾਉਣੀ

due (ਡਯੂ) *a adv n* ਦੇਣਯੋਗ ਬਕਾਇਆ, ਉਚਿਤ, ਮੁਨਾਸਬ, ਨਿਸ਼ਚਤ, ਦੀ ਵਜ੍ਹਾ ਨਾਲ, ਦੇ ਕਾਰਨ, ਬਿਲਕੁਲ, ਸਿੱਧਾ, ਹੱਕ, ਅਧਿਕਾਰ, ਦਾਅਵਾ; ਉਧਾਰ, ਕਰਜ਼ਾ; ਮਹਿਸੂਲ

duel (ਡਯੂਅਲ) *n v* ਦਵੰਦ, ਦਵੱਲੀ ਲੜਾਈ;

duffer (ਡਅੱਫ਼ਅ*) *n* ਨਿਕੰਮਾ ਆਦਮੀ, ਲੋਲ੍ਹਾ, ਬੰਦਾ, ਬੁਧੂ, ਬਗਲੋਲ

dull (ਡਅੱਲ) *a v* ਮੋਟੀ ਮੱਤ ਵਾਲਾ, ਮੂਰਖ, ਮੂਤੂ; ਖੁੰਢਾ; ਸੁਸਤ, ਮੱਠਾ, ਫਿੱਲਾ; ਜੜੂ; ਧੁੰਦਲਾ; ਮੱਤ

ਮਾਰ ਦੇਣੀ, ਮੂਰਖ ਬਣਾ ਦੇਣਾ; ਖੁੰਢਾ ਕਰਨਾ, ਮੰਦਾ ਪਾ ਦੇਣਾ, ਫਿੱਕਾ ਹੋਣਾ, ਬੇ-ਸੁਆਦ ਹੋਣਾ; ਫਿੱਕਾ ਜਾਂ ਤੇਜਹੀਣ ਹੋਣਾ; ~**ard** ਮੂਰਖ ਮਨੁੱਖ, ਮੂਤੂ ਵਿਅਕਤੀ, ਮੱਤਹੀਣ ਬੰਦਾ, ਮੋਟੀ ਮੱਤ ਵਾਲਾ ਆਦਮੀ, ਬੁੱਧੂ, ਲੋਲ੍ਹਾ

duly (ਡਯੂਲਿ) *adv* ਉਚਿਤ ਰੂਪ ਵਿਚ, ਠੀਕ-ਠੀਕ, ਕਾਇਦੀ, ਤੋਰ ਤੇ, ਯਥਾ ਸਮੇਂ, ਯਥਾ ਸੰਭਵ

dumb (ਡਅੱਮ) *adv* ਗੁੰਗਾ, ਚੁੱਪ, ਹੈਰਾਨ-ਪਰੇਸ਼ਾਨ, ਹੱਕਾ-ਬੱਕਾ; ਮੂਰਖ, ਉੱਜਡ; ਬੇਜ਼ਬਾਨ ਬਣਾ ਦੇਣਾ, ਗੁੰਗਾ ਬਣਾ ਦੇਣਾ; ਚੁੱਪ ਕਰਾ ਦੇਣਾ; ~**found** ਗੁੰਗਾ ਕਰ ਦੇਣਾ, ਚੁੱਪ ਕਰਾ ਦੇਣਾ, ਘਬਰਾ ਦੇਣਾ

dummy (ਡਅੱਮਿ) *n a* ਮਿੱਟੀ ਦਾ ਮਾਧੋ, ਕਠਪੁਤਲੀ; ਮੂਰਖ, ਮੋਟੀ ਮੱਤ ਵਾਲਾ, ਕਾਠ ਦਾ ਉੱਲੂ, ਮਾਨਵੀ, ਬੁੱਤ, ਲੱਕੜੀ ਦਾ ਢਾਂਚਾ, ਬਣਾਉਟੀ, ਨਕਲੀ, ਜਾਅਲੀ, ਫ਼ਰਜ਼ੀ, ਕਲਪਤ

dump (ਡਅੱਪ) *v n* ਢੇਰ ਲਾਉਣਾ; (ਕੂੜਾ ਆਦਿ) ਇਕ ਥਾਂ ਸੁੱਟਣਾ, ਜਮ੍ਹਾਂ ਕਰਨਾ; ਪੱਕਾ, ਠੋਕਰ, ਠੁੰਡਾ; ਧਮਾਕਾ, ਧੜੰਮ ਦਾ ਆਵਾਜ਼; ਕੋਈ ਤੁੱਛ ਵਸਤੂ, ਛੋਟੀ ਮੋਟੀ ਚੀਜ਼

dunce (ਡਅੱਸ) *n* ਮੂਰਖ ਮਨੁੱਖ, ਮੂਤੂ, ਘੁੰਗੂ, ਭੌਂਦੂ, ਉੱਜਡ

dunderhead (ਡਅੰਡਅਹੈੱਡ) *n* ਘਰ ਦਿਮਾਗ਼, ਭੌਂਦੂ

dung (ਡਅੰਙ) *n* ਗੋਹਾ, ਲਿੱਦ; ਰੂੜੀ; ਗੰਦ-ਮੰਦ; ਰੂੜੀ ਪਾਉਣੀ

duo (ਡਯੂਅਉ) *n* ਜੋੜਾ, ਸੰਗੀਤੱਗਾਂ ਦੀ ਜੋੜੀ

dupe (ਡਯੂਪ) *v n* ਧੋਖਾ ਦੇਣਾ; ਠੱਗਣਾ; ਛਲਣਾ; ਮੁੰਠਨਾ; ਮੁੰਛਣਾ; ਭੋਲਾ-ਪਾਤਸ਼ਾਹ, ਧੋਖੇ ਦਾ ਸ਼ਿਕਾਰ; ਸਿੱਧਤ ਮਨੁੱਖ

duplex (ਡਯੂਪਲੈੱਕਸ) *a v* ਦੋਹਰਾ, ਦੂਣਾ, ਦੁੱਗਣਾ; ਦੁਤਰਫ਼ੀ, ਦੁਹਰਾਉਣਾ; ਦੁੱਗਣਾ ਕਰਨਾ

duplicate (ਡਯੂਪਲਿਕੇਇਟ) *a n v* ਦੂਹਰਾ, ਜੋੜਾ; ਹੂਬਹੂ, ਉਹੋ ਜੇਹਾ, (ਕਿਸੇ ਦੂਜੇ) ਵਰਗਾ, ਪ੍ਰਤੀਰੂਪ; ਉਤਾਰਾ, ਨਕਲ, ਪ੍ਰਤੀਲਿਪੀ

duplicating ('ਡਯੂਪਲਿਕੇਇਟਿਙ) *n* ਪ੍ਰਤੀਲਿਪੀਕਰਨ, ਉਤਾਰਾਕਰਨ

duplication ('ਡਯੂਪਲਿ'ਕੇਇਸ਼ਨ) *n* ਉਤਾਰਾ ਕਰਨਾ, ਪ੍ਰਤੀਲਿਪੀਕਰਨ; ਦੁਗਣਾ ਕਰਨ

duplicity (ਡਯੂ'ਪਲਿਸਅਟਿ) *n* ਧੋਖੇਬਾਜ਼ੀ, ਚਾਲਬਾਜ਼ੀ, ਛਲ, ਕਪਟ, ਦੁਰੰਗੀ, ਦੁਬਾਜਰਾਪਣ

durability (ਡਯੂਅਰਅ'ਬਿਲਅਟਿ) *n* ਪਕਿਆਈ, ਹੰਢਣਸਾਰਤਾ, ਪਾਏਦਾਰੀ, ਸਥਿਰਤਾ, ਟਿਕਾਊ

durable ('ਡਯੂਅਰਅਬਲ) *a* ਹੰਢਣਸਾਰ, ਪਾਇਦਾਰ, ਪੱਕਾ, ਚਿਰ-ਸਥਾਈ

duration (ਡਯੂ'ਰੇਇਸ਼ਨ) *n* ਮਿਆਦ, ਅਵਧੀ, ਮੁਕਰਰ ਸਮਾਂ, ਨਿਸ਼ਚਤ ਸਮਾਂ

duress (ਡਯੂ(ਅ)'ਰਿਸ) *n* ਨਾਜਾਇਜ਼ ਦਬਾਉ; ਧਮਕੀ, ਸਖ਼ਤੀ; ਧੱਕਾਸ਼ਾਹੀ

during ('ਡਯੂਅਰਿਙ) *perp* ਦੇ ਵਿਚ, ਵਿਚ, ਸਮੇਂ ਵਿਚ, ਤਕ, ਵੇਲੇ, ਵੇਲੇ ਤਕ, ਤਦ ਤਕ, ਜਦ ਤਕ, ਦੌਰਾਨ

dusk (ਡਅੱਸਕ) *n v* ਘੁਸਮੁਸਾ; ਧੁੰਦਲਾਪਣ, ਤ੍ਰਿਕਾਲਾਂ, ਸੰਧਿਆ, ਹਨੇਰਾ ਹੋਣਾ, ਧੁੰਦਲਾ ਹੋਣਾ

dust (ਡਅੱਸਟ) *n v* ਧੂੜ, ਘੱਟਾ, ਮਿੱਟੀ, ਗਰਦਾ, ਖੇਹ, ਕੂੜਾ ਕਰਕਟ; ਫੁੱਲਾਂ ਦਾ ਬੂਰ, ਪਰਾਗਾ, ਕੇਸਰ; ਮਨੁੱਖੀ ਸਰੀਰ, ਗੜਬੜ, ਰੌਲਗੌਲਾ, ਝੰਬੇਲਾ; (ਅਪ) ਧੂੜ ਝਾੜਨਾ, ਸਫ਼ਾਈ ਕਰਨਾ; ਧੂੜ ਪਾਉਣੀ, ਖੇਹ ਉਡਾਉਣਾ, ਮਿੱਟੀਓ-ਮਿੱਟੀ ਕਰਨਾ; ਛਿੜਕਣਾ, ਧੂੜਨਾ; **~bin** ਕੂੜਾਦਾਨ; **~colour** ਹਲਕਾ ਭੂਰਾ; **~er** ਝਾੜਨ, ਪਰੋਲਾ

ਝਾੜਨ ਵਾਲਾ

duty ('ਡਯੂਟਿ) *n* ਫ਼ਰਜ਼, ਕਰਤੱਵ; ਕੰਮ, ਸੇਵਾ, ਫ਼ਰਜ਼ ਦੀ ਅਦਾਇਗੀ; ਇਖ਼ਲਾਕੀ ਪਾਬੰਦੀ; ਮਹਿਸੂਲ, ਚੁੰਗੀ

dwarf (ਡਵੋਰਫ) *n v a* ਬੌਣਾ, ਠਿਗਣਾ, ਗਿਠਮੁੱਠੀਆ, ਨਿੱਕਾ ਬਣਾਉਣਾ ਜਾਂ ਕਰਨਾ; **~ish** ਕੁਝ ਛੋਟਾ, ਬੌਣੇ ਵਰਗਾ, ਨਿੱਕਾ, ਛੁਟੇਰਾ

dwell (ਡਵੈੱਲ) *v* ਰਹਿਣਾ, ਵਸਣਾ, ਰਿਹਾਇਸ਼ ਕਰਨਾ, ਧਿਆਨ ਜਮਾਉਣਾ, ਧਿਆਨ ਕੇਂਦਰਤ ਕਰਨਾ; **~er** ਵਾਸੀ, ਨਿਵਾਸੀ, ਵਸਨੀਕ, ਬਾਸ਼ਿੰਦਾ; **~ing** ਨਿਵਾਸ, ਰਿਹਾਇਸ਼, ਵਾਸਾ, ਵਸੇਬਾ, ਨਿਵਾਸ-ਸਥਾਨ, ਰਿਹਾਇਸ਼ ਦੀ ਜਗ੍ਹਾ

dwindle (ਡਵਿੰਡਲ) *v* ਘੱਟ ਹੋਣਾ, ਘਟਦੇ ਜਾਣਾ, ਸੁੰਗੜਨਾ, ਘੁਲਣਾ; ਢਲਣਾ; ਪਤਲੇ ਹੋਣਾ, ਮਾੜੇ ਪੈਣਾ; ਮਹੱਤਾ ਜਾਂਦੀ ਰਹਿਣੀ, ਸਿਤਾਰਾ ਢਲਣਾ

dye (ਡਾਇ) *n v* ਰੰਗ, ਰੰਗ ਚਾੜ੍ਹਨ ਵਾਲੀ ਚੀਜ਼, ਰੰਗ ਚਾੜ੍ਹਨ ਵਾਲਾ ਮਸਾਲਾ; ਰੰਗਣਾ, ਰੰਗ ਲਾਉਣਾ; **~r** ਲਲਾਰੀ, ਰੰਗਸਾਜ਼, ਰੰਗਰੇਜ਼

dying ('ਡਾਇਇਙ) *n* ਮਰਨ, ਖ਼ਾਤਮਾ, ਅੰਤ

dynamic (ਡਾਇ'ਨੈਮਿਕ) *n a* (ਸੰਚਾਲਕ) ਸ਼ਕਤੀ, ਵੇਗ, ਗਤੀ; ਗਤੀ-ਆਤਮਕ, ਗਤੀਸ਼ੀਲ, ਵੇਗਵਾਨ, ਸ਼ਕਤੀਮਾਨ, ਪ੍ਰਭਾਵਸ਼ੀਲ, ਗਤੀ-ਵਿਗਿਆਨ ਸਬੰਧੀ

dynamite (ਡਾਇਨਅਮਾਇਟ) *v n* ਬਾਰੂਦ ਨਾਲ ਉਡਾਉਣਾ, (ਵਿਸ਼ੇਸ਼ ਪ੍ਰਕਾਰ ਦਾ) ਬਾਰੂਦ

dynasty (ਡਿਨਅਸਟਿ) *n* ਰਾਜਵੰਸ਼, ਸ਼ਾਹੀ ਖ਼ਾਨਦਾਨ, ਸ਼ਾਹੀ ਘਰਾਣਾ

dysentery ('ਡਿਸੰਟਰਿ) *n* ਪੇਚਿਸ, ਮਰੋੜ, ਸੰਗ੍ਰਹਿਣੀ, ਅਤਿਸਾਰ

E

E, e (ਈ) *n* ਰੋਮਨ ਵਰਟਮਾਲਾ ਦਾ ਪੰਜਵਾਂ ਅੱਖਰ

each (ਈਚ) *a pron* ਹਰ, ਹਰ ਇਕ, ਪ੍ਰਤੀ, ਛੀ, ਇਕ ਇਕ, ਹਰੇਕ

eager ('ਈਗਆ*) *a* ਅਭਿਲਾਸ਼ੀ, ਉਤਸ਼ਾਹੀ, ਤਾਂਘੀ, ਜੋਸ਼ੀਲਾ, ਮੁਸ਼ਤਾਕ, ਵਿਆਕੁਲ; **~ness** ਅਭਿਲਾਸ਼ਾ, ਉਤਸ਼ਾਹ, ਰੀਝ, ਤਾਂਘ, ਸਰਗਰਮੀ

eagle ('ਈਗਲ) *n* ਉਕਾਬ, ਸ਼ਾਹੀਨ; **~eyed** ਤੀਖਣ ਦ੍ਰਿਸ਼ਟੀ ਵਾਲਾ, ਬਾਜ਼ ਨਜ਼ਰ

ear (ਇਅ*) *n* ਕੰਨ; ਸੁਣਨ ਦੀ ਯੋਗਤਾ; ਕਟਕ ਜਾਂ ਹੋਰ ਅਨਾਜ ਦੀ ਬੱਲੀ, ਸਿੱਟਾ; **~drum** ਕੰਨਾਂ ਦਾ ਪੜਦਾ; **~ring** ਕੰਨਾਂ ਦੀਆਂ ਵਾਲੀਆਂ, ਮੁੰਦਰਾਂ; **~wax** ਕੰਨਾਂ ਦੀ ਮੈਲ; **give~ to** ਧਿਆਨ ਦੇਣਾ

early ('ਅ:ਲਿ) *a adv* ਅਗੇਤਾ, ਸੁਵੇਲੇ, ਪਹਿਲਾਂ, ਛੇਤੀ; ਆਰੰਭਕ, ਮੁਢਲਾ, ਪੁਰਾਤਨ

earn (ਅ:ਨ) *v* ਖੱਟਣਾ, ਕਮਾਉਣਾ, ਪ੍ਰਾਪਤ ਕਰਨਾ; ਪੈਦਾ ਕਰਨਾ; **~ed** ਕਮਾਇਆ, ਪ੍ਰਾਪਤ; **~ing** ਆਮਦਨੀ, ਕਮਾਈ

earnest ('ਅ:ਨਿਸਟ) *a n* ਗੰਭੀਰ, ਉੱਦਮੀ, ਤੀਬਰ, ਸੱਚਾ; ਗੰਭੀਰਤਾ, ਸਾਂਈ, ਬਿਆਨਾ; **~ly** ਗੰਭੀਰਤਾ ਨਾਲ, ਸੱਚੇ ਦਿਲੋਂ; **~ness** ਗੰਭੀਰਤਾ, ਸੰਜੀਦਗੀ, ਸਚਾਈ

earth (ਅ:ਥ) *n v* ਭੁਇੰ, ਭੋਂ, ਧਰਤੀ, ਜ਼ਮੀਨ, ਪ੍ਰਿਥਵੀ, ਭੂਮੀ, ਖ਼ਾਕ; ਮੁਲਕ, ਦੱਬਣਾ, ਧਰਤੀ ਹੇਠਾਂ ਲੁਕਾਉਣਾ; **~en** ਮਿੱਟੀ ਦਾ ਬਣਿਆ, ਕੱਚਾ, ਮਿਟਿਆਲਾ; **~en ware** ਮਿੱਟੀ ਦੇ ਭਾਂਡੇ; **~quake** ਭੁਚਾਲ, ਭੂ-ਕੰਪ

ease (ਈਜ਼) *n v* ਸੌਖ, ਆਰਾਮ, ਤਸਕੀਨ; ਸੁਖ ਦੇਣਾ, ਸੌਖੇ ਹੋਣਾ, ਸੁਸਤਾਉਣਾ, ਢਿੱਲਾ ਕਰਨਾ; **stand at~** (ਸੈਨਕ ਆਦੇਸ਼) ਸੌਖੇ ਖੜੋਵੋ! **~ness** ਸੁਗਮਤਾ, ਸੁਖੈਨਤਾ, ਸੌਖ, ਸਰਲਤਾ; ਚੈਨ, ਸੁਖ

east (ਈਸਟ) *n a adv* ਪੂਰਬ, ਪੂਰਬ ਕੇ ਦੇਸ਼, ਚੜ੍ਹਦਾ ਪਾਸਾ; **~ern** ਪੂਰਬੀਆ, ਪੂਰਬੀ

easter (ਈਸਟ*) *n* ਇਸਾਈਆਂ ਦਾ ਤਿਉਹਾਰ, ਹਜ਼ਰਤ ਈਸਾ ਦਾ ਮੁੜ ਜੀਵਤ ਹੋਣ ਦਾ ਦਿਵਸ

easy ('ਈਜ਼ੀ) *a n adv* ਸੌਖਾ, ਸੁਖਾਲਾ, ਸੁਖੈਨ, ਸਹਿਲਾ, ਸਹਿਲ, ਸੁਗਮ; ਸੁਖੀ, ਸੁਖਾਵਾਂ; ਸੁਖਦਾਈ, ਬੇਫ਼ਿਕਰ; ਉਹ ਜਿਨਸ ਜਿਸ ਦੀ ਮੰਗ ਘੱਟ ਹੋਵੇ; ਆਸਾਨੀ ਨਾਲ, ਸਰਲਤਾ ਨਾਲ ਸੁਵਿਧਾਪੂਰਵਕ; **~chair** ਆਰਾਮ ਕੁਰਸੀ; **~going** ਸੁੱਖ ਰਹਿਣਾ, ਆਰਾਮ ਤਲਬ; **take it~** ਘਬਰਾਓ ਨਹੀਂ, ਤਸੱਲੀ ਰੱਖੋ

eat (ਈਟ) *v* ਖਾਣਾ, ਚੱਥਣਾ, ਨਿਗਲਣਾ, ਹਜ਼ਮ ਕਰਨਾ; **~away** ਖਾ ਜਾਣਾ; **~humble pie** ਜ਼ਲੀਲ ਹੋਣਾ; **~one's heart out** ਅੰਦਰ-ਅੰਦਰ ਕੁੜ੍ਹਨਾ; **~able** ਖਾਧ-ਪਦਾਰਥ; **~inghouse** ਢਾਬਾ, ਅੰਨਪੂਰਨਾ

eccentric (ਇਕ'ਸੈਂਟਰਿਕ) *n a* ਵਿਕੇਂਦਰੀ ਚੱਕਰ, ਅਕੇਂਦਰੀ; ਖਬਤੀ, ਵਹਿਮੀ, ਵਚਿੱਤਰ

echo ('ਐਕਅਉ) *n v* ਗੂੰਜ, ਧੁਨੀ, ਪ੍ਰਤੀਧੁਨੀ; ਗੂੰਜਣਾ, ਗੂੰਜਾਉਣਾ

eclipse (ਇ'ਕਲਿਪਸ) *n v* ਗ੍ਰਹਿਣ; ਤੇਜ ਘਟਾਉਣਾ, ਮਾਣ ਘਟਾਉਣਾ

ecological ('ਇਕਅ'ਲੌਜਿਕਲ) *a* ਪਰਿਆਵਰਤਕ

ecology (ਈ'ਕੌਲਅਜਿ) *n* ਵਾਤਾਵਰਣ ਵਿਗਿਆਨ, ਪਰਿਆਵਰਤ ਵਿਗਿਆਨ

economic ('ਈਕਅੱਨੌਮਿਕ) *a* ਆਰਥਕ, ਕਿਫ਼ਾਇਤੀ, ਮਾਲੀ ਲਾਭਦਾਇਕ; ~al ਸਸਤਾ; ~s ਅਰਥ-ਸ਼ਾਸਤਰ

economist (ਇ'ਕੌਨਮਿਸਟ) *n* ਅਰਥ-ਸ਼ਾਸਤਰੀ, ਅਰਥ-ਵਿਗਿਆਨੀ

economize (ਇ'ਕੌਨਮਾਇਜ਼) *v* ਬਚਾਉਣਾ, ਬੱਚਤ ਕਰਨਾ, ਸੰਜਮ ਕਰਨਾ

economy (ਇ'ਕੌਨਮੀ) *n* ਅਰਥ-ਪ੍ਰਬੰਧ, ਆਰਥਕ ਦਸ਼ਾ, ਬੱਚਤ

ecstasy ('ਐਕਸਟਅਸੀ) *n* ਉਤਸਾਹ, ਤਰੰਗ, ਪਰਮਾਨੰਦ

ecstatic (ਇਕ'ਸਟੈਟਿਕ) *a* ਉਤਸਾਹਪੂਰਨ, ਮਸਤ, ਤਰੰਗਮਈ

edacious (ਇ'ਡੇਇਸ਼ਅਸ) *a* ਖਾਊ-ਪੀਊ, ਪੇਟੂ, ਲਾਲਚੀ, ਭੁੱਖੜ, ਲੋਭੀ

edacity (ਇ'ਡੈਸਅਟਿ) *n* ਭੁੱਖਾਪਣ, ਲਾਲਚੀਪਣ, ਪੇਟੂਪਣ

edge (ਐੱਜ) *n v* ਹਾਸ਼ੀਅ; ਝਾਲਰ; ਦੌਰ, ਕੰਢਾ, ਧਾਰ, ਕਿਨਾਰਾ; ਹਾਸ਼ੀਆ ਲਾਉਣਾ, ਧਾਰ ਬਣਾਉਣਾ; ਕੰਨੀ ਕਤਰ ਕੇ ਟੁਰਨਾ, ਤਰਕਾਉਣਾ, ਉਕਸਾਉਣਾ ~d ਤਿੱਖਾ; ਕਿਨਾਰੇਦਾਰ ~less ਖੁੰਢਾ, ਕੁੰਠਤ

edible ('ਐੱਡਿਬਲ) *a* ਖਾਣਯੋਗ, ਸੁਆਦਲਾ

edify ('ਐੱਡਿਫ਼ਾਇ) *v* (ਜੀਵਾਂ ਦਾ) ਉਦਾਰ ਕਰਨਾ, ਸਿੱਖਿਆ ਦੇਣੀ, ਚਿਤਾਰਣਾ; ~ing ਗਿਆਨ-ਵਰਧਕ, ਉਪਦੇਸ਼ਕ

edit ('ਐੱਡਿਟ) *v* ਸੰਪਾਦਨ ਕਰਨਾ, ਕਾਟ ਛਾਂਟ ਕਰਨਾ; ~ing ਸੰਪਾਦਨ; ~ion ਸੰਸਕਰਨ, ਸੰਪਾਦਨ, ਜਿਲਦ, ਪ੍ਰਕਾਸ਼ਨ; ~or ਸੰਪਾਦਕ; ~orial ਸੰਪਾਦਕੀ

educand ('ਐੱਜੁਕਅੰਡ) *n* ਚੇਲਾ, ਸ਼ਿਸ਼,

ਸਿੱਖਿਆਰਥੀ

educate ('ਐੱਜੁਕੇਇਟ) *v* ਸਿਖਾਉਣਾ, ਪੜ੍ਹਾਉਣਾ, ਵਿੱਦਿਆ ਦੇਣਾ; ~d ਸਿੱਖਿਅਤ, ਸਿਖਾਇਆ, ਪੜ੍ਹਿਆ-ਲਿਖਿਆ

education ('ਐੱਜ'ਕੇਇਸ਼ਨ) *n* ਸਿੱਖਿਆ, ਪੜ੍ਹਾਈ-ਲਿਖਾਈ; ~al ਸਿੱਖਿਆ ਸਬੰਧੀ, ਵਿੱਦਿਅਕ

educator ('ਐੱਜੁਕੇਟਾ*) *n* ਸਿੱਖਿਅਕ, ਅਧਿਆਪਕ

efface (ਇ'ਫ਼ੇਇਸ) *v* ਮੇਸਣਾ, ਮਾਤ ਪਾਉਣਾ, ਕਲਮ ਫੇਰਨੀ; ਮਲੀਆਮੇਟ ਕਰਨਾ, ਨੇਸਤੇ-ਨਾਬੂਦ ਕਰਨਾ, ਭੁਲਾ ਦੇਣਾ; ~ment ਮਲੀਆ-ਮੇਟ, ਨੇਸਤੇ-ਨਾਬੂਦ, ਫ਼ਨਾ, ਨਾਸ

effect (ਇ'ਫ਼ੈੱਕਟ) *n v* ਸਿੱਟਾ, ਫਲ, ਅਸਰ; ਤਾਸੀਰ, ਨਤੀਜਾ, ਕਮਾਲ, ਉਦੇਸ਼, ਮਾਲ, ਵਸਤੂ; ਕਰ ਦਿਖਾਉਣਾ, ਪੂਰਾ ਕਰਨਾ, ਪੈਦਾ ਕਰਨਾ; ~ive ਪ੍ਰਭਾਵਸ਼ਾਲੀ, ਕਾਰਗਰ, ਸਾਰਥਕ; ਸ਼ਕਤੀਮਾਨ; ਅਸਰਦਾਰ

efficiency (ਇ'ਫ਼ਿਸ਼ਅੰਸੀ) *n* ਸਮਰੱਥਾ, ਕੁਸ਼ਲਤਾ, ਨਿਪੁੰਨਤਾ, ਯੋਗਤਾ, ਕਮਾਲ ਕਾਬਲੀਅਤ

efficient (ਇ'ਫ਼ਿਸ਼ਅੰਟ) *a* ਸਮਰੱਥ, ਨਿਪੁੰਨ, ਪ੍ਰਵੀਨ, ਗੁਣਕਾਰੀ, ਲਾਇਕ, ਕਾਮਲ

effigy ('ਐੱਫ਼ਿਜਿ) *n* ਪੁਤਲਾ, ਗੁੱਡਾ, ਮੂਰਤੀ

effloresce (ਐੱਫ਼ਲੋ'ਰੈੱਸ) *v* ਕਲੀਆਂ ਖਿੜਨੀਆਂ, ਫੁੱਲਣਾ, ਜੋਬਨ ਤੇ ਆ ਜਾਣਾ; ~nce (ਫੁੱਲਾਂ ਦਾ) ਖੇੜਾ, ਖਿੜਨ, ਸ਼ਗੁਫ਼ਤਗੀ; ~nt ਖਿੜਿਆ, ਫੁੱਲਾਂ ਲੱਦਿਆ

effluence (ਐੱਫ਼ਲੂਅੰਸ) *n* ਨਿਕਾਸ, ਬਹਾਉ, ਹੌਂ

effort (ਐੱਫ਼ਅ*ਟ) *n* ਜਤਨ, ਘਾਲ, ਕੋਸ਼ਸ਼, ਨੱਠ-ਭੱਜ, ਸਰਗਰਮੀ

egalitarian (ਇ'ਗੈਲਿ'ਟੇਅਰਿਅਨ) *a* ਸਮਾਨਤਾਵਾਦੀ

egg (ਐੱਗ) *n v* ਅੰਡਾ, ਆਂਡਾ; ਚੁੱਕਣਾ, ਉਕਸਾਉਣਾ; **in the~** ਗਰਭ ਵਿਚ, ਸ਼ੁਰੂ ਦੀ ਹਾਲਤ ਵਿਚ

ego ('ਐੱਗਅਉ) *n* ਆਪਾ, ਅਹੰ, ਖ਼ੁਦੀ, ਹਉਸੈ, ਅਹੰਕਾਰ; **~ism** ਅਹੰਕਾਰਵਾਦ, ਹਉਮੈਵਾਦ, ਅਹੰਵਾਦ; **~ist** ਅਹੰਕਾਰੀ, ਹਉਮੈਵਾਦੀ, ਖ਼ੁਦਗਰਜ਼

either ('ਆਇਦਆ*) *pron a adv* ਜਾਂ ਤਾਂ, ਭਾਵੇਂ, ਇਹ, ਇਕ ਤਾਂ, ਦੋ ਵਿਚੋਂ ਇਕ, ਕੋਈ ਇਕ; ਦੋਹਾਂ ਹਾਲਤਾਂ ਵਿਚ

ejaculate (ਇ'ਜੈਕਯੂਲੇਇਟ) *v* ਛੁਟਣਾ, ਖ਼ਲਾਸ ਕਰਨਾ, ਛੁੱਟ ਪੈਣਾ, ਬੋਲ ਉੱਠਣਾ, ਜਪਣਾ, ਬਾਹਰ ਕੱਢਣਾ

ejaculation (ਇ'ਜੈਕਯੂ'ਲੇਇਸ਼ਨ) *n* ਬਾਹਰ ਨਿਕਲਣ, ਛੁਟਣ

eject (ਇ'ਜੈਕਟ, 'ਈਜੈਕਟ) *v n* ਬਾਹਰ ਕੱਢਣਾ; ਬੇਦਖ਼ਲ ਕਰਨਾ, ਖ਼ਾਰਜ ਕਰਨਾ, ਹਟਾ ਦੇਣਾ; **~ion** ਕਢਾਈ, ਬੇਦਖ਼ਲੀ, ਹੁਕਮਨਾਮਾ ਬੇਦਖ਼ਲੀ, ਦੇਸ਼-ਨਿਕਾਲਾ, ਜਲਾਵਤਨੀ; **~ment** ਬੇਦਖ਼ਲੀ

elaborate (ਇ'ਲੈਬ(ਅ)ਰਅਟ, ਇ'ਲੈਬਅਰੇਇਟ) *a v* ਵਿਸਤਰਤ; ਜਟਲ, ਵਿਸਤਾਰ ਸਹਿਤ ਦੱਸਣਾ

elaboration (ਇ'ਲੈਬਅ'ਰੇਇਸ਼ਨ) *n* ਵਿਸਤਾਰ, ਸੰਪੰਨਤਾ

elastic (ਇ'ਲੈਸਟਿਕ) *a* ਲਚਕਵਾਂ, ਢਿਲਕਵਾਂ, ਮੌਜੀ, ਤਰੰਗੀ; ਲਚਕਦਾਰ, ਲਚਕੀਲਾ

elasticity ('ਇਲ'ਸਟਿਸਅਟਿ) *n* ਲਚਕ, ਅਨੁਕੂਲਣ-ਸ਼ੀਲਤਾ

elbow ('ਐੱਲਬਅਉ) *n* ਕੁਹਣੀ, ਅਰਕ, ਕੁਹਣੀ-ਮੋੜ; ਕੁਹਣੀ ਮਾਰਨੀ, ਘੁਸੜਨਾ, ਹੂਝ ਮਾਰਨਾ; **at one's~** ਕੋਲ ਹੀ, ਨੇੜੇ ਹੀ

elder *a n* ਵਡੇਰਾ (ਆਦਮੀ), ਵੱਡ-ਵਡੇਰਾ, ਵਡਿਕਾ; ਬਜ਼ੁਰਗਾ; **~erly** ਬੁੱਢਾ, ਵੱਡੀ ਉਮਰ

ਦਾ, ਪੁਰਾਣੇ ਸਮੇਂ ਦਾ

El Dorado (ਐੱਲਡਆ'ਰਾਡਅਉ) *n* ਸਵਰਨ-ਭੂਮੀ, ਸੋਨ ਨਗਰੀ; ਸੋਨੇ ਦੀ ਕਲਪਤ ਨਗਰੀ

elect (ਇ'ਲੈੱਕਟ) *v* ਚੁਣ ਲੈਣਾ, ਚੁਣਨਾ, ਚੋਣ ਕਰਨੀ; ਚੋਣਵਾਂ, ਚੁਣਵਾਂ, ਵਧੀਆ; ਨਾਮਜ਼ਦ; **~ed** ਚੁਣਿਆ, ਨਿਰਵਚਤ

election (ਇ'ਲੈੱਕਸ਼ਨ) *n* ਚੋਣ, ਨਿਰਵਾਚਨ

electoral (ਇ'ਲੈੱਕਟ(ਅ)ਰ(ਅ)ਲ) *a* ਚੋਣ-ਸਬੰਧੀ, ਨਿਰਵਾਚਨ

electorate (ਇ'ਲੈੱਕਟ(ਓ)ਰਅਟ) *n a* ਚੋਣ-ਹਲਕਾ, ਚੋਣ ਖੇਤਰ; ਚੋਣਕਾਰ, ਵੋਟਰ

electric (ਇ'ਲੈੱਕਟਰਿਕ) *n* ਬਿਜਲੀ; ਬਿਜਲੀ ਦਾ, ਬਿਜਲੀ ਨਾਲ ਸਬੰਧਤ; **~al** ਬਿਜਲਈ; ਦਾਮਨਿਕ, ਬਰਕੀ; **~ity** ਬਿਜਲੀ, ਦਾਮਨੀ, ਬਰਕ

electrification (ਇ'ਲੈੱਕਟਰਿਫ਼ਿ'ਕੇਇਸ਼ਨ) *n* ਬਿਜਲੀਕਰਨ

electrify (ਇ'ਲੈੱਕਟਰਿਫ਼ਾਇ) *v* ਬਿਜਲੀ ਪਹੁੰਚਾਉਣੀ; ਉਤੇਜਤ ਕਰਨਾ

electrocute (ਇ'ਲੈੱਕਟਰਅਕਯੂਟ) *n* ਬਿਜਲੀ ਨਾਲ ਮਰਨਾ

electrocution (ਇ'ਲੈੱਕਟਰਅ'ਕਯੂਸ਼ਨ) *n* ਬਿਜਲੀ ਦੁਆਰਾ ਮੌਤ

elegance, elegancy ('ਐੱਲਿਗਅੰਸ, ਐੱਲਿਗਅੰਸਿ) *n* ਛਬ, ਸ਼ਾਨ, ਸ਼ੋਭਾ, ਠਾਠ-ਬਾਠ

elegant ('ਐੱਲਿਗਅੰਟ) *a* ਛਬੀਲਾ, ਸ਼ਾਨਦਾਰ

element ('ਐੱਲਿਮਅੰਟ) *n* ਤੱਤ, ਸਾਰ, ਸਾਰ-ਤੱਤ, ਅੰਸ਼, ਹਿੱਸਾ, ਮੂਲ, ਅਸਲਾ; **~ary** ਮੁੱਢਲਾ, ਆਧਾਰੀ, ਮੂਲ, ਆਰੰਭਕ, ਮੌਲਕ

elephant ('ਐੱਲਿਫ਼ਅੰਟ) *n* ਹਾਥੀ, ਪੀਲ ਜਾਂ ਫ਼ੀਲ, ਗਜ; **~driver** ਮਹਾਵਤ

elevate (ਐੱਲਿਵੇਇਟ) *v* ਉਚਿਆਉਣਾ,

ਵਡਿਆਉਣਾ, ਉੱਚਾ ਚੁੱਕਣਾ; ਪਦਵੀ ਉੱਚੀ
ਕਰਨੀ, ਤਰੱਕੀ ਦੇਣੀ

elevation ('ਐਲਿ'ਵੇਇਸ਼ਨ) *n* ਉਚਾਈ, ਵਡਿਆਈ,
ਉਚਾਣ, ਬੁਲੰਦੀ; **~d** ਉੱਨਤ, ਉੱਚ ਉਥਾਪਤ

elevator (ਐਲਿਵੇਇਟਰਅ*) *n* ਉੱਚਾ ਚੁੱਕਣ ਵਾਲਾ
ਲਿਫਟ

eleven (ਇ'ਲੈੱਵਨ) *a n* ਗਿਆਰਾਂ, ਇਕਾਦਸ਼,
ਯਾਰਾਂ; **~th** ਗਿਆਰਵਾਂ, ਯਾਰ੍ਹਵਾਂ

elf (ਐਲਫ਼) *n* ਪਰੇਤ, ਛਲੇਡਾ, ਪਰੀ, ਜਿਨ੍ਹਰਾ; ਬੌਣਾ

elicit (ਇ'ਲਿਸਿਟ) *v* ਕਢਵਾ ਲੈਣਾ, ਗੱਲ ਕਢਵਾ
ਲੈਣੀ, ਸਿੱਟਾ ਕੱਢਣਾ

eligibility ('ਐਲਿਜਅ'ਬਿਲਅਟਿ) *n* ਪਾਤਰਤਾ,
ਹੱਕ, ਯੋਗਤਾ, ਕਾਬਲੀਅਤ

eligible ('ਐਲਿਜਅਬਲ) *a* ਪਾਤਰ, ਲਾਇਕ

eleminate (ਇ'ਲੀਮਿਨੇਇਟ) *v* ਕੱਢ ਦੇਣਾ, ਕੱਟ
ਦੇਣਾ, ਕੱਢਾ ਕੱਢ ਦੇਣਾ, ਵਿਚੋਂ ਕੱਢਣਾ, ਖ਼ਾਰਜ
ਕਰਨਾ

elimination (ਇ'ਲਿਮਿਨੇਸ਼ਨ) *n* ਨਿਕਾਸ, ਲੋਪ

elision (ਇ'ਲਿਯ਼ਨ) *n* ਛੋਟ, ਲੋਪ, ਅੱਖਰ-ਲੋਪ,
ਸਵਰ-ਲੋਪ

elite (ਏਇ'ਲੀਟ) (*F*) *n* ਸ਼੍ਰੇਸ਼ਠ ਵਰਗ

elixir (ਇ'ਲਿਕਸਅ*) *n* ਸੰਜੀਵਨੀ, ਅਕਸੀਰ,
ਸ਼ਰਬਤ

elk (ਐਲਕ) *n* ਬਾਰਾਸਿੰਗਾ

elocution ('ਐਲਅ'ਕਯ਼ੁਸ਼ਨ) *n* ਭਾਸ਼ਣਕਲਾ,
ਭਾਸ਼ਣ-ਕਾਰੀ; **~ary** ਸੁਵਕਤਤਾ

elongate ('ਈਲੋਙਗੋਇਟ) *v* ਵਧਾਉਣਾ,
ਫੈਲਾਉਣਾ, ਲੰਬਾ ਕਰਨਾ, ਪਤਲਾ ਹੋਣਾ; **~d**
ਬਿਆਇਆ, ਦੀਰਘਕ੍ਰਿਤ, ਪਰਸਾਰਿਆ

elongation ('ਇਲੋਙ'ਗੋਇਸ਼ਨ) *n* ਫੈਲਾਉ,
ਲੰਬਾਨ, ਖਿਚਾਉ, ਵਿਸਤਰਤੀ

elope (ਇ'ਲਅਉਪ) *v* ਉੱਧਲਣਾ, ਲੋਪ ਹੋਣਾ,
ਚੋਰੀ ਭੱਜ ਨਿਕਲਣਾ, ਫ਼ਰਾਰ ਹੋਣਾ; **~ment**
ਉਧਾਲਾ

eloquence ('ਐਲਅਕਵਅੰਸ) *a* ਸੁਭਾਸ਼ਤਾ, ਖ਼ੁਸ਼-
ਬਿਆਨੀ

eloquent ('ਐਲਅ'ਕਵਅੰਟ) *a* ਸੁਭਾਸ਼ੀਆ, ਖ਼ੁਸ਼-
ਬਿਆਨ

else (ਐਲਸ) *adv* ਕੋਈ ਹੋਰ, ਹੋਰ ਭੀ, ਪਰ ਨਹੀਂ
ਤਾਂ, ਵਰਨਾ, ਜਾਂ; **~where** ਹੋਰ ਤਾਂ, ਦੂਜੇ ਢੰਗ
ਨਾਲ; **~wise** ਨਹੀਂ ਤਾਂ, ਦੂਜੇ ਢੰਗ ਨਾਲ;
what~ ਹੋਰ ਕੀ?

elucidate (ਇ'ਲੂਸਿਡੇਇਟ) *v* ਵਿਆਖਿਆ
ਕਰਨੀ, ਸਪਸ਼ਟੀਕਰਨ ਕਰਨਾ; ਚਾਨਣ ਪਾਉਣਾ

elucidation (ਇ'ਲੂਸਿਡੇਇਸ਼ਨ) *n* ਵਿਆਖਿਆ,
ਵਿਸਤਾਰ, ਸਪਸ਼ਟੀਕਰਨ, ਵਿਵਰਨ

elucidative, elucidatory (ਇ'ਲੂਸਿਡੇਇਟਿਵ੍,
ਇ'ਲੂਸਿਡੇਇਟ(ਅ)ਰਿ) *a* ਵਿਆਖਿਆਤਮਕ,
ਵਿਸਤਰਤ, ਸਪਸ਼ਟੀਕ੍ਰਿਤ

elude (ਇ'ਲੂਡ) *v* ਖਿਸਕ ਜਾਣਾ, ਟਾਲ ਜਾਣਾ,
ਅੱਖ ਬਚਾ ਕੇ ਨਿਕਲ ਜਾਣਾ, ਬਚ ਨਿਕਲਣਾ

elusion (ਇ'ਲੂਯ਼ਨ) *n* ਘੁਸਾਈ, ਅੱਖ ਬਚਾਈ,
ਧੋਖਾ, ਮੁਗਾਲਤਾ

elusive (ਇ'ਲੂਸਿਵ੍) *a* ਹੱਥ ਨਾ ਆਉਣ ਵਾਲਾ,
ਤਿਲਕਵਾਂ; **~ness** ਕਪਟ; ਛਲ, ਭਰਾਂਤੀ;
ਬਚਾਉ

emaciate (ਇ'ਮੇਇਸ਼ਿਏਇਟ) *v a* ਲਿੱਸਾ ਹੋਣਾ,
ਨਿਰਬਲ ਹੋਣਾ, ਸੁੱਕਣਾ, ਘੁਲਣਾ, ਕਮਜ਼ੋਰ ਪੈਣਾ;
ਨਿਰਬਲ, ਦੁਬਲਾ-ਪਤਲਾ, ਸੁੱਕਿਆ, ਕਮਜ਼ੋਰ

emaciation (ਇ'ਮੇਸ਼ਿ'ਏਇਸ਼ਨ) *n* ਨਿਰਬਲਤਾ
ਦੁਬਲਾਪਨ, ਨਿਤਾਂਤੀ, ਸਿਥਲਤਾ, ਕਮਜ਼ੋਰੀ

emaculate (ਇ'ਮੈਕਯੁਲੇਇਟ) *v* ਦਾਗ਼

ਹਟਾਉਣਾ, ਧੱਬਾ ਹਟਾਉਣਾ (ਚਿਹਰੇ ਤੋਂ)

emancipate ('ਇ'ਮੈਂਸਪੇਇਟ) *v* ਛੁਡਾਉਣਾ, ਸੁਤੰਤਰ ਕਰਵਾਉਣਾ; ਬਰੀ ਕਰਨਾ, ਛੁਟਕਾਰਾ ਦੇਣਾ, ਨਿਸਤਾਰਾ ਕਰਨਾ

emancipation (ਇ'ਮੈਂਸਿ'ਪੇਇਸ਼ਨ) *n* ਮੁਕਤੀ, ਛੁਟਕਾਰਾ, ਨਿਸਤਾਰਾ, ਖ਼ਲਾਸੀ, ਨਿਜਾਤ

emancipatory (ਇ'ਮੈਂਸਿ'ਪੇਇਟਅਰਿ) *a* ਮੁਕਤੀ-ਸਬੰਧੀ, ਛੁਟਕਾਰੇ-ਸਬੰਧੀ, ਉਧਾਰਕ

emasculate (ਇ'ਮੈਸਕਯੁਲਿਟ, ਇ'ਮੈਸਕਯੁਲੇਇਟ) *a* ਖੱਸੀ; ਹਿਜੜਾ, ਨਾਮਰਦ; ਨਪੁੰਸਕ, ਨਿਤਾਣਾ; ਖੱਸੀ ਕਰਨਾ, ਨਸੁੰਪਕ ਕਰਨਾ; ਕਮਜ਼ੋਰ ਕਰਨਾ, ਨਿਤਾਣਾ ਕਰਨਾ

emasculation (ਇ'ਮੈਸਕਯੁ'ਲੇਇਸ਼ਨ) *n* ਖੱਸੀਪੁਣਾ, ਨਪੁੰਸਕਤਾ, ਨਿਤਾਣਤਾ, ਨਾਮਰਦੀ

embalm (ਇਮ'ਬਾਮ) *v* ਲਾਸ਼ ਨੂੰ ਸੁਰੱਖਿਅਤ ਰੱਖਣ ਲਈ ਮਸਾਲੇ ਲਾਉਣੇ; ਸੁਗੰਧਿਤ ਕਰਨਾ, ਸੁਰੱਖਿਅਤ

embank (ਇਮ'ਬੈਂਕ) *n* ਬੰਨ੍ਹ ਬੰਨ੍ਹਣਾ; ਪਟੜੀ ਬੰਨ੍ਹਣੀ, ਦਰੇਸੀ ਬਣਾਉਣੀ; ~ment ਬੰਨ੍ਹ, ਪਟੜੀ, ਦਰੇਸੀ

embargo (ਐਮ'ਬਾਅਗੋ) *n v* ਵਪਾਰ ਦੀ ਮਨਾਹੀ, ਨਾਕਾਬੰਦੀ; ਅਧਿਕਾਰ ਵਿਚ ਲੈਣਾ, ਨਾਕਾਬੰਦੀ ਕਰਨਾ

embarrass (ਇ'ਮਬੈਰਅਸ) *v* ਪਰੇਸ਼ਾਨੀ ਵਿਚ ਪਾਉਣਾ; ਉਲਝਾਉਣਾ, ਪਰੇਸ਼ਾਨ ਕਰਨਾ, ਭੇੜਾ ਪਾਉਣਾ; ~ing ਪਰੇਸ਼ਾਨਕਾਰੀ; ~ment ਉਲਝਣ, ਅੜਿੱਕਾ, ਪਸ਼ੇਮਾਨੀ, ਘਬਰਾਹਟ

embassy ('ਐਮਬਅਸਿ) *n* ਸਿਫ਼ਾਰਤਖ਼ਾਨਾ, ਦੂਤਾਵਾਸ, ਸਿਫ਼ਾਰਤ

embellish (ਇਮ'ਬੈਲਿਸ਼) *v* ਸ਼ਿੰਗਾਰਨਾ, ਸਜਾਉਣਾ

embezzie (ਇਮ'ਬੈਂਜ਼ਲ) *v* ਗਬਨ ਕਰਨਾ, ਖੁਰਦ-ਬੁਰਦ ਕਰਨਾ, ਘਾਲਾ-ਮਾਲਾ ਕਰਨਾ, ਗੋਲ-ਮਾਲ ਕਰਨਾ

emblem ('ਐਮਬਲਅਮ) *v n* ਨਿਸ਼ਾਨ, ਚਿੰਨ੍ਹ, ਅਲਾਮਤ; ਨਿਸ਼ਾਨ ਬਣਾਉਣਾ, ਪ੍ਰਤੀਕ ਰਾਹੀਂ ਪਰਗਟ ਕਰਨਾ

embodiment (ਇਮ'ਬੋਡਿਮਅੰਟ) *n* ਸਾਕਾਰ ਰੂਪ; ਪ੍ਰਤੱਖ ਰੂਪ, ਸਾਖਿਆਤ ਦਰਸ਼ਨ, ਰੂਪ, ਪੁੰਜ

embody (ਇਮ'ਬੋਡ਼ਿ) *v* ਸਾਕਾਰ ਕਰਨਾ, ਰੂਪ ਦੇਣਾ; ਨਿਰੂਪਣ ਕਰਨਾ, ਸ਼ਾਮਲ ਕਰਨਾ; ਵਿਚਾਰ ਨੂੰ ਪਰਗਟ ਰੂਪ ਦੇਣਾ, ਅਸੂਲ ਨੂੰ ਅਮਲ ਵਿਚ ਲਿਆਉਣਾ

embrace (ਇਮ'ਬਰੇਇਸ) *v n* ਜੱਫੀ ਪਾਉਣੀ, ਗਲ ਲਾਉਣਾ; ਧਾਰਨ ਕਰਨਾ, ਗ੍ਰਹਿਣ ਕਰਨਾ; ਜੱਫੀ, ਗਲਵੱਕੜੀ; ਧਾਰਨਾ

emerge (ਇ'ਮਅਃਜ) *v* ਫੁੱਟਣਾ, ਉਤਰਨਾ, ਪਰਗਟ ਹੋਣਾ; ~nce ਨਿਕਾਸ, ਉਭਾਰ, ਉਗਮਣ, ਪਰਗਟਾਉ

emergency (ਇਮਅਃਜਅੰਸੀ) *n* ਸੰਕਟ, ਔਖਾ ਸਮਾਂ, ਅਪਾਤਕਾਲ, ਇਤਫ਼ਾਕਿਆ ਲੋੜ

emeritus (ਇ'ਮੈੱਟਿਅਸ) *a* ਸਨਮਾਨਤ ਪੈਨਸ਼ਨ ਪ੍ਰਾਪਤ, ਸੇਵਾਮੁਕਤ, ਅਵਕਾਸ਼ ਪ੍ਰਾਪਤ (ਅਧਿਆਪਕ)

emigrant ('ਐਮਿਗਰਅੰਟ) *a n* ਪਰਵਾਸੀ, ਪਰਦੇਸ ਵਾਸੀ

emigration ('ਐਮਿ'ਗਰੇਇਸ਼ਨ) *n* ਪਰਵਾਸ, ਹਿਜਰਤ, ਜਲਾਵਤਨ

eminence ('ਐਮਿਨਅੰਸ) *n* ਸਿਖਰ, ਟਿੱਲਾ, ਉਚਾਈ; ਮਹਾਨਤਾ; ਵਡਿਆਈ; ਨਾਮਵਰੀ; ਗੌਰਵ; ਪ੍ਰਸਿੱਧੀ, ਸ੍ਰੇਸ਼ਠਤਾ

eminent ('ਐਮਿਨਅੰਟ) *a* ਉੱਚ ਕੋਟੀ ਦਾ, ਪ੍ਰਤਾਪੀ,

ਮਹਾਨ, ਉੱਚਾ; ਬੁਲੰਦ, ਮੁਮਤਾਜ਼; ਨੁਮਾਇਆਂ, ਪ੍ਰਸਿੱਧ, ਗੌਰਵਸ਼ਾਲੀ

emissary ('ਐੱਮਿਸ(ਅ)ਰਿ) *n* ਦੂਤ, ਕਾਸਦ, ਸਫ਼ੀਰ, ਏਲਚੀ

emission (ਇ'ਮਿਸ਼ਨ) *n* ਨਿਕਾਸ, ਉਦਗਾਰ, (ਮਨੋ) ਸੁਪਨ-ਦੇਸ਼

emit (ਇ'ਮਿਟ) *v* (ਪ੍ਰਕਾਸ਼ ਦੀਆਂ ਕਿਰਨਾਂ) ਛੱਡਣਾ, ਕੱਢਣਾ

emolument (ਇ'ਮੋਲਯੁਮੰਟ) *n* ਵੇਤਨ, ਤਨਖ਼ਾਹ, ਤਲਬ

emotion (ਇ'ਮਅਉਸ਼ਨ) *n* ਤਰੰਗ, ਭਾਵ, ਵਲਵਲਾ, ਜਜ਼ਬਾ, ਜੋਸ਼, ਉਤੇਜਨਾ, ਸੰਵੇਗ; ~al ਭਾਵੁਕ, ਉਤੇਜਤ, ਭਾਵਪੂਰਨ

emotive (ਇ'ਮਅਉਟਿਵ) *a* ਭਾਵਾਤਮਕ

empathy ('ਐੱਮਪਅਥਿ) *n* (ਦਰਸ਼) ਹਮਦਰਦੀ, ਸਹਾਨੁਭੂਤੀ

emperor ('ਐੱਮਪ(ਅ)ਰਅ*) *n* ਸਮਰਾਟ, ਸ਼ਹਿਨਸ਼ਾਹ, ਸੁਲਤਾਨ, ਬਾਦਸ਼ਾਹ

emphasis ('ਐੱਮਫ਼ਅਸਿਸ) *n* ਬਲ, ਜ਼ੋਰ

emphasize ('ਐੱਮਫ਼ਅਸਾਇਜ਼) *v* ਜ਼ੋਰ ਦੇਣਾ, ਦਬਾਉ ਦੇਣਾ

emphatic (ਇਮ'ਫ਼ੈਟਿਕ) *a* ਜ਼ੋਰਦਾਰ, ਪ੍ਰਭਾਵਸ਼ਾਲੀ, ਦਿੜ੍ਹ; (ਵਿਆ) ਦਬਾਵਾਚਕ

empire ('ਐੱਮਪਾਇਅ*) *n* ਸਾਮਰਾਜ, ਸਲਤਨਤ, ਬਾਦਸ਼ਾਹੀ

empiric (ਇਮ'ਪਿਰਿਕ) *a n* ਅਮਲੀ, ਪ੍ਰਯੋਗਕ; ਸਿਖਾਂਦਰੂ, ਵੈਦਜ਼ਾ, ਨੀਮ-ਹਕੀਮ; ~al ਅਨੁਭਾਵਕ, ਅਨੁਭਵਵਾਦੀ, ਪ੍ਰਯੋਗ-ਸਿੱਧ

emplane (ਇਮ'ਪਲੇਇਨ) *v* ਹਵਾਈ ਜਹਾਜ਼ ਵਿਚ ਸਵਾਰ ਹੋਣਾ ਜਾਂ ਮਾਲ ਲੱਦਣਾ

employ (ਇਮ'ਪਲੋਇ) *v* ਭਰਤੀ ਕਰਨਾ, ਕੰਮ ਦੇਣਾ,

ਰੁਜ਼ਗਾਰ ਉੱਤੇ ਲਾਉਣਾ; ਪ੍ਰਯੋਗ ਕਰਨਾ, ਵਰਤਨਾ; ~ed ਨਿਯੁਕਤ, ਲੱਗਿਆ, ਰੁੱਝਿਆ; ~ee ਨੌਕਰ, ਮੁਲਾਜ਼ਮ, ਕਰਮਚਾਰੀ; ~er ਮਾਲਕ, ਸੁਆਮੀ; ~ment ਨੌਕਰੀ, ਤਨਖ਼ਾਹ ਵਾਲੀ ਮੁਲਾਜ਼ਮਤ, ਰੁਜ਼ਗਾਰ, ਪੇਸ਼ਾ

emporium (ਐੱਮ'ਪੋਰਿਅਮ) *n* ਹੱਟ, ਤਿਜਾਰਤਗਾਹ, ਬਜ਼ਾਰ

empower (ਇਮ'ਪਾਉਅ*) *v* ਇਖ਼ਤਿਆਰ ਦੇਣਾ, ਅਧਿਕਾਰ ਸੌਂਪਣਾ, ਸੱਤਾ ਦੇਣੀ, ਮੁਖ਼ਤਿਆਰ ਬਣਾਉਣਾ

empress ('ਐੱਮਪਰਿਸ) *n* ਮਹਾਰਾਣੀ, ਮਲਕਾ, ਸਮਰਾਟ ਦੀ ਪਤਨੀ

emptiness ('ਐੱਮ(ਪ)ਟਿਨਿਸ) *n* ਸੁੰਵਾਪਣ, ਵਿਹਲ, ਖ਼ਲਾਅ, ਥੋਥਾਪਣ, ਸੰਖਣਾਪਣ

empty ('ਐੱਮ(ਪ)ਟਿ) *a v* ਵਿਹਲਾ, ਸੱਖਣਾ, ਸੁੰਨਾ, ਖ਼ਾਲੀ, ਥੋਥਾ, ਫੋਕਾ, ਭੁੱਖਾ, ਨਿਕੰਮਾ, ਨਿਰਾਰਥਕ; ਖ਼ਾਲੀ ਕਰਨਾ, ਖ਼ਾਲੀ ਹੋਣਾ

emulate ('ਐੱਮਯੁਲੇਇਟ) *v* ਰਸ਼ਕ ਕਰਨਾ, ਬਰਾਬਰੀ ਕਰਨੀ, ਰੀਸ ਕਰਨੀ, ਹੋੜ ਕਰਨਾ

emulation ('ਐੱਮਯੁ'ਲੇਇਸ਼ਨ) *n* ਬਰਾਬਰੀ, ਮੁਕਾਬਲਾ, ਰੀਸ, ਰਸ਼ਕ

enable (ਇ'ਨੇਇਬਲ) *v* ਯੋਗ ਬਣਾਉਣਾ, ਸਮੱਰਥ ਕਰਨਾ, ਕਾਬਲ ਕਰਨਾ

enact (ਇ'ਨੈਕਟ) *v* ਕਨੂੰਨ ਪਾਸ ਕਰਨਾ, ਬਣਾਉਣਾ, (ਨਾਟਕ) ਖੇਡਣਾ, ਐਕਟਿੰਗ ਕਰਨਾ; ~ment ਕਨੂੰਨ ਦਾ ਰੂਪ

enamel (ਇ'ਨੈਮਲ) *n v* ਮੁਲੰਮਾ, ਝਾਲ; ਮੀਨਾਕਾਰੀ; ਮੁਲੰਮਾ ਕਰਨਾ, ਝਾਲ ਫੇਰਨੀ, ਮੀਨਾਕਾਰੀ ਕਰਨੀ

en bloc (ਆਨ'ਬਲੈਕ) (*F*) *a* ਸਮੂਹਕ, ਰੂਪ ਵਿਚ, ਸਾਰੇ ਦੇ ਸਾਰੇ

encage, incage (ਇਨ'ਕੋਇਜ) *v* ਪਿੰਜਰੇ ਵਿਚ ਰੱਖਣਾ, ਬੰਦ ਕਰਨਾ, ਕੈਦ ਕਰਨਾ

encamp (ਇਨ'ਕੈਂਪ) *v* ਡੇਰਾ ਜਾਂ ਛਾਉਣੀ ਪਾਉਣਾ, ਪੜਾਉ ਪਾਉਣਾ, ਪੜਾ ਵਿਚ ਠਹਿਰਨਾ, ਤੰਬੂ ਖੜ੍ਹਾ ਕਰਨਾ; ~ment ਛਾਉਣੀ, ਡੇਰਾ, ਪੜਾਉ, ਤੰਬੂ, ਖ਼ੈਮਾ

encase, incase (ਇਨ'ਕੋਇਸ) *v* ਢਕਣਾ, ਬਕਸੇ ਵਿਚ ਰੱਖਣਾ, ਲਪੇਟਣਾ, ਖ਼ਾਨੇ ਵਿਚ ਰੱਖਣਾ

encash (ਇਨ'ਕੈਸ਼) *v* ਨਕਦ ਰੁਪਏ ਦੇਣਾ, ਹੁੰਡੀ ਜਾਂ ਚੈੱਕ ਤੁੜਾਉਣਾ, ਵਸੂਲਣਾ

encave (ਇਨ'ਕੋਇਵੂ) *v* ਗੁਫ਼ਾ ਵਿਚ ਲੁਕਾਉਣਾ, ਕੰਦਰਾਂ ਵਿਚ ਰੱਖਣਾ

enchain (ਇਨ'ਚੇਇਨ) *v* ਜੰਜੀਰ ਨਾਲ ਬੰਨ੍ਹਣਾ; ਕੜੀ-ਬੱਧ ਕਰਨਾ, ਕਸ ਕੇ ਬੰਨ੍ਹਣਾ; ਧਿਆਨ ਖਿੱਚਣਾ, ਵੱਸ ਵਿਚ ਕਰਨਾ

enchant (ਇਨ'ਚਾਂਟ) *v* ਜਾਦੂ ਕਰਨਾ, ਟੂਣਾ ਕਰਨਾ ਲੁਭਾਉਣਾ, ਰੀਝਾਉਣਾ, ਮੁਗਧ ਕਰਨਾ; ~ing ਮੋਹਕ, ਦਿਲਕਸ਼; ~ment ਜਾਦੂ, ਟੂਣਾ, ਇੰਦਰਜਾਲ, ਸੰਮੋਹਨ ਮਾਇਆ

encharge (ਇਨ'ਚਾਜ) *v* ਸੌਂਪਣਾ, ਸਪੁਰਦ ਕਰਨਾ

encircle (ਇਨ'ਸਅਃਕਲ) *v* ਵਲ ਲੈਣਾ, ਘੇਰ ਲੈਣਾ, ਵਲਗਣਾ, ਬੰਦ ਕਰਨਾ, ਘੇਰਾ ਪਾਉਣਾ, ਵਾੜ ਲਾਉਣਾ

enclose, inclose (ਇਨ'ਕਲਅਉਜ਼) *v* ਘੇਰਨਾ, ਬੰਦ ਕਰਨਾ, ਵਾੜ ਲਗਾਉਣਾ; ~d ਘੇਰਿਆ, ਬੰਦ, ਨੱਥੀ ਕੀਤਾ

enclosure (ਇਨ'ਕਲਅਉਯ਼ਅ*) *n* ਵਲਗਣ, ਘੇਰਾ, ਵਾੜ, ਇਹਾਤਾ; ਨੱਥੀ ਕਾਗ਼ਜ਼; ਸਹਿ-ਪੱਤਰ

enclothe (ਇਨ'ਕਲਅਉਦ) *v* ਕੱਪੜੇ ਪੁਆਉਣਾ, ਵਸਤਰ ਪਹਿਨਾਉਣਾ

encode (ਇਨ'ਕਅਉਡ) *v* ਕੋਡ ਵਿਚ ਬਦਲਣਾ

encompass (ਇਨ'ਕਾੱਮਪਅਸ) *v* ਘੇਰ ਲੈਣਾ, ਸ਼ਾਮਲ ਕਰਨਾ, ਵਿਆਪਤ ਕਰਨਾ, ਵਲ੍ਹੇਟਣਾ, ਧਰਨਾ

encore ('ਔਡਕੋ*) *int* ਮੁਕਰਰ

encounter (ਇਨ'ਕਾਉਂਟਅ*) *n v* ਟਾਕਰਾ, ਮੁਕਾਬਲਾ, ਮੁੱਠ-ਭੇੜ, ਸੰਗਰਾਮ, ਸਮਾਗਮ, ਅਚਾਨਕ, ਮੇਲ; ਟਾਕਰਾ ਕਰਨਾ, ਜੁਝਣਾ, ਭਿੜਨਾ, ਲੜਨਾ

encourage (ਇਨ'ਕਅੱਰਿਜ) *v* ਉਤਸ਼ਾਹ ਦੇਣਾ, ਦਿਲ ਵਧਾਉਣਾ, ਹੌਸਲਾ ਦੇਣਾ, ਹੁੱਕ ਦੇਣੀ, ਪਿੱਠ ਠੋਕਣੀ, ਪਰੇਰਨਾ ਦੇਣੀ, ਉਕਸਾਉਣਾ; ~ment ਉਤਸਾਹ, ਧਰਵਾਸ, ਪਰੇਰਨਾ

encouraging (ਇਨ'ਕਅੱਰਿਜਿਙ) *a* ਉਤਸ਼ਾਹਜਨਕ

encroach (ਇਨ'ਕਰਅਉਚ) *v* (ਅਯੋਗ) ਦਖ਼ਲ ਦੇਣਾ, ਅਨੁਚਿਤ ਅਧਿਕਾਰ ਜਮਾਉਣਾ, ਲੱਤ ਅੜਾਉਣੀ; ~ment ਅਯੋਗ ਦਖ਼ਲ, ਨਾਜਾਇਜ਼ ਕਬਜ਼ਾ

encumber (ਇਨ'ਕਅੱਮਬਅ*) *v* ਭਾਰ ਪਾਉਣਾ; ਰੋੜਾ ਅਟਕਾਉਣਾ, ਵਿਘਨ ਪਾਉਣਾ, ਅਟਕਾਉਣਾ; ਕਰਜ਼ਾਈ ਕਰਨਾ

encumbrance (ਇਨ'ਕਅੱਮਬਰਅੰਸ) *n* ਭਾਰ, ਬੋਝ, ਵਿਘਨ, ਦੁੱਖ, ਰੋੜਾ

encyclopaedia (ਇਨ'ਸਾਇਕਲਅ(ਉ)'ਪੀਡ-ਯਅ) *n* ਵਿਸ਼ਵ-ਕੋਸ਼

end (ਐਂਡ) *n v* ਅੰਤ, ਸੀਮਾ, ਹੱਦ, ਸਿਰਾ; ਟੋਟਾ; ਸਮਾਪਤੀ, ਬਰਬਾਦੀ, ਮਿਰਤੂ, ਨਤੀਜਾ, ਉਦੇਸ਼, ਮਨੋਰਥ; ਸਮਾਪਤ ਕਰਨਾ, ਅੰਤ ਕਰਨਾ, ਪੂਰਾ ਕਰਨਾ, ਨਸ਼ਟ ਕਰਨਾ, ਖ਼ਤਮ ਹੋਣਾ, ਨਤੀਜਾ ਨਿਕਲਣਾ, ਸਿੱਟਾ ਕੱਢਣਾ; **in the~** ਆਖ਼ਰਕਾਰ, ਅੰਤ ਨੂੰ; **make both~s meet** ਡੰਗ

ਟਪਾਉਣਾ, ਗੁਜ਼ਾਰਾ, ਕਰਨਾ; ~less ਅਨੰਤ, ਅਪਾਰ, ਨਿਰੰਤਰ, ਬੇ-ਇੰਤਹਾ

endanger (ਇਨ'ਡੇਂਜਿਅ*) *n* ਖ਼ਤਰੇ ਵਿਚ ਪਾਉਣਾ, ਆਪੱਤੀ ਵਿਚ ਪਾਉਣਾ

endear (ਇਨ'ਡਿਅ*) *v* ਪਿਆਰਾ ਬਣਾਉਣਾ, ਲਾਡਲਾ ਬਣਾਉਣਾ; ~ment ਪ੍ਰੀਤ, ਪਿਆਰ, ਪਰੇਮ, ਲਾਡ-ਦੁਲਾਰ

endeavour (ਇਨ'ਡੈਵਅ*) *n v* ਜਤਨ, ਘਾਲ, ਹੰਭਲਾ, ਵਾਹ, ਜਾਨਮਾਰੀ, ਉੱਦਮ, ਕੋਸ਼ਸ਼; ਜਤਨ ਕਰਨਾ, ਉੱਦਮ ਕਰਨਾ

endorse (ਇਨ'ਡੋਸ) *v* ਸਕਾਰਨਾ, ਤਸਦੀਕ ਕਰਨੀ, ਪਿਠਾਂਕਣ ਕਰਨਾ, ਪੁਸ਼ਟੀ ਕਰਨੀ; ~ment ਸਹੀ, ਤਸਦੀਕ, ਪਿਠਾਂਕਤ, ਸਮਰਥਨ, ਅਨੁਮੋਦਨ

endow (ਇਨ'ਡਾਉ) *v* ਝੇਟਾ ਕਰਨਾ, ਨਾਉਂ ਲਾਉਣਾ ਵਕਫ ਕਰਨਾ, ਧਰਮ ਅਰਥ ਦੇਣਾ, ਦਾਨ ਦੇਣਾ, ਝੇਟ ਦੇਣਾ, ਸਮੱਰਥ ਬਣਾਉਣਾ; ~ment ਧਰਮ ਅਰਥ ਝੇਟਾ, ਧਰਮਦਾਨ; ਦਹੇਜ, ਸਮੱਰਥਾ, ਪ੍ਰਤਿਭਾ; ਯੋਗਤਾ

endurance (ਇਨ'ਡਯੁਅਰਨਸ) *n* ਜੇਰਾ, ਸਹਾਰਨ-ਸ਼ਕਤੀ, ਧੀਰਜ, ਸਹਿਣਸ਼ੀਲਤਾ, ਬੁਰਦਬਾਰੀ, ਸਬਰ

endure (ਇਨ'ਡਯੁਅ*) *v* ਝੋਗਣਾ, ਸਹਾਰਨਾ, ਝੱਲਣਾ, ਸਹਿਣਾ, ਭੁਗਤਣਾ, ਟਿਕਣਾ, ਠਹਿਰੇ ਰਹਿਣਾ

enduring (ਇਨ'ਡਯੁਅਰਿਙ) *a* ਚਿਰਸਥਾਈ, ਟਿਕਾਊ, ਸਹਿਨਸ਼ੀਲ

enemy (ਐਨਅਮਿ) *n a* ਵੈਰੀ, ਦੁਸ਼ਮਨ, ਵਿਪੱਖੀ, ਸ਼ੱਤਰੂ, ਵਿਰੋਧੀ

energetic (ਐਨਅ'ਜੈਟਿਕ) *n a* ਤੇਜਵਾਨ, ਬਲਵਾਨ, ਪ੍ਰਬੱਲ, ਸ਼ਕਤੀਸ਼ਾਲੀ, ਮਿਹਨਤੀ,

ਉਤਸ਼ਾਹੀ

energize (ਐਨਅ:ਜਾਇਜ਼) *v* ਸ਼ਕਤੀ ਦਾ ਸੰਚਾਰ ਕਰਨਾ, ਬਲ ਪ੍ਰਦਾਨ ਕਰਨਾ, ਸ਼ਕਤੀ ਭਰਨਾ; ਜਾਨ ਪਾ ਦੇਣਾ

energy (ਐਨਅ:ਜਿ) *n* ਬਲ, ਜ਼ੋਰ, ਸ਼ਕਤੀ, ਦਮ, ਊਰਜਾ, ਤੇਜ, ਜੀਵਨ-ਸ਼ਕਤੀ ਕਿਰਿਆਸ਼ੀਲਤਾ, ਯੋਗਤਾ

enfeeble (ਇਨ'ਫ਼ੀਬਲ) *v* ਸ਼ਕਤੀਹੀਨ ਕਰਨਾ, ਨਿਤਾਣਾ ਕਰਨਾ, ਦੁਰਬਲ ਕਰਨਾ

enfold, infold (ਇਨ'ਫ਼ਅਉਲਡ) *v* ਜੱਫ਼ੀ ਵਿਚ ਲੈਣਾ, ਗਲ ਲਾਉਣਾ, ਘੁੱਟਣਾ, ਵਲੇਟਣਾ, ਤਹਿ ਕਰਨਾ

enforce (ਇਨ'ਫ਼ੋਸ) *v* ਚਾਲੂ ਕਰਨਾ, ਲਾਗੂ ਕਰਨਾ, ਹੁਕਮ ਜਾਂ ਕਨੂੰਨ ਅਮਲ ਵਿਚ ਲਿਆਉਣਾ, ਜਾਰੀ ਕਰਨਾ, ਪ੍ਰਚਲਤ ਕਰਨਾ, (ਹੁਕਮ) ਚਲਾਉਣਾ; ~ment ਪ੍ਰਦਾਨ, ਦ੍ਰਿੜੀਕਰਨ, ਪਾਲਣ, ਤਾਮੀਲ

enfranchise (ਇਨ'ਫ਼ਰੈਨਚਾਇਜ਼) *v* ਆਜ਼ਾਦ ਕਰਨਾ, ਰਿਹਾ ਕਰਨਾ; ਸ਼ਹਿਰੀ ਹੱਕ ਦੇਣੇ, ਵੋਟ ਦਾ ਹੱਕ ਦੇਣਾ; ~ment ਮੁਕਤੀਦਾਨ, ਵੋਟ ਅਧਿਕਾਰ

engage (ਇਨ'ਗੇਇਜ) *v* ਵਚਨ-ਬੱਧ ਹੋਣਾ, ਇਕਰਾਰ; ~d ਰੁੱਝਿਆ; ਮੰਗਣੀ, ਕੁੜਮਾਈ ਕਰਨੀ, ਕੰਮ ਤੇ ਲਾ ਦੇਣਾ; ਆਹਰੇ ਲਾਉਣਾ, ਜੁਟ ਜਾਣਾ, ਲਾ ਰਖਣਾ, ਕੱਸ ਕੇ ਫੜਨਾ; ਭਿੜਨਾ; ~ment ਇਕਰਾਰ, ਵਚਨ-ਬੰਧੇਜ; ਰੁਝੇਵਾਂ, ਕੰਮ, ਧੰਦਾ; ਸੰਗਤੀ, ਕੁੜਮਾਈ; ਘੁੱਠ-ਭੇੜ, ਝੜਪ

engender (ਇਨ'ਜੈਂਡਅ*) *v* ਪੈਦਾ ਕਰਨਾ, ਉਤਪੰਨ ਕਰਨਾ, ਬੱਚਾ ਜਣਨਾ

engine ('ਐਨੱਜਿਨ) *n v* ਇੰਜਣ, ਕਲ, ਮਸ਼ੀਨ, ਜੰਤਰ

engineer ('ਐਨਜਿ'ਨਿਅ*) *n v* ਇੰਜਨਸਾਜ਼,

ਇੰਜਨੀਅਰ, ਨਿਰਮਾਤਾ; ਨਿਰਮਾਨ ਕਰਨਾ, ਇੰਜੀਨੀਅਰੀ ਦਾ ਕੰਮ ਕਰਨਾ, ਕਾਢ ਕੱਢਣੀ, ਪ੍ਰਬੰਧ ਕਰਨਾ, ਜੁਗਤ ਕੱਢਣੀ, ਮਨਸੂਬਾ ਬੰਨ੍ਹਣਾ; ~ing ਇੰਜੀਨੀਅਰੀ, ਜੰਤਰਸ਼ਾਸਤਰ

engrave (ਇਨ'ਗਰੇਇਵ) v ਮੀਨਾਕਾਰੀ ਕਰਨਾ, ਨੱਕਾਸ਼ੀ ਕਰਨਾ, ਉਘਾੜਨਾ, ਉਕਰਨਾ

engraving (ਇਨ'ਗਰੇਇਵਿਙ) n ਖੁਦਾਇ, ਨੱਕਾਸ਼ੀ, ਖੁਦਨ

engross (ਇਨ'ਗਰਅਉਸ) v ਮੋਟੇ ਅੱਖਰਾਂ ਵਿਚ ਲਿਖਣਾ, ਕਾਨੂੰਨ ਦੇ ਰੂਪ ਵਿਚ ਜ਼ਾਹਰ ਕਰਨਾ, ਸਾਰਾ ਭੰਡਾਰ ਖ਼ਰੀਦ ਲੈਣਾ; ਧਿਆਨ ਵਿਚ ਲੀਨ ਕਰਨਾ

engulf (ਇਨ'ਗਅੱਲਫ਼) v ਲਪੇਟ ਵਿਚ ਲੈਣਾ; ~ed ਲੀਨ, ਇਕਾਗਰਚਿੱਤ, ਮਗਨ

enhance (ਇਨ'ਹਾਂਸ) v ਵਧਾਉਣਾ, (ਕੀਮਤ) ਚੜ੍ਹਾਉਣੀ, ਉੱਚਾ ਕਰਨਾ; ~ment ਵਾਧਾ, ਵਧਾ-ਚੜ੍ਹ, ਤੀਬਰਤਾ

enigma (ਇ'ਨਿਗਮਅ) n ਬੁਝਾਰਤ, ਅਣਾਉਣੀ, ਪਹੇਲੀ, ਉਲਝਣ

enigmatic ('ਇਨਿਗ'ਮੈਟਿਕ) a ਗੁੱਝਾ, ਪੇਚੀਦਾ

enjoin (ਇਨ'ਜੌਇਨ) v ਲਾਗੂ ਕਰਨਾ, ਨਿਰਧਾਰਤ ਕਰਨਾ, ਹੁਕਮ ਦੇਣਾ, ਨਿਰਦੇਸ਼ ਕਰਨਾ

enjoy (ਇਨ'ਜੌਇ) v ਭੋਗਣਾ, ਮਾਣਨਾ, ਆਨੰਦ ਲੁੱਟਣਾ, ਉਪਯੋਗ ਕਰਨਾ; ਲਾਭ ਉਠਾਉਣਾ; ~ment ਵਾਧਾ, ਸਮਰਿਧੀ, ਸੰਪੰਨਤਾ

enkindle (ਇਨ'ਕਿੰਡਲ) v ਪ੍ਰਚੰਡ ਕਰਨਾ, ਭੜਕਾਉਣਾ, ਉਤੇਜਤ ਕਰਨਾ, ਜਲਾਉਣਾ, ਭਾਵਾਂ ਨੂੰ ਤੀਬਰ ਕਰਨਾ, ਅੱਗ ਲਾਉਣਾ

enlarge (ਇਨ'ਲਾਜ) v ਵਧਾਉਣਾ, ਫੈਲਾਉਣਾ, ਵਿਸਤਰਤ ਕਰਨਾ, ਇਜ਼ਾਫ਼ਾ ਕਰਨਾ, (ਫੋਟੋ) ਵੱਡੀ ਕਰਨੀ; ~ment ਵਾਧਾ, ਵ੍ਰਿਧੀ, ਫੈਲਾਉ

enlighten (ਇਨ'ਲਾਇਟਨ) v ਸਿੱਖਿਆ ਦੇਣਾ, ਪ੍ਰਕਾਸ਼ ਪਾਉਣਾ, ਸਪਸ਼ਟ ਕਰਨਾ, ਉਪਦੇਸ਼ ਦੇਣਾ, ਗਿਆਨ ਦੇਣਾ; ~ed ਪ੍ਰਬੁੱਧ, ਪ੍ਰਕਾਸ਼ਤ, ਗਿਆਨ-ਉੱਦੀਪਤ; ~ment ਬੋਧ, ਗਿਆਨ ਪ੍ਰਕਾਸ਼ਨ, ਸਪਸ਼ਟੀਕਰਨ, ਗਿਆਨ ਦਾਨ

enlist (ਇਨ'ਲਿਸਟ) v ਸੂਚੀਬੱਧ ਕਰਨਾ, ਭਰਤੀ ਕਰਨਾ ਜਾਂ ਹੋਣਾ; ਸਹਿਯੋਗ ਪ੍ਰਾਪਤ ਕਰਨਾ; ~ment ਭਰਤੀ

enmity ('ਐਨਮਅਟਿ) n ਵੈਰ, ਦੁਸ਼ਮਨੀ, ਰੰਜ਼ਕ, ਵੈਰ-ਭਾਵ, ਵਿਰੋਧ

enormous (ਇ'ਨੋਮਅਸ) a ਵੱਡਾ ਸਾਰਾ, ਮਹਾਨ, ਭੀਸ਼ਟ, ਅਤਿਅਧਿਕ, ਅਸਾਧਾਰਨ

enough (ਇ'ਨਅੱਫ਼) a adv int ਚੋਖਾ, ਕਾਫ਼ੀ, ਉਚਿਤ; ਬਹੁਤ ਸਾਰਾ, ਬੱਸ! ਹੱਦ ਤੇ ਗਈ

eouire, iouire (ਇਨ'ਕਵਾਇਅ*) v ਜਾਂਚ ਕਰਨਾ, ਪੁੱਛ ਗਿੱਛ ਕਰਨਾ, ਪੁੱਛਣਾ

eouiry, iouiry (ਇਨ'ਕਵਾਇਅਰਿ) n ਪੁੱਛ ਗਿੱਛ, ਜਾਂਚ, ਖੋਜ, ਤਹੀਕੀਕਾਤ

enrich (ਇਨ'ਰਿਚ) v ਸੰਪੰਨ ਬਣਾਉਣਾ, ਨਿਹਾਲ ਕਰ ਦੇਣਾ, ਵਧੀਆ ਬਣਾਉਣਾ; ਸਮਰਿਧ ਬਣਾਉਣਾ; ਜ਼ਰਖੇਜ ਕਰਨਾ; ਅਲੰਕਰਤ ਕਰਨਾ, ਸਜਾਉਣਾ; ~ment ਵਾਧਾ, ਸਮਰਿਧੀ, ਸੰਪੰਨਤਾ

enrol, enroll (ਇਨ'ਰਅਉਲ) v ਨਾਂ ਚੜ੍ਹਾਉਣਾ, ਦਰਜ ਕਰਨਾ, ਦਾਖ਼ਲ ਕਰਨਾ, ਭਰਤੀ ਕਰਨਾ; ~ment ਇੰਦਰਾਜ, ਦਾਖ਼ਲਾ, ਭਰਤੀ, ਸੂਚੀ, ਫ਼ਰਦ

en route (ਆਨ'ਰੂਟ) (F) adv ਥਰਾਸਤਾ, ਰਾਹ ਜਾਂਦਿਆਂ

enshrine (ਇਨ'ਸ਼ਰਾਇਨ) v ਪਵਿੱਤਰ ਥਾਂ ਤੇ ਰੱਖਣਾ, ਪਵਿੱਤਰ ਸਮਝ ਕੇ ਸੁੱਰਖਿਅਤ ਰੱਖਣਾ

enslave (ਇਨ'ਸਲੇਇਵ) v ਗ਼ੁਲਾਮ ਬਣਾਉਣਾ, ਵੱਸ ਵਿਚ ਕਰਨਾ; ~ment ਗ਼ੁਲਾਮੀ, ਦਾਸਤਾ

ensue (ਇਨ'ਸਯੂ) *v* ਸਿੱਟਾ ਨਿਕਲਣਾ, ਖੋਜ ਕਰਨਾ, ਪਿੱਛਾ ਕਰਨਾ, ਪਿੱਛੇ ਚੱਲਣਾ

ensuing (ਇਨ'ਸਯੂਇੰਗ) *a* ਆਗਾਮੀ, ਆਉਣ ਵਾਲਾ, ਉੱਤਰ-ਕਾਲੀਨ

entangle (ਇਨ'ਟੈਂਗਲ) *v* ਉਲਝਾਉਣਾ, ਫਸਾ ਲੈਣਾ, ਅੜਾਉਣਾ, ਹੈਰਾਨ ਪਰੇਸ਼ਾਨ ਕਰਨਾ; ~**ment** ਉਲਝੇਵਾਂ, ਝਮੇਲਾ, ਜੰਜਾਲ, ਅੜਿਚਨ

enter ('ਔਨਟਾ*) *v* ਵੜਨਾ, ਅੰਦਰ ਆਉਣਾ, ਦਾਖ਼ਲ ਹੋਣਾ, ਪ੍ਰਵੇਸ਼ ਕਰਨਾ, ਘੁਸੜਨਾ, ਦਰਜ ਕਰਨਾ; ਨਾਂ ਲਿਖਣਾ, ਦਾਖ਼ਲਾ ਕਰਨਾ, ਕਦਮ ਰੱਖਣਾ

enterprise ('ਔਨਟ'ਅਪਰਾਇਜ਼) *n* ਮੁਹਿੰਮ, ਔਖਾ ਕੰਮ, ਉਦਯੋਗ, ਉੱਦਮ, ਹਿੰਮਤ, ਹੌਸਲਾ

enterprising ('ਔਨਟਾ*ਪਰਾਇਜ਼ਿੰਗ) *a* ਉੱਦਮੀ, ਉਦਯੋਗੀ, ਮਨਚਲਾ, ਦਲੇਰ

entertain ('ਔਨਟਾ'ਟੇਇਨ) *v* ਚੱਲਣਾ ਜਾਰੀ ਰੱਖਣਾ; ਆਉ-ਭਗਤ ਕਰਨੀ, ਪਰਚਾਉਣਾ, ਧਾਰਨਾ; ~**ing** ਮਨੋਰੰਜਕ, ਦਿਲਚਸਪ, ਰੋਚਕ; ~**ment** ਖ਼ਾਤਰ ਆਉ-ਭਗਤ, ਦਿਲ-ਪਰਚਾਵਾ, ਮੌਜ-ਮੇਲਾ, ਮਨੋਰੰਜਨ

enthrone (ਇਨ'ਥਰਅਉਨ) *v* ਗੱਦੀ ਉੱਤੇ ਬਿਠਾਉਣਾ, ਤਖ਼ਤ ਤੇ ਬਿਠਾਉਣਾ

enthuse (ਇਨ'ਥਯੂਜ਼) *v* ਜੋਸ਼ ਦੁਆਉਣਾ; ਉਤਸਾਹਤ ਕਰਨਾ, ਉਮੰਗ ਪੈਦਾ ਕਰਨੀ, ਉਤਸ਼ਾਹਤ ਹੋਣਾ

enthusiasm (ਇਨ'ਥਯੂਜ਼ਿਐਜ਼(ਅ)ਮ) *n* ਜੋਸ਼, ਉਤਸ਼ਾਹ, ਸਰਗਰਮੀ, ਉਮਾਹ, ਉਮੰਗ, ਜਲਾਲ

enthusiast (ਇਨ'ਥਯੂਜ਼ਿਐਸਟ) *n* ਉਤਸਾਹੀ, ਉਤਸੁਕ, ਅਨੁਰਾਗੀ, ਜੋਸ਼ੀਲਾ (ਵਿਅਕਤੀ); ~**ic**, ~**ical** ਜੋਸ਼ੀਲਾ, ਉਤਸ਼ਾਹੀ, ਸਰਗਰਮ, ਪ੍ਰਜੋਸ਼, ਉਮੰਗੀ, ਅਨੁਰਾਗੀ

entice (ਇਨ'ਟਾਇਸ) *v* ਲੁਭਾਉਣਾ, ਭਰਮਾਉਣਾ, ਵਰਗਲਾਉਣਾ, ਬਹਿਕਾਉਣਾ, ਫਸਾਉਣਾ

entire (ਇਨ'ਟਾਇਅ*) *a n* ਸਾਰਾ, ਸਮੁੱਚਾ, ਸਾਬਤ, ਸਗਲ, ਸਮਗਰ, ਸਕਲ, ਸਮਸਤ, ਜਿਉਂ ਦਾ ਤਿਉਂ, ਸ਼ੁੱਧ

entitle (ਔਨਟਾਇਟਲ) *v* ਸਿਰਲੇਖ ਦੇਣਾ, ਨਾਂ ਰਖਣਾ, ਖਿਤਾਬ ਦੇਣਾ, ਹਕ ਦੇਣਾ; ~**d** ਅਧਿਕਾਰੀ, ਹੱਕਦਾਰ, ਅਧਿਕ੍ਰਿਤ; ਸੀਰਸ਼ਕ

entity (ਔਨਟਅਟਿ) *n* ਹੋਂਦ, ਹਸਤੀ, ਜ਼ਾਤ, ਅਸਤਿਤਵ; ਅਸਲੀਅਤ, ਮੌਜੂਦਗੀ, ਵਜੂਦ

entomology (ਔਨਟਅ(ਉ)'ਮੌਲਅਜਿ) *n* ਕੀਟ-ਵਿਗਿਆਨ

entrance ('ਔਨਟਰ(ਅ)ਨਸ) *n* ਦਾਖ਼ਲਾ, ਪ੍ਰਵੇਸ਼, ਪ੍ਰਵੇਸ਼-ਦੁਆਰ

entrap (ਇਨ'ਟਰੈਪ) *v* ਜਾਲ ਵਿਚ ਫਸਾਉਣਾ, ਮੁਗਧ ਕਰਨਾ, ਖਿੱਚਣਾ, ਬਹਿਕਾਉਣਾ

entreat (ਇਨ'ਟਰੀਟ) *v* ਮਿੰਨਤ ਕਰਨੀ, ਹਾੜੇ ਕੱਢਣੇ, ਤਰਲਾ ਕਰਨਾ, ਵਾਸਤਾ ਪਾਉਣਾ, ਗਿੜਗਿੜਾਉਣਾ

entrench (ਇਨ'ਟਰੈੱਨਚ) *v* ਮੋਰਚਾ ਬੰਨ੍ਹਣਾ, ਪੈਰ ਜਮਾਉਣਾ, ਡਟ ਜਾਣਾ

entrepreneur ('ਔਨਟਰਅਪਰਅ'ਨਅਃ*) *n* ਉੱਦਮਕਰਤਾ, ਉਦਯੋਗਪਤੀ, ਕਾਰਖ਼ਾਨੇਦਾਰ; ~**ship** ਉੱਦਮ

entrust (ਇਨ'ਟਰਅੱਸਟ) *v* ਸਪੁਰਦ ਕਰਨਾ, ਸੌਂਪਣਾ

entry ('ਔਨਟਰਿ) *n* ਦਾਖ਼ਲਾ, ਆਮਦ, ਰਸਾਈ; ਪ੍ਰਵੇਸ਼, (ਕਾ) ਦਖ਼ਲ, ਕਬਜ਼ਾ, ਲਾਂਘਾ, ਪ੍ਰਵੇਸ਼-ਦੁਆਰ; ਇੰਦਰਾਜ

enumerate (ਇ'ਨਯੂਮਅਰੇਇਟ) *v* ਗਿਨਣਾ, ਗਿਣਤੀ ਕਰਨੀ; ਨਿਰਦੇਸ਼ ਕਰਨਾ, ਵਿਵਰਣ ਦੇਣਾ,

ਸ਼ੁਮਾਰ ਕਰਨਾ

enumeration (ਇ'ਨਯੁਮਅ'ਰੇਇਸ਼ਨ) *n* ਗਿਣਤੀ, ਗਣਨਾ, ਸ਼ੁਮਾਰ, ਨਿਰਦੇਸ਼ਨ

enunicate (ਇ'ਨਅੱਨਸਿਏਇਟ) *v* ਘੋਸ਼ਣਾ ਕਰਨੀ, ਐਲਾਨ ਕਰਨਾ, ਉਚਾਰਨ ਕਰਨਾ, ਉਚਾਰਨਾ

enunciation (ਇ'ਨਅੱਨਸਿ'ਏਇਸ਼ਨ) *n* ਕਥਨ, ਉਚਾਰਨ, ਵਰਣਨ, ਪ੍ਰਸਤੁਤੀਕਰਨ

envelop (ਇਨ'ਵ੍ਹੈਲਪ) *v* ਵਲ੍ਹੇਟਣਾ, ਵਿਹੜਨਾ, ਢਕਣਾ, ਕੱਜਣਾ, ਲਿਫ਼ਾਫ਼ੇ ਵਿਚ ਪਾਉਣਾ; ~ment ਵਿਹੜ, ਲਪੇਟ, ਘੇਰਾ, ਆਵਰਣ

envelope ('ਐਨਵ੍ਅਲਅਉਪ) *n* ਲਿਫ਼ਾਫ਼ਾ, ਆਵਰਣ

enviable ('ਐਨਵ੍ਿਅਬਲ) *a* ਰਸ਼ਕਯੋਗ, ਰੀਸਯੋਗ, ਈਰਖਾਯੋਗ

environment (ਇਨ'ਵ੍ਾਇਅਰ(ਅ)ਨਮੇਂਟ) *n* ਵਾਤਾਵਰਣ, ਚੁਗਿਰਦਾ, ਪਰਿਸਥਿਤੀ, ਵਾਯੂਮੰਡਲ, ਚੁਫੇਰਾ; ਦੁਆਲਾ, ਪਰਿਵੇਸ਼; ਮਾਹੌਲ; ~al ਵਾਤਾਵਰਣ ਸਬੰਧੀ, ਵਾਯੂਮੰਡਲ ਸਬੰਧੀ, ਪਰਿਸਥਿਤੀ ਸਬੰਧੀ

envisage (ਇਨ'ਵ੍ਿਜ਼ਿਜ) *v* ਸਾਮੂਣੇ ਹੋਣਾ ਰੂਬਰੂ ਹੋਣਾ; ਵਿਚਾਰ ਵਿਚ ਲਿਆਉਣਾ

envoy ('ਐਨਵ੍ਓਇ) *n* ਕਾਸਦ, ਪ੍ਰਤੀਨਿਧ; ਏਲਚੀ, ਛੋਟਾ ਸਫ਼ੀਰ ਜਾਂ ਦੂਤ

envy ('ਐਨਵ੍ਿ) *n v* ਸਾੜਾ, ਈਰਖਾ, ਈਰਖਾ ਕਰਨੀ, ਹਸਦ ਕਰਨਾ

enzyme ('ਐਨਜ਼ਾਇਮ) *n* ਪਾਚਕ ਰਸ, ਰਸਾਇਣੀ ਖ਼ਮੀਰ

epic ('ਐਪਿਕ) *n a* (ਕਾਵਿ) ਮਹਾਂਕਾਵਿਕ, ਬੀਰਕਾਵਿ, ਵੀਰ-ਗਾਥਾ; ~al ਮਹਾਂਕਾਵਿਕ, ਮਹਾਂਕਾਵਿ ਸਬੰਧੀ

epidemic ('ਐਪਿ'ਡੈਮਿਕ) *n a* ਵਿਆਪਕ ਬੀਮਾਰੀ, ਮਹਾਂਮਾਰੀ, ਫੂਤ ਰੋਗ, ਸੰਚਾਰੀ

epilepsy ('ਐਪਿਲੈਂਪਸਿ) *n* ਮਿਰਗੀ, ਮੂਰਛਾ ਰੋਗ

epilogue ('ਐਪਿਲੌਗ) *n* ਉਪਸੰਹਾਰ, ਸਾਹਿਤ-ਰਚਨਾ ਦਾ ਅੰਤਮ ਭਾਗ

episode ('ਐਪਿਸਅਉਡ) *n* ਪ੍ਰਸੰਗ, ਉਪ-ਕਥਾ; ਕਥਾ-ਮਾਲਾ; ਸੰਯੋਗੀ ਘਟਨਾ

epitaph ('ਐਪਿਟਾਫ਼) *n* ਸਮਾਧੀ-ਲੇਖ, ਸਿਮਰਤੀ-ਲੇਖ, ਕਬਰ ਦਾ ਕੁਤਬਾ

epithet ('ਐਪਿਥੈੱਟ) *n* ਵਿਸ਼ੇਸ਼ਣ, ਉਪਾਧੀ, ਉਪਨਾਮ

epitome (ਇ'ਪਿਟਅਮਿ) *n* ਪੁਸਤਕ ਦਾ ਸਾਰ, ਖ਼ੁਲਾਸਾ, ਤੱਤ, ਅੰਸ਼ ਸਾਰਾਂਸ਼, ਨਿਚੋੜ

epitomize (ਇ'ਪਿਟਅਮਾਇਜ਼) *v* ਤੱਤ ਕੱਢਣਾ, ਸੰਖੇਪ ਕਰਨਾ, ਸਾਰ ਸੰਗ੍ਰਹ ਕਰਨਾ

epoch ('ਈਪੌਕ) *n* ਯੁੱਗ, ਕਾਲ, ਜ਼ਮਾਨਾ, ਦੌਰ

equal ('ਈਕਵ੍(ਅ)ਲ) *a n v* ਸਮ, ਤੁੱਲ, ਸਮਰੂਪ ਇਕਰੂਪ, ਸੰਤੁਲਤ, ਸਮਾਨ ਹੋਣਾ, ਬਰਾਬਰੀ ਕਰਨਾ, ਇਕ ਜਿਹਾ ਕਰਨਾ; ~ity ਬਰਾਬਰੀ, ਤੁੱਲਤਾ, ਸਮਾਨਤਾ, ਸਮਤਾ; ~ize ਬਰਾਬਰ ਕਰਨਾ, ਸਮੀਕਰਨ ਕਰਨਾ

equate (ਇ'ਕਵੇਇਟ) *v* ਬਰਾਬਰ ਕਰਨਾ, ਬਰਾਬਰੀ ਦੱਸਣੀ, ਸਮੀਕਰਨ ਕਰਨਾ, ਸਮੀਕ੍ਰਿਤ ਕਰਨਾ, ਤੁੱਲਤਾ ਦਿਖਾਉਣੀ, ਸਮਾਨ ਰੂਪ ਮੰਨਣਾ

equation (ਇ'ਕਵੇਇਯ਼ਨ) *n* ਸਮੀਕਰਨ, ਤੁੱਲਕਰਨ; ਸੰਤੁਲਨ, ਬਰਾਬਰੀ, (ਗਣਿ)

equator (ਇ'ਕਵੇਇਟਅ*) *n* ਭੂ-ਮੱਧ-ਰੇਖਾ

equilibrium ('ਈਕਵ੍ਿ'ਲਿਬਰਿਅਮ) *n* ਸਮਤੋਲ, ਸੰਤੁਲਨ, ਸੰਤੁਲਨ ਅਵਸਥਾ, ਤੁੱਲ ਭਾਰਤਾ

equip (ਇ'ਕਵ੍ਿਪ) *v* ਲੈਸ ਕਰਨਾ, ਸਾਜ਼ੋ-ਸਮਾਨ ਦਾ

ਪ੍ਰਬੰਧ ਕਰਨਾ, ਸੰਦਬੱਧ ਕਰਨਾ, ਸੁਆਰਨਾ, ਸਜਾਉਣਾ; ਤਿਆਰ ਕਰਨਾ, ਠੀਕ ਠਾਕ ਕਰਨਾ; ~ped ਸੁਸੱਜਤ, ਸਾਜ਼-ਸਾਮਾਨ ਨਾਲ ਲੈਸ; ~ment ਸਮਗਰੀ, ਸਾਜ਼ੋ-ਸਾਮਾਨ, ਬੋਰੀਆ-ਬਿਸਤਰਾ

equity ('ਐੱਕਵਅਟਿ) *n* ਨਿਆਂ, ਹੱਕ; ਨਿਰਪੱਖਤਾ; (ਕਾ) ਸੁਨੀਤੀ, ਉਹ ਹੁੰਡੀਆਂ ਜਾਂ ਸ਼ੇਅਰ ਜਿਨ੍ਹਾਂ ਤੇ ਨਿਸ਼ਚਤ ਸੂਦ ਨਹੀਂ ਮਿਲਦਾ

equivalence (ਇ'ਕਵਿਵ੍ਅਲਅੰਸ) *n* ਤੁੱਲਤਾ, ਸਮਾਨਤਾ, ਸਮਾਨਾਰਥਕਤਾ, ਸਮਫਲਤਵ, ਸਮੂਲਤਾ

equivalent (ਇ'ਕਵਿਵ੍ਅਲਅੰਟ) *n a* ਤੁੱਲਾ ਰਾਸ਼ੀ, ਪਰਯਾਯ, ਤੁੱਲਾਰਥ ਸ਼ਬਦ; ਸਮਾਨ ਸਮਮੁੱਲ, ਸਮਪ੍ਰਭਾਵੀ; ਤੁੱਲਾਰਥਕ, ਸਮਾਨਾਰਥਕ

era ('ਇਅਰਅ) *n* ਸੰਮਤ, ਸੰਨ, ਸਾਕਾ

eradicate (ਇ'ਰੈਡ੍ਇਕੇਇਟ) *v* ਜੜ੍ਹੋਂ ਉਖੇੜਨਾ ਨਸ਼ਟ ਕਰਨਾ, ਨਿਰਮੂਲ ਕਰਨਾ, ਕੱਢ ਦੇਣਾ, ਹਟਾ ਦੇਣਾ, ਉਜਾੜਨਾ

eradication (ਇ'ਰੈਡ੍ਇ'ਕੇਇਸ਼ਨ) *n* ਮਲੀਆਮੇਟ, ਸਫ਼ਾਈ, ਖ਼ਾਤਮਾ, ਸਤਿਆਨਾਸ

erase (ਇ'ਰੇਇਜ਼) *v* ਰਬੜ ਨਾਲ ਮਿਟਾਉਣਾ, ਖੁਰਚਣਾ, ਪੂੰਝਣਾ, ਮੇਸਣਾ; ~r ਰਬੜ (ਮਿਟਾਉਣ ਵਾਲੀ), ਖੁਰਚਨੀ

erect (ਇ'ਰੈੱਕਟ) *v a* ਸਿੱਧਾ ਕਰਨਾ, ਖੜ੍ਹਾ ਕਰਨਾ, ਉਠਾਉਣਾ, ਨਿਰਮਾਣ ਕਰਨਾ, ਖਲੋਤਾ, ਖੜ੍ਹਾ, ਰੋਮਾਂਚਤ; ~ion ਨਿਰਮਾਣ, ਉਠਾਨ, ਖੜਾ ਕਰਨਾ, ਰਚਨਾ, ਸੰਸਥਾਪਨ; ਇਮਾਰਤ

erode (ਇ'ਰਅਉਡ) *v* ਢਹਿਣਾ, ਖੋਰਨਾ, ਨਸ਼ਟ ਕਰਨਾ, ਹੌਲੀ ਹੌਲੀ ਖੈ ਕਰਨਾ, ਚੱਟ ਜਾਣਾ; ਖਾ ਜਾਣਾ

erosion (ਇ'ਰਅਉਯ਼ਨ) *n* ਢਾਹ, ਖੋਰ, ਕਾਟ, ਖੈ,

ਖੈ ਕਰਨ

erotic (ਇ'ਰੋਟਿਕ) *n a* ਸ਼ਿੰਗਾਰ-ਕਾਵਿ, ਪਰੇਮ-ਕਾਵਿ; ਇਸ਼ਕੀਆ, ਸ਼ਿੰਗਾਰਾਤਮਕ; ਪਰੇਮਾਤਮਕ; ਕਾਮੁਕ, ਵਾਸ਼ਨਾ-ਪੂਰਨ

err (ਅ:*) *v* ਗ਼ਲਤੀ ਕਰਨੀ, ਭੁੱਲ ਕਰਨੀ; ਅਸ਼ੁੱਧ ਹੋਣਾ, ਭੁੱਲ ਹੋਣੀ; ~ata *pl* ਸ਼ੁੱਧੀ-ਪੱਤਰ ਅਸ਼ੁੱਧ ਲਿਖਤ, ਅਸ਼ੁੱਧੀ ਲਿਖਤ; ~atic ਅਨਿਸ਼ਚਤ, ਅਨਿਯਤ, ਡਾਵਾਂਡੋਲ, ਚੰਚਲ, ਬੇਕਾਇਦਾ, ਅਸਥਿਰ, ਕ੍ਰਮਹੀਨ; ~oneous ਅਸ਼ੁੱਧ, ਗ਼ਲਤ, ਭਰਾਂਤੀਪੂਰਨ ਤਰੁਟੀਪੂਰਨ, ਮਿਥਿਆ; ~or ਅਸ਼ੁੱਧੀ, ਗ਼ਲਤੀ, ਗ਼ਲਤ ਗੱਲ, ਭੁੱਲ; ਦੋਸ਼

erupt (ਇ'ਰਅੱਪਟ) *v* (ਮਸੂੜ੍ਹਿਆਂ ਵਿੱਚੋਂ ਲਹੂ ਦਾ) ਫੁੱਟ ਨਿਕਲਣਾ, (ਜੁਆਲਾਮੁਖੀ ਪਹਾੜ ਦੀ) ਫੁੱਟ ਪੈਣਾ; ~ion ਸਫੋਟ, ਵਿਸਫੋਟ, ਫੋੜਾ; ਨਿਕਾਸ

escalator ('ਐੱਸਕਅਲੇਇਟਅ*) *n* ਬਿਜਲਈ ਪੌੜੀ, ਟੁਰਦੀ ਪੌੜੀ

escape (ਇ'ਸਕੇਇਪ) *n v* ਪਲਾਇਨ, ਬਚਾਉ; ਛੁਟਕਾਰਾ; ਫਰਾਰ ਹੋਣਾ, ਭੱਜਣਾ; ਸਾਫ਼ ਬਚਨਾ

escapism (ਇ'ਸਕੇਇਪਿਜ਼(ਅ)ਮ) *n* ਪਲਾਇਨਵਾਦ, ਭਾਂਜਵਾਦ

escapist (ਇ'ਸਕੇਇਪਿਸਟ) *n* ਪਲਾਇਨਵਾਦੀ

eschew (ਇਸ'ਚੂ) *v* (ਤੋਂ) ਪਰਹੇਜ਼ ਕਰਨਾ, ਬਾਝ ਰਹਿਣਾ

escort ('ਐੱਸਕੋਟ, ਇ'ਸਕੋਟ) *n v* ਰੱਖਿਅਕ, ਰਖਵਾਲਾ, ਰਾਖੀ; ਪਹਿਰਾ; ਰੱਖਿਆ ਕਰਨੀ, ਅਗਵਾਈ ਕਰਨੀ

esoteric ('ਐੱਸਅ(ਉ)'ਟੈਰਿਕ) *a* ਗੁੱਝੂ, ਗੁਪਤ, ਬਾਤਨੀ

especial (ਇ'ਸਪੈੱਸ਼ਲ) *a* ਉੱਤਮ, ਪ੍ਰਮੁੱਖ; ਖ਼ਾਸ, ਵਿਸ਼ੇਸ਼

espionage ('ਐੱਸਪਿਅਨਾਯ਼) *n* (ਜਾਸੂਸਾਂ ਵਲੋਂ

ਕੀਤੀ), ਤੇਜ਼-ਫੇੜ੍ਹ

espousal (ਇ'ਸਪਉੁਜ਼ਲ) *n* ਹਿਮਾਇਤ, ਵਕਾਲਤ, ਵਿਆਹ, ਨਿਕਾਹ; ਮੰਗਣੀ

espy (ਇ'ਸਪਾਇ) *v* ਤਾੜਨਾ, ਪਤਾ ਲਗਾਉਣਾ, ਭੇਦ ਪਾਉਣਾ

esquire (ਇ'ਸਕਵਾਇਅ*) *n* ਨਾਂ ਦੇ ਸਨਮਾਨਾਰਥ ਪਦ, ਪਿਛੇ ਲਿਖਿਆ ਜਾਂਦਾ ਹੈ, ਸਰਦਾਰ ਜੀ ਸ੍ਰੀਮਾਨ ਆਦਿ

essay (ਏ'ਸੇਇ, ਐਸੇ) *n v* ਨਿਬੰਧ, ਸਾਹਿਤਕ ਰਚਨਾ ਜਾਂ ਲੇਖ, ਜਤਨ; ਪਰਖ, ਜਾਂਚ; ਪਰਖਣਾ, ਕਸਣਾ, ਕੋਸ਼ਸ਼ ਕਰਨੀ; ~**ist** ਨਿਬੰਧਕਾਰ, ਨਿਬੰਧ ਲੇਖਕ

essence (ਏ'ਸਅੰਸ) *a n* ਸਾਰ, ਮੂਲ, ਮੂਲ ਪ੍ਰਕਿਰਤੀ, ਖ਼ਾਸੀਅਤ; ਤੱਤ, ਮੂਲ ਵਸਤੂ, ਮਹਿਕ, ਖ਼ੁਸ਼ਬੂ

essential (ਇ'ਸੈਂਸ਼ਲ) *a n* ਮੂਲ; ਅਵੱਸ਼ਕ, ਤਾਤਵਕ, ਸਾਰਭੂਤ, ਵਾਸਤਵਿਕ; ~**ly** ਜ਼ਰੂਰੀ ਹੀ, ਅਵੱਸ਼ਕ ਰੂਪ ਨਾਲ, ਯਥਾਰਥਕ ਰੂਪ ਨਾਲ

establish (ਇ'ਸਟੈਬਲਿਸ਼) *v* ਸਥਾਪਤ ਕਰਨਾ, ਜਮਾਉਣਾ, ਬਾਪਣਾ, ਬਿਠਾਉਣਾ, ਸਿਧ ਕਰਨਾ, ਸਾਬਤ ਕਰਨਾ, ਨੀਂਹ ਰੱਖਣੀ; ~**ed** ਸਥਾਪਤ, ਸਿਧ, ਪ੍ਰਮਾਣਤ, ਸਰਵਸੰਮਤ; ~**ment** ਸੰਸਥਾਪਨ, ਕਾਇਮੀ, ਚਾਕਰ ਮੰਡਲ, ਦਫ਼ਤਰ ਦਾ ਅਮਲਾ; ਵਪਾਰੀ ਫ਼ਰਮ, ਘਰ-ਬਾਰ, ਘਰ-ਗ੍ਰਹਿਸਥੀ

estate (ਇ'ਸਟੇਇਟ) *n* ਜਾਇਦਾਦ; ਇਲਾਕਾ, ਜਾਗੀਰ, ਸ਼ਾਸਕ ਵਰਗਾ, (ਪ੍ਰ) ਦਸ਼ਾ, ਹਾਲਤ, ਸੰਪਤੀ, ਜਾਗੀਰ, ਰਿਆਸਤ

esteem (ਇ'ਸਟੀਮ) *v n* ਆਦਰ ਮਾਨ ਕਰਨਾ, ਚੰਗਾ ਸਮਝਣਾ, ਖ਼ਿਆਲ ਕਰਨਾ; ਆਦਰ ਸਨਮਾਨ, ਮਾਣ

estimate (ਏ'ਸਟਿਮਅਟ, 'ਏਸਟਿਮੇਇਟ) *n v* ਅਨੁਮਾਨ (ਗਿਣਤੀ, ਮਿਕਦਾਰ, ਰਕਮ ਆਦਿ ਦਾ) ਤਖ਼ਮੀਨਾ, ਅੱਟਾ ਸੱਟਾ, ਅੰਦਾਜ਼ਾ ਲਾਉਣਾ, ਅਨੁਮਾਨ ਲਾਉਣਾ

estimation ('ਏਸਟਿ'ਮੇਇਸ਼ਨ) *n* ਪਰਿਮਾਪ, ਮੁੱਲਾਂਕਣ, ਅਨੁਮਾਨ, ਅਟਕਲ ਮੱਤ, ਮੂਲ ਨਿਰੂਪਣ

estrange (ਇ'ਸਟਰੇਇੰਜ) *v* ਰੁਸਾਉਣਾ, ਨਾਰਾਜ਼ ਕਰਨਾ, ਚਿਤ ਹਟਾਉਣਾ, ਬੇਮੁਖ ਕਰਨਾ

eternal (ਇ'ਟਅਃਨਲ) *a* ਅਮਰ, ਸਨਾਤਨ, ਨਿਤ, ਨਿਰੰਤਰ

eternity (ਇ'ਟਅਃਨਅਟਿ) *n* ਸਦੀਵਤਾ, ਅਨੰਤਤਾ, ਅਮਿਟ ਸਚਾਈ

ether ('ਇਥਅ*) *n* ਆਕਾਸ਼, ਆਕਾਸ਼ ਤੋਂ ਪਰ੍ਹੇ ਆਕਾਸ਼, ਬੇਹੋਸ਼ ਕਰ ਦੇਣ ਵਾਲੀ ਦਵਾਈ; ਇਕ ਰਸਾਇਨਕ ਪਦਾਰਥ

ethic, ethics ('ਏਥਿਕ, 'ਏਥਿਕਸ) *n* ਨੀਤੀ ਵਿਗਿਆਨ; ਨੈਤਕਤਾ, ਨੈਤਕਨਿਯਮ; ਸਦਾਚਾਰ; ~**al** ਨੈਤਕ, ਨੀਤੀ-ਸ਼ਾਸਤਰੀ; ਆਚਾਰਕ

ethnic ('ਏਥਨਿਕ) *a* ਜਾਤੀ, ਨਸਲੀ; ਨਾਸਤਕ

etiquette ('ਏਟਿਕੈੱਟ) *n* ਸ਼ਿਸ਼ਟਾਚਾਰ, ਲੋਕਾਚਾਰ, ਸੁਚੱਜ, ਸੰਭਿਆਚਾਰ, ਵਿਧੀ; ਅਦਬੋ-ਆਦਾਬ; ਦਰਬਾਰੀ ਅਦਬੋ-ਆਦਾਬ, ਤਕੱਲਫ਼

eulogize ('ਯੂਲਅਜਾਇਜ਼) *n* ਉਸਤਤੀ ਕਰਨੀ, ਜਸ ਗਾਉਣਾ, ਕੀਰਤੀ ਕਰਨੀ

eulogy ('ਯੂਲਅਜਿ) *n* ਉਸਤਤੀ, ਪ੍ਰਸੰਸਾ, ਵਡਿਆਈ; ਕਸੀਦਾ, ਕੀਰਤੀ, ਸਲਾਹੁਤਾ

eunuch ('ਯੂਨਅਕ) *n* ਹੀਜੜਾ, ਖੁਸਰਾ, ਜਨਖਾ; ਨਾਮਰਦ

euphony ('ਯੂਫ਼ਅਨਿ) *n* ਮਧੁਰ ਧੁਨ, ਸੁਰਸ਼੍ਰੇਸ਼ਟਾ, ਸੁਰੀਲਾਪਨ, ਸੁਸ਼ਬਦ

evacuate (ਇ'ਵੈਕਯੁਏਇਟ) *v* ਕੱਢਣਾ, ਖ਼ਾਲੀ

ਕਰਨਾ; ਛੱਡ ਦੇਣਾ, ਪਰੇ ਲਿਜਾਣਾ, ਪਰਿਤਿਆਗ
ਕਰਨਾ, ਹਟਾਉਣਾ; ਵਿਰੇਚਨ ਕਰਨਾ

evacution (ਇਵੈਕਯ'ਏਇਸ਼ਨ) *n* ਨਿਕਾਸ,
ਤਿਆਗ, ਮਲ ਤਿਆਗ

evade (ਇਵ੍ਏਡ) *v* ਟਾਲ ਜਾਣਾ, ਬਚ ਜਾਣਾ,
ਟਾਲਮਟੋਲ ਕਰਨਾ, ਭੱਜਣਾ, ਖਿਸਕਣਾ

evaluation (ਇਵ੍ਐਲਯੁ'ਏਇਸ਼ਨ) *n* ਮੁਲੱ-
ਨਿਰਧਾਰਨ

evaporate (ਇਵ੍ਐਪਅਰੋਇਟ) *v* ਭਾਫ਼ ਬਣਨਾ,
ਭਾਫ਼ ਬਣਾਉਣਾ, ਲੋਪ ਹੋ ਜਾਣਾ, ਨਮੀ ਜਾਂ ਤਰੀ
ਕੱਢ ਦੇਣੀ

evoporation (ਇਵ੍ਐਪਅ'ਰੇਇਸ਼ਨ) *n* ਵਾਸ਼ਪਨ,
ਵਾਸ਼ਪੀਕਰਨ, ਭਾਫ਼ਣ; ਭਾਫ਼

evasion (ਇਵ੍ਐਇਯਨ) *a* ਟਾਲਮਟੋਲ, ਬਹਾਨਾ,
ਘੁੱਤਾ

evasive (ਇਵ੍ਏਇਸਿਵ੍) *a* ਛਲੀ, ਕਪਟੀ, ਟਾਲੂ

Eve (ਈਵ੍) *n* (1) ਹੱਵਾ, ਆਦਿ ਨਾਰੀ; (e~)
(2) ਔਰਤ; (3) ਪੂਰਬ, ਦਿਵਸ, ਘਟਨਾ
ਵਿਸ਼ੇਸ਼; ਸੰਧਿਆ; ਪੂਰਬ-ਸੰਧਿਆ

even (ਈਵਨ) *adv* ਇਕ ਰਸ, ਸਮਤਲ, ਸਮ,
ਬਰਾਬਰ, ਬਿਨਾ ਰਿਆਇਤ; ਸ਼ਾਂਤ; ਜੋੜ, ਯੁਗਮ,
ਯੁਗਤ; ਭੀ, ਵੀ, ਤਕ, ਇਥੋਂ ਤਕ ਕਿ

evening (ਈਵਨਿਙ) *n* ਸੰਝ, ਸੰਧਿਆ, ਸ਼ਾਮ

event (ਇਵ੍ਏਂਟ) *n* ਘਟਨਾ, ਵਾਰਦਾਤ,
ਮਹੱਤਵਪੂਰਨ ਵਾਕਿਆ

eventual (ਇਵ੍ਐਨੱਚੁਅਲ) *a* ਅੰਤਮ, ਆਖ਼ਰੀ,
ਸੰਭਾਵਤ; **~ity** ਸੰਭਾਵਨਾ, ਸੰਭਵ ਘਟਨਾ; **~ly**
ਆਖ਼ਰਕਾਰ, ਅੰਤ ਵਿਚ

ever (ਔਵ੍ਅ*) *adv* ਨਿੱਤ, ਨਿਰੰਤਰ; ਸਦਾ
ਸਦੀਵੀ, ਲਗਾਤਾਰ, ਕਦੇ, ਕਿਸੇ ਵੇਲੇ, ਹਰ ਵੇਲੇ;
~after ਉਦੋਂ ਤੋਂ, ਉਦੋਂ ਲੈ ਕੇ; **~green** ਸਦਾ-

ਬਹਾਰ, ਬਾਰਾ ਮਾਸੀ; **~lasting** ਨਿੱਤਤਾ;
ਸਥਾਈ, ਨਿੱਤ, ਅੰਨਤ, ਅਜਰ, ਚਿਰਸਥਾਈ;
for~ ਸਦਾ ਲਈ

every (ਔਵ੍ਰਿ) *a* ਹਰ, ਹਰ ਇਕ, ਪ੍ਰਤੀ, ਪ੍ਰਤੀ
ਇਕ, ਇਕ ਇਕ

evict (ਇਵ੍ਇਕਟ) *v* (ਮਕਾਰੇ ਨੂੰ) ਬੇਦਖ਼ਲ ਕਰਨਾ,
ਕੱਢ ਦੇਣਾ; **~ion** ਬੇਦਖ਼ਲੀ

evidence ('ਔਵ੍ਇਡਅੰਸ) *a* ਸਪਸ਼ਟਤਾ; ਸੰਕੇਤ,
ਪਰਮਾਣ, ਗਵਾਹੀ, ਸ਼ਹਾਦਤ, ਸਬੂਤ; ਪਰਮਾਣਤ
ਕਰਨਾ, ਪਰਗਟ ਕਰਨਾ, ਸਾਬਤ ਕਰਨਾ,
ਸ਼ਹਾਦਤ ਦੇਣਾ

evident ('ਔਵ੍ਇਡਅੰਟ) *a* ਪ੍ਰਤੱਖ ਜ਼ਾਹਰ, ਖੁੱਲ੍ਹਾ,
ਸਪਸ਼ਟ

evil ('ਇਵ੍ਲ) *a n* ਬੁਰਾ, ਮੰਦਾ, ਮਨਹੂਸ, ਨਕਾਰਾ,
ਹਾਨੀਕਾਰਕ, ਬਦੀ, ਗੁਨਾਹ, ਬੁਰਾਈ; **~doer**
ਬਦਕਾਰ, ਦੁਸ਼ਟ

evocation ('ਔਵ੍ਅ(ਉ)'ਕੇਇਸ਼ਨ) *n* ਜਜ਼ਬਾਤ
ਦਾ ਉਭਾਰ, ਸੱਦਾ, ਪੁਕਾਰ

evocative, evocatory (ਇਵ੍ੌਕਅਟਿਵ੍
ਇਵ੍ੌਕਅਟਰਿ) *a* ਭਾਵਨਾਮਈ,
ਭਾਵਨਾਉਪਜਾਇਕ

evoke (ਇਵ੍ਅਉਕ) *v* ਬੁਲਾਉਣਾ, ਸੱਦਣਾ,
(ਜਜ਼ਬਾਤ) ਉਭਾਰਨਾ, ਵੱਡੀ ਅਦਾਲਤ ਵਿਚ
ਤਲਬ ਕਰਨਾ, ਚੇਤਨ ਕਰਨਾ, ਜਗਾਉਣਾ

evolution ('ਈਵ੍ਅ'ਲੂਸ਼ਨ) *n* ਵਿਕਾਸ, ਚਾਲ

evolve (ਇਵ੍ੌਲਵ੍) *v* ਉਤਪੰਨ ਕਰਨਾ; ਫੈਲਾਉਣਾ,
ਫੈਲਣਾ, ਤਰਤੀਬ ਦੇਣਾ; (ਗਰਮੀ ਦਾ) ਖ਼ਾਰਜ
ਕਰਨਾ; ਵਿਕਾਸ ਕਰਨਾ, ਪੁਸ਼ਟੀ ਹੋਣੀ, ਵਧਾਉਣਾ,
ਵੱਧਣਾ

exact (ਇਗਜ਼ੈਕਟ) *a v* ਠੀਕ, ਸਹੀ, ਜਚਵਾਂ,
ਢੁਕਵਾਂ, ਸੁਨਿਸ਼ਚਿਤ; ਕਠੋਰ, ਤਕਾਜ਼ਾ ਕਰਨਾ,

ਜ਼ੋਰ ਪਾਉਣਾ; ~ly ਐਨ, ਬਰਾਬਰ, ਠੀਕ ਵਕਤ, ਉੱਤੇ, ਦਰੁਸਤ

exaggerate (ਇਗਾ'ਜ਼ੈਜਅਰੇਇਟ) v ਅੱਤਕਥਨੀ ਕਰਨੀ, ਵਧਾ ਚੜ੍ਹਾ ਕੇ ਦੱਸਣਾ, ਮਿਰਚ ਮਸਾਲਾ ਲਾ ਕੇ ਦੱਸਣਾ

exaggeration (ਇਗਾ'ਜ਼ੈਜਅ'ਰੇਇਸ਼ਨ) n ਅੱਤਕਥਨੀ; ਮੁਬਾਲਗਾ, ਵਾਕ-ਵਿਸਤਾਰ

exalt (ਇਗਾ'ਜ਼ੋਲਟ) v ਵਧਾਉਣਾ, ਉਚਿਆਉਣਾ, ਉੱਚਾ ਕਰਨਾ, ਵਡਿਆਈ ਕਰਨੀ; ਉਸਤਤੀ ਕਰਨੀ; ~ation ਉਚਾਣ, ਉੱਚਪਦ, ਉੱਨਤੀ, ਉੱਚਤਾ, ਬੁਲੰਦੀ, ਆਨੰਦ, ਉੱਲਾਸ, ਉਮੰਗ; ਤੀਬਰਤਾ

examination (ਇਗਾ'ਜ਼ੈਮਿ'ਨੇਇਸ਼ਨ) n ਪਰੀਖਿਆ, ਇਮਤਿਹਾਨ, ਪਰਖ; ਨਿਰੀਖਣ; ਮੁਆਇਨਾ, ਜਾਂਚ-ਪੜਤਾਲ

examine (ਇਗਾ'ਜ਼ੈਮਿਨ) n ਪੜਤਾਲਣਾ, ਪਰੀਖਿਆ ਲੈਂਟੀ, ਜਾਂਚ ਕਰਨੀ, ਪਰਖਣਾ; ਪੜਤਾਲ ਕਰਨੀ; ਛਾਣਬੀਣ ਕਰਨੀ; ਜਾਂਚ ਕਰਨੀ, ਪੁੱਛ-ਗਿੱਛ ਕਰਨੀ; ~e ਪਰੀਖਿਆਰਥੀ; ~r ਪਰੀਖਿਅਕ, ਪੜਤਾਲੀਆ

example (ਇਗਾ'ਜ਼ਾਂਪਲ) n ਦ੍ਰਿਸ਼ਟਾਂਤ, ਉਦਾਹਰਣ, ਮਿਸਾਲ; ਨਮੂਨਾ

exasperate (ਇਗਾ'ਜ਼ੈਸਪਅਰੇਇਟ) v ਖਿਝਾਉਣਾ, ਉਤੇਜਤ ਕਰਨਾ, ਕਰੋਧ ਦੁਆਉਣਾ, ਚਿੜ੍ਹਾਉਣਾ, ਅੱਗ ਬਗੋਲਾ ਕਰਨਾ

excavate ('ਐਕਸਕਅਵੇਇਟ) v ਖੋਤਣਾ, ਪੁੱਟਣਾ, ਖੁੱਟਣਾ; ਖ਼ਾਲੀ ਕਰਨਾ; ਪੋਲਾ ਕਰਨਾ, ਥੋਥਾ ਕਰਨਾ

exceed (ਇਕ'ਸੀਡ) v ਵਧ ਜਾਣਾ, ਅੱਗੇ ਨਿਕਲ ਜਾਣਾ, ਅੱਤ ਕਰਨੀ, ਹੱਦ ਟੱਪਣੀ; ਮਾਤ ਕਰਨਾ, ਉਲੰਘਣਾ; ~ingly ਅਤੀ ਅਧਿਕ; ਬਹੁਤ, ਬੇਹੱਦ, ਬਹੁਤ ਹੀ

excellence (ਇਕ'ਸੈਲਅੰਸ) v ਅੱਗੇ ਨਿਕਲ ਜਾਣਾ, ਵਧ ਜਾਣਾ, ਬਾਜ਼ੀ ਲੈ ਜਾਣਾ, ਮਾਤ ਕਰਨਾ

excellent (ਇਕ'ਸੈਲਅੰਟ) a ਉਤਕ੍ਰਿਸ਼ਟ, ਪਰਮ, ਸ੍ਰੇਸ਼ਠ, ਉੱਤਮ, ਮਹੱਤਵ-ਪੂਰਨ, ਪ੍ਰਤਿਸ਼ਠਤ

except (ਇਕਸੈਪੱਟ) v perp ਛੱਡਣਾ, ਗਿਣਤੀ ਵਿਚ ਨਾ ਲਿਆਉਣਾ, ਆਪੱਤੀ ਕਰਨੀ, ਇਤਰਾਜ਼ ਕਰਨ, ਕੱਢਣਾ; ਪਰੰਤੂ; ~ion ਵਰਜਨ, ਵਿਵਰਜਨ, ਛੋਟ, ਤਿਆਗ; ~ional ਅਸਧਾਰਨ, ਅਨੋਖਾ

excerpt ('ਐਂਕਸਅ:ਪਟ, ਇਕ'ਸਅ:ਪਟ) n v ਪੁਸਤਕ ਵਿਚੋਂ ਹਵਾਲਾ, ਟੂਕ, ਪੁਸਤਕ, ਸੰਕਲਨ; ਚੋਣ, ਖ਼ੁਲਾਸਾ ਕਰਨਾ, ਚੋਣ ਕਰਨਾ

excess (ਇਕ'ਸੈਂਸ) n a ਅੱਤਿਆਚਾਰ; ਵਧੀਕੀ, ਵਾਧਾ, ਅਧਿਕਤਾ, ਬਹੁਤਾਤ; ~ive ਅਤੀ, ਅਤੀਅੰਤ, ਬੇਹਿਸਾਬ, ਬੇਸ਼ੁਮਾਰ

exchange (ਇਕਸ'ਚੇਇੰਜ) n v (1) ਤਬਾਦਲਾ ਵਟਾਂਦਰਾ, ਸਿੱਕੇ ਦਾ ਵਟਾਂਦਰਾ, ਹੁੰਡੀ ਦੁਆਰਾ ਲੈਣ-ਦੇਣ, ਆਦਾਨਪ੍ਰਦਾਨ; (2) ਕੇਂਦਰ; ਵਟਾਂਦਰਾ ਕਰਨਾ, ਬਦਲਨਾ, ਲੈਣ ਦੇਣ ਕਰਨਾ, ਨਿਗਾਹਾਂ ਮਿਲਾਉਣੀਆਂ

exchequer (ਇਕਸ'ਚੈੱਕਅ*) n ਰਾਜ-ਕੋਸ਼, ਸਰਕਾਰੀ ਖ਼ਜ਼ਾਨਾ, ਮਹਿਕਮਾ ਮਾਲ, ਵਿੱਤ-ਵਿਭਾਗ

excise ('ਐਕਸਾਇਜ਼, ਐਕ'ਸਾਇਜ਼) v ਉਤਪਾਦਨ ਕਰ, ਚੁੰਗੀ, ਸਰਕਾਰੀ ਮਹਿਸੂਲ, ਆਬਕਾਰੀ; ਚੁੰਗੀ ਲੈਣਾ, ਮਹਿਸੂਲ ਲੈਣਾ; ਕੱਟ ਦੇਣਾ, ਉਡਾ ਦੇਣਾ

excite (ਇਕ'ਸਾਇਟ) v ਉਕਸਾਉਣਾ, ਉਭਾਰਨਾ, ਗਰਮਾਉਣਾ, ਟੁੰਬਣਾ; ਭੜਕ ਪੈਣਾ, ਗਰਮ ਹੋ ਜਾਣਾ; ~ment ਜੋਸ਼, ਖਲਬਲੀ ਉਤੇਜਨਾ, ਆਵੇਸ਼, ਸਨਸਨੀ

exciting (ਇਕ'ਸਾਇਟਿੰਡ) a ਭੜਕਾਊਣ ਵਾਲਾ, ਉਕਸਾਊਣ ਵਾਲਾ, ਉਤੇਜਕ

exclaim (ਇਕ'ਸਕਲੇਇਮ) v ਪੁਕਾਰ ਉੱਠਣਾ, ਚੀਕ ਉੱਠਣਾ, ਦੁਹਾਈ ਪਾਉਣਾ

exclamation ('ਔਕਸਕਲਆ'ਮੇਇਸ਼ਨ) n ਪੁਕਾਰ, ਦੁਹਾਈ, ਹਾਏ ਹਾਏ; ਵਿਸਮਕ ਚਿੰਨ੍

exclamatory (ਔਕ'ਸਕਲੈਮਅਟ(ਅ)ਰਿ) a ਅਸਚਰਜ-ਜਨਕ, ਵਿਸਮੈ-ਜਨਕ

exclude (ਇਕ'ਸਕਲੂਡ) v ਬਾਹਰ ਰੱਖਣਾ, ਪਰੇ ਰੱਖਣਾ, ਕੱਢ ਦੇਣਾ; ਛੱਡ ਦੇਣਾ; ਰੋਕਣਾ

excluding (ਇਕ'ਸਕਲੂਡਿਙ) n ਬਿਨਾ, ਤੋਂ ਰਹਿਤ, ਨੂੰ ਛੱਡ ਕੇ

exclusion (ਇਕ'ਸਕਲੂਯ਼ਨ) n ਵਰਜਨ, ਅਲਹਿਦਗੀ

exclusive (ਇਕ'ਸਕਲੂਸਿਵ਼) a ਨਿਵੇਕਲਾ; ਰਾਖਵਾਂ; ਵੱਖਰਾ

excreta (ਇਕ'ਸਕਰੀਟਆ) n pl ਵਿਸ਼ਟਾ, ਗੋਹਾ, ਮਲ-ਮੂਤਰ, ਟੱਟੀ

excrete (ਇਕ'ਸਕਰੀਟ) v ਵਿਸ਼ਟਾ, ਗੋਹਾ, ਮੈਲਾ ਆਦਿ ਤਿਆਗਣਾ, ਟੱਟੀ ਕਰਨਾ, ਹੱਗਣਾ

excretion (ਇਕ'ਸਕਰੀਸ਼ਨ) n ਮਲ-ਮੂਤਰ

excurse (ਇਕ'ਸਕਘ:ਸ) v ਮਟਰ-ਗਾਸ਼ਤ ਕਰਨੀ, ਘੁੰਮਣਾ, ਸੈਰ-ਸਪਾਟਾ ਕਰਨਾ

excursion (ਇਕ'ਸਕਘ:ਸ਼ਨ) n ਸਫ਼ਰ; ਸੈਰ-ਸਪਾਟਾ, ਹਵਾਖੋਰੀ, ਮਟਰ-ਗਾਸ਼ਤ, ਭੁਮਣ

excursive (ਇਕ'ਸਕਘ:ਸਿਵ਼) a ਭੁਮਣਸ਼ੀਲ, ਸੈਲਾਨੀ

excuse (ਇਕ'ਸਕਯੂਸ) n v ਦੋਸ਼-ਮੁਕਤੀ, ਖਿਮਾ, ਬਹਾਨਾ; ਖਿਮਾ ਕਰਨਾ, ਉਜ਼ਰ ਕਰਨਾ, ਖਿਮਾ ਮੰਗਣੀ

execrate (ਐਕੱਸਿਕਰੇਇਟ) v ਅਤੀਅੰਤ ਘਿਰਨਾ ਕਰਨਾ, ਸਰਪ ਦੇਣਾ, ਸਰਾਪਣਾ, ਕੋਸਣਾ, ਲਾਨ੍ਤ ਪਾਉਣਾ

execration (ਐਕੱਸਿ'ਕਰੇਇਸ਼ਨ) n ਘਿਰਨਾ, ਨਫ਼ਰਤ, ਲਾਨ੍ਤ, ਦੁਰਾਸੀਸ, ਸਰਪ

execute (ਐਕੱਸਿਕਯੂਟ) v ਲਾਗੂ ਕਰਨਾ; ਪਾਲਟਾ ਕਰਨੀ, ਅਮਲ ਕਰਨਾ; ਬਜਾ ਲਿਆਉਣਾ; ਸ਼ਿਖ ਦੇਣਾ, ਸਹੀ ਪਾਉਣੀ; ਜਾਇਦਾਦ ਜਾਂ ਮੁਲਕ ਦੇ ਦੇਣਾ; ਕਰਤੱਵ ਪਾਲਣਾ, ਫ਼ਾਂਸੀ ਦੇਣਾ, (ਸੰਗੀ) ਵਜਾਉਣਾ

execution (ਐਕੱਸਿ'ਕਯੂਸ਼ਨ) n ਪਾਲਣ, ਮੂਰਤੀ, ਤਾਮੀਲ; ਨਿਭਾ, ਚੁਸਤੀ, ਹੁਸ਼ਿਆਰੀ, ਜ਼ਬਤ; ਪ੍ਰਾਣ-ਦੰਡ, ਸੂਲੀ, ਫ਼ਾਂਸੀ

executive (ਇਗਜ਼ੈਂਕਯੂਟਿਵ਼) a n ਪ੍ਰਬੰਧਕ, ਪ੍ਰਬੰਧ-ਅਧਿਕਾਰੀ

exegesis (ਐਕੱਸਿ'ਜੀਸਿਸ) n ਵਿਆਖਿਆ, ਟੀਕਾ; ਭਾਸ਼

exemplify (ਇਗਜ਼ੈਂਪਲਿਫ਼ਾਇ) v ਦ੍ਰਿਸ਼ਟਾਂਤ ਦੁਆਰਾ, ਮਿਸਾਲ ਦੇਣਾ, ਮਿਸਾਲ ਬਣਨਾ,

exempt (ਇਗਜ਼ੈਂਪਟ) a n v ਮੁਕਤ, ਰਿਹਾ, ਛੱਡਿਆ ਹੋਇਆ; ਮੁਕਤ ਕਰਨਾ, ਛੱਡ ਦੇਣਾ

exercise (ਐਕੱਸਅ:ਸਾਇਸ) n v ਪ੍ਰਯੋਗ; ਅਭਿਆਸ, ਮਸ਼ਕ, ਕਸਰਤ; ਪ੍ਰਸ਼ਨਮਾਲਾ, ਪੂਜਾ-ਪਾਠ, ਪ੍ਰਯੋਗ ਕਰਨਾ; ਅਭਿਆਸ ਕਰਨਾ; ਸੇਵਨ ਕਰਨਾ, ਕਸਰਤ ਕਰਨੀ; ਸਿੱਖਿਆ ਦੇਣੀ; ਵਰਤੋਂ ਕਰਨੀ

exert (ਇਗਜ਼ਅ:ਟ) v ਜ਼ੋਰ ਮਾਰਨਾ; ਕੰਮ ਲੈਣਾ, ਪ੍ਰਯਤਨ ਕਰਨਾ, ਚੇਸ਼ਟਾ ਕਰਨੀ, ਪ੍ਰਯਾਸ ਕਰਨਾ; ~ion ਪ੍ਰਯਤਨ, ਜਤਨ, ਪਰਿਸ਼੍ਰੱਮ, ਉੱਦਮ, ਕੋਸ਼ਿਸ਼, ਸਰਗਰਮੀ

exgratia (ਐਕੱਸ'ਗਰੇਇਸ਼ਅ) (L) (phr) ਬਖ਼ਸ਼ਸ਼ ਵਜੋਂ

exhale (ਐਕੱਸ'ਹੇਇਲ) v (ਧੂੰਆਂ ਜਾਂ ਹਵਾੜ੍) ਬਾਹਰ ਕੱਢਣਾ, ਸਾਹ ਬਾਹਰ ਕੱਢਣਾ, ਹੌਲੀ ਹੌਲੀ

ਬੋਲਣਾ, ਪ੍ਰਾਣ ਤਿਆਗਣੇ

exhaust (ਇਗਜ਼ਾਸਟ) *v n* ਸੱਖਣਾ ਕਰਨਾ; ਖ਼ਰਚ ਕਰ ਦੇਣਾ, ਸਿਲੰਡਰ ਵਿਚੋਂ ਭਾਫ਼ ਦਾ ਨਿਕਲਣਾ; ~ion ਸੱਖਣਾਪਣ, ਨਿਕਾਸ; ਖੀਣਤਾ, ਥਕਾਵਟ

exhibit (ਇਗਜ਼ਿਬਿਟ) *v* ਵਿਖਾਉਣਾ, ਪਰਗਟ ਕਰਨਾ, ਪੇਸ਼ ਕਰਨਾ, ਨੁਮਾਇਸ਼ ਕਰਨੀ; ਉਜਾਗਰ ਕਰਨਾ; ~ion ਪਰਦਰਸ਼ਨ, ਪ੍ਰਤੱਖ, ਨਿਰੂਪਣ, ਪਰਦਰਸ਼ਨੀ, ਨੁਮਾਇਸ਼; ~ive ਵਿਸਤਰਤ, ਵਿਆਪਕ, ਪੂਰਨ, ਸਰਵਾਂਗੀਨ

exhilarate (ਇਗਜ਼ਿਲਅਰੇਇਟ) *v* ਆਨੰਦ ਕਰਨਾ, ਹੁਲਸਾਉਣਾ, ਮਗਨ ਕਰਨਾ, ਖ਼ੁਸ਼ ਕਰਨਾ

exhilaration (ਇਗਜ਼ਿਲਅਾ'ਰੇਇਸ਼ਨ) *n* ਪ੍ਰਫੁਲਤਾ, ਆਹਲਾਦ, ਉਲੱਾਸ, ਖੇੜਾ, ਆਨੰਦ

exigence, exigency (ਐਕਸਿਜਅੰਸ, ਐਕਸਿਜਅੰਸੀ) *n* ਸਖ਼ਤ ਲੋੜ; ਮੁਤਾਲਬਾ; ਫੌਰੀ ਲੋੜ, ਔਕੜ

exile (ਐਕ'ਸਾਇਲ) *n v* ਦੇਸ਼-ਨਿਕਾਲਾ, ਪਰਵਾਸ, ਜਲਾਵਤਨੀ, ਬਨਵਾਸੀ ਬਨਵਾਸ, ਜਲਾਵਤਨ (ਮਨੁੱਖ); ਦੇਸ਼ ਨਿਕਾਲਾ ਦੇਣਾ, ਜਲਾਵਤਨ ਕਰਨਾ; ਜਲਾਵਤਨ

exist (ਇਗਜ਼ਿਸਟ) *v* ਹੋਣਾ, ਮੌਜੂਦ ਹੋਣਾ; ਰਹਿਣਾ, ਅਸਤਿਤਵ ਰੱਖਣਾ, ਘਟਣ ਹੋਣਾ; ~ence ਹੋਂਦ, ਮੌਜੂਦਗੀ; ਹਸਤੀ, ਪੈਦਾਇਸ਼, ਅਸਤਿਤਵ, ਪ੍ਰਾਣ, ਜੀਵ; ~ent ਵਿੰਦਮਾਨ, ਵਰਤਮਾਨ, ਵਾਸਤਵਿਕ, ਜੀਵਤ, ਪ੍ਰਚਲਤ

exit (ਐਕਸਿਟ) *n* ਪ੍ਰਸਥਾਨ; ਕੂਚ; ਵਿਦਾ, ਨਿਕਾਸ, ਬਾਹਰ ਜਾਣ ਦਾ ਰਸਤਾ

exodus (ਐਕਸਅਡਅਸ) *n* ਨਿਕਾਲਾ, ਕੂਚ, ਪ੍ਰਦੇਸ-ਜਾਣ, ਹਿਜਰਤ

ex-officio (ਐਕੱਸਅ'ਫ਼ਿਸ਼ਿਅਉ) (L) *a* ਅਹੁਦੇ ਦੇ ਨਾਤੇ, ਪਦ ਅਨੁਸਾਰ

exonerate (ਇਗਜ਼ੌਨਅਰੇਇਟ) *v* ਭਾਰ ਮੁਕਤ ਕਰਨਾ, ਨਿਵਿਰਤ ਕਰਨਾ, ਭਾਰ ਲਾਹੁਣਾ; ਨਿਰਦੋਸ਼ ਠਹਿਰਾਉਣਾ; (ਸੇਵਾ ਤੋਂ) ਛੁੱਟੀ ਦੇਣੀ

exorbitant (ਇਗਜ਼ੌ*ਬਿਟਅੰਟ) *a* ਬੇਜਾ, ਅਨੁਚਿਤ, ਅਤੀਅੰਤ

exotic (ਇਗਜ਼ੌਟਿਕ) *a* ਬਿਦੇਸ਼ੀ; ਵਚਿੱਤਰ

expand (ਇਕਸਪੈਂਡ) *v* ਚਾਰੇ ਪਾਸੇ ਫੈਲਣਾ, ਵਿਆਖਿਆ ਕਰਨੀ, ਵਧਣਾ, ਵਧਾਉਣਾ, ਫੁਲਾਉਣਾ, ਪਸਾਰਨਾ

expansion (ਐਕਸਪੈਨਸ਼ਨ) *n* ਫੈਲਾਉ; ਕਾਰੋਬਾਰ ਦਾ ਫੈਲਾਉ; ਵਿਸਤਾਰ ਪ੍ਰਚਾਰ, ਵਿਆਪਤੀ

expatiate (ਐਕ'ਸਪੇਇਸ਼ਿਏਇਟ) *v* (ਕਿਸੇ ਵਿਸ਼ੇ ਉੱਤੇ) ਰੱਜ ਕੇ ਬੋਲਣਾ; ਬੇਰੋਕ-ਟੋਕ ਘੁੰਮਣਾ, ਫਿਰਨਾ, ਵਿਚਰਨਾ

expatriate (ਐਕਸ'ਪੇਟਰਿਏਇਟ, ਐਕੱਸ'ਪੇਟਰਿਅਟ) *v a* ਪਰਵਾਸ ਕਰਨਾ, ਦੇਸ਼ ਤਿਆਗ ਕਰਨਾ, ਦੇਸ਼ ਨਿਕਾਲਾ ਦੇਣਾ, ਪਰਵਾਸੀ, ਜਲਾਵਤਨੀ

expatriation (ਐਕੱਸ'ਪੇਟਰਿ'ਏਇਸ਼ਨ) *n* ਪਰਵਾਸ, ਦੇਸ਼ਤਿਆਗ, ਦੇਸ਼-ਨਿਕਾਲਾ

expect (ਇਕਸਪੈੱਕਟ) *v* ਆਸ ਰੱਖਣੀ; ਉਮੀਦ ਕਰਨੀ; ਰਾਹ ਵੇਖਣਾ, ਉਡੀਕਣਾ, ਖ਼ਿਆਲ ਕਰਨਾ; ~ancy ਆਸ਼ਾ, ਸੰਭਾਵਨਾ, ਭਵਿੱਖ, ਆਸ, ਉਮੀਦਵਾਰੀ; ~ant mother ਗਾਰਭਵਤੀ ਇਸਤਰੀ

expedience, expediency (ਇਕ'ਸਪੀਡਯਅੰਸ, ਇਕ'ਸਪੀਡਯਅੰਸਿ) *n* ਉਪਯੋਗਤਾ, ਉਚਿਤਤਾ; ਹਿਕਮਤ; ਸਿਆਣਪ

expedient (ਇਕ'ਸਪੀਡਯਅੰਟ) *n a* ਉਪਯੋਗੀ

expedite (ਐਕੱਸਪਿਡਾਇਟ) *v* (ਕੰਮ) ਛੇਤੀ ਕਰ ਦੇਣਾ, ਤੁਰਤ ਕਰਨਾ, ਝਟਪਟ ਕਰਨਾ, ਸ਼ੀਘਰ

ਘੱਲਣਾ

expedition (ਐਕੱਸਪਿ'ਡਿਸ਼ਨ) *n* ਮੁਹਿੰਮ, ਚਤੁਰਾਈ

expel (ਇਕ'ਸਪੈੱਲ) *v* ਜ਼ੋਰ ਨਾਲ ਬਾਹਰ ਕੱਢਣਾ, ਬਰਾਦਰੀ ਜਾਂ ਸਕੂਲ ਅਥਵਾ ਕਾਲਜ ਵਿਚੋਂ ਕੱਢ ਦੇਣਾ, ਛੇਕਣਾ, ਨਾਂ ਕੱਟ ਦੇਣਾ, ਖਾਰਜ ਕਰਨਾ

expend (ਇਕ'ਸਪੈੱਡ) *v* ਪ੍ਰਯੋਗ ਕਰ ਲੈਣਾ, ਖ਼ਰਚ ਕਰਨਾ, ਲਗਾਉਣਾ, ਖਪਾਉਣਾ; **~iture** ਖ਼ਰਚ, ਖਪਾਉ, ਖ਼ਰਚੀ ਰਕਮ

expense (ਇਕ'ਸਪੈੱਸ) *n* ਖ਼ਰਚ, ਮੁੱਲ, ਲਾਗਤ

expensive (ਇਕ'ਸਪੈੱਨਸਿਵ਼) *a* ਮਹਿੰਗਾ, ਕੀਮਤੀ, ਮੁੱਲਵਾਨ, ਖ਼ਰਚੀਲਾ

experience (ਇਕ'ਸਪਿਅਰਿੰਸ) *n v* ਅਨੁਭਵ, ਤਜਰਬਾ, ਅਨੁਭਵ ਕਰਨਾ, ਸਿੱਖਣਾ, ਮਾਲੂਮ ਕਰਨਾ, ਪਰਖਣਾ, ਮਹਿਸੂਸ ਕਰਨਾ; **~d** ਅਨੁਭਵੀ, ਤਜਰਬੇਕਾਰ, ਕੁਸ਼ਲ

experiment (ਇਕ'ਸਪੈਰਿਮੈਂਟ, ਇਕ'ਸਪੈਰਿਮੈਂਟ) *n v* ਪ੍ਰਯੋਗ, ਤਜਰਬਾ, ਜਾਂਚ, ਪਰਖ; ਪ੍ਰਯੋਗ ਕਰਨਾ, ਤਜਰਬਾ ਕਰਨਾ, ਪਰੀਖਿਆ ਕਰਨੀ, ਜਾਂਚਣਾ; **~al** ਪ੍ਰਯੋਗਾਤਮਕ ਅਨੁਭੂਤੀਮੂਲਕ,

expert (ਐਕੱਸਪਅ:ਟ) *a* ਮਾਹਰ, ਵਿਸ਼ੇਸ਼ੱਗ

expertise (ਐੱਕਸਪਅ:ਟੀਜ਼) *n* ਨਿਪੁੰਨਤਾ, ਵਿਸ਼ੇਸ਼ੱਗਤਾ, ਮੁਹਾਰਤ

expire (ਇਕ'ਸਪਾਇਅ*) *v* (ਫੇਫੜਿਆਂ ਦੀ) ਹਵਾ ਬਾਹਰ ਕੱਢਣੀ: (ਅੱਗ ਦਾ) ਬੁੱਝ ਜਾਣਾ; ਮਰਨਾ, ਖ਼ਤਮ ਹੋਣਾ

expiry (ਇਕ'ਸਪਾਇਅਰਿ) *n* ਅੰਤ, ਖ਼ਾਤਮਾ

explain (ਇਕ'ਸਪਲੇਇਨ) *v* ਵਿਆਖਿਆ ਕਰਨੀ, ਸਪਸ਼ਟ ਕਰਨਾ, ਵਿਸਤਾਰ ਨਾਲ ਸਮਝਾਉਣਾ, ਜਵਾਬਦੇਹੀ ਕਰਨੀ, ਸਫ਼ਾਈ ਦੇਣਾ

explanation (ਐੱਕਸਪਲ'ਨੇਇਸ਼ਨ) *n* ਵੇਰਵਾ, ਵਿਆਖਿਆਤਮਕ, ਸਪਸ਼ਟੀਕਰਨ, ਸਫ਼ਾਈ,

ਜਵਾਬ ਤਲਬੀ

explanatory (ਇਕ'ਸਪੈੱਲਨਅਟ(ਅ)ਰਿ) *a* ਵਿਆਖਿਆਤਮਕ, ਸਪਸ਼ਟੀਕਰਨ, ਵੇਰਵੇਪੂਰਨ

explicable (ਇਕ'ਸਪਲਿਕਅਬਲ) *a* ਵਿਆਖਿਆ ਯੋਗ, ਸਪਸ਼ਟ ਕਰਨ ਯੋਗ

explicate (ਐਕਸਪਲਿਕੇਇਟ) *v* ਸਪਸ਼ਟ ਕਰਨਾ, ਅਰਥ ਖੋਲ੍ਹਣਾ, ਸਮਝਾਉਣਾ

explication (ਐੱਕਸਪਲਿ'ਕੇਇਸ਼ਨ) *n* ਸਪਸ਼ਟੀਕਰਨ, ਅਰਥ-ਵਿਸਤਾਰ

explicit (ਇਕ'ਸਪਲਿਸਿਟ) *n a* ਸੁਸਪਸ਼ਟ, ਸਾਫ਼, ਖਰਾ

explode (ਇਕ'ਸਪਲਅਉਡ) *v* ਵਿਸਫੋਟ ਹੋਣਾ, ਆਵਾਜ਼ ਜਾਂ ਧਮਾਕੇ ਨਾਲ ਫਟਣਾ; ਖੰਡਨ ਕਰਨਾ; ਬਦਨਾਮ ਕਰਨਾ

exploit (ਐਕਸਪਲੋਇਟ) *n v* ਵਰਤਣਾ, ਸ਼ੋਸ਼ਣ ਕਰਨਾ, ਲੁੱਟ ਕਰਨੀ, ਆਪਣਾ ਮਤਲਬ ਕੱਢਣਾ; **~ation** ਦੁਰ-ਉਪਯੋਗ; ਸ਼ੋਸ਼ਣ

exploration (ਐਕਸਪਲੋਅ'ਰੇਇਸ਼ਨ) *n* ਖੋਜ; ਛਾਣਬੀਨ, ਖੋਜ ਪੜਤਾਲ

explore (ਇਕ'ਸਪਲੋ*) *v* ਜਾਂਚ ਪੜਤਾਲ ਕਰਨੀ, ਛਾਣਬੀਨ ਕਰਨੀ, ਖੋਜ ਕੱਢਣੀ, ਢੂੰਡ ਭਾਲ ਕਰਨੀ; ਟੋਹਣਾ, ਖੋਜਨਾ, ਗਾਹਣਾ

explosion (ਇਕ'ਸਪਲਅਉਯਨ) *n* ਧਮਾਕਾ, ਭੜਾਕਾ; ਸਫੋਟ, ਵਿਸਫੋਟ; ਕ੍ਰੋਧ ਨਾਲ ਭੜਕ ਉਠਣਾ

explosive (ਇਕ'ਸਪਲਉਸਿਵ਼) *n* ਸਫੋਟਕ ਪਦਾਰਥ; ਸਫੋਟਕ ਧੁਨੀ; ਸਫੋਟਕ; ਵਿਸਫੋਟਕ

exponent (ਇਕ'ਸਪਅਉਨੈਂਟ) *n* ਵਿਆਖਿਆਤਾ, ਵਿਆਖਿਆਕਾਰ, ਪੈਰੋਕਾਰ

export (ਐਕਸਪੋਟ, ਇਕ'ਸਪੋਟ) *n v* ਨਿਰਯਾਤ, ਬਰਾਮਦ, ਬਾਹਰ ਘੱਲਣਾ, ਨਿਰਯਾਤ ਕਰਨਾ

expose (ਇਕ'ਸਪਅਉੱਜ਼) v ਨੰਗਾ ਰੱਖਣਾ, ਖੁੱਲ੍ਹਾ ਛੱਡਣਾ, ਬਰਬਾਦ ਹੋਣ ਦੇਣਾ; ਨੁਮਾਇਸ਼ ਲਈ ਰੱਖਣਾ; (ਭੇਦ) ਪਰਗਟ ਕਰਨਾ, ਨਸ਼ਰ ਕਰਨਾ

exposition (ਐਕਸਪਆ(ਉ)ਜ਼ਿਸ਼ਨ) n ਸਪਸ਼ਟੀਕਰਨ, ਪ੍ਰਤੀਪਾਦਨ, ਪ੍ਰਸਤੁਤੀਕਰਨ, ਭਾਸ਼, ਆਲੋਚਨਾ, ਟੀਕਾ, ਵਿਆਖਿਆ

exposure (ਇਕ'ਸਪਅਉਜਅ*) n ਭੇਦ ਆਦਿ ਦਾ ਪਰਗਟੀਕਰਨ, ਪੱਖ, ਹਵਾ ਲੁਆਉਣ; ਪਰਗਟਾਉ, ਪ੍ਰਭਾਵ; (ਫੋਟੋ) ਪ੍ਰਕਾਸ਼ਨ

expound (ਇਕ'ਸਪਾਉੱਡ) v ਵਿਆਖਿਆ ਕਰਨੀ, ਬਿਆਨ ਕਰਨਾ, ਸਪਸ਼ਟ ਕਰਨਾ, ਪਰਗਟ ਕਰਨਾ, ਵਿਸਤਾਰ ਨਾਲ ਦੱਸਣਾ

express (ਇਕ'ਸਪਰੈੱਸ) n v a adv ਅਭਿਵਿਅਕਤ ਕਰਨਾ, ਪਰਗਟ ਕਰਨਾ, ਸੂਚਤ ਕਰਨਾ, ਖੋਲ੍ਹਣਾ, ਜ਼ਾਹਰ ਕਰਨਾ, ਨਿਚੋੜਨਾ; ਅਭਿਵਿਅਕਤ, ਸਪਸ਼ਟ, ਸਾਫ਼; ਸਟੀਕ, ਠੀਕ, ਤੇਜ਼ੀ ਨਾਲ; ~ion ਅਭਿਵਿਅੰਜਨਾ, ਅਭਿਵਿਅਕਤੀ, ਪਦਾਵਲੀ, ਕਥਨ, ਮੁਹਾਵਰਾ, ਵਿਅੰਜਨਾਸ਼ੈਲੀ, ਭਾਵ-ਅਭਿਵਿਅਕਤੀ; ~ive ਅਭਿਵਿਅੰਜਨਾਤਮਕ, ਅਰਥ-ਪੂਰਨ, ਭਾਵ-ਪੂਰਨ, ਵਿਅੰਜਕ

expulsion (ਇਕ'ਸਪੱਲਸ਼ਨ) n ਬਾਹਰ ਕੱਢਣ ਦੇਣ, ਨਿਰਵਾਸਨ

expunge (ਇਕ'ਸਪਅੰਨਜ) v ਕੱਢ ਦੇਣਾ, ਰੱਦ ਕਰਨਾ, ਲੋਪ ਕਰਨਾ, ਕੱਟ ਦੇਣਾ, ਮਿਟਾ ਦੇਣਾ

exquisite (ਐਂਕਸਕਵਿਜ਼ਿਟ) a n ਉੱਤਮ, ਨਫ਼ੀਸ, ਤੇਜ਼, ਤੀਬਰ, ਬਾਂਕਾ

extempore (ਐਕ'ਸਟੈਂਪਅਰਿ) adv a ਤਤਕਾਲਕ ਭਾਸ਼ਨ, ਬਿਨਾ ਸੋਚੇ, ਬਿਨਾ ਤਿਆਰੀ ਤੋਂ ਦਿੱਤਾ ਗਿਆ (ਭਾਸ਼ਣ)

extemporize (ਇਕ'ਸਟੈਂਪਅਰਾਇਜ਼) v ਪਹਿਲਾਂ ਸੋਚੇ ਬਿਨਾ ਬੋਲਣਾ, ਸਮੇਂ ਦੇ ਅਨੁਸਾਰ ਬੋਲ ਜਾਣਾ, ਬਿਨਾ ਤਿਆਰੀ ਬੋਲਣਾ

extend (ਇਕ'ਸਟੈੱਡ) v ਪੂਰਾ ਫੈਲਾਉਣਾ, ਵਿਸਤਾਰ ਸਹਿਤ ਲਿਖਣਾ; ਪਹੁੰਚਣਾ, ਪਹੁੰਚਾਉਣਾ; (ਮਿਆਦ) ਵਧਾਉਣਾ

extension (ਇਕ'ਸਟੈੱਨਸ਼ਨ) n ਵਾਧਾ, ਵਿਸਤਾਰ, ਮਿਆਦ ਵਿਚ ਵਾਧਾ, ਪ੍ਰਸਾਰ

extensive (ਇਕ'ਸਟੈੱਨਸਿਵ੍) n ਵਿਆਪਕ, ਵਿਸਤਰਤ, ਵਿਸ਼ਾਲ, ਵੱਡਾ

extent (ਇਕ'ਸਟੈੱਟ) n ਸੀਮਾ, ਹੱਦ, ਵਿਸਤਾਰ, ਫੈਲਾਉ

exterior (ਇਕ'ਸਟਿਅਰਿਅ*) a n ਬਾਹਰੀ, ਬਾਹਰਲਾ, ਖਾਰਜੀ, ਬੈਰੂਨੀ

exterminate (ਇਕ'ਸਟਅਃਮਿਨੇਇਟ) v ਜੜ੍ਹੋਂ ਪੁੱਟਣਾ, ਨਸ਼ਟ ਕਰਨਾ, ਮਿਟਾਉਣਾ, ਉਖੇੜਨਾ, ਬਰਬਾਦ ਕਰਨਾ

external (ਇਕ'ਸਟਅਃਨਲ) n a ਬਾਹਰੀ, ਬੈਰੂਨੀ, ਵਿਦੇਸ਼ੀ ਪਰਰਾਸਟਰੀ

extinct (ਇਕ'ਸਟਿੰਕ(ਕ)ਟ) a ਬੁਝਿਆ, ਨਸ਼ਟ, ਮੁਰਦਾ; ਲੁਪਤ, ਅਪ੍ਰਚਲੱਤ; ~ion ਲੋਪ, ਨਾਸ, ਨਿਰਵਾਣ; ਪਰਿਸਮਾਪਤੀ, ਸੱਤਿਆਨਾਸ, ਵਿਨਾਸ਼

extinguish (ਇਕ'ਸਟਿਡ੍ਗਵਿਸ਼) v ਬੁਝਾਉਣਾ, ਮਿਟਾਉਣਾ, ਦਬਾ ਦੇਣਾ, ਦਮਨ ਕਰਨਾ, ਠੰਡਾ ਕਰਨਾ; ~er ਵਿਨਾਸ਼-ਕਰਤਾ, ਬੁਝਾਉਣ ਵਾਲਾ, ਅਗਨੀ ਰੋਧਕ

extort (ਇਕ'ਸਟੋਟ) v (ਸ਼ਬਦਾਂ ਦੇ ਅਰਥਾਂ ਨੂੰ) ਤੋੜਨਾ ਮਰੋੜਨਾ, (ਅੱਖਰਿਆਂ ਦੇ) ਘੁਮਾ ਫਿਰਾ ਕੇ ਸਿੱਟੇ ਕੱਢਣੇ, ਖਿੱਚੋਤਾਨ ਕਰਕੇ ਅਰਥ ਕੱਢਣੇ

extra (ਐਂਕਸਟਰਆ) n a adv ਵਾਧੂ ਤੇ ਫ਼ਾਲਤੂ ਚੀਜ਼, ਅਧਿਕ ਵਸਤੂ, ਫ਼ਾਲਤੂ, ਵਾਧੂ, ਵਿਸ਼ੇਸ਼, ਵੱਡਾ; ਸਧਾਰਨ ਤੋਂ ਅਧਿਕ, ਅਤੀ, ਜ਼ਿਆਦਾ

extract (ਐਕੱਸਟਰੈਕਟ) *n v* ਰਸ, ਤੱਤ, ਨਿਚੋੜ,
ਸਤ, ਅਰਕ; ਜ਼ਿੰਟਾ, ਸਾਰ, ਸਾਰਾਂਸ਼, ਸੰਖੇਪ,
ਖ਼ੁਲਾਸਾ; ਅਰਕ ਕੱਢਣਾ, ਸਾਰ ਕੱਢਣਾ, ਨਿਚੋੜਨਾ,
ਬਲ ਨਾਲ ਹਟਾਉਣਾ, ਦੰਦ ਕੱਢਣਾ (ਉਖੇੜਨਾ)

etraneous (ਇਕ'ਸਟਰੇਇਨਯਅਸ) *a* ਭਿੰਨ;
ਅਸੰਬੱਧ, ਅਸੰਗਤ, ਬਾਹਰੀ

extraordinary (ਇਕ'ਸਟਰੋਡਨਰਿ) *n a* ਵਿਸ਼ੇਸ਼,
ਅਸਾਧਾਰਨ, ਵਿਲੱਖਣ, ਅਨੋਖਾ, ਨਿਰਾਲਾ, ਮਹਾਨ

extravagance (ਇਕ'ਸਟਕੈਵੁਅਰਗਾਂਸ) *n*
ਫ਼ਜ਼ੂਲ ਖ਼ਰਚੀ, ਫ਼ਜ਼ੂਲੀਅਤ, ਬੇਤੁਕਾਪਨ

extravagant (ਇਕ'ਸਟਰੈਵੁਅਗਾਂਟ) *a* ਫ਼ਜ਼ੂਲ-
ਖ਼ਰਚ, ਉਡਾਊ, ਖ਼ਰਚੀਲਾ

extravaganza (ਐਕ'ਸਟਰੈਵੁਅ'ਰੌਂਜ਼ਅ) *n*
ਅਲੋਕਕਤਾ, ਧੂਮ-ਧੱੜਕਾ

extreme (ਇਕ'ਸਟਰੀਮ) *a n* ਅਧਿਕ, ਅੰਤਮ,
ਆਖ਼ਰੀ ਸਿਰੇ ਦਾ, ਕੱਟੜ, ਸੰਕੀਰਣ, ਇੰਤਹਾਪਸੰਦ
ਚਰਮਸੀਮਾ, ਹੱਦ, ਸਿਰਾ; ~**ly** ਬਹੁਤ ਹੀ ਹੱਦ ਤੋ
ਜ਼ਿਆਦਾ, ਅਤੀਅਧਿਕ, ਬੇਹੱਦ; ~**ness** ਅਤਤਾ,
ਬਹੁਤਾਤ, ਚਰਮਸਥਿਤੀ; ਉਗਰਤਾ

extremism (ਇਕ'ਸਟਰੀਮਿਜ਼(ਅ)ਮ) *n*
ਅੱਤਵਾਦ, ਇੰਤਹਾਪਸੰਦੀ

extremist (ਇਕ'ਸਟਰੀਮਿਸਟ) *n* ਕੱਟੜ,
ਇੰਤਹਾਪਸੰਦ, ਉਗਰਵਾਦੀ, ਅੱਤਵਾਦੀ

extremity (ਇਕ'ਸਟਰੈੱਮਅਟਿ) *n* ਸਿਰਾ, ਹੱਦ,
ਤੇਜ਼ੀ, ਤੀਬਰਤਾ; (*In pl*) ਹੱਥ ਪੈਰ

extricate ('ਔਕਸਟਰਿਕੇਇਟ) *v* ਨਿਸਤਾਰਨਾ,
ਛੁਡਾਉਣਾ, ਉਧਾਰ ਕਰਨਾ, ਮੁਕਤ ਕਰਨਾ,
ਸੁਲਝਾਉਣਾ

extrication ('ਔਕਸਟਰਿ'ਕੇਇਸ਼ਨ) *n* ਨਿਸਤਾਰਾ,
ਛੁਟਕਾਰਾ, ਮੁਕਤੀ, ਸੁਲਝਾਉ

extrinsic (ਔਕ'ਸਟਰਿੰਸਿਕ) *a* ਅਣਅਵੱਸ਼ਕ,
ਅਪ੍ਰਧਾਨ, ਗ਼ੈਰ-ਜ਼ਰੂਰੀ; ਬਾਹਰੀ, ਅਸੰਬਧਤ

extrovert ('ਔਕਸਟਰਆ(ਉ)ਵਅ:ਟ) *v n* ਬਾਹਰ
ਵੱਲ ਨਿਕਲਣਾ, ਬਾਹਰਮੁਖੀ

exuberant (ਇਗਾ'ਜ਼ੂਬ(ਅ)ਰਅੰਟ) *a* ਸੰਪੰਨ,
ਸਮਰਿਧ, ਬਹੁਤ ਜ਼ਿਆਦਾ; ਜ਼ਿੰਦਾ-ਦਿਲ, ਉੱਲਾਸ-
ਪੂਰਨ, ਓਜਪੂਰਨ, ਸ਼ਬਦ-ਆਡੰਬਰਪੂਰਨ (ਭਾਸ਼ਾ);
ਤੀਬਰ, ਭਰਪੂਰ

exuberate (ਇਗਾ'ਜ਼ੂਬਅਰੇਇਟ) *v* ਝੂਲ੍ਹ ਝੂਲ੍ਹ
ਪੈਣਾ; ਸਮਰਿਧ ਜਾਂ ਪਰਿਪੂਰਨ ਹੋਣਾ, ਬਹੁਲਤਾ
ਹੋਣੀ, ਭਰਪੂਰ ਹੋਣਾ, ਹਰਿਆ ਭਰਿਆ ਹੋਣਾ

eye (ਆਇ) *n* ਅੱਖ, ਨੈਣ, ਨੇਤਰ, ਦ੍ਰਿਸ਼ਟੀ;
ਅੱਖ ਦਾ ਤਾਰਾ; ਧਿਆਨ, ਮੋਰ ਦੇ ਖੰਭਾਂ ਦੀ ਟਿੱਕੀ;
~**ball** ਅੱਖ ਦਾ ਡੇਲਾ, ਆਨਾ; ~**brow** ਭਾਊਂ,
ਭਰਵੱਟਾ; ~**drop** ਅੱਥਰੂ, ਹੰਝੂ; ~**lash**
ਝਿੰਮਣੀ, ਪਲਕ; ~**lid** ਪਪੋਟਾ, ਅੱਖ ਦਾ
ਉੱਪਰਲਾ ਪਰਦਾ; ~**sight** ਨਜ਼ਰ, ਜੋਤ,
ਬੀਨਾਈ, ਦ੍ਰਿਸ਼ਟੀ; ~**wash** ਅੱਖਾਂ ਦੀ ਦਾਰੂ,
ਮੂੰਹ ਰੱਖਣੀ, ਉਪਰੀ ਫੱਕੇਸਲਾ; ~**witness**
ਸਾਖੀ, ਚਸ਼ਮਦੀਦ ਗਵਾਹ

F

F, f (ਐਫ਼) *n* ਰੋਮਨ ਵਰਨਮਾਲਾ ਦਾ ਛੇਵਾਂ ਅੱਖਰ; (ਸੰਗੀ) ਚੌਥੀ ਸੁਰ

fable ('ਫ਼ੇਇਬਲ) *n v* ਪੁਰਾਟਕ ਕਥਾ, ਕਿੱਸਾ, ਕਹਾਣੀ; (ਨਾਟਕ ਦਾ) ਕਥਾਨਕ, ਪਸ਼ੂ-ਪੰਛੀਆਂ ਦੀ ਸਿੱਖਿਆਦਾਇਕ ਕਹਾਣੀ (ਪੰਚਤੰਤਰ ਦੀ ਵਾਰਤਾ); ਬਣਾਵਟੀ ਕਿੱਸਾ ਦੱਸਣਾ, ਮਨਘੜਤ ਕਹਾਣੀ ਸੁਣਾਉਣੀ; ਕਲਪਤ ਵਾਰਤਾ ਪੇਸ਼ ਕਰਨੀ

fabric ('ਫ਼ੈਬਰਿਕ) *n* ਢਾਂਚਾ, ਫ਼ਰੇਮ; ਉਸਾਰੀ; ਬੁਣਤੀ ਕੱਪੜਾ

fabricate ('ਫ਼ੈਬਰਿਕੇਇਟ) *v* ਬਣਾਉਣਾ, ਘੜਨਾ, ਉਣਨਾ, ਨਿਰਮਾਣ ਕਰਨਾ, ਰਚਨਾ ਕਰਨੀ; ਬਣਾਉਟੀ ਗੱਲ ਘੜਨੀ, ਜਾਅਲਸਾਜ਼ੀ ਕਰਨੀ; ~d ਘੜੀ ਹੋਈ, ਝੂਠੀ, ਕੂੜੀ

fabrication ('ਫ਼ੈਬਰਿ'ਕੇਇਸ਼ਨ) *n* ਬਣਾਉਟੀ, ਗੱਲ, ਝੂਠੀ ਕਹਾਣੀ; ਮਨਘੜਤ ਬਿਰਤਾਂਤ, ਜਾਅਲਸਾਜ਼ੀ

fabricator ('ਫ਼ੈਬਰਿਕੇਇਟਆਅ*) *n* ਝੂਠਾ, ਧੋਖੇਬਾਜ਼, ਮਿਥਿਆਵਾਦੀ

fabulous ('ਫ਼ੈਬਯੂਲ਼ਅਸ) *a* ਝੂਠਾ, ਕਲਪਤ, ਨਿਰਾਧਾਰ, ਮਿਥਿਆਕਾਰੀ, ਚਮਤਕਾਰੀ

face (ਫ਼ੇਇਸ) *n v* ਚਿਹਰਾ-ਮੋਹਰਾ, ਮੁਹਾਂਦਰਾ, ਮੂੰਹ-ਮੱਥਾ, ਮੂੰਹ, ਮੁੱਖ, ਹੁਲੀਆ, ਨੁਹਾਰ; ਦਿਖਾਵਾ, ਟੀਪ-ਟਾਪ; ਸਾਮੁਣੇ ਆਉਣਾ; ਮੁਕਾਬਲਾ ਕਰਨਾ, ਡਟੇ; ਰਹਿਣਾ; ~cloth ਕੱਫਣ, ਮੂੰਹ ਢੋਣ ਲਈ ਪ੍ਰਯੋਗ ਕੀਤਾ ਕੱਪੜਾ; ~down (ਸਖ਼ਤੀ ਨਾਲ) ਦੇਖਣ ਨਾਲ ਹੀ ਸ਼ਰਮਿੰਦਾ ਕਰਨਾ; ~lifting ਪੋਚਾ ਪਾਚੀ; ~value ਅੰਕਤ ਮੁੱਲ, ਪ੍ਰਤੱਖ ਮੁੱਲ; ~to ਆਮੁਨੇ-ਸਾਮੁਨੇ; **having two ~s** ਬਹੁਰੂਪੀਆ ਹੋਣਾ, ਆਪਣੀ ਗੱਲ ਵਿਚ ਸੱਚਾ ਨਾ ਹੋਣਾ; **on the ~of it** ਜ਼ਾਹਰਾ ਤੌਰ ਤੇ, ਉਪਰੇ ਤੌਰ ਤੇ; **pull a long ~** ਮੂੰਹ ਬਣਾਉਣਾ, ਮੂੰਹ ਫੁਲਾਉਣਾ; **show one's~** ਹਾਜ਼ਰ ਹੋਣਾ

facet ('ਫ਼ੈਸਿਟ) *n* ਮੱਥਾ, ਪੱਖ, ਪਹਿਲੂ

facial ('ਫ਼ੇਇਸ਼ਲ) *a* ਮੂੰਹ ਦਾ, ਚਿਹਰੇ ਦਾ

facile ('ਫ਼ੈਸਾਇਲ) *a* ਸੁਖਾਲਾ, ਸੌਖਾ, ਸਰਲ, ਆਸਾਨ, ਸੁਗਮ, ਸਿੱਧਾ; ਨੇਕ, ਸਰਲ ਸੁਭਾਅ, ਉਦਾਰ, ਭਲਾਮਾਣਸ, ਨਿਮਰਤਾ ਵਾਲਾ

facilitate (ਫ਼ਅ'ਸਿਲਿਟੇਇਟ) *v* ਸੁਖਾਲਾ ਕਰਨਾ, ਸਰਲ ਕਰ ਦੇਣਾ, ਸੁਵਿਧਾ ਦੇਣੀ, ਸਹੂਲਤ ਦੇਣੀ

facility (ਫ਼ਅ'ਸਿਲ਼ਅਟਿ) *n* ਸਹੂਲਤ, ਸੌਖ, ਸੁਵਿਧਾ, ਆਸਾਨੀ; ਲਚਕ; ਮੁਹਾਰਤ

facing ('ਫ਼ੇਇਸਿਙ) *n* ਮੋਹਰਾ, ਅਗਾੜੀ, ਮੱਥਾ

facsimile (ਫ਼ਕ'ਸਿਮਿਲੀ) *n v* ਹੂਬਹੂ ਨਕਲ, ਪ੍ਰਤੀਲਿਪੀ, ਪ੍ਰਤੀਰੂਪ; ਉਤਾਰਾ ਕਰਨਾ, ਪ੍ਰਤੀਲਿਪੀ ਬਣਾਉਟੀ; ~**signature** ਚਿਤਰ-ਹਸਤਾਖ਼ਰ

fact (ਫ਼ੈਕਟ) *n* ਤੱਥ, ਤੱਤ, ਸਚਾਈ, ਅਸਲੀਅਤ ਵਾਸਤਵਿਕਤਾ, ਯਥਾਰਥਤਾ, ਹਕੀਕਤ; **in~** ਅਸਲ ਵਿਚ, ਦਰਅਸਲ, ਸੰਖੇਪ ਵਿਚ

faction (ਫ਼ੈਕਸ਼ਨ) *n* ਧੜਾ, ਫ਼ਿਰਕਾ, ਸਿਰ, ਪਾਸਾ, ਪੱਖਪਾਤ; ~**al, factious** ਪੜ੍ਹੇਬਾਜ਼ੀ ਵਾਲਾ, ਪੱਖਪਾਤੀ, ਦਲ ਸਬੰਧੀ, ਫ਼ਸਾਦੀ, ਉਪੱਦਰ ਮਚਾਉ; ~**alism** ਦਲਬੰਦੀ, ਗੁਟਬੰਦੀ, ਪੜ੍ਹੇਬਾਜ਼ੀ; ~**ary** ਪੜ੍ਹੇਬਾਜ਼, ਗੁੱਟਬਾਜ਼

factitious (ਫ਼ੈਕ'ਟਿਸ਼ਅਸ) *a* ਨਕਲੀ, ਜਾਅਲੀ, ਕ੍ਰਿਤਿਮ, ਬਣਾਉਟੀ, ਕਲਪਤ

factor ('ਫ਼ੈਕਟਆ*) *n* ਗੁਣਨਖੰਡ, ਜੁਜ਼, ਗਣਿਕ,

ਕਾਰਕ, ਉਪਾਦਾਨ, ਭਾਗ, ਪੱਖ, ਅੰਗ, ਅੰਸ਼;
ਕਾਰਿੰਦਾ, ਆਤੂਤੀ; ਪ੍ਰਤੀਨਿਧ; **~ise** ਗੁਟਨਖੰਡ
ਕਰਨਾ, ਜੁੜ ਬਣਾਉਟੇ, ਵਿਭਾਗ ਕਰਨਾ

factory ('ਫ਼ੈਕਟ(ਅ)ਰਿ) *n* ਕਾਰਖ਼ਾਨਾ

factual ('ਫ਼ੈਕਚੁਅਲ) *a* ਵਾਸਤਵਿਕ, ਯਥਾਰਥ,
ਤੱਥ

faculty ('ਫ਼ੈਕਅਲਟਿ) *n* ਯੋਗਤਾ, ਕਾਰਜਕੁਸ਼ਲਤਾ,
ਪ੍ਰਬੰਧ ਦੀ ਯੋਗਤਾ; ਮਾਨਸਕ ਸ਼ਕਤੀ; ਵਿੰਦਿਆ-
ਵਿਭਾਗ, ਫ਼ੈਕਲਟੀ, (ਯੂਨੀਵਰਸਿਟੀ ਦਾ) ਪਰਤਾਗਾ

fade (ਫ਼ੈਡਿ) *v* ਬਟਾਉਟੀ, ਮੁਰਝਾਉਣਾ,
ਕੁਮਲਾਉਣਾ, ਸੁੱਕਣਾ, ਫ਼ਿਕਾ ਪੈਣਾ, ਪੀਲਾ ਹੋ
ਜਾਣਾ, ਝੌਂ ਜਾਣਾ, ਰੰਗ ਉੱਡਣਾ, ਹੌਲੀ ਹੌਲੀ ਲੋਪ
ਹੋਣਾ, ਰੰਗ ਉਡਾਉਣਾ, ਘੱਟ ਹੋਣਾ, ਮਾੜਾ ਪੈਣਾ;
~less ਸਦਾ-ਬਹਾਰ, ਹਰਿਆ-ਭਰਿਆ

faecal ('ਫ਼ੀਕਲ) *a* ਗੰਦ ਦਾ, ਵਿਸ਼ਟਾ ਦਾ, ਕੀਟ
ਦਾ; **~matter** ਗੰਦ, ਟੱਟੀ

fag (ਫ਼ੈਗ) *n v* ਮਿਹਨਤ, ਕਠਨ ਪਰਿਸ਼ਰੱਮ, ਵਗਾਰ
ਦਾ ਕੰਮ, ਵਾਪੂ ਵਗਾਰ, ਚੱਟੀ ਦਾ ਕੰਮ; ਥੱਕ ਜਾਣਾ,
ਥਕਾ ਦੇਣਾ, ਵਗਾਰ ਦਾ ਕੰਮ ਕਰਨਾ; ਸਖ਼ਤ
ਮਿਹਨਤ ਕਰਨੀ, ਜਾਨ ਮਾਰ ਕੇ ਕੰਮ ਕਰਨਾ, ਬਹੁਤ
ਕਸ਼ਟ ਸਹਿਣਾ; ਸਿਥਲ ਕਰ ਦੇਣਾ; **~end** ਆਖ਼ਰੀ
ਹਿੱਸਾ, ਨਿਕੰਮਾ, ਭਾਗ ਜਾਂ ਸਿਰਾ

fail (ਫ਼ੈਇਲ) *n v* ਨਿਰਸੰਦੇਹ; ਅਸਫਲਤਾ, ਅਸਫਲ
ਹੋਣਾ, ਸਿਰੇ ਨਾ ਚੜ੍ਹਨਾ, (ਕੋਈ ਕੰਮ) ਨਾ ਕਰ
ਸਕਣਾ, ਹਾਰ ਜਾਣਾ, ਉੱਕਣਾ, ਟੁੱਟ ਜਾਣਾ,
ਦੀਵਾਲਾ ਨਿਕਲਣਾ, ਘੱਟ ਹੋਣਾ, ਪੂਰਾ ਨਾ
ਉਤਰਨਾ, ਹਿੰਮਤ ਹਾਰ ਜਾਣਾ, ਨਸ਼ਟ ਹੋ ਜਾਣਾ,
ਨਿਰਾਸ਼ ਕਰਨਾ; **~ing** ਘਾਟਾ, ਕਮੀ, ਕਮਜ਼ੋਰੀ,
ਦੁਰਬਲਤਾ, ਉਕਾਈ, ਢਿੱਲ, ਭੁੱਲ, ਕਸੂਰ; **~ure**
ਅਸਫਲਤਾ, ਨਾਕਾਮਯਾਬੀ, ਹਾਰ, ਨਾਕਾਮੀ,
ਉਕਾਈ, ਭੁੱਲ; ਘਾਟਾ, ਟੋਟਾ, ਕਮੀ, ਅਭਾਵ;

ਹਾਰਿਆ ਹੋਇਆ, ਨਿਸਫਲ ਜਤਨ; ਨੁਕਸਾਨ;
ਦੀਵਾਲਾ; **without~** ਨਿਸ਼ਚਤ ਰੂਪ ਨਾਲ,
ਜ਼ਰੂਰੀ, ਅਵੱਸ਼ਕ

faint (ਫ਼ੇਇੰਟ) *a n v* ਮੱਧਮ, ਧੀਮਾ, ਫ਼ਿਕਾ,
ਅਸਪਸ਼ਟ, ਕਮਜ਼ੋਰ, ਨਿਢਾਲ, ਬੇਹੋਸ਼, ਮੂਰਛਾ,
ਬੇਸੁਰਤੀ, ਗਸ਼; ਬੇਸੁਰਤ ਹੋਣਾ, ਗਸ਼ ਪੈਣੀ,
ਮੂਰਛਾ ਆਉਣੀ, ਸਿਥਲ ਪੈਣਾ, ਨਿਢਾਲ ਹੋ
ਜਾਣਾ, ਹਿੰਮਤ ਹਾਰਨਾ, ਹੌਸਲਾ ਛੱਡਣਾ, ਡਰ
ਜਾਣਾ, ਕਾਇਰਤਾ ਵਿਖਾਉਣਾ; **~heart**
~hearted ਡਰਪੋਕ, ਕਾਇਰ, ਕਮਜ਼ੋਰ

fair (ਫ਼ੇਅ*) *n a v* (1) ਮੇਲਾ, ਨੁਮਾਇਸ, ਮੰਡੀ;
(2) ਤੀਵੀਂ, ਜ਼ਨਾਨੀ; ਸੋਹਣਾ, ਸੁੰਦਰ, ਸਾਫ਼,
ਉੱਜਲ, ਸੁਥਰਾ, ਬੇਦਾਗ਼, ਨਿਆਂਕਾਰੀ, ਨਿਰਪੱਖ,
ਵਾਜਬ, ਉਚਿਤ, ਮੁਨਾਸਬ, ਜਚਵਾਂ, ਨਾਜ਼ੁਕ,
ਸਧਾਰਨ ਸਤਰ ਦਾ; ਔਸਤ ਦਰਜੇ ਦਾ; ਅਨੁਕੂਲ
ਹੋਣਾ, ਠੀਕ ਬੈਠਣਾ, ਰਾਸ ਹੋਣਾ; ਠੀਕ ਠੀਕ
ਨਕਲ ਉਤਾਰਨਾ; **~ and square**
ਈਮਾਨਦਾਰ, ਸਾਫ਼ ਨੀਤ ਵਾਲਾ; **~copy** ਸ਼ੁੱਧ
ਪ੍ਰਤਿ; **~minded** ਨਿਰਪੱਖ; **the ~sex** ਨਾਰੀ
ਜਾਤੀ; **~ness** ਨਿਰਪੱਖਤਾ, ਹੱਕ-ਨਿਆਂ,
ਸੁਅੱਛਤਾ, ਸੁੰਦਰਤਾ

fairy ('ਫ਼ੇਅਰਿ) *n a* ਪਰੀ, ਅਪੱਛਰਾ, ਸੁੰਦਰ
ਮੁਟਿਆਰ; ਫ਼ਰਜ਼ੀ, ਖ਼ਿਆਲੀ; ਜਾਦੂ ਦੀ; ਮੋਹਣੀ,
ਕੋਮਲ ਨਾਜ਼ੁਕ; **~tale** ਪਰੀ-ਕਥਾ, ਅਦਭੁਤ
ਕਹਾਣੀ, ਕਲਪਤ ਕਿੱਸਾ

fait accompli ('ਫ਼ੇਇਟਅ'ਕੌਂਪਲੀ) (*F*) *n*
ਨਿਭਿਆ ਮਾਮਲਾ

faith (ਫ਼ੇਇਥ) *n int v* ਧਰਮ, ਮੱਤ, ਸ਼ਰਧਾ, ਨਿਸ਼ਚਾ,
ਵਿਸ਼ਵਾਸ, ਈਮਾਨ, ਭਰੋਸਾ; **in good~** ਸਚਾਈ
ਨਾਲ, ਨਿਸ਼ਚੇ ਨਾਲ, ਈਮਾਨਦਾਰੀ ਨਾਲ; **~ful**
ਨਿਸ਼ਠਾਵਾਨ, ਦੀਨਦਾਰ, ਸਿਦਕੀ, ਵਫ਼ਾਦਾਰ,

ਵਿਸ਼ਵਾਸਪਾਤਰ, ਭਰੋਸੇਯੋਗ; ~less ਸ਼ਰਧਾਹੀਨ, ਧਰਮਹੀਨ, ਨਾਸਤਕ, ਕਾਫ਼ਰ, ਬੇਈਮਾਨ, ਬਦਨੀਤ, ਵਿਸ਼ਵਾਸਘਾਤੀ

fake (ਫ਼ੇਇਕ) *n* ਨਕਲੀ ਮਾਲ, ਛਲ, ਕਪਟ, ਧੋਖਾ, ਚਾਲਬਾਜ਼ੀ

falcon ('ਫ਼ੋਲਕਅਨ) *n* ਬਾਜ਼, ਸ਼ਿਕਰਾ

fall (ਫ਼ੋਲ) *v n* ਡਿਗਣਾ, ਢਹਿਣਾ, ਲਹਿਣਾ, ਉੱਤਰਨਾ, ਝੜਨਾ, ਉੱਖੜ ਕੇ ਡਿਗਣਾ, ਟੁੱਟ ਕੇ ਡਿਗਣਾ, ਵਾਪਰਨਾ, ਨੀਂਵੀ ਹੋਣਾ; ਮੂੰਹ ਭਾਰ ਡਿਗਣਾ, ਮੁਸੀਬਤ ਵਿਚ ਫਸਣਾ; ਗਿਰਾਵਟ, ਪਤਨ; ਉਤਾਰ, ਢਲਾਣ, ਨਿਵਾਣ, ਢਾਲ; ਝਰਨਾ, ਆਬਸ਼ਾਰ; ~across ਕਿਸੇ ਨਾਲ ਅਚਾਨਕ ਮੁਲਾਕਾਤ ਹੋ ਜਾਣੀ; ~off ਘੱਟ ਹੋਣਾ; ~out ਵਾਪਰਨਾ; ਛੱਡ ਦੇਣਾ; ~short ਥੁੜਨਾ, ਘੱਟ ਹੋ ਜਾਣਾ; ~upon ਹਮਲਾ ਕਰਨਾ, ਭਿੜਨਾ; to ~ a prey to ਸ਼ਿਕਾਰ ਹੋ ਜਾਣਾ, ਕਿਸੇ ਹੱਥੀ ਚੜ੍ਹ ਜਾਣਾ, ਵਾਦੀ ਹੋ ਜਾਣਾ

fallacy ('ਫ਼ੈਲਅਸਿ) *n* ਭੁਲਾਵਾ, ਭਰਮ, ਧੋਖਾ, ਛਲ, ਭਰਾਂਤੀ, ਫ਼ਰੇਬ, ਭੁਲੇਖਾ, ਵਾਕਛਲ, ਮਿਥਿਆ ਗਿਆਨ

false (ਫ਼ੋਲਸ) *a adv* ਝੂਠਾ, ਕੂੜਾ; ਨਕਲੀ, ਜਾਅਲੀ, ਖੋਟਾ, ਬੇਵਫ਼ਾ, ਦਗ਼ਾਬਾਜ਼, ਕਪਟੀ; ਧੋਖੇ ਨਾਲ, ਦਗ਼ਾ ਕਰਕੇ; ~hood, ~ness ਝੂਠ, ਧੋਖਾ, ਫ਼ਰੇਬ, ਦਗ਼ਾ, ਕਪਟਤਾ; ਝੂਠ-ਮੂਠ, ਝੂਠੀ ਗੱਲ

falsify ('ਫ਼ੋਲਸਿਫ਼ਾਇ) *v* ਝੂਠਾ ਸਿੱਧ ਕਰਨਾ, ਝੁਠਲਾਉਣਾ, ਅਸੁੱਧ ਕਰਨਾ, ਵਿਗਾੜਨਾ, ਦੂਸ਼ਤ ਕਰਨਾ

fame (ਫ਼ੇਇਮ) *n* ਜਸ, ਮਸ਼ਹੂਰੀ, ਪ੍ਰਸਿੱਧੀ, ਨੇਕਨਾਮੀ, ਕੀਰਤੀ; ~d ਮਸ਼ਹੂਰ, ਪ੍ਰਸਿੱਧ, ਜਸ-ਪ੍ਰਾਪਤ

familiar (ਫ਼ਅ'ਮਿਲਯਅ*) *a n* ਜਾਣੂ, ਪਰਿਚਿਤ, ਵੇਖਿਆ-ਚਾਖਿਆ; ਸਧਾਰਨ, ਮਾਮੂਲੀ, ਪ੍ਰਚਲਤ; ਬੇ-ਤਕੱਲੁਫ਼, ਨਿੱਝਕ; ~ity ਜਾਣ-ਪਛਾਣ, ਵਾਕ-ਫ਼ੀਅਤ, ਪਰਿਚੈ; ਅਪੱਣਤ, ਬੇ-ਤਕੱਲਫ਼ੀ; ~ize ਵਾਕਫ਼ੀਅਤ ਕਰਾ ਦੇਣੀ, ਜਾਣ-ਪਛਾਣ ਕਰਵਾਉਣੀ; ਅਭਿਆਸ ਕਰਾਉਣਾ; ਮਸ਼ਹੂਰ ਕਰਨਾ

family ('ਫ਼ੈਮ(ਅ)ਲਿ) *n* ਟੱਬਰ, ਪਰਵਾਰ, ਕੁਟੰਬ, ਕੋੜਮਾ; ਖ਼ਾਨਦਾਨ, ਘਰਾਣਾ; ~man ਟੱਬਰਦਾਰ, ਗ੍ਰਹਿਸਤੀ; ~tree ਬੰਸਾਵਲੀ, ਕੁਰਸੀਨਾਮਾ; in the~ way ਗਰਭਵਤੀ

famine ('ਫ਼ੈਮਿਨ) *n* ਕਾਲ, ਕਹਤ, ਥੁੜ੍ਹ, ਟੋਟ, ਅਭਾਵ; ~stricken ਕਾਲ-ਪੀੜਤ, ਕਾਲ ਦੇ ਮਾਰੇ; ~ment ਭੁਖਮਰੀ, ਕਾਲ ਪੀੜਾ

famous ('ਫ਼ੇਇਮਅਸ) *a* ਮਸ਼ਹੂਰ, ਪ੍ਰਸਿੱਧ, ਨਾਮੀ; ਵਧੀਆ

fan (ਫ਼ੈਨ) *n v* (1) ਪੱਖਾ; ਅਨਾਜ ਉਡਾਉਣ ਵਾਲੀ ਮਸ਼ੀਨ; (2) ਪਰੇਮੀ, ਰਸੀਆ, ਚੇਟਕੀ; ਪੱਖਾ ਝੱਲਣਾ; ਅੱਗ ਬਾਲਣ ਲਈ ਹਵਾ ਕਰਨੀ, ਅੱਗ ਭੜਕਾਉਣਾ, ਉਤੇਜਤ ਕਰਨਾ; ~out (ਸੈਨਾ ਆਦਿ ਦਾ) ਖਿਲਰ ਜਾਣਾ

fanatic (ਫ਼ਅ'ਨੈਟਿਕ) *a n* ਹਠ-ਧਰਮੀ, ਤੁੱਅੱਸਬੀ, ਜਨੂਨੀ; ~al ਕੱਟੜ, ਉਨਮਾਦਮਈ; ~ism ਧਰਮ-ਉਨਮਾਦ, ਕੱਟੜਤਾ; ਹਠ-ਧਰਮੀ ਦੀਵਾਨਾਪਣ

fanciful ('ਫ਼ੈਂਸਿਫ਼ੁਲ) *a* ਖ਼ਿਆਲੀ, ਕਾਲਪਨਕ, ਵਹਿਮੀ, ਬਣਾਉਟੀ; ਵਚਿੱਤਰ, ਅਨੋਖਾ, ਮੌਜੀ, ਸਨਕੀ

fancy ('ਫ਼ੈਂਸਿ) *n a v* ਖ਼ਿਆਲ, ਭਾਵਨਾ, ਅਨੁਮਾਨ, ਕਲਪਨਾ, ਕਿਆਸ; ਭਰਮ, ਮਾਇਆ, ਵਹਿਮ ਸਨਕ; ਕਲਪਤ, ਤੱਤਹੀਣ, ਮੌਜੀ, ਸਨਕੀ, ਵਹਿਮੀ; ਵਿਚਰਨਾ, ਖ਼ਿਆਲ ਕਰਨਾ, ਕਲਪਨਾ

ਕਰਨੀ, ਕਿਆਸ ਕਰਨਾ, ਮਨ ਵਿਚ ਕਲਪਤ ਚਿੱਤਰ ਬਣਾਉਣਾ; ~dress ਸਾਂਗ-ਵਸਤਰ; ~fair ਮੀਨਾ-ਬਜ਼ਾਰ; ~man ਦੱਲਾ, ਭੜੂਆ; ~woman ਰੰਡੀ, ਬਜ਼ਾਰੀ ਤੀਵੀਂ, ਬਦਚਲਨ ਵਿਸਤਰੀ

fantasy, phantasy ('ਫੈਂਟਅਸਿ) n ਕਲਪਨਾ-ਸ਼ਕਤੀ; ਤਰੰਗ, ਮਨਮੌਜ, ਸਨਕ

far (ਫ਼ਾ*) adv a n ਦੂਰ, ਦੂਰੇਡ਼ੇ, ਬਹੁਤ ਦੂਰ; ਬਹੁਤ ਜ਼ਿਆਦਾ, ਬੜਾ; ਗਾਇਬ, ਲੁਪਤ; ਕਲਪਨਾਮਈ, ਦੂਰੋਂ, ਦੂਰੀ ਤੋਂ; ਦੂਰ ਦਾ, ਦੂਰਵਰਤੀ; ~and near ਹਰੇਕ ਥਾਂ ਤੇ, ਚਾਰੇ ਪਾਸੇ; ~away ਬਹੁਤ ਦੂਰ, ਦੂਰ ਸਾਰੇ, ਪਰੇ-ਪਰੇੜੇ; ~reaching ਦੂਰਗਾਮੀ; ~sighted ਦੂਰ-ਅੰਦੇਸ਼, ਦੂਰ-ਦਰਸੀ

farce (ਫ਼ਾ*ਸ) n v ਨਕਲ, ਸਾਂਗ, ਹਾਸਾ ਠੱਠਾ, ਮਸ਼ਕਰੀ, ਮਖੌਲ; ਮਸਾਲੇਦਾਰ ਬਣਾਉਣਾ, ਹਾਸਰਸੀ ਬਣਾਉਣਾ

fare (ਫ਼ੇਅ*) n v ਭਾੜਾ, ਕਿਰਾਇਆ (ਸਫ਼ਰ); ਖ਼ੁਰਾਕ, ਪੈਂਡਾ ਕਰਨਾ, ਸਫ਼ਰ ਕਰਨਾ, ਨਿਬੜਨਾ; ਭੋਜਨ ਖਾਣਾ

farewell ('ਫ਼ੇਅ*ਵੈੱਲ) n int ਵਿਦਾ, ਵਿਦਾਇਗੀ, ਅਲਵਿਦਾ

farm (ਫ਼ਾ*ਮ) n v ਖੇਤ, ਖੇਤੀ, ਸ਼ਿਸ਼ੂ-ਨਿਕੇਤਨ; ਪਟਾ, ਠੇਕਾ ; ਖੇਤੀ ਕਰਨਾ, ਵਾਹੀ ਕਰਨਾ; ਠੇਕਾ ਲੈਣਾ; ~house ਖੇਤ ਵਿਚਲਾ ਮਕਾਨ, ਹਵੇਲੀ; ~er ਕਿਸਾਨ, ਜ਼ਿਮੀਂਦਾਰ, ਕਾਸ਼ਤਕਾਰ, ਵਾਹੀਕਾਰ, ਫ਼ਸਿਕ; ~ing ਵਾਹੀ-ਜੋਤੀ, ਖੇਤੀ, ਕਾਸ਼ਤਕਾਰੀ, ਕਿਰਸਾਨੀ

farther ('ਫ਼ਾ*ਦਅ*) a adv ਵਧੇਰੇ, ਵੱਧ, ਹੋਰ ਜ਼ਿਆਦਾ, ਭੀ, ਵੀ, ਅਤੇ ਇਸ ਤੋਂ ਇਲਾਵਾ, ਅਗੇਰੇ, ਹੋਰ ਅੱਗੇ; ~most ਸਭ ਤੋਂ ਦੂਰ, ਦੂਰਤਮ, ਦੂਰਵਰਤੀ

farthest ('ਫ਼ਾਦਿਸਟ) ਸਭ ਤੋਂ ਦੂਰੇਡ਼ਾ

fascinate ('ਫ਼ੈਸਿਨੇਇਟ) v ਮੋਹ ਲੈਣਾ, ਮੁਗਧ ਕਰਨਾ, ਮੋਹਤ ਕਰਨਾ; ਵੱਸ ਵਿਚ ਕਰ ਲੈਣਾ, ਬੁਰੀ ਨਜ਼ਰ ਰੱਖਣੀ, ਧਿਆਨ ਆਕਰਸ਼ਤ ਕਰਨਾ

fascinating ('ਫ਼ੈਸਿਨੇਇਟਿਙ) a ਮਨਮੋਹਣਾ, ਦਿਲ-ਖਿਚਵਾਂ, ਮਨੋਹਰ, ਰੀਝਾਉਣਾ, ਆਕਰਸ਼ਕ

fascination ('ਫ਼ੈਸਿ'ਨੇਇਸ਼ਨ) n ਖਿਚ, ਆਕਰਸ਼ਨ, ਵਸ਼ੀਕਰਨ

fashion ('ਫ਼ੈਸ਼ਨ) n v ਵੇਸ, ਭੇਸ, ਸਜਧਜ, ਢੰਗ, ਰੂਪ, ਪ੍ਰਕਾਰ, ਸ਼ੈਲੀ, ਪਰਣਾਲੀ, ਪ੍ਰਥਾ, ਰੀਤ, ਰਸਮ; ਬਣਾਉਣਾ, ਸਜਾਣਾ, ਢਾਲਣਾ; ~able ਫ਼ੈਸ਼ਨ-ਪਰਸਤ, ਆਧੁਨਿਕ ਜੀਵਨ ਵਾਲਾ ਵਿਅਕਤੀ, ਪ੍ਰਚਲਤ ਸ਼ੈਲੀ, ਅਨੁਯਾਈ, ਸ਼ੋਭਾਚਾਰੀ, ਲੋਕਚਾਰੀ

fast (ਫ਼ਾਸਟ) n a adv. v ਵਰਤ, ਨਾਗਾ, ਫ਼ਾਕਾ, ਰੋਜ਼ਾ, ਉਪਵਾਸ; ਤੇਜ਼, ਤਿੱਖਾ; ਕੱਸਿਆ, ਕਸ ਕੇ ਬੱਧਾ; ਪੱਕਾ (ਰੰਗ ਆਦਿ), ਝਟਪਟ, ਤੁਰਤ, ਛੇਤੀ ਛੇਤੀ; ਨੇੜੇ, ਕੋਲ, ਦ੍ਰਿੜਤਾ ਨਾਲ, ਕਸ ਕੇ, ਵਰਤ ਰੱਖਣਾ, ਰੋਜ਼ਾ ਰੱਖਣਾ; ~friend ਪੱਕਾ ਮਿੱਤਰ, ਜਿਗਰੀ ਦੋਸਤ; ~en ਬੰਨ੍ਹਣਾ, ਜਕੜਨਾ, ਜੁੜਨਾ, ਪੱਕਾ ਹੋਣਾ, ਮਜ਼ਬੂਤ ਹੋਣਾ, ਸਥਾਈ ਹੋਣਾ, ਅਧਿਕਾਰ ਕਰਨਾ; ਕਬਜ਼ਾ ਜਮਾ ਲੈਣਾ; ~ener ਕਸਣ ਵਾਲਾ, ਜਕੜਨੀ, ਹੁੱਕ, ਚਿਟਕਨੀ, ਬੰਨ੍ਹਣ ਵਾਲਾ; ~ness ਤੇਜ਼ੀ, ਸ਼ੀਘਰਤਾ, ਦ੍ਰਿੜਤਾ

fat (ਫ਼ੈਟ) a n v ਮੋਟਾ, ਮੋਟਾ-ਤਾਜ਼ਾ, ਪਲਿਆ ਹੋਇਆ, ਭਾਰੀ (ਜ਼ਮੀਨ); ਮੋਟੀ ਅਕਲ ਵਾਲਾ, ਗੰਵਾਰ, ਬੁੱਧੂ

fatal ('ਫ਼ੇਇਟਲ) a ਘਾਤਕ, ਕਾਰੀ, ਮਾਰੂ, ਹਤਿਆਰ, ਹਾਨੀਕਾਰਕ; ~ity ਵਿਨਾਸ਼ੀ ਪ੍ਰਭਾਵ, ਵਿਨਾਸ਼ਕਤਾ, ਬਿਪਤਾ, ਕਸ਼ਟ

fate (ਫ਼ੇਇਟ) n v ਭਾਗ, ਲੇਖ, ਮੁਕੱਦਰ, ਨਸੀਬ, ਕਿਸਮਤ, ਤਕਦੀਰ

father ('ਫ਼ਾਦਅ*) *n v* ਪਿਤਾ, ਬਾਪ, ਪਿਉ; ਵਡੇਰਾ, ਜਨਮਦਾਤਾ, ਪ੍ਰਮੁੱਖ ਵਿਅਕਤੀ, **(F~)** ਪਰਮਾਤਮਾ; ਲਾਟ ਪਾਦਰੀ ਦਾ ਖ਼ਿਤਾਬ; ਜਨਮ ਦੇਣਾ, ਪੈਦਾ ਕਰਨਾ; ਪਿਤਾ ਬਣਨਾ; **~in law** ਸਹੁਰਾ; **~less** ਅਨਾਥ, ਯਤੀਮ; **grand~** ਦਾਦਾ, ਨਾਨਾ, ਪੁਰਖਾ

fathom ('ਫ਼ੈਦਅਮ) *n v* ਪਾਣੀ ਦੀ ਡੂੰਘਾਈ ਨਾਪਣੀ, ਬਾਹ ਲੈਣੀ, ਤਹਿ ਤਕ ਪੁੱਜਣਾ; ਬਾਹਵਾਂ ਨਾਲ ਘੇਰ ਲੈਣਾ; **~less** ਅਥਾਹ, ਅਟੱਲ

fatigue (ਫ਼ਅ'ਟੀਗ) *n v* ਥਕੇਵਾਂ, ਥਕਾਵਟ, ਵਗਾਰ, ਸਿਥਲ ਕਰ ਦੇਣਾ; ਧਾਤ ਨੂੰ ਕੁੱਟ ਕੁੱਟ ਕੇ ਪਤਲਾ ਕਰ ਦੇਣਾ

fatty ('ਫ਼ੈਟੀ) *a n* ਚਰਬੀਲਾ, ਮੋਟਾ ਤਾਜ਼ਾ

fault (ਫ਼ੋਲਟ) *n v* ਭੁੱਲ, ਗਲਤੀ, ਕਸੂਰ, ਦੋਸ਼, ਨੁਕਸ, ਤੇਡ; ਦਰਾੜ ਪਾਉਣੀ, ਟੁੱਟ ਜਾਣਾ; **~finding** ਨੁਕਤਾਚੀਨੀ, ਦੋਸ਼ ਦੇਖਣ ਦੀ ਰੁਚੀ; **~less** ਬੇਕਸੂਰ, ਨਿਰਦੋਸ਼, ਨਿਸ਼ਕਲੰਕ; **~y** ਅਸ਼ੁੱਧ, ਗਲਤ, ਨੁਕਸਦਾਰ, ਦੋਸ਼ਪੂਰਨ, ਦੋਸ਼ੀ, ਕਸੂਰਵਾਰ

fauna ('ਫ਼ੋਨਅ) *n pl* ਜੀਵ ਜੰਤੁ; ਜੀਵ ਜੰਤੁ ਵਰਗ, ਜੀਵ-ਸ਼ਾਸਤਰ

favour ('ਫ਼ੇਇਵ਼ਅ*) *n v* ਉਪਕਾਰ, ਲਿਹਾਜ਼, ਪੱਖਦਾਰੀ ਰਿਆਇਤ; ਅਨੁਕੂਲਤਾ; ਮੂੰਹ-ਮੁਹਾਂਦਰਾ, ਚਿਹਰਾ-ਮੁਹਰਾ; ਲਿਹਾਜ਼ ਕਰਨਾ, ਤਰਫ਼ਦਾਰੀ ਕਰਨੀ, ਅਨੁਕੂਲਤਾ ਪਰਗਟ ਕਰਨੀ; ਮਿਹਰਬਾਨੀ ਕਰਨੀ; ਸਵੀਕਾਰ ਕਰਨਾ, ਸਰਲ ਕਰ ਦੇਣਾ, ਸਹਾਰਾ ਦੇਣਾ; **~able** ਅਨੁਕੂਲ, ਸਹਾਇਕ, ਹਿਤਕਾਰੀ, ਮੁਆਫ਼ਕ; ਉਪਕਾਰਕ; **~ite** ਲਾਡਲਾ, ਮੂੰਹ ਚੜ੍ਹਿਆ, ਲਿਹਾਜ਼ੀ, ਵਿਸ਼ੇਸ਼ ਨਿਕਟਵਰਤੀ ਵਿਅਕਤੀ; ਪਿਆਰਾ, ਮਨਪਸੰਦ, ਮਨਭਾਉਣਾ; **~itism** ਤਰਫ਼ਦਾਰੀ, ਪੱਖਪਾਤ, ਲਿਹਾਜ਼, ਮੁਲਾਹਜ਼ਾ

fawn (ਫ਼ੋਨ) *n v* ਹਿਰਨ ਦਾ ਬੱਚਾ, ਹਿਰਨੇਟਾ; ਲਾਡਕਰਨਾ; ਚਾਪਲੂਸੀ ਕਰਨੀ; **~ing** ਖ਼ੁਸ਼ਾਮਦੀ, ਚਾਪਲੂਸ; ਖ਼ੁਸ਼ਾਮਦ, ਚਾਪਲੂਸੀ

fear (ਫ਼ਿਅ*) *n* ਡਰ ਭੌ, ਪਰੇਸ਼ਾਨੀ; ਡਰਨਾ ਜਾਂ ਡਰਾਉਣਾ, ਭੈਭੀਤ ਕਰਨਾ, ਸ਼ੰਕਾ ਹੋਣਾ; ਰੱਬ ਤੋਂ ਡਰਨਾ; **~ful** ਡਰਾਉਣਾ, ਭਿਅੰਕਰ, ਭਿਆਨਕ, ਘੋਰਨਾਕ; **~less** ਨਿਡਰ, ਨਿਧੜਕ, ਦਲੇਰ

feasibility ('ਫ਼ੀਜ਼ਅ'ਬਿਲਟੀ) *n* ਸੰਭਵਤਾ, ਯੋਗਤਾ, ਨਿਭਣਯੋਗਤਾ

feasible ('ਫ਼ੀਜ਼ਅਬਲ) *a* ਹੋਣ ਯੋਗ, ਉਚਿਤ, ਨਿਭਣਯੋਗ, ਉਪਯੋਗੀ

feast (ਫ਼ੀਸਟ) *n v* ਪਰੀਤੀਭੋਜ, ਦਾਅਵਤ, ਭੰਡਾਰਾ, ਜ਼ਿਆਫ਼ਤ, ਤਿਉਹਾਰ, ਪਰਬ, ਉਤਸਵ, ਧਾਰਮਕ, ਉਤਸਵ; ਰਜ ਕੇ ਖਾਣਾ ਜਾਂ ਖਵਾਉਣਾ, ਤ੍ਰਿਪਤ ਕਰਨਾ, ਭੰਡਾਰਾ ਕਰਨਾ, ਪਰਬ ਮਨਾਉਣਾ

feat (ਫ਼ੀਟ) *n a* ਸਾਹਸੀ ਕੰਮ, ਅਸਾਧਾਰਨ ਕੰਮ, ਅਸਚਰਜ ਕੰਮ, ਕਮਾਲ, ਕਾਰੀਗਰੀ, ਹੱਥ ਦੀ ਸਫ਼ਾਈ; ਪ੍ਰਵੀਨ, ਨਿਪੁੰਨ, ਚੁਸਤ, ਫੁਰਤੀਲਾ

feather ('ਫ਼ੈਦ਼ਅ*) *n v* ਖੰਭ, ਪਰ; ਬਹੁਤ ਹੌਲੀ ਵਸਤੁ; ਖੰਭ ਲਾਉਣਾ, ਖੰਭ ਚਿਪਕਾਉਣਾ; **in high~** ਬੜੇ ਜੋਸ਼ ਵਿਚ, ਪੂਰੇ ਉਤਸਾਹ ਨਾਲ

feature ('ਫ਼ੀਚਅ*) *n* ਚਿਹਰਾ-ਮੁਹਰਾ, ਹੁਲੀਆ, ਰੂਪ, ਰੰਗ-ਰੂਪ, ਨਕਸ਼, ਸ਼ਕਲ-ਸੂਰਤ; ਵਿਸ਼ੇਸ਼ਤਾ, ਲੱਛਣ; (ਅਖ਼ਬਾਰ ਦਾ) ਵਿਸ਼ੇਸ਼ ਲੇਖ; ਪ੍ਰਮੁੱਖ ਹੋਣਾ, ਰੂਪ ਦੇਣਾ, ਸ਼ਕਲ ਦੇਣੀ, ਰੂਪ-ਰੇਖਾ ਬਣਾਉਣੀ, ਨਕਸ਼ਾ ਖਿਚਣਾ, ਖ਼ਾਕਾ ਜਾਂ ਢਾਂਚਾ ਤਿਆਰ ਕਰਨਾ; **~film** ਕਥਾ-ਚਿੱਤਰ; **~less** ਆਕ੍ਰਿਤੀਹੀਣ, ਆਕਰਸ਼ਣਹੀਣ, ਫਿੱਕਾ ਤੇ ਕੋਝਾ, ਅਲਪਝ ਜਿਹਾ

federal ('ਫ਼ੈੱਡ(ਅ)ਰ(ਅ)ਲ) *a* ਸੰਘੀ

federation ('ਫ਼ੈੱਡਅ'ਰੇਇਸ਼ਨ) *n* ਸੰਘ, ਸੰਗਠਨ, ਸੰਧੀ

fee (ਫ਼ੀ) *n* ਫ਼ੀਸ, ਉਜਰਤ, ਮਿਹਨਤਾਨਾ,

feeble ('ਫ਼ੀਬਲ) *a* ਕਮਜ਼ੋਰ, ਮਾੜਾ, ਨਿਰਬਲ
ਦੁਰਬਲ, ਲਿੱਸਾ, ਬੁੱਧੀਹੀਣ, ਪ੍ਰਭਾਵਹੀਣ

feed (ਫ਼ੀਡ) *v n* ਖੁਆਉਣਾ, ਚੋਗਾ ਪਾਉਣਾ,
ਚਰਨਾ, ਚੁਗਣਾ, ਖ਼ੁਰਾਕ ਪੂਰੀ ਕਰਨੀ; ਖ਼ੁਰਾਕ,
ਗ਼ਿਜ਼ਾ, ਭੋਜਨ; **~back** ਪਰਤੀ ਸੂਚਨਾ,

feel (ਫ਼ੀਲ) *v n* ਟੋਹਣਾ; ਅਨੁਭਵ ਕਰਨਾ,
ਮਹਿਸੂਸ ਕਰਨਾ, ਟਟੋਲਣਾ, ਟੋਹ ਕੇ ਲੱਭਣਾ;
ਜਾਪਣਾ, ਪ੍ਰਤੀਤ ਹੋਣਾ, ਭਾਸਣਾ; ਸਮਝਣਾ; ਜਾਂਚ
ਪੜਤਾਲ ਕਰਨੀ, ਸੂਝ ਹੋਣੀ, ਪਤਾ ਹੋਣਾ;
ਪ੍ਰਭਾਵਤ ਹੋਣਾ; ਵਿਸ਼ਵਾਸ ਹੋਣਾ; ਸਪਰਸ਼,
ਪਰਖ, ਛੂਹ ਦੁਆਰਾ ਪੜਤਾਲ; **~the pulse of**
ਨਬਜ਼ ਵੇਖਣੀ, ਭੇਦਾਂ ਜਾਂ ਵਿਚਾਰਾਂ ਨੂੰ ਸਮਝਣਾ;
~ing ਭਾਵ, ਇਹਿਸਾਸ, ਵਿਚਾਰ, ਜਜ਼ਬਾ;
ਦਰਦ, ਵੇਦਨਾ; ਹਮਦਰਦੀ, ਵਿਸ਼ਵਾਸ

feign (ਫ਼ੇਇਨ) *v* ਬਹਾਨਾ ਕਰਨਾ, ਮਕਰ ਕਰਨਾ,
ਮਚਲੇ ਹੋਣਾ; ਘੜਨਾ

felicitate (ਫ਼ਲ'ਲਿਸਿਟੇਇਟ) *v* ਵਧਾਈ ਦੇਣੀ;
ਪਰਸੰਨ ਕਰਨਾ, ਨਿਹਾਲ ਕਰਨਾ, ਅਭਿਨੰਦਨ
ਕਰਨਾ

felicitation (ਫ਼ਅ'ਲਿਸਿ'ਟੇਇਸ਼ਨ) *n* ਵਧਾਈ,
ਮੁਬਾਰਕਬਾਦ, ਅਭਿਨੰਦਨ

felicity (ਫ਼ਅ'ਲਿਸਅਟਿ) *n* ਆਨੰਦ, ਪਰਮਾਨੰਦ,
ਹੁਲਾਸ, ਸੁਭਾਗ

fellow ('ਫ਼ੈੱਲਅਉ) *n* ਸਾਥੀ, ਜੋਟੀਦਾਰ, ਸਹਿਯੋਗੀ,
ਸੰਗੀ, ਆੜੀ, ਦੋਸਤ, ਭਾਈ-ਬੰਦ; ਸਮਕਾਲੀ,
(ਯੂਨੀਵਰਸਿਟੀ ਦਾ) ਫ਼ੈਲੋ, ਬੰਦਾ; **~ship**
ਭਾਈਚਾਰਾ, ਬਰਾਦਰੀ, ਭਿਆਲੀ, ਮਿੱਤਰਤਾ;
ਮਿੱਤਰ-ਭਾਵ; ਸਾਥੀ-ਸੰਘ; ਕਾਲਜ ਜਾਂ
ਯੂਨੀਵਰਸਿਟੀ ਦਾ ਵਜ਼ੀਫ਼ਾ; ਯੂਨੀਵਰਸਿਟੀ ਦੀ
ਸਦੱਸਤਾ

female ('ਫ਼ੀਮੇਇਲ) *n a* ਮਦੀਨ, ਮਾਦਾ,
ਇਸਤਰੀ, ਮਹਿਲਾ, ਔਰਤ; ਜਨਾਨਾ; **~friend**
ਸਹੇਲੀ, ਸੱਖੀ

feminine ('ਫ਼ੈਮਿਨਿਨ) *a* ਜਨਾਨਾ, ਤੀਵੀਆਂ ਦਾ;
ਜਨਾਨੜਾ, ਤੀਵੀਆਂ ਵਰਗਾ

femininity, feminism, femineity ('ਫ਼ੈਮਿ-
ਨਿਨਅਟਿ, 'ਫ਼ੈਮਿਨਿਜ਼(ਅ)ਮ, 'ਫ਼ੈਮਿਨੀਅਟਿ) *n*
ਨਾਰੀਤਵ, ਇਸਤਰੀਪਣ, ਨਾਰੀਪਣ, ਇਸਤਰੀ-
ਵਾਦ

feminist ('ਫ਼ੈਮਿਨਿਸਟ) *a* ਨਾਰੀਵਾਦੀ; ਨਾਰੀਆਂ
ਸਬੰਧੀ

fence (ਫ਼ੈੱਸ) *n v* ਵਾੜ, ਜੰਗਲਾ, ਵਲਗਣ, ਘੇਰਾ,
ਅਹਾਤਾ; ਪੌਤੜਾ; ਪੱਟਾ; ਘੇਰਾ ਵਲਣਾ; ਵਲਗਣ
ਬਣਾਉਣਾ, ਵਾੜ ਲਾਉਣਾ; ਬਚਾ ਕਰਨਾ,
ਗਤਕਾ ਖੇਡਣਾ, ਚੋਰੀ ਦਾ ਮਾਲ ਖ਼ਰੀਦਣਾ ਤੇ
ਵੇਚਣਾ

fencing ('ਫ਼ੈੱਸਿਡ) *n* ਜੰਗਲਾ, ਵਾੜ, ਘੇਰਾ
ਚਾਰਦੀਵਾਰੀ; ਚੋਰੀ ਦੇ ਸਾਮਾਨ ਦਾ ਗੁਦਾਮ;
ਗਤਕਾ

fend (ਫ਼ੈੱਡ) *v* ਪ੍ਰਬੰਧ ਕਰਨਾ, ਇਕੱਤਰ ਕਰਨਾ;
ਬਚਾਉਣਾ, ਰੱਖਿਆ ਕਰਨੀ, ਸੰਭਾਲ ਕੇ ਰੱਖਣਾ,
ਬਚਾ ਕੇ ਰੱਖਣਾ; ਨਿਵਾਰਨ ਕਰਨਾ, ਹਟਾਉਣਾ,
ਦੂਰ ਭਜਾ ਦੇਣਾ

ferment ('ਫ਼ਅ'ਮੈਂਟ, ਫ਼ਅ'ਮੈਂਟ) *n v* ਖ਼ਮੀਰ,
ਜਾਮਨ, ਉਬਾਲ, ਗੜਬੜ; ਉਬਲਣਾ, ਖ਼ਮੀਰ
ਉਠਨਾ, ਉਤੇਜਤ ਕਰਨਾ, ਫ਼ਸਾਦ ਕਰਾਉਣਾ,
ਜੋਸ਼ ਵਿਚ ਆਉਣਾ, ਭੜਕ ਉੱਠਨਾ; **~ation**
ਖ਼ਮੀਰ, ਜਾਮਨ, ਉਬਾਲ, ਉਤੇਜਨਾ; ਫ਼ਸਾਦ

ferocious (ਫ਼ਅ'ਰਅਉਸ਼ਅਸ) *a* ਵਹਿਸ਼ੀ, ਹਿੰਸਕ,
ਦਰਿੰਦਾ, ਖ਼ੂੰਖਾਰ, ਕਰੂਰ, ਭਿਆਂਕਰ, ਘੇਰਹਿਮ

ferocity (ਫ਼ਅ'ਰੌਸਅਟਿ) *n* ਵਹਿਸ਼ੀਪਣ,

ਨਿਰਦਇਤਾ, ਕਰੂਰਤਾ, ਹਿੰਸਕਤਾ, ਜੰਗਲੀਪਨ

ferry ('ਫੈਰਿ) *n v* ਪੱਤਣ, ਘਾਟ, ਬੇੜੀ-ਘਾਟ, ਬੇੜੀ; ਬੇੜੀ ਦਾ ਭਾੜਾ; ਬੇੜੀ ਵਿਚ ਪਾਰ ਜਾਣਾ, ਬੇੜੀ ਵਿਚ ਪਾਰ ਲੈ ਜਾਣਾ; ਹਵਾਈ; **~boat** ਯਾਤਰੀਆਂ ਦੀ ਬੇੜੀ, ਪੱਤਣ ਦੀ ਬੇੜੀ, ਘਾਟ ਵਾਲੀ ਨੌਕਾ; **~man** ਮਾਂਝੀ, ਪਾਤਣੀ

fertile ('ਫ਼ਅਃਟਾਇਲ) *a* ਉਪਜਾਊ, ਜ਼ਰਖੇਜ਼, ਫਲਦਾਇਕ; ਬਹੁਫਲਨੀ

fertility (ਫ਼ਅਃਟਿਲਅਟਿ) *n* ਉਪਜਾਊਤ, ਉਪਜਾਊ-ਸ਼ਕਤੀ, ਜਣਨ-ਸ਼ਕਤੀ, ਜ਼ਰਖੇਜ਼ੀ

fertilize ('ਫ਼ਅਃਟਅਲਾਇਜ਼) *v* ਉਪਜਾਊ ਬਣਾਉਣਾ, ਫਲਦਾਰ ਬਣਾਉਣਾ; ਜ਼ਰਖੇਜ਼ ਕਰਨਾ; **~er** ਰੂੜੀ, ਖਾਦ

fervent ('ਫ਼ਅਃਵ਼ੰਟ) *a* ਪ੍ਰਚੰਡ, ਜੋਸ਼ੀਲਾ ਗਰਮਾਗਰਮ, ਭਖਦਾ, ਤੱਤਾ

fervid ('ਫ਼ਅਃਵਿਡ) *a* ਉਤਸੁਕ, ਪ੍ਰਚੰਡ, ਮਘਦਾ; **~ness** ਉਤਸੁਕਤਾ, ਪ੍ਰਚੰਡਤਾ; ਉਤਕੰਠਾ

fervour, fervency ('ਫ਼ਅਃਵ਼ਅ*, 'ਫ਼ਅਃਵ਼ੰਸਿ) *n* ਤੀਬਰਤਾ, ਪ੍ਰਚੰਡਤਾ, ਉਤਸਾਹ, ਗਰਮੀ, ਤਪੱਸ, ਤਾਅ

festival ('ਫ਼ਐਸਟਅਵ਼ਲ) *n a* ਉਤਸਵ, ਪੁਰਬ, ਤਿਉਹਾਰ, ਜਸ਼ਨ

festive ('ਫ਼ੈਸਟਿਵ਼) *a* ਖੁਸ਼ ਖੁਸ਼, ਰੰਗੀਨਤ, ਪਰਸੰਨ, ਖੁਸ਼ੀ ਵਾਲਾ, ਆਨੰਦਦਾਇਕ; ਜ਼ਿੰਦਾ-ਦਿਲ, ਵਿਨੋਦੀ

festivity (ਫ਼ੈੱਸ'ਟਿਵ਼ਅਟਿ) *n* ਰੌਣਕ, ਸਜ-ਧਜ, ਰੰਗ-ਰਲੀਆਂ; ਉਤਸਵ, ਪੁਰਬ, ਤਿਉਹਾਰ, ਮੇਲਾ, ਰਾਗ-ਰੰਗ, ਜਸ਼ਨ

festoon (ਫ਼ੈੱਸਟੂਨ) *n v* ਹਾਰ, ਸਜਾਵਟ ਲਈ ਲਾਈਆਂ ਝੰਡੀਆਂ; ਹਾਰਾਂ, ਝੰਡੀਆਂ ਆਦਿ ਨਾਲ ਸਜਾਉਣਾ, ਹਾਰ ਪਾਉਣਾ

fetch (ਫ਼ੈੱਚ) *v n* ਲਿਆਉਣਾ, ਚੁੱਕਣਾ; ਮੁੱਲ ਮਿਲਣਾ, ਕੁਝ ਪ੍ਰਾਪਤ ਹੋਣਾ; ਪ੍ਰਭਾਵਤ ਕਰਨਾ; ਧੋਖਾ, ਕਪਟ, ਫ਼ਰੇਬ, ਹੱਥਫੇਰੀ

fete (ਫ਼ੇਇਟ) *n v* ਉਤਸਵ; ਮੇਲਾ; ਤਿਉਹਾਰ ਜਾਂ ਉਤਸਵ ਮਨਾਉਣਾ, ਮੌਜ-ਮੇਲਾ ਕਰਨਾ; ਮੇਲਾ ਲਾਉਣਾ

fetter ('ਫ਼ੈੱਟਅ*) *n v* ਬੇੜੀ, ਪੈਂਖੜ, ਰੋਕ, ਰੁਕਾਵਟ, ਗਰਿਫ਼ਤਾਰੀ, ਬੇੜੀ ਪਾਉਣਾ, ਬੰਧਨ ਲਾਉਣਾ, ਬੰਨ੍ਹ ਦੇਣਾ

feud (ਫ਼ਯੂਡ) *n* ਖ਼ਾਨਦਾਨੀ ਵੈਰ, ਜੱਦੀ ਦੁਸ਼ਮਨੀ, ਦੰਗਾ, ਦੁਸ਼ਮਨੀ; ਜਾਗੀਰ; **~al** ਜਾਗੀਰੀ, ਸਾਮੰਤ-ਵਾਦੀ, ਸਾਮੰਤੀ, ਭੂਪਵਾਦੀ; **~alism** ਜਾਗੀਰ-ਦਾਰੀ, ਬਿਸਵੇਦਾਰੀ, ਸਾਮੰਤਵਾਦ, ਰਾਜਵਾੜਾਸ਼ਾਹੀ; **~alist** ਜਾਗੀਰਦਾਰ, ਸਾਮੰਤਵਾਦੀ

fever ('ਫ਼ੀਵ਼ਅ*) *n v* ਤਾਪ, ਬੁਖ਼ਾਰ, ਉਤੇਜਨਾ; ਤਾਪ ਚੜ੍ਹਾਉਣਾ; **~ish** ਤਾਪਲ, ਸਰਗਰਮ, ਭਖਦਾ

few (ਫ਼ਯੂ) *a n* ਕੁਝ, ਥੋੜ੍ਹੇ ਜਿਹੇ, ਕੁਝ ਕੁ, ਕੋਈ ਕੋਈ, ਟਾਂਵਾਂ ਟਾਂਵਾਂ, ਇਕ ਅੱਧਾ; **not a~** ਬਹੁਤ ਸਾਰੇ; **the~** ਕੁਝ ਥੋੜ੍ਹੀ ਗਿਲਤੀ ਦੇ, ਚੋਟਵੇਂ

fiasco (ਫ਼ਿ'ਐਸਕਅਓ) *n v* ਅਸਫਲਤਾ, ਨਾਕਾਮਯਾਬੀ, ਬਹੁਤ ਬੁਰੀ ਵਿਫਲਤਾ

fiat ('ਫ਼ਾਇਐਟ) *n v* ਹੁਕਮ, ਫ਼ਰਮਾਨ, ਆਗਿਆ, ਆਦੇਸ਼; ਅਧਿਕਾਰ ਦੇਣਾ, ਮੁਖ਼ਤਿਆਰ ਬਣਾਉਣਾ

fibre ('ਫ਼ਾਇਬਅ*) *n* ਰੇਸ਼ਾ; ਸੂਤ, ਤੰਦ; ਢੰਗ, ਢਾਂਚਾ, ਸ਼ਕਲ; ਸੁਭਾਅ; **~d** ਰੇਸ਼ੇਦਾਰ, ਤੰਦਾਂ ਵਾਲਾ, ਤਾਰਦਾਰ

fibrous ('ਫ਼ਿਇਬਰਅਸ) *a* ਰੇਸ਼ੇਦਾਰ; ਪੱਕਾ, ਮਜ਼ਬੂਤ

fickle ('ਫ਼ਿਕਲ) *a* ਚੰਚਲ, ਅਸਥਿਰ, ਚਪਲ, ਡੋਲਵਾਂ, ਪਰਿਵਰਤਨਸ਼ੀਲ; **~minded** ਚੰਚਲ

ਮਨ ਵਾਲਾ, ਅਟਿਕਵਾਂ ਵਿਅਕਤੀ; **~ness**
ਚੰਚਲਤਾ, ਅਸਥਿਰਤਾ

fiction ('ਫ਼ਿਕਸ਼ਨ) *n* ਗਲਪ, ਨਾਵਲ ਕਹਾਣੀ
ਆਦਿ ਕਥਾ-ਸਾਹਿਤ; ਕਲਪਤ ਕਥਾ, ਝੂਠਾ
ਕਿੱਸਾ, ਕਲਪਨਾ, ਗੱਪ, ਝੂਠ; **~al** ਗਲਪਈ,
ਕਲਪਤ, ਕਹਾਣੀ ਜਾਂ ਨਾਵਲ ਸਬੰਧੀ

fictitious (ਫ਼ਿਕ'ਟਿਸ਼ਅਸ) *a* ਬਣਾਉਟੀ, ਨਕਲੀ,
ਘੋਟਾ, ਫ਼ਰਜ਼ੀ, ਕਲਪਤ, ਅਵਾਸਤਵਿਕ,

fidelity (ਫ਼ਿ'ਡੈੱਲਅਟਿ) *n* ਵਫ਼ਾਦਾਰੀ, ਨਿਸ਼ਠਾ;
ਦ੍ਰਿੜਤਾ; ਸਥਿਰ ਵਿਸ਼ਵਾਸ, ਪੱਕੀ ਸ਼ਰਧਾ

fie (ਫ਼ਾਇ) *int* ਫਿਟੇ ਮੂੰਹ, ਲੱਖ ਲਾਨ੍ਹਤ, ਧਿਕਾਰ

fief (ਫ਼ੀਫ਼) *n* ਜਾਗੀਰ

field (ਫ਼ੀਲਡ) *n v* (1) ਖੇਤ, ਚਰਾਗਾਹ; ਭੋਂ,
ਜ਼ਮੀਨ; (2) ਰਣਭੂਮੀ, ਜੁੱਧ-ਖੇਤਰ; (3) ਹਾਕੀ,
ਫ਼ੁਟਬਾਲ, ਕ੍ਰਿਕਟ ਆਦਿ ਖੇਡਾਂ ਦੇ ਮੈਦਾਨ; ਗੇਂਦ
ਰੋਕਣਾ ਤੇ ਮੋੜਨਾ; ਖਿਡਾਰੀਆਂ ਨੂੰ ਹੱਲਾ ਸ਼ੇਰੀ
ਦੇਣੀ, ਉਤਸ਼ਾਹ ਵਧਾਉਣਾ, ਕਾਰਜ ਕਰਨਾ;
hold the~ ਡਟੇ ਰਹਿਣਾ, ਪੈਰ ਪਿੱਛੇ ਨਾ
ਕਰਨਾ; **keep the~** ਅੰਦੋਲਨ ਜਾਰੀ ਰੱਖਣਾ,
ਆਪਣੀ ਗੱਲ ਪੱਕੀ ਕਰਨਾ; **take the~** ਮੈਦਾਨ
ਵਿਚ ਨਿਤਰਨਾ, ਲੜਾਈ ਸ਼ੁਰੂ ਕਰਨੀ

fiend (ਫ਼ੀਂਡ) *n* ਭੂਤਨਾ, ਪਰੇਤ; ਸ਼ੈਤਾਨ, ਦੁਸ਼ਟ,
ਚੰਡਾਲ, ਉਪੱਦਰੀ

fierce (ਫ਼ਿਅਃਸ) *a* ਤੀਬਰ, ਤੁੰਦ, ਪ੍ਰਚੰਡ; ਘੋਰ,
ਉਗਰ ਭਿਆਨਕ, ਕਰੂਰ; ਜੋਸ਼ੀਲਾ, ਨਿਰਦਈ,
ਬੇਰਹਿਮ

fiery ('ਫ਼ਾਇਅਰਿ) *a* ਅਗਨਮਈ, ਦਗਦਾ, ਭਖਦਾ;
ਜੋਸ਼ੀਲਾ, ਲੜਾਕਾ, ਅੱਗ ਦੀ ਨਾੜ, ਕਰੋਪੀ; ਅੱਗ
ਵਰਗਾ, ਤਪਦਾ, ਲਾਲ ਅੰਗਾਰ; ਭੜਕਾਊ,
ਉਤੇਜਤ ਕਰਨ ਵਾਲਾ, ਅੱਗ ਵਾਂਗ ਭਖਾ ਦੇਣ
ਵਾਲਾ; ਧੂੰਆਂਧਾਰ (ਭਾਸ਼ਣ)

fiesta (ਫ਼ਿ'ਐੱਸਟਅ) *n* ਮੇਲਾ

fifteen ('ਫ਼ਿੱਫ਼'ਟੀਨ) *a n* ਪੰਦਰ੍ਹਾਂ; **~th** ਪੰਦਰਵਾਂ

fifth (ਫ਼ਿੱਫ਼ਥ) *a n* ਪੰਜਵਾਂ; ਪੰਜ ਤਾਰੀਖ਼; ਪੰਜਵੀਂ
ਥਿੱਤ, ਪੰਜਵੀਂ ਸੁਰ (ਰਾਗ ਵਿਚ), ਪੰਚਮ;
ਘਟੀਆ ਚੀਜ਼, ਰੱਦੀ ਵਸਤੂ; **~column**
ਦੇਸ਼ਧਰੋਹੀ ਸੰਸਥਾ, ਘਰ ਦਾ ਭੇਤੀ, ਦੇਸ਼ਧਰੋਹੀ;
~columnist ਦੇਸ਼ਧਰੋਹੀ, ਗ਼ੱਦਾਰ

fifty ('ਫ਼ਿੱਫ਼ਟਿ) *a n* ਪੰਜਾਹ (50), ਪੰਜਾਹਵਾਂ ਦਾ
ਸਮੂਹ; ਬਹੁਤ ਸਾਰੇ, ਕਈ, ਲੋੜ ਤੋਂ ਵਧੇਰੇ

fig (ਫ਼ਿਗ) *n* (1) ਅੰਜੀਰ, ਮਾਮੂਲੀ ਚੀਜ਼, ਤੁੱਛ
ਵਸਤੂ; (2) ਹਾਲਤ, ਦਸ਼ਾ, ਅਵਸਥਾ

fight (ਫ਼ਾਇਟ) *n v* ਲੜਨਾ, ਝਗੜਨਾ, ਜੁੱਧ ਕਰਨਾ,
ਜੰਗ ਕਰਨਾ; ਟੱਕਰ ਲੈਣੀ, ਮੁਕਾਬਲਾ ਕਰਨਾ;
ਮੁਕੱਦਮਾ ਲੜਨਾ; ਖੁਲ੍ਹਣਾ; ਲੜਾਈ ਮੁੱਠ-ਭੇੜ,
ਟੱਕਰ, ਕੁਸ਼ਤੀ, ਜੁੱਧ, ਜੰਗ; ਸੰਘਰਸ਼, ਜਤਨ;
ਲਗਾਤਾਰ ਕੋਸ਼ਿਸ਼; **~out** ਲੜ ਝਗੜ ਕੇ ਮਾਮਲਾ
ਨਜਿੱਠਣਾ; **~er** ਜੋਧਾ, ਲੜਾਕਾ, ਸੂਰਬੀਰ

figment ('ਫ਼ਿਗਮਅੰਟ) *n* ਕਲਪਨਾ, ਵਹਿਮ,
ਮਨਘੜਤ, ਥਿਆਨ

figure ('ਫ਼ਿਗਾ*) *n v* ਸ਼ਕਲ, ਖ਼ਾਕਾ, ਆਕਾਰ,
ਬਾਹਰੀ ਰੂਪ, ਸਰੀਰ, ਡੌਲ, ਕਾਠੀ, ਮੂਰਤੀ, ਬੁੱਤ;
(ਗਣਿਤ ਆਦਿ ਵਿਚ) ਸੰਖਿਆ, ਗਿਣਤੀ; ਅੰਗ,
ਚਿੰਨ੍ਹ, ਛਾਪ, ਉਪਮਾ, ਅੱਲਕਾਰ, ਸਦ੍ਰਿਸ਼ਤਾ;
ਅਨੁਮਾਨ; ਵੇਲ-ਬੂਟੇ ਪਾਉਣੇ; ਗਿਣਤੀ ਕਰਨੀ;
ਕੁੱਲ ਜੋੜ ਕਰਨਾ; **~head** ਦਿਖਾਵੇ ਦਾ ਮੁਖੀ, ਨਾਂ
ਦਾ ਪ੍ਰਧਾਨ; **~of speech** ਅਲੰਕਾਰ (ਰੂਪਕ,
ਅੱਤਕਥਨੀ ਆਦਿ); **~less** ਨਿਰਾਕਾਰ,
ਆਕਾਰਹੀਨ, ਬੇਢੰਗਾ, ਭੱਦਾ, ਬੇਡੌਲ

filament ('ਫ਼ਿਲਅਮਅੰਟ) *n* ਰੇਸ਼ਾ, ਤਾਰ, ਤੰਦ, ਸੂਤ;
ਪਰਾਗ ਕੇਸਰ, ਕਿੰਜਲਕ; ਬਲਬ ਦੀ ਤਾਰ; **~ary**
ਰੇਸ਼ੇ ਦਾ, ਤੰਦਾਂ ਵਾਲਾ; ਕੇਸਰ ਜਾਂ ਕਿੰਜਲਕ ਵਾਲਾ

file (ਫ਼ਾਇਲ) *n v* ਫ਼ਾਇਲ, ਪੁਲੰਦਾ, ਮਿਸਲ; ਪੰਗਤੀ, ਕਤਾਰ, ਖ਼ਾਨੇ, ਘਰ, ਰੇਤੀ ਚੋਸਾ; ਕਪਟੀ ਮਨੁੱਖ, ਚਲਾਕ ਬੰਦਾ; ਨੱਥੀ ਕਰਨਾ ਕ੍ਰਮਵਾਰ ਕਾਗ਼ਜ਼ ਰੱਖਣਾ; ਮਿਸਲ ਬਣਾਉਣੀ, ਰੇਤੀ ਨਾਲ ਪੱਧਰਾ ਕਰਨਾ; ਸਾਫ਼ ਕਰਨਾ, ਸੁਧਾਰਨਾ, ਮੁਲਾਇਮ ਕਰਨਾ, ਰਗੜਨਾ, ਘਿਸਾਉਣਾ; ਪਾਲ ਬੰਨ੍ਹਣੀ, ਪੰਗਤੀਆਂ ਵਿਚ ਕੂਚ ਕਰਨਾ; **~a suit** ਦਾਅਵਾ ਦਾਇਰ ਕਰਨਾ; **rank and~** ਪਿਛਲੱਗਾ, ਆਮ ਲੋਕ, ਸਰਬ

fill (ਫ਼ਿਲ) *v n* ਭਰਨਾ, ਭਰ ਜਾਣਾ, ਪੂਰਾ ਕਰਨਾ, ਪੂਰਨਾ, ਪੂਰੇ ਜਾਣਾ, ਦਫ਼ਤਰ ਦੇ ਕੰਮ ਨਿਭਾਉਣੇ; ਕਿਸੇ ਅਹੁਦੇ ਤੇ ਹੋਣਾ; ਰੱਜ ਕੇ ਖਾਣਾ, ਤੁਸਣਾ; ਪੂਰਤੀ, ਮਾਪ, ਭਰਤੀ, ਰੱਜ, ਤ੍ਰਿਪਤੀ; **~in** ਖ਼ਾਨਾ ਪੂਰੀ ਕਰਨਾ, ਲਿਖਣਾ; **~up** ਪੂਰੀ ਤਰ੍ਹਾਂ ਵਧ ਜਾਣਾ, ਵੱਡਾ ਹੋ ਜਾਣਾ, ਖ਼ਾਲੀ ਥਾਂ ਨੂੰ ਭਰਨਾ; **~er** ਭਰਨ ਵਾਲਾ, ਪੂਰਕ; **~ing** ਭਰਤ, ਭਰਾਈ; ਦੰਦ ਵਿਚ ਭਰੀ ਗਈ ਵਸਤੁ

fillet ('ਫ਼ਿਲਿਟ) *n v* ਕਿਸੇ ਚੀਜ਼ ਦਾ ਪਤਲਾ ਜਿਹਾ ਟੁਕੜਾ, ਸਿਰ ਨੂੰ ਬੰਨ੍ਹਣ ਲਈ ਫ਼ੀਤਾ, ਪਰਾਂਦਾ, ਜਾਨਵਰਾਂ ਦੀ ਕਮਰ, ਕੁੱਲ੍ਹਾ, ਸਿਰ ਉੱਤੇ ਪੱਟੀ, ਫ਼ੀਤਾ ਆਦਿ ਬੰਨ੍ਹਣਾ, ਮੱਛੀ ਦੇ ਟੁਕੜ ਕਰਨੇ

fillip ('ਫ਼ਿਲਿਪ) *n v* ਠੋਲ੍ਹਾ ਮਾਰਨਾ, ਉਂਗਲ ਦੀ ਚੁਟਕੀ, ਹਿਲਕੋਰਨਾ; ਪਰੇਰਨਾ, ਉਕਸਾਹਟ; ਹੱਲਾਸ਼ੇਰੀ ਦੇਣੀ; ਨਹੁੰ ਜਾਂ ਉਂਗਲ ਦਾ ਤੁਟਕਾ ਮਾਰਨਾ

film (ਫ਼ਿਲਮ) *n v* ਚਲਚਿੱਤਰ, ਫ਼ਿਲਮ, ਪਰਦਾ, ਝਿੱਲੀ, ਪਤਲੀ, ਤਹਿ; ਅੱਖ ਦਾ ਜਾਲਾ; ਫ਼ਿਲਮ ਬਣਾਉਣਾ

filter ('ਫ਼ਿਲਟਾ*) *n v* ਤਰਲ ਪਦਾਰਥਾਂ ਨੂੰ ਛਾਣਨ ਵਾਲਾ ਜੰਤਰ, ਪੁਣਨਾ, ਛਾਣਨਾ (ਤਰਲ ਪਦਾਰਥ ਦਾ), ਸਾਫ਼ ਕਰਨਾ; ਛਣ ਕੇ ਲੰਘਣਾ, ਚੋਣਾ,

ਚੁਆਉਣਾ; ਫੁੱਟ ਕੇ ਨਿਕਲਣਾ; ਫੁੱਟ ਨਿਕਲਣਾ

filth (ਫ਼ਿਲਥ) *n* ਗੰਦ, ਗੰਦ-ਮੰਦ, ਗੰਦਗੀ, ਮੈਲ; ਮਲ ਰੂੜੀ, ਕੂੜਾ; ਅਸ਼ਲੀਲਤਾ, ਭ੍ਰਿਸ਼ਟਤਾ

filtrate ('ਫ਼ਿਲਟਰੇਇਟ) *n v* ਪੁਣ ਕੇ ਸਾਫ਼ ਕੀਤੀ ਸ਼ਰਾਬ; ਪੁਣਨਾ, ਸਾਫ਼ ਕਰਨਾ

filtration ('ਫ਼ਿਲਟ'ਰੇਇਸ਼ਨ) *n* ਛਣਾਈ, ਛਾਨਣ

fin (ਫ਼ਿਨ) *n* ਮੱਛੀ ਦਾ ਖੰਭ, ਖੰਭ

final ('ਫ਼ਾਇਨਲ) *a n* ਫ਼ੈਸਲਾ, ਅੰਤਮ, ਅੰਤਲਾ; **~e** (ਸੰਗੀ) ਅੰਤਮ, ਗਤੀ, (ਨਾਟਕ) ਅੰਤਮ ਝਾਕੀ, ਅੰਤ, ਸਮਾਪਤੀ; **~ly** ਆਖ਼ਰ ਵਿਚ, ਅੰਤਮ ਰੂਪ ਵਿਚ

finance (ਫ਼ਾਇਨੈਂਸ) *a* ਵਿੱਤ, ਅਰਥ, ਮਾਲ, ਪੂੰਜੀ, ਆਰਥਕ ਸਾਧਨ; ਆਰਥਕ ਪ੍ਰਬੰਧ; ਪੂੰਜੀ ਲਾਉਣੀ, (ਕਿਸੇ ਵਿਹਾਰ ਵਿਚ) ਪੈਸਾ ਲਾਉਣਾ, ਆਰਥਕ ਪ੍ਰਬੰਧ ਕਰਨਾ, ਪੂੰਜੀ ਇਕੱਤਰ ਕਰਨਾ; **~r** ਸ਼ਾਹੂਕਾਰ; ਪੂੰਜੀਪਤੀ, ਸਰਮਾਏਦਾਰ

financial (ਫ਼ਾਇਨੈਂਸ਼ਲ) *a* ਆਰਥਕ, ਮਾਲੀ ਵਿੱਤ ਸਬੰਧੀ, ਆਮਦਨੀ ਬਾਰੇ

financier (ਫ਼ਾਇਨੈਂਸਿਅ*) *n* ਆਰਥਕ ਪ੍ਰਬੰਧ ਵਿਚ ਪ੍ਰਵੀਨ, ਪੂੰਜੀਕਾਰ, ਸ਼ਾਹੂਕਾਰ, ਸਰਮਾਏਦਾਰ, ਕੋਸ਼-ਅਧਿਅਕਸ਼

find (ਫ਼ਾਇੰਡ) *v* ਲੱਭਣਾ, ਪ੍ਰਾਪਤ ਕਰਨਾ, ਹੱਥ ਲੱਗਣਾ, ਮਾਲੂਮ ਹੋਣਾ, ਜਾਨਣਾ; ਖੋਜ ਕਰਨੀ; ਵੇਖਣਾ, ਨਜ਼ਰ ਆਉਣਾ; ਅਨੁਭਵ ਕਰਨਾ, ਮਹਿਸੂਸ ਕਰਨਾ, ਸਮਝਣਾ; **~fault with** ਨੁਕਸ ਕੱਢਣੇ; **~ing** ਨਿਰਣਾ, ਉਪਲਬਧੀ, ਨਿਸ਼ਕਰਸ਼, ਖੋਜ

fine (ਫ਼ਾਇਨ) *n v* ਜੁਰਮਾਨਾ, ਚੱਟੀ, ਤਾਵਾਨ; ਨਜ਼ਰਾਨਾ; ਜੁਰਮਾਨਾ ਕਰਨਾ; ਚੰਗਾ, ਵਧੀਆ, ਉੱਤਮ, ਸੋਹਣਾ, ਮਨੋਹਰ, ਨਿਰਦੋਸ਼, ਨਿਰਮਲ, ਸ਼ੁੱਧ, ਚੁਸਤ; ਟੀਪ-ਟਾਪ ਵਾਲਾ, ਭੜਕੀਲਾ;

ਪਤਲਾ, ਬਾਰੀਕ, ਮਹੀਨ, ਸੂਖਮ; ਨੋਕਦਾਰ, ਤੇਜ਼, ਤਿੱਖਾ; **~art** ਲਲਿਤ ਕਲਾ

finger ('ਫ਼ਿੰਗਰਾਅ*) *n v* ਉੱਗਲ, ਉਂਗਲੀ; **~print** ਉਂਗਲਾਂ ਦੇ ਨਿਸ਼ਾਨ

finish ('ਫ਼ਿਨਿਸ਼) *v n* ਪੂਰਾ ਕਰਨਾ, ਸਮਾਪਤ ਹੋਣਾ, ਮੁੱਕਣਾ ਜਾਂ ਮੁਕਾਉਣਾ, ਸਿਰੇ ਚਾੜ੍ਹਨਾ, ਬਣਾਉਣਾ ਸਜਾਉਣਾ; ਅੰਤ, ਸਮਾਪਤੀ, ਖ਼ਾਤਮਾ; **~ed** ਸਮਾਪਤ, ਸੰਪੂਰਨ, ਤਿਆਰ

finite ('ਫ਼ਾਇਨਾਇਟ) *a* ਸੀਮਤ, ਸੀਮਾਬੰਧ, ਨਿਸ਼ਚਤ; ਅਜਿਹੀ ਕਿਰਿਆ

fire (ਫ਼ਾਇਅ*) *n v* ਅੱਗ, ਅਗਨੀ; ਭਾਂਬੜ ਅੰਗਾਰਾ; ਤਪਸ਼, ਸਾੜ; ਅੱਗ ਲਗਾਣਾ, ਭੜਕ ਉੱਠਣਾ; ਤੋਪ ਦਾਗਣੀ, ਗੋਲੀ ਚਲਾਉਣੀ, ਅੱਗ ਦੇਣੀ; **~place** ਚੁੱਲ੍ਹਾ; **~work** ਆਤਸ਼ਬਾਜ਼ੀ; **catch~, take~** ਅੱਗ ਲੱਗਣਾ

firing ('ਫ਼ਾਇਰਿਙ) *n* ਗੋਲਾਬਾਰੀ, ਭਾਂਬੜ, ਜਲਾਉਣ ਦਾ ਲੱਕੜੀ

firm (ਫ਼ਅ:ਮ) *n a v* ਵਪਾਰੀ-ਸੰਸਥਾ, ਕੰਪਨੀ; ਪੱਕਾ, ਦ੍ਰਿੜ, ਮਜ਼ਬੂਤ, ਤਕੜਾ; ਨਿਸ਼ਚਤ; ਕਰੜਾ ਦ੍ਰਿੜ ਕਰਨਾ, ਠੋਸ ਕਰਨਾ; **~ness** ਪਕਿਆਈ, ਦ੍ਰਿੜਤਾ

first (ਫ਼ਅ:ਸਟ) *n a adv* ਪਹਿਲੀ ਤਾਰੀਖ਼; ਪਹਿਲਾ ਸਥਾਨ; ਵਧੀਆ ਕਿਸਮ; ਪਹਿਲਾ; ਪ੍ਰਮੁੱਖ, ਪ੍ਰਧਾਨ; ਪ੍ਰਾਰੰਭਕ, ਸਭ ਤੋਂ ਪਹਿਲਾਂ; **~aid** ਫੱਟਣ ਦਾ ਆਰੰਭਕ ਇਲਾਜ, ਤੁਰਤ ਸਹਾਇਤਾ; **~born** ਪਲੇਠੀ ਦਾ ਜੇਠਾ; **~day** ਐਤਵਾਰ; **~person** (ਵਿਆ) ਉੱਤਮ ਪੁਰਖ; **~rate** ਵਧੀਆ, ਸ੍ਰੇਸ਼ਠ, ਉੱਤਮ; **~ly** ਸਭ ਤੋਂ ਪਹਿਲਾਂ, ਅੱਵਲ

fisc, fisk (ਫ਼ਿਸਕ) *n* ਸਰਕਾਰੀ ਖ਼ਜ਼ਾਨਾ; **~al** ਆਰਥਕ, ਵਿੱਤ ਸਬੰਧੀ, ਰਾਜ ਦੋਸ਼ ਸਬੰਧੀ

fish (ਫ਼ਿਸ਼) *n v* ਮੱਛੀ, ਮੱਛੀ ਦਾ ਮਾਸ; ਮੱਛੀਆਂ

ਫੜਨਾ, (ਪਾਣੀ ਦੀ ਤਹਿ ਵਿੱਚੋਂ) ਮੱਛੀਆਂ, ਮੋਤੀ, ਮੂੰਗੇ ਆਦਿ ਕੱਢ ਲਿਆਉਣਾ; **~in troubled waters** ਬਿਪਤਾ ਵੇਲੇ ਆਪਣਾ ਕੰਮ ਕੱਢਣਾ, ਗੜਬੜ ਵਿਚ ਆਪਣਾ ਦਾਅ ਲਾਉਣਾ; **~market** ਮੱਛੀ ਬਜ਼ਾਰ, ਰੌਲੇ ਵਾਲੀ ਥਾਂ; **~monger** ਮੱਛੀ ਵੇਚਣ ਵਾਲਾ; **~erman** ਮਾਛੀ; **~ery** ਮੱਛੀਆਂ ਵਾਲੀ ਥਾਂ, ਮੱਛੀਆਂ ਫੜਨ ਦਾ ਪੇਸ਼ਾ ਜਾਂ ਵਿਹਾਰ, ਮੱਛੀਆਂ ਦਾ ਵਟਜ

fist (ਫ਼ਿਸਟ) *n v* ਮੁੱਕੀ, ਘਸੁੰਨ; ਮੁੱਕੀ ਮਾਰਨੀ

fistula ('ਫ਼ਿਸਟਯੂਲ) *n* ਭਗੰਦਰ, ਡੂੰਘਾ ਜ਼ਖ਼ਮ

fit (ਫ਼ਿਟ) *a n adv v* (1) ਯੋਗ, ਢੁੱਕਵਾਂ, ਜਚਵਾਂ, ਤੰਦਰੁਸਤ, ਸੁਅਸਥ; (2) ਬੀਮਾਰੀ ਦਾ ਦੌਰਾ, ਬੇਹੋਸ਼ੀ, ਡੋਬ; ਤਰੰਗ; ਯੋਗਤਾ ਦੇਣੀ; ਠੀਕ-ਠਾਕ ਜੜ ਦੇਣਾ; ਠੀਕ ਬੈਠਣਾ, ਜਚਣਾ; ਮੁਨਾਸਬ ਹੋਣਾ, ਅਨੁਕੂਲ ਹੋਣਾ, ਫ਼ਿਟ ਹੋਣਾ; **~ness** ਉਚਿਤਤਾ, ਸੰਗਤੀ, ਅਨੁਰੂਪਤਾ; **~ting** (ਬ ਵ) ਸਾਮਾਨ, ਸਾਜ ਸਾਮਾਨ; ਠੀਕ ਉਚਿਤ, ਯੋਗ, ਢੁਕਵਾਂ ਮੁਨਾਸਬ

five (ਫ਼ਾਇਵ੍) *a n* ਪੰਜ; ਪਾਂਜਾ; ਪੰਜ ਦੀ ਸੰਖਿਆ; **~fold** ਪੰਜ ਗੁਣਾ; **~o'clock** ਪੰਜ ਵਜੇ

fix (ਫ਼ਿਕਸ) *v n* ਨਿਸ਼ਚਤ ਕਰਨਾ, ਨਿਰਧਾਰਤ ਕਰਨਾ, ਸਿੱਥਣਾ, ਨਿਯਤ ਕਰਨਾ; ਪੱਕਾ ਕਰਨਾ; ਕਰੜੇ ਹੋਣਾ, ਪੱਥਰਾ ਜਾਣਾ, ਤਿਆਰ ਕਰਨਾ, ਅਹੁਦਾ ਸੰਭਾਲਣਾ, ਰਾਏ ਕਾਇਮ ਕਰਨਾ, ਫ਼ੈਸਲਾ ਕਰਨਾ; ਪੂਰ ਕਰਨਾ; ਨਿਯੁਕਤ ਕਰਨਾ; ਔਖ, ਔਕੜ, ਉਲਝਣ, ਜੰਜਾਲ; ਕਠਨਾਈ; **~ation** ਸਥਿਰੀਕਰਨ, ਸਥਿਰਤਾ, ਦ੍ਰਿੜਨਾ, ਪਕਿਆਈ; ਟਿਕਟਿਕੀ; **~ed** ਨਿਸ਼ਚਤ, ਸਥਿਰ, ਨਿਯਤ, ਮਿਆਦੀ; **~edness** ਦ੍ਰਿੜਤਾ, ਸਥਿਰਤਾ, ਅਚਲਤਾ

fizzle ('ਫ਼ਿਜਲ) *v n* ਸੂੰ ਸੂੰ ਕਰਕੇ ਨਿਕਲਣਾ, ਠੁੱਸ ਹੋ ਜਾਣਾ; ਅਸਫਲਤਾ; **~out** ਅਸਫਲ ਹੋਣਾ, ਠੁਸ ਹੋਣਾ

flag (ਫ਼ਲੈਗ) *n v* (1) ਝੰਡਾ; ਫ਼ਾਇਲ ਵਿਚ ਨਿਸ਼ਾਨੀ ਲਈ ਲਾਈ ਪਰਚੀ; (2) ਫ਼ਰਸ਼ ਵਿਚ ਲਾਉਣ ਵਾਲੀ ਸਿਲ ; ਫ਼ਰਸ਼ੀ ਪੱਥਰ (3) ਪੰਛੀ ਦੇ ਖੰਭ ਦੀ ਬਣੀ ਕਲਮ ; (4) ਝੰਡਾ ਲਾਉਣਾ, ਝੰਡਾ ਚੜ੍ਹਾਉਣਾ; (5) ਪੱਥਰ ਦੀਆਂ ਬਣੀਆਂ ਸਿਲਾਂ ਫ਼ਰਸ਼ ਵਿਚ ਲਾਉਣੀਆਂ (6) ਉਤਸ਼ਾਹਹੀਣ ਹੋਣਾ, ਸਿਥਲ ਹੋ ਜਾਣਾ, ਮੁਰਝਾਉਣਾ, ਦਿਲਚਸਪੀ ਨਾ ਰਹਿਣੀ

flake (ਫ਼ਲੇਇਕ) *n v* ਤੂੰਬਾ, ਫੰਬਾ, ਪੇਪੜੀ, ਪਤਲੀ ਪਰਤ; ਥੋੜ੍ਹਾ ਥੋੜ੍ਹਾ ਕਰਕੇ ਬਾਹਰ ਨਿਕਲਣਾ, ਟੋਟੇ ਟੋਟੇ ਕਰਕੇ ਬਾਹਰ ਕੱਢਣਾ

flambeau ('ਫ਼ਲੈਮਬਅਉ) *n* ਮਸ਼ਾਲ, ਬੱਤੀ

flamboyance, flamboyancy (ਫ਼ਲੈਮ'ਬੋਇਅੰਸ, ਫ਼ਲੈਮ'ਬੌਇਅੰਸਿ) *n* ਭੜਕੀਲਾਪਣ, ਤੜਕ-ਭੜਕ

flame (ਫ਼ਲੇਇਮ) *n v* ਭਾਂਬੜ, ਲਾਟ, ਜੋਤ; ਤੇਜ਼ ਰੌਸ਼ਨੀ; ਬਲਣਾ, ਬਲ ਉੱਠਣਾ, ਲਾਟਾਂ ਉੱਠਣੀਆਂ, ਕਰੋਧ ਨਾਲ ਭੜਕ ਉੱਠਣਾ

flank (ਫ਼ਲੈਂਕ) *n v* ਵੱਖੀ, ਪਾਸਾ, ਫ਼ੌਜ ਦੀ ਟੁਕੜੀ ਦੇ ਸੱਜੇ-ਖੱਬੇ ਦਾ ਪਾਸਾ; ਇਕ ਕਿਨਾਰਾ, ਦਿਸ਼ਾ; ਫ਼ੌਜ ਦੇ ਕਿਸੇ ਪਾਸੇ ਨੂੰ ਮਜ਼ਬੂਤ ਕਰਨਾ

flannel ('ਫ਼ਲੈਨਲ) *n a* ਫਲਾਲੈਣ, ਇਕ ਪ੍ਰਕਾਰ ਦਾ ਊਨੀ ਕੱਪੜਾ, ਫਲਾਲੈਣ ਦੇ ਕੱਪੜੇ; ਫਲਾਲੈਣ ਦੀਆਂ ਪੱਟੀਆਂ

flap (ਫ਼ਲੈਪ) *v n* ਫੜਫੜਾਉਣਾ, ਖੰਭ ਮਾਰਨੇ, ਖੰਭ ਫਟਕਣੈ; ਥਪਕਣਾ, ਉਡਾਉਣਾ; ਗੜੇ ਕੱਢਣੇ; ਡੋਲਣਾ, ਝੂਲਣਾ

flare (ਫ਼ਲੇਅ*) *v n* ਭੜਕਣਾ, ਭੜਕ ਉੱਠਣਾ, ਚਮਕਣਾ; ਫੁੱਲਣਾ, ਖਿੱਲਰਨਾ, ਫੁਲਾਉਣਾ, ਸੜਨਾ; ਭਾਂਬੜ, ਭੜਕ; ਤਿੱਖੀ ਰੌਸ਼ਨੀ, ਪ੍ਰਕਾਸ਼-ਗੋਲਾ, ਅੱਖਾਂ ਚੁੰਧਿਆ ਦੇਣ ਵਾਲਾ ਪ੍ਰਕਾਸ਼; ਤੜਕ ਭੜਕ, ਆਡੰਬਰ

flash (ਫ਼ਲੈਸ਼) *v n a* ਚਮਕਣਾ, ਲਿਸ਼ਕਣਾ, ਭੜਕ ਉੱਠਣਾ, ਅਚਾਨਕ ਚਮਕ ਪੈਣਾ; ਤੇਜ਼ੀ ਨਾਲ ਚੱਲਣਾ; ਚਮਕ, ਲਿਸ਼ਕ, ਝਲਕਾਰਾ, ਚਾਨਣ ਦੀ ਲਪਟ; ਅਭਿਮਾਨ ਭਰੀ ਗੱਲ-ਬਾਤ ਬਣਾਉਟੀ, ਭੜਕੀਲਾ; **~house** ਰੰਡੀਖ਼ਾਨਾ

flask (ਫ਼ਲਾਸਕ) *n* ਸੁਰਾਹੀ, ਝੱਜਰ

flat (ਫ਼ਲੈਟ) *n a adv v* (1) ਇਕ ਹੀ ਛੱਤ ਦੇ ਰਿਹਾਇਸ਼ੀ ਕਮਰਿਆਂ ਦੀ ਪਾਲ; ਰਹਿਣ ਵਾਲਾ ਕਮਰਾ; (2) ਪੱਧਰਾ, ਮੈਦਾਨ; ਹਥੇਲੀ; ਫ਼ਰਸ਼; ਖਿਲਰਿਆ; ਸਪਸ਼ਟ, ਸਾਫ਼; ਪ੍ਰਭਾਵਹੀਣ, ਸ਼ਕਤੀ-ਹੀਣ, ਨਿਰਬਲ; ਮੁਲਾਇਮ ਕਰਨਾ, ਚੀਕਣਾ ਕਰਨਾ

flatter ('ਫ਼ਲੈਟਅ*) *v n* ਝੂਠੀ ਪ੍ਰਸੰਸਾ ਕਰਨੀ; ਚਾਪਲੂਸੀ ਕਰਨੀ, ਖ਼ੁਸ਼ਾਮਦ ਕਰਨੀ; ਝੂਠੀ ਆਸ ਬਨਾਉਣੀ; **~y** ਖ਼ੁਸ਼ਾਮਦ, ਚਾਪਲੂਸੀ, ਝੂਠੀ ਪ੍ਰਸੰਸਾ

flatulent ('ਫ਼ਲੈਟਯੁਲਅੰਟ) *a* ਵਾਈ ਵਾਲਾ, ਬਾਦੀ, ਹਵਾ ਪੈਦਾ ਕਰਨ ਵਾਲਾ; ਫੁੱਲਿਆ; ਬਹਾਨੇ ਖੋਰ, ਕਪਟੀ

flavour ('ਫ਼ਲੇਇਵ੍ਅ*) *a* ਸੁਆਦ, ਸ਼ੀਰੀਂ ਮਹਿਕ, ਰਸ, ਲੱਜ਼ਤ; ਸੁਗੰਧਤ ਕਰਨਾ; **~less** ਸੁਆਦਹੀਣ, ਬੇਸੁਆਦ, ਬੇਲੱਜ਼ਤ

flavorous ('ਫ਼ਲੇਇਵ੍ਅਰਅਸ) *a* ਸੁਆਦੀ, ਮਹਿਕਦਾਰ, ਸ਼ੀਰੀਂ, ਖ਼ੁਸ਼ਬੂਦਾਰ

flaw (ਫ਼ਲੋ) *n v* ਦੋਸ਼, ਨੁਕਸ, ਔਗੁਣ, ਤਰੁਟੀ, ਕਮੀ, ਘਾਟ, ਤੇੜ, (ਕਾ) ਕਲੰਕ, ਵਿਗਾੜਨਾ, ਨੁਕਸ ਪੈਦਾ ਕਰਨਾ; **~less** ਬੇਨੁਕਸ, ਬੇਐਬ, ਬੇਦਾਗ਼, ਨਿਸ਼ਕਲੰਕ

flawn (ਫਲੋਨ) *n* ਤਲਨ ਵਾਲਾ ਭਾਂਡਾ, ਕੜਾਹੀ, ਖੁੱਲ੍ਹਾ ਪਤੀਲਾ

flay (ਫਲੇਇ) *v* ਖੱਲ ਲਾਹੁਣੀ, ਛਿੱਲਣਾ, ਉਧੇੜਨਾ; ਕਰੜੀ ਆਲੋਚਨਾ ਕਰਨੀ, ਛਾਂਟ ਕੇ ਠੀਕ ਕਰਨਾ

flee (ਫਲੀ) *v* ਨਸ ਜਾਣਾ; ਫਰਾਰ ਹੋ ਜਾਣਾ; ਖਿਸਕ ਜਾਣਾ, ਲੋਪ ਹੋ ਜਾਣਾ, ਕਤਰਾਉਣਾ, ਤਿਆਗਣਾ

fleece (ਫਲੀਸ) *n v* ਉੱਨ, ਪਸ਼ਮ, ਇਕ ਵਾਰੀ ਵਿਚ ਲਾਹੀ ਹੋਈ ਉੱਨ; ਲੱਛਾ, ਡਿੱਗਦੀ ਹੋਈ ਬਰਫ਼ ਆਦਿ; ਉਨ ਲਾਹੁਣੀ, ਭੇਡ, ਬੱਕਰੀ ਆਦਿ ਮੁੰਨਣੀ; ਠੱਗ ਲੈਣਾ, ਮੁੰਨਣਾ, ਛਿਲ ਲਾਹੁਣੀ, ਖੋਹ ਲੈਣਾ

fleet (ਫਲੀਟ) *n a v* (1) ਜਹਾਜ਼ੀ ਬੇੜਾ, ਬੱਸਾਂ ਜਾਂ ਟੈਕਸੀਆਂ ਆਦਿ ਦਾ ਸਮੂਹ, ਫਰਾਰ ਹੋ ਜਾਣਾ, ਚੁਸਤ; (2) ਖਾੜੀ

flesh (ਫਲੈੱਸ਼) *n a v* (ਕੱਚਾ) ਮਾਸ, ਗੋਸ਼ਤ, ਮੁਟਾਪਾ, ਚਰਬੀ; ਸਰੀਰ, ਸਿਖਾਉਣਾ; ਮੂੰਹ ਨੂੰ ਲਹੂ ਲਾਉਣਾ; **~and blood** ਵਾਸਤਵਿਕ ਰੂਪ ਵਿਚ ਜੀਵਤ

flex (ਫਲੈੱਕਸ) *n v* ਬਿਜਲੀ ਦੀ ਲਚਕਦਾਰ ਤਾਰ; **~ibility** ਲਚਕ, ਨਿਮਰਤਾ, **~ible** ਲਿਫਵਾਂ, ਲਚਕਦਾਰ; ਮੌਕੇ ਦੇ ਮੁਤਾਬਕ ਢਾਲ ਲੈਣਾ

flick (ਫਲਿਕ) *n v* ਹੌਲਾ ਜੇਹਾ ਧੱਕਾ; ਝਟਕਾ; ਸੱਟ ਮਾਰਨੀ, ਚਾਬਕ ਮਾਰਨਾ; ਝਾੜਨਾ, ਝਟਕ ਦੇਣਾ, ਤਿੜਤਿੜ ਕਰਨਾ

flight (ਫਲਾਇਟ) *n v* ਉਡਾਰੀ, ਉਡਾਣ, ਭਾਜੜ, ਪਲਾਇਨ, ਬਾਜ਼ ਦੀ ਸ਼ਿਕਾਰ ਉੱਤੇ ਝਪਟ

flimsy (ਫਲਿਮਜ਼ਿ) *n a* ਪਤਲਾ ਕਾਗਜ਼; ਨਿਗੁਣਾ, ਤੁੱਛ

flinch (ਫਲਿੰਚ) *v* ਘਬਰਾਉਣਾ, ਬੇਚੈਨ ਹੋਣਾ, ਅਸ਼ਾਂਤ ਹੋਣਾ, ਹਾਰ ਮੰਨਣਾ, ਪਿੱਠ ਦਿਖਾਉਣੀ

fling (ਫਲਿੰਡ) *v n* ਵਗਾਹ ਕੇ ਮਾਰਨਾ, ਸੁੱਟ ਦੇਣਾ,

ਚੁੱਕ ਕੇ ਮਾਰਨਾ; ਗਾਲ੍ਹ ਕੱਢਣੀ; ਡਾਂਟਣਾ, ਬੁਰਾ ਭਲਾ ਕਹਿਣਾ, ਝਪਟ, ਵੇਗਮਈ ਚਾਲ

flip (ਫਲਿਪ) *v n* ਉਂਗਲੀਆਂ ਨਾਲ ਉਛਾਲਣਾ; ਹੌਲੀ ਜੇਹੀ ਉਂਗਲ ਮਾਰਨੀ; ਧੱਕਾ, ਤੁਨਕਾ, ਝਟਕਾ

flirt (ਫਲਅੱਟ) *v n* ਨਖਰੇ ਕਰਨ, ਚੁਹਲ-ਮੁਹਲ ਕਰਨਾ; ਅੱਖ-ਮਟੱਕਾ ਕਰਨਾ; ਨਾਜ਼ੋ, ਚੋਚਲੋ; **~ation** ਨਖਰੇਬਾਜ਼ੀ, ਪਿਆਰ ਦਾ ਦਿਖਾਵਾ

flisk (ਫਲਿਸਕ) *v n* ਬੇਚੈਨ ਹੋਣਾ, ਇੱਧਰ ਉੱਧਰ ਨੱਚਣਾ, ਟੱਪਣਾ; ਵਹਿਮ, ਖ਼ਬਤ

flit (ਫਲਿਟ) *v n* ਛੋਟੀ ਉਡਾਰੀ ਮਾਰਨੀ, ਸਰਕਣਾ, ਖਿਸਕਣਾ; ਨੱਸ ਜਾਣਾ, ਡੁੰਮਣਾ

float (ਫਲੋਅਊਟ) *v n* ਤਾਰਨਾ, ਠੇਲ੍ਹਣਾ, ਵਹਾਉਣਾ, ਵਹਿਣ ਦੇ ਨਾਲ ਤਰਨਾ; **~able** ਤਰਨਯੋਗ

floating (ਫਲਅਊਟਿੰਙ) *a* ਤਰਦਾ, ਠਿੱਲ੍ਹਦਾ, ਪਾਣੀ ਨਾਲ ਵਹਿੰਦਾ; ਅਸਥਿਰ

flock (ਫਲੋੱਕ) *n v n* ਇੱਜੜ, ਸਮੂਹ, ਝੁੰਡ; (ਮਨੁੱਖਾਂ ਦਾ) ਜੱਥਾ, ਟੋਲਾ; ਰੂੰ ਜਾਂ ਉੱਨ ਦਾ ਫਹਿਆ ਜਾਂ ਗੋਹੜਾ, ਛੱਟੀ, ਗੁੱਛਾ, ਲਿਟ; (ਬ ਵ) ਗੱਦੇ-ਗੱਦੀਆਂ ਨੂੰ ਭਰਨ ਲਈ ਵਰਤੇ ਜਾਣ ਵਾਲੇ ਬਚੀ-ਖੁਚੀ ਉੱਨ ਦੇ ਗੁੱਛੇ; ਕਾਗਜ਼ ਬਣਾਉਣ ਲਈ ਵਰਤਿਆ ਜਾਣ ਵਾਲਾ ਉੱਨ ਦਾ ਲੌਗੜ; ਇਕੱਤਰ ਹੋਣਾ, ਇਕੱਠੇ ਹੋਣਾ,

flog (ਫਲੋਗਾ) *v* ਚਾਬਕ ਮਾਰਨਾ, ਛਮਕਾ ਮਾਰਨੀਆਂ, (ਘੋੜੇ ਨੂੰ) ਹਿੱਕਣਾ; ਝੰਬਣਾ

flood (ਫਲੱਅੱਡ) *n v* ਹੜ੍ਹ; ਕਾਂਗ; ਹੜ੍ਹ ਆ ਜਾਣਾ, ਹੜ੍ਹ ਲਿਆਉਣਾ; ਡੋਬ ਦੇਣਾ; ਪਾਣੀ ਪਾਣੀ ਕਰ ਦੇਣਾ; **~gate** ਮੋਘਾ, ਨਹਿਰ ਦਾ ਫਾਟਕ; **~light** ਪ੍ਰਕਾਸ਼ ਪੁੰਜ ਰੌਸ਼ਨੀ

floor (ਫਲੋਅ*) *n v* ਫ਼ਰਸ਼; ਥੱਲਾ, ਤਹਿ; ਧਰਤੀ-ਤਲ;

ਮੰਜ਼ਲ, ਸਭਾ-ਸਦਨ, ਮੰਚ; ਫ਼ਰਸ਼ ਬਣਾਉਣਾ, ਵਿਆਕੁਲ ਕਰ ਦੇਣਾ

flop (ਫ਼ਲੌਪ) *n v* ਧੜੰਮ ਦੀ ਅਵਾਜ਼; ਠੁੱਸ, ਤਿਰਡ਼ਫਿਸ, ਅਸਫਲਤਾ; ਧੜੰਮ ਕਰਕੇ ਡਿਗਣਾ

flora (ਫ਼ਲੋਰਾ) *n* ਕਿਸੇ ਇਲਾਕੇ ਜਾਂ ਸਮੇਂ ਦੀ ਬਨਸਪਤੀ (F) ਫੁੱਲਾਂਰਾਣੀ; **~design** ਫੁੱਲਕਾਰੀ, **~l** ਫੁੱਲਾਂ ਸਬੰਧੀ, ਫੁੱਲਾਂ ਦਾ; ਬਨਸਪਤੀ ਬਾਰੇ

florist (ਫ਼ਲੋਰਿਸਟ) *n* ਫੁੱਲ-ਵਿਗਿਆਨੀ; ਫੁੱਲ ਵੇਚਨ ਵਾਲਾ

flour (ਫ਼ਲਾਉਅ*) *n v* ਆਟਾ, ਮੈਦਾ; **~mill** ਆਟਾ ਪੀਹਣ ਦੀ ਚੱਕੀ

flourish (ਫ਼ਲਅੱਰਿਸ਼) *v n* ਵਧਨਾ; ਜੋਬਨ ਵਿਚ ਹੋਣਾ; ਹਰੇ ਭਰੇ ਹੋਣਾ; ਵਿਕਾਸ, ਵਾਧਾ, ਪਰਤਾਪ, ਖ਼ੁਸ਼ਹਾਲੀ

flout (ਫ਼ਲਾਉਟ) *v n* ਅਵੱਗਿਆ ਕਰਨੀ, ਹੁਕਮ ਅਦੂਲੀ ਕਰਨਾ, ਹੁਕਮ ਅਦੂਲੀ, ਉਲੰਘਣਾ

flow (ਫ਼ਲਅਉ) *v n* ਵਗਣਾ, ਵਹਿਣਾ, ਫੁੱਟਣਾ, ਫੁੱਟ ਨਿਕਲਣਾ; (ਖ਼ੂਨ ਦਾ ਸਰੀਰ ਵਿਚ) ਦੌਰਾ ਕਰਨਾ; ਫ਼ਲਕ ਪੈਣਾ, ਉਛਲੋ ਕੇ ਵਗਣਾ; ਰਵਾਨੀ; ਪਾਣੀ ਦਾ ਰੁੜੂ; **~ing** ਪਰਵਾਹਪੂਰਨ, ਸਰਲ

flower (ਫ਼ਲਾਉਅ*) *n v* ਫੁੱਲ, ਪੁਸ਼ਪ; ਕਲੀ; ਵਿਕਾਸ, ਜੋਬਨ; ਤੱਤ, ਸਾਰ, ਫੁੱਲਣਾ, ਖਿੜਨਾ, ਫੁੱਲ ਲਾਉਣੇ, ਖਿੜਨ ਦੇਣਾ; ਕੱਪੜੇ ਆਦਿ ਉੱਤੇ ਬੂਟੀਆਂ ਕੱਢਣੀਆਂ, ਫੁੱਲਾਂ ਨਾਲ ਸਜਾਉਣਾ; ਖ਼ਮੀਰ ਦਾ ਝੱਗ ਛੱਡਣਾ; **~bed** ਫੁੱਲਾਂ ਦੀ ਕਿਆਰੀ; **~bud** ਕਲੀ; **~pot** ਗਮਲਾ; **~et** ਛੋਟਾ ਫੁੱਲ, ਨਿੱਕ ਜੇਹਾ ਫੁੱਲ

flu (ਫ਼ਲੂ) *n* ਫ਼ਲੂ ਰੋਗ, ਇਨਫ਼ਲੂਐਂਜ਼ਾ

fluctuating (ਫ਼ਲਅੱਕਚੁਏਇਟਿਙ) *a* ਅਸਥਿਰ, ਚੰਚਲ, ਘਟਦਾ-ਵਧਦਾ, ਉਤਰਦਾ-ਚੜੂਦਾ

fluctuation (ਫ਼ਲਅੱਕਚੁ'ਏਇਸ਼ਨ) *n* ਅਸਥਿਰਤਾ, ਉਤਾਰ-ਚੜੂਾਉ, ਘਾਟਾ-ਵਾਧਾ, ਅਨਿਯਮਤਤਾ

fluency (ਫ਼ਲੂਅੰਸਿ) *n* ਰਵਾਨੀ, ਇਕਸਾਰ ਵਹਾ, ਬੇਅਟਕ ਚਾਲ

fluent ('ਫ਼ਲੂਅੰਟ) *a* (ਭਾਸ਼ਨ ਜਾਂ ਸ਼ੈਲੀ) ਰਵਾਂ, ਸਰਲ ਪਰਵਾਹਸ਼ੀਲ

fluid (ਫ਼ਲੂਇਡ) *a n* ਤਰਲ, ਦ੍ਰਵ; **~ity** ਤਰਲਤਾ, ਦ੍ਰਵਤਾ

flush (ਫ਼ਲਅੱਸ਼) *v n a* (1) ਪੰਛੀਆਂ ਨੂੰ ਉਡਾਉਣਾ, ਉੱਡ ਜਾਣਾ, ਖੰਭ ਖੋਲ ਕੇ ਉੱਡਣਾ; (2) (ਨਾਲੀ ਆਦਿ ਨੂੰ) ਪਾਣੀ ਨਾਲ ਧੋਣਾ, ਪਾਣੀ ਵਗਾਉਣਾ; ਖੇਤ ਨੂੰ ਪਾਣੀ ਨਾਲ ਭਰ ਦੇਣਾ, ਤਰੋ-ਤਰ ਕਰ ਦੇਣਾ, (ਚਿਹਰੇ ਦਾ) ਲਾਲ ਹੋ ਜਾਣਾ, ਚਮਕਣਾ, ਚਮਕਾਉਣਾ, ਤਾਜ਼ਗੀ; ਲਾਲੀ, ਚਮਕ; ਚਿਹਰੇ ਦੀ ਲਾਲੀ, ਸਮਰਿਧ; (3) ਤਾਸ਼ ਦੀ ਇਕ ਖੇਡ

flute (ਫ਼ਲੂਟ) *n v* ਵੰਝਲੀ, ਬੰਸਰੀ, ਬੰਸਰੀ ਤੋਂ ਕੋਈ ਸੁਰ ਕੱਢਟੀ

flutter (ਫ਼ਲਅੱਟਅ*) *v n* ਖੰਭ ਮਾਰਨਾ, ਖੰਭ ਫੜਫੜਾਉਣਾ, ਝੰਡੇ ਦਾ ਲਹਿਰਨਾ; ਘੇਚੈਨ ਕਰਨਾ, ਪਰੇਸ਼ਾਨ ਕਰਨਾ, ਤੜਫਣਾ; ਫੜਫੜਾਹਟ, ਫ਼ਰਾਟਾ, ਝੰਡੇ ਆਦਿ ਦੇ ਲਹਿਰਨ (ਦੀ ਕਿਰਿਆ), ਕਾਂਬਾ; ਉਤੇਜਨਾ, ਮਾਨਸਕ ਵੇਗ

flux (ਫ਼ਲਅੱਕਸ) *v n* ਦ੍ਰਵਤ ਕਰਨਾ, ਪਾਣੀ ਵਰਗਾ ਬਣਾਉਣਾ; ਪੰਘਰਨਾ, ਗਲਣਾ; ਬੜੀ ਮਾਤਰਾ ਵਿਚ ਵਗਣਾ; ਖ਼ੂਨ ਵਗਣਾ; ਮੋਕ, ਦਸਤ, ਪੇਚਸ, ਭੁਕਟੀ

fly (ਫ਼ਲਾਇ) *n v a* ਮੱਖੀ; ਉੱਡਣਾ, ਉਡਾਉਣਾ, ਹਵਾਈ ਜਹਾਜ਼ ਵਿਚ ਸਫ਼ਰ ਕਰਨਾ; ਲਹਿਰਾਉਣਾ; ਫੁਰਤੀ ਨਾਲ ਲੰਘ ਜਾਣਾ; ਨੱਸ ਕੇ ਨਿਕਲ ਜਾਣਾ, ਤੀਰ ਹੋ ਜਾਣਾ; ਸਾਵਧਾਨ, ਖ਼ਬਰਦਾਰ,

ਸਚੇਤ; ~at upon ਟੁਟ ਕੇ ਪੈ ਜਾਣਾ; ~ing bridge ਕਿਸ਼ਤੀਆਂ ਦਾ ਆਰਜ਼ੀ ਪੁਲ; ~ing club ਹਵਾਈ ਜਹਾਜ਼ਾਂ ਨੂੰ ਚਲਾਉਣ ਦੀ ਸਿਖਲਾਈ ਦੀ ਸੰਸਥਾ ਜਾਂ ਸਕੂਲ; ~ing colours ਸ਼ਾਨਦਾਰ ਸਫਲਤਾ; ~in the face of ਨਿਰਾਦਰ ਕਰਨਾ, ਗੁਸਤਾਖ਼ੀ ਕਰਨਾ; ~out ਗੁੱਸਾ ਕਰਨਾ; ~past ਹਵਾਈ ਜਹਾਜ਼ ਦੀ ਸਲਾਮੀ

foam (ਫ਼ੋਮ) *n v* ਝੱਗ; ਝੱਗ ਛੱਡਣੀ; ਪਾਣੀ ਆਦਿ ਉੱਤੇ ਝੱਗ ਆਉਣੀ; ~y ਝੱਗਦਾਰ

focal (ਫ਼ੋਕਲ) *a* ਇਕੱਤਰਤ, ਨਾਭੀ ਸਬੰਧੀ, ਕੇਂਦਰ ਬਿੰਦੂ ਸਬੰਧੀ, ਫ਼ੋਕਸੀ

focus (ਫ਼ੋਕਸ) *n v* ਪਰਵ-ਬਿੰਦੂ, ਕਾਰਜ-ਕੇਂਦਰ, ਮੁੱਖ ਖੇਤਰ; (ਰੋਗ ਆਦਿ ਦਾ) ਕੇਂਦਰਤ ਕਰਨਾ, ਕੇਂਦਰ ਵੱਲ ਫੇਰਨਾ, ਫ਼ੋਕਸ ਹੇਠ ਲੈਣਾ

fodder (ਫ਼ੱਡਾ*) *n v* ਪਸ਼ੂਆਂ ਦਾ ਚਾਰਾ, ਤੂੜੀ; ਚਾਰਾ ਦੇਣਾ

foe (ਫ਼ੋ) *n* (ਕਾਵਿ) ਵੈਰੀ, ਸ਼ੱਤਰੁ, ਦੁਸ਼ਮਨ

f(o)etal (ਫ਼ੀਟਲ) *a* ਗਰਭ-ਸਬੰਧੀ, ਗਰਭਸਥ, ਭਰੂਣ-ਸਬੰਧੀ; ~period ਗਰਭ-ਅਵਧੀ, ਗਰਭ-ਸਮਾਂ

foetation (ਫ਼ੀ'ਟੇਇਸ਼ਨ) *n* ਗਰਭ-ਅਵਸਥਾ, ਗਰਭ-ਧਾਰਨ

foetus ('ਫ਼ੀਟਸ) *n* ਗਰਭ-ਅਵਸਥਾ, ਚਾਰ ਮਹੀਨਿਆਂ ਤੋਂ ਜਨਮ ਤਕ ਦਾ ਗਰਭ ਵਿਚ ਬੱਚਾ

fog (ਫ਼ੋਗ) *n v* ਧੁੰਦ, ਕੁਹਰਾ, ਕੁਹਾਸਾ; ਧੁੰਦਲਾ ਕਰਨਾ, ਢਕੇ ਜਾਣਾ; ਹੈਰਾਨ ਕਰ ਦੇਣਾ; ~in ਪਰੇਸ਼ਾਨ, ਘਬਰਾਇਆ, ਹੈਰਾਨ; ~gy ਧੁੰਦਲਾ, ਅਸਪਸ਼ਟ

foil (ਫ਼ੋਇਲ) *n v* (1) ਪੱਤਰਾ, ਸੋਨੇ ਚਾਂਦੀ ਆਦਿ ਨੂੰ ਕੁਟਕੇ ਬਣਾਏ) ਵਰਕ; ਖਿੜਕੀ ਦੀ ਉਤਲੀ

ਡਾਟ (2) ਖੁੰਢੀ ਤਲਵਾਰ; ਅਸਫਲਤਾ, ਹਾਰ; ਬੇਅਸਰ ਕਰ ਦੇਣਾ, ਹਰਾ ਦੇਣਾ; ਮਾਰ ਕੇ ਭਜਾ ਦੇਣਾ

fold (ਫ਼ੋਲਡ) *n v* (1) ਵਾੜਾ; ਕੋਈ ਧਰਮ-ਸੰਘ, ਪੰਥ, ਤਹਿ ਕਰਨਾ, ਮੋੜਨਾ, ਮੁੜਨਾ, ਦੋਹਰਾ ਕਰਨਾ; ਮੋੜ ਪਾ ਕੇ ਦੋਹਰਾ ਕਰਨਾ; ਢਕਣਾ, ਵਲੇਟਣਾ, ਲਪੇਟਣਾ; (ਹੱਥ) ਜੋੜਨੇ; ਚਿਰੰਕਣਾ, (2) ਮੋੜ, ਪਰਤ; ਤਹਿ, ਵਲੇਟ, ਲਪੇਟ, ਕੁੰਡਲ, ਬੰਦ ਕਰਨਾ; ~er ਮੋੜਨ ਵਾਲਾ, ਦੋਹਰਾ ਕਰਨ ਵਾਲਾ, ਤਹਿ ਲਾਉਣ ਵਾਲਾ; ~ing ਮੋੜ, ਤਹਿ, ਸਲਵਟ; ਠੱਪਵਾਂ, ਮੁੜਵਾਂ, ਫ਼ੋਲਡਿੰਗ

folio (ਫ਼ੋਲਿਓ) *n v* ਪੰਨਾ, ਸਫ਼ਾ; ਪੰਨੇ ਲਗਾਉਣਾ

folk (ਫ਼ੋਕ) *n* ਲੋਕ, ਜਨਤਾ; ~lore ਲੋਕ-ਪਰੰਪਰਾ, ਲੋਕ-ਵਾਰਤਾ, ਲੋਕ-ਕਥਾ, ਲੋਕਪਰਾ; ~song ਲੋਕ-ਗੀਤ

follow (ਫ਼ੋਲਅਓ) *v* ਪਿੱਛਾ ਕਰਨਾ, ਪਿੱਛੇ ਲੱਗਣਾ; ਪਿੱਛੋਂ ਆਉਣਾ; ਆਗਿਆ ਦਾ ਪਾਲਣ ਕਰਨਾ; ਪੇਸ਼ਾ ਅਪਨਾਉਣਾ; (ਕਿਸੇ ਵਿਚਾਰ ਜਾਂ ਗੱਲ ਤੇ) ਦ੍ਰਿੜ੍ਹ ਰਹਿਣਾ; ਪਾਲਣਾ ਕਰਨੀ; ~on (ਕ੍ਰਿਕਟ) ਪਹਿਲੀ ਵਾਰੀ ਦੇ ਮੁਕਦਿਆਂ ਹੀ ਦੂਜੀ ਵਾਰੀ ਦੀ ਖੇਡ; ~up ਕਿਸੇ ਕਾਰਜ ਨੂੰ ਸਿਰੇ ਚਾੜ੍ਹਨ ਲਈ ਪਿੱਛੇ ਲੱਗੇ ਰਹਿਣਾ; ~er ਸ਼ਰਧਾਲੂ, ਸੇਵਕ, ਅਨੁਯਾਈ, ਚੇਲਾ; ਸੈਨਾ ਵਿਚ ਧੋਬੀ, ਨਾਈ, ਲਾਂਗਰੀ ਆਦਿ ਗੈਰ-ਲੜਾਕੇ ਕਰਮਚਾਰੀ; ~ing ਸਿੱਖੀ, ਸੇਵਕੀ, ਉੱਮਤ, ਅਨੁਯਾਈ-ਸਮੂਹ; ਹੇਠ ਲਿਖਿਆ, ਪਿੱਛੋਂ ਆਉਣ ਵਾਲਾ, ਨਿਮਨਲਿਖਤ

folly ('ਫ਼ੋਲਿ) *n* ਮੂਰਖਤਾ, ਬੇਵਕੂਫ਼ੀ, ਅਗਿਆਨ, ਹਾਸੋਹੀਣੀ, ਗੱਲ

foment (ਫ਼ਅ(ਓ)ਮੇਂਟ) *v* ਸੇਕਣਾ, ਟਕੋਰ ਕਰਨੀ, ਤੱਤੇ ਪਾਣੀ ਨਾਲ ਧੋਣਾ ਜਾਂ ਸੇਕਣਾ; ਉਤੇਜਤ

ਕਰਨਾ, ਭੜਕਾਉਣਾ, ਉਕਸਾਉਣਾ

fond (ਫ਼ੌਂਡ) *a* ਪਰੇਮੀ, ਚਾਹਵਾਨ, ਲਾਡਲਾ; ਸਿੰਧਰ;
~**ie** ਲਾਡ ਕਰਨਾ, ਪੁਚਕਾਰਨਾ, ਪਿਆਰ ਨਾਲ
ਘੱਟਣਾ; ~**ling** ਪਿਆਰਾ ਬੱਚਾ, ਲਾਡਲਾ, ਦੁਲਾਰਾ;
~**ness** ਪਰੇਮ, ਚਾਅ, ਮੋਹ

food (ਫ਼ੂਡ) *n* ਅੰਨ, ਖ਼ੁਰਾਕ, ਭੋਜਨ, ਆਹਾਰ, ਖਾਣਾ

fool (ਫ਼ੂਲ) *n a v* ਮੂਰਖ, ਮੂਡ੍ਹ, ਬੁੱਧੂ, ਬੇਵਕੂਫ,
ਠੱਗਣਾ; ਬੇਵਕੂਫ ਬਣਾਉਣਾ; ~**s paradise**
ਹਵਾਈ ਮਹਿਲ; ~**ish** ਮੂਰਖ, ਬੇਅਕਲ, ਬੁੱਧੂ,
ਮੰਤਹੀਣ; ~**ishness** ਮੂਰਖਤਾ, ਉਜੱਡਤਾ,
ਮੂਡ੍ਹਤਾ, ਬੇਵਕੂਫੀ

foot (ਫ਼ੁਟ) *n v* ਪੈਰ, ਚਰਨ, ਪਗ, ਖੁਰ, ਪੈਦਲ
ਫ਼ੌਜ; ਧਾਵਾ; ਫ਼ੁੱਟ (12 ਇੰਚ ਦਾ ਨਾਪ); ਲੱਤ
ਮਾਰਨਾ, ਠੁੰਡਾ ਮਾਰਨਾ; ~**board** ਪਾਏਦਾਨ;
~**fall** ਪੈਰਾਂ ਦੀ ਆਵਾਜ਼, ਟੁਰਨ ਦੀ ਆਵਾਜ਼;
~**man** ਪਿਆਦਾ, ਪੈਦਲ ਫ਼ੌਜ ਦਾ ਫ਼ੌਜੀ,
ਬਾਵਰਦੀ ਨੌਕਰ; ~**path** ਪਟੜੀ, ਪਗਡੰਡੀ,
ਡੰਡੀ; ~**rest** ਪਾਏਦਾਨ; ~**rule** ਫ਼ੁੱਟ; ~**step**
ਚਾਲ; ਕਦਮ; ਪਾਏਦਾਨ; ~**wear** ਜੁੱਤੀ, ਬੂਟ;
have one~ in grave ਮੌਤ ਨੇੜੇ ਹੋਣਾ,
ਕਬਰ ਵਿਚ ਲੱਤਾਂ ਹੋਣੀਆਂ; **put one's
best~foremost** ਪੂਰਾ ਜਤਨ ਕਰਨਾ; ~**ing**
ਪਕੜ, ਪੈਰ-ਜਮਾ, ਪੈਂਡਾ, ਆਧਾਰ; ਸਬੰਧ, ਨਾਤਾ;
ਹੈਸੀਅਤ

footle ('ਫ਼ੂਟਲ) *n v* (ਅਪ) ਮੂਰਖਤਾ, ਮੂਡ੍ਹਤਾ,
ਬੇਵਕੂਫੀ, ਨੀਚ ਕੰਮ ਕਰਨਾ

for (ਫ਼ੋ*) *prep conj* ਵਾਸਤੇ, ਲਈ, ਜੋਗਾ,
ਕਿਉਂਕਿ, ਦੀ ਥਾਂ; ਮੁਕਾਬਲੇ ਵਿਚ; ਖ਼ਾਤਰ; ਵੱਲ
ਨੂੰ, ਪਾਸ ਨੂੰ; ~**good** ਸਦਾ ਲਈ; ~**the
present** ਅਜੇ, ਹਾਲਾਂ, ਹਾਲੀਂ; **once ~ all**
ਸਦਾ ਲਈ, ਹਮੇਸ਼ਾ ਵਾਸਤੇ; **take ~ granted**

ਯਕੀਨ ਕਰ ਲਵੇ, ਪੱਕਾ ਸਮਝੋ; **word ~word**
ਲਫ਼ਜ਼-ਬ-ਲਫ਼ਜ਼, ਅੱਖਰੋ-ਅੱਖਰੀ, ਸ਼ਾਬਦਕ

forbear (ਫ਼ੋ'ਬੇਅ*) *v* ਸਹਿ ਜਾਣਾ, ਸਹਾਰਾ ਲੈਣਾ,
ਧੀਰਜ ਰੱਖਣਾ; ਬਚਾਉਣਾ; ~**ance** ਧੀਰਜ,
ਹੌਸਲਾ, ਜੇਰਾ, ਬਚਾਉ; ~**ing** ਸਹਿਨਸ਼ੀਲ,
ਖਿਮਾਸ਼ੀਲ, ਧੀਰਜਵਾਨ

forbid (ਫ਼ਅ'ਬਿਡ) *v* ਰੋਕਣਾ; ਵਰਜਣਾ, ਹੋਡਨਾ,
ਮਨਾ ਕਰਨਾ; ~**den** ਵਰਜਤ

force (ਫ਼ੋ:ਸ) *n v* ਸ਼ਕਤੀ, ਤਾਣ, ਜੋਰ, ਬਲ; ਫ਼ੌਜੀ
ਟੁਕੜੀ, ਪੁਲੀਸ; ਜੋਸ਼, ਆਵੇਗ, ਪ੍ਰਚੰਡਤਾ; ਧੱਕਾ
ਦੇਣਾ, ਸਵੀਕਾਰ ਕਰਨ ਲਈ ਮਜਬੂਰ ਕਰਨਾ;
ਖੋਹ ਲੈਣਾ, ਧੱਕੇ ਨਾਲ ਲੈ ਲੈਣਾ; **in great ~**
ਸ਼ਕਤੀਪੂਰਨ, ਚੜ੍ਹਦੀ ਕਲਾ ਵਿਚ; ~**ful** ਜੋਰਦਾਰ,
ਪਰ੍ਭਾਵਦਾਰ, ਸ਼ਕਤੀਸ਼ਾਲੀ

forcible (ਫ਼ੋ:ਸਅਬਲ) *a* ਬਲਪੂਰਨ, ਪਰਬਲ,
ਜਬਰਦਸਤੀ, ਜਬਰੀ

ford (ਫ਼ੋਡ) *n v* ਪੱਤਣ, ਲਾਂਘਾ; ਪਾਰ ਕਰਨਾ, ਪਾਰ
ਲੰਘਣਾ; ~**able** ਪਾਰ ਲੰਘਣ ਯੋਗ

fordo (ਫ਼ੋ'ਡੂ) *v* ਨਸ਼ਟ ਕਰਨਾ, ਤਬਾਹ ਕਰਨਾ

fordone (ਫ਼ੋ'ਡਅੱਨ) *a* ਥੱਕਿਆ, ਹੁੱਸਿਆ, ਥੱਕਿਆ
ਟੁੱਟਿਆ, ਨਸ਼ਟ

fore (ਫ਼ੋ*) *adv prep a n* ਸਾਮ੍ਹਣੇ, ਅੱਗੇ;
ਮੂਹਰੇ; ~**bear** ਪਿਤਰ, ਵਡੇਰੇ, ਪੁਰਵਜ, ਬਾਪ-
ਦਾਦੇ; ~**cast** ਪਹਿਲਾਂ, ਤੋਂ ਲਾਇਆ ਕਿਆਸ,
ਪੇਸ਼ੀਨਗੋਈ, ਪੂਰਵ-ਅਨੁਮਾਨ; ਅਗੇਤਾ ਕਿਆਸ
ਕਰਨਾ, ਪੂਰਵ-ਕਲਪਨਾ ਕਰਨੀ; ~**father**
ਵਡੇਰੇ, ਬਜ਼ੁਰਗ, ਦਾਦੇ-ਪੜਦਾਦੇ, ਪੁਰਵਜ,
ਪਿਤਰ; ~**finger** ਅਗਰੀ ਉਂਗਲ, ਅੰਗੂਠੇ ਨਾਲ
ਦੀ ਉਂਗਲ ਤਰਜਨੀ; ~**front** ਸਭ ਤੋਂ ਅਗਲਾ
ਹਿੱਸਾ, ਮੂਹਰਲਾ ਭਾਗ; ~**go** ਪਹਿਲਾਂ ਹੋਣਾ, ਸਮੇਂ
ਜਾਂ ਸਥਾਨ ਵਿਚ ਅੱਗੇ ਹੋਣਾ; ਛੱਡਣਾ,

ਤਿਆਗਣਾ; ~going ਉਪਰੋਕਤ, ਉੱਪਰਲਾ, ਉੱਤੇ ਆਇਆ, ਪੁਰਵਵਰਣਤ; ~gone ਅਗੇਤਰਾ, ਪਹਿਲਾਂ ਹੀ, ਪੂਰਵ ਨਿਸ਼ਚਤ; ~ground ਅਗਵਾੜਾ, ਅਗਰ ਭੂਮੀ; ~head ਮੱਥਾ, ਮਸਤਕ; ~man ਫੋਰਮੈਨ, ਮਜ਼ਦੂਰਾਂ ਦਾ ਦਰੋਗਾ, ਅਧਿਅਕਸ਼, ਸਰਦਾਰ, ਮੁਖੀ; ~most ਪ੍ਰਮੁੱਖ, ਪ੍ਰਧਾਨ, ਪਹਿਲਾ; ਸਭ ਤੋਂ ਪਹਿਲਾ; ~noon ਦੁਪਹਿਰ ਤੋਂ ਪਹਿਲਾਂ ਦਾ ਵੇਲਾ, ਪੂਰਵ ਦੁਪਹਿਰ; ~run ਪੂਰਵ ਸੂਚਨਾ ਦੇਂਦੀ, ਪਹਿਲਾਂ ਆਉਣਾ, ਅਗਵਾਈ ਕਰਨੀ; ~shore ਮੰਢ, ਕੱਛਾਰ; ~side ਅਗਲਾ ਹਿੱਸਾ, ਅਗਲਾ ਭਾਗ; ~sight ਦੂਰ-ਦ੍ਰਿਸ਼ਟੀ, ਦੂਰ-ਅੰਦੇਸ਼ੀ, ਦੂਰ-ਦ੍ਰਿਸ਼ਟਤਾ, ਦੂਰ ਦੀ ਸੋਝੀ; ਭਵਿੱਖ ਦੀ ਚਿੰਤਾ; ~sighted ਦੂਰ-ਦਰਸ਼ੀ, ਦੂਰ-ਅੰਦੇਸ਼ੀ, ਲੰਮੀ; ਸੋਚ ਵਾਲਾ; ~stall ਪੇਸ਼ਬੰਦੀ ਕਰਨਾ, ਰੋਕ ਦੇਣਾ; ~tell ਅੱਗੋਂ ਦੱਸ ਦੇਣਾ, ਭਵਿੱਖਬਾਣੀ ਕਰਨੀ, ਪੇਸ਼ੀਨਗੋਈ ਕਰਨੀ; ~teller ਭਵਿੱਖਬਾਣੀ-ਕਰਤਾ, ਜੋਤਸ਼ੀ; ~warning ਪੂਰਵ-ਚਿਤਾਵਨੀ, ਪੂਰਵ-ਸਾਵਧਾਨੀ, ਖ਼ਬਰਦਾਰੀ; ~word ਪੁਸਤਕ ਦਾ ਮੁੱਖਬੰਦ, ਭੂਮਕਾ, ਪ੍ਰਸਤਾਵਨਾ

foreign (ਫ਼ੋਰਨ) a n ਵਿਦੇਸ਼ੀ (ਬਿਦੇਸ਼ੀ), ਪਰਦੇਸੀ, ਵਲਾਇਤੀ, ਬਾਹਰਲਾ, ਉਪਰਾ, ਬਿਗਾਨਾ; ਅਜੋੜ, ਅਮੇਲ

forensic (ਫ਼ਅਰੈਂਸਿਕ) a ਅਪਰਾਧ ਦੀ ਵਿਗਿਆਨਕ ਜਾਂਚ ਸਬੰਧੀ

forest ('ਫ਼ੋਰਿਸਟ) n v ਜੰਗਲ, ਵਨ, ਬੀੜ; ਜੰਗਲ ਲਾਉਣਾ; ~ation ਜੰਗਲਾਉਣਾ; ~ry ਵਣ-ਵਿਗਿਆਨ; ਜੰਗਲੀ ਇਲਾਕਾ

forever (ਫ਼ਅ'ਰੇਵ਼ਅ*) adv ਹਮੇਸ਼ਾ, ਸਦਾ ਲਈ, ਸਰਵਥਾ; ~more ਜ਼ਰੂਰ ਹੀ, ਅਨੰਤ ਕਾਲ ਤਕ

forfeit ('ਫ਼ੋ*ਫ਼ਿਟ) v a n ਗੁਆ ਬੈਠਣਾ, ਵਾਂਝਿਆਂ ਹੋ ਜਾਣਾ, ਖੁਹਾ ਲੈਣਾ; ਜੁਰਮਾਨਾ ਭਰਨਾ, ਜ਼ਬਤ ਕੀਤਾ, ਖੋਹਿਆ ਗਿਆ, ਦੰਡ, ਜੁਰਮਾਨਾ

forfend (ਫ਼ੋ'ਫ਼ੈਂਡ) v ਰੋਕਣਾ, ਟਾਲਣਾ, ਦੂਰ ਰੱਖਣਾ, ਹਟਵਾਂ ਰੱਖਣਾ, ਟਾਲ ਦੇਣਾ

forfex ('ਫ਼ੋ'ਫ਼ੈਕਸ) n ਕੈਂਚੀ

forgather (ਫ਼ੋ'ਗੈਦਅ*) v ਇਕੱਤਰ ਹੋਣਾ, ਇੱਕਠੇ ਹੋ ਕੇ ਬੈਠਣਾ; ਸਮਾਗਮ ਕਰਨਾ

forge (ਫ਼ੋਜ) v n ਘੜਨਾ, ਅੱਗ ਨਾਲ ਗਰਮ ਕਰਕੇ ਅਤੇ ਕੁੱਟ ਕੇ ਕੋਈ ਰੂਪ ਦੇਣਾ; ਨਕਲੀ ਬਣਾਉਣਾ; ਹੌਲੀ ਹੌਲੀ ਜਾਂ ਕਠਿਨਾਈ ਨਾਲ ਅਗਾਂਹ ਵਧਣਾ; ਜਾਅਲੀ, ਲੁਹਾਰ ਦੀ ਭੱਠੀ; ~d ਜਾਅਲੀ, ਨਕਲੀ; ~r ਲੁਹਾਰ, ਠਠਿਆਰ; ਜਾਅਲਸਾਜ਼, ਦਗ਼ਾਬਾਜ਼; ~ry ਜਾਅਲੀ ਦਸਖ਼ਤ ਜਾਂ ਦਸਤਾਵੇਜ਼, ਜਾਅਲਸਾਜ਼ੀ, ਕਪਟ, ਫ਼ਰੇਬ

forget (ਫ਼ਅ'ਗੈਟ) v ਭੁੱਲਣਾ, ਵਿਸਾਰ ਦੇਣਾ; ਖ਼ਿਆਲ ਛੱਡ ਦੇਣਾ; ਉਪੇਖਿਆ ਕਰਨੀ; ~ful ਭੁੱਲਕੜ, ਭੁੱਲੜ

forgive (ਫ਼ਅ'ਗਿਵ਼) v ਮਾਫ਼ ਕਰਨਾ, ਖ਼ਿਮਾ ਕਰਨਾ, ਬਖ਼ਸ਼ ਦੇਣਾ; ~ness ਮਾਫ਼ੀ, ਖ਼ਿਮਾ, ਛੁਟਕਾਰਾ

forgiving (ਫ਼ਅ'ਗਿਵ਼ਿਙ) n ਬਖ਼ਸ਼ਣਹਾਰ, ਖਿਮਾਸ਼ੀਲ

forgo (ਫ਼ੋ'ਗਅਉ) v (ਹੱਕ, ਦਾਅਵਾ ਆਦਿ) ਛੱਡ ਦੇਣਾ, ਤਿਆਗ ਦੇਣਾ

fork (ਫ਼ੋ:ਕ) n v ਕਾਂਟਾ (ਖਾਣੇ ਲਈ ਵਰਤਣ ਵਾਲਾ); ਤ੍ਰੰਗਲੀ; ਸਾਂਗਾਂ ਹੋਣੀਆਂ ਜਾਂ ਫੁੱਟਣੀਆਂ; ਸਾਂਗਾਂ ਵਾਲੇ ਜੰਦ ਨਾਲ ਭੋਂ ਪੋਲੀ ਕਰਨੀ

forlorn (ਫ਼ਅ'ਲੋ:ਨ) a ਘੇਸਹਾਰਾ, ਨਿਆਸਰਾ, ਦੀਨ, ਅਨਾਥ; ਸੱਖਣਾ, ਬੇਆਬਾਦ

form (ਫ਼ੋ:ਮ) n v ਰੂਪ, ਸ਼ਕਲ, ਸੂਰਤ, ਆਕਾਰ,

ਡੋਲ, ਢਾਂਚਾ, ਬਣਾਵਟ; ਸ਼੍ਰੇਣੀ; ਛਾਪੇਖਾਨੇ ਦਾ ਫ਼ਰਮਾ; ਨਿਯਮਾਨੁਕੂਲ ਲਿਖਤ ਜਾਂ ਦਸਤਾਵੇਜ਼, ਕਿਸਮ, ਪ੍ਰਕਾਰ; ਸ਼ਬਦਾਂ ਦੀ ਰਚਨਾ; ਕੋਈ ਰੂਪ ਦੇਣਾ ਜਾਂ ਬਣਾਉਣਾ, ਢਾਲਣਾ; ~**ed** ਰਹਿਤ, ਨਿਰਮਤ, ਬਣਿਆ; ~**less** ਨਿਰਾਕਾਰ, ਨਿਰੂਪ, ਆਕਾਰਹੀਨ, ਰੂਪਹੀਨ

formal ('ਫ਼ੋ:ਮਲ) *a* ਰਸਮੀ, ਰਿਵਾਜੀ, ਲੋਕਾਚਾਰ ਵਾਲਾ, ਉਚੇਚਤਾਪੂਰਨ; ~**ise** /~**ize** ਰੀਤ ਅਨੁਸਾਰ ਕਰਨਾ, ਵਿਸ਼ੇਸ਼ ਆਕਾਰ ਜਾਂ ਰੂਪ ਦੇਣਾ; ~ **ism** ਲੋਕਾਚਾਰ, ਉਚੇਚ, ਸ਼ਿਸ਼ਟਾਚਾਰ ਬਾਰੇ ਕਰੜਾਈ; ਰੂਪਵਾਦ; ~**ly** ਰੀਤ ਨਾਲ, ਵਿੱਧੀਵਤ ਰੂਪ ਵਿਚ, ਰਸਮੀ ਤਰੀਕੇ ਨਾਲ; ~**ity** ਦਸਤੂਰ, ਰੀਤ, ਰਸਮ, ਮਰਯਾਦਾ; ਉਚੇਚ, ਤਕੱਲਫ਼

format ('ਫ਼ੋ:ਮੈਟ) *n* ਕਿਤਾਬ ਦਾ ਬਾਹਰੀ ਰੂਪ, ਪੁਸਤਕ ਦਾ ਫ਼ਰਮਾ

formation (ਫ਼ੋ'ਮੇਇਸ਼ਨ) *n* ਬਣਾਵਟ, ਰਚਨਾ, ਨਿਰਮਾਣ; ਚਟਾਨਾਂ ਦਾ ਜਮਾਉ

formative ('ਫ਼ੋ:ਮਅਟਿਵੑ) *n a* ਬਣਾਉਣ ਵਾਲਾ, ਤਰਤੀਬ ਦੇਣ ਵਾਲਾ; ਰਚਨਾਤਮਕ, ਨਿਰਮਾਣਾਤਮਕ

former ('ਫ਼ੋ:ਮਅ*) *a pron* ਪਹਿਲਾਂ, ਪੂਰਵਲਾ, ਭੂਤਪੂਰਵ

formidable ('ਫ਼ੋ:ਮਿਡਅਬਲ) *a* ਡਰਾਉਣਾ; ਭਿਆਨਕ, ਬਹੁਤ ਵੱਡਾ; ਪਰਬਲ

formula ('ਫ਼ੋ:ਮਯੁਲ਼ਅ) *n* ਗੁਰ, ਸੂਤਰ, ਫ਼ਾਰਮੂਲਾ; ਦਸਤੂਰ, ਰੀਤੀ, ਵਿਧੀ, ਨਿਯਮ; ~**tion** ਵਿਵਸਥਿਤ ਕਰਨ; ਸਥਾਪਨਾ; ਸੂਤਰੀਕਰਨ

formulise ('ਫ਼ੋ:ਮਯੁਲ਼ਾਇਜ਼) *v* ਨਿਯਮਤ ਰੂਪ ਵਿਚ ਕਹਿਣਾ, ਸੂਤਰਬੱਧ ਕਰਨਾ

formulism ('ਫ਼ੋ:ਮਯੁਲ਼ਿਜ਼(ਅ)ਮ) *n* ਰੂੜ੍ਹੀਵਾਦ,

formulist ('ਫ਼ੋ:ਮਯੁਲ਼ਿਸਟ) *n* ਰੂੜ੍ਹੀਵਾਦੀ

forsake (ਫ਼ਅ'ਸੇਇਕ) *v* ਛੱਡ ਦੇਣਾ, ਤਿਆਗਣਾ, ਛੱਡ ਬੈਠਣਾ; ਮਿੱਤਰਤਾ ਤੋੜ ਲੈਣੀ; ~**n** ਤਿਆਗਿਆ, ਛੱਡਿਆ

fort (ਫ਼ੋ:ਟ) *n* ਕਿਲ੍ਹਾ, ਗੜ੍ਹ, ਦੁਰਗ, ਕੋਟ; ~**ification** ਮਜ਼ਬੂਰੀ, ਪੁਸ਼ਟੀਕਰਨ; ਕਿਲ੍ਹਾਬੰਦੀ, ਮੋਰਚਾਬੰਦੀ; ~**ify** ਕਿਲ੍ਹਾਬੰਦੀ ਕਰਨੀ, ਮੋਰਚਾਬੰਦੀ ਕਰਨੀ; ~**itude** ਹਿੰਮਤ, ਹੌਸਲਾ, ਸਾਹਸ, ਸਹਿਨਸ਼ਕਤੀ, ਤਾਕਤ, ਜਿਗਰਾ; ~**ress** ਗੜ੍ਹੀ, ਕੋਟ

forte ('ਫ਼ੋ:ਟੇਇ) *n* ਕਿਸੇ ਮਨੁੱਖ ਦਾ ਕੋਈ ਵਿਸ਼ੇਸ਼ ਗੁਣ, ਕੋਈ ਇਖ਼ਲਾਕੀ ਜਾਂ ਦਿਮਾਗ਼ੀ ਸ਼ਕਤੀ; ਤਲਵਾਰ ਦਾ ਉੱਪਰਲਾ ਭਾਗ

forth (ਫ਼ੋ:ਥ) *adv* ਅਗਾਂਹ, ਅੱਗੇ ਵੱਲ; ਅਗਾਂਹ ਨੂੰ, ਹੁਣ ਤੋਂ, ਬਾਹਰ, ਅੱਗੇ; ਅਗਾੜੀ; ~**coming** ਆਉਣ ਵਾਲਾ, ਅਗਾਂਹ ਨੂੰ ਹੋਣ ਵਾਲਾ, ਆਗਾਮੀ; ~**right** ਸਿੱਧਾ ਰਾਹ; ਪ੍ਰਵੀਣ, ਚਤਰ; ਅਟਲ, ਸਪਸ਼ਟ, ਖਰਾ, ਖਰੀ ਖਰੀ ਕਹਿਣ ਵਾਲਾ, ਮੂੰਹਫਟ; ਤੁਰਤ; ~**with** ਤੁਰਤ, ਫੌਰਨ, ਝਟਪਟ, ਹੁਣੇ, ਇਸੇ ਵੇਲੇ

fortunate ('ਫ਼ੋ:ਚਅਨਅਟ) *a* ਸੁਭਾਗਾ, ਚੰਗੀ ਕਿਸਮਤ ਵਾਲਾ, ਭਾਗਾਂ ਵਾਲਾ, ਨਸੀਬਾਂ ਵਾਲਾ, ਖ਼ੁਸ਼ਕਿਸਮਤ

fortune ('ਫ਼ੋ:ਚੁਨ) *n* ਕਿਸਮਤ, ਭਾਗ, ਨਸੀਬ, ਹੋਣੀ; ~**teller** ਜੋਤਸ਼ੀ, ਨਜੂਮੀ

fortunize ('ਫ਼ੋ:ਟਅਨਾਇਜ਼) *v* ਸੁਖੀ ਬਣਾਉਣਾ, ਸੁਖ ਦੇਣਾ

forum ('ਫ਼ੋਰਅਮ) *n* ਲੋਕ-ਚਰਚਾ ਦੀ ਥਾਂ, ਗੋਸ਼ਟੀ-ਸਥਾਨ, ਗੋਸ਼ਟੀ, ਸਮਾਰੋਹ, ਜਨ-ਸਭਾ, ਚੌਪਾਲ; ਅਖਾੜਾ, ਅਦਾਲਤ

forward ('ਫ਼ੋ:ਵਅਡ) *a n adv v* ਅਗਲਾ, ਮੂਹਰਲਾ, ਅਗੇਤਰਾ, ਅਗਾਂਹ ਵਧਿਆ ਹੋਇਆ;

ਪਹਿਲੇ ਸਮੇਂ ਦਾ; ਮੂਹਰੇ ਲਾਉਣਾ, ਅੱਗੇ ਵਧਾਉਣਾ; ਅਗਾਂਹ ਭੇਜਣਾ, ਅੱਗੇ ਟੋਰਨਾ; ਉੱਨਤੀ ਦੀ ਚਾਲ ਤੇਜ਼ ਕਰਨੀ; (ਚਿੱਠੀ ਆਦਿ) ਅਗਲੇ ਪਤੇ ਤੇ ਭੇਜਣੀ; ਘੱਲਣਾ, ਰਵਾਨਾ ਕਰਨਾ

fossil ('ਫ਼ੌਸਲ) *a n* ਪਥਰਾਇਆ, ਪਥਰਾਈ; ਰੁੜ੍ਹੀਵਾਦੀ; ~**ize** ਪਥਰਾਉਣਾ, ਪੱਥਰਾਏ ਜਾਣਾ, ਪੱਥਰ ਰੂਪ ਕਰਨਾ ਜਾਂ ਹੋਣਾ

foster ('ਫ਼ੌਸਟਅ*) *v a* ਪਾਲਣਾ-ਪੋਸਣਾ, ਪਾਲਣਾ ਕਰਨੀ; ਦੁੱਧ ਚੁੰਘਾਉਣਾ; ਅਗਾਂਹ ਵਧਾਉਣਾ; ~**er** ਪਾਲਕ, ਪੋਸ਼ਕ, ਪਰੋਉਤਸ਼ਾਹਕ

foul (ਫ਼ਾਉਲ) *a n adv v* ਗੰਦਾ, ਮੈਲਾ, ਲਿਬੜਿਆ, ਅਪਵਿੱਤਰ, ਬਦਬੂਦਾਰ, ਗੰਦ ਬਕਣ ਵਾਲਾ; ਬਦਸੂਰਤ, ਕੋਝੀ ਸੂਰਤ ਵਾਲਾ; ਖੇਡ ਦੇ ਨਿਯਮਾਂ ਦੇ ਵਿਰੁੱਧ, ਅਨੇਮਾ; ~**play** ਧੋਖੇਬਾਜ਼ੀ; **through fair and~** ਜਿਵੇਂ ਕਿਵੇਂ

found (ਫ਼ਾਉਂਡ) *v* ਨੀਂਹ ਰੱਖਣੀ, ਮਕਾਨ (ਆਦਿ) ਬਣਾਉਣਾ, ਆਰੰਭ ਕਰਨਾ, ਉਸਾਰਨਾ, ਸਥਾਪਨਾ ਕਰਨੀ; ਕੋਈ ਸੰਸਥਾ ਆਰੰਭ ਕਰਨੀ, ਖੜੀ ਕਰਨੀ; ਕਾਇਮ ਕਰਨੀ, ਨੀਂਹ ਜਾਂ ਆਧਾਰ ਹੋਣਾ; ਆਸ਼ਰਤ ਹੋਣਾ; (ਧਾਤ ਆਦਿ ਨੂੰ) ਗਾਲ ਕੇ ਢਾਲਣਾ, ਢਲਾਈ ਕਰਨੀ; ~**ation** ਨੀਂਹ, ਬੁਨਿਆਦ; ਆਧਾਰ, ਸਹਾਰਾ; ਨਿਰਮਾਣ, ਰਚਨਾ, ਆਰੰਭ; ਮੂਲ ਸਿਧਾਂਤ; ~**ation stone** ਨੀਂਹ-ਪੱਥਰ; ~**er** ਨੀਂਹ ਰੱਖਣ ਵਾਲਾ, ਆਰੰਭ ਕਰਨ ਵਾਲਾ, ਮੋਢੀ, ਸੰਚਾਲਕ

foundling ('ਫ਼ਾਉਨਡਲਿਙ) *n* ਅਨਾਥ, ਯਤੀਮ

fount ('ਫ਼ਾਉਂਟ) *n* ਇਕੋ ਸਾਈਜ਼ (ਨਾਪ) ਦੇ ਅੱਖਰ, ਟਾਈਪ-ਵਰਗਾ, ਲੈਂਪ (ਲਾਲਟੇਨ) ਦਾ ਬੱਲਾ ਜਿਸ ਵਿੱਚ ਤੇਲ ਭਰਿਆ ਜਾਂਦਾ ਹੈ; ਸਰੋਤ

fountain ('ਫ਼ਾਉਨਟਿਨ) *n* ਫ਼ੁਹਾਰਾ, ਝਰਨਾ, ਚਸ਼ਮਾ; ਸੋਮਾ; ~**head** ਮੂਲ ਸਰੋਤ, ਮੁੱਢ; ਮੂਲ ਕਾਰਨ

four (ਫ਼ੋ*) *n a* ਚਾਰ ਦੀ ਗਿਣਤੀ; ~**fold** ਚਾਰ ਗੁਣਾ; ~**square** ਸਥਿਰ, ਮਜ਼ਬੂਤ; ਵਰਗਾਕਾਰ; ~**th** ਚੌਥਾ; (ਬ ਵ) ਚੌਥੇ ਦਰਜੇ ਦੀਆਂ ਵਸਤਾਂ

fourteen ('ਫ਼ੋ'ਟੀਨ) *a* ਚੌਦਾਂ (14); ~**th** ਚੌਦਵਾਂ

fox (ਫ਼ੌਕਸ) *n v* ਲੂੰਬੜ, ਲੂੰਬੜੀ; ਚਲਾਕ ਆਦਮੀ, ਘਾਗ, ਚਲਤਾ ਪੁਰਜਾ; ਚਲਾਕੀ ਕਰਨੀ; ਧੋਖਾ ਦੇਣਾ, ਛਲ ਕਰਨਾ; ~**iness** ਚਾਲਬਾਜ਼ੀ, ਮੱਕਾਰੀ, ਚਲਾਕੀ

fraction ('ਫ਼ਰੈਕਸ਼ਨ) *n* ਹਿੱਸਾ, ਭਾਗ, ਖੰਡ, ਅੰਸ਼, ਟੁਕੜਾ; ~**al** ਬਟੇ ਵਾਲਾ, ਭਿੰਨਾਤਮਕ, ਕਸਰ; ਨਿਗੁਣਾ

fracture ('ਫ਼ਰੈਕਚਅ*) *n v* ਹੱਡੀ ਟੁੱਟਣਾ, ਹੱਡੀ ਤਿੜਕਣਾ; ਹੱਡੀ ਦਾ ਟੁੱਟਣ

fragile ('ਫ਼ਰੈਜਾਇਲ) *a* ਨਾਜ਼ਕ, ਕਮਜ਼ੋਰ, ਭੁਰਭੁਰਾ

fragility (ਫ਼ਰਅ'ਜਿਲਅਟਿ) *n* ਭੁਰਭੁਰਾਪਨ, ਟੁੱਟਪੁਣਾ

fragment ('ਫ਼ਰੈਗਮਅੰਟ) *n* ਟੋਟਾ, ਟੁਕੜਾ, ਫਾੜ, ਖੰਡ, ਅੰਸ਼, ਭਾਗ; ~**ary** ਟੋਟੇ ਟੋਟੇ, ਵੱਖੋ-ਵੱਖ, ਖੰਡਤ

fragmentation ('ਫ਼ਰੈਗਮੈਨ'ਟੇਇਸ਼ਨ) *n* ਟੋਟੇ ਟੋਟੇ ਹੋਣਾ, ਵਿਖੰਡਨ

fragrance ('ਫ਼ਰੇਇਗਰਅੰਸ) *a* ਖ਼ੁਸ਼ਬੂ, ਸਿੱਠੀ ਸੁਗੰਧ, ਮਹਿਕ

fragrant ('ਫ਼ਰੇਇਗਰਅੰਟ) *a* ਖ਼ੁਸ਼ਬੁਦਾਰ, ਮਹਿਕਦਾ

frail (ਫ਼ਰੇਇਲ) *a* ਕਮਜ਼ੋਰ, ਮਾੜਾ, ਲਿੱਸਾ; ~**ty** ਕਮਜ਼ੋਰੀ, ਦੁਰਬਲਤਾ; ਔਗੁਣ ਕਰਨ ਵਾਲੀ ਰੁਚੀ

frame (ਫ਼ਰੇਇਮ) *v n* ਬਣਾਉਣਾ, ਘੜਨਾ, ਸਾਜਨਾ; ਜੜਨਾ, ਠੇਕਣਾ, ਠੀਕ ਬੈਠਾਉਣਾ; ਢਾਲਣਾ; (ਕਿਸੇ ਨੂੰ ਕਿਸੇ ਕੰਮ ਲਈ) ਤਿਆਰ ਕਰਨਾ; ਸੋਚਣਾ,

ਕਲਪਨਾ ਕਰਨੀ; ਢਾਂਚਾ, ਪਿੰਜਰ, ਚੁਗਾਠ, ਚੌਖਟਾ; ਹਾਲਤ, ਦਸ਼ਾ; ਕਾਠੀ, ਸ਼ਰੀਰ, ਕਾਇਆ; ਰਚਨਾ, ਨਿਰਮਾਨ, ਬਣਾਵਟ; **~work** ਢਾਂਚਾ, ਚੌਖਟਾ

franc (ਫਰੈਂਕ) *n* ਫ਼ਰਾਂਸ ਦਾ ਇਕ ਸਿੱਕਾ, ਫ਼ਰਾਂਕ

franchise ('ਫ਼ਰੈਨਚਾਇਜ਼) *n* ਵੋਟ ਦੇਣ ਦਾ ਅਧਿਕਾਰ, ਮੱਤ-ਅਧਿਕਾਰ, ਨਾਗਰਿਕਤਾ

frank (ਫਰੈਂਕ) *a v n* ਬੇਲਾਗ, ਨਿਰਛਲ, ਸਾਫ਼-ਸਾਫ਼, ਖਰਾ, ਬੇਲਾਗ, ਭੋਲਾ, ਸਾਦਾ

frantic ('ਫਰੈਨਟਿਕ) *a* ਕਰੋਧ ਨਾਲ ਭਰਿਆ; ਦੀਵਾਨਾ, ਬਦਹਵਾਸ, ਉਤੇਜਨਾ ਪੂਰਨ

franternal (ਫ਼ਰਾਅ'ਟਅ:ਨਲ) *a.* ਬਰਾਦਰਾਨਾ, ਸੁਹਿਰਦਕ, ਭਾਈਬੰਦੀ ਦਾ

fraternity (ਫ਼ਰਅ'ਟਅ:ਨਅਟਿ) *n* ਭਾਈਚਾਰਾ, ਭਾਈਬੰਦੀ, ਭਰਾਤਰੀ-ਭਾਵ, ਮੰਡਲੀ

fraternize ('ਫ਼ਰੈਟਅਨਾਇਜ਼) *v* ਭਾਈਚਾਰਾ ਪਾਉਣਾ, ਭਾਈਬੰਦੀ ਕਰਨੀ, ਮੇਲਜੋਲ ਕਰਨਾ, ਮਿਲਣਾ-ਜੁਲਣਾ

fraud (ਫ਼ਰੋਡ) *n* ਧੋਖਾ, ਛਲ, ਫ਼ਰੇਬ, ਕਪਟ, ਚਾਲਬਾਜ਼ੀ; ਚਾਤਰੀ, ਛਲ, ਠੱਗੀ; **~ulence** ਧੋਖੇਬਾਜ਼ੀ, ਮੱਕਾਰੀ, ਕਪਟਤਾ, ਚਾਲਬਾਜ਼ੀ, ਛਲ; **~ulent** ਮੱਕਾਰੀ ਵਾਲੀ, ਕਪਟੀ, ਫ਼ਰੇਬੀ, ਛਲੀਆ, ਮੱਕਾਰ, ਧੋਖੇਬਾਜ਼

fray ('ਫ਼ਰੇਇ) *v n* ਝਗੜਾ, ਕਲਹ, ਹੰਗਾਮਾ, ਬਖੇੜਾ, ਦੰਗਾ, ਫ਼ਸਾਦ, ਸ਼ੋਰ-ਸ਼ਰਾਬਾ; ਪਤਲਾ ਕਰਨਾ, ਰਗੜਨਾ

freak (ਫ਼ਰੀਕ) *n* ਖ਼ਿਆਲ, ਤਰੰਗ, ਮੌਜ, ਵਹਿਮ, ਖ਼ਬਤ, ਅਨੂਭਾ

free (ਫ਼ਰੀ) *a* ਆਜ਼ਾਦ, ਸੁਤੰਤਰ, ਸਵਾਧੀਨ; ਸਪਸ਼ਟ, ਸਾਫ਼; ਖੁੱਲ੍ਹਾ-ਡੁੱਲ੍ਹਾ, ਬੰਧਨਹੀਨ; (ਹਵਾ) ਤੁਕਾਂਤ ਰਹਿਤ, ਛੁੰਟਿਆ; ਮੁਫ਼ਤ;, ਫ਼ੀਨ, ਨਿਰਲੱਜ, ਬੇ-ਹਯਾ; ਬੇ-ਪੜ੍ਹਕ; **~forall** ਖੁੱਲ੍ਹੀ

ਲੜਾਈ, ਲੱਗਦੀ ਲਾਉਣਾ; **~hold** ਪੂਰੀ ਮਾਲਕੀ; **~thinker** ਸੁਤੰਤਰ ਚਿੰਤਕ; ਆਜ਼ਾਦ ਖਿਆਲ; **~trade** ਖੁੱਲ੍ਹਾ ਵਪਾਰ **~dom** ਆਜ਼ਾਦੀ, ਸੁਤੰਤਰਤਾ, ਸਵਾਧੀਨਤਾ

freeze (ਫ਼ਰੀਜ਼) *v* ਜੰਮ ਕੇ ਬਰਫ਼ ਬਣ ਜਾਣਾ; ਠੰਡਾ ਹੋ ਜਾਣਾ; ਸਰਦੀ ਦੇ ਕਾਰਨ ਆਕੜ ਜਾਣਾ; **~r** ਬਰਫ਼ ਜਮਾਉਣ ਦਾ ਜੰਤਰ; (ਫ਼ਰਿਜ ਦਾ) ਬਰਫ਼ ਜਮਾਉਣ ਦਾ ਖ਼ਾਨਾ

freezing ('ਫ਼ਰੀਜ਼ਿਡ) *a* ਬਹੁਤ ਠੰਢਾ; **~point** ਜਮਾਉ ਦਰਜਾ, ਯਖੀਨ ਦਰਜਾ, ਹਿਮਾਂਕ

freight (ਫ਼ਰੇਇਟ) *n v* ਭਾੜਾ, ਮਾਲ-ਢੁਆਈ ਸਾਮਾਨ ਭੇਜਣ ਦਾ ਕਿਰਾਇਆ; **~age** ਭਾੜਾ, ਮਾਲ ਲੈ ਜਾਣ ਦਾ ਕਿਰਾਇਆ, ਮਹਿਸੂਲ; **~er** ਮਾਲ-ਵਾਹਕ ਜਹਾਜ਼

French (ਫ਼ਰੈਂਚ) *a n* ਫ਼ਰਾਂਸੀਸੀ ਭਾਸ਼ਾ, ਬੋਲੀ; **~bean** ਲੋਬੀਆ; **~letter** ਨਿਰੋਧ

frenzy ('ਫ਼ਰੈਨਜ਼ਿ) *n v* ਝੱਲ, ਜਨੂਨ, ਸਨਕ

frequency ('ਫ਼ਰਿਕਵਅੰਸਿ) *n* ਵਾਰਵਾਰਤਾ, ਗਿਣਤੀ ਦਾ ਅਨੁਪਾਤ

frequent ('ਫ਼ਰਿਕਵਅਨਟ) *a v* ਵਾਰ-ਵਾਰ ਆਉਣ ਵਾਲਾ, ਆਮ, ਬਹੁਤ; (ਨਬਜ਼) ਤੇਜ਼, ਤੀਬਰ; ਅਕਸਰ, ਆਮ ਪ੍ਰਚਲਤ; ਘੜੀ-ਮੁੜੀ ਜਾਣਾ, ਬਾਰੰਬਾਰ ਜਾਣਾ

fresh (ਫ਼ਰੈਸ਼) *a adv a* ਨਿਰਮਲ, ਚਮਕਦਾਰ (ਚਿਹਰਾ-ਮੁਹਰਾ); ਤਾਜ਼ਾ, ਜੋ ਬਾਸੀ ਨਾ ਹੋਵੇ (ਖਾਣਾ); ਤਾਜ਼ਾ ਚੁਸਤ, ਫੁਰਤੀਲਾ; ਨਵਾਂ ਆਧੁਨਿਕ; (ਜਲਵਾਯੂ) ਕੱਚਾ; ਵਗਦਾ (ਪਾਣੀ); ਅਗਲਾ, ਹੋਰ ਨਵਾਂ; **~en** ਤਾਜ਼ਾ ਦਮ ਹੋਣਾ ਜਾਂ ਕਰਨਾ, ਤਾਜ਼ਾ ਹੋਣਾ ਜਾਂ ਕਰਨਾ; **~er** ਨਵਾਂ ਵਿਅਕਤੀ; ਨਵਾਂ ਵਿਦਿਆਰਥੀ

fret (ਫ਼ਰੈੱਟ) *v n* (1) ਤੰਗ ਕਰਨਾ, ਗੁੱਸਾ

ਦਿਵਾਉਣਾ, ਖਿਝਾਉਣਾ; ਕੁਤਰਨਾ, ਚਬਾਉਣਾ; (2) ਨੱਕਾਸ਼ੀ ਕਰਨੀ, ਚਿਤਰਕਾਰੀ ਕਰਨੀ; ਜਾਲੀਦਾਰ ਨੱਕਾਸ਼ੀ; ~ful ਖਿਝ, ਪਰੇਸ਼ਾਨੀ, ਝੁੰਝਲਾਹਟ, ਝਗੜਾਲੂਪਣ, ਕਰੋਧ, ਚਿੜਚੜਾਪਣ

fricative ('ਫ਼ਰਿਕਅਟਿਵ਼) *a n* (ਭਾਸ਼ਾ) ਸੰਘਰਸ਼ੀ, ਘਰਸੀ

friction ('ਫ਼ਰਿਕਸ਼ਨ) *n* ਰਗੜ, ਘਿਸਰ, ਮਾਲਸ਼, ਘਰਸ਼ਣ, ਸੰਘਰਸ਼, ਮੱਤਭੇਦ, ਝਗੜਾ; ~al ਰਗੜ-ਸਬੰਧੀ, ਰਗੜਵਾਲਾ, ਘਰਸੀ, ਸੰਘਰਸ਼ੀ

Friday ('ਫ਼ਾਇਡਿ) *n* ਸ਼ੁੱਕਰਵਾਰ

friend (ਫ਼ਰੈਂਡ) *n v* ਯਾਰ, ਦੋਸਤ, ਮਿੱਤਰ, ਮਿੱਤਰ ਬਣਾਉਣਾ, ਸਹਾਇਤਾ ਦੇਣੀ; ~less ਮਿੱਤਰਹੀਨ, ਬੇਮਦਦਗਾਰ; ~ly ਮਿੱਤਰਤਾ-ਪੂਰਨ, ਦੋਸਤਾਨਾ, ਅਪੱਣਤਵਾਲਾ; ~ship ਮਿੱਤਰਤਾ, ਦੋਸਤੀ, ਯਾਰੀ

frig, fridge (ਫ਼ਰਿਜ) *n* ਫ਼ਰਿੱਜ, ਰੈਫ਼ਿਗਰੇਟਰ; ਚੀਜ਼ਾਂ ਠੰਡੀਆਂ ਰੱਖਣ ਲਈ ਬਿਜਲੀ ਦੀ ਅਲਮਾਰੀ, ਠੰਡਾ, ਠੰਡਾ-ਠਾਰ ਜੰਮਿਆ; ਰੁੱਖਾ, ਫਿੱਕਾ

frigate ('ਫ਼ਰਿਗਅਟ) *n* ਗਸ਼ਤੀ ਜਹਾਜ਼; ਤੋਪਾਂ ਵਾਲਾ ਜੰਗੀ ਜਹਾਜ਼

fright (ਫ਼ਰਾਇਟ) *n v* ਭੈ, ਡਰ, ਡਰਾਉਣਾ ਭੈਭੀਤ ਕਰਨਾ; ~ened ਭੈਭੀਤ, ਸਹਿਮਿਆ, ਡਰਿਆ; ~ful ਭਿਆਨਕ, ਡਰਾਉਣਾ, ਭਿਆਂਕਰ, ਭੈਭੀਤ

frill (ਫ਼ਰਿਲ) *n v* ਝਾਲਰ, ਕੰਨੀ, ਪਲੇਟ, ਪਸ਼ੂਆਂ ਵਿਖਾਵਾ, ਟੀਪ-ਟਾਪ; ਝਾਲਰ ਲਾਉਣੀ, ਕਿਨਾਰੀ ਲਾ ਕੇ ਸਜਾਉਣਾ; ਵਿਖਾਵਾ ਕਰਨਾ, ਅਡੁੱਕਵੀਂ ਸਜਾਵਟ ਕਰਨੀ

fringe (ਫ਼ਰਿੰਜ) *n v* ਕੰਨੀ, ਕਿਨਾਰੀ, ਮਗ਼ਜ਼ੀ, ਕੋਰ, ਝਾਲਰ; ਹਾਸ਼ੀਆ, ਕਿਨਾਰਾ, ਕੰਨੀ ਜਾਂ ਕਿਨਾਰੀ ਲਾਉਣੀ, ਮਗ਼ਜ਼ੀ ਲਾਉਣੀ

frizzle ('ਫ਼ਰਿਜ਼ਲ) *n v* ਕੁੰਡਲਦਾਰ ਵਾਲ, ਘੁੰਗਰਾਲੇ ਵਾਲ ਘੁੰਗਰਾਲੇ ਬਣਾਉਣੇ ਵਾਲਾਂ ਵਿਚ ਕੁੰਡਲ ਬਣਾਉਣੇ

fro (ਫ਼ਰਅਉ) *adv prep* ਪਰੇ, ਪਿੱਛੇ; ਪਿੱਛੇ ਵੱਲ

frock (ਫ਼ਰੌਕ) *n v* ਬੱਚੇ ਦੀ ਵਿਸ਼ੇਸ਼ ਕਮੀਜ਼, ਫ਼ਰਾਕ; ਇਸਾਈ ਸਾਧੂਆਂ ਦਾ ਲੰਮਾ ਚੋਗਾ

frog (ਫ਼ਰੌਗ) *n* ਡੱਡੂ, ਦਾਦਰ, ਮੈਂਡਕ; ~man ਗੋਤਾਖ਼ੋਰ

frolic ('ਫ਼ਰੌਲਿਕ) *n v a* ਕਲੋਲ, ਚੋਜ, ਅਨੰਦ, ਪ੍ਰਸੰਨਤਾ, ਰੰਗ-ਰਲੀਆਂ, ਚੁਲਬੁਲਾਹਟ, ਚੰਚਲਤਾ, ਖੇਡ-ਕੁੱਦ; ਕਲੋਲਾਂ ਕਰਨੀਆਂ, ਟੱਪਣਾ, ਨੱਚਣਾ, ਖ਼ੁਸ਼ੀਆਂ ਮਨਾਉਣੀਆਂ; ਕਲੋਲੀ, ਆਨੰਦਤ, ਪ੍ਰਸੰਨ, ਚੁਲਬੁਲਾ, ਚੰਚਲ, ਖਿਡਾਰੀ

from (ਫ਼ਰੌਮ) *perp* ਤੋਂ, ਆਰੰਭ ਤੋਂ, ਦੂਰੀ ਉੱਤੇ, ਤੋਂ ਲੈ ਕੇ, ਕੋਲੋਂ, ਪਾਸੋਂ, ਰਾਹੀਂ, ਵਿਚੋਂ; ~day to day ਹਰ ਰੋਜ਼, ਪ੍ਰਤੀਦਿਨ

front (ਫ਼ਰਅੰਟ) *n v* ਅੱਗਾ, ਅਗਾੜੀ, ਮੁਹਰਾ, ਮੱਥਾ, ਸਨਮੁਖ ਭਾਗ, ਮੋਰਚਾ, ਸੰਗਠਤ ਸੰਸਥਾ; ਮੂੰਹ, ਮਸਤਕ, ਲਲਾਟ, ਮੱਥਾ; ਅੱਗੇ ਹੋਣਾ, ਅਗਾੜੀ ਹੋਣਾ, ਸਨਮੁਖ ਹੋਣਾ, ਮੂੰਹ ਕਰਨਾ, ਸਾਮ੍ਹਣਾ ਕਰਨਾ, ਭਿੜਨਾ, ਡਟਣਾ; ~age ਮੁਖ-ਦਿਸ਼ਾ ਮਕਾਨ ਦੀ ਅਗਾੜੀ; ਮੁੱਖ ਭਾਗ, ਖ਼ਾਸ ਹਿੱਸਾ; ~al ਸਾਮੂਣੇ ਦਾ. ਮੱਥੇ ਦਾ, ਅਗਾੜੀ ਵਾਲਾ, ਸਿੱਧਾ, ਸ਼ਿੰਗਾਰ-ਪੱਟੀ

frontier ('ਫ਼ਰਅੰਟਿਅ*) *n* ਹੱਦ, ਸਰਹੱਦ, ਸੀਮਾ; ਸੂਬਾ ਜਾਂ ਪ੍ਰਾਂਤ; ਮੁੱਢਲਾ

frost (ਫ਼ਰੌਸਟ) *n v* ਕੱਕਰ, ਕੋਰਾ, ਤੁਖਾਰ ਪਾਲਾ, ਉਤਸ਼ਾਹਹੀਨਤਾ, ਫਿੱਕਾ, ਸੜ ਜਾਣਾ; ਕੋਰੇ ਨਾਲ ਢੱਕਿਆ ਜਾਣਾ; ~y ਕੱਕਰੀਲਾ; ਰੁੱਖਾ, ਕੋਰਾ

frown (ਫ਼ਰਅਉਨ) *n v* ਤਿਉੜੀ, ਮੱਥੇ ਦੇ ਵੱਟ, ਚੜ੍ਹੀ ਹੋਈ ਭੌਂ; ਨਰਾਜ਼ਗੀ; ਕਰੋਧ; ਤਿਉੜੀ ਚੜ੍ਹਾਉਣਾ, ਕੋਂਛਣਾ, ਮੱਥੇ ਵੱਟ ਪਾਉਣਾ, ਭੌਂਹਾਂ (ਭਵਾਂ) ਚੜ੍ਹਾਉਣਾ

fruit (ਫ਼ਰੂਟ) *n v* ਫਲ, ਮੇਵਾ, ਪਰਿਣਾਮ, ਸੰਤਾਨ; ਆਮਦਨੀ; ਫਲਣਾ, ਫਲ ਦੇਣਾ; **~arain** ਫਲਹਾਰੀ; **~ful** ਉਪਜਾਊ; ਸਫਲ, ਸਾਰਥਕ ਸਕਾਰਥਕ; ਲਾਭਦਾਇਕ, ਉਤਪਾਦਕ; **~less** ਬਾਂਝ, ਬੇਫਲ, ਨਿਸਫਲ, ਫਲਹੀਨ, ਨਿਰਰਥਕ, ਫ਼ਜ਼ੂਲ

frustrate (ਫ਼ਰਅੱਸਟਰੇਇਟ) *v* ਨਿਰਾਸ਼ ਕਰਨਾ, ਮਾਯੂਸ ਕਰਨਾ; ਆਸ ਭੰਗ ਕਰਨਾ, ਨਿਸਫਲ ਕਰਨਾ; ਤੋੜ ਦੇਣਾ

frustration (ਫ਼ਰਅੱਸਟਰੇਇਸ਼ਨ) *n* ਨਿਰਾਸਤਾ, ਫ਼ਹਿੰਦੀ ਕਲਾ, ਵਿਸ਼ਾਦ, ਨਿਸ਼ਫਲਤਾ, ਕੁੰਠਾ, ਨਿਰਾਸ਼ਾ

fry (ਫ਼ਰਾਇ) *n v* ਭੁੰਨਿਆ, ਮਾਸ, ਤਲਿਆ ਮਾਸ; ਭੁੰਨਣਾ, ਭੁੰਜਣਾ, ਤਲਣਾ; **~ing** ਤਲੀ ਚੀਜ਼, ਭੁੰਨੀ ਵਸਤੁ

fuddle ('ਫ਼ਅੱਡਲ) *n v* ਮਸਤੀ, ਨਸ਼ਾ; ਵਿਆਕੁਲਤਾ; ਮਸਤ ਕਰਨਾ, ਮਖ਼ਮੂਰ ਕਰਨਾ, ਮਦਹੋਸ਼ ਕਰਨਾ ਜਾਂ ਹੋਣਾ, (ਸ਼ਰਾਬ ਪਿਆ ਕੇ) ਬੇਸੁਧ ਕਰ ਦੇਣਾ ਜਾਂ ਹੋਣਾ; ਬਹੁਤ ਸ਼ਰਾਬ ਪੀਤੀ ਜਾਂ ਪਿਆਉਣੀ, ਵਿਆਕੁਲ ਕਰਨਾ

fudge (ਫ਼ਅੱਜ) *n v* ਛੋਟਾ ਕਿੱਸਾ; ਫ਼ਜ਼ੂਲ ਗੱਲਾਂ, ਯੱਕੜ, ਗੱਪ, ਨਿਰਰਥਕ ਵਾਰਤਾਲਾਪ; ਛਪਦਿਆਂ ਛਪਦਿਆਂ ਪ੍ਰਕਾਸ਼ਤ ਸਮਾਚਾਰ; ਦੁੱਧ ਖੰਡ ਦੇ ਦਾਣਿਆਂ ਨਾਲ ਬਣਿਆ ਭੋਜਨ; ਕੁੱਚਜ ਘੋਲਣਾ

fudgy (ਫ਼ਅੱਜਿ) *a* ਭੈੜਾ, ਬੁਰਾ, ਕਰੂਪ

fuel (ਫ਼ਯੂਅਲ) *n v* ਬਾਲਣ, ਲੱਕੜੀ; ਉਤੇਜਨਾ, ਭੜਕਾਊ ਪਦਾਰਥ; ਬਾਲਣ ਪਾਉਣਾ

fulfil (ਫ਼ੁਲ'ਫ਼ਿਲ) *v* (*U S fulfill*) ਭਰਨਾ; ਪੂਰਾ ਕਰਨਾ; ਪੂਰਨ ਕਰਨਾ, (ਵਚਨ ਆਦਿ) ਪਾਲਣਾ, ਨਿਭਾਉਣਾ, ਸੰਤੁਸ਼ਟ ਕਰਨਾ, ਹੋਣਾ, ਸਿੱਧ ਕਰਨਾ; **~ment** ਪੂਰਤੀ, ਪੂਰਨਤਾ, ਸੰਪੰਨਤਾ, ਸੰਤੁਸ਼ਟੀ,

ਪਾਲਣਾ

fulgency ('ਫ਼ਅੱਲਜਅੰਸਿ) *n* ਚਮਕ, ਚਮਕੀਲਾਪਣ, ਉਜਲਤਾ, ਆਭਾ

fulgent ('ਫ਼ਅੱਜਲਅੰਟ) *a* ਚਮਕਦਾਰ, ਚਮਕੀਲਾ, ਉਜਲਾ

fulgor ('ਫ਼ਅੱਲਗਾਅੱ) *n* ਚਮਕ, ਆਭਾ, ਕਾਂਤੀ; **~ous** ਚਮਕਦਾਰ, ਚਕਾਚੌਂਧ ਕਰਨ ਵਾਲਾ

full (ਫ਼ੁਲ) *a* ਪੂਰਨ, ਭਰਪੂਰ, ਪੂਰਾ; ਸ਼ਰਾਬੋਰ, ਅਧਿਕ; ਫੁੱਲਿਆ, (ਮਨੁੱਖ) ਰੱਜਿਆ; ਤੀਬਰ, ਪ੍ਰਚੰਡ, ਕਲਫ਼ ਲਾਉਣਾ; **~er** ਧੋਬੀ, ਕੱਪੜਿਆਂ ਨੂੰ ਕਲਫ਼ ਲਾਉਣ ਵਾਲਾ, ਲਿਲਾਰੀ; **~ness, fulness** ਭਰਪੂਰਤਾ, ਪੂਰਨਤਾ, ਸੰਪੂਰਨਤਾ, ਸਮਗਰਤਾ, ਬਹੁਲਤਾ; **~y** ਪੂਰਾ ਪੂਰਾ, ਪੂਰੀ ਤਰ੍ਹਾਂ, ਪੂਰਨ ਤੌਰ ਤੇ, ਸਾਰੇ ਦਾ ਸਾਰਾ

fume (ਫ਼ਯੂਮ) *v n* ਵਾਸ਼ਪ, ਭਾਫ਼; ਕਰੋਧ ਦਾ ਆਵੇਸ਼; ਧੂਣੀ ਦੇਣੀ, ਧੂੰਆਂ ਕਰਨਾ, ਭਾਫ਼ ਕੱਢਣਾ; ਗੁੱਸੇ ਹੋਣਾ

fumigate ('ਫ਼ਯੂਮਿਗੇਇਟ) *v* ਧੂਣੀ ਦੇਣੀ

fumigation ('ਫ਼ਯੂਮਿ'ਗੇਇਸ਼ਨ) *n* ਧੂਣੀ, ਧੂਪ, ਧੂੰਆਂ ਕਰਨ ਦੀ ਕਿਰਿਆ

fumy ('ਫ਼ਯੂਮਿ) *a* ਧੂੰਆਦਾਰ, ਵਾਸ਼ਪਯੁਕਤ, ਭਾਫ਼ ਵਾਲਾ

fun (ਫ਼ਅੱਨ) *n v* ਖੇਡ, ਤਮਾਸ਼ਾ, ਕੌਤਕ, ਕ੍ਰੀੜਾ, ਸਾਂਗ, ਹਾਸਾ-ਠੱਠਾ, ਦਿਲਲਗੀ; ਖੇਡ ਤਮਾਸ਼ਾ ਕਰਨਾ, ਹਾਸਾ ਉਡਾਉਣਾ, ਉੱਲੂ ਬਣਾਉਣਾ; **~fair** ਮੇਲਾ

function ('ਫ਼ਅੱਙਕਸ਼ਨ) *n v* (1) ਸਮਾਗਮ, ਸਮਾਰੋਹ, ਉਤਸਵ, ਸਮਾਜਕ ਸੰਮੇਲਨ, ਅਧਿਕਾਰ; (2) ਕੰਮ; ਕ੍ਰਿਤ, ਕਰਮ, ਕੰਮ ਕਰਨਾ, ਕਰਤੱਵ ਪਾਲਣਾ; **~al** (ਰੋਗ) ਕਿਰਿਆਸ਼ੀਲ, ਕਾਰਜਾਤਮਕ; ਬਿਰਤੀ ਮੂਲਕ; ਫਲ ਸਬੰਧੀ

fund (ਫ਼ੰਡ) *n v* ਖ਼ਜ਼ਾਨਾ, ਪੂੰਜੀ, ਸਰਮਾਇਆ, ਧਨ-ਕੋਸ਼; ਰਕਮ, ਰਾਸ਼ੀ, ਭੰਡਾਰ; ਇਕੱਤਰ ਕਰਨਾ, ਜਮ੍ਹਾਂ ਕਰਨਾ, ਸੰਚਤ ਕਰਨਾ, ਰੁਪਈਆ ਲਾਉਣਾ

fundamental ('ਫ਼ੰਡਾਮਅੰਟਲ) *n a* ਮੂਲ ਤੱਤ, ਸਾਰ, ਮੂਲ ਸਿਧਾਂਤ, ਆਧਾਰੀ ਨਿਯਮ; ਮੌਲਕ, ਮੂਲਭੂਤ, ਪ੍ਰਮੁੱਖ ਮੁਖੀ; ~alism ਮੂਲਵਾਦ; ~ally ਮੁਖ ਰੂਪ ਵਿਚ, ਮੌਲਕ ਰੂਪ ਵਿਚ, ਬੁਨਿਆਦੀ ਤੌਰ ਤੇ

funeral ('ਫ਼ਯੂਨ(ਅ)ਨ(ਅ)ਲ) *n a* ਜਨਾਜ਼ਾ, ਅੰਤਮ ਸੰਸਕਾਰ, ਦਾਹ ਸੰਸਕਾਰ, ਕਿਰਿਆ ਕਰਮ; ਮਾਤਮੀ

fungus (ਫ਼ੰਡਗਾਸ) *n pl* ਉੱਲੀ; ਖੁੰਬ ਵਾਂਗ ਉੱਗ ਪੈਣ ਦਾ ਭਾਵ, ਖੁੰਬ

funicle (ਫ਼ਯੂਨਿਕਲ) *n* ਡੋਰੀ, ਰੱਸੀ, ਸੂਤ ਦੀ ਤੰਦ

funnel ('ਫ਼ੰਨਲ) *n* ਪੁੱਆਰਾ; ਪੁੰ-ਕਸ਼; ਝਰੋਖਾ, ਖਿੜਕੀ, ਰੋਸ਼ਨਦਾਨ

funny ('ਫ਼ੰਨਿ) *n a* ਛੋਟੀ ਕਿਸ਼ਤੀ; ਹਾਸੇ ਭਰਿਆ, ਕੌਤਕੀ, ਰਸਕ; ਅਜੀਬ, ਨਿਰਾਲਾ

fur (ਫ਼ਅ:*) *n* ਪੋਸਤੀਨ, ਖੱਲ ਦਾ ਅਸਤਰ; ਖੱਲ ਦਾ ਕੰਪੜਾ

furiosity ('ਫ਼ਯੂਰਿ'ਔਸਅਟਿ) *n* ਕਰੋਧ, ਪਾਗਲਪਨ, ਵਿਆਕੁਲਤਾ

furious ('ਫ਼ਯੂਅਰਿਅਸ) *a* ਤੇਜ਼, ਕਰੋਧ-ਗ੍ਰਸਤ, ਪ੍ਰਚੰਡ, ਤੀਬਰ, ਭਿਆਂਕਰ

furl (ਫ਼ਅ:ਲ) *v* ਵਲੇੑਟਨਾ, ਤਹਿ ਕਰਨਾ; ਸੁੰਗੋੜਨਾ, ਤਰੋੜਨਾ ਮਰੋੜਨਾ; ਬੰਦ ਹੋਣਾ

furlong ('ਫ਼ਅ:ਲੋਂਡ) *n* ਫ਼ਰਲਾਂਗ, ਮੀਲ ਦਾ ਅੱਠਵਾਂ ਭਾਗ, 220 ਗਜ਼ ਦੀ ਲੰਬਾਈ

furlough ('ਫ਼ਅ:ਲਅਊ) *n* ਲੰਮੀ ਛੁੱਟੀ, ਆਰਜ਼ੀ ਬੇਰੁਜ਼ਗਾਰੀ

furnace ('ਫ਼ਅ:ਨਿਸ) *n v* ਭੱਠੀ, ਤੰਦੂਰ, ਅੰਗੀਠੀ, ਭੱਠੀ ਵਿਚ ਤਾਅ ਦੇਣਾ

furnish ('ਫ਼ਅ:ਨਿਸ਼) *v* ਸਜਾਉਣਾ, ਜੁਗਤ ਨਾਲ ਰੱਖਣਾ, ਜੁਟਾਉਣਾ, ਪੇਸ਼ ਕਰਨਾ, ਪ੍ਰਸਤੁਤ ਕਰਨਾ, ਦੇਣਾ, ਲਿਆ ਦੇਣਾ

furniture ('ਫ਼ਅ:ਨਿਚਅ*) *n* ਸਜਾਵਟ-ਸਮਗਰੀ, ਕੁਰਸੀਆਂ-ਮੇਜ਼ ਆਦਿ; ਘਰ ਦੇ ਅੰਦਰ ਦਾ ਸਾਮਾਨ

furore (ਫ਼ਯੂ(ਅ)ਰੋਰਿ) *n* ਹਲਚਲ, ਹੰਗਾਮਾ, ਕੁਹਰਾਮ

furrow ('ਫ਼ਔਰਅਊ) *n v* ਸਿਆੜ; ਪਹੀਏ ਦੀ ਲੀਹ, ਨਾਲੀ, ਲੀਕ, ਡੂੰਘੀ, ਝਰੀ; ਪਹਾੜਾਂ ਵਿਚ ਖੁੱਲ੍ਹਾ ਹਿੱਸਾ; ਲੀਕ ਪਾਉਣੀ, ਝਰੀਆਂ ਪਾਉਣਾ, ਝਰੀਦਾਰ ਬਣਾਉਣਾ

further ('ਫ਼ਅ:ਦਅ*) *v a adv* ਅੱਗੇ ਵਧਾਉਣਾ; ਉਤਸ਼ਾਹਤ ਕਰਨਾ, ਉੱਨਤ ਕਰਨਾ; ਅਗਲਾ, ਅਗੇਰੇ ਹੋਰ ਦੂਰ, ਇਸ ਤੋਂ ਅੱਗੇ; ਹੋਰ ਦੂਰ, ਇਸ ਤੋਂ ਅੱਗੇ; ਹੋਰ ਅੱਗੇ; ਇਸ ਤੋਂ ਪਰੇ; ~more ਇਸ ਤੋਂ ਇਲਾਵਾ; ~most ਦੂਰਤਮ, ਬਹੁਤ ਦੂਰ; ~ance ਉੱਨਤੀ, ਵਾਧਾ

fury ('ਫ਼ਯੂਅਰਿ) *n* ਭਿਆਂਕਰ ਕਰੋਧ; ਪ੍ਰਬਲਤਾ, ਭੀਸ਼ਣਤਾ, ਚੰਡੀ, ਜੁੱਧ ਦੀ ਉਗਰਤਾ

fuse (ਫ਼ਯੂਜ਼) *n v* ਫ਼ਿਊਜ਼ ਪਲੀਤਾ, ਪਟਾਖ਼ਾ ਜਾਂ ਵਿਸਫੋਟਸ਼ੀਲ ਪਦਾਰਥ ਨਾਲ ਲੱਗੀ ਡੋਰੀ, ਬੱਤੀ, ਨਲਕੀ; ਗਾਲਣਾ, ਪਿਘਲਾਉਣਾ, ਪੰਘਾਰਨਾ; ਪਲੀਤਾ ਦਾਗਣਾ

fusion ('ਫ਼ਯੂਯ਼ਨ) *n* ਮਿਸ਼ਰਨ; ਇਕਰੂਪਤਾ; ਦ੍ਵੈ ਪਦਾਰਥਾਂ ਦਾ ਮੇਲ; (ਭਾਸ਼ਾ) ਸੰਸ਼ਲੇਸ਼ਨ

fuss (ਫ਼ਅਸ) *n v* ਹਲਚਲ, ਖਲਬਲੀ, ਗੜਬੜ ਕਰਨਾ, ਹਲਚਲ ਮਚਾਉਣਾ; ਹੱਲਾ-ਗੁੱਲਾ ਕਰਨਾ; ~iness ਖਲਬਲੀ, ਗੜਬੜ; ~y ਹਲਚਲ

ਕਰਨ ਵਾਲਾ, ਰੌਲਾ ਪਾਉਣ ਵਾਲਾ; ਹੰਗਾਮਾ ਮਚਾਉਣ ਵਾਲਾ, ਗੜਬੜ ਕਰਨ ਵਾਲਾ

futile ('ਫ਼ਯੂਟਾਇਲ) *a* ਵਿਅਰਥ, ਨਿਰਰਥਕ, ਤੁੱਛ, ਬੇਕਾਰ

futility (ਫ਼ਯੂ'ਟਿਲਅਟਿ) *n* ਵਿਅਰਥਤਾ, ਨਿਰਰਥਕਤਾ, ਤੁੱਛਤਾ

future ('ਫ਼ਯਚਅ*) *n a* ਭਵਿੱਖ, ਉੱਤਰਕਾਲ, ਭਵਿੱਖ ਕਾਲ

futurism ('ਫ਼ਯੂਅਰਿਜ਼(ਅ)ਮ) *n* ਭਵਿੱਖਵਾਦ

futurist ('ਫ਼ਯੂਚਅਰਿਸਟ) *n* ਭਵਿੱਖਵਾਦੀ

fuzz (ਫ਼ਅੱਜ਼) *n* ਲੂੰਈ, ਨਰਮ ਤੇ ਘੁੰਘਰਾਲੇ ਵਾਲ; **~y** ਲੂੰਇਦਾਰ, ਅਸਪਸ਼ਟ, ਧੁੰਦਲਾ; ਧੱਬੇਦਾਰ

G

G, g (ਜੀ) *n* ਰੋਮਨ ਵਰਨਮਾਲਾ ਦਾ ਸੱਤਵਾਂ ਅੱਖਰ; (ਸੰਗੀ) ਸਪਤਕ ਦੀ ਪੰਜਵੀਂ ਸੁਰ

gab (ਗੈਬ) *n* ਬਕਵਾਸ, ਬਕ-ਬਕ, ਗੱਪ-ਸ਼ੱਪ; **~ble** ਬਕਣਾ, ਬਕ-ਬਕ ਕਰਨਾ, ਬੁੜਬੁੜਾਉਣਾ, ਗਰਬਲ-ਗਰਬਲ ਕਰਨਾ; ਬਕਵਾਸ, ਬੜ-ਬੜਾਹਟ, ਬਕ-ਬਕ

gaby ('ਗੇਇਬਿ) *n* ਮੂਰਖ, ਬੁੱਧੂ, ਬੇਵਕੂਫ਼, ਅਹਿਮਕ (ਵਿਅਕਤੀ)

gad (ਗੈਡ) *v* ਭਟਕਣਾ, ਅਵਾਰਾ ਫਿਰਨਾ, ਟੱਕਰਾਂ ਮਾਰਦੇ ਫਿਰਨਾ

gaffe (ਗੈਫ਼) *n* ਵੱਡੀ ਭੁੱਲ

gaffer ('ਗੈਫ਼ਅ*) *n* ਚੌਧਰੀ, ਸਰਦਾਰ, ਆਗੂ, ਮੁਖੀਆ; ਬਿਰਧ ਪੁਰਸ਼, ਬੁੱਢਾ; ਬੁੱਧੂ, ਗੰਵਾਰ

gag (ਗੈਗ) *n v* ਮੂੰਹ ਵਿਚ ਠੂੰਨਿਆ ਕੱਪੜਾ, ਬੁੱਜਾ; ਮਖੌਲ, ਮਜ਼ਾਕ; ਮੂੰਹ ਬੰਦ ਕਰਨਾ, ਚੁੱਪ ਕਰਾਉਣਾ; ਝੂਠ ਬੋਲਣਾ, ਪਖੰਡ ਰਚਣਾ

gaga ('ਗਾਗਾ) *a* ਮੂਰਖ, ਗੰਵਾਰ, ਬੇਵਕੂਫ਼

gaiety ('ਗੇਇਅਟਿ) *n* ਜਸ਼ਨ, ਧੂਮ-ਧਾਮ ਦਾ ਅਵਸਰ, ਰੰਗ ਰਲੀਆਂ, ਆਨੰਦ, ਦਿਲਲਗੀ, ਚਮਕ-ਦਮਕ

gain (ਗੇਇਨ) *v n* ਲਾਭ ਹੋਣਾ ਜਾਂ ਲੈਣਾ, ਵਾਧਾ ਹੋਣਾ; ਖੱਟਣਾ, ਕਮਾਉਣਾ, ਲਾਭ, ਵਾਧਾ; ਮੁਨਾਫ਼ਾ; **~ings** ਪ੍ਰਾਪਤੀਆਂ, ਸਫਲਤਾਵਾਂ, ਉਪਲਬਧੀਆਂ

gait (ਗੇਇਟ) *n* ਚਾਲ, ਚਾਲ-ਢਾਲ, ਟੋਰ, ਚੱਲਣ ਦਾ ਅੰਦਾਜ਼

gala ('ਗਾਲਅ) *n* ਪੁਰਬ, ਤਿਉਹਾਰ, ਉਤਸਵ, ਜਸ਼ਨ, ਸਮਾਰੋਹ

galaxy ('ਗੈਲਅਕਸਿ) *n* ਆਕਾਸ਼, ਗੰਗਾ, ਕਹਿਕਸ਼ਾ; ਰਤਨ-ਮੰਡਲ; ਇੰਦਰ ਦਾ ਅਖਾੜਾ; ਮਹਾਂਪੁਰਸ਼

gale (ਗੇਇਲ) *n* ਝੱਖੜ, ਬਹੁਤ ਤੇਜ਼ ਹਵਾ, ਸਮੀਰ

gall (ਗੋਲ) *n v* ਪਿੱਤਾ; ਕਿੜ, ਕੀਨਾ; ਛਾਲਾ, ਫਫੋਲਾ, ਘਾਉ; ਰਗੜ; ਜ਼ਖ਼ਮ ਹੋਣਾ, ਤੰਗ ਕਰਨਾ, ਝੱਲੀਲ ਕਰਨਾ, ਹੈਰਾਨ ਕਰਨਾ; **~blad-der** ਪਿਤ ਦੀ ਪੱਥਰੀ; **~stone** ਪਿੱਤੇ ਦੀ ਪੱਥਰੀ

gallant ('ਗੈਲਅੰਟ) *a n* ਸੂਰਮਾ, ਜਾਨਬਾਜ਼, ਜਵਾਨ-ਮਰਦ, ਸ਼ੁਕੀਨ, ਦਰਸ਼ਨੀ, ਸ਼ਾਨਦਾਰ, ਨਫ਼ੀਸ; ਬਾਂਕਾ, ਆਸ਼ਕ ਮਿਜ਼ਾਜ, ਰਸੀਆ; **~ry** ਬਹਾਦਰੀ, ਵੀਰਤਾ, ਦਿਖਾਵਾ

gallery ('ਗੈਲਅਰਿ) *n* ਛੱਜਾ, ਬਰਾਂਡਾ, ਦਲਾਨ, ਬਰਾਮਦਾ; ਚਿੱਤਰਸ਼ਾਲਾ, ਚਿਤਰ ਪਰਦਰਸ਼ਨੀ-ਕਮਰਾ, ਰੰਗ ਮਹਿਲ, (ਥੀਏਟਰ) ਗੈਲਰੀ

gallop ('ਗੈਲਅਪ) *n v* ਸਰਪਟ, ਸਰਪਟ ਚੌਕੜੀ, ਵੇਗ ਦੀ ਦੌੜ, ਸਰਪਟ ਸਵਾਰੀ; ਸਰਪਟ ਦੌੜਨਾ ਜਾਂ ਦੁੜਾਉਣਾ

gallows ('ਗੈਲਅਉਜ਼) *n pl* ਫਾਂਸੀ ਦਾ ਤਖ਼ਤਾ, ਸੂਲੀ, ਫਾਂਸੀ ਦੀ ਸਜ਼ਾ

gamble ('ਗੈਮਬਲ) *v n* ਜੂਆ ਖੇਡਣਾ, ਜੋਖਮ ਉਠਾਉਣਾ, ਜੂਆਬਾਜ਼ੀ; ਜੋਖਮ ਦਾ ਕੰਮ; **~r** ਜੂਆਰੀ

gambling ('ਗੈਂਬਲਿਙ) *n* ਜੂਆ

game (ਗੇਇਮ) *n v a* ਖੇਡ, ਬਾਜ਼ੀ; ਦਿਲਲਗੀ, ਜੂਏ ਵਿਚ ਉਡਾਉਣਾ; ਸਾਹਸੀ, ਦਲੇਰ, ਲੜਾਕਾ, ਲੰਗੜਾ; **~ster** ਸ਼ਿਕਾਰੀ, ਜੁਆਰੀ, ਖਿਡਾਰੀ

gammy ('ਗੈਮਿ) *a* (ਅਪ) ਲੰਗੜਾ

gamut ('ਗੈਮਅਟ) *n* ਖੇਤਰ, ਸਰਗਮ, ਸੰਪੂਰਨ

ਸੁਰ; ਧੁਨੀ ਜਾਂ ਸਾਜ਼ ਦਾ ਘੇਰਾ ਜਾਂ ਵ੍ਰਿਤ

gander ('ਗੈਂਡਅ*) *n* (ਨਰ) ਹੰਸ; ਮੂਰਖ, ਬੁੱਧੂ

gang (ਗੈਙ) *n* ਟੋਲੀ, ਮੰਡਲੀ, ਦਲ, ਝੁੰਡ, ਜੁੱਟ, ਜੁੰਡਲੀ

gaol, jail (ਜੋਇਲ) *n v* ਜੇਲ੍ਹ, ਜੇਲ੍ਹਖ਼ਾਨਾ, ਕਾਰਾਵਾਸ, ਬੰਦੀਖ਼ਾਨਾ; ਕੈਦ, ਜੇਲ੍ਹ ਭੇਜਣਾ, ਜੇਲ੍ਹ ਵਿਚ ਬੰਦ ਕਰਨਾ; ~**bird** ਆਦਿ ਕੈਦੀ, ਪੁਰਾਣਾ ਬਦਮਾਸ਼, ਨਿਤ ਦਾ ਅਪਰਾਧੀ; ~**er** ਜੇਲ੍ਹ ਦਾ ਵੱਡਾ ਅਫ਼ਸਰ, ਦਰੋਗ਼ਾ; ਜੇਲ੍ਹਰ

gap (ਗੈਪ) *n* ਅੰਤਰ, ਵਿੱਥ, ਫ਼ਰਕ

garage ('ਗੈਰਾਜ਼) *n* ਮੋਟਰ-ਘਰ, ਮੋਟਰਖ਼ਾਨਾ; ਗਰਾਜ

garb (ਗਾਬ) *n* ਵੇਸ, ਪਹਿਰਾਵਾ, ਵਸਤਰ, ਪੁਸ਼ਾਕ

garbage ('ਗਾਬਿਜ) *n* ਕੂੜਾ, ਗੰਦਗੀ, ਮੈਲ, ਮਲ, ਰੱਦੀ, ਗੰਦ-ਮੰਦ

garble ('ਗਾਬਲ) *v* ਸਭ ਤੋਂ ਚੰਗੀ ਚੀਜ਼ ਛਾਂਟ ਲੈਣਾ ਦਾ ਚੋਰੀ ਚੁੱਕ ਲੈਣਾ; ਛਾਣਨਾ, ਛਾਣ-ਬੀਣ ਕਰਨਾ

garden ('ਗਾ*ਡਨ) *n v* ਫੁਲਵਾੜੀ, ਬਗ਼ੀਚਾ, ਗੁਲਸ਼ਨ ਗੁਲਜ਼ਾਰ; ~**er** ਮਾਲੀ, ਬਾਗ਼ਬਾਨ

gargle ('ਗਾ*ਗਲ) *v n* ਗਰਾਰੇ ਕਰਨਾ; ਗਰਾਰਾ, ਕੁੱਲਾ

garland ('ਗਾ*ਲਅੰਡ) *n v* ਮਾਲਾ, ਹਾਰ, ਗਜਰਾ, ਸਿਹਰਾ; ਹਾਰ ਪਾਉਣਾ

garlic ('ਗਾਲਿਕ) *n* ਲਸਣ, ਥੋਮ

garment ('ਗਾਰਮੰਟ) *n v* ਵੇਸ, ਲਿਬਾਸ, ਪੁਸ਼ਾਕ, ਕੱਪੜੇ, ਵਸਤਰ, ਕੱਪੜੇ ਪੁਆਉਣਾ, ਵੇਸ ਧਾਰਨਾ, ਪੁਸ਼ਾਕ ਪਹਿਨਣਾ

garner ('ਗਾਨਅ*) *n v* (ਕਣਕ ਦਾ) ਕੋਠਾ, ਸਟੋਰ, ਜ਼ਖ਼ੀਰਾ, ਗੁਦਾਮ; ਇਕੱਤਰ ਕਰਨਾ, ਅਨਾਜ ਭਰਨਾ

garnet ('ਗਾਨਿਟ) *n* ਲਾਲ ਜਵਾਹਰ, ਲਾਲ ਮਣੀ; ਲਹੂ-ਰੰਗਾ ਕੀਮਤੀ ਪੱਥਰ

garnish ('ਗਾਨਿਸ਼) *v n* ਸਜਾਉਣਾ ਖਾਣਾ ਲਗਾਉਣਾ; ਚਮਕਾਉਣਾ; ਸੰਮਨ ਤਾਮੀਲ ਕਰਨਾ, ਸ਼ਿੰਗਾਰ, ਸਜਾਵਟ, ਨਕਸ਼-ਨਿਗਾਰ

garrison ('ਗੈਰਿਸਨ) *n v* ਸ਼ਹਿਰ ਜਾਂ ਕਿਲ੍ਹੇ ਦੀ ਰੱਖਿਆ ਕਰਨ ਵਾਲੀ ਫ਼ੌਜ, ਰੱਖਿਆ ਸੈਨਾ, ਮੋਰਚਾਬੰਦੀ ਕਰਨਾ, ਕਿਲ੍ਹੇਬੰਦੀ ਕਰਨਾ

garrulous ('ਗੈਰਅਲਅਸ) *a* ਗੱਪੀ, ਗਾਲੜੀ, ਬਾਤੂਨੀ, ਗੱਪੰ-ਸੰਖ, ਗੱਪੌੜੀ

gas (ਗੈਸ) *n v* (ਬੋਲ) ਗੈਸ, ਪੈਟਰੋਲ, ਗੈਸੋਲੀਨ; ਗੈਸ ਵਰਗਾ ਦ੍ਰਵ; ਗੈਸ ਦੇਣਾ ਜਾਂ ਚੜ੍ਹਾਉਣਾ; ~**sy** ਗੈਸ ਨਾਲ ਭਰਿਆ, ਫੁੱਲਿਆ; ਗਾਲੜੀ, ਗੱਪੀ, ਬਾਤੂਨੀ; ਸ਼ਬਦ-ਬਹੁਲਤਾ

gasolene, gasoline ('ਗੈਸਅ(ਉ)ਲੀਨ) *n* (ਅਮਰੀਕੀ) ਪੈਟਰੋਲ, ਪੈਟਰੋਲੀਅਮ ਤੋਂ ਪ੍ਰਾਪਤ ਤਰਲ ਵਸਤੁ, ਗੈਸੋਲੀਨ

gastric ('ਗੈਸਟਰਿਕ) *a* ਪੇਟ ਦਾ, ਮਿਹਦੇ ਦਾ, ਢਿੱਡ ਸਬੰਧੀ, ਜਠਰੀ

gate (ਗੇਇਟ) *n* ਲਾਂਘਾ, ਫਾਟਕ, ਕਿਵਾੜ, ਕਪਾਟ; ਰਾਹ, ਰਸਤਾ, ਦੱਰਾ, ਘਾਟੀ ਲੱਕੜ ਜਾਂ ਲੋਹੇ ਦਾ ਜੰਗਲਾ

gather ('ਗੈਦਅ*) *v* ਇੱਕਤਰ ਕਰਨਾ, ਜਮ੍ਹਾਂ ਕਰਨਾ, ਬਟੋਰਨਾ; ਪ੍ਰਾਪਤ ਕਰਨਾ, ਇਕੱਠੇ ਹੋਣਾ, ਸੰਗਠਤ ਹੋਣਾ, ਧਨ ਜੋੜਨਾ, ਵਧਣਾ

gaud (ਗੋਡ) *n pl* ਭੜਕੀਲੇ ਕੱਪੜੇ, ਨੁਮਾਇਸ਼ੀ ਜ਼ੇਵਰ ਜਾਂ ਲਿਬਾਸ; ਭੜਕੀਲੀਆਂ ਚੀਜ਼ਾਂ; ਉਤਸਵ, ਸਮਾਰੋਹ, ਧੂਮ-ਧਾਮ; ਰੰਗ ਰਲੀਆਂ

gauge (ਗੇਇਜ) *n v* ਮਾਪ, ਪੈਮਾਨਾ, ਸਮਰੱਥਾ, ਗੁੰਜਾਇਸ਼, ਮਿਕਦਾਰ, ਵਿਸਤਾਰ, ਰੇਲ ਦੀ ਪਟੜੀ ਦੀ ਚੌੜਾਈ ਜਾਂ ਅੰਤਰ; ਸਮਾਈ ਨਾਪਟੀ, ਗੁੰਜਾਇਸ਼ ਮਾਲੂਮ ਕਰਨੀ, ਇਕ ਜਿਹੀ ਕਰਨੀ;

ਅਨੁਮਾਨ ਲਗਾਉਣਾ, ਜਾਂਚਣਾ, ਅੰਦਾਜ਼ਾ ਕਰਨਾ

gaunt (ਗੌਂਟ) *a* ਦੁਬਲਾ, ਪਤਲਾ ਮਰੀਅਲ; ਬੰਜਰ

gauzy ('ਗੋਜ਼ਿ) *a* ਜਾਲੀਦਾਰ

gay (ਗੇਇ) *a n* ਖ਼ੁਸ਼, ਹੱਸਮੁਖ; ਭੜਕੀਲਾ

gaze (ਗੇਇਜ਼) *v n* ਘੂਰਨਾ, ਤਾੜਨਾ, ਟਿਕਟਿਕੀ ਲਾ ਕੇ ਵੇਖਣਾ, ਦ੍ਰਿਸ਼ਟੀ ਜਮਾਉਣੀ, ਧਿਆਨ ਨਾਲ ਵੇਖਣਾ; ਟਿਕਟਿਕੀ, ਤਾਕ

gazette (ਗਅ'ਜ਼ੈਟ) *n v* ਰੋਜ਼ਨਾਮਾ, ਰਾਜ-ਪੱਤਰ, ਘੋਸ਼ਣਾ-ਪੱਤਰ, ਸੂਚਨਾ-ਪੱਤਰ, ਸਮਾਚਾਰ ਪੱਤਰਿਕਾ

gear (ਗਿਅ*) *n v* (ਪ੍ਰਾ) ਸਾਮਾਨ, ਵਸਤਰ; ਸਮਗਰੀ, ਬਰਤਨ, ਭਾਂਡਾ, ਪੁਰਜ਼ੇ, ਕਲ, ਔਜ਼ਾਰ; ਮਸ਼ੀਨ ਵਿਚ ਪੁਰਜ਼ੇ ਜੋੜਨਾ ਜਾਂ ਲਗਾਉਣਾ, ਸਾਜ਼ ਲਗਾਉਣਾ

gem (ਜੈੱਮ) *n* ਹੀਰਾ, ਨਗ, ਨਗੀਨਾ, ਇਕ ਕੀਮਤੀ ਪੱਥਰ, ਜਵਾਹਰ, ਰਤਨ, ਮਣੀ

gaminate ('ਜੈਮਿਨੇਇਟ) *v a* ਦੁਗਣਾ ਕਰਣਾ, ਦੁਹਰਾਉਣਾ; ਜੋੜਾ, ਜੁੱਟ, ਜੁੱਟਾਂ ਵਿਚ ਬੱਝਾ

gemination ('ਜੈਮਿ'ਨੇਇਸ਼ਨ) *a* ਜੋੜਿਆਂ ਵਿਚ ਰੱਖਣਾ, ਯੁਗਮੀਕਰਨ; (ਭਾਸ਼ਾ) ਦੁੱਤੀਕਰਨ

Gemini ('ਜੈਮਿਨਾਇ) *n* ਮਿਥੁਨ ਰਾਸ਼ੀ

gender ('ਜੈਂਡਅ*) *n* (ਵਿਆ) ਲਿੰਗ

genealogical ('ਜੀਨਯਅ'ਲੌਜਿਕਲ) *a* ਵੰਸ਼-ਪਰੰਪਰਾਗਤ, ਬੰਸਾਵਲੀ ਸਬੰਧੀ

general ('ਜੈਨ(ਅ)ਰ(ਅ)ਲ) *a n* ਆਮ, ਸਧਾਰਨ, ਵਿਆਪਕ, ਪ੍ਰਚਲਤ; ਸਿਪਾਹਸਲਾਰ; **~ization** ਸਧਾਰਨੀਕਰਨ; ਸਧਾਰਨ, ਅਨੁਮਾਨ; **~ize** ਸਧਾਰਨੀਕਰਨ ਕਰਨਾ; ਸਧਾਰਨ ਭਾਵ ਪ੍ਰਦਾਨ ਕਰਨਾ, ਸਧਾਰਨ ਨਿਯਮ ਤੋਂ ਨਿਰਣਾ ਕੱਢਣਾ; ਆਮ ਵਰਤੋਂ ਵਿਚ ਲਿਆਉਣਾ; ਅਸਪਸ਼ਟ ਬੋਲਣਾ ਜਾਂ ਆਖਣਾ; **~ized** ਵਿਆਪਕ, ਸਧਾਰਨੀਕ੍ਰਿਤ; **~ly** ਆਮ ਤੌਰ ਤੇ, ਸਧਾਰਨ, ਨਿਯਮ ਦੇ ਰੂਪ ਵਿਚ; ਸਧਾਰਨ ਅਰਥਾਂ ਵਿਚ, ਸਰਸਰੀ ਤੌਰ ਤੇ, ਵਿਆਪਕ ਰੂਪ ਵਿਚ, ਅਕਸਰ

generate ('ਜੈੱਨਅਰੇਇਟ) *v* ਪੈਦਾ ਕਰਨਾ, ਉਤਪੰਨ ਕਰਨਾ, ਉਪਜਾਉਣਾ

generating ('ਜੈੱਨਅਰੇਇਟਿਙ) *n a* ਉਤਪਾਦਕ, ਜਨਕ

generation ('ਜੈੱਨਅ'ਰੇਇਸ਼ਨ) *a* ਨਸਲ, ਪੌਦ, ਸੰਤਾਨ, ਵੰਸ਼; ਪੈਦਾਇਸ਼, ਉਤਪਾਦਨ, ਜਣਨ

generative ('ਜੈੱਨਅਰਅਟਿਵ਼) *a* ਉਪਜਾਊ, ਜਣਨਸ਼ੀਲ, ਉਤਪਾਦਕ

generator ('ਜੈੱਨਅਰੇਇਟਅ*) *n* ਉਪਜਾਉਣ ਵਾਲਾ, ਉਤਪਾਦਕ, ਜਨਮ ਦਾਤਾ; (ਵਾਸ਼ਪ, ਬਿਜਲੀ, ਗੈਸ ਆਦਿ ਦਾ) ਉਤਪਾਦਕ ਜੰਤਰ, ਜੈਨਰੇਟਰ

generic (ਜਿ'ਨੈਰਿਕ) *a* ਆਮ, ਸਧਾਰਨ; ਜਿਨਸੀ, ਵਰਗੀ, ਜਾਤੀਗਤ; ਵਿਆਪਕ

generosity ('ਜੈੱਨਅ'ਰੌਸਅਟਿ) *n* ਉਦਾਰਤਾ, ਸਖ਼ਾਵਤ, ਦਾਨ-ਪੁੰਨ

generous ('ਜੈੱਨਅਰਅਸ) *a* ਉਦਾਰ, ਸਖੀ, ਦਾਨੀ, ਖੁੱਲ-ਦਿਲਾ(ਮਨੁੱਖ), ਦਾਨਸ਼ੀਲ

genetic (ਜਿ'ਨੈਟਿਕ) *a* ਜਣਨ ਬਾਰੇ, ਉਤਪਤੀ ਸਬੰਧੀ, ਆਨੁਵੰਸ਼ਕ

genius ('ਜੀਨਯਅਸ) *n* ਪ੍ਰਤਿਭਾ, ਕੁਦਰਤੀ, ਯੋਗਤਾ, ਪ੍ਰਤਿਭਾਸ਼ੀਲ ਵਿਅਕਤੀ; ਸਹਿਜਯੋਗਤਾ, ਭਾਸ਼ਾ ਦੇ ਮੂਲ ਤੱਤ, ਕਿਸੇ ਕਾਨੂੰਨ ਦੀ ਪੱਧਤੀ

genocide ('ਜੈੱਨਅ(ਉ)ਸਾਇਡ) *n* ਕੁਲ-ਨਾਸ; ਨਸਲਕੁਸ਼ੀ

genre ('ਯ਼ਾਨਰਅ) *n* ਪ੍ਰਕਾਰ, ਕਿਸਮ, ਭੇਦ; ਸ਼ੈਲੀ, ਢੰਗ, ਸਾਹਿਤ ਰੂਪ

gentle ('ਜੈਂਟਲ) *a n* ਭੱਦਰ, ਪਤਵੰਤਾ, ਕੁਲਵੰਤ, ਕੁਲੀਨ, ਖ਼ਾਨਦਾਨੀ; ਧੀਮਾ, ਨਰਮ, ਹਲੀਮ,

ਦਇਆਵਾਨ, ਨਰਮ ਦਿਲ, ਕੋਮਲ, ਕਿਰਪਾਲੂ;
~**ness** ਨਰਮੀ, ਨਿਮਰਤਾ, ਕੋਮਲਤਾ, ਭੱਦਰਤਾ

gentleman ('ਜੈਂਟਲਮਅਨ) *n* ਸੱਜਨ, ਭੱਦਰ
ਪੁਰਸ਼, ਰਈਸ; ਸਰਦਾਰ; ~**like** ਸੱਭਿਅ, ਸ਼ਿਸ਼ਟ,
ਵਿਨੀਤ, ਸਾਊਆਂ ਵਰਗਾ; ~**liness** ਸ਼ਿਸ਼ਟਤਾ,
ਕੁਲੀਨਤਾ, ਸੱਜਨਤਾ, ਸ਼ਰਾਫ਼ਤ, ਰਈਸੀ

gently ('ਜੈਂਟਲਿ) *adv* ਨਰਮੀ ਨਾਲ, ਹੌਲੇ ਜਿਹੇ,
ਧੀਰੇ-ਧੀਰੇ

gentry ('ਜੈਂਟਰਿ) *n* ਭੱਦਰ ਪੁਰਸ਼, ਭਲੇਮਾਣਸ

genuine ('ਜੈਨੱਯੁਇਨ) *a* ਅਸਲੀ, ਖਰਾ,
ਯਥਾਰਥਕ, ਵਾਸਤਵਿਕ, ਸੱਚਾ; ~**ness**
ਵਾਸਤਵਿਕਤਾ, ਅਸਲੀਅਤ, ਮੌਲਕਤਾ,
ਵਿਸ਼ੁੱਧਤਾ, ਸੱਚਾਪਣ, ਖਰਾਪਣ

genus ('ਜੀਨਅਸ) *n* ਸ਼੍ਰੇਣੀ, ਵਰਗ, ਜਾਤੀ,
ਤਬਕਾ, ਜਿਨਸ, ਕਬੀਲਾ, ਕਿਸਮ; ਭੇਦ; ਪ੍ਰਕਾਰ,
ਕ੍ਰਮ

geography (ਜਿ'ਔਗਰਅਫ਼ਿ) *n* ਭੂਗੋਲ,
ਜੁਗਰਾਫ਼ੀਆ, ਭੂਮੀ ਬਿਰਤਾਂਤ

geological ('ਜਿਅਾ(ਉ)'ਲੌਜਿਕਲ) *a* ਭੂ-
ਵਿਗਿਆਨਕ, ਭੂ-ਗਾਰਤੀ

geologist (ਜਿ'ਔਲਅਜਿਸਟ) *n* ਭੂ-ਵਿਗਿਆਨਕ

geology (ਜਿ'ਔਲਅਜਿ) *n* ਭੂ-ਵਿਗਿਆਨ

geometric, -al (ਜਿਅਾ(ਉ)'ਮੈਟਰਿਕ,
ਜਿਅ(ਉ)'ਮੈਟਰਿਕਲ) *a* ਜਿਆਮਿਤੀ, ਰੇਖਾ-
ਗਣਿਤ

geometry (ਜਿ'ਔਮਅਟਰਿ) *n* ਰੇਖਾ-ਗਣਿਤ, ਭੂ-
ਮਿਤੀ; ਰੇਖਕੀ, ਜਿਆਮਿਤੀ

germ (ਜਅ:ਮ) *n* ਕਿਰਮ, ਕੀਟਾਣੂ, ਜੀਵਾਣੀ,
ਰੋਗਾਣੂ, ਸੂਖਮ ਜੰਤੂ; ਮੂਲ ਸਿਧਾਂਤ, ਸਰੋਤ;
~**inate** ਉਪਜਣਾ ਜਾਂ ਉਪਜਾਉਣਾ, ਉਗਣਾ ਜਾਂ
ਉਗਾਉਣਾ, ਉਤਪੰਨ ਹੋਣਾ ਜਾਂ ਕਰਨਾ, ਨਿਕਲਣਾ

ਜਾਂ ਪੈਦਾ ਕਰਨਾ; ~**ination** ਪੁੰਗਰਨ, ਅੰਕੁਰਣ,
ਉਦਭਵ, ਉਪਜਣ; ~**inator** ਉਤਪੰਨ ਕਰਨ
ਵਾਲਾ, ਉਗਾਉਣ ਵਾਲਾ

gerund ('ਜੈਰੱਅੰਡ) *n* (ਵਿਆ) ਕਿਰਿਆ-ਵਾਚੀ
ਨਾਂਵ, ਅੰਗਰੇਜੀ ਕਿਰਿਆ ਵਿਚ ਜੋੜ ਕੇ
ਬਣਾਇਆ ਗਿਆ ਨਾਉਂ

gest, geste ('ਜੈਸਟ) *n* ਸੰਕੇਤ, ਇਸ਼ਾਰਾ
ਵਿਹਾਰ, ਵਰਤਾਉ, ਸਲੂਕ, ਆਚਰਣ

gestation (ਜੈਸ'ਟੇਇਸ਼ਨ) *n* ਗਰਭ-ਅਵਸਥਾ,
ਗਰਭ-ਕਾਲ, ਗਰਭ, ਹਮਲ

gesticulate (ਜੈਸਟਿਕਯੁਲੇਇਟ) *v* ਅੰਗਾਂ ਨੂੰ
ਹਿਲਾ ਕੇ ਸੰਕੇਤ ਕਰਨਾ, ਅਭਿਨੇ ਕਰਨਾ, ਹਾਵ-
ਭਾਵ ਵਿਅਕਤ ਕਰਨਾ

gesture ('ਜੈਸਚਅਾ*) *n* ਇਸ਼ਾਰਾ, ਸੈਨਤ, ਇੰਗਿਤ;
ਸੰਕੇਤ, ਹਾਵ-ਭਾਵ ਦਰਸਾਉਣ ਲਈ ਸਰੀਰ ਦੇ
ਅੰਗਾਂ ਦਾ ਪ੍ਰਯੋਗ

get (ਗੈਟ) *v* ਲੈਣਾ, ਪ੍ਰਾਪਤ ਕਰਨਾ, ਉਪਲਬਧ ਕਰਨਾ,
ਮਿਲਣਾ, ਵਸੂਲ ਕਰਨਾ, ਰੱਖਣਾ, ਮਾਲੂਮ ਕਰਨਾ,
ਲੱਗ ਜਾਣਾ, ਸਹਿਤ, ਭੁਗਤਣਾ; ਪਕੜਨਾ,
ਫਸਾਉਣਾ; ਸਮੇਟਣਾ, ਬਟੋਰਨਾ, ਘੇਰਵੱਸ ਕਰ ਦੇਣਾ;
ਜਣਨਾ, ਬੱਚਾ ਦੇਣਾ; ਤਿਆਰ ਕਰਨਾ; ਹੋ ਜਾਣਾ;
~**along** ਨਿਰਵਾਹ ਕਰਨਾ; ~**on** ਪਹਿਨਣਾ; ਕੰਮ
ਚਲਾਉਣਾ, ਗੁਜ਼ਾਰਾ ਕਰਨਾ, ਤਰੱਕੀ ਕਰਨਾ

geyser ('ਗੀਜ਼ਅਾ*) *n* ਪਾਣੀ ਦਾ ਚਸ਼ਮਾ; ਹਮਾਮ

ghastly ('ਗਾਸਟਲਿ) *a* ਭਿਆਨਕ, ਡਰਾਉਣਾ;
ਭੀਸ਼ਣ, ਬੁਰਾ

ghost ('ਗਾਉਸਟ) *n* ਜਿੰਨ, ਪਰੇਤ, ਭੂਤ, ਰੂਹ,
ਵਹਿਮ, ਪ੍ਰਤੀਛਾਇਆ, ਪਰਛਾਵਾਂ, ਛਾਇਆ;
ਪਿੰਜਰ; ਗੁਪਤ ਲੇਖਕ; ~**ly** (ਪ੍ਰ) ਰੂਹਾਨੀ,
ਆਤਮਕ, ਮਜ਼ਹਬੀ, ਦੀਨੀ, ਗ਼ੈਰ-ਸਰੀਰੀ, ਭੂਤ-
ਪਰੇਤ ਸਬੰਧੀ, ਭੂਤ ਵਰਗਾ

giant ('ਜਾਇਅੰਟ) *n a* ਰਾਖ਼ਸ਼, ਦੈਂਤ, ਦੇਉ, ਦਾਨਵ; ਅਸਧਾਰਨ ਸ਼ਕਤੀ

giddy ('ਗਿੱਡਿ) *a v* ਜਿਸ ਦਾ ਸਿਰ ਚਕਰਾਉਂਦਾ ਹੋਵੇ, ਚੱਲਿਤਕਾਰੀ, ਬੇਸੁਧ, ਹੋਛਾ; ਚਕਰਾਉਣਾ, ਘੇਰਨੀ, ਪੈਣੀ, ਬੇ-ਸੁਧ ਹੋਣਾ

gift (ਗਿਫ਼ਟ) *n v* ਬਖ਼ਸ਼ਸ਼, ਦਾਨ, ਉਪਹਾਰ, ਤੋਹਫ਼ਾ, ਨਜ਼ਰਾਨਾ, ਸੁਗਾਤ, ਢੋਆ; (ਕਾ) ਦਾਨ, ਭੇਟ ਕੁਦਰਤੀ ਕਮਾਲ; ਦਾਨ ਦੇਣਾ, ਸੁਗਾਤ ਵਜੋਂ ਦੇਣਾ; **~ed** ਗੁਣੀ, ਪ੍ਰਤਿਭਾਸ਼ਾਲੀ, ਗੁਣਵਾਨ, ਵਰੋਸਾਇਆ

gig (ਗਿਗ) *n* ਤਾਂਗਾ, ਟਮਟਮ; ਹੌਲੀ, ਬੇੜੀ, ਹਲਕੀ ਕਿਸ਼ਤੀ

gigantic (ਜਾਇ'ਗੈਂਟਿਕ) *a* ਬਹੁਤ ਵੱਡਾ, ਦਿਉ-ਕੱਦ; ਸ਼ਾਨਦਾਰ, ਬਹੁਤ ਭਾਰੀ, ਵਿਰਾਟ

giggle ('ਗਿਗਲ) *v n* ਬਦ-ਤਮੀਜ਼ੀ ਨਾਲ ਹੱਸਣਾ, ਦੰਦ ਕੱਢਣਾ; ਖੀ-ਖੀ ਕਰਨਾ, ਹਿਚ- ਹਿਚ ਕਰਨਾ; ਹਿਚ-ਹਿਚ, ਅਸ਼ਿਸ਼ਟ ਹਾਸਾ

gigolo (ਜਿਗਅਲਅਉ) *n* ਭਾੜੇ ਦਾ ਯਾਰ

gild (ਗਿਲਡ) *v n* ਸੋਨੇ ਦੀ ਝਾਲ ਚੜ੍ਹਾਉਣੀ, ਸੋਨੇ ਦਾ ਪੱਤਰਾ ਮੜ੍ਹਨਾ, ਮੁਲੰਮਾ ਕਰਨਾ; ਪੈਸਿਆਂ ਨਾਲ ਐਬ ਕੱਜਣੇ, ਸ਼ਬਦ-ਆਡੰਬਰ ਕਰਨਾ, ਸ਼ਬਦਾਂ ਨਾਲ ਸਜਾਵਟ ਕਰਨੀ; ਖ਼ੱਸੀ ਘੋੜਾ

gilt (ਗਿਲਟ) *n a* (1) ਮੁਲੰਮਾ, ਝੋਲ; ਉਪਰੀ ਸੁੰਦਰਤਾ (2) ਸੂਰ ਦਾ ਮਾਦਾ ਬੱਚਾ

gimmick ('ਗਿਮਿਕ) *n* (ਅਪ) ਢਕੌਂਸਲਾ, ਢਕਵੰਜ

gin (ਜਿਨ) *n v* (1) ਫੰਦਾ, ਜਾਲ, ਕੁੜੱਕੀ ਵੇਲਣਾ, ਭਾਰ ਚੁੱਕਣ ਵਾਲਾ ਵਿਸ਼ੇਸ਼ ਜੰਤਰ; ਫੰਧੇ ਵਿਚ ਫਸਾਉਣਾ; ਜਾਲ ਵਿਚ ਪਕੜਨਾ; (2) ਇਕ ਕਿਸਮ ਦੀ ਸ਼ਰਾਬ, ਜਿਨ

ginger ('ਜਿੰਜਅ*) *n v* ਅਦਰਕ, ਸੁੰਢ, ਜੋਸ਼; ਉਤਸ਼ਾਹ, ਉਤੇਜਨਾ; ਉਤਾਰਨਾ, ਉਕਸਾਉਣਾ;

ਘੋੜੇ ਨੂੰ ਚਾਬੁਕ ਲਾਉਣਾ; **dry~** ਸੁੰਢ

gingerly ('ਜਿੰਜਅ:ਲਿ) *a adv* ਸੰਕੋਚ ਸਹਿਤ, ਬੜੀ ਸਾਵਧਾਨੀ ਨਾਲ, ਡਰਦੇ ਡਰਦੇ; ਸੰਭਲ ਕੇ

gipsy, gypsy ('ਜਿਪਸਿ) *n* ਖ਼ਾਨਾਬਦੋਸ਼ ਜਾਤੀ, ਚੰਗੜ; ਸਿਕਲੀਗਰ, ਸ਼ਰਾਰਤੀ, ਚੰਚਲ, ਨਖ਼ਰੇਲੋ

gird (ਗਅ:ਡ) *v n v* (1) ਮਜ਼ਾਕ ਕਰਨਾ; ਤਾਅਨਾ ਮਾਰਨਾ, ਅਵਾਜ਼ ਕਸਣਾ; (2) ਪੇਟੀ ਕੱਸਣਾ; ਕਮਰਬੰਦ ਆਦਿ ਚਾਰੇ ਪਾਸੇ ਲਪੇਟਣਾ, ਪੇਟੀ ਬੰਨ੍ਹਣੀ; ਪੱਕਾ ਕਰਨਾ; ਜਕੜਨਾ; ਮਜ਼ਾਕ, ਵਿਅੰਗ, ਹਾਸਾ-ਠੱਠਾ; **~le** ਪੇਟੀ, ਕਮਰਬੰਦ; ਘੇਰਾ, ਦਰਖ਼ਤ ਦੀ ਛਾਲ, ਚਿੱਪਣੀ; ਪੇਟੀ ਬੰਨ੍ਹਣਾ

girder ('ਗਅ:ਡਅ*) *n* ਸ਼ਤੀਰ, ਕੜੀ; ਲੋਹੇ ਜਾਂ ਫ਼ੌਲਾਦ ਦਾ ਗਾਰਡਰ; ਛੱਤ ਜਾਂ ਪੁਲ ਦੀ ਡਾਟ

girl (ਗਅ:ਲ) *n* ਲੜਕੀ, ਬੱਚੀ, ਕੁੜੀ, ਨੱਢੀ, ਮੁਟਿਆਰ, ਕੰਨਿਆ; ਛੋਕਰੀ; **~hood** ਬਾਲ-ਅਵਸਥਾ, ਕੰਨਿਆਪਣ

gist (ਜਿਸਟ) *n* ਨਚੋੜ; ਭਾਵ, ਸਾਰ, ਸਾਰੰਸ਼

give (ਗਿਵ੍) *v* ਦੇਣਾ, ਭੇਟਾ ਕਰਨਾ, ਪੇਸ਼ ਕਰਨਾ, ਪਿਲਾਉਣਾ (ਦਵਾਈ); ਪਰਗਟ ਕਰਨਾ; ਕਾਰਨ ਹੋਣਾ; ਮੁਕੱਰਰ ਕਰਨਾ, ਰੱਖਣਾ (ਨਾਂ); ਪੈਦਾ ਕਰਨਾ, ਦੇਣਾ, ਨਿਕਲਣਾ; ਢਿਗ ਪੈਣਾ, ਬੈਠ ਜਾਣਾ; **~away** ਭੇਦ ਖੋਲ੍ਹ ਦੇਣਾ; ਪ੍ਰਦਾਨ ਕਰਨਾ; ਝੁਕ ਜਾਣਾ; **~n** ਦਿੱਤਾ, ਪ੍ਰਦੱਤ

giving ('ਗਿਵ੍ਇੰ) *n a* ਦਿੱਤੀ ਹੋਈ ਵਸਤ; ਸਮਰਪਣ; ਦੇਣ ਵਾਲਾ, ਪ੍ਰਦਾਤਾ

glacier ('ਗਲੇਇਸਯਅ*) *a* ਬਰਫ਼ਾਨੀ, ਬਰਫ਼ੀਲਾ

glad (ਗਲੈਡ) *a* ਖ਼ੁਸ਼, ਪ੍ਰਸੰਨ, ਅਨੰਦਤ, ਤੁਸ਼ਟ, ਪ੍ਰਸੰਨ-ਚਿੱਤ; **~den** ਖ਼ੁਸ਼ ਕਰਨਾ, ਪ੍ਰਸੰਨ ਕਰਨਾ, ਸੰਤੁਸ਼ਟ ਕਰਨਾ; **~dening** ਆਨੰਦਾਇਕ, ਪ੍ਰਸੰਨਤਾਦਾਇਕ; **~some** ਖ਼ੁਸ਼, ਪ੍ਰਸੰਨ, ਸੰਤੁਸ਼ਟ

glamorous ('ਗਲੈਮਅਰਅਸ) *a* ਦਿਲਖਿੱਚਵਾਂ,

ਠਾਠਦਾਰ, ਆਕਰਸ਼ਕ, ਮਨਮੋਹਨਾ, ਮੋਹਕ

glamour (ਗਲੈਮਆ*) *n v* ਠਾਠ-ਬਾਠ, ਆਕਰਸ਼ਟ; ਜਾਦੂ; ਮੋਹ ਲੈਣਾ; ਆਕਰਸ਼ਤ ਕਰਨਾ, ਜਾਦੂ ਕਰਨਾ

glance (ਗਲਾਂਸ) *n v* ਝਾਤ, ਤੱਕਣੀ, ਉੱਡਦੀ ਨਜ਼ਰ; ਚਮਕ; ਵੇਖਣਾ, ਨਜ਼ਰ ਮਾਰਨੀ; ਝਾਤ ਮਾਰਨਾ, ਚਮਕਣਾ, ਲਿਸ਼ਕਣਾ

gland (ਗਲੈਂਡ) *n* ਗਿਲਟੀ, ਗਲੈਂਡ, ਗੰਢੀ

glare (ਗਲੇਅ*) *v n* ਘੂਰੀ ਪਾ ਕੇ ਵੇਖਣਾ, ਅੱਖਾਂ ਗੱਡ ਕੇ ਤੱਕਣਾ; ਲਿਸ਼ਕਾਰਾ ਮਾਰਨਾ; ਤੇਜ਼ ਰੌਸ਼ਨੀ, ਚਮਕ, ਤਿੱਖਾ ਪ੍ਰਕਾਸ਼, ਅੱਖਾਂ ਚੁੰਧਿਆ ਦੇਣ ਵਾਲੀ ਰੌਸ਼ਨੀ

glaring (ਗਲੇਅਰਿੰਗ) *a* ਪ੍ਰਤੱਖ, ਸੁਸਪਸ਼ਟ, ਚਮਕਦਾਰ, ਉੱਜਲ, ਉੱਘੜਵਾਂ

glass (ਗਲਾਸ) *n v* ਸ਼ੀਸ਼ਾ, ਕੱਚ, ਸ਼ੀਸ਼ੇ ਦਾ ਗਲਾਸ, ਆਇਨਾ, ਸ਼ੀਸ਼ਾ ਜੜਨਾ; ਪ੍ਰਤੀਬਿੰਬ ਸੁੱਟਣਾ; ਸ਼ੀਸ਼ੇ ਵਿਚ ਬੰਦ ਕਰਨਾ

glaucoma (ਗਲੋ'ਕਅਉਮਅ) *n* ਮੋਤੀਆ ਬਿੰਦ

glaze (ਗਲੇਇਜ਼) *v n* ਸ਼ੀਸ਼ੇ ਜੜਨੇ, ਲਿਸ਼ਕਾਉਣਾ, ਰਗੜ ਕੇ ਚਮਕਾਉਣਾ; ਪਾਲਸ਼ ਜਾਂ ਰੋਗਨ ਕਰਨਾ; ਸ਼ੀਸ਼ੇ ਦਾ ਰੋਗਨ ਫੇਰਨਾ, (ਅੱਖ) ਪਥਰਾ ਜਾਣੀ, ਤੇਜਹੀਨ ਹੋ ਜਾਣੀ; ਪਾਲਸ਼, ਰੋਗਨ, ਸ਼ੀਸ਼ੇ ਦਾ ਪਾਣੀ, ਕਿਸੇ ਚਮਕਦਾਰ ਚੀਜ਼ ਦਾ ਪਾਣੀ; ਚਿਕਨਾਈ; ਚਮਕ, ਲਿਸ਼ਕ ਅੱਖ ਦਾ ਜਾਲਾ; ~d ਚਮਕੀਲਾ, ਚਮਕਾਈ ਹੋਈ, ਚਮਕਦਾਰ; ਸ਼ੀਸ਼ੇਦਾਰ

gleam (ਗਲੀਮ) *n v* ਝਲਕ, ਲਿਸ਼ਕਾਰਾ, ਚਮਕ, ਆਬ; ਝਲਕ ਦੇਣੀ, ਲਿਸ਼ਕਾਰਾ ਮਾਰਨਾ

glide (ਗਲਾਇਡ) *v n* ਸਰਕਣਾ, ਤਿਲਕਣਾ, ਹੌਲੀ-ਹੌਲੀ ਖਿਸਕਣਾ, ਵਗਣਾ; ਹੌਲੀ ਲੰਘਣਾ, ਹੌਲੀ ਵਗਣਾ; ਗਾਉਂਦਿਆਂ-ਗਾਉਂਦਿਆਂ ਸੁਰ ਜਾਂ ਤਰਜ਼ ਬਦਲਣਾ; ~r ਹਲਕਾ ਜਿਹਾ ਹਵਾਈ

ਜਹਾਜ਼, ਗਲਾਈਡਰ

glimmer (ਗਲਿਮਅ*) *v n* ਝਿਲਮਿਲਾਉਣਾ, ਝਿਲਮਿਲ ਝਿਲਮਿਲ ਕਰਨਾ, ਟਿਮਟਿਮਾਉਣਾ, ਝਿਲਮਿਲ, ਟਿਮਟਿਮਾਹਟ, ਝਲਕ

glimpse (ਗਲਿੰਪਸ) *n v* ਝਲਕ, ਝਾਕੀ, ਨਜ਼ਰ, ਝਿਟ; ਝਲਕ ਦੇਣੀ, ਝਾਤ ਪਾਉਣੀ, ਸਰਸਰੀ ਨਜ਼ਰ ਮਾਰਨੀ, ਝਲਕ ਵਿਖਾਉਣੀ

glitter ('ਗਲਿਟਅ*) *v n* ਲਿਸ਼ਕਣਾ, ਜ਼ੋਰ ਦੀ ਚਮਕ ਮਾਰਨੀ, ਜਗਮਗ ਜਗਮਗ ਕਰਨਾ, ਝਲੂਕਣਾ; ਭੜਕੀਲਾ ਹੋਣਾ, ਲਿਸ਼ਕ, ਚਮਕ, ਜਗਮਗਾਹਟ

glitz (ਗਲਿਟਸ) *n* ਤੜਕ-ਭੜਕ

global ('ਗਲਅਉਬਲ) *a* ਵਿਸ਼ਵ ਵਿਆਪੀ, ਸਰਬ ਵਿਆਪੀ, ਵਿਆਪਕ

globe (ਗਲਅਉਬ) *n* ਭੂ-ਮੰਡਲ, ਧਰਤੀ ਦਾ ਇਕ ਗੋਲੇ ਉੱਤੇ ਬਣਾਇਆ ਨਕਸ਼ਾ; ਧਰਤੀ, ਪ੍ਰਿਥਵੀ, ਨਛੱਤਰ

gloom (ਗਲੂਮ) *n v* ਹਨੇਰਾ, ਧੁੰਦਲਾਪਣ; ਅਸਪਸ਼ਟਤਾ, ਉਦਾਸੀ, ਨਿਰਾਸ਼ਾ; ਧੁੰਦਲਾ ਕਰ ਦੇਣਾ, ਨਿਰਾਸ਼ ਕਰ ਦੇਣਾ; ਉਦਾਸ ਹੋ ਜਾਣਾ; ~y ਉਦਾਸ, ਅਸੰਤੁਸ਼ਟ; ਅੰਧਕਾਰਪੂਰਨ, ਉਦਾਸੀਨ, ਗ਼ਮਗੀਨ

glorification ('ਗਲੋਰਿਫ਼ਿ'ਕੇਇਸ਼ਨ) *n* ਸ਼ੋਭਾ, ਪ੍ਰਸੰਸਾ, ਉਸਤਤੀ, ਮਹਿਮਾ, ਵਡਿਆਈ

glorify ('ਗਲੋਰਿਫ਼ਾਇ) *v* ਵਡਿਆਉਣਾ, ਮਹਿਮਾ ਦੱਸਣੀ; ਗੌਰਵਮਈ ਬਣਾਉਣਾ, ਗੁਣ ਗਾਉਣੇ, ਜਸ ਗਾਉਣਾ

glorious ('ਗਲੋਰਿਅਸ) *a* ਸ਼ਾਨਦਾਰ, ਪ੍ਰਤਾਪੀ, ਤੇਜਸਵੀ; ਮਹਾਨ; ਸਨਮਾਨਯੁਕਤ, ਮਹਿਮਾ ਵਾਲਾ

glory ('ਗਲੋਰਿ) *n* ਵਡਿਆਈ, ਸ਼ਾਨ, ਮਹਿਮਾ,

ਤੇਜ ਪ੍ਰਤਾਪ, ਗੌਰਵ

gloss (ਗਲੇਸ) *n v* (1) ਟਿੱਪਣੀ, ਵਿਆਖਿਆ, ਟੀਕਾ, ਸ਼ਬਦਾਂ ਦਾ ਕੋਸ਼; (2) ਲਿਸ਼ਕ, ਚਮਕ- ਦਮਕ; ਮੁਲੰਮਾ; ਚਮਕਦਾਰ ਬਣਾਉਣਾ, ਲਿਸ਼ਕਾਉਣਾ, ਤੇਜ਼-ਮਰੋੜ ਕਰਨੇ, ਹੋਰ ਦੇ ਹੋਰ ਅਰਥ ਕੱਢਣੇ; ~**ary** ਔਖੇ ਸ਼ਬਦਾਂ ਦੀ ਅਰਥਾਵਲੀ, ਪਰਿਭਾਸ਼ਕ ਸ਼ਬਦਾਵਲੀ

glottis ('ਗਲੈਟਿਸ) *n* ਘੰਡੀ ਦਾ ਮੂੰਹ, ਕੰਠਦੁਆਰ

glove (ਗਲਅੱਵ) *n v* ਦਸਤਾਨਾ; ਬਾਕਸਿੰਗ (ਮੁੱਕੇਬਾਜ਼ੀ) ਵਿਚ ਪਾਇਆ ਜਾਣ ਵਾਲਾ ਚਮੜੇ ਦਾ ਦਸਤਾਨਾ

glow (ਗਲਅਉ) *v n* ਚਮਕਣਾ, ਦਮਕਣਾ, ਭਖਣਾ, ਲਾਲ ਹੋਣਾ, ਪ੍ਰਫੁਲਤ ਹੋਣਾ; ਚਮਕ, ਲਾਲੀ, ਚਾਉ, ਜੋਸ਼, ਆਵੇਸ਼; ~**ing** ਪ੍ਰਦੀਪਤ, ਉੱਜਲ, ਸ਼ੋਖ਼; ~**worm** ਟਟਿਹਣਾ, ਜੁਗਨੂੰ

glue (ਗਲੂ) *n v* ਸਰੇਸ਼, ਗੁੰਦ (ਚਿਪਕਾਉਣ ਵਾਲੀ), ਗੁੰਦ ਨਾਲ ਚਿਪਕਾਉਣਾ, ਪੱਕੀ ਤਰ੍ਹਾਂ ਬੰਦ ਕਰਨਾ; ~**pot** ਗੁੰਦਦਾਨੀ; ~**y** ਚਿਪਚਪ, ਚਿਪਕਾਉਣ ਵਾਲਾ

gnash (ਨੈਸ਼) *v* ਦੰਦ ਪੀਹਣੇ, ਦੰਦ ਕਰੀਚਣੇ, ਕਰੀਚੀ ਵੱਟਣੀ

gnaw (ਨੋ) *v* ਟੁੱਕਣਾ, ਕੁਤਰਨਾ, ਚੱਬਦੇ ਰਹਿਣਾ; ਘੁਣ ਵਾਂਗ ਲੱਗਣਾ, ਦੁੱਖ ਦੇਣਾ, ਹੌਲੀ ਹੌਲੀ ਨਾਸ ਕਰਨਾ

go (ਗਅਉ) *v* ਜਾਣਾ, ਚਲੇ ਜਾਣਾ, ਟੁਰਨਾ, ਰਵਾਨਾ ਹੋਣਾ; ਪ੍ਰਸਥਾਨ ਕਰਨਾ, ਫਾਇਰ ਹੋਣਾ, ਚੱਲਣਾ; ~**ahead** ਅੱਗੇ ਵਧਣ ਦਾ ਸੰਕੇਤ; ~**between** ਵਿਚੋਲਾ, ਪੰਚ, ਦਲਾਲ; ~**by** ਅਨੁਸਰਣ ਕਰਨਾ, ਦੇ ਵੱਲ ਚੱਲਣਾ; ~**off** ਨੱਠ ਜਾਣਾ, ਨਿਕਲ ਜਾਣਾ, ਬੰਧੁਕ ਆਦਿ ਦਾ ਚੱਲਣਾ, ਫਾਇਰ ਹੋਣਾ; ਗੁੰਮ ਹੋ ਜਾਣਾ, ਚਲਾਣਾ ਕਰ ਜਾਣਾ; ~**er** ਚੱਲਣ ਵਾਲਾ,

ਟੁਰਨ(ਤੁਰਨ) ਵਾਲਾ; ਹਿੰਮਤੀ ਮਨੁੱਖ, ਇਰਾਦੇ ਦਾ ਪੱਕਾ; ~**ing** ਚਾਲ, ਗਮਨ, ਜਾਣ, ਰਵਾਨਗੀ, ਪ੍ਰਸਥਾਨ

goal (ਗਅਉਲ) *n* ਟੀਚਾ, ਨਿਸ਼ਾਨਾ, ਉਦੇਸ਼; (ਫੁਟਬਾਲ, ਹਾਕੀ ਆਦਿ ਵਿਚ) ਬਾਜ਼ੀ, ਗੋਲ, ਦੌੜ ਸਮਾਪਤ ਹੋਣ ਵਾਲੀ ਥਾਂ; ~**keeper** (ਫੁਟਬਾਲ ਜਾਂ ਹਾਕੀ ਦੀ ਖੇਡ ਵਿਚ) ਗੋਲਚੀ, ਗੋਲੀ

goat (ਗਅਉਟ) *n* ਬੱਕਰੀ, ਬੱਕਰਾ; ਕਾਮੀ ਜਾਂ ਵਿਭਚਾਰੀ ਵਿਅਕਤੀ; ਮਕਰ ਰਾਸ਼ੀ ਦਾ ਚਿੰਨ੍ਹ; ~**y** ਦੁਰਾਚਾਰੀ

gobble ('ਗੌਬਲ) *v* ਕਾਹਲੀ ਕਾਹਲੀ ਖਾਣਾ, ਹਪੁੰ- ਹਪੁੰ ਕਰਕੇ ਖਾਣਾ, ਹੜੱਪ ਕਰ ਜਾਣਾ; ਗੁੱਸੇ ਵਿਚ ਕੜਕਣਾ

God (ਗੌਡ) *n* ਭਗਵਾਨ, ਖ਼ੁਦਾ, ਰੱਬ; **G~ forsaken** ਰੱਬ ਮਾਰਿਆ, ਅਭਾਗਾ, ਗੁਣਹੀਣ; **G~fearing** ਰਹਿਮ-ਦਿਲ, ਖ਼ੁਦਾ ਤਰਸ

god *n* ਦੇਵ, ਦੇਵਤਾ, ਮੂਰਤੀ, ਬੁੱਤ; ~**dess** ਦੇਵੀ; ਪੂਜਣਯੋਗ ਇਸਤਰੀ; ~**father** ਧਰਮ ਪਿਤਾ, ਮੋਢੀ; ~**less** ਨਾਸਤਕ, ਮੁਨਕਰ, ਬੇਦੀਨ, ਪਾਪੀ, ਦੁਸ਼ਟ; ~**ly** ਪਵਿੱਤਰ, ਧਰਮਾਤਮਾ, ਧਰਮੀ

godown ('ਗਅਉਡਾਉਨ) *n* ਗੁਦਾਮ, ਭੰਡਾਰ, ਮਾਲਖ਼ਾਨਾ

goggle ('ਗੌਗਲ) *v n pl* ਤਿਰਛੀ ਅੱਖ ਨਾਲ ਵੇਖਣਾ, ਘੂਰ ਕੇ ਵੇਖਣਾ, ਕਨਖੀਆਂ ਨਾਲ ਵੇਖਣਾ, ਡੇਲੇ ਘੁਮਾਉਣੇ; ਚਸ਼ਮਾ, ਧੁੱਪ-ਐਨਕ

Golconda (ਗੌਲ'ਕੌਨਡਾ) *n* (ਅਲੰਕਾਰ ਵਜੋਂ) ਧਨ ਦੀ ਖਾਨ, ਧਨ-ਕੁਬੇਰ

gold (ਗਅਉਲਡ) *n a* ਸੋਨਾ, ਧਨ, ਮਾਲ, ਦੌਲਤ; ਸੋਨੇ ਦਾ ਸਿੱਕਾ; ਸੁਨਹਿਰੀ ਰੰਗ; ਸੋਨੇ ਦਾ ਪਾਣੀ, ਸ਼ਾਨਦਾਰ ਚੀਜ਼; ਸੁਨਹਿਰੀ; ~**en** ਸੁਨਹਿਰਾ, ਸੋਨੇ

ਵਰਗਾ; ਅਮੋਲਕ, ਬਹੁਮੁੱਲਾ; ~**leaf** ਸੋਨੇ ਦਾ ਵਰਕ; ~**smith** ਸੁਨਿਆਰਾ

good (ਗੁੜ) *a n* ਚੰਗਾ, ਅੱਛਾ, ਨੇਕ, ਸਦਾਚਾਰੀ, ਭਲਾ; ਸੋਹਣਾ, ਉਚਿਤ, ਮੁਨਾਸਬ; ਕਾਬਲ; ਗੁਣਕਾਰੀ, ਲਾਭਦਾਇਕ, ਗੁਣਵਾਨ, ਸਿੱਧਾ-ਸਾਦਾ; ਦਿਆਵਾਨ; ਕਾੜੀ, ਬਘੇਰਾ; ਪੁੰਨ, ਧਰਮ; ~**bye** ਨਮਸਤੇ; ਸ਼ੁਭ ਵਿਦਾਇਗੀ, ਰੱਬ-ਰਾਖਾ; ~**for nothing** ਨਿਕੰਮਾ, ਵਿਅਰਥ; ~**looking** ਸੋਹਣਾ, ਸੁਨੱਖਾ, ਦਰਸ਼ਨੀ; ~**morning** ਸ਼ੁਭ ਪ੍ਰਭਾਤ, ਨਮਸਤੇ; ~**natured** ਚੰਗੇ ਸੁਭਾਅ ਵਾਲਾ, ਨੇਕ, ਸੁਸ਼ੀਲ, ਭਲਾ; ~**night** ਸ਼ੁਭ ਰਾਤਰੀ, ਨਮਸਤੇ; ~**will** ਸ਼ੁਭ ਇੱਛਾ, ਸਦਭਾਵਨਾ, ਸਦਭਾਵ; ~**ly** ਸੋਹਣਾ, ਸੁੰਦਰ; ਉੱਤਮ, ਮਹਾਨ; ਕਾੜੀ; ~**ness** ਨੇਕੀ, ਚੰਗਿਆਈ, ਭਲਾਈ, ਸ੍ਰੇਸ਼ਠਤਾ; ਉਦਾਰਤਾ

goody -goody ('ਗੁਡ਼ਿ,ਗੁਡ਼ਿ) *n* ਬਣਾਵਟੀ ਤੌਰ ਵਿਚ ਭਲਾ ਚਾਹੁਣ ਵਾਲਾ, ਭਲਾਈ ਕਰਨ ਦਾ ਵਿਖਾਵਾ ਕਰਨ

goose (ਗੂਸ) *n* ਹੰਸ, ਹੰਸਨੀ; ਸਿੰਮਪੁੜ, ਮੂਰਖ, ਘੁੱਲੂ

gorge (ਗੋਜ) *n v* ਖੱਡ, ਡੂੰਘੀ ਘਾਟੀ; ਪਹਾੜਾਂ ਵਿਚੋਂ ਤੰਗ ਰਸਤਾ; ਮੱਛੀ ਦੀ ਖੁਰਾਕ; ਕਿਲ੍ਹੇ ਦਾ ਪਿਛਲਾ ਦਰਵਾਜ਼ਾ, ਬੁਰਜ ਦਾ ਰਸਤਾ; ਤੁੜਨਾ, ਗਲ ਤਕ ਭਰ ਦੇਣਾ; ਬਹੁਤ ਖਾਣਾ

gorgeous ('ਗੋਜਅਸ) *a* ਸ਼ਾਨਦਾਰ, ਭੜਕੀਲਾ, ਉੱਜਲ, ਸੱਜਿਆ, ਫੱਬਿਆ, ਅਲੰਕਰਤ, ਚਮਕਦਾਰ, ਲਿਸ਼ਕਦਾ

gorilla (ਗਾ'ਰਿਲਅ) *n* ਬਣ ਮਾਨਸ; ਵਹਿਸ਼ੀ ਬੰਦਾ

gospel ('ਗੋਸਪਲ) *n* ਇੰਜੀਲ, ਬਾਈਬਲ, ਇਸਾਈਆਂ ਦਾ ਧਰਮ-ਗ੍ਰੰਥ; ਈਸਾ ਦੁਆਰਾ

ਪਰਗਟ ਕੀਤਾ ਸ਼ੁਭ ਸਮਾਚਾਰ; ਮੱਤ, ਈਮਾਨ, ਧਰਮ-ਸਿਧਾਂਤ

gossip ('ਗੋਸਿਪ) *n v* ਗੱਪ, ਗੱਪ-ਸ਼ੱਪ, ਵਾਧੂ ਗੱਲ; ਗੱਪੀ, ਗਾਲੜੀ; ਗੱਪਾਂ ਮਾਰਨੀਆਂ, ਫ਼ਜੂਲ ਬਕਵਾਸ ਕਰਨਾ; ~**y** ਗੱਪੀ, ਗਾਲੜੀ, ਬਕਵਾਸੀ

gourmand ('ਗੁਅਮਅੰਡ) *n* ਪੇਟੂ, ਚਟੋਰਾ

gout (ਗਾਉਟ) *n* ਗਠੀਆ, ਜੋੜਾਂ ਵਿਚ ਪੀੜ ਤੇ ਸੋਜ ਦਾ ਰੋਗ

govern ('ਗਅੱਵਨ) *v* ਪ੍ਰਬੰਧ ਕਰਨਾ, ਇੰਤਜ਼ਾਮ ਕਰਨਾ; ਰਾਜ ਪ੍ਰਬੰਧ ਕਰਨਾ, ਰੱਖਣਾ; ~**ed** ਸ਼ਾਸਤ, ਅਧੀਨ, ਨਿਯੰਤਰਤ; ~**ess** ਅਧਿਆਪਕਾ, ਮਾਸਟਰਨੀ, ਉਸਤਾਨੀ; ਸ਼ਾਸਕਾ; ~**ment** ਸਰਕਾਰ, ਰਾਜ, ਹਕੂਮਤ, ਗੌਰਮਿੰਟ, ਸ਼ਾਸਨ; ~**or** ਰਾਜਪਾਲ, ਪ੍ਰਦੇਸ਼ਪਾਲ, ਹਾਕਮ, ਸੂਬੇਦਾਰ

gown (ਗਾਉਨ) *n v* ਚੋਲਾ, ਖੱਲਾ ਤੇ ਲੰਮਾ, ਕੁੜਤਾ; ਫਰਾਕ-ਕੋਟ; ਗਾਉਨ

grab (ਗਰੈਬ) *v n* ਲੁੱਟਣਾ, ਝਮੱਟ ਮਾਰਨੀ; ਝਪਟ ਕੇ ਫੜਨਾ; ਲੁੱਟ-ਖਸੁੱਟ ਜਾਂ ਝਪਟ; ਗਾਰਿਫ਼ਤ, ਦਸਤ-ਦਰਾਜ਼ੀ

grace (ਗਰੇਇਸ) *n v* ਸੁੰਦਰਤਾ, ਛਬ, ਸ਼ੋਭਾ, ਅਦਾ, ਖੂਬੀ, ਹੁਸਨ, ਅੰਦਾਜ਼; ਬਖ਼ਸ਼ਸ਼, ਰਿਆਇਤ; ਰੱਬੀ ਮਿਹਰ, ਖ਼ੁਦਾਈ ਕਰਮ; ਸਜਾਉਣਾ, ਸ਼ਿੰਗਾਰਨਾ; ਮਾਣ ਬਖ਼ਸ਼ਣਾ; ~**ful** ਸੁੰਦਰ, ਛਬੀਲਾ, ਹੁਸੀਨ, ਖ਼ੂਬਸੂਰਤ, ਦਿਲਰੁਬਾ; ~**less** ਅਸੁੰਦਰ, ਛਬੀਹੀਣ, ਕੋਝਾ, ਫੂਹੜ; ਨਿਰਲੱਜ

gracious ('ਗਰੇਇਸ਼ਅਸ) *a* ਮਿਹਰਬਾਨ, ਦਿਆਲੂ, ਬਖ਼ਸ਼ਿੰਦ; ਸੁੰਦਰ; ਧਾਰਮਕ; ਕਾਮਲ

gradation (ਗਰਾਅ'ਡੇਇਸ਼ਨ) *n* ਦਰਜੇਬੰਦੀ, ਗ੍ਰੇਡਬੰਦੀ, ਦਰਜੇ ਅਨੁਸਾਰ ਦਿੱਤੀ ਗਈ ਤਰਤੀਬ; ~**al** ਦਰਜੇਬੰਦੀ ਸਬੰਧੀ, ਕ੍ਰਮਬੰਦੀ ਦਾ, ਗ੍ਰੇਡਬੰਦੀ ਨਾਲ ਸਬੰਧਤ

grading ('ਗਰੇਇਡਿਙ) *n* ਦਰਜਾਬੰਦੀ, ਸ਼੍ਰੇਣੀਕਰਨ, ਕੋਟੀਕਰਨ, ਕੋਟੀ-ਕ੍ਰਮ; ਨਿਰਧਾਰਣ

gradual ('ਗਰੇਜੁਅਲ) *a n* ਦਰਜੇਵਾਰ, ਸਿਲਸਲੇਵਾਰ; ਗਿਰਜੇ ਵਿਚ ਗਾਏ ਜਾਣ ਵਾਲੇ ਵਿਸ਼ੇਸ਼ ਗੀਤ; **~ly** ਹੌਲੀ-ਹੌਲੀ ਸਹਿਜੇ-ਸਹਿਜੇ

graduate ('ਗਰੈਜੁਅਟ, 'ਗਰੇਜੂਏਇਟ) *n v* ਸਨਦਯਾਫਤਾ (ਵਿਅਕਤੀ); ਡਿਗਰੀ ਪ੍ਰਾਪਤ ਕਰਨੀ, ਸਨਦ ਲੈਣੀ; ਦਰਜੇ ਲਾਉਣੇ

graduation ('ਗਰੇਜੁ'ਏਇਸ਼ਨ) *n* ਡਿਗਰੀ ਪ੍ਰਾਪਤ ਕਰਨ ਦਾ ਕਾਰਜ, ਅੰਕ ਲਾਉਣ

grain (ਗਰੇਇਨ) *n v* ਦਾਣਾ, ਅਨਾਜ; ਬੀਂ, ਤੁਖ਼ਮ; ਟੁਕੜਾ, ਕਿਣਕਾ, ਜ਼ੱਰਾ ਜਾਂ ਦਾਣੇਦਾਰ ਬਣਾਉਣਾ; ਲਾਲ ਰੰਗ ਚਾੜ੍ਹਨਾ; ਖੱਲ ਦੇ ਵਾਲ ਉਤਾਰਨੇ

gram (ਗਰੈਮ) *n* (1) ਛੋਲੇ; ਘੋੜਿਆਂ ਦਾ ਦਾਣਾ; ਗੁੱਸਾ; (2) ਗਰਾਮ; ਕਿਲੋਗ੍ਰਾਮ ਦਾ ਹਜ਼ਾਰਵਾਂ ਹਿੱਸਾ

grammar ('ਗਰੈਮਅ*) *n* ਵਿਆਕਰਣ; (ਵਿਆਕਰਣ ਦੀ) ਪੁਸਤਕ; ਵਿਆਕਰਣ ਦੇ ਸਿਧਾਂਤਾਂ ਦਾ ਪ੍ਰਯੋਗ, ਭਾਸ਼ਾ ਦੇ ਮੁਹਾਵਰੇ; **~ian** ਵਿਆਕਰਣ ਸ਼ਾਸਤਰੀ, ਵਿਆਕਰਣ ਆਚਾਰੀਆ

grammatical (ਗਰਅ'ਮੈਟਿਕਲ) *a* ਵਿਆਕਰਣਕ

granary ('ਗਰੈਨਅਰਿ) *n* ਅਨਾਜ-ਭੰਡਾਰ, ਅਨਾਜ ਦਾ ਗੁਦਾਮ, ਭੜੋਲਾ, ਬੁਖਾਰੀ

grand (ਗਰੈਂਡ) *a* ਸ਼ਾਨਦਾਰ; ਅਸਲੀ; ਠਾਠ-ਬਾਠ ਵਾਲਾ, ਉੱਚਾ, ਵੱਡਾ; **~eur** ਵਡਿਆਈ, ਸ਼ੋਭਾ, ਸ਼ਾਨ, ਚੜ੍ਹਤ, ਮਹਿਮਾ, ਤੇਜ, ਪ੍ਰਤਾਪ, ਪ੍ਰਤਿਸ਼ਠਾ

granite ('ਗਰੈਨਿਟ) *n* ਇਕ ਸਖ਼ਤ ਦਾਣੇਦਾਰ ਪੱਥਰ

granny ('ਗਰੈਨਿ) *n* (ਮੋਹ ਨਾਲ) ਦਾਦੀ ਜਾਂ ਨਾਨੀ; ਬੁੱਢੀ ਤੀਵੀਂ

grant (ਗਰਾਂਟ) *v n* ਮਨਜ਼ੂਰ ਕਰਨਾ; ਕਬੂਲ ਕਰਨਾ; ਮੰਨ ਲੈਣਾ, ਅਤਾ ਕਰਨਾ, ਬਖ਼ਸ਼ਣਾ; ਅਨੁਦਾਨ, ਮਾਫ਼ੀ, ਸਰਕਾਰੀ ਸਹਾਇਤਾ; ਮਨਜ਼ੂਰੀ

grape ('ਗਰੇਇਪ) *n* ਅੰਗੂਰ, ਦਾਖ

grapevine ('ਗਰੇਇਪਵਾਇਨ) *n* ਅੰਗੂਰੀ ਸ਼ਰਾਬ; ਅਫ਼ਵਾਹ

graph (ਗਰਾਫ਼) *n v* ਰੇਖਾ, ਖ਼ਾਕਾ; ਚਿੱਤਰ; **~ic** ਨਕਸ਼ੇ ਦਾ, ਲਿਖਤ ਸਬੰਧੀ, ਚਿੱਤਰਕਾਰੀ ਤੇ ਬੁੱਤ ਤਰਾਸ਼ੀ ਸਬੰਧੀ, ਹੂਬਹੂ

grapple ('ਗਰੈਪਲ) *n v* ਕੁੰਡਾ, ਕਮੰਦ; ਮੁੱਠ-ਭੇੜ, ਹੱਥੋ-ਪਾਈ; ਫੜਨਾ, ਉਲਝਾਉਣਾ, ਗੁੱਥਮ-ਗੁੱਥਾ ਹੋਣਾ, ਹੱਥੋ-ਪਾਈ ਕਰਨੀ

grasp (ਗਰਾਸਪ) *v n* ਝਮੁੱਟ ਮਾਰਨੀ, ਝਪਟਣਾ, ਘੁੱਟ ਕੇ ਫੜਨਾ; ਕਾਬੂ, ਕਬਜ਼ਾ, ਪਕੜ; **~ing** ਪਕੜ, ਲਾਲਚੀ

grass (ਗਰਾਸ) *n v* ਘਾਹ, ਚਾਰਾ; ਚਰਾਗਾਹ; **~roots** ਜਨ ਸਧਾਰਨ, ਆਧਾਰ, ਬੁਨਿਆਦ; **~y** ਹਰਾ-ਭਰਾ, ਘਾਹ ਵਾਲਾ

grateful ('ਗਰੇਇਟਫ਼ੁਲ) *a* ਸਵੀਕਾਰ ਕਰਨ ਯੋਗ, ਸੁਹਾਵਣਾ, ਦਿਲ-ਪਸੰਦ; ਧੰਨਵਾਦੀ, ਇਹਸਾਨਮੰਦ, ਕ੍ਰਿਤੱਗ, ਆਭਾਰੀ; **~ness** ਕ੍ਰਿਤੱਗਤਾ, ਇਹਸਾਨਮੰਦੀ, ਆਭਾਰ

gratification ('ਗਰੈਟਿਫ਼ਿ'ਕੇਇਸ਼ਨ) *n* ਇੱਛਾ-ਪੂਰਤੀ, ਖ਼ੁਸ਼ੀ, ਪ੍ਰਸੰਨਤਾ, ਤ੍ਰਿਪਤੀ, ਤੁਸ਼ਟੀ; ਵੱਢੀ

gratify ('ਗਰੈਟਿਫ਼ਾਇ) *v* ਰੀਝਉਣਾ, ਰੀਝ ਪੂਰੀ ਕਰਨੀ, ਖ਼ੁਸ਼ ਕਰਨਾ; ਫ਼ੀਸ ਦੇਣੀ, ਮੁੱਠੀ ਗਰਮ ਕਰਨੀ, ਵੱਢੀ ਦੇਣੀ

gratis ('ਗਰੈਇਟਿਸ) *adv a* ਇਨਾਮ ਵਿਚ ਦਿਤਾ, ਪੁਰਸਕਾਰ ਵਜੋਂ ਦਿਤਾ; ਬਿਨਾ ਮੁੱਲ ਤੋਂ, ਮੁਫ਼ਤ, ਨਿਰਮੁੱਲ

gratitude ('ਗਰੈਟਿਟਯੂਡ) *n* ਸ਼ੁਕਰੀਆ, ਧੰਨਵਾਦ, ਸ਼ੁਕਰ, ਇਹਸਾਨ, ਕਿਰਪਾ, ਇਹਸਾਨਮੰਦੀ

gratutious (ਗਰਅਾ'ਟਯੂਇਟਅਸ) *a* ਬਿਨਾ ਮੁੱਲ ਤੋਂ ਪ੍ਰਾਪਤ, ਮੁਫ਼ਤ ਦਾ, ਅਟਕਮਾਇਆ, ਵਿਅਰਥ, ਫੋਕਟ, ਬਿਨਾ ਅਧਿਕਾਰ

gratuity (ਗਰਅਾ'ਟਯੂਅਟੀ) *n* ਧੰਨ-ਦਾਨ; ਉਪਦਾਨ; ਮਜ਼ਦੂਰੀ, ਤਨਖ਼ਾਹ

grave (ਗਰੇਇਵ਼) *n v a* (1) ਕਬਰ, ਸਮਾਧ, ਮੜੀ, ਸੁਨਸਾਨ ਥਾਂ; ਮਿਰਤੂ, ਅੰਤ, ਨਾਸ, (2) ਦੱਬਣਾ, ਦਫ਼ਨਾਉਣਾ; ਤਰਾਸ਼ਣਾ, ਰੂਪ ਬਣਾਉਣਾ, ਨੱਕਾਸ਼ੀ ਕਰਨੀ, ਉੱਕਰਨਾ; (3) ਗੰਭੀਰ, ਭਾਰੀ, ਮਹਾਨ, ਜ਼ਰੂਰੀ, ਧੀਰਜਵਾਨ, ਸੰਗੀਨ, ਭਿਆਨਕ, ਡਰਾਉਣਾ, ਸ਼ਖ਼ਤ, ਸੰਜੀਦਾ; ~**clothes** ਕਫ਼ਨ, ਖੱਫ਼ਣ; ~**yard** ਮੜੀਆਂ, ਕਬਰਸਤਾਨ

gravitate ('ਗਰੈਵ਼ਿਟੇਇਟ) *v* ਆਕਰਸ਼ਣ-ਕੇਂਦਰ ਵੱਲ ਖਿਚਣਾ, ਆਕਰਸ਼ਤ ਹੋਣਾ, ਥੱਲੇ ਵੱਲ ਝੁਕਣਾ

gravitation ('ਗਰੈਵ਼ਿ'ਟੇਇਸ਼ਨ) *n* ਗੁਰੂਤਾ ਖਿੱਚ, ਕੇਂਦਰੀ ਖਿੱਚ, ਖਿਚਾਉ, ਕਸ਼ਸ਼, ਆਕਰਸ਼ਣ ਸ਼ਕਤੀ; ~**al** ਗੁਰੂਤਾ ਖਿੱਚ ਸੰਬਧੀ, ਆਕਰਸ਼ਕ, ਕਸ਼ਸ਼ ਭਰਿਆ

gravity ('ਗਰੈਵ਼ਅਟੀ) *n* ਆਕਰਸ਼ਣ-ਸ਼ਕਤੀ, ਭੂਮੀ ਦੀ ਖਿੱਚ, ਗੁਰੂਤਾ; ਗੁਰੂਤਵ, ਭਾਰ, ਭਾਰਾਪਣ, ਗੰਭੀਰਤਾ; ਅਹਿਮੀਅਤ, ਸੰਜੀਦਗੀ

graze (ਗਰੇਇਜ਼) *n v* ਛਿੱਲਣਾ, ਛਿੱਲਿਆ ਜਾਣਾ; ਪਸ਼ੂਆਂ ਨੂੰ ਚਾਰਨਾ, ਘਾਹ ਚਾਰਨਾ

grazing ('ਗਰੇਇਜ਼ਿਙ) *n* ਚਰਾਈ, ਚਰਗਾਹ, ਚਰਾਂਦ; ਚਰਵਾਹਗੀਰੀ

grease (ਗਰੀਸ, ਗਰੀਜ਼) *n v* ਚਰਬੀ; ਸਨੇਹ; ਚਿਕਨਾਈ, ਗਾਰੀਜ਼ੀ ਚਰਬੀ ਲਾਉਣੀ; ਚੀਕਟਾ ਕਰਨਾ; ਗਰੀਜ਼ ਲਾਉਣੀ

great (ਗਰੇਇਟ) *n a* ਉੱਤਮ, ਮਹਾਨ, ਅਸਧਾਰਨ, ਤੇਜਵਾਨ, ਸ਼ਾਨਦਾਰ; ਪ੍ਰਮੁੱਖ;

ਅਸਧਾਰਨ; ਸੰਪੰਨ, ~**ness** ਮਹਾਨਤਾ, ਗੁਰੂਤਾ, ਗੌਰਵਤਾ, ਵਡਿਆਈ

greed (ਗਰੀਡ) *n* ਲੋਭ, ਲਾਲਚ, ਹਿਰਸ, ਤਮ੍ਹਾਂ; ~**y** ਲੋਭੀ, ਲਾਲਚੀ, ਹਿਰਸੀ, ਪੇਟੂ, ਭੁੱਖਾ

green (ਗਰੀਨ) *a n v* ਹਰਾ, ਸਾਵਾ, ਹਰਿਆ-ਭਰਿਆ, ਹਰਿਆਲਾ, ਸਬਜ਼, ਨਰਮ, ਮੁਲਾਇਮ; ਅਨਾੜੀ; ਜਿਉਂਦਾ ਜਾਗਦਾ, ਤਾਜ਼ਾ (ਜ਼ਖ਼ਮ ਲਈ), ਸਾਗ ਸਬਜ਼ੀ; ਘਾਹ ਦਾ ਮੈਦਾਨ; ਜੋਬਨ, ਉਤਪਾਦਨ-ਸ਼ਕਤੀ; ਹਰਾ ਹੋਣਾ, ਹਰਾ ਕਰਨਾ, ਹਰੇ ਰੰਗ ਵਿਚ ਰੰਗਣਾ, ਠੱਗਣਾ, ਲੁੱਟਣਾ; ~**eye** ਈਰਖਾ, ਸਾੜਾ, ਰਸ਼ਕ; ~**grocer** ਕੁੰਜੜਾ, ਸਬਜ਼ੀ ਵਾਲਾ; ~**horn** ਅਨਾੜੀ, ਅੱਲ੍ਹੜ; ~**room** ਨੇਪਥਸ਼ਾਲਾ, ਸ਼ਿੰਗਾਰ ਕਮਰਾ; ~**ery** ਹਰਿਆਲੀ, ਬਨਸਪਤੀ, ਸਬਜ਼ੀ, ਤਰਕਾਰੀ

greet (ਗਰੀਟ) *v* ਸੁਆਗਤ ਕਰਨਾ, ਜੈ ਜੈ ਕਾਰ ਕਰਨੀ, ਸ਼ਾਬਾਸ਼ ਦੇਣੀ; ਆਦਾਬ ਕਰਨਾ, ਪ੍ਰਣਾਮ ਕਰਨਾ, ਨਮਸਕਾਰ ਕਰਨਾ, ਸਲਾਮ ਕਰਨਾ; ~**ing** ਨਮਸਕਾਰ, ਪ੍ਰਣਾਮ, ਸੁਆਗਤ, ਹਰਸ਼ ਧੁਨੀ

grenade (ਗਰਅਾ'ਨੇਇਡ) *n* ਬਾਰੂਦ ਦਾ ਹੱਥ-ਗੋਲਾ; ਕੱਚ ਦਾ ਬੰਬ

grey, gray (ਗਰੇਇ) *n v a* ਸਲੇਟੀ; ਸਲੇਟੀ ਕਰਨਾ ਜਾਂ ਹੋਣਾ, ਮਿਟਿਆਲਾ, ਭੂਰਾ, ਸੁਆਹ ਰੰਗਾ, ਉਦਾਸ; ਬੁੱਢਾ ਹੁੰਦਾ ਹੋਇਆ; ਸਿਆਣਾ, ਪੁਰਾਣੇ ਜ਼ਮਾਨੇ ਦਾ; ~**hound** ਸ਼ਿਕਾਰੀ ਕੁੱਤਾ; ~**ness** ਭੂਰਾਪਣ, ਧੁੰਦਲਾਪਣ

grief (ਗਰੀਫ਼) *n* ਸੋਗ, ਗ਼ਮ, ਸ਼ੋਕ, ਅਫ਼ਸੋਸ, ਦੁੱਖ

grievance ('ਗਰੀਵ਼ੰਸ) *n* ਸ਼ਿਕਾਇਤ, ਗਿਲਾ, ਉਲਾਂਭਾ; ਔਕੜ, ਔਖਿਆਈ, ਥਿਪਤਾ

grieve (ਗਰੀਵ਼) *v* ਦੁੱਖ ਦੇਣਾ ਜਾਂ ਦੁਖੀ ਹੋਣਾ, ਦਿਲ ਦੁਖਾਉਣਾ ਜਾਂ ਦੁਖਣਾ, ਸੋਗ ਪਾਉਣਾ ਜਾਂ ਪੈਣਾ

grievous ('ਗਰੀਵ਼ਅਸ) *a* ਦੁਖਦਾਇਕ, ਸ਼ਖ਼ਤ,

ਘੋਰ, ਹਾਨੀਕਾਰਕ, ਦੁਸ਼ਟ; ਡਾਢਾ

grill (ਗਰਿਲ) *n v* ਮਾਸ ਭੁੰਨਣ ਲਈ ਸੀਖਦਾਰ ਚੁੱਲ੍ਹਾ; ਭੁੰਨਣਾ, ਕਬਾਬ ਕਰਨਾ; ਕਰੜੀ ਪੁੱਛ-ਗਿੱਛ ਕਰਨਾ

grim (ਗਰਿਮ) *a* ਨਿਰਦਈ, ਸਖ਼ਤ, ਕਰੜਾ, ਕਠੋਰ; ਡਰਾਉਣਾ, ਭਿਆਨਕ, ਦੁਖੀ, ਕਰੂਪ; **~y** ਮੈਲਾ, ਗੰਦਾ, ਕਾਲਖ ਨਾਲ ਭਰਿਆ

grind (ਗਰਾਇੰਡ) *v n* ਪੀਹਣਾ; ਚੱਬਣਾ; ਪਿਹਾਉਣਾ, ਸਾਣ ਚੜ੍ਹਾਉਣਾ; ਜ਼ੁਲਮ ਕਰਨਾ, ਸਤਾਉਣਾ; ਤਿੱਖਾ ਕਰਨਾ, ਤੇਜ਼ ਕਰਨਾ; ਚੱਕੀ ਪੀਹਣਾ; **~er** ਪੀਹਣ ਵਾਲਾ; ਪੀਹਣ ਦੀ ਮਸ਼ੀਨ, ਗਰਾਈਂਡਰ; ਸਾਣ ਦੀ ਮਸ਼ੀਨ; **~stone** ਸਾਣ, ਸਾਣ ਲਾਉਣ ਦਾ ਪੱਥਰ

grip (ਗਰਿਪ) *n v* ਪਕੜ, ਪੰਜਾ; ਕਬਜ਼ਾ, ਮੁਹਾਰਤ, ਦਸਤਾ, ਹੱਥਾ, ਮੁੱਠਾ; ਮਜ਼ਬੂਤੀ ਨਾਲ ਪਕੜਨਾ, ਡੂੰਘੀ ਪਕੜ ਰੱਖਣਾ, ਮੁੱਠੀ ਵਿਚ ਲੈਣਾ, ਜਕੜ ਕੇ ਫੜਨਾ

gripe (ਗਰਾਇਪ) *v n* ਕਸ ਕੇ ਫੜਨਾ, ਪੱਕਾ ਜਕੜਨਾ, ਦਬੋਚਣਾ; ਅੱਤਿਆਚਾਰ ਕਰਨਾ, ਤਕਲੀਫ਼ ਦੇਣੀ; ਕਸ਼ਟ ਦੇਣਾ; ਦਬਾਉਣਾ, ਮਰੋੜਨਾ; ਮਰੋੜ ਪੈਣਾ

groan (ਗਰਅਉਨ) *v n* ਕਰਾਹੁਣਾ, ਤੜਫਣਾ, ਤਾਂਘਣਾ, ਹਉਕਾ ਲੈਣਾ, ਆਹ ਭਰਨੀ, ਲਾਲਸਾ ਕਰਨੀ; ਅੰਦਰੋਂ ਦੁੱਖ ਹੋਣਾ; ਕਰਾਹ, ਚੀਸ, ਤੜਪ, ਹਉਕਾ, ਆਹ

grocer (ʹਗਰਅਉਸਅ*) *n* ਪੰਸਾਰੀ, ਕਰਿਆਨੇ ਵਾਲਾ, ਪਰਚੂਨੀਆ, ਹੱਟਵਾਣੀਆ; **~y** ਪੰਸਾਰੀ ਦੀ ਦੁਕਾਨ, ਕਰਿਆਨੇ ਦੀ ਹੱਟੀ, ਕਰਿਆਨੇ ਦਾ ਸਾਮਾਨ

groom (ਗਰੂਮ) *n v* ਲਾੜਾ, ਦੁਲ੍ਹਾ, ਵਰ; ਦਰੋਗਾ; ਘੋੜੇ ਦਾ ਸਾਈਸ; ਦਾਣਾ-ਘਾਹ ਪਾਉਣਾ,

ਦੇਖ-ਭਾਲ ਕਰਨੀ, ਸਾਂਈਸੀ ਕਰਨੀ

gross (ਗਰਅਉਸ) *n a* ਗੁਰਸ, ਬਾਰਾਂ ਦਰਜਨ, ਸੰਪੂਰਨ, ਭਰਿਆ, ਵਾਧੂ, ਅਤੀ ਅਧਿਕ; ਮੋਟਾ, ਫੁੱਲਿਆ; (ਗਲਤੀ ਆਦਿ) ਸਖ਼ਤ, ਭਾਰੀ; ਸਮੁੱਚਾ, ਕੁੱਲ, ਸਾਰਾ, ਸਮਸਤ; ਮੋਟਾ, ਭੱਦਾ, ਗੰਵਾਰ, ਅਸ਼ਲੀਲ, ਅਸ਼ਿਸ਼ਟ, ਗਲੀਜ਼; ਮੈਲਾ, ਖ਼ਰਾਬ (ਖਾਣਾ); ਸੁਸਤ

grotto (ʹਗਰੌਟਅਉ) *n* ਸੁੰਦਰ ਗੁੱਫਾ ਜਾਂ ਗ਼ਾਰ, ਸੁੰਦਰ ਦਿਸ਼ਾਂ ਵਾਲੀ ਕੰਦਰਾ

ground (ਗਰਾਉਂਡ) *n v* ਭੋਂ, ਜ਼ਮੀਨ, ਮੈਦਾਨ; ਧਰਤੀ, ਧਰਾਤਲ, ਤਲ, ਭੂਮੀ; ਨੀਂਹ, ਆਧਾਰ; ਨੀਂਹ ਰੱਖਣੀ; ਨੀਂਹ ਪੱਕੀ ਕਰਨੀ; ਜ਼ਮੀਨ ਉੱਤੇ ਉੱਤਰਨਾ; **~floor** ਹੇਠਲੀ ਮੰਜ਼ਲ; **~(s)man** ਕ੍ਰਿਕਟ ਦੇ ਮੈਦਾਨ ਦੀ ਦੇਖ-ਭਾਲ ਕਰਨ ਵਾਲਾ; **~nut** ਮੂੰਗਫਲੀ; **~ing** ਮੁਢਲੀ ਸਿੱਖਿਆ, ਬੁਨਿਆਦੀ ਤਾਲੀਮ

group (ਗਰੁਪ) *n v* ਸਮੂਹ ਝੁੰਡ, ਮੰਡਲੀ, ਟੋਲੀ, ਢਾਣੀ, ਸੰਸਥਾ, ਜਮਾਤ; ਜੱਥਾ, ਇਕੱਠ; ਇਕੱਤਰ ਕਰਨਾ ਜਾਂ ਹੋਣਾ, ਜਮ੍ਹਾਂ ਕਰਨਾ ਜਾਂ ਹੋਣਾ, ਵਰਗੀਕਰਨ ਕਰਨਾ; **~ing** ਵਰਗੀਕਰਨ, ਸਮੂਹਣ, ਸਮੂਹੀਕਰਨ, ਵਰਗਵੰਡ

grouse (ਗਰਾਉਸ) *v n* ਸ਼ਿਕਾਇਤ ਜਾਂ ਗਿਲਾ ਕਰਨਾ; ਸ਼ਿਕਾਇਤ, ਅਸੰਤੋਸ਼, ਗਿਲਾ

grove (ਗਰਅਉਵ) *n* ਦਰਖ਼ਤਾਂ ਦਾ ਸਮੂਹ, ਝਿੜੀ, ਝੰਜ, ਉਪਵਣ

grovel (ʹਗਰੌਵਲ) *v* ਰੀਂਗਣਾ, ਗੋਡੇ ਟੇਕਣਾ, ਗਿੜਗਿੜਾਉਣਾ

grow (ਗਰਅਉ) *v* ਉਗਣਾ; ਫੁੱਟਣਾ; ਉਪਜਾਉਣਾ; ਪੈਦਾ ਕਰਨਾ; ਵੱਡਾ ਹੋਣਾ; ਉਗਾਉਣਾ; **~er** ਕਿਸਾਨ, ਕਾਸ਼ਤਕਾਰ; **~ing** ਵੱਧਦਾ ਹੋਇਆ, ਵਰਧਮਾਨ, ਵਿਕਾਸਸ਼ੀਲ; **~th** ਜਨਮ,

ਉਤਪਤੀ; ਫ਼ਸਲ; ਤਰੱਕੀ, ਵਿਕਾਸ, ਵਾਧਾ, ਖੇਤੀ, ਕਾਸ਼ਤ, ਉਪਜ

growl (ਗਰਾਉਲ) *n v* ਬੁੜਬੁੜਾਹਟ, ਗੜਗੜਾਹਟ; ਗਿਲਾ, ਸ਼ਿਕਾਇਤ; ਬੁੜਬੁੜਾਉਣਾ, ਸ਼ਿਕਾਇਤ ਕਰਨੀ, ਗਿਲਾ ਕਰਨਾ; **~er** ਗਰਜਨ ਵਾਲਾ; ਬੁੜਬੁੜਾਉਣ ਵਾਲਾ; ਚੁਪਹੀਆ ਗੱਡੀ

grub (ਗਰਅੱਬ) *v n* ਉਖਾੜਨਾ, (ਜੜ੍ਹ ਆਦਿ ਭੂਮੀ ਤੋਂ) ਬਾਹਰ ਕੱਢਣਾ; ਭਾਲਣਾ, ਛਾਣਬੀਣ ਕਰਨੀ, ਖੋਜਣਾ, ਕਿਰਾਏ ਦਾ ਘੋੜਾ ਜਾਂ ਟੱਟੂ; (ਪ੍ਰਚਲਤ) ਭੋਜਨ, ਦਾਣਾ; ਮਜ਼ਦੂਰ, ਬੌਣਾ

grudge (ਗਰਅੱਜ) *v n* (ਕੋਈ ਚੀਜ਼ ਦੇਣ ਤੋਂ) ਸੰਕੋਚ ਕਰਨਾ, ਮੰਗਣਾ, ਖਾਰ ਖਾਣੀ, ਖੁਣਸ ਖਾਣਾ; ਰੰਜਕ, ਲਾਗ, ਵੈਰ-ਭਾਵ

gruesome (ਗਰੂਸਅਮ) *a* ਭਿਆਨਕ, ਭੀਸ਼ਣ, ਡਰਾਉਣਾ; ਬਹੁਤ ਬੁਰਾ

grumble (ਗਰਅੰਬਲ) *n v* ਬੁੜ ਬੁੜ; ਚਿੜ ਚਿੜ; ਗਿਲਾ, ਸ਼ਿਕਾਇਤ, ਸ਼ਿਕਵਾ; ਬੁੜ-ਬੁੜਾਉਣਾ; ਚਿੜਚੜਾਉਣਾ, ਚਿੜਨਾ

guarantee (ਗੈਰਅੰਟੀ) *n v* ਜ਼ਾਮਨ, ਜ਼ੁੰਮੇਵਾਰ; ਜ਼ਮਾਨਤ, ਗਾਰੰਟੀ; ਜ਼ਾਮਨ ਹੋਣਾ, ਜ਼ੁੰਮੇਵਾਰੀ ਲੈਣਾ, ਗਾਰੰਟੀ ਦੇਣਾ

guarantor (ਗੈਰਅੰਟੇ*) *n* ਜ਼ਾਮਨ, ਜ਼ੁੰਮੇਵਾਰ, ਗਾਰੰਟੀ ਦੇਣ ਵਾਲਾ

guaranty (ਗੈਰਅੰਟਿ) *n* ਜ਼ਮਾਨਤ, ਜ਼ਮਾਨਤਨਾਮਾ, ਜ਼ਾਮਨੀ

guard (ਗਾਡ) *n v* ਚੌਕੀਦਾਰ, ਪਹਿਰੇਦਾਰ, ਸੰਤਰੀ, ਰੁਕਾਵਟ, ਕਟਹਿਰਾ, ਰੇਲ ਦਾ ਗਾਰਡ; ਸਾਵਧਾਨੀ, ਚੌਕਸੀ, ਖ਼ਬਰਦਾਰੀ, ਪਹਿਰੇਦਾਰੀ; ਚੌਕੀਦਾਰੀ ਕਰਨਾ, ਰਖਵਾਲੀ ਕਰਨੀ, ਨਿਗਰਾਨੀ ਰੱਖਣੀ, ਸਾਵਧਾਨੀ ਵਰਤਣੀ; **~ed** ਸੁਰੱਖਿਅਤ,

ਸਚੇਤ, ਸਾਵਧਾਨ, ਚੁਕੰਨਾ

guardian ('ਗਾਡਯਅਨ) *n* ਰੱਖਿਅਕ, ਰਖਵਾਲਾ; ਵਾਲੀ, ਸਰਬਰਾਹ, ਸਰਪਰਸਤ, ਗਾਰਡੀਅਨ

guava ('ਗਵਾਵ਼ਅ) *n* ਅਮਰੂਦ (ਫਲ ਜਾਂ ਦਰਖਤ)

guess (ਗੈੱਸ) *v n* ਅਨੁਮਾਨ ਲਾਉਣਾ; ਅੰਦਾਜ਼ਾ ਲਾਉਣਾ; ਅੱਟਾ-ਸੱਟਾ ਲਾਉਣਾ; ਰਾਇ ਕਾਇਮ ਕਰਨਾ, ਖ਼ਿਆਲ ਕਰਨਾ; ਤਾੜਨਾ; **~work** ਅਟਕਲ-ਪੱਚੂ, ਅਨੁਮਾਨ ਉੱਤੇ ਆਧਾਰਤ ਕਾਰਵਾਈ

guest (ਗੈੱਸਟ) *n* ਪਰਾਹੁਣਾ, ਮਹਿਮਾਨ, ਅਤਿਥੀ; **~house** ਨਿਵਾਸ-ਸਥਾਨ, ਮਹਿਮਾਨਖ਼ਾਨਾ

guidance ('ਗਾਇਡੰਸ) *n* ਅਗਵਾਈ, ਅਗਵਾਨੀ, ਰਾਹ-ਦਿਖਾਈ, ਮਾਰਗ-ਦਰਸ਼ਨ, ਨਿਰਦੇਸ਼, ਰਹਿ-ਨੁਮਾਈ, ਰਾਹਬਰੀ

guile (ਗਾਇਲ) *n* ਧੋਖਾ, ਛਲ, ਫ਼ਰੇਬ, ਚਲਾਕੀ, ਮੱਕਾਰੀ; **~ful** ਕਪਟੀ, ਮੱਕਾਰ, ਦਗਾਬਾਜ਼

guillotine ('ਗਿਲ਼ਅ'ਟੀਨ) *n v* ਫਾਂਸੀ ਦੇਣ ਦਾ ਇਕ ਜੰਤਰ, ਸਿਰ-ਕੱਟ ਟੇਕਾ, (ਡਾਕਟਰੀ) ਚੀਰਫਾੜ ਦਾ ਜੰਤਰ

guilt (ਗਿਲਟ) *n* ਦੋਸ਼, ਅਪਰਾਧ, ਕਸੂਰ, ਗੁਨਾਹ, ਖ਼ਤਾ, ਜੁਰਮ; **~less** ਨਿਰਦੋਸ਼, ਬੇਗੁਨਾਹ, ਮਾਸੂਮ, ਨਿਰਅਪਰਾਧ; **~y** ਪਾਪੀ, ਦੋਸ਼ੀ, ਅਪਰਾਧੀ, ਮੁਜਰਮ, ਖ਼ਤਾਵਾਰ, ਗੁਨਹਗਾਰ, ਕਸੂਰਵਾਰ

guinea ('ਗਿਨਿ) *n* (ਇਤਿ) ਇਕ ਸੋਨੇ ਦਾ ਸਿੱਕਾ, ਅਸ਼ਰਫ਼ੀ

guise (ਗਾਇਜ਼) *n* (ਪ੍ਰਾ) ਲਿਬਾਸ, ਪੁਸ਼ਾਕ, ਭੇਸ, ਰੂਪ; ਬਾਹਰੀ ਰੂਪ, ਬਾਹਰੀ ਦਸ਼ਾ; ਸਾਂਗ

gulf (ਗਅੱਲਫ਼) *n v* ਖਾੜੀ, ਡੂੰਘੀ ਖੱਡ; ਪਾੜਾ, ਭੰਵਰ; ਗਰਦਾਬ; ਸਮੁੰਦਰ, ਸਾਗਰ

gulp (ਗਅੱਲਪ) *v n* ਨਿਗਲਣਾ, ਹੜਪ ਕਰ ਜਾਣਾ, ਦਮ ਘੁੱਟਣਾ; ਨਿਗਲਣਾ, ਡੀਕ, ਸੁੜ੍ਹਾਕਾ

gum (ਗਅੱਮ) *n v* (1) ਮਸੂੜਾ, ਬੁੱਟ (2) ਗੂੰਦ,

ਰੀਤੁ, ਸਰੇਸ਼; ਚੋਟਾ; ਚਿਪਕਾਉਣਾ, ਰੇਪਣਾ, ਜੋੜਨਾ; ਗੁੰਦ ਨਾਲ ਪੱਕਾ ਕਰਨ; ~my ਲੇਸਲਾ, ਚਿਪਚਪਾ, ਗੁੰਦ ਵਾਲਾ, ਸੁੱਜਿਆ, ਫੁੱਲਿਆ

gun (ਗਅੱਨ) *n* ਬੰਦੂਕ, ਤੋਪ; ਰਾਈਫਲ, ਤੁਫੰਗ; **~man** ਸ਼ਸਤਰਧਾਰੀ ਡਾਕੂ; ਅਰਦਲੀ; ਬੰਦੂਕਚੀ; **~powder** ਬਾਰੂਦ, ਦਾਰੂ-ਸਿੱਕਾ; **~ner** ਬੰਦੂਕਚੀ, ਤੋਪਚੀ, ਗੋਲਾਂਦਾਜ਼

gunny ('ਗਅੱਨਿ) *n* ਟਾਟ ਦਾ ਥੈਲਾ, ਬੋਰਾ, ਬੋਰੀ, ਗੁਣ

gurgle ('ਗਅਃਗਲ) *n v* ਗਰਾਰੇ, ਗੁੜਗੁੜ੍ਹਾਉਣਾ; ਗੁੜ ਗੁੜ ਕਰਨਾ

gush (ਗਅੱਸ਼) *n v* ਉਮਾਹ; ਜੋਸ਼, ਭਾਵ-ਵੇਗ; ਉੱਛਲਣਾ, ਫੁੱਟ ਨਿਕਲਣਾ, ਉਛਾਲਣਾ, ਫ਼ੁਹਾਰਾ ਬਣਾਉਣਾ

gust (ਗਅੱਸਟ) *n* (1) (ਹਵਾ, ਧੂੰਆਂ) ਜ਼ੋਰ ਦਾ ਝੋਂਕਾ, ਝੱਖੜ, ਪ੍ਰਬਲ ਆਵੇਗਾ, ਜੋਸ਼, ਉਮੰਗ; (ਸਧਾਰਨ) ਜੋਸ਼, ਜ਼ੋਰ, ਝਪਟ (2) ਸੌਂਦਰਯ-ਬੋਧ, ਲੱਜ਼ਤ, ਸੁਗੰਧ; **~y** ਜੰਸ਼ੀਲਾ

gut (ਗਅੱਟ) *n v* ਆਂਦਰਾਂ, ਅੰਤੜੀਆਂ; ਮਿਹਦੇ ਦੀ ਨਾਲੀ, (ਬ ਵ) ਮਿਹਦਾ; ਤੰਦਾਂ; ਤੰਗ ਰਸਤਾ, ਖਾਈ; ਨਦੀ ਦਾ ਮੋੜ; ਪਾਣੀ ਦੀ ਤੰਗ ਨਾਲੀ; ਜਾਨ, ਹਿੰਮਤ, ਹੀਆ; ਆਂਦਰਾਂ ਕੱਢ ਕੇ ਸਾਫ਼ ਕਰਨਾ (ਮੱਛੀ); ਲਾਲਚ ਨਾਲ ਖਾਣਾ, ਹੜੱਪਣਾ; (ਪੁਸਤਕ ਆਦਿ ਦਾ) ਸਾਰ ਭਾਵ ਜਾਂ ਤੱਤ ਕੱਢ ਲੈਣਾ; (ਸਾਮਾਨ) ਲੁੱਟ ਲੈ ਜਾਣਾ, ਨਸ਼ਟ ਕਰ ਦੇਣਾ

guy (ਗਾਇ) *n v* (1) ਜਹਾਜ਼ ਦਾ ਰੱਸਾ (2) ਹਊਆ; (3) ਬੰਦਾ, ਜਣਾ, ਸਾਥੀ; ਠੱਠਾ ਕਰਨਾ, ਮਜ਼ਾਕ ਉਡਾਉਣਾ, ਖਿਸਕ ਜਾਣਾ, ਪੁਤਲਾ ਬਣਾਉਣਾ

gymnast (ਜਿਮਨੈਸਟ) *n* ਕਸਰਤੀ, ਜਿਮਨਾਸਟਿਕ ਦਾ ਮਾਹਰ, ਵਰਜ਼ਸ਼ ਦਾ ਮਾਹਰ

gynaecology (ਗਾਇਨਅ'ਕੋਲਅਜਿ) *n* ਨਾਰੀ-ਰੋਗ-ਵਿਗਿਆਨ

gyve (ਜਾਇਵ) *n v* ਰੁਕਾਵਟ, ਬਾਧਾ; ਹੱਥਕੜੀ, ਬੇੜੀ, ਜੰਜੀਰ; ਰੁਕਾਵਟ ਪਾਉਣੀ, ਮੁਸ਼ਕਾਂ ਕੱਸਣਾ

H

H, h (ਏਇਚ) *n* ਰੋਮਨ ਵਰਣਮਾਲਾ ਦਾ ਅੱਠਵਾਂ ਅੱਖਰ

ha (ਹਾ) *int* ਓਹ, ਓਹੋ, ਹਾਏ

habeas corpus (ਹੇਇਬਯਅਸ 'ਕੋਪਅਸ) *n* (ਕਾ) ਦੋਸ਼ੀ ਨੂੰ ਅਦਾਲਤ ਦੇ ਸਾਮ੍ਹਣੇ ਪੇਸ਼ ਕਰਨ ਦਾ ਲਿਖਤੀ ਆਦੇਸ਼, ਜਿਸਮਾਨੀ ਹਾਜ਼ਰੀ

haberdasher (ਹੈਬਅਡੈਸ਼ਅ*) *n* ਮਨਿਆਰ, ਬਸਾਤੀ, ਕਰਿਆਨੇ ਦਾ ਦੁਕਾਨਦਾਰ, ਫੁਟਕਲ ਮਾਲ ਵੇਚਣ ਵਾਲਾ

habit ('ਹੈਬਿਟ) *n* ਆਦਤ, ਇੱਲਤ, ਸੁਭਾਅ, ਵਿਹਾਰ, ਚਾਲ-ਢਾਲ, ਢੰਗ; ਰਹਿਣਾ, ਵਸੇਬਾ ਕਰਨਾ, ਗਿੱਝਣਾ; **~ability** ਵਾਸਯੋਗਤਾ, ਰਿਹਾਇਸ਼ਯੋਗਤਾ;ਚਚ **~able** ਵਸੋਂ ਅਨੁਕੂਲ, ਰਹਿਣ ਯੋਗ; **~ual** ਪ੍ਰਚਲਤ, ਸੁਭਾਵਕ, ਵਿਹਾਰਕ; ਅਭਿਆਸੀ, ਆਦੀ; ਪੁਰਾਣਾ; **~uate** ਗਿਝਾਉਣਾ, ਆਦਤ ਬਣਾਉਣਾ, ਸਿਖਾਉਣਾ; **~uation** ਵਾਦੀ, ਗੇਝ, ਆਦੀ ਹੋਣ; **~ude** ਰੀਤ, ਗੇਝ, ਰਿਵਾਜ, ਸੁਭਾਅ, ਸ਼ਰੀਰਕ ਜਾਂ ਮਾਨਸਕ ਬਣਤਰ

hackney ('ਹੈਕਨਿ) *n v* ਟੱਟੂ, ਭਾੜੇ ਦਾ ਟੱਟੂ; ਮਜ਼ਦੂਰ; ਕਿਰਾਏ ਉੱਤੇ ਦੇਣਾ, ਆਮ ਕਰ ਦੇਣਾ; **~ed** ਜ਼ੀਰਣ, ਜਰਜਰ, ਸਿਥਲ; ਸਧਾਰਨ; ਭਾੜੇ ਦਾ; ਬਜ਼ਾਰੀ, ਚਾਲੂ, ਘਸਿਆ ਪਿਟਿਆ

haemoglobin (ਹੀਮਅ(ਉ)'ਗਲਅਉਬਿਨ) *n* ਰਕਤਾਣੂ

haemorrhage, hemorrhage ('ਹੈੱਮਅਰਿਜ) *n* ਰਕਤ-ਪਰਵਾਹ

hag (ਹੈਗ) *n* ਬੁੱਢੜੀ, ਕਰੂਪ ਬੁੱਢੀ ਤੀਵੀਂ, ਚੁੜੇਲ, ਭੂਤਨੀ

haggard ('ਹੈਗਅਡ) *a n* ਮਾੜੂਆ; ਮੰਦੇ ਹਾਲ, ਥੱਕਿਆ-ਹਾਰਿਆ; ਚਿਹਰਾ ਝੱਵਿਆ; ਜੰਗਲੀ ਬਾਜ਼

haggle ('ਹੈਗਲ) *v n* (ਮੁੱਲ ਕਰਦਿਆਂ) ਝੇੜਾ ਪਾਉਣਾ, ਝਗੜਨਾ, ਮੁੱਲ ਕਰਨਾ; ਝਗੜਾ

hail (ਹੇਇਲ) *n v* (1) ਗੜਾ, ਵਾਛੜ; ਗਾਲ੍ਹਾਂ; ਗੜੇ ਪੈਣੇ, ਸਵਾਲਾਂ ਆਦਿ ਦੀ ਵਾਛੜ ਕਰਨੀ (2) ਨਮਸਕਾਰ, ਸ਼ਾਬਾਸ਼, ਧੰਨ ਧੰਨ; ਸ਼ਾਬਾਸ਼ ਦੇਣਾ, ਬੱਲੇ ਬੱਲੇ ਕਹਿਣਾ, ਸੁਆਗਤ ਕਰਨਾ, ਜੀਉ ਆਇਆਂ, ਆਖਣਾ; **~storm** ਗੜਿਆਂ ਦਾ ਤੂਫ਼ਾਨ

hair (ਹੇਅ*) *n* ਵਾਲ, ਕੇਸ, ਲੂੰ, ਰੋਮ; ਜੱਤ, ਉੱਨ, ਪਸ਼ਮ; **~breadth** ਵਾਲ ਭਰ, ਜ਼ਰਾ ਜਿੰਨਾ, ਬਿਲਕੁਲ ਮਾਮੂਲੀ ਫ਼ਾਸਲਾ; **~raising** ਰੋਮਾਂਚਕਾਰੀ; **~less** ਗੰਜਾ, ਰੋਡਾ, ਘੋਨਾ, ਵਾਲਰਹਿਤ; **~y** ਵਾਲਦਾਰ, ਸੰਘਣੇ ਵਾਲ

hale (ਹੇਲ) *a v* ਤੰਦਰੁਸਤ, ਨਿਰੋਗ, ਤਕੜਾ, ਰਿਸ਼ਟ-ਪੁਸ਼ਟ, ਮੋਟਾ-ਤਾਜ਼ਾ; ਬਦੋਬਦੀ ਘਸੀਟਣਾ; **~and hearty** ਰਾਜ਼ੀ-ਬਾਜ਼ੀ, ਤੰਦਰੁਸਤ, ਤਕੜਾ; **~ness** ਰਿਸ਼ਟ-ਪੁਸ਼ਟਤਾ, ਤੰਦਰੁਸਤੀ, ਹੱਟਾ-ਕੱਟਾਪਣ

half (ਹਾਫ਼) *n a adv* ਅੱਧ,.ਅੱਧਾ; ਛਿਮਾਹੀ; **~ and ~** ਅੱਧੋ-ਅੱਧ, ਅੱਧਾ-ਅੱਧਾ, ਬਰਾਬਰ-ਬਰਾਬਰ, ਇਕੋ ਜਿਹਾ; **~baked** ਅੱਧ-ਪੱਕਾ ਅੱਧ-ਕੱਚਾ; **~brother, ~sister** ਮਤਰੇਇਆ ਭਰਾ, ਭੈਣ; **~hearted** ਬੇਦਿਲਾ, ਉਤਸ਼ਾਹਹੀਣ; **~mast** ਅੱਧੀ ਉਚਾਈ ਤੋਂ, ਸੋਗ ਵਜੋਂ ਝੰਡੇ ਦਾ ਝੁਕਾਓ; **~witted** ਮੂਰਖ, ਵਲੱਲਾ, ਬੁੱਧੂ, ਭੋਂਦੂ, ਸ਼ੁਦਾਈ; **better~** ਘਰ ਵਾਲੀ, ਇਸਤਰੀ, ਤੀਵੀਂ, ਵਹੁਟੀ

hall (ਹੌਲ) *n* ਵੱਡਾ ਕਮਰਾ, ਹਾਲ; ਵੱਡਾ ਮਕਾਨ,

ਦੀਵਾਨਖ਼ਾਨਾ, ਮਹੱਲ; ਸਭਾ ਭਵਨ; ~mark ਪ੍ਰਮਾਣਕਤਾ ਦਾ ਚਿੰਨ੍ਹ

hallo (ਹਾ'ਲਅਉ) *int* *v* ਸੰਬੋਧਨ ਕਰਨ ਲਈ ਜਾਂ ਹੈਰਾਨੀ ਪਰਗਟ ਕਰਨ ਲਈ ਬੋਲਿਆ ਜਾਣ ਵਾਲਾ ਸ਼ਬਦ, ਹੇ, ਜੀ, ਓ, ਹੋ; ਹਾਕ ਮਾਰਨਾ, ਬੁਲਾਉਣਾ, ਪੁਕਾਰਨਾ; ਕੁੱਤੇ ਨੂੰ ਤੂ-ਤੂ ਕਰਨਾ, ਲਲਕਾਰਨਾ; ਵਾਵੇਲਾ ਮਚਾਣਾ, ਸ਼ੋਰ ਪਾਉਣਾ

hallow (ਹੈਲਅਉ) *n* *v* ਸੰਤ, ਸਾਧੂ, ਮਹਾਤਮਾ; (1) ਪੂਜਣਾ, ਪਵਿੱਤਰ ਕਰਨਾ; (2) ਉਤੇਜਤ ਕਰਨਾ, ਲਲਕਾਰਦੇ ਹੋਏ ਪਿੱਛਾ ਕਰਨਾ

hallucinate (ਹਅ'ਲੂਸਿਨੇਇਟ) *v* ਉਲਟੇ ਰਾਹ ਪੈਣਾ, ਭਰਾਂਤੀ ਜਾਂ ਛਾਇਆ ਪੈਣੀ

hallucination (ਹਅ'ਲੂਸਿ'ਨੇਇਸ਼ਨ) *n* ਅੱਖਾਂ ਦਾ ਧੋਖਾ, ਵਹਿਮ, ਮਨੋਭਰਾਂਤੀ

halo ('ਹੇਇਲਅਉ) *n* *v* ਪ੍ਰਭਾ-ਮੰਡਲ, ਪ੍ਰਕਾਸ਼-ਕੁੰਡਲ, ਪਰਵਾਰ, ਹਾਲਾ; ਚਾਨਣ ਦਾ ਘੇਰਾ ਪਾਉਣਾ, ਵਡਿਆਈ ਦੇਣੀ, ਜਸ ਕਰਨਾ

halt (ਹੋਲਟ) *n* *v* *a* ਠਹਿਰ, ਡੇਰਾ, ਮੁਕਾਮ, ਮੰਜ਼ਲ; ਰੋਕ, ਠਹਿਰਾਉ, ਰੁਕਣਾ, ਅਟਕਣਾ, ਠਹਿਰਨਾ, ਕੰਮ ਬੰਦ ਕਰਨਾ, ਪੜਾਉ ਕਰਨਾ; ~ing ਲੰਗੜਾਪਣ, ਵਿਰਾਮ, ਠਹਿਰਾ; ~ingly ਰੁਕ ਰੁਕ ਕੇ

halve (ਹਾਵ੍) *v* ਅੱਧੋ-ਅੱਧ ਕਰਨਾ; ਦੋ ਟੋਟੇ ਕਰਨਾ, ਬਰਾਬਰ ਦਾ ਸਾਂਝੀਵਾਲ ਹੋਣਾ

hamburgh ('ਹੈਮਬਅ:ਗ) *n* ਕਾਲਾ ਅੰਗੂਰ, ਅੰਗੂਰ ਦੀ ਇਕ ਪ੍ਰਕਾਰ; ਇਕ ਵਿਸ਼ੇਸ਼ ਨਸਲ ਦਾ ਕੁੱਕੜ; ਗਾਂ ਦੇ ਮਾਸ ਦਾ ਕੀਮਾ; ~er ਇਕ ਖਾਧ ਪਦਾਰਥ

hamlet ('ਹੈਮਲਿਟ) *n* ਛੋਟਾ ਪਿੰਡ, ਪਿੰਡੋਰੀ

hammer ('ਹੈਮਅ*) *n* *v* ਹਥੌੜਾ; ਮੁੰਗਲੀ; ਨੀਲਾਮੀ ਵੇਲੇ ਖ਼ਰੀਦਾਲ ਉੱਤੇ ਮਾਰੀ ਜਾਣ ਵਾਲੀ ਮੁੰਗਲੀ, ਹਥੌੜਾ ਮਾਰਨਾ; ਠੋਕਣਾ, ਗੋਡਣਾ

hamper (ਹੈਂਪਅ*) *n* *v* (1) ਛਾਬਾ (2) ਰੁਕਾਵਟ,

ਰੋਕ, ਪ੍ਰਤੀਬੰਧ; (3) ਜਹਾਜ਼ ਦਾ ਭਾਰਾ ਸਾਮਾਨ, ਰੁਕਾਵਟ ਪਾਉਣੀ, ਅੜਿੱਕਾ ਡਾਹੁਣਾ, ਰੋਕਣਾ

hand (ਹੈਂਡ) *n* *v* ਹੱਥ, ਦਸਤ; ਪਸ਼ੂਆਂ ਦਾ ਅਗਲਾ ਪੈਰ; ਲਿਖਾਈ, ਦਸਤਖ਼ਤ; ਸੂਈ; ਪ੍ਰਭਾਵ, ਸੱਤਾ, ਪਾਸਾ, ਦਿਸ਼ਾ; ਹੱਥ ਦੇਣਾ, ਸੌਂਪਣਾ, ਦੇ ਦੇਣਾ; ਵਿਰਾਸਤ ਦੇ ਰੂਪ ਵਿਚ ਦੇ ਦੇਣਾ; ਬਖ਼ਸ਼ ਦੇਣਾ; ~and foot ਪੂਰੀ ਤਰ੍ਹਾਂ, ਪੱਕਾ ਕਰਕੇ (ਬੰਨ੍ਹਣਾ); ~bill ਇਸ਼ਤਿਹਾਰ, ਪਰਚਾ, ਦੁਪੱਤਰੀ; ~book ਕਿਤਾਬਛੀ, ਛੋਟੀ ਜਿਹੀ ਕਿਤਾਬ; ~cuff ਹੱਥਕੜੀ; ਹੱਥਕੜੀ ਲਾਉਣੀ; ~ in ~ ਇਕ ਦੂਜੇ ਦਾ ਹੱਥ ਫੜੀ, ਹੱਥ ਵਿਚ ਹੱਥ ਪਾਈ; ~shake ਹੱਥ ਮਿਲਾਉਣਾ; ~s up ਵਿਰੋਧੀ ਨੂੰ ਹਥਿਆਰ ਸੁੱਟਣ ਜਾਂ ਹੱਥ ਖੜੇ ਕਰਨ ਦਾ ਹੁਕਮ; ~ to ~ ਹੱਥੋ-ਹੱਥੀ, ਹੱਥੋ-ਹੱਥ, ਆਮ੍ਹੋ-ਸਾਮ੍ਹਣੇ; ~writing ਲਿਖਤ, ਹੱਥ ਦੀ ਲਿਖਾਈ; ਲਿਖਤ ਦਾ ਢੰਗ; ~ful ਬੁੱਕ ਭਰ, ਰੁੱਗ ਭਰ, ਮੁੱਠ ਭਰ; ਬਹੁਤ ਥੋੜੇ, ਥੋੜ੍ਹੀ ਗਿਣਤੀ; ਔਖਾ ਕੰਮ

handicap (ਹੈਂਡਿਕੈਪ) *n* *v* ਅਪੰਗਤਾ; ਸੀਮਾ ਕਮਜ਼ੋਰੀ, ਅੜਚਣ, ਪਾਬੰਦੀ ਲਾਉਣੀ, ਅਸੁਵਿਧਾ ਕੋਈ ਰੁਕਾਵਟ ਜਾਂ ਪ੍ਰਤੀਬੰਧ ਲਾਉਣਾ

handicraft ('ਹੈਂਡਿਕਰਾਫ਼ਟ) *n* ਦਸਤਕਾਰੀ, ਹੱਥ-ਸ਼ਿਲਪ, ਕਾਰੀਗਰੀ; ਹੁਨਰ-ਸ਼ਿਲਪ-ਵਿੱਦਿਆ

handiwork ('ਹੈਂਡਿ,ਵਅਃਕ) *n* ਦਸਤਕਾਰੀ, ਹੱਥ-ਸ਼ਿਲਪ, ਹੱਥ ਦਾ ਪੰਧਾ

handkerchief ('ਹੈਙਕਅਚਿਫ਼) *n* ਰੁਮਾਲ

handle ('ਹੈਂਡਲ) *n* *v* ਹੱਥਾ, ਦਸਤਾ; ਮੁੱਠਾ, ਕਬਜ਼ਾ; ਸੰਭਾਲਣਾ, ਪ੍ਰਬੰਧ ਕਰਨਾ, ਚਲਾਉਣਾ, ਨਿਭਾਉਣਾ

handsome ('ਹੈਨਸਅਮ) *a* ਸੋਹਣਾ, ਸੁਨੱਖਾ, ਰੂਪਵਾਨ, ਸੁੰਦਰ, ਖ਼ੁਬਸੂਰਤ; ਚੋਖਾ, ਚੰਗਾ; ~ness ਸੁੰਦਰਤਾ, ਖ਼ੁਬਸੂਰਤੀ, ਉਦਾਰਤਾ

hang (ਹੈਙ) *n* *v* ਲਟਕਣ; ਢਾਲ, ਝੁਕਾਉ, ਲਮਕਾਉ,

ਲਟਕਾਉ; ਗ੍ਰਹਿਣ ਕਰਨ ਦਾ ਭਾਵ, ਟੰਗਣਾ,
ਲਮਕਾਉਣਾ; ~man ਜੱਲਾਦ

hanky ('ਹੈਂਕਿ) *n* ਰੁਮਾਲ

hap (ਹੈਪ) *n v* ਸੰਜੋਗ, ਢੋਅ ਅਵਸਰ ਹੋਣਾ, ਅਚਾਨਕ
ਹੋ ਜਾਣਾ, ਇਤਫਾਕੀਆ ਹੋਣਾ, ਢੋਅ-ਢੁੱਕਣਾ;
~hazard ਸੰਜੋਗਮਾਤਰ, ਇਤਫਾਕ, ਸੰਜੋਗੀ,
ਇਤਫਾਕੀਆ, ਅਵਿਵਸਥਿਤ, ਉਲਜਲੂਲ

happen ('ਹੈਪ(ਅ)ਨ) *v* ਹੋਣਾ, ਵਾਪਰਨਾ, ਘਟਣਾ,
ਪੇਸ਼ ਆਉਣਾ, ਸਾਮ੍ਹਣੇ ਆਉਣਾ, ਵਰਤਣਾ; ~ed
ਘਟਿਤ, ਬੀਤਿਆ, ਵਾਪਰਿਆ; ~ing ਘਟਣਾ,
ਵਾਰਦਾਤ

happiness ('ਹੈਪਿਨਿਸ) *n* ਖ਼ੁਸ਼ਹਾਲੀ, ਸਮਰਿਧੀ,
ਖ਼ੁਸ਼ੀ, ਪ੍ਰਸੰਨਤਾ, ਸੁਖ, ਆਨੰਦ, ਚੈਨ

happy ('ਹੈਪਿ) *a* ਪ੍ਰਸੰਨ, ਖ਼ੁਸ਼, ਆਨੰਦ; ਸੁਖੀ,
ਰਾਜ਼ੀਬਾਜ਼ੀ

harass ('ਹੈਰਅਸ) *v* ਤੰਗ ਕਰਨਾ, ਦਿਕ ਕਰਨਾ,
ਜ਼ਿਚ ਕਰਨਾ, ਸਤਾਉਣਾ, ਦੁੱਖ ਦੇਣਾ; ~ment
ਪਰੇਸ਼ਾਨੀ, ਕਲੇਸ਼, ਤਕਲੀਫ਼

harbour ('ਹਾਬਅ*) *n v* ਬੰਦਰਗਾਹ, ਗੋਦੀ;
ਆਸਰਾ, ਸਹਾਰਾ, ਆਸਰਾ ਦੇਣਾ, ਪਨਾਹ ਦੇਣੀ;
ਥਾਂ ਦੇਣੀ; ਬੰਦਰਗਾਹ ਵਿਚ ਰੁਕਣਾ, ਲੰਗਰ ਸੁੱਟਣਾ

hard (ਹਾ*ਡ) *a* ਕਰੜਾ, ਸਖ਼ਤ, ਪੱਕਾ, ਠੋਸ, ਪੀੜਾ;
ਔਖਾ, ਕਠਨ, ਮੁਸ਼ਕਲ; ਨਿਰਦਈ; ਠੋਰ, ਸਖ਼ਤ;
~bitten ਹਠੀਲਾ, ਹਠੀ, ਘੁਲਾਟੀਆ;
~headed ਅਭਾਵੁਕ; ਕਿਰਿਆਸ਼ੀਲ, ਮਿਹਨਤੀ;
~hearted ਸਖ਼ਤ ਦਿਲ, ਨਿਰਦਈ, ਬੇਰਹਿਮ;
~labour ਮੁਸ਼ੱਕਤ, ਸਖ਼ਤ ਮਿਹਨਤ ~of hearing ਬੋਲਾ, ਜਿਸ ਨੂੰ ਉੱਚਾ ਸੁਣਦਾ ਹੋਵੇ; ~times
ਔਖੇ ਦਿਨ, ਬੇਰੁਜ਼ਗਾਰੀ ਦਾ ਸਮਾਂ; ~up (ਪੈਸੇ ਦੀ)
ਤੰਗੀ, ਔਖ; ~en ਸਖ਼ਤ ਕਰਨਾ, ਕਠੋਰ ਕਰਨਾ,
ਦ੍ਰਿੜ ਕਰਨਾ, ਪੱਕਾ ਕਰਨਾ; ~ened ਦ੍ਰਿੜ, ਪੱਕਾ,

ਕਠੋਰ, ਸਖ਼ਤ; ~lines ਮੰਦਭਾਗੀ, ਬਦਕਿਸਮਤੀ;
~ly ਮਸਾਂ, ਮਸਾਂ ਜਿਹੇ, ਸ਼ਾਇਦ ਹੀ; ~ness
ਕਠੋਰਤਾ, ਕਰੜਾਈ; ~ship ਤੰਗੀ, ਔਖਿਆਈ;
ਮੁਸੀਬਤ, ਬਿਪਤਾ; ਕਸ਼ਟ; ~ware ਧਾਤ ਦਾ
ਸਾਮਾਨ; ਹਥਿਆਰ; ਕੰਪਿਊਟਰ ਦੀ ਮਸ਼ੀਨਰੀ;
~water ਭਾਰਾ ਪਾਣੀ; ~y ਕਰੜਾ, ਸਖ਼ਤ,
ਤਕੜਾ, ਮਜ਼ਬੂਤ, ਹਿੰਮਤੀ, ਦਲੇਰ; ਨਿਡਰ

hare (ਹੇਅ*) *n* ਸੇਹਾ, ਖ਼ਰਗੋਸ਼

harem ('ਹਾਰੀਮ) *n* ਰਨਵਾਸ, ਜ਼ਨਾਨਖ਼ਾਨਾ, ਹਰਮ

harm (ਹਾਮ) *n v* ਹਾਨੀ, ਨੁਕਸਾਨ; ਨੁਕਸਾਨ
ਕਰਨਾ, ਹਾਨੀ ਪਹੁੰਚਾਉਣੀ; ਕਸ਼ਟ ਦੇਣਾ; ~ful
ਹਾਨੀਕਾਰਕ, ਦੁੱਖਦਾਈ

harmonic (ਹਾ'ਮੌਨਿਕ) *a* ਸੁਰਮੇਲ ਵਾਲਾ,
ਸਮਸਵਰ; ਇਕ ਸੁਰ, ਇਕਤਾਲ

harmonious (ਹਾ'ਮਅਉਨਯਅਸ) *a* ਮਿਲਵਾਂ,
ਇਕਸਰਤਾ ਵਾਲਾ ਇਕ ਸੁਰ, ਇਕ ਤਾਲ;
ਸੁਰੀਲਾ

hormonize ('ਹਾ'ਮਅਨਾਇਜ਼) *v* ਇਕਸੁਰ ਕਰਨਾ,
ਇਕਸਰਤਾ ਲਿਆਉਣੀ ਸੰਗਤ ਕਰਨਾ, ਸੁਰਾਂ
ਮਿਲਾਉਣੀਆਂ

harmony ('ਹਾ'ਮਅਨਿ) *n* ਇਕਸੁਰਤਾ,
ਇਕਸਰਤਾ, ਸੁਰਮੇਲ, ਸੰਗਤੀ; ਸਮਤਾਲ

harp (ਹਾ'ਪ) *n v* (ਸਿਤਾਰ ਵਰਗਾ) ਵਾਜਾ,
ਦਿਲਰੁਬਾ; ਇਹ ਸਾਜ਼ ਵਜਾਉਣਾ; ~er ਸਿਤਾਰ
ਵਜਾਉਣ ਵਾਲਾ

harry ('ਹੈਰਿ) *v* ਉਜਾੜਨਾ, ਤਬਾਹ ਕਰਨਾ, ਵੀਰਾਨ
ਕਰਨਾ, ਲੁੱਟ-ਮਾਰ ਮਚਾਉਣਾ; ਦਿਕ ਕਰਨਾ

harsh (ਹਾ'ਸ਼) *a* ਰੁੱਖਾ, ਸਖ਼ਤ, ਖ਼ਰਵਾ, ਕਰਖ਼ਤ,
ਕਰੜਾ, ਨਾਪਸੰਦ, ਸਖ਼ਤ ਦਿਲ, ਪੱਥਰ ਚਿਤ

harvest ('ਹਾਵਿਸਟ) *n v* ਪੱਕੀ ਹੋਇ ਫ਼ਸਲ,
ਉਪਜ ਝਾੜ; ਫ਼ਸਲ ਕੱਟਣੀ, ਵਾਢੀ ਕਰਨੀ,

ਫ਼ਸਲ ਇਕੱਠੀ ਕਰਨੀ

hashish ('ਹੈਸ਼ੀਸ਼) *n* ਹਸ਼ੀਸ਼, ਗਾਂਜਾ

haste (ਹੇਇਸਟ) *n v* ਕਾਹਲ, ਛੇਤੀ, ਉਤਾਵਲ, ਜਲਦੀ, ਤੇਜ਼ੀ; ਕਾਹਲ ਕਰਨੀ, ਉਤਾਵਲ ਕਰਨੀ; ~n ਕਾਹਲ ਕਰਨੀ, ਛੇਤੀ ਕਰਨੀ, ਕਾਹਲਾ ਟੁਰਨਾ

hasty ('ਹੇਇਸਟਿ) *a* ਕਾਹਲਾ, ਉਤਾਵਲਾ, ਤੇਜ਼, ਤਿੱਖਾ; ਚਿੜਚੜਾ, ਉਜੱਡ

hat (ਹੈਟ) *n* ਟੋਪ, ਟੋਪੀ, ਅੰਗਰੇਜ਼ੀ ਟੋਪ

hatchet ('ਹੈਚਿਟ) *n* ਕੁਹਾੜੀ, ਗੰਡਾਸਾ

hate (ਹੇਇਟ) *n v* ਘਿਰਨਾ, ਨਫ਼ਰਤ, ਤਿਰਸਕਾਰ; ਘਿਰਨਾ ਕਰਨੀ, ਨਫ਼ਰਤ ਕਰਨੀ; ~ful ਘਿਰਨਾਯੋਗ, ਘਿਰਨਾਜਨਕ

hatred ('ਹੇਇਟਰਿਡ) *n* ਘਿਰਨਾ, ਨਫ਼ਰਤ, ਦਵੈਖ

haughty ('ਹੋਟਿ) *a* ਘਮੰਡੀ, ਅਭਿਮਾਨੀ, ਹੰਕਾਰੀ

haul (ਹੋਲ) *v n* ਖਿਚਣਾ, ਧੂਹਣਾ, ਘਸੀਟਣਾ; ਖਿਚ, ਘਸੀਟ; ਲੱਭਤ; ~age ਖਿਚਾਈ; ਢੁਹਾਈ; ਘਸੀਟ

haunt (ਹੋਟ) *v n* ਘੜੀ ਮੁੜੀ ਆਉਣਾ, ਮੁੜ ਮੁੜ ਆਉਣਾ, ਆਉਣ ਜਾਣ ਰੱਖਣਾ; ਭੂਤ-ਵਾਸ, ਭੂਤ-ਘਰ, ਅੱਡਾ

have (ਹੈਵ੍) *v aux n* ਕੋਲ ਹੋਣਾ, ਅਧਿਕਾਰ ਵਿਚ ਹੋਣਾ; ਲੈਣਾ, ਫੜਨਾ, ਪ੍ਰਾਪਤ ਕਰਨੀ; ਪਾਉਣਾ; ਧਨਵਾਨ; ਛਲ, ਕਪਟ; ~not (usu. in *pl*) (ਬੋਲ) ਨਿਰਧਨ, ਗ਼ਰੀਬ

haven ('ਹੋਇਵ੍ਨ) *n* ਬੰਦਰਗਾਹ; ਪਨਾਹਗਾਹ

having ('ਹੈਵ੍ਇਡ) *n* ਧਨ-ਸੰਪੱਤੀ, ਜਾਇਦਾਦ, ਸਮਗਰੀ, ਸਾਮਾਨ, ਅਸਬਾਬ

havoc ('ਹੈਵ੍ਅਕ) *n* ਤਬਾਹੀ, ਬਰਬਾਦੀ, ਵਿਨਾਸ਼, ਸਰਵਨਾਸ਼, ਪਰਲੋ

hawk (ਹੋਕ) *n v* ਬਾਜ਼, ਸ਼ਿਕਰਾ; ਜਾਬਰ ਅਤਿਆਚਾਰੀ; ਡਾਕੂ, ਲੁਟੇਰਾ; ~er ਫੇਰੀ ਵਾਲਾ, ਡੱਗੀ ਵਾਲਾ

hay (ਹੇਇ) *n* ਸੁੱਕਾ ਘਾਹ, ਤੂੜੀ

hazard ('ਹੈਜ਼ਅਡ) *n v* ਸੰਕਟ, ਖ਼ਤਰਾ; ਦੇਵਨੇਤ, ਘਟਨਾ, ਸੋਕਾ; ਪਾਸੇ ਦੀ ਇਕ ਖੇਡ, ਜੂਆ; ਸੰਕਟ ਵਿਚ ਫਸਾਉਣਾ, ਦਿਲ ਤਕੜਾ ਕਰ ਕੇ ਆਖਣਾ; ~ous ਸੰਕਟਮਈ; ਜੋਖੋਂ ਵਾਲਾ, ਬਿਪਤਾਪੂਰਨ, ਖ਼ਤਰਨਾਕ

haze (ਹੇਇਜ਼) *n v* ਧੁੰਦ, ਕੁਹਰਾ; ਧੁੰਦਲਾਪਣ; ਪਰੇਸ਼ਾਨੀ, ਨਿਰਾਸਤਾ; ਧੁੰਦਲਾ ਕਰਨਾ, ਧੁੰਦ ਪਾਉਣੀ; ਤੰਗ ਕਰਨਾ

hazy ('ਹੇਇਜ਼ਿ) *a* ਧੁੰਦਲਾ, ਅਸਪਸ਼ਟ, ਸ਼ੱਕ ਵਾਲਾ

head (ਹੈੱਡ) *n v* (1) ਸਿਰ, ਸੀਸ, ਬੁੱਧੀ; (ਸਿੱਕੇ ਉੱਤੇ ਬਣਿਆ) ਚਿਹਰਾ; ਸਿਰਾ ਜਾਂ ਅਗਲਾ ਹਿੱਸਾ; (2) ਸਰਦਾਰ, ਮੁਖੀਆ, ਪ੍ਰਧਾਨ, ਮੁੱਖ ਅਧਿਕਾਰੀ; ਸਿਰਲੇਖ; ਵਿਅਕਤੀ, ਜਨਾ; ਨੇਕ ਕੱਢਣੀ, ਸਿਰਾ ਬਣਾਉਣਾ, ਮੂੰਹ ਬਣਾਉਣਾ; ਛਾਂਗਣਾ, ਲਾਪਰਨਾ, ਅੱਗੇ ਹੋਣਾ; ਸਿਰਲੇਖ ਹੋਣਾ; ਉੱਨਤੀ ਕਰਨੀ; ਸਿਖਰ ਤੇ ਪੁੱਜਣਾ; ~ache ਸਿਰ-ਪੀੜ; ਸਿਰਦਰਦੀ, ਔਖੀ ਸਮੱਸਿਆ; ~line ਸੁਰਖੀ; ~master ਵੱਡਾ ਮਾਸਟਰ, ਮੁੱਖ ਅਧਿਆਪਕ; ~quarters ਮੁੱਖ ਦਫ਼ਤਰ; ਦਫ਼ਤਰ ਸਦਰ; ~man ਜੱਲਾਦ; ~ing ਸਿਰਲੇਖ, ਸੁਰਖੀ, ਸੀਰਸ਼ਕ, ਉਨਵਾਨ; ~ship ਸਰਦਾਰੀ, ਮੁਖੀ ਦਾ ਪਦ; ~y ਪ੍ਰਚੰਡ, ਪ੍ਰਬਲ, ਵੇਗਵਾਨ

heal (ਹੀਲ) *v* ਤੰਦਰੁਸਤ ਹੋਣਾ ਜਾਂ ਕਰਨਾ, ਰਾਜ਼ੀ ਹੋਣਾ ਜਾਂ ਕਰਨਾ, ਜ਼ਖਮ ਭਰਨਾ

health (ਹੈੱਲਥ) *n* ਸਿਹਤ, ਤੰਦਰੁਸਤੀ, ਸੁਅਸਥ, ਅਰੋਗਤਾ; ~y ਸਿਹਤਮੰਦ, ਨਿਰੋਗ, ਸੁਅਸਥ

heap (ਹੀਪ) *n v* ਢੇਰ, ਢੇਰੀ, ਸਮੂਹ, ਜਖੀਰਾ; ਢੇਰ ਲਾਉਣਾ, ਇਕੱਤਰ ਕਰਨਾ, ਜਮ੍ਹਾਂ ਕਰਨਾ

hear (ਹਿਅ*) *v* ਸੁਨਣਾ; ਸੁਣ ਲੈਣਾ; ਕੰਨ ਲਾਉਣਾ; ~say ਅਫ਼ਵਾਹ, ਸੁਣੀ-ਸੁਣਾਈ ਗੱਲ; ~ing

~ing ਸੁਣਵਾਈ; ਪੇਸ਼ੀ

hearse (ਹਅ:ਸ) *n* ਬਬਾਣ, ਲਾਸ਼ ਲੈ ਜਾਣ ਵਾਲੀ ਗੱਡੀ

heart (ਹਾ'ਟ) *n* ਦਿਲ, ਜੀਅ, ਮਨ, ਹਿਰਦਾ; ਛਾਤੀ, ਸੀਨਾ; ਹੌਸਲਾ, ਦਲੇਰੀ, ਸਾਹਸ; ~and soul ਜੋਸ਼ ਨਾਲ, ਉਤਸ਼ਾਹ ਨਾਲ, ਤਨੋਮਨੋ; ~beat ਦਿਲ ਦੀ ਧੜਕਣ; ~breaking ਦਿਲ-ਤੋੜ; ~burning ਸਾੜਾ, ਈਰਖਾ, ਦਵੈਖ; ~felt ਸੱਚੇ ਦਿਲੋਂ, ਹਾਰਦਿਕ; ~of hearts ਸੱਚੇ ਦਿਲ ਨਾਲ; ~rending ਅਤੀ ਦੁਖਦਾਈ, ਹਿਰਦੇ-ਵੇਧਕ; ~less ਬੇਰਹਿਮ, ਨਿਰਦਈ, ਪੱਥਰ-ਦਿਲ; ~en ਉਤਸ਼ਾਹਤ ਕਰਨਾ, ਢਾਰਸ ਦੇਣਾ, ਦਿਲ ਵਧਾਉਣਾ; ~ily ਖ਼ੁਸ਼ੀ ਖ਼ੁਸ਼ੀ, ਸੱਚੇ ਦਿਲੋਂ; ਜੀ ਖੋਲ੍ਹ ਕੇ

hearth (ਹਾ'ਥ) *n* ਚੁੱਲ੍ਹਾ, ਅੰਗੀਠੀ, ਘਰਬਾਰ, ਬਾਲ-ਬੱਚੇ, ਪਰਵਾਰ

heat (ਹੀਟ) *n v* ਗਰਮੀ, ਤਾਅ, ਤਪਸ਼; ਹੁਣ੍ਹਾਲ; ਜੋਸ਼, ਉਤੇਜਨਾ, ਕਰੋਧ, ਰੋਸ; ਤਪਾਉਣਾ, ਤੱਤਾ ਕਰਨਾ, ਭਖਾਉਣਾ, ਸੇਕਣਾ; ਤਪਣਾ; ਭੜਕਣਾ, ਗੁੱਸੇ ਵਿਚ ਆਉਣਾ; ~stroke ਲੂ-ਲਗਾੱਟ; ~ed ਤਪਤ, ਉਤੇਜਤ

heave (ਹੀਵ੍) *n v* ਲੰਮਾ ਸਾਹ, ਹਊਕਾ; ਉਭਾਰ; ਹਊਕਾ ਭਰਨਾ, ਠੰਢਾ ਸਾਹ ਲੈਣਾ

heaven (ਹੈੱਵ੍ਨ) *n* ਸੁਰਗ; ਬਹਿਸ਼ਤ, ਜੰਨਤ, ਦੇਵ-ਲੋਕ; ਇਸ਼ਵਰ; ਅੰਬਰ, ਆਕਾਸ਼, ਅਸਮਾਨ; ਵਾਯੂ-ਮੰਡਲ; ~ly ਦਿਵਯ, ਸੁਰਗੀ; ਆਕਾਸ਼ੀ, ਆਸਮਾਨੀ; ਚੰਗਾ, ਵਧੀਆ

heaviness (ਹੈੱਵ੍ਿਨਿਸ) *n* ਭਾਰ, ਗੁਰੂਤਾ; ਪ੍ਰਚੰਡਤਾ, ਭਾਰਾਪਣ

heavy (ਹੈੱਵ੍ਿ) *a* ਭਾਰਾ, ਬੋਝਲ, ਵਜ਼ਨੀ; ਵੱਡਾ; ਭਰਪੂਰ; ਲੱਦਿਆ; ਸੋਕਮਈ, ਵਿਸ਼ਾਦਪੂਰਨ; ਨਿਰਾਸ

heed (ਹੀਡ) *n v* ਸਾਵਧਾਨੀ, ਚੌਕਸੀ, ਧਿਆਨ;

ਚੌਕਸੀ ਕਰਨੀ, ਪਰਵਾਹ ਕਰਨੀ, ਧਿਆਨ ਕਰਨਾ; ~ful ਸਚੇਤ, ਸਾਵਧਾਨ, ਚੌਕਸ; ~less ਅਚੇਤ, ਅਸਾਵਧਾਨ, ਲਾਪਰਵਾਹ

heel (ਹੀਲ) *n v* ਅੱਡੀ, ਪਸ਼ੂਆਂ ਦੇ ਖੁਰ, ਪਿਛਲੀਆਂ ਲੱਤਾਂ; ਅੱਡੀ ਲਾਉਣੀ; ਪਿੱਛੇ ਪਿੱਛੇ ਲੱਗੋ ਫਿਰਨ

hefty (ਹੈੱਫਟਿ) *a* ਰਿਸ਼ਟ-ਪੁਸ਼ਟ, ਹੱਟਾ-ਕੱਟਾ, ਮੋਟਾ ਤਾਜ਼ਾ

height (ਹਾਇਟ) *n* ਉਚਾਈ, ਬੁਲੰਦੀ; ਕੱਦ, ਲੰਬਾਈ; ਚੜ੍ਹਦੀ ਕਲਾ, ਚੋਟੀ; ਟਿੱਲਾ, ਸਿਖਰ; ~en ਉੱਚਾ ਕਰਨਾ, ਉਭਾਰਨਾ, ਡੂੰਘਾ ਕਰਨਾ, ਉਠਾਉਣਾ, ਚੜ੍ਹਾਉਣਾ

heinous (ਹੋਇਨਅਸ) *a* ਘਿਰਨਾਯੋਗ, ਘਿਰਣਤ

heir (ਏਅ*) *n* ਵਾਰਸ, ਉਤਰਾਧਿਕਾਰੀ, ਜਾਂਨਸ਼ੀਨ, ਵਾਲੀ ਵਾਰਸ; ~less ਲਾਵਾਰਸ

hell (ਹੈੱਲ) *n* ਪਾਤਾਲ, ਨਰਕ, ਦੋਜ਼ਖ਼, ਜਹੰਨਮ; ਯਮਲੋਕ, ਰਸਾਤਲ

helmet (ਹੈੱਲਮਿਟ) *n* ਲੋਹੇ ਦੀ ਟੋਪੀ; ਧੁੱਪ ਨੂੰ ਰੋਕਣ ਵਾਲੀ ਛੱਜੇਦਾਰ ਟੋਪੀ

help (ਹੈੱਲਪ) *n v* ਸਹਾਇਤਾ, ਮਦਦ, ਸਹਾਰਾ; ਉਪਾਉ; ਸਹਾਇਤਾ ਕਰਨਾ, ਸਹਾਇਕ ਹੋਣਾ, ਸਹਾਰਾ ਦੇਣਾ, ਹਿਮਾਇਤ ਕਰਨੀ, ਹੱਥ ਵਟਾਉਣਾ; ~mate ਹਮਦਮ, ਸਹਾਇਕ; ~ful ਸਹਾਇਕ, ਲਾਭਦਾਇਕ; ~ing ਸਹਾਇਤਾ ਕਰਨੀ, ਸਹਾਇਕ; ~less ਨਿਆਸਰਾ, ਨਿਤਾਣਾ, ਬੇਚਾਰਾ, ਬੇ-ਸਹਾਰਾ, ਮਜਬੂਰ

helter-skelter (ਹੈੱਲਟਅ'ਸਕੈੱਲਟਅ*) *adv* ਖਲਬਲੀ

hemisphere (ਹੈੱਮਿ'ਸਫ਼ਿਅ*) *n* ਅਰਧਗੋਲਾ, ਗੋਲਾਰਧ

hemlock (ਹੈੱਮਲੋਕ) *n* ਧਤੂਰਾ

hemp (ਹੈੱਪ) *n* ਸਣ, ਪੱਟ, ਸੂਤਲੀ, ਭੰਗ, ਗਾਂਜਾ, ਸੁੱਖਾ

hen (ਹੈਨੰ) *n* ਕੁਕੜੀ, ਮੁਰਗੀ; ਡਰਪੋਕ ਬੰਦਾ;
~**pecked** ਰੰਨ-ਸੁਰੀਦ, ਜੋਰੂ ਦਾ ਗ਼ੁਲਾਮ;
~**nery** ਮੁਰਗੀਖ਼ਾਨਾ, ਪੋਲਟਰੀ ਫ਼ਾਰਮ

hence (ਹੈੱਸ) *adv* ਇਸ ਲਈ; ਏਥੋਂ, ਇਸ
ਥਾਂ ਤੋਂ, ਹੁਣ ਤੋਂ; ~**forth**, ~**forward** ਮੁੜ, ਹੁਣ
ਤੋਂ, ਇਸ ਤੋਂ ਮਗਰੋਂ

henchman (ਹੈੱਚਮਅਨ) *n* ਮੁੱਖ ਸੇਵਕ, ਦਾਸ;
ਪਿੱਠੂ, ਚਮਚਾ

henna (ਹੈੱਨਅ) *n* ਮਹਿੰਦੀ, ਹਿਨਾ

herald (ਹੈੱਰ(ਅ)ਲਡ) *n v* ਦੂਤ, ਸੰਦੇਸ਼ਵਾਹਕ;
ਨਕੀਬ; ਹਰਕਾਰਾ; ਮੁਨਾਦੀ; ਆਰੰਭ ਕਰਨਾ

herb (ਹਅੱਬ) *n a* ਔਸ਼ਧੀ, ਜੜੀ ਬੂਟੀ, ਸਾਗ;
~**al** ਜੜੀ ਬੂਟੀਆਂ ਦਾ ਬਣਿਆ

herd (ਹਅੱਡ) *n v* ਦਲ, (ਪਸ਼ੂਆਂ ਦਾ) ਚੌਣਾ,
ਵੱਗ, ਇੱਜੜ, ਝੁੰਡ, (ਜਨ-ਸਮੂਹ); ਗਵਾਲਾ,
ਆਜੜੀ, ਪਸ਼ੂ-ਪਾਲਕ; ਪਸ਼ੂ ਚਾਰਨੇ; ਸਮੂਹ ਵਿਚ
ਚੱਲਣਾ; ~**sman** ਆਜੜੀ, ਚਰਵਾਹਾ, ਗਵਾਲਾ,
ਪਾਲੀ

here (ਹਿਅ*) *n adv* ਇਸ ਥਾਂ, ਇਹ ਜਗ੍ਹਾ, ਇੱਧਰ;
~**about** ਇੱਧਰ ਉੱਧਰ, ਨੇੜੇ ਹੀ; ~**and there**
ਥਾਂ, ਥਾਂ, ਇਥੇ ਉਥੇ, ਇੱਧਰ ਉੱਧਰ; ~**by** ਇੰਝ
ਕਰਕੇ; ~**in** ਇਸ ਥਾਂ (ਇਸ ਪੁਸਤਕ ਵਿਚ); ~**in**
after ਇਸ ਤੋਂ ਮਗਰੋਂ, ਅੱਗੇ; ~**to** ਇਸ ਵਾਸਤੇ,
ਇਸ ਗੱਲ ਵਿਚ; ~**to fore** ਇਸ ਤੋਂ ਪਹਿਲਾਂ;
~**upon** ਇਸ ਤੋਂ ਮਗਰੋਂ, ਇਸ ਲਈ; ~**with**
ਇਸ ਦੇ ਨਾਲ, ਇਸ ਨਾਲ ਨੱਥੀ

hereditary (ਹਿ'ਰੈਡਿਟ(ਅ)ਰਿ) *a* ਜੱਦੀ, ਪੁਸ਼ਤੀ,
ਵੰਸ਼ ਦਾ, ਵੰਸ਼ਗਤ, ਕੁਲ ਦਾ; ਪੈਤਰਿਕ

heredity (ਹਿ'ਹੈੱਡਅਟਿ) *n* ਵਿਰਾਸਤ, ਪੈਤਰਿਕ
ਗੁਣ, ਵੰਸ਼ ਪਰੰਪਰਾ

heresy (ਹੈੱਰਅਸਿ) *n* ਕੁਫ਼ਰ, ਪਖੰਡ

heretic (ਹੈੱਰਅਟਿਕ) *n* ਕਾਫ਼ਰ, ਧਰਮ ਵਿਰੋਧੀ,
ਪਖੰਡੀ, ਨਾਸਤਕ

heritage (ਹੈੱਰਿਟਿਜ) *n* ਪਿਤਰੀ ਧਨ, ਪੈਤਰਿਕ
ਪੂੰਜੀ, ਵਿਰਾਸਤ ਮੀਰਾਸ, ਉਤਰਾਧਿਕਾਰ

hermit ('ਹਅੱਮਿਟ) *n* ਸੰਨਿਆਸੀ, ਬਨਵਾਸੀ,
ਤਪਸਵੀ, ਬਾਨਪ੍ਰਸਥ, ਇਕਾਂਤਵਾਸੀ; ~**age**
ਆਸ਼ਰਮ, ਕੁਟੀਆ, ਮੱਠ, ਇਕਾਂਤਵਾਸ,
ਗੋਸ਼ਾਨਸ਼ੀਨੀ

hero ('ਹਿਅਰਅਉ) *n* ਪਰਮ ਮਨੁੱਖ, ਦੇਵਤਿਆਂ
ਵਰਗਾ ਮਨੁੱਖ; ਵੀਰ, ਜੋਧਾ, ਸੂਰਬੀਰ, ਬਹਾਦਰ
ਨਾਇਕ; ਸੂਰਮਾ; ਰਾਸ਼ਟਰ ਜੋਧਾ; ~**ine** ਨਾਇਕਾ;
~**ism** ਸੂਰਬੀਰਤਾ

heroic (ਹਿ'ਰੋਇਕ) *n a* ਵੀਰ-ਕਾਵਿ ਵਿਚ
ਪ੍ਰਯੁਕਤ ਛੰਦ; ਵੀਰਤਾਪੂਰਨ; ਵੀਰਰਸ ਪ੍ਰਧਾਨ;
ਤੇਜਸਵੀ, ਵੀਰ

hesitance,   hesitancy   ('ਹੈਜ਼ਿਟਅੰਸ,
'ਹੈਜ਼ਿਟਅੰਸਿ) *n* ਦੁਬਧਾ, ਸੰਕੋਚ, ਝੱਕ, ਝਸ਼ੋਪੰਜ,
ਝਿਜਕ, ਹਿਚਕਚਾਹਟ

hesitant ('ਹੈਜ਼ਿਟ(ਅ)ਨਟ) *a* ਝਿਜਕਦਾ, ਦੁਚਿਤਾ

hesitate   ('ਹੈਜ਼ਿਟੇਇਟ)   *v*   ਝਿਜਕਣਾ,
ਹਿਚਕਚਾਉਣਾ, ਸ਼ਸ਼ੋਪੰਜ ਵਿਚ ਪੈਣਾ, ਦੁਬਧਾ
ਵਿਚ ਪੈਣਾ, ਸੰਕੋਚ ਕਰਨਾ

hesitation ('ਹੈਜ਼ਿ'ਟੇਇਸ਼ਨ) *n* ਝਿਜਕ, ਦੁਬਧਾ,
ਸੰਕੋਚ, ਦੁਚਿਤੀ

heterodox ('ਹੈੱਟ(ਅ)ਰਅ(ਉ)ਡੌਕਸ) *n a* ਭਿੰਨ-
ਮੱਤ; ਭਿੰਨ-ਮਤੀਆ, ਮਨਮਤੀਆ

heterogeneous ('ਹੈੱਟਅਰਅ(ਉ)'ਜ਼ੀਨਯਅਸ) *a*
ਵਿਖਮ, ਵਿਰੋਧੀ; ਭਿੰਨ, ਵਿਜਾਤੀ, ਭਿੰਨ ਜਾਤੀ

hexagon ('ਹੈੱਕਸਅਗਾਅਨ) *n* ਛੇ ਭੁਜ

hexameter (ਹੈੱਕ'ਸੈਮਿਟਅ*) *n* (ਕਾਵਿ) ਛੇ ਪਦੀ
(ਛੰਦ)

hiccup ('ਹਿਕਅੱਪ) *n v* ਹਿੱਚਕੀ; ਹਿੱਚਕੀ ਲੱਗਣੀ; ਹਿੱਚਕੀ ਆਉਣੀ

hide (ਹਾਇਡ) *n v* ਪਸ਼ੂਆਂ ਦਾ ਚੰਮ, ਖੱਲ, ਚਮੜਾ, ਲੁਕਾਉਣਾ ਜਾਂ ਲੁਕਣਾ; ~out (ਬੋਲ) ਲੁਕਣ ਦੀ ਥਾਂ

hideous ('ਹਿਡ਼ਿਅਸ) *a* ਭਿਆਨਕ, ਘਿਨਾਉਣਾ, ਘੋਰ

hierarch ('ਹਾਇਅਰਾਕ) *n* ਪਰੋਹਤ, ਇਮਾਮ, ਪ੍ਰਧਾਨ ਪਾਦਰੀ, ਮਹਾਅਚਾਰੀਆ; ~y ਦੇਵ ਸ੍ਰੇਣੀ, ਮਹੰਤੀ, ਮਹੰਤਸ਼ਾਹੀ

high (ਹਾਇ) *a* ਉੱਚਾ, ਉੱਨਤ, ਬੁਲੰਦ, ਉੱਤੇ; ਉੱਤਮ, ਉਤਕ੍ਰਿਸ਼ਟ, ਅਤੀ ਅਧਿਕ; ~born ਕੁਲੀਨ, ਸੁਜਾਤ; ~caste ਉੱਚੀ ਜਾਤ; ~court ਉੱਚ ਅਦਾਲਤ; ~handedness ਧਾਂਦਲੀ, ਆਪੂਦਰਾਪਣ, ਉਦੰਡਤਾ; ~way ਸ਼ਾਹ-ਰਾਹ; ~wayman ਵੱਟ-ਮਾਰ; ~ten ਉੱਨਤ ਕਰਨਾ, ਉੱਚਾ ਕਰਨਾ, ਤੀਬਰ ਕਰਨਾ, ਵਧਾਉਣਾ

hijacker ('ਹਾਇਜੈਕਅ*) *n* ਅਪਹਰਣਕਰਤਾ

hijacking ('ਹਾਇਜੈਕਿਙ) *n* ਠੱਗੀ; (ਜਹਾਜ਼ ਬੱਸ ਆਦਿ ਦਾ) ਅਪਹਰਨ

hike (ਹਾਇਕ) *n v* ਪੈਦਲ ਸੈਰ; ਲੰਮੀ ਪਦ ਯਾਤਰਾ; ਲੰਮੀ ਪਦ ਯਾਤਰਾ ਕਰਨਾ, ਤੇਜ਼ ਚੱਲਣਾ

hilarious (ਹਿ'ਲੇਅਰਿਅਸ) *a* ਪ੍ਰਫੁੱਲਤ, ਪ੍ਰਸੰਨ, ਉੱਲਾਸਮਈ, ਆਨੰਦਪੂਰਨ; ~ness ਪ੍ਰਫੁੱਲਤਾ, ਪ੍ਰਸੰਨਤਾ, ਉੱਲਾਸ, ਆਨੰਦ, ਮਗਨਤਾ, ਖ਼ੁਸ਼ੀ

hill (ਹਿਲ) *n* ਡੂਗਰ, ਪਹਾੜੀ; ਟਿੱਲਾ, ਟਿੱਬਾ, ਢਿਗ; ~ock ਛੋਟੀ ਪਹਾੜੀ; ਟਿੱਬਾ, ਟਿੱਲਾ, ਢੱਕੀ

hilly billy ('ਹਿਲਿਬਿਲਿ) *n* ਗਵਾਰੂ, ਉਜੱਡ; ਇਕ ਲੋਕ-ਗੀਤ

hind (ਹਾਇੰਡ) *n a* ਹਿਰਨੀ, ਮੂਨ, ਮੀਰਗਟੀ; ਗੰਵਾਰ, ਪੇਂਡੂ ਪਿਛਲੇ ਪਾਸੇ ਦਾ, ਪਿੱਠ-ਪਿਛਲਾ;

~er ਰੋਕਣਾ, ਵਿਘਨ ਪਾਉਣਾ, ਅੜਚਨ ਪਾਉਣਾ, ਅਟਕਾਉਣਾ, ਪ੍ਰਤੀਬੰਧ ਲਾਉਣਾ; ~erance, ~rance ਅੜਚਨ, ਰੁਕਾਵਟ, ਵਿਘਨ; ਨਿਸ਼ੇਧ, ਪ੍ਰਤੀਬੰਧ

hinge (ਹਿੰਜ) *n v* ਚੂਲ, ਕਬਜ਼ਾ, ਜੋੜ; ਕੋਰ; ਕੇਂਦਰ, ਮੂਲ, ਜੜ੍ਹ; ਸਿਧਾਂਤ

hint (ਹਿੰਟ) *n v* ਸੰਕੇਤ, ਸੂਚਨਾ, ਸੁਝਾਉ, ਭਿਣਕ, ਇਸ਼ਾਰਾ; ਸੰਕੇਤ ਜਾਂ ਸੂਚਨਾ ਦੇਣਾ, ਸੁਝਾਉ ਦੇਣਾ

hip (ਹਿਪ) *n v int* ਕੁੱਲਾ, ਚੂਲਾ, ਢਹਿੰਦੀ ਕਲਾ; ਸ਼ਾਬਾਸ਼ ਦੇਣਾ, ਹਿਪ ਹਿਪ ਹੁੱਰਾ ਕਰਨਾ, ਉਤਸ਼ਾਹ ਦੇਣਾ

hippocampus ('ਹਿਪਅ'ਕੈਂਪਅਸ) *n* ਸਮੁੰਦਰੀ ਘੋੜਾ, ਇਕ ਤਰ੍ਹਾਂ ਦੀ ਮੱਛੀ

hippopotamus ('ਹਿਪਅ'ਪੌਟਅਮਅਸ) *n* ਦਰਿਆਈ ਘੋੜਾ

hire ('ਹਾਇਅ*) *n v* ਭਾੜਾ, ਕਿਰਾਇਆ; ਮਿਹਨਤਾਨਾ, ਮਜ਼ਦੂਰੀ, ਕਿਰਾਏ ਤੇ ਲੈਣਾ, ਮਿਹਨਤਾਨਾ ਦੇ ਕੇ ਲਾਉਣਾ

hiss (ਹਿਸ) *n v* ਫੁੰਕਾਰਾ, ਛੁਟਕਾਰ, ਹਿੱਛ; ਫੁੰਕਾਰਾ ਮਾਰਨਾ, ਛਟਕਾਰ ਪੈਣੀ

historian (ਹਿ'ਸਟੋਰਿਅਨ) *n* ਇਤਿਹਾਸਕਾਰ, ਤਾਰੀਖ਼ਦਾਨ

historic (ਹਿ'ਸਟੌਰਿਕ) *a* ਇਤਿਹਾਸਕ, ਇਤਿਹਾਸ ਪ੍ਰਸਿੱਧ, ਇਤਿਹਾਸ ਅਨੁਸਾਰ, ਮਹੱਤਵਪੂਰਨ; ~al ਇਤਿਹਾਸਕ, ਇਤਿਹਾਸ ਸਬੰਧੀ, ਤਾਰੀਖ਼ੀ

history ('ਹਿਸਟ(ਅ)ਰਿ) *n* ਇਤਿਹਾਸ, ਤਾਰੀਖ਼

hit (ਹਿਟ) *n v* ਚੋਟ, ਮਾਰ, ਵਾਰ, ਘਾਉ; ਚੋਟ ਲਾਉਣੀ, ਮਾਰਨਾ, ਵਾਰ ਕਰਨਾ, ਜ਼ਰਬ ਪਹੁੰਚਾਉਣਾ; ~below the belt ਮਰਯਾਦਾ ਭੰਗ ਕਰਨੀ, ਕੋਝਾ ਵਾਰ ਕਰਨਾ; ~upon ਸੁੱਝਣਾ

hither ('ਹਿਦਅ*) *adv* ਨੇੜੇ, ਹੋਰ ਨੇੜੇ; ਇੱਧਰ,

ਇਸ ਪਾਸੇ, ਇਸ ਥਾਂ; ~and thither ਇੱਧਰ ਉੱਧਰ; ~to ਹੁਣ ਤੋੜੀ, ਹੁਣ ਤੀਕ

hive ('ਹਾਇਵ੍ਹ) *n v* ਮਖਿਆਲ, ਸ਼ਹਿਦ ਦੀਆਂ ਮੱਖੀਆਂ ਦਾ ਛੱਤਾ; ਭੀੜ; ਸ਼ਹਿਦ ਦੀਆਂ ਮੱਖੀਆਂ ਪਾਲਣਾ

hives (ਹਾਇਵ੍ਜ਼) *n pl* ਛਪਾਕੀ

hoard (ਹੋਡ) *n v* ਖ਼ਜ਼ਾਨਾ, ਭੰਡਾਰ, ਜ਼ਖ਼ੀਰਾ; ਖ਼ਜ਼ਾਨਾ ਜੋੜਨਾ; ~**ing** ਦੱਬੀ ਹੋਈ ਮਾਇਆ, ਗੁਪਤ ਸੰਗ੍ਰਹ

hoarse (ਹੋ'ਸ) *a* ਬੈਠਿਆ (ਗਲਾ), ਘੱਗੀ (ਅਵਾਜ਼), ਬੇਸੁਰੀ (ਅਵਾਜ਼); ~**n** (ਗਲ ਜਾਂ ਅਵਾਜ਼ ਦਾ) ਬੈਠਣਾ, ਘਗਿਆਉਣਾ, ਭਰੜਾਉਣਾ, ਪਾਟਣਾ; ~**ness** ਘਿੱਗੀ, ਭਰੜਾਹਟ, ਭਾਰਾਪਣ (ਬੋਲ ਜਾਂ ਅਵਾਜ਼ ਦਾ)

hoax (ਹਅਉਕਸ) *v n* ਝਾਂਸਾ ਦੇਣਾ, ਬੁੱਧੂ ਬਣਾਉਣਾ; ਝਾਂਸਾ

hob (ਹੌਬ) *n* ਪੇਂਡੂ, ਗੰਵਾਰ; **to play~** ਖਲਬਲੀ ਮਚਾਉਣਾ, ਗੜਬੜ ਪਾਉਣੀ

hobby ('ਹੌਬਿ) *n* ਸ਼ੌਕੀਆ ਕੰਮ, ਸ਼ੁਗਲ; ~**horse** ਬੱਚਿਆਂ ਦਾ ਲੱਕੜ ਦਾ ਘੋੜਾ

hobnob ('ਹੌਬਨੌਬ) *v* ਹਮ-ਪਿਆਲਾ ਹੋਣਾ, ਇਕੱਠੇ ਸ਼ਰਾਬ ਪੀਣੀ

hocus-pocus ('ਹਅਉਕਅਸ'ਪਅਉਕਅਸ) *n v* ਛਲ, ਧੋਖਾ, ਚਕਮਾ; ਇੰਦਰ-ਜਾਲ, ਛਲਣਾ, ਚਕਮਾ ਦੇਣਾ

hoist (ਹੋਇਸਟ) *n v* ਉਠਾਅ, ਚੜ੍ਹਾਅ; ਲਹਿਰਾਉਣਾ, ਖੜ੍ਹਾ ਕਰਨਾ, ਉਠਾਉਣਾ

hold (ਹਅਉਲਡ) *n v* ਬੰਨ੍ਹਣ, ਪਕੜ; ਕਬਜ਼ੀ, ਅਧਿਕਾਰ, ਪ੍ਰਭਾਵ; ਫੜਨਾ, ਫੜੀ ਰੱਖਣਾ; ਕਬਜ਼ਾ ਕਰਨਾ, ਰੋਕੀ ਰੱਖਣਾ; ~**on** ਪ੍ਰਭਾਵ, ਅਸਰ; ~**up** ਰੁਕਾਵਟ, ਅਟਕਾਅ; ਡਾਕੂਆਂ ਵੱਲੋਂ ਰਾਹ ਘੇਰਨਾ, ਰਾਹਮਾਰੀ; ~**with** ਸਵੀਕਾਰ ਕਰਨਾ

hole (ਹਅਉਲ) *n v* ਛੇਕ, ਸੁਰਾਖ਼, ਛਿਦਰ, ਮੋਰੀ; ਟੋਆ ਪੁੱਟਣਾ, ਛੇਕ ਕਰਨਾ; ਖੁੱਤੀ ਜਾਂ ਘੁੱਤੀ ਵਿਚ ਗੇਂਦ ਜਾਂ ਗੋਲੀ ਪਾਉਣੀ; ਸੁਰੰਗ ਬਣਾਉਣਾ

holiday ('ਹੌਲਿਡੇਇ) *n* ਛੁੱਟੀ

holiness ('ਹਅਉਲਿਨਿਸ) *n* ਸੁੱਚਮ, ਪਵਿੱਤਰਤਾ, ਪਾਵਨਤਾ, ਪੁਨੀਤਤਾ

hollow ('ਹੌਲਅਉ) *n a adv* ਖੋਹ, ਖਾਲਾ; ਖੋਖਲਾ, ਪੋਲਾ; ਸੁੰਨ; ਭੁੱਖਾ; ਥੋਥਾ, ਕਪਟੀ; ~**ness** ਖੋਖਾਪਣ, ਸੁੰਨਾਪਣ

holocaust ('ਹੌਲਅਕੋਸਟ) *n* ਕਤਲਾਮ, ਹੱਤਿਆ ਕਾਂਡ, ਘੱਲੂਘਾਰਾ; ਸਰਬਨਾਸ਼, ਤਬਾਹੀ

holy ('ਹਅਉਲਿ) *a* ਪਾਵਨ, ਪੱਵਿਤਰ, ਪੁਨੀਤ, ਪਾਕ; ਧਰਮਾਤਮਾ, ਮਹਾਤਮਾ

homage ('ਹੌਮਿਜ) *n* ਸਨਮਾਨ; ਸ਼ਰਧਾਂਜਲੀ

home (ਹਅਉਮ) *n a adv* ਘਰ, ਗ੍ਰਹਿ, ਰਿਹਾਇਸ਼, ਨਿਵਾਸ, ਸੁਦੇਸ਼, ਭਵਨ, ਮਕਾਨ, ਘਰ-ਬਾਰ; ਘਰੇਲੂ, ਸੁਦੇਸ਼ੀ; ਘਰ ਮੁੜਨਾ, ਘਰ ਭੇਜਣਾ; ਵਾਸ ਕਰਨਾ; ਘਰ ਬਣਾ ਦੇਣਾ; ~**land** ਮਾਤ ਭੂਮੀ; ~**spun** ਘਰ ਦਾ ਬੁਣਿਆ (ਕੱਪੜਾ); ਸਾਦਮੁਰਾਦਾ; ~**less** ਬੇਘਰਾ, ਨਿਰਆਸਰਾ, ਗ੍ਰਹਿਹੀਣ, ਅਨਾਥ; ~**like** ਘਰੇਲੂ, ਘਰ ਵਾਂਗ, ਜਾਣੀ ਪਛਾਣੀ, ਪਰਿਚਤ; ~**ly** ਘਰੇਲੂ, ਸਧਾਰਨ; ਪੁਰਾਤਨ; ਸਿਧਾ-ਸਾਦਾ

homicide ('ਹੌਮਿਸਾਇਡ) *n* ਮਾਨਵ-ਹੱਤਿਆ; ਹੱਤਿਆਰਾ

homogeneous ('ਹੌਮਅ'ਜੀਨਿਯਅਸ) *a* ਸਜਾਤੀ, ਇਕਸਾਰ, ਸਮਰੂਪ, ਹਮਜਿਨਸ; ਸਮਾਨ, ਸਮ-ਅੰਗ, ਸਦ੍ਰਿਸ਼, ਇਕ ਰੂਪ; ~**ness, homogenity** ਸਜਾਤੀਅਤ, ਸਮਰੂਪਤਾ, ਸਦ੍ਰਿਸ਼ਤਾ

homonym ('ਹੌਮਅਨਿਮ) *n* ਸਮ-ਰੂਪਕ, ਸ਼ਬਦ, ਇਕੋ ਜਿਹੇ ਰੂਪ ਪਰ ਭਿੰਨ ਭਿੰਨ ਅਰਥਾਂ ਵਾਲੇ ਸ਼ਬਦ

Homo sapiens ('ਹਅਉਮਅਓ, 'ਸੈਪਿਐਂਨਜ਼) *n* ਮਾਨਵਜਾਤੀ

homosexual ('ਹੈਮਅਉ'ਸੈਕਸਯੁਅਲ) *a n* ਸਮਲਿੰਗ, ਸਮਲਿੰਗੀ; **~ity** ਸਮਲਿੰਗ ਕਾਮੁਕਤਾ

honest ('ਔਨਿਸਟ) *a* ਈਮਾਨਦਾਰ, ਖਰਾ, ਨੇਕਨੀਅਤ, ਦਿਆਨਤਦਾਰ; ਸ਼ੁੱਧਆਤਮਾ

honey ('ਹਅੱਨਿ) *n* ਮਾਖਿਉਂ, ਮਧੂ, ਸ਼ਹਿਦ; ਮਹਿਬੂਬਾ, ਪਿਆਰੀ; **~moon** ਵਿਆਹ ਤੋਂ ਪਿਛੋਂ ਮਨਾਇਆ ਜਾਣ ਵਾਲਾ ਸੁਹਾਗ-ਸਮਾਂ

honorarium ('ਔਨਅ'ਰੇਅਰਿਅਮ) *n* ਮਾਨ-ਭੱਤਾ, ਕਾਰਜ-ਸ਼ੁਲਕ, ਸੇਵਾ-ਫਲ, ਕਿਰਤ-ਫਲ

honorary ('ਔਨ(ਅ)ਰਅਰਿ) *a* ਸਨਮਾਨ-ਸੂਚਕ, ਮਾਨ-ਅਰਥ, ਬਿਨਾ ਤਨਖ਼ਾਹ ਦੇ, ਮਾਣ-ਸੇਵੀ

honorific ('ਔਨਅ'ਰਿਫ਼ਿਕ) *a n* ਸਨਮਾਨ ਸੂਚਕ (ਉਪਾਧੀ)

honoris causa or gratia (ਹੋ'ਨੋਰਿਸ'ਕਾਉਜ਼ਾ) *(L) adv phr* ਸਨਮਾਨਕ

honour ('ਔਨਅ*) *n v* ਮਾਣ, ਆਦਰ; ਇੱਜ਼ਤ, ਸਤਿਕਾਰ; ਸ਼ਾਨ, ਵਡਿਆਈ, ਬਜ਼ੁਰਗੀ, ਕੀਰਤੀ, ਗੌਰਵ; ਇੱਜ਼ਤ ਕਰਨੀ, ਸਤਿਕਾਰ ਕਰਨਾ, ਇੱਜ਼ਤ ਬਖ਼ਸ਼ਣੀ, ਵਡਿਆਉਣਾ; ਹੁੰਡੀ ਸਵੀਕਾਰ ਕਰਨੀ; ਸਮੇਂ ਸਿਰ ਦੇਣਾ, ਕਰਜ਼ਾ ਚੁਕਾਉਣਾ; **~able** ਮਾਣਯੋਗ, ਪੂਜ, ਆਦਰਣੀਯ; ਦਿਆਨਤਦਾਰ, ਸਚਿਆਰ, ਸ਼ਾਖ਼ ਵਾਲਾ, ਪੂਜਨੀਕ

hooch (ਹੁਚ) *n* ਤਾੜੀ, ਸ਼ਰਾਬ, ਠੱਰਾ

hood (ਹੁਡ) *n v* ਕੰਟੋਪ; (ਸੱਪ ਦਾ, ਫੰਨ੍ਹ); (ਬਾਜ਼ ਲਈ) ਚਮੜੇ ਦੀ ਟੋਪੀ; (ਗੱਡੀ ਦਾ) ਟੱਪ; ਕੱਜਣਾ, ਲੁਕਾਉਣਾ; ਚੜ੍ਹਾਉਣੀ

hoodlum ('ਹੂਡਲਅਮ) *n* ਗੁੰਡਾ, ਲਫ਼ੰਗਾ, ਬਦਮਾਸ਼

hoof (ਹੂਫ਼) *n v* ਖੁਰ, ਟਾਪ, ਸੁਮ, ਪੌੜ; ਠੋਕਰ

hook (ਹੁਕ) *n v* ਕਾਂਟਾ, ਅੰਕੁਸ਼, ਕੁੰਡਾ; ਜਾਲ, ਘੰਡੀ; ਦਾਤੀ, ਦਾਤਰੀ; ਮੁੜਨਾ, ਝੁਕਣਾ; ਮੋੜਨਾ, ਝੁਕਾਉਣਾ, ਵਿੰਗਾ ਕਰਨਾ; **~in, ~up** ਉਲਝਾਉਣਾ, ਫਾਹੁਣਾ; **~on** ਸਹਾਰਾ ਦੇਣਾ; **~worm** ਪੇਟ ਦਾ ਕੀੜਾ; **by~ or by crook** ਕਿਵੇਂ ਨਾ ਕਿਵੇਂ, ਕਿਸੇ ਨਾ ਕਿਸੇ ਤਰ੍ਹਾਂ; **~ed** ਟੇਢਾ, ਹੁੱਕਦਾਰ ਹੋਣ ਦਾ ਗੁਣ

hooligan ('ਹੂਲਿਗਅਨ) *n* ਗੁੰਡਾ, ਬਦਮਾਸ਼; **~ism** ਗੁੰਡਾਪਣ, ਗੁੰਡਪਣਾ, ਬਦਮਾਸ਼ੀ

hoop (ਹੂਪ) *n v* ਪਹੀਆਂ ਆਦਿ ਨੂੰ ਜਕੜਨ ਲਈ ਗੋਲ ਲੋਹੇ ਦਾ ਚੱਕਰ, ਕੜਾ; ਲਚਕੀਲੀ ਪੇਟੀ; ਮੁੰਦਰੀ, ਅੰਗੂਠੀ, (ਕਾਲੀ ਖਾਂਸੀ ਵਿਚ) ਖਊਂ-ਖਊਂ, ਠਉਂ-ਠਊਂ ਆਦਿ; ਲੋਹੇ ਦੀ ਪੱਤਰੀ ਨਾਲ ਜਕੜਨਾ, ਖਊਂ-ਖਊਂ ਕਰਨਾ; **~ing cough** ਕਾਲੀ ਖੰਘ, ਕੁੱਤਾ-ਖੰਘ

hoot (ਹੂਟ) *n v* ਤਿਰਸਕਾਰ ਵਜੋਂ ਹੂ-ਹੂ, ਲੂ-ਲੂ, ਬੂ-ਬੂ, ਓਏ-ਓਏ, ਭੂੰ-ਭੂੰ; ਉੱਲੂ-ਬੋਲੀ ਓਏ-ਓਏ ਕਰਨਾ, ਭੂੰ-ਭੂੰ ਕਰਨਾ, ਛੀ-ਛੀ ਕਰਨਾ, ਧਿਕਾਰਨਾ; ਲੂ-ਲੂ ਕਰਕੇ ਭਜਾ ਦੇਣਾ; ਚਿੱਲਾਉਣਾ, ਸ਼ੋਰ ਪਾਉਣਾ

hope (ਹਅਉਪ) *n v* ਉਮੀਦ, ਭਰੋਸਾ, ਆਸ, ਆਸਰਾ; ਸੰਭਾਵਨਾ, ਵਿਸ਼ਵਾਸ, ਉਮੀਦ ਕਰਨੀ, ਆਸ ਕਰਨੀ ਜਾਂ ਲਾਉਣਾ, ਚਾਹੁਣਾ, ਭਰੋਸਾ ਕਰਨਾ; **~fulness** ਆਸ਼ਾ, ਪੂਰਨਤਾ, ਆਸਵੰਦੀ; **~less** ਨਿਰਾਸ, ਨਾਉਮੀਦ, ਮਾਯੂਸ, ਨਿਰਾਸ਼ਾਜਨਕ; ਨਿਕੰਮਾ

horizon (ਹਅ'ਰਾਇਜ਼ਨ) *n* ਦਿਸ-ਹੱਦਾ, ਦਿਗ-ਮੰਡਲ; **~tal** ਦਿਸ-ਹੱਦੇ ਦਾ, ਦਿਗ-ਮੰਡਲੀ, ਸਮਤਲ ਪਈ ਰੇਖਾ, ਲੇਟਵੀਂ ਰੇਖਾ

horn (ਹੋ*ਨ) *v* ਸਿੰਗ; ਨਰਸਿੰਘਾ, ਸਿੰਗੀ, ਸਮਰਿਧੀ ਦਾ ਪ੍ਰਤੀਕ; ਉੱਲੂ ਦੀ ਕਲਗ਼ੀ; ਹਾਰਨ, ਭੋਂਪੂ; ਸਿੰਗ ਮਾਰਨਾ, ਸਿੰਗ ਚਲਾਉਣਾ; ਸਿੰਗੀ ਵਜਾਉਣੀ; ਦਖ਼ਲ ਦੇਣਾ; ਰੋਕਣਾ; **~in** ਵਿਘਨ ਪਾਉਣਾ,

ਰੋਕਣਾ, ਦਖ਼ਲਅੰਦਾਜ਼ੀ ਕਰਨੀ; ~mad ਪੂਰਾ ਪਾਗਲ

hornet ('ਹੋਨਿਟ) *n* ਭੂੰਡ, ਭਰਿੰਡ, ਡ੍ਹਮੂ

horoscope (ਹੋਰੌਸਕਅਉਪ) *n* ਨਖੱਤਰ ਨਿਰੀਖਣ; ਟੇਵਾ, ਜਨਮ-ਪਤਰੀ, ਜਨਮ-ਕੁੰਡਲੀ, ਕੁੰਡਲੀ

horoscopy (ਹੋਰੌਸਕਅਪਿ) *n* ਜੋਤਸ਼, ਜੋਤਸ਼-ਵਿੰਦਿਆ

horrible ('ਹੋਰਅਬਲ) *a* ਘੋਰ, ਪ੍ਰਚੰਡ; ਭਿਆਨਕ, ਡਰਾਉਣਾ, ਵਿਕਰਾਲ, ਭਿਅੰਕਰ

horrid ('ਹੋਰਿਡ) *a* ਭਿਅੰਕਰ, ਵਿਕਰਾਲ, ਡਰਾਉਣਾ; ਕਠੋਰ; ~ness ਭਿਅੰਕਰਤਾ, ਵਿਕਰਾਲਤਾ; ਕਠੋਰਤਾ

horrific (ਹੋਰਿਫ਼ਿਕ) *a* ਭਿਅੰਕਰ, ਭਿਆਨਕ

horrified ('ਹੋਰਿਫ਼ਾਇਡ) *a* ਭੈਭੀਤ, ਜੀ-ਡ੍ਹਿਆਣ

horrify ('ਹੋਰਿਫ਼ਾਇ) *v* ਡਰਾ ਦੇਣਾ, ਭੈਭੀਤ ਕਰਨਾ, ਦਿਲ ਦੁਖਾਉਣਾ, ਧੱਕਾ ਪਹੁੰਚਾਉਣਾ

horror ('ਹੋਰਅ*) *n* ਡ੍ਹੈ; ਖੋਡ, ਡਰ; ਘਿਰਣਾ, ਨਫ਼ਰਤ; ਭੈਦਾਇਕ ਚੀਜ਼

horse (ਹੋ'ਸ) *n v* ਘੋੜਾ; ਰਿਸਾਲਾ, ਘੋੜ- ਸਵਾਰ ਫ਼ੌਜ; ਘੋੜੇ ਤੇ ਚੜ੍ਹਨਾ; ~laugh ਉੱਚਾ ਹਾਸਾ, ਠਹਾਕਾ; ~power ਸ਼ਕਤੀ ਦਾ ਮਾਪ; ~shoe ਨਾਲ੍ਹ, ਘੋੜੇ ਦੀ ਨਾਲ੍ਹ; ~trading ਸੂਝ ਨਾਲ ਕੀਤੀ ਗਈ ਸੌਦੇਬਾਜ਼ੀ

horticulture ('ਹੋਟਿਕਅੱਲਚਅ*) *n* ਬਾਗ਼ਬਾਨੀ, ਬਾਗ਼ਬਾਨੀ-ਵਿਗਿਆਨ

horticulturist ('ਹੋਟਿ'ਕਅੱਲਚ(ਅ)ਰਿਸਟ) *n* ਬਾਗ਼ਬਾਨੀ ਦਾ ਮਾਹਰ, ਬਾਗ਼ਬਾਨੀ-ਵਿਗਿਆਨੀ

hosier ('ਹਅਉਜ਼ਿਅ*) *n* ਜੁਰਾਬਾਂ, ਬੁਨੈਣਾਂ ਆਦਿ ਵੇਚਣ ਵਾਲਾ, ਜੁਰਾਬਫ਼ਰੋਸ਼; ~y ਜੁਰਾਬਾਂ ਬੁਨੈਣਾਂ ਆਦਿ ਦੀ ਦੁਕਾਨ ਜਾਂ ਕਾਰਖ਼ਾਨਾ

hospitable (ਹੋ'ਸਪਿਟਅਬਲ) *a* ਮਹਿਮਾਨ ਨਿਵਾਜ਼, ਖ਼ਾਤਰਦਾਰ; ~ness ਮਹਿਮਾਨ ਨਿਵਾਜ਼ੀ, ਖ਼ਾਤਰਦਾਰੀ

hospital ('ਹੋਸਪਿਟਲ) *n* ਹਸਪਤਾਲ, ਸ਼ਫ਼ਾਖ਼ਾਨਾ; (ਇਤਿ) ਮਹਿਮਾਨਖ਼ਾਨਾ; ~ism ਚਿਕਿਤਸਾ-ਪ੍ਰਬੰਧ, ਹਸਪਤਾਲੀ, ਪ੍ਰਬੰਧ; ਹਸਪਤਾਲੀਪੁਣਾ; ~ization ਚਿਕਿਤਸਾ ਲਈ ਹਮਪਤਾਲ ਵਿਚ ਕੀਤੀ ਭਰਤੀ; ~ize ਚਿਕਿਤਸਾ ਲਈ ਹਸਪਤਾਲ ਵਿਚ ਭਰਤੀ ਕਰਨਾ, ਦਾਖ਼ਲ ਕਰਨਾ

hospitality ('ਹੋਸਪਿ'ਟੈਲਅਟਿ) *n* ਪਰਾਹੁਣਾਚਾਰੀ, ਮਹਿਮਾਨ ਨਿਵਾਜ਼ੀ, ਖ਼ਾਤਰਦਾਰੀ

host (ਹਅਉਸਟ) *n* ਜਜਮਾਨ; ~el ਛਾਤਰਾਵਾਸ; ਸਰਾਂ, ਧਰਮਸ਼ਾਲਾ

hostage ('ਹੋਸਟਿਜ) *n* ਬੰਧਕ ਵਿਅਕਤੀ, ਯਰਗਮਾਲ

hostess ('ਹਅਉਸਟਿਸ) *n* ਮੇਜ਼ਬਾਨ ਔਰਤ; ਏਅਰ ਹੋਸਟੈੱਸ

hostile ('ਹੋਸਟਾਇਲ) *a* ਵਿਰੋਧੀ; ਪ੍ਰਤੀਕੂਲ; ਉਲਟ

hostility (ਹੋ'ਸਟਿਲਅਟਿ) *n* ਵਿਰੋਧ; ਵੈਰ, ਵੈਰ-ਭਾਵ, ਦੁਸ਼ਮਣੀ, ਲੜਾਈ-ਝਗੜਾ

hot (ਹੋਟ) *a* ਗਰਮ, ਤਪਿਆ ਹੋਇਆ, ਤੱਤਾ; ਕੌੜਾ, ਕਰਾਰਾ, ਚਟਪਟਾ; ਤੀਬਰ; ਗੁਸੈਲਾ; ਪ੍ਰਚੰਡ, ਜੋਸ਼ ਵਿਚ; ਉਤੇਜਤ; (ਖ਼ਬਰਾਂ ਆਦਿ) ਤਾਜ਼ਾ, ਗਰਮਾ-ਗਰਮ, ਨਵੀਆਂ; ~brained, ~headed ਗਰਮ ਮਿਜ਼ਾਜ, ਕਰੋਧੀ; ~line ਸੰਕਟਕਾਲੀ ਸੰਚਾਰ ਸਾਧਨ; ~water ਮੁਸੀਬਤ; ~ness ਗਰਮੀ, ਤਾਪ, ਤੀਖਣਤਾ, ਕਰੋਧ, ਪ੍ਰਚੰਡਤਾ

hotel (ਹਅ(ਉ)'ਟੈੱਲ) *n* ਤੋਜਨ ਖਾਣ ਦੀ ਥਾਂ, ਕਿਰਾਏ ਤੇ ਰਹਿਣ ਦੀ ਥਾਂ, ਵੱਡੀ ਸਰਾਂ ਜਾਂ ਮੁਸਾਫ਼ਰਖ਼ਾਨਾ

hound (ਹਾਉਂਡ) *n v* ਸ਼ਿਕਾਰੀ ਕੁੱਤਾ; ਨੀਚ ਆਦਮੀ, ਕਮੀਨਾ ਆਦਮੀ; ਕੁੱਤਿਆਂ ਨੂੰ ਲੈ ਕੇ ਸ਼ਿਕਾਰ ਖੇਡਣਾ, ਹੁਸਕਾਰਨਾ, (ਕੁੱਤੇ ਨੂੰ ਸ਼ਿਕਾਰ ਦੇ ਪਿੱਛੇ) ਛੱਡਣਾ

hour ('ਆਉਅ*) *n* ਘੰਟਾ; ਸੱਠ ਮਿੰਟ ਦੇ ਬਰਾਬਰ

ਦਾ ਸਮਾਂ; ਬੋੜ੍ਹਾ ਸਮਾਂ; ਘੜੀ ਭਰ ਸਮਾਂ; ਮੁਕੱਰਰ ਵਕਤ; *at the eleventh~* ਆਖ਼ਰੀ ਵਕਤ ਤੇ, ਅੰਤਮ ਸਮੇਂ ਤੇ; *small ~s* ਅੰਮ੍ਰਿਤ ਵੇਲਾ

house (ਹਾਊਸ) *n v* (1) ਮਕਾਨ, ਘਰ, ਨਿਵਾਸ-ਸਥਾਨ, ਧਾਮ; ਘਰਬਾਰ; (2) ਖ਼ਾਨਦਾਨ, ਘਰਾਣਾ, ਵੰਸ਼, ਕੁਲ, ਕੁਟੰਬ; ਥਾਂ ਦੇਣੀ, ਠਹਿਰਾਉਣਾ, ਸ਼ਰਨ ਦੇਣਾ, ਉਤਾਰਨਾ, ਗੁਦਾਮ ਵਿਚ ਰੱਖਣਾ; **~hold** ਘਰਬਾਰ, ਕੁਟੰਬ, ਗ੍ਰਹਿਸਥ; **~holder** ਘਰਬਾਰ ਵਾਲਾ, ਕੁਟੰਬ ਵਾਲਾ, ਗ੍ਰਹਿਸਥੀ (ਮੱਨੁਖ); **~keeper** ਗ੍ਰਹਿਣੀ, ਸੁਆਣੀ, ਨਿਗਰਾਨ; **~maid** ਨੌਕਰਾਨੀ; **~wife** ਗ੍ਰਹਿਣੀ, ਸੁਆਣੀ

housing ('ਹਾਊਜ਼ਿੰਙ) *n* ਸ਼ਰਨ, ਥਾਂ, ਘਰ, ਬਸੇਰਾ

hover ('ਹੌਵਅ*') *n v* ਮੰਡਲਾਉਣ; ਦੁਬਧਾ, ਅਨਿਸ਼ਚਾ; ਮੰਡਲਾਉਣਾ, ਚੱਕਰ ਕੱਟਣਾ

how (ਹਾਊ) *adv n* ਕਿਸ ਤਰ੍ਹਾਂ, ਕਿਵੇਂ, ਕਿਸ ਕਾਰਨ, ਕੀਕਣ, ਕਿੰਦਾਂ, ਕਿਤਨਾ, ਕਿਹਾ, ਕਿੰਨਾ ਕੁ; **~ever** ਪਰ ਕੁਝ ਵੀ ਹੋਵੇ, ਹਰ ਹਾਲਤ ਵਿਚ; ਫਿਰ ਵੀ; ਕਿੰਨਾ ਹੀ; **~soever** ਜਿਵੇਂ ਕਿਵੇਂ, ਜਿਉਂ ਤਿਉਂ, ਜਿਹਾ-ਕਿਹਾ; ਕਿਵੇਂ ਨਾ ਕਿਵੇਂ, ਕਿਸੇ ਤਰ੍ਹਾਂ ਵੀ

howl (ਹਾਊਲ) *n v* ਅਰੂਕ, ਚੀਖ, ਆਵਾਜ਼; ਆਹ ਦਾ ਨਾਅਰਾ; ਹਾਸੇ ਠੱਠੇ ਦੀ ਆਵਾਜ਼; (ਜਾਨਵਰਾਂ ਦਾ) ਹਵਾਂਕਣਾ, ਅਰੂਕਣਾ, ਚਾਂਗਰਨਾ, ਭੌਂਕਣਾ; (ਆਦਮੀਆਂ ਦਾ) ਦਰਦ ਨਾਲ ਚੀਖਣਾ, ਚਿੱਲਾ ਕੇ ਰੋਣਾ; **~ing** ਚੀਕ ਚਿਹਾੜਾ, ਹਾਲ ਪਾਹਰਿਆ; **~er** ਚਿਲਾਉਣ ਵਾਲਾ; ਘੋਰ ਗ਼ਲਤੀ

howlet ('ਹਾਊਲਿਟ) *n* ਉੱਲੂ, ਉੱਲੂ ਦਾ ਬੱਚਾ

hub (ਹੱਬ) *n* (ਪਹੀਏ ਦੀ) ਨਾਭ, ਨਾਭੀ, ਧੁਰਾ, ਵਿਚਕਾਰ ਦਾ ਹਿੱਸਾ; ਕੇਂਦਰ

hubble-bubble ('ਹੱਬਲ-ਬਅੱਬਲ) *n* ਹੁੱਕਾ, ਗੁੜਗੁੜੀ; ਹੁੱਕੇ ਦੀ ਗੁੜਗੁੜ

huddle ('ਹਅੱਡਲ) *n v* (ਲੋਕਾਂ ਦਾ) ਉੱਗੜ-ਦੁੱਗੜ ਇਕੱਠ; ਗੜਬੜ, ਘੜਮੱਸ, ਭੀੜ-ਭਾੜ, ਉੱਗੜ-ਦੁੱਗੜ; ਢੇਰ ਲਗਾ ਦੇਣਾ

hue (ਹਯੂ) *n* (1) ਰੰਗ, ਛਬ, ਆਭਾ, ਰੰਗਤ; (2) ਸ਼ੋਰ, ਹੱਲਾ-ਰਫਾ, ਚਿੱਲਾਹਟ; **~less** ਰੰਗਹੀਨ

huff (ਹਅੱਫ) *n v* ਰੋਹ, ਗੁੱਸਾ, ਤਾਅ, ਕਾਵੜ੍ਹ; ਸ਼ੇਖ਼ੀ ਮਾਰਨੀ; ਤੈਸ਼ ਵਿਚ ਆਉਣਾ, ਗੁੱਸੇ ਵਿਚ ਹੋਣਾ; ਨਰਾਜ਼ ਕਰਨਾ

hug (ਹਅੱਗ) *n v* ਜੱਫੀ, ਗਲ ਲਾਉਣਾ, ਕਲਾਵੇ ਵਿਚ ਲੈਣਾ, ਜੱਫੀ ਪਾਉਣੀ; ਕਾਇਮ ਰਹਿਣਾ, ਆਪਣੇ ਮੂੰਹ ਮੀਆਂ-ਮਿੱਠੂ ਬਣਨਾ

huge (ਹਯੂਜ) *a* ਬਹੁਤ ਵੱਡਾ, ਵਿਸ਼ਾਲ, ਵਿਰਾਟ, ਭਾਰੀ; **~ly** ਵਿਸ਼ਾਲ ਰੂਪ ਵਿਚ

hull (ਹਅੱਲ) *n v* ਛਿਲਕਾ, ਛਿੱਲੜ, ਫੋਕੜ; ਖੋਖ, ਖੋਲ; ਜਹਾਜ਼ ਦਾ ਢਾਂਚਾ, ਧੜ; ਛਿੱਲਣਾ, ਛਿਲਕਾ ਲਾਹੁਣਾ; ਪਰਦਾ ਲਾਹੁਣਾ, ਪਰੇ ਕਰਨਾ, ਹਟਾਉਣਾ

hum (ਹਅੱਮ) *n v int* ਭਿਣਕ, ਭਿਣ-ਭਿਣ, ਭੀਂ-ਭੀਂ, ਭਿਣਭਿਣਾਹਟ, ਘੂੰ-ਘੂੰ, ਹੈਰਾਨੀ ਦੀ ਅਵਾਜ਼; **~ming** ਭਿਣ-ਭਿਣ ਕਰਨ ਵਾਲਾ, ਗੂੰਜਣ ਵਾਲਾ

human ('ਹਯੂਮਅਨ) *n a* ਮੱਨੁਖ, ਮਾਨਵ, ਇਨਸਾਨ; ਮਨੁੱਖੀ, ਇਨਸਾਨੀ, ਮਾਨਵੀ; **~being** ਮਾਨਵ, ਇਨਸਾਨ; **~kind** ਮਾਨਵ ਜਾਤੀ; **~ism** ਮਾਨਵਤਾ, ਮੈਤਰੀ-ਭਾਵ, ਇਨਸਾਨੀ ਦੋਸਤੀ; ਮਾਨਵਵਾਦ; ਮਾਨਵ-ਵਿੱਦਿਆ; **~itraian** ਮਨੁੱਖਤਾਵਾਦੀ, ਖਲਕ-ਦੋਸਤ, ਜਨ-ਸੇਵੀ, ਲੋਕ-ਉਪਕਾਰੀ; **~itarianism** ਮਾਨਵਹਿਤਵਾਦ, ਪਰਉਪਕਾਰਵਾਦ, ਜਨ-ਸੇਵਾਵਾਦ; **~ity** ਮਨੁੱਖਤਾ, ਆਦਮਜਾਤ, ਮਾਨਵਤਾ, ਮਨੁੱਖਜਾਤੀ; ਹਮਦਰਦੀ, ਦਰਦਵੰਦੀ, ਦਿਆਲਤਾ; **~ize** ਮਨੁੱਖੀ ਰੂਪ ਦੇਣਾ, ਆਦਮੀ ਬਣਾਉਣਾ, ਮਨੁੱਖਤਾ ਸਿਖਾਉਣਾ, ਇਨਸਾਨੀ ਸਿਫ਼ਤਾਂ ਵਾਲਾ ਬਣਾਉਣਾ; **~ness**

ਇਨਸਾਨੀਅਤ, ਮਾਨਵਤਾ, ਮਨੁੱਖਤਾ

humane (ਹਯੂ'ਮੇਇਨ) *a* ਦਿਆਲੂ, ਮਾਨਵ ਹਿਤੈਸ਼ੀ; ਹਮਦਰਦ, ਮੈਤਰੀ ਭਾਵ ਵਾਲਾ, ਤਰਸਵਾਨ, ਨਰਮਦਿਲ; **~ness** ਦਇਆਲਤਾ, ਕਿਰਪਾਲਤਾ, ਮਾਨਵੀਕਤਾ, ਸੁੰਦਰਤਾ

humble ('ਹਅੱਮਬਲ) *a v* ਨਿਮਾਣਾ, ਮਸਕੀਨ, ਨਾਚੀਜ਼, ਘਮੰਡ ਰਹਿਤ, ਨਿਰਹੰਕਾਰ; ਤੁੱਛ; ਮਾਣ ਤੋੜਨਾ, ਹੀਣ ਕਰਨਾ, ਨੀਵਾਂ ਕਰਨਾ, ਨਿਵਾਉਣਾ; **~ness** ਤੁੱਛਤਾ, ਸਧਾਰਨਤਾ, ਮਾਮੂਲੀਪਣ; ਨਿਮਰਤਾ

humbug ('ਹਅੱਮਬਅੱਗ) *n a v* ਦੰਭ, ਪਖੰਡ, ਧੋਖਾ, ਠੱਗੀ; ਬਕਵਾਸ, ਉਟਪਟਾਂਗ, ਗੁੱਲ-ਜਲੂਲ ਧੋਖਾ ਦੇਣਾ, ਠੱਗਣਾ; ਛਲਣਾ; **~gery** ਛਲ, ਕਪਟ

humdrum ('ਹਅੱਮਡਰਅੱਮ) *n a* ਨੀਰਸਤਾ, ਫਿੱਕਾਪਣ; ਤੁੱਛ ਵਿਅਕਤੀ; ਨੀਰਸ, ਫਿੱਕਾ, ਬੇਸੁਆਦਾ, ਸਧਾਰਨ

humiliate (ਹਯੂ'ਮਿਲਿਏਇਟ) *v* ਮਾਣ ਤੋੜਨਾ, ਨੀਵਾਂ ਦਿਖਾਉਣਾ, ਬੇਇੱਜ਼ਤ ਕਰਨਾ, ਜ਼ਲੀਲ ਕਰਨਾ

humiliating (ਹਯੂ'ਮਿਲਿਏਇਟਿਙ) *a* ਬੇਇੱਜ਼ਤੀ ਭਰਿਆ, ਹੌਛਾ, ਤੁੱਛ, ਅਪਮਾਨਜਨਕ

humiliation (ਹਯੂ'ਮਿਲਿ'ਏਇਸ਼ਨ) *n* ਬੇਇੱਜ਼ਤੀ, ਅਪਮਾਨ, ਤਿਰਸਕਾਰ

humility (ਹਯੂ'ਮਿਲਅਟਿ) *n* ਨਿਮਰਤਾ, ਅਧੀਨਗੀ, ਨਿਰਮਾਣਤਾ; ਦੀਨਤਾ

humorous ('ਹਯੂਮਅਰਅਸ) *a* ਵਿਨੋਦਮਈ, ਹਾਸੇ ਭਰਿਆ, ਮਸਖ਼ਰਾ, ਮਜ਼ਾਕੀਆ

humour, humor ('ਹਯੂਮਅ*) *n* ਹਾਸ-ਰਸ; ਵਿਲਾਸ, ਵਿਨੋਦ, ਮੌਜ, ਲਹਿਰ, ਮਜ਼ਾਕ; ਸੁਭਾਅ, ਮਿਜ਼ਾਜ

hunger ('ਹਅੱਙਗਅ*) *n v* ਭੁੱਖ, ਭੋਖੜਾ, ਹਾਬੜੀ; ਤੀਬਰ ਇਛਿਆ, ਭੁੱਖਾ ਹੋਣਾ, ਭੁੱਖ ਲੱਗਣੀ,

---

ਫਾਕੇ ਕਰਾਉਣੇ

hungriness ('ਹਅੱਙਗਰਿਨਿਸ) *n* ਭੁੱਖਾਪਣ

hungry ('ਹਅੱਙਗਰਿ) *a* ਭੁੱਖ, ਭੁੱਖਾ-ਭਾਣਾ; ਭੁੱਖੜ, ਲਾਲਸਾਵਾਨ

hunt (ਹਅੰਟ) *n v* ਸ਼ਿਕਾਰ, ਤਲਾਸ਼, ਖੋਜ, ਪਿੱਛਾ; **~er** ਸ਼ਿਕਾਰੀ, ਸ਼ਿਕਾਰੀ ਕੁੱਤਾ; **~ing** ਸ਼ਿਕਾਰ

hurdle ('ਹਅਃਡਲ) *n* ਰੋਕ, ਰੁਕਾਵਟ, ਅੜਿੱਕਾ, ਬਾਧਾ, ਅੜੀ, ਜੰਗਲਾ

hurl (ਹਅਃਲ) *n v* (ਪੱਥਰ ਆਦਿ) ਵਗਾਹ ਕੇ ਸੁੱਟਣਾ, ਧੱਕਣਾ, ਢੇਰ ਦੇਣਾ; ਸੋਟ, ਉਛਾਲ

hurrah, hurra (ਹੁ'ਰਾ) *int n* (ਪ੍ਰਸੰਸਾ ਤੇ ਖ਼ੁਸ਼ੀ ਦੇ ਪਰਗਟਾਉ ਵਜੋਂ) ਆਹਾ!, ਵਾਹ-ਵਾਹ!, ਵਾਹਵਾ, ਜੈਕਾਰਾ, ਹਰਸ਼-ਨਾਦ

hurricane ('ਹਅੱਰਿਕਅਨ) *n* ਤੂਫ਼ਾਨ, ਝੱਖੜ

hurried ('ਹਅੱਰਿਡ) *a* ਝਬਦੇ, ਤੁਰਤ; ਸੀਘਰ, ਉਤਾਵਲਾ; **~ness** ਸ਼ੀਘਰਤਾ, ਜਲਦਬਾਜ਼ੀ, ਫੁਰਤੀ, ਉਤਾਵਲਾਪਣ

hurry ('ਹਅੱਰਿ) *n* ਜਲਦੀ, ਛੇਤੀ, ਜਲਦਬਾਜ਼ੀ, ਕਾਹਲੀ, ਉਤਾਵਲ, ਬੇਚੈਨੀ

hurt (ਹਅਃਟ) *n v a* ਸੱਟ, ਜ਼ਰਬ, ਚੋਟ; ਘਾਉ, ਜ਼ਖਮ, ਸਦਮਾ, ਨੁਕਸਾਨ; ਜ਼ਖ਼ਮੀ ਕਰਨਾ; ਦੁੱਖ ਪਹੁੰਚਾਉਣਾ, ਦਰਦ ਹੋਣਾ

hurtle ('ਹਅਃਟਲ) *v* ਭਿੜਨਾ; ਰਿੜ੍ਹਨਾ, ਰੇੜ੍ਹਨਾ; ਪੂਰਮ ਕਰਕੇ ਡਿਗਣਾ

husband ('ਹਅੱਜ਼ਬਅੰਡ) *n v* ਪਤੀ, ਘਰ ਵਾਲਾ, ਖਾਵੰਦ, ਕੰਤ, ਸੁਆਮੀ; **~ry** ਕਿਸਾਨੀ, ਵਾਹੀ-ਖੇਤੀ, ਖੇਤੀ, ਕਾਸ਼ਤਕਾਰੀ, ਕਾਸ਼ਕਾਰੀ, ਕਾਸ਼ਤ, ਘਰੇਲੂ ਪ੍ਰਬੰਧ; **animal ~ry** ਪਸ਼ੂ-ਪਾਲਣ

hush (ਹਅੱਸ਼) *v int* ਚੁੱਪ-ਚਾਂ, ਸ਼ਾਂਤੀ, ਖ਼ਮੋਸ਼ੀ; ਚੁੱਪ ਕਰਾਉਣਾ ਜਾਂ ਹੋਣਾ, ਦਬ ਵੱਟਣੀ, ਸ਼ਾਂਤ ਕਰਨਾ

husk (ਹਅੱਸਕ) *n v* ਛਿਲਕਾ, ਭੂਸੀ, ਫੱਕ, ਸੂਰਜ

ਛਿਲੜ; ਛਿਲਕਾ ਲਾਹੁਣਾ, ਛੱਟਣਾ, ਛੜਨਾ,
ਛਿਲਕਾ; --ed ਛਿਲਕੇਦਾਰ

hustle (ਹੱਸਲ) *n v* ਧਕੱਮ-ਧੱਕਾ, ਟੱਕਰ,
ਜਲਦੀ, ਤੀਬਰਤਾ; ਜ਼ੋਰ ਨਾਲ ਧੱਕਾ ਮਾਰਨਾ,
ਧੱਕਮ-ਧੱਕਾ ਕਰਨਾ

hut (ਹਅੱਟ) *n v* ਝੁੱਗੀ, ਝੁੱਪੜੀ, ਟੱਪਰੀ, ਛੱਪਰੀ,
ਕੁੱਲੀ, (ਸੈਨਾ) ਪੜਾਉ, ਅਸਥਾਈ ਟਿਕਾਣਾ;
ਝੁੱਗੀ ਵਿਚ ਰਹਿਣਾ ਜਾਂ ਰੱਖਣਾ; ~ment ਫ਼ੌਜਾਂ
ਲਈ ਲੱਕੜੀ ਦਾ ਮਕਾਨ, ਬੈਰਕ, ਡੇਰਾ

hyaena, hyena (ਹਾਇ'ਈਨਅ) *n* ਲੱਕੜਬੱਗਾ,
ਬਘਿਆੜ ਵਰਗਾ ਇਕ ਮਾਸਖੋਰਾ ਜੰਗਲੀ ਪਸ਼ੂ;
(ਅਲੰਕਾਰਕ) ਜ਼ਾਲਮ, ਬੇਰਹਿਮ, ਨਿਰਦਈ ਮਨੁੱਖ

hybrid ('ਹਾਇਬਰਿਡ) *n a* ਦੋਗਲਾਪਣ, ਦੋਗਲਾ,
ਦੋ-ਨਸਲਾ; ~ism, ~ity ਦੋਗਲਾਪਣ; ~ize ਦੋ-

ਨਸਲਾ ਜਾਂ ਦੋਗਲਾ ਬਣਾਉਣਾ

hygiene ('ਹਾਇਜੀਨ) *n* ਸਿਹਤ-ਵਿਗਿਆਨ,
ਅਰੋਗ-ਵਿਗਿਆਨ; ਸਰੀਰ ਰੱਖਿਆ ਨਿਯਮ

hymn (ਹਿਮ) *n v* ਭਜਨ, ਪੂਜਾ ਦੇ ਗੀਤ, ਸ਼ਬਦ;
ਭਜਨ ਕਰਨਾ; ਸ਼ਬਦ ਗਾਉਣਾ

hypocrisy (ਹਿ'ਪੌਕਰਅਸਿ) *n* ਪਖੰਡ, ਛਲ, ਦੰਭ,
ਮੋਮੋਠਗਣੀ

hypocrite ('ਹਿਪਅਕਰਿਟ) *n* (ਵਿਅਕਤੀ) ਕਪਟੀ,
ਪਖੰਡੀ, ਛਲੀਆ, ਦੰਭੀ, ਮੱਕਾਰ

hypothesis (ਹਾਇ'ਪੌਥਿਸਿਸ) *n* ਅਨੁਮਾਨ,
ਕਲਪਨਾ; ਮਿਥੀ ਸਥਾਪਨਾ, ਫ਼ਰਜ਼ੀ ਮਨੌਤ,
ਕਲਪਤ ਵਿਚਾਰ, ਪਰਿਕਲਪਨਾ

hysteria (ਹਿ'ਸਟਿਅਰਿਅ) *n* ਝੱਲ, ਪਾਗਲਪਣ,
ਉਨਮਾਦ

I, i (ਆਇ) ਰੋਮਨ ਵਰਨਮਾਲਾ ਦਾ ਨੌਵਾਂ ਅੱਖਰ

I *pron n* ਮੈਂ, ਅਹੰ; ਹਉਂ, ਆਪਾ, ਅਰੰਵਾਦ

ibidem, ibid ('ਇਬਿਡ੍ਰੈਮ, 'ਇਬਿਡ੍) (*L*) *adv* ਉਹੀ, ਉਕਤ, ਉਸੇ (ਪੁਸਤਕ, ਅਧਿਆਇ ਜਾਂ ਪੈਰੇ) ਵਿਚ

ice (ਆਇਸ) *n v* ਬਰਫ਼, ਹਿਮ; (ਬ ਵ) ਕੁਲਫ਼ੀ, ਆਈਸ ਕ੍ਰੀਮ; ਬਰਫ਼ ਵਿਚ ਲਾ ਕੇ ਠੰਢਾ ਕਰਨਾ; ~**berg** ਬਰਫ਼ ਦਾ ਤੋਦਾ, ਹਿਮ-ਪਰਬਤ; ਭਾਵਹੀਨ ਮਨੁੱਖ

icon ('ਆਇਕੋਨ) *n* ਬੁੱਤ, ਮੂਰਤੀ, ਚਿੱਤਰ; ~**oclasm** ਬੁੱਤ-ਭੰਜਨ, ਮੂਰਤੀ-ਖੰਡਨ; ~**ography** ਮੂਰਤੀ ਕਲਾ; ~**olater** ਮੂਰਤੀ ਪੂਜਨ, ਬੁੱਤ ਪੂਜਾ ਕਰਨ ਵਾਲਾ; ~**olatry** ਮੂਰਤੀ-ਪੂਜਾ-ਵਿਰੋਧ

idea (ਆਇ'ਡ੍ਰਿਆ) *n* ਵਿਚਾਰ, ਖ਼ਿਆਲ, ਆਸ਼ਾ, ਭਾਵ; ਮਾਨਸਕ ਰੂਪ-ਰੇਖਾ, ਢਾਂਚਾ, ਨਕਸ਼ਾ; ਯੋਜਨਾ, ਤਜਵੀਜ਼, ਯੁਕਤੀ

ideal (ਆਇ'ਡ੍ਰਿਅਲ) *a n* ਆਦਰਸ਼, ਨਮੂਨੇ ਦਾ, ਪ੍ਰਮਾਣਕ; ਖਿਆਲੀ, ਆਦਰਸ਼, ਵਿਚਾਰ-ਪਰਦਰਸ਼ਕ; ~**ism** ਆਦਰਸ਼ਵਾਦ, ਕਲਪਨਾਵਾਦ; ~**ist** ਆਦਰਸ਼ਵਾਦੀ, ਕਲਪਨਾਵਾਦੀ; ~**ize** ਆਦਰਸ਼ਿਉਣਾ, ਆਦਰਸ਼ ਰੂਪ ਦੇਣਾ

identic (ਆਇ'ਡੈਂਟਿਕ) *a* ਠੀਕ ਉਹੋ ਜਿਹਾ, ਸਗਵਾਂ, ਸਮਾਨ, ਸਰਬੰਗ, ਸਮ

identification (ਆਇ'ਡੈਂਟਿਫ਼ਿ'ਕੇਇਸ਼ਨ) *n* ਪਛਾਣ, ਸ਼ਨਾਖ਼ਤ, ਅਭੇਦਤਾ, ਤਦਰੂਪਤਾ

identity (ਆਇ'ਡੈਂਟਅਟਿ) *n* ਪਛਾਣ; ਅਭੇਦਤਾ,

ਇਕਾਤਮਕਤਾ, ਤਦਰੂਪਤਾ, ਇਕਰੂਪਤਾ, ਸਮਾਨਤਾ

ideologist ('ਆਇਡਿ'ਔਲਅਜਿਸਟ) *n* ਵਿਚਾਰ-ਵੇਤਾ, ਸਿਧਾਂਤਕਾਰ

ideology ('ਆਇਡਿ'ਔਲਅਜਿ) *n* ਭਾਵ-ਵਿਗਿਆਨ, ਵਿਚਾਰਧਾਰਾ, ਵਿਚਾਰ-ਪੱਧਤੀ, ਚਿੰਤਨ-ਸ਼ੈਲੀ, ਭਾਵ-ਪ੍ਰਣਾਲੀ; ਸਿਧਾਂਤ-ਸਮੂਹ

idiom ('ਇਡ੍ਰਿਅਮ) *n* ਮੁਹਾਵਰਾ; ਬੋਲ-ਚਾਲ, ਭਾਸ਼ਾ ਦੀ ਕੋਈ ਵਿਸ਼ੇਸ਼ਤਾ; ~**atic** ਮੁਹਾਵਰੇਦਾਰ, ਠੇਠ; ਬੋਲ-ਚਾਲ ਸਬੰਧੀ

idiot ('ਇਡ੍ਰਿਅਟ) *n* ਮੂਰਖ, ਮੂੜ੍ਹ, ਅਹਿਮਕ, ਬੁੱਧੂ, ਬੁਝੜ; ~**ic** ਮੂਰਖਤਾ ਭਰਿਆ, ਅਹਿਮਕਾਨਾ

idle ('ਆਇਡ੍ਲ) *a v* ਵਿਹਲਾ, ਬੇਕਾਰ, ਨਿਕੰਮਾ; ਨਕਾਰਾ, ਆਲਸੀ, ਸੁਸਤ; ਨਿਰਮੂਲ ਹੋਣਾ, ਨਿਰਥਕ ਹੋਣਾ; ਵਿਹਲੇ ਹੋਣਾ, ਬੇਕਾਰ ਹੋਣਾ, ਨਿਕੰਮੇ ਰਹਿਣਾ

idol ('ਆਇਡ੍ਲ) *n* ਬੁੱਤ, ਮੂਰਤੀ, ਪ੍ਰਤਿਮਾ; ~**ater** ਬੁੱਤ-ਪੂਜ, ਮੂਰਤੀ-ਉਪਾਸ਼ਕ; ~**atry** ਬੁੱਤ-ਪੂਜਾ, ਮੂਰਤੀ-ਪੂਜਾ

if (ਇਫ਼) *n conj* ਜੇਕਰ, ਅਗਰ; ਸ਼ਰਤ

ignite (ਇਗ'ਨਾਇਟ) *v* ਅੱਗ ਲਾਉਣੀ ਜਾਂ ਲੱਗਣੀ, ਬਾਲਣਾ ਜਾਂ ਬਲਣਾ; ਚੁਆਤੀ ਲਾਉਣੀ, ਬਲ ਉੱਠਣਾ, ਭਖਾਉਣਾ

ignition (ਇਗ'ਨਿਸ਼ਨ) *n* ਸੜਨ, ਬਲਣ, ਜਲਣ, ਭਖਣ

ignoble (ਇਗ'ਨਅਉਬਲ) *a* ਨੀਚ ਜਾਤ ਵਾਲਾ, ਹੀਣੀ ਜਾਤ ਦਾ, ਅਕੁਲੀਨ; ਕਮੀਨਾ, ਹੀਣਾ, ਨੀਚ, ਹੋਛਾ

ignorance ('ਇਗਨ(ਅ)ਰਅੰਸ) *n* ਅਗਿਆਨ, ਬੇਸਮਝੀ, ਨਾਦਾਨੀ

ignorant ('ਇਗਨ(ਅ)ਰਅੰਟ) *a* ਅਗਿਆਨੀ, ਅਲਪੱਗ, ਅਟਜਾਟ, ਬੇਸਮਝ, ਨਾਦਾਨ, ਅਬੋਧ, ਮੂਰਖ, ਮੂੜ੍ਹ

ill (ਇਲ) *a n adv* ਬੀਮਾਰ, ਰੋਗੀ, ਅਸੁਅਸਥ; ਬੁਰਾ, ਭੈੜਾ; ਨਾਮੁਆਫ਼ਕ, ਅਸ਼ੁਭ; ਦੁਖਦਾਈ; ਮੁਸ਼ਕਲ; ਕੋਝਾ; ਅਸੰਗਤ; ਅਨੁਚਿਤ; ਬੁਰਾਈ, ਭੈੜ, ਦੋਸ਼; ਵਿਕਾਰ, ਵਿਗਾੜ; **~bred** ਕੁਢੰਜਾ, ਭੈੜਾ, ਬਦਤਮੀਜ਼; **~favoured** ਕੋਝਾ, ਬਦਸ਼ਕਲ; **~natured** ਭੈੜੇ ਸੁਭਾਅ ਵਾਲਾ, ਚਿੜਚੜਾ, ਅਵੈੜਾ, ਬਦਮਜਾਜ਼; **~omened** ਕੁਸ਼ਗਨਾ, ਬਦਸ਼ਗਨਾ; **~tempered** ਅਵੈੜਾ, ਅਤੁਰ, ਕਰੋਪੀ; **~treat, ~use** ਬਦਸਲੂਕੀ ਕਰਨੀ; **~treatment** ਬਦਸਲੂਕੀ, ਦੁਰਵਿਚਾਰ, ਦੁਰਵਰਤੋਂ; **~ness** ਬੀਮਾਰੀ, ਰੋਗ, ਅਸੁਅਸਥਤਾ; ਬੁਰਾਈ, ਦੋਸ਼

illegal (ਇ'ਲੀਗਲ) *a* ਗ਼ੈਰਕਾਨੂੰਨੀ, ਅਵੈਧ, ਨਾਜਾਇਜ਼; **~ity** ਅਵੈਧਤਾ

illegibillity (ਇਲੇਜਿ'ਬਿਲਅਟਿ) *n* (ਪੜ੍ਹਨ ਵਿਚ) ਅਸਪਸ਼ਟਤਾ

illegible (ਇ'ਲੈਜਾਅਬਲ) *a* ਅਸਪਸ਼ਟ, ਜਿਹੜਾ ਚੰਗੀ ਤਰ੍ਹਾਂ ਪੜ੍ਹਿਆ ਨਾ ਜਾ ਸਕੇ

illegitimacy ('ਇਲਿ'ਜਿਟਅਮਅਸਿ) *n* ਅਯੋਗਤਾ, ਅਨੁਚਿਤਤਾ, ਹਰਾਮੀਪਣ

illegitimate (ਇਲਿ'ਜਿਟਿਮਅਟ) *a* ਅਯੋਗ, ਨਾਮੁਨਾਸਬ; ਗ਼ੈਰਕਾਨੂੰਨੀ, ਅਵੈਧ; ਹਰਾਮੀ

illicit (ਇ'ਲਿਸਿਟ) *a* ਵਰਜਤ, ਗ਼ੈਰਕਾਨੂੰਨੀ; ਅਨੁਚਿਤ, ਨਾਮੁਨਾਸਬ, ਨਾਜਾਇਜ਼

illiteracy (ਇ'ਲਿਟ(ਅ)ਰਅਸਿ) *n* ਅਨਪੜ੍ਹਤਾ, ਨਿਰੱਖਰਤਾ

illiterate (ਇ'ਲਿਟ(ਅ)ਰਅਟ) *a* ਅਨਪੜ੍ਹ, ਅਸਿੱਖਿਅਤ, ਉਜੱਡ

illogical (ਇ'ਲੌਜਿਕਲ) *a* ਤਰਕਹੀਨ, ਤਰਕ-ਵਿਰੁੱਧ, ਨਿਆਂਵਿਰੁੱਧ, ਅਸੰਗਤ, ਅਢੁੱਕਵਾਂ

illuminate (ਇ'ਲੂਮਿਨੇਇਟ) *v* ਚਾਨਣ ਕਰਨਾ, ਰੋਸ਼ਨ ਕਰਨਾ, ਪ੍ਰਕਾਸ਼ਮਾਨ ਕਰਨਾ; ਜ਼ਾਹਰ ਕਰਨੀ

illumination (ਇ'ਲੂਮਿ'ਨੇਇਸ਼ਨ) *n* ਚਾਨਣ, ਪ੍ਰਕਾਸ਼, ਰੌਸ਼ਨੀ

illumine (ਇ'ਲੂਮਿਨ) *v* ਗਿਆਨ ਦੇਣਾ, ਸੋਝੀ ਕਰਾਉਣੀ; ਚਾਨਣ ਕਰਨਾ, ਰੌਸ਼ਨੀ ਕਰਨੀ, ਪ੍ਰਕਾਸ਼ਮਾਨ ਕਰਨਾ

illusion (ਇ'ਲੂਯਨ) *n* ਭਰਮ, ਵਹਿਮ, ਭੁਲਾਵਾ; ਛਲ, ਮਾਇਆ, ਇੰਦਰ-ਜਾਲ, ਭੁਲੇਖਾ; **~ism** ਮਾਇਆਵਾਦੀ, ਭਰਮਵਾਦ

illusive (ਇ'ਲੂਸਿਵ) *a* (ਸਿੱਖਿਆ) ਭਰਮਾਤਮਕ, ਭੁਲਾਵਾ, ਛਲਰੂਪ

illusory (ਇ'ਲੂਸਅਰਿ) *a* ਭਰਮ ਪਾਉਣ ਵਾਲਾ, ਭਰਮ ਉਪਜਾਉ; ਮਾਇਆਮਈ, ਛਲਰੂਪ

illustrate ('ਇਲਅਸਟਰੇਇਟ) *v* ਸਪਸ਼ਟ ਕਰਨਾ, ਉਦਾਹਰਣ ਦੇ ਕੇ ਸਮਝਾਉਣਾ, ਚਿੱਤਰਾਂ ਨਾਲ ਸਮਝਾਉਣਾ; ਵਿਆਖਿਆ ਕਰਨੀ, ਚਿੱਤਰਯੁਕਤ ਕਰਨਾ; **~d** ਉਦਾਹਰਣਯੁਕਤ, ਸਚਿੱਤਰ

illustration ('ਇਲਅ'ਸਟਰੇਇਸ਼ਨ) *n* ਵਿਆਖਿਆ, ਸਪਸ਼ਟੀਕਰਨ; ਉਦਾਹਰਣ, ਮਿਸਾਲ, ਦ੍ਰਿਸ਼ਟਾਂਤ; ਚਿਤਰ, ਤਸਵੀਰ

illustrative ('ਇਲਅਸਟਰਅਟਿਵ੍) *a* ਚਿਤਰਮਈ; ਉਦਾਹਰਣਯੁਕਤ; ਦ੍ਰਿਸ਼ਟਾਂਤਯੁਕਤ; ਵਿਆਖਿਆ ਵਾਲਾ

illustrious (ਇ'ਲਅੱਸਟਰਿਅਸ) *n* ਪ੍ਰਸਿੱਧ, ਮਸ਼ਹੂਰ, ਨਾਮੀ, ਨੇਕਨਾਮ, ਕੀਰਤੀਵਾਨ, ਜਸਵੰਤ; **~ness** ਕੀਰਤੀ, ਪ੍ਰਸਿੱਧੀ, ਜਸ, ਗੌਰਵ

image ('ਇਮਿਜ) *n v* ਸ਼ਕਲ, ਆਕਾਰ, ਰੂਪ, ਤਸਵੀਰ; ਮੂਰਤੀ, ਪ੍ਰਤਿਮਾ; ਪ੍ਰਤਿਬਿੰਬ, ਬਿੰਬ, ਹੂ-ਬਹੁ ਉਤਾਰਾ; ਚਿਤਰ ਬਣਾਉਣਾ, ਮੂਰਤੀ ਬਣਾਉਣੀ; ਮੂਰਤੀਮਾਨ ਕਰਨਾ, ਕੋਈ ਰੂਪ ਦੇਣਾ; ਕਲਪਨਾ ਕਰਨੀ, ਖ਼ਿਆਲ ਬੰਨ੍ਹਣਾ; ~ry ਅਲੰਕਾਰ, ਅਲੰਕਾਰਮਈ ਚਿੱਤਰਨ ਜਾਂ ਨਿਰੂਪਨ, ਬਿੰਬਾਵਲੀ, ਬਿੰਬ-ਵਿਧਾਨ, ਮੂਰਤੀ-ਨਿਰਮਾਨ

imaginary (ਇ'ਮੈਜਿਨ(ਅ)ਰਿ) *a* ਖ਼ਿਆਲੀ, ਕਲਪਤ, ਕਿਆਸੀ, ਕਾਲਪਨਕ, ਮਨਘੜੰਤ

imagination (ਇ'ਮੈਜਿ'ਨੇਇਸ਼ਨ) *n* ਕਲਪਨਾ, ਭਾਵਨਾ, ਸੰਕਲਪ, ਕਲਪਨਾ, ਸ਼ਕਤੀ, ਨਿਰੂਪਨ-ਸ਼ਕਤੀ, ਤਸੱਵਰ

imaginative (ਇ'ਮੈਜਿਨਅਟਿਵ) *a* ਕਲਪਨਾਮਈ, ਕਲਪਤ, ਭਾਵਨਾਪੂਰਨ, ਭਾਵਨਾਮਈ, ਉਸਾਰੂ ਖ਼ਿਆਲ

imagine (ਇ'ਮੈਜਿਨ) *v* ਕਲਪਨਾ ਕਰਨੀ, ਵਿਚਾਰ ਕਰਨਾ, ਖ਼ਿਆਲ ਬੰਨ੍ਹਣਾ, ਸੋਚਣਾ; ਅਨੁਮਾਨ ਲਾਉਣਾ, ਖ਼ਿਆਲ- ਉਡਾਰੀ ਲਾਉਣੀ;

imagism ('ਇਮਿਜਿਜ਼(ਅ)ਮ) *n* ਬਿੰਬਵਾਦ, ਚਿੱਤਰਨ-ਵਾਦ

imbibe (ਇਮ'ਬਾਇਬ) *v* ਗ੍ਰਹਿਣ ਕਰਨਾ, ਲੈ ਲੈਣਾ; ਮਨ ਵਿਚ ਧਾਰਨ ਕਰਨਾ, ਦਿਲ ਵਿਚ ਵਸਾਉਣਾ, ਆਪਣੇ ਅੰਦਰ ਰਚਾ ਲੈਣਾ; ਜਜ਼ਬ ਕਰ ਲੈਣਾ

imbroglio (ਇਮ'ਬਰਾਉਗਲਿਅਉ) *n* ਝਮੇਲਾ, ਝੰਜਟ, ਉਲਝਣ, ਔਕੜ, ਭੈੜੀ ਅਵਸਥਾ

imitate ('ਇਮਿਟੇਇਟ) *v* ਨਕਲ ਕਰਨੀ, ਸਾਂਗ ਲਾਉਣੀ, ਅਨੁਕਰਨ ਕਰਨਾ; ਅਨੁਸਰਨ ਕਰਨਾ, ਕਦਮਾਂ ਤੇ ਚੱਲਣਾ, ਰੀਸ ਕਰਨੀ; ਨਕਲ ਉਤਾਰਨੀ

imitation ('ਇਮਿ'ਟੇਇਸ਼ਨ) *n* ਨਕਲ, ਸਾਂਗ, ਅਨੁਕਰਨ; ਰੀਸ; ਨਕਲੀ, ਪ੍ਰਤੀਲਿਪੀ

imitative ('ਇਮਿਟਅਟਿਵ) *a* ਨਕਲੀ (ਜੋ ਮੌਲਕ ਨਹੀਂ), ਅਨੁਕਰਨੀ, ਅਨੁਕਰਨਾਤਮਕ, ਬਣਾਉਤੀ; ਨਕਲੀਆ

imitator ('ਇਮਿਟੇਇਟਅ*) *n* ਨਕਲੀਆ, ਅਨੁਗਾਮੀ, ਅਨੁਸਾਰੀ

immaculate (ਇ'ਮੈਕਯੂਲਅਟ) *a* ਪਵਿੱਤਰ, ਨਿਰਮਲ, ਸ਼ੁੱਧ, ਪੁਨੀਤ, ਬੇਦਾਗ਼, ਨਿਰਦੋਸ਼

immanence immanency ('ਇਮਅਨਅੰਸ, ਇਮਅਨੰਸੀ) *n* (ਪਰਮਾਤਮਾ ਦੀ) ਸਰਵ-ਵਿਆਪਕਤਾ, ਵਿਆਪਕਤਾ, ਅੰਤਰਭੂਤੀ

immanent ('ਇਮਅਨੰਟ) *a* ਸਰਵਵਿਆਪੀ, ਵਿਆਪਕ, ਸਰਵਅੰਤਰਜਾਮੀ

immaterial ('ਇਮਅ'ਟਿਅਰਿਅਲ) *a* ਅਸਰੀਰੀ, ਅਮੂਰਤ, ਨਿਗੁਣਾ; ਮਹੱਤਾਹੀਨ, ਮਾਮੂਲੀ

immature ('ਇਮਅ'ਟਯੂਅ*) *a* ਕੱਚਾ, ਅਣਪੱਕਾ, ਅਪੂਰਨ, ਅਧੂਰਾ, ਅਪ੍ਰੌੜ

immaturity ('ਇਮਅ'ਟਯੂਅਰਅਟਿ) *n* ਕੱਚਿਆਈ, ਅਪੂਰਤਾ, ਅਪ੍ਰੌੜਤਾ

immeasurable ('ਇ'ਮੈਜ(ਅ)ਰਅਬਲ) *a* ਅਮਿੱਤ, ਬੇਹੱਦ, ਬੇਅੰਤ, ਅਪਾਰ, ਅਨੰਤ, ਅਥਾਹ

immediate (ਇ'ਮੀਡਯਟ) *a* ਫੌਰੀ, ਤਤਕਾਲਕ, ਤੁਰਤ, ਨਜ਼ਦੀਕੀ, ਅਪਰੋਖ, ਸਿੱਧਾ; ~ly ਤਤਕਾਲ, ਤੁਰਤ ਹੀ, ਝੱਟ-ਪਟ; ਉਸੇ ਵੇਲੇ, ਫੌਰਨ

immemorial ('ਇਮਿ'ਮੋਰਿਅਲ) *a* ਸਮਰਨ-ਅਤੀਤ; ਬਹੁਤ ਪੁਰਾਣਾ, ਕਦੀਮੀ, ਅਤੀ ਪ੍ਰਾਚੀਨ

immense (ਇ'ਮੈਂਸ) *a* ਬੇਹੱਦ, ਅਪਾਰ, ਅਸੀਮ, ਅਮਿੱਤ; ਬਹੁਤ ਵੱਡਾ

immensity (ਇ'ਮੈਂਸਅਟਿ) ਅਸੀਮਤਾ, ਅਮਿੱਤਤਾ, ਅਪਾਰਤਾ; ਵਿਸ਼ਾਲਤਾ, ਮਹਾਨਤਾ; ਉੱਤਮਤਾ

immensurability (ਇਮ'ਮੈੱਨਸੁਰਅ'ਬਿਲਅਟਿ) *n* ਅਸੀਮਤਾ, ਵਿਸ਼ਾਲਤਾ, ਉਤਕ੍ਰਿਸ਼ਟਤਾ

immerse (ਇ'ਮਅ:ਸ) *v* ਡੋਬਣਾ, ਡੋਬ ਦੇਣਾ; ਜਲ-ਪਰਵਾਹ ਕਰਨਾ, ਡੋਬਾ ਦੇਣਾ; ਲੀਨ ਕਰਨਾ (ਵਿਚਾਰ, ਫ਼ਿਕਰ ਆਦਿ ਵਿਚ) ਮਗਨ ਕਰਨਾ

immersion (ਇ'ਮਅ:ਸ਼ਨ) *n* ਜਲ-ਪਰਵਾਹ; ਡੋਬਾ, ਗੋਤਾ; ਮਗਨਤਾ, ਲੀਨਤਾ

immigrant ('ਇਮਿਗਰਅੰਟ) *a n* ਆਵਾਸੀ, ਪਰਵਾਸੀ

immigrate ('ਇਮਿਗਰੇਇਟ) *v* ਆ ਵੱਸਣਾ, ਆਵਾਸੀ ਬਣਨਾ

immigration ('ਇਮਿ'ਗਰੇਇਸ਼ਨ) *n* ਆਵਾਸ, ਪਰਵਾਸ

imminence, imminency ('ਇਮਿਨਅੰਸ 'ਇਮਿਨਅੰਸਿ) *n* ਨਿਕਟਤਾ, ਸਮੀਪਤਾ

imminent ('ਇਮਿਨਅੰਟ) *a* ਹੋਣ ਵਾਲਾ, ਅਟੱਲ, ਸਿਰ ਤੇ ਆਈ (ਬਿਪਤਾ, ਬਲਾ, ਔਕੜ ਆਦਿ), ਕੋਲ ਪੁੱਜਿਆ, ਲਾਗੇ ਹੀ, ਨਿਕਟਵਰਤੀ

immobile (ਇ'ਮਅਉਬਾਇਲ) *a* ਅਚੱਲ, ਸਥਿਰ, ਅਟੱਲ, ਨਿਸ਼ਚਲ

immobility ('ਇਮਅ(ਉ)'ਬਿਲਅਟਿ) *n* ਅਚੱਲਤਾ, ਸਥਿਰਤਾ, ਨਿਸ਼ਚੱਲਤਾ

immobilize (ਇ'ਮਅਉਬਿਲਾਇਜ਼) *v* ਅਚੱਲ ਕਰਨਾ, ਸਥਿਰ ਕਰਨਾ, ਬੇਹਰਕਤ ਕਰਨਾ

immolate ('ਇਮਅ(ਉ)ਲੇਇਟ) *v* ਬਲੀ ਦੇਣੀ; ਕੁਰਬਾਨੀ ਦੇਣੀ, ਆਹੂਤੀ ਦੇਣੀ

immolation ('ਇਮਅ(ਉ)'ਲੇਇਸ਼ਨ) *n* ਬਲੀ, ਕੁਰਬਾਨੀ, ਭੇਟਾ

immoral (ਇ'ਮੌਰ(ਅ)ਲ) *a* ਭ੍ਰਿਸ਼ਟਾਚਾਰੀ, ਦੁਰਵਿਹਾਰੀ, ਬਦ, ਬੁਰਾ, ਅਨੈਤਕ; ਕੁਕਰਮੀ, ਬਦਕਾਰ, ਦੁਰਾਚਾਰੀ, ਬਦਚਲਨ; **~ity** ਬਦਚਲਨੀ, ਬਦੀ, ਭ੍ਰਿਸ਼ਟਤਾ, ਦੁਰਾਚਾਰ, ਆਚਾਰਹੀਣਤਾ, ਅਨੈਤਕਤਾ

immortal (ਇ'ਮੋਟਲ) *a n* ਅਮਰ ਅਵਿਨਾਸ਼ੀ, ਅਕਾਲ; ਅਮਰ ਵਿਅਕਤੀ; **~ity** ਅਮਰਤਵ, ਅਵਿਨਾਸ਼ਤਾ; ਸਦੀਵਤਾ

immovable (ਇ'ਮੂਵ੍ਅਬਲ) *a* ਅਚੱਲ, (ਜਾਇਦਾਦ) ਗਤੀਹੀਣ, ਸਥਾਈ, ਅਟੱਲ

immovability (ਇ'ਮੂਵ੍ਅ'ਬਿਲਅਟਿ) *n* ਅਚੱਲਤਾ, ਅਹਿਲਤਾ, ਗਤੀਹੀਣਤਾ, ਸਥਿਰਤਾ, ਅਪਰਿਵਰਤਨਸ਼ੀਲਤਾ

immune (ਇ'ਮਯੂਨ) *a* ਮੁਕਤ, ਸੁਰੱਖਿਅਤ

immunity (ਇ'ਮਯੂਨਅਟਿ) *n* ਬਚਾਉ, ਸੁਰੱਖਿਆ; ਛੁਟਕਾਰਾ; ਮੁਕਤੀ

immunize ('ਇਮਯੂਨਾਇਜ਼) *v* (ਰੋਗ ਆਦਿ ਤੋਂ) ਸੁਰੱਖਿਅਤ ਕਰਨਾ, ਬਚਾਉ ਕਰ ਦੇਣਾ, ਛੁਟਕਾਰਾ ਕਰਾਉਣਾ

immutable (ਇ'ਮਯੂਟਅਬਲ) *a* ਅਟੱਲ, ਅਪਰਿਵਰਤਨਸ਼ੀਲ; ਸਥਿਰ, ਨਿਸ਼ਚੱਲ; ਨਿਰਵਿਕਾਰ

impact ('ਇਮਪੈਕਟ) *n v* ਟੱਕਰ, ਧੱਕਾ, ਸੱਟ, ਆਘਾਤ, ਅਸਰ, ਪ੍ਰਭਾਵ; ਟੱਕਰ ਮਾਰਨੀ ਜਾਂ ਮਰਵਾ ਦੇਣੀ

impair (ਇਮ'ਪੇਅ*) *v* ਵਿਗਾੜਨਾ, ਖ਼ਰਾਬ ਕਰਨਾ, ਵਿਕਾਰ ਪਾਉਣਾ, ਤੋੜ-ਮਰੋੜ ਦੇਣਾ; ਕਮਜ਼ੋਰ ਕਰਨਾ; **~ed** ਅਸਮਰਥ

impalpability (ਇਮ'ਪੈਲਪਅ'ਬਿਲਅਟਿ) *n* ਦੁਰਬੋਧਤਾ, ਅਸਪਰਸ਼ਤਾ

impalpable (ਇਮ'ਪੈਲਪਅਬਲ) *a* ਅਗੋਚਰ, ਦੁਰਬੋਧ, ਅਤੀ ਸੂਖ਼ਮ

impanel (ਇਮ'ਪੈਨਲ) *v* ਸੂਚੀ (ਲਿਸਟ) ਵਿਚ ਦਾਖ਼ਲ ਕਰਨਾ, ਸੂਚੀ ਵਿਚ ਲਿਖ ਲੈਣਾ

impart (ਇਮ'ਪਾ:ਟ) v ਦੇਣਾ, ਬਖ਼ਸ਼ਣਾ, ਪ੍ਰਦਾਨ ਕਰਨਾ ਦੇਣਾ, ਪ੍ਰਕਾਸ਼ਤ ਕਰਨਾ, ਪਹੁੰਚਾਉਣਾ

impartial (ਇਮ'ਪਾ'ਸ਼ਲ) a ਨਿਰਪੱਖ, ਬੇਲਾਗਾ; ਨਿਆਂਕਾਰੀ, ਇਨਸਾਫ਼ਪਸੰਦ; ਧੜੇਬਾਜ਼ੀ ਤੋਂ ਉੱਪਰ, ਸਮਦਰਸ਼ੀ; ~ity ਨਿਰਪੱਖਤਾ, ਸਮ-ਦਰਸ਼ਤਾ; ਨਿਆਂਕਰਤਾ

impassability (ਇਮ'ਪਾਸਅ'ਬਿਲਅਟਿ) n ਦੁਰਗਮਤਾ, ਅਗਮਤਾ

impassable (ਇਮ'ਪਾਸਅਬਲ) a ਦੁਰਗਮ, ਅਗਮ, ਅਲੰਘ

impasse (ਐਮ'ਪਾਸ) n ਬੰਦ ਗਲੀ; ਉਲਝਣ, ਔਕੜ, ਘੋਰ ਸੰਕਟ, ਗਤੀਰੋਧ

impassibility (ਇਮ'ਪਾਸਅ'ਬਿਲਅਟਿ) n ਜੜ੍ਹਤਾ, ਅਚੇਤਨਤਾ, ਭਾਵਹੀਨਤਾ

impassible (ਇਮ'ਪਾਸਅਸਿਬਲ) a ਚੇਤਨਾਹੀਨ, ਜੜ੍ਹ; ਰਾਗਾਤੀਤ, ਸੁੱਖ-ਦੁੱਖਰਹਿਤ

impassionate (ਇਮ'ਪੈਸ਼ਨਅਟ) a ਆਤੁਰ, ਆਵੇਸ਼ਪੂਰਨ

impassioned (ਇਮ'ਪੈਸ਼ੰਡ) a ਜੋਸ਼ੀਲਾ, ਭੜਕਿਆ, ਆਵੇਗਪੂਰਨ, ਆਵੇਸ਼-ਪੂਰਨ

impassive (ਇਮ'ਪੈਸਿਵ) a ਭਾਵਹੀਨ, ਭਾਵਨਾਰਹਿਤ, ਨਿਰਵੇਗ, ਸਥਿਰ, ਅਡੋਲ, ਬੇਹਿੱਸ

impassivity (ਇਮਪੈ'ਸਿਵਅਟਿ) n ਭਾਵਹੀਨਤਾ, ਨਿਰਵੇਗਤਾ; ਸਥਿਰਤਾ, ਅਡੋਲਤਾ

impatience (ਇਮ'ਪੇਇਸ਼ੰਸ) n ਬੇਸਬਰੀ, ਬੇਤਾਬੀ, ਬੇਚੈਨੀ, ਕਾਹਲ, ਉਤਾਵਲ, ਵਿਆਕੁਲਤਾ

impatient (ਇਮ'ਪੇਇਸ਼ੰਟ) a ਬੇਸਬਰ, ਕਾਹਲਾ, ਬੇਚੈਨ, ਉਤਾਵਲਾ, ਅਧੀਰ, ਵਿਆਕੁਲ

impawn (ਇਮ'ਪੌਨ) v ਗਹਿਣੇ ਪਾਉਣਾ, ਗਿਰਵੀ ਕਰਨਾ, ਰਹਿਨ ਰੱਖਣਾ; ਵਚਨ ਦੇਣਾ

impeach (ਇਮ'ਪੀਚ) v ਦੋਸ਼ ਲਾਉਣਾ, ਨੁਕਤਾਚੀਨੀ ਕਰਨੀ, ਅਪਰਾਧੀ ਸਿੱਧ ਕਰਨਾ, ਮਹਾਂਦੋਸ਼ ਲਾਉਣਾ; ~ment ਮਹਾਂਦੋਸ਼; ਕਿਸੇ ਅਦਾਲਤ ਦੇ ਸਾਮ੍ਹਣੇ ਜਾਂ ਸੰਸਦ ਵਿਚ ਵੱਡੇ ਅਧਿਕਾਰੀ ਦੇ ਆਚਰਨ ਬਾਰੇ ਵਾਦਵਿਵਾਦ

impeccability (ਇਮ'ਪੈੱਕਅ'ਬਿਲਅਟਿ) n ਪਾਪਹੀਨਤਾ, ਨਿਰਦੋਸ਼ਤਾ, ਮਾਸੂਮੀਅਤ

impeccable (ਇਮ'ਪੈੱਕਅਬਲ) a ਬੇ-ਐਬ, ਨਿਸ਼ਪਾਪ; ਨਿਰਦੋਸ਼ ਬੇਗੁਨਾਹ, ਮਾਸੂਮ

impecuniosity ('ਇਮਪਿ'ਕਯੂਨਿ'ਔਸਅਟਿ) n ਗ਼ਰੀਬੀ, ਕੰਗਾਲੀ, ਨਿਰਧਨਤਾ

impecunious ('ਇਮਪਿ'ਕਯੂਨਯਅਸ) a ਨਿਰਧਨ, ਕੰਗਾਲ; ਗ਼ਰੀਬ

impedance (ਇਮ'ਪੀਡਅੰਸ) n ਅਡ਼ਿੱਕਾ, ਰੁਕਾਵਟ, ਰੋਕ

impede (ਇਮ'ਪੀਡ) v ਰੁਕਾਵਟ ਪਾਉਣੀ, ਅੜਿੱਕਾ ਡਾਹੁਣਾ, ਵਿਘਨ ਪਾਉਣਾ, ਅੜਚਨ ਪਾਉਣੀ

impedient (ਇਮ'ਪੀਡਯਅੰਟ) a ਰੁਕਾਵਟੀ, ਵਿਘਨਪਾਊ, ਅਟਕਾਊ

impediment (ਇਮ'ਪੈਡਿਮਅੰਟ) n ਵਿਘਨ, ਰੁਕਾਵਟ

impel (ਇਮ'ਪੈੱਲ) v ਉਕਸਾਉਣਾ, ਜ਼ੋਰ ਪਾਉਣਾ, ਮਜਬੂਰ ਕਰਨਾ; ਉਤੇਜਤ ਕਰਨਾ, ਉਤਸਾਹਤ ਕਰਨਾ; ਚਲਾਉਣਾ, ਰੇੜ੍ਹਨਾ

impenetrable (ਇਮ'ਪੈਨਿਟਰਅਬਲ) a ਅਛੇਦ, ਅਟਛਿੱਦ, ਕਰੜਾ; ਠੋਸ; ਅਥਾਹ, ਅਸਗਾਹ, ਅਪਾਰ; ਵਿਚਾਰਾਂ ਤੋਂ ਪਰੇ, ਬੁੱਧੀ ਦੀ ਪਹੁੰਚ ਤੋਂ ਬਾਹਰਾ, ਗੁੜ੍ਹ

impenetrate (ਇਮ'ਪੈਨਿਟਰੇਇਟ) v ਦਾਖ਼ਲ ਕਰਨਾ, ਪ੍ਰਵੇਸ਼ ਕਰਨਾ, ਧੁਰ ਤਾਈਂ ਜਾਣਾ, ਡੂੰਘਾ

ਧਸਣਾ, ਖੁਸ ਜਾਣਾ

imperative (ਇਮ'ਪੈੱਰਅਟਿਵ੍) *a n* (ਵਿਆ)
ਆਗਿਆਆਵਾਚਕ, ਆਗਿਆਅਰਥ, ਆਦੇਸ਼ਾਤਮਕ,
ਹੁਕਮੀ; ਅਤੀ ਅਵੱਸ਼ਕ

imperfect (ਇਮ'ਪਅਃਫ਼ਿਕਟ) *a* ਅਧੂਰਾ, ਅਪੂਰਨ,
ਅਸਮਾਪਤ, ਨਾਕਸ, ਦੋਸ਼ਪੂਰਨ; **~ion**
ਅਪੂਰਨਤਾ, ਅਸਮਾਪਤੀ; ਕਸਰ, ਨੁਕਸ, ਤਰੁਟੀ

imperial (ਇਮ'ਪਿਅਰਿਅਲ) *a n* ਸ਼ਾਹੀ, ਰਾਜਸੀ;
ਸਹਿਨਸ਼ਾਹੀ; ਸਾਮਰਾਜੀ; **~ism** ਸਾਮਰਾਜਵਾਦ,
ਸ਼ਹਿਨਸ਼ਾਹੀਅਤ; **~ist** ਸਾਮਰਾਜਵਾਦੀ

imperil (ਇਮ'ਪੈੱਰ(ਅ)ਲ) *v* ਖ਼ਤਰੇ ਵਿਚ ਪਾਉਣਾ,
ਜੋਖੋਂ ਵਿਚ ਪਾਉਣਾ

imperishable (ਇਮ'ਪੈੱਰਿਸ਼ਅਬਲ) *a* ਅਮਰ,
ਅਵਿਨਾਸ਼ੀ, ਅਮਿਟ

impersonal (ਇਮ'ਪਅਃਸਨਲ) *a*
ਅਵਿਅਕਤੀਗਤ, ਅਨਿੱਜੀ, ਗ਼ੈਰਸ਼ਖ਼ਸੀ; **~verb**
(ਵਿਆ) ਭਾਵਵਾਚੀ ਕਿਰਿਆ

impersonation (ਇਮ'ਪਅਃਸਆ'ਨੇਇਸ਼ਨ) *n*
ਮਾਨਵੀ-ਕਰਨ; ਰੂਪ ਧਾਰਨ, ਭੇਸ ਬਦਲਣਾ

impersonify ('ਇਮਪਅ'ਸੌਨਿਫ਼ਾਇ) *v*
ਮਾਨਵੀਕਰਨ ਕਰਨਾ, ਮੂਰਤੀਕਰਨ ਕਰਨਾ

impertinence (ਇਮ'ਪਅਃਟਿਨਅੰਸ) *n*
ਬੇਅਦਬੀ, ਗੁਸਤਾਖ਼ੀ, ਅਸ਼ਿਸ਼ਟਤਾ, ਨਿਰਰਥਕਤਾ

impertinent (ਇਮ'ਪਅਃਟਿਨਅੰਟ) *a* ਗੁਸਤਾਖ਼,
ਬੇਅਦਬ

impetuous (ਇਮ'ਪੈੱਚੁਅਸ) *a* ਵੇਗਵਾਨ,
ਜੋਸ਼ੀਲਾ, ਬੜਾ ਜੋਸ਼, ਪ੍ਰਚੰਡ

impetus ('ਇਮਪਿਟਅਸ) *n* ਜ਼ੋਰ, ਵੇਗ, ਗਤੀ-
ਸ਼ਕਤੀ, ਚਾਲ ਦਾ ਜ਼ੋਰ, ਤੇਜ਼ੀ, ਪਰੇਰਨਾ

impious ('ਇਮਪਿਅਸ) *a* ਅਧਰਮੀ, ਸ਼ਰਧਾਹੀਨ,
ਨਾਸਤਕ, ਅਪਵਿੱਤਰ, ਭ੍ਰਿਸ਼ਟ

implacability (ਇਮ'ਪਲੈਕਅ'ਬਿਲਅਟਿ) *n*
ਕਰੜਾਈ, ਸਖ਼ਤੀ, ਨਿਰਦਇਤਾ

implacable (ਇਮ'ਪਲੈਕਅਬਲ) *a* ਸਖ਼ਤ,
ਕਰੜਾ; ਸਖ਼ਤ ਦਿਲ, ਨਿਰਦਈ

implant (ਇਮ'ਪਲਾਂਟ) *v* ਗੱਡਣਾ; ਬੀਜਣਾ,
(ਬੂਟਾ) ਲਾਉਣਾ; ਦਿਲ ਵਿਚ ਬਿਠਾਉਣਾ, ਧਾਰ
ਲੈਣਾ, ਗ੍ਰਹਿਣ ਕਰਾ ਦੇਣਾ; **~ation** (ਪੌਦੇ ਦੀ)
ਗਡਾਈ; ਬਿਜਾਈ

implement ('ਇਮਪਲੀਮਅੰਟ, 'ਇਮਪਲਿਮੈਂਟ) *n*
v ਸੰਦ, ਹਥਿਆਰ, ਜੰਤਰ; ਸਾਧਨ, ਵਸਤੂ, ਪੂਰਾ
ਕਰਨ, ਨਿਭਾਉਣਾ, ਸਾਜ਼-ਸਾਮਾਨ; ਲਾਗੂ ਕਰਨਾ,
ਪਾਲਣਾ ਕਰਨੀ; ਅਮਲ ਵਿਚ ਲਿਆਉਣਾ, (ਉੱਤੇ)
ਅਮਲ ਕਰਨਾ; **~ation** ਪਾਲਣ, ਅਮਲ, ਕਾਰਜ
ਰੂਪ ਦੇਣ ਦੀ ਕਿਰਿਆ

implicate ('ਇਮਪਲਿਕੇਇਟ) *v* ਫਸਾਉਣਾ,
ਉਲਝਾਉਣਾ, ਫਸਾ ਲੈਣਾ; ਭਾਵ-ਅਰਥ ਹੋਣੇ

implication ('ਇਮਪਲਿ'ਕੇਇਸ਼ਨ) *n* ਉਲਝਣ,
ਅੜ੍ਹਿੰਕਾ, ਅੜਚਨ; ਭਾਵ-ਅਰਥ, ਅਰਥ-
ਸੰਭਾਵਨਾ

implicit (ਇਮ'ਪਲਿਸਿਟ) *a* ਲੁਪਤ, ਨਿਹਿਤ;
ਸੰਕੇਤਤ; ਨਿਸਚਤ

implied (ਇਮ'ਪਲਾਇਡ) *a* ਅਰਥਯੁਕਤ,
ਸੰਕੇਤਤ, ਨਿਹਿਤ, ਅੰਤਰਨਿਹਿਤ; ਅਵਿਅਕਤ,
ਅਸਪਸ਼ਟ

implore (ਇਮ'ਪਲੋ*) *v* ਬੇਨਤੀ ਕਰਨੀ, ਮਿਨਤ
ਕਰਨੀ, ਤਰਲਾ ਕਰਨਾ; ਜਾਚਨਾ

implosion (ਇਮ'ਪਲਅਉਯ਼ਨ) *n* ਅੰਤਰ ਵਿਸਫੋਟ

imply (ਇਮ'ਪਲਾਇ) *v* ਅਰਥ ਹੋਣਾ, ਭਾਵ ਹੋਣਾ,
ਤਾਤਪਰਜ ਨਿਕਲਣਾ

impolite ('ਇਮਪਅ'ਲਾਇਟ) *a* ਅਸੱਭਿਅ,
ਅਸ਼ਿਸ਼ਟ, ਬਦਤਮੀਜ਼; ਉਜੱਡ, ਗੰਵਾਰ; **~ness**

ਅਸੱਭਿਅਤਾ, ਅਸ਼ਿਸ਼ਟਤਾ, ਉਜੱਡਪੁਣਾ

import (ਇਮ'ਪੋਟ, ਇਮਪੋਟ) *v n* ਦਰਾਮਦ ਕਰਨਾ, ਆਯਾਤ ਕਰਨਾ; ਅਰਥ ਦੇਣਾ, ਸੰਕੇਤ ਕਰਨਾ; ਬਾਹਰੋਂ ਆਉਂਦਾ ਮਾਲ, ਆਯਾਤ, ਦਰਾਮਦ; ਅਰਥ, ਭਾਵ; ~ed ਆਯਾਤ ਕੀਤਾ, ਦਰਾਮਦ ਕੀਤਾ

importance (ਇਮਪੋ:ਟੰਸ) *n* ਮਹੱਤਾ, ਮਹੱਤਵ; ਕਦਰ, ਗੌਰਵ, ਪ੍ਰਤਿਸ਼ਠਾ, ਦੰਭ; ਜ਼ਰੂਰਤ

important (ਇਮਪੋ:ਟੰਟ) *a* ਜ਼ਰੂਰੀ, ਮਹੱਤਵਪੂਰਨ, ਅਵੱਸ਼ਕ; ਸਨਮਾਨਤ

impose (ਇਮ'ਪਅਉਜ਼) *v* ਸਥਾਪਤ ਕਰਨਾ, ਉੱਪਰ ਰੱਖਣਾ; ਸਿਰ ਮੜ੍ਹਨਾ, ਠੋਸਣਾ

imposing (ਇਮ'ਪਅਉਜ਼ਿਙ) *a n* ਪ੍ਰਭਾਵਸ਼ਾਲੀ, ਪਤੁੱਲੇਦਾਰ, ਰੋਹਬਦਾਬ ਵਾਲਾ

imposition ('ਇਮਪਅ'ਜ਼ਿਸ਼ਨ) *n* ਭਾਰ; ਟੈਕਸ, ਕਰ, ਲਗਾਨ; ਦੰਡ; ਧੋਖਾ, ਕਪਟ ਆਰੋਪਣ

impossibility (ਇਮ'ਪੱਸਅ'ਬਿਲਅਟਿ) *n* ਅਸੰਭਵਤਾ, ਅਸੰਭਾਵਨਾ, ਅਣਹੋਣੀ, ਕਠਨਤਾ

impossible ('ਇਮ'ਪੱਸਅਬਲ) *a* ਅਸੰਭਵ, ਅਸਾਧ, ਅਣਹੋਣਾ, ਅਤੀ ਕਰੋਪੀ

impost ('ਇਮਪਅਉਸਟ) *n* ਕਰ, ਟੈਕਸ, ਲਗਾਨ, ਮਹਿਸੂਲ

impostor (ਇਮ'ਪੱਸਟਅ*) *n* ਪਖੰਡੀ, ਕਪਟੀ, ਠੰਗ, ਧੋਖੇਬਾਜ਼, ਛਲੀਆ; ਮਜ਼੍ਹਬੂਰੀ

impotence, impotency ('ਇਮਪਅਟਅੰਸ, 'ਇਮਪਅਟਅੰਸਿ) *n* ਨਾਮਰਦੀ, ਨਪੁੰਸਕਤਾ; ਕਮਜ਼ੋਰੀ, ਲਾਚਾਰੀ, ਮਜ਼੍ਹਬੂਰੀ

impotent ('ਇਮਪਅਟਅੰਟ) *a* ਨਾਮਰਦ, ਨਪੁੰਸਕ; ਕਮਜ਼ੋਰ, ਨਿਤਾਣਾ, ਹੀਣਾ, ਦੁਰਬਲ

impound (ਇਮ'ਪਾਉਂਡ) *v* ਰੋਕ ਲਾ ਲੈਣੀ, ਰੋਕ ਰੱਖਣਾ, ਪਾਬੰਦੀ ਲਾ ਦੇਣਾ; ਕਾਨੂੰਨੀ ਢੰਗ ਨਾਲ ਕਬਜ਼ੇ ਵਿਚ ਲੈ ਲੈਣਾ, ਖੋਹ ਲੈਣਾ; (ਪਸ਼ੂਆਂ ਨੂੰ)

ਕਾਂਜੀ ਹਾਊਸ ਵਿਚ ਬੰਦ ਕਰ ਦੇਣਾ

impoverish (ਇਮ'ਪੌਵ(ਅ)ਰਿਸ਼) *v* ਕੰਗਾਲ ਕਰ ਦੇਣਾ, ਨਿਰਧਨ ਕਰ ਦੇਣਾ, ਸਾਧਨਹੀਨ ਕਰ ਦੇਣਾ; ~ment ਗ਼ਰੀਬੀ, ਕੰਗਾਲੀ; ਨਿਰਧਨਤਾ; ਬਲਹੀਨਤਾ, ਸ਼ਕਤੀਹੀਨਤਾ

impracticablity (ਇਮ'ਪਰੈਕਟਿਕਅ'ਬਿਲਟਿ) *n* ਅਵਿਹਾਰਕਤਾ; ਦੁਸ਼ਕਰਤਾ; ਦੁਰਗਮਤਾ

impracticable (ਇਮ'ਪਰੈਕਟਿਕਅਬਲ) *a* ਅਵਿਹਾਰਕ, ਗ਼ੈਰ-ਅਮਲੀ, ਲਾਇਲਾਜ, ਨਾਕਾਬਲੇ-ਅਮਲ; ਅਸਾਧ; ਔਖਾ, ਦੁਰਗਮ

imprecate ('ਇਮਪਰਿਕੇਇਟ) *v* ਬਦਅਸੀਸ ਦੇਣੀ, ਬਦਦੁਆ ਦੇਣੀ, ਸਰਾਪ ਦੇਣਾ; ਫਿਟ-ਕਾਰਨਾ, ਲਾਨ੍ਹਤ ਪਾਉਣੀ, ਕੋਸਣਾ

imprecision ('ਇਮਪਰਿ'ਸਿਯਨ) *n* ਅਸਪਸ਼ਟਤਾ, ਅਨਿਸ਼ਚਤਤਾ

impregnability (ਇਮ'ਪਰੈਗਨਅ'ਬਿਲਅਟਿ) *n* ਮਜ਼ਬੂਤੀ, ਪਕਿਆਈ, ਅਜਿੱਤਤਾ, ਅਭੇਦਤਾ

impregnable (ਇਮ'ਪਰੈਗਨਅਬਲ) *a* ਅਜਿੱਤ, ਅਭੇਦ, ਪੱਕਾ, ਮਜ਼ਬੂਤ

impregnate ('ਇਮਪਰੈਗਨੇਇਟ) *v a* ਗਰਭ ਕਰਨਾ; ਭਰ ਦੇਣਾ, ਸੰਚਾਰ ਕਰਨਾ, (ਭਾਵ, ਗੁਣ ਆਦਿ) ਕੁੱਟ-ਕੁੱਟ ਕੇ ਭਰ ਦੇਣਾ, ਦਿਲ ਵਿਚ ਬਿਠਾ ਦੇਣਾ; ਗਰਭਵਤੀ

impress (ਇਮ'ਪਰੈੱਸ, 'ਇਮਪਰੈੱਸ) *v n* (1) ਮੋਹਰ ਲਾਉਣੀ, ਠੱਪਾ ਲਾਉਣਾ; ਅੰਕਤ ਕਰਨਾ, ਨਿਸ਼ਾਨ ਲਾਉਣਾ; ਪ੍ਰਭਾਵਤ ਕਰਨਾ; ਮਨ ਵਿਚ ਬਿਠਾ ਦੇਣਾ; (2) ਜ਼ਬਤ ਕਰਨਾ, ਜ਼ਬਰੀ ਭਰਤੀ ਕਰਨਾ; ਠੱਪਾ, ਛਾਪ, ਮੋਹਰ, ਸਿੱਕਾ, ਵਿਸ਼ੇਸ਼ਤਾ; ~ed ਅੰਕਤ, ਚਿੰਨ੍ਹਤ, ਮੁਦ੍ਰਿਤ, ਛਪਿਆ ਪ੍ਰਭਾਵਤ; ਆਰੋਪਤ; ~ible ਪ੍ਰਭਾਵਸ਼ੀਲ; ~ion ਠੱਪਾ, ਛਾਪ, ਮੋਹਰ, ਚਿੰਨ੍ਹ,

ਨਿਸ਼ਾਨ; ਪ੍ਰਭਾਵ, ਵਿਚਾਰ, ਰਾਇ; ~ionable ਸੰਵੇਦਨਸ਼ੀਲ, ਪ੍ਰਭਾਵਸ਼ੀਲ; ~ionist ਪ੍ਰਭਾਵਵਾਦੀ; ਭਾਵ-ਚਿੱਤਰ, ~ive ਪ੍ਰਭਾਵਸ਼ਾਲੀ, ਅਸਰ ਪਾਉਣ ਵਾਲਾ

imprest ('ਇਮਪਰੈੱਸਟ) *n* ਪੇਸ਼ਗੀ ਧਨ, ਪੇਸ਼ਗੀ ਤਨਖ਼ਾਹ

imprint (ਇਮ'ਪਰਿੰਟ) *v n* ਠੱਪਾ ਲਾਉਣਾ, ਮੋਹਰ ਲਾਉਣਾ, ਠੇਕਣਾ, ਨਿਸ਼ਾਨ ਲਾਉਣਾ; (ਪੁਸਤਕ ਉੱਤੇ) ਪ੍ਰਕਾਸ਼ਕ ਅਤੇ ਮੁਦ੍ਰਿਕ ਦਾ ਵੇਰਵਾ, ਠੱਪਾ, ਛਾਪਾ

imprison (ਇਮ'ਪਰਿਜ਼ਨ) *v n* ਕੈਦ ਕਰਨਾ, ਜੇਲ੍ਹ ਵਚ ਸੁੱਟਣਾ; ਘੇਰ ਲੈਣਾ, ਬੰਦ ਕਰਨਾ, ਡੱਕ ਲੈਣਾ; ~ ment ਕੈਦ, ਬੰਦੀ, ਜੇਲ੍ਹ-ਖਾਨਾ

improbability (ਇਮ'ਪਰੌਬਅ'ਬਿਲਅਟਿ) *n* ਅਸੰਭਾਵਤਾ, ਦੁਰਘਟਤਾ

improbable (ਇਮ'ਪਰੌਬਅਬਲ) *a* ਅਸੰਭਾਵੀ

improper (ਇਮ'ਪਰੌਪਅ*) *a* ਨਾਵਾਜਬ, ਅਯੋਗ, ਅਨੁਚਿਤ; ਗ਼ਲਤ, ਕੋਝਾ, ਕੁਵੱਲਾ

impropriety (ਇਮਪਰਅ'ਪਰਾਇਅਟਿ) *n* ਅਨੁਚਿੱਤਤਾ, ਅਯੋਗਤਾ; ਬੇਹੁਦਗੀ ਅਸ਼ਿਸ਼ਟਤਾ

improve (ਇਮ'ਪਰੂਵ) *v* ਸੁਧਾਰਨਾ, ਸੁਧਰਨਾ, ਉੱਨਤੀ ਕਰਾਉਣੀ, ਠੀਕ ਕਰਨਾ, ਵਧਾ-ਫੁੱਲਣਾ; ਅਵਸਰ ਦਾ ਠੀਕ ਲਾਭ ਉਠਾਉਣਾ; ਮੱਤ ਦੇਣੀ, ਉਚਿਤ ਸਿੱਖਿਆ ਦੇਣਾ; ~d ਸੰਸ਼ੋਧਤ, ਉੰਨਤ, ਉਤਕ੍ਰਿਸ਼ਟ, ਸੁਧਰਿਆ; ~ment ਸੁਧਾਰ, ਉੰਨਤੀ, ਬਿਹਤਰੀ

improvidence (ਇਮ'ਪਰੌਵਿਡਅੰਸ) *a* ਲਾਪਰਵਾਹ, ਅਸਾਵਧਾਨ; ਨਾ-ਦੂਰਦਰਸ਼ੀ, ਫ਼ਜ਼ੂਲ ਖ਼ਰਚ

improvident (ਇਮ'ਪਰੌਵਿਡਅੰਟ) *a* ਲਾਪਰਵਾਹ, ਅਸਾਵਧਾਨ; ਨਾ-ਦੂਰਦਰਸ਼ੀ, ਫ਼ਜ਼ੂਲ ਖ਼ਰਚ

improving (ਇਮ'ਪਰੂਵਿਙ) *a* ਵਿਕਾਸਮਾਨ, ਵਰਧਮਾਨ, ਅੱਛਾ ਹੋਣਾ ਜਾਂ ਹੋਣ ਵਾਲਾ

imprudence (ਇਮ'ਪਰੂਡਅੰਸ) *n* ਅਸਾਵਧਾਨੀ, ਅਵਿਵੇਕ, ਬੇਸਮਝ

imprudent (ਇਮਪਰੂਡਅੰਟ) *n* ਬੇਸਮਝੀ, ਅਸਾਵਧਾਨੀ, ਅਵਿਵੇਕੀ

impudence (ਇਮਪਯੂਡਅੰਸ) *n* ਬੇਅਦਬੀ, ਗੁਸਤਾਖ਼ੀ, ਬੇਹਯਾਈ, ਢੀਠਤਾ, ਨਿੱਲਜਤਾ

impudent (ਇਮਪਯੂਡਅੰਟ) *n* ਗੁਸਤਾਖ਼, ਬੇਅਦਬ; ਢੀਠ, ਨਿੱਲਜ; ਬੇਹਯਾ

impulse (ਇਮਪਅੱਲਸ) *n* ਮਨੋਵੇਗ, ਤਰੰਗ, ਅੰਤਰ ਪਰੇਰਨਾ; ਮਾਨਸਕ ਪਰੇਰਨਾ; ਗਤੀ, ਚਾਲ; ਆਵੇਗ

impulsion (ਇਮ'ਪਅੱਲਸ਼ਨ) *n* ਮਾਨਸਕ ਪਰੇਰਨਾ; ਉਕਸਾਹਟ

impulsive (ਇਮ'ਪਅੱਲਸਿਵ੍) *a* ਮਨੋਵੇਗੀ, ਵੇਗਵਾਨ, ਤਰੰਗੀ

impunity (ਇਮ'ਪਯੂਨਅਟਿ) *n* ਸਜ਼ਾ ਤੋਂ ਛੋਟ, ਦੰਡ ਮੁਕਤੀ, ਮਾਫ਼ੀ

impure (ਇਮ'ਪਯੂਅ*) *a* ਅਪਵਿੱਤਰ, ਮੈਲਾ, ਗੰਦਾ; ਭ੍ਰਿੰਟਿਆ, ਨਾਪਾਕ; ਨਿੰਦਾਯੋਗ

impurity (ਇਮ'ਪਯੂਅਰਅਟਿ) *n* ਅਪਵਿੱਤਰਤਾ; ਮੈਲਾਪਣ, ਗੰਦਗੀ; ਮਿਲਾਵਟ, ਖੋਟ, ਅਸ਼ੁੱਧਤਾ

imputation (ਇਮਪਯੂ'ਟੇਸ਼ਨ) *n* ਉੱਜ, ਆਰੋਪ, ਤੁਹਮਤ, ਇਲਜ਼ਾਮ

impute (ਇਮ'ਪਯੂਟ) *v* ਜ਼ੁੰਮੇ ਲਾਉਣਾ, ਸਿਰ ਮੜ੍ਹਨਾ, ਤੁਹਮਤ ਲਾਉਣੀ, ਆਰੋਪਣਾ

in (ਇਨ) *perp adv a n* ਵਿਚ, ਅੰਦਰ; ਉੱਤੇ; ਅੰਦਰ ਨੂੰ, ਅੰਦਰ ਵੱਲ, ਅੰਦਰਲਾ

inability (ਇਨਅ'ਬਿਲਅਟਿ) *n* ਅਸਮਰੱਥਾ, ਅਯੋਗਤਾ, ਨਾਲਾਇਕੀ; ਨਿਰਬਲਤਾ; ਬੇਵੱਸੀ

in absentia ('ਇਨਐਬ'ਸੈਂਟਿਆ) (L) adv
ਗ਼ੈਰਹਾਜ਼ਰੀ ਵਿਚ

inaccessibility ('ਇਨਅਕ'ਸੈੱਸਿਆ'ਬਿਲਅਟਿ) n
ਦੁਰਲੱਭਤਾ, ਦੁਰਗਮਤਾ

inaccessible ('ਇਨਐਕ'ਸੈੱਸਿਅਬਲ) a ਪਹੁੰਚ ਤੋਂ
ਪਰੇ, ਅਪਹੁੰਚ; ਦੁਰਗਮ; ਅਗਮ, ਦੁਰਲੱਭ

inaccuracy (ਇਨ'ਐਕਯੁਰਅਸਿ) n ਅਸ਼ੁੱਧੀ,
ਅਯਥਾਰਥ; ਦੋਸ਼

inaccurate (ਇਨ'ਐਕਯੁਰਅਟ) a ਅਸ਼ੁੱਧ,
ਗ਼ਲਤ, ਅਯਥਾਰਥ; ਦੋਸ਼ਪੂਰਨ

inaction (ਇਨ'ਐਕਸ਼ਨ) n ਆਲਸ, ਸੁਸਤੀ;
ਦਲਿੱਦਰ; ਨਿਸ਼ਕਿਰਿਆਤਾ

inactive (ਇਨ'ਐਕਟਿਵ) a ਸੁਸਤ, ਬੇਹਿੰਮਤ,
ਆਲਸੀ, ਦਲਿੱਦਰੀ, ਨਿਕੰਮਾ, ਬੇਕਾਰ,
ਨਿਸ਼ਕਿਰਿਆ

inactivity ('ਇਨਐਕ'ਟਿਵਅਟਿ) n ਆਲਸ,
ਸੁਸਤੀ; ਬੇਕਾਰੀ, ਨਿਸ਼ਕਿਰਿਆਤਾ

inadequacy (ਇਨ'ਐਡਿਕਵਅਸਿ) n ਥੁੜ੍ਹ, ਘਾਟ,
ਅਲਪਤਾ, ਅਪੂਰਨਤਾ

inadequate (ਇਨ'ਐਡਿਕਵਅਟ) a ਨਾ ਕਾਫ਼ੀ;
ਥੋੜ੍ਹਾ, ਘੱਟ; ਅਪੂਰਨ; ਅਯੋਗ, ਅਸਮਰੱਥ

inadmissibility ('ਇਨਅਡ'ਮਿਸਅ'ਬਿਲਅਟਿ) n
ਅਪ੍ਰਵਾਨਤਾ, ਨਾ ਮੰਨਣਯੋਗਤਾ, ਅਸਵੀਕਾਰਤਾ

inadmissible ('ਇਨਅਡ'ਮਿਸਅਬਲ) a ਨਾ
ਮੰਨਣਯੋਗ, ਅਪ੍ਰਵੇਸ਼ੀ

in aeternum (ਇਨ'ਐਟਅਨਅਮ) (L) adv
ਸਦਾ, ਸਦੈਵ

inanimate (ਇਨ'ਐਨਿਮਅਟ) a ਬੇਜਾਨ,
ਨਿਰਜੀਵ, ਪ੍ਰਾਣਹੀਨ, ਅਚੇਤਨ, ਜੜ੍ਹ, ਮੁਰਦਾਦਿਲ

inanimation (ਇਨ'ਐਨ'ਮੇਇਸ਼ਨ) n
ਪਰਾਧੀਨਤਾ, ਨਿਰਜੀਵਤਾ, ਜੜ੍ਹਤਾ, ਅਚੇਤਨਤਾ

inapplicable (ਇਨ'ਐਪਲਿਕਅਬਲਅ) a
ਅਛੁੱਕਵਾਂ, ਲਾਗੂ ਨਾ ਹੋਣ ਯੋਗ, ਅਨੁਚਿਤ,
ਨਾਵਾਜਬ

inappropriate ('ਇਨਅ'ਪਰਅਉਪਰਿਅਟ) a
ਅਛੁੱਕਵਾਂ, ਅਨੁਚਿਤ, ਬੇਮੇਲ; ਅਸੰਗਤ, ਬੇਮੌਕਾ

inapt (ਇਨ'ਐਪਟ) a ਅਯੋਗ, ਨਾਲਾਇਕ,
ਨਾਮੁਨਾਸਬ; ~itude ਅਯੋਗਤਾ, ਨਾਲਾਇਕੀ

inasmuch (ਜ'ਇਨਅਜ਼'ਮਅੱਚ) adv ਜਿਥੋਂ ਤਕ
ਕਿ

inattentive ('ਇਨਅਟੈਂਟਿਵ) a ਬੇਧਿਆਨਾ,
ਘੇਸਲਾ, ਮਚਲਾ, ਲਾਪਰਵਾਹ

inaugural (ਇਨੋਗਯੂਰ(ਅ)ਲ) v ਉਦਘਾਟਨੀ,
ਉਦਘਾਟਨਕਾਰੀ; ~function ਉਦਘਾਟਨ-
ਸਮਾਰੋਹ

inaugurate (ਇਨੋਗਯੂਰੇਇਟ) v ਉਦਘਾਟਨ
ਕਰਨਾ, ਮਹੂਰਤ ਕਰਨਾ; ਚੱਠ ਕਰਨੀ

inauguration (ਇ'ਨੋਗਯੁ'ਰੇਇਸ਼ਨ) n
ਉਦਘਾਟਨ, ਮਹੂਰਤ, ਚੱਠ; ਆਰੰਭ

inauspicious ('ਇਨਓ'ਸਪਿਸ਼ਅਸ) a ਅਸ਼ੁਭ,
ਕੁਸ਼ਗਨਾ, ਦੁਰਭਾਗ ਸੂਚਕ

inborn, inbred (ਇਨ'ਬੋਨ, ਇਨ'ਬਰੈੱਡ) a
ਜਮਾਂਦਰੂ, ਜਨਮ ਤੋਂ ਹੀ, ਸੁਭਾਵਕ, ਕੁਦਰਤੀ,
ਜਨਮਜਾਤ, ਸਹਿਜ

incamera ('ਇਨ'ਕੈਮਅਰਅ) (L) a ਗੁਪਤ

incapability (ਇਨ'ਕੇਇਪਅ'ਬਿਲਅਟਿ) n
ਅਸਮਰੱਥਾ, ਅਯੋਗਤਾ, ਨਾਲਾਇਕ, ਨਿਰਬਲਤਾ

incapable (ਇਨ'ਕੇਇਪਅਬਲ) a ਅਸਮਰੱਥ,
ਅਯੋਗ, ਨਾਲਾਇਕ, ਨਾਕਾਬਲ; ਸ਼ਕਤੀਹੀਨ

incapacity (ਇਨਕਅ'ਪੈਸਅਟਿ) n ਅਸਮਰੱਥਾ,
ਅਯੋਗਤਾ, ਨਾਲਾਇਕੀ; ਅਧਿਕਾਰਹੀਨਤਾ

incarnate ('ਇਨਕਾਨੇਇਟ, ਇਨ'ਕਾਨਅਟ) v a

ਅਵਤਾਰ ਧਾਰਨਾ, ਜਨਮ ਲੈਣਾ; ਸਾਕਾਰ ਰੂਪ ਵਿਚ ਰੱਖਣਾ; ਸਾਕਾਰ, ਸਾਖਿਆਤ, ਸਰੂਪ, ਮੂਰਤੀਮਾਨ

incarnation ('ਇਨਕਾ'ਨੇਇਸ਼ਨ) *n* ਅਵਤਾਰ ਧਾਰਨ, ਅਵਤਾਰ; ਦੇਹਧਾਰੀ ਹੋਣ ਦੀ ਦਸ਼ਾ

incense (ਇਨ'ਸੈਂਸ) *v n* ਧੂਪ ਦੇਣਾ, ਧੂਣੀ ਦੇਣੀ, ਸੁਗੰਧੀ ਧੁਖਾਉਣੀ, ਮਹਿਕਾਉਣਾ; ਧੂਪ ਗੁੱਸਾ ਚੜ੍ਹਾਉਣਾ, ਕਰੋਧ ਚੜ੍ਹਾਉਣਾ; ਉਤੇਜਤ ਕਰਨਾ

incentive (ਇਨ'ਸੈਂਟਿਵ੍) *n a* ਉਤਸਾਹ, ਪਰੇਰਨਾ, ਉਤੇਜਨਾ, ਉਕਸਾਹਟ; ਪਰੇਰਕ, ਉਤੇਜਕ

incept (ਇਨ'ਸੈਪਟ) *v* ਗ੍ਰਹਿਣ ਕਰਨਾ, ਚੂਸ ਲੈਣਾ, ਸੁਕਾਉਣਾ; ~**ion** ਮੁੱਢ, ਆਰੰਭ, ਸ਼ੁਰੂਆਤ, ਸ਼ੁਰੂ; ~**ive** ਮੁੱਢਲਾ, ਆਰੰਭਕ, ਸ਼ੁਰੂ ਦਾ, ਆਰੰਭ ਸੂਚਕ

incertain (ਇਨ'ਸਅਃਟਨ) *a* ਅਨਿਸ਼ਚਤ, ਸੰਦੇਹਯੁਕਤ, ਸੰਦਿਗਧ

incessant (ਇਨ'ਸੈਸੰਟ) *a* ਅਟੁੱਟ, ਇਕਤਾਰ, ਲਗਾਤਾਰ, ਨਿਰੰਤਰ

inch (ਇੰਚ) *n* ਇੰਚ, ਗਜ਼ ਦਾ ਛੱਤੀਵਾਂ ਭਾਗ

incidence ('ਇਨਸਿਡ਼ਅੰਸ) *n* ਘਟਨਾ, ਸਥਿਤੀ, ਵਾਪਰਨ, ਮਾਜਰਾ, ਹਾਦਸਾ, ਵਾਕਿਆ

incident ('ਇਨਸਿਡ਼ਅੰਟ) *n a* ਘਟਨਾ, ਵਾਕਿਆ, ਬਿਰਤਾਂਤ, ਮਾਜਰਾ; ਪ੍ਰਸੰਗ; ~**al** ਇਤਫ਼ਾਕੀਆ, ਆਰਜ਼ੀ

incipient (ਇਨ'ਸਿਪਿਅੰਟ) *a* ਮੁੱਢਲਾ, ਆਰੰਭਕ

incisive (ਇਨ'ਸਾਇਸਿਵ੍) *a* ਸਮਝਦਾਰ, ਬੁੱਧੀਵਾਨ, ਤੀਖਣ (ਬੁੱਧੀ), ਤਿੱਖਾ, ਬਾਰੀਕ

incite (ਇਨ'ਸਾਇਟ) *v* ਭੜਕਾਉਣਾ, ਉਕਸਾਉਣਾ, ਉਭਾਰਨਾ, ਉਤੇਜਤ ਕਰਨਾ, ਵਰਗਲਾਉਣਾ; ~**ment, incitation** ਉਕਸਾਹਟ, ਉਭਾਰ, ਉਤੇਜਨਾ, ਭੜਕਾਹਟ

inclination ('ਇਨਲਕਲਿ'ਨੇਇਸ਼ਨ) *n* ਢਾਲ, ਝੁਕਾਉ, ਰੁਝਾਨ, ਪ੍ਰਵਿਰਤੀ, ਰੁਚੀ, ਇੱਛਾ

incline (ਇਨ'ਕਲਾਇਨ) *v n* ਰੌ ਹੋਣਾ, ਝੁਕਾਉਣਾ, ਝੁਕਟਾ; ਇੱਛਾ ਰੱਖਣੀ; ਮੁੜਨਾ, ਮੋੜਨਾ; ~**d** ਝੁਕਿਆ, ਢਾਲਵਾਂ, ਪ੍ਰਵਿਰਤ

include (ਇਨ'ਕਲੂਡ) *v* ਸ਼ਾਮਲ ਕਰਨਾ, ਜੋੜਨਾ, ਸੰਮਿਲਤ ਕਰਨਾ, ਮਿਲਾਉਣਾ; ਦਾਖ਼ਲ ਕਰਨਾ; ~**d** ਅੰਤਰਗਤ, ਅੰਤਰਭੂਤ, ਸੰਮਿਲਤ

inclusion (ਇਨ'ਕਲੂਯ਼ਨ) *n* ਸੰਮਿਲਨ, ਦਾਖ਼ਲਾ

inclusive (ਇਨ'ਕਲੂਸਿਵ੍) *a* ਸਹਿਤ, ਸੰਮਿਲਤ; ~**ness** ਅੰਤਰ ਭਾਵ, ਸਮਾਵੇਸ਼ਨ

incognito ('ਇਨਕੋਗਨ'ਨੀਟਅਉ) *a n adv* ਬਹੁਰੂਪੀਆ; ਗੁਮਨਾਮ, ਅਗਿਆਤ

incongnizable (ਇਨ'ਕੋਗਨਿਜ਼ਅਬਲ) *a* ਅਬੋਧ, ਅਗੋਚਰ, ਅਗੰਮ

incoherence (ਇਨਕਅਅ(ਉ)'ਹਿਅਰਅੰਸ) *n* ਅਜੋੜਤਾ, ਅਸੰਗਤੀ, ਅਸਬੰਧਤਾ, ਅਜੋੜ

incoherent (ਇਨਕਅਅ(ਉ)'ਹਿਅਰਅੰਟ) *a* ਅਸੰਗਤ, ਅਜੋੜ, ਅਰਥਹੀਨ, ਉਘੜ-ਦੁੱਘੜ

incohesive (ਇਨਕਅਅ(ਉ)'ਹੀਸਿਵ੍) *a* ਅਸੰਗਤ, ਅਸੰਬੱਧ, ਬੇਮੇਲ

income ('ਇਢਕਅੱਮ) *n* ਆਮਦਨੀ, ਕਮਾਈ, ਆਮਦ, ਆਯ; ਲਾਭ

incoming ('ਇਨ'ਕੱਅਮਿਢ਼) *n* ਆਗਮਨ, ਆਮਦਨੀ, ਧਨ-ਆਗਮ; ਆਪੂਵਾਸੀ, ਆਗਾਮੀ

incommensurate ('ਇਨਕਅਅ'ਮੈਨ੍ਸ(ਅ)ਰਅਟ) *a* ਅਤੁੱਲ, ਅਸਮਾਨ; ਘੱਟ

incommunicable ('ਇਨਕਅਅ'ਮਯੂਨਿਕਅਬਲ) *a* ਅਕੱਥ, ਅਕਬਨੀ, ਅਵਰਲਨੀ

incompatibility ('ਇਨਕਅਮਪੈਟਅਅ'ਬਿਲਅਟਿ) *n* ਅਢੁੱਕਵਾਂਪਣ, ਅਸੰਗਤੀ

incompatible ('ਇਨਕਮਪੈਟਅਬਲ) *a* ਵਿਰੁੱਧ, ਅਸੰਗਤ, ਅਢੁੱਕਵਾਂ, ਬੇਮੇਲ

incompetence, incompetency (ਇਨ'ਕੌਮਪਿਟਅੰਸ, ਇਨ'ਕੌਮਪਿਟਅੰਸਿ) *n* ਅਸਮਰਥਤਾ, ਅਯੋਗਤਾ, ਨਾਲਾਇਕੀ

incompetent (ਇਨ'ਕੌਮਪਿਟਅੰਟ) *a* ਅਸਮਰੱਥ, ਅਯੋਗ, ਨਾਲਾਇਕ, ਨਾਕਾਬਲ

incomplete ('ਇਨਕਮਪਲੀਟ) *a* ਅਧੂਰਾ, ਅਪੂਰਨ, ਨਾਮੁਕੰਮਲ; ~ly ਅਧੂਰੇ ਤੌਰ ਤੇ

incompliance ('ਇਨਕਮਪਲਾਇਅੰਸ) *n* ਅਵੱਗਿਆ, ਅਸਵੀਕ੍ਰਿਤੀ

incomprehensibilty, incomprehensiveness (ਇਨ'ਕੌਮਪਰਿਹੈੱਸਅ'ਬਿਲਿਅਟਿ, ਇਨ'ਕੌਮਪਰਿਹੈੱਸਿਵਨਿਸ) *n* ਦੁਰਬੋਧਤਾ, ਗੁੜ੍ਹਤਾ; ਅਪਾਰਤਾ

incomprehensible (ਇਨ'ਕੌਂਪਰਿ'ਹੈੱਸਅਿਬਲ) *n* ਅਬੋਧ, ਦੁਰਬੋਧ, ਗੁੜ੍ਹ; ਅਨੰਤ, ਅਪਾਰ

incomprehension (ਇਨ'ਕੌਂਪਰਿ'ਹੈੱਸ਼ਨ) *n* ਅਬੋਧਤਾ, ਅਗਿਆਨ, ਨਾਸਮਝੀ, ਗੁੜ੍ਹਤਾ, ਅਸੀਮਤਾ

incomprehensive (ਇਨ'ਕੌਂਪਰਿਹੈੱਸਿਵ) *a* ਸੰਕੀਰਨ, ਸੀਮਤ, ਤੰਗ; ਦੁਰਬੋਧ, ਅਬੋਧ

inconclusive ('ਇਨਕਅਨ'ਕਲੂਸਿਵ) *a* ਅਨਿਸਚਤ, ਫੈਸਲਾਰਹਿਤ, ਅਸਪਸ਼ਟ; ~ness ਅਨਿਸਚਤਤਾ, ਅਨਿਰਨਾ, ਅਨਿਸ਼ਚਾ, ਸੰਦੇਹਸ਼ੀਲਤਾ, ਸੰਦਿਗੱਧਤਾ

incongruity ('ਇਨਕੌਂਗ੍ਰੂਅਟਿ) *n* ਅਸੰਗਤੀ, ਅਸੰਬੱਧਤਾ, ਵਿਰੋਧ, ਬੇਤੁਕਾਪਣ, ਬੇਢੰਗਾ

incongruous (ਇਨ'ਕੌਂਗਰੁਅਸ) *a* ਅਸਬੰਧਤ, ਅਸੰਗਤ, ਬੇਮੇਲ; ਵਿਰੋਧੀ, ਬੇਢੰਗਾ, ਬੇਡੌਲ, ਬੇਤੁਕਾ, ਬੇਮੌਕਾ, ਨਾਮੁਨਾਸਬ

inconsiderate ('ਇਨਕਅਨ'ਸਿਡ(ਅ)ਰਅਟ) *a* ਅਵਿਵੇਕੀ, ਬੁੱਧੀਹੀਨ, ਭਾਵਨਾਹੀਨ, ਬੇਪਰਵਾਹ, ਬੇ-ਲਿਹਾਜ਼ਾ ਕੋਰਾ; ~ness, inconsideration ਅਵਿਵੇਕ, ਬੁੱਧੀ-ਹੀਨਤਾ, ਬੇਪਰਵਾਹੀ, ਬੇਲਿਹਾਜ਼ੀ

inconsistence, inconsistency ('ਇਨਕਅਨ'ਸਿਸਟਅੰਸ, ਇਕਅਨ'ਸਿਸਟਅੰਸਿ) *n* ਸਵੈ-ਵਿਰੋਧ; ਵਿਪਰੀਤਤਾ, ਅਸੰਗਤਾ, ਅਪ੍ਰਸੰਗਕਤਾ, ਬੇਅਸੂਲਪਨ

inconsistent ('ਇਨਕਅਨ'ਸਿਸਟਅੰਟ) *a* ਵਿਪਰੀਤ; ਬੇਮੇਲ; ਅਜੋੜ, ਅਸੰਗਤ, ਬੇਅਸੂਲ ਪ੍ਰਤੀਕੂਲ

inconsonance (ਇਨ'ਕੌਨਸਅਨਅੰਸ) *n* ਬੇਸੁਰਾਪਨ, ਅਸੰਗਤੀ

inconspicuous ('ਇਨਕਅਨ'ਸਪਿਕਯੁਅਸ) *a* ਅਪ੍ਰਤੱਖ, ਅਸਪਸ਼ਟ, ਅਪਰਗਟ; ~ness ਅਪ੍ਰਤੱਖਤਾ, ਅਸਪਸ਼ਟਤਾ, ਅਪਰਗਟਾ, ਪੀਲਾਪਨ

inconvenience ('ਇਨਕਅਨ'ਵੀਨਯਅੰਸ) *n v* ਔਖਿਆਈ, ਤਕਲੀਫ਼, ਖੇਚਲ, ਦਿੱਕਤ; ਕਸ਼ਟ, ਜ਼ਹਿਮਤ, ਅਸੁਵਿਧਾ; ਦਿੱਕਤ ਦੇਣੀ, ਕਸ਼ਟ ਦੇਣਾ, ਹਰਜ ਕਰਨਾ

inconvenient ('ਇਨਕਅਨ'ਵੀਨਯਅੰਟ) *a* ਤਕਲੀਫ਼-ਦੇਹ, ਬੇਮੌਕਾ, ਬੇਜਾ, ਨਾਮੁਨਾਸਬ, ਨਾਮੁਆਫ਼ਕ, ਅਸੁਵਿਧਾਪੂਰਨ

incorporate ('ਇਨ'ਕੌਪਅਰਇਟ) *v* ਇਕੱਠਾ ਕਰਨਾ, ਇਕ ਜਾਨ ਕਰਨਾ, ਸੰਮਿਲਤ ਕਰਨਾ, ਸੰਯੁਕਤ ਹੋਣਾ, ਸੰਯੁਕਤ ਕਰਨਾ; ~d ਸੰਮਿਲਤ, ਸੰਸਥਾਪਤ, ਨਿਗਮਤ

incorrect ('ਇਨਕਅ'ਰੈਕਟ) *a* ਗਲਤ, ਅਸ਼ੁੱਧ, ਝੂਠ, ਅਯੋਗ, ਤਰੁਟੀਪੂਰਨ, ਅਨੁਚਿਤ

incorrigibility (ਇਨ'ਕੌਰਿਗਿ'ਬਿਲਿਅਟਿ) *n*

ਅਸਾਪਤਾ

incorrigible (ਇਨ'ਕੌਰਿਜਿਅਬਲ) *a* ਅਸਾਧ

increase (ਇਨ'ਕਰੀਸ, 'ਇਨਕਰੀਸ) *v n* ਅਧਿਕ ਹੋਣਾ, ਵਧਣਾ, ਵਧਾਉਣਾ, ਉੱਨਤ ਹੋਣਾ; ਅਧਿਕਤਾ, ਵਾਧਾ, ਉੱਨਤ; ~**d** ਵਧਿਆ

increasing (ਇਨ'ਕਰੀਸਿੰਡ) *a* ਵਰਧਮਾਨ, ਵਧਣ ਵਾਲਾ

increment ('ਇਨਕਰਿਮ਄੍ਟ) *n* ਵਿਸਤਾਰ, ਵਾਧਾ, ਵ੍ਰਿਧੀ; ਲਾਭ, ਮੁਨਾਫ਼ਾ, ਤਰੱਕੀ

inculcate (ਇਨਕਅੱਲਕੇਇਟ) *v* ਗ੍ਰਹਿਣ ਕਰਾਉਣਾ, ਜ਼ਿਹਨ ਵਿਚ ਬਿਠਾਉਣਾ, ਮੁੜ-ਮੁੜ ਸਮਝਾਉਣਾ, ਤਾਕੀਦ ਕਰਨੀ

inculpable (ਇਨ'ਕਅੱਲਪਅਬਲ) *a* ਨਿਰਦੋਸ਼, ਅਕਲੰਕ, ਬੇਦੋਸ਼ਾ

incumbent (ਇਨ'ਕਅੱਮਬਅੰਟ) *a n* ਉਚਿਤ, ਅਤੀ ਅਵੱਸ਼ਕ, ਬਹੁਤ ਜ਼ਰੂਰੀ, ਨਿਰਭਰ; ਅਹੁਦੇਦਾਰ, ਪਦਧਾਰੀ, ਉਹ ਵਿਅਕਤੀ ਜਿਸਨੇ ਪਦ ਗ੍ਰਹਿਣ ਕੀਤਾ ਹੋਵੇ

incur (ਇਨ'ਕਅਾਃ*) *v* ਗ੍ਰਸਤ ਹੋਣਾ, ਆਪਣੇ ਉੱਤੇ ਲੈਣਾ; ਉਠਾਉਣਾ

incurable (ਇਨ'ਕਯੁਅਰਅਬਲ) *a n* ਅਸਾਧ, ਲਾ-ਇਲਾਜ

indebted (ਇਨ'ਡੈਟਿਡ) *a* ਰਿਣੀ, ਦੇਣਦਾਰ; ਕਿਰਤੱਗ, ਇਹਸਾਨਮੰਦ, ਕਰਜ਼ਈ; ~**ness** ਰਿਣਗ੍ਰਸਤਤਾ, ਕਰਜ਼ਦਾਰੀ; ਕ੍ਰਿਤੱਗਤਾ, ਇਹਸਾਨਮੰਦੀ

indecency (ਇਨ'ਡੀਸੰਸਿ) *n* ਗੰਵਾਰੂਪਣ, ਅਸ਼ਿਸ਼ਟਤਾ; ਅਭੱਦਰਤਾ; ਅਸ਼ਲੀਲਤਾ; ਅਣਉਚਿਤਤਾ

indecent (ਇਨ'ਡੀਸੰਟ) *a* ਗੰਵਾਰ, ਅਸ਼ਿਸ਼ਟ, ਅਭਦਰ; ਬਦਤਮੀਜ਼, ਅਣਉਚਿਤ

indeed (ਇਨ'ਡੀਡ) *adv int* ਸਚੱਮੁਚ, ਯਕੀਨੀ ਤੌਰ ਤੇ, ਦਰਅਸਲ, ਨਿਰਸੰਦੇਹ, ਬੇਸ਼ੱਕ, ਠੀਕ

indefinite (ਇਨ'ਡੈੱਫ਼ਨਿਟ) *a* ਅਸਪਸ਼ਟਤਾ, ਅਨਿਸ਼ਚਤਤਾ, ਸੰਦੇਹਪੂਰਨ, ਬੇਹੱਦ; ~**ly** ਅਨਿਸ਼ਚਤ ਤੌਰ ਤੇ, ਅਟਮਿੰਥੇ ਤੌਰ ਤੇ; ~**ness** ਅਸਪਸ਼ਟਤਾ, ਸੰਦਿਗਧਤਾ, ਅਸੀਮਤਾ, ਗੋਲ-ਮਾਲ

indent ('ਇਨਡੈੱਟ, ਇਨ'ਡੈੱਟ) *n v* ਦੰਦੀਕਰਨ; ਟੱਕ; ~**ure** ਵਸਤੂ-ਸੂਚੀ; ਇਕਰਾਰਨਾਮਾ ਦੰਦਾ; ਮੰਗ-ਪੱਤਰ; ਦੰਦੇ ਕੱਢਣਾ, ਨਿਸ਼ਾਨ ਲਾਉਣੇ, ਠੱਪਾ ਲਾਉਣਾ, ਹਾਸ਼ੀਏ ਤੋਂ ਦੂਰ ਸ਼ੁਰੂ ਕਰਨਾ

independence ('ਇੰਡਿ'ਪੈਂਡਅੰਸ) *n* ਸੁਤੰਤਰਤਾ, ਸਵਾਧੀਨਤਾ, ਆਜ਼ਾਦੀ

independent (ਇੰਡਿਪੈਂਡਅੰਟ) *a n* ਸੁਤੰਤਰ, ਆਜ਼ਾਦ, ਸਵਾਧੀਨ; ਨਿਰਪੇਖ

index ('ਇਨਡੈੱਕਸ) *n v* ਸੂਚਕ ਨਿਸ਼ਾਨ, ਦਲੀਲ, ਚਿੰਨ੍ਹ; ~**finger** ਤਰਜਨੀ, ਅੰਗੂਠੇ ਦੇ ਨਾਲ ਦੀ ਉਂਗਲੀ

indian ('ਇਨਡਯਅਨ) *n* ਭਾਰਤੀ, ਹਿੰਦੁਸਤਾਨੀ

indicate ('ਇਨਡਿਕੇਇਟ) *v* ਸੁਝਾਉਣਾ, ਪ੍ਰਸਤਾਵਤ ਕਰਨਾ, ਪ੍ਰਤੀਕ ਹੋਣਾ, ਸੰਕੇਤ ਕਰਨਾ, ਇਸ਼ਾਰਾ ਕਰਨਾ, ਘੋਸ਼ਣਾ ਕਰਨੀ, ਦੱਸਣਾ, ਜਤਾਉਣਾ, ਪਰਗਟ ਕਰਨਾ; ~**d** ਸੂਚਤ, ਸੰਕੇਤਤ, ਨਿਰਦਿਸ਼ਟ

indication ('ਇਨਡਿ'ਕੇਇਸ਼ਨ) *n* ਚਿੰਨ੍ਹ, ਲੱਛਣ, ਪਰਦਰਸ਼ਕ ਸੰਕੇਤ, ਇਸ਼ਾਰਾ

indicative (ਇਨ'ਡਿਕਅਟਿਵ੍) *a n* (ਵਿਆ) ਨਿਸ਼ਚੇਵਾਚਕ; ਬੋਧਕ, ਸੁਝਾਊ, ਸੂਚਕ, ਸੰਦੇਤਕ ਸਵੀਕਾਰ ਸੂਚਕ; ਨਿਸ਼ਰੇ ਅਰਥ

indicator ('ਇਨਡਿਕੇਇਟ*) *n* ਸੂਚਕ, ਬੋਧਕ, ਨਿਰਦੇਸ਼ਕ, (ਜੰਤਰ ਦੀ) ਸੂਈ

indict (ਇਨ'ਡਿਕਟ) v ਦੋਸ਼ ਲਾਉਣਾ, ਅਪਰਾਧੀ
ਠਹਿਰਾਉਣਾ; ~able ਦੋਸ਼ ਲਾਉਣ ਜੋਗ,
ਅਪਰਾਧੀ ਠਹਿਰਾਉਣ ਜੋਗ; ~ment ਦੋਸ਼-
ਆਰੋਪਣ, ਆਰੋਪਣ-ਵਿਧੀ, ਕਾਨੂੰਨੀ ਦਾਅਵਾ

indifference (ਇਨ'ਡਿਫਰਾਂਸ) n ਬੇਪਰਵਾਹੀ,
ਬੇ-ਵਾਸਤਾ, ਉਦਾਸੀਨਤਾ, ਮਹੱਤਵਹੀਨਤਾ

indifferent (ਇਨ'ਡਿਫਰਾਂਟ) a ਉਦਾਸੀਨ,
ਵਿਰਕਤ, ਬੇਲਾਗ, ਬੇਪਰਵਾਹ, ਅਲਗਰਜ਼

indigenous (ਇਨ'ਡਿਜਿਨਅਸ) a ਸੁਦੇਸ਼ੀ, ਦੇਸੀ

indigestion (ਇਨਡਿ'ਜੇਸ਼ੱਨ) n ਬਦਹਜ਼ਮੀ,
ਅਜੀਰਣਤਾ, ਅਪਚਾ

indignity (ਇਨ'ਡਿਗਨਅਟਿ) n ਨਿਰਾਦਰ,
ਅਨਾਦਰ, ਖੁਆਰੀ, ਅਵੱਗਿਆ, ਅਪਮਾਨ, ਹੱਤਕ,
ਹੇਠੀ, ਤਿਰਸਕਾਰ, ਫਿਕਾਰ; ਅਸ਼ਿਸ਼ਟ ਆਚਰਨ

indigo (ਇਨਡਿਗਾਓ) n ਨੀਲ

indirect (ਇਨਡਿ'ਰੈਕੱਟ) a ਟੇਢਾ, ਵਿੰਗਾ,
ਅਸਿੱਧਾ, ਫੇਰਵਾਂ, ਵਕਰ, ਕੁਟਲ, ਚੱਕਰਦਾਰ,
ਟੇਢਾ-ਮੇਢਾ; ਅਸਰਲ

indiscipline (ਇਨਡਿ'ਸਿਪਲਿਨ) n ਬੇਜ਼ਬਤੀ,
ਅਨੁਸ਼ਾਸਨਹੀਣਤਾ, ਅਸੰਜਮ

indiscretion (ਇਨਡਿ'ਸਕਰੈਸ਼ੱਨ) n
ਚਿੰਤਨਹੀਣਤਾ; ਨਾਦਾਨੀ, ਅਵਿਵੇਕ

indiscreet (ਇਨਡਿ'ਸਕਰੀਟ) a ਅਸਾਵਧਾਨ,
ਸੂਝ ਰਹਿਤ

indiscriminate (ਇਨਡਿ'ਸਕਰਿਮਿਨਅਟ) a
ਨਿਰਪਛਾਣ, ਵਿਵੇਕਹੀਨ, ਅੰਧਾਧੁੰਦ, ਰਲਿਆ-
ਮਿਲਿਆ; ~ness ਨਿਰਪਛਾਤਾ, ਵਿਵੇਕਹੀਣਤਾ;
ਗੋਂਡ-ਮੰਡ

indispensability (ਇਨਡਿ'ਸਪੈਂਸਆ'ਬਿਲਅਟਿ)
n ਅਵੱਸ਼ਕਤਾ

indispensable (ਇਨਡਿ'ਸਪੈਂਸਅਬਲ) a
ਲਾਜ਼ਮੀ, ਜ਼ਰੂਰੀ, ਅਵੱਸ਼ਕ

indispose (ਇਨਡਿ'ਸਪਅਓਜ਼) v ਢਿੱਲਾ ਕਰਨਾ,
ਅਸੁਅਸਥ ਕਰਨਾ, ਅਯੋਗ ਕਰਨਾ; ਬੇਮੁਖ
ਕਰਨਾ, ਵਿਰਕਤ ਬਣਾਉਣਾ, ਅਰੁਚੀ ਪੈਦਾ
ਕਰਨੀ, ਦਿਲ ਫੇਰ ਦੇਣਾ; ~d ਢਿੱਲਾ, ਅਸੁਅਸਥ,
ਬੀਮਾਰ

indispostion ('ਇਨਡਿਸਪਅ'ਜ਼ਿਸ਼ਨ) n ਢਿੱਲ,
ਕਸਰ, ਨਾਸਾਜ਼ਗੀ; ਬੇਦਿਲੀ, ਅਰੁਚੀ

indisputable ('ਇਨਡਿ'ਸਪਯੂਟਅਬਲ) a
ਨਿਰਵਿਵਾਦ, ਨਿਸਚਤ

indistinct ('ਇਨਡਿ'ਸਟਿਙ(ਕ)ਟ) a ਅਸਪਸ਼ਟ,
ਧੁੰਦਲਾ

individual ('ਇਨਡਿ'ਵਿਜੁਅਲ) n a ਵਿਅਕਤੀ,
ਜਣਾ, ਜਨ, ਆਦਮੀ; ਜਾਤੀ, ਸ਼ਖਸੀ; ਇੱਕਲਾ,
ਅੱਡੋ-ਅੱਡ; ਵਿਸ਼ੇਸ਼, ਵਿਅਕਤੀਗਤ; ~ism
ਵਿਅਕਤੀਵਾਦ, ਅਹੰਵਾਦ, ਨਿਜਵਾਦ; ~ist
ਵਿਅਕਤੀਵਾਦੀ, ਅਹੰਵਾਦੀ, ਨਿਜਵਾਦੀ,
ਨਿਜਤਵਵਾਦੀ; ~ity ਆਪਾ, ਸ਼ਖਸੀਅਤ, ਜਾਤ

indivisibility ('ਇਨਡਿ'ਵਿਜ਼ਅ'ਬਿਲਅਟਿ) n
ਅਵੰਡਤਾ, ਅਖੰਡਤਾ

indivisible ('ਇਨਡਿ'ਵਿਜ਼ਅਬਲ) a n ਅਵੰਡ,
ਅੱਖੰਡ, ਅਭੇਦੀ

indolence ('ਇਨਡਅਲਅੰਸ) n ਆਲਸ, ਸੁਸਤੀ,
ਵਿਮੁੱਖਤਾ

indolent ('ਇਨਡਅਲਅੰਟ) a ਆਲਸੀ, ਸੁਸਤ,
ਪੀੜ-ਰਹਿਤ

indologist (ਇਨ'ਡੋਲਅਜਿਸਟ) n ਭਾਰਤ ਸਬੰਧੀ
ਗਿਆਨ ਵੇਤਾ, ਭਾਰਤ-ਵਿਗਿਆਨੀ

indology (ਇਨ'ਡੋਲਅਜਿ) n ਭਾਰਤ-ਵਿਗਿਆਨ

indomitable (ਇਨ'ਡੋਮਿਟਅਬਲ) a ਅਜਿਤ,
ਹਠੀ, ਜ਼ਿੱਦੀ, ਬੇਕਾਬੂ, ਹਠੀਲਾ

indoor ('ਇਨਡੋਂ*) *a* ਅੰਤਰਵਾਸੀ, ਅੰਦਰਲਾ, ਭੀਤਰੀ, ਨਿਵਾਸੀ (ਰੋਗੀ)

indubious (ਇਨ'ਡਯੂਬਯਅਸ) *a* ਨਿਸ਼ਚਤ, ਸੰਦੇਹਹੀਣ

induce (ਇਨ'ਡਯੂਸ) *v* ਪਰੇਰਨਾ, ਲੁਭਾ ਲੈਣਾ, ਫੁਸਲਾ ਦੇਣਾ, ਮੰਨਣਾ; ਲਿਆਉਣਾ, ਪੈਦਾ ਕਰਨਾ; ਕਾਰਨ ਬਣਨਾ; ~**ment** ਲੋੜ, ਉਤਸ਼ਾਹ

induct (ਇਨ'ਡਅੱਕਟ) *v* ਅਧਿਕਾਰ ਦੇਣਾ; ਕਬਜ਼ਾ ਦੇਣਾ; ਭਰਤੀ ਕਰਨਾ, ਪ੍ਰਵੇਸ਼ ਕਰਾਉਣਾ; ਪ੍ਰਾਰੰਭ ਕਰਨਾ; ~**ion** ਪ੍ਰਵੇਸ਼, ਭੂਮਕਾ, ਪ੍ਰਸਤਾਵਨਾ; (ਨਿਆਂ) ਆਗਮਨ; ~**ive** ਆਗਮਨਾਤਮਕ, ਅਨੁਮਾਨਾਤਮਕ

indulge (ਇਨ'ਡਅੱਲਜ) *v* ਕ੍ਰਿਪਤ ਕਰਨਾ ਜਾਂ ਹੋਣਾ, ਸਲਾਹ ਦੇਣਾ; ਭੋਗਣਾ; ਸ਼ੌਕ ਵਧਣਾ; ~**nce** ਮਜ਼ਾ, ਆਤਮਕ੍ਰਿਪਤੀ, ਆਤਮ-ਸੰਤੋਸ਼; ਅਤੀਭੋਗ; ~**nt** ਦਿਆਲੂ, ਕਿਰਪਾਲੂ, ਦਇਆਵਾਨ, ਮਿਹਰਬਾਨ; ਸ਼ੁਕੀਨ; ਆਸਕਤ, ਲਿਪਤ

industrial ('ਇਨ'ਡਅੱਸਟਰਿਅਲ) *a* ਉੱਦਮੀ (ਆਦਮੀ) ਉੱਦਮ ਸਬੰਧੀ, ਉੱਦਯੋਗਕ; ~**isation** ਉਦਯੋਗੀਕਰਨ, ਸਨਅਤੀਕਰਨ; ~**ism** ਉਦਯੋਗਵਾਦ, ਸਨਅਤਵਾਦ; ~**ist** ਕਾਰਖ਼ਾਨੇਦਾਰ, ਉਦਯੋਗਪਤੀ, ਉਦਯੋਗਵਾਦੀ, ਉਦਯੋਗ ਵਿਸ਼ੇਸ਼ੱਗ; ~**ize** ਉਦਯੋਗੀਕਰਨ ਕਰਨਾ

industrious (ਇਨ'ਡਅੱਸਟਰਿਅਸ) *a* ਮਿਹਨਤੀ ਉਦਯੋਗੀ, ਉੱਦਮੀ

industry ('ਇਨਡਅਸਟਰਿ) *n* ਮਿਹਨਤ, ਉੱਦਮ, ਕਰਮ-ਨਿਸ਼ਠਾ; ਉਦਯੋਗ, ਸਨਅਤ, ਦਸਤਕਾਰੀ

indwell ('ਇਨ'ਡਵੈੱਲ) *v* ਰਹਿਣਾ, ਨਿਵਾਸ ਕਰਨਾ, ਘੁਸਣਾ, ਅਧਿਕਾਰ ਜਮਾਉਣਾ

ineffable (ਇਨ'ਐੱਫਅਬਲ) *a* ਅਕੱਥ, ਅਕਹੀ, ਪ੍ਰਸੰਸਾ ਤੋਂ ਬਾਹਰ

ineffaceable ('ਇਨਿ'ਫ਼ੇਇਸਅਬਲ) *a* ਅਮਿਟ, ਅਮੇਸ, ਪੱਕਾ

ineffective (ਇਨਿ'ਫ਼ੈੱਕਟਿਵ੍) *a* ਪ੍ਰਭਾਵਹੀਨ, ਬੇਅਸਰ, ਨਿਕੰਮਾ, ਵਿਅਰਥ; ~**ness** ਅਪ੍ਰਭਾਵਤਾ, ਨਿਸਫਲਤਾ; ਵਿਅਰਥਤਾ, ਅਯੋਗਤਾ

inefficient ('ਇਨਿ'ਫ਼ਿਸ਼ੰਟ) *a* ਅਕੁਸ਼ਲ, ਨਾਲਾਇਕ; ਨਿਸਫਲ, ਨਿਰਰਥਕ

inelastic ('ਇਨਿ'ਲੈਸਟਿਕ) *a* ਲਚਕਹੀਨ, ਬੇਲਚਕ, ਅਕ੍ਰੀਅਲ; ~**ity** ਲਚਕਹੀਨਤਾ, ਲੋਚਹੀਨਤਾ; ਮੁੱਲ-ਨਿਰਲੇਪਤਾ, ਹਠ

inept (ਇ'ਨੈੱਪਟ) *a* ਅਢੁੱਕਵਾਂ, ਬੇਤੁਕਾ; ਕੁਥਾਂਈ; ਅਸੰਗਤ

inequality ('ਇਨਿ'ਕਵੱਲਅਟਿ) *n* ਨਾਬਰਾਬਰੀ, ਅਸਮਾਨਤਾ, ਅਸਮਤਾ, ਕਮੀ-ਬੇਸ਼ੀ, ਵਾਧਾ ਘਾਟਾ

inertia (ਇ'ਨਅਃਸ਼ਅ) *n* ਗਤੀਹੀਨਤਾ (ਭੌ) ਜੜ੍ਹਤਾ, ਸਥਿਰਤਾ, ਨਿਸ਼ਚਤਤਾ, ਸਿਥਲਤਾ

inesse (ਇਨ'ਐੱਸਿ) (*L*) *adv* ਅਸਲ ਵਿਚ, ਵਾਸਤਵ ਵਿਚ

inevitable (ਇਨ'ਐੱਵਿਟਅਬਲ) *a* ਅੱਟਲ, ਅਮਿਟ, ਲਾਜ਼ਮੀ

inexperience ('ਇਨਿਕ'ਸਪਿਅਰਿਅੰਸ) *n* ਨਾਤਜਰਬੇਕਾਰੀ, ਅਨਾੜੀਪਨ, ਅੱਲੂਝਪਨਾ, ਅਨੁਭਵਹੀਨਤਾ; ~**d** ਅਨਾੜੀ, ਅਨੁਭਵਹੀਨ

infancy ('ਇਨਫ਼ੰਸਿ) *n* ਵਿਕਾਸ ਦੀ ਆਰੰਭਕ ਅਵਸਥਾ; ਬਾਲਪਨ, ਬਚਪਨ; ਨਾਬਾਲਗਾ

infant ('ਇਨਫ਼ੰਟ) *n* ਬਾਲ, ਬਾਲਕ; ਬੱਚਾ, ਨਿਆਣਾ, ਮਾਸੂਮ, ਇਆਣਾ, ਅੰਵਾਣਾ, ਗੀਗਾ,

ਨਿੱਕੜਾ, ਨਾਬਾਲਗ਼ਾ

infantry (*ਇਨਫ਼ਅੰਟਰਿ*) *n* ਪਿਆਦਾ ਫ਼ੌਜ, ਪੈਦਲ
ਸੈਨਾ

infer (*ਇਨ'ਫ਼ਅ:*) *v* ਅਨੁਮਾਨ ਲਾਉਣਾ, ਦਲੀਲ
ਦੇਂਦੀ, ਅਰਥ ਦੇਣਾ, ਸੂਚਤ ਕਰਨਾ, ਭਾਵ ਲੈਣਾ;
~able ਅਨੁਮਾਨ ਲਾਉਣ ਯੋਗ, ਅਰਥ ਦੇਣ
ਯੋਗ, ਸੂਚਤ ਕਰਨ ਯੋਗ; **~ence** ਅਨੁਮਾਨ,
ਨਿਰਨਾ, ਪਰਿਣਾਮ; ਨਿਰਣੀਤ ਵਿਸ਼ਾ

inferior (ਇਨ'ਫ਼ਿਅਰਿਆ*) *n a* ਮਾਤਹਿਤ; ਤੁੱਛ,
ਛੋਟਾ, ਨੀਵਾਂ, ਅਸ੍ਰੇਸ਼ਠ, ਘਟੀਆ; **~ity** ਹੀਣਤਾ,
ਤੁੱਛਤਾ, ਛੋਟਪਣ, ਨੀਵਾਂਪਣ, ਅਸ੍ਰੇਸ਼ਠਤਾ,
ਘਟੀਆਪਣ; **~ity complex** ਹੀਣਤਾ-ਭਾਵ,
ਹੀਨ-ਭਾਵਨਾ, ਆਤਮ-ਹੀਣਤਾ

inferno (ਇਨ'ਫ਼ਅ:ਨਾਉ) *n* ਨਰਕ, ਦੋਜ਼ਖ

infidel (*ਇਨਫ਼ਿਡ(ਅ)ਲ*) *n a* ਨਾਸਤਕ, ਕਾਫ਼ਰ,
ਅਨੀਸ਼ਵਰਵਾਦੀ,   ਧਰਮ-ਨਿੰਦਕ;   **~ity**
ਵਿਸ਼ਵਾਸਘਾਤ,   ਨਾਸਤਕਤਾ,   ਧਰਮ-ਧਰੋਹ
ਸ਼ਰਧਾਹੀਣਤਾ

infiltrate (*ਇਨਫ਼ਿਲਰੇਇਟ*) *v* ਅੰਦਰ ਘੁਸਣਾ,
ਘੁਸਪੈਠ ਕਰਨੀ, ਪ੍ਰਵੇਸ਼ ਕਰਨਾ, ਵਿਆਪਤ ਹੋਣਾ

infiltration (*ਇਨਫ਼ਿਲ'ਟਰੇਇਸ਼ਨ*) *n* ਚੋਰੀ- ਛਿੱਪੇ
ਘੁਸਣ ਦੀ ਕਿਰਿਆ, ਘੁਸਪੈਠ

infinite (*ਇਨਫ਼ਿਨਅਟ*) *a* ਅਸੀਮ, ਅਨੰਤ,
ਅਪਾਰ, ਬੇਹੱਦ; ਅਣਗਿਣਤ

infirm (ਇਨ'ਫ਼ਅ:ਮ) *a* ਨਿਰਬਲ, ਦੁਰਬਲ
ਕਮਜ਼ੋਰ, ਨਿਤਾਣਾ, ਛੀਣ, ਸਿਥਲ; **~ity**
ਨਿਰਬਲਤਾ, ਦੁਰਬਲਤਾ, ਕਮਜ਼ੋਰੀ, ਨਿਤਾਣਾਪਣ
ਖੀਣਤਾ

infix (*ਇਨਫ਼ਿਕਸ, ਇਨ'ਫ਼ਿਕਸ*) *n v* (ਭਾਸ਼ਾ)
ਪ੍ਰਤਯ; ਵਿਚ ਜੜਨਾ; ਟਿਕਾਉਣਾ

inflame (ਇਨ'ਫ਼ਲੇਇਮ) *v* ਅੱਗ ਲਾਉਣੀ;

ਉਤੇਜਤ ਕਰਨਾ; ਭੜਕਾਉਣਾ, ਉਭਾਰਨਾ; ਤੇਜ਼
ਕਰਨਾ, ਅੱਗ ਉਠਣਾ

inflammation (*ਇਨ'ਫ਼ਲਅਮੇਇਸ਼ਨ*) *n* ਦਾਹ,
ਤਾਪ, ਜਲਣ, ਸੋਜ਼ਸ਼

inflammatory (ਇਨਫ਼ਲਅਮਅਟ(ਅ)ਰਿ) *a* ਅੱਗ-
ਲਾਊ, ਭੜਕਾਊ; ਸੋਜ਼ਸ਼ਕਾਰੀ

inflate (ਇਨ'ਫ਼ਲੇਇਟ) *v* ਫੂਕ ਦੇਣੀ, ਫੁਲਾਉਣਾ,
ਹਵਾ ਭਰਨੀ; ਅਭਿਮਾਨੀ ਬਣਾ ਦੇਣਾ

inflation (ਇਨ'ਫ਼ਲੇਇਸ਼ਨ) *n* ਫੈਲਾਉ, ਮੁਦ੍ਰਾ
ਫੈਲਾਉ

inflect (ਇਨ'ਫ਼ਲੈੱਕਟ) *v* ਸ਼ਬਦ ਦਾ ਰੂਪ
ਬਦਲਾਉਣਾ, ਰੂਪ ਸਾਧਨਾ ਕਰਨੀ; **~ion,
inflexion** (ਵਿਆ) ਵਿਭਕਤੀ; (ਸੰਗੀ) ਸੁਰ
ਦਾ ਉਤਾਰ-ਚੜ੍ਹਾ

inflexible (ਇਨ'ਫ਼ਲੈੱਕਸਅਬਲ) *a* ਲਚਕਹੀਨ,
ਬੇਲਚਕ, ਆਕੜਿਆ, ਤਰਿੰਗ, ਕਰੜਾ

inflexional (ਇਨ'ਫ਼ਲੈੱਕਸ਼ਨਲ) *a* (ਭਾਸ਼ਾ)
ਵਿਕਾਰੀ

influence (*ਇਨਫ਼ਲੂਅੰਸ*) *n v* ਪ੍ਰਭਾਵ, ਅਸਰ,
ਰਸੂਖ, ਪ੍ਰਭਾਵਤ ਕਰਨਾ, ਅਸਰ ਪਾਉਣਾ

influential (*ਇਨਫ਼ਲੂ'ਐਂਸ਼ਲ*) *a* ਪ੍ਰਭਾਵਸ਼ਾਲੀ,
ਪ੍ਰਭਾਵ-ਪੂਰਨ, ਪ੍ਰਭਾਵੀ

influenza (*ਇਨਫ਼ਲੂ'ਐਂਜ਼ਾ*) *n* ਨਜ਼ਲਾ, ਫਲੂ,
ਸਰਦੀ-ਜ਼ੁਕਾਮ ਨਾਲ ਤਾਪ

influx (*ਇਨਫ਼ਲਅੱਕਸ*) *n* ਅੰਦਰ ਨੂੰ ਵਹਿਣ;
ਅੰਤਰ-ਪਰਵਾਹ, ਅੰਤਰ ਆਗਮ

inform (ਇਨ'ਫ਼ੋਮ) *v* ਪਤਾ ਦੇਣਾ, ਖ਼ਬਰ ਦੇਣੀ,
ਸੂਹ ਦੇਣੀ, ਸੂਚਤ ਕਰਨਾ; ਇਲਜ਼ਾਮ ਲਾਉਣਾ;
ਪਰੇਰਤ ਕਰਨਾ

informal (ਇਨ'ਫ਼ੋ'ਮਲ) *a* ਗ਼ੈਰ-ਰਸਮੀ,
ਅਨੁਪਚਾਰਕ, ਸਾਦੀ, ਬੇਕਾਇਦਾ

informant (ਇਨ'ਫ਼ੋਮਅੰਟ) *n* ਮੁਖ਼ਬਰ; ਸੂਚਕ, ਸੰਦੇਸ਼ਵਾਹਕ

information ('ਇਨਫ਼ਅ'ਮੇਇਸ਼ਨ) *n* (ਕਾ) ਸ਼ਿਕਾਇਤ; ਸੂਚਨਾ, ਇਤਲਾਹ, ਸਮਾਚਾਰ, ਖ਼ਬਰ ਜਾਣਕਾਰੀ

infraction (ਇਨ'ਫ਼ਰੈਕਸ਼ਨ) *n* ਉਲੰਘਣਾ; ਭੰਗ ਕਰਨ (ਦਾ ਕਾਰਜ)

infuriate (ਇਨ'ਫ਼ਯੁਅਰਿਏਇਟ) *v* ਕਰੋਧ ਦੁਆਉਣਾ, ਗੁੱਸਾ ਚੜ੍ਹਾਉਣਾ

infuriation (ਇਨ'ਫ਼ਯੁਅਰਿ'ਏਇਸ਼ਨ) *n* ਕਰੋਧ, ਤੈਸ਼, ਝੁੰਜਲਾਹਟ

infuse (ਇਨ'ਫ਼ਯੂਜ਼) *v* ਉਲੱਦਣਾ, ਭਰਨਾ; ਜਾਨ ਪਾ ਦੇਣੀ, ਪਰੇਰਨਾ ਦੇਣੀ; ਭਿੱਜਣਾ, ਤਰ ਹੋਣਾ

infusion (ਇਨ'ਫ਼ਯੂਯ਼ਨ) *n* ਕਾੜ੍ਹਾ; ਸੰਚਾਰਨ; ਘੋਲ, ਨਚੋੜ

ingredient (ਇਨ'ਗਰੀਡਯਅੰਟ) *n* ਅੰਗ, ਅੰਸ਼; ਮੂਲ ਸਮਗਰੀ, ਸੰਘਟਕ ਅੰਸ਼

inhabit (ਇਨ'ਹੈਬਿਟ) *v* ਵੱਸਣਾ, ਰਹਿਣਾ, ਵਾਸ ਕਰਨਾ; ਅਧਿਕਾਰ ਕਰਨਾ

inhale (ਇਨ'ਹੇਇਲ) *v* ਸਾਹ ਅੰਦਰ ਖਿੱਚਣਾ, ਸਾਹ ਲੈਣਾ; ਕਸ਼ ਖਿੱਚਣਾ (ਸਿਗਰਟ ਜਾਂ ਹੁੱਕੇ ਦਾ), ਦਮ ਲਾਉਣਾ

inherit (ਇਨ'ਹੈਰਿਟ) *v* ਵਿਰਸੇ ਵਿਚ ਮਿਲਣਾ; ਉੱਤਰਾਧਿਕਾਰ ਵਿਚ ਪ੍ਰਾਪਤ ਕਰਨਾ; ~ance ਉੱਤਰਾਧਿਕਾਰ; ਵਿਰਸਾ, ਵਿਰਾਸਤ

inhibit (ਇਨ'ਹਿਬਿਟ) *v* ਰੁਕਾਵਟ ਪਾਉਣਾ, ਵਿਘਨ ਪਾਉਣਾ, ਰੋਕਣਾ ਮਨ੍ਹਾਂ ਕਰਨਾ, ਵਰਜਣਾ; ~ion ਨਿਰੋਧ, ਨਿਰੋਧਣ, (ਕਾ) ਨਿਰੋਧ-ਲੇਖ; ਰੋਕ, ਮਨਾਹੀ

inhuman (ਇਨ'ਹਯੂਮਅਨ) *a* ਅਮਾਨਵੀ, ਅਣਮਨੁੱਖੀ, ਗ਼ੈਰ-ਇਨਸਾਨੀ; ਵਹਿਸ਼ੀ

inhumane ('ਇਨਹਯੁ'ਮੇਇਨ) *a* ਨਿਰਦਈ, ਕਠੋਰ

initial (ਇ'ਨਿਸ਼ਲ) *n v a* (ਬ ਵ) ਨਾਉਂ-ਅੱਖਰ, ਨਾਉਂ ਦੇ ਪਹਿਲੇ ਅੱਖਰ; ਹਸਤਾਖ਼ਰ ਕਰਨੇ, ਛੋਟੇ ਦਸਤਖ਼ਤ ਕਰਨੇ, ਨਾਉਂ ਦੇ ਪਹਿਲੇ ਅੱਖਰ ਪਾਉਣੇ; ਮੁੱਢਲਾ, ਆਦਿ, ਪ੍ਰਾਰੰਭਕ

initiate (ਇ'ਨਿਸ਼ਿਅਟ, ਇ'ਨਿਸ਼ਿਏਇਟ) *v a* ਆਰੰਭ ਕਰਨਾ, ਦੀਖਿਆ ਦੇਣੀ, ਚਾਲੂ ਕਰਨਾ; ਸਿਰਜਣ ਕਰਨਾ, ਦੀਖਿਅਤ

initiation (ਇ'ਨਿਸ਼ਿ'ਏਇਸ਼ਨ) *n* ਆਰੰਭ, ਸ੍ਰੀਗਣੇਸ਼, ਦੀਖਿਆ, ਪ੍ਰਵੇਸ਼

initiative (ਇ'ਨਿਸ਼ਿਅਟਿਵ੍) *n a* ਪਹਿਲ, ਆਰੰਭ, ਪਹਿਲਾ ਕਦਮ, ਆਰੰਭਕ, ਪ੍ਰਾਰੰਭਕ

initio (ਇ'ਨਿਸ਼ਿਅਉ) (*L*) *adv* ਸ਼ੁਰੂ ਵਿਚ

inject (ਇਨ'ਜੈੱਕਟ) *v* ਟੀਕਾ ਲਾਉਣਾ, ਸੂਆ ਲਾਉਣਾ, ਸੂਈ ਲਾਉਣੀ, ਇੰਜੈਕਸ਼ਨ ਦੇਣਾ; ਭਰਨਾ, ਪਾਉਣਾ

injunction (ਇਨ'ਜਅੱਙਕਸ਼ਨ) *n* ਹੁਕਮ, ਆਗਿਆ, ਆਦੇਸ਼, ਹਿਦਾਇਤ; (ਕਾ) ਮਨਾਹੀ ਦਾ ਹੁਕਮ

injure ('ਇਨਜਅ*) *v* ਘਾਇਲ ਕਰਨਾ, ਸੱਟ-ਫੇਟ ਮਾਰਨੀ, ਚੋਟ ਲਾਉਣੀ; ਹਰਜ ਪਹੁੰਚਾਉਣਾ, ਨੁਕਸਾਨ ਕਰਨਾ

injurious (ਇਨ'ਜੁਅਰਿਅਸ) *a* ਅੱਤਿਆਚਾਰ-ਪੂਰਨ, ਅਪਮਾਨਜਨਕ, ਘਾਤਕ, ਦੁੱਖਦਾਇਕ, ਹਿੰਸਕ

injustice (ਇਨ'ਜਅੱਸਟਿਸ) *n* ਅਨਿਆਂ, ਬੇਇਨਸਾਫ਼ੀ; ਅਧਰਮੀ ਕਾਰਜ

ink (ਇਙਕ) *n v* ਸਿਆਹੀ, ਮੱਸ, ਮਸੀ, ਰੌਸ਼ਨਾਈ; ਸਿਆਹੀ ਲਾਉਣੀ

inkling ('ਇਙਕਲਿਙ) *n* ਸੰਕੇਤ, ਝਲਕ, ਇਸ਼ਾਰਾ,

ਬਿਟਕ, ਆਭਾਸ

inland (ਇਨਲੈਂਡ) *n a adv* ਦੇਸ਼ ਦਾ ਅੰਦਰਲਾ ਭਾਗ, ਦੇਸ-ਅਭਿਅੰਤਰ; ਅੰਤਰਦੇਸ਼ੀ, ਦੇਸ ਦੇ ਅੰਦਰਲਾ; ਅੰਦਰ

in-laws (ਇਨਲੋਜ਼) *n pl* ਸਹੁਰੇ, ਸਹੁਰਾ ਘਰ, ਸੁਸਰਾਲ ਵਾਲੇ

inmate (ਇਨਮੇਇਟ) *n* ਵਾਸੀ, ਵਸਨੀਕ, ਸਹਿਵਾਸੀ

in memoriam (ਇਨਮਿ'ਮੋਰਿਅੱਮ) (*L*) *adv* ਯਾਦ ਵਿਚ, ਸਿਮਰਤੀ

inn (ਇਨ) *n* ਸਰਾਂ, ਧਰਮਸ਼ਾਲਾ

innate (ਇਨ'ਨੇਇਟ) *a* ਅੰਤਰੀਵ; ਜਮਾਂਦਰੂ, ਅੰਦਰਲਾ, ਸਹਿਜ, ਜਨਮਜਾਤ, ਸੁਭਾਵਕ

inner (ਇਨਅ*) *a* ਅੰਦਰਲਾ, ਅੰਦਰੂਨੀ, ਆਂਤਰਕ, ਭੀਤਰੀ

innings (ਇਨਿਡ਼ਗਜ਼) *n* (ਕ੍ਰਿਕਟ ਆਦਿ ਵਿਚ) ਪਾਲ, ਸਿਤ, ਵਾਰੀ; ਇਨਿੰਗ

innocence (ਇਨਅਸਅੱਸ) *n* ਸਰਲਤਾ, ਮਾਸੂਮੀਅਤ, ਨਿਰਦੋਸ਼ਤਾ, ਅਗਿਆਨ, ਭੋਲਾਪਣ

innocent (ਇਨਅਸੰਟ) *a n* ਅਣਜਾਣ, ਅਜਾਣ, ਭੋਲਾ, ਸਰਲ ਚਿਤ, ਸਿਧਾ; ਮੂੜ੍ਹ, ਬੁੱਧੂ ਆਦਮੀ

innovate (ਇਨਅ(ਉ)ਵੇਇਟ) *v* ਕਾਢ ਕੱਢਣੀ, ਨਵੀਂ ਰੀਤ ਚਲਾਉਣੀ, ਪਰਿਵਰਤਨ ਲਿਆਉਣਾ

innovation (ਇਨਅ'ਵੇਇਸ਼ਨ) *n* ਕਾਢ, ਘਾੜਤ, ਨਵੀਂ ਰੀਤ

innovative (ਇਨਅਵ੍ਵਅਟਿਵ੍) *a* ਨਵੀਨਤਾਕਾਰੀ

in nuce (ਇਨ'ਨਯੂਸੇਇ) (*L*) *adv* ਸੰਖੇਪ ਵਿਚ

innumerable (ਇ'ਨਯੂਮ(ਅ)ਰਅਬਲ) *a* ਅਣਗਿਣਤ, ਅਸੰਖ, ਬੇਹਿਸਾਬ, ਬੇਸ਼ੁਮਾਰ

inoculate (ਇ'ਨੌਕਯੁਲੇਇਟ) *v* ਟੀਕਾ ਲਾਉਣਾ,

ਸੂਆ ਲਾਉਣਾ

inoculation (ਇ'ਨੌਕਯੁ'ਲੇਇਸ਼ਨ) *n* ਟੀਕਾ, ਲੋਦਾ; ਕਲਮ

inordinate (ਇਨਓਡ਼ਿਨੇਟ) *a* ਅਤੀ ਅਧਿਕ, ਬੇਹੱਦ, ਹੱਦੋਂ ਵੱਧ, ਅਤੀਮਾਤਰ

input (ਇਨਪੁਟ) *n* ਅੰਤਰਗਾਮੀ; ਨਿਵੇਸ਼, ਆਦਾਨ

inquire, enquire (ਇਨ'ਕਵਾਇਅ*) *v* ਖੋਜਣਾ, ਖੋਜ ਕਰਨਾ, ਪੁੱਛ-ਗਿੱਛ ਕਰਨੀ; ਪ੍ਰਸ਼ਨ ਕਰਨਾ, ਪੱਚਣਾ, ਜਾਂਚ ਕਰਨੀ; ਤਹਿਕੀਕਾਤ ਕਰਨੀ

inquiry (ਇਨ'ਕਵਾਇਅਰਿ) *n* ਖੋਜ, ਪੁੱਛ-ਗਿੱਛ; ਪਤਾ, ਜਾਂਚ, ਤਹਿਕੀਕਾਤ

inquisition (ਇਨਕਵਿ'ਜ਼ਿਸ਼ਨ) *n* ਖੋਜ; ਪੁੱਛ, ਜਾਂਚ, ਤਹਿਕੀਕਾਤ

inquisitive (ਇਨ'ਕਵਿਜ਼ਅਟਿਵ੍) *a* ਜਿਗਿਆਸੂ, ਜਾਨਣ ਲਈ ਉਤਸੁਕ; ਖੋਜੀ

insane (ਇਨ'ਸੇਇਨ) *a* ਪਾਗਲ, ਦੀਵਾਨਾ, ਭਰਾਂਤੀਚਿਤ, ਮੂੜ੍ਹ

insanitation (ਇਨ'ਸੈਨਿ'ਟੇਇਸ਼ਨ) *a* ਅਸੁਅੱਛਤਾ, ਗੰਦਗੀ

insanitary (ਇਨ'ਸੈਨਿਟ(ਅ)ਰਿ) *a* ਗੰਦਗੀ ਭਰਿਆ, ਅਸੁਅਸਥਕਾਰੀ

insanity (ਇਨ'ਸੈਨਿਟਿ) *n* ਮਨੋਰੋਗ, ਪਾਗਲਪਣ, ਦੀਵਾਨਗੀ, ਭਰਾਂਤੀ-ਚਿੱਤਤਾ, ਬੁੱਧੀਹੀਨਤਾ

inscribe (ਇਨ'ਸਕਰਾਇਬ) *v* ਉਕਰਨਾ, ਲਿਖਣਾ, ਅੰਕਤ ਕਰਨਾ, ਚਿੰਨ੍ਹਣਾ; ਕਰਜ਼ੇ ਦਾ ਕੁਝ ਹਿੱਸਾ ਚੁਕਾਉਣਾ

inscription (ਇਨ'ਸਕਰਿਪਸ਼ਨ) *n* ਸ਼ਿਲਾ-ਲੇਖ, ਸਿੱਕਿਆਂ ਦੀ ਲਿਖਤ, ਮੁਦ੍ਰਾ-ਲੇਖ

insect (ਇਨਸੈਕਟ) *n* ਕੀੜਾ, ਪਤੰਗਾ, ਮੱਕੋੜਾ, ਕੀਟ; **~icide** ਕੀਟਨਾਸ਼ਕ ਦਵਾਈ; ਕੀਟਨਾਸ਼ਕ; ਕੀੜੇ ਮਾਰ

insecure ('ਇਨਸਿ'ਕਯੂਅ*) *a* ਅਸੁਰੱਖਿਅਤ, ਅਦਿੜ੍ਹ, ਕੱਚਾ, ਪੋਲਾ

insecurity ('ਇਨਸਿ'ਕਯੂਅਰਅਟਿ) *n* ਅਸੁਰੱਖਿਅਤਾ, ਭੈ, ਸ਼ੰਕਾ

insensible (ਇਨ'ਸੈਂਸਅਬਲ) *a* ਅਤੀ ਸੂਖਮ; ਅਚੇਤਨ, ਚੇਤਨਾ ਰਹਿਤ; ਅਟਭਿੰਜ, ਅਸੰਵੇਦਨਸ਼ੀਲ

insensitive (ਇਨ'ਸੈਂਸਅਟਿਵ) *a* ਅਸੰਵੇਦਨਸ਼ੀਲ, ਸੰਵੇਦਨਾ ਰਹਿਤ, ਭਾਵਹੀਨ, ਅਨੁਭੂਤੀਹੀਨ

insensuous (ਇਨ'ਸੈਂਸਯੂਅਸ) *a* ਅਕਾਮੁਕ, ਅਵਿਲਾਸੀ

insert (ਇਨ'ਸਅਃਟ) *v* ਸੰਮਿਲਤ ਕਰਨਾ, ਜੋੜਨਾ; ਦਰਜ ਕਰਨਾ, ਬਿਠਾ ਦੇਣਾ, ਜਮਾ ਦੇਣਾ, ਘੁਸੇੜਨਾ, ਫ਼ਿੱਟ ਕਰਨਾ

inside ('ਇਨ'ਸਾਇਡ) *adv n a* ਅੰਦਰ, ਅੰਦਰਲੀ, ਅੰਦਰੂਨੀ; ਅੰਤਰ; ਆਂਤਰਕ, ਭੀਤਰੀ

insight ('ਇਨਸਾਇਟ) *n* ਸੂਝ, ਨੀਝ, ਅੰਤਰਦ੍ਰਿਸ਼ਟੀ

insignia (ਇਨ'ਸਿਗਨਿਆ) *n* (ਬ ਵ) ਅਧਿਕਾਰ ਚਿੰਨ੍ਹ, ਨਿਸ਼ਾਨ, ਬਿੱਲਾ, ਤਮਗ਼ਾ

insignificant ('ਇਨਸਿਗ'ਨਿਫ਼ਿਕਅੰਟ) *a* ਤੁੱਛ, ਹੇਚ; ਛੋਟਾ, ਮਹੱਤਵਹੀਨ; ਵਿਅਰਥ, ਬੇਕਾਰ

insist (ਇਨ'ਸਿਸਟ) *v* ਹਠ ਕਰਨਾ, ਰਿਹਾੜ ਕਰਨੀ, ਜ਼ਿੱਦ ਕਰਨੀ, ਅੜ ਜਾਣਾ; ਜ਼ੋਰ ਪਾਉਣਾ; ~ence ਹਠ, ਜ਼ਿੱਦ, ਆਗ੍ਰਹ, ਅਨੁਰੋਧ; ਜ਼ੋਰ

inspect (ਇਨ'ਸਪੈੱਕਟ) *v* ਜਾਂਚਣਾ; ਛਾਣਬੀਨ ਕਰਨੀ; ਨਿਰੀਖਣ ਕਰਨਾ, ਮੁਆਇਨਾ ਕਰਨਾ, ਦੇਖ-ਭਾਲ ਕਰਨੀ; ~ion ਜਾਂਚ, ਛਾਣਬੀਨ, ਨਿਰੀਖਣ, ਮੁਆਇਨਾ; ~or ਨਿਰੀਖਕ

inspiration ('ਇਨਸਪਅ'ਰੇਇਸ਼ਨ) *n* ਪਰੇਰਨਾ, ਉਤੇਜਨਾ ਪ੍ਰੇਤਸਾਹਨ, ਆਵੇਸ਼; ਸਾਹ ਖਿਚਣਾ

inspire (ਇਨ'ਸਪਾਇਅ*) *v* ਸਾਹ (ਅੰਦਰ ਨੂੰ) ਲੈਣਾ; ਰੂਹ ਫੂਕ ਦੇਣੀ, ਉਤਸ਼ਾਹਤ ਕਰਨਾ, ਪਰੇਰਨਾ ਦੇਣੀ, ਜਮਾ ਦੇਣਾ

instability ('ਇਨਸਟਅ'ਬਿਲਅਟਿ) *n* ਅਸਥਿਰਤਾ, ਅਨਿੱਤਤਾ, ਛਿਣਭੰਗਰਤਾ, ਅਸਥਾਈਤਵ

install (ਇਨਸਟੱੋਲ) *v* ਸਥਾਪਨਾ, ਪ੍ਰਕਾਸ਼ ਕਰਨਾ, ਗੱਦੀ ਉੱਤੇ ਬਿਠਾਉਣਾ, ਜਮਾਉਣਾ, ਗੱਡਣਾ, (ਮਸ਼ੀਨ) ਲਾਉਣਾ; ~ation ਨਿਵੇਸ਼, ਅਭਿਸ਼ੇਕ, ਨਿਰੂਪਣ, ਸਥਾਪਨਾ, ਲਗਾਈ

instalment (ਇਨ'ਸਟੋਲਮਅੰਟ) *n* ਕਿਸ਼ਤ, ਕਿਸ਼ਤਬੰਦੀ

instance ('ਇਨਸਟਅੰਸ) *n v* ਮਿਸਾਲ, ਦ੍ਰਿਸ਼ਟਾਂਤ, ਪ੍ਰਮਾਣ ਦੇਣਾ, ਉੱਲੇਖ ਕਰਨਾ

instant ('ਇਨਸਟਅੰਟ) *a n* ਅਤੀ ਜ਼ਰੂਰੀ; ਤਤਕਾਲੀ; ਝਟਪਟੀ, ਇਸ ਖਿਣ, ਵਰਤਮਾਨ, ਤੁਰੰਤ, ਤਤਕਾਲਕ; ~aneous ਤਤਕਾਲੀ, ਝਟਪਟੀ; ~ly ਤਤਕਾਲ, ਉਸੇ ਵੇਲੇ, ਤੁਰੰਤ, ਝਟਪਟ

in status quo (ਇਨ'ਸਟੇਇਟਅਸ'ਕਵਅਉ) (L) *adv* ਪਹਿਲੀ ਜੇਹੀ ਅਵਸਥਾ ਵਿਚ

instead (ਇਨ'ਸਟੈੱਡ) *adv* ਬਜਾਏ, ਦੀ ਥਾਂ ਤੇ, ਇਸ ਦੇ ਬਦਲੇ, ਇਸ ਦੇ ਵੱਟੇ

instigate ('ਇਨਸਟਿਗੇਇਟ) *v* ਉਕਸਾਉਣਾ, ਉਭਾਰਨਾ, ਸ਼ਹਿ ਦੇਣੀ, ਚੁੱਕਣਾ; ਉਤੇਜਤ ਕਰਨਾ; (ਫ਼ਸਾਦ, ਬਗ਼ਾਵਤ ਆਦਿ) ਫੁਸਲਾ ਕੇ ਕਰਾਉਣਾ

instigation ('ਇਨਸਟਿ'ਗੇਇਸ਼ਨ) *n* ਉਕਸਾਹਟ, ਉਤਸ਼ਾਹਨ, ਚੁੱਕ, ਉਭਾਰ

instigator (ਇਨਸਟਿਗੇਇਟਆ*) *n* ਉਕਸਾਉਣ ਵਾਲਾ, ਭੜਕਾਊ

instil(l) (ਇਨ'ਸਟਿਲ) v ਟਪਕਾਉਣਾ, ਬੂੰਦ-ਬੂੰਦ
ਕਰ ਕੇ ਪਾਉਣਾ, ਦਿਲ ਵਿਚ ਬਿਠਾਉਣਾ, ਦ੍ਰਿੜ੍ਹ
ਕਰਾਉਣਾ, ਪੱਕਾ ਕਰਾਉਣਾ; ਚਿੱਤ ਵਿਚ
ਸਮਾਉਣਾ

instinct ('ਇਨਸਟਿੰਕਟ, ਇਨ'ਸਟਿੰਕਟ) n a
ਕੁਦਰਤੀ ਸੂਝ, ਮੂਲ ਪ੍ਰਵਿਰਤੀ, ਫ਼ਿਤਰਤ, ਅੰਤਰ
ਪਰੇਰਨਾ, ਸਹਿਜ ਪਰੇਰਨਾ, ਸਹਿਜ ਗਿਆਨ,
ਅਨੁਭਵਤਾ; ਪੂਰਨ; ~ive ਕੁਦਰਤੀ, ਮੂਲ,
ਪ੍ਰਵਿਰਤਕ; ਸਹਿਜ, ਅੰਤਰ-ਪਰੇਰਨਾ ਸਬੰਧੀ

institute ('ਇਨਸਟਿਟਯੂਟ) v n ਸਥਾਪਣਾ,
ਕਾਇਮ ਕਰਨਾ, (ਪੜਤਾਲ ਆਦਿ) ਸ਼ੁਰੂ
ਕਰਾਉਣੀ, ਮੁਕੱਰਰ ਕਰਨਾ; ਵਿਦਿਆਲੇ ਦਾ
ਭਵਨ ਜਾਂ ਦਫ਼ਤਰ, ਸਭਾ, ਸੰਸਥਾ; ਰੀਤੀ-ਸੰਗ੍ਰਹ,
ਵਿਧੀ-ਸਾਰ

institution ('ਇਨਸਟਿ'ਟਯੂਸ਼ਨ) n ਸੰਸਥਾ,
ਆਸ਼ਰਮ; (ਪਾਦਰੀ ਆਦਿ ਦੀ) ਨਿਯੁਕਤੀ,
ਸਥਾਪਨ, ਦਸਤੂਰ, ਰਿਵਾਜ, ਸੰਸਥਾ-ਭਵਨ; ~al
ਸੰਸਥਾਗਤ, ਸੰਸਥਾਨਕ, ਸੰਗਠਾਤਮਕ

instruct (ਇਨ'ਸਟਰਅੱਕਟ) v ਸਿਖਾਉਣਾ,
ਪੜ੍ਹਾਉਣਾ; ਦੱਸਣਾ; ਜ਼ਰੂਰੀ ਗੱਲਾਂ ਸਮਝਾਉਣਾ;
ਹਦਾਇਤ ਦੇਣੀ; ~ion ਸਿਖਿਆ, ਪੜ੍ਹਾਈ,
ਵਿਦਿਆਦਾਨ; ਸੂਚਨਾ, ਇਤਲਾਹ, ਨਿਰਦੇਸ਼;
~ive ਸਿਖਿਆਦਾਇਕ; ~or ਸਿਖਿਅਕ, ਗੁਰੂ,
ਅਧਿਆਪਕ, ਨਿਰਦੇਸ਼ਕ

instrument (ਇਨਸਟਰੂ'ਮਅੰਟ) n ਹਥਿਆਰ,
ਔਜ਼ਾਰ; ਹੱਥਠੇਕਾ, ਸਾਜ਼; (ਵਿਗਿਆਨ ਵਿਚ
ਵਰਤਿਆ ਜਾਣ ਵਾਲਾ) ਜੰਤਰ, (ਕਾ) ਲਿਖਤ ਜਾਂ
ਕਾਗਜ਼, ਇਖ਼ਤਿਆਰ-ਪੱਤਰ, ਦਸਤਾਵੇਜ਼

instrumental (ਇਨਸਟਰੂ'ਮੈਂਟਲ) a ਸਹਾਇਕ,
ਵਸੀਲਾ ਬਣਨ ਵਾਲਾ; (ਸੰਗੀ) ਸਾਜ਼ ਦਾ; ਸੰਗੀਤ
ਦਾ; ਜੰਤਰ ਸਬੰਧੀ; ~case ਕਰਣ ਕਾਰਕ;

~ist ਸਾਜ਼-ਵਾਦਕ

insubordinate (ਇਨਸਅ'ਬੋਡਿਨਅਟ) a
ਅਵੱਗਿਆਕਾਰੀ ਬਾਗੀ, ਨਾਬਰ

insubordination (ਇਨਸਅ'ਬੋਡਿ'ਨਿਇਸ਼ਨ) n
ਨਾਬਰੀ, ਅੱਵਗਿਆ, ਆਗਿਆ-ਭੰਗ, ਆਕੀਪੁਣਾ,
ਨਾ ਫ਼ਰਮਾਨੀ

insufficient (ਇਨਸਅ'ਫ਼ਿਸ਼ੰਟ) a ਥੋੜ੍ਹਾ, ਘੱਟ,
ਕਸਰਵੰਦਾ, ਨਾਕਾਫ਼ੀ, ਅਲਪ

insulator (ਇਨਸਯੁਲੇਇਟਅ*) n ਤਾਪ ਰੋਕ,
ਇਨਸੁਲੇਟਰ

insult (ਇਨਸਅੱਲਟ, ਇਨ'ਸਅੱਲਟ) n v ਹੇਠੀ,
ਹੱਤਕ, ਨਿਰਾਦਰੀ, ਅਪਮਾਨ; ਹੇਠੀ ਕਰਨੀ; ਹੱਤਕ
ਕਰਨੀ, ਤਿਰਸਕਾਰ ਕਰਨਾ, ਅਪਮਾਨ ਕਰਨਾ;
~ing ਅਪਮਾਨਜਨਕ, ਅਨਾਦਰਜਨਕ, ਬੇਇੱਜ਼ਤੀ
ਵਾਲਾ

insurance (ਇਸ'ਸ਼ੋਰਅੰਸ) n ਬੀਮਾ; ਬੀਮੇ ਦੀ
ਕਰਮ; ~policy ਬੀਮਾ-ਪਾਲਸੀ, ਬੀਮਾ-ਪੱਤਰ

insure (ਇਸ'ਸ਼ੋ*) v ਬੀਮਾ ਕਰਨਾ, ਬੀਮੇ ਰਾਹੀਂ
ਜਾਇਦਾਦ ਆਦਿ ਸੁਰੱਖਿਅਤ ਕਰਾਉਣੀ

insurgent (ਇਨ'ਸਅਃਜਅੰਟ) a n ਆਕੀ,
ਬਾਗੀ, ਵਿਦਰੋਹੀ; (ਸਮੁੰਦਰ ਆਦਿ) ਚੈਲਾਬੀ,
ਅੱਗੇ ਵੱਧਦਾ, ਉਤਰਦਾ; ਬਾਗੀ ਆਦਮੀ,
ਵਿਦਰੋਹੀ ਵਿਅਕਤੀ

insurrection (ਇਨਸਅ'ਰੈਕਸ਼ਨ) n ਬਗਾਵਤ,
ਵਿਦਰੋਹ, ਸਾਜ਼ਸ਼, ਬਗ਼ਾਵਤ ਦੀ ਲਹਿਰ

intact (ਇਨ'ਟੈਕਟ) n ਜਿਸ ਨੂੰ ਹੱਥ ਨਾ ਲਾਇਆ
ਹੋਵੇ, ਅਛੋਹ; ਸਾਲਮ, ਪੂਰਨ, ਠੀਕ

intake (ਇਨਟੇਇਕ) n ਹਵਾ ਪਹੁੰਚਾਉਣ ਦਾ
ਰਸਤਾ; ਵਟਕ; ਅੰਦਰ ਆਉਣ ਵਾਲਾ
ਵਿਅਕਤੀ, ਕਾਸ਼ਤ ਕਰਨਯੋਗ, ਭੂਮੀ; ਅੰਤਰ-
ਗ੍ਰਹਿਣ

integral (ਇਨਟਿਗਰ(ਅ)ਲ) *a* ਅਖੰਡ ਵਸਤੂ ਦਾ; ਪੂਰਾ (ਹਿੱਸਾ); ਕੁਲ, ਸਮੁੱਚਾ

integrate (ਇਨਟਿਗਰੇਇਟ) *v a* ਪੂਰਾ ਕਰਨਾ, ਏਕੀਕਰਨ ਕਰਨਾ, ਸਮੁੱਚਾ

integration (ਇਨਟਿ'ਗਰੇਇਸ਼ਨ) *n* ਮਿਲਾਪ, ਏਕਤਾ, ਮੇਲ, ਏਕੀਕਰਨ, ਅਨੁਕੂਲਣ

integrity (ਇਨ'ਟੈਂਗਰਅਟਿ) *n* ਪੂਰਨਤਾ; ਅਖੰਡਤਾ; ਨੇਕ-ਨੀਤੀ, ਇਮਾਨਦਾਰੀ, ਦਿਆਨਤਦਾਰੀ

intellect (ਇਨਟਅਲੈੱਕਟ) *n* ਸਮਝ, ਸੂਝ, ਬੁੱਧੀ; ਬੁੱਧੀਮਾਨ, ਸਿਆਣਾ; ~**ual** ਬੋਧਕ, ਅਕਲੀ; ਬੁੱਧੀਮਾਨ, ਬੁੱਧੀਜੀਵੀ; ~**ualist** ਬੁੱਧੀਵਾਦੀ

intelligence (ਇਨ'ਟੈਲਿਜਾਂਸ) *n* ਅਕਲ, ਸਮਝ, ਬੁੱਧੀ, ਗਿਆਨ, ਸੁੰਘੜਤਾ, ਸੂਝ; ਗੁਪਤ ਸੂਚਨਾ

intelligent (ਇਨ'ਟੈਲਿਜਅੰਟ) *a* ਸੁੰਘੜ, ਸੁਝਵਾਨ, ਸਮਝਦਾਰ, ਅਕਲਮੰਦ; ~**sia** ਬੁੱਧੀਜੀਵੀ, ਪੜ੍ਹੇ-ਲਿਖੇ ਲੋਕ

intelligibility (ਇਨ'ਟੈਲਿਜਅ'ਬਿਲਅਟਿ) *n* ਸੁਗਮਤਾ, ਸੁਬੋਧਤਾ

intelligible (ਇਨ'ਟੈਲਿਜਬਲ) *a* ਸੁਗਮ, ਸੁਬੋਧ, ਸਪਸ਼ਟ, ਸਮਝ ਵਿਚ ਆਉਣ ਵਾਲਾ

intend (ਇਨ'ਟੈਂਡ) *v* ਚਾਹੁਣਾ, ਚਿਤਵਣਾ, ਮਨ ਬਣਾਉਣਾ, ਠਾਣ ਲੈਣਾ; ਸੰਕਲਪ ਕਰਨਾ, ਇਰਾਦਾ ਕਰਨਾ; ਨਿਸ਼ਚਤ ਹੋਣਾ; ਮਤਲਬ ਹੋਣਾ, ਅਰਥ ਲਾਉਣਾ, ਭਾਵ ਹੋਣਾ

intense (ਇਨ'ਟੈਂਸ) *a* ਡੂੰਗਾ, ਤੀਬਰ, ਬਹੁਤ ਜ਼ਿਆਦਾ, ਤੀਖਣ, ਜ਼ੋਰਦਾਰ, ਪ੍ਰਬਲ, ਭਾਵਮਈ

intensification (ਇਨ'ਟੈਂਸਿਫ਼ਿ'ਕੇਇਸ਼ਨ) *n* ਤੀਬਰੀਕਰਨ, ਡੂੰਘਾ ਕਰਨ, ਗੂੜ੍ਹਾ ਕਰਨ

intensify (ਇਨ'ਟੈਂਸਿਫ਼ਾਇ) *v* ਡੂੰਘਾ ਕਰਨਾ ਜਾਂ

ਹੋਣਾ, ਵਧਾਉਣਾ, ਭਾਵੁਕ ਹੋਣਾ

intensity (ਇਨ'ਟੈਂਸਅਟਿ) *n* ਤੀਬਰਤਾ, ਗੰਭੀਰਤਾ, ਡੂੰਘਾਈ, ਪ੍ਰਚੰਡਤਾ, ਪ੍ਰਬਲਤਾ, ਭਾਵੁਕਤਾ

intensive (ਇਨ'ਟੈਂਸਿਵ੍) *a* ਤੀਬਰ, ਪ੍ਰਚੰਡ, ਡੂੰਘਾ; ਘਣੀ ਖੇਤੀ

intent (ਇਨ'ਟੈਂਟ) *n a* ਇਰਾਦਾ, ਉਦੇਸ਼, ਨੀਤ, ਆਸ਼ਾ, ਸੰਕਲਪ, ਮੁਰਾਦ, ਮਤਲਬ, ਮਨਸ਼ਾ, ਇੱਛਿਆ; ਜੁੱਟਿਆ, ਤਤਪਰ

inter ('ਇੰਟਅ*) *prep v* ਗੱਡਣਾ, ਦੱਬਣਾ; ਵਿਚ, ਦਰਮਿਆਨ, ਅੰਤਰ, ਪਰਸਪਰ; ~**alia** (*L*) ਹੋਰ ਗੱਲਾਂ ਨਾਲ; ~**se** ਆਪੋ ਵਿਚ; ~**action** ਪਰਸਪਰ ਪ੍ਰਭਾਵ; ~**caste** ਅੰਤਰਜਾਤੀ; ~**cede** ਵਿਚ ਪੈਣਾ, ਵਿਚੋਲਾ ਬਣਨਾ, ਝਗੜਾ ਨਿਪਟਾਉਣਾ; ਦਖ਼ਲ ਦੇਣਾ

intercept (ਇੰਟਅ'ਸੈੱਪਟ) *v* ਵਿਚਕਾਰ ਰੋਕਣਾ; ਰਾਹ ਵਿਚ ਰੋਕਣਾ, ਰਸਤੇ ਵਿਚ ਪਕੜਨਾ; ~**ion** ਰੋਕ

intercession (ਇਨਟਅ'ਸੈਸ਼ਨ) *n* ਵਿਚੋਲਗੀ, ਸਾਲਸੀ, ਵਕਾਲਤ

interchange (ਇਨਟਅ'ਚੇਇੰਜ) *v* ਅਦਲਾ-ਬਦਲੀ ਕਰਨੀ, ਅਦਲ-ਬਦਲ; ~**able** ਬਦਲਣਾ, ਬਦਲਣਯੋਗ

intercommunicate (ਇਨਟਅ'ਕਅਮਯੂਨਿ'ਕੇਇਟ) *v* ਆਪਸੀ ਆਵਾਜਾਈ ਕਰਨੀ, ਪਰਸਪਰ ਮੇਲ-ਜੋਲ ਰੱਖਣਾ

intercommunication (ਇਨਟਅ'ਕਅਮਯੂਨਿ'ਕੇਇਸ਼ਨ) *n* ਆਵਾਜਾਈ, ਅੰਤਰ ਸੰਚਾਰ, ਪਰਸਪਰ ਮੇਲ-ਜੋਲ

intercourse (ਇਨਟਅਕੋਸ) *n* ਮੇਲ-ਜੋਲ, ਵਰਤੋਂ-ਵਿਹਾਰ; ਬੋਲ-ਚਾਲ; ਸੰਭੋਗ, ਮੈਥੁਨ

interdepend (ਇਨਟਅਡਿ'ਪੈਂਡ) *v* ਅੰਤਰ-
ਸਬਧਿਤ ਹੋਣਾ, ਪਰਸਪਰ ਨਿਰਭਰ ਹੋਣਾ, ਇਕ
ਦੂਜੇ ਉੱਤੇ ਨਿਰਭਰ ਹੋਣਾ, ਇਕ ਦੂਜੇ ਨਾਲ ਬੱਝੇ
ਹੋਣਾ; **~ence** ਅੰਤਰ-ਸਬੰਧ, ਪਰਸਪਰ
ਨਿਰਭਰਤਾ, ਇਕ ਦੂਜੇ ਦਾ ਆਸਰਾ; **~ent**
ਇਕ ਦੂਜੇ ਤੇ ਨਿਰਭਰ, ਪਰਸਪਰ, ਆਸਰਤ,
ਅੰਤਰ-ਸਬੰਧਤ

interest (ਇਨਟਰੈੱਸਟ) *n v* (1) ਅਧਿਕਾਰ,
ਸਬੰਧ, ਭਲਾਈ, ਲਾਭ, ਫ਼ਾਇਦਾ, ਹਿਤ; (2)
ਸੁਆਰਥ, ਸਰੋਕਾਰ, ਦਿਲਚਸਪੀ, ਰੁਚੀ, ਸ਼ੌਕ;
(3) ਸੂਦ, ਵਿਆਜ; ਦਿਲਚਸਪੀ ਪੈਦਾ ਕਰਨੀ,
ਪਰੇਰਨਾ ਦੇਣੀ, ਉਤਸੁਕਤਾ ਪੈਦਾ ਕਰਨੀ; **~ing**
ਦਿਲਚਸਪ, ਰੋਚਕ, ਮਨੋਰੰਜਕ, ਸੁਆਦੀ

interfere (ਇਨਟਅ'ਫ਼ਿਅ*) *v* ਦਖ਼ਲ ਦੇਣਾ;
ਵਿਘਨ ਪਾਉਣਾ, ਰੁਕਾਵਟ ਪਾਉਣੀ; **~nce**
ਦਖ਼ਲ; ਵਿਘਨ, ਰੋਕ-ਟੋਕ

interfuse (ਇਨਟਅ'ਫ਼ਯੂਜ਼) *v* ਇਕ ਦੂਜੇ ਵਿਚ
ਮਿਲਣਾ

interim (ਇਨਟਅਰਿਮ) *n a adv* ਵਿਚਕਾਰਲਾ
ਸਮਾਂ, ਆਰਜ਼ੀ ਸਮਾਂ; ਵਿਚਕਾਰਲਾ, ਅੰਤਰਮ,
ਆਰਜ਼ੀ

interior (ਇਨ'ਟਿਅਰਿਅ*) *a n* ਅੰਦਰੂਨੀ,
ਅੰਦਰਲਾ, ਘਰੇਲੂ; ਮਾਨਸਕ, ਆਂਤਰਕ; ਅੰਦਰਲਾ
ਭਾਗ, ਹਿਰਦਾ, ਅੰਤਹਕਰਣ, ਹੀਆ, ਆਤਮਾ

interjacent (ਇਨਟਅ'ਜੋਇਸਅੰਟ) *a*
ਵਿਚਕਾਰਲਾ; ਵਿਚਲਾ, ਦਰਮਿਆਨੀ

interject ('ਇਨਟਅ'ਜੈਕਟ) *v* ਟੋਕ ਦੇਣਾ, ਵਿਚੋਂ
ਬੋਲ ਪੈਣਾ, ਗੱਲ ਟੁੱਕਣੀ; ਘੁਸੇੜ ਦੇਣਾ; **~ion**
(ਵਿਆ) ਵਿਸਮਕ, ਹੈਰਾਨੀ, ਅਫ਼ਸੋਸ ਆਦਿ ਦਾ
ਸੂਚਕ ਸ਼ਬਦ

interlock (ਇਨਟਅ'ਲੌਕ) *v* ਇਕ ਦੂਜੇ ਵਿਚ

ਫ਼ਸਣਾ, ਅੜਾਉਣਾ, ਫਸਾ ਕੇ ਜੋੜਨਾ, ਗੰਠਨਾ

interlocution (ਇਨਟਅਲਅ(ਉ)'ਕਯੂਸ਼ਨ) *n*
ਗੱਲਬਾਤ, ਵਾਰਤਾਲਾਪ

interlope (ਇਨਟਅ'ਲਅਉਪ) *v* ਟੰਗ ਅੜਾਉਣਾ,
ਦਖ਼ਲ ਦੇਣਾ

intermarriage (ਇਨਟਅ'ਮੈਰਿਜ) *n* ਅੰਤਰਜਾਤੀ
ਵਿਆਹ

intermediate (ਇਨਟਅ'ਮੀਡ਼ਯਅਟ) *a v*
ਵਿਚਕਾਰਲਾ, ਵਿਚਲਾ; ਵਿਚ ਪੈਣਾ, ਵਿਚ-
ਵਿਚਾਉ ਕਰਨਾ

intermediation (ਇਨਟਅ'ਮੀਡ਼ਿ'ਏਇਸ਼ਨ) *n*
ਮਧਿਅਸਥਤਾ, ਵਿਚੋਲਗੀ, ਸਾਲਸੀ

intermingle (ਇਨਟਅ'ਮਿੰਗਲ) *v* ਰਲਾ-ਮਿਲਾ
ਦੇਣਾ; ਰਲ-ਮਿਲ ਜਾਣਾ, ਗੱਡ-ਮੱਡ ਹੋ ਜਾਣਾ,
ਆਪਸ ਵਿਚ ਮਿਲ ਜਾਣਾ

intermission (ਇਨਟਅ'ਮਿਸ਼ਨ) *n* ਵਕਫ਼ਾ,
ਛੁੱਟੀ

intermix (ਇਨਟਅ'ਮਿਕਸ) *v* ਰਲਾ-ਮਿਲਾ ਦੇਣਾ,
ਰਲ ਮਿਲ ਜਾਣਾ, ਆਪਸ ਵਿਚ ਮਿਲਣਾ, ਗੱਡ-
ਮੱਡ ਹੋ ਜਾਣਾ

intern (ਇਨ'ਟਅ:ਨ,'ਇਨਟਅ:ਨ) *v n* ਨਜ਼ਰਬੰਦ
ਕਰਨਾ, ਨਿਗਰਾਨੀ ਹੇਠ ਰੱਖਣਾ; ਸਿਖਲਾਈ
ਅਧੀਨ ਡਾਕਟਰ; **~ment** ਨਜ਼ਰਬੰਦੀ

internal (ਇਨ'ਟਅ:ਨਲ) *a* ਅੰਦਰਲਾ, ਵਿਚਲਾ
ਭੀਤਰੀ, ਆਂਤਰਕ; ਮੁਲਕੀ

international (ਇਨਟਅ'ਨੈਸ਼ਨਲ) *a n* ਅੰਤਰ-
ਰਾਸ਼ਟਰੀ, ਕੌਮਾਂਤਰੀ

interpol (ਇਨਟਅ:ਪੋਲ) *n* ਅੰਤਰ-ਰਾਸ਼ਟਰੀ

interpolar (ਇਨਟਅ'ਪਅਉਲਅ*) *a* ਅੰਤਰ-
ਧਰੁਵੀ

interpret (ਇਨ'ਟਅ:ਪਰਿਟ) *v* ਭਾਵ ਕੱਢਣਾ;

ਵਿਆਖਿਆ ਕਰਨੀ, ਅਰਥ ਕੱਢਣਾ; ਅਨੁਵਾਦ
ਕਰਨਾ, ਤਰਜਮਾਨੀ ਕਰਨਾ; ~ation ਭਾਵ-
ਅਰਥ; ਵਿਆਖਿਆ; ਅਨੁਵਾਦ; ~er ਟੀਕਾਕਾਰ;
ਦੋ-ਭਾਸ਼ੀਆ

interprovincial (ਇਨਟਅਪਰਅ'ਵਿਨਸ਼ਲ) *a*
ਅੰਤਰ-ਪ੍ਰਾਂਤੀ

interracial (ਇਨਟਅ'ਰੇਇਸ਼ਲ) *a* ਅੰਤਰ-ਜਾਤੀ

interrelated (ਇਨਟਅਰਿ'ਲੇਇਟਿਡ) *a* ਪਰਸਪਰ
ਸਬੰਧਤ

interrogate (ਇਨ'ਟੈੱਰਅਉਗੇਇਟ) *v* ਸਵਾਲ
ਕਰਨਾ, ਪੁੱਛਣਾ, ਪੁੱਛ-ਗਿੱਛ ਕਰਨੀ, ਤਫ਼ਤੀਸ਼
ਕਰਨੀ

interrogation (ਇਨਟੈੱਰਅ(ਉ)ਗੇਇਸ਼ਨ) *n*
ਸਵਾਲ, ਪੁੱਛ, ਪੁੱਛ-ਗਿੱਛ, ਪੁੱਛ-ਪੜਤਾਲ

interrogative (ਇਨਟਅ'ਰੋਗਅਟਿਵ) *a* *n*
ਸਵਾਲੀਆ, ਪ੍ਰਸ਼ਨਵਾਚੀ; ਕੀ, ਕੌਣ ਆਦਿ
ਸਰਵਨਾਮ

interrogator (ਇਨਟੈੱਰਅਉਗੇਇਟਅ*) *n*
ਸਵਾਲ ਕਰਨ ਵਾਲਾ, ਪੁੱਛ ਗਿੱਛ ਕਰਨ ਵਾਲਾ

interrupt (ਇਨਟਅ'ਰਅੱਪਟ) *v* ਰੋਕਣਾ; ਰੋੜਾ
ਅਟਕਾਉਣਾ, ਵਿਘਨ ਪਾਉਣਾ, ਖਲਲ ਪਾਉਣਾ;
ਗੱਲ ਟੁੱਕਣਾ; ~ion ਰੁਕਾਵਟ, ਵਿਘਨ, ਟੇਕ

intersect (ਇਨਟਅ'ਸੈੱਕਟ) *v* ਕੱਟਣਾ, ਕੱਟ ਕੇ
ਲੰਘਣਾ, ਵਿਚੋਂ ਲੰਘਣਾ; ~ion ਲਾਂਘਾ; ਚੀਰ,
ਕਾਟ (ਰੇਖਾ)

intertwine ('ਇਨਟਅ'ਟਵਾਇਨ) *v* ਗੁੰਦਣਾ,
ਵੱਟਣਾ, ਵਲੇਟਣਾ, ਉਲਝਾਉਣਾ

interval (ਇਨਟਅ'ਵ਼ਲ) *n* ਵਕਫ਼ਾ; ਮਧਿਆਂਤਰ,
ਵਿਚਲਾ ਸਮਾਂ, ਖ਼ਾਲੀ ਥਾਂ, (ਸੰਗੀ) ਧੁਨੀ-ਅੰਤਰ;
ਫ਼ਰਕ

intervene (ਇਨਟਅ'ਵ਼ੀਨ) *v* ਵਿਚ ਪੈਣਾ;

(ਇਸ) ਸਮੇਂ ਵਿਚਕਾਰ ਹੋਣਾ; ਦਖ਼ਲ ਦੇਣਾ,
ਵਿਘਨ ਪਾਉਣਾ

intervening (ਇਨਟਅ'ਵ਼ੀਨਿਙ) *a* ਮੱਧਵਰਤੀ,
ਅੰਤਰਵਰਤੀ

intervention (ਇਨਟ'ਅਵ਼ੈੱਨੱਸ਼ਨ) *n v* ਦਖ਼ਲ,
ਵਿਘਨ, ਰੁਕਾਵਟ

interview (ਇਨਟਅ'ਵ੍ਯੂ) *n v* ਮੁਲਾਕਾਤ, ਭੇਂਟ;
ਮੁਲਾਕਾਤ ਕਰਨੀ, ਭੇਂਟ ਕਰਨੀ

intimacy (ਇੰਟਿਮਅਸਿ) *n* ਨੇੜ, ਨਿਕਟਤਾ,
ਮਿੱਤਰਤਾਈ, ਅਪਣੱਤ, ਯਾਰਾਨਾ

intimate (ਇੰਟਿਮੇਇਟ) *a n v* ਗੂੜ੍ਹਾ (ਮਿੱਤਰ),
ਜਿਗਰੀ, ਨਿਕਟ, ਦਿਲੀ; ਨਿਝੱਕ, ਯਾਰ,
ਲੰਗੋਟੀਆ; ਪਤਾ ਦੇਣਾ, ਸੂਚਤ ਕਰਨਾ, ਖ਼ਬਰ
ਦੇਣੀ, ਜਾਣੂ ਕਰਨਾ, ਗਿਆਤ ਕਰਨਾ, ਇਤਲਾਹ
ਦੇਣੀ; ਹੁਸ਼ਿਆਰ ਕਰਨਾ, ਇਸ਼ਾਰਾ ਦੇਣਾ

intimation (ਇਨਟਿ'ਮੇਇਸ਼ਨ) *n* ਸੰਦੇਸ਼, ਪਤਾ,
ਖ਼ਬਰ, ਇਤਲਾਹ, ਸੂਚਨਾ, ਇਸ਼ਾਰਾ

intimidate (ਇਨ'ਟਿਮਿਡੇਇਟ) *v* ਡਰਾਉਣਾ,
ਧਮਕਾਉਣਾ, ਭੈਭੀਤ ਕਰਨਾ, ਦਬਕਾਉਣਾ

intimidation (ਇਨ'ਟਿਮਿ'ਡੇਇਸ਼ਨ) *n* ਡਰ,
ਧਮਕੀ, ਭੈ, ਡਾਂਟ-ਡਪਟ

intolerable (ਇਨ'ਟੌਲਅਰ(ਅ)ਬਲ) *a* ਅਸਹਿ,
ਬਰਦਾਸ਼ਤ ਤੋਂ ਬਾਹਰ, ਬੇਹੱਦ

intolerance (ਇਨ'ਟੌਲਅਰਅੰਸ) *n* ਤੰਗਦਿਲੀ,
ਅਸਹਿਨਸ਼ੀਲਤਾ

intolerant (ਇਨ'ਟੌਲਅਰਅੰਟ) *a* ਅਸਹਿਨਸ਼ੀਲ,
ਤੰਗ-ਦਿਲ, ਕੱਟੜ

intonation (ਇਨਟਅ(ਉ)'ਨੇਇਸ਼ਨ) *n* ਰਹਾ;
ਅਲਾਪ, ਸੁਰ-ਲਹਿਰ

in toto (ਇਨ'ਟਅਉਟਅਉ) *(L) adv* ਪੂਰਨ ਰੂਪ
ਵਿਚ

intoxicant (ਇਨ'ਟੈਕਸਿਕਅੰਟ) *a n* ਨਸ਼ੀਲਾ,
ਨਸ਼ੀਲੀ; ਮਾਦਕ ਪਦਾਰਥ

intoxication (ਇਨ'ਟੈਕਸਿ'ਕੇਇਸ਼ਨ) *n* ਨਸ਼ਾ,
ਮਸਤੀ, ਖੁਮਾਰ, ਖੁਮਾਰੀ; ਮਦਹੋਸ਼ੀ

intraouility (ਇਨਟਰੈਨ'ਕਵਿਲਅਟਿ) *n* ਬੇਚੈਨੀ,
ਅਸ਼ਾਂਤੀ

intransitive (ਇਨ'ਟਰੈਂਸਅਟਿਵ੍) *a n* ਅਕਰਮਕ,
(ਵਿਆ) ਅਕਰਮਕ ਕਿਰਿਆ

intra vires ('ਇਨਟਰਆ,ਵ੍ਹਾਇਰਜ਼) (*L*) *a*
ਅਧਿਕਾਰਗਤ, ਅਧਿਕਾਰ ਅਨੁਕੂਲ, ਵਸੀਕਾਰ ਦੇ
ਅੰਦਰ

intrepid (ਇਨ'ਟਰੈਪਿਡ) *a* ਨਿਡਰ, ਬਹਾਦਰ,
ਦਲੇਰ, ਨਿਧੜਕ, ਨਿਰਡੈ, ਸਾਹਸੀ

intricacy (ਇਨਟਰਿਕਅਸਿ) *n* ਗੁੰਝਲ, ਪੇਚੀਦਗੀ,
ਅਸਪਸ਼ਟਤਾ, ਜਟਿਲਤਾ, ਵਿਖਮਤਾ, ਦੁਰਬੋਧਤਾ,
ਗੁੜ੍ਹਤਾ

intricate (ਇਨ'ਟਰਿਕਅਟ) *a* ਗੁੰਝਲਦਾਰ,
ਵਲਾਵਾਂ, ਪੇਚੀਦਾ; ਅਸਪਸ਼ਟ

intrigue (ਇਨ'ਟਰੀਗ) *n v* ਆਸ਼ਨਾਈ, ਗੁਪਤ
ਪ੍ਰੇਮ; ਸਾਜ਼ਸ਼; ਲੁਕਵਾਂ ਸਬੰਧ ਪੈਦਾ ਕਰਨਾ,
ਵਿਤਕਰਾ ਕਰਨਾ, ਆਸ਼ਨਾਈ ਰੱਖਣੀ; ਗੰਢ-ਸੰਢ
ਕਰਨਾ, ਸਾਜ਼ਸ਼ ਕਰਨੀ; ਭਰਮ ਪੈਦਾ ਕਰਨਾ

intrinsic (ਇੰ'ਟਰਿੰਸਿਕ) *a* ਅੰਤਰੀਵ, ਭੀਤਰੀ;
ਸੁਭਾਵਕ, ਅਸਲੀ, ਵਾਸਤਵਿਕ, ਯਥਾਰਥਕ

introduce ('ਇੰਟਰਅ'ਡਯੂਸ) *v* ਜਾਣ ਪਛਾਣ
ਦੇਣੀ, ਪਰਿਚਯ ਦੇਣਾ ਜਾਂ ਕਰਾਉਣਾ, ਉਪਸਥਿਤ
ਕਰਨਾ, ਦਾਖ਼ਲ ਕਰਨਾ; ਪ੍ਰਸਤੁਤ ਕਰਨਾ, ਸ਼ੁਰੂ
ਕਰਨਾ, ਪ੍ਰਚਲਤ ਕਰਨਾ, ਪੇਸ਼ ਕਰਨਾ (ਬਿਲ);
ਭੂਮਕਾ ਬੰਨ੍ਹਣੀ, ਪ੍ਰਸਤਾਵਨਾ ਲਿਖਣੀ

introduction (ਇੰਟਰਅ'ਡਅੱਕਸ਼ਨ) *n* ਜਾਣ-
ਪਛਾਣ; ਅਸਥਾਪਨ; ਆਰੰਭ; ਪ੍ਰਚਲਣ; ਭੂਮਕਾ,

ਮੁੱਖ-ਬੰਧ

introductory (ਇੰਟਰਅ'ਡਅੱਕਟ(ਅ)ਰਿ) *a*
ਜਾਣ-ਪਛਾਣ ਦੇ ਤੌਰ ਤੇ, ਪ੍ਰਵੇਸ਼ ਸਾਧਕ;
ਪੁਰੰਭਕ; ਆਰੰਭਕ, ਭੂਮਕਾ ਸਵਰੂਪ

introgression (ਇੰਟਰਅ'ਗਰੈਸ਼ਨ) *n* ਅੰਦਰੂਨੀ
ਗਤੀ, ਅੰਤਰਗਮਨ

introspect (ਇੰਟਰਅ(ਉ)'ਸਪੈੱਕਟ) *v* ਚਿਤੰਨ
ਕਰਨਾ, ਅੰਦਰ ਧਿਆਨ ਕਰਨਾ, ਅੰਤਰ-ਧਿਆਨ
ਕਰਨਾ, ਅੰਤਰ-ਧਿਆਨ ਹੋਣਾ, ਅੰਤਰ-ਦ੍ਰਿਸ਼ਟੀ
ਕਰਨੀ; **~ion** ਆਤਮ-ਚੀਨਣ, ਅੰਤਰ-ਧਿਆਨ,
ਅੰਤਰ-ਦ੍ਰਿਸ਼ਟੀ; **~ive** ਚਿੰਤਨਾਤਮਕ, ਅੰਤਰ-
ਧਿਆਨਾਤਮਕ, ਅੰਤਰ-ਦ੍ਰਿਸ਼ਟੀ ਸਬੰਧੀ

introvert ('ਇੰਟਰਅ(ਉ)'ਵ੍ਅੰ:ਟ) *v n* ਮਨ ਨੂੰ
ਅੰਦਰ ਮੋੜਨਾ, ਅੰਤਰ-ਮੁਖੀ ਹੋਣਾ, ਅੰਤਰ-ਮੁਖੀ
ਵਿਅਕਤੀ

intrusion (ਇੰ'ਟਰੂਯ਼ਨ) *n* ਬਿਨਾ ਆਗਿਆ
ਪ੍ਰਵੇਸ਼; ਅਯੋਗ ਦਖ਼ਲ, ਵਿਘਨ

intuition (ਇੰਟਯੂ'ਇਸ਼ਨ) *n* ਅਨੁਭਵ, ਅੰਤਰ-
ਪੇਰਨਾ; ਅੰਤਰ-ਦ੍ਰਿਸ਼ਟੀ; ਸਹਿਜ-ਗਿਆਨ,
ਸਹਿਜ-ਬੋਧ; **~al** ਅਨੁਭਵੀ; ਅੰਤਰ-
ਗਿਆਨਾਤਮਕ; ਸਹਿਜ ਬੋਧਾਤਮਕ

intuitive (ਇਨ'ਟਯੁਇਟਿਵ੍) *a* ਅਨੁਭਵੀ; ਅੰਤਰ-
ਦ੍ਰਿਸ਼ਟੀਗਤ

invade (ਇਨ'ਵ੍ਏਇਡ) *v* ਹੱਲਾ ਕਰਨਾ, ਚੜ੍ਹਾਈ
ਕਰਨੀ, ਚੜ੍ਹ ਆਉਣਾ, ਧਾਵਾ ਕਰਨਾ; ਘੁਸਣਾ;
~r ਹੱਲਾ ਕਰਨ ਵਾਲਾ, ਚੜ੍ਹਾਈ ਕਰਨ ਵਾਲਾ,
ਹਮਲਾਵਰ

invalid (ਇਨ'ਵ੍ਅਲਿਡ, ਇਨਵ੍ਅਲਿਡ) *a n v*
ਨਕਾਰਾ, ਅਪਾਹਜ, ਦੁਰਬਲ, ਅਸਮਰੱਥ, ਅਯੋਗ;
ਰੋਗੀ, ਬਲਹੀਨ ਮਨੁੱਖ; ਨਕਾਰਾ ਕਰ ਦੇਣਾ

invaluable (ਇਨ'ਵ੍ਐਲਯੁਅਬਲ) *a* ਅਮੋਲਕ,

ਬਹੁਮੁੱਲੀ, ਅਟਮੇਲ, ਅਮੇਲ

invariable (ਇਨ'ਵੇਅਰਿਅਬਲ) *a* ਅਡੋਲ, ਪੱਕਾ, ਸਥਿਰ, ਅੱਚਲ, ਇਕਸਾਰ; (ਗਤਿ) ਅਟੱਲ, ਸਥਿਰ, ਅਪਰਿਵਰਤਨੀ

invariant (ਇਨ'ਵੇਅਰਿਅੰਟ) *a* ਸਥਿਰ, ਅਡੋਲ, ਪੱਕਾ, ਇਕਸਾਰ; ਅਟੱਲ, ਅਚੱਲ

invasion (ਇਨ'ਵੇਇਯਨ) *n* ਹੱਲਾ, ਆਕਰਮਣ, ਚੜ੍ਹਾਈ, ਧਾਵਾ; ਵਿਘਨ

invent (ਇਨ'ਵੈਂਟ) *v* ਕਾਢ ਕੱਢਣੀ, ਵਿਉਂਤਣਾ, ਈਜਾਦ ਕਰਨੀ, ਆਵਿਸ਼ਕਾਰ ਕਰਨਾ; ਘੜ ਲੈਣੀ; ~ion ਈਜਾਦ, ਆਵਿਸ਼ਕਾਰ; ਕਾਢ, ਵਿਉਂਤ

invert (ਇਨ'ਵਅਃਟ) *v* ਉਲਟਣਾ, ਪਲਟਣਾ, ਪੁੱਠਾ ਕਰ ਦੇਣਾ, ਸਿਲਸਲਾ ਤੋੜਨਾ; ਕ੍ਰਮ ਭੰਗ ਕਰਨਾ

invest (ਇਨ'ਵੈਸੰਟ) *v* ਰੁਪਿਆ ਲਾਉਣਾ, ਰਕਮ ਲਾਉਣੀ, ਧਨ ਲਾਉਣਾ; ਘੇਰਨਾ, ਘੇਰਾ ਘੱਤਣਾ; ~ment ਨਿਵੇਸ਼ ਲਾਗਤ, ਲਾਈ ਰਕਮ; ਲਿਬਾਸ; ਘੇਰਾ

investigate (ਇਨ'ਵੈਸੰਟਿਗੇਇਟ) *v* ਖੋਜ ਕਰਨੀ; ਛਾਣ-ਬੀਨ ਕਰਨੀ, ਪਤਾ ਲਾਉਣਾ, ਜਾਂਚ-ਪੜਤਾਲ ਕਰਨੀ, ਤਫ਼ਤੀਸ਼ ਕਰਨੀ

investigation (ਇਨ'ਵੈਸੰਟਿ'ਗੇਇਸ਼ਨ) *n* ਖੋਜ, ਛਾਣ-ਬੀਨ, ਜਾਂਚ-ਪੜਤਾਲ, ਪੁੱਛ-ਗਿੱਛ, ਤਹਿਕੀਕਾਤ, ਤਫ਼ਤੀਸ਼

investigator (ਇਨ'ਵੈਸੰਟਿਗੇਇਟਅ*) *n* ਖੋਜਕਾਰ, ਤਫ਼ਤੀਸ਼ਕਾਰ

inviable (ਇਨ'ਵਾਇਅਬਲ) *a* ਨਾ ਜਿਉਣ ਯੋਗ

invigilate (ਇਨ'ਵਿਜਿਲੇਇਟ) *v* (ਇਮਤਿਹਾਨ ਦੇਣ ਵਾਲਿਆਂ ਦੀ) ਨਿਗਰਾਨੀ ਕਰਨੀ

invigilation (ਇਨ'ਵਿਜਿ'ਲੇਇਸ਼ਨ) *n* ਨਿਗਰਾਨੀ, ਨਿਰੀਖਣ, ਦੇਖ-ਭਾਲ

invigilator (ਇਨ'ਵਿਜਿਲੇਇਟਅ*) *n* ਨਿਗਰਾਨ, ਨਿਰੀਖਕ

invisible (ਇਨ'ਵਿਜ਼ਿਬਲ) *a* ਅਦਿੱਖ, ਅਡਿੱਠ; ਅਦਿਸਵੀਂ, ਲੋਪ, ਨਿਰਾਕਾਰ

invitation (ਇਨਵਿ'ਟੇਇਸ਼ਨ) *n* ਸੱਦਾ, ਬੁਲਾਵਾ, ਨਿਉਤਾ, ਦਾਅਵਤ, ਨਿਮੰਤਰਨ

invite (ਇਨ'ਵਾਇਟ) *v* ਸੱਦਣਾ, ਦਾਅਵਤ ਦੇਣੀ, ਬੁਲਾਉਣਾ, ਨਿਉਤਾ ਦੇਣਾ, ਆਕਰਸ਼ਤ ਕਰਨਾ, ਖਿੱਚਣਾ; ~e ਨਿਮੰਤਰਤ ਵਿਅਕਤੀ

invocation (ਇਨਵੁਅ'ਕੇਇਸ਼ਨ) *n* ਅਰਦਾਸ; ਪ੍ਰਾਰਥਨਾ, ਮੰਗਲਾਚਰਨ, ਦੇਵ-ਉਸਤਤੀ

invoice (ਇਨਵੋਇਸ) *n v* ਬੀਚਕ, ਚਲਾਨ; (ਮਾਲ ਦਾ) ਬੀਚਕ ਬਣਾਉਣਾ, ਚਲਾਨ ਤਿਆਰ ਕਰਨਾ

invoke (ਇਨ'ਵਅਉਕ) *v* ਆਵਾਹਨ ਕਰਨਾ, ਵਾਸਤਾ ਪਾਉਣਾ, ਜਾਚਨਾ ਕਰਨੀ, ਅਰਦਾਸ ਕਰਨੀ, ਬੇਨਤੀ ਕਰਨੀ

involuntarily (ਇਨ'ਵੋੱਲਅਨਟ(ਅ)ਰਿਲਿ) *adv* ਆਪਣੇ ਆਪ, ਬਿਨਾ ਮਰਜੀ ਦੇ

involuntary (ਇਨ'ਵੋੱਲਅਨਟ(ਅ)ਰਿ) *a* ਮਜਬੂਰਨ, ਅਟਇੱਛਤ

involve (ਇਨ'ਵੌਲਵ) *v* ਉਲਝਾਉਣਾ; ਫਸਾਉਣਾ; ਲਪੇਟ ਵਿਚ ਲੈਣਾ, ਅਤ੍ਰੰਝਣਾ; ਅੰਦਰ ਵੱਲ ਚੱਕਰ ਦੇਣਾ; ਸੰਕੇਤ ਕਰਨਾ; ਸ਼ਾਮਲ ਕਰਨਾ, ਮਿਲਾਉਣਾ; ~ment ਲਪੇਟ, ਉਲਝਣ; ਸਮੱਸਿਆ

invulnerability (ਇਨ'ਵਅੱਲਨ(ਅ)ਰਾ'ਬਿਲਅਟਿ) *n* ਸੁਰੱਖਿਅਤਾ, ਅਖੰਡਤਾ, ਅਭੰਜਤਾ, ਅਜਿੱਤਤਾ

invulnerable (ਇਨ'ਵਅੱਲਨ(ਅ)ਰਅਬਲ) *a*

ਸੁਰੱਖਿਅਤ, ਅਖੰਡ, ਅਜਿੱਤ

inward (ਇਨਵ'ਅਡ) *a n* ਅੰਦਰਲਾ, ਆਂਤਰਕ, ਅੰਤਰੀਵ, ਆਗਾਮੀ, ਆਉਣ ਵਾਲਾ, (ਬ ਵ) ਆਂਦਰਾਂ; ~**ly** ਅੰਦਰੋ-ਅੰਦਰ, ਅੰਦਰੋਂ, ਦਿਲ ਵਿਚ

iota (ਆਈਆਉਟਾ) *n* ਯੂਨਾਨੀ ਲਿਪੀ ਦਾ ਇਕ ਅੱਖਰ; ਕਣ, ਭੋਗ, ਕਣ ਮਾਤਰ, ਬਹੁਤ ਥੋੜ੍ਹੀ ਮਿਕਦਾਰ

ipso facto (ਇਪਸਆਉ-ਫੈਕਟਆਉ) (*L*) *adv* ਆਪਣੇ-ਆਪ, ਤਦ ਅਨੁਸਾਰ

iron (ਆਇਅਨ) *n a v* ਲੋਹਾ; ਕਰੜਾਈ; ਲੋਹੇ ਦਾ ਜੰਤਰ ਇਸਤਰੀ (ਕੱਪੜੇ ਪ੍ਰੈਸ ਕਰਨ ਲਈ); (ਬ ਵ) ਹੱਥਕੜੀ, ਜੰਜੀਰ; ਪੱਕੇ ਇਰਾਦੇ ਵਾਲਾ; ਸਖ਼ਤ, ਮਜ਼ਬੂਤ; ਬੇਦਰਦ; ਲੋਹੇ ਨਾਲ ਮੜ੍ਹਨਾ; ਕੱਪੜੇ ਇਸਤਰੀ ਕਰਨਾ; ਹੱਥਕੜੀ

ironical (ਆਇਰੌਨਿਕਲ) *a* ਵਿਅੰਗਮਈ, ਕਾਟਵਾਂ

irony ('ਆਇ(ਅ)ਰਅਨਿ) *n a* ਵਿਅੰਗ, ਭਾਸ਼ਾ ਦੀ ਵਿਅੰਗਮਈ ਵਰਤੋਂ; ਦੁਰਘਟਨਾ; ਕਿਸਮਤ ਦਾ ਖੇਲ, ਵਿਡੰਬਣਾ; ਲੋਹੇ ਵਾਂਗੂ, ਲੋਹੇ ਵਰਗਾ

irrational (ਇ'ਰੈਸ਼ਨਲ) *a* ਅਨੁਚਿਤ, ਅਤਾਰਕਿਕ, ਗ਼ੈਰਵਾਜਬ, ਅਵਿਵੇਕੀ; ਤਰਕਹੀਣ; ~**ity** ਅਨੁਚਿੱਤਤਾ, ਨਾ-ਮਾਲੂਕੀਅਤ, ਤਰਕਹੀਣਤਾ; ਬੇਹੂਦਗੀ

irrefutable ('ਇਰਿ'ਫ਼ਯੂਟਅਬਲ) *a* ਅਖੰਡਨੀ, ਅਕੱਟ, ਜਿਸ ਨੂੰ ਝੁਠਲਾਇਆ ਨਾ ਜਾ ਸਕੇ

irregular (ਇ'ਰੈਗਯੂਲਅ*) *a n pl* ਅਸੰਗਤ, ਬੇਕਾਇਦਾ, ਬੇਨਿਯਮਾ, ਬੇਢੰਗਾ, ਕਸੂਤਾ; ਬੇਕਾਇਦਾ ਫ਼ੌਜੀ ਦਸਤੇ; ~**ity** ਬੇਕਾਇਦਗੀ

irrelevance (ਇ'ਰੈਲਿਅਵਅੰਸ) *n* ਅਸੰਗਤੀ, ਅਸੰਬੰਧਤਾ, ਅਪ੍ਰਸੰਗਕਤਾ

irrelevant (ਇ'ਰੈਲਿਅਵਅਨਟ) *a* ਅਸਬੰਧਤ, ਅਸੰਗਤ, ਗ਼ੈਰ-ਮੁਨਾਸਬ

irrepressible ('ਇਰਿ'ਪਰੈਸਅਬਲ) *a* ਨਾ ਦਬਣ ਵਾਲਾ, ਨਾ ਰੁਕਣ ਵਾਲਾ, ਮੂੰਹਜ਼ੋਰ, ਅੱਖੜ

irrespective ('ਇਰਿ'ਸਪੈੱਕਟਿਵ੍) *a* ਬਿਨਾ ਪਰਵਾਹ ਦੇ, ਬਿਨਾ ਲਿਹਾਜ

irresponsibility ('ਇਰਿ'ਸਪੌਂਸਿ'ਬਿਲਅਟਿ) *n* ਗ਼ੈਰ-ਜ਼ਿੰਮੇਵਾਰੀ

irresponsible ('ਇਰਿ'ਸਪੌਂਸਅਬਲ) *a* ਗ਼ੈਰ-ਜ਼ਿੰਮੇਵਾਰ, ਲਾਪਰਵਾਹ

irrigate ('ਇਰਿਗੇਇਟ) *v* ਸਿੰਚਣਾ, ਆਬਪਾਸ਼ੀਕਰਨੀ, ਪਾਣੀ ਦੇਣਾ

irrigation ('ਇਰਿ'ਗੇਇਸ਼ਨ) *n* ਸਿੰਚਾਈ, ਸੇਚਨ, ਆਬਪਾਸ਼ੀ

irritate ('ਇਰਿਟੇਇਟ) *v* ਗੁੱਸਾ ਦਿਵਾਉਣਾ, ਖਿਝਾਉਣਾ; ਚਿੜਾਉਣਾ, ਤੰਗ ਕਰਨਾ, ਉਤੇਜਤ ਕਰਨਾ; ਜਲਨ ਪੈਦਾ ਕਰਨੀ

irritation ('ਇਰਿ'ਟੇਇਸ਼ਨ) *n* ਉਤੇਜਨਾ, ਜਲਨ, ਚਿੜਚੜਾਹਟ, ਖਿਝ

island (ਆਇਲਅੰਡ) *n* ਟਾਪੂ, ਦੀਪ, ਜਜ਼ੀਰਾ

isle (ਆਇਲ) *n* ਟਾਪੂ, ਦੀਪ; ~**t** ਛੋਟਾ ਟਾਪੂ

isogloss ('ਆਇਸਅਉਗਲੌਸ) *n* (ਭਾਸ਼ਾ) ਸਮਵਿਕਾਰ ਰੇਖਾ

isolate ('ਆਇਸਅਲੇਇਟ) *v* ਦੂਜਿਆਂ ਤੋਂ ਵੱਖ ਕਰਨਾ, ਵਿਤਰੇਕ ਕਰਨਾ; ਵੱਖਰਾ ਕਰਨਾ, ਨਵੇਕਲਾ ਰੱਖਣਾ, ਨਿਖੇੜਨਾ, ਅਲੱਗ ਕਰਨਾ

isolating ('ਆਇਸਅਲੇਇਟਿਙ) *a* ਅਯੋਗਾਤਮਕ

isolation ('ਆਇਸਅ'ਲੇਇਸ਼ਨ) *n* ਅੱਡਰਾਪਨ, ਵੱਖਰਤਾ, ਵਖਰੇਵਾਂ

issue ('ਇਸ਼ੂ) *n v* ਨਿਕਾਸ, ਨਤੀਜਾ, ਅੰਤ; ਸੰਤਾਨ, ਔਲਾਦ; ਅੰਕ ਪਰਚਾ (ਅਖ਼ਬਾਰ ਦਾ); (ਨਦੀ ਦਾ) ਮੂੰਹ; ਨਿਕਲਣਾ, ਪੈਦਾ ਹੋਣਾ, ਫੁੱਟਣਾ, ਨਤੀਜਾ ਨਿਕਲਣਾ; ਜਾਰੀ ਕਰਨਾ, ਕੱਢਣਾ,

ਪ੍ਰਕਾਸ਼ਤ ਕਰਨ; **~less** ਨਿਰਸੰਤਨ

itch (ਇਚ) *n v* ਖਾਜ, ਖੁਜਲੀ, ਖ਼ਾਰਸ਼, ਜਲੂਟ; ਤੀਬਰ
ਇੱਛਾ; ਖਾਜ ਹੋਣੀ, ਜਲਨ ਹੋਣੀ ਜਾਂ ਉੱਠਣੀ,
ਖੁਰਕਣਾ

item ('ਆਇਟਮ) *n adv* ਮੱਦ, ਨਗ; (ਅਖਬਾਰ
ਆਦਿ ਵਿਚ) ਸਮਾਚਾਰ, ਖ਼ਬਰ, ਮਜ਼ਮੂਨ

itineracy, itinerancy (ਇ'ਟਿਨ(ਅ)ਰਅਸਿ,

ਇ'ਟਿਨ(ਅ)ਰਅੰਸਿ) *n* ਖ਼ਾਨਾਬਦੋਸ਼ੀ,
ਭ੍ਰਮਣਸ਼ੀਲਤਾ, ਸੈਲਾਨੀਪਣ

itinerant (ਇ'ਟਿਨ(ਅ)ਰਅੰਟ) *a* ਫਿਰਤੂ, ਸਫ਼ਰੀ,
(ਜੱਜ) ਦੌਰੇ ਤੇ

ivory ('ਆਇਵ੍(ਅ)ਰਿ) *n* ਹਾਥੀ-ਦੰਦ, ਦੰਦ-ਖੰਡ;
(ਬ ਵ) ਬਿਲਿਅਰਡ-ਬਾਲ; **~tower** ਖ਼ਿਆਲੀ
ਮਹਿਲ

J

J, j (ਜੇਇ) *n* ਰੋਮਨ ਵਰਨਮਾਲਾ ਦਾ ਦਸਵਾਂ ਅੱਖਰ

jabber ('ਜੈਬਅ*) *v n* ਬੁੜਬੁੜਾਉਣਾ; ਕਾਹਲੀ ਕਾਹਲੀ ਬੋਲਣਾ, ਬਕ ਬਕ ਕਰਨਾ; ਚੀਕਾਂ-ਕੂਕਾਂ ਮਾਰਨੀਆਂ; ਬਕਵਾਸ, ਬਕੜਵਾਹ; ਅਸਪਸ਼ਟ ਗੱਲ; **~ing** ਬਕਵਾਸ, ਬਕ-ਬਕ, ਗਿਟਮਿਟ, ਬੁੜਬੁੜ, ਚੂੰ ਚਾਂ, ਬਕੜਵਾਹ

jackal ('ਜੈਕੋਲ) *n v* ਗਿੱਦੜ; ਅਤਿਨੈ ਕਰਨਾ

jacket ('ਜੈਕਿਟ) *n* ਕੁੜਤੀ, ਫਤੂਹੀ, ਪੋਸਤੀਨ; ਗਿਲਾਫ਼

jade (ਜੇਇਡ) *n v* ਹੁੱਸਿਆ ਤੇ ਮਰੀਅਲ ਘੋੜਾ, ਮਾੜਾ ਟੱਟੂ; ਕੰਜਰੀ, ਵੇਸਵਾ, ਕਮਜ਼ਾਤ; ਹਰਾ, ਨੀਲਾ ਜਾਂ ਚਿੱਟਾ ਕੀਮਤੀ ਪੱਥਰ; ਥੱਕਣਾ, ਥੱਕਾਉਣਾ, ਘਸਣਾ, ਰਗੜਨਾ; **~d** ਹੁੱਸਿਆ, ਥੱਕਿਆ, ਮੰਦਾ ਪਿਆ

jaggery ('ਜੈਗਅਰਿ) *n* ਗੁੜ

jaguar ('ਜੈਗਯੁਆ*) *n* ਚਿਤਕਬਰਾ ਜੰਗਲੀ ਬਿੱਲਾ, ਬਾਗਾਤਬਿੱਲਾ

jail, gaol (ਜੇਇਲ) *n v* ਜੇਲ੍ਹ, ਬੰਦੀਖ਼ਾਨਾ, ਕੈਦਖ਼ਾਨਾ; ਬੰਦੀ ਬਣਾਉਣਾ, ਜੇਲ੍ਹ ਵਿਚ ਦੇਣਾ, ਕੈਦ ਕਰਨਾ

jalousie ('ਜੈਲੂਝ਼ਿ) *n* ਖਿੜਕੀ ਦਾ ਪਰਦਾ, ਝਿਲਮਿਲ

jam (ਜੈਮ) *v n* (ਮਸ਼ੀਨ ਦੇ ਕਿਸੇ ਪੁਰਜ਼ੇ ਦਾ) ਜਾਮ ਹੋ ਜਾਣਾ; (ਰਸਤਾ) ਬੰਦ ਹੋ ਜਾਣਾ (ਭੀੜ ਆਦਿ ਦੇ ਕਾਰਨ); ਰਾਹ ਰੋਕਣਾ, ਰੁਕਾਵਟ ਪਾਉਣੀ, ਬੰਦ ਕਰਨਾ; ਜੰਮ ਕੇ ਬੈਠ ਜਾਣਾ; ਦੱਬ ਕੇ ਸਤ ਕਫ਼ੜਾ, ਨਚੋੜਨਾ; ਫੇਹ ਕੇ ਇਕ ਕਰਨਾ; ਪੀਹਣਾ; ਜੰਜਾਲ; ਦਬਾਅ, ਰੋਕ; ਭੀੜ; ਮੁਰੱਬਾ,

ਜਾਮ; **~packed** ਖਚਾਖਚ ਭਰਿਆ

jangle ('ਜੈਂਡਗਲ) *n v* ਝੁਣਕਾਰ, ਠਣਕਾਰ; ਤਕਰਾਰ, ਝਗੜਾ, ਫ਼ਸਾਦ; ਬੇਸੁਰੀ ਅਵਾਜ਼ ਕੱਢਣੀ, ਘੰਟੀ ਦਾ ਟਣ-ਟਣ ਕਰਨਾ; ਝਗੜਨਾ, ਤਕਰਾਰ ਕਰਨੀ; **~r** ਹੁੱਜਤੀ, ਝਗੜਾਲੂ, ਲੜਾਕਾ, ਫ਼ਸਾਦੀ ਆਦਮੀ

jangling ('ਜੈਂਡਗਲਿਙ) *n* ਝੱਖ, ਝਗੜਾ, ਧਿਖੇੜਾ, ਲੜਾਈ, ਬਹਿਸ-ਮੁਬਾਹਸਾ

jar (ਜਾ*) *v n* ਝਗੜਾ ਕਰਨਾ, ਤਕਰਾਰ ਕਰਨਾ; ਸਹਿਮਤ ਨਾ ਹੋਣਾ, ਬਹਿਸ ਵਿਚ ਪੈਣਾ; (ਕਿਸੇ ਅੰਗ ਵਿਚ) ਕੰਬਣੀ ਆਉਣੀ; ਗੂੰਜ ਪੈਣੀ, ਝਟਕਾਰ ਪੈਣੀ, ਕਰਖ਼ਤ ਅਵਾਜ਼ ਕੱਢਣੀ, ਕੰਨ ਖਾਣੇ; (1) ਝਗੜਾ, ਤਕਰਾਰ; ਵਿਰੋਧ, ਕਰਖ਼ਤ ਅਵਾਜ਼; (2) ਮਰਤਬਾਨ, ਘੜਾ, ਮੱਘਾ, ਗਾੜਵਾਂ

jargon ('ਜਾ'ਗਅਨ) *n* ਸਮਝ ਵਿਚ ਨਾ ਆਉਂਦ ਵਾਲੀ ਬੋਲੀ, ਗਿਟਮਿਟ

jaundice ('ਜੋਨਡਿਸ) *n v* ਯਰਕਾਨ, ਪਰਨੇਹ, ਪੀਲੀਆ; ਸਾੜਾ; ਨਜ਼ਰ ਨੁਕਸ; ਯਰਕਾਨ ਦਾ ਰੋਗੀ ਹੋਣਾ; ਈਰਖਾ, ਭਰ ਦੇਣੀ

javelin ('ਜੈਵ੍ਲਿਨ) *n* ਬਰਛਾ, ਬੱਲਮ, ਨੇਜ਼ਾ

jaw (ਜੋ) *n v* ਹੜਬ, ਜਬਾੜਾ; ਤਕਰਾਰ, ਝਗੜਾ, ਝਗੜਨਾ, ਤਕਰਾਰ ਕਰਨੀ, ਵਾਧੂ ਗੱਲਾਂ ਮਾਰਨੀਆਂ; ਲਗਾਤਾਰ ਬੋਲਦੇ ਜਾਣਾ, ਵਿਆਖਿਆਨ ਦੇਣਾ

jay (ਜੇਇ) *n* (1) ਨੀਲਕੰਠ; (2) ਗਾਲੜੀ, ਗੱਪੀ, ਖੱਪੀ; (3) ਮੂਰਖ, ਸਿੰਪਲ

jealous ('ਜੈਲਅਸ) *a* ਈਰਖਾਈ, ਦਵੈਖੀ; ਕੱਟੜ; **~y** ਈਰਖਾ, ਸਾੜਾ; ਦਵੈਖ

jeer (ਜਿਅ*) *v n pl* ਮਖੌਲ ਉਡਾਉਣਾ, ਮਸ਼ਕਰੀ ਕਰਨੀ; ਤਾਅਨਾ ਮਾਰਨਾ, ਬੋਲੀ ਮਾਰਨੀ; ਹਾਸਾ, ਮਸ਼ਕਰੀ, ਤਾਅਨਾ, ਬੋਲੀ

jejune (ਜਿ'ਜੂਨ) *a* ਬੰਜਰ, ਅਣ-ਉਪਜਾਉ; ਰਸਹੀਨ, ਖ਼ੁਸ਼ਕ, ਰੁੱਖਾ; ਬਹੁਤ ਥੋੜ੍ਹਾ, ਨਾਕਾਫ਼ੀ; **~ness** ਰਸਹੀਨਤਾ ਖ਼ੁਸ਼ਕੀ, ਰੁੱਖਾਪਨ, ਨੀਰਸਤਾ, ਫਿੱਕਾਪਨ

jelly ('ਜੈਲਿ) *n* ਇਕ ਲੇਸਵੀਂ ਮਿੱਠੀ ਚਟਨੀ, ਮੁਰੱਬਾ, ਜੈਲੀ

jeopard, jeopardize ('ਜੈੱਪਅਡ,'ਜੈਪਅ:-ਡਾਇਜ਼) *v* ਖ਼ਤਰੇ ਵਿਚ ਪਾਉਣਾ, ਬਿਪਤਾ ਵਿਚ ਫਸਾਉਣਾ; **~ous** ਸੰਕਟ ਭਰਿਆ, ਸੰਕਟਮਈ, ਖ਼ਤਰਨਾਕ

jerk (ਜਅਃਕ) *n v* ਧੱਕਾ, ਝਟਕਾ, ਮੋਚ, ਖਿਚ, ਤਣਾਉ; ਝਟਕਾ ਦੇਣਾ ਜਾਂ ਲੱਗਣਾ; ਝਟਕੇ ਨਾਲ ਖਿਚਣਾ; **~iness** ਝਟਕਾ, ਧੱਕਾ; ਸੰਕੋਚ

jest (ਜੈੱਸਟ) *n v* ਹਾਸਾ, ਠੱਠਾ, ਮਸ਼ਕਰੀ, ਮਖੌਲ, ਛੇੜ-ਛਾੜ, ਮਸ਼ਕਰੀ ਕਰਨੀ, ਹਾਸਾ-ਠੱਠਾ ਕਰਨਾ, ਛੇੜ-ਛਾੜ ਕਰਨੀ, ਦਿਲਲਗੀ ਕਰਨੀ; **~book** ਚੁਟਕਲਿਆਂ ਦੀ ਕਿਤਾਬ; **~er** ਮਖੌਲੀਆ, ਦਿਲਲਗੀਬਾਜ਼; ਭੰਡ, ਵਿਦੂਸ਼ਕ; **~ful** ਠੱਠੇ ਦਾ, ਮਜ਼ਾਕੀਆ, ਮਖੌਲੀਆ, ਹਸੰਦੜਾ

jetty ('ਜੈੱਟਿ) *n* ਜਹਾਜ਼ ਤੋਂ ਮਾਲ ਲਾਹੁਣ ਵਾਲਾ ਘਾਟ, ਪੱਕਾ ਘਾਟ, ਜੈਟੀ; ਬੰਦਰਗਾਹ ਦੀ ਰੱਖਿਆ ਲਈ ਬਣਾਇਆ ਗਿਆ ਬੰਨ੍ਹ

jew (ਜੂ) *n v* ਯਹੂਦੀ; (ਬੋਲ) ਸੂਦ-ਖੋਰ

jewel ('ਜੂਅਲ) *n v* ਹੀਰਾ, ਨਗ, ਮਣੀ, ਰਤਨ, ਲਾਲ; ਬਹੁਮੁੱਲੀ ਵਸਤੂ, ਜੜਾਉ ਗਹਿਣਾ; ਰਤਨਾਂ ਨਾਲ ਅਲੰਕਰਤ ਕਰਨਾ, ਜੜਾਉ ਬਣਾਉਣਾ; **~ler, ~er** ਜੌਹਰੀ, ਸਰਾਫ਼ ਰਤਨਾਂ ਦਾ ਵਪਾਰੀ, ਲਾਲਾਂ ਦਾ ਵਣਜਾਰਾ; **~lery,ery** ਜ਼ੇਵਰ,

ਗਹਿਣੇ, ਭੂਸ਼ਣ; ਜੜਾਉ ਹੀਰੇ, ਰਤਨਾਂ ਦਾ ਵਪਾਰ, ਜੌਹਰਾਂ ਦੀ ਸੌਦਾਗਰੀ

jiggle ('ਜਿਗਲ) *n v* (ਹੌਲੀ ਹੌਲੀ ਦਿੱਤਾ) ਧੱਕਾ, ਝਟਕਾ

jill (ਜਿਲ) *n* ਮੁਟਿਆਰ, ਕੁੜੀ, ਯੁਵਤੀ; **~flirt** ਛਿਨਾਲ, ਭੈੜੇ ਚਰਿੱਤਰ ਵਾਲੀ ਕੁੜੀ; **~et** ਛਿਨਾਲ ਔਰਤ; ਅਵਾਰਾ ਔਰਤ

jilit (ਜਿਲਟ) *n v* ਬੇਵਫ਼ਾਈ; ਬੇਵਫ਼ਾਈ ਕਰਨੀ

jimmy ('ਜਿਮਿ) *n* ਅਸ਼ਰਫ਼ੀ, ਪੌਂਡ

jingle ('ਜਿਙਗਲ) *n v* ਝਣਕਾਰ, ਟੁਣਕਾਰ, ਛਣਕਾਰ; ਅਨੁਪ੍ਰਾਸ, ਝਣ-ਪਣ ਕਰਨਾ

jingo ('ਜਿਙਗਅਉ) *n a int* ਜੰਗਬਾਜ਼, ਲੜਾਈ-ਝਗੜੇ ਦੀ ਨੀਤੀ ਨੂੰ ਅਪਣਾਉਣ ਵਾਲਾ; ਆਡੰਬਰੀ, ਡੰਡੀ; ਧੋਖੇਬਾਜ਼; (y~)

jink (ਜਿਙਕ) *n v* ਟਾਲ ਮਟੋਲ; ਟਾਲਣਾ, ਟਲਣਾ, ਖਿਸਕਣਾ, ਖਿਸਕਾਉਣਾ

jitter ('ਜਿਟਅ*) *v* ਘਬਰਾਉਣਾ

job (ਜੌਬ) *n* ਆਸਾਮੀ, ਨੌਕਰੀ; ਕੰਮ, ਰੁਜ਼ਗਾਰ, ਧੰਦਾ; ਪੇਸ਼ਾ; ਕਿਰਤ, ਮਜ਼ਦੂਰੀ; **~ber** ਦਲਾਲ; **~bery** ਦਲਾਲੀ, ਆੜ੍ਹਤ; ਬੇਈਮਾਨੀ ਵੱਢੀ-ਖੋਰੀ; ਸੁਆਰਥ

jocund ('ਜੌਕਅੰਡ) *a* ਹਸਮੁਖ, ਜ਼ਿੰਦਾਦਿਲ, ਪ੍ਰਸੰਨ-ਚਿੱਤ, ਮੌਜੀ, ਰੰਗੀਲਾ; **~ity** ਜ਼ਿੰਦਾਦਿਲੀ, ਰੰਗੀਲਾਪਨ, ਖੇੜਾ, ਪ੍ਰਸੰਨਤਾ, ਖ਼ੁਸ਼-ਮਿਜ਼ਾਜੀ

jog (ਜੌਗ) *v n* ਔਖਾ ਤੁਰਨਾ, ਡਿਗਦੇ-ਢਹਿੰਦੇ ਤੁਰਨਾ, ਹੌਲੀ ਚੱਲਣਾ; ਰੇਤਾ ਆਉਣਾ, ਠੁੰਗਾ ਮਾਰਨਾ, ਝੰਜੋੜਨਾ, ਹਲੂਣਨਾ; ਚਲੇ ਜਾਣਾ, ਤੁਰ ਪੈਣਾ; ਸੁਸਤ ਚਾਲ, ਮੱਠੀ ਚਾਲ

join (ਜੌਇਨ) *v n* ਜੋੜਨਾ ਜਾਂ ਜੁੜਨਾ, ਮਿਲਣਾ, ਇਕੱਠੇ ਹੋਣਾ, ਸਾਂਝ ਪਾਉਣੀ, ਭਿਆਲੀ ਕਰਨੀ; ਹਿੱਸਾ ਪਾਉਣਾ; ਮਿਲਣ ਵਾਲੀ ਥਾਂ, ਜੋੜ-ਰੇਖਾ;

ਸੰਗਮ, ਜੋੜ-ਬਿੰਦੂ; **~ing time** ਕਾਰਜ ਗੁਹਿਣ-ਕਾਲ

joint ('ਜੋਇੰਟ) *n a v* ਜੋੜ, ਗੰਢ, ਟਾਂਕਾ, ਹੱਡੀਆਂ ਦਾ ਜੋੜ; ਜੋੜ-ਬਿੰਦੂ, ਚੂਲ; ਕਬਜ਼ਾ; ਸਾਂਝਾ; ਇਕੱਠਾ; ਮਿਲਵਾਂ, ਭਿਆਲੀ ਵਾਲਾ; ਜੋੜ ਬਿਠਾਉਣਾ, ਟਾਂਕਾ ਲਾਉਣਾ; ਚੂਲ ਲਾਉਣੀ; **~family** ਸਾਂਝਾ ਪਰਵਾਰ; **~secretary** ਸੰਯੁਕਤ-ਸਕੱਤਰ; **~stock** ਸਾਂਝੀ ਪੂੰਜੀ, ਸਾਂਝਾ ਧਨ

joke (ਜਾਉਕ) *n v* ਮਖੌਲ, ਮਸ਼ਕਰੀ, ਹਾਸਾ-ਠੱਠਾ; ਚੁਟਕਲਾ, ਲਤੀਫ਼ਾ; ਹਸਾਉਣੀ ਗੱਲ, ਮਖੌਲ ਕਰਨਾ, ਦਿਲਲਗੀ ਕਰਨੀ, ਮਸ਼ਕਰੀ ਕਰਨੀ; **~let** ਘਟੀਆ, ਮਸ਼ਕਰੀ; **~r** ਮਖੌਲੀਆ, ਹਸਾਊ, ਦਿਲਲਗੀਬਾਜ਼; ਭੰਡ, ਵਿਦੂਸ਼ਕ

jollification ('ਜੌਲਿਫ਼ਿ'ਕੇਇਸ਼ਨ) *n* ਰੰਗ-ਰਲੀਆਂ, ਮੌਜ-ਮੇਲਾ

jolify ('ਜੌਲਿਫ਼ਾਇ) *v* ਖ਼ੁਸ਼ੀਆਂ ਮਨਾਉਣੀਆਂ, ਰੰਗ-ਰਲੀਆਂ ਮਨਾਉਣੀਆਂ, ਖ਼ੁਸ਼ ਹੋਣਾ ਜਾਂ ਕਰਨਾ, ਮਸਤ ਹੋਣਾ ਜਾਂ ਕਰਨਾ

jolly ('ਜੌਲਿ) *a n adv* ਰੰਗੀਲਾ, ਰੌਂਕੀ, ਮੌਜੀ, ਖ਼ੁਸ਼, ਆਨੰਦ ਵਿਚ; ਜ਼ਿੰਦਾਦਿਲ

jolt (ਜਾਉਲਟ) *v n* ਹੁੱਝਕਾ ਮਾਰਨਾ, ਹਲੂਟਨਾ, ਝੰਜੋਟਨਾ; ਹੁੱਝਕਾ, ਹਲੂਣਾ, ਧੱਕਾ

jostle ('ਜੌਸਲ) *v n* ਹੁੱਝਕਾ ਵੱਜਣਾ, ਧੱਕੋ-ਧੱਕੀ ਹੋਣਾ, ਝਟਕਾ ਮਾਰਨਾ; ਹੁੱਝਕਾ, ਹਲੂਣਾ, ਧੱਕਾ, ਝਟਕਾ

journal ('ਜਅਃਨਲ) *n* ਰਸਾਲਾ, ਪੱਤਰ, ਅਖ਼ਬਾਰ ਰੋਜ਼ਨਾਮਚਾ; **~ism** ਪੱਤਰਕਾਰੀ, ਅਖ਼ਬਾਰ-ਨਵੀਸੀ, ਪੱਤਰਕਾਰਤਾ; **~ist** ਪੱਤਰਕਾਰ, ਅਖ਼ਬਾਰ ਨਵੀਸ

journey ('ਜਅਃਨਿ) *n v* ਪੈਂਡਾ; ਸਫ਼ਰ, ਸਾਰ,

ਯਾਤਰਾ; ਪੈਂਡਾ ਕਰਨਾ ਜਾਂ ਮਾਰਨਾ, ਸਫ਼ਰ ਕਰਨਾ, ਯਾਤਰਾ ਕਰਨੀ

jovial ('ਜਾਉਵ੍ਯਕਾਅਲ) *a* ਹਸਮੁੱਖ, ਖ਼ੁਸ਼ਦਿਲ, ਜ਼ਿੰਦਾਦਿਲ, ਮੌਜੀ, ਪ੍ਰਸੰਨ-ਚਿੱਤ; ਆਨੰਦਮਈ; **~ity** ਹਸਮੁੱਖਤਾ, ਜ਼ਿੰਦਾਦਿਲੀ, ਖ਼ੁਸ਼ਦਿਲੀ, ਪ੍ਰਸੰਨਤਾ

joy (ਜੋਇ) *n v* ਖ਼ੁਸ਼ੀ, ਹੁਲਾਸ, ਪ੍ਰਸੰਨਤਾ; ਆਨੰਦਦਾਇਕ ਵਸਤੂ; **~ful** ਖ਼ੁਸ਼, ਪ੍ਰਸੰਨ, ਆਨੰਦਤ; **~fulness** ਪ੍ਰਸੰਨਤਾ, ਆਨੰਦ, ਖ਼ੁਸ਼ੀ, ਮੌਜ; **~ous** ਆਨੰਦਮਈ, ਖ਼ੁਸ਼ੀ ਭਰਿਆ; ਖ਼ੁਸ਼, ਆਨੰਦ, ਪ੍ਰਸੰਨ

jubilance, jubilation ('ਜੁਬਿਲਅੰਸ, ਜੁਬਿ'ਲੇਇਸ਼ਨ) *n* ਖ਼ੁਸ਼ੀ, ਮੌਜ-ਮੇਲਾ, ਰੰਗ-ਰਲੀਆਂ

jubilant ('ਜੁਬਿਲਅੰਟ) *a* ਖ਼ੁਸ਼, ਪ੍ਰਸੰਨ; ਹਸੂੰ ਹਸੂੰ ਕਰਨਾ

jubilate ('ਜੁਬਿਲੇਇਟ) *v* ਖ਼ੁਸ਼ੀ ਮਨਾਉਣੀ, ਖਿੜੇ ਮੱਥੇ ਹੋਣਾ, ਆਨੰਦਤ ਹੋਣਾ

jubilee ('ਜੁਬਿਲੀ) *n* ਖ਼ੁਸ਼ੀ ਦਾ ਜਸ਼ਨ, ਆਨੰਦ-ਉਤਸਵ; ਜਰੰਤੀ

judaism ('ਜੁਡੇਇਇਜ਼ਮ) *n* ਯਹੂਦੀ ਮੱਤ, ਯਹੂਦੀਵਾਦ, ਯਹੂਦੀਅਤ, ਯਹੂਦੀ

judaist ('ਜੁਡੇਇਇਸਟ) *n* ਯਹੂਦੀ

judge (ਜੱਜ) *n v* ਜੱਜ, ਮੁਨਸਫ਼, ਨਿਆਂਅਧਿਕਾਰੀ; ਪਾਰਖੂ, ਪੰਚ, ਨਿਰਣਾਇਕ ਫ਼ੈਸਲਾ ਕਰਨਾ, ਨਿਰਣੈ ਕਰਨਾ; (ਕਿਸੇ ਬਾਰੇ) ਅਨੁਮਾਨ ਲਾਉਣਾ, ਪਰਖ ਕਰਨੀ; ਮੁਕੱਦਮਾ ਸੁਣਨਾ; **~ment, judgment** ਫ਼ੈਸਲਾ, ਨਿਰਣੈ; ਰਾਇ; ਵਿਚਾਰ-ਸ਼ਕਤੀ, ਸੂਝ, ਸਮਝ, ਵਿਵੇਕ; **~ship** ਜੱਜੀ, ਜੱਜ ਦੀ ਪਦਵੀ

judicate ('ਜੁਡ੍ਰਿਕੇਇਟ) *v* ਇਨਸਾਫ਼ ਕਰਨਾ, ਨਿਆਂ

ਕਰਨਾ, ਵਿਵੇਚਨ ਕਰਨਾ, ਮੁਨਸਫ਼ੀ ਕਰਨਾ

judicial (ਜੂ'ਡਿਸ਼ਲ) *a* ਅਦਾਲਤੀ, ਕਚਹਿਰੀ ਬਾਰੇ, ਨਿਆਂ ਸਬੰਧੀ; ਨਿਰਪੱਖ, ਨਿਆਂਪੂਰਨ; ਮੁਨਸਫ਼ ਦਾ, ਜੱਜੀ; ਅਦਾਲਤ ਵੱਲੋਂ ਕੀਤਾ ਗਿਆ

judiciary (ਜੂ'ਡਿਸ਼ਅਰਿ) *n* ਨਿਆਂਪਾਲਕਾ, ਨਿਆਂਵਿਵਸਥਾ; ਨਿਆਂ-ਵਿਭਾਗ; ਅਦਾਲਤੀ ਅਮਲਾ

jug (ਜਅੱਗ) *n v* ਜੱਗ, ਗੰਗਾ ਸਾਗਰ; (ਅਪ) ਕੈਦਖ਼ਾਨਾ; ਚਹਿਕਣਾ, ਚੀਂ ਚੀਂ ਕਰਨਾ, ਚਹਿਚਹਾਉਣਾ

juggle ('ਜਅੱਗਲ) *v n* ਹੱਥ-ਫੇਰੀ ਕਰਨੀ, ਚਲਾਕੀ ਕਰਨੀ; ਧੋਖਾ ਕਰਨਾ, ਛਲ ਕਰਨਾ; ਹੱਥ ਫੇਰੀ, ਚਲਾਕੀ; ਬਾਜ਼ੀਗਰੀ, ਜਾਦੂਗਰੀ, ਮਦਾਰੀ ਦਾ ਖੇਲ; **~r** ਮਦਾਰੀ, ਜਾਦੂਗਰ; ਧੋਖੇਬਾਜ਼

jugglery ('ਜਅੱਗਲਰਿ) *n* ਹੱਥ-ਫੇਰੀ, ਚਲਾਕੀ; ਜਾਦੂਗਰੀ; **~of words** ਸ਼ਬਦ ਚਤਰਤਾ, ਸ਼ਬਦਜਾਲ, ਸ਼ਬਦਾਂ ਦਾ ਜਾਦੂ

juggling ('ਜਅੱਗਲਿਙ) *n* ਹੱਥ-ਫੇਰੀ, ਹੱਥ ਦੀ ਸਫ਼ਾਈ, ਜਾਦੂਗਰੀ; ਧੋਖਾ, ਮੱਕਾਰੀ, ਛਲਾਵਾ

juice (ਜੂਸ) *n* ਰਸ, ਨਚੋੜ, ਸਾਰ

juiciness ('ਜੂਸਿਨਿਸ) *n* ਰਸਿਕਤਾ, ਤਾਤਵਿਕਤਾ, ਰਸਦਾਇਕਤਾ, ਰੋਚਕਤਾ

juicy ('ਜੂਸਿ) *a* ਰਸਦਾਰ, ਰਸਦਾਇਕ; ਰੋਚਕ, ਮਨੋਰੰਜਕ; (ਗੱਲ) ਚੋਂਦੀ ਚੋਂਦੀ

jumbal ('ਜਅੰਬਲ) *n* ਖੰਡ ਦੀ ਟਿੱਕੀ; ਮਿੱਠੀ ਟਿੱਕੀ; ਨਾਨ-ਖਤਾਈ

jump (ਜਅੰਪ) *v n* ਛਾਲ ਮਾਰਨੀ, ਟਪੱਣਾ, ਛੜੱਪਾ ਮਾਰਨਾ, ਕੁੱਦਣਾ, ਭੁੜਕਣਾ, (ਮੁੱਲ) ਅਚਾਨਕ ਵਧ ਜਾਣਾ; ਅਨੁਕੂਲ ਹੋਣਾ; ਝਪਟਾ ਮਾਰਨਾ; ਝੱਟ ਕਥਜ਼ਾ ਕਰ ਲੈਣਾ; ਸਰਸਰੀ ਨਜ਼ਰ ਨਾਲ ਵੇਖਣਾ; ਉਲੰਘਣ; ਅਚਾਨਕ ਕਿਸੇ ਨਿਰਣੈ ਤੇ ਪੁੱਜਣਾ; ਛਾਲ; **~in** ਗੱਡੀ ਵਿਚ ਕਾਹਲੀ ਨਾਲ ਚੜ੍ਹਨਾ; **~upon** ਧਮਕਾਉਣਾ, ਡਾਂਟਣਾ, ਧੌਂਸ ਦੇਣਾ; ਟੁੱਟ ਕੇ ਪੈਣਾ, ਚੜ੍ਹ ਜਾਣਾ; **~ing** ਹੁਭਕੀ, ਟਪੂਸੀ, ਛਾਲ, ਹੰਭਲਾ

junction ('ਜਅੱਙਕਸ਼ਨ) *n* ਦੁਮੇਲ ਸੰਗਮ, ਜੰਕਸ਼ਨ; ਸੰਧੀ ਜੋੜ

juncture ('ਜਅੱਙਕਚਅ*) *n* ਅਵਸਰ, ਮੌਕਾ; ਜੋੜ

jungle ('ਜਅੱਙਗਲ) *n* ਜੰਗਲ; ਵਣ; ਘੜਮਸ

junior ('ਜੂਨਯਅ*) *n a* ਜੂਨੀਅਰ (ਕਰਮਚਾਰੀ), ਛੋਟਾ, ਨਿੱਕਾ, ਨੀਵੀਂ ਸ਼੍ਰੇਣੀ ਜਾਂ ਪਦਵੀ ਦਾ (ਵਿਅਕਤੀ)

junk (ਜਅੱਙਕ) *n v* ਪੁਰਾਣਾ ਮਾਲ, ਕਬਾੜ, ਟੋਟਾ, ਟੁਕੜਾ; ਟੁਕੜੇ ਟੁਕੜੇ ਕਰਨਾ

junto ('ਜਅੰਟਅਉ) *n* ਦਲ, ਟੋਲਾ, ਮੰਡਲੀ (ਰਾਜਨੀਤੀ), ਜੁੰਡੀ, ਜੁੰਡਲੀ

jupiter ('ਜੂਪਿਟਅ*) *n* (ਰੋਮਨ) ਦੇਵਰਾਜ; ਜੂਪੀਟਰ; ਬ੍ਰਿਹਸਪਤੀ ਨਖੱਤਰ, ਗੁਰੂ

jurisdiction ('ਜੁਅਰਿਸ'ਡਿਕਸ਼ਨ) *n* ਅਮਲਦਾਰੀ, ਅਧਿਕਾਰ-ਖੇਤਰ, ਨਿਆਂ-ਅਧਿਕਾਰ, ਨਿਆਂ-ਵਿਵਸਥਾ

jurisprudence ('ਜੁਅਰਿਸ'ਪਰੂਡਅੰਸ) *n* ਨਿਆਂ ਸ਼ਾਸਤਰ ਧਰਮ-ਸ਼ਾਸਤਰ; ਨਿਆਂ-ਪ੍ਰਵੀਣਤਾ, ਕਾਨੂੰਨ-ਦਾਨੀ

jurisprudent ('ਜੁਅਰਿਸ'ਪਰੂਡਅੰਟ) *n a* ਨਿਆਂ-ਸ਼ਾਸਤਰੀ, ਕਾਨੂੰਨ ਦਾ ਮਾਹਰ, ਕਾਨੂੰਨਦਾਨ; **~ial** ਨਿਆਂ-ਸ਼ਾਸਤਰ ਬਾਰੇ

jurist ('ਜੁਅਰਿਸਟ) *n* ਕਾਨੂੰਨਦਾਨ; ਵਕੀਲ, ਐਡਵੋਕੇਟ, ਨਿਆਂ-ਨਿਪੁੰਨ, ਵਿਧਾਨਕਾਰ, ਨਿਆਇਕ, ਵਿਧੀ-ਵਿਦਿਆਰਥੀ

jury ('ਜੁਅਰਿ) *n* ਅਦਾਲਤੀ ਪੰਚਾਇਤ, ਜਿਊਰੀ; **~man** ਪੰਚ, ਨਿਆਂ ਸਭਾ ਦਾ ਮੈਂਬਰ

just (ਜਅੱਸਟ) *a adv* ਠੀਕ, ਵਾਜਬ, ਮੁਨਾਸਬ, ਉਚਿਤ; ਨਿਆਂਪੂਰਨ, ਨਿਆਂਕਾਰੀ, ਅਦਲੀ, ਨਿਰਪੱਖ, ਸੱਚਾ, ਨਿਸ਼ਕਪਟ, ਈਮਾਨਦਾਰ; ਉਸੇ ਵੇਲੇ, ਠੀਕ ਉਦੋਂ, ਹੁਣੇ ਹੁਣੇ ਹੀ; ਜਿਉਂ ਹੀ; ਕੁਝ-ਕੁਝ; ਕੇਵਲ, ਮੁਸ਼ਕਲ ਨਾਲ; ~**now** ਹੁਣੇ, ਤੁਰਤ

justice ('ਜਅੱਸਟਿਸ) *n* ਨਿਆਂ, ਇਨਸਾਫ਼, ਅਦਾਲਤੀ ਕਾਰਵਾਈ; ਨਿਆਂ-ਸੰਗਤੀ, ਨਿਰਪੱਖਤਾ

justifiability, justifiableness ('ਜਅੱਸਟਿ-ਫ਼ਾਇਬਲਅਟਿ' ਅੱਸਟਿਫ਼ਾਇਬਲਨਿਸ) *n* ਨਿਆਂ-ਸਿੱਧੀ, ਨਿਆਂ ਸਮਰਥਨ, ਨਿਆਂਖਮਤਾ, ਨਿਆਂ ਸੰਗਤੀ

justifiable ('ਜਅੱਸਟਿਫ਼ਾਇਬਲ) *a* ਉਚਿਤ, ਨਿਆਂ ਅਨੁਸਾਰ, ਠੀਕ

justification ('ਜਅੱਸਟਿਫ਼ਿ'ਕੇਇਸ਼ਨ) *n* ਉਚਿਤਤਾ, ਸਫ਼ਾਈ, ਸਮਰਥਨ, ਪ੍ਰਮਾਣਕਤਾ

justified ('ਜਅੱਸਟਿਫ਼ਾਇਡ) *a* ਉਚਿਤ, ਯੋਗ

justify ('ਜਅੱਸਟਿਫ਼ਾਇ) *v* ਠੀਕ ਸਿੱਧ ਕਰਨ, ਉਚਿਤ ਠਹਿਰਾਉਣਾ, ਹੱਕ ਵਿਚ ਦਲੀਲਾਂ ਦੇਣੀਆਂ; ਸਚਾਈ ਦਾ ਪ੍ਰਮਾਣ ਦੇਣਾ; ਸਮਰਥਨ ਕਰਨ; ਨਿਆਂ-ਸੰਗਤ ਸਿੱਧ ਕਰਨ

jute (ਜੂਟ) *n* ਪਟਸਨ, ਸਣ, ਸਨੁਕੜਾ

juvenescence ('ਜੂਵ੍ਅਨੈੱਸੰਸ) *n* ਜਵਾਨੀ ਦਾ ਉਭਾਰ, ਚੜ੍ਹਦੀ ਜਵਾਨੀ

juvenescent ('ਜੂਵ੍ਅਨੈੱਸੰਟ) *a* ਚੜ੍ਹਦੀ ਜਵਾਨੀ ਵਾਲਾ, ਮਸਫੁੱਟ (ਗੱਭਰੂ)

juvenile ('ਜੂਵ੍ਅਨਾਇਲ) *a n* ਨੌਜਵਾਨ, ਗਭਰੇਟ ਬਾਲਕ, ਅਲੂਆਂ ਮੁੰਡਾ, ਅੱਲੜ ਬੱਚਾ; ~**ness**, **juvenility** ਅੱਲੂੜ੍ਹਪੁਣਾ; ਬਾਲਪਨ, ਚੜ੍ਹਦੀ ਜਵਾਨੀ

juxtapose ('ਜਅੱਕਸਟਅ'ਪਅਉਜ਼) *v* ਨਾਲ ਨਾਲ ਰੱਖਣਾ, ਕੋਲ ਕੋਲ ਰੱਖਣਾ

juxtaposition ('ਜਅੱਕਸਟਅਪਅ'ਜ਼ਿਸ਼ਨ) *n* ਨਿਕਟਤਾ, ਸਮੀਪਤਾ

K

K, k (ਕੇਇ) *n* ਰੋਮਨ ਵਰਨਮਾਲਾ ਦਾ ਗਿਆਰਵਵਾਂ ਅੱਖਰ

kago ('ਕਾਗਅਉ) *n* ਡੋਲੀ, ਪਾਲਕੀ

kar(r)oo (ਕਅ'ਰੂ) *n* ਪਠਾਰ

keck (ਕੈੱਕ) *v n* ਉਲਟੀ ਕਰਨੀ; ਕੈ ਕਰਨੀ; ਕੈ, ਉਲਟੀ

keen (ਕੀਨ) *a n* (1) ਚਾਹਵਾਨ, ਅਭਿਲਾਖੀ, ਇੱਛੁਕ; (2) ਭਾਵੁਕ, ਤਿੱਖੀ ਬੁੱਧ ਵਾਲਾ; (3) ਸਖ਼ਤ, ਬਹੁਤ ਜ਼ਿਆਦਾ; (4) (ਇੱਛਾ) ਤੀਬਰ, ਭਾਰੀ; ਵਿਰਲਾਪ; ਵੈਣ; **~ness** ਉਤਸੁਕਤਾ, ਸ਼ੋਕ, ਉਤਕੰਠਾ, ਚਿੰਤਾ, ਬੇਚੈਨੀ; ਤੀਖਣਤਾ, ਤੀਬਰਤਾ, ਤੇਜ਼ੀ

keep (ਕੀਪ) *v n* ਰੱਖਣਾ, ਰਹਿਣਾ; ਧਿਆਨ ਰੱਖਣਾ, ਖ਼ਿਆਲ ਰੱਖਣਾ; ਪਾਲਣਾ ਕਰਨੀ, ਜ਼ੁੰਮੇ ਲੈਣਾ, ਹੱਥ ਵਿਚ ਲੈਣਾ; ਚਲਾਉਣਾ; ਹਿਸਾਬ-ਕਿਤਾਬ ਰੱਖਣਾ; ਰਘੇਲ ਰੱਖਣਾ; ਰੋਕਣਾ; ਗੁਪਤ ਰੱਖਣਾ, ਛੁਪਾਉਣਾ; ਡਟੇ ਰਹਿਣਾ; ਰਖੇਲ, ਧਰੇਲ; ਗੁਜ਼ਾਰਾ; **~away** ਨੇੜੇ ਨਾ ਢੁੱਕਣ ਦੇਣਾ; **~back** ਛੁਪਾਉਣਾ, ਗੁਪਤ ਰੱਖਣਾ; ਦੂਰ ਰਹਿਣਾ; **~body & soul together** ਜੀਉਂਦਾ ਰਹਿਣਾ; **~down** ਦਬਾਉਣਾ; **~from** (ਤੋਂ) ਦੂਰ ਰਹਿਣਾ; **~in** ਵੱਸ ਵਿਚ ਰੱਖਣਾ; **~on** ਚਲੰਦਾ ਰੱਖਣਾ; **~track** ਪਿੱਛਾ ਕਰਨਾ, ਪੈੜ ਦਬਣਾ

keg (ਕੈੱਗ) *n* ਪੀਪਾ (ਦਸ ਗੈਲਨ ਤੋਂ ਘੱਟ ਦਾ), ਛੋਟਾ ਢੋਲ

kell (ਕੈੱਲ) *n* ਮੱਕੜੀ ਦਾ ਜਾਲਾ

ken (ਕੈੱਨ) *v n* ਵੇਖ ਕੇ ਪਛਾਣਨਾ; ਬੁੱਝਣਾ, ਸਮਝਣਾ, ਜਾਣ ਲੈਣਾ; ਦ੍ਰਿਸ਼ਟੀ-ਸੀਮਾ, ਸੂਝ, ਗਿਆਨ-ਖੇਤਰ; **~ning** ਨਿਗਾਹ, ਦ੍ਰਿਸ਼ਟੀ; ਜਾਣਕਾਰੀ, ਗਿਆਨ, ਪਛਾਣ

kennel ('ਕੈੱਨਲ) *n* ਕੁੱਤੇਖ਼ਾਨਾ; ਘਟੀਆ ਮਕਾਨ; ਪਰਨਾਲਾ; ਪਾਣੀ ਦੀ ਮੋਰੀ

kernel ('ਕਅ:ਨਲ) *n* ਗਿਰੀ, ਮਗ਼ਜ਼, ਗਿਟਕ; ਸਾਰ, ਮੂਲ, ਤੱਤ; ਕੇਦਰ-ਬਿੰਦੂ, ਅੰਦਰ

kerosene ('ਕੈਰੋਅਸੀਨ) *n* ਮਿੱਟੀ ਦਾ ਤੇਲ

kersey ('ਕਅ:ਜ਼ਿ) *n* ਪਟੂ; ਮੋਟਾ ਉਨੀ ਕੱਪੜਾ

ketchup ('ਕੈੱਟਅਪ) *n* ਟਮਾਟਰਾਂ ਆਦਿ ਦੀ ਚਟਨੀ, ਸਾਸ, ਚਾਟ

kettle ('ਕੈੱਟਲ) *n* ਦੇਗਚੀ, ਪਤੀਲੀ, ਕੇਤਲੀ, ਚਾਹਦਾਨੀ

key (ਕੀ) *n a v* ਕੁੰਜੀ, ਚਾਬੀ; ਟੀਕਾ; ਹੱਲ; ਵਸੀਲਾ, ਰਾਹ, ਸਾਧਨ, ਪੋਪ ਦੇ ਅਧਿਕਾਰ; ਸਮੁੰਦਰੀ ਚੌਕੀ, (ਸੰਗੀ) ਸੁਰ; **~note** ਮੁੱਖ ਸੁਰ, ਮੂਲ ਸੁਰ, ਤਾਨ; ਮੂਲ ਭਾਵ; **~less** ਸਾਧਨਹੀਨ

kibble ('ਕਿਬਲ) *n v* ਡੋਲ, ਬਾਲਟੀ; ਪੀਹਣਾ, ਕੁਚਲਣਾ

kick (ਕਿਕ) *v n* ਲੱਤ ਮਾਰਨੀ, ਠੁੱਡਾ ਮਾਰਨਾ, ਦੁਲੱਤਾ (ਬੰਦੂਕ ਦਾ) ਧੱਕਾ ਮਾਰਨਾ; (ਫੁੱਟਬਾਲ ਨੂੰ) ਕਿੱਕ ਮਾਰਨੀ; ਧੱਕੇ ਮਾਰ ਕੇ ਕੱਢਣਾ, ਠੁੱਡਾ, ਦੁਲੱਤਾ, ਪਰਛੰਡਾ, (ਬੰਦੂਕ ਦਾ) ਧੱਕਾ, (ਫੁੱਟਬਾਲ ਵਿਚ) ਕਿੱਕ; **~back** (ਅਪ) ਵੱਢੀ; **~up** ਉਡਾ ਦੇਣਾ

kickshaw ('ਕਿਕਸ਼ੋ) *n* ਚੰਗਾ-ਚੋਖਾ (ਖਾਣਾ), ਸੁਆਦਲਾ ਖਾਣਾ, ਨਗੂਣੀ ਚੀਜ਼, ਤੁੱਛ ਵਸਤੂ, ਖਿਡੌਣਾ

kid (ਕਿਡ)*n* ਮੇਮਣਾ, ਬੱਕਰੀ ਦਾ ਬੱਚਾ, ਨਿਆਣਾ; **~dy** ਨਿੱਕਾ ਨਿਆਣਾ, ਛੋਟਾ ਬੱਚਾ; **~ling** ਪਠੋਰਾ, ਮੇਮਣਾ, ਬਕਰੋਟਾ

kidnap ('ਕਿਡਨੈਪ) *v* ਕੱਢ ਕੇ ਲੈ ਜਾਣਾ, (ਮਨੁੱਖ ਨੂੰ) ਜ਼ਬਰਦਸਤੀ ਚੁੱਕ ਲੈ ਜਾਣਾ; ਅਪਹਰਣ ਕਰਨਾ, ਅਗਵਾ ਕਰਨਾ; **~per** ਬਾਲ-ਚੋਰ, ਅਪਹਰਣ-ਕਰਤਾ

kidney ('ਕਿਡਨਿ) *n* ਗੁਰਦਾ; ਸੁਭਾਅ, ਤਬੀਅਤ; **~bean** ਲੋਬੀਆ

kill (ਕਿਲ) *v* ਮਾਰ ਸੁੱਟਣਾ, ਮਾਰ ਦੇਣਾ, ਕਤਲ ਕਰਨਾ; ਸ਼ਿਕਾਰ ਕਰਨਾ, ਝਟਕਾਉਣਾ, ਹਲਾਲ ਕਰਨਾ; **~er** ਹਤਿਆਰਾ, ਖ਼ੂਨੀ, ਕਾਤਲ, ਘਾਤਕ

kiln ('ਕਿਲਨ) *n* ਭੱਠਾ, ਆਵਾ

kilogram, kilogramme ('ਕਿਲਅ(ਉ)ਗਰੈਮ) *n* ਕਿਲੋਗਰਾਮ, ਇਕ ਹਜ਼ਾਰ ਗਰਾਮ

kilometre ('ਕਿਲਅਮੀਟਅ*) *n* ਕਿਲੋਮੀਟਰ, ਇਕ ਹਜ਼ਾਰ ਮੀਟਰ

kin (ਕਿਨ) *n a* ਸਾਕ-ਸਬੰਧੀ, ਗੋਤ-ਭਾਈ, ਸਮਜਾਤੀ; ਇਕੋ ਜਿਹੇ ਸੁਭਾਅ ਵਾਲੇ; **~sman** ਰਿਸ਼ਤੇਦਾਰ, ਗੋਤੀ, ਨਿਕਟ ਸਬੰਧੀ, ਸਗੋਤਰ ਨਾਤੇਦਾਰ; **~ship** ਖ਼ੂਨ ਦਾ ਰਿਸ਼ਤਾ, ਸਾਕ, ਸਾਕਾਦਾਰੀ, ਰਿਸ਼ਤੇਦਾਰੀ

kind (ਕਾਈਂਡ) *n a* ਕਿਸਮ, ਪ੍ਰਕਾਰ, ਵੰਨਗੀ, ਭਾਂਤ; ਨਸਲ, ਕਿਰਪਾਲੂ, ਦਿਆਲੂ; ਮਿਹਰਬਾਨ, ਰਹਿਮਦਿਲ; ਪਿਆਰਾ, ਪਰੇਮੀ; ਸ਼ੀਲਵਾਨ; **~hearted** ਕੋਮਲ-ਚਿੱਤ, ਨਰਮ ਦਿਲ; **~liness** ਉਦਾਰਤਾ, ਕਿਰਪਾਲਤਾ, ਦਇਆਲਤਾ, ਰਹਿਮਦਿਲੀ, ਕੋਮਲਚਿੱਤਤਾ; **~ness** ਕਿਰਪਾਲਤਾ, ਦਇਆਲਤਾ, ਮਿਹਰਬਾਨੀ, ਮਿਹਰ, ਦਇਆ, ਹਮਦਰਦੀ

kindergarten ('ਕਿੰਡਅ'ਗਾਟਨ) *n* ਬਾਲਵਾੜੀ, ਕਿੰਡਰਗਾਰਟਨ

kindle ('ਕਿੰਡਲ) *v* ਬਾਲਣਾ, ਮਘਾਉਣਾ; ਪ੍ਰਜ੍ਵਲਤ ਕਰਨਾ, ਚਮਕਾਉਣਾ; ਉਤਸ਼ਾਹਤ ਕਰਨਾ, ਉਤੇਜਤ ਕਰਨਾ, ਭਖਾਉਣਾ, ਭੜਕ ਉੱਠਣਾ, ਬਲ ਉੱਠਣਾ

kinematic ('ਕਿਨਿ'ਮੈਟਿਕ) *a* ਗਤੀ-ਆਤਮਕ, ਗਤੀ ਸਬੰਧੀ; **~s** ਗਤੀ-ਵਿਗਿਆਨ, ਚਾਲ-ਵਿਦਿਆ

kinetic (ਕਿ'ਨੈਟਿਕ) *a* ਗਤੀਆਤਮਕ

king (ਕਿਙ) *n v* ਬਾਦਸ਼ਾਹ, ਭੂਪ, ਨਰੇਸ਼, ਰਾਜਾ; **~fisher** ਬਿਰ੍ਹੀ ਜਾਂ ਬਹਿਰੀ, ਸ਼ਿਕਾਰੀ ਪੰਛੀ; **~wood** ਸਾਗਵਾਨ ਦੀ ਲੱਕੜ; **~dom** ਬਾਦਸ਼ਾਹੀ, ਬਾਦਸ਼ਾਹਤ, ਸਲਤਨਤ, ਰਾਜ; ਰਾਜਧਾਨੀ; ਰੱਬੀ; **~hood** ਬਾਦਸ਼ਾਹੀ, ਰਾਜ-ਪਦ, ਰਾਜ; **~let, ~ling** ਰਜਵਾੜਾ **~ship** ਬਾਦਸ਼ਾਹੀ, ਰਾਜ; ਰਾਜ-ਪਦ, ਰਾਜ-ਅਧਿਕਾਰ

kiosk ('ਕੀਔਸਕ) *n* ਖੁੱਲ੍ਹਾ ਤੰਬੂ, ਛੋਟਾ ਸ਼ਾਮਿਆਨਾ; ਖੋਖਾ

kip (ਕਿਪ) *n* (1) ਛੋਟੇ ਪਸ਼ੂ ਦੀ ਖਲੜੀ, ਮੇਮਣੇ ਦੀ ਖੱਲ, ਨਰਮ ਚਮੜਾ; (2) ਟਿਕਾਣਾ, ਆਸਰਾ

kiss (ਕਿਸ) *n v* ਚੁੰਮਣ, ਚੁੰਮੀ, ਬੁੱਘੀ; ਚੁੰਮਣਾ, ਚੁੰਮੀ ਲੈਣੀ; ਪਿਆਰ ਕਰਨਾ; **~curl** ਜ਼ੁਲਫ; **~ing** ਚੁੰਮਣ, ਚੁੰਮੀ, ਚੁੰਮਾ-ਚੱਟੀ

kit (ਕਿਟ) *n v* (1) ਵਸਤ-ਵਲੇਵਾ, ਸਾਜ਼-ਸਾਮਾਨ; ਫ਼ੌਜੀਆਂ ਦੇ ਹਥਿਆਰਾ ਦੀ ਕਿੱਟ; ਬਿਸਤਰਾ, ਕਾਰੀਗਰ ਦੇ ਸੰਦ; ਸਫ਼ਰੀ ਸਾਮਾਨ; (2) ਬਲੂੰਗੜਾ ਸਜਣਾ, ਸਜਾਉਣਾ; ਤਿਆਰੀ ਕਰਨੀ; **~bag** ਸਿਪਾਹੀ ਦਾ ਜਾਂ ਯਾਤਰੀ ਦਾ ਸਾਮਾਨ ਵਾਲਾ ਝੋਲਾ

kit-cat ('ਕਿਟਕੈਟ) *n* ਗੁੱਲੀ-ਡੰਡਾ

kitchen ('ਕਿਚਨ) *n* ਰਸੋਈ, ਲੰਗਰ; **~garden** ਘਰੋਗੀ ਬਗ਼ੀਚਾ; **~stuff** ਰਸੋਈ ਦਾ ਸਾਮਾਨ,

ਰਸਦ-ਪਾਣੀ

kite (ਕਾਇਟ) *n v* (1) ਇੱਲ੍ਹ; (2) ਲੋਭੀ ਮਨੁੱਖ;
(3) ਪਤੰਗ, ਗੁੱਡੀ; ਹਵਾਈ ਜਹਾਜ਼; **~flying**
ਪਤੰਗਬਾਜ਼ੀ; ਫੁਰਲੀ

kith (ਕਿਥ) *n* ਸੱਕੇ-ਸਬੰਧੀ, ਸੱਜਣ-ਮਿੱਤਰ,
ਰਿਸ਼ਤੇਦਾਰ, ਭਾਈਬੰਦੀ

kitten ('ਕਿਟਨ) *n v* ਬਲੂੰਗੜਾ, ਬਲੂੰਗਾ; ਚੰਚਲ
ਕੁੜੀ, ਨਖਰੇਬਾਜ਼ ਕੁੜੀ;

klick (ਕ'ਲਿਕ) *v* ਟਿਕ-ਟਿਕ ਕਰਨਾ

knag (ਨੈਗ) *n* ਲੱਕੜੀ ਦੀ ਗੰਢ; ਟਾਹਣੀ ਦਾ ਮੁੱਢ

knave (ਨੇਇਵ) *n* ਲੁੱਚਾ, ਬਦਮਾਸ਼, ਲਫੰਗਾ, ਠੱਗ,
ਬੇਇਮਾਨ; **~ry, knavishness** ਲੁੱਚਪੁਣਾ,
ਬਦਮਾਸ਼ੀ

knavish ('ਨੇਇਵ਼ਿਸ਼) *a* ਬਦਮਾਸ਼, ਲੁੱਚਾ; ਠੱਗ,
ਧੋਖੇਬਾਜ਼, ਫ਼ਰੇਬੀ

knee (ਨੀ) *n v* ਗੋਡਾ; ਗੋਡਾ ਛੁਹਾਉਣਾ

knickers ('ਨਿਕਅਜ਼) *n pl knickerbocker*
ਦਾ ਛੋਟਾ ਰੂਪ, ਨਿਕਰ; ਤੀਵੀਆਂ ਦਾ ਕੱਛਾ

knife (ਨਾਇਫ਼) *n v* ਚਾਕੂ, ਕਰਦ, ਛੁਰੀ; ਚਾਕੂ
ਮਾਰਨਾ, ਛੁਰਾ ਮਾਰਨਾ; ਛੁਰੀ ਨਾਲ ਵੱਢਣਾ;
~grinder ਸਾਣ, ਪੱਥਰੀ ਜਿਸ ਉੱਤੇ ਚਾਕੂ
ਛੁਰੀਆਂ ਤਿੱਖੀਆਂ ਕਰਦੇ ਹਨ; **war to the~**
ਘੋਰ ਜੁਧ, ਘਮਸਾਨ ਲੜਾਈ

knight (ਨਾਇਟ) *n v* ਨਾਇਕ, ਹਥਿਆਰਬੰਦ
ਸੂਰਮਾ, ਬਹਾਦਰ ਸਿਪਾਹੀ, ਘੋੜ-ਸਿਪਾਹੀ; ਫ਼ੌਜੀ
ਸਰਦਾਰ; ਨਾਈਟ; ਕੌਮੀ ਸੇਵਾ ਲਈ ਦਿੱਤਾ
ਗਿਆ ਸਨਮਾਨ ਵਾਲਾ ਪਦ; ਨਾਈਟ ਜਾਂ
ਸਰਦਾਰ ਬਣਾਉਣਾ, ਨਾਈਟ ਬਾਪਣਾ; **~age**
ਸਾਮੰਤ ਵਰਗ, ਨਾਈਟਾਂ ਦੀ ਸੂਚੀ, ਸ਼ਾਹੀ
ਸਰਦਾਰਾਂ ਦਾ ਵੇਰਵਾ; **~like, ~ly** ਬੀਰਤਾ
ਪੂਰਨ, ਸਾਮੰਤ ਵਰਗ ਦਾ; **~liness**

ਸਾਮੰਤਸ਼ਾਹੀ, ਸਰਦਾਰੀ; ਸੂਰਬੀਰਤਾ

knit (ਨਿਟ) *v* ਉਣਨਾ, ਬੁਣਨਾ; **~wear** ਬੁਣੇ
ਕੱਪੜੇ; **~ting** ਬੁਣਤੀ, ਬੁਣਾਈ; ਜੋੜ ਮੇਲ

knob (ਨੌਬ) *n* ਲਾਟੂ, ਮੁੰਨਾ, ਡੂਡਨਾ; ਦਸਤਾ, ਹੱਥੀ;
ਗੁੜ ਦੀ ਰੋੜੀ

knock (ਨੌਕ) *v* ਖੜਕਾਉਣਾ; ਖੜਾਕ ਕਰਨਾ,
ਦਸਤਕ ਦੇਣੀ, ਕੁੰਡੀ ਖੜਕਾਉਣੀ, ਠੱਕ-ਠੱਕ
ਕਰਨਾ; ਸੱਟ ਮਾਰਨੀ, ਹਥੌੜੇ ਆਦਿ ਨਾਲ
ਠੋਕਣਾ; ਹੈਰਾਨ ਕਰ ਦੇਣਾ; **~down** ਕਰਾਰੀ
(ਸੱਟ), ਚਿੱਤ ਹੋਣ ਦਾ ਭਾਵ; ਨਿਲਾਮੀ ਵਿਚ
ਰਾਖਵੀਂ ਕੀਮਤ; **~about** ਅਵਾਰਾ ਫਿਰਨਾ;
~off ਕੰਮ ਛੱਡ ਬੈਠਣਾ; **~out** ਪਛਾੜਨਾ; **~ing**
ਦਰਵਾਜ਼ੇ ਤੇ ਹੋਈ ਠੱਕ-ਠੱਕ; ਧੱਕਾ ਦੇਣ ਵਾਲਾ,
ਪਛਾੜਨ ਵਾਲਾ

knot (ਨੌਟ) *n v* ਗੰਢ; (ਧਾਗੇ ਦੀ) ਹਰੜ, ਹਰੀੜ;
ਜੁੜਾ, ਰੁੰਡਾ; ਘੁੰਡੀ, ਮਰੋੜੀ; ਸਮੁੰਦਰੀ ਮੀਲ
(6080 ਫੁਟ); ਝਮੇਲਾ, ਕਠਨਾਈ, ਔਕੜ; ਗੰਢ
ਦੇਣੀ, ਹਰੜ ਪਾਉਣੀ, ਜੁੜਾ ਕਰਨਾ, ਘੁੰਡੀ
ਪਾਉਣੀ, ਮਰੋੜੀ ਦੇਣੀ; **~ted** ਗੰਢਦਾਰ, ਗੁੰਝ,
ਵਿਖਮ, ਪੇਚਕਾਰ, ਪੇਚੀਦਾ; **~tiness** ਜਟਲਤਾ,
ਗੁੰਝਲਪੁਰਨਤਾ; **~ty** ਗੁੰਝਲਦਾਰ, ਔਖਾ, ਟੇਢਾ
ਗੰਢਦਾਰ; ਗੰਢ ਵਾਲਾ

know (ਨਅਉ) *v* ਜਾਣਨਾ, ਪਛਾਣਨਾ, ਸਮਝਣਾ,
ਵਾਕਫੀਅਤ ਹੋਣੀ, ਜਾਣੂ ਹੋਣਾ, ਗਿਆਨ ਹੋਣਾ;
~ing ਵਾਕਫ, ਜਾਣਕਾਰ, ਸਿਆਨਾ, ਸੁਝਵਾਨ;
ਚੁਸਤ; **~ingly** ਜਾਣ-ਬੁੱਝ ਕੇ ਵਿਸ਼ੇਸ਼ ਇਰਾਦੇ
ਨਾਲ; **~ingness** ਚੌਕਸੀ, ਚਤਰਾਈ,
ਜਾਣਕਾਰੀ, ਸਮਝਦਾਰੀ, ਸਿਆਣਪ, ਹੁਸ਼ਿਆਰੀ;
~n ਮਸ਼ਹੂਰ, ਪ੍ਰਸਿੱਧ, ਉੱਘਾ; ਜਾਣਿਆ,
ਪਛਾਣਿਆ; ਮਾਲੂਮ

knowledge ('ਨੌਲਿਜ) *n* ਗਿਆਨ, ਸੂਝ, ਸੋਝੀ,

ਵਿੱਦਿਆ, ਜਾਣਕਾਰੀ, ਵਾਕਫ਼ੀ; ਪਛਾਣ, ਪਰਿਚਯ; ਆਮ ਸੂਝ-ਬੂਝ, ਅਨੁਭਵ; ਸਮਾਚਾਰ; *a little ~ is dangerous thing* ਨੀਮ ਹਕੀਮ ਖ਼ਤਰਾ ਜਾਨ; **~able** ਜਾਣਕਾਰ, ਸੂਝਵਾਨ, ਸੋਝੀ ਵਾਲਾ; ਬੁੱਧੀਮਾਨ; ਸਚੇਤ, ਚੇਤਨ

kodak ('ਕਅਉਡੈਕ) *n v* 'ਕੋਦਕ' ਨਾਮ ਦਾ ਕੈਮਰਾ; ਕੋਦਕ ਕੈਮਰੇ ਨਾਲ ਫੋਟੋ ਖਿੱਚਣੀ; ਝਟਪਟ ਫੜਨਾ, ਗ੍ਰਹਿਣ ਕਰਨਾ; ਸਪਸ਼ਟ ਵਰਣਨ ਕਰਨਾ

kulak ('ਕੂਲੇਕ) *n* ਧਨੀ ਜਾਂ ਖ਼ੁਸ਼ਹਾਲ ਕਿਸਾਨ

kyphotic (ਕਾਇ'ਫ਼ੌਟਿਕ) *a* ਕੁੱਬਾ, ਕੁੱਬ

L

L, l (ਐੱਲ) *n* ਰੋਮਨ ਵਰਨਮਾਲਾ ਦਾ ਬਾਰ੍ਹਵਾਂ ਅੱਖਰ; (ਰੋਮਨ) ਗਿਣਤੀ ਵਿਚ 50 ਦਾ ਅੰਕ

labarum (ਲੈਬਅਰਅਮ) *n* ਝੰਡਾ, ਨਿਸ਼ਾਨ

label (ਲੇਇਬਲ) *n v* ਲੇਬਲ, ਚਿਟ, ਚੇਪੀ, ਫੱਟੀ; ਲੇਬਲ ਚਿਪਕਾਉਣਾ, ਚੇਪੀ ਲਗਾਉਣੀ; ਨਾਂ ਦੇਣਾ; ~**led** ਅੰਕਤ, ਚਿੰਨ੍ਹਤ, ਲੇਬਲ ਲੱਗਾ

laboratory (ਲਾਅੱਬੋਰਅਟ(ਅ)ਰਿ) *n* ਪ੍ਰਯੋਗਸ਼ਾਲਾ

laborious (ਲਅਾੱਬੋਰਿਅਸ) *a* ਮਿਹਨਤੀ; ਮੁਸ਼ਕਲ, ਕਠਨ; (ਸ਼ੈਲੀ) ਉਰਚ ਭਰੀ; ~**ness** ਮਿਹਨਤ, ਮੁਸ਼ਕਲ ਭਰਪੂਰਤਾ, ਕਠਨਤਾ

labour (ਲੇਇਬਅ*) *n v* (1) ਮਿਹਨਤ; ਮਜ਼ਦੂਰੀ, ਕਿਰਤ; ਮਜ਼ਦੂਰ , ਕੁਲੀ; ਮਜ਼ਦੂਰ-ਪੇਸ਼ਾ ਜਮਾਤ, (2) ਪ੍ਰਸੂਤ ਪੀੜਾਂ, ਮੁਸ਼ਕਲ ਕੰਮ; ਕਸ਼ਟ, ਕਲੇਸ਼; ਮਿਹਨਤ ਕਰਨਾ; ਮਜ਼ਦੂਰੀ ਕਰਨਾ; ਕਸ਼ਟ ਸਹਿਣਾ; ~**of love** ਨਿਸ਼ਕਾਮ ਸੇਵਾ ਦਾ ਕੰਮ; forced~ ਵਗਾਰ, ~**er** ਮਜ਼ੂਰ, ਕਿਰਤੀ, ਮਜ਼ਦੂਰ, ਕਾਮਾ, ਕੁਲੀ, ਸ਼ਰੰਮਕ; ~**ing** ਮਜ਼ਦੂਰ

labrum (ਲੇਇਬਰਅਮ) *n* ਬੁੱਲ੍ਹ, ਹੋਂਠ

labyrinth (ਲੈਬਅਰਿੰਥ) *n* ਭੁੱਲ-ਭੁਲੱਈਆ, ਚੱਕਰ, ਗੋਰਖਪੰਦਾ, ਪੇਚੀਦਗੀ, ਉਲਝਿਆ, ਮਾਮਲਾ, ਉਲਝਣ

lac, lakh (ਲੈਕ) *n* ਲੱਖ

lace (ਲੇਇਸ) *n v* ਫੀਤਾ, ਲੇਸ; ਝਾਲਰ, ਕਿੰਗਰੀ; ਕਿਨਾਰੀ; ਫੀਤਾ ਜਾਂ ਕਿਨਾਰੀ ਲਾਉਣੀ; ਤਸਮੇ ਨਾਲ ਕੱਸਣਾ (ਬੂਟ ਆਦਿ ਨੂੰ); ਕਮਰ ਨੂੰ ਕੱਸ ਕੇ ਬੰਨ੍ਹਣਾ

laches (ਲੇਇਚਿਜ਼) *n* ਹੁਕਮ ਅਦੂਲੀ, ਗ਼ਫ਼ਲਤ;

ਲਾਪਰਵਾਹੀ, ਢਿੱਲ

lack (ਲੈਕ) *n v* ਅਣਹੋਂਦ; ਘਾਟਾ, ਕਮੀ, ਬੁੜ, ਅਭਾਵ, ਤਰੁਟੀ; ਮੁਥਾਜੀ; ਘਾਟਾ ਹੋਣਾ, ਬੁੜ ਹੋਣੀ; ਮੁਥਾਜੀ ਹੋਣੀ; ~**ing** ਰਹਿਤ, ਹੀਣ, ਘਾਟ ਵਾਲਾ, ਕਮੀ ਵਾਲਾ

lackadaisical (ਲੈਕਅਾੱਡੇਇਜ਼ਿਕਲ) *a* ਨਿਸਤੇਜ, ਬੇਜਾਨ; ਨਿਰਉਤਸ਼ਾਹ

lackey, lacquey (ਲੈਕਿ) *n v* ਝੋਲੀ ਚੁੱਕ, ਜੁੱਤੀ-ਚੰਟ, ਪਿਛਲੱਗਾ; ਝੋਲੀ-ਚੁੱਕਣੀ, ਚਾਪਲੂਸੀ ਕਰਨੀ

lactation (ਲੈਕਟੇਇਸ਼ਨ) *n* ਦੁੱਧ ਪਿਲਾਉਣਾ, ਦੁੱਧ ਦੇਣਾ

lactic (ਲੈਕਟਿਕ) *a* ਦੁੱਧ ਦਾ, ਦੁਧੀਆ

lacuna (ਲਅਾੱਕਯੂਨਅ) *n* (ਪੁਰਾਤਨ ਲਿਖਤਾਂ ਵਿਚ) ਪਾਠ-ਲੋਪ; ਵਿਰਲ, ਖ਼ਲਾਅ, ਛੋਟ, ਛਿਦਰ

lacy (ਲੇਇਸਿ) *a* ਝਾਲਰਦਾਰ, ਲੇਸਦਾਰ, ਫੀਤੇਦਾਰ

lad (ਲੈਡ) *n* ਬਾਲਕ, ਲੜਕਾ, ਨੱਢਾ, ਛੋਕਰਾ, ਬਾਲ; ਜਟਾ, ਸ਼ਖ਼ਸ

ladder (ਲੈਡਅ*) *n v* ਪੌੜੀ; ਜ਼ੀਨਾ, ਵਸੀਲਾ (ਤਰੱਕੀ ਦਾ); ਚੜ੍ਹਤ ਹੋਣੀ

laddie (ਲੈਡਿ) *n* ਬੱਚੂ

lade (ਲੇਇਡ) *v* ਲੱਦਣਾ, ਮਾਲ ਭਰਨਾ; ~**n** ਲੱਦਿਆ ਹੋਇਆ, ਲਾਦੂ

lading (ਲੇਇਡਿਙ) *n* ਸਾਮਾਨ, ਮਾਲ-ਅਸਬਾਬ, ਬੋਝ, ਮਾਲ ਲੱਦ

ladle (ਲੇਇਡਲ) *n v* ਕੜਛੀ, ਵੱਡਾ ਚਮਚਾ, ਕੜਛੀ ਨਾਲ ਕੱਢਣਾ

lady (ਲੇਇਡਿ) *n* ਇਸਤਰੀ, ਮਹਿਲਾ; ਨਾਰੀ,

ਬੀਬੀ; ਘੇਗਮ; ਘਰ-ਵਾਲੀ, ਵਹੁਟੀ; ~finger ਲਿੰਡੀ

lag (ਲੈਗ) v n (1) ਮੱਠੀ ਚਾਲ ਚੱਲਣਾ, ਹੌਲੀ ਹੌਲੀ ਚੱਲਣਾ, ਪਿੱਛੇ ਰਹਿ ਜਾਣਾ, ਪਛੜਨਾ, ਢਿੱਲ, ਪੱਛੜੇਵਾਂ; (2) ਪਕੜਨਾ; ਗਰਿਫ਼ਤਾਰ ਕਰਨਾ; ਮੁਜਰਮ, ਦੋਸ਼ੀ; ~gard ਢਿੱਲਾ, ਮੱਠਾ, ਸੁਸਤ, ਢਿੱਲੜ; ~ging ਮੰਦਗਾਮੀ, ਪਛੜਿਆ

lake (ਲੇਇਕ) n ਝੀਲ, ਸਰੋਵਰ, ਸਰ, ਵੱਡਾ ਤਲਾਅ

laliation (ਲੈ'ਲੇਇਸ਼ਨ) n ਤੋਤਲਾ ਉਚਾਰਨ, ਥਥਲਾ ਉਚਾਰਨ

lama ('ਲਾਮਾ) n ਤਿੱਬਤੀ ਬੋਧੀ ਗੁਰੂ, ਲਾਮਾ

lamb (ਲੈਮ) n v ਮੇਮਣਾ; ਲੇਲਾ, ਭਡੂਰ, ਦੁੰਭਾ, ਗਊ ਆਦਮੀ

lambaste (ਲੈਮ'ਬੇਇਸਟ) v ਕਰੜੀ ਆਲੋਚਨਾ ਕਰਨੀ, ਝੰਬ ਲਾਹੁਣੀ

lame (ਲੇਇਮ) a v ਲੰਙਾ; ਅਸੰਤੋਸ਼ਜਨਕ; ਭੌਰਤਸੱਲੀ-ਬਖ਼ਸ਼; (ਛੰਦ) ਗਤੀਹੀਨ, ਰਵਾਨੀ ਤੋਂ ਬਿਨਾ; ਲੰਙਾ ਕਰ ਦੇਣਾ; ਨਕਾਰਾ ਕਰ ਦੇਣਾ, ਵਿਗਾੜ ਦੇਣਾ; ~ness ਲੰਗੜਾਹਟ, ਲੰਗੜਾਪਣ; ਅਸੰਤੁਸ਼ਟਤਾ

lament (ਲਾ'ਮੈਂਟ) n v ਵਿਰਲਾਪ, ਰੁਦਨ, ਰੋਣ-ਧੋਣ, ਕੀਰਨਾ, ਵੈਣ, ਰੋਣਾ, ਰੋਣਾ-ਧੋਣਾ, ਕੁਰਲਾਉਣਾ, ਕੀਰਨੇ ਪਾਉਣੇ, ਰੁਦਨ ਕਰਨਾ; ~able ਵਿਰਲਾਪ-ਯੋਗ; ~ation ਵਿਰਲਾਪ, ਕੀਰਨੇ, ਹਾਹਾਕਾਰ, ਵੈਣ, ਮਾਤਮ, ਰੋਣ-ਪਿੱਟਣ, ਕੁਰਲਾਹਟ, ਅਲਾਹੁਣੀ

lamp (ਲੈਂਪ) n ਲੈਂਪ, ਦੀਵਾ, ਦੀਪਕ, ਦੀਪ, ਪ੍ਰਕਾਸ਼, ਜੋਤੀ

lance (ਲਾਂਸ) n v ਨੇਜ਼ਾ, ਬਰਛਾ, ਭਾਲਾ; ਨੇਜ਼ੇਬਾਜ਼ ਸਿਪਾਹੀ; ਨੇਜ਼ਾ ਮਾਰਨਾ, ਚੀਰਨਾ

land (ਲੈਂਡ) n v ਧਰਤੀ, ਜ਼ਮੀਨ, ਭੋਂ, ਭੂਮੀ, ਖ਼ੁਸ਼ਕੀ, ਥਲ; ਦੇਸ਼, ਜਾਗੀਰ; ਇਲਾਕਾ; ਜਹਾਜ਼ ਆਦਿ ਤੋਂ ਉਤਰਨਾ ਜਾਂ ਉਤਾਰਨਾ; ~holder ਜ਼ਿਮੀਂਦਾਰ, ਪੱਟੇਦਾਰ; ~lady ਮਾਲਕਣ; ~slide ਢਾਰ, ਚਟਾਨਾਂ ਦਾ ਖਿਸਕਣ; ~ing ਧਰਤੀ ਉੱਤੇ ਉਤਾਰਾ (ਹਵਾਈ ਜਹਾਜ਼); ~less ਭੂਮੀਹੀਨ, ਬੇਜ਼ਮੀਨ

lane (ਲੇਇਨ) n ਗਲੀ, ਕੂਚਾ, ਤੰਗ ਰਸਤਾ

language ('ਲੈਂਙਗਵੇਜ) n ਜ਼ਬਾਨ, ਭਾਸ਼ਾ, ਬੋਲੀ, ਭਾਖਾ; national~ ਰਾਸ਼ਟਰ ਭਾਸ਼ਾ; regional~ ਪ੍ਰਾਦੇਸ਼ਕ ਭਾਸ਼ਾ

languish ('ਲੈਂਙਗਵਿਸ਼) v ਨਿਢਾਲ ਹੋਣਾ, ਮੁਰਝਾਉਣਾ, ਜ਼ੋਰ ਘਟਣਾ

languor ('ਲੈਂਙਗਾ*) n ਕਮਜ਼ੋਰੀ; ਨਿਰਬਲਤਾ, ਸੁਸਤੀ, ਢਿੱਲਪਣ, ਥਕੇਵਾਂ; ਬੇਦਿਲੀ

lantern ('ਲੈਨਟਅ:ਨ) n ਲਾਲਟੈਨ, ਬੱਤੀ, ਲੈਂਪ, ਫ਼ਾਨੂਸ

lap (ਲੈਪ) v n ਝੋਲੀ ਪਾਉਣਾ; ਪਲਟਣਾ, ਗੋਦੀ ਵਿਚ ਲੈਣਾ; ਝੋਲੀ, ਪੱਲਾ, ਗੋਦੀ; (ਕੱਪੜੇ ਦਾ) ਪੱਲੂ; ਦਾਮਨ

lapse (ਲੈਪਸ) n v ਉਕਾਈ ਭੁੱਲ, ਅਣਗਹਿਲੀ; ਉੱਤਰਨਾ, ਘਟਣਾ, ਸਮੇਂ ਦਾ ਲੰਘਣਾ; ~d ਪਤਿਤ, ਭ੍ਰਿਸ਼ਟ; ਸਮਾਪਤ, ਬੀਤਿਆ, ਪੁੰਗਿਆ

large (ਲਾ*ਜ) a adv ਵੱਡਾ, ਖੁੱਲ੍ਹਾ; ਮੋਕਲਾ; ਵਿਸਤਾਰ ਪੂਰਵਕ, ਵਿਆਪਕ; at~ ਸੁਤੰਤਰ, ਆਜ਼ਾਦ; (ਬਿਆਨ ਆਦਿ) ਵੇਰਵੇ ਸਹਿਤ; ~ly ਆਮ ਕਰਕੇ, ਜ਼ਿਆਦਾਤਰ; ~ness ਵਿਸਤਾਰ, ਬਹੁਲਤਾ, ਬਹੁਤਤ, ਵਿਆਪਕਤਾ

lark (ਲਾ:ਕ) n v (1) ਭੂਰੇ ਮਿੱਟਿਆਲੇ ਰੰਗ ਦ ਪੰਛੀਆਂ ਦੀਆਂ ਕਿਸਮਾਂ ਜਿਨ੍ਹਾਂ ਦੇ ਪੈਰਾਂ ਦੀਆਂ ਪਿਛਲੀਆਂ ਉਂਗਲਾਂ ਵੱਡੀਆਂ ਹੁੰਦੀਆਂ ਹਨ; (2)

ਹਾਸਾ, ਦਿਲਲਗੀ, ਚੁਹਲ; ਮਜ਼ੇ ਦੀ ਗੱਲ,
ਦਿਲਚਸਪ ਘਟਨਾ, ਚੁਹਲ ਕਰਨੇ, ਖੇਡਣਾ-ਕੁੱਦਣਾ

larynx ('ਲੈਰਿੰਕਸ) *n* ਗਲ, ਘੰਡੀ

lash (ਲੈਸ਼) *v n* ਚਾਬਕ ਜਾਂ ਕੋਰੜੇ ਮਾਰਨੇ; ਟੁੱਟ
ਪੈਣਾ, ਝਪਟਣਾ; ਜ਼ੋਰ ਨਾਲ ਹਮਲਾ ਕਰਨਾ;
ਉਬਲ ਪੈਣਾ; ~out ਉਦਮ ਮਚਾਉਣਾ; ~ing
ਕੋਰੜੇ ਦੀ ਮਾਰ; ਬੰਧਨ, ਰੱਸੀਆਂ

lass, lassie (ਲੈਸ, 'ਲੈਸਿ) *n* ਮੁਟਿਆਰ, ਜਵਾਨ
ਕੁੜੀ; ਪਰੇਮਕਾ, ਪਰੀਤਮਾ

lassitude ('ਲੈਸਿਟਯੂਡ) *n* ਸੁਸਤੀ, ਥਕਾਵਟ,
ਸ਼ਕਤੀਹੀਣਤਾ, ਥਕੇਵਾਂ, ਬੇਦਿਲੀ

last (ਲਾਸਟ) *a adv n* ਅੰਤਮ, ਆਖ਼ਰੀ,
ਅਖੀਰਲਾ, ਛੇਕੜਲਾ, ਘਟਿਆ, ਸਭ ਤੋਂ ਨੀਵੇਂ
ਦਰਜੇ ਦਾ; ਅਢੁੱਕਵਾਂ; ਉੱਕਾ; ਸਭ ਤੋਂ ਪਿੱਛੇ,
ਅਖੀਰ ਵਿਚ; ਆਖ਼ਰੀ ਵਾਰ, ਆਖ਼ਰ, ਛੇਕੜ;
at~ ਅਖੀਰ, ਆਖ਼ਰਕਾਰ; ~ly ਅੰਤ ਵਿਚ, ਅੰਤ
ਨੂੰ, ਅੰਤ ਤੇ, ਅਖੀਰ ਵਿਚ

late (ਲੇਇਟ) *a adv* ਪਛੜਿਆ, ਪਿਛੇਤਾ,
ਚਿਰਾਕਾ, ਬੇਵਕਤ, ਕਵੇਲੜਾ, ਕਦੀਮ; ਸੁਰਗੀ,
ਮਰਹੂਮ; ਦੇਰ ਕਰਕੇ, ਵਕਤ ਤੋਂ ਪਿੱਛੇ; ਬਹੁਤ
ਦਿਨਾਂ ਪਿੱਛੋਂ, ਆਖ਼ਰੀ ਜ਼ਮਾਨੇ ਵਿਚ; ਬਹੁਤ ਦੇਰੀ
ਨਾਲ; of~ years ਕੁਝ ਸਾਲਾਂ ਤੋਂ; ~ly ਪਿੱਛੋਂ
ਜਿਹੇ, ਹੁਣੇ ਹੁਣੇ, ਕੁਝ ਦਿਨ ਪਹਿਲਾਂ; ~st
ਨਵੀਨ, ਅਜੋਕਾ, ਆਧੁਨਿਕਤਮ; ਅੰਤਮ

latent ('ਲੇਇਟਅੰਟ) *a* ਛੁਪਿਆ, ਗੁਪਤ, ਨਿਹਿਤ;
ਦਬਿਆ, ਭੀਤਰੀ

latex ('ਲੇਇਟੈਕਸ) *n* ਬਨਸਪਤੀ ਦੁੱਧ, ਬੂਟਿਆਂ
ਦਾ ਦੁੱਧ, ਕੱਚੀ ਰਬੜ

lathe (ਲੇਇਦ) *n* ਖਰਾਦ

lather ('ਲਾਦਆ*) *n v* ਝੱਗ; ਝੱਗ ਆਉਂਦੀ, ਝੱਗ
ਉੱਠਦੀ, ਛਲਕਣਾ; ਮੁਰੰਮਤ ਕਰਨਾ

lathy ('ਲਾਥਿ) *a* ਦੁਬਲਾ-ਪਤਲਾ, ਕਮਜ਼ੋਰ

latitude ('ਲੈਟਿਟਯੂਡ) *n* ਵਿਥ-ਕਾਰ, ਅਕਸ਼ਾਂਸ਼;
ਚੌੜਾਈ, ਫੈਲਾਉ, ਵਿਸਤਾਰ ਖੇਤਰ; ਪੂਰਾ
ਦਾਇਰਾ; ਆਜ਼ਾਦ, ਛਿਆਲੀ, ਵਿਚਾਰ ਸੁਤੰਤਰਤਾ

latrine ('ਲੈਟਰੀਨ) *n* ਟੱਟੀ, ਝੌਂਚਾਲਾ

latter ('ਲੈਟਆ*) *a* ਦੂਜਾ; ਪਿੱਛਲਾ, ਬਾਅਦ ਦਾ,
ਪਿੱਛਲੇਰਾ, ਮਗਰਲਾ, ਆਧੁਨਿਕ

lattice ('ਲੈਟਿਸ) *n* ਜਾਲੀ; ~d ਜਾਲੀਦਾਰ

laud (ਲੋਡ) *n v* ਸ਼ਲਾਘਾ, ਸਲਾਹੁਤਾ, ਪ੍ਰਸੰਸਾ,
ਸ਼ਲਾਘਾ ਕਰਨੀ, ਪ੍ਰਸੰਸਾ ਕਰਨੀ, ਗੁਣ ਗਾਉਣੇ;
~able ਸ਼ਲਾਘਾਯੋਗ; ਚੰਗਾ; ਠੀਕ

laugh (ਲਾਫ਼) *v n* ਹੱਸਣਾ; ਲਹਿਰਾਉਣਾ; ਹੱਸਣਾ,
ਦਿਲਲਗੀ ਕਰਨੀ, (ਮਖੌਲ ਕਰ ਕੇ ਕਿਸੇ ਦੀ);
~at ਮਜ਼ਾਕ ਉਡਾਉਣਾ; ~in one's sleeves
ਅੰਦਰੇ-ਅੰਦਰ ਖ਼ੁਸ਼ ਹੋਣਾ; ~off ਹੱਸ ਕੇ ਟਾਲਣਾ;
~ing ਹਾਸਾ; ~ing stock ਹਾਸੇ ਦਾ ਨਿਸ਼ਾਨਾ,
ਮੌਜੂ; ~ter ਹਾਸਾ, ਖਿੱਲੀ, ਖਿੜਖਿੜ, ਮੁਸਕਾਣ

launch (ਲਾਂਚ) *v n* (ਜਹਾਜ਼) ਠੇਲ੍ਹਣਾ, ਵਗਾਉਣਾ,
(ਮੁਹਿੰਮ ਤੇ) ਸ਼ੁਰੂ ਕਰਨਾ, ਸਖ਼ਤ-ਸੁਸਤ ਕਹਿਣਾ;
ਸੈਲਾਨੀ ਕਿਸ਼ਤੀ, ਲਾਂਚ-ਬੋਟ, ਵੱਡੀ ਕਿਸ਼ਤੀ;
ਠੇਲ੍ਹ, ਠੇਲ੍ਹਣ; (ਜਹਾਜ਼ ਦੀ) ਉਤਰਾਈ, ਜਲ-
ਅਵਤਰਨ

launder (ਲਾਂਡਆ*) *v* ਕੱਪੜੇ ਧੋਣਾ, ਇਸਤਰੀ
ਕਰਨਾ; ~er ਧੋਬੀ

laundry (ਲਾਂਡਰਿ) *n* ਧੋਬੀ ਦੀ ਦੁਕਾਨ, ਧੋਬੀਖ਼ਾਨਾ,
ਲਾਂਡਰੀ

laura (ਲੋਰਾ) *n* ਕੁਟੀਆ, ਝੁੱਗੀ, ਆਸ਼ਰਮ

laureate ('ਲੋਰਿਅਟ) *a n* ਲਾਰਲ ਦਾ, ਲਾਰਲ ਦੇ
ਹਾਰ ਨਾਲ ਸਜਿਆ ਹੋਇਆ; ਸਨਮਾਨਤ;
poet~ ਰਾਜ-ਕਵੀ; ਮਹਾਂਕਵੀ; ~ship
ਰਾਜਕਵੀ ਦੀ ਪਦਵੀ

laurel ('ਲੋਰ(ਅ)ਲ) *n v* ਚਮਕੀਲੀਆਂ ਪੱਤੀਆਂ ਵਾਲੀ ਸਦਾਬਹਾਰ ਝਾੜੀ; ਪੁਸ਼ਪ-ਮੁਕਟ, ਜੈ-ਮਾਲਾ; ਲਾਰਲ ਦਾ ਮੁਕਟ ਕਿਸੇ ਦੇ ਸਿਰ ਤੇ ਰੱਖਣਾ

lava (ਲਾਵ੍ਹਾ) *n* ਲਾਵਾ, ਜੁਆਲਾਮੁਖੀ ਦਾ ਉਬਾਲ

lavation (ਲੈ'ਵ੍ਹੇਇਸ਼ਨ) *n* ਪੰਜ-ਇਸ਼ਨਾਨਾ, ਮੂੰਹ-ਹੱਥ ਧੋਣਾ, ਸਫ਼ਾਈ

lavatory (ਲੈਵ੍ਹਅਟ(ਅ)ਰਿ) *n* ਟੱਟੀ, ਗੁਸਲਖ਼ਾਨਾ

lavish (ਲੈਵ੍ਹਿਸ਼) *a v* ਸ਼ਾਹ-ਖ਼ਰਚ, ਫ਼ਜ਼ੂਲ-ਖ਼ਰਚ, ਵਾਫ਼ਰ, ਬੇ-ਅੰਦਾਜ਼ਾ, ਬਹੁਤਾ; ਪਾਣੀ ਵਾਂਗ ਰੋੜ੍ਹਨਾ, ਬਹੁਤਾ ਖ਼ਰਚ ਕਰਨਾ; ~ment, ~ness ਫ਼ਜ਼ੂਲ-ਖ਼ਰਚੀ

law (ਲਾ) *n* ਕਾਨੂੰਨ, ਵਿਧਾਨ, ਵਿਧੀ; ਕਾਇਦਾ, ਜ਼ਾਬਤਾ; ~ablding ਕਾਨੂੰਨ ਪਾਲਕ; ~and order ਅਮਨ-ਕਾਨੂੰਨ; ~court ਕਚਹਿਰੀ; ~suit ਮੁਕੱਦਮਾ, ਦਾਅਵਾ; to go to~ ਦਾਅਵਾ ਕਰਨਾ, ਮੁਕੱਦਮਾ ਕਰਨਾ; ~ful ਕਾਨੂੰਨੀ, ਵਿਧੀਪੂਰਨ, ਵਿਧੀ ਅਨੁਸਾਰ; ~fulness ਵਿਧੀਪੂਰਨਤਾ, ਵੈਧਤਾ; ~less ਗ਼ੈਰ-ਕਾਨੂੰਨੀ, ਵਿਧੀਹੀਨ, ਅਵੈਧ, ਨਿਆਂ ਵਿਰੁੱਧ; ~yer ਵਕੀਲ; ਕਾਨੂੰਨਦਾਨ

lax (ਲੈਕਸ) *a* ਢਿੱਲਾ, ਘੋਲੀ, ਕੋਮਲ, ਨਰਮ, ਲਚਕੀਲਾ; ~ation ਢਿੱਲ, ਸਿਥਲਤਾ; ~ative ਜੁਲਾਬੀ; ਜੁਲਾਬ; ~ity ਢਿੱਲ; ਨਰਮੀ; ਅਸਪਸ਼ਟਤਾ; ਆਚਰਨਹੀਣਤਾ, ਲਾਪਰਵਾਹੀ

lay (ਲੇਇ) *v n a* ਰੱਖਣਾ, ਧਰਨਾ, ਲਿਟਾ ਦੇਣਾ; ਲੰਮਾ ਪਾ ਦੇਣਾ; ਗੀਤ, ਨਗ਼ਮਾ; ਸੰਸਾਰੀ, ਗ੍ਰਹਿਸਥੀ; ~down · ਨਿਰਧਾਰਤ ਕਰਨਾ; ~man ਸਧਾਰਨ ਵਿਅਕਤੀ, ਗ਼ੈਰਮਾਹਰ; ~out ਖ਼ਾਕਾ, ਰੂਪ-ਰੇਖਾ; ~waste ਨਸ਼ਟ ਕਰਨਾ

layer (ਲੇਇਅ*) *n v* ਤਹਿ, ਪਰਤ; ਦਾਬ; ਫ਼ਸਲ

ਦਾ ਫਹਿ ਜਾਣਾ; ਦਾਬ ਲਾਉਣੀ

laze (ਲੇਇਜ਼) *v n* ਆਲਸ ਕਰਨਾ, ਸੁਸਤ ਹੋਣਾ; ਸੁਸਤੀ, ਆਲਸ

laziness (ਲੇਇਜ਼ਿਨਿਸ) *n* ਆਲਸ, ਸੁਸਤੀ, ਦਲਿੱਦਰ, ਨੇਸਤੀ

lazy ('ਲੇਇਜ਼ਿ) *a v* ਸੁਸਤ, ਆਲਸੀ, ਢਿੱਲਾ; ਕੰਮਚੋਰ; ਸੁਸਤੀ ਕਰਨੀ, ਆਲਸ ਵਿਚ ਸਮਾਂ ਬਿਤਾਉਣਾ

leach (ਲੀਚ) *v* ਟਪਕਾਉਣਾ, ਚੁਆਉਣਾ

lead (ਲੀਡ) *v n* ਸਿੱਕੇ ਦਾ ਚੌਖਟਾ ਜੜਨਾ; ਅਗਵਾਈ ਕਰਨੀ, ਸਮਝਾਉਣਾ; (ਜ਼ਿੰਦਗੀ) ਬਿਤਾਉਣੀ, ਗੁਜ਼ਾਰਨੀ; ਆਰੰਭ ਕਰਨਾ, ਅੱਗੇ ਹੋਣਾ; ਦੌੜ ਵਿਚ ਅੱਗੇ ਹੋਣਾ, ਆਗੂ ਹੋਣਾ, ਲੀਡਰ ਹੋਣਾ; ਸਿੱਕਾ; ਪਟਸਾਲ, ਸੰਧੂਰ; (ਛਾਪੇ ਦਾ) ਲੈਡ, ਸਿੱਕੇ ਦੀ ਪੱਤੀ; ਅਗਵਾਈ; ਮਿਸਾਲ; ~en ਸਿੱਕੇ ਵਰਗਾ, ਭਾਰੀ, ਘੋਝਲ; ~astray ਬਹਿਕਾਉਣਾ, ਗੁਮਰਾਹ ਕਰਨਾ, ~the way ਅਗਵਾਈ ਕਰਨਾ

leader (ਲੀਡਅ*) *n* ਆਗੂ, ਨੇਤਾ, ਮੁਖੀਆ, ਸਰਦਾਰ, ਸਰਕਾਰੀ ਅਧਿਕਾਰੀ; ~of the opposition ਵਿਰੋਧੀ ਦਲ ਦਾ ਨੇਤਾ; ~of the house ਸਦਨ ਦਾ ਨੇਤਾ; ~ship ਅਗਵਾਈ, ਅਗਵਾਨੀ, ਲੀਡਰੀ

leading (ਲੀਡਿਙ) *a* ਵੱਡਾ, ਪ੍ਰਧਾਨ, ਮੁੱਖ, ਉੱਤਮ, ਉੱਘਾ, ਅਗਲਾ; ~artical ਸੰਪਾਦਕੀ ਲੇਖ

leaf (ਲੀਫ਼) *n* ਪੱਤਰਾ, ਪੱਤਾ, ਪੰਖੜੀ, ਪੱਤਰ (ਰੁੱਖ ਦਾ); (ਚਾਹ ਦੀ) ਪੱਤੀ; (ਕਿਤਾਬ ਦਾ) ਵਰਕਾ; (ਚਾਂਦੀ, ਸੋਨੇ ਦਾ) ਵਰਕ; ~let ਛੋਟਾ ਪੱਤਾ, ਪੱਤੀ; ਕੋੱਪਲ, ਨਵੀਂ ਪੱਤੀ; ਦੁਪੱਤਰੀ

league (ਲੀਗ) *n v* ਮੇਲ; ਸੰਗਠਨ, ਏਕਤਾ; ਸੰਘ, ਦਲ, ਲੀਗ; ਮਿਲਾਉਣਾ, ਮਿਲਣਾ, ਇਕ

ਹੋਣਾ, ਗਠਜੋੜ ਕਰਨਾ; L~ of Nations ਰਾਸ਼ਟਰਸੰਘ

leak (ਲੀਕ) *n v* ਛੇਕ, ਸੁਰਾਖ, ਦਰਾੜ, ਰਿਸਣਾ, ਟਪਕਣਾ, ਚੋਣਾ; (ਭੇਤ) ਪਤਾ ਲੱਗ ਜਾਣਾ, ਭੇਤ ਖੋਲ੍ਹਣਾ; **~age** ਚੋਆ, ਖੋਰ, ਰਸਾ, ਟਪਕਾ; ਟੁੱਟ-ਭੱਜ

lean (ਲੀਨ) *a v n* ਦੁਬਲਾ, ਲਿੱਸਾ, ਸੁਕੜ, ਦੁਰਬਲ, ਕਮਜ਼ੋਰ; ਢੋਹ ਲਾਉਣੀ, ਟੇਕ ਲੈਣੀ, ਟਿਕਿਆ ਹੋਣਾ; ਭਰੋਸਾ ਕਰਨਾ; ਝੁਕਣਾ, ਝੁਕਾਉਣਾ; ਝੁਕਾਉ ਹੋਣਾ, ਹਾਮੀ ਹੋਣਾ; ਝੁਕਾਉ; **~ing** ਝੁਕਾਉ, ਪ੍ਰਵਿਰਤੀ

leap (ਲੀਪ) *v n* ਕੁੱਦਣਾ, ਛਾਲ ਮਾਰਨੀ, ਉਛਲਣਾ, ਟੱਪਣਾ, ਟੱਪ ਜਾਣਾ, ਉਲਾਂਘਣਾ, ਛਲਾਂਗ, ਚੁੰਗ, ਚੌਕੜੀ; **~year** ਲੌਂਦੀ ਵਰ੍ਹਾ, ਲੀਪ ਦਾ ਸਾਲ, 366 ਦਿਨਾਂ ਦਾ ਸਾਲ; **by ~s and bounds** ਅਤੀ ਸ਼ੀਘਰਤਾ ਨਾਲ, (ਤੁਰਕੀ) ਦਿਲ ਦੂਹੀ ਰਾਤ ਚੌਗੁਣੀ, ਝਟਪਟ

learn (ਲ੍ਰਅ:ਨ) *v* ਸਿੱਖਿਆ ਲੈਣੀ; ਗਿਆਨ ਪ੍ਰਾਪਤ ਕਰਨਾ, ਜਾਣਨਾ, ਪੜ੍ਹਨਾ; ਸੂਚਨਾ ਹੋਣੀ, ਪਤਾ ਲੱਗਣਾ; **~ed** ਵਿਦਵਾਨ, ਆਲਮ, ਗਿਆਨੀ; **~er** ਵਿਦਿਆਰਥੀ; ਸਿਖਾਂਦਰੂ, ਚੇਲਾ; **~ing** ਗਿਆਨ, ਵਿੱਦਿਆ, ਇਲਮ, ਸਿੱਖਿਆ, ਪੜ੍ਹਾਈ

lease (ਲੀਸ) *n v* ਪੱਟਾ, ਠੇਕਾ; ਚਕੌਤਾ, ਪੱਟੇ ਦੇਣਾ, ਠੇਕੇ ਤੇ ਦੇਣਾ; **~hold** ਪੱਟੇਦਾਰੀ, ਠੇਕਾ; ਪੱਟੇ ਤੇ ਲਈ ਜ਼ਮੀਨ; **~holder** ਪੱਟੇਦਾਰ, ਠੇਕੇਦਾਰ

least (ਲੀਸਟ) *a adv n* ਘੱਟ ਤੋਂ ਘੱਟ, ਛੋਟੇ ਤੋਂ ਛੋਟਾ, ਸਭ ਤੋਂ ਛੋਟਾ; **at~** ਘੱਟੋ-ਘੱਟ, ਹੋਰ ਨਹੀਂ ਤਾਂ; **at the~** ਘੱਟ ਤੋਂ ਘੱਟ; **in the~** ਜ਼ਰਾ ਵੀ, ਬੇਹੂਦਾ ਵੀ, ਕੁਝ ਵੀ, ਉੱਕਾ

leather (ਲੈੱਦਅ*) *n v* ਚਮੜਾ, ਚੰਮ; ਪੋੜੀ; ਪੱਕਾ

ਚਮੜਾ; ਚਮੜੇ ਦਾ ਸਾਮਾਨ; ਚਮੜਾ ਚੜ੍ਹਾਉਣਾ; ਤੰਤੜਾਂ ਦੀ ਮਾਰ ਦੇਣੀ

leave (ਲੀਵ) *n v* ਆਗਿਆ; ਅਨੁਮਤੀ; ਇਜਾਜ਼ਤ; ਛੁੱਟੀ; ਵਿਦਾ, ਵਿਦਾਈ; ਛੱਡ ਦੇਣਾ, ਰਹਿਤ ਦੇਣਾ, ਰਵਾਨਾ ਹੋਣਾ; **~taking** ਵਿਦਾ, ਵਿਦਾਇਗੀ; **~out** ਭੁੱਲ ਜਾਣਾ; **~to take** ਵਿਦਾ ਹੋਣਾ

lecher (ਲੈੱਚਅ*) *n* ਲੱਚਰ, ਕਾਮੀ, ਭੋਗੀ, ਵਿਤਚਾਰੀ, ਲੁੱਚਾ; **~ous** ਕਾਮੀ, ਲੰਪਟ, ਲੁੱਚਾ; **~ousness** ਕਾਮੁਕਤਾ, ਕਾਮਵਾਸ਼ਨਾ, ਲੁੱਚਪੁਣਾ; **~y** ਵਿਤਚਾਰ, ਲੁੱਚਪੁਣਾ

lection (ਲੈੱਕਸ਼ਨ) *n* ਪਾਠ, ਪੜ੍ਹਾਈ; **~ary** ਪ੍ਰਾਰਥਨਾ-ਪੁਸਤਕ, ਭਜਨ-ਮਾਲਾ, ਉਸਤਤੀ-ਸੰਗ੍ਰਹ

lector (ਲੈੱਕਟਅ*) *n* ਪਾਦਰੀ

lecture (ਲੈੱਕਚਅ*) *n v* ਭਾਸ਼ਣ ਵਿਆਖਿਆਨ; ਤਕਰੀਰ ਕਰਨਾ; ਵਿੱਦਿਆ ਦੇਣੀ, ਜ਼ਬਾਨੀ ਸਬਕ ਦੇਣਾ; ਡਾਂਟਣਾ; **~r** ਵਕਤਾ, ਵਿਆਖਿਆਨੀ

ledger (ਲੈੱਜਅ*) *n* ਵਹੀ-ਖਾਤਾ, ਖਾਤਾ

leech (ਲੀਚ) *n* (1) (ਪ੍ਰਾ) ਹਕੀਮ, ਤਬੀਬ; (2) ਜੋਕ; ਲਹੂ-ਚੂਸ, ਰੱਤ-ਪੀਣਾ; ਮੁਨਾਫ਼ੇਖੋਰ

leer (ਲਿਅ*) *n v* ਬੁਰੀ ਨਜ਼ਰ, ਭੁੱਖੀ ਨਜ਼ਰ; **~y** ਚਲਾਕ, ਚੌਕਸ, ਚੁਕੰਨਾ

left (ਲੈੱਫ਼ਟ) *a adv n* ਖੱਬਾ; ਖੱਬੇ ਪਾਸੇ ਦਾ; ਉਲਟਾ ਹੱਥ; ਵਾਮ ਮਾਰਗੀ ਸੰਪਰਦਾਇ; ਖੱਬੇ-ਪੱਖੀ (ਰਾਜਨੀਤੀ); **~leave** ਦਾ ਭੁਤਕਾਲ ਰੂਪ; **~handed** ਖੱਬਚੂ, ਖੱਬੂ; ਬੇ-ਤੁਕਾ, ਦੁਬਾਜਰਾ, ਦੋ-ਰੁਖਾ

leg (ਲੈੱਗ) *n* ਲੱਤ, ਟੰਗ, ਜੰਘ; ਚਰਨ; (ਮੰਜੇ, ਕੁਰਸੀ ਆਦਿ ਦਾ) ਪਾਵਾ; **to pull one's~** ਲੱਤ ਖਿੱਚਣਾ

legacy (ਲੈੱਗਾਸਿ) *n* ਵਿਰਸਾ, ਸੰਪੱਤੀ

legal (ਲੀਗਲ) *a* ਕਾਨੂੰਨੀ; ਵਿਧੀ-ਮੂਲਕ; ਨਿਯਮਕ; ਉਚਿਤ, ਜਾਇਜ਼; ~ist ਕਾਨੂੰਨਦਾਨ, ਕਾਨੂੰਨੀ ਪੰਡਤ; ~ity ਕਾਨੂੰਨੀ ਹੈਸੀਅਤ, ਨਿਯਮਕਤਾ; ~ize ਜਾਇਜ਼ ਠਹਿਰਾਉਣਾ, ਪ੍ਰਮਾਣਤ ਕਰਨਾ, ਕਾਨੂੰਨੀ ਰੂਪ ਦੇਣਾ; ~ly ਵਿਧੀਪੂਰਬਕ ਕਾਨੂੰਨ ਦੀ ਦ੍ਰਿਸ਼ਟੀ ਵਿਚ

legend (ਲੈੱਜਅੰਡ) *n* ਲੋਕ-ਕਥਾ, ਦੰਦ-ਕਥਾ, ਪੁਰਾਣਕ ਕਥਾ, ਰਵਾਇਤ, ਕਿੱਸਾ- ਕਹਾਣੀ; ਦੇਵ-ਕਹਾਣੀ; ~ary ਪੁਰਾਣਕ, ਪ੍ਰਸਿੱਧ; ਕਾਲਪਨਕ, ਸਿਖਿਆ, ਪੁਰਾਣ

legible (ਲੈੱਜਅਬਲ) *a* ਸਪੱਸ਼ਟ, ਪੜ੍ਹਿਆ ਜਾ ਸਕਣ ਵਾਲਾ; ~hand ਖ਼ੁਸ਼ਖ਼ਤ, ਸੁਲੇਖ

legislate (ਲੈੱਜਿਸਲੇਇਟ) *v* ਕਾਨੂੰਨ ਬਣਾਉਣਾ, ਵਿਧਾਨ ਬਣਾਉਣਾ, ਨਿਯਮ ਬਣਾਉਣਾ

legislation (ਲੈੱਜਿਸ'ਲੇਇਸ਼ਨ) *n* ਵਿਧੀ- ਨਿਰਮਾਨ, ਵਿਧਾਨਕਾਰੀ, ਵਿਧੀ-ਵਿਵਸਥਾ, ਕਾਨੂੰਨ-ਨਿਰਮਾਣ, ਵਿਧਾਨ

legislative (ਲੈੱਜਿਸਲਅਟਿਵ) *a* ਵਿਧਾਨੀ, ਨਿਯਮ ਸਬੰਧੀ, ਵਿਧਾਨਕ

legislator (ਲੈੱਜਿਸਲੇਇਟਅ*) *n* ਵਿਧਾਇਕ ਵਿਧੀਕਰਤਾ, ਵਿਵਸਥਾਪਕ

legislature (ਲੈੱਜਿਸਲੇਇਚ*) *n* ਵਿਧਾਨ ਸਭਾ, ਵਿਧਾਨ-ਮੰਡਲ

legitimacy (ਲਿ'ਜਿਟਿਮਅਸਿ) *n* ਯੋਗਤਾ, ਉਚਿਤਤਾ; ਵਿਧੀ ਅਨੁਕੂਲਤਾ; ਸਚਾਈ, ਖਰਾਪਣ

legitimate (ਲਿ'ਜਿਟਿਮਅਟ, ਲਿ'ਜਿਟਿਮੇਇਟ) *a v* ਨਿਯਮਕ, ਵਿਧੀ ਅਨੁਕੂਲ,ਕਾਨੂੰਨੀ; ਜਾਇਜ਼ (ਔਲਾਦ); ਯਥਾਰਥ, ਸੱਚਾ, ਅਸਲੀ; ਵਿਧੀ ਅਨੁਕੂਲ ਸਿੱਧ ਕਰਨਾ

legitimise (ਲਿ'ਜਿਟਿਮਾਇਜ਼) *v* ਵਿਧੀ ਅਨੁਕੂਲ

ਕਰਨਾ, ਪ੍ਰਮਾਣਕ-ਕਰਨਾ

leisure (ਲੈੱਯ਼ਅ*) *n* ਵਿਸ਼੍ਰਾਮ, ਫ਼ੁਰਸਤ, ਛੁੱਟੀ; ਖ਼ਾਲੀ ਸਮਾਂ; ~ly ਹੌਲੀ, ਮੰਦ; ਫ਼ੁਰਸਤ ਦਾ; ਸੋਚਿਆ-ਸਮਝਿਆ; ਹੌਲੀ-ਹੌਲੀ, ਸਾਵਧਾਨੀ ਨਾਲ

lemon (ਲੈੱਮਅਨ) *n* ਨਿੰਬੂ; ਨਿੰਬੂ ਦਾ ਬੂਟਾ; ਹਲਕਾ ਪੀਲਾ (ਰੰਗ)

lend (ਲੈੱਡ) *v* ਉਧਾਰ ਦੇਣਾ; ਦੇਣਾ, ਕਿਰਾਏ ਦੇ ਦੇਣਾ; ~a hand ਹੱਥ ਵਟਾਉਣਾ; ~an ear ਸੁਣਨਾ, ਕੰਨ ਧਰਨੇ

length (ਲੈੱਡਥ) *n* ਲੰਬਾਈ, ਵਿਸਤਾਰ, ਫੈਲਾਉ, ਦੂਰੀ, ਅੰਤਮ ਸੀਮਾ, ਅੱਖਰਾਂ ਦੀ ਮਾਤਰਾ; **at an arm's**~ ਪਰੇ, ਦੂਰ; **at**~ ਵਿਸਤਾਰ ਪੂਰਬਕ; ~en ਲੰਮਾ ਕਰਨਾ, ਵਧਾਉਣਾ, ਵਧਨਾ, ਫੈਲਾਉਣਾ; ~y ਲੰਮਾ, ਦੀਰਘ

lenience, leniency (ਲੀਨਯਅੰਸ, ਲੀਨਯਅੰਸਿ) *n* ਨਰਮੀ, ਕੋਮਲਤਾ, ਹਲੀਮੀ, ਦਇਆਲਤਾ

lenient (ਲੀਨਯਅੰਟ) *a* ਨਰਮ, ਦਿਆਲੂ, ਉਦਾਰ

Leo (ਲੀਅਉ) *n* ਸਿੰਘ ਰਾਸ਼ੀ

leopard (ਲੈੱਪਅਡ) *n* ਚਿੱਤਰਾ, ਚੀਤਾ

leper (ਲੈੱਪਅ*) *n* ਕੋੜ੍ਹੀ, ਕੋੜ੍ਹ ਦਾ ਰੋਗੀ, ਕੁਸ਼ਟ- ਰੋਗੀ

lepra (ਲੈੱਪਰਅ) *n* ਕੋੜ੍ਹ, ਕੁਸ਼ਟ

leprosy (ਲੈੱਪਰਅਸਿ) *n* ਕੋੜ੍ਹ; ਇਖ਼ਲਾਕੀ ਗਿਰਾਵਟ

leprous (ਲੈੱਪਰਅਸ) *a* ਕੋੜ੍ਹੀ

less (ਲੈੱਸ) *a adv n prep* ਘੱਟ, ਥੋੜ੍ਹਾ, ਊਣਾ; ਘੱਟ ਗਿਣਤੀ; ਘਟਾ ਕੇ, ਕੱਢ ਕੇ, ਬਿਨਾ; ~en ਘਟਣਾ, ਘਟਾਉਣਾ, ਹੌਲਾ ਹੋਣਾ, ਥੋੜ੍ਹਾ ਕਰਨਾ

lessee (ਲੈੱਸੀ) *n* ਪੱਟੇਦਾਰ, ਕਿਰਾਏਦਾਰ

lesson (ਲੈੱਸਨ) *n v* ਪਾਠ, ਸਬਕ, ਪੜ੍ਹਾਈ, ਸਿੱਖਿਆ, ਉਪਦੇਸ਼, ਸਖ਼ਤ ਦੰਡ; ਸਿਖਾਉਣਾ,

ਪੜ੍ਹਾਉਣਾ

lest (ਲੈੱਸਟ) *conj* ਮਤਾਂ, ਮਤੇ, ਇਉਂ ਨਾ ਹੋਵੇ ਕਿ

let (ਲੈੱਟ) *v n* ਰੁਕਾਵਟ ਪਾਉਣੀ, ਅੜਿੱਕਾ ਢਾਹੁਣਾ; ਨਿਕਲਣ ਦੇਣਾ, ਜਾਣ ਦੇਣਾ; ਹੋਣ ਦੇਣਾ; ਕਰਨ ਦੇਣਾ, ਛੱਡਣਾ; ਰੁਕਾਵਟ, ਰੋਕ-ਟੇਕ, ਕਿਰਾਏਦਾਰੀ, ~**alone** ਦਖ਼ਲ ਨਾ ਦੇਣਾ; ~**down** ਨੀਵਾਂ ਕਰਨਾ, ਨਿਰਾਸ ਕਰਨਾ; ~**into** ਟੁੱਟ ਕੇ ਪੈਣਾ; ~**on** ਰਿਹਾ ਕਰਨਾ, ਛੱਡਣਾ; ~**one know** ਮੁਖ਼ਬਰੀ ਕਰਨਾ, ਭੇਦ ਦੱਸਣਾ

lethal (ਲੀਥਲ) *a* ਘਾਤਕ, ਮਾਰੂ, ਮੁਹਲਕ, ਜਾਨ ਲੇਵਾ, (ਹਥਿਆਰ ਆਦਿ)

lethargic (ਲਬਾ'ਥਾਜਿਕ) *a* ਸੁਸਤ, ਆਲਸੀ, ਕੰਮਚੋਰ, ਮੱਠਾ, ਸਾਹ ਸਤ-ਹੀਣ

lethargy (ਲੈੱਥਅਜਿ) *n* ਆਲਸ, ਸੁਸਤੀ, ਕੰਮਚੋਰੀ; ਸਾਹ ਸਤ-ਹੀਣਤਾ

letter (ਲੈੱਟਅ) *n v* ਚਿੱਠੀ, ਪੱਤਰ, ਖ਼ਤ; ਅੱਖਰ, ਵਰਣ, ਹਰਫ਼; (ਛਾਪੇ ਵਿਚ) ਟਾਈਪ; ਵਿੱਦਿਆ, ਸਾਹਿਤ, ਗਿਆਨ; ਅੱਖਰ ਉੱਕਰਨੇ; ਠੱਪਾ ਲਾਉਣਾ; ~**ed** ਵਿਦਵਾਨ, ਗਿਆਨੀ, ਪੰਡਤ, ਪੜ੍ਹਿਆ-ਲਿਖਿਆ; ~**ing** ਅੱਖਰ-ਲੇਖਣ, ਨਾਮ ਅੰਕਣ, ਲਿਖਾਵਟ

level (ਲੈੱਵ਼ਲ) *n a v* ਪੱਧਰ, ਸਤਰ, ਦਰਜਾ, ਮਿਆਰ; ਸਮਤਾ; ਸੰਤੁਲਤ; ਫ਼ਰਕ ਮਿਟਾ ਕੇ ਬਰਾਬਰ ਕਰਨਾ; ਮਰਯਾਦਾ ਅਨੁਕੂਲ ਕਰਨਾ; ਮਿੱਟੀ ਵਿਚ ਮਿਲਾ ਦੇਣਾ, ਮਲੀਆਮੇਟ ਕਰ ਦੇਣਾ; ਸ਼ਿਸਤ ਬੰਨ੍ਹੀਂ; ਦੋਸ਼ ਲਾਉਣਾ; ~**crossing** ਪੱਧਰਾ ਲਾਂਘਾ, ਰੇਲਵੇ ਫਾਟਕ; **to do one's~ best** ਪੂਰਾ ਕਰਨਾ, ਟਿੱਲ ਲਾਉਣਾ; ~**ling** ਪੱਧਰਾ ਕਰਨ ਦਾ ਕੰਮ, ਪੱਧਰ ਕਰਨ ਵਾਲਾ

lever (ਲੀਵ਼ਅ*) *n v* ਤੁਲ; ਲੀਵਰ; (ਬੰਦੂਕ ਆਦਿ

ਦਾ) ਤੋੜਾ; ਤੁਲ ਦੇਣੀ, ਲੀਵਰ ਲਾਉਣਾ, ਤੋੜਾ ਦੱਬਣਾ

levy (ਲੈੱਵ਼ਿ) *n v* ਲਗਾਨ, ਮਹਿਸੂਲ, ਚੰਦਾ, ਉਗਰਾਹੀ; ਲਗਾਨ ਦੀ ਮਾਤਰਾ ਜਾਂ ਦਰ; ਰੰਗਰੂਟਾਂ ਦੀ ਟੋਲੀ; ਵਸੂਲ ਕਰਨਾ, ਉਗਰਾਹੁਣਾ; (ਕਰ ਆਦਿ) ਲਾਉਣਾ; ਜੁੱਧ ਛੇੜਨਾ

lewd (ਲਯੂਡ) *a* ਹੋਛਾ; ਬਦਮਾਸ਼; ਵਿਸ਼ਈ, ਕਾਮੀ; ~**ness** ਲੁੱਚਪਨ, ਬਦਕਾਰੀ, ਕਾਮੁਕਤਾ

lexical (ਲੈੱਕਸਿਕਲ) *a* ਕੋਸ਼ੀ, ਕੋਸ਼ਗਤ

lexicographer (ਲੈੱਕਸਿ'ਕੋਗਰਅਫ਼ਅ*) *n* ਕੋਸ਼ਕਾਰ, ਕੋਸ਼ ਬਣਾਉਣ ਵਾਲਾ

lexicography (ਲੈੱਕਸਿ'ਕੋਗਰਅਫ਼ਿ) *n* ਕੋਸ਼ਕਾਰੀ

lexicon (ਲੈੱਕਸਿਕੱਨ) *n* ਕੋਸ਼, ਸ਼ਬਦ ਭੰਡਾਰ, ਸ਼ਬਦਾਵਲੀ

liability, liableness (ਲਾਇਅ'ਬਿਲਅਟਿ, ਲਾਇਬਲਨਿਸ) *n* ਜ਼ੁੰਮੇਵਾਰੀ, ਉੱਤਰਦਾਇਤਵ; ਦੇਤਦਾਰੀ; ਭਾਗ, ਕਰਜ਼, ਉਧਾਰ, ਸਿਰ ਪਈ ਰਕਮ

liable (ਲਾਇਬਲ) *a* ਦੇਣਦਾਰ; ਜ਼ੁੰਮੇਵਾਰ, ਕਰ ਵਾਲਾ, (ਕੋਈ ਕੰਮ ਕਰਨ ਲਈ) ਬੇਵੱਸ, ਯੋਗ, ਯੋਗਤਾ ਰਖੱਣ ਵਾਲਾ; ਜ਼ਰੂਰੀ, ਅਵੱਸ਼ਕ

liaise (ਲਿ'ਏਇਜ਼) *v* ਸੰਧੀ ਕਰਨਾ, ਅਹਿਦਨਾਮਾ ਕਰਨਾ

liaison (ਲਿ'ਏਇਜ਼(ਅ)ਨ) *n* ਸਪੰਰਕ, ਤਾਲਮੇਲ, ਦੋਹਾਂ ਧਿਰਾਂ ਵਿਚਾਲੇ ਸਬੰਧ; ਨਾਜਾਇਜ਼ ਸਬੰਧ, ਯਾਰੀ; ~**officer** ਤਾਲਮੇਲ ਅਫ਼ਸਰ, ਸਪੰਰਕ ਅਧਿਕਾਰੀ

liar (ਲਾਇਅ*) *n* ਝੂਠਾ, ਝੂਠ ਬੋਲਣ ਵਾਲਾ

Lib (ਲਿਬ) *n* (*Women's Liberation* ਦਾ ਸੰਖੇਪ), ਨਾਰੀ ਮੁਕਤੀ

liberal (ਲਿਬ(ਅ)ਰ(ਅ)ਲ) *a n* ਖੁੱਲ੍ਹਦਿਲਾ, ਵੱਡੇ

ਦਿਲ ਵਾਲਾ, ਆਜ਼ਾਦ ਖ਼ਿਆਲ, ਉਦਾਰਚਿੱਤ, ਸਖੀ, ਦਾਨੀ; ਧਾਰਮਕ ਕੱਟੜਤਾ ਤੋਂ ਬਾਹਰ; ~ism ਖੁੱਲ੍ਹ-ਖ਼ਿਆਲੀ, ਨਰਮ ਵਿਚਾਰ, ਉਦਾਰਵਾਦ; ~ist ਉਦਾਰਵਾਦੀ; ~ity ਆਜ਼ਾਦ ਖ਼ਿਆਲੀ, ਉਦਾਰਤਾ; ਸਖ਼ਾਵਤ; ~ize ਨਰਮ ਕਰਨਾ, ਢਿੱਲਾ ਕਰਨਾ, ਉਦਾਰ ਬਣਾਉਣਾ

liberate ('ਲਿਬਅਰੇਇਟ) *v* ਆਜ਼ਾਦ ਕਰਨਾ, ਸੁੰਤਤਰ ਕਰਨਾ, ਮੁਕਤ ਕਰਨਾ; ਰਿਹਾ ਕਰਨਾ, ਛੁਟਕਾਰਾ ਦੇਣਾ; ~d ਰਿਹਾ, ਮੁਕਤ, ਆਜ਼ਾਦ

liberation (ਲਿਬਅ'ਰੇਇਸ਼ਨ) *n* ਆਜ਼ਾਦੀ, ਸੁਤੰਤਰਤਾ, ਛੁਟਕਾਰਾ, ਰਿਹਾਈ

liberator (ਲਿਬਅਰੇਇਟਅ*) *n* ਛੁਟਕਾਰਾ ਦੇਣ ਵਾਲਾ, ਮੁਕਤੀਦਾਤਾ, ਰਿਹਾ ਕਰਨ ਵਾਲਾ, ਸੁਤੰਤਰਤਾ ਦੇਣ ਵਾਲਾ

iiberty (ਲਿਬਅਟਿ) *n* ਛੁਟਕਾਰਾ, ਮੁਕਤੀ, ਆਜ਼ਾਦੀ, ਸਵਾਧੀਨਤਾ, ਸੁਤੰਤਰਤਾ; **at~** ਰਿਹਾ, ਮੁਕਤ, ਸੁਤੰਤਰ

libido (ਲਿ'ਬਿਡਅਊ) *n* (ਮਨੋ) ਕਾਮ-ਸ਼ਕਤੀ, ਕਾਮ-ਤ੍ਰਿਪਤੀ, ਕਾਮ-ਵਾਸ਼ਨਾ, ਕਾਮ-ਉਤੇਜਨਾ

Libra (ਲਾਇਬਰਅ) *n* ਤੁਲਾ ਰਾਸ਼ੀ

librarian (ਲਾਇ'ਬਰੇਅਰਿਅਨ) *n* ਪੁਸਤਕ-ਪਾਲ

library (ਲਾਇਬਰਅਰਿ) *n* ਪੁਸਤਕਾਲਾ, ਕਿਤਾਬ-ਘਰ, ਗ੍ਰੰਥ-ਘਰ, ਲਾਇਬਰੇਰੀ

licence, license (ਲਾਇਸਅੰਸ) *n v* ਲਾਇਸੰਸ, ਆਗਿਆ, ਅਨੁਮਤੀ, ਆਗਿਆ-ਪੱਤਰ, ਸਨਦ; ਛੋਟ; ਲਾਈਸੈਂਸ ਦੇਣਾ, ਆਗਿਆ ਦੇਣੀ, ਖੁੱਲ੍ਹ ਦੇਣੀ

licensee (ਲਾਇਸਅੰਸੀ) *n* ਲਾਈਸੈਂਸਦਾਰ

lick (ਲਿਕ) *v n* ਜੀਭ ਨਾਲ ਚੱਟਣਾ, ਕੁੱਟਣਾ, ਠੋਕਣਾ; ਚੱਟਣਾ; **~one's shoes** ਝੋਲੀ ਚੁੱਕਣਾ, ਚਾਪਲੂਸੀ ਕਰਨਾ, ਜੁੱਤੀ ਚੱਟਣਾ; **~ing**

ਮਾਰ-ਕੁਟਾਈ, ਹਾਰ; ਦੰਡ

lid (ਲਿਡ) *n* ਢੱਕਣ, ਢੱਕਣਾ, ਚੱਪਣੀ; ਛੱਪਰ, (ਅੱਖਾਂ ਦੀ) ਪਲਕ, ਪਪੋਟਾ; ~ded ਢੱਕਣਦਾਰ

lie (ਲਾਇ) *n v* ਝੂਠ, ਮਿਥਿਆ-ਕਥਨ, ਝੂਠੀ ਗੱਲ; ਛਲ, ਅਸਤ; ਝੂਠ ਬੋਲਣਾ, ਲੇਟਣਾ, ਪੈਣਾ, ਪਏ ਹੋਣਾ; ਹਮਬਿਸਤਰ ਹੋਣਾ; **white~** ਮਾਮੂਲੀ ਝੂਠ

lien (ਲਿਅਨ) *n* ਹੱਕ-ਰਖਾਈ, ਅਧਿਕਾਰ ਗ੍ਰਹਿਣ, ਅਧਿਕਾਰ, ਕਾਨੂੰਨੀ ਅਧਿਕਾਰ, ਪੁਨਰ ਗ੍ਰਹਿਣ ਅਧਿਕਾਰ, ਪੀਲੀਆ, ਤਿੱਲੀ, ਤਾਪਤਿੱਲੀ

lieu, in~ of (ਲਯੂ) *n* ਦੀ ਬਾਂ, ਦੀ ਜਗ੍ਹਾ, ਬਦਲੇ ਵਿਚ

lieutenant (ਲੈੱਫ਼'ਟੈਨਅੰਟ) *n* ਲੈਫ਼ਟੀਨੈਂਟ ਨਾਇਬ, ਲਫ਼ਟੈਨ; ਪ੍ਰਤੀਨਿਧੀ; ਉਪ; **~governor** ਉਪ-ਰਾਜਪਾਲ

life (ਲਾਇਫ਼) *n* ਜ਼ਿੰਦ, ਜਾਨ, ਪ੍ਰਾਣ; ਆਯੂ, ਜੀਵਨਕਾਲ, ਜੀਵਨ; ਦਮ, ਸਜੀਵਤਾ, ਜ਼ਿੰਦਾ-ਦਿਲੀ; ਜੀਵ, ਪਰਾਣ ਸ਼ਕਤੀ, ਜ਼ਿੰਦਗੀ; **~long** ਜੀਵਨ ਤਰ (ਦਾ); **~sentence** ਉਮਰ ਕੈਦ; **come to~** ਜਿਉਂਦਾ ਹੋਣਾ; **~ful** ਜੀਊਂਦਾ ਜਾਗਦਾ, ਬਲਵਾਨ, ਬਲਸ਼ਾਲੀ, ਸਜੀਵ; **~less** ਨਿਰਜਿੰਦ, ਨਿਸ਼ਪ੍ਰਾਣ, ਨਿਰਜੀਵ, ਮੁਰਦਾ

lift (ਲਿਫ਼ਟ) *n v* ਉਠਾਉ, ਉੱਥਾਪਨ; ਚੜ੍ਹਾਉ, ਚੁੱਕ, ਉਠਾਨ, ਉਠਾਉਣਾ; ਉੱਥਾਪਨ ਕਰਨਾ, ਉਠਾਰਨਾ, ਉੱਚਾ ਕਰਨਾ; ਉਤਾਰ ਦੇਣਾ, ਲਾਹ ਦੇਣਾ, ਚੁੱਕ ਦੇਣਾ (ਪਰਦਾ ਆਦਿ); ਉਪੇਖਣਾ

light (ਲਾਇਟ) *n v a* ਲੋਅ, ਚਾਨਣ, ਪ੍ਰਕਾਸ਼, ਜੋਤ, ਰੌਸ਼ਨੀ; ਉਜਾਲਾ; ਦੀਵਾ, ਚਿਰਾਗ, ਚਾਨਣ ਦਾ ਖੰਡਾ; ਰੌਸ਼ਨੀ ਕਰਨੀ; ਹਲਕਾ, ਹੌਲਾ, ਬਰੀਕ; **bring to~** ਪ੍ਰਕਾਸ਼ਤ ਕਰਨਾ, ਪਰਗਟ ਕਰਨਾ; **come to~** ਪ੍ਰਕਾਸ਼ਤ ਹੋਣਾ, ਪਰਗਟ ਹੋਣਾ;

~en ਚਾਨਣ ਹੋਣ, ਪ੍ਰਕਾਸ਼ਤ ਹੋਣ; ਰੌਸ਼ਨੀ ਪਾਉਣੀ, ਚਾਨਣ ਪਾਉਣਾ; ਚਮਕਾਉਣਾ; ਹੌਲਾ ਕਰਨ ਜਾਂ ਹੋਣ, ਪੀਰਜ ਦੇਣਾ, ਜੀ ਹੌਲਾ ਕਰਨਾ; ~er ਦੀਵਾ; ਹੌਲੀ ਕਿਸ਼ਤੀ, ਮਾਲਬੋਟ; ~ning ਬਿਜਲੀ ਦੀ ਲਿਸ਼ਕ, ਲਿਸ਼ਕੋਰ; ਚਮਕ; ਅਸਮਾਨੀ ਬਿਜਲੀ; ~some ਸੁੰਦਰ, ਹੌਲਾ, ਸੌਜੀ, ਖੁਸ਼ਦਿਲ, ਪ੍ਰਸੰਨ; ਫੁਰਤੀਲਾ, ਚਮਕੀਲਾ

like (ਲਾਇਕ) *n v a adv conj* ਰੁਚੀ, ਪਸੰਦ, ਚਾਹ; ਚੰਗਾ ਲੱਗਣਾ, ਚਾਹੁਣਾ, ਅਨੁਕੂਲ ਹੋਣਾ; ਸਮਾਨ, ਤੁੱਲ, ਅਨੁਸਾਰ, ਬਰਾਬਰ, ਵਰਗਾ; ਸੰਭਵ ਤੌਰ ਤੇ, ਉਸੇ ਢੰਗ ਨਾਲ; ਜਿਵੇਂ, ਜਿਹੇ ਜਿਹਾ; ~lihood ਸੰਭਾਵਨਾ, ਸੰਭਵਤਾ; ~ly ਸੰਭਵ, ਯੋਗ, ਉਪਯੋਗੀ; ~n ਉਪਮਾ ਦੇਣੀ, ਤੁਲਨਾ ਦੇਣੀ, ਮੇਲ ਕਰਨਾ, ਮਿਲਾਉਣਾ; ~ness ਸਮਾਨਤਾ, ਇਕਰੂਪਤਾ, ਸਮਰੂਪਤਾ, ਉਪਮਾ, ਪ੍ਰਤੀਰੂਪ, ਅਨੁਰੂਪਤਾ

liking ('ਲਾਇਕਿਡ਼) *n* ਪੱਸਦ ਦੀ ਵਸਤੁ; ਰੁਚੀ, ਪਸੰਦ; ਇੱਛਾ; ਪਰੀਤ, ਤੁਸ਼ਟੀ

Lilliputian ('ਲਿਲਿ'ਪਯੂਸ਼ਨ) *a n* ਬੌਣਾ, ਨਾਟਾ, ਠਿਗਣਾ, (ਕਲਪਤ ਪ੍ਰਦੇਸ਼) ਲਿਲੀਪੁਟ ਦਾ ਵਸਨੀਕ, ਵਾਮਨ-ਦੇਸ

lily ('ਲਿਲਿ) *n* ਦੁੱਧ ਵਰਗੀ ਚਿੱਟੀ ਚੀਜ਼; ਲਿੱਲੀ, ਕੁਮੁਦਿਨੀ, ਨਲਿਨੀ; ਬਹੁਤ ਚਿੱਟੀ ਵਸਤੁ; ਅਤੀ ਸ਼ੁੱਧ ਵਿਅਕਤੀ; ਸਫੈਦ, ਦੁਧੀਆ ਪਦਾਰਥ

limb (ਲਿਮ) *n v* ਅੰਗ-ਉਪਾਂਗ, ਹੱਥ-ਪੈਰ; ਸ਼ਰਾਰਤੀ ਮੁੰਡਾ, ਸ਼ੈਤਾਨ ਲੜਕਾ; ਹੱਥ-ਪੈਰ ਕੱਟਣੇ, ਅੰਗ ਭੰਗ ਕਰਨੇ, ਅੰਗ ਛੇਦਨ ਕਰਨਾ; ~less ਅਪਾਹਜ, ਅੰਗਹੀਨ, ਲੂਲ੍ਹਾ

limbo ('ਲਿੰਬਅਉ) *n* ਨਰਕ, ਕੈਦ; ਭੁੱਲਣ ਦੀ ਦਸ਼ਾ; ਕਬਾੜ੍ਹਖਾਨਾ

lime (ਲਾਇਮ) *n v* ਚੂਨਾ, ਸਫੈਦੀ, ਚੂਨੇ ਦਾ ਪੱਥਰ;

ਲਾਸਾ; ਕਲੀ ਕਰਨੀ; (ਖੱਲਾ ਨੂੰ) ਚੂਨੇ ਦੇ ਪਾਣੀ ਵਿਚ ਭਿਉਣਾ; ਜੋਤਨਾ, ਚਿਪਕਾਉਣਾ; ~juice ਨਿੰਬੂ ਦਾ ਰਸ; ~light ਪ੍ਰਸਿੱਧੀ, ਮਸ਼ਹੂਰੀ; ਤੇਜ਼ ਰੌਸ਼ਨੀ; ~stone ਚੂਨੇ ਦਾ ਪੱਥਰ

limit ('ਲਿਮਿਟ) *n v* ਹੱਦ; ਸੀਮਾ, ਅਵਧੀ; ਸੀਮਾ-ਰੇਖਾ, ਸੀਮਤ ਕਰਨਾ, ਹੱਦਬੰਦੀ ਕਰਨੀ; ਸੀਮਾ-ਬੱਧ ਕਰਨਾ; ਪ੍ਰਤੀਬੰਧ ਲਾਉਣਾ, ਰੋਕਣਾ; ~ed ਸੀਮਿਤ, ਤੰਗ, ਪਾਬੰਦ; ਸੰਕੀਰਣ; ~ing ਸੀਮਾਕਾਰੀ, ਸੀਮਾਂਤ; ਚਰਮ; ~less ਬੇਹੱਦ, ਅਮਿਤ, ਅਨੰਤ, ਅਟੱਲ, ਅਸੀਮ

limp (ਲਿੰਪ) *n v* ਲੰਗਤਾਹਟ, ਲੰਗ; ਲੰਗੜਾਉਣਾ; ~er ਲੰਗਾ, ਲੰਗੜਾ ਕੇ ਟੁਰਨ ਵਾਲਾ; ~ing ਲੰਗੜਾਹਟ; ਲੰਗੜਾ; ~ness ਲੰਗੜਾਹਟ, ਲੰਗੜਾਪਣ

line (ਲਾਇਨ) *n v* ਪੰਗਤ, ਪੰਗਤੀ, ਕਤਾਰ; ਸਿਲਸਲਾ; ਦਿਸ਼ਾ; ਪਾਸਾ; ਅਸਤਰ ਲਗਾਉਣਾ, ਲੀਕ ਖਿੱਚਣਾ; dividing~ ਸਰਹੱਦ; hard ~s ਕਰੜੀ ਨੀਤੀ ਅਪਨਾਉਣ ਵਾਲਾ; to come into~ ਅਨੁਕੂਲ ਹੋਣਾ; toe the~ (ਕਿਸੇ ਦੀ) ਨੀਤੀ ਅਪਣਾਉਣਾ, ਪਿੱਠੂ ਬਣਨਾ; ~age, lineage ਪੰਗਤੀ-ਬੰਧਨ, ਪੰਗਤੀ-ਕਰਨ; ਵੰਸ਼, ਵੰਸ਼-ਪਰੰਪਰਾ, ਕੁਲ, ਨਸਲ; ਜੰਦ

lineal ('ਲਿਨਿਅਲ) *a* ਪਿਤਰੀ, ਵੰਸ਼ ਦਾ, ਪਰੰਪਰਾਗਤ, ਕੁਲ ਦਾ, ਨਸਲ ਦਾ, ਖ਼ਾਨਦਾਨੀ, ਜੱਦੀ; ~ity ਕੁਲ, ਜਾਤ, ਗੋਤ, ਪਿੱਤਰ, ਵੰਸ਼, ਪਰੰਪਰਾ

linger ('ਲਿੰਗਗਾ*) *v* ਲਟਕਾਉਣਾ, ਲਮਕਣਾ, ਪਛੜਾਉਣਾ; ਢਿੱਲ ਕਰਨੀ, ਠਹਿਰਨਾ; ~ing ਦੀਰਘਕਾਲ, ਚਿਰ, ਦੇਰ; ਦੀਰਘਕਾਲੀਨ, ਚਿਰਕਾਲੀਨ

linguafranca ('ਲਿੰਗਵਾਂ'ਫਰੈਂਕਅਾ) *n* ਸੰਪਰਕ

ਭਾਸ਼ਾ; ਭਾਸ਼ਾ ਮਿਸ਼ਰਣ, ਸਾਂਝੀ ਭਾਸ਼ਾ

linguist ('ਲਿਙਗਵਿਸਟ) *a* ਭਾਸ਼ਾ-ਵਿਗਿਆਨੀ; **~ics** ਭਾਸ਼ਾ-ਵਿਗਿਆਨ

link (ਲਿਙਕ) *n v* ਲੜੀ; ਕੜੀ, ਜੋੜ; ਸੰਜੋਗੀ ਭਾਗ, ਸੰਬੰਧ ਜੋੜਨ ਵਾਲਾ, ਜੋੜਨਾ, ਸ੍ਰੇਣੀ-ਬੱਧ ਕਰਨਾ, ਗੰਢਣਾ, ਤਰੁੱਪਣਾ; ਸੰਯੁਕਤ ਕਰਨਾ, ਸੰਬੰਧ ਕਰਨਾ; **~boy** ਮਸ਼ਾਲਚੀ ਮੁੰਡਾ; **~age** ਕੜੀ, ਸ਼ਰਿੰਖਲਾ; **~ed** ਜੁੜਿਆ, ਸੰਯੁਕਤ, ਸੰਬੰਧ

lion ('ਲਾਇਅਨ) *n* ਸ਼ੇਰ, ਬੱਬਰ ਸ਼ੇਰ, ਸ਼ੀਂਹ, ਕੇਸਰ ਸਿੰਘ, ਸਾਰਦੂਲ; **~ess** ਸ਼ੇਰਨੀ, ਸ਼ੀਹਣੀ

lip (ਲਿਪ) *n v* ਬੁੱਲ੍ਹ; ਹੋਂਠ, ਚੁੰਝ, ਚੁੰਚ; ਬੇਅਦਬੀ; ਬੁੱਲ੍ਹਾਂ ਨਾਲ ਲਾਉਣਾ; ਚੁੰਮਣ ਲੈਣਾ, ਚੁੰਮਣਾ, ਪਿਆਰ ਕਰਨਾ, ਘੁਸਰ-ਮੁਸਰ ਕਰਨਾ; ਮਿਣਮਿਣਾਉਣਾ; **~service** ਮੂੰਹ ਰੱਖਣੀ

liquid ('ਲਿਕਵਿਡ) *n a* ਦ੍ਰਵ, ਤਰਲ, ਦ੍ਰਵ ਰੂਪ, ਪਾਣੀ ਵਰਗਾ, ਪਤਲਾ; ਪਾਰਦਰਸ਼ੀ, ਚਮਕੀਲਾ; **~ity, ~ness** ਤਰਲਤਾ; ਬੈਂਕ ਨਕਦੀ; **~ize** ਪਿਘਲਾਉਣਾ, ਤਰਲ ਬਣਾਉਣਾ

liquidate ('ਲਿਕਵਿਡੇਇਟ) *n* ਰਿਣ ਚੁਕਾਉਣਾ, ਕਰਜ਼ਾ ਲਾਹੁਣਾ; ਹਿਸਾਬ ਸਾਫ਼ ਕਰਨਾ; ਦਿਵਾਲਾ ਨਿਕਲਣਾ; **~d** ਸਮਾਪਤ, ਨਿਰਧਾਰਤ, ਨਿਰਣੀਤ, ਮੁਕਤ

liquidation ('ਲਿਕਵਿ'ਡਇਸ਼ਨ) *n* ਭੁਗਤਾਨ, ਚੁਕਤਾ; ਕਾਰੋਬਾਰ ਬੰਦ ਕਰਨ ਦਾ ਕਾਰਜ; ਦੀਵਾਲਾ, ਸਫ਼ਾਇਆ

liquor ('ਲਿਕਅ*) *n v* ਸ਼ਰਾਬ, ਮਦਰਾ, ਸੁਰਾ, ਮਦਪਾਨ ਕਰਨਾ

lisp (ਲਿਸਪ) *n v* ਤੋਤਲਾਪਣ, ਤੁਤਲਾਹਟ; ਤੁਤਲਾਉਣਾ, ਤੁਤਲਾ ਕੇ ਬੋਲਣਾ, ਲੱਲ੍ਹਾ ਮਾਰਨਾ

list (ਲਿਸਟ) *n v* ਪੰਗਤੀ; ਸੂਚੀ-ਪੱਤਰ, ਸੂਚੀ, ਕੰਨੀ ਲਾਉਣੀ, ਕਿਨਾਰੀ ਬਣਾਉਣਾ; ਸੂਚੀ ਬਣਾਉਣਾ; **~ed** ਸੂਚੀਬੱਧ; **~ing** ਸੂਚੀਕਰਨ; **~er** ਸਰੋਤਾ, ਸੁਣਨ ਵਾਲਾ

literacy ('ਲਿਟ(ਅ)ਰਅਸਿ) *n* ਸਾਖਰਤਾ, ਅੱਖਰ-ਗਿਆਨ

literal ('ਲਿਟ(ਅ)ਰ(ਅ)ਲ) *a* ਸ਼ਾਬਦਕ, ਅੱਖਰੀ, ਅੱਖਰਬੱਧ; ਮੂਲ ਅਰਥਕ, ਤੱਥਵਾਦੀ

literary ('ਲਿਟ(ਅ)ਰਅਰਿ) *a* ਸਾਹਿਤਕ; ਲੇਖਕਾਂ ਦੁਆਰਾ ਪ੍ਰਯੁਕਤ, ਸਾਹਿਤਕ ਭਾਸ਼ਾ, ਸ਼ਾਸਤਰੀ

literature ('ਲਿਟ(ਅ)ਰਅਚਅ*) *n* ਸਾਹਿਤ, ਅਦਬ; ਸਾਹਿਤ-ਖੇਤਰ

litigate ('ਲਿਟਿਗੇਇਟ) *v* ਮੁਕੱਦਮਾ ਲੜਨਾ, ਵਾਦਵਿਵਾਦ ਕਰਨਾ, ਦਾਅਵਾ ਕਰਨਾ, ਨਾਲਸ਼ ਕਰਨੀ

litigation ('ਲਿਟਿ'ਗੇਇਸ਼ਨ) *v* ਮੁਕੱਦਮਾ, ਦਾਅਵਾ, ਮੁਕੱਦਮੇਬਾਜ਼ੀ

litre ('ਲੀਟਅ*) *n* ਲਿਟਰ, ਮੀਟਰ ਪੱਧਤੀ ਵਿਚ ਧਾਰਤਾ ਜਾਂ ਸਮਾਈ ਦੀ ਇਕ ਇਕਾਈ

litter ('ਲਿਟਅ*) *v n* ਪਰਾਲੀ ਵਿਛਾਉਣੀ, ਘਾਹ ਵਿਛਾਉਣਾ; ਉਘੜ-ਦੁੱਘੜ ਸੁੱਟ ਦੇਣਾ; ਕੂੜਾ ਗੋਹਾ; ਉਤਸ਼ਾਹਹੀਣਤਾ; ਗੜਬੜ; ਝੋਲੀ

litterateur ('ਲਿਟਅਰਾ'ਟਅ*) (*F*) *n* ਸਾਹਿਤਕਾਰ, ਅਦੀਬ, ਲੇਖਕ, ਸਾਹਿਤਕਾਰ

little ('ਲਿਟਲ) *a* ਛੋਟਾ, ਨਿੱਕਾ, ਨੰਨ੍ਹਾ, ਲਘੂ ਅਲਪ, ਥੋੜ੍ਹਾ, ਕੁਝ, ਕੁਛ, ਘੱਟ, ਕਮ; ਅਲਪ ਕਾਲਕ, ਠਿੰਗਣਾ, ਬੌਣਾ, ਨਾਟਾ; **~worth** ਬੇਕਾਰ, ਨਿਕੰਮਾ, ਵਿਅਰਥ; **~ness** ਛੁਟਿਆਈ, ਛੋਟਾਪਣ, ਨਿੱਕਾਪਣ, ਕਮੀ, ਲਘੁਤਾ; ਦੀਨਤਾ, ਤੁੱਛਤਾ, ਸੁਆਰਥ

live (ਲਿਵ਼, ਲਾਇਵ) *v a* ਜੀਉਂਦੇ ਹੋਣਾ, ਜੀਉਣਾ, (ਕਿਸੇ ਚੀਜ਼ ਉੱਤੇ) ਨਿਰਬਾਹ ਕਰਨਾ; ਕਾਇਮ ਰਹਿਣਾ; ਵਿਹਾਰ ਕਰਨਾ; ਨਿਵਾਸ ਕਰਨਾ, ਵੱਸਣਾ,

ਰਹਿਣਾ; ਸਜੀਵ, ਜੀਵਤ, ਜ਼ਿੰਦਾ; ~and let ~ ਜਿਓ ਤੇ ਜੀਣ ਦਿਓ; ~ stock ਪਸ਼ੂ ਧਨ; ~d ਜੀਵਤ, ਜੀਵਨਯੁਕਤ; ~lihood ਰੋਜ਼ੀ, ਰੋਟੀ, ਰੁਜ਼ਗਾਰ, ਨਿਰਬਾਹ, ਰਿਜ਼ਕ, ਜੀਵਨਾ, ਉਪਜੀਵਕਾ, ਜੀਵਨ-ਸਾਧਨ; ~long (ਕਾਵਿ) ਸਾਰਾ ਦਿਨ; ~ly ਜਿਓਂਦਾ-ਜਾਗਦਾ, ਹੂਬਹੂ, ਵਾਸਤਵਿਕ, ਯਥਾਰਥਕ; ਸਜੀਵ, ਪਰਾਣਮਈ; ਫੁਰਤੀਲਾ, ਪ੍ਰਸੰਨਚਿੱਤ, ਪ੍ਰਫੁੱਲਤ, ਆਨੰਦਮਈ; ~n (ਬੋ) ਮਘਣਾ, ਮਘਾਉਣਾ

liver ('ਲਿਵ਼ਅ*) n ਜਿਗਰ, ਕਲੇਜਾ, ਕਲੇਜੀ; ~y (ਨੌਕਰਾਂ ਜਾਂ ਛੋਟੇ ਕਰਮਚਾਰੀ ਦੀ) ਵਰਦੀ ਤੇ ਖ਼ੁਰਾਕ, ਜਿਗਰ ਦਾ, ਜਿਗਰੀ; ਚੀਕਣਾ, ਸੁਸਤ, ਚਿੜਚਿੜਾ

living ('ਲਿਵ਼ਿੰਗ) n a ਵਾਸ, ਰੋਜ਼ੀ, ਨਿਰਬਾਹ, ਰੁਜ਼ਗਾਰ, ਰੋਟੀ; ਸਮਕਾਲੀ, ਸਮਕਾਲਕ, ਵਿੰਦਮਾਨ; ਯਥਾ-ਤੱਥ; ਪਰਾਣਮਈ, ਪਰਾਟਧਾਰੀ, ਸਜੀਵ, ਜੀਵਤ, ਜਿਓਂਦਾ; ~ness ਸਜੀਵਤਾ; ਸਮਕਾਲੀਨਤਾ

lizard ('ਲਿਜ਼ਅਡ) n ਛਿਪਕਲੀ, ਕਿਰਲੀ

load (ਲਅਉਡ) n v ਦਬਾਉ, ਦਾਬਾ, ਭਾਰ, ਬੋਝ, ਮਾਲ-ਅਸਬਾਬ, ਲੱਦ, ਖੇਪ; ਰੁਕਾਵਟ; ਬਿਜਲੀ ਦੀ ਮਾਤਰਾ; (ਜ਼ੁੰਮੇਵਾਰੀ ਜਾਂ ਚਿੰਤਾ ਦਾ) ਭਾਰ; ਅਧਿਕਤਾ, ਬਹੁਤਾਤ; ~stone ਚੁੰਬਕ, ਲੋਹਮਣੀ, ਲੋਹਕਾਂਤ; ~ed ਭਾਰਾ, ਭਰਿਆ, ਲੱਦਿਆ; ~ing ਲੱਦਣ ਵਾਲਾ, ਭਰਨ ਵਾਲਾ; ਭਾਰ, ਬੋਝ; ਲਦਾਈ, ਭਰਾਈ

loaf (ਲਅਉਫ਼) n v ਨਾਨ, ਰੋਟੀ, ਡਬਲਰੋਟੀ; ਅਵਾਰਾਗਰਦੀ, ਮਟਰਗਸ਼ਤ; ਅਵਾਰਾਗਰਦੀ ਕਰਨੀ; ~er ਅਵਾਰਾਗਰਦ, ਬਦਮਾਸ਼

loan (ਲਅਉਨ) n v ਰਿਣ, ਉਧਾਰ, ਤਕਾਵੀ, ਕਰਜ਼; ਰਿਣ ਦੇਣਾ, ਉਧਾਰ ਦੇਣਾ

loath, loth (ਲਅਉਥ) a ਵਿਮੁਖ, ਵਿਰਕਤ; ਅਟਇੱਛਕ

loathe (ਲਅਉਦ) v ਘਿਰਨਾ ਕਰਨੀ; ਨਫ਼ਰਤ ਕਰਨੀ, ਪਸੰਦ ਨਾ ਕਰਨਾ

lobby ('ਲੌਬਿ) n v ਦਲਾਨ, ਡਿਓਢੀ; ਸਭਾ-ਮੰਡਲ, ਸਦੱਸ-ਗੈਲਰੀ, ਲਾਂਬੀ; ਪ੍ਰਭਾਵ ਮੰਡਲ; ਮੁਲਾਕਾਤੀ ਕਮਰਾ

local ('ਲਅਉਕਲ) a n ਸਥਾਨਕ; ਅਲਪ ਵਿਸਤਰਤ, ਦੇਸੀ; ~e ਘਟਨਾ-ਸਥਲ, ਸਥਾਨ, ਮੌਕਾ; ~ity ਸਥਾਨ, ਸਥਿਤੀ, ਪ੍ਰਦੇਸ਼, ਇਲਾਕਾ; ~ize ਸਥਾਨਕ ਬਣਾਉਣਾ, ਇਕ ਦੇਸ਼ ਦਾ ਬਣਾਉਣਾ, ਕੇਂਦਰਤ ਕਰਨਾ

locate (ਲਅ(ਉ)'ਕੇਇਟ) v ਪਤਾ ਕੱਢਣਾ, ਸੂਹ ਲਾਉਣੀ, ਸਥਾਨ ਦੱਸਣਾ, ਬਿਠਾਉਣਾ, ਰੱਖਣਾ

locative ('ਲੌਕਅਟਿਵ਼) n a (ਵਿਆ) ਅਧਿਕਰਨ ਕਾਰਕ, ਸੱਤਵੀਂ ਵਿਭਕਤੀ, ਸਥਾਨ ਨਿਰਦੇਸ਼ਕ

lock (ਲੌਕ) n v ਲਿੰਟ, ਲਟ, ਕੇਸਾਂ ਦਾ ਗੁੱਛਾ, ਅਲਕਾ, ਸ਼ਿਖਾ, ਜ਼ੁਲਫ਼, ਜੰਦਰਾ; ਬੰਦੂਕ ਦਾ ਘੋੜਾ, ਨਹਿਰ ਦਾ ਬੰਨ੍ਹ; ਆਲਿੰਗਨ; ਤਾਲਾ ਲਾਉਣਾ, ਜੰਦਰਾ ਮਾਰਨਾ; ਬੰਦ ਕਰਨਾ, ਜਕੜ ਲੈਣਾ; ਗੁੰਨ੍ਹਣਾ, ਫ਼ਾਹੁਣਾ, ਉਲਝਾਉਣਾ, ਵਲ੍ਹੇਟਣਾ; under ~and key ਜਿੰਦੇ ਅੰਦਰ, ਤਾਲਾ ਲਾ ਕੇ; ~er ਤਾਲੇਦਾਰ ਅਲਮਾਰੀ, (ਬੈਂਕ ਦਾ) ਲਾਕਰ; ਕੋਠਾ; ~out ਤਾਲਾਬੰਦੀ ਕਰਨਾ; ~up ਹਵਾਲਾਤ

locket ('ਲੌਕਿਟ) n ਲੋਹੇ ਦੀ ਪੱਟੀ; ਸੋਨੇ ਜਾਂ ਚਾਂਦੀ ਦਾ ਕੁੰਡਾ, ਢੋਲਣ; ਲਾਕਟ, ਇਕ ਪ੍ਰਕਾਰ ਦਾ ਹਾਰ

locomotion ('ਲਅਉਕਅਮਅ'ਮਅਉਸ਼ਨ) n ਗਮਨ, ਚਲਨ, ਗਤੀਸ਼ੀਲਤਾ, ਹਰਕਤ; ਯਾਤਰਾ ਪੱਧਤੀ

locomotive ('ਲਅਉਕਅਮਅ'ਮਅਉਟਿਵ਼) n a ਰੇਲ-ਇੰਜਣ, ਚੱਲਟਸ਼ੀਲ, ਗਤੀਸ਼ੀਲ, ਗਤੀ

ਉਤਪਾਦਕ

locus ('ਲਾਉਕੁਅਸ) n ਮੌਕਾ; ਵਕੂਅ; ਠੀਕ ਥਾਂ,
ਸਥਾਨ, ਸੰਸਥਿਤੀ; ਬਿੰਦੂ-ਪੱਥ; ~standi (L)
ਦਖ਼ਲ-ਅੰਦਾਜ਼ੀ ਜਾਂ ਪੱਖ ਪੇਸ਼ ਕਰਨ ਦਾ ਅਧਿਕਾਰ

locust ('ਲਾਉਕਅਸਟ) n ਟਿੱਡੀ, ਟਿੱਡੀ-ਦਲ

locution (ਲਾ(ਉ)'ਕਯੂਸ਼ਨ) n ਭਾਸ਼ਣ-ਸ਼ੈਲੀ,
ਮੁਹਾਵਰਾ, ਅੰਦਾਜ਼ੇ ਤਕਰੀਰ, ਤਰਜ਼ੇ ਗੁਫ਼ਤਗੂ;
ਵਾਕ, ਉਕਤੀ, ਪਦ, ਸ਼ਬਦ

lodge (ਲੱਜ) n v ਰਿਹਾਇਸ਼, ਵਾਸ, ਛੋਟਾ ਮਕਾਨ;
ਤੰਬੂ, ਖੇਮਾ; ਰਿਹਾਇਸ਼ ਦੇਣੀ, ਰੱਖਣਾ, ਵਸਾਉਣਾ,
ਨਿਵਾਸ ਦੇਣਾ, ਧਾਰਨਾ, ਰੱਖਣਾ, ਟਿਕਾਉਣਾ,
ਠਹਿਰਾਉਣਾ; ਵਸੱਣਾ, ਬਸੇਰਾ ਕਰਨਾ, ਰਾਤ ਕੱਟਣਾ

lodging ('ਲੌਜਿਙ) n ਰਿਹਾਇਸ਼, ਵਾਸ-ਗ੍ਰਿਹ,
ਆਵਾਸ

loft (ਲੌਫ਼ਟ) n v ਮੰਮਟੀ, ਅਟਾਰੀ, ਛੱਤਰੀ,
ਕਬੂਤਰਖ਼ਾਨਾ; ਗੋਂਦ ਨੂੰ ਉੱਚਾ ਸੁੱਟਣਾ; ~y ਉੱਚਾ,
ਉੱਚ, ਉਤੰਗ, ਉੱਨਤ

log (ਲੌਗ) n v ਲੱਕੜ ਦਾ ਕੁੰਦਾ, ਖੁੰਢ, ਗੋਲੀ,
ਗੱਟਾ; ਮੰਜ਼ਲ ਤੈ ਕਰਨਾ, ਜੁਰਮਾਨਾ ਕਰਨਾ, ਦੰਡ
ਦੇਣਾ; ~book ਰੋਜ਼ਨਾਮਚਾ, ਜਾਤਰੂ ਦੀ ਡਾਇਰੀ

logarithm ('ਲੌਗਅਰਿਦ(ਅ)ਮ) n (ਸੰਖੇਪ log)
(ਹਿਸਾਬ) ਲਾਗ, ਲਾਗਰਿਥਮ, ਲਘੂਗਣਕ, ਛੇਦ;
ਘਾਤ (ਜਿਸ ਤਕ ਸੰਖਿਆ ਨੂੰ ਵਧਾਉਣਾ ਚਾਹੀਦੇ
ਜਿਵੇਂ ਦੋ ਦੀ ਤਿੰਨ ਘਾਤ=2^3)

logger ('ਲੌਗਅ*) n ਲੱਕੜਹਾਰਾ; ~head ਮੂੜ੍ਹ,
ਵਿਅਕਤੀ, ਉੱਲੂ; ਲੋਹੇ ਦਾ ਜੰਤਰ

logic ('ਲੌਜਿਕ) n ਤਰਕ-ਸ਼ਾਸਤਰ, ਨਿਆਇ-
ਸ਼ਾਸਤਰ, ਤਰਕ, ਮੰਤਕ; ~al ਤਾਰਕਕ, ਤਰਕ-
ਸ਼ਾਸਤਰ ਸਿਬੰਧੀ; ਤਰਕ-ਪੂਰਨ, ਯੁਕਤੀ-ਯੁਕਤ;
ਤਰਕਸਿੱਧ

logos ('ਲੌਗੌਸ) n ਸ਼ਬਦ; (cap) ਸ਼ਬਦ-ਬ੍ਰਹਮ

loin (ਲੌਇਨ) n ਕੁੱਲ੍ਹਾ, ਕਮਰ, ਪੁੱਠਾ, ਪੁੱਠ; ~cloth
ਧੋਤੀ; ਲੰਗੋਟ, ਜਾਂਘੀਆਂ

loiter ('ਲੌਇਟਅ*) v ਮਟਰ-ਗਸ਼ਤ ਕਰਨਾ,
ਟਹਿਲਣਾ, ਵਿਅਰਥ ਸਮਾਂ ਨਸ਼ਟ ਕਰਨਾ, ਮਾਰੇ-
ਮਾਰੇ ਫ਼ਿਰਨ; ~over one's work ਜੀ
ਚੁਰਾਉਣਾ, ਕੰਮ-ਚੋਰ ਹੋਣਾ

lollipop ('ਲੌਲਿਪੌਪ) n (ਬ ਵ) ਮਿਠਿਆਈਆਂ;
ਖੰਡ ਦਾ ਰੂਪਾ, ਲਾਲੀਪਾਪ

lone, lonely (ਲਅਉਨ, 'ਲਅਉਨਲਿ) a n
ਇਕੱਲਾ, ਨਿਆਸਰਾ, ਬੇਆਸਰਾ; ਸੁੰਵਾ, ਉਜਾੜ,
ਉਦਾਸ; ~liness ਇਕੱਲ, ਸੁੰਨਾਪਨ, ਵੀਰਾਨਾ,
ਉਜਾੜ; ਤਨਹਾਈ; ਇਕਲਾਪਾ

long (ਲੌਙ) n v adv ਲੰਬਾ; ਦੀਰਘ ਕਾਲ, ਲੰਮੀ
ਅਵਧੀ; ਵਿਸਤਾਰ, ਵੇਰਵਾ; ਬਹੁਤ ਚਾਹੁਣਾ,
ਲਾਲਸਾ ਹੋਣੀ; ਤਾਂਘਣਾ, ਰੀਝਣਾ, ਲੰਮਾ, ਦੂਰ
ਦਾ, ਅਤੀਤ ਕਾਲੀਨ; ਚਿਰਕਾਲੀ, ਲੰਮੇ ਸਮੇਂ ਤੋਂ,
ਚਿਰ ਤੋਂ; ~cloth ਲੱਠਾ; ~eared ਮੂਰਖ, ਗਧਾ,
ਲਮਕੰਨਾ; ~standing ਚਿਰਕਾਲੀ, ਚਿਰੋਕਣਾ,
ਪੁਰਾਣਾ; in the ~run ਅਖੀਰ ਨੂੰ, ਅਖ਼ਰਕਾਰ;
~evity ਚਿਰੰਜੀਵਤਾ, ਦੀਰਘ, ਆਯੂ; ~ing
ਤਾਂਘ, ਅਕਾਂਖਿਆ; ਉਤਸੁਕ, ਅਭਿਲਾਸ਼ੀ

longitude (ਲੌਙੀਟਯੂਡ) n ਲੰਮਾਈ; ਤੂਲ,
(ਭੂਗੋ.) ਰੇਖਾਂਸ਼, (ਗਣਿ, ਜੋ) ਖਗੋਲੀ ਰੇਖਾਂਸ਼

longitudinal (ਲੌਙੀਟਯੂਡੁਨਅਲ) a ਲੰਮਾ,
ਲੰਮਾਈ ਸਬੰਧੀ, ਦੇਸ਼ਾਂਤਰੀ; ਭੋਗ ਸਬੰਧੀ

loof (ਲੂਫ਼) n ਹਥੇਲੀ

look (ਲੁਕ) v n ਤੱਕਣਾ, ਦਰਸ਼ਨ ਕਰਨਾ, ਤਾੜਨਾ,
ਵੇਖਣਾ; ਨਿਰੀਖਣ ਕਰਨਾ, ਪਰੀਖਿਆ ਕਰਨੀ,
ਸੁੱਝਣਾ, ਦਿਸਣਾ; ਰਾਹ ਵੇਖਣਾ; ਆਭਾ, ਛੱਬ, ਰੂਪ,
ਸੂਰਤ, ਅੰਦਾਜ਼, ਚਿਹਰਾ-ਮੁਹਰਾ, ਨੈਣ-ਨਕਸ਼, ਦਿਖ;
ਦਰਸ਼ਨ; ~about ਖ਼ਬਰਦਾਰ ਹੋਣਾ; ~after ਦੇਖ

ਭਾਲ ਕਰਨ; ~down (up) on ਨਫ਼ਰਤ ਕਰਨੀ;
~into ਨਿਰੀਖਣ ਕਰਨ; ~on ਤਮਾਸ਼ਾ ਵੇਖਣ;
~to ਵੱਲ ਧਿਆਨ ਦੇਣ; ~through ਘੋਖਣਾ,
ਚੰਗੀ ਤਰ੍ਹਾਂ ਪੜਤਾਲਣਾ; ~ing ਦ੍ਰਿਸ਼ਟੀ, ਦਰਸ਼ਨ

loom (ਲੂਮ) n ਕਰਘਾ, ਖੱਡੀ, ਕੱਪੜਾ ਬੁਨਣ ਦੀ
ਮਸ਼ੀਨ

loop (ਲੂਪ) n v (ਰੱਸੇ, ਡੋਰੀ ਆਦਿ ਦਾ) ਵਲ;
ਘੁੰਡੀ; (ਮੁੰਠੀ ਦਾ ਕੰਮ ਦੇਣ ਵਾਲਾ) ਚੱਕਰ, ਧਾਤ
ਦੀ ਅੰਗੂਠੀ; ਨਿਰੋਧਕ ਛੱਲਾ; ਫੰਧਾ ਪਾਉਣਾ;
ਚੱਕਰ ਵਿਚ ਫਸਣਾ; ~hole ਝਰੋਖਾ, ਛਿਦਰ,
ਰੰਧਰ; ਮਘੋਰਾ, ਚੋਰ ਰਸਤਾ, ਬਚਾਉ ਦਾ ਰਾਹ

loose (ਲੂਸ) v a ਸੁੰਤਰ ਕਰਨਾ, ਛੱਡਣਾ, ਖੋਲ੍ਹਣਾ;
ਢਿੱਲਾ ਕਰਨਾ, ਉਤਾਰਨਾ; ਦਾਗਣਾ; ਬੰਧਨ-ਮੁਕਤ,
ਖੁੱਲ੍ਹਾ ਹੋਇਆ; ਸੁਤੰਤਰ, ਮੁਕਤ, ਬੇਰੋਕ; ਅਸਥਿਰ,
ਅਦ੍ਰਿੜ੍ਹ, ਢਿੱਲਾ; ਅਸਪਸ਼ਟ; (ਅਨੁਵਾਦ) ਅਸ਼ਲੀਲ,
ਅਵਾਰਾ; ~n ਸੁਤੰਤਰ ਕਰਨਾ, ਮੁਕਤ ਕਰਨਾ, ਢਿੱਲਾ
ਕਰਨਾ, ਛੱਡਣਾ; ਦਸਤ ਲੱਗਾਲੇ; ਜ਼ਾਬਤਾ ਢਿੱਲਾ ਕਰ
ਦੇਣਾ; ~ness ਢਿੱਲ, ਸਿਥਲਤਾ, ਢਿੱਲਾਪਣ;
ਵਿਤਚਾਰ, ਦੁਰਾਚਾਰ; ਮਰੋੜ, ਦਸਤ, ਪੇਚਸ਼

loot (ਲੂਟ) n v ਲੁੱਟ, ਲੁੱਟ ਦਾ ਮਾਲ; ਲੁੱਟਣਾ

lord (ਲੋਡ) n v (L~) ਇਸ਼ਵਰ, ਪ੍ਰਭੂ; ਸੁਆਮੀ,
ਮਾਲਕ, ਸਾਹਿਬ, ਸਰਦਾਰ; ਸਾਮੰਤ, ਨਵਾਬ,
ਜਾਗੀਰਦਾਰ, ਲਾਟ; ਰਈਸ; ਨੇਤਾ; ਪਤੀ, ਨਾਥ;
ਸ਼ਾਸਨ ਕਰਨਾ, ਹੁਕਮ ਚਲਾਉਣਾ; ਲਾਰਡ ਦੀ
ਉਪਾਧੀ ਦੇਣੀ, ਲਾਰਡ ਬਣਾਉਣਾ; ~ship
ਪ੍ਰਭਾਵਤ, ਸਰਦਾਰੀ, ਸਾਹਿਬਪੁਣਾ, ਸੁਆਮੀਤੁਤਵ;
ਰਾਜ, ਜਾਗੀਰ

lorn (ਲੋਨ) n ਉਜਾੜ, ਵੀਰਾਨ, ਇਕੱਲਾ, ਅਨਾਥ,
ਲਾਚਾਰ, ਵਿਚਾਰਾ, ਬੇਕਸ

lorry ('ਲੋਰਿ) n ਠੇਲ੍ਹਾ, ਟਰੱਕ; ਮੋਟਰ ਲਾਰੀ,
ਛਕੜਾ, ਲਾਰੀ

lose (ਲੂਜ਼) v ਗੁਆਉਣਾ, ਗੁਆਚਣਾ, ਵਾਂਝਿਆਂ
ਹੋਣਾ; ਲੁਪਤ ਹੋਣਾ, ਮਰ ਜਾਣਾ; ~one's
temper ਕਰੋਧ ਵਿਚ ਆਉਣਾ; ਗੁੱਸੇ ਹੋਣਾ

loss (ਲੌਸ) n ਘਾਟਾ, ਟੋਟਾ, ਨੁਕਸਾਨ, ਹਾਨੀ

lot (ਲੌਟ) n ਤਕਦੀਰ, ਨਸੀਬ, ਲੇਖ, ਭਾਗ,
ਕਿਸਮਤ; ਹਾਲਤ; ਥੋਕ ਮਾਲ, ਢੇਰ, ਨੀਲਾਮੀ
ਲਈ ਢੇਰੀ; ਟੁਕੜੀ; ~tery ਲਾਟਰੀ; ਕਿਸਮਤ
ਦੀ ਗੱਲ, ਭਾਗਾਂ ਦੀ ਖੇਡ, ਜੁਆ

lotus ('ਲਾਓਟਅਸ) n ਕੰਵਲ, ਕਮਲ, ਪਦਮ,
ਪੰਕਜ; ਕੁਮੁਦਿਨੀ, ਨਲਿਨੀ

loud (ਲਾਉਡ) a adv ਉੱਚ, ਉੱਚਾ, ਭਾਰਾ; ਜੋਰਦਾਰ;
ਭੜਕੀਲਾ; ~ness ਉੱਚੀ ਅਵਾਜ਼, ਜ਼ੋਰ-ਸ਼ੋਰ

lounge (ਲਾਉਨਜ) v n ਮਟਕ ਮਟਕ ਕੇ ਟੁਰਨਾ,
ਟਹਿਲਣਾ, ਅਵਾਰਾਗਰਦੀ ਕਰਨੀ; ਆਲਸ ਵਿਚ
ਸਮਾਂ ਗੁਆਉਣਾ, ਸੁਸਤਾਉਣਾ; ਮਟਰਗਸ਼ਤ;
ਸੋਫ਼ਾ, ਸੈਰਗਾਹ; ਡਿਉੜੀ, ਬੈਠਕ, ਲਾਉਂਜ

louse (ਲਾਉਸ) n ਜੂੰ

lout (ਲਾਉਟ) n v ਪੇਂਡੂ; ਗੰਵਾਰ, ਉਜੱਡ, ਅਨਾੜੀ
ਬੰਦਾ; ਆਦਰ ਨਾਲ ਝੁਕਣਾ, ਸਲਾਮ ਕਰਨਾ

love (ਲਅੱਵ੍) n v ਪਿਆਰ, ਪਰੇਮ, ਮੁਹੱਬਤ, ਇਸ਼ਕ,
ਪਰੀਤ, ਸਨੇਹ, ਚਾਹ; ਕਾਮਵਾਸ਼ਨਾ; ਪਿਆਰ
ਕਰਨਾ, ਮੁੱਹਬਤ ਕਰਨਾ; ~d ਪਿਆਰਾ, ਪ੍ਰਿਯ; ~ly
ਪਿਆਰਾ, ਲਲਿਤ, ਰਮਣੀਕ, ਹੁਸੀਨ, ਦਿਲਕਸ਼;
~r ਪਰੇਮੀ, ਅਨੁਰਾਗੀ, ਆਸ਼ਕ, ਆਸ਼ਨਾ

loving ('ਲਾਅੱਵਿਙ) a ਪਿਆਰਾ, ਨਿੱਘਾ, ਪ੍ਰਿਯ, ਸਨੇਹੀ

low (ਲਅੱਉ) n v a adv ਨੀਵਾਂ, ਹੇਠਲਾ, ਛੋਟਾ;
ਨੀਚ, ਹੋਛਾ; ਨਿਸਤੇਜ, ਦਲਿਤ; (ਸਵਰ) ਕੋਮਲ,
ਮੱਧਮ, ਹੇਠਾਂ, ਥੱਲੇ, ਧੀਰੇ ਧੀਰੇ, ਹੌਲੀ ਹੌਲੀ;
~lying ਨੀਵਾਂ; ~er ਉਤਾਰਨਾ, ਝੁਕਾਉਣਾ,
ਨੀਵਾਂ ਕਰਨਾ; ਲੰਬਾਈ ਘਟਾਉਣੀ, ਉਚਾਈ
ਘਟਾਉਣੀ; (ਮੁੱਲ ਆਦਿ ਦਾ) ਘਟਣਾ, ਡਿੱਗਣਾ,

ਹੇਠਾਂ ਆਉਣਾ; ਹੇਠਲਾ, ਹੋਰ ਹੇਠਾਂ ਦਾ

loyal ('ਲੋਇ(ਅ)ਲ) *a* ਵਫ਼ਾਦਾਰ, ਬਾਵਫ਼ਾ;
ਸਾਦਿਕ, ਨਮਕਹਲਾਲ

lubricant ('ਲੂਬਰਿਕਅੰਟ) *n* ਸਨੇਹਕ, ਚੋਪੜ,
ਗਰੀਸ, ਚਿਕਨਾਈ

lubricate ('ਲੂਬਰਿਕੇਇਟ) *v* ਤੇਲ ਦੇਣਾ, ਚੋਪੜਨਾ,
ਵਾਂਗਣਾ; ਮੁਸ਼ਕਲਾਂ ਨੂੰ ਸੌਖਿਆਂ ਪਾਰ ਕਰ ਲੈਣਾ

lucid ('ਲੂਸਿਡ) *a* ਪ੍ਰਕਾਸ਼ਮਈ, ਉੱਜਲ, ਸੁਅੱਛ,
ਨਿਰਮਲ, ਨਿਖਰਿਆ, ਸਾਫ਼, ਚਮਕੀਲਾ; **~ity**
ਸੁਅੱਛਤਾ, ਉੱਜਲਤਾ, ਸਪਸ਼ਟਤਾ, ਸਫ਼ਾਈ,
ਚਮਕ; **~ly** ਸਪਸ਼ਟ ਰੂਪ ਵਿਚ

luck (ਲੱਕ) *n* ਭਾਗ, ਲੇਖ, ਕਿਸਮਤ, ਤਕਦੀਰ,
ਨਸੀਬ; ਸੁਭਾਗ, **~y** ਭਾਗਸ਼ਾਲੀ, ਸੁਭਾਗਵਾਨ,
ਖ਼ੁਸ਼ਕਿਸਮਤ, ਧੰਨ

luggage ('ਲੱਗਿਜ) *n* ਸਫ਼ਰੀ ਸਾਮਾਨ,
ਅਸਬਾਬ, ਬੋਰੀਆ-ਬਿਸਤਰਾ, ਗੰਢੜੀ, ਪੋਟਲੀ

lukewarm ('ਲੂਕ'ਵੋਮ) *a* ਕੋਸਾ, ਨਿੱਘਾ; ਨੀਮ
ਗਰਮ; ਉਦਾਸੀਨ (ਆਦਮੀ); **~ness**
ਕੋਸਾਪਣ, ਨਿੱਘ, ਨੀਮ-ਗਰਮੀ; ਨਿਰਉਤਸ਼ਾਹ

luminous ('ਲੂਮਿਨਅਸ) *a* ਨੂਰਾਨੀ, ਤੇਜਮਈ,
ਚਮਕੀਲਾ, ਚਮਕਦਾਰ, ਪ੍ਰਕਾਸ਼ਵਾਨ; **~ness**
ਤੇਜ, ਚਮਕ, ਪ੍ਰਕਾਸ਼

lump (ਲੰਪ) *n v* ਇਕ ਕੰਢੇਦਾਰ ਸੁਰਮਈ ਮੱਛੀ;
ਘਾਟ, ਡਲਾ, ਡੇਲੀ, ਪਿੰਡ, ਢੇਲਾ; ਪੇੜਾ (ਆਟਾ),
ਪਿੰਨਾ (ਮੱਖਣ), ਪਿੰਨੀ, ਢੇਰ, ਅਧਿਕਤਾ; ਮਿੱਟੀ ਦਾ
ਮਾਧੋ, ਗੋਬਰ-ਗਟੇਸ਼; ਇੱਕਤਰ ਕਰਨਾ, ਢੇਰ
ਲਾਉਣਾ, ਢੇਰ ਹੋਣਾ; ਬਰਾਬਰ ਸਮਝਣਾ; ਸਾਰਾ
ਧਨ ਲਾ ਦੇਣਾ, ਬੇਢੰਗੀ ਟੋਰ ਟੁਰਨਾ; **~sum** ਇਕ
ਮੁਸ਼ਤ ਰਾਸ਼ੀ

lunacy ('ਲੂਨਅਸਿ) *n* ਪਾਗਲਪਣ, ਉਨਮਾਦ;
ਸੁਦਾਅ, ਸੁਦਾਈਪਣ, ਝੱਲ, ਝੱਲਾਪਣ

lunar ('ਲੂਨਅ*) *n a* ਚੰਦ ਦੀ ਦੂਰੀ; ਫਿੱਕਾ,
ਹਲਕਾ, ਮੱਧਮ

lunatic ('ਲੂਨਅਟਿਕ) *a* ਪਾਗਲ, ਦੀਵਾਨਾ,
ਬਾਵਲਾ, ਖ਼ਬਤੀ; **~asylum** ਪਾਗਲਖ਼ਾਨਾ

lunch, luncheon (ਲੰਚ, 'ਲੰਚ(ਅ)ਨ) *n v*
ਲੰਚ ਦੁਪਿਹਰ ਦਾ ਖਾਣਾ; ਭੋਜਨ ਦੇਣਾ, ਲੰਚ ਦੇਣਾ

lung (ਲੰਡ) *n* ਫੇਫੜਾ, ਫਿੱਫਰਾ

lurch (ਲਅਃਚ) *n* ਬਿਪਤਾ, ਸੰਕਟ, ਮੁਸੀਬਤ,
ਆਪਤਕਾਲ; ਝਟਕਾ; ਜ਼ਖ਼ਮ; **leave in the~**
ਮੁਸੀਬਤ ਵਿਚ ਛੱਡ ਜਾਣਾ

lure (ਲੂਅ*) *n v* ਆਕਰਸ਼ਨ, ਲੁਭਾਉਣਾ, ਝਾਂਸਾ,
ਫੁਸਲਾਹਟ; ਲੋੜ ਵਿਚ ਪਾਉਣਾ, ਫੁਸਲਾਉਣਾ,
ਝਾਂਸਾ ਦੇਣਾ, ਚਕਮਾ ਦੇਣਾ

lust (ਲਅਸਟ) *n v* ਕਾਮ-ਵਾਸ਼ਨਾ; ਹਵਸ; ਆਵੇਗ-
ਪੂਰਨ ਕਾਮਨਾ ਕਰਨੀ, ਹਾਬੜਨਾ, ਹਵਸ ਕਰਨੀ;
~ful ਲਾਲਸੀ, ਹਾਬੜਿਆ; **~fulness**
ਕਾਮੁਕਤਾ, ਕਾਮ ਆਤੁਰਤਾ, ਲਾਲਸਾ; **~y** ਰਿਸ਼ਟ-
ਪੁਸ਼ਟ, ਤੱਗੜਾ

lustre ('ਲਅਸਟਅ*) *n v* ਚਮਕ; ਆਭਾ, ਆਬ;
ਤੇਜ, ਸ਼ੋਭਾ, ਮਹਿਮਾ; ਚਮਕਣਾ

luxurious (ਲਅੱਗਾ'ਯੂਅਰਿਅਸ) *a* ਵਿਲਾਸੀ, ਸੁਖ
ਭੋਗੀ, ਸੁਖਰਾਇਣ; ਵਿਲਾਸਮਈ, ਅਤੀ
ਸੁਖਾਵਾਂ, ਆਨੰਦਪੂਰਨ; **~ness** ਵਿਲਾਸ, ਸੁਖ
ਭੋਗ; ਆਨੰਦਪੂਰਨਤਾ, ਭਰਪੂਰਤਾ

luxury ('ਲਅੱਕਸ਼(ਅ)ਰਿ) *n* ਐਯਾਸ਼ੀ, ਰੰਗ-ਰਾਸ;
ਵਿਲਾਸ, ਸੁਆਦ, ਸੁਖ

lyric ('ਲਿਰਿਕ*) *n a* ਗੀਤ, ਗੀਤ ਕਾਵਿ; ਵੀਨਾ ਦਾ,
ਵੈਣਿਕ, ਵੀਨਾ ਸਬੰਧੀ, ਗੀਤਾਤਮਕ, ਗੀਤਮਈ;
~al ਸਰੋਦੀ; **~ism** ਗੀਤਾਤਮਕਤਾ, ਸਰੋਦੀਪੁਣਾ;
~ist ਗੀਤਕਾਰ

lyrist ('ਲਿਰਿਸਟ) *n* ਵੀਨਾਵਾਦਕ, ਗੀਤਕਾਰ

M

M, m (ਐਮ) *n* ਰੋਮਨ ਵਰਣਮਾਲਾ ਦਾ ਤੇਰ੍ਹਵਾਂ ਅੱਖਰ; ਰੋਮਨ ਗਿਣਤੀ ਦਾ ਇਕ ਹਜ਼ਾਰ ਦਾ ਅੰਕ

M. A. ('ਐਮ 'ਏਇ) Master of Arts, ਐਮ. ਏ. ਦੀ ਡਿਗਰੀ

ma (ਮਾ) *n* ਅੰਮੀ, ਮੰਮੀ, ਮਾਂ

machine (ਮਅ'ਸ਼ੀਨ) *n v* ਮਸ਼ੀਨ, ਕਲ, ਜੰਤਰ, ਪੁਰਜ਼ਾ; ਸਾਧਨ; ਮਸ਼ੀਨ ਚਲਾਉਣਾ; ~ry ਮਸ਼ੀਨਾਂ, ਕਲਾਂ ਜੰਤਰਾਂ ਦਾ ਸਮੂਹ; ਜੰਤਰਾਂ ਦਾ ਕਾਰਜ, ਕਲ ਦੀ ਬਣਾਵਟ; ਕਲ-ਪੁਰਜ਼ੇ, ਮਸ਼ੀਨਰੀ

machinist (ਮਅ'ਸ਼ੀਨਿਸਟ) *n* ਮਿਸਤਰੀ, ਮਸ਼ੀਨ-ਸਾਜ਼; ਮਸ਼ੀਨ ਚਾਲਕ

mad (ਮੈਡ) *a v* ਪਾਗਲ, ਝੱਲਾ, ਸੁਦਾਈ, ਦੀਵਾਨਾ, ਕਮਲਾ, ਬਾਉਲਾ, ਖ਼ਬਤੀ; ਪਾਗਲ ਬਣਾਉਣਾ ਜਾਂ ਹੋਣਾ, ਮੂਰਖ ਹੋਣਾ ਜਾਂ ਕਰਨਾ; ~cap ਮਸਤਾਨਾ, ਸਿਰ ਫਿਰਿਆ, ਭਾਵੂਕ; ~house ਪਾਗਲਖ਼ਾਨਾ; ~den ਝੱਲਾ ਕਰ ਦੇਣਾ, ਸੁਦਾਈ ਬਣਾ ਦੇਣਾ; ~ly ਪਾਗਲਾਂ ਵਾਂਗੂ, ਸੁਦਾਈਆਂ ਵਰਗਾ ; ~ness ਪਾਗਲਪਣ, ਝੱਲ, ਮੂਰਖਤਾ

madam ('ਮੈਡਅਮ) *n* ਸ਼੍ਰੀਮਤੀ, ਬੇਗਮ, ਮੇਮ ਸਾਹਿਬ

mafia ('ਮੈਫ਼ਿਅ) *n* ਮਾਫ਼ੀਆ, ਨਾਜਾਇਜ਼ ਧੰਦਾ ਕਰਨ ਵਾਲਿਆਂ ਦਾ ਗਰੋਹ

mag (ਮੈਗ) *n v* ਬਕਵਾਸ; ਬਕਵਾਸ ਕਰਨਾ, ਗੱਪ ਮਾਰਨਾ, ਬੁੜਬੁੜ ਕਰਨਾ

magazine ('ਮੈਗਅ'ਜ਼ੀਨ) *n* (1) ਰਸਾਲਾ, ਪਰਚਾ, ਪਤੱਰਕਾ; (2) ਸਟੋਰ, ਭੰਡਾਰ; ਖ਼ਜ਼ਾਨਾ, ਗੁਦਾਮ; (3) ਅਸਲਾਖ਼ਾਨਾ, ਸ਼ਸਤਰ-ਘਰ, ਬਾਰੂਦਖ਼ਾਨਾ

magic ('ਮੈਜਿਕ) *n* ਜਾਦੂ; ਜਾਦੂਗਰੀ, ਟੂਣਾ; ~al ਜਾਦੂ ਦਾ; ~ian ਜਾਦੂਗਰ, ਟੂਣੇਹਾਰ, ਬਾਜ਼ੀਗਰ

magisterial ('ਮੈਜਿ'ਸਟਿਅਰਿਅਲ) *a* ਮੈਜਿਸਟਰੇਟੀ, ਮੈਜਿਸਟਰੇਟ ਦਾ, ਹਾਕਮਾਨਾ, ਅਫ਼ਸਰਾਨਾ

magistrate ('ਮੈਜਿਸਟਰੇਇਟ) *n* ਮੈਜਿਸਟਰੇਟ, ਦੰਡ ਅਧਿਕਾਰੀ

magmatic (ਮੈਗ'ਮੈਟਿਕ) *a* ਚਿਪਚਪਾ, ਲੇਸਦਾਰ

magna C(h)arta ('ਮੈਗਨਅ'ਕਾਟਅ) *n* (ਸੰਨ 1512 ਈ. ਵਿਚ ਇੰਗਲੈਂਡ ਦੇ ਬਾਦਸ਼ਾਹ ਰਾਹੀਂ ਪ੍ਰਦਾਨ ਕੀਤਾ) ਮਹਾਂ ਅਧਿਕਾਰ ਪੱਤਰ

magnanimity ('ਮੈਗਨਅ'ਨਿਮਅਟਿ) *n* ਉਦਾਰਤਾ, ਖ਼ੁਸ਼ਦਿਲੀ

magnanimous (ਮੈਗ'ਨੈਨਿਮਅਸ) *a* ਉਦਾਰ-ਚਿੱਤ, ਸਖੀ, ਖੁੱਲ੍ਹਦਿਲਾ, ਜਿਗਰੇ ਵਾਲਾ, ਉਦਾਰ-ਆਤਮਾ

magnate ('ਮੈਗਨੇਇਟ) *n* ਧਨਾਢ, ਰਈਸ, ਧਨੀ

magnet ('ਮੈਗਨਿਟ) *n* ਚੁੰਬਕ, ਮਿਕਨਾਤੀਸ; ਕੁਤਬਨੁਮਾ; (ਅਲੰਕਾਰਕ) ਆਕਰਸ਼ਕ ਵਸਤੂ; ~ic ਚੁੰਬਕੀ, ਮਿਕਨਾਤੀਸ, ਖਿਚਵਾਂ, ਆਕਰਸ਼ਟਸ਼ੀਲ; ~ize ਚੁੰਬਕ-ਸ਼ਕਤੀ ਦੇਣਾ, ਆਕਰਸ਼ਟ ਸ਼ਕਤੀ ਦੇਣਾ, ਚੁੰਬਕ ਸ਼ਕਤੀ ਵਾਲਾ ਹੋਣਾ; ~ized ਚੁੰਬਕ ਯੁਕਤ

magneto (ਮੈਗ'ਨੀਟਅਉ) *n* ਚੁੰਬਕੀ-ਸ਼ਕਤੀ ਦੇਣ ਵਾਲਾ ਜੰਤਰ

magnified ('ਮੈਗ'ਨਿਫ਼ਾਇਡ) *n* ਵਿਸਤਰਤ, ਵਿਸ਼ਾਲ

magnify ('ਮੈਗਨਿਫ਼ਾਇ) v ਵਡਿਆਉਣਾ,
ਵਧਾਉਣਾ, ਵੱਡਾ ਕਰਨਾ; ਵਧਾ ਕੇ ਦਸੱਣਾ;
ਮਹਿਮਾ ਕਰਨੀ; ~ing ਆਵਰਧਕ, ਆਵਰਧਨ

magnitude ('ਮੈਗਨਿਟਯੂਡ) n ਆਕਾਰ, ਕੱਦ,
ਮਾਤਰ; ਵਡੱਪਣ, ਮਹੱਤਾ, ਮਹੱਤਵ

magnum ('ਮੈਗਨਅਮ) n ਅੱਧੇ ਗੈਲੱਨ ਦੀ
ਬੋਤਲ, ਵੱਡੀ ਬੋਤਲ

magus ('ਮੇਇਗਾਅਸ) n ਜਾਦੂਗਰ, ਸਿਆਣਾ

maid (ਮੇਇਡ) n ਕੰਨਿਆ, ਕੁਆਰੀ ਲੜਕੀ,
ਮੁਟਿਆਰ; ਨੌਕਰਾਨੀ, ਦਾਸੀ, ਗੋਲੀ; ~en
ਕੰਨਿਆ, ਕੁਆਰੀ ਲੜਕੀ; (ਕ੍ਰਿਕਟ) ਖ਼ਾਲੀ
ਓਵਰ, ਨਵੀਂ; ਅਛੂਤੀ, ਕੋਰੀ; ਪਲੇਠਾ, ਪਹਿਲਾ;
~en speech ਪਹਿਲੀ ਤਕਰੀਰ, ਪ੍ਰਥਮ
ਭਾਸ਼ਣ; ~enhood ਕੁਆਰਾਪਣ, ਅਛੂਤਾਪਣ

mail (ਮੇਇਲ) n v ਡਾਕ, ਡਾਕ ਦਾ ਥੈਲਾ; ਡਾਕ
ਵਿਚ ਪਾਉਣਾ (ਖ਼ਤ)

maim (ਮੇਇਮ) v ਅੰਗ-ਭੰਗ ਕਰਨਾ, ਕੱਟਣਾ,
ਲੂਲ੍ਹਾ ਜਾਂ ਟੁੰਡਾ ਕਰ ਦੇਣਾ; ਨਿਕੰਮਾ ਕਰਨਾ,
ਬੇਕਾਰ ਕਰਨਾ

main ('ਮੇਇਨ) a ਪਰਮ, ਉੱਤਮ, ਪ੍ਰਮੁੱਖ, ਮੁੱਖ,
ਅਸਲੀ, ਪ੍ਰਧਾਨ, ਵੱਡਾ; ~land ਮਹਾਂਦੀਪ;
~yard ਚਬੂਤਰਾ (ਮੁੱਖ ਮਸਤੂਲ ਦੇ ਹੇਠਾਂ ਦਾ);
~ly ਮੁੱਖ ਤੌਰ ਤੇ, ਬਹੁਤ ਕਰਕੇ, ਪ੍ਰਮੁੱਖ ਰੂਪ ਵਿਚ

maintain (ਮੇਇਨ'ਟੇਇਨ) v ਕਾਇਮ ਰੱਖਣਾ,
ਕਰਦੇ ਰਹਿਣਾ; ਸੰਭਾਲੀ ਰੱਖਣਾ, ਕਬਜ਼ੇ ਵਿਚ
ਰੱਖਣਾ, ਨਿਰਬਾਹ ਕਰਨਾ, ਪਾਲਾ ਕਰਨੀ; ~ed
ਪੋਸ਼ਤ; ਰੱਖਿਆ ਹੋਇਆ, ਪੁਸ਼ਟ

maintenance ('ਮੇਇਨਟਅਨਅੰਸ) n ਦੇਖ-ਭਾਲ,
ਰੱਖਿਆ; ਪਾਲਣ-ਪੋਸ਼ਣ, ਸਹਾਰਾ, ਨਿਰਬਾਹ

maize (ਮੇਇਜ਼) n ਮੱਕੀ

majestic (ਮਅ'ਜੈੱਸਟਿਕ) a ਸ਼ਾਹੀ, ਸ਼ਾਹਾਨਾ,
ਗੌਰਵਸ਼ਾਲੀ, ਸ਼ਾਨਦਾਰ, ਆਲੀਸ਼ਾਨ, ਤੇਜੱਸਵੀ

majesty ('ਮੈਜਅਸਟਿ) n ਸ਼ਾਨ; ਸ਼ੋਭਾ,
ਦਬਦਬਾ, ਵਕਾਰ; ਰਾਜ-ਪ੍ਰਤਾਪ; ਮਹਾਂਬਲੀ

major ('ਮੇਇਜਅ*) n a ਪ੍ਰਧਾਨ, ਮੁੱਖ
(ਵਿਅਕਤੀ) ਸ੍ਰੇਸ਼ਠ, ਵੱਡਾ (ਆਦਮੀ), ਬਾਲਗ਼,
ਮੇਜਰ (ਫ਼ੌਜੀ ਅਫ਼ਸਰ); ਗੰਭੀਰ; ~ship ਮੇਜਰ
ਦੀ ਪਦਵੀ; ਪ੍ਰਮੁੱਖਤਾ, ਵਡੱਪਣ

majority (ਮਅ'ਜੌਰਅਟਿ) n ਬਹੁ-ਸੰਮਤੀ, ਬਹੁ-ਮੱਤ;
ਪ੍ਰਚੂਤਾ

make (ਮੇਇਕ) v n ਬਣਾਉਣਾ; ਪੈਦਾ ਕਰਨਾ;
ਰਚਨਾ; ਤਿਆਰ ਕਰਨਾ (ਚਾਹ ਆਦਿ); ਵਿਛਾਉਣਾ
(ਬਿਸਤਰਾ ਆਦਿ);   ਕਰਨਾ, ਅਮਲ ਵਿਚ
ਲਿਆਉਣਾ; ਕਾਇਮ ਕਰਨਾ; ਆਕਾਰ, ਰੂਪ,
ਆਕ੍ਰਿਤੀ, ਰਚਨਾ, ਕ੍ਰਿਤੀ; ~good ਘਾਟਾ ਪੂਰਾ
ਕਰਨਾ; ~up ਕਸਰ ਪੂਰੀ ਕਰਨੀ; ਭੇਸ ਬਦਲਣਾ;
ਸ਼ਿੰਗਾਰ ਸਮਗਰੀ; ਮਨਘੜਤ (ਕਿੱਸਾ); ਇਕੱਤਰ
ਕਰਨਾ (ਪੈਸੇ ਆਦਿ); ~r ਕਰਤਾ; ਪਾਲਕ
ਨਿਰਮਾਤਾ

making ('ਮੇਇਕਿਙ) n ਰਚਨਾ,   ਬਣਾਵਟ,
ਆਮਦਨੀ

maladjustment ('ਮੈਲਅ'ਜਅੱਸ(ਟ)ਮਅੰਟ) n
ਅਣਜੋੜ, ਬੇਤਰਤੀਬੀ, ਕੁਵਿਵਸਥਾ, ਭੈੜਾ ਪ੍ਰਬੰਧ

maladministration   ('ਮੈਲਅਡ'ਮਿ-
ਨਿ'ਸਟਰੇਇਸ਼ਨ) n ਬਦਅਮਨੀ, ਬਦਇੰਤਜ਼ਾਮੀ,
ਭੈੜਾ ਰਾਜ-ਪ੍ਰਬੰਧ, ਕੁਸ਼ਾਸਨ

maladroit ('ਮੈਲਅ'ਡਰੋੱਇਟ) a ਬਦਤਮੀਜ਼,
ਭੱਦਾ, ਅਨਾੜੀ; ~ness ਭੱਦਾਪਣ, ਅਨਾੜੀਪਣ,
ਬੇਢੰਗਾਪਣ

malady ('ਮੈਲਅਡਿ) n ਵਿਕਾਰ, ਰੋਗ, ਬੀਮਾਰੀ

mala fide ('ਮੇਇਲਅ'ਫ਼ਾਇਡਿ) a adv
ਬਦਨੀਤੀ ਵਾਲੀ, ਖੋਟੀ ਭਾਵਨਾ ਨਾਲ

malaise (ਮੈ'ਲੇਇਜ਼) *n* ਬੇਚੈਨੀ, ਸਰੀਰਕ ਕਸ਼ਟ (ਬਿਨਾ ਕਿਸੇ ਵਿਸ਼ੇਸ਼ ਬੀਮਾਰੀ ਦੇ), ਖ਼ਰਾਬੀ, ਵਿਗਾੜ

malaria (ਮਅ'ਲੇਅਰਿਆ) *n* ਮਲੇਰਿਆ, ਮੌਸਮੀ ਬੁਖ਼ਾਰ, ਕਾਂਬੇ ਦਾ ਤਾਪ

malconduct (ਮੈਲ'ਕੌਂਡਅਕਟ) *n* ਦੁਰਵਿਹਾਰ, ਬੁਰੀ ਵਰਤੋਂ

maldistribution (ਮੈਲ'ਡਿਸਟਰਿ'ਬਯੂਸ਼ਨ) *n* ਕਾਣੀ ਵੰਡ

male (ਮੇਇਲ) *n a* ਨਰ, ਪੁਰਸ਼; ਪੁਲਿੰਗ, ਨਰ-ਜਾਤੀ, ਮਰਦਾਵਾਂ

maledict ('ਮੈਲਿ'ਡਿਕਟ) *v a* ਸਰਾਪ ਦੇਣਾ, ਸਰਾਪਣਾ; ਸਰਾਪਿਆ; ~**ion** ਸਰਾਪ, ਬਦ-ਦੁਆ, ਬਦ-ਅਸੀਸ

malevolence (ਮਅ'ਲੈੱਵਅਲਅੰਸ) *n* ਮੰਦਭਾਵਨਾ, ਦੁਰਇੱਛਾ, ਵੈਰ, ਪ੍ਰਦੋਹ, ਦੇਖ

malevolent (ਮਅ'ਲੈੱਵਲਅੰਟ) *a* ਮੰਦਇੱਛਿਤ, ਦੁਰਭਾਵਨਾ-ਪੂਰਨ; ਦੁਰਆਤਮਾ, ਵੈਰੀ

malice ('ਮੈਲਿਸ) *n* ਵੈਰ, ਈਰਖਾ, ਦੇਖ, ਖਾਰ, ਖੁਟਸ, ਬਦਨੀਤੀ

malicious (ਮਅ'ਲਿਸ਼ਅਸ) *a* ਵੈਰੀ, ਦੋਖੀ, ਖੁਟਸੀ; ਬਦਨੀਤੀ ਦਾ; ਪਾਪ-ਆਤਮਾ ਵਾਲਾ; ~**ness** ਖੁਟਸ, ਦੋਖ, ਵੈਰ

malign (ਮਅ'ਲਾਇਨ) *v a* ਨਿੰਦਾ ਕਰਨੀ, ਬੁਰਾਈ ਕਰਨੀ, ਬਦਨਾਮ ਕਰਨਾ, ਅਸ਼ੁੱਭ, ਘਾਤਕ; ~**ance**, ~**ancy** (ਰੋਗ ਦੀ) ਘਾਤਕਤਾ, ਪ੍ਰਚੰਡਤਾ; ਈਰਖਾ; ਕਪਟ

mall (ਮੈਲ) *n* ਠੰਢੀ ਸੜਕ, ਜਨਪਥ, ਛਾਂ-ਦਾਰ ਮਾਰਗ

malnutrition ('ਮੈਲਨਯੂ'ਟਰਿਸ਼ਨ) *n* ਅਪੂਰਨ ਖ਼ੁਰਾਕ, ਅਸੰਤੁਲਤ ਭੋਜਨ

malodour (ਮੈਲ'ਅਉਡਅਆ*) *n* ਬਦਬੂ, ਦੁਰਗੰਧ

malpractice ('ਮੈਲ'ਪਰੈਕਟਿਸ) *n* ਬਦਚਲਨ, ਭ੍ਰਿਸ਼ਟਾਚਾਰ, ਦੁਰਾਚਾਰ; ਬੇ-ਪਰਵਾਹੀ, ਗਫ਼ਲਤ; ਖਿਆਨਤ

malpractitioner (ਮੈਲ'ਪਰੈਕਟਿਸ਼ਨਅ*) *n* ਬਦਚਲਨ, ਭ੍ਰਿਸ਼ਟਾਚਾਰੀ, ਕੁਕਰਮੀ, ਬੇਇਮਾਨ, ਦੁਰਾਚਾਰੀ; ਬੇਪਰਵਾਹ, ਗਾਫ਼ਿਲ

maltreat ('ਮੈਲ'ਟਰੀਟ) *v* ਬੁਰਾ ਸਲੂਕ ਕਰਨਾ, ਬੁਰਾ ਵਰਤਾਉ ਕਰਨਾ, ਦੁਰਵਿਹਾਰ ਕਰਨਾ, ਬਦਸਲੂਕੀ ਕਰਨੀ; ~**ment** ਦੁਰਾਚਾਰ, ਦੁਰਵਿਹਾਰ, ਬਦਸਲੂਕੀ

mamma (ਮਅ'ਮਾ) *n* ਅੰਮੀ, ਅੰਬੜੀ, ਮਾਂ ਜੀ, ਬੀ ਜੀ; ਬੀਬੀ ਜੀ; ~**l** ਥਣਧਾਰੀ ਪ੍ਰਾਣੀ, ਦੁੱਧ ਪਿਲਾਉਣ ਵਾਲੇ ਜੀਵ

mammon ('ਮੈਮਅਨ) *n* ਧਨ-ਦੇਵਤਾ, ਕੁਬੇਰ, ਮਾਇਆ, ਦੌਲਤ

mammoth ('ਮੈਮਅਥ) *a n* ਵਿਸ਼ਾਲ, ਬਹੁਤ ਵੱਡਾ, ਮਹਾਨ

mammy ('ਮੈਮਿ) *n* ਮਾਂ, ਮੰਮੀ, ਅੰਬੜੀ; ਆਯਾ

man (ਮੈਨ) *n v* ਪੁਰਸ਼, ਆਦਮੀ, ਨਰ, ਇਨਸਾਨ, ਮਾਨਵ; ਮੰਨੁਖ ਜਾਤੀ; ਦਾਸ, ਸੇਵਕ, ਸੈਨਕ ਜਵਾਨ; ਪਤੀ, ਖਾਵੰਦ; ਸੁਰੱਖਿਆ ਲਈ ਆਦਮੀ ਹੋਣਾ; ਹੌਸਲਾ ਵਧਾਉਣਾ, ਦਿਲ ਮਜ਼ਬੂਤ ਕਰਨਾ; ~**at-arms** ਸਿਪਾਹੀ, ਸੈਨਕ; ਜੋਧਾ, ਸੈਨਕ; ~**ful** ਬਹਾਦਰ, ਸੂਰਬੀਰ, ਦਲੇਰ, ਸਾਹਸੀ; ~**fulness** ਮਰਦਾਨਗੀ, ਸੂਰਬੀਰਤਾ, ਬਹਾਦਰੀ, ਦਲੇਰੀ; ਦ੍ਰਿੜ੍ਹਤਾ; ~**kind** ਮਾਨਵ-ਜਾਤੀ; ਪੁਰਸ਼, ਮੰਨੁਖ, ਮਾਨਵ; ~**less** ਉਜਾੜ, ਸੁੰਞਾ, ਨਿਰਜਨ; ~**like** ਮਾਨਵ ਰੂਪ; ਇਨਸਾਨੀ; ਮਰਦਾਨਗੀ ਭਰਿਆ, ਨਰ-ਰੂਪ; ~**power** ਮੰਨੁਖੀ ਸ਼ਕਤੀ

manacle ('ਮੈਨਅਕਲ) *n v* ਹਥਕੜੀ, ਬੇੜੀ, ਜੰਜ਼ੀਰ, ਸੰਗਲ; ਰੁਕਾਵਟ; ਹੱਥਕੜੀ ਪਹਿਨਾਉਣੀ, ਜੰਜ਼ੀਰ ਨਾਲ ਕੱਸਣਾ

manage ('ਮੈਨਿਜ) *n v* ਸਿਖਲਾਈ; ਪ੍ਰਬੰਧ ਕਰਨਾ, ਬੰਦੋਬਸਤ ਕਰਨਾ, ਇੰਤਜ਼ਾਮ ਕਰਨਾ; ਦੇਖ-ਭਾਲ ਕਰਨੀ, ਸੰਭਾਲਣਾ; ਚਲਾਉਣਾ; ~able ਅਧੀਨ, ਵੱਸ (ਪ੍ਰਬੰਧ ਵਿਚ); ~ment ਪ੍ਰਬੰਧ, ਇੰਤਜ਼ਾਮ, ਬੰਦੋਬਸਤ, ਉਪਾਉ, ਫ਼ਲ, ਜੁਗਤੀ; ਸ਼ਾਸਨ, ਪ੍ਰਬੰਧਨ; ~r ਪ੍ਰਬੰਧਕ, ਸੰਚਾਲਕ, ਮੈਨੇਜਰ; ~rial ਪ੍ਰਬੰਧਕੀ, ਪ੍ਰਬੰਧ-ਸਬੰਧੀ

managing ('ਮੈਨਿਜ਼ਿਡ) *n a* ਪ੍ਰਬੰਧ ਕਰਨ, ਪ੍ਰਬੰਧ; ਪ੍ਰਬੰਧਕ, ਚਾਲਕ; ~body ਪ੍ਰਬੰਧਕੀ ਸੰਸਥਾ; ~committee ਪ੍ਰਬੰਧਕੀ ਕਮੇਟੀ; ~director ਪ੍ਰਬੰਧ ਨਿਰਦੇਸ਼ਕ

mandate ('ਮੈਨਡੇਇਟ) *n v* ਫ਼ਰਮਾਨ, ਸਰਕਾਰੀ ਆਦੇਸ਼, ਅਧਿਆਦੇਸ਼, ਅਗਿਆ-ਪੱਤਰ; ਸੌਂਪਣਾ, ਸਮਰਪਣ ਕਰਨਾ

mandatory ('ਮੈਨਡਅਟ(ਅ)ਰਿ) *a* ਅਧਿਦੇਸ਼ਾਤਮਕ, ਅਧਿਦੇਸ਼ੀ; ਅਨਿਵਾਰਜ, ਲਾਜ਼ਮੀ, ਅਵੱਸ਼ਕ

mandrill ('ਮੈਨਡਰਿਲ) *n* ਬਣ-ਮਾਨਸ, ਵੱਡਾ ਲੰਗੂਰ

mango ('ਮੈਙਗਅਉ) *n* ਅੰਬ

manhandle ('ਮੈਨ'ਹੈਂਡਲ) *v* ਹੱਥੋਪਾਈ ਕਰਨੀ

mania ('ਮੇਇਨਯਾ) *n* ਖ਼ਬਤ, ਸਨਕ; ~c ਖ਼ਬਤੀ, ਸ਼ੁਦਾਈ, ਸਨਕੀ, ਦੀਵਾਨਾ, ਸਿਰਫ਼ਿਰੀ, ਪਾਗਲ (ਆਦਮੀ)

manifest ('ਮੈਨਿਫ਼ੈੱਸਟ) *n v a* ਪਾਲਸੂਚੀ; ਪਰਗਟਾਉਣਾ, ਪ੍ਰਤੱਖ ਕਰਨਾ, ਉਘਾੜਨਾ; ਸਿੱਧ ਕਰਨਾ, ਸਾਖਿਆਤ ਕਰਨਾ, ਅਭਿਵਿਕਤ ਕਰਨਾ; ਪਰਕਟ, ਸਪਸ਼ਟ; ~ation ਅਭਿਵਿਅੰਜਨ,

ਪ੍ਰਕਾਸ਼, ਜ਼ਹੂਰ; ~ed ਸਪਸ਼ਟ, ਪਰਗਟ; ~o ਮਨੋਰਥ-ਪੱਤਰ, ਘੋਸ਼ਣਾ-ਪੱਤਰ, ਨੀਤੀ-ਘੋਸ਼, ਮੈਨੀਫ਼ੈਸਟੋ; ਪ੍ਰਵਿਅੰਜਨਾ

manifold ('ਮੈਨਿਫ਼ਅਉਲਡ) *v a* ਬਹੁ-ਗੁਣਾ ਕਰਨਾ, ਬਹੁ-ਵਿਧੀ ਬਣਾਉਣਾ; ਬਹੁ-ਭਾਂਤੀ, ਬਹੁ-ਵਿਧ, ਨਾਨਾ-ਵਿਧ, ਵੰਨ-ਸੁਵੰਨਾ

manipulate (ਮਅ'ਨਿਪਯੁਲੇਇਟ) *v* ਹੱਥਾਂ ਨਾਲ ਚਲਾਉਣਾ, ਕੰਮ ਵਿਚ ਲਿਆਉਣਾ; ਆਪਣੇ ਹਿਤ ਵਿਚ ਵਰਤਣਾ; ਜੋੜ-ਤੋੜ ਕਰਨਾ

manipulation (ਮਅ'ਨਿਪਯੁ'ਲੇਇਸ਼ਨ) *n* ਹੱਥ ਫੇਰੀ, ਜੁਗਤ; ਜੋੜ-ਤੋੜ; ਪੱਤੇਬਾਜ਼ੀ, ਹੁਸ਼ਿਆਰੀ

manipulative (ਮਅ'ਨਿਪਯੁਲਅਟਿਵ) *a* ਫ਼ਲ ਭਰਿਆ

manipulator (ਮਅ'ਨਿਪਯੁਲੇਇਟਾ*) *n* ਪੱਤੇਬਾਜ਼, ਫ਼ਲੀਸ਼ਾ, ਸਾਜ਼-ਬਾਜ਼ ਕਰਨ ਵਾਲਾ

manner ('ਮੈਨਅ*) *n* ਵਿਧੀ, ਢੱਬ, ਤਰਜ਼, ਤੌਰ, ਤਰੀਕਾ, ਆਚਾਰ, ਸ਼ਿਸ਼ਟਾਚਾਰੂ, ਵਿਹਾਰ (ਬ ਵ) ਚੋਜ, ਰੀਤ, ਢੰਗ, ਰੀਤੀ, ਦਸਤੂਰ; ~ed ਸੁਸ਼ੀਲ, ਭੱਦਰ, ਸ਼ਿਸ਼ਟ, ਵਿਨੀਤ; ~ism ਸ਼ਿਸ਼ਟਤਾ, ਆਚਾਰ, ਆਚਰਨ, ਵਿਹਾਰ; ~less ਕੁਚੱਜਾ, ਅਸ਼ਿਸ਼ਟ, ਦੁਰਾਚਾਰੀ

manoeuvrability (ਮਅ'ਨੁਵਰਅ'ਬਿਲਅਟਿ) *n* ਜੁੱਧ-ਅਭਿਆਸ ਵਿਚ ਨਿਪੁੰਨਤਾ

manoeuvre (ਮਅ'ਨੂਵਾ*) *n* ਪੈਂਤੜੇ-ਬਾਜ਼ੀ, ਚਲਾਕੀ, ਜੁਗਤੀ, ਦਾਅ, ਚਾਲ, ਉਪਾਉ, ਤੋੜ-ਜੋੜ; ਜੁੱਧ ਅਭਿਆਸ ਕਰਨਾ; ਦਾਅ ਲਾਉਣਾ

manor ('ਮੈਨਅ*) *n* ਜਾਗੀਰ, ਮਿਲਖ, ਤਅੱਲੁਕਾ, ਜ਼ਿਮੀਂਦਾਰੀ

mansion ('ਮੈਨਸ਼ਨ) *n* ਹਵੇਲੀ, ਮਹਲ, ਕੋਠੀ, ਭਵਨ

mantle ('ਮੈਨਟਲ) *n v* ਚੋਗਾ, ਲਬਾਦਾ; ਦੁਪੱਟਾ,

ਨਕਾਬ; ਜਾਲੀ, ਕੱਜਣ; ਚੋਗਾ ਜਾਂ ਲਬਾਦਾ
ਪਾਉਣਾ, ਚੋਗੇ ਨਾਲ ਢੱਕ ਲੈਣਾ, ਢਕ ਲੈਣਾ,
ਛੁਪਾ ਲੈਣਾ, ਪਰਦਾ ਪਾਉਣਾ

manual ('ਮੈਨਯੂਅਲ) *n a* ਕਿਤਾਬੜੀ, ਪੁਸਤਕਾ,
ਗੁਟਕਾ, ਨੇਮਾਵਲੀ, ਮੈਨੂਅਲ; ਦਸਤੀ, ਹੱਥ-
ਸਬੰਧੀ, ਹੱਥ ਦਾ, ਸਰੀਰਕ; **~art** ਹਸਤ-ਕਲਾ;
~excercise ਸਰੀਰਕ ਕਸਰਤ; **~labour**
ਸਰੀਰਕ ਕਿਰਤ; **~work** ਹੱਥ ਦਾ ਕੰਮ

manufactory ('ਮੈਨਯੂ'ਫੈਕਟ(ਅ)ਰਿ) *n*
ਕਾਰਖ਼ਾਨਾ, ਸ਼ਿਲਪਗ੍ਰਿਹ, ਸ਼ਿਲਪਸ਼ਾਲਾ,
ਨਿਰਮਾਣਸ਼ਾਲਾ

manufacture ('ਮੈਨਯੂ'ਫੈਕਚਅ*) *n v*
ਕਾਰੀਗਰੀ, ਸ਼ਿਲਪਕਾਰੀ, ਨਿਰਮਾਣ, ਨਿਰਮਾਣ
ਕਰਨਾ, ਰਚਨਾ, ਬਣਾਉਣਾ; **~d** ਰਚਿਆ ਗਿਆ,
ਬਣਾਇਆ ਗਿਆ, ਨਿਰਮਤ; **~r** ਉਤਪਾਦਕ,
ਨਿਰਮਾਤਾ, ਕਾਰਖ਼ਾਨੇਦਾਰ; ਕਾਰੀਗਰ

manure (ਮਅ'ਨਯੂਅ*) *n v* ਰੂੜੀ, ਖਾਦ; ਰੂੜੀ
ਪਾਉਣੀ, ਖਾਦ ਪਾਉਣੀ

manuscript ('ਮੈਨਯੂਸਕਰਿਪਟ) *n a* ਹੱਥ-ਲਿਖਤ
ਮਸੌਦਾ, ਦਸਤਾਵੇਜ਼; ਹੱਥ-ਲਿਖਤ, ਲਿਖਤੀ,
ਕਲਮੀ, ਦਸਤੀ

Many ('ਮੈਨਿ) *a n* ਬਹੁਤ, ਬਹੁਤੇ, ਅਨੇਕ, ਕਈ;
ਅਧਿਕ; **~ sided** ਬਹੁ-ਪੱਖੀ; **as ~** ਜਿੰਨੇ, ਉੰਨੇ,
ਜਿਤਨੇ, ਉਤਨੇ; **how~** ਕਿੰਨੇ, ਕਿਤਨੇ

map (ਮੈਪ) *n v* ਨਕਸ਼ਾ ਮਾਨ-ਚਿੱਤਰ; ਨਕਸ਼ਾ
ਵਾਹੁਣਾ, ਚਿੱਤਰ ਖਿਚਣਾ; **~out** ਉਲੀਕਣਾ,
ਵਿਉਂਤਣਾ, ਯੋਜਨਾ ਬਣਾਉਣੀ; **off the ~**
ਮਹੱਤਵਹੀਣ **on the ~** ਮਹੱਤਵਪੂਰਨ

mar (ਮਾ*) *v* ਵਿਗਾੜਨਾ, ਖ਼ਰਾਬ ਕਰਨਾ,
ਉਜਾੜਨਾ, ਨੁਕਸਾਨ ਪੰਹੁਚਾਉਣਾ

marathon ('ਮੈਰਅਥਨ) *n* (ਕਈ ਮੀਲ ਦੀ)

ਲੰਮੀ ਦੌੜ; ਲੰਮੇ ਦਮ ਵਾਲਾ ਕੰਮ

maraud (ਮਅ'ਰੋੜ) *v* ਲੁੱਟ-ਮਾਰ ਕਰਨੀ, ਠੱਗੀ
ਕਰਨੀ, ਚੋਰੀ ਕਰਨੀ, ਲੁੱਟਣਾ, ਡਾਕਾ ਮਾਰਨਾ

marble ('ਮਾਬਲ) *n v* ਸੰਗਮਰਮਰ; ਅਬਰੀ
ਬਣਾਉਣਾ; **~d** ਸੰਗਮਰਮਰ ਦੀ ਤਰ੍ਹਾਂ,
ਅਬਰੀਕਾਰ

March (ਮਾ'ਚ) *n v* (1) ਅੰਗਰੇਜ਼ੀ ਸਾਲ ਦਾ
ਤੀਜਾ ਮਹੀਨਾ; (2) ਕੂਚ, ਰਵਾਨਗੀ,
(3) (ਇਤਿ) ਸੀਮਾ, ਸਰਹੱਦ; ਕੂਚ ਕਰਨਾ,
ਮਾਰਚ ਕਰਨਾ, ਚਲਾਉਂਦੇ ਜਾਣਾ, ਵਧਾਉਂਦੇ
ਜਾਣਾ; **~past** ਸਲਾਮੀ ਦੇਂਦੇ ਲੰਘਣਾ

mare (ਮੇਅ*) *n* ਘੋੜੀ

margin ('ਮਾਜਿਨ) *n v* ਹਾਸ਼ੀਆ ਕਿਨਾਰੀ, ਕੰਨੀ,
ਕੋਰ; ਕੰਢਾ, ਕਿਨਾਰਾ; ਗੁੰਜਾਇਸ਼; ਹਾਸ਼ੀਆ
ਰੱਖਣਾ, ਹਾਸ਼ੀਆ ਮਾਰਨਾ; **~al** ਕੰਨੀ ਦਾ;
ਹਾਸ਼ੀਏ ਦਾ; ਮਾਮੂਲੀ

marigold ('ਮੈਰਿਗਅਉਲ਼ਡ) *n* (ਪੌਦਾ ਜਾਂ ਫੁੱਲ਼)
ਗੇਂਦਾ, ਗੁੱਟਾ

marine (ਮਅ'ਰੀਨ) *n a* ਵਪਾਰੀ ਜਹਾਜ਼; ਜਹਾਜ਼ੀ
ਬੇੜਾ; ਜਹਾਜ਼ੀ; ਸਮੁੰਦਰੀ; **~r** ਮੱਲਾਹ, ਜਹਾਜ਼ੀ,
ਜਹਾਜ਼ਰਾਨ

marish ('ਮੈਰਿਸ਼) *n a* ਦਲਦਲ, ਚਿੱਕੜ; ਦਲਦਲੀ

marital ('ਮੈਰਿਟਲ) *a* ਵਿਵਾਹਕ, ਵਿਆਹ-ਸਬੰਧੀ,
ਦੰਪਤੀ-ਸਬੰਧੀ

maritime ('ਮੈਰਿਟਾਇਮ) *a* ਸਮੁੰਦਰੀ, ਸਾਗਰੀ,
ਸਾਗਰ-ਸਬੰਧੀ

mark (ਮਾਕ) *n v* ਨਿਸ਼ਾਨ; ਅੰਕ, ਚਿੰਨ੍ਹ, ਮੁਹਰ,
ਤਮਗਾ, ਪੱਟਾ; ਬਿੰਦੂ, ਕਲੰਕ, ਦਾਗ, ਧੱਬਾ;
ਨਿਸ਼ਾਨ ਲਾਉਣਾ; ਨਾਂ ਲਿਖਣਾ; ਮੁਹਰ ਲਾਉਣੀ,
ਚਿੰਨ੍ਹ ਲਾਉਣਾ; ਵੇਖਣਾ, ਧਿਆਨ ਕਰਨਾ;
(ਫੁਟਬਾਲ); **~ed** ਵਿਸ਼ਿਸ਼ਟ, ਅੰਕਤ; ਸਪਸ਼ਟ;

~edly ਉਘੇ ਤੌਰ ਤੇ; ~er ਨਿਸ਼ਾਨ ਲਗਾਉਣ ਵਾਲਾ, ਅੰਕਕ; ਮੁਨੀਮ; ~ing ਨਿਸ਼ਾਨ; ਅੰਕਣ; ਰੰਗਣ; ~s manship ਨਿਸ਼ਾਨੇਬਾਜ਼ੀ

market ('ਮਾਕਿਟ) *n v* ਬਜ਼ਾਰ, ਮੰਡੀ, ਮਾਰਕੀਟ; ਖ਼ਰੀਦੋ-ਫ਼ਰੋਖ਼ਤ ਕਰਨਾ, ਬਜ਼ਾਰ ਵਿਚ ਚੀਜ਼ਾਂ ਵੇਚਣਾ-ਖ਼ਰੀਦਣਾ; ~ing ਲੈਣ-ਦੇਣ, ਖ਼ਰੀਦੋ-ਫ਼ਰੋਖ਼ਤ, ਵਪਾਰ

maroon (ਮਅ'ਰੂਨ) *n a v* ਪਟਾਕਾ, ਆਤਸ਼ਬਾਜ਼ੀ; ਉਨਾਬੀ (ਰੰਗ), ਗੂੜ੍ਹਾ ਲਾਲ (ਰੰਗ), ਮੈਰੂਨ (ਰੰਗ); ਅਵਾਰਾਗਰਦੀ ਕਰਨੀ, ਲੋਫਰਾਂ ਵਾਂਗ ਫਿਰਨਾ

marriage ('ਮੈਰਿਜ) *n* ਵਿਆਹ, ਸ਼ਾਦੀ, ਨਿਕਾਹ; ਲਾਵਾਂ-ਫੇਰੇ; (ਅਲੰਕਾਰਕ) ਏਕਤਾ, ਸੰਜੋਗ, ਇਤਫ਼ਾਕ; ~procession ਬਰਾਤ, ਜੰਞ, ਜਨੇਤ; civil ~ ਅਦਾਲਤੀ ਸ਼ਾਦੀ

married (ਮੈਰਿਡ) *a* ਸ਼ਾਦੀ-ਸ਼ੁਦਾ, ਵਿਆਹੁਤਾ, ਵਿਆਹਿਆ; ~ couple ਜੋੜੀ, ਦੰਪਤੀ

marry ('ਮੈਰਿ) *v* ਵਿਆਹੁਣਾ; ਵਿਆਹ ਕਰਨਾ, ਸ਼ਾਦੀ ਕਰਨੀ, ਹੱਥ ਪੀਲੇ ਕਰਨੇ, ਵਰਣਾ; (ਅਲੰਕਾਰਕ) ਅਧਿਕ ਪਿਆਰ ਕਰਨਾ, ਡੂੰਘੇ ਸਬੰਧ ਜੋੜਨੇ

Mars (ਮਾਜ਼) *n* ਮੰਗਲ (ਤਾਰਾ) ਜੁੱਧ ਦਾ ਦੇਵਤਾ

marsh (ਮਾਸ਼) *n* ਖੋਭਾ, ਖੁਭਣ, ਦਲਦਲ, ਦਲਦਲੀ ਜ਼ਮੀਨ; ~iness ਦਲਦਲੀ ਸਥਿਤਿ; ~y ਦਲਦਲੀ, ਖੋਭਵਾਲਾ, ਜਿਲਣ ਭਰਿਆ

marshal ('ਮਾਸ਼ਲ) *n v* ਸੈਨਾਪਤੀ, ਮਾਰਸ਼ਲ; ਇੱਕਤਰ ਕਰਨਾ, ਇਕੱਠਾ ਕਰਨਾ; ਕ੍ਰਮਵਾਰ ਰੱਖਣਾ, ਅੱਗੇ ਚੱਲਣਾ; ~ship ਮਾਰਸ਼ਲ ਦਾ ਅਹੁਦਾ, ਸੈਨਾਪਤੀ ਦੀ ਪਦਵੀ

mart (ਮਾ:ਟ) *n* ਮੰਡੀ, ਬਜ਼ਾਰ, ਵੰਪਾਰ ਕੇਂਦਰ; ਨੀਲਾਮੀ ਦਾ ਕੇਂਦਰ

martial (ਮਾ'ਸ਼ਲ) *a* ਜੰਗੀ, ਫ਼ੌਜੀ, ਸੈਨਕ, ਲੜਾਕੂ; ~law ਫ਼ੌਜੀ ਕਾਨੂੰਨ, ਮਾਰਸ਼ਲ ਲਾਅ

martyr ('ਮਾਟਅ*) *n* ਸ਼ਹੀਦ, ਆਤਮ-ਬਲੀਦਾਨੀ ਧਰਮ ਲਈ ਪ੍ਰਾਣ ਦੇਣਾ, ਸ਼ਹੀਦ ਕਰਨਾ, ਆਤਮ-ਬਲੀਦਾਨ ਦੇਣਾ; ~dom ਸ਼ਹੀਦੀ, ਸ਼ਹਾਦਤ, ਆਤਮ-ਬਲੀਦਾਨ

marvel ('ਮਾਵ੍ਲ) *n v* ਕਮਾਲ, ਅਜੂਬਾ, ਅਦਭੁਤ, ਅਸਚਰਜ, ਅਚੰਭਾ, ਹੈਰਾਨ ਹੋਣਾ, ਅਚੰਭੇ ਵਿਚ ਪੈਣਾ; ~lous ਅਜੀਬ, ਅਸਚਰਜ, ਅਦਭੁਤ, ਅਨੋਖਾ, ਅਨੂਠਾ; ~lousness ਅਦਭੁਤਤਾ, ਅਸਚਰਜਤਾ ਵਚਿੱਤਰਤਾ, ਅਨੋਖਾਪਣ; ਅਲੌਕਕਤਾ

marxism (ਮਾਕਸਿਜ਼(ਅ)ਮ) *n* ਮਾਰਕਸਵਾਦ

masculine (ਮੈਸਕਯੁਲਿਨ) *a n* ਮਰਦਾਵਾਂ, ਨਰ, ਆਦਮੀ ਜਿਹਾ, ਤਕੜਾ, ਬਲਵਾਨ; ~gender ਪੁਲਿੰਗ

masculinity (ਮੈਸਕਯੁ'ਲਿਨਅਟਿ) *n* ਮਰਦਊਪੁਣਾ, ਮਰਦਾਨਗੀ, ਪੁਰਸ਼ਤਾ

mash (ਮੈਸ਼)*n v a* ਕਚੂਮਰ, ਭੜਥਾ; ਜੌਂ ਅਤੇ ਗਰਮ ਪਾਣੀ ਦਾ ਘੋਲ, ਘੋੜੇ ਦਾ ਦਾਣਾ ਜਾਂ ਉਬਲਿਆ ਦਲੀਆ; ਫ਼ੇਹਣਾ, ਕਚੂਮਰ ਕੱਢਣਾ; ਮੋਹ ਲੈਣਾ; ਜਾਨੀ, ਮਨਮੋਹਕ; ~er ਰੰਗੀਲਾ, ਰਸੀਆ, ਛੈਲ-ਛਬੀਲਾ; ਛੈਲਾ

mask (ਮਾਸਕ) *n v* ਪਰਦਾ, ਨਕਾਬ, ਬੁਰਕਾ, ਕੱਜਣ; (ਅਲੰਕਾਰਕ) ਸਾਂਗ, ਮਖੌਟਾ, ਬਹੁਰੂਪੀਆ; ਨਕਾਬਪੋਸ਼; ਪਰਦਾ ਪਾਉਣਾ, ਕੱਜਣਾ; ਲੁਕਾਉਣਾ; ~ed ਗੁਪਤ, ਭੇਖੀ; ~er masquer ਬਹੁਰੂਪੀਆ, ਨਕਾਬਪੋਸ਼

mason ('ਮੇਇਸਨ) *n* ਰਾਜ, ਚਿਣਾਈਗਰ, ਸੰਗ-ਤਰਾਸ਼

masque (ਮਾਸਕ) *n* ਮੂਕ ਰਾਸਲੀਲਾ; ~rade

ਮਖੌਟੀ ਨਾਚ; ਦਿਖਾਵਾ, ਭੇਖ

mass (ਮੈਸ) *n v* ਪੂਜਾ-ਸਮਾਰੋਹ; ਢੇਰ, ਪੁੰਜ, ਸਮੂਹ; ਇਕੱਠ, ਇਕੱਠੇ ਹੋਣਾ; ਢੇਰ ਲਾਉਣਾ

massacre (ਮੈਸਅਕਆ*) *n v* ਖ਼ੂਨ-ਖ਼ਰਾਬਾ, ਕਤਲਾਮ, ਹੱਤਿਆ, ਤਬਾਹੀ, ਕਤਲ; ਖ਼ੂਨ-ਖ਼ਰਾਬਾ ਕਰਨਾ, ਕਤਲਾਮ ਕਰਨਾ, ਹੱਤਿਆ ਕਰਨੀ

massage (ਮੈਸਾਯ਼) *n v* ਮਾਲਸ਼ (ਸਰੀਰ ਦੀ); ਮਾਲਸ਼ ਕਰਨੀ, ਹੱਥ-ਪੈਰ ਦਬਾਉਣਾ

masseur, masseuse (ਮੈ'ਸਅः, ਮੈ'ਸਅःਜ਼) *n* ਮਾਲਸ਼ੀ, ਮਾਲਸ਼ੀਆ

massive (ਮੈਸਿਵ) *a* ਭਾਰੀ, ਵੱਡਾ, ਭਾਰਾ, ਵਜ਼ਨੀ, ਠੋਸ, ਸਥੂਲ; ਸ਼ਾਨਦਾਰ; ਵਿਸ਼ਾਲ (ਗ੍ਰੰਥ); **~ness** ਸਥੂਲਤਾ, ਵਿਸ਼ਾਲਤਾ

mast (ਮਾਸਟ) *n* ਥੰਮੀ, ਸ਼ਤੀਰ, ਮਸਤੂਲ

master (ਮਾਸਟਅ*) *n v* ਮਾਲਕ, ਆਕਾ, ਵਪਾਰਕ ਜਹਾਜ਼ ਦਾ ਕਪਤਾਨ, ਹਾਕਮ, ਉਸਤਾਦ, ਸਿਖਿਅਕ, ਮਾਸਟਰ; ਜਿੱਤ ਲੈਣਾ, ਅਧੀਨ ਕਰਨਾ, ਹੁਕਮ ਚਲਾਉਣਾ, ਵਿਸ਼ੇਸ਼ਗ ਬਣਨਾ, ਮੁਹਾਰਤ ਪ੍ਰਾਪਤ ਕਰਨੀ, ਚੰਗੀ ਤਰ੍ਹਾਂ ਸਿੱਖ ਲੈਣਾ; **~piece** ਸ਼ਾਹਕਾਰ; **~ly** ਨਿਪੁੰਨ, ਪ੍ਰਵੀਨ, ਕਮਾਲ ਦੀ; ਅਦੁੱਤੀ, ਅਤੀ ਉੱਤਮ; **~y** ਮੁਹਾਰਤ, ਹਕੂਮਤ, ਕਾਰੀਗੀਰੀ, ਕਮਾਲ; ਪ੍ਰਭੁਤਾ, ਅਧਿਕਾਰ, ਕਾਬੂ

masturbate (ਮੈਸਟਅਬੇਇਟ) *v* ਮੁੱਠ ਮਾਰਨੀ, ਹੱਥਰਸੀ ਕਰਨੀ, ਹਸਤ-ਮੈਥੁਨ ਕਰਨਾ

masturbation (ਮੈਸਟਅ'ਬੇਇਸ਼ਨ) *n* ਮੁੱਠਬਾਜ਼ੀ, ਹੱਥਰਸੀ, ਹਸਤ-ਮੈਥੁਨ

mat, matt (ਮੈਟ) *a v n* ਮੱਧਮ, ਮੈਲਾ; ਮੈਲਾ ਕਰਨਾ, ਚਮਕ ਮਾਰਨਾ; ਸੱਫ ਵਿਛਾਉਂਦੀ, ਫੁਹੜੀ ਪਾਉਣੀ; ਚਟਾਈ, ਟਾਟ, ਸੱਫ; **~ting** ਚਟਾਈ ਬਣਾਉਣ ਦਾ ਕੰਮ; **~tress** ਫੁਹੜੀ, ਗੱਦਾ

matador (ਮੈਟਅਡੋ*) *n* ਸਾਨੂੰਮੱਲ, ਸਾਨੂੰ ਨਾਲ ਲੜਨ ਵਾਲਾ ਪਹਿਲਵਾਨ; ਤਾਸ਼ ਦਾ ਵੱਡਾ ਪੱਤਾ

match (ਮੈਚ) *n v* (1) ਮਾਚਸ, ਅੱਗ ਬਾਲਣ ਵਾਲੀ ਤੀਲੀ; ਪਲੀਤਾ; (2) ਮੈਚ, ਖੇਡ, ਟਾਕਰਾ; ਜੋੜ, ਮੁਕਾਬਲੇ ਦਾ; (3) ਨਾਤਾ, ਵਿਆਹ-ਸਬੰਧ; ਵਰ (ਲਾੜਾ ਜਾਂ ਲਾੜੀ), ਜੋੜਾ; ਵਾਰੇ ਆਉਣਾ; ਬਰਾਬਰ ਹੋਣਾ, ਜੋੜ ਦਾ ਹੋਣਾ, ਮੇਲ ਮਿਲਾਉਣਾ; ਟੱਕਰਨਾ, ਭਿੜਨਾ, ਮਿਲਣਾ; ਵਿਆਹ ਕਰਾਉਣਾ; **~box** ਤੀਲੀਆਂ ਦੀ ਡੱਬੀ; **~ed** ਵਿਆਹਤ, ਅਨੁਰੂਪ, ਸੁਮੇਲ, ਮੇਲ ਖਾਂਦਾ ਹੋਇਆ; **~ing** ਸੁਮੇਲ, ਤੁੱਲ, ਢੁੱਕਵਾਂ; **~less** ਅਨੁਪਮ, ਅਤੁੱਲ, ਅਦੁੱਤੀ, ਅਨੋਖਾ; **~lessness** ਅਨੁਪਮਤਾ, ਅਨ-ਅਨੁਰੂਪਤਾ, ਅਤੁਲਨੀਅਤ

mate (ਮੇਇਟ) *n v* ਮਿੱਤਰ, ਸਖਾ, ਸਖੀ, ਯਾਰ, ਦੋਸਤ, ਸਹੇਲੀ, ਹਮਜੋਲੀ, ਸੰਗੀ, ਸਾਥੀ, ਜੀਵਨ ਸਾਥੀ; ਮੁਖੀਆ, ਜਹਾਜ਼ ਦਾ ਮੇਟ; ਜੋੜੇ ਦਾ ਮਿਲਣਾ, ਜੋੜੇ ਦਾ ਮਿਲਾਉਣਾ, ਸਾਥੀ ਬਣਾਉਣਾ, ਸੰਗ ਕਰਨਾ; ਵਿਆਹ ਹੋਣਾ

mater (ਮੇਇਟਅ*) *n* ਅੰਮਾ, ਮਾਂ, ਮਾਤਾ

material (ਮਅ'ਟਿਅਰਿਅਲ) *n a* ਸਾਮਾਨ, ਸਮਗਰੀ, ਮਾਲ, ਵਸਤੂ, ਭੌਤਕ ਦ੍ਰਵ; ਸਥੂਲ, ਪਦਾਰਥਕ, ਭੌਤਕ, ਸੰਸਾਰਕ; ਦੁਨਿਆਵੀ, ਮਾਇਕ; **~ism** ਪਦਾਰਥਵਾਦ, ਮਾਦਾ-ਪਰਸਤੀ; ਜੜ੍ਹਵਾਦ, ਅਨਾਤਮਵਾਦ; ਭੌਤਕਵਾਦੀ; **~ist** ਭੌਤਕਵਾਦੀ, ਪਦਾਰਥਵਾਦੀ, ਮਾਦਾਵਾਦੀ, ਜੜ੍ਹਵਾਦੀ; **~istic** ਭੌਤਕਵਾਦੀ, ਪਦਾਰਥਵਾਦੀ; **~ize** ਸਾਕਾਰ ਕਰਨਾ, ਭੌਤਕ ਰੂਪ ਪ੍ਰਦਾਨ ਕਰਨਾ

maternal (ਮਅ'ਟਅःਨਲ) *a* ਮਾਤਰੀ, ਨਾਨਕਾ, ਮਾਂ ਦੇ ਰਿਸ਼ਤੇ ਦਾ; **~grand father** ਨਾਨਾ; **~uncle** ਮਾਮਾ, ਮਾਸੜ

maternity (ਮਅ'ਟਅःਨਅਟਿ) *n* ਜਣੇਪਾ; ਪ੍ਰਸੂਤ;

~home ਵਿਆਮਸ਼ਾਲਾ, ਪ੍ਰਸੂਤ-ਘਰ; ~nurse ਦਾਈ, ਨਰਸ

mathematical (ਮੈਥਅ'ਮੈਟਿਕਲ) *a* ਗਣਿਤਕ, ਗਣਿਤ-ਸ਼ਾਸਤਰੀ, ਹਿਸਾਬੀ, ਗਣਿਤੀ, ਸਥਿਰ, ਨਿਸ਼ਚਤ; ~ly ਗਣਿਤ ਅਨੁਸਾਰ, ਹਿਸਾਬ ਦੇ ਨੁਕਤੇ ਤੋਂ

mathematician (ਮੈਥ(ਅ)ਮਅ'ਟਿਸ਼ਨ) *n* ਗਣਿਤਸਾਸ਼ਤਰੀ, ਹਿਸਾਬਦਾਨ

mathematics (ਮੈਥ(ਅ)ਮੈਟਿਕਸ) *n* ਹਿਸਾਬ, ਗਣਿਤ-ਸ਼ਾਸਤਰ, ਗਣਿਤ, ਗਣਨਾ

matin ('ਮੈਟਿਨ) *n pl a* ਪ੍ਰਾਤਕਾਲ, ਅੰਮ੍ਰਿਤ-ਵੇਲਾ

matinee (ਮੈਟਿਨੇਇ) *n* ਲੌਢੇ ਵੇਲੇ ਦਾ ਤਮਾਸ਼ਾ (ਸਿਨਮੇ ਜਾਂ ਥੀਏਟਰ ਦਾ)

matins (ਮੈਟਿਨਜ਼) *n* ਪ੍ਰਾਤਕਾਲ ਦੀ ਪ੍ਰਾਰਥਨਾ

matriarch (ਮੇਇਟਰਿਆਕ) *n* ਰਾਜ ਮਾਤਾ, ਪ੍ਰਧਾਨ ਇਸਤਰੀ; ~al ਮਾਤਾ ਪ੍ਰਧਾਨ (ਸਮਾਜ); ~y ਮਾਤਰੀ-ਰਾਜ, ਇਸਤਰੀ-ਪ੍ਰਧਾਨ ਸਮਾਜ

matricide (ਮੈਟਰਿ'ਸਾਇਡ) *n* ਮਾਤ-ਹੱਤਿਆ, ਮਾਤਰ ਘਾਤੀ, ਮਾਤਰ-ਘਾਤਕ, ਮਾਂ ਦਾ ਕਤਲ

matriculate (ਮਅ'ਟਰਿਕਯੂਲੇਇਟ) *n a* ਮੈਟਰਿਕ ਪਾਸ ਵਿਦਿਆਰਥੀ; ਦਸਵੀਂ ਦਰਜਾ ਪਾਸ

matrimonial (ਮੈਟਰਿ'ਮਅਉਨਯਅਲ) *n a* ਵਿਵਾਹਕ, ਵਿਆਹ-ਸਬੰਧੀ

matrimony (ਮੈਟਰਿਮ(ਅ)ਨਿ) *n* ਵਿਆਹ, ਸ਼ਾਦੀ

matrix ('ਮੇਇਟਰਿਕਸ) *n* ਕੁੱਖ, ਘੰਰੇਦਾਨੀ, (ਛਾਪੇ ਦਾ) ਸੰਚਾ, ਕਾਲਬ

matron (ਮੇਇਟਰ(ਅ)ਨ) *n* ਵਿਆਹੁਤਾ ਨਾਰੀ, ਮਾਈ; ਮਾਤਾ, ਪ੍ਰਧਾਨ ਪ੍ਰਚਾਰਕਾ, ਦਾਈ; ਦਵਾਈਖ਼ਾਨੇ ਦੀ ਨਿਗਰਾਨ; ਸਕੂਲ ਦੀ ਪ੍ਰਬੰਧਕ ਮੈਟਰਨ; ~age ਗ੍ਰਹਿਣੀ-ਪਦ, ਦਾਈਪੁਣਾ

matter (ਮੈਟਅ*) *n v* ਪਦਾਰਥ, ਵਿਸ਼ੈ-ਵਸਤੂ, ਵਿਚਾਰ-ਸਮਗਰੀ; ਸਾਰ, ਪੁਸਤਕ-ਸਾਰ; ਪ੍ਰਕਰਣ, ਮਾਮਲਾ

maturation (ਮੈਟਯੁ'ਰੇਇਸ਼ਨ) *n* ਪਕਿਆਈ, ਪਰਿਪੱਕਤਾ; ਪ੍ਰੌਢਤਾ, ਸਿਆਣਪ

mature (ਮਅ'ਟਯੂਅ*) *a n v* ਪੱਕਾ, ਭਰਵਾਂ, ਪੱਕਿਆ; ਗੱਭਰੂ, ਬਾਲਗ਼ਾ, ਪੂਰੀ ਹੋਈ, ਗੱਭਰੂ ਹੋਣਾ, ਬਾਲਗ਼ ਜਾਂ ਮੁਟਿਆਰ ਹੋਣਾ; ~ness, maturity ਪਕਿਆਈ, ਪ੍ਰੌਢਤਾ, ਪੱਕੀ ਉਮਰ, ਸਿਆਣੀ ਉਮਰ, ਪਰਿਪੱਕਤਾ

mausoleum (ਮੌਸਅ'ਲਿਅਮ) *n* ਦੇਹਰਾ, ਸਮਾਧ, ਮਕਬਰਾ, ਰੋਜ਼ਾ

maxim (ਮੈਕਸਿਮ) *n* (ਪ੍ਰਸਿੱਧ) ਲੋਕੋਕਤੀ, ਕਹਾਵਤ, ਅਖੌਤ, ਨੀਤੀ-ਵਚਨ, ਤੱਤ; ਸੂਤਰ, ਸਿਧਾਂਤ; ~al ਅਧਿਕਤਮ

maximum (ਮੈਕਸਿਮਮ) *n* ਵੱਧ ਤੋਂ ਵੱਧ, ਅਧਿਕਤਮ

May (ਮੇਇ) *v aux n* ਸੰਭਵ ਹੋਣਾ, ਕਰ ਸਕਣਾ; (1) ਮਈ, ਅੰਗਰੇਜ਼ੀ ਸਾਲ ਦਾ ਪੰਜਵਾਂ ਮਹੀਨਾ; (2) ਬਹਾਰ, ਨਵ-ਜੋਬਨ, ਭਰ-ਜਵਾਨੀ; ਕੁਮਾਰੀ, ਕੁਆਰੀ, ਬਾਲਾ; ~day ਪਹਿਲੀ ਮਈ ਦਾ ਦਿਨ, ਮਈ ਦਿਵਸ, ਕਿਰਤੀ ਦਿਵਸ

mayor (ਮੇਅ*) *n* ਮੇਅਰ, ਨਗਰ-ਨਾਇਕ, ਨਗਰਪਤੀ

maze (ਮੇਇਜ਼) *n v* ਭੁੱਲ-ਭੱਲਈਆ, ਭੰਵਰਜਾਲ, ਜੰਜਾਲ, ਉਲਝਣ, ਗੁੰਝਲ, ਗੋਰਖ-ਧੰਦਾ, ਵਿਆਕੁਲ

mazy (ਮੇਇਜ਼ੀ) *a* ਗੁੰਝਲਦਾਰ, ਵਲੇਵੇਂਦਾਰ, ਕੁਟਲ, ਜਟਿਲ

meadow (ਮੈੱਡਅਉ) *n* ਚਰਾਗਾਹ, ਸਬਜ਼ਾਜ਼ਾਰ, ਤਰਾਈ, ਉਪਜਾਊ ਜ਼ਮੀਨ

meagre ('ਮੀਗਅ*) *a* ਥੋੜ੍ਹਾ, ਘੱਟ, ਪਤਲਾ, ਲਿੱਸਾ; ਅਧੂਰਾ, ਅਪੂਰਨ; **~ness** ਥੁੜ੍ਹ, ਘਾਟ, ਪਤਲਾਪਣ, ਅਪੂਰਨਤਾ, ਉਣਾ

meal (ਮੀਲ) *n v* ਖਾਣਾ, ਭੋਜਨ, ਆਹਾਰ; ਸੈਦਾ, ਆਟਾ, ਸੱਤੂ; ਰੋਟੀ ਖਾਣੀ, ਭੋਜਨ ਕਰਨਾ

mean (ਮੀਨ) *n v* (ਗਤਿ) ਮੱਧਮਾਨ, ਔਸਤ, ਮੱਧਵਰਤੀ; ਸਾਧਨ, ਉਪਾਉ; ਉਦੇਸ਼ ਰੱਖਣਾ, ਅਰਥ ਹੋਣਾ, ਭਾਵ ਹੋਣਾ; ਚਾਹੁਣਾ, ਅਰਥ ਕਰਨਾ, ਸੂਚਤ ਕਰਨਾ, ਪਰਗਟ ਕਰਨਾ; **by all ~s** ਅਵੱਸ਼ ਹੀ, ਹਰ ਤਰ੍ਹਾਂ ਨਾਲ; **by no ~s** ਕਿਸੇ ਤਰ੍ਹਾਂ ਵੀ ਨਹੀਂ; **~time** ਇੰਚਰ, ਇੰਨੇ ਵਿਚ; **~while** ਇਸ ਸਮੇਂ ਵਿਚ, ਇੰਨੇ ਨੂੰ; **~ness** ਨੀਚਤਾ, ਹੋਛਾਪਣ, ਕਮੀਨਪਣ; **~ing** ਅਰਥ, ਭਾਵ, ਮਤਲਬ, ਪ੍ਰਯੋਜਨ, ਤਾਤਪਰਜ; **~ingful** ਅਰਥਪੂਰਣ; **~ingless** ਨਿਰਾਰਥਕ, ਅਰਥਹੀਨ

meander (ਮਿਐਂਡਅ*) *n v* (ਬ ਵ) ਚੱਕਰ, ਭੁੱਲ-ਭੁੱਲਈਆ; ਵਿੰਗਵਲਾਵੇਂ ਵਾਲਾ ਰਾਹ; ਚੱਕਰਦਾਰ ਯਾਤਰਾ; ਪੇਚ, ਮੋੜ, ਕੁਟਲਤਾ; ਚੱਕਰ ਖਾਣਾ, ਆਵਾਰਾਗਰਦੀ ਕਰਨੀ, ਫਿਰਦੇ ਰਹਿਣਾ; **~ed** ਭੁੱਲ-ਭੁੱਲਈਆਂ ਵਾਲਾ, ਮੋੜਦਾਰ, ਵਿੰਗ-ਤੜਿੰਗਾ

measles (ਮੀਜ਼ਲਜ਼) *n pl* ਖਸਰਾ, ਧੱਸਲ; ਛੋਟੀ ਚੇਚਕ, ਦੇਵੀ, ਛੋਟੀ ਸੀਤਲਾ; ਵਫੋਲੇ

measurable (ਮੈੱਯੁਅਰਅਬਲ) *a* ਮਾਪਣ ਯੋਗ, ਨਾਪਣ ਯੋਗ; ਅਨੁਮਾਨ ਯੋਗ

measure (ਮੈੱਯੂਅ*) *n v* ਮਾਪ, ਨਾਪ, ਪੈਮਾਨਾ, ਤੋਲ, ਮਾਤਰਾ; ਮਾਪਕ, ਫ਼ੀਤਾ; ਉਪਾਉ, ਕੰਮ; ਮਾਪਣ ਦਾ ਢੰਗ, ਅਨੁਮਾਨ, ਅੰਦਾਜ਼ਾ; ਮਾਪਣਾ, ਨਾਪਣਾ, ਪੈਮਾਇਸ਼ ਕਰਨੀ, ਤੋਲਣਾ, (ਕੱਪੜਿਆਂ ਲਈ) ਨਾਪ ਲੈਣਾ, ਮੇਚ ਲੈਣਾ; ਅਜ਼ਮਾਉਣਾ;

ਕੱਛਣਾ; **~d** ਮਾਪਿਆ ਤੋਲਿਆ; ਸੰਤੁਲਤ, ਧਿਆਨ; **~ment** ਪੈਮਾਇਸ਼, ਨਾਪ, ਮਾਪ, ਅਨੁਮਾਨ

meat (ਮੀਟ) *n* ਮਾਸ, ਗੋਸ਼ਤ; **~less** ਨਿਰਮਾਸ, ਮਾਸ ਰਹਿਤ

mechanic (ਮਿ'ਕੈਨਿਕ) *n* ਕਾਰੀਗਰ, ਮਿਸਤਰੀ, ਮਸ਼ੀਨਸਾਜ਼; ਮਕੈਨਿਕ; **~al** ਮਕਾਨਕੀ, ਮਸ਼ੀਨੀ, ਜੰਤਰਕ ਵਿਗਿਆਨ ਸਬੰਧੀ; **~ally** ਜੰਤਰਵਤ, ਮਸ਼ੀਨ ਵਾਂਗ; **~s** ਜੰਤਰ-ਵਿਗਿਆਨ, ਮਸ਼ੀਨ ਬਣਾਉਣ, ਜੰਤਰ-ਸ਼ਾਸਤਰ

mechanism ('ਮੇੱਕਅਨਿੱਜ਼(ਅ)ਮ) *n* ਜੰਤਰ-ਵਿਧੀ, ਬਣਤਰ, ਪੁਰਜ਼ੇ; ਰਚਨਾ

mechanist ('ਮੇੱਕਅਨਿਸਟ) *n* ਕਾਰੀਗਰ, ਮਸ਼ੀਨ ਬਣਾਉਣ ਵਾਲਾ; ਜੰਤਰ-ਵਿਗਿਆਨੀ

mechanization (ਮੇੱਕਅਨਾਇ'ਜ਼ੇਇਸ਼ਨ) *n* ਮਸ਼ੀਨੀਕਰਨ, ਜੰਤਰੀਕਰਨ

mechanize (ਮੇੱਕਅਨਾਇਜ਼) *v* ਮਸ਼ੀਨ ਵਾਂਗ ਬਣਾਉਣਾ, ਜੰਤਰ-ਪ੍ਰਯੋਗ ਕਰਨਾ; **~d** ਜੰਤਰ-ਭ੍ਰਿਤ, ਜੰਤਰ-ਚਾਲਤ

medal (ਮੈੱਡਲ) *n* ਮੈਡਲ, ਤਮਗਾ, ਤਕਮਾ

meddle (ਮੈੱਡਲ) *v* ਦਖ਼ਲ ਦੇਣਾ, ਟੰਗ ਅੜਾਉਣੀ

meddling (ਮੈੱਡਲਿੰਡ) *a* ਵਿਘਨਕਾਰਕ

media (ਮੀਡਿਅ) *n* ਸੰਚਾਰ ਸਾਧਨ; **~n** ਮੱਧ, ਮੱਧਵਰਤੀ, ਦਰਮਿਆਨੀ; ਮੱਧਮ, ਮਾਧਿਅਕ; **~te** ਮੱਧ-ਵਰਤੀ, ਮਧਿਅਸਥ, ਮੱਧ-ਸਥਿਤ; ਵਿਚ ਪੈਣਾ, ਸਮਝੌਤਾ ਕਰਾਉਣਾ, ਵਸੀਲਾ ਬਣਨਾ, ਮਧਿਅਸਥ ਬਣਨਾ; **~tion** ਮਧਿਅਸਥਤਾ, ਸਾਲਸੀ; **~tor** ਮਧਿਅਸਥ, ਵਿਚੋਲਾ, ਸਾਲਸ

medieval, mediaeval (ਮੈੱਡਿ'ਈਵ਼ਲ) *a* ਮੱਧਕਾਲੀਨ, ਮੱਧ-ਜੁਗੀ, ਮੱਧ-ਕਾਲ ਦਾ; **~ism**

ਮੱਧਕਾਲੀਨਤਾ, ਮੱਧਯੁਗੀਨਤਾ, ਮੱਧਕਾਲੀਨ ਰੀਤਾਂ

medical (ਮੈਡੀਕਲ) *a n* ਚਿਕਿਤਸਕੀ, ਡਾਕਟਰੀ; ਔਸ਼ਧੀ; ਚਿਕਿਤਸਾ ਸਬੰਧੀ

medicate (ਮੈਡ੍ਰਿਕੇਟ) *v* ਦਵਾ ਦੇਣਾ, ਦਵਾ-ਦਾਰੂ ਕਰਨਾ, ਦਵਾਈ ਕਰਨੀ, ਇਲਾਜ ਕਰਨਾ; ਦਵਾਈ ਮਿਲਾਉਣੀ

mediocre (ਮੀਡ੍ਰਿ'ਅਉਕਅ*) *a* (ਵਿਅਕਤੀ) ਸਧਾਰਨ, ਵਿਚਕਾਰਲਾ, ਮਾਮੂਲੀ, ਔਸਤ ਦਰਜੇ

meditate (ਮੈਡਿਟੇਇਟ) *v* ਲਿਵਲੀਨ ਹੋਣਾ, ਧਿਆਨ ਲਾਉਣਾ, ਮਗਨ ਹੋਣਾ, ਵਿਚਰਨਾ, ਇਕਾਗਰ ਚਿੱਤ ਹੋਣਾ, ਸਮਾਧੀ ਲਾਉਣੀ; ~d ਚਿੰਤਤ, ਨਿਰਧਾਰਤ

meditation (ਮੈਡਿਟੇਇਸ਼ਨ) *n* ਧਿਆਨ, ਮਨਨ, ਚਿੰਤਨ, ਮਗਨਤਾ, ਇਕਾਗਰਤਾ, ਸਮਾਧੀ, ਅਰਾਧਨਾ; ~ness ਮਗਨਸ਼ੀਲਤਾ, ਚਿਤੰਨਸ਼ੀਲਤਾ, ਧਿਆਨਸ਼ੀਲਤਾ, ਵਿਚਾਰ ਮਗਨਤਾ, ਲਿਵਲੀਨਤਾ

meditator (ਮੈਡਿਟੇਇਟਅ*) *n* ਧਿਆਨੀ, ਮਨਨ ਕਰਤਾ, ਚਿੰਤਕ

medium (ਮੀਡ੍ਯਅਮ) *n a* ਮਾਧਿਅਮ; ਵਿਚਲਾ ਗੁਣ, ਵਿਚਲਾ-ਮੇਲ, ਵਿਚਲਾ ਦਰਜਾ, ਵਿਚਲੀ ਚੀਜ਼; ਸਾਧਨ, ਵਸੀਲਾ, ਮਾਰਗ

meek (ਮੀਕ) *a* ਨਿਰਮਾਣ, ਮਸਕੀਨ, ਨਿਮਾਣਾ, ਦੀਨ, ਸ਼ਾਂਤ, ਬੇਜ਼ਬਾਨ; ~ly ਨਿਮਰਤਾ ਪੂਰਬਕ, ਚੁਪਚਾਪ

meet (ਮੀਟ) *n a v* ਇਕੱਤਰਤਾ, ਜੋੜ-ਮੇਲ, ਇਕੱਠ; ਮੀਟਿੰਗ; ਉਚਿਤ, ਯੋਗ, ਠੀਕ, ਉਪਯੁਕਤ; ਮਿਲਣਾ, ਮੇਲ ਹੋਣਾ, ਜਾਣ-ਪਛਾਣ ਕਰਨੀ; ਗ੍ਰਹਿਣ ਕਰਨਾ, ਪ੍ਰਾਪਤ ਕਰਨਾ; ~ing ਸਮਾਗਮ, ਜਲਸਾ, ਸਭਾ, ਸੰਮੇਲਨ, ਗੋਸ਼ਠੀ, ਇਕੱਠ; ਮਿਲਾਵਾ, ਸੰਗਮ

mega (ਮੈਗਾ) *a* ਮਹਾਂ, ਵਿਸ਼ਾਲ, ਵੱਡਾ

melancholic (ਮੈਲ੍ਅਨ'ਕੌਲਿਕ) *a* ਉਦਾਸ, ਵਿਸ਼ਾਦੀ, ਦਿਲਗੀਰ

melancholy (ਮੈਲ੍ਅਨਕਅਲਿ) *n a* ਵਿਸ਼ਾਦ, ਚਿੰਤਾ, ਉਦਾਸੀ, ਦਿਲਗੀਰੀ

melee (ਮੈਲੇਇ) (*F*) *n* ਮੁੱਠ-ਭੇੜ, ਝਪਟ; ਲੜਾਈ, ਸੰਗਰਾਮ, ਝਗੜਾ, ਦੰਗਾ

mellorate (ਮੀਲਿਅਰੇਇਟ) *v* ਸੁਧਾਰਨਾ, ਸੰਵਾਰਨਾ, ਚੰਗਾ ਬਣਾਉਣਾ, ਬਿਹਤਰ ਬਣਾਉਣਾ; ਸੁਧਰਨਾ

melioration (ਮੀਲਿਅ'ਰੇਇਸ਼ਨ) *n* ਸੁਧਾਰ, ਉੱਨਤੀ, ਚੰਗਿਆਈ

mellow (ਮੈਲ੍ਅਉ) *a* ਰਸੀਲਾ, ਨਰਮ, ਰਸਿਆ (ਫੱਲ), ਮਿੱਠਾ, ਪੱਕਿਆ ਹੋਇਆ; ਕੂਲੀ, ਮੱਧਮ, ਮਿਲਾਪੜਾ, ਖ਼ੁਸ਼ ਮਿਜ਼ਾਜ; ਕੋਮਲ ਬਣਾਉਣਾ, ਪ੍ਰਸੰਨ ਕਰਨਾ; ਪੱਕਣਾ; ਰਸਣਾ; ~ness ਕੋਮਲਤਾ, ਰਸੀਲਾਪਣ, ਮਤਵਾਲਾਪਣ; ~y ਕੋਮਲ, ਰਸੀਲਾ, ਮਧੁਰ; ਪੱਕਿਆ

melodic (ਮਿ'ਲੌਡਿਕ) *a* ਮਧੁਰ, ਮਿੱਠਾ, ਸੁਰੀਲਾ

melodious (ਮਿ'ਲਅਉਡ੍ਯਅਸ) *a* ਸੁਰੀਲਾ, ਮਧੁਰ, ਸੰਗੀਤਮਈ, ਰਸੀਲਾ, ਮਿੱਠਾ

melodrama ('ਮੈਲ੍ਅ(ਉ)ਡਰਾਮਅ) *n* ਅਤੀ ਭਾਵੁਕਤਾ ਭਰਪੂਰ ਨਾਟਕ, ਸਨਸਨੀ ਭਰਿਆ ਨਾਟਕ; ਸੰਗੀਤਮਈ ਨਾਟਕ

melody (ਮੈਲ੍ਅਡਿ) *n* ਧੁਨ; ਸੁਰੀਲਾ ਗੀਤ; ਤਰਾਨਾ

melon (ਮੈਲ੍ਅਨ) *n* ਖਖੜੀ, ਫੁੱਟ, ਖਰਬੂਜਾ

melt (ਮੈਲਟ) *n v* ਪਿਘਲੀ ਧਾਤ; ਪਿਘਲਣਾ, ਪੰਘਰਨਾ; ਘੁਲਣਾ; ਪਸੀਜਣਾ, ਢਲਣਾ; ਰੋਣ ਲਗਣਾ; (ਧੁਨੀ ਦਾ) ਕੋਮਲ ਹੋਣਾ; ~away ਘੁਲਣਾ, ਪਿਘਲ ਜਾਣਾ; ~into tears ਫਿੱਸ

ਪੈਣਾ, ਰੋ ਪੈਣਾ

melting (ਮੈੱਲਟਿਙ) *n a* ਦ੍ਵਣ, ਗਲਣ, ਪਿਘਲਣ, ਪਿਘਲਾਉਣ, ਦ੍ਵਣਸ਼ੀਲ, ਗਲਣਾ; **~point** ਦ੍ਵ ਅੰਕ, ਪਿਘਲਣ ਅੰਕ; **~pot** ਕੁਠਾਲੀ

member ('ਮੈੱਮਬਅ*) *n* ਸਦੱਸ, ਸਭਾ-ਸਦੱਸ; ਭਾਗ, ਅੰਸ਼, ਅੰਗ (ਖ਼ਾਸ ਕਰਕੇ ਹੱਥ ਪੈਰ); **~ship** ਸਦੱਸਤਾ

membrane (ਮੈੱਮਬਰੇਇਨ) *n* ਝਿੱਲੀ, ਪਰਦਾ

membranous (ਮੈੱਮ'ਬਰੇਇਨਅਸ) *a* ਝਿੱਲੀਦਾਰ

memo (ਮੈੱਮਅਉ) *n* ਯਾਦ-ਪੱਤਰ, ਸਿਮਰਤੀ- ਪੱਤਰ, ਯਾਦਗਾਰ, ਸਮਾਰਕ

memoir (ਮੈੱਮਵਾ:) *n* ਬਿਰਤਾਂਤ, ਵਿਵਰਣ; ਯਾਦਦਾਸ਼ਤ, ਸੰਸਮਰਣ, ਨਿਜੀ ਗਿਆਨ

memorable (ਮੈੱਮ(ਅ)ਰਅਬਲ) *a* ਯਾਦਗਾਰੀ, ਨਾਮਵਰ, ਪ੍ਰਸਿੱਧ, ਮਸ਼ਹੂਰ

memorandum (ਮੈੱਮਅ'ਰੈਂਡਅਮ) *n* ਯਾਦਦਾਸ਼ਤ, ਸਿਮਰਤੀ-ਪੱਤਰ; (ਕਾ) ਦਸਤਾਵੇਜ਼; ਪੱਤਰ, ਯਾਦ-ਪੱਤਰ

memorial (ਮਅ'ਮੋਰਿਅਲ) *n a* ਯਾਦਗਾਰ, ਸਿਮਰਤੀ ਚਿੰਨ੍ਹ, ਸਮਾਰਕ; ਯਾਦਗਾਰੀ ਲੇਖ

memorize (ਮੈੱਮਅਰਾਇਜ਼) *v* ਯਾਦ ਕਰਨਾ, ਚੇਤੇ ਕਰਨਾ

memory (ਮੈੱਮਅਰਿ) *n* ਚੇਤਾ, ਯਾਦ, ਯਾਦਦਾਸ਼ਤ, ਸਿਮਰਤੀ

menace (ਮੈੱਨਅਸ) *n v* ਧਮਕੀ, ਡਰਾਵਾ, ਖ਼ਤਰਾ; ਧਮਕਾਉਣਾ, ਡਰਾਉਣਾ, ਖ਼ਤਰੇ ਵਿਚ ਪਾਉਣਾ

mend (ਮੈਂਡ) *v n* ਸੁਧਾਰਨਾ ਜਾਂ ਸੁਧਰਨਾ, ਠੀਕ ਕਰਨਾ ਜਾਂ ਹੋਣਾ, ਸੋਧ ਕਰਨੀ, ਸੰਵਾਰਨਾ, ਮੁਰੰਮਤ ਕਰਨਾ: ਗੰਢਣਾ-ਤਰੁੱਪਣਾ; **~able** ਸੌਂਪਣ ਯੋਗ, ਮੁਰੰਮਤ ਲਾਇਕ; **~ing** ਸੁਧਾਰ,

ਉੱਧਾਰ, ਮੁਰੰਮਤ

mendicant (ਮੈਂਡਿਕਅੰਟ) *n* ਫ਼ਕੀਰ, ਜਾਚਕ, ਮੰਗਤਾ,

menial (ਮੀਨਯਅਲ) *n a* ਕੰਮੀ, ਕਮੀਨ, ਘਰੇਲੂ ਨੌਕਰ, ਸੇਵਕ, ਦਾਸ; ਨੌਕਰ-ਚਾਕਰ; ਹੀਣਾ, ਨੀਵਾਂ, ਨੀਚ

meningitis (ਮੈਨਿਨ'ਜਾਇਟਿਸ) *n* ਗਰਦਨ-ਤੋੜ ਬੁਖ਼ਾਰ; ਦਿਮਾਗ਼ ਦੇ. ਨੇੜੇ ਸੋਜ ਹੋ ਜਾਣ ਦਾ ਰੋਗ

menses (ਮੈਂਸੀਜ਼) *n pl* ਮਾਹਵਾਰੀ, ਮਾਸਕ ਧਰਮ

menstruate (ਮੈੱਨਸਟਰੁ'ਏਇਟ) *n* ਮਾਹਵਾਰੀ ਆਉਣੀ

menstruation (ਮੈੱਨਸਟਰੁ'ਏਇਸ਼ਨ) *n* ਮਾਹਵਾਰੀ, ਮਾਸਕ ਧਰਮ

mensuration (ਮੈਂਸਯੁਅ'ਰੇਇਸ਼ਨ) *n* ਜ਼ਮੀਨ ਦੀ ਪੈਮਾਇਸ਼, ਮਾਪ

mental (ਮੈਂਟਲ) *a* ਦਿਮਾਗ਼ੀ, ਮਾਨਸਕ; **~ity** ਸੁਭਾਅ, ਖਸਲਤ, ਮਿਜ਼ਾਜ; ਮਾਨਸਕ ਅਵਸਥਾ, ਮਨੋਬਿਰਤੀ

menthol (ਮੈੱਥੋਲ) *n* ਪੁਦੀਨੇ ਦਾ ਸਤ, ਮੈਂਥੋਲ

mention (ਮੈਨਸ਼ਨ) *v n* ਜ਼ਿਕਰ ਕਰਨਾ, ਉੱਲੇਖ ਕਰਨਾ, ਨਾਂ ਲੈਣਾ, ਕਹਿਣਾ; ਜ਼ਿਕਰ, ਉੱਲੇਖ, ਕਥਨ, ਵਰਨਣ; **~able** ਉੱਲੇਖਨੀਯ, ਜ਼ਿਕਰ ਲਾਇਕ, ਹਵਾਲੇ ਯੋਗ; **~ed** ਕਥਿਤ, ਨਿਰਦਿਸ਼ਟ, ਨਿਰਦੇਸ਼ਤ, ਉਲਿਖਤ, ਵਰਤਣ

menu (ਮੈੱਨਯੂ) *n* ਭੋਜਨ-ਸੂਚੀ, ਮੀਨੂ

mercantile (ਮਅ:ਕਅੰਟਾਇਲ) *a* ਵਪਾਰਕ, ਤਜਾਰਤੀ, ਵਣਜੀ

mercenary (ਮਅ:ਸਿਨ(ਅ)ਰਿ) *a n* ਸੁਆਰਥੀ; ਭਾੜੇ ਦਾ ਟੱਟੂ

merchandise ('ਮਅ:ਚਅੰਡਾਇਜ਼) *n* ਵਪਾਰਕ

ਮਾਲ, ਤਜਾਰਤੀ ਸਾਮਾਨ

merchant ('ਮਅਃਚਅੰਟ) *n* ਵਪਾਰੀ, ਸੌਦਾਗਰ

merciful ('ਮਅਃਸਿਫ਼ੁਲ) *a* ਦਿਆਲੂ, ਦਇਆਵਾਨ, ਕਿਰਪਾਲੂ, ਮਿਹਰਬਾਨ

merciless ('ਮਅਃਸਿਲਿਸ) *a* ਬੇਰਹਿਮ, ਬੇਤਰਸ, ਨਿਰਦਈ, ਨਿਸ਼ਠੁਰ, ਬੇਦਰਦ, ਪੱਥਰਦਿਲ

mercury ('ਮਅਃਕ਼ਯੁਰਿ) *n* ਪਾਰਾ, ਚੰਚਲਤਾ, ਚੁਸਤੀ, ਫੁਰਤੀ; (ਗੁਹਿ) ਬੁੱਧ

mercy ('ਮਅਃਸਿ) *n* ਦਇਆ, ਮਿਹਰ, ਰਹਿਮ, ਕਿਰਪਾ, ਦਇਆਲਤਾ, ਤਰਸ, ਕਰੁਣਾ

mere (ਮਿਅ*) *n v a* (ਕਾਵਿਕ, ਪ੍ਰ) ਤਲਾ, ਝੀਲ, ਛੰਭ; ਹੱਦ, ਸੀਮਾ; ਹੱਦਬੰਦੀ ਕਰਨਾ; ਸਿਰਫ਼, ਕੇਵਲ, ਨਿਰਾ, ਨਿਰਾਪੁਰਾ, ਉੱਕਾ; ~ly ਸਿਰਫ਼, ਕੇਵਲ, ਨਿਰਾ

merge (ਮਅਃਜ) *v* ਵਿਲੀਨ ਹੋਣਾ, ਅਭੇਦ ਕਰਨਾ ਜਾਂ ਹੋਣਾ, ਸ਼ਾਮਲ ਹੋਣਾ ਜਾਂ ਕਰਨਾ, ਸਮਾ ਜਾਣਾ; ~d ਵਿਲੀਨ, ਸਮਾਵਿਸ਼ਟ

merit ('ਮੈਰਿਟ) *n* ਯੋਗਤਾ, ਕਾਬਲੀਅਤ, ਪ੍ਰਵੀਨਤਾ, ਚੰਗਿਆਈ; ਖ਼ੂਬੀ, ਸਿਫ਼ਤ; ਉੱਤਮਤਾ; ~orious ਗੁਣਵਾਨ, ਗੁਣੀ, ਕਾਬਲ; ਪ੍ਰਸੰਸਾਯੋਗ, ਨੇਕ, ਭਲਾ; ~oriousness ਯੋਗਤਾ, ਭਲਾਈ, ਨੇਕੀ

merriment ('ਮੈਰਿਮਅੰਟ) *n* ਹਾਸ-ਵਿਲਾਸ, ਖੇਡ-ਤਮਾਸ਼ਾ, ਹਾਸਾ-ਮਸ਼ਕਰੀ, ਖ਼ੁਸ਼ੀ, ਆਨੰਦ, ਮੌਜਮੇਲਾ

merry ('ਮੈਰਿ) *a* ਖ਼ੁਸ਼, ਪ੍ਰਸੰਨ, ਖਿੜਿਆ-ਫੁੱਲਿਆ; ਰੰਗੀਲਾ, ਹੱਸਮੁੱਖ, ਮੌਜੀ, ਰੌਂਟਕੀ; ~making ਰੰਗ-ਰਲੀਆਂ, ਮੌਜ-ਮੇਲਾ

mesmerism ('ਮੈਜ਼ਮਅਰਿਜ਼(ਅ)ਮ) *n* ਵਸੀਕਰਨ, ਵਸਤੀਕਰਨ-ਵਿੱਦਿਆ, ਸੰਮੋਹਨ

mesmerize ('ਮੈਜ਼ਮਅਰਾਇਜ਼) *v* ਬੇਹੋਸ਼

ਕਰਨਾ, ਬੇਸੁਧ ਕਰਨਾ, ਮੂਰਛਤ ਕਰਨਾ, ਮੈਸਮਰਿਜ਼ਮ ਨਾਲ ਪ੍ਰਭਾਵਤ ਕਰਨਾ

mess (ਮੈੱਸ) *n v* ਮਿਲਗੋਭਾ, ਮਿਸ਼ਰਣ, ਰਲਮਿਲਾ; ਰੋਲਘਚੋਲਾ; ਪੁਆੜਾ, ਝੰਜਟ, ਬਖੇੜਾ; (ਫ਼ੌਜੀ) ਲੰਗਰ; ਸਾਂਝਾ ਲੰਗਰ; ਰਲਾ-ਮਿਲਾ ਦੇਣਾ; ਗੜਬੜ ਪਾ ਦੇਣੀ; ਲੰਗਰ ਵਿਚ ਖਾਣਾ, ਇੱਕਠੇ ਖਾਣਾ

message ('ਮੈੱਸਿਜ) *n* ਸੁਨੇਹਾ, ਸੰਦੇਸ਼ਾ, ਬਿਰਤਾਂਤ, ਖ਼ਬਰ

messenger ('ਮੈੱਸਿੰਜਅ*) *n* ਕਾਸਦ, ਹਰਕਾਰਾ, ਦੂਤ, ਸੰਦੇਸ਼ਵਾਹਕ

Messiah (ਮਿ'ਸਾਇਆ) *n* ਹਜ਼ਰਤ ਈਸਾ; ਈਸਾ ਮਸੀਹ, ਮਸੀਹਾ, ਮੁਕਤੀ ਦਾਤਾ

Messianic ('ਮੈੱਸਿ'ਐਨਿਕ) *a* ਮਸੀਹੀ, ਈਸਾ-ਸਬੰਧੀ

Messrs ('ਮੈੱਸਅਜ਼) *n* mister (Mr) ਦਾ ਬਹੁਵਚਨ, ਸਰਵਸ੍ਰੀ

metal ('ਮੈੱਟਲ) *n v* ਧਾਤ; ਸੜਕ ਬਣਾਉਣ ਵਾਲੀ ਬਜਰੀ ਜਾਂ ਰੋੜੀ; ਧਾਤ ਲਾਉਣੀ, ਧਾਤ ਨਾਲ ਮੜ੍ਹਨਾ; ਪੱਕੀ ਸੜਕ ਬਣਾਉਣੀ; ਸੜਕ ਤੇ ਰੋੜੀ ਪਾਉਣੀ; ~lic ਧਾਤਵੀ, ਧਾਤ ਦਾ, ਧਾਤ ਨਾਲ ਬਣਿਆ; (ਸੜਕ) ਪੱਕੀ; ਧਾਤ ਵਰਗਾ; ~lurgy ਧਾਤ-ਵਿੱਦਿਆ, ਧਾਤ ਨੂੰ ਸਾਫਣ ਜਾਂ ਸ਼ੁਧ ਕਰਨ ਦੀ ਵਿੱਦਿਆ; ਧਾਤ ਦਾ ਕੰਮ; ਧਾਤ-ਕਰਮ

metaphor ('ਮੈੱਟਅਫ਼ਅ*) *n* ਰੂਪਕ, ਰੂਪਕ ਅਲੰਕਾਰ; ~ical ਰੂਪਕ ਦਾ, ਅੰਲਕਾਰ

metaphrase ('ਮੈੱਟਅ'ਫ਼ਰੇਇਜ਼) *n v* ਸ਼ਬਦ-ਅਨੁਵਾਦ; ਲਫ਼ਜ਼ੀ ਤਰਜਮਾ ਕਰਨਾ

metaphysical ('ਮੈੱਟਅ'ਫ਼ਿਜ਼ਿਕਲ) *a* ਅਧਿਆਤਮਕ, ਪਰਾਭੌਤਕ, ਅਮੂਰਤ, ਸੂਖਮ,

ਤਾਤਵਿਕ, ਪਾਰਲੌਕਿਕ

metaphysics ('ਮੈਟਅ'ਫ਼ਿਜ਼ਿਕਿਸ) *n pl* ਅਧਿਆਤਮਵਾਦ; ਪਰਾਭੌਤਕ ਗਿਆਨ, ਗੂੜ੍ਹ ਵਿਚਾਰ

meterology ('ਮੀਟਯਅ'ਰੌਲਿਅਜਿ) *n* ਜਲ ਵਾਯੂ-ਵਿਗਿਆਨ, ਮੌਸਮ-ਵਿਗਿਆਨ

meter ('ਮੀਟਅ*) *n* ਨਾਪਕ, ਮਾਪਕ, ਨਾਪਣ ਵਾਲਾ; ਮੀਟਰ, ਇਕ ਮਾਪ

method ('ਮੈਥਅਡ) *n* ਤਰੀਕਾ, ਢੰਗ, ਵਿਧੀ, ਜਾਚ, ਪ੍ਰਣਾਲੀ, ਕ੍ਰਮ, ਤਰਤੀਬ; ਵਿਵਸਥਾ, ਬਾਕਾਇਦਗੀ; ~**ical** ਵਿਧੀ-ਅਨੁਸਾਰ, ਵਿਧੀਬੱਧ, ਵਿਵਸਥਿਤ, ਕ੍ਰਮ-ਅਨੁਸਾਰ, ਢੁੱਕਵਾਂ; ~**ist** ਦ੍ਰਿੜ੍ਹ ਧਾਰਮਕ, ਵਿਚਾਰਾਂ ਵਾਲਾ ਵਿਅਕਤੀ, ਕੱਟੜ; ਇਸਾਈਆਂ ਦੀ ਵਿਸ਼ੇਸ਼ ਸੰਪਰਦਾਇ ਦਾ ਸਦੱਸ; ~**ology** ਵਿਧੀ-ਵਿਗਿਆਨ, ਕਾਰਜ-ਵਿਧੀ, ਵਿਧੀ-ਸ਼ਾਸਤਰ

meticulous (ਮਿ'ਟਿਕਯੂਲਅਸ) *a* ਅਤੀ ਸਾਵਧਾਨ, ਸੌਂਘਾ, ਬਾਰੀਕਬੀਨ; ~**ness** ਅਤੀ ਸਾਵਧਾਨਤਾ

metre ('ਮੀਟਅ*) *n* ਲੰਬਾਈ ਦਾ ਨਾਪ, ਮੀਟਰ; ਕਵਿਤਾ ਦੀ ਬਹਿਰ, ਛੰਦ

metric ('ਮੈਟਰਿਕ) *a* ਮੀਟਰ ਸਬੰਧੀ; ਦਸ ਅੰਸ਼ੀ, ਦਾਸ਼ਮਿਕ; ~**al** ਛੰਦ ਸਬੰਧੀ

metropolis (ਮਿ'ਟਰੌਪਲਿਸ) *n* ਮਹਾਂਨਗਰ; ਮੁੱਖ ਸ਼ਹਿਰ, ਰਾਜਧਾਨੀ, ਕਾਰਜ-ਕੇਂਦਰ

metropolitan ('ਮੈਟਰਅ'ਪੌਲਿਟ(ਅ)ਨ) *a* ਮੁੱਖ ਨਗਰ ਦਾ, ਰਾਜਧਾਨੀ ਦਾ

mettle ('ਮੈਟਲ) *n* ਹਿੰਮਤ, ਜੋਰ, ਜਿਗਰਾ; ਸੁਭਾਅ, ਤਬੀਅਤ; ~**d**, ~**some** ਹਿੰਮਤੀ, ਹੌਸਲੇ ਵਾਲਾ, ਸਾਹਸੀ, ਵੱਡੇ ਜਿਗਰੇ ਵਾਲਾ

mica (ਮਾਇਕਅ) *n* ਅਬਰਕ

miche (ਮਿਚ) *v n* ਗੁਪਤ ਰੱਖਣਾ, ਛੁਪਾਉਣਾ, ਲੁਕਾਉਣਾ; ਸ਼ਰਮਿੰਦਾ ਹੋਣਾ; ਅਵਾਰਾਗਰਦੀ ਕਰਨਾ; ~**r** ਗੁਪਤ ਰੱਖਣ ਵਾਲਾ, ਅਵਾਰਾ

micro ('ਮਾਇਕਰਅਉ) *a* ਸੂਖਮ, ਦਸ ਲੱਖਵਾਂ ਭਾਗ

microbiological ('ਮਾਇਕਰਅ'ਬਾਇਅ-ਲੌਜਿਕਲ) *a* ਸੂਖਮ-ਜੀਵ-ਵਿਗਿਆਨ ਸਬੰਧੀ

microbiology ('ਮਾਇਕਰਅਬਾਇ'ਔਲਅਜਿ) *n* ਅਣੂ-ਵਿਗਿਆਨ, ਸੂਖਮ ਜੀਵ-ਵਿਗਿਆਨ

microfilm ('ਮਾਇਕਰਅ(ਉ)ਫ਼ਿਲਮ) *n* ਛੋਟੀ ਫ਼ਿਲਮ

microscope ('ਮਾਇਕਰੋਸਕਅਉਪ) *n* ਖ਼ੁਰਦਬੀਨ, ਸੂਖਮ ਦਰਸ਼ਕ ਜੰਤਰ, ਅਣੁਦਰਸ਼ਕ ਜੰਤਰ

microscopic ('ਮਾਇਕਰਅ'ਸਕੌਪਿਕ) *a* ਖ਼ੁਰਦਬੀਨ ਦਾ, ਖ਼ੁਰਦਬੀਨੀ, ਸੂਖਮ, ਸੂਖਮ-ਦਰਸ਼ੀ; ~**al** ਖ਼ੁਰਦਬੀਨੀ, ਸੂਖਮ ਦਰਸ਼ਕ ਜੰਤਰ ਸਬੰਧੀ; ਅਤੀ ਸੂਖਮ

microwave ('ਮਾਇਕਰਅਵੇਇਵ਼) *n* ਸੂਖਮ ਲਹਿਰ, (ਹਵਾ ਦੀ) ਸੂਖਮ ਤਰੰਗ

mid (ਮਿਡ) *a prep* ਦਰਮਿਆਨਾ, ਮੰਝਲਾ, ਮੱਧਵਰਤੀ, ਮੱਧ ਸਹਿਤ, ਵਿਚਕਾਰ ਦਾ; ~**day** ਦੁਪਹਿਰ; ~**night** ਅੱਧੀ ਰਾਤ, ਘੁੱਪ ਹਨੇਰਾ; ~**way** ਮੱਧ ਮਾਰਗ, ਵਿਚਕਾਰਲਾ ਰਸਤਾ

middle ('ਮਿਡਲ) *n a* ਮੱਧ ਦੇਸ਼, ਮੱਧ-ਵਰਤੀ ਅੰਤਰ, ਵਿਚਕਾਰ; ਦਰਮਿਆਨੀ, ਮਰਕਜ਼ੀ, ਔਸਤ ਦਰਜੇ ਦਾ; ~**man** ਦਲਾਲ, ਵਿਚੋਲਾ, ਆੜ੍ਹਤੀ

middling ('ਮਿਡਲਿੰਡ) *adv a* ਸਧਾਰਨ ਤੌਰ ਤੇ; ਕੁਝ ਕੁਝ; ਮੱਧ ਦਾ; ਮੱਧ ਸ਼੍ਰੇਣੀ ਦਾ, ਦੂਜੇ ਦਰਜੇ ਦਾ

midst (ਮਿਡਸਟ) *a* ਮੱਧ (ਵਿਚ); ਵਿਚਕਾਰ; ਦਰਮਿਆਨ

midwife ('ਮਿਡਵਾਇਫ਼) *n* ਦਾਈ

might (ਮਾਇਟ) *n v aux* ਬਲ ਸ਼ਕਤੀ; ਜ਼ੋਰ, ਤਾਣ, ਤਾਕਤ; may ਦਾ ਭੂਤ ਕਾਲ; ~y ਜ਼ੋਰਾਵਰ, ਜ਼ਬਰਦਸਤ, ਪ੍ਰਬਲ, ਬਲਵਾਨ, ਸ਼ਕਤੀਮਾਨ, ਬਲੀ, ਸਮਰੱਥ, ਮਹਾਨ; ਅਤੀਅੰਤ, ਬਹੁਤ

migraine ('ਮੀਗਰੇਇਨ) *n* ਅੱਧੇ ਸਿਰ ਦੀ ਪੀੜ

migrant ('ਮਾਇਗਰਾਂਟ) *n a* ਮੌਸਮੀ ਪੰਛੀ

migrate (ਮਾਇ'ਗਰੇਇਟ) *v* ਪਰਵਾਸ ਕਰਨਾ, ਥਾਂ ਬਦਲਣਾ; ਹਿਜਰਤ ਕਰਨਾ

migration (ਮਾਇ'ਗਰੇਇਸ਼ਨ) *n* ਪਰਵਾਸ, ਹਿਜਰਤ

milch (ਮਿਲਚ) *a* ਦੁੱਧ ਦੇਣ ਵਾਲੀ, ਦੁੱਧੈਲ; ਲਾਭ-ਸਰੋਤ; ਲਾਭ ਦਾ ਸਾਧਨ

mild (ਮਾਇਲਡ) *a* ਸ਼ਾਂਤ, ਦਿਆਲੂ, ਹਲੀਮ, ਹਲਕਾ, ਨਰਮ; ਸੋਮਦਿਲ; ਦੁਰਬਲ, ਕਮਜ਼ੋਰ; ~ness ਸ਼ਾਂਤੀ, ਦਇਆਲਤਾ, ਕਿਰਪਾਲਤਾ, ਕੋਮਲਤਾ, ਨਰਮੀ, ਮਧੁਰਤਾ, ਦੁਰਬਲਤਾ, ਕਮਜ਼ੋਰੀ

mile (ਮਾਇਲ) *n* ਮੀਲ, 1760 ਗਜ਼ ਦੀ ਵਿਥ; ~stone ਮੀਲ-ਪੱਥਰ, ਮਾਰਗ-ਸ਼ਿਲਾ, ਮਹੱਤਵਪੂਰਨ ਘਟਨਾ

milk (ਮਿਲਕ) *n v* ਦੁੱਧ, ਖੀਰ; ਦੁੱਧ ਚੋਣਾ, ਦੋਹਣਾ; ~y ਦੁਧੀਆ

mill (ਮਿਲ) *n v* ਚੱਕੀ, ਕਾਰਖ਼ਾਨਾ, ਮਿਲ; ਪੀਹਣਾ, ਪੀਸਣਾ

millet ('ਮਿਲਿਟ) *n* ਬਾਜਰਾ, ਮੋਟਾ ਅਨਾਜ

milleu ('ਮੀਲਯਅ:) *n* ਸਮਾਜਕ ਵਾਤਾਵਰਨ, ਮਾਹੌਲ

milli ('ਮਿਲਿ) *n* ਹਜ਼ਾਰਵਾਂ ਭਾਗ, ਜਿਵੇਂ ਕਿ ਮੀਟਰਕ; ~gram ਗਰਾਮ ਦਾ ਹਜ਼ਾਰਵਾਂ ਭਾਗ;

~litre ਲਿਟਰ ਦਾ ਹਜ਼ਾਰਵਾਂ ਭਾਗ

million ('ਮਿਲਯਅਨ) *n a* ਦਸ ਲੱਖ; ~aire ਲੱਖਪਤੀ, ਕਰੋੜਪਤੀ; ਧਨਵਾਨ

millitant ('ਮਿਲਿਟਅੰਟ) *a* ਲੜਾਕਾ, ਜੰਗੀ, ਜੋਧਾ, ਖਾੜਕੂ, ਜੁਝਾਰ, ਮੁਜਾਹਦ, ਜੰਗਜੂ

millitary ('ਮਿਲਿਟ(ਅ)ਰਿ) *n* ਸੈਨਾ, ਫ਼ੌਜ, ਲਸ਼ਕਰ, ਜੰਗੀ, ਫ਼ੌਜੀ, ਸਿਪਾਹੀਆਨਾ, ਸੈਨਕ

millitate ('ਮਿਲਿਟੇਇਟ) *v* ਜੁੱਧ ਕਰਨਾ, ਜੰਗ ਕਰਨਾ; ਲੜਨਾ, ਵਿਰੋਧ ਕਰਨਾ; ਪ੍ਰਭਾਵ ਪਾਉਣਾ

millitia (ਮਿ'ਲਿਸ਼ਅ) *n* ਦੇਸ਼-ਰੱਖਿਅਕ ਸੈਨਾ, ਰਾਸ਼ਟਰੀ ਸੈਨਾ, ਰਜ਼ਾਕਾਰ ਫ਼ੌਜ

mimic ('ਮਿਮਿਕ) *n a v* ਬਹੁਰੂਪੀਆ, ਨਕਲੀਆ, ਭੰਡ, ਸਾਂਗੀ; ਨਕਲੀ, ਮਜ਼ਾਕੀਆ; ਨਕਲ ਉਤਾਰਨਾ; ~ry ਸਾਂਗ, ਨਕਲ, ਅਨੁਕਰਨ, ਭੰਡੋਤੀ

minar (ਮਿਨਾ*) *n* ਮੀਨਾਰ, ਲਾਠ, ਬੁਰਜ, ਚਾਨਣ-ਮੁਨਾਰਾ; ~et ਛੋਟਾ ਮੀਨਾਰ, ਬੁਰਜ, ਚਾਨਣ-ਮੁਨਾਰਾ

mince (ਮਿੰਸ) *v* ਕੀਮਾ; ਕੀਮਾ ਬਣਾਉਣਾ, ਟੁਕੜੇ ਕਰਨਾ

mind (ਮਾਇਨਡ) *n v* ਮਨ, ਚਿੱਤ, ਮਨਸ਼ਾ; ਮੱਤ, ਬੁੱਧ, ਸਮਝ, ਬੁੱਧੀ, ਚੇਤਾ, ਯਾਦਦਾਸ਼ਤ; ਖ਼ਿਆਲ, ਰੁਚੀ; ਵਿਚਾਰਧਾਰਾ, ਹਿਰਦਾ, ਜੀਅ, ਦਿਲ; ਅੰਤਹਕਰਨ; ਵਿਚ ਦਿਲ ਲਗਾਣਾ; *to make up one's* ~ ਫ਼ੈਸਲਾ ਕਰਨਾ, ਦ੍ਰਿੜਤਾ ਧਾਰਨ ਕਰਨੀ, ਨਿਸਚਾ ਕਰਨਾ, ਪੱਕਾ ਇਰਾਦਾ ਬਣਾਉਣਾ; ~ful ਹੁਸ਼ਿਆਰ, ਸਾਵਧਾਨ, ਖ਼ਬਰਦਾਰ, ਚੌਕੰਨਾ; ~less ਮੂਢ, ਮੂਰਖ, ਬੇਵਕੂਫ਼, ਬੁੱਧੀਹੀਨ

mine (ਮਾਇਨ) *pron n v* ਮੇਰਾ; ਮੇਰਾ ਭਾਗ, ਮੇਰਾ ਹਿੱਸਾ; ਖਾਣ; ਸੁਰੰਗ; ਖ਼ਜ਼ਾਨਾ, ਭੰਡਾਰ; ਖਾਣ ਪੁੱਟਣਾ; ~ral ਖਾਣਾਂ ਦੀ (ਧਾਤ), ਧਾਤ ਸਬੰਧੀ;

ਬਣਾਉਟੀ ਖਣਿਜ-ਜਲ; **~ralogy** ਖਣਿਜ-ਵਿਗਿਆਨ, ਧਾਤ-ਵਿੱਦਿਆ; ਧਾਤੂ-ਪਰੀਖਿਅਣ-ਸ਼ਾਸਤਰ

Minerva (ਮਿ'ਨਅ:ਵ੍ਅ) *n* ਰੋਮ ਦੀ ਵਿੱਦਿਆ ਦੇਵੀ, ਸਰਸਵਤੀ

mingle ('ਮਿਙਗਲ) *v* ਘੁਲਮਿਲ ਜਾਣਾ, ਮਿਲਾਉਣਾ, ਮੇਲ ਕਰਨਾ, ਮਿਲਣਾ, ਮਿਸ਼ਰਤ ਕਰਨਾ; **~d** ਮਿਸ਼ਰਤ, ਮਿਲਿਆ ਹੋਇਆ

miniature ('ਮਿਨਅਚਅ*) *n a* ਲਘੂ-ਚਿੱਤਰ, ਲਘੂਕ੍ਰਿਤ ਚਿੱਤਰ; ਬੌਣਾ, ਵਾਮਨ; ਛੋਟਾ

minimal (ਮਿਨਿਮਲ) *a* ਅਲਪਤਮ, ਨਿਊਨਤਮ, ਘੱਟ ਤੋਂ ਘੱਟ

minimize (ਮਿਨਿਮਾਇਜ਼) *v* ਘਟਾਉਣਾ, ਅਲਪੀਕਰਨ ਕਰਨਾ, ਮਾਤਰਾ ਘੱਟ ਕਰਨੀ, ਛੋਟਾ ਕਰਨਾ, ਘੱਟ ਕਰਨਾ

mining ('ਮਾਇਨਿਙ) *n* ਖਾਣ ਦੀ ਖੁਦਾਈ, ਸੁਰੰਗ ਦੀ ਪੁਟਾਈ

minister ('ਮਿਨਿਸਟਅ*) *n v* ਮੰਤਰੀ, ਵਜ਼ੀਰ, ਦੀਵਾਨ; ਪਰੋਹਤ, ਪਾਦਰੀ; ਆਚਾਰੀਆ; ਸੇਵਾ ਕਰਨੀ, ਸਹਾਇਤਾ ਕਰਨੀ, ਪ੍ਰਬੰਧ ਕਰਨਾ

ministerial ('ਮਿਨਿ'ਸਟਿਅਰਿਅਲ) *a* ਵਜ਼ਾਰਤੀ, ਮੰਤਰੀ ਦਾ; ਰਾਜਕੀ, ਸਰਕਾਰੀ ਪੱਖ ਦਾ; ਪਾਦਰੀ ਸਬੰਧੀ

ministration ('ਮਿਨਿ'ਸਟਰੇਇਸ਼ਨ) *n* ਦੇਖ-ਭਾਲ, ਖਿਦਮਤ; ਸੇਵਾ

ministry ('ਮਿਨਿਸਟਰਿ) *n* ਮੰਤਰੀ ਸਭਾ, ਵਜ਼ਾਰਤ, ਮੰਤਰਾਲਿਆ; ਮੰਤਰੀ-ਮੰਡਲ, ਮੰਤਰੀ-ਪਰਿਸ਼ਦ, ਮੰਤਰੀਗਣ; ਪਰੋਹਤਪਣ

minor ('ਮਾਇਨਅ*) *n a* ਬਾਲ, ਨਾਬਾਲਗ਼ ਸੇਂਟ; ਫਰਾਂਸਿਸ ਦੇ ਸਮੇਂ ਅਤੇ ਸੰਪਰਦਾਇ ਦਾ ਇਕ ਸੰਨਿਆਸੀ; ਸਧਾਰਨ; **~ity** ਅਲਪ ਸੰਖਿਆ, ਅਲਪ ਸੰਖਿਅਕ; ਲੜਕਪਣ, ਨਾਬਾਲਗ਼ੀ, ਬਾਲਪਣ, ਬਾਲ-ਅਵਸਥਾ; ਘੱਟ ਗਿਣਤੀ ਦੀ ਜਮਾਤ, ਅਲਪ ਸੰਖਿਅਕ

minster ('ਮਿੰਨਸਟਰ*) *n* ਮੱਠ, ਆਸ਼ਰਮ, ਵੱਡਾ ਗਿਰਜਾ

minstrel ('ਮਿਨਸਟਰ(ਅ)ਲ) *n* ਭੱਟ, ਗਵੱਈਆ, ਕੀਰਤਨੀਆ, ਗਾਇਕ

mint (ਮਿੰਟ) *n v* ਟਕਸਾਲ; ਕੋਸ਼ ਖ਼ਜ਼ਾਨਾ; ਖਾਣ; ਪੁਦੀਨਾ; ਟਕਸਾਲਣਾ, ਢਾਲਣਾ, ਸਿੱਕੇ ਬਣਾਉਣਾ, ਸ਼ਬਦਾਂ ਆਦਿ ਦੀ ਕਾਢ ਕੱਢਣਾ; **~age** ਸਿੱਕਾ ਢਲਾਈ, ਠੱਪਾ ਲੁਆਈ; ਢਲਾਈ (ਦਰ), ਢਲਿਆ ਹੋਇਆ ਸਿੱਕਾ

minus ('ਮਾਇਨਅਸ) *prep a n* ਬਿਨਾ, ਬਾਕੀ, ਨਫ਼ੀ, ਨਫ਼ੀ ਦਾ ਨਿਸ਼ਾਨ, ਰਿਣ-ਚਿੰਨ੍ਹ, ਰਿਣ ਘੱਟ

minute ('ਮਿਨਿਟ) *n v a* (1) ਮਿੰਟ, ਘੰਟੇ ਦਾ ਸੱਠਵਾਂ ਹਿੱਸਾ; ਛਿਣ, ਪਲ; (2) ਸਧਾਰਨ ਲੇਖ, ਕਾਰਵਾਈ, (ਬ ਵ) ਕਾਰਜ-ਵੇਰਵਾ (ਕਿਸੇ ਸਭਾ ਆਦਿ ਦਾ); ਸੰਖੇਪ ਵੇਰਵਾ ਲਿਖਣਾ; ਮਸੌਦਾ ਤਿਆਰ ਕਰਨਾ; ਸਬੂਤ ਤਿਆਰ ਕਰਨਾ, ਠੀਕ ਸਮੇਂ ਦਾ ਪਤਾ ਲਾਉਣਾ; ਅਤੀ ਅਲਪ; ਸੂਖਮ, ਅਤੀ ਲਘੂ, ਮਹੀਨ, ਬਾਰੀਕ; **~ly** ਛਿਣ ਦਾ, ਮਿੰਟ ਮਿੰਟ ਦਾ, ਸੂਖਮ ਨਾਲ

minx (ਮਿਙਕਸ) *n* ਸ਼ੋਖ਼ ਅੱਖਾਂ ਵਾਲੀ ਕੁੜੀ, ਚੰਚਲ ਕੁੜੀ

miracle ('ਮਿਰਅਕਲ) *n* ਕਰਾਮਾਤ, ਕ੍ਰਿਸ਼ਮਾ, ਕਮਾਲ, ਚਮਤਕਾਰ

miraculous (ਮਿ'ਰੈਕਯੁਅਲਸ) *a* ਦਿੱਬ, ਦੈਵੀ, ਕਰਾਮਾਤੀ, ਚਮਤਕਾਰੀ; ਅਲੌਕਕ, ਅਦਭੁਤ

mirador ('ਮਿਰਅ'ਡੋ*) *n* ਘੰਟਾਘਰ, ਬੁਰਜ, ਚਬੂਤਰਾ

mirage ('ਮਿਰਾਯ਼) *n* ਮ੍ਰਿਗ-ਤ੍ਰਿਸ਼ਨਾ, ਮਰੀਚਕਾ,

ਮ੍ਰਿਗ-ਜਾਲ, ਨਜ਼ਰ ਦਾ ਧੋਖਾ

mire ('ਮਾਇਆ*) *n v* ਚਿੱਕੜ, ਦਲਦਲ, ਖੋਤਾ;
ਚਿੱਕੜ ਵਿਚ ਫਸਣਾ, ਮੈਲਾ ਕਰਨਾ

mirror ('ਮਿਰਆ*) *n v* ਸ਼ੀਸ਼ਾ, ਆਰਸੀ, ਆਇਨਾ;
ਦਰਪਣ, ਹੂ-ਬਹੂ ਅਕਸ ਜਾਂ ਨਕਸ਼ਾ, ਪ੍ਰਤੀਬਿੰਬਤ
ਕਰਨਾ, ਅਕਸ ਦਿਖਾਉਣਾ

mirth (ਮਅਃਥ) *n* ਖੁਸ਼ੀ, ਦਿਲਲਗੀ, ਹਾਸਾ,
ਆਨੰਦ, ਹੁਲਾਸ; ~**ful** ਪ੍ਰਸੰਨ, ਖ਼ੁਸ਼, ਰੰਗੀਲਾ,
ਮੌਜੀ; ~**less** ਉਦਾਸ, ਅਪ੍ਰਸੰਨ

miry ('ਮਾਇਰਿ) *a* ਚਿੱਕੜ ਭਰਿਆ; ਲਿਬੜਿਆ,
ਜ਼ਲੀਲ, ਨੀਚ, ਗੰਦਾ

misapply ('ਮਿਸਅ'ਪਲਾਇ) *v* ਦੁਰਉਪਯੋਗ
ਕਰਨਾ, ਮਿਥਿਆ ਪ੍ਰਯੋਗ ਕਰਨਾ, ਅਯੋਗ ਵਰਤੋਂ
ਕਰਨੀ

misapprehend ('ਮਿਸ'ਐਪਰਿ'ਹੈਂਡ) *v* ਉਲਟਾ
ਜਾਂ ਗਲਤ ਸਮਝਣਾ

misapprehension ('ਮਿਸ'ਐਪਰਿ'ਹੈਨਸ਼ਨ) *n*
ਮਿਥਿਆ-ਬੋਧ, ਭਰਮ, ਭੁੱਲ, ਗ਼ਲਤ-ਫ਼ਹਿਮੀ

misappropriate ('ਮਿਸਅ'ਪਰਅਉਪਰਿਏਇਟ)
v (ਪਰਾਏ ਧਨ ਦਾ) ਗ਼ਬਨ ਕਰਨਾ, ਖ਼ੁਰਦ-ਬੁਰਦ
ਕਰਨਾ, ਨਾਜਾਇਜ਼ ਖ਼ਰਚ ਕਰਨਾ, ਗ਼ਲਤ ਕੰਮ
ਵਿਚ ਖ਼ਰਚ ਕਰਨਾ

misappropriation ('ਮਿਸਅ'ਪਰਅਉਪਰਿ-
'ਏਇਸ਼ਨ) *n* ਕੁਵਰਤੋਂ, ਘਾਲਮਾਲਾ,
ਦੁਰਉਪਯੋਗ, (ਰੁਪਏ ਦਾ) ਗ਼ਬਨ

misarrange ('ਮਸਅ'ਰੇਇੰਜ) *v* ਬੇਤਰਤੀਬੀ ਨਾਲ
ਰੱਖਣਾ, ਬਿਨਾ ਕ੍ਰਮ ਦੇ ਰੱਖਣਾ, ਬਿਨਾ ਸਿਲਸਲੇ
ਦੇ ਰੱਖਣਾ

misbecome ('ਮਿਸਬਿ'ਕੱਮ) *v* ਅਯੋਗ ਹੋਣਾ,
ਅਣਉਪਯੋਗੀ ਹੋਣਾ, ਸ਼ੋਭਾ ਨਾ ਦੇਣਾ, ਸ਼ਾਨ ਦੇ
ਖ਼ਿਲਾਫ਼ ਹੋਣਾ

misbecoming ('ਮਿਸਬਿ'ਕੱਮਿੰਗ) *a*
ਅਸ਼ੋਭਨੀਕ, ਅਯੋਗ, ਅਣਉਪਯੋਗੀ

misbehave ('ਮਿਸਬਿ'ਹੇਇਵ) *v* ਦੁਰਵਿਹਾਰ
ਕਰਨਾ, ਬੁਰਾ ਵਰਤਾਉ ਕਰਨਾ; ~**d** ਅਸੱਭਿਆ,
ਬਦਚਲਨ, ਬਦਤਮੀਜ਼

misbehaviour ('ਮਿਸਬਿ'ਹੇਇਵ੍ਯਅ*) *n*
ਦੁਰਵਿਹਾਰ, ਦੁਰਾਚਾਰ, ਬਦਤਮੀਜ਼ੀ, ਕੁਚਾਲ

misbelief ('ਮਿਸਬਿ'ਲੀਫ਼) *v* ਗ਼ਲਤ ਧਾਰਨਾ;
ਦੂਰ-ਵਿਸ਼ਵਾਸ; ਗ਼ਲਤ-ਰਾਇ

miscalculate ('ਮਿਸ'ਕੈਲਕੁਯੁਲੇਇਟ) *v* ਗ਼ਲਤ
ਹਿਸਾਬ ਲਾਉਣਾ, ਝੂਠਾ ਅਨੁਮਾਨ ਲਾਉਣਾ

miscalculation ('ਮਿਸ'ਕੈਲਕਯੁ'ਲੇਇਸ਼ਨ) *n*
ਗ਼ਲਤ ਹਿਸਾਬ, ਝੂਠਾ ਅਨੁਮਾਨ, ਭੁੱਲ-ਚੁੱਕ

miscarriage ('ਮਿਸ'ਕੈਰਿਜ) *n* ਪਤੇ ਤੇ ਨਾ
ਪਹੁੰਚਣਾ, ਅਸਫਲਤਾ; ਗਰਭਪਾਤ

miscarry ('ਮਿਸ'ਕੈਰਿ) *v* ਗਰਭ ਡਿੱਗਣਾ; ਤੁਟਾ;
ਨਿਸਫਲ ਹੋਣਾ, ਭਟਕ ਜਾਣਾ

miscellaneous ('ਮਿਸਅ'ਲੇਇਨਯਅਸ) *a*
ਫੁਟਕਲ, ਅਨੇਕ, ਵਿਭਿੰਨ, ਵਿਵਿਧ (ਵਿਅਕਤੀ),
ਭਿੰਨ ਭਿੰਨ ਪ੍ਰਕਾਰ ਦੇ

mischief ('ਮਿਸਚਿਫ਼) *n* ਸ਼ਰਾਰਤ; ਉਪੱਦਰ,
ਖ਼ਰਾਬੀ, ਛੇੜਖ਼ਾਨੀ, ਇਲਤ

mischievous ('ਮਿਸਚਿਵ੍ਅਸ) *a* ਉਪੱਦਰੀ,
ਖ਼ਰਾਬ, ਇਲੱਤੀ, ਸ਼ਰਾਰਤੀ

misconceive ('ਮਿਸਕਅੰ'ਸੀਵ੍) *v* ਗ਼ਲਤ
ਸਮਝਣਾ, ਉਲਟ ਸਮਝਣਾ, ਮਿਥਿਆ ਧਾਰਨ
ਕਰਨਾ, ਗ਼ਲਤ ਮਤਲਬ ਲੈਣਾ; ਗ਼ਲਤ ਰਾਇ
ਕਾਇਮ ਕਰਨਾ

misconception ('ਮਿਸਕਅੰ'ਸੈੱਪਸ਼ਨ) *n* ਗ਼ਲਤ
ਧਾਰਨਾ, ਗ਼ਲਤ-ਫ਼ਹਿਮੀ, ਭਰਾਂਤੀ

misconduct ('ਮਿਸ'ਕੌਂਡਅੱਕਟ, ਮਿਸਕਅੰ-

'ਡਾਂਕਟ) *n v* ਕੁਕਰਮ; ਦੁਰਾਚਾਰ; ਬਦਸਲੂਕੀ; ਕੁਚਾਲ, ਬਦਇੰਤਜ਼ਾਮੀ; ਭੈੜਾ ਪ੍ਰਬੰਧ ਕਰਨਾ

miconstrue ('ਮਿਸਕਅੰ'ਸਟਰੂ) *v* ਅਰਥ ਦਾ ਅਨਰਥ ਕਰਨਾ, ਅਰਥ ਠੀਕ ਨਾ ਲਾਉਣਾ; (ਵਿਅਕਤੀ ਨੂੰ) ਗਲਤ ਸਮਝਣਾ

miscreant ('ਮਿਸਕਰਿਅੰਟ) *n* ਸ਼ਰਾਰਤੀ, ਬਦਮਾਸ਼, ਗੁੰਡਾ, ਬਦਜ਼ਾਤ

misdeed ('ਮਿਸ'ਡੀਡ) *n* ਕੁਕਰਮ, ਕਰਤੂਤ, ਦੁਰਾਚਾਰ, ਬੁਰਾ ਕੰਮ, ਬਦਕਾਰੀ

misdirect ('ਮਿਸਡਿ'ਰੈਕਟ) *v* ਗਲਤ ਰਾਹ ਦੱਸਣਾ; ਕੁਰਾਹੇ ਪਾਉਣਾ, ਚੁੰਕਣਾ, ਬਹਿਕਾਉਣਾ

misdo ('ਮਿਸ'ਡੂ) *v* ਬੁਰਾ ਕੰਮ ਕਰਨਾ, ਕੁਕਰਮ ਕਰਨਾ, ਅਪਰਾਧ ਕਰਨਾ, ਕਰਤੂਤ ਘੋਲਣੀ; **~er** ਦੋਸ਼ੀ, ਕੁਕਰਮੀ; **~ing** ਕਰਤੂਤ, ਕਾਰਾ, ਦੁਰਾਚਾਰ, ਕੁਚਾਲ

miser ('ਮਾਇਜ਼ਅ*) *n* ਸੂਮ, ਕੰਜੂਸ, ਚੀਪੜ, ਮੱਖੀਚੂਸ; **~liness** ਕੰਜੂਸੀ, ਸੂਮਪੁਣਾ, ਲੋਭ

miserable ('ਮਿਜ਼(ਅ)ਰਅਬਲ) *a* ਦੁਖੀ, ਪੀੜਤ, ਦਰਦਵੰਦ; ਮੰਦਭਾਗਾ, ਅਭਾਗਾ, ਨਿਰਧਨ, ਕਮੀਨਾ, ਜ਼ਲੀਲ, ਹਕੀਰ

misery ('ਮਿਜ਼(ਅ)ਰਿ) *n* ਸੰਤਾਪ, ਵੇਦਨਾ, ਦੁੱਖ, ਦੀਨਤਾ, ਦੁਰਦਸ਼ਾ, ਪਰੇਸ਼ਾਨੀ, ਦੁਰਗਤੀ; ਕਲੇਸ਼, ਕਸ਼ਟ, ਮੁਸੀਬਤ, ਆਫ਼ਤ, ਬਦਕਿਸਮਤੀ

misfit ('ਮਿਸਫ਼ਿਟ) *n* ਅਣਮਿਲਵਾਂ ਕੱਪੜਾ, ਕਸੂਤਾ ਆਦਮੀ

misgive ('ਮਿਸ'ਗਿਵ) *v* ਸੰਦੇਹ ਕਰਨਾ, ਮੱਥਾ ਠਨਕਣਾ; (ਦਿਲ ਵਿਚ) ਖ਼ਤਰਾ ਪੈਦਾ ਹੋਣਾ

misgiving (ਮਿਸ'ਗਿਵਙ) *n* ਸੰਦੇਹ, ਸ਼ੰਕਾ, ਤੌਖਲਾ, ਧੁੜਕੂ, ਡਰ

misgovern ('ਮਿਸ'ਗਅੱਵਅਨ) *v* ਬੁਰਾ ਪ੍ਰਬੰਧ ਕਰਨਾ, ਕੁਸ਼ਾਸਨ ਕਰਨਾ, ਚੰਗੀ ਤਰ੍ਹਾਂ ਰਾਜ ਨਾ

ਕਰਨਾ; **~ment** ਕੁਸ਼ਾਸਨ, ਅਨਿਆਈ ਰਾਜ

misguide ('ਮਿਸ'ਗਾਇਡ) *v* ਬਹਿਕਾਉਣਾ, ਕੁਰਾਹੇ ਪਾਉਣਾ; ਗੁਮਰਾਹ ਕਰਨਾ

mishandle ('ਮਿਸ'ਹੈਂਡਲ) *v* ਦੁਰਉਪਯੋਗ ਕਰਨਾ, ਗਲਤ ਢੰਗ ਨਾਲ ਵਰਤਣਾ; (ਕੰਮ) ਬੁਰੀ ਤਰ੍ਹਾਂ ਕਰਨਾ, ਬੁਰਾ ਸਲੂਕ ਕਰਨਾ

mishap ('ਮਿਸਹੈਪ) *n* ਹਾਦਸਾ, ਦੁਰਘਟਨਾ; ਬਿਪਤਾ, ਆਪੱਤੀ, ਮੁਸੀਬਤ, ਉਪੱਦਰ, ਆਫ਼ਤ

misinform ('ਮਿਸਇਨ'ਫ਼ੋਮ) *v* ਗਲਤ ਖ਼ਬਰ ਹੋਣੀ, ਝੂਠਾ ਸਮਾਚਾਰ ਦੱਸਣਾ; ਧੋਖ ਦੇਣਾ, ਬਹਿਕਾਉਣਾ, ਗਲਤਫਹਿਮੀ ਵਿਚ ਪਾਉਣਾ

misinterpret ('ਮਿਸਇਨ'ਟਅਃਪਰੈੱਟ) *v* ਝੂਠਾ ਅਰਥ ਲਾਉਣਾ, ਗਲਤ ਅਰਥ ਕੱਢਣਾ, ਗਲਤ ਸਿੱਟਾ ਕੱਢਣਾ; **~ation** ਮਿਥਿਆ ਅਰਥ, ਅਨਰਥ, ਗਲਤ ਨਤੀਜਾ, ਗਲਤ ਵਿਆਖਿਆ

misjudge ('ਮਿਸ'ਜਅੱਜ) *v* ਗਲਤ ਨਿਰਣੈ ਦੇਣਾ, ਗਲਤ ਧਾਰਨਾ ਬਣਾਉਣੀ, ਗਲਤ ਅੰਦਾਜ਼ਾ ਲਾਉਣਾ; **~ment** ਗਲਤ ਫ਼ੈਸਲਾ, ਦੁਰ-ਨਿਰਣਾ

mislead ('ਮਿਸ'ਲੀਡ) *v* ਧੋਖਾ ਦੇਣਾ, ਗੁਮਰਾਹ ਕਰਨਾ, ਕੁਰਾਹੇ ਪਾਉਣਾ, ਟਪਲਾ ਲਾਉਣਾ; ਗਲਤਫਹਿਮੀ ਵਿਚ ਪਾਉਣਾ; **~ing** ਭਰਾਂਤੀਜਨਕ, ਟਪਲਾ ਲਾਊ

mismanage ('ਮਿਸ'ਮੈਨਿਜ) *v* ਬਦਇੰਤਜ਼ਾਮੀ ਕਰਨੀ, ਵਿਗਾੜਨਾ; **~ment** ਭੈੜਾ ਪ੍ਰਬੰਧ, ਬਦਇੰਤਜ਼ਾਮੀ

misplace ('ਮਿਸ'ਪਲੇਇਸ) *v* ਗਲਤ ਥਾਂ ਤੇ ਰੱਖਣਾ, ਕੁਥਾਵੇਂ ਰੱਖਣਾ, ਗਲਤ ਹੱਥਾਂ ਵਿਚ ਦੇਣਾ; **~d** ਖੋਹਿਆ ਹੋਇਆ, ਬੇਠਿਕਾਨੇ, ਭ੍ਰਿਸ਼ਟ

misprint ('ਮਿਸਪਰਿੰਟ, ਮਿਸ'ਪਰਿੰਟ) *n v* ਛਪਾਈ ਦੀ ਭੁੱਲ; ਅਸ਼ੁੱਧ ਛਾਪਣਾ, ਗਲਤ ਛਾਪਣਾ, ਛਾਪਣ ਵਿਚ ਗਲਤੀ ਕਰਨੀ

misquote ('ਮਿਸ'ਕਅਉਟ) *v* ਅਸ਼ੁਧ ਹਵਾਲਾ ਦੇਣਾ

misreport ('ਮਿਸਰਿ'ਪੋਟ) *v n* ਗ਼ਲਤ ਖ਼ਬਰ ਦੇਣੀ; ਗ਼ਲਤ ਬਿਆਨੀ ਕਰਨੀ; ਗ਼ਲਤ ਬਿਆਨੀ

misrepresent ('ਮਿਸਰਿ'ਪੋਰਿ'ਜੈਂਟ) *v* ਗ਼ਲਤ ਪੇਸ਼ ਕਰਨਾ, ਗ਼ਲਤ ਬਿਆਨੀ ਕਰਨੀ, ਤੋੜ-ਮਰੋੜ ਕੇ ਦੱਸਣਾ; ਉਲਟਾ ਅਰਥ ਕੱਢਣਾ; ~ation ਗ਼ਲਤ ਬਿਆਨੀ, ਮਿਥਿਆਵਾਦ, ਅਪਕਥਨ, ਝੂਠ

misrule ('ਮਿਸ'ਰੂਲ) *n* ਹਕੂਮਤ ਜਾਂ ਸ਼ਾਸਨ ਦੀ ਖ਼ਰਾਬੀ, ਕੁਸ਼ਾਸਨ, ਅੰਧੇਰਗਰਦੀ, ਬਦਅਮਨੀ, ਬਦਇੰਤਜ਼ਾਮੀ

miss (ਮਿਸ) *v n* ਅਸਫਲ ਹੋਣਾ, ਪ੍ਰਾਪਤ ਨਾ ਕਰਨਾ; ਨਿਸ਼ਾਨਾ ਚੁੱਕ ਜਾਣਾ; ਛੱਡ ਜਾਣਾ; (ਗੱਡੀ) ਨਿਕਲ ਜਾਣੀ, ਨਾ ਮਿਲਨੀ; ਅਵਸਰ ਹੱਥ ਨਾ ਆਉਣਾ; ਗ਼ਲਤੀ; ਕੁਆਰੀ, ਅਵਿਵਾਹਤ ਕੁੜੀ ਜਾਂ ਬੀਬੀ; ~ing ਲੁਕਿਆ, ਲੁਪਤ, ਗੁੰਮ, ਗੁਆਚਿਆ, ਗ਼ਾਇਬ

missile ('ਮਿਸਾਇਲ) *n a* ਮਿਸਾਈਲ, ਗੋਲਾ, ਹਥਿਆਰ, ਅਸਤਰ

mission ('ਮਿਸ਼ਨ) *n* ਦੂਤ ਮੰਡਲ, ਪ੍ਰਚਾਰਕ ਮੰਡਲ, ਧਰਮ-ਪ੍ਰਚਾਰਕ, ਸੰਸਥਾ, ਮਿਸ਼ਨ; ਧਰਮ-ਪ੍ਰਚਾਰ, ਧਾਰਮਿਕ-ਸੇਵਾ; ~ary ਮਿਸ਼ਨ ਦਾ, ਮਿਸ਼ਨਰੀ; ਪਾਦਰੀ, ਧਰਮ-ਪ੍ਰਚਾਰਕ

mist (ਮਿਸਟ) *n v* ਧੁੰਦ, ਕੁਹਰਾ; ਧੁੰਦ ਪੈਣੀ, ਧੁੰਦਲਾ ਕਰਨਾ

mistake (ਮਿ'ਸਟੇਇਕ) *n v* ਭੁੱਲ, ਗ਼ਲਤੀ; ਭਰਾਂਤੀ, ਅਸ਼ੁੱਧੀ; ਤਰੁਟੀ, ਦੋਸ਼, ਭੁਲੇਖਾ, ਟਪਲਾ, ਉਕਾਈ, ਖ਼ਤਾ; ਗ਼ਲਤੀ ਲੱਗਣੀ, ਉੱਕਣਾ, ਖ਼ਤਾ ਕਰਨੀ; ~n ਭਰਾਂਤ, ਭਰਮਪੂਰਨ, ਅਸ਼ੁੱਧ

mister ('ਮਿਸਟਅ*) *n* ਜਨਾਬ, ਸ਼੍ਰੀਮਾਨ

mistreat ('ਮਿਸ'ਟਰੀਟ) *v* ਬੁਰਾ ਵਰਤਾਉ ਕਰਨਾ, ਦੁਰਵਿਹਾਰ ਕਰਨਾ, ਬਦਸਲੂਕੀ ਕਰਨਾ

mistress ('ਮਿਸਟਰਿਸ) *n* ਸ਼੍ਰੀਮਤੀ; ਬੀਬੀ; ਉਸਤਾਨੀ; ਗ੍ਰਹਿਣੀ, ਗ੍ਰਹਿਸਥਣ, ਬੇਗਮ, ਘਰ ਵਾਲੀ, ਮਾਲਕਣ

misturst ('ਮਿਸ'ਟਰਅੱਸਟ) *v n* ਅਵਿਸ਼ਵਾਸ ਕਰਨਾ, ਇਤਬਾਰ ਨਾ ਕਰਨਾ, ਭਰੋਸਾ ਨਾ ਕਰਨਾ, ਬਦਝਨ ਹੋਣਾ

misty ('ਮਿਸਟਿ) *a* ਮਿਟਿਆਲਾ, ਅੰਧਕਾਰਮਈ, ਧੁੰਦਲਾ; ਅਸਪਸ਼ਟ, ਅਨਿਸ਼ਚਤ

misunderstand ('ਮਿਸਅੰਡਅ'ਸਟੈਂਡ) *v* ਉਲਟਾ ਜਾਂ ਗ਼ਲਤ ਸਮਝਣਾ; ਅਨਰਥ ਕਰਨਾ, ਉਲਟਾ ਅਰਥ ਸਮਝਣਾ, ਕੁਝ ਦਾ ਕੁਝ ਸਮਝਣਾ; ~ing ਗ਼ਲਤਫ਼ਹਿਮੀ, ਗ਼ਲਤ ਸੋਚ, ਭੁਲੇਖਾ, ਭਰਮ

misuse ('ਮਿਸ'ਯੂਜ਼) *v n* ਅਸ਼ੁੱਧ ਪ੍ਰਯੋਗ ਕਰਨਾ; ਦੁਰਵਰਤੋਂ ਕਰਨੀ; ਇਸਤੇਮਾਲ ਕਰਨਾ;

mix (ਮਿਕਸ) *v* ਮਿਲਾਉਣਾ, ਮਿਲਣਾ, ਘੋਲਣਾ, ਰਲਾਉਣਾ, ਰਲਣਾ, ਮਿਸ਼ਰਨ ਕਰਨਾ; ਸੰਯੁਕਤ ਕਰਨਾ; ~ed ਮਿਲਿਆ, ਘੁਲਿਆ, ਮਿਸ਼ਰਤ, ਸੰਯੁਕਤ, ਮਿਲਿਆ ਜੁਲਿਆ; ~ture ਰਲਾਵਟ, ਮਿਲਾਵਟ, ਮਿਸ਼ਰਣ, ਘੋਲ; ~up ਘਾਲਾ ਮਾਲਾ

mizzle ('ਮਿਜ਼ਲ) *n v* (ਪਾਣੀ ਦੀ) ਫੁਹਾਰ, ਨਿੱਕੀ ਨਿੱਕੀ ਕਣੀ; ਦੌੜ ਜਾਣਾ, ਨੱਸ ਜਾਣਾ, ਫਰਾਰ ਹੋ ਜਾਣਾ

moan (ਮਅਉਨ) *n v* ਸਿਸਕੀ, ਸਿਸਕਣ ਵਿਰਲਾਪ; ਮਾਤਮ; ਮਾਤਮ ਕਰਨਾ; ਵਿਰਲਾਪ ਕਰਨਾ, ਅਫ਼ਸੋਸ ਕਰਨਾ; ਕਰਾਹੁਣਾ; ਆਹ ਭਰਨੀ; ~ful ਵਿਰਲਾਪਮਈ, ਸ਼ੋਕਯੁਕਤ, ਸਿਸਕੀਆਂ ਭਰਿਆ

mob (ਮੌਬ) *n v* ਜਨ-ਸਮੂਹ, ਜਮਘਟਾ, ਭੀੜ, ਮਜਮਾ; ਭੀੜ-ਭਾੜ; ਅਵਾਮ, ਜਨਤਾ; ਭੀੜ

ਹੋਣੀ ਜਾਂ ਕਰਨੀ, ਮਜਮਾ ਲੱਗਣਾ ਜਾਂ ਲਾਉਣਾ

mobile ('ਮਅਉਬਾਇਲ) *a n* ਗਤੀਸ਼ੀਲ, ਚਲਣਸ਼ੀਲ, ਚਲੰਤ, ਚੰਚਲ, ਚਲਦਾ-ਫਿਰਦਾ; ਗਤੀਸ਼ੀਲ ਦਸਤਾ

mobility (ਮਅ(ਉ)'ਬਿਲਅਟਿ) *n* ਗਤੀਸ਼ੀਲਤਾ, ਚੱਲਣਸ਼ੀਲਤਾ; ਚਪਲਤਾ

mock (ਮੌਕ) *n v a* ਮਸ਼ਕਰੀ, ਠੱਠਾ, ਹਾਸਾ, ਨਕਲ, ਠੱਠਾ-ਮਸ਼ਕਰੀ ਕਰਨਾ, ਮਖੌਲ ਉਡਾਉਣਾ, ਖਿੱਲੀ ਉਡਾਉਣੀ; ਨਕਲ ਉਤਾਰਨੀ; ਝੂਠਾ, ਨਕਲੀ; **~ery** ਹਾਸਾ, ਮਜ਼ਾਕ; ਝੂਠਾ ਦਿਖਾਵਾ, ਨਕਲ

modal ('ਮਅਉਡਲ) *a* ਦਿਖਾਵੇ ਦਾ; ਰੀਤੀ ਦਾ, ਰੀਤੀਆਤਮਕ; ਵਿਧੀਗਤ

mode (ਮਅਉਡ) *n* ਵਿਧੀ, ਪੱਧਤੀ, ਪ੍ਰਣਾਲੀ; ਤਰੀਕਾ, ਢੰਗ, ਤਰਜ਼, ਅੰਦਾਜ਼, ਤੌਰ; ਦਸਤੂਰ

moderate ('ਮੌਡ(ਅ)ਰਅਟ, ਮੌਡਅਰੇਇਟ) *a v* ਉਦਾਰ ਵਿਚਾਰਾਂ ਵਾਲਾ; ਨਰਮ ਖ਼ਿਆਲੀਆ; ਸੰਜਮੀ, ਸੰਤੁਲਤ; ਔਸਤ ਦਰਜੇ ਦਾ; ਮੱਧਮ ਪੈਣਾ ਜਾਂ ਪਾਉਣਾ; **~ness** ਨਰਮ ਖ਼ਿਆਲੀ, ਸੰਜਮਤਾ

moderation ('ਮੌਡਅ'ਰੇਇਸ਼ਨ) *n* ਸੰਤੁਲਨ; ਨਿਯੰਤਰਨ; ਨਰਮੀ, ਸੰਜਮ, ਹਲਕਾਪਣ

moderator ('ਮੌਡਅਰੇਇਟਅ*) *n* ਵਿਚੋਲਾ, ਮਧਿਅਸਥ, ਪੰਚ

modern ('ਮੌਡ(ਅ)ਨ) *a* ਆਧੁਨਿਕ, ਅਜੋਕਾ, ਵਰਤਮਾਨ; ਨਵੀਨ, ਨਵਾਂ; **~ism** ਆਧੁਨਿਕਤਾ, ਨਵੀਨਤਾ, ਆਧੁਨਿਕ ਵਿਚਾਰ; **~ist** ਆਧੁਨਿਕਤਾ ਵਾਦੀ, ਨਵੀਨਤਾਵਾਦੀ; **~ity** ਆਧੁਨਿਕਤਾ, ਨਵੀਨਤਾ; **~ization** ਆਧੁਨਿਕੀਕਰਨ, ਨਵੀਨੀਕਰਨ; **~ize** ਆਧੁਨਿਕ ਕਾਲ ਦੀਆਂ ਲੋੜਾਂ ਦੇ ਅਨੁਸਾਰ ਬਣਾਉਣਾ

modest ('ਮੌਡਿਸਟ) *a* ਸ਼ਰਮਾਕਲ, ਸੰਗਾਊ, ਸੰਕੋਚਵਾਨ, ਲੱਜਾਵਾਨ; ਸਰਲ, ਸਾਦਾ; ਨਮਰ; **~y** ਲੱਜਾਸ਼ੀਲਤਾ, ਲੱਜਾ, ਸ਼ਰਮੀਲਾਪਣ, ਨਿਮਰਸ਼ੀਲਤਾ, ਕਾਜ

modification ('ਮੌਡਿਫ਼ਿ'ਕੇਇਸ਼ਨ) *n* ਪਰਿਵਰਤਨ, ਸੁਧਾਈ, ਤਰਮੀਮ, ਸੰਸ਼ੋਧਨ

modify ('ਮੌਡਿਫ਼ਾਇ) *v* ਬਦਲਣਾ, (ਸਵਰ) ਪਰਿਵਰਤਨ ਕਰਨਾ; ਸੁਧਾਰਨਾ, ਸੁਧਾਈ ਕਰਨੀ, ਠੀਕ ਕਰਨਾ; ਤਰਮੀਮ ਕਰਨੀ

modulate ('ਮੌਡਯੁਲੇਇਟ) *v* (ਸੰਗੀ) ਸੁਰ ਨੂੰ ਉੱਚਾ ਨੀਵਾਂ ਕਰਨਾ; ਸੁਰ ਨੂੰ ਠੀਕ ਠੀਕ ਕਰਨਾ, ਸਾਧਣਾ; ਲੋੜ ਅਨੁਸਾਰ ਬਦਲਣਾ, ਘਟਾਉਣਾ ਜਾਂ ਵਧਾਉਣਾ

modulation ('ਮੌਡਯੁ'ਲੇਇਸ਼ਨ*) *n* ਸੁਰ ਦਾ ਲਹਿਰਾਉ, ਅਵਾਜ਼ ਦਾ ਉਤਰਾ-ਚੜ੍ਹਾ, ਅਲਾਪ

module ('ਮੌਡਯੂਲ) *n* ਛੋਟੀ ਮਾਤਰਾ, ਲੰਮਾਈ ਦੇ ਅਨੁਪਾਤ ਨੂੰ ਪਰਗਟ ਕਰਨ ਵਾਲੀ ਇਕਾਈ, ਨਾਪਕ ਦੀ ਇਕਾਈ

modulus ('ਮੌਡਯੂਲ) *n* ਗੁਣਾਂਕ, ਮਾਪਾਂਕ, ਗੁਣਕ

modus operandi ('ਮਅਉਡਅਸ' ਔਪਅ'ਰੈਨਡੀ) (L) ਕਾਰਜ ਵਿਧੀ

moist (ਮੌਇਸਟ) *a* ਭਿੱਜਿਆ ਹੋਇਆ, ਸਿੱਲ੍ਹਾ, ਨਮ, ਗਿੱਲਾ, ਤਰ; **~en** ਭਿਉਣਾ, ਸਿੱਲ੍ਹਾ ਕਰਨਾ, ਨਮ ਦੇਣੀ, ਗਿੱਲਾ ਕਰਨਾ, ਤਰ ਕਰਨਾ; ਭਿੱਜਣਾ, ਗਿੱਲਾ ਹੋਣਾ; **~ure** ਨਮੀ, ਸਿੱਲ੍ਹ, ਤਰੀ, ਗਿੱਲਾਪਣ

moke (ਮਅਉਕ) *n* (ਅਪ) ਗਧਾ, ਖੋਤਾ, ਖ਼ਰ; ਟੱਟੂ

moiasses (ਮਅ(ਉ)'ਲੈਸਿਜ਼) *n* ਸੀਰਾ

molecular (ਮਅ(ਉ)'ਲੈਕਯੁਅਲ*) *a* ਆਣਵਿਕ, ਆਟਵੀ

molecule ('ਮੌਲਿਕਯੂਲ) *n* (ਭੌ ਅਤੇ ਰਸਾ) ਅਣੂ,

ਕਟ, ਕਿਟਕਾ, ਰੇਜ਼ਾ, ਕਿਰਚ

molest (ਮਅ(ਉ)ਲੈੱਸਟ) *v* ਛੇੜਨਾ, ਛੇੜ-ਛਾੜ ਕਰਨੀ, ਔਖਾ ਕਰਨਾ, ਸਤਾਉਣਾ, ਦਿੱਕ ਕਰਨ, ਦਖ਼ਲ ਦੇਣਾ; ~**ation** ਔਖਿਆਈ, ਪਰੇਸ਼ਾਨੀ, ਛੇੜ-ਛਾੜ

molification ('ਮੌਲਿਫ਼ਿ'ਕੇਇਸ਼ਨ) *n* ਸ਼ਾਂਤੀ, ਕੋਮਲਤਾ, ਨਰਮੀ, ਮੁਲਾਇਮਤਾ

mollify ('ਮੌਲਿਫ਼ਾਇ) *v* ਸ਼ਾਂਤ ਕਰਨਾ, ਪ੍ਰਸੰਨ ਕਰਨਾ; ਠੰਢਾ ਕਰਨਾ; ਕੋਮਲ ਕਰਨਾ, ਮੁਲਾਇਮ ਕਰਨਾ; ਸ਼ਿੱਦਤ ਘਟਾ ਦੇਲੀ

moment ('ਮਅਉਮਅੰਟ) *n* ਛਿਣ, ਖਿਨ, ਝਟ, ਨਿਮਖ, ਪਲ, ਦਮ, ਲਮਹਾ; ~**ary** ਅਸਥਾਈ, ਛਿਣ-ਭੰਗੁਰ, ਛਿਣ-ਸਥਾਈ; ~**ous** ਮਹੱਤਵਪੂਰਨਤਾ, ਅਵੱਸ਼ਕ; ~**ousness** ਮਹੱਤਵਪੂਰਨਤਾ, ਅਵੱਸ਼ਕਤਾ

momentum (ਮਅ(ਉ)'ਮੌਨਟਅਮ) *n* (ਭੌ) ਗਤੀ-ਮਾਤਰਾ, ਸੰਵੇਗ

monarch ('ਮੌਨਅਃਕ) *n* ਸਮਰਾਟ, ਰਾਜਾ, ਰਾਜ, ਅਧਿਰਾਜ, ਸੁਲਤਾਨ, ਬਾਦਸ਼ਾਹ; ~**y** ਰਾਜ, ਬਾਦਸ਼ਾਹੀ, ਰਾਜ-ਤੰਤਰ

monastery ('ਮੌਨਅਸਟ(ਅ)ਰਿ) *n* ਈਸਾਈ ਮੱਠ, ਖ਼ਾਨਕਾਹ, ਆਸ਼ਰਮ; ਵਿਹਾਰ

monastic (ਮਅ'ਨੈਸਟਿਕ) *a* ਮੱਠ-ਸਬੰਧੀ, ਆਸ਼ਰਮ-ਸਬੰਧੀ, ਸੰਨਿਆਸੀਆਂ ਦਾ; ~**ism** ਵਿਰਕਤ ਜੀਵਨ, ਤਿਆਗੀ ਜੀਵਨ, ਮੱਠਵਾਸ, ਵਾਨਪ੍ਰਸਥ, ਸੰਨਿਆਸ, ਵਿਰਾਗ

Monday ('ਮਅੰਡਿ) *n* ਸੋਮਵਾਰ

monetary ('ਮਅੱਨਿਟ(ਅ)ਰਿ) *a* ਮੁਦਰਾ ਸਬੰਧੀ, ਵਿੱਤੀ; ਆਰਥਕ, ਧਨ ਸਬੰਧੀ, ਮਾਲੀ

monetization ('ਮਅੱਨਿਟਾਇ'ਜ਼ੇਇਸ਼ਨ) *n* ਮੁਦਰੀਕਰਨ, ਧਾਤ ਦਾ ਸਿੱਕਾ ਬਣਾਉਣ ਦੀ ਕਿਰਿਆ

money (ਮਅੱਨਿ) *n* ਧਨ, ਰੁਪਏ, ਪੈਸੇ, ਮੁਦਰਾ; ਵਿੱਤ, ਸਿੱਕਾ, ਧਨ-ਰਾਸ਼ੀ, ਦੌਲਤ, ਪੂੰਜੀ, ਨਕਦੀ; ~**lending** ਸ਼ਾਹੂਕਾਰਾ, ਮਹਾਜਨੀ

monger ('ਮਅੰਡਗਅ*) *n* ਦੁਕਾਨਦਾਰ, ਵਪਾਰੀ

mongoose ('ਮੌਡਗੁਸ) *n* ਨਿਉਲਾ

monitor ('ਮੌਨਿਟਅ*) *n v* ਮਾਨੀਟਰ, ਉਪਦੇਸ਼ਕ ਨਿਰੀਖਕ, ਬੋਧਕ, ਖ਼ਤਰੇ ਦੀ ਖ਼ਬਰ ਦੇਣ ਵਾਲਾ ਵਿਅਕਤੀ; ਜੰਗੀ ਜਹਾਜ਼; ਨਿਰੀਖਣ ਕਰਨਾ; ~**y** ਪਾਦਰੀ ਦਾ ਉਪਦੇਸ਼ਾਤਮਕ ਪੱਤਰ

monk (ਮਅੱਡਕ) *n* ਜੋਗੀ, ਸਾਧੂ, ਸੰਨਿਆਸੀ, ਮੱਠਵਾਸੀ, ਉਦਾਸੀ, ਫ਼ਕੀਰ, ਦਰਵੇਸ਼, ਵਿਰਾਗੀ, ਤਿਆਗੀ

monkey ('ਮਅੱਡਕਿ) *n v* ਬਾਂਦਰ, ਵਾਨਰ; ਸੁਰਾ-ਪਾਤਰ, ਸ਼ਰਾਬ ਵਾਲਾ ਭਾਂਡਾ; ਹਾਸਾ ਉਡਾਉਣਾ, ਨਕਲ ਲਾਉਣੀ

monocracy (ਮਅ'ਨੌਕਰਅਸਿ) *n* ਤਾਨਾਸ਼ਾਹੀ, ਇਕਪੁਰਖੀ ਰਾਜ

monocrat ('ਮੌਨਅਕਰੈਟ) *n* ਤਾਨਾਸ਼ਾਹ

monogamy (ਮੌ'ਨੌਗਅਮਿ) *n* ਇਕ ਪਤਨੀਤਵ; ਇਕ ਵਿਆਹ ਕਰਨ ਦੀ ਪ੍ਰਥਾ

monolatry (ਮੌ'ਨੌਲਅਟਰਿ) *n* ਇਕ ਇਸ਼ਟ-ਪੂਜਾ

monologue ('ਮੌਨਅਲੌਗ) *n* ਮਨ-ਬਚਨੀ, ਸਵੈਗਤ ਕਥਨ

moncpolist (ਮਅ'ਨੌਪਅਲਿਸਟ) *n* ਇਜਾਰਾਦਾਰ, ਏਕਅਧਿਕਾਰ ਦਾ ਪੱਖੀ, ਏਕਅਧਿਕਾਰੀ

monopolize (ਮਅ'ਨੌਪਅਲਾਇਜ਼) *v* ਇਜਾਰਾਦਾਰੀ ਚਲਾਉਣੀ

monopoly (ਮਅ'ਨੌਪਅਲਿ) *n* ਇਜਾਰਾਕਾਰੀ, ਏਕਅਧਿਕਾਰ

monotonous (ਮਅ'ਨੌਟਅਨਅਸ) *a* ਇਕ ਲੈਅ,

ਇਕ ਸੁਰ; ਇਕ ਰਸ, ਨੀਰਸ; ਅਕਾਉ;
~ness, monotony ਇਕਸਾਰਤਾ,
ਇਕਸੁਰਤਾ, ਅਕੇਵਾਂ, ਉਕਤਾਹਟ, ਨੀਰਸਤਾ

monsieur (ਮਸ਼ਿਅਯਮਃ) (F) *n* ਸੀ, ਸ੍ਰੀਮਾਨ

monsoon ('ਮੋਨ'ਸੂਨ) *n* ਮੋਨਸੂਨ, ਮੌਸਮੀ ਹਵਾ;
ਵਰਖਾ, ਵਰਖਾ, ਰੁੱਤ

monster ('ਮੌਂਸਟਅ*) *a n* ਰਾਖਸ਼, ਦਾਨਵ,
ਦੁਰਾਤਮਾ; ਅਤੀ ਵਿਸ਼ਾਲ

monstrous ('ਮੌਂਸਟਰਅਸ) *a adv* ਰਾਖਸ਼ੀ,
ਬਹੁਤ ਵੱਡਾ, ਦਿਉ ਵਰਗਾ; ਅਜੀਬ, ਵੀਤਰਸ,
ਡਰਾਉਣਾ, ਘੋਰ; ਹਰ ਤਰ੍ਹਾਂ ਅਯੋਗ, ਸਰਾਸਰ
ਗਲਤ; ਬਹੁਤ ਜ਼ਿਆਦਾ

month (ਮਅੰਥ) *n* ਮਹੀਨਾ, ਮਾਹ, ਮਾਸ; ਮਹੀਨੇ
ਦੇ

monument ('ਮੌਨਯੂਮਅੰਟ) *n* ਪੁਰਾਤਨ
ਇਮਾਰਤ, ਸਮਾਰਕ, ਸਮਾਰਕ ਚਿੰਨ੍ਹ; ~al
ਯਾਦਗਾਰੀ; ਸ਼ਾਨਦਾਰ; ਮਹਾਨ; ਸਮਾਰਕੀ

mooch (ਮੂਚ) *v* (ਉਪ) ਮੁੱਛਣਾ, ਚੁੱਕ ਲੈਣਾ, ਚੁਰਾ
ਲੈਣਾ, ਉਡਾ ਲੈਣਾ; ਇਧਰ ਉੱਧਰ ਐਵੇਂ ਫਿਰਨਾ,
ਮਟਰ-ਗਸ਼ਤ ਕਰਨੀ, ਵਿਹਲਾ ਫਿਰਨਾ

mood (ਮੂਡ) *n* ਮਿਜਾਜ, ਬਿਰਤੀ, ਮਨੋਦਸ਼ਾ, ਚਿੱਤ,
ਜੀਅ, ਭਾਵ, ਭਾਵੁਕ ਦਸ਼ਾ; ਕਿਰਿਆ ਦੇ ਰੂਪ;
~y ਦਿਲਗੀਰ, ਉਦਾਸ; ਮਨਮੌਜੀ, ਮਨਚਲਾ;
ਗੁਸੈਲਾ, ਚਿੜਚਿੜਾ

moon (ਮੂਨ) *n* ਚੰਨ, ਚੰਦ, ਚੰਦਰਮਾ, ਸਸਿ, ਸ਼ਸ਼ੀ,
ਮਹਿਤਾਬ; ~calf ਜਮਾਂਦਰੂ ਮੂਰਖ; ~face ਚੰਦਰ
ਮੁਖ; ~light ਚੰਦ ਦੀ ਚਾਨਣੀ, ਚੰਦਰਕਾ, ਚੰਦਰ
ਪ੍ਰਭਾ, ਜਯੋਤਸਨਾ; full ~ ਪੂਰਨਮਾਸ਼ੀ ਦਾ ਚੰਨ,
ਪੂਰਾ ਚੰਨ

mop (ਮੌਪ) *n v* ਪੂੰਝਣ, ਪੂੰਝਣਾ, ਸਾਫ਼ ਕਰਨਾ,
ਬੁਹਾਰਨਾ, ਮੂੰਹ ਚੜ੍ਹਾਉਣਾ

mope (ਮਅਉਪ) *n v* ਉਦਾਸ ਆਦਮੀ, ਦਿਲਗੀਰ
ਹੋਣਾ, ਉਦਾਸ ਰਹਿਣਾ, ਗੁਆਚਿਆ ਗੁਆਚਿਆ
ਰਹਿਣਾ

moped (ਮਅਉਪੈਂਡ) *n* ਇੰਜਨਦਾਰ ਸਾਈਕਲ,
ਪੈਡਲ ਵਾਲਾ ਮੋਟਰ ਸਾਈਕਲ, ਮੋਪੈਡ

moral (ਮੌਰ(ਅ)ਲ) *a* ਨੀਤੀ ਬਚਨ, ਉਪਦੇਸ਼;
ਅਖ਼ਲਾਕੀ, ਨੈਤਕ; ~ity ਆਚਾਰ, ਨੀਤੀ,
ਨੈਤਕਤਾ, ਸਦਾਚਾਰ

morale (ਮੌ'ਰਾਲ) *n* (ਸੈਨਕ ਆਦਿ ਦਾ) ਹੌਸਲਾ,
ਮਨੋਬਲ, ਧੀਰਜ

moratorium (ਮੋਰਅ'ਟੋਰਿਅਮ) *n* ਰਿਣ ਜਾਂ
ਕਰਜਾ ਚੁਕਾਉਣ ਦੀ ਕਾਨੂੰਨੀ ਮੁਹਲਤ; ਰੋਕ,
ਬੰਦਸ਼, ਬੰਦੀ

morbid ('ਮੌਬਿਡ) *a* (ਚਿਕਿ) ਰੋਗੀ, ਰੋਗ-ਗ੍ਰਸਤ;
ਸੰਬੰਧੀ; ਵਿਕ੍ਰਿਤ, ਦੂਸ਼ਤ, ਬੀਮਾਰ; ~ity,
~ness ਅਸੁਅਸਥਤਾ, ਵਿਗਾੜ, ਵਿਕ੍ਰਿਤੀ,
ਰੋਗਗ੍ਰਸਤਤਾ

morbus (ਮੌਬਅਸ) *n* ਰੋਗ, ਬੀਮਾਰੀ, ਵਿਕਾਰ

more (ਮੋ*) *n a adv* ਅਧਿਕਤਾ; ਅਧਿਕ, ਬਹੁਤ
ਜ਼ਿਆਦਾ; ਹੋਰ ਜ਼ਿਆਦਾ; ਅਧਿਕ ਮਾਤਰਾ ਵਿਚ;
~over ਇਸ ਤੋਂ ਛੁੱਟ, ਇਸ ਦੇ ਅਤਿਰਿਕਤ,
ਇਸ ਦੇ ਸਿਵਾਇ; ਪਰ, ਬਲਕਿ

morgue (ਮੋਗ) *n* ਹੰਕਾਰ, ਅਭਿਮਾਨ, ਘਮੰਡ

moribund (ਮੌਰਿਬਅੰਡ) *a* ਅੰਤਲੇ ਦਮਾਂ ਤੇ,
ਅਖੀਰਲੇ ਸੁਆਸਾਂ ਤੇ, ਮਰਨ ਕਿਨਾਰੇ, ਮੌਤ ਦੇ
ਕੰਢੇ ਤੇ

morning (ਮੋ'ਨਿਙ) *n* ਸਵੇਰਾ, ਪ੍ਰਭਾਤ, ਵੱਡਾ ਵੇਲਾ,
ਅੰਮ੍ਰਿਤ ਵੇਲਾ, ਪਹੁ-ਫੁਟਾਲਾ, ਤੜਕਾ, ਤੋਰ; ਉਸ਼ਾ
ਕਾਲ; ~good ਸ਼ੁਭ ਸਵੇਰ, ਨਮਸਕਾਰ

morsel (ਮੌਂਸਲ) *n* ਗਰਾਹੀ, ਟੁੱਕ, ਟੁੱਕਰ, ਬੁਰਕੀ,
ਲੁਕਮਾ, ਨਿਵਾਲਾ; ਟੁਕੜਾ

mortal (ਮੋਂ'ਟਲ) *n a* ਮਰਨਹਾਰ ਜੀਵ, ਮਨੁੱਖ, ਜਨ, ਨਾਸਵਾਨ, ਵਿਨਾਸ਼ੀ, ਮਰਨਹਾਰ, ਮਰਨਧਰਮੀ; (ਦੁਸ਼ਮਣ) ਜਾਨੀ, ਜਾਨ ਲੇਵਾ

mortar (ਮੋਂਟਾ*) *n v* ਉੱਖਲੀ, ਖਰਲ, ਕੁੰਡਾ; ਛੋਟੀ ਮਾਰਟਰ ਬੰਦੂਕ; ਗਾਰਾ, ਚੂਨਾ, ਮਸਾਲਾ, ਤੋਪਾਂ ਨਾਲ ਹਮਲਾ ਕਰਨਾ, ਗੋਲਾਬਾਰੀ ਕਰਨੀ, ਗਾਰੇ ਨਾਲ ਜੋੜਨਾ

mortgage (ਮੋਗਿਜ) *n v* ਗਿਰਵੀ, ਰਹਿਣ; ਗਿਰਵੀ ਰੱਖਣਾ ਰਹਿਣੇ ਰੱਖਣਾ

mortification (ਮੋਟਿਫ਼ਿ'ਕੇਇਸ਼ਨ) *n* ਆਤਮ-ਦਮਨ; ਸੰਜਮ, ਤਪੱਸਿਆ; ਅਪਮਾਨ

mortify (ਮੋਟਿਫ਼ਾਇ) *v* (ਸਰੀਰ ਜਾਂ ਭਾਵਾਂ ਨੂੰ) ਵੱਸ ਵਿਚ ਕਰਨਾ, ਇੰਦਰੀਆਂ ਦਾ ਦਮਨ ਕਰਨਾ, ਮਨ ਮਾਰਨਾ; ਹੰਕਾਰ ਤੋੜਨਾ, ਅਪਮਾਨ ਕਰਨਾ, ਭਾਵਾਂ ਨੂੰ ਠੇਸ ਪਹੁੰਚਾਉਣਾ

mortuary (ਮੋਚੁਅਰਿ) *n a* ਮੁਰਦਾਘਾਟ, ਲਾਸ਼-ਘਰ, ਮੁਰਦਾਖ਼ਾਨਾ

mortum (ਮੋਂਟਅਮ) *n* ਮਿਰਤੂ, ਮੌਤ, ਮਰਨ

mosque (ਮੌਸਕ) *n* ਮਸੀਤ, ਮਸਜਦ

mosquito (ਮਅ'ਸਕੀਟਅਉ) *n* ਮੱਛਰ; ~**net** ਮੱਛਰਦਾਨੀ, ਮੱਛਹਿਰੀ

moss (ਮੌਸ) *n v* ਚਿੱਕੜ, ਦਲਦਲ, ਚਲ੍ਹ; ਗਿੱਲੀ ਧਰਤੀ; ਕਾਈ; ਕਾਈ ਉੱਗਣੀ

most (ਮਅਉਸਟ) *a adv* ਸਭ ਤੋਂ ਜ਼ਿਆਦਾ, ਸਭ ਤੋਂ ਵੱਧ, ਵੱਧ ਤੋਂ ਵੱਧ, ਅਧਿਕਤਮ, ਸਭ ਤੋਂ ਵੱਧ ਕੇ

mot (ਮਅਉ) *n* ਚੁਟਕਲਾ, ਲਤੀਫ਼ਾ

mote (ਮਅਉਟ) *n* ਧੂੜ, ਧੂੜ-ਕਣ, ਅਣੂ, ਕਣ, ਰਵਾ, ਮਿੱਟੀ ਦਾ ਜ਼ੱਰਾ

motel (ਮਅਉ'ਟੈੱਲ) *n* ਮਾਟਲ, ਹੋਟਲ ਜਿਥੇ ਮੋਟਰਾਂ ਵਾਲੇ ਰਾਤ ਠਹਿਰ ਸਕਦੇ ਹਨ

moth (ਮੌਥ) *n* ਭੰਬਟ, ਪਤੰਗਾ, ਪਰਵਾਨਾ; ਲੋਭੀ ਆਦਮੀ

mother (ਮਅੱਦਅ*) *n v* ਮਾਤਾ, ਅੰਮਾ, ਮਾਈ, ਜਣਨੀ; ਧਾਰਮਕ ਸੰਘ ਦੀ ਪ੍ਰਧਾਨ ਇਸਤਰੀ; ਮਾਂ ਵਾਂਗ ਰੱਖਿਆ ਕਰਨੀ; ਗੋਦੀ ਲੈਣਾ, ਪਾਲਣਾ ਪੋਸਣਾ; ਜਨਮ ਦੇਣਾ; ~**in law** ਸੱਸ; ~**land** ਮਾਤ-ਭੂਮੀ; ~**of peare** ਸਿੱਪੀ; ~**tongue** ਮਾਤ-ਭਾਸ਼ਾ, ਮਾਦਰੀ ਜ਼ਬਾਨ; ~**less** ਮਾਤਹੀਣ, ਅਨਾਥ

motif (ਮਅਉ'ਟੀਫ਼) *n* ਆਧਾਰੀ ਗੁਣ ਜਾਂ ਵਿਚਾਰ; ਬੂਟੀ

motion (ਮਅਉਸ਼ਨ) *v* (1) ਚਾਲ, ਗਤੀ, ਕਿਰਿਆ, ਚੱਲਣ, ਹਰਕਤ; ਪ੍ਰਸਤਾਵ; (2) ਅੰਤੜੀਆਂ ਦਾ ਮਰੋੜਾ, ਢਿੱਡ ਪੀੜ, ਵੱਟ, ਮੱਲ-ਤਿਆਗਾ; ~**less** ਗਤੀਹੀਣ, ਸਥਿਰ, ਨਿਸ਼ਚਲ, ਅੱਚਲ

motivation (ਮਅਉਟਿਵ'ਵੇਇਸ਼ਨ) *n* ਪਰੇਰਨਾ, ਪ੍ਰੇਤਸਾਹਨ, ਕਾਰਨ, ਪ੍ਰਯੋਜਨ

motive (ਮਅਉਟਿਵ) *n a v* ਪਰੇਰਨਾ; ਕਾਰਜ, ਨਿਮਿੱਤ, ਪ੍ਰਯੋਜਨ, ਮਨੋਰਥ, ਅਰਥ, ਮਨਸ਼ਾ, ਗਰਜ਼, ਮਕਸਦ; ਪਰੇਰਕ, ਪ੍ਰਵਰਤਕ; ਪਰੇਰਤ ਕਰਨਾ; ਕਾਰਨ ਹੋਣਾ

motivity (ਮਅਉ'ਟਿਵੁਅਟਿ) *n* ਪਰੇਰਨਾ; ਚਾਲਕਤਾ, ਚਾਲਕ ਸ਼ਕਤੀ

motor (ਮਅਉਟਅ*) *n v a* ਗੱਡੀ, ਮੋਟਰ, ਪਰੇਰਕ, ਸੰਚਾਲਕ, ਗਾਮੀ, ਚਾਲਕ; ਚਾਲਕ ਨਾੜੀ; ~**cade** ਮੋਟਰਾਂ ਦਾ ਕਾਫ਼ਲਾ

motto (ਮੌਟਅਉ) *n* ਆਦਰਸ਼ ਵਾਕ, ਲੋਕੋਕਤੀ; ਮੁਦਰਾਲੇਖ; ਨੀਤੀ ਵਾਕ; ਟੇਕ, ਵਾਕ-ਖੰਡ

mould (ਮਅਉਲਡ) *n v* ਕਾਲਬ (ਉਸਾਰੀ); ਨਮੂਨਾ, ਤਰਾਸ਼, ਉੱਲੀ; ਢਾਲਣਾ, ਸਾਂਚੇ ਵਿਚ

ਵਾਲਣਾ, ਨਮੂਨਾ ਬਣਾਉਣਾ, ਗੁੰਨ੍ਹਣਾ, ਮਿਲਾਉਣਾ; ਸੁਆਰਨਾ, ਮਾਡਲ ਬਣਾਉਣਾ

mound (ਮਾਊਂਡ) *n v* ਮੋਰਚਾ; ਟਿੱਲਾ; ਮਿੱਟੀ ਦਾ ਢੇਲਾ; ਪਹਾੜੀ; ਟਿੱਲ੍ਹਿਆਂ ਨਾਲ ਘੇਰਨਾ, ਢੇਰ ਲਾਉਣਾ; ਮੋਰਚਾ ਬੰਦੀ ਕਰਨਾ

mount (ਮਾਊਂਟ) *v n* ਚੜ੍ਹਨਾ; (ਘੋੜੇ ਤੇ) ਸਵਾਰ ਹੋਣਾ; ਵਧਣਾ; ~ed ਚੜ੍ਹਿਆ ਹੋਇਆ, ਸਵਾਰ

mountain (ਮਾਊਨਟਿਨ) *n* ਪਰਬਤ, ਪਹਾੜ, ਕੋਹ

mourn (ਮੋ'ਨ) *v* ਸੋਗ ਮਨਾਉਣਾ; ਸੰਤਾਪ ਕਰਨਾ; ਮਾਤਮ ਕਰਨਾ, ਵਿਰਲਾਪ ਕਰਨਾ; ਦੁਖੀ ਹੋਣਾ; ~er ਸੋਗ ਮਨਾਉਣ ਵਾਲਾ, ਮਾਤਮ ਕਰਨ ਵਾਲਾ; ~ful ਮਾਤਮੀ, ਸੋਗੀ, ਸੋਗਵਾਨ; ~ing ਸੋਕ, ਸੋਗ, ਖੇਦ, ਦੁੱਖ, ਰੰਜ, ਗਾਮ, ਮਾਤਮ, ਵਿਰਲਾਪ, ਰੁਦਨ

mouse (ਮਾਊਸ) *n* ਚੂਹਾ, ਮੂਸਾ, ਮੂਸ; ਸ਼ਰਮਾਕਲ ਆਦਮੀ

moustache (ਮਅ'ਸਟਾਸ਼) *n* ਮੁੱਛ

mouth (ਮਾਊਥ) *n v* ਮੁੱਖ, ਚਿਹਰਾ, ਮੂੰਹ

move (ਮੂਵ਼) *v* ਚੱਲਣਾ, ਟੁਰਨਾ, ਹਰਕਤ ਕਰਨੀ, ਹਿੱਲਣਾ, ਕਾਰਵਾਈ ਕਰਨੀ; ਅਰਜੀ ਦੇਣਾ, (ਸਰੀਰ ਦੇ ਅੰਗ ਨੂੰ) ਹਿਲਾਉਣਾ, ਉੱਨਤੀ ਕਰਨਾ, ਅੱਗੇ ਵਧਣਾ; ਟੱਟੀ ਕਰਨੀ; ~ability ਗਾਮਨਸ਼ੀਲਤਾ, ਹਿੱਲਣ ਜਾਂ ਚੱਲਣ ਦੀ ਸਮਰੱਥਾ, ਚੱਲਤਾ; ~able ਚੱਲ-ਸੰਪਤੀ; ਸਾਮਾਨ; ਚੱਲਣਸ਼ੀਲ, ਚਲਾਇਮਾਨ; ~d ਪਰੇਰਤ, ਚਲਤ; ਪ੍ਰਸਤੁਤ, ਪ੍ਰਸਤਾਵਤ; ਪ੍ਰਭਾਵਤ; ~ment ਚਾਲ, ਟੋਰ, ਹਰਕਤ; ਗਤੀ; ਕਾਰਵਾਈ; ਅੰਦੋਲਨ, ਹਲਚਲ; ਹਿਲਜੁਲ, ਭਾਵਨਾ; ਗਤੀ-ਵਿਧੀ

movie (ਮੂਵ਼ਿ) *a* ਚਲਚਿੱਤਰ ਸਬੰਧੀ, ਫ਼ਿਲਮ ਸਬੰਧੀ; ~s ਚਲਚਿੱਤਰ, ਸਿਨੇਮਾ

moving (ਮੂਵ਼ਿੰਗ) *a* ਚੱਲਦਾ-ਫਿਰਦਾ, ਚੱਲਤ,

ਗਤੀਮਾਨ, ਗਤੀਸ਼ੀਲ; ਕਰੁਣਾਮਈ, ਪ੍ਰਭਾਵਸ਼ਾਲੀ

much (ਮੱਚ) *a adv* ਚੋਖਾ, ਢੇਰ, ਬਹੁਤਾ, ਬਾਹਲਾ; ਅਤੀਅੰਤ, ਅਧਿਕ ਮਾਤਰਾ ਵਿਚ

mucous (ਮਯੂਕਅਸ) *a* ਚਿਪਚਿਪਾ, ਲੇਸਦਾਰ; ਕਫ਼ਦਾਰ

mucus (ਮਯੂਕਅਸ) *n* ਰੀਂ੍ਹ, ਕਫ਼, ਬਲਗਾਮ, ਚਿਪਚਿਪਾ, ਪੇਚਸ

mud (ਮੱਡ) *n* ਚਿੱਕੜ, ਦਲਦਲ, ਭੱਦੀ ਗੱਲ, ਗੰਦਗੀ; ~dy ਗੰਧਲਾ, ਚਿੱਕੜ ਭਰਿਆ; ਧੁੰਦਲਾ, ਮੈਲਾ, ਅਸਪਸ਼ਟ; ਗੰਧਲਾ ਕਰਨਾ, ਲਬੇੜਨਾ, ਧੁੰਦਲਾ ਕਰਨਾ

muddle (ਮਅੱਡਲ) *v n* ਕੰਮ ਨੂੰ ਵਿਗਾੜ ਦੇਣਾ, ਖ਼ਰਾਬ ਕਰ ਦੇਣਾ, ਰਲਗੱਡ ਕਰ ਦੇਣਾ; ਨਸ਼ੇ ਨਾਲ ਚੂਰ ਕਰਨਾ; ~some ਕੰਮ-ਵਿਗਾੜੂ, ਗੜਬੜ ਕਰਨ ਵਾਲਾ

muffle ('ਮਅੱਫ਼ਲ) *n v* ਉਂਗਲਾਂ ਤੋਂ ਬਿਨਾ ਦਸਤਾਨਾ; ਭੱਠੀ ਦਾ ਖ਼ਾਨਾ; ਗਲ ਢਕਣਾ (ਗਰਮ ਰੱਖਣ ਲਈ), ਗਲੂ-ਬੰਦ ਪਾਉਣਾ; ਅਵਾਜ਼ ਦਬਾਉਣਾ; ~r ਗਲੁਬੰਦ, ਮਫ਼ਲਰ; ਮੋਟਾ ਦਸਤਾਨਾ

mug (ਮਅੱਗ) *n v* ਜਲ-ਪਾਤਰ, ਲੋਟਾ, ਗੜਵਾ, ਮੱਗ; ਠੰਢਾ ਸ਼ਰਬਤ; ਮੂਫ਼ੂ, ਆਦਮੀ, ਮੂਰਖ-ਬੰਦਾ; ਕਿਸੇ ਵਿਸ਼ੇ ਦਾ ਡੂੰਘਾ ਅਧਿਐਨ ਕਰਨਾ, ਬਹੁਤ ਪੜ੍ਹਨਾ, ਰਟ ਲੈਣਾ

muggy (ਮਅੱਗਿ) *n a* ਘੁਟਣ; ਗਲਾ ਘੋਟਣ ਵਾਲਾ, ਸਾਹ-ਘੋਟੂ, ਹੁਸੜ ਵਾਲਾ

mule (ਮਯੂਲ) *n* ਖੱਚਰ, ਦੋਗਲਾ ਜਾਨਵਰ, ਅਸ਼ੀਅਲ ਟੱਟੂ; ਮੂਰਖ ਆਦਮੀ; ~teer ਖੱਚਰ ਵਾਲਾ

multi (ਮਅੱਲਟਿ) *a* ਅਨੇਕ, ਬਹੁਤ

multicellular (ਮਅ'ਲਟਿ'ਸੈਲਯੁਲਅ*) *a* ਬਹੁਕੋਸ਼ਕੀ, ਬਹੁਕੋਸ਼ੀ

multicolour (ਮਅਲਟਿ'ਕਅੱਲਅ*) *n* ਬਹੁਰੰਗ, ਕਈ ਰੰਗ, ਅਨੇਕ ਵਰਨ

multifarious (ਮਅਲਟਿ'ਫ਼ੇਅਰਿਅਸ) *a* ਰੰਗ-ਬਰੰਗਾ, ਬਹੁਮੁਖੀ, ਬਹੁਰੂਪ

multifold (ਮਅੱਲਟਿਫ਼ਅਉਲਡ) *a* ਬਹੁਗੁਨ

multimillionaire (ਮਅੱਲਟਿਮਿਲਯਨਅ'ਨੇਅ*) *n* ਕਰੋੜਪਤੀ, ਬਹੁਤ ਧਨਵਾਨ (ਬਹੁਲੱਖਪਤੀ)

multinational (ਮਅੱਲਟਿ'ਨੈਸ਼ਨਲ) *n a* ਬਹੁਰਾਸ਼ਟਰੀ (ਕੰਪਨੀ)

multiple (ਮਅੱਲਟਿ'ਪਲ) *n a* ਗੁਣਜ; ਅਨੇਕ ਤੱਤੀ, ਬਹੁ ਭਾਗੀ, ਕਿਸਮ ਕਿਸਮ ਦਾ

multiplicity (ਮਅੱਲਟਿ'ਪਲਿਸਅਟਿ) *n* ਬਹੁਲਤਾ, ਵਿਵਿਧਤਾ

multiply (ਮਅੱਲਟਿਪਲਾਇ) *v* (ਗਣਿ) ਗੁਣਾ ਕਰਨਾ, ਜ਼ਰਬ ਦੇਣੀ

multipurpose (ਮਅੱਲਟਿ'ਪਅ:ਪਅਜ਼) *n a* ਬਹੁ-ਪੱਖੀ, ਬਹੁ-ਪ੍ਰਯੋਜਨ, ਬਹੁ-ਮਨੋਰਥੀ

multitude (ਮਅੱਲਟਿਟਯੁਡ) *n* ਅਧਿਕ ਗਿਣਤੀ, ਬਹੁ ਸੰਖਿਆ, ਬਹੁਲਤਾ, ਵਿਵਿਧਤਾ, ਬਹੁਰੂਪਤਾ

mum (ਮਅੱਮ) *n int a v* ਖ਼ਾਮੋਸ਼, ਚੁੱਪ, ਸ਼ਾਂਤ; ਚੁੱਪ ਰਹਿਣਾ, ਚੁੱਪ ਕਰਕੇ (ਮੂਕ) ਐਕਟਿੰਗ ਕਰਨੀ

mumble (ਮਅੱਮਬਲ) *n v* ਬੁੜਬੁੜਾਹਟ, ਗੁਟਗੁਟਾਹਟ, ਅਸਪਸ਼ਟ ਵਚਨ, ਅਵਿਅਕਤ ਬਾਣੀ; ਅਸਪਸ਼ਟ ਬੋਲਣਾ, ਮੂੰਹ ਵਿਚ ਗੱਲਾਂ ਕਰਨੀਆਂ, ਗੁਟਗੁਟਾਉਨਾ, ਬੁੜਬੁੜਾਉਨਾ

mummy (ਮਅੱਮੀ) *n* ਲਾਸ਼ ਜੋ ਮਸਾਲੇ ਲਾ ਕੇ ਸੁਰੱਖਿਅਤ ਰੱਖੀ ਜਾਵੇ, ਪੁਰਾਤਨ ਲਾਸ਼, ਸੁਰੱਖਿਅਤ

mump (ਮਅੱਮਪ) *v* ਸ਼ਾਂਤ ਰੂਪ ਧਾਰਨਾ, ਚੁੱਪ ਕਰਨਾ, ਚੁੱਪਚਾਪ ਬੈਠਣਾ; ਮਨ ਵਿਚ ਕੁੜ੍ਹਨਾ, ਬੁੜਬੁੜਾਉਨਾ; ~s ਕਨੇਡੂ, ਕੰਨ ਪੇੜੇ; ਰੁਸੇਵਾਂ, ਮੂੰਹ-ਮੁਟਾਪਾ, ਰੋਸਾ

mumpish ('ਮਅੱਮਪਿਸ਼) *a* ਤੁਨਕਮਿਜ਼ਾਜ

munch (ਮਅੱਚ) *v* ਚੱਬਣਾ (ਦਾਂਤੇ); ਕਰਚ ਕਰਚ ਕਰਕੇ ਖਾਣਾ, ਮੁਰਚ ਮੁਰਚ ਚੱਬਣਾ; ਚਿੱਥਣਾ

mundane (ਮਅੰ'ਡੇਇਨ) *a* ਦੁਨਿਆਵੀ, ਲੌਕਕ, ਸੰਸਾਰਕ; ਵਿਸ਼ਵ ਸਬੰਧੀ, ਸ੍ਰਿਸ਼ਟੀ ਸਬੰਧੀ; ~ness ਲੌਕਕਤਾ, ਸੰਸਾਰਕਤਾ

municipal (ਮਯੁ'ਨਿਸਿਪਲ) *a* ਨਗਰਪਾਲਕਾ, ਨਗਰਪਾਲਕਾ ਨਾਲ ਸਬੰਧਤ; ਸ਼ਹਿਰੀ; ~ity ਨਗਰਪਾਲਕਾ, ਨਗਰ ਸਭਾ

munificence (ਮਯੁ'ਨਿਫ਼ਿਸੰਸ) *n* ਦਇਆਲਤਾ, ਉਦਾਰਤਾ, ਸਖਾਵਤ, ਖੁੱਲ੍ਹਦਿਲੀ

munificent (ਮਯੁ'ਨਿਫ਼ਿਸੰਟ) *n* ਦਿਆਲੂ, ਸਖੀ, ਦਾਤਾ, ਦਾਨੀ

munify (ਮਯੁਨਿਫ਼ਾਇ) *v* ਸੁਰੱਖਿਅਤ ਕਰਨਾ, ਮਜ਼ਬੂਤ ਕਰਨਾ, ਕਿਲ੍ਹਾਬੰਦੀ ਕਰਨਾ

munition (ਮਯੁ'ਨਿਸ਼ਨ) *n v* ਅਸਲਾ, ਗੋਲਾਬਾਰੂਦ; ਜੁੱਧ-ਸਮਗਰੀ, ਲੜਾਈ ਦਾ ਸਾਮਾਨ; ਜੁੱਧ-ਸਮਗਰੀ ਇਕੱਠੀ ਕਰਨੀ, ਗੋਲਾ-ਬਾਰੂਦ ਜਮ੍ਹਾਂ ਕਰਨਾ

murder (ਮਅ:ਡਅ*) *n v* ਖ਼ੂਨ, ਹੱਤਿਆ, ਘਾਤ, ਹਿੰਸਾ, ਕਤਲ; ਖ਼ੂਨ ਕਰਨਾ, ਹੱਤਿਆ ਕਰਨੀ, ਘਾਤ ਕਰਨਾ, ਕਤਲ ਕਰਨਾ, ਮਾਰ ਸੁੱਟਣਾ; ~er ਕਾਤਲ, ਖ਼ੂਨੀ, ਹੱਤਿਆਰਾ

murmur (ਮਅ:ਮਅ*) *n v* ਕਾਨਾਫੂਸੀ; ਮਰਮਰ ਧੁਨੀ, ਕਲਕਲ, ਬਿਣਬਿਣ, ਸਰਸਰਾਉਨਾ

muscle (ਮਅੱਸਲ) *n* ਪੱਠਾ; ਜ਼ੋਰ, ਬਾਹੁਬਲ

muscular (ਮਅੱਸਕਯੁਲਅ*) *a* ਪੱਠੇਦਾਰ;

ਗਠੀਲਾ, ਗੰਢਿਆ, ਪੁਸ਼ਟ

muse (ਮਯੂਜ਼) *n v* (ਕਾਵਿ) ਕਵੀ, ਸ਼ਾਇਰ; ਸਰਸਵਤੀ; ਕਾਵਿ-ਪ੍ਰਤਿਭਾ, ਧਿਆਨ; ਗੰਭੀਰ ਵਿਚਾਰ ਵਿਚ ਪੈਣਾ, ਮਨਨ ਕਰਨਾ, ਚਿੰਤਨ ਕਰਨਾ; ~ful ਧਿਆਨ ਮਗਨ, ਚਿੰਤਤ; ~less ਵਿਚਾਰਹੀਨ, ਅਭਾਵਕ

museum (ਮਯੂਜ਼ਿਅਮ) *n* ਅਜਾਇਬ ਘਰ, ਅਜਾਇਬਘਰਾਨਾ

mushroom (ਮਸ਼ਰੁਮ) *n v* ਖੁੰਭ, ਕੁਕਰਮੁੱਤਾ; ਨਵਾਂ ਨਵਾਬ, ਕੱਲ ਦਾ ਰਈਸ; ਖੁੰਭਾਂ ਤੇਡਣਾ

music (ਮਯੂਜ਼ਿਕ) *n* ਸੰਗੀਤ; ਸੰਗੀਤਸ਼ਾਸਤਰ, ਸੁਰ, ਰਾਗਾ; ~ian ਸੰਗੀਤ-ਸ਼ਾਸਤਰੀ, ਸੰਗੀਤੱਗ, ਵਾਦਕ; ਗਾਇਕ; ~ologist ਸੰਗੀਤ-ਸ਼ਾਸਤਰੀ; ~ology ਸੰਗੀਤ-ਸ਼ਾਸਤਰ, ਸੰਗੀਤ-ਵਿਗਿਆਨ

musk (ਮਅਸਕ) *n* ਕਸਤੂਰੀ, ਮੁਸ਼ਕ; ~y ਕਸਤੂਰੀ ਦੀ ਵਾਸ਼ਨਾ ਵਾਲਾ, ਕਸਤੂਰੀ ਯੁਕਤ, ਸੁਗੰਧਿਤ; ਖੁਸ਼ਬੁਦਾਰ

musket (ਮਅਸਕਿਟ) *n* ਪੁਰਾਣੇ ਵੇਲੇ ਦੀ ਬੰਦੂਕ; ~eer ਬੰਦੂਕ ਲੈ ਕੇ ਚੱਲਣ ਵਾਲਾ ਸਿਪਾਹੀ, ਬੰਦੂਕਚੀ

muslin (ਮਅਜ਼ਲਿਨ) *n a* ਮਲਮਲ, ਪਤਲਾ ਕੱਪੜਾ

musquash (ਮਅਸਕਵੈਸ਼) *n* ਛਛੂੰਦਰ

must (ਮਅਸਟ) *n v aux a* ਕੱਚੀ ਸ਼ਰਾਬ; ਉੱਲੀ, ਫਫੂੰਦੀ, ਭਕਰੀ; ਉੱਲੀ ਲੱਗਣੀ, ਚਾਹੀਦਾ ਹੈ; ਅਵੱਸ਼, ਲਾਜ਼ਮੀ

mustard (ਮਅਸਟਅਡ) *n* ਰਾਈ, ਸਰ੍ਹੋਂ; ਸੁਆਦੀ ਚੀਜ਼, ਦਿਲਚਸਪ ਆਦਮੀ

muster (ਮਅਸਟਅ*) *n v* ਗਿਣਤੀ, ਹਾਜ਼ਰੀ, ਜੋਡ; ਸਮਾਗਮ, ਸਮੂਹ, ਜਮਘਟ; ਗਿਣਤੀ ਕਰਨੀ; ਹਾਜ਼ਰੀ ਲੈਣੀ, ਇਕੱਠ ਕਰਨਾ ਜਾਂ ਹੋਣਾ;

ਸ਼ਕਤੀ ਇਕੱਠੀ ਕਰਨੀ, ਸਾਹਸ ਕਰਨਾ

mutability (ਮਯੂਟਅ'ਬਿਲਾਅਟਿ) *n* ਚੰਚਲਤਾ, ਅਸਥਿਰਤਾ; ਪਰਿਵਰਤਨਸ਼ੀਲਤਾ

mutation (ਮਯੂ'ਟੇਇਸ਼ਨ) *n* ਅਦਲ-ਬਦਲ, ਤਬਦੀਲੀ, ਪਰਿਵਰਤਨ

mute (ਮਯੂਟ) *a n v* ਖਾਮੋਸ਼ ਜਾਂ ਗੂੰਗਾ; ਅਵਾਕ, ਮੂਕ, ਚੁੱਪ; ਮੌਨ, ਖਾਮੋਸ਼; ਸਪਰਸ਼ ਵਿਅੰਜਨ; ਮੂਕ ਐਕਟਰ; ਧੀਮਾ ਕਰਨਾ, ਦਬਾਉਣਾ; ~ness ਧੁਨੀਹੀਨਤਾ, ਮੂਕ ਭਾਵ, ਖਮੋਸ਼ੀ, ਗੂੰਗਾਪਣ

mutilate ('ਮਯੂਟਿਲੇਇਟ) *v* ਕੋਈ ਅੰਗ ਕੱਟ ਦੇਣਾ, ਹੱਥ-ਪੈਰ ਕੱਟ ਦੇਣਾ, ਅੰਗ ਭੰਗ ਕਰਨਾ, ਪੁਸਤਕ ਦਾ ਕੋਈ ਹਿੱਸਾ ਕੱਟ ਦੇਣਾ, ਖੰਡਤ ਕਰਨਾ; ~d ਵਿਕ੍ਰਿਤ, ਭਿੰਨ ਭਿੰਨ, ਖੰਡਤ, ਲੰਗੜਾ-ਲੂਲਾ, ਕੱਟਿਆ-ਵੱਢਿਆ

mutilation ('ਮਯੂਟਿ'ਲੇਇਸ਼ਨ) *n* ਅੰਗ-ਭੰਗ, ਖੰਡਨ, ਕਾਂਟ-ਛਾਂਟ

mutineer (ਮਯੂਟਿ'ਨਿਅ*) *n* ਗਦਰੀ, ਵਿਦਰੋਹੀ, ਬਾਗੀ

mutiny (ਮਯੂਟਿਨਿ) *n v* (ਫੌਜੀ) ਗਦਰ, ਬਗਾਵਤ, ਕਰਾਂਤੀ, ਵਿਦਰੋਹ, ਗਦਰ ਕਰਨਾ, ਬਗਾਵਤ ਕਰਨੀ, ਵਿਦਰੋਹ ਕਰਨਾ

mutt (ਮਅੱਟ) *n* ਗਧਾ, ਬੇਵਕੂਫ਼, ਬੁੱਧੂ, ਬੇਅਕਲ

mutter (ਮਅੱਟਅ*) *n v* ਅਸਪਸ਼ਟ ਉਚਾਰਨ, ਗੁਣਗੁਣਾਹਟ, ਬੁੜਬੁੜਾਉਣਾ; ਮੂੰਹ ਵਿਚ ਬੋਲਣਾ, ਕਾਨਾਫ਼ੂਸੀ ਕਰਨੀ, ਘੁਸਰ-ਫੁਸਰ ਕਰਨ; ~ing ਅਸਪਸ਼ਟ ਭਾਸ਼ਣ, ਅਵਿਅਕਤ ਉਚਾਰਨ, ਬੁੜਬੁੜ

mutton (ਮਅੱਟਨ) *n* ਭੇਡ ਜਾਂ ਬੱਕਰੀ ਦਾ ਮਾਸ

mutual ('ਮਯੂਚੁਅਲ) *a* ਪਰਸਪਰ, ਆਪਸੀ, ਬਾਹਮੀ, ਸਾਂਝਾ, ਸੰਮਿਲਤ; ~ity ਪਰਸਪਰਤਾ; ~ly ਆਪਸ ਵਿਚ, ਪਰਸਪਰ

muzziness (ਮਅੱਜ਼ਿਨਿਸ) *n* ਸੁਸਤੀ, ਆਲਸ, ਉਤਸ਼ਾਹੀਣਤਾ

muzzle (ਮਅੱਜ਼ਲ) *n v* ਥੁਥਨੀ; ਬੁੱਲੀ, ਬੰਦੂਕ ਦੀ ਨਾਲੀ ਦਾ ਮੂੰਹ, ਮੋਰੀ; ਦਹਾਨਾ; ਜ਼ਬਾਨਬੰਦੀ ਕਰਨੀ, ਬੋਲਣ ਦੇ ਲਿਖਣ ਦੀ ਮਨਾਹੀ ਕਰਨੀ

my (ਮਾਇ) *pron* ਮੇਰਾ, ਮੇਰੀ, ਮੇਰੇ; ~self ਆਪਣੇ ਆਪ, ਖ਼ੁਦ, ਆਪਣੇ ਆਪ ਨੂੰ, ਮੈਂ ਖ਼ੁਦ

myopia, myopy (ਮਾਇ'ਅਉਪਯਾ, ਮਾਇਅਉਪਿ) *n* ਨਿਕਟ ਦ੍ਰਿਸ਼ਟੀ, ਅਲਪ ਦ੍ਰਿਸ਼ਟੀ

myriad (ਮਿਰਿਅਡ) *n a* ਬਹੁਤ ਵੱਡੀ ਸੰਖਿਆ; ਅਣਗਿਣਤ, ਅਸੰਖ, ਬੇਸ਼ੁਮਾਰ

mysterious (ਮਿ'ਸਟਿਅਰਿਅਸ) *a* ਭੇਦ-ਭਰਿਆ, ਭੇਦ-ਯੁਕਤ, ਰਹੱਸਪੂਰਨ, ਰਹੱਸਮਈ; ~ness ਅਸਪਸ਼ਟਤਾ, ਰਹੱਸਪੂਰਨਤਾ, ਗੁੜ੍ਹਤਾ ਦੁਰਬੋਧਤਾ

mystery (ਮਿਸਟ(ਅ)ਰਿ) *n* ਰਹੱਸ, ਭੇਦ, ਰਾਜ਼, ਦੁਰਬੋਧਤਾ, ਅਸਪਸ਼ਟਤਾ, ਗੁੜ੍ਹਤਾ

mystic (ਮਿਸਟਿਕ) *a n* ਰਹੱਸਮਈ, ਸੂਫ਼ੀਆਨਾ, ਰਹੱਸਾਤਮਕ; ਅਲੌਕਕ, ਜੋਗੀ; ~ism ਰਹੱਸਵਾਦ, ਅਧਿਆਤਮ-ਵਿੱਦਿਆ

mystify (ਮਿਸਟੀਫ਼ਾਇ) *v* ਰਹੱਸਮਈ ਬਣਾ ਦੇਣਾ, ਗੁੜ੍ਹ ਕਰਨ ਦੇਣਾ; ਭੇਦਪੂਰਨ ਬਣਾਉਣਾ; ਵਿਸਮਿਤ ਕਰਨਾ

mystique (ਮਿ'ਸਟੀਕ) *n* ਰਹੱਸ

myth (ਮਿਥ) *n* ਮਿੱਥ, ਮਿਥਿਆ, ਪੁਰਾਣ ਕਥਾ; ~ical ਮਿਥਕ, ਪੁਰਾਣਕ; ਕਾਲਪਨਕ; ~ological ਮਿਥਹਾਸਕ, ਪੁਰਾਣਕ, ਪੁਰਾਣ ਸਬੰਧੀ, ਪੁਰਾਣ ਉਕਤ; ~ology ਮਿਥਹਾਸ, ਪੁਰਾਣ; ਪੁਰਾਣ, ਵਿੱਦਿਆ, ਪੁਰਾਣ ਕਥਾ-ਸ਼ਾਸਤਰ; ~onomy ਪੁਰਾਣ-ਸ਼ਾਸਤਰ

N

N, n (ਐੱਨ) *n* ਰੋਮਨ ਵਰਨਮਾਲਾ ਦਾ ਚੌਦ੍ਹਵਾਂ ਅੱਖਰ; ਮਾਪ ਦੀ ਇਕਾਈ; (ਗਣਿ) ਅਨਿਸ਼ਚਤ ਸੰਖਿਆ

nab (ਨੈਬ) *v n* ਫੜਨਾ, ਫੜ ਲੈਣਾ; ਗਿਰਿਫ਼ਤਾਰ ਕਰਨਾ, ਰੰਗੇ ਹੱਥੀਂ ਫੜ ਲੈਣਾ; ਪਹਾੜ ਦੀ ਸਿਖਰ, ਚੋਟੀ

nacarat (ਨੈਕਅਰੈਟ) *n* ਸੰਤਰੀ ਰੰਗ, ਜੋਰਗੀਆ, ਰੰਗ, ਭਗਵਾ ਹੰਗ

nag (ਨੈਗ) *n* ਟੱਟੂ, ਛੋਟਾ ਘੋੜਾ; ~gy ਲੜਾਕਾ, ਝਗੜਾਲੂ

naiad (ਨਾਇਐਡ) *n* ਜਲ-ਦੇਵੀ, ਜਲ-ਪਰੀ

nail (ਨੇਇਲ) *n v* ਨਹੁੰ; ਨਹੁੰਦਰ; (ਪਸ਼ੂਆਂ ਦਾ) ਪੰਜਾ, ਕਿੱਲ, ਮੇਖ, ਕੋਕਾ; ਬਿਰੰਜੀ; ਲੰਮਾਈ ਦਾ ਇਕ ਮਾਪ; ਕਿੱਲ ਠੋਕਣਾ, ਕੱਸਣਾ, ਫੜ ਲੈਣਾ

naive (ਨਾਈ'ਈਵ਼) *a* ਭੋਲਾ-ਭਾਲਾ, ਸਿੱਧਾ-ਸਾਦਾ, ਸਿੱਧਪੱਤ

naivety (ਨਾਇ'ਈਵ਼ਟਿ) *n* ਭੋਲਪਣ, ਨਿਰਛਲਤਾ, ਸਰਲਤਾ, ਸਾਦਗੀ

naked (ਨੇਇਕਿਡ) *a* ਨੰਗਾ, ਅਟਕੋਜਿਆ, ਨਗਨ; ਬੇਪਰਦਾ; ਸਪਸ਼ਟ, ਸਾਫ਼ ਸਾਫ਼; ਸਾਦਾ; ~ness ਨੰਗਾਪਣ, ਨਗਨਤਾ, ਨੰਗੇਜ, ਬੇਪਰਦਗੀ

name (ਨੇਇਮ) *n v* ਨਾਂ, ਨਾਮ; ਯਾਦਗਾਰ; ਪ੍ਰਤਿਸ਼ਠਤ ਵਿਅਕਤੀ; ਪ੍ਰਸਿੱਧੀ, ਸ਼ੁਹਰਤ, ਨਾਮਣਾ; ਕੁਲ, ਵੰਸ਼; ਨਾਂ ਰੱਖਣਾ; ਨਾਂ ਲੈਣਾ; ਜ਼ਿਕਰ ਕਰਨਾ, ਚਰਚਾ ਕਰਨੀ; **to call ~s** ਗਾਲ੍ਹਾਂ ਕੱਢਣਾ; ~d ਪ੍ਰਸਿੱਧ, ਨਾਮੀ; ~less ਅਪ੍ਰਸਿੱਧ, ਨਾਮਹੀਣ, ਗੁਮਨਾਮ, ਅਗਿਆਤ; ~ly ਅਰਥਾਤ, ਭਾਵ ਇਹ ਕਿ; ~sake ਹਮਨਾਮ, ਇਕੋ ਨਾਂ ਵਾਲਾ

naming (ਨੇਇਮਿਙ) *n* ਨਾਮਕਰਨ

nancy (ਨੈਂਸਿ) *a* ਜਨਾਨੜਾ, ਜਨਾਨੇ ਸੁਭਾਅ ਵਾਲਾ (ਆਦਮੀ)

naos (ਨੇਇਔਸ) *n* ਮੰਦਰ ਦਾ ਅੰਦਰਲਾ ਹਿੱਸਾ, ਗਰਭ-ਗ੍ਰਿਹਿ

nap (ਨੈਪ) *v n* ਪਲ ਭਰ ਅੱਖ ਲਾਉਂਦੀ; ਠੁੱਕਾ ਲਾਉਂਟਾ; ਠੁੱਕਾ; ਬਾਜ਼ੀ, ਚਾਲ; ਤਾਸ਼ ਦੀ ਇਕ ਖ਼ਾਸ ਖੇਡ; ਮੱਸ, ਕੱਪੜੇ ਦੀ ਬੂਰ ਜਾਂ ਲੂੰਈਂ

nape (ਨੇਇਪ) *n* ਧੌਣ ਦਾ ਪਿਛਲਾ ਪਾਸਾ, ਗਿੱਚੀ

napkin (ਨੈਪਕਿਨ) *n* ਤੌਲੀਆ, ਰੁਮਾਲ, ਅੰਗੋਛਾ

narcotic (ਨਾ'ਕੌਟਿਕ) *a n* ਨਸ਼ੀਲੀ, ਮੂਰਛਾਕਾਰ; ਨੀਂਦ ਲਿਆਉਂਦ ਵਾਲੀ ਦਵਾਈ, ਨਸ਼ੀਲੀ ਚੀਜ਼

narcotization ('ਨਾ'ਕਅਟਾਇ'ਜ਼ੇਇਸ਼ਨ) *n* ਬੇਹੋਸ਼ੀ, ਬੇਸੁੱਧੀ, ਨਸ਼ੇ ਦੀ ਹਾਲਤ, ਸੁੰਨਤਾ

narcotize ('ਨਾ'ਕਅਟਾਇਜ਼) *v* ਬੇਹੋਸ਼ ਕਰਨਾ, ਨਸ਼ਾ ਚੜ੍ਹਾ ਦੇਣਾ, ਸੁੰਨ ਕਰਨਾ, ਬੇਹਿੱਸ ਕਰਨਾ

narrate (ਨਅ'ਰੇਇਟ) *v* ਵਰਨਣ ਕਰਨਾ, ਬਿਆਨ ਕਰਨਾ, ਸੁਣਾਉਂਟਾ

narration (ਨਅ'ਰੇਇਸ਼ਨ) *n* ਵਰਨਣ, ਬਿਆਨ, ਕਥਨ, ਕਥਾ, ਕਿੱਸਾ, ਵਿਆਖਿਆ

narrative (ਨੈਰਅਟਿਵ਼) *n a* ਬਿਰਤਾਂਤ, ਵਰਨਣ, ਕਥਾ, ਕਿੱਸਾ; ਵਰਨਨਾਤਮਕ

narrator (ਨਅ'ਰੇਇਟਅ*) *n* ਬਿਆਨ ਕਰਨ ਵਾਲਾ, ਦੱਸਣ ਵਾਲਾ, ਕਥਾਵਾਚਕ

narrow (ਨੈਰਅਉ) *a n v* ਤੰਗ, ਭੀੜ, ਸੌੜਾ, ਸੀਮਤ, ਸੰਕੁਚਤ; ਛੋਟਾ; ਤੰਗਦਿਲ, ਤੁੱਛਸਭੀ, ਸੁਆਰਥੀ; ਤੰਗ ਨਜ਼ਰੀਆ; ਸੰਖੇਪ ਕਰਨਾ; ਸੁਕੜਨਾ; ~escape ਬਾਲ ਬਾਲ ਬਚਣਾ; ~ly

ਮਸਾਂ ਹੀ, ਮਸਾਂ; ਮੁਸ਼ਕਲ ਨਾਲ, ਬਾਰੀਕੀ ਨਾਲ; ~minded ਤੰਗਦਿਲ, ਤੁਅੱਸਬੀ, ਸੁਆਰਥੀ, ਹੋਛਾ; ~ness ਸੌੜ, ਸੰਕੀਰਣਤਾ, ਤੰਗੀ, ਸੰਕੋਚ

nasal ('ਨੇਇਜ਼ਲ) *a* ਨਾਸਕੀ, ਅਨੁਨਾਸਕ; ਨੱਕ ਦਾ, ਨੱਕ ਜਾਂ ਨਾਸ ਸਬੰਧੀ

nascent (ਨੈਸੰਟ) *a* ਨਵ-ਜਨਮਿਆ, ਉਸਰਦਾ; ਵਿਕਾਸਸ਼ੀਲ

nasty ('ਨਾਸਟਿ) *a* ਗੰਦਾ, ਭੈੜਾ, ਕੋਝਾ, ਘਿਰਣਾਯੋਗ; ਅਸ਼ੁੱਧ, ਅਸ਼ਲੀਲ; ਲੱਚਰ; ਹੋਛਾ

natal ('ਨੇਇਟਲ) *a* ਪ੍ਰਸੂਤ ਸਬੰਧੀ; ਜਨਮ ਸਬੰਧੀ; ~ty ਜਨਮ, ਪੈਦਾਇਸ਼, ਉਤਪਤੀ

nation ('ਨੇਇਸ਼ਨ) *n* ਕੌਮ, ਜਾਤੀ, ਰਾਸ਼ਟਰ; ਪਰਜਾ; ~al ਰਾਸ਼ਟਰੀ, ਕੌਮੀ; ਕੌਮ ਦਾ ਬੰਦਾ; ਵਸਨੀਕ; ~alism ਰਾਸ਼ਟਰਵਾਦ, ਕੌਮਪਰਸਤੀ, ਵਤਨਪਰਸਤੀ; ~alist ਰਾਸ਼ਟਰਵਾਦੀ, ਕੌਮਪਰਸਤ, ਦੇਸ਼ ਭਗਤ; ~ality ਕੌਮੀਅਤ, ਰਾਸ਼ਟਰੀਅਤਾ; ਰਾਸ਼ਟਰੀ ਭਾਵਨਾ, ਕੌਮੀ ਜਜ਼ਬਾ; ~alization ਰਾਸ਼ਟਰੀਕਰਨ; ~alize ਰਾਸ਼ਟਰੀਕਰਨ ਕਰਨਾ, ਰਾਸ਼ਟਰੀ ਜਾਂ ਕੌਮੀ ਬਣਾਉਣਾ; ~alized ਰਾਸ਼ਟਰੀਕ੍ਰਿਤ

native ('ਨੇਇਟਿਵ਼) *n a* ਵਾਸੀ, ਵਸਨੀਕ; ਦੇਸ਼-ਵਾਸੀ; ਦੇਸੀ ਮਨੁੱਖ

nativity (ਨਾ'ਟਿਵ਼ਅਟਿ) *n* ਜਨਮ, ਪੈਦਾਇਸ਼, ਉਤਪਤੀ; n~ ਹਜ਼ਰਤ ਈਸਾ, ਮਾਤਾ ਮਰੀਅਮ ਜਾਂ ਯੂਹਨਾ ਦਾ ਜਨਮ; ਜਨਮ-ਉਤਸਵ; ਜਨਮ-ਪੱਤਰੀ, ਕੁੰਡਲੀ

natural ('ਨੈਚਰ(ਅ)ਲ) *a n* ਕੁਦਰਤੀ, ਸੁਭਾਵਕ; ਪ੍ਰਕਿਰਤਕ; ਅਸਲੀ; ਮੂਲ, ਭੌਤਕ; ~ism ਪ੍ਰਕਿਰਤੀਵਾਦ; ਕੁਦਰਤੀ ਧਰਮ, ਨਾਸਤਕਤਾ; ਪ੍ਰਕਿਰਤਕ ਜੀਵਨ ਦੇ ਸਿਧਾਂਤ; ਯਥਾਰਥਵਾਦੀ ਪੱਧਤੀ; ਆਜ਼ਾਦ ਖ਼ਿਆਲੀ; ~istic ਪ੍ਰਕਿਰਤਕ

ਇਤਿਹਾਸ ਬਾਰੇ; ਪਸ਼ੂ-ਜੀਵਨ-ਸ਼ਾਸਤਰ ਬਾਰੇ; ਪ੍ਰਕਿਰਤੀਵਾਦੀ; ~ization ਦੇਸੀਕਰਨ, ਰਾਸ਼ਟਰੀਕਰਨ, ਨਾਗਰੀਕਰਨ; ~ize ਕੁਦਰਤੀ ਬਣਾਉਣਾ; ਰਸਮ-ਰੀਤੀ ਤੋਂ ਮੁਕਤ ਕਰਨਾ; (ਕਿਸੇ ਵਿਦੇਸ਼ੀ ਨੂੰ) ਨਾਗਰਿਕਤਾ ਦੇ ਅਧਿਕਾਰ ਦੇਣੇ; (ਬੇਗਾਨੀ) ਰਸਮ-ਰੀਤੀ ਆਦਿ ਨੂੰ ਅਪਨਾਉਣਾ; ~ly ਕੁਦਰਤੀ ਤੌਰ ਤੇ, ਸੁਭਾਵਕ ਤੌਰ ਤੇ; ਹਾਂ, ਠੀਕ; ~ness ਸੁਭਾਵਕਤਾ, ਸਹਿਜਤਾ, ਵਾਸਤਵਿਕਤਾ

nature ('ਨੇਇਚਅ*) *n* ਕੁਦਰਤ, ਪ੍ਰਕਿਰਤੀ, ਸ੍ਰਿਸ਼ਟੀ; ਸੁਭਾ, ਤਬੀਅਤ; ਖ਼ਸਲਤ; ਜਾਤੀ, ਵਰਗ, ਕਿਸਮ, ਪ੍ਰਕਾਰ; by ~ ਸੁਭਾਅ ਵੱਲੋਂ; in a state of ~ ਨੰਗਾ

naturing ('ਨੇਇਚਅਰਿੰਗ) *a* ਰਚਨਾਤਮਕ, ਸਿਰਜਣਾਤਮਕ, ਉਤਪਾਦਕ

naturopathy (ਨੇਇਚਅ'ਰੌਪਅਥਿ) *n* ਕੁਦਰਤੀ ਇਲਾਜ, ਪ੍ਰਕਿਰਤਕ ਚਿਕਿਤਸਾ

naught (ਨੈਟ) *n a* ਕੁਝ ਨਹੀਂ; (ਅੰਕ) ਸਿਫ਼ਰ, ਸੂਨ, ਜ਼ੀਰੋ; ਨਗੂਣਾ, ਹੀਣਾ; to come to ~ ਅਸਫਲ ਹੋਣਾ; ~iness ਢੀਠਾਈ, ਦੁਸ਼ਟਤਾ, ਉਪੱਦਰਸ਼ੀਲਤਾ, ਸ਼ਰਾਰਤ; ~y ਸ਼ਰਾਰਤੀ, ਨਟਖਟ (ਬੱਚਾ), ਜ਼ਿੱਦੀ, ਹਠੀ; ਬਦਮਾਸ਼

nausea ('ਨੌਸਯਅ) *n* ਮਤਲੀ; ਕਚਿਆਣ, ਘਿਰਨਾ, ਅਰੁਚੀ

nautical ('ਨੌਟਿਕਲ) *a* ਸਮੁੰਦਰੀ; ਜਹਾਜ਼ੀ, ਜਹਾਜ਼ ਸਬੰਧੀ, ਜਹਾਜ਼ਰਾਨੀ ਬਾਰੇ

naval (ਨੇਇਵ਼ਲ) *a* ਜਲ-ਸੈਨਾ ਸਬੰਧੀ, ਸਮੁੰਦਰੀ ਫ਼ੌਜ ਲਈ; ਜਹਾਜ਼ੀ; ~force ਜਲ-ਸੈਨਾ, ਨੌ-ਸੈਨਾ, ਸਮੁੰਦਰੀ ਬੇੜਾ

nave (ਨੇਇਵ਼) *n* ਨਾਭੀ; ਪਹੀਏ ਦੀ ਪੁਰੀ; ਗਿਰਜੇ ਦਾ ਵਿਚਕਾਰਲਾ ਭਾਗ; ~l ਨਾਭੀ, ਨਾਡ; ਧੁੰਨੀ,

ਧਰਨ; ਕੇਂਦਰ-ਬਿੰਦੂ

navigate ('ਨੈਵਿਗੇਇਟ) v ਜਹਾਜ਼ ਚਲਾਉਣਾ, ਜਹਾਜ਼ ਵਿਚ ਸਫ਼ਰ ਕਰਨਾ

navigator ('ਨੈਵਿਗੇਇਟਆ*) n ਜਹਾਜ਼ ਚਲਾਉਣ ਵਾਲਾ; ਮਾਰਗ-ਨਿਰਦੇਸ਼ਕ

navy ('ਨੇਇਵਿ) n ਜੰਗੀ ਜਹਾਜ਼ਾਂ ਦਾ ਬੇੜਾ, ਜਲ-ਸੈਨਾ, ਨੌ-ਸੈਨਾ; (ਕਵਿਤਾ) ਬੇੜਾ

nay (ਨੇਇ) n adv ਨਹੀਂ, ਨਾ; ਇੰਜ ਨਹੀਂ, ਕਿਉਂ ਨਹੀਂ, ਨਾ ਨਾ

near (ਨਿਅ*) adv prep a v ਨੇੜੇ, ਲਾਗੇ, ਕੋਲ; ਲਗਭਗ, ਕਰੀਬ-ਕਰੀਬ; ਲਾਗਲਾ, ਨੇੜੇ ਦਾ, ਨਜ਼ਦੀਕੀ; ਨੇੜੇ ਆਉਣਾ, ਲਾਗੇ ਪੁੱਜਣਾ, ਕੋਲ ਪਹੁੰਚਣਾ; ~ly ਲਗਭਗ, ਕਰੀਬ-ਕਰੀਬ, ਨੇੜੇ-ਨੇੜੇ; ~ness ਨੇੜ, ਨੇੜਤਾ, ਨਿਕਟਤਾ, ਸਮੀਪਤਾ

neat (ਨੀਟ) a n ਸਾਫ਼, ਸੁਅੱਛ, ਸੁਥਰਾ; ਉੱਜਲ; ਸੁੱਧ, ਖ਼ਾਲਸ; ਰੋਕਾ ਪਸ਼ੂ; ਗਾਂ ਜਾਂ ਬਲਦ; ~ness ਸੁਅੱਛਤਾ, ਨਿਰਮਲਤਾ, ਸੁੱਧਤਾ

neath (ਨੀਥ) prep ਥੱਲੇ, ਹੇਠਾਂ

necessary ('ਨੈਸਅਸ(ਅ)ਰਿ) a n ਜ਼ਰੂਰੀ, ਲੋੜੀਂਦਾ, ਅਵੱਸ਼ਕ

necessitate (ਨਿ'ਸੈਸਿਟੇਇਟ) v ਅਵੱਸ਼ਕ ਬਣਾ ਦੇਣਾ; ਜ਼ਰੂਰੀ ਨਤੀਜਾ ਹੋਣਾ; ਮਜਬੂਰ ਕਰ ਦੇਣਾ, ਬੇਵਸ ਕਰ ਦੇਣਾ

necessity (ਨਿ'ਸੈਸਅਟਿ) n ਲੋੜ, ਜ਼ਰੂਰਤ, ਅਵੱਸ਼ਕਤਾ; ਲੋੜੀਂਦੀ ਵਸਤੂ; ਕਾਰਨ, ਸਬੰਧ; ਰੁਕਾਵਟ; ਬੇਵਸੀ, ਲਾਚਾਰੀ, ਮਜਬੂਰੀ

neck (ਨੈੱਕ) n v ਧੌਣ, ਗਲਾ, ਗਰਦਨ; ਗਲ ਘੁੱਟਣਾ, ਗਲ ਲਾਉਣਾ; ~cloth ਗਲੂਬੰਦ; ~lace ਹਾਰ, ਗਲ ਪਾਉਣ ਵਾਲੀ ਗਾਨੀ, ਕੰਠਾ, ਕੰਠੀ; ~tie ਟਾਈ, ਨਕਟਾਈ

nector (ਨੈਕਟਆ*) n ਅੰਮ੍ਰਿਤ; ਆਘੇ-ਹਯਾਤ

Neddy (ਨੈੱਡਿ) n (ਬੋਲ) ਖੱਚਰ, ਖੋਤਾ

nee (ਨੇਇ) a ਪੇਕਿਆਂ ਦਾ (ਗੋਤ ਜਾਂ ਨਾਂ); ਕੁਆਰੀ ਹੁੰਦੀ ਦਾ ਨਾਂ; ਕੁਆਰਾ ਨਾਂ

need (ਨੀਡ) n ਲੋੜ, ਜ਼ਰੂਰਤ; ਥੁੜ, ਤੰਗੀ, ਸੰਕਟ, ਕਸ਼ਟ, ਮੁਥਾਜੀ, ਦੁੱਖ; ਕੰਗਾਲੀ, ਗ਼ਾਰੀਬੀ; ਇੱਛਾ, ਆਕਾਂਖਿਆ; ~ful ਜ਼ਰੂਰੀ, ਅਵੱਸ਼ਕ, ਲੋੜੀਂਦੀ; ਯੋਗ, ਉਚਿਤ, ਮੁਨਾਸਬ (ਕਾਰਵਾਈ); ~iness ਲੋੜ, ਜ਼ਰੂਰਤ, ਤੰਗੀ; ~y ਲੋੜਵੰਦ, ਥੁੜਿਆ ਹੋਇਆ, ਗ਼ਾਰੀਬ, ਮੁਥਾਜ

needle ('ਨੀਡਲ) n v ਸੂਈ, ਸੂਆ; ਸਲਾਈ; ਨੋਕਦਾਰ ਪੱਥਰ; ਸਿਊਣਾ; ਚੋਭਣਾ; ਨੋਕਦਾਰ ਪੱਥਰ ਬਣਾਉਣਾ; ਅੰਦਰ ਵੜ ਜਾਣਾ; ਚੀਰ-ਫਾੜ ਕਰਨੀ; ਛੇਕ ਕਰਨਾ; ~work ਸੀਣਾ ਪਰੋਣਾ, ਸਿਲਾਈ-ਕਢਾਈ ਦਾ ਕੰਮ; ਕਸੀਦਾ

nefarious (ਨਿ'ਫੇਅਰਿਅਸ) n a ਬਦ, ਭੈੜਾ, ਬੁਰਾ; ~ness ਦੁਸ਼ਟਤਾ

negate (ਨਿ'ਗੇਇਟ) v ਰੱਦਣਾ, ਮਿਟਾਉਣਾ, ਮੇਸਣਾ, ਨਿਸਫਲ ਕਰਨਾ, ਅਸਵੀਕਾਰ ਕਰਨਾ; ਖੰਡਨ ਕਰਨਾ

negation (ਨਿ'ਗੇਇਸ਼ਨ) n ਨਿਖੇਧ, ਨਾਕਾਰਾਤਮਕ, ਕਥਨ, ਇਨਕਾਰ; ਅਸਵੀਕਰਨ; ਤਰਦੀਦ

negative (ਨੈਗਅਟਿਵ) a n v ਨਿਖੇਧੀਪੂਰਨ; ਇਨਕਾਰੀ; (ਗਣਿ) ਨਫ਼ੀ; ਅਸਵੀਕਾਰ ਕਰਨਾ, ਨਾਮਨਜ਼ੂਰ ਕਰਨਾ; ਰੱਦ ਕਰਨਾ, ਖੰਡਨ ਕਰਨਾ

neglect (ਨਿ'ਗਲੈੱਕਟ) n v ਅਣਗਹਿਲੀ, ਉਪੇਖਿਆ, ਲਾਪਰਵਾਹੀ; ਭੁੱਲ, ਉਕਾਈ; ਅਣਗਹਿਲੀ ਕਰਨੀ, ਉਕਾਈ ਕਰਨੀ; ਅਸਾਵਧਾਨੀ ਵਰਤਣੀ, ਧਿਆਨ ਨਾ ਦੇਣਾ; ~able ਛੱਡਣਯੋਗ, ਭੁੱਲਣ ਯੋਗ,

ਵਿਸਾਰਨਯੋਗ; ~ed ਭੁੱਲਿਆ ਹੋਇਆ,
ਵਿਸਰਿਆ, ਉਪੇਖਿਅਤ, ਅਣਗੌਲਿਆ

negligence (ਨੈੱਗਲਿਜਅੰਸ) *n* ਲਾਪਰਵਾਹੀ,
ਅਣਗਹਿਲੀ, ਕੁਤਾਹੀ, ਅਸਾਵਧਾਨੀ, ਉਕਾਈ;
ਭੁੱਲ; ਉਪੇਖਿਆ, ਗਫਲਤ

negligent (ਨੈੱਗਲਿਜਅੰਟ) *a* ਲਾਪਰਵਾਹ,
ਅਸਾਵਧਾਨ, ਆਲਸੀ, ਅਵੇਸਲਾ, ਗਫਲਤ
ਭਰਿਆ, ਉਪੇਖਿਆਕਾਰੀ

negligible (ਨੈੱਗਲਿਜਅਬਲ) *a* ਨਗੂਣਾ, ਤੁੱਛ,
ਨਾਂ-ਮਾਤਰ; ਬਹੁਤ ਥੋੜ੍ਹਾ, ਜ਼ਰਾ ਕੁ

negotiable (ਨਿ'ਗਅਊਸ਼ਯਅਬਲ) *a* ਸਮਝੌਤੇ
ਯੋਗ, (ਹੁੰਡੀ) ਸਕਾਰਨ ਯੋਗ

negotiate (ਨਿ'ਗਅਊਸ਼ਿਏਇਟ) *v* (ਸਮਝੌਤੇ
ਲਈ) ਗੱਲਬਾਤ ਕਰਨੀ; (ਮੁਆਮਲਾ)
ਨਜਿੱਠਣਾ; (ਕਾਰ-ਵਿਹਾਰ ਦਾ) ਪ੍ਰਬੰਧ ਕਰਨਾ;
ਵੇਚਣਾ, ਵਪਾਰ ਕਰਨਾ

Negro ('ਨੀਗਰਅਊ) *n a* ਹਬਸ਼ੀ; ਹਬਸ਼ੀ ਜਾਤੀ
ਦਾ; ਕਾਲਾ-ਸਿਆਹ

neigh (ਨੇਇ) *v n* ਹਿਣਕਣਾ; ਹਿਣਕ (ਘੋੜੇ ਦੀ);
~ing ਹਿਣਹਿਣਾਹਟ

neighbour, neighbor ('ਨੇਇਬਅ*) *n v*
ਗੁਆਂਢੀ, ਪੜੋਸੀ, ਹਮਸਾਇਆ; ਗੁਆਂਢ ਵਿਚ
ਹੋਣਾ, ਕੋਲ ਹੋਣਾ; ~hood ਗੁਆਂਢ; ਆਂਢ-
ਗੁਆਂਢ, ਚੁਫੇਰਾ, ਚੁਗਿਰਦਾ; ~ing ਗੁਆਂਢ
ਦਾ; ਨਾਲ ਲੱਗਦਾ; ਸਾਂਝੀ ਬੰਨੀ ਵਾਲਾ;
~liness ਨੇੜਤਾ, ਨਿਕਟਤਾ, ਗੁਆਂਢ

neither ('ਨਾਇਦਅ*) *conj adv a pron* ਨਾ,
ਨਾ ਹੀ; ਬਿਲਕੁਲ ਨਹੀਂ, ਕੋਈ ਵੀ ਨਹੀਂ

neo ('ਨੀਅਊ) (ਸੰਯੁਕਤ ਰੂਪ) ਨਵ, ਨਵਾਂ, ਨਵੀਂ

neologist (ਨੀ'ਔਲਅਜਿਸਟ) *n* ਨਵੀਨਤਾਵਾਦੀ;
ਬੁੱਧੀਵਾਦੀ; ਨਵੇਂ ਸ਼ਬਦ ਘੜਨ ਵਾਲਾ

nephew ('ਨੈੱਵ੍ਯੂ) *n* ਭਤੀਜਾ; ਭਾਂਜਾ

nepotism ('ਨੈੱਪਅਟਿਜ਼(ਅ)ਮ) *n* ਭਾਈ-
ਭਤੀਜਾਵਾਦ, ਕੁੰਬਾਪਰਸਤੀ

Neptune ('ਨੈੱਪਟਯੂਨ) *n* ਸਾਗਰ-ਦੇਵ, ਵਰੁਣ

nerve (ਨਅੱਵ) *n v* ਤੰਤੂ, ਨਸ, ਰਗ ਘੇਚੈਨੀ;
ਸਾਹਸ ਵਧਾਉਣਾ; ~less ਮੱਠਾ, ਢਿੱਲਾ;
ਨਿਢਰਿਆ, ਸਿਥਲ

nervous ('ਨਅੱਵ੍ਅਸ) *a* ਬੇਚੈਨ, ਭਾਵੁਕ,
ਘਬਰਾਇਆ ਹੋਇਆ, ਪਰੇਸ਼ਾਨ; ~system
ਨਸ-ਪ੍ਰਬੰਧ; ~ness ਬੇਚੈਨੀ, ਘਬਰਾਹਟ,
ਪਰੇਸ਼ਾਨੀ

nest (ਨੈੱਸਟ) *n v* ਆਲ੍ਹਣਾ, ਆਸ਼ਿਆਨਾ, ਘੁਰਨਾ,
ਖੁੱਡਾ; ਰੈਣ ਬਸੇਰਾ; ਡੇਰਾ; ਘਰ ਬਣਾਉਣਾ,
ਆਲ੍ਹਣਾ ਪਾਉਣਾ ~le ਰਹਿਣਾ, ਵਸਣਾ,
ਟਿਕਾਣਾ ਬਣਾਉਣਾ; ਸ਼ਰਨ ਲੈਣੀ; ਪਾਲਣਾ

net (ਨੈੱਟ) *n a* ਜਾਲ, ਜਾਲੀ; ਫਾਹੀ, ਫੰਧਾ; ਧੋਖਾ;
ਭਰਮ; ਮੂਲ, ਅਸਲ, ਉੱਕਾ, ਨਿਰੋਲ, ਖ਼ਾਲਸ,
ਉੱਕਾ-ਪੁੱਕਾ, ਨਿਰਾ; ਜਾਲ ਵਿਚ ਫਸਾਉਣਾ;
~work ਜਾਲੀ ਦਾ ਕੰਮ; ਜਾਲੀ; ਜਾਲੀਦਾਰ
ਲਕੀਰਾਂ, (ਰੇਲਾਂ, ਸੜਕਾਂ, ਪ੍ਰਸਾਰਨ ਆਦਿ ਦਾ)
ਜਾਲ; ~ting ਜਾਲ, ਜਾਲੀ ਦਾ ਕੰਮ; ਜਾਲ
ਲਾਉਣਾ

neurology ('ਨਯੁਅ'ਰੌਲਅਜਿ) *n* ਤੰਤਰ-
ਵਿਗਿਆਨ, ਚੇਤਾ ਵਿਗਿਆਨ

neuropathy ('ਨਯੁਅ'ਰੌਪਅਥਿ) *n* ਤੰਤੂ-ਰੋਗ

neurosis ('ਨਯੁਅਰਉਸਿਸ) *n* ਤੰਤੂ ਵਿਕਾਰ,
ਨਾੜਾਂ ਵਿਚ ਕੋਈ ਵਿਗਾੜ; ਪਾਗਲਪਨ;
ਮਾਨਸਕ ਬੇਚੈਨੀ

neutral ('ਨਯੂਟਰ(ਅ)ਲ) *a* ਨਿਰਪੱਖ, ਥੋਥਾਂਗਾ;
ਅਨਿਸਚਤ; ਵੱਖਰਾ, ਅਲਿੰਗ; ~ity ਨਿਰਪੱਖਤਾ,
ਉਦਾਸੀਨਤਾ; ਨਪੁੰਸਕਤਾ; ~ization

ਨਿਰਾਕਰਣ, ਪ੍ਰਭਾਵਹੀਣਤਾ; ~ize ਬਰਾਬਰ ਕਰਨਾ, ਪ੍ਰਭਾਵਹੀਣ ਕਰਨਾ, ਉਦਾਸੀਨ ਕਰਨਾ; ਨਿਰਪੱਖ ਬਣਾਉਣਾ

never (ਨੇੱਵ੍ਅਾ*) *adv* ਕਦੇ ਨਹੀਂ, ਉੱਕਾ ਹੀ ਨਹੀਂ; ~**more** ਫੇਰ ਕਦੇ ਨਹੀਂ, ਮੁੜ ਕੇ ਨਹੀਂ, ਬੱਸ ਫੇਰ ਨਹੀਂ; ~**theless** ਤਾਂ ਵੀ, ਫੇਰ ਵੀ; ਪਰੇ

new (ਨਯੂ) *a adv* ਨਵਾਂ, ਨਵੀਨ, ਆਧੁਨਿਕ, ਅਜੋਕਾ, ਨਵੇਂ ਸਿਰੇ ਤੋਂ, ਨਵੇਂ ਢੰਗ ਨਾਲ; ~**comer** ਨੌਵਾਰਦ; ~**ly** ਨਵਾਂ ਨਵਾਂ, ਹੁਣੇ ਹੁਣੇ, ਬੋਤੂ ਚਿਰ ਤੋਂ

news (ਨਯੂਜ਼) *n* ਖ਼ਬਰ, ਸਮਾਚਾਰ; ਹਾਲਚਾਲ; ਬਿਰਤਾਂਤ; ~**paper** ਅਖ਼ਬਾਰ, ਸਮਾਚਾਰ-ਪੱਤਰ

next (ਨੈਕਸਟ) *a adv prep n* ਅਗਲਾ, ਦੂਜਾ; ਆਗਾਮੀ; ਉਪਰੰਤ; ਕੋਲ, ਲਾਗੇ, ਨੇੜੇ, ਠੀਕ ਅੱਗੇ, ਠੀਕ ਪਿੱਛੇ

nexus (ਨੈਕਸੱਸ) *n* ਸਬੰਧ, ਮੇਲ; ਗੱਠਜੋੜ

nib (ਨਿਬ) *n* ਨੋਕ; ਚੁੰਝ, ਜੀਭ, ਨੋਕ ਜਾਂ ਜੀਭ

nice (ਨਾਇਸ) *a adv* ਸੁਚੱਜਾ, ਸੁਘੜ, ਚੰਗਾ, ਸੋਹਣਾ; ਪਿਆਰਾ; ~**ty** ਖੂਬੀ, ਚੰਗਿਆਈ; ਸੁਖਮਤਾ, ਬਾਰੀਕੀ; ਕੋਮਲਤਾ

niche (ਨਿਚ) *n v* ਆਲਾ, ਤਾਕ; ਟਿਕਾਣਾ, ਸਥਾਨ; ਆਲ਼ੇ ਵਿਚ ਰੱਖਣਾ; ਸਾਂਟਣਾ

nick (ਨਿਕ) *n v* ਵੱਢਾ; ਦੰਦਾ; ਸੁਭ ਸਮਾਂ; ਦੰਦੇਦਾਰ ਬਣਾਉਣਾ; ਦੰਦੇ ਕੱਢਣੇ; ਨਿਸ਼ਾਨ ਜਾਂ ਚਿੰਨੑ ਲਾਉਣਾ; ~**er** ਗੰਢ ਕੱਪ, ਜੇਬ ਕਤਰਾ; ਉਚਕਾ; ਹਿਟਕਣਾ, ਹਿਣਹਿਣਾਉਣਾ

nickle (ਨਿਕਲ) *n v a* ਰੁਪਾ, ਗਿਲਟ, ਨਿਕਲ, ਕਲੲਈ, ਮੁਲੰਮਾ; ਨਿਕਲ ਚੜ੍ਹਾਉਣਾ

nickname (ਨਿਕਨੇਇਮ) *n v* ਉਪ-ਨਾਂ; ਅੱਲ ਪਾਉਣੀ, ਨਾਂ ਪਾਉਣਾ

nid nod (ਨਿਡ'ਨੌਡ) *v* ਸਿਰ ਹਿਲਣਾ ਜਾਂ

ਹਿਲਾਉਣਾ

niece (ਨੀਸ) *n* ਭਤੀਜੀ, ਭਾਣਜੀ

niffy ('ਨਿਫ਼ਿ) *a* (ਅਪ) ਬਦਬੁਦਾਰ

nifty ('ਨਿਫ਼ਟਿ) *a* ਚੁਸਤ, ਫੁਰਤੀਲਾ, ਫ਼ੈਸ਼ਨਦਾਰ

niggard ('ਨਿਗਾਅ:ਡ) *n a* ਸੂਮ, ਕੰਜੂਸ; ~**liness** ਕੰਜੂਸੀ; ~**ly** ਸੂਮ, ਕੰਜੂਸ

niggling ('ਨਿਗਲਿੑਡ) *a* ਘਟੀਆ, ਨਗੂਣਾ, ਤੁੱਛ, ਨੀਚ

nigh (ਨਾਇ) *adv a prep* ਨੇੜੇ, ਲਾਗੇ, ਕੋਲ, ਨੇੜੇ ਦਾ

night (ਨਾਇਟ) *n* ਰਾਤ, ਹਨੇਰਾ; ~**and day** ਰਾਤ ਦਿਨੇ, ਨਿਸਦਿਨ; ~**blindness** ਅੰਧਰਾਤਾ

nightingale ('ਨਾਇਟਿੑਗੇਇਲ) *n* ਬੁਲਬੁਲ

nil (ਨਿਲ) *n* ਸਿਫ਼ਰ, ਕੁਝ ਨਹੀਂ

nimble ('ਨਿੰਬਲ) *a* ਫੁਰਤੀਲਾ, ਚੁਸਤ; ਹੁਸ਼ਿਆਰ; ~**ness** ਫੁਰਤੀ, ਚੁਸਤੀ; ਨਿਪੁੰਨਤਾ

nine (ਨਾਇਨ) *a n* ਨੌਂ; (ਤਾਸ਼ ਦਾ) ਨਹਿਲਾ; ~**day's wonder** ਚਹੁੰ ਦਿਨਾਂ ਦੀ ਚਾਨਣੀ; ~**teen** ਉੱਨੀ; ~**ty** ਨੱਬੇ

nip (ਨਿਪ) *v n* ਚੁੰਢੀ ਵੱਢਣੀ; ਖੋਹਣਾ; ਕਤਰਨਾ, ਛਾਂਟਣਾ; ਨਾਸ ਕਰਨਾ; ਤਾਅਨੇ ਮਾਰਨੇ; ਜਿੱਚ ਕਰਨਾ; ਦਬਾਉ; ਚੁਸਕੀ; *to ~ in the bud* ਜੰਮਦਿਆਂ ਹੀ ਕੁਚਲ ਦੇਣਾ

nipple ('ਨਿਪਲ) *n* ਥਣ ਦੀ ਚੁਚੀ, ਡੋਡੀ, ਨਿਪਲ

nit (ਨਿਟ) *n* ਲੀਖ, ਜੂੰ

no (ਨਾਉ) *a adv n* ਨਹੀਂ, ਨਾ; ਕੋਈ ਨਹੀਂ, ਕੁਝ ਨਹੀਂ; ~**where** ਕਿਸੇ ਥਾਂ ਵੀ ਨਹੀਂ, ਕਿਧਰੇ ਵੀ ਨਹੀਂ; *by* ~**means** ਕਿਸੇ ਤਰ੍ਹਾਂ ਵੀ ਨਹੀਂ

nobility (ਨਾ(ਉ)'ਬਿਲ਼ਅਟਿ) *n* ਕੁਲੀਨਤਾ, ਸਾਉਪੁਣਾ, ਵਡੱਤਣ

noble ('ਨਾਉਬਲ) *a n* ਕੁਲੀਨ, ਸ੍ਰੇਸ਼ਠ;

ਖ਼ਾਨਦਾਨੀ, ਉਦਾਰ, ਸੁਖੀ, ਸ਼ਰੀਫ਼; ਪ੍ਰਭਾਵਸ਼ਾਲੀ; ਅਮੀਰ; **~man** ਅਮੀਰ, ਸਰਦਾਰ; ਦਰਬਾਰੀ; **~ness** ਖ਼ਾਨਦਾਨੀ, ਕੁਲੀਨਤਾ, ਸ੍ਰੇਸ਼ਠਤਾ

nod (ਨੌਡ) *v n* ਸਿਰ ਹਿਲਾਉਣਾ, ਸਵੀਕਾਰ ਕਰਨਾ; ਉਂਘਲਾਉਣਾ; ਸਿਰ ਦਾ ਇਸ਼ਾਰਾ, ਸਿਰ, ਨੀਂਦ ਦੀ ਝੌਂਕ; **~ding** ਸਿਰ ਹਿਲਾਉਣ, ਨਮਸਕਾਰ ਕਰਨ, ਸਿਰ ਨਿਵਾਉਣ; **~dle** (ਬੋਲ) ਸਿਰ, ਖੋਪਰੀ, ਮੁੰਡੀ; ਸਿਰ ਹਿਲਾਉਣਾ, ਸਿਰ ਮਾਰਨਾ ਜਾਂ ਝੁਕਾਉਣਾ

node (ਨਾਉਡ) *n* ਗੰਢ; ਘੁੰਡੀ; ਕਟਾਣ-ਬਿੰਦੂ; ਕੇਂਦਰੀ-ਬਿੰਦੂ

nodus (ਨੌਉਡ੍ਅਸ) *n* ਗੁੰਝਲ, ਔਕੜ, ਕਠਨਾਈ

noise (ਨੋਇਜ਼) *n* ਰੌਲਾ, ਸ਼ੋਰ; ਰੌਲਾਗੌਲਾ, ਸ਼ੋਰ ਸਰਾਬਾ; ਧੁੰਮ

noisy (ਨੌਇਜ਼ਿ) *v* ਹੁੱਲੜਬਾਜ਼, ਖਰੂਦੀ; ਰੌਲੇ-ਗੌਲੇ ਵਾਲਾ; ਸ਼ੋਰ-ਸਰਾਬੇ ਵਾਲਾ

nomenclator (ਨਾਉਮੈਨਕਲੇਇਟਾ*) *n* ਨਾਮਦਾਤਾ, ਨਾਂ ਰੱਖਣ ਵਾਲਾ, ਨਾਮਦਾਤਾ, ਮੁਨਕਿਲ

nomenclature (ਨਾਉਮੈਨਕਲਚਾ*) *n* ਨਾਮ, ਪਾਰਿਭਾਸ਼ਕ ਸ਼ਬਦਾਵਲੀ; ਨਾਮਾਵਲੀ; ਨਾਮ-ਸੂਚੀ

nominal (ਨੌਮਿਨਲ) *n* ਨਾਂ ਬਾਰੇ, ਨਾਮ ਦਾ; ਨਾਂ ਵਰਗਾ, ਫ਼ਰਜ਼ੀ; ਸ਼ਾਬਦਕ

nominate (ਨੌਮਿਨੇਇਟ) *v* ਨਾਮਜ਼ਦ ਕਰਨਾ, ਮਨੋਨੀਤ ਕਰਨਾ; **~d** ਨਾਮਜ਼ਦ ਨਿਯੁਕਤ

nomination (ਨੌਮਿਨੇਇਸ਼ਨ) *n* ਨਾਮਜ਼ਦਗੀ; ਨਿਯੁਕਤੀ

nominee (ਨੌਮਿਨੀ) *n* ਨਾਮਜ਼ਦ, ਆਦਮੀ, ਮਨੋਨੀਤ ਵਿਅਕਤੀ

non (ਨੌਨ) *pref* ਸ਼ਬਦਾਂ ਨਾਲ ਲਾਇਆ ਜਾਣ ਵਾਲਾ ਅਗੇਤਰ ਜੋ ਨਾ, ਅਣ-, ਅਨ-, ਅ-, ਨਿਰ-, ਬੇ-, ਗ਼ੈਰ ਆਦਿ ਦੇ ਅਰਥਾਂ ਵਿਚ ਆਉਂਦਾ ਹੈ

non-aligned (ਨੌਨ-ਅਲਾਇੰਡ) *a* ਗੁਟ ਨਿਰਖੇਪ, ਗ਼ੈਰ-ਜਾਨਬਦਾਰ

non-aggression (ਨੌਨ-ਅਗਰੈੱਸ਼ਨ) *n* ਅਨ-ਆਕਰਮਣ

non-attendance (ਨੌਨ-ਅਟੈਂਡਅੰਸ) *n* ਗ਼ੈਰ-ਹਾਜ਼ਰੀ

non-being (ਨੌਨਬੀਇੰਡ) *n* ਅਣਹੋਂਦ, ਅਭਾਵ

non-committal (ਨੌਨ-ਕਅਮਿਟਲ) *a* ਬੰਧਨ, ਮੁਕਤ; ਪ੍ਰਤਿਬੰਧਤਾ ਰਹਿਤ

non-compliance (ਨੌਨ-ਕਅਮਪਲਾਇਅੰਸ) *n* ਅਪਾਲਣਾ

non-conservative (ਨੌਨ-ਕਅੰਸਅ:-ਵ੍ਅਟਿਵ੍) *a* ਰੂੜੀ ਵਿਰੋਧੀ

non-cooperation (ਨੌਨ-ਕਅਉਅੱਪਅ-ਰੇਇਸ਼ਨ) *a* ਨਾ-ਮਿਲਵਰਤਨ

none (ਨੱਨ) *pron a adv* ਕੋਈ ਨਹੀਂ, ਕੋਈ ਵੀ ਨਾ; ਨਹੀਂ, ਜ਼ਰਾ ਵੀ ਨਹੀਂ

nonentity (ਨੌਨੈੱਨਟਅਟਿ) *n* ਅਣਅਸਤਿਤਵ, ਅਭਾਵ; ਅਸਤਿਤਵਹੀਨਤਾ; ਨਾਚੀਜ਼, ਤੁੱਛ ਵਿਅਕਤੀ

non-essential (ਨੌਨਇ'ਸੈਂਸ਼ਲ) *a* ਗ਼ੈਰ-ਜ਼ਰੂਰੀ, ਅਨਾਵੱਸ਼ਕ

non-existent (ਨੌਨਿਗਜ਼ਿਸਟਅੰਟ) *a* ਹੋਂਦ ਰਹਿਤ, ਅਸਤਿਤਵਹੀਨ

non-official (ਨੌਨਅਫ਼ਿਸ਼ਲ) *a* ਗ਼ੈਰ-ਸਰਕਾਰੀ

non-recurring (ਨੌਨਰਿਕਅ:ਰਿਡ) *a* ਮੁੜ ਨਾ ਹੋਣ ਵਾਲਾ

ਮਨੋਨੀਤ ਵਿਅਕਤੀ

non-resident ('ਨੌਨ'ਰੈਜ਼ਿਡਅੰਟ) *n a* ਅਸਥਾਈ ਵਸਨੀਕ

nonsense ('ਨੌਨਸਅੱਸ) *n a* ਅਰਥਹੀਨ (ਵਾਕ), ਬੇਸੁਰੀ (ਗੱਲ), ਬੇਮੌਕਾ (ਕਥਨ), ਉਲ-ਜਲੂਲ; ਬਕਵਾਸ, ਫ਼ਜ਼ੂਲ (ਗੱਲ), ਵਾਹਯਾਤ

nonsensical (ਨੌਨ'ਸੈਂਅੰਸਿਕਲ) *a* ਅਰਥਹੀਨ, ਬੇਸੁਰਾ, ਬੇਤੁਕਾ, ਫ਼ਜ਼ੂਲ

nonstop ('ਨੌਨ'ਸਟੌਪ) *a* ਲਗਾਤਾਰ, ਨਿਰੰਤਰ

non-vegetarian ('ਨੌਨ'ਵੈਜਿ'ਟੇਅਰਿਅਨ) *a* ਮਾਸਾਹਾਰੀ

non-violence ('ਨੌਨ'ਵਾਇਅਲਅੰਸ) *a* ਅਹਿੰਸਾ

non-violent ('ਨੌਨ'ਵਾਇਲੰਟ) *a* ਅਹਿੰਸਕ, ਅਹਿੰਸਾਤਮਕ

noodle ('ਨੂਡਲ) *n* (1) ਇਕ ਪ੍ਰਕਾਰ ਦੀਆਂ ਸੇਵੀਆਂ, ਨੂਡਲ; (2) ਮੂਰਖ, ਲੋਲ੍ਹੂ, ਬੁੱਧੂ; ਉੱਲੂਘਾਟਾ, ਗੰਵਾਰ, ਅਨਾੜੀ; **~dom** ਮੂਰਖਤਾ, ਲੋਲ੍ਹੂਪਨ, ਬੁੱਧੀਹੀਨਤਾ; ਅਬੋਧਤਾ

nook (ਨੁਕ) *n* ਨੁੱਕਰ, ਗੁੱਠ; ਆਲਾ; ਵੱਖਰੀ ਥਾਂ

noon (ਨੂਨ) *n a* ਦੁਪਹਿਰ, **~day** ਦੁਪਹਿਰ, ਅੱਧਾ ਦਿਨ

nor (ਨੋ*) *adv conj* ਅਤੇ ਨਾ ਹੀ, ਦੋਹਾਂ ਵਿਚੋਂ ਇਕ ਵੀ ਨਾ

norm (ਨੋ'ਮ) *n* ਮਾਪ, ਪ੍ਰਤੀਮਾਨ, ਕਸਵੱਟੀ; ਆਦਰਸ਼, ਨਮੂਨਾ

normal ('ਨੌਮਲ) *a* ਸਧਾਰਨ, ਆਮ; ਸੁਭਾਵਕ, ਕੁਦਰਤੀ; ਨਿਯਮਤ, ਸੰਗਤ; **~cy** ਸਧਾਰਨਤਾ, ਸੁਭਾਵਕਤਾ; **~ize** ਇਕ ਸਾਰ ਕਰਨਾ; ਨਮੂਨੇ ਦਾ ਬਣਾਉਣਾ; ਸਧਾਰਨ ਹਾਲਤ ਵਿਚ ਲਿਆਉਣਾ; **~ly** ਸਧਾਰਨ ਤੌਰ ਤੇ, ਆਮ ਤੌਰ ਤੇ, ਅਨੁਮਾਨ

north (ਨੋਥ) *n a adv* ਉੱਤਰ, ਸ਼ਮਾਲ, (ਕਿਸੇ

ਦੇਸ਼ ਦਾ) ਉੱਤਰੀ ਭਾਗ; ਉੱਤਰ ਵੱਲ; **~ern** ਉੱਤਰੀ

nose (ਨਾਉਜ਼) *n v* ਨੱਕ; ਨਾਸ; ਸੁੰਘਣ ਦੀ ਸ਼ਕਤੀ; ਸੁੰਘਣਾ, ਸੁੰਘ ਕੇ ਜਾਂਚਣਾ; ਨੱਕ ਨਾਲ ਰਗੜਨਾ; ਜ਼ੋਰ ਨਾਲ ਸਾਹ ਲੈਣਾ; ਖੋਜ ਕਰਨੀ, ਪਤਾ ਕਰਨਾ; **~gay** ਗੁਲਦਸਤਾ, ਫੁੱਲਾਂ ਦਾ ਗੁੱਛਾ; **to turn one's ~ at** ਨੱਕ ਚੜ੍ਹਾਉਣਾ; **~less** ਨਕਟਾ, ਨੱਕਹੀਨ

not (ਨੌਟ) *adv* ਨਹੀਂ, ਨਾ

notable ('ਨਾਉਟਅਬਲ) *a n* ਪ੍ਰਸਿੱਧ, ਵਰਨਣਯੋਗ, ਦੱਸਣਯੋਗ, ਸ੍ਰੇਸ਼ਠ, ਵਿਸ਼ੇਸ਼; ਉੱਘਾ, ਪਤਵੰਤਾ, ਅਸਧਾਰਨ

notably ('ਨਾਉਟਅਬਲਿ) *adv* ਖ਼ਾਸ ਤੌਰ ਤੇ

notch (ਨੌਚ) *n v* ਦੰਦਾ; ਖੰਘਾ; ਤੰਗ ਰਸਤਾ; ਛੇਕ; ਟੱਕ, ਕਾਟ, ਕਤਰ; ਛੇਕ ਕਰਨਾ, ਦਰਾੜ ਪਾਉਣੀ

note (ਨਾਉਟ) *n v* ਟਿੱਪਣੀ, ਨੋਟ; ਸੂਚਨਾ, ਚੇਤਾਵਨੀ, ਐਲਾਨ; ਟੀਕਾ, ਵਿਆਖਿਆ, ਕੁੰਜੀ; ਟੀਕਾ ਕਰਨਾ; **~worthy** ਧਿਆਨਯੋਗ, ਵਿਚਾਰਨਯੋਗ; **~d** ਪ੍ਰਸਿੱਧ, ਮਸ਼ਹੂਰ, ਉੱਘਾ, ਨਾਮੀ, ਨਾਮਵਰ

nothing ('ਨੱਥਿਙ) *n adv* ਕੁਝ ਨਾ, ਕੱਖ ਨਹੀਂ; ਬਿਲਕੁਲ ਮਾਮੂਲੀ ਚੀਜ਼, ਮੂਲੋਂ ਨਹੀਂ, ਕਿਸੇ ਤਰ੍ਹਾਂ ਵੀ ਨਹੀਂ, ਕਦੇ ਵੀ ਨਹੀਂ; **~ness** ਅਣਹੋਂਦ, ਅਭਾਵ, ਸੁੰਨਤਾ; ਅਸਾਰਤਾ, ਗੌਰਵਹੀਨਤਾ; ਨਿਰਾਰਥਕਤਾ

notice ('ਨਾਉਟਿਸ) *n v* ਚੇਤਾਵਨੀ; ਸੂਚਨਾ; ਸੂਚਨਾ-ਪੱਤਰ, ਖ਼ਬਰ, ਇਤਲਾਹ; ਐਲਾਨ; ਤਵੱਜੋ; ਧਿਆਨ ਦੇਣਾ, ਵਿਚਾਰਨਾ; ਸੂਚਨਾ ਦੇਣੀ; ਨੋਟਿਸ ਦੇਣਾ, ਟੀਕਾ-ਟਿੱਪਣੀ ਕਰਨੀ; **to bring to ~** ਧਿਆਨ ਵਿਚ ਲਿਆਉਣਾ

notification ('ਨਾਉਟਿਫ਼ਿ'ਕੇਇਸ਼ਨ) *n*

ਅਧਿਸੂਚਨਾ, ਐਲਾਨ, ਘੋਸ਼ਣਾ; ਐਲਾਨਨਾਮਾ, ਘੋਸ਼ਣਾ-ਪੱਤਰ

notify ('ਨਾਉਟਿਫ਼ਾਇ) *v* ਸੂਚਤ ਕਰਨਾ, ਖ਼ਬਰ ਦੇਣੀ; ਐਲਾਨ ਕਰਨਾ

noting ('ਨਾਉਟਿਙ) *n* ਟਿਪਣ, ਟਿਪਣੀ, ਨੋਟ

notion ('ਨਾਉਸ਼ਨ) *n* ਖ਼ਿਆਲ, ਧਾਰਨਾ, ਸੰਕਲਪ; ਭਾਵ; ਭਾਵਨਾ, ਮਨੋਭਾਵ; ਮੱਤ, ਵਿਚਾਰ, ਰਾਇ; ~al ਕਲਪਤ, ਸਿਧਾਂਤਕ; ਅਨੁਮਾਨਤ; ਖ਼ਿਆਲੀ

notoriety ('ਨਾਉਟਾ'ਰਾਇਅਟਿ) *n* ਬਦਨਾਮੀ

notorious (ਨਾ(ਉ)'ਟੋਰਿਅਸ) *a* ਬਦਨਾਮ, ਨਾਮੀ (ਭੈੜੇ ਅਰਥਾਂ ਵਿਚ)

notwithstanding ('ਨੋਟਵਿਥ'ਸਟੈਂਡ਼ਿਙ) *prep adv conj* ਦੇ ਬਾਵਜੂਦ, ਭਾਵੇਂ, ਤਾਂ ਵੀ, ਹੁੰਦਿਆਂ ਹੋਇਆਂ, ਹੁੰਦਿਆਂ-ਸੁੰਦਿਆਂ

noun (ਨਾਉਨ) *n* ਨਾਂ, ਨਾਮ, ਸੰਗਿਆ

nourish ('ਨਅ:ਰਿਸ਼) *v* ਪਾਲਣਾ, ਪਾਲਣਾ-ਪੋਸਣਾ; ਪਾਲਣਾ ਕਰਨੀ; ਖ਼ੁਰਾਕ ਦੇਣੀ

novel ('ਨੌਵ਼ਲ) *a n* ਨਵਾਂ, ਨਵੀਨ; ਨਿਰਾਲਾ, ਅਨੋਖਾ; ਉਪਨਿਆਸ ਨਾਵਲ, ਨਾਵਲ ਸਾਹਿਤ; ~ist ਨਾਵਲਕਾਰ, ਉਪਨਿਆਸਕਾਰ; ~ty ਅਨੋਖੀ, ਵਸਤੂ, ਨਵੀਨਤਾ, ਨਵਾਂਪਣ

novice ('ਨੌਵ਼ਿਸ) *n* ਸਿਖਾਂਦਰੂ; ਨਵਾਂ ਚੇਲਾ; ਪਾਦਰੀ ਪਦ ਦਾ ਉਮੀਦਵਾਰ

now (ਨਾਉ) *a conj adv n* ਹੁਣੇ ਹੁਣੇ, ਅੱਜਕਲ, ਹੁਣ ਤਕ; ਤਤਕਾਲ, ਫ਼ੌਰਨ, ਝਟ-ਪਟ ਤੁਰਤ; ~a~days ਅੱਜਕਲ, ਇਸ ਸਮੇਂ ਵਿਚ, ਇਨ੍ਹੀ ਦਿਨੀਂ

nowhere ('ਨਾਉਵ਼ੇਅ*) *a* ਕਿਧਰੇ ਨਹੀਂ, ਕਿਤੇ ਨਹੀਂ,

nozzle ('ਨੌਜ਼ਲ) *n* ਟੂਟੀ; ਮੂੰਹ, ਨੋਕ;

nuance ('ਨਯੁਆਂਸ) *n* ਸੂਖਮ ਅੰਤਰ, ਬਾਰੀਕ ਫ਼ਰਕ

nuclear ('ਨਯੁਕਲ਼ਿਆ*) *a* ਕੇਂਦਰੀ; ਨਿਉਕਲੀ

nucleus ('ਨਯੁਕਲ਼ਿਅਸ) *n* ਨਾਭ, ਕੇਂਦਰ-ਬਿੰਦੂ, ਮੂਲ ਕੇਂਦਰ; ਬੀਜ-ਕੇਂਦਰ, ਅੰਦਰਲਾ ਹਿੱਸਾ, ਮਗ਼ਜ਼; (ਬਨ) ਅੰਕੁਰ ਮੁੰਢ

nude (ਨਯੂਡ) *a n* ਨੰਗਾ, ਨਗਨ, ਨੰਗ-ਮੁਨੰਗਾ; ਨੰਗੀ ਤਸਵੀਰ; ~ness, nudity ਨੰਗੇਜ਼, ਨਗਨਤਾ

nuisance ('ਨਯੁਸੰਸ) *n* ਪੁਆੜਾ, ਖੱਭ; ਦੁੱਖਦਾਈ ਵਸਤੂ

null (ਨੱਲ) *a n v* ਮਨਸੂਖ, ਰੱਦ; ਨਾਜਾਇਜ਼, ਝੂਠਾ, ਗ਼ੈਰਕਾਨੂੰਨੀ; ~ify ਨਿਸਫਲ ਕਰਨਾ, ਰੱਦ ਕਰਨਾ, ਮਨਸੂਖ ਕਰਨਾ, ਮਿਟਾ ਦੇਣਾ

nullah ('ਨੱਲ੍ਹਾ) *n* ਛੋਟੀ ਨਦੀ, ਨਾਲਾ

numb (ਨੱਮ) *a v* ਸਿਥਲ, ਸੁੰਨ, ਅਚੇਤਨ ਬੇਹਿੱਸ, ਜੜ੍ਹ; ਸੁੰਨ ਕਰਨਾ, ਚੇਤਨਾਹੀਣ ਕਰਨਾ; ~ness ਸਿਥਲਤਾ, ਸੁੰਨ; ਅਚੇਤਨਾ, ਬੇਹਿਸੀ, ਜੜ੍ਹਤਾ

number ('ਨੰਮਬਅ*) *n v* ਸੰਖਿਆ, ਗਿਣਤੀ; ਅੰਕ, ਹਿੰਦਸਾ; ਨੰਬਰ; ਜੋੜ; ਰਕਮ, ਰਾਸ; ਗਿਣਨਾ, ਗਿਣਤੀ ਕਰਨੀ, ਗਿਣਤੀ ਦਾ ਨਿਸ਼ਚਾ ਕਰਨਾ; ਗਿਣਤੀ ਵਿਚ ਆਉਣਾ; ਨੰਬਰ ਲਾਉਣੇ, ਸ਼ਾਮਲ ਕਰਨਾ; ~ing ਗਣਨ, ਗਣਨਾ, ਅੰਕਣ, ਕ੍ਰਮਾਂਕਣ; ~less ਅਣਗਿਣਤ, ਬੇਸ਼ੁਮਾਰ, ਅਸੰਖ, ਬਿਨਾ ਨੰਬਰ ਤੋਂ

numerable ('ਨਯੂਮ(ਅ)ਰਅਬਲ) *a* ਗਿਣਨਯੋਗ

numeral ('ਨਯੂਮ(ਅ)ਰ(ਅ)ਲ) *a n* ਸੰਖਿਆਸੂਚਕ; ਸੰਖਿਆ, ਹਿੰਦਸਾ, ਅੰਕੜਾ, ਗਿਣਤੀ-ਬੋਧਕ ਸ਼ਬਦ

numerate ('ਨਯੂਮਅਰੇਇਟ) *v* ਗਿਣਨਾ, ਗਿਣਤੀ ਕਰਨਾ

numerical (ਨਯੂ'ਮੈਰਿਕਲ) *a* ਸੰਖਿਆਵਾਚੀ; ਗਿਣਤੀ ਵਾਲਾ, ਸੰਖਿਆਤਮਕ, ਅੰਕੀ

numerosity ('ਨਯੂਮਅ'ਰੌਸਅਟਿ) *n* ਬਹੁਲਤਾ, ਅਧਿਕਤਾ, ਬਹੁਤਾਤ, ਅਕਸਰੀਅਤ

numerous ('ਨਯੂਮਅਰਅਸ) *a* ਅਨੇਕ, ਅਣਗਿਣਤ, ਵਿਸ਼ਾਲ, ਭਾਰੀ ਗਿਣਤੀ ਵਾਲਾ; ~**ness** ਬਹੁਲਤਾ, ਬਹੁਤਾਤ

nummet ('ਨੱਮਿਟ) *n* (ਉਪ) ਦੁਪਹਿਰ ਦਾ ਭੋਜਨ, ਲੰਚ

numskull ('ਨੱਮਸਕੱਲ) *n* ਮੂਰਖ, ਬੁੱਧੂ, ਲੋਲ੍ਹੂ, ਭੌਂਦੂ, ਗੰਵਾਰ, ਉਜੱਡ

nun (ਨੱਨ) *n* (ਇਸਾਈ) ਸੰਤਣੀ, ਯੋਗਣ, ਸਾਧਣੀ, ਨਨ; ~**clo** ਪੋਪ ਦਾ ਦੂਤ; ~**nery** ਆਸ਼ਰਮ, ਮੱਠ, ਵਿਹਾਰ

nuptial ('ਨੱਪਸ਼ਲ) *a n* ਵਿਆਹ ਸਬੰਧੀ, ਵਿਆਹ, ਵਿਆਹ ਦੀ ਰਸਮ, ਵਿਆਹ-ਉਤਸਵ

nurse (ਨਅਃਸ) *n v* ਦਾਈ, ਪਾਲਕਾ, ਰੋਗੀ ਸੇਵਕਾ, ਨਰਸ; ਪਾਲਣਾ-ਪੋਸਣਾ, ਦੁੱਧ ਚੁੰਘਾਉਣਾ; ਖਿਡਾਵੀ ਦਾ ਕੰਮ ਕਰਨਾ; ਰੋਗੀ ਦੀ ਸੇਵਾ ਕਰਨੀ; ~**ry**

ਬਾਲਵਾੜੀ, ਪਨੀਰੀ, ਖੇਤ; ਜ਼ਖ਼ੀਰਾ

nursing ('ਨਅਃਸਿਙ) *n* ਪਾਲਣ ਪੋਸਣ; ਸੇਵਾ

nurture ('ਨਅਃਚਅ*) *n v* ਪਾਲਣ-ਪੋਸਣ; ਪਾਲਣਾ ਕਰਨੀ, ਖੁਆਉਣਾ-ਪਿਆਉਣਾ, ਉਤਸ਼ਾਹਤ ਕਰਨਾ; ਪੜ੍ਹਾਉਣਾ-ਸਿਖਾਉਣਾ

nut (ਨੱਟ) *n v* ਗਿਰੀ ਮੇਵਾ; ਸਨਕੀ, ਪਾਗਲ; ਢਿਬਰੀ; ਮਾਰੂਆ ਵਿਅਕਤੀ; ਗਿਰੀਦਾਰ ਫਲ ਇਕੱਠੇ ਕਰਨਾ; ਲੱਭਣਾ; ~**oil** ਗਿਰੀ ਦਾ ਤੇਲ; *hard ~ to crack* ਔਖਾ ਸੁਆਲ; ਅਤੁਬ ਬੰਦਾ

nutrition (ਨਯੂ'ਟਰਿਸ਼ਨ) *a* ਪਾਲਣ-ਪੋਸਣ; ਪੁਸ਼ਟ ਭੋਜਨ; ਆਹਾਰ ਪੁਸ਼ਟੀ

nutritious (ਨਯੂ'ਟਰਿਸ਼ਅਸ) *a* ਪੁਸ਼ਟੀਕਰ, ਬਲਵਰਧਕ, ਨਰੋਆ

nutritive ('ਨਯੂਟਰਅਟਿਵ੍) *a n* ਪੁਸ਼ਟ, ਪੁਸ਼ਟੀਕਰ; ਆਹਾਰ, ਭੋਜਨ, ਖ਼ੁਰਾਕ, ਗਿਜ਼ਾ

nutshell ('ਨੱਟਸ਼ੈੱਲ) *n* ਅਖਰੋਟ ਆਦਿ ਦਾ ਛਿਲਕਾ; ਸੰਖੇਪ, ਖ਼ੁਲਾਸਾ

nymph (ਨਿੰਫ਼) *n* ਪਰੀ; ਅਪੱਛਰਾਂ; ਹੂਰ; (ਕਾਵਿ) ਸੁੰਦਰ ਮੁਟਿਆਰ, ਸੁੰਦਰ ਕੰਨਿਆ

O

O, o (ਅਓ) *n* ਰੋਮਨ ਲਿਪੀ ਦਾ ਪੰਦਰਵਾਂ ਅੱਖਰ; ੦ ਰੂਪੀ ਚਿੰਨ੍ਹ; ਚੱਕਰ, ਦਾਇਰਾ; ਸਿਫ਼ਰ, ਜ਼ੀਰੋ

O, oh (ਅਓ) *int* ਹੈ! ਉਹ! ਉਫ!

oar (ਓ*) *n v* ਚੱਪੂ, ਪਤਵਾਰ; ਮੁਹਾਣਾ; ਚੱਪੂ ਚਲਾਉਣਾ, ਬੇੜੀ ਚਲਾਉਣਾ; ~**sman** ਮੱਲਾਹ

oasis (ਅਓ'ਏਇਸਿਸ) *n* ਨਖ਼ਲਿਸਤਾਨ

oast ('ਅਓਸਟ) *n* ਭੱਠੀ

oat (ਅਓਟ) *n* ਜਵੀ; ~**cake** ਜਵੀ ਦੀ ਰੋਟੀ

oath (ਅਓਥ) *n* ਸੌਂਹ, ਕਸਮ, ਸੌਗੰਧ, ਸ਼ਪਥ, ਹਲਫ਼

obdurate ('ਔਬਡਯੁਰਅਟ) *a* ਹਠੀ, ਅੜੀਅਲ, ਜ਼ਿਦੀ, ਢੀਠ

obedience (ਅ'ਬੀਡਯਅੰਸ) *n* ਆਗਿਆ-ਪਾਲਣ, ਆਗਿਆਕਾਰਤਾ, ਤਾਬੇਦਾਰੀ

obedient (ਅ'ਬੀਡਯਅੰਟ) *a* ਆਗਿਆਕਾਰ, ਆਗਿਆਕਾਰੀ, ਤਾਬੇਦਾਰ; ~**ly** ਆਗਿਆ ਅਨੁਸਾਰ

obeisance (ਅ(ਓ)'ਬੇਇਸਅੰਸ) *n* ਨਮਸਕਾਰ, ਪ੍ਰਣਾਮ; ਸ਼ਰਧਾਂਜਲੀ, ਸਨਮਾਨ

obese (ਅ(ਓ)'ਬੀਸ) *a* ਮੋਟਾ, ਵੱਡੇ ਸਰੀਰ ਵਾਲਾ, ਢਿੱਡਲ

obesity (ਅ(ਓ)'ਬਿਸਅਟਿ) *n* ਮੋਟਾਪਾ, ਸਰੀਰ ਦਾ ਭਾਰਾਪਣ

obey (ਅ'ਬੇਇ) *v* ਆਖੇ ਲੱਗਣਾ, ਕਿਹਾ ਮੰਨਣਾ, ਆਗਿਆ ਦਾ ਪਾਲਨ ਕਰਨਾ, ਹੁਕਮ ਮੰਨਣਾ; ਮੰਨ ਲੈਣਾ; ਤਾਬੇਦਾਰੀ ਕਰਨੀ

object ('ਔਬਜਿਕਟ, ਅਬ'ਜੈੱਕਟ) *n v* ਵਸਤੂ, ਪਦਾਰਥ, ਚੀਜ਼; (ਮਖੌਲ ਦਾ) ਪਾਤਰ, ਮੌਜੂ;

ਮੰਤਵ, ਮਨੋਰਥ, ਉਦੇਸ਼ ਪ੍ਰਯੋਜਨ (ਫ਼ਿਲਾਸਫ਼ੀ) ਵਿਸ਼ਾ; ਇਤਰਾਜ਼ ਕਰਨਾ, ਸ਼ੰਕਾ ਕਰਨਾ, ਉਜ਼ਰ ਕਰਨਾ, ਵਿਰੋਧ ਕਰਨਾ; ~**ion** ਇਤਰਾਜ਼, ਸ਼ੰਕਾ, ਉਜ਼ਰ ਵਿਰੋਧ, ਹੁੱਜਤ, ਆਪੱਤੀ; ~**ionable** ਇਤਰਾਜ਼ਯੋਗ, ਆਪੱਤੀਜਨਕ; ਅਨੁਚਿਤ, ਨਾਮੁਨਾਸਬ; ~**ive** *a* ਬਾਹਰਮੁਖੀ, ਬਾਹਰਲਾ, ਵਾਸਤਵਿਕ, ਵਸਤੁਪਰਕ, ਯਥਾਰਥਕ, ਕਰਮ ਕਾਰਕ; ਕਰਮ ਬਾਰੇ; (ਸੈਨਾ) ਟੀਚਾ (ਜਿਥੇ ਪੁੱਜਣਾ ਹੋਵੇ), ਉਦੇਸ਼, ਮੰਤਵ, ਮਨੋਰਥ; ~**ivity** ਵਾਤਵਿਕਤਾ; ਯਥਾਰਥਕਤਾ, ਬਾਹਰਮੁਖਤਾ

objurgate ('ਔਬਜਅਗੋਇਟ) *v* ਫਿਟਕਾਰਨਾ, ਝਿੜਕਣਾ, ਫਿਟਲਾਨ੍ਹਤਾ ਕਰਨੀ, ਬੁਰਾ-ਭਲਾ ਕਹਿਣਾ, ਤਾੜਨਾ, ਡਾਂਟਣਾ

objurgation ('ਔਬਜਅ'ਗੋਇਸ਼ਨ) *n* ਫਿਟਕਾਰ, ਝਿੜਕ, ਡਾਂਟ-ਡਪਟ, ਝਾੜ-ਝੰਬ, ਧਿੱਕਾਰ, ਲਾਨ੍ਹਤ-ਮਲਾਮਤ

obligate ('ਔਬਲਿਗੋਇਟ) *v* ਇਹਸਾਨ ਕਰਨਾ, (ਕਾਨੂੰਨੀ ਜਾਂ ਅਖ਼ਲਾਕੀ) ਬੰਦਸ਼ ਲਾ ਦੇਂਦੀ

obligation ('ਔਬਲਿ'ਗੋਇਸ਼ਨ) *n* ਜ਼ਿੰਮੇਵਾਰੀ, ਭਾਰ, ਫ਼ਰਜ਼, ਕਾਨੂੰਨੀ ਜਾਂ ਅਖ਼ਲਾਕੀ ਬੰਦਸ਼, ਇਕਰਾਰਨਾਮਾ, ਪ੍ਰਤਿਗਿਆ-ਪੱਤਰ, ਇਹਸਾਨ, ਉਪਕਾਰ

obligatory (ਅ'ਬਲਿਗਅਟ(ਅ)ਰਿ) *a* ਜ਼ਰੂਰੀ, ਅੱਵਸ਼ਕ, (ਕਾ) ਲਾਗੂ, ਪੱਕਾ

oblige (ਅ'ਬਲਾਇਜ) *v* ਉਪਕਾਰ ਕਰਨਾ, ਇਹਸਾਨ ਕਰਨਾ, ਮਜਬੂਰ ਕਰਨਾ, (ਕੋਈ ਕੰਮ) ਬਦੋਬਦੀ ਕਰਾਉਣਾ; ਬੰਦਸ਼ ਲਾਉਣੀ; (ਬੋਲ) ਦਿਲਪਰਚਾਵਾ ਕਰਨਾ; ~**d** ਮਜਬੂਰ, ਕਰਤਗ, ਆਭਾਰੀ

obliging (ਅ'ਬਲਾਇਜਿਙ) *a* ਮਿਲਾਪੜਾ, ਮਿੱਠੇ ਸੁਭਾਅ ਵਾਲਾ, ਉਪਕਾਰੀ, ਨਿਮਰਤਾ ਵਾਲਾ, ਆਭਾਰੀ, ਇਹਸਾਨ ਕਰਨ ਵਾਲਾ

oblique (ਅ'ਬਲੀਕ) *a v* ਟੇਢਾ, ਤਿਰਛਾ, ਆਡਾ; ਟੇਢੀ ਚਾਲ ਨਾਲ ਵਧਟਾ, ਕੁਟਿਲ ਨੀਤੀ ਨਾਲ ਅੱਗੇ ਵਧਟਾ

oblivion (ਅ'ਬਲਿਵਿਅਨ) *n* ਭੁਲਾਵਾਂ ਗੁਮਨਾਮੀ; ਉਪੇਖਿਆ

oblong ('ਔਬਲੌਙ) *a* ਚੌਰਸ, ਚੌਕੋਰ; ਲੰਬੂਤਰਾ; ਆਇਤ

obnoxious (ਅਬ'ਨੌਕਸ਼ਅਸ) *a* ਘਿਰਣਾਯੋਗ, ਨਿੰਦਣਯੋਗ, ਵਰਜਤ, ਇਤਰਾਜ਼ਯੋਗ, ਬੇਹੂਦਾ, ਕੋਝਾ

obscene (ਅਬ'ਸੀਨ) *a* ਅਸ਼ਲੀਲੀ, ਲੱਚਰ, ਫ਼ਾਹਸ਼

obsenity (ਅਬ'ਸੈਨਅਟਿ) *n* ਅਸ਼ਲੀਲਤਾ

obscure (ਅਬ'ਸਕਯੂਅ*) *a n v* ਧੁੰਦਲਾ, ਘਸਮੇਲਾ; ਹਨੇਰਾ; ਅਸਪਸ਼ਟ, ਤੇਜਹੀਣ; ਗੁੱਝੂ, ਦੁਰਬੋਧ, ਕਠਨ, ਗੁਪਤ, ਅਗਿਆਤ, ਗੁਮਨਾਮ; ਧੁੰਦਲਾਪਣ; ਅਸਪਸ਼ਟਤਾ

obscurity (ਅਬ'ਸਕਯੂਅਰਅਟਿ) *n* ਧੁੰਦਲਾਪਣ, ਹਨੇਰਾ; ਗੁੜ੍ਹਤਾ, ਦੁਰਬੋਧਤਾ, ਗੁਮਨਾਮੀ, ਅਪ੍ਰਸਿੱਧੀ; ਤੇਜਹੀਣਤਾ

obsecrate ('ਔਬਸਿਕਰੇਇਟ) *n* ਬੇਨਤੀ ਕਰਨੀ, ਪ੍ਰਾਥਨਾ ਕਰਨੀ, ਹਾੜ੍ਹੇ ਕੱਢਣੇ, ਮਿੰਨਤ ਕਰਨੀ

obsecration ('ਔਬਸਿ'ਕਰੇਇਸ਼ਨ) *n* ਬੇਨਤੀ, ਪ੍ਰਾਥਨਾ, ਅਰਦਾਸ, ਮਿੰਨਤ-ਤਰਲਾ

obsequies ('ਔਬਸਿਕਵਿਜ਼) *n* ਅੰਤਮ ਸੰਸਕਾਰ, ਦਾਹ-ਸੰਸਕਾਰ, ਕਿਰਿਆ-ਕਰਮ

observance (ਅਬ'ਜ਼ਅਵੰਸ) *n* ਪਾਬੰਦੀ, ਪਾਲਣ (ਰੀਤੀ-ਰਿਵਾਜ, ਕਾਨੂੰਨ ਆਦਿ ਦੀ); ਮਨੌਤ;

(ਪ੍ਰ) ਕਰਮ-ਕਾਂਡ, ਧਾਰਮਕ ਰੀਤੀ

observation ('ਔਬਜ਼ਅ'ਵੇਇਸ਼ਨ) *n* ਦੇਖ-ਭਾਲ; ਨਿਰੀਖਣ, ਪੜਚੋਲ, ਟਿੱਪਣੀ, ਆਲੋਚਨਾ; ਵਿਚਾਰ, ਸੋਚ; ਰਾਇ, ਕਥਨ, ਉਕਤੀ

observatory (ਅਬ'ਜ਼ਅਵਟਅਰਿ) *n* ਜੰਤਰ-ਮੰਤਰ, ਨੀਝਸ਼ਾਲਾ, ਨਿਰੀਖਣਸ਼ਾਲਾ

observe (ਅਬ'ਜ਼ਅ:ਵ) *v* ਪਾਲਣਾ ਕਰਨੀ (ਨਿਯਮ, ਰੀਤੀ ਆਦਿ ਦੀ); ਮਨਾਉਣਾ; ਵੇਖਣਾ, ਨਿਰੀਖਣ ਕਰਨਾ, ਪੜਚੋਲ ਕਰਨੀ; ਧਿਆਨ ਦੇਣਾ, ਅਨੁਭਵ ਕਰਨਾ; ਸਤਰਕ ਹੋਣਾ, ਸਾਵਧਾਨ ਹੋਣਾ; **~d** ਨਿਰੀਖਤ, ਦੇਖਿਆ, ਦ੍ਰਿਸ਼ਟ, ਅਵਲੋਕਿਤ; **~r** ਨਿਰੀਖਕ; ਵੇਖਣ ਵਾਲਾ, ਦਰਸ਼ਕ; ਆਲੋਚਕ

obsolesce ('ਔਬਸਅ'ਲੈੱਸ) *v* ਪੁਰਾਣਾ ਪੈ ਜਾਣਾ, ਬੇਕਾਰ ਹੋ ਜਾਣਾ, ਅਪ੍ਰਚਲਤ ਹੋਣਾ; **~nce** ਅਪ੍ਰਚਲਨ

obsolete ('ਔਬਸਅਲੀਟ) *a* ਅਪ੍ਰਚਲਤ, ਅਵਿਹਾਰੀ, ਪੁਰਾਣਾ, ਲੁਪਤ

obstacle ('ਔਬਸਟਅਕਲ) *n* ਰੁਕਾਵਟ, ਅੜਿਕਾ, ਵਿਘਨ, ਰੋਕ, ਅੜਚਨ

obstinacy ('ਔਬਸਟਿਨਅਸਿ) *n* ਢੀਠਤਾ; ਸਿਰੜ, ਜ਼ਿਦ, ਹਠ, ਚੀਚ੍ਰਪਟ, ਅੜੀ

obstinate ('ਔਬਸਟਿਨਅਟ) *a* ਜ਼ਿੱਦੀ, ਢੀਠ, ਸਿਰੜ, ਹਠੀ, ਚੀੜ੍ਹਾ; ਕਰੜਾ, ਦ੍ਰਿੜ੍ਹ; ਹਠਵਾਦੀ

obstruct (ਅਬ'ਸਟਰਅੱਕਟ) *v* ਰੋਕ ਪਾਉਣੀ, ਅੜਿਕਾ ਡਾਹੁਣਾ, ਰਾਹ ਰੋਕਣਾ; ਗਤੀਰੋਧ ਕਰਨਾ, ਵਿਘਨ ਪਾਉਣਾ, ਗੜਬੜ ਕਰਨੀ; **~ed** ਅਵਰੁੱਧ, ਰੋਕਿਆ ਹੋਇਆ; **~ion** ਰੋਕ, ਰੁਕਾਵਟ, ਗਤੀਰੋਧ, ਅੜਿਕਾ, ਅੜਿੱਚਨ, ਵਿਘਨ, ਅਟਕਾਉ; **~ive** ਵਿਘਨਕਾਰੀ, ਗਤੀਰੋਧਕ; **~ing** ਪ੍ਰਚਲਤ, ਪ੍ਰਵਰਤ, ਪ੍ਰਪਤ

obtrude (ਅਬ'ਟਰੂਡ) v ਦਖ਼ਲ ਦੇਣਾ, ਘੁਸਣਾ, ਦਖ਼ਲ-ਅੰਦਾਜ਼ੀ ਕਰਨਾ; ਗਲ ਮੜ੍ਹਨਾ, ਥੋਪਣਾ

obtrusion (ਅਬ'ਟਅੂਰੂਯ਼ਨ) n ਨਾਜਾਇਜ਼ ਦਖ਼ਲ, ਠੋਸਣ

obtuse (ਅਬ'ਟਯੂਸ) a ਮੰਦ, ਖੁੰਢਾ, ਮੁਠ੍ਹ; (ਪੱਤਾ) ਗੋਲ, (ਰੇਖਾ) ਸਮਕੋਣ ਤੋਂ ਵੱਡਾ ਕੋਣ, ਅਧਿਕਕੋਣ

obvert (ਔਬ'ਵ੍ਅ:ਟ) v ਉਲਟਾ ਦੇਣਾ, ਉਲਟਾ ਕਰਨਾ, ਮੂਧਾ ਕਰਨਾ; ਫੇਰ ਦੇਣਾ

obviate (ਔਬਵਿਏਇਟ) v (ਲੋੜ ਆਦਿ) ਦੂਰ ਕਰਨੀ, ਨਿਵਾਰਨਾ, ਛੁਟਕਾਰਾ ਦਿਵਾਉਣਾ, ਖਹਿੜਾ ਛੁਡਾਉਣਾ

obvious (ਔਬਵਿਅਸ) a ਸਪਸ਼ਟ, ਜ਼ਾਹਰ, ਪ੍ਰਤੱਖ, ਪਰਗਟ

occasion (ਅ'ਕੇਇਯ਼ਨ) n ਅਵਸਰ, ਮੌਕਾ, ਚੋਅ; ਸਮਾਂ, ਵੇਲਾ; ਕਾਰਨ, ਸਬੱਬ, ਪ੍ਰਯੋਜਨ, ਲੋੜ; ~al ਖ਼ਾਸ ਮੌਕੇ ਦਾ; ਵਿਸ਼ੇਸ਼ ਅਵਸਰ ਦਾ; ਅਨਿਯਮਤ; ~ally ਕਦੇ-ਕਦੇ, ਕਦੇ-ਕਦਾਈਂ; ਮੌਕੇ-ਮੌਕੇ ਤੇ, ਗਾਹੇਬਗਾਹੇ, ਖ਼ਾਸ ਖ਼ਾਸ ਮੌਕਿਆਂ ਤੇ; ਪ੍ਰਸੰਗਵਸ

occupancy (ਔਕਯੁਪਅੰਸਿ) a ਕਬਜ਼ਾ, ਅਧਿਕਾਰ, ਦਖ਼ਲ, ਕਿਰਾਏਦਾਰੀ, ਪਟਕਾਰੀ; ਰਿਹਾਇਸ਼

occupant ('ਔਕਯੁਪਅੰਟ) n ਕਾਬਜ਼, ਕਬਜ਼ਾਦਾਰ, ਨਿਵਾਸੀ, ਰਿਹਾਇਸ਼ ਕਰਨ ਵਾਲਾ; ਕਿਰਾਏਦਾਰ, ਪਟੇਦਾਰ

occupation (ਔਕਯੁ'ਪੇਇਸ਼ਨ) n ਪੇਸ਼ਾ, ਧੰਦਾ, ਕਾਰ-ਵਿਹਾਰ; ਕਬਜ਼ਾਦਾਰੀ, ਅਧਿਕਾਰ, ਕਬਜ਼ਾ; ~al ਵਿਵਸਾਇਕ

occupy (ਔਕਯੁਪਾਇ) v ਕਬਜ਼ਾ ਕਰਨਾ, ਅਧਿਕਾਰ ਵਿਚ ਲੈ ਲੈਣਾ, ਮੱਲਣਾ; ਸਾਂਭ ਲੈਣਾ; ਪਟਕਾਰ ਹੋਣਾ, ਕਿਰਾਏਦਾਰ ਹੋਣਾ; ਰਿਹਾਇਸ਼

ਰੱਖਣੀ, ਰਹਿਣਾ; ਥਾਂ ਮੱਲਣੀ

occur (ਅ'ਕਅ:*) v ਵਾਪਰਨਾ, ਹੋਣਾ; ਪੇਸ਼ ਆਉਣਾ; ਸੁੱਝਣਾ, ਔੜਨਾ, ਫੁਰਨਾ, ਚੇਤੇ ਆਉਣਾ; ~rence ਘਟਨਾ, ਵਾਰਦਾਤ, ਉਤਪਤੀ, ਸੰਯੋਗ

ocean (ਅਉਸ਼ਨ) n ਸਮੁੰਦਰ, ਮਹਾਂਸਾਗਰ; ~ography ਸਾਗਰ-ਵਿਗਿਆਨ

octagon ('ਔਕਟਅਗਅਨ) n ਅੱਠਕੋਣੀ, ਅੱਠਬਾਹੀ

octave (ਔਕਟਿਵ) n ਅਸ਼ਟਪਦੀ, ਅੱਠਾਂ ਵਸਤੂਆਂ ਦਾ ਸਮੂਹ, ਅਸ਼ਟਮੀ

octogenarian (ਔਕਟਅਉਜਿ'ਨੇਅਰਿਅਨ) a n ਅੱਸੀ ਸਾਲ ਦੀ ਉਮਰ ਵਾਲਾ

octopod (ਔਕਟਅਪੌਡ) n ਅੱਠ ਪੈਰਾਂ ਵਾਲਾ, ਅੱਠ-ਪਦ-ਜੰਤੂ, ਅੱਠਪਾਦ

octroi (ਔਕਟਰਵਾ) n ਚੁੰਗੀ, ਮਹਿਸੂਲ, ਮਸੂਲ; ਚੁੰਗੀ-ਘਰ

ocular (ਔਕਯੁਲਅ*) a ਅੱਖਾਂ ਦਾ; ਅੱਖੀਂ ਡਿੱਠਾ

oculist (ਔਕਯੁਲਿਸਟ) n ਅੱਖਾਂ ਦਾ ਡਾਕਟਰ; ਅੱਖਾਂ ਦੇ ਰੋਗਾਂ ਦਾ ਮਾਹਰ

odd (ਔਡ) a n ਵਿੱਲਖਣ, ਅਨੋਖਾ, ਵਚਿੱਤਰ, ਅਸਧਾਰਨ; ਬੇਜੋੜ, ਬਿਖਮ, ਫੁਟਕਲ; ਬਾਕੀ; ~ity ਵਿਲੱਖਣਤਾ, ਅਨੋਖਾਪਨ, ਅਸਧਾਰਨਤਾ; ~s ਅਣਮੇਲ, ਫ਼ਰਕ, ਵਿਰੋਧ, ਅਸਮਾਨਤਾ; ਵੈਰ, ਵਿਰੋਧ; ਮੁਖ਼ਾਲਫ਼ਤ

ode (ਅਉਡ) n ਗੀਤ-ਕਾਵਿ

odorous (ਅਉਡਅਰਅਸ) a ਖ਼ੁਸ਼ਬੂਦਾਰ, ਸੁਗੰਧਮਈ

odour (ਅਉਡਅ*) n ਖ਼ੁਸ਼ਬੂ, ਮਹਿਕ, ਸੁਗੰਧ; ਮਸ਼ਹੂਰੀ; ਰੰਗ; ~less ਗੰਧਹੀਨ, ਨਿਰਗੰਧ, ਬੇਮਹਿਕ

off (ਔਫ) *adv prep a n v* ਦੂਰ, ਪਰ੍ਹਾਂ, ਵੱਖਰਾ, ਲਾਂਭੇ, ਅਸਬੰਧਤ; ਲੋਪ, ਅਪ੍ਰਾਪਤ, ਪਰਲਾ, ਦੂਰ ਦਾ; (ਕ੍ਰਿਕਟ ਵਿਚ) ਖੇਡਣ ਵਾਲੇ ਦਾ ਸੱਜਾ ਪਾਸਾ; ਮੁਕਰਨਾ, ਬੇਮੁਖ ਹੋਣਾ; ~**hand** ਬਿਨਾ ਤਿਆਰੀ, ਵੇਲੇ ਦੇ ਵੇਲੇ

offence (ਅ'ਫੈਂਸ) *n* ਦੋਸ਼, ਅਪਰਾਧ, ਕਸੂਰ

offend (ਅ'ਫੈਂਡ) *v* ਨਾਰਾਜ਼ ਕਰਨਾ, ਗੁੱਸੇ ਕਰਨਾ; ਅਪਰਾਧ ਕਰਨਾ, ਉਲੰਘਣਾ ਕਰਨੀ; ~**er** ਅਪਰਾਧੀ, ਕਸੂਰਵਾਰ, ਦੋਸ਼ੀ; ~**ing** ਅੱਤਿਆਚਾਰੀ, ਅਪਰਾਧੀ

offensive (ਅ'ਫ਼ੈਨਸਿਵ੍) *a n* ਘਿਰਣਾਜਨਕ, ਦੁਰਗੰਧਕ; ਦੁੱਖਮਈ, ਅਪਮਾਨਜਨਕ; ਵਧੀਕੀ ਭਰਿਆ; ਹਮਲਾਵਰ; ਹਮਲਾ; ਆਕਰਮਣ

offer (ਔਫ਼ਅ*) *v n* ਪੇਸ਼ ਕਰਨਾ, ਦੇਣਾ, ਅੱਗੇ ਰੱਖਣਾ; ਭੇਟ ਕਰਨਾ, ਚੜ੍ਹਾਨਾ, ਅਰਪਣਾ, ਸੌਂਪ ਦੇਣਾ; ਜ਼ਾਹਰ ਹੋਣਾ; ਰਾਇ, ਪ੍ਰਸਤਾਵ, ਪੇਸ਼ਕਸ਼, ਭੇਟ

office (ਔਫ਼ਿਸ) *n* ਦਫ਼ਤਰ, ਪਦਵੀ, ਅਹੁਦਾ; ਫ਼ਰਜ਼, ਉਪਕਾਰ, ਸਰਕਾਰੀ ਮਹਿਕਮਾ ਜਾਂ ਵਿਭਾਗ; ~**bearer** ਅਹੁਦੇਦਾਰ, ਪਦ-ਅਧਿਕਾਰੀ; ~**r** ਅਫ਼ਸਰ, ਪਦ-ਅਧਿਕਾਰੀ, ਕਰਮਚਾਰੀ

official (ਅ'ਫ਼ਿਸ਼ਲ) *a n* ਸਰਕਾਰੀ, ਦਫ਼ਤਰੀ, ਕਾਨੂੰਨੀ, ਅਹੁਦੇ ਨਾਲ ਸਬੰਧਤ, ਪਦ ਸਬੰਧੀ; ਸਰਕਾਰੀ ਮੁਲਾਜ਼ਮ, ਕਿਸੇ ਦਫ਼ਤਰ ਦਾ ਅਧਿਕਾਰੀ; ~**dom** ਅਫ਼ਸਰੀ; ਅਧਿਕਾਰੀ ਵਰਗ, ਅਫ਼ਸਰ ਲੋਕ; ~**ism** ਅਫ਼ਸਰੀ ਸ਼ਾਨ, ਅਫ਼ਸਰਸ਼ਾਹੀ

officiate (ਅ'ਫ਼ਿਸ਼ਿਏਇਟ) *v* ਕਾਇਮ-ਮੁਕਾਮ ਹੋਣਾ, ਕਿਸੇ ਦੀ ਥਾਂ ਕੰਮ ਕਰਨਾ, ਕਾਰਜਕਾਰੀ ਬਣਨਾ

offing (ਔਫ਼ਿੰਙ) *n* ਦ੍ਰਿਸ਼ਟਮਾਨ ਦੂਮੇਲ; ਸਾਗਰ-ਖੰਡ; **in the ~** ਸੰਭਾਵਤ ਘਟਨਾ

offset (ਔਫ਼ਸੈਟ) *n v* ਆਫ਼ਸੈਟ ਛਪਾਈ; ਰਵਾਨਗੀ, ਪ੍ਰਸਥਾਨ; ਆਰੰਭ; ਹਰਜਾਨਾ; ਹਰਜਾਨਾ ਭਰਨਾ, ਬਰਾਬਰ ਕਰਨਾ

offshoot (ਔਫ਼ਸ਼ੂਟ) *n* ਟਾਹਣੀ, ਅੱਖ (ਟਹਣੀ ਵਿਚੋਂ ਫੁੱਟੀ), ਗੋਣ ਵਸਤੂ, ਵਿਉਤਪੱਤ ਵਸਤੂ

offspring (ਔਫ਼ਸਪਰਿਙ) *n* ਸੰਤਾਨ, ਬਾਲ-ਬੱਚੇ, ਵੰਸ਼

oft (ਔਫ਼ਟ) *adv* ਕਈ ਵਾਰ, ਬਹੁਤ ਵੇਰਾਂ, ਬਹੁਤ ਕਰਕੇ, ਬਹੁਤਾ; ~**en** ਬਹੁਤਾ, ਬਹੁਤ ਕਰਕੇ, ਕਈ ਵਾਰ, ਥੋੜ੍ਹੀ ਥੋੜ੍ਹੀ ਦੇਰ ਨਾਲ, ਅਕਸਰ

ogle (ਅਉਗਲ) *v n* ਅੱਖ ਮਾਰਨੀ, ਅੱਖ ਮਟੱਕਾ ਕਰਨਾ; ਲਲਚਾਈ ਨਜ਼ਰ

oil (ਔਇਲ) *n v* ਤੇਲ, ਰੋਗਨ; ਤੇਲ ਦੇਣਾ, ਤੇਲ ਪਾਉਣਾ; ~**cake** ਖਲ; ~**painting** ਤੇਲ-ਚਿੱਤਰ; **burn the midnight ~** ਬਹੁਤ ਰਾਤ ਤਕ ਪੜ੍ਹਨ ਲਿਖਣਾ; **pour ~ on the waters** ਮਾਮਲੇ ਨੂੰ ਠੰਡਾ ਜਾਂ ਸ਼ਾਂਤ ਕਰਨਾ; ~**y** ਚਿਕਣਾ, ਤੇਲ ਯੁਕਤ, ਤੇਲ ਪੂਰਨ; ਅਸਥਿਰ; ਖੁਸ਼ਾਮਦੀ

ointment (ਔਇੰਟਮਅੰਟ) *n* ਮੱਲ੍ਹਮ, ਲੇਪ

O.K., okay (ਅਉ'ਕੇਇ) *adv a* ਸਭ ਠੀਕ ਹੈ, ਸੁਖ ਸਾਂਦ ਹੈ, ਸਭ-ਅੱਛਾ, ਪ੍ਰਵਾਨ

old (ਅਉਲ੍ਡ) *a n* ਬੁੱਢਾ, ਬਿਰਧ, ਸਿਆਣਾ, ਬਜ਼ੁਰਗ, ਪੁਰਾਣਾ, ਹੰਢਿਆ, ਮੁੱਢਲਾ, ਆਰੰਭਕ; ਅਪ੍ਰਚਲਤ; ~**fashioned** ਅਪ੍ਰਚਲਤ, ਪੁਰਾਣੀ ਸ਼ੈਲੀ ਦਾ, ਪੁਰਾਣਪੰਥੀ, ਦਕਿਆਨੂਸੀ; ~**en** ਪੁਰਾਣੇ ਸਮੇਂ ਦਾ, ਪੁਰਾਤਨ, ਪ੍ਰਾਚੀਨ ਕਾਲ ਦਾ; ਪੁਰਾਨਾ, ਪ੍ਰਾਚੀਨ; ~**ness** ਬੁਢਾਪਾ, ਪ੍ਰਾਚੀਨਤਾ, ਪੁਰਾਤਨਤਾ, ਜਰਜਰਤਾ

ombudsman ('ਔਮਬੁਡੁਜ਼ਮਅਨ) *n* ਲੋਕਪਾਲ

omelet, omelette ('ਔਮਲਿਟ) *n* ਅੰਡਿਆਂ ਦਾ
ਪੂੜਾ, ਆਮਲੇਟ

omen ('ਅਉਮੈਨ) *n* ਸ਼ਗਨ (ਚੰਗਾ ਜਾਂ ਬੁਰਾ)

omission (ਅ'ਮਿਸ਼ਨ) *n* ਭੁੱਲ, ਭੁੱਲ-ਚੁੱਕ,
ਗ਼ਲਤੀ, ਉਕਾਈ, ਤਰੁਟੀ

omit (ਅ'ਮਿਟ) *v* ਛੱਡ ਜਾਣਾ, ਖੁੰਝਾ ਦੇਣਾ, ਸ਼ਾਮਲ
ਨਾ ਕਰਨਾ, ਭੁੱਲ ਜਾਣਾ

omniform ('ਔਮਨਿਫ਼ੋਮ) *a* ਸਰਬ ਰੂਪੀ

omnipotent (ਔਮ'ਨਿਪੋਅਟਅੰਟ) *a* ਸਰਬ-
ਸ਼ਕਤੀਮਾਨ

omnipresent ('ਔਮਨਿ'ਪਰੈੱਜ਼ੰਟ) *a*
ਸਰਬਵਿਆਪਕ, ਸਰਬਵਿਆਪੀ

omniscient (ਔਮ'ਨਿਸਿਅੰਟ) *a* ਸਰਬੱਗ,
ਸਰਬਗਿਆਤਾ, ਸਰਬਦਰਸ਼ੀ, ਤ੍ਰੈਕਾਲ-ਦਰਸ਼ੀ

on (ਔਨ) *prep a adv* ਉੱਤੇ, ਉੱਪਰ, ਵਿਚ, ਨੂੰ;
ਉਦੇਸ਼, ਪ੍ਰਯੋਜਨ, ਮੰਤਵ, ਅਭਿਪ੍ਰਾਯ; ਆਧਾਰ,
ਕੇਂਦਰ, ਧੁਰਾ; ਨੇੜੇ, ਕੋਲ, ਲਾਗੇ, ਪਾਸ, ਸਾਮ੍ਹਣੇ,
ਅਗੇ ਵੱਲ, ਠੀਕ ਪਿੱਛੇ, ਠੀਕ ਉੱਤੇ ਜਾਂ ਉੱਪਰ,
ਪ੍ਰਭਾਵ ਪਾਉਂਦੇ ਹੋਏ;   ਨਿਰੰਤਰ, ਲਗਾਤਾਰ,
ਅਵਿਰਾਮ, ਪਰ

once (ਵਅੰਸ) *adv conj n* ਇਕ ਵਾਰ, ਇਕ
ਵਾਰੀ, ਇਕ ਮੌਕਾ

one (ਵਅੰਨ) *a n pron* ਇਕ, ਇਕੋ, ਬਰਾਬਰ,
ਸਮਾਨ, ਕੇਵਲ ਇਕ, ਕੋਈ ਇਕ; ~eyed
ਕਾਣਾ; ~ness ਏਕਤਾ, ਇਕਰੂਪਤਾ,
ਇਕਜੁੰਟਤਾ, ਅਭਿੰਨਤਾ

onerous ('ਔਨਰਅਸ) *a* ਔਖਾ, ਕਠਨ, ਦੁੱਭਰ;
ਭਾਰਾ

ongoings ('ਔਨਗਾਉਇੰਗਜ਼) *n pl*
ਕਾਰਵਾਈਆਂ

onion ('ਅੰਨਯਅਨ) *a* ਗੰਢਾ, ਗੰਠਾ, ਪਿਆਜ਼

onlooker ('ਔਨਲੁਕਅ*) *n* ਦਰਸ਼ਕ

only ('ਅਉਨਲਿ) *a adv conj* ਕੇਵਲ, ਸਿਰਫ਼,
ਨਿਰਾ

onomatopoeia ('ਔਨਅ(ਉ)'ਸੈਟਅ(ਉ)'ਪੀਅ) *n*
ਨਾਦ-ਅਲੰਕਾਰ, ਧੁਨੀ-ਅਨੁਕਰਨ

onset ('ਔਨਸੈੱਟ) *n* ਸਖ਼ਤ ਹਮਲਾ, ਜੋਸ਼ੀਲਾ
ਧਾਵਾ, ਚੜ੍ਹਾਈ

onsalught ('ਔਨਸਲੋਟ) *n* ਧਾਵਾ ਹਮਲਾ, ਪ੍ਰਚੰਡ
ਆਕਰਮਣ; ਕਰਾਰਾ ਵਾਰ

onus ('ਅਉਨਅਸ) *n* ਜ਼ੁੰਮੇਵਾਰੀ, ਫ਼ਰਜ਼; ਕਰਤੱਵ

onward ('ਔਨਵਅ:ਡ) *a* ਅਗਲਾ, ਅੱਗੇ ਵਧਣ
ਵਾਲਾ; ~s ਅੱਗੇ, ਅਗਾਂਹ, ਅਗੇਰੇ

oof (ਉਫ਼) *n* (ਬੋਲ) ਰੁਪਿਆ-ਪੈਸਾ, ਦੌਲਤ; ਨਕਦ

opacity (ਅਉ'ਪੈਸਅਟਿ) *n* ਧੁੰਦਲਾਪਣ; ਅਪਾਰ-
ਦਰਸ਼ਕਤਾ; ਮੰਦ-ਬੁੱਧੀ, ਮੋਟੀ ਅਕਲ; ਅਰਥ ਦੀ
ਅਸਪਸ਼ਟਤਾ

opaque (ਅ(ਉ)'ਪੇਇਕ) *a n* ਧੁੰਦਲਾ, ਅਸਪਸ਼ਟ;
ਅਪਾਰਦਰਸ਼ੀ, ਅੰਨ੍ਹਾ ਸ਼ੀਸ਼ਾ

open ('ਅਉਪਨ) *a n v* ਖੁੱਲ੍ਹਾ, ਮੋਕਲਾ, ਚੌੜਾ,
ਜ਼ਾਹਰ, ਪਰਗਟ, ਅਟਕੱਜਿਆ, ਖੁੱਲ੍ਹਮ-ਖੁੱਲ੍ਹਾ;
ਆਮ (ਖ਼ਾਸ ਦੇ ਵਿਰੋਧ ਵਿਚ); ਖਿਲਰਿਆ
ਹੋਇਆ, ਫੈਲਿਆ ਹੋਇਆ; ਖਿੜਿਆ ਹੋਇਆ,
ਆਰੰਭ ਕਰਨਾ, ਉਦਘਾਟਨ ਕਰਨਾ; ~eyed
ਸਚੇਤ, ਹੁਸ਼ਿਆਰ; ਸਾਵਧਾਨ; ~ended (ਭਾਸ਼ਾ)
ਖੁੱਲ੍ਹਾ; ਚੱਲਦੀ, ਜਾਰੀ (ਗੱਲਬਾਤ); ~faced ਸਾਫ਼
ਦਿਲ; ~handed ਸਖੀ, ਦਾਨੀ, ਉਦਾਰ;
~hearted ਸਾਫ਼ ਦਿਲ, ਮਿਲਣਸਾਰ;
~minded ਨਿਰਪੱਖ, ਖੁੱਲ੍ਹ-ਦਿਲਾ, ਘੇਤੁਅੱਸਥ;
~ing ਵਿਰਲ, ਛੇਕ, ਮੂੰਹ, ਗਾਲੀ; ਉਦਘਾਟਨ;
~ly ਖੁੱਲ੍ਹਮ-ਖੁੱਲ੍ਹਾ; ਖੁੱਲ੍ਹੇ ਤੌਰ ਤੇ, ਸਪਸ਼ਟ ਰੂਪ

ਵਿਚ, ਸਰੇ-ਆਮ

opera ('ਔਪ(ਅ)ਰਅ) *n* ਗੀਤ-ਨਾਟ, ਓਪੇਰਾ

operate ('ਔਪਅਰੇਇਟ) *v* ਅਮਲ ਕਰਨਾ, ਅਮਲ ਵਿਚ ਲਿਆਉਣਾ; ਕਿਰਿਆਸ਼ੀਲ ਕਰਨਾ, ਚਲਾਉਣਾ

operation ('ਔਪਅ'ਰੇਇਸ਼ਨ) *n* ਓਪਰੇਸ਼ਨ, ਚੀਰ-ਫਾੜ; ਕਾਰਵਾਈ, ਕਿਰਿਆ-ਪ੍ਰਣਾਲੀ ਕਾਰੋਬਾਰ, ਕੰਮ-ਕਾਜ; ਕਾਰਜ-ਖੇਤਰ, ਪ੍ਰਭਾਵ-ਖੇਤਰ; ਉੱਦਮ; ਸੈਨਕ ਕਾਰਵਾਈ

operative ('ਔਪ(ਅ)ਰਅਟਿਵ੍) *a n* ਕਾਰਜਸ਼ੀਲ, ਕਰਮਕਾਰੀ, ਅਸਰਦਾਇਕ, ਫਲਦਾਇਕ, ਲਾਗੂ, ਮਜ਼ਦੂਰ

operator ('ਔਪਅਰੇਇਟਅ*) *n* ਚਾਲਕ; ਕਰਮਕਾਰੀ; ਓਪਰੇਸ਼ਨ (ਚੀਰ-ਫਾੜ) ਕਰਨ ਵਾਲਾ

ophthalmology ('ਔਫਥੈਲ'ਮੌਲਅਜਿ) *n* ਅੱਖ ਰੋਗ ਵਿਗਿਆਨ, ਨੇਤਰ-ਚਿਕਿਤਸਾ

opine (ਅ(ਉ)ਪਾਇਨ) *v* ਰਾਇ ਹੋਣੀ, ਰਾਇ ਦੇਣੀ; ਵਿਚਾਰ ਹੋਣਾ

opinion (ਅ'ਪਿਨਯਅਨ) *n* ਰਾਇ, ਮੱਤ, ਸੰਮਤੀ, ਖ਼ਿਆਲ

opium ('ਅਉਪਯਅਮ) *n* ਅਫ਼ੀਮ, ਫ਼ੀਮ

opponent (ਅ'ਪਅਉਨਅੰਟ) *n a* ਵਿਰੋਧੀ, ਵੈਰੀ, ਦੁਸ਼ਮਣ

opportune ('ਔਪਅਟਯੂਨ) *a* ਠੀਕ, ਉਚਿਤ, ਅਨੁਕੂਲ, ਯੋਗ; ਢੁੱਕਵਾਂ

opportunism ('ਔਪਅਟਯੂਨਿਜ਼(ਅ)ਮ) *n* ਮੌਕਾ-ਪਰਸਤੀ, ਅਵਸਰਵਾਦ, ਜ਼ਮਾਨਾਸਾਜ਼ੀ

opportunist ('ਔਪਅਟਯੂਨਿਸਟ) *a* ਮੌਕਾਪਰਸਤ, ਜ਼ਮਾਨਾਸਾਜ਼, ਅਵਸਰਵਾਦੀ

opportunity ('ਔਪਅ'ਟਯੂਨਅਟਿ) *n* ਮੌਕਾ,

ਅਵਸਰ; ਢੋਅ, ਸੰਜੋਗ, ਦਾਅ

oppose (ਅ'ਪਅਉਜ਼) *v* ਵਿਰੋਧ ਕਰਨਾ, ਮੁਖ਼ਾਲਫ਼ਤ ਕਰਨੀ; ਟਾਕਰੇ ਤੇ ਲਿਆਉਣਾ; ਵਿਰੋਧੀ ਪੱਖ ਲੈਣਾ

opposite ('ਔਪਅਜ਼ਿਟ) *a n prep* ਵਿਰੋਧੀ, ਉਲਟਾ; ਵਿਪਰੀਤ, ਪ੍ਰਤੀਕੂਲ

opposition ('ਔਪਅ'ਜ਼ਿਸ਼ਨ) *n* ਵਿਰੋਧ, ਮੁਖ਼ਾਲਫ਼ਤ, ਟਾਕਰਾ; ਦੁਸ਼ਮਨੀ; ਵਿਰੋਧੀ ਧੜਾ, ਵਿਰੋਧੀ ਪੱਖ; ਤੁਲਨਾ, ਪ੍ਰਤੀਕੂਲਤਾ

oppress (ਅ'ਪਰੈਸ) *v* ਸਤਾਉਣਾ, ਦੁੱਖ ਦੇਣਾ, ਜਿਚ ਕਰਨਾ, ਦਬਾਉਣਾ, ਜ਼ੁਲਮ ਕਰਨਾ, ਦਮਨ ਕਰਨਾ; **~ion** ਸਖ਼ਤੀ, ਜਬਰ, ਅੱਤਿਆਚਾਰ, ਜ਼ੁਲਮ, ਵਧੀਕੀ, ਜ਼ੋਰਾਵਰੀ; **~ive** ਅੱਤਿਆਚਾਰੀ, ਜਾਬਰ

opt (ਔਪਟ) *v* ਆਪਣੀ ਪਸੰਦ ਦੱਸਣੀ, ਆਪਣੀ ਇੱਛਾ ਪਰਗਟ ਕਰਨਾ, ਆਪਣੀ ਮਰਜ਼ੀ ਦੱਸਣੀ; **~ative** (ਵਿਆ) ਇੱਛਾਸੂਚਕ; **~ion** ਚੁਨਣ ਦਾ ਅਧਿਕਾਰ, ਚੋਣ, ਇੱਛਾ, ਸਵੈਇੱਛਾ, ਇਖ਼ਤਿਆਰ, ਮਰਜ਼ੀ; **~ional** ਇੱਛਕ, ਵਿਕਲਪਕ, ਇਖ਼ਤਿਆਰੀ

optimism ('ਔਪਟਿਮਿਜ਼(ਅ)ਮ) *n* ਆਸ਼ਾਵਾਦ, ਚੜ੍ਹਦੀ ਕਲਾ, ਖ਼ੁਸ਼ ਉਮੀਦੀ

optimist ('ਔਪਟਿਮਿਸਟ) *n* ਆਸ਼ਾਵਾਦੀ, ਖ਼ੁਸ਼ ਉਮੀਦ; **~ic** ਆਸ਼ਾਵਾਦੀ

optimum ('ਔਪਟਿਮਅਮ) *a* ਸਰਵੋਤਮ, ਆਦਰਸ਼ਕ, ਅਨੁਕੂਲਤਮ

opulence ('ਔ ... ਅਮੀਰੀ, ਹੁ ...

opulent ('ਔ ... ਮਾਲਦਾਰ, ...

opus ('ਅਉਪਅ... ਸ਼ਾਹਕਾਰ

ਉਪ

oracle ('ਔਰਕਲ) *n* ਦੇਵ-ਬਾਣੀ, ਇਲਹਾਮ, ਅਗੰਮੀ ਸੂਝ; ਭਵਿੱਖ-ਵਕਤਾ; ਮਾਰਗ-ਦਰਸ਼ਕ; ਲਾਲ-ਬੁਝੱਕੜ

oracular (ਔ'ਰੈਕਯੁਲਅ*) *a* ਅਗੰਮੀ, ਇਲਹਾਮੀ; ਭੇਦ-ਭਰਿਆ; ਗੁੜ੍ਹ

oral ('ਓਰ(ਅ)ਲ) *a* ਜ਼ਬਾਨੀ, ਮੂੰਹ-ਜ਼ਬਾਨੀ, ਮੌਖਕ

orange ('ਔਰਿੰਜ) *n a* ਸੰਤਰਾ, ਸੰਤਰੇ ਰੰਗਾ, ਭਗਵਾਂ; ~**ry** ਸੰਤਰਿਆਂ ਦਾ ਬਾਗ਼

orate (ਓ'ਰੇਇਟ) *v* ਭਾਸ਼ਣ ਦੇਣਾ, ਤਕਰੀਰ ਕਰਨੀ

oration (ਓ'ਰੇਇਸ਼ਨ) *n* ਪ੍ਰਵਚਨ, ਭਾਸ਼ਣ, ਸੁਭਾਸ਼ਣ, ਵਿਆਖਿਆਨ, ਤਕਰੀਰ; ਲੈਕਚਰ

orator ('ਔਰਅਟਅ*) *n* ਵਕਤਾ, ਵਿਆਖਿਆਤਾ

oratory ('ਔਰਅਟ(ਅ)ਰਿ) *n* ਉਪਾਸਨਾ-ਗ੍ਰਿਹ, ਛੋਟਾ ਗਿਰਜਾ; ਭਾਸ਼ਣ-ਕਲਾ

orb (ਓਬ) *n v* ਨੇਤਰ, ਅੱਖ ਦੀ ਪੁਤਲੀ ਪ੍ਰਿਥਵੀ-ਮੰਡਲ, ਗੋਲਾ; (ਜੋਤਸ਼) ਪਿੰਡ; ਚੰਦਰ-ਮੰਡਲ, ਚੱਕਰ, ਘੇਰਾ, ਵ੍ਰਿਤ; ਘੇਰਨਾ, ਪਰਕਰਮਾ ਕਰਨਾ; ~**it** ਗ੍ਰਿਹ-ਪਥ, ਕਾਰਜ-ਮੰਡਲ, ਚੱਕਰ; ਅੱਖ ਦੀ ਕਟੋਰੀ

orchard ('ਓਚਅਡ) *n* ਵਾੜੀ, ਬਗ਼ੀਚੀ, ਚਮਨ, ਬਗ਼ੀਚਾ; ~**man** ਮਾਲੀ

orchestra ('ਓਕਿਸਟਰਅ) *n* ਰਕਸ ਗਾਹ, ਸਰੋਦ ਗਾਹ, ਵਾਦਕ ਦਲ, ਗਾਉਣ ਵਜਾਉਣ ਵਾਲੀ ਮੰਡਲੀ; ਬਾਂਸਰੀ, ਸਾਰੰਗੀ; ਸਾਰੰਗੀ ਤੇ ਹੋਰ ਵਾਜਿਆਂ ਦਾ ਸੰਜੋਗ, ਆਰਕੈਸਟਰਾ

ordeal (ਓ'ਡੀਲ) *n* ਕਰੜੀ ਅਜ਼ਮਾਇਸ਼, ਅਗਨੀ-ਪਰੀਖਿਆ; ਦੈਵੀ ਕਰੋਪੀ

order ('ਓਡਅ*) *n v* ਹੁਕਮ, ਆਗਿਆ, ਆਦੇਸ਼; ਜੁਗਤ, ਕਰੀਨਾ, ਕ੍ਰਮ, ਸਿਲਸਲਾ; ਸ਼੍ਰੇਣੀ, ਵਰਗ, ਰਜਾ, ਪਦ, ਪੰਗਤੀ; ਤਰਕੀਬ; ਕਿਸਮ; ਤਬਕਾ, ਧੰਧ; ਬਿੱਲਾ ਜਾਂ ਤਮਗ਼ਾ; ਰੀਤੀ, ਰਿਵਾਜ;

ਆਦੇਸ਼ ਦੇਣਾ; ਮਾਲ ਮੰਗਵਾਉਣ ਵਾਸਤੇ ਹੁਕਮ ਭੇਜਣਾ; ਤਰਤੀਬ ਨਾਲ ਰੱਖਣਾ, ਅਧਿਕਾਰ ਜਤਾਉਣਾ; ~**ly** ਸੈਨਾ-ਆਦੇਸ਼-ਪਾਲ, ਅਰਦਲੀ; ਸੁਡੌਲ, ਅਨੁਸ਼ਾਸਨਪਾਲਕ; ਸਲੀਕਾ ਪਸੰਦ

ordinance ('ਓਡਿਨਅੰਸ) *n* ਫ਼ਰਮਾਨ, ਅਧਿਆਦੇਸ਼; ਧਰਮ-ਵਿਧੀ

ordinary ('ਓਡਨਰਿ) *a* ਸਧਾਰਨ, ਰਿਵਾਜੀ, ਮਾਮੂਲੀ, ਰੀਤੀਗਤ, ਪ੍ਰਥਾਗਤ

ordnance ('ਓਡਨਅੰਸ) *n* ਸਰਕਾਰੀ ਜੁੱਧ-ਵਿਭਾਗ; ਗੋਲਾ-ਬਾਰੂਦ; ਤੋਪਖ਼ਾਨਾ

ordure ('ਓ'ਡਯੁਅ*) *n* ਗੋਹਾ, ਲਿੰਦ, ਵਿੱਠ, ਮਲ; ਭੈੜੇ ਸ਼ਬਦ

ore (ਓ*) *n* ਕੱਚੀ ਧਾਤ

organ ('ਓਗਅਨ) *v* ਅੰਗ, ਇੰਦਰੀ, ਅੰਸ਼ (ਪਾਰਟੀ ਆਦਿ ਦੇ) ਸੰਚਾਰ ਸਾਧਨ; ~**ic** ਅੰਗ-ਸਬੰਧੀ, ਕਾਇਕ, ਸਰੀਰ ਤੇ ਪ੍ਰਭਾਵ ਪਾਉਣ ਵਾਲਾ; ਸਜੀਵੀ, ਬਨਸਪਤੀ ਜਗਤ ਜਾਂ ਜੀਵ ਸਬੰਧੀ; ਸੰਗਠਿਤ; ਕਾਰਬਨ ਯੁਕਤ, ਕਾਰਬਨਿਕ

organization ('ਓਗਅਨਾਇਸ਼ਨ) *v* ਜਥੇਬੰਦੀ, ਸੰਗਠਨ, ਰਚਨਾ

organize ('ਓਗਅਨਾਇਜ਼) *v* ਜਥੇਬੰਦ ਕਰਨਾ, ਪ੍ਰਬੰਧ ਕਰਨਾ; ਸੰਗਠਤ ਕਰਨਾ; ~**d** ਸੰਗਠਤ, ਵਿਵਸਥਿਤ; ~**r** ਸੰਗਠਕ, ਜਥੇਦਾਰ, ਪ੍ਰਬੰਧਕ, ਵਿਵਸਥਾਪਕ, ਆਯੋਜਕ

orient (ਓਰਿਐਂਟ) *n a* ਮੋਤੀ ਦੀ ਝਲਕ, ਪੂਰਬ ਦੇਸ਼, ਚੜ੍ਹਦਾ ਸੂਰਜ, ਆਬ, ਚਮਕ (ਸ਼ੀਸ਼ੇ ਜਾਂ ਜ਼ੇਵਰ ਆਦਿ ਦੀ), ਉਜਲ, ਨਿਰਮਲ, ਆਬਦਾਰ, ਚਮਕਦਾਰ, ਚਮਕੀਲਾ, ਪੂਰਬੀ; ~**al** ਪੂਰਬ-ਵਾਸੀ, ਪੂਰਬ ਦੇਸ਼ਾਂ ਦੀ ਸੰਸਕ੍ਰਿਤੀ ਸਬੰਧੀ, ਪੂਰਬੀ (ਭਾਸ਼ਾ)

origin ('ਔਰਿਜਅਨ) *n* ਮੂਲ, ਉਤਪਤੀ, ਉਦਭਵ; ਬੀਜ, ਆਰੰਭ, ਜਨਮ, ਆਦਿ, ਬੁਨਿਆਦ, ਸਰੋਤ;

~al ਮੂਲ, ਮੌਲਕ; ਨਵੀਨ; ~ality ਮੌਲਕਤਾ; ਰਚਨਾਤਮਕਤਾ; ~ate ਉਤਪੰਨ ਹੋਣਾ ਜਾਂ ਕਰਨਾ, ਵਿਉਤਪੰਨ ਹੋਣਾ ਜਾਂ ਕਰਨਾ, ਪੈਦਾ ਕਰਨਾ ਜਾਂ ਹੋਣਾ; ਆਰੰਭ ਕਰਨਾ; ਜਨਮ ਦੇਣਾ; ~ating ਆਰੰਭਕ, ਉਦਭਾਵਕ; ~ator ਉਤਪਾਦਕ, ਜਨਮਦਾਤਾ

ornament ('ਓਨਅਮਅੰਟ) n v ਗਹਿਣਾ, ਜ਼ੇਵਰ, ਭੂਸ਼ਣ, ਅੰਲਕਾਰ; ਸ਼ੋਭਾ; ਸ਼ਿੰਗਾਰ, ਸਜਾਵਟ; ~al ਸਜਾਵਟੀ, ਅਲੰਕਾਰਕ

ornithology ('ਓਨਿਥਅਲੋਜਿ) n ਪੰਛੀ-ਵਿਗਿਆਨ, ਖਗ-ਵਿਗਿਆਨ, ਵਿਹਗ-ਸ਼ਾਸਤਰ

orphan ('ਓ:ਫ਼ਨ) a n v ਯਤੀਮ, ਅਨਾਥ; ਅਨਾਥ ਬਣਾਉਣਾ; ~age ਯਤੀਮਖ਼ਾਨਾ, ਅਨਾਥ-ਆਸ਼ਰਮ, ਅਨਾਥਾਲਿਆ

orthodox ('ਓਥਅਡੌਕਸ) a ਕੱਟੜ, ਰੂੜ੍ਹੀਬੱਧ, ਪਰੰਪਰਾਗਤ, ਸਨਾਤਨੀ ਮੱਤ

orthography (ਓ'ਥੋਗਰਅਫ਼ਿ) n ਸ਼ੁੱਧ ਲੇਖਣ, ਸ਼ੁੱਧ ਅੱਖਰਜੋੜ

oscillate ('ਔਸਿਲੇਇਟ) v ਅਸਥਿਰ ਹੋਣਾ, ਕੰਬਣਾ, ਡਾਵਾਂ-ਡੋਲ ਹੋਣਾ; ਝੂਲਣਾ, ਝੁਲਾਉਣਾ, ਹਲਾਉਣਾ, ਡੋਲਣਾ

oscillation ('ਔਸਿ'ਲੇਇਸ਼ਨ) n ਅਸਥਿਰਤਾ, ਕੰਬਣ, ਝੂਲਣ, ਡੋਲਣ, ਘੁਮਾਉ

ostensible (ਔ'ਸਟੈਨਸਅਬਲ) a ਆਡੰਬਰਪੂਰਨ, ਪਖੰਡਪੂਰਨ, ਦੰਭਪੂਰਨ, ਬਣਾਉਟੀ

ostentation ('ਔਸਟੈਂਟ'ਇਸ਼ਨ) n ਦਿਖਾਵਾ, ਠਾਠ-ਬਾਠ, ਦੰਭ, ਆਤਮ-ਸ਼ਲਾਘਾ, ਆਤਮ-ਪਰਦਰਸ਼ਨ; ਆਡੰਬਰਪੂਰਨ, ਤੜਕ-ਭੜਕ

ostrich ('ਔਸਟਰਿਚ) n ਸ਼ੁਤਰ ਮੁਰਗ

other ('ਅਦਅ*) n ਹੋਰ, ਦੂਜਾ, ਅਗਲਾ, ਕੋਈ ਹੋਰ; ਭਿੰਨ; ~wise ਨਹੀਂ ਤਾਂ, ਵਰਨਾ, ਜਾਂ

otto ('ਔਟਅਉ) n ਇਤਰ, ਅਤਰ

ouch (ਆਉਚ) n int (ਪ੍ਰ) ਜੜਾਉ, ਬਕਸੂਆ, ਨਗੀਨਾ ਛੇਕ; ਉਹ!, ਹਾਇ!

oust (ਆਉਸਟ) v ਕੱਢ ਦੇਣਾ; ਬੇਦਖ਼ਲ ਕਰਨਾ, ਹਟਾਉਣਾ, ਵੰਚਤ ਕਰਨਾ

out (ਆਉਟ) n v a adv int ਖੁੱਲ੍ਹਾ ਮੈਦਾਨ; ਬੇਦਖ਼ਲ ਕਰਨਾ; ਬਾਹਰ ਕਰਨਾ; ਬਾਹਰ ਦਾ; ਬਾਹਰ, ਪਰੇ; ਦੂਰ ਹੋ; ~break ਜੁੱਧ ਦਾ ਆਰੰਭ; ਵਿਦਰੋਹ, ਫ਼ਸਾਦ; ~burst ਉਬਾਲ; ਭੜਕਾ; ~cast ਅਧਰਮੀ, ਭ੍ਰਿਸ਼ਟ, ਨਿਕੰਮਾ; ~caste (ਬਰਾਦਰੀ ਵਿੱਚੋਂ) ਛੇਕਿਆ, ਨਿਥਾਵਾਂ ਬਰਾਦਰੀ ਵਿਚੋਂ ਕੱਢ ਦੇਣਾ; ~come ਨਤੀਜਾ, ਫਲ, ਪਰਿਣਾਮ, ਨਿਸ਼ਕਰਸ; ~cry ਹਾਹਾਕਾਰ, ਚੀਕ-ਚਿਹਾੜਾ; ਦੁਹਾਈ, ਰੌਲਾ-ਰੱਪਾ; ~date ਪੁਰਾਣਾ ਕਰ ਦੇਣਾ; ~dated ਅਪ੍ਰਚਲਤ, ਪੁਰਾਣਾ; ~door ਬਾਹਰਲਾ, ਬਾਹਰੀ, ਮੈਦਾਨੀ, ਖੁੱਲ੍ਹਾ; ~doors ਅਸਮਾਨ ਥੱਲੇ, ਖੁੱਲ੍ਹੀ ਹਵਾ ਵਿਚ; ~fall ਮੁਹਾਣਾ, ਦਹਾਨਾ; ~goings ਖ਼ਰਚ, ਲਾਗਤ; ~lay ਲਾਗਤ, ਖ਼ਰਚ; ਖ਼ਾਕਾ; ~let ਨਿਕਾਸ, ਮੋਰੀ; ਲਾਂਘਾ; ~line ਰੂਪ-ਰੇਖਾ, ਖ਼ਾਕਾ, ਰੇਖਾ-ਚਿੱਤਰ; ਸੰਖੇਪ ਸਾਰ-ਅੰਸ਼; ~look ਨਜ਼ਰਿਆ, ਦ੍ਰਿਸ਼ਟੀਕੋਣ; ਰੰਗ-ਢੰਗ; ~lying ਦੂਰ-ਦੁਰਾਡਾ, ਬਾਹਰਵਰਤੀ, ਸੀਮਾਵਰਤੀ; ~moded ਅਪ੍ਰਚਲਤ; ~number ਗਿਣਤੀ ਵਿਚ ਵੱਧ ਹੋਣਾ; ~patient ਬਾਹਰੀ ਰੋਗੀ; ~post ਸਰਹੱਦੀ ਚੌਕੀ; ਸੈਨਾ-ਦਲ; ਸੀਮਾ-ਸਥਾਨ; ~put ਉਪਜ, ਉਤਪਾਦਨ; (ਕੰਪਿਊਟਰ) ਆਉਟਪੁੱਟ; ~rage ਉਪੱਦਰ, ਅਤਿਆਚਾਰ; ਘੋਰ ਅਪਮਾਨ, ਹੱਤਕ; ~rageous (ਅਤੀ) ਨਿਰਦਈ, ਉਪੱਦਰੀ, ਭ੍ਰਿਸ਼ਟਾਚਾਰੀ; ~right ਕਟਈ, ਸਰਾਸਰ, ਪੱਕਾ; ~run ਹੱਦ ਲੰਘ ਜਾਣਾ,

ਸੀਮਾ ਪਾਰ ਕਰ ਜਾਣਾ, ਹੋਰ ਤੇਜ਼ ਦੌੜਨਾ; ~side ਬਾਹਰਲਾ ਤਲ, ਬਾਹਰੀ ਭਾਗ, ਅਸੰਮਿਲਤ, ਅਸੰਯੁਕਤ; ~sider ਪਰਦੇਸੀ, ਅਪਰਿਚਿਤ ਆਦਮੀ; ~spoken ਮੂੰਹਫਟ, ਖਰਾ, ਸਾਫ਼ਗੋ, ਬੇਬਾਕ; ~standing ਬਕਾਇਆ, ਬਾਕੀ, ਪ੍ਰਮੁਖ, ਸਿਰਮੌਰ; ~ing ਛੋਟੀ ਸੈਰ, ਟਹਿਰੀਹੀ ਸਫ਼ਰ, ਹਵਾਖੋਰੀ; ~ward ਬਾਹਰ, ਬਾਹਰ ਦਾ, ਬੈਰੂਨੀ; ਬਾਹਰਮੁਖੀ; ~wardly ਬਾਹਰ, ਬਾਹਰ ਤੋਂ, ਬਾਹਰੋਂ; ~wards ਬਾਹਰੀ ਰੂਪ ਵਿਚ, ਬਾਹਰ ਬਾਹਰ ਵੱਲ

oval ('ਅਉਵਲ) *a n* ਅੰਡਾਕਾਰ; ਅੰਡਾਕਾਰ ਵਸਤੂ

ovary ('ਅਉਵਅਰਿ) *n* ਅੰਡਕੋਸ਼; ਬੀਜ-ਕੋਸ਼

oven ('ਅਵਨ) *n* ਤੰਦੂਰ, ਚੁੱਲ੍ਹਾ, ਭੱਠੀ

over ('ਅਉਵਅ*) *n adv a prep* ਅਧਿਕਤਾ; ਵਾਧਾ; ਮੁੜ ਮੁੜ, ਵਾਰ ਵਾਰ, ਇਕ ਵੇਰ ਫੇਰ; ਬਾਹਰ ਵੱਲ, ਉੱਪਰ; ਅੱਗੇ, ਅਗਲੇ ਪਾਰ; (ਕ੍ਰਿਕਟ) ਓਵਰ; ~act ਅਤਿ ਅਭਿਨੈ ਕਰਨਾ; ~age ਨਿਰਧਾਰਤ ਉਮਰ ਤੋਂ ਵੱਧ; ~all ਸਮੁੱਚੇ ਤੌਰ ਤੇ, ਕੁੱਲ ਮਿਲਾ ਕੇ; ~bridge ਉੱਪਰਲਾ ਪੁਲ; ~burden ਹੋਰ ਲੱਦ ਦੇਣਾ, ਦੱਬ ਦੇਣਾ; ~cast ਬਦਲਵਾਈ, ਛਾਇਆ ਹੋਇਆ, ਅੰਧਕਾਰ ਕਰ ਦੇਣਾ, ਢਕਣਾ, ਛਾ ਜਾਣਾ; ~charge ਵਧੇਰੇ ਭਾਰ; ਵਧੇਰੇ ਪੈਸੇ ਲੈਣੇ; ~coat ਫ਼ਰਗਲ, ਵੱਡਾ ਕੋਟ, ਓਵਰ ਕੋਟ; ~come ਜਿੱਤਣਾ, ਕਾਬੂ ਪਾਉਣਾ, ਛਾ ਜਾਣਾ, ਸਰ ਕਰਨਾ; ~date ਪਿਛਲੀ ਤਾਰੀਖ਼ ਪਾਉਣਾ; ~do ਅੰਤ ਕਰਨਾ, ਬਹੁਤ ਦੂਰ ਤਕ ਚਲੇ ਜਾਣਾ; ~dose (ਦਵਾਈ ਦੀ) ਅਧਿਕ ਮਾਤਰਾ, ਅਜਿਹੀ ਖ਼ੁਰਾਕ ਦੇਣੀ; ~draft ਵਾਪੂ ਵਸੂਲੀ; ~draw ਵਧਾ ਚੜ੍ਹ ਕੇ ਦੱਸਣਾ, ਵਧੇਰੇ ਲੈਣਾ; ~due ਮਿਆਦ ਪੁੱਗਿਆ; ~estimate ਅਤੀ ਅਨੁਮਾਨ,

ਬਹੁਤ ਅਧਿਕ ਅਨੁਮਾਨ ਕਰਨਾ, ਅਧਿਕ ਅੰਕਣਾ; ~flow ਛਲਕਾਉ, ਛਲਕ; ~haul ਨਵਾਂ ਕਰਨਾ, ਕਾਇਆ-ਕਲਪ ਕਰਨੀ; ~head ਉਤਲਾ, ਉੱਪਰਲਾ, ਉੱਚਾ, ਉੱਪਰਲਾ (ਖ਼ਰਚ); ~hear ਚੋਰੀ ਛਿਪੇ ਸੁਣ ਲੈਣਾ; ~lapping ਪਰਸਪਰ ਵਿਆਪੀ, ਉੱਪਰ ਚੜ੍ਹੀ ਹੋਈ; ~load ਅਤੀ ਬੋਝ, ਅਤੀ ਭਾਰ; ਭਾਰੀ ਕਰਨਾ, ਵੱਧ ਭਾਰ ਲੱਦਣਾ; ~look ਅਣਦੇਖੀ ਕਰ ਜਾਣਾ; ਨਜ਼ਰ-ਅੰਦਾਜ਼ ਕਰਨਾ; ਨਿਗਰਾਨੀ ਕਰਨੀ; ~night ਪਿਛਲੀ ਰਾਤ ਦਾ; ਰਾਤੇ-ਰਾਤ ਭਰ ਦਾ; ~payment ਅਧਿਕ ਭੁਗਤਾਨ; ~rule (ਫ਼ੈਸਲੇ ਜਾਂ ਤਜਵੀਜ਼ ਨੂੰ) ਰੱਦਣਾ, ਰੱਦ ਕਰਨਾ, ਮਨਸੂਖ ਕਰਨਾ; ~sea(s) ਸਮੁੰਦਰੋਂ ਪਾਰ ਦੇਸ਼; ਵਿਦੇਸ਼ੀ, ਸਮੁੰਦਰ ਪਾਰਲਾ; ~see (ਕਰਮਚਾਰੀਆਂ ਦੇ ਕੰਮ ਦੀ) ਦੇਖ-ਭਾਲ ਕਰਨੀ, ਨਿਗਰਾਨੀ ਕਰਨੀ; ~seer ਨਿਗਰਾਨ, ਨਿਗਾਹਬਾਨ, ਦਰੋਗ਼ਾ, ਓਵਰਸੀਅਰ, ਸਰਵੇਖਕ; ~set ਉਲਟਣਾ, ਮੂਧਾ ਕਰਨਾ, ਪਲਟਣਾ, ਰੇਹਾਂ ਡਿਗਣਾ; ~shadow ਛਾਂ ਕਰਨੀ, ਧੁੱਪ ਤੋਂ ਬਚਾਉਣਾ, ਢਕ ਦੇਣਾ; ~sight ਨਿਰੀਖਣ, ਦੇਖ-ਭਾਲ, ਨਿਗਰਾਨੀ; ਅਣਗਹਿਲੀ; ~take ਜਾ ਕੇ ਫੜ ਲੈਣਾ, ਬਰਾਬਰ ਆ ਜਾਣਾ; (ਮੁਸੀਬਤ ਦਾ) ਅਚਾਨਕ ਆ ਪੈਣਾ; ~time ਅਧਿ-ਸਮਾਂ, ਵਾਧੂ ਸਮੇਂ ਲਈ ਕੀਤੀ ਅਦਾਇਗੀ; ~weight ਅਤੀ ਭਾਰ, ਜ਼ਿਆਦਾ ਬੋਝ; *throw* ~ ਛੱਡਣਾ, ਤਿਆਗਣਾ, ਤਿਰਸਕਾਰਨਾ

overt ('ਅਉਵਅ:ਟ) *a* ਸਪਸ਼ਟ, ਖੁੱਲ੍ਹਾ, ਪਰਗਟ, ਪ੍ਰਤੱਖ, ਖੁੱਲ੍ਹਾ-ਖੁੱਲ੍ਹਾ ਕੀਤਾ; ~ness ਸਪਸ਼ਟਤਾ, ਖੁੱਲ੍ਹਾਪਣ

owe (ਅਉ) *n* ਰਿਣੀ ਹੋਣਾ, ਦੇਣਦਾਰ ਹੋਣਾ

owing ('ਅਉਇਙ) *pred a* ਬਾਕੀ, ਰਿਣਬੱਧ, ਫਲਸਰੂਪ, ਕਾਰਨ ਕਰਕੇ, ਦੇ ਕਾਰਨ

owl (ਆਉਲ) *n* ਉੱਲੂ, ਘੁੱਗੂ, ਆਡੰਬਰਪੂਰਨ ਵਿਅਕਤੀ

own (ਅਉਨ) *v a* ਅਧਿਕਾਰ ਰੱਖਣਾ, ਹੱਕਦਾਰ ਹੋਣਾ, ਇਕਬਾਲ ਕਰਨਾ, ਮੰਨਣਾ; ਨਿੱਜੀ, ਵਿਅਕਤੀਗਤ; ~er ਮਾਲਕ, ਸੁਆਮੀ; ~ership ਮਲਕੀਅਤ, ਮਾਲਕੀ, ਪ੍ਰਭੁਤਾ

ox (ਔਕਸ) *n* ਬਲਦ, ਬੈਲ

oxygen ('ਔਕਸਿਜ(ਅ)ਨ) *n* ਆਕਸੀਜਨ ਗੈਸ, ਪ੍ਰਾਣਵਾਯੂ

oyster ('ਔਇਸਟਅ*) *n* ਇਕ ਤਰ੍ਹਾਂ ਦੀ ਝੀਂਗਾ ਮੱਛੀ, ਘੋਗਾ

ozone ('ਅਉਜ਼ਅਉਨ) *n* ਆਕਸੀਜਨ ਵਰਗੀ ਇਕ ਗੈਸ, ਆਨੰਦਦਾਇਕ ਪ੍ਰਭਾਵ

P

P, p (ਪੀ) *n* ਰੋਮਨ ਵਰਟਮਾਲਾ ਦਾ ਸੋਲ੍ਹਵਾਂ ਅੱਖਰ

pace (ਪੇਇਸ) *n v* ਕਦਮ, ਪਗ, ਡਗ, ਪਦ, ਚਾਲ, ਗਤੀ, ਰਫ਼ਤਾਰ (ਚਲੱਣ ਜਾਂ ਦੌੜਨ ਦੀ); ਪ੍ਰਗਤੀ, ਟੁਰਨਾ, ਘ੍ਰਿੰਮਣਾ; **~maker** ਗਤੀ ਨਿਰਧਾਰਕ; (ਦਿਲ ਦੀ ਗਤੀ ਦਾ) ਨਿਰਧਾਰਕ ਜੰਤਰ; **~setter** ਗਤੀ-ਨਿਰਧਾਰਕ; **keep ~** ਸਮਾਨ ਗਤੀ ਨਾਲ ਟੁਰਨਾ; ਕਦਮ ਮਿਲਾ ਕੇ ਚੱਲਣਾ

pacific (ਪਅ'ਸਿਫ਼ਿਕ) *a* ਸ਼ਾਂਤ, ਪ੍ਰਸ਼ਾਂਤ, ਸ਼ਾਂਤਮਈ

pacification ('ਪੈਸਿਫ਼ਿ'ਕੇਇਸ਼ਨ) *n* ਸੁਲ੍ਹਾਨਾਮਾ, ਸੰਧੀਨਾਮਾ; ਸ਼ਾਂਤੀ ਸਥਾਪਨ

pacificist (ਪੈਸਿਫ਼ਾਇਸਿਸਟ) *n* ਅਮਨਪਸੰਦ, ਸ਼ਾਂਤੀਵਾਦੀ

pacify ('ਪੈਸਿਫ਼ਾਇ) *v* ਸ਼ਾਂਤ ਕਰਨਾ, ਢਾਰਸ ਦੇਣੀ, ਮਨਾਉਣਾ

pack (ਪੈਕ) *n v* ਪੋਟਲੀ, ਥੁਰਾਚਾ, ਗੰਢੜੀ, ਗੰਢ, ਸਮੂਹ, ਗੁੱਟ, ਡੱਬਿਆਂ ਵਿਚ ਬੰਦ ਕਰਨਾ, ਠੋਸ ਦੇਣਾ, ਖਚਖਚ ਭਰ ਦੇਣਾ, ਤੁੰਨਣਾ, ਥੋਰੀਆ ਖਿਸਤਰ ਬੰਨ੍ਹ ਕੇ ਤਿਆਰ ਹੋਣਾ, ਗਠੜੀ ਜਾਂ ਪੰਡ ਸਣੇ ਭੱਜ ਪੈਣਾ; **~age** ਗੰਢ, ਗਠੜੀ, ਬੰਡਲ, ਪੁੰਲਦਾ; ਗੰਢ ਬੰਨ੍ਹਣੀ, ਪੁਲੰਦਾ ਬਣਾਉਣਾ, ਪਾਰਸਲ ਕਰਨਾ, ਵਲੇਟਣਾ; **~et** ਪੁਲੰਦਾ, ਛੋਟਾ ਬੰਡਲ, ਪੁੜਾ, ਪੁੜੀ, ਮੁੱਠਾ, ਪੈਕਟ; **~ing** ਪੈਕਿੰਗ; ਪੁਲੰਦਾ ਬੰਨ੍ਹਣ ਦਾ ਕੰਮ; ਬੰਨ੍ਹਾਈ, ਭਰਾਈ

pact (ਪੈਕਟ) *n v* ਸੰਧੀ, ਅਹਿਦਨਾਮਾ, ਸੁਲ੍ਹਾਨਾਮਾ; ਸੰਧੀ (ਕਰਨੀ), ਸਮਝੌਤਾ (ਕਰਨਾ)

pad (ਪੈਡ) *n v* ਜੀਨ, ਨਰਮ ਕਾਠੀ, ਗੱਦਾ, ਗੱਦੀ; **~ding** ਭਰਾਈ

paddle ('ਪੈਡਲ) *n v* ਚੁੱਪੂ, ਕਿਸ਼ਤੀ ਦਾ ਡੰਡਾ, ਛੋਟਾ ਬੇਲਚਾ, ਹੌਲੀ-ਹੌਲੀ ਕਿਸ਼ਤੀ ਚਲਾਉਣੀ, ਖੰਭਾਂ ਨਾਲ ਪਾਣੀ ਵਿਚ ਤਰਨਾ, ਜਲ-ਕ੍ਰੀੜਾ ਕਰਨਾ, ਠੁਮਕ-ਠੁਮਕ ਟੁਰਨਾ, ਚੱਲਣਾ; **~r** ਚਲਾਉਣ ਵਾਲਾ, ਚਾਲਕ, ਖੇਵੱਈਆ, ਮੱਲਾਹ

paddy ('ਪੈਡਿ) *n v* ਧਾਨ, (ਉਪ) ਰੋਸਾ, ਖਿਝ

padlock ('ਪੈਡਲੌਕ) *n v* ਜੰਦਰਾ, ਤਾਲਾ, ਕੁਫ਼ਲ; ਤਾਲਾ ਲਾਉਣਾ, ਕੁਫ਼ਲਬੰਦ ਕਰਨਾ

paean ('ਪੀਅਨ) *n* ਵਿਜੈ-ਗੀਤ, ਜੈ-ਧੁਨੀ, ਉਸਤਤ ਗਾਨ; ਸ਼ੁਕਰਾਨੇ ਦਾ ਗੀਤ, ਸੋਹਲਾ

paederast ('ਪੈਡੇਅਰੈਸਟ) *n* ਮੁੰਡੇਬਾਜ਼, ਲੌਂਡੇਬਾਜ਼

paediatric ('ਪੀਡਿ'ਐਟਰਿਕ) *a* ਬਾਲ ਚਿਕਿਤਸਾ-ਸਬੰਧੀ, ਬਾਲ ਰੋਗ-ਸਬੰਧੀ

pagan ('ਪੇਇਗਅਨ) *n a* ਕਾਫ਼ਰ, ਨਾਸਤਕ, ਅੰਧਵਿਸ਼ਵਾਸੀ, ਮੂਤੂ

page (ਪੇਇਜ) *n v* ਪੰਨਾ, ਸਫ਼ਾ; ਚਾਕਰ; ਸਾਕਾ; ਸਫ਼ੇ ਲਾਉਣਾ, ਬੁਲਾਵਾ ਘੱਲਣਾ

pagination ('ਪੈਜਿ'ਨੇਇਸ਼ਨ) *n* ਪੰਨਾ-ਸੰਖਿਆ, ਪੰਨਿਆਂ ਦੀ ਕੁੱਲ ਗਿਣਤੀ

pagoda (ਪਅ'ਗਅਉਡਅ) *n* ਸ਼ਿਵਾਲਾ, ਦੇਵਾਲਾ, (ਦੱਖਣੀ ਭਾਰਤ ਦਾ ਪ੍ਰਾਚੀਨ) ਸੋਨੇ ਦਾ ਸਿੱਕਾ

paid (ਪੇਇਡ) *a* ਭੁਗਤਾਨ ਕੀਤਾ, ਚੁਕਾ ਦਿੱਤਾ

pail (ਪੇਇਲ) *n* ਤੌੜਾ, ਬਾਲਟੀ, ਡੋਲ

pain (ਪੇਇਨ) *n v* ਦਰਦ, ਦੁੱਖ, ਪੀੜ, ਸੰਤਾਪ, ਵੇਦਨਾ, ਤਕਲੀਫ਼, ਪ੍ਰਸਵ-ਵੇਦਨਾ; ਸਤਾਉਣਾ, ਦੁੱਖ ਦੇਣਾ, ਪੀੜਾ ਦੇਤੀ, ਬੇਚੈਨ ਕਰਨਾ; **~killer** ਪੀੜ-ਨਾਸਕ; **~ed** ਪੀੜਤ, ਦੁੱਖੀ; **~ful** ਦੁੱਖੀ, ਕਸ਼ਟਦਾਇਕ, ਦੁਖਦਾਈ; ਕਠਨ; **~less**

ਪੀੜਾਹੀਣ, ਕਸ਼ਟ-ਰਹਿਤ, ਦੁੱਖਹੀਣ

paint (ਪੇਇੰਟ) *n v* ਰੰਗ, ਲੇਪ; ਰੋਗਨ; ਰੰਗਣਾ, ਰੰਗ ਲਾਉਣਾ ਜਾਂ ਭਰਨਾ; **~er** ਚਿੱਤਰਕਾਰ, ਰੰਗ-ਲੇਖਕ, ਰੰਗਸਾਜ਼, ਨੱਕਾਸ਼, ਮੁਸੱਵਰ; ਰੰਜਕ; **~ing** ਚਿੱਤਰਕਾਰੀ, ਨੱਕਾਸ਼ੀ, ਰੰਗਾਈ; ਚਿੱਤਰ

pair (ਪੇਅ*) *n* ਜੋੜ, ਜੁੱਟ, ਜੋੜਾ, ਜੋੜੀ, ਜੋਟਾ; ਦੰਪਤੀ, ਪਤੀ-ਪਤਨੀ, ਜੋੜੀਦਾਰ, ਜੋੜ ਜੋੜਨਾ, ਜੋੜੀ ਬਣਾਉਣਾ

pal (ਪੈਲ) *n v* ਸੰਗੀ, ਸਾਥੀ, ਮਿੱਤਰ; ਦੋਸਤ ਬਣਨਾ; ਮਿਲਣਾ-ਜੁਲਣਾ

palace ('ਪੈਲਿਸ) *n* ਰਾਜ-ਭਵਨ, ਸ਼ਾਹੀ ਮਹੱਲ; ਹਵੇਲੀ, ਸ਼ਾਨਦਾਰ ਇਮਾਰਤ

palaeography ('ਪੈਲਿ'ਔਗਰਅਫ਼ਿ) *n* ਪੁਰਾ-ਲੇਖ-ਸ਼ਾਸਤਰ

palaestra (ਪੈ'ਲੀਸਟਰਅ) *n* ਅਖਾੜਾ, ਕਸਰਤ ਘਰ

palanquin ('ਪੈਲਅਨ'ਕੀਨ) *n* ਡੋਲੀ, ਪਾਲਕੀ

palatable ('ਪੈਲਅਟਅਬਲ) *a* ਸੁਆਦੀ, ਜ਼ਾਇਕੇਦਾਰ, ਮਜ਼ੇਦਾਰ, ਸੁਆਦਿਸ਼ਟ

palate ('ਪੈਲਅਟ) *n* ਤਾਲੂ; ਸੁਆਦ, ਜ਼ਾਇਕਾ

palatial ('ਪਅ'ਲੇਇਸ਼ਲ) *a* ਮਹੱਲ ਵਰਗਾ; ਆਲੀਸ਼ਾਨ, ਸ਼ਾਨਦਾਰ, ਵਿਸ਼ਾਲ, ਸ਼ਾਹੀ

pall (ਪੇਲ) *n v* ਖੱਫ਼ਣ, ਮੁਰਦੇ ਨੂੰ ਢਕਣ ਵਾਲਾ ਕੱਪੜਾ; ਪਰਦਾ; ਚੋਗਾ; ਬੇਮਜ਼ਾ ਹੋ ਜਾਣਾ; ਹਿੰਮਤ ਹਾਰਨਾ, ਜੀ ਚੁਰਾਉਣਾ; **~bearer** (ਅਰਥੀ ਨੂੰ) ਮੋਢਾ ਦੇਣਾ ਵਾਲਾ

palm (ਪਾਮ) *n v* (1) ਤਾੜ, (ਵਿਜੈ-ਚਿੰਨ੍ਹ ਵਜੋਂ) ਤਾੜ ਦਾ ਪੱਤਾ, ਸਰਬਸ੍ਰੇਸ਼ਠਤਾ, ਸਰਬਉੱਚਤਾ; (2) ਤਲੀ, ਹਥੇਲੀ; ਫੜਨਾ; ਰਿਸ਼ਵਤ ਦੇਣੀ, ਮੁੱਠੀ ਗਰਮ ਕਰਨੀ; **~ist** ਹੱਥ ਵੇਖਣ ਵਾਲਾ, ਪਾਂਡਾ

palpitate ('ਪੈਲਪਿਟੇਇਟ) *v* (ਦਿਲ ਦਾ) ਧੜਕਣਾ, ਧਕ ਧਕ ਕਰਨਾ; (ਨਬਜ਼ ਜਾਂ ਨਾੜ ਦਾ) ਫੜਕਣਾ; ਖਟਖਟਉਣਾ, ਫੜਕ ਉੱਠਣਾ

palpitation ('ਪੈਲਪਿ'ਟੇਇਸ਼ਨ) *n* ਧੜਕਣ, ਧਕ ਧਕ, ਕਾਂਬਾ, ਥਰਥਰਾਹਟ

paltry ('ਪੋਲਟਰਿ) *a* ਤੁੱਛ, ਘਟੀਆ, ਮਾਮੂਲੀ

pamper ('ਪੈਂਪਅ*) *v* ਪੁਚ ਪੁਚ ਕਰਨਾ, ਆਦਤ ਵਿਗਾੜ ਦੇਣੀ; **~ed** ਵਿਗੜਿਆ, ਚਾਂਭਲਿਆ

pamphlet ('ਪੈਂਫ਼ਲਿਟ) *n* ਛੋਟਾ ਰਸਾਲਾ, ਪੱਤਰਕਾ, ਪੁਸਤਕਾ, ਕਿਤਾਬਚਾ, ਪੈਂਫਲਿਟ, ਚੌਪੰਨਾ

pan (ਪੈਨ) *n v pref* ਕੜਾਹੀ; ਤਸਲਾ; ਤੱਕੜੀ ਦਾ ਪਲੜਾ; ਖੋਪੜੀ

panacea ('ਪੈਨਅ'ਸਿਅ) *n* ਸਰਬਰੋਗ ਔਖਧ, ਅਕਸੀਰ, ਹਰ ਮਰਜ਼ ਦੀ ਦਵਾ

pandemonium ('ਪੈਂਡਿ'ਮਅਉਨਯਅਮ) *n* ਭੂਤ-ਘਰ; ਪਰੇਤਵਾਸ; ਅਸ਼ਾਂਤੀਪੂਰਨ ਥਾਂ, ਧਮੱਚੜ, ਸ਼ੋਰ-ਸ਼ਰਾਬਾ, ਕਾਵਾਂ-ਰੌਲੀ, ਮੱਛੀ-ਬਜ਼ਾਰ; ਉਪੱਦਰ, ਗੜਬੜ

pander ('ਪੈਂਡਅ*) *n v* ਭੜੂਆ, ਦਲਾਲ, ਬੁਰੇ ਕੰਮ ਵਿਚ ਸਹਾਇਤਾ ਦੇਣੀ

panel ('ਪੈਨਲ) *n v* ਵਿਅੱਕਤੀਆਂ ਦੇ ਨਾਵਾਂ ਦੀ ਸੂਚੀ; ਪੰਚ ਜਿਊਰੀ; ਡਾਕਟਰਾਂ ਦੀ ਟੋਲੀ; ਸੂਚੀ, ਕ੍ਰਮਣਿਕਾ; ਦਲ; ਕਾਠੀ ਕੱਸਣੀ; ਚੌਖਟਾ ਬਣਾਉਣਾ

pang (ਪੈਙ) *n* ਵੇਦਨਾ; ਪੀੜਾ, ਦਰਦ, ਚੀਸ

panic (ਪੈਨਿਕ) *n v* ਅਤੀਅੰਤ ਭੈ, ਦਹਿਸ਼ਤ, ਤ੍ਰਾਸ, ਸੰਤ੍ਰਾਸ, ਆਂਤਕ; ਦਹਿਲਣਾ, ਦਹਿਸ਼ਤ ਵਿਚ ਪੈਣਾ, ਤ੍ਰਾਸ ਵਿਚ ਹੋਣਾ; **~stricken** ਭੈਭੀਤ; **~ky** ਭੈਭੀਤ, ਤ੍ਰਾਸਤ

panorama ('ਪੈਨਅ'ਰਾਮਅ) *n* ਵਿਸ਼ਾਲ-ਦ੍ਰਿਸ਼, ਚਿੱਤਰਾਵਲੀ; ਫਿਰਨ ਵਾਲੀ ਤਸਵੀਰ

pant (ਪੈਂਟ) *n v* ਧੜਕਣ, ਹੌਂਕਣੀ ਹਫਣੀ; ਧੜਕਣਾ, ਸਾਹ ਫੁੱਲਣਾ, ਕਾਮਨਾ ਰੱਖਣੀ

pantaloon (ਪੈਂਟਆ'ਲੂਨ) *n* ਪਤਲੂਨ, ਪੈਂਟ

panther (ਪੈਂਥਅ*) *n* ਚੀਤਾ, ਬਾਘ

pantomime (ਪੈਂਟਅਮਾਇਮ) *n v* ਮੂਕ ਅਭਿਨੈ, ਮੂਕ ਨਾਚ; ਮੂਕ ਅਭਿਨੇਤਾ; ਮੂਕ ਅਭਿਨੈ ਕਰਨਾ; ਮੂਕ ਨਾਚ ਨੱਚਣਾ

pantomimist (ਪੈਂਟਅਮਿਮਿਸਟ) *n* ਮੂਕ ਅਭਿਨੇਤਾ

pantomorphic (ਪੈਂਟਅ'ਮੋਰਫ਼ਿਕ) *a* ਬਹੁਰੂਪੀਆ

pantry (ਪੈਂਟਰਿ) *n* ਪੈਂਟਰੀ, ਭੰਡਾਰ, ਰਸਦਖ਼ਾਨਾ

papa (ਪਅ'ਪਾ) *n* ਪਾਪਾ, ਡਾਡਾ, ਬਾਪੂ

papacy (ਪੇਇਪਅਸਿ) *n* ਪੋਪ-ਪਦ, ਪੋਪ-ਤੰਤਰ, ਪੋਪ-ਪ੍ਣਾਲੀ

paper (ਪੇਇਪਅ*) *n* ਪੱਤਰ; ਕਾਗ਼ਜ਼ੀ, ਧਨ, ਹੁੰਡੀ, ਨੋਟ, ਪ੍ਮਾਣ-ਪੱਤਰ; ਪ੍ਸ਼ਨ ਪੱਤਰ, ਸਮਾਚਾਰ-ਪੱਤਰ; ਨਿਬੰਧ, ਲੇਖ; **~back** ਕਾਗ਼ਜ਼ੀ ਜਿਲਦ ਵਾਲੀ ਪੁਸਤਕ; **~ing** (ਪੁਸਤਕਾ ਆਦਿ ਉੱਤੇ) ਕਾਗ਼ਜ਼ੀ ਮੜ੍ਹਾਈ, ਕਾਗ਼ਜ਼ੀ ਸਜਾਵਟ

pappy (ਪੈਪਿ) *a* ਨਰਮ, ਪਿਲਪਿਲਾ, ਪਿਲ- ਪਿਲ ਕਰਦਾ; ਅਤੀਅੰਤ ਸਿੱਧਾ

par (ਪਾ*) *n* ਸਮਾਨਤਾ, ਬਰਾਬਰੀ, ਸਮਤਾ, ਤੁਲਨਾ; ਬਰਾਬਰ ਮਾਤਰਾ, ਔਸਤ ਪਰਿਣਾਮ ਜਾਂ ਰਾਸ਼ੀ

para (ਪੈਰਅ) *n* ਪੈਰਾ, ਪੈਰਾਗ੍ਰਾਫ

parachute (ਪੈਰਅਸ਼ੂਟ) *n v* ਹਵਾਈ ਛਤਰੀ, ਪੈਰਾਸ਼ੂਟ; ਪੈਰਾਸ਼ੂਟ ਨਾਲ ਉਤਰਨਾ

parade (ਪਅ'ਰੇਇਡ) *n v* ਦਿਖਾਵਾ, ਪਰਦਰਸ਼ਨ; ਕਵਾਇਦ, ਪਰੇਡ; ਸੈਨਾ ਪਰਦਰਸ਼ਨ ਕਰਨਾ, ਆਡੰਬਰ ਦਿਖਾਉਣਾ

paradigm (ਪੈਰਅਡਾਇਮ) *n* ਮਿਸਾਲ; ਨਕਸ਼ਾ, ਨਮੂਨਾ, ਸ਼ਬਦ ਰੂਪਾਵਲੀ

paradise (ਪੈਰਅਡਾਇਸ) *n* ਜੰਨਤ, ਬਹਿਸ਼ਤ, ਸੁਰਗ

paradox (ਪੈਰਅਡੌਕਸ) *n* ਵਿਰੋਧਾਭਾਸ, ਅਸੰਗਤ ਕਥਨ, ਉੱਲਟੀ ਗੱਲ; **~ical** ਵਿਰੋਧਾਭਾਸੀ

paragraph (ਪੈਰਅਗਰਾਫ਼) *n v* ਖੰਡ, ਪੈਰਾ, ਪੈਰਾਗ੍ਰਾਫ; ਪੈਰਾ ਲਿਖਣਾ, ਲੇਖ ਨੂੰ ਪੈਰਿਆਂ ਵਿਚ ਵੰਡਣਾ

parallel (ਪੈਰਅਲੈੱਲ) *n v a* ਅਕਸ਼ਾਂਸ ਰੇਖਾ; ਸਮਾਨਾਂਤਰ, ਤੁਲਨਾ; ਸਦਿੱਸ਼ ਵਿਅਕਤੀ ਜਾਂ ਵਸਤੂ; ਸਮਾਨਾਂਤਰ ਅਵਸਥਾ, ਸਮਾਨਾਂਤਰ ਰੇਖਾ ਜਾਂ ਸਥਿਤੀ; ਤੁਲਨਾ ਸਮਾਨਤਾ; ਸਮਾਨ ਦਿਖਾਉਣਾ, ਤੁਲਨਾ ਕਰਨੀ; ਸਮਾਨਾਂਤਰ ਕਰਨਾ; ਬਰਾਬਰ ਕਰਨਾ, ਮਿਲਾਉਣਾ; ਸਦਿੱਸ਼, ਸਮਾਨ; **~ism** ਸਮਾਨਾਂਤਰਤਵ, ਸਮਾਨਾਂਤਰਤਾ; ਸਮਾਨਾਂਤਰਵਾਦ; ਸਮਾਨਤਾ, ਤੁਲਨਾ, ਬਰਾਬਰੀ

paralyse (ਪੈਰਅਲਾਇਜ਼) *v* ਲਕਵਾ ਮਾਰਨਾ, ਅਧਰੰਗ ਹੋਣਾ; ਗਤੀਹੀਨ ਕਰਨਾ, ਸ਼ਕਤੀਹੀਨ ਕਰਨਾ, ਲੂਲ੍ਹਾ ਲੰਗੜਾ ਬਣਾ ਦੇਣਾ

paralysis (ਪਅ'ਰੈਲਿਸਿਸ) *n* ਲਕਵਾ, ਅਧਰੰਗ; ਅਤੀ ਸ਼ਕਤੀ-ਹੀਨਤਾ

parameter (ਪਅ'ਰੈਮਿਟਅ*) *n* (ਗਣਿ) ਪੈਰਾਮੀਟਰ; ਮਾਪਦੰਡ

paramilitary (ਪੈਰਅ'ਮਿਲਿਟਰਿ) *a* ਅਰਧ-ਸੈਨਕ, ਨੀਮ ਫ਼ੌਜੀ

paramount (ਪੈਰਅਮਾਉਂਟ) *a* ਪਰਮ, ਸਰਬਸ੍ਰੇਸ਼ਠ, ਸਰਬੋਤਮ, ਸਰਬਉੱਚ, ਪ੍ਮੁਖ

paramour (ਪੈਰਅ'ਮੁਅ*) *n* ਯਾਰ, ਧਗੜਾ, ਯਾਰਨੀ, ਆਸ਼ਨਾ

paraphernalia (ਪੈਰਅਫਅ'ਨੇਇਲਯਅ) *n pl* ਨਿੱਕਸੁੱਕ, ਟਿੰਡ-ਫਹੁੜੀ, ਨਿੱਜੀ ਸਾਮਾਨ, ਲੀੜੇ-ਲੱਤੇ; ਸਾਜ਼ੋ-ਸਾਮਾਨ; ਮਸ਼ੀਨ ਦੇ ਕਲ-ਪੁਰਜ਼ੇ

paraphrase (ਪੈਰਅਫਰੇਇਜ਼) *n v* ਸ਼ਬਦਾਰਥ, ਭਾਵ ਅਨੁਵਾਦ; ਟੀਕਾ, ਵਿਆਖਿਆ, ਅਰਥ-ਪ੍ਰਕਾਸ਼; ਭਾਸ਼, ਤਸ਼ਰੀਹ, ਭਾਸ਼ ਲਿਖਣਾ, ਟੀਕਾ ਲਿਖਣਾ, ਵਿਆਖਿਆ ਕਰਨੀ, ਭਾਵ ਪ੍ਰਕਾਸ਼ਤ ਕਰਨਾ; ~r ਵਿਆਖਿਆਕਾਰ, ਅਨੁਵਾਦਕ

parasite (ਪੈਰਅਸਾਇਟ) *n* ਪਰਜੀਵੀ; ਸੁਆਰਥੀ; ਪਿਛਲੱਗ, ਚਾਪਲੂਸ

parathesis (ਪਅ'ਰੈਥਿਸਿਸ) *n* ਸੰਯੋਜਤ, ਏਕਤਾ, ਸਮਾਨਤਾ

parcel (ਪਾਸਲ) *n v adv* ਪੁਲੰਦਾ, ਪੋਟਲੀ, ਅੰਸ਼, ਖੰਡ, ਭਾਗਾ, ਬੁਰਚਾ, ਪਾਰਸਲ; (ਵਪਾਰ) ਮਾਲ ਦਾ ਚਾਲਾਨ, ਮਾਲ ਦੀ ਇਕ ਖੇਪ; ਖੰਡਤ ਕਰਨਾ, ਵੰਡਣਾ; ਪੁਲੰਦਾ ਜਾਂ ਪਾਰਸਲ ਬੰਨ੍ਹਣਾ

pardon (ਪਾਡਨ) *n v* ਖਿਮਾ, ਛੁਟਕਾਰਾ, ਮਾਫ਼ੀ, ਦੋਸ਼-ਮੁਕਤੀ; ਖਿਮਾ ਕਰਨਾ, ਦੋਸ਼-ਮੁਕਤ ਕਰਨਾ

pare (ਪੇਅ*) *v* ਛਾਂਗਣਾ, ਛਾਂਟਣਾ, ਸੁਡੌਲ ਬਣਾਉਣਾ, ਤਰਾਸ਼ਣਾ; ਛਿੱਲਣਾ, ਛਿੱਲ ਲਾਹੁਣੀ, ਕੱਟਣਾ, ਕਤਰਨਾ, ਮੁੱਢਣਾ

parent (ਪੇਅਰੰਟ) *n* ਮਾਂ-ਪਿਉ, ਮਾਂ-ਬਾਪ, ਮਾਤਾ-ਪਿਤਾ, ਪਿਤਰ; ਬਜ਼ੁਰਗ, ਵੱਡ-ਵਡੇਰੇ, ਪੁਰਖੇ; (ਬਨ); ~al ਪਿਤਰੀ, ਪੈਤ੍ਰਿਕ

parenthesis (ਪਅ'ਰੈਂਥਿਸਿਸ) *n* ਉਪਵਾਕ, ਅਪ੍ਧਾਨ ਵਾਕ; ਬ੍ਰੈਕਟਾਂ ਦੁਆਰਾ ਚਿੰਨ੍ਹਿਆ ਸ਼ਬਦ-ਸਮੂਹ; ਛੋਟੀ ਬ੍ਰੈਕਟ (); ਮੱਧਵਰਤੀ ਘਟਨਾ, ਵਕਫ਼ਾ, ਵਿਰਾਮ

par excellence (ਪਾਰ'ਐਕਸਅ'ਲਾਂਸ) (*F*) *adv* ਸ੍ਰੇਸ਼ਠ, ਸਭ ਤੋਂ ਵਧੀਆ, ਪਰਮ ਉਤਕ੍ਰਿਸ਼ਟ

parity (ਪੈਰਅਟਿ) *n* ਬਰਾਬਰੀ, ਤੁਲਨਾ, ਸਮਾਨਤਾ; ਅਨੁਰੂਪਤਾ, ਸਮਾਨਾਂਤਰਤਾ

park (ਪਾਕ) *n v* ਪਾਰਕ, ਉਪਵਣ, ਉਦਿਆਨ; ਵਾੜਾ; ਮੈਦਾਨ; ਪੜਾਉ, ਕੈਂਪ; ਪਾਰਕ ਬਣਾਉਣੀ; ਮੋਟਰ ਖੜੀ ਕਰਨੀ (ਚੌਕ ਆਦਿ ਵਿਚ); ~ing ਗੱਡੀਆਂ ਖੜਾਉਣ ਦਾ ਥਾਂ, ਪਾਰਕਿੰਗ

parlance (ਪਾਲਅੰਸ) *n* ਸੰਵਾਦ, ਸਮਭਾਸ਼ਟ, ਭਾਸ਼ਾ, ਸ਼ਬਦਾਵਲੀ, ਬੋਲ-ਚਾਲ, ਮੁਹਾਵਰਾ

parley (ਪਾਲਿ) *n* (ਵਿਵਾਦੀ ਮਾਮਲਿਆਂ ਨੂੰ ਹਲ ਕਰਨ ਲਈ ਬੁਲਾਇਆ) ਸੰਮੇਲਨ; ਵਾਰਤਾ, ਵਾਰਤਾਲਾਪ, ਬਹਿਸ, ਵਿਵਾਦ

parliament (ਪਾਲਅਮਅੰਟ) *n* ਪਾਰਲੀਮੈਂਟ, ਸੰਸਦ, ਵਿਚਾਰ ਸਭਾ; ~arian ਸੰਸਦੀ ਸੰਸਦਵਾਦੀ; ~ary ਸੰਸਦੀ; ਅਧਿਨਿਯਮਤ ਜਾਂ ਸਥਾਪਤ; ਸੱਭਿਆ, ਸ਼ਿਸ਼ਟ

parlour (ਪਾ*ਲਅ*) *n* ਦੀਵਾਨਖ਼ਾਨਾ, ਬੈਠਕ, ਖ਼ਿਲਵਤਖ਼ਾਨਾ; ਸਥਾਨ

parlous (ਪਾ*ਲਅਸ) *a adv* ਸੰਕਟਪੂਰਨ, ਭਿਅੰਕਰ, ਖ਼ਤਰਨਾਕ; ਕਠਨ, ਕਰੜਾ, ਹੁਸ਼ਿਆਰ

parody (ਪੈਰਅਡਿ) *n v* ਪੈਰੋਡੀ, ਵਿਅੰਗ ਕਾਵਿ, ਨਕਲ, ਸੁਆਂਗ

parrot (ਪੈਰਅਟ) *n v* ਤੋਤਾ, ਸ਼ੁਕ

parson (ਪਾ*ਸਨ) *n* ਪਾਦਰੀ, ਪਰੋਹਤ; ਸਿੱਖਿਅਕ, ਮੁੱਖ ਸਿੱਖਿਅਕ

part (ਪਾ*ਟ) *n v* ਹਿੱਸਾ, ਅੰਗ, ਅੰਸ਼, ਖੰਡ, ਟੁਕੜਾ; (ਅਭਿਨੈ) ਰੋਲ; ਇਲਾਕਾ, ਪ੍ਰਦੇਸ, ਦਲ, ਪੱਖ; ਕਾਂਡ; ਹਿੱਸੇ ਕਰਨਾ; ਵੰਡਣਾ, ਟੁੱਟਣਾ, ਅੱਡ ਕਰਨਾ ਜਾਂ ਹੋਣਾ; ~of speech ਸ਼ਬਦ-ਸ਼੍ਰੇਣੀ; ~ly ਅੰਸ਼ ਰੂਪ ਵਿਚ, ਕੁਝ ਕੁਝ, ਕਿਸੇ ਕਦਰ; ਕੁਝ ਹੱਦ ਤਕ

partake (ਪਾ*ਟੇਇਕ) *v* ਸ਼ਾਮਲ ਹੋਣਾ, ਹਿੱਸਾ ਲੈਣਾ, ਸ਼ਰੀਕ ਹੋਣਾ, ਗ੍ਰਹਿਣ ਕਰਨਾ, ਲੈ ਲੈਣਾ

partial (ਪਾ*ਸ਼ਲ) *n a* (ਸੰਗੀ) ਅੰਸ਼ੁਕ ਸੁਰ; ਤਰਫ਼ਦਾਰ; ਪੱਖਪਾਤੀ; ਅਪੂਰਾ, ਅਪੂਰਨ; ~ity

ਪੱਖ-ਪਾਤ, ਤਰਫ਼ਦਾਰੀ; ਅਨੁਚਿਤ ਲਗਾਓੁ

participant (ਪਾ*ਟਿਸਿਪਅੰਟ) *n* ਭਾਈਵਾਲ, ਸਾਂਝੀਦਾਰ, ਹਿੱਸੇਦਾਰ, ਭਾਗੀ, ਸਹਿਭਾਗੀ

participate (ਪਾ*ਟਿਸਿਪੇਇਟ) *v* ਸ਼ਾਮਲ ਹੋਣਾ, ਭਾਗ ਲੈਣਾ, ਸੰਮਿਲਤ ਹੋਣਾ

participation (ਪਾ*ਟਿਸਿ'ਪੇਇਸ਼ਨ) *n* ਸਾਂਝੇਦਾਰੀ, ਸਹਿਤਗਤਾ, ਸ਼ਮੂਲੀਅਤ, ਸ਼ਿਰਕਤ, ਭਾਗ

particle ('ਪਾ*ਟਿਕਲ) *n* ਕਣ, ਅਣੂ; ਅਲਪਤਮ ਅੰਸ਼, (ਵਿਆ) ਅੰਸ਼ਕ

particular (ਪਅ*ਟਿਕਯੁਲਅ*) *n a* ਬਿਓਰਾ; ਵਿਸ਼ੇਸ਼, ਖ਼ਾਸ, ਵਿਲੱਖਣ, ਅਸਧਾਰਨ; ~ity ਵਿਸ਼ੇਸ਼ਤਾ; ਵਿਸ਼ੇਸ਼ ਕਥਨ, ਵਿਸ਼ੇਸ਼ ਨਿਰਦੇਸ; ਅਸਧਾਰਨਤਾ; ਨਿਰਾਲਾਪਣ

partisan (ਪਾ*ਟਿਜ਼ੈਨ) *n* ਪੱਖਪਾਤੀ, ਤਰਫ਼ਦਾਰੀ; ~ship ਪੱਖਪਾਤ, ਹਿਮਾਇਤ, ਤਰਫ਼ਦਾਰੀ

partition (ਪਾ*ਟਿਸ਼ਨ) *n v* ਬਟਵਾਰਾ, ਵਿਭਾਜਨ, ਵੰਡ, ਭਾਗ, ਖੰਡ; ਵਿਭਾਗ, ਵਿਭਾਗੀਕਰਨ; ਬਟਵਾਰਾ ਕਰਨਾ, ਵਿਭਾਜਨ ਕਰਨਾ, ਵੰਡਣਾ; ~ed ਵਿਭਾਜਤ, ਵਿਭਕਤ, ਵੰਡਿਆ

partner ('ਪਾ*ਟਨਅ*) *n* ਸਾਂਝੀਦਾਰ, ਸਾਥੀ, ਭਾਈਵਾਲ, ਭਾਗੀ, ਹਿੱਸੇਦਾਰ, ਪੱਤੀਦਾਰ; ਜੀਵਨ ਸਾਥੀ; ਜੋੜਾ; ਸੰਗੀ ਬਣਨਾ, ਸਾਥੀ ਹੋਣਾ, ਸਹਿਭਾਗੀ ਬਣਨੀ, ਹੱਥ ਵਟਾਉਣਾ; ~ship ਸਾਂਝ, ਸਹਿਭਾਗਤਾ, ਪੱਤੀਦਾਰੀ, ਸਾਂਝੇਦਾਰੀ

partridge ('ਪਾ*ਟਰਿਜ) *n* ਤਿੱਤਰ

party ('ਪਾ*ਟਿ) *n a* ਗਰੁੱਟ, ਪੱਖ, ਦਲ, ਸੰਘ, ਜੱਥਾ, ਜੁੱਟ, ਮੰਡਲੀ, ਟੋਲੀ, ਪ੍ਰੀਤੀ-ਭੋਜ, ਪਰਵਾਰਕ ਸਮਾਰੋਹ; ਵਾਦੀ, ਪ੍ਰਤੀਵਾਦੀ, ਸਹਾਇਕ, ਅਪਰਾਧ ਸਹਿਕਾਰੀ; ~ism ਦਲਵਾਦ, ਪਾਰਟੀਬਾਜ਼ੀ

pass (ਪਾਸ) *n v* ਸਫਲਤਾ; ਨਾਜ਼ੁਕ ਹਾਲਤ,

ਸੰਕਟਮਈ ਦਸ਼ਾ; ਆਗਿਆ-ਪੱਤਰ, ਪਾਸ, ਵਾਰ, ਚੋਟ, ਸੱਟ; ਅੱਗੇ ਵਧਣਾ, ਟੁਰਨਾ; ਪ੍ਰਚਲਤ ਹੋਣਾ; ਭੇਜਿਆ ਜਾਣਾ; ਪਾਰ ਹੋਣਾ, ਕੱਟੇ ਜਾਣਾ, ਚਲੇ ਜਾਣਾ; ਮਨਜ਼ੂਰ ਹੋਣਾ, ਪਾਸ ਹੋਣਾ; ਨਿਰਣ ਕਰਨਾ; ~able ਲੰਘਣਯੋਗ, ਕੰਮ ਚਲਾਊ; ~ed ਬੀਤ ਚੁਕਿਆ, ਗੁਜ਼ਰਿਆ, ਲੰਘ ਚੁਕਿਆ

passage (ਪੈਸਿਜ) *n* ਲਾਂਘਾ, ਮਾਰਗ; ਰਾਹਦਾਰੀ; ਗੁਜ਼ਰ, ਗਮਨ; ਜਲ-ਯਾਤਰਾ ਦਾ ਭਾੜਾ; (ਬਿੱਲ ਦੀ) ਸਵੀਕ੍ਰਿਤੀ; ਬਰਾਮਦਾ, ਵਰਾਂਡਾ; ਗੁਜ਼ਰਗਾਹ

passenger ('ਪੈਸਿੰਜਅ*) *n* ਪਾਂਧੀ, ਯਾਤਰੀ, ਰਾਹਗੀਰ, ਮੁਸਾਫ਼ਰ

passing ('ਪਾਸਿਙ) *n a adv* ਸਵੀਕਰਨ, ਪਾਸ; ਗਮਨ, ਚਲਣ; ਮੌਤ, ਮਿਰਤੂ; ਅਸਥਾਈ, ਛਿਣ-ਭੰਗਰ; ਬਾਹਰੀ; ਇਤਫ਼ਾਕੀਆ, ਸਰਸਰੀ

passion ('ਪੈਸ਼ਨ) *n v* ਆਵੇਗ, ਮਨੋਵੇਗ, ਗੁੱਸਾ, ਜੋਸ਼, ਰੋਸਾ, ਸੰਤਾਪ; ਤੀਬਰ ਲਾਲਸਾ; ਆਵੇਸ਼, ਕਾਮ-ਉਨਮਾਦ; ਕਾਮ

passive ('ਪੈਸਿਵ) *a n* ਉਦਾਸੀਨ, ਨਿਸ਼ਕਿਰਿਆ; (ਵਿਆ) ਅਕਰਮਕ; ਸਿਥਲ, ਸੁਸਤ

passport ('ਪਾਸਪੋ*ਟ) *n* ਪਾਸਪੋਰਟ, ਪਰਵਾਨਾ, ਰਾਹਦਾਰੀ

past (ਪਾਸਟ) *a prep adv* ਭੂਤ ਕਾਲਕ, ਪੂਰਵ ਕਾਲਕ, ਅਤੀਤ ਕਾਲੀਨ, ਅਤੀਤ, ਵਿਗਤ, ਗਤ, ਪਹਿਲਾ; ਭੂਤ ਕਾਲ, ਪੂਰਵਕਾਲ, ਅਤੀਤ ਕਾਲ; ~master ਉਸਤਾਦ

paste ('ਪੇਇਸਟ) *n v* ਲੇਵੀ, ਲੇਪੀ, ਘੁਲੀ ਹੋਈ ਗੁੰਦ, ਗਾਰਾ; ਲੇਵੀ ਨਾਲ ਚੇਪਣਾ, ਮੜ੍ਹਨਾ, ਢਕਣਾ, (ਅਪ) ਕੁੱਟਣਾ

pasture ('ਪਾਸਚਅ*) *n v* ਚਰਾਗਾਹ, ਚਰਾਂਦ, ਗੋਚਰ; ਚਾਰਾ, ਘਾਹ, ਪੱਠਾ; ਚਾਰਨਾ, ਚਾਰਨ ਲਈ ਲੈ ਜਾਣਾ

patch (ਪੈਚ) *n v* ਟੁਕੜਾ, ਖੰਡ, ਡੂ-ਖੰਡ; ਫਹਿਆ, ਪੱਟੀ, ਪਿਉਂਦ, ਜੋੜ; (ਸਤ੍ਹਾ ਦੇ) ਵੱਡੇ ਦਾਗ਼; ਤਰੁੱਪਣਾ, ਟਾਂਕਾ ਲਾਉਣਾ; ਟਾਂਕਣਾ, ਪਿਉਂਦ ਲਾਉਣੀ; ਜੋੜ ਲਾਉਣਾ; (ਸਤ੍ਹਾ ਉੱਤੇ) ਵੱਡੇ ਵੱਡੇ ਦਾਗ਼ ਦਿਸਣੇ; ਮੁਰੰਮਤ ਕਰਨਾ; ਨਿਪਟਾਉਣਾ, ਨਿਬੇੜਨਾ, (ਝਗੜਾ ਆਦਿ)

path (ਪਾਥ) *n* ਪਾਥ, ਪੰਧ, ਮਾਰਗ, ਰਾਹ, ਰਸਤਾ, ਵਾਟ, ਪਗਡੰਡੀ; ਪੱਧਤੀ

pathetic (ਪਅ'ਥੈਟਿਕ) *n a* ਦਰਦ ਭਰਿਆ, ਕਰੁਣਾਮਈ, ਭਾਵਨਾਪੂਰਨ, ਮਾਰਮਕ, ਹਿਰਦੇ-ਵੇਦਕ, ਅਫ਼ਸੋਸਨਾਕ

patience (ਪੇਇਸ਼ੰਸ) *n* ਸਬਰ, ਧੀਰਜ, ਸ਼ਾਂਤੀ ਠਹਮਲ, ਸਹਿਣਸ਼ੀਲਤਾ, ਸਹਿਣ-ਸ਼ਕਤੀ

patois (ਪੈਟਵਾ) *n* ਲੋਕ-ਬੋਲੀ, ਸਥਾਨਕ ਬੋਲੀ

patriarch (ਪੇਇਟਰਿਆਕ) *n* ਪਿਤਾਮਾ, ਨਾਇਕ ਪਿਤਾ, ਕੁਲਪਤੀ; ਮੁਖੀਆ, ਸਰਦਾਰ; ~y ਪਿਤਰਤੰਤਰ, ਪੈਤ੍ਰਕ ਵਿਵਸਥਾ; ਪਿਤਾ-ਪ੍ਰਧਾਨ-ਤੰਤਰ, ਪੈਤ੍ਰਕ ਸਮਾਜ

patrimony (ਪੈਟਰਿਮਅਨਿ) *n* ਵਿਰਾਸਤ, ਵਿਰਸਾ; ਪੈਤ੍ਰਕ ਸੰਪੱਤੀ; ਪਿਤਰੀ ਧਨ

patriot (ਪੈਟਰਿਅਟ) *n v* ਦੇਸ਼-ਭਗਤ, ਦੇਸ਼-ਬੰਧੂ, ਵਤਨਪਰਸਤ; ~ic ਦੇਸ਼-ਭਗਤੀਪੂਰਨ; ~ism ਦੇਸ਼-ਪ੍ਰੇਮ, ਦੇਸ਼-ਭਗਤੀ

patrol (ਪਅ'ਟਰਅਉਲ) *n* ਪੈਟਰੋਲ, ਗਸ਼ਤ; ਪੁਲੀਸ ਦਾ ਪਹਿਰੇਦਾਰ ਸਿਪਾਹੀ; ਪਹਿਰਾ ਦੇਣਾ, ਗਸ਼ਤ ਕਰਨੀ, ਨਿਗਰਾਨੀ ਕਰਨੀ, ਚੌਕਸ ਰਹਿਣਾ

patron (ਪੇਇਟਰ(ਅ)ਨ) *n* ਸਰਪਰਸਤ, ਵਲੀ, ਰੱਖਿਅਕ; ਪਾਲਣਹਾਰਾ, ਪਾਲਕ; ~age ਸਰਪਰਸਤੀ, ਹਿਮਾਇਤ, ਰੱਖਿਆ, ਪਾਲਣ; ~ize ਆਸਰਾ ਦੇਣਾ, ਸਹਾਇਤਾ ਦੇਣੀ, ਪਾਲਣਾ ਕਰਨੀ, ਸਰਪਰਸਤੀ ਕਰਨਾ, ਉਤਸਾਹਤ ਕਰਨਾ

pattern (ਪੈਟਅ*ਨ) *n* ਨਮੂਨਾ, ਵੰਨਗੀ, ਆਦਰਸ਼; ਆਦਰਸ਼ ਮਨੁੱਖ; ਸ਼ੈਲੀ

paucity (ਪੋਸਅਟਿ) *n* ਥੁੜ੍ਹ, ਕਮੀ, ਘਾਟ, ਕਿੱਲਤ

pauper (ਪੋਪਅ*) *n* ਮੁਥਾਜ, ਕੰਗਾਲ, ਅਨਾਥ, ਭਿਖਮੰਗਾ

pause (ਪੋਜ਼) *n v* ਰੁਕਾਵਟ, ਰੋਕ, ਅਟਕ, ਵਕਫ਼ਾ, ਠਹਿਰਾਉ, ਵਿਰਾਮ; ਅੰਤਰ, ਅੰਤਰਕਾਲ, ਵਿਸ਼ਰਾਮ; ਰੁਕਣਾ, ਠਹਿਰਨਾ, ਅਟਕਣਾ, ਵਕਫ਼ਾ ਦੇਣਾ

pave (ਪੇਇਵ) *v* ਫ਼ਰਸ਼ਬੰਦੀ ਕਰਨੀ, ਫ਼ਰਸ਼ ਬੰਨ੍ਹਣਾ ਜਾਂ ਲਾਉਣਾ, ਫ਼ਰਸ਼ ਤੇ ਪੱਥਰ ਜਾਂ ਇੱਟਾਂ ਜੜਨੀਆਂ, ਖੜੰਜਾ ਲਾਉਣਾ, ਪਧ-ਬੰਧ ਕਰਨਾ; ~ment ਪਟੜੀ, ਪੱਕਾ ਰਾਹ, ਪਗਡੰਡੀ

pavilion (ਪਅ'ਵਿਲਯਅਨ) *n v* ਮੰਡਪ; ਤੰਬੂ, ਖੇਮਾ, ਡੇਰਾ; ਮੰਡਪ ਉਸਾਰਨਾ; ਇਮਾਰਤ ਦੇ ਬਾਹਰ ਸਜਾਵਟ ਕਰਨੀ

paw (ਪੋ) *n v* (ਪਸ਼ੂ ਦਾ) ਪੰਜਾ, ਚੰਗਲ, ਨਹੁੰਦਰਾਂ ਵਾਲਾ ਪੈਰ, ਚਪੇੜ, ਹੱਥ; ਪੰਜਾ ਮਾਰਨਾ

pawn (ਪੋਨ) *n v* ਸ਼ਤਰੰਜ ਦਾ ਪਿਆਦਾ; ਮੁਹਰਾ, ਕੱਠਪੁਤਲੀ; ਅਮਾਨਤ; ਗਹਿਣਾ, ਗਿਰਵੀ, ਧਰੋਹਰ; ਅਮਾਨਤ ਰੱਖਣੀ, ਗਿਰਵੀ ਰੱਖਣਾ; ~broker ਸ਼ਾਹੂਕਾਰ

pay (ਪੇਇ) *v n* ਵੇਤਨ, ਤਨਖ਼ਾਹ ਜਾਂ ਮਜ਼ਦੂਰੀ ਦੇਣੀ; ਅਦਾ ਕਰਨਾ, ਭੁਗਤਾਉਣਾ, ਚੁਕਾਉਣਾ; ~able ਭੁਗਤਾਨਯੋਗ, ਅਦਾਇਗੀ; ~ee ਲੈਣ ਵਾਲਾ, ਭੁਗਤਾਨ ਕਰਤਾ; ~er ਦੇਣ ਵਾਲਾ, ਪ੍ਰਾਪਤ ਕਰਨਾ; ~ing ਲਾਭਦਾਇਕ, ਫ਼ਾਇਦੇਮੰਦ; ~ment ਭੁਗਤਾਨ, ਅਦਾਇਗੀ

pea (ਪੀ) *n* ਮਟਰ

peace (ਪੀਸ) *n* ਅਮਨ, ਸ਼ਾਂਤੀ, ਮੇਲ-ਮਿਲਾਪ, ਜੁੱਧਬੰਦੀ; ਮਿੱਤਰਤਾ, ਸੁਲ੍ਹਾ; ਸਕੂਨ; ~ful ਸ਼ਾਂਤੀ-

ਪਰੇਮੀ, ਸ਼ਾਂਤ, ਸ਼ਾਂਤੀ-ਪੂਰਨ

peach (ਪੀਚ) *n v* ਆੜੂ; ਅਤੀ ਸੁੰਦਰ ਕੁੜੀ;
ਜਾਸੂਸ ਬਣਨਾ, ਮੁਖ਼ਬਰ ਹੋਣਾ; **~er** ਜਾਸੂਸ,
ਮੁਖ਼ਬਰ

peacock (ਪੀਕੌਕ) *n v* ਮੋਰ, ਤਾਊਸ

peahen (ਪੀਹੈਨੑ) *n* ਮੋਰਨੀ

peak (ਪੀਕ) *n* ਚੋਟੀ, ਸਿਖਰ, ਸਿਰਾ, ਕੂਟ, ਪਰਬਤ
ਦੀ ਟੀਸੀ, ਨੋਕ

peanut (ਪੀਨਅੱਟ) *n* ਮੂੰਗਫਲੀ

pear (ਪੇਅ*) *n* ਨਾਸ਼ਪਾਤੀ

pearl (ਪਅ:ਲ) *n* ਮੋਤੀ, ਮਟੀ, ਰਤਨ, ਬਹੁਮੁੱਲਾ
ਪਦਾਰਥ

peasant (ਪੈੱਜ਼ੰਟ) *n* ਕਿਸਾਨ, ਹਲਵਾਹਕ, ਪੇਂਡੂ;
~ry ਕਿਸਾਨੀ, ਕਿਸਾਨ-ਵਰਗ

pebble (ਪੈੱਬਲ) *n* ਠੀਕਰੀ, ਰੋੜਾ, ਕੰਕਰ, ਕੰਕਰੀ,
ਛੋਟਾ ਟੁਕੜਾ

peccable (ਪੈੱਕਅਬਲ) *a* ਪਾਪੀ, ਅਪਰਾਧੀ ਪਾਪ-
ਅਧੀਨ, ਪਾਪ-ਵੱਸ

peculiar (ਪਿ'ਕਯੂਲਿਅ*) *n a* ਵਿਸ਼ੇਸ਼, ਨਿੱਜੀ,
ਵਿਸ਼ੇਸ਼ ਅਧਿਕਾਰ; ਵਿਸ਼ੇਸ਼ ਸੁਵਿਧਾ, ਨਿਜੀ
ਜਾਇਦਾਦ; **~ity** ਵਿਸ਼ੇਸ਼ਤਾ, ਵਿਲੱਖਣਤਾ,
ਅਸਧਾਰਨਤਾ, ਅਨੋਖਾਪਣ

pecuniary (ਪਿ'ਕਯੂਨਯਅਰਿ) *a* ਆਰਥਕ, ਮਾਲੀ,
ਰੁਪਏ ਪੈਸੇ ਦਾ, ਧਨ-ਸਬੰਧੀ, ਆਰਥਕ ਦੰਡ
ਸਬੰਧੀ; ਤਾਵਾਨੀ

pedal (ਪੈਡਲ) *n v a* ਪਦ-ਜੰਤਰ; ਪਾਇਦਾਨ;
ਸਾਈਕਲ ਆਦਿ ਦਾ ਪੈਡਲ; ਵਾਜੇ ਨੂੰ
ਵਜਾਉਣਾ, ਪੈਡਲ ਨੂੰ ਚਲਾਉਣਾ; ਪੈਰ ਦਾ

peddle (ਪੈੱਡਲ) *v* ਘਟੀਆ ਕੰਮਾਂ ਵਿਚ ਰੁੱਝੇ
ਰਹਿਣਾ; ਫੁਟਕਲ ਵੇਚਣਾ, ਫੇਰੀ ਲਾਉਣੀ; ਹੌਲੀ-
ਹੌਲੀ ਵਿਚਾਰ ਪਰਗਟ ਕਰਨਾ

pedestal (ਪੈਡਿਸਟਲ) *n v* ਚੌਕੀ ਆਧਾਰ, ਨੀਂਹ,
ਬੁਨਿਆਦ; ਆਧਾਰਤ ਕਰਨਾ, ਪਾਵੇ ਦੇ ਸਹਾਰੇ
ਟਿਕਾਉਣਾ ਜਾਂ ਸਥਿਰ ਕਰਨਾ, ਬੈਠਣਾ; ਸਹਾਰਾ
ਦੇਣਾ

pedestrian (ਪਿ'ਡੈਸਟਰਿਅਨ) *n a* ਪੈਦਲ
(ਜਾਤਰੀ), ਪਿਆਦਾ (ਵਿਅਕਤੀ)

peel (ਪੀਲ) *n v* ਸਰਹੱਦੀ ਮੀਨਾਰ, ਸੀਮਾ-ਥੰਮੂ,
ਨਾਨਬਾਈ ਦੀ ਕੜਛੀ, ਰੋਟੀ ਵਾਲੇ ਦੀ ਰੱਸੀ;
ਛਿਲਕਾ; ਫਲ ਦਾ ਛਿੱਲੜ ਲਾਹੁਣਾ; ਛਿੱਲਣਾ;
ਉੱਧੇੜਨਾ; ਉੱਧੜਨਾ

peep (ਪੀਪ) *n* ਲੁਕਵੀਂ ਨਜ਼ਰ, ਝਾਤੀ, ਚੋਰ-ਅੱਖ;
'ਚੀ'-'ਚੀ' ਕਰਨਾ, ਚੀਕਣਾ; ਚੋਰ-ਅੱਖ ਨਾਲ
ਵੇਖਣਾ, ਲੁਕ ਕੇ ਵੇਖਣਾ, ਝਾਕਣਾ

peer (ਪਿਅ*) *n v* (ਪਦ, ਸ਼੍ਰੇਣੀ ਆਦਿ ਦੇ ਪੱਖੋਂ)
ਬਰਾਬਰ ਦਾ ਆਦਮੀ; ਕੁਲੀਨ, ਰਈਸ, ਬਰਾਬਰ
ਕਰਨਾ ਜਾਂ ਹੋਣਾ; ਕਿਸੇ ਆਦਮੀ ਨੂੰ ਸੱਭਿਅ
ਸਮਾਜ ਵਿਚ ਸ਼ਾਮਲ ਕਰਨਾ; ਤੱਕਣਾ, ਝਾਕਣਾ,
ਧਿਆਨ ਨਾਲ ਵੇਖਣਾ

peeve (ਪੀਵ) *v* ਦੁਖੀ ਹੋਣਾ, ਉਤੇਜਤ ਕਰਨਾ,
ਸੜਨਾ ਜਾਂ ਸਾੜਨਾ, ਕੁੜ੍ਹਨਾ

peevish (ਪੀਵਿਸ਼) *a* ਖਿਝੂ, ਰੁੱਖਾ, ਚਿੜਚੜਾ

peg (ਪੈੱਗ) *n v* ਮੇਖ, ਕਿੱਲ, ਕਿੱਲੀ, ਖੁੰਟੀ, ਖੁੰਟਾ;
ਸ਼ਰਾਬ ਦਾ ਪਿਆਲਾ, ਪੈੱਗ; ਕਿੱਲ ਨਾਲ ਜੜਨਾ,
ਮੇਖ ਨਾਲ ਜੜਨਾ

pejorate (ਪਿਜੋਰੇਇਟ) *v* ਕਿਸੇ ਨੂੰ ਘਟੀਆ ਸਿੱਧ
ਕਰਨਾ, ਗੁਣ ਘਟਾਉਣਾ, ਦੋਸ਼ਪੂਰਨ ਬਣਾਉਣਾ

pelican (ਪੈੱਲਿਕਨ) *n* ਪੈਲੀਕਨ, ਇਕ ਜਲ-ਪੰਛੀ

pen (ਪੈੱਨ) *n v* ਕਿਲਕ, ਕਲਮ, ਹੋਲਡਰ, ਲੇਖਣੀ,
ਖੰਭ ਦੀ ਕਲਮ, ਪੈੱਨ; ਨਿਬੰਧ, ਲੇਖ, ਰਚਨਾ;
ਰਚਨਾਸ਼ੈਲੀ

penal (ਪੀਨਲ) *a n* ਦੰਡਾਤਮਕ, ਤਾਜ਼ੀਰੀ, ਸਜ਼ਾ

ਪਾਉਣਯੋਗ, ਦੰਡਯੋਗ; ~code ਦੰਡ-ਸੰਹਿਤਾ;
~ize ਦੰਡ ਦੇਣਾ, ਸਜ਼ਾ ਦੇਣੀ; ~ty ਜੁਰਮਾਨਾ,
ਦੰਡ, ਹਰਜਾਨਾ, ਤਾਵਾਨ

penance ('ਪੈੱਨਅੰਸ) *n v* ਪ੍ਰਾਸ਼ਚਤ, ਪਛਤਾਵਾ,
ਪਸ਼ਚਾਤਾਪ; ਆਤਮ-ਨਿਗ੍ਰਹਿ; ਤਪੱਸਿਆ;
ਪ੍ਰਾਸ਼ਚਤ ਕਰਨਾ, ਤਪ ਕਰਨਾ

pencil ('ਪੈੱਸਲ) *n v* ਕੂਚੀ, ਬੁਰਸ਼, ਨੱਕਾਸ਼ੀ,
ਚਿੱਤਰਕਾਰੀ ਦੀ ਸ਼ੈਲੀ, ਚਿੱਤਰਕਾਰਤਾ, ਪੈਨਸਿਲ,
ਰੇਖਾ-ਸੂਚੀ; ਪੈਨਸਿਲ ਨਾਲ ਚਿੰਨ੍ਹਣਾ, ਨਿਸ਼ਾਨ
ਲਾਉਣਾ, ਲਿਖ ਰੱਖਣਾ, ਦਰਜ ਕਰਨਾ

pendant ('ਪੈੱਨਡਅੰਟ) *n a* ਲਮਕਣ ਵਾਲਾ
ਗਹਿਣਾ, ਝੁਮਕੇ, ਕਾਂਟੇ; ਜਹਾਜ਼ ਦਾ ਤਿਕੋਣਾ ਝੰਡਾ

pendent ('ਪੈੱਨਡਅੰਟ) *a* ਲਟਕਦਾ, ਅਗਾਂਹ ਨੂੰ
ਵਧਿਆ, ਅਨਿਸ਼ਚਤ, ਵਿਚਾਰ-ਅਧੀਨ

pending ('ਪੈੱਨਡਿਙ) *a prep* ਲੰਬਤ, ਸਥਗਤ,
ਵਿਚਾਰ-ਅਧੀਨ; ਅਨਿਸ਼ਚਤ, ਅਪੂਰਨ

pendulous ('ਪੈੱਨਡਯੁਲਅਸ) *a* ਝੂਲਦਾ,
ਲਟਕਦਾ, ਅਸਥਿਰ

pendulum ('ਪੈੱਨਡਯੁਲਅਮ) *n* (ਘੜੀ ਜਾਂ
ਕਲਾਕ ਆਦਿ ਦਾ) ਪੈਂਡੂਲਮ, ਲਟਕਣ, ਲੰਗਰ;
ਲਟਕਣ ਵਾਲੀ ਚੀਜ਼

penelope (ਪਅ'ਨੈੱਲਪਿ) *n* ਪਤੀਬਰਤਾ ਇਸਤਰੀ,
ਸਤੀ ਸਵਿਤਰੀ; ਸਤਵੰਤੀ; ਇਕ ਪੰਛੀ

penetrate ('ਪੈੱਨਿਟਰੇਇਟ) *v* ਆਰ-ਪਾਰ ਲੰਘਣਾ,
ਛੇਕਣਾ, ਮੋਰੀ ਕਰਨੀ, ਦਾਖ਼ਲ ਹੋਣਾ, ਪ੍ਰਵੇਸ਼
ਕਰਨਾ, ਵਿੰਨ੍ਹਣਾ, ਘੁੰਮਣਾ, ਰੁੱਤਣਾ

penetrating ('ਪੈੱਨਿ'ਟਰੇਇਟਿਙ) *a* ਭੇਦਕਾਰੀ,
ਭੇਦਕ, ਅੰਤਰਪ੍ਰਵੇਸ਼ੀ, ਤੀਖਣ

penetration ('ਪੈੱਨਿ'ਟਰੇਇਸ਼ਨ) *v* ਪ੍ਰਵੇਸ਼,
ਘੁਮੜਨ, ਭੇਦਕਰਨ; ਬੁੱਧੀ ਦੀ ਤੀਖਣਤਾ

penguin ('ਪੈੱਙਗਵਿਨ) *n* ਪੈਂਗੁਇਨ, ਇਕ

ਸਮੁੰਦਰੀ ਪੰਛੀ

peninsula (ਪਅ'ਨਿਨਸੁਲਅ) *n* ਟਾਪੂਨਮਾ,
ਪ੍ਰਾਇਦੀਪ, ਦੀਪ ਕਲਪ

penitence ('ਪੈੱਨਿਟਅੰਸ) *n* ਪਛਤਾਵਾ, ਪ੍ਰਾਸ਼ਚਤ,
ਪਸ਼ਚਾਤਾਪ

penitent ('ਪੈੱਨਿਟਅੰਟ) *n a* ਪ੍ਰਾਸ਼ਚਤਮਾਨ,
ਪਸ਼ਚਾਤਾਪੀ, ਤੋਬਾ ਕਰਨ ਵਾਲਾ, ਪਛਤਾਉਣ
ਵਾਲਾ

penniless ('ਪੈੱਨਿਲਿਸ) *a* ਮੁਹਾਜ, ਨਦਾਰ,
ਨਿਰਧਨ, ਗ਼ਰੀਬ

pension ('ਪੈੱਨਸ਼ਨ) *n v* ਪੈਨਸ਼ਨ, ਵਜ਼ੀਫ਼ਾ,
ਰੀਟਾਇਰ ਹੋਣ ਪਿੱਛੋਂ ਮਿਲਦੀ ਰਹਿਣ ਵਾਲੀ
ਤਨਖ਼ਾਹ; ਪੈਨਸ਼ਨ ਦੇਣੀ

pensive ('ਪੈੱਸਿਵ੍) *n* ਸੋਚੀਂ-ਡੁੱਬਾ, ਧਿਆਨ-ਮਗਨ;
ਉਦਾਸ, ਗ਼ਾਮਗੀਨ; ~ness ਧਿਆਨ-ਮਗਨਤਾ,
ਉਦਾਸੀ

pentagon ('ਪੈੱਟਅਗਾਅਨ) *n* ਪੰਚਕੋਣ, ਪੰਚਭੁਜ,
ਪੰਚਕੋਨਾ

penury ('ਪੈੱਨਯੁਰਿ) *n* ਨਿਰਧਨਤਾ, ਕੰਗਾਲੀ,
ਤੰਗਦਸਤੀ, ਗ਼ਰੀਬੀ; ਘਾਟਾ, ਕਮੀ, ਥੁੜ੍ਹ

peon (ਪਯੂਨ) *n* ਚਪੜਾਸੀ, ਹਰਕਾਰਾ, ਸਿਪਾਹੀ,
ਸੇਵਾਦਾਰ, ਸੇਵਕ, ਅਰਦਲੀ

people ('ਪੀਪਲ) *n v* ਲੋਕ, ਲੋਕੀਂ, ਜਨ, ਜਨਤਾ,
ਜਨ-ਸਧਾਰਨ, (in *pl*) ਪਰਜਾ; ਆਬਾਦ ਕਰਨਾ;
ਵੱਸਣਾ

pepper ('ਪੈੱਪਅ*) *n* ਕਾਲੀ ਮਿਰਚ, ਗੋਲ ਮਿਰਚ;
ਕੌੜੀ ਚੀਜ਼; ਮਿਰਚਾਂ ਛਿੜਕਣਾ, ਮਿਰਚਾਂ ਪਾਉਣਾ;
~mint ਪੇਪਰਮੈਂਟ; ਪੁਦੀਨਾ

per (ਪਅ:*) *perp* ਤੋਂ, ਦੁਆਰਾ, ਦੀ ਸਹਾਇਤਾ
ਨਾਲ, ਦੇ ਸਾਧਨ ਦੁਆਰਾ; ਪ੍ਰਤੀ, ਫ਼ੀ, ਹਰ ਇਕ

perambulate (ਪਅ'ਰੈਂਬਯੁਲੇਇਟ) *v* ਗਸ਼ਤ

करनी, ਚੱਕਰ ਲਾਉਣਾ, ਗਸ਼ਤ ਲਾਉਣੀ; ਸਫ਼ਰ
ਕਰਨਾ, ਘੁੰਮਣਾ, ਫਿਰਨ ਚੱਲਣਾ, ਪ੍ਰਦੱਖਣਾ
ਕਰਨੀ, ਪਰਿਕਰਮਾ ਕਰਨੀ

perambulation (ਪਅ'ਰੈਬਯੁ'ਲੇਇਸ਼ਨ) *n*
ਗਸ਼ਤ, ਪ੍ਰਦੱਖਣ, ਪਰਿਕਰਮਾ, ਵਿਚਰਣ; ਸਫ਼ਰ

per annum (L) (ਪਅਰ'ਐਨਅਮ) *adv* ਪ੍ਰਤੀ
ਵਰ੍ਹਸ, ਵਾਰਸ਼ਕ

per bearer (ਪਅ'ਬੇਇਰਅ*) *adv* ਦਸਤੀ, ਕਿਸੇ
ਦੇ ਹੱਥੀਂ

perceive (ਪਅ'ਸੀਵ) *v* ਧਿਆਨ ਦੇਣਾ; ਸਮਝਣਾ;
ਅਨੁਭਵ ਕਰਨਾ, ਪ੍ਰਤੱਖ ਗਿਆਨ ਪ੍ਰਾਪਤ ਕਰਨਾ,
ਪ੍ਰਤੀਤ ਕਰਨਾ, ਪਛਾਣਨਾ, ਵਿਚਾਰਨਾ; ~d
ਗਿਆਤ, ਵਿਦਿਤ, ਅਨੁਭੂਤ, ਦੇਖਿਆ ਹੋਇਆ

per cent, per centum (ਪਅ'ਸੈਂਟ, ਪਅ-
'ਸੈਂਟਅਮ) (L) *adv* ਪ੍ਰਤੀ ਸੈਂਕੜਾ, ਫ਼ੀ ਸਦੀ,
ਪ੍ਰਤੀਸ਼ਤ; ~age ਫ਼ੀ ਸਦੀ, ਫ਼ੀ ਸੈਂਕੜਾ, ਪ੍ਰਤੀ
ਸੈਂਕੜਾ, ਪ੍ਰਤੀਸ਼ਤਤਾ

percept ('ਪਅ:ਸੈਂਪਟ) *n* ਪ੍ਰਤੱਖ ਗਿਆਨ,
ਪ੍ਰਤੀਤੀ-ਬੋਧ; ਅਨੁਭੂਤੀ, ਅਨੁਭਵ; ~ible
ਅਨੁਭਵਯੋਗ, ਗ੍ਰਹਿਣ ਕਰਨ ਯੋਗ, ਸਪਸ਼ਟ,
ਵਿਅਕਤ; ਗੋਚਰ; ~ion ਪ੍ਰਤੱਖ ਗਿਆਨ,
ਅਨੁਭੂਤੀ, ਅਨੁਭਵ, ਸੋਝੀ, ਬੋਧ, ਗ੍ਰਹਿਣ-ਸ਼ਕਤੀ,
ਸਹਿਜ-ਅਨੁਭੂਤੀ, ਪ੍ਰਤੀਤੀ

perchance (ਪਅ'ਚਾਂਸ) *adv* (ਪੁ) ਸੰਯੋਗ
ਨਾਲ, ਸਬੱਬੀ, ਇਤਫ਼ਾਕਨ, ਸੰਯੋਗਵੱਸ

pericipient (ਪਅ'ਸਿਪਿਅੰਟ) *n a* ਪ੍ਰਤੱਖ, ਪ੍ਰਤੱਖ
ਬੋਧ (ਰੱਖਣ ਵਾਲਾ), ਪ੍ਰਤੱਖ-ਦਰਸ਼ੀ (ਵਿਅਕਤੀ),
ਪ੍ਰਤੱਖ ਗਿਆਨੀ, ਅਨੁਭਵੀ (ਪੁਰਸ਼), ਸੁਝਵਾਨ,
ਅਨੁਭੂਤੀਸ਼ੀਲ

percolate ('ਪਅ:ਕਅਲੇਇਟ) *v* ਨਿਤਰਨਾ;
ਝਰਨਾ, ਨੁੱਚੜਨਾ, ਰਿਸਣਾ, ਚੋਣਾ, ਨੁਚੜਾਉਣਾ,

ਰਿਸਾਉਣਾ; ਚੁਆਉਣਾ, ਛਾਣਨਾ

perennial (ਪਅ'ਰੈਨਯਅਲ) *n a* ਨਿਰੰਤਰ,
ਲਗਾਤਾਰ ਰਹਿਣ ਵਾਲਾ, ਚਿਰਜੀਵੀ, ਬਾਰਾਂ
ਮਾਸੀ, ਨਿੱਤ

perfect ('ਪਅ:ਫ਼ਿਕਟ, ਪਅ'ਫ਼ੈਕਟ) *n v* ਪੂਰਨ
ਕਾਲ; ਪੂਰਨ, ਸੰਪੂਰਨ, ਸੰਪੰਨ, ਪੂਰਾ, ਭਰਪੂਰ,
ਨਿਪੁੰਨ, ਸਿੱਧ; ਵਾਸਤਵਿਕ, ਸੱਚਾ; ਉੱਤਮ; ਪੂਰਾ
ਕਰਨਾ, ਸੰਪੂਰਨ ਕਰਨਾ; ~ion ਪੂਰਨਤਾ, ਸਿੱਧੀ,
ਸਮਾਪਤੀ, ਸੰਪੰਨਤਾ, ਪੂਰਤੀ, ਪ੍ਰਵੀਨਤਾ,
ਕੌਸ਼ਲਤਾ, ਪਰਿਪੱਕਤਾ; ਪੂਰਨੀਕਰਨ,
ਨਿਰਦੇਸ਼ੀਕਰਨ; ~ly ਪੂਰੇ ਤੌਰ ਤੇ, ਮੁਕੰਮਲ ਤੌਰ
ਤੇ

perfidy ('ਪਅ:ਫ਼ਿਡਿ) *n* ਕਪਟ, ਛਲ, ਧੋਖ,
ਬੇਈਮਾਨੀ, ਵਿਸ਼ਵਾਸਘਾਤ; ਗੱਦਾਰੀ, ਬੇਵਫ਼ਾਈ

perforate ('ਪਅ:ਫ਼ਅਰੇਇਟ) *v* ਛੇਕਣਾ, ਵਿੰਨ੍ਹਣਾ,
ਵਰਮੇ ਨਾਲ ਛੇਕ ਕਰਨਾ, ਮੋਰੀ ਕਰਨੀ, ਰੰਧਰ
ਬਣਾਉਣਾ; ਪਾੜਨਾ, ਘਰ ਬਣਾਉਣਾ, ਰਾਹ
ਬਣਾਉਣਾ; ~d ਛਿਦਰੀ, ਛੇਕਾਂ ਵਾਲਾ, ਛਿਦਕਤ,
ਛੇਕਦਾਰ

perforation ('ਪਅ:ਫ਼ਅ'ਰੇਇਸ਼ਨ) *n* ਸੁਰਾਖਣ,
ਸੁਰਾਖ਼, ਛਿਦਰ, ਛੇਦ, ਛੇਦਨ

perforator ('ਪਅ:ਫ਼ਅਰੇਇਟਅ*) *n* ਵੇਧਕ,
ਛੇਦਕ, ਵਰਮਾ, ਮੋਰੀ ਕਰਨ ਵਾਲਾ ਔਜ਼ਾਰ

perforce (ਪਅ'ਫ਼ੋਸ) *adv* ਬਲ ਪੂਰਵਕ,
ਜਬਰਨ, ਜਬਰਦਸਤੀ; ਮਜਬੂਤੀ ਨਾਲ, ਬੇਵੱਸੀ
ਨਾਲ, ਲਾਚਾਰੀ ਨਾਲ

perform (ਪਅ'ਫ਼ੋਮ) *v* ਪੂਰਨ ਕਰਨਾ, ਪਾਲਣਾ
ਕਰਨੀ, ਤਾਮੀਲ ਕਰਨੀ, ਪੂਰਾ ਕਰਨਾ;
ਨਿਭਾਉਣਾ, ਨਿਰਬਾਹ ਕਰਨਾ; ਅਭਿਨੈ ਕਰਨਾ,
ਕੌਤਕ ਦਿਖਾਉਣਾ, ਕਰਤਬ ਦਿਖਾਉਣਾ; ~ance
ਪੂਰਤੀ, ਪਾਲਣ, ਤਾਮੀਲ; ਨਿਭਾਉ, ਤਕਮੀਲ;

ਕਾਰਜ, ਕਰਤਬ, ਹੁਨਰ; ਕੌਤਕ, ਤਮਾਸ਼ਾ; ਪਰਦਰਸ਼ਨ, ਅਭਿਨੈ, ਅਦਾਕਾਰੀ; ~er ਪੂਰਕ, ਪਾਲਕ; ਕਰਤਾ, ਕੰਮ ਕਰਨ ਵਾਲਾ, ਅਭਿਨੇਤਾ, ਪਰਦਰਸ਼ਕ, ਕਰਤਬੀ

perfume ('ਪਅਃਫ਼ਯੂਮ, ਪਅ'ਫ਼ਯੂਮ) *n v* ਖ਼ੁਸ਼ਬੂ, ਮਹਿਕ, ਅਤਰ, ਸੁਗੰਧੀ; ਸੁਗੰਧਿਤ ਕਰਨ, ਮਹਿਕਾਉਣਾ; ~d ਸੁਗੰਧਿਤ, ਖ਼ੁਸ਼ਬੂਦਾਰ

perfuse (ਪਅ'ਫ਼ਯੂਜ਼) *v* ਛਿੜਕਣਾ, ਤਰੌਂਕਣਾ; ਫੈਲਾਉਣਾ; ਤਰਨਾ

perhaps (ਪਅ'ਹੈਪਸ) *adv* ਖ਼ਬਰੇ, ਸ਼ਾਇਦ; ਸੰਭਵ ਤੌਰ ਤੇ

peril ('ਪੈੱਰੱਅਲ) *n* ਸੰਕਟ, ਖ਼ਤਰਾ, ਜੋਖਮ, ਵਿਪੱਤੀ, ਆਸ਼ੰਕਾ; ਜੋਖੋਂ ਵਿਚ ਪਾਉਣਾ, ਸੰਕਟ ਵਿਚ ਪਾਉਣਾ; ~ous ਸੰਕਟਪੂਰਨ, ਸੰਕਟਮਈ, ਜੋਖਮਮਈ, ਖ਼ਤਰਨਾਕ

period ('ਪਿਅਰਿਅਡ) *n* ਸਮਾਂ, ਅਵਧੀ, ਮੁੰਦਤ, ਦੌਰ, ਜ਼ਮਾਨਾ, ਅਉਧ, ਅਉਧੀ, ਮਿਆਦ; (in *pl*) ਮਾਸਕ ਧਰਮ, ਮਾਹਵਾਰੀ; ਯੁਗ, ਕਾਲ

periphery (ਪਅ'ਰਿਫ਼ਅਰਿ) *n* ਘੇਰ, ਘੇਰਾ, ਪਰਿਧੀ; ਦਾਇਰਾ

perish ('ਪੈਰਿਸ਼) *v n* ਫ਼ਨਾ ਹੋਣਾ, ਨਸ਼ਟ ਕਰਨਾ, ਮਿਟਣਾ, ਮਿਟਾਉਣਾ; ਬਰਬਾਦ ਹੋਣਾ; ਵਿਨਾਸ਼ ਹੋਣਾ; ~able ਨਾਸਵਾਨ (ਵਸਤੂ), ਵਿਕਾਰੀ, ਵਿਗੜਨ ਵਾਲਾ, ਪਤਨਸ਼ੀਲ (ਪਦਾਰਥ ਆਦਿ)

perjure ('ਪਅਃਜਅ*) *v refl* ਝੂਠੀ ਸੁਗੰਧ ਖਾਣੀ, ਝੂਠੀ ਗਵਾਹੀ ਦੇਣੀ, ਹਲਫ਼ ਚੁੱਕਣਾ

perk (ਪਅਃਕ) *n v a* ਉੱਪਰਲੀ ਆਮਦਨੀ, ਤਨਖਾਹ ਤੋਂ ਇਲਾਵਾ ਸਹੂਲਤ, ਭੱਤਾ, ਦਸਤੂਰੀ; ਆਕੜ ਕੇ ਟੁਰਨਾ; ~iness ਆਕੜ; ਜ਼ਿੰਦਾਦਿਲੀ; ~y ਢੀਠ, ਬੇਅਦਬ; ਅਹੰਕਾਰੀ, ਅਭਿਮਾਨੀ

permanence ('ਪਅਃਮ(ਅ)ਨਅੰਸ) *n* ਨਿੱਤਤਾ; ਸਥਾਈਪੁਣਾ, ਸਥਿਰਤਾ; ਟਿਕਾਉਪੁਣਾ, ਪਾਇਦਾਰੀ

permanent ('ਪਅਃਮ(ਅ)ਨਅੰਟ) *a* ਸਥਾਈ, ਸਥਿਰ, ਨਿੱਤ, ਅੱਟਲ, ਚਿਰਸਥਾਈ, ਟਿਕਾਉ, ਪੱਕਾ

permeate ('ਪਅਃਮਿਏਇਟ) *v* ਪ੍ਰਵੇਸ਼ ਕਰਨਾ, ਰਮ ਜਾਣਾ; ਸਮਾਉਣਾ, ਭਰ ਦੇਣਾ

permeation ('ਪਅਃਮਿ'ਏਇਸ਼ਨ) *n* ਫੈਲਾਉ, ਪ੍ਰਸਾਰ, ਵਿਆਪਤੀ; ਰਚਣ

per mensum (ਪਅਃਮੈੱਨਸਅਮ) (*L*) *adv* ਮਾਸਕ, ਪ੍ਰਤੀ ਮਾਸ

permissible (ਪਅਃਮਿਸਅਬਲ) *a* ਉਚਿਤ, ਯੁਕਤ, ਜਾਇਜ਼, ਯੋਗ, ਰਵਾ, ਮੁਨਾਸਬ

permission (ਪਅ*ਮਿਸ਼ਨ) *n* ਆਗਿਆ, ਅਨੁਮਤੀ, ਸਵੀਕ੍ਰਿਤੀ, ਇਜਾਜ਼ਤ, ਰਜਾਮੰਦੀ

permit (ਪਅਃਮਿਟ, ਪਅ'ਮਿਟ) *n v* ਇਜਾਜ਼ਤ, ਆਗਿਆ, ਅਨੁਮਤੀ; ਆਗਿਆ-ਪੱਤਰ, ਇਜਾਜ਼ਤਨਾਮਾ, ਪਰਚੀ, ਪਰਮਟ; ਪਰਵਾਨਾ; ਇਜਾਜ਼ਤ ਦੇਣੀ

permutation ('ਪਅਃਮਿਯੂ'ਟੇਇਸ਼ਨ) *n* ਕ੍ਰਮ-ਪਰਿਵਰਤਨ, ਪਰਿਵਰਤਨ; (ਪ੍ਰ) ਵਸਤੂ ਵਟਾਂਦਰਾ

pernicious (ਪਅ'ਨਿਸ਼ਅਸ) *a* ਘਾਤਕ, ਵਿਨਾਸ਼ੀ, ਨਾਸਕ; ~ness ਵਿਨਾਸ਼ਕਤਾ, ਘਾਤਕਤਾ, ਦੁਸ਼ਟਤਾ

perpendicular ('ਪਅਃਪੈਂ'ਡਿਕਯੂਲ*) *a* ਲੰਬ ਰੂਪ, ਖੜਾ, ਸਰਲ, ਬਿਲਕੁਲ ਸਿੱਧਾ; ਲੰਬ ਮਾਪਕ; ਸਮਕੋਣਕ, ਰੇਖਾ, ਖੜੀ ਰੇਖਾ, ਲੰਬ; ~ity ਲੰਬਰੂਪਤਾ, ਸਮਕੋਣਤਾ, ਖੜ੍ਹਾਪਣ

perpetual (ਪਅਃਪੈੱਚੁਅਲ) *a* ਨਿੱਤ, ਨਿਰੰਤਰ,

ਸਥਾਈ, ਚਿਰਸਥਾਈ, ਚਿਰੋਕਣਾ, ਸਨਾਤਨ, ਸਰਵਕਾਲਕ, ਕ੍ਰਮਬੱਧ

perpetuate (ਪਅ'ਪੈਂਚੁਏਇਟ) *v* ਸਥਾਈ ਬਣਾਉਣਾ, ਚਿਰਸਥਾਈ ਕਰਨਾ, ਕਾਇਮ ਰੱਖਣਾ, ਬਣਾਈ ਰੱਖਣਾ, ਅਮਰ ਕਰਨਾ

perplex (ਪਅ'ਪਲੈੱਕਸ) *v* ਵਿਆਕੁਲ ਕਰਨਾ, ਭਟਕਾਉਣਾ, ਉਲਝਾਉਣਾ, ਹੈਰਾਨ ਕਰਨਾ, (ਵਿਸ਼ੇ ਨੂੰ) ਸੰਦਿਗਧ ਕਰਨਾ, ਔਖਾ ਕਰਨਾ, ਪੇਚੀਦਾ ਬਣਾਉਣਾ; ~ity ਹੈਰਾਨੀ, ਅਸਚਰਜਤਾ, ਉਲਝਣ, ਅੜਾਉਣੀ, ਭਟਕਣ; ਕਠਨਾਈ, ਪੇਚੀਦਾਪਣ; ਵਿਆਕੁਲਤਾ

perquisite (ਪਅਃਕਵਿਜ਼ਿਟ) *n* ਉੱਪਰਲੀ ਆਮਦਨੀ, ਭੱਤਾ, ਦਸਤੂਰੀ, ਬਾਲਾਈ ਆਮਦਨੀ; ਬਖ਼ਸ਼ੀਸ਼, ਇਨਾਮ

perquisition (ਪਅਃਕਵਿ'ਜ਼ਿਸ਼ਨ) *n* ਪ੍ਰੱਛ-ਪੜਤਾਲ, ਗੰਭੀਰ ਪੁੱਛ-ਗਿੱਛ, ਤਫ਼ਤੀਸ਼

persecute (ਪਅਃਸਿਕਯੂਚਟ) *v* (ਵਿਸ਼ੇਸ਼ ਕਰਕੇ ਵਿਰੋਧੀ ਵਿਚਾਰ ਵਾਲਿਆਂ ਨੂੰ) ਕਸ਼ਟ ਦੇਣਾ, ਪੀੜਤ ਕਰਨਾ, ਸਿਤਮ ਕਰਨਾ, ਅਤਿਆਚਾਰ ਕਰਨਾ, ਸਤਾਉਣਾ, ਜ਼ੁਲਮ ਕਰਨਾ; ਤਸੀਹੇ ਦੇਣਾ

persecution (ਪਅਃਸਿ'ਕਯੂਸ਼ਨ) *n* ਅਤਿਆਚਾਰ, ਜ਼ੁਲਮ, ਤੰਗੀ, ਸਖ਼ਤੀ, ਤਸੀਹਾ

perseverance (ਪਅਃਸਿ'ਵਿਅਰਅੰਸ) *n* ਉੱਦਮ, ਅਟਕੱਕ ਪ੍ਰਯਤਨ, ਮਿਹਨਤ; ਦਿੜ੍ਹਤਾ, ਸਾਬਤ ਕਦਮੀ

persevere (ਪਅਃਸਿ'ਵਿਅ*) *v* ਸਾਬਤ ਕਦਮ ਰਹਿਣਾ, ਧੀਰਜ ਕਰਨਾ, ਦ੍ਰਿੜ੍ਹ ਰਹਿਣਾ, ਉੱਦਮਸ਼ੀਲ ਰਹਿਣਾ, ਪੱਕੀ ਲਗਨ ਨਾਲ ਕੰਮ ਕਰਨਾ, ਡਟੇ ਰਹਿਣਾ

persevering (ਪਅਃਸਿ'ਵਿਅਰਿੰਗ) *a* ਦ੍ਰਿੜ੍ਹ, ਉੱਦਮੀ, ਧੀਰਜਵਾਨ, ਧੁਨ ਦਾ ਪੱਕਾ

persist (ਪਅ'ਸਿਸਟ) *v* ਅੱਟਲ ਰਹਿਣਾ, ਅੱਚਲ ਹੋਣਾ, ਸਥਿਰ ਰਹਿਣਾ, ਪੱਕੇ ਰਹਿਣਾ, ਜੰਮ ਕੇ ਰਹਿਣਾ, ਡਟੇ ਰਹਿਣਾ, ਬਣੇ ਰਹਿਣਾ; ~ence ਅੱਟਲਤਾ, ਸਥਿਰਤਾ, ਪਕਿਆਈ, ਹਠ, ਜ਼ਿਦ; ~ent ਅੱਟਲ, ਸਥਿਰ, ਪੱਕਾ, ਹਠੀ, ਜ਼ਿੱਦੀ; ਸਥਾਈ, ਪ੍ਰਯਤਨਸ਼ੀਲ, ਚਿਰਜੀਵੀ

person ('ਪਅਃਸਨ) *n* ਪੁਰਸ਼, ਪੁਰਖ, ਮਨੁੱਖ, ਆਦਮੀ, ਵਿਅਕਤੀ; ~al ਵਿਅਕਤੀਗਤ ਸਮਾਚਾਰ; ਨਿੱਜੀ; ਆਪਣਾ, ਦੇਹੀ; ~ality ਸ਼ਖ਼ਸੀਅਤ, ਵਿਅਕਤਿੱਤਵ; ਮਨੁੱਖਤਵ, ਨਿੱਜੀ ਅਸਤਿੱਤਵ; ਨਿੱਜੀਪਨ, ਆਪਾਪਨ; ~ally ਖ਼ੁਦ, ਆਪ, ਨਿੱਜੀ ਰੂਪ ਵਿਚ, ਜਾਤੀ ਤੌਰ ਤੇ, ਵਿਅਕਤੀਗਤ ਰੂਪ ਵਿਚ; ਬਜਾਤੇ ਖ਼ੁਦ; ~ification ਮਾਨਵੀਕਰਨ, ਪ੍ਰਤੀਬਿੰਬ; ~ify ਮਾਨਵੀਕਰਨ ਕਰਨਾ, ਮੂਰਤੀਕਰਨ ਕਰਨਾ; (ਗੁਣ ਆਦਿ ਦਾ) ਰੂਪਮਾਨ ਹੋਣਾ; ~nel ਕਰਮਚਾਰੀ-ਵਰਗ, ਕਾਰਜ-ਕਰਤਾ ਵਰਗ, ਸੇਵਾ-ਦਲ, ਅਮਲਾ

perspective (ਪਅ'ਸਪੈੱਕਟਿਵ੍) *n a* ਪਰਿਪੇਖ, ਚਿੱਤਰ; ਦ੍ਰਿਸ਼ਟੀਕੋਣ; ਅਵਲੋਕਨ; ਦ੍ਰਿਸ਼ਟੀ-ਸੀਮਾ

perspiration (ਪਅਃਸਪਿ'ਰੇਇਸ਼ਨ) *n* ਪਸੀਨਾ, ਮੁੜ੍ਹਕਾ

perspire (ਪਅ*ਸਪਾਇਅ*) *v* ਮੁੜ੍ਹਕਾ ਆਉਣਾ, ਪਸੀਨਾ ਆਉਣਾ, ਪਸਿੱਜਣਾ

persuade (ਪਅ*ਸਵੇਇਡ) *v* ਪਰੇਰਨਾ, ਮਨਾਉਣਾ, ਰਾਜ਼ੀ ਕਰਨਾ, ਪਰੇਰਤ ਕਰਨਾ; ਉਤੇਜਤ ਕਰਨਾ, ਉਭਾਰਨਾ

persuasion (ਪਅ*ਸਵੇਇਸ਼ਨ) *n* ਪਰੇਰਨਾ, ਪ੍ਰੋਤਸਾਹਨ; ਸੰਪਰਦਾਈ, ਫ਼ਿਰਕਾ, ਵਿਸ਼ਵਾਸ

pertain (ਪਅ*ਟੇਇਨ) *v* ਵਹ ਪੈਣਾ, ਸਬੰਧ

ਰੱਖਣਾ, ਮੇਲ ਹੋਣਾ; ਮਿਲਣਾ, ਉਪਯੁਕਤ ਹੋਣਾ

pertinacious ('ਪਅਃਟਿਨੇਇਸ਼ਅਸ) *a* ਹੱਠੀ, ਜ਼ਿੱਦੀ, ਜ਼ਿੱਦਲ, ਦ੍ਰਿੜ੍ਹ, ਅੜੀਅਲ, ਪੱਕਾ; **~ness** ਹਠ, ਜ਼ਿੱਦ, ਦ੍ਰਿੜ੍ਹਤਾ, ਅੜੀ, ਪਕਿਆਈ

pertinence (ਪਅਃਟਿਨਅੰਸ) *n* ਪ੍ਰਸੰਗਕਤਾ, ਢੁਕਵਾਂਪਣ; ਉਚਿਤਤਾ

pertinent ('ਪਅਃਟਿਨਅੰਟ) *n a* ਸੁਲੱਗ, ਸੰਗਤ, ਸਬੰਧਤ; ਯੋਗ, ਠੀਕ, ਉਚਿਤ, ਢੁਕਵਾਂ

perturb (ਪਅ*ਟਅਃਬ) *v* ਪਰੇਸ਼ਾਨ ਹੋਣਾ; ਗੜੋ-ਮੜੋ ਕਰਨਾ, ਤਰਤੀਬ ਭੰਨਣੀ, ਉਲਟ ਫੇਰ ਕਰਨਾ, ਤਿੱਤਰ-ਬਿੱਤਰ ਕਰਨਾ; ਉਪੱਦਰ ਕਰਨਾ, ਅਰਾਜਕਤਾ ਉਤਪੰਨ ਕਰਨੀ, ਹੁੱਲੜ ਮਚਾਉਣਾ; ਪਰੇਸ਼ਾਨ ਕਰਨਾ, ਬੇਚੈਨ ਕਰਨਾ; **~ed** ਵਿਆਕੁਲ, ਬੇਚੈਨ, ਘਬਰਾਇਆ

pertussis (ਪਅ*ਟਅੱਸਿਸ) *n* ਕਾਲੀ ਖਾਂਸੀ, ਕੁੱਤੇ-ਖੰਘ

perusal (ਪਅ'ਰੂਜ਼ਲ) *n* ਮੁਤਾਲਿਆ, ਪਠਨ, ਪੜ੍ਹਾਈ, ਅਧਿਐਨ; ਨਿਰੀਖਣ, ਪਰਖ, ਪੜਚੋਲ

pervade (ਪਅ'ਵੇਇਡ) *v* ਸਮਾਉਣਾ, ਵਿਆਪਣਾ, ਸੰਚਰਨਾ, ਰਸਣਾ, ਪ੍ਰਸਾਰ ਕਰਨਾ, ਪੱਸਰਨਾ

perverse (ਪਅ'ਵਅਃਸ) *a* ਪਤਿਤ; ਪੁੱਠਾ, ਅਵੱਲਾ, ਅੜੀਅਲ, ਅਮੋੜ, ਜ਼ਿੱਦੀ, ਉਲਟਾ

perversion (ਪਅ'ਵਅਃਮਨ) *n* ਉਲਟ-ਫੇਰ; ਵਿਗਾੜ, ਆਚਾਰ-ਭ੍ਰਿਸ਼ਟਤਾ, ਪਥ-ਭ੍ਰਿਸ਼ਟਤਾ

pervert (ਪਅ'ਵਅਃਟ, 'ਪਅਃਵਅਃਟ) *v n* ਵਿਗਾੜਨਾ, ਪੁੱਠੇ ਰਾਹ ਪਾਉਣਾ; ਵਿਗੜਿਆ ਆਦਮੀ, ਪੁੱਠਾ ਆਦਮੀ, ਪਤਿਤ ਪੁਰਸ਼, ਪਥ-ਭ੍ਰਿਸ਼ਟ ਆਦਮੀ, ਆਚਾਰ-ਭ੍ਰਿਸ਼ਟ ਬੰਦਾ

pessimism ('ਪੈਸਿਮਿਜ਼(ਅ)ਮ) *n* ਨਿਰਾਸ਼ਾਵਾਦ, ਢਹਿੰਦੀ ਕਲਾ, ਨਿਰਾਸਤਾ

pessimist ('ਪੈਸਿਮਿਸਟ) *a* ਨਿਰਾਸ਼ਾਵਾਦੀ,

ਨਿਰਾਸ਼; **~ic** ਨਿਰਾਸ਼ਾਵਾਦੀ, ਦੁਖੀ, ਦੁੱਖਵਾਦੀ

pest (ਪੈੱਸਟ) *n* ਬਲਾ, ਜ਼ਹਿਮਤ; ਵਿਨਾਸ਼ਕਾਰੀ ਕੀੜਾ ਜਾਂ ਕਿਰਮ; **~icide** ਕੀੜੇ ਮਾਰ ਦਵਾਈ; **~iferous** ਦੁਸ਼ਟਕਾਰੀ; ਹਾਨੀਕਾਰਕ; ਘਾਤਕ, ਵਿਨਾਸ਼ਕ, ਦੁਰਾਚਾਰੀ

pet (ਪੈੱਟ) *n a v* ਪਾਲਤੂ ਪਸ਼ੂ, ਪਾਲਿਆ ਜਾਨਵਰ; ਚਿਤਚੜ੍ਹਾਪਣ; ਲਾਡਲਾ, ਲਾਡਲੀ; ਲਾਡ ਲੜਾਉਣਾ, ਲਾਡ ਪਿਆਰ ਕਰਨਾ; **~name** ਲਾਡਲਾ ਨਾਂ

petal ('ਪੈੱਟਲ) *n* ਫੁੱਲ-ਪੱਤੀ, ਪੰਖੜੀ

petition (ਪਅ'ਟਿਸ਼ਨ) *n v* ਅਰਜੀ, ਪ੍ਰਾਰਥਨਾ-ਪੱਤਰ; ਜਾਚਨਾ, ਆਵੇਦਨ; ਉਜਰਦਾਰੀ; ਪ੍ਰਾਰਥਨਾ ਕਰਨੀ, ਦਰਖ਼ਾਸਤ ਦੇਣੀ; **~er** ਪ੍ਰਾਰਥਕ, ਜਾਚਕ, ਉਜਰਦਾਰ

petrify ('ਪੈੱਟਰਿਫ਼ਾਇ) *v* ਪਥਰਾਉਣਾ, ਕਰੜਾ ਕਰਨਾ, ਕਠੋਰ ਕਰਨਾ; ਸੁੰਨ ਹੋ ਜਾਣਾ; (ਅੱਖਾਂ) ਪਥਰਾ ਜਾਣੀਆਂ, ਨਿਰਜੀਵ ਕਰਨਾ, ਅਚੇਤਨ ਹੋਣਾ

petrol ('ਪੈੱਟਰੋਲ) *n* ਪੈਟਰੋਲ, (ਮੋਟਰਾਂ, ਕਾਰਾਂ ਆਦਿ ਵਿਚ ਪਾਉਣ ਵਾਲਾ) ਤੇਲ; **~eum** ਕੱਚਾ ਪੈਟਰੋਲ, ਖਣਿਜ ਤੇਲ, ਮਿੱਟੀ ਦਾ ਤੇਲ

petticoat ('ਪੈੱਟਿਕਅਉਟ) *n* ਪੇਟੀਕੋਟ (ਸਾੜ੍ਹੀ ਹੇਠਲਾ) ਲਹਿੰਗਾ, ਘੱਗਰੀ; (ਬੋਲ) ਔਰਤ, ਜਨਾਨੀ; **~Government** ਜ਼ਨਾਨਾ ਸਰਕਾਰ, ਰੰਨਾਂ ਦੀ ਹਕੂਮਤ, ਰੰਡੀ ਸ਼ਾਸਨ, ਤ੍ਰੀਆ ਰਾਜ

pettines ('ਪੈੱਟਿਨਿਸ) *n* ਤੁੱਛਤਾ, ਅਲਪਤਾ, ਸੰਕੀਰਣਤਾ, ਛੋਟਾਪਣ

pettish ('ਪੈੱਟਿਸ਼) *a* ਚਿੜਚੜਾ, ਖਿਝਿਆ, ਖਿਝੂ, ਤੁਨਕ ਮਿਜ਼ਾਜ; ਹਠੀਲਾ, ਜ਼ਿੱਦੀ

petty ('ਪੈੱਟਿ) *a* ਨਿੱਕਾ, ਛੋਟਾ, ਮਾਮੂਲੀ; ਤੁੱਛ, ਤੰਗਦਿਲ

phallic ('ਫੈਲਿਕ) *a* ਲਿੰਗਰੂਪ, ਲਿੰਗ-ਪੂਜਾ ਸਬੰਧੀ; ~**ism** ਲਿੰਗ-ਪੂਜਾ

phantasm ('ਫੈਂਟੈਜ਼(ਅ)ਮ) *n* ਫ਼ਲਾਵਾ, ਭਰਾਂਤੀ; ਫ਼ਲੇਫ਼ਾ, ਮਿਥਿਆਭਾਸ, ਮਾਇਆ

phantom ('ਫੈਂਟਅਮ) *n* ਬੇਤਾਲ, ਪਿਸ਼ਾਚ; ਪਰੇਤ, ਫ਼ਾਂ, ਫ਼ਾਇਆ, ਭੂਤ-ਪਰੇਤ; ਕਲਪਨਾ; ਮਨੋ ਲੀਲ੍ਹਾ, ਮਾਇਆ

pharmacology ('ਫ਼ਾਮਅ'ਕੌਲਅਜਿ) *n* ਔਸ਼ਧੀ-ਵਿਗਿਆਨ

pharmacist ('ਫ਼ਾਮਅਸਿਸਟ) *n* ਦਵਾ-ਫ਼ਰੋਸ਼

pharmacy ('ਫ਼ਾਮਅਸਿ) *n* ਦਵਾਈ-ਘਰ, ਦਵਾਖ਼ਾਨਾ, ਔਸ਼ਧਾਲਿਆ

phase (ਫ਼ੇਇਜ਼) *n* ਚਰਨ, ਪੱਖ, ਪਹਿਲੂ, ਅਵਸਥਾ

phenomenal (ਫ਼ਅ'ਨੌਮਿਨਲ) *a* ਦ੍ਰਿਸ਼ਟਮਾਨ, ਪ੍ਰਤੱਖ, ਨਜ਼ਰ ਬਾਰੇ; ਜ਼ਾਹਰ ਕੁਦਰਤ ਬਾਰੇ, ਅਨੋਖਾ, ਅਸਚਰਜ, ਅਲੌਕਕ, ਸ਼ਾਨਦਾਰ; ~**ist** ਦ੍ਰਿਸ਼ਟੀ-ਗਿਆਨ, ਪ੍ਰਤੱਖ ਗਿਆਨਵਾਦੀ, ਵਾਦੀ

phenomenology (ਫ਼ਅ'ਨੌਮਿ'ਨੌਲਅਜਿ) *n* (ਸਿੱਖਿਆ) ਘਟਨਾ-ਕਿਰਿਆ-ਵਿਗਿਆਨ

phenomenon (ਫ਼ਅ'ਨੌਮਿਨਅਨ) *n* ਗੋਚਰ ਪਦਾਰਥ, ਪ੍ਰਤੱਖ ਵਸਤੂ; ਘਟਨਾ, ਤੱਥ; ਕ੍ਰਿਸ਼ਮਾ

philanthropist (ਫ਼ਿ'ਲੈਨਥਰਅਪਿਸਟ) *n* ਜਨ-ਹਿਤੈਸ਼ੀ, ਸਮਾਜ-ਸੇਵਕ, ਲੋਕ-ਪਰੇਮੀ, ਪਰਉਪਕਾਰੀ, ਮਾਨਵਪਰੇਮੀ ਵਿਅਕਤੀ

philanthropy (ਫ਼ਿ'ਲੈਨਥਰਅਪਿ) *n* ਲੋਕ-ਹਿੱਤ, ਪਰਉਪਕਾਰ, ਲੋਕ-ਭਲਾਈ; ਮਨੁੱਖ ਜਾਤੀ ਪ੍ਰਤੀ ਭਰਾਤਰੀ ਭਾਵ; ਉਦਾਰਤਾ, ਹਮਦਰਦੀ

philatelic ('ਫ਼ਿਲਅ'ਟੈਲਿਕ) *a* ਟਿਕਟ-ਸੰਗ੍ਰਹਨ ਬਾਰੇ, ਟਿਕਟਾਂ ਇਕੱਠੀਆਂ ਕਰਨ ਸਬੰਧੀ

philologist (ਫ਼ਿ'ਲੌਲਅਜਿਸਟ) *n* ਭਾਸ਼ਾ-ਵਿਗਿਆਨੀ; ਭਾਸ਼ਾ ਸਾਹਿਤ-ਪਰੇਮੀ

philology (ਫ਼ਿ'ਲੌਲਅਜਿ) *n* ਭਾਸ਼ਾ-ਵਿਗਿਆਨ, ਭਾਸ਼ਾ-ਸ਼ਾਸਤਰ; ਭਾਸ਼ਾ-ਤੱਤ; ਵਿੱਦਿਆ ਪਰੇਮ

philosopher (ਫ਼ਿ'ਲੌਸਅਫ਼ਅ*) *n* ਦਾਰਸ਼ਨਕ, ਫ਼ਿਲਸਫ਼ਰ; ਗਿਆਨੀ, ਪੰਡਤ

philosophy (ਫ਼ਿ'ਲੌਸਅਫ਼ਿ) *n* ਫ਼ਲਸਫ਼ਾ, ਦਰਸ਼ਨ, ਫ਼ਿਲਾਸਫ਼ੀ, ਤੱਤ-ਗਿਆਨ

phlegm (ਫ਼ਲੈੱਮ) *n* ਬਲਗਮ, ਖੰਗਾਰ, ਕਫ਼, ਢਿੱਲੜਪੁਣਾ

phobia ('ਫ਼ਅਉਬਿਅ) *n* ਤ੍ਰਾਸ, ਭੈ

phoneme ('ਫ਼ਅਉਨੀਮ) *n* ਧੁਨੀ-ਗ੍ਰਾਮ

phonetic (ਫ਼ਅ'ਨੈੱਟਿਕ) *a* ਧੁਨੀ ਸਬੰਧੀ, ਸ਼੍ਰੁਤੀ; ਧੁਨੀਆਤਮਕ; ~**s** ਧੁਨੀ-ਵਿੱਦਿਆ, ਧੁਨੀ-ਵਿਗਿਆਨ, ਸਵਰ-ਵਿਗਿਆਨ

phonic ('ਫ਼ਅਉਨਿਕ) *a* ਧੁਨੀ ਦਾ; ਧੁਨੀਯੁਕਤ, ਸੁਰ ਸਬੰਧੀ; ਸ਼ਬਦੀ, ਸ਼ਾਬਦਕ

phonogram ('ਫ਼ਅਉਨਅਗਰਾਮ) *n* ਫ਼ੋਨੋਗ੍ਰਾਫ਼ ਨਾਲ ਰਿਕਾਰਡ ਕੀਤੀ ਹੋਈ ਅਵਾਜ਼; ਧੁਨੀ ਅੰਕਟ, ਧੁਨੀ-ਸੰਕੇਤ; ਧੁਨੀ-ਲੇਖ; ਸੰਖਿਪਤ ਰੂਪ ਵਿਚ ਧੁਨੀ-ਚਿੰਨ੍ਹ; ਫ਼ੋਨੇਗ੍ਰਾਮ

photo ('ਫ਼ਅਉਟਅਉ) *n v* ਫ਼ੋਟੋ, ਫ਼ੋਟੋਗ੍ਰਾਫ਼, ਪ੍ਰਕਾਸ਼-ਚਿੱਤਰ, ਆਲੋਕ-ਚਿੱਤਰ, ਅਕਸੀ ਤਸਵੀਰ; ਫ਼ੋਟੋ ਖਿੱਚਣੀ; ~**stat** ਕਿਸੇ ਲਿਖਤ ਦੀ ਫ਼ੋਟੋ ਕਾਪੀ; ~**graph** ਅਕਸੀ ਤਸਵੀਰ, ਫ਼ੋਟੋਗ੍ਰਾਫ਼

phrase (ਫ਼ਰੇਇਜ਼) *n v* ਵਾਕਾਂਸ਼, ਉਕਤੀ, ਕਥਨ; ਬਿਆਨ ਕਰਨਾ, ਵਰਨਣ ਕਰਨਾ, ਕਹਿਣਾ, ਸ਼ਬਦਾਂ ਵਿਚ ਬੀਜਣਾ; ~**less** ਉਕਤੀ-ਰਹਿਤ, ਵਰਨਣ-ਅਤੀਤ; ਅਵਰਨਨੀ

physic ('ਫ਼ਿਜ਼ਿਕ) *n v* ਹਿਕਮਤ, ਡਾਕਟਰੀ, ਵੈਦਗੀ; ਚਿਕਿਤਸਾ ਸ਼ਾਸਤਰ; ਦਵਾਈ, ਔਸ਼ਧੀ ਦਵਾਈ ਦੇਣੀ; ਇਲਾਜ ਕਰਨਾ; ~**ian** ਡਾਕਟਰ,

ਹਕੀਮ, ਵੈਦ; ਚਿਕਿਤਸਕ

physical ('ਫ਼ਿਜ਼ਿਕਲ) *a* ਪਦਾਰਥਕ, ਭੌਤਕ, ਸਥੂਲ, ਜੜੁ, ਸਾਕਾਰ; ਸੰਸਾਰਕ; ਸਰੀਰ-ਸਬੰਧੀ, ਸਰੀਰਕ; ਕੁਦਰਤੀ, ਪ੍ਰਕਿਰਤਕ; ਭੌਤਕ-ਵਿਗਿਆਨ ਸਬੰਧੀ

physicist ('ਫ਼ਿਜ਼ਿਸਿਸਟ) *n* ਭੌਤਕ-ਵਿਗਿਆਨੀ, ਭੌਤਕ-ਵਿਗਿਆਨ-ਸ਼ਾਸਤਰੀ; ਪਦਾਰਥਵਾਦੀ

physics ('ਫ਼ਿਜ਼ਿਕਸ) *n pl* ਭੌਤਕ-ਵਿਗਿਆਨ, ਭੌਤਕੀ-ਪਦਾਰਥ-ਵਿਗਿਆਨ

physiologist (ਫ਼ਿਜ਼ਿ'ਔਲਅਜਿਸਟ) *n* ਸਰੀਰ-ਵਿਗਿਆਨ

physiology (ਫ਼ਿਜ਼ਿ'ਔਲਅਜਿ) *n* ਸਰੀਰ-ਵਿਗਿਆਨ, ਸਰੀਰ-ਕਿਰਿਆ-ਵਿਗਿਆਨ

physique (ਫ਼ਿ'ਜ਼ੀਕ) *n* ਸਰੀਰਕ ਬਣਤਰ, ਕਾਇਆ, ਦੇਹ, ਜੁੱਸਾ

piano, pianoforte (ਪਿ'ਐਨਅਊ, ਪਿ'ਐਨਅ(ਊ)-'ਫ਼ੋਟਿ) *n* ਪਿਆਨੋ, ਇਕ ਸੰਗੀਤਕ ਸਾਜ਼, ਵਾਜਾ

pice (ਪਾਇਸ) *v* ਪੈਸਾ

pick (ਪਿਕ) *v* ਚੁਨਣਾ, ਛਾਂਟਣਾ, ਇਕੱਠ ਕਰਨਾ; ਸਾਫ਼ ਕਰਨਾ; ਪੁੱਟਣਾ, ਟੋਆ ਕੱਢਣਾ; ~**pocket** ਜੇਬ-ਕਤਰਾ

picket ('ਪਿਕਿਟ) *n v* ਪਿਕਟ, ਕੁਮਕ, ਰੱਖਿਆ ਦਲ; ਕੰਮ ਤੇ ਜਾਣ ਤੋਂ ਰੋਕਣ ਵਾਲੇ ਵਿਅਕਤੀ; ਧਰਨਾ ਮਾਰਨਾ, ਰੁਕਾਵਟ ਪਾਉਣੀ; ~**eer** ਪਿਕਟਿੰਗ ਕਰਨ ਵਾਲਾ ਵਿਅਕਤੀ, ਧਰਨਾ ਮਾਰਨ ਵਾਲਾ; ~**ing** ਧਰਨਾ

pickle ('ਪਿਕਲ) *n v* (1) ਅਚਾਰ, ਸਿਰਕਾ; (2) ਸ਼ਰਾਰਤੀ ਮੁੰਡਾ; ਅਚਾਰ ਪਾਉਣਾ

picnic ('ਪਿਕਨਿਕ) *n v* ਪਿਕਨਿਕ, ਸੈਰ-ਸਪਾਟਾ; ਪਿਕਨਿਕ ਕਰਨੀ

pictorial (ਪਿਕ'ਟੋਰਿਅਲ) *a n* ਸਚਿੱਤਰ,

ਚਿੱਤਰਮਈ; ਤਸਵੀਰਾਂ ਵਾਲਾ, ਮੂਰਤਾਂ ਵਾਲਾ

picture ('ਪਿਕਚਅ*) *n v* ਤਸਵੀਰ, ਮੂਰਤ, ਚਿੱਤਰ; ਤਸਵੀਰ ਖਿੱਚਣੀ, ਚਿਤਰਨ ਕਰਨਾ; ~**gallery** ਚਿਤਰਸ਼ਾਲਾ, ਤਸਵੀਰ-ਘਰ; ~**sque** ਚਿੱਤਰਮਈ, ਚਿੱਤਰਵਤ, ਤਸਵੀਰ ਵਾਂਗ, ਸਜੀਵ, ਕੁਦਰਤੀ ਰੂਪ ਵਾਲਾ

pidgin, pigeon ('ਪਿਜੀਨ) *n* (ਬੋਲ) ਕਾਰੋਬਾਰ; ਵਾਸਤਾ; ਦੋ ਭਾਸ਼ਾਵਾਂ ਦਾ ਮਿਸ਼ਰਿਤ ਰੂਪ; ~**English** ਵਿਹਾਰਕ ਅੰਗਰੇਜੀ, ਕਾਰੋਬਾਰੀ ਅੰਗਰੇਜੀ, ਮਿਸ਼ਰਤ ਅੰਗਰੇਜੀ, ਖਿਚੜੀ ਅੰਗਰੇਜੀ

piece (ਪੀਸ) *n v* ਟੁਕੜਾ, ਟੋਟਾ, (ਕਾਗ਼ਜ਼ ਦਾ) ਫ਼ਡਕਾ, ਕਤਰ; ਭੋਂ ਦਾ ਟੋਟਾ, ਅੰਸ਼, ਅੰਗ; ਜੋੜ ਲਾਉਣਾ; ~**meal** ਥੋੜ੍ਹਾ ਥੋੜ੍ਹਾ ਕਰਕੇ, ਥੋਰਾ-ਥੋਰਾ ਕਰਕੇ, ਟੋਟਿਆਂ ਵਿਚ, ਟੁਕੜਿਆਂ ਵਿਚ; ~**work** ਠੇਕੇ ਦਾ ਕੰਮ, ਉਜਰਤੀ ਕੰਮ

pierce ('ਪਿਅ:ਸ) *n a* ਵਿੰਨ੍ਹਣਾ, ਖੋਭਣਾ ਜਾਂ ਖੁਭਣਾ, ਚੋਭਣਾ ਜਾਂ ਚੁੱਭਣਾ

piercing ('ਪਿਅ:ਸਿਙ) *n a* ਵੇਧਨ, ਭੇਦਨ; ਤੀਖਣ, ਵੇਧਕ, ਵੇਧਨਸ਼ੀਲ; ਚੀਕਵੀਂ (ਅਵਾਜ਼); ਘੋਖਵੀਂ (ਨਜ਼ਰ)

pig (ਪਿਗ) *n v* ਸੂਰ; ਸੂਰ ਦਾ ਮਾਸ; ਮੈਲਾ, ਗੰਦਾ (ਮਨੁੱਖ); ਲਾਲਚੀ ਆਦਮੀ, ਲੋਭੀ ਵਿਅਕਤੀ; ਗੰਦੇ ਰਹਿਣਾ, ਸੂਰ ਵਾਂਗ ਰਹਿਣਾ; ~**iron** ਕੱਚਾ ਲੋਹਾ, ਲੋਹੇ ਦਾ ਢੱਲਾ; ~**jump** (ਘੋੜੇ ਦੀ) ਛਲਾਂਗ, ਚੌਕੜੀ; ~**gery** ਸੂਰਖ਼ਾਨਾ, ਸੂਰਾਂ ਦਾ ਵਾੜਾ; ਗੰਦੀ ਥਾਂ, ਕੂੜੇ ਵਾਲੀ ਥਾਂ; ਹੋਛਾਪਣ, ਕਮੀਨਾਪਣ

pigeon ('ਪਿਜੀਨ) *n v* ਕਬੂਤਰ; ਘੁੱਗੂ, ਭੌਂਦੂ, ਲੋੱਲੂ; ਠੱਗਣਾ, ਧੋਖਾ ਦੇਣਾ; ~**hole** ਕੰਧ ਦੀ ਮੋਰੀ ਜਾਂ ਆਲਾ ਜਿਸ ਵਿਚ ਕਬੂਤਰ ਬੈਠ ਜਾਂਦੇ ਹਨ; ਕਾਗ਼ਜ਼ ਆਦਿ ਰੱਖਣ ਲਈ ਬਣਾਏ ਖ਼ਾਨੇ;

~ry ਕਬੂਤਰਖ਼ਾਨਾ, ਕਬੂਤਰਾਂ ਦਾ ਆਲ੍ਹਣਾ

pigmy ('ਪਿਗਮਿ) *n a* ਬੌਣਾ, ਬਹੁਤ ਛੋਟੇ ਕੱਦ ਦਾ; ਥੋੜ੍ਹੀ ਅਕਲ ਵਾਲਾ

pike (ਪਾਇਕ) *n* ਬਰਛੀ, ਭਾਲਾ, ਨੇਜ਼ਾ; (ਪਹਾੜ ਦੀ) ਨੋਕਦਾਰ ਟੀਸੀ; ਚੁੰਗੀ ਘਰ, ਚੁੰਗੀ, ਮਹਿਸੂਲ

pile (ਪਾਇਲ) *n v* (1) ਢੇਰ, ਥਹੀ, ਧਾਕ; (ਬੋਲ) ਬਹੁਤ ਜ਼ਿਆਦਾ ਧਨ; (2) ਕਿੱਲੀ, ਕਿੱਲ, ਕਿੱਲਾ; (3) ਬਵਾਸੀਰ; (4) (ਭੇਡ ਦੀ) ਲੂੰਈ, ਲੂੰ; ਢੇਰ ਲਾਉਣਾ, ਇਕੱਠਾ ਕਰਨਾ; ਭਰਨਾ, ਤੁੰਨਣਾ, ਮੂੰਹੋ ਮੂੰਹ ਭਰਨਾ

pilfer ('ਪਿਲਫ਼ਅ*) *v* ਨਿੱਕੀ-ਮੋਟੀ ਚੋਰੀ ਕਰਨੀ, ਹੇਰਾ ਫੇਰੀ ਕਰਨੀ, ਹੱਥ ਮਾਰਨਾ, ਠੁੰਗ ਲੈਣਾ; ~age ਨਿੱਕੀ-ਮੋਟੀ ਚੋਰੀ

pilgarlic (ਪਿਲ'ਗਾਲਿਕ) *n* ਗੰਜਾ ਸਿਰ, ਰੋਡਾ ਸਿਰ; ਗੰਜਾ ਵਿਅਕਤੀ; ਨਿਰਧਨ ਵਿਅਕਤੀ

pilgrim ('ਪਿਲਗਰਿਮ) *n v* ਯਾਤਰੀ, ਤੀਰਥ-ਯਾਤਰੀ, ਹਾਜੀ, ਜ਼ਿਆਰਤੀ; ਤੀਰਥ-ਯਾਤਰਾ ਕਰਨਾ, ਹੱਜ ਕਰਨਾ; ~age ਤੀਰਥ-ਯਾਤਰਾ; ਜ਼ਿਆਰਤ, ਹੱਜ, ਤੀਰਥ-ਕਰਨਾ

pill (ਪਿਲ) *n v* (ਦਵਾਈ ਦੀ) ਗੋਲੀ; ਕੋੜੀ ਤੇ ਅਸਹਿ ਗੱਲ; ਪੱਤਾ ਕਟਣਾ; ਲੁੱਟਣਾ

pillar ('ਪਿਲਅ*) *n* ਥੰਮ੍ਹ, ਥਮੂਲਾ, ਥੰਮ੍ਹੀ; ਮਦਦਗਾਰ, ਸਹਾਇਕ

pillion ('ਪਿਲਯਅਨ) *n* ਸਾਈਕਲ ਜਾਂ ਮੋਟਰ ਸਾਈਕਲ ਦੀ ਪਿਛਲੀ ਕਾਠੀ

pillow ('ਪਿਲਅਉ) *n v* ਸਿਰ੍ਹਾਣਾ; ਸਹਾਰਾ, ਟੇਕ, ਢੋਹ; ਸਹਾਰਾ ਲੈਣਾ, ਢੋਹ ਲਾਉਣੀ

pilot ('ਪਾਇਲਅਟ) *n v* ਹਵਾਈ ਜਹਾਜ਼ ਦਾ ਚਾਲਕ, ਪਾਇਲਟ; ਜਹਾਜ਼ਰਾਨ

pimp (ਪਿੰਪ) *n v* ਦੱਲਾ, ਦਲਾਲ, ਭੜੂਆ; ਦੱਲਪੁਣਾ ਕਰਨਾ

pimple ('ਪਿੰਪਲ) *n* ਫਿੰਸੀ, ਫੋੜਾ; ਕਿੱਲ, ਮੁਹਾਂਸਾ; ~d ਫੋੜਿਆਂ ਵਾਲਾ, ਮੁਹਾਂਸਿਆਂ ਵਾਲਾ

pin (ਪਿਨ) *n v* ਪਿਨ (ਕਾਗ਼ਜ਼ ਨੱਥੀ ਕਰਨ ਵਾਲਾ), ਸੂਈ, ਕੰਡਾ; ਮੇਖ, ਕਿੱਲ; ~money ਘਰ ਵਾਲੀ ਦਾ ਨਿੱਜੀ ਖ਼ਰਚ, ਜੇਬ-ਖ਼ਰਚ; ~point ਸੁਨਿਸ਼ਚਤ (ਕਰਨਾ), ਠੀਕ ਨਿਸ਼ਾਨ (ਲਾਉਣਾ); ~prick ਚੁਭਵੀਂ ਗੱਲ ਜਾਂ ਕਾਰਵਾਈ

pinch (ਪਿੰਚ) *v n* ਚੁੰਢੀ ਵੱਢਣੀ; (ਭੁੱਖ, ਠੰਢ ਆਦਿ ਦਾ) ਕਸ਼ਟ ਹੋਣਾ; ਦੁੱਖ ਹੋਣਾ, ਔਖਿਆਂ ਕਰਨਾ; (ਜੁੱਤੀ) ਲੱਗਣੀ

pine (ਪਾਇਨ) *v n* ਵਿਆਕੁਲ ਹੋਣਾ, ਝੂਰਨਾ, ਦੁਖੀ ਹੋਣਾ; ਵਿਆਕੁਲਤਾ, ਕਲੇਸ਼, ਦੁੱਖ; ਚੀੜ੍ਹ, ਦਿਆਰ; ~apple ਅਨਾਨਾਸ

pink (ਪਿੰਕ) *n a v* ਗੁਲਾਬੀ ਰੰਗ, ਪਿਆਜ਼ੀ ਰੰਗ; ਗੁਲਾਬੀ, ਪਿਆਜ਼ੀ; ਵਾਰ ਕਰਨਾ, ਸਜਾਉਣਾ, ਅਲੰਕਰਤ ਕਰਨਾ; (ਇੰਜਨ ਦਾ) ਪਟਾਕੇ ਮਾਰਨਾ; ~ing ਖੜਖੜਾਹਟ; ~y ਗੁਲਾਬੀ, ਪਿਆਜ਼ੀ

pinnacle ('ਪਿਨਅਕਲ) *n v* ਬੁਰਜ, ਗੁੰਬਦ; ਸਿਖਰ, ਚੋਟੀ, ਟਿੱਲਾ, ਸਿਰਾ, ਕਲਸ

pioneer ('ਪਾਇਅ'ਨਿਅ*) *n v* ਆਗੂ, ਮੋਢੀ, ਨੇਤਾ, ਸੰਸਥਾਪਕ, ਪ੍ਰਵਰਤਕਾਰ; ਅਗਵਾਈ ਕਰਨੀ, ਰਾਹ ਵਿਖਾਉਣਾ; ਅੱਗੇ ਚਲਣਾ, ਪਹਿਲ ਕਰਨੀ; ਰਾਹ ਸਾਫ਼ ਕਰਨਾ

pious ('ਪਾਇਅਸ) *a* ਧਰਮੀ, ਸਦਾਚਾਰੀ, ਪਵਿੱਤਰ, ਧਰਮਾਤਮਾ, ਨੇਕ; ~ness ਪਵਿੱਤਰਤਾ, ਪੁੰਨਸ਼ੀਲਤਾ, ਭਗਤੀ, ਸਦਾਚਾਰਤਾ

pipe (ਪਾਇਪ) *n v* ਨਾਲ, ਨਲਕੀ, ਨਲਕਾ, ਪਾਈਪ, ਵੰਝਲੀ, ਬੰਸਰੀ; ਹੁੱਕਾ, ਨੜੀ; ~line ਨਲ ਪ੍ਰਬੰਧ, ਪਾਈਪ ਲਾਈਨ

piquancy ('ਪੀਕਅੰਸਿ) *n* ਤੀਖਣਤਾ,

ਚਟਪਟਾਪਨ, ਕਰਾਰਾਪਨ, ਰੋਚਕਤਾ, ਤੇਜੀ

piquant ('ਪੀਕਅੰਟ) a ਰੁਚੀਕਰ, ਸੁਆਦੀ; ਕਰਾਰਾ, ਮਜੇਦਾਰ, ਮਸਾਲੇਦਾਰ, ਚਟਪਟਾ

pique (ਪੀਕ) v n ਖਿਝਾਉਣਾ, ਚਿੜਾਉਣਾ, ਗੁੱਸਾ ਚੜ੍ਹਾਉਣਾ, ਸਤਾਉਣਾ; ਚਿੜ, ਖਿਝ

piracy ('ਪਾਇ(ਅ)ਰਅਸਿ) n ਸਮੁੰਦਰੀ ਡਾਕਾ; ਸਾਹਿਤਕ ਚੋਰੀ

pirate ('ਪਾਇ(ਅ)ਰਅਟ) n v ਸਮੁੰਦਰੀ ਡਾਕੂ, ਲੁਟੇਰਾ; ਸਾਹਿਤਕ ਚੋਰ; ਚੋਰੀ (ਕਿਤਾਬ) ਛਾਪਣੀ, ਡਾਕਾ ਮਾਰਨਾ, ਲੁੱਟ-ਮਾਰ ਕਰਨੀ

pisiculture ('ਪਿਸਿਕਅਲਚਅ*) n ਮੱਛੀ-ਪਾਲਣ

pish (ਪਿਸ਼) v int ਫਿਟਕਾਰਨਾ, ਦੁਰਕਾਰਨਾ, ਛੀ ਛੀ ਕਰਨਾ; ਥੂ ਥੂ, ਛੀ ਛੀ

piss (ਪਿਸ) n v (ਉਪ) ਮੂਤਰ, ਪਿਸ਼ਾਬ, ਮੂਤ; ਪਿਸ਼ਾਬ ਕਰਨਾ, ਮੂਤਰਨਾ

pistol ('ਪਿਸਟਲ) n v ਪਿਸਤੌਲ; ਪਿਸਤੌਲ ਚਲਾਉਣਾ

pit (ਪਿਟ) n v ਟੋਆ, ਖਤਾਨ, ਖੱਡ, ਖਾਈ, ਖੁੰਤੀ; ਛੇਕ, ਮੋਰੀ; ਟੋਆ ਪੁੱਟਣਾ, ਛੇਕ ਕਰਨਾ, ਮੋਰੀ ਕਰਨੀ; ਦਾਗ਼ ਪੈਣਾ; ~**fall** ਜੰਗਲੀ ਜਾਨਵਰਾਂ ਨੂੰ ਫੜਨ ਲਈ ਚੋਰ-ਟੋਆ; ਲੁਕਿਆ ਖ਼ਤਰਾ

pitch (ਪਿਚ) n v (1) ਲੁੱਕ; (2) (ਕ੍ਰਿਕਟ) ਗੇਂਦ ਸੁੱਟਣ ਦਾ ਢੰਗ; ਕ੍ਰਿਕਟ ਦੀਆਂ ਵਿਕਟਾਂ ਦੇ ਵਿਚਕਾਰਲੀ ਥਾਂ; ਤਬੂੰ ਲਾਉਣਾ; ਕੈਂਪ ਲਾਉਣਾ, ਪੜਾਉ ਕਰਨਾ; ਸਥਾਪਤ ਕਰਨਾ, ਕਾਇਮ ਕਰਨਾ, ਨੁਮਾਇਸ਼ ਲਈ ਰੱਖਣਾ; ਲੁੱਕ ਲਾਉਣੀ; ਮੂੰਹ ਭਾਰ ਡਿਗਣਾ; ਭਿਆਨਕ ਹਮਲਾ ਕਰਨਾ; ~**ed** ਸਥਿਰ, ਜੰਮਿਆ, ਪੱਕਾ; ~**ed battle** ਘਮਸਾਨ ਦਾ ਜੁੱਧ, ਘੋਰ ਜੁੱਧ; ~**ed roof** ਢਲਵੀਂ ਛੱਤ

pitcher ('ਪਿਚਅ*) n ਘੜਾ, ਮਟਕਾ, ਝੱਜਰ;

ਕਲਸ ਪੱਤਰ

piteous ('ਪਿਟਿਅਸ) a ਤਰਸਯੋਗ, ਦੁੱਖ ਭਰੀ, ਦਰਦਨਾਕ, ਅਫ਼ਸੋਸਨਾਕ, ਕਰੁਣਾਜਨਕ

pith (ਪਿਥ) n ਗੁੱਦਾ; ਤੱਤ, ਸਾਰ, ਨਿਚੋੜ; ਗਿਰੀ; ਬਲ, ਤਾਕਤ, ਹਿੰਮਤ, ਉਤਸ਼ਾਹ

pitiable ('ਪਿਟਿਅਬਲ) a ਤਰਸਯੋਗ, ਕਰੁਣਾ-ਜਨਕ, ਦਇਆਯੋਗ; ਦੁੱਖ ਭਰਿਆ

pitiful ('ਪਿਟਿਫ਼ੁਲ) a ਦਿਆਲੂ, ਦਇਆਵਾਨ, ਕਿਰਪਾਲੂ, ਰਹਿਮ-ਦਿਲ, ਦਰਦਮੰਦ; ਤਰਸਵਾਨ

pitiless ('ਪਿਟਿਲਿਸ) a ਬੇਤਰਸ, ਨਿਰਦਈ, ਬੇਰਹਿਮ, ਕਠੋਰ-ਚਿੱਤ, ਕਰੜਾ

pity ('ਪਿਟਿ) n v ਤਰਸ, ਰਹਿਮ, ਦਇਆ, ਕਿਰਪਾ, ਹਮਦਰਦੀ; ਹਮਦਰਦੀ ਵਿਖਾਉਣਾ, ਰਹਿਮ ਕਰਨਾ, ਦਇਆ ਕਰਨੀ; ਅਫ਼ਸੋਸ ਕਰਨਾ

pivot (ਪਿਵ੍ਅਟ) n v ਚੂਲ, ਚੂਬੀ, ਧੁਰਾ; ਕਿੱਲੀ (ਜਿਵੇਂ ਚੱਕੀ ਦੀ); ਕੇਂਦਰ-ਬਿੰਦੂ, ਮੂਲ-ਆਧਾਰ, ਮੂਲ ਸਮੱਸਿਆ; ~**al** ਕੇਂਦਰੀ; ਧੁਰੇ ਦਾ; ਮੂਲ ਸਮੱਸਿਆ ਵਾਲਾ

placard ('ਪਲੈਕਾੜ) n v ਫੱਟਾ, ਬੋਰਡ, ਪਲੈਕਾਰਡ; ਇਸ਼ਤਿਹਾਰ, ਐਲਾਨ, ਵਿਗਿਆਪਨ-ਪੱਤਰ; ਇਸ਼ਤਿਹਾਰ ਲਗਾਉਣਾ, ਪਰਚੀ ਵੰਡਣਾ

placate ('ਪਲਅ'ਕੇਇਟ) v ਤਸੱਲੀ ਕਰਾਉਣੀ, ਸੰਤੁਸ਼ਟ ਕਰਨਾ, ਮਨਾ ਲੈਣਾ, ਸ਼ਾਂਤ ਕਰਨਾ

place (ਪਲੇਇਸ) n v ਥਾਂ, ਜਗ੍ਹਾ, ਠਾਹਰ, ਟਿਕਾਣਾ, ਪਿੰਡ, ਸਥਾਨ; ਹੈਸੀਅਤ, ਪਦਵੀ; ਲਾਉਣਾ, ਸਥਾਪਨ ਕਰਨਾ; ਥਾਂ ਦੇਣੀ, ਟਿਕਾਉਣਾ, ਰੱਖਣਾ, ਧਰਨਾ; ਨਿਯੁਕਤ ਕਰਨਾ, ਤਾਇਨਾਤ ਕਰਨਾ; ~**man** ਸਰਕਾਰੀ ਨੌਕਰ; ~**ment** ਸਥਾਪਨਾ; (ਰਾਜ) ਆਸਣ-ਅਵਸਥਾ; ਰੁਜ਼ਗਾਰ ਦਿਵਾਉਣ ਦਾ ਅਮਲ

placid ('ਪਲੈਸਿਡ) a ਸ਼ਾਂਤ, ਗੰਭੀਰ; ~**ity** ਸ਼ਾਂਤੀ,

ਨਿਮਰਤਾ, ਠਰੰਮ੍ਹਾ, ਧੀਰਜ, ਗੰਭੀਰਤਾ

plagiarism ('ਪਲੇਇਜਯਅਰਿਜ਼(ਅ)ਮ) *n* ਸਾਹਿਤ-ਚੋਰੀ, ਵਿਚਾਰ-ਚੋਰੀ

plagiarist ('ਪਲੇਇਜਯਅਰਿਸਟ) *n* ਸਾਹਿਤ-ਚੋਰ; ਵਿਚਾਰ-ਚੋਰ

plagiarize ('ਪਲੇਇਜਯਰਾਇਜ਼) *v* ਕਿਸੇ ਦੀ ਰਚਨਾ ਜਾਂ ਵਿਚਾਰ ਚੁਰਾ ਲੈਣਾ, ਸਾਹਿਤ-ਚੋਰੀ ਕਰਨੀ

plague (ਪਲੇਇਗ) *n* ਪਲੇਗ, ਤਾਊਨ; ਬਿਪਤਾ, ਦੁੱਖ, ਰੱਬੀ ਮਾਰ, ਆਫ਼ਤ

plain (ਪਲੇਇਨ) *a adv n* ਸਾਦਾ, ਸਰਲ, ਆਸਾਨ, ਸਿੱਧਾ-ਸਾਦਾ, ਬੇਰੰਗ, ਬਿਨਾ ਸਜਾਵਟ; ਖਰਾ; ਮਾਮੂਲੀ, ਘਰੇਲੂ; ਮੈਦਾਨੀ ਇਲਾਕਾ, ਮੈਦਾਨ, ਪੱਧਰ; **~spoken** ਖਰੀ ਖਰੀ ਸੁਣਾਉਣ ਵਾਲਾ; **~ness** ਸਾਦਗੀ, ਸਰਲਤਾ, ਸਪਸ਼ਟਤਾ

plaint (ਪਲਇੰਟ) *n* ਅਰਜ਼ੀ-ਦਾਅਵਾ, ਨਾਲਿਸ਼; ਸ਼ਿਕਾਇਤ, ਸ਼ਿਕਵਾ, ਫ਼ਰਿਆਦ; **~iff** ਮੁੱਦਈ, ਦਾਅਵੇਦਾਰ, ਵਾਦੀ

plaintive ('ਪਲੇਇਨਟਿਵ੍) *a* ਸੋਗ ਵਾਲਾ, ਸੋਗਵਾਨ, ਸੋਗਸੂਚਕ, ਮਾਤਮੀ, ਦੁੱਖ ਭਰਿਆ

plan (ਪਲੈਨ) *n v* ਯੋਜਨਾ, ਤਜਵੀਜ਼, ਮਨਸੂਬਾ; ਤਰਤੀਬ, ਵਿਵਸਥਾ, ਨਕਸ਼ਾ; ਖ਼ਾਕਾ, ਢਾਂਚਾ; ਯੋਜਨਾ ਬਣਾਉਣੀ; ਨਕਸ਼ਾ ਬਣਾਉਣਾ; ਢਾਂਚਾ ਤਿਆਰ ਕਰਨਾ; **~ned** ਵਿਉਂਤਬੱਧ, ਯੋਜਨਾਬੱਧ, ਆਯੋਜਤ; **~ner** ਵਿਉਂਤਕਾਰ, ਯੋਜਕ, ਆਯੋਜਕ; **~ning** ਆਯੋਜਨ, ਵਿਉਂਤਬੰਦੀ, ਯੋਜਨਾਬੰਦੀ; ਉਪਾਉ, ਪਰਿਕਲਪਨਾ

plane (ਪਲੇਇਨ)*n v* (1) ਰੰਦਾ; ਤਲ, ਸਤ੍ਹਾ, ਪਟੜੀ; (2) ਫੱਟਾ; (3) ਪੱਧਰ, ਮੈਦਾਨ, ਪੱਧਰਾ ਇਲਾਕਾ; (4) ਹਵਾਈ ਜਹਾਜ਼; ਰੰਦਾ ਫੇਰਨਾ, ਰੰਦੇ ਨਾਲ ਛਿੱਲਣਾ

planet ('ਪਲੈਨਿਟ) *n* ਗ੍ਰਹਿ

plank (ਪਲੈਂਕ) *n v* ਤਖ਼ਤਾ, ਫੱਟਾ, ਪਟੜਾ, ਪਟੜੀ, ਚੌਂਕੀ; ਰਾਜਨੀਤਕ ਯੋਜਨਾ; ਤਖ਼ਤੇ ਲਾਉਣੇ

plant (ਪਲਾਂਟ) *n v* (1) ਬੂਟਾ, ਪੌਦਾ; (2) ਮਸ਼ੀਨ; (3) ਕਾਰਖ਼ਾਨਾ; (4) ਫ਼ਰੇਬ; ਸਾਜਸ਼; ਬੂਟਾ ਲਾਉਣਾ, ਬੀਜਣਾ; **~ation** ਫ਼ਾਰਮ; ਖੇਤੀ; ਬਸਤੀ, ਚੱਕ, ਆਬਾਦੀ; **~er** ਹਲਵਾਹ, ਕਿਰਸਾਣ, ਕਾਸ਼ਤਕਾਰ; ਮਾਲੀ; **~ing** ਪੌਦਾ ਲਾਉਣ ਦਾ ਕਾਰਜ, ਖਿਜਾਈ; ਬਗ਼ੀਚਾ, ਬਾਗ਼, ਖੇਤੀ

plaster ('ਪਲਾਸਟਅ*) *n v* ਲੇਪ, ਪਲਸਤਰ, ਲੇਅ, ਪੋਚਾ; ਗੋਹਾ-ਮਿੱਟੀ; ਲੇਪ ਕਰਨਾ, ਪਲਸਤਰ ਲਾਉਣਾ

plate (ਪਲੇਇਟ) *n v* ਤਖ਼ਤੀ, ਤਖ਼ਤਾ; (ਧਾਤ ਦੀ) ਪੱਤਰੀ, ਚਾਦਰ, ਧਾਤ ਦੇ ਭਾਂਡੇ; ਤਸ਼ਤਰੀ, ਥਾਲੀ, ਰਕਾਬੀ, ਪਲੇਟ; ਛੱਤ ਜਾਂ ਸ਼ਤੀਰ; ਪੱਤਰਾ ਚਾੜ੍ਹਨਾ, ਸੋਨੇ ਚਾਂਦੀ ਦਾ ਪਾਣੀ ਫੇਰਨਾ

plateau ('ਪਲੈਟਅਉ) *n* ਪੱਬੀ, ਪਠਾਰ

platform ('ਪਲੈਟਫ਼ੋ:ਮ) *n* (ਰੇਲ ਦਾ) ਪਲੇਟ-ਫ਼ਾਰਮ; ਥੜ੍ਹਾ, ਚਬੂਤਰਾ, ਚੌਂਤਰਾ, ਰੰਗਮੰਚ, ਸਭਾ-ਮੰਚ, ਮੰਚ; ਆਸਣ

platoon (ਪਅਲ'ਟੂਨ) *n* (ਇਤਿ) ਪੈਦਲ ਫ਼ੌਜ ਦੀ ਛੋਟੀ ਟੁਕੜੀ, ਪਲਟਨ

platter ('ਪਲੈਟਅ*) *n* ਥਾਲੀ, ਤਸ਼ਤਰੀ, ਪਲੇਟ; ਕਠੌਤੀ, ਕਠਾਰੀ; ਪ੍ਰਾਤ

plausible ('ਪਲੋਜ਼ਿਬਲ) *a* ਨਿਆਇਸੰਗਤ, ਯੁਕਤੀਸੰਗਤ, ਤਰਕਸ਼ੀਲ; ਸਪਸ਼ਟਵਾਦੀ, ਸਤਿਵਾਦੀ

play (ਪਲੇਇ) *n* ਖੇਡ, ਤਮਾਸ਼ਾ, ਸ਼ੁਗਲ, ਮਜ਼ਾਕ, ਦਿਲਲਗੀ; ਨਾਟਕ, ਡਰਾਮਾ, ਖੇਡ-ਤਮਾਸ਼ਾ; ਖੇਡਣਾ; ਉਛਲਣਾ, ਫੁਦਕਣਾ; ਕਲੋਲ ਕਰਨਾ;

(ਕਿਸੇ ਨਾਲ) ਚਾਲ ਚੱਲਣਾ; ਰੰਗ ਰਲੀਆਂ ਮਨਾਉਣਾ, ਆਨੰਦ ਮਨਾਉਣਾ; ਨਾਟਕ ਵਿਚ ਭਾਗ ਲੈਣਾ, ਅਭਿਨੇ ਕਰਨਾ; **~boy** ਅੱਯਾਸ਼ੀ ਬੰਦਾ (ਵਿਸ਼ੇਸ ਕਰਕੇ ਨੌਜਵਾਨ), ਐਸ਼ੀ-ਪੱਠਾ; **~ful** ਖਿਡਾਰੂ, ਚੰਚਲ, ਸ਼ੁਗਲੀ, ਹਸਮੁਖ, ਜ਼ਿੰਦਾਦਿਲ; ਰੌਣਕੀ; **~ground** ਖੇਡ ਦਾ ਮੈਦਾਨ; **~house** ਰੰਗਸ਼ਾਲਾ, ਤਮਾਸ਼ਾਘਰ; **~mate** ਸਾਥੀ, ਜੋੜੀਦਾਰ, ਆੜੀ; ਲੰਗੋਟੀਆ ਯਾਰ; **~wright** ਨਾਟਕਕਾਰ; **~fullness** ਖਿਡਾਰੂਪਣ; ਚੰਚਲਤਾ, ਮੌਜ-ਮੇਲਾ, ਦਿਲਲਗੀ, ਮਖੌਲ

player ('ਪਲੇਇਅ*) *n* ਖਿਡਾਰੀ; ਜੁਆਰੀਆ; ਗਾਇਕ; ਅਭਿਨੇਤਾ

plaza ('ਪਲਾਜ਼ਾ) *n* ਬਜ਼ਾਰ ਦਾ ਚੌਕ, ਜਨ-ਸਥਾਨ

plea (ਪਲੀ) *n* ਦਲੀਲ, ਤਰਕ; ਜਵਾਬ-ਦੇਹੀ, ਪ੍ਰਤੀਵਾਦ, ਪ੍ਰਤੀਕਥਨ

plead (ਪਲੀਡ) *v* ਦਲੀਲ ਪੇਸ਼ ਕਰਨੀ, ਤਰਕ ਕਰਨਾ; ਵਕਾਲਤ ਕਰਨੀ; **~er** ਵਕੀਲ, ਪਲੀਡਰ; **~ing** ਸਫ਼ਾਈ, ਬਚਾਉ ਲਈ ਬਿਆਨ, ਪੱਖ ਦਾ ਸਮਰਥਨ

pleasant ('ਪਲੈਜ਼ਅੰਟ) *a* ਸੁਹਾਵਣਾ, ਰਮਣੀਕ, ਮਨੋਹਰ, ਸੁਖਦਾਈ, ਮਜ਼ੇਦਾਰ; **~ry** ਹਾਸਵਿਨੋਦ, ਵਿਨੋਦਸ਼ੀਲਤਾ; ਠੱਠਾ, ਦਿਲਲਗੀ, ਹਾਸਾ, ਮਖੌਲ; ਵਿਅੰਗ

please (ਪਲੀਜ਼) *v adv* ਸੰਤੁਸ਼ਟ ਕਰਨਾ, ਤ੍ਰਿਪਤ ਕਰਨਾ; ਖ਼ੁਸ਼ ਕਰਨਾ, ਪ੍ਰਸੰਨ ਕਰਨਾ ਜਾਂ ਹੋਣਾ; ਕਿਰਪਾ ਕਰਕੇ, ਕਿਰਪਾਪੂਰਵਕ; **~d** ਖ਼ੁਸ਼, ਪ੍ਰਸੰਨ, ਤ੍ਰਿਪਤ, ਸੰਤੁਸ਼ਟ, ਆਨੰਦਤ

pleasing ('ਪਲੀਜ਼ਿੰਗ) *a* ਸੁਹਾਵਣਾ, ਸੁਖਦਾਈ, ਮਨੋਹਰ, ਆਨੰਦਦਾਇਕ

pleasurable ('ਪਲੈਯ਼ਿ(ਅ)ਰਅਬਲ) *a* ਸੁਖਦਾਈ, ਆਨੰਦਦਾਇਕ, ਸੁਖਾਵਾਂ

pleasure ('ਪਲੈਯ਼ਅ*) *n* ਖ਼ੁਸ਼ੀ, ਆਨੰਦ, ਪ੍ਰਸੰਨਤਾ, ਤ੍ਰਿਪਤੀ, ਸੁਖ, ਮਜ਼ਾ; ਮੌਜ-ਮੇਲਾ

plebiscite ('ਪਲੈਬਿਸਿਟ) *n* ਲੋਕ-ਮੰਤ, ਜਨ-ਮੰਤ, ਜਨਤਾ ਦੀ ਰਾਇ, ਜਨ-ਮੰਤ-ਸੰਗ੍ਰਹ

pledge (ਪਲੈੱਜ) *n v* ਪ੍ਰਤਿਗਿਆ, ਪ੍ਰਣ, ਸਹੁੰ, ਵਾਅਦਾ, ਇਕਰਾਰ, ਵਚਨ; ਪ੍ਰਤਿਗਿਆ ਕਰਨੀ, ਪ੍ਰਣ ਕਰਨਾ; **~d** ਵਚਨਬੱਧ

plenary ('ਪਲੀਨਅਰਿ) *a* ਪੂਰਾ, ਸਮੁੱਚਾ, ਕੁੱਲ, ਸਾਰਾ, ਸਗਲਾ, ਅਖਿਲ

plenty ('ਪਲੈਂਟਿ) *n adv* ਬਹੁਤਾਤ, ਬਹੁਲਤਾ, ਅਧਿਕਤਾ, ਭਰਮਾਰ, ਪ੍ਰਫੁੱਲਤਾ; ਬਿਲਕੁਲ, ਕਾਫ਼ੀ

pliable, pliant ('ਪਲਾਇਬਲ, 'ਪਲਾਇਅੰਟ) *a* ਨਰਮ, ਲਚਕਦਾਰ, ਲਿਫਵਾਂ

plight (ਪਲਾਇਟ) *n v* ਦੁਰਦਸ਼ਾ, ਦੁਰਗਤੀ, ਦਸ਼ਾ, ਅਵਸਥਾ, ਸਥਿਤੀ; ਵਚਨ, ਪ੍ਰਣ; ਪ੍ਰਤਿਗਿਆ ਕਰਨੀ, ਵਚਨ ਦੇਣਾ; ਕਿਸੇ ਨਾਲ ਸਾਕ ਕਰਨਾ

plot (ਪਲੌਟ) *n v* (1) ਜ਼ਮੀਨ ਜਾ ਟੁਕੜਾ, ਕਿਆਰਾ, ਪਲਾਟ; (2) (ਨਾਟਕ ਆਦਿ ਦਾ) ਕਥਾਨਕ; (3) ਛਲ, ਸਾਜ਼ਸ਼, ਗੁਪਤ ਯੋਜਨਾ; ਸਾਜ਼ਸ਼ ਕਰਨੀ, ਸਾਜ਼-ਬਾਜ਼ ਕਰਨੀ; ਖ਼ਾਕਾ ਖਿੱਚਣਾ, ਰੂਪ-ਰੇਖਾ ਬਣਾਉਣੀ

plough (ਪਲਾਉ) *n v* ਹਲ; ਵਾਹਨ, ਵਾਹੀ ਹੋਈ ਭੋਂ; ਹਲ ਵਾਹੁਣਾ; **~man** ਹਾਲੀ, ਹਲਵਾਹ

ploy (ਪਲੋਇ) *n* (ਬੋਲ) ਕੰਮ, ਕਾਰਜ, ਧੰਦਾ; ਪੇਸ਼ਾ, ਕਿਰਤ; ਮੁਹਿਮ

pluck (ਪਲਅੱਕ) *v n* ਤੋੜਨਾ (ਫੁੱਲ ਆਦਿ), ਮਰੋੜਨਾ, ਖੋਹਣਾ, ਨੋਚਣਾ, ਝਪਟਣਾ, ਖਿੱਚਣਾ; ਜਿਗਰਾ, ਹੌਸਲਾ, ਕਲੇਜੀ

plug (ਪਲਅੱਗ) *n v* ਡੱਟਾ, ਗੱਟਾ, ਡਾਟ, ਘੁੰਡਾ; ਕਾਗ; ਮਸ਼ੀਨ ਦਾ ਪਲੱਗ; ਡੱਟਾ ਦੇਣਾ, ਡਾਟ ਲਾਉਣੀ

plumber (ਪਲਅੱਮਅ*) *n* ਨਲਸਾਜ਼; ਨਲਕੇ ਲਾਉਣ ਵਾਲਾ; ~y ਨਲਕੇ ਨਾਲਾਂ ਆਦਿ ਫਿਟ ਕਰਨ ਦਾ ਕੰਮ

plump (ਪਲਅੱਪ) *n a adv v* ਦਸਤਾ, ਜੱਥਾ; ਸਮੂਹ, ਦਲ, ਮੋਟਾ-ਤਾਜ਼ਾ, ਗੁਦਗੁਦਾ, ਰਿਸ਼ਟ-ਪੁਸ਼ਟ; ਸਪਸ਼ਟਤਾ ਨਾਲ, ਖਰੇ ਢੰਗ ਨਾਲ; ਧਰੰਮ ਡਿਗਣਾ, ਕੁੱਟਣਾ, ਗੋਤਾ ਲਾਉਣਾ; ਫੁਲਾਉਣਾ, ਤਕੜਾ ਕਰਨਾ

plunder (ਪਲਅੰਡ੍ਅ*) *n* ਲੁੱਟ ਦਾ ਮਾਲ, ਲੁੱਟਮਾਰ ਕਰਨੀ; ~er ਡਾਕੂ, ਲੁਟੇਰਾ, ਅਪਹਰਣ-ਕਰਤਾ

plunge (ਪਲਅੱਜ) *v n* ਡੁਬਕੀ ਮਾਰਨੀ, ਡੋਬਣਾ, ਗੋਤਾ ਦੇਣਾ; ਛਾਲ; ਔਖਾ ਕੰਮ

plural (ਪਲੂਅਰ(ਅ)ਲ) *a n* ਬਹੁਵਚਨ, ਅਨੇਕ; ~ity ਬਹੁਲਤਾ, ਅਧਿਕਤਾ, ਅਨੇਕਤਾ; ਬਹੁਤ ਜ਼ਿਆਦਾ ਗਿਣਤੀ

plus (ਪਲੱਸ) *prep n a* ਜਮ੍ਹਾਂ, ਜੋੜ ਕੇ, ਅਤੇ, ਨਾਲੇ, ਹੋਰ; ਵਾਧੂ; ਜੋੜ ਦਾ ਨਿਸ਼ਾਨ (+)

pluto (ਪਲੂਟਅਉ) *n* ਕੁਬੇਰ, ਯਮ, ਪਲੂਟੋ, ਨਰਕ ਦਾ ਦੇਵਤਾ; ~cracy ਪੂੰਜੀਪਤੀ ਰਾਜ; ਸਾਮੰਤ-ਵਰਗ, ਸ਼ਾਸਕ-ਵਰਗ, ਅਮੀਰਾਂ ਦਾ ਰਾਜ, ਧਨਾਢ ਤੰਤਰ; ~crat ਕੁਬੇਰ, ਸਾਮੰਤ, ਮਹਾਜਨ; ਧਨਾਢ, ਧਨਾਢ ਸ਼ਾਸਕ

ply (ਪਲਾਇ) *n v* (ਕੱਪੜੇ ਦੀ) ਤਹਿ, ਪਰਤ, ਮੁਟਾਈ; ਝੁਕਾਉ; ਚਲਾਉਣਾ (ਹਥਿਆਰ ਆਦਿ) ਲਗਾਤਾਰ ਵਰਤਣਾ, ਵਰਤੋਂ ਵਿਚ ਲਿਆਉਣਾ, ਕਾਰਜ ਕਰਨਾ

pocket (ਪਅਕਿਟ) *n v* ਜੇਬ, ਖੀਸਾ, ਬੋਝਾ; ਥੈਲੀ, ਗੁਥਲੀ, ਝੋਲਾ; ਆਮਦਨੀ, ਆਰਥਕ ਸਾਧਨ; ਹੜੱਪ ਕਰਨਾ, ਹਜ਼ਮ ਕਰ ਜਾਣਾ; (ਵਧੀਕੀ, ਬੇਇੱਜ਼ਤੀ ਆਦਿ) ਸਹਾਰ ਜਾਣਾ; ~book ਜੇਬੀ ਕਿਤਾਬ, ਛੋਟੇ ਆਕਾਰ ਦੀ ਕਿਤਾਬ, ਗੁਟਕਾ; ~money ਜੇਬ ਖ਼ਰਚ

podex (ਪਅਉਡਿਕਸ) *n* (ਸਰੀਰ ਦਾ) ਪਿਛਲਾ ਹਿੱਸਾ; ਚੂਤੜ, ਚੂਈ; ਗੁਦਾ

podium (ਪਅਉਡਿਅਮ) *n* ਮੰਚ, ਚਬੂਤਰਾ

poem (ਪਅਉਇਮ) *n* ਕਵਿਤਾ, ਕਾਵਿ-ਰਚਨਾ, ਪਦ, ਛੰਦ-ਬਧ ਰਚਨਾ

poesy (ਪਅਉਇਜ਼ਿ) *n* (ਪੁ) ਕਾਵਿ-ਕਲਾ, ਕਾਵਿ-ਰਚਨਾ, ਛੰਦ-ਰਚਨਾ; ਕਾਵਿ-ਸੰਗ੍ਰਹ

poet (ਪਅਉਇਟ) *n* ਕਵੀ, ਸ਼ਾਇਰ, ਛੰਦਕਾਰ, ਗੀਤਕਾਰ; ~aster ਤੁਕਬੰਦ, ਕਵੀਸ਼ਰ, ਘਟੀਆ ਸ਼ਾਇਰ; ~ess ਕਵਿਤਰੀ; ~ic, ~ical ਕਾਵਿਕ, ਕਾਵਿਮਈ, ਕਾਵਿ-ਆਤਮਕ; ~ics ਕਾਵਿ-ਸ਼ਾਸਤਰ, ਛੰਦ-ਸ਼ਾਸਤਰ, ਅੱਲਕਾਰ-ਸ਼ਾਸਤਰ, ਅੱਲਕਾਰ-ਸ਼ਾਸਤਰ, ਕਾਵਿ-ਵਿੰਦਿਆ, ਰੀਤੀ-ਸ਼ਾਸਤਰ; ~ry ਕਾਵਿ, ਕਾਵਿ-ਰਚਨਾ

poignancy (ਪੌਇਨਯਅੱਸਿ) *n* (ਸੁਆਦ, ਗੰਧ ਦੀ) ਤੁਰਸ਼ੀ; ਚੋਭ, ਤੀਖਣਤਾ

poignant (ਪੌਇਨਯਅੰਟ) *a* ਤੀਖਣ, ਤੀਬਰ, ਤੇਜ਼, ਚਟਪਟੀ, ਤਿੱਖੀ; ਚੁਭਵਾਂ

point (ਪੌਇੰਟ) *n v* ਬਿੰਦੀ, ਨੁਕਤਾ, ਨੋਕ, ਦਸ਼ਮਲਵ-ਚਿੰਨ੍ਹ, ਥਾਂ, ਟਿਕਾਣਾ; ਵਿਸ਼ੈ; ਗੱਲ; ਦਰਜਾ, ਨੰਬਰ; ਇਸ਼ਾਰਾ ਕਰਨਾ, ਸੰਕੇਤ ਕਰਨਾ; ਨਿਸ਼ਾਨ ਲਾਉਣਾ; ~ed ਨੋਕਦਾਰ, ਨੋਕ ਵਾਲਾ, ਤਿੱਖੀ ਨੋਕ ਵਾਲਾ, ਚੁਭਵੀਂ, ਸਾਫ਼ ਸਾਫ਼, ਖਰੀ ਖਰੀ; ~edly ਵਿਸ਼ੇਸ਼ ਜ਼ੋਰ ਦੇ ਕੇ, ਸਾਫ਼ ਸਾਫ਼ ਦੱਸ ਕੇ, ਸਪਸ਼ਟ ਸੰਕੇਤ ਕਰ ਕੇ; ~less ਨਿਰਰਥਕ, ਸਾਰਹੀਨ

poison (ਪੌਇਜ਼ਨ) *n v* ਜ਼ਹਿਰ, ਵਿਸ਼, ਵਿਹੁ; ਵਿਗਾੜਨਾ; ਵਿਖਨ ਪਾਉਣਾ, ਬਾਧਾ ਪਾਉਣੀ; ~ous ਜ਼ਹਿਰੀਲਾ, ਜ਼ਹਿਰੀ, ਵਿਸ਼ੈਲਾ, ਵਿਹੁਲਾ

poke (ਪਅਉਕ) *v* ਹੁੱਝ ਮਾਰਨੀ, ਖੋਭਣਾ, ਚੋਭਣਾ; ਧੱਕਾ ਦੇਣਾ; ਅਰਕ ਮਾਰਨੀ

polar (ਪਲਉਲਅ*) *a* ਧਰੁੱਵੀ, ਧਰੁੱਵਾਂ ਦਾ; ਕੁਤਬੀ; **~bear** ਧਰੁੱਵੀ ਰਿੱਛ; **~ity** ਧਰੁੱਵੀ ਉਲਾਰ, ਧਰੁੱਵੀਪਨ

pole (ਪਅੋਉਲ) *n v* (ਉੱਤਰੀ ਜਾਂ ਦੱਖਣੀ) ਧਰੁੱਵ; ਥੰਮੂ, ਖੰਭਾ; ਵੰਝ, ਬਾਂਸ; ਪੋਲੈਂਡ ਦਾ ਵਸਨੀਕ; ਖੰਭਾ ਗੱਡਣਾ, ਬੱਲੀ ਲਾਉਣਾ

police (ਪਅ'ਉਲੀਸ) *n v* ਪੁਲੀਸ; ਪੁਲੀਸ-ਵਿਭਾਗ; ਪੁਲੀਸ ਕਰਮਚਾਰੀ, ਪੁਲਸੀਏ; ਪੁਲੀਸ ਨਿਯੁਕਤ ਕਰਨੀ, ਪੁਲੀਸ ਲਾਉਣੀ; ਪ੍ਰਬੰਧ ਕਰਨਾ; **~man** ਪੁਲੀਸ ਦਾ ਸਿਪਾਹੀ, ਪੁਲੀਸ ਕਰਮਚਾਰੀ

policy (ਪੌਲਅਸਿ) *n* ਨੀਤੀ, ਜੁਗਤ, ਢੰਗ, ਰੀਤ, ਵਿਧੀ; ਬੀਮਾ-ਪੱਤਰ, ਪਾਲਿਸੀ

polio (ਪਅਉਲਿਅਉ) *n* ਪੋਲਿਓ ਦੀ ਬੀਮਾਰੀ

polish (ਪੌਲਿਸ਼) *v n* ਪਾਲਸ਼ ਕਰਨੀ, ਰੋਗਨ ਕਰਨਾ; ਚਮਕਾਉਣਾ, ਲਿਸ਼ਕਾਉਣਾ; ਪਾਲਸ਼, ਰੋਗਨ, ਚਮਕ, ਲਿਸ਼ਕ; ਸ਼ਿਸ਼ਟਤਾ; **~ed** ਪਰਿਸ਼ਕ੍ਰਿਤ, ਸ਼ਿਸ਼ਟ, ਪਾਲਸ਼ਦਾਰ

polite (ਪਅ'ਲਾਇਟ) *a* ਨਿਮਰਤਾ ਵਾਲਾ, ਸ਼ਿਸ਼ਟ, ਸੱਤਿਅ, ਸੁਸ਼ੀਲ; **~ness** ਨਿਮਰਤਾ, ਸ਼ਿਸ਼ਟਤਾ, ਸੁਸ਼ੀਲਤਾ

politic (ਪੌਲਅਟਿਕ) *a* ਸਿਆਣਾ, ਬੁੱਧੀਮਾਨ; ਮੌਕਾਸ਼ਨਾਸ; ਨੀਤੀਵਾਨ, ਨੀਤੀਕੁਸ਼ਲ; ਅਨੁਭਵੀ, ਤਜਰਬਾਕਾਰ

political (ਪਅ'ਲਿਟਿਕਲ) *a n* ਰਾਜਨੀਤਕ, ਸਿਆਸੀ; ਰਾਜਸੀ, ਸ਼ਾਸਕੀ, ਰਾਜ ਪ੍ਰਬੰਧ ਸਬੰਧੀ

politician (ਪੌਲਿ'ਟਿਸ਼ਨ) *n* ਸਿਆਸਤਦਾਨ; ਰਾਜਨੀਤੀਵਾਨ; ਪੇਸ਼ਾਵਰ ਰਾਜਨੀਤੀਵੇਤਾ

politicking (ਪੌਲਿਟਿਕਿੜ) *n* ਸਿਆਸਤ ਬਾਜ਼ੀ

politics (ਪੌਲਿਟਿਕਸ) *n* ਰਾਜਨੀਤੀ-ਸ਼ਾਸਤਰ, ਰਾਜਨੀਤੀ-ਵਿਗਿਆਨ; ਸਿਆਸਤ

polity (ਪੌਲਅਟਿ) *n* ਰਾਜ-ਪ੍ਰਬੰਧ, ਰਾਜ-ਵਿਵਸਥਾ, ਸ਼ਾਸਨ-ਪ੍ਰਣਾਲੀ

poll (ਪਅਉਲ) *n v* ਵੋਟ ਗਿਣਨ, ਵੋਟ ਪਾਉਣ, ਵੋਟਾਂ ਦੀ ਗਿਣਤੀ; ਵੋਟ ਸਵੀਕਾਰ ਹੋਣਾ; **~ing** ਮੱਤਦਾਨ; **~ing station** ਮੱਤਦਾਨ ਕੇਂਦਰ

pollute (ਪਅ'ਲੂਟ) *v* ਵਿਗਾੜਨਾ, ਖ਼ਰਾਬ ਕਰਨਾ, ਗੰਦਾ ਕਰਨਾ, ਅਪਵਿੱਤਰ ਕਰਨਾ, ਪਲੀਤ ਕਰਨਾ, ਮੈਲਾ ਕਰਨਾ; **~d** ਦੂਸ਼ਤ, ਅਪਵਿੱਤਰ, ਗੰਧਲਾ, ਗੰਦਾ

pollution (ਪਅ'ਲੂਸ਼ਨ) *n* ਗੰਦਾਪਣ, ਦੂਸ਼ਣ, ਭ੍ਰਿਸ਼ਟਤਾ

polo (ਪਅਉਲਅਉ) *n* ਚੁਗਾਨ, ਪੋਲੋ

polyandry (ਪੌਲਿਅੈਂਡਰਿ) *n* ਬਹੁ-ਕੰਤੀ, ਬਹੁ-ਪਤੀਤਵ, ਇਕ ਤੀਵੀਂ ਦੇ ਇਕ ਤੋਂ ਵਧੇਰੇ ਪਤੀ ਹੋਣ ਦੀ ਪ੍ਰਥਾ

polygamy (ਪਅ'ਲਿਗਾਮਿ) *n* ਬਹੁ-ਵਿਆਹ, ਬਹੁ-ਪਤਨੀਤਵ

polyglot (ਪੌਲਿਗਲੌਟ) *a n* ਬਹੁ-ਭਾਸ਼ਾਈ; ਬਹੁ-ਭਾਸ਼ੀ ਮਨੁੱਖ

polysemy (ਪਅ'ਲਿਸਅਮਿ) *n* ਬਹੁਅਰਥਕਾ, ਅਨੇਕ ਅਰਥਕਤਾ

pomegranate (ਪੌਮਿ'ਗਰੈਨਿਟ) *n* ਅਨਾਰ

pomp (ਪੌਪ) *n* ਠਾਠ-ਬਾਠ, ਸਜ-ਧਜ, ਧੂਮ-ਧਾਮ, ਸ਼ਾਨ, ਸ਼ੋਭਾ, ਚਮਕ-ਦਮਕ, ਆਡੰਬਰ

pomposity (ਪੌਮ'ਪੌਸਅਟਿ) *n* ਸ਼ਾਨ, ਠਾਠ, ਚਮਕ-ਦਮਕ; ਅਲੰਕਾਰਕਤਾ

pompous (ਪੌਮਪਅਸ) *a* ਸ਼ਾਨਦਾਰ, ਭੜਕੀਲਾ, ਲੱਛੇਦਾਰ, ਸ਼ੋਭਾ ਵਾਲਾ

pond (ਪੌਡ) *n* ਟੋਭਾ, ਤਲਾਅ, ਸਰੋਵਰ; ਛੱਪੜ

ponder ('ਪੌਂਡਅ*) *v* ਵਿਚਾਰਨਾ, ਸੋਚਣਾ, ਗੌਲਣਾ; ਧਿਆਨ ਦੇਣਾ, ਗਹੁ ਕਰਨਾ, ਜਾਚਣਾ; **~able** ਭਾਰ, ਬੋਝਲ; ਵਜ਼ਨੀ; **~ous** ਔਖਾ, ਕਠਨ, ਬੇਢੱਬਾ, (ਸ਼ੈਲੀ) ਨੀਰਸ, ਖੁਸ਼ਕ, ਰੁੱਖੀ, ਸ਼ਬਦ-ਆਡੰਬਰ ਵਾਲੀ

pony ('ਪਅਉਨਿ) *n* ਟੱਟੂ, ਛੋਟੇ ਕੱਦ ਦਾ ਘੋੜਾ

pooh-pooh ('ਪੂ-'ਪੂ) *v* ਤਿਰਸਕਾਰਨਾ; ਦੁਰਕਾਰਨਾ, ਥੂਹ-ਥੂਹ ਕਰਨਾ

pool (ਪੂਲ) *n v* ਤਲਾਅ, ਕੁੰਡ, ਛੱਪੜ, ਟੋਭਾ, ਸਰ; ਸਾਂਝੀ ਪੂੰਜੀ, ਸਾਂਝਾ ਧਨ; ਵਿਹਾਰਕ ਸਾਧਨ ਸਾਂਝੇ ਕਰ ਲੈਣੇ; **~ed** ਇਕੱਤਰਤ, ਸੰਗ੍ਰਹਤ, ਸੰਚਤ

poor (ਪੁਅ*) *a* ਗ਼ਰੀਬ, ਕੰਗਾਲ, ਨਿਰਧਨ; ਮਾੜਾ, ਹੀਣਾ, ਨਿਮਾਣਾ, ਮੰਦੀ ਹਾਲਤ ਵਿਚ, ਬਲਹੀਣ, ਕਮਜ਼ੋਰ; **~ly** ਥੁੜ੍ਹ ਨਾਲ; ਘਟੀਆ ਤਰੀਕੇ ਨਾਲ

pop (ਪੌਪ) *n v* ਠਾਹ ਦੀ ਅਵਾਜ਼, ਟੱਕ ਦੀ ਅਵਾਜ਼, ਅਚਾਨਕ ਫਟਣ ਜਾਂ ਧਮਾਕੇ ਨਾਲ ਖੁੱਲ੍ਹਣ ਦੀ ਅਵਾਜ਼; ਟੱਕ ਕਰਕੇ ਖੋਲ੍ਹਣਾ; ਪਿਸਤੌਲ, ਬੰਦੂਕ ਆਦਿ ਚਲਾਉਣੀ; ਠਾਹ ਦੀ ਅਵਾਜ਼ ਹੋਣਾ; ਅਚਾਨਕ ਕੋਈ ਸਵਾਲ ਕਰ ਦੇਣਾ; ਟੁੱਟ ਕੇ ਪੈਣਾ; ਮੱਕੀ ਦੀਆਂ ਖਿੱਲਾਂ ਕਰਨੀਆਂ, (ਬੋਲ) ਪੌਪ, ਇਕ ਲੋਕ ਸੰਗੀਤ; **~corn** ਮੱਕੀ ਦੀਆਂ ਖਿੱਲਾਂ

pope (ਪਅਉਪ) *n* ਰੋਮਨ ਕੈਥੋਲਿਕ ਇਸਾਈਆਂ ਦਾ ਸਭ ਤੋਂ ਵੱਡਾ ਪਾਦਰੀ, ਧਰਮ-ਅਧਿਅਕਸ਼, ਪੋਪ; ਮਹਾਤਮਾ, ਧਰਮਾਤਮਾ, ਦੇਵਤਾ

poppy ('ਪੌਪਿ) *n* ਪੋਸਤ ਦਾ ਬੂਟਾ, ਖਸਖਸ

populace ('ਪੌਪਯੁਅਲਸ) *n* ਆਮ ਲੋਕ, ਜਨਤਾ, ਭੀੜ

popular ('ਪੌਪਯੁਲਅ*) *a* ਲੋਕ-ਪ੍ਰਿਯ, ਪ੍ਰਸਿੱਧ, ਮਸ਼ਹੂਰ, ਸਰਬਪ੍ਰਿਯ; ਪ੍ਰਚਲਤ; **~ity** ਲੋਕ-ਪ੍ਰਿਯਤਾ; ਪ੍ਰਸਿੱਧੀ; ਮਸ਼ਹੂਰੀ, ਸਰਬਮਾਨਤਾ

populate ('ਪੌਪਯੁਲੇਇਟ) *v* ਵੱਸਣਾ, (ਕਿਸੇ ਥਾਂ ਨੂੰ) ਵਸਾਉਣਾ, ਆਬਾਦ ਕਰਨਾ, ਆਬਾਦ ਹੋਣਾ

population ('ਪੌਪਯੁ'ਲੇਇਸ਼ਨ) *n* ਵੱਸੋਂ, ਆਬਾਦੀ; ਜਨ-ਸੰਖਿਆ, ਜਨਤਾ

populism ('ਪੌਪਯੁਲਿਜ਼(ਅ)ਮ) *n a* ਸੋਸ਼ੇਬਾਜ਼ੀ, ਸਸਤੀ ਸ਼ੋਹਰਤ

populous ('ਪੌਪਯੁਲਅਸ) *a* ਵੱਸਦਾ, ਘੁੱਗ ਵੱਸਦਾ, ਸੰਘਣੀ ਵੱਸੋਂ ਵਾਲਾ, ਘਣੀ ਆਬਾਦੀ ਵਾਲਾ, ਜਨਪੂਰਨ

porcelain ('ਪੋਸ(ਅ)ਲਿਨ) *n* ਚੀਨੀ, ਮਿੱਟੀ, ਚੀਨੀ ਦੇ ਭਾਂਡੇ; ਕੋਮਲ, ਨਾਜ਼ਕ, ਟੁੱਟਣਹਾਰ

porch (ਪੋ'ਚ) *n* ਡਿਓਡੀ; ਮਕਾਨ ਦੇ ਸਾਹਵੇਂ ਪਾਇਆ ਛੱਜਾ

pornography (ਪੋ'ਨੌਗਰਅਫ਼ਿ) *n* ਫਾਅਸ਼ ਲਿਖਤ, ਅਸ਼ਲੀਲ ਸਾਹਿਤ, ਕਾਮ ਉਕਸਾਊ ਰਚਨਾ

port (ਪੋ'ਟ) *n* (1) ਬੰਦਰਗਾਹ; (2) ਫ਼ਾਟਕ, ਮੁੱਖ ਦੁਆਰ, ਸਦਰ ਦਰਵਾਜ਼ਾ; (3) ਮਿੱਠੀ, ਲਾਲ ਰੰਗ ਦੀ ਅਤੇ ਤੇਜ਼-ਨਸ਼ੇ ਵਾਲੀ ਇਕ ਸ਼ਰਾਬ; ਜਹਾਜ਼ ਦੇ ਖੱਬੇ ਪਾਸੇ ਵੱਲ ਲੈ ਜਾਣਾ

portable ('ਪੋਟਅਬਲ) *a* ਚੁੱਕਵਾਂ, ਸਫ਼ਰੀ

portage ('ਪੋਟਿਜ) *n v* ਢੁਆਈ, ਢੋਆ-ਢੁਆਈ; ਢੋਣਾ, ਲੈ ਜਾਣਾ

porter ('ਪੋਟਅ*) *n* ਕੁਲੀ, ਭਾਰ ਮਜ਼ਦੂਰ, ਪਾਂਡੀ; ਦਰਬਾਨ, ਡਿਉਢੀਦਾਰ; **~house** ਸ਼ਰਾਬਖ਼ਾਨਾ, ਮੈਖਾਨਾ, ਸ਼ਰਾਬ ਦੀ ਦੁਕਾਨ, ਠੇਕਾ

portfolio ('ਪੋਟ'ਫ਼ਅਉਲਿਅਉ) *n* ਬਸਤਾ, ਵਜ਼ਾਰਤ ਦਾ ਅਹੁਦਾ, ਵਜ਼ਾਰਤ ਦਾ ਵਿਭਾਗ, ਮੰਤਰੀ-ਪਦ

portion ('ਪੋਸ਼ਨ) *n v* ਹਿੱਸਾ, ਵੰਡ, ਪੱਤੀ, ਦਾਜ, ਵੰਡਣਾ, ਵੰਡ ਪਾਉਣੀ, ਹਿੱਸਾ ਦੇਣਾ, ਦਾਜ ਦੇਣਾ

portmanteau ('ਪੋਟ'ਮੈਨਟਅਉ) *n* ਚਮੜੇ ਦਾ

ਬਕਸਾ, ਚਮੜੇ ਦਾ ਥੈਲਾ, ਸੰਯੁਕਤ ਸ਼ਬਦ, ਸਮਾਸ

portrait (’ਪੋਟਰੇਇਟ) *n* ਤਸਵੀਰ, ਚਿੱਤਰ, ਮੂਰਤ; ਹੂ-ਬਹੂ ਸ਼ਕਲ; **~ure** ਚਿੱਤਰਕਾਰੀ, ਤਸਵੀਰ-ਸਾਜ਼ੀ, ਚਿੱਤਰਣ, ਸ਼ਬਦ-ਚਿੱਤਰ

portray (ਪੋ’ਟਰੇਇ) *v* ਚਿੱਤਰ ਬਣਾਉਣਾ, ਤਸਵੀਰ ਖਿਚਣੀ; ਉਲੀਕਣਾ, ਸ਼ਬਦ-ਚਿੱਤਰ ਉਲੀਕਣਾ

pose (ਪਅਉਜ਼) *v n* (ਸਵਾਲ) ਪੇਸ਼ ਕਰਨਾ, ਸਾਮ੍ਹਣੇ ਰੱਖਣਾ; ਦਿਖਾਵਾ ਕਰਨਾ, ਦੰਭ ਕਰਨਾ; ਢੌਂਗ ਰਚਣਾ; ਅੰਦਾਜ਼, ਢੰਗ, ਰੂਪ, ਸਥਿਤੀ, ਰੌਂ, ਢੌਂਗ; ਦਿਖਾਵਾ

position (ਪਅ’ਜ਼ਿਸ਼ਨ) *n v* ਹਾਲਤ, ਅਵਸਥਾ, ਦਸ਼ਾ, ਥਾਂ, ਟਿਕਾਣਾ, ਮੌਕਾ, ਸਥਿਤੀ; ਸਿਧਾਂਤ; ਦ੍ਰਿਸ਼ਟੀਕੋਣ; ਬਿਠਾਉਣਾ, ਟਿਕਾਉਣਾ, ਥਾਂ ਸਿਰ ਰੱਖਣਾ, ਮੋਰਚੇ ਤੇ ਡਟਣਾ; ਪਦ ਸੰਭਾਲਣਾ

positive (’ਪੌਜ਼ਅਟਿਵ੍) *n a* (ਗਣਿ) ਧਨ, (ਰਿਣ ਦੇ ਵਿਰੋਧ ਵਿਚ) ਸਕਾਰਾਤਮਕ, (ਵਿਆ) ਸਧਾਰਨ ਵਿਸ਼ੇਸ਼ਣ, ਅਵੱਸ਼ਕ, ਸਪਸ਼ਟ, ਨਿਰਸੰਦੇਹ, ਸੱਚਾ, ਨਿਸ਼ਚੇਆਤਮਕ, ਅਸਲੀ, ਭੌਤਕ

positivism (’ਪੌਜ਼ਅਟਿਵ੍ਜ਼(ਅ)ਮ) *n* ਪ੍ਰਤੱਖਵਾਦ, ਪ੍ਰਮਾਣਵਾਦ

possess (ਪਅ’ਜ਼ੈਸ) *v* ਮਾਲਕ ਹੋਣਾ, ਸੁਆਮੀ ਹੋਣਾ, ਅਧਿਕਾਰ ਰੱਖਣਾ, ਕਬਜ਼ਾ ਕਰਨਾ, ਯੁਕਤ ਹੋਣਾ, (ਭੂਤ ਪਰੇਤ ਦਾ) ਚੰਬੜੇ .ਹੋਣਾ; **~ion** ਅਧਿਕਾਰ, ਮਾਲਕੀ, (ਕਾ) ਦਖ਼ਲ, ਕਾਨੂੰਨੀ ਕਬਜ਼ਾ, ਮਲਕੀਅਤ, ਮਿਲਖ, ਜਾਇਦਾਦ, ਧਨ-ਮਾਲ ਦੌਲਤ; **~ive** (ਵਿਆ) ਸਬੰਧ-ਵਾਚੀ, ਸਬੰਧ (ਕਾਰਕ), ਅਧਿਕਾਰਾਤਮਕ, ਕਬਜ਼ੇ ਦਾ

possibility (’ਪੌਸਅ’ਬਿਲਅਟਿ) *n* ਸੰਭਵਤਾ, ਸੰਭਾਵਨਾ, ਹੋਣਹਾਰੀ, ਸੰਭਵ ਘਟਨਾ, ਸੰਭਵ ਅਵਸਥਾ

possible (’ਪੌਸਅਬਲ) *a n* ਸੰਭਵ, ਮੁਮਕਨ, ਹੋ ਸਕਣ ਵਾਲਾ, ਹੋਣਹਾਰ, ਮਾਕੂਲ

possibly (’ਪੌਸਅਬਲਿ) *a n* ਸ਼ਾਇਦ, ਸੰਭਾਵਨਾ ਦੇ ਰੂਪ ਵਿਚ

post (ਪਅਉਸਟ) *n v adv* (1) ਥੰਮ੍ਹਾ, ਥਮ੍ਹਲਾ, ਖੰਭਾ, ਕੌਲਾ, ਮੁੰਨਾ, ਕਿੱਲਾ; (2) ਡਾਕ ਰਾਹੀਂ ਚਿੱਠੀਆਂ ਪਹੁੰਚਾਉਣਾ; ਮੁਕੱਰਰ ਕੀਤੀਆਂ ਚੌਕੀਆਂ; ਮੋਰਚਾ, ਕਿਲ੍ਹਾ, ਗੜ੍ਹ, ਕੋਟ, ਵਪਾਰਕ ਕੇਂਦਰ, ਡਿਊਟੀ ਦੀ ਥਾਂ, ਆਸਾਮੀ, ਪਦ, ਨੌਕਰੀ, ਅਹੁਦਾ, ਕਾਗ਼ਜ਼ ਦਾ ਆਕਾਰ; (3) ਮਗਰਲਾ, ਉੱਤਰ-ਕਾਲੀਨ, ਪਿੱਛੋਂ, ਮਗਰੋਂ ਪਿਛਲਾ; ਚਿੱਠੀਆਂ ਆਦਿ ਡਾਕ ਵਿਚ ਪਾਉਣੀਆਂ, ਡਾਕ ਰਾਹੀਂ ਭੇਜਣਾ, ਚਿਪਕਾਉਣਾ, ਪ੍ਰਚਾਰ ਕਰਨਾ; ਕਾਹਲ ਕਰਨੀ (ਪਦਵੀ ਉੱਤੇ) ਨਿਯੁਕਤ ਕਰਨਾ, (ਹਿਸਾਬ ਵਾਲੀ ਵਹੀ ਉੱਤੇ) ਚੜ੍ਹਾ ਦੇਣਾ, ਸੂਚਨਾ ਦੇਣੀ; ਕਾਹਲ ਵਿਚ; ਤੇਜ਼ੀ ਨਾਲ; **~card** ਪੱਤਰ, ਡਾਕ ਦਾ ਕਾਰਡ; **~man** ਡਾਕੀਆ, ਹਰਕਾਰਾ; **~office** ਡਾਕਖ਼ਾਨਾ, ਡਾਕਘਰ, ਟੱਪਾਘਰ; **by return of~** ਵਾਪਸੀ ਡਾਕ; **~age** ਡਾਕ ਦਾ ਮਹਿਸੂਲ, ਡਾਕ-ਭਾਰ; **~ing** ਡਾਕ ਵਿਚ ਭੇਜਣ, ਸਥਾਪਨਾ, ਨਿਯੁਕਤੀ; ਤੈਨਾਤੀ, ਰਜਿਸਟਰ ਵਿਚ ਚੜ੍ਹਾਉਣਾ; **~al** ਡਾਕ ਸਬੰਧੀ, ਡਾਕਖ਼ਾਨੇ ਸਬੰਧੀ; **~date** ਆਗਾਮੀ ਮਿਤੀ ਪਾਉਣੀ; **~war** ਜੁੱਧ-ਉਪਰੰਤ

poster (’ਪਅਉਸਟਅ*) *n* ਇਸ਼ਤਿਹਾਰ, ਵਿਗਿਆਪਨ-ਪੱਤਰ

posterior (ਪੌਸ’ਟਿਅਰਿਅ*) *a n* ਪਿੱਛੋਂ ਦਾ, ਮਗਰਲਾ, ਚਿੱਤੜ, ਪਿੱਛਾ, ਉੱਤਰ-ਵਰਤੀ

posterity (ਪੌ’ਸਟੈਰੱਅਟਿ) *n* (ਦਰਸ਼) ਵੰਸ਼, ਸੰਤਾਨ, ਔਲਾਦ, ਆਉਣ ਵਾਲੀਆਂ ਨਸਲਾਂ

post-facto (’ਪਅਉਸਟ’ਫੈਕਟਅਉ) *n* ਘਟਨਾ ਤੋਂ

ਪਿਛੋਂ, ਕੰਮ ਹੋਣ ਦੇ ਬਾਦ

posthumous ('ਪੌਸਟਯੁਮਅਸ) *a* ਮਰਨ ਉਪਰੰਤ

postmeridiem ('ਪਅਉਸਟਮਅ'ਰਿਡੀਅਮ) *adv* ਛੋਟਾ ਰੂਪ P.M., ਦੁਪਹਿਰ ਮਗਰੋਂ

post-mortem ('ਪਅਉਸਟ'ਮੋਟਅਮ) *n* ਲਾਸ਼ ਦਾ ਮੁਆਇਨਾ, ਸ਼ਵ-ਪਰੀਖਿਆ

post-nuptial ('ਪਅਉਸਟ'ਨਅੱਪਸ਼ਯਅਲ) *n* ਵਿਵਾਹ-ਉਪਰੰਤ

postpone ('ਪਅਉਸ(ਟ)'ਪਅਉਨ) *v* ਸਥਗਤ ਕਰਨਾ, ਮੁਲਤਵੀ ਕਨਰਾ, ਟਾਲਣਾ; ~**d** ਸਥਗਤ, ਅੱਗੇ ਪਾਇਆ; ~**ment** ਟਾਲ-ਮਟੋਲ, ਸਥਗਨ

postposition ('ਪਅਉਸਟਪਅ'ਜ਼ਿਸ਼ਨ) *n* ਪਰਸਰਗ

postulate ('ਪੌਸਟਯੁਲਅਟ, 'ਪੌਸਟਯੁਲੇਇਟ) *n v* ਬੁਨਿਆਦੀ ਅਸੂਲ, ਆਧਾਰ-ਤੱਤ, ਪੂਰਵ-ਅਨੁਮਾਨ, ਪੂਰਵ-ਧਾਰਟਾ; ਮੰਨ ਲੈਣਾ, ਸ਼ਰਤ ਲਾ ਦੇਣਾ, ਪ੍ਰਤੀਬੰਧ ਲਾਉਣਾ, ਜ਼ਰੂਰੀ ਸ਼ਰਤ ਸਵੀਕਾਰ ਕਰਨੀ, ਦਾਵਵਾ ਕਰਨ

postulation ('ਪੌਸਟਯੁ'ਲੇਇਸ਼ਨ) *n* ਮੂਲ ਸ਼ਰਤ; ਆਧਾਰ ਤੱਤ

posture ('ਪੌਸਚਅ*) *n v* ਪੈਂਤੜਾ, ਅਦਾ, ਅੰਦਾਜ਼, ਸਥਿਤੀ, ਆਸਨ (ਯੋਗ ਦਾ), ਮੁਦਰਾ; ਬੈਠਕ; ਬੈਠਣ ਦਾ ਢੰਗ; ਢੰਗ ਬਣਨਾ

pot (ਪੌਟ) *n v* ਭਾਂਡਾ, ਬਰਤਨ, ਪਤੀਲਾ; ਗਾਮਲਾ; ਚਾਹਦਾਨੀ; ~**belly** ਗੋਗੜ, ਗੋਗੜੀਆ

potato (ਪਅ'ਟੇਇਟਅਉ) *n* ਆਲੂ; ~**chips** ਤਲੇ ਹੋਏ ਆਲੂਆਂ ਦੇ ਪਤਲੇ ਪਤਲੇ ਟੁਕੜੇ

potency ('ਪਅਉਟਅੰਸਿ) *n* ਬਲ, ਸ਼ਕਤੀ, ਸਮਰੱਥਾ, ਪ੍ਰਭਾਵਸ਼ੀਲਤਾ

potent ('ਪਅਉਟਅੰਟ) *a* ਬਲਵਾਨ, ਸ਼ਕਤੀਵਾਨ,

ਤਕੜਾ, ਜ਼ੋਰਦਾਰ; ~**ial** ਹੋ ਸਕਣ ਵਾਲਾ, ਹੋਣ ਵਾਲਾ; ਸੰਭਾਵੀ; ~**iality** ਸ਼ਕਤੀ ਬਲ, ਸਮਰੱਥਾ, ਯੋਗਤਾ; ਸੰਭਾਵਨਾ, ਸੰਭਵਤਾ, ਸੰਭਵ ਸ਼ਕਤੀ, ਸਿਖਰੀ ਬਲ

potter (ਪੌਟਅ*) *n v* ਕੁਮ੍ਹਾਰ, ਘੁਮਿਆਰ, ਕੁੰਭਕਾਰ; ਨਿਕੰਮੇ ਰਹਿਣਾ, ਝੱਖ ਮਾਰਨੀ, ਟੱਕਰਾਂ ਮਾਰਨੀਆਂ; ~**y** ਕੁੰਭਕਾਰੀ, ਕੁਮ੍ਹਾਰ ਦੀ ਦੁਕਾਨ, ਕਰਾਕਰੀ ਦਾ ਕਾਰਖਾਨਾ

pouch (ਪਾਊਚ) *n v* ਥੈਲੀ, ਜੇਬ, ਖੀਸਾ, ਗੁਥਲੀ; (ਪ੍ਰ) ਕਬਝੇ ਵਿਚ ਲੈਣਾ; ਹੱਥ ਵਿਚ ਲੈਣਾ; (ਬੋਲ) ਇਨਾਮ ਦੇਣਾ, ਭੇਟਾ ਕਰਨਾ, ਗੁਥਲੀ ਵਾਂਗੂੰ ਲਮਕਾਉਣਾ; ਹੜੱਪ ਕਰ ਜਾਣਾ, ਮਾਰ ਲੈਣਾ

pounce (ਪਾਊਂਸ) *v* ਝਪਟਣਾ, ਝਪਟ ਮਾਰਨੀ; ਤਾੜ ਲੈਣਾ, ਜਾਣ ਜਾਣਾ; ਪੰਜਾ, ਨਹੁੰਦਰ, ਝਪਟ

pound (ਪਾਊਂਡ) *v n* ਫੇਹਣਾ, ਚਿੱਥਣਾ, ਘੋਟਣਾ, ਕੁੱਟਣਾ, ਪੀਹਣਾ; (1) ਬਰਤਾਨੀਆ ਦਾ ਸੋਨੇ ਦਾ ਸਿੱਕਾ, ਪੌਂਡ; (2) ਤੋਲ ਦਾ ਇਕ ਵੱਟਾ, 16 ਔਂਸ; (3) ਕਾਂਜੀ ਹਾਊਸ, ਫਾਟਕ, ਕੈਦਖਾਨਾ; ਵਾੜਾ ਅਹਾਤਾ; ਔਖੀ ਘਾਟੀ

pour (ਪੋ*) *v* ਵਗਾਉ, ਡੋਲ੍ਹਣਾ, ਉਲੱਦਣਾ, ਪਲਟਣਾ, ਧਾਰ ਵਗਾਉਣੀ; ਵਗਾ ਦੇਣਾ, ਵਹਾ ਦੇਣਾ, ਪਰਵਾਹਤ ਕਰਨਾ; ਡੁਲ੍ਹਣਾ, ਵਗਣਾ, ਵਹਿਣਾ; ਪਾਉਣਾ, ਕਰਨਾ; (ਸੰਗੀਤ ਨਾਲ) ਸੁਰਾਂ ਕੱਢਣੀਆਂ; ਬਹੁਤ ਮਾਤਰਾ ਵਿਚ ਆਉਣਾ

poverty ('ਪੌਵਅਟਿ) *n* ਗ਼ਰੀਬੀ, ਕੰਗਾਲੀ, ਨਿਰਧਨਤਾ; (ਗੁਣ ਆਦਿ) ਅਣਹੋਂਦ, ਅਭਾਵ

powder ('ਪਾਉਡਅ*) *n v* ਪਾਊਡਰ, ਵਟਣਾ, ਧੂੜਾ; ਬੂਰਾ, ਚੂਰਾ, ਧੂੜ; ਚੂਰਨ, ਫੱਕੀ; ਬਾਰੂਦ; ਤਾਕਤ, ਸ਼ਕਤੀ; ਪਾਊਡਰ ਮਲਣਾ; ਪਾਊਡਰ ਜਾਂ ਧੂੜਾ ਛਿੜਕਣਾ, ਪੀਹਣਾ

power ('ਪਾਉਅ*) *n* ਸ਼ਕਤੀ, ਬਲ; ਤਾਕਤ, ਜ਼ੋਰ, ਪ੍ਰਤਿਭਾ; ਤੇਜ, ਓਜ, ਰੋਹਬ; ਸੱਤਾ, ਰਾਜ, ਹਕੂਮਤ, ਸ਼ਾਸਨ; ਅਧਿਕਾਰ; ~house, ~station ਬਿਜਲੀ ਘਰ; ~ful ਸ਼ਕਤੀਮਾਨ, ਬਲਵਾਨ, ਜ਼ੋਰਾਵਰ, ਤਾਕਤਵਰ; ਸਮਰੱਥ; ~less ਨਿਰਬਲ, ਦੁਰਬਲ, ਮਾੜਾ, ਨਿਤਾਣਾ, ਹੀਣਾ, ਅਸਮਰੱਥ

practicability ('ਪਰੈਕਟਿਕ'ਬਿਲਅਟਿ) *n* ਵਿਹਾਰਕਤਾ, ਉਪਯੋਗਤਾ; ਸੰਭਵਤਾ, ਸੰਭਾਵਨਾ

practicable ('ਪਰੈਕਟਿਕਅਬਲ) *a* ਹੋਣ ਯੋਗ, ਵਿਹਾਰਕ, ਵਰਤੋਂ ਵਿਚ ਲਿਆਇਆ ਜਾ ਸਕਣ ਵਾਲਾ, ਸੰਭਵ

practical ('ਪਰੈਕਟੀਕਲ) *a n* ਅਮਲੀ, ਵਿਹਾਰਕ, ਕਿਰਿਆਤਮਕ, ਅਤਿਆਸ-ਸਿੱਧ; ~ity ਵਿਹਾਰਕਤਾ; ਕਿਰਿਆਤਮਕਤਾ; ~ly ਅਮਲੀ ਤੌਰ ਤੇ; ਵਾਸਤਵ ਵਿਚ, ਅਮਲ ਵਿਚ

practice ('ਪਰੈਕਟਿਸ) *n* ਅਭਿਆਸ, ਮਸ਼ਕ; ਵਿਹਾਰ, ਆਚਾਰ, ਘਾਸ, ਵਰਤੋਂ, ਰੀਤ, ਦਸਤੂਰ, ਪ੍ਰਥਾ, ਪੱਧਤੀ, ਰਿਵਾਜ; ਕਾਰਜ-ਪ੍ਰਣਾਲੀ, ਚਲਨ

practise ('ਪਰੈਕਟਿਸ) *v* ਅਭਿਆਸ ਕਰਨਾ, ਮਸ਼ਕ ਕਰਨੀ; ਵਿਹਾਰਕ ਰੂਪ ਦੇਣਾ; ਕੰਮ ਵਿਚ ਲਿਆਉਣਾ; ਅਮਲ ਕਰਨਾ, ਵਰਤੋਂ ਕਰਨੀ; ~d ਅਭਿਆਸਤ, ਅਨੁਭਵੀ, ਗਿਆਨ-ਵਿਦੁ

practising ('ਪਰੈਕਟਿਸਿਙ) *a* ਕਿਰਿਆਸ਼ੀਲ, ਅਭਿਆਸੀ

practitioner ('ਪਰੈਕਟਿਸ਼ਨਾ*) *n* ਅਭਿਆਸੀ, ਪੇਸ਼ਾਵਰ; ਧੰਦਾ ਕਰਨ ਵਾਲਾ

pragmatic, ~al (ਪਰੈਗਾ'ਮੈਟਿਕ, ਪਰੈਗਾ'ਮੈਟਿਕਲ) *a n* ਯਥਾਰਥੀ, ਅਮਲੀ, ਕਿਰਿਆਤਮਕ, ਵਿਹਾਰਕ; ਅਸਲੀ; ਕੱਟੜ, ਪਰਿਣਾਮਵਾਦੀ, ਹਠਵਾਦੀ

pragmatist ('ਪਰੈਗਮਅਟਿਸਟ) *n* ਯਥਾਰਥਵਾਦੀ, ਵਸਤੂਵਾਦੀ, ਪ੍ਰਯੋਗਵਾਦੀ

praise (ਪਰੇਇਜ਼) *n v* ਵਡਿਆਈ, ਸਿਫ਼ਤ, ਗੁਣ, ਪ੍ਰਸੰਸਾ, ਉਸਤਤੀ, ਕੀਰਤੀ, ਮਹਿਮਾ, ਸ਼ਲਾਘਾ, ਸਲਾਹੁਤੀ; ਵਡਿਆਈ ਕਰਨੀ, ਸਿਫ਼ਤ ਦੱਸਣੀ, ਗੁਣ ਗਾਉਣੇ, ਪ੍ਰਸੰਸਾ ਕਰਨੀ, ਉਸਤਤੀ ਗਾਉਣੀ, ਕੀਰਤੀ ਕਰਨੀ; ~worthy ਪ੍ਰਸੰਸਾਯੋਗ, ਵਡਿਆਉਣਯੋਗ

pray (ਪਰੇਇ) *v* ਬੇਨਤੀ ਕਰਨੀ, ਅਰਜ਼ ਕਰਨੀ, ਅਰਦਾਸ ਕਰਨੀ, ਪੂਜਾ ਕਰਨੀ, ਉਪਾਸਨਾ ਕਰਨੀ; ~er ਪ੍ਰਾਰਥਨਾ, ਬੇਨਤੀ, ਅਰਜ਼, ਅਰਦਾਸ, ਜਾਚਨਾ, ਅਰਾਧਨਾ, ਉਪਾਸਨਾ, ਅਰਾਧਕ, ਪੁਜਾਰੀ, ਉਪਾਸਕ

preach (ਪਰੀਚ) *n v* ਉਪਦੇਸ਼, ਸਿੱਖਿਆ, ਪ੍ਰਵਚਨ; ਉਪਦੇਸ਼ ਦੇਣਾ; ਸਿੱਖਿਆ ਦੇਣੀ; ਦੀਖਿਆ ਦੇਣੀ; ਸਿਖਾਉਣਾ, ਪਾਠ ਪੜ੍ਹਾਉਣਾ, ਧਾਰਮਕ ਵਿਆਖਿਆ ਕਰਨੀ; ~er ਉਪਦੇਸ਼ਕ, ਪ੍ਰਚਾਰਕ

preamble (ਪਰੀ'ਐਮਬਲ) *n* ਪ੍ਰਾਕਥਨ, ਉੱਥਾਨਕਾ, ਪ੍ਰਸਤਾਵਨਾ, ਭੂਮਕਾ; ਮੁੱਖਬੰਧ ਲਿਖਣਾ

precarious (ਪਰਿ'ਕੇਅਰਿਅਸ) *a* (ਪ੍ਰ) ਸੰਕਟਪੂਰਨ, ਅਨਿਸ਼ਚਤ; ਖ਼ਤਰਨਾਕ

precaution (ਪਰਿ'ਕੋਸ਼ਨ) *n* ਸਾਵਧਾਨੀ, ਸਤਰਕਤਾ, ਖ਼ਬਰਦਾਰੀ; ~ary ਸਤਰਕਤਾਪੂਰਨ, ਖ਼ਬਰਦਾਰੀ ਵਾਲਾ

precautious (ਪਰਿ'ਕੋਸ਼ਅਸ) *a* ਸਾਵਧਾਨ, ਚੌਕਸ, ਖ਼ਬਰਦਾਰ, ਜਾਗਰੂਕ

precede (ਪਰੀ'ਸੀਡ) *v* ਪਹਿਲਾਂ ਹੋਣਾ ਜਾਂ ਵਾਪਰਨਾ, ਅੱਗੋਂ ਲਾਉਣਾ; ਪਹਿਲ ਕਰਨੀ; ਰਾਹ ਵਿਖਾਉਣਾ; ਪੂਰਵਵਰਤੀ ਹੋਣਾ; ~nce ਪਹਿਲ, ਪ੍ਰਮੁੱਖਤਾ, ਤਰਜੀਹ, ਪ੍ਰਾਥਮਕਤਾ; ~nt ਪੂਰਵ-

ਪ੍ਰਮਾਣ, ਦ੍ਰਿਸ਼ਟਾਂਤ, ਮਿਸਾਲ

preceding (ਪਰੀ'ਸੀਡਿਙ) *a* ਪੂਰਬਲਾ, ਪਹਿਲਾ, ਪੂਰਵ-ਵਰਤੀ, ਪੂਰਵਗਾਮੀ

precept ('ਪਰੀਸੈੱਪਟ) *n* ਉਪਦੇਸ਼, ਸਿੱਖਿਆ, ਨਸੀਹਤ

precinct (ਪਰਿਸਿਙ(ਕ)ਟ) *n* ਅਹਾਤਾ, ਵਲਗਣ, ਚੁਫੇਰਾ, ਚੁਗਿਰਦਾ; ਸਰਹੱਦ

precious ('ਪਰੈੱਸ਼ਅਸ) *a* ਬਹੁਮੁੱਲਾ, ਕੀਮਤੀ, ਅਮੁੱਲਾ; ਅਤੀ ਉੱਤਮ, ਸ੍ਰੇਸ਼ਠ

precipitance,   precipitancy (ਪਰਿ'ਸਿਪਿਟਅੰਸ, ਪਰਿ'ਸਿਪਿਟਅੰਸਿ) *n* ਕਾਹਲੀ, ਹਫੜਾ-ਦਫੜੀ, ਉਤਾਵਲ, ਘਾਬਰ; ਅੰਨ੍ਹੇ-ਵਾਹੀ; ਘੇਤਹਾਸ਼ਾਪਣ

precipitate (ਪਰਿ'ਸਿਪਿਟੇਇਟ) *v a* ਸੁੱਟਣਾ, ਡੇਗਣਾ; ਨਾਜ਼ਕ ਸਿਰੇ ਤਕ ਪਹੁੰਚਾਉਣਾ; ਮੂੰਹ ਭਾਰ, ਸਿਰ ਭਾਰ

precipitation (ਪਰਿ'ਸਿਪਿ'ਟੇਇਸ਼ਨ) *n* ਉਤਾਵਲਾਪਣ, ਕਾਹਲ, ਹਫੜਾ-ਦਫੜੀ; ਘੇਸਮੜੀ

precis ('ਪਰੇਇਸੀ) *n* ਸਾਰ, ਸਾਰਾਂਸ਼, ਤੱਤ, ਨਿਚੋੜ

precise (ਪਰਿ'ਸਾਇਸ) *a* ਅਸਲੀ, ਯਥਾਰਥ, ਵਾਸਤਵਿਕ; ਠੀਕ-ਠੀਕ, ਪੂਰਾ-ਪੂਰਾ, ਸ਼ੁੱਧ, ਸਹੀ; ~**ly** ਹੂ-ਬਹੂ, ਯਥਾਰਥ ਤੌਰ ਤੇ, ਅਸਲ ਵਿਚ; ~**ness** ਸੁਨਿਸ਼ਚਤਾ, ਸ਼ੁੱਧਤਾ

precision (ਪਰਿ'ਸਿਯ਼ਨ) *n* ਸੁਨਿਸ਼ਚਤਤਾ, ਵਿਸ਼ੁੱਧਤਾ, ਸ਼ੁੱਧਤਾ, ਠੀਕ ਦਰੁੱਸਤ

preclude (ਪਰਿ'ਕਲੂਡ) *v* ਰੋਕਣਾ, ਬੰਦ ਕਰਨਾ; ਪਰੇ ਰੱਖਣਾ, ਬਾਹਰ ਰੱਖਣਾ, ਵੱਖਰਾ ਕਰਨਾ

preconceive ('ਪਰੀ'ਕਅੱਨਸੀਵ਼) *n* ਪੂਰਵ ਸੰਕਲਪ ਬਣਾਉਣਾ, ਪੂਰਵ ਕਲਪਨਾ ਕਰਨੀ, ਪੂਰਵ ਨਿਰਣੇ ਕਰਨਾ, ਪੂਰਵ ਧਾਰਨਾ ਬਣਾਉਣਾ; ~**d** ਪੂਰਵ-ਚਿੰਤਤ, ਪੂਰਵ ਅਨੁਮਾਨਤ, ਪੂਰਵ

ਨਿਰਣੀਤ

preconception ('ਪਰੀਕਅੰ'ਸੈੱਪਸ਼ਨ) *n* ਮਨ ਦੀ ਗੰਢ, ਭਰਮ, ਬਦਗੁਮਾਨੀ, ਤਰਫ਼ਦਾਰੀ; ਪੂਰਵ-ਬੋਧ, ਪੂਰਵ-ਚਿੰਤਨ, ਪੂਰਵ-ਕਲਪਨਾ, ਪੂਰਵ-ਧਾਰਣਾ

precursive (ਪਰੀ'ਕਅਃਸਿਵ਼) *a* ਪੂਰਵ-ਵਰਤੀ, ਪਹਿਲਾ, ਮੁੱਢਲਾ

precursor (ਪਰੀ'ਕਅਃਸਅ*) *n* ਮੋਹਰੀ, ਪੂਰਵਗਾਮੀ, ਅਗਰਦੂਤ

predesignate ('ਪਰੀ'ਡੈਜ਼ਿਗਨੇਇਟ) *a v* ਪੂਰਵ-ਨਿਯਤ, ਪੂਰਵ-ਨਿਰਦਿਸ਼ਟ, ਪੂਰਵ-ਨਿਯੁਕਤ; ਪਹਿਲਾਂ ਨਿਯਤ ਕਰਨਾ

predetermine ('ਪਰੀਡਿ'ਟਅਃਮਿਨ) *v* ਅਗਾਊਂ ਮਿਥਣਾ, ਪਹਿਲਾਂ ਹੀ ਨਿਰਣੇ ਕਰ ਲੈਣਾ, ਪੂਰਵ-ਨਿਸ਼ਚੇ ਕਰਨਾ, ਪੂਰਵ-ਨਿਰਧਾਰਨ ਕਰਨਾ

predicate ('ਪਰੈੱਡਿਕੇਇਟ, 'ਪਰੈੱਡਿਕਅਟ) *v n* ਦਾਅਵੇ ਨਾਲ ਕਹਿਣਾ; ਵਿਧੇਯ

predication (ਪਰਿ'ਡਿਕੇਸ਼ਨ) *n* ਨਿਰੂਪਣ, ਪੁਸ਼ਟੀ; ਪੂਰਕ ਕਥਨ

predict (ਪਰਿ'ਡਿਕਟ) *v* ਪੂਰਵ-ਸੂਚਤ ਕਰਨਾ, ਭਵਿੱਖ-ਵਾਕ ਕਹਿਣਾ; ~**ability** ਹੋਣੀ, ਭਵਿੱਖ-ਬਾਣੀ, ਭਵਿੱਖ-ਵਾਕ; ~**ion** ਭਵਿੱਖ-ਵਾਕ, ਅਗੇਤੀ ਖ਼ਬਰ, ਭਾਵੀ ਕਥਨ, ਪੂਰਵ-ਸੂਚਨਾ

predominance (ਪਰਿ'ਡੋਮਿਨਅੰਸ) *n* ਜ਼ੋਰ, ਦਬਾਉ, ਦਬਦਬਾ, ਪ੍ਰਭੁਤਾ; ਅਧਿਕਤਾ; ਬੋਲਬਾਲਾ

predominant (ਪਰਿ'ਡੋਮਿਨਅੰਟ) *a* ਭਾਰੂ, ਪ੍ਰਬਲ, ਹਾਵੀ, ਪ੍ਰਮੁਖ, ਪ੍ਰਧਾਨ

predominate (ਪਰਿ'ਡੋਮਿਨੇਇਟ) *v* (ਕਿਸੇ ਉੱਤੇ) ਅਧਿਕਾਰ ਜਮਾਉਣਾ, ਭਾਰੂ ਹੋਣਾ, ਜ਼ੋਰ ਪਕੜਨਾ, ਪ੍ਰਬਲ ਹੋਣਾ, ਦਬਾਉਣਾ, ਪ੍ਰਭੁਤਾ ਜਮਾਉਣੀ, ਹਾਵੀ ਹੋਣਾ

predomination ('ਪਰਿ'ਡੋਮਿ'ਨੇਇਸ਼ਨ) *n*
ਅਧਿਕਾਰ, ਪ੍ਰਭੁਤਾ, ਦਬਦਬਾ, ਪ੍ਰਬਲਤਾ,
ਪ੍ਰਧਾਨਤਾ

preface ('ਪਰੇਫ਼ਿਸ) *n v* ਭੂਮਕਾ, ਉਠਾਨਕਾ,
ਪ੍ਰਸਤਾਵਨਾ, ਮੁੱਖ-ਬੰਧ; ਮੁੱਖ-ਬੰਧ ਲਿਖਟਾ;
ਪ੍ਰਾਰੰਭ ਕਰਨਾ

prefer ('ਪਰਿਫ਼ਅ*) *n v* ਤਰੱਕੀ ਦੇਟੀ; ਵਾਧਾ
ਦੇਟਾ, ਵਧਾਉਟਾ; ਬਹੁਤਾ ਪਸੰਦ ਕਰਨਾ, ਪਹਿਲ
ਦੇਟੀ, ਤਰਜੀਹ ਦੇਟੀ; **~able** ਚੰਗੇਰਾ, ਉੱਤਮ,
ਅਧਿਕ ਅੱਛਾ; **~ably** ਚੰਗੇਰਾ ਸਮਝ ਕੇ,
ਤਰਜੀਹ ਦੇ ਕੇ; **~ence** ਤਰਜੀਹ, ਲਿਹਾਜ਼,
ਵਿਸ਼ੇਸ਼ਤਾ; ਪਸੰਦ; ਆਦਰ, ਸਤਿਕਾਰ; **~ential**
ਤਰਜੀਹੀ, ਲਿਹਾਜ਼ੀ, ਰਿਆਇਤੀ, ਵਿਸ਼ੇਸ਼

prefigure ('ਪਰੀ'ਫ਼ਿਗਾਅ*) *v* ਪੂਰਬ-ਚਿਤਰਨ
ਕਰਨਾ, ਝਲਕ ਪਾਉਟਾ, ਪੂਰਬ ਆਭਾਸ ਦੇਟਾ

prefix ('ਪਰੀ'ਫ਼ਿਕਸ) *v n* ਅਗੇਤਰ ਲਾਉਟਾ,
ਉਪਸਰਗ ਲਾਉਟਾ; ਅੱਗੇ ਜੋੜਨਾ; ਉਪਸਰਗ,
ਅਗੇਤਰ

preform ('ਪਰੀ'ਫ਼ੋਮ) *v n* ਪਹਿਲਾਂ ਤੋਂ ਰਚਨਾ
ਕਰਨੀ, ਪੂਰਵ-ਰਚਨਾ ਕਰਨਾ, ਪੂਰਵ-ਨਿਰਮਾਣ
ਕਰਨਾ; **~ation** ਪੂਰਵ-ਨਿਰਮਾਣ, ਪੂਰਵ-ਰਚਨਾ

pregnancy ('ਪਰੇਗਾਨਅੰਸਿ) *n* ਗਰਭ, ਹਮਲ

pregnant ('ਪਰੇਗਾਨਅੰਟ) *a* ਹਮਲਾ, ਗਰਭਵਤੀ;
ਗੱਭਣ, ਆਸ ਲੱਗੀ, ਭਾਵਪੂਰਨ, ਕਲਪਨਾਸ਼ੀਲ;
ਗੁੱਝੂ, ਅਰਥ-ਪੂਰਵ

prejudge ('ਪਰੀ'ਜਾਅੱਜ) *v* (ਬਿਨਾ ਪੁੱਛ-ਪੜਤਾਲ
ਤੋਂ) ਫ਼ੈਸਲਾ ਕਰਨਾ, ਪੂਰਵ-ਨਿਰਣੈ ਕਰਨਾ,
ਪੂਰਵ-ਨਿਸ਼ਕਰਸ ਕੱਢਣਾ, ਪਹਿਲਾਂ ਤੋਂ ਹੀ ਮਨ
ਬਣਾ ਲੈਣਾ

prejudice ('ਪਰੈ'ਜੁਡ੍ਰਿਸ) *n v* ਪੱਖਪਾਤ,
ਤਰਫਦਾਰੀ, ਵਿਗਾੜ; ਹਰਜ; ਪੱਖਪਾਤ ਕਰਨਾ,

ਤਰਫਦਾਰੀ ਕਰਨੀ; ਵਿਗਾੜ ਦੇਟਾ; **~d** ਪੱਖਪਾਤ
ਵਾਲਾ

prejudicial ('ਪਰੈਜਾ'ਡਿਸ਼ਲ) *a* ਪੱਖਪਾਤੀ;
ਹਾਨੀਕਾਰਕ, ਵਿਰੁੱਧ

preliminary (ਪਰਿ'ਲਿਮਿਨਅਰਿ) *a n* ਪ੍ਰਾਰੰਭਕ,
ਮੁੱਢਲੀ, ਪ੍ਰਾਰੰਭਕ ਵਿਵਸਥਾ; ਤਿਆਰੀ

prelude ('ਪਰੈੱਲਯੂਡ) *n v* ਉਠਾਨਕਾ,
ਪ੍ਰਸਤਾਵਨਾ, ਆਮੁਖ, ਮੁੰਢ, ਆਰੰਭ, ਭੂਮਕਾ;
ਭੂਮਕਾ ਬੰਨ੍ਹਣੀ; ਮੰਗਲਾਚਰਨ ਦੇ ਤੌਰ ਤੇ
ਵਰਤਣਾ

prelusive (ਪਰਿ'ਲਯੂਸਿਵ਼) *a* ਆਰੰਭਕ, ਮੁਢਲਾ,
ਭੂਮਕਾ ਸਰੂਪ; ਪੂਰਵ-ਸੂਚਨਾਤਮਕ

premature ('ਪਰੈੱਮਅਟਯੂਅ*) *a* ਅਗੇਤਰਾ
ਅਧੂਰਾ, ਕੱਚਾ, ਅਕਾਲ-ਪੋਢੂ, ਕਚਰੋਈ; **~ly**
ਅਗੇਤਰੇ ਹੀ, ਵਕਤ ਤੋਂ ਪਹਿਲਾਂ, ਕਾਹਲੀ ਕਾਹਲੀ

premeditate ('ਪਰੀ'ਮੈੱਡੀਟੇਇਟ) *v a* ਪੂਰਵ-
ਵਿਚਾਰ ਕਰਨਾ, ਪੂਰਵ-ਚਿੰਤਨ ਕਰਨਾ, (ਮਨ
ਵਿਚ) ਨੀਂਹ ਬੰਨ੍ਹਣੀ, ਮਨਸੂਬਾ ਬੰਨ੍ਹਣਾ; **~d**
ਪੂਰਵ-ਚਿੰਤਤ, ਜਾਣ-ਬੁੱਝੀ, ਪੂਰਵ-ਕਲਪਤ

premeditation (ਪਰੀ'ਮੈੱਡਿ'ਟੇਇਸ਼ਨ) *n* ਪੂਰਵ-
ਸੰਕਲਪ, ਅਗਾਊਂ ਚਿਤਵਣ

premier ('ਪਰੈੱਮਯਅ*) *n a* ਪ੍ਰਧਾਨ-ਮੰਤਰੀ,
ਪ੍ਰਮੁੱਖ, ਮੁਖੀਆ, ਆਗੂ; ਪ੍ਰਧਾਨ, ਸ੍ਰੇਸ਼ਠ, ਸਰਵ-
ਸ੍ਰੇਸ਼ਠ; **~ship** ਪ੍ਰਧਾਨ-ਮੰਤਰੀ ਪਦ, ਪ੍ਰਧਾਨ-
ਮੰਤਰੀ ਕਾਲ

premise ('ਪਰੈੱਸਿ) *n v* ਆਧਾਰ-ਵਾਕ, ਪੂਰਵ-
ਵਾਕ, ਪੂਰਵ-ਕਥਿਤ ਤੱਥ; ਚਾਰ ਦੀਵਾਰੀ,
ਅਹਾਤਾ

premium ('ਪਰੀਮਯਅਮ) *n* ਪ੍ਰਤੀਫਲ;
ਇਵਜ਼ਾਨਾ; ਘੋਨਸ, ਲਾਭ-ਅੰਸ਼; ਬੀਮੇ ਦੀ
ਕਿਸ਼ਤ, ਸਿਖਵਾਈ, ਪੜ੍ਹਵਾਈ, ਕਿਸੇ ਕਿੱਤੇ ਨੂੰ

ਸਿੱਖਣ ਦੀ ਫ਼ੀਸ; ਬਦਲਵਾਈ

promonition ('ਪ੍ਰੈੱਮੱਅਨਿਸ਼ਅਨ) *n* ਪੂਰਵ-ਸੂਚਨਾ, ਅਗੇਤੀ ਚੇਤਾਵਨੀ, ਅਗਾਊਂ ਸੂਹ, ਖੁੜਕ, ਪ੍ਰਬੋਧ, ਪੂਰਵ-ਬੋਧ

prenatal ('ਪ੍ਰੀਨੇਇਟਲ) *a* ਗਰਭ ਅਵਸਥਾ ਸਬੰਧੀ, ਜਨਮ ਤੋਂ ਪਹਿਲੇ, ਜਨਮ-ਪੂਰਵ

prentice ('ਪ੍ਰੈੱਨਟਿਸ) *a* ਅਨੁਭਵਹੀਨ, ਅਨਾੜੀ, ਅਲੂਣ, ਅਣਜਾਣ, ਮੁੱਢ

preoccupation (ਪ੍ਰੀ'ਔਕਯੁ'ਪੇਇਸ਼ਅਨ) *n* ਪੂਰਵ-ਧਾਰਨਾ, ਪੂਰਵ-ਨਿਰਣੈ; ਅਗੇਤਾ ਕਬਜ਼ਾ, ਪੂਰਵ ਰੁਝੇਵਾਂ, ਧਿਆਨ-ਮਗਨਤਾ

preoccupy ('ਪ੍ਰੀਔਕਯੁਪਾਇ) *v* ਕਬਜ਼ੇ ਵਿਚ ਕਰ ਲੈਣਾ, ਪੂਰਵ-ਅਧਿਕਾਰ ਕਰਨਾ, ਅਗਾਊਂ ਕਬਜ਼ਾ ਕਰਨਾ, ਸੋਚਾਂ ਵਿਚ ਡੋਬ ਰੱਖਣਾ, ਰੁੱਝਿਆ ਰੱਖਣਾ, ਪੂਰਵ-ਅਧਿਕਾਰ ਕਰਨਾ, ਵਿਚਾਰ-ਮਗਨ ਹੋਣਾ

prepaid ('ਪ੍ਰੀਪੇਇਡ) *a* ਪਹਿਲਾਂ ਦਿੱਤਾ ਗਿਆ, ਪਹਿਲੋਂ ਅਦਾ ਕੀਤਾ

preparation ('ਪ੍ਰੈੱਪਅਰੇਇਸ਼ਨ) *n* ਤਿਆਰੀ, ਪੂਰਵ-ਵਿਵਸਥਾ ਇੰਤਜ਼ਾਮ, ਥੰਦੋਬਸਤ, ਸਾਜ਼-ਸਾਮਾਨ, ਸਬਕ ਪੜ੍ਹਨ ਦੀ ਤਿਆਰੀ

preparatory (ਪਰਿ'ਪਰੈਅਟ(ਅ)ਰਿ *a* ਆਯੋਜਨਾਤਮਕ, ਤਿਆਰੀ; ਆਰੰਭਕ; ਪ੍ਰਾਰੰਭਕ

prepare (ਪਰਿ'ਪੇਅ*) *v* ਤਿਆਰ ਕਰਨਾ; ਤੱਤਪਰ ਕਰਨਾ; ਪ੍ਰਸਤੁਤ ਕਰਨਾ; ਸਿੱਧ ਕਰਨਾ; ~d ਤਿਆਰ, ਤੱਤਪਰ; ਉਤਪੰਨ; ਪ੍ਰਾਪਤ, ਸੁਸੱਜਤ; ~dness ਤਿਆਰੀ, ਤੱਤਪਰਤਾ

preponderance (ਪਰਿ'ਪੌਨਡ਼(ਅ)ਰਅੰਸ) *n* ਪ੍ਰਬਲਤਾ, ਪ੍ਰਧਾਨਤਾ, ਅਧਿਕਤਾ, ਬਹੁਲਤਾ

preposition ('ਪ੍ਰੈੱਪਅ'ਜ਼ਿਸ਼ਨ) *n* ਪੂਰਵ-ਸਰਗਾ, ਸੰਬਧ ਸੂਚਕ ਸ਼ਬਦ; ~al ਸਬੰਧਕੀ, ਪੂਰਵ-

---

ਸੰਗੀ

prerequisite ('ਪ੍ਰੀ'ਰੈਕਵਿਜ਼ਿਟ) *a n* ਬਹੁਤ ਜ਼ਰੂਰੀ, ਅਤੀ ਲੋੜੀਂਦਾ, ਪਰਤ, ਪਹਿਲੀ ਲੋੜ, ਪੂਰਵ-ਆਕਾਂਖਿਆ, ਪ੍ਰਮੁੱਖ ਅਵੱਸ਼ਕਤਾ

prerogative (ਪਰਿ'ਰੌਗਅਟਿਵ*) *n* ਸ਼ਾਹੀ ਇਖ਼ਤਿਆਰ, ਪਰਮ-ਅਧਿਕਾਰ, ਜਨਮ-ਸਿੱਧ ਅਧਿਕਾਰ, ਪ੍ਰਭੂਸਤਾ, ਸਹਿਜ-ਸ਼ਕਤੀ; ਵਿਸ਼ੇਸ਼ ਅਧਿਕਾਰ ਵਾਲਾ

prescribe (ਪਰਿ'ਸਕਰਾਇਬ) *v* ਨਿਰਦੇਸ਼ ਕਰਨਾ, ਤਜਵੀਜ਼ ਕਰਨੀ; ਹੁਕਮ ਦੇਣਾ; ਆਗਿਆ ਕਰਨੀ; ਨੁਸਖਾ ਲਿਖਣਾ, ਨਿਯਤ ਕਰਨਾ; ~d ਨਿਯਤ; ਨਿਸ਼ਚਤ, ਨਿਰਦਿਸ਼ਟ; ਪ੍ਰਕਲਪਤ

prescription (ਪਰੀ'ਸ਼ਕਰਿਪਸ਼ਨ) *n* ਨੁਸਖਾ, ਤਜਵੀਜ਼; ਨਿਰਧਾਰਨ, ਨਿਰਦੇਸ਼ਨ, ਵਿਧੀ; ਪਰਿਪਾਟੀ

prescriptive (ਪਰੀ'ਸਕਰਿਪਟਵ੍) *a* ਨਿਰਧਾਰਨਾਤਮਕ, ਆਗਿਆ ਅਨੁਸਾਰ, ਵਿਧੀਪੂਰਵਕ

presence ('ਪ੍ਰੈੱਜ਼ੰਸ) *n* ਹਾਜ਼ਰੀ, ਮੌਜੁਦਗੀ, ਉਪਸਥਿਤੀ

present ('ਪ੍ਰੈੱਜ਼ੰਟ) *a n v* (1) ਹਾਜ਼ਰ, ਮੌਜੂਦ, ਅਜੋਕਾ, ਵਰਤਮਾਨ; (2) ਭੇਟਾ, ਬਖ਼ਸ਼ੀਸ਼, ਤੋਹਫ਼ਾ, ਦੱਛਣਾ, ਪੁਰਸਕਾਰ, ਉਪਹਾਰ; ਮਿਲਾਉਣਾ, ਭੇਟ ਕਰਾਉਣਾ, ਅੱਗੇ ਰੱਖਣਾ, ਸਾਖਿਆਤ ਕਰਨਾ, ਹਾਜ਼ਰ ਹੋਣਾ, ਉਪਸਥਿਤ ਹੋਣਾ; ~able ਸੁਡੌਲ, ਵੇਖਣਯੋਗ, ਪੇਸ਼ ਕਰਨਯੋਗ; ~ation ਭੇਟਾ, ਦਾਨ, ਉਪਹਾਰ, ਦੱਛਣਾ, ਅਰਪਣ

presently ('ਪ੍ਰੈੱਜ਼ੰਟਲਿ) *adv* ਹੁਣੇ ਹੀ, ਹੁਣ; ਥੋੜੀ ਦੇਰ ਨੂੰ, ਛੇਤੀ ਹੀ, ਤਤਕਾਲ, ਤੁਰੰਤ

preservation ('ਪ੍ਰੈੱਜ਼ਅ'ਵ਼ੇਇਸ਼ਨ) *n* ਸੰਭਾਲ,

ਸੁਰੱਖਿਆ, ਬਚਾਉ, ਰੱਖਿਆ, ਕਾਇਮੀ

preserve (ਪਰਿ'ਜ਼ਅਵ੍) *v n* (ਖ਼ਰਾਬ ਜਾਂ ਨੁਕਸਾਨ ਤੋਂ) ਬਚਾਉ ਰੱਖਣਾ, ਰੱਖਿਆ ਕਰਨੀ, ਸਹੀ ਸਲਾਮਤ ਰੱਖਣਾ, ਬਰਕਰਾਰ ਰੱਖਣਾ, ਕਾਇਮ ਰੱਖਣਾ; ~d ਸੁਰੱਖਿਅਤ, ਮਹਿਫ਼ੂਜ਼

preside (ਪਰਿ'ਜ਼ਾਇਡ੍) *v* ਸਭਾਪਤੀ ਬਣਨਾ, ਪ੍ਰਧਾਨਗੀ ਕਰਨੀ; ਪ੍ਰਮੁੱਖ ਹੋਣਾ; ~ncy ਪ੍ਰਧਾਨਗੀ, ਪ੍ਰਧਾਨਤਾ, ਰਾਜ, ਮਹਾਂ ਪ੍ਰਾਂਤ; ~nt ਪ੍ਰਧਾਨ, ਰਾਸ਼ਟਰਪਤੀ, ਸਭਾਪਤੀ, ਅਧਿਕਰਸ; ~ntial ਪ੍ਰਧਾਨਗੀ, ਰਾਸ਼ਟਰਪਤੀ ਸਬੰਧੀ

presiding (ਪਰਿ'ਜ਼ਾਇਡਿਡ੍) *a* ਪ੍ਰਧਾਨਗੀ ਕਰਨ ਵਾਲਾ; ~officer ਨਿਰਵਾਚਨ ਅਫ਼ਸਰ

presidium (ਪਰਿ'ਸਿਡ੍ਰਿਅਮ) *n* ਸਭਾਪਤੀ-ਮੰਡਲ, ਪ੍ਰਧਾਨਗੀ-ਮੰਡਲ, (ਸਾਮਵਾਦੀ ਦੇਸ਼ਾਂ ਦੀ) ਸਹਾਈ ਸੰਮਤੀ

press (ਪਰੈੱਸ) *n v* (1) ਛਾਪਾਖ਼ਾਨਾ, ਛਾਪਾ, ਮਸ਼ੀਨ; (2) ਕੱਪੜੇ ਇਸਤਰੀ ਕਰਨ ਵਾਲਾ ਲੋਹਾ; (3) ਪੱਤਰਕਾਰੀ; (4) ਸ਼ਿਕੰਜਾ, ਦਬਾਉਣਾ; ਦੱਬਣਾ, ਦਬਾਉਣਾ, ਨੱਪਣਾ, ਜ਼ੋਰ ਪਾਉਣਾ, ਸ਼ਿਕੰਜੇ ਵਿਚ ਰੱਖਣਾ; ~conference ਪੱਤਰਕਾਰੀ-ਸੰਮੇਲਨ; ~man ਪੱਤਰਕਾਰ; ਛਪਾਈ ਕਰਮਚਾਰੀ; ~ing ਅਤੀ ਜ਼ਰੂਰੀ; ਪ੍ਰਬਲ; ਜ਼ੋਰਦਾਰ; ਭਾਰੀ; ~ure ਦਬਾਉ; ਦਾਬ; ਜ਼ੋਰ; ਤੰਗੀ; ਮੁਸੀਬਤ; ਸਖ਼ਤੀ; ਤਕਲੀਫ਼; ਜ਼ਬਰ, ਜ਼ਬਰਦਸਤੀ; ਨਪੀੜ; ~urize ਦਬਾਉ ਪਾਉਣਾ; ਜ਼ੋਰ ਪਾਉਣਾ

prestige (ਪਰੈਸੱਟੀਜ਼) *n* ਪ੍ਰਤਿਸ਼ਠਾ; ਰਤੁਤਲ; ਇੱਜ਼ਤ, ਮਾਣ, ਸ਼ਾਖ਼, ਪ੍ਰਤਾਪ, ਗੌਰਵ

presumably (ਪਰਿ'ਜ਼ਯੂਮਅਬਲਿ) *adv* ਸੰਭਵ ਤੌਰ ਤੇ, ਮਿਥਤ ਰੂਪ ਵਿਚ

presume (ਪਰਿ'ਜ਼ਯੂਮ) *v* ਪਰਿਕਲਪਨਾ ਕਰਨੀ,

ਫ਼ਰਜ਼ ਕਰਨਾ, ਕਿਆਸ ਕਰਨਾ, ਮੰਨਣਾ

presumption (ਪਰਿ'ਜ਼ਅੰ(ਪ)ਸ਼ਨ) *n* ਕਿਆਸ, ਗੁਮਾਨ, ਪਰਿਕਲਪਨਾ, ਖ਼ਿਆਲ, ਸੰਭਾਵਨਾ; ਗੁਸਤਾਖ਼ੀ

presumptive (ਪਰਿ'ਜ਼ਅੰ(ਪ)ਟਿਵ੍) *a* ਕਿਆਸੀ; ਫ਼ਰਜ਼ੀ, ਅਨੁਮਾਨੀ

presumptuous (ਪਰਿ'ਜ਼ਅੰ(ਪ)ਚੁਅਸ) *a* ਗੁਸਤਾਖ਼, ਸ਼ੋਖ, ਜ਼ਿੱਦੀ, ਹਠੀ, ਢੀਠ ਅਤਿ ਅਭਿਮਾਨੀ

presuppose ('ਪਰੀ'ਸਅੱਪਅਊਜ਼) *v* ਪੂਰਵ ਧਾਰਨਾ ਬਣਾਉਟੀ, ਪੂਰਵ ਅਨੁਮਾਨ ਲਾਉਣਾ

presupposition (ਪਰੀ'ਸਅੱਪਅ'ਜ਼ਿਸ਼ਨ) *n* ਪੂਰਵ-ਅਨੁਮਾਨ, ਪੂਰਵ-ਧਾਰਣਾ

pretence (ਪਰਿ'ਟੈਂਸ) *n* ਬਹਾਨਾ, ਛਲ, ਕਪਟ; ਅਡੰਬਰ

pretend (ਪਰਿ'ਟੈਂਡ) *v* ਬਹਾਨਾ ਕਰਨਾ, ਮਕਰ ਕਰਨਾ, ਢੌਂਗ ਕਰਨਾ, ਦਿਖਾਵਾ ਕਰਨਾ

pretension (ਪਰਿ'ਟੈਂਨਸ਼ਨ) *n* ਦਾਅਵਾ; ਬਹਾਨਾ, ਡੀਂਗ, ਫਤੂ, ਆਂਡਬਰ; ਦੰਤ

pretext ('ਪਰੀਟੈੱਕਸਟ) *n v* ਛਲ, ਕਪਟ, ਬਹਾਨਾ, ਝੁੱਚਰ, ਹੀਲ-ਹੁੱਜਤ, ਕਪਟ ਕਰਨਾ, ਹੀਲ-ਹੁੱਜਤ ਕਰਨੀ

pretty ('ਪਰਿਟਿ) *a adv* (ਬੱਚੇ ਜਾਂ ਤੀਵੀਂ ਲਈ) ਸੁੰਦਰ, ਮਲੂਕ, ਬਾਂਕਾ, ਅਲਬੇਲਾ; (ਗੀਤ) ਉੱਤਮ;

prevail (ਪਰਿ'ਵ੍ਰੇਇਲ) *v* ਹਾਵੀ ਹੋਣਾ, ਛਾ ਜਾਣਾ, ਗ਼ਾਲਬ ਹੋਣਾ, ਪ੍ਰਬਲ ਹੋਣਾ, ਭਾਰੂ ਹੋਣਾ, ਜ਼ੋਰ ਫੜਨਾ; ~ing ਪ੍ਰਚਲਤ; ਪ੍ਰਧਾਨ, ਪ੍ਰਬਲ, ਸਰਬ ਸਧਾਰਨ

prevalence ('ਪਰੈੱਵ੍ਅਲਅੰਸ) *a* ਪ੍ਰਚਲਨ; ਬੋਲ-ਬਾਲਾ, ਹੋਂਦ

prevalent (ਪਰੈੱਵਅਲਅੰਟ) *a* ਪ੍ਰਚਲਤ, ਵਿਆਪਕ

prevent (ਪਰਿਵੈੱਟ) *v* ਰੋਕਣਾ, ਹੋਣਾ, ਵਰਜਣਾ, ਨਿਸ਼ੇਧ ਕਰਨਾ, ਮਨ੍ਹਾ ਕਰਨਾ; ~ion ਰੋਕ, ਵਿਘਨ, ਰੁਕਾਵਟ, ਨਿਰੋਧ, ਠਾਕ, ਅਟਕਾ; ~ive ਨਿਵਾਰਕ, ਨਿਰੋਧਕ, ਨਿਸ਼ੇਧਕ

previous ('ਪਰੀਵੂਅਸ) *a* ਪਿਛਲਾ, ਪੂਰਵ, ਬੀਤਿਆ; ~ly ਪਹਿਲਾਂ, ਪੂਰਵ

prey (ਪਰੇਇ) *n v* ਸ਼ਿਕਾਰ; ਬਲੀ; ਸ਼ਿਕਾਰ ਮਾਰਨਾ ਜਾਂ ਕਰਨਾ

price (ਪਰਾਇਸ) *n v* ਮੁੱਲ, ਕੀਮਤ, ਦਰ; ਭਾਅ; ਮੁੱਲ ਲਾਉਣਾ; ~less ਅਮੋਲ, ਅਣਮੋਲ

prick (ਪਰਿਕ) *v n* ਚੋਭਣਾ ਜਾਂ ਚੁੱਭਣਾ, ਵਿੰਨ੍ਹਣਾ, ਗੱਡਣਾ; ਬਿੰਧਣਾ, ਚੋਭ, ਸੁਰਾਖ, ਛਿਦਰ, ਛੇਕ; ~le ਨੋਕਦਾਰ ਕੰਡਾ; ਕੰਡਾ ਚੁਭਣਾ ਜਾਂ ਚੁਭਾਉਣਾ; ਸੱਲਣਾ; ਵਿੰਨ੍ਹਣਾ; ~ly ਕੰਡਿਆਲੀ (ਝਾੜੀ); ਕੰਡੇਦਾਰ; ਖਿਝੂ, ਚਿੜਚੜਾ (ਵਿਅਕਤੀ); ~ly heat ਪਿੱਤ

pride (ਪਰਾਇਡ) *n v* ਅਭਿਮਾਨ, ਘਮੰਡ; ਗੁਮਾਨ; ਅਹੰਕਾਰ; ਘਮੰਡ ਕਰਨਾ; ਅਭਿਮਾਨ ਕਰਨਾ

priest (ਪਰੀਸਟ) *n* ਪਾਦਰੀ; ਪੁਜਾਰੀ, ਪਰੋਹਤ, ਇਮਾਮ; ~craft ਪਰੋਹਤਾਈ; ~hood ਪਰੋਹਤਪਣ, ਪਾਦਰੀਗੀਰੀ

prima ('ਪਰੀਮਆ) *a* ਪ੍ਰਮੁੱਖ, ਪ੍ਰਧਾਨ, ਪ੍ਰਥਮ; ~cy ਪ੍ਰਧਾਨਤਾ, ਪ੍ਰਮੁੱਖਤਾ, ਲਾਟ, ਪਾਦਰੀ ਦਾ ਪਦ

prima facie ('ਪਰਾਇਮ'ਫੇਇਸੀ) (L) *adv a* ਪਹਿਲੀ ਦ੍ਰਿਸ਼ਟੀ ਨਾਲ, ਪ੍ਰਤੱਖ, ਪਰਗਟ ਤੌਰ ਤੇ

primarily ('ਪਰਾਇਮ(ਅ)ਰਅਲਿ) *adv* ਮੂਲ ਰੂਪ ਵਿਚ, ਮੁੱਖ ਰੂਪ ਵਿਚ, ਪ੍ਰਧਾਨ, ਵੱਡਾ

primary ('ਪਰਾਇਮਅਰਿ) *a* ਪ੍ਰਾਰੰਭਕ, ਮੁੱਢਲਾ, ਪ੍ਰਥਮ; ਬੁਨਿਆਦੀ, ਮੂਲਕ, ਮੂਲ

prime ('ਪਰਾਇਮ) *a n v* ਪ੍ਰਧਾਨ, ਪ੍ਰਮੁੱਖ,

ਮਹੱਤਵਪੂਰਨ; ਉੱਤਮ, ਸਰਵਸ੍ਰੇਸ਼ਠ, ਪ੍ਰਥਮ, ਮੌਲਕ, ਪ੍ਰਾਥਮਕ; ~cost ਮੂਲ ਲਾਗਤ; ~minister ਪ੍ਰਧਾਨ ਮੰਤਰੀ

primer ('ਪਰਾਇਮਅ*) *n* ਬਾਲ-ਬੋਧ, ਕਾਇਦਾ, ਪ੍ਰਾਇਮਰ

primitive ('ਪਰਿਮਿਟਿਵੂ) *a n* ਪ੍ਰਾਚੀਨ, ਪ੍ਰਾਰੰਭਕ, ਆਦਿ ਕਾਲੀਨ; ਆਦਿ ਵਾਸੀ; ਬੁਨਿਆਦੀ ਮੂਲ; ~ness ਪ੍ਰਾਚੀਨਤਾ, ਪ੍ਰਾਤਨਤਾ, ਸਾਦਾਪਣ, ਮੌਲਕਤਾ

primitivism ('ਪਰਿਮਿਟਿਵਿਜ਼(ਅ)ਮ) *n* ਪ੍ਰਾਚੀਨਤਾਵਾਦ, ਆਦਿਮਤਾਵਾਦ

prince (ਪਰਿੰਸ) *n* ਸ਼ਹਿਜ਼ਾਦਾ, ਰਾਜ-ਕੁਮਾਰ, ਯੁਵਰਾਜ, ਅਧਿਰਾਜ, ਟਿੱਕਾ; ~ly ਸ਼ਾਹੀ; ਅਮੀਰੀ, ਰਈਸੀ; ਸ਼ਾਨਦਾਰ; ~ss (ਯੂ) ਸ਼ਹਿਜ਼ਾਦੀ, ਰਾਜਕੁਮਾਰੀ, ਰਾਜ-ਦੁਲਾਰੀ; ਰਾਣੀ, ਮਲਕਾ; ਯੁਵਰਾਨੀ

principal ('ਪਰਿੰਸਅਪਲ) *a n* (1) ਪ੍ਰਧਾਨ, ਮੁੱਖ, ਮੁਖੀ, ਸਰਦਾਰ, ਹੁਕਮਰਾਨ, ਅਧਿਅਕਸ਼, ਪ੍ਰਿੰਸੀਪਲ; (2) ਮੂਲ ਰਾਸ਼ੀ, ਮੂਲ, ਅਸਲ

principle ('ਪਰਿੰਸਅਪਲ) *n* ਨਿਯਮ, ਸਿਧਾਂਤ, ਅਸੂਲ, ਵਿਧੀ, ਵਿਵਸਥਾ

print (ਪਰਿੰਟ) *n v* ਛਾਪ, ਨਿਸ਼ਾਨ, ਠੱਪਾ, ਮੋਹਰ, ਚਿੰਨ੍ਹ; ਛਾਪਣਾ; ਛਪਵਾਉਣਾ; ਛਪਵਾ ਕੇ ਪ੍ਰਕਾਸ਼ਤ ਕਰਨਾ; ਛਿੱਬਣਾ; ਠੇਕਣਾ; ~ed matter ਛਪੀ ਹੋਈ ਸਮਗਰੀ; ~er ਛਾਪਕ, ਛਾਪਕਾਰ, ਮੁਦਰਕ; ਛਪਾਈ ਮਸ਼ੀਨ; ~ing ਛਪਾਈ, ਛਾਪਣ ਕਲਾ, ਮੁਦਰਣ

prior ('ਪਰਾਇਅ*) *a adv n* ਪਹਿਲਾ, ਪਹਿਲੋਂ ਦਾ, ਅਗੇਤਰਾ, ਪੂਰਵ-ਵਰਤੀ, ਪ੍ਰਥਮ; ਪਹਿਲੋਂ; ~ity ਪਹਿਲ, ਅਗੇਤ, ਪ੍ਰਥਮਤਾ, ਪੂਰਵਵਰਤਤਾ

prism (ਪਰਿਜ਼(ਅ)ਮ) *n* ਰੰਗਾਵਲੀ ਸ਼ੀਸ਼ਾ,

(ਬ ਵ) ਇੰਦਰ-ਧਨੁਸ਼ ਦਾ ਰੰਗ, ਸਪਤ-ਵਰਣ

prison (ਪਰਿਜ਼ਨ) *n v* ਜੇਲ੍ਹਖਾਨਾ, ਬੰਦੀਖ਼ਾਨਾ, ਕੈਦਖ਼ਾਨਾ, ਹਵਾਲਾਤ, ਕਾਰਾਵਾਸ, ਬੰਦੀ-ਗ੍ਰਹਿ; ਕੈਦ ਕਰਨਾ, ਬੰਦੀ ਬਣਾਉਣਾ, ਡੱਕਣਾ; **~er** ਕੈਦੀ, ਬੰਦੀਵਾਨ

prittle-prattle ('ਪਰਿਟਲ-'ਪਰੈਟਲ) *n* ਚੀਕ ਚਿਹਾੜਾ, ਬਕ-ਬਕ, ਝੱਖ

privacy ('ਪਰਿਵ੍ਹਅਸਿ) *n* ਇਕਾਂਤ; ਪਰਦਾ, ਰਹੱਸ, ਇਕਾਂਤ ਥਾਂ

private ('ਪਰਾਇਵ੍ਹਿਟ) *n a* ਇਕਾਂਤ, ਸੁੰਨਸਾਨ; ਗੁਪਤ ਅੰਗ, ਗੁਪਤ, ਲੁਕਵੀਂ, ਇਕਾਂਤਵਾਸੀ; **~ly** ਗੁਪਤ ਤੌਰ ਤੇ, ਨਿਜੀ ਤੌਰ ਤੇ, ਲੁਕਵੇਂ ਢੰਗ ਨਾਲ

privation (ਪਰਾਇ'ਵ੍ਹਇਸ਼ਨ) *n* ਥੁੜ੍ਹ, ਕਮੀ, ਤੰਗੀ, ਅਭਾਵ, ਕੰਗਾਲੀ

privilege ('ਪਰਿਵ੍ਹਿਲਿਜ) *n v* ਵਿਸ਼ੇਸ਼ ਅਧਿਕਾਰ; ਉਚੇਚਾ ਹੱਕ, ਰਿਆਇਤ; ਅਧਿਕਾਰ ਦੇਣਾ; **~ed** ਵਿਸ਼ੇਸ਼ਾਧਿਕ੍ਰਿਤ

privy ('ਪਰਿਵ੍ਹਿ) *a n* ਲੁਕਵੀਂ, ਗੁਪਤ, ਆਪਣੀ; ਟੱਟੀ-ਖ਼ਾਨਾ; **~purse** ਰਾਜ-ਭੱਤਾ, ਨਿਜੀ ਖ਼ਰਚ; **~seal** ਸਰਕਾਰੀ ਮੋਹਰ

prize (ਪਰਾਇਜ਼) *n* (1) ਇਨਾਮ, ਪੁਰਸਕਾਰ; (2) ਲੁੱਟ ਦਾ ਮਾਲ; ਲਭਤ

pro (ਪਰਅਉ) *prep* ਲਈ, ਵਾਸਤੇ, ਵਜੋਂ, ਪਤੀ; **~s and cons** ਹੱਕ ਵਿਚ ਅਤੇ ਵਿਰੋਧੀ (ਦਲੀਲਾਂ); ਪੱਖ-ਵਿਪੱਖ ਤਰਕ

probability ('ਪਰੌਬਅ'ਬਿਲਅਟਿ) *n* ਸੰਭਾਵਨਾ, ਸੰਭਵ ਗੱਲ; ਸੰਭਾਵਤ

probable ('ਪਰੌਬਅਬਲ) *a* ਸੰਭਵ, ਸੰਭਾਵੀ, ਅਨੁਮਾਨਕ

probably ('ਪਰੌਬਅਬਲਿ) *adv* ਸ਼ਾਇਦ, ਸੰਭਾਵਨਾ ਹੈ ਕਿ, ਆਸ ਹੈ ਕਿ, ਗ਼ਾਲਬਨ

probation (ਪਰਅ'ਬੇਇਸ਼ਨ) *n* ਪਰਤਾਵਾ, ਪਰਖ; ਪਰੀਖਿਆ, ਅਜ਼ਮਾਇਸ਼; **on~** ਪਰਤਾਵੇ ਦੇ ਤੌਰ ਤੇ, ਪਰਖ ਅਧੀਨ, ਪਰਖ ਤੇ; **~ary** ਅਜ਼ਮਾਇਸ਼ੀ (ਸਮਾ); **~er** ਸਿਖਾਂਦਰੂ, ਪਰੀਖਿਆ-ਅਧੀਨ

probe ('ਪਰਅਉਬ) *n v* ਜਾਂਚ, ਛਾਣਬੀਣ; ਟਟੋਲਣਾ; ਛਾਣਬੀਣ ਕਰਨੀ; ਜਾਂਚ ਕਰਨੀ; ਪੜਤਾਲ ਕਰਨੀ, ਫਰੋਲਣਾ, ਖਰੋਚਨਾ

problem ('ਪਰੌਬਲਅਮ) *n* ਸਮੱਸਿਆ, ਪ੍ਰਸ਼ਨ, ਉਲਝਣ, ਧਰਮ-ਸੰਕਟ, ਗੁੰਝਲ; **~atic (al)** ਸਮੱਸਿਆਤਮਕ, ਸ਼ੱਕੀ, ਅਨਿਸ਼ਚਤ, ਸੰਦੇਹੀ

procedure (ਪਰਅ'ਸੀਜਅ*) *n* ਕਾਰਜ-ਪ੍ਰਣਾਲੀ, ਪ੍ਰਕਿਰਿਆ; ਕਾਰਵਾਈ, ਅਮਲ.

proceed (ਪਰਅ'ਸੀਡ) *v* ਅੱਗੇ ਵਧਣਾ, ਨਿਕਲਣਾ (ਮਕਾਨ ਤੋਂ), ਅੱਗੇ ਚਲੱਣਾ, ਵਧਣਾ (ਕਿਸੇ ਕੰਮ ਜਾਂ ਲੇਖ ਆਦਿ ਵਿਚ) ਸ਼ੁਰੂ ਕਰਨਾ, ਕਾਰਵਾਈ ਕਰਨੀ, ਜਾਰੀ ਰੱਖਣਾ; **~ing** ਕਾਰਵਾਈ, ਆਚਰਨ, ਵਿਹਾਰ

proceeds ('ਪਰਅਉਸੀਡਜ਼) *n (pl)* ਵੱਟਕ, ਪ੍ਰਾਪਤੀ, ਪੈਦਾਵਾਰ, ਆਮਦਨੀ, ਮੁਨਾਫ਼ਾ, ਵਾਧਾ, ਬਚਤ

process ('ਪਰਅਉਸੈੱਸ) *n v* ਪ੍ਰਕਿਰਿਆ, ਅਮਲ, ਤਰੀਕਾ, ਕਾਨੂੰਨੀ ਕਾਰਵਾਈ, ਇਤਲਾਹਨਾਮਾ, ਅਦਾਲਤੀ ਹੁਕਮਨਾਮਾ; ਮੁਕੱਦਮਾ ਚਲਾਉਣਾ; ਅਮਲ ਕਰਨਾ

procession (ਪਰਅ'ਸੈੱਸ਼ਨ) *n v* ਜਲੂਸ, ਸਵਾਰੀ; ਜਲੂਸ ਕੱਢਣਾ; **~al** ਜਲੂਸੀ

proclaim (ਪਰਅ'ਕਲੇਇਮ) *v* ਐਲਾਨ ਕਰਨਾ, ਘੋਸ਼ਣਾ ਕਰਨੀ, ਡੌਂਡੀ ਪਿੱਟਣੀ, ਇਸ਼ਤਿਹਾਰ ਦੇਣਾ; ਜੰਗ ਦਾ ਐਲਾਨ ਕਰਨਾ; **~ed** ਘੋਸ਼ਤ, ਐਲਾਨ ਕੀਤਾ, ਪ੍ਰਚਾਰਤ

proclamation ('ਪਰੋਕਲਮਾ'ਮੇਇਸ਼ਨ) *n* ਐਲਾਨ, ਫ਼ਰਮਾਨ; ਦੰਢੋਰਾ; ਹੋਕਾ; ਐਲਾਨ, ਘੋਸ਼ਣਾ, ਮੁਨਾਦੀ, ਡੌਂਡੀ; ਸ਼ਾਹੀ ਐਲਾਨ

procuration ('ਪਰੋਕਯੁ'ਰੇਇਸ਼ਨ) *n* ਪ੍ਰਾਪਤੀ, ਵਸੂਲੀ, ਉਪਲਬਧੀ, ਅਧਿਕਾਰ-ਪੱਤਰ, ਮੁਖ਼ਤਾਰਨਾਮਾ

procurator ('ਪਰੋਕਯੁਰੇਇਟਾ*) *n* ਖ਼ਜ਼ਾਨਾ ਅਫ਼ਸਰ, ਕਾਰਿੰਦਾ, ਗੁਮਾਸ਼ਤਾ, ਪ੍ਰਤੀਨਿਧੀ, ਮੁਖ਼ਤਾਰ

procure (ਪਰਾ'ਕਯੁਅ*) *a* ਪ੍ਰਾਪਤ ਕਰਨਾ, ਪਾਉਣਾ, ਉਪਲਬਧ ਕਰਨਾ, ਹਾਸਲ ਕਰਨਾ; ~**ment** ਪ੍ਰਾਪਤੀ, ਵਸੂਲੀ, ਉਪਲਬਧੀ

prodigal ('ਪਰੋਡਿਗਲ) *a* ਸ਼ਾਹ-ਖ਼ਰਚ, ਉਡਾਊ, ਉਜਾੜੂ, ਫ਼ਜ਼ੂਲ ਖ਼ਰਚ; ਮੁਕਤ-ਹੱਥ; ~**ity** ਸ਼ਾਹ-ਖ਼ਰਚੀ, ਫ਼ਜ਼ੂਲ ਖ਼ਰਚੀ; ਖੁੱਲ੍ਹ-ਖ਼ਰਚੀ

prodigious (ਪਰਾ'ਡਿਜਅਸ) *a* ਅਦਭੁਤ, ਅਲੋਕਿਕ, ਵਚਿੱਤਰ, ਅਜੀਬ, ਬਹੁਤ ਸਾਰਾ; ਵਿਰਾਟ, ਮਹਾਨ, ਜ਼ਬਰਦਸਤ; ਤੀਬਰ, ਅਸਾਧਾਰਨ

produce (ਪਰਾ'ਡਯੂਸ, 'ਪਰੋਡਯੂਸ) *v n* ਪੇਸ਼ ਕਰਨਾ, ਹਾਜ਼ਰ ਕਰਨਾ; ਪ੍ਰਕਾਸ਼ਤ ਕਰਨਾ; (ਰੇਖਾ) ਲਕੀਰ ਵਧਾਉਣੀ; ਪੈਦਾ ਕਰਨਾ, ਉਪਜਾਉਣਾ; (ਨਾਟਕ, ਤਮਾਸ਼ਾ) ਖੇਡਣਾ; ਪੈਦਾਵਾਰ, ਉਪਜ, ਉਤਪਤੀ; ਪ੍ਰਾਪਤੀ, ਆਮਦਨੀ; ~**d** ਉਤਪੰਨ, ਉਤਪਾਦਤ; ~**r** ਪੈਦਾ ਕਰਨ ਵਾਲਾ, ਪੇਸ਼ ਕਰਨ ਵਾਲਾ, ਉਤਪਾਦਕ, (ਵਸਤੂਆਂ) ਬਣਾਉਣ ਵਾਲਾ; (ਨਾਟਕ, ਤਮਾਸ਼ੇ) ਨਿਰਮਾਤਾ

producibility (ਪਰਾ'ਡਯੂਸਅ'ਬਿਲਅਟਿ) *n* ਉਤਪਾਦਨ-ਸ਼ਕਤੀ

product ('ਪਰੋਡਅੱਕਟ) *n* ਪੈਦਾਵਾਰ, ਉਪਜ, ਉਤਪਤੀ; ਫਲ, ਲਾਭ; (ਹਿਸਾਬ) ਗੁਣਨ-ਫਲ;

~**ion** ਪੈਦਾਵਾਰ, ਉਤਪਤੀ; ਉਪਜ; ਨਿਰਮਾਣ, ਕਲਾਕ੍ਰਿਤੀ; ~**ive** ਉਪਜਾਊ, ਉਤਪਾਦੀ; ~**ivity** ਉਤਪਾਦਤਾ; ਉਪਜਾਉਪਣ

profess (ਪਰਾ'ਫ਼ੈੱਸ) *v* ਦਾਅਵਾ ਕਰਨਾ, ਪਰਗਟ ਕਰਨਾ; ਪ੍ਰਚਾਰ ਕਰਨਾ, ਖੁੱਲ੍ਹੇ ਆਮ ਕਹਿਣਾ; ਘੋਸ਼ਣਾ ਕਰਨੀ; ਸਵੀਕਾਰ ਕਰਨਾ, ਅੰਗੀਕਾਰ ਕਰਨਾ, ਮੰਨਣਾ; ~**ion** ਧੰਦਾ, ਪੇਸ਼ਾ, ਰੁਜ਼ਗਾਰ, ਉਪਜੀਵਕਾ, ਕਿਰਤ-ਵਿਰਤ; ~**ional** ਪੇਸ਼ੇਵਰ, ਪੇਸ਼ੇ ਦਾ; ~**or** ਆਚਾਰੀਆ, ਪ੍ਰਾਧਿਆਪਕ, ਪ੍ਰੋਫ਼ੈਸਰ; ਨਿਸ਼ਰੇਧਾਰੀ

proficiency (ਪਰਾ'ਫ਼ਿਸ਼੍ਇੰਸਿ) *n* ਨਿਪੁੰਨਤਾ, ਪਰਿਪੱਕਤਾ, ਪ੍ਰਵੀਨਤਾ, ਮੁਹਾਰਤ

proficient (ਪਰਾ'ਫ਼ਿਸ਼੍ਅੰਟ) *a n* ਨਿਪੁੰਨ; ਮਾਹਰ, ਲਾਇਕ; ਪ੍ਰਵੀਨ

profile ('ਪਰੋਫ਼ਾਉਫ਼ਾਇਲ) *n v* ਇਕ-ਰੁਖੀ ਤਸਵੀਰ; ਇਕ-ਪਾਸੀ ਤਸਵੀਰ, ਇਕ-ਰੁਖਾ ਖ਼ਾਕਾ; ਸਿਟੀ ਦਾ ਬੰਨ੍ਹ; ਕਿਲੇ ਦਾ ਵਿੰਗਾ ਖੜ੍ਹਾ ਭਾਗਾ; ਇਕ-ਪਾਸੀ ਤਸਵੀਰ ਬਣਾਉਣਾ; ਰੇਖਾ-ਚਿਤਰ ਲਿਖਣਾ

profit ('ਪਰੋਫ਼ਿਟ) *n v* ਲਾਭ, ਨਫ਼ਾ; ਵਾਧਾ; ਲਾਭ ਲੈਣਾ, ਫ਼ਾਇਦਾ ਉਠਾਉਣਾ; ~**able** ਲਾਭਦਾਇਕ, ਲਾਹੇਵੰਦ, ਲਾਭਵੰਦ, ਉਪਯੋਗੀ; ~**eer** ਮੁਨਾਫ਼ਾਖੋਰੀ, ਨਾਜਾਇਜ਼ ਲਾਭ ਲੈਣਾ, ਨਫ਼ਾਖੋਰੀ ਕਰਨੀ; ~**eering** ਮੁਨਾਫ਼ਾਖੋਰੀ, ਨਫ਼ਾਖੋਰੀ, ਸੂਦਖੋਰੀ; ~**less** ਲਾਭਰਹਿਤ, ਨਿਰਾਰਥਕ, ਬੇਫ਼ਾਇਦਾ, ਬੇਕਾਰ

profound (ਪਰਾ'ਫ਼ਾਉਂਡ) *a n* ਡੂੰਘਾ, ਗੁੜ੍ਹਾ, (ਭਾਵ) ਘੂਕ, (ਨੀਂਦ) ਘੁੱਪ (ਹਨੇਰਾ); ਭਰਵਾਂ, ਅਤੀਅੰਤ, ਅਤੀਅਧਿਕ, ਤੀਬਰ; ਹਾਰਦਿਕ; ਗੰਭੀਰਤਾ, ਡੂੰਘਾਈ, ਤੀਬਰਤਾ; ~**ness**, ~**ity** ਗੁੜ੍ਹਤਾ, ਅਗਾਧਤਾ, ਘਣੱਪਣ; ਤੀਬਰਤਾ

profuse (ਪਰਅ'ਫ਼ਯੂਜ਼) *a* ਸਖੀ, ਉਦਾਰ, ਲੁਟਾਉ; ਭਰਪੂਰ, ਬਹੁਤ ਅਧਿਕ

progeny ('ਪਰੌਜਅਨਿ) *n* ਸੰਤਾਨ; ਨਸਲ, ਨਤੀਜਾ; ਫਲ

programme ('ਪਰਅਉਗਰੈਮ) *n v* ਕਾਰਜਕ੍ਰਮ, ਯੋਜਨਾ, ਕਾਰਜ-ਸੂਚੀ; ਪ੍ਰੋਗਰਾਮ ਬਣਾਉਣਾ, ਯੋਜਨਾ ਬਣਾਉਣੀ; ~d ਯੋਜਨਾਬੱਧ, ਕਾਰਜ-ਕ੍ਰਮਬੱਧ, ਪੂਰਵ-ਯੋਜਤ

progress ('ਪਰਅਉਗਰੈੱਸ, ਪਰਅ(ਉ)'ਗਰੈੱਸ) *n v* ਤਰੱਕੀ, ਉੱਨਤੀ, ਵਾਧਾ, ਪ੍ਰਗਤੀ, ਵਿਕਾਸ-ਅਵਸਥਾ; ਜਾਰੀ ਰਹਿਣਾ, ਚੱਲ ਰਿਹਾ, ਹੋਣਾ; ਪ੍ਰਗਤੀ ਕਰਨੀ, ਅੰਗੇ ਵਧਣਾ; ~ion ਵਿਕਾਸ, ਉੱਨਤੀ, ਪ੍ਰਗਤੀ ਸਿਲਸਲਾ; ~ive ਪ੍ਰਗਤੀਵਾਦੀ, ਅਗਾਂਹ-ਵਧੂ, ਤਰੱਕੀ-ਪਸੰਦ, ਅਗਾਰਗਾਮੀ, ਵਿਕਾਸਵਾਦੀ, ਸਿਲਸਲੇਵਾਰ, ਪ੍ਰਗਤੀਸ਼ੀਲ

prohibit (ਪਰਅ'ਹਿਬਿਟ) *v* ਵਰਜਤ ਕਰਨਾ, ਰੋਕਣਾ, ਹਟਕਣਾ, ਮਨ੍ਹਾ ਕਰਨਾ, ਵਰਜਣਾ, ਪ੍ਰਤੀਬੰਧ ਲਾਉਣਾ; ~ed ਵਰਜਤ; ਮਨ੍ਹਾ; ~ion ਵਰਜਨ, ਬੰਧੇਜ; ਮਨਾਹੀ; ਨਸ਼ੇਬੰਦੀ, ਸ਼ਰਾਬਬੰਦੀ; ~ory ਨਿਸ਼ੇਧਾਤਮਕ, ਨਿਸ਼ੇਧੀ, ਨਿਸ਼ੇਧਵਾਦੀ

project (ਪਰਅ'ਜੈੱਕਟ, 'ਪਰੌਜੈੱਕਟ) *v n* ਸੁੱਟਣਾ, ਤਜਵੀਜ਼ ਕਰਨੀ, ਵਿਉਂਤ ਬਣਾਉਣੀ, ਯੋਜਨਾ ਤਿਆਰ ਕਰਨਾ; ਤਜਵੀਜ਼, ਖ਼ਾਕਾ, ਯੋਜਨਾ; ~or ਚਲਚਿੱਤਰ ਜੰਤਰ, ਪ੍ਰੋਜੈਕਟਰ; ਯੋਜਨਾਕਾਰ, ਨਿਰੂਪਕ

proliferate (ਪਰਅ(ਉ)'ਲਿਫ਼ਅਰੇਇਟ) *v* ਪਸਰਨਾ, ਵਾਧਾ ਹੋਣਾ

proliferation (ਪਰਅ(ਉ)'ਲਿਫ਼ਅ'ਰੇਇਸ਼ਨ) *n* ਵਾਧਾ, ਪਸਾਰ, ਪਲਰਨ

prolific (ਪਰਅ(ਉ)'ਲਿਫ਼ਿਕ) *a* ਉਪਜਾਊ, ਫਲਦਾਇਕ; ਬਹੁ-ਉਪਜਾਊ; ਭਰਿਆ; ਭਰਵਾਂ;

~ation ਕ੍ਰਮਕ ਵਿਕਾਸ; ਕ੍ਰਮਬੱਧ ਵਾਧਾ; ਸਿਲਸਲੇਵਾਰ ਤਰੱਕੀ

prologue ('ਪਰਅਉਲੋਗ) *n* ਮੁੱਖ-ਬੰਧ, ਪ੍ਰਸਤਾਵਨਾ, ਮੰਗਲਾਚਰਨ, ਭੂਮਕਾ

prolong (ਪਰਅ(ਉ)'ਲੋਙ) *v* ਲਮਕਾਉਣਾ, ਵਿਸਤਾਰ ਦੇਣਾ, ਦੀਰਘ ਕਰਨਾ, ਵਧਾ ਦੇਣਾ, ਪ੍ਰਸਾਰਤ ਕਰਨਾ; ~ation ਲਮਕਾਉ, ਵਧਣ, ਵਿਸਤਾਰ, ਫੈਲਾਉ

prominence, prominency ('ਪਰੌਮਿਨਅੰਸ, 'ਪਰੌਮਿਨਅੰਸਿ) *n* ਮਹੱਤਾ, ਮਸ਼ਹੂਰੀ, ਪ੍ਰਸਿੱਧੀ, ਉੱਭਾਰ; ਵਧਾਣ; ਪ੍ਰਧਾਨਤਾ, ਪ੍ਰਮੁੱਖਤਾ, ਵਿਸ਼ਿਸ਼ਟਤਾ

prominent ('ਪਰੌਮਿਨਅੰਟ) *a* ਉੱਭਰਿਆ; ਅੱਗੇ ਵਧਿਆ; ਉਨਤ, ਪ੍ਰਸਿੱਧ, ਉੱਘਾ, ਮਸ਼ਹੂਰ, ਸ੍ਰੇਸ਼ਠ, ਵਿਸ਼ਿਸ਼ਟ

promise ('ਪਰੌਮਿਸ) *n v* ਵਚਨ, ਇਕਰਾਰ, ਕੌਲ, ਪ੍ਰਣ; ਪ੍ਰਤਿਗਿਆ; ਇਕਰਾਰ ਕਰਨਾ; ~d ਸੰਭਾਵਤ, ਕਲਪਤ

promising ('ਪਰੌਮਿਸਿਙ) *a* ਹੋਣਹਾਰ, ਸੰਭਾਵਨਾ ਪੂਰਨ, ਆਸ਼ਾਜਨਕ

promissory ('ਪਰੌਮਿਸਅਰਿ) *a* ਆਸ਼ਾਪੂਰਨ, ਸੰਭਾਵਨਾ-ਪੂਰਨ; ~note ਪਰੌਨੋਟ, ਵਚਨ-ਪੱਤਰ

promote (ਪਰਅ'ਮਅਉਟ) *v* ਵਧਾਉਣਾ, ਤਰੱਕੀ ਦੇਣੀ, ਦਰਜਾ ਵਧਾਉਣਾ, ਪਦ-ਉੱਨਤੀ ਕਰਨਾ, ਅਨੁਪ੍ਰਾਣਤ ਕਰਨਾ; ~r ਸਮਰਥਕ, ਉਤੇਜਤ ਕਰਨ ਵਾਲਾ; ਉਤਸਾਹਕ

prompt (ਪਰੌ(ਪ)ਟ) *a v* ਤਿਆਰ, ਤਤਪਰ, ਤਿਆਰ-ਬਰ-ਤਿਆਰ, ਝਟਪਟ, ਤੁਰੰਤ; ਉਕਸਾਉਣਾ, ਚੁੱਕਣਾ; ~er ਉਤੇਜਕ, ਪਰੇਰਕ, ਪ੍ਰਾਮਪਟਰ; ~ing ਪਰੇਰਨਾ, ਟੂੰਬਣ, ਉਤੇਜਨਾ, ਅਨੁਬੋਧਨ, ਪ੍ਰਾਪਟਿੰਗ

promulgate ('ਪ੍ਰੌਮਅਲਗੇਇਟ) v ਐਲਾਨ ਕਰਨਾ, ਘੋਸ਼ਤ ਕਰਨਾ; (ਕਾ) ਲਾਗੂ ਕਰਨਾ, ਜਾਰੀ ਕਰਨਾ

promulgation ('ਪ੍ਰੌਮਅਲਗੇਇਸ਼ਨ) n ਪ੍ਰਕਾਸ਼ਨ, ਘੋਸ਼ਣਾ, ਡੌਂਡੀ, ਮੁਨਾਦੀ, ਐਲਾਨ

prone (ਪ੍ਰਅਉਨ) a ਮੂਧਾ, ਉਂਧੀ, ਮੂੰਹ-ਭਾਰ; ਰੁਫ਼ਾਲ, ਚਿੱਤ

pronoun ('ਪ੍ਰਅਉਨਉਨ) n (ਵਿਆ) ਸਰਵਨਾਮ, ਪੜਨਾਂਵ

pronounce (ਪ੍ਰਅ'ਨਾਉਂਸ) v ਉਚਾਰਨਾ, ਬੋਲਣਾ, ਕਹਿਣਾ, ਪੜ੍ਹਨਾ; ਐਲਾਨ ਕਰਨਾ; ਨਿਰਣਾ ਦੇਣਾ; ~d ਉਚਾਰਨ, ਸਪਸ਼ਟ, ਨਿਸ਼ਚਤ, ਘੋਸ਼ਤ

pronunciation (ਪ੍ਰਅ'ਨਅੰਨਸਿ'ਏਇਸ਼ਨ) n ਉਚਾਰਨ, ਉਚਾਰਨ-ਵਿਧੀ

proof (ਪ੍ਰੂਫ਼) n v ਸਬੂਤ, ਪ੍ਰਮਾਣ, ਗਵਾਹੀ, ਸਾਖੀ, ਸਿੱਧੀ; ਸੋਧ ਕਰਨੀ, ਸਿੱਧ ਬਣਾਉਣਾ, ਨਿਸ਼ਪ੍ਰਭਾਵੀ ਬਣਾਉਣਾ; ~reader ਪ੍ਰੂਫ਼-ਰੀਡਰ, ਸੋਧਨ-ਕਰਤਾ

prop (ਪ੍ਰੌਪ) n v ਥੰਮ੍ਹੀ, ਟੇਕ, ਆਸਰਾ, ਢੋਹ, ਸਹਾਰਾ, ਆਸਰਾ; ਥੰਮ੍ਹੀ ਦੇਣੀ, ਢੋਹ ਲਾਉਣੀ, ਟੇਕ ਦੇਣੀ, ਆਸਰਾ ਦੇਣਾ, ਸੰਭਾਲਣਾ

propaganda ('ਪ੍ਰੌਪਅ'ਗੈਂਡਅ) n ਪ੍ਰਚਾਰ, ਪ੍ਰਸਾਰ

propagandist (ਪ੍ਰੌਪਅ'ਗੈਂਡਿਸਟ) n ਪ੍ਰਚਾਰਕ, ਪ੍ਰਸਾਰਕ

propagate (ਪ੍ਰੌਪਅਗੇਇਟ) v ਪ੍ਰਚਾਰ ਕਰਨਾ, ਪ੍ਰਕਾਸ਼ਤ ਕਰਨਾ; ਅੱਗੇ ਵਧਾਉਣਾ; ਵਧਾਉਣਾ, ਫੈਲਾਉਣਾ

propagation ('ਪ੍ਰੌਪਅ'ਗੇਇਸ਼ਨ) n ਵਧਣ-ਫੁੱਲਣ, ਵਰਧਨ, ਖਿਲਾਰ

propagator ('ਪ੍ਰੌਪਅਗੇਇਟਅ*) n ਉਤਪਾਦਕ, ਪ੍ਰਚਾਰਕ, ਪ੍ਰਸਾਰਕ

propel (ਪ੍ਰਅ'ਪੈੱਲ) v ਪ੍ਰੇਰਤ ਕਰਨਾ, ਅੱਗੇ ਧੱਕਣਾ, ਠੇਲ੍ਹਣਾ, ਰੇੜ੍ਹਨਾ; ~ler ਪ੍ਰੇਰਕ, ਪ੍ਰਵਰਤਕ

proper (ਪ੍ਰੌਪਅ*) a ਵਾਸਤਵਿਕ, ਯੋਗ, ਸਹੀ, ਉਚਿਤ, (ਪ੍ਰ) ਨਿੱਜੀ, ਸੰਗਤ, ਯਥਾਰਥ, ਠੀਕ-ਠਾਕ; ~ly ਉਚਿਤ ਰੀਤੀ ਨਾਲ, ਠੀਕ ਤਰ੍ਹਾਂ, ਸਾਊ ਢੰਗ ਨਾਲ

property (ਪ੍ਰੌਪਅਟਿ) n ਜਾਇਦਾਦ; ਸੰਪੱਤੀ, ਮਾਲ-ਧਨ, ਮਲਕੀਅਤ

prophecy ('ਪ੍ਰੌਫ਼ਿਸਿ) n ਭਵਿੱਖਬਾਣੀ; ਇਲਹਾਮ

prophesy ('ਪ੍ਰੌਫ਼ਿਸਾਇ) v ਭਵਿੱਖ ਬਾਰੇ ਦੱਸਣਾ, ਭਵਿੱਖਬਾਣੀ ਕਰਨੀ, ਪੂਰਵ-ਸੂਚਨਾ ਦੇਣੀ

prophet ('ਪ੍ਰੌਫ਼ਿਟ) n ਈਸ਼ਵਰ-ਦੂਤ, ਭਵਿੱਖ-ਵਕਤਾ, ਪੈਗੰਬਰ; ~ic, ~ical ਅਗੰਮੀ; ਇਲਹਾਮੀ, ਪੈਗੰਬਰੀ

propitious (ਪ੍ਰਅ'ਪਿਸ਼ਅਸ) a ਸੁਲੱਖਣਾ, ਅਨੁਕੂਲ, ਸ਼ੁਭ (ਲਗਨ), ਕਿਰਪਾਲੂ, ਕਲਿਆਣਕਾਰੀ

proportion (ਪ੍ਰਅ'ਪੋਸ਼ਨ) n ਅਨੁਪਾਤ; ਨਿਸਬਤ; ~able ਤੁਲ, ਸਮ-ਤੋਲ, ਤੁਲਵਾਂ; ~al ਅਨੁਰੂਪ; ਤੁਲ ਨਿਸਬਤੀ, ਸਮ-ਤੁਲ; ~ate ਸਮ-ਤੋਲ, ਤੁਲਵਾਂ, ਅਨੁਰੂਪ

proposal (ਪ੍ਰਅ'ਪਅਉਜ਼ਲ) n ਪ੍ਰਸਤਾਵ, ਸੁਝਾਉ, ਪ੍ਰਸਥਾਪਨਾ, ਤਜਵੀਜ਼, ਵਿਆਹ-ਪ੍ਰਸਤਾਵ

propose (ਪ੍ਰਅ'ਪਅਉਜ਼) v ਤਜਵੀਜ਼ ਕਰਨਾ, ਪ੍ਰਸਤਾਵ ਰੱਖਣਾ, ਇਰਾਦਾ ਰੱਖਣਾ, ਸੁਝਾਉ ਦੇਣਾ, ਮਤਾ ਪੇਸ਼ ਕਰਨਾ; ~d ਪ੍ਰਸਤਾਵਤ; ਪ੍ਰਸਥਾਪਤ; ~r ਪ੍ਰਸਤਾਵਕ, ਇੱਛਾ ਪਰਗਟ ਕਰਨ ਵਾਲਾ

propound (ਪ੍ਰਅ'ਪਾਉਂਡ) v ਪੇਸ਼ ਕਰਨਾ,

ਦੇਣਾ, ਤਨਖ਼ਾਹ ਦੇਣੀ

sale (ਸੇਇਲ) *n* ਵੇਚ, ਵਿਕਰੀ; ਵੰਟਕ; ਬੋਲੀ; ~**sman** ਵੇਚਣ ਵਾਲਾ

salient (ਸੇਇਲੀਅੰਟ) *n a* ਪ੍ਰਮੁਖ, ਮੁੱਖ; ਉੱਘੜਵਾਂ, ਮਹੱਤਵਪੂਰਨ

saline (ਸੇਇਲਾਇਨ) *a n* ਖਾਰਾ, ਲੂਣਾ, ਨਮਕੀਨ

saliva (ਸਅ'ਲਾਇਵ੍ਹਅ) *n* ਲਾਰ, ਥੁੱਕ, ਲੂਆਬ

saloon (ਸਅ'ਲੂਨ) *n* ਹਾਲ, ਬੈਠਕ; ਸਭਾ; ਸੈਲੂਨ; ਰੇਲ ਦਾ ਪਹਿਲੇ ਦਰਜੇ ਦਾ ਡੱਬਾ

salt (ਸੋਲਟ) *n a v* ਲੂਣ, ਨਮਕ, ਕੱਟਤਾ, ਉਤੇਜਕਤਾ, ਤੀਬਰਤਾ; ਲੂਣ-ਮਿਰਚ ਲਾਉਣਾ, ਨਮਕ ਛਿੜਕਣਾ

salutary (ਸੈਲਯੁਟ(ਅ)ਰਿ) *a* ਸਿਹਤਮੰਦ ਕਲਿਆਣਕਾਰੀ, ਹਿਤਕਾਰੀ ਉਪਯੋਗੀ,

salutation (ਸੈਲਯੂ'ਟੈਇਸ਼ਨ) *n* ਨਮਸਕਾਰ, ਪ੍ਰਣਾਮ, ਸਲਾਮ, ਅਭਿਵਾਦਨ, ਬੰਦਗੀ

salute (ਸਅ'ਲੂਟ) *n v* ਸਲਾਮ, ਅਭਿਨੰਦਨ, ਨਮਸਕਾਰ, ਪ੍ਰਣਾਮ; (ਸੈਨਾ) ਤੋਪਾਂ ਦੀ ਸਲਾਮੀ, ਫ਼ੌਜੀ ਸਨਮਾਨ; ਸਲਾਮ ਕਰਨਾ, ਨਮਸਕਾਰ ਕਰਨੀ, ਸੁਆਗਤ ਕਰਨਾ

salvage (ਸੈਲਵਿਜ) *n v* ਬਚਾਉ, ਨਿਸਤਾਰਾ; ਸਮਗਰੀ, ਸਾਮਾਨ; ਮਿਹਨਤਾਨਾ; ਨਸ਼ਟ ਹੋਣ ਤੋਂ ਬਚਾਉਣਾ

salvation (ਸੈਲ'ਵੇਇਸ਼ਨ) *n* ਰੱਖਿਆ; ਨਿਸਤਾਰਾ, ਮੋਖ, ਮੁਕਤੀ, ਨਿਰਵਾਣ, ਨਜਾਤ

same (ਸੇਇਮ) *a pron adv* ਸਮਾਨ, ਉਹ, ਉਸੇ ਵਰਗਾ, ਉਸੇ ਤਰ੍ਹਾਂ ਨਾਲ ਨਾਲ, ਉਹੀ ਗੱਲ, ਉਹੀ ਚੀਜ਼; ਸਮਾਨ ਰੂਪ ਵਿਚ, ਉਸੇ ਤਰ੍ਹਾਂ, ਉਸੇ ਢੰਗ ਨਾਲ

sample (ਸਾਂਪਲ) *n v* ਵੰਨਗੀ; ਉਦਾਹਰਣ, ਨਮੂਨਾ; ਨਮੂਨਾ ਲੈਣਾ

Samson (ਸੈਮਸਅਨ) *n* ਸ਼ਕਤੀਸ਼ਾਲੀ ਆਦਮੀ, ਬਲਵਾਨ ਪੁਰਸ਼

sanatorium (ਸੈਨਅ'ਟੋਰਿਅਮ) *n* ਅਰੋਗਤਾ-ਸਥਾਨ, ਸੈਨੇਟੋਰੀਅਮ

sanctify (ਸੈਙ(ਕ)ਟਿਫ਼ਾਇ) *v* ਪਵਿੱਤਰ ਕਰਨਾ, ਪਾਵਨ ਕਰਨਾ, ਪਵਿੱਤਰਤਾ ਵਧਾਉਣੀ, ਸ਼ੁੱਧ ਕਰਨਾ, ਪਾਕੀਜ਼ਾ ਕਰਨਾ

sanctimony (ਸੈਙ(ਕ)ਟਿਮਅਨਿ) *n* ਦੰਭ; ਕਪਟ, ਪਖੰਡ, ਢੌਂਗ

sanction (ਸੈਙ(ਕ)ਸ਼ਨ) *n v* (1) ਸਵੀਕ੍ਰਿਤੀ, ਮਨਜ਼ੂਰੀ; (2) ਪ੍ਰਤੀਬੰਧ, ਪਾਬੰਦੀ; ਦੰਡ, ਸਜ਼ਾ, ਦੰਡ ਦੀ ਕਾਨੂੰਨੀ ਧਾਰਾ; ਅਧਿਕਾਰ ਦੇਣਾ, ਮਨਜ਼ੂਰੀ ਦੇਣੀ; ~**ed** ਮਨਜ਼ੂਰ, ਸਵੀਕ੍ਰਿਤ

sanctity (ਸੈਙ(ਕ)ਟਅਟਿ) *n* ਪਵਿੱਤਰਤਾ, ਧਾਰਮਕਤਾ; ਪਾਵਨਤਾ

sanctuary (ਸੈਙ(ਕ)ਚੁਅਰਿ) *n* ਧਰਮ-ਸਥਾਨ, ਮੰਦਰ, ਦਰਗਾਹ; ਪਨਾਹਗਾਰ

sanctum (ਸੈਙ(ਕ)ਟਅਮ) *n* ਉਪਾਸਨਾ-ਗ੍ਰਿਹ, ਇਕਾਂਤ ਕਮਰਾ; ਤੀਰਥ; ਪਵਿੱਤਰ ਆਸਨ

sand (ਸੈਂਡ) *n v* ਰੇਤ, ਪੂੜ, ਰੇਤ ਦੇ ਕਿਣਕੇ; ਰੇਤਲੀ ਧਰਤੀ, ਰੇਗਿਸਤਾਨ, ਰੇਤੇ ਵਿਚ ਗੱਡਣਾ; ਰੇਗਮਾਰ ਮਾਰਨਾ, ਘਸਾਉਣਾ; ~**y** ਰੇਤਲਾ ਰੇਗਿਸਤਾਨੀ; ਕੱਚਾ, ਬੂਰਾ, ਭੂਰਾ

sandal (ਸੈਂਡਲ) *n* ਸੰਦਲ, ਚੰਦਨ; ਸੈਂਡਲ; ~**wood** ਚੰਦਨ ਦੀ ਲੱਕੜੀ, ਚਿੱਟਾ ਚੰਦਨ

sandwich (ਸੈਨਵਿਜ) *n v* ਸੈਂਡਵਿਚ, ਘੁਸੇੜਨਾ, ਠੋਸਣਾ; ਨਪੀੜਨਾ

sane (ਸੇਇਨ) *a* ਸਮਝਦਾਰ, ਸਿਆਣਾ; ਉਦਾਰ

sanitary (ਸੈਨਿਟ(ਅ)ਰਿ) *a* ਸਫ਼ਾਈ ਬਾਰੇ; ਨਿਰੋਗਤਾ ਸਬੰਧੀ, ਅਰੋਗ ਰੱਖਿਅਕ; ਸੁਆਸਥ-ਵਰਧਕ

sanitation ('ਸੈਨਿ'ਟੇਇਸ਼ਨ) *n* ਸਫ਼ਾਈ, ਅਰੋਗ-ਪ੍ਰਬੰਧ

sanity ('ਸੈਨਅਟਿ) *n* ਸਿਹਤ, ਸੁਅਸਥ, ਦਿਮਾਗ਼ੀ ਸਿਹਤ

sans (ਸੈਂਜ਼) *prep* ਬਿਨਾਂ, ਬਗ਼ੈਰ, ਹੀਨ, ਰਹਿਤ, ਬਿਲਾ, ਵਿਹੀਨ

sap (ਸੈਪ) *n* ਰਸ; ਸਤ, ਸਾਰ, ਤੱਤ, (ਪੌਦਿਆਂ ਦਾ) ਦੁੱਧ, ਦ੍ਰਵ; ਰਸ ਸੁੱਕਣਾ, ਰਸ ਨਚੋੜਨਾ, ਸਤ ਕੱਢਣਾ, ਸਾਰ ਜਾਂ ਤੱਤ ਕੱਢ ਲੈਣਾ, ਸਾਹ-ਸਤ ਕੱਢਣਾ

sapling ('ਸੈਪਲਿਙ) *n* ਬਰੂਟਾ, ਨਵਾਂ ਪੌਦਾ; ਬਿਰਵਾ, ਨੌਨਿਹਾਲ, ਯੁਵਕ

sapphire ('ਸੈਫ਼ਾਇਅ*) *n a* ਨੀਲਮ, ਨੀਲ-ਕਾਂਤਮਣੀ, ਨੀਲਮਣੀ

sarcasm ('ਸਾਕੈਜ਼(ਅ)ਮ) *n* ਚੁਭਣ ਵਾਲੀ ਗੱਲ, ਕਟਾਕਸ਼, ਵਿਅੰਗ-ਵਾਕ, ਵਿਅੰਗ

sarcastic (ਸਾ'ਕੈਸਟਿਕ) *a* ਵਿਅੰਗਪੂਰਨ, ਵਿਅੰਗਮਈ; ਤੀਖਣ

Satan ('ਸੇਇਟ(ਅ)ਨ) *n* ਸ਼ੈਤਾਨ, ਇਬਲੀਸ

satellite ('ਸੈਟਅਲਾਇਟ) *n* ਉਪਗ੍ਰਹਿ; ਪਿਛਲੱਗ, ਅਨਗਾਮੀ, ਅਨੁਯਾਈ, ਸਹਾਇਕ

satire ('ਸੈਟਾਇਅ*) *n* ਵਿਅੰਗ, ਵਿਅੰਗ-ਲੇਖ, ਵਿਅੰਗ ਉਕਤੀ, ਵਿਅੰਗ-ਕਾਵਿ

satiric (ਸਾ'ਟਿਰਿਕ) *a* ਵਿਅੰਗਪੂਰਨ, ਵਿਅੰਗ-ਸਾਹਿਤ, ਨਿੰਦਾਤਮਕ

satirist ('ਸੈਟਅਰਿਸਟ) *n* ਵਿਅੰਗਕਾਰ, ਨਿੰਦਕ

satisfaction ('ਸੈਟਿਸ'ਫ਼ੈਕਸ਼ਨ) *n* ਸੰਤੋਖ, ਸੰਤੁਸ਼ਟੀ, ਤ੍ਰਿਪਤੀ, ਤੁਸ਼ਟੀ, ਇੱਛਾ-ਪੂਰਤੀ

satisfactory ('ਸੈਟਿਸ'ਫ਼ੈਕਟ(ਅ)ਰਿ) *a* ਸੰਤੋਖਜਨਕ, ਤਸੱਲੀਬਖ਼ਸ਼

satisfied ('ਸੈਟਿਸਫ਼ਾਇਡ) *a* ਸੰਤੁਸ਼ਟ, ਤ੍ਰਿਪਤ

satisfy ('ਸੈਟਿਸਫ਼ਾਇ) *v* ਸੰਤੁਸ਼ਟ ਕਰਨਾ, ਸੰਤੋਖ ਦੇਣਾ, ਤ੍ਰਿਪਤਾਉਣਾ, ਤ੍ਰਿਪਤ ਕਰਨਾ; ਮੰਨਣਾ, ਖ਼ੁਸ਼ ਹੋਣਾ, ਰਾਜ਼ੀ ਹੋਣਾ

saturation ('ਸੈਚਾ'ਰੇਇਸ਼ਨ) *n* ਸੰਤ੍ਰਿਪਤੀ, ਸੰਪੂਰਤੀ, ਤਵਾਰਤ, ਰਜਾਓ

Saturday ('ਸੈਟਅਡਿ) *n* ਸਨਿੱਚਰਵਾਰ, ਸ਼ਨੀਵਾਰ

sauce (ਸੋਸ) *n v* ਚਟਨੀ; ਲੂਣ ਘੋਲ; ਸੁਆਦ, ਰਸ ਮਜ਼ਾ, ਗੁਸਤਾਖ਼ੀ, ਸ਼ੇਖੀ; ਮਸਾਲੇਦਾਰ ਬਣਾਉਣਾ, ਚਟਪਟਾ ਬਣਾਉਣਾ

saucer ('ਸੋਸਅ*) *n* (ਚਾਹ ਦੀ) ਪਲੇਟ; ਤਸ਼ਤਰੀ; ਰਕਾਬੀ

saucy ('ਸੋਸਿ) *a* ਚੰਚਲ, ਮੂੰਹ ਫਟ, ਗੁਸਤਾਖ਼, ਸ਼ੋਖ਼; ਚੁਸਤ, ਜ਼ਿੰਦਾਦਿਲ

savage (ਸੈਵਿਜ਼) *a n v* ਜੰਗਲੀ, ਦਰਿੰਦਾ ਖੂੰਖਾਰ, ਅਸੱਭਿਅ, ਰਾਖਸ਼ੀ, ਅੱਖੜ; ਰਾਖਸ਼, ਅੱਖੜ ਬੰਦਾ; ਜੰਗਲੀ ਬਣਾਉਣਾ; **~ness** ਅਸੱਭਿਅਤਾ, ਜੰਗਲੀਪਨ; ਬਰਬਰਤਾ, ਬੇਰਹਿਮੀ, ਵਹਿਸ਼ੀਪਨ; **~ry** ਬਰਬਰਤਾ, ਨਿਸ਼ਠੁਰਤਾ, ਵਹਿਸ਼ੀਪਨ, ਦਰਿੰਦਗੀ

savant ('ਸੈਵਅੰਟ) *n* ਬੁੱਧੀਵਾਨ ਲੋਕ, ਵਿਦਵਾਨ ਪੁਰਸ਼, ਮਹਾਂ ਪੰਡਤ, ਗਿਆਨੀ

save (ਸੇਇਵ) *v n prep* ਬਚਾਉਣਾ, ਬੱਚਤ ਕਰਨੀ; ਰੱਖ ਲੈਣਾ, ਜੋੜਨਾ, ਜਮ੍ਹਾਂ ਕਰਨਾ; ਨਾ ਦੇਣਾ, ਗ੍ਰਹਿਣ ਕਰਨਾ; (ਫੁਟਬਾਲ) ਗੋਲ ਦਾ ਬਚਾਓ; ਧਨ ਬਚਾਉਣਾ; ਪਰ, ਲੇਕਿਨ, ਕਿੰਤੂ, ਬਿਨਾ

saving ('ਸੇਇਵਙ਼) ਬਚਤ, ਜੋੜਿਆ ਧਨ; ਬਚਾਓ, ਕਿਫ਼ਾਇਤ

saviour ('ਸੇਇਵਯਅ*) *n* ਰਾਜ-ਰੱਖਿਅਕ, ਮੁਕਤੀਦਾਤਾ

savour ('ਸੇਇਵਅ*) *n v* ਗੰਧ, ਮਹਿਕ; ਬਾਸ;

ਸੁਆਦ, ਮਜ਼ਾ; ਜ਼ਾਇਕਾ; ਸੁਆਦੀ ਬਣਾਉਣਾ, ਸੁਗੰਧਿਤ ਕਰਨਾ; ~y ਸੁਆਦੀ ਮਸਾਲੇਦਾਰ, ਚਟਪਟਾ

savvy ('ਸੈਵ਼ਿ) *n* (ਅਪ) ਚਤਰਾਈ, ਹੁਸ਼ਿਆਰੀ, ਸਮਝ

saw (ਸੋ) *n* ਆਰਾ, ਆਰੀ, ਕਲਵੱਤਰ; ਆਰਾ ਚਲਾਉਣਾ, ਚੀਰਨਾ; (ਜਿਲਦਸਾਜ਼ੀ) ਚੀਰ ਦੇਣਾ; ~ing ਚਿਰਾਈ

say (ਸੇਇ) *n v* ਕਥਨ, ਮੱਤ, ਕਹਿਤੀ, ਗੱਲ-ਬਾਤ; ਉਚਾਰਨਾ, ਆਖਣਾ; ਬੋਲਣਾ, ਟਿੱਪਣੀ ਦੇਣੀ; ਵਚਨ ਦੇਣਾ; ਵਰਨਣ ਕਰਨਾ; ~ing ਉਕਤੀ, ਕਥਨ, ਬਾਣੀ, ਮੱਤ, ਅਖਾਣ, ਬਚਨ; ਕਹਾਵਤ, ਮੁਹਾਵਰਾ, ਲੋਕੋਕਤੀ; ਮਿਸਾਲ

scale (ਸਕੇਇਲ) *n v* ਤਰਾਜੂ ਦਾ ਪਲੜਾ, ਤੁਲਾ; ਸਧਾਰਨ ਤੱਕੜੀ; ਪੰਗਤੀ, ਦਰਜਾ; ਅੰਕਾਂ ਦਾ ਪੈਮਾਨਾ, ਅੰਕਨ ਚਿੰਨ੍ਹ; ਮਾਪ-ਦੰਡ; ਪ੍ਰਤੀਮਾਨ, ਜਾਂਚਨਾ, ਤੱਕੜੀ ਵਿਚ ਤੋਲਣਾ, ਜੋਖਣਾ, ਪੈਮਾਇਸ ਕਰਨੀ; ਮਾਪਣਾ

scalp (ਸਕੈਲਪ) *n v* ਖੋਪੜੀ, ਸਿਰ ਦਾ ਉਤਲਾ ਭਾਗ; ਖੋਪੜੀ ਲਾਹੁਣੀ, ਸਿਰ ਕਲਮ ਕਰਨਾ

scam (ਸਕੈਮ) *n* (ਅਪ) ਘੋਟਾਲਾ

scamble ('ਸਕੈਂਬ਼ਲ) *v* ਸੰਘਰਸ਼ ਕਰਨਾ, ਧੱਕਮ-ਧੱਕਾ ਕਰਨਾ, ਗੋਡਿਆਂ ਆਸਰੇ ਚੜ੍ਹਨਾ

scamp (ਸਕੈਂਪ) *n v* ਲੁੱਚਾ, ਬਦਮਾਸ਼, ਕੰਮਚੋਰ; ਵਗਾਰ ਟਾਲਣੀ

scan (ਸਕੈਨ) *v* ਤਕਤੀਹ ਕਰਨੀ; ਛੰਦ ਦੀਆਂ ਮਾਤਰਾਂ ਗਿਨਣਾ; ਪਰਖਣਾ, ਜਾਂਚਣਾ; ~ning ਬਾਰੀਕ ਜਾਂਚ, ਪਰੀਖਣ

scandal ('ਸਕੈਂਡਲ) *n* ਘੋਟਾਲਾ, ਕੁਕਰਮ, ਬੁਰਾਈ, ਲੋਕ-ਨਿੰਦਿਆ, ਨਿੰਦਾ

scant (ਸਕੈਂਟ) *v a* ਸੀਮਤ ਕਰਨਾ, ਘੱਟ ਘੱਟ

ਦੇਣਾ; ਬਹੁਤ ਘੱਟ, ਬਹੁਤ ਥੋੜ੍ਹਾ, ਨਾਕਾਫ਼ੀ, ਬਰਾਏ ਨਾਮ; ~y ਵਿਰਲਾ, ਘੱਟ, ਨਾਕਾਫ਼ੀ ਦੁਰਲੱਭ

scapegoat ('ਸਕੇਇਪਗਾਉਟ) *a* ਕੁਰਬਾਨੀ ਦਾ ਬੱਕਰਾ, ਬਲੀ

scar (ਸਕਾ*) *n* ਦਾਗ਼, ਬੀਜ-ਨਾਭੀ; ਨਿਸ਼ਾਨ, ਖਰੀਂਢ, ਝਰੀਟ, ਧੱਬਾ; ਦਾਗ਼; ਰਾਜ਼ੀ ਹੋਣਾ; ਜ਼ਖ਼ਮ ਤੇ ਖਰੀਂਢ ਆਉਣਾ, ਦਾਗ਼ ਲੱਗਣਾ

scarce (ਸਕੇਅ:ਸ) *a* ਮਸਾਂ, ਮੁਸ਼ਕਲ ਨਾਲ, ਅਲਪ, ਬਹੁਤ ਘੱਟ; ਥੋੜ੍ਹਾ; ~ly ਮੁਸ਼ਕਲ ਨਾਲ; ਬਿਲਕੁਲ ਨਹੀਂ, ਨਾਂਹ ਦੇ ਬਰਾਬਰ; ਸ਼ਾਇਦ, ਹੁਣੇ ਹੁਣੇ

scarcity ('ਸਕੇਅ:ਸਅਟਿ) *n* ਥੁੜ੍ਹ, ਤੰਗੀ, ਟੋਟ, ਦੁਰਲੱਭਤਾ, ਅਭਾਵ

scare (ਸਕੇਅ*) *n v* ਸਹਿਮ, ਡਰ, ਦਹਿਲ, ਧੁੜਕੂ, ਅਚਾਨਕ ਭੈਭੀਤ ਕਰਨਾ, ਡਰਾਉਣਾ

scarf (ਸਕਾ:ਫ਼) *n v* ਦੁਪੱਟਾ, ਪਟਕਾ, ਰੁਮਾਲ, ਗਲੂਬੰਦ, ਸਕਾਰਫ਼; ਚੂਲ ਬੈਠਾਉਣਾ, ਮੇਲ ਮਿਲਾਉਣਾ

scarlet ('ਸਕਾ:ਲਅਟ) *n a* ਲਾਲ ਰੰਗ ਦਾ ਕੱਪੜਾ; ਸੰਧੂਰੀ, ਗੁਲਨਾਰੀ, ਕਿਰਮਚੀ

scatter ('ਸਕੈਟਅ*) *v* ਖਿੰਡਾਉਣਾ, ਖਿੰਡਣਾ; ਖਿਲਾਰਨਾ, ਬਿਖੇਰਨਾ, ਤਿੱਤਰ-ਬਿੱਤਰ ਕਰਨਾ; ਫੈਲਾਉਣਾ, ਭਗਦੜ ਮਚਾਉਣੀ; ~ed ਬਿਖਰਿਆ, ਤਿੱਤਰ-ਬਿੱਤਰ

scavenge ('ਸਕੈਵ਼ਿੰਜ) *v* ਕੂੜਾ-ਕਰਕਟ ਉਠਾਉਣਾ, ਸਫ਼ਾਈ ਕਰਨਾ; ~r ਮਿਹਤਰ, ਜਮਾਂਦਾਰ, ਸੜਕਾਂ ਸਾਫ਼ ਕਰਨ ਵਾਲਾ; ਅਸ਼ਲੀਲ ਲੇਖਕ, ਲੱਚਰ ਲੇਖਕ

scene (ਸੀਨ) *n* ਦ੍ਰਿਸ਼, ਘਟਨਾ ਸਥਾਨ; ਰੰਗ-ਮੰਚ, ਰੰਗ-ਭੂਮੀ, ਰੰਗਸ਼ਾਲਾ, ਪਰਦਰਸ਼ਨ-ਭੂਮੀ;

ਨਾਟਕ ਦੇ ਅੰਕ ਦਾ ਭਾਗ; ਝੜਪ; **~ry** ਦਿਸ਼

ਦਿਸ਼ਾਵਲੀ, ਕੁਦਰਤੀ ਦਿਸ਼

scenic ('ਸੀਨਿਕ) *a* ਰਮਣੀਕ, ਸਜੀਵ, ਰੰਗਮੰਚੀ

scent (ਸੈਂਟ) *n v* ਸੁਗੰਧੀ, ਮਹਿਕ, ਖ਼ੁਸ਼ਬੂ; ਅਤਰ, ਫ਼ੁਲੇਲ; ਅਤਰ ਲਾਉਣਾ, ਸੁਗੰਧਿਤ ਕਰਨਾ

schedule ('ਸੈਂਡਯੂਲ) *n v* ਸੂਚੀ, ਸਾਰਨੀ, ਫ਼ਰਦ, ਪੱਟੀ, ਸਮਾਂ-ਸੂਚੀ, ਕਾਰਜ-ਕ੍ਰਮ, ਨਾਮਾਵਲੀ; ਚਿੰਠਾ, ਯੋਜਨਲੇਖ; ਸੂਚੀ ਬਣਾਉਣੀ, ਅਨੁਸੂਚਤ ਕਰਨਾ; **~d** ਅਨੁਸੂਚਤ, ਨਿਯਤ

schema ('ਸਕੀਮਅ) *n* ਯੋਜਨਾ, ਖ਼ਾਕਾ, ਨਕਸ਼ਾ, ਆਕਾਰ

scheme (ਸਕੀਮ) *n v* ਯੋਜਨਾ, ਪ੍ਰਬੰਧ, ਜੁਗਤ, ਉਪਾਉ, ਮਨਸੂਬਾ, ਚਾਲ, ਸਾਜ਼ਸ਼; ਸੂਚੀ, ਵੇਰਵਾ, ਰੂਪ-ਰੇਖਾ, ਨਕਸ਼ਾ; ਯੋਜਨਾ ਬਣਾਉਣੀ; ਰੂਪ-ਰੇਖਾ ਬਣਾਉਣਾ

schism (ਸਕਿਜ਼(ਅਮ) *n* ਪੜੇਬੰਦੀ, ਫੁੱਟ, ਮੱਤ-ਭੇਦ; ਸੰਪਰਦਾਇਕ ਵਖਰੇਵਾਂ; ਫ਼ਿਰਕੇਬੰਦੀ

scholar ('ਸਕੌਲਅ*) *n* ਵਿਦਵਾਨ, ਪੰਡਤ, ਗਿਆਨੀ; ਵਿਦਿਆਰਥੀ, ਸ਼ਾਗਿਰਦ; **~ly** ਵਿਦਵਾਨ-ਵਰਗਾ; ਵਿਦਵਤਾਪੂਰਨ; **~ship** ਵਜ਼ੀਫ਼ਾ; ਵਿਦਵਤਾ ਗਿਆਨ

school (ਸਕੂਲ) *n* (1) ਵਿਦਿਆਲਾ, ਮਦਰਸਾ, ਪਾਠਸ਼ਾਲਾ; (2) ਸੰਪਰਦਾਇ, ਫ਼ਿਰਕਾ; (3) ਮੱਤ, ਵਾਦ, ਪੰਥ, ਮਾਰਗ, ਵਰਗ

schwa (ਸ਼ਵਾ) *n* (ਵਿਆ) ਲਘੁ ਸਵਰ ਧੁਨੀ

science ('ਸਾਇੰਸ) *n* ਵਿਗਿਆਨ, ਗਿਆਨ, ਵਿੱਦਿਆ ਸ਼ਾਸਤਰੀ

scientific ('ਸਾਇਅੰਟਿਫ਼ਿਕ) *a* ਵਿਗਿਆਨਕ, ਸ਼ਾਸਤਰ-ਅਨੁਕੂਲ; ਵਿਵਸਥਿਤ, ਕ੍ਰਮਬੱਧ

scientist ('ਸਾਇਅੰਟਿਸਟ) *n* ਵਿਗਿਆਨੀ, ਸਾਇੰਸਦਾਨ

sciolism ('ਸਾਇਅ(ਉ)ਲਿਜ਼(ਅ)ਮ *n* ਸਧਾਰਨ ਗਿਆਨ, ਗਿਆਨ ਦਾ ਝੂਠਾ ਅਹੰਕਾਰ, ਪਖੰਡ

scissor ('ਸਿਜ਼ਅ*) *v* ਕੱਟਣਾ, ਕਤਰਨਾ, ਛਾਂਟਣਾ, ਕੈਂਚੀ ਨਾਲ ਕਤਰਨਾ; **~s** ਕੈਂਚੀ, ਕਾਤੀ, ਕਤਰਨੀ

scissure ('ਸਿਜ਼ਅ*) *n* ਚੀਰਾ, ਚੀਰ, ਘਾਉ

scoff (ਸਕੌਫ਼) *n v* ਖਿੱਲੀ, ਟਿੱਚਰ, ਮਸਖ਼ਰੀ, ਮਖ਼ੌਲ; ਗੁੱਡਾ; ਉਪਹਾਸ; ਮਜ਼ਾਕ, ਠੱਠਾ; ਹਾਸਾ-ਠੱਠਾ ਕਰਨਾ, ਮਜ਼ਾਕ ਉਡਾਉਣਾ, ਤਿਰਸਕਾਰ ਕਰਨਾ

scold (ਸਕਅਉਲਡ) *n v* ਤਾੜਨਾ, ਝਿੜਕਣਾ, ਡਾਂਟਣਾ, ਧਮਕਾਉਣਾ; ਬੁਰਾ-ਭਲਾ ਆਖਣਾ, ਖ਼ਬਰ ਲੈਂਦੀ, ਲਿਤਾੜਨਾ; **~ing** ਨਿੰਦਾ, ਧਿੱਕਾਰ, ਝਿੜਕ, ਡਾਂਟ-ਡਪਟ, ਡਾਂਟ-ਫਿਟਕਾਰ

scoop (ਸਕੂਪ) *n v* ਕੜਛੀ; ਕੋਲੇ ਪਾਉਣ ਵਾਲਾ ਬੇਲਚਾ, ਤਕੜਾ ਲਾਭ; ਤਾਜ਼ਾ ਖ਼ਬਰ, ਚਪੇੜ, ਮਾਰ-ਕੁੱਟ; (ਡੋਈ ਨਾਲ) ਕੱਢਣਾ, ਖੋਖਲਾ ਕਰਨਾ; ਅਫ਼ਵਾਹ ਫੈਲਾਉਣਾ

scoot (ਸਕੂਟ) *v* ਭੱਜ ਜਾਣਾ, ਰਫ਼ੂਚਕਰ ਹੋਣਾ, ਭੱਜ ਨਿਕਲਣਾ; ਝਪਟਣਾ; **~er** ਗੱਡੀ, ਯਾਨ, ਸਕੂਟਰ, ਮੋਟਰ ਬੋਟ

scope (ਸਕਅਉਪ) *n* (rare) ਮੰਤਵ, ਗੁੰਜਾਇਸ਼; ਕਾਰਜ-ਖੇਤਰ, ਪਹੁੰਚ

score (ਸਕੋ*) *n v* ਵੀਹ ਦੀ ਗਿਣਤੀ, ਕੋੜੀ, ਬੀਸੀ; ਅੰਕ ਬਣਾਉਣੇ, ਪੁਆਇੰਟ ਜਿੱਤਣੇ; ਗੋਲ ਕਰਨਾ, ਰਨ ਬਣਾਉਣਾ

scorn (ਸਕੌਨ) *a v* ਘਿਰਣਾ, ਨਫ਼ਰਤ, ਹਿਕਰਤ; ਨਫ਼ਰਤ ਕਰਨੀ; **~ful** ਤਿਰਸਕਾਰਪੂਰਨ, ਅਪਮਾਨਜਨਕ, ਘਿਰਾਉਣਾ

scorpio (ਸਕੌਪਿਅਉ) *n* ਬਿਰਖ ਰਾਸ਼ੀ; **~n** ਬਿੱਛੂ, ਠੂਹਾਂ, ਅਠੂਹਾਂ; ਬ੍ਰਿਸ਼ਚਕ ਰਾਸ਼ੀ

scoundrel ('ਸਕਅਉਨਡਰ(ਅ)ਲ *n* ਲੁੱਚਾ, ਗੁੰਡਾ,

ਪਾਜੀ, ਬਦਮਾਸ਼, ਸ਼ੋਹਦਾ

scour ('ਸਕਾਉਅ*) *n v* ਸਫ਼ਾਈ, ਰੁਆਈ; ਮਾਂਜਣਾ, ਰਗੜਨਾ, ਮਲਣਾ, ਸਾਫ਼ ਕਰਨਾ, ਚਮਕਾਉਣਾ; ਧੋਣਾ

scourge (ਸਕਅ:ਜ) *n v* ਝੰਡਾ, ਕੋਰੜਾ, ਚਾਬੁਕ; ਅੱਤਿਆਚਾਰ ਕਰਨਾ, ਕਸ਼ਟ ਦੇਣਾ, ਝੰਬਣਾ, ਝੰਬਣਾ, ਬੌਤਾਂ ਲਾਉਣੀਆਂ

scout (ਸਕਾਉਟ) *n v* ਸਕਾਊਟ; ਮੁਖਬਰ ਗੁਪਤਚਰ; ਪਹਿਰੇਦਾਰ; ਜਾਸੂਸੀ ਕਰਨੀ, ਭੇਤ ਲਾਉਣਾ, ਦੇਖਣਾ; ਤਿਰਸਕਾਰ ਕਰਨਾ; ਹਾਸਾ ਉਡਾਉਣਾ, ਨਾਮਨਜ਼ੂਰ ਕਰਨਾ

scrab (ਸਕਰੈਬ) *v* ਖੁਰਚਣਾ, ਖਾਜ ਕਰਨੀ, ਖੁਜਲਾਉਣਾ, ਰਗੜਨਾ

scrabble ('ਸਕਰੈਬਲ) *n v* ਚੀਂਘੜ-ਮੀਂਘੜ ਲਿਖਣ; ਹਨੇਰੇ ਵਿਚ ਭਾਲਣਾ, ਟੋਲਣਾ, ਧੱਕਮ-ਧੱਕੀ ਹੋਣਾ; ਅਸਪਸ਼ਟ ਲਿਖਣਾ

scramble ('ਸਕਰੈਂਬਲ) *n v* ਧੱਕਾ-ਮੁੱਕੀ, ਹਫੜਾ-ਦਫੜੀ, ਦੌੜ-ਭੱਜ; ਧੱਕਮ-ਧੱਕਾ ਕਰਨਾ

scrape (ਸਕਰੇਇਪ) *n v* ਰਗੜਨ ਦੀ ਅਵਾਜ਼, ਘਸਣ ਦੀ ਅਵਾਜ਼; ਰਗੜ; ਰਗੜਨਾ, ਘਸਾਉਣਾ; ਇਕਸਾਰ ਪੱਧਰਾ ਕਰਨਾ

scratch (ਸਕਰੈਚ) *n v a* ਵਲੂੰਧਰ, ਖਰੁੰਢ, ਖਰੁੰਢ, ਝਰੀਟ, ਰਗੜ, ਖੁਰਚਣ; ਖੁਰਕਣ; ਖਰੋਚਣਾ, ਖੁਰਕਣਾ; ਘਿੱਚਮਿੱਚ ਲਿਖਣਾ

scream (ਸਕਰੀਮ) *v* ਚੀਕਣਾ, ਕੂਕਣਾ, ਡਡਿਆਉਣਾ, ਕਿਲਕਾਰੀਆਂ ਮਾਰਨੀਆਂ, ਲੇਰਾਂ ਮਾਰਨੀਆਂ; ਕਰਾਹੁਣਾ, ਢਾਹਾਂ ਮਾਰਨੀਆਂ

screen (ਸਕਰੀਨ) *n v* ਪਰਦਾ, ਓਟ, ਆੜ, ਖੱਸ ਦੀ ਟੱਟੀ; ਪਰਦਾ, ਕਨਾਤ, ਚਿਕ, ਚਿਲਮਨ; ਸੂਚਨਾ-ਪਟ; ਚਿੰਤਰਪਟ; ਸਿਨੇਮਾ ਦਾ ਚਿੱਟਾ ਪਰਦਾ; ਲੁਕਾਉਣਾ, ਬਚਾਉਣਾ, ਪਰਦਾ ਪਾਉਣਾ,

ਅੱਖਾਂ ਤੋਂ ਓਝਲ ਕਰਨਾ; ~**ing** ਐਕਸ-ਰੇ ਪ੍ਰੇਖਣ, ਛਾਣ-ਬੀਣ

screw (ਸਕਰੂ) *n v* ਪੇਚ ਦੀ ਮਰੋੜੀ; ਤਮਾਕੂ ਆਦਿ ਦਾ ਛੋਟਾ ਮਰੋੜਿਆ ਹੋਇਆ ਕਾਗਜ਼; ਤਨਖ਼ਾਹ ਦੀ ਰਕਮ, ਸੂਮ; ਪੇਚਾਂ ਨਾਲ ਪੀਚਣਾ, ਕੱਸਣਾ; ~**driver** ਪੇਚਕੱਸ

scribble ('ਸਕਰਿਬਲ) *n v* ਚੀਂਘੜ-ਮੀਂਘੜ ਲਿਖਤ ਲਿਖਣਾ, ਅਸਪਸ਼ਟ ਤੇ ਭੱਦਾ ਲਿਖਣਾ, ਊਟ-ਪਟਾਂਗ ਲਿਖਣਾ, ਕੁਲੇਖ ਲਿਖਣਾ; ਕਲਮ ਘਸਾਉਣਾ : ਘਸੀਟ

scribe (ਸਕਰਾਇਬ) *n v* ਲਿਖਾਰੀ, ਮੁਨਸ਼ੀ, ਮੁਹੱਰਰ, ਕਾਤਿਬ, ਕਲਰਕ, ਲੇਖਕ, ਲਿਪੀਕਾਰ, ਨਕਲਨਵੀਸ; ਲਕੀਰਨ, ਨਿਸ਼ਾਨ ਲਾਉਣੇ, ਅੰਕਤ ਕਰਨਾ, ਲਿਖਣਾ

scrimmage ('ਸਕਰਿਮਿਜ) *n v* ਹੱਥੋ-ਪਾਈ, ਗੁੱਥਮ-ਗੁੱਥਾ, ਖਿੰਚੋਤਾਣ; ਖਿੰਚੋਤਾਣ ਕਰਨੀ, ਗੁੱਥਮ-ਗੁੱਥਾ ਹੋਣਾ, ਤੇੜਾ-ਖੋਹੀ ਕਰਨੀ, ਸੰਘਰਸ਼ ਕਰਨਾ

script (ਸਕਰਿਪਟ) *n* ਲਿਪੀ, ਵਰਣਮਾਲਾ

scripture ('ਸਕਰਿਪਚਅ*) *n* ਧਰਮ-ਗ੍ਰੰਥ, ਪਵਿੱਤਰ ਗ੍ਰੰਥ

scroll (ਸਕਰਅਉਲ) *n v* (ਪੁ) ਫਹਿਰਿਸਤ, ਸੂਚੀ, ਤਾਲਕਾ; ਗੋਲ ਵਸਤੂਟਾ, ਵੇਲ-ਬੂਟੇ ਕੱਢਣੇ, ਵੇਲ-ਬੂਟਿਆਂ ਨਾਲ ਸਜਾਉਣਾ

scrub (ਸਕਰਅੱਬ) *n v* ਝਾੜ-ਬਰੋਟਾ; ਖੜ੍ਹੀਆਂ ਮੁੱਛਾਂ, ਅਜਿਹਾ ਬੁਰਸ਼; ਤੁੱਛ ਵਿਅਕਤੀ, ਕੂਚੀ ਮਾਂਜਣਾ, ਝੜਨਾ, ਪੂੰਝਣਾ, ਮਲਣਾ, ਘਸਾਉਣਾ, ਰਗੜਨਾ; ਝਾੜੂ ਦੇਣਾ, ਬੁਰਸ਼ ਕਰਨਾ

scrutinize ('ਸਕਰੂਟਿਨਾਇਜ਼) *v* ਸੂਖਮ ਪਰੀਖਿਆ ਕਰਨਾ, ਪੜਤਾਲਣਾ, ਜਾਚਨਾ, ਛਾਣ-ਬੀਣ ਕਰਨੀ

scrutiny ('ਸਕਰੁਟਿਨਿ) *n* ਦੇਖ-ਭਾਲ, ਪਰਖ, ਪੜਤਾਲ, ਪਰੀਖਿਆ, ਨਿਰੀਖਣ, ਖੋਜ

scuffle ('ਸਕਅੱਫਲ) *n v* ਹੱਥੋ-ਪਾਈ, ਗੁੱਥਮ-ਗੁੱਥਾ, ਧੱਕਮ-ਧੱਕਾ, ਧੀਗਾ-ਮੁਸ਼ਤੀ, ਹੱਥੋ-ਪਾਈ ਹੋਣੀ; ਗੁੱਥਮ-ਗੁੱਥਾ ਹੋਣਾ, ਭਿੜਨਾ

sculp (ਸਕਅੱਲਪ) *v* ਨੱਕਾਸ਼ੀ ਕਰਨਾ, ਸੰਗਤਰਾਸ਼ੀ ਕਰਨਾ; ~ture ਬੁੱਤ-ਤਰਾਸ਼ੀ, ਸੰਗਾ-ਤਰਾਸ਼ੀ; ਮੂਰਤੀ ਕਲਾ; ਮੂਰਤੀ ਪ੍ਰਤਿਮਾ; ~tor ਸੰਗ-ਤਰਾਸ਼; ਮੂਰਤੀਕਾਰ

scum (ਸਕਅੱਮ) *n v* ਝੱਗ, ਮੈਲ, ਰਹਿੰਦ-ਖੂੰਹਦ; ਝੱਗ ਉਠਨਾ

scuttle ('ਸਕਅੱਟਲ) *n v* ਨੱਠ-ਭੱਜ; ਝੱਗ ਆਉਣੀ; ਨਾਕਾਮ ਬਣਾਉਣਾ; ਖਿਸਕਣਾ, ਭੱਜ ਜਾਣਾ, ਹਵਾ ਹੋਣਾ, ਚੱਲਦੇ ਬਣਨਾ

sea (ਸੀ) *n* ਸਮੁੰਦਰ, ਸਾਗਰ, ਤਰੰਗ, ਵਿਸ਼ਾਲਤਾ, ਫੈਲਾਉ, ਵਿਸਤਾਰ; ~man ਜਹਾਜ਼ੀ; ~shore ਸਾਗਰ-ਤੱਟ; ~sickness ਕਚਿਆਣ

seal (ਸੀਲ) *n v* ਛਾਪ, ਮੁਹਰ, ਠੱਪਾ, ਮੁਦਰਾ, ਸੀਲ; ਸਬੂਤ; ਸੀਲ ਮੱਛੀ; ਸ਼ਿਕਾਰ ਕਰਨਾ, ਮੁਹਰ ਲਾਉਣਾ, ਠੱਪਾ ਲਾਉਣਾ, ਪੱਕਾ ਕਰਨਾ; ਸੱਚਾ ਪਰੇਮ ਜਤਲਾਉਣਾ; ~ed ਮੁਹਰਬੰਦ, ਮੁਹਰ ਲੱਗਿਆ; ਬੰਦ ਕੀਤਾ

search (ਸਅ਼ਚ) *n v* ਖੋਜ, ਢੂੰਡ, ਜਾਂਚ, ਤਲਾਸ਼, ਦੇਖ-ਭਾਲ; ਭਾਲਣਾ, ਖੋਜਣਾ, ਢੂੰਡਣਾ, ਜਾਂਚਣਾ, ਤਲਾਸ਼ ਕਰਨੀ, ਦੇਖ-ਭਾਲ ਕਰਨੀ

season ('ਸੀਜ਼ਨ) *n v* ਰੁੱਤ, ਮੌਸਮ, ਅਨੁਕੂਲ ਅਵਸਰ; ਛੌਂਕਣਾ; ~al ਮੌਸਮੀ

seat (ਸੀਟ) *n* ਆਸਨ, ਗੱਦੀ, ਕੁਰਸੀ; ਆਧਾਰ ਪੇਂਦਾ; ਟਿਕਾਣਾ, ਕੇਂਦਰ; ਕਾਠੀ

secession (ਸਿ'ਸੈੱਸ਼ਨ) *n* ਸਮਾਜ-ਤਿਆਗ; ਸਬੰਧ-ਤਿਆਗ; ਅਲਹਿਦਗੀ, ਵਖਰੇਵਾਂ

seclude (ਸਿ'ਕਲੂਡ) *v* ਇਕਾਂਤ ਵਿਚ ਰੱਖਣਾ, ਲੋਕ-ਸੰਪਰਕ ਤੋਂ ਦੂਰ ਰੱਖਣਾ, ਸੁਤੰਤਰ ਰੱਖਣਾ; ~d ਦੂਰਸਥਾਪਤ, ਨਿਰਜਨ, ਇਕਾਂਤ

seclusion (ਸਿ'ਕਲੂਯ਼ਨ) *n* ਇਕਾਂਤਵਾਸ, ਨਿਰਜਨ ਥਾਂ, ਸੁੰਨੀ ਥਾਂ, ਇਕਾਂਤਤਾ; ~ist ਇਕਾਂਤਵਾਦੀ, ਨਿਰਜਨਤਾ-ਪ੍ਰਿਯ

second ('ਸੈਕਅੰਡ) *n a v* ਪਿੱਛੇ ਆਇਆ ਆਦਮੀ, ਦੂਜਾ ਆਦਮੀ ਜਾਂ ਦਰਜਾ; ਛਿਣ, ਮਿੰਟ ਦਾ 1/60 ਭਾਗ, ਸੈਕੰਡ; ਤਾਈਦ ਕਰਨੀ; ~ary ਗੌਣ, ਅਪ੍ਰਧਾਨ, ਅਮੁੱਖ, ਘੱਟ ਮਹੱਤਵ ਵਾਲਾ; ਮਗਰੋਂ ਵਾਲਾ; ~er ਅਨੁਮੋਦਕ, ਪ੍ਰਸਤਾਵ-ਸਮਰਥਕ; ~ly ਦੂਜੇ ਨੰਬਰ ਤੇ, ਦੂਜੀ ਥਾਂ ਤੇ, ਦੂਜੇ

secrecy ('ਸੀਕਰਅਸਿ) *n* ਗੁੱਝਾਪਣ, ਗੁਪਤਾ, ਰਹੱਸ, ਰਹੱਸਪੂਰਨਤਾ, ਲੁਕਾਉ-ਛਿਪਾਉ, ਭੇਤ, ਰਾਜ਼

secret ('ਸੀਕਰਿਟ) *n a* ਭੇਤ; ਰਾਜ਼, ਗੁਪਤ, ਗੁੱਝ, ਅਦ੍ਰਿਸ਼ਟ, ਖੁਫੀਆ; ਨਿੱਜੀ

secretarial ('ਸੈੱਕਰਿ'ਟੇਅਰਿਅਲ) *a* ਸੱਕਤਰੇਤ ਦਾ, ਸੱਕਤਰੇਤ ਸਬੰਧੀ; ਸਕੱਤਰ ਸਬੰਧੀ

secretariat(e) ('ਸੈੱਕਰਿ'ਟੇਰਿਅਟ) *a* ਸਕੱਤਰੇਤ, ਸਰਕਾਰ ਦਾ ਵੱਡਾ ਦਫ਼ਤਰ

secretion (ਸਿ'ਕਰੀਸ਼ਨ) *n* ਰਹੱਸ, ਲੁਕਾਉ, ਛਿਪਾਉ

secretive (ਸੀਕਰਅਟਿਵ) *a* ਰਹੱਸਪੂਰਨ, ਲੁਕਵਾਂ; ਛਿਪਵਾਂ, ਚੁੱਪ-ਚੁਪੀਤਾ, ਕ੍ਰਮੋਸ਼

sect (ਸੈੱਕਟ) *n* (1) ਪੰਥ, ਫ਼ਿਰਕਾ, ਮਾਰਗ, ਮੱਤ; ਧਾਰਮਕ ਸੰਪਰਦਾਇ; (2) ਛੇਦਨ, ਵਿਨ੍ਹੰਣ; ~arian ਸੰਪਰਦਾਇਕ, ਫ਼ਿਰਕਾਪਰਸਤ, ਸੰਕੀਰਨ, ਫ਼ਿਰਕੂ; ~or ਖੇਤਰ, ਖੰਡ; ਸ਼ਹਿਰ ਦਾ ਇਕ ਹਿੱਸਾ

section (ਸੈੱਕਸ਼ਨ) *n v* ਵਿਭਾਜਨ, ਕਾਟ; ਭਾਗ,

ਖੰਡ, ਹਿੱਸਾ; ਅਨੁਭਾਗ, ਮੰਡਲ, ਸੈਕਸ਼ਨ; **~al** ਵਿਭਾਗੀ, ਅੰਸ਼ਕ, ਅਨੁਭਾਗੀ, ਵਰਗੀ

secular ('ਸੈੱਕਯੁਲਅ*) *n a* ਅਸੰਪਰਦਾਇਕ; ਧਰਮ-ਨਿਰਪੇਖ; **~ism** ਧਰਮ-ਨਿਰਪੇਖਤਾ, ਧਰਮ-ਨਿਰਪੇਖਵਾਦ, ਅਧਾਰਮਕਤਾ

secure (ਸਿ'ਕਯੁਅ*) *v a* ਸੁਰੱਖਿਅਤ ਰੱਖਣਾ; ਪੱਕਾ ਕਰਨਾ, ਪੁਖਤਾ ਕਰਨਾ; ਪ੍ਰਾਪਤ ਕਰਨਾ, ਬੇਫ਼ਿਕਰ, ਬੇਪਰਵਾਹ; ਦੁਬਧਾਹੀਣ; **~d** ਸੁਰੱਖਿਅਤ

security (ਸਿ'ਕਯੁਅਰਅਟਿ) *n* ਸੁਰੱਖਿਆ, ਸਲਾਮਤੀ, ਬਚਾਉ; ਰੱਖਿਅਕ; ਜ਼ਾਮਨੀ; ਜ਼ਮਾਨਤਨਾਮਾ, ਜ਼ਮਾਨਤ, ਸਾਖ-ਪੱਤਰ; ਰਿਣ-ਪੱਤਰ

sedation (ਸਿ'ਡੇਇਸ਼ਨ) *n* ਸ਼ਾਂਤੀਕਰਨ, ਸੀਤਲੀਕਰਨ

sediment ('ਸੈਡਿਮਅੰਟ) *n* ਫੋਗ, ਤਲਛਟ; **~ary** ਗਾਦ-ਭਰਿਆ, ਮੈਲ ਵਾਲਾ, ਤਲਛਟੀ

sedition (ਸਿ'ਡਿਸ਼ਨ) *n* ਬਗ਼ਾਵਤ; ਵਿਦਰੋਹ; ਰਾਜ-ਸੱਤਾ, ਵਿਦਰੋਹ, ਅੰਦੋਲਨ

seduce (ਸਿ'ਡਯੂਸ) *v* ਇਸਤਰੀ ਨੂੰ ਛਲਣਾ, ਬਹਿਕਾਉਣਾ; ਸਤ ਭੰਗ ਕਰਨਾ; ਗੁਮਰਾਹ ਕਰਨਾ, ਦੂਸ਼ਤ ਕਰਨਾ, ਪਤਿਤ ਕਰਨਾ

seduction (ਸਿ'ਡਅੱਕਸ਼ਨ) *n* ਝਾਂਸਾ, ਵਰਗਲਾਹਟ

see (ਸੀ) *v* ਤੱਕਣਾ, ਵੇਖਣਾ, ਦਿਸਣਾ, ਦਰਸ਼ਨ ਕਰਨਾ, ਦ੍ਰਿਸ਼ਟੀਗਤ ਕਰਨਾ; ਧਿਆਨ ਕਰਨਾ, ਗੌਰ ਕਰਨਾ, ਪਰਖਣਾ, ਨਿਰੀਖਣ ਕਰਨਾ; ਮਹਿਸੂਸ ਕਰਨਾ, ਮੁਲਾਕਾਤ ਕਰਨੀ

seed (ਸੀਡ) *n v* ਤੁਖਮ, ਨਸਲ, ਬੀਜ, ਦਾਣਾ, ਬੀਜਾਣੂ; ਮਣੀ, ਵੀਰਜ; ਮੁੱਢ, ਸ਼ੁਰੂਆਤ, ਬੀਂ ਬੀਜਣਾ, ਛਿੜਕਣਾ

seek (ਸੀਕ) *v* ਭਾਲਣਾ, ਖੋਜਣਾ, ਪਤਾ ਲਾਉਣਾ, ਢੂੰਡਣਾ; ਯਾਚਨਾ ਕਰਨੀ, ਪ੍ਰਾਰਥਨਾ ਕਰਨੀ

seem (ਸੀਮ) *v* ਪ੍ਰਤੀਤ ਹੋਣਾ, ਗਿਆਤ ਹੋਣਾ, ਲੱਗਣਾ, ਅਨੁਭਵ ਹੋਣਾ; ਦਿਸਣਾ, ਨਜ਼ਰ ਆਉਣਾ, ਜ਼ਾਹਰ ਹੋਣਾ; **~ly** ਭੱਦਰ, ਉੱਤਮ; ਉਚਿਤ, ਸ਼ਿਸ਼ਟ, ਉਪਯੁਕਤ, ਸੁਸੰਗਤ, ਸੁੰਦਰ

seep (ਸੀਪ) *v* ਰਿਸਣਾ, ਟਪਕਣਾ, ਸਿੰਮਣਾ

seer ('ਸੀਅ*) *n* ਭਵਿੱਖ-ਦ੍ਰਸ਼ਟਾ; ਰਿਸ਼ੀ; ਸਿੱਧ ਪੁਰਸ਼; ਪੈਗ਼ੰਬਰ, ਨੱਬੀ

seesaw ('ਸੀਸੋ) *n v* ਪੀਲ-ਪਲਾਂਘਾ; ਝੂਲਾ; ਬਰਾਬਰ ਦਾ ਮੁਕਾਬਲਾ; ਝੁਮ-ਝੁਮਾ ਖੇਲਣਾ

seethe (ਸੀਦ) *v* ਤਾਉ ਦੇਣਾ, ਜੋਸ਼ ਦੁਆਉਣਾ; ਕਰੋਧ ਵਿਚ ਆਉਣਾ; ਉਤੇਜਤ ਕਰਨਾ

segment ('ਸੈੱਗਮਅੰਟ, ਸੈੱਗ'ਮੈਂਟ) *n v* ਭਾਗ; ਖੰਡ, ਟੁਕੜਾ; ਫਾਂਕ; ਵਿਭਾਜਤ ਕਰਨਾ; **~ation** ਵਿਭਾਜਨ, ਵਿਛੇਦ

segregate ('ਸੈੱਗਰਿਗੇਇਟ) *v* ਅੱਡ ਕਰਨਾ, ਅੱਲਗ ਕਰਨਾ; ਕੱਟਣਾ, ਹਟਾਉਣਾ

segregation ('ਸੈੱਗਰਿ'ਗੇਇਸ਼ਨ) *n* ਵਿਯੋਗ, ਅਲਹਿਦਾਪਣ; ਵਿਤਕਰਾ, ਭੇਦਭਾਵ

seize (ਸੀਜ਼) *v* (ਕਾ) ਅਧਿਕਾਰ ਵਿਚ ਲੈਣਾ, ਕਾਬੂ ਕਰਨਾ, ਕਬਜ਼ਾ ਕਰਨਾ

seizure ('ਸੀਯ਼ਅ*) *n* ਕਬਜ਼ਾ; ਪਕੜ; ਧਾਰਣ; ਹਮਲਾ, ਅਵੇਸ਼

seldom ('ਸੈੱਲਡਅਮ) *adv* ਵਿਰਲਾ ਹੀ; ਕਦੀ-ਕਦਾਈਂ, ਬਹੁਤ ਘੱਟ; ਕਦਾਚਿਤ; ਕਦੇ ਕਦੇ

select (ਸਿ'ਲੈੱਕਟ) *v a* ਚੁਣਨਾ, ਛਾਂਟਣਾ, ਪਸੰਦ ਕਰਨਾ; ਮਨੋਨੀਤ ਕਰਨਾ; ਚੋਣਵਾਂ; **~ed** ਵਧੀਆ; ਚੁਣਿਆ, ਪਵਿੱਤਰ; **~ion** ਚੋਣ; ਮਨੋਨੀਤ; ਚੁਣਾਉ; ਛਾਂਟ; **~ive** ਚੁਣਨਯੋਗ, ਚੋਣਸ਼ੀਲ; ਵਰਣਾਤਮਕ

self (ਸੈੱਲਫ਼) *n a* ਆਪਾ, ਖ਼ੁਦੀ, ਅਹੰ, ਆਤਮ ਭਾਵ, ਨਿਜੀ ਹੋਂਦ; ਨਿਜ; ~abandoned ਵਿਲਾਸੀ, ਭੋਗੀ, ਵਿਸ਼ਈ; ~acquired ਸਵੈ-ਪ੍ਰਾਪਤ; ~centred ਸਵੈ-ਕੇਂਦਰਤ, ਸੁਆਰਥੀ, ਮਤਲਬੀ; ~confidence ਆਤਮ-ਵਿਸ਼ਵਾਸ; ~ish ਸੁਆਰਥੀ, ਮਤਲਬੀ, ਖ਼ੁਦਗ਼ਰਜ਼; ~ishness ਸੁਆਰਥ, ਖ਼ੁਦਗ਼ਰਜ਼ੀ; ~less ਸੁਆਰਥਹੀਨ, ਬੇਗਰਜ਼, ਤਿਆਗੀ; ~sufficiency ਆਤਮ-ਨਿਰਭਰਤਾ;

sell (ਸੈੱਲ) *v* ਵੇਚਣਾ, ਵਿਕਰੀ ਕਰਨੀ, ਫ਼ਰੋਖ਼ਤ ਕਰਨਾ; ਵਿਕਣਾ; ਠੱਗਣਾ, ਧੋਖਾ ਦੇਣਾ, ਝਾਂਸਾ ਦੇਣਾ; ~er ਵਿਕ੍ਰੇਤਾ, ਵੇਚਣ ਵਾਲਾ

semantics (ਸਿ'ਮੈਂਟਿਕਸ) *n* ਅਰਥ-ਵਿਗਿਆਨ, ਅਰਥਕੀ

semblance ('ਸੈੱਬਲਅੰਸ) *n* ਬਾਹਰੀ ਰੂਪ, ਸਮਾਨਤਾ, ਝਲਕ, ਆਭਾਸ

semen ('ਸੀਮੈੱਨ) *n* ਵੀਰਜ, ਬੀਜ, ਮਨੀ; ਧਾਤ

semester (ਸਿ'ਮੈੱਸਟਅ*) *n* ਛਿਮਾਹੀ ਪਾਠ-ਕ੍ਰਮ; ਛਿਮਾਹੀ

semi ('ਸੈੱਮੀ) *pref* ਅੱਧ, ਅਰਧ (ਅਗੇਤਰ ਰੂਪ); ਨੀਮ; ਅਪੂਰਣ; ~colon ਅਰਧਵਿਰਾਮ

seminar ('ਸੈੱਮਿਨਾ*) *n* ਗੋਸ਼ਟੀ, ਵਿਚਾਰ-ਗੋਸ਼ਟੀ

seminary ('ਸੈੱਮਿਨਅਰਿ) *n* ਸਿੱਖਿਆਲਾ, ਸਕੂਲ, ਪਾਠਸ਼ਾਲਾ, ਵਿਦਿਆਲਾ,

semiotics ('ਸੈੱਮਿ'ਔਟਿਕਸ) *n* ਚਿੰਨ੍ਹ ਵਿਗਿਆਨ

semolina ('ਸੈੱਮਅ'ਲੀਨਅ) *n* ਸੂਜੀ

senate ('ਸੈੱਨਿਟ) *n* ਉੱਚ-ਸਦਨ; ਵਿਧਾਨ-ਸਭਾ, ਵੱਡੀ ਸਭਾ; ਵਿਸ਼ਵ-ਵਿਦਿਆਲਾ ਦੀ ਪ੍ਰਬੰਧ-ਸੰਮਤੀ, ਪ੍ਰਸ਼ਾਸਨ ਸੰਮਤੀ

send (ਸੈਂਡ) *v* ਘੱਲਣਾ, ਭੇਜਣਾ, ਪਹੁੰਚਾਉਣਾ, ਵਿਦਾ ਕਰਨਾ, ਟੋਰਨਾ, ਰਵਾਨਾ ਕਰਨਾ; ਚਲਾਉਣਾ, ਭਜਾਉਣਾ, ਧੱਕਣਾ, ਠੇਲ੍ਹਣਾ; ~off ਵਿਦਾਇਗੀ

senility (ਸਿ'ਨਿਲਅਟਿ) *n* ਬਿਰਧ ਅਵਸਥਾ, ਬੁਢਾਪਾ; ਕਮਜ਼ੋਰੀ

senior ('ਸੀਨਯਅ*) *n a* ਜਠੇਰਾ, ਬਿਰਧਜਨ, ਵੱਡਾ; ਪ੍ਰਧਾਨ, ਉੱਚ, ਸ੍ਰੇਸ਼ਠ; ~ity ਉੱਚਤਾ, ਵੱਡਪਣ, ਬਜ਼ੁਰਗੀ, ਸਿਆਣਾਪਾ, ਜੇਠਾਪਣ

sensation (ਸੈੱਨ'ਸੇਇਸ਼ਨ) *n* ਸੰਵੇਦਨਾ, ਉਦਵੇਗ, ਤੀਬਰ ਅਨੁਭਵ, ਸਨਸਨੀ, ਚੇਤਨਤਾ, ਅੰਤਰ-ਅਨੁਭਵ; ਸਮਝ, ਇਹਸਾਸ; ਝਰਨਾਹਟ, ਲਹਿਰ; ~al ਸਨਸਨੀਖੇਜ਼, ਉਤੇਜਨਾਪੂਰਨ, ਸੰਵੇਦਨਾਤਮਕ

sense (ਸੈੱਸ) *n* ਵਿਵੇਕ, ਸਹਿਜ ਬੁਧੀ, ਹੋਸ਼; ਗਿਆਨ ਇੰਦਰੀ, ਚੇਤਨਤਾ, ਸੰਵੇਦਨਾ; ਸਧਾਰਨ ਗਿਆਨ, ਵਿਚਾਰਕਤਾ, ਵਿਚਾਰਕ ਗਿਆਨ, ਸਮਝਦਾਰੀ; ਭਾਵਨਾ, ਵਿਚਾਰ, ਭਾਵੁਕਤਾ; ਤਾਤਪਰਜ, ਅਰਥ; ਭਾਵ, ਮਤਲਬ; ਤੱਤ; ~less ਚੇਤਨਾਹੀਨ, ਬੇਹੋਸ਼; ਬੁੱਧੀਹੀਨ, ਨਾਸਮਝ, ਨਾਦਾਨ, ਮੂਰਖ

sensible ('ਸੈੱਸਅਬਲ) *a* ਸੰਵੇਦਨਸ਼ੀਲ; ਵਿਚਾਰਕ; ਗਿਆਨਵਾਨ, ਵਿਵੇਕੀ, ਸਮਝਦਾਰ

sensitive ('ਸੈੱਸਿਟਿਵ੍) *n a* ਸੰਵੇਦੀ, ਸੰਵੇਦਨਸ਼ੀਲ, ਸਚੇਤ, ਚੇਤਨਾਸ਼ੀਲ, ਸੂਖਮਗ੍ਰਾਹੀ, ਭਾਵੁਕ, ਨਾਜ਼ੁਕ ਮਿਜ਼ਾਜ, ਛੁਈਮੁਈ; ~ness ਸੰਵੇਦਨਸ਼ੀਲਤਾ, ਭਾਵੁਕਤਾ, ਭਾਵਗ੍ਰਾਹਿਕਤਾ, ਨਾਜ਼ੁਕ-ਮਿਜ਼ਾਜੀ

sensory ('ਸੈੱਸਅਰਿ) *a* ਸੰਵੇਦੀ, ਸੰਵੇਦਕ, ਸੰਵੇਦਨਾਤਮਕ, ਅਨੁਭੂਤੀ ਸਬੰਧੀ

sensual ('ਸੈੱਸਯੂਅਲ) *a* ਪ੍ਰਤੱਖਵਾਦੀ, ਸੰਵੇਦਨਾਵਾਦੀ; ਕਾਮੁਕ; ਵਾਸਨਾਤਮਕ

sensuos ('ਸੈੱਸਯੂਅਸ) *a* ਇੰਦਰੀ-ਭੋਗ ਸਬੰਧੀ,

ਇੰਦਰੀ-ਗਤ

sentence ('ਸੈੱਟਅੰਸ) *n v* ਵਾਕ; ਸੂਤਰ, (ਪ੍ਰ) ਕਹਾਵਤ; ਨਿਰਣੈ; ਜਿਊਰੀ ਦਾ ਫ਼ੈਸਲਾ; ਸਜ਼ਾ ਦਾ ਹੁਕਮ; ਫ਼ੈਸਲਾ ਦੱਸਣਾ, ਨਿਰਣੈ ਦੇਣਾ, ਹੁਕਮ ਸੁਣਾਉਣਾ

sentiment ('ਸੈੱਟਿਮਅੰਟ) *n* ਭਾਵਨਾ, ਮਨੋਭਾਵ, ਭਾਵਾਤਮਕ ਵਿਚਾਰ, ਜਜ਼ਬਾ; ~**al** ਭਾਵੁਕ, ਜਜ਼ਬਾਤੀ

sentinel, sentry ('ਸੈੱਟਿਨਲ, 'ਸੈੱਟਰਿ) *n v* ਸੰਤਰੀ, ਰੱਖਿਅਕ, ਪਹਿਰੇਦਾਰ; ਪਹਿਰਾ ਦੇਣਾ, ਰੱਖਿਆ ਕਰਨੀ

separable ('ਸੈੱਪ(ਅ)ਰਅਬਲ) *a* ਨਿੱਖੜਵਾਂ, ਅੱਡ ਹੋਣ ਯੋਗ, ਅਲੱਗ ਕਰਨ ਯੋਗ

separate ('ਸੈੱਪਅਰਅਟ, 'ਸੈੱਪਅਰੇਇਟ) *n a v* ਵੱਖ; ਸੁਤੰਤਰ, ਨਿਜੀ, ਆਪਣਾ; ਵਖਰਾਉਣਾ, ਅੱਡ ਕਰਨਾ, ਵਿਯੁਕਤ ਕਰਨਾ, ਵਿਭਕਤ ਕਰਨਾ, ਭੇਦ ਕਰਨਾ, ਅੱਲਗ ਕਰਨਾ, ਜੁਦਾ ਕਰਨਾ, ਵਿਛੜਨਾ

separation ('ਸੈੱਪਅ'ਰੇਇਸ਼ਨ) *n* ਜੁਦਾਈ; ਵਿਯੁਕਤੀ, ਵਿਯੋਗ, ਬਿਰਹ, ਵਿਭੇਦ

sepoy ('ਸੀਪੌਇ) *n* ਸੈਨਕ, ਸਿਪਾਹੀ

sequel ('ਸੀਕਵ(ਅ)ਲ) *n* ਸਮਾਪਤੀ, ਅੰਤਮ ਰੂਪ, ਉੱਤਰ, ਬਾਕੀ, ਬਚਿਆ ਹਿੱਸਾ, ਪਰਿਣਾਮ

sequence ('ਸੀਕਵਅੰਸ) *n* ਕੜੀ, ਸਿਲਸਲਾ, ਤਰਤੀਬ

seraglio (ਸੇਰਾਗਲਾਉ) *n* ਹਰਮ, ਰਣਵਾਸ

serape (ਸੈਰਾਪਿ) *n* ਸ਼ਾਲ, ਦੁਸ਼ਾਲਾ, ਓਢੂਨਾ

serene (ਸਿ'ਰੀਨ) *n v a* ਸ਼ਾਂਤ ਵਿਸਥਾਰ; ਸ਼ਾਂਤ ਕਰਨਾ; ਸਥਿਰ; ਨਿਰਮਲ, ਸ਼ੁੱਧ, ਪ੍ਰਸੰਨ; ਨਿਖਰਿਆ, ਉੱਜਲ

serf (ਸਅਃਫ਼) *n* ਪੀੜਤ ਵਿਅਕਤੀ; ਗ਼ੁਲਾਮ,

ਵਗਾਰੀ; ~**dom** ਦਾਸ ਪ੍ਰਥਾ, ਦਾਸਤਾ

serial ('ਸਿਅਰਿਅਲ) *n a* ਪ੍ਰਕਾਸ਼ਨ ਲੜੀ; ਲੜੀਦਾਰ, ਧਾਰਾਵਾਹਕ, ਸਿਲਸਲੇਵਾਰ; ~**number** ਲੜੀ ਨੰਬਰ, ਕ੍ਰਮ ਸੰਖਿਆ; ~**ly** ਕ੍ਰਮ ਅਨੁਸਾਰ, ਕ੍ਰਮ ਪੂਰਵਕ, ਸਿਲਸਲੇਵਾਰ

sericulture ('ਸੈਰਿ'ਕਅੱਲਚਅ*) *n* ਰੇਸ਼ਮ-ਉਤਪਾਦਨ

series ('ਸਿਅਰੀਜ਼) *n* ਲੜੀ, ਕੜੀ, ਮਾਲਾ, ਸਿਲਸਲਾ; ਸ਼੍ਰੇਣੀ; ਅੰਕਮਾਲਾ, ਲੇਖਮਾਲਾ, ਪੁਸਤਕਮਾਲਾ

serious ('ਸਿਅਰਿਅਸ) *a* ਗੰਭੀਰ, ਧੀਰ, ਸੰਜੀਦਾ ਚਿੰਤਨਸ਼ੀਲ, ਵਿਚਾਰਸ਼ੀਲ, ਧਿਆਨ, ਮਗਨ; ~**ness** ਗੰਭੀਰਤਾ, ਸੰਜੀਦਗੀ, ਵਿਚਾਰਸ਼ੀਲਤਾ, ਉਤਸੁਕਤਾ

sermon ('ਸਅਃਮਅਨ) *n v* ਪ੍ਰਵਚਨ, ਉਪਦੇਸ਼, ਧਰਮ-ਉਪਦੇਸ਼, ਧਰਮ-ਵਿਆਖਿਆਨ; ਵਿਆਖਿਆਨ ਦੇਣਾ, ਸਿੱਖਿਆ ਦੇਤੀ

serpent ('ਸਅਃਪਅੰਟ) *n* ਸੱਪ, ਨਾਗ, ਭੁਜੰਗ; ਵਿਸ਼ਵਾਸਘਾਤੀ ਆਦਮੀ, ਧੋਖੇਬਾਜ਼ ਆਦਮੀ

servant ('ਸਅਃਵਅੰਟ) *n* ਕਰਮਚਾਰੀ, ਨੌਕਰ, ਮੁਲਾਜ਼ਮ, ਸੇਵਕ, ਦਾਸ

serve (ਸਅਃਵ) *v* ਸੇਵਾ ਕਰਨੀ, ਨੌਕਰੀ ਕਰਨੀ, ਕੰਮ ਕਰਨਾ, ਖ਼ਿਦਮਤ ਕਰਨੀ; ਲਾਭਦਾਇਕ ਹੋਣਾ, ਉਪਯੋਗੀ ਹੋਣਾ, ਕੰਮ ਆਉਣਾ; ਮਤਲਬ ਪੂਰਾ ਕਰਨਾ, ਸੰਤੁਸ਼ਟ ਕਰਨਾ; ਟਹਿਲ ਕਰਨੀ

service ('ਸਅਃਵਿਸ) *n v* ਸੇਵਾ, ਨੌਕਰੀ, ਖ਼ਾਤਰ, ਖ਼ਿਦਮਤ, ਮੁਲਾਜ਼ਮਤ; ਉਪਕਾਰ, ਪਰਉਪਕਾਰ, ਸੇਵਾ-ਭਾਵ; ਸਹਾਇਤਾ; ਪੂਜਾ-ਪਾਠ; ਮੁਰੰਮਤ ਕਰਨੀ, ਸਫ਼ਾਈ ਕਰਨੀ; ~**able** ਉਪਕਾਰੀ ਹਿੱਤਕਾਰੀ, ਸੇਵਾ ਯੋਗ, ਟਿਕਾਊ, ਮਜ਼ਬੂਤ

serviette ('ਸਅਃਵਿ'ਐੱਟ) *n* ਰੁਮਾਲ, ਤੌਲੀਆ

servile ('ਸਅਃਵ੍ਾਇਲ) *a* ਨੀਚ, ਤੁੱਛ; ਹੀਣ; ਖੁਸ਼ਾਮਦੀ; ਕਮੀਨਾ; ਜੀ ਹਜ਼ੂਰੀਆ, ਚਾਪਲੂਸ

servitude ('ਸਅਃਵ੍ਿਟਯੂਡ) *n* ਦਾਸਤਾ; ਗ਼ੁਲਾਮੀ, ਸੇਵਾ ਭਾਵ

sesame ('ਸੈੱਸਅਮਿ) *n* ਤਿਲ

session ('ਸੈੱਸ਼ਨ) *n* ਵਿਧਾਨ ਸਭਾ ਦੀ ਬੈਠਕ, ਸਭਾ, ਵਿਸ਼ਵਵਿਦਿਆਲੇ ਦਾ ਸਿੱਖਿਆ-ਕਾਲ, ਅਧਿਆਪਨ ਵਰ੍ਹਾ; ਅਜਲਾਸ

set (ਸੈੱਟ) *n v* ਜੁੱਟ; ਸੂਰਜ ਦਾ ਢਲਣਾ; ਢਾਂਚਾ, ਬਣਾਵਟ; ਧਾਰਾ, ਵਹਾਉ; ਬੈਠਾਉਣਾ, ਜੜਨਾ; ਸਥਾਪਤ ਕਰਨਾ; ਨਿਰਣੈ ਕਰਨਾ, ਨਿਸ਼ਚਤ ਕਰਨਾ, ਨਿਯਤ ਕਰਨਾ; ਪੱਕਾ ਕਰਨਾ, ਠਾਣ ਲੈਣਾ; ਠੀਕ ਕਰਨਾ; **~ting** ਯੋਜਨਾ; ਸਥਾਪਨ, ਜੜਾਉ, ਬੈਠਾਉ; ਦ੍ਰਿਸ਼ਪਟ, ਚੁਗਿਰਦਾ, ਵਾਤਾਵਰਨ

settle ('ਸੈੱਟਲ) *v* ਸਥਾਪਨ ਕਰਨਾ, ਲਾਉਣਾ, ਜਮਾਉਣਾ; ਸ਼ਾਂਤ ਕਰਨਾ, ਸੁਲਝਣਾ, ਸੁਲਝਾਉਣਾ; ਫ਼ੈਸਲਾ ਕਰਨਾ; ਨਿਸ਼ਚੈ ਕਰਨਾ, ਠਾਨਣਾ, ਨਿਯੁਕਤ ਕਰਨਾ; ਸਹਿਮਤ ਕਰਨਾ; ਰਾਜੀ ਹੋਣਾ; **~d** ਨਿਸ਼ਚਤ, ਨਿਯਤ, ਸਥਾਪਤ, ਚੁਕਤਾ ਕੀਤਾ, ਚੁਕਾਇਆ; **~ment** ਨਿਰਣਾ, ਨਿਸ਼ਰਾ; ਨਿਪਟਾਰਾ; ਸਥਾਪਨ; ਸਮਾਧਾਨ, ਸਮਝੌਤਾ; ਉਪਨਿਵੇਸ਼; ਬਸਤੀ

seven ('ਸੈਵ੍ਨ) *a n* ਸੱਤ; ਸੱਤਵਾਂ; ਸੱਤ ਦੀ ਗਿਣਤੀ, ਸੱਤਾਂ ਦਾ ਇੱਕਠ; **~fold** ਸੱਤ-ਗੁਣਾ; **~teen** ਸਤਾਰਾਂ; **sweet ~teen** ਨਵਯੁਵਤੀ ਦਾ ਸੁੰਦਰਤਾ-ਕਾਲ, ਸਤਾਰਾਂ ਸਾਲਾ ਸੁੰਦਰੀ; **~th** ਸੱਤਵਾਂ ਭਾਗ; ਸੱਤਵਾਂ; **~ty** ਸੱਤਰ ਦੀ ਸੰਖਿਆ ਜਾਂ ਅੰਕ; ਸੱਤਰਵਾਂ

several (ਸੈੱਵ੍ਅ*ਲ) *a pron* ਤੋੜਨਾ (ਸਬੰਧ) ਅੱਡ ਕਰਨਾ, ਵੱਖ ਕਰਨਾ, ਅੱਲਗਾ ਕਰਨਾ;

ਅਲਹਿਦਾ, ਨਿਆਰਾ, ਭਿੰਨ, ਸੁਤੰਤਰ, ਵਿਭਿੰਨ, ਵਿਸ਼ੇਸ਼, ਅਨੇਕ, ਨਾਨਾ ਪ੍ਰਕਾਰ

severe (ਸਿਵ੍ਿਆ*) *a* ਘੋਰ, ਅਤੀਅੰਤ, ਬੇਹੱਦ, ਪ੍ਰਚੰਡ, ਉਗਰ, ਤੀਬਰ, ਤੀਖਣ, ਅਸਹਿ, ਭਾਰੀ, ਸਖ਼ਤ; ਦੰਡਸ਼ੀਲ; ਤਿੱਖਾ, ਕੌੜਾ

severity (ਸਿ'ਵ੍ੈੱਅਟਿ) *n* ਤੀਖਣਤਾ, ਤੀਬਰਤਾ, ਗਰਮੀ, ਤੇਜ਼ੀ, ਨਿਰਦਇਤਾ, ਕਠੋਰਤਾ, ਨਿਸ਼ਠੁਰਤਾ

sew (ਸਅਉ) *v* ਸਿਉਣਾ, ਸੀਣਾ, ਸਿਲਾਈ ਕਰਨਾ; **~er** ਦਰਜ਼ੀ; **~ing** ਸਿਲਾਈ, ਸਿਉਣ

sewage ('ਸੂਇਜ) *n* ਗੰਦੀ ਨਾਲੀ ਦਾ ਪਾਣੀ, ਮਲ-ਪਰਵਾਹ

sewer (ਸੂਅ*) *n* (ਇਤਿ) ਖਾਨਸਾਮਾ; ਗੰਦਾ ਨਾਲਾ

sex (ਸੈੱਕਸ) *n* ਲਿੰਗ, ਲਿੰਗ ਭੇਦ, ਯੋਨੀ, ਕਾਮ; **~ology** ਲਿੰਗ-ਵਿਗਿਆਨ, ਕਾਮ-ਵਿਗਿਆਨ; **~ual** ਲਿੰਗੀ, ਮੈਥੁਨੀ, ਲਿੰਗ ਮੂਲਕ, ਯੋਨੀ ਸਬੰਧੀ, ਇਸਤਰੀ-ਪੁਰਸ਼ ਸਬੰਧੀ; **~uality** ਕਾਮਵਾਸਨਾ, ਕਾਮੁਕਤਾ; **~y** ਅਤੀ ਕਾਮੀ, ਅਤੀ ਵਿਲਾਸੀ, ਕਾਮੁਕ

shabby ('ਸ਼ੈਬੀ) *a* ਖੁੱਥੜ; ਪਾਟਿਆ, ਪੁਰਾਣਾ, ਲੀਚੜ, ਨੀਚ, ਕੰਜੂਸ; ਹੋਛਾ

shack (ਸ਼ੈਕ) *n* ਝੁੱਗੀ, ਟਪਰੀ

shackle ('ਸ਼ੈਕਲ) *n v* ਹੱਥਕੜੀ; (in *pl* s) ਰੁਕਾਵਟ; ਬੰਧਨ, ਕੁੰਡਾ; ਜੋੜਨਾ, ਮਿਲਾਉਣਾ; ਸੰਗਲ ਪਾਉਣਾ; ਰੋੜਾ ਅਟਕਾਉਣਾ

shade (ਸ਼ੇਇਡ) *n v* ਪਰਛਾਈਂ, ਛਾਂ, ਛਾਂ-ਦਾਰ ਥਾਂ; ਘੁਸਮੁਸਾ; ਭਰਾਂਤੀ; ਹਨੇਰਾ ਕਰਨਾ, ਧੁੰਦਲਾ ਕਰਨਾ; ਛਾਂ ਕਰਨੀ, ਧੁੱਪ ਤੋਂ ਬਚਾਉਣਾ; ਪਰਦਾ ਪਾਉਣਾ, ਲੁਕਾਉਣਾ; **~d** ਛਾਇਆ ਛ੍ਰਿਤ, ਥੋੜ੍ਹਾ ਘਟਾਇਆ

shadow ('ਸ਼ੈਡਅਉ) *n v* ਛਾਂ; ਪ੍ਰਤੀਬਿੰਬ,

ਸਹਿਚਰ, ਸਹਿਗਾਮੀ, ਸੰਗੀ, ਪ੍ਰਤੀਰੂਪ, ਛਾਇਆ;
ਝਲਕ, ਹਲਕਾ ਖ਼ਾਕਾ; ਛਾਉਣਾ, ਛਾ ਜਾਣਾ,
ਲੁਕਾ ਲੈਣਾ; ਧੁੰਦਲਾ ਖ਼ਾਕਾ ਖਿੱਚਣਾ; ਛਾਂ
ਪਾਉਣੀ, ਛਾਂ ਕਰਨੀ

shady ('ਸ਼ੇਇਡ੍ਰਿ) *a* ਛਾਂਦਾਰ, ਛਾਇਆਮਈ;
ਘਣਾ; ਅਪਰਗਟ, ਗੁਪਤ, ਨਿੰਧਿੰਗ

shake (ਸ਼ੇਇਕ) *n v* ਹਲੂਣਾ, ਹੁਝਕਾ, ਥਰਕਣ,
ਝਟਕਾ, ਧੱਕਾ, ਹਿਚਕੋਲਾ; ਕੰਬਣ, ਥਰਕਣਾ,
ਡੋਲਣਾ; ਕੰਬਾਉਣਾ, ਘੁਮਾਉਣਾ

shaky ('ਸ਼ੇਇਕਿ) *a* ਅਸਥਿਰ, ਨਿਰਬਲ,
ਭਾਵਾਂਡੋਲ, ਸੰਦੇਹ-ਪੂਰਨ, ਕੰਬਣ ਵਾਲਾ,
ਝਿੱਜਕਦਾ; ਹਿੱਲਦਾ ਅਟਿੱਕਵਾਂ, ਢਿੱਲਾ

shallow ('ਸ਼ੈਲਅਉ) *n v a* ਕਛਾਰ, ਘੱਟ ਪਾਣੀ
ਦੀ ਥਾਂ; ਹੋਛਾ ਹੋਣਾ; ਤੁੱਛ, ਸਾਰਹੀਣ, ਹੋਛਾ;
~ness ਹੋਛਾਪਣ, ਥੋੜ੍ਹਾਪਣ, ਹਲਕਾਪਣ

shamble ('ਸ਼ੈਂਬਲ) *n v* ਭੱਦੀ ਚਾਲ, ਵਿਰੂਪ
ਗਤੀ, ਬੇਢੰਗੀ ਦੌੜ, ਡਿਗਦੇ ਢਹਿੰਦੇ ਤੁਰਨਾ,
ਲੜਖੜਾਂਦੇ ਹੋਏ ਚੱਲਣਾ

shambles ('ਸ਼ੈਂਬਲਜ਼) *n* ਬੁਚੜਖ਼ਾਨਾ; ਰੋਲ
ਘਚੋਲਾ; ਦੁਰਦਸ਼ਾ, ਤਬਾਹੀ

shame (ਸ਼ੇਇਮ) *n v* ਲੱਜਾ, ਲਾਜ, ਸ਼ਰਮ,
ਝਿਜਕ, ਝੇਂਪ, ਹਿਆ, ਗ਼ੈਰਤ; ਸ਼ਰਮਿੰਦਗੀ,
ਲਾਨ੍ਹਤ; ਸ਼ਰਮਿੰਦਾ ਕਰਨਾ; ਨੀਵਾਂ ਦਿਖਾਉਣਾ,
ਅਪਮਾਨਤ ਕਰਨਾ; ~full ਸ਼ਰਮਨਾਕ,
ਲੱਜਾਜਨਕ; ਅਸ਼ਲੀਲ, ਖ਼ਰਾਬ; ~less ਬੇਸ਼ਰਮ,
ਬੇਹਯਾ, ਲੱਜਹੀਣ, ਨਿਰਲੱਜ, ਢੀਠ

shanty ('ਸ਼ੈਨਟਿ) *n* ਛੱਪਰੀ, ਟੱਪਰੀ, ਕੁਟੀਆ,
ਕੁਟੀਰ, ਝੁੱਪੜੀ

shape (ਸ਼ੇਇਪ) *n v* ਰਚਨਾ, ਰੂਪ, ਡੀਲ-ਡੌਲ,
ਬਣਾਵਟ, ਆਕਾਰ, ਆਕ੍ਰਿਤੀ, ਸੂਰਤ, ਸ਼ਕਲ;
ਰੰਗ-ਰੂਪ, ਪ੍ਰਕਾਰ; ਸਿਰਜਣਾ, ਰੂਪ ਦੇਣਾ, ਸ਼ਕਲ

ਦੇਣੀ; ਸ਼ਕਲ ਇਖ਼ਤਿਆਰ ਕਰਨੀ; ਨਿਰਮਾਣ
ਕਰਨਾ, ਸਾਂਚੇ ਵਿਚ ਢਾਲਣਾ; ~d ਸਾਕਾਰ,
ਸਰੂਪ, ਰੂਪਯੁਕਤ; ਆਕਾਰਯੁਕਤ

share (ਸ਼ੇਅ*) *n v* ਵੰਡਾਈ, ਬਟਾਈ, ਹਿੱਸਾ;
ਵੰਡ, ਅੰਸ਼; ਹਿੱਸਾ ਲੈਣਾ, ਸ਼ਾਮਲ ਹੋਣਾ,
ਸਹਿਭਾਗੀ ਹੋਣਾ

shark (ਸ਼ਾਕ) *n v* ਸਮੁੰਦਰੀ ਮੱਛੀ, ਵੱਡਾ ਮੱਛ;
ਧੋਖੇਬਾਜ਼ ਸ਼ਖ਼ਸ; ਠਗਾਂਟ, ਚਾਰ ਸੌ ਵੀਹ ਕਰਨੀ

sharp (ਸ਼ਾਪ) *a v* ਤਿੱਖਾ, ਤੇਜ਼, ਧਾਰਦਾਰ, ਬਾਰੀਕ,
ਨੋਕੀਲਾ, ਨੋਕਦਾਰ, ਅਣਿਆਲਾ, ਤਤਪਰ;
ਹੁਸ਼ਿਆਰ, ਚੌਕਸ, ਸੰਵੇਦਨਸ਼ੀਲ, ਚਲਾਕ; ਤੁਰਤ-
ਫੁਰਤ ਕਰਨ ਵਾਲਾ; ਤਿੱਖਾ ਕਰਨਾ, ਤੇਜ਼ ਕਰਨਾ,
ਧਾਰ ਬਣਾਉਣਾ; ~en ਤੇਜ਼ ਕਰਨਾ ਜਾਂ ਹੋਣਾ, ਧਾਰ
ਲਗਾਉਣਾ, ਸਾਣ ਉੱਤੇ ਚੜ੍ਹਾਉਣਾ; ਸਪਸ਼ਟ
ਕਰਨਾ; ਉਤਸੁਕ ਕਰਨਾ; ਕਾਇਆਂ ਹੋਣਾ;
~ness ਤੀਖਣਤਾ, ਤੇਜ਼ੀ, ਤੀਬਰਤਾ, ਨੁਕੀਲਾ-
ਪਣ, ਪ੍ਰਚੰਡਤਾ; ਕਠੋਰਤਾ, ਤੀਬਰ ਦ੍ਰਿਸ਼ਟੀ,
ਸਤਰਕਤਾ; ਸੰਵੇਦਨਸ਼ੀਲਤਾ

shatter ('ਸ਼ੈਟਅ*) *v* ਛਿੰਨ-ਭਿੰਨ ਕਰਨਾ,
ਉਲਟਣਾ-ਪੁਲਟਣਾ, ਬਰਬਾਦ ਕਰਨਾ, ਧੱਜੀਆਂ
ਉਡਾਉਣਾ, ਖਿਲਾਰਨਾ

shave (ਸ਼ੇਇਵ) *n v* ਹਜਾਮਤ; ਹਜਾਮਤ ਕਰਨੀ,
ਮੁੰਨਣਾ; ਵਾਲ ਬਣਾਉਣਾ, ਵਾਲ ਕੱਟਣਾ; ~r
ਨਾਈ, ਹੱਜਾਮ; ਮੁੰਡਾ; ਛੋਕਰਾ, ਲੁਟੇਰਾ

shaving ('ਸ਼ੇਇਵਿਙ) *n* ਕਤਰਨਾਂ; ਛਿੱਲਤਰਾਂ

shawl (ਸ਼ੋਲ) *n* ਚਾਦਰ, ਗਰਮ ਲੋਈ ਜਾਂ ਭੂਰੀ,
ਸ਼ਾਲ, ਦੁਸ਼ਾਲਾ

sheaf (ਸ਼ੀਫ਼) *n v* ਦੱਥਾ, ਭਰੀ, ਪੂਲਾ, ਪੂਲੰਦਾ,
ਮੁੱਠ; ਪੂਲਾ ਬੰਨ੍ਹਣਾ

sheath (ਸ਼ੀਥ) *n* ਮਿਆਨ, ਗਿਲਾਫ਼, ਕੋਸ, ਖੋਲ;
~e ਮਿਆਨ ਵਿਚ ਪਾਉਣਾ, ਗਿਲਾਫ਼ ਚੜ੍ਹਾਉਣਾ,

ਖੋਲ ਚੜ੍ਹਾਉਣਾ; ਮੜ੍ਹਨਾ; ਸੁਰੱਖਿਅਤ ਕਰਨਾ;
ਬਕਸੇ ਵਿਚ ਬੰਦ ਕਰਨਾ

shed (ਸ਼ੈੱਡ) *n v* ਛੰਨ, ਛੱਪਰ, ਢਾਰਾ; ਉਤਾਰਨਾ,
ਲਾਹੁਣਾ

sheep (ਸ਼ੀਪ) *n* ਭੇਡ; ਮੀਢਾ; ਮੇਖ (ਰਾਸ਼ੀ);
ਸੰਕੋਚੀ, ਸ਼ਰਮਾਕਲ ਮਨੁੱਖ; **~ish** ਦੱਬੂ

sheer (ਸ਼ਿਅਰ*) *a adv* (ਢਲਾਨ) ਸਿੱਧੀ ਖੜ੍ਹਵੀਂ;
ਨਿਰਾ, ਨਿਪਟ, ਸਰਾਸਰ; ਸਿਰਫ਼, ਖੜ੍ਹਵੇਂ ਢੰਗ
ਨਾਲ; ਪ੍ਰਤੱਖ ਤੌਰ ਤੇ

sheet (ਸ਼ੀਟ) *n v* ਚਾਦਰ, ਪਲੰਘ-ਪੋਸ਼; ਝਾਲਰ;
ਅਖ਼ਬਾਰ, ਪਰਚਾ, ਕਾਗ਼ਜ਼; ਚਾਦਰ ਲੈਣੀ, ਚਾਦਰ
ਵਿਛਾਉਣੀ

shelf (ਸ਼ੈੱਲਫ਼) *n* ਕਿਤਾਬਖ਼ਾਨਾ, ਅਲਮਾਰੀ ਦਾ
ਖ਼ਾਨਾ; ਰਖਣਾ

shell (ਸ਼ੈੱਲ) *n v* (1) ਖੋਲ, ਖੇਪਰੀ; (2) ਸੰਖ,
ਸਿੱਪੀ, ਘੋਗਾ; (3) ਛਿਲੜ, ਪਰਤ, ਤਹਿ; (4)
ਰੂਪ-ਰੇਖਾ, ਖ਼ਾਕਾ; (5) ਫ਼ੌਜੀ ਸਿਪਾਹੀ ਦੀ ਜਾਕਟ
ਜਾਂ ਝੱਗੀ; ਛਿਲਣਾ, ਹੋਲੇ ਸੁੱਟਣਾ

shelter (ਸ਼ੈੱਲਟਾ*) *n v* ਆਸਰਾ, ਸ਼ਰਨ, ਬਚਾਉ,
ਓਟ, ਆੜ, ਝੌਂਪੜੀ, ਸ਼ੈੱਡ; ਛਤਰ; ਪਨਾਹ; ਆਸਰਾ
ਲੈਣਾ, ਸ਼ਰਨ ਵਿਚ ਆਉਣਾ; **~less** ਬੇਆਸਰਾ,
ਬੇਸਹਾਰਾ, ਨਿਰਾਧਾਰ, ਸ਼ਰਨਹੀਨ, ਅਨਾਥ

shelve (ਸ਼ੈੱਲਵ਼) *v* ਪੁਸਤਕ ਆਦਿ ਨੂੰ ਅਲਮਾਰੀ ਵਿਚ
ਰੱਖਣਾ, ਤਾਕ ਤੇ ਰੱਖਣਾ; ਮੁਲਤਵੀ ਕਰਨਾ, ਛੱਡ
ਦੇਣਾ; (ਕਿਸੇ ਆਦਮੀ ਨੂੰ) ਕੱਢ ਦੇਣਾ, ਕੰਮ ਤੋਂ
ਹਟਾਉਣਾ; ਅਲਮਾਰੀ ਦੇ ਤਖ਼ਤੇ ਜਾਂ ਦਰਾਜ਼
ਬਣਵਾਉਣਾ

shield (ਸ਼ੀਲਡ) *n v* ਢਾਲ, ਆਸਰਾ, ਸ਼ਰਨ;
ਰੱਖਿਆ ਕਰਨੀ, ਲੁਕਾਉਣਾ, ਬਚਾਉ ਕਰਨਾ

shift (ਸ਼ਿਫ਼ਟ) *v n* ਬਦਲਣਾ; ਬਦਲੀ ਕਰਨੀ;
ਪਲਟਾਉਣਾ; ਤਬਦੀਲੀ, ਬਦਲੀ, ਜੋੜ-ਤੋੜ;

~ing ਪਰਿਵਰਤਨ; ਸਥਾਨਾਂਤਰਨ

shimmer (ਸ਼ਿਮਅ*) *n v* ਝਿਲਮਿਲ,
ਟਿਮਟਿਮਾਹਟ, ਝਿਲਮਿਲਾਹਟ; ਟਿਮਟਿਮਾਣਾ,
ਝਿਲਮਿਲ ਕਰਨਾ; ਝਲਕਣਾ

shine (ਸ਼ਾਇਨ) *v n* ਚਮਕਣਾ, ਲਿਸ਼ਕਣਾ;
ਝਲਕਣਾ, ਜਗਮਗਾਉਣਾ, ਪ੍ਰਕਾਸ਼ਤ ਹੋਣਾ;
ਚਮਕਾਉਣਾ; ਚਮਕ, ਝਲਕ, ਲਿਸ਼ਕ; ਸਾਫ਼
ਮੌਸਮ

shining (ਸ਼ਾਇਨਿੰਗ) *a* ਪ੍ਰਕਾਸ਼ਮਾਨ, ਚਮਕੀਲਾ,
ਚਮਕਦਾਰ; ਤੇਜਸਵੀ

shiny (ਸ਼ਾਇਨਿ) *a* ਚਮਕਦਾ, ਲਿਸ਼ਕਦਾਰ

ship (ਸ਼ਿਪ) *n v* ਜਹਾਜ਼, ਸਮੁੰਦਰੀ ਜਹਾਜ਼; ਜਹਾਜ਼
ਤੋਂ ਭੇਜ ਦੇਣਾ; **~wright** ਜਹਾਜ਼ ਸਾਜ਼; **~ping**
ਜਹਾਜ਼ਰਾਨੀ, ਜਹਾਜ਼ ਦੀ ਲਦਾਈ ਜਾਂ ਭਰਾਈ

shirk (ਸ਼ਅਕ) *v* ਘੁਮਾਈ ਮਾਰਨੀ, ਜੀ ਚੁਰਾਉਣਾ,
ਕੰਮ-ਚੋਰੀ ਕਰਨੀ

shirt (ਸ਼ਅੱਟ) *n* ਕਮੀਜ਼, ਕੁੜਤਾ, ਝੱਗਾ

shit (ਸ਼ਿਟ) *n v* ਗੂੰਹ, ਗੰਦ, ਵਿਸ਼ਟਾ; ਹੱਗਣਾ,
ਜੰਗਲ ਜਾਣਾ, ਟੱਟੀ ਕਰਨੀ

shiver (ਸ਼ਿਵਅ*) *v n* (1) ਕੰਬਣਾ, ਕਾਂਬਾ ਪੈਣਾ,
ਥਰਥਰਾਉਣਾ; ਕਾਂਬਾ, ਕੰਬਟੀ; ਝੁਟਝੁਟੀ;
(2) ਟੁਕੜੇ ਕਰਨੇ, ਭੰਨ ਸੁੱਟਣਾ, ਚੂਰਾ ਕਰ
ਦੇਣਾ; ਟੁਕੜਾ, ਟੋਟਾ, ਚੂਰਾ

shock (ਸ਼ੌਕ) *n v* ਝਟਕਾ; ਮਾਨਸਕ ਸੱਟ, ਸਦਮਾ,
ਅਚਾਨਕ ਪਿਆ ਦੁੱਖ; ਧੱਕਾ; ਝਟਕਾ ਵੱਜਣਾ

shoe (ਸ਼ੂ) *n v* ਜੁੱਤੀ; ਘੋੜੇ ਦੀ ਖੁਰੀ; ਖੁਰੀਆਂ
ਲਾਉਣੀਆਂ; ਸੁੰਮ ਚੜ੍ਹਾਉਣਾ; **~maker** ਮੋਚੀ

shoot (ਸ਼ੂਟ) *v* ਜ਼ੋਰ ਨਾਲ ਨਿਕਲਣਾ, ਅਚਾਨਕ
ਨਿਕਲਣਾ; ਬੰਦੂਕ ਚਲਾਉਣੀ; ਜ਼ੋਰ ਨਾਲ
ਸੁੱਟਣਾ; ਸਿਨੇਮਾ ਦੀ ਤਸਵੀਰ ਲੈਣੀ; **~er**
ਬੰਦੂਕਚੀ, ਨਿਸ਼ਾਨੇਬਾਜ਼; **~ing** ਨਿਸ਼ਾਨੇਬਾਜ਼ੀ,

ਤੀਰਅੰਦਾਜ਼ੀ, ਸ਼ਿਕਾਰੀ; ਸਿਨਮੇ ਦੀ ਤਸਵੀਰ ਲੈਣ ਦਾ ਅਮਲ; ~out (ਬੋਲ) ਗੋਲੀਬਾਰੀ

shop (ਸ਼ੌਪ) *n v* ਦੁਕਾਨ, ਹੱਟੀ, ਸ਼ਾਲਾ, ਮਹਿਕਮਾ, ਵਿਭਾਗ; ਸੌਦਾ-ਸੁਲਫ਼ ਲੈਣਾ, ਹੱਟੀ ਤੇ ਜਾਣਾ, (ਕੁਝ) ਖ਼ਰੀਦਣਾ; ~ping ਖ਼ਰੀਦਦਾਰੀ, ਬਜ਼ਾਰ ਜਾਣਾ, ਸੌਦਾ-ਸੁਲਫ਼ਾ ਲੈਣ (ਦਾ ਕਾਰਜ)

shore (ਸ਼ੋ*) *n* (ਸਮੁੰਦਰ ਦਾ) ਕੰਢਾ, ਕਿਨਾਰਾ, ਤਟ, ਸਾਹਿਲ; ਥੁਹਟੀ, ਸਹਾਰਾ; ਥੰਮੀ ਲਾਉਣੀ

short (ਸ਼ੌਟ) *a adv n* ਨਿੱਕਾ, ਛੋਟਾ, ਸੰਖਿਪਤ, ਮਧਰਾ; ਥੋੜ੍ਹਾ, ਘੱਟ; ਨਿਗੁਣਾ, ਮਾਮੂਲੀ; ਨਾਕਾਫ਼ੀ, ਅਪੂਰਨ, ਹ੍ਰਸਵ; ਨਿੱਠਰ, ਕੱਢ; ~coming ਘਾਟ, ਕਮਜ਼ੋਰੀ, ਊਣਤਾਈ; ~hand ਸੰਕੇਤ, ਲਿਪੀ, ਸ਼ਾਰਟਹੈਂਡ; ~lived ਅਲਪਕਾਲਕ; ਅਸਥਿਰ, ਅਨਿੱਤ; ~sighted ਤੰਗ-ਨਜ਼ਰ, ਤੰਗ ਸੁਝ ਵਾਲਾ; ~sighted-ness ਤੰਗ-ਨਜ਼ਰੀਆ, ਅਲਪਦ੍ਰਿਸ਼ਟੀ, ਤੰਗ-ਸੂਝ; ~tempered ਚਿਤਚੜ੍ਹਾ, ਖਿਝੂ, ਤਲਖ਼ ਸੁਭਾਅ ਵਾਲਾ; ~age ਘਾਟਾ, ਘਾਟ, ਥੁੜ੍ਹ, ਕਮੀ, ਅਭਾਵ, ਤੋੜਾ; ~en ਘੱਟ ਹੋਣਾ; ਸੰਖਿਪਤ ਕਰਨਾ; ~ly ਛੇਤੀ ਹੀ, ਹੁਣੇ ਹੀ; ਥੋੜ੍ਹਾ ਚਿਰ ਪਹਿਲਾਂ ਜਾਂ ਮਗਰੋਂ; ਸੰਖੇਪ ਵਿਚ, ਥੋੜ੍ਹੇ ਸ਼ਬਦਾਂ ਵਿਚ, ਮੁੱਕਦੀ ਗੱਲ

shot (ਸ਼ੌਟ) *n v* ਬੰਦੂਕ ਦੀ ਗੋਲੀ, ਤੋਪ ਦਾ ਗੋਲਾ, ਛੱਰਾ; ਬੰਦੂਕ ਤੋਪ ਆਦਿ ਦਾ ਫ਼ਾਇਰ; ਨਿਸ਼ਾਨਾ; ਨਿਸ਼ਾਨੇਬਾਜ਼, ਨਿਸ਼ਾਨੇਮਾਰ; (ਅਲੰਕਾਰਕ) ਅੰਦਾਜ਼ਾ; ਗੋਲੀ ਭਰਨੀ, ਗੋਲਾ ਭਰਨਾ, ਛੱਰੇ ਭਰਨੇ

shoulder (ਸ਼ਾਉਲਡਅ*) *n v* ਮੋਢਾ; ਕੰਧਾ, ਮੋਰ; ਮੋਢੇ ਨਾਲ ਧੱਕਣਾ; ਜ਼ੁੰਮੇਵਾਰੀ ਲੈਣੀ; ਮੋਢੇ ਤੇ ਭਾਰ ਸੰਭਾਲਣਾ

shout (ਸ਼ਾਉਟ) *n v* ਚੀਕਣਾ, ਕੂਕਣਾ, ਜ਼ੋਰ ਦੀ ਅਵਾਜ਼ ਮਾਰਨੀ; ਰੌਲਾ ਪਾਉਣਾ; ਚੀਕ, ਕੂਕ, ਜ਼ੋਰ ਦੀ ਅਵਾਜ਼, ਰੌਲਾ

shove (ਸ਼ਅੱਵ) *v n* ਧੱਕਣਾ, ਧੱਕਾ ਦੇਣਾ, ਰੇੜ੍ਹਨਾ; ਧੱਕੇ ਮਾਰ ਕੇ ਹਟਾਉਣਾ; ਅੱਗੇ ਖਿਸਕਾਉਣਾ ਜਾਂ ਖਿਸਕਣਾ; ਧਾਉਣਾ, ਰੰਖਣਾ; ਧੱਕਾ

shovel (ਸ਼ਅੱਵ੍ਲ) *n v* ਬੇਲਚਾ

show (ਸ਼ਅਉ) *v n* ਵਿਖਾਉਣਾ; ਪੇਸ਼ ਕਰਨਾ, ਪਰਗਟ ਕਰਨਾ, ਪ੍ਰਕਾਸ਼ਤ ਕਰਨਾ, ਜ਼ਾਹਰ ਕਰਨਾ; ਸਾਖਿਆਤ ਹੋਣਾ; ਵਿਖਾਵਾ, ਪਰਦਰਸ਼ਨ, ਨੁਮਾਇਸ਼, ਪਰਦਰਸ਼ਨੀ, ਦ੍ਰਿਸ਼, ਪਰਗਟਾਉ; ਆਡੰਬਰ, ਠਾਠ-ਬਾਠ; ਬਾਹਰੀ ਰੂਪ; ~y ਭੜਕੀਲਾ, ਚਮਕੀਲਾ, ਦਿਖਾਵਟੀ, ਆਡੰਬਰਪੂਰਨ

shower (ਸ਼ਾਉਅ*) *n* ਵਾਛੜ; ਫੁਹਾਰ; ਝੜੀ

shrewd (ਸ਼ਰੂਡ) *a* ਸੁਝਵਾਨ, ਸਿਆਣਾ, ਚਤਰ, ਸੁਲਝੇ ਵਿਚਾਰਾਂ ਵਾਲਾ

shriek (ਸ਼ਰੀਕ) *v n* ਚੀਕਣਾ, ਲੇਰ ਕੱਢਣੀ, ਚਾਂਗਰ ਮਾਰਨੀ, ਡਾਡ ਮਾਰਨੀ; ਚੀਕ, ਕੂਕ

shrine (ਸ਼ਰਾਇਨ) *n* ਮੰਦਰ, ਮੱਠ, ਦਰਗਾਹ, ਖ਼ਾਨਗਾਹ, ਸਮਾਧ; ਬਲੀਦਾਨ ਸਥਾਨ; ਪਵਿੱਤਰ ਸਮਾਰਕ, ਯਾਦਗਾਰ; ਅਸਥੀ-ਪਾਤਰ

shrink (ਸ਼ਰਿੰਕ) *n v* ਸੰਕੁਚਨ, ਸਿਮਟਨ; ਸੁੰਗੜਨ; ਝਿਜਕ; ਸਿਮਟਣਾ, ਸੰਕੁਚਤ ਹੋਣਾ, ਛੋਟਾ ਹੋ ਜਾਣਾ; ਝੁਰੀਆਂ ਪੈਣੀਆਂ, ਸੁਕੜਾ ਦੇਣਾ, ਸੰਕੋਚ ਕਰਨਾ

shrive (ਸ਼ਰਾਇਵ੍) *v* (ਕਿਸੇ ਇਸਾਈ ਪਾਦਰੀ ਦੇ ਸਾਮ੍ਹਣੇ) ਗੁਨਾਹ ਸਵੀਕਾਰ ਕਰਨਾ; ਤੋਬਾ ਕਰਨੀ; ਗੁਨਾਹ ਬਖ਼ਸ਼ਵਾਉਣਾ

shrub (ਸ਼ਰਅੱਬ) *n* ਝਾੜੀ; ~by ਝਾੜੀਦਾਰ

shudder (ਸ਼ਅੱਡਅ*) *v n* ਕੰਬਣੀ ਛਿੜਨੀ, ਕੰਥ ਉੱਠਣਾ, ਸਹਿਮ ਜਾਣਾ; ਕੰਬਣੀ, ਥਰਥਰਾਹਟ

shuffle ('ਸ਼ਅੱਫ਼ਲ) *v n* ਘਿਸਰ ਕੇ ਚਲੱਣਾ, ਪੈਰ ਘਸੀਟਣੇ, ਵਿਆਕੁਲ ਹੋਣਾ; ਇਕ ਗੱਲ ਤੇ ਨਾ ਟਿਕਣਾ; ਬਿਤਕਣਾ, ਡੋਲਣਾ; ਟਾਲ-ਮਟੋਲ ਕਰਨਾ; ਢਾਵਾਂ-ਢੋਲ ਹੋਣਾ; ਘਸੀਟ, ਰਗੜ, ਖਿਸਕਣ, ਸਰਕਣ; ਅਦਲਾ-ਬਦਲੀ

shun (ਸ਼ਅੱਨ) *v* ਦੂਰ ਰਹਿਣਾ, ਪਰ੍ਹਾਂ ਰਹਿਣਾ; ਬਚਣਾ; ਕਤਰਾਉਣਾ; ਪਰਹੇਜ਼ ਕਰਨਾ

shunt (ਸ਼ਅੱਟ) *v n* ਲਾਂਭੇ ਹੋ ਜਾਣਾ; ਰਾਹ ਛੱਡਣਾ; ਬਦਲਣਾ; ਪਟੜੀ ਬਦਲਣਾ, ਲਾਂਭੇ ਹੋਣ (ਦਾ ਕਾਰਜ); ਬਿਜਲੀ ਦੀ ਲਾਈਨ ਬਦਲਣ ਵਾਲਾ ਜੰਤਰ; ~er ਪਟੜੀ ਬਦਲਣ ਵਾਲਾ, ਲਾਈਨ ਬਦਲਣ ਵਾਲਾ

shut (ਸ਼ਅੱਟ) *v* ਬੰਦ ਕਰਨਾ (ਮੂੰਹ); ਬੰਦ ਹੋਣਾ; ਨਿਰਾਸ ਕਰਨਾ; ਵਾਂਝਿਆਂ ਕਰਨਾ; ਬੰਦ ਅਵਸਥਾ ਵਿਚ ਡਿਗਣਾ ਜਾਂ ਸੁੰਗੜਨਾ; ਮੀਟਿਆ

shuttle ('ਸ਼ਅੱਟਲ) *n* ਨਲੀ, ਫਿਰਕੀ, ਜੁਲਾਹੇ ਦੀ ਨਾਲ, ਸਟਿਲ; ਛੋਟੇ ਰੂਟ ਦੀ ਬੱਸ; ~cock ਬੈਡਮਿੰਟਨ ਦੀ ਚਿੜੀ; ~train ਸਥਾਨਕ ਰੇਲ ਗੱਡੀ

shy (ਸ਼ਾਇ) *a v n* ਸੰਗਾਊ, ਸ਼ਰਮੀਲਾ; ਕਤਰਾਉਣ ਵਾਲਾ; ਭੜਕ ਉੱਠਣਾ, ਚੌਂਕ ਉੱਠਣਾ; ਨਿਸ਼ਾਨਾ, ਸੁੱਟਣ ਦੀ ਕੋਸ਼ਿਸ਼

sibling (ਸਿਬਲਿਡ) *n* ਇੱਕੋ ਮਾਂ ਬਾਪ ਦੇ ਬੱਚੇ, ਸਹੋਦਰ, ਭਰਾ-ਭੈਣ

sick (ਸਿਕ) *a* ਰੋਗੀ, ਬੀਮਾਰ; ਖਿਝਿਆ, ਅੱਕਿਆ; ਉਚਾਟ; ~en ਸ਼ਰੀਰ ਕੁਝ ਢਿੱਲਾ ਹੋਣਾ, ਬੀਮਾਰ ਹੁੰਦੇ ਜਾਪਣਾ; ~ly ਰੋਗੀ ਜਿਹਾ, ਬੀਮਾਰਾਂ ਵਰਗਾ

sickle (ਸਿਕਲ) *n* ਦਾਤਰੀ, ਦਾਤੀ

side (ਸਾਇਡ) *n v* ਪਾਸਾ, ਬੰਨਾ, ਦਿਸ਼ਾ; ਰੁਖ, ਪੱਖ; ਪੜਾ; ਬਾਹੀ, ਭੁਜਾ; ਕੰਢਾ, ਕਿਨਾਰਾ; ਪੱਖ ਲੈਣਾ, ਸਾਥ ਦੇਣਾ, ਨਾਲ ਹੋਣਾ; ~effect ਗੌਣ

ਪ੍ਰਭਾਵ (ਆਮ ਕਰਕੇ ਮਾੜਾ); ~track ਮੁੱਖ ਸੜਕ ਦੇ ਨਾਲ ਰਸਤਾ ਜਾਂ ਛੋਟੀ ਸੜਕ; ਰੇਲ ਦੀ ਲਾਂਭੇ ਵਾਲੀ ਪਟੜੀ; ਟਾਲ ਦੇਣਾ; ਲਾਂਭੇ ਲੈ ਜਾਣਾ

siege (ਸੀਜ) *n v* ਘੇਰਾ, ਕਿਲ੍ਹਾਬੰਦੀ, ਨਾਕਾਬੰਦੀ; ਪਿੱਛੇ ਪੈ ਜਾਣਾ; ਘੇਰਾ ਪਾਉਣਾ

sigh (ਸਾਇ) *v* ਹਉਕਾ ਲੈਣਾ, ਠੰਡਾ ਸਾਹ ਲੈਣਾ, ਸਿਸਕਣਾ

sight (ਸਾਇਟ) *n v* ਨਜ਼ਰ ਨਿਗਾਹ, ਦ੍ਰਿਸ਼ਟੀ ਤੱਕਣੀ; ਨਜ਼ਾਰਾ, ਦਿੱਸ, ਦਰਸ਼ਨ; ਦ੍ਰਿਸ਼ਟੀ-ਸੀਮਾ; ਵੇਖਣਾ, ਵੇਖ ਲੈਣਾ; ~seer ਸੈਲਾਨੀ, ਦਰਸ਼ਕ

sign (ਸਾਇਨ) *n v* ਨਿਸ਼ਾਨ, ਚਿੰਨ੍ਹ, ਪ੍ਰਤੀਕ, ਪ੍ਰਮਾਣ, ਲੱਛਣ; ਝੰਡਾ; ਇਸ਼ਾਰਾ, ਸੰਕੇਤ; ਦਸਤਖ਼ਤ ਕਰਨੇ; ~ed ਹਸਤਾਖ਼ਰਤ

signature ('ਸਿਗਨਅਚਅ*) *n* ਦਸਤਖ਼ਤ, ਹਸਤਾਖ਼ਰ, ਸਹੀ

significant (ਸਿਗ'ਨਿਫ਼ਿਕਅੰਟ) *a* ਵਿਸ਼ੇਸ਼, ਜ਼ਰੂਰੀ, ਪ੍ਰਭਾਵਸ਼ਾਲੀ, ਅਰਥਪੂਰਨ, ਭਾਵਪੂਰਨ

signification ('ਸਿਗਨਿਫ਼ਿ'ਕੇਇਸ਼ਨ) *n* ਭਾਵ, ਤਾਤਪਰਜ, ਅਰਥ, ਭਾਵਾਰਥ; ਸਾਰਥਕਤਾ, ਸ਼ਬਦ-ਸ਼ਕਤੀ

signify ('ਸਿਗਨਿਫ਼ਾਇ) *v* ਪਰਗਟ ਕਰਨਾ, ਜ਼ਾਹਰ ਕਰਨਾ; ਅਰਥ ਦੇਣਾ, ਭਾਵ ਦੇਣਾ

silence ('ਸਾਇਲਅੰਸ) *n v* ਸ਼ਾਂਤੀ, ਚੁੱਪ-ਚਾਪ, ਮੌਨ, ਖ਼ਮੋਸ਼ੀ, ਸੰਨਾਟਾ; ਚੁੱਪ ਕਰਾ ਦੇਣਾ, ਸ਼ਾਂਤ ਕਰ ਦੇਣਾ

silent ('ਸਾਇਲਅੰਟ) *a* ਚੁੱਪ, ਸ਼ਾਂਤ, ਖ਼ਾਮੋਸ਼, ਮੌਨ; ਚੁਪ-ਚਾਪ

silk (ਸਿਲਕ) *n* ਰੇਸ਼ਮ, ਰੇਸ਼ਮੀ ਕੱਪੜਾ; ~worm ਰੇਸ਼ਮ ਦਾ ਕੀੜਾ; ~y ਰੇਸ਼ਮ ਵਰਗਾ ਕੋਮਲ ਤੇ ਨਰਮ; ਚਮਕਦਾਰ

silly ('ਸਿਲਿ) a ਮੂਰਖ, ਬੇਵਕੂਢ, ਬੁੱਧੂ, ਬੇਅਕਲ, ਸਿੰਧਤ, ਭੋਲਾ-ਭਾਲਾ

silt (ਸਿਲਟ) n v ਭੱਲ, ਵਗਦੇ ਪਾਣੀ ਦੇ ਹੇਠਾਂ ਬੈਠੀ ਮਿੱਟੀ, ਗਾਰ, ਤਲਛਟ, ਰੇਤ ਆਦਿ; ਭੱਲ ਪੈਣੀ

silver ('ਸਿਲਵ੍ਅਾ*) n a v ਚਾਂਦੀ, ਚਾਂਦੀ ਦਾ ਸਿੱਕਾ; ਚਾਂਦੀ ਦਾ; ਚਾਂਦੀ ਚੜ੍ਹਾਉਣਾ; ~paper ਵਰਕ; ~tongued ਮਿਠਬੋਲਾ, ਪ੍ਰਭਾਵਸ਼ਾਲੀ ਲੈਕਚਰ ਕਰਨ ਵਾਲਾ

similar ('ਸਿਮਿਲਅਾ*) a ਵਰਗਾ, ਜਿਹਾ, ਮਿਲਦਾ ਜੁਲਦਾ, ਸਮਾਨ; ~ity ਸਮਰੂਪਤਾ, ਸਾਰੂਪਤਾ, ਸਮਾਨਤਾ, ਸਮਤਾ; ~ly ਉਸੇ ਤਰ੍ਹਾਂ ਸਮਾਨ ਰੂਪ ਵਿਚ

simile ('ਸਿਮਿਲਿ) n ਉਪਮਾ, ਤਸ਼ਬੀਹ, ਉਪਮਾ-ਅਲੰਕਾਰ

simple ('ਸਿੰਪਲ) a n ਸਾਦਾ, ਸਿੱਧਾ, ਸਰਲ ਸਿੱਧਾ-ਸਾਦਾ, ਸਧਾਰਨ; ਭੋਲਾ-ਭਾਲਾ, ਖ਼ਾਲਸ

simpleton ('ਸਿੰਪਲਟ(ਅ)ਨ) n ਸਿੱਧੜ, ਸਿੱਧਾ-ਸਾਦਾ, ਲੋਲ੍ਹਾ, ਮੂਰਖ, ਬੁੱਧੂ

simplicity (ਸਿੰ'ਪਲਿਸਅਟਿ) n ਸਾਦਗੀ, ਸਰਲਤਾ; ਸ਼ੁੱਧਤਾ; ਅਸੰਗੁਕਤਤਾ; ਨਿਸ਼ਕਪਟਤਾ, ਭੋਲਾਪਣ

simplification ('ਸਿਮ'ਪਲਿਫ਼ਿ'ਕੇਇਸ਼ਨ) n ਸਰਲੀਕਰਨ

simplify ('ਸਿੰਪਲਿਫ਼ਾਇ) v ਸੌਖਾ ਕਰਨਾ, ਸਰਲ ਬਣਾਉਣਾ; ਸਾਦਾ ਕਰਨਾ; ਗੁੰਝਲ ਦੂਰ ਕਰਨੀ; ਸੁਬੋਧ ਬਣਾਉਣਾ

simulate ('ਸਿਮਯੁਲੇਇਟ) v ਸਾਂਗ ਕਰਨਾ, ਢੌਂਗ ਰਚਨਾ, ਝੂਠਾ ਰੂਪ ਬਣਾਉਣਾ; ਨਕਲ ਕਰਨੀ; ਭੇਸ ਬਦਲਣਾ, ਰੂਪ ਧਾਰਨਾ

simulation ('ਸਿਮਯੁ'ਲੇਇਸ਼ਨ) n ਬਹਾਨਾ, ਢੌਂਗ; ਨਕਲ, ਰੀਸ, ਸਾਂਗ; ਪਖੰਡ

simultaneity ('ਸਿਮ(ਅ)ਲਟ(ਅ)'ਨਿਅਟਿ) n ਸਮਕਾਲੀਪਨ, ਸਮਕਾਲੀਨਤਾ

simultaneous ('ਸਿਮ(ਅ)ਲ'ਟੇਇਨਯਅਸ) a ਸਮਕਾਲੀ, ਸਮਕਾਲਕ; ~ly ਨਾਲ ਨਾਲ, ਇਕੋ ਸਮੇਂ ਵਿਚ

sin (ਸਿਨ) n v ਪਾਪ, ਗੁਨਾਹ; ਕੁਕਰਮ, ਅਧਰਮ; ਪਾਪ ਕਰਨਾ, ਗੁਨਾਹ ਕਰਨਾ, ਦੁਰਾਚਾਰ ਕਰਨਾ; ~ner ਗੁਨਹਗਾਰ, ਪਾਪੀ, ਅਪਰਾਧੀ

since ('ਸਿੰਸ) prep conj adv ਤੋਂ, ਤੋਂ ਲੈ ਕੇ, ਤੋਂ ਹੁਣ ਤਕ; ਕਿਉਂਕਿ, ਇਸ ਲਈ ਕਿ; ਇਹ ਵੇਖਦੇ ਹੋਏ

sincere ('ਸਿੰਸਿਅ*) a ਸੱਚਾ, ਖਰਾ; ਨਿਰਛਲ, ਨਿਸ਼ਕਪਟ; ਈਮਾਨਦਾਰ

sincerity (ਸਿੰ'ਸੇਰਅਟਿ) n ਨਿਸ਼ਕਪਟਤਾ, ਨਿਰਛਲਤਾ, ਸਾਫ਼-ਦਿਲੀ, ਸਚਾਈ, ਈਮਾਨਦਾਰੀ

sine (ਸਾਇਨ) prep ਬਿਨਾ, ਬਗ਼ੈਰ, ਬਾਝ; ~die (L) ਅਨਿਮੰਥੇ ਸਮੇਂ ਲਈ, ਦਿਨ ਨਿਸ਼ਚਤ ਕੀਤੇ ਬਿਨਾ; ~qua non (L) ਜ਼ਰੂਰੀ ਸ਼ਰਤ

sinew ('ਸਿਨਯੂ) n v ਜਾਨ; ਸਰੀਰਕ ਬਲ, ਸਾਧਨ, ਵਸੀਲੇ; ਜੋੜੀ ਰੱਖਣਾ, ਸੰਗਠਤ ਰੱਖਣਾ; ਧਾਰਨਾ, ਗੰਢਣਾ; ~y ਤਕੜਾ; ਮਜ਼ਬੂਤ; ਬਲਵਾਨ

sing (ਸਿੰਡ) v n ਗਾਉਣਾ, ਰਾਗ ਅਲਾਪਣਾ; ਗੁੰਜਣਾ; ~er ਗਾਇਕ, ਗੱਵਈਆ, ਰਾਗੀ; ~ing ਗਾਣਾ, ਗੀਤ, ਗਾਇਨ

single ('ਸਿੰਗਲ) a n v ਇੱਕਲਾ, ਕੱਲਮ-ਕੱਲਾ; ਇਕਹਿਰਾ, ਇਕਵੱਲੀ ਦਾ; ਬੇਸਹਾਰਾ; ਕੰਵਾਰਾ, ਅਟਵਿਆਹਿਆ; ਨਿਤਾਰਨਾ, ਵੱਖ ਕਰਨਾ; ~handed ਬਿਨਾ ਕਿਸੇ ਸਹਾਇਤਾ ਦੇ ਇਕ-ਹੱਥਾ; ~hearted ਬਿਨਾ ਦੁਬਧਾ; ਖਰਾ, ਥੇਲਾਗ਼; ~minded ਇਕਾਗਰ ਚਿੱਤ, ਇਕ ਮਨ, ਦ੍ਰਿੜ

ਇਰਾਦੇ ਵਾਲਾ

singlet ('ਸਿੰਗਲਿਟ) *n* ਬੁਨੈਣ, ਫ਼ਤੂਹੀ

singular ('ਸਿੰਗਾਗੁਯਲਅ*) *n a* (ਵਿਆ) ਇਕਵਚਨ; ਨਿਰਾਲਾ, ਅਨੋਖਾ, ਅਦੁੱਤੀ, ਅਸਧਾਰਨ, ਬੇਤੁਕਾ; **~ity** ਇਕਮਾਤਰਤਾ, ਇਕੱਲਾਪਣ; ਵਿਸ਼ਿਸ਼ੰਟਤਾ, ਵਿਲੱਖਣਤਾ

sink (ਸਿੰਕ) *n v* ਡੁੱਬਣਾ ਜਾਂ ਡੋਬਣਾ; (ਭੋ ਦਾ) ਹੇਠਾਂ ਬੈਠ ਜਾਣਾ, ਦਿਲ ਘਟਣਾ, ਹੌਸਲਾ ਢਿਗਣਾ; ਖ਼ਤਮ ਹੋਣਾ; ਹੌਲੀ ਹੌਲੀ ਮੁੱਕਣਾ; ਗੰਦਗੀ ਜਾਂ ਗੰਦਾ ਪਾਣੀ ਸੁੱਟਣ ਵਾਲਾ ਟੋਆ ਜਾਂ ਚੁਬੱਚਾ; **~ing** ਦਿਲ ਘਟਣ ਦੀ ਅਵਸਥਾ

sip (ਸਿਪ) *v n* ਘੁੱਟ ਭਰਨਾ, ਘੁੱਟੋ-ਵੱਟੀ ਪੀਣਾ

sir (ਸਅ:*) *n* ਸ੍ਰੀਮਾਨ, ਜਨਾਬ, ਹਜ਼ੂਰ, ਮਹਾਰਾਜ

sire ('ਸਾਇਅ*) *n* ਪਿਤਾ ਜਾਂ ਵਡੇਰਾ, ਖ਼ਾਨਦਾਨ ਦਾ ਬਜ਼ੁਰਗਾ; ਸ੍ਰੀਮਾਨ, ਜਨਾਬ

sissy ('ਸਿਸਿ) *n* ਜ਼ਨਾਣਾ, ਕੁੜੀਆਂ ਵਰਗਾ ਮੁੰਡਾ

sister ('ਸਿਸਟਅ*) *n* ਭੈਣ; ਸਹੇਲੀ, ਸਖੀ; ਸਤ-ਸੰਗਣ, ਧਰਮ-ਭੈਣ; **~in law** ਸਾਲੀ; ਨਣਾਣ; ਭਰਜਾਈ; ਸਾਲੇਹਾਰ, ਦਰਾਣੀ, ਜਿਠਾਣੀ

sit (ਸਿਟ) *v* ਬੈਠਣਾ, ਬਹਿਣਾ; ਬਿਠਾਉਣਾ; ਟਿਕਾਉਣਾ; **~ting** ਸਭਾ, ਬੈਠਕ, ਲਗਾਤਾਰ ਬੈਠਣ ਜਾ ਸਮਾਂ, ਇਜਲਾਸ; **~ting member** ਚੱਲਦਾ ਆ ਰਿਹਾ ਮੈਂਬਰ; **~ting room** ਬੈਠਕ, ਦੀਵਾਨਖ਼ਾਨਾ

site (ਸਾਇਟ) *n* ਥਾਂ, ਮੌਕਾ

situate(d) ('ਸਿਟਯੁਏਇਟਿਡ) *a* ਸਥਿਤ; ਸਬਾਪਤ

situation ('ਸਿਟਯੂ'ਏਇਸ਼ਨ) *n* ਥਾਂ, ਮੌਕਾ, ਜਗ੍ਹਾ, ਸਥਿਤੀ; ਹਾਲ, ਹਾਲਤ, ਦਸ਼ਾ

six (ਸਿਕਸ) *n* ਛੇ, ਛੇ ਦਾ ਅੰਕ; ਛੀਕਾ; **~fold** ਛੇ ਗੁਣਾ; **~er** ਛੱਕਾ; **~teen** ਸੋਲਾਂ ਸੋਲਾਂ ਦੀ

ਸੰਖਿਆ; **~teenth** ਸੋਲ੍ਹਵਾਂ; **~th** ਛੇਵਾਂ ਭਾਗ, ਛੇਵਾਂ; **~ty** ਸੱਠ

sizable ('ਸਾਇਜ਼ਅਬਲ) *a* ਉਪਯੁਕਤ ਆਕਾਰ ਦਾ, ਲੰਮਾ-ਚੌੜਾ, ਬੜਾ, ਕਾਫ਼ੀ

size (ਸਾਇਜ਼) *n* (1) ਆਕਾਰ; ਕੱਦ; ਨਾਪ, ਪਰਿਮਾਣ, ਲੰਮਾਈ-ਚੌੜਾਈ; (2) ਮਾਵਾ, ਕਲਫ਼

sizy ('ਸਾਇਜ਼ਿ) *a* ਚਿਪਚਿਪਾ, ਲੇਸਦਾਰ

skeleton ('ਸਕੈਲਿਟਨ) *n* ਹੱਡੀਆਂ ਦਾ ਪਿੰਜਰ; ਢਾਂਚਾ, ਖ਼ਾਕਾ, ਸੰਖੇਪ, ਸੰਖਿਪਤ ਰੂਪ, ਸਾਰ

skelter ('ਸਕੈਲਟਅ*) *n* ਹਫੜਾ-ਦਫੜੀ, ਹੜਬੜੀ, ਹਫੜਾ-ਦਫੜੀ ਮਚਾਉਣਾ

sketch (ਸਕੈੱਚ) *n v* ਖ਼ਾਕਾ, ਢਾਂਚਾ, ਰੇਖਾ-ਚਿੱਤਰ, ਰੂਪ ਰੇਖਾ; ਸੰਖੇਪ ਬਿਆਨ; ਖ਼ਾਕਾ ਤਿਆਰ ਕਰਨਾ, ਰੂਪ-ਰੇਖਾ ਬਣਾਉਣੀ, ਸੰਖੇਪ ਵਿਚ ਬਿਆਨ ਕਰਨਾ; **~y** ਖ਼ਾਕਾ ਜਿਹਾ, ਢਾਂਚਾ ਮਾਤਰ, ਸਧਾਰਨ ਰੂਪ-ਰੇਖਾ ਵਿਚ

skill (ਸਕਿਲ) *n* ਮੁਹਾਰਤ, ਨਿਪੁੰਨਤਾ, ਸੁੱਚਜ, ਕੌਸ਼ਲ; **~ed** ਜਾਂਚ ਵਾਲਾ, ਚੱਜ ਵਾਲਾ, ਕੁਸ਼ਲ, ਮਾਹਰ, ਨਿਪੁੰਨ, ਪ੍ਰਵੀਣ

skim (ਸਕਿਮ) *n v* ਝੱਗ, ਮਲਾਈ, ਪੇਪੜੀ; (ਦੁੱਧ ਉੱਤੋਂ) ਮਲਾਈ ਲਾਹੁਣੀ, ਝੱਗ ਲਾਹੁਣੀ, ਪੇਪੜੀ ਲਾਹੁਣੀ; ਸਰਸਰੀ ਨਜ਼ਰ ਮਾਰਨੀ; **~med milk** ਸਪਰੇਟਾ, ਕਰੀਮ ਕੱਢਿਆ ਦੁੱਧ

skin (ਸਕਿਨ) *n v* ਖੱਲ, ਖੱਲੜੀ, ਚਮੜੀ, ਛਿੱਲ, ਛਿੱਲੜ; ਖੱਲ ਲਾਹੁਣੀ; ਛਿੱਲਣਾ; **~deep** ਉਤਲਾ-ਉਤਲਾ, ਮਾਮੂਲੀ; **~flint** ਕੰਜੂਸ, ਸੂਮ; **~ny** ਪਤਲਾ, ਲਿੱਸਾ, ਮਾੜੂਆ

skip (ਸਕਿਪ) *n* ਟੱਪਣਾ, ਕੁੱਦਣਾ, ਛੜੱਪੇ ਮਾਰਨੇ; ਰੱਸੀ ਟੱਪਣਾ; (ਬੋਲ) ਨੱਸ ਜਾਣਾ, ਭੱਜ ਨਿਕਲਣਾ; (ਕੋਈ ਕੰਮ) ਵਿਚੋਂ ਛੱਡ ਛੱਡ ਕੇ ਕਰਨ

skirt (ਸਕਅਃਟ) *n v* ਲਹਿੰਗਾ, ਘਗੱਰਾ; ਤੀਵੀਂ; ਕਿਨਾਰਾ, ਸੀਮਾ

skull (ਸਕਅੱਲ) *n* ਖੋਪਰੀ, ਕਪਾਲ

sky (ਸਕਾਇ) *n v* ਆਕਾਸ਼, ਅਸਮਾਨ; ਉੱਚਾ ਟੰਗਣਾ; ~blue ਅਸਮਾਨੀ (ਰੰਗ)

slab (ਸਲੈਬ) *n a* ਸਿਲ, ਫੱਟੀ, ਲੇਸਦਾਰ, ਚਿਪਚਿਪਾ

slack (ਸਲੈਕ) *a n v* ਸੁਸਤ, ਢਿੱਲਾ, ਢਿੱਲੜ, ਆਲਸੀ; ਮੰਦਵਾੜਾ, ਵਪਾਰ ਦੀ ਮੰਦਗੀ; (ਬ ਵ) ਪਾਜਾਮਾ ਜਾਂ ਪਤਲੂਨ; ਮੱਧਮ ਕਰਨਾ, ਸੁਸਤਾਉਣਾ, ਮਠੇ ਪੈਣਾ, ਆਲਸ ਕਰਨਾ; ~en ਢਿੱਲਾ ਕਰਨਾ, ਢਿੱਲਾ ਛੱਡ ਦੇਣਾ; ਸੁਸਤ ਹੋ ਜਾਣਾ; ~ness ਆਲਸ, ਸੁਸਤੀ, ਢਿੱਲ

slang (ਸਲੈਙ) *n v* ਵਰਗ ਭਾਸ਼ਾ, ਬਜ਼ਾਰੀ ਬੋਲੀ, ਬੋਲ-ਕੁਬੋਲ, ਅਪਭਾਸ਼ਾ; ਗਾਲ੍ਹ ਕਢਣੀ

slant (ਸਲਾਂਟ) *v n* ਤਿਰਛਾ ਹੋਣਾ, ਢਾਲਵਾਂ ਬਣਾਉਣਾ; ਢਾਲ, ਢਲਾਣ, ਤਿਰਛਾਪਣ

slap (ਸਲੈਪ) *n v* ਚਪੇੜ, ਧੱਫਾ, ਲੱਫੜ, ਧੌਲ; ਚਪੇੜ ਮਾਰਨੀ

slash (ਸਲੈਸ਼) *v n* (ਤਲਵਾਰ, ਚਾਬੁਕ ਆਦਿ ਨਾਲ) ਅਨੇਕਾਂਵਾਰ ਕਰਨਾ, ਵਾਢੀ ਲਾਉਣਾ, ਵੱਢਣਾ, ਪੜਛੇ ਲਾਹੁਣੇ, ਚੀਰਨਾ; ਚੀਰਾ

slaughter (ਸਲੋਟਅ*) *v n* ਵੱਢਣਾ, ਝਟਕਾਉਣਾ; ਕਤਲ-ਏ-ਆਮ ਕਰਨਾ, ਵੱਢ-ਟੁੱਕ ਕਰਨੀ; ਕਤਲ ਕਰਨਾ, ਖੂਨ ਕਰਨਾ; ਵੱਢਣ, ਝਟਕਾਉਣ (ਦੀ ਕਿਰਿਆ); ਕਤਲ-ਏ-ਆਮ, ਕਤਲ, ਹੱਤਿਆ

slave (ਸਲੇਇਵ) *n v* ਗ਼ੁਲਾਮ, ਗੋਲਾ, ਬਰਦਾ, ਦਾਸ, ਨੀਚ ਕੰਮ ਕਰਨਾ ~ry ਗ਼ੁਲਾਮੀ, ਦਾਸਤਾ; ਦਾਸ-ਪ੍ਰਥਾ

slaver (ਸਲੇਵ੍ਅ*) *n v* (1) ਲਾਲ੍ਹਾਂ, ਥੁੱਕ;

(2) ਹੋਛੀ ਖ਼ੁਸ਼ਾਮਦ, ਤੁੱਛ ਚਾਪਲੂਸੀ; ਲਾਲ੍ਹਾਂ ਵਗਾਣੀਆਂ; ਚਾਪਲੂਸੀ ਕਰਨੀ

slavish ('ਸਲੇਇਵੀਸ਼) *a* ਹੋਛਾ, ਨੀਚ, ਤੁੱਛ; ਗ਼ੁਲਾਮਾਂ ਵਰਗਾ

slay (ਸਲੇਇ) *v* ਕਤਲ ਕਰਨਾ, ਮਾਰ ਸੁੱਟਣਾ, ਵੱਢ ਦੇਣਾ

sleek ('ਸਲੀਕ) *a v* ਕੂਲਾ, ਕੋਮਲ, ਨਰਮ, ਮੁਲਾਇਮ, ਚਿਕਣਾ; ਗੁਦਗੁਦਾ; ਮੁਲਾਇਮ ਕਰਨਾ; ਗੁਦਗੁਦਾ ਬਣਾਉਣਾ

sleep (ਸਲੀਪ) *n v* ਨੀਂਦਰ, ਸੌਣ; ਮੌਸੀ; ਆਰਾਮ; ਸੌਣਾ, ਸੌਂ ਜਾਣਾ, ਅੱਖ ਲੱਗਣੀ; ਠੰਢੇ ਪੈਣਾ; ~er ਸੁੱਤਾ ਵਿਅਕਤੀ; ਲੱਕੜੀ ਦੇ ਗੱਟੂ ਜਿਨ੍ਹਾਂ ਉੱਤੇ ਰੇਲ ਪਟੜੀ ਵਿਛਾਈ ਜਾਂਦੀ ਹੈ, ਸਲੀਪਰ

sleeve (ਸਲੀਵ) *n* ਆਸਤੀਨ

slender ('ਸਲੈਂਡਅ*) *a* ਪਤਲਾ; ਮਾੜਾ; ਥੋੜ੍ਹਾ, ਸੂਖਮ, ਨਾਜ਼ੁਕ, ਕਮਜ਼ੋਰ

slice (ਸਲਾਇਸ) *n v* ਡਬਲ ਰੋਟੀ ਜਾਂ ਪਤਲਾ ਟੁਕੜਾ, ਟੋਟਾ, ਫਾੜੀ, ਗਰਾਹੀ, ਡੱਕਰਾ, ਹਿੱਸਾ, ਭਾਗ, ਅਸ਼ੂ; ਟੁਕੜੇ ਕੱਟਣੇ, ਫਾੜੀਆਂ ਕਰਨੀਆਂ

slick (ਸਲਿਕ) *adv a* ਪੂਰੀ ਤਰ੍ਹਾਂ ਠੀਕ-ਠਾਕ, ਸਿੱਧਾ; ਸਫ਼ਾਈ ਵਾਲਾ, ਫੁਰਤੀਲਾ; ਚੁੰਟ, ਚਤਰ

slide (ਸਲਾਇਡ) *v n* ਤਿਲਕਣਾ, ਖਿਸਕਣਾ; ਸਰਕਣਾ; ਸਰਕਾਉਣਾ, ਰੇਂੜੁਨਾ; ਬਰਫ਼ ਉੱਤੇ ਰਿੜ੍ਹਨ ਕਰਕੇ ਬਣਿਆ ਰਾਹ; ਤਿਲਕਵੀਂ ਢਲਾਨ; ਖਿਸਕਣ; ਰਿੜ੍ਹਨ

slight (ਸਲਾਇਟ) *a v n* ਥੋੜ੍ਹਾ ਜਿਹਾ, ਮਾੜਾ ਜਿਹਾ, ਮਾਮੂਲੀ, ਕਮਜ਼ੋਰ; ਹੇਠੀ ਕਰਨੀ; ਤੁੱਛ ਸਮਝਣਾ; ਲਾਪਰਵਾਹੀ ਕਰਨੀ; ਹੇਠੀ, ਅਵੱਗਿਆ

slip (ਸਲਿਪ) *n v* ਕਾਗ਼ਜ਼ ਦੀ ਚਿਟ; ਲੱਕੜੀ ਦੀ ਫੱਟੀ; ਪੱਤਰੀ; ਕਾਗ਼ਜ਼ ਦੀ ਲੰਮੀ ਕਤਰ; ਭੁੱਲ,

ਭੁੱਲ-ਚੁਕ, ਉਕਾਈ, ਤਰੁਟੀ; ਤਿਲਕਣਾ, ਖਿਸਕਣਾ, ਢਿਲਕਣਾ, ਸਰਕਣਾ; ਅੱਖ ਬਚਾ ਕੇ ਨਿਕਲ ਜਾਣਾ, ਚੁੱਪ-ਚਾਪ ਸਰਕ ਜਾਣਾ; ਖਿਡਕਣਾ, ਭੁੱਲ ਕਰਨੀ; ~per ਸਲਿਪਰ (ਪੈਰੀਂ ਪਾਉਣ ਵਾਲਾ); ~pery ਤਿਲਕਵਾਂ; ਅਸਥਿਰ; ਚਲਾਕ, ਬੇਇਤਬਾਰਾ

slit (ਸਲਿਟ) v n ਚੀਰਨਾ, ਚੀਰ ਪਾਉਣਾ, ਪਾੜਨਾ; ਚੀਰ, ਰਗੜ

slogan ('ਸਲਆਉਗਾਅਨ) n ਨਾਅਰਾ; ਸੰਕੇਤਕ ਸ਼ਬਦ, ਨੀਤੀਵਾਕ; ਇਸ਼ਤਿਹਾਰਬਾਜੀ ਵਿਚ ਵਰਤੇ ਜਾਣ ਵਾਲੇ ਚੁਸਤ ਵਾਕ

slope (ਸਲਅਉਪ) n v ਢਾਲ, ਢਲਵਾਨ, ਢਲਵੀਂ ਜਮੀਨ; ਟਹਿਲਣਾ, ਘੁੰਮਣਾ-ਫਿਰਨਾ, ਨੱਸ ਜਾਣਾ; ਤਿਰਛਾ ਕਰਨਾ, ਢਾਲਵਾਂ ਕਰਨਾ

sloppy ('ਸਲੌਪਿ) a ਚੂਹੜ, ਖੁੱਥੜ, ਵੱਲਲਾ

slow (ਸਲਅਉ) a adv v ਮੱਠਾ, ਢਿੱਲਾ, ਸੁਸਤ, ਮੱਧਮ, ਆਲਸੀ; ਹੌਲੀ ਹੌਲੀ; ਸੁਸਤ ਹੋ ਜਾਣਾ; ਢਿੱਲੇ ਪੈ ਜਾਣਾ

slum (ਸਲਅੱਮ) n ਝੁੱਗੀ-ਝੌਂਪੜੀ; ਗੰਦਾ ਮਹੱਲਾ

slumber ('ਸਲਅੰਬਅ*) n v ਨੀਂਦ, ਸੌਣ ਦੀ ਦਸ਼ਾ; ਸੌਂ ਜਾਣਾ; ~ous ਸੁੱਤਾ, ਆਲਸੀ ਆਦਮੀ, ਸੁਸਤ-ਮਨੁੱਖ

slur (ਸਲਅ:*) v n ਕਲੰਕ ਲਾਉਣਾ, ਦਾਗ ਲਾਉਣਾ; ਦੂਸ਼ਤ ਕਰਨਾ; ਤੁਹਮਤ ਲਾਉਣੀ; ਇਲਜਾਮ ਲਾਉਣਾ; ਕਲੰਕ; ਬਦਨਾਮੀ, ਦੋਸ਼, ਇਲਜ਼ਾਮ

sly (ਸਲਾਇ) a ਛਰੋਬੀ, ਦਗ਼ੋਬਾਜ਼, ਪੱਤੋਬਾਜ਼, ਖਚਰਾ; ਗੁੱਝਾ, ਵਿਅੰਗ ਭਰਿਆ

small (ਸਮੋਲ) a ਨਿੱਕਾ, ਛੋਟਾ, ਮਧਰਾ; ਥੋੜ੍ਹਾ, ਮਾੜਾ, ਬਾਰੀਕ, ਪਤਲਾ; ~hours ਰਾਤ ਦਾ ਤੀਜਾ ਜਾਂ ਚੌਥਾ ਪਹਿਰ; ~pox ਚੀਚਕ, ਮਾਤਾ,

ਸੀਤਲਾ

smart (ਸਮਾਟ) a v n ਚੁਸਤ, ਫੁਰਤੀਲਾ; ਜ਼ੋਰਦਾਰ; ~ness ਚਤਰਤਾ, ਹੁਸ਼ਿਆਰੀ, ਸਜੀਵਤਾ, ਤੀਖਣਤਾ, ਫੁਰਤੀ, ਤੇਜੀ, ਚੁਸਤੀ

smash (ਸਮੈਸ਼) v n ਭੰਨ ਦੇਣਾ, ਤੋੜ ਦੇਣਾ, ਟੋਟੇ ਟੋਟੇ ਕਰ ਦੇਣਾ; ਸਖ਼ਤ ਸੱਟ ਮਾਰਨੀ; ਟੱਕਰ (ਟੈਨਿਸ ਵਿਚ); ਬਰਬਾਦੀ (ਵੈਪਾਰ ਆਦਿ ਦੀ)

smear (ਸਮਿਅ*) v n ਲਿਬੇੜਨਾ; ਮਲਣਾ, ਪੁੰਦਲਾ ਕਰਨਾ, ਅਸਪਸ਼ਟ ਬਣਾ ਦੇਣਾ; ਦਾਗੀ ਕਰਨਾ; ਵਿਗਾੜਨਾ; ਬਦਨਾਮ ਕਰਨਾ; ਦਾਗ, ਧੱਬਾ, ਕਲੰਕ; ਲੇਪ

smell (ਸਮੈਲ) n v ਸੁਗੰਧ, ਗੰਧ, ਬੁ, ਮੁਸ਼ਕ, ਸੁੰਘਣਾ; ਖ਼ੁਸ਼ਬੂ ਦੇਣੀ, ਗੰਧਯੁਕਤ ਹੋਣਾ; ਸੜ ਜਾਣਾ, ਸੜ੍ਹਾਂਦ ਮਾਰਨੀ; ਸੂਹ ਕੱਢ ਲੈਣੀ, ਖੋਜ ਕੱਢਣਾ; ~ing ਗੰਧ, ਬਾਸ, ਗੰਧਯੁਕਤ, ਖ਼ੁਸ਼ਬੂਦਾਰ

smelt v ਕੱਚੀ ਧਾਤ ਨੂੰ ਗਾਲਣਾ (ਪੰਘਲਾਉਣਾ)

smicker ('ਸਮਿਕਅ*) n v ਬਣਾਉਟੀ ਹਾਸਾ; ਹੱਸਣਾ; ਮੂਰਖਾਂ ਵਾਂਗ ਹੱਸਣਾ, ਦੰਦ ਕੱਢਣਾ

smile (ਸਮਾਇਲ) n v ਮੁਸਕਾਨ, ਮੁਸਕਰਾਹਟ; ਮੁਸਕਾਉਣਾ, ਖ਼ੁਸ਼ ਹੋਣਾ, ਪ੍ਰਸੰਨਤਾ ਵਿਚ ਹੋਣਾ

smog (ਸਮੌਗ) ਧੁਆਂਖੀ ਧੁੰਦ

smoke (ਸਮਅਉਕ) n v ਧੂੰਆਂ, ਸਿਗਰਟ ਪੀਣ ਦੀ ਕਿਰਿਆ; (ਬੋਲ) ਸਿਗਰਟ; ਦਮ, ਹੁੱਕੇ ਦੇ ਸੂਟੇ; (ਚਿਮਨੀ ਦਾ) ਧੂੰ ਕੱਢਣਾ; ਧੁਖਣਾ; ਤਾੜ ਜਾਣਾ, ਸਮਝ ਜਾਣਾ; ~y ਧੁਆਂਖਿਆ, ਧੂੰ ਨਾਲ ਭਰਿਆ

smooth (ਸਮੂਦ) a v ਸਮਤਲ; ਚਿਕਣਾ, ਮੁਲਾਇਮ; ਕੁਲਾ; (ਪਾਣੀ ਦਾ ਤਲ) ਸ਼ਾਂਤ; ਰਵਾਂ; ਸੁਹਾਵਣਾ, (ਸਫ਼ਰ) ਨਿਰਵਿਘਨ; ਮਿਲਣਸਾਰ (ਸੁਭਾਅ, ਵਿਹਾਰ); ਸਮਤਲ ਕਰਨਾ, ਚਿਕਨਾ ਬਣਾਉਣਾ, ਹਮਵਾਰ ਕਰਨਾ; ~spoken,

~tongued ਮਿਠਬੋਲਾ; ਖ਼ੁਸ਼ਾਮਦੀ

smother ('ਸਮਅੱਦਆ*) v ਗਲ ਘੁੱਟਣਾ; ਸਾਹ ਘੁੱਟ ਕੇ ਮਾਰ ਦੇਣਾ; (ਮੁਆਮਲੇ ਨੂੰ) ਦਬਾਈ ਰੱਖਣਾ; ਜ਼ਾਹਰ ਨਾ ਹੋਣ ਦੇਣਾ

smuggle ('ਸਮਅੱਗਲ) v (ਕਾਨੂੰਨ ਵਿਰੁਧ) ਮਾਲ ਦੇਸ਼ ਤੋਂ ਬਾਹਰ ਭੇਜਣਾ ਜਾਂ ਅੰਦਰ ਲਿਆਉਣਾ, ਛੁਪਾ ਦੇਣਾ; ਚੁੰਗੀ ਚੋਰੀ ਕਰਨੀ; ਤਸਕਰੀ ਕਰਨੀ

smuggling ('ਸਮਅੱਗਲਿੜ) n ਚੁੰਗੀ ਚੋਰੀ, ਚੋਰੀ ਛਿਪਾ ਵਪਾਰ, ਕਾਨੂੰਨ ਵਿਰੁੱਧ ਮਾਲ ਅਯਾਤ ਨਿਰਯਾਤ

snack (ਸਨੈਕ) n ਹਿੱਸਾ, ਅੰਸ਼; ਹਲਕਾ ਭੋਜਨ

snag (ਸਨੈਗ) n ਖੁੰਢ, ਕੱਟਿਆ ਨੋਕਦਾਰ ਮੁੱਢ; ਗੰਢ

snake (ਸਨੇਇਕ) n v ਸੱਪ; ਦਗ਼ੋਬਾਜ਼ ਮਨੁੱਖ

snap (ਸਨੈਪ) v n ਅਚਨਚੇਤ ਵੱਢ ਲੈਣਾ, ਕਿਸੇ ਦੀ ਗੱਲ ਟੁੱਕਣੀ; ਅਚਾਨਕ ਖਿਝ ਕੇ ਬੋਲਣਾ; ਭੰਨ ਫੋਟੋ ਲੈ ਲੈਣੀ; ਕੜਾਕਾ, ਖੜਾਕ; ਫੁਰਤੀ, ਜੋਸ਼; ਸਧਾਰਨ ਫੋਟੋ

snare (ਸਨੇਅ*) n v ਫਾਹੀ, ਕੁੜੱਕੀ, ਜਾਲ, ਫੰਦਾ; ਧੋਖੇ ਨਾਲ ਅੜਾ ਦੇਣਾ, ਫਸਾ ਦੇਣਾ

snatch (ਸਨੈਚ) v n ਖੋਹਣਾ, ਖੋਹ ਲੈਣਾ, ਝਪਟ ਮਾਰਨੀ; ਲੈ ਕੇ ਭੱਜ ਜਾਣਾ; ਅਚਨਚੇਤ ਫੜਨਾ, ਥੋੜੇ ਸਮੇਂ ਦਾ ਆਵੇਸ਼

sneer (ਸਨਿਅ*) v ਮਖੌਲ ਉਡਾਉਣਾ, ਹਾਸਾ ਉਡਾਉਣਾ; ਨੀਚ ਸਮਝਣਾ, ਤੁੱਛ ਸਮਝਣਾ; ਤਾਅਨਾ ਮਾਰਨਾ

sneeze (ਸਨੀਜ਼) n v ਛਿੱਕ, ਨਿੱਛ; ਛਿੱਕਣਾ, ਨਿੱਛ ਮਾਰਨੀ

sniff (ਸਨਿਫ਼) v n ਨਕ ਵਿਚ ਚੜ੍ਹਾਉਣਾ, ਸਾਹ ਨਾਲ ਨੱਕ ਵਿਚ ਅੰਦਰ ਨੂੰ ਖਿੱਚਣਾ; ਸੁਰੜ-ਸੁਰੜ ਕਰਨਾ; ਨੱਕ ਵਿਚ ਅੰਦਰ ਨੂੰ ਖਿੱਚਿਆ ਸਾਹ; ~y ਹਕਾਰਤ ਭਰਿਆ; ਬਦਬੂ ਵਾਲਾ

snivel ('ਸਨਿਵਲ) v n ਨੱਕ ਵਗਣਾ, ਸੂੰ-ਸੂੰ ਕਰਨਾ, ਨੱਕ ਨਾਲ ਸੁਰੜ-ਸੁਰੜ ਕਰਨਾ; ਭੁਸਕਣਾ, ਬੁਸਕਣਾ; ਨੱਕ ਦੀ ਸੁਰੜ-ਸੁਰੜ

snob (ਸਨੌਬ) n ਬੜੀ ਫੂੰ-ਫਾਂ ਵਾਲਾ, ਆਕੜਖ਼ਾਨ, ਪਾਟੇਖ਼ਾਂ, ਹੇਛਾ, ਨੀਵੇਂ ਵਿਚਾਰਾਂ ਵਾਲਾ; ~bery ਘਮੰਡ, ਫੂੰ-ਫਾਂ, ਫੋਕੀ ਆਕੜ

snocp (ਸਨੂਪ) v ਲੁਕੇ-ਛਿਪੇ ਆਉਣਾ ਜਾਣਾ, ਮੁਖਬਰੀ ਕਰਨਾ, ਨਾਜਾਇਜ਼ ਦਖ਼ਲ ਦੇਣਾ

snooze (ਸਨੂਜ਼) v n ਥੋੜੂੰ ਚਿਰ ਲਈ ਸੌਣਾ; ਉਂਘਲਾਉਣਾ; ਉਂਘ

snore (ਸਨੋ*) n v ਘੁਰਾੜੇ; ਘੁਰਾੜੇ ਮਾਰਨੇ

snout (ਸਨਾਉਟ) n ਥੁਥਨੀ, ਥੁੱਨੀ; ਬੂਥੀ

snow (ਸਨਅਉ) n v ਬਦਲਾਂ ਵਿਚੋਂ ਡਿਗਣ ਵਾਲੀ ਬਰਫ਼; ਬਰਫ਼ ਪੈਣੀ, ਬਰਫ਼ ਡਿੱਗਣੀ; ~fall ਬਰਫ਼ਬਾਰੀ

snub (ਸਨਅੱਬ) v n ਝਿੜਕ ਦੇਣਾ, ਝਾੜ ਦੇਣਾ, ਡਾਂਟਣਾ; ਝਿੜਕ, ਝਾੜ, ਡਾਂਟ

snuff v n ਨਸਵਾਰ ਲੈਣੀ; ਨਸਵਾਰ

so (ਸਅਉ) adv conj int pron ਏਨਾ, ਇੰਨਾ; ਇੰਝ, ਇਸ ਤਰ੍ਹਾਂ; ਇਸ ਲਈ, ਇਸ ਕਰਕੇ, ਸੱਚ-ਮੁਚ ਹੀ, ਅਸਲ ਵਿਚ; ਇਹੋ ਗੱਲ; ~and so ਫਲਾਣਾ ਆਦਮੀ, ਫਲਾਣੀ ਚੀਜ਼; ਫਲਾਣਾ-ਢਿਮਕਾ; ~called ਕਥਿਤ, ਨਾਮ ਨਿਹਾਦ; ~far as ਜਿਥੋਂ ਤਕ ਕਿ; ~so (ਬੋਲ) ਠੀਕ-ਠਾਕ, ਨਾ ਚੰਗਾ ਨਾ ਮਾੜਾ, ਗੁਜ਼ਾਰੇ ਮੁਆਫ਼ਕ

soak (ਸਅਉਕ) v n ਭਿਊਂਣਾ, ਪਾਣੀ ਵਿਚ ਡੋਬਣਾ; ਪੂਰੀ ਤਰ੍ਹਾਂ ਭਿੱਜ ਜਾਣਾ; ਰੱਜ ਕੇ ਪੀਣਾ; ਡੁਬਾਉ; ਜ਼ੋਰ ਦੀ ਬਰਸਾਤ

soap (ਸਅਉਪ) n v ਸਾਬਣ; ਸਾਬਣ ਨਾਲ ਧੋਣਾ; ਚਾਪਲੂਸੀ ਕਰਨੀ

soar (ਸੋ*) v ਹਵਾ ਵਿਚ ਤਰਨਾ; ਉੱਚੀ ਸੋਚ-

ਉਡਾਰੀ ਲਾਉਣੀ; ਉਚਾਈ ਤੇ ਚੜ੍ਹਨਾ

sob (ਸੋਬ) *n v* ਡੁਸਕੀ, ਸਿਸਕੀ; ਡੁਸਕਣਾ; ਬੁਸਕਣਾ, ਸਿਸਕੀਆਂ ਲੈਣੀਆਂ, ਹੌਕੇ ਭਰਨੇ

sober ('ਸਅਉਬਅ*) *a v* ਗੰਭੀਰ, ਸੁਝਵਾਨ, ਸੰਜਮੀ; ਸ਼ਾਂਤ ਕਰਨਾ, ਹੋਸ਼ ਵਿਚ ਹੋਣਾ; ~**ness** ਸਥਿਰ ਬੁੱਧੀ, ਗੰਭੀਰਤਾ, ਸਥਿਰਤਾ, ਵਿਚਾਰ-ਸ਼ੀਲਤਾ

sociable ('ਸਅਉਸ਼ਅਬਲ) *a n* ਮਿਲਣਸਾਰ, ਮਿਲਾਪੜਾ, ਸਨੇਹੀ, ਆਪਸੀ, ਦੋਸਤਾਨਾ; ਵਾਧੂ ਸ਼ਿਸ਼ਟਾਚਾਰ ਤੋਂ ਬਿਨਾ

social ('ਸਅਉਸ਼ਲ) *a n* ਸਮਾਜਕ, ਸਮਾਜੀ ਮਿਲਾਪੜਾ, ਆਪਸੀ; ~**security** ਸਮਾਜਕ ਸੁਰੱਖਿਆ; ~**ism** ਸਮਾਜਵਾਦ, ਸਾਂਝੀਵਾਲਤਾ ~**ist** ਸਮਾਜਵਾਦੀ ~**ize** ਸਮਾਜੀਕਰਨ ਕਰਨਾ

society (ਸਅ'ਸਾਇਅਟਿ) *n* ਸਮਾਜ, ਭਾਈਚਾਰਾ; ਬਿਰਾਦਰੀ; ਉਚ ਵਰਗ; ਵੱਡੇ ਲੋਕ; ਸਭਾ, ਪਰਿਸ਼ਦ, ਸਮਿਤੀ, ਸੰਘ; ਸੰਗਤ

sociology ('ਸਅਉਸਿ'ਔਲਅਜਿ) *n* ਸਮਾਜ-ਵਿਗਿਆਨ, ਸਮਾਜ-ਸ਼ਾਸਤਰ

sock (ਸੌਕ) *n v* ਜੁਰਾਬ, ਪਤਾਵਾ; ਢੀਮ ਮਾਰਨੀ, ਕੋਈ ਚੀਜ਼ ਵਗਾਹ ਕੇ ਮਾਰਨੀ

sodomite ('ਸੌਡਅਮਾਇਟ) *n* ਲੌਂਡੇਬਾਜ਼, ਮੁੰਡੇਬਾਜ਼; ਪਸ਼ੂ-ਸੰਭੋਗੀ

sodomy ('ਸੌਡਅਮਿ) *n* ਮੁੰਡੇਬਾਜ਼ੀ, ਲੌਂਡੇਬਾਜ਼ੀ

soft (ਸੌਫਟ) *a adv* ਕੂਲਾ, ਨਰਮ, ਮੁਲਾਇਮ, ਚਿਕਨਾ; ਲਚਕਦਾਰ, ਢਿੱਲਵਾਂ, ਸੁਹਾਵਣਾ, ਨਿਰਬਲ, ਪੋਲਾ, ਜ਼ਨਾਨਾ; (ਰਾਗ) ਮੱਧਮ, ਧੀਮੀ ਸੁਰ ਵਿਚ; ~**currency** ਨਾ-ਬਦਲਣਯੋਗ ਮੁਦਰਾ; ~**en** ਨਰਮ ਹੋਣਾ, ਢਲਣਾ, ਮੋਮ ਹੋਣਾ, ਢਾਲਣਾ; ਮੱਧਮ ਕਰਨਾ, ਧੀਮਾ ਕਰਨਾ; ~**ness** ਕੋਮਲਤਾ, ਨਰਮੀ, ਨਿਮਰਤਾ; ~**ware**

ਕਮਪਿਊਟਰ ਦਾ ਪ੍ਰੋਗਰਾਮ ~**y** ਸਿੱਧਫ, ਸਿੱਧਾ-ਸਾਦਾ (ਆਦਮੀ), ਭੋਲਾ-ਭਾਲਾ (ਮਨੁੱਖ); ਮੂਰਖ ਕਮਜ਼ੋਰ (ਵਿਅਕਤੀ); ਢਿੱਲੀ ਕੁਲੱਛੀ

soil (ਸੌਇਲ) *v n* ਮੈਲਾ ਕਰਨਾ, ਲਿਬੇੜਨਾ; ਦਾਗ਼ ਪੈ ਜਾਣਾ; ਧੱਬਾ; ਮਿੱਟੀ, ਜ਼ਮੀਨ; ਦੇਸ, ਵਤਨ

sojourn ('ਸੌਜਅ:ਨ) *n v* ਥੋੜ੍ਹੇ ਸਮੇਂ ਦਾ ਡੇਰਾ; ਠਹਿਰਨਾ, ਰੁਕਣਾ, ਡੇਰਾ ਕਰਨਾ; ਟਿਕਣਾ

solace ('ਸੌਲਅਸ) *n v* ਦਿਲਾਸਾ, ਢਾਰਸ, ਧੀਰਜ, ਤਸੱਲੀ, ਹੌਸਲਾ; ਦਿਲਾਸਾ ਦੇਣਾ, ਤਸੱਲੀ ਦੇਣੀ; ~**ment** ਢਾਰਸ; ਤਸੱਲੀ; ਦਿਲਾਸਾ

solar ('ਸਅਉਲ*) *a* ਸੂਰਜ ਦਾ, ਸੂਰਜੀ; ~**system** ਸੌਰ-ਮੰਡਲ

solder ('ਸੌਲਡਅ*) *n v* ਧਾਤ ਦਾ ਟਾਂਕਾ; ਜੋੜ; ਟਾਂਕਾ ਲਾਉਣਾ; ਜੋੜ ਲਾਉਣਾ

soldier ('ਸਅਉਲਜਅ*) *n* ਫ਼ੌਜੀ ਸੈਨਕ; ਫ਼ੌਜ ਦਾ ਸਿਪਾਹੀ

sole (ਸਅਉਲ) *n a v* ਜੁੱਤੀ ਦਾ ਤਲਾ, (ਕਿਸੇ ਚੀਜ਼ ਦਾ) ਥੱਲਾ, ਪੇਂਦਾ, ਆਧਾਰ; ਇੱਕਲਾ, ਇਕੱ-ਇਕ, ਸਿਰਫ਼; (ਕਾ) ਕੰਵਾਰਾ, ਛੜਾ; ਜੁੱਤੀ ਦਾ ਤਲਾ ਲਾਉਣਾ

solemn ('ਸੌਲਅਮ) *a* ਗੰਭੀਰ, ਸੰਜੀਦਾ; ਵਿਧੀ-ਅਨੁਕੂਲ; ਮਰਯਾਦਾਪੂਰਵਕ, ਰਸਮ; ~**ity** ਗੰਭੀਰਤਾ, ਸੰਜੀਦਗੀ; ਮਹਾਨਤਾ, ਠਾਠ; ਧਾਰਮਕ ਰਸਮ, ਧਾਰਮਕ ਸੰਸਕਾਰ; ਪਵਿੱਤਰਤਾ; ~**ize** ਮਨਾਉਣਾ (ਤਿਉਹਾਰ, ਉਤਸਵ ਆਦਿ); (ਰੀਤੀ, ਰਸਮ) ਵਿਧੀ ਅਨੁਸਾਰ ਨਿਭਾਉਣੀ

solicit (ਸਅ'ਲਿਸਿਟ) *v* ਬੇਨਤੀ ਕਰਨੀ, ਯਾਚਨਾ ਕਰਨੀ, ਅਰਜ਼ ਕਰਨੀ; ~**ation** ਬੇਨਤੀ, ਮਿੰਨਤ, ਯਾਚਨਾ; ~**or** ਯਾਚਕ; ਉਪਵਕੀਲ, ਮੁਕਦਮਾ ਚਲਾਣ ਦੀ ਰਾਇ ਦੇਣ ਵਾਲਾ

solid ('ਸੌਲਿਡ) *a* ਠੋਸ, ਨਿੱਗਰ; ਪੱਕਾ, ਦ੍ਰਿੜ੍ਹ,

ਮਜ਼ਬੂਤ; ਸੁਧ; ਤਰਕਸੰਗਤ, ਪ੍ਰਮਾਣਤ; ਸੱਚਾ,
ਵਾਸਤਵਿਕ, ਅਸਲੀ; ~arity ਏਕਤਾ,
ਸੰਗਠਨ, ਇਕਜੁੱਟਤਾ

solitary ('ਸੋਲਿਟ(ਅ)ਰਿ) *a n* ਇੱਕਲਾ, ਇਕੋ-
ਇਕ, ਕੱਲਮ-ਕੱਲਾ; ਲੁੱਗਾ, ਸੁੰਨਸਾਨ; ਇਕਾਂਤ,
ਇਕਾਂਤਵਾਸੀ; ਵੈਰਾਗੀ

solitude ('ਸੋਲਿਟਯੂਡ) *n* ਇਕਾਂਤ, ਸੁੰਵ,
ਸੁੰਨਸਾਨ; ਇੱਕਲਾਪਨ

soluble ('ਸੋਲਯੁਬਲ) *a* ਘੁਲਣਹਾਰ; ਹੱਲ ਕਰਨ
ਯੋਗ, ਸੁਲਝਾਉਣ ਯੋਗ

solution (ਸਅਲੂਸ਼ਨ) *n* ਘੋਲ, ਘੁਲਣ, ਘੁਲਾਈ,
(ਸਮੱਸਿਆ ਦਾ) ਉਪਾਉ; ਸੁਲਝਾਉ; (ਗਣਿ)
ਹੱਲ; ਮੁਕਤੀ

solve (ਸੋਲਵ) *v* (ਗਣਿ) ਸਵਾਲ ਹੱਲ ਕਰਨਾ;
ਬੁੱਝਣਾ, ਹੱਲ ਕੱਢਣਾ; (ਸਮੱਸਿਆ) ਸੁਲਝਾਉਣੀ,
ਖੋਲ੍ਹਣੀ

sombre ('ਸੋਮਬਆ*) *a* ਹਨੇਰਾ, ਧੁੰਦਲਾ, ਕਾਲਾ;
ਉਦਾਸ, ਮੁਰਝਾਇਆ

some (ਸਅਮ) *a pron adv* ਕੋਈ; ਕੁਝ,
ਕਈ, ਕਿੰਨੇ ਹੀ, ~**how** ਕਿਸੇ ਨਾ ਕਿਸੇ ਤਰ੍ਹਾਂ,
ਕਿਸੇ ਤਰ੍ਹਾਂ, ਕਿਵੇਂ ਨਾ ਕਿਵੇਂ; ~**one** ਕੋਈ, ਕੋਈ
ਆਦਮੀ; ~**thing** ਕੁਝ, ਕੋਈ, ਕੁਝ ਨਾ ਕੁਝ,
ਕੁਝ ਕੁ; ~**time** ਕੁਝ ਚਿਰ, ਥੋੜ੍ਹਾ ਸਮਾਂ; ਕਿਸੇ
ਵੇਲੇ; ~**what** ਕੁਝ ਕੁ, ਥੋੜ੍ਹਾ ਜਿਹਾ, ਕੋਈ
ਚੀਜ਼; ~**where** ਕਿਤੇ, ਕਿੱਧਰੇ, ਕਿਸੇ ਪਾਸੇ

somersault ('ਸਅਮਅਸੋਲਟ) *n* ਪੁੱਠੀ ਛਾਲ,
ਉਲਟ-ਚੱਕਰ, ਬਾਜ਼ੀ (ਪਾਉਣੀ), ਬਾਜ਼ੀਆਂ
(ਪਾਉਣੀਆਂ), ਕਲਾਬਾਜ਼ੀ

son (ਸਅੱਨ) *n* ਪੁੱਤਰ, ਬੇਟਾ, ਸੰਤਾਨ; ~**in law**
ਜਵਾਈ, ਦਾਮਾਦ

sonant ('ਸਅਉਨਅੰਟ) *a n* ਧੁਨੀਪੂਰਨ, ਨਾਦੀ,

ਸੁਰੀਲਾ

song (ਸੌਂਡ) *n* ਗੀਤ; ਪਦ; ਗਾਉਣ

soon (ਸੂਨ) *adv* ਛੇਤੀ, ਤੁਰੰਤ, ਝ਼ੀਘਰ, ਹੁਣੇ ਹੀ,
ਥੋੜ੍ਹੇ ਚਿਰ ਨੂੰ

soot (ਸੁਟ) *n v* ਧੁਆਂਖ, ਕਾਲਖ; ਧੁਆਂਖਣਾ, ਕਾਲਾ
ਕਰਨਾ, ਕਾਲਖ ਲਾਉਣੀ

soothe (ਸੂਦ) *v* (ਗੁੱਸਾ) ਠੰਢਾ ਕਰਨਾ; ਸ਼ਾਂਤ
ਕਰਨਾ, (ਪੀੜ) ਘਟ ਕਰਨੀ, ਖ਼ੁਸ਼ਾਮਦ ਕਰਨੀ

sophistic, ~al (ਸਆਫ਼ਿਸਟਿਕ,
ਸਆਫ਼ਿਸਟਿਕਲ) *a* ਝੂਠੀ ਦਲੀਲ ਵਾਲਾ;
ਕੁਤਰਕੀ, ਧੋਖੇ ਵਾਲਾ; ~**ated** ਦੁਨੀਆਦਾਰ;
ਸਿਆਣਪ, ਭਰਪੂਰ, ਵਿਵੇਕਪੂਰਤ; ਨਫ਼ੀਸ;
~**ation** ਦੁਨੀਆਦਾਰੀ, ਸਿਆਣਪ, ਸੂਝ;
ਨਫ਼ਾਸਤ

sordid ('ਸੋਡ਼ਿਡ) *a* ਝੋਹਦਾ, ਸੂਮ; ਹੋਛਾ, ਨੀਚ
ਘਿਣਾਉਣਾ, ਭੈੜਾ

sore ('ਸੋ*) *a n adv* ਦੁਖਦਾ; ਖਿਝਿਆ, ਔਖਿਆ,
ਦੁੱਖੀ; (ਗੋਲ) ਰੁੱਠਵੀਂ; ਜ਼ਖ਼ਮ; ਫੱਟ

sorrow ('ਸੌਰਅਉ) *n* ਉਦਾਸੀ, ਸੋਗ, ਗ਼ਮ,
ਅਫ਼ਸੋਸ; ਕਲੇਸ਼, ਚਿੰਤਾ, ਦੁੱਖ; ਬਿਪਤਾ, ਸੰਕਟ:
~**ful** ਉਦਾਸ, ਗ਼ਮਗੀਨ, ਸੋਗੀ

sorry ('ਸੋਰਿ) *a* ਦੁੱਖੀ, ਉਦਾਸ, ਗ਼ਮਗੀਨ;
ਪਛਤਾਉਂਦਾ, ਦਿਲਗੀਰ; ਹੀਣਾ

sort (ਸੋਟ) *n v* ਪ੍ਰਕਾਰ, ਕਿਸਮ, ਵੰਨਗੀ; ਵੱਖ ਵੱਖ
ਕਰਨਾ, ਛਾਂਟਣਾ; ~**ing** ਛੰਟਾਈ, ਛਾਂਟ,
ਪ੍ਰਿਥਕਕਰਨ, ਵਰਗੀਕਰਨ

soul (ਸਅਉਲ) *n* ਆਤਮਾ, ਰੂਹ; ਅੰਤਹਕਰਨ,
ਆਪਾ, ਮਨ, ਚਿੱਤ, ਦਿਲ; ਜੀਵ; ~**less**
ਨਿਰਜੀਵ, ਪ੍ਰਾਣਹੀਨ; ਉਤਸ਼ਾਹਹੀਨ; ਥੋੜਮੀਰਾ

sound (ਸਾਊਂਡ) *a adv* ਆਵਾਜ਼, ਧੁਨੀ, ਖੜਾਕ;
ਉਚਾਰਨ; ਆਵਾਜ਼ ਨਿਕਲਣੀ, ਧੁਨੀ ਉਤਪੰਨ

ਹੋਣੀ; ਰਾਜ਼ੀ-ਬਾਜ਼ੀ, ਤੰਦਰੁਸਤ, ਚੰਗਾ-ਭਲਾ; ਠੀਕ ਹਾਲਤ ਵਿਚ

soup (ਸੂਪ) *n* ਤਰੀ, ਸ਼ੋਰਬਾ, ਸੂਪ

sour ('ਸਾਉਅ*) *a v* ਖੱਟਾ (ਸੁਆਦ); (ਰੋਟੀ) ਬੁਸੀ ਹੋਈ, ਖ਼ਮੀਰੀ; (ਵਾਸ਼ਨਾ) ਖ਼ਮੀਰ ਵਰਗੀ

source (ਸੋਸ) *n* ਸਰੋਤ, ਨਿਕਾਸ, ਪੈਦਾ ਹੋਣ ਵਾਲੀ ਥਾਂ; ਮੂਲ, ਮੁੱਢ

south (ਸਾਉਥ) *n a adv* ਦੱਖਣ, ਦੱਖਣ ਦਿਸ਼ਾ; ਦੱਖਣੀ

souvenir ('ਸੂਵੑ(ਅ)'ਨਿਅ*) *n* ਯਾਦਗਾਰ, ਨਿਸ਼ਾਨੀ, ਸਮਾਰਕ

sovereign ('ਸੌਵੑਰਿਨ) *a n* ਉੱਤਮ, ਉੱਚਤਮ, ਸਿਰਮੌਰ, ਸਿਰਤਾਜ; ਸਰਬ-ਸੱਤਾਧਾਰੀ; **~ty** ਰਾਜਗੀਰੀ, ਹਕੂਮਤ; ਸਰਬ ਸਮਰੱਥਾ, ਪ੍ਰਭੁਤਾ

sow (ਸੌਅਉ) *v* ਬੀਜਣਾ, ਬੀ ਪਾਉਣਾ; ਪ੍ਰਚਾਰ ਕਰਨਾ

space (ਸਪੇਇਸ) *n v* ਖ਼ਾਲੀ ਥਾਂ, ਵਿੱਥ; ਪੁਲਾੜ, ਆਕਾਸ਼, ਖ਼ਲਾਅ; ਵਿਸਤਾਰ; ਵਿਚਾਲੇ ਦਾ ਸਮਾਂ, ਸਮੇਂ ਦਾ ਅੰਤਰ; ਵਿੱਥ ਤੇ ਰੱਖਣਾ, ਵਿੱਥ ਦੇਣੀ; **~craft** ਪੁਲਾੜੀ ਜਹਾਜ਼; **~man** ਪੁਲਾੜੀ ਯਾਤਰੀ

spacious ('ਸਪੇਇਸ਼ਅਸ) *a* ਖੁੱਲ੍ਹਾ, ਮੋਕਲਾ, ਵਿਸ਼ਾਲ, ਲੰਮਾ-ਚੌੜਾ; **~ness** ਵਿਸਤਾਰ, ਫੈਲਾਉ, ਲੰਮਾਈ-ਚੌੜਾਈ, ਗੁੰਜਾਇਸ

spade (ਸਪੇਇਡ) *n* ਬੇਲਚਾ, ਫਾਉੜਾ, ਕਹੀ; **~work** ਮੁਢੱਲਾ ਸਖ਼ਤ ਕੰਮ, ਕਰੜੀ ਮਿਹਨਤ ਵਾਲਾ ਆਰੰਭਕ ਕੰਮ, ਮੋਟਾ ਮੋਟਾ ਕੰਮ

spado ('ਸਪੇਇਡਅਉ) *a* ਕਮਜ਼ੋਰ ਆਦਮੀ, ਨਪੁੰਸਕ ਵਿਅਕਤੀ; ਹੀਜੜਾ

span (ਸਪੈਨ) *n v* ਗਿੱਠ, ਅਵਧੀ, ਕਾਲ; ਥੋੜ੍ਹਾ ਸਮਾਂ ਜਾਂ ਥੋੜ੍ਹੀ ਦੂਰੀ; ਪੂਰਾ ਵਿਸਤਾਰ ਜਾਂ

ਖਿਲਾਰ; 9 ਇੰਚ; ਗਿੱਠਾਂ ਨਾਲ ਮਿਤਨਾ; ਦਰਿਆ ਆਦਿ ਉੱਤੇ ਪੁਲ ਬਣਾਉਣਾ; ਆਰਪਾਰ ਫੈਲਣਾ

spare (ਸਪੇਅ*) *a v* ਵਾਧੂ, ਫ਼ਾਲਤੂ; ਵਿਹਲਾ, ਖ਼ਾਲੀ (ਸਮਾਂ); ਲੋੜ ਨਾ ਸਮਝਣੀ, ਛੱਡਣਾ, ਵਿਹਲਾ ਕਰਨਾ, ਛੋਟ ਕਰਨੀ, ਵਰਤੋਂ ਵਿਚ ਨਾ ਲਿਆਉਣਾ, ਲਾਂਭੇ ਰੱਖਣਾ; ਬਚਾ ਰੱਖਣਾ; **~part** ਫ਼ਾਲਤੂ ਪੁਰਜ਼ੇ

spark (ਸਪਾ:ਕ) *n v* ਚਿੰਗਾ; ਬਿਜਲੀ ਦੀ ਚੰਗਿਆੜੀ; (ਗੁਣ ਦੀ) ਝਲਕ; ਚੰਗਿਆੜੀਆਂ ਨਿਕਲਣੀਆਂ; **~ie** ਲਿਸ਼ਕਣਾ, ਚਮਕਣਾ, ਝਲਕ ਮਾਰਨੀ; ਚੰਗਿਆੜੇ ਛੱਡਣੇ; ਲਿਸ਼ਕ, ਚਮਕ, ਝਲਕ, ਲਿਸ਼ਕਾਰਾ

sparrow ('ਸਪੈਰਅਉ) *n* ਚਿੜੀ

spawl (ਸਪੋਲ) *n v* ਥੁੱਕ, ਲਾਰ; ਥੁੱਕਣਾ, ਲਾਰਾਂ ਛੱਡਣੀਆਂ

speak (ਸਪੀਕ) *v* ਬੋਲਣਾ, ਕਹਿਣਾ, ਦੱਸਣਾ; ਗੱਲਬਾਤ ਕਰਨੀ; **~er** ਵਕਤਾ, ਬੋਲਣ ਵਾਲਾ

spear (ਸਪਿਅ*) *v* ਬਰਛਾ, ਬੱਲਮ, ਨੇਜ਼ਾ, ਬਰਛਾ ਮਾਰਨਾ; **~head** ਅੱਗੇ ਵਧਾਉਣਾ, ਆਗੂ, ਹਰਾਵਲ; **~mint** ਪੁਦਨਾ

special (ਸਪੈੱਸ਼ੱਲ) *a* ਖ਼ਾਸ, ਵਿਸ਼ੇਸ਼, ਵਿਸ਼ਿਸ਼ਟ; ਅਸਾਧਾਰਨ; **~ist** ਵਿਸ਼ੇਸ਼ੱਗ; **~ity** ਵਿਸ਼ੇਸ਼ ਗੁਣ; ਵਿਸ਼ੇਸ਼ਤਾ; **~ization** ਵਿਸ਼ੇਸ਼ੱਗਤਾ, ਮੁਹਾਰਤ; **~ize** ਵਿਸ਼ੇਸ਼ਤਾ ਦੇਣੀ; **~ized** ਵਿਸ਼ਿਸ਼ਟ, ਵਿਸ਼ੇਸ਼ੀਕ੍ਰਿਤ

species ('ਸਪੀਸ਼ੀਜ਼) *n* ਜਾਤੀ, ਉਪ-ਜਾਤੀ, ਨਸਲ; ਸ੍ਰੇਣੀ, ਕੋਟੀ, ਵਰਗ

specific (ਸਪਿਅ'ਸਿਫ਼ਿਕ) *a* ਵਿਸ਼ੇਸ਼, ਖ਼ਾਸ, ਉਚੇਰਾ; ਨਿਸ਼ਚਤ; ਜਿਨਸੀ, ਜਾਤੀਗਤ; **~ation** ਸਪਸ਼ਟਤਾ; ਵਿਸ਼ੇਸ਼ ਵਿਵਰਨ

specified ('ਸਪੈੱਸਿਫ਼ਾਇਡ) *a* ਨਿਸ਼ਚਤ ਉੱਲਿਖਤ

specify ('ਸਪੈੱਸਿਫ਼ਾਇ) *v* ਸਪਸ਼ਟ ਕਰਨਾ, ਨਿਸ਼ਚਤ ਕਰਨਾ; ਵਿਸ਼ੇਸ਼ ਢੰਗ ਨਾਲ ਕਹਿਣਾ

specimen ('ਸਪੈੱਸਿਮਅਨ) *n* ਨਮੂਨਾ, ਵੰਨਗੀ, ਉਦਾਹਰਣ

spectacle (ਸਪੈੱਕਟਅਲ) *n* ਨਜ਼ਾਰਾ, ਝਾਕੀ, (ਬਵ) ਐਨਕ; ~d ਐਨਕ ਵਾਲਾ, ਚਸ਼ਮਾਧਾਰੀ

spectator (ਸਪੈੱਕ'ਟੇਇਟਅ*) *n* ਦਰਸ਼ਕ, ਤਮਾਸ਼ਬੀਨ, ਦ੍ਰਸ਼ਟਾ

spectrum ('ਸਪੈੱਕਟਰਅਮ) *n* ਕਿਰਨ-ਪਰਛਾਈਂ, ਵਰਣ-ਕ੍ਰਮ; ਰੰਗ-ਦ੍ਰਿਸ਼; ਸਿਲਸਲਾ

speculate ('ਸਪੈੱਕਯੁਲੇਇਟ) *v* ਅਨੁਮਾਨ ਲਾਉਣਾ, ਅੰਦਾਜ਼ਾ ਲਾਉਣਾ, ਖ਼ਿਆਲੀ ਘੋੜੇ ਦੁੜਾਉਣੇ

speculation ('ਸਪੈੱਕਯੁ'ਲੇਇਸ਼ਨ) *n* ਅਨੁਮਾਨ, ਅੰਦਾਜ਼ਾ, ਕਿਆਸ, ਸੱਟਾਬਾਜ਼ੀ; ਚਿੰਤਨ

speculative ('ਸਪੈੱਕਯੁਲਅਟਿਵ) *a* ਕਾਲਪਨਕ, ਖ਼ਿਆਲੀ, ਕਿਆਸੀ, ਵਿਚਾਰਸ਼ੀਲ; ਸੱਟੇ ਵਿਚ ਲੱਗਿਆ

speech (ਸਪੀਚ) *n* ਭਾਸ਼ਣ, ਤਕਰੀਰ, ਕਥਨ-ਸ਼ਕਤੀ; ਬੋਲ, ਬੋਲੀ; ~less ਬੇਜ਼ਬਾਨ, ਗੁੰਗਾ, ਚੁੱਪ, ਮੌਨ, ਖ਼ਮੋਸ਼; ਅਵਾਕ

speed (ਸਪੀਡ) *n v* ਗਤੀ, ਚਾਲ; ਫੁਰਤੀ, ਤੇਜ਼ੀ, ਤੀਬਰਤਾ; ਫੁਰਤੀ ਵਖਾਉਣੀ; ਛੇਤੀ ਘੱਲਣਾ; ਉੱਨਤੀ ਕਰਨੀ; ~y ਵੇਗਵਾਨ, ਵੇਗਪੂਰਨ, ਤੀਬਰ

spell (ਸਪੈੱਲ) *n v* ਮੰਤਰ, ਟੂਣਾ, ਆਕਰਸ਼ਣ; ਕੁਝ ਚਿਰ; ਸ਼ਬਦ-ਜੋੜ ਕਰਨਾ, ਹਿੱਜੇ ਕਰਨਾ; ~bound ਕੀਲਿਆ, ਮੋਹਤ, ਮੰਤਰ-ਮੁਗਧ; ~ing ਹਿੱਜੇ, ਸ਼ਬਦ-ਜੋੜ, ਵਰਣ-ਵਿਨਿਆਸ

spend (ਸਪੈੱਡ) *v* ਖ਼ਰਚਣਾ, ਖ਼ਰਚ ਕਰਨਾ, ਖ਼ਰਚ ਹੋ ਜਾਣਾ; ~thrift ਫ਼ਜ਼ੂਲ ਖ਼ਰਚ

sperm (ਸਪਅ:ਮ) *n* ਨਰ ਦਾ ਵੀਰਜ; ਮਣੀ, ਸ਼ੁਕਰਾਣੂ

sphere ('ਸਫ਼ਿਅ*) *n* ਖੇਤਰ, ਦਾਇਰਾ; ਗੋਲਾ, ਆਕਾਸ਼ੀ ਪਿੰਡ

sphinx (ਸਫ਼ਿੰਡਕਸ) *n* ਨਰਸਿੰਘ, ਗੁੱਝਾ ਮਨੁੱਖ

spice (ਸਪਾਇਸ) *n v* ਮਸਾਲਾ, ਮਿਰਚ-ਮਸਾਲਾ; ਮਸਾਲੇਦਾਰ ਬਣਾਉਣਾ

spick and span ('ਸਪਿਕ ਅਨ'ਸਪੈਨ) *a* ਨਵਾਂ, ਕੋਰਾ, ਤਾਜ਼ਾ; ਨਵਾਂ-ਨਿਕੋਰ, ਚੁਸਤ

spicy ('ਸਪਾਇਸਿ) *a* ਮਸਾਲੇਦਾਰ; ਕਰਾਰਾ; ਚਟਕੀਲਾ, ਲੱਛੇਦਾਰ

spider ('ਸਪਾਇਡਅ*) *n* ਮੱਕੜੀ

spike (ਸਪਾਇਕ) *n v* ਤਿੱਖੀ ਨੋਕ; ਲੰਮਾ ਕਿੱਲ; ਨੋਕਦਾਰ ਸੀਖ; ਜੁੱਤੀ ਦੇ ਥੱਲੇ ਲੱਗੀ ਮੇਖ; ਸੁੰਬਾ; ਮੇਖਾਂ ਲਾਉਣੀਆਂ

spile (ਸਪਾਇਲ) *n v* ਕਿੱਲ, ਤਿੱਖੀ ਮੇਖ; ਕਿੱਲ ਲਾਉਣਾ, ਮੇਖ ਗੱਡਣੀ

spill (ਸਪਿਲ) *v n* ਡੋਲ੍ਹਣਾ, ਰੋੜ੍ਹਨਾ; ਡੁੱਲ੍ਹਣਾ; ਰੁੜ੍ਹਨਾ; ਵਗਣਾ; ਕਾਗਜ਼ ਜਾਂ ਲਕੜੀ ਦੀ ਬੱਤੀ

spin (ਸਪਿਨ) *v n* ਕੱਤਣਾ, ਪੂਣੀਆਂ ਕੱਤਣੀਆਂ, ਚਰਖਾ ਕੱਤਣਾ, ਤੱਕਲੀ ਨਾਲ ਵੱਟਣਾ; ਚੱਕਰੀ; ~ning ਕਤਾਈ, ਕੱਤਣ, ਬੁਨਣ; ਘੁਮਾਈ, ਚੱਕਰ; ~dle ਤੱਕਲਾ (ਚਰਖੇ ਦਾ); ਤੱਕਲੀ (ਵਾਟ; ਸੂਤ ਆਦਿ ਵੱਟਣ ਵਾਲੀ), ਫੇਰਨੀ; ਜੁਲਾਹੇ ਦੀ ਨਲੀ; ਧੁਰਾ, ਧੁਰੀ, ਲੱਠ (ਚਰਖੇ ਦੀ)

spinal ('ਸਪਾਇਨਲ) *a* ਰੀੜ੍ਹ ਦੀ ਹੱਡੀ ਦਾ; ~cord ਰੀੜ੍ਹ ਦੀ ਹੱਡੀ

spine (ਸਪਾਇਨ) *n* ਕੰਗਰੋੜ੍ਹ, ਸੂਲ; ਉੱਭਰਵਾਂ ਹਿੱਸਾ; ~less *a* ਬਿਨਾ ਕਮਰੋੜ, ਰੀੜ੍ਹ ਦੀ ਹੱਡੀ ਬਿਨਾ; ਨਿਤਾਣਾ, ਡਰਪੋਕ, ਕਮਜ਼ੋਰ

spinster ('ਸਪਿੰਸਟਅ*) *n* ਅਣਵਿਆਹੀ ਤੀਵੀਂ,

ਛੜੀ, ਬੁੱਢ-ਕੁਆਰੀ

spiral ('ਸਪਾਇਰਲ) *a n* ਚੱਕਰਦਾਰ, ਕੁੰਡਲਦਾਰ, ਚੂੜੀਦਾਰ; ਚੱਕਰਦਾਰ ਕਮਾਨੀ

spirit ('ਸਪਿਰਿਟ) *n v* ਆਤਮਾ, ਰੂਹ, ਜੀਵ-ਆਤਮਾ, ਪ੍ਰਾਣ, ਬ੍ਰਹਮ, ਪਰਮਾਤਮਾ; ਭੂਤ, ਪਰੇਤ; ਹਿੰਮਤ, ਹੌਸਲਾ, ਜੋਸ਼, ਖ਼ੁਸ਼ਦਿਲੀ, ਜ਼ਿੰਦਾਦਿਲੀ, ਚੜ੍ਹਦੀ ਕਲਾ ਵਾਲੀ ਦਸ਼ਾ; ਸਤ, ਸ਼ਰਾਬ; ਸਪਿਰਿਟ, (ਕਿਸੇ ਨੂੰ) ਪ੍ਰਸੰਨ ਕਰਨਾ, ਉਤਸ਼ਾਹਤ ਕਰਨਾ; ~**less** ਮੁਰਦਾਦਿਲ, ਬੇਹੌਸਲਾ, ਢਿੱਲੜ, ਫੋਸੜ; ਉਦਾਸ; ~**ual** ਆਤਮਕ, ਰੂਹਾਨੀ, ਆਤਮਾ ਸਬੰਧੀ, ਅਧਿਆਤਮਕ, ਮਨੁੱਖੀ, ਪਰਮਾਰਥਕ, ਅਸਰੀਰੀ, ਅਮੂਰਤ; ~**ualism** ਆਤਮਵਾਦ, ਅਧਿਆਤਮਵਾਦ, ਅਧਿਆਤਮਕਤਾ; ~**ualist** ਅਧਿਆਤਮਵਾਦੀ, ਬ੍ਰਹਮਵਾਦੀ; ~**uality** ਅਧਿਆਤਮਕਤਾ, ਅਧਿਆਤਮ, ਰੂਹਾਨੀਅਤ

spit (ਸਪਿਟ) *v n* ਥੁੱਕਣਾ, ਥੁੱਕ ਸੁੱਟਣਾ; ਗੁੱਸੇ ਵਿਚ ਮੂੰਹੋਂ ਕੱਢਣਾ; ਸੀਖ ਨਾਲ ਕਬਾਬ ਚੰਬੇੜਨਾ; ਫੁੰਕਾਰ, ਥੁੱਕ; ~**tie** ਥੁੱਕ, ਉਗਾਲ; ~**toon** ਪੀਕਦਾਨ, ਥੁੱਕਦਾਨ, ਉਗਾਲਦਾਨ

spite (ਸਪਾਇਟ) *n v* ਲਾਗਤਬਾਜ਼ੀ, ਲਾਗ-ਡਾਟ; ਦਵੈਸ਼; ਖੁਨਸ, ਈਰਖਾ, ਸਾੜਾ; ਵੈਰ; ਲਾਗਤਬਾਜ਼ੀ ਕਰਨੀ

splash (ਸਪਲੈਸ਼) *v n* ਪਾਣੀ ਦੇ ਛਿੱਟੇ ਉਡਣੇ, (ਕਿਸੇ ਉੱਤੇ) ਛਿੱਟੇ ਪਾਉਣੇ; ਛਿੰਟ, ਛਿੱਟਾ, ਧੱਬਾ

spleen (ਸਪਲੀਨ) *n* ਤਿੱਲੀ, ਕੌੜਾ ਸੁਭਾਅ, ਅਰੂਬਪੁਣਾ, ਖਿਝ; ਗੁੱਸਾ

splendid ('ਸਪਲੈਂਡਿਡ) *n* ਸ਼ਾਨਦਾਰ, ਪ੍ਰਭਾਵ-ਸ਼ਾਲੀ, ਪ੍ਰਸੰਸਾਯੋਗ, ਗੌਰਵਮਈ, ਸ਼ਾਹਾਨਾ, ਆਲੀਸ਼ਾਨ; ~**ness** ਪ੍ਰਭਾਵਸ਼ੀਲਤਾ, ਗੌਰਵ

splendour ('ਸਪਲੈਂਡਅ*) *n* ਸ਼ਾਨ, ਠਾਠ, ਠਾਠ-

ਬਾਠ, ਸਜਧਜ; ਗੌਰਵ

split (ਸਪਲਿਟ) *v n* ਵੱਖਰਾ ਹੋਣਾ; ਪਾੜਨਾ; ਵੰਡਣਾ, ਫਟਣਾ; ਫਟ ਕੇ ਟੁਕੜੇ ਉਡ ਜਾਣੇ; ਦਰਾੜ, ਝੀਰੀ, ਧਾਤ ਦੀ ਇਕ ਫੜ੍ਹ

spoil (ਸਪੋਇਲ) *n v* ਲੁਟ, ਨਫ਼ਾ, ਖ਼ਰਾਬ ਕਰਨਾ, ਵਿਗਾੜਨਾ; ਲੁੱਟਣਾ, ਲੁੱਟ ਲੈਣਾ; ~**ed** ਵਿਗੜਿਆ, ਦੁਸ਼ਟ, ਵਿਜਿਤ

spoke (ਸਪਅਉਕ) *n v* (ਪਹੀਏ ਦੀ) ਅਰ, ਤਾਰ; ਰੁਕਾਵਟ ਪਾਉਣੀ

spokesman ('ਸਪਅਉਕਸਮਅਨ) *n* ਪ੍ਰਵਕਤਾ; ਬੁਲਾਰਾ, ਪ੍ਰਤੀਨਿਧ, ਨੁਮਾਇੰਦਾ

sponge ('ਸਪਅੰਜ) *n v* ਸਪੰਜ; ਅਸਪੰਜ; ਸਪੰਜ ਨਾਲ ਸਫ਼ਾਈ ਕਰਨਾ; ਖ਼ੁਸ਼ਾਮਦ ਨਾਲ ਕੰਮ ਕੱਢਣਾ; ~**r** ਮੁਫਤਖੋਰ, ਸਪੰਜ ਨਾਲ ਸਾਫ ਕਰਨ ਵਾਲਾ

spongy ('ਸਪਅੰਜੀ) *a* ਸਪੰਜ ਵਰਗਾ, ਗੁਦਗੁਦਾ

sponsor ('ਸਪੌਂਸਅ*) *n* ਸਰਪਰਸਤ; ਜ਼ਾਮਨ ਪੇਸ਼ਕਾਰ, ਨਾਂ ਪੇਸ਼ ਕਰਨਾ; ~**ship** ਸਰਪਰਸਤੀ, ਜ਼ਾਮਨੀ

spontaneity ('ਸਪੌਂਅ'ਨੇਇਅਟਿ) *n* ਸਵੈ-ਇੱਛਾ, ਆਪਮੁਹਾਰਤਾ, ਸੁਭਾਵਕਤਾ, ਕੁਦਰਤੀਪਨ

spontaneous (ਸਪੌਂ'ਟੇਇਨਯਅਸ) *a* ਕੁਦਰਤੀ, ਸੁਭਾਵਕ, ਸਵੈਚਾਲਕ, ਬਿਨਾ, ਇਰਾਦੇ, ਸਵੈ-ਪਰੇਰਤ

spoon (ਸਪੂਨ) *n v* ਚਮਚਾ, ਕੜਛੀ, ਡੋਈ; ਚਮਚੇ ਨਾਲ ਕੱਢਣਾ; ~**feed** ਮੂੰਹ ਵਿੱਚ ਪਾਉਣਾ, ਚਮਚੇ ਨਾਲ ਖੁਆਉਣਾ; ~**y** ਆਸ਼ਕ; ਭੌਂਦੂ, ਵੱਲੱਲਾ

sporadic (ਸਪਅ'ਰੈਡਿਕ) *a* ਕਦੇ ਕਦੇ, ਕਦੇ ਕਦਾਈਂ, ਇਕਾਦੁਕਾ; ਇਤਫਾਕੀਆ, ਖਿੱਲਰਿਆ, ਵੱਖਰਾ ਵੱਖਰਾ; ~**al** ਕਿਤੇ ਕਿਤੇ ਮਿਲਣ ਵਾਲਾ

sport (ਸਪੋਃਟ) *n v* ਖੇਡ, ਮਨੋਰੰਜਨ, ਹਾਸਾ-ਠੱਠਾ, ਦਿਲਲਗੀ; ਖੇਡਣਾ; ਦਿਲ-ਪਰਚਾਵਾ ਕਰਨਾ, ਹਾਸਾ-ਮਖੌਲ ਕਰਨਾ; ~**ing** ਖਿਡਾਰੀ, ਖੇਡਾਂ ਦਾ ਸ਼ੁਕੀਨ; ~**ive** ਖੇਡਣ ਦਾ ਸ਼ੁਕੀਨ, ਵਿਨੋਦੀ; ~**sman** ਖਿਡਾਰੀ; ~**smanship** ਖੇਡ, ਖਿਡਾਰੀ ਰੁਚੀ, ਨਿਆਂਕਾਰੀ ਸੁਭਾਅ

spot (ਸਪੌਟ) *n v* ਦਾਗ਼, ਡੱਬ, ਨਿਸ਼ਾਨ, ਧੱਬਾ, ਤਿਲ, ਟਿਮਕਣਾ; ਜਗ੍ਹਾ; ਮੌਕਾ, ਨਿਸ਼ਚਤ ਸਥਾਨ, ਸਥਿਤੀ; ਐਬ, ਕਲੰਕ, ਮੱਛੀ ਤੇ ਪਾਲਵੇਂ ਕਬੂਤਰਾਂ ਦੀ ਕਿਸਮ; (ਕਿਸੇ ਚੀਜ਼ ਦੀ) ਥੋੜੀ ਜਿਹੀ ਮਾਤਰਾ, ਥੋਰਾ ਕੁ; ਦਾਗ਼ ਲਾਉਣਾ, ਧੱਬਾ ਪਾਉਣਾ, ਲੱਭ ਲੈਣਾ, ਪਛਾਣ ਲੈਣਾ; ~**less** ਨਿਰਮਲ, ਬੇਦਾਗ਼, ਕਲੰਕਰਹਿਤ; ਨਿਸ਼ਕਲੰਕ

spouse (ਸਪਾਉੱਜ਼) *n* ਪਤੀ ਜਾਂ ਪਤਨੀ

spout (ਸਪਾਉਟ) *n v* (ਭਾਂਡੇ ਦੀ) ਟੂਟੀ; ਬੂੰਬੂ, ਧਾਰ, ਤਤੀਰੀ; ਫੁਹਾਰਾ; ਤਤੀਰੀ ਛੁੱਟਣੀ, ਜ਼ੋਰ ਦੀ ਧਾਰ ਪੈਣੀ

sprain (ਸਪਰੇਇਨ) *v n* ਮਚਕੋੜਨਾ, ਮਰੋੜਾ ਚਾੜੂ ਦੇਣਾ, ਵਲ ਪੈ ਜਾਣਾ; ਸੋਚ

spray (ਸਪਰੇਇ) *n v* ਫੁਹਾਰ, ਛਿੜਕਾ; ਛਿੜਕਣਾ

spread (ਸਪਰੈੱਡ) *v n* ਖਿਲਾਰਨਾ; ਵਿਛਾਉਣਾ; ਖਿੱਲਰਨਾ, ਵਿਛਣਾ; ਤਾਣਨਾ ਪਸਾਰਨਾ, ਖਿਲਾਰ, ਵਿਸਤਾਰ, ਪਸਾਰਾ; ਪ੍ਰਸਾਰ

sprightly (ਸਪਰਾਇਟਲਿ) *a* ਫੋਹਲਾ, ਚੁਸਤ, ਉਤਸ਼ਾਹੀ, ਸਜੀਵ; ਖ਼ੁਸ਼, ਖਿੜਿਆ

spring (ਸਪਰਿਙ) *v n* ਥੁੜਕਣਾ, ਟੱਪਣਾ, ਭੜਕਣਾ; ਸਰੋਤ, ਚਸ਼ਮਾ; ਲਚਕ; ਕਮਾਨੀ, ਸਪਿੰਗ; ਬਸੰਤ ਰੁੱਤ

sprinkle (ਸਪਰਿਙਕਲ) *v n* ਛਿੜਕਣਾ, ਤਰੌਂਕਾ ਦੇਣਾ, ਤਰੌਂਕਣਾ; ਤਰੌਂਕਾ

spur (ਸਪਅਃ*) *v* ਅੱਡੀ ਮਾਰਨੀ; ਜੋਸ਼ ਦਿਵਾਉਣਾ, ਉਤਸਾਹ ਵਧਾਉਣਾ

spurious (ਸਪਯੂਅਰਿਅਸ) *a* ਖੋਟਾ, ਝੂਠਾ, ਬਣਾਉਟੀ, ਨਕਲੀ (ਸਿੱਕਾ ਆਦਿ)

spurt, spirt (ਸਪਅਃਟ) *v n* ਥੜੀ ਤੇਜ਼ੀ ਨਾਲ ਵਧਣਾ, ਫਰਾਟਾ ਭਰ ਕੇ ਨਿਕਲ ਜਾਣਾ; ਫਰਾਟਾ, ਸਰਨਾਟਾ, ਉਬਾਲ

sputum (ਸਪਯੂਟਅਮ) *n* ਥੁੱਕ, ਖੰਘਾਰ

spy (ਸਪਾਇ) *n v* ਜਾਸੂਸ, ਸੂਹੀਆ; ਜਾਸੂਸੀ ਕਰਨੀ, ਭੇਦ ਲੈਣਾ

squab (ਸਕਵੌਬ) *n a* ਗੋਲ-ਮਟੋਲ, ਗੀਢਾ, ਮਠੂੰਨ; ਮੋਟਾ ਤੇ ਮਧਰਾ

squabble (ਸਕਵੌਬਲ) *n v* ਝਗੜਾ, ਲੜਾਈ; ਤੂ-ਤੂ ਮੈਂ-ਮੈਂ; SlSs G[s Ej`s

squad (ਸਕਵੌਡ) *n* ਜੱਥਾ, ਦਸਤਾ, ਫ਼ੌਜੀਆਂ ਦੀ ਨਿੱਕੀ ਟੋਲੀ

squall (ਸਕਵੌਲ) *v n* ਚੀਕਣਾ; ਚੀਕ-ਚਿਹਾੜਾ, ਚੀਕਣ ਦੀ ਅਵਾਜ਼; ਹਨੇਰੀ, ਝੱਖੜ; ~**y** ਮੀਂ-ਹਨੇਰੀ ਵਾਲਾ (ਮੌਸਮ)

squander (ਸਕੌਵੰਡਅ*) *v* ਉਡਾਉਣਾ, ਗੁਆਉਣਾ, ਫ਼ਜ਼ੂਲ-ਖ਼ਰਚੀ ਕਰਨੀ, ਅੰਨ੍ਹੇਵਾਹ ਖ਼ਰਚਣਾ; ~**ing** ਫ਼ਜ਼ੂਲ-ਖ਼ਰਚੀ

square (ਸਕਵੇਅ*) *a adv n v* ਵਰਗਾਕਾਰ, ਬਰਾਬਰ ਲੰਮਾਈ-ਚੌੜਾਈ ਤੇ ਸਮਕੋਣਾਂ ਵਾਲਾ; ਟਿਕਾਣੇ ਸਿਰ, ਉਚਿਤ ਵਿਧੀ ਨਾਲ; ਵਰਗਾ, ਮੁਰੱਬਾ (ਸ਼ਕਲ), ਬਰਾਬਰ ਬਾਹੀਆਂ ਤੇ ਦੋਟਾਂ ਵਾਲੀ ਚੌਕੋਰ, ਚੌਕ; ਠੀਕ ਕਰਨਾ, ਸੰਵਾਰਨਾ, ਅਨੁਕੂਲ ਹੋਣਾ; ~**root** ਵਰਗ ਮੂਲ

squash (ਸਕਵੌਸ਼) *v n* ਮਿੱਧਣਾ, ਫੇਹਣਾ, ਚਿੱਥਣਾ; ਦਰੜਨਾ; ਨਚੋੜਨਾ; ਮੂੰਹ ਤੋੜ ਜਵਾਬ ਦੇਣਾ; ਦੱਬੇ ਜਾਣਾ, ਫਸ ਜਾਣਾ; ਭੀੜ-ਭਾੜ, ਭੁਰਤਾ, ਸ਼ਰਬਤ

squeeze (ਸਕਵੀਜ਼) v n ਨਚੋੜਨਾ, ਫੇਹਣਾ, ਘੁਟਣਾ; ਮਲਣਾ, ਦਬਾਉਣਾ; ਜ਼ਬਰਦਸਤੀ ਵਸੂਲੀ ਕਰਨੀ; ਮਜਬੂਰ ਕਰਨਾ, ਦਬਾਅ ਪਾਉਣਾ; ਦਬਾਉ, ਨਚੋੜ

squint (ਸਕਵਿੰਟ) n v ਭੈਂਗਾ, ਟੀਰਾ; ਭੈਂਗਾਪਣ, ਤੱਕਣੀ, ਝਾਤ; ਟੀਰ ਕੱਢਣਾ, ਟੀਰਾ ਤੱਕਣਾ

squirrel ('ਸਕਵਿਰ(ਅ)ਲ) n ਗਾਲ੍ਹੜੂ, ਕਾਟੋ, ਗਾਲ੍ਹਿਰੀ

stability (ਸਟਅ'ਬਿਲਅਟਿ) n ਮਜ਼ਬੂਤੀ, ਸਥਿਰਤਾ, ਪਕਿਆਈ, ਸੰਤੁਲਨ

stabilization ('ਸਟੇਇਬਅਲਾਇ'ਜ਼ੇਇਸ਼ਨ) n ਸਥਿਤੀ-ਕਰਨ, ਸਥਾਈਕਰਨ, ਦ੍ਰਿੜ੍ਹੀਕਰਨ

stabilize ('ਸਟੇਇਬਅਲਾਇਜ਼) v ਮਜ਼ਬੂਤ ਕਰਨਾ, ਪੱਕਾ ਕਰਨਾ, ਸਥਿਰਤਾ ਦੇਣੀ

stable ('ਸਟੇਇਬਲ) a n ਪੱਕਾ, ਮਜ਼ਬੂਤ; ਟਿਕਾਊ; ਤਬੇਲਾ, ਅਸਤਬਲ

stadium ('ਸਟੇਇਡਯਅਮ) n ਦੌੜ ਦਾ ਮੈਦਾਨ, ਖੇਡ ਦਾ ਮੈਦਾਨ

staff (ਸਟਾਫ਼) n v ਸਰਕਾਰੀ ਅਧਿਕਾਰੀ ਜਾਂ ਕਰਮਚਾਰੀ; ਸੋਟਾ, ਡੰਡਾ, ਸੋਟੀ; ਸਹਾਰਾ; ਕਰਮਚਾਰੀ ਰਖਣਾ

stag (ਸਟੈਗ) n ਬਾਰਾਂ-ਸਿੰਗਾ

stage (ਸਟੇਇਜ) n v ਬੱਜ੍ਹਾ, ਚਬੂਤਰਾ, ਡਾਇਸ; ਰੰਗ-ਮੰਚ; ਨਾਟ-ਕਲਾ; ਅਖਾੜਾ

stagger ('ਸਟੈਗਾਅ*) v n ਡਗਮਗਾਉਣਾ; ਲੜਖੜਾਉਣਾ; ਹਿਚਕਾਉਣਾ, ਸ਼ਸ਼ੋਪੰਜ ਵਿਚ ਪੈਣਾ; ਚਕਰਾਉਣਾ; ਡਗਮਗਾਹਟ, ਲੜਖੜਾਹਟ

stagnant ('ਸਟੈਗਨਅੰਟ) a ਗਤੀਹੀਣ, ਰੁਕਿਆ, ਖਲੋਤਾ, ਸਥਿਰ, ਪਰਵਾਹਹੀਣ

stagnate ('ਸਟੈਗਨੇਇਟ) v (ਪਾਣੀ ਆਦਿ ਦਾ) ਖੜਾ ਰਹਿਣਾ, ਗਤੀਹੀਣ ਹੋਣਾ, ਖਲੋਤਾ ਰਹਿਣਾ

stagnation (ਸਟੈਗ'ਨੇਇਸ਼ਨ) n ਗਤੀਹੀਣਤਾ,

ਸਥਿਰਤਾ; ਪਰਵਾਹਹੀਣਤਾ; ਖੜੋਤ, ਨਿਸਚਲਤਾ

stain (ਸਟੇਇਨ) v n ਧੱਬਾ ਲਾਉਣਾ, ਡੱਬ ਪਾ ਦੇਣੇ, ਮੈਲਾ ਹੋਣਾ; ਕਲੰਕ ਲਾਉਣਾ; ਵੱਟਾ, ਕਲੰਕ; ~less ਬੇਦਾਗ਼, ਬੇਐਬ, ਨਿਰਮਲ;

stair (ਸਟੇਅ*) n ਪੌੜੀ, ਸੀੜ੍ਹੀ; ~case ਪੌੜੀਆਂ, ਜ਼ੀਨਾ

stake (ਸਟੇਇਕ) n v ਕਿੱਲ, ਮੇਖ, ਖੁੰਟਾ, ਚੋਭ, ਖੰਡਾ; ਸਹਾਰਾ ਦੇਣਾ; ਦਾਅ ਤੇ ਲਾਉਣਾ

stale (ਸਟੇਇਲ) a n v ਘਿਸਿਆ ਪਿਟਿਆ, ਬਾਸੀ, ਨੀਰਸ; ਪਸ਼ੂਆਂ ਦਾ ਪਿਸ਼ਾਬ; ਮੂਤਣਾ (ਪਸ਼ੂਆਂ ਦਾ)

stalemate ('ਸਟੇਇਲਮੇਇਟ) n v ਗਤੀਰੋਧ, ਅਟਕਾਉ; ਅਟਕਾਉ ਪੈਦਾ ਕਰਨਾ, ਜਮੂਦ ਪੈਦਾ ਕਰਨਾ

stall (ਸਟੌਲ) n v ਸਾਮਾਨ ਵੇਚਣ ਦੀ ਦੁਕਾਨ, ਖੋਖਾ, ਹੱਟ; ਠੱਪ ਹੋ ਜਾਣਾ; ਰੁਕਾਵਟ ਪਾਉਣਾ, ਦੇਰ ਕਰਨਾ, ਰੋੜਾ ਅਟਕਾਉਣਾ

stamina (ਸਟੈਮਿਨਅ) n ਬਲ, ਤੇਜ, ਸਰੀਰਕ ਸ਼ਕਤੀ, ਦਮ

stammer ('ਸਟੈਮਅ*) v n ਥਥਲਾਉਣਾ, ਤੋਤਲਾ ਹੋਣਾ; ਹਕਲਾਉਣਾ; ਥਥਲਾਹਟ, ਤੁਤਲਾਹਟ, ਹਕਲਾਹਟ

stamp (ਸਟੈਂਪ) v n ਮੁਹਰ ਲਗਾਉਣਾ, ਠੱਪਾ ਲਗਾਉਣਾ, ਛਾਪਣਾ; ਸਿੱਕਾ ਬਣਾਉਣਾ; ਠੋਕਣਾ, ਠੱਪਾ, ਛਾਪਾ; ਸਰਕਾਰੀ ਮੁਹਰ ਦਾ ਠੱਪਾ; ਟਿਕਟ, ਰਸੀਦੀ ਟਿਕਟ; ਅਸ਼ਟਾਮ

stampede (ਸਟੈਂ'ਪੀਡ) n ਭਾਜੜ, ਖਲਬਲੀ, ਹਫੜਾ-ਦਫੜੀ

stand (ਸਟੈਂਡ) v n ਖੜ੍ਹਾ ਹੋਣਾ, ਖਲੋਣਾ; ਰੱਖ ਦੇਣਾ; ਕਾਇਮ ਹੋਣਾ; ਸਹਾਰਨਾ; (ਖਰਚ) ਬਰਦਾਸ਼ਤ ਕਰਨਾ, ਆਪਣੇ ਸਿਰ ਲੈਣਾ, ਭਰ

ਦੇਣਾ; ਘੜਵੰਜੀ, ਥੜ੍ਹਾ; ਅੱਡਾ; ਚਬੂਤਰਾ; ~ **by** ਸਾਥ ਦੇਣਾ ਜਾਂ ਨਿਭਾਉਣਾ; ਕਾਇਮ ਰਹਿਣਾ, ਨੇੜੇ ਰਹਿਣਾ; **~point** ਵਿਚਾਰ, ਨਜ਼ਰੀਆ, ਦ੍ਰਿਸ਼ਟੀਕੋਣ; **~still** ਸਥਿਰ, ਅਹਿਲ, ਠਹਿਰਾਉ

standard ('ਸਟੈਂਡਅ:ਡ) *n* ਪੱਧਰ, ਸਤਰ, ਦਰਜਾ, ਕੋਟੀ, ਮਿਆਰ; ਆਦਰਸ਼; **~ization** ਪ੍ਰਮਾਣੀਕਰਨ, ਮਿਆਰੀਕਰਨ; **~ize** ਮਿਆਰ ਕਾਇਮ ਕਰਨਾ, ਟਕਸਾਲਣਾ

standing ('ਸਟੈਂਡਿਙ) *a n* ਸਥਾਈ, ਪੱਕੀ; ਖੜ੍ਹੀ (ਫ਼ਸਲ); ਕੋਟੀ, ਸਤਰ; **~orders** ਸਥਾਈ ਆਦੇਸ਼

stanza ('ਸਟੈਂਜ਼ਅ) *n* ਬੰਦ, ਸ਼ਲੋਕ, ਛੰਦ

staple ('ਸਟੇਇਪਲ) *n v* (ਕਾਗ਼ਜ਼ ਨੱਥੀ ਕਰਨ ਵਾਲਾ) ਕੁੰਡੀ, ਛੱਲਾ, ਸਟੇਪਲ; ਕੱਚਾ ਮਾਲ; ਮੁੱਖ ਸਮਗਰੀ; ਤਾਰ ਨਾਲ ਨੱਥੀ ਕਰਨਾ; ਵਰਗੀਕਰਨ ਕਰਨਾ, ਅਲੱਗ ਅਲੱਗ ਛਾਂਟਣਾ

star (ਸਟਾ*) *n* ਤਾਰਾ; ਸਿਤਾਰਾ; (ਨਾਟਕ ਜਾਂ ਫ਼ਿਲਮ ਦਾ) ਵਧੀਆ ਐਕਟਰ; ਉੱਘਾ ਆਦਮੀ; ਤਾਰਿਆਂ ਨਾਲ ਸਜਾਉਣਾ, ਤਾਰੇ ਜੜਨਾ

starch (ਸਟਾਚ) *n v* ਨਸ਼ਾਸਤਾ, ਕਲਫ਼, ਸਟਾਰਚ; ਮਾਇਆ, ਪਾਣ, ਪਾਹ; ਆਕੜ; ਕਲਫ਼ ਲਗਾਣਾ

stare (ਸਟੇਅ*) *v n* ਅੱਖਾਂ ਫਾੜ ਫਾੜ ਕੇ ਤੱਕਣਾ, ਘੂਰਨਾ, ਝਾਕਣਾ; ਤਾੜ, ਸਥਿਰ ਦ੍ਰਿਸ਼ਟੀ, ਟਿਕਟਿਕੀ

stark (ਸਟਾਕ) *a adv* ਸਖ਼ਤ ਆਕੜਿਆ; ਅਟੱਲ, ਕਠੋਰ; ਘੋਰ; ਨਿਰਾ

start (ਸਟਾਟ) *n v* ਪ੍ਰਸਥਾਨ, ਆਰੰਭ; ਸ੍ਰੀ ਗਣੇਸ਼, ਸ਼ੁਰੂਆਤ; ਕੂਚ ਕਰਨਾ, ਚੱਲਣਾ, ਨਿਕਲਣਾ

startle ('ਸਟਾ'ਟਲ) *v n* ਡਰਾ ਦੇਣਾ, ਘਬਰਾ ਦੇਣਾ; ਚੌਂਕ

stravation (ਸਟਾ'ਵੇਇਸ਼ਨ) *n* ਭੁਖਮਰੀ, ਕੰਗਾਲੀ, ਭੋਖੜਾ, ਫ਼ਾਕਾ, ਨਾਗਾ

starve (ਸਟਾਵ੍) *v* ਭੁੱਖਿਆਂ ਮਾਰਨਾ ਜਾਂ ਫ਼ਾਕੇ ਕੱਟਣੇ; ਅਤੀ ਗ਼ਰੀਬ ਜਾਂ ਮੁਹਤਾਜ ਹੋਣਾ; (ਬੋਲ) ਭੁੱਖ ਲੱਗਣੀ

state (ਸਟੇਇਟ) *n a v* (1) ਹਾਲ, ਹਾਲਤ, ਅਵਸਥਾ; (2) ਰਿਆਸਤ, ਸਲਤਨਤ, ਰਾਜ, ਸਰਕਾਰ; (3) ਪ੍ਰਦੇਸ਼; (4) ਰੁਤਬਾ; ਠਾਠ-ਬਾਠ, ਸਰਕਾਰੀ; ਰਸਮੀ ਕਥਨ ਕਰਨਾ, ਮੁਕਰਰ ਕਰਨਾ; **~ly** ਸ਼ਾਨਦਾਰ; **~ment** ਬਿਆਨ, ਕਥਨ; **~sman** ਨੀਤੀਵਾਨ, ਸਿਆਸਤਦਾਨ, ਰਾਜਨੀਤੀਵੇਤਾ; **~smanship** ਰਾਜਨੀਤਗਤਾ, ਸਿਆਣਪ, ਸਿਆਸਤਦਾਨੀ

static ('ਸਟੈਟਿਕ) *a* ਗਤੀਹੀਣ, ਸਥਿਰ, ਨਿਸ਼ਚਲ; **~al** ਗਤੀਹੀਣ, ਸਥਿਰ, ਅਹਿੱਲ

station ('ਸਟੇਇਸ਼ਨ) *n v* ਸਟੇਸ਼ਨ, ਰੇਲ-ਘਰ; ਅੱਡਾ, ਟਿਕਾਣਾ, ਥਾਂ ਦੇਣੀ, ਰੱਖਣਾ; **~ary** ਟਿਕਿਆ, ਸਥਿਰ, ਸਥਿਤ, ਅਹਿੱਲ, ਟਿਕਾਉ

stationer ('ਸਟੇਇਸ਼ਨਅ*) *n* ਲਿਖਣ ਸਮਗਰੀ ਵੇਚਣ ਵਾਲਾ, ਸਟੇਸ਼ਨਰ; **~y** ਲਿਖਣ-ਸਮਗਰੀ (ਕਾਗ਼ਜ਼, ਕਲਮ, ਦਵਾਤ ਆਦਿ)

statistics (ਸਟੇਟਿਸਟਿਕਸ) *n* ਸਾਖਿਅਕੀ

statistician (ਸਟੈਟਿ'ਸਟਿਸ਼ਨ) *n* ਅੰਕੜਾ-ਵਿਗਿਆਨੀ; **~ical** ਅੰਕੜਿਆਂ ਸਬੰਧੀ, ਸਾਂਖਿਅਕੀ; **~ics** ਅੰਕੜਾ-ਵਿਗਿਆਨ

statue ('ਸਟੈਚੂ) *n* ਮੂਰਤੀ, ਬੁੱਤ; **~tte** ਛੋਟੀ ਮੂਰਤੀ, ਛੋਟਾ ਬੁੱਤ

stature ('ਸਟੈਚਅ*) *n* ਕੱਦ, ਡੀਲ, ਕੱਦ-ਕਾਠ; ਰੁਤਬਾ

status ('ਸਟੇਇਟਅਸ) *n* ਪਦ, ਪਦਵੀ, ਅਹੁਦਾ, ਦਰਜਾ, ਰੁਤਬਾ, ਹੈਸੀਅਤ; ਅਵਸਥਾ, ਦਸ਼ਾ, ਹਾਲਤ; **~quo, ~quo ante** (*L*) ਜਿਉਂ ਦੀ

ਤਿਉਂ ਹਾਲਤ, ਯਥਾ-ਸਥਿਤੀ

statute ('ਸਟੈਟਯੂਟ) *n* ਵਿਧਾਨ-ਸਭਾ ਦਾ ਲਿਖਤੀ ਕਾਨੂੰਨ, ਅਧਿਨਿਯਮ; ਰੱਬੀ ਕਾਨੂੰਨ, ਦੈਵੀ ਵਿਧਾਨ

statutory ('ਸਟੈਟਯੂਟ(ਅ)ਰਿ) *a* ਕਾਨੂੰਨੀ, ਕਾਨੂੰਨ-ਅਨੁਸਾਰੀ

staunch (ਸਟੌਂਚ) *a* ਪੱਕਾ, ਨਿਸ਼ਚੇਵਾਨ, ਸਿਦਕਵਾਨ, ਵਫ਼ਾਦਾਰ

stay (ਸਟੇਇ) *n v* ਡੇਰਾ, ਬਸੇਰਾ, ਅਟਕਾਉ, ਰੋਕ; ਬੰਧਨ, ਸੰਜਮ; ਆਸਰਾ, ਸਹਾਰਾ; ਅਟਕਾਉਣਾ, ਠਹਿਰਾਉਣਾ; ਰੁਕ ਜਾਣਾ, ਸਹਿਣਾ, ਬਰਦਾਸ਼ਤ ਕਰਨਾ; ਉੜੀਕਣਾ; ~ing ਨਿਵਾਸ ਠਹਿਰਾਉ

stead (ਸਟੈੱਡ) *n* ਭੂਮੀ; ਸਥਾਨ, ਦਸ਼ਾ; ਪਲੱਖ

steadfast ('ਸਟੈੱਡਫ਼ਾਸਟ) *a* ਦ੍ਰਿੜ੍ਹ, ਅਟੱਲ, ਸਥਿਰ, ਪੱਕਾ, ਸਾਬਤ-ਕਦਮ

steady (ਸਟੈੱਡ੍ਰਿ) *a v* ਅਚੱਲ, ਅਟੱਲ, ਇਕਾਗਰ, ਸਥਿਰ, ਟਿਕਵਾਂ, ਦ੍ਰਿੜ੍ਹ, ਟਿਕਿਆ, ਠਹਿਰਿਆ; ਸੰਤੁਲ ਜਾਣਾ; ਟਿਕਾਉਣਾ

steal (ਸਟੀਲ) *v* ਚੁਰਾਉਣਾ, ਚੋਰੀ ਲੈਣਾ, ਚੁਪ ਚੁਪ ਕੇ ਲੈ ਜਾਣਾ, ਮੋਹ ਲੈਣਾ, ਲੁਭਾ ਲੈਣਾ; ~th ਚੋਰੀ; ਛਲ; ~thy ਗੁਪਤ, ਲੁਕਵੀਂ, ਗੁੱਝੀ, ਚੁੱਪ-ਚਾਪ, ਖੁਫ਼ੀਆ ਤੌਰ ਤੇ

steam (ਸਟੀਮ) *n v* ਭਾਫ਼, ਹਵਾੜ੍ਹ; ਭਾਫ਼ ਦੇਣੀ, ਭਾਫ਼ ਛੱਡਣੀ

steel (ਸਟੀਲ) *n v* ਫ਼ੌਲਾਦ, ਇਸਪਾਤ; ਤਕੜਾ ਕਰਨਾ; ~y ਫ਼ੌਲਾਦੀ, ਕਰੜਾ, ਬੰਜਰ, ਸਖ਼ਤ, ਬੇਦਰਦ

steep (ਸਟੀਪ) *v n a* ਭਿਉਣਾ, ਤਰ ਕਰਨਾ, ਡੋਬਾ ਦੇਣਾ; ਡੋਬਾ, ਢਲਾਨ (ਖੜ੍ਹਵੀਂ), ਦੰਦੀ; ਢਲਵਾਂ ~ness ਢਲਾਨ, ਢਲਵਾਂਪਣ, ਦੁਰਗਮਤਾ

steer (ਸਟਿਅ*) *n* ਕਿਸੇ ਖ਼ਾਸ ਦਸ਼ਾ ਵਿਚ ਚੱਲਣਾ,

(ਜਹਾਜ਼ ਨੂੰ) ਖੇਉਣਾ, ਚਲਾਉਣਾ ਵੱਢਾ, ਵਛੜਾ; ~sman ਵਾਹਕ, ਨਾਵਕ

stem (ਸਟੈੱਮ) *n v* ਤਣਾ, ਡੰਡੀ, ਸ਼ਬਦ-ਮੂਲ, ਧਾਤੂ; ਗਤੀ ਰੋਕਣਾ

stench (ਸਟੈਂਚ) *n* ਦੁਰਗੰਧ, ਸੜ੍ਹਾਂਦ, ਬਦਬੂ, ਹੁਮਕ

step ('ਸਟੈੱਪ) *v n pref* ਕਦਮ ਚੁੱਕਣਾ, ਹਿੱਲਣਾ; ਕਦਮ; (ਪੈਰ ਦਾ) ਖੜਾਕ ਪੈਰ-ਚਿੰਨ੍ਹ; ਚਾਲ ਦਾ ਢੰਗ; (ਦੂਜਿਆਂ ਨਾਲ) ਕਦਮ ਮਿਲਾ ਕੇ ਚੱਲਣਾ; ਤਦਬੀਰ, ਕਾਰਵਾਈ; ਇਕ ਅਗੇਤਰ, ਮਤਰੇਈ, ਮਤਰੇਆ ਦੇ ਅਰਥਾਂ ਵਿਚ; ~ping-stone ਪਤੁੱਲ, ਅੱਡਾ; ਲਾਂਘੇ ਦਾ ਪੱਥਰ; ਸਾਧਨ, ਵਸੀਲਾ; ~up ਅੱਗੇ ਆਉਣਾ, ਤੇਜ਼ ਕਰਨਾ, ਵਧਾਉਣਾ; ~child ਮਤਰੇਆ ਬੱਚਾ; ~daughter ਮਤਰੇਈ ਧੀ; ~son ਮਤਰੇਆ ਪੁਤਰ

stepney ('ਸਟੈੱਪਨਿ) *n* ਵਾਧੂ ਟਾਇਰ ਅਤੇ ਟਿਊਬ, ਵਾਧੂ ਪਹੀਆ

sterile ('ਸਟੈੱਰਾਇਲ) *a* ਬੰਜਰ, (ਜ਼ਮੀਨ); ਬਾਂਝ (ਜੀਵ)

sterility (ਸਟਅ'ਰਿਲਅਟਿ) *n* ਬਾਂਝਪਣ; ਅਫਲਤਾ

sterilize ('ਸਟੈੱਰਅਲਾਇਜ਼) *v* ਬਾਂਝ ਕਰਨਾ, ਜਰਮ ਰਹਿਤ ਕਰਨਾ

stern (ਸਟਅਃਨ) *a* ਕਰੜੀ, ਸਖ਼ਤ, ਤੁਰਸ਼, ਬੇਦਰਦ, ਕਠੋਰ, ਨਿਰਦਈ; ~ness ਨਿਰਦਇਤਾ, ਨਿਸ਼ਠੁਰਤਾ, ਕਠੋਰਤਾ, ਕਰੜਾਈ

steward ('ਸਟਯੂਅਃਡ) *n* ਮੁਖਤਾਰ ਜਾਇਦਾਦ; ਠੇਕੇਦਾਰ, ਭੰਡਾਰੀ, ਸੇਵਾਦਾਰ,

stick (ਸਟਿਕ) *v* ਚੋਭਣਾ; ਲੱਗਣਾ, ਲਗਾਉਣਾ (ਬੋਲ) ਰੱਖਣਾ, ਜੰਮਣਾ, ਜਮਾਉਣਾ; ਡੱਟ ਜਾਣਾ; ਚਿਪਕਣਾ, ਚਿਪਕਾਉਣਾ, ਲੱਗੇ ਰਹਿਣਾ; ਅਟਕ ਜਾਣਾ, ਅੜ ਜਾਣਾ; ਸੋਟੀ, ਡਾਂਗ, ਬੀਂਤ, ਡੰਡਾ;

(ਲਾਖ ਦੀ) ਬੱਤੀ; (ਡੋਬੀ ਦੀ) ਤੀਲੀ; ਫੋਸਤ; ~y ਲੇਸਲਾ, ਚਿਪਚਿਪਾ, ਪਿਚ-ਪਿਚ ਕਰਨਾ, ਚਿਕਣਾ

stiff (ਸਟਿਫ਼) a ਸਖ਼ਤ, ਕਰੜਾ, ਅੜੀਅਲ, ਅੱਖੜ, ਗਾੜ੍ਹਾ, ਸੰਘਣਾ; ~**necked** ਘਮੰਡੀ, ਆਕੜਖਾਨ, ਹੈਂਕੜਬਾਜ਼; ~**en** ਆਕੜ ਜਾਣਾ; ਕਠੋਰ ਬਣਾਉਣਾ, ਅੱਖੜ ਜਾਂ ਜ਼ਿੰਦੀ ਹੋਣਾ; ਗਾੜ੍ਹਾ ਕਰਨਾ

stifle (ਸਟਾਇਫ਼ਲ) v n ਕੁਚਲਣਾ, ਗਲਾ ਘੁੱਟਣਾ; ਪੱਠਾ

stigma (ਸਟਿਗਮਅ) n ਦਾਗ਼, ਕਲੰਕ; ~**tize** ਦਾਗ਼ ਲਾਉਣਾ, ਕਲੰਕਤ ਕਰਨਾ, ਬਦਨਾਮ ਕਰਨਾ

still a n v adv ਸ਼ਾਂਤ, ਅਹਿੱਲ, ਠਹਿਰਿਆ, ਬੰਦ; ਖੜਾ (ਪਾਣੀ); ਚੁੱਪ-ਚੁਪੀਤਾ, ਬੇਜਾਨ; ਖੜੀ ਫ਼ਿਲਮ ਜਾਂ ਤਸਵੀਰ; ਠੰਢਾ ਕਰਨਾ; ਉਸ ਵਕਤ ਤੀਕ, ਫਿਰ ਵੀ, ਬਾਵਜੂਦ ਇਸ ਦੇ; ~**born** ਮੁਰਦਾ ਬੱਚਾ; ~**room** ਸ਼ਰਾਬ ਕੱਢਣ ਦੀ ਥਾਂ

stimulate (ਸਟਿਮਯੂਲੇਇਟ) v ਉਤੇਜਕ ਕਰਨਾ, ਜੋਸ਼ ਦਿਵਾਉਣਾ, ਨਸ਼ਾ ਚਾੜ੍ਹਨਾ ਜਾਂ ਲਿਆਉਣਾ; ਉਤਾਰਨਾ, ਉਕਸਾਉਣਾ

stimulation (ਸਟਿਮਯੂ'ਲੇਇਸ਼ਨ) n ਉਤੇਜਨਾ, ਨਸ਼ਾ, ਉਕਸਾਹਟ, ਟੂੰਬ

stimulus ('ਸਟਿਮਯੁਲਅਸ) n ਉਤਸ਼ਾਹ, ਉਕਸਾਹਟ, ਟੂੰਬ

sting ('ਸਟਿੰਗ) n v ਡੰਗ; ਕੰਡਾ, ਕਸੀਰ; ਡੰਗ ਮਾਰਨ (ਬਿੱਛੂ ਜਾਂ ਸੱਪ ਦਾ); ਰੁੜਨਾ (ਸੂਲ ਦਾ); ਜਲਣ ਹੋਣੀ, ਦਰਦ ਕਰਨਾ, ਚੀਸ ਉਠਣੀ

stingy ('ਸਟਿੰਜਿ) a ਕੰਜੂਸ, ਲੀਚੜ

stink (ਸਟਿੰਕ) v n ਬੂ ਮਾਰਨਾ, ਚੁਕਣਾ, ਦੁਰਗੰਧ ਛੱਡਣਾ, ਸੜ੍ਹਿਆਂਧ ਮਾਰਨੀ; ਬਦਬੂ, ਦੁਰਗੰਧ,

ਸੜ੍ਹਿਆਂਧ

stint (ਸਟਿੰਟ) v n ਥੋੜ੍ਹਾ ਦੇਣਾ, ਕਸਰ ਰੱਖਣੀ, ਭੁੱਖਾ ਰੱਖਣਾ, ਹੱਥ ਘੁਟਣਾ, ਸੰਕੋਚ ਕਰਨਾ; ਕਸਰ, ਸੰਕੋਚ, ਕੰਜੂਸੀ

stipend ('ਸਟਾਇਪੈਂਡ) n ਵਜ਼ੀਫ਼ਾ, ਭੱਤਾ

stipulate ('ਸਟਿਪਯੁਲੇਇਟ) v ਸਮਝੌਤਾ ਕਰਨਾ ਜਾਂ ਸੌਦਾ ਕਰਨਾ, ਬੰਧੇਜ ਕਰਨਾ, ਸ਼ਰਤ ਕਰ ਲੈਣੀ, ਬਿਦਣਾ

stipulation ('ਸਟਿਪਯੁ'ਲੇਇਸ਼ਨ) n ਸ਼ਰਤ, ਇਕਰਾਰ-ਨਾਮਾ, ਬਾਂਧ, ਬੰਧਾਨ

stir (ਸਟਅਃ*) v n ਚਲਾਉਣਾ, ਹਿਲਾਉਣਾ, ਸਰਕਣਾ, ਹਰਕਤ ਕਰਨੀ, ਹਰਕਤ ਦੇਣੀ; ਅੰਦੋਲਨ ਕਰਨਾ; ਜਾਗਰਤੀ ਪੈਦਾ ਕਰਨੀ, ਪ੍ਰੇਰਨਾ ਦੇਣੀ, ਉਠਾਉਣਾ; ਉਕਸਾਉਣਾ, ਭੜਕਾਉਣਾ; ਉਤਸ਼ਾਹਤ ਕਰਨਾ, ਹਲਚਲ, ਗੜਬੜੀ, ਖਲਬਲੀ, ਹੰਗਾਮਾ; ਗਤੀ, ਹਰਕਤ

stitch (ਸਟਿਚ) n ਰੇਤ, ਹੋਕ, ਟਾਂਕਾ (ਫੱਟ ਦਾ); ਤੋਪਾ, ਤਰੋਪਾ, ਨਗੰਦਾ, ਬਖੀਆ; ਸਿਲਾਈ; ਟਾਂਕਾ ਲਗਾਉਣਾ, ਟਾਂਕਣਾ; ਤੋਪਾ ਮਾਰਨਾ; ~**ing** ਸਿਲਾਈ, ਸਿਉਣ

stock (ਸਟੋਕ) n ਜ਼ਖੀਰਾ; ਮਾਲ ਸਾਮਾਨ, ਕੱਚਾ ਮਾਲ; (ਸੰਦ ਦਾ) ਦਸਤਾ, ਮੁੱਠੀ, ਕੁੰਦਾ; ਸਟਾਕ, ਹੁੰਡੀ; (ਕੰਪਨੀ ਦੀ) ਸਾਂਝੀ ਪੂੰਜੀ, ਭੰਡਾਰ; ਮੂਲ ਧਨ; ~**broker** ਸਟਾਕ ਦਲਾਲ; ~**exchange** ਸਰਾਫ਼ਾ ਬਜ਼ਾਰ, ਸਟਾਕ ਐਕਸਚੇਂਜ

stocking ('ਸਟੋਕਿਙ) n ਵੱਡੀ ਜੁਰਾਬ; ਮਾਲ ਇੱਕਤਰ ਕਰਨ (ਦੀ ਕਿਰਿਆ)

stoke (ਸਟਅਉਇਕ) v (ਭੱਠੀ) ਝੋਕਣਾ; ਕੋਲੇ ਪਾਉਣੇ; (ਬੋਲ) ਜਲਦੀ ਜਲਦੀ ਖਾਣਾ ਨਿਗਲਣਾ

stomach ('ਸਟਅੱਮਅਕ) n ਪੇਟ, ਉਦਰ, ਢਿੱਡ; ਮਿਹਦਾ, ਓਝਰੀ, ਪੋਟਾ (ਪੰਛੀਆ ਦਾ); ਭੁੱਖ,

ਉਤਸ਼ਾਹ

stone (ਸਟਅਉਨ) *n a v* ਪੱਥਰ; ਹੀਰਾ; ਗੁਠਲੀ, ਗਿਟਕ; (ਅੰਗੂਰਾਂ ਦਾ) ਬੀਜ; ਗੜਾ; ਪੱਥਰ ਦਾ; ਪਥਰਾਉਣਾ; ਪੱਥਰਾਂ ਨਾਲ ਮਾਰਨਾ; ਗਿਟਕਾਂ ਕੱਢਣੀਆ; ਪੱਥਰ ਲਗਾਉਣੇ

stony ('ਸਟਅਉਨਿ) *a* ਪਥਰੀਲਾ, ਗਿਟਕ ਵਾਲਾ; ਕਰੜਾ

stool (ਸਟੂਲ) *n* (1) ਚੌਕੀ, ਸਟੂਲ, ਤਿਪਾਈ, ਪੀੜ੍ਹੀ; (2) ਖੁੱਡੀ; (3) ਟੱਟੀ, ਪਖ਼ਾਨਾ

stoop (ਸਟੂਪ) *v n* ਝੁਕਣਾ ਜਾਂ ਝੁਕਾਉਣਾ, ਕੋਡਾ ਹੋਣਾ ਜਾਂ ਕਰਨਾ, ਕੁੱਬਾ ਹੋਣਾ; ਝਪਟਣਾ, ਝਪਟਾ ਮਾਰਨਾ, ਟੁੱਟ ਪੈਣਾ; (1) ਝੁਕਾਅ; ਕੁੱਬ; (ਪ) ਬਾਜ਼ ਦਾ ਝਪਟਾ (2) ਘਰ ਦੇ ਸਾਹਮਣੇ ਦਾ ਖੁੱਲ੍ਹਾ ਚਬੂਤਰਾ

stop (ਸਟੋਪ) *n v* ਪ੍ਰਤੀਬੰਧ, ਵਿਰਾਮ, ਠਹਿਰਾਉ, ਅਟਕਾਉ, ਰੁਕਾਵਟ, ਅਟਕਣਾ, ਅਟਕਾਉਣਾ, ਠਹਿਰਨਾ, ਠਹਿਰਾਉਣਾ, ਟਿਕਣਾ, ਟਿਕਾਉਣਾ, ਬੱਸ ਕਰਨੀ, ਡੇਰਾ ਕਰਨਾ; ~**cock** ਟੂਟੀ; ~**gap** ਵੇਲਾ ਟਪਾਉ, ਕੰਮ ਟਪਾਉ; ~**press** ਤਾਜ਼ੀ ਖ਼ਬਰ, ਛਾਪਦਿਆਂ ਛਾਪਦਿਆਂ ਆਈ ਖ਼ਬਰ; ~**page** ਅਟਕਾਉ, ਠਹਿਰਾਉ, ਰੋਕ, ਅਟਕ; ਮੁਕਾਮ; ~**per** ਡੱਕਾ, ਡਾਟ, ਡੱਟ, ਗੱਟਾ, ਬੁੱਜਾ, ਰੋਕੂ, ਰੋਕ, ਅੜਾ

storage ('ਸਟੋਰਿਜ) *n* ਭੰਡਾਰ, ਗੁਦਾਮ; ਮਾਲ ਭਰਾਈ ਦਾ ਮਹਿਸੂਲ

store (ਸਟੋ*) *n v* ਜ਼ਖੀਰਾ, ਗੁਦਾਮ, ਭੰਡਾਰ; ਸੰਚਤ ਕਰਨਾ, ਜੋੜਨਾ, ਜ਼ਖ਼ੀਰਾ ਕਰਨਾ; ~**house** ਖਾਤਾ, ਕੋਠੀ, ਗੁਦਾਮ; ਖ਼ਜ਼ਾਨਾ; ~**keeper** ਮੋਦੀ, ਭੰਡਾਰੀ, ਦੁਕਾਨਦਾਰ

storey (ਸਟੋਰਿ) *n* ਮੰਜ਼ਲ, ਛੱਤ

stork (ਸਟੋਕ) *n* ਸਾਰਸ, ਲਕਲਕ, ਕਰੌਂਚ

storm (ਸਟੋਮ) *n v* ਝੱਖੜ, ਤੇਜ਼ ਹਨੇਰੀ, ਤੁਫ਼ਾਨ; ਧਮੱਚੜ, ਘੜੰਮਸ, ਹੁੱਲੜ; ਹਨੇਰੀ ਵਾਂਗ ਗਰਜਣਾ, ਡਾਂਟਣਾ; ਕਿਲ੍ਹੇ ਤੇ ਸਿੱਧਾ ਧਾਵਾ ਬੋਲ ਕੇ ਕਬਜ਼ੇ ਵਿਚ ਕਰ ਲੈਣਾ; ~**y** ਤੁਫ਼ਾਨੀ, ਝੱਖੜ ਵਾਲੀ (ਰੁੱਤ); ਕਰੋਪੂਰਨ, ਕਰੋਪੀ, ਤੇਜ਼, ਹੁੱਲੜੀ

story ('ਸਟੋਰਿ) *n* ਕਿੱਸਾ ਵਾਰਤਾ; ਕਹਾਣੀ; ਬਣਾਈ ਹੋਈ ਗੱਲ, ਗੱਪ; ~**teller** ਕਥਾਕਾਰ, ਕਹਾਣੀ-ਕਾਰ, ਕਹਾਣੀ-ਲੇਖਕ, ਵਾਰਤਾਕਾਰ

stout (ਸਟਾਉਟ) *a n* ਪੱਕਾ; ਵਫ਼ਾਦਾਰ ਮਜ਼ਬੂਤ, ਤਾਕਤਵਰ, ਮੁਸ਼ਟੰਡਾ; ਹੱਟਾ-ਕੱਟਾ

stove *n* ਚੁੱਲ੍ਹਾ, ਅੰਗੀਠੀ, ਗਰਮ-ਘਰ

straight ('ਸਟਰੇਇਟ) *a n adv* ਸਿੱਧਾ, ਟਿੱਕਵਾਂ (ਨਿਸ਼ਾਨਾ, ਵਾਰ, ਨਜ਼ਰ, ਤਰੀਕਾ ਆਦਿ); ਖਰਾ, ਬੇਲਾਗ (ਵਿਹਾਰ, ਹਿਸਾਬ); ਠੀਕ, ਹਮਵਾਰ, ਦਰੁਸਤ; ਠੀਕ ਤਰ੍ਹਾਂ; ~**forward** ਖਰਾ, ਸਪੱਸ਼ਟ, ਸੁਖਾਲਾ, ਸਿੱਧਾ; ~**way** ਅਚਾਨਕ ਹੀ, ਉਸੇ ਵੇਲੇ, ਉਸੇ ਵਕਤ, ਫ਼ੌਰਨ; ~**en** ਠੀਕ ਕਰਨਾ, ਦਰੁਸਤ ਕਰਨਾ, ਸੁਲਝਾਉਣਾ, ਸੁਲਝਣਾ, ਸਿੱਧਾ ਹੋਣਾ; ~**ness** ਸਿੱਧਾਪਣ, ਸਰਲਤਾ; ਸਚਾਈ, ਨਿਸ਼ਕਪਟਤਾ

strain (ਸਟਰੇਇਨ) *n* ਤਣਾਉ, ਖਿੱਚ; ਜ਼ੋਰ, ਦਬਾਅ; ਕੱਸਣਾ, ਤਣਨਾ, ਦੱਬਣਾ; ਖਿੱਚਣਾ; ਜ਼ੋਰ ਪਾਉਣਾ, ਜ਼ੋਰ ਖਾ ਜਾਣਾ, ਥਕਾ ਦੇਣਾ

strange (ਸਟਰੇਇੰਜ) *a* ਅਜੀਬ, ਅਦਭੁਤ, ਅਸਧਾਰਨ, ਨਿਰਾਲਾ, ਪਰਦੇਸੀ, ਓਪਰਾ, ਪਰਾਇਆ; ~**ness** ਅਨੋਖਾਪਨ, ਵਚਿੱਤਰਤਾ, ਨਿਰਾਲਾਪਨ, ਨਵਾਂਪਣ; ~**r** ਅਜਨਬੀ, ਪਰਦੇਸੀ, ਓਪਰਾ, ਪਰਾਇਆ, ਨਵਾਂ ਵਿਅਕਤੀ; ਅਨੁਭਵ-ਹੀਨ, ਅਲਗਾਣ, ਅਨਾੜੀ ਵਿਅਕਤੀ

strangle ('ਸਟਰੈਂਗਲ) *v* ਸੰਘੀ, ਘੁੱਟਣੀ, ਗਲਾ ਘੁੱਟ ਕੇ ਮਾਰ ਦੇਣਾ, ਗਲਾ ਘੋਟਣਾ

strangulate ('ਸਟਰੈਂਗਾਯੁਲੇਇਟ) *v* ਸੰਘੀ
ਘੁੱਟਣਾ, ਗਲਾ ਘੁੱਟਣਾ; ਦਬਾ ਕੇ ਲਹੂ ਦਾ
ਗੇੜ ਰੋਕਣਾ

strap (ਸਟਰੈਪ) *n v* ਚਮੜੇ ਦੀ ਪੇਟੀ, ਫ਼ੀਤਾ,
ਪੱਟਾ; ਕੱਸਣਾ, ਬੰਨ੍ਹਣਾ; ~**ping** ਰਿਸ਼ਟ-ਪੁਸ਼ਟ,
ਹੱਟਾ-ਕੱਟਾ, ਮੁਸ਼ੰਟਡਾ

strategic, ~**al** (ਸਟਰਾਅ'ਟੀਜਿਕ,
ਸਟਰਾਅ'ਟੀਜਿਕਲ) *a* ਜੁੱਧ-ਕਲਾ ਸਬੰਧੀ,
ਫ਼ੌਜੀ ਨੁਕਤਾ, ਜੁੱਧਨੀਤਕ

strategy ('ਸਟਰੈਟਿਜਿ) *n* ਕਾਰਜਨੀਤੀ, ਜੁੱਧ-ਨੀਤੀ

stratify ('ਸਟਰੈਟਿਫ਼ਾਇ) *v* ਪਰਤ ਤੇ ਪਰਤ
ਜਮਾਉਣੀ, ਤਹਿ ਤੇ ਤਹਿ ਜਮਾਉਣੀ; ਦਰਜਾਬੰਦੀ
ਕਰਨਾ

stratum ('ਸਟਰਾਟਅਮ) *n* ਤਹਿ, ਪਰਤ, ਤਬਕਾ;
ਸਤਰ, ਵਰਗ, ਸ਼੍ਰੇਣੀ

straw (ਸਟਰੋ) *n* ਤੁੜੀ, ਭੋਹ; ਕੱਖ, ਤੀਲਾ; ਪਰਾਲੀ,
ਨੀਰਾ

stray (ਸਟਰੇਇ) *v a n* ਭਟਕਦੇ ਫਿਰਨਾ, ਅਵਾਰਾ
ਫਿਰਨਾ, ਟੱਕਰਾਂ ਮਾਰਨੀਆਂ; ਭੁੱਲਿਆ-ਭਟਕਿਆ,
ਅਵਾਰਾ (ਪਸ਼ੂ); ਲਾਵਾਰਸ ਵਸਤੂ; ਅਵਾਰਾ
ਆਦਮੀ

streak (ਸਟਰੀਕ) *n v* ਧਾਰੀ, ਲੀਕ, (ਖ਼ਾਸ ਕਰ
ਰੰਗਦਾਰ); ਝਲਕਾਰਾ (ਬਿਜਲੀ ਦਾ); ਧਾਰੀਆਂ
ਪਾਉਣੀਆਂ; ~**y** ਧਾਰੀਦਾਰ; ਘਰਾਲੀ

stream (ਸਟਰੀਮ) *n v* ਨਦੀ, ਛੋਟੀ ਨਹਿਰ,
ਨਾਲਾ, ਧਾਰਾ, ਸਰੋਤ, ਪਰਵਾਹ, ਲੋਕਾਂ ਦੀ ਵਧਦੀ
ਭੀੜ; ਵਹਿਣਾ ਜਾਂ ਵਗਣਾ

street (ਸਟਰੀਟ) *n* ਸਰਵਜਨਕ ਰਸਤਾ; ਗਲੀ,
ਸੜਕ, ਨਗਰ-ਮਾਰਗਾ

strength ('ਸਟਰੈਂਥ) *n* ਤਾਕਤ, ਜ਼ੋਰ, ਬਲ
ਮਜ਼ਬੂਤੀ, ਤਕੜਾਈ, ਪਕਿਆਈ; ~**en** ਤਕੜਾ

ਕਰਨਾ ਜਾਂ ਹੋਣਾ; ~**ening** ਮਜ਼ਬੂਤ ਬਣਾਉਣ
ਵਾਲਾ, ਬਲਕਾਰੀ, ਸ਼ਕਤੀਦਾਇਕ

strenuous ('ਸਟਰੈਨਯੁਅਸ) *a* ਕਠਨ, ਕਰੜਾ,
(ਜਤਨ), ਜਾਨਮਾਰ

stress (ਸਟਰੈੱਸ) *n v* ਭਾਰ, ਦਬਾਉ, ਤਣਾਉ,
ਖਿਚਾਉ; ਜ਼ੋਰ ਦੇਣਾ, ਮੰਹਤਵ ਪ੍ਰਦਾਨ ਕਰਨਾ

stretch (ਸਟੈਰੱਚ) *v n* ਖਿੱਚ ਕੇ ਸਿੱਧਾ ਕਰਨਾ,
ਤਾਣਨਾ, ਪਸਾਰਨਾ, ਫੈਲਾਉਣਾ, ਫੈਲਣਾ, ਖਿੱਚਣਾ;
ਖਿਲਾਰ, ਲਮਕਾਅ; ~**er** ਵਿਸਤਾਰਕ, ਫੈਲਾਉਣ
ਵਾਲਾ, ਕੱਸਣ ਵਾਲਾ, ਸਟਰੈੱਚਰ

strew (ਸਟਰੂ) *v* ਛਿੜਕਣਾ (ਰੇਤ ਆਦਿ); ਬਖੇਰਨਾ

stricken ('ਸਟਰਿਕਨ) *a* ਮਾਰਿਆ, ਘਾਇਲ
ਪੀੜਤ

strict (ਸਟਰਿਕਟ) *a* ਕੜੀ, ਬਾਜ਼ਾਬਤਾ, ਸਖ਼ਤ,
ਕਠੋਰ (ਨਿਗਰਾਨੀ); ਕਰੜਾ, ਜ਼ਬਤੀ; ~**ly**
ਬਿਲਕੁਲ, ਠੀਕ ਠੀਕ; ~**ly speaking** ਠੀਕ
ਠੀਕ ਅਰਥਾਂ ਵਿਚ, ਸੱਚ ਪੁੱਛੋ ਤਾਂ, **ਵਾਸਤਵ**
ਵਿਚ, ਅਸਲ ਵਿਚ, ਪੱਕੇ ਤੌਰ ਤੇ; ~**ness**
ਨਿਸ਼ਚਤਤਾ, ਸਖ਼ਿਰਤਾ, ਦ੍ਰਿੜ੍ਹਤਾ, **ਕਠੋਰਤਾ,**
ਕਰੜਾਈ, ਸਖ਼ਤੀ

stricture ('ਸਟਰਿਕਚਅ*) *n* ਕਰੜੀ ਨੁਕਤਾਚੀਨੀ,
ਟੀਕਾ-ਟਿੱਪਣੀ; ਨਾੜੀ ਦਾ ਸੁੰਗੜਾਉ

stride (ਸਟਰਾਇਡ) *v n* ਲੰਮੇ ਕਦਮ ਰੱਖਣਾ,
ਉਲਾਂਘਣ, ਉਲਾਂਘ ਭਰਨੀ, ਡਗ ਭਰਨਾ; ਟੱਪ
ਜਾਣਾ, ਉਲਾਂਘ; ਕਦਮ

strident ('ਸਟਰਾਇਡੰਟ) *a* ਕਰਖ਼ਤ, ਕੜਕਵੀਂ

strife (ਸਟਰਾਇਫ਼) *n* ਲੜਾਈ-ਭਿੜਾਈ, ਝੇੜਾ,
ਬਖੇੜਾ, ਝੰਜਟ, ਵਿਵਾਦ, ਕਲਹ

strike ('ਸਟਰਾਇਕ) *v n* ਮਾਰਨਾ, ਵਾਰ ਕਰਨਾ,
ਧਿਆਨ ਖਿੱਚਣਾ; ਖ਼ਿਆਲ ਆਉਣਾ; ਸੁੱਝਣਾ;
ਪੁੱਟਣਾ; ਹਾਰ ਮੰਨਣਾ, ਹਥਿਆਰ ਸੁੱਟਣਾ;

(ਮਜ਼ਦੂਰਾਂ ਦਾ) ਹੜਤਾਲ ਕਰਨ; ਕੰਮ ਛੱਡ ਦੇਣ; (ਘੰਟਾ) ਵਜਾਉਣਾ; (ਚਾਕੂ ਆਦਿ) ਖੋਭਣਾ; ਹੜਤਾਲ; ਹਮਲਾ, ਹਵਾਈ ਹਮਲਾ

striking ('ਸਟਰਾਇਕਿਡ੍ਹ) *a* ਚਮਤਕਾਰੀ, ਉੱਘੜਵਾਂ

string ('ਸਟਰਿੱਡ੍ਹ) *n v* ਡੋਰੀ, ਸੂਤਲੀ, ਧਾਗਾ, ਤੰਦ, ਤਣੀ; ਤਾਰ, ਤੰਦੀ, ਲੜੀ ਪਰੋਣਾ; ਛਿੱਲਣਾ; ਧਾਗੇ ਕੱਢਣੇ

stringency ('ਸਟਰਿਨਜਾਅੰਸਿ) *n* ਸਖ਼ਤੀ, ਕਠੋਰਤਾ, ਕਰੜਾਪਨ; ਦਰਿਦ੍ਰਤਾ

stringent ('ਸਟਰਿਨਜਾਅੰਟ) *a* ਸਖ਼ਤ, ਕਰੜਾ (ਨੇਮ, ਪਾਬੰਦੀ), ਤੰਗ ਹਾਲ

strip (ਸਟਰਿਪ) *v* ਨੰਗਾ ਕਰਨਾ, ਕੱਪੜੇ ਉਛਾੜ ਆਦਿ ਲਾਹੁਣੇ; (ਦਰਖ਼ਤ ਦੀ) ਛਾਲ ਲਾਹੁਣੀ; ਸੰਖਣਾ ਕਰਨਾ, ਵਾਂਝਿਆਂ ਕਰਨਾ; ਲੈ ਲੈਣਾ

stripe (ਸਟਰਾਇਪ) *n* ਚੌੜੀ ਧਾਰੀ, ਫਾਂਟ, ਪੱਟੀ; (ਪ੍ਰ) ਚਾਬਕ ਦੀ ਮਾਰ; (ਬ ਵ) ਬੈਂਤ ਦੀ ਸਜ਼ਾ; **~d** ਧਾਰੀਦਾਰ, ਪੱਟੀਦਾਰ, ਲਹਿਰੀਏ ਵਾਲਾ

strive (ਸਟਰਾਇਵ੍ਹ) *v* ਜਤਨ ਕਰਨਾ, ਘਾਲਣਾ; ਜ਼ੋਰ ਲਾਉਣਾ ਜਾਂ ਮਾਰਨਾ, ਵਾਹ ਲਾਉਣੀ; ਸੰਘਰਸ਼ ਕਰਨਾ, ਟਾਕਰਾ ਕਰਨਾ, ਭਿੜਨਾ

stroke (ਸਟਰਅਉਕ) *n v* ਥਪਕੀ, ਥਾਪੜੀ, ਟਕੋਰਾ; ਵਾਰ, ਚੋਟ, ਮਾਰ, ਹੱਲਾ; ਥਾਪੜੀ ਦੇਣੀ, ਥਪਕੀ ਮਾਰਨੀ, ਥਾਪੜਨਾ

stroll (ਸਟਰੋਲ੍ਹ) *v n* ਸੈਰ ਕਰਨਾ, ਟਹਿਲਣਾ, ਇੱਧਰ-ਉੱਧਰ ਘੁੰਮਣਾ, ਮਟਰ-ਗਸ਼ਤ ਕਰਨੀ; ਚਹਿਲ-ਕਦਮੀ, ਸੈਰ, ਹਵਾਖੋਰੀ; **~er** ਘੁਮੱਕੜ, ਟਹਿਲਣ ਵਾਲਾ, ਮਟਰ-ਗਸ਼ਤ ਕਰਨ ਵਾਲਾ

strong (ਸਟਰੌਡ੍ਹ) *a* ਰਿਸ਼ਟ-ਪੁਸ਼ਟ, ਤਾਕਤਵਰ, ਬਲਵਾਨ, ਤਕੜਾ; ਮਜ਼ਬੂਤ, ਪੱਕਾ; **~box,** **room** ਤਿਜੌਰੀ, ਤਹਿਖ਼ਾਨਾ; **~hold** ਗੜ੍ਹ, ਕੋਟ, ਕਿਲ੍ਹਾ

structure ('ਸਟਰਅੱਕਚਾ*) *n* ਬਣਾਵਟ, ਬਣਤਰ, ਬਣਤ, ਰਚਨਾ

struggle ('ਸਟਰਅੱਗਲ) *v n* (ਘੁੱਟਣ ਲਈ) ਸਖ਼ਤ ਕੋਸ਼ਸ਼ ਕਰਨਾ, ਹੱਥ-ਪੈਰ ਮਾਰਨੇ; ਵਾਹ ਲਾਉਣੀ, ਜ਼ੋਰ ਮਾਰਨਾ, ਜਾਂ ਲਾਉਣਾ; (ਵਿਰੋਧੀ ਨਾਲ) ਸੰਘਰਸ਼ ਕਰਨਾ, ਕਸ਼ਮਕਸ਼ ਕਰਨਾ; ਟਿੱਲ, ਜ਼ੋਰ, ਸੰਘਰਸ਼, ਦੰਦ-ਭੰਜ, ਜਦੋਜਹਿਦ

strumpet ('ਸਟਰਅੱਪਿਟ) *n* ਵੇਸਵਾ, ਰੰਡੀ, ਕਸਬਣ

stubborn ('ਸਟਅੱਬਅਨ) *a* ਹਠੀ, ਜ਼ਿੱਦੀ, ਹਠੀਲਾ, ਅੜੀਅਲ, ਕਰੜਾ, ਸਖ਼ਤ; ਸਿਰੜੀ; **~ness** ਹਠ, ਦ੍ਰਿੜ੍ਹਤਾ, ਕੱਟੜਤਾ, ਕਠੋਰਤਾ, ਜ਼ਿੱਦ, ਅੜੀ

stud (ਸਟਅੱਡ) *n v* ਕੋਕਾ, ਕਿੱਲ, (ਸਜਾਵਟ ਲਈ) ਫੁੱਲਦਾਰ ਕਿੱਲ; ਬੁਧੀਆਂ ਜੜਨੀਆਂ; ਸਟੱਡ ਲਗਾਉਣਾ

student ('ਸਟਯੂਡਅੰਟ) *n* ਵਿਦਿਆਰਥੀ, ਛਾਤਰ, ਸਿਖਿਆਰਥੀ, ਚੇਲਾ, ਸ਼ਾਗਿਰਦ

studio ('ਸਟਯੂਡ੍ਹਿਅਉ) *n* ਕਲਾ-ਮੰਦਰ, ਚਿੱਤਰਸ਼ਾਲਾ, ਸਟੂਡੀਓ; ਸਿਨੇਮਾ ਸਟੂਡੀਓ

studious ('ਸਟਯੂਡ੍ਹਯਅਸ) *a* ਮਿਹਨਤੀ, ਪੜ੍ਹਾਕੂ; ਉਤਸ਼ਾਹੀ, ਤਤਪਰ, ਉਤਸ਼ਾਹ-ਪੂਰਨ

study ('ਸਟਅੱਡਿ) ਪੜ੍ਹਾਈ, ਪਾਠ; ਅਭਿਆਸ, ਪੜ੍ਹਾਈ ਕਰਨੀ; ਸਬਕ ਯਾਦ ਕਰਨਾ; ਘੋਖਣਾ, ਤਾੜ ਵਿਚ ਰਹਿਣਾ; ਚਿੰਤਨ ਕਰਨਾ

stuff (ਸਟਅੱਫ) *n v* ਪਦਾਰਥ, ਵਸਤੂ, ਮੂਲ, ਧਾਤੂ ਤੱਤ, ਜਿਨਸ, ਕੱਚਾ ਮਾਲ; ਫ਼ਜ਼ੂਲ ਗੱਲ; ਹਾਬੜ ਕੇ ਖਾਣਾ; ਝੂਠ ਬੋਲ ਕੇ ਧੋਖਾ ਦੇਣਾ, ਛਲਣਾ; **~y** ਵੱਟ ਵਾਲਾ, ਹੁੰਮਸੀ, ਸਾਹ-ਘੋਟੂ, ਨਾਰਾਜ਼, ਗੁੱਸਿਆ

stumble (ਸਟਅੱਮਬਲ) *v n* ਠੋਕਰ ਖਾਣਾ, ਠੇਡਾ ਖਾਣਾ; ਚੁੱਕ ਜਾਣਾ; ਦੁਬਧਾ ਵਿਚ ਪੈਣਾ; ਠੋਕਰ,

ਠੂੰਡਾ, ਭਾਰੀ ਭੁੱਲ

stump (ਸਟਅੱਪ) *n v* ਕ੍ਰਿਕਟ ਦੀਆਂ ਤਿੰਨ
ਡੰਡੀਆਂ ਵਿਚੋਂ ਇਕ; ਮੁੱਢ, ਖੁੱਢ; ਟੁੱਟੇ ਹੋਏ ਦੰਦ
ਦੀ ਜੜ੍ਹ; ਹੱਥ ਜਾਂ ਪੈਰ ਦਾ ਟੁੰਡ, ਡੂੰਡ; ਸਿਗਾਰ
ਦਾ ਟੋਟਾ; (ਕ੍ਰਿਕਟ) ਵਿਕਟ ਆਉਟ ਕਰਨਾ;
ਵਿਕਟ-ਕੀਪਰ (ਬੋਲ); ਮੁਤਾਲਬਾ ਪੂਰਾ ਕਰਨਾ,
ਮੰਗ ਪੂਰੀ ਕਰਨੀ

stun (ਸਟਅੱਨ) *v* ਬੇਹੋਸ਼ ਕਰ ਦੇਣਾ, ਹੋਸ਼
ਗੁਆਉਣੇ, ਚਕਰਾ ਦੇਣਾ, ਸੁਰਤ ਭੁਲਾ ਦੇਣੀ;
~**ning** ਹੋਸ਼-ਗੁਆਉਂ; ਸ਼ਾਨਦਾਰ, ਚਮਤਕਾਰੀ

stunt (ਸਟਅੰਟ) *v n* ਵਿਕਾਸ ਰੋਕਣਾ; ਉੱਨਤੀ
ਰੋਕ ਦੇਣੀ; ਇਸ਼ਤਿਹਾਰਬਾਜ਼ੀ, ਉਸ਼ਟੰਡ, ਸ਼ੋਸ਼ਾ

stupendous (ਸਟਯੂੰਪੈਂਡਅਸ) *a*
ਅਸਚਰਜਮਈ, ਬਹੁਤ ਵੱਡਾ, ਬਹੁਤ ਭਾਰੀ,
ਸ਼ਾਨਦਾਰ; ਜ਼ਬਰਦਸਤ (ਕੰਮ, ਭੁੱਲ)

stupid (ਸਟਯੂਪਿਡ) *a* ਬੇਵਕੂਫ਼ (ਆਦਮੀ), ਮੂਰਖ
(ਵਿਅਕਤੀ), ਮੂੜ੍ਹ (ਮਨੁੱਖ); ਬੁੱਧ, ਨਿਰਬੁੱਧ,
ਪਗਲਾ, ਖਰ-ਦਿਮਾਗ਼ਾ, ਉਜੱਡ;~**ity** ਮੂਰਖਤਾ,
ਬੇਵਕੂਫ਼ੀ, ਉਤਪੁਟਾ, ਉੱਜਡਪੁਟਾ

sturdy (ਸਟਅਃਡਿ) *a* ਮਜ਼ਬੂਤ, ਤਕੜਾ, ਕਾਠਾ,
ਹੱਟਾ-ਕੱਟਾ

stutter (ਸਟਅੱਟਅˇ) *v n* ਥਥਲਾਉਣਾ,
ਥਥਿਆਉਣਾ, ਥਥਲਾ ਕੇ ਬੋਲਣਾ, ਅਟਕ ਅਟਕ
ਕੇ ਬੋਲਣਾ; ਥਥਲਾਹਟ, ਥੱਥ

style (ਸਟਾਇਲ) *n* ਸ਼ੈਲੀ, ਢੰਗ, ਪੱਧਤੀ, ਰੀਤੀ,
ਤਰਜ਼; ਵਿਸ਼ੇਸ਼ਤਾਵਾਂ; ਚੰਗਿਆਈਆਂ; ਠਾਠ

stylish (ਸਟਾਇਲਿਸ਼) *a* ਛਬੀਲਾ, ਲੱਛੇਦਾਰ,
ਫ਼ੈਸ਼ਨਦਾਰ

suave (ਸਵਾਵ੍) *a* ਮਧੁਰ, ਸੁਹਾਵਾ, ਨਰਮ,
ਮਿੱਠਾ, ਸੁਆਦੀ, ਮਿੱਠਬੋਲੜਾ

sub (ਸਅੱਬ) *prep pref* ਹੇਠਾਂ, ਥੱਲੇ, ਅਧੀਨ;

ਨਿਚਲਾ, ਉਪ, ਲਘੁ, ਛੋਟਾ; ~**class**
ਉਪਵਰਗ; ~**conscious** ਅਵਚੇਤਨ

subdue (ਸਅੱਬ'ਡਯੂ) *v* ਵੱਸ ਕਰਨਾ, ਕਾਬੂ
ਕਰਨਾ, ਅਧੀਨ ਕਰਨਾ, ਦਬਾ ਲੈਣਾ; ਜਿੱਤ ਲੈਣਾ,
ਹਲਕਾ ਕਰਨਾ, ਘੱਟ ਕਰਨਾ

subject ('ਸਅੱਬਜੈਕਟ) *a n v* ਅਧੀਨ; ਪਰਜਾ;
ਰਈਅਤ; ਮਜ਼ਮੂਨ, ਵਿਸ਼ਾ, ਪ੍ਰਕਰਣ; (ਵਿਆ)
ਕਰਤਾ; ਅਧੀਨ ਕਰਨਾ, ਹੇਠ ਕਰਨਾ, ਵਸ਼ੀਕਾਰ
ਕਰਨਾ, (ਠੰਢੇ, ਮਘੌਲ ਦਾ) ਵਿਸ਼ਾ ਬਣਾਉਣਾ,
ਨਿਸ਼ਾਨਾ ਬਣਾਉਣਾ; ~**ion** ਅਧੀਨਤਾ, ਦਾਸਤਾ,
ਵਸ਼ੀਕਰਨ; ~**ive** (ਦਰਸ਼) ਅੰਤਰਮੁਖੀ;
ਕਾਲਪਨਕ, ਖ਼ਿਆਲੀ; ਕਰਤਾ; ~**ive case**
ਕਰਤਾ ਕਾਰਕ; ~**ivity** ਆਤਮਨਿਸ਼ਠਤਾ,
ਅੰਤਰਮੁੱਖਤਾ

sub-judice ('ਸਅੱਬ'ਜੁਡਿਸ) (*L*) *a* ਪੇਸ਼
ਅਦਾਲਤ, ਵਿਚਾਰ ਅਧੀਨ, ਨਿਆਇ ਅਧੀਨ

subjugate (ਸਅੱਬਜੁਗੇਇਟ) *v* ਵੱਸ ਵਿਚ
ਕਰਨਾ, ਅਧੀਨ ਕਰਨਾ, ਜਿੱਤ ਲੈਣਾ, ਕਾਬੂ ਵਿਚ
ਕਰਨਾ, ਦਬਾ ਲੈਣਾ, ਦਮਨ ਕਰਨਾ

subjugation ('ਸਅੱਬਜੁˇ'ਗੋਇਸ਼ਨ) *a* ਵਸ਼ੀਕਰਨ,
ਅਧੀਨਤਾ, ਦਮਨ, ਦਬਾਉ, ਤਾਬੇਦਾਰੀ

sublimation ('ਸਅੱਬਲਿ'ਮੇਇਸ਼ਨ) *n* ਜੌਹਰ-
ਉਡਾਈ; ਸੁਧਤਾਈ, ਉਚਿਆਉਣ

sublime (ਸਅ'ਬਲਾਇਮ) *a v* ਉਦਾਤ,
ਸ਼ਿਰੋਮਣੀ, ਗੌਰਵਮਈ, ਸ਼ਾਨਦਾਰ, ਜੌਹਰ
ਉਡਾਉਣਾ, ਉੱਪਰ ਚੁੱਕਣਾ; ਮਹਾਨ ਜਾਂ
ਪ੍ਰਭਾਵਸ਼ਾਲੀ ਬਣਾਉਣਾ

sublimity (ਸਅ'ਬਲਿਮਅਟਿ) *n* ਮਹਾਨਤਾ,
ਪ੍ਰਭਾਵਸ਼ੀਲਤਾ, ਗੌਰਵਤਾ, ਉੱਚਤਾ; ਉਦਾਤਤਾ

submarine (ਸਅੱਬਮੈਰਿਨ) *n* ਜਲਵਰਤੀ,
ਡੁਬਕਣੀ, ਪਣ ਡੁਬਕੀ

submerge (ਸਅਬ'ਮਅਃਜ) *v* ਪਾਣੀ ਵਿਚ ਡੋਬਣਾ ਜਾਂ ਡੁੱਬਣਾ, ਗਰਕ ਕਰਨਾ ਜਾਂ ਹੋਣਾ; ~nce ਡੋਬ, ਡੋਬਾ, ਡੁਬਕੀ, ਜਲ-ਪਰਵਾਹ; ਗੋਤਾ

submission (ਸਅਬ'ਮਿਸ਼ਨ) *n* ਅਧੀਨਗੀ, ਤਾਬੇਦਾਰੀ; (ਕਾ) ਬੇਨਤੀ

submissive (ਸਅਬ'ਮਿਸਿਵ਼) *a* ਆਗਿਆਪਾਲ, ਆਗਿਆਕਾਰ, ਤਾਬੇਦਾਰ, ਦੀਨ, ਸੁਸ਼ੀਲ; ਨਿਮਰ, ਹੁਕਮਬਰਦਾਰ

submit (ਸਅਬ'ਮਿਟ) *v* ਹਵਾਲੇ ਕਰਨਾ, ਸ਼ਰਨ ਲੈਣਾ, ਅਧੀਨ ਹੋਣਾ, ਪੇਸ਼ ਕਰਨਾ; ਅੱਗੇ ਰੱਖਣਾ ਬੇਨਤੀ ਕਰਨਾ; ਝੁਕ ਜਾਣਾ, ਮੰਨ ਲੈਣਾ

subordinate (ਸਅਬ਼ਾ*ਡਇਨੇਟ) *a n v* ਅਧੀਨ, ਸਹਾਇਕ, ਮਾਤਹਿਤ; ਹੇਠਲਾ, ਅਧੀਨ ਵਿਅਕਤੀ; ਮਾਤਹਿਤ ਬਣਾਉਣਾ

subordination (ਸਅਬ਼ਾ*ਡਇਨੇਸ਼ਨ) *n* ਅਧੀਨਗੀ, ਮਾਤਹਿਤੀ

subscribe (ਸਅਬ'ਸਕਰਾਇਬ) *v* ਹਾਮੀ ਭਰਨੀ, ਤਾਈਦ ਕਰਨੀ; ਚੰਦਾ ਦੇਣਾ, ਗਾਹਕ ਬਣਨਾ; ~r ਸਹੀਕਾਰ; ਗਾਹਕ, ਚੰਦਾ ਦੇਣ ਵਾਲਾ

subscript (ʼਸਅੱਬਸਕਰਿਪਟ) *a* ਹੇਠ ਲਿਖਿਆ, ਨਿਮਨਲਿਖਤ; ~ion ਚੰਦਾ, ਦਾਨ; ਮੁੱਲ, ਕੀਮਤ, ਨਾਮ ਲੇਖਨ

subsequence (ʼਸਅੱਬਸਿਕਵਅੰਸ) *n* ਉੱਤਰਵਰਤਾ, ਪਰਿਣਾਮ

subsequent (ʼਸਅੱਬਸਿਕਵਅੰਟ) *a* ਉੱਤਰਵਰਤੀ, ਉੱਤਰਕਾਲੀਨ, ਆਗਾਮੀ, ਅਗਲਾ, ਪਿੱਛੋਂ ਦਾ; ~ly ਬਾਅਦ, ਵਿਚ, ਪਿੱਛੋਂ

subservient (ਸਅਬ'ਸਅਃਵ਼ਿਅੰਟ) *a* ਉਪਯੋਗੀ, ਕਾਰਕ ਸਹਾਇਕ, ਹੱਥ-ਠੇਕਾ

subside (ਸਅਬ'ਸਾਇਡ) *v* (ਪਾਣੀ) ਉੱਤਰ ਜਾਣਾ, ਬੱਲੇ ਆ ਜਾਣਾ, ਘਟ ਜਾਣਾ, ਗਾਇਬ ਹੋ ਜਾਣਾ

subsidiary (ਸਬਹਾ'ਸਿਡਯਅਰਿ) *a n* ਸਹਾਇਕ, ਅਧੀਨ, ਉਪਸੰਗੀ; ਮਾਤਹਿਤ

subsidize (ʼਸਅੱਬਸਿਡਾਇਜ਼) *v* ਮਾਲੀ ਸਹਾਇਤਾ ਕਰਨੀ, ਅਰਥ-ਸਹਾਇਤਾ ਦੇਣੀ

subsidy (ʼਸਅੱਬਸਿਡਿ) *n* ਆਰਥਕ ਸਹਾਇਤਾ, ਇਮਦਾਦੀ ਰਕਮ; ਅਨੁਦਾਨ

subsist (ਸਅਬ'ਸਿਸਟ) *v* ਜੀਉਂਦੇ ਰਹਿਣਾ, ਰਹਿਣਾ, ਟਿਕਣਾ; ਖੁਆਉਣਾ-ਪਿਆਉਣਾ, ਜੀਵਨ-ਨਿਰਬਾਹ ਕਰਨਾ, ਜ਼ਿੰਦਾ ਰਹਿਣਾ, ਜੀਊਣਾ; ~ence ਉਪਜੀਵਕਾ, ਜੀਵਨ-ਨਿਰਬਾਹ, ਰੋਜ਼ੀ, ਗੁਜ਼ਾਰਾ

substance (ʼਸਅੱਬਸਟਅੰਸ) *n* ਸਾਰ, ਸਾਰਾਂਸ਼, ਭਾਵ, ਨਚੋੜ; ਅਸਲੀ ਮਤਲਬ; ਵਿਸ਼ਾ-ਵਸਤੂ; ਵਾਸਤਵਿਕਤਾ

substandard (ʼਸਅੱਬ'ਸਟੈਂਡਅਃਡ) *a* ਮਿਆਰ ਤੋਂ ਡਿੱਗਿਆ, ਘਟਿਆ

substantial (ਸਅਬ'ਲਟੈਨਸ਼ਲ) *a n* ਮਹੱਤਪੂਰਨ, ਠੋਸ, ਨਿੱਗਰ; ਵਾਸਤਵਿਕ, ਧਨਵਾਨ, (ਬ ਵ) ਮਹੱਤਵਪੂਰਨ ਅੰਗ; ~ity ਵਾਸਤਵਿਕਤਾ, ਯਥਾਰਥਕਤਾ, ਸਾਰ, ਸਚਾਈ; ਮੱਹਤਵਪੂਰਨਤਾ; ~ly ਉਚਿਤ ਰੂਪ ਵਿਚ

substantiate (ਸਅਬ'ਸਟੈਂਸ਼ਿਏਇਟ) *v* ਸਚਾਈ ਸਿੱਧ ਕਰਨਾ, ਸਾਬਤ ਕਰਨਾ, ਸਬੂਤ ਦੇਣਾ, ਪ੍ਰਮਾਣ ਦੇਣਾ

substantive (ʼਸਅੱਬਸਟਅੰਟਿਵ਼) *a n* ਸੁਤੰਤਰ, ਵਾਸਤਵਿਕ, ਮੌਲਕ, ਅਸਲੀ

substitute (ʼਸਅੱਬਸਟਿਟਯੂਟ) *n v* ਇਵਜ਼, ਬਦਲ, ਪ੍ਰਤੀਸ਼ਾਪਨ; ਬਦਲ ਕੇ ਰੱਖਣਾ, ਵਟਾ ਕੇ ਰੱਖਣਾ; ਅਦਲਾ-ਬਦਲੀ ਕਰਨੀ

substiution (ʼਸਅੱਬਸਟਿʼਟਯੂਸ਼ਨ) *n* ਅਦਲਾ-ਬਦਲੀ, ਬਦਲੀ, ਪ੍ਰਤੀਸ਼ਾਪਨ

substratum ('ਸੱਬਾਬ'ਸਟਰਾਟਅਮ) *n* ਆਧਾਰ, ਨੀਂਹ; ਨਿਮਨ ਵਰਗ

subterranean ('ਸੱਬਟਅਾ'ਰੇਇਨਯਅਨ) *a* ਥੱਲੇ ਦਾ, ਜ਼ਮੀਨ ਦੇ ਹੇਠਾਂ ਦਾ, ਭੂਮੀਗਤ

subtle ('ਸੱਟਲ) *a* ਸੂਖਮ; ਪਤਲਾ, ਵਿਰਲਾ, ਲਤੀਫ, ਰਹੱਸਮਈ, ਬਾਰੀਕ; ਤੀਬਰ; ਮੱਕਾਰ; **~ty** ਵਿਰਲਤਾ; ਸੂਖਮਤਾ; ਤੀਖਣਤਾ

subtract (ਸਅਬ'ਟਰੈਕਟ) *v* ਘਟਾਉਣਾ, ਤਫ਼ਰੀਕ ਕਰਨਾ, ਮਨਫ਼ੀ ਕਰਨਾ, ਕੱਢਣਾ; **~ion** ਘਟਾਉ, ਤਫ਼ਰੀਕ, ਮਨਫ਼ੀ; **~or** ਘਟਾਉਣ ਵਾਲਾ, ਤਫ਼ਰੀਕ ਕਰਨ ਵਾਲਾ, ਕੱਢਣ ਵਾਲਾ

suburb ('ਸੱਬਅਃਬ) *n* ਸ਼ਹਿਰ ਦੇ ਆਸ-ਪਾਸ ਦਾ ਇਲਾਕਾ, ਸ਼ਹਿਰ ਦਾ ਚੁਗਿਰਦਾ, ਉਪ-ਨਗਰ; **~an** ਆਲੇ-ਦੁਆਲੇ ਸਬੰਧੀ; ਉਪ-ਨਗਰ ਸਬੰਧੀ

subvent (ਸੱਬ'ਵੈਂਟ) *v* ਸਹਾਇਤਾ ਕਰਨਾ, ਮਾਲੀ ਸਹਾਇਤਾ ਕਰਨਾ, ਪਰਮਾਰਥ ਸਹਾਇਤਾ ਦੇਣੀ

subversion (ਸਅਬ'ਵਅਃਸ਼ਨ) *n* ਉਲਟ-ਪੁਲਟ, ਭੰਨ-ਤੋੜ, ਵਿਨਾਸ਼, ਉਲਟ-ਫੇਰ

subvert (ਸਅਬ'ਵਅਃਟ) *v* ਉਲਟ-ਪੁਲਟ ਦੇਣਾ, ਨਸ਼ਟ ਕਰਨਾ, ਸਤਿਆਨਾਸ ਕਰਨਾ; ਵਿਗਾੜਨਾ ਖ਼ਰਾਬ ਕਰਨਾ

subway ('ਸੱਬਵੇਇ) *n* ਭੂਮੀ ਥੱਲੇ ਦਾ ਮਾਰਗ

succeed (ਸਅਕ'ਸੀਡ) *v* ਸਫਲ ਹੋਣਾ, ਮਨੋਰਥ ਪੂਰਾ ਹੋਣਾ; (ਕਿਸੇ ਦੀ) ਥਾਂ ਲੈਣੀ; ਉੱਤਰਾਧਿਕਾਰੀ ਹੋਣਾ, ਗੱਦੀ ਤੇ ਬਹਿਣਾ, ਜਾਨਸ਼ੀਨ ਹੋਣਾ; **~ing** ਆਗਾਮੀ; ਉੱਤਰਵਰਤੀ

success (ਸਅਕ'ਸੈਸ) *n* (1) ਸਫਲਤਾ, ਕਾਮਯਾਬੀ, (2) ਰਟੂ ਤੋਤਾ; **~ful** ਸਫਲ, ਕਾਮਯਾਬ; **~ion** ਉੱਤਰ-ਅਧਿਕਾਰ, ਜਾਨਸ਼ੀਨੀ; ਵਿਰਾਸ, ਸਿਲਸਲਾ; **~ive** ਕ੍ਰਮ-ਅਨੁਸਾਰ, ਸਿਲਸਲੇਵਾਰ, ਲਗਾਤਾਰ; **~or** ਉੱਤਰਾਧਿਕਾਰੀ;

ਜਾਨਸ਼ੀਨ, ਵਾਰਸ; **nothing succeeds like~** ਚਲਦੀ ਦਾ ਨਾਂ ਗੱਡੀ

succinct (ਸਅਕ'ਸਿਙ(ਕ)ਟ) *a* ਸੰਖੇਪ, ਥੋੜ੍ਹੇ ਸ਼ਬਦਾਂ ਦਾ, ਸੰਖਿਪਤ

succour ('ਸਅੱਕਅ*) *v n* (ਮੁਸ਼ਕਲ ਸਮੇਂ) ਸਹਾਇਤਾ ਦੇਣਾ, ਮਦਦ ਕਰਨਾ, ਆਸਰਾ ਦੇਣਾ; ਸਹਾਇਤਾ, ਮਦਦ, ਆਸਰਾ, ਬਹੁੜੀ

succumb (ਸਅ'ਕਅੱਮ) *v* ਹਾਰ ਜਾਣਾ, ਹਥਿਆਰ ਸੁੱਟ ਦੇਣਾ, ਸ਼ਿਕਸਤ ਖਾਣਾ, ਮਰ ਜਾਣਾ; ਸ਼ਿਕਾਰ ਹੋਣਾ (ਰੋਗ, ਲਾਲਚ, ਦਬਾਉ ਦਾ)

such (ਸਅੱਚ) *a pron* ਇਸ ਤਰ੍ਹਾਂ ਦਾ, ਅਜਿਹਾ, ਇਤਨਾ, ਇਸ ਢੰਗ ਦਾ; (ਕ) ਪਹਿਲਾਂ ਕਿਹਾ; ਫਲਾਂ-ਫਲਾਂ; ਉਹ ਲੋਕ, ਇਹ; ਅਜਿਹੀਆਂ ਚੀਜ਼ਾਂ; **~and such** ਫਲਾਂ-ਫਲਾਂ, ਫਲਾਨਾ, ਢਿਮਕਾ

suck (ਸਅੱਕ) *v n* ਚੁੰਘਣਾ; ਚੁਸਕੀ ਲਾਉਣੀ; ਚੂਪਟਾ; ਜੀਭ ਫੇਰਨਾ, ਸੁੜਕਣਾ; ਚੁਸਕੀ, ਸੁੜਕਾ; **~in** (ਭੰਵਰ ਆਦਿ ਦਾ) ਹੜੱਪ ਜਾਣਾ, ਗਾਰਕ ਕਰ ਦੇਣਾ

suckle ('ਸਅੱਕਲ) *v* ਦੁੱਧ ਪਿਆਉਣਾ, ਚੁੰਘਾਉਣਾ; ਦੁੱਧ ਪੀਣਾ, ਚੁੰਘਣਾ

suction ('ਸਅੱਕਸ਼ਨ) *n* ਚੁੰਘ, ਚੁੰਘਾਈ

sudden ('ਸਅੱਡਨ) *a n* ਅਚਾਨਕ, ਅਚਨਚੇਤੀ, ਬਹੁਤ ਤੇਜ਼; **~ly** ਅਚਾਨਕ, ਅਕਸਮਾਤ, ਛੇਤੀ ਨਾਲ, ਤੇਜ਼ੀ ਨਾਲ

sue (ਸੂ) *v* ਮੁੱਕਦਮਾ ਚਲਾਉਣਾ, ਦਾਅਵਾ ਕਰਨਾ, ਦਰਖ਼ਾਸਤ ਕਰਨਾ,

suffer ('ਸਅੱਫਅ*) *v* ਨੁਕਸਾਨ ਸਹਿਣਾ, ਸਹਾਰਨਾ; ਝੱਲਣਾ, ਭੋਗਣਾ, ਭੁਗਤਣਾ, ਦੁੱਖ ਪਾਉਣਾ; **~ing** ਦੁਖੜਾ, ਵੇਦਨਾ, ਪੀੜਾ, ਸੰਤਾਪ, ਕਸ਼ਟ ਕਲੇਸ਼, ਜਫਰ

suffice (ਸਅ'ਫ਼ਾਇਸ) *v* ਪੂਰਾ ਹੋਣਾ, ਕਾਫ਼ੀ ਹੋਣਾ,

ਬਹੁਤ ਹੋਣਾ, ਸਰਨਾ, ਕੰਮ ਚਲਾਉਣਾ

sufficiency (ਸਅ'ਫ਼ਿਸ਼ੰਸਿ) *n* ਰੱਜ-ਪੁੱਜ, ਬਹੁਤਾਤ, ਖ਼ੁਸ਼ਹਾਲੀ, ਯੋਗਤਾ

sufficient (ਸਅ'ਫ਼ਿਸ਼ਅੰਟ) *a* ਕਾਫ਼ੀ, ਰੱਜਵਾਂ, ਪੂਰਾ, ਚੋਖਾ, ਸਮਰੱਥ; ਯੋਗ

suffix ('ਸਅਫ਼ਿਕਸ) *n v* ਪਿਛੇਤਰ, ਪ੍ਰਤਯ; ਪਿਛੇਤਰ ਲਾਉਣਾ

suffocate ('ਸਅਫ਼ਅਕੇਇਟ) *v* ਸਾਹ ਰੋਕਣਾ, ਸਾਹ ਰੁਕਣਾ, ਸਾਹ ਘੋਟਣਾ, ਗਲਾ ਦਬਾਉਣਾ, ਦਮ ਘੋਟਣਾ, ਦਮ ਘੁੱਟਣਾ

suffocation ('ਸਅਫ਼ਅ'ਕੇਇਸ਼ਨ) *n* ਸਾਹ-ਰੋਧ, ਦਮਘੁਟੀ

sugar ('ਸੁਗਾ*) *n v* ਸ਼ਕੱਰ, ਖੰਡ, ਚੀਨੀ; ਚਾਪਲੂਸੀ; ਖੰਡ ਪਾਉਣੀ; ਖੰਡ ਚਾੜ੍ਹਨੀ, ਗਲੇਫਣਾ; ~cane ਗੰਨਾ; ~plum ਪਤਾਸਾ, ਮਿੱਠੀ ਗੋਲੀ

suggest (ਸਅ'ਜੇਸਟ) *v* ਸੁਝਾਉ ਦੇਣਾ, ਸੁਝਾਉਣਾ, ਸੰਕੇਤ ਕਰਨਾ; ਰਾਇ ਦੇਤੀ, ਤਜਵੀਜ਼ ਕਰਨਾ, ਪ੍ਰਸਤਾਵ ਕਰਨਾ; ~ion ਸੁਝਾਉ, ਤਜਵੀਜ਼; ਉਪਦੇਸ਼, ਰਾਇ, ਸਲਾਹ; ਆਤਮ-ਪੇਰਨਾ; ~ive ਸੁਝਾਉਣ ਵਾਲਾ, ਸੰਕੇਤਕ, ਸੂਚਕ; ਸੰਕੇਤ-ਪੂਰਨ

suicidal (ਸੁਇ'ਸਾਇਡਲ) *a* ਆਤਮਘਾਤੀ, ਆਤਮਨਾਸੀ, ਆਤਮ-ਹੱਤਿਆ ਸਬੰਧੀ

suicide ('ਸੁਇਸਾਇਡ) *n* ਆਤਮ-ਹੱਤਿਆ, ਖ਼ੁਦਕਸ਼ੀ

suit (ਸੂਟ) *n v* (1) ਮੁਕੱਦਮਾ, ਦਾਅਵਾ, ਕਾਨੂੰਨੀ ਜਾਂ ਅਦਾਲਤੀ; (2) ਕੱਪਿਆਂ ਦਾ ਜੋੜਾ, ਸੂਟ (ਜਿਸ ਵਿਚ ਕੋਟ, ਪਤਲੂਨ ਆਦਿ ਇਕੇ ਹੀ ਕੱਪੜੇ ਦੇ ਹੋਣ); ਜਾਚਨਾ, ਪ੍ਰਰਥਨਾ; ਸ਼ਾਦੀ ਦੀ ਗੱਲਬਾਤ; ਮੇਲ ਖਾਣਾ, ਫਬਣਾ, ਸਜਣਾ,

ਅਨੁਕੂਲ ਬਣਾਉਣਾ; ਅਨੁਸਾਰ ਬਣਾਉਣਾ, ਰਾਸ ਆਉਣਾ; ~case ਸੂਟ ਕੇਸ, ਛੋਟਾ ਬਕਸਾ; ~ability ਠੁੱਕ, ਅਨੁਕੂਲਤਾ, ਯੋਗਤਾ, ਢੁਕਾਉ; ~able ਉਚਿਤ, ਅਨੁਕੂਲ, ਮਿਲਦਾ-ਜੁਲਦਾ, ਮੁਆਫ਼ਕ, ਜਚਦਾ, ਢੁੱਕਵਾਂ, ਫੱਬਵਾਂ

suite (ਸਵੀਟ) *n* (1) (ਕਮਰਿਆਂ, ਫ਼ਰਨੀਚਰ ਆਦਿ ਦਾ) ਇਕ ਸਿਲਸਲਾ, ਨੌਕਰ-ਚਾਕਰ, ਲਾਮ-ਡੋਰੀ; (2) (ਸੰਗੀ) ਵਾਦਕ ਸੰਗੀਤ ਸਬੰਧੀ ਕ੍ਰਿਤੀ

sullen ('ਸਅੱਲਅਨ) *a* ਉਦਾਸ, ਚਿੰਤਤ, ਚਿੜਚੜਾ, ਮੂੰਹ ਵੱਟਿਆ

sully ('ਸੁਅੱਲਿ) *v* (ਕਾਵਿਕ) ਬਦਨਾਮ ਕਰਨਾ, ਧੱਬਾ ਲਾਉਣਾ; ਭੁਸ਼ਟ ਕਰਨਾ, ਮੈਲਾ ਕਰਨਾ

sultry ('ਸਅੱਲਟਰਿ) *a* (ਹਵਾ ਜਾਂ ਰੁੱਤ) ਹੁੰਮਸੀ, ਗਰਮ; (ਸੁਭਾਅ) ਤੇਜ਼, ਤੀਖਣ, ਉਤੇਜਨਾਸ਼ੀਲ

sum ('ਸਅੱਮ) *n v* ਕੁੱਲ, ਜੋੜ, ਮਿਜ਼ਾਨ, ਯੋਗਫਲ; ਜੋੜ ਕਰਨਾ, ਜੋੜਨਾ; ~total ਕੁੱਲ ਜੋੜ

summarize ('ਸਅੱਮਅਰਾਇਜ਼) *v* ਸਾਰ ਦੇਣਾ, ਸੰਖੇਪ ਕਰਨਾ, ਖ਼ੁਲਾਸਾ ਕਰਨਾ, ਸਾਰਾਂਸ਼ ਕੱਢਣਾ

summary ('ਸਅੱਮਅਰਿ) *a n* ਸੰਖੇਪ; ਸਾਰ, ਸਾਰਾਂਸ਼; ਖ਼ੁਲਾਸਾ, ਨਚੋੜ, ਤਾਤਪਰਜ

summer ('ਸਅੱਮਅ*) *n v* ਗਰਮੀਆਂ, ਗਰਮੀ ਦੀ ਰੁੱਤ, ਹੁਨਾਲਾ; ਗਰਮੀ ਕੱਟਣੀ

summit ('ਸਅੱਮਿਟ) *n* ਚੋਟੀ, ਸਿਖਰ, ਸਿਖਰ ਸੰਮੇਲਨ

summon ('ਸਅੱਮਅਨ) *v* ਸੱਦਣਾ, ਬੁਲਾ ਭੇਜਣਾ; ਤਲਬ ਕਰਨਾ, ਪੁਕਾਰਨਾ, ਯਾਦ ਕਰਨਾ; (ਕਾ) ਸੰਮਨ ਭੇਜ ਕੇ ਤਲਬ ਕਰਨਾ; ~s ਅਦਾਲਤੀ ਸੱਦਾ, ਤਲਖ਼ੀ, ਹੁਕਮਨਾਮਾ, ਸੰਮਨ, ਬੁਲਾਵਾ

sumptuous ('ਸਅੰਪਚੁਅਸ) *a* ਖੁੱਲ੍ਹਾ-ਡੁੱਲ੍ਹਾ, ਸ਼ਾਹਾਨਾ, ਅਮੀਰਾਨ, ਕੀਮਤੀ, ਸ਼ਾਹ ਖ਼ਰਚ ਵਾਲਾ

sun (ਸਅੱਨ) *n v* ਸੂਰਜ, ਰਵੀ, ਆਫ਼ਤਾਬ; ਦਿਨ;

ਧੁੱਪ; ਧੁੱਪ ਸੇਕਟੀ, ਧੁੱਪੇ ਬਹਿਣਾ, ਧੁੱਪ ਲੁਆਈ; ~**bath** ਧੁੱਪ ਇਸ਼ਨਾਨ; ~**beam** ਸੂਰਜ ਦੀ ਕਿਰਨ; ~**down** ਸੂਰਜ-ਡੁੱਬੇ, ਦਿਨ-ਲੱਥੇ; ~**flower** ਸੂਰਜਮੁਖੀ; ~**rise** ਪਹੁ-ਫੁਟਾਲਾ; ~**set** ਅਸਤ, ਆਥਣ; ~**shine** ਧੁੱਪ; ਖੇੜਾ; ~**stroke** ਗਰਮੀ ਦਾ ਧੱਕਾ, ਲੂ, ਲੂਹਾ

Sunday ('ਸਅੰਡਿ) *n* ਐਤਵਾਰ

sunder ('ਸਅੰਡਅ*) *v* ਅਲੱਗ ਕਰਨਾ ਜਾਂ ਹੋਣਾ, ਵੱਖ ਕਰਨਾ ਜਾਂ ਹੋਣਾ, ਨਿਖੇੜਨਾ ਜਾਂ ਨਿਖੜਨਾ; ਤੋੜਨਾ, ਅਲੱਗ ਰੱਖਣਾ

sundry ('ਸਅੰਡਰਿ) *a n* (ਪ੍ਰ) ਕਈ, ਅਨੇਕ, ਕਈ ਇਕ; ਨਿੱਕ-ਸੁੱਕ, ਉਰਲੀਆਂ-ਪਰਲੀਆਂ ਚੀਜ਼ਾਂ

sup (ਸਅੱਪ) *v n* ਘੁੱਟ ਘੁੱਟ ਪੀਣਾ, ਸੁੜਕਣਾ, ਘੋਤੂ ਘੋਤੂ ਪੀਣਾ; ਘੁੱਟ; ਚੁਸਕੀ

super ('ਸੂਪਅ*) *n a pref* ਵੱਡਾ ਆਦਮੀ; ਵਧੀਆ ਕਿਸਮ ਦਾ ਕੱਪੜਾ ਜਾਂ ਵਸਤੂ; ਵਾਧੂ, ਐਰਾ-ਗੈਰਾ; ਬਹੁਤ ਵਧੀਆ; ਅੰਗੋਤਰ, ਉਤਲਾ', ਪਾਰਲਾ', ਪਰਾ'; ~**fine** ਅਤੀ ਉੱਤਮ, ਬਹੁਤ ਹੀ ਵਧੀਆ; ਮਹੀਨ, ਬਾਰੀਕ (ਕੱਪੜਾ); ~**human** ਦੈਵੀ, ਅਲੌਕਿਕ; ~**man** ਮਹਾਂ-ਮਾਨਵ; ਪਰਮ ਪੁਰਸ਼, ਬ੍ਰਹਮ-ਗਿਆਨੀ; ~**natural** ਦੈਵੀ, ਅਲੌਕਿਕ, ਪ੍ਰਾਸਰੀਰਕ, ਅਸਚਰਜਤਾਮਈ; ~**structure** ਉੱਤਲੀ ਉਸਾਰੀ, ਉੱਪਰਲਾ ਢਾਂਚਾ; ~**tax** ਵਾਧੂ ਕਰ, ਅਧਿ-ਕਰ

superannuate ('ਸੂਪਅ'ਰੈਨਯੂਏਇਟ) *v* ਬੁਢਾਪੇ ਕਾਰਨ ਨੌਕਰੀ ਤੋਂ ਮੁਕਤ ਕਰਨਾ, ਪੈਨਸ਼ਨ ਦੇ ਕੇ ਮੁਕਤ ਕਰਨਾ

superannuation ('ਸੂਪਅ'ਰੈਨਯੂ'ਏਇਸ਼ਨ) *n* ਬੁਢਾਪੇ ਕਾਰਨ ਕੰਮ ਯੋਗ ਨਾ ਰਹਿਣਾ, ਬੁਢਾਪੇ ਦੀ ਪੈਨਸ਼ਨ

superb (ਸ'ਪਅਃਬ) *a* ਸ਼ਾਨਦਾਰ; ਅਤੀ ਚੰਗਾ, ਵਧੀਆ; ਗ਼ਜ਼ਬ ਦਾ

superficial ('ਸੂਪਅ'ਫ਼ਿਸ਼ਲ) *a* ਬਾਹਰ-ਬਾਹਰ ਦਾ, ਉੱਪਰਲਾ-ਉੱਪਰਲਾ, ਦਿਖਾਵੇ ਦਾ, ਮੋਟਾ-ਮੋਟਾ, ਥੋਥਾ, ਹਲਕਾ

superficiality ('ਸੂਪਅ'ਫ਼ਿਸਿ'ਐਲਅਟਿ) *n* ਉੱਪਰ-ਲਾਪਟ, ਦਿਖਾਵਾ, ਥੋਥਾਪਣ, ਕਚਿਆਈ, ਹਲਕਾਪਣ

superfluous (ਸੂ'ਪਅਃਫ਼ਲੁਸ) *a* ਨਿਰਰਥਕ, ਬੋਲੇਝਾ, ਫ਼ਾਲਤੂ

superintend ('ਸੂਪ(ਅ)ਰਿਨ'ਟੈਂਡ) *v* ਪ੍ਰਬੰਧ ਕਰਨਾ, ਦੇਖ-ਭਾਲ ਕਰਨੀ; ~**ence** ਪ੍ਰਬੰਧ, ਨਿਗਰਾਨੀ, ਦੇਖ-ਭਾਲ; ~**ent** ਪ੍ਰਬੰਧਕ, ਸੰਚਾਲਕ, ਸੁਪਰਿਟੈਂਡੈਂਟ

superior (ਸੂ'ਪਿਅਰਿਅ*) *a n* ਵੱਡਾ ਉੱਤਮ, ਵੱਡਾ; ਵਧੀਆ, ਬਿਹਤਰ, ਸ੍ਰੇਸ਼ਠ, ਬਜ਼ੁਰਗਾ; ਅਸਧਾਰਨ ਪ੍ਰਮੁੱਖ; ~**ity** ਉੱਤਮਤਾ, ਪ੍ਰਮੁੱਖਤਾ, ਵਿਸ਼ੇਸ਼ ਯੋਗਤਾ, ਵਡਿਆਈ; ਉੱਚਤਾ; ਗੁਮਾਨ

supersede ('ਸੂਪਅ'ਸੀਡ) *v* ਮਨਸੂਖ ਕਰਨਾ, ਛੱਡ ਦੇਣਾ, ਉਲੰਘਣਾ, ਬਦਲਣਾ, ਥਾਂ ਮੱਲਣਾ

supersession ('ਸੂਪਅ'ਸੈਸ਼ਨ) *n* ਪ੍ਰਤੀਸਥਾਪਨ, ਇਕ ਦੀ ਉਲੰਘਣਾ ਕਰਕੇ ਕਿਸੇ ਦੂਜੇ ਦੀ ਨਿਯੁਕਤੀ

supersitition ('ਸੂਪਅ'ਸਟਿਸ਼ਨ) *n* ਵਹਿਮ, ਭਰਮਜਾਲ, ਅੰਧ-ਸਰਧਾ, ਅੰਧ-ਵਿਸ਼ਵਾਸ

supervise (ਸੂਪਅਵ੍ਹਾਇਜ਼) *v* ਦੇਖ-ਰੇਖ ਕਰਨਾ, ਦੇਖ-ਭਾਲ ਕਰਨੀ, ਤਾਕ ਰੱਖਣੀ, ਨਿਗਰਾਨੀ ਕਰਨੀ

supervision ('ਸੂਪਅ'ਵ੍ਹਿਜਨ) *n* ਦੇਖ-ਰੇਖ, ਦੇਖ-ਭਾਲ, ਨਿਗਰਾਨੀ, ਪਿਆਨ

supervisor ('ਸੂਪਅ'ਵ੍ਹਾਇਜ਼ਅ*) *n* ਨਿਗਰਾਨ,

ਨਿਰੀਖਕ

supper ('ਸਅੱਪਅ*) *n* ਰਾਤ ਦਾ ਖਾਣਾ

supplement ('ਸਅੱਪਲਿਮਅੰਟ, 'ਸਅੱਪਲਿਮੈਂਟ) *n* (ਹਿਸਾਬ) ਸਮਪੂਰਕ, (ਅਖ਼ਬਾਰ ਦਾ) ਪੂਰਕ-ਪੱਤਰ, ਅਤੀਰਿਕਤ ਅੰਸ਼; ਸੰਪੂਰਨ ਕਰਨਾ, ਵਧਾਉਣਾ, ਲਗਾਉਣਾ, ਵਾਧਾ ਕਰਨਾ;~**al,** ~**ary** ਪੂਰਕ, ਸਮਪੂਰਕ; ਪਿੱਛੋਂ ਜੁੜਿਆ, ਜ਼ਮੀਮੀ

supplicate ('ਸਅੱਪਲਿਕੇਇਟ) *v* ਬੇਨਤੀ ਕਰਨੀ, ਅਰਜ਼ ਕਰਨੀ, ਤਰਲੇ ਕੱਢਣੇ, ਮਿੰਨਤ ਕਰਨੀ, ਹਾੜ੍ਹੇ ਕੱਢਣੇ

supplication ('ਸਅੱਪਲਿ'ਕੇਇਸ਼ਨ) *n* ਬੇਨਤੀ, ਅਰਜ਼, ਤਰਲਾ, ਮਿੰਨਤ, ਵਾਸਤਾ, ਜਾਚਨਾ

supplier (ਸਅੱ'ਪਲਾਇਅ*) *n* ਭੰਡਾਰੀ, ਪੂਰਤੀਕਰਤਾ, ਮੁਹਯਾ ਕਰਨ ਵਾਲਾ,

supply (ਸਅ'ਪਲਾਇ) *v n* ਰਸਦ ਪਹੁੰਚਾਉਣੀ, ਲੋੜ ਪੂਰੀ ਕਰਨੀ; ਪੂਰਾ ਕਰਨੀ; ਭਰਤੀ ਕਰਨਾ; ਭੰਡਾਰ, ਰਸਦ; ਪੂਰਤੀ; ਰਸਦ-ਪਾਣੀ

support (ਸਅ'ਪੋਟ) *v n* ਸਮਰਥਨ ਕਰਨਾ, ਸਹਾਰਾ ਦੇਣਾ; ਥੰਮ੍ਹਣਾ, ਹਿਮਾਇਤ ਕਰਨੀ; ਸੰਭਾਲਣਾ, ਭਾਰ ਉਠਾਉਣਾ; (ਮਤੇ ਦੀ) ਪੁਸ਼ਟੀ ਕਰਨੀ; ਪਿੱਠ ਠੋਕਣੀ, ਪਾਲਣ-ਪੋਸਣ ਕਰਨਾ; ਹਾਮੀ, ਪੁਸ਼ਟੀ, ਹਿਮਾਇਤ; ਆਸਰਾ; ~**ed** ਸਮਰਥਤ; ~**er** ਪੁਸ਼ਟੀਕਾਰ; ਸਹਾਇਕ, ਸਹਾਈ, ਅੰਗਪਾਲ; ਹਿਮਾਇਤੀ, ਮਦਦਗਾਰ; ~**ing** ਸਮਰਥਕ, ਸਹਾਇਕ, ਸਹਾਈ

suppose ('ਸਅ'ਪਅਉਜ਼) *v* ਮੰਨ ਲੈਣਾ, ਸਮਝਣਾ, ਕਲਪਤ ਕਰਨਾ, ਅਨੁਮਾਨ ਕਰਨਾ; ਸੋਚ ਲੈਣਾ; ~**d** ਅਨੁਮਾਨਤ, ਕਲਪਤ, ਮੰਨਿਆ

supposition ('ਸਅਪਅ'ਜ਼ਿਸ਼ਨ) *n* ਅਨੁਮਾਨ, ਮਨੌਤ, ਧਾਰਨਾ, ਅੰਦਾਜ਼ਾ; ਸਮਝ

suppress (ਸਅ:ਪਰੈੱਸ) *v* ਦਬਾਉਣਾ, ਬੰਦ ਕਰਨਾ, ਰੋਕ ਦੇਣਾ, ਕੁਚਲ ਦੇਣਾ; ਪ੍ਰਕਾਸ਼ਤ ਨਾ ਹੋਣ ਦੇਣਾ; ~**ion,** ~**or** ਦਬਾਈ, ਦਮਨ; ਜ਼ਬਤੀ, ਬੰਦਸ਼; ਲੁਕਾਅ

supremacy (ਸ'ਪਰੈੱਮਅਸਿ) *n* ਸਰਦਾਰੀ, ਸ੍ਰੇਸ਼ਠਤਾ, ਪ੍ਰਮੁੱਖਤਾ, ਬੋਲਬਾਲਾ

supreme (ਸੁ'ਪਰੀਮ) *a* ਸਰਵ-ਉੱਚ, ਸਰਵ-ਸ੍ਰੇਸ਼ਠ, ਸਰਵ-ਪ੍ਰਧਾਨ; ਸ਼ਰੋਮਣੀ, ਸਰਬੋਤਮ, ਸਰਵ-ਉੱਚ, ਉੱਚਤਮ (ਅਦਾਲਤ); ਮਹੱਤਵਪੂਰਨ

surcharge ('ਸਅ:ਚਾਜ, ਸਅ:'ਚਾਜ) *n v* ਅਧਿਕ ਕਿਰਾਇਆ, ਭਾੜਾ ਜਾਂ ਮਹਿਸੂਲ; ਵਾਧੂ ਭਾਰ ਪਾਉਣਾ, ਚੱਟੀ ਲਾਉਣੀ

sure (ਸ਼ੋ*) *a adv* ਅਚੁਕ; ਨਿਸ਼ਚਤ, ਦ੍ਰਿੜ੍ਹ, ਪੱਕਾ, ਵਿਸ਼ਵਾਸੀ, ਭਰੋਸੇ ਯੋਗ, ਬਿਨਾ ਸ਼ੱਕ, ਬਿਲਕੁਲ ਸੱਚ; ~**ly** ਯਕੀਨੀ ਤੌਰ ਤੇ, ਪੱਕੀ ਤਰ੍ਹਾਂ, ਜ਼ਰੂਰ; ~**ty** ਜ਼ਾਮਨ, ਜ਼ਮਾਨਤ ਦੇਣ ਵਾਲਾ; ਮੁਚੱਲਕਾ, ਜ਼ਮਾਨਤ; ਯਕੀਨ, ਨਿਸ਼ਚਾ

surface ('ਸਅ:ਫ਼ਿਸ) *n a* ਤਲ, ਭੂ-ਤਲ, ਸਤ੍ਹਾ; ਉੱਪਰਲਾ-ਉੱਪਰਲਾ

surge (ਸਅ:ਜ) *v n* ਠਾਠਾਂ ਮਾਰਦਾ, ਲਹਿਰ ਉੱਠਣੀ, ਲਹਿਲਾਉਣਾ; ਚੜ੍ਹਨਾ, ਉਭਰਨਾ; ਲਹਿਰ, ਤਰੰਗ, ਮੌਜ

surname ('ਸਅ:ਨੇਇਮ) *n* ਉਪ-ਨਾਂ, ਕੁਲ ਨਾਂ, ਖ਼ਾਨਦਾਨੀ ਨਾਂ; ਉਪਾਧੀ

surpass (ਸਅ'ਪਾਸ) *v* ਅੱਗੇ ਵਧ ਜਾਣਾ, ਪਿੱਛੇ ਛੱਡ ਜਾਣਾ

surplus ('ਸਅ:ਪਲਅਸ) *n a* ਬਚਤ, ਰੋਕੜ, ਵਾਧੂ ਮਿਕਦਾਰ, ਵਾਧਾ, ਫ਼ਾਲਤੂ, ਅਤਿਰਿਕਤ

surprise (ਸਅ'ਪਰਾਇਜ਼) *n v* ਹੈਰਾਨੀ, ਅਸਚਰਜਤਾ, ਅਸਚਰਜ, ਅਚੰਭਾ; ਪਰੇਸ਼ਾਨ ਕਰਨਾ; ਹੈਰਾਨ ਕਰਨਾ, ਅਚੰਭਤ ਕਰਨਾ

surprising (ਸਅ'ਪਰਾਇਜ਼ਙ) *a* ਅਨੋਖਾ, ਵਚਿੱਤਰ

surrender (ਸਅ'ਰੈਂਡਅ*) v n (ਤਾਕਤ ਜਾਂ ਕਬਜ਼ਾ) ਸੌਂਪ ਦੇਣਾ, ਹਵਾਲੇ ਕਰਨਾ, ਛੱਡਣਾ, ਤਿਆਗਣਾ, ਹਥਿਆਰ ਸੁੱਟਣੇ, ਹਾਰ ਮੰਨੰਟੀ; ਹਾਰ, ਸਮਰਪਣ, ਆਤਮ-ਸਮਰਪਣ

surround (ਸਅ'ਰਾਉਂਡ) v ਘੇਰਨਾ, ਦੁਆਲੇ ਹੋਣਾ, ਘੇਰਿਆ ਹੋਣਾ; ਚੌਤਰਫੀ ਹੋਣਾ; ~ings ਆਸ-ਪਾਸ ਦਾ ਵਾਤਾਵਰਣ, ਚੁਗਿਰਦਾ, ਅੜੋਸ-ਪੜੋਸ

surveillance (ਸਰਵ:'ਵੇਇਲਅੰਸ) n ਰਖਵਾਲੀ, ਨਿਗਰਾਨੀ, ਦੇਖ-ਭਾਲ

survey (ਸਅ'ਵੇਇ, 'ਸਅ:ਵੇਇ) v n ਪੜਤਾਲ ਕਰਨੀ, ਨਿਰੀਖਣ ਕਰਨਾ; ਦੇਖਣਾ, ਜਾਂਚ ਕਰਨੀ; ਪੈਮਾਇਸ਼ ਕਰਨੀ, ਕੱਛਣਾ; ਸਰਵੇ, ਪੈਮਾਇਸ਼, ਕੱਛ; ਜਾਂਚ, ਪੜਤਾਲ; ~or ਸਰਵੇ ਕਰਨ ਵਾਲਾ, ਪੈਮਾਇਸ਼ ਕਰਨ ਵਾਲਾ ਅਫ਼ਸਰ

survival (ਸਅ'ਵ਼ਾਇਵ਼ਲ) n ਯਾਦਗਾਰ, ਉੱਤਰਜੀਵਤਾ, ਬਚਾਉ; ~of the fittest ਯੋਗਤਮ ਦੀ ਜੈ

survive (ਸਅਵ਼ਾਇਵ਼) v ਬਚਿਆ ਰਹਿਣਾ, ਟਿਕਿਆ ਰਹਿਣਾ, ਜੀਉਂਦੇ ਰਹਿਣਾ

survivor (ਸਅ'ਵ਼ਾਇਵਅ*) n ਬਚਿਆ ਰਹਿਣ ਵਾਲਾ; (ਬ ਵ) ਪਿਛਲੇ ਰਹਿੰਦੇ, ਉੱਤਰਜੀਵੀ

susceptibility (ਸਅ'ਸੈਪਟਅ'ਬਿਲਅਟਿ) n ਗੁੰਜਾਇਸ਼, ਸੰਭਾਵਨਾ, ਗ੍ਰਹਿਣਸ਼ੀਲਤਾ

susceptible (ਸਅ'ਸੈਪਟਅਬਲ) a ਭਾਵਗ੍ਰਾਹੀ, ਗ੍ਰਹਿਣਸ਼ੀਲ, ਗੁੰਜਾਇਸ਼ ਵਾਲਾ; ਭਾਵੁਕ, ਪ੍ਰਭਾਵਕ, ਸੰਵੇਦਨਸ਼ੀਲ

suspect ('ਸਅੱਸਪੈੱਕਟ) v a n ਸ਼ੱਕ ਕਰਨਾ, (ਕਿਸੇ ਗੱਲ ਦਾ) ਅੰਦੇਸ਼ਾ ਹੋਣਾ, ਸ਼ੱਕ ਹੋਣਾ; ਸ਼ੁਬ੍ਹਾ ਹੋਣਾ, ਗੁਮਾਨ ਹੋਣਾ; ਸੰਦੇਹਪੂਰਨ; ਸ਼ੱਕ, ਸੰਦੇਹ

suspend (ਸਾਅ'ਸਪੈਂਡ) v ਮੁਅੱਤਲ ਕਰਨਾ; ਰੋਕ ਰੱਖਣਾ, ਟੰਗਣਾ; ਲਮਕਾਉਣਾ, ਲਟਕਾਉਣਾ

suspense (ਸਅ'ਸਪੈੱਂਸ) n ਦੋ-ਚਿੱਤੀ, ਦੋ-ਦਿਲੀ, ਦੁਬਧਾ, ਜੱਕੋਤਕੀ, ਸਸ਼ੋਪੰਜ

suspension (ਸਅ'ਸਪੈਨਸ਼ਨ) n ਲਮਕਾਅ, ਲਟਕਾਉ; ਮੁਅੱਤਲੀ; ਰੁਕਾਅ

suspicion (ਸਅ'ਸਪਿਸ਼ਨ) n ਸੰਦੇਹ, ਸ਼ੰਕਾ, ਖਟਕਾ

suspicious (ਸਅ'ਸਪਿਸ਼ਅਸ) a ਸ਼ੱਕੀ, ਸੰਦੇਹੀ, ਸ਼ੰਕਾਵਾਦੀ

sustain (ਸਅ'ਸਟੇਇਨ) v ਸਹਾਰਾ ਦੇਣਾ, ਭਾਰ ਉਠਾਉਣਾ; ਜੀਉਂਦਾ ਰੱਖਣਾ, ਹਿੰਮਤ ਕਾਇਮ ਰੱਖਣਾ; ਮੁਕਾਬਲਾ ਕਰਨਾ, ਤਸਦੀਕ ਕਰਨਾ, ਪੁਸ਼ਟੀ ਕਰਨੀ, ਪ੍ਰੋੜ੍ਹਤਾ ਕਰਨੀ; ਜਾਰੀ ਰੱਖਣਾ; ~d ਪ੍ਰਮਾਣਤ, ਦੀਰਘਕਾਲਕ; ਲਗਾਤਾਰ

sustenance ('ਸਅੱਸਟਿਨਅੰਸ) n ਜੀਵਕਾ, ਗੁਜ਼ਾਰਾ, ਆਹਾਰ; ਪਾਲਣ-ਪੋਸਣ, ਖ਼ੁਰਾਕ

swag (ਸਵੈਗ) n (ਅਪ) ਚੋਰੀ ਦਾ ਮਾਲ, ਲੁੱਟ ਦਾ ਧਨ

swagger ('ਸਵੈਗਅ*) v a ਫੜ ਮਾਰਨੀ; ਆਕੜ ਕੇ ਚੱਲਣਾ, ਠਾਠ ਨਾਲ ਚੱਲਣਾ; ਧੌਂਸ ਜਮਾਉਂਟੀ, ਡੀਂਗ ਮਾਰਨੀ; ਫੁਰਤੀਲਾ, ਤੇਜ, ਰੋਹਬ ਵਾਲਾ

swallow ('ਸਵੈੱਲਅਉ) v ਹੜੱਪ ਕਰਨਾ; ਨਿਗਲਣਾ, ਖਾ ਲੈਣਾ, ਹੱਪਣਾ, ਨਿਘਾਰਨਾ, ਹੜਪਣਾ; ਨਸ਼ਟ ਕਰਨਾ, ਸਹਿਣਾ, ਪੀ ਜਾਣਾ

swan (ਸਵੈਨ) n ਹੰਸ; ਰਾਜਹੰਸ

swap (ਸਵੈਪ) n v ਅਦਲਾ-ਬਦਲੀ, ਅਦਲਾ-ਬਦਲੀ ਕਰਨਾ

sway (ਸਵੇਇ) v n ਉੱਲਰਨਾ; ਡੁਲਾਉਣਾ; ਲਚਕਾ ਖਾਣਾ; ਝੂਮਣਾ, ਝੂਟਣਾ, ਝੁਲਾਰਨਾ; ਅਸਰ ਪਾਉਣਾ; ਸਿੱਕਾ ਬਿਠਾਉਣਾ; ਰਾਜ ਕਰਨਾ; ਉਲਾਰ; ਝਟਕਾ; ਅਸਰ

swear (ਸਵੈਰੋ*) v n ਸੰਹੁ ਖਾਣੀ ਜਾਂ ਚੁੱਕਣੀ,

ਕਸਮ ਖਾਣੀ, ਸੌਗੰਦ ਖਾਣੀ, ਸਹੁੰ ਖੁਆਣੀ; ਸਹੁੰ, ਸੌਗੰਦ, ਕਸਮ; ~ing ਹਲਫ਼ ਉਠਾਉਣ, ਸਹੁੰ, ਸੌਗੰਦ, ਕਸਮ

sweat (ਸਵੈੱਟ) *n v* ਪਸੀਨਾ, ਮੁੜ੍ਹਕਾ, ਪਰਸੇਉ; ਪਸੀਨਾ ਆਉਣਾ; ਤੇਲ ਕੱਢਣਾ, ਕਰੜੀ ਮਿਹਨਤ ਕਰਨੀ; ~er ਕਰੜੀ ਮਿਹਨਤ ਕਰਨ ਵਾਲਾ; ਸਵੈਟਰ

sweep (ਸਵੀਪ) *v n* ਝਾੜੂ ਦੇਣਾ, ਸੁੰਬਰਨਾ, ਝਾੜਨਾ, ਬੁਹਾਰਨਾ, ਹੂੰਝਣਾ, ਝਪਟਣਾ; ਸਫ਼ਾਈ; ~er ਮਿਹਤਰ, ਸਫ਼ਾਈ ਕਰਨ ਵਾਲਾ; ~ing ਦੂਰਗਾਮੀ; ਵਿਆਪਕ; ਮਹੱਤਵਪੂਰਨ

sweet (ਸਵੀਟ) *a n* ਮਿੱਠਾ; ਸੁਆਦੀ, ਸੁਰੀਲਾ; ਪਰੀਤਮ; ~heart ਪਰੇਮੀ ਪਰੇਮ ਕਾ, ਜਾਨੀ ਢੋਲਾ, ਦਿਲਦਾਰ; ~potato ਸ਼ਕਰਕੰਦੀ

swell (ਸਵੈੱਲ) *v a n* ਸੁੱਜਣਾ, ਸੁਜਾਉਣਾ, ਸੁੱਜ ਜਾਣਾ, ਫੈਲਣਾ, ਉਭਾਰ ਦੇਣਾ; ਫੁਲਣਾ ਜਾਂ ਫੁਲਾਉਣਾ, ਸੋਜ, ਉਭਾਰ, ਉਫ਼ਾਰ, ਉਮੜ ਉੱਛਾਲਾ; ਹੁਲਾਰਾ; ~ing ਸੋਜ, ਫੁਲਾਉ, ਉਭਾਰ; ਉਠਾਅ, ਪੱਫੜ

swift (ਸਵਿਫ਼ਟ) *a adv* ਤੀਬਰ, ਤੇਜ਼; ਫੁਰਤੀਲਾ, ਵੇਗਵਾਨ; ਤੀਬਰਤਾ ਨਾਲ, ਤੇਜ਼ੀ ਨਾਲ; ਜਲਦੀ ਨਾਲ; ~ness ਤੀਬਰਤਾ, ਤੇਜ਼ੀ, ਸਫ਼ੁਰਤੀ, ਤਤਪਰਤਾ

swim (ਸਵਿਮ) *v n* ਤਰਨਾ, ਤਾਰੀ ਲਾਉਣੀ, ਪਾਰ ਕਰਨਾ; ਤੈਰਾਕੀ; ~mer ਤਾਰੂ, ਤੈਰਾਕ;

swindle (ਸਵਿੰਡਲ) *v n* ਛਲ ਕਰਨਾ, ਠੱਗਣਾ, ਲੁੱਟ ਲੈਣਾ, ਮੁੱਠਣਾ, ਮੁੱਛਣਾ, ਛਲ ਲੈਣਾ; ਕਪਟ, ਛਲ, ਧੋਖਾ, ਠੱਗੀ, ਫ਼ਰੇਬ

swine (ਸਵਾਇਨ) *n* ਸੂਰ; ਲਾਲਚੀ ਆਦਮੀ, ਲੋਭੀ ਵਿਆਕਤੀ, ਨੀਚ ਆਦਮੀ

swing (ਸਵਿੰਡ) *v n* ਝੂਲਣਾ, ਝੁਲਾਉਣਾ;

ਹੁਲਾਰਨਾ, ਹੁਲਾਰੇ ਖਾਣਾ, ਪੀਂਘ ਝੂਟਣਾ; ਫੇਰਨਾ, ਝੁਲਾਰਨਾ (ਬਾਂਹ); ਘੁਮਾਉਣਾ, ਝੂਮਦੇ ਹੋਏ ਚੱਲਣਾ; ਝੂਮਣਾ; ਫਾਂਸੀ ਤੇ ਲਟਕਣਾ, ਝੂਲਾ; ਝੂਟਾ, ਹੂਟਾ; ਹੁਲਾਰਾ, ਝਲ

sword (ਸੋਡ) *n* ਤਲਵਾਰ, ਤੇਗਾ, ਸ਼ਮਸ਼ੀਰ, ਖੜਗ, ਕਿਰਪਾਨ

sycophancy ('ਸਿਕਅਫ਼ਅੰਸਿ) *n* ਖ਼ੁਸ਼ਾਮਦ, ਚਾਪਲੂਸੀ, ਜੀ-ਹਜ਼ੂਰੀ

sycophant ('ਸਿਕਅਫ਼ਅੰਟ) *n* ਚਾਪਲੂਸ, ਖ਼ੁਸ਼ਾਮਦੀ ਟੁੱਟ, ਜੀ ਹਜ਼ੂਰੀਆ

syllable ('ਸਿਲਅਬਲ) *n v* ਉਚਾਰਖੰਡ; ਸਾਫ਼ ਸਾਫ਼ ਬੋਲਣਾ, ਇਕ ਇਕ ਸ਼ਬਦਾਂਸ਼ ਬੋਲਣਾ

syllabus ('ਸਿਲਅਬਅਸ) *n* ਵਿਸ਼ੇ-ਪ੍ਰਣਾਲੀ, ਸਾਰਾਂਸ਼, ਸਾਰ-ਸੰਗ੍ਰਹ, ਖ਼ਾਕਾ

symbol (ਸਿੰਬਲ) *n* ਸੰਕੇਤ, ਨਿਸ਼ਾਨ, ਪ੍ਰਤੀਕ, ਚਿੰਨ੍ਹ; ~ic, ~ical ਸੰਕੇਤਕ; ਚਿੰਨ੍ਹ ਮਾਤਰਾ; ਲਿਪੀ ਚਿੰਨ੍ਹ ਪ੍ਰਤੀਕਾਤਮਕ; ~ism ਚਿੰਨ੍ਹਵਾਦ, ਸੰਕੇਤਕਤਾ, ਸੰਕੇਤ-ਪੱਧਤੀ, ਪ੍ਰਤੀਕਵਾਦ

symmetric, -al (ਸਿ'ਮੇਟਰਿਕ, ਸਿ'ਮੇਟੱਰਿਕਲ) *a* ਸਡੌਲ, ਮੇਲ ਖਾਂਦਾ, ਸਮ-ਮਾਪੀ, ਸਮਰੂਪੀ

symmetry ('ਸਿਮਅਟਰਿ) *n* ਸੁਡੌਲਤਾ, ਸਮਤਾ, ਮੇਲ, ਸਮ-ਤੁਲਨਾ, ਸਮਰੂਪ

sympathetic ('ਸਿੰਪਅ'ਥੈਟਿਕ) *a* ਹਮਦਰਦ, ਦਰਦਵੰਦ, ਹਮਦਮ, ਦਿਆਲੂ; ਹਿਮਾਇਤੀ

sympathize ('ਸਿੰਪਥਾਇਜ਼) *v* ਹਮਦਰਦੀ ਰੱਖਣੀ, ਹਮਦਰਦੀ ਪਰਗਟ ਕਰਨੀ; ਦਰਦ ਵੰਡਾਉਣਾ; ਦਇਆ ਕਰਨਾ

sympathy ('ਸਿੰਪਅਥਿ) *n* ਹਮਦਰਦੀ, ਦਰਦਵੰਦੀ; ਸੰਮਤੀ, ਤਾਈਦ, ਹਿਮਾਇਤ

symptom ('ਸਿੰਮ(ਪ)ਟਅਮ) *n* (ਰੋਗ ਦੀ) ਨਿਸ਼ਾਨੀ; ਲੱਛਣ, ਸੰਕੇਤ; ~atic ਲਾਖਣਿਕ,

ਚਿੰਨ੍ਹ-ਮਾਤਰ, ਬੋਧਕ

synchronize ('ਸਿਡ਼ਕਰਅਨਾਇਜ਼) *v*
ਸਮਕਾਲਵਰਤੀ ਹੋਣਾ

synopsis (ਸਿ'ਨੌਪਸਿਸ) *n* ਖੁਲਾਸਾ, ਸੰਖੇਪ,
ਸਾਰਾਂਸ਼, ਰੁਪ-ਰੇਖਾ, ਵਸਤੁਸਾਰ

syntax ('ਸਿੰਟੈਕਸ) *n* ਵਾਕ-ਰਚਨਾ, ਵਾਕ-ਵਿਉਂਤ

syrup, sirup ('ਸਿਰਅਪ) *n* ਸੀਰਾ, ਚਾਸ਼ਨੀ;
ਸ਼ਰਬਤ

system ('ਸਿਸਟਅਮ) *n* ਪ੍ਰਣਾਲੀ, ਪਧੱਤੀ,
ਤਰੀਕਾ, ਚਾਲ; ਜਗਤ, ਸੰਸਾਰ; ਕ੍ਰਮ;
ਸਿਲਸਲਾ, ਵਿਵਸਥਾ, ਯੋਜਨਾ, ਤੰਤਰ,
ਸਮੁਦਾਇ; **~atic** ਕ੍ਰਮਬੱਧ, ਵਿਵਸਥਿਤ,
ਨਿਯਮਤ, ਵਿਧੀਪੂਰਵਕ, ਰੀਤੀਬੱਧ,
ਸਿਲਸਿਲੇਵਾਰ, ਬਾਕਾਇਦਾ

T

T, t (ਟੀ) *n* ਰੋਮਨ ਵਰਨਮਾਲਾ ਦਾ ਵੀਹਵਾਂ ਅੱਖਰ; *cross the ~ 's* ਪੂਰੀ ਤਰ੍ਹਾਂ ਠੀਕ ਕਰ ਦੇਣਾ

tab (ਟੈਬ) *n* ਤਸਮਾ; ਟੈਪੀ ਦਾ ਕੰਨ-ਪਟਾ; ਤਸਮੇ ਦਾ ਛੱਲਾ; (ਬੋਲ) ਜਾਂਚ, ਹਿਸਾਬ-ਕਿਤਾਬ, ਨਿਰੀਖਣ; *keep ~s on* ਹਿਸਾਬ-ਕਿਤਾਬ, ਨਿਰੀਖਣ

table ('ਟੇਇਬਲ) *n v* ਮੇਜ਼, ਖਾਣੇ ਦੀ ਮੇਜ਼, ਚੌਕੀ; ਪਟੜਾ, ਪਟੜੀ; ਸਾਰਨੀ ਸੂਚੀ; ਮੇਜ਼ ਉੱਤੇ ਰੱਖਣਾ, ਪਰੋਸਣਾ; ~**land** ਪਠਾਰ, ਪੱਬੀ

tableau ('ਟੈਬਲਅਉ) *n* ਦ੍ਰਿਸ਼, ਝਾਕੀ, ਸਚਿੱਤਰ ਪੇਸ਼ਕਾਰੀ; ~**curtains** ਕਨਾਤੀ ਪਰਦੇ

tabloid ('ਟੈਬਲੌਇਡ) *n* ਸਮਾਚਾਰ-ਪੱਤਰ; ਪੱਤਰਕਾ, ਛੋਟੇ ਆਕਾਰ ਦੀ ਅਖ਼ਬਾਰ

taboo, tabu (ਟਅ'ਬੂ) *n a v* ਮਨਾਹੀ; ਵਿਵਰਜਤ; ਮਨਾਹੀ ਕਰਨੀ, ਵਿਵਰਜਤ ਠਹਿਰਾਉਣਾ; ਪਰੇ ਰੱਖਣਾ

tabor ('ਟੇਇਬਅ*) *n v* (ਇਤਿਹਾਸਕ) ਢੋਲਕੀ; ਤਬਲਾ; ਤਬਲਾ ਵਜਾਉਣਾ

tabulate ('ਟੈਬਯੁਲਅ) *v a* ਸੂਚੀ ਬਣਾਉਣਾ, ਸਾਰਨੀਬੱਧ ਕਰਨਾ, ਖ਼ਾਨੇ ਵਾਹੁਣਾ; ਸਾਰਨੀਬੱਧ, ਤਾਲਿਕਾਬੱਧ

tabulation ('ਟੈਬਯੁ'ਲੇਇਸ਼ਨ) *n* ਸਾਰਨੀਕਰਨ

tacit ('ਟੈਸਿਟ) *a* ਗੁਪਤ, ਅਣਕਿਹਾ, ਗੁੱਝਾ; ਬਿਨਬੋਲਿਆ; ਖ਼ਮੋਸ਼

tack (ਟੈਕ) *n v* ਕਿੱਲ, ਕੋਕਾ, ਬਿਰੰਜੀ; (ਬ ਵ) ਕੱਚੀ ਸਿਲਾਈ, ਟੋਪੇ, ਨਗੰਦੇ; ਟਾਂਕਣਾ, ਨੱਥੀ ਕਰਨਾ; (ਜਹਾਜ਼ ਦਾ) ਰਾਹ ਬਦਲਣਾ, ਰੁਖ ਫੇਰਨਾ; ~**ing** ਕਿੱਲ ਠੋਕਣਾ; ਬਖ਼ੀਆ ਕਰਨਾ,

ਟੋਪੇ ਲਾਉਣਾ; ਕ੍ਰਮਬੱਧ ਕਰਨਾ, ਇਕੱਤਰਤ ਕਰਨਾ

tackle ('ਟੈਕਲ) *v* ਬਹਿਸ ਕਰਨਾ, ਤਕਰਾਰ ਕਰਨਾ; ਟਿਪਟਾਉਣ ਦਾ ਜਤਨ ਕਰਨਾ, ਨਿਜਿੱਠਣਾ, ਸਿੱਝਣਾ; ਮੁਕਾਬਲਾ ਕਰਨਾ

tact (ਟੈਕਟ) *n* ਸੁੱਚਜ, ਜੁਗਤ, ਢੰਗ, ਵਿਧੀ, ਸਿਆਣਪ; ~**ful** ਸੁੱਚਜਾ, ਸਿਆਣਾ, ਵਿਓਂਤੀਆ, ਜੁਗਤੀ, ਚਤਰ; ~**ical** ਯੁਕਤੀਪੂਰਨ; ~**ics** ਜੁੱਧ-ਕਲਾ, ਜੰਗੀ ਚਾਲਾਂ, ਦਾਅ-ਪੇਚ, ਨਿਪੁੰਨਤਾ, ਚਾਤਰੀ, ਪ੍ਰਪੰਚ, ਚਾਲਬਾਜ਼ੀ, ਤਰਕੀਬ

tag (ਟੈਗ) *n v* ਨੱਥੀ, ਜੋੜ; ਫੀਤਾ, ਤਸਮਾ, ਨੱਥੀ ਕਰਨਾ, ਟਾਂਕਣਾ, ਜੋੜ ਦੇਣਾ; ਜੋੜ ਲਾਉਣਾ; ਤੁਕ ਜੋੜਨੀ

tail (ਟੇਇਲ) *n v* ਪੂਛ, ਪੂਛਲ, ਦੁਮ; ਅੰਤ, ਪਿੱਛਾ, ਪਿਛਾੜੀ; ਹੇਠਲਾ ਭਾਗ, ਸਿਰਾ; ਦੋ ਸਿਰੇ ਤਰਾਸ਼ ਦੇਣਾ; ਜੋੜਨਾ; ਜੁੜਨਾ, ਲੱਗਣਾ

tailor ('ਟੇਇਲਅ*) *n v* ਦਰਜ਼ੀ, ਸਿਲਾਈ ਕਰਨ ਵਾਲਾ; ਕਪੜੇ ਸੀਉਂਣੇ; ~**ing** ਦਰਜ਼ੀਗੀਰੀ, ਸਿਲਾਈ ਦਾ ਕੰਮ

taint ('ਟੇਇੰਟ) *n* ਕਲੰਕ; ਦੋਸ਼, ਖਰਾਬੀ, ਧੱਬਾ, ਦਾਗ਼, ਨਿਸ਼ਾਨ, ਬਦਮਾਸ਼ੀ ਦਾ ਟਿੱਕਾ; ਛੂਤ; ~**ed** ਦੂਸ਼ਤ, ਬਦਨਾਮ, ਕਲੰਕਤ, ਭ੍ਰਿਸ਼ਟ, ਗੰਦਾ; ~**less** ਨਿਰਦੋਸ਼, ਨਿਸ਼ਕਲੰਕ, ਬੇਦਾਗ਼ਾ, ਸਾਫ਼

take (ਟੇਇਕ) *n v* ਸ਼ਿਕਾਰ; ਆਮਦਨੀ, ਰੋਕੜ; ਲੈਣਾ, ਫੜਨਾ, ਕਬਜ਼ਾ ਕਰ ਲੈਣਾ, ਅਧਿਕਾਰ ਵਿਚ ਲੈ ਆਉਣਾ; ਲੈ ਲੈਣਾ, ਪ੍ਰਾਪਤ ਕਰ ਲੈਣਾ ~**action** ਕਾਰਵਾਈ ਕਰਨਾ; ~**after** ਕਿਸੇ ਵਰਗਾ ਹੋਣਾ; ~**arms** ਹਥਿਆਰ ਚੁੱਕਣਾ; ~**in**

hand ਆਰੰਭ ਕਰਨਾ, ਸੁਰੂ ਕਰਨਾ ; **~off** ਨਕਲ, ਵਿਅੰਗ-ਚਿੱਤਰ, ਲਾਹ ਲੈਣਾ, ਘਟਾ ਦੇਣਾ; ਹਵਾਈ ਜਹਾਜ਼ ਦੀ ਚੜ੍ਹਾਈ; ਛਾਲ ਮਾਰਨ ਦਾ ਅੱਡਾ; **~out** ਵੱਖਰਾ ਕਰਨਾ, ਬਾਹਰ ਲੈ ਜਾਣਾ; ਕੱਢਣਾ; **~to task** ਡਾਂਟਣਾ, ਝਾੜ-ਝੰਬ ਕਰਨਾ, ਝਾੜਨਾ; **~up with** ਨਾਲ ਰਹਿਣਾ

taking ('ਟੇਇਕਿਙ) *n a* ਲੈਣ, ਲੈ ਜਾਣ; ਪਕੜ, ਗਰਿਫ਼ਤਾਰੀ; ਬੇਚੈਨੀ; ਦਿਲ-ਖਿੱਚਵਾਂ

tale (ਟੇਇਲ) *n* ਕਹਾਣੀ, ਅਫ਼ਸਾਨਾ; ਕਿੱਸਾ; **~bearer** ਚੁਗ਼ਲ ਖ਼ੋਰ

talent ('ਟੈਲਅੰਟ) *n* ਯੋਗਤਾ, ਪ੍ਰਤਿਭਾ, ਬੁੱਧੀ; **~ed** ਪ੍ਰਤਿਭਾਸੀਲ, ਗੁਣਵਾਨ, ਬੁੱਧੀਵਾਨ

tailsman ('ਟੈਲਿਜ਼ਮਅਨ) *n* ਤਾਵੀਜ਼, ਜੰਤਰ; ਰੱਖ; ਤਲਿਸਮ, ਜਾਦੂ

talk (ਟੋਕ) *n v* ਵਾਰਤਾ; ਬੋਲ; ਗੱਲ-ਕੱਥ; ਬੋਲਣਾ, ਗੱਲ ਕਰਨੀ, ਵਾਰਤਾਲਾਪ ਕਰਨੀ; ਗੱਪ ਮਾਰਨੀ; **~ative** ਬੜਬੋਲਾ ਗਾਲੜੀ, ਗਲਾਦਰੜ; **~er** ਵਾਰਤਾਕਾਰ, ਵਕਤਾ, ਗੱਪੀ, ਸ਼ੇਖੀਬਾਜ਼; **~ing** ਬੋਲਣ ਵਾਲਾ

tall (ਟੋਲ) *a adv* ਲੰਮਾ, ਉੱਚਾ, ਵੱਡਾ; ਹੱਦ ਤੋਂ ਵਧ; **~ness** ਲੰਬਾਈ, ਉਚਾਈ, ਬੁਲੰਦੀ, ਕੱਦ

tally ('ਟੈਲਿ) *n v* (ਇਤਿ) ਲੇਖਾ-ਪੱਟੀ, ਹਿਸਾਬ, ਲੇਖਾ; ਹੋਣਾ, (ਲੇਖ) ਮੇਲ ਖਾਣਾ, ਬਰਾਬਰ ਹੋਣਾ, ਠੀਕ ਨਿਕਲਣਾ, ਮਿਲਣਾ

tame (ਟੇਇਮ) *a v* ਘਰੇਲੂ, ਪਾਲਿਆ, ਪਾਲਤੂ; ਪ੍ਰਭਾਹੀਣ; ਫਿੱਕਾ, ਬੇਅਸਰ, ਸਿਧਾਉਣਾ, ਪਾਲਤੂ ਬਣਾ ਲੈਣਾ; ਵੱਸ ਕਰਨਾ, ਕਾਬੂ ਕਰਨਾ

tamper ('ਟੈਮਪਅ*) *v* ਦਖ਼ਲ ਦੇਣਾ, ਤੋੜ-ਮਰੋੜ ਕਰਨਾ; ਪ੍ਰਭਾਵ ਪਾਉਣਾ

tangible ('ਟੈਂਜਅਬਲ) *a* ਸਪਰਸ਼ੀ; ਸਥੂਲ,

ਨਿੱਗਰ, ਯਥਾਰਥ, ਸਪਸ਼ਟ; ਵਾਸਤਵਿਕ, ਭੌਤਕ, ਸਰੀਰਕ, ਨਿਸ਼ਚਤ; **~ness** ਸਪਰਸ਼ਤਾ, ਸਥੂਲਤਾ, ਵਾਸਤਵਿਕਤਾ, ਭੌਤਕਤਾ; **~d** ਜਟਿਲ, ਪੇਚੀਦਾ, ਗੁਝੰਲਦਾਰ, ਉਲਝਿਆ ਹੋਇਆ

tank (ਟੈਙਕ) *n* ਟੈਂਕੀ, ਹੌਜ਼, ਟੈਂਕ, ਸਰੋਵਰ, ਤਲਾਬ, ਜੰਗੀ ਮੋਟਰ ਗੱਡੀ; **~er** ਤੇਲ ਦਾ ਜਹਾਜ਼, ਟੈਂਕੀ ਵਾਲਾ ਜਹਾਜ਼

tantalize ('ਟੈਂਟਅਲਾਇਜ਼) *v* ਤਰਸਾਉਣਾ, ਕਲਪਾਉਣਾ, ਝੂਠੀਆਂ ਆਸਾਂ ਦੇਣੀਆਂ, ਮਾਨਸਕ ਕਸ਼ਟ ਦੇਣਾ; ਚਿੜ੍ਹਾਉਣਾ

tantamount ('ਟੈਂਟਅਮਾਉਂਟ) *a* ਤੁੱਲ, ਸਮਾਨ, ਬਰਾਬਰ, ਤੁਲਾਰਥ

tap (ਟੈਪ) *n v* (1) ਨਲ, ਬੰਬਾ; ਡਾਟ, ਡੱਟਾ; ਖੜਕਾਰ, (2) ਖਟ-ਖਟ, ਟਕੋਰ; ਟੂਟੀ ਲਾਉਣੀ, ਖੜਕਾਉਣਾ

tape (ਟੇਇਪ) *n v* ਫ਼ੀਤਾ, ਨਵਾਰ, ਟੇਪ; ਫ਼ੀਤੇ ਲਗਾਉਣਾ

tar (ਟਾ*) *n v* ਲੁੱਕ, ਤਾਰਕੋਲ, ਕੋਲਤਾਰ; ਲੁੱਕ ਮਲਣੀ, ਲੁੱਕ ਵਿਛਾਉਣੀ (ਸੜਕ ਉੱਤੇ); ਕਾਲਾ ਕਰਨਾ

tardiness ('ਟਾਡਿਨਿਸ) *n* ਸੁਸਤੀ, ਆਲਸ, ਮੰਦਤਾ, ਢਿੱਲ, ਹਿਚਕਚਾਹਟ, ਟਾਲ-ਮਟੋਲ

tardo ('ਟਾਡੋਅਉ) *a* ਹੌਲੀ-ਹੌਲੀ, ਆਹਿਸਤਾ-ਆਹਿਸਤਾ, ਮੰਦ-ਮੰਦ

tardy ('ਟਾਡਿ) *a* ਆਲਸੀ, ਸੁਸਤ, ਢਿੱਲਾ, ਮੱਠਾ, ਮੰਦ

target ('ਟਾਗਿਟ) *n* ਨਿਸ਼ਾਨਾ, ਟੀਚਾ

tariff ('ਟੈਰਿਫ਼) *n v* ਮਹਿਸੂਲ, ਚੁੰਗੀ, ਕਰ, ਨਿਰਖ਼ਨਾਮਾ; ਮੁੱਲ ਲਿਖਣਾ

tarnish ('ਟਾਨਿਸ਼) *n v* ਦਾਗ਼, ਬੱਜ; ਬਦਰੰਗ

ਕਰਨਾ ਜਾਂ ਹੋਣਾ, ਸ਼ਕਲ ਵਿਗਾੜਨੀ ਜਾਂ ਵਿਗਾੜਨੀ; ~ed ਕਲੰਕਤ, ਦਾਗ਼ੀ, ਬੇਆਬਰੂ

taro ('ਟਾਰਅਉ) *n* ਕਚਾਲੂ

tarpaulin (ਟਾ'ਪੋਲਿਨ) *n* ਤਿਰਪਾਲ; ਮੱਲਾਹ

task (ਟਾਸਕ) *n v* ਕੰਮ; ਸੌਂਪਿਆ ਕੰਮ; ਧੰਦਾ, ਘਾਲ; ਬੋਝ ਪਾਉਣਾ, ਕੰਮ ਉੱਤੇ ਲਾਉਣਾ, ਕੰਮ ਲੈਣਾ, ਮਿਹਨਤ ਕਰਾਉਣੀ; ~master ਕੰਮ ਲੈਣ ਵਾਲਾ, ਮਾਲਕ, ਸੁਆਮੀ

taste (ਟੇਇਸਟ) *n v* ਸੁਆਦ, ਰਸ, ਜ਼ਾਇਕਾ; ਰੁਚੀ, ਸ਼ੌਕ, ਸੁਆਦ ਲੈਣਾ, ਚੱਖਣਾ, ਮਜ਼ਾ ਚੱਖਣਾ; ਆਨੰਦ ਲੈਣਾ, ਲੁਤਫ਼ ਲੈਣਾ; ~ful *a* ਮਿੱਠਾ, ਮਜ਼ੇਦਾਰ, ਸੁਆਦੀ (ਵਸਤੂ); ਰੋਚਕ, ਰਸਿਕ (ਵਿਅਕਤੀ); ~less ਫਿੱਕਾ, ਅਲੂਣਾ, ਬੇਸੁਆਦਾ

tasty ('ਟੇਇਸਟਿ) *a* ਸੁਆਦੀ, ਸੁਆਦਲਾ, ਮਜ਼ੇਦਾਰ, ਰਸੀਲਾ

taunt (ਟੌਂਟ) *n v a* ਮਿਹਣਾ, ਮਲਾਮਤ, ਉਲ੍ਹਾਂਭਾ; ਮਿਹਣਾ ਮਾਰਨਾ, ਬੋਲੀ ਮਾਰਨੀ, ਨਿੰਦਾ ਕਰਨੀ; ਉੱਚਾ, ਲੰਮਾ ਉੱਚਾ, ਬੁਲੰਦ

tautologize (ਟੋ'ਟੌਲਅਜਾਇਜ਼) *v* ਦੁਹਰਾਉਣਾ, ਪੁਨਰ-ਉਕਤੀ ਕਰਨਾ

tautology (ਟੋ'ਟੌਲਅਜਿ) *n* ਦੁਹਰਾਉ, ਪੁਨਰ-ਉਕਤੀ

tavern ('ਟੈਵੑ(ਅ)ਨ) *n* ਸ਼ਰਾਬਖ਼ਾਨਾ, ਕਲਾਲ ਖ਼ਾਨਾ, ਠੇਕਾ

tax (ਟੈਕਸ) *n v* ਕਰ, ਮਹੀਸੂਲ, ਟੈਕਸ, ਲਗਾਨ; ਕਰ ਲਾਉਣਾ; ਭਾਰ ਪਾਉਣਾ; ~payer ਕਰ-ਦਾਤਾ; ~ation ਕਰਾਧਾਨ, ਲਗਾਨਬੰਦੀ, ਮਹਿਸੂਲਬੰਦੀ

taxi ('ਟੈਕਸਿ) *n v* ਟੈਕਸੀ, ਕਿਰਾਏ ਦੀ ਮੋਟਰ; ਟੈਕਸੀ ਵਿਚ ਜਾਣਾ

tea (ਟੀ) *n* ਚਾਹ, ਚਾਹ ਦੀ ਪੱਤੀ, ਚਾਹ ਦਾ ਪੌਦਾ

teach (ਟੀਚ) *v* ਪੜ੍ਹਾਉਣਾ, ਪੜ੍ਹਾਈ ਕਰਾਉਣੀ, ਅਧਿਆਪਨ ਕਰਨਾ, ਸਿਖਾਉਣਾ, ਦਿਮਾਗ਼ ਵਿਚ ਬਿਠਾਉਣਾ; ~er ਅਧਿਆਪਕ, ਸਿਖਿਅਕ, ਗੁਰੂ, ਉਸਤਾਦ, ਪ੍ਰਚਾਰਕ; ~ing ਅਧਿਆਪਨ, ਸਿਖਿਅਣ, ਸਿਖਲਾਈ; ਸਿੱਖਿਆ, ਉਪਦੇਸ਼

teak (ਟੀਕ) *n* ਸਾਗਵਾਨ ਦੀ ਲਕੜੀ, ਸਾਲ

team (ਟੀਮ) *n* (ਖਿਡਾਰੀਆਂ ਦੀ) ਟੀਮ; ਜੁੱਟ, ਜੋਟੀ, ਝੁੰਡ, ਸਮੂਹ, ਗਰੋਹ, ਟੋਲੀ

tear (ਟੇਅ*) *v n* ਪਾੜਨਾ, ਟੋਟੇ ਕਰਨਾ, ਫਾੜਨਾ ਜਾਂ ਫਟਨਾ, ਚੀਰਨਾ, ਅੱਲਗ ਅੱਲਗ ਕਰਨਾ, ਚਾਕ ਕਰਨਾ, ਚੀਰਾ ਲਾਉਣਾ; ਚੀਰ; ਅੱਥਰੂ, ਹੰਝੂ, ਕਤਰਾ; ~gas ਅੱਥਰੂ ਗੈਸ; ~ful ਹੰਝੂਆਂ ਨਾਲ ਭਰਿਆ, ਸੱਜਲ; ਰੋਣਹਾਕਾ; ~ing ਚੀਰਨ ਵਾਲਾ, ਫਾੜਨ ਵਾਲਾ

tease (ਟੀਜ਼) *v* ਛੇੜਨਾ, ਸਤਾਉਣਾ, ਤੰਗ ਕਰਨਾ, ਹੈਰਾਨ ਕਰਨਾ; ਚਿੜਾਉਣਾ, ਖਪਾਉਣਾ, ਖਿਝਾਉਣਾ, ਪਿੱਛੇ ਪੈ ਜਾਣਾ; ਝਕਾਉਣਾ

teat (ਟੀਟ) *n* ਪਸ਼ੂਆਂ ਦਾ ਥਣ, ਖੀਰੀ; ਚੂਚੀ, ਚੁੰਘਣੀ, ਨਿਪਲ

technical ('ਟੈਕਨਿਕਲ) *a* ਤਕਨੀਕੀ; ਜੰਤਰਕ ਪਰਿਭਾਸ਼ਕ; ~ity ਤਕਨੀਕੀਪੁਣਾ, ਪਰਿਭਾਸ਼ਕਤਾ, ਸ਼ਾਸਤਰੀਅਤਾ

technician (ਟੈਕ'ਨਿਸ਼ਨ) *a* ਤਕਨੀਕੀ ਮਾਹਰ, ਮਿਸਤਰੀ

technicolor ('ਟੈਕਨਿ'ਕਅੱਲਅ*) *n* ਚਲਚਿੱਤਰ ਨੂੰ ਰੰਗੀਨ ਬਣਾਉਣ ਦੀ ਵਿਧੀ

technique (ਟੈਕ'ਨੀਕ) *n* ਤਕਨੀਕ, ਪੱਧਤੀ, ਰੀਤੀ, ਵੱਲ, ਕਾਰੀਗਰੀ; ਚਾਤਰਤਾ

technology (ਟੈਕ'ਨੌਲਅਜਿ) *n* ਸ਼ਿਲਪ-ਵਿਗਿਆਨ, ਉਦਯੋਗ-ਵਿਗਿਆਨ

tedious ('ਟੀਡੀਅਸ) *a* ਹੰਢਾਊ, ਅਕਾਊ, ਅਰੋਚਕ, ਉਕਤਾਊਂਟ ਵਾਲ਼ਾ; ~ness ਥਕਾਵਟ, ਥਕੇਵਾਂ, ਅਕੇਵਾਂ, ਉਕਤਾਹਟ

teen (ਟੀਨ) *n* (ਅਪ) ਦੁੱਖ, ਕਸ਼ਟ, ਕਲੇਸ਼

teens (ਟੀਨਜ਼) *n* ਕਿਸ਼ੋਰ ਅਵਸਥਾ; ਲੜਕਪਨ

teetotal (ਟੀ'ਟਉਟਲ) *n* ਨਸ਼ੇ-ਵਿਰੋਧੀ, ਨਸ਼ੇ-ਵਿਰੋਧ ਸਬੰਧੀ; ~ism ਨਸ਼ਾ-ਵਿਰੋਧ, ਨਸ਼ਾ-ਤਿਆਗ, ਸੁਧੀਪੁਣਾ; ~ler ਨਸ਼ਿਆਂ ਦਾ ਕੱਟੜ ਵਿਰੋਪੀ; ਸੂਧੀ

telecommunication(s) ('ਟੈਲਿਕਅਮਯੂਨਿ'ਕੇਇਸ਼ਨ(ਜ਼)) *n pl* ਦੂਰ ਸੰਚਾਰ

telegram ('ਟੈਲਿਗਰਾਮ) *n* ਤਾਰ (ਸੁਨੇਹਾ), ਦੂਰ ਸੰਵਾਦ, ਦੂਰ ਲੇਖ

telegraph ('ਟੈਲਿਗਰਾਫ਼) *v* ਤਾਰ-ਪ੍ਰਬੰਧ, ਤਾਰ-ਜੰਤਰ; ~y ਤਾਰ ਪ੍ਰਣਾਲੀ

telepathy (ਟਿ'ਲੈੱਪਅਥਿ) *n* ਦੂਰ-ਸੰਵੇਦਨ, ਟੈਲੀਪੈਥੀ

telephone ('ਟੈਲਿਫ਼ਅਉਨ) *n v* ਦੂਰਭਾਸ਼, ਟੇਲੀਫ਼ੋਨ; ਫ਼ੋਨ ਕਰਨਾ

teleprint ('ਟੈਲਿਪਰਿੰਟ) *v* ਦੂਰ ਲੇਖੀ ਦੁਆਰਾ ਲਿਖਣਾ, ਟੈਲੀਪ੍ਰਿੰਟਰ ਦੁਆਰਾ ਛਾਪਣਾ; ~er ਤਾਰ ਲੇਖੀ, ਦੂਰ ਮੁਦ੍ਰਕ

telescope ('ਟੈਲਿਸਕਅਉਪ) *n v* ਦੂਰਦਰਸ਼ਕ ਜੰਤਰ, ਦੂਰਦਰਸ਼ੀ, ਦੂਰਬੀਨ; ਘੁੱਸ ਜਾਣਾ, ਟਿਕ ਜਾਣਾ

television ('ਟੈਲਿ'ਵਿਯ਼ਨ) *n* ਦੂਰਦਰਸਨ, ਪਰੋਖਾ ਦ੍ਰਿਸ਼

tell (ਟੈੱਲ) *v* ਕਹਿਣਾ, ਵਰਨਣ ਕਰਨਾ, ਸੁਣਾਉਣਾ, ਬਿਆਨ ਕਰਨਾ, ਪਰਗਟ ਕਰਨਾ, ਸਮਝਾਉਣਾ, ਦੱਸਣਾ; ~tale ਚੁਗਲ, ਭੇਤ-ਪਰਗਟਾਊ

temblor (ਟੈੱਬਲਅਾ*) *n* ਭੂਚਾਲ, ਭੂਕੰਪ

temper ('ਟੈੱਪਅਾ*) *n v* ਸੁਭਾਅ, ਮਿਜ਼ਾਜ; ਕਰੋਧ, ਚਿੜਚੜਾਪਣ; ਨਰਮ ਕਰਨਾ; ਜ਼ੋਰ ਘਟਾਉਣਾ; ~ament ਸੁਭਾਅ, ਪ੍ਰਕਿਰਤੀ, ਮਿਜ਼ਾਜ, ਤਬੀਅਤ; ~ature ਤਾਪਮਾਨ, ਤਾਪ, ਬੁਖ਼ਾਰ, ਗਰਮੀ

tempest ('ਟੈੱਪਿਸਟ) *n* ਝੱਖੜ, ਤੂਫ਼ਾਨ, (ਬੋਲ) ਉੱਪਦਰ, ਹਲਚਲ, ਹੰਗਾਮਾ, ਹੁੱਲੜ, ਸ਼ੋਰ-ਸ਼ਰਾਬਾ

temple ('ਟੈੱਪਲ) *n* (1) ਮੰਦਰ, ਸ਼ਿਵਾਲਾ, ਦੇਵ ਮੰਦਰ ਗਿਰਜਾ-ਘਰ, ਪੂਜਾ-ਸਥਾਨ, ਠਾਕਰ-ਦੁਆਰਾ; (2) ਪ੍ਰੱਜਪੜੀ, ਕਨਪਟੀ

tempo ('ਟੈੱਪਅਉ) *n* ਤਾਲ; ਗਤੀ, ਚਾਲ; ਜੋਸ਼

temporal ('ਟੈੱਪ(ਅ)ਰ(ਅ)ਲ) *a* ਕਨਪਟੀ ਸਬੰਧੀ; ਸੰਸਾਰੀ, ਸੰਸਾਰਕ, ਦੁਨਿਆਵੀ, ਕਾਲ-ਸੂਚਕ; ਲੌਕਿਕ, ਭੌਤਕ

temporary ('ਟੈੱਪ(ਅ)ਰਅਰਿ) *a* ਕੱਚੀ, ਆਰਜ਼ੀ, ਵਕਤੀ, ਕੰਮ-ਚਲਾਊ, ਵੇਲਾ-ਟਪਾਊ

temporize ('ਟੈੱਪਅਪਰਾਇਜ਼) *v* ਵੇਲਾ ਟਪਾਉਣਾ, ਢੰਗ ਟਪਾਈ, ਵਕਤ ਟਾਲਣਾ, ਟਾਲਮਟੋਲ ਕਰਨਾ; ਦੁਨੀਆਸਾਜ਼ੀ ਕਰਨਾ

tempt (ਟੈੱ(ਪ)ਟ) *v* ਵਰਗਲਾਉਣਾ. ਭਰਮਾਉਣਾ, ਲੁਭਾਉਣਾ; ਕੋਸ਼ਸ਼ ਕਰਨੀ; ~ation ਲਾਲਚ, ਲੋਭ, ਚਕਮਾ, ਭਰਮਾਉਣਾ, ਭੁਲਾਵਾ

ten (ਟੈੱਨ) *a n* ਦਸ; ਦਹਾਕਾ, ਦਹਾਈ, ਦਹਾ

tenable (ਟੈੱਨਅਬਲ) *a* ਚਾਲੂ, ਟਿਕਾਊ, ਤਰਕ-ਸੰਗਤ

tenacious (ਟਿ'ਨੇਇਸ਼ਅਸ) *a* ਮਜ਼ਬੂਤ, ਪੱਕਾ, ਕੱਟੜ, ਦ੍ਰਿੜ-ਸਿਧਾਂਤਵਾਦੀ; ਕੰਜੂਸ, ਸੂਮ, ਹਠੀ, ਚੀੜ੍ਹਾ; ਤਕੜਾ; ~ness, tenacity ਮਜ਼ਬੂਤੀ, ਪਕਿਆਈ, ਦ੍ਰਿੜਤਾ, ਹਠ

tenancy (ਟੈੱਨਅੰਸਿ) *n* ਕਿਰਾਏਦਾਰੀ; ਭਾੜੇਦਾਰੀ; ਲਗਾਨਦਾਰੀ, ਕਾਸ਼ਤਕਾਰੀ

tenant ('ਟੈਨੰਅੰਟ) *n v* ਕਿਰਾਏਦਾਰ, ਪੱਟੇਦਾਰ, ਮੁਜ਼ਾਰਾ; ਲਗਾਨਦਾਰ; ਵੱਸਣਾ, ਕਬਜ਼ਾ ਕਰਨਾ; ਕਿਰਾਏ ਤੇ ਲੈਣਾ

tend (ਟੈਂਡ) *v* (ਬੀਮਾਰੀ ਦੀ) ਸੇਵਾ ਕਰਨੀ, ਟਹਿਲ ਕਰਨੀ, ਨਾਲ ਰਹਿਣਾ, ਖ਼ਬਰਗੀਰੀ ਕਰਨੀ, ਨਿਗਰਾਨੀ ਕਰਨੀ, ਤੀਮਰਦਾਰੀ ਕਰਨੀ; ਦੇਖਭਾਲ ਕਰਨੀ

tendency (ਟੈਂਡੈਂਸੀ) *n* ਝੁਕਾਉ; ਰੁਖ, ਰੁਝਾਨ, ਪ੍ਰਵਿਰਤੀ

tender ('ਟੈਂਡਅ*) *n v a* ਠੇਕਾ, ਟੈਂਡਰ; ਪੇਸ਼ ਕਰਨਾ, ਬੇਟਾ ਦੇਣਾ; ਤਖ਼ਮੀਨਾ ਪੇਸ਼ ਕਰਨਾ, ਅਨੁਮਾਨ ਪੇਸ਼ ਕਰਨਾ (ਠੇਕੇਦਾਰ ਵੱਲੋਂ); ਨਰਮ, ਮੁਲਾਇਮ; ਨਾਜ਼ੁਕ, ਕੁਲਾ; ~foot ਕੋਮਲ; ਨਵਾਂ ਆਦਮੀ, ਸਿਖਾਂਦੜ

tenement (ਟੈਨੱਅਮਅੰਟ) *n* ਮਕਾਨ ਨਿਵਾਸ ਸਥਾਨ, ਹਵੇਲੀ; ਜਾਇਦਾਦ

tenor (ਟੈਨੱਅ*) *n* ਚਾਲ, ਵਿਧੀ, ਤਰੀਕਾ; ਤਰਜ਼

tense ('ਟੈਂਸ) *a v n* ਤਣਿਆ, ਖਿੱਚਿਆ, ਆਕਰਸ਼ਿਆ, ਕੱਸਿਆ; ਬੇਚੈਨ, ਉਤੇਜਤ; ਤਾਣਨਾ, ਖਿੱਚਣਾ, ਕੱਸਣਾ; (ਵਿਆ) ਕਾਲ

tension ('ਟੈਨੱਸ਼ਨ) *n* ਤਣਾਉ, ਕੱਸ, ਖਿੱਚ, ਖਿਚਾਉ, ਕਸਾਉ, ਫੈਲਾਉ; ਤਣਾਤਣੀ, ਖਿੱਚੋਤਾਣ

tent (ਟੈਂਟ) *n* ਤੰਬੂ, ਖੇਮਾ, ਫੋਲਦਾਰੀ; ਡੇਰਾ ਲਾਉਣਾ; ~ed ਤੰਬੂਦਾਰ, ਖੇਮੇ ਵਾਲਾ

tenuous ('ਟੈਨੱਯੂਅਸ) *a* ਮਹੀਨ, ਬਾਰੀਕ, ਪਤਲਾ, ਸੂਖਮ, ਅਲਪ

tenure ('ਟੈਂਨਯੂਅ*) *a* ਮਿਆਦ ਅਧਿਕਾਰ-ਕਾਲ, ਕਾਰਜ-ਕਾਲ ਮਲਕੀਅਤ, ਕਬਜ਼ਾ, ਦਖ਼ਲ

term (ਟਅਃਮ) *n v* ਮਿਆਦ, ਮੁੱਦਤ, ਅਵਧੀ; ਸਿੱਖਿਆ-ਕਾਲ; ਹੱਦ, ਸੀਮਾ; ਨਿਜਤ ਦਿਵਸ, ਨਿਸ਼ਚਤ ਤਿਥੀ; (ਕਾ) ਮਿਆਦੀ ਕਬਜ਼ਾ (ਭਾਸ਼ਾ) ਸ਼ਬਦ, ਪਦ; ਬੰਧਨ; ਸ਼ਰਤ; ਕਹਿਣਾ, ਨਾਮਜ਼ਦ ਕਰਨਾ

terminal ('ਟਅਃਮਿਨਲ) *a n* ਅੰਤਲਾ, ਮਿਆਦੀ; ਅਖੀਰੀ; ਮਾਤਰਕ (ਖ਼ਰਚ); ਫੇਕਜ਼ਲਾ; ਹੱਦ, ਧੁਰ, ਅੰਤ, ਸਿਰਾ

terminate ('ਟਅਃਮਿਨੇਇਟ) *v a* ਅੰਤ ਕਰਨਾ ਜਾਂ ਖ਼ਤਮ ਕਰਨਾ ਜਾਂ ਹੋਣਾ; ਸੀਮਤ ਕਰਨਾ, ਹੱਦ ਬੰਨ੍ਹਣਾ; ਖ਼ਤਮ ਹੋਣ ਵਾਲਾ; ਸੀਮਿਤ

termination ('ਟਅਃਮਿ'ਨੇਇਸ਼ਨ) *n* ਅੰਤ, ਖ਼ਾਤਮਾ, ਸੀਮਾ, ਹੱਦਬੰਦੀ

terminology ('ਟਅਃਮਿ'ਨੌਲਅਜਿ) *n* ਪਰਿਭਾਸ਼ਾ-ਵਿਗਿਆਨ, ਪਰਿਭਾਸ਼ੀ, ਪਰਿਭਾਸ਼ਕ ਸ਼ਬਦਾਵਲੀ

terminus ('ਟਅਃਮਿਨਅਸ) *n* ਅੰਤਲਾ ਸਟੇਸ਼ਨ

termite ('ਟਅਃਮਾਇਟ) *n* ਦੀਮਕ, ਸਿਉਂਕ

terrace ('ਟੈਰੱਅਸ) *n* ਚਬੂਤਰਾ, ਚੌਤਰਾ; ਖੁੱਲ੍ਹੀ ਛੱਤ

terrain (ਟੈ'ਰੇਇਨ) *n* ਜ਼ਮੀਨ ਦਾ ਭਾਗ, ਖੇਤਰ, ਧਰਾਤਲ

terrible ('ਟੈਰੱਅਬਲ) *a* ਭਿਆਨਕ, ਵਿਕਰਾਲ, ਭਿਅੰਕਰ, ਡਰਾਉਣਾ; ਤੀਬਰ, ਅਤੀ ਪ੍ਰਚੰਡ, ਬਹੁਤ ਤੇਜ਼, ਬੜਾ ਭਾਰੀ, ਡਾਢਾ

terrific (ਟਅ'ਰਿਫ਼ਿਕ) *a* ਭਿਅੰਕਰ, ਵਿਕਰਾਲ, ਡਰਾਉਣਾ, ਭਿਆਨਕ, ਘੋਰ, ਡਾਢਾ

terrify ('ਟੈਰਿਫ਼ਾਇ) *v* ਭੈਭੀਤ ਕਰਨਾ, ਡਰਾਉਣਾ, ਭੈ ਦੇਣਾ

territorial ('ਟੈਰਅ'ਟੋਰਿਅਲ) *n* ਪ੍ਰਦੇਸ਼ਕ, ਰਾਜ-ਖੇਤਰੀ

territory ('ਟੈਰੱਅਟ(ਅ)ਰਿ) *n* ਪ੍ਰਦੇਸ਼, ਰਾਜ, ਰਾਜਖੇਤਰ, ਇਲਾਕਾ, ਖੰਡ

terror ('ਟੈਰੱਅ*) *n* ਡਰ, ਖੌਫ਼, ਤਰਾਸ, ਹੌਲ; ~sticken ਭੈਭੀਤ, ਡਰ ਮਾਰਿਆ; ~ism

ਆਤੰਕਵਾਦ; **~ist** ਆਤੰਕਵਾਦੀ, ਦਹਿਸ਼ਤ ਪਸੰਦ; **~ize** ਭੈਭੀਤ ਕਰਨਾ, ਡਰਾਉਣਾ

terse (ਟਾਃਸ) *a* ਸਪਸ਼ਟ, ਸਾਫ਼-ਸੁਥਰਾ, ਸੰਖਿਪਤ

tertiary (ਟਾਃਸ਼ਅਰਿ) *a n* ਤੀਜੇ ਦਰਜੇ ਦਾ; ਤੀਜਾ; (ਭੂ) ਤੀਜਾ ਯੁੱਗ

test (ਟੈੱਸਟ) *n v* ਪਰਖ, ਪਰੀਖਿਆ, ਜਾਂਚ, ਇਮਤਿਹਾਨ; ਕਸੌਟੀ; ਆਧਾਰ; ਕੁਠਾਲੀ; ਪਰੀਖਿਆ ਕਰਨਾ, ਪਰਖਣਾ, ਅਜ਼ਮਾਉਣਾ, ਇਮਤਿਹਾਨ ਲੈਣਾ

Testament (ਟੈੱਸਟਅਮੰਟ) *n* ਪੁਰਾਣਾ ਧਰਮ ਨੇਮ, ਨੇਮ-ਪੱਤਰ; ਵਸੀਅਤ, ਇੱਛਾ-ਪੱਤਰ

testicle ('ਟੈੱਸਟਿਕਲ) *n* ਅੰਡਕੋਸ਼, ਅੰਡ, ਟੱਟਾ, ਨਲ, (ਬੱਕਰੇ ਦਾ) ਕਪੂਰਾ

testify ('ਟੈੱਸਟਿਫ਼ਾਇ) *v* ਪ੍ਰਮਾਣ ਦੇਣਾ, ਗਵਾਹੀ ਦੇਣੀ, ਸਬੂਤ ਦੇਣਾ, ਸਾਬਤ ਕਰਨਾ, ਸਿੱਧ ਕਰਨਾ

testimonial ('ਟੈੱਸਟਿ'ਮਅਉਨਯਅਲ) *n* ਸਨਦ, ਪ੍ਰਮਾਣ-ਪੱਤਰ; ਪ੍ਰਸੰਸਾ-ਪੱਤਰ, ਚਰਿੱਤਰ ਪੱਤਰ; ਉਪਹਾਰ

testimony ('ਟੈੱਸਟਿਅਮਅਨਿ) *n* (ਕਾ) ਸ਼ਹਾਦਤ, ਹਲਫ਼ੀਆ ਬਿਆਨ, ਸਬੂਤ, ਪ੍ਰਮਾਣ

testy ('ਟੈੱਸਟਿ) *a* ਕਰੋਪੀ, ਚਿੜਚਿੜਾ, ਖਿਝੂ

tete-a-tete ('ਟੇਇਟਾ'ਟੇਇਟ) *n a adv* ਗੁਪਤ ਵਾਰਤਾਲਾਪ, ਘੁਸਰ-ਮੁਸਰ, ਘੋਰ-ਮਸੌਰਾ; ਗੁਪਤ, ਇਕਾਂਤ, ਆਮੂਣੇ-ਸਾਮੁਣੇ; ਨਿੱਜੀ ਤੌਰ ਤੇ, ਅੰਦਰਖ਼ਾਨੇ

tetter ('ਟੈਟਅ*) *n v* ਖੁਜਲੀ, ਦੰਦ, ਧੱਦਰ, ਚੰਬਲ (ਬੀਮਾਰੀਆਂ); ਖਾਜ ਕਰਨਾ, ਖੁਜਲੀ ਕਰਨਾ

text (ਟੈੱਕਸਟ) *n* ਮੂਲ ਪਾਠ, ਵਿਸ਼ਾ-ਵਸਤੂ, ਪਾਠ-ਪੁਸਤਕ, ਸੂਤਰ, ਵਚਨ, ਗ੍ਰੰਥ ਦਾ ਸਾਰ; **~book** ਪਾਠ-ਪੁਸਤਕ; **~ual** ਪਾਠ-ਸਬੰਧੀ, ਪਾਠਗਤ

textile ('ਟੈੱਕਸਟਾਇਲ) *a n* ਬੁਣਾਈ ਸਬੰਧੀ, ਬੁਣਿਆ; ਕੱਪੜਾ, ਬੁਣੀ ਸਮਗਰੀ

texture ('ਟੈੱਕਸਚਅ*) *n* ਰਚਨਾ, ਬੁਣਤ, ਬੁਣਾਈ, ਜੜਤ, ਗਠਨ

than (ਦੈਨ) *conj prep* ਕੋਲੋਂ, ਨਾਲੋਂ, ਪਾਸੋਂ, ਬਨਿਸਬਤ, ਤੁਲਨਾ ਵਜੋਂ

thank (ਥੈਂਕ) *n v* ਧੰਨਵਾਦ, ਸ਼ੁਕਰੀਆ; ਧੰਨਵਾਦ ਕਰਨਾ; **~ful** ਧੰਨਵਾਦੀ, ਕ੍ਰਿਤੱਗ, ਮਸ਼ਕੂਰ, ਇਹਸਾਨਮੰਦ; **~less** ਨਾਸ਼ੁਕਰਾ, ਅਕ੍ਰਿਤਘਣ; ਨਮਕ ਹਰਾਮ

thatch (ਥੈਚ) *n v* ਛੱਪਰ; ਘਾਹ, ਫੂਸ; ਛੱਪਰ ਪਾਉਣਾ; ਛੱਪਰ ਨਾਲ ਢਕਣਾ

theatre (ਥਿ'ਐਟਅ*) *n* ਰੰਗਭੂਮੀ, ਨਾਟਕ-ਗ੍ਰਿਹ, ਥੀਏਟਰ, ਨਾਟਘਰ, ਲੈਕਚਰ ਹਾਲ

theft (ਥੈਫ਼ਟ) *n* ਚੋਰੀ, ਲੁੱਟ

theism ('ਥੀਇਜ਼(ਅ)ਮ) *n* ਆਸਤਕਤਾ, ਈਸ਼ਵਰਵਾਦ, ਆਸਤਕਵਾਦ, ਖ਼ੁਦਾਪਰਸਤੀ

theist ('ਥੀਇਸਟ) *n* ਆਸਤਕ, ਇਸ਼ਵਰਵਾਦ-ਸਬੰਧੀ, ਖ਼ੁਦਾਪਰਸਤੀ ਦਾ

thematic (ਥੀ'ਮੈਟਿਕ) *a* ਵਿਸ਼ੇਗਤ, ਆਤਮਕ ਵਿਸ਼ੇ ਸਬੰਧੀ, ਵਿਕਰਣ-ਯੁਕਤ

theme (ਥੀਮ) *n* ਵਿਸ਼ਾ-ਵਸਤੂ, ਪ੍ਰਕਰਣ, ਕਥਾ-ਪ੍ਰਸੰਗ; ਰਚਨਾ, ਨਿਬੰਧ

thence (ਦੈਂਸ) *adv* (ਪ੍ਰ) ਉਸ ਥਾਂ ਤੋਂ, ਉੱਥੋਂ, ਉਸ ਸਮੇਂ ਤੋਂ, ਤਦ ਤੋਂ, ਉਧਰੋਂ; **~forth** ਉਦੋਂ ਅੱਗੋਂ, ਤਦ ਤੋਂ; **~forward** ਉਦੋਂ ਅੱਗੋਂ, ਤਦ ਤੋਂ

theocracy (ਥਿ'ਔਕਰਅਸਿ) *n* ਦੀਨੀ ਹਕੂਮਤ, ਧਰਮ-ਤੰਤਰ, ਇਸ਼ਵਰਤੰਤਰ

theology (ਥਿ'ਔਲਅਜਿ) *n* ਧਰਮ-ਸ਼ਾਸਤਰ

theorem ('ਥਿਅਰਅਮ) *n* (ਗਣਿ) ਮਸਲਾ; ਪ੍ਰਮੇਯ, ਸੂਤਰ

theoretic-al (ਥਿਆ'ਰੈਟਿਕ, ਥਿਆ'ਰੈਟਿਕਲ) *a* ਸਿਧਾਂਤਕ; ਇਲਮੀ; ਵਿਚਾਰਾਤਮਕ, ਦਿਮਾਗ਼ੀ

theorist ('ਥਿਅਰਿਸਟ) *n* ਸਿਧਾਂਤੀ, ਸਿਧਾਂਤਕਾਰ; ਗ਼ੈਰ-ਅਮਲੀ ਆਦਮੀ

theorize ('ਥਿਅਰਾਇੱਜ਼) *v* ਸਿਧਾਂਤ ਘੜਨੇ, ਨਿਯਮ ਬਣਾਉਣਾ, ਮੱਤ ਸਥਾਪਤ ਕਰਨਾ, ਅਨੁਮਾਨ ਲਾਉਣਾ

theory ('ਥਿਅਰਿ) *n* ਸਿਧਾਂਤ; ਮੱਤ; ਅਸੂਲ, ਨੇਮ; ਵਿਚਾਰ, ਕਲਪਨਾ; ਸ਼ਾਸਤਰ, ਵਿੱਦਿਆ

theosophy (ਥਿ'ਔਸਅਫ਼ਿ) *n* ਬ੍ਰਹਮ-ਵਿਗਿਆਨ, ਬ੍ਰਹਮ-ਵਿੱਦਿਆ, ਬ੍ਰਹਮਵਾਦ, ਇਸ਼ਵਰਵਾਦ

therapy (ਥਰੈਂਪਿ) *n* ਇਲਾਜ, ਚਿਕਿਤਸਾ

there (ਦੇਆ*) *adv n int* ਉਥੇ; ਉਹ ਥਾਂ; ਹੱਛਾ ਹੱਛਾ! ~about(s) ਉਥੇ, ਕਿਥੇ, ਨੇੜੇ, ਤੇੜੇ, ਉਸ ਦੇ ਆਸ ਪਾਸ; ਉੱਨਾ ਕੁ; ~after ਉਸ ਤੋਂ ਪਿਛੋਂ; ~at ਇਸ ਤੇ; ~by ਇੰਜ ਕਰਕੇ; ~fore ਤਾਹੀਓਂ, ਇਸ ਲਈ, ਤਦੇ ਹੀ; ~in ਉਸ ਵਿਚ; ~of ਉਸ ਦਾ; ~upon ਉਸ ਤੇ; ਫਲਸਰੂਪ; ਫ਼ੌਰਨ, ਤਤਕਾਲ; ~with (ਪ੍ਰ) ਉਸ ਦੇ ਨਾਲ, ਨਾਲੇ, ਨਾਲ ਹੀ

thermal (ਥਅ:ਮ) *n a* ਤਾਪ; ਗਰਮੀ ਦਾ, ਤਾਪਕ, ਤਾਪੀ, ਥਰਮ ਸਬੰਧੀ

thermometer (ਥਅ:ਮੌਮਿਟਅ*) *n* ਤਾਪਮਾਪੀ, ਤਾਪਮਾਨ ਜੰਤਰ, ਥਰਮਾਮੀਟਰ

thesis ('ਥੀਸਿਸ) *n* ਪ੍ਰਤਿਗਿਆ, ਵਾਦ; ਖੋਜ-ਪ੍ਰਬੰਧ

thick (ਥਿਕ) *a adv* ਮੋਟਾ, ਸਥੂਲ; ਘਚਾਪੀਚ, ਗੁੰਨ੍ਹਿਆ, ਗੁੰਦਿਆ, ਲੱਦਿਆ; ਠੋਸ, ਗਾੜ੍ਹਾ; ਅਸਪਸ਼ਟ, ਧੁੰਦਲਾ; ਮੂਰਖ; ਮੋਟੇ ਤੋਰ ਤੇ, ਲਗਾਤਾਰ; ~skinned ਮੋਟੀ ਚਮੜੀ ਵਾਲਾ; ~ness ਸਥੂਲਤਾ, ਮੁਟਾਪਾ, ਮੁਟਾਈ, ਘਟਤਾ, ਗਾੜ੍ਹਾਪਣ; ਮੂੜ੍ਹਤਾ; ਬੁੱਧੂਪਣ

thicket ('ਥਿਕਿਟ) *n* ਝਾੜੀ, ਝੁੰਡ, ਝੁਰਮਟ

thief (ਥੀਫ਼) *n* ਚੋਰ, ਉਚੱਕਾ, ਲੁਟੇਰਾ, ਸੰਨ੍ਹਮਾਰ

thieve (ਥੀਵ਼) *v* ਚੋਰੀ ਕਰਨਾ, ਚੁਰਾਉਣਾ

thigh (ਥਾਇ) *n* ਪੱਟ, ਜੰਘ

thin (ਥਿਨ) *a v* ਮਹੀਨ, ਬਾਰੀਕ; ਸੂਖਮ, ਪਤਲਾ; ਦੁਬਲਾ; ਵਿਰਲਾ, ਝਿਰਝਿਰਾ; ਪਾਰਦਰਸ਼ੀ; ਘਟਾਉਣਾ, ਘੱਟ ਕਰਨਾ, ਪਤਲਾ ਕਰਨਾ ਜਾਂ ਪੈਣਾ

thing (ਥਿਙ) *n* ਸ਼ੈ, ਵਸਤੂ, ਚੀਜ਼, ਜਿਨਸ, ਸਮਗਰੀ, ਪਰਸਥਿਤਿ; ਵਿਸ਼ਾ, ਗੱਲ, ਮਾਮਲਾ

think (ਥਿਙਕ) *v* ਵਿਚਾਰ ਕਰਨਾ, ਖ਼ਿਆਲ ਕਰਨਾ, ਗਿਆਨ ਹੋਣਾ, ਖ਼ਬਰ ਹੋਣੀ, ਸਮਝਣਾ ਸੋਚਣਾ, ਵਿਚਾਰਨਾ; ~highly of ਬਹੁਤ ਜ਼ਿਆਦਾ ਸਨਮਾਨ ਦੇਣਾ; ~of ਕਲਪਨਾ ਕਰਨਾ, ਵਿਚਾਰਨਾ, ਸੋਚਣਾ; ~out ਸੋਚ ਵਿਚਾਰ ਕਰਕੇ ਫ਼ੈਸਲਾ ਕਰਨਾ; ~er ਚਿੰਤਕ, ਵਿਚਾਰਕ, ਦਾਰਸ਼ਨਕ; ~ing ਚਿੰਤਨ, ਸੋਚ-ਵਿਚਾਰ, ਵਿਚਾਰ-ਕਿਰਿਆ

third (ਥਅ:ਡ) *a n* ਤੀਜਾ; ਤਿਹਾਈ

thirst (ਥਅ:ਸਟ) *n v* ਤ੍ਰਿਖਾ, ਤਰੇਹ, ਚਾਹ; ਤੇਹ ਲੱਗਣੀ, ਪਿਆਸ ਲੱਗਣੀ

thirteen ('ਥਅ:'ਟੀਨ) *n* ਤੇਰ੍ਹਾਂ

thirty ('ਥਅ:ਟਿ) *n* ਤੀਹ

thorax ('ਥੋਰੈਕਸ) *n* ਛਾਤੀ, ਸੀਨਾ

thorn (ਥੋਨ) *n* ਸੂਲ; ਖਾਰ, ਕੰਡਾ

thorough ('ਥਅੱਰਅ) *n a* ਅੱਤਵਾਦੀ ਨੀਤੀ; ਸੰਪੂਰਨ, ਪੂਰਨ, ਪੂਰਾ ਤਮਾਮ; ਸੁੱਧ (ਆਦਮੀ); ~fare ਸਰੇ ਆਮ, ਆਮ, ਲਾਂਘਾ

though (ਦਅਉ) *adv* ਭਾਵੇਂ, ਚਾਹੇ, ਹਾਲਾਂ ਕਿ, ਖੈਰ

thought (ਥੋਟ) *n* ਚਿੰਤਨ, ਵਿਚਾਰ, ਧਿਆਨ,

ਮਨਨ, ਸੋਚ, ਇਰਾਦਾ, ਧਾਰਨਾ ਸਮਝ, ਵਿਵੇਕ;
~ful ਵਿਚਾਰਸ਼ੀਲ, ਮਨਨਸ਼ੀਲ, ਧਿਆਨਮਗਨ,
ਗੰਭੀਰ; ਸੁਹਿਰਦ, ਹਮਦਰਦ; ~less ਵਿਚਾਰ-
ਹੀਨ, ਮਨਨਹੀਨ, ਬੇਖ਼ਬਰ

thousand ('ਥਾਉਜ਼ਅੰਡ) *a n* ਹਜ਼ਾਰ; ਸਹੰਸਰ,
ਬੇਸ਼ੁਮਾਰ

thrash (ਥਰੈਸ਼) *v* ਝੰਬਣਾ, ਫੰਡਣਾ, ਠੋਕਣਾ;
ਕੁੱਟਣਾ, ਪਿੱਟਣਾ; ਫਾਂਟੀ ਚਾੜ੍ਹਨਾ, ਹਰਾਉਣਾ

thread (ਥਰੈੱਡ) *n v* ਧਾਗਾ, ਡੋਰੀ, ਸੂਤ, ਸੂਤਰ,
ਤੰਦ, ਤਾਰ; ਕਢਾਈ ਕਰਨੀ

threat (ਥਰੈੱਟ) *n* ਧਮਕੀ, ਤੜੀ, ਦਾਬਾ, ਧੌਂਸ,
ਘੁਰਕੀ, ਖਟਕਾ; ~en ਧਮਕਾਉਣਾ, ਡਰਾਉਣਾ;
(ਦੀ) ਧਮਕੀ ਦੇਣਾ

threshold ('ਥਰੈੱਸ਼(ਹ)ਅਉਲਡ) *n* ਚੌਖਟ, ਦੇਹਰੀ;
ਸਰਦਲ, ਮੁਹਾਠ, ਪ੍ਰਵੇਸ਼, ਸ਼ੁਰੂਆਤ

thrice (ਥਰਾਇਸ) *adv* ਤਿੰਨ ਵਾਰੀ, ਤਿਗੁਣਾ,
ਤਿੰਨ ਗੁਣਾ

thrift (ਥਰਿਫ਼ਟ) *n* ਕਿਰਸ, ਸੰਜਮ, ਕਿਫ਼ਾਇਤਸ਼ਾਰੀ;
(ਪ੍ਰ) ਖ਼ਸ਼ਹਾਲੀ

thrill (ਥਰਿਲ) *n v* ਰੋਮਾਂਚ; ਪੁੜਕਣ; ਝਰਨਾਹਟ;
ਕੰਬਣੀ; ਝਰਨਾਹਟ ਛਿੜਨੀ; ਰੋਮਾਂਚ ਹੋਣਾ

thrive (ਥਰਾਇਵ੍) *v* ਫੁੱਲਣਾ-ਫਲਣਾ, ਵਾਧਾ ਹੋਣਾ,
ਉੱਨਤੀ ਕਰਨੀ, ਫਲਣਾ, ਹਰਿਆ ਭਰਿਆ ਹੋਣਾ

throat (ਥਰਅਉਟ) *n* ਸੰਘ, ਗਲ, ਕੰਠ

throb (ਥਰੌਬ) *v n* ਫ਼ਰਿਕਣਾ; ਟੀਸਣਾ, ਚਸਕਣਾ,
ਟੀਸ ਪੈਣੀ; ਫੜਕਣਾ, ਪੜਕਣਾ; ਜਜ਼ਬਾਤੀ
ਹੋਣਾ; ਪੜਕਣ, ਟੀਸ, ਚੀਸ, ਫੜਕਣ

throe (ਥਰਅਉ) *n v* ਜੰਮਣ ਪੀੜਾਂ, ਦਰਦਾਂ, ਪ੍ਰਸੂਤ
ਵੇਦਨਾ, ਸੰਤਾਪ, ਕਸ਼ਟ, ਪੀੜਾ; ਕਸ਼ਟ ਪਾਉਣਾ,
ਪੀੜ ਹੋਣੀ

throne (ਥਰਅਉਨ) *n v* ਤਖ਼ਤ, ਰਾਜ-ਗੱਦੀ,

ਸਿੰਘਾਸਨ; ਪ੍ਰਭੂ-ਸੱਤਾ, ਰਾਜ-ਸੱਤਾ, ਹਕੂਮਤ;
ਤਖ਼ਤ ਉੱਤੇ ਬਿਠਾਉਣਾ

throng (ਥਰੌਂਗ) *n v* ਭੀੜ, ਜਮਘਟਾ, ਇੱਕਠ;
ਭੀੜ ਹੋਣੀ ਜਾਂ ਕਰਨੀ, ਜਮਘਟਾ ਜੰਮਣਾ

throttle ('ਥਰੌੱਟਲ) *n v* ਸੰਘ, ਗਲਾ, ਸਾਹ-ਨਾਲੀ;
ਗਲ ਘੁੱਟਣਾ

through (ਥਰੂ) *prep adv a* ਵਿਚੋਂ ਦੀ, ਆਰ-
ਪਾਰ, ਦੇ ਰਾਹੀਂ, ਦੇ ਦੁਆਰਾ, ਦੇ ਕਾਰਨ, ਮਾਰਫ਼ਤ;
ਬਿਲਕੁਲ; ~out ਪੂਰੀ ਤਰ੍ਹਾਂ, ਸਾਰੇ ਦਾ ਸਾਰਾ,
ਮੁੱਢੋਂ ਅਖੀਰ ਤਕ

throw (ਥਰਅਉ) *n v* ਟੱਪਾ, ਉਛਾਲ; ਫੈਂਕ,
ਸੁੱਟਣਾ, ਡੇਗਣਾ, ਟੱਪਣਾ, ਦੇਣਾ ਜਾਂ ਦਿਵਾਉਣਾ;
ਧੱਕਣਾ, ਭੁੰਜੇ ਸੁੱਟਣਾ; ~away ਵਰਤ ਕੇ
ਸੁੱਟਣਯੋਗ

thrust (ਥਰਅਸਟ) *n v* ਘੁਸੇੜ, ਚੋਭ, ਖੋਭ; ਤੇਜ਼
ਹੁੱਝ; ਘੁਸੇੜਨਾ, ਖੋਭਣਾ, ਖੁਭਣਾ, ਵਿਨ੍ਹਣਾ, ਧੱਕਾ
ਦੇਣਾ, ਹਟਾਉਣਾ

thud (ਥਅੱਡ) *n v* ਧੜੰਮ, ਧੜੰਮ ਦੀ ਅਵਾਜ਼,
ਖੜਾਕ; ਧਮਾਕਾ (ਹੋਣਾ), ਧੜੰਮ ਕਰਕੇ ਡਿਗਣਾ

thug (ਥਅੱਗ) *n* ਗੁੰਡਾ, ਠਗਾ, ਖੂਨੀ; ਹਤਿਆਰਾ

thumb (ਥਅੱਮ) *n v* ਅਗੂੰਠਾ; ਠੂਠ; ਅੰਗੂਠੇ ਨਾਲ
ਘਸਾਉਣਾ, ਦਬਾਉਣਾ

thump (ਥਅੱਪ) *n v* ਮੁੱਕਾ (ਮਾਰਨਾ), ਘੱਪੜ;
ਲੱਫੜ (ਲਾਉਣਾ); ਡੰਡਾ (ਮਾਰਨਾ); ਕੁੱਟਣਾ

thunder ('ਥਅੰਡਅ*) *n v* ਗੜਗੜਾਹਟ, ਕੜਕ,
ਗੜਗੱਜ, ਬਤੁਕ, ਭਬਕ; ਗੜਗੜਾਉਣਾ,
ਗੱਜਣਾ, ਗਰਜਣਾ, ਗੜੁਕਣਾ, ਕੜਕਣਾ; ~bolt
(ਬਿਜ) ਅਸਮਾਨੀ ਗੋਲਾ

tick (ਟਿਕ) *n v* (ਘੜੀ ਦੀ) ਟਿਕ-ਟਿਕ, ਖਟਖਟ;
ਛਿਣ, ਪਲ; ਟਿੱਕਣ ਚਿੰਨ੍ਹ (√), ਟਿੱਕ ਮਾਰਕ;
ਚੰਮ ਜੂੰ, ਚਿੱਚੜ, (ਘੜੀ ਦਾ) ਟਿਕ-ਟਿਕ ਕਰਨ;

ਸਹੀ ਲਾਉਣੀ

ticket ('ਟਿਕਿਟ) *n v* ਟਿਕਟ, ਪ੍ਰਵੇਸ਼-ਪੱਤਰ; ਟਿਕਟ ਦੇਣਾ; (ਵੇਚਣ ਲਈ) ਲੇਬਲ ਲਾਉਣਾ

tickle ('ਟਿਕਲ) *n v* ਕੁਤਕੁਤਾੜੀ, ਕੁਤਕੁਤੀ, ਕੁਤਕੁਤਾਹਟ; ਪਲੋਸਣਾ, ਕੁਤਕੁਤਾਉਣਾ

tickling ('ਟਿਕਲਿੜ) *n* ਕੁਤਕੁਤਾਹਟ

tide (ਟਾਇਡ) *n* ਜਵਾਰਭਾਟਾ; ਅਵਸਰ; ਮੌਸਮ; (ਵਕਤ ਦੀ) ਚਾਲ, ਗੋੜ, ਕਾਲ-ਚੱਕਰ

tidy ('ਟਾਇਡਿ) *n a v* ਸਮੇਂ ਅਨੁਕੂਲ; ਸੁਅੱਛ, ਸੁਥਰਾ, ਸਾਫ਼, ਠੀਕ-ਠਾਕ, ਅਤੀ-ਅਧਿਕ, ਕਾਫ਼ੀ; ਚੰਗਾ-ਭਲਾ, ਤੰਦਰੁਸਤ; ਸੱਜਿਆ, ਸਲੀਕੇਦਾਰ; ਸਜਾਉਣਾ, ਠੀਕ-ਠਾਕ ਕਰਨਾ, ਸਾਫ਼-ਸੁਥਰਾ ਰੱਖਣਾ

tie (ਟਾਇ) *n v* ਗੰਢ, ਜੋੜ; ਬੰਨ੍ਹਟ, ਰੱਸੀ, ਸੂਤਲੀ, ਡੋਰੀ; ਯੋਗ; (ਸੰਗੀ) ਮੇਲ-ਚਿੰਨ੍ਹ; ਡੰਡਾ; ਰੇਲ ਦਾ ਸਲੀਪਰ; ਨੇਕਟਾਈ; ਗੰਢਣਾ, ਮਿਲਾਉਣਾ, ਪੱਕਾ ਕਰਨਾ, ਦ੍ਰਿੜ ਬਣਾਉਣਾ, ਜਕੜਨਾ, ਦੱਸਣਾ

tiffin (ਟਿਫ਼ਿਨ) *v* ਖਾਣਾ, ਟਿਫ਼ਿਨ; ਲੰਚ ਕਰਨਾ, ਰੋਟੀ ਖਾਣੀ, ਖਾਣਾ ਖਾਣਾ

tiger ('ਟਾਇਗਅ*) *n* ਸ਼ੇਰ, ਸ਼ੀਹ, ਬਾਘ, ਚੀਤਾ

tight (ਟਾਇਟ) *n a* ਘੁੱਟਵੇਂ; ਦ੍ਰਿੜ, ਠੋਸ, ਗੰਢਿਆ; ਅਭੇਦ; ਸੁਰੱਖਿਅਤ, ਕੱਸਿਆ; ਤੰਗ; ਸਡੌਲ; ਤਣਿਆ; ~**fisted** ਮੁੱਠੀ ਘੁੱਟ ਕੇ ਰੱਖਣ ਵਾਲਾ, ਕੰਜੂਸ; ~**lipped** ਚੁੱਪ ਸਾਧ

tile ('ਟਾਇਲ) *n v* ਖਪਰੈਲ, ਪਟੜੀ, ਚੌਂਕੀ; ਟਾਈਲਾਂ ਲਾਉਣੀਆਂ, ਪਟੜੀਬੰਦ ਬਣਾਉਣਾ

till (ਟਿਲ) *n v prep conj* ਦੁਕਾਨ ਦੀ ਗੋਲਕ, ਗੱਲਾ; ਤਦ, ਜਦ ਤਕ; ਜਦ ਤਕ ਕਿ, ਜਦ ਕਿ, ਇਥੋਂ ਤਕ ਕਿ; ਖੇਤੀ ਕਰਨਾ, ਹਲ ਚਲਾਉਣਾ, ਵਾਹੁਣਾ, ਜੋਤਣਾ, ਕਾਸ਼ਤ ਕਰਨਾ; ~**er** ਕਿਸਾਨ, ਕਾਸ਼ਤਕਾਰ

tilt (ਟਿਲਟ) *n v* ਢਾਲ, ਉਲਾਰ, (ਵੈਰੀ ਉੱਤੇ) ਵਾਰ, ਹਮਲਾ, ਮੁਠਭੇੜ, ਨੇਜ਼ੇਬਾਜ਼ੀ, ਹੱਥੋਂ, ਚੰਦੇਆ ਲਾਉਣਾ, ਟੇਢਾ ਕਰਨਾ

timber ('ਟਿੰਬਅ*) *n* ਕਾਠ, ਲੱਕੜ, ਇਮਾਰਤੀ ਲੱਕੜ; ਜੰਗਲ, ਵਣ; ਕੜੀ, ਸ਼ਹਿਤੀਰ

time (ਟਾਇਮ) *n* ਸਮਾਂ, ਵਕਤ, ਯੁੱਗ, ਕਾਲ, ਅਵਧੀ, ਫ਼ੁਰਸਤ, ਮਿਰਤੂ ਕਾਲ; ਮੌਕਾ; ਜ਼ਮਾਨਾ, ਜੀਵਨ-ਦਸ਼ਾ, ਦਫ਼ਾ; ਮਿਆਦ, ਜੀਵਨ-ਦਸ਼ਾ, ਮੁਹਲਤ; ~**table** ਸਮਾਂ ਸਾਰਨੀ, ਟਾਇਮ ਟੇਬਲ; ~**server** ਮੌਕਾਪਰਸਤ, ਜ਼ਮਾਨਾਸਾਜ਼; ~**ly** ਸਮੇਂ ਅਨੁਸਾਰ, ਵੇਲੇ ਸਿਰ

timid ('ਟਿਮਿਡ) *a* ਡਰਾਕਲ, ਡਰਪੋਕ, ਬੁਜ਼ਦਿਲ, ਝੱਪੂ, ਦੀਨ; ~**ity**, ~**ness** ਸਾਹਸ-ਹੀਨਤਾ, ਕਾਇਰਤਾ, ਬੁਜ਼ਾਦਿਲੀ; ਦੀਨਤਾ

timing ('ਟਾਇਮਿਙ) *n* ਸਮਾਂ, ਵਕਤ, ਸਮਾਂ-ਮਾਨ, ਸਮਾਂ-ਨਿਰਧਾਰਨ, ਸਮੇਂ ਦਾ ਹਿਸਾਬ

tin (ਟਿਨ) *n v* ਕਲੀ, ਕਲੀ ਵਾਲੀ ਲੋਹੇ ਦੀ ਚਾਦਰ, (ਬੋਲ) ਟੀਨ; ਪੀਪੀ, ਪੀਪਾ; ਕਲੀ ਕਰਨਾ

ting (ਟਿਙ) *n v* ਟਿਨਟਿਨਾਹਟ, ਖਿਣਖਿਣਾਹਟ; ਟਿਨਟਿਨਾਉਣਾ, ਖਿਣਖਿਣਾਉਣਾ

tinge (ਟਿੰਜ) *n v* ਰੰਗਤ, ਭਾਹ, ਆਭਾ, ਝਲਕ, ਹਲਕਾ ਰੰਗ; ਰੰਗਤ ਦੇਣੀ, ਪੁੱਠ ਚੜ੍ਹਨੀ, ਝਲਕ ਮਾਰਨੀ

tingle ('ਟਿਙਗਲ) *n v* ਖੁਤਖੁਤੀ, ਧੁਖਧੁਖੀ, ਝੁਟਝੁਟੀ; ਛੋਟਾ ਕਿੱਲ, ਸਿੱਕੇ ਦਾ ਕਲਿੱਪ; ਟਣ-ਟਣ, ਛਣ-ਛਣ; ਧੁਖਧੁਖੀ ਲੱਗਣੀ, ਵੱਜਣਾ; ਸਨਸਨੀ ਪੈਦਾ ਕਰਨਾ

tinsel ('ਟੀਨਸਲ) *n v* ਗੋਟਾ, ਕਿਨਾਰੀ, ਸਲਮਾ, ਪੰਨਾ; ਚਮਕ-ਦਮਕ, ਤੜਕ-ਭੜਕ, ਟੀਪ-ਟਾਪ; ਗੋਟਾ ਲਾਉਣਾ, ਸਲਮਾ ਸਿਤਾਰਾ ਜੜਨਾ

tip (ਟਿਪ) *n v a adv* ਸਿਰਾ, ਨੋਕ, ਮੂੰਹ; ਕੂਚੀ,

ਬੁਰਸ਼; ਇਨਾਮ, ਬਖ਼ਸ਼ੀਸ਼, ਟਿਪ; ਗੁਰ; ਥਾਪੀ; ਪੱਕਾ; ਝੁਕਾਉ; ਝੁਕਾਉਣਾ; ਟੇਢਾ ਕਰਨਾ; ਉਲਟਣਾ, ਉਲਟਾਉਣਾ; **~top** ਬਹੁਤ ਵਧੀਆ, ਟਿਕਣ

tire ('ਟਾਇਅ*) *v n* (1) ਸ਼ਿੰਗਾਰ ਕਰਨਾ, ਸਜਾਉਣਾ; (2) ਥਕਾਉਣਾ, ਥੱਕਣਾ, (3) ਉਕਤਾ ਜਾਣਾ; ਵੇਸ, ਪੁਸ਼ਾਕ, ਕਪੜੇ; **~some** ਥਕਾਊ

tit (ਟਿਟ) *n* ਮਰੀਅਲ ਘੋੜਾ, ਟੱਟੂ; ਪਿੰਡਾ

Titan ('ਟਾਇਟਨ) *n* (ਯੂਨਾਨ ਦਾ) ਸੂਰਜ ਦੇਵਤਾ, ਮਹਾਂ ਮਾਨਵ, ਦੈਂਤ

titbit ('ਟਿਟਬਿਟ) *n* ਸੁਆਦਲਾ ਭੋਜਨ; ਚੁਟਕਲਾ; ਚਟਪਟੀ ਖ਼ਬਰ

title ('ਟਾਇਟਲ) *n* ਸ਼ੀਰਸ਼ਕ; ਪਦਵੀ, ਖ਼ਿਤਾਬ; ਹੱਕ-ਮਾਲਕੀ, ਸਿਰਲੇਖ; ਅਧਿਕਾਰ-ਪੱਤਰ, ਦਸਤਾਵੇਜ਼

tittle-tattle ('ਟਿਟਲ*-ਟੈਟਲ) *n v* ਬਕਵਾਸ (ਕਰਨਾ), ਗੱਪ (ਮਾਰਨਾ), ਬੜਬੜ ਕਰਨਾ

toad (ਟਅਉਡ) *n* ਡੱਡੂ ਵਰਗਾ ਜੀਵ; ਘਿਰਣਤ ਵਿਅਕਤੀ; **~stool** ਕੁਕਰ ਮੁੱਤਾ; **~y** ਚਾਪਲੂਸੀ, ਟੁਕੜਖੋਰੀ; ਖ਼ੁਸ਼ਾਮਦ ਕਰਨਾ

toast (ਟਅਉਸਟ) *v n* ਸਿਹਤ ਦਾ ਜਾਮ ਪੀਣਾ; ਡਬਲ ਰੋਟੀ ਦਾ ਟੁਕੜਾ ਭੁੰਨਣਾ, ਸੇਕਣਾ; ਸੇਕਿਆ ਡਬਲ ਰੋਟੀ ਦਾ ਟੁਕੜਾ, ਟੋਸਟ

toddle ('ਟੌਡਲ) *n v* ਠੁਮਕ-ਠੁਮਕ ਚਾਲ, ਠੁਮਕੀ ਟੋਰ, ਡਿੰਕ-ਡੋਲਾ, ਡਗਮਗਾਉਂਦੀ ਟੋਰ; ਚੁਹਲ-ਕਦਮੀ, ਮਟਰਗਸ਼ਤੀ; ਠੁਮਠੁਮ ਕਰਕੇ ਟੁਰਨਾ, ਚੁਹਲ ਕਦਮੀ ਕਰਨਾ, ਮਟਰਗਸ਼ਤੀ ਕਰਨਾ

toe (ਟਅਉ) *n v* ਪੈਰ ਦੀ ਉਂਗਲ, ਪੰਜੇ ਲਾਉਣਾ, ਖੁਰਾਂ ਵਿਚ ਖੁਰੀਆਂ

together (ਟਅ'ਗੈੱਦਅ*) *adv* ਇੱਕਠੇ; ਲਗਾਤਾਰ

toil (ਟੌਇਲ) *n* ਸਖ਼ਤ ਮਿਹਨਤ (ਕਰਨੀ), ਫੰਦਾ, ਜਾਲ

toilet ('ਟੌਇਲਿਟ) *n* ਇਸ਼ਨਾਨ ਗ੍ਰਿਹ; ਮੂੰਹ-ਹੱਥ ਧੋਣਾ, ਟੱਟੀ, ਗੁਸਲਖ਼ਾਨਾ; ਬਣਾਉ-ਸ਼ਿੰਗਾਰ, ਕੰਘੀ-ਪੱਟੀ; ਕੱਪੜਾ-ਲੱਤਾ

token ('ਟਅਉਕ(ਅ)ਨ) *n* ਨਿਸ਼ਾਨੀ, ਯਾਦ-ਚਿੰਨ੍ਹ, ਪ੍ਰਤੀਕ, ਲੱਛਣ, ਪ੍ਰਮਾਣ; ਸਿੱਕਾ

tolerable ('ਟੌਲਅਰਅਬਲ) *a* ਸਹਿਣਸ਼ੀਲ, ਸਹਿਣ ਯੋਗ, ਚੰਗਾ, ਤਸੱਲੀਬਖ਼ਸ਼, ਸੰਤੋਖਜਨਕ, ਸਧਾਰਨ

tolerance ('ਟੌਲਅਰਅੰਸ) *n* ਧੀਰਜ, ਸਹਿਣਸ਼ੀਲਤਾ, ਉਦਾਰਤਾ, ਬਰਦਾਸ਼ਤ

tolerant ('ਟੌਲਅਰਅੰਟ) *a* ਖਿਮਾਸ਼ੀਲ, ਸਹਿਣ-ਸ਼ੀਲ, ਉਦਾਰ

tolerate ('ਟੌਲਅਰੇਇਟ) *v* ਬਰਦਾਸ਼ਤ ਕਰਨਾ, ਸਹਿਣਾ, ਝੱਲਣਾ, ਸਹਾਰਨਾ

toleration ('ਟੌਲਅ'ਰੇਇਸ਼ਨ) *n* ਉਦਾਰਤਾ, ਸਹਿਣ-ਸ਼ੀਲਤਾ, ਬਰਦਾਸ਼ਤ

toll (ਟਅਉਲ) *n v* ਪੱਥ-ਕਰ; ਟਲੀ ਜਾਂ ਘੰਟੀ ਦੀ ਅਵਾਜ਼, ਚੁੰਗੀ ਲੈਣਾ, ਮਹਿਸੂਲ ਲੈਣਾ

tomato (ਟਅ'ਮਾਟਅਉ) *n* ਟਮਾਟਰ

tomb (ਟੂਮ) *n v* ਸਮਾਧ; ਕਬਰ, ਮਕਬਰਾ; ਮਜ਼ਾਰ, ਦਰਗਾਹ; ਦੱਬਣਾਉਣਾ, ਲੁਕਾਉਣਾ

tomfool ('ਟੋਮਫ਼ੂਲ) *n* ਮਹਾਂਮੂਰਖ

tomorrow (ਟਅ'ਮੌਰਅਉ) *n* ਕੱਲ੍ਹ, ਆਉਣ ਵਾਲਾ ਦਿਨ, ਆਗਾਮੀ ਦਿਵਸ

ton (ਟੱਨ) *n* ਟਨ, 2240 ਪੌਂਡ ਜਾਂ 1000 ਕਿਲੋਗ੍ਰਾਮ ਦਾ ਭਾਰ

tone (ਟਅਉਨ) *n v* ਤਰਜ਼, ਅੰਦਾਜ਼, ਲਹਿਜਾ; ਟੋਨ, ਸਵਰਾਘਾਤ; (ਸੰਗੀ) ਧੁਨ, ਨਾਦ; ਧੁਨੀ ਉਤਪੰਨ ਕਰਨਾ, ਤਾਨ ਭਰਨਾ, ਉਚਿਤ ਰੰਗ ਭਰਨਾ; ਸੁਰ ਮਿਲਾਉਣਾ; ਸਾਜ਼ ਸੁਰ ਕਰਨਾ

tonga ('ਟੌਂਗਾਅ) *n* ਟਾਂਗਾ, ਯੱਕਾ

tongs (ਟੌਂਗੁਜ਼) *n pl* ਚਿਮਟਾ, ਸੰਨ੍ਹੀ, ਚਿਮਟੀ

tongue (ਟਅੰਗ) *n v* ਜੀਭ, ਰਸਨਾ, ਜ਼ਬਾਨ; ਭਾਸ਼ਾ, ਬੋਲੀ, ਬਾਣੀ, ਜ਼ਬਾਨ ਖੋਲ੍ਹਣਾ, ਗੱਲ ਕਰਨੀ

tonight (ਟਅ'ਨਾਇਟ) *adv* ਅੱਜ ਦੀ ਰਾਤ, ਅੱਜ ਰਾਤ ਨੂੰ

tonsil ('ਟੌਂਸਲ) *n* ਗਲਾ, ਗਲ ਦੇ ਕੰਡੇ; ਟਾਨਸਿਲ

tony ('ਟਾਉਨਿ) *a* ਸੁਰੀਲਾ, ਮੂਰਖ, ਬੇਵਕੂਫ਼

too (ਟੂ) *adv* ਬਹੁਤ ਵਧੇਰੇ, ਅਤੀਅੰਤ, ਅਤੀ ਅਧਿਕ

tool (ਟੂਲ) *n v* ਸੰਦ, ਕਲ, ਜੰਤਰ; ਜੁੱਧ-ਸਮਗਰੀ, ਗੋਲੀ-ਸਿੱਕਾ, ਗੋਲਾ-ਬਾਰੂਦ; ਸਾਧਨ; ਹੱਕਣਾ, ਚਲਾਉਣਾ, ਸਵਾਰੀ ਕਰਨੀ

tooth (ਟੂਥ) *n v* ਦੰਦ; ਦੰਦਾ (ਆਰੀ ਜਾਂ ਕੰਘੀ ਦਾ); ਚਰਖੀ, ਆਰੀ; ਦੰਦੇ ਕੱਢਣੇ

top (ਟੌਪ) *n v a* ਟੀਸੀ, ਸਿਖਰ, ਚੋਟੀ, ਸਿਰਾ; ਸਿਖਰ ਤੇ ਅਪੜਨਾ; ਕੱਦ ਵਿਚ ਲੰਮਾ ਹੋਣਾ; ਵਧ ਜਾਣਾ, ਬਾਜ਼ੀ ਲੈ ਜਾਣੀ; ਮੁਖੀਆ, ਸ਼੍ਰੇਸ਼ਠ, ਸਰਵ-ਉੱਚ

topaz (ਟਾਉਪੈੱਜ਼) *n* ਪੁਖਰਾਜ

topple ('ਟੌਪਲ) *v* ਡਗਮਗਾ ਕੇ ਡਿਗਣਾ; ਡੇਗਣਾ, ਗਿਰਾਉਣਾ

topsyturvy ('ਟੌਪਸਿ'ਟਅːਵਿ) *n v a adv* ਉਲਟ-ਪੁਲਟ; ਉਲਟਣਾ, ਪੁਲਟਣਾ, ਥੱਲੇ-ਉੱਤੇ ਕਰਨ, ਗੜਬੜ ਕਰਨਾ; ਉਲਟਾ-ਪੁਲਟਾ

torch (ਟੋਚ) *n* ਟਾਰਚ, ਬੱਤੀ, ਮਸ਼ਾਲ, ਜੋਤ; ਚਾਨਣ

torment ('ਟੋਮੈਂਟ, ਟ'ਮੈਂਟ) *n v* ਤਸੀਹਾ, ਦੁੱਖ, ਕਸ਼ਟ; ਘੋਰ ਸੰਤਾਪ ਦੇਣਾ, ਬਹੁਤ ਦੁੱਖ ਦੇਣਾ, ਕਸ਼ਟ ਦੇਣਾ

tornado (ਟੋ'ਨੇਇਡਅਉ) *n* ਝੱਖੜ, ਤੇਜ਼ ਤੁਫ਼ਾਨ, ਵਾਛੜ

torpedo (ਟੋ'ਪੀਡਅਉ) *n v* ਡੁਬਕਣੀ ਕਿਸ਼ਤੀ, ਟਾਰਪੀਡੋ; ਵਿਸਫੋਟਕ, ਸੁਰੰਗ, ਟਾਰਪੀਡੋ ਨਾਲ ਮਾਰਨਾ; ਅਸਫਲ ਕਰਨਾ, ਵਿਅਰਥ ਕਰਨਾ

tortoise ('ਟੋਟਅਸ) *n* ਕੱਛੂ ਕੁੰਮਾ, ਕੱਛੂ

tortuous ('ਟੋਚੁਅਸ) *a* ਵਲੇਵੇਂਦਾਰ; ਟੇਢਾ-ਮੇਢਾ, ਪੇਚੀਦਾ

torture (ਟੋਚਅ*) *n v* ਤਸੀਹਾ, ਅਜ਼ਾਬ, ਮਾਨਸਕ ਪੀੜਾ, ਕਸ਼ਟ; ਤਸੀਹਾ ਦੇਣਾ; ਸਤਾਉਣਾ; ਤੜਨਾ-ਮਰੋੜਨਾ

toss (ਟੌਸ) *n v* ਸਿੱਕੇ ਦਾ ਉਛਾਲ, ਸਿੱਕਾ ਸੁੱਟਣ ਦੀ ਕਿਰਿਆ, ਟਾਸ; (ਹਵਾ ਦਾ) ਬੁੱਲਾ; ਉਥਲ-ਪੁਥਲ; ਉਛਾਲ; ਸਿੱਕਾ ਸੁੱਟਣਾ; ਹਿੱਲਣਾ-ਜੁਲਣਾ; ਡਾਵਾਂ-ਡੋਲ ਹੋਣਾ

total ('ਟਾਉਟਲ) *n a v* ਜੋੜ, ਜੋੜ-ਫਲ, ਜਮ੍ਹਾਂ, ਕੁੱਲ, ਸਾਰਾ, ਸਮੁੱਚਾ; ਉੱਕਾ; ਜੋੜ ਕਰਨਾ, ਜੋੜ ਹੋਣਾ; ~itarian ਸਰਵ ਅਧਿਕਾਰਵਾਦੀ, ਸਰਵ ਸੱਤਾਵਾਦੀ, ਇਕ ਦਲਵਾਦੀ, ਤਾਨਾਸ਼ਾਹੀ; ~ity ਪੂਰਨਤਾ, ਸਮਗਰਤਾ, ਕੁੱਲ ਜੋੜ; ਕੁੱਲ ਸੰਖਿਆ

totty ('ਟੌਟਿ) *a* ਹੱਕਾ-ਬੱਕਾ, ਚੁੰਧਿਆਇਆ, ਲੜਖੜਾਉਂਦਾ, ਨਸ਼ੇ ਵਿਚ ਚੂਰ

touch (ਟਅੱਚ) *n v* ਛੋਹ, ਸਪਰਸ਼, ਸੰਪਰਕ, ਲਗਾਉ; ਹੱਥ ਲਾਉਣਾ, ਛੋਹਣਾ; ਹੌਲੀ-ਹੌਲੀ ਦੱਬਣਾ, ਤੀਰ ਵਾਂਗ ਲੱਗਣਾ, ਸੁੱਤਾ ਕਰੋਧ ਜਗਾਉਣਾ; (ਤਕ) ਪਹੁੰਚਣਾ; (ਨਾਲ) ਲੱਗਣਾ; ~ing ਦਰਦਨਾਕ, ਦਿੱਲ ਟੁੰਬਵਾਂ; ~y ਚਿੜਚੜਾ, ਸੜੀਅਲ ਮਿਜਾਜ਼

tough (ਟਅੱਫ) *a n* ਸਖ਼ਤ, ਕਰੜਾ, ਮਜ਼ਬੂਤ, ਔਖਾ; ਗੁੰਡਾ, ਬਦਮਾਸ਼

tour (ਟੁਅ*) *n v* ਦੌਰਾ (ਕਰਨਾ), ਯਾਤਰਾ (ਕਰਨੀ),

ਭ੍ਰਮਣ (ਕਰਨਾ)

tournament ('ਟੌਨਅਮਅੰਟ) *n* ਖੇਡਾਂ ਦਾ ਮੁਕਾਬਲਾ, ਖੇਡ ਪ੍ਰਤੀਯੋਗਤਾ; ਫ਼ੌਜੀ ਨੁਮਾਇਸ਼; ਮੁਕਾਬਲਾ

tout (ਟਾਉਟ) *n v* ਦਲਾਲ; ਦਲਾਲੀ ਕਰਨਾ

toward, towards ('ਟਅਉਅਡ, ਟਅ'ਵੋਡਜ਼) *a prep* ਵੱਲ, ਪਾਸੇ, ਦੀ ਦਿਸ਼ਾ ਵਿਚ, ਦੇ ਪ੍ਰਤੀ, ਦੇ ਵਿਸ਼ੇ ਵਿਚ

towel ('ਟਾਉਅਲ) *n v* ਤੌਲੀਆ, ਪਰਨਾ; ਸਰੀਰ ਪੂੰਝਣਾ; ਠੋਕਣਾ, ਰਗੜਨਾ

tower (ਟਾਉਅ*) *n v* ਬੁਰਜ, ਮੁਨਾਰਾ; ਉੱਚਾ ਉਠਣਾ ਜਾਂ ਚੜ੍ਹਨਾ, ਹਵਾ ਵਿਚ ਖੜ੍ਹਾ ਹੋਣਾ

town (ਟਾਉਨ) *n* ਕਸਬਾ, ਸ਼ਹਿਰ, ਨਗਰ; **~ship** ਨਗਰ ਖੇਤਰ, ਨਵੀਂ ਬਸਤੀ

toxic ('ਟੈਕਸਿਕ) *a* ਜ਼ਹਿਰੀਲਾ; ਜ਼ਹਿਰ-ਸਬੰਧੀ; **~ant** ਜ਼ਹਿਰ, ਵਿਸ਼ੈਲਾ ਜ਼ਹਿਰੀਲਾ

toy (ਟੌਇ) *n v* ਖਿਡੌਣਾ; ਘੁੱਗੂ-ਘੋੜਾ, ਖੇਡ; ਮਨੋਰੰਜਨ ਕਰਨਾ, ਦਿਲ ਬਹਿਲਾਉਣਾ

trace (ਟਰੇਇਸ) *n v* ਖੁਰਾ-ਖੋਜ, ਚਿੰਨ੍ਹ, ਨਿਸ਼ਾਨ, ਪਦ-ਚਿੰਨ੍ਹ, ਸੁਰਾਗ; ਰੂਪ-ਰੇਖਾ ਉਲੀਕਣੀ, ਖ਼ਾਕਾ ਖਿੱਚਣਾ; ਟ੍ਰੇਸ ਕਰਨਾ, ਨਕਲ ਕਰਨੀ, ਭਾਲਣਾ, ਲੱਭਣਾ; ਸੁਰਾਗ ਲਾਉਣਾ

trachoma (ਟਰਅ'ਕਅਉਮਅ) *n* ਕੁੱਕਰੇ

track (ਟਰੈਕ) *n* ਮਾਰਗ, ਪਥ; ਪਟੜੀ, ਰੇਲ ਦੀ ਪਟੜੀ; ਪੈੜ ਪਗਡੰਡੀ, ਖੁਰਾਂ ਦੇ ਨਿਸ਼ਾਨ, ਚਿੰਨ੍ਹ; ਪੈੜ ਕਢਣੀ

tract (ਟਰੈਕਟ) *n* ਭੂ-ਖੰਡ ਖੇਤਰ, ਅਰਸਾ; ਛੋਟਾ ਗ੍ਰੰਥ, ਛੋਟਾ ਪੱਤਰ, ਟਰੈਕਟ; **~ion** ਖਿਚਾਉ, ਖਿੱਚ, ਆਕਰਸ਼ਣ; **~or** ਟਰੈਕਟਰ, ਹਲਵਾਹਕ ਇੰਜਣ

trade (ਟਰੇਇਡ) *n* ਧੰਦਾ, ਕਾਰੋਬਾਰ, ਪੇਸ਼ਾ; ਵਣਜ, ਵਪਾਰ, ਤਿਜਾਰਤ, ਸੌਦਾਗਰੀ; ਵਪਾਰ ਕਰਨਾ, ਕਾਰੋਬਾਰ ਕਰਨਾ, ਤਿਜਾਰਤ ਕਰਨੀ; **~mark** ਮਾਰਕਾ; ਵਿੱਲਖਣਤਾ

tradition (ਟਰਅ'ਡਿਸ਼ਨ) *n* ਰਿਵਾਜ, ਪਰੰਪਰਾ, ਰੀਤ, ਰਵਾਇਤ, ਦਸਤੂਰ, ਦੈਵੀ ਸਿਧਾਂਤ

traffic ('ਟਰੈਫ਼ਿਕ) *n* ਆਵਾਜਾਈ, ਆਉਣ-ਜਾਣਾ, ਆਮਦੋ-ਰਫ਼ਤ; ਧੰਦਾ, ਵਣਜ, ਲੈਣ-ਦੇਣ; ਸੌਦਾ ਕਰਨਾ, ਲੈਣ-ਦੇਣ ਕਰਨਾ

tragedy (ਟਰੈਜਅਡਿ) *n* ਬੜੀ ਸ਼ੋਕਮਈ ਦੁਰਘਟਨਾ, ਦੁਖਾਂਤ ਨਾਟਕ; ਦੁਖਾਂਤਕ ਰਚਨਾ; ਵੱਡੀ ਆਫ਼ਤ, ਭਾਰੀ ਮੁਸੀਬਤ

tragic, -al ('ਟਰੈਜਿਕ 'ਟਰੈਜਿਕਲ) *a* ਸ਼ੋਕਮਈ, ਸੋਗ ਭਰਿਆ, ਦੁਖਦਾਈ; ਦਰਦਨਾਕ; ਦੁਖਾਂਤ ਨਾਟਕ ਦਾ

trail (ਟਰੇਇਲ) *n v* ਪਗਡੰਡੀ, ਪੈੜ, ਲੀਹ, ਪੇਹਾ; ਤੋਪ ਨੂੰ ਖਿੱਚਣ ਵਾਲੀ ਮੋਟਰ ਗੱਡੀ ਦਾ ਹੇਠਲਾ ਹਿੱਸਾ; ਖੋਜ ਕੱਢਣਾ; (ਘਾਹ ਆਦਿ ਨੂੰ) ਪੈਰਾਂ ਨਾਲ ਲਿਤਾੜਨਾ; ਪਿੱਛੇ ਘਸੀਟੇ ਜਾਣਾ

train (ਟਰੇਇਨ) *v n* ਸਿਖਾਉਣਾ, ਸਿਖਲਾਈ ਦੇਣੀ; ਅਭਿਆਸ ਕਰਾਉਣਾ; ਲਾਮ-ਡੋਰੀ; ਪਿਛਲੱਗ; ਰੇਲ-ਗੱਡੀ; **~down** (ਕਸਰਤ ਰਾਹੀਂ) ਭਾਰ ਘਟਾਉਣਾ; **~with** ਸਾਥੀ ਬਣਨਾ; **~ee** ਸਿਖਿਆਰਥੀ; **~ing** ਸਿਖਲਾਈ

trait (ਟਰੇਇਟਅ) *n* ਗੁਣ, ਲੱਛਣ, ਵਿਸ਼ੇਸ਼ਤਾ

traitor ('ਟਰੇਇਟਅ*) *n* ਦਰੋਹੀ, ਦੇਸ਼-ਧਰੋਹੀ

trample ('ਟਰੈਂਪਲ) *v n* ਮਿੱਧਣਾ, ਲਿਤਾੜਨਾ; ਲਿਤਾੜ ਦੇਣਾ; ਪਦ-ਦਲਨ; **~d** ਲਿਤਾੜਿਆ, ਕੁਚਲਿਆ; ਦਬਾਇਆ, ਅਪਮਾਨਤ

trance (ਟਰਾਂਸ) *n v* ਸਮਾਧੀ, ਅੰਤਰਲੀਨਤਾ, ਵਜਦ, ਪਰਮ-ਆਨੰਦ ਦੀ ਅਵਸਥਾ, ਵਿਚ ਲੈ ਆਉਣਾ

tranquil ('ਟਰੈਂਕਵਿਲ) *a* ਸ਼ਾਂਤ, ਚੁੱਪ-ਚਾਪ, ਟਿਕਿਆ; ~ity ਟਿਕਾਅ, ਸ਼ਾਂਤੀ, ਅਮਨ-ਚੈਨ, ਸਕੂਨ; ~lize ਸ਼ਾਂਤ ਕਰਨਾ, ਟਿਕਾਉ ਵਿਚ ਲਿਆਉਣਾ, ਸ਼ਾਂਤੀ ਸਥਾਪਤ ਕਰਨੀ; ਧੀਰਜ ਦੇਣਾ

transact (ਟਰੈਂਜ਼ੈਕਟ) *v* ਅਮਲ ਕਰਨਾ, ਨੇਪਰੇ ਚਾੜੂਨਾ, ਨਿਬਾਹੁਣਾ, ਪੂਰਾ ਕਰਨਾ; ਪ੍ਰਬੰਧ ਕਰਨਾ; ~ion ਸੌਦਾ, ਮੁਆਮਲਾ, ਕਾਰਵਾਈ; ਸਮਝੌਤਾ, ਸੁਲ੍ਹਾ-ਸਫ਼ਾਈ; ਨਿਰਵਾਹ; ਕਾਰਜ-ਪ੍ਰਬੰਧ; ਵਿਧਾਨਕ ਕਾਰਵਾਈ

transcend (ਟਰੈਂਸੈਂਡ) *v* ਮਨੁੱਖੀ ਅਨੁਭਵ ਤੋਂ ਪਰ੍ਹੇ ਹੋਣਾ; ਕਮਾਲ ਤੇ ਪਹੁੰਚਣਾ; ਪਾਰਗਾਮੀ ਹੋਣਾ; ~ence, ~ency (ਇੰਦਰੀਆਂ ਦੀ ਪਹੁੰਚ ਤੋਂ ਪਾਰ ਦੀ ਦਸ਼ਾ; ਪਾਰਗਮਨ; ~ent ਅਤੀ ਉੱਚਾ, ਪਾਰਗਾਮੀ, ਅਨੁਭਵ-ਅਤੀਤ-ਤੱਤਵ, ਸੂਝ ਤੇ ਅਨੁਭਵ ਤੋਂ ਪਰਾਂ ਦਾ

transcribe (ਟਰਾਂਸਕਰਾਇਬ) *v* ਪ੍ਰਤੀਲਿਪੀ ਬਣਾਉਣੀ; (ਲਿਖਤ ਨੂੰ) ਨਕਲ ਕਰਨਾ, ਉਤਾਰਾ ਲੈਣਾ

transcript ('ਟਰਾਂਸਕਰਿਪਟ) *n* ਪ੍ਰਤੀਲਿਪੀ; ਨਕਲ (ਲਿਖਤ ਦੀ), ਉਤਾਰਾ; ~ion ਲਿਪੀ-ਅੰਤਰਣ ਪ੍ਰਤੀਲਿਪੀ, ਨਕਲ

transect (ਟਰੈਂਸੈਕਟ) *v* ਨਿਖੇੜਨਾ, ਪਾੜਨਾ, ਵੱਖ ਕਰਨਾ, ਭਿੰਨ-ਭਿੰਨ ਕਰਨਾ, ਵਿਭਾਜਤ ਕਰਨਾ; ~ion ਨਿਖੇੜਾ, ਵਿਭਾਜਤ, ਵੰਡ

transfer (ਟਰਾਂਸ'ਫ਼ੇਆ*, 'ਟਰੈਨਸਫ਼ੇਆ*) *v n* ਬਦਲਣਾ, ਤਬਦੀਲ ਕਰਨਾ, ਸਥਾਨ-ਅੰਤਰਣ ਕਰਨਾ; ਸੌਂਪ ਦੇਣਾ, ਹਵਾਲੇ ਕਰਨਾ; ਤਬਦੀਲੀ, ਸਥਾਨ-ਅੰਤਰਣ; ਇੰਤਕਾਲ; ਨਕਸ਼ੇ ਆਦਿ ਦਾ ਉਤਾਰਾ; ~ence ਤਬਦੀਲੀ, ਬਦਲੀ; ਇੰਤਕਾਲ; ਨਕਲ

transform (ਟਰਾਂਸ'ਫ਼ੋਮ) *v* ਰੂਪ ਬਦਲ ਦੇਣਾ, ਕਾਇਆ ਪਲਟ ਦੇਣੀ, (ਵਿਆ) ਰੂਪਾਂਤਰ ਕਰਨਾ; ~er (ਬਿਜਲੀ) ਪਰਿਵਰਤਨ ਜੰਤਰ, ਪਰਿਮਾਣਕ ਜੰਤਰ; ਪਰਿਵਰਤਨ ਕਰਤਾ

transgress (ਟਰੈਂਸ'ਗਰੈੱਸ) *v* ਉਲੰਘਣਾ ਕਰਨੀ, ਅਵੱਗਿਆ ਕਰਨੀ; ਭੁੱਲ ਕਰਨੀ, ਪਾਪ ਕਰਨਾ; ~ion ਉਲੰਘਣਾ, ਅਵਗਿਆ, ਜੁਰਮ, ਅਪਰਾਧ

transit ('ਟਰਾਂਸਿਟ) *n v* ਗੁਜ਼ਰ, ਲਾਂਘਾ, ਆਊਣ-ਜਾਣ, ਪਾਰਗਮਨ; ~ion ਪਰਿਵਰਤਨ, ਬਦਲੀ; ~ional ਅਸਥਾਈ, ਥੋੜ੍ਹੇ ਚਿਰ ਲਈ, ਆਰਜ਼ੀ; ~ory ਅਸਥਿਰ, ਛਿਣ-ਭੰਗੁਰ; ਅਲਪਕਾਲੀ, ਅਸਥਾਈ

translate (ਟਰੈਂਸ'ਲੇਇਟ) *v* ਅਨੁਵਾਦ ਕਰਨਾ, ਉਲਥਾ ਕਰਨਾ; ਤਾਤਪਰਜ ਕੱਢਣਾ, ਵਿਆਖਿਆ ਕਰਨੀ

translation (ਟਰੈਂਸ'ਲੇਇਸ਼ਨ) *n* ਅਨੁਵਾਦ, ਉਲਥਾ; ਤਰਜਮਾ

translator (ਟਰੈਂਸ'ਲੇਇਟਆ*) *n* ਅਨੁਵਾਦਕ, ਉਲਥਾਕਾਰ

transliterate (ਟਰੈਂਜ਼'ਲਿਟਅਰੇਇਟ) *v* ਲਿਪੀ-ਅੰਤਰਣ, ਵਰਣਾਂਤਰ

transmission (ਟਰੈਂਜ਼'ਮਿਸ਼ਨ) *n* ਲਾਂਘਾ, ਸੰਚਾਰਣ; ਪਾਰਗਮਨ

transmit (ਟਰੈਂਜ਼'ਮਿਟ) *v* ਭੇਜਣਾ, ਘੱਲਣਾ, ਪਹੁੰਚਾਣਾ; ਖ਼ਬਰ ਭੇਜਣੀ ਜਾਂ ਪਹੁੰਚਾਉਣੀ

transmutation ('ਟਰੈਂਜ਼ਮਯੂ'ਟੇਇਸ਼ਨ) *n* ਕਾਇਆ-ਕਲਪ, ਰੂਪ-ਬਦਲੀ, ਰੂਪਾਂਤਰਣ; ਗੁਣ-ਪਰਿਵਰਤਨ

transparence (ਟਰੈਂਜ਼'ਪੈਰਅੰਸ) *n* ਪਾਰਦਰਸ਼ਤਾ; ਨਿਰਮਲਤਾ, ਸੁਅੱਛਤਾ

transparency (ਟਰੈਂਜ਼'ਪੈਰਅੰਸਿ) *n* ਪਾਰਦਰਸ਼ੀ

ਚਿੱਤਰ

transparent (ਟਰੈਂਜ਼'ਪੈਰਅੰਟ) *a* ਪਾਰਦਸ਼ੀ ਨਿਰਮਲ; ਖਰਾ, ਸਪਸ਼ਟ

transpire (ਟਰੈਂਸ'ਪਾਇਅ*) *v* ਅਵਾਈ ਉਡਣੀ, ਪਤਾ ਲੱਗਣਾ; ਵਾਪਰਨਾ, ਹੋਣਾ

transplant (ਟਰੈਂਸ'ਪਲਾਂਟ) *v* ਇਕ ਥਾਂ ਤੋਂ ਪੁਟ ਕੇ ਦੂਜੀ ਥਾਂ ਬੀਜਣਾ; (ਸਰੀਰ ਦੇ ਅੰਗ ਦਾ) ਦੂਜੇ ਥਾਂ ਜਾਂ ਦੂਜੇ ਸਰੀਰ ਵਿਚ ਲਾਉਣਾ; **~ation** ਅੰਗ ਦੀ ਪਿਉਂਦ; **~ing** ਪਿਉਂਦ ਲਾਉਣੀ, ਪਨੀਰੀ ਲਾਉਣੀ

transport (ਟਰੈਂ'ਸਪੋਟ) *v n* ਢੋਣਾ; ਦੇਸ਼ ਨਿਕਾਲਾ ਦੇਣਾ; ਢੁਆਈ; ਆਵਾਜਾਈ; ਵਾਹਣ; ਦੇਸ਼-ਨਿਕਾਲਾ; ਵਜਦ; ਢੁਆਈ ਦਾ ਸਾਧਨ, ਆਵਾਜਾਈ ਲਈ ਵਰਤੀਆਂ ਜਾਣ ਵਾਲੀਆਂ ਗੱਡੀਆਂ ਆਦਿ; **~ation** ਢੋਆ-ਢੁਆਈ; ਦੇਸ਼-ਨਿਕਾਲਾ; ਸਫ਼ਰ

transverbate (ਟਰੈਂਜ਼'ਵ੍ਅ:ਬੇਇਟ) *v* ਸ਼ਬਦ-ਅਨੁਵਾਦ ਕਰਨਾ; ਅਨੁਵਾਦ ਕਰਨਾ

transverse ('ਟਰੈਨਜ਼ਵ੍ਅ:ਸ) *a* ਤਿਰਛਾ, ਆਡੇ ਰੁਖ, ਟੇਢੇ ਰੁਖ

trap (ਟਰੈਪ) *n v* (1) ਛਲ, ਕਪਟ; (2) ਕੁੜਿੱਕੀ, ਫਾਹੀ, ਫੰਧਾ; (3) ਖਿੜਕੀਦਾਰ ਪਿੰਜਰਾ; (4) ਸਾਜ਼-ਸਾਮਾਨ; ਧੋਖੇ ਨਾਲ ਕਾਬੂ ਕਰਨਾ; **~s** ਸਾਮਾਨ, ਸਮਗਰੀ, ਉਪਕਰਣ, ਅਸਬਾਬ

travail ('ਟਰੈਵ੍ਇਲ) *n v* ਪ੍ਰਸੂਤ ਪੀੜਾਂ, ਵਿਅੰਮ ਦੀ ਪੀੜ; ਕਸ਼ਟ; ਸਖ਼ਤ ਮਿਹਨਤ; ਦੁੱਖ ਝੱਲਣਾ, ਕਸ਼ਟ ਸਹਿਣਾ

travel ('ਟਰੈਵ੍ਲ) *v n* ਸਫ਼ਰ ਕਰਨਾ, ਯਾਤਰਾ ਕਰਨੀ, ਘੁਮਾਉਣਾ-ਫਿਰਾਉਣਾ; ਸਫ਼ਰ, ਯਾਤਰਾ, ਘੁੰਮਣ-ਘੁਮਾਉਣ; ਚਾਲ, ਗਤੀ; **~ler** ਯਾਤਰੀ, ਪਾਂਧੀ, ਮੁਸਾਫ਼ਰ, ਰਾਹਗੀਰ; **~ling** ਸਫ਼ਰ, ਯਾਤਰਾ, ਭ੍ਰਮਣ; ਸਫ਼ਰ ਦਾ ਸਾਮਾਨ, ਸਫ਼ਰੀ, ਚੱਲਦਾ-ਫਿਰਦਾ; **~ogue** ਸਫ਼ਰਨਾਮਾ

traverse ('ਟਰੈਵ੍ਅਸ) *v n* ਆਰ-ਪਾਰ ਕਰਨਾ; (ਵਿਸ਼ੈ ਦੇ) ਹਰ ਪੱਖ ਤੇ ਨਜ਼ਰ ਮਾਰਨੀ; (ਕਚਹਿਰੀ ਵਿਚ) ਕਿਸੇ ਮੁਆਮਲੇ ਨੂੰ ਰੱਦ ਕਰਨਾ; ਵਿਰੋਧ ਕਰਨਾ; ਖੰਡਨ, ਇਨਕਾਰ

travesty ('ਟਰੈਵ੍ਅਸਟਿ) *n v* ਪ੍ਰਹਸਨ, ਹਾਸੋਹੀਣੀ ਨਕਲ, ਘਟੀਆ ਨਕਲ; ਮੁਖੌਟਾ; ਨਕਲ ਲਾਹੁਣੀ, ਮਜ਼ਾਕ ਉਡਾਉਣਾ

tray (ਟਰੇਇ) *n* ਥਾਲੀ, ਤਸ਼ਤਰੀ, ਟ੍ਰੇ

treacher (ਟਰੈੱਚਅ*) *n* ਵਿਸਾਹਘਾਤੀ, ਧਰੋਹੀ, ਗ਼ੱਦਾਰ, ਕਿਰਤਘਣ; **~y** ਧੋਖਾ, ਫ਼ਰੇਬ, ਧਰੋਹ, ਵਿਸਾਹਘਾਤ, ਗ਼ੱਦਾਰੀ, ਕਪਟ

tread (ਟਰੈੱਡ) *v n* ਟੁਰਨਾ, ਚੱਲਣਾ, ਪੈਰ ਰੱਖਣਾ; ਲਿਤਾੜਨਾ, ਮਿੱਧਣਾ; ਸਮਾਪਤ ਕਰਨਾ, ਸੰਪੂਰਨ ਕਰਨਾ; ਚਾਲ, ਗਤੀ; ਕਦਮ

treason ('ਟਰੀਜ਼ਨ) *n* ਵਿਦਰੋਹ, ਬਗ਼ਾਵਤ, ਗ਼ਦਰ, ਰਾਜ-ਧਰੋਹ, ਗ਼ੱਦਾਰੀ; ਵਿਸਾਹਘਾਤ

treasure (ਟਰੈਜ਼ਅ*) *n v* ਖ਼ਜ਼ਾਨਾ, ਕੋਸ਼; ਦੌਲਤ, ਮਾਲ; ਕਦਰ ਕਰਨੀ, ਸਾਂਭ ਕੇ ਰੱਖਣਾ; ਯਾਦ-ਦਾਸ਼ਤ ਵਿਚ ਰੱਖਣਾ; **~r** ਖ਼ਜ਼ਾਨਚੀ, ਕੋਸ਼-ਅਧਿਕਾਰੀ, ਕੋਸ਼ਪਾਲ

treasury ('ਟਰੈੱਯ਼ਅਰਿ) *n* ਕੋਸ਼, ਕੋਸ਼ਗ੍ਰਹਿ, ਖ਼ਜ਼ਾਨਾ, ਮਹਿਕਮਾ ਮਾਲ; ਗਿਆਨ ਭੰਡਾਰ

treat (ਟਰੀਟ) *v n* ਵਰਤਾਅ ਕਰਨਾ, ਸਲੂਕ ਕਰਨਾ, ਵਿਹਾਰ ਕਰਨਾ; ਉਪਚਾਰ ਕਰਨਾ, ਨਿਭਾਉ ਕਰਨਾ; ਦਾਅਵਤ ਦੇਣੀ, ਦਾਵਅਤ; ਮੌਜ-ਮੇਲਾ, ਮਨੋਰੰਜਨ, ਆਨੰਦ; **~ment** ਵਰਤਾਉ, ਸਲੂਕ, ਵਤੀਰਾ, ਭੋਜ਼, ਬੰਦੋਬਸਤ, ਪ੍ਰਬੰਧ, ਨਿਰੂਪਣ

treble ('ਟਰੈਬੱਲ) *a v n* ਤਿਹਰਾ; ਤਿਗੁਣਾ;

ਤਿਗੁਣਾ ਕਰਨਾ

treddle ('ਟਰੈਡੱਲ) *n v* ਪਾਇਦਾਨ, ਪੈਡਲ; ਪੈਡਲ ਮਾਰਨਾ, ਪੈਰ ਨਾਲ ਚਲਾਉਣਾ

tree (ਟਰੀ) *n* ਰੁੱਖ, ਬਿਰਛ, ਦਰਖ਼ਤ; ਵੰਸਾਵਲੀ

trek (ਟਰੈੱਕ) *n v* ਸਫ਼ਰ; ਪੈਂਡਾ, ਯਾਤਰਾ; ਬੈਲ-ਗੱਡੀ ਉੱਤੇ ਸਫ਼ਰ; ਲੰਮੀ ਯਾਤਰਾ, ਪੈਂਡੇ ਪੈਣਾ, ਪੰਧ ਮਾਰਨਾ, ਸਪਾਟਾ ਕਰਨਾ; **~ker** ਪਾਂਧੀ, ਮੁਸਾਫ਼ਰ, ਘੁਮੱਕੜ, ਯਾਤਰੀ

tremble ('ਟਰੈਂਬਲ) *v n* ਕਬੰਣਾ, ਕਬੰਣੀ ਆਉਣੀ, ਥਰਥਰਾਉਣਾ; ਡਗਮਗਾਉਣਾ; ਭੈਭੀਤ ਹੋ ਜਾਣਾ; ਕੰਬਣੀ, ਕਾਂਬਾ, ਥਰਥਰਾਹਟ, ਥਰਥਰੀ

tremendous (ਟਰਿਮੈਂਨੱਡਅਸ) *a* ਡਰਾਉਣਾ, ਭਿਆਨਕ; ਡਾਢਾ, ਪ੍ਰਬਲ, ਬਹੁਤ ਜ਼ਿਆਦਾ; ਬੜਾ ਵੱਡਾ

tremor ('ਟਰੈੱਮਅ*) *n* ਕਬੰਣੀ, ਕਾਂਬਾ, ਥਰਥਰਾਹਟ; ਹਲਕਾ ਭੁਚਾਲੀ ਝਟਕਾ

trench (ਟਰੈੱਟਚ) *n v* ਖਾਈ; ਮੋਰਚਾ, ਖੰਦਕ; ਖਾਈ ਪੁੱਟਣੀ; ਮੋਰਚਾ ਪੁੱਟਣਾ, ਖੰਦਕ ਬਣਾਉਣੀ

trend (ਟਰੈਂਡ) *n v* ਰੁਝਾਨ, ਪ੍ਰਵਿਰਤੀ, ਰੌਂ, ਰੁਖ; ਖਾਸ ਰੁਝਾਨ ਰਖਣਾ

trespass ('ਟਰੈੱਸਪਅਸ) *v n* ਨਾਜਾਇਜ਼ ਜਾ ਵੜਨਾ, ਨਾਜਾਇਜ਼ ਦਖ਼ਲ ਦੇਣਾ, ਮਰਯਾਦਾ ਦਾ ਉਲੰਘਣ ਕਰਨਾ, ਅਵੱਗਿਆ ਕਰਨੀ; ਉਲੰਘਣ, ਅਵੱਗਿਆ

trial ('ਟਰਾਇ(ਅ)ਲ) *n* ਪਰਖ, ਅਜ਼ਮਾਇਸ਼, ਪਰੀਖਿਆ; ਅਜ਼ਮਾਇਸ਼ੀ ਮੁਕਾਬਲਾ

triangle ('ਟਰਾਇਐਂਗਲ) *n* ਤਿਕੋਣ, ਤ੍ਰਿਭੁਜ, ਤਿਕੋਣ ਜੰਤਰ

triangular (ਟਰਾਇ'ਐਂਗਯੁਲਅ*) *a* ਤਿਕੋਣਾ

tribal ('ਟਰਾਇਬਲ) *a* ਕਬੀਲੇ ਦਾ, ਕਬਾਇਲੀ; ਗੋਤ

tribe ('ਟਰਾਇਬ) *a* ਜਾਤੀ, ਕਬੀਲਾ; ਟੱਬਰ, ਉਪਵੰਸ਼, ਉਪਕੁਲ

tribulation ('ਟਰਿਬਯੁ'ਲੇਇਸ਼ਨ) *n* ਕਸ਼ਟ, ਦੁੱਖ, ਸੰਤਾਪ, ਤਸੀਹਾ, ਮੁਸੀਬਤ

tribunal (ਟਰਾਇ'ਬਯੂਨਲ) *n* ਕਚਹਿਰੀ, ਅਦਾਲਤ, ਨਿਆਂ-ਸਭਾ, ਵਿਸ਼ੇਸ਼ ਅਦਾਲਤ

tribune ('ਟਰਿਬਯੂਨ) *n* (1) ਲੋਕ-ਨੇਤਾ, ਲੋਕਪ੍ਰਿਅ ਆਗੂ, ਮੰਚ; ਅਦਾਲਤ ਵਿਚ ਜੱਜ ਦੇ ਬੈਠਣ ਦੀ ਕੁਰਸੀ ਜਾਂ ਥਾਂ

tributary ('ਟਰਿਬਯੁਟ(ਅ)ਰਿ) *n a* ਸਹਾਇਕ ਨਦੀ; ਅਧੀਨ ਰਾਜਾ, ਸ਼ਾਖ਼ਾ; ਅਪ੍ਰਧਾਨ, ਸਹਾਇਕ

tribute ('ਟਰਿਬਯੂਟ) *n* ਸ਼ਰਧਾਂਜਲੀ; ਨਜ਼ਰਾਨਾ, ਖਿਰਾਜ

trick (ਟਰਿਕ) *n v* ਦਾਅ, ਚਾਲ, ਚਲਾਕੀ, ਫ਼ਰੇਬ, ਧੋਖਾ, ਛਲ, ਕਪਟ; ਚਤਰਾਈ, ਹੱਥ-ਫ਼ੇਰੀ; ਧੋਖਾ ਕਰਨਾ, ਕਪਟ ਕਰਨਾ, ਹੱਥ-ਫੇਰੀ ਕਰਨੀ; **~y** ਧੋਖੇਬਾਜ਼, ਛਲੀ, ਕਪਟੀ, ਚਾਲਬਾਜ਼

trickle ('ਟਰਿਕਲ) *n v* ਹੌਲੀ-ਹੌਲੀ ਵਹਿਣ ਵਾਲੀ ਧਾਰਾ; ਮੰਦ ਪਰਵਾਹ; ਪਤਲੀ ਧਾਰ; ਤੁਪਕੇ ਡਿਗਣੇ, ਤੁਪਕਾ ਤੁਪਕਾ ਕਰਕੇ ਚੋਣਾ

tricolour ('ਟਰਾਇਕਲ*) *a n* ਤਿਰੰਗਾ, ਤਿੰਨ ਰੰਗਾਂ ਵਾਲਾ; ਭਾਰਤ ਦਾ ਰਾਸ਼ਟਰੀ ਝੰਡਾ

trident ('ਟਰਾਇਡੰਟ) *n* ਤਿੰਨ ਸਾਂਗਾ, ਹਥਿਆਰ, ਤ੍ਰਿਸ਼ੂਲ

triennial (ਟਰਾਇ'ਐਨਯਅਲ) *a n* ਤਿੰਨ-ਵਰਸ਼ੀ, ਤ੍ਰੈ-ਵਾਰਸ਼ਕ

trifle ('ਟਰਾਇਫ਼ਲ) *n v* ਨਿਗੂਣੀ ਚੀਜ਼, ਤੁੱਛ ਵਸਤੂ; ਮਾਮੂਲੀ ਰਕਮ; ਛੋਟਾ ਖਿਡਾਉਣਾ; ਹੋਛੀਆਂ ਗੱਲਾਂ ਕਰਨੀਆਂ, ਘਟੀਆ ਕੰਮ ਕਰਨਾ

trigger ('ਟਰਿਗਅ*) *n* (ਬੰਦੂਕ, ਪਿਸਤੌਲ ਆਦਿ ਦਾ) ਘੋੜਾ

trigonometry ('ਟਰਿਗਾਅ'ਨੌਮਅਟਰਿ) *n* ਤਿਕੋਣ-ਮਿਤੀ

trillingual (ਟਰਾਇ'ਲਿਡਗਵ(ਅ)ਲ) *a* ਤ੍ਰੈਭਾਸ਼ੀ, ਤਿੰਨਾਂ ਭਾਸ਼ਾਵਾਂ ਦਾ

trim (ਟਰਿਮ) *a v* ਸਾਫ਼ ਸੁਥਰਾ, ਸੱਜਿਆ ਸੰਵਰਿਆ, ਬਣਿਆ-ਠਣਿਆ, ਸੁਅੰਡ, ਲਤਰਨ-ਲਾਪਰਨ, ਸਾਫ਼-ਸੁਥਰਾ ਕਰਨਾ, (ਪੁਸ਼ਾਕ) ਸੰਵਾਰਨੀ; (ਦਾੜ੍ਹੀ) ਕਤਰਨੀ; ਖ਼ਤ ਕੱਢਣਾ

trio (ਟਰੀਅਉ) *n pl* ਤਿਗੜੀ, ਤਿੰਨਾਂ ਜਣਿਆਂ ਦੀ ਮੰਡਲੀ, ਤਿੰਨ ਗਾਇਕਾਂ ਦੀ ਟੋਲੀ, ਵਿਸ਼ੇਸ਼ ਭਾਂਤ ਦਾ ਨਾਚ

trip (ਟਰਿਪ) *v n* ਕਾਹਲੇ-ਕਾਹਲੇ ਟੁਰਨਾ, ਸੈਰ-ਸਪਾਟਾ ਕਰਨਾ, ਕਿਸੇ ਥਾਂ ਨੂੰ ਵੇਖਣ ਲਈ ਜਾਣਾ, ਖਿੜਕਣਾ; ਚੱਕਰ, ਠੋਕਰ, ਖਿੜਕ, ਉਕਾਈ

triple ('ਟਰਿਪਲ) *a v* ਤਿਹਰਾ, ਤੀਨਾ, ਤਿੰਨ ਗੁਣਾ; ਤਿਹਰਾ ਹੋਣਾ ਜਾਂ ਕਰਨਾ

triplicate ('ਟਰਿਪਲਿਕੇਇਟ) *v a* ਤਿਹਰਾ ਕਰਨਾ, ਤਿੰਨ ਕਾਪੀਆਂ ਬਣਾਉਣੀਆਂ; ਤਿਗੁਣਾ; ਤੀਜੀ ਨਕਲ

triumph ('ਟਰਾਇਅੰਫ਼) *n v* ਜਿੱਤ, ਵਿਜੈ, ਫ਼ਤਿਹ, ਜਿੱਤ ਪ੍ਰਾਪਤ ਕਰਨੀ, ਫ਼ਤਿਹ ਪਾਉਣੀ; **~ant** ਵਿਜੇਤਾ, ਜਿੱਤਿਆ, ਕਾਮਯਾਬ

trivial ('ਟਰਿਵਿਅਲ) *a* ਤੁੱਛ, ਨਿਗੁਣਾ, ਥੋਥਾ, ਬਹੁਤ ਮਾਮੂਲੀ; ਨਿਕੰਮਾ; **~ity** ਤੁੱਛ ਚੀਜ਼, ਨਿਗੁਣੀ ਵਸਤੂ; ਤੁੱਛਤਾ, ਨਿਗੁਣਾਪਣ

Trojan ('ਟਰਅਉਜ(ਅ)ਨ) *a* ਸੂਰਮਾ, ਵੀਰ, ਸਾਹਸੀ

trolley ('ਟੌਰਲਿ) *n* ਠੇਲ੍ਹਾ, ਸਟੇਸ਼ਨ ਤੇ ਸਾਮਾਨ ਢੋਣ ਵਾਲੀ ਰੇੜ੍ਹੀ; ਰੇਲ ਦੀ ਪਟੜੀ ਤੇ ਚਲਾਇਆ ਜਾਣ ਵਾਲਾ ਠੇਲ੍ਹਾ; ਟਰਾਲੀ

troop (ਟਰੂਪ) *n v* ਟੋਲੀ, ਮੰਡਲੀ, ਜੁੰਡਲੀ; ਫ਼ੌਜ, ਸੈਨਾ; ਇੱਕਠਾ ਹੋਣਾ, ਇੱਕਤਰ ਕਰਨਾ, ਜੱਥਾ ਬਣਾਉਣਾ; ਫ਼ੌਜ ਨੂੰ ਟੁਕੜੀਆਂ ਵਿਚ ਵੰਡਣਾ

trophy ('ਟਰਅਉਫ਼ਿ) *n* ਫ਼ਤਿਹ ਦੀ ਨਿਸ਼ਾਨੀ; ਜਿੱਤ ਦਾ ਇਨਾਮ, ਵਿਜੈ ਪੁਰਸਕਾਰ

trouble ('ਟਰਅੰਬਲ) *n v* ਦੁੱਖ, ਕਸ਼ਟ ਤਕਲੀਫ਼, ਬਿਪਤਾ, ਸੰਕਟ; ਰੋਗ, ਬੀਮਾਰੀ; ਔਕੜ, ਅਸੁਵਿਧਾ; ਤਕਲੀਫ਼ ਦੇਣੀ, ਕਸ਼ਟ ਦੇਣਾ

trounce (ਟਰਅਉਂਸ) *v* ਛੱਕੇ ਛੁਡਾ ਦੇਣਾ, ਸਜ਼ਾ ਦੇਣੀ, ਭੁਗਤ ਸੁਆਰਨੀ; ਬੁਰੀ ਤਰ੍ਹਾਂ ਹਰਾਉਣਾ, ਖੁੰਬ ਠੱਪਣੀ

troupe (ਟਰੂਪ) *n* ਅਭਿਨੇਤਾ-ਦਲ, ਨਾਟ-ਮੰਡਲੀ, ਐਕਟਰਾਂ ਦੀ ਮੰਡਲੀ

trousers ('ਟਰਅਉਜ਼ਅਃਜ਼) *n pl* ਪਤਲੂਨ

truancy ('ਟਰੂਅੰਸਿ) *n* ਅਵਾਰਾਪਣ, ਕੰਮ-ਚੋਰੀ, ਘੁਸਾਈ

truant ('ਟਰੂਅੰਟ) *a n* ਸਕੂਲ ਤੋਂ ਭੱਜਿਆ (ਬੱਚਾ); ਕੰਮ ਚੋਰ (ਬੱਚਾ); ਨਿਕੰਮਾ; ਭਗੌੜਾ (ਬੱਚਾ), ਅਵਾਰਾ

truck (ਟਰਅੱਕ) *v n* ਵੱਟਾ-ਸੱਟਾ ਕਰਨਾ; ਅਦਲਾ-ਬਦਲੀ ਕਰਨੀ, ਸੌਦਾ ਕਰਨਾ, ਵਪਾਰ ਕਰਨਾ; (ਮਾਲ) ਵੇਚਦੇ ਫਿਰਨਾ; ਲੈਣ-ਦੇਣ; ਮਾਲ ਢੋਣ ਵਾਲੀ ਮੋਟਰ ਗੱਡੀ, ਟਰੱਕ

true (ਟਰੂ) *a n* ਸੱਚਾ, ਖਰਾ, ਸ਼ੁੱਧ; ਸੱਚ, ਸਤਿਵਾਦੀ, ਅਸਲੀ, ਵਾਸਤਵਿਕ; ਠੀਕ; ਵਫ਼ਾਦਾਰ, ਈਮਾਨਦਾਰ, ਵਿਸ਼ਵਾਸਯੋਗ

truly (ਟਰੂਅੱਲੀ) *adv* ਅਸਲ ਵਿਚ; ਵਾਸਤਵ ਵਿਚ, ਸੱਚ-ਮੁੱਚ, ਈਮਾਨਦਾਰੀ ਨਾਲ, ਸੱਚੇ ਦਿਲੋਂ

trump (ਟਰਅੱਪ) *n v* (ਤਾਸ਼ ਵਿਚ) ਰੰਗ ਦਾ ਪੱਤਾ, ਤੁਰਪ ਦਾ ਪੱਤਾ; (ਬੋਲ) ਬੜਾ ਸੂਰਮਾ, ਉੱਤਮ ਮਨੁੱਖ, ਅੰਤਮ ਸਾਧਨ, ਆਖ਼ਰੀ ਚਾਲ, ਤੁਰਪ

ਲਾਉਣਾ, ਚਾਲ ਚੱਲਣੀ

trumpet ('ਟਰਅੰਪਿਟ) *n v* ਬਿਗਲ, ਤੁਰ੍ਹੀ, ਤੁਰਮ, ਨਰਸਿੰਘਾ; ਬਿਗਲ ਵਜਾਉਣਾ, ਡੌਂਡੀ ਪਿੱਟਣੀ; (ਹਾਥੀ ਦਾ) ਚਿੰਘਾੜਨ

truncate ('ਟਰਅੱਨਕੇਇਟ) *v a* ਛਾਂਗਣਾ (ਰੁਖ ਆਦਿ ਨੂੰ); ਹੱਥ-ਪੈਰ ਵੱਢਣੇ (ਮਨੁੱਖ ਦੇ)

truncation (ਟਰਅੰਡ'ਕੇਇਸ਼ਨ) *n* ਛੰਗਾਈ, ਕਟਾਈ, ਮੁਛਾਈ, ਕਾਂਟ-ਛਾਂਟ

trunk (ਟਰਅੱਡਕ) *n* ਰੁਖ ਦਾ ਤਣਾ; (ਮਨੁੱਖ ਦਾ) ਧੜ; ਮੁੱਖ ਰੇਲ ਲਾਈਨ, ਸੜਕ; ਬਕਸਾ, ਸੰਦੂਕ, ਟਰੰਕ; ਹਾਥੀ ਦੀ ਸੁੰਡ; ~**call** ਟੈਲੀਫ਼ੋਨ ਤੇ ਦੂਸਰੇ ਸ਼ਹਿਰ ਨੂੰ ਸੰਦੇਸ਼; ~**line,** ~**road** ਮੁੱਖ ਸੜਕ, ਜਰਨੈਲੀ ਸੜਕ, ਸ਼ਾਹ ਰਾਹ

trust (ਟਰਅੱਸਟ) *n v* ਵਿਸ਼ਵਾਸ, ਭਰੋਸਾ, ਯਕੀਨ, ਪ੍ਰਤੀਤੀ; ਪੱਕੀ ਆਸ; ਅਮਾਨਤ; ਨਿਆਸ; (ਵਪਾਰ) ਵਪਾਰੀ ਸੰਘ, ਟਰਸਟ; ਵਿਸ਼ਵਾਸ ਕਰਨਾ, ਯਕੀਨ ਕਰਨਾ, ਭਰੋਸਾ ਰੱਖਣਾ; ~**deed** ਸਾਖ-ਪੱਟਾ, ਵਸੀਕਾਨਾਮਾ, ਅਮਾਨਤਨਾਮਾ; ~**worthy** ਇਤਬਾਰਯੋਗ, ਵਿਸ਼ਵਾਸਯੋਗ, ਭਰੋਸੇਯੋਗ; ~**ee** ਨਿਆਸੀ, ਨਿਆਸਧਾਰੀ, ਟਰਸਟੀ, ਸਰਕਾਰੀ ਅਮੀਨ, ਅਮਾਨਤਦਾਰ; ~**ful** ਸੱਚਾ, ਸਤਿਵਾਦੀ, ਈਮਾਨਦਾਰ, ਵਿਸ਼ਵਾਸਯੋਗ; ਅਸਲੀ, ਵਾਸਤਵਿਕ; ~**y** ਵਿਸ਼ਵਾਸਯੋਗ, ਇਤਬਾਰੀ, ਈਮਾਨਦਾਰ

truth (ਟਰੂਥ) *n* ਸੱਚ, ਸਚਾਈ, ਅਸਲੀਅਤ ਵਾਸਤ-ਵਿਕਤਾ, ਹਕੀਕਤ, ਯਥਾਰਥਕਤਾ, ਈਮਾਨਦਾਰੀ; ~**ful** ਸੱਚਾ, ਸਤਿਵਾਦੀ, ਈਮਾਨਦਾਰ, ਵਿਸ਼ਵਾਸ-ਯੋਗ; ਅਸਲੀ, ਵਾਸਤਵਿਕ

try (ਟਰਾਇ) *v n* ਕੋਸ਼ਿਸ਼ ਕਰਨੀ, ਜਤਨ ਕਰਨਾ; ਅਜ਼ਮਾਉਣਾ, ਪਰਤਾਵਾ ਲੈਣਾ, ਪਰਖਣਾ, ਜਾਂਚਣਾ; ਮੁੱਕਦਮਾ ਚਲਾਉਣਾ; ਕੋਸ਼ਿਸ਼, ਉਪਰਾਲਾ; ~**out**

ਪਰਖਣਾ, ਅਜ਼ਮਾ ਕੇ ਵੇਖਣਾ; ਆਜ਼ਮਾਇਸ਼; ~**ing** ਔਖਾ, ਕਰੜਾ, ਕਠਨ, ਮੁਸ਼ਕਲ, ਦੁੱਖਦਾਈ, ਕਸ਼ਟਕਾਰੀ

tub (ਟਅੱਬ) *n v* ਟੱਬ ਵਿਚ ਕੀਤਾ ਇਸ਼ਨਾਨ; ਟੱਬ ਵਿਚ ਨਹਾਉਣਾ

tube (ਟਯੂਬ) *n* ਨਕਲੀ, ਨਾਲ; ਨਲੀ; ਸੁਰੰਗ; ਨਾੜ

tuberculosis (ਟਯੂ'ਬਅ:ਕਯੁ'ਲਅਉਸਿਸ) *n* ਤਪਦਿਕ, ਖਈ ਰੋਗ, ਖੰਘ-ਤਾਪ, ਟੀ ਬੀ

tuck (ਟਅੱਕ) *n v* (ਕਪੜੇ ਦਾ) ਪਲੇਟ; (ਅਪ) ਮਿਠਿਆਈ, ਛੋਟੇ ਕੇਕ ਆਦਿ; ~**in** ਰੱਜ ਕੇ ਖਾਣਾ, ਸੰਘ ਤਕ ਭਰ ਲੈਣਾ; ~**shop** ਮਿਠਿਆਈ ਆਦਿ ਦੀ ਦੁਕਾਨ

Tuesday ('ਟਯੂਜ਼ਡਿ) *n* ਮੰਗਲਵਾਰ

tug (ਟਅੱਗ) *v n* ਧੂਹਣਾ, ਘਸੀਟਣਾ, ਝਟਕਾ ਕੇ ਖਿੱਚਣਾ; (ਦਿਲ ਨੂੰ) ਧੂਹ ਪਾਉਣੀ; (ਕਿਸੇ ਵਿਸ਼ੇ ਨੂੰ) ਖਿੱਚ, ਧੂ, ਘਸੀਟ; ਝਟਕਾ, ਕਠੋਰ ਜਤਨ; ~**of war** ਰੱਸਾ ਖਿੱਚਣ ਦਾ ਮੁਕਾਬਲਾ

tuition (ਟਯੂ'ਇਸ਼ਨ) *n* ਪੜ੍ਹਾਈ, ਟਿਊਸ਼ਨ, ਨਿਜੀ ਪੜ੍ਹਾਈ ਦੀ ਫ਼ੀਸ

tumour ('ਟਯੂਮਅ*) *n* ਗਰੰਥੀ, ਰਸੌਲੀ, ਗੰਢ, ਗਿਲਟੀ

tumult ('ਟਯੂਮਅੱਲਟ) *n* ਸ਼ੋਰ-ਸ਼ਰਾਬਾ, ਰੌਲਾ-ਗੌਲਾ, ਦੰਗਾ-ਫ਼ਸਾਦ, ਹੰਗਾਮਾ, ਅਸ਼ਾਂਤੀ; ਉਤੇਜਨਾ; ~**uous** ਖਰੂਦੀ, ਫ਼ਸਾਦੀ, ਦੰਗੇਬਾਜ਼, ਵੈਡ਼ਾ, ਕੱਬਾ

tune (ਟਯੂਨ) *n v* ਸੁਰ, ਲੈਅ, ਤਰਜ਼, ਧੁਨ, ਤਾਲ; ਰਾਗ; ਤਰੰਨਮ, ਸੁਰ-ਸੰਗੀਤ; ਅਨੁਕੂਲਤਾ, ਉਪ-ਯੁਕਤਤਾ; ਅਨੁਕੂਲ ਬਣਾਉਣਾ; (ਕਾਵਿ) ਗਾਉਣਾ; ਰਾਗ ਛੋਹਣਾ

tunnel ('ਟਅੱਨਲ) *n v* ਸੁਰੰਗ, ਸੁਰੰਗ ਕੱਢਣੀ; ਸੁਰੰਗ ਵਿਚੋਂ ਲੰਘਣਾ

turban ('ਟਅਃਬਅਨ) *n* ਪੱਗ, ਪਗੜੀ, ਦਸਤਾਰ

turbulence ('ਟਅਃਬਯੁਲਅੰਸ) *n* ਖਲਬਲੀ, ਗੜਬੜ, ਖਰੂਦ, ਫ਼ਸਾਦ, ਦੰਗਾ, ਹੰਗਾਮਾ

turbulent ('ਟਅਃਬਯੁਲਅੰਟ) *a* ਖਰੂਦੀ, ਉਪੱਦਰੀ, ਫ਼ਸਾਦੀ; ਅਸ਼ਾਂਤ, ਵਿਆਕੁਲ, ਬੇਚੈਨ

turmeric ('ਟਅਃਮਅਰਿਕ) *n* ਹਲਦੀ

turmoil ('ਟਅਃਮੋਇਲ) *n v* ਗੜਬੜ, ਰੌਲਾ-ਗੌਲਾ, ਹਫੜਾ-ਦਫੜੀ; ਅਸ਼ਾਂਤੀ, ਬੇਚੈਨੀ, ਹਲਚਲ, ਖਲਬਲੀ; ਹਲਚਲ ਮਚਾਉਣਾ

turn (ਟਅਃਨ) *v n* ਮੋੜਨਾ, ਮੁੜਨਾ, ਘੁਮਾਉਣਾ, ਘੁੰਮਣਾ, ਫੇਰਨਾ ਜਾਂ ਫਿਰਨਾ, ਗੋੜਨਾ ਜਾਂ ਗਿੜਨਾ; ਭੁਆਉਣਾ ਜਾਂ ਭੌਣਾ, ਪਰਤਨਾ ਜਾਂ ਪਰਤ ਜਾਣਾ, ਪਾਸਾ ਬਦਲਣਾ; ਉਲਟਣਾ; ਮੋੜ, ਚੱਕਰ, ਮੋੜਾ; ਰੁਚੀ, ਰੁਝਾਨ; ਰੱਸੇ ਦਾ ਵਲਾਵਾਂ; ~coat ਦਲ-ਬਦਲੂ, ਚੱਕਵਾਂ-ਚੁਲ੍ਹਾ, ਆਇਆ-ਰਾਮ ਗਿਆ-ਰਾਮ; ~down ਨਾਮਨਜ਼ੂਰ ਕਰਨਾ, ਰੱਦ ਕਰ ਦੇਣਾ; ~out ਕੱਢ ਦੇਣਾ; ਬਾਹਰ ਵੱਲ ਮੋੜਨਾ; ਕੰਮ ਤੇ ਪੁੱਜਣਾ; ਪੈਦਾਵਾਰ, ਉਪਜ; ਹਾਜ਼ਰੀ, ਇਕੱਠ; ~over ਉਲੱਟਣਾ, ਉਲਟਾਉਣਾ, ਪਲਟਾਉਣਾ; ਉਲਟ ਜਾਣਾ, ਮੁਧੇ ਹੋ ਜਾਣਾ; ~round ਪਿੱਛੇ ਨੂੰ ਮੁੜਨਾ, ਆਪਣੀ ਨੀਤੀ ਬਦਲ ਦੇਣੀ; ~turtle ਮੁਧਾ ਹੋ ਜਾਣਾ, ਉਲਟ ਜਾਣਾ; ~ing-point ਮੋੜ

turnip ('ਟਅਃਨਿਪ) ਗੋਗਲੂ

turtle ('ਟਅਃਟਲ) *n* ਘੁੱਗੀ; ~dove ਘੁੱਗੀ

tusk (ਟਅਸਕ) *n v* ਹਾਥੀ-ਦੰਦ, ਹਾਥੀ ਦਾ ਲੰਮਾ ਦੰਦ, ਦੰਦ ਚੁਭਾਉਣਾ

tussle ('ਟਅਸਲ) ·*n v* ਖਿੱਚ-ਧੂਹ, ਝੜਪ, ਲੜਾਈ-ਝਗੜਾ, ਸੰਘਰਸ਼; ਝਗੜਾ ਕਰਨਾ, ਲੜਾਈ ਕਰਨੀ

tutor ('ਟਯੂਟਅ*) *n v* ਨਿਜੀ ਤੌਰ ਤੇ ਪੜ੍ਹਾਉਣ

ਵਾਲਾ; ਉਸਤਾਦ; ਨਾਬਾਲਗ਼ ਬੱਚੇ ਦਾ ਸਰ-ਪਰਸਤ; ਬੱਚੇ ਦੀ ਵਿੱਦਿਆ ਲਈ ਜ਼ੁੰਮੇਵਾਰ ਹੋਣਾ, ਟਿਊਟਰ ਹੋਣਾ; ~ship ਕਿਸੇ ਬੱਚੇ ਦੀ ਪੜ੍ਹਾਈ ਲਈ ਜ਼ੁੰਮੇਵਾਰੀ, ਨਿਗਰਾਨੀ

twelfth ('ਟਵੈਲੱਫ਼ਥ) *a n* ਬਾਰ੍ਹਵਾਂ; ਬਾਰ੍ਹਵਾਂ ਹਿੱਸਾ

twelve (ਟਵੈੱਲਵ਼) *a n* ਬਾਰਾਂ, ਬਾਰਾਂ ਦੀ ਸੰਖਿਆ

twentieth ('ਟਵੈਨੱਟਿਅਥ) *a* ਵੀਹਵਾਂ

twenty ('ਟਵੈਨਿਟ) *a n* ਵੀਹ, ਵੀਹ ਦੀ ਗਿਣਤੀ; ~fold ਵੀਹ ਗੁਣਾ

twice (ਟਵਾਇਸ) *adv* ਦੋ ਵਾਰੀ, ਦੋ ਗੁਣਾ

twilight ('ਟਵਾਇਲਾਇਟ) *n v* ਸੰਝ, ਸ਼ਾਮ, ਸਵੇਰ ਜਾਂ ਤ੍ਰਿਕਾਲਾਂ ਦਾ ਘੁਸਮੁਸਾ, ਝਟਪਟਾ; ਮੱਧਮ ਰੌਸ਼ਨੀ ਕਰਨਾ, ਧੁੰਦਲੇ ਪ੍ਰਕਾਸ਼ ਨਾਲ ਪ੍ਰਕਾਸ਼ਤ ਕਰਨਾ

twin (ਟਵਿਨ) *n a* ਜੋੜੇ, ਜੋੜੇ ਜੰਮੇ ਹੋਏ ਬੱਚੇ ਜਾਂ ਵਿਅਕਤੀ; ਜੌੜਾ ਜੰਮਿਆ

twine (ਟਵਾਇਨ) *n v* ਰੱਸੀ, ਡੋਰੀ, ਧਾਗਾ, ਵਾਟਵੀਂ ਰੱਸੀ; ਵਲ, ਪੇਚ, ਮਰੋੜੀ; ਧਾਗਾ ਜਾਂ ਰੱਸੀ ਵੱਟਮੀ, ਵੱਟ ਚੜ੍ਹਾਉਣਾ, ਵਲ੍ਹੇਟਣਾ

twink (ਟਵਿੰਕ) *n v* ਘੜੀ, ਪਲ, ਪਲਕ ਮਾਤਰ, ਅੱਖ ਦਾ ਫੋਰ; ਝਮਕਣਾ, ਪਲਕ ਮਾਰਨਾ; ਟਿਮ-ਟਿਮਾਉਣਾ, ਜਗਮਗਾਉਣਾ; ~le ਚਮਕਣਾ, ਲਿਸ਼ਕਣਾ, ਟਿਮਟਿਮਾਉਣਾ, ਮਟਕਾਉਣਾ; ਚਮਕ, ਲਿਸ਼ਕ, ਲਿਸ਼ਕਾਰਾ

twirl (ਟਵਅਃਲ) *v n* ਘੁਮਾਉਣਾ, ਭੁਆਉਣਾ, ਭੁਆਟਣੀ ਦੇਣੀ, ਕਾਹਲੀ-ਕਾਹਲੀ ਚੱਕਰ ਦੇਣਾ; ਮੁੱਛਾਂ ਨੂੰ ਤਾਅ ਦੇਣਾ; ਭੁਆਂਟਣੀ, ਚੱਕਰ, ਘੁਮਾਉ

twist (ਟਵਿਸਟ) *v n* ਮਰੋੜਨਾ, ਮਰੋੜੀ ਦੇਣਾ, ਮੇਲਣਾ, ਵੱਟ ਚਾੜ੍ਹਨ, ਵੱਟਣਾ; ਟਵਿਸਟ ਨਾਚ ਨੱਚਣਾ; ਗੁੰਦਣਾ; ਮਰੋੜ; ਵੱਟਿਆ ਧਾਗਾ

twitter ('ਟਵਿਟਅ*) *n* ਚਹਿਕਣਾ; ਫੜਕਣਾ; ਹੌਲੀ

ਅਵਾਜ਼ ਵਿਚ ਬੋਲਣਾ; ਚਹਿਚਹਾਟ, ਫੜਫੜਾਹਟ

type (ਟਾਇਪ) *n v* ਪ੍ਰਕਾਰ, ਕਿਸਮ, ਵੰਨਗੀ, ਮਿਸਾਲ, ਨਮੂਨਾ; ਕਿਸੇ ਵੰਨਗੀ ਦਾ ਨਮੂਠਾ ਹੋਣਾ, ਟਾਈਪ ਕਰਨਾ

typhoid ('ਟਾਇਫ਼ੌਇਡ) *a* ਮੂਹਰਕਾ ਤਾਪ, ਮਿਆਦੀ ਬੁਖ਼ਾਰ, ਟਾਈਫ਼ਾਈਡ

typhoon (ਟਾਇ'ਫ਼ੂਨ) *n* ਜ਼ੋਰਦਾਰ ਹਨੇਰੀ, ਸਖ਼ਤ ਝੱਖੜ; ਸਮੁੰਦਰੀ ਝੱਖੜ; ਪ੍ਰਚੰਡ ਤੂਫ਼ਾਨ

typify (ਟਿਪਿਫ਼ਾਇ) *v* ਉਦਾਹਰਣ ਦੇ ਕੇ ਸਪਸ਼ਟ ਕਰਨਾ, ਨਮੂਨਾ ਪੇਸ਼ ਕਰਨਾ; ਨਮੂਨੇ ਵਜੋਂ ਹੋਣਾ

typist ('ਟਾਇਪਿਸਟ) *n* ਟਾਈਪ ਕਰਨ ਵਾਲਾ, ਟਾਈਪਿਸਟ

tyrannical (ਟਿ'ਰੈਨਿਕਲ) *a* ਅਤਿਆਚਾਰੀ, ਜਾਬਰ, ਸਿਤਮਗਰ, ਨਿਰਦਈ, ਕਹਿਰਵਾਨ, ਡਾਢਾ, ਤਾਨਾਸ਼ਾਹ

tyrannize ('ਟਿਰਅਨਾਇਜ਼) *v* ਜਬਰ ਕਰਨਾ, ਜ਼ੁਲਮ ਕਰਨਾ, ਧੱਕਾ ਕਰਨਾ

tyranny ('ਟਿਰਅਨਿ) *n* ਜ਼ੁਲਮ, ਅਤਿਆਚਾਰ, ਜਾਬਰ, ਧੱਕੇਸ਼ਾਹੀ

tyrant ('ਟਾਇ(ਅ)ਰਅੰਟ) *n* ਜ਼ਾਲਮ, ਜਾਬਰ, ਅਤਿਆਚਾਰੀ; ਜ਼ਾਲਮ ਰਾਜਾ

tyre, tyro (ਟਾਇ'ਅ, 'ਟਾਇ(ਅ)ਰਅਉ) *n* (1) ਸਿਖਾਂਦਰੂ, ਨਵਾਂ ਸਿਖਿਆ, (2) ਟਾਇਰ (ਮੋਟਰ, ਸਾਈਕਲ ਆਦਿ ਦਾ)

U

U, u (ਯੂ) *n* ਰੋਮਨ ਵਰਣਮਾਲਾ ਦਾ ਇਕੀਵਾਂ ਅੱਖਰ

ubiquitous (ਯੂ'ਬਿਕਵਿਟਾਅਸ) *a* ਸਰਵਵਿਆਪਕ, ਸਰਵਵਿਆਪੀ

ugh (ਅੱਖ਼) *int* ਉਹ! ਉਫ! ਤੋਬਾ

ugliness (ਅੱਗਲਿਨਿਸ) *n* ਕਰੂਪਤਾ, ਕੋਜਮ, ਕੁੱਢਬ

ugly ('ਅੱਗਲਿ) *a* ਕਰੂਪ, ਬਦਸ਼ਕਲ, ਬਦਸੂਰਤ, ਕੋਹਜਾ, ਅੱਸਭਿਅ, ਅਸ਼ਿਸ਼ਟ, ਭੱਦਾ, ਬੁਰਾ

ulcer ('ਅਲੱਸਅੱ) *n* ਫੋੜਾ, ਨਾਸੂਰ, ਅਲਸਰ; ਵਿਭਚਾਰ, ਦੁਰਾਚਾਰ; ਗੰਦਗੀ

ulterior (ਅੱਲ'ਟਿਅਰਿਅੱ) *a* ਦੂਰੇੜਾ, ਪਰਲਾ, ਪਰੇ ਸਥਿਤ, ਦੂਰਵਰਤੀ; (ਮਨੋਰਥ ਆਦਿ) ਗੁਪਤ, ਅਪੂਤੱਖ, ਗੁੱਝਾ

ultimate ('ਅੱਲਟਿਮਅਟ) *a* ਮੁੰਢਲਾ, ਮੂਲ; ਕੱਟਈ; ਅੰਤਲਾ, ਆਖ਼ਰੀ; ~**ly** ਆਖ਼ਰ ਨੂੰ, ਸਿੱਟੇ ਵਜੋਂ

ultimatum ('ਅੱਲਟਿ'ਮੇਇਟਅਮ) *n* ਮੌਲਕ ਸਿਧਾਂਤ; ਅਤੰਮ ਚੇਤਾਵਨੀ, ਅੰਤਮ ਗੱਲ

ultra ('ਅੱਲਟਰਾ) *n* ਅੱਤ-ਪੱਖੀ, ਅੱਤਵਾਦੀ, ਉਗਰਪੰਥੀ ਪ੍ਰਗਤੀਵਾਦੀ

ultra-sonics ('ਅੱਲਟਰਾ'ਸੌਨਿਕਸ) *n* ਪਰਾ-ਧੁਨਿਕ ਵਿਗਿਆਨ

ultra-rays ('ਅੱਲਟਰਾ'ਰੇਇਜ਼) *n* ਪਰਾਕਿਰਨਾਂ

umbrage ('ਅੱਮਬਰਿਜ) *n* (ਕਾਵਿ) ਦਰਖ਼ਤ ਦੀ ਛਾਂ, ਛਾਇਆ; ਨਾਰਾਜ਼ਗੀ, ਗੁੱਸਾ; ~**ous** ਛਾਇਆਮਈ, ਛਾਂ-ਦਾਰ, ਨਾਰਾਜ਼, ਖੜਾ

umbrella (ਅੱਮਬਰੈੱਲਅ) *n* ਛਤਰੀ, ਛਾਤ; ਛਤਰ

umlaut ('ਉਮਲਾਉਟ) *n v* (ਵਿਆ) ਸਵਰ-ਪਰਿਵਰਤਨ

umpire ('ਅੱਮਪਾਇਅੱ) *n* ਨਿਰਣਾਯਕ; ਪੰਚ, ਅਮਪਾਇਰ, ਰੈਫਰੀ, (ਕਾ) ਸਰਪੰਚ, ਸਾਲਸ; ਅਮਪਾਇਰੀ ਜਾਂ ਸਾਲਸੀ ਕਰਨੀ

umpteen ('ਅੱਮ(ਪ)ਟੀਨ) *a* (ਅਪ) ਅਨੇਕ, ਬੇਹਿਸਾਬ

un (ਅੱਨ) *pref* 'ਨਾ' ਦੇ ਅਰਥਾਂ ਵਿਚ ਅਗੇਤਰ

unabashed (ਅੱਨਬੈਸ਼ੱਡ) *a* ਨਿਰਲੱਜ, ਬੇਸ਼ਰਮ

unabated (ਅਨਬੈਟਇੱਡ) *a* ਲਗਾਤਾਰ, ਬੇਰੋਕ

unable (ਅਨੇਬਲ) *a* ਅਸਮਰੱਥ, ਅਯੋਗ, ਨਾਕਾਬਲ

unacceptable (ਅਨ'ਅਕਸੇਪੱਟਬਲ) *a* ਅਸਵੀਕ੍ਰਿਤ, ਨਾਪਸੰਦ

unaccustomed (ਅੱਨ'ਅਕਸਟਮੱਡ) *a* ਅਨਜਾਣ, ਅਪਰਿਚਿਤ; ਅਸਧਾਰਨ

unaffected (ਅੱਨ'ਅਫੇਕਟਿੱਡ) *a* ਅਪ੍ਰਭਾਵਤ, ਅਣਭਿੱਜ; ਨਿਸ਼ਕਪਟ, ਸਹਿਜ, ਸੁਭਾਵਕ

unanimity, unanimousness ('ਯੂਨਅੱ'ਨਿਮਅਟਿ, ਯੂ'ਨੈਨਿਮਸਨਿਸ) *a* ਇਕ ਰਾਇ, ਇਕ ਮੱਤ, ਸਰਵ-ਸੰਮਤੀ

unanimous (ਯੂ'ਨੈਨਿਮਅੱਸ) *a* ਇਕ ਰਾਇ, ਮੁਤਫ਼ਿਕ, ਇਕ ਵਿਚਾਰ

unanswerable (ਅੱਨ-ਆਨਸਰੇਬੱਲ) *a* ਲਾਜਵਾਬ; ਨਿਰੁੱਤਰ, ਅਖੰਡਨੀ

unarmed (ਅੱਨ-ਆਅੱਮਡ) *a* ਨਿਹੱਥਾ, ਖ਼ਾਲੀ ਹੱਥ, ਨਿਸ਼ਸਤਰ

unashamed (ਅੱਨ(ਅ)ਸ਼ੇਮਡ) *a* ਨਿਰਲੱਜ, ਬੇਹਯਾ

unassuming (ਅਨ(ਅ)ਸਯੂਮਇਡ) *a* ਸਰਲ, ਸਾਦਾ

unauthorised (ਅਨ-ਆਥਰਾਇਜ਼ਡ) *a* ਨਾਜਾਇਜ਼, ਅਟ-ਅਧਿਕ੍ਰਿਤ

unavoidable (ਅਨ(ਅ)ਵ੍ਹਾਡੇਬਲ) *a* ਅਵੱਸ਼ਕ, ਅਨਿਵਾਰੀ, ਲਾਜ਼ਮੀ

unaware (ਅਨ(ਅ)ਵੇ*) *a* ਅਚੇਤ, ਅਚਿੰਤ, ਬੇਖ਼ਬਰ, ਅਨਜਾਣ, ਗਾਫ਼ਿਲ

unbalanced (ਅਨਬੈਲੰਸਡ) *a* ਥਿੜਕਿਆ, ਉਖੜਿਆ-ਪੁਖੜਿਆ; ਅਸੰਤੁਲਤ

unbearable (ਅਨਬੇਅਰੇਬਲ) *a* ਦੁੱਭਰ, ਅਸਹਿ

unbecoming (ਅਨ-ਬਿਕਮ-ਇੰਙ) *a* ਅਨੁਚਿਤ, ਬੁਰਾ, ਅਜੋਗ, ਅੱਢੁਕਵਾਂ

unbelieving (ਅਨ-ਬਿਲੀਇਵਙ) *a* ਅਧਰਮੀ, ਨਾਸਤਕ, ਅਵਿਸ਼ਵਾਸੀ

unbias(s)ed (ਅਨਬਾਇਅਸਡ) *a* ਨਿਰਪੱਖ, ਪੱਖਪਾਤਹੀਨ

unblemished (ਅਨ-ਬਲੇਮਇਸ਼ਡ) *a* ਨਿਹਕਲੰਕ, ਬੇਦਾਗ਼, ਨਿਰਦੋਸ਼

unbounded (ਅਨ-ਬਾਉਂਡਿਡ) *a* ਅਨੰਤ, ਅਪਾਰ, ਬੇਹੱਦ, ਅਸੀਮਿਤ, ਬੇਅੰਤ

uncertain (ਅਨਸਃਟੰਨ) *a* ਡਾਵਾਂ-ਡੋਲ, ਦੁੱਚਿਤਾ, ਗ਼ੈਰ-ਯਕੀਨੀ; ~ty ਅਨਿਸ਼ਚਤਤਾ, ਸੰਦੇਹ

uncle ('ਅੰਡਕਲ) *n* ਚਾਚਾ, ਤਾਇਆ, ਮਾਮਾ, ਮਾਸੜ, ਫੁੱਫੜ

Uncle Sam ('ਅੰਡਕਲ'ਸੈਮ) *n* ਅਮਰੀਕੀ ਸਰਕਾਰ

uncomfortable (ਅਨਕਮਫ਼ਟੇਬਲ) *a* ਬੇਆਰਾਮ, ਕਸ਼ਟਦਾਇਕ, ਅਸੁਵਿਧਾਜਨਕ

uncommon (ਅਨਕਾਮਨ) *a* ਅਸਧਾਰਨ, ਵਿਸ਼ੇਸ਼, ਨਿਰਾਲਾ, ਅਨੋਖਾ

uncompromising (ਅਨਕਾਂਪ੍ਰਮਾਜ਼ਿਙ) *a* ਹਠਧਰਮੀ, ਅੱਟਲ, ਕਰੜਾ

unconcern (ਅਨਕੰਸ*ਨ) *n* ਉਦਾਸੀਨਤਾ, ਨਿਸ਼ਚਿੰਤਤਾ, ਬੇਪਰਵਾਹੀ

unconcerned (ਅਨਕੰਸਨ*ਡ) *a* ਉਦਾਸੀਨ, ਅਸੰਬੰਧਤ, ਬੇਪਰਵਾਹ, ਬੇਫ਼ਿਕਰ

unconditional (ਅਨਕੰਡਿਸ਼ਨਲ) *a* ਉੱਕਾ, ਸੁਤੰਤਰ, ਨਿਰਪੇਖ, ਬਿਨਾ, ਸ਼ਰਤ

unconfirmed (ਅਨਕਫ਼*ਮਡ) *a* ਅਪੁਸ਼ਟ, ਅਪ੍ਰਮਾਣਤ

unconscious (ਅਨਕਾੱਨਸ਼ਸ) *a* ਅਚੇਤ, ਬੇਸੁਧ, ਬੇਖ਼ਬਰ, ਬੇਹੋਸ਼

unconstitutional (ਅੱਨ-ਕਾਂਸਟਿ-ਟਯੂ-ਸ਼ਨਲ) *a* ਸੰਵਿਧਾਨ ਵਿਰੁੱਧ, ਅਵਿਧਾਨਕ

unconstrained (ਅਨਕਨਸਟਰੇਂਡ) *a* ਆਜ਼ਾਦ, ਬਿਨਾ ਰੋਕ, ਪਾਬੰਦੀਰਹਿਤ

unconventional (ਅਨਕਨਵੇਂਸ਼ਨਲ) *a* ਰੁੜ੍ਹੀਮੁਕਤ, ਗ਼ੈਰ-ਰਵਾਇਤੀ

uncover (ਅਨਕਵ*) *v* ਪਰਗਟ ਕਰਨਾ, ਪਰਦਾ ਹਟਾਉਣਾ, ਨੰਗਾ ਕਰਨਾ, ਢੱਕਣ ਉਤਾਰਨਾ

undefined (ਅਨ-ਡਿਫ਼ਾਇੰਡ) *a* ਅਨਿਸ਼ਚਤ; ਅਸਪਸ਼ਟ; ਅਪਰਿਭਾਸ਼ਤ, ਪਰਿਭਾਸ਼ਾਰਹਿਤ

under ('ਅੰਡਅ*) *a prep* ਹੇਠਲਾ; ਘੱਟ, ਥੋੜ੍ਹਾ; ਦੇ ਅਧੀਨ, (ਨਿਯਮ ਆਦਿ ਦੇ) ਅਨੁਸਾਰ, ਵਿਚ-ਵਿਚ, ਅੰਦਰ, ਮਾਤਹਿਤ

underconsideration (ਅੰਡਅ*ਕੰਸੀਡ'ਰੇਸ਼ਨ) *n* ਵਿਚਾਰ ਅਧੀਨ

undercurrent (ਅੰਡਅ*ਕਰੰਟ) *a* ਅੰਤਰ-ਧਾਰਾ, ਅੰਤਰ-ਪਰਵਾਹ; ਅਦ੍ਰਿਸ਼ਟ ਪ੍ਰਭਾਵ; ਗੁਪਤ

underdeveloped (ਅੰਡਅ*ਡਿਵੇ਼ਲਪਡ) *a* ਪਿੱਛੇ ਰਿਹਾ, ਪਛੜਿਆ, ਘੱਟ ਵਿਕਸਤ, ਅਰਧ-

ਵਿਕਸਤ, ਘੱਟ ਉੱਨਤ

underemployment (ਅੰਡਅ*ਇਮ'ਪਲੌਇ-ਮਅੰਟ) *n* ਅਪੂਰਨ ਰੁਜ਼ਗਾਰ, ਯੋਗਤਾ ਨਾਲੋਂ ਛੋਟੇ ਕੰਮ ਤੇ ਲਗਾ

underestimate (ਅੰਡਅ*ਏਸਟਿਮੇਟ) *v* ਗਲਤ ਅੰਦਾਜ਼ਾ ਕਰਨਾ; ਅਸਲ ਨਾਲੋਂ ਘੱਟ ਸਮਝਣਾ, ਅਲਪ ਅਨੁਮਾਨ ਕਰਨਾ

undergo (ਅੰਡਅ*ਗੋ) *v* ਬਰਦਾਸ਼ਤ ਕਰਨਾ, ਸਹਿਣਾ, ਝੱਲਣਾ, ਭੋਗਣਾ

undergraduate (ਅਡੰਅ*ਗਰੇਡਯੂਇਟ) ਡਿਗਰੀ ਅਪ੍ਰਾਪਤ ਵਿਦਿਆਰਥੀ; ਪੂਰਵਸਨਾਤਕ

underground (ਅੰਡ:ਗਰਾਉਂਡ) *a* ਪਦਤੀ ਦੇ ਤਲ ਦੇ ਹੇਠਾਂ, ਜ਼ਮੀਨਦੋਜ਼, (ਨਹਿਰ, ਰੇਲ); (ਬੋਲ) ਗੁਪਤ, ਛੁਪਿਆ

underline (ਅੰਡ:ਲਾਇਨ) *a* ਪੁਸਤਕ ਜਾਂ ਚਿੱਠੀ ਦੇ ਜ਼ਰੂਰੀ ਵਾਕਾਂ ਨੂੰ ਲਕੀਰਨਾ; ਰੇਖਾ ਅਕੰਤ ਕਰਨਾ, ਮੱਹਤਵ ਦੇਣਾ

underlying (ਅੰਡ:ਲਾਇੰਗ) *a* ਬੁਨਿਆਦੀ; ਅੰਤਰੀਵ, ਅੰਦਰਲਾ

undermentioned (ਅੰਡ:ਮੇਨਸ਼ੰਡ) *a* ਨਿਮਨ ਲਿਖਤ

undermine (ਅੰਡ:ਮਾਇਨ) *v* ਨਸ਼ਟ ਕਰਨਾ, ਕਮਜ਼ੋਰ ਬਣਾਉਣਾ, ਨੀਂਹ ਖੋਖਲੀ ਕਰ ਦੇਣੀ, ਅੰਦਰੋਂ-ਅੰਦਰ ਸੁਰੰਗ ਪੁੱਟਣੀ (ਦਰਿਆ ਆਦਿ ਦੀ)

underneath (ਅੰਡ:ਨੀਥ) *n a* ਹੇਠਲਾ ਤਲ, ਨੀਵੀਂ ਸਤ੍ਹਾ; ਨੀਵੇਂ ਥਾਂ ਉੱਤੇ; ਥੱਲੇ; ਹੇਠਲਾ

underproduction (ਅੰਡ:ਪਰਡਕਸ਼ਨ) *n* ਨਾਕਾਫ਼ੀ ਉਪਜ, ਘੱਟ ਪੈਦਾਵਾਰ, ਅਲਪ ਉਤਪਾਦਨ

underquote (ਅੰਡ:ਕਵੋਟ) *v* (ਦੂਜੇ ਦੇ ਮੁਕਾਬਲੇ ਦੇ) ਘੱਟ ਕੀਮਤ ਲਗਾਉਣੀ (ਮਾਲ ਆਦਿ ਦੀ)

underrate (ਅੰਡ:ਰੇਟ) *v* ਘੱਟ ਮੁੱਲ ਲਗਾਉਣਾ

under ripe (ਅੰਡ:ਰਾਇਪ) *a* ਕੱਚਾ, ਅੱਧ-ਪੱਕਾ

under secretary (ਅੰਡ:ਸੇਕਰਿਟਰਿ) *a* ਉਪ-ਸੱਕਤਰ

undersigned (ਅੰਡ:ਸਾਇੰਡ) *n* ਨਿਮਨ-ਹਸਤਾਖ਼ਰੀ, ਹੇਠਾਂ ਦਸਤਖ਼ਤ ਕਰਨ ਵਾਲਾ

undersized (ਅੰਡ:ਸਾਇਜ਼ਡ) *a* ਛੋਟਾ, ਠਿਗਣਾ, ਗਿਠ-ਮੁੱਠਾ, ਬੌਣਾ

understamped (ਅੰਡ:ਸਟੈਂਪਡ) *a* ਥੋੜ੍ਹੀਆਂ ਟਿਕਟਾਂ ਵਾਲਾ, ਅਲਪਮੁਦਰਾ ਅਕੰਤ (ਲਿਫ਼ਾਫ਼ਾ ਜਾਂ ਕਾਰਡ)

understate (ਅੰਡ:ਸਟੇਟ) *v* ਘੱਟ ਦੱਸਣਾ; **~ment** ਘੱਟ ਬਿਆਨ

understock (ਅੰਡ:ਸਟਾਕ) *v* (ਦੁਕਾਨ ਜਾਂ ਕਾਰਖ਼ਾਨੇ ਵਿਚ) ਘੱਟ ਸਾਮਾਨ ਰੱਖਣਾ

undertake (ਅੰਡ:ਟੇਕ) *v* (ਕਿਸੇ ਕੰਮ ਨੂੰ ਕਰਨ ਦਾ) ਵਚਨ ਦੇਣਾ, ਹਾਮੀ ਭਰਨੀ; ਕਿਸੇ ਨੂੰ ਵਿਚ ਲੈਣਾ, ਕਬੂਲ ਕਰਨਾ, ਬੀੜਾ ਚੁੱਕਣਾ, ਆਪਣੇ ਜ਼ੁੰਮੇ ਲੈਣਾ; **~taking** ਕਾਰੋਬਾਰ; ਅੰਗੀਕਾਰ (ਕੰਮ ਦੇ ਭਾਰ ਨੂੰ), ਵਚਨ, ਪ੍ਰਤਿੱਗਿਆ; ਜ਼ੁੰਮੇਵਾਰੀ; ਅੰਤਮ-ਸੰਸਕਾਰ-ਪ੍ਰਬੰਧ

undertone (ਅੰਡ:ਟੋਨ) *n* ਧੀਮਾ ਸੁਰ; ਪਤਲਾ ਜਾਂ ਹਲਕਾ ਰੰਗ

undertrial (ਅੰਡ:ਟਰਾਇਲ) *a* ਪਰੀਖਿਆ-ਅਧੀਨ

underwear (ਅੰਡ:ਵੇਅ*) *n* ਕੱਛੀ, ਲੰਗੋਟੀ

underweight (ਅੰਡ:ਵੇਟ) *n* (ਔਸਤ ਤੋਂ) ਘੱਟ ਭਾਰ, ਘਟ ਵਜ਼ਨ

underwork (ਅੰਡ:ਵ'ਕ) *n* ਇਮਦਾਦੀ ਕੰਮ, ਸਹਾਇਤਾ ਕਾਰਜ; ਹੌਲਾ ਕੰਮ, ਹੌਲਾ ਕੰਮ ਕਰਨਾ

underworld (ਅੰਡ:ਵ'ਲਡ) *n* ਨਰਕ, ਰਸਾਤਲ; ਪਾਤਾਲ-ਲੋਕ, ਤਹਿ, ਗੁਪਤਸਤਾਨ ਅਪਰਾਧੀ-ਜਗਤ

understand ('ਅੰਡਅ'ਸਟੈਂਡ) *v* ਅਰਥ ਕੱਢਣਾ;
ਬੁੱਝਣਾ, ਗੱਲ ਸਮਝਣਾ; ਅਨੁਮਾਨ ਕਰ ਲੈਣਾ;
ਜਾਣਨਾ; ~ing ਸਮਝ, ਗਿਆਨ, ਬੋਧਸ਼ਕਤੀ;
ਰਜ਼ਾਮੰਦੀ, ਸਹਿਮਤੀ, ਇਕਮੱਤਤਾ

undeserving (ਅਨ-ਡਿਜ਼ਰਵਿਙ) *a* ਅਣਧਿਕਾਰੀ,
ਅਪਾਤਰ

undesirable (ਅਨ-ਡਿਜ਼ਾਇਅਰੇਬਲ) *a*
ਅਣਚਾਹਿਆ (ਵਿਅਕਤੀ); ਅਣਇਛੱਤ

undivided (ਅਨ-ਡਿਵਾਇਡਿਡ) *a* ਅੰਵਡ,
ਅਣਵੰਡਿਆ, ਅਭਿੰਨ, ਇਕਾਗਰ, ਸਮੁੱਚਾ,
ਸਾਰਾ, ਸਬੂਤਾ, ਸਾਲਮ

undo (ਅੰਡੂ) *v* ਬਰਬਾਦ ਕਰਨਾ, ਨਸ਼ਟ ਕਰਨਾ,
ਤਬਾਹ ਕਰਨਾ, ਵਿਗਾੜਨਾ; ਮਿਟਾਉਣਾ

undone (ਅਨਡਨ) *a* ਬਰਬਾਦ, ਤਬਾਹ, ਨਸ਼ਟ

undoubtedly (ਅਨਡਾਉਟਿਡਲੀ) *a* ਨਿਰਸੰਦੇਹ,
ਬੇਸ਼ਕ, ਯਕੀਨੀ

undressed (ਅਨਡਰੈਸਡ) *a* ਨੰਗਾ, ਨੰਗਾ-ਧੜੰਗਾ,
ਵਸਤਰਹੀਨ

undue (ਅਨ'ਡਯੂ) *a* ਨਾਜਾਇਜ਼, ਨਾ-ਮੁਨਾਸਬ;
ਅਸੰਤੁਲਤ

unduly (ਅਨਡਯੂਲਿ) *adv* ਅਸਧਾਰਨ, ਰੂਪ ਵਿਚ;
ਅਵ-ਅਵਸ਼ਕ ਰੂਪ ਵਿਚ

unearned (ਅਨਅੱ*ਡ) *a* ਅਣਕਮਾਇਆ;
ਨਾਜਾਇਜ਼; ਹਰਾਮ ਦਾ, ਮੁਫ਼ਤ ਦਾ

unearth (ਅਨਅੱ*ਥ) *v* ਪਤਾ ਕੱਢਣਾ, ਸੂਹ ਕੱਢਣੀ;
ਜ਼ਮੀਨ ਤੋਂ ਬਾਹਰ ਕੱਢਣਾ

uneasy (ਅਨ-ਇਜ਼ਾਇ) *a* ਬੇਚੈਨ, ਬੇਆਰਾਮ,
ਵਿਆਕੁਲ, ਪਰੇਸ਼ਾਨ

uneconomic (ਅਨਇਕਨਾਮਇਕ) *a* ਲਾਭਰਹਿਤ,
ਬੇਫਾਇਦਾ

unempolyed (ਅਨਇਮਪਲਾਇਡ) *a* ਬੇਕਾਰ,
ਬੇਰੁਜ਼ਗਾਰ

unempolyment (ਅਨਇੰਪਲਾਇਮੰਟ) *n*
ਬੇਕਾਰੀ, ਬੇਰੁਜ਼ਗਾਰੀ

unending (ਅਨਐਂਡਿਙ) *a* ਅਨੰਤ; ਅਮੁੱਕ,
ਨਿਰੰਤਰ, ਅਖੰਡ, ਬੇਅੰਤ

unequal (ਅਨ'ਇਕਵਲ) *a* ਬੇਮੇਲ, ਅਸਮਾਨ,
ਨਾਬਰਾਬਰ

unequivocal (ਅਨ'ਇਕਵਿਵੋੱਕਲ) *a* ਸਪਸ਼ਟ,
ਸਾਫ਼, ਸੰਦੇਹ ਰਹਿਤ, ਖ਼ਰਾ ਖ਼ਰਾ

unerring (ਅਨ'ਅਰਿੰਗ) *a* ਅਭੁੱਲ, ਅਚੁੱਕ

uneven (ਅਨ'ਈਵਨ) *a* ਉੱਚਾ-ਨੀਵਾਂ; ਅਪਧੱਰਾ,
ਉੱਘੜ-ਦੁੱਘੜ, ਅਸਮਾਨ

unexampled (ਅਨਿਗਜ਼ਾਂ'ਪਲਡ) *a* ਅਦੁੱਤੀ,
ਅਨੂਪ; ਲਾਸਾਨੀ, ਬੇਨਜ਼ੀਰ

unexceptionable (ਅਨਿਕਸੇਪਸ਼ਨੇਬਲ) *a*
ਤੱਸਲੀਬਖ਼ਸ਼

unexceptional (ਅਨਿਕਸੇਪਸ਼ਨਲ) *a* ਮਾਮੂਲੀ,
ਸਾਧਾਰਨ

unexpected (ਅਨਿਕਸੇਪਕਟਿਡ) *a* ਅਚਾਨਕ,
ਅਕਾਸਮਕ

unexperienced (ਅਨਿਕਸੇਪਿਅਰਇੰਸਡ) *a*
ਅਨੁਭਵਹੀਨ, ਨਾਤਜਰਬੇਕਾਰ

unfair (ਅਨੱਫੇਅ*) *a* ਬੇਜਾ, ਖੋਟਾ, ਨਾਵਾਜਬ,
ਅਨੁਚਿਤ

unfaithful (ਅਨਫ਼ੇਥਫ਼ੁਲ) *a* ਬੇਵਫ਼ਾ, ਨਮਕ
ਹਰਾਮ, ਕਿਰਤਘਨ, ਝੂਠਾ

unfasten (ਅਨਫ਼ਾੱਸਨ) *v* ਖੋਲ੍ਹਣਾ, ਢਿੱਲਾ ਕਰਨਾ

unfavourable (ਅਨਫ਼ੇਵਰਬਲ) *a* ਵਿਰੋਧੀ,
ਪ੍ਰਤੀਕੂਲ, ਵਿਖਮ

unfit (ਅਨਫ਼ਿਟ) *a v* ਅਯੋਗ, ਅਢੁੱਕਵਾਂ, ਅਨੁਚਿਤ,
ਨਿਕੰਮਾ, ਨਕਾਰਾ; ਨਕਾਰਾ ਬਣਾ ਦੇਣਾ; ~ting

ਅਢੁੱਕਵਾਂ, ਕਸੁਤਾ

unfortunate (ਅਨਫ਼ਾ:ਚਨਿਟ) *a* ਅਭਾਗਾ ਵਿਅਕਤੀ; ਭਾਰਹੀਨ, ਅਭਾਗਾ, ਬਦਨਸੀਬ, ਬਦਕਿਸਮਤ; ਮੰਦਭਾਗਾ, ਨਾਮੁਰਾਦ

unfounded (ਅਨਫ਼ਾਉਂਡਿਡ) *a* ਨਿਰਮੂਲ, ਮਿਥਿਆ, ਬੇਬੁਨਿਆਦ, ਸਰਾਸਰ ਗ਼ਲਤ

unfurl (ਅਨਫ਼ੰਲ) *v* ਖੋਲ੍ਹਣਾ, ਸੁੱਟਣਾ ਜਾਂ ਖੁੱਲ੍ਹਣਾ; ਪਸਾਰਨਾ, ਲਹਿਰਾਉਣਾ, ਫੈਲਾਉਣਾ, ਫੈਲਣਾ

unfurnished (ਅਨਫ਼ੰਰਨਿਸ਼ਡ) *a* ਖ਼ਾਲੀ, ਅੱਸਜਿਤ, ਬਿਨਾ ਸਜਾਵਟ ਤੋਂ

ungracious (ਅਨਗਰੇਸ਼ਅਸ) *a* ਨੀਚ, ਦੁਸ਼ਟ, ਕਠੋਰ

ungrammatical (ਅਨਗਰਮੈਟਿਕਲ) *a* ਵਿਆਕਰਨ-ਵਿਰੁੱਧ, ਵਿਆਕਰਨ-ਵਿਪਰੀਤ

ungrounded (ਅਨਗਰਾਉਂਡਿਡ) *a* ਨਿਰਮੂਲ, ਬੇ-ਬੁਨਿਆਦੀ, ਫ਼ਜ਼ੂਲ, ਨਿਰਆਧਾਰ

unguarded (ਅਨਗਾ*ਡਿਡ) *a* ਵਿਚਾਰ-ਰਹਿਤ, ਅਚੇਤ, ਬੇਧਿਆਨ (ਪ੍ਰਗਟਾਉ), ਅਰੱਖਿਅਤ

unhappy (ਅਨਹੈਪਿ) *a* ਨਾਮੁਰਾਦਾ; ਦੁਖੀ; ਅਪ੍ਰਸੰਨ, ਨਾਖ਼ੁਸ਼, ਉਦਾਸ

unhealthy (ਅਨਹੈਲਥਿ) *a* ਅਸੁਅਸਥ, ਰੋਗੀ, ਬੀਮਾਰ; ਹਾਨੀਕਾਰਕ

unheard (ਅਨਹ:ਡ) *a* ਅਣਸੁਣਿਆ, ਅਣਜਾਣਿਆ, ਅਗਿਆਤ

unholy (ਅਨਹੋਲੀ) *a* ਅਪਵਿੱਤਰ, ਨਾਪਾਕ, ਅਸ਼ੁੱਧ, ਭ੍ਰਿਸ਼ਟ, ਮਲੀਨ

unhuman (ਅਨਹਯੂਮਨ) *a* ਅਮਨੁੱਖੀ, ਨਿਰਦਈ, ਅਮਾਨਵੀ

unicameral (ਯੂਨਿ'ਕੈਮਅਰਲ) *a* ਇਕ-ਘਰਾ, ਇਕ-ਕਕਸ਼ੀ, ਇਕ ਸਦਨੀ (ਪਾਰਲੀਮੈਂਟ)

unification (ਯੂਨਿਫ਼ਿ'ਕੇਇਸ਼ਨ) *n* ਮੇਲ, ਇਤਿਹਾਦ, ਮਿਲਾਉਣੀ, ਏਕੀਕਰਨ

uniform (ਯੂਨਿਫ਼ੋਮ) *a* ਇਕਸਾਰ, ਬਰਾਬਰ, ਇਕ ਸਮਾਨ; ਨਿਰੰਤਰ; ਵੇਸ, ਭੇਸ, ਵਰਦੀ; ~**ity** ਸਮਤਾ, ਸਮਰੂਪਤਾ, ਇਕਸਾਰਤਾ, ਇਕਰੂਪਤਾ, ਮੇਲ

unify (ਯੂਨਿਫ਼ਾਇ) *v* ਇਕਰੂਪ ਕਰਨਾ, ਇਕ ਰੰਗ ਕਰਨਾ, ਇਕ ਕਰ ਦੇਣਾ

unilateral (ਯੂਨਿ'ਲੈਟ(ਅ)ਰ(ਅ)ਲ) *a* ਇਕ ਪੱਖੀ, ਇਕ ਤਰਫ਼ਾ

unimpeachable (ਅਨਇੰਪੀਚਬਲ) *a* ਨਿਰਦੋਸ਼, ਬੇਕਸੂਰ, ਨਿਰਅਪਰਾਧ, ਸੱਚਾ

unimportant (ਅਨਿਪਾ*ਟੰਟ) *a* ਗ਼ੈਰ-ਜ਼ਰੂਰੀ, ਅਲਵੱਸ਼ਕ, ਮਹੱਤਵਹੀਨ

uninformed (ਅਨਇਨਫ਼ਾ*ਮਡ) *a* ਅਸੂਚਤ, ਅਣਜਾਣ, ਨਾਦਾਨ, ਬੇ-ਖ਼ਬਰ

uninhabited (ਅਨਇਨਹੈਬਿਟਿਡ) *a* ਨਿਰਜਨ, ਗ਼ੈਰ-ਆਬਾਦ, ਵੀਰਾਨ, ਉਜੜਿਆ-ਪੁੱਜੜਿਆ

unintelligibillity (ਅਨਇੰਟੇਲਿਜਿਬਿਲਿਟੀ) *n* ਅਸਪਸ਼ਟਤਾ, ਅਬੋਧਤਾ, ਅਬੁੱਝਤਾ

unintelligible (ਅਨਇੰਟੇਲਿਜਿਬਲ) *a* ਅਸਪਸ਼ਟ, ਅਬੋਧ

uninterrupted (ਅਨਇੰਟਰਪਟਿਡ) *a* ਨਿਰਵਿਘਨ, ਅਖੰਡ, ਨਿਰੰਤਰ, ਲਗਾਤਾਰ

union (ਯੂਨਯਅਨ) *n* ਸੰਘ, ਸਭਾ-ਭਵਨ, ਸਭਾ, ਸਮਾਗਮ, ਜਥੇਬੰਦੀ, ਜੋੜ; ਮੇਲ; ਵਿਆਹ, ਏਕਾ

unique (ਯੂ'ਨੀਕ) *a* ਅਨੋਖਾ, ਅਨੂਠਾ, ਨਿਰਾਲਾ, ਬੇਜੋੜ, ਲਾਜਵਾਬ; ~**ness** ਅਨੇਖਾਪਣ, ਅਨੂਠਾਪਣ, ਨਿਰਾਲਾਪਣ, ਅਨੁਪਤਾ

unisexual (ਯੂਨਿ'ਸੈਕਸੁਅਲ) *a* ਇਕ-ਲਿੰਗੀ

unison (ਯੂਨਿਸ਼ਨ) *n* ਧੁਨੀਆਂ ਜਾਂ ਸੁਰਾਂ ਵਿਚ ਤਾਲ ਦੀ ਏਕਤਾ; ਸੁਰ-ਮੇਲ, ਏਕਤਾ, ਮੇਲ-ਮਿਲਾਪ

unit ('ਯੂਨਿਟ) *n* ਇਕ, ਇਕਾਈ; ਮਾਤਰਕ, ਇਕਾਈ ਦਾ ਪਰਿਮਾਨ (ਬਿਜਲੀ); ਦਲ, ਟੁਕੜੀ, ਯੂਨਿਟ (ਫ਼ੌਜ), ਸ਼ਾਖ਼ਾ

unitary ('ਯੂਨਿਟ(ਅ)ਰਿ) *a* ਏਕਾਤਮਕ, ਇਕਾਈ ਦਾ

unite ('ਯੂਨਾਇਟ) *v* ਮਿਲ ਕੇ ਕੰਮ ਕਰਨਾ, ਜੁੜਨਾ, ਪਰਸਪਰ ਮਿਲਾਉਣਾ ਜਾਂ ਮਿਲਣਾ, ਜੋੜਨਾ, ਇਕ ਕਰਨਾ ਜਾਂ ਹੋਣਾ; ਵਿਆਹ ਬੰਧਨ ਵਿਚ ਬੰਨ੍ਹਣਾ; ~d ਸੰਯੁਕਤ, ਯੁਕਤ, ਸਾਂਝਾ

unity ('ਯੂਨਅਟਿ) *n* ਮੇਲ, ਸਮਰੂਪਤਾ; ਸਮਾਨਤਾ, ਸੰਗਤੀ; ਏਕਤਾ, ਏਕਾ (ਗਣਿ) ਇਕਾਈ

universal ('ਯੂਨਿ'ਵ੍ਵਅ:ਸਲ) *a* ਵਿਆਪਕ, ਸਾਮਾਨਯ, ਸਰਵਵਿਆਪਕ, ਸੰਪੂਰਨ, ਕੁੱਲ; ~ity ਵਿਆਪਕਤਾ, ਸਰਵ-ਵਿਆਪਕਤਾ; ~ize ਵਿਸ਼੍ਵ-ਵਿਆਪੀ ਬਣਾਉਣਾ; ਸਰਵ-ਦੇਸੀ ਬਣਾਉਣਾ

universe ('ਯੂਨਿਵ੍ਵਅ:ਸ) *n* ਬ੍ਰਹਿਮੰਡ, ਵਿਸ਼੍ਵ, ਸ੍ਰਿਸ਼ਟੀ, ਜਗਤ

university ('ਯੂਨਿ'ਵ੍ਵਅ:ਸਅਟਿ) *n* ਵਿਸ਼੍ਵਵਿਦਿਆਲਾ

unjust (ਅਨਜਸਟ) *a* ਨਿਆਂਹੀਨ, ਅਨੁਚਿਤ, ਅਨਿਆਂਪੂਰਨ; ~ified ਨਾਵਾਜਬ, ਅਯੋਗ, ਅਨੁਚਿਤ, ਨਿਆਂਰਹਿਤ

unkind (ਅਨਕਾਇੰਡ) *a* ਬੇਰਹਿਮ, ਬੇਦਰਦ, ਨਿਰਦਈ, ਕਠੋਰ, ਨਿਸ਼ਠੁਰ

unknown (ਅਨਨੋਨ) *a* ਅਣਜਾਣ, ਨਾਮਲੂਮ; ਬੇਗਾਨਾ, ਅਜਨਬੀ, ਓਪਰਾ

unlawful (ਅਨਲਾਫ਼ੁਲ) *a* ਗ਼ੈਰ-ਕਾਨੂੰਨੀ, ਅਵੈਧ, ਹਰਾਮੀ

unlearned (ਅਨਲੰ:ਡ) *a* ਅਣਜਾਣ; ਮੂਰੁ, ਅਗਿਆਨ

unless (ਅਨ'ਲੈਸ) *conj* ਜਦ ਤੀਕ ਨਾ, ਨਹੀਂ ਤਾਂ, ਜੇ ਕਰ ਨਾ; ਇਸ ਨੂੰ ਛੱਡ ਕੇ, ਸਿਵਾਏ ਇਸ ਦੇ

unlettered (ਅਨਲੇਟ:ਡ) *a* ਨਿਰੱਖਰ, ਅਨਪੜ੍ਹ, ਬੇਇਲਮ

unlike (ਅਨਲਾਇਕ) *a* ਭਿੰਨ, ਅਣਮਿਲਦਾ, ਪ੍ਰਤੀਕੂਲ; ~ly ਅਸੰਭਾਵੀ

unlimited (ਅਨਲਿਮਿਟਿਡ) *a* ਅਪਾਰ, ਅਸੀਮਤ, ਬੇਹੱਦ, ਬੇਅੰਤ, ਅਤੀ ਅਧਿਕ

unload (ਅਨਲੋਡ) *v* ਭਾਰ ਲਾਹੁਣਾ, ਭਾਰਮੁਕਤ ਕਰਨਾ, ਖ਼ਾਲੀ ਕਰ ਦੇਣਾ, ਮਾਲ ਲਾਹੁਣਾ

unlock (ਅਨਲੋਕ) *v* ਜੰਦਾ ਖੋਲ੍ਹਣਾ; (ਬੋਲ) ਦਿਲ ਦੀ ਗੱਲ ਖੋਲ੍ਹਣੀ, ਫੁੱਟ ਪੈਣਾ

unlucky (ਅਨੱਲਕੀ) *a* ਭਾਗਹੀਨ, ਅਭਾਗਾ, ਅਸ਼ੁਭ, ਅਸਫਲ, ਨਾਮੁਰਾਦ, ਬਦਕਿਸਮਤ

unmanageable (ਅਨਮੈਨਿਜਬਲ) *a* ਕਾਬੂ ਤੋਂ ਬਾਹਰ, ਬੇਕਾਬੂ, ਪ੍ਰਬੰਧ ਰਹਿਤ

unmanly (ਅਨਮੈਨਲਿ) *a* ਜਨਾਨੜਾ; ਬੁਜ਼ਦਿਲ, ਬੋਦਾ

unmannerly (ਅਨਮੈਨ:ਲਿ) *adv* ਕੁਚੱਜਾ, ਬਦਤਮੀਜ਼, ਬੇਹੂਦਾ, ਅਸ਼ਿਸ਼ਟ, ਗੰਵਾਰ

unmarried (ਅਨਮੈਰਿਡ) *a* ਕੁਆਰਾ, ਕੁਆਰੀ, ਅਵਿਵਾਹਤ

unmatched (ਅਨਮੈਚਡ) *a* ਅਢੁੱਕਵਾਂ, ਬੇਜੋੜਾ

unmentioned (ਅਨਮੈਨਸ਼ੰਡ) *a* ਅੱਕਥ ਨਾ-ਕਥਨ ਯੋਗ, ਅਨੁਲਿਖਤ

unnatural (ਅਨਨੈਚਰਲ) *a* ਗ਼ੈਰ-ਕੁਦਰਤੀ, ਅਸੁਭਾਵਕ, ਬਣਾਉਟੀ, ਨਾਜਾਇਜ਼, ਹਰਾਮੀ

unnecessary (ਅਨਨੇਸਿਸਰਿ) *a* ਬੇਲੋੜਾ, ਅਲਾਵਸ਼ੱਕ

unnumbered (ਅਨੰਬਃਡ) *a* ਅਣਗਿਣਤ,

ਬੇਹੱਦ, ਬੇਸ਼ੁਮਾਰ

unofficial (ਅੱਨਅਫ਼ਿਸ਼ਲ) *a* ਗ਼ੈਰ-ਸਰਕਾਰੀ, ਗ਼ੈਰਰਸਮੀ

unopposed (ਅਨਪੌਸਡ) *a* ਬਿਨਾ ਮੁਕਾਬਲੇ ਤੋਂ, ਬਿਨਾ ਮੁਕਾਬਲਾ, ਨਿਰਵਿਰੋਧ

unpaid (ਅਨਪੇਡ) *a* ਅਦਾ ਨਾ ਕੀਤਾ

unparalleled (ਅਨਪੈਰਲਲਡ) *a* ਅਨੂਠਾ, ਬੇਨਜ਼ੀਰ, ਲਾਸਾਨੀ, ਨਿਰਾਲਾ

unparliamentary (ਅਨਪਾਃਲਮੇਂਟਰਿ) *a* ਸਭਾ ਦੇ ਨੇਮ-ਵਿਰੁੱਧ, ਅਸੰਸਦੀ; ਅਸ਼ਲੀਲ, ਅਸ਼ਿਸ਼ਟ

unpleasant (ਅਨਪਲੇਜ਼ੰਟ) *a* ਬੇਮਜ਼ਾ, ਬੁਰਾ, ਨਾਗਵਾਰ

unpopular (ਅਨਪਾਪੂਯੂਲ*) *a* ਬਦਨਾਮ, ਅਪ੍ਰਸਿੱਧ

unprecedented (ਅਨਪ੍ਰੇਸਿਡੇਂਟਡ) *a* ਅਨੋਖਾ; ਨਵੇਕਲਾ, ਬੇਮਿਸਾਲ

unprejudiced (ਅਨਪਰਿਜੁਡਿਸਡ) *a* ਬੇਲਾਗ, ਪੱਖਪਾਤ-ਰਹਿਤ, ਨਿਰਪੱਖ

unprepared (ਅਨਪਰਿਪੇਅਃਡ) *a* ਬਿਨਾ ਤਿਆਰੀ ਕੀਤੇ, ਅਸਿੱਧ; ਪਹਿਲਾਂ ਨਾ ਸੋਚਿਆ

unpresentable (ਅਨਪਰਿਜ਼ੇਂਟਬਲ) *a* ਭੱਦਾ, ਅਪਰਦਰਸ਼ਨੀ

unpresumptuous (ਅਨਪਰਿਜ਼ਸਟਯੂਅਸ) *a* ਸਰਲ, ਸਾਦਾ; ਨਿਮਰਤਾ ਭਰਪੂਰ

unprincipled (ਅਨਪਰਿੰਸਪਲਡ) · *a* ਬੇਅਸੂਲਾ, ਸਦਾਚਾਰਹੀਨ, ਚਰਿੱਤਰਹੀਨ, ਸਿਧਾਂਤਹੀਨ

unproductive (ਅਨਪਰਡਕਟਿਵ) *a* ਬਾਂਝ, ਬੰਜਰ, ਬੇਕਾਰ, ਅਟਉਪਜਾਊ

unprofitable (ਅਨਪਰਾਫ਼ਿਟਬਲ) *a* ਵਿਅਰਥਤਾ, ਲਾਭਹੀਨਤਾ

unpublished (ਅਨਪਬਲਿਸ਼ਡ) *a* ਅਟਛਪਿਆ,

ਅਪ੍ਰਕਾਸ਼ਤ, ਗੁਪਤ

unquestionable (ਅਨਕਵੇਸਚਨਬਲ) *a* ਨਿਰਸੰਦੇਹ, ਨਿਰਵਿਵਾਦ; ~questioned ਨਿਰਵਿਵਾਦ, ਨਿਸ਼ਚਤ

unreal (ਅਨਰਿਅਲ) *a* ਝੂਠਾ, ਅਵਾਸਤਵਿਕ, ਨਕਲੀ

unregistered (ਅਨਰੇਜਿਸਟ'ਡ) *a* ਗ਼ੈਰ-ਰਜਿਸਟਰੀ-ਸ਼ੁਦਾ, ਸਧਾਰਨ (ਪੱਤਰ ਆਦਿ)

unrest (ਅਨਰੇਸਟ) *n* ਬੇਚੈਨੀ, ਗੜਬੜ, ਅਸ਼ਾਂਤੀ, ਫ਼ਸਾਦ

unriddle (ਅਨਰਿਡੱਲ) *a* (ਅੜਾਉਂਤੀ, ਗੁੰਝਲ, ਬੁਝਾਰਤ, ਸੱਮਸਿਆ ਆਦਿ) ਖੋਲ੍ਹਣੀ, ਹੱਲ ਕਰਨੀ

unrighteous (ਅਨਰਾਇਚਸ) *a* ਅਧਰਮੀ, ਪਾਪੀ, ਬੇਈਮਾਨ; ~ness ਅਧਰਮ, ਬੁਰਾਈ, ਦੁਸ਼ਟਤਾ, ਬੇਈਮਾਨੀ

unripe (ਅਨਰਾਇਪ) *a* ਕੱਚਾ, ਹਰਾ, ਅਟਪੱਕਿਆ, ਅਵਿਕਸਤ; ਨਾਬਾਲਗ਼

unruly (ਅਨਰੂਲਿ) *a* ਨੇਮ ਰਹਿਤ, ਮੂੰਹਜ਼ੋਰ, ਤੁਫ਼ਾਨੀ

unsatisfied (ਅਨਸੈਟਿਸਫ਼ਾਇਡ) *a* ਅਸੰਤੁਸ਼ਟ, ਅਤ੍ਰਿਪਤ

unscientific (ਅਨਸਾਂਇਟਫ਼ਿਕ) *a* ਅਵਿਗਿਆਨਕ, ਨਿਯਮ-ਵਿਰੁੱਧ, ਸਿਧਾਂਤਹੀਨ

unscrupulous (ਅਨਸਕਰੁਪਯੂਲਸ) *a* ਚਰਿੱਤਰਹੀਨ; ਬੇਅਸੂਲਾ; ਬੇਸ਼ਰਮ

unseasonable (ਅਨਸੀਜ਼ਨਬਲ) *a* ਬੇਮੌਸਮ (ਬਾਰਸ਼ ਆਦਿ), ਬੇਮੌਕਾ

unseat (ਅਨਸੀਟ) *v* ਥਾਂ ਤੋਂ ਹਟਾਉਂਾ; ਮੈਂਬਰੀ ਤੋਂ ਹਟਾਉਣਾ

unseen (ਅਨਸੀਨ) *a* ਅਣਦੇਖਿਆ, ਅਡਿੱਠ, ਨਾ ਪੜ੍ਹਿਆ ਹੋਇਆ ਪਾਠ

unsophisticated (ਅਨਸਫ਼ਿਸਟਿਕੇਟਿਡ) *a*
ਨਿਰਛਲ; ਸਿੱਧਾ-ਸਾਦਾ, ਭੋਲਾ, ਸਰਲ

unspent (ਅਨਸਪੈਂਟ) *a* ਅਣਖ਼ਰਚਿਆ,
ਅਣਵਰਤਿਆ, ਅਣਬੀਤਿਆ

unstable (ਅਨਸਟੇਬਲ) *a* ਅਸਥਾਈ, ਅਸਥਿਰ

unstitch (ਅਨਸਟਿਚ) *v* ਟਾਂਕਾ ਘੋਲ੍ਹਣਾ, ਬਖ਼ੀਆ
ਉਪੇੜਨਾ

until (ਅਨਟਿਲ) *prep conj* ਜਦ ਤੀਕ, ਤੀਕ,
ਇਸ ਹੱਦ ਤੀਕ, ਜਦ ਤੀਕ ਨਾ

unto (ਅੱਨਟੂ) *prep* ਤੀਕ ਨੂੰ; ਵੇਖੋ *to*

untimely (ਅਨਟਾਇਮਲਿ) *a* ਅਕਾਲਕ, ਸਮੇਂ ਤੋਂ
ਪਹਿਲਾਂ; ਬੇਮੌਕਾ, ਕੁਵੇਲੇ

untold (ਅਨਟੋਲਡ) *a* ਅੱਕਥ; ਅਣਵਰਤਤ; ਬੇਹੱਦ

untouchability (ਅਨਟੱਚਬਿਲਇਟਿ) *n* ਛੁਆ-
ਛੂਤ, ਛੂਤ-ਛਾਤ; ~touchable ਅਛੂਤ;
ਹਰੀਜਨ

untoward (ਅਨਟੋਅੱਡ) *a* ਭੈੜਾ, ਕਸੂਤਾ;
ਅਵੱਲਾ, ਅਵੈੜਾ

untrained (ਅਨਟਰੇਂਡ) *a* ਅਣਸਿੱਖਿਆ, ਨਾ
ਸਿਖਲਾਇਆ

unusual (ਅਨਯੂਜ਼ੂਅਲ) *a* ਅਭਰਿੱਠ, ਅਸਧਾਰਨ,
ਅਨੋਖ, ਅਲੌਕਕ

unwanted (ਅਨਵਾਂਟਿਡ) *a* ਅਣਚਾਹਿਆ,
ਬੇਲੋੜਾ, ਵਾਧੂ, ਅਣਅਵੱਸ਼ਕ

unwell (ਅਨਵੈਲ) *a* ਅਸੁਅਸਥ, ਬੀਮਾਰ

unwilling (ਅਨਵਿਲਇੰਗ) *a* ਅਣਇੱਛੁਕ,
ਬੇਦਿਲ; ਅਸਹਿਮਤ; ~ness ਨਾਰਾਜ਼ਮੰਦੀ,
ਅਸਹਿਮਤੀ

unwise (ਅਨਵਾਇਜ਼) *a* ਅਗਿਆਨੀ, ਬੇਸਮਝ,
ਕੁਵੱਲਾ (ਕੰਮ)

unworldly (ਅਨਵ:ਲਡੱਲਿ) *a* ਅਸੰਸਾਰਕ;

ਪਰਮਾਰਥੀ

unworthy (ਅਨਵ:ਦਿ) *a* ਅਯੋਗ, ਨਿਖਿੱਧ,
ਨਾਲਾਇਕ, ਨਿਗੁਣਾ

unwritten (ਅਨਰਿਟਨ) *a* ਅਟਲਿਖਿਆ,
ਅਲਿਖਤ, ਮੌਖਕ, ਜ਼ਬਾਨੀ

unyielding (ਅਨਯੀਲਡ੍ਰਿੰਗ) *a* ਅੜੀਅਲ, ਜ਼ਿੱਦੀ,
ਪੱਕਾ, ਬੇਲੋਚ

up (ਅੱਪ) *n v a adv prep* ਉੱਨਤੀ, ਉਚਾਈ;
ਉੱਪਰ ਉੱਠ ਕੇ ਖਲੋਣਾ; ਸਮਾਪਤ; ਉੱਪਰਲਾ,
ਉੱਚਾ; ਉੱਤੇ, ਉੱਪਰ ਨੂੰ, ਉੱ ਪਰ ਤਕ; ਤਰਤੀਬ
ਵਿਚ

upbringing (ਅਪਬਰਿੰਗਿੰਗ) *n* ਪ੍ਰਾਰੰਭਿਕ
ਸਿੱਖਿਆ, ਪਾਲਣਾ, ਪਾਲਣ-ਪੋਸਣ

update (ਅਪਡੇਟ) *v* ਆਧੁਨਿਕ ਬਣਾਉਣਾ

upgrade (ਅਪਗਰੇਡ) *n v* ਪਦ-ਉੱਨਤੀ, ਪਦ
ਉੱਨਤ, ਉੱਨਤ ਕਰਨਾ, ਕਰਜਾ ਵਧਾਉਣਾ

uphill (ਅਪਹਿਲ) *adv a* ਪਹਾੜ ਦੇ ਉੱਪਰ ਵੱਲ;
ਕਠਨ, ਕਰੜਾ

uphold (ਅਪਹੋਲਡ) *v* ਪੁਸ਼ਟੀ ਕਰਨਾ; ਸਿੱਧਾ ਖੜਾ
ਰੱਖਣਾ, ਉੱਪਰ ਚੁੱਕੀ ਰੱਖਣਾ; ਕਾਇਮ ਰੱਖਣਾ,
(ਫ਼ੈਸਲਾ ਆਦਿ) ਬਹਾਲ ਰੱਖਣਾ, ਯਥਾਪੂਰਵ
ਰੱਖਣਾ

upkeep (ਅਪਕੀਪ) *n* ਪਾਲਣ-ਪੋਸਣ, ਨਿਗਰਾਨੀ,
ਸੰਭਾਲ

uplift (ਅੱਪਲਿਫ਼ਟ) *v n* ਉੱਚਾ ਕਰਨਾ, ਉੱਪਰ ਨੂੰ
ਚੁੱਕਣਾ, ਸੁਧਾਰਨਾ; ਸੁਧਾਰ, ਉੱਨਤੀ

upper (ਅਪਅ*) *n a* ਉਤਲਾ, ਉਤੇਰਾ; ਵੱਡਾ
(ਪਦਵੀ ਵਿਚ)

uppermost (ਅਪ*ਮੋਸਟ) *a* ਸਾਰਿਆਂ ਤੋਂ ਇਪਰ
ਦਾ; ਸਭ ਤੋਂ ਉੱਤੇ

upright (ਅਪਰਾਇਟ) *a* ਸਿੱਧਾ; ਖੜਾ, ਸਰਲ,

ਸਾਦਾ; ਈਮਾਨਦਾਰ

uprising (ਅਪਰਾਇਜ਼ਿੰਗ) *n* ਉਭਾਰ; ਝਗੜਾ, ਬਲਵਾ, ਬਗਾਵਤ, ਕਰਾਂਤੀ

uproar (ਅਪਰੋਅ*) *n* ਰੌਲਾ, ਰੌਲਾ-ਰੱਪਾ, ਹੱਲੜ, ਹੱਲਾ-ਗੁੱਲਾ

uproot (ਅਪਰੂਟ) *v* ਜੜੋਂ ਉਖਾੜਨਾ, ਬਰਬਾਦ ਕਰਨਾ

upset (ਅਪਸੇਟ) *v n* ਉਲਟਨਾ; ਉਲਟ-ਪੁਲਟ ਕਰਨਾ, ਪਰੇਸ਼ਾਨ ਕਰਨਾ; ਗੜਬੜ; (ਨੀਲਾਮੀ ਵਿਚ) ਸਰਕਾਰੀ ਕੀਮਤ

upshot (ਅਪਸ਼ਾਟ) *n* ਸਿੱਟਾ, ਨਤੀਜਾ, ਅੰਤ

upside (ਅਪਸਾਇਡ) *n* ਉਪਰਲਾ ਹਿੱਸਾ, ਉਪਰੀ ਸਤ੍ਹਾ; **~down** ਉਲਟਾ, ਉਲਟਾ-ਪੁਲਟਾ, ਪਰਿਤਆ, ਪੁੱਠਾ, ਮੂਧਾ; **~to** (ਅਪ-ਟੂ-ਡੇਟ) (ਅਪ-ਟੂ) ਤੀਕ, ਤਾਈਂ, ਤੀਕਰ, ਤਕ; **~to date** ਆਧੁਨਿਕ; ਸਮੇਂ ਦਾ ਹਾਣੀ

upward(s) (ਅਪਵ:ਡ(ਜ਼)) *adv a* ਉੱਪਰ ਦਾ, ਉੱਪਰ ਵੱਲ; ਵਧਤ ਦਾ, ਤੱਰਕੀ ਦਾ; ਬਹੁਤਾ

upon (ਅ'ਪੌਨ) *prep* ਉੱਤੇ, ਉੱਪਰ, ਉੱਪਰ ਵੱਲ; ਪਿੱਛੇ; ਪਾਸ; ਬਾਬਤ

Uranus (ਯੂਅਰਅਨਅਸ) *n* ਮੰਗਲ-ਗ੍ਰਹਿ

urban ('ਅ:ਬਅਨ) *a* ਸ਼ਹਿਰਿ, ਨਾਗਰਿਕ; ਸੁਘੜ; **~e** ਸੁਘੜ, ਸਾਊ; ਸ਼ੀਲਵਾਨ, ਸੁਸ਼ੀਲ, ਸ਼ਿਸ਼ਟ; **~ity** ਸੁਘੜਤਾ, ਸਾਊਪੁਣਾ, ਸ਼ਿਸ਼ਟਤਾ, ਨਾਗਰਿਕ ਜੀਵਨ

urchin ('ਅ:ਚਿਨ) *n* ਮੁੰਡਾ, ਲੜਕਾ, ਛੋਹਰ; ਸ਼ਰਾਰਤੀ ਲੜਕਾ; ਜੰਗਲੀ ਚੂਹਾ

urea (ਯੁ(ਅ)'ਰਿਅ) *n* (ਰਸਾ) ਘੁਲਣਸ਼ੀਲ, ਰੰਗਹੀਨ ਅਤੇ ਰਵੇਦਾਰ ਯੋਗਕ

urge (ਅ:ਜ) *v n* ਪਰੇਰਨਾ, ਉਤੇਜਤ ਕਰਨਾ, ਤਾਕੀਦ ਕਰਨਾ, ਵਾਹ; **~ncy** ਅਤੀ ਅਵਸ਼ੱਕਤਾ,

ਲੋੜਵੰਦੀ, ਤਾਂਗ, ਤੀਬਰ, ਮਹੱਤਵ; (ਟੱਟੀ-ਪਿਸ਼ਾਬ ਦੀ) ਹਾਜਤ; **~nt** ਜ਼ਰੂਰੀ, ਅਵਸ਼ੱਕ, ਬਹੁਤ ਲੋੜੀਂਦਾ

urinal ('ਯੂਅਰਿਨਲ) *a n* ਮੂਤਰਾਲਾ; ਪਿਸ਼ਾਬ-ਘਰ

urine ('ਯੂਅਰੀਨ) *n* ਪਿਸ਼ਾਬ, ਮੂਤਰ, ਮੂਤ

urn (ਅ:ਨ) *n v* ਕਲਸ; ਅਸਥੀ-ਪਾਤਰ; ਵੱਡੀ ਚਾਦਾਨੀ

usage ('ਯੂਸਿਜ) *n* ਰੀਤੀ, ਪਰਿਪਾਟੀ, ਰਿਵਾਜ, ਰਸਮ, ਦਸਤੂਰ

use ('ਯੂਸ) *n v* ਵਰਤੋਂ ਦੀ ਸ਼ਕਤੀ; ਲਾਭ; ਵਰਤੋਂ ਕਰਨਾ; ਕੰਮ ਵਿਚ ਲਿਆਉਣਾ; ਖ਼ਰਚ ਕਰਨਾ ਜਾਂ ਹੋਣਾ; **~ful** ਉਪਯੋਗੀ; ਉਪਕਾਰੀ, ਹਿਤਕਾਰੀ, ਲਾਭਦਾਇਕ; **~less** ਨਿਰਰਥਕ, ਵਿਅਰਥ, ਨਿਸਫਲ; ਘਟੀਆ

usher ('ਅਸ਼ਅ*) *n v* (ਕਿਸੇ ਮਹਿਮਾਨ ਨੂੰ) ਅੰਦਰ ਲਿਆਉਣਾ

ususal ('ਯੂਯੁਅਲ) *a* ਪ੍ਰਚਲਤ, ਰਿਵਾਜੀ, ਆਮ; **~ly** ਆਮ ਤੌਰ ਤੇ, ਸਧਾਰਨ ਤੌਰ ਤੇ

usurer ('ਯੂਯੁਨ(ਅ)ਰਅ*) *n* ਸੂਦਖੋਰ

utensil (ਯੁ'ਟੈਨਸਲ) ਬਰਤਨ, ਭਾਂਡਾ

uterus ('ਯੂਟਅਰਅਸ) *n* ਗਰਭ-ਕੋਸ਼, ਗਰਭਾਸ਼ਯ, ਬੱਚੇਦਾਨੀ, ਗਰਭ

utiltraian ('ਯੂਟਿਲਿ'ਟੇਅਰਿਅਨ) *n a* ਉਪਯੋਗਤਾ-ਵਾਦੀ; ਉਪਯੋਗੀ, ਸੁਆਰਥੀ; **~ism** ਉਪਯੋਗਤਾਵਾਦ, ਸੁਆਰਥਵਾਦ

utility (ਯੂ'ਟਿਲਅਟਿ) *n* ਉਪਯੋਗ, ਲਾਭ, ਉਪਯੋਗਤਾ

utilization ('ਯੂਟਿਲਾਇ'ਜ਼ੇਇਸ਼ਨ) *n* ਉਪਯੋਗਤਾ

utilize ('ਯੂਟਿਲਆਇਜ਼) *v* ਕੰਮ ਵਿਚ ਲਿਆਉਣਾ, ਉਪਯੋਗ ਕਰਨਾ

utmost ('ਅੱਟਮਅਉਸਟ) *a* ਅਤੀਅੰਤ, ਅਧਿਕ,

ਬੇਹੱਦ, ਅਤੀ

Utopia (ਯੁ'ਟਅਉਪਯਅ) *n* ਯੂਟੋਪੀਆ ਆਦਰਸ਼-
ਚਿੱਤਰ, ਕਾਲਪਨਕ, ਸੁਖ-ਚਿੱਤਰ, ਸ਼ੇਖ਼-ਚਿੱਲੀ ਦਾ
ਸੁਪਨਾ; ~n ਕਾਲਪਨਕ, ਮਾਨਸਕ, ਖ਼ਿਆਲੀ,
ਅਵਿਹਾਰਕ; ~ly ਸਰਾਸਰ, ਨਿਪਟ, ਨਿਰਾ,
ਉੱਕਾ, ਬਿਲਕੁਲ

utter (ਅੱਟਅ*) *v* ਕਹਿਣਾ, ਉਚਾਰਨ, ਕਰਨ;
ਜਾਰੀ ਕਰਨਾ; ~ance ਉਚਾਰਨ, ਬੋਲ; ਵਾਕ-
ਸ਼ਕਤੀ, ਬੋਲੀ

uvula ('ਯੂਵ੍ਯੁਲਅ) *n* ਗਲੇ ਦੀ ਘੰਡੀ, ਕਾਂ, ਕਾਂਉ

uxorious (ਅੱਕ'ਸੋਰਿਅਸ) *a* ਜਨ-ਮੁਰੀਦ, ਜੋਰੂ ਦਾ
ਗ਼ੁਲਾਮ

V

V, v (ਵੀ) *n* ਰੋਮਨ ਵਰਨਮਾਲਾ ਦਾ ਬਾਈਵਾਂ ਅੱਖਰ; ਰੋਮਨ ਅੰਕਾਂ ਵਿਚੋਂ ਪੰਜ ਦਾ ਅੰਕ; ਆਕਾਰ; ਵਿਜੈ ਦਾ ਨਿਸ਼ਾਨ

vacancy (ਵੇਇਕਅੰਸਿ) *n* ਖ਼ਾਲੀ ਥਾਂ; ਖ਼ਾਲੀ ਅਸਾਮੀ; ਖ਼ਲਾਅ, ਫ਼ੁਰਸਤ

vacant ('ਵੇਇਕਅੰਟ) *a* ਖ਼ਾਲੀ; ਸੁੰਵਾ; ਵਿਹਲਾ

vacate (ਵਅ'ਕੇਇਟ) *v* ਖ਼ਾਲੀ ਕਰਨਾ, ਵਿਹਲਾ ਕਰਨਾ, ਰੱਦ ਕਰਨਾ, ਬੇਕਾਰ ਕਰਨਾ; ਖੰਡਨ ਕਰਨਾ; ~d ਖ਼ਾਲੀ ਕੀਤਾ, ਖ਼ਾਲੀ

vacation (ਵਅ'ਕੇਇਸ਼ਨ) *n* ਵਿਹਲ, ਫ਼ੁਰਸਤ; ਲੰਮੀਆਂ ਛੁੱਟੀਆਂ; ਵਕਫ਼ਾ

vaccary ('ਵੈਕਅਰਿ) *n* ਗਊਸ਼ਾਲਾ

vaccinate ('ਵੈਕਸਿਨੇਇਟ) *v* ਲੋਦਾ ਲਾਉਣਾ, ਟੀਕਾ ਲਾਉਣਾ (ਚੀਚਕ ਦਾ)

vaccine ('ਵੈਕਸੀਨ) *n* ਚੀਚਕ ਦੇ ਟੀਕੇ ਦੀ ਦਵਾਈ, ਵੈਕਸੀਨ

vacillate ('ਵੈਸਇਲੇਇਟ) *v* ਡੋਲਣਾ, ਦੁਚਿੰਤੀ ਵਿਚ ਪੈਣਾ, ਜੱਕੋ-ਤੱਕੀ ਕਰਨਾ

vacillation ('ਵੈਸਇ'ਲੇਇਸ਼ਨ) *n* ਜੱਕੋ-ਤੱਕੀ, ਦੁਚਿੰਤੀ, ਅਸਥਿਰਤਾ

vacuum ('ਵੈਕਯੁਅਮ) *n* ਖ਼ਲਾਅ, ਸੁੰਨ-ਸਥਾਨ

vagabond ('ਵੈਗਅਬੌਂਡ) *a n v* ਅਵਾਰਾ, ਲੋਫ਼ਰ; ਅਵਾਰਾਗਰਦ, ਲੁਚਾ; ਅਵਾਰਾ ਫਿਰਨਾ, ਬਦਮਾਸ਼ੀ ਕਰਨਾ

vagarious (ਵਅ'ਗੇਇਰਿਅਸ) *a* ਵਹਿਮੀ, ਸਨਕੀ, ਮੌਜੀ, ਖ਼ਬਤੀ

vagary ('ਵੇਇਗਅਰਿ) *n* ਤਰੰਗ, ਮੌਜ, ਲਹਿਰ, ਖ਼ਿਆਲ, ਵਹਿਮ

vagina (ਵਅ'ਜਾਇਨਅ) *n* ਭਗ, ਯੋਨੀ; (ਇਸਤਰੀ ਦਾ) ਗੁਪਤ ਅੰਗ; ਘੋਲ

vagrancy ('ਵੇਇਗਰਅੰਸਿ) *n* ਅਵਾਰਾਗਰਦੀ, ਲਟੋਰਪੁਣਾ

vagrant ('ਵੇਇਗਰਅੰਟ) *a n* ਅਵਾਰਾ, ਭੌਂਦੂ; ਲਟੋਰ, ਖ਼ਾਨਾ-ਬਦੋਸ਼, ਸੈਲਾਨੀ, ਹਰਜਾਈ

vague (ਵੇਇਗ) *a* ਅਸਪਸ਼ਟ, ਧੁੰਦਲਾ ਜਿਹਾ, ਸ਼ੱਕੀ; ~ness ਸੰਦੇਹ, ਅਸਪਸ਼ਟਤਾ, ਧੁੰਦਲਾਪਣ

vail (ਵੇਇਲ) *n* (ਪ੍ਰ) ਲਾਭ, ਇਨਾਮ, ਬਖ਼ਸ਼ੀਸ਼; ਸਿਰ ਝੁਕਾਉਣਾ; ਲਾਭ ਉਠਾਉਣਾ, ਸਹਾਈ ਹੋਣਾ

vain (ਵੇਇਨ) *a* ਅਭਿਮਾਨੀ, ਘਮੰਡੀ, ਬਿਰਥਾ, ਵਿਅਰਥ, ਨਿਸਫਲ, ਥੋਥਾ; in~ ਬੇਫ਼ਾਇਦਾ, ਫ਼ਜ਼ੂਲ, ਨਿਸਫਲ, ਅਜਾਈ

vale (ਵੇਇਲ) *n* (ਕਾਵਿਕ) ਘਾਟੀ, ਵਾਦੀ

valediction ('ਵੈਲਿ'ਡਿਕਸ਼ਨ) *n* ਵਿਦਾ, ਅਲਵਿਦਾ, ਵਿਦਾਇਗੀ, ਰੁਖ਼ਸਤ

valedictory ('ਵੈਲਿ'ਡਿਕਟ(ਅ)ਰਿ) *a n* ਅਲਵਿਦਾਈ; ਵਿਦਾਇਗੀ ਭਾਸ਼ਨ

valiance ('ਵੈਲਯਅੰਸ) *n* ਸੂਰਵੀਰਤਾ, ਬਹਾਦਰੀ, ਦਲੇਰੀ, ਜਵਾਂਮਰਦੀ

valiant ('ਵੈਲਯਅੰਟ) *a* ਸੂਰਵੀਰ, ਯੋਧਾ, ਦਲੇਰ, ਬਹਾਦਰ, ਜਵਾਂਮਰਦ, ਸੂਰਮਾ

valid ('ਵੈਲਿਡ) *a* ਯੋਗ, ਉਚਿਤ, ਜਾਇਜ਼, ਦਰੁਸਤ, ਠੀਕ, ਵਾਜਬ; ~ate ਪੱਕਾ ਕਰਨਾ, ਪ੍ਰਮਾਣਤ ਕਰਨਾ; ~ity ਪ੍ਰਮਾਣਕਤਾ, ਉਚਿਤਤਾ, ਵੈਧਤਾ

valley ('ਵੈਲਿ) *n* ਵਾਦੀ, ਘਾਟੀ, ਦੂਨ

valorous ('ਵੈਲਅਰਅਸ) *a* ਬਹਾਦਰ, ਜਵਾਂਮਰਦ,

ਦਲੇਰ, ਵੀਰ, ਸੂਰਮਾ

valour ('ਵੈਲਅ*) *n* ਬਹਾਦਰੀ, ਜਵਾਂਮਰਦੀ, ਦਲੇਰੀ, ਵੀਰਤਾ, ਵੀਰ-ਰਸ

valuable ('ਵੈਲਯੂਅਬਲ) *a n* ਬਹੁ-ਮੁੱਲਾ, ਕੀਮਤੀ, ਮਾਨਯੋਗ; ਕੀਮਤੀ ਸਾਮਾਨ

valuate ('ਵੈਲਯੂਏਇਟ) *v* ਮੁੱਲਾਂਕਣ ਕਰਨਾ, ਮੁੱਲ ਨਿਸ਼ਚਤ ਕਰਨਾ, ਮੁੱਲ ਨਿਰਧਾਰਤ ਕਰਨਾ

valuation ('ਵੈਲਯੂਏਇਸ਼ਨ) *n* ਮੁੱਲ-ਨਿਰਧਾਰਣ, ਮੁੱਲਾਂਕਣ

value ('ਵੈਲਯੂ) *n v* ਲਾਭ, ਗੁਣ, ਮਹੱਤਵ; ਮੁੱਲ, ਕੀਮਤ; ਮਾਲੀਅਤ; ਭਾਵ

vamp (ਵੈਂਪ) *n v* ਜੋੜ, ਗੰਢ-ਤੁੱਪ (ਜੁੱਤੀ); ਪੰਜਾ ਲਾਉਣਾ; ਗੰਢ-ਤੁੱਪ ਕਰਨਾ; ਤੱਤਕਾਲੀ ਸੰਗੀਤ ਦੇਣਾ; ~er ਮੋਚੀ; ਗੰਢਣ ਵਾਲਾ; ਫਸਾਉਣਾ; ਫੁਸਲਾਉਣਾ, ਲੁਭਾਉਣਾ; ~ire ਅਤਿਆਚਾਰੀ, ਲੁਟੇਰਾ, ਠੱਗ

van (ਵੈਨ) *n* (1) ਬੰਦ ਛਕੜਾ, (ਰੇਲ ਵਿਚ) ਮਾਲ ਡੱਬਾ; (2) (ਫੌਜ ਦਾ) ਅਗਲਾ ਹਿੱਸਾ, ਹਰਾਵਲ ਦਸਤਾ, ਆਗੂ; (3) (ਪ੍ਰ) ਖੰਭ, ਪੰਖ; ਬਾਂਹ

vanish ('ਵੈਨਿਸ਼) *n v* ਲੋਪ ਹੋ ਜਾਣਾ, ਓਹਲੇ ਹੋ ਜਾਣਾ, ਲੁਕਟਾ, ਗਾਇਬ ਹੋ ਜਾਣਾ, ਨਸ਼ਟ ਹੋ ਜਾਣਾ

vanity ('ਵੈਨਅਟਿ) *n* ਸਾਰਹੀਨਤਾ, ਵਿਅਰਥਤਾ, ਨਿਰਾਰਥਕਤਾ ਦਿਖਾਵਾ, ਫੂੰ ਫਾਂ, ਅਡੰਬਰ; ~case ਸ਼ਿੰਗਾਰਦਾਨੀ

vanquish ('ਵੈਂਕਵਿਸ਼) *v* ਹਰਾਉਣਾ, ਜਿੱਤਣਾ, ਕਾਬੂ ਪਾਉਣਾ

vaporization ('ਵੇਇਪਅਰਾਇ'ਜ਼ੇਇਸ਼ਨ) *n* ਵਾਸ਼ਪੀ-ਕਰਨ, ਭਾਫ਼ਣ

vaporize ('ਵੇਇਪਅਰਾਇਜ਼) *v* ਵਾਸ਼ਪ ਵਿਚ ਬਦਲਣਾ, ਭਾਫ਼ ਬਣਨਾ ਜਾਂ ਬਣਾਉਣਾ, ਉਡ

ਜਾਣਾ, ਹਵਾਤਰਨਾ

vapour ('ਵੇਇਪਅ*) *n* (ਹਵਾ ਵਿਚ) ਵਾਸ਼ਪ, ਭਾਉ, ਕੁਹਰਾ, ਧੂੰਆ; ਕਾਲਪਨਕ ਵਸਤੁ, ਮਿਥਿਆ ਅਭਿਮਾਨ, ਹੰਕਾਰ; ~y ਵਾਸ਼ਪੀ, ਭਾਫ਼ਦਾਰ, ਕੁਹਰੇਦਾਰ; ਧੁੰਦਲਾ

variability ('ਵੇਅਰਿਅ'ਬਿਲਅਟਿ) *n* ਅਨਿੱਤਤਾ ਅਸਥਿਰਤਾ; ਪਰਿਵਰਤਤਾ, ਹੇਰ-ਫੇਰ

variable ('ਵੇਅਰਿਅਬਲ) *a n* ਪਰਿਵਰਤਨਸ਼ੀਲ, ਅਸਥਿਰ, ਚੰਚਲ, ਬਦਲਣਹਾਰ, ਅਸਥਾਈ; (ਗਣ) ਭਿੰਨ-ਭਿੰਨ

variance ('ਵੇਅਰਿਅੰਸ) *n* ਭੇਦ, ਵਖੇਵਾਂ, ਵਿਭਿੰਨਤਾ, ਅੰਤਰ; ਮੱਤ-ਭੇਦ, ਅਸੰਮਤੀ; ਫੁੱਟ; ਭਿੰਨਤਾ

variant ('ਵੇਅਰਿਅੰਟ) *a n* ਵੱਖਰਾ, ਭਿੰਨ, ਪਰਿਵਰਤਨਸ਼ੀਲ

variation ('ਵੇਅਰਿ'ਏਇਸ਼ਨ) *n* ਭੇਦ, ਅੰਤਰ; ਤਬਦੀਲੀ, ਉਤਾਰ-ਚੜ੍ਹਾਉ; (ਵਿਆ) ਰੂਪਾਂਤਰ

varied ('ਵੇਅਰਿਡ) *a* ਵਿਭਿੰਨ, ਵਿਵਿਧ; ਪਰਿਵਰਤਤ

variegated ('ਵੇਅਰਿਗੇਇਟਿਡ) *a* ਰੰਗ-ਬਰੰਗਾ, ਵੰਨ-ਸੁਵੰਨਾ, ਬਹੁਰੰਗਾ, ਚਿਤਕਬਰਾ

variety (ਵਅ'ਰਾਇਅਟਿ) *n* ਰੰਗਾ-ਰੰਗ, ਬਹੁਰੰਗੀ, ਕਿਸਮ; ਵਚਿੱਤਰ; ਅਨੇਕਤਾ

various ('ਵੇਅਰਿਅਸ) *a* ਅਨੇਕ, ਤਰ੍ਹਾਂ-ਤਰ੍ਹਾਂ ਦਾ, ਨਾਨਾ

varnish ('ਵਾ*ਨਿਸ਼) *n v* ਰੋਗਨ, ਵਾਰਨਿਸ਼; ਬਟਾਉਟੀ ਚਮਕ-ਦਮਕ, ਟੀਪ-ਟਾਪ, ਰੋਗਨ ਕਰਨਾ, ਵਾਰਨਿਸ਼ ਕਰਨੀ

varsity ('ਵਾਸਅਟਿ) *n* (ਬੋਲ) ਵਿਸ਼ਵਵਿਦਿਆਲਾ

vary ('ਵੇਅਰਿ) *v* ਬਦਲਣਾ, ਪਲਟਣਾ, ਘਟਣਾ, ਵਧਣਾ, ਘਟਾਉਣਾ-ਵਧਾਉਣਾ, ਤਬਦੀਲ ਕਰਨਾ;

ਨਾਨਾ ਰੂਪ ਕਰਨਾ ਜਾਂ ਹੋਣਾ, ਭਿੰਨ-ਭਿੰਨ ਕਰਨਾ
ਜਾਂ ਹੋਣਾ, ਰੂਪ ਬਦਲਣਾ

vascular ('ਵ੍ਸਕਯੁਲਅ*) *a* ਖ਼ੂਨ ਵਗਣ ਵਾਲੀ
(ਨਾਲੀ), ਵਾਹਿਕ ਸਬੰਧੀ, ਨਾੜੀ ਸਬੰਧੀ

vase (ਵ੍ਾਜ਼) *n* ਫੁੱਲਦਾਨ, ਗੁਲਦਾਨ, ਸਜਾਵਟੀ
ਗਲਾਸ

vasectomy (ਵਅ'ਸੈਕਟਅਮਿ) *n* (ਮਰਦਾਂ
ਸਬੰਧੀ) ਨਲਬੰਦੀ

vast (ਵ੍ਾਸਟ) *a n* ਵਿਸ਼ਾਲ, ਅਪਾਰ, ਬਹੁਤ ਵੱਡਾ,
ਭਾਰੀ; ਖੁੱਲ੍ਹੀ ਥਾਂ; **~ness** ਵਿਸ਼ਾਲਤਾ,
ਅਪਾਰਤਾ, ਲੰਬਾਈ-ਚੌੜਾਈ

vault (ਵ੍ਾਲਟ) *n v* (1) ਕਮਾਨੀਦਾਰ ਛੱਤ; ਗੁੰਬਜ;
ਤਹਿਖ਼ਾਨਾ, ਗੁਦਾਮ (ਸ਼ਰਾਬ ਆਦਿ ਲਈ),
ਡਾਟਦਾਰ ਬਣਾਉਣਾ; ਤਹਿਖ਼ਾਨਾ ਬਣਾਉਣਾ; (2)
ਛਾਲ, ਪਲਾਂਘਣ, ਉਛਾਲ, ਉੱਛਲ-ਕੁੱਦ; ਛਾਲ
ਮਾਰਨਾ, ਉਛਲਣਾ ਜਾਂ ਉਛਾਲਣਾ

vaunt (ਵ੍ਾਂਟ) *v n* ਘਮੰਡ ਕਰਨਾ; ਡੀਂਗ, ਸ਼ੇਖੀ,
ਹੰਕਾਰ, ਫੜ੍ਹ

veer (ਵ੍ਿਅ*) *v* ਦਿਸ਼ਾ ਬਦਲਣਾ, ਘੁੰਮਣਾ,
ਘੁਮਾਉਣਾ, ਮੁੜਨਾ, ਰੁਖ ਫੇਰਨਾ, ਪਾਸਾ
ਪਰਤਾਉਣਾ; ਦਿਮਾਗ਼ ਫਿਰਨਾ ਜਾਂ ਫੇਰਨਾ;
(ਨੇਵੀ) ਢਿੱਲਾ ਕਰਨਾ, ਛੱਡਣਾ

vegetable ('ਵੈੱਜਟਅਬਲ) *n a* ਸਾਗ-ਭਾਜੀ,
ਸਬਜ਼ੀ ਤਰਕਾਰੀ; ਸਾਗ-ਭਾਜੀ ਦਾ, ਤਰਕਾਰੀ ਦਾ

vegetarian ('ਵੈਜਿ'ਟੇਅਰਿਅਨ) *n* ਵੈਸ਼ਨੂ,
ਸ਼ਾਕਾਹਾਰੀ

vegetate ('ਵੈਜਿਟੇਇਟ) *v* (ਪੌਦਿਆਂ ਦਾ) ਉੱਗਣਾ,
ਲੱਗਣਾ, ਵਧਣਾ; (ਬੋਲ) ਪਏ-ਪਏ ਜੀਵਨ
ਬਿਤਾਉਣਾ

vehemence ('ਵ੍ੀਅਮਅੰਸ) *n* ਜੋਸ਼, ਜ਼ੋਰ, ਵੇਗ,
ਤੀਬਰਤਾ, ਪ੍ਰਚੰਡਤਾ

vehement ('ਵ੍ੀਅਮਅੰਟ) *a* (ਭਾਵਨਾ, ਵਿਚਾਰ)
ਜੋਸ਼ੀਲੀ, ਧੜੱਲੇਦਾਰ, ਜ਼ੋਰਦਾਰ, ਉਤਸ਼ਾਹੀ;
ਤੀਬਰ, ਤੇਜ਼, ਪ੍ਰਬਲ (ਹਵਾ ਆਦਿ)

vehicle ('ਵ੍ਿਅਕਲ) *n* ਸਵਾਰੀ, ਵਾਹਨ, ਰੱਥ,
ਗੱਡੀ; ਮਾਧਿਅਮ

vehicular (ਵ੍ਿ'ਹਿਕਯੁਲਅ*) *a* ਸਵਾਰੀ ਦਾ;
ਮਾਧਿਅਮ ਰੂਪ

veil (ਵ੍ੇਇਲ) *n v* ਘੁੰਡ, ਪੱਲਾ, ਪਰਦਾ, ਬੁਰਕਾ,
ਨਕਾਬ, ਦੁਪੱਟਾ; ਗ਼ਿਲਾਫ਼; ਓਟ, ਆੜ, ਓਹਲਾ,
ਬਚਾਣਾ; ਘੁੰਡ ਕੱਢਣਾ, ਕੱਜਣਾ, ਲੁਕਾਉਣਾ

vein (ਵ੍ੇਇਨ) *n* ਸਿਰਾ; (ਆਮ ਵਰਤੋਂ ਵਿਚ)
ਨਾੜੀ, ਰਗ, ਲਹਿਰ, ਮੌਜ

velocity (ਵ੍ਿ'ਲੌਸਅਟਿ) *n* ਵੇਗ, ਰਫ਼ਤਾਰ, ਜ਼ੋਰ
ਦੀ ਚਾਲ

velvet ('ਵ੍ੈਲਵਿਟ) *n a* ਮਖਮਲ, ਪੱਲਛ;
ਮਖਮਲੀ, ਕੋਮਲ, ਗੁਦਗੁਦਾ

vend (ਵ੍ੈਂਡ) *v* ਵੇਚਣਾ, ਵਿਕਰੀ ਕਰਨਾ; **~ee**
ਖ਼ਰੀਦਾਰ; **~or** ਵੇਚਣ ਵਾਲਾ, ਫੇਰੀ ਵਾਲਾ,
ਛਾਬੜੀ ਵਾਲਾ

vendetta (ਵ੍ੈਨ'ਡੈੱਟਅ) *n* ਜੱਦੀ ਵੈਰ, ਵੈਰ

venerability ('ਵ੍ੈਨ੍(ਅ)ਰਅ'ਬਿਲਅਟਿ) *n* ਸ਼ਰਧਾ,
ਆਦਰ, ਸਤਿਕਾਰਯੋਗਤਾ

venerable ('ਵ੍ੈਨੱ(ਅ)ਰਅਬਲ) *a* ਆਦਰਯੋਗ,
ਸਤਿਕਾਰਯੋਗ, ਪੂਜਨੀਕ; **~ness**
ਸਤਿਕਾਰਯੋਗਤਾ

venerate ('ਵ੍ੈਨਅਰੇਇਟ) *v* ਸਤਿਕਾਰਨਾ, ਮਾਨਤਾ
ਕਰਨੀ, ਪੂਜਾ ਕਰਨੀ, ਆਦਰ ਕਰਨਾ, ਸਨਮਾਨ
ਕਰਨਾ, ਪੂਜਣਾ

veneration ('ਵ੍ੈਨਅਰੇਇਸ਼ਨ) *n* ਆਦਰ, ਮਾਣ,
ਪੂਜਾ, ਭਗਤੀ

venereal (ਵ੍ਅ'ਨਿਅਰਿਅਲ) *a* ਜਿਨਸੀ; ਲਿੰਗ-

ਰੋਗ ਸਬੰਧੀ, ਗੁਪਤ ਰੋਗ ਸਬੰਧੀ

venery ('ਵੈਨੱਅਰਿ) *n* (ਪ੍ਰ') ਸ਼ਿਕਾਰ; ਵਿਸ਼ੇ-ਭੋਗ, ਕਾਮ-ਭੋਗ

vengeance ('ਵੈਨੱਜਅੰਸ) *n* ਬਦਲਾ, ਵੈਰ

venom ('ਵੈਨੱਅਮ) *n* ਜ਼ਹਿਰ, ਵਿਹੁ, ਵਿਸ; (ਬੋਲ) ਵੈਰ, ਈਰਖਾ; ~ous ਜ਼ਹਿਰੀ, ਵਿਹੁਲਾ, ਵਿਸੈਲਾ, ਜ਼ਹਿਰੀਲਾ

vent (ਵੈਂਟ) *n v* ਵਿਰਲ, ਮੋਰੀ, ਸੁਰਾਖ਼; ਮੇਘਾ; (ਬੋਲ) ਨਿਕਾਸ; ਮੋਰੀ ਕਰਨੀ; ~**age** ਸੁਰਾਖ਼, ਮੋਰੀ, ਗਾਲੀ, ਛੇਕ, ਛਿਦਰ

ventilate ('ਵੈਂਟਿਲੇਇਟ) *v* ਹਵਾ ਨਾਲ ਸ਼ੁੱਧ ਕਰਨਾ, ਹਵਾਦਾਰ ਕਰਨਾ, ਪਰਗਟ ਕਰਨਾ, ਹਵਾੜ੍ਹ ਕੱਢਣਾ

ventilation ('ਵੈਂਟਿ'ਲੇਇਸ਼ਨ) *n* ਹਵਾ ਦੀ ਆਵਾਜਾਈ, ਹਵਾਦਾਰੀ

ventilator ('ਵੈ'ਨਟਿਲੇਇਟਅਾ*) *n* ਰੌਸ਼ਨਦਾਨ, ਵਾਯੂਮਾਰਗ, ਪੰਖਾ

venture ('ਵੈਨੱਚਅਾ*) *n v* ਖ਼ਤਰੇ ਵਾਲਾ ਕੰਮ, ਔਖਾ ਕੰਮ, ਖ਼ਤਰਾ, ਸੰਕਟ; ਹਿੰਮਤ ਕਰਨਾ, ਖ਼ਤਰੇ ਵਿਚ ਪੈਣਾ; ਬਾਜ਼ੀ ਲਾਉਣੀ

venue ('ਵੈਨੱਯੂ) *n* (ਕਾ) ਮੌਕਾ, ਘਟਨਾ ਸਥਾਨ, ਸੰਮੇਲਨ ਸਥਾਨ

Venus ('ਵੀਨਅਸ) *n* ਹੁਸਨ-ਇਸ਼ਕ ਦੀ ਦੇਵੀ; ਸੁੰਦਰੀ, ਰੂਪਵਤੀ, ਹੁਸੀਨਾ; ਸ਼ੁਕੱਰ (ਤਾਰਾ)

veracious (ਵਅ'ਰੇਇਸ਼ਅਸ) *a* ਸੱਚਾ, ਈਮਾਨਦਾਰ, ਸਤਿਵਾਦੀ

veracity (ਵਅ'ਰੈਸਅਟਿ) *n* ਸਚਾਈ, ਯਥਾਰਥਕਤਾ

veranda(h) (ਵਅ'ਰੈਂਡਅ) *n* ਵਰਾਂਡਾ, ਪਸਾਰ

verb (ਵਅਃਬ) *n* ਕਿਰਿਆ (ਵਿਆ); ~**al** ਕਿਰਿਆਵੀ, ਅੱਖਰੀ, ਸ਼ਾਬਦਕ ਜ਼ਬਾਨੀ (ਸਨੇਹਾ); ਸ਼ਾਬਦਕ; ~**ally** ਲਫ਼ਜ਼-ਬਲਫ਼ਜ਼

ਸ਼ਬਦ-ਸ਼ਬਦ; ਜ਼ਬਾਨੀ; ~**atim** ਅੱਖਰ-ਅੱਖਰ, ਸ਼ਾਬਦਕ; ~**ose** ਸ਼ਬਦ-ਬਹੁਤਲਤਾ, ਸ਼ਬਦ-ਅਧਿਕਤਾ, ਸ਼ਬਦ-ਅਡੰਬਰ; ~**osity** ਸ਼ਬਦ-ਅਡੰਬਰ

verdict ('ਵਅਃਡ਼ਿਕਟ) *n* ਅਦਾਲਤੀ ਫ਼ੈਸਲਾ, ਫ਼ਤਵਾ, ਅੰਤਮ ਨਿਰਣਾ

verecund ('ਵੈਰਿਕਅੰਡ) *a* ਸ਼ਰਮਾਕਲ, ਸ਼ਰਮੀਲਾ ਲੱਜਾਵਾਨ

verge (ਵਅਃਜ) *n v* ਕੰਢਾ; ਸਿਰਾ ਝੁਕਣਾ, ਢਲਣਾ (ਕਿਸੇ ਸਿਰੇ ਵੱਲ)

verification ('ਵੈਰਿਫ਼ਿ'ਕੇਇਸ਼ਨ) *n* ਜਾਂਚ, ਪੜਤਾਲ, ਤਸਦੀਕ

verify ('ਵੈਰਿਫ਼ਾਇ) *v* ਨਿਤਾਰਾ ਕਰਨਾ, ਪੜਤਾਲ ਕਰਨੀ, ਸਚਾਈ ਦੀ ਛਾਣਬੀਣ ਕਰਨੀ; ਯਥਾਰਥ ਖੋਜਣਾ; ਮਿਲਾਉਣਾ, ਤਸਦੀਕ ਕਰਨਾ, ਸਹੀ ਕਰਨਾ

verily ('ਵੈਰੱਅਲਿ) *a* ਦਰਅਸਲ, ਸੱਚਮੁੱਚ, ਅਸਲ ਵਿਚ, ਵਾਸਤਵ ਵਿਚ, ਨਿਸ਼ਚੇ ਹੀ, ਅਵੱਸ਼

vermilion (ਵਅ'ਮਿਲਯਅਨ) *n a v* ਸੰਧੂਰ, ਲਾਲ ਰੰਗ; ਸਿੰਗਰਫ਼ੀ, ਸੰਧੂਰੀ; ਸੰਧੂਰ ਲਾਉਣਾ

versatile ('ਵਅਃਸਅਟਾਇਲ) *a* (ਲੇਖਕ) ਬਹੁਮੁਖੀ, ਬਹੁਪੱਖੀ ਪ੍ਰਤਿਭਾਸ਼ਾਲੀ, ਛੇਤੀ ਹੀ ਪਰਿਵਰਤਨਸ਼ੀਲ; ~**ness**, **versatility** ਬਹੁਮੁਖੀ, ਪ੍ਰਤਿਭਾ, ਚਪਲਤਾ, ਅਸਥਿਰਤਾ

verse (ਵਅਃਸ) *n* ਸਲੋਕ ਕਵਿਤਾ; ਕਵਿਤਾਉਣਾ, ਪਦਬੱਧ ਕਰਨਾ, ਕਵਿਤਾ ਕਰਨਾ

versification ('ਵਅਃਸਿਫ਼ਿ'ਕੇਇਸ਼ਨ) *n* ਕਾਵਿ-ਰਚਨਾ, ਕਾਵਿ-ਸਿਰਜਨਾ

versifier ('ਵਅਃਸਿਫ਼ਾਇਅਾ*) *n* ਕਵੀ, ਸ਼ਾਇਰ

versify ('ਵਅਃਸਿਫ਼ਾਇ) *v* ਨਜ਼ਮਾਉਣਾ, ਛੰਦਬੱਧ ਕਰਨਾ, ਕਵਿਤਾ ਰਚਣੀ, ਤੁਕਬੰਦੀ ਕਰਨੀ

version ('ਵ੍ਹਾ:ਸ਼ਨ) *n* ਪਾਠਾਂਤਰ, ਤਰਜਮਾ, ਭਾਸ਼ਾਂਤਰ, ਅਨੁਵਾਦ, ਉਲਥਾ; ਸੰਸਕਰਣ

versus ('ਵ੍ਹਾ:ਸਾਅਸ) *prep* ਟਾਕਰੇ ਉੱਤੇ, ਪ੍ਰਤੀ, ਬਨਾਮ

vertex ('ਵ੍ਹਾ:ਟੈਕਸ) *n* ਟੀਸੀ, ਸਿਰਾ, ਸਿਖਰ, ਚੋਟੀ

vertical ('ਵ੍ਹਾ:ਟਿਕਲ) *n a* ਸਿੱਧੀ (ਰੇਖਾ) ਸਿਖਰਲਾ, ਚੋਟੀ ਦਾ, ਖੜ੍ਹਾ; ~**ly** ਖੜ੍ਹਵੇਂ ਪਾਸੇ, ਖੜ੍ਹੇਤੇ ਢੰਗ ਨਾਲ

vertigo ('ਵ੍ਹਾ:ਟਿਗਾਅਉ) *n* ਘੇਰਨੀ, ਘੁਮਾਟੀ, ਭੁਆਂਟਨੀ, ਭੌਂ, ਚੱਕਰ

very ('ਵ੍ਹੈਰਿ) *a adv* ਅਤੀਅੰਤ, ਅਧਿਕ, ਬਹੁਤ, ਬਹੁਤ ਹੀ, ਅਸਲੀ, ਖ਼ਰਾ, ਠੀਕ, ਸਹੀ, ਸੱਚਾ, ਵਾਸਤਵਿਕ; ਸੰਪੂਰਨ ਰੂਪ ਵਿਚ

vesicotomy ('ਵ੍ਹੈਸਿ'ਕੌਟਅਮਿ) *n* ਨਸਬੰਦੀ, ਮਸਾਨੇ ਦਾ ਉਪਰੇਸ਼ਨ

vessel ('ਵ੍ਹੈਸਲ) *n* ਭਾਂਡਾ, ਪਾਤਰ, ਬਰਤਨ; ਬੇੜੀ; ਕਿਸ਼ਤੀ, ਜਹਾਜ਼; ਨਾੜ, ਵਾਹਿਨੀ; *weaker~* ਅਬਲਾ ਔਰਤ, ਨਾਰੀ

vest ('ਵ੍ਹੈਸਟ) *n v* ਅੰਗੀ, ਚੋਲੀ, ਬੰਡੀ, ਬੁਨੈਣ; ਸਪੁਰਦ ਕਰਨਾ, ਹਵਾਲੇ ਕਰਨਾ; ਕੱਪੜੇ ਪਾਉਣੇ ਜਾਂ ਪੁਆਉਣੇ; ~**in** ਅਧਿਕਾਰ ਵਿਚ ਦੇਣਾ, ਕਬਜ਼ੇ ਵਿਚ ਦੇਣਾ, ਸੌਂਪਣਾ; ~**ed** ਸਥਿਤ, ਨਿਹਿਤ; ~**ing** ਬੁਨੈਟ, ਕਮੀਜ਼ ਤੋਂ ਹੇਠਾਂ ਪਹਿਨਣ ਵਾਲਾ ਵਸਤਰ

veteran ('ਵ੍ਹੈਟ(ਅ)ਰ(ਅ)ਨ) *v a* ਅਨੁਭਵੀ, ਨਿਪੁੰਨ ਤੇ ਕੁਸ਼ਲ ਮਨੁੱਖ; ਸਾਬਕਾ ਫ਼ੌਜੀ; ਪੁਰਾਣਾ ਖੁੰਢ; ਤਜਰਬਾਕਾਰ, ਨਿਪੁੰਨ, ਕੁਸ਼ਲ

veterinary ('ਵ੍ਹੈਟ(ਅ)ਰਿਨ(ਅ)ਰਿ) *a n* ਪਸੂ ਚਿਕਿਤਸਕ

veto ('ਵ੍ਹੀਟਅਉ) *n v* ਰੱਦ ਕਰਨ ਦੀ ਕਿਰਿਆ, ਅਸਵੀਕ੍ਰਿਤੀ ਨਿਖੇਪੀ, ਰੋਕ, ਵੀਟੋ; ਨਿਖੇਪੀ-ਪੱਤਰ; ਨਿਖੇਪੀ ਕਰਨੀ, ਨਾਮਨਜ਼ੂਰ ਕਰਨੀ

vex ('ਵ੍ਹੈਕਸ) *v* ਛੇੜਨਾ, ਤੰਗ ਕਰਨਾ, ਜਿਚ ਕਰਨਾ, ਔਖਾ ਕਰਨਾ; ~**ation** ਪਰੇਸ਼ਾਨੀ, ਚਿੜ੍ਹ, ਤੰਗੀ, ਖਿਝ, ਕਲੇਸ਼

via ('ਵ੍ਹਾਇਅ) *a prep* ਰਾਹੀਂ, ਦੁਆਰਾ, ਬਰਾਸਤਾ

viable ('ਵ੍ਹਾਇਅਬਲ) *a* ਜੀਉਣਯੋਗਾ; ਵਿਚਰਕ

viability ('ਵ੍ਹਾਇਅ'ਬਿਲਅਟਿ) *n* ਜੀਉਣਯੋਗਤਾ, ਜੀਵਨ-ਸਮਰੱਥਾ, ਵਿਚਰਕਤਾ

via media ('ਵ੍ਹਾਇਅ'ਮੀਡ੍ਹਿਅ) *n* ਵਿਚਕਾਰਲਾ ਰਾਹ, ਮੰਧ ਮਾਰਗ

viaticum (ਵ੍ਹਾਇ'ਐਟਿਕਅਮ) *n* ਸਫ਼ਰ-ਖਰਚ, ਭੱਤਾ, ਸਫਰ-ਭੱਤਾ

vibrate (ਵ੍ਹਾਇ'ਬਰੇਇਟ) *v* ਕੰਬਣਾ, ਥੱਰਾਉਣਾ, ਥਰਕਣਾ; ਹਿੱਲਣਾ, ਡੋਲਣਾ, ਲਹਿਰਾਉਣਾ, ਪੈਂਡੁਲਮ ਦਾ ਹਿੱਲਣਾ, ਟਿਕ-ਟਿਕ ਕਰਨਾ

vibration (ਵ੍ਹਾਇ'ਬਰੇਇਸ਼ਨ) *n* ਕਾਂਬਾ, ਥੱਰਾਹਟ, ਥਰਕ, ਲਰਜ਼

vice (ਵ੍ਹਾਇਸ) *n v perp* ਦੁਰਾਚਾਰ, ਭ੍ਰਿਸ਼ਟਤਾ; ਕਲੰਕ, ਦਾਗ਼; ਔਗੁਣ; ਬਦੀ, ਐਬ, ਖ਼ਰਾਬੀ; ਵਿਕਾਰ; ਸ਼ਿਕੰਜੇ ਵਿਚ ਕੱਸਣਾ; ਬਦਲੇ ਵਿਚ; ਉਪ (ਜਿਵੇਂ vice chairman, vice principle ਆਦਿ)

vice versa ('ਵ੍ਹਾਇਸਿ'ਵ੍ਹਾ:ਸਅ) *adv* ਦੂਜੇ ਪਾਸੇ, ਦੂਜੀ ਤਰ੍ਹਾਂ, ਵਿਪਰੀਤ ਤੌਰ ਤੇ, ਇਸ ਦੇ ਉਲਟ

vicinity (ਵ੍ਹਿ'ਸਿਨਅਟਿ) *n* ਨੇੜਤਾ, ਨਜ਼ਦੀਕੀ, ਗੁਆਂਢ, ਪੜੋਸ, ਇਰਦ-ਗਿਰਦ ਦਾ ਇਲਾਕਾ

viciosity, viciousness ('ਵ੍ਹਿਸਿ'ਔਸਅਟਿ, 'ਵ੍ਹਿਸ਼ਿਸਨਿਸ) *n* ਪਾਪ, ਨੀਚਤਾ, ਦੁਸ਼ਟਤਾ, ਬੁਰਾਈ, ਕੁਕਰਮ, ਬਦਕਾਰੀ

vicious ('ਵਿਸ਼ਅਸ) a ਪਾਪੀ, ਨੀਚ, ਦੁਸ਼ਟ, ਬੁਰਾ, ਦੁਰਆਤਮਾ, ਦੁਰਾਚਾਰੀ, ਬਦਕਾਰ, ਐਬੀ, ਖੋਟਾ; ਥੋਥੀ; ਚਿੜਚਿੜਾ, ਦਵੈਸ਼ ਭਰਿਆ

victim ('ਵਿਕਟਿਮ) n ਬਲੀ, ਭੇਟ, ਸ਼ਿਕਾਰ, ਬਲੀ ਦਾ ਬੱਕਰਾ; ~ization ਬਲੀਦਾਨ ਅਤਿਆਚਾਰ, ਦੰਡਣ; ~ize ਸ਼ਿਕਾਰ ਬਣਾਉਣਾ, ਬਲੀ ਦਾ ਬੱਕਰਾ ਬਣਾਉਣਾ

victor ('ਵਿਕਟਅ*) n ਜੇਤੂ, ਵਿਜਈ; ~ious ਵਿਜੇਤਾ, ਫ਼ਤਿਹ ਕਰਨ ਵਾਲਾ; ~y ਜਿੱਤ, ਵਿਜੇ, ਫ਼ਤਿਹ

vide ('ਵਾਇਡੀ) v imp ਹਵਾਲਾ ਦੇਣ ਲਈ ਆਖਣਾ ਜਾਂ ਲਿਖਣਾ, ਸੰਕੇਤ ਵਜੋਂ (ਵੇਖੋ)

viduity (ਵਿ'ਡ੍ਯੂਅਟਿ) n ਵਿਧਵਾਪਣ, ਰੰਡੇਪਾ

vie (ਵਾਇ) v ਬੁਰਦ ਲਾਉਣੀ, ਵਾਰੀ ਲੈਣੀ, ਬਿਦਣਾ, ਮੁਕਾਬਲਾ ਕਰਨਾ, ਬਰਾਬਰੀ ਕਰਨੀ, ਰੀਸ ਕਰਨੀ

view (ਵ੍ਯੂ) n v ਨਿਰੀਖਣ, ਅਵਲੋਕਨ; (ਕਾ') ਮੁਆਇਨਾ; ਦ੍ਰਿਸ਼ਟੀ-ਦਿੱਖ, ਸਮੀਖਿਆ ਕਰਨੀ, ਪਰਖਣਾ; ~point ਦ੍ਰਿਸ਼ਟੀ ਬਿੰਦੂ, ਨੁਕਤਾ-ਨਿਗਾਹ, ਦ੍ਰਿਸ਼ਟੀਕੋਣ; in ~ of ਇਹ ਦੇਖਦੇ ਹੋਏ, ਇਸ ਖ਼ਿਆਲ ਨਾਲ

vigil ('ਵਿਜਿਲ) n ਜਾਗਰਤੀ, ਚੌਂਕਸੀ; ਸਜਗਤਾ; ~ance ਸਾਵਧਾਨੀ, ਚੌਂਕਸੀ, ਹੁਸ਼ਿਆਰੀ, ਖ਼ਬਰਦਾਰੀ; ~ant ਸਾਵਧਾਨ, ਹੁਸ਼ਿਆਰ, ਚੌਂਕਸ

vigorous ('ਵਿਗਅਰਅਸ) a ਜ਼ੋਰਦਾਰ, ਪਰਫੁੱਲੇਦਾਰ, ਪ੍ਰਬਲ, ਸ਼ਕਤੀਵਾਨ, ਤੀਖਣ; ~ness ਸ਼ਕਤੀ, ਬਲ, ਜ਼ੋਰ-ਪਰਫੁੱਲੇਦਾਰੀ, ਪ੍ਰਬਲਤਾ

vigour, vigor ('ਵਿਗਅ*) n ਬਲ, ਸ਼ਕਤੀ, ਜ਼ੋਰ; ਸਜੀਵਤਾ; ਜੀਵਨ ਸ਼ਕਤੀ; ਮਾਨਸਕ ਸ਼ਕਤੀ

vile (ਵਾਇਲ) a (ਪ੍ਰ) ਬੇਕਾਰ, ਨਿਕੰਮਾ; ਨੀਚ, ਕਮੀਨਾ, ਘਟੀਆ; ਦੁਸ਼ਟ, ਪਾਜੀ

vilification ('ਵਿਲਿਫ਼ਿ'ਕੇਇਸ਼ਨ) n ਭੰਡੀ, ਨਿੰਦਾ ਬਦਨਾਮੀ, ਬੁਰਾਈ

vilify ('ਵਿਲਿਫ਼ਾਇ) v ਭੰਡਣਾ, ਬਦਨਾਮੀ ਕਰਨੀ, ਨਿੰਦਣਾ, ਬੁਰਾ ਭਲਾ ਆਖਣਾ

villa ('ਵਿਲਅ) n ਪਿੰਡ ਦਾ ਬੰਗਲਾ ਜਾਂ ਹਵੇਲੀ, ਗ੍ਰਾਮ-ਨਿਵਾਸ

village ('ਵਿਲੀਜ) n ਪਿੰਡ, ਗਿਰਾਂ, ਦੇਹਾਤ; ~r ਪੇਂਡੂ ਗਿਰਾਈਂ, ਦੇਹਾਤੀ

villain ('ਵਿਲਅਨ) n a ਦੁਸ਼ਟ, ਦੁਰਜਨ; ਸ਼ੈਤਾਨ, ਲੁੱਚਾ; ਗੰਵਾਰ

vim (ਵਿਮ) n ਜਾਨ, ਸ਼ਕਤੀ, ਬਲ, ਉਤਸਾਹ

vincible ('ਵਿੰਸਅਬਲ) a ਜਿੱਤਣਯੋਗ, ਸਰ ਕਰਨਯੋਗ

vindicate ('ਵਿੰਡਿਕੇਇਟ) v ਖੋਰੀ, ਖੁਨਸੀ; ਬਦਲਾ ਭਰਿਆ

vindictive ('ਵਿੰ'ਡਿਕਟਿਵ) a ਖੋਰੀ, ਖੁਨਸੀ; ਬਦਲੇ ਭਰਿਆ

vine (ਵਾਇਨ) n ਅੰਗੂਰ ਦੀ ਵੇਲ; ~yard ਅੰਗੂਰਾਂ ਦਾ ਬਾਗ਼; ~ry ਅੰਗੂਰ-ਖੇਤਰ ਅੰਗੂਰਸਤਾਨ

vinegar ('ਵਿਨਿਗਅ*) n ਸਿਰਕਾ; ਖਟਾਸ; ਸਿਰਕਾ ਮਿਲਾਉਣਾ

vintage ('ਵਿੰਟਿਜ) n ਦਾਖ, ਅੰਗੂਰ; ਅੰਗੂਰਾਂ ਦਾ ਝਾੜ; ਵਡੀਆ, ਉੱਤਮ

violate ('ਵਾਇਅਲੇਇਟ) v ਉਲੰਘਣਾ ਕਰਨੀ; ਭ੍ਰਿਸ਼ਟ ਕਰਨਾ, ਦੁਰਵਿਹਾਰ ਕਰਨਾ; ਵਿਘਨ ਪਾਉਣਾ; ਜ਼ਬਰਦਸਤੀ ਕਰਨੀ, ਸਤੀਤਵ ਭੰਗ ਕਰਨਾ

violation ('ਵਾਇਅ'ਲੇਇਸ਼ਨ) n ਉਲੰਘਣਾ, ਖੰਡਨ; ਦੂਸ਼ਨ; ਜ਼ਬਰਦਸਤੀ; ਸਤ ਭੰਗ

violence ('ਵਾਇਅਲਅੰਸ) n ਹਿੰਸਾ, ਤਸ਼ਦੱਦ,

ਉਪੰਦਰ, ਡਾਢਾਪਣ, ਪ੍ਰਚੰਡਤਾ; ਜਬਰਦਸਤੀ

violent ('ਵਾਇਅਲਅੰਟ) *a* ਹਿੰਸਕ ਹਿੰਸਾਤਮਕ, ਹਿੰਸਾਪੂਰਨ ਜਬਰਦਸਤੀ ਵਾਲ਼ਾ; ਪ੍ਰਚੰਡ

violet ('ਵਾਇਅਲਅਟ) *n a* ਬਨਫਸ਼ਾ, ਜਾਮਨੀ ਰੰਗ, ਵੈਂਗਣੀ ਰੰਗ; •ਵੈਂਗਣੀ, ਜਾਮਨੀ

violin ('ਵਾਇਅ'ਲਿਨ) *n* ਸਾਰੰਗੀ, ਵੀਨਾ, ਛੇਤਾਰਾ

virago (ਵਿ'ਰਾਗਾਉ) *n* ਚੰਡੀ, ਵੀਰਾਂਗਣਾਂ, ਮਰਦਾਵੀਂ ਔਰਤ

viral ('ਵਾਇਅਰ(ਅ)ਲ) *a* ਵਿਹੁਲਾ, ਜ਼ਹਿਰੀਲਾ, ਵਿਸੈਲਾ

virgin ('ਵੁਅ:ਜਿਨ) *n a* ਕੰਨਿਆ, ਕੰਜਕ ਕੁਆਰੀ, ਕੁਮਾਰੀ, ਪਵਿੱਤਰ, ਬੇਦਾਗ਼; ~hood, ~ity ਸ਼ੁਧਤਾ, ਪਵਿੱਤਰਤਾ, ਕੁਆਰਾਪਣ

Virgo ('ਵੁਅ:ਰਾਗਉ) *n* ਕੰਨਿਆ ਰਾਸ਼ੀ

virile ('ਵਿਰਾਇਲ) *a* ਮਰਦਾਵਾਂ, ਨਰ, ਹਿਸਟ-ਪੁਸ਼ਟ, ਤਕੜਾ, ਬਲਵਾਨ

virility (ਵਿ'ਰਿਲਅਟਿ) *n* ਵੀਰਜ, ਮਰਦਾਉਪੁਣਾ, ਮਰਦਾਨਗੀ; ਨਰਤਵ, ਪੁਰਸ਼ਾਰਥ

virose ('ਵਾਇਰਅਉਸ) *a* ਵਿਹੁਲਾ, ਵਿਸੈਲਾ, ਜ਼ਹਿਰੀਲੀ; ਬਦਬੂਦਾਰ

virous ('ਵਾਇਰਅਸ) *a* ਵਿਹੁਲਾ, ਵਿਸੈਲਾ, ਜ਼ਹਿਰੀਲਾ

virtual ('ਵੁਅ:ਚੁਅਲ) *a* ਅਮਲੀ, ਅਮਲੀ, ਸੱਚੀ-ਮੁੱਚੀ

virtue ('ਵੁਅ:ਚੂ) *n* ਸਦਾਚਾਰ, ਨੈਤਕਤਾ, ਉੱਤਮਤਾ, ਨੇਕੀ, ਭਲਾਈ; *by* (*in*) *~ of* ਨਾਲ, ਦੇ ਜ਼ੋਰ ਨਾਲ; ਦੇ ਸਦਕੇ, ਦੀ ਬਦੌਲਤ, ਦੇ ਕਾਰਨ

virtuous ('ਵੁਅ:ਚੁਅਸ) *a* ਸਦਾਚਾਰੀ, ਧਰਮਾਤਮਾ, ਨੇਕ ਪਵਿੱਤਰ; ~ness ਸਦਾਚਾਰ, ਸੱਜਣਤਾ, ਧਾਰਮਕਤਾ, ਨੇਕੀ ਭਲਾਈ, ਚੰਗਿਆਈ

virus ('ਵਾਇਅਰਅਸ) *n* ਜ਼ਹਿਰੀਲਾ ਮਾਦਾ, ਵਿਹੁ,

ਵਾਇਰਸ; ਮਲੀਨਤਾ; ਕੁਰੱਤਣ, ਕੜਵਾਹਟ

vis (ਵਿਸ) *n* ਤਾਣ, ਬਲ, ਜ਼ੋਰ, ਸ਼ਕਤੀ

visa ('ਵੀਜ਼ਅ) *n* ਰਾਹਦਾਰੀ, ਵੀਜ਼ਾ

vis-a-vis ('ਵੀਜ਼ਾ'ਵੀ) *n a adv* ਆਮੂਨੇ-ਸਾਮ੍ਹਣੇ ਬੈਠੇ ਵਿਅਕਤੀ, ਸਨਮੁਖ, ਆਮੂਨੇ-ਸਾਮ੍ਹਣੇ; ਵਿਸੈ ਵਿਚ, ਸਬੰਧ ਵਿਚ, ਮੁਕਾਬਲੇ

viscid ('ਵਿਸਿਡ) *a* ਲੇਸਦਾਰ, ਚਿਪਚਿਪ, ਲਿਸਲਿਸਾ, ਲੁਆਬਦਾਰ; ~ity ਚਿਪਚਿਪਾਹਟ

viscose ('ਵਿਸਕਅਉਸ) *n a* ਮਾਵਾ, ਕਲਫ਼, ਮਾਇਆ; ਲੇਸਦਾਰ, ਚਿਪਚਿਪਾ

viscosity (ਵਿ'ਸਕੌਸਅਟਿ) *n* ਲੇਸ, ਲੁਆਬ, ਚਿਪਚਿਪਾਪਣ

visibility ('ਵਿਜ਼ਅ'ਬਿਲਅਟਿ) *n* ਦ੍ਰਿਸ਼ਟਵਾ, ਦ੍ਰਿਸ਼ਮਾਨਤਾ, ਸਪਸ਼ਟਤਾ, ਪ੍ਰਤਖਤਾ

visible ('ਵਿਜ਼ਅਬਲ) *a* ਦਿਸਦਾ, ਦ੍ਰਿਸ਼ਟੀਗੋਚਰ, ਦ੍ਰਿਸ਼ਮਾਨ, ਜ਼ਾਹਰ, ਪ੍ਰਤਖ, ਪਰਗਟ, ਵਿਅਕਤ

vision ('ਵਿਯਨ) *n v* ਦ੍ਰਿਸ਼ਟੀ, ਨਜ਼ਰ, ਨਿਗਾਹ; ਝਲਕ, ਝਾਕੀ, ਆਭਾਸ; ਸੁਪਨਾ, ਮ੍ਰਿਗਾ-ਤ੍ਰਿਸ਼ਨਾ, ਮਾਇਆ; ਸੁਪਨਾ ਦੇਖਣਾ, ਕਲਪਨਾ ਕਰਨਾ; ~ary ਮਾਇਆਗ੍ਰਸਤ ਗ਼ੈਰ-ਅਮਲੀ, ਕਾਲਪਨਕ, ਖ਼ਿਆਲੀ; ~less ਦ੍ਰਿਸ਼ਟੀਹੀਨ, ਅੰਨ੍ਹਾ, ਜੋਤਹੀਨ

visit ('ਵਿਜ਼ਿਟ) *n v* ਮੁਲਾਕਾਤ, ਦਰਸ਼ਨ, ਭੇਟ, ਮੇਲ; ਦੌਰਾ, ਫੇਰੀ; ਨਿਰੀਖਣ, ਮੁਆਇਨਾ; ਮੁਲਾਕਾਤ ਕਰਨੀ, ਦਰਸ਼ਨ ਕਰਨਾ; ਮਿਲਣਾ; ~ation ਦੌਰਾ, ਮੁਆਇਨਾ; ਰੱਬੀ ਮਾਰ, ਅਜ਼ਾਬ; ~ing ਮੁਲਾਕਾਤ, ਦਰਸ਼ਨ, ਨਿਰੀਖਣ, ਮੁਆਇਨਾ; ~ing card ਮੁਲਾਕਾਤੀ-ਪੱਤਰ; ~ing hours ਮੁਲਾਕਾਤੀ ਸਮਾਂ; ~ing professor ਮਹਿਮਾਨ ਪ੍ਰੋਫ਼ੈਸਰ; ~or ਮੁਲਾਕਾਤੀ, ਦਰਸ਼ਕ, ਮਹਿਮਾਨ; ~ors gallery ਦਰਸ਼ਕ-ਗੈਲਰੀ

vista ('ਵ੍ਹਿਸਟਾ) *n* ਦ੍ਰਿਸ਼, ਪਹਿਲਾਂ ਵਾਪਰ ਚੁੱਕੀਆਂ ਘਟਨਾਵਾਂ ਦੀ ਝਾਕੀ, ਦੂਰ-ਝਾਤ

visual ('ਵ੍ਹਿਜ਼ੂਅਲ) *a* ਦ੍ਰਿਸ਼ਟੀਗਤ, ਦ੍ਰਿਸ਼ਟੀ ਸਬੰਧੀ, ਦਰਸ਼ਨੀ; **~ity** ਨਜ਼ਰ, ਦ੍ਰਿਸ਼ਟੀ; **~ization** ਸਪਸ਼ਟੀਕਰਨ, ਸਪਸ਼ਟ ਦਰਸ਼ਨ; ਦ੍ਰਿਸ਼ਟੀਗਤ ਚਿਤਰਣ; **~ize** ਦ੍ਰਿਸ਼ਟੀਗੋਚਰ ਕਰਨ; ਬਾਹਰਲਾ ਰੂਪ ਦੇਖਣਾ, ਵਿਅਕਤ ਕਰਨ

vital ('ਵਾਇਟਲ) *a* (in *pl*) ਜਾਨਦਾਰ, ਜੀਵਨਮਈ, ਮਹੱਤਵਪੂਰਨ, ਅਤੀ ਲੋੜੀਂਦਾ, ਨਾਜ਼ੁਕ ਮਾਰਮਕ; **~ity** ਸਜੀਵਤਾ, ਜੀਵਨ ਤੱਤ, ਪ੍ਰਾਣ-ਸ਼ਕਤੀ, ਜਾਨ ਜੀਵਨ ਸ਼ਕਤੀ

vitiate ('ਵ੍ਹਿਸ਼ੀਏਇਟ) *v* ਵਿੱਟਣਾ, ਦੂਸ਼ਤ ਕਰਨਾ, ਭ੍ਰਿਸ਼ਟ ਕਰਨਾ, ਵਿਗਾੜਨਾ, ਖ਼ਰਾਬ ਕਰਨਾ

viva ('ਵੀਵ੍ਹਾ) ਜ਼ਿੰਦਾਬਾਦ, ਜੁਗ ਜੁਗ ਜੀਵੇ!

vivacious (ਵਿ'ਵ੍ਹੇਇਸ਼ਅਸ) *a* ਰਹਿਣਾ, ਮੌਜੀ, ਸਜੀਵ, ਪ੍ਰਫੁੱਲਤ, ਉੱਲਾਸਪੂਰਨ, ਉਤਸ਼ਾਹਪੂਰਨ, ਜੋਸ਼ੀਲਾ, ਜ਼ਿੰਦਾਦਿਲ; **~ness** ਉਤਸਾਹ, ਜ਼ਿੰਦਾਦਿਲੀ

vivacity (ਵਿ'ਵ੍ਹੈਸਅਟਿ) *n* ਜ਼ਿੰਦਾਦਿਲੀ, ਸਜੀਵਤਾ, ਉਤਸਾਹ, ਪ੍ਰਫੁੱਲਤਾ, ਜੋਸ਼

viva voce ('ਵ੍ਹਾਇਵ੍ਹਾ'ਵ੍ਹਾਉਸਿ) *n a adv* ਜ਼ਬਾਨੀ ਪਰੀਖਿਆ, ਮੌਖਿਕ ਪਰੀਖਿਆ; ਜ਼ਬਾਨੀ, ਮੌਖਿਕ; ਮੌਖਿਕ ਤੌਰ ਤੇ

vive, viva (ਵੀਵ੍ਹ) *(F) int* ਜ਼ਿੰਦਾਬਾਦ! ਅਮਰ ਰਹੇ!

vivid ('ਵ੍ਹਿਵ੍ਹਿਡ) *a* ਜੀਉਂਦੀ, ਸਜੀਵ; ਸਪਸ਼ਟ; ਭੜਕੀਲਾ, ਚਟਕੀਲਾ, ਚਮਕਦਾਰ; ਬਲਸ਼ਾਲੀ, ਸ਼ਕਤੀਸ਼ਾਲੀ; **~ity**, **~ness** ਜ਼ਿੰਦਾਦਿਲੀ, ਸਜੀਵਤਾ; ਸਪਸ਼ਟਤਾ, ਚਟਕ-ਮਟਕ, ਭੜਕ

vivify ('ਵ੍ਹਿਵ੍ਹਿਫ਼ਾਈ) *v* ਜੀਵਨ ਦੇਣਾ, ਜੀਵਤ ਕਰਨਾ, ਸਜੀਵ ਕਰਨਾ, ਜਾਨ ਪਾਉਣੀ, ਪ੍ਰਾਣ

ਪਾਉਣੇ

vocable ('ਵ੍ਹਾਉਕਲਅਬਲ) *n* ਨਾਉਂ; ਪਦ, ਸ਼ਬਦ, ਬੋਲ

vocabulary (ਵ੍ਹਅ(ਉ)'ਕੈਬਯੁਲਅਰਿ) *n* ਸ਼ਬਦਾਵਲੀ, ਸ਼ਬਦ-ਸੰਗ੍ਰਹ; ਸ਼ਬਦ-ਕੋਸ਼

vocal ('ਵ੍ਹਾਉਕਲ) *a n* ਉਚਰਤ, ਵਾਚਕ; ਸਵਰ, ਉਚਾਰਨ; **~cord** ਸਵਰ-ਤੰਤੂ

vocation (ਵ੍ਹਅ(ਉ)'ਕੇਇਸ਼ਨ) *n* ਪੁਕਾਰ, ਮੁਨਾਦੀ, ਬੁਲਾਵਾ; ਪੇਸ਼ਾ, ਜੀਵਨ ਨਿਰਬਾਹ; **~al** ਪੇਸ਼ੇ ਜਾਂ ਰੁਜ਼ਗਾਰ ਸਬੰਧੀ, ਵਿਵਸਾਇਕ

vociferate (ਵ੍ਹਅ(ਉ)'ਸਿੱਫ਼ਅਰੇਇਟ) *v* ਚਿਚਿਆਉਣਾ, ਕੂਕਣਾ, ਕਿਲਕਾਰੀਆਂ ਮਾਰਨੀਆਂ, ਚੀਕਣਾ, ਚਿਲਾਉਣਾ, ਰੌਲਾ ਪਾਉਣਾ

vogue (ਵ੍ਹਾਉਗ) *n* ਚਾਲ, ਦਸਤੂਰ, ਰਿਵਾਜ; *in~* ਪ੍ਰਚਲਤ ਫ਼ੈਸ਼ਨ ਵਿਚ, ਵਰਤੋਂ ਵਿਚ

voice ('ਵ੍ਹੋਇਸ) *n v* ਬਾਣੀ, ਧੁਨੀ, ਸ਼ਬਦ, ਬੋਲ, ਅਵਾਜ਼; ਆਖਣਾ, ਬੋਲਣਾ, ਕਹਿਣਾ; ਰਾਇ ਦੇਦੀ, ਵਿਚਾਰ ਜ਼ਾਹਰ ਕਰਨਾ; *active~* ਕਰਤਰੀ ਵਾਚ; *with one~* ਸਰਬ ਸੰਮਤੀ ਨਾਲ, ਇਕ ਮੱਤ ਹੋ ਕੇ

void (ਵ੍ਹੋਇਡ) *a n v* ਖ਼ਾਲੀ, ਸੁੰਨ, ਵੀਰਾਨ, ਸੁੰਨਾ, ਨਾਜਾਇਜ਼; ਨਿਸਫਲ, ਨਿਰਥਕ; *null and~* ਰੱਦ, ਮਨਸੂਖ

volcano (ਵ੍ਹੋੱਲ'ਕੇਇਨਅਉ) *n* ਜੁਆਲਾਮੁਖੀ ਪਹਾੜ

volition (ਵ੍ਹਅ(ਉ)'ਲਿਸ਼ਨ) *n* ਸੰਕਲਪ; ਇੱਛਾ-ਸ਼ਕਤੀ, ਕਾਮਨ-ਸ਼ਕਤੀ; ਮਰਜੀ, ਪਸੰਦ

volte ('ਵ੍ਹੋਲਟਿ) *n* ਪੱਤਰਤ, ਪੱਤਰੇਬਾਜੀ; **~face** ਪਾਸਾ ਬਦਲੀ, ਪਲਟ; (ਸਿਆਸਤ ਵਿਚ) ਪਾਸਾ ਬਦਲਣ, ਉਲਟਾ, ਪੱਤਰਾ

volume ('ਵ੍ਹੋਲਯੂਮ) *n* ਥੀੜ, ਗ੍ਰੰਥ, ਸੈਂਚੀ; ਭਾਗ, ਖੰਡ, ਗ੍ਰੰਥ-ਖੰਡ, ਜਿਲਦ, ਪੁਸਤਕਾਂ ਦਾ ਪ੍ਰਾਚੀਨ

ਰੂਪ; ਘਟਫਲ, ਆਇਤਨ, ਜਸਾਮਤ, ਸਮਾਈ, ਘਟਤਾ; ਮਾਤਰਾ, ਰਾਸ਼ੀ

voluminous (ਵ੍ਯਾ'ਲ੍ਯੂਮਿਨਸ) *a* ਕੁੰਡਲਦਾਰ, ਪੇਚਦਾਰ, ਚੱਕਰਦਾਰ; ਕਈ ਖੰਡਾਂ ਦਾ, ਅਨੇਕ ਹਿੱਸਿਆਂ ਦਾ; ਵਿਸਤਾਰਮਈ, ਲੰਮਾ-ਚੌੜਾ

voluntarily ('ਵ੍ਹੋਲਅੰਟ(ਅ)ਰਿਲਿ) *adv* ਮਰਜ਼ੀ ਨਾਲ, ਆਪਣੇ, ਆਪ, ਮਨ ਤੋਂ, ਸਵੈਇੱਛਾ ਪੂਰਵਕ

voluntary ('ਵ੍ਹੋਲਅੰਟ(ਅ)ਰਿ) *n a* ਸਵੈਇੱਛਤ, ਮਨ-ਮਰਜ਼ੀ ਦਾ

volunteer ('ਵ੍ਹੋਲਅੰ'ਟਿਅਰ*) *n v* ਸਵੈਸੇਵਕ; ਸਵੈਇੱਛਕ ਸੈਨਾ, ਵਲੰਟੀਅਰ; ਬਿਨਾ ਮੰਗਿਆਂ ਦੇਣਾ, ਅਰਪਣ ਕਰਨਾ

voluptuary (ਵ੍ਯਾ'ਲਅੱਪਟ੍ਯੂਅਰਿ) *n a* ਵਿਸ਼ਈ, ਵਿਲਾਸੀ, ਭੋਗੀ, ਕਾਮੀ, ਵਿਤਕਾਰੀ, ਅੱਯਾਸ਼

voluptuous (ਵ੍ਯਾ'ਲਅੱਪਚੁਅਸ) *a* ਐਸ਼ ਭਰਿਆ, ਕਾਮਕ, ਵਾਸ਼ਨਾਮਈ

volution (ਵ੍ਯਾ'ਲੂਸ਼ਨ) *n* ਵਲ, ਵਲੇਵਾਂ, ਵਲਾਵਾਂ, ਕੁੰਡਲੀ, ਚੱਕਰ, ਲਪੇਟ

vomit ('ਵੌਮਿਟ) *n v* ਕੈ, ਉੱਲਟੀ, ਉਪਰਛੱਲ (ਆਉਣੀ)

voracious (ਵ੍ਯਾ'ਰੇਇਸ਼ਅਸ) *a* ਹਾਬੜਿਆ, ਭੁੱਖਾ, ਭੁੱਖੜ, ਖਾਊ ਪੇਟੂ

vote (ਵ੍ਯਅਉਟ) *n v* ਮੱਤ; ਵੋਟ; ਰਾਇ, ਸੰਮਤੀ, ਵੋਟ ਪਾਉਣੀ, ਰਾਇ ਦੇਣੀ ਮੱਤ ਦੇਣਾ; ਵਿਧਾਨ ਬਣਾਉਣਾ; ~of censure ਨਿੰਦਾ ਪ੍ਰਸਤਾਵ; *casting~* ਨਿਰਣਾਇਕ ਵੋਟ; ~*r* ਵੋਟਰ, ਮੱਤਦਾਤਾ

voting ('ਵ੍ਯਅਉਟ) ਮੱਤਦਾਨ

vouch (ਵ੍ਯਾਉਚ) *v* ਪੁਸ਼ਟੀ ਕਰਨੀ, ਸਾਖੀ ਭਰਨੀ, ਗਵਾਹੀ ਦੇਣੀ; ਜ਼ਮਾਨਤ ਦੇਣੀ, ਜ਼ਾਮਨ ਹੋਣਾ; ~er ਪ੍ਰਮਾਣ-ਪੱਤਰ, ਆਧਾਰ-ਪੱਤਰ, ਬੀਚਕ, ਖ਼ਰਚ ਦਾ ਕਾਗ਼ਜ਼, ਵਾਉਚਰ

vouchsafe (ਵ੍ਯਾਉਚ'ਸੇਇਫ਼) *n v* ਕਿਰਪਾ ਕਰਨੀ, ਦਇਆ ਕਰਨੀ; ਮਨਜ਼ੂਰ ਕਰਨਾ, ਮੰਨ ਲੈਣਾ, ਕਿਰਪਾ ਪੂਰਵਕ ਦੇ ਦੇਣਾ

vow (ਵ੍ਯਾਉ) *n v* ਮੰਨੌਤ, ਸੁੱਖਣਾ, ਸੰਕਲਪ; ਵਾਅਦਾ, ਪ੍ਰਤਿੱਗਿਆ, ਪ੍ਰਣ, ਇਕਰਾਰ, ਵਚਨ; ਸੰਕਲਪ ਕਰਨਾ, ਪ੍ਰਤੀਗਿਆ ਕਰਨੀ, ਪ੍ਰਣ ਕਰਨਾ

vowel ('ਵ੍ਯਾਉ(ਅ)ਲ) *n* ਸਵਰ, ਅ, ਬ, ਅਥਾਤ a, e, i, o, u

vox populi ('ਵ੍ਹੋਕਸ'ਪੋਪਯੂਲਿ) (*L*) *n* ਲੋਕਾਂ ਦੀ ਅਵਾਜ਼, ਜਨਤਾ ਦੀ ਰਾਇ

voyage ('ਵ੍ਹੋਇਇਜ) *n v* ਜਲ-ਯਾਤਰਾ; ਸਮੁੰਦਰ ਦੀ ਯਾਤਰਾ; ਜਲ-ਯਾਤਰਾ ਕਰਨੀ, ਲੰਮਾ ਸਫ਼ਰ ਕਰਨਾ

vulgar ('ਵ੍ਯਅੱਲਗਾਅ*) *a* ਅਸ਼ਲੀਲ, ਗੰਵਾਰ, ਪੇਂਡੂ ਅਸ਼ਿਸ਼ਟ, ਦੇਹਾਤੀ

vulnerability,   vulnerableness ('ਵ੍ਯਅੱਲਨ(ਅ)ਰਅ'ਬਿਲਅਟਿ, 'ਵ੍ਯਅੱਲਨ(ਅ)ਰ ਅਬਲਨਿਸ) *n* ਨਿਰਬਲਤਾ, ਦੁਰਬਲਤਾ

vulnerable ('ਵ੍ਯਅੱਲਨਅਰਅਬਲ) *a* ਕਮਜ਼ੋਰ, ਆਲੋਚਨਾਯੋਗ, ਸਮੀਖਿਆਯੋਗ

vulture ('ਵ੍ਯਅੱਲਚਅ*) *n* ਗਿਰਝ, ਗਿੱਧ; ਲੋਭੀ ਆਦਮੀ

vulva ('ਵ੍ਯਅੱਵਅ) *n* ਭਗਾ-ਦੁਆਰ, ਯੋਨੀ, ਜਟਨ-ਅੰਗ

W

W, w ('ਡਅੱਬਲਯੂ) *n* ਰੋਮਨ ਵਰਨਮਾਲਾ ਦਾ ਤੇਈਵਾਂ ਅੱਖਰ

wacky ('ਵੈਕਿ) *a n* (ਅਪ) ਸਨਕੀ, **ਖ਼ਬਤੀ** (ਬੰਦਾ)

wafer ('ਵੇਇਫ਼ਾ*) *n v* ਪੇਪੜੀ, ਪਾਪੜ, ਪਤਲਾ ਬਿਸਕੁਟ

wage ('ਵੇਇਜ) *n v* ਦਿਹਾੜੀ, ਉਜਰਤ, ਮਿਹਨਤਾਨਾ, ਮਜ਼ਦੂਰੀ; ਪੁਰਸਕਾਰ; ਬਾਜ਼ੀ ਲਾਉਣਾ, ਦਾਉ ਲਾਉਣਾ

waggery ('ਵੈਗਅਰਿ) *n* ਖਿੱਲੀ, ਠੱਠਾ, ਹਾਸਾ-ਮਜ਼ਾਕ, ਵਿਦੂਸ਼ਕਤਾ

wag(g)on ('ਵੈਗਅਨ) *n* ਮਾਲ ਗੱਡੀ ਦਾ ਡੱਬਾ; ਛਕੜਾ, ਗੱਡਾ

wail (ਵੇਇਲ) *n v* ਵਿਰਲਾਪ, ਕੁਰਲਾਹਟ, ਵੈਣ, ਰੁਦਨ; ਵਿਰਲਾਪ ਕਰਨਾ, ਰੁਦਨ ਕਰਨਾ, ਚੀਕਣਾ, ਰੋਣਾ ਪਿੱਟਣਾ, ਮਾਤਮ ਕਰਨਾ

waist (ਵੇਇਸਟ) *n* ਲੱਕ, ਕਮਰ, ਵਿਚਾਲਾ; ਕਮਰਬੰਦ, ਮੇਖਲਾ, ਚੋਲੀ, ਅੰਗੀ; ~**cloth** ਧੋਤੀ, ਲੁੰਗੀ, ਲੰਗੋਟੀ; ~**coat** ਕੁੜਤੀ, ਵਾਸਕਟ

wait (ਵੇਇਟ) *v n* ਤੱਕਣਾ, ਰਾਹ ਦੇਖਣਾ, ਵਾਟ ਜੋਹਣਾ; ਠਹਿਰਨਾ, ਰੁਕਣਾ; ਆਸ ਕਰਨੀ, ਆਸਰਾ ਤਕਣਾ; ਚਿਰ ਲਾਉਣਾ, ਉਡੀਕ, ਨਿਗਰਾਨੀ, ਗੁਪਤ ਥਾਂ; ਦੇਰੀ, ਚਿਰ; ~**er** ਬੈਰਾ, ਖਿਦਮਤਗਾਰ, ਸੇਵਾ ਕਰਨ ਵਾਲਾ ਆਦਮੀ, ਉਡੀਕਤ ਵਾਲਾ ਆਦਮੀ

wake (ਵੇਇਕ) *n v* (1) ਜਾਗਰਤੀ; ਜਗਰਾਤਾ; ਪਦ-ਚਿੰਨ੍ਹ; ਜਾਗਣਾ; ਜਗਾਉਣਾ, ਉਠਾਉਣਾ, ਸਚੇਤ ਰਹਿਣਾ

walk (ਵੋਕ) *n v* ਟੋਰ, ਚਾਲ, ਗਮਨ; ਚੁਹਲ ਕਦਮੀ; ਘੁੰਮਣ-ਫਿਰਨ, ਹਵਾ ਖੋਰੀ; ਸੈਰਗਾਹ; ਟਹਿਲਣਾ, ਚੱਲਣਾ, ਭੁਮਣ ਕਰਨਾ, ਘੁੰਮਣਾ, ਗਸ਼ਤ ਕਰਨੀ, ਸੈਰ ਕਰਨੀ; ਵਿਹਾਰ ਕਰਨਾ; ~**out** ਸਭਾ-ਤਿਆਗ; ~**way** ਰਾਹ, ਮਾਰਗ, ਰਸਤਾ, ਪਗਡੰਡੀ; ~**ing** ਟੁਰਨ ਸਬੰਧੀ, ਟਹਿਲਣ ਬਾਰੇ

wall (ਵੋਲ) *n v* ਕੰਧ, ਦੀਵਾਰ, ਭਿੱਤੀ; ਕਿਲ੍ਹਾ, ਮੋਰਚਾਬੰਦੀ, ਕਿਲ੍ਹਾਬੰਦੀ; ਕੰਧ ਖੜੀ ਕਰਨੀ ਜਾਂ ਖਿੱਚਣੀ

wallet ('ਵੱਲਿਟ) *n* (ਸਫ਼ਰੀ) ਝੋਲਾ, ਥੈਲਾ, ਥੈਲੀ; ਚਮੜੇ ਦੀ ਪੇਟੀ ਜਾਂ ਬਟੂਆ

walnut ('ਵੋਲਨਅੱਟ) *n* ਅਖਰੋਟ

wamble ('ਵੱਬੱਲ) *n v* ਕੰਬਣਾ, ਥਰਥਰਾਹਟ, ਕੰਬਣਾ, ਥਰਥਰਾਉਣਾ; ਚਿੱਤ ਕੱਚਾ ਹੋਣਾ

wand (ਵੌਂਡ) *n* ਡੰਡਾ, ਸੋਟਾ; ਜਾਦੂ ਦਾ ਡੰਡਾ, ਝੁਰਲੂ

wander ('ਵੌਂਡਅ*) *v* ਵਿਚਰਨਾ, ਭੁਮਣ ਕਰਨ, ਘੁਮੰਣਾ, ਭੌਂਦੇ ਫਿਰਨ, ਭਟਕਣਾ, ਮਾਰੇ-ਮਾਰੇ ਫਿਰਨਾ; ਡੋਲਣਾ; ਬੇ-ਸਿਰ ਪੈਰ ਬੋਲਣਾ; ~**lust** ਅਵਾਰਗੀ ਦਾ ਚਸਕਾ

wane (ਵੇਇਨ) *n v* ਕਮੀ, ਘਾਟਾ, ਉਤਾਰ, ਹ੍ਰਾਸ; ਖੀਣ ਹੋਣਾ, ਘੈ ਹੋਣਾ, ਢਲ ਜਾਣਾ

want (ਵੌਂਟ) *n v* ਮੰਗ, ਇੱਛਾ, ਭੁਤੂ, ਮੁਥਾਜੀ, ਅਣਹੋਂਦ, ਅਭਾਵ, ਘਾਟਾ, ਕਮੀ, ਅਵਸ਼ਕੰਤਾ; ਦਲਿੱਦਰ, ਗ਼ਰੀਬੀ; ਜ਼ਰੂਰੀ ਲੋੜ; ਲੋੜੀਂਦੀ ਚੀਜ਼; ਚਾਹੁਣਾ, ਮੰਗਣਾ, ਕਾਮਨਾ ਕਰਨੀ ਅਭਾਵ ਹੋਣਾ, ਘਟਣਾ; ਲੋੜ ਹੋਣੀ

wanton ('ਵੌਂਟਅਨ) *n a v* ਬਹੁਤ ਕਾਮੀ, ਅਵਾਰਾ; ਲੁੱਚਾ; ਸਨਕੀ, ਬੇਲਗਾਮ, ਸ਼ੋਖ, ਚੰਚਲ, ਚਪਲ, ਕ੍ਰੀੜਾ-ਪ੍ਰਿਅ; ਕਲੋਲ ਕਰਨਾ, ਕ੍ਰੀੜਾ ਕਰਨਾ, ਵਿਹਰ ਕਰਨਾ, ਅਵਾਰਾ ਫਿਰਨਾ; ਛੇੜਨਾ

war (ਵੋ*) *n v* ਸੰਗ੍ਰਾਮ, ਰਣ, ਜੁੱਧ, ਜੰਗ, ਲੜਾਈ; ਜੰਗ ਲੜਨਾ, ਲੜਾਈ ਕਰਨੀ; **~fare** ਜੁੱਧ, ਸੰਗ੍ਰਾਮ, ਲੜਾਈ; **~ship** ਜੰਗੀ ਜਹਾਜ਼; **civil~** ਖ਼ਾਨਾਜੰਗੀ, ਘਰੇਲੂ ਜੁੱਧ, ਗ੍ਰਹਿ ਜੁੱਧ; **cold~** ਸੀਤ ਜੁੱਧ, ਠੰਢੀ ਜੰਗ

ward (ਵੋਡ) *n v* ਰੱਖਿਆ, ਨਿਗਰਾਨੀ, ਜ਼ਿੰਮਾ, ਚੌਕੀਦਾਰ, ਇਹਾਤਾ, ਹਲਕਾ; ਨਿਗਰਾਨੀ ਰੱਖਣੀ; ਪਹਿਰਾ ਦੇਣਾ, ਚੌਕੀਦਾਰੀ ਕਰਨੀ; **~off** ਬਚਾਉ ਕਰਨਾ, ਰੋਕਥਾਮ ਕਰਨਾ; **~robe** ਕੱਪੜੇ ਰੱਖਣ ਵਾਲੀ ਅਲਮਾਰੀ; ਵਸਤਰ, ਲਿਬਾਸ; **~room** ਜੰਗੀ ਜਹਾਜ਼ ਵਿਚ ਅਫ਼ਸਰ ਦਾ ਕਮਰਾ; **~en** ਰਖਵਾਲਾ ਜਾਂ ਨਿਗ੍ਰਾਬਾਨ; ਛਾਤਰਾਵਾਸ ਦਾ ਅਧਿਅਕਸ਼, ਪ੍ਰਬੰਧਕ, ਨਿਗਰਾਨ

ware (ਵੇਅ*) *n a v* ਭਾਂਡੇ, ਬਰਤਨ; ਪਦਾਰਥ; ਸੌਦਾ, ਸੌਦਾ-ਪੱਤਾ, ਸਾਮਾਨ; **~house** ਮਾਲ ਗੁਦਾਮ, ਮਾਲਖ਼ਾਨਾ, ਭੰਡਾਰ

warm (ਵੋਮ) *a v n* ਨਿੱਘਾ, ਗਰਮ, ਕੋਸਾ; ਉਤਸਾਹੀ, ਸਰਗਰਮ, ਜੋਸ਼ੀਲਾ; ਸਜੀਵ, ਭੜਕਾਉਣਾ, ਭੜਕਣਾ; ਉਕਸਾਉਣਾ; ਤੱਤਾ ਹੋਣਾ, ਧੁੱਪ ਲੁਆਉਣੀ; ਸੰਵੇਦਨਸ਼ੀਲ ਹੋਣਾ ਜਾਂ ਕਰਨਾ; ਗਰਮੀ, ਤਾਪ, ਤਪਸ਼

warn (ਵੋਨ) *v* ਸਾਵਧਾਨ ਕਰਨਾ, ਸਚੇਤ ਕਰਨਾ, ਚੇਤਾਵਣੀ ਦੇਣਾ, ਸੂਚਨਾ ਦੇਣਾ; **~ing** ਚੇਤਾਵਣੀ, ਤਾੜਨਾ, ਇਤਲਾਹ, ਆਗਾਹੀ

warrant ('ਵੌਰੰਟ) *n v* ਅਧਿਕਾਰ-ਪੱਤਰ, ਆਦੇਸ਼-ਪੱਤਰ, ਫ਼ਰਮਾਨ, ਹੁਕਮਨਾਮਾ; ਸਨਦ; ਜ਼ਮਾਨਤ; ਨਿਸਚਾ ਕਰਨਾ; ਵਿਸ਼ਵਾਸ ਦੁਆਉਣਾ; ਸੰਭਾਲਟਾ,

ਸਹਾਰਾ ਦੇਣਾ, ਥੰਮ੍ਹਣਾ; **~y** ਇਕ ਤਰ੍ਹਾਂ ਦੀ ਗਾਰੰਟੀ; ਅਧਿਕਾਰ

warrior ('ਵੌਰਿਅ*) *n* ਸੂਰਬੀਰ; ਲੜਾਕੀ ਕੌਮ, ਜੁੱਧਪ੍ਰਿਯ

wary ('ਵੇਅਰਿ) *a* ਚਤਰ, ਸਾਵਧਾਨ, ਖ਼ਬਰਦਾਰ, ਚੌਕਸ, ਹੁਸ਼ਿਆਰ, ਚੁਕੰਨਾ

wash (ਵੌਸ਼) *n v* ਧੋਣ, ਧੁਆਈ; ਧੋਣਾ, ਨਹਾਉਣਾ, ਧੋ ਕੇ ਸਾਫ਼ ਕਰਨਾ, ਹੰਗਾਲਣਾ; **~basin** ਚਿਲਮਚੀ; **~erman** ਧੋਬੀ; **~erwoman** ਧੋਬਣ

wasp (ਵੌਸਪ) *n* ਭਰਿੰਡ, ਧਮੂੜੀ, ਬੱਰ

wastage ('ਵੇਇਸਟਿਜ) *n* ਫ਼ਜ਼ੂਲਖ਼ਰਚੀ, ਨੁਕਸਾਨ, ਹਾਨੀ; ਨਾਸ, ਉਜਾੜਾ, ਬਰਬਾਦੀ

waste (ਵੇਇਸਟ) *a v n* ਵੀਰਾਨ, ਉਜਾੜ; ਨਿਕੰਮੀ; ਬਰਬਾਦ, ਨਸ਼ਟ, ਰਹਿੰਦ-ਖੂੰਹਦ; ਉੜਾ ਦੇਣਾ, ਫ਼ਜ਼ੂਲ ਖ਼ਰਚੀ ਕਰਨੀ; ਦੁਰਬਲ ਹੋਣਾ; ਕੂੜਾ-ਕਰਕਟ, ਲੀਰਾਂ; ਫ਼ਜ਼ੂਲ-ਖ਼ਰਚੀ; **~land** ਬੰਜਰ ਧਰਤੀ, ਵੀਰਾਨ ਧਰਤੀ; **~paper basket** ਰੱਦੀ ਦੀ ਟੋਕਰੀ

watch (ਵੌਚ) *n v* ਘੜੀ; ਜਗਰਾਤਾ; ਸਾਵਧਾਨੀ, ਰੱਖਿਆ, ਨਿਗਰਾਨੀ, ਪਹਿਰਾ, ਚੌਕੀ; ਪਹਿਰਾ ਦੇਣਾ, ਜਾਗਦੇ ਰਹਿਣਾ, ਚੌਕਸ ਹੋਣਾ; ਰਾਤ ਜਾਗਣਾ, ਜਗਰਾਤਾ ਕਰਨਾ; **~and ward** ਪਹਿਰਾ ਚੌਕੀ; **~dog** ਰਾਖਾ ਕੁੱਤਾ; ਨਿਗਰਾਨ, ਰਖਵਾਲ; **~man** ਰਾਖਾ, ਪਹਿਰੇਦਾਰ ਚੌਕੀਦਾਰ; **~tower** ਅਟਾਰੀ; **~word** (ਸੈਨਕ ਪਹਿਰੇ ਲਈ) ਸੰਕੇਤ ਸ਼ਬਦ; ਨਾਰਾ; **on the~** ਖ਼ਬਰਦਾਰ; **~ful** ਖ਼ਬਰਦਾਰ, ਚੌਕਸ; **~fulness** ਚੌਕਸੀ, ਖ਼ਬਰਦਾਰੀ, ਸਾਵਧਾਨੀ

water ('ਵੋਟਅ*) *n v* ਪਾਣੀ, ਜਲ, ਨੀਰ; ਪਿਸ਼ਾਬ; ਹੰਝੂ; ਰਾਲ, ਚਮਕ, ਆਭਾ, ਆਬ; ਸਿੰਜਣਾ,

ਸਿੰਚਾਈ ਕਰਨੀ, ਪਾਣੀ ਦੇਣਾ, ਆਬਪਾਸ਼ੀ ਕਰਨੀ, ਛਿੜਕਾ ਕਰਨਾ; ਤਰ ਕਰਨਾ, ਭਿਊਣਾ, ਗਿੱਲਾ ਕਰਨਾ, ਪਿਆਉਣਾ; ਪਾਣੀ ਆ ਜਾਣਾ; ਮੂਤਣਾ, ਪਿਸ਼ਾਬ ਕਰਨਾ; ਵਧਾਉਣਾ, ਵਾਧਾ ਕਰਨਾ; ~bearer ਕਹਾਰ, ਪਨਹਾਰ, ਝਿਊਰ; ~course ਜਲਮਾਰਗ; ~craft ਬੇੜੀ, ਨਈਆ ਜਾਂ ਜਹਾਜ਼; ~fall ਝਰਨਾ, ਆਬਸ਼ਾਰ; ~fowl ਮੁਰਗਾਬੀ, ਜਲ-ਪੰਛੀ; ~lily ਕੰਵਲ, ਕਮਲ, ਕੁਮਦਨੀ; ~melon ਮਤੀਰਾ, ਤਰਬੂਜ਼, ਹਦਵਾਣਾ; ~nymph ਜਲਪਰੀ; ~proof ਬਰਸਾਤੀ; ਅਭਿੱਜ; ~tight ਜਲ ਰੋਕ; (ਸੂਚਨਾ-ਨਾਮਾ) ਸ਼ੰਕਾ ਰਹਿਤ; in hot~ ਔਖ ਵਿਚ, ਔਕੜ ਵਿਚ; make ~ pass ਮੂਤਣਾ, ਪਿਸ਼ਾਬ ਕਰਨਾ; rose~ ਅਰਕ ਗੁਲਾਬ; throw cold ~ on ਪਾਣੀ ਫੇਰਨਾ, ਦਬਾਉਣਾ; ~y ਪਨਿਆਲਾ; ਸਜਲ

wave (ਵੇਇਵ੍) *n v* ਛੱਲ, ਲਹਿਰ, ਤਰੰਗ, ਹਿਚਕੋਲਾ; ਹਿੱਲਣਾ, ਹਿਲੋਰੇ ਖਾਣੇ; ਹੱਥ ਹਿਲਾਉਣਾ; ਲਹਿਰਾਂ ਉਠਈਆਂ

wavy ('ਵੇਇਵਿ) *n a* ਲਹਰੀਆਦਾਰ, ਲਹਿਰਦਾਰ; ਤਰੰਗਤ, ਤਰੰਗਮਈ, ਕਲੋਲਮਈ; ਘੁੰਗਰਾਲਾ

wax ('ਵੈਕਸ) *n* ਮੋਮ; ਕੰਨਾਂ ਦੀ ਮੈਲ; ਮੋਮੀ ਬਣਾਉਣਾ, ਮੋਮ ਲਾਉਣੀ, ਮੋਮ ਦੀ ਤਹਿ ਦੇਣੀ; ਲਾਖ ਨਾਲ ਜੋੜਨਾ; ਚੰਦ ਦਾ ਆਕਾਰ ਵਧਣਾ; ਉੱਨਤੀ ਕਰਨਾ; ~y ਮੋਮੀ, ਮੋਮਦਾਰ; ਚਿਪਚਿਪਾ, ਨਰਮ, ਕੂਲਾ; ਛੇਤੀ ਨਾਰਾਜ਼ ਹੋਣ ਵਾਲਾ

way (ਵੇਇ) *n* ਰਾਹ, ਰਸਤਾ, ਮਾਰਗ, ਪੱਥ, ਡਗਰ; ਵੀਹੀ; ਗਲੀ, ਸੜਕ; ਜੁਗਤ, ਉਪਾਉ, ਰੀਤ, ਵਿਧੀ, ਤਰਕੀਬ, ਢੰਗ, ਢਬ, ਕਾਇਦਾ; ~farer ਪੈਦਲ ਯਾਤਰਾ ਕਰਨ ਵਾਲਾ, ਪਾਂਧੀ; by ~ of ਤੌਰ ਤੇ; by the~ ਐਵੇਂ

weak (ਵੀਕ) *a* ਕਮਜ਼ੋਰ, ਨਿਰਬਲ, ਢਿੱਲਾ, ਨਿਤਾਣਾ, ਨਿਸੱਤਾ, ਖੀਣ; ਮੱਧਮ, ਹਲਕਾ; ~character ਕਮਜ਼ੋਰ ਆਚਰਨ ਵਾਲਾ; the ~er sex ਨਾਰੀ, ਔਰਤ ਜ਼ਾਤ, ਅਬਲਾ; ~ness ਕਮਜ਼ੋਰੀ, ਦੁਰਬਲਤਾ, ਸ਼ਕਤੀਹੀਣਤਾ, ਸੁਸਤੀ; ਤਰੁਟੀ, ਐਬ, ਬੁਰਾਈ

weal (ਵੀਲ) *n* ਖ਼ੁਸ਼ਹਾਲੀ, ਵਾਧਾ, ਸਮਰਿਧੀ; ਭਲਾਈ, ਕਲਿਆਨ; ਅਨੰਦ, ਪ੍ਰਸੰਨਤਾ; ਚੰਗੀ ਕਿਸਮਤ, ਚੰਗਿਆਈ, ਅੱਛਾਈ

wealth (ਵੈੱਲਥ) *n* ਧਨ, ਧਨ-ਸੰਪੱਤੀ, ਅਮੀਰੀ, ਦੌਲਤਮੰਦੀ; ਅਨੰਦ, ਸੁਭਾਗਾ; ਬਹੁਤਾਤ; ~y ਧਨਵਾਨ, ਅਮੀਰ, ਦੌਲਤਮੰਦ, ਮਾਲਦਾਰ

weapon ('ਵੈੱਪਅਨ) *n* ਹਥਿਆਰ, ਸ਼ਸਤਰ, ਅਸਤਰ-ਸ਼ਸਤਰ

wear (ਵੇਅ*) *n v* ਪੁਸ਼ਾਕ, ਲਿਬਾਸ, ਵੇਸ, ਪਹਿਰਾਵਾ; ਘਟਾਉਣਾ, ਨੁਕਸਾਨ ਕਰਨਾ; ਘਸਣਾ, ਰਗੜ ਖਾਣੀ, ਘਸਾਉਣਾ, ਰਗੜਨਾ; ਥੱਕਣਾ, ਫੇਰਨਾ, ਘੁਕਣਾ, ਘੁਕਾਉਣਾ; ਘੁਮਾਉਣਾ, ਘੁੰਮਣਾ, ਮੁੜ ਜਾਣਾ; ~and tear ਟੁੱਟ ਭੱਜ; ~down ਰਗੜ ਦੇਣਾ, ਕਮਜ਼ੋਰ ਕਰਨਾ; ~off ਘਸਾ ਦੇਣਾ; ~iness ਥਕਾਵਟ; ~y ਥਕਿਆ, ਅੱਕਿਆ, ਉਚਾਟ; ਨਿਰਾਸ, ਉਦਾਸੀਨ

weather ('ਵੈੱਦਅ*) *n a* ਰੁੱਤ, ਮੌਸਮ; ਹਵਾ ਵਾਲੇ ਪਾਸੇ ਸਥਿਤ, ਹਵਾ ਦੀ ਦਿਸ਼ਾ ਦਾ; ~cock ਪੌਣ-ਕੁੱਕੜ; ਫ਼ਸਲੀ ਬਟੇਰਾ

weave (ਵੀਵ੍) *n v* ਬੁਣਤੀ, ਬੁਣਨਾ; ਕੱਪੜਾ ਬਣਾਉਣਾ, ਤਾਣੀ ਬੁਣਨਾ; ਗੰਢਣਾ; ਘੜਨਾ, ਗੁੰਦਣਾ; ~r ਜੁਲਾਹਾ; ਬਈਆ

web (ਵੈੱਬ) *n* ਜਾਲ; ਜਾਲਾ (ਮੱਕੜੀ ਦਾ); ਕੱਪੜਾ, ਤਾਣਾ, ਰੇਜਾ

webster ('ਵੈੱਬਸਟਆ*) *n* ਜੁਲਾਹਾ

wed (ਵੈੱਡ) *v* ਵਰ ਲੈਣਾ, ਵਿਆਹ ਕਰਨਾ, ਵਿਆਹੁਣਾ, ਨਿਕਾਹ ਕਰਨਾ, ਪਰਨਾਉਣਾ, ਪਰਾਏ ਜਾਣਾ, ਜੋੜਨਾ, ਮਿਲਾਉਣਾ; **~ding** ਵਿਆਹ, ਨਿਕਾਹ, ਸ਼ਾਦੀ, ਪਰਣੇਵਾਂ

wedlock ('ਵੈੱਡਲੌਕ) *n* ਵਿਆਹ, ਬੰਧਨ, ਗਠਜੋੜ

Wednesday ('ਵੈੱਨੱਜ਼ਡਿ) *n* ਬੁੱਧਵਾਰ

wee (ਵੀ) *n* ਨਿੱਕ, ਨੰਨ੍ਹਾ, ਛੋਟਾ

weed (ਵੀਡ) *n v* ਘਾਵ-ਪੱਤਾ; ਨਦੀਨ ਮਰੀਅਲ ਘੋੜਾ; ਗੁੱਡਣਾ, ਗੋਡੀ ਕਰਨੀ, ਛਾਂਟਣਾ, ਛਾਂਟੀ ਕਰਨੀ, ਕੱਢਣਾ, ਪੁੱਟਣਾ

week (ਵੀਕ) *n* ਹਫ਼ਤਾ, ਸਪਤਾਹ; **~ly** ਹਫ਼ਤਾਵਾਰ, ਸਪਤਾਹਕ

weep (ਵੀਪ) *v* ਰੋਣਾ, ਵਿਰਲਾਪ ਕਰਨਾ, ਅੱਖਾਂ ਭਰਨੀਆਂ; ਸੋਗ ਮਨਾਉਣਾ, ਅਫ਼ਸੋਸ ਕਰਨਾ; ਚੋਣਾ, ਰਿਸਣਾ; **~ing** ਰੋਣ-ਧੋਣ, ਰੁਦਨ, ਵਿਰਲਾਪ; ਅੱਥਰੂਪੂਰਨ

weigh (ਵੇਇ) *v* ਭਾਰ ਤੋਲਣਾ, ਤੁੱਲ ਹੋਣਾ, ਬਰਾਬਰ ਹੋਣਾ; ਅੰਕਣਾ, ਜਾਚਣਾ, ਮੁੱਲਾਂਕਣ ਕਰਨਾ, ਅਨੁਮਾਨ ਲਾਉਣਾ, ਮਹੱਤਵ ਹੋਣਾ; **~t** ਵਜ਼ਨ, ਭਾਰ, ਬੋਝ, ਤੋਲ, ਵੱਟਾ; ਭਾਰੀ ਚੀਜ਼; ਮਹੱਤਵ, ਪ੍ਰਭਾਵ, ਪ੍ਰਧਾਨਤਾ; ਮਹੱਤਾ

welcome ('ਵੈੱਲਕਅਮ) *n v a int* ਸੁਆਗਤ, ਸਤਿਕਾਰ, ਆਓਭਗਤ; ਸੁਆਗਤ ਕਰਨਾ, ਸਤਿਕਾਰ ਕਰਨਾ; ਸੁਖਾਵਾਂ; ਜੀ ਆਇਆਂ ਨੂੰ; **~address** ਅਭਿਨੰਦਨ-ਪੱਤਰ, ਸੁਆਗਤੀ ਭਾਸ਼ਣ

weld (ਵੈੱਲਡ) *v* ਢਾਲ ਕੇ ਜੋੜਨਾ, ਸੰਯੁਕਤ ਕਰਨਾ; ਸਰੂਪ ਬਣਾਉਣਾ; **~ing** ਗਰਮ ਕਰਕੇ ਜੋੜਨਾ, ਵੈਲਡਿੰਗ

welfare ('ਵੈੱਲਫ਼ੇਅ*) *n* ਕਲਿਆਣ, ਭਲਾਈ; ਸੁੱਖ; ਉੱਨਤੀ

welkin ('ਵੈੱਲਕਿਨ) *n* (ਕਾਵਿ) ਅੰਬਰ, ਗਗਨ, ਆਕਾਸ਼, ਨਭ

well (ਵੈੱਲ) *n v adv int* ਖੂਹ, ਬਾਉਲੀ; ਸੋਤਾ, ਚਸ਼ਮਾ; ਉੱਬਲਣਾ, ਉਮੜਨਾ, ਉੱਭਾਰਨਾ, ਫੁਹਾਰਾ ਚੱਲਣਾ; ਤਰੰਗੜਤ, ਚੰਗਾ ਭਲਾ, ਠੀਕ-ਠਾਕ; ਤਸੱਲੀਬਖ਼ਸ਼ ਰੂਪ ਵਿਚ; ਭਲੀ-ਭਾਂਤੀ, ਚੰਗੀ ਤਰ੍ਹਾਂ; ਬਖ਼ੂਬੀ, ਨਿਰਾ; ਨਿਪਟ, ਬਿਲਕੁਲ; **~behaved** ਆਚਰਨਸ਼ੀਲ, ਸੁੱਘੜ, ਸੁਸ਼ੀਲ; **~being** ਭਲਾਈ, ਖੈਰ, ਸਲਾਮਤੀ

welt (ਵੈੱਲਟ) *n v* ਕਿਨਾਰੀ, ਗੋਟਾ; ਮਗ਼ਜ਼ੀ; ਗੋਟਾ ਲਾਉਣਾ; ਛਾਂਟੇ ਮਾਰਨੇ, ਲਾਸਾਂ ਪਾ ਦੇਣੀਆਂ, ਨੀਲ ਪਾ ਦੇਣੇ; **~ing** ਗੋਟਾ ਲਾਉਣਾ; ਕੋਰੜਿਆਂ ਦੀ ਮਾਰ, ਕੁਟਾਈ

wench (ਵੈਂਚ) *n v* ਛੋਕਰੀ, ਪੱਠੀ; ਵੇਸਵਾ, ਰੰਡੀ, ਵੇਸਵਾ ਗਮਨ ਕਰਨਾ, ਰੰਡੀਬਾਜ਼ੀ ਕਰਨਾ

wend (ਵੈਂਡ) *v* ਬਦਲਣਾ, ਚਲੇ ਜਾਣਾ, ਗੁਜ਼ਰਨਾ; ਰਾਹ ਪੈਣਾ

west (ਵੈਸਟ) *n a adv* ਪੱਛਮ; ਪੱਛਮੀ ਦੇਸ਼; ਪੱਛਮੀ; ਪੱਛਮ ਵਾਲੇ ਪਾਸੇ; **~ern** ਪੱਛਮੀ, ਪੱਛਮ ਦਾ ਨਿਵਾਸੀ

wet (ਵੈੱਟ) *n a v* ਗਿੱਲਾ, ਨਮੀ, ਤਰੀ, ਸੇਜਲ, ਸਿੱਲ੍ਹ; ਗਿੱਲਾ ਕਰਨਾ, ਤਰ ਕਰਨਾ, ਨਮ ਦੇਣਾ; **~lands** ਛੰਭ; **~weather** ਵਰਖਾ ਰੁੱਤ

wharf (ਵੋਫ਼) *n v* ਜਹਾਜ਼ ਦਾ ਘਾਟ; ਘਾਟ ਤੇ ਮਾਲ ਲਾਹੁਣਾ

what (ਵੌਟ) *a pron* ਕਿਹੜਾ, ਕਿਹੋ ਜਿਹਾ, ਕਿੱਡਾ, ਕੌਣ; ਕਿੰਨਾ; ਕੀ; **~ever** ਕਿਹੋ ਜਿਹਾ, ਕੈਸਾ, ਕੁਝ ਵੀ, ਜੋ ਵੀ, ਕੁਝ; ਕਿਸੇ ਤਰ੍ਹਾਂ ਦਾ

wheat (ਵੀਟ) *n* ਕਣਕ, ਗੰਦਮ, ਗੋਹੂੰ; **~en** ਕਣਕੰਨਾ, ਗੰਦਮੀ, ਗੋਹੂੰ ਦੇ ਰੰਗ ਦਾ

wheel (ਵੀਲ) *n v* ਚੱਕਾ, ਪਹੀਆ, ਚੱਕਰ; ਚਰਖਾ, ਚਰਖੀ; ਫਿਰਕੀ; ਬੈੜ, ਘਿਰਨੀ; ਟੇਢੇ ਵਿੰਗੇ ਟੁਰਨ; ਸਾਈਕਲ ਚਲਾਉਣਾ

whelm (ਵੈੱਲਮ) *v* ਮਗਨ ਕਰਨਾ, ਘੇਰਨਾ; ਪ੍ਰਭਾਵਤ ਕਰਨਾ; ਲਪੇਟ ਵਿਚ ਲੈਣਾ

whelp (ਵੈੱਲਪ) *n v* ਕਤੂਰਾ, ਕੁੱਤੇ ਦਾ ਬੱਚਾ, ਪਿੱਲਾ; ਜਣਨਾ, ਵਿਆਣਾ; (ਮਨਸੂਬਾ) ਘੜਨਾ

when (ਵੈੱਨ) *adv pron n* ਕਦ, ਕਿਸੇ ਵੇਲੇ, ਕਦੋਂ; ਜਦ; ਜਿਸ ਵੇਲੇ, ਜਿਉਂ ਹੀ, ਜਦ ਕਿ; ਕਿੰਨੇ ਵਜੇ, ਕਿਸ ਸਮੇਂ; ਅਵਸਰ, ਵੇਲਾ; **~ever** ਜਦ ਕਦੇ, ਜਿਸ ਸੌਕੇ ਤੇ, ਜਿਉਂ ਹੀ

whence (ਵੈੱਸ) *n pron adv* ਕਿਥੋਂ; ਜਿੱਥੋਂ; ਕਿਸ ਮਾਧਿਅਮ ਦੁਆਰਾ, ਕਿਸ ਤਰ੍ਹਾਂ ਕਿੱਧਰੋਂ, ਕਿਵੇਂ; ਜਿਵੇਂ

where (ਵੇਅ*) *n pron adv* ਕਿੱਥੇ, ਕਿਹੜੀ ਥਾਂ; ਜਿੱਥੇ, ਜਿਹੜੀ ਥਾਂ, ਕਿਸ ਸਥਿਤੀ ਵਿਚ; ਕਿਸ ਥਾਂ; ਜਿਸ ਥਾਂ; ਜਿਧਰ ਨੂੰ, ਜਿੱਧਰ; **~abouts** ਪੱਤਾ, ਥਾਂ-ਟਿਕਾਣਾ; **~as** ਜਦ ਕਿ, ਜਦੋਂ; ਪਰੰਤੂ, ਚੁਨਾਂਚਿ; ਇਸ ਦੇ ਉਲਟ

whether (ਵੈੱਦਅ*) *pron conj a* ਦੋਹਾਂ ਵਿਚੋਂ ਕਿਹੜਾ; ਭਾਵੇਂ, ਚਾਹੇ

whey (ਵੇਇ) *n a* ਫਿਟਾਏ ਦੁੱਧ ਦਾ ਪਾਣੀ, ਦਹੀਂ ਵਿਚਲਾ ਪਾਣੀ; ਲੱਸੀ ਵਰਗਾ

which (ਵਿਚ) *a pron* ਕੌਣ, ਜਿਹੜਾ, ਜੋ, ਜਿਹੜੀ ਚੀਜ਼; ਕਿਹੜੀ ਚੀਜ਼; ਜਿਸ ਨੂੰ; **~ever**, **soever** ਜਿਹੜਾ ਵੀ, ਜੋ ਵੀ, ਜੋ ਕੋਈ ਵੀ

while (ਵਾਇਲ) *n v conj* ਸਮਾਂ, ਵੇਲਾ, ਵਕਤ; ਵੇਲਾ ਗਵਾਉਣਾ, ਵੇਲਾ ਟਪਾਉਣਾ; ਜਦ, ਜਦ ਤਕ, ਜਿਸ ਸਮੇਂ ਵਿਚ, ਤਦ ਤਕ

whim (ਵਿਮ) *n* ਮਨ-ਮੌਜ, ਤਰੰਗ, ਖ਼ਬਤ, ਸਨਕ, ਖ਼ਿਆਲ, ਵਹਿਮ; **~sical** ਮਨ-ਮੌਜੀ, ਤਰੰਗੀ,

ਵਹਿਮੀ, ਖ਼ਬਤੀ; **~sy** ਮੌਜ, ਤਰੰਗ, ਵਹਿਮ, ਖ਼ਬਤ

whinny (ਵਿਨਿ) *v n* ਹਿਣਹਿਣਾਹਟ; ਹਿਣਕਣਾ

whip (ਵਿਪ) *n v* ਕੋਰੜਾ, ਚਾਬੁਕ, ਹੰਟਰ, ਛਾਂਟਾ; ਕੋਰਵਾਨ; ਪ੍ਰਧਿਪਕ, ਰਾਜਸੀ ਦਲ ਦਾ ਸਚੇਤਕ, ਖ਼ਬਰਦਾਰ ਕਰਨ ਵਾਲਾ; ਕੋਰੜਾ ਮਾਰਨਾ, ਚਾਬੁਕ ਨਾਲ ਮਾਰਨਾ; ਭੱਜ ਕੇ ਨਿਕਲ ਜਾਣਾ

whirl (ਵਅਃਲ) *v n* ਭਵਾਉਣਾ ਜਾਂ ਭੌਣਾ, ਚੱਕਰ ਦੇਣੇ ਜਾਂ ਚੱਕਰ ਖਾਣਾ, ਘੁਕਾਉਣਾ ਜਾਂ ਘੁਰਨਾ, ਘੁਮਾ ਕੇ ਸੁੱਟਣਾ, ਘੁਮਾ ਕੇ ਵਗ੍ਹਾ ਮਾਰਨਾ; ਤੇਜ਼ ਚੱਕਰ, ਘੁਮਾਈ

whisper ('ਵਿਸਪਅ*) *v* ਕਾਨਾਫੂਸੀ ਕਰਨੀ, ਘੁਸਰਮੁਸਰ ਕਰਨੀ, ਕੰਨ ਵਿਚ ਕਹਿਣਾ

whistle ('ਵਿਸਲ) *n v* ਸੀਟੀ, ਸੀਟੀ ਦੀ ਅਵਾਜ਼; ਸਾਂ ਦੀ ਅਵਾਜ਼; ਸੀਟੀ ਵਜਾਉਣੀ, ਸਾਂ-ਸਾਂ ਦੀ ਅਵਾਜ਼ ਨਿਕਲਣੀ ਜਾਂ ਕੱਢਣੀ

white (ਵਾਇਟ) *a n v* ਚਿੱਟਾ, ਧੌਲਾ, ਬੱਗਾ; ਸਫ਼ੈਦ; ਅੰਡੇ ਦੀ ਸਫ਼ੈਦੀ; ਗੋਰੇ ਰੰਗ ਵਾਲੀ ਜਾਤੀ; ਚਿੱਟਾ ਕਰਨਾ, ਸਾਫ਼ ਕਰਨਾ, ਸਫ਼ੈਦੀ ਕਰਨੀ; **~alloy** ਨਕਲੀ ਚਾਂਦੀ; **~ant** ਸਿਉਂਕ, ਦੀਮਕ; **~lie** ਮਾਮੂਲੀ ਝੂਠ; **~livered** ਕਾਇਰ, ਬੁਜ਼ਦਿਲ; **~man** ਗੋਰਾ, ਫ਼ਰੰਗੀ; **~Paper** ਲੋਕਾਂ ਦੀ ਜਾਣਕਾਰੀ ਲਈ ਛਪੀ ਸਰਕਾਰੀ ਰਿਪੋਰਟ; **~smith** ਕਲੀਗਰ; **~wash** ਸਫ਼ੈਦੀ (ਕਰਨਾ), ਲਿੰਬਾਈ, ਸਫ਼ਾਈ (ਕਰਨੀ); **~n** ਚਿੱਟਾ ਕਰਨਾ, ਚਿੱਟਾ ਹੋ ਜਾਣਾ; **~ning** ਚਿਟਿਆਉਣ; ਕਲੀ, ਸਫ਼ੈਦੀ, ਚਿੱਟੀ ਮਿੱਟੀ

whither ('ਵਿਦਅ*) *adv n* ਕਿੱਧਰ, ਕਿੱਧਰ ਨੂੰ, ਕਿੱਥੇ, ਕਿਹੜੇ ਪਾਸੇ; ਜਿੱਧਰ, ਜਿੱਥੇ; ਲਕਸ਼

who (ਹੂ) *pron* ਕੌਣ, ਕਿਹੜਾ; ਕਿਹੜੇ; ਕਿਨ,

ਕਿਨ੍ਹਾਂ, ਜਿਨ, ਜਿਨ੍ਹਾਂ; **~ever** ਜੋ ਕੋਈ ਵੀ, ਜੋ
ਵੀ; **~soever** ਜਿੰਨੇ ਵੀ, ਜਿਨੇ ਕਿਨੇ, ਜਿਸ
ਕਿਸੇ, ਜੋ ਕੋਈ ਵੀ, ਜਿਹੜਾ ਕੋਈ ਵੀ

whole (ਹਅਉਲ) *a n* ਸਾਰਾ, ਪੂਰਾ, ਸਮੁਚਾ, ਪੂਰੇ
ਦਾ ਪੂਰਾ; ਸਬੂਤ; **~hearted** ਪੂਰੇ ਦਿਲ ਨਾਲ,
ਸੱਚੇ ਦਿਲੋਂ; **~sale** ਥੋਕ ਵਿਕਰੀ, ਥੋਕ;
~some ਨਿਰੋਆ, ਪੌਸ਼ਟਿਕ, ਲਾਭਕਾਰੀ,
ਗੁਣਕਾਰੀ, ਹਿਤਕਾਰੀ

wholly (ਹਅਉਲਿ) *adv* ਪੂਰੇ ਦਾ ਪੂਰਾ, ਸਾਰੇ ਦਾ
ਸਾਰਾ, ਸਮੁਚਾ, ਸਮੁੱਚੇ ਰੂਪ ਵਿਚ; ਪੂਰੀ ਤਰ੍ਹਾਂ;
ਬਿਲਕੁਲ; ਮੂਲੋਂ ਹੀ ਮੁੱਢੋਂ

whom (ਹੂਮ) *pron* ਵੇਖੋ who,ਕਿਸ ਨੂੰ; ਜਿਸ
ਨੂੰ; **~soever** ਜਿਸ ਨੂੰ, ਜਿਸ ਨੇ ਵੀ, ਜਿਨ੍ਹਾਂ
ਨੂੰ ਵੀ

whoop (ਹੂਪ) *n* ਖਊਂ-ਖਊਂ ਕਰਨ ਦੀ ਕਿਰਿਆ,
ਖੰਘ ਦਾ ਗੋਤਾ; ਚਾਂਗਰ; **~ing, ~ping**
cough ਕਾਲੀ ਖਾਂਸੀ, ਕੁੱਤਾ ਖਾਂਸੀ

whore (ਹੋ*) *pron* ਵੇਸਵਾ, ਕੰਜਰੀ; ਲੁੱਚਪੁਣਾ
ਕਰਨਾ, ਬਦਮਾਸ਼ੀ ਕਰਨਾ; **~dom** ਰੰਡੀਬਾਜ਼ੀ,
ਵੇਸ਼ਵਾਪੁਣਾ

whose (ਹੂਜ਼) *pron* ਕੀਹਦਾ, ਕਿਸ ਦਾ, ਕਿਨ੍ਹਾਂ
ਦਾ; ਜੀਹਦਾ, ਜਿਸ ਦਾ, ਜਿਨ੍ਹਾਂ ਦਾ

why (ਵਾਇ) *adv int n* ਕਿਉਂ, ਕਿਸ ਲਈ,
ਕਿਸ ਕਾਰਨ, ਕਿਸ ਕਰਕੇ; ਜਿਸ ਲਈ, ਜਿਸ
ਕਰਕੇ; ਕੀ ਇਹ ਵੀ ਹੋ ਸਕਦਾ ਹੈ; ਕਾਰਨ;
ਵਿਆਖਿਆ

wicked (ਵਿਕਿਡ) *a* ਬਦਮਾਸ਼, ਬਦਚਲਨ, ਬਦ,
ਬੁਰਾ, ਦੁਸ਼ਟ, ਪਾਪੀ, ਦੁਰਾਚਾਰੀ; **~ness**
ਬਦਮਾਸ਼ੀ, ਬਦਚਲਨੀ, ਬਦੀ, ਬੁਰਾਈ, ਦੁਸ਼ਟਤਾ

wicket (ਵਿਕਿਟ) *n* ਫਾਟਕ, ਖਿੜਕ, ਵਿਕਟ;
ਵਿਕਟ; **~gate** ਛੋਟਾ ਦਰਵਾਜ਼ਾ, ਉਪ-ਦੁਆਰ

wide (ਵਾਇਡ) *adv a* ਖੁੱਲ੍ਹਾ; ਚੌੜਾ, ਮੋਕਲਾ, ਦੂਰ
ਤਕ ਪਸਰਿਆ; ਕਾਫ਼ੀ, ਚੋਖਾ; **~awake** ਪੂਰੀ
ਤਰ੍ਹਾਂ ਸਚੇਤ; **~eyed** ਹੈਰਾਨ, ਹੱਕਾ-ਬੱਕਾ;
~spread ਦੂਰ ਤਕ ਪਸਰਿਆ; ਵਿਸਤਰਤ,
ਵਿਸ਼ਾਲ; **~n** ਖੁੱਲ੍ਹਾ ਕਰਨਾ, ਮੋਕਲਾ ਹੋਣਾ,
ਵਿਸਤਾਰ ਦੇਣਾ

widow (ਵਿਡਅਉ) *n v* ਵਿਧਵਾ; ਰੰਡੀ ਕਰ
ਦੇਣਾ; **~er** ਰੰਡਾ; **~hood** ਰੰਡੇਪਾ, ਵਿਧਵਾਪਣ

width (ਵਿਡਥ) *n* ਚੌੜਾਈ; ਬਰ (ਕੱਪੜੇ ਦਾ),
ਅਰਜ਼; ਵਿਸਤਾਰ, ਵਿਆਪਕਤਾ, ਉਦਾਰਤਾ;
ਉੱਚਤਾ

wife (ਵਾਇਫ਼) *n* ਵਹੁਟੀ, ਪਤਨੀ, ਘਰ ਵਾਲੀ,
ਤੀਵੀਂ, ਜ਼ਨਾਨੀ

wig (ਵਿਗ) *n v* ਵਿਗ, ਸਿਰ ਦੇ ਨਕਲੀ ਵਾਲ;
ਜੱਜਾਂ ਅਤੇ ਵਕੀਲਾਂ ਦੇ ਪਦ ਦਾ ਚਿੰਨ੍ਹ; ਡਾਂਟਣਾ,
ਤਾੜਨਾ, ਝਾੜਝੰਬ ਕਰਨੀ; **~ging** ਡਾਟ, ਝਾੜ-
ਝੰਬ, ਡਿੱਟ-ਲਨ੍ਹਤ

wiggle (ਵਿਗਲ) *v* ਇੱਧਰ ਉੱਧਰ ਘੁਮਾਉਣਾ,
ਫੇਰਨਾ

wild (ਵਾਇਲਡ) *a adv n* ਜੰਗਲੀ, ਜਾਂਗਲੀ;
ਵਹਿਸ਼ੀ, ਝੱਲਾ; ਬੇਕਾਬੂ, ਬੇ-ਲਗਾਮ; ਬੇ-
ਤਰਤੀਬ, ਅਵਿਵਸਥਿਤ; ਉਜਾੜ, ਬੀਆਬਾਨ;
~cat ਸ਼ੇਰ, ਚੀਤਾ ਆਦਿ; **~goose** ਜੰਗਲੀ
ਹੰਸ; ਮੂਰਖ ਆਦਮੀ; **~goose chase** ਫ਼ਜ਼ੂਲ
ਕੋਸ਼ਸ਼, ਅਸੰਭਵ ਕੰਮ ਲਈ ਜਤਨ; **~life**
ਜੰਗਲੀ ਜਾਨਵਰ

wile (ਵਾਇਲ) *n v* (*in pl*) ਫ਼ਰੇਬ, ਮਕਰ,
ਚਲਿੱਤਰ, ਕਪਟ; ਫ਼ਰੇਬ ਕਰਨਾ, ਮਕਰ ਕਰਨਾ,
ਛਲ ਕਰਨਾ

wilful (ਵਿਲਫੁਲ) *a* ਮਨਮਰਜ਼ੀ ਦਾ, ਜਾਣ ਬੁੱਝ
ਕੇ, ਜਾਣਦਿਆਂ ਹੋਇਆਂ; ਜ਼ਿੱਦੀ

will (ਵਿਲ) *v aux n* ਭਵਿੱਖਵਾਰੀ ਸਹਾਇਕ ਕਿਰਿਆ, (ਗਾ, ਗੇ, ਗੀ, ਗੀਆਂ ਆਦਿ); ਇੱਛਾ ਕਰਨ, ਇਰਾਦਾ ਹੋਣਾ, ਮਰਜ਼ੀ ਹੋਣਾ; ਚਾਹੁਣ; ਇੱਛਾ; ~**power** ਇੱਛਾ-ਸ਼ਕਤੀ; *at*~ ਮਰਜ਼ੀ ਨਾਲ; *good*~ ਸ਼ੁਭਭਾਵਨਾ, ਸਦਭਾਵਨਾ; *ill*~ ਦੁਰਭਾਵਨਾ; ~**ing** ਰਾਜ਼ੀ, ਰਜ਼ਾਮੰਦ, ਸਹਿਮਤ; ~**ness** ਰਜ਼ਾਮੰਦੀ, ਸਹਿਮਤੀ; ਇੱਛਾ; ਸ਼ੌਕ

willy ('ਵਾਇਲਿ) *a* ਚਾਲਬਾਜ਼, ਚਲਾਕ

willy-nilly ('ਵਿਲਿ'ਨਿਲਿ) *adv* ਚਾਹੇ-ਅਣਚਾਹੇ, ਔਖੇ-ਸੌਖੇ; ਰੋਂਦੇ-ਧੋਂਦੇ

wimp (ਵਿੰਪ) *n* (ਅਪ) ਲੱਲੂ

win (ਵਿਨ) *v n* ਜਿੱਤਣਾ, ਫ਼ਤਿਹ ਪਾਉਣੀ; ਸਫ਼ਲ ਹੋਣਾ; ਜਿੱਤ, ਵਿਜੈ; ~**prize** ਇਨਾਮ ਹਾਸਲ ਕਰਨਾ; ~**out** ਸਫ਼ਲ ਹੋਣਾ, ਕਾਮਯਾਬ ਹੋਣਾ; ~**ner** ਜੇਤੂ, ਵਿਜਈ; ~**ning** ਜਿੱਤ, ਵਿਜੈ, ਫ਼ਤਿਹ, ਸਫ਼ਲਤਾ; ਵਿਜਈ

wind (ਵਿੰਡ) *n v* ਹਵਾ, ਵਾਯੂ; ਝੱਖੜ, ਵਾਈ, ਬਾਈ ਜਾਂ ਵਾ ਦਾ ਰੋਗ, ਵਾਤ-ਰੋਗ; ਗੰਧ, ਵਾਸਨਾ, ਸਾਹ ਚੜ੍ਹਨਾ; ਸਾਹ ਕੱਢਣਾ; ~**fall** ਹਵਾ ਨਾਲ ਡਿੱਗਾ ਫਲ, ਟਪਕਾ; ~**mill** ਪੌਣ-ਚੱਕੀ; ~**pipe** ਸਾਹ-ਨਾਲੀ; *take, get*~ ਪ੍ਰਸਿੱਧ ਹੋਣਾ, ਉੱਘਾ ਹੋਣਾ

wind (ਵਾਇੰਡ) *v n* ਚੱਕਰ ਖਾਣਾ, ਵਲ ਖਾਣੇ, ਚੱਕਰ ਖਾਂਦਿਆਂ ਵਧਣਾ, ਵਲ੍ਹੇਟਣਾ, ਲੱਛਾ ਬਟਾਉਣਾ; ~~**up** ਪੂਰਾ-ਪੂਰਾ ਵਲੇਟ ਦੇਣਾ, ਸਾਰਾ ਇੱਕਠਾ ਕਰ ਲੈਣਾ; ਸਮੇਟ ਦੇਣਾ, ਸਮਾਪਤ ਕਰਨਾ; ਭੜਕਾਉਣਾ; ~**ing up** ਸਮਾਪਤਕਾਰੀ

window ('ਵਿੰਡਅਉ) *n* ਬਾਰੀ, ਖਿੜਕੀ, ਤਾਕੀ, ਝਰੋਖਾ; ~**shopping** ਦੁਕਾਨਾਂ ਦੀ ਸੈਰ

wine (ਵਾਇਨ) *n v* ਸ਼ਰਾਬ; ~**bowl** ਜਾਮ, ਪਿਆਲਾ; ~**cup** ਜਾਮ

wing (ਵਿੰਙ) *n v* (ਪੰਛੀ ਦਾ) ਖੰਭ; ਕਿਸੇ ਚੀਜ਼ ਦਾ ਬਾਹਰ ਨੂੰ ਵਧਿਆ ਇੱਕ ਪਾਸਾ, ਬਾਹੀ, ਖੰਡ ਲਾਉਣੇ; (ਤੀਰ) ਚਲਾਉਣਾ; ਉਡ ਕੇ ਜਾਣਾ; *on the ~* ਉੱਡਦਾ ਹੋਇਆ

wink (ਵਿੰਡਕ) *v n* ਅੱਖ ਝਮਕਣੀ, ਪਲਕ ਫਰਕਣੀ; ਅੱਖ ਨਾਲ ਇਸ਼ਾਰਾ ਕਰਨਾ; (ਤਾਰੇ ਦਾ) ਟਿਮਟਿਮਾਉਣਾ; ਝਪਕਾ, ਇਸ਼ਾਰਾ

winter ('ਵਿੰਟਅ*) *n* ਸਿਆਲ, ਸਰਦੀ ਦੀ ਰੁੱਤ

wipe (ਵਾਇਪ) *v* ਪੂੰਝਣਾ, ਮਾਂਜਣਾ, ਰਗੜ ਕੇ ਸਾਫ਼ ਕਰਨਾ ਜਾਂ ਮਿਟਾਉਣਾ; ਧੋ ਦੇਣਾ; ~**out** ਮਿਟਾਉਣਾ, ਸਫ਼ਾਇਆ ਕਰਨਾ

wire ('ਵਾਇਅ*) *n v* ਤਾਰ; ਤਾਰ ਲਾਉਣੀ; ਤਾਰ ਭੇਜਣੀ; ~**less** ਬੇਤਾਰ, ਆਕਾਸ਼ਬਾਣੀ

wisdom ('ਵਿਜ਼ਡਅਮ) *n* ਬੁੱਧੀਮਾਨੀ, ਅਕਲ, ਮੱਤ, ਸਿਆਣਪ, ਦਾਨਾਈ, ਅਕਲਮੰਦੀ, ਗਿਆਨ, ਵਿਵੇਕ; ~**tooth** ਅਕਲ-ਦਾੜ੍ਹ; *god of*~ ਗਣੇਸ਼

wise (ਵਾਇਜ਼) *a* ਬੁੱਧੀਮਾਨ, ਅਕਲਮੰਦ, ਸਿਆਣਾ; ਗਿਆਨਵਾਨ, ਵਿਵੇਕੀ, ਦੂਰਦਰਸ਼ੀ, ਸੂਝਵਾਨ

wish (ਵਿਸ਼) *v n* ਚਾਹੁਣਾ, ਇੱਛਾ ਕਰਨੀ, ਇਰਾਦਾ ਕਰਨਾ

wit (ਵਿਟ) *n v* ਸੂਝ, ਸਮਝ; ਹਾਜ਼ਰ-ਜਵਾਬੀ, ਸਿਆਣਾ, ਬੁੱਧੀਵਾਨ, ਸੂਝਵਾਨ ਵਿਅਕਤੀ; ਮਖੌਲੀਆ, ਹਾਜ਼ਰ ਜਵਾਬ

witch (ਵਿਚ) *n v* (1) ਜਾਦੂਗਰਨੀ, ਟੂਣੇਹਾਰੀ; ਡੈਣ; (2) ਸੁੰਦਰ ਮੁਟਿਆਰ; ਮੁਗਧ ਕਰਨਾ, ਮੋਹਤ ਕਰਨਾ, ਜਾਦੂ ਕਰਨਾ; ~**craft** ਜਾਦੂ, ਟੂਣਾ, ਜਾਦੂਗਰੀ; ~**ery** ਜਾਦੂ, ਟੂਣਾ; ~**hunt** ਵਿਰੋਧੀਆਂ ਦਾ ਸ਼ਿਕਾਰ

with (ਵਿਦ) *prep* ਨਾਲ; ਸਣੇ, ਸਮੇਤ; ਕੋਲ; ਕਾਰਨ, ਕਰਕੇ; ਹੁੰਦਿਆਂ ਵੀ

withdraw (ਵਿਦ'ਡਰੋ) v ਹਟਾ ਲੈਣਾ ਜਾਂ ਹਟ ਜਾਣਾ, ਮੋੜ ਲੈਣਾ ਜਾਂ ਮੁੜ ਜਾਣਾ, ਕੱਢ ਲੈਣਾ ਜਾਂ ਨਿਕਲ ਜਾਣਾ; ਲਾਂਭੇ ਹੋਣਾ, ਇਕ ਪਾਸੇ ਹੋ ਜਾਣਾ; ~al ਵਾਪਸੀ; ਪਰਤਾਉ, (ਪੈਸਾ) ਕੱਢਣ

wither ('ਵਿਦਅ*) v ਕੁਮਲਾ ਜਾਣਾ, ਮੁਰਝਾ ਜਾਣਾ, ਸੁੱਕ ਜਾਣਾ; ~ed ਨੀਰਸ, ਖ਼ੁਸ਼ਕ, ਕੁਮਲਾਇਆ, ਮੁਰਝਾਇਆ

withheld (ਵਿਦ'ਹੇਲੱਡ) a ਰੋਕਿਆ, ਦਬਾਇਆ

withhold (ਵਿਦ'ਹਅਉਲੱਡ) v ਰੋਕ ਲੈਣਾ, ਅਟਕਾ ਲੈਣਾ, ਰੋਕੀ ਰੱਖਣ, ਦਬਾਈ ਰੱਖਣਾ

within (ਵਿ'ਦਿਨ) adv prep ਅੰਦਰ, ਅੰਦਰਵਾਰ; ਅੰਦਰੋਂ, ਅੰਦਰਲੇ ਤੋਰ ਤੇ; ਵਿਚ, ਅੰਦਰ; ਸੀਮਾ ਵਿਚ, ਸਮੇਂ ਦੇ ਅੰਦਰ

without (ਵਿ'ਦਾਉਟ) adv prep ਬਿਨਾ, ਬਗ਼ੈਰ, ਰਹਿਤ, ਸਿਵਾ; ਬਾਹਰ, ਬਾਹਰੀ, ਬਾਹਰੀ ਤੋਰ ਤੇ

withstand (ਵਿਦ'ਸਟੈਂਡ) v ਟਾਕਰਾ ਕਰਨਾ, ਸਾਮ੍ਹਣਾ ਕਰਨਾ

witness (ਵਿਟਨਿਸ) n v ਗਵਾਹੀ, ਸ਼ਹਾਦਤ; ਸਬੂਤ, ਪ੍ਰਮਾਣ; ਗਵਾਹ, ਸਾਖੀ; ਗਵਾਹੀ ਦੇਣੀ, ਸ਼ਹਾਦਤ ਦੇਣੀ; ਪ੍ਰਮਾਣ ਜਾਂ ਸਬੂਤ ਦੇਣਾ; eye~ ਚਸ਼ਮਦੀਦ ਗਵਾਹ, ਮੌਕੇ ਦਾ ਗਵਾਹ

witticism ('ਵਿਟਿਸਿਜ਼(ਅ)ਮ) n ਹਾਸੇ ਵਾਲੀ ਗੱਲ, ਮਿੱਠਾ-ਮਖੌਲ, ਰਸਮਈ ਵਾਕ, ਬੁੱਧੀ-ਵਿਲਾਸ

wittingly ('ਵਿਟਿਙਲਿ) adv ਜਾਣ ਬੁੱਝ ਕੇ, ਜਾਣਦਿਆਂ, ਸਮਝਦਿਆਂ

witty ('ਵਿਟਿ) a ਮਖੌਲੀਆ, ਮਸਕਰਾ, ਹਾਸੇ-ਮਖੌਲ ਭਰਿਆ, ਰਸਿਕ

wizard ('ਵਿਜ਼ਅਃਡ) n a ਜਾਦੂਗਰ, ਪੂਰਾ ਨਿਪੁੰਨ, ਮਾਹਰ

woe (ਵਅਉ) n (ਕਾਵਿਕ) ਕਸ਼ਟ, ਦੁੱਖ, ਮੁਸੀਬਤ,

ਗ੍ਰਾਮ; ~ful ਦੁੱਖ ਭਰਿਆ, ਸੋਗ ਵਾਲਾ, ਸ਼ੋਕਮਈ; ਗ੍ਰਾਮਗੀਨ; ਦੁਖੀ, ਅਭਾਗਾ; ਅਨੁਚਿਤ; ~fulness ਦੁੱਖ ਭਰਪੂਰਤਾ, ਗ੍ਰਾਮਗੀਨੀ

wolf (ਵੁਲਫ) n v ਬਘਿਆੜ; ਲੋਭੀ ਮਨੁੱਖ

woman ('ਵੁਮਅਨ) n ਤੀਵੀਂ, ਜ਼ਨਾਨੀ, ਇਸਤਰੀ, ਨਾਰੀ, ਔਰਤ; ~hood ਜਨਨਾਪਨ, ਨਾਰੀਤਵ; ਕੋਮਲਤਾ, ਇਸਤਰੀ ਜਾਤੀ, ਨਾਰੀ ਵਰਗਾ, ਤੀਵੀਂਆਂ, ਜ਼ਨਾਨੀਆਂ; ~ish (ਘਿਰਣਾ ਵਿਚ, ਮਰਦ ਲਈ) ਜ਼ਨਾਨਾ, ਤੀਵੀਂਆਂ ਜਿਹਾ; ਤੀਵੀਂਆਂ ਵਰਗਾ; ~ly ਜ਼ਨਾਨਾ, ਇਸਤਰੀਆਂ ਵਾਲਾ, ਕੋਮਲ, ਸਨੇਹਮਈ; ਨਿੱਘਾ

womb (ਵੂਮ) n ਕੁੱਖ, ਬੱਚੇਦਾਨੀ; ਢਿੱਡ; fruit of the~ ਔਲਾਦ

wonder ('ਵਅੰਡਅ*) v n ਹੈਰਾਨ ਹੋਣਾ, ਚਕਿਤ ਹੋਣਾ, ਅਚੰਭਾ ਹੋਣਾ; ਹੈਰਾਨੀ, ਅਚੰਭਾ, ਅਸਚਰਜਤਾ; ਕਰਾਮਾਤ, ਕੌਤਕ, ਚਮਤਕਾਰ; ਅਸਧਾਰਨ ਘਟਨਾ; ~land ਪਰੀਲੋਕ; ~ful ਅਜੀਬ, ਅਸਚਰਜ, ਨਿਰਾਲਾ, ਅਨੋਖਾ, ਅਦਭੁਤ, ਉੱਤਮ, ਪ੍ਰਸੰਸਾਯੋਗ, ਬਹੁਤ ਵਧੀਆ

wondrous ('ਵਅੰਡਰਅਸ) a ਅਦਭੁਤ, ਅਜੀਬ, ਨਿਰਾਲਾ, ਵਚਿੱਤਰ; ਬਹੁਤ ਹੀ ਚੰਗਾ, ਬੜਾ ਹੀ ਵਧੀਆ

woo (ਵੂ) v ਪਿਆਰ ਜਤਾਉਣਾ, ਪਰੇਮ ਕਰਨਾ, ਇਸ਼ਕਬਾਜ਼ੀ ਕਰਨੀ; ਪਿੱਛੇ ਪੈਣਾ

wood (ਵੁਡ) n (pl) ਜੰਗਲ, ਬੀੜ, ਵਣ; ਲੱਕੜ; ਲੱਕੜੀ, ਰੁੱਖ; ~craft ਲੱਕੜੀ ਦਾ ਕੰਮ; ~land ਜੰਗਲੀ ਇਲਾਕਾ; ~man ਜੰਗਲ ਦਾ ਦਰੋਗਾ; ਲੱਕੜਹਾਰਾ; ਜੰਗਲੀ; ~en ਲਕੜੀ ਦਾ, ਲੱਕੜੀ ਤੋਂ ਬਣਾਇਆ; ਸਖ਼ਤ, ਕਾਠਾ; ਪ੍ਰਾਚੀਨ, ਬੇਰੌਣਕ, ਬੇਲੋਚ

wool (ਵੁਲ) n ਉੱਨ, ਪਸ਼ਮ; ਉੱਨੀ ਧਾਗਾ; pull

the ~ over one's eyes ਝਾਂਸਾ ਦੇਣਾ;
~len ਉੱਨੀ, ਉੱਨ ਦਾ, ਪਸ਼ਮ ਦਾ; ਉੱਨੀ
ਕੱਪੜਾ, ਗਰਮ ਕੱਪੜਾ; ~ly ਉੱਨਦਾਰ, ਰੂੰਈ
ਵਾਲਾ, ਅਸਪਸ਼ਟ, ਧੁੰਦਲਾ; ਢਿੱਕ; ਉੱਨੀ ਕੱਪੜੇ

word (ਵਅਃਡ) *n* ਸ਼ਬਦ, ਲਫ਼ਜ਼, ਪਦ; ਗੱਲ,
ਕਥਨ; ਸਮਾਚਾਰ, ਆਗਿਆ, ਆਦੇਸ਼; ਵਾਅਦਾ
ਬਚਨ; **a ~ to the wise** ਅਕਲਮੰਦ ਨੂੰ
ਇਸ਼ਾਰਾ ਕਾਫ਼ੀ ਹੈ; **keep one's~** ਵਚਨ
ਪਾਲਣਾ; ~iness ਸ਼ਬਦ-ਜਾਲ, ਵਾਕ-ਜਾਲ,
ਸ਼ਬਦ-ਅਡੰਬਰ; ~ing ਸ਼ਬਦ-ਚੋਣ, ਸ਼ੈਲੀ, ਵਾਕ
ਰਚਨਾ, ਵਰਤਨ-ਸ਼ੈਲੀ; ਸ਼ਬਦ, ਸ਼ਬਦਾਵਲੀ

work (ਵਅਃਕ) *n v* ਕੰਮ, ਕਾਰ; ਧੰਦਾ, ਪੇਸ਼ਾ
ਕਾਰੀਗਰੀ, ਕੁਸ਼ਲਤਾ; ਰਚਨਾ, ਕਿਰਤ, ਲਿਖੀ
ਹੋਈ ਕਿਤਾਬ; ਕਾਰਖ਼ਾਨਾ; ਵਿਭਾਗ, ਮਹਿਕਮਾ;
ਕੰਮ ਕਰਨਾ; ਘਾੜਤ ਕਰਨੀ, ਕਿਸੇ ਚੀਜ਼ ਦਾ
ਕਾਰੀਗਰ ਹੋਣਾ; ਮਸ਼ੀਨ ਦਾ ਚਾਲੂ ਹੋਣਾ;
ਪਾਉਣਾ, ਅਸਰ ਕਰਨਾ; ਪ੍ਰਭਾਵ ਪਾਉਣਾ, ਅਸਰ
ਕਰਨਾ; ~house ਅਨਾਥ ਘਰ; ~load ਕੰਮ
ਦਾ ਭਾਰ; ~man ਮਜ਼ਦੂਰ; ਮਿਸਤਰੀ,
ਕਾਰੀਗਰ; ~manship ਕਾਰੀਗਰੀ, ਕੁਸ਼ਲਤਾ,
ਨਿਪੁੰਨਤਾ; ਰਚਨਾ, ਘਾੜਤ; ~out ਹਿਸਾਬ
ਲਾਉਣਾ; ਹੱਲ ਕਰਨਾ, ਕੱਢਣਾ (ਸਵਾਲ ਆਦਿ);
~shop ਕਾਰਖ਼ਾਨਾ, ਕਰਮਸ਼ਾਲਾ, ਦੁਕਾਨ; *set
to* ~ ਕੰਮ ਵਿਚ ਜੁੱਟ ਜਾਣਾ, ਕੰਮ ਅਰੰਭਣਾ;
~er ਕਿਰਤੀ, ਕਾਮਾ, ਮਜ਼ਦੂਰ, ਸੇਵਕ; ~ing
ਪ੍ਰਬੰਧ, ਕਾਰਜ-ਸੰਚਾਲਨ; ਕਾਰਜ ਪ੍ਰਣਾਲੀ; ਕੰਮ-
ਚਲਾਊ, ਚਲੰਤ, ਉਦਯੋਗੀ, ਚਾਲੂ, ਕਿਰਿਆ-
ਸ਼ੀਲ, ਕਾਰਜਕਾਰੀ; ਕੰਮ ਦਾ

workaholic ('ਵਅਃਕਅ'ਹੌਲਿਕ) *n* ਕੰਮ ਦਾ ਕੀੜਾ

world (ਵਅਃਲਡ) *n* ਸੰਸਾਰ, ਦੁਨੀਆ, ਜਗਤ,
ਜਹਾਨ; ਦੁਨਿਆਵੀ ਧੰਦੇ, ਜੀਵਨ ਦੇ ਕਾਰ-

ਵਿਹਾਰ; ਬ੍ਰਹਿਮੰਡ, ਬਾਹਰੀ ਦੁਨੀਆ; **lower~**
ਪਾਤਾਲ, ਨਰਕ; ~liness ਸੰਸਾਰਕਤਾ,
ਲੋਕਕਤਾ, ਦੁਨੀਆਦਾਰੀ, ਲੋਕਾਚਾਰੀ, ਪ੍ਰਪੰਚ,
ਪਾਰਖਿਵਤਾ; ~ly ਸੰਸਾਰੀ, ਲੌਕਕ, ਦੁਨਿਆਵੀ,
ਸੰਸਾਰਕ, ਐਸ਼ਪਰਸਤੀ ਵਾਲਾ, ਵਿਹਾਰਕ

worm (ਵਅਃਮ) *n* ਕੀੜਾ, ਕਿਰਮ; ਨਿਗੁਣਾ ਜਾਂ
ਘਟੀਆ ਆਦਮੀ

worried ('ਵਅੱਰਿਡ) *a* ਚਿੰਤਾਤੁਰ, ਪਰੇਸ਼ਾਨ,
ਵਿਆਕੁਲ

worry ('ਵਅੱਰਿ) *v n* ਚਿੰਤਾ ਕਰਨੀ, ਫ਼ਿਕਰ
ਕਰਨੀ; ਪਰੇਸ਼ਾਨ ਕਰਨਾ, ਦਿੱਕ ਕਰਨਾ; ਚਿੰਤਾ,
ਫ਼ਿਕਰ, ਪਰੇਸ਼ਾਨੀ, ਬਿਪਤਾ

worse (ਵਅਃਸ) *a adv n* (ਕਿਸੇ ਹੋਰ ਨਾਲੋਂ)
ਭੈੜਾ, ਬੁਰਾ, ਘਟੀਆ, ਨਿਕੰਮਾ, ਮਾੜਾ; ~n ਹੋਰ
ਭੈੜੀ ਹਾਲਤ ਕਰ ਦੇਣੀ ਜਾਂ ਹੋ ਜਾਣੀ, ਹੋਰ
ਵਿਗਾੜ ਦੇਣਾ ਜਾਂ ਵਿਗੜ ਜਾਣਾ, ਹੋਰ ਖ਼ਰਾਬ
ਕਰ ਦੇਣਾ ਜਾਂ ਹੋ ਜਾਣਾ

worship ('ਵਅਃਸ਼ਿਪ) *v* ਪੂਜਾ, ਅਰਾਧਨਾ,
ਉਪਾਸਨਾ; ਭਜਨ; ਪੂਜਾ ਕਰਨੀ, ਉਪਾਸਨਾ
ਕਰਨੀ, ਅਰਾਧਨਾ ਕਰਨੀ

worst (ਵਅਃਸਟ) *a adv n* ਸਭ ਤੋਂ ਬੁਰਾ,
ਨਿਕੰਮਾ, ਖ਼ਰਾਬ; ਨੀਚਤਮ; ਬਹੁਤ ਬੁਰਾ, ਭੈੜੇ ਤੋਂ
ਭੈੜਾ; ਬਹੁਤ ਬੁਰੀ ਤਰ੍ਹਾਂ; ਮੰਦੀ ਤੋਂ ਮੰਦੀ ਹਾਲਤ

worsted (ਵੁਸਟਿਡ) *n* ਉੱਨੀ ਧਾਗਾ; ਉੱਨੀ ਧਾਗੇ
ਨਾਲ ਉਣਿਆ ਕੱਪੜਾ

worth (ਵਅਃਥ) *a n* ਦੇ ਮੁੱਲ ਦਾ, ਕੀਮਤ ਦਾ;
ਯੋਗ, ਜੋਗਾ, ਲਾਇਕ, ਉਚਿਤ; ਦੇ ਬਰਾਬਰ;
ਹੈਸੀਅਤ ਵਾਲਾ, ਸੰਪੱਤੀ ਵਾਲਾ; ਮੁੱਲ; ਮਹੱਤਾ;
ਕਦਰ; ~while ਉਚਿਤ; ~less ਨਿਕੰਮਾ,
ਫ਼ਜ਼ੂਲ, ਬੇਕਾਰ, ਖ਼ਰਾਬ; ਨਿਗੁਣਾ, ਤੁੱਛ ਘਟੀਆ;
~y ਯੋਗ, ਕਾਬਲ, ਲਾਇਕ, ਉਚਿਤ; ਪੂਜਨੀਕ,

ਸਤਿਕਾਰਯੋਗ, ਸ੍ਰੇਸ਼ਠ ਮਨੁੱਖ

would-be ('ਵੁਡਬੀ) *a adv* ਹੋਣ ਵਾਲਾ, ਆਗਾਮੀ, ਭਾਵੀ

wound (ਵੂੰਡ) *n v* ਜਖਮ, ਘਾਓ, ਸੱਟ, ਫੱਟ; ਠੇਸ; ਜ਼ਖਮ ਕਰਨਾ, ਸੱਟ ਲਾਉਣੀ; ਮਾਨਸਕ ਕਸ਼ਟ ਦੇਣਾ; ~ed ਘਾਇਲ; ਜ਼ਖਮੀ; ਜਰਜਰ

wrack (ਰੈਕ) *n* ਵਿਨਾਸ਼, ਤਬਾਹੀ, ਬਰਬਾਦੀ; ਜਹਾਜ਼ ਦੇ ਗਾਰਕਣ ਦੀ ਕਿਰਿਆ; ~ful ਟੁੱਟਿਆ-ਭੱਜਿਆ

wrangle ('ਰੈਙਗਲ) *n* ਝਗੜਾ, ਤੂੰ-ਤੂੰ ਮੈਂ-ਮੈਂ, ਘਖੇੜਾ, ਵਿਵਾਦ, ਤਕਰਾਰ; ਝਗੜਨਾ, ਤਕਰਾਰ ਕਰਨੀ

wrap (ਰੈਪ) *v* ਵਲ੍ਹੇਟਣਾ, ਢਕਣਾ (ਕੱਪੜੇ ਆਦਿ ਵਿਚ); ਬੰਨ੍ਹਣਾ, ਪੈਕ ਕਰਨਾ, ਬੰਡਲ ਬਣਾਉਣਾ; ਢਕ ਲੈਣਾ, ਕੱਜ ਦੇਣਾ; ~per ਵਲ੍ਹੇਟਣ ਵਾਲਾ; ਸਿਰ ਦਾ ਲੀੜਾ; ਵਲ੍ਹੇਟਣ ਵਾਲਾ ਕੱਪੜਾ; (ਕਿਤਾਬ ਦੀ) ਜਿਲਦ ਉੱਤੇ ਚਾੜ੍ਹਿਆ ਕਾਗ਼ਜ਼

wrath (ਰੋਥ) *n* ਗੁੱਸਾ, ਕਰੋਧ, ਨਾਰਾਜ਼ਗੀ; ~ful ਗੁੱਸੇਖੋਰ, ਕਰੋਪੀ, ਗੁਸੈਲਾ

wreath (ਰੀਥ) *n* ਹਾਰ, ਫੁੱਲਮਾਲਾ, ਮੁਕਟ

wreathe (ਰੀਦ) *v* ਗੁੰਦਣਾ, ਹਾਰ ਬਣਾਉਣਾ; ਹਾਰ ਪਾਉਣਾ

wreck (ਰੈੱਕ) *n v* ਤਬਾਹੀ, ਬਰਬਾਦੀ, ਵਿਨਾਸ਼; ਜਹਾਜ਼ ਦੇ ਗਾਰਕ ਹੋਣ; ਟੁੱਟਾ ਤੇ ਬਰਬਾਦ ਹੋਇਆ ਜਹਾਜ਼; ਢੱਠਾ ਘਰ; ਬਰਬਾਦ ਕਰਨਾ, ਤਬਾਹੀ ਕਰਨੀ; ~age ਮਲਬਾ; ~ing ਤਬਾਹ ਕਰਨਾ, ਬਰਬਾਦੀ, ਵਿਨਾਸ਼

wrench (ਰੈਂਚ) *n v* ਜ਼ੋਰ ਦਾ ਝਟਕਾ, ਮਰੋੜ; ਪੇਚਕਸ, ਸੰਨ੍ਹੀ, ਰੈਂਚ; ਝਟਕਾ ਦੇਣਾ, ਮਰੋੜ ਦੇਣਾ

wrest (ਰੈੱਸਟ) *v* ਤੋੜ-ਮਰੋੜ ਕਰਨੀ, ਕਾਂਟ-ਛਾਂਟ ਕਰਨੀ; ਵਿਗਾੜਨੀ; ਖੋਹ-ਖਾਹੀ ਕਰਨੀ

wrestle ('ਰੈੱਸਲ) *n v* ਘੋਲ, ਕੁਸ਼ਤੀ, ਦੰਗਲ; ਸਖ਼ਤ ਮੁਕਾਬਲਾ; ਘੁਲਣਾ, ਕੁਸ਼ਤੀ ਕਰਨੀ; ~r ਬਲਵਾਨ, ਪਹਿਲਵਾਨ, ਘੁਲਣ ਵਾਲਾ

wrestling ('ਰੈੱਸਲਿਙ) *n* ਘੋਲ, ਕੁਸ਼ਤੀ

wretch (ਰੈੱਚ) *n* ਬੇਨਸੀਬ, ਕਰਮਾਂ ਮਾਰਿਆ, ਅਭਾਗਾ ਆਦਮੀ; ਵਿਚਾਰਾ; ਹੀਣ ਆਦਮੀ; ~ed ਬੇਨਸੀਬ, ਕਿਸਮਤ ਦਾ ਮਾਰਿਆ, ਕਰਮਾਂ ਮਾਰਿਆ; ਪੀੜਤ, ਅਭਾਗਾ, ਦਲਿੰਦਰੀ; ~edness ਬਦਨਸੀਬੀ, ਬੇਨਸੀਬੀ, ਬਦਕਿਸਮਤੀ

wriggle ('ਰਿਗਲ) *v n* ਪਲਸੇਟੇ ਮਾਰਨੇ, ਪਾਸੇ ਮਰੋੜਨੇ, ਵਲ ਪਾਉਂਦੇ ਜਾਣਾ, ਵਲ-ਵਲੇਵੇਂ ਖਾਂਦੇ ਜਾਣਾ, ਸੱਪ ਵਾਂਗ ਘਸੀਟਦੇ ਚੱਲਣਾ; ਵੱਟ, ਪਲਸੇਟਾ

wright (ਰਾਇਟ) *n* ਕਾਰੀਗਰ, ਮਿਸਤਰੀ, ਸ਼ਿਲਪੀ

wring (ਰਿਙ) *v n* ਮਰੋੜਨਾ, ਮਰੋੜਾ ਦੇਣਾ; ਮਰੋੜ ਦੇ ਤੋੜ ਦੇਣਾ; ਮਲਣਾ; ਨਚੋੜਨਾ (ਕੱਪੜਾ); ਮਰੁੰਡਣਾ; (ਪੈਸਾ) ਨਚੋੜਨ, ਮਰੋੜਾ

wrinkle ('ਰਿਙਕਲ) *n v* ਝੁਰੜੀ; ਝੁਰੜੀਆਂ ਪੈ ਜਾਣੀਆਂ

wrist (ਰਿਸਟ) *n* ਵੀਣੀ, ਗੁੱਟ; ~let ਕੜਾ, ਕੰਗਣ; ਹੱਥਕੜੀ

writ (ਰਿਟ) *n* (ਅਦਾਲਤੀ) ਪਰਵਾਨਾ, ਹੁਕਮਨਾਮਾ; ਲਿਖਤ, ਲਿਖਿਆ

write (ਰਾਇਟ) *v* ਲਿਖਣਾ; ਦਰਜ ਕਰਨਾ; ਰਜਿਸਟਰ, ਵਹੀ ਆਦਿ ਤੇ ਚੜ੍ਹਾਉਣਾ, ਰਚਨਾ ਕਰਨੀ; ~off ਵੱਟੇ ਖਾਤੇ ਪਾਉਣਾ, ਕਲਮ ਫੇਰ ਦੇਣਾ; ~r ਲੇਖਕ, ਲਿਖਾਰੀ; (ਕਿਤਾਬ ਦਾ) ਕਰਤਾ, ਗ੍ਰੰਥਕਾਰ, ਮੁਨਸ਼ੀ, ਕਲਰਕ

writhe (ਰਾਇਦ) *v n* ਤੜਫਣਾ, ਸਰੀਰ ਨੂੰ ਮਰੋੜਨਾ; ਬੜਾ ਕਸ਼ਟ ਹੋਣਾ, ਅਤੀ ਦੁਖੀ ਹੋਣਾ; ਤਿਲਮਲਾਹਟ

writing ('ਰਾਇਟਿਙ) *n* ਲਿਖਾਈ, ਲੇਖ; ਦਸਤਾਵੇਜ਼, ਸਨਦ; ਲ਼ਿਤੀ, ਰਚਨਾ, ਪੁਸਤਕ

wrong (ਰੌਙ) *a adv n* ਗ਼ਲਤ, ਅਸ਼ੁੱਧ; ਖਰਾਬ, ਨਾਜਾਇਜ਼, ਅਨੁਚਿਤ, ਨਾਵਾਜਬ; ਉਲਟਾ; ਗ਼ਲਤੀ; ~ful ਅਯੋਗ, ਅਨੁਚਿਤ, ਨਾਜਾਇਜ਼, ਬੇਜਾ, ਦੋਸ਼ਪੂਰਨ

wrought (ਰੋਟ) *n v* ਉਤੇਜਤ, ਪ੍ਰਭਾਵਤ, ਹਾਵੀ; ਘੜਿਆ, ਕੁੱਟ ਕੇ ਬਣਾਇਆ; ਕੱਢਿਆ, ਸਜਾਇਆ; ~on ਪ੍ਰਭਾਵਤ, ਹਾਵੀ; ~up ਉਤੇਜਤ, ਭੜਕਿਆ

wry (ਰਾਇ) *a* (ਮੂੰਹ) ਵਿੰਗਾ, ਟੇਢਾ, ਝੀਵਿਆ, ਵਿਗੜਿਆ

X

X, x (ਐਕੱਸ) *n* ਰੋਮਨ ਵਰਨਮਾਲਾ ਦਾ ਚੌਵੀਵਾਂ ਅੱਖਰ, (ਰੋਮਨ ਅੰਕਾਂ ਵਿਚ) ਦਸ; ਅਗਿਆਤ ਵਿਅਕਤੀ, ਪਹਿਲੀ ਰਾਸ਼ੀ ਜਾਂ ਵਸਤੁ

xanthic (ਜ਼ੈਨਥਿਕ) *a* ਬਸੰਤੀ, ਪੀਲਾ, ਖੱਟਾ

xanthichromia ('ਜ਼ੈਨਥਅ(ਉ)'ਕਰਅਉਮਿਅ) *n* ਪੀਲੀਆ, ਚਮੜੀ ਦਾ ਪੀਲਾਪਣ, ਪਿਲਤਣ

Xantippe (ਜ਼ੈਨ'ਟਿਪਿ) *n* ਲੜਾਕੀ ਔਰਤ, ਕਲਹਿਣੀ ਤੀਵੀਂ

xenium (ਜ਼ੀਨਿਅਮ) *n* (ਰਾਜਦੂਤਾਂ ਜਾਂ ਪਰਾਹੁਣੇ ਨੂੰ ਦਿੱਤਾ ਜਾਣ ਵਾਲਾ) ਨਜ਼ਰਾਨਾ, ਭੇਟਾ

xenodochy (ਜ਼ਿ'ਨੌਡ਼ਅਕਿ) *n* ਮਹਿਮਾਨ-ਨਿਵਾਜ਼ੀ, ਅਤਿਥੀ-ਸਤਿਕਾਰ

Xmas ('ਕਰਿਸਮਅਸ) *n* ਕ੍ਰਿਸਮਿਸ, ਵੱਡਾ ਦਿਨ

X-ray ('ਐਕੱਸਰੇਇ) *v* ਐਕਸ-ਰੇ ਲੈਣਾ, ਐਕਸ-ਰੇ ਦਾ ਚਿੱਤਰ ਲੈਣਾ; ~s ਐਕਸ-ਰੇਜ਼, ਕ੍ਰਾਸ਼-ਕਿਰਨਾਂ, ਰੁੰਟਜਨ ਕਿਰਨਾਂ

xylophagous (ਜ਼ਾਇ'ਲੌਫ਼ਅਗਾਅਸ) *a* ਕਾਠ-ਭੱਖੀ, ਲੱਕੜ ਖਾਣ ਵਾਲਾ

xyster ('ਜ਼ਿਸਟਾ*) *n* (ਹੱਡੀਆਂ ਖੁਰਚਣ ਲਈ) ਖੁਰਚਣੀ

Y

Y, y (ਵਾਇ) *n* ਰੋਮਨ ਵਰਨਮਾਲਾ ਦਾ ਪੰਝੀਵਾਂ ਅੱਖਰ, ਦੂਜੀ ਅਗਿਆਤ ਰਾਸ਼ੀ ਜਾਂ ਵਸਤੁ

yacht (ਯੌਟ) *n v* ਸੈਰ-ਸਪਾਟੇ ਲਈ ਜਾਂ ਦੌੜਾਂ ਲਈ ਪੱਲ੍ਹਾਂ ਵਾਲੀ ਬੇੜੀ, ਡੌਂਗੀ; ਬੇੜੀਆਂ ਦੀ ਦੌੜ ਵਿਚ ਸ਼ਾਮਲ ਹੋਣਾ; **~er** ਬੇੜੀ ਜਾਂ ਡੌਂਗੀ ਦਾ ਮਲਾਹ, ਪਾਤਨੀ, ਖੇਵਟ; **~ing** ਡੌਂਗੀ ਜਾਂ ਬੇੜੀ ਦੀ ਯਾਤਰਾ; ਡੌਂਗੀ ਜਾਂ ਬੇੜੀ ਬਾਰੇ

yackety-yack ('ਯੈਕਟਿ'ਯੈਕ) *n* (ਅਪ) ਚਪੜ ਚਪੜ, ਬਕਵਾਸ

yam (ਯੈਮ) *n* ਰਤਾਲੂ, ਕਚਾਲੂ; ਅਰਬੀ

yap (ਯੈਪ) *v n* ਘਬਰਾਹਟ ਵਿਚ ਜਾਂ ਚਿੜ ਕੇ ਭੌਂਕਟਾ; ਬਕਟਾ, ਬਕਵਾਸ ਕਰਨਾ; ਭੌਂਕਣ ਦੀ ਉੱਚੀ ਅਵਾਜ਼

yard (ਯਾਡ) *n* ਗਜ਼, ਤਿੰਨ ਫੁੱਟ ਦੀ ਲੰਬਾਈ; ਵਿਹੜਾ; ਅਹਾਤਾ; ਵਾੜਾ, ਵਲਗਣ; **~stick** ਗਜ਼; ਕਸਵੱਟੀ, ਪੈਮਾਨਾ

yarn (ਯਾਨ) *n v* ਸੂਤ; ਤੰਦ, ਤਾਰ, ਧਾਗਾ; ਊਨੀ ਧਾਗਾ; ਕਿੱਸਾ ਘੜਨਾ

yawn (ਯੌਨ) *v n* ਉਬਾਸੀ ਲੈਣੀ, ਉਬਾਸੀ ਆਉਣੀ; ਉਬਾਸੀ; **~ing** ਉਬਾਸੀ, ਉਬਾਸੀ ਲੈਂਦਾ ਹੋਇਆ

yea (ਯੇਇ) *partical* (ਪ੍ਰ) ਹਾਂ; ਅਵੱਸ਼, ਜ਼ਰੂਰ; ਠੀਕ; ਸੱਚਮੁਚ; ਸਗੋਂ

yeah (ਯੇਅ) *adv* (ਬੋਲ) ਹਾਂ

year (ਯਿਅ*) *n* ਵਰ੍ਹਾ, ਸਾਲ; ਲੰਮੀ ਮੁਦੱਤ; ਸੰਨ, ਸੰਮਤ; **~book** ਸਾਲਨਾਮਾ, ਵਰ੍ਹਾ-ਕੋਸ਼, ਵਰ੍ਹਾ-ਪੁਸਤਕ; **~ly** ਵਾਰਸ਼ਕ, ਸਾਲਾਨਾ; ਸਾਲ ਭਰ ਦਾ, ਹਰ ਸਾਲ, ਪ੍ਰਤੀ ਵਰ੍ਹਾ, ਵਰ੍ਹੇ ਦੇ ਵਰ੍ਹੇ

yearn (ਯਾਅ:ਨ) *v* ਤਾਂਘ ਹੋਣੀ, ਤੀਬਰ ਇੱਛਾ ਹੋਣੀ, ਉਤਸੁਕ ਹੋਣਾ, ਵਿਆਕੁਲ ਹੋਣਾ; **~ful** ਦੁੱਖਦਾਈ, ਸੋਗੀ, ਅਫ਼ਸੋਸਨਾਕ; **~ing** ਤ੍ਰਿਸ਼ਨਾ, ਉਤਸੁਕਤਾ, ਲਾਲਸਾ, ਇੱਛਾ; ਪਿਆਰ, ਤ੍ਰਿਸ਼ਨਾਪੂਰਨ, ਇੱਛਾਪੂਰਨ

yeast (ਯੀਸਟ) *n* ਖ਼ਮੀਰ, ਖ਼ਮੀਰ ਉੱਠਣ ਨਾਲ ਆਈ ਝੱਗ

yell (ਯੈੱਲ) *v n* ਚੀਕਣਾ, ਚਾਂਗਰ ਮਾਰਨੀ, ਚੰਘਾੜ ਮਾਰਨੀ; ਚੀਕ; ਚਾਂਗਰ; ਰੌਲਾ

yellow ('ਯੈੱਲਅਉ) *a* ਪੀਲਾ; ਖੱਟਾ, (ਪ੍ਰ) ਈਰਖਾਲੂ

yelp (ਯੈੱਲਪ) *n v* ਕੁੱਤੇ ਦੇ ਭੌਂਕਣ ਦੀ ਅਵਾਜ਼, ਚਿਚਲਾਉਣਾ, ਰੁਕਣਾ; ਉੱਚੀ ਅਵਾਜ਼ ਵਿਚ ਗੱਲ ਕਰਨੀ, ਚੀਕਣਾ

yeoman ('ਯਅਉਮਅਨ) *n* (ਇਤਿ) ਸ਼ਾਹੀ ਘਰਾਣੇ ਦਾ ਨੌਕਰ; ਕਿਸਾਨ, ਛੋਟਾ ਜ਼ਿਮੀਂਦਾਰ; ਆਮ ਮਨੁੱਖ; **~ly** ਕੱਟੜ, ਪੱਕਾ; ਬਹਾਦਰਾਂ ਵਾਂਗ

yes (ਯੇਸ) *particle n* ਹਾਂ, ਚੰਗਾ, ਹੱਛਾ; ਹੂੰ, ਹਾਹੋ, ਹਾਂ ਜੀ; **~man** ਜੀ-ਹਜ਼ੂਰੀਆ

yesterday ('ਯੈਸਟਅਡਿ) *n adv* ਕੱਲ (ਬੀਤ ਚੁੱਕਾ), ਕੱਲ ਦਾ ਦਿਨ; ਕੱਲ੍ਹ ਨੂੰ, ਕੱਲ ਦਿਨੇ

yesteryear ('ਯੈਸਟਅ'ਯਿਅ*) *n* ਪਿਛਲਾ ਸਾਲ, ਪਿਛਲੇ ਸਾਲ, ਬੀਤੇ ਸਾਲ

yet (ਯੈੱਟ) *adv conj* ਅਜੇ, ਅਜੇ ਤਕ, ਹੁਣ ਤਕ, ਹਾਲਾਂ, ਹਾਲੇ; ਅਜੇ ਵੀ, ਹੋਰ ਵੀ; ਪਰ ਇਸ ਨਾਲ

yex (ਯੈੱਕਸ) *n v* ਹਿਚਕੀ (ਲੈਣਾ)

yield (ਯੀਲਡ) *v n* (ਫ਼ਸਲ ਆਦਿ) ਉਪਜਾਉਣਾ

ਪੈਦਾ ਕਰਨਾ; ਝਾੜ ਹੋਣਾ; ਹਾਰ ਮੰਨ ਲੈਣੀ, ਹੀਣਾ ਹੋਣਾ; ਪੈਦਾਵਾਰ, ਉਪਜ, ਫਸਲ; ਮੁਨਾਫ਼ਾ; ~ing ਉਪਜ, ਉਤਪਾਦਨ, ਲਾਭ; ਆਤਮ-ਸਮਰਪਣ; ਨਰਮ; ਅਨੁਕੂਲ

yoghurt ('ਯੋਗਅ:ਟ) *n* ਦਹੀਂ

yoke (ਯਅਉਕ) *n v* ਜੂਲਾ, ਪੰਜਾਲੀ; ਨਰੜ; ਜੋੜਨਾ; ਜਕੜਨਾ, ਅਧੀਨ ਬਣਾਉਣਾ, ਦਾਸ ਬਣਾਉਣਾ

yolk, yelk (ਯਅਉਕ, ਯੈਲੱਕ) *n* ਅੰਡੇ ਦਾ ਪੀਲਾ ਅੰਸ਼, ਜ਼ਰਦੀ

younder ('ਯੌਂਡਅ*) *adv a* ਪਰ੍ਹਾਂ, ਦੂਰ, ਉਥੇ, ਓਧਰ; ਸਾਹਵੇਂ, ਸਾਮ੍ਹਣੇ; ਪਰਲਾ; ਸਾਮ੍ਹਣਾ, ਸਾਮ੍ਹਣੇ ਵਾਲਾ

yore (ਯੋ*) *n* ਪ੍ਰਾਚੀਨ ਕਾਲ, ਪੁਰਾਣਾ ਜ਼ਮਾਨਾ

young (ਯਅੱਙ) *a n* ਗੱਭਰੂ, ਗਭਰੇਟ, ਨਿੱਕਾ,

ਚੜ੍ਹਦੀ ਜਵਾਨੀ ਵਾਲਾ; ਅੱਲ੍ਹੜ ਜਵਾਨ; ~**man** ਗੱਭਰੂ, ਨੌਜਵਾਨ; ~**woman** ਮੁਟਿਆਰ, ਜਵਾਨ ਤੀਵੀਂ; ~**er** ਛੋਟਾ (ਬੱਚਾ), ਨੱਢਾ; ~**ster** ਬੱਚਾ, ਮੁੰਡਾ

your (ਯੋ*) *pro* ਤੁਹਾਡਾ; ਤੇਰਾ; ਆਪ ਜੀ ਦਾ; ~**self** ਤੁਸੀਂ ਆਪ, ਤੁਸੀਂ ਖ਼ੁਦ, ਆਪਣੇ ਆਪ ਨੂੰ

youth (ਯੂਥ) *n* ਜਵਾਨੀ; ਜੋਬਨ ਕਾਲ, ਚੜ੍ਹਦੀ ਜਵਾਨੀ; ਜਵਾਨ, ਗਭਰੂ, ਯੁਵਕ; ਨੌਜਵਾਨ ਮੁੰਡੇ-ਕੁੜੀਆਂ; ~**ful** ਨੌਜਵਾਨ, ਚੜ੍ਹਦੀ ਜਵਾਨੀ ਵਾਲਾ; ਜਵਾਨੀ ਦਾ; ~**fulness** ਜਵਾਨੀ, ਜੋਬਨ, ਜਵਾਨੀ ਦਾ ਸਮਾਂ, ਗੱਭਰੇਟਪਣ, ਨੌਜਵਾਨੀ

yule (ਯੂਲ) *n* ਕ੍ਰਿਸਮਿਸ ਦਾ ਦਿਨ, ਵੱਡਾ ਦਿਨ, ਕ੍ਰਿਸਮਿਸ ਦਾ ਪੁਰਬ

yummy ('ਯਅੱਮਿ) *a* (ਬਾਲ ਬੋਲੀ) ਮਿੱਠੀ, ਸੁਆਦੀ

Z

Z, z (ਜ਼ੈੱਡ) *n* ਰੋਮਨ ਵਰਣਮਾਲਾ ਦਾ ਛੱਬੀਵਾਂ ਤੇ ਅੰਤਲਾ ਅੱਖਰ, ਤੀਜੀ ਅਗਿਆਤ ਰਾਸ਼ੀ

zany ('ਜ਼ੋਇਨਿ) *n* ਭੰਡ, ਮਖੌਲੀਆ, ਵਿਦੂਸ਼ਕ; ਮੂਰਖ, ਲੋਲੂ ਆਦਮੀ; **~ism** ਭੰਡੀ, ਵਿਦੂਸ਼ਕਤਾ, ਭੰਡਪੁਣਾ, ਮਸ਼ਕਰਾਪਣ

zeal (ਜ਼ੀਲ) *n* ਉਤਸ਼ਾਹ, ਜੋਸ਼, ਸ਼ੋਕ, ਸਰਗਰਮੀ ਲਗਨ; **~ful** ਉਤਸ਼ਾਹਪੂਰਣ, ਉਤਸੁਕ, ਜੋਸ਼ੀਲਾ, ਸਰਗਰਮ, ਧੁਨ ਦਾ ਪੱਕਾ; **~less** ਉਤਸ਼ਾਹੀਨ, ਸੁਸਤ; **~ous** ਤੇਜ਼, ਤਿੱਖਾ, ਤੀਬਰ; ਉਤਸ਼ਾਹਪੂਰਨ, ਜੋਸ਼ੀਲਾ, ਉਦੱਮੀ, ਸ਼ੁਕੀਨ, ਸਰਗਰਮ; **~ousness** ਤਿੱਖਾਪਣ, ਉਤਸ਼ਾਹਪੂਰਨਤਾ, ਜੋਸ਼ੀਲਾਪਣ, ਸਰਗਰਮੀ, ਲਗਨਪੂਰਨਤਾ

zebra ('ਜ਼ੀਬੁਰਾ) *n* ਜ਼ੈਬਰਾ, ਘੋੜੇ ਵਰਗਾ ਧਾਰੀਆਂ ਵਾਲਾ ਜਾਨਵਰ; **~crossing** ਪੈਦਲ ਚੱਲਣ ਵਾਲਿਆਂ ਲਈ ਬਣਾਇਆ ਧਾਰੀਦਾਰ ਰਸਤਾ

zenith (ਜ਼ੈਨਿਥ) *n* ਆਕਾਸ਼ ਵਿਚ ਉਹ ਬਿੰਦੂ ਜਿਹੜਾ ਵੇਖਣ ਵਾਲੇ ਦੇ ਸਿਰ ਦੇ ਉੱਪਰ ਹੋਵੇ; ਸਿਖਰ-ਬਿੰਦੂ, ਉੱਚ-ਸੀਮਾ; ਕਮਾਲ, ਵੱਧ ਤੋਂ ਵੱਧ ਉੱਨਤੀ, ਉੱਥਾਨ

zephyr ('ਜ਼ੈਫ਼ਅ*) *n* ਬਸੰਤ ਰੁੱਤ ਦੀ ਵਾਯੂ, ਸਮੀਰ, ਤਿੱਨੀ-ਤਿੱਨੀ ਹਵਾ, ਪੱਛਮ ਦੀ ਹਵਾ; ਜਾਲੀਦਾਰ ਕੱਪੜਾ; ਪਵਨ ਦੇਵ Also **Zephyrus**

zero ('ਜ਼ਿਅਰਅਉ) *n* ਸਿਫ਼ਰ, ਸ਼ੂਨ; ੦ ਦਾ ਅੰਕ; ਮਾਪਦੰਡ ਦਾ ਅਰੰਭਲਾ ਬਿੰਦੂ, ਨੀਵੇਂ ਤੋਂ ਨੀਵਾਂ ਬਿੰਦੂ; ਅਣਹੋਂਦਿਆ, ਨਾ ਹੋਇਆ ਮਨੁੱਖ; **~hour** ਅਰੰਭ-ਬਿੰਦੂ; ਅਰੰਭ-ਕਾਲ, ਸ਼ੂਨ ਕਾਲ

zest (ਜ਼ੈਸੱਟ) *n v* ਚਾਅ, ਰੀਝ, ਦਿਲਚਸਪੀ, ਸੁਆਦ, ਚਸਕਾ; ਮਜ਼ਾ ਦੇਣਾ, ਸੁਆਦ ਦੇਣਾ

zigzag ('ਜ਼ਿਗਜ਼ੈਗ) *a n adv v* ਵਲਾਵੇਂਦਾਰ, ਵਿੰਗਾ-ਟੇਢਾ, ਵਿੰਗ-ਤੜਿੰਗਾ; ਵਿੰਗੀ ਟੇਢੀ ਲਕੀਰ; ਵਲਾਵੇਂ ਖਾਂਦਾ; ਟੇਢਾ ਚੱਲਣਾ, ਤੇੜ-ਮੇੜ ਦੇਣਾ

zinc ('ਜ਼ਿਬਕ) *n v* ਜਿਸਤ, ਜ਼ਿੰਕ; ਜਿਸਤ ਦੀ ਪਾਲਸ਼ ਕਰਨਾ

Zingaro ('ਜ਼ਿੰਡ਼ਗਾਅਰਅਉ) *n* ਖ਼ਾਨਾਬਦੋਸ਼ ਫਿਰਤੂ ਲੋਕ, ਜਿਪਸੀ

zingiber ('ਜ਼ਿੰਜਿਬਅ*) ਸੁੰਢ, ਅਦਰਕ

zippy ('ਜ਼ਿਪਿ) *n* ਜਾਨਦਾਰ, ਜੀਵਤ, ਫੁਰਤੀਲਾ, ਸਜੀਵ

zodiac ('ਜ਼ਾਉਡ਼ਿਐਕ) *n* (ਆਕਾਸ਼ ਦਾ) ਰਾਸ਼ੀ-ਮੰਡਲ, ਰਾਸ਼ੀ

zonal ('ਜ਼ਾਉਨਲ) *n a* ਖੇਤਰੀ, ਮੰਡਲੀ, ਇਲਾਕਾਈ, ਪ੍ਰਦੇਸ਼ਕ

zone (ਜ਼ਾਉਨ) *n* ਮੰਡਲ, ਘੇਰਾ, ਚੱਕਰ; ਪੱਟੀ, ਧਾਰੀ; ਖੇਤਰ, ਇਲਾਕਾ, ਖੰਡ, ਪ੍ਰਦੇਸ਼, ਭੂ-ਮੰਡਲ; ਕਮਰਬੰਦ, ਕਮਰ ਪੇਟੀ

zoo (ਜ਼ੂ) *n* ਚਿੜੀਆਘਰ; **~logical garden** ਚਿੜੀਆਘਰ; **~logist** ਜੰਤੂ ਵਿਗਿਆਨੀ; **~logy** ਜੰਤੂ ਵਿਗਿਆਨ

zoom (ਜ਼ੂਮ) *v n* ਹਵਾਈ ਜਹਾਜ਼ ਦਾ ਤਿੱਖੀ ਗਤੀ ਨਾਲ ਉਡਣਾ; ਕੀਮਤਾਂ ਚੜ੍ਹਨਾ; ਸ਼ੋਰ ਕਰਨਾ

zymosis (ਜ਼ਾਇ'ਮਅਉਸਿਸ) *n* ਖ਼ਮੀਰ; ਖਲਬੀ ਦੀ ਇਕ ਛੂਤ ਦੀ ਬੀਮਾਰੀ